CALIFORNIA
HEALTH AND SAFETY CODE
(1/3)

2020 EDITION

Revised December 30, 2019
By Sacramento Legal Publishing

CALIFORNIA LEGISLATURE

GENERAL PROVISIONS

(General Provisions enacted by Stats. 1939, Ch. 60.)

1.
This act shall be known as the Health and Safety Code.
(Enacted by Stats. 1939, Ch. 60.)

2.
The provisions of this code in so far as they are substantially the same as existing statutory provisions relating to the same subject matter shall be construed as restatements and continuations, and not as new enactments.
(Enacted by Stats. 1939, Ch. 60.)

3.
All persons who, at the time this code takes effect, hold office under any of the acts repealed by this code, which offices are continued by this code, continue to hold them according to their former tenure.
(Enacted by Stats. 1939, Ch. 60.)

4.
Any action or proceeding commenced before this code takes effect, and any right accrued, is not affected by this code, but all procedure thereafter taken therein shall conform to the provisions of this code as far as possible.
(Enacted by Stats. 1939, Ch. 60.)

5.
Unless the provision or the context otherwise requires, these definitions, rules of construction, and general provisions shall govern the construction of this code.
(Enacted by Stats. 1939, Ch. 60.)

6.
Division, part, chapter, article, and section headings do not in any manner affect the scope, meaning, or intent of the provisions of this code.
(Enacted by Stats. 1939, Ch. 60.)

7.
Whenever a power is granted to, or a duty is imposed upon, a public officer, the power may be exercised or the duty may be performed by a deputy of the officer or by a person authorized, pursuant to law, by the officer, unless this code expressly provides otherwise.
(Enacted by Stats. 1939, Ch. 60.)

8.
Writing includes any form of recorded message capable of comprehension by ordinary visual means. Whenever any notice, report, statement, or record is required or authorized by this code, it shall be made in writing in the English language unless it is expressly provided otherwise.
(Enacted by Stats. 1939, Ch. 60.)

9.
Whenever reference is made to any portion of this code or of any other law of this State, the reference applies to all amendments and additions now or hereafter made.
(Enacted by Stats. 1939, Ch. 60.)

10.
"Section" means a section of this code unless some other statute is specifically mentioned. Subdivision means a subdivision of the section in which that term occurs unless some other section is expressly mentioned.
(Enacted by Stats. 1939, Ch. 60.)

11.
The present tense includes the past and future tenses; and the future, the present.
(Enacted by Stats. 1939, Ch. 60.)

12.
The masculine gender includes the feminine and neuter.
(Enacted by Stats. 1939, Ch. 60.)

12.2.
"Spouse" includes "registered domestic partner," as required by Section 297.5 of the Family Code.
(Added by Stats. 2016, Ch. 50, Sec. 51. (SB 1005) Effective January 1, 2017.)

13.
The singular number includes the plural, and the plural the singular.
(Enacted by Stats. 1939, Ch. 60.)

14.
"County" includes city and county.
(Enacted by Stats. 1939, Ch. 60.)

15.
Unless expressly otherwise provided, any notice required to be given to any person by any provision of this code may be given by mailing notice, postage prepaid, addressed to the person to be notified, at his residence or principal place of business in this State. The affidavit of the person who mails the notice, stating the facts of such mailing, is prima facie evidence that the notice was thus mailed.
(Enacted by Stats. 1939, Ch. 60.)

16.
"Shall" is mandatory and "may" is permissive.
(Enacted by Stats. 1939, Ch. 60.)

17.
"Oath" includes affirmation.
(Enacted by Stats. 1939, Ch. 60.)

18.
"Signature" or "subscription" includes mark when the signer or subscriber can not write, such signer's or subscriber's name being written near the mark by a witness who writes his own name near the signer's or subscriber's name; but a signature or subscription by mark can be acknowledged or can serve as a signature or subscription to a sworn statement only when two witnesses so sign their own names thereto.
(Enacted by Stats. 1939, Ch. 60.)

19.
"Person" means any person, firm, association, organization, partnership, business trust, corporation, limited liability company, or company.
(Amended by Stats. 1994, Ch. 1010, Sec. 151. Effective January 1, 1995.)

20.
"State department" or "department" means State Department of Health Services. Commencing July 1, 2007, any reference to the former State Department of Health Services regarding a function vested by Chapter 2 (commencing with Section 131050) of Part 1 of Division 112, in the State Department of Public Health is deemed to, instead, refer to the State Department of Public Health, and any reference to the former State Department of Health Services regarding a function not vested by Chapter 2 (commencing with Section 131050) of Part 1 of Division 112, in the State Department of Public Health, is deemed to, instead, refer to the State Department of Health Care Services.
(Amended by Stats. 2006, Ch. 241, Sec. 8. Effective January 1, 2007. Operative July 1, 2007, by Sec. 37 of Ch. 241.)

21.
"Director" means "State Director of Health Services." Commencing July 1, 2007, any reference to the former State Director of Health Services regarding a function vested by Chapter 2 (commencing with Section 131050) of Part 1 of Division 112, in the State Department of Public Health is deemed to, instead, refer to the State Public Health Officer.
(Amended by Stats. 2006, Ch. 241, Sec. 9. Effective January 1, 2007. Operative July 1, 2007, by Sec. 37 of Ch. 241.)

22.
"Board" or "State Board of Public Health" means "State Department of Health Services," with respect to regulatory functions heretofore performed by the State Board of Public Health or the "Advisory Health Council" with respect to all other functions heretofore performed by the board.
(Amended by Stats. 1977, Ch. 1252.)

23.
"State" means the State of California, unless applied to the different parts of the United States. In the latter case, it includes the District of Columbia and the territories.
(Enacted by Stats. 1939, Ch. 60.)

24.
If any provision of this code, or the application thereof to any person or circumstance, is held invalid, the remainder of the code, or the application of such provision to other persons or circumstances, shall not be affected thereby.
(Enacted by Stats. 1939, Ch. 60.)

25.
Wherever, pursuant to this code, any state department, officer, board, agency, committee, or commission is authorized to adopt rules and regulations, such rules and regulations which are building standards, as defined in Section 18909 of the Health and Safety Code, shall be adopted pursuant to the provisions of Part 2.5 (commencing with Section 18901) of Division 13 of the Health and Safety Code unless the provisions of Sections 18930, 18933, 18938, 18940, 18943, 18944, and 18945 of the Health and Safety Code are expressly excepted in the provision of this code under which the authority to adopt the specific building standard is delegated. Any building standard adopted in violation of this section shall have no force or effect. Any building standard adopted prior to January 1, 1980, pursuant to this code and not expressly excepted by statute from such provisions of the State Building Standards Law shall remain in effect only until January 1, 1985, or until adopted, amended, or superseded by provisions published in the State Building Standards Code, whichever occurs sooner.
(Added by Stats. 1979, Ch. 1152.)

27.
For purposes of this code:
(a) "Communicable Disease Prevention and Control Act" means Sections 104730, 104830 to 104860, inclusive, 113150, 113155, Part 1 (commencing with Section 120100) of, Chapter 1 (commencing with Section 120325, but excluding Section 120380) of Part 2 of, Part 3 (commencing with Section 120500) of, and Part 5 (commencing with Section 121350) of, Division 105.
(b) "Hereditary Disorders Act" means Article 1 (commencing with Section 124975) of Chapter 1 of Part 5 of Division 106, and Sections 125050, 125055, 125060, and 125065.
(c) "Maternal and Child Health Program Act" means Section 120380, Chapter 4 (commencing with Section 103925) of Part 2 of Division 102, Article 4 (commencing with Section 116875) of Chapter 5 of Part 12 of Division 104, Article 1 (commencing with Section 123225) of Chapter 1 of Part 2 of Division 106, Article 2 (commencing with Section 125000) of Chapter 1 of Part 5 of Division 106, and Sections 125075 to 125110, inclusive.
(d) "Miscellaneous Food, Food Facility, and Hazardous Substances Act" means Chapter 4 (commencing with Section 108100), Chapter 6 (commencing with Section 108675), and Chapter 7 (commencing with Section 108750) of Part 3 of, Chapter 3 (commencing with Section 111940), Chapter 4 (commencing with Section 111950), Chapter 5

(commencing with Section 112150), Chapter 6 (commencing with Section 112350), Chapter 7 (commencing with Section 112500), Chapter 8 (commencing with Section 112650), Chapter 9 (commencing with Section 112875), Chapter 10 (commencing with Section 113025), and Article 3 (commencing with Section 113250) of Chapter 11, of Part 6 of, and Chapter 4 (commencing with Section 113700) of Part 7 of, Division 104.
(e) "Primary Care Services Act" means Chapter 1 (commencing with Section 124400), Chapter 2 (commencing with Section 124475), Chapter 3 (commencing with Section 124550), Chapter 4 (commencing with Section 124575), Chapter 5 (commencing with Section 124600), Chapter 6 (commencing with Section 124800), and Article 1 (commencing with Section 124875) of Chapter 7 of, Part 4 of Division 106.
(f) "Radiologic Technology Act" means Sections 106965 to 107120, inclusive, and Chapter 6 (commencing with Section 114840) of Part 9 of Division 104.
(Added by Stats. 1995, Ch. 415, Sec. 1. Effective January 1, 1996.)
28.
For the purposes of this code, "recycled water" or "reclaimed water" has the same meaning as recycled water as defined in subdivision (n) of Section 13050 of the Water Code.
(Added by renumbering Section 27 (as added by Stats. 1995, Ch. 28) by Stats. 1996, Ch. 1023, Sec. 105. Effective September 29, 1996.)

DIVISION 1. ADMINISTRATION OF PUBLIC HEALTH [135 - 1179.102]

(Division 1 enacted by Stats. 1939, Ch. 60.)

PART 0.5. California Health and Human Services Agency Departments: Public Notice Requirements [135- 135.]

(Part 0.5 added by Stats. 2015, Ch. 296, Sec. 1.)
135.
If a department within the California Health and Human Services Agency has received approval of an operational state plan by a federal agency, or has applied and has been approved for a waiver from a federal law or federal regulation, the department shall make any and all approved plans and waivers available to the public by publishing a hyperlink to that information on the homepage of the department's Internet Web site.
(Added by Stats. 2015, Ch. 296, Sec. 1. (AB 294) Effective January 1, 2016.)

PART 1. STATE DEPARTMENT OF HEALTH SERVICES [137 - 429.997]
(Heading of Part 1 amended by Stats. 1980, Ch. 676.)

CHAPTER 1.3. Women's Health [137 - 138.6]
(Chapter 1.3 added by Stats. 1994, Ch. 760, Sec. 2.)
137.
(a) The State Department of Public Health shall develop a coordinated state strategy for addressing the health-related needs of women, including implementation of goals and objectives for women's health.
(b) The approved programmatic costs associated with this strategy shall be the responsibility of the State Department of Public Health unless otherwise provided by law.
(Amended by Stats. 2012, Ch. 23, Sec. 8. (AB 1467) Effective June 27, 2012.)
138.4.
(a) The State Department of Public Health shall place priority on providing information to consumers, patients, and health care providers regarding women's gynecological cancers, including signs and symptoms, risk factors, the benefits of early detection through appropriate diagnostic testing, and treatment options.
(b) In exercising the powers under this section, the State Department of Public Health shall consult with appropriate health care professionals and providers, consumers, and patients, or organizations representing them.
(c) The duties of the State Department of Public Health pursuant to this section are contingent upon the receipt of funds appropriated for this purpose.
(d) The State Department of Public Health may adopt any regulations necessary and appropriate for the implementation of this section.
(Amended by Stats. 2012, Ch. 23, Sec. 10. (AB 1467) Effective June 27, 2012.)
138.6.
(a) The State Department of Public Health shall include in any literature that it produces regarding breast cancer information that shall include, but not be limited to, all of the following:
(1) Summarized information on risk factors for breast cancer in younger women, including, but not limited to, information on the increased risk associated with a family history of the disease.

(2) Summarized information regarding detection alternatives to mammography that may be available and more effective for at-risk women between the ages of 25 and 40 years.
(3) Information on Internet Web sites of relevant organizations, government agencies, and research institutions where information on mammography alternatives may be obtained.
(b) The information required by subdivision (a) shall be produced consistent with the department's protocols and procedures regarding the production and dissemination of information on breast cancer, including, but not limited to, the following factors:
(1) Restrictions imposed by space limitation on materials currently produced and distributed by the department.
(2) Future regular production and replacement schedules.
(3) Translation standards governing the number of languages and literacy levels.
(4) The nature, content, and purpose of the material into which this new information will be incorporated.
(c) It is the intent of the Legislature that subdivisions (a) and (b) apply to information that is distributed by any branch of the department, including, but not limited to, the Cancer Detection Section and the Office of Health Equity.
(Amended by Stats. 2012, Ch. 23, Sec. 11. (AB 1467) Effective June 27, 2012.)

CHAPTER 1.5. Multicultural Health [152- 152.]

(Chapter 1.5 added by Stats. 1999, Ch. 146, Sec. 3.)
152.
(a) The State Department of Public Health Office of Health Equity shall do all of the following:
(1) Perform strategic planning to develop departmentwide plans for implementation of goals and objectives to close the gaps in health status and access to care among the state's diverse racial and ethnic communities, women, persons with disabilities, and the lesbian, gay, bisexual, transgender, queer, and questioning (LGBTQQ) communities.
(2) Conduct departmental policy analysis on specific issues related to multicultural health.
(3) Coordinate projects funded by the state that are related to improving the effectiveness of services to ethnic and racial communities, women, and the LGBTQQ communities.
(4) Identify the unnecessary duplication of services and future service needs.
(5) Communicate and disseminate information and perform a liaison function within the department and to providers of health, social, educational, and support services to racial and ethnic communities, women, persons with disabilities, and the LGBTQQ communities. The department shall consult regularly with representatives from diverse racial and ethnic communities, women, persons with disabilities, and the LGBTQQ communities, including health providers, advocates, and consumers.
(6) Perform internal staff training, an internal assessment of cultural competency, and training of health care professionals to ensure more linguistically and culturally competent care.
(7) Serve as a resource for ensuring that programs collect and keep data and information regarding ethnic and racial health statistics, including those statistics described in reports released by Healthy People 2020, and information based on sexual orientation, gender identity, and gender expression, strategies and programs that address multicultural health issues, including, but not limited to, infant and maternal mortality, cancer, cardiovascular disease, diabetes, human immunodeficiency virus (HIV), acquired immunodeficiency syndrome (AIDS), child and adult immunization, osteoporosis, menopause, and full reproductive health, asthma, unintentional and intentional injury, and obesity, as well as issues that impact the health of racial and ethnic communities, women, and the LGBTQQ communities, including substance abuse, mental health, housing, teenage pregnancy, environmental disparities, immigrant and migrant health, and health insurance and delivery systems.
(8) Encourage innovative responses by public and private entities that are attempting to address multicultural health issues.
(9) Provide technical assistance to counties, other public entities, and private entities seeking to obtain funds for initiatives in multicultural health, including identification of funding sources and assistance with writing grants.
(b) Notwithstanding Section 10231.5 of the Government Code, the State Department of Public Health shall biennially prepare and submit a report to the Legislature on the status of the activities required by this chapter. This report shall be included in the report required under paragraph (1) of subdivision (d) of Section 131019.5.
(Amended by Stats. 2012, Ch. 23, Sec. 14. (AB 1467) Effective June 27, 2012.)

CHAPTER 2. Powers and Duties [416 - 429.997]

(Chapter 2 enacted by Stats. 1939, Ch. 60.)

ARTICLE 7.5. Conservatorship and Guardianship for Developmentally Disabled Persons [416 - 416.23]
(Heading of Article 7.5 amended by Stats. 1973, Ch. 546.)
416.
The Director of Developmental Services may be appointed as either guardian or conservator of the person and estate, or person or estate, of any developmentally disabled person, who is either of the following:
(1) Eligible for the services of a regional center.

(2) A patient in any state hospital, and who was admitted or committed to such hospital from a county served by a regional center.

Any reference in this article to the Director of Health shall be deemed a reference to the Director of Developmental Services.

(Amended by Stats. 1977, Ch. 1252.)

416.1.

Unless exceptions are expressly made in this article, the provisions of Division 4 (commencing with Section 1400) of the Probate Code shall apply to guardianship and conservatorship appointments made under this article.

(Amended by Stats. 1979, Ch. 730.)

416.5.

The director may be nominated by any one of the following to act as guardian or conservator for any developmentally disabled person; (1) who is or may become eligible for the services of a regional center, or (2) who is a patient in any state hospital, and who was admitted or committed to such hospital from a county served by a regional center:

(a) A parent, relative or friend.

(b) The guardian or conservator of the person or estate, or person and estate, of the developmentally disabled person to act as his successor.

(c) The developmentally disabled person.

Such nomination shall be in writing and may provide that the authority of the director is to take effect at some date or occurrence in the future that may be fixed in the nomination. The director shall promptly accept or reject such nomination in writing. His acceptance shall be binding upon him and his successors. Any nomination to take effect in the future may be withdrawn by the nominator before its effective date.

(Amended by Stats. 1973, Ch. 546.)

416.6.

In every case in which he has agreed to do so, the director may petition for his appointment to act as conservator or guardian of the alleged developmentally disabled person and his estate or his person or estate in the superior court of the county where the main administrative office of the regional center serving such developmentally disabled person is located.

(Amended by Stats. 1973, Ch. 546.)

416.7.

If the alleged developmentally disabled person is within the state and is able to attend, he shall be present at the hearing. If he is unable to attend by reason of physical or other inability, such inability shall be evidenced by the affidavit or certificate of a duly licensed medical practitioner as provided in Section 1825 of the Probate Code. Such affidavit or certificate shall be filed no later than 10 days prior to the time of the hearing.

(Amended by Stats. 1979, Ch. 730.)

416.8.

In addition to the requirements of Division 4 (commencing with Section 1400) of the Probate Code, the court shall be provided by the regional center with a complete evaluation of the developmentally disabled person for whose protection the appointment is sought. The report shall include a current diagnosis of his physical condition prepared under the direction of a licensed medical practitioner and a report of his current mental condition and social adjustment prepared by a licensed and qualified social worker or psychologist. The evaluation report required by this section shall not be made part of the public record of the guardianship or conservatorship proceedings and shall be open to inspection only by court personnel, the person who is the subject of the proceeding, his parents, guardian or conservator, the attorneys for such parties, and such other persons as may be designated by the court. If an affidavit or certificate has been filed as provided in Section 416.7 evidencing the inability of the alleged developmentally disabled person to be present at the hearing, the psychologist or social worker who assists in preparing the report shall visit the alleged developmentally disabled person and be prepared to testify as to his present condition.

(Amended by Stats. 1979, Ch. 730.)

416.9.

The court may appoint the Director of Developmental Services as guardian or conservator of the person and estate or person or estate of a minor or adult developmentally disabled person. The preferences established in Section 1812 of the Probate Code for appointment of a conservator shall not apply. An appointment of the Director of Developmental Services as conservator shall not of itself constitute a judicial finding that the developmentally disabled person is legally incompetent. The petition for the appointment of the Director of Developmental Services as conservator of an adult developmentally disabled person may include a request that the court adjudge the developmentally disabled person to be legally incompetent or such an adjudication may be made subsequently upon a petition made, noticed, and heard by the court in the same manner as a petition for the appointment of the director as conservator. If the Director of Developmental Services is serving as the guardian of an adult developmentally disabled person on December 31, 1980, after that date such appointment shall be deemed to be the appointment of a conservator and the conservatee shall be deemed to have been adjudged to be legally incompetent.

(Amended by Stats. 1979, Ch. 730.)

416.95.

Prior to the appointment of the Director of Developmental Services as guardian or conservator of the person or estate of a minor or adult developmentally disabled person, the court shall inform the person of the nature and purpose of the guardianship or conservatorship proceedings and the effect of the proceedings on the basic rights of the person. After communicating the information to the alleged developmentally disabled person and prior to the appointment of the Director of Developmental Services as

guardian or conservator, the court shall consult with the person to determine the person's opinion concerning the appointment.

Any adult developmentally disabled person for whom guardianship or conservatorship is sought pursuant to this article shall be informed by a member or designee of the regional center and by the court of the person's right to counsel; and if the person does not have an attorney for the proceedings the court shall immediately appoint the public defender or other attorney to represent the person. The person shall pay the cost for such legal service if able.

If an affidavit or certificate has been filed, as provided in Section 416.7, evidencing the inability of the alleged developmentally disabled person to be present at the hearing, the psychologist or social worker assisting in preparing the report and who is required to visit each person as provided in Section 416.8 shall communicate such information to the person during the visit, consult the person to determine the person's opinion concerning the appointment, and be prepared to testify as to the person's opinion, if any.

(Amended by Stats. 1979, Ch. 730.)

416.10.

No appointment of both the Director of Developmental Services and a private guardian or conservator shall be made for the same person and estate, or person or estate. The Director of Developmental Services may be appointed as provided in this article to succeed an existing guardian or conservator upon the death, resignation or removal of such guardian or conservator.

(Amended by Stats. 1977, Ch. 1252.)

416.11.

No costs or fees shall be charged or received by the county clerk for the filing of any conservatorship or guardianship petition as provided in this article, or for any official services performed by him in the course of the proceeding under this article.

(Added by Stats. 1968, Ch. 1099.)

416.12.

The Director of Developmental Services shall file an official bond in no event less than twenty-five thousand dollars ($25,000), which bond shall inure to the joint benefit of the several guardianship or conservatorship estates and the State of California, and the Director of Developmental Services shall not be required to file bonds in individual cases.

(Amended by Stats. 1978, Ch. 429.)

416.13.

The appointment by the court of the Director of Developmental Services as conservator or guardian shall be by the title of his office. The authority of the Director of Developmental Services as conservator or guardian shall cease upon the termination of his term of office as such Director of Developmental Services and his authority shall vest in his successor or successors in office without further court proceedings. The Director of Developmental Services shall not resign as conservator or guardian unless his resignation is approved by the court.

(Amended by Stats. 1977, Ch. 1252.)

416.14.

The Director of Developmental Services shall:

(a) Consult with developmentally disabled persons and their families with respect to the services the director offers.

(b) Act as adviser for those developmentally disabled persons who request the director's advice and guidance or for whose benefit it is requested.

(c) Accept appointment as guardian or conservator of the person and estate, or person or estate, of those developmentally disabled persons who need the director's assistance and protection.

(Amended by Stats. 1979, Ch. 730.)

416.15.

The Director of Developmental Services, when acting as adviser, may provide advice and guidance to the developmentally disabled person without prior appointment by a court. The provision for such services shall not be dependent upon a finding of incompetency, nor shall it abrogate any civil right otherwise possessed by the developmentally disabled person.

(Amended by Stats. 1977, Ch. 1252.)

416.16.

The Director of Developmental Services shall have the same powers and duties as those established for guardians and conservators in Division 4 (commencing with Section 1400) of the Probate Code and shall succeed the State Director of Health as guardian or conservator of developmentally disabled individuals for whom the State Director of Health was appointed guardian or conservator.

(Amended by Stats. 1979, Ch. 730.)

416.17.

It is the intent of this article that the director when acting as guardian or conservator of the person of a developmentally disabled person through the regional center as provided in Section 416.19 of this article, shall maintain close contact with the developmentally disabled person no matter where such person is living in this state; shall act as a wise parent would act in caring for his developmentally disabled child; and shall permit and encourage maximum self-reliance on the part of the developmentally disabled person under his protection.

(Amended by Stats. 1973, Ch. 546.)

416.18.

The director shall provide for at least an annual review in writing of the physical, mental, and social condition of each developmentally disabled person for whom he has been appointed conservator or guardian, or for whom he is otherwise acting in his official

capacity under this article. These records shall be confidential but may be made available to persons approved by the director or the court.
(Amended by Stats. 1973, Ch. 546.)

416.19.
The services to be rendered by the director as adviser or as guardian or conservator of the person shall be performed through the regional centers or by other agencies or individuals designated by the regional centers.
(Amended by Stats. 1975, Ch. 694.)

416.20.
The director shall receive such reasonable fees for his services as guardian or conservator of the estate as the court allows and such fees shall be paid into the General Fund of the State Treasury.
(Added by Stats. 1968, Ch. 1099.)

416.23.
This article does not authorize the care, treatment, or supervision or any control over any developmentally disabled person without the written consent of his parent or guardian or conservator.
(Amended by Stats. 1979, Ch. 730.)

ARTICLE 9. Air Sanitation [425- 425.]
(Article 9 repealed and added by Stats. 1967, Ch. 1545.)

425.
The State Department of Health Services shall submit to the State Air Resources Board recommendations for ambient air quality standards reflecting the relationship between the intensity and composition of air pollution and the health, illness, irritation to the senses, and the death of human beings.
(Amended by Stats. 1977, Ch. 1252.)

ARTICLE 21. Mandated County Advisory Boards [429.997- 429.997.]
(Article 21 added by Stats. 1993, Ch. 64, Sec. 2.)

429.997.
Notwithstanding any provision of state law, and unless prohibited by federal law, a county may eliminate or consolidate any health advisory boards that are required by state law or regulation, or in any existing contract with the department. Where advisory boards are required only by contract between the department and a county, that contract shall be amended by the department, upon written request of the county, to remove a requirement for an advisory board from the contract.
(Added by Stats. 1993, Ch. 64, Sec. 2. Effective June 30, 1993.)

PART 1.5. Office of the Surgeon General [438 - 439]
(Part 1.5 added by Stats. 2019, Ch. 38, Sec. 12.)

438.
The Office of the Surgeon General is hereby established within the California Health and Human Services Agency. The office shall be responsible for all of the following:
(a) Raising public awareness on and coordinating policies governing scientific screening and treatment for toxic stress and adverse childhood events.
(b) Advising the Governor, the Secretary of the California Health and Human Services Agency, and policymakers on a comprehensive approach to address health issues and challenges, including toxic stress and adverse childhood events, as effectively and early as possible.
(c) Marshalling the insights and energy of medical professionals, scientists, and other academic experts, public health experts, public servants, and everyday Californians to solve our most pressing health challenges, including toxic stress and adverse childhood events.
(Added by Stats. 2019, Ch. 38, Sec. 12. (SB 78) Effective June 27, 2019.)

439.
(a) The Surgeon General shall be appointed by the Governor and shall be the director of the Office of the Surgeon General.
(b) On and after July 1, 2019, the appointment of the Surgeon General shall be subject to confirmation by the Senate.
(c) The salary of the Surgeon General shall be fixed in accordance with state law.
(Added by Stats. 2019, Ch. 38, Sec. 12. (SB 78) Effective June 27, 2019.)

PART 1.6. HEALTH RESEARCH FAIRNESS [439.900 - 439.906]
(Part 1.6 added by Stats. 1991, Ch. 792, Sec. 1.)

439.900.
This act shall be known and may be cited as the Health Research Fairness Act.
(Added by Stats. 1991, Ch. 792, Sec. 1.)

439.901.
The Legislature finds and declares all of the following:
(a) The National Institutes of Health (NIH), the nation's major source of funding for medical research conducted in the United States, spends approximately 13 percent of its budget for research on conditions and diseases that are primarily women's health issues. Although it is true that the great majority of the NIH research funds are expended for studies of diseases that affect both men and women, or for fundamental research that has significance for diseases affecting all segments of our population, women have not been adequately represented in research populations in major NIH-funded studies of diseases which affect both men and women.
(b) Today many medical treatments currently used on women are based on studies conducted entirely on men. For example, although cardiovascular illness is the number one cause of death and disability in American women, women have consistently been excluded from major research studies in this area.
(c) It is estimated that 175,000 American women will develop breast cancer, and 44,000 women will die from the disease this year. Currently, one in nine women born in the United States will develop breast cancer in her lifetime.
(d) Women constitute 11 percent of all reported AIDS cases. Eighty percent of all HIV-infected women are women of color.
(e) Osteoporosis, a condition characterized by excessive loss of bone tissue, affects an estimated 24 million Americans and results annually in an estimated $10 billion in direct medical costs. The cost of this disease will continue to escalate as the population ages and the incidence of osteoporosis increases. If current trends continue, the cost of osteoporosis treatment could be as much as $62 billion by the year 2020.
(f) Eighty percent of individuals affected by osteoporosis are women. One-half of all women over age 45 years, and 90 percent of all women over age 75 years, suffer from osteoporosis.
(g) Nearly one million couples seek medical advice or treatment for infertility. In the last 20 years, the number of infertility-related visits to doctors has nearly quadrupled. The risk of infertility is one and one-half times greater for blacks than for whites.
(h) Despite these facts, women's health issues—which are defined as diseases or conditions that are unique to women, are more prevalent or more serious in women, or for which specific risk factors or interventions differ for women—have received insufficient attention both in terms of funding and research.
(i) The best way to treat women's health problems is to prevent them from occurring, or to catch them in their earliest stages when they are most treatable. Without research into the causes and cures of diseases affecting women, these diseases cannot be effectively treated.
(j) On August 24, 1990, the NIH published a revised, strengthened "NIH/ADHMA Policy Concerning Inclusion of Women in Study Populations." That policy clearly stated that adequate numbers of women must be included in NIH-funded clinical studies, in proportion to the prevalence of the condition under study, unless an appropriate justification is provided. The revised policy also states that NIH will not fund grants that do not comply with its provisions.
(k) The majority of biomedical research funded by, or based at, the University of California is fundamental research that investigates basic life processes and disease mechanisms, often at the cellular or molecular level, and that yields benefits for all segments of our population.
(Added by Stats. 1991, Ch. 792, Sec. 1.)

439.902.
(a) On or before June 30, 1992, state agencies shall adopt, and it is the intent of the Legislature that the Regents of the University of California adopt, policies based on the publication "NIH/ADHMA Policy Concerning Inclusion of Women in Study Populations," so that women and members of minority groups are appropriately included as subjects of health research projects carried out by state agencies or University of California researchers. The review of research proposals funded by state agencies or the University of California should include consideration of the appropriateness of the composition of research populations.
(b) On or before September 30, 1992, state agencies and the University of California shall transmit to the Legislature copies of the policies adopted pursuant to this section, along with copies of the specific procedures put in place to carry out those policies.
(Added by Stats. 1991, Ch. 792, Sec. 1.)

439.903.
State agencies shall, and it is the intent of the Legislature that the University of California:
(a) Provide special opportunities for funding research projects devoted to diseases, disorders, or other health conditions of particular concern to women and minorities, or in health research areas in which women and minorities have been traditionally underrepresented.
(b) At the same time, ensure that funding will enable researchers to adapt to changing population distribution of diseases.
(Added by Stats. 1991, Ch. 792, Sec. 1.)

439.904.
(a) State agencies and the University of California shall report, consistent with available data, on the extent to which state funds administered by those agencies and the University of California are used to support research on diseases, disorders, or other health conditions that meet one or more of the following criteria, as determined by the state agency or the University of California:
(1) Are unique to women or minorities, more prevalent in women or minorities, or more serious for women or minorities.
(2) For which the risk factors or interventions are different for women or minorities.
(b) On or before June 30, 1992, state agencies and the University of California shall adopt procedures for collecting and classifying data on the extent to which state-funded research projects address medical issues of particular concern to women and minorities. On and after June 30, 1993, information concerning the extent to which research supported by particular programs of state agencies and the University of California addresses medical issues of particular concern to women and minorities shall be incorporated into the appropriate periodic program reports required under existing law.
(Added by Stats. 1991, Ch. 792, Sec. 1.)

439.905.

It is the intent of the Legislature to encourage research on the effectiveness of RU-486 (mifepristone) in treating breast and ovarian cancer, meningioma, endometriosis, Cushing's syndrome, osteoporosis, diabetes, and AIDS.

(Added by Stats. 1991, Ch. 792, Sec. 1.)

439.906.

For purposes of this part, "state agency" has the same meaning as defined in Section 11000 of the Government Code.

(Added by Stats. 1991, Ch. 792, Sec. 1.)

[PART 1.7. HEALTH FACILITIES DISCLOSURE ACT] [440.10 - 440.50]

(Heading of Part 1.7 amended by Stats. 1974, Ch. 1171.)

440.10.

"Health facility," as used in this chapter, means any general acute care hospital required to be licensed pursuant to Chapter 2 (commencing with Section 1250) of Division 2.

(Added by Stats. 1993, Ch. 1049, Sec. 1. Effective January 1, 1994.)

440.20.

Within seven days after completion of the patient's itemized bill, every health facility shall provide to the primary attending health care practitioner a copy, upon written request specifying the individual patient, of the complete itemized charges for services rendered by the health facility to the health care practitioner's patient when the primary attending health care practitioner is not employed by the health facility nor is a member of an integrated group practice that provided the health facility services.

(Added by Stats. 1993, Ch. 1049, Sec. 2. Effective January 1, 1994.)

440.30.

The primary attending health care practitioner's written request to the health facility shall specify the records to be copied pursuant to Section 440.20 and shall include a fee to defray the cost of copying, not to exceed twenty-five cents ($0.25) per page, plus any reasonable costs of clerical services incurred in locating and making the records available.

(Added by Stats. 1993, Ch. 1049, Sec. 3. Effective January 1, 1994.)

440.40.

The primary attending health care practitioner shall obtain prior written consent from each patient for whom a billing is requested, authorizing the release of the patient's billing. A copy of this signed patient consent form shall be forwarded to the health care facility as part of the written request for itemized billings.

(Added by Stats. 1993, Ch. 1049, Sec. 4. Effective January 1, 1994.)

440.50.

No information, other than the itemized billing set forth in Section 440.20, that is prohibited from being released by any other provision of law shall be made available pursuant to Section 440.20.

(Added by Stats. 1993, Ch. 1049, Sec. 5. Effective January 1, 1994.)

PART 1.8. END-OF-LIFE CARE [442 - 442.7]

(Part 1.8 added by Stats. 2008, Ch. 683, Sec. 2.)

442.

For the purposes of this part, the following definitions shall apply:

(a) "Actively dying" means the phase of terminal illness when death is imminent.

(b) "Disease-targeted treatment" means treatment directed at the underlying disease or condition that is intended to alter its natural history or progression, irrespective of whether or not a cure is a possibility.

(c) "Health care provider" means an attending physician and surgeon. It also means a nurse practitioner or physician assistant practicing in accordance with standardized procedures or protocols developed and approved by the supervising physician and surgeon and the nurse practitioner or physician assistant.

(d) "Hospice" means a specialized form of interdisciplinary health care that is designed to provide palliative care, alleviate the physical, emotional, social, and spiritual discomforts of an individual who is experiencing the last phases of life due to the existence of a terminal disease, and provide supportive care to the primary caregiver and the family of the hospice patient, and that meets all of the criteria specified in subdivision (b) of Section 1746.

(e) "Palliative care" means medical treatment, interdisciplinary care, or consultation provided to a patient or family members, or both, that has as its primary purpose the prevention of, or relief from, suffering and the enhancement of the quality of life, rather than treatment aimed at investigation and intervention for the purpose of cure or prolongation of life as described in subdivision (b) of Section 1339.31. In some cases, disease-targeted treatment may be used in palliative care.

(f) "Refusal or withdrawal of life-sustaining treatment" means forgoing treatment or medical procedures that replace or support an essential bodily function, including, but not limited to, cardiopulmonary resuscitation, mechanical ventilation, artificial nutrition and hydration, dialysis, and any other treatment or discontinuing any or all of those treatments after they have been used for a reasonable time.

(Added by Stats. 2008, Ch. 683, Sec. 2. Effective January 1, 2009.)

442.5.

(a) When a health care provider makes a diagnosis that a patient has a terminal illness, the health care provider shall do both of the following:

(1) Notify the patient of his or her right, or, when applicable, the right of another person authorized to make health care decisions for the patient, to comprehensive information and counseling regarding legal end-of-life options. This notification may be provided at the time of diagnosis or at a subsequent visit in which the provider discusses treatment options with the patient or the other authorized person.

(2) Upon the request of the patient or another person authorized to make health care decisions for the patient, provide the patient or other authorized person with comprehensive information and counseling regarding legal end-of-life care options pursuant to this section. When a terminally ill patient is in a health facility, as defined in Section 1250, the health care provider, or medical director of the health facility if the patient's health care provider is not available, may refer the patient or other authorized person to a hospice provider or private or public agencies and community-based organizations that specialize in end-of-life care case management and consultation to receive comprehensive information and counseling regarding legal end-of-life care options.

(b) If a patient or another person authorized to make health care decisions for the patient, requests information and counseling pursuant to paragraph (2) of subdivision (a), the comprehensive information shall include, but not be limited to, the following:

(1) Hospice care at home or in a health care setting.

(2) A prognosis with and without the continuation of disease-targeted treatment.

(3) The patient's right to refusal of or withdrawal from life-sustaining treatment.

(4) The patient's right to continue to pursue disease-targeted treatment, with or without concurrent palliative care.

(5) The patient's right to comprehensive pain and symptom management at the end of life, including, but not limited to, adequate pain medication, treatment of nausea, palliative chemotherapy, relief of shortness of breath and fatigue, and other clinical treatments useful when a patient is actively dying.

(6) The patient's right to give individual health care instruction pursuant to Section 4670 of the Probate Code, which provides the means by which a patient may provide written health care instruction, such as an advance health care directive, and the patient's right to appoint a legally recognized health care decisionmaker.

(c) The information described in subdivision (b) may, but is not required to, be in writing. Health care providers may utilize information from organizations specializing in end-of-life care that provide information on factsheets and Internet Web sites to convey the information described in subdivision (b).

(d) Counseling may include, but is not limited to, discussions about the outcomes for the patient and his or her family, based on the interest of the patient. Information and counseling, as described in subdivision (b), may occur over a series of meetings with the health care provider or others who may be providing the information and counseling based on the patient's needs.

(e) The information and counseling sessions may include a discussion of treatment options in a culturally sensitive manner that the patient and his or her family, or, when applicable, another person authorized to make health care decisions for the patient, can easily understand. If the patient or other authorized person requests information on the costs of treatment options, including the availability of insurance and eligibility of the patient for coverage, the patient or other authorized person shall be referred to the appropriate entity for that information.

(f) The notification made pursuant to paragraph (1) of subdivision (a) shall not be required if the patient or other person authorized to make health care decisions, as defined in Section 4617 of the Probate Code, for the patient has already received the notification.

(g) For purposes of this section, "health care decisions" has the meaning set forth in Section 4617 of the Probate Code.

(h) This section shall not be construed to interfere with the clinical judgment of a health care provider in recommending the course of treatment.

(Amended by Stats. 2015, Ch. 303, Sec. 245. (AB 731) Effective January 1, 2016.)

442.7.

If a health care provider does not wish to comply with his or her patient's request or, when applicable, the request of another person authorized to make health care decisions, as defined in Section 4617 of the Probate Code, for the patient for information on end-of-life options, the health care provider shall do both of the following:

(a) Refer or transfer a patient to another health care provider that shall provide the requested information.

(b) Provide the patient or other person authorized to make health care decisions for the patient with information on procedures to transfer to another health care provider that shall provide the requested information.

(Amended by Stats. 2014, Ch. 568, Sec. 2. (AB 2139) Effective January 1, 2015.)

PART 1.85. End of Life Option Act [443 - 443.22]

(Part 1.85 added by Stats. 2015, 2nd Ex. Sess., Ch. 1, Sec. 1.)

443.

This part shall be known and may be cited as the End of Life Option Act.

(Added by Stats. 2015, 2nd Ex. Sess., Ch. 1, Sec. 1. (AB 15 2x) Effective June 9, 2016. Repealed as of January 1, 2026, pursuant to Section 443.215.)

443.1.

As used in this part, the following definitions shall apply:

(a) "Adult" means an individual 18 years of age or older.

(b) "Aid-in-dying drug" means a drug determined and prescribed by a physician for a qualified individual, which the qualified individual may choose to self-administer to bring about his or her death due to a terminal disease.

(c) "Attending physician" means the physician who has primary responsibility for the health care of an individual and treatment of the individual's terminal disease.

(d) "Attending physician checklist and compliance form" means a form, as described in Section 443.22, identifying each and every requirement that must be fulfilled by an attending physician to be in good faith compliance with this part should the attending physician choose to participate.

(e) "Capacity to make medical decisions" means that, in the opinion of an individual's attending physician, consulting physician, psychiatrist, or psychologist, pursuant to Section 4609 of the Probate Code, the individual has the ability to understand the nature and consequences of a health care decision, the ability to understand its significant benefits, risks, and alternatives, and the ability to make and communicate an informed decision to health care providers.

(f) "Consulting physician" means a physician who is independent from the attending physician and who is qualified by specialty or experience to make a professional diagnosis and prognosis regarding an individual's terminal disease.

(g) "Department" means the State Department of Public Health.

(h) "Health care provider" or "provider of health care" means any person licensed or certified pursuant to Division 2 (commencing with Section 500) of the Business and Professions Code; any person licensed pursuant to the Osteopathic Initiative Act or the Chiropractic Initiative Act; any person certified pursuant to Division 2.5 (commencing with Section 1797) of this code; and any clinic, health dispensary, or health facility licensed pursuant to Division 2 (commencing with Section 1200) of this code.

(i) "Informed decision" means a decision by an individual with a terminal disease to request and obtain a prescription for a drug that the individual may self-administer to end the individual's life, that is based on an understanding and acknowledgment of the relevant facts, and that is made after being fully informed by the attending physician of all of the following:

(1) The individual's medical diagnosis and prognosis.

(2) The potential risks associated with taking the drug to be prescribed.

(3) The probable result of taking the drug to be prescribed.

(4) The possibility that the individual may choose not to obtain the drug or may obtain the drug but may decide not to ingest it.

(5) The feasible alternatives or additional treatment opportunities, including, but not limited to, comfort care, hospice care, palliative care, and pain control.

(j) "Medically confirmed" means the medical diagnosis and prognosis of the attending physician has been confirmed by a consulting physician who has examined the individual and the individual's relevant medical records.

(k) "Mental health specialist assessment" means one or more consultations between an individual and a mental health specialist for the purpose of determining that the individual has the capacity to make medical decisions and is not suffering from impaired judgment due to a mental disorder.

(l) "Mental health specialist" means a psychiatrist or a licensed psychologist.

(m) "Physician" means a doctor of medicine or osteopathy currently licensed to practice medicine in this state.

(n) "Public place" means any street, alley, park, public building, any place of business or assembly open to or frequented by the public, and any other place that is open to the public view, or to which the public has access.

(o) "Qualified individual" means an adult who has the capacity to make medical decisions, is a resident of California, and has satisfied the requirements of this part in order to obtain a prescription for a drug to end his or her life.

(p) "Self-administer" means a qualified individual's affirmative, conscious, and physical act of administering and ingesting the aid-in-dying drug to bring about his or her own death.

(q) "Terminal disease" means an incurable and irreversible disease that has been medically confirmed and will, within reasonable medical judgment, result in death within six months.

(Added by Stats. 2015, 2nd Ex. Sess., Ch. 1, Sec. 1. (AB 15 2x) Effective June 9, 2016. Repealed as of January 1, 2026, pursuant to Section 443.215.)

443.2.

(a) An individual who is an adult with the capacity to make medical decisions and with a terminal disease may make a request to receive a prescription for an aid-in-dying drug if all of the following conditions are satisfied:

(1) The individual's attending physician has diagnosed the individual with a terminal disease.

(2) The individual has voluntarily expressed the wish to receive a prescription for an aid-in-dying drug.

(3) The individual is a resident of California and is able to establish residency through any of the following means:

(A) Possession of a California driver's license or other identification issued by the State of California.

(B) Registration to vote in California.

(C) Evidence that the person owns or leases property in California.

(D) Filing of a California tax return for the most recent tax year.

(4) The individual documents his or her request pursuant to the requirements set forth in Section 443.3.

(5) The individual has the physical and mental ability to self-administer the aid-in-dying drug.

(b) A person shall not be considered a "qualified individual" under the provisions of this part solely because of age or disability.

(c) A request for a prescription for an aid-in-dying drug under this part shall be made solely and directly by the individual diagnosed with the terminal disease and shall not be made on behalf of the patient, including, but not limited to, through a power of attorney, an advance health care directive, a conservator, health care agent, surrogate, or any other legally recognized health care decisionmaker.

(Amended by Stats. 2017, Ch. 561, Sec. 99. (AB 1516) Effective January 1, 2018. Repealed as of January 1, 2026, pursuant to Section 443.215.)

443.3.

(a) An individual seeking to obtain a prescription for an aid-in-dying drug pursuant to this part shall submit two oral requests, a minimum of 15 days apart, and a written request to his or her attending physician. The attending physician shall directly, and not through a designee, receive all three requests required pursuant to this section.

(b) A valid written request for an aid-in-dying drug under subdivision (a) shall meet all of the following conditions:

(1) The request shall be in the form described in Section 443.11.

(2) The request shall be signed and dated, in the presence of two witnesses, by the individual seeking the aid-in-dying drug.

(3) The request shall be witnessed by at least two other adult persons who, in the presence of the individual, shall attest that to the best of their knowledge and belief the individual is all of the following:

(A) An individual who is personally known to them or has provided proof of identity.

(B) An individual who voluntarily signed this request in their presence.

(C) An individual whom they believe to be of sound mind and not under duress, fraud, or undue influence.

(D) Not an individual for whom either of them is the attending physician, consulting physician, or mental health specialist.

(c) Only one of the two witnesses at the time the written request is signed may:

(1) Be related to the qualified individual by blood, marriage, registered domestic partnership, or adoption or be entitled to a portion of the individual's estate upon death.

(2) Own, operate, or be employed at a health care facility where the individual is receiving medical treatment or resides.

(d) The attending physician, consulting physician, or mental health specialist of the individual shall not be one of the witnesses required pursuant to paragraph (3) of subdivision (b).

(Added by Stats. 2015, 2nd Ex. Sess., Ch. 1, Sec. 1. (AB 15 2x) Effective June 9, 2016. Repealed as of January 1, 2026, pursuant to Section 443.215.)

443.4.

(a) An individual may at any time withdraw or rescind his or her request for an aid-in-dying drug, or decide not to ingest an aid-in-dying drug, without regard to the individual's mental state.

(b) A prescription for an aid-in-dying drug provided under this part may not be written without the attending physician directly, and not through a designee, offering the individual an opportunity to withdraw or rescind the request.

(Added by Stats. 2015, 2nd Ex. Sess., Ch. 1, Sec. 1. (AB 15 2x) Effective June 9, 2016. Repealed as of January 1, 2026, pursuant to Section 443.215.)

443.5.

(a) Before prescribing an aid-in-dying drug, the attending physician shall do all of the following:

(1) Make the initial determination of all of the following:

(A) (i) Whether the requesting adult has the capacity to make medical decisions.

(ii) If there are indications of a mental disorder, the physician shall refer the individual for a mental health specialist assessment.

(iii) If a mental health specialist assessment referral is made, no aid-in-dying drugs shall be prescribed until the mental health specialist determines that the individual has the capacity to make medical decisions and is not suffering from impaired judgment due to a mental disorder.

(B) Whether the requesting adult has a terminal disease.

(C) Whether the requesting adult has voluntarily made the request for an aid-in-dying drug pursuant to Sections 443.2 and 443.3.

(D) Whether the requesting adult is a qualified individual pursuant to subdivision (o) of Section 443.1.

(2) Confirm that the individual is making an informed decision by discussing with him or her all of the following:

(A) His or her medical diagnosis and prognosis.

(B) The potential risks associated with ingesting the requested aid-in-dying drug.

(C) The probable result of ingesting the aid-in-dying drug.

(D) The possibility that he or she may choose to obtain the aid-in-dying drug but not take it.

(E) The feasible alternatives or additional treatment options, including, but not limited to, comfort care, hospice care, palliative care, and pain control.

(3) Refer the individual to a consulting physician for medical confirmation of the diagnosis and prognosis, and for a determination that the individual has the capacity to make medical decisions and has complied with the provisions of this part.

(4) Confirm that the qualified individual's request does not arise from coercion or undue influence by another person by discussing with the qualified individual, outside of the presence of any other persons, except for an interpreter as required pursuant to this part, whether or not the qualified individual is feeling coerced or unduly influenced by another person.

(5) Counsel the qualified individual about the importance of all of the following:

(A) Having another person present when he or she ingests the aid-in-dying drug prescribed pursuant to this part.

(B) Not ingesting the aid-in-dying drug in a public place.

(C) Notifying the next of kin of his or her request for an aid-in-dying drug. A qualified individual who declines or is unable to notify next of kin shall not have his or her request denied for that reason.

(D) Participating in a hospice program.

(E) Maintaining the aid-in-dying drug in a safe and secure location until the time that the qualified individual will ingest it.

(6) Inform the individual that he or she may withdraw or rescind the request for an aid-in-dying drug at any time and in any manner.

(7) Offer the individual an opportunity to withdraw or rescind the request for an aid-in-dying drug before prescribing the aid-in-dying drug.

(8) Verify, immediately before writing the prescription for an aid-in-dying drug, that the qualified individual is making an informed decision.

(9) Confirm that all requirements are met and all appropriate steps are carried out in accordance with this part before writing a prescription for an aid-in-dying drug.

(10) Fulfill the record documentation required under Sections 443.8 and 443.19.

(11) Complete the attending physician checklist and compliance form, as described in Section 443.22, include it and the consulting physician compliance form in the individual's medical record, and submit both forms to the State Department of Public Health.

(12) Give the qualified individual the final attestation form, with the instruction that the form be filled out and executed by the qualified individual within 48 hours prior to the qualified individual choosing to self-administer the aid-in-dying drug.

(b) If the conditions set forth in subdivision (a) are satisfied, the attending physician may deliver the aid-in-dying drug in any of the following ways:

(1) Dispensing the aid-in-dying drug directly, including ancillary medication intended to minimize the qualified individual's discomfort, if the attending physician meets all of the following criteria:

(A) Is authorized to dispense medicine under California law.

(B) Has a current United States Drug Enforcement Administration (USDEA) certificate.

(C) Complies with any applicable administrative rule or regulation.

(2) With the qualified individual's written consent, contacting a pharmacist, informing the pharmacist of the prescriptions, and delivering the written prescriptions personally, by mail, or electronically to the pharmacist, who may dispense the drug to the qualified individual, the attending physician, or a person expressly designated by the qualified individual and with the designation delivered to the pharmacist in writing or verbally.

(c) Delivery of the dispensed drug to the qualified individual, the attending physician, or a person expressly designated by the qualified individual may be made by personal delivery, or, with a signature required on delivery, by United Parcel Service, United States Postal Service, Federal Express, or by messenger service.

(Added by Stats. 2015, 2nd Ex. Sess., Ch. 1, Sec. 1. (AB 15 2x) Effective June 9, 2016. Repealed as of January 1, 2026, pursuant to Section 443.215.)

443.6.

Before a qualified individual obtains an aid-in-dying drug from the attending physician, the consulting physician shall perform all of the following:

(a) Examine the individual and his or her relevant medical records.

(b) Confirm in writing the attending physician's diagnosis and prognosis.

(c) Determine that the individual has the capacity to make medical decisions, is acting voluntarily, and has made an informed decision.

(d) If there are indications of a mental disorder, refer the individual for a mental health specialist assessment.

(e) Fulfill the record documentation required under this part.

(f) Submit the compliance form to the attending physician.

(Added by Stats. 2015, 2nd Ex. Sess., Ch. 1, Sec. 1. (AB 15 2x) Effective June 9, 2016. Repealed as of January 1, 2026, pursuant to Section 443.215.)

443.7.

Upon referral from the attending or consulting physician pursuant to this part, the mental health specialist shall:

(a) Examine the qualified individual and his or her relevant medical records.

(b) Determine that the individual has the mental capacity to make medical decisions, act voluntarily, and make an informed decision.

(c) Determine that the individual is not suffering from impaired judgment due to a mental disorder.

(d) Fulfill the record documentation requirements of this part.

(Added by Stats. 2015, 2nd Ex. Sess., Ch. 1, Sec. 1. (AB 15 2x) Effective June 9, 2016. Repealed as of January 1, 2026, pursuant to Section 443.215.)

443.8.

All of the following shall be documented in the individual's medical record:

(a) All oral requests for aid-in-dying drugs.

(b) All written requests for aid-in-dying drugs.

(c) The attending physician's diagnosis and prognosis, and the determination that a qualified individual has the capacity to make medical decisions, is acting voluntarily, and has made an informed decision, or that the attending physician has determined that the individual is not a qualified individual.

(d) The consulting physician's diagnosis and prognosis, and verification that the qualified individual has the capacity to make medical decisions, is acting voluntarily, and has made an informed decision, or that the consulting physician has determined that the individual is not a qualified individual.

(e) A report of the outcome and determinations made during a mental health specialist's assessment, if performed.

(f) The attending physician's offer to the qualified individual to withdraw or rescind his or her request at the time of the individual's second oral request.

(g) A note by the attending physician indicating that all requirements under Sections 443.5 and 443.6 have been met and indicating the steps taken to carry out the request, including a notation of the aid-in-dying drug prescribed.

(Added by Stats. 2015, 2nd Ex. Sess., Ch. 1, Sec. 1. (AB 15 2x) Effective June 9, 2016. Repealed as of January 1, 2026, pursuant to Section 443.215.)

443.9.

(a) Within 30 calendar days of writing a prescription for an aid-in-dying drug, the attending physician shall submit to the State Department of Public Health a copy of the qualifying patient's written request, the attending physician checklist and compliance form, and the consulting physician compliance form.

(b) Within 30 calendar days following the qualified individual's death from ingesting the aid-in-dying drug, or any other cause, the attending physician shall submit the attending physician followup form to the State Department of Public Health.

(Added by Stats. 2015, 2nd Ex. Sess., Ch. 1, Sec. 1. (AB 15 2x) Effective June 9, 2016. Repealed as of January 1, 2026, pursuant to Section 443.215.)

443.10.

A qualified individual may not receive a prescription for an aid-in-dying drug pursuant to this part unless he or she has made an informed decision. Immediately before writing a prescription for an aid-in-dying drug under this part, the attending physician shall verify that the individual is making an informed decision.

(Added by Stats. 2015, 2nd Ex. Sess., Ch. 1, Sec. 1. (AB 15 2x) Effective June 9, 2016. Repealed as of January 1, 2026, pursuant to Section 443.215.)

443.11.

(a) A request for an aid-in-dying drug as authorized by this part shall be in the following form:

REQUEST FOR AN AID-IN-DYING DRUG TO END MY LIFE IN A HUMANE AND DIGNIFIED MANNER I, ..., am an adult of sound mind and a resident of the State of California.

I am suffering from ...., which my attending physician has determined is in its terminal phase and which has been medically confirmed.

I have been fully informed of my diagnosis and prognosis, the nature of the aid-in-dying drug to be prescribed and potential associated risks, the expected result, and the feasible alternatives or additional treatment options, including comfort care, hospice care, palliative care, and pain control.

I request that my attending physician prescribe an aid-in-dying drug that will end my life in a humane and dignified manner if I choose to take it, and I authorize my attending physician to contact any pharmacist about my request.

INITIAL ONE:

.... I have informed one or more members of my family of my decision and taken their opinions into consideration.

.... I have decided not to inform my family of my decision.

.... I have no family to inform of my decision.

I understand that I have the right to withdraw or rescind this request at any time.

I understand the full import of this request and I expect to die if I take the aid-in-dying drug to be prescribed. My attending physician has counseled me about the possibility that my death may not be immediately upon the consumption of the drug.

I make this request voluntarily, without reservation, and without being coerced.

Signed:..

Dated:..

DECLARATION OF WITNESSES

We declare that the person signing this request:

(a) is personally known to us or has provided proof of identity;

(b) voluntarily signed this request in our presence;

(c) is an individual whom we believe to be of sound mind and not under duress, fraud, or undue influence; and

(d) is not an individual for whom either of us is the attending physician, consulting physician, or mental health specialist.

..........................Witness 1/Date

..........................Witness 2/Date

NOTE: Only one of the two witnesses may be a relative (by blood, marriage, registered domestic partnership, or adoption) of the person signing this request or be entitled to a portion of the person's estate upon death. Only one of the two witnesses may own, operate, or be employed at a health care facility where the person is a patient or resident.

(b) (1) The written language of the request shall be written in the same translated language as any conversations, consultations, or interpreted conversations or consultations between a patient and his or her attending or consulting physicians.
(2) Notwithstanding paragraph (1), the written request may be prepared in English even when the conversations or consultations or interpreted conversations or consultations were conducted in a language other than English if the English language form includes an attached interpreter's declaration that is signed under penalty of perjury. The interpreter's declaration shall state words to the effect that:

I, (INSERT NAME OF INTERPRETER), am fluent in English and (INSERT TARGET LANGUAGE).

On (insert date) at approximately (insert time), I read the "Request for an Aid-In-Dying Drug to End My Life" to (insert name of individual/patient) in (insert target language).

Mr./Ms. (insert name of patient/qualified individual) affirmed to me that he/she understood the content of this form and affirmed his/her desire to sign this form under his/her own power and volition and that the request to sign the form followed consultations with an attending and consulting physician.

I declare that I am fluent in English and (insert target language) and further declare under penalty of perjury that the foregoing is true and correct.

Executed at (insert city, county, and state) on this (insert day of month) of (insert month), (insert year).

X_____Interpreter signature

X_____Interpreter printed name

X_____Interpreter address

(3) An interpreter whose services are provided pursuant to paragraph (2) shall not be related to the qualified individual by blood, marriage, registered domestic partnership, or adoption or be entitled to a portion of the person's estate upon death. An interpreter whose services are provided pursuant to paragraph (2) shall meet the standards promulgated by the California Healthcare Interpreting Association or the National Council on Interpreting in Health Care or other standards deemed acceptable by the department for health care providers in California.
(c) The final attestation form given by the attending physician to the qualified individual at the time the attending physician writes the prescription shall appear in the following form:

FINAL ATTESTATION FOR AN AID-IN-DYING DRUG TO END MY LIFE IN A HUMANE AND DIGNIFIED MANNER I, ..., am an adult of sound mind and a resident of the State of California.

I am suffering from ...., which my attending physician has determined is in its terminal phase and which has been medically confirmed.

I have been fully informed of my diagnosis and prognosis, the nature of the aid-in-dying drug to be prescribed and potential associated risks, the expected result, and the feasible alternatives or additional treatment options, including comfort care, hospice care, palliative care, and pain control.

I have received the aid-in-dying drug and am fully aware that this aid-in-dying drug will end my life in a humane and dignified manner.

INITIAL ONE:

.... I have informed one or more members of my family of my decision and taken their opinions into consideration.

.... I have decided not to inform my family of my decision.

.... I have no family to inform of my decision.

My attending physician has counseled me about the possibility that my death may not be immediately upon the consumption of the drug.

I make this decision to ingest the aid-in-dying drug to end my life in a humane and dignified manner. I understand I still may choose not to ingest the drug and by signing this form I am under no obligation to ingest the drug. I understand I may rescind this request at any time.

Signed:...

Dated:...

Time:...

(1) Within 48 hours prior to the individual self-administering the aid-in-dying drug, the individual shall complete the final attestation form. If aid-in-dying medication is not returned or relinquished upon the patient's death as required in Section 443.20, the completed form shall be delivered by the individual's health care provider, family member, or other representative to the attending physician to be included in the patient's medical record.
(2) Upon receiving the final attestation form the attending physician shall add this form to the medical records of the qualified individual.
(Added by Stats. 2015, 2nd Ex. Sess., Ch. 1, Sec. 1. (AB 15 2x) Effective June 9, 2016. Repealed as of January 1, 2026, pursuant to Section 443.215.)
443.12.
(a) A provision in a contract, will, or other agreement executed on or after January 1, 2016, whether written or oral, to the extent the provision would affect whether a person may make, withdraw, or rescind a request for an aid-in-dying drug is not valid.
(b) An obligation owing under any contract executed on or after January 1, 2016, may not be conditioned or affected by a qualified individual making, withdrawing, or rescinding a request for an aid-in-dying drug.
(Added by Stats. 2015, 2nd Ex. Sess., Ch. 1, Sec. 1. (AB 15 2x) Effective June 9, 2016. Repealed as of January 1, 2026, pursuant to Section 443.215.)
443.13.

(a) (1) The sale, procurement, or issuance of a life, health, or annuity policy, health care service plan contract, or health benefit plan, or the rate charged for a policy or plan contract may not be conditioned upon or affected by a person making or rescinding a request for an aid-in-dying drug.

(2) Pursuant to Section 443.18, death resulting from the self-administration of an aid-in-dying drug is not suicide, and therefore health and insurance coverage shall not be exempted on that basis.

(b) Notwithstanding any other law, a qualified individual's act of self-administering an aid-in-dying drug shall not have an effect upon a life, health, or annuity policy other than that of a natural death from the underlying disease.

(c) An insurance carrier shall not provide any information in communications made to an individual about the availability of an aid-in-dying drug absent a request by the individual or his or her attending physician at the behest of the individual. Any communication shall not include both the denial of treatment and information as to the availability of aid-in-dying drug coverage. For the purposes of this subdivision, "insurance carrier" means a health care service plan as defined in Section 1345 of this code or a carrier of health insurance as defined in Section 106 of the Insurance Code.

(Added by Stats. 2015, 2nd Ex. Sess., Ch. 1, Sec. 1. (AB 15 2x) Effective June 9, 2016. Repealed as of January 1, 2026, pursuant to Section 443.215.)

443.14.

(a) Notwithstanding any other law, a person shall not be subject to civil or criminal liability solely because the person was present when the qualified individual self-administers the prescribed aid-in-dying drug. A person who is present may, without civil or criminal liability, assist the qualified individual by preparing the aid-in-dying drug so long as the person does not assist the qualified person in ingesting the aid-in-dying drug.

(b) A health care provider or professional organization or association shall not subject an individual to censure, discipline, suspension, loss of license, loss of privileges, loss of membership, or other penalty for participating in good faith compliance with this part or for refusing to participate in accordance with subdivision (e).

(c) Notwithstanding any other law, a health care provider shall not be subject to civil, criminal, administrative, disciplinary, employment, credentialing, professional discipline, contractual liability, or medical staff action, sanction, or penalty or other liability for participating in this part, including, but not limited to, determining the diagnosis or prognosis of an individual, determining the capacity of an individual for purposes of qualifying for the act, providing information to an individual regarding this part, and providing a referral to a physician who participates in this part. Nothing in this subdivision shall be construed to limit the application of, or provide immunity from, Section 443.16 or 443.17.

(d) (1) A request by a qualified individual to an attending physician to provide an aid-in-dying drug in good faith compliance with the provisions of this part shall not provide the sole basis for the appointment of a guardian or conservator.

(2) No actions taken in compliance with the provisions of this part shall constitute or provide the basis for any claim of neglect or elder abuse for any purpose of law.

(e) (1) Participation in activities authorized pursuant to this part shall be voluntary. Notwithstanding Sections 442 to 442.7, inclusive, a person or entity that elects, for reasons of conscience, morality, or ethics, not to engage in activities authorized pursuant to this part is not required to take any action in support of an individual's decision under this part.

(2) Notwithstanding any other law, a health care provider is not subject to civil, criminal, administrative, disciplinary, employment, credentialing, professional discipline, contractual liability, or medical staff action, sanction, or penalty or other liability for refusing to participate in activities authorized under this part, including, but not limited to, refusing to inform a patient regarding his or her rights under this part, and not referring an individual to a physician who participates in activities authorized under this part.

(3) If a health care provider is unable or unwilling to carry out a qualified individual's request under this part and the qualified individual transfers care to a new health care provider, the individual may request a copy of his or her medical records pursuant to law.

(Added by Stats. 2015, 2nd Ex. Sess., Ch. 1, Sec. 1. (AB 15 2x) Effective June 9, 2016. Repealed as of January 1, 2026, pursuant to Section 443.215.)

443.15.

(a) Subject to subdivision (b), notwithstanding any other law, a health care provider may prohibit its employees, independent contractors, or other persons or entities, including other health care providers, from participating in activities under this part while on premises owned or under the management or direct control of that prohibiting health care provider or while acting within the course and scope of any employment by, or contract with, the prohibiting health care provider.

(b) A health care provider that elects to prohibit its employees, independent contractors, or other persons or entities, including health care providers, from participating in activities under this part, as described in subdivision (a), shall first give notice of the policy prohibiting participation under this part to the individual or entity. A health care provider that fails to provide notice to an individual or entity in compliance with this subdivision shall not be entitled to enforce such a policy against that individual or entity.

(c) Subject to compliance with subdivision (b), the prohibiting health care provider may take action, including, but not limited to, the following, as applicable, against any individual or entity that violates this policy:

(1) Loss of privileges, loss of membership, or other action authorized by the bylaws or rules and regulations of the medical staff.

(2) Suspension, loss of employment, or other action authorized by the policies and practices of the prohibiting health care provider.

(3) Termination of any lease or other contract between the prohibiting health care provider and the individual or entity that violates the policy.

(4) Imposition of any other nonmonetary remedy provided for in any lease or contract between the prohibiting health care provider and the individual or entity in violation of the policy.

(d) Nothing in this section shall be construed to prevent, or to allow a prohibiting health care provider to prohibit, any other health care provider, employee, independent contractor, or other person or entity from any of the following:

(1) Participating, or entering into an agreement to participate, in activities under this part, while on premises that are not owned or under the management or direct control of the prohibiting provider or while acting outside the course and scope of the participant's duties as an employee of, or an independent contractor for, the prohibiting health care provider.

(2) Participating, or entering into an agreement to participate, in activities under this part as an attending physician or consulting physician while on premises that are not owned or under the management or direct control of the prohibiting provider.

(e) In taking actions pursuant to subdivision (c), a health care provider shall comply with all procedures required by law, its own policies or procedures, and any contract with the individual or entity in violation of the policy, as applicable.

(f) For purposes of this section:

(1) "Notice" means a separate statement in writing advising of the prohibiting health care provider policy with respect to participating in activities under this part.

(2) "Participating, or entering into an agreement to participate, in activities under this part" means doing or entering into an agreement to do any one or more of the following:

(A) Performing the duties of an attending physician as specified in Section 443.5.

(B) Performing the duties of a consulting physician as specified in Section 443.6.

(C) Performing the duties of a mental health specialist, in the circumstance that a referral to one is made.

(D) Delivering the prescription for, dispensing, or delivering the dispensed aid-in-dying drug pursuant to paragraph (2) of subdivision (b) of, and subdivision (c) of, Section 443.5.

(E) Being present when the qualified individual takes the aid-in-dying drug prescribed pursuant to this part.

(3) "Participating, or entering into an agreement to participate, in activities under this part" does not include doing, or entering into an agreement to do, any of the following:

(A) Diagnosing whether a patient has a terminal disease, informing the patient of the medical prognosis, or determining whether a patient has the capacity to make decisions.

(B) Providing information to a patient about this part.

(C) Providing a patient, upon the patient's request, with a referral to another health care provider for the purposes of participating in the activities authorized by this part.

(g) Any action taken by a prohibiting provider pursuant to this section shall not be reportable under Sections 800 to 809.9, inclusive, of the Business and Professions Code. The fact that a health care provider participates in activities under this part shall not be the sole basis for a complaint or report by another health care provider of unprofessional or dishonorable conduct under Sections 800 to 809.9, inclusive, of the Business and Professions Code.

(h) Nothing in this part shall prevent a health care provider from providing an individual with health care services that do not constitute participation in this part.

(Added by Stats. 2015, 2nd Ex. Sess., Ch. 1, Sec. 1. (AB 15 2x) Effective June 9, 2016. Repealed as of January 1, 2026, pursuant to Section 443.215.)

443.16.

(a) A health care provider may not be sanctioned for any of the following:

(1) Making an initial determination pursuant to the standard of care that an individual has a terminal disease and informing him or her of the medical prognosis.

(2) Providing information about the End of Life Option Act to a patient upon the request of the individual.

(3) Providing an individual, upon request, with a referral to another physician.

(b) A health care provider that prohibits activities under this part in accordance with Section 443.15 shall not sanction an individual health care provider for contracting with a qualified individual to engage in activities authorized by this part if the individual health care provider is acting outside of the course and scope of his or her capacity as an employee or independent contractor of the prohibiting health care provider.

(c) Notwithstanding any contrary provision in this section, the immunities and prohibitions on sanctions of a health care provider are solely reserved for actions of a health care provider taken pursuant to this part. Notwithstanding any contrary provision in this part, health care providers may be sanctioned by their licensing board or agency for conduct and actions constituting unprofessional conduct, including failure to comply in good faith with this part.

(Added by Stats. 2015, 2nd Ex. Sess., Ch. 1, Sec. 1. (AB 15 2x) Effective June 9, 2016. Repealed as of January 1, 2026, pursuant to Section 443.215.)

443.17.

(a) Knowingly altering or forging a request for an aid-in-dying drug to end an individual's life without his or her authorization or concealing or destroying a withdrawal or rescission of a request for an aid-in-dying drug is punishable as a felony if the act is done with the intent or effect of causing the individual's death.

(b) Knowingly coercing or exerting undue influence on an individual to request or ingest an aid-in-dying drug for the purpose of ending his or her life or to destroy a withdrawal or rescission of a request, or to administer an aid-in-dying drug to an individual without his or her knowledge or consent, is punishable as a felony.

(c) For purposes of this section, "knowingly" has the meaning provided in Section 7 of the Penal Code.

(d) The attending physician, consulting physician, or mental health specialist shall not be related to the individual by blood, marriage, registered domestic partnership, or adoption, or be entitled to a portion of the individual's estate upon death.

(e) Nothing in this section shall be construed to limit civil liability.

(f) The penalties in this section do not preclude criminal penalties applicable under any law for conduct inconsistent with the provisions of this act.

(Amended by Stats. 2017, Ch. 269, Sec. 3. (SB 811) Effective January 1, 2018. Repealed as of January 1, 2026, pursuant to Section 443.215.)

443.18.

Nothing in this part may be construed to authorize a physician or any other person to end an individual's life by lethal injection, mercy killing, or active euthanasia. Actions taken in accordance with this part shall not, for any purposes, constitute suicide, assisted suicide, homicide, or elder abuse under the law.

(Added by Stats. 2015, 2nd Ex. Sess., Ch. 1, Sec. 1. (AB 15 2x) Effective June 9, 2016. Repealed as of January 1, 2026, pursuant to Section 443.215.)

443.19.

(a) The State Department of Public Health shall collect and review the information submitted pursuant to Section 443.9. The information collected shall be confidential and shall be collected in a manner that protects the privacy of the patient, the patient's family, and any medical provider or pharmacist involved with the patient under the provisions of this part. The information shall not be disclosed, discoverable, or compelled to be produced in any civil, criminal, administrative, or other proceeding.

(b) On or before July 1, 2017, and each year thereafter, based on the information collected in the previous year, the department shall create a report with the information collected from the attending physician followup form and post that report to its Internet Web site. The report shall include, but not be limited to, all of the following based on the information that is provided to the department and on the department's access to vital statistics:

(1) The number of people for whom an aid-in-dying prescription was written.

(2) The number of known individuals who died each year for whom aid-in-dying prescriptions were written, and the cause of death of those individuals.

(3) For the period commencing January 1, 2016, to and including the previous year, cumulatively, the total number of aid-in-dying prescriptions written, the number of people who died due to use of aid-in-dying drugs, and the number of those people who died who were enrolled in hospice or other palliative care programs at the time of death.

(4) The number of known deaths in California from using aid-in-dying drugs per 10,000 deaths in California.

(5) The number of physicians who wrote prescriptions for aid-in-dying drugs.

(6) Of people who died due to using an aid-in-dying drug, demographic percentages organized by the following characteristics:

(A) Age at death.

(B) Education level.

(C) Race.

(D) Sex.

(E) Type of insurance, including whether or not they had insurance.

(F) Underlying illness.

(c) The State Department of Public Health shall make available the attending physician checklist and compliance form, the consulting physician compliance form, and the attending physician followup form, as described in Section 443.22, by posting them on its Internet Web site.

(Added by Stats. 2015, 2nd Ex. Sess., Ch. 1, Sec. 1. (AB 15 2x) Effective June 9, 2016. Repealed as of January 1, 2026, pursuant to Section 443.215.)

443.20.

A person who has custody or control of any unused aid-in-dying drugs prescribed pursuant to this part after the death of the patient shall personally deliver the unused aid-in-dying drugs for disposal by delivering it to the nearest qualified facility that properly disposes of controlled substances, or if none is available, shall dispose of it by lawful means in accordance with guidelines promulgated by the California State Board of Pharmacy or a federal Drug Enforcement Administration approved take-back program.

(Added by Stats. 2015, 2nd Ex. Sess., Ch. 1, Sec. 1. (AB 15 2x) Effective June 9, 2016. Repealed as of January 1, 2026, pursuant to Section 443.215.)

443.21.

Any governmental entity that incurs costs resulting from a qualified individual terminating his or her life pursuant to the provisions of this part in a public place shall have a claim against the estate of the qualified individual to recover those costs and reasonable attorney fees related to enforcing the claim.

(Added by Stats. 2015, 2nd Ex. Sess., Ch. 1, Sec. 1. (AB 15 2x) Effective June 9, 2016. Repealed as of January 1, 2026, pursuant to Section 443.215.)

443.215.

This part shall remain in effect only until January 1, 2026, and as of that date is repealed, unless a later enacted statute, that is enacted before January 1, 2026, deletes or extends that date.

(Added by Stats. 2015, 2nd Ex. Sess., Ch. 1, Sec. 1. (AB 15 2x) Effective June 9, 2016. Repealed as of January 1, 2026, by its own provisions. Repeal affects Part 1.85, comprising Sections 443 to 443.22.)

443.22.

(a) The Medical Board of California may update the attending physician checklist and compliance form, the consulting physician compliance form, and the attending physician

followup form, based on those provided in subdivision (b). Upon completion, the State Department of Public Health shall publish the updated forms on its Internet Web site.

(b) Unless and until updated by the Medical Board of California pursuant to this section, the attending physician checklist and compliance form, the consulting physician compliance form, and the attending physician followup form shall be in the following form:

* *

NOTICE OF INCOMPLETE TEXT: The physician compliance and follow-up forms appear in the published chaptered bill. See Sec. 1 of Chapter 1 (pp. 18–25), 2nd Ex. Session, Statutes of 2015.

* *

(Added by Stats. 2015, 2nd Ex. Sess., Ch. 1, Sec. 1. (AB 15 2x) Effective June 9, 2016. Repealed as of January 1, 2026, pursuant to Section 443.215. Note: See published bill for complete section text. The physician compliance forms appear on pages 18 to 25 of Ch. 1 (2nd Ex.).)

PART 1.9. MEDICAL REFERRAL SERVICES [445- 445.]

(Part 1.9 added by Stats. 1973, Ch. 923.)

445.

No person, firm, partnership, association or corporation, or agent or employee thereof, shall for profit refer or recommend a person to a physician, hospital, health-related facility, or dispensary for any form of medical care or treatment of any ailment or physical condition. The imposition of a fee or charge for any such referral or recommendation creates a presumption that the referral or recommendation is for profit.

The provisions of this section shall not apply to referrals or recommendations which are made under the crippled children services program or prepaid health plans.

A physician, hospital, health-related facility or dispensary shall not enter into a contract or other form of agreement to accept for medical care or treatment any person referred or recommended for such care or treatment by a medical referral service business located in or doing business in another state if the medical referral service business would be prohibited under this part if the business were located in or doing business in this state.

A violation of the provisions of this section shall constitute a misdemeanor and upon conviction thereof may be punished by imprisonment in the county jail for not longer than one year, or a fine of not more than five thousand dollars ($5,000), or by both such fine and imprisonment.

Any violation of this section may be enjoined in a civil action brought in the name of the people of the State of California by the Attorney General, except that the plaintiff shall not be required to allege facts necessary to show or tending to show lack of adequate remedy at law or to show or tending to show irreparable damage or loss.

(Amended by Stats. 1974, Ch. 1333.)

PART 2. LOCAL ADMINISTRATION [851- 851.]

(Part 2 enacted by Stats. 1939, Ch. 60.)

CHAPTER 5. Local Health and Safety Regulations [851- 851.]

(Chapter 5 enacted by Stats. 1939, Ch. 60.)

851.

Any board of supervisors may adopt such rules and regulations with regard to keeping and storing of every description of gunpowder, hercules powder, giant powder, or other explosives or combustible material, as the safety and protection of the lives and property of individuals may require.

(Enacted by Stats. 1939, Ch. 60.)

PART 4. Healthy California for All Commission [1000 - 1005]

(Heading of Part 4 amended by Stats. 2019, Ch. 67, Sec. 1.)

1000.

(a) The Legislature finds and declares all of the following:

(1) Health care is a human right and it is in the public interest that all Californians have access to health care that improves health outcomes, manages and lowers health care costs for the state and its residents, and reduces health disparities.

(2) With the implementation of the federal Patient Protection and Affordable Care Act (Public Law 111-148) and other state efforts, California has reduced the uninsured share of its population to less than 10 percent.

(3) As of 2016, nearly three million Californians remained uninsured, 21 percent of Californians remained underinsured, and 11 percent of California adults went without health care because of cost.

(4) The United States spends more per capita than any other industrialized nation on health care, but has low rankings based on many metrics, including access to care, equity, efficiency, and healthy lives.

(5) California has a primary care physician shortage, and the geographic distribution of physicians across California is uneven.

(6) According to the federal Centers for Medicare and Medicaid Services, national health spending is projected to grow 5.5 percent annually, on average, through 2026, representing 19.7 percent of the economy in 2026.

(b) It is the intent of the Legislature to establish a health care delivery system that provides coverage and access through a unified financing system for all Californians.

(c) It is the intent of the Legislature to control health care costs so that California is able to achieve a sustainable health care system with more equitable access to quality health care.

(d) It is the intent of the Legislature that rising health care costs be mitigated and administrative costs be limited so that more money is spent on direct care to patients and less on profits and overhead.

(e) It is the intent of the Legislature that all Californians receive high-quality health care, with positive health care outcomes, regardless of age, income, race, ethnicity, immigration status, gender or gender nonconforming status, sexual orientation, geographic location, health status, or ability.

(f) It is the intent of the Legislature that all Californians have access to affordable health coverage, including health coverage with reasonable out-of-pocket costs relative to household income, or being eligible for appropriate cost-sharing assistance.

(g) It is the intent of the Legislature that California train and employ an adequate number of primary care physicians, specialty care physicians, mental and behavioral health professionals, and allied health care professionals to meet the health care needs of the state.

(h) It is the intent of the Legislature that the health care system ensure that all Californians have timely access to necessary health care, including access that addresses language and geographic barriers.

(Added by Stats. 2018, Ch. 34, Sec. 3. (AB 1810) Effective June 27, 2018. Repealed as of January 1, 2022, pursuant to Section 1005.)

1001.

(a) Effective July 1, 2019, there is hereby established the Healthy California for All Commission as an independent body to develop a plan that includes options for advancing progress toward achieving a health care delivery system in California that provides coverage and access through a unified financing system, including, but not limited to, a single-payer financing system, for all Californians.

(b) The commission shall meet for the first time on or before September 1, 2019, and shall convene meetings at least quarterly at locations that are easily accessible to the public in accordance with the Bagley-Keene Open Meeting Act (Article 9 (commencing with Section 11120) of Chapter 1 of Part 1 of Division 3 of Title 2 of the Government Code).

(c) (1) The commission shall be comprised of 13 members as follows:

(A) The Secretary of California Health and Human Services, or the secretary's designee, who shall serve as the chairperson.

(B) Eight members who shall be appointed by the Governor.

(C) Two members who shall be appointed by the Senate Committee on Rules.

(D) Two members who shall be appointed by the Speaker of the Assembly.

(2) There shall also be five ex officio, nonvoting members of the commission who shall be the Executive Director of the California Health Benefit Exchange, the Director of Health Care Services, the Chief Executive Officer of the Public Employees' Retirement System, and the chairs of the health committees of the Senate and the Assembly, or their officially designated representatives.

(3) The appointees shall have appropriate knowledge and experience regarding health care coverage or financing, or other relevant expertise.

(4) The members of the commission shall serve without compensation, but shall be reimbursed for necessary traveling and other expenses incurred in performing their duties and responsibilities.

(d) The commission may establish advisory committees that include members of the public with knowledge and experience in health care that support stakeholder engagement and an analytical process by which key design options are developed. A member of an advisory committee need not be a member of the commission.

(e) The commission and each advisory committee shall keep official records of all of their proceedings.

(Amended by Stats. 2019, Ch. 67, Sec. 2. (SB 104) Effective July 9, 2019. Repealed as of January 1, 2022, pursuant to Section 1005.)

1002.

(a) On or before July 1, 2020, the commission shall submit a report to the Legislature and the Governor with options that include all of the following:

(1) An analysis of California's existing health care delivery system, including cost, quality, workforce, and provider consolidation trends and how they impact the state's ability to provide all Californians with timely access to high-quality, affordable health care.

(2) Options for additional steps California can take to prepare for transition to a unified financing system, including, but not limited to, a single-payer financing system, including, but not limited to, administrative changes, reorganization of state programs, federal waivers, and statutory and constitutional changes.

(3) Options for coverage expansions, including potential funding sources. Options shall include expansion for full-scope Medi-Cal to individuals over 64 years of age, regardless of immigration status.

(b) On or before February 1, 2021, the commission shall submit a report to the Legislature and the Governor that includes options for key design considerations for a unified financing system, including, but not limited to, a single-payer financing system, including all of the following:

(1) Eligibility and enrollment.

(2) Covered benefits and services.

(3) Provider participation.

(4) Purchasing arrangements.

(5) Provider payments, including consideration of global budgets.

(6) Cost containment.

(7) Quality improvement.

(8) Participant cost sharing.

(9) Quality monitoring and disparities reduction.

(10) Information technology systems and financial management systems.

(11) Data sharing and transparency.

(12) Governance and administration, including integration of federal funding sources.

(c) The reports required under this section shall be submitted in compliance with Section 9795 of the Government Code, and shall be posted on the California Health and Human Services Agency's internet website.

(d) The commission shall provide an update detailing its progress in developing the reports required by subdivisions (a) and (b) to the Governor and the health committees of the Senate and the Assembly on or before January 1, 2020, and shall update those committees every six months thereafter.

(Repealed and added by Stats. 2019, Ch. 67, Sec. 4. (SB 104) Effective July 9, 2019.)

1002.5.

(a) The council shall prepare an analysis and evaluation, known as a feasibility analysis, to determine the feasibility of a public health insurance plan option to increase competition and choice for health care consumers.

(b) At a minimum, the feasibility analysis shall include all of the following:

(1) An actuarial and economic analysis of a public health insurance plan.

(2) A plan to expand the participation of public health plans, including state-licensed county organized health systems and local health plans.

(3) A state developed public health insurance plan.

(4) A list of necessary federal waivers for a state-developed public health insurance plan.

(5) A discussion of potential funding and state costs for a public health insurance plan.

(6) An analysis of the extent to which a new public health insurance plan option could address the underlying factors that limit health plan choices in some regions.

(c) In developing the feasibility analysis, the council shall consult with key stakeholders, including, but not limited to, consumer advocates, health care providers, and health plans, including, but not limited to, county organized health systems and local health plans.

(d) (1) The council shall submit the feasibility analysis to the Legislature and the Governor on or before October 1, 2021. The feasibility analysis shall be submitted in compliance with Section 9795 of the Government Code.

(2) The council shall provide an update detailing its progress in developing the feasibility analysis to the Governor and the health committees of the Senate and the Assembly on or before January 1, 2020, and shall update those committees every six months thereafter.

(e) This section does not authorize the council to apply for a waiver under Section 1332 of the federal Patient Protection and Affordable Care Act (Public Law 111-148), as amended by the federal Health Care and Education Reconciliation Act of 2010 (Public Law 111-152), and any amendments to, or regulations or guidance issued under, those acts.

(Added by Stats. 2018, Ch. 677, Sec. 2. (AB 2472) Effective January 1, 2019.)

1003.

This part shall not be construed to authorize the commission to implement any provision of the reports developed pursuant to Section 1002 until there is further action by the Legislature and the Governor.

(Amended by Stats. 2019, Ch. 67, Sec. 5. (SB 104) Effective July 9, 2019. Repealed as of January 1, 2022, pursuant to Section 1005.)

1004.

(a) The California Health and Human Services Agency is authorized to provide staff support to implement this part.

(b) For purposes of implementing this part, including, but not limited to, hiring staff and consultants, facilitating and conducting meetings, conducting research and analysis, and developing the required plan and updates, the California Health and Human Services Agency may enter into exclusive or nonexclusive contracts on a bid or negotiated basis. Contracts entered into or amended pursuant to this section shall be exempt from Chapter 6 (commencing with Section 14825) of Part 5.5 of Division 3 of Title 2 of the Government Code, Section 19130 of the Government Code, and Part 2 (commencing with Section 10100) of Division 2 of the Public Contract Code and shall be exempt from the review or approval of any division of the Department of General Services.

(Added by Stats. 2018, Ch. 34, Sec. 3. (AB 1810) Effective June 27, 2018. Repealed as of January 1, 2022, pursuant to Section 1005.)

1005.

This part shall remain in effect only until January 1, 2022, and as of that date is repealed.

(Added by Stats. 2018, Ch. 34, Sec. 3. (AB 1810) Effective June 27, 2018. Repealed as of January 1, 2022, by its own provisions. Note: Repeal affects Part 4, commencing with Section 1000.)

PART 5. OFFICE OF RURAL HEALTH [1179 - 1179.6]

(Part 5 added by Stats. 1995, Ch. 305, Sec. 1.)

1179.

The Legislature finds and declares all of the following:

(a) Outside of California's four major metropolitan areas, the majority of the state is rural. In general, the rural population is older, sicker, poorer, and more likely to be unemployed, uninsured, or underinsured. The lack of primary care, specialty providers and transportation continue to be significant barriers to access to health services in rural areas.

(b) There is no coordinated or comprehensive plan of action for rural health care in California to ensure the health of California's rural residents. Most of the interventions that have taken place on behalf of rural communities have been limited in scope and purpose and were not conceived or implemented with any comprehensive or systematic approach in mind. Because health planning tends to focus on approaches for population centers, the unique needs of rural communities may not be addressed. A comprehensive plan and approach is necessary to obtain federal support and relief, as well as to realistically institute state and industry interventions.

(c) Rural communities lack the resources to make the transition from present practices to managed care, and to make other changes that may be necessary as the result of health care reform efforts. With numerous health care reform proposals being debated and with the extensive changes in the current health care delivery system, a comprehensive and coordinated analysis must take place regarding the impact of these proposals on rural areas.

(d) Rural areas lack the technical expertise and resources to improve and coordinate their local data collection activities, which are necessary for well-targeted health planning, program development, and resource development. Data must be available to local communities to enable them to plan effectively.

(e) The Legislature recognizes the need to take a comprehensive approach to strengthen and coordinate rural health programs and health care delivery systems in order to:

(1) Facilitate access to high quality health care for California's rural communities.

(2) Promote coordinated planning and policy development among state departments and between the State and local public and private providers.

(Added by Stats. 1995, Ch. 305, Sec. 1. Effective August 3, 1995.)

1179.1.

(a) The Secretary of the Health and Welfare Agency shall establish an Office of Rural Health, or an alternative organizational structure, in one of the departments of the Health and Welfare Agency to promote a strong working relationship between state government and local and federal agencies, universities, private and public interest groups, rural consumers, health care providers, foundations, and other offices of rural health, as well as to develop health initiatives and maximize the use of existing resources without duplicating existing effort. The office or alternative organizational structure shall serve as a key information and referral source to promote coordinated planning for the delivery of health services in rural California.

(b) To the extent funds are appropriated by the Legislature, these efforts may include:

(1) Educating the public and recommending appropriate public policies regarding the viability of rural health care in California.

(2) Monitoring and working with state and federal agencies to assess the impact of proposed rules and regulations on rural areas.

(3) Promoting community involvement and community support in maintaining, rebuilding, and diversifying local health services in rural areas.

(4) Encouraging and evaluating the use of advanced communications technology to provide access to health promotion and disease prevention information, specialty expertise, clinical consultation, and continuing education for health professionals.

(5) Encouraging the development of regional health care and public health networks and collaborative efforts, including, but not limited to, emergency transportation networks.

(6) Working with state and local agencies, universities, and private and public interest groups to promote research on rural health issues.

(7) Soliciting the assistance of other offices or programs of rural health in California to carry out the duties of this part.

(8) Disseminating information and providing technical assistance to communities, health care providers, and consumers of health care services.

(9) Promoting strategies to improve health care professional recruitment and retention in rural areas.

(10) Encouraging innovative responses by public and private entities to address rural health issues.

(Added by Stats. 1995, Ch. 305, Sec. 1. Effective August 3, 1995.)

1179.3.

(a) (1) The Office of Statewide Health Planning and Development shall develop and administer a competitive grants program for projects located in rural areas of California.

(2) The office shall define "rural area" for the purposes of this section after receiving public input and upon recommendation of the Interdepartmental Rural Health Coordinating Committee and the Rural Health Programs Liaison.

(3) The purpose of the grants program shall be to fund innovative, collaborative, cost-effective, and efficient projects that pertain to the delivery of health and medical services in rural areas of the state.

(4) The office shall develop and establish uses for the funds to fund special projects that alleviate problems of access to quality health care in rural areas and to compensate public and private health care providers associated with direct delivery of patient care. The funds shall be used for medical and hospital care and treatment of patients who cannot afford to pay for services and for whom payment will not be made through private or public programs.

(5) The office shall administer the funds appropriated by the Legislature for purposes of this section. Entities eligible for these funds shall include rural health providers served by the programs operated by the office, the Emergency Medical Services Authority, the State Department of Health Care Services, the State Department of Public Health, and the Managed Risk Medical Insurance Board. The grant funds shall be used to expand existing services or establish new services and shall not be used to supplant existing levels of service. Funds appropriated by the Legislature for this purpose may be expended in the fiscal year of the appropriation or the subsequent fiscal year.

(b) The Office of Statewide Health Planning and Development shall establish the criteria and standards for eligibility to be used in requests for proposals or requests for application, the application review process, determining the maximum amount and number of grants to be awarded, preference and priority of projects, compliance monitoring, and the measurement of outcomes achieved after receiving comment from the public at a meeting held pursuant to the Bagley-Keene Open Meeting Act (Article 9 (commencing with Section 11120) of Chapter 1 of Part 1 of Division 3 of Title 2 of the Government Code).

(c) The Office of Statewide Health Planning and Development shall make information regarding the status of the funded projects available at the public meetings described in subdivision (b).

(Amended by Stats. 2013, Ch. 22, Sec. 13. (AB 75) Effective June 27, 2013. Operative July 1, 2013, by Sec. 110 of Ch. 22.)

1179.6.

(a) (1) In order to provide improved delivery of services to the families of agricultural workers, the State Department of Health Services shall review and survey the extent to which agricultural workers and their families utilize those public health programs for which they are eligible. In conducting the survey, the department shall ensure the full participation of entities that provide services to agricultural workers, including clinics, community-based agencies, public health departments, and organizations and associations involved with agricultural worker health and well-being. Programs considered in the survey shall include, but shall not be limited to, all of the following:

(A) The Medi-Cal program.

(B) The Healthy Families program.

(C) The Early and Periodic Screening, Diagnostic, and Treatment Program (EPSDT).

(D) The Child Health and Disability Prevention Program (CHDP).

(E) Health clinics.

(F) Public health prevention programs.

(G) Immunization programs.

(H) Community mental health programs.

(I) Programs funded under the California Children and Families Program.

(J) Parenting programs.

(K) Teen pregnancy prevention and case management programs.

(L) Domestic violence and child abuse prevention programs.

(M) Any other relevant programs available in communities of agricultural workers.

(2) The department shall use the results of the survey to prepare an implementation plan that maximizes access and streamlines service delivery, in order to make comprehensive family wellness programs readily available to agricultural workers and their families. In developing the implementation plan, the department shall ensure the full participation of entities contributing to the survey of available services. The implementation plan shall be based on the principles set forth in subdivision (g) of Section 50517.5, including all of the following:

(A) Involvement of agricultural workers and their families in program design and delivery.

(B) Community collaboration on the local level among available public and private agencies.

(C) Coordination with the provision of adequate housing.

(b) (1) The survey shall address the extent to which outreach programs are directed to, and succeed in, reaching agricultural workers and their families, and shall identify any geographical, cultural, linguistic, or other barriers that may prevent full utilization of available services.

(2) The survey shall place significant emphasis on actual experiences of agricultural workers and their families.

(c) The department shall report the results of the survey required by this section to the Legislature on or before March 1, 2001, and shall present the Legislature with the implementation plan required by paragraph (2) of subdivision (a) on or before December 31, 2001.

(Added by Stats. 2000, Ch. 312, Sec. 1. Effective September 7, 2000.)

PART 6. CHILDREN'S HOSPITAL BOND ACT OF 2004 [1179.10 - 1179.43]

(Part 6 added November 2, 2004, by initiative Proposition 61, Sec. 1, a bond act.)

CHAPTER 1. General Provisions [1179.10 - 1179.11]

(Chapter 1 added November 2, 2004, by initiative Proposition 61.)

1179.10.

This part shall be known and may be cited as the Children's Hospital Bond Act of 2004.

(Added November 2, 2004, by initiative Proposition 61.)

1179.11.

As used in this part, the following terms have the following meanings:

(a) "Authority" means the California Health Facilities Financing Authority established pursuant to Section 15431 of the Government Code.

(b) "Children's hospital" means either:

(1) A University of California general acute care hospital described below:

(A) University of California, Davis Children's Hospital.

(B) Mattel Children's Hospital at University of California, Los Angeles.

(C) University Children's Hospital at University of California, Irvine.

(D) University of California, San Francisco Children's Hospital.

(E) University of California, San Diego Children's Hospital.

(2) A general acute care hospital that is, or is an operating entity of, a California nonprofit corporation incorporated prior to January 1, 2003, whose mission of clinical care, teaching, research, and advocacy focuses on children, and that provides comprehensive pediatric services to a high volume of children eligible for governmental programs and to children with special health care needs eligible for the California Children's Services program and:

(A) Provided at least 160 licensed beds in the categories of pediatric acute, pediatric intensive care and neonatal intensive care in the fiscal year ending between June 30, 2001, and June 29, 2002, as reported to the Office of Statewide Health Planning and Development on or before July 1, 2003.

(B) Provided over 30,000 total pediatric patient (census) days, excluding nursery acute days, in the fiscal year ending between June 30, 2001, and June 29, 2002, as reported to the Office of Statewide Health Planning and Development on or before July 1, 2003.

(C) Provided medical education of at least eight (rounded to the nearest integer) full-time equivalent pediatric or pediatric subspecialty residents in the fiscal year ending between June 30, 2001, and June 29, 2002, as reported to the Office of Statewide Health Planning and Development on or before July 1, 2003.

(c) "Committee" means the Children's Hospital Bond Act Finance Committee created pursuant to Section 1179.32.

(d) "Fund" means the Children's Hospital Fund created pursuant to Section 1179.20.

(e) "Grant" means the distribution of money in the fund by the authority to children's hospitals for projects pursuant to this part.

(f) "Program" means the Children's Hospital Program established pursuant to this part.

(g) "Project" means constructing, expanding, remodeling, renovating, furnishing, equipping, financing, or refinancing of a children's hospital to be financed or refinanced with funds provided in whole or in part pursuant to this part. "Project" may include reimbursement for the costs of constructing, expanding, remodeling, renovating, furnishing, equipping, financing, or refinancing of a children's hospital where such costs are incurred after January 31, 2003. "Project" may include any combination of one or more of the foregoing undertaken jointly by any participating children's hospital that qualifies under this part.

(Added November 2, 2004, by initiative Proposition 61.)

CHAPTER 2. The Children's Hospital Program [1179.20 - 1179.25]

(Chapter 2 added November 2, 2004, by initiative Proposition 61.)

1179.20.

The proceeds of bonds issued and sold pursuant to this part shall be deposited in the Children's Hospital Fund, which is hereby created.

(Added November 2, 2004, by initiative Proposition 61.)

1179.21.

The purpose of the Children's Hospital Program is to improve the health and welfare of California's critically ill children, by providing a stable and ready source of funds for capital improvement projects for children's hospitals. The program provided for in this part is in the public interest, serves a public purpose, and will promote the health, welfare, and safety of the citizens of the state.

(Added November 2, 2004, by initiative Proposition 61.)

1179.22.

The authority is authorized to award grants to any children's hospital for purposes of funding projects, as defined in subdivision (g) of Section 1179.11.

(Added November 2, 2004, by initiative Proposition 61.)

1179.23.

(a) Twenty percent of the total funds available for grants pursuant to this part shall be awarded to children's hospitals as defined in paragraph (1) of subdivision (b) of Section 1179.11.

(b) Eighty percent of the total funds available for grants pursuant to this part shall be awarded to children's hospitals as defined in paragraph (2) of subdivision (b) of Section 1179.11.

(Added November 2, 2004, by initiative Proposition 61.)

1179.24.

(a) The authority shall develop a written application for the awarding of grants under this part within 90 days of the adoption of this act. The authority shall award grants to eligible children's hospitals, subject to the limitations of this part and to further the purposes of this part based on the following factors:

(1) The grant will contribute toward expansion or improvement of health care access by children eligible for governmental health insurance programs and indigent, underserved, and uninsured children.

(2) The grant will contribute toward the improvement of child health care or pediatric patient outcomes.

(3) The children's hospital provides uncompensated or undercompensated care to indigent or public pediatric patients.

(4) The children's hospital provides services to vulnerable pediatric populations.

(5) The children's hospital promotes pediatric teaching or research programs.

(6) Demonstration of project readiness and project feasibility.

(b) An application for funds shall be submitted to the authority for approval as to its conformity with the requirements of this part. The authority shall process and award grants in a timely manner, not to exceed 60 days.

(c) A children's hospital identified in paragraph (1) of subdivision (b) of Section 1179.11 shall not apply for, and the authority shall not award to that children's hospital, a grant that would cause the total amount of grants awarded to that children's hospital to exceed one-fifth of the total funds available for grants to all children's hospitals pursuant to subdivision (a) of Section 1179.23. Notwithstanding this grant limitation, any funds available under subdivision (a) of Section 1179.23 that have not been exhausted by June 30, 2014, shall become available for an application from any children's hospital identified in paragraph (1) of subdivision (b) of Section 1179.11.

(d) A children's hospital identified in paragraph (2) of subdivision (b) of Section 1179.11 shall not apply for, and the authority shall not award to that children's hospital, a grant that would cause the total amount of grants awarded to that children's hospital to exceed seventy-four million dollars ($74,000,000) from funds available for grants to all children's hospitals pursuant to subdivision (b) of Section 1179.23. Notwithstanding this grant limitation, any funds available under subdivision (b) of Section 1179.23 that have not been exhausted by June 30, 2014, shall become available for an application from any children's hospital defined in paragraph (2) of subdivision (b) of Section 1179.11.

(e) In no event shall a grant to finance a project exceed the total cost of the project, as determined by the children's hospital and approved by the authority.

(f) All projects that are awarded grants shall be completed within a reasonable period of time. If the authority determines that the children's hospital has failed to complete the project under the terms specified in awarding the grant, the authority may require remedies, including the return of all or a portion of the grant. A children's hospital receiving a grant under this part shall submit certification of project completion to the authority.

(g) Grants shall only be available pursuant to this section if the authority determines that it has sufficient money available in the fund. Nothing in this section shall require the authority to award grants if the authority determines that it has insufficient moneys available in the fund to do so.

(h) The authority may annually determine the amount available for purposes of this part. Administrative costs for this program shall not exceed the actual costs or one percent, whichever is less.

(Added November 2, 2004, by initiative Proposition 61.)

1179.25.

The Bureau of State Audits may conduct periodic audits to ensure that bond proceeds are awarded in a timely fashion and in a manner consistent with the requirements of this part, and that awardees of bond proceeds are using funds in compliance with applicable provisions of this part.

(Added November 2, 2004, by initiative Proposition 61.)

CHAPTER 3. Fiscal Provisions [1179.30 - 1179.43]

(Chapter 3 added November 2, 2004, by initiative Proposition 61.)

1179.30.

Bonds in the total amount of seven hundred fifty million dollars ($750,000,000), not including the amount of any refunding bonds, may be issued and sold to provide a fund to be used for carrying out the purposes expressed in this part and to reimburse the General Obligation Bond Expense Revolving Fund pursuant to Section 16724.5 of the Government Code. The bonds, when sold, shall be and constitute a valid and binding obligation of the State of California, and the full faith and credit of the State of California is hereby pledged for the punctual payment of the principal of, and interest on, the bonds as the principal and interest become due and payable.

(Added November 2, 2004, by initiative Proposition 61.)

1179.31.

The bonds authorized by this part shall be prepared, executed, issued, sold, paid, and redeemed as provided in the State General Obligation Bond Law (Chapter 4 (commencing with Section 16720) of Part 3 of Division 4 of Title 2 of the Government Code), and all of the provisions of that law apply to the bonds and to this part and are hereby incorporated in this part as though set forth in full in this part.

(Added November 2, 2004, by initiative Proposition 61.)

1179.32.

(a) Solely for the purpose of authorizing the issuance and sale pursuant to the State General Obligation Bond Law of the bonds authorized by this part, the Children's Hospital Bond Act Finance Committee is hereby created. For purposes of this part, the Children's Hospital Bond Act Finance Committee is "the committee" as that term is used in the State General Obligation Bond Law. The committee consists of the Controller, Director of Finance, and the Treasurer, or their designated representatives. The Treasurer shall serve as chairperson of the committee. A majority of the committee may act for the committee.

(b) The authority is designated the "board" for purposes of the State General Obligation Bond Law, and shall administer the fund pursuant to this part.

(Added November 2, 2004, by initiative Proposition 61.)

1179.33.

The committee shall determine whether or not it is necessary or desirable to issue bonds authorized pursuant to this part in order to carry out the actions specified in Section 1179.21 and, if so, the amount of bonds to be issued and sold. Successive issues of bonds may be authorized and sold to carry out those actions progressively, and it is not necessary that all of the bonds be issued or sold at any one time.

(Added November 2, 2004, by initiative Proposition 61.)

1179.34.

There shall be collected each year and in the same manner and at the same time as other state revenue is collected, in addition to the ordinary revenues of the state, a sum in an amount required to pay the principal of, and interest on, the bonds each year. It is the duty of all officers charged by law with any duty in regard to the collection of the revenue to do and perform each and every act that is necessary to collect that additional sum.

(Added November 2, 2004, by initiative Proposition 61.)

1179.35.

Notwithstanding Section 13340 of the Government Code, there is hereby appropriated continuously from the General Fund in the State Treasury, for the purposes of this part, an amount that will equal the total of the following:

(a) The sum annually necessary to pay the principal of, and interest on, bonds issued and sold pursuant to this part, as the principal and interest become due and payable.

(b) The sum necessary to carry out Section 1179.36, appropriated without regard to fiscal years.

(Added November 2, 2004, by initiative Proposition 61.)

1179.36.

For the purposes of carrying out this part, the Director of Finance may authorize the withdrawal from the General Fund of an amount not to exceed the amount of the unsold bonds that have been authorized by the committee to be sold for the purpose of carrying out this part. Any amounts withdrawn shall be deposited in the fund. Any money made available under this section shall be returned to the General Fund from proceeds received from the sale of bonds for the purpose of carrying out this part.

(Added November 2, 2004, by initiative Proposition 61.)

1179.37.

All money deposited in the fund that is derived from premium and accrued interest on bonds sold shall be reserved in the fund and shall be available for transfer to the General Fund as a credit to expenditures for bond interest.

(Added November 2, 2004, by initiative Proposition 61.)

1179.38.

Pursuant to Chapter 4 (commencing with Section 16720) of Part 3 of Division 4 of Title 2 of the Government Code, the cost of bond issuance shall be paid out of the bond proceeds. These costs shall be shared proportionally by each program funded through this bond act.

(Added November 2, 2004, by initiative Proposition 61.)

1179.39.

The authority may request the Pooled Money Investment Board to make a loan from the Pooled Money Investment Account in accordance with Section 16312 of the Government Code, for purposes of carrying out this part. The amount of the request shall not exceed the amount of the unsold bonds that the committee, by resolution, has authorized to be sold for the purpose of carrying out this part. The authority shall execute any documents required by the Pooled Money Investment Board to obtain and repay the loan. Any amounts loaned shall be deposited in the fund to be allocated by the board in accordance with this part.

(Added November 2, 2004, by initiative Proposition 61.)

1179.40.

The bonds may be refunded in accordance with Article 6 (commencing with Section 16780) of Chapter 4 of Part 3 of Division 4 of Title 2 of the Government Code, which is a part of the State General Obligation Bond Law. Approval by the voters of the state for the issuance of the bonds described in this part includes the approval of the issuance of any bonds issued to refund any bonds originally issued under this part or any previously issued refunding bonds.

(Added November 2, 2004, by initiative Proposition 61.)

1179.41.

Notwithstanding any other provision of this part, or of the State General Obligation Bond Law, if the Treasurer sells bonds pursuant to this part that include a bond counsel opinion to the effect that the interest on the bonds is excluded from gross income for federal tax purposes, subject to designated conditions, the Treasurer may maintain separate accounts for the investment of bond proceeds and for the investment of earnings on those proceeds. The Treasurer may use or direct the use of those proceeds or earnings to pay any rebate, penalty, or other payment required under federal law or take any other action with respect to the investment and use of those bond proceeds required or desirable under federal law to maintain the tax-exempt status of those bonds and to obtain any other advantage under federal law on behalf of the funds of this state.

(Added November 2, 2004, by initiative Proposition 61.)

1179.42.

The people hereby find and declare that, inasmuch as the proceeds from the sale of bonds authorized by this part are not "proceeds of taxes" as that term is used in Article XIII B of the California Constitution, the disbursement of these proceeds is not subject to the limitations imposed by that part.

(Added November 2, 2004, by initiative Proposition 61.)

1179.43.

Notwithstanding any other provision of this part, the provisions of this part are severable. If any provision of this part or its application is held invalid, that invalidity shall not affect other provisions or applications that can be given effect without the invalid provision or application.

(Added November 2, 2004, by initiative Proposition 61.)

PART 6.1. CHILDREN'S HOSPITAL BOND ACT OF 2008 [1179.50 - 1179.72]

(Part 6.1 added November 4, 2008, by initiative Proposition 3, a bond act.)

CHAPTER 1. General Provisions [1179.50 - 1179.51]

(Chapter 1 added November 4, 2008, by initiative Proposition 3.)

1179.50.

(a) This part shall be known and may be cited as the Children's Hospital Bond Act of 2008.

(b) California's network of regional children's hospitals provide vital health care services to children facing life-threatening illness or injury. Over one million times each year, children are cared for at these hospitals without regard to their family's ability to pay.

(c) Children's hospitals also provide specialized treatment and care that has increased the survival of children suffering from serious diseases and illnesses such as childhood leukemia, cancer, heart defects, diabetes, sickle cell anemia, and cystic fibrosis.

(d) Children's hospitals also provide essential training for pediatricians, pediatric specialists and others who treat children, and they conduct critically important medical research that benefits all of California's children.

(e) However, the burden of providing uncompensated care and the increasing costs of health care seriously impair our children's hospitals' ability to modernize and expand their facilities and to purchase the latest medical technologies and special medical equipment necessary to take care of sick children.

(f) Therefore, the people desire to provide a steady and ready source of funds for capital improvement programs for children's hospitals to improve the health, welfare, and safety of California's children.

(Added November 4, 2008, by initiative Proposition 3.)

1179.51.

As used in this part, the following terms have the following meanings:

(a) "Authority" means the California Health Facilities Financing Authority established pursuant to Section 15431 of the Government Code.

(b) "Children's hospital" means either of the following:

(1) A University of California general acute care hospital described below:

(A) University of California, Davis Children's Hospital.

(B) Mattel Children's Hospital at University of California, Los Angeles.

(C) University Children's Hospital at University of California, Irvine.

(D) University of California, San Francisco Children's Hospital.

(E) University of California, San Diego Children's Hospital.

(2) A general acute care hospital that is, or is an operating entity of, a California nonprofit corporation incorporated prior to January 1, 2003, whose mission of clinical care, teaching, research, and advocacy focuses on children, and that provides comprehensive pediatric services to a high volume of children eligible for governmental programs and to children with special health care needs eligible for the California Children's Services program and that meets all of the following:

(A) The hospital had at least 160 licensed beds in the categories of pediatric acute, pediatric intensive care and neonatal intensive care in the fiscal year ending between June 30, 2001, and June 29, 2002, as reported to the Office of Statewide Health Planning and Development on or before July 1, 2003.

(B) The hospital provided over 30,000 total pediatric patient (census) days, excluding nursery acute days, in the fiscal year ending between June 30, 2001, and June 29, 2002, as reported to the Office of Statewide Health Planning and Development on or before July 1, 2003.

(C) The hospital provided medical education to at least eight, rounded to the nearest whole integer, full-time equivalent pediatric or pediatric subspecialty residents in the fiscal year ending between June 30, 2001, and June 29, 2002, as reported to the Office of Statewide Health Planning and Development on or before July 1, 2003.

(c) "Committee" means the Children's Hospital Bond Act Finance Committee created pursuant to Section 1179.61.

(d) "Fund" means the Children's Hospital Bond Act Fund created pursuant to Section 1179.53.

(e) "Grant" means the distribution of money in the fund by the authority to children's hospitals for projects pursuant to this part.

(f) "Program" means the Children's Hospital Program established pursuant to this part.

(g) "Project" means constructing, expanding, remodeling, renovating, furnishing, equipping, financing, or refinancing of a children's hospital to be financed or refinanced with funds provided in whole or in part pursuant to this part. "Project" may include reimbursement for the costs of constructing, expanding, remodeling, renovating, furnishing, equipping, financing, or refinancing of a children's hospital where these costs are incurred after January 31, 2008. "Project" may include any combination of one or more of the foregoing undertaken jointly by any participating children's hospital that qualifies under this part.

(Added November 4, 2008, by initiative Proposition 3.)

CHAPTER 2. The Children's Hospital Program [1179.53 - 1179.58]

(Chapter 2 added November 4, 2008, by initiative Proposition 3.)
1179.53.
The proceeds of bonds issued and sold pursuant to this part shall be deposited in the Children's Hospital Bond Act Fund, which is hereby created.
(Added November 4, 2008, by initiative Proposition 3.)
1179.54.
The purpose of the Children's Hospital Program is to improve the health and welfare of California's critically ill children, by providing a stable and ready source of funds for capital improvement projects for children's hospitals. The program provided for in this part is in the public interest, serves a public purpose, and will promote the health, welfare, and safety of the citizens of the state.
(Added November 4, 2008, by initiative Proposition 3.)
1179.55.
The authority is authorized to award grants to any children's hospital for purposes of funding projects, as defined in subdivision (g) of Section 1179.51.
(Added November 4, 2008, by initiative Proposition 3.)
1179.56.
(a) Twenty percent of the total funds available for grants pursuant to this part shall be awarded to children's hospitals as defined in paragraph (1) of subdivision (b) of Section 1179.51.
(b) Eighty percent of the total funds available for grants pursuant to this part shall be awarded to children's hospitals as defined in paragraph (2) of subdivision (b) of Section 1179.51.
(Added November 4, 2008, by initiative Proposition 3.)
1179.57.
(a) The authority shall develop a written application for the awarding of grants under this part within 90 days of the adoption of this act. The authority shall award grants to eligible children's hospitals, subject to the limitations of this part and to further the purposes of this part based on the following factors:
(1) The grant will contribute toward expansion or improvement of health care access by children eligible for governmental health insurance programs and indigent, underserved, and uninsured children.
(2) The grant will contribute toward the improvement of child health care or pediatric patient outcomes.
(3) The children's hospital provides uncompensated or undercompensated care to indigent or public pediatric patients.
(4) The children's hospital provides services to vulnerable pediatric populations.
(5) The children's hospital promotes pediatric teaching or research programs.
(6) Demonstration of project readiness and project feasibility.
(b) (1) An application for funds shall be submitted to the authority for approval as to its conformity with the requirements of this part.
(2) The authority shall process and award grants in a timely manner, not to exceed 60 days.
(c) A children's hospital identified in paragraph (1) of subdivision (b) of Section 1179.51 shall not apply for, and the authority shall not award to that children's hospital, a grant that would cause the total amount of grants awarded to that children's hospital to exceed one-fifth of the total funds available for grants to all children's hospitals pursuant to subdivision (a) of Section 1179.56. Notwithstanding this grant limitation, any funds available under subdivision (a) of Section 1179.56 that have not been exhausted by June 30, 2018, shall become available for an application from any children's hospital identified in paragraph (1) of subdivision (b) of Section 1179.51.
(d) A children's hospital identified in paragraph (2) of subdivision (b) of Section 1179.51 shall not apply for, and the authority shall not award to that children's hospital, a grant that would cause the total amount of grants awarded to that children's hospital to exceed ninety-eight million dollars ($98,000,000) from funds available for grants to all children's hospitals pursuant to subdivision (b) of Section 1179.56. Notwithstanding this grant limitation, any funds available under subdivision (b) of Section 1179.56 that have not been exhausted by June 30, 2018, shall become available for an application from any children's hospital defined in paragraph (2) of subdivision (b) of Section 1179.51.
(e) In no event shall a grant to finance a project exceed the total cost of the project, as determined by the children's hospital and approved by the authority.
(f) All projects that are awarded grants shall be completed within a reasonable period of time. If the authority determines that the children's hospital has failed to complete the project under the terms specified in awarding the grant, the authority may require remedies, including the return of all or a portion of the grant. A children's hospital receiving a grant under this part shall submit certification of project completion to the authority.
(g) Grants shall only be available pursuant to this section if the authority determines that it has sufficient money available in the fund. Nothing in this section shall require the authority to award grants if the authority determines that it has insufficient moneys available in the fund to do so.
(h) The authority may annually determine the amount available for purposes of this part. Administrative costs for this program shall not exceed the actual costs or 1 percent, whichever is less.
(Added November 4, 2008, by initiative Proposition 3.)
1179.58.

The Bureau of State Audits may conduct periodic audits to ensure that bond proceeds are awarded in a timely fashion and in a manner consistent with the requirements of this part, and that awardees of bond proceeds are using funds in compliance with applicable provisions of this part.
(Added November 4, 2008, by initiative Proposition 3.)

CHAPTER 3. Fiscal Provisions [1179.59 - 1179.72]

(Chapter 3 added November 4, 2008, by initiative Proposition 3.)
1179.59.
Bonds in the total amount of nine hundred eighty million dollars ($980,000,000), not including the amount of any refunding bonds, may be issued and sold to provide a fund to be used for carrying out the purposes expressed in this part and to reimburse the General Obligation Bond Expense Revolving Fund pursuant to Section 16724.5 of the Government Code. The bonds, when sold, shall be and constitute a valid and binding obligation of the State of California, and the full faith and credit of the State of California is hereby pledged for the punctual payment of the principal of, and interest on, the bonds as the principal and interest become due and payable.
(Added November 4, 2008, by initiative Proposition 3.)
1179.60.
The bonds authorized by this part shall be prepared, executed, issued, sold, paid, and redeemed as provided in the State General Obligation Bond Law (Chapter 4 (commencing with Section 16720) of Part 3 of Division 4 of Title 2 of the Government Code), and all of the provisions of that law apply to the bonds and to this part and are hereby incorporated in this part as though set forth in full in this part.
(Added November 4, 2008, by initiative Proposition 3.)
1179.61.
(a) Solely for the purpose of authorizing the issuance and sale pursuant to the State General Obligation Bond Law of the bonds authorized by this part, the Children's Hospital Bond Act Finance Committee is hereby created. For purposes of this part, the Children's Hospital Bond Act Finance Committee is "the committee" as that term is used in the State General Obligation Bond Law. The committee consists of the Controller, Director of Finance, and the Treasurer, or their designated representatives. The Treasurer shall serve as chairperson of the committee. A majority of the committee may act for the committee.
(b) The authority is designated the "board" for purposes of the State General Obligation Bond Law, and shall administer the program pursuant to this part.
(Added November 4, 2008, by initiative Proposition 3.)
1179.62.
The committee shall determine whether or not it is necessary or desirable to issue bonds authorized pursuant to this part in order to carry out the actions specified in Section 1179.54 and, if so, the amount of bonds to be issued and sold. Successive issues of bonds may be authorized and sold to carry out those actions progressively, and it is not necessary that all of the bonds be issued or sold at any one time.
(Added November 4, 2008, by initiative Proposition 3.)
1179.63.
There shall be collected each year and in the same manner and at the same time as other state revenue is collected, in addition to the ordinary revenues of the state, a sum in an amount required to pay the principal of, and interest on, the bonds each year. It is the duty of all officers charged by law with any duty in regard to the collection of the revenue to do and perform each and every act that is necessary to collect that additional sum.
(Added November 4, 2008, by initiative Proposition 3.)
1179.64.
Notwithstanding Section 13340 of the Government Code, there is hereby appropriated continuously from the General Fund in the State Treasury, for the purposes of this part, an amount that will equal the total of the following:
(a) The sum annually necessary to pay the principal of, and interest on, bonds issued and sold pursuant to this part, as the principal and interest become due and payable.
(b) The sum necessary to carry out Section 1179.65, appropriated without regard to fiscal years.
(Added November 4, 2008, by initiative Proposition 3.)
1179.65.
For the purposes of carrying out this part, the Director of Finance may authorize the withdrawal from the General Fund of an amount not to exceed the amount of the unsold bonds that have been authorized by the committee to be sold for the purpose of carrying out this part. Any amounts withdrawn shall be deposited in the fund. Any money made available under this section shall be returned to the General Fund from proceeds received from the sale of bonds for the purpose of carrying out this part.
(Added November 4, 2008, by initiative Proposition 3.)
1179.66.
All money deposited in the fund that is derived from premium and accrued interest on bonds sold shall be reserved in the fund and shall be available for transfer to the General Fund as a credit to expenditures for bond interest.
(Added November 4, 2008, by initiative Proposition 3.)
1179.67.
Pursuant to Chapter 4 (commencing with Section 16720) of Part 3 of Division 4 of Title 2 of the Government Code, the cost of bond issuance shall be paid out of the bond proceeds. These costs shall be shared proportionally by each children's hospital funded through this bond act.

(Added November 4, 2008, by initiative Proposition 3.)

1179.68.

The authority may request the Pooled Money Investment Board to make a loan from the Pooled Money Investment Account, including other authorized forms of interim financing that include, but are not limited to, commercial paper, in accordance with Section 16312 of the Government Code, for purposes of carrying out this part. The amount of the request shall not exceed the amount of the unsold bonds that the committee, by resolution, has authorized to be sold for the purpose of carrying out this part. The authority shall execute any documents required by the Pooled Money Investment Board to obtain and repay the loan. Any amounts loaned shall be deposited in the fund to be allocated by the board in accordance with this part.

(Added November 4, 2008, by initiative Proposition 3.)

1179.69.

The bonds may be refunded in accordance with Article 6 (commencing with Section 16780) of Chapter 4 of Part 3 of Division 4 of Title 2 of the Government Code, which is a part of the State General Obligation Bond Law. Approval by the voters of the state for the issuance of the bonds described in this part includes the approval of the issuance of any bonds issued to refund any bonds originally issued under this part or any previously issued refunding bonds.

(Added November 4, 2008, by initiative Proposition 3.)

1179.70.

Notwithstanding any other provision of this part, or of the State General Obligation Bond Law, if the Treasurer sells bonds pursuant to this part that include a bond counsel opinion to the effect that the interest on the bonds is excluded from gross income for federal tax purposes, subject to designated conditions, the Treasurer may maintain separate accounts for the investment of bond proceeds and for the investment of earnings on those proceeds. The Treasurer may use or direct the use of those proceeds or earnings to pay any rebate, penalty, or other payment required under federal law or take any other action with respect to the investment and use of those bond proceeds required or desirable under federal law to maintain the tax-exempt status of those bonds and to obtain any other advantage under federal law on behalf of the funds of this state.

(Added November 4, 2008, by initiative Proposition 3.)

1179.71.

The people hereby find and declare that, inasmuch as the proceeds from the sale of bonds authorized by this part are not "proceeds of taxes" as that term is used in Article XIII B of the California Constitution, the disbursement of these proceeds is not subject to the limitations imposed by that part.

(Added November 4, 2008, by initiative Proposition 3.)

1179.72.

Notwithstanding any other provision of this part, the provisions of this part are severable. If any provision of this part or its application is held invalid, that invalidity shall not affect other provisions or applications that can be given effect without the invalid provision or application.

(Added November 4, 2008, by initiative Proposition 3.)

PART 6.2. Naloxone Grant Program [1179.80- 1179.80.]

(Part 6.2 added by Stats. 2016, Ch. 30, Sec. 2.)

1179.80.

(a) In order to reduce the rate of fatal overdose from opioid drugs including heroin and prescription opioids, the State Department of Public Health shall, subject to an appropriation for this purpose in the Budget Act of 2016, award funding to local health departments, local government agencies, or on a competitive basis to community-based organizations, regional opioid prevention coalitions, or both, to support or establish programs that provide Naloxone to first responders and to at-risk opioid users through programs that serve at-risk drug users, including, but not limited to, syringe exchange and disposal programs, homeless programs, and substance use disorder treatment providers.

(b) The department may award grants itself or enter into contracts to carry out the provisions of subdivision (a). The award of contracts and grants is exempt from Part 2 (commencing with Section 10100) of Division 2 of the Public Contract Code and is exempt from approval by the Department of General Services prior to their execution.

(c) Not more than 10 percent of the funds appropriated shall be available to the department for its administrative costs in implementing this section. If deemed necessary by the department, the department may allocate funds to other state departments to assist in the implementation of subdivision (a).

(Added by Stats. 2016, Ch. 30, Sec. 2. (SB 833) Effective June 27, 2016.)

PART 6.3. CHILDREN'S HOSPITAL BOND ACT OF 2018 [1179.81 - 1179.102]

(Part 6.3 added November 6, 2018, by initiative Proposition 4, Sec. 1.)

CHAPTER 1. General Provisions [1179.81 - 1179.82]

(Chapter 1 added November 6, 2018, by initiative Proposition 4, Sec. 1.)

1179.81.

(a) This part shall be known, and may be cited, as the Children's Hospital Bond Act of 2018.

(b) California's network of regional children's hospitals provide vital health care services to children facing life-threatening illness or injury. Over one million times each year, children are cared for at these hospitals without regard to their family's ability to pay.

(c) Children's hospitals also provide specialized treatment and care that has increased the survival of children suffering from serious diseases and illnesses such as childhood leukemia, cancer, heart defects, diabetes, sickle cell anemia, and cystic fibrosis.

(d) Children's hospitals also provide essential training for pediatricians, pediatric specialists and others who treat children, and they conduct critically important medical research that benefits all of California's children.

(e) However, the burden of providing uncompensated care and the increasing costs of health care seriously impair our children's hospitals' ability to modernize and expand their facilities and to purchase the latest medical technologies and special medical equipment necessary to take care of sick children.

(f) Therefore, the people desire to provide a steady and ready source of funds for capital improvement programs for children's hospitals to improve the health, welfare, and safety of California's children.

(Added November 6, 2018, by initiative Proposition 4, Sec. 1. Effective December 19, 2018.)

1179.82.

As used in this part, the following terms have the following meanings:

(a) "Authority" means the California Health Facilities Financing Authority established pursuant to Section 15431 of the Government Code.

(b) "Children's hospital" means either of the following:

(1) A University of California general acute care hospital described below:

(A) University of California, Davis Children's Hospital.

(B) Mattel Children's Hospital at University of California, Los Angeles.

(C) University Children's Hospital at University of California, Irvine.

(D) University of California, San Francisco Children's Hospital.

(E) University of California, San Diego Children's Hospital.

(2) A general acute care hospital that is, or is an operating entity of, a California nonprofit corporation that received a grant or grants pursuant to Part 6 (commencing with Section 1179.10) or Part 6.1 (commencing with Section 1179.50) that provides comprehensive pediatric services to a high volume of children eligible for governmental programs and to children with special health care needs eligible for the California Children's Services Program.

(c) "Committee" means the Children's Hospital Bond Act Finance Committee created pursuant to Section 1179.91.

(d) "Fund" means the Children's Hospital Bond Act Fund created pursuant to Section 1179.83.

(e) "Grant" means the distribution of money in the fund by the authority to children's hospitals for projects pursuant to this part or to an eligible hospital pursuant to this part.

(f) "Program" means the Children's Hospital Program established pursuant to this part.

(g) "Project" means constructing, expanding, remodeling, renovating, furnishing, equipping, financing, or refinancing of a children's hospital to be financed or refinanced with funds provided in whole or in part pursuant to this part. "Project" may include reimbursement for the costs of constructing, expanding, remodeling, renovating, furnishing, equipping, financing, or refinancing of a children's hospital where these costs are incurred after January 1, 2018. "Project" may include any combination of one or more of the foregoing undertaken jointly by two or more participating children's hospitals that qualify under this part.

(Added November 6, 2018, by initiative Proposition 4, Sec. 1. Effective December 19, 2018.)

CHAPTER 2. The Children's Hospital Program [1179.83 - 1179.88]

(Chapter 2 added November 6, 2018, by initiative Proposition 4, Sec. 1.)

1179.83.

The proceeds of bonds issued and sold pursuant to this part shall be deposited in the Children's Hospital Bond Act Fund, which is hereby created.

(Added November 6, 2018, by initiative Proposition 4, Sec. 1. Effective December 19, 2018.)

1179.84.

The purpose of the Children's Hospital Program is to improve the health and welfare of California's critically ill children by providing a stable and ready source of funds for capital improvement projects for children's hospitals. The program provided for in this part is in the public interest, serves a public purpose, and will promote the health, welfare, and safety of the citizens of the state.

(Added November 6, 2018, by initiative Proposition 4, Sec. 1. Effective December 19, 2018.)

1179.85.

The authority is authorized to award grants to any children's hospital for purposes of funding projects, as defined in subdivision (g) of Section 1179.82, or to a hospital pursuant to subdivision (c) of Section 1179.86.

(Added November 6, 2018, by initiative Proposition 4, Sec. 1. Effective December 19, 2018.)

1179.86.

(a) Eighteen percent of the total funds available for grants pursuant to this part shall be awarded to children's hospitals as defined in paragraph (1) of subdivision (b) of Section 1179.82.

(b) Seventy-two percent of the total funds available for grants pursuant to this part shall be awarded to children's hospitals as defined in paragraph (2) of subdivision (b) of Section 1179.82.

(c) Ten percent of the total funds available for grants pursuant to this part shall be available for grants to hospitals that provide pediatric services to children eligible for the California Children's Services Program that are either (1) a public hospital as defined in paragraph (25) of subdivision (a) of Section 14105.98 of the Welfare and Institutions Code, or (2) a general acute care hospital licensed pursuant to Section 1250 of this code that is, or is an operating entity of, a California nonprofit corporation. The funds shall be used solely for constructing, expanding, remodeling, renovating, furnishing, or equipping the pediatric program of an eligible hospital. A children's hospital as defined in subdivision (b) of Section 1179.82 shall not be eligible for grants under this subdivision, except that any funds available under this subdivision that have not been exhausted by June 30, 2033, shall become available for an application from any such children's hospital. The authority shall award grants under procedures it shall adopt to further the purposes of this subdivision.

(Added November 6, 2018, by initiative Proposition 4, Sec. 1. Effective December 19, 2018.)

1179.87.

(a) The authority shall develop a written application for the awarding of grants under this part within 90 days of the adoption of this act. The authority shall award grants to eligible children's hospitals, subject to the limitations of this part and to further the purposes of this part, based on the following factors:

(1) The grant will contribute toward expansion or improvement of health care access by children eligible for governmental health insurance programs and indigent, underserved, and uninsured children.

(2) The grant will contribute toward the improvement of child health care or pediatric patient outcomes.

(3) The children's hospital provides uncompensated or undercompensated care to indigent or public pediatric patients.

(4) The children's hospital provides services to vulnerable pediatric populations.

(5) The children's hospital promotes pediatric teaching or research programs.

(6) Demonstration of project readiness and project feasibility.

(b) (1) An application for funds shall be submitted to the authority for approval as to its conformity with the requirements of this part.

(2) The authority shall process and award grants in a timely manner, not to exceed 60 days.

(c) A children's hospital identified in paragraph (1) of subdivision (b) of Section 1179.82 shall not apply for, and the authority shall not award to that children's hospital, a grant that would cause the total amount of grants awarded to that children's hospital to exceed one-fifth of the total funds available for grants to all children's hospitals pursuant to subdivision (a) of Section 1179.86. Notwithstanding this grant limitation, any funds available under subdivision (a) of Section 1179.86 that have not been exhausted by June 30, 2033, shall become available for an application from any children's hospital identified in paragraph (1) of subdivision (b) of Section 1179.82.

(d) A children's hospital identified in paragraph (2) of subdivision (b) of Section 1179.82 shall not apply for, and the authority shall not award to that children's hospital, a grant that would cause the total amount of grants awarded to that children's hospital to exceed one hundred thirty-five million dollars ($135,000,000) from funds available for grants to all children's hospitals pursuant to subdivision (b) of Section 1179.86. Notwithstanding this grant limitation, any funds available under subdivision (b) of Section 1179.86 that have not been exhausted by June 30, 2033, shall become available for an application from any children's hospital defined in paragraph (2) of subdivision (b) of Section 1179.82.

(e) In no event shall a grant to finance a project exceed the total cost of the project, as determined by the children's hospital and approved by the authority.

(f) All projects that are awarded grants shall be completed within a reasonable period of time. If the authority determines that the children's hospital has failed to complete the project under the terms specified in awarding the grant, the authority may require remedies, including the return of all or a portion of the grant. A children's hospital receiving a grant under this part shall submit certification of project completion to the authority.

(g) Grants shall only be available pursuant to this section if the authority determines that it has sufficient money available in the fund. Nothing in this section shall require the authority to award grants if the authority determines that it has insufficient moneys available in the fund to do so.

(h) The authority may annually determine the amount available for purposes of this part. Administrative costs for this program shall not exceed the actual costs or 1 percent, whichever is less.

(Added November 6, 2018, by initiative Proposition 4, Sec. 1. Effective December 19, 2018.)

1179.88.

The California State Auditor may conduct periodic audits to ensure that bond proceeds are awarded in a timely fashion and in a manner consistent with the requirements of this part and that awardees of bond proceeds are using funds in compliance with applicable provisions of this part.

(Added November 6, 2018, by initiative Proposition 4, Sec. 1. Effective December 19, 2018.)

CHAPTER 3. Fiscal Provisions [1179.89 - 1179.100]

(Chapter 3 added November 6, 2018, by initiative Proposition 4, Sec. 1.)

1179.89.

Bonds in the total amount of one billion five hundred million dollars ($1,500,000,000), not including the amount of any refunding bonds, may be issued and sold to provide a fund to be used for carrying out the purposes expressed in this part and to reimburse the General Obligation Bond Expense Revolving Fund pursuant to Section 16724.5 of the Government Code. The bonds, when sold, shall be and constitute a valid and binding obligation of the state, and the full faith and credit of the state is hereby pledged for the punctual payment of the principal of, and interest on, the bonds as the principal and interest become due and payable.

(Added November 6, 2018, by initiative Proposition 4, Sec. 1. Effective December 19, 2018.)

1179.90.

The bonds authorized by this part shall be prepared, executed, issued, sold, paid, and redeemed as provided in the State General Obligation Bond Law (Chapter 4 (commencing with Section 16720) of Part 3 of Division 4 of Title 2 of the Government Code), and all provisions of that law apply to the bonds and to this part and are hereby incorporated in this part as though set forth in full in this part.

(Added November 6, 2018, by initiative Proposition 4, Sec. 1. Effective December 19, 2018.)

1179.91.

(a) Solely for the purpose of authorizing the issuance and sale pursuant to the State General Obligation Bond Law (Chapter 4 (commencing with Section 16720) of Part 3 of Division 4 of Title 2 of the Government Code) of the bonds authorized by this part, the Children's Hospital Bond Act Finance Committee is hereby created. For purposes of this part, the Children's Hospital Bond Act Finance Committee is the "committee" as that term is used in the State General Obligation Bond Law. The committee consists of the Controller, the Director of Finance, and the Treasurer, or their designated representatives. The Treasurer shall serve as chairperson of the committee. A majority of the committee may act for the committee.

(b) The authority is designated the "board" for purposes of the State General Obligation Bond Law (Chapter 4 (commencing with Section 16720) of Part 3 of Division 4 of Title 2 of the Government Code), and shall administer the program pursuant to this part.

(Added November 6, 2018, by initiative Proposition 4, Sec. 1. Effective December 19, 2018.)

1179.92.

The committee shall determine whether or not it is necessary or desirable to issue bonds authorized pursuant to this part in order to carry out the actions specified in Section 1179.84 and, if so, the amount of bonds to be issued and sold. Successive issues of bonds may be authorized and sold to carry out those actions progressively, and it is not necessary that all of the bonds be issued or sold at any one time.

(Added November 6, 2018, by initiative Proposition 4, Sec. 1. Effective December 19, 2018.)

1179.93.

There shall be collected each year and in the same manner and at the same time as other state revenue is collected, in addition to the ordinary revenues of the state, a sum in an amount required to pay the principal of, and interest on, the bonds each year. It is the duty of all officers charged by law with any duty in regard to the collection of the revenue to do and perform each and every act that is necessary to collect that additional sum.

(Added November 6, 2018, by initiative Proposition 4, Sec. 1. Effective December 19, 2018.)

1179.94.

Notwithstanding Section 13340 of the Government Code, there is hereby appropriated continuously from the General Fund in the State Treasury, for the purposes of this part, an amount that equals the total of the following:

(a) The sum annually necessary to pay the principal of, and interest on, bonds issued and sold pursuant to this part, as the principal and interest become due and payable.

(b) The sum necessary to carry out Section 1179.95, appropriated without regard to fiscal years.

(Added November 6, 2018, by initiative Proposition 4, Sec. 1. Effective December 19, 2018.)

1179.95.

For the purposes of carrying out this part, the Director of Finance may authorize the withdrawal from the General Fund of an amount not to exceed the amount of the unsold bonds that have been authorized by the committee to be sold for the purpose of carrying out this part. Any amounts withdrawn shall be deposited in the fund. Any money made available under this section shall be returned to the General Fund from proceeds received from the sale of bonds for the purpose of carrying out this part.

(Added November 6, 2018, by initiative Proposition 4, Sec. 1. Effective December 19, 2018.)

1179.96.

All money deposited in the fund that is derived from premium and accrued interest on bonds sold shall be reserved in the fund and shall be available for transfer to the General Fund as a credit to expenditures for bond interest.

(Added November 6, 2018, by initiative Proposition 4, Sec. 1. Effective December 19, 2018.)

1179.97.

Pursuant to Chapter 4 (commencing with Section 16720) of Part 3 of Division 4 of Title 2 of the Government Code, the cost of bond issuance shall be paid out of the bond proceeds. These costs shall be shared proportionally by each children's hospital funded through this bond act.

(Added November 6, 2018, by initiative Proposition 4, Sec. 1. Effective December 19, 2018.)

1179.98.

The authority may request the Pooled Money Investment Board to make a loan from the Pooled Money Investment Account, including other authorized forms of interim financing that include, but are not limited to, commercial paper, in accordance with Section 16312 of the Government Code, for purposes of carrying out this part. The amount of the request shall not exceed the amount of the unsold bonds that the committee, by resolution, has authorized to be sold for the purpose of carrying out this part. The authority shall execute any documents required by the Pooled Money Investment Board to obtain and repay the loan. Any amounts loaned shall be deposited in the fund to be allocated by the board in accordance with this part.

(Added November 6, 2018, by initiative Proposition 4, Sec. 1. Effective December 19, 2018.)

1179.99.

The bonds may be refunded in accordance with Article 6 (commencing with Section 16780) of Chapter 4 of Part 3 of Division 4 of Title 2 of the Government Code, which is a part of the State General Obligation Bond Law. Approval by the voters of the state for the issuance of the bonds described in this part includes the approval of the issuance of any bonds issued to refund any bonds originally issued under this part or any previously issued refunding bonds.

(Added November 6, 2018, by initiative Proposition 4, Sec. 1. Effective December 19, 2018.)

1179.100.

Notwithstanding any other provision of this part, or of the State General Obligation Bond Law (Chapter 4 (commencing with Section 16720) of Part 3 of Division 4 of Title 2 of the Government Code), if the Treasurer sells bonds pursuant to this part that include a bond counsel opinion to the effect that the interest on the bonds is excluded from gross income for federal tax purposes, subject to designated conditions, the Treasurer may maintain separate accounts for the investment of bond proceeds and for the investment of earnings on those proceeds. The Treasurer may use or direct the use of those proceeds or earnings to pay any rebate, penalty, or other payment required under federal law or take any other action with respect to the investment and use of those bond proceeds required or desirable under federal law to maintain the tax-exempt status of those bonds and to obtain any other advantage under federal law on behalf of the funds of this state.

(Added November 6, 2018, by initiative Proposition 4, Sec. 1. Effective December 19, 2018.)

CHAPTER 4. General Provisions [1179.101 - 1179.102]

(Chapter 4 added November 6, 2018, by initiative Proposition 4, Sec. 1.)

1179.101.

The people hereby find and declare that, inasmuch as the proceeds from the sale of bonds authorized by this part are not "proceeds of taxes" as that term is used in Article XIII B of the California Constitution, the disbursement of these proceeds is not subject to the limitations imposed by that article.

(Added November 6, 2018, by initiative Proposition 4, Sec. 1. Effective December 19, 2018.)

1179.102.

Notwithstanding any other provision of this part, the provisions of this part are severable. If any provision of this part or its application is held invalid, that invalidity shall not affect other provisions or applications that can be given effect without the invalid provision or application.

(Added November 6, 2018, by initiative Proposition 4, Sec. 1. Effective December 19, 2018.)

DIVISION 1.5. USE OF SECLUSION AND BEHAVIORAL RESTRAINTS IN FACILITIES [1180 - 1180.6]

(Division 1.5 added by Stats. 2003, Ch. 750, Sec. 2.)

1180.

(a) The California Health and Human Services Agency, in accordance with their mission, shall provide the leadership and coordination necessary to reduce the use of seclusion and behavioral restraints in facilities that are licensed, certified, or monitored by departments that fall within its jurisdiction.

(b) The agency may make recommendations to the Legislature for additional facilities, or for additional units or departments within facilities, that should be included within the requirements of this division in the future, including, but not limited to, emergency rooms.

(c) At the request of the secretary, the involved state departments shall provide information regarding existing training protocols and requirements related to the utilization of seclusion and behavioral restraints by direct care staff who work in facilities within their jurisdiction. All involved state departments shall cooperate in implementing any training protocols established pursuant to this division. It is the intent of the Legislature that training protocols developed pursuant to this division be incorporated into existing training requirements and opportunities. It is further the intent of the Legislature that, to the extent feasible, the training protocols developed pursuant to Section 1180.2 be utilized in the development of training protocols developed pursuant to Section 1180.3.

(d) The secretary, or his or her designee, is encouraged to pursue federal and private funding to support the development of a training protocol that can be incorporated into the existing training activities for direct care staff conducted by the state, facilities, and educational institutions in order to reduce the use of seclusion and behavioral restraints.

(e) The secretary or his or her designee shall make recommendations to the Legislature on how to best assess the impact of serious staff injuries sustained during the use of seclusion or behavioral restraints, on staffing costs, and on workers' compensation claims and costs.

(f) The agency shall not be required to implement this section if implementation cannot be achieved within existing resources, unless additional funding for this purpose becomes available. The agency and involved departments may incrementally implement this section in order to accomplish its goals within existing resources, through the use of federal or private funding, or upon the subsequent appropriation of funds by the Legislature for this purpose, or all of these.

(Added by Stats. 2003, Ch. 750, Sec. 2. Effective January 1, 2004.)

1180.1.

For purposes of this division, the following definitions apply:

(a) "Behavioral restraint" means "mechanical restraint" or "physical restraint" as defined in this section, used as an intervention when a person presents an immediate danger to self or to others. It does not include restraints used for medical purposes, including, but not limited to, securing an intravenous needle or immobilizing a person for a surgical procedure, or postural restraints, or devices used to prevent injury or to improve a person's mobility and independent functioning rather than to restrict movement.

(b) "Containment" means a brief physical restraint of a person for the purpose of effectively gaining quick control of a person who is aggressive or agitated or who is a danger to self or others.

(c) "Mechanical restraint" means the use of a mechanical device, material, or equipment attached or adjacent to the person's body that he or she cannot easily remove and that restricts the freedom of movement of all or part of a person's body or restricts normal access to the person's body, and that is used as a behavioral restraint.

(d) "Physical restraint" means the use of a manual hold to restrict freedom of movement of all or part of a person's body, or to restrict normal access to the person's body, and that is used as a behavioral restraint. "Physical restraint" is staff-to-person physical contact in which the person unwillingly participates. "Physical restraint" does not include briefly holding a person without undue force in order to calm or comfort, or physical contact intended to gently assist a person in performing tasks or to guide or assist a person from one area to another.

(e) "Seclusion" means the involuntary confinement of a person alone in a room or an area from which the person is physically prevented from leaving. "Seclusion" does not include a "timeout," as defined in regulations relating to facilities operated by the State Department of Developmental Services.

(f) "Secretary" means the Secretary of California Health and Human Services.

(g) "Serious injury" means significant impairment of the physical condition as determined by qualified medical personnel, and includes, but is not limited to, burns, lacerations, bone fractures, substantial hematoma, or injuries to internal organs.

(Amended by Stats. 2008, Ch. 179, Sec. 135. Effective January 1, 2009.)

1180.2.

(a) This section shall apply to the state hospitals operated by the State Department of State Hospitals and facilities operated by the State Department of Developmental Services that utilize seclusion or behavioral restraints.

(b) The State Department of State Hospitals and the State Department of Developmental Services shall develop technical assistance and training programs to support the efforts of facilities described in subdivision (a) to reduce or eliminate the use of seclusion and behavioral restraints in those facilities.

(c) Technical assistance and training programs should be designed with the input of stakeholders, including clients and direct care staff, and should be based on best practices that lead to the avoidance of the use of seclusion and behavioral restraints, including, but not limited to, all of the following:

(1) Conducting an intake assessment that is consistent with facility policies and that includes issues specific to the use of seclusion and behavioral restraints as specified in Section 1180.4.

(2) Utilizing strategies to engage clients collaboratively in assessment, avoidance, and management of crisis situations in order to prevent incidents of the use of seclusion and behavioral restraints.

(3) Recognizing and responding appropriately to underlying reasons for escalating behavior.

(4) Utilizing conflict resolution, effective communication, deescalation, and client-centered problem solving strategies that diffuse and safely resolve emerging crisis situations.

(5) Individual treatment planning that identifies risk factors, positive early intervention strategies, and strategies to minimize time spent in seclusion or behavioral restraints. Individual treatment planning should include input from the person affected.

(6) While minimizing the duration of time spent in seclusion or behavioral restraints, using strategies to mitigate the emotional and physical discomfort and ensure the safety of the person involved in seclusion or behavioral restraints, including input from the person about what would alleviate his or her distress.

(7) Training in conducting an effective debriefing meeting as specified in Section 1180.5, including the appropriate persons to involve, the voluntary participation of the person who has been in seclusion or behavioral restraints, and strategic interventions to engage affected persons in the process. The training should include strategies that result in maximum participation and comfort for the involved parties to identify factors that lead to the use of seclusion and behavioral restraints and factors that would reduce the likelihood of future incidents.

(d) (1) The State Department of State Hospitals and the State Department of Developmental Services shall take steps to establish a system of mandatory, consistent, timely, and publicly accessible data collection regarding the use of seclusion and behavioral restraints in facilities described in this section. It is the intent of the Legislature that data be compiled in a manner that allows for standard statistical comparison.

(2) The State Department of State Hospitals and the State Department of Developmental Services shall develop a mechanism for making this information publicly available on the Internet.

(3) Data collected pursuant to this section shall include all of the following:

(A) The number of deaths that occur while persons are in seclusion or behavioral restraints, or where it is reasonable to assume that a death was proximately related to the use of seclusion or behavioral restraints.

(B) The number of serious injuries sustained by persons while in seclusion or subject to behavioral restraints.

(C) The number of serious injuries sustained by staff that occur during the use of seclusion or behavioral restraints.

(D) The number of incidents of seclusion.

(E) The number of incidents of use of behavioral restraints.

(F) The duration of time spent per incident in seclusion.

(G) The duration of time spent per incident subject to behavioral restraints.

(H) The number of times an involuntary emergency medication is used to control behavior, as defined by the State Department of State Hospitals.

(e) A facility described in subdivision (a) shall report each death or serious injury of a person occurring during, or related to, the use of seclusion or behavioral restraints. This report shall be made to the agency designated in subdivision (i) of Section 4900 of the Welfare and Institutions Code no later than the close of the business day following the death or injury. The report shall include the encrypted identifier of the person involved, and the name, street address, and telephone number of the facility.

(f) A facility described in subdivision (a) and that is operated by the State Department of Developmental Services shall not place any individual with a developmental disability in seclusion.

(g) (1) On a monthly basis, a facility described in subdivision (a) that is operated by the State Department of Developmental Services shall report to the protection and advocacy agency described in subdivision (i) of Section 4900 all of the following:

(A) The number of incidents of the use of behavioral restraints and the duration of time spent per incident of restraint.

(B) The number of times an involuntary emergency medication is used to control behavior.

(2) The reports required pursuant to paragraph (1) shall include the name, street address, and telephone number of the facility.

(Amended by Stats. 2017, Ch. 18, Sec. 2. (AB 107) Effective June 27, 2017.)

1180.3.

(a) This section shall apply to psychiatric units of general acute care hospitals, acute psychiatric hospitals, psychiatric health facilities, crisis stabilization units, community treatment facilities, group homes, skilled nursing facilities, intermediate care facilities, community care facilities, and mental health rehabilitation centers.

(b) (1) The secretary or his or her designee shall develop technical assistance and training programs to support the efforts of facilities to reduce or eliminate the use of seclusion and behavioral restraints in those facilities that utilize them.

(2) Technical assistance and training programs should be designed with the input of stakeholders, including clients and direct care staff, and should be based on best practices that lead to the avoidance of the use of seclusion and behavioral restraints. In order to avoid redundancies and to promote consistency across various types of facilities, it is the intent of the Legislature that the technical assistance and training program, to the extent possible, be based on that developed pursuant to Section 1180.2.

(c) (1) The secretary or his or her designee shall take steps to establish a system of mandatory, consistent, timely, and publicly accessible data collection regarding the use of seclusion and behavioral restraints in all facilities described in subdivision (a) that utilize seclusion and behavioral restraints. In determining a system of data collection, the secretary should utilize existing efforts, and direct new or ongoing efforts, of associated state departments to revise or improve their data collection systems. The secretary or his or her designee shall make recommendations for a mechanism to ensure compliance by facilities, including, but not limited to, penalties for failure to report in a timely manner. It is the intent of the Legislature that data be compiled in a manner that allows for standard

statistical comparison and be maintained for each facility subject to reporting requirements for the use of seclusion and behavioral restraints.

(2) The secretary shall develop a mechanism for making this information, as it becomes available, publicly available on the Internet. For data currently being collected, this paragraph shall be implemented as soon as it reasonably can be achieved within existing resources. As new reporting requirements are developed and result in additional data becoming available, this additional data shall be included in the data publicly available on the Internet pursuant to this paragraph.

(3) At the direction of the secretary, the departments shall cooperate and share resources for developing uniform reporting for all facilities. Uniform reporting of seclusion and behavioral restraint utilization information shall, to the extent possible, be incorporated into existing reporting requirements for facilities described in subdivision (a).

(4) Data collected pursuant to this subdivision shall include all of the data described in paragraph (3) of subdivision (d) of Section 1180.2.

(5) The secretary or his or her designee shall work with the state departments that have responsibility for oversight of the use of seclusion and behavioral restraints to review and eliminate redundancies and outdated requirements in the reporting of data on the use of seclusion and behavioral restraints in order to ensure cost-effectiveness.

(d) Neither the agency nor any department shall be required to implement this section if implementation cannot be achieved within existing resources, unless additional funding for this purpose becomes available. The agency and involved departments may incrementally implement this section in order to accomplish its goals within existing resources, through the use of federal or private funding, or upon the subsequent appropriation of funds by the Legislature for this purpose, or all of these.

(Added by Stats. 2003, Ch. 750, Sec. 2. Effective January 1, 2004.)

1180.4.

(a) A facility described in subdivision (a) of Section 1180.2 or subdivision (a) of Section 1180.3 shall conduct an initial assessment of each person prior to a placement decision or upon admission to the facility, or as soon thereafter as possible. This assessment shall include input from the person and from someone whom the person desires to be present, such as a family member, significant other, or authorized representative designated by the person, and if the desired third party can be present at the time of admission. This assessment shall also include, based on the information available at the time of initial assessment, all of the following:

(1) A person's advance directive regarding deescalation or the use of seclusion or behavioral restraints.

(2) Identification of early warning signs, triggers, and precipitants that cause a person to escalate, and identification of the earliest precipitant of aggression for persons with a known or suspected history of aggressiveness, or persons who are currently aggressive.

(3) Techniques, methods, or tools that would help the person control the person's behavior.

(4) Preexisting medical conditions or any physical disabilities or limitations that would place the person at greater risk during restraint or seclusion.

(5) Any trauma history, including any history of sexual or physical abuse that the affected person feels is relevant.

(b) A facility described in subdivision (a) of Section 1180.2 or subdivision (a) of Section 1180.3 may use seclusion or behavioral restraints for behavioral emergencies only when a person's behavior presents an imminent danger of serious harm to self or others.

(c) A facility described in subdivision (a) of Section 1180.2 or subdivision (a) of Section 1180.3 shall not use either of the following:

(1) A physical restraint or containment technique that obstructs a person's respiratory airway or impairs the person's breathing or respiratory capacity, including techniques in which a staff member places pressure on a person's back or places the staff member's body weight against the person's torso or back.

(2) A pillow, blanket, or other item covering the person's face as part of a physical or mechanical restraint or containment process.

(d) A facility described in subdivision (a) of Section 1180.2 or subdivision (a) of Section 1180.3 shall not use physical or mechanical restraint or containment on a person who has a known medical or physical condition and there is reason to believe that the use would endanger the person's life or seriously exacerbate the person's medical condition.

(e) (1) A facility described in subdivision (a) of Section 1180.2 or subdivision (a) of Section 1180.3 shall not use prone mechanical restraint on a person at risk for positional asphyxiation as a result of one of the following risk factors that are known to the provider:

(A) Obesity.

(B) Pregnancy.

(C) Agitated delirium or excited delirium syndromes.

(D) Cocaine, methamphetamine, or alcohol intoxication.

(E) Exposure to pepper spray.

(F) Preexisting heart disease, including, but not limited to, an enlarged heart or other cardiovascular disorders.

(G) Respiratory conditions, including emphysema, bronchitis, or asthma.

(2) Paragraph (1) shall not apply when written authorization has been provided by a physician, made to accommodate a person's stated preference for the prone position or because the physician judges other clinical risks to take precedence. The written authorization may not be a standing order, and shall be evaluated on a case-by-case basis by the physician.

(f) A facility described in subdivision (a) of Section 1180.2 or subdivision (a) of Section 1180.3 shall avoid the deliberate use of prone containment techniques whenever possible, utilizing the best practices in early intervention techniques, such as deescalation. If prone containment techniques are used in an emergency situation, a staff member shall observe the person for any signs of physical duress throughout the use of prone containment. Whenever possible, the staff member monitoring the person shall not be involved in restraining the person.

(g) A facility described in subdivision (a) of Section 1180.2 or subdivision (a) of Section 1180.3 shall not place a person in a facedown position with the person's hands held or restrained behind the person's back.

(h) A facility described in subdivision (a) of Section 1180.2 or subdivision (a) of Section 1180.3 shall not use physical restraint or containment as an extended procedure. A facility described in subdivision (a) of Section 4684.80 or paragraph (1) of subdivision (a) of Section 4698 of the Welfare and Institutions Code that is licensed by the State Department of Social Services shall not use physical restraint or containment for more than 15 consecutive minutes. The department may, by regulation, authorize an exception to the 15-minute maximum duration if necessary to protect the immediate health and safety of residents or others from risk of imminent serious physical harm and the use of physical restraint or containment conforms to the facility program plan approved by the State Department of Developmental Services pursuant to subdivision (i) of Section 4684.81 or subdivision (d) of Section 4698, as applicable, of the Welfare and Institutions Code.

(i) A facility described in subdivision (a) of Section 1180.2 or subdivision (a) of Section 1180.3 shall keep under constant, face-to-face human observation a person who is in seclusion and in any type of behavioral restraint at the same time. Observation by means of video camera may be utilized only in facilities that are already permitted to use video monitoring under federal regulations specific to that facility.

(j) A facility described in subdivision (a) of Section 1180.2 or subdivision (a) of Section 1180.3 shall afford to persons who are restrained the least restrictive alternative and the maximum freedom of movement, while ensuring the physical safety of the person and others, and shall use the least number of restraint points.

(k) A person in a facility described in subdivision (a) of Section 1180.2 and subdivision (a) of Section 1180.3 has the right to be free from the use of seclusion and behavioral restraints of any form imposed as a means of coercion, discipline, convenience, or retaliation by staff. This right includes, but is not limited to, the right to be free from the use of a drug used in order to control behavior or to restrict the person's freedom of movement, if that drug is not a standard treatment for the person's medical or psychiatric condition.

(Amended by Stats. 2019, Ch. 28, Sec. 1. (SB 81) Effective June 27, 2019.)
1180.5.

(a) A facility described in subdivision (a) of Section 1180.2 or subdivision (a) of Section 1180.3 shall conduct a clinical and quality review for each episode of the use of seclusion or behavioral restraints.

(b) A facility described in subdivision (a) of Section 1180.2 or subdivision (a) of Section 1180.3 shall, as quickly as possible but no later than 24 hours after the use of seclusion or behavioral restraints, conduct a debriefing regarding the incident with the person, and, if the person requests it, the person's family member, domestic partner, significant other, or authorized representative, if the desired third party can be present at the time of the debriefing at no cost to the facility, as well as with the staff members involved in the incident, if reasonably available, and a supervisor, to discuss how to avoid a similar incident in the future. The person's participation in the debriefing shall be voluntary. The purposes of the debriefing shall be to do all of the following:

(1) Assist the person to identify the precipitant of the incident, and suggest methods of more safely and constructively responding to the incident.

(2) Assist the staff to understand the precipitants to the incident, and to develop alternative methods of helping the person avoid or cope with those incidents.

(3) Help treatment team staff devise treatment interventions to address the root cause of the incident and its consequences, and to modify the treatment plan.

(4) Help assess whether the intervention was necessary and whether it was implemented in a manner consistent with staff training and facility policies.

(c) The facility shall, in the debriefing, provide both the person and staff the opportunity to discuss the circumstances resulting in the use of seclusion or behavioral restraints, and strategies to be used by the staff, the person, or others that could prevent the future use of seclusion or behavioral restraints.

(d) The facility staff shall document in the person's record that the debriefing session took place and any changes to the person's treatment plan that resulted from the debriefing.

(Added by Stats. 2003, Ch. 750, Sec. 2. Effective January 1, 2004.)
1180.6.

The State Department of Public Health, the State Department of State Hospitals, the State Department of Social Services, the State Department of Developmental Services, and the State Department of Health Care Services shall annually provide information to the Legislature, during Senate and Assembly budget committee hearings, about the progress made in implementing this division. This information shall include the progress of implementation and barriers to achieving full implementation.

(Amended by Stats. 2013, Ch. 23, Sec. 6. (AB 82) Effective June 27, 2013.)

DIVISION 2. LICENSING PROVISIONS [1200 - 1797.8]

(Division 2 enacted by Stats. 1939, Ch. 60.)

CHAPTER 1. Clinics [1200 - 1245]

(Chapter 1 repealed and added by Stats. 1978, Ch. 1147.)

ARTICLE 1. Definitions and General Provisions [1200 - 1211]
(Article 1 added by Stats. 1978, Ch. 1147.)
1200.

(a) As used in this chapter, "clinic" means an organized outpatient health facility that provides direct medical, surgical, dental, optometric, or podiatric advice, services, or treatment to patients who remain less than 24 hours, and that may also provide diagnostic or therapeutic services to patients in the home as an incident to care provided at the clinic facility. Nothing in this section shall be construed to prohibit the provision of nursing services in a clinic licensed pursuant to this chapter. In no case shall a clinic be deemed to be a health facility subject to the provisions of Chapter 2 (commencing with Section 1250). A place, establishment, or institution that solely provides advice, counseling, information, or referrals on the maintenance of health or on the means and measures to prevent or avoid sickness, disease, or injury, where that advice, counseling, information, or referral does not constitute the practice of medicine, surgery, dentistry, optometry, or podiatry, shall not be deemed a clinic for purposes of this chapter.

(b) For purposes of this chapter:

(1) "Primary care clinics" means all the types of clinics specified in subdivision (a) of Section 1204, including community clinics and free clinics.

(2) "Specialty clinics" means all the types of clinics specified in subdivision (b) of Section 1204, including surgical clinics, chronic dialysis clinics, and rehabilitation clinics.

(3) "Clinic corporation" means a nonprofit organization that operates one or more primary care clinics, as defined in paragraph (1) of subdivision (a) of Section 1204, that are required to be licensed under Section 1205, one or more mobile health care units required to be licensed or approved pursuant to the Mobile Health Care Services Act (Chapter 9 (commencing with Section 1765.101)) and operated as primary care clinics, or one or more primary care clinics and one or more mobile health care units.

(4) "Department" means the Licensing and Certification Division of the State Department of Public Health, or its successor.

(5) "Centralized applications unit" means the centralized applications unit in the Licensing and Certification Division of the department, or a successor entity.

(Amended by Stats. 2010, Ch. 502, Sec. 2. (SB 442) Effective January 1, 2011.)
1200.1.

(a) As used in this chapter, "clinic" also means an organized outpatient health facility which, pursuant to Section 1204.1, provides direct psychological advice, services, or treatment to patients who remain less than 24 hours, and which may also provide diagnostic or therapeutic services authorized under Chapter 6.6 (commencing with Section 2900) of Division 2 of the Business and Professions Code to patients in the home as an incident to care provided at the clinic facility.

(b) Psychological clinics, as defined in Section 1204.1, shall not be considered primary care clinics for the purposes of any state grants, state loans, or other state aid. Nothing contained in this section shall prohibit psychological clinics from receiving payment to which they are otherwise entitled from the state or in which the state participates financially, for services rendered pursuant to their license.

(c) Any reference in any statute to Section 1200 shall be deemed and construed to also be a reference to this section.

(Added by Stats. 1980, Ch. 1315.)
1201.

"License" means a basic permit to operate a clinic. A license may only be granted to a clinic of a type enumerated in Section 1204 or 1204.1, and the license shall not be transferable. However, the issuance of a license upon a change of ownership shall not of itself constitute a project within the meaning of Section 127170.

(Amended by Stats. 1996, Ch. 1023, Sec. 148. Effective September 29, 1996.)
1201.5.

"Nonprofit speech and hearing center" means a nonprofit agency which provides an integrated program of speech pathology and audiology services in an outpatient setting designed to improve the functioning of persons with communicative disorders. A nonprofit speech and hearing center provides diagnostic and therapeutic services for such individuals, together with related counseling, pursuant to policies and procedures governing all aspects of the program formulated with the aid of one or more physicians and surgeons, who shall additionally serve on separate committees which determine patient care policy and perform utilization review functions. A multidisciplinary panel, which includes one or more physicians and surgeons, shall serve as a consulting advisory body to the center. All patients of the center shall be referred by a physician and surgeon, or by a dentist or psychologist as appropriate. A center shall prepare, maintain, and revise, as necessary, a treatment plan for all active patients, and shall provide periodic progress reports to the physician and surgeon or other professional referring the patient. A center shall maintain a complete record of all services rendered with respect to each patient.

(Added by Stats. 1979, Ch. 478.)
1202.

"Special permit" means a permit issued in addition to a license authorizing the clinic to offer one or more special services, as defined in Section 1203 or regulations adopted pursuant thereto.

(Repealed and added by Stats. 1978, Ch. 1147.)
1203.

"Special service" means a functional division, department, or unit of a clinic, or a clinic that is organized, staffed, and equipped to provide a specific type or types of care which have been identified by this section or by regulations of the state department, and for which the state department has established special standards for ensuring the quality of such care. Special services shall include, but need not be limited to, birth services. (Repealed and added by Stats. 1978, Ch. 1147.)

1204.

Clinics eligible for licensure pursuant to this chapter are primary care clinics and specialty clinics.

(a) (1) Only the following defined classes of primary care clinics shall be eligible for licensure:

(A) A "community clinic" means a clinic operated by a tax-exempt nonprofit corporation that is supported and maintained in whole or in part by donations, bequests, gifts, grants, government funds or contributions, that may be in the form of money, goods, or services. In a community clinic, any charges to the patient shall be based on the patient's ability to pay, utilizing a sliding fee scale. No corporation other than a nonprofit corporation, exempt from federal income taxation under paragraph (3) of subsection (c) of Section 501 of the Internal Revenue Code of 1954 as amended, or a statutory successor thereof, shall operate a community clinic; provided, that the licensee of any community clinic so licensed on the effective date of this section shall not be required to obtain tax-exempt status under either federal or state law in order to be eligible for, or as a condition of, renewal of its license. No natural person or persons shall operate a community clinic.

(B) A "free clinic" means a clinic operated by a tax-exempt, nonprofit corporation supported in whole or in part by voluntary donations, bequests, gifts, grants, government funds or contributions, that may be in the form of money, goods, or services. In a free clinic there shall be no charges directly to the patient for services rendered or for drugs, medicines, appliances, or apparatuses furnished. No corporation other than a nonprofit corporation exempt from federal income taxation under paragraph (3) of subsection (c) of Section 501 of the Internal Revenue Code of 1954 as amended, or a statutory successor thereof, shall operate a free clinic; provided, that the licensee of any free clinic so licensed on the effective date of this section shall not be required to obtain tax-exempt status under either federal or state law in order to be eligible for, or as a condition of, renewal of its license. No natural person or persons shall operate a free clinic.

(2) Nothing in this subdivision shall prohibit a community clinic or a free clinic from providing services to patients whose services are reimbursed by third-party payers, or from entering into managed care contracts for services provided to private or public health plan subscribers, as long as the clinic meets the requirements identified in subparagraphs (A) and (B). For purposes of this subdivision, any payments made to a community clinic by a third-party payer, including, but not limited to, a health care service plan, shall not constitute a charge to the patient. This paragraph is a clarification of existing law.

(b) The following types of specialty clinics shall be eligible for licensure as specialty clinics pursuant to this chapter:

(1) A "surgical clinic" means a clinic that is not part of a hospital and that provides ambulatory surgical care for patients who remain less than 24 hours. A surgical clinic does not include any place or establishment owned or leased and operated as a clinic or office by one or more physicians or dentists in individual or group practice, regardless of the name used publicly to identify the place or establishment, provided, however, that physicians or dentists may, at their option, apply for licensure.

(2) A "chronic dialysis clinic" means a clinic that provides less than 24-hour care for the treatment of patients with end-stage renal disease, including renal dialysis services.

(3) A "rehabilitation clinic" means a clinic that, in addition to providing medical services directly, also provides physical rehabilitation services for patients who remain less than 24 hours. Rehabilitation clinics shall provide at least two of the following rehabilitation services: physical therapy, occupational therapy, social, speech pathology, and audiology services. A rehabilitation clinic does not include the offices of a private physician in individual or group practice.

(4) An "alternative birth center" means a clinic that is not part of a hospital and that provides comprehensive perinatal services and delivery care to pregnant women who remain less than 24 hours at the facility.
(Amended by Stats. 2000, Ch. 27, Sec. 1. Effective January 1, 2001.)
1204.1.

In addition to the primary care clinics and specialty clinics specified in Section 1204, clinics eligible for licensure pursuant to this chapter include psychology clinics. A "psychology clinic" is a clinic which provides psychological advice, services, or treatment to patients, under the direction of a clinical psychologist as defined in Section 1316.5, and is operated by a tax-exempt nonprofit corporation which is supported and maintained in whole or in part by donations, bequests, gifts, grants, government funds, or contributions which may be in the form of money, goods, or services. In a psychology clinic, any charges to the patient shall be based on the patient's ability to pay, utilizing a sliding fee scale. No corporation other than a nonprofit corporation, exempt from federal taxation under paragraph (3), subsection (c) of Section 501 of the Internal Revenue Code of 1954, as amended, or a statutory successor thereof, shall operate a psychology clinic.

Each psychology clinic licensed pursuant to this section shall comply with the provisions of Part 2 (commencing with Section 13100) of Division 12.

Only a psychology clinic may be licensed under this chapter to exclusively provide psychological advice, services, or treatment. However, nothing in this subdivision precludes clinics specified in Section 1204 from providing psychological advice, services, or treatment as included within, or adjunctive to, medical advice, services, or treatment provided by such clinics. Failure to comply with the requirements of this section may be grounds for denial, revocation, or suspension of the license.

(Amended by Stats. 1987, Ch. 456, Sec. 1.)
1204.2.

(a) Notwithstanding any other law, and except as provided in subdivision (c), a primary care clinic described in subdivision (a) of Section 1204 that is licensed pursuant to this chapter shall not be required to enter into a written transfer agreement with a nearby hospital as a condition of licensure.

(b) (1) A primary care clinic shall send with each patient at the time of transfer, or in the case of an emergency, as promptly as possible, copies of all medical records related to the patient's transfer. To the extent practicable and applicable to the patient's transfer, the medical records shall include current medical findings, diagnoses, laboratory results, medications provided prior to transfer, a brief summary of the course of treatment provided prior to transfer, ambulation status, nursing and dietary information, name and contact information for the treating physician at the clinic, and, as appropriate, pertinent administrative and demographic information related to the patient, including name and date of birth.

(2) The requirements in paragraph (1) do not apply if the primary care clinic has entered into a written transfer agreement with a local hospital that provides for the transfer of medical records.

(c) A primary care clinic licensed pursuant to subdivision (a) of Section 1204 that provides services as an alternative birth center shall, as a condition of licensure, be required to maintain a written transfer agreement with a local hospital. The transfer agreement shall include provisions for communication and transportation to meet medical emergencies. Essential personal, health, and medical information shall either accompany the patient upon transfer or be transmitted immediately by telephone to the receiving facility. This section does not modify or supersede the requirements imposed on alternative birth centers described in Section 1204.3.

(d) This section shall become operative on January 1, 2018.
(Amended (as added by Stats. 2015, Ch. 704, Sec. 2) by Stats. 2016, Ch. 86, Sec. 171. (SB 1171) Effective January 1, 2017.)
1204.3.

(a) An alternative birth center that is licensed as an alternative birth center specialty clinic pursuant to paragraph (4) of subdivision (b) of Section 1204 shall, as a condition of licensure, and a primary care clinic licensed pursuant to subdivision (a) of Section 1204 that provides services as an alternative birth center shall, meet all of the following requirements:

(1) Be a provider of comprehensive perinatal services as defined in Section 14134.5 of the Welfare and Institutions Code.

(2) Maintain a quality assurance program.

(3) Meet the standards for certification established by the American Association of Birth Centers, or at least equivalent standards as determined by the state department.

(4) In addition to standards of the American Association of Birth Centers regarding proximity to hospitals and presence of attendants at births, meet both of the following conditions:

(A) Be located in proximity, in time and distance, to a facility with the capacity for management of obstetrical and neonatal emergencies, including the ability to provide cesarean section delivery, within 30 minutes from time of diagnosis of the emergency.

(B) Require the presence of at least two attendants at all times during birth, one of whom shall be a physician and surgeon, a licensed midwife, or a certified nurse-midwife.

(5) Have a written policy relating to the dissemination of the following information to patients:

(A) A summary of current state laws requiring child passenger restraint systems to be used when transporting children in motor vehicles.

(B) A listing of child passenger restraint system programs located within the county, as required by Section 27362 of the Vehicle Code.

(C) Information describing the risks of death or serious injury associated with the failure to utilize a child passenger restraint system.

(b) The state department shall issue a permit to a primary care clinic licensed pursuant to subdivision (a) of Section 1204 certifying that the primary care clinic has met the requirements of this section and may provide services as an alternative birth center. Nothing in this section shall be construed to require that a licensed primary care clinic obtain an additional license in order to provide services as an alternative birth center.

(c) (1) Notwithstanding subdivision (a) of Section 1206, no place or establishment owned or leased and operated as a clinic or office by one or more licensed health care practitioners and used as an office for the practice of their profession, within the scope of their license, shall be represented or otherwise held out to be an alternative birth center licensed by the state unless it meets the requirements of this section.

(2) Nothing in this subdivision shall be construed to prohibit licensed health care practitioners from providing birth related services, within the scope of their license, in a place or establishment described in paragraph (1).
(Amended by Stats. 2013, Ch. 665, Sec. 8. (AB 1308) Effective January 1, 2014.)
1204.4.

The State Department of Health Services shall provide information to the California Health Facilities Financing Authority with respect to primary care clinic grant applicants for capital outlay projects as specified in Section 15438.6 of the Government Code.
(Added by Stats. 2000, Ch. 99, Sec. 3. Effective January 1, 2001.)
1204.5.

A primary care clinic may submit verification of certification from the Joint Commission, the Accreditation Association for Ambulatory Health Care (AAAHC), or any other accrediting organization recognized by the department to the Licensing and Certification Division within the State Department of Public Health for entry into the electronic Licensing

Management System for purposes of data collection and extraction for licensing and certification fee calculations.

(Amended by Stats. 2013, Ch. 583, Sec. 1. (AB 297) Effective January 1, 2014.)

1205.

Except as provided in Section 1206, no person, firm, partnership, association, corporation, or public agency shall operate, establish, manage, conduct or maintain a clinic in this state without first obtaining a license therefor as provided in this chapter; nor shall any such person, firm, partnership, association, corporation, or public agency provide any special service without obtaining a special permit therefor. However, any licensed clinic offering any service which is later designated by regulation of the state department as a special service shall be allowed to continue offering such service until the state department evaluates the quality of such service and issues a special permit therefor or notifies the licensee that it is not eligible for a special permit and must cease and desist from offering such service.

(Repealed and added by Stats. 1978, Ch. 1147.)

1205.5.

A clinic that has been verified by the Licensing and Certification Division of the State Department of Health Services and the Office of Statewide Health Planning and Development as having (1) provided chronic dialysis and (2) been licensed as an outpatient clinic, before September 26, 1978, shall not be required to have a certificate of need pursuant to Chapter 1 (commencing with Section 127125) of Part 2 of Division 107 in order to obtain licensure as a chronic dialysis clinic. A clinic that has been verified by the Licensing and Certification Division of the State Department of Health Services and the Office of Statewide Health Planning and Development as having (1) provided surgical services, (2) been licensed as an outpatient clinic and (3) been eligible to receive Medi-Cal reimbursement as an outpatient clinic in connection with the surgical services, before September 26, 1978, shall not be required to have a certificate of need pursuant to Chapter 1 (commencing with Section 127125) of Part 2 of Division 107 in order to obtain licensure as a surgical clinic.

Nothing in this section shall, however, be construed to exempt a clinic subject to this section from the requirement for a certificate of need with respect to projects specified in subdivision (c), (d), or (e) of Section 127170, or with respect to changes of licensure category occurring subsequent to initial licensure as a specialty clinic pursuant to this section.

A clinic that has been verified by the Licensing and Certification Division of the State Department of Health Services and the Office of Statewide Health Planning and Development as having (1) provided surgical services, (2) been licensed as an outpatient clinic and (3) been eligible to receive Medi-Cal reimbursement as an outpatient clinic in connection with the surgical services, before September 26, 1978, and that meets the requirements for licensure as a surgical clinic, need not operate on an open-staff basis in order to be licensed as a surgical clinic.

A clinic that has been verified by the Licensing and Certification Division of the State Department of Health Services and the Office of Statewide Health Planning and Development as having (1) provided rehabilitation service and (2) been licensed as an outpatient clinic, a community clinic, or free clinic, before September 26, 1978, shall not be required to have a certificate of need pursuant to Chapter 1 (commencing with Section 127125) of Part 2 of Division 107 in order to obtain licensure as a rehabilitation clinic.

(Amended by Stats. 1996, Ch. 1023, Sec. 149. Effective September 29, 1996.)

1206.

This chapter does not apply to the following:

(a) Except with respect to the option provided with regard to surgical clinics in paragraph (1) of subdivision (b) of Section 1204 and, further, with respect to specialty clinics specified in paragraph (2) of subdivision (b) of Section 1204, any place or establishment owned or leased and operated as a clinic or office by one or more licensed health care practitioners and used as an office for the practice of their profession, within the scope of their license, regardless of the name used publicly to identify the place or establishment.

(b) Any clinic directly conducted, maintained, or operated by the United States or by any of its departments, officers, or agencies, and any primary care clinic specified in subdivision (a) of Section 1204 that is directly conducted, maintained, or operated by this state or by any of its political subdivisions or districts, or by any city. Nothing in this subdivision precludes the state department from adopting regulations that utilize clinic licensing standards as eligibility criteria for participation in programs funded wholly or partially under Title XVIII or XIX of the federal Social Security Act.

(c) (1) Any clinic conducted, maintained, or operated by a federally recognized Indian tribe or tribal organization, as defined in Section 450 or 1603 of Title 25 of the United States Code, that is located on land recognized as tribal land by the federal government.

(2) Any clinic conducted, maintained, or operated by a federally recognized Indian tribe or tribal organization, as defined in Section 450 or 1603 of Title 25 of the United States Code, under a contract with the United States pursuant to the Indian Self-Determination and Education Assistance Act (Public Law 93-638), regardless of the location of the clinic, except that if the clinic chooses to apply to the State Department of Public Health for a state facility license, then the State Department of Public Health will retain authority to regulate that clinic as a primary care clinic as defined by subdivision (a) of Section 1204.

(d) Clinics conducted, operated, or maintained as outpatient departments of hospitals.

(e) Any facility licensed as a health facility under Chapter 2 (commencing with Section 1250).

(f) Any freestanding clinical or pathological laboratory licensed under Chapter 3 (commencing with Section 1200) of Division 2 of the Business and Professions Code.

(g) A clinic operated by, or affiliated with, any institution of learning that teaches a recognized healing art and is approved by the state board or commission vested with responsibility for regulation of the practice of that healing art.

(h) A clinic that is operated by a primary care community or free clinic and that is operated on separate premises from the licensed clinic and is only open for limited services of no more than 40 hours a week. An intermittent clinic as described in this subdivision shall, however, meet all other requirements of law, including administrative regulations and requirements, pertaining to fire and life safety.

(i) The offices of physicians in group practice who provide a preponderance of their services to members of a comprehensive group practice prepayment health care service plan subject to Chapter 2.2 (commencing with Section 1340).

(j) Student health centers operated by public institutions of higher education.

(k) Nonprofit speech and hearing centers, as defined in Section 1201.5. Any nonprofit speech and hearing clinic desiring an exemption under this subdivision shall make application therefor to the director, who shall grant the exemption to any facility meeting the criteria of Section 1201.5. Notwithstanding the licensure exemption contained in this subdivision, a nonprofit speech and hearing center shall be deemed to be an organized outpatient clinic for purposes of qualifying for reimbursement as a rehabilitation center under the Medi-Cal Act (Chapter 7 (commencing with Section 14000) of Part 3 of Division 9 of the Welfare and Institutions Code).

(l) A clinic operated by a nonprofit corporation exempt from federal income taxation under paragraph (3) of subsection (c) of Section 501 of the Internal Revenue Code of 1954, as amended, or a statutory successor thereof, that conducts medical research and health education and provides health care to its patients through a group of 40 or more physicians and surgeons, who are independent contractors representing not less than 10 board-certified specialties, and not less than two-thirds of whom practice on a full-time basis at the clinic.

(m) Any clinic, limited to in vivo diagnostic services by magnetic resonance imaging functions or radiological services under the direct and immediate supervision of a physician and surgeon who is licensed to practice in California. This shall not be construed to permit cardiac catheterization or any treatment modality in these clinics.

(n) A clinic operated by an employer or jointly by two or more employers for their employees only, or by a group of employees, or jointly by employees and employers, without profit to the operators thereof or to any other person, for the prevention and treatment of accidental injuries to, and the care of the health of, the employees comprising the group.

(o) A community mental health center, as defined in Section 5667 of the Welfare and Institutions Code.

(p) (1) A clinic operated by a nonprofit corporation exempt from federal income taxation under paragraph (3) of subsection (c) of Section 501 of the Internal Revenue Code of 1954, as amended, or a statutory successor thereof, as an entity organized and operated exclusively for scientific and charitable purposes and that satisfied all of the following requirements on or before January 1, 2005:

(A) Commenced conducting medical research on or before January 1, 1982, and continues to conduct medical research.

(B) Conducted research in, among other areas, prostatic cancer, cardiovascular disease, electronic neural prosthetic devices, biological effects and medical uses of lasers, and human magnetic resonance imaging and spectroscopy.

(C) Sponsored publication of at least 200 medical research articles in peer-reviewed publications.

(D) Received grants and contracts from the National Institutes of Health.

(E) Held and licensed patents on medical technology.

(F) Received charitable contributions and bequests totaling at least five million dollars ($5,000,000).

(G) Provides health care services to patients only:

(i) In conjunction with research being conducted on procedures or applications not approved or only partially approved for payment (I) under the Medicare program pursuant to Section 1359y(a)(1)(A) of Title 42 of the United States Code, or (II) by a health care service plan registered under Chapter 2.2 (commencing with Section 1340), or a disability insurer regulated under Chapter 1 (commencing with Section 10110) of Part 2 of Division 2 of the Insurance Code; provided that services may be provided by the clinic for an additional period of up to three years following the approvals, but only to the extent necessary to maintain clinical expertise in the procedure or application for purposes of actively providing training in the procedure or application for physicians and surgeons unrelated to the clinic.

(ii) Through physicians and surgeons who, in the aggregate, devote no more than 30 percent of their professional time for the entity operating the clinic, on an annual basis, to direct patient care activities for which charges for professional services are paid.

(H) Makes available to the public the general results of its research activities on at least an annual basis, subject to good faith protection of proprietary rights in its intellectual property.

(I) Is a freestanding clinic, whose operations under this subdivision are not conducted in conjunction with any affiliated or associated health clinic or facility defined under this division, except a clinic exempt from licensure under subdivision (m). For purposes of this subparagraph, a freestanding clinic is defined as "affiliated" only if it directly, or indirectly through one or more intermediaries, controls, or is controlled by, or is under common control with, a clinic or health facility defined under this division, except a clinic exempt from licensure under subdivision (m). For purposes of this subparagraph, a freestanding clinic is defined as "associated" only if more than 20 percent of the directors or trustees of the clinic are also the directors or trustees of any individual clinic or health facility defined under this division, except a clinic exempt from licensure under subdivision (m). Any activity by a clinic under this subdivision in connection with an affiliated or associated entity shall fully comply with the requirements of this subdivision. This subparagraph shall not apply to agreements between a clinic and any entity for purposes of coordinating medical research.

(2) By January 1, 2007, and every five years thereafter, the Legislature shall receive a report from each clinic meeting the criteria of this subdivision and any other interested party concerning the operation of the clinic's activities. The report shall include, but not be limited to, an evaluation of how the clinic impacted competition in the relevant health care market, and a detailed description of the clinic's research results and the level of acceptance by the payer community of the procedures performed at the clinic. The report shall also include a description of procedures performed both in clinics governed by this subdivision and those performed in other settings. The cost of preparing the reports shall be borne by the clinics that are required to submit them to the Legislature pursuant to this paragraph.

(Amended by Stats. 2018, Ch. 279, Sec. 1. (AB 2204) Effective January 1, 2019.)

1206.1.

The provisions of this chapter do not require licensure of any place or establishment owned or leased and operated as a clinic or office by one or more licensed psychologists and used as an office for the practice of psychology, regardless of the name used publicly to identify such place or establishment.

(Added by Stats. 1980, Ch. 1315.)

1207.

The state department shall inspect and license clinics, and shall inspect and approve clinics to offer special services.

(Added by Stats. 1978, Ch. 1147.)

1208.

The state department may provide consulting services upon request to any clinic to assist in the identification or correction of deficiencies or the upgrading of the quality of care provided by the clinic.

(Added by Stats. 1978, Ch. 1147.)

1209.

This chapter does not authorize any person other than a licensed practitioner of a healing art, or any corporation except charitable or professional corporations as expressly provided in this chapter, to furnish to any person any advice, services, or treatment within the scope of such professional licensure.

This chapter does not authorize any person, other than a licentiate of a healing art acting within the scope of his or her license, to engage directly or indirectly in the practice of medicine and surgery, dentistry, optometry, podiatry, psychology, or pharmacy.

This chapter does not regulate, govern, or affect in any manner the practice of medicine and surgery, pharmacy, dentistry, optometry, chiropractic, podiatry, psychology, or drugless healing by any person duly licensed to engage in such practice.

(Amended by Stats. 1980, Ch. 1315.)

1211.

(a) Notwithstanding any other law, a clinic licensed pursuant to Section 1204 may operate in shared clinic space with a clinic exempt from licensure pursuant to subdivision (b) of Section 1206 under the following conditions:

(1) Each clinic uses signage that clearly identifies which clinic is operating during the hours of operation.

(2) The licensed clinic reports the operating hours of both clinics.

(3) Each clinic maintains separate medical records.

(4) Each clinic maintains separate drug storage.

(5) Both clinics are licensed by the California State Board of Pharmacy pursuant to Section 4180.5 of the Business and Professions Code.

(b) The department may enter and inspect the shared space at any time pursuant to Section 1227 of the Health and Safety Code, including accessing records. The exempt clinic shall allow the department to access and inspect its records.

(c) The licensed clinic shall be responsible for any statutory or regulatory violations occurring on the premises.

(d) Notwithstanding the rulemaking provisions of the Administrative Procedure Act (Chapter 3.5 (commencing with Section 11340) of Part 1 of Division 3 of Title 2 of the Government Code), the department may implement, interpret, or make specific this section by means of all-facility letters, or similar instructions, without taking regulatory action.

(e) This section shall become inoperative on January 1, 2021, and as of that date is repealed.

(Added by Stats. 2017, Ch. 548, Sec. 10. (AB 401) Effective January 1, 2018. Repealed as of January 1, 2021, by its own provisions.)

ARTICLE 2. Administration [1212 - 1220]

(Article 2 added by Stats. 1978, Ch. 1147.)

1212.

(a) Any person, firm, association, partnership, or corporation desiring a license for a clinic or a special permit for special services under the provisions of this chapter, shall file with the department a verified application on forms prescribed and furnished by the department, containing the following:

(1) Evidence satisfactory to the department that the applicant is of reputable and responsible character. If the applicant is a firm, association, partnership, trust, corporation, or other artificial or legal entity, like evidence shall be submitted as to the members, partners, trustees or shareholders, directors, and officers thereof and as to the person who is to be the administrator of, and exercise control, management, and direction of the clinic for which application is made.

(2) If the applicant is a partnership, the name and principal business address of each partner, and, if any partner is a corporation, the name and principal business address of each officer and director of the corporation and name and business address of each stockholder owning 10 percent or more of the stock thereof.

(3) If the applicant is a corporation, the name and principal business address of each officer and director of the corporation, and if the applicant is a stock corporation, the name and principal business address of each stockholder holding 10 percent or more of the applicant's stock and, if any stockholder is a corporation, the name and principal business address of each officer and director of the corporate stockholder.

(4) Evidence satisfactory to the department of the ability of the applicant to comply with the provisions of this chapter and rules and regulations promulgated under this chapter by the department.

(5) The name and address of the clinic, and if the applicant is a professional corporation, firm, partnership, or other form of organization, evidence that the applicant has complied with the requirements of the Business and Professions Code governing the use of fictitious names by practitioners of the healing arts.

(6) The name and address of the professional licentiate responsible for the professional activities of the clinic and the licentiate's license number and professional experience.

(7) The class of clinic to be operated, the character and scope of advice and treatment to be provided, and a complete description of the building, its location, facilities, equipment, apparatus, and appliances to be furnished and used in the operation of the clinic.

(8) Sufficient operational data to allow the department to determine the class of clinic that the applicant proposes to operate and the initial license fee to be charged.

(9) Any other information as may be required by the department for the proper administration and enforcement of this chapter, including, but not limited to, evidence that the clinic has a written policy relating to the dissemination of the following information to patients:

(A) A summary of current state laws requiring child passenger restraint systems to be used when transporting children in motor vehicles.

(B) A listing of child passenger restraint system programs located within the county, as required by Section 27360 or 27362 of the Vehicle Code.

(C) Information describing the risks of death or serious injury associated with the failure to utilize a child passenger restraint system.

(b) (1) No application is required if a licensed primary care clinic adds a service that is not a special service, as defined in Section 1203, or any regulation adopted under that section, or remodels or modifies, or adds an additional physical plant maintained and operated on separate premises to, an existing primary care clinic site. However, the clinic shall notify the department, in writing, of the change in service or physical plant no less than 60 days prior to adding the service or remodeling or modifying, or adding an additional physical plant maintained and operated on a separate premises to, an existing primary care clinic site. Nothing in this subdivision shall be construed to limit the authority of the department to conduct an inspection at any time pursuant to Section 1227, in order to ensure compliance with, or to prevent a violation of, this chapter, or any regulation adopted under this chapter.

(2) If applicable city, county, or state law obligates the primary care clinic to obtain a building permit with respect to the remodeling or modification to be performed by the clinic, or the construction of a new physical plant, the primary care clinic shall provide a signed certification or statement as described in Section 1226.3 to the department within 60 days following completion of the remodeling, modification, or construction project covered by the building permit.

(c) In the course of fulfilling its obligations under Section 1221.09, the department shall ensure that any application form utilized by a primary care clinic, requiring information of the type specified in paragraph (1), (4), (8), or (9) of subdivision (a), is consistent with the requirements of Section 1225, including the requirement that rules and regulations for primary care clinics be separate and distinct from the rules and regulations for specialty clinics. Nothing in this section shall be construed to require the department to issue a separate application form for primary care clinics.

(d) (1) The department, upon written notification by a primary care clinic or an affiliate clinic of its intent to add an additional physical plant maintained and operated on separate premises, as described in paragraph (1) of subdivision (b) and upon payment of a licensing fee for each additional physical plant added, shall review the information provided in the notification, and if the information submitted is in compliance with the requirements specified in this subdivision, the department shall approve the additional physical plant within 30 days of all information being submitted and shall amend the primary care clinic or affiliate clinic's license to include the additional physical plant as part of a single consolidated license. If the notification does not include the information required by this subdivision, the department shall notify the licensee of the need for additional information and shall not amend the license to add the additional physical plant until the additional information is received and reviewed by the department.

(2) Written notification shall include evidence that the primary care clinic or affiliate clinic is licensed in good standing and otherwise meets the criteria specified in this subdivision. In issuing the single consolidated license, the department shall specify the location of each physical plant.

(3) The written notification shall demonstrate compliance with all of the following criteria:

(A) There is a single governing body for all the facilities maintained and operated by the licensee.

(B) There is a single administration for all the facilities maintained and operated by the licensee.

(C) There is a single medical director for all the facilities maintained and operated by the licensee, with a single set of bylaws, rules, and regulations.

(D) The additional physical plant meets minimum construction standards of adequacy and safety for clinics found in the most recent version of the California Building Standards Code and prescribed by the Office of Statewide Health Planning and Development, as required in subdivision (b) of Section 1226. Compliance with the minimum construction standards of adequacy and safety may be established as specified in Section 1226.3.

(E) The additional physical plant meets fire clearance standards.

(4) The written notification required to be submitted pursuant to this subdivision shall include all of the following documentation:

(A) The name and address of the licensee's corporation administrative office, including the name and contact information for the corporation's chief executive officer or executive director.

(B) The name and address of, and the hours of operation and services provided by, the additional physical plant.

(C) A copy of any document confirming the corporation's authority to control the additional physical plant. Examples of acceptable documentation include, but shall not be limited to, a lease or purchase agreement, grant deed, bill of sale, sublease, rental agreement, or memorandum of understanding between the owner of the property and the proposed licensee.

(5) A primary care clinic or an affiliate clinic may add additional physical plants pursuant to this section that are no more than one-half mile from the licensed clinic adding the additional physical plant under a consolidated license.

(6) Upon renewal of a consolidated license approved pursuant to this subdivision, a licensee fee shall be required for each additional physical plant approved on the license.
(Amended by Stats. 2016, Ch. 639, Sec. 1. (AB 2053) Effective January 1, 2017.)
1213.
A person, firm, association, partnership, corporation, or other legal entity desiring a license for a clinic shall be exempt from the requirements of Chapter 2 (commencing with Section 16000) of Division 12.5.
(Amended by Stats. 2010, Ch. 502, Sec. 3. (SB 442) Effective January 1, 2011.)
1214.
Each application under this chapter for an initial license, renewal license, license upon change of ownership, or special permit shall be accompanied by a Licensing and Certification Program fee, as follows:

(a) For all primary care clinics licensed pursuant to this chapter, the annual fee shall be set in accordance with Section 1266.

(b) For all specialty clinics licensed pursuant to this chapter, the annual fee shall be set in accordance with Section 1266.

(c) For all rehabilitation clinics, the annual fee shall be set in accordance with Section 1266.
(Amended by Stats. 2006, Ch. 74, Sec. 2. Effective July 12, 2006.)
1214.1.
Notwithstanding the provisions of Section 1214, each application for a surgical clinic or a chronic dialysis clinic under this chapter for an initial license, renewal license, license upon change of ownership, or special permit shall be accompanied by an annual Licensing and Certification Program fee set in accordance with Section 1266.
(Amended by Stats. 2006, Ch. 74, Sec. 3. Effective July 12, 2006.)
1214.5.
Each application under this chapter for an initial license, renewal license, license upon change of ownership, or special permit for a psychology clinic shall be accompanied by a Licensing and Certification Program fee set in accordance with Section 1266.
(Amended by Stats. 2006, Ch. 74, Sec. 4. Effective July 12, 2006.)
1215.
Each new license issued pursuant to this chapter shall expire 12 months from the date of its issuance, and each special permit shall expire on the expiration date of the underlying license. The state department shall transmit to the licensee a renewal fee invoice at least 45 days prior to the expiration date of the license. Failure by the clinic licensee to make timely payment of the renewal fee shall result in the expiration of the license and special permit, if any. A renewal license or special permit may be issued for a period not to exceed two years if the holder of the license or special permit has not been found to be in violation of any statutory requirements, regulations, or standards during the preceding license period. In all other cases, the renewal license or special permit shall be issued for a period not to exceed one year. Timely application for renewal, accompanied by the necessary fee, shall be deemed equivalent to renewal of a license or special permit, where the department is unable to issue a renewal license or special permit on or before the expiration date.
(Repealed and added by Stats. 1978, Ch. 1147.)
1216.
(a) Every clinic holding a license shall, on or before the 15th day of February each year, file with the Office of Statewide Health Planning and Development upon forms to be furnished by the office, a verified report showing the following information relating to the previous calendar year:

(1) Number of patients served and descriptive information, including age, gender, race, and ethnic background of patients.

(2) Number of patient visits by type of service, including all of the following:

(A) Child health and disability prevention screens, treatment, and followup services.

(B) Medical services.

(C) Dental services.

(D) Other health services.

(3) Total clinic operating expenses.

(4) Gross patient charges by payer category, including Medicare, Medi-Cal, the Child Health Disability Prevention Program, county indigent programs, other county programs, private insurance, self-paying patients, nonpaying patients, and other payers.

(5) Deductions from revenue by payer category, bad debts, and charity care charges.

(6) Additional information as may be required by the office or the department.

(b) In the event a clinic fails to file a timely report, the department may suspend the license of the clinic until the report is completed and filed with the office.

(c) In order to promote efficient reporting of accurate data, the office shall consider the unique operational characteristics of different classifications of licensed clinics, including, but not limited to, the limited scope of services provided by some specialty clinics, in its design of forms for the collection of data required by this section.

(d) For the purpose of administering funds appropriated from the Cigarette and Tobacco Products Surtax Fund for support of licensed clinics, clinics receiving those funds may be required to report any additional data the office or the department may determine necessary to ensure the equitable distribution and appropriate expenditure of those funds. This shall include, but not be limited to, information about the poverty level of patients served and communicable diseases reported to local health departments.

(e) This section shall apply to all primary care clinics.

(f) This section shall apply to all specialty clinics, as defined in paragraph (2) of subdivision (a) of Section 1204 of the Health and Safety Code that receive tobacco tax funds pursuant to Article 2 (commencing with Section 30121) of Chapter 2 of Part 13 of Division 2 of the Revenue and Taxation Code.

(g) Specialty clinics that are not required to report pursuant to subdivision (f) shall report data as directed in Section 1216 as it existed prior to the enactment of Chapter 1331 of the Statutes of 1989 and Chapter 51 of the Statutes of 1990.
(Amended by Stats. 1991, Ch. 278, Sec. 5. Effective July 30, 1991.)
1217.
(a) An applicant for a license to operate a primary care clinic, as specified in subdivision (a) of Section 1204 that meets all requirements for licensure under this chapter, except that it proposes to operate its clinic out of an existing facility that does not satisfy all of the applicable building requirements for the physical plant, other than fire and life safety requirements, shall be issued a license by the state department if both of the following requirements are met:

(1) The applicant establishes, by evidence satisfactory to the state department, that, where possible and feasible, the applicable building requirements have been met.

(2) The applicant submits a plan of modernization acceptable to the state department that sets forth the proposed changes to be made, during a period not to exceed three years from the date of initial licensure, to bring the applicant's facility into substantial conformance with applicable building requirements.

(b) Failure to complete the plan of modernization as approved and within the time allowed shall constitute a basis for revocation or nonrenewal of the applicant's license unless the applicant earlier applies for and obtains a waiver from the department. The director shall waive building requirements for primary care clinics where he or she determines all of the following conditions are met:

(1) That the requirements cannot be met by an applicant, or that they can be met only at an unreasonable and prohibitive cost.

(2) That the requirements are not essential to protect the health and safety of the clinic staff or the public it serves.

(3) That the granting of the waiver applied for is in the public interest.
(Amended by Stats. 2003, Ch. 602, Sec. 3. Effective January 1, 2004.)
1218.
Upon the filing of an application for a license or for a special permit, or for renewal of a license or special permit, the state department shall investigate the facts set forth in the application and, if the state department finds that the statements contained in the application are true, that the establishment or the continued operation of the clinic and any special services it provides are in conformity with the intent and purpose of this chapter, and that the applicant is in compliance with the provisions of this chapter and the rules and regulations of the state department, the state department shall issue to the applicant the license or special permit, or renewal thereof, applied for. However, if the director finds that the statements contained in the application are not true, or that the establishment or the continued operation of the clinic, or its special services, is not in conformity with the intent and purpose of this chapter, or that applicant is not in compliance with the provisions of this chapter and the rules and regulations promulgated hereunder, he shall deny the applicant the license or special permit or renewal thereof applied for. The state department shall either grant or deny a license or special permit within 100 days of the filing of a completed application for such license or special permit.
(Added by Stats. 1978, Ch. 1147.)
1218.1.
(a) A clinic corporation on behalf of a primary care clinic that has held a valid, unrevoked, and unsuspended license for at least the immediately preceding five years, with no demonstrated history of repeated or uncorrected violations of this chapter or a regulation adopted under this chapter that pose immediate jeopardy to a patient, as defined in subdivision (f), and that has no pending action to suspend or revoke its license, may file an affiliate clinic application under this section to establish a primary care clinic at an additional site or a mobile health care unit, either of which shall hereafter be referred to as the affiliate clinic. The department, upon receipt of the completed affiliate clinic application submitted by the clinic corporation, shall approve a license for the affiliate clinic, without the necessity of first conducting an initial onsite survey, if all of the following conditions are met:

(1) The clinic corporation that operates the existing licensed primary care clinic, which shall hereafter be referred to as the parent clinic, has submitted a completed affiliate clinic application and the associated application fee.

(2) The parent and affiliate clinics' corporate officers, as specified in Section 5213 of the Corporations Code, are the same.

(3) The parent and affiliate clinics are owned and operated by the same nonprofit organization with the same board of directors.

(4) The parent and affiliate clinics have the same medical director or directors and medical policies, procedures, protocols, and standards.

(b) The affiliate clinic application shall consist solely of a simple form and required supporting documents giving the following information:

(1) The name and address of the clinic corporation's administrative office.

(2) The name and contact information of the clinic corporation's chief executive officer or executive director.

(3) The name and address of the new affiliate primary care clinic site or the location of the new affiliate mobile health care unit.

(4) The name and contact information of the administrator of the new affiliate primary care clinic site or mobile health care unit.

(5) The expected days and hours of operation and the services to be provided at the new affiliate primary care clinic site or mobile health care unit.

(6) Evidence that the new affiliate mobile health care unit meets the requirements of the Mobile Health Care Services Act (Chapter 9 (commencing with Section 1765.101)).

(7) The type and the manufacturer of the new affiliate mobile health care unit and the proposed area or areas where the new affiliate mobile health care unit will be providing services.

(8) To the extent otherwise required by law, evidence of compliance with the minimum construction standards for adequacy and safety of the new affiliate clinic's physical plant, pursuant to the OSHPD 3 requirements of the most recent version of the California Building Code applicable to clinics and subdivision (b) of Section 1226. The compliance may be established in the form prescribed by Section 1226.3.

(9) Evidence of fire clearance for the new affiliate clinic site.

(10) A copy of the lease or purchase agreement for the new affiliate clinic site.

(11) A copy of the transfer agreement between the new affiliate clinic and a local hospital.

(12) A current list of clinic corporation board members.

(c) The affiliate clinic application shall be signed by an officer of the clinic corporation's board of directors or the clinic corporation's chief executive officer or executive director.

(d) The department shall issue a clinic license under this section within 30 days of receipt of a completed affiliate clinic application. If approved, a clinic license shall be issued within seven days of approval. If the department determines that an applicant does not meet the conditions stated in subdivision (a), it shall identify, in writing and with particularity, the grounds for that determination, and shall instead process the application in accordance with the time specified in Section 1218.

(e) Nothing in this section shall prohibit the department from conducting a licensing inspection of the affiliate clinic at any time after receipt of the completed affiliate clinic application.

(f) For purposes of this section, "immediate jeopardy to a patient" means a situation in which the clinic's noncompliance with one or more requirements of licensure has caused, or is likely to cause, serious injury, harm, impairment, or death to a patient.
(Amended by Stats. 2010, Ch. 502, Sec. 4. (SB 442) Effective January 1, 2011.)
1218.2.
Notwithstanding any other provision of law, two or more primary care clinics that are operated by a single nonprofit corporation shall be entitled to consolidate their administrative functions within the State of California without first obtaining the approval of the department. The department shall have access to offsite records. Upon request for access by the department, offsite records shall either be transferred to a clinic or administrative site or be available at the offsite facility within 48 hours. The administrative functions are limited to the following:

(a) Offsite storage and maintenance of patient medical records that have been inactive for at least three years.

(b) Offsite storage and maintenance of personnel records, except that copies of specific records documenting the employees' date of hire, general qualifications, proof of current licensure if applicable, training, and annual health checks shall be kept at the site at which the employee provides all or a majority of his or her services.

(c) Billing and related financial functions.

(d) Purchasing functions.
(Added by Stats. 2003, Ch. 602, Sec. 5. Effective January 1, 2004.)
1218.3.
(a) In order to reduce paperwork, eliminate errors, and streamline communications between the department and licensed primary care clinics, a clinic corporation that operates one or more affiliate clinics shall, on behalf of all licensed clinics it operates, act as the administrative headquarters for purposes of receiving from and submitting to the department communications regarding primary care clinic license applications or license renewals, primary care clinic operations, requests for prior approval, additions of services, primary care clinic relocations, required reports of changes in primary care clinic administration and board of directors, notices of deficiencies, and all communications from the department to primary care clinics licensed by the department including communications by mail, e-mail, facsimile, or any other electronic or telephonic means.

(b) The department shall maintain a complete corporate file containing information about each clinic corporation operating one or more affiliate clinics, including all of the following:

(1) A copy of the clinic corporation's articles of incorporation and bylaws.

(2) Unless exempt under paragraph (1) of subdivision (a) of Section 1204, a copy of the determination letter to show the clinic corporation's exempt status under paragraph (3) of subsection (c) of the Internal Revenue Code of 1954, as amended.

(3) A copy of the clinic corporation's organizational chart.

(4) Information identifying the clinic corporation's governing body, including the clinic corporation's board of directors and corporate officers and required documents.

(5) Information identifying the clinic corporation's administrators, including the chief executive officer or executive director and medical director.

(c) A clinic corporation shall not be required to resubmit information, materials, or documents identified in subdivision (b) as part of an affiliate clinic application, unless the information, materials, or documents are necessary to complete the corporate file.

(d) A clinic corporation shall submit to the department, on behalf of all licensed primary care clinics operated by the clinic corporation, a single report of change that is applicable to all primary care clinics operated by the clinic corporation, including a change in a principal officer or general manager of the governing body, the medical director, and the clinic administrator, as required by law.

(e) A clinic corporation may submit to the department, on behalf of all licensed primary care clinics operated by the clinic corporation that are within the same license renewal month, a single payment for all primary care clinic licensure renewal fees.
(Added by Stats. 2010, Ch. 502, Sec. 5. (SB 442) Effective January 1, 2011.)
1218.4.
(a) A licensed primary care community or free clinic shall report to the department, when renewing its license, whether it is currently operating an intermittent clinic, the location of any intermittent clinic, and the estimated hours of operation of any intermittent clinic.

(b) For the purposes of this section "intermittent clinic" means a clinic described in subdivision (h) of Section 1206.
(Added by Stats. 2015, Ch. 412, Sec. 2. (AB 1130) Effective January 1, 2016.)
1219.
(a) Except for affiliate clinics, as defined in Section 1218.1, if a clinic or an applicant for a license has not been previously licensed, the department may only issue a provisional license to the clinic as provided in this section.

(b) A provisional license to operate a clinic shall terminate six months from the date of issuance.

(c) Within 30 days prior to the termination of a provisional license, the department shall give the clinic a full and complete inspection, and, if the clinic meets all applicable requirements for licensure, a regular license shall be issued. If the clinic does not meet the requirements for licensure but has made substantial progress towards meeting such requirements, as determined by the department, the initial provisional license shall be renewed for six months.

(d) If the department determines that there has not been substantial progress towards meeting licensure requirements at the time of the first full inspection provided by this section, or, if the department determines upon its inspection made within 30 days of the termination of a renewed provisional license that there is a lack of full compliance with such requirements, no further license shall be issued.

(e) If an applicant for a provisional license to operate a clinic has been denied by the department, the applicant may contest the denial by filing a statement of issues, as provided in Section 11504 of the Government Code. The proceedings to review the denial shall be conducted pursuant to the provisions of Chapter 5 (commencing with Section 11500) of Part 1 of Division 3 of Title 2 of the Government Code.
(Amended by Stats. 2008, Ch. 90, Sec. 1. Effective January 1, 2009.)
1219.1.
(a) The state department may issue a provisional license to a clinic if:

(1) The clinic and the applicant for licensure substantially meet the standards specified by this chapter and regulations adopted pursuant to this chapter.

(2) No violation of this chapter or regulations adopted under this chapter exists in the clinic which jeopardizes the health or safety of patients.

(3) The applicant has adopted a plan for correction of any existing violations which is satisfactory to the state department.

(b) A provisional license issued under this section shall expire not later than six months after the date of issuance, or at such earlier time as determined by the state department at the time of issuance, and may not be renewed.
(Added by Stats. 1987, Ch. 1456, Sec. 2.)
1220.
Immediately upon the denial of any application for a license or special permit or a renewal thereof, the state department shall notify the applicant in writing. Within 15 days after the state department mails the notice, the applicant may present his written petition for a hearing to the state department. Upon receipt by the state department of the petition in proper form, such petition shall be set for hearing. The proceedings shall be conducted in accordance with Chapter 5 (commencing with Section 11500) of Part 1 of Division 3 of Title 2 of the Government Code, and the state department has all powers granted therein. The director may issue a temporary license to operate a community clinic or free clinic when the director determines that the facility is in compliance with the provisions of this chapter, except that the facility has applied for but not yet been granted an exemption from federal taxation as required by subdivision (a) of Section 1204. In such cases, the prospective licensee shall submit to the director a copy of its application for exemption from federal taxation which it has sent to the federal Internal Revenue Service. The director shall request the Franchise Tax Board to review the application and to render an opinion regarding whether it is likely that the exemption will be granted. If the Franchise Tax Board so determines, the director may proceed to issue a temporary license. Such temporary license shall expire 12 months from the date of its issuance or upon the facility

being granted such exemption from federal taxation. The director shall issue no more than three successive temporary licenses to one facility.
(Added by Stats. 1978, Ch. 1147.)

ARTICLE 2.5. Licensing of Clinics [1221 - 1221.19]
(Article 2.5 added by Stats. 2001, Ch. 525, Sec. 2.)
1221.
For purposes of this article, the following definitions shall apply:
(a) "Centralized applications unit" means the centralized applications unit in the Licensing and Certification Division of the State Department of Health Services, or a successor entity.
(b) "Clinic" means nonprofit primary care clinics, nonprofit community health centers, nonprofit community clinics, and free clinics.
(Added by Stats. 2001, Ch. 525, Sec. 2. Effective January 1, 2002.)
1221.05.
Commencing July 1, 2002, all new applications for licenses for clinics shall be reviewed by the centralized applications unit.
(Added by Stats. 2001, Ch. 525, Sec. 2. Effective January 1, 2002.)
1221.09.
Commencing January 1, 2002, the centralized applications unit shall work with organizations that are among and advocate on behalf of, clinics to streamline application forms and clarify information needed to qualify as completed.
(Added by Stats. 2001, Ch. 525, Sec. 2. Effective January 1, 2002.)
1221.11.
Commencing January 1, 2002, a telephone number shall be provided for applicants to verify receipt of their application by the Licensing and Certification Division.
(Added by Stats. 2001, Ch. 525, Sec. 2. Effective January 1, 2002.)
1221.13.
All new applications submitted to the centralized applications unit shall be reviewed within two weeks for completeness. The centralized applications unit shall resolve minor issues directly with the applicant.
(Added by Stats. 2001, Ch. 525, Sec. 2. Effective January 1, 2002.)
1221.15.
(a) Commencing January 1, 2002, the Licensing and Certification Division shall designate at least one surveyor in each of the four regions to specialize in clinic surveys and complaint investigations. The program shall cross-train additional staff in this specialty.
(b) Commencing January 1, 2002, all completed packages forwarded by the centralized applications unit to the regional clinic specialists shall be scheduled for survey within 30 days of receipt.
(Added by Stats. 2001, Ch. 525, Sec. 2. Effective January 1, 2002.)
1221.17.
The Licensing and Certification Program training unit shall work with organizations that are among and advocate on behalf of clinics and other stakeholders to develop a training curriculum on clinic specialization, including the special needs of rural clinics.
(Added by Stats. 2001, Ch. 525, Sec. 2. Effective January 1, 2002.)
1221.19.
The centralized applications unit and regional offices shall be routinely reviewed by the department beginning January 31, 2003, to determine if applications for clinic licenses are processed in a timely and effective manner.
(Added by Stats. 2001, Ch. 525, Sec. 2. Effective January 1, 2002.)

ARTICLE 2.6. Provider Enrollment for Clinics [1222- 1222.]
(Article 2.6 added by Stats. 2004, Ch. 449, Sec. 1.)
1222.
The department shall, on or before July 1, 2005, implement a process that allows an applicant for licensure as a primary care clinic, as defined in subdivision (a) of Section 1204, at the applicant's option, to submit an application for review of the clinic's qualifications for participation in any of the following programs simultaneous with any review for enrollment and certification as a provider in the Medi-Cal program, and if approved for participation in a program, to be enrolled or certified, or both, as a provider in the program, subsequent to certification and enrollment as a provider in the Medi-Cal program:
(a) Medi-Cal Presumptive Eligibility under Section 14148.7 of the Welfare and Institutions Code.
(b) Child Health and Disability Prevention Program provided for pursuant to Article 6 (commencing with Section 124025) of Chapter 3 of Part 2 of Division 106.
(c) Perinatal Services Program provided for pursuant to Article 4.7 (commencing with Section 14148) of Chapter 7 of Part 3 of Division 9 of the Welfare and Institutions Code.
(d) Family Planning, Access, Care, and Treatment (Family PACT) Waiver Program provided for pursuant to subdivision (aa) of Section 14132 of the Welfare and Institutions Code.
(Added by Stats. 2004, Ch. 449, Sec. 1. Effective January 1, 2005.)

ARTICLE 3. Regulations [1225 - 1234]
(Article 3 added by Stats. 1978, Ch. 1147.)
1225.
(a) The department shall adopt, and may from time to time amend or repeal, in accordance with Chapter 3.5 (commencing with Section 11340) of Part 1 of Division 3 of Title 2 of the Government Code, such reasonable rules and regulations as may be necessary or proper to carry out the purposes and intent of this chapter and to enable the department to exercise the powers and perform the duties conferred upon it by this chapter, not inconsistent with any of the provisions of any statute of this state. The rules

and regulations for primary care clinics shall be separate and distinct from the rules and regulations for specialty clinics.
(b) All regulations relating to licensed clinics in effect on December 31, 1977, which were adopted by the department, shall remain in full force and effect until altered, amended, or repealed by the director.
(c) A chronic dialysis clinic, a surgical clinic, or a rehabilitation clinic licensed or seeking licensure shall comply with the following federal certification standards in effect immediately preceding January 1, 2018:
(1) A chronic dialysis clinic shall comply with federal certification standards for an end-stage renal disease clinic, as specified in Sections 494.1 to 494.180, inclusive, of Title 42 of the Code of Federal Regulations.
(2) A surgical clinic, as defined in subdivision (b) of Section 1204, shall comply with federal certification standards for an ambulatory surgical clinic, as specified in Sections 416.1 to 416.54, inclusive, of Title 42 of the Code of Federal Regulations.
(3) A rehabilitation clinic shall comply with federal certification standards for a comprehensive outpatient rehabilitation facility, as specified in Sections 485.50 to 485.74, inclusive, of Title 42 of the Code of Federal Regulations.
(Amended by Stats. 2018, Ch. 34, Sec. 4. (AB 1810) Effective June 27, 2018.)
1226.
(a) The regulations shall prescribe the kinds of services which may be provided by clinics in each category of licensure and shall prescribe minimum standards of adequacy, safety, and sanitation of the physical plant and equipment, minimum standards for staffing with duly qualified personnel, and minimum standards for providing the services offered. These minimum standards shall be based on the type of facility, the needs of the patients served, and the types and levels of services provided.
(b) The Office of Statewide Health Planning and Development, in consultation with the Community Clinics Advisory Committee, shall prescribe minimum construction standards of adequacy and safety for the physical plant of clinics as found in the California Building Standards Code.
(c) A city or county, as applicable, shall have plan review and building inspection responsibilities for the construction or alteration of buildings described in paragraph (1) and paragraph (2) of subdivision (b) of Section 1204 and shall apply the provisions of the latest edition of the California Building Standards Code in conducting these plan review responsibilities. For these buildings, construction and alteration shall include conversion of a building to a purpose specified in paragraphs (1) and (2) of subdivision (b) of Section 1204.
Upon the initial submittal to a city or county by the governing authority or owner of these clinics for plan review and building inspection services, the city or county shall reply in writing to the clinic whether or not the plan review by the city or county will include a certification as to whether or not the clinic project submitted for plan review meets the standards as propounded by the office in the California Building Standards Code.
If the city or county indicates that its review will include this certification it shall do all of the following:
(1) Apply the applicable clinic provisions of the latest edition of the California Building Standards Code.
(2) Certify in writing, to the applicant within 30 days of completion of construction whether or not these standards have been met.
(d) If upon initial submittal, the city or county indicates that its plan review will not include this certification, the governing authority or owner of the clinic shall submit the plans to the Office of Statewide Health Planning and Development who shall review the plans for certification whether or not the clinic project meets the standards, as propounded by the office in California Building Standards Code.
(e) When the office performs review for certification, the office shall charge a fee in an amount that does not exceed its actual costs.
(f) The office of the State Fire Marshal shall prescribe minimum safety standards for fire and life safety in surgical clinics.
(g) Notwithstanding subdivision (c), the governing authority or owner of a clinic may request the office to perform plan review services for buildings described in subdivision (c). If the office agrees to perform these services, after consultation with the local building official, the office shall charge an amount not to exceed its actual costs. The construction or alteration of these buildings shall conform to the applicable provisions of the latest edition of the California Building Standards Code for purposes of the plan review by the office pursuant to this subdivision.
(h) Regulations adopted pursuant to this chapter establishing standards for laboratory services shall not be applicable to any clinic that operates a clinical laboratory licensed pursuant to Section 1265 of the Business and Professions Code.
(Amended by Stats. 1997, Ch. 732, Sec. 1. Effective January 1, 1998.)
1226.1.
(a) A primary care clinic shall comply with the following requirements regarding health examinations and other public health protections for individuals working in a primary care clinic:
(1) An employee working in a primary care clinic who has direct contact with patients shall have a health examination within six months prior to employment or within 15 days after employment. Each examination shall include a medical history and physical evaluation. A written examination report, signed by the person performing the examination, shall verify that the employee is able to perform his or her assigned duties.
(2) At the time of employment, testing for tuberculosis shall consist of a purified protein derivative intermediate strength intradermal skin test or any other test for tuberculosis infection recommended by the federal Centers for Disease Control and Prevention (CDC) and licensed by the federal Food and Drug Administration (FDA). If a positive reaction is

obtained from the skin test, or any other test for tuberculosis infection recommended by the CDC and licensed by the FDA, the employee shall be referred to a physician to determine if a chest X-ray is necessary. Annual examinations shall be performed only when medically indicated.

(3) The clinic shall maintain a health record for each employee that includes reports of all employment-related health examinations. These records shall be kept for a minimum of three years following termination of employment.

(4) An employee known to have or exhibiting signs or symptoms of a communicable disease shall not be permitted to work until he or she submits a physician's certification that the employee is sufficiently free of the communicable disease to return to his or her assigned duties.

(b) Any regulation adopted before January 1, 2004, that imposes a standard on a primary care clinic that is more stringent than described in this section is void.
(Amended by Stats. 2007, Ch. 24, Sec. 3. Effective January 1, 2008.)
1226.2.

The Community Clinics Advisory Committee provided for in subdivision (b) of Section 1226 shall meet on an ad hoc basis and shall be comprised of at least 15 individuals who are employed by, or under contract to provide service to, a community clinic on a full-time basis, either directly or as a representative of a clinic association. Members of the committee shall be appointed by the three statewide primary care clinic associations in California that represent the greatest number of community or free clinic sites.
(Added by Stats. 2003, Ch. 602, Sec. 7. Effective January 1, 2004.)
1226.3.

A primary care clinic may establish compliance with the minimum construction standards of adequacy and safety for the physical plant described in subdivision (b) of Section 1226 by submitting a written certification, as described in Section 5536.26 of the Business and Professions Code, from a licensed architect or a written statement from a local building department that the applicable construction, remodeling, alteration, or other applicable modification of the physical plant is in compliance with these standards. No particular form of certification or statement shall be required by the department. Any form of statement utilized by a city or county building department, or certification by a licensed architect, indicating that the premises conform to the requirements of the California Building Standards Code, shall be accepted by the department as sufficient proof of compliance. Enforcement of compliance with applicable provisions of the California Building Standards Code, pursuant to subdivision (b) of Section 1226, shall be within the exclusive jurisdiction of the local building department.
(Added by Stats. 2003, Ch. 602, Sec. 8. Effective January 1, 2004.)
1226.5.

(a) It is the intent of the Legislature to establish seismic safety standards for facilities licensed as surgical clinics pursuant to this chapter, and for facilities certified for participation in the federal Medicare program as ambulatory surgical centers, which accommodate surgical patients under general anesthesia, but are not required to remain open and usable after an earthquake to accommodate emergency patients.

(b) A facility described in subdivision (a) which, after January 1, 1991, anchors fixed medical equipment to the floor or roof of the facility with a gross operating weight of more than 400 pounds or anchors fixed medical equipment to the walls or ceiling with a gross operating weight of more than 20 pounds shall retain the services of an architect licensed in California, a structural engineer licensed in California, or a civil engineer registered in California to assure that the equipment is anchored in such a manner to meet the requirements of an occupancy importance factor of 1.00, as set forth in Title 24 of the California Code of Regulations.

(c) A facility described in subdivision (a) which retains the services of an architect or engineer for the anchorage of fixed medical equipment shall keep available for inspection by the department for a period of five years following the installation, a current written certification from the architect or engineer that the equipment is mounted in accordance with the applicable requirements.
(Added by Stats. 1990, Ch. 1579, Sec. 1.)
1227.

Any duly authorized officer, employee, or agent of the state department may upon presentation of proper identification, enter and inspect any building or premises at any time, with or without advance notice, to secure compliance with, or to prevent a violation of, any provision of this chapter or any regulations adopted pursuant to this chapter.
(Added by Stats. 1978, Ch. 1147.)
1228.

(a) Except as provided in subdivision (c), every clinic for which a license or special permit has been issued shall be periodically inspected. The frequency of inspections shall depend upon the type and complexity of the clinic or special service to be inspected. Inspections shall be conducted no less often than once every three years and as often as necessary to ensure the quality of care being provided.

(b) (1) During inspections, representatives of the department shall offer any advice and assistance to the clinic as they deem appropriate. The department may contract with local health departments for the assumption of any of the department's responsibilities under this chapter. In exercising this authority, the local health department shall conform to the requirements of this chapter and to the rules, regulations, and standards of the department.

(2) The department shall reimburse local health departments for services performed pursuant to this section, and these payments shall not exceed actual cost. Reports of each inspection shall be prepared by the representative conducting it upon forms prepared and furnished by the department and filed with the department.

(c) This section shall not apply to any of the following:

(1) A rural health clinic.

(2) A primary care clinic accredited by the Joint Commission on Accreditation of Healthcare Organizations (JCAHO), the Accreditation Association for Ambulatory Health Care (AAAHC), or any other accrediting organization recognized by the department.

(3) An ambulatory surgical center.

(4) An end stage renal disease facility.

(5) A comprehensive outpatient rehabilitation facility that is certified to participate either in the Medicare program under Title XVIII (42 U.S.C. Sec. 1395 et seq.) of the federal Social Security Act, or the medicaid program under Title XIX (42 U.S.C. Sec. 1396 et seq.) of the federal Social Security Act, or both.

(d) Notwithstanding paragraph (2) of subdivision (c), the department shall retain the authority to inspect a primary care clinic pursuant to Section 1227, or as necessary to ensure the quality of care being provided.
(Amended by Stats. 2003, Ch. 602, Sec. 9. Effective January 1, 2004.)
1229.

The state department shall notify any clinic of all deficiencies in its compliance with the provisions of this chapter or the rules and regulations adopted hereunder, which are discovered or confirmed by inspection, and the clinic shall agree with the state department upon a plan of correction which shall give the clinic a reasonable time to correct such deficiencies. During such allotted time, a list of deficiencies and the plan of correction shall be conspicuously posted in a clinic location accessible to public view. If at the end of the allotted time, as provided in the plan of correction, the clinic has failed to correct the deficiencies, the state department shall assess the licensee a civil penalty not to exceed fifty dollars ($50) per day, until the state department finds the clinic in compliance. In such case, the state department may also initiate action against the clinic to revoke or suspend the license. Nothing in this chapter shall be deemed to prohibit a clinic which is unable to correct the deficiencies, as specified in a plan of corrections, for reasons beyond its control from voluntarily surrendering its license pursuant to Section 1245 prior to the assessment of any civil penalty or the initiation of any revocation or suspension proceeding.
(Repealed and added by Stats. 1978, Ch. 1147.)
1229.1.

No notification of deficiency, civil or criminal penalty, fine, sanction, or denial, suspension, or revocation of licensure, may be imposed against a primary care clinic, or any person acting on behalf of the clinic, for a violation of a regulation, as defined in Section 11342.600 of the Government Code, including every rule, regulation, order, or standard of general application, or the amendment, supplement, or revision of any rule, regulation, order, or standard adopted by a state agency to implement, interpret, or make specific the law enforced or administered by it, or to govern its procedure, unless the regulation has been adopted pursuant to Chapter 3.5 (commencing with Section 11340) of Part 1 of Division 3 of Title 2 of the Government Code.
(Added by Stats. 2003, Ch. 602, Sec. 10. Effective January 1, 2004.)
1230.

Reports on the results of each inspection shall be kept on file in the state department along with the plan of correction and clinic comments. The inspection report may include a recommendation for reinspection. All inspection reports, lists of deficiencies, and plans of correction shall be public records open to public inspection.
(Added by Stats. 1978, Ch. 1147.)
1231.

(a) All clinics shall maintain compliance with the licensing requirements. These requirements shall not, however, prohibit the use of alternate concepts, methods, procedures, techniques, space, equipment, personnel qualifications, or the conducting of pilot projects, provided these exceptions are carried out with provision for safe and adequate patient care and with prior written approval of the department. A written request and substantiating evidence supporting the request shall be submitted by the applicant or licensee to the state department. Where a licensee submits a single program flexibility request and substantiating evidence on behalf of more than one similarly situated primary care clinic, the department may approve the program flexibility request as to each of the primary care clinics identified in the request. The department shall approve or deny any request within 60 days of submission. This approval shall be in writing and shall provide for the terms and conditions under which the exception is granted. A denial shall be in writing and shall specify the basis therefor.

(b) Substantiating evidence of a shortage of a specific health care professional that is submitted in support of a request for utilization of alternatives to personnel requirements contained in regulations adopted under this chapter may include documentation that the clinic is located in a geographic area that is either deemed under federal law, or designated by the Office of Statewide Health Planning and Development, as a medically underserved area, a health professional shortage area, or as serving, in whole or in part, a medically underserved population.

(c) If after investigation the department determines that a clinic granted a waiver pursuant to this section is operating in a manner contrary to the terms or conditions of the waiver, the director shall immediately revoke the waiver as to that clinic site.
(Amended by Stats. 2003, Ch. 602, Sec. 11. Effective January 1, 2004.)
1231.5.

The department may grant to a PACE program, as defined in Chapter 8.75 (commencing with Section 14591) of Part 3 of Division 9 of the Welfare and Institutions Code, exemptions from the provisions contained in this chapter in accordance with the requirements of Section 100315.
(Amended by Stats. 2011, Ch. 367, Sec. 1. (AB 574) Effective January 1, 2012.)
1232.

No clinic which permits sterilization operations for contraceptive purposes to be performed therein, nor the medical staff of such clinic, shall require the individual upon whom such a sterilization operation is to be performed to meet any special nonmedical qualifications, which are not imposed on individuals seeking other types of operations in the clinic. Such prohibited nonmedical qualifications shall include, but not be limited to, age, marital status, and number of natural children.

Nothing in this section shall prohibit requirements relating to the physical or mental condition of the individual or affect the right of the attending physician to counsel or advise his patient as to whether or not sterilization is appropriate. This section shall not affect existing law with respect to individuals below the age of majority.
(Added by Stats. 1978, Ch. 1147.)

1233.

A surgical clinic may restrict use of its facilities to members of the medical staff of the surgical clinic and other physicians and surgeons approved by the medical staff to practice at the clinic.
(Added by Stats. 1979, Ch. 1186.)

1233.5.

By June 30, 1995, a licensed clinic board of directors and its medical director shall establish and adopt written policies and procedures to screen patients for purposes of detecting spousal or partner abuse. The policies shall include procedures to accomplish all of the following:

(a) Identifying, as part of its medical screening, spousal or partner abuse among patients.

(b) Documenting in the medical record patient injuries or illnesses attributable to spousal or partner abuse.

(c) Providing to patients who exhibit signs of spousal or partner abuse a current referral list of private and public community agencies that provide, or arrange for, the evaluation, counseling, and care of persons experiencing spousal or partner abuse, including, but not limited to, hot lines, local battered women's shelters, legal services, and information about temporary restraining orders.

(d) Designating licensed clinical staff to be responsible for the implementation of these guidelines.

It is the intent of the Legislature that clinics, for purposes of satisfying the requirements of this section, adopt guidelines similar to those developed by the American Medical Association regarding domestic violence detection and referral. The Legislature recognizes that while guidelines evolve and change, the American Medical Association's guidelines may serve, at this time, as a model for clinics to follow.
(Amended by Stats. 1994, Ch. 147, Sec. 4. Effective July 11, 1994.)

1234.

(a) Smoking a tobacco product shall not be permitted in patient areas of a clinic except those rooms designated for occupancy exclusively by smokers.

(b) Clearly legible signs shall either:

(1) State that smoking is unlawful and be conspicuously posted by, or on behalf of, the owner or manager of such clinic, in all areas of a clinic where smoking is unlawful.

(2) Identify "smoking permitted" areas, and be posted by, or on behalf of, the owner or manager of such clinic, only in areas of a clinic where smoking is lawfully permitted.

If "smoking permitted" signs are posted, there shall also be conspicuously posted, near all major entrances, clearly legible signs stating that smoking is unlawful except in areas designated "smoking permitted."

(c) This section shall not apply to skilled nursing facilities, intermediate care facilities, and intermediate care facilities for the developmentally disabled.

(d) For purposes of this section, "smoking" has the same meaning as in subdivision (c) of Section 22950.5 of the Business and Professions Code.

(e) For purposes of this section, "tobacco product" means a product or device as defined in subdivision (d) of Section 22950.5 of the Business and Professions Code.
(Amended by Stats. 2016, 2nd Ex. Sess., Ch. 7, Sec. 11. (SB 5 2x) Effective June 9, 2016.)

ARTICLE 4. Offenses [1235 - 1238]

(Article 4 added by Stats. 1978, Ch. 1147.)

1235.

(a) Except as provided in subdivision (b), any person who violates any of the provisions of this chapter or who willfully or repeatedly violates any rule or regulation promulgated under this chapter is guilty of a misdemeanor, and upon conviction thereof shall be punished by a fine not to exceed one thousand dollars ($1,000) or by imprisonment in the county jail for a period not to exceed 180 days or by both such fine and imprisonment.

(b) Any person who violates the provisions of Section 1234 is guilty of an infraction and shall be punished by a fine of not more than one hundred dollars ($100).
(Amended by Stats. 1983, Ch. 1092, Sec. 144. Effective September 27, 1983. Operative January 1, 1984, by Sec. 427 of Ch. 1092.)

1236.

The director may bring an action to enjoin the violation or threatened violation of Section 1205 in the superior court in and for the county in which the violation occurred or is about to occur. Any proceeding under the provisions of this section shall conform to the requirements of Chapter 3 (commencing with Section 525) of Title 7 of Part 2 of the Code of Civil Procedure, except that the director shall not be required to allege facts necessary to show or tending to show lack of adequate remedy at law or irreparable damage or loss.
(Repealed and added by Stats. 1978, Ch. 1147.)

1237.

Any action brought by the director against a clinic shall not abate by reason of a sale or other transfer of ownership of the facility which is a party to the action, except with express written consent of the director.
(Repealed and added by Stats. 1978, Ch. 1147.)

1238.

The district attorney of every county shall, upon application by the state department or its authorized representative, institute and conduct the prosecution of any action for violation within his county of any provision of this chapter or regulations adopted hereunder.
(Added by Stats. 1978, Ch. 1147.)

ARTICLE 5. Suspension and Revocation [1240 - 1245]

(Article 5 added by Stats. 1978, Ch. 1147.)

1240.

The state department may suspend or revoke any license or special permit issued under the provisions of this chapter upon any of the following grounds and in the manner provided in this chapter:

(a) Violation by the licensee or holder of a special permit of any of the provisions of this chapter or of the rules and regulations promulgated under this chapter.

(b) Aiding, abetting, or permitting the violation of any provision of this chapter or of the rules and regulations promulgated under this chapter.

(c) Conduct inimical to the public health, welfare, or safety of the people of the State of California in the maintenance and operation of the premises or services for which a license or special permit is issued.
(Added by Stats. 1978, Ch. 1147.)

1241.

Proceedings for the suspension, revocation, or denial of licenses or special permits under this chapter shall be conducted in accordance with the provisions of Chapter 5 (commencing with Section 11500) of Part 1 of Division 3 of Title 2 of the Government Code, and the state department shall have all the powers granted by such provisions. In the event of conflict between the provisions of this chapter and such provisions of the Government Code, the provisions of the Government Code shall prevail.
(Added by Stats. 1978, Ch. 1147.)

1242.

The director may temporarily suspend any license issued to a specialty clinic or special permit prior to any hearing, when in his opinion such action is necessary to protect the public welfare. The director shall notify the licensee or holder of a special permit of the temporary suspension and the effective date thereof, and at the same time shall serve such provider with an accusation. Upon receipt of a notice of defense by the licensee or holder of a special permit, the director shall set the matter for hearing within 30 days after receipt of such notice. The temporary suspension shall remain in effect until such time as the hearing is completed and the director has made a final determination on the merits; provided, however, that the temporary suspension shall be deemed vacated if the director fails to make a final determination on the merits within 60 days after the original hearing has been completed.

If the provisions of this chapter or the rules or regulations promulgated by the director are violated by a licensed surgical clinic or chronic dialysis clinic or holder of a special permit which is a group, corporation, or other association, the director may suspend the license or special permit of such organization or may suspend the license or special permit as to any individual person within such organization who is responsible for such violation.
(Added by Stats. 1978, Ch. 1147.)

1243.

The withdrawal of an application for a license or a special permit after it has been filed with the state department, shall not, unless the state department consents in writing to such withdrawal, deprive the state department of its authority to institute or continue a proceeding against the applicant for the denial of the license or special permit upon any ground provided by law, or to enter an order denying the license or special permit upon any such ground.

The suspension, expiration, or forfeiture by operation of law of a license or a special permit issued by the state department, or its suspension, forfeiture or cancellation by order of the state department or by order of a court of law, or its surrender without the written consent of the state department, shall not deprive the state department of its authority to institute or continue a disciplinary proceeding against the licensee or holder of a special permit upon any ground provided by law or to enter an order suspending or revoking the license or special permit or otherwise taking disciplinary action against the licensee or holder of a special permit on any such ground.
(Added by Stats. 1978, Ch. 1147.)

1244.

Any license or special permit revoked pursuant to this chapter may be reinstated pursuant to the provisions of Section 11522 of the Government Code.
(Added by Stats. 1978, Ch. 1147.)

1245.

Any licensee or holder of a special permit may, with the approval of the state department, surrender his license or special permit for suspension by the state department for a temporary period not to exceed 24 consecutive months. Any license or special permit suspended pursuant to this section may be reinstated by the state department on receipt of an application and after an inspection showing full compliance with all applicable licensing requirements.
(Added by Stats. 1978, Ch. 1147.)

CHAPTER 1.3. Outpatient Settings [1248 - 1248.85]

(Chapter 1.3 added by Stats. 1994, Ch. 1276, Sec. 2.)

1248.

For purposes of this chapter, the following definitions shall apply:

(a) "Division" means the Medical Board of California. All references in this chapter to the division, the Division of Licensing of the Medical Board of California, or the Division of Medical Quality shall be deemed to refer to the Medical Board of California pursuant to Section 2002 of the Business and Professions Code.

(b) (1) "Outpatient setting" means any facility, clinic, unlicensed clinic, center, office, or other setting that is not part of a general acute care facility, as defined in Section 1250, and where anesthesia, except local anesthesia or peripheral nerve blocks, or both, is used in compliance with the community standard of practice, in doses that, when administered have the probability of placing a patient at risk for loss of the patient's life-preserving protective reflexes.

(2) "Outpatient setting" also means facilities that offer in vitro fertilization, as defined in subdivision (b) of Section 1374.55.

(3) "Outpatient setting" does not include, among other settings, any setting where anxiolytics and analgesics are administered, when done so in compliance with the community standard of practice, in doses that do not have the probability of placing the patient at risk for loss of the patient's life-preserving protective reflexes.

(c) "Accreditation agency" means a public or private organization that is approved to issue certificates of accreditation to outpatient settings by the board pursuant to Sections 1248.15 and 1248.4.

(Amended by Stats. 2011, Ch. 645, Sec. 2. (SB 100) Effective January 1, 2012.)

1248.1.

No association, corporation, firm, partnership, or person shall operate, manage, conduct, or maintain an outpatient setting in this state, unless the setting is one of the following:

(a) An ambulatory surgical center that is certified to participate in the Medicare program under Title XVIII (42 U.S.C. Sec. 1395 et seq.) of the federal Social Security Act.

(b) Any clinic conducted, maintained, or operated by a federally recognized Indian tribe or tribal organization, as defined in Section 450 or 1601 of Title 25 of the United States Code, and located on land recognized as tribal land by the federal government.

(c) Any clinic directly conducted, maintained, or operated by the United States or by any of its departments, officers, or agencies.

(d) Any primary care clinic licensed under subdivision (a) and any surgical clinic licensed under subdivision (b) of Section 1204.

(e) Any health facility licensed as a general acute care hospital under Chapter 2 (commencing with Section 1250).

(f) Any outpatient setting to the extent that it is used by a dentist or physician and surgeon in compliance with Article 2.7 (commencing with Section 1646) or Article 2.8 (commencing with Section 1647) of Chapter 4 of Division 2 of the Business and Professions Code.

(g) An outpatient setting accredited by an accreditation agency approved by the division pursuant to this chapter.

(h) A setting, including, but not limited to, a mobile van, in which equipment is used to treat patients admitted to a facility described in subdivision (a), (d), or (e), and in which the procedures performed are staffed by the medical staff of, or other healthcare practitioners with clinical privileges at, the facility and are subject to the peer review process of the facility but which setting is not a part of a facility described in subdivision (a), (d), or (e).

Nothing in this section shall relieve an association, corporation, firm, partnership, or person from complying with all other provisions of law that are otherwise applicable.

(Added by Stats. 1994, Ch. 1276, Sec. 2. Effective January 1, 1995.)

1248.15.

(a) The board shall adopt standards for accreditation and, in approving accreditation agencies to perform accreditation of outpatient settings, shall ensure that the certification program shall, at a minimum, include standards for the following aspects of the settings' operations:

(1) Outpatient setting allied health staff shall be licensed or certified to the extent required by state or federal law.

(2) (A) Outpatient settings shall have a system for facility safety and emergency training requirements.

(B) There shall be onsite equipment, medication, and trained personnel to facilitate handling of services sought or provided and to facilitate handling of any medical emergency that may arise in connection with services sought or provided.

(C) In order for procedures to be performed in an outpatient setting as defined in Section 1248, the outpatient setting shall do one of the following:

(i) Have a written transfer agreement with a local accredited or licensed acute care hospital, approved by the facility's medical staff.

(ii) Permit surgery only by a licensee who has admitting privileges at a local accredited or licensed acute care hospital, with the exception that licensees who may be precluded from having admitting privileges by their professional classification or other administrative limitations, shall have a written transfer agreement with licensees who have admitting privileges at local accredited or licensed acute care hospitals.

(iii) Submit for approval by an accrediting agency a detailed procedural plan for handling medical emergencies that shall be reviewed at the time of accreditation. No reasonable plan shall be disapproved by the accrediting agency.

(D) The outpatient setting shall submit for approval by an accreditation agency at the time of accreditation a detailed plan, standardized procedures, and protocols to be followed in the event of serious complications or side effects from surgery that would place a patient at high risk for injury or harm or to govern emergency and urgent care situations. The plan shall include, at a minimum, that if a patient is being transferred to a local accredited or licensed acute care hospital, the outpatient setting shall do all of the following:

(i) Notify the individual designated by the patient to be notified in case of an emergency.

(ii) Ensure that the mode of transfer is consistent with the patient's medical condition.

(iii) Ensure that all relevant clinical information is documented and accompanies the patient at the time of transfer.

(iv) Continue to provide appropriate care to the patient until the transfer is effectuated.

(E) All physicians and surgeons transferring patients from an outpatient setting shall agree to cooperate with the medical staff peer review process on the transferred case, the results of which shall be referred back to the outpatient setting, if deemed appropriate by the medical staff peer review committee. If the medical staff of the acute care facility determines that inappropriate care was delivered at the outpatient setting, the acute care facility's peer review outcome shall be reported, as appropriate, to the accrediting body or in accordance with existing law.

(3) The outpatient setting shall permit surgery by a dentist acting within his or her scope of practice under Chapter 4 (commencing with Section 1600) of Division 2 of the Business and Professions Code or physician and surgeon, osteopathic physician and surgeon, or podiatrist acting within his or her scope of practice under Chapter 5 (commencing with Section 2000) of Division 2 of the Business and Professions Code or the Osteopathic Initiative Act. The outpatient setting may, in its discretion, permit anesthesia service by a certified registered nurse anesthetist acting within his or her scope of practice under Article 7 (commencing with Section 2825) of Chapter 6 of Division 2 of the Business and Professions Code.

(4) Outpatient settings shall have a system for maintaining clinical records.

(5) Outpatient settings shall have a system for patient care and monitoring procedures.

(6) (A) Outpatient settings shall have a system for quality assessment and improvement.

(B) (i) Members of the medical staff and other practitioners who are granted clinical privileges shall be professionally qualified and appropriately credentialed for the performance of privileges granted. The outpatient setting shall grant privileges in accordance with recommendations from qualified health professionals, and credentialing standards established by the outpatient setting.

(ii) Each licensee who performs procedures in an outpatient setting that requires the outpatient setting to be accredited shall be, at least every two years, peer reviewed, which shall be a process in which the basic qualifications, staff privileges, employment, medical outcomes, or professional conduct of a licensee is reviewed to make recommendations for quality improvement and education, if necessary, including when the outpatient setting has only one licensee. The peer review shall be performed by licensees who are qualified by education and experience to perform the same types of, or similar, procedures. The findings of the peer review shall be reported to the governing body, which shall determine if the licensee continues to meet the requirements described in clause (i). The process that resulted in the findings of the peer review shall be reviewed by the accrediting agency at the next survey to determine if the outpatient setting meets applicable accreditation standards pursuant to this section.

(C) Clinical privileges shall be periodically reappraised by the outpatient setting. The scope of procedures performed in the outpatient setting shall be periodically reviewed and amended as appropriate.

(7) Outpatient settings regulated by this chapter that have multiple service locations shall have all of the sites inspected.

(8) Outpatient settings shall post the certificate of accreditation in a location readily visible to patients and staff.

(9) Outpatient settings shall post the name and telephone number of the accrediting agency with instructions on the submission of complaints in a location readily visible to patients and staff.

(10) Outpatient settings shall have a written discharge criteria.

(b) Outpatient settings shall have a minimum of two staff persons on the premises, one of whom shall be a licensed physician and surgeon or a licensed health care professional with current certification in advanced cardiac life support (ACLS), as long as a patient is present who has not been discharged from supervised care. Transfer to an unlicensed setting of a patient who does not meet the discharge criteria adopted pursuant to paragraph (10) of subdivision (a) shall constitute unprofessional conduct.

(c) An accreditation agency may include additional standards in its determination to accredit outpatient settings if these are approved by the board to protect the public health and safety.

(d) No accreditation standard adopted or approved by the board, and no standard included in any certification program of any accreditation agency approved by the board, shall serve to limit the ability of any allied health care practitioner to provide services within his or her full scope of practice. Notwithstanding this or any other provision of law, each outpatient setting may limit the privileges, or determine the privileges, within the appropriate scope of practice, that will be afforded to physicians and allied health care practitioners who practice at the facility, in accordance with credentialing standards established by the outpatient setting in compliance with this chapter. Privileges may not be arbitrarily restricted based on category of licensure.

(e) The board shall adopt standards that it deems necessary for outpatient settings that offer in vitro fertilization.

(f) The board may adopt regulations it deems necessary to specify procedures that should be performed in an accredited outpatient setting for facilities or clinics that are outside the definition of outpatient setting as specified in Section 1248.

(g) As part of the accreditation process, the accrediting agency shall conduct a reasonable investigation of the prior history of the outpatient setting, including all licensed physicians and surgeons who have an ownership interest therein, to determine whether there have been any adverse accreditation decisions rendered against them. For the purposes of this section, "conducting a reasonable investigation" means querying the Medical Board of California and the Osteopathic Medical Board of California to ascertain if either the outpatient setting has, or, if its owners are licensed physicians and surgeons, if those physicians and surgeons have, been subject to an adverse accreditation decision.

(Amended by Stats. 2015, Ch. 287, Sec. 3. (SB 396) Effective January 1, 2016.)

1248.2.

(a) Any outpatient setting may apply to an accreditation agency for a certificate of accreditation. Accreditation shall be issued by the accreditation agency solely on the basis of compliance with its standards as approved by the board under this chapter.

(b) The board shall obtain and maintain a list of accredited outpatient settings from the information provided by the accreditation agencies approved by the board, and shall notify the public, by placing the information on its Internet Web site, whether an outpatient setting is accredited or the setting's accreditation has been revoked, suspended, or placed on probation, or the setting has received a reprimand by the accreditation agency.

(c) The list of outpatient settings shall include all of the following:

(1) Name, address, and telephone number of any owners, and their medical license numbers.

(2) Name and address of the facility.

(3) The name and telephone number of the accreditation agency.

(4) The effective and expiration dates of the accreditation.

(d) Accrediting agencies approved by the board shall notify the board and update the board on all outpatient settings that are accredited.

(Amended by Stats. 2011, Ch. 645, Sec. 4. (SB 100) Effective January 1, 2012.)

1248.25.

If an outpatient setting does not meet the standards approved by the board, accreditation shall be denied by the accreditation agency, which shall provide the outpatient setting notification of the reasons for the denial. An outpatient setting may reapply for accreditation at any time after receiving notification of the denial. The accreditation agency shall report within three business days to the board if the outpatient setting's certificate for accreditation has been denied.

(Amended by Stats. 2011, Ch. 645, Sec. 5. (SB 100) Effective January 1, 2012.)

1248.3.

(a) Certificates of accreditation issued to outpatient settings by an accreditation agency shall be valid for not more than three years.

(b) The outpatient setting shall notify the accreditation agency within 30 days of any significant change in ownership, including, but not limited to, a merger, change in majority interest, consolidation, name change, change in scope of services, additional services, or change in locations.

(c) Except for disclosures to the division or to the Division of Medical Quality under this chapter, an accreditation agency shall not disclose information obtained in the performance of accreditation activities under this chapter that individually identifies patients, individual medical practitioners, or outpatient settings. Neither the proceedings nor the records of an accreditation agency or the proceedings and records of an outpatient setting related to performance of quality assurance or accreditation activities under this chapter shall be subject to discovery, nor shall the records or proceedings be admissible in a court of law. The prohibition relating to discovery and admissibility of records and proceedings does not apply to any outpatient setting requesting accreditation in the event that denial or revocation of that outpatient setting's accreditation is being contested. Nothing in this section shall prohibit the accreditation agency from making discretionary disclosures of information to an outpatient setting pertaining to the accreditation of that outpatient setting.

(Added by Stats. 1994, Ch. 1276, Sec. 2. Effective January 1, 1995.)

1248.35.

(a) Every outpatient setting that is accredited shall be inspected by the accreditation agency and may also be inspected by the Medical Board of California. The Medical Board of California shall ensure that accreditation agencies inspect outpatient settings.

(b) Unless otherwise specified, the following requirements apply to inspections described in subdivision (a).

(1) The frequency of inspection shall depend upon the type and complexity of the outpatient setting to be inspected.

(2) Inspections shall be conducted no less often than once every three years by the accreditation agency and as often as necessary by the Medical Board of California to ensure the quality of care provided. After the initial inspection for accreditation, subsequent inspections may be unannounced. For unannounced routine inspections, the accreditation agency shall notify the outpatient setting that the inspection will occur within 60 days.

(3) The Medical Board of California or the accreditation agency may enter and inspect any outpatient setting that is accredited by an accreditation agency at any reasonable time to ensure compliance with, or investigate an alleged violation of, any standard of the accreditation agency or any provision of this chapter.

(c) If an accreditation agency determines, as a result of its inspection, that an outpatient setting is not in compliance with the standards under which it was approved, the accreditation agency may do any of the following:

(1) Require correction of any identified deficiencies within a set timeframe. Failure to comply shall result in the accrediting agency issuing a reprimand or suspending or revoking the outpatient setting's accreditation.

(2) Issue a reprimand.

(3) Place the outpatient setting on probation, during which time the setting shall successfully institute and complete a plan of correction, approved by the board or the accreditation agency, to correct the deficiencies.

(4) Suspend or revoke the outpatient setting's certification of accreditation.

(d) (1) Except as is otherwise provided in this subdivision, before suspending or revoking a certificate of accreditation under this chapter, the accreditation agency shall provide the outpatient setting with notice of any deficiencies and the outpatient setting shall agree with the accreditation agency on a plan of correction that shall give the outpatient setting reasonable time to supply information demonstrating compliance with the standards of the accreditation agency in compliance with this chapter, as well as the opportunity for a hearing on the matter upon the request of the outpatient setting. During the allotted time to correct the deficiencies, the plan of correction, which includes the deficiencies, shall be conspicuously posted by the outpatient setting in a location accessible to public view. Within 10 days after the adoption of the plan of correction, the accrediting agency shall send a list of deficiencies and the corrective action to be taken to the board and to the California State Board of Pharmacy if an outpatient setting is licensed pursuant to Article 14 (commencing with Section 4190) of Chapter 9 of Division 2 of the Business and Professions Code. The accreditation agency may immediately suspend the certificate of accreditation before providing notice and an opportunity to be heard, but only when failure to take the action may result in imminent danger to the health of an individual. In such cases, the accreditation agency shall provide subsequent notice and an opportunity to be heard.

(2) If an outpatient setting does not comply with a corrective action within a timeframe specified by the accrediting agency, the accrediting agency shall issue a reprimand, and may either place the outpatient setting on probation or suspend or revoke the accreditation of the outpatient setting, and shall notify the board of its action. This section shall not be deemed to prohibit an outpatient setting that is unable to correct the deficiencies, as specified in the plan of correction, for reasons beyond its control, from voluntarily surrendering its accreditation prior to initiation of any suspension or revocation proceeding.

(e) The accreditation agency shall, within 24 hours, report to the board if the outpatient setting has been issued a reprimand or if the outpatient setting's certification of accreditation has been suspended or revoked or if the outpatient setting has been placed on probation. If an outpatient setting has been issued a license by the California State Board of Pharmacy pursuant to Article 14 (commencing with Section 4190) of Chapter 9 of Division 2 of the Business and Professions Code, the accreditation agency shall also send this report to the California State Board of Pharmacy within 24 hours.

(f) The accreditation agency, upon receipt of a complaint from the board that an outpatient setting poses an immediate risk to public safety, shall inspect the outpatient setting and report its findings of inspection to the board within five business days. If an accreditation agency receives any other complaint from the board, it shall investigate the outpatient setting and report its findings of investigation to the board within 30 days.

(g) Reports on the results of any inspection shall be kept on file with the board and the accreditation agency along with the plan of correction and the comments of the outpatient setting. The inspection report may include a recommendation for reinspection. All final inspection reports, which include the lists of deficiencies, plans of correction or requirements for improvements and correction, and corrective action completed, shall be public records open to public inspection.

(h) If one accrediting agency denies accreditation, or revokes or suspends the accreditation of an outpatient setting, this action shall apply to all other accrediting agencies. An outpatient setting that is denied accreditation is permitted to reapply for accreditation with the same accrediting agency. The outpatient setting also may apply for accreditation from another accrediting agency, but only if it discloses the full accreditation report of the accrediting agency that denied accreditation. Any outpatient setting that has been denied accreditation shall disclose the accreditation report to any other accrediting agency to which it submits an application. The new accrediting agency shall ensure that all deficiencies have been corrected and conduct a new onsite inspection consistent with the standards specified in this chapter.

(i) If an outpatient setting's certification of accreditation has been suspended or revoked, or if the accreditation has been denied, the accreditation agency shall do all of the following:

(1) Notify the board of the action.

(2) Send a notification letter to the outpatient setting of the action. The notification letter shall state that the setting is no longer allowed to perform procedures that require outpatient setting accreditation.

(3) Require the outpatient setting to remove its accreditation certification and to post the notification letter in a conspicuous location, accessible to public view.

(j) The board may take any appropriate action it deems necessary pursuant to Section 1248.7 if an outpatient setting's certification of accreditation has been suspended or revoked, or if accreditation has been denied.

(Amended by Stats. 2015, Ch. 287, Sec. 4. (SB 396) Effective January 1, 2016.)

1248.4.

(a) It is the intent of the Legislature that an accreditation agency operating on or before January 1, 1995, or a successor thereof, or an accreditation agency thereafter operating as part of a joint program granted temporary certification as an accreditation agency by the division, whether operating as part of a joint program or independently, and meeting the standards set forth in this chapter, as determined by the division, not be required to go through the entire application process with the division. Therefore, the division may grant a temporary certificate of approval to such an accreditation agency. The temporary approval issued to an accreditation agency under this subdivision shall expire on January 1, 1998. In order to continue its status as an accreditation agency, an accreditation agency approved by the division under this subdivision shall apply for renewal of approval by the division on or before January 1, 1998, and shall establish that it is in compliance with the standards set forth in this chapter and any regulations adopted pursuant thereto.

(b) Each accreditation agency approved by the division shall, on and after January 1, 1995, promptly forward to the division a list of each outpatient setting to which it has granted a certificate of accreditation, as well as settings that have lost accreditation or were denied accreditation.

(c) The division shall approve an accreditation agency that applies for approval on a form prescribed by the division, accompanied by payment of the fee prescribed by this chapter and evidence that the accreditation agency meets the following criteria:

(1) Includes within its accreditation program, at a minimum, the standards for accreditation of outpatient settings approved by the division as well as standards for patient care and safety at the setting.

(2) Submits its current accreditation standards to the division every three years, or upon request for continuing approval by the division.

(3) Maintains internal quality management programs to ensure quality of the accreditation process.

(4) Has a process by which accreditation standards can be reviewed and revised no less than every three years.

(5) Maintains an available pool of allied health care practitioners to serve on accreditation review teams as appropriate.

(6) Has accreditation review teams that shall do all of the following:

(A) Consist of at least one physician and surgeon who practices in an outpatient setting; any other members shall be practicing actively in these settings.

(B) Participate in formal educational training programs provided by the accreditation agency in evaluation of the certification standards at least every three years.

(7) The accreditation agency shall demonstrate that professional members of its review team have experience in conducting review activities of freestanding outpatient settings.

(8) Standards for accreditation shall be developed with the input of the medical community and the ambulatory surgery industry.

(9) Accreditation reviewers shall be credentialed and screened by the accreditation agency.

(10) The accreditation agency shall not have an ownership interest in nor be involved in the operation of a freestanding outpatient setting, nor in the delivery of health care services to patients.

(d) Accreditation agencies approved by the division shall forward to the division copies of all certificates of accreditation and shall notify the division promptly whenever the agency denies or revokes a certificate of accreditation.

(e) A certification of an accreditation agency by the division shall expire at midnight on the last day of a three-year term if not renewed. The division shall establish by regulation the procedure for renewal. To renew an unexpired approval, the accreditation agency shall, on or before the date upon which the certification would otherwise expire, apply for renewal on a form, and pay the renewal fee, as prescribed by the division.

(Amended by Stats. 1997, Ch. 769, Sec. 1. Effective October 8, 1997.)
1248.5.
The board shall evaluate the performance of an approved accreditation agency no less than every three years, or in response to complaints against an agency, or complaints against one or more outpatient settings accreditation by an agency that indicates noncompliance by the agency with the standards approved by the board.

(Amended by Stats. 2011, Ch. 645, Sec. 7. (SB 100) Effective January 1, 2012.)
1248.55.
(a) If the accreditation agency is not meeting the criteria set by the division, the division may terminate approval of the agency.

(b) Before terminating approval of an accreditation agency, the division shall provide the accreditation agency with notice of any deficiencies and reasonable time to supply information demonstrating compliance with the requirements of this chapter, as well as the opportunity for a hearing on the matter in compliance with Chapter 5 (commencing with Section 11500) of Part 1 of Division 3 of Title 2 of the Government Code.

(c) (1) If approval of the accreditation agency is terminated by the division, outpatient settings accredited by that agency shall be notified by the division and, except as provided in paragraph (2), shall be authorized to continue to operate for a period of 12 months in order to seek accreditation through an approved accreditation agency, unless the time is extended by the division for good cause.

(2) The division may require that an outpatient setting, that has been accredited by an accreditation agency whose approval has been terminated by the division, cease operations immediately in the event that the division is in possession of information indicating that continued operation poses an imminent risk of harm to the health of an individual. In such cases, the division shall provide the outpatient setting with notice of its action, the reason underlying it, and a subsequent opportunity for a hearing on the matter. An outpatient setting that is ordered to cease operations under this paragraph may reapply for a certificate of accreditation after six months and shall notify the division promptly of its reapplication.

(Added by Stats. 1994, Ch. 1276, Sec. 2. Effective January 1, 1995.)
1248.6.

(a) The Division of Licensing shall establish by regulation a reasonable fee for an application for approval as an accreditation agency in an amount that is reasonably necessary to recover the cost of implementing and administering this chapter, and not to exceed five thousand dollars ($5,000). The division shall establish by regulation a reasonable fee for a temporary certificate of approval, as outlined in subdivision (a) of Section 1248.4, not to exceed two thousand dollars ($2,000). The division shall also establish a reasonable fee for renewal. The renewal fee shall be proportionate to the number of outpatient settings accredited by the approved accrediting body seeking renewal, and shall not exceed one hundred dollars ($100) per outpatient setting accreditation reviewed.

(b) All fees paid to and received by the division or the Medical Board of California under this chapter shall be paid into the State Treasury and shall be credited to a special fund that is hereby created as the Outpatient Setting Fund of the Medical Board of California. Funds in the Outpatient Setting Fund of the Medical Board of California shall be expended by the board for the purpose of implementing and administering this chapter upon appropriation by the Legislature. No surplus in the fund shall be deposited in or transferred to the General Fund or any other fund.

(Added by Stats. 1994, Ch. 1276, Sec. 2. Effective January 1, 1995.)
1248.65.
It shall constitute unprofessional conduct for a physician and surgeon to willfully and knowingly violate this chapter.

(Added by Stats. 1994, Ch. 1276, Sec. 2. Effective January 1, 1995.)
1248.7.

(a) The board shall investigate all complaints concerning a violation of this chapter. With respect to any complaints relating to a violation of Section 1248.1, or upon discovery that an outpatient setting is not in compliance with Section 1248.1, the board shall investigate and, where appropriate, the board, through or in conjunction with the local district attorney, shall bring an action to enjoin the outpatient setting's operation. The board or the local district attorney may bring an action to enjoin a violation or threatened violation of any other provision of this chapter in the superior court in and for the county in which the violation occurred or is about to occur. Any proceeding under this section shall conform to the requirements of Chapter 3 (commencing with Section 525) of Title 7 of Part 2 of the Code of Civil Procedure, except that the Division of Medical Quality shall not be required to allege facts necessary to show or tending to show lack of adequate remedy at law or irreparable damage or loss.

(b) With respect to any and all actions brought pursuant to this section alleging an actual or threatened violation of any requirement of this chapter, the court shall, if it finds the allegations to be true, issue an order enjoining the person or facility from continuing the violation. For purposes of Section 1248.1, if an outpatient setting is operating without a certificate of accreditation, this shall be prima facie evidence that a violation of Section 1248.1 has occurred and additional proof shall not be necessary to enjoin the outpatient setting's operation.

(Amended by Stats. 2011, Ch. 645, Sec. 8. (SB 100) Effective January 1, 2012.)
1248.75.
(a) Except as may otherwise be provided in this section, before the Division of Medical Quality may seek an injunction as provided under Section 1248.7, the Division of Medical Quality shall notify the outpatient setting of all deficiencies in its compliance with this chapter, and any rules and regulations adopted pursuant to this chapter, and the Division of Medical Quality and the outpatient setting shall reach an agreement upon a plan of correction that shall give the outpatient setting reasonable time to correct the deficiencies. The Division of Medical Quality shall also inform the outpatient setting that failure to reach an agreement or to correct deficiencies may lead to corrective action by the Division of Medical Quality, which may include imposition of fines under Section 1248.8. If at the end of the allotted time the division and the outpatient setting have failed to reach an agreement or the outpatient setting has failed to correct the deficiencies, as revealed by inspection, the Division of Medical Quality may take corrective action to include, as appropriate, seeking an injunction under Section 1248.7, revoking or requesting that the accreditation agency revoke accreditation, or communicating with any agency that has oversight authority over the outpatient setting, such as the Department of Health Services or other appropriate licensing authority, to request that the agency take corrective action against the outpatient setting.

(b) For purposes of this section, and at the sole discretion of the Division of Medical Quality, any notifications, inspections, and corrective action plans of the Division of Medical Quality relating to outpatient settings that have been accredited by an accreditation agency may be performed or coordinated by the accreditation agency rather than by the Division of Medical Quality.

(c) If the Division of Medical Quality determines that an outpatient setting poses an immediate and substantial hazard to the health or safety of the patient, that may not reasonably be corrected through a plan of correction, the Division of Medical Quality may immediately institute injunction proceedings pursuant to Section 1248.7.

(Added by Stats. 1994, Ch. 1276, Sec. 2. Effective January 1, 1995.)
1248.8.

(a) Any person or entity that willfully violates this chapter or any rule or regulation adopted under this chapter shall be guilty of a misdemeanor and subject to a fine not to exceed one thousand dollars ($1,000) per day of violation.

(b) In determining the punishment to be imposed under this section, the court shall consider all relevant facts, including, but not limited to, the following:

(1) Whether the violation exposed a patient or other individual to the risk of death or serious physical harm.

(2) Whether the violation had a direct or immediate relationship to health, safety, or security of a patient or other individual.

(3) Evidence, if any, of willfulness in the violation.

(4) The presence or absence of good faith efforts by the outpatient setting to prevent the violation.

(c) For purposes of this section, "willfully" or "willful" means that the person doing an act or omitting to do an act intends the act or omission, and knows the relevant circumstances connected with the act or omission.

(d) The district attorney of every county shall, upon application by the Division of Medical Quality or its authorized representative, institute and conduct the prosecution of any action or violation within the county of any provisions of this chapter.

(Added by Stats. 1994, Ch. 1276, Sec. 2. Effective January 1, 1995.)

1248.85.

This chapter shall not preclude an approved accreditation agency from adopting additional standards consistent with Section 1248.15, establishing procedures for the conduct of onsite inspections, selecting onsite inspectors to perform accreditation onsite inspections, or establishing and collecting reasonable fees for the conduct of accreditation onsite inspections.

(Amended by Stats. 2011, Ch. 645, Sec. 9. (SB 100) Effective January 1, 2012.)

CHAPTER 2. Health Facilities [1250 - 1339.59]

(Chapter 2 repealed and added by Stats. 1973, Ch. 1202.)

ARTICLE 1. General [1250 - 1264]

(Article 1 added by Stats. 1973, Ch. 1202.)

1250.

As used in this chapter, "health facility" means a facility, place, or building that is organized, maintained, and operated for the diagnosis, care, prevention, and treatment of human illness, physical or mental, including convalescence and rehabilitation and including care during and after pregnancy, or for any one or more of these purposes, for one or more persons, to which the persons are admitted for a 24-hour stay or longer, and includes the following types:

(a) "General acute care hospital" means a health facility having a duly constituted governing body with overall administrative and professional responsibility and an organized medical staff that provides 24-hour inpatient care, including the following basic services: medical, nursing, surgical, anesthesia, laboratory, radiology, pharmacy, and dietary services. A general acute care hospital may include more than one physical plant maintained and operated on separate premises as provided in Section 1250.8. A general acute care hospital that exclusively provides acute medical rehabilitation center services, including at least physical therapy, occupational therapy, and speech therapy, may provide for the required surgical and anesthesia services through a contract with another acute care hospital. In addition, a general acute care hospital that, on July 1, 1983, provided required surgical and anesthesia services through a contract or agreement with another acute care hospital may continue to provide these surgical and anesthesia services through a contract or agreement with an acute care hospital. The general acute care hospital operated by the State Department of Developmental Services at Agnews Developmental Center may, until June 30, 2007, provide surgery and anesthesia services through a contract or agreement with another acute care hospital. Notwithstanding the requirements of this subdivision, a general acute care hospital operated by the Department of Corrections and Rehabilitation or the Department of Veterans Affairs may provide surgery and anesthesia services during normal weekday working hours, and not provide these services during other hours of the weekday or on weekends or holidays, if the general acute care hospital otherwise meets the requirements of this section.

A "general acute care hospital" includes a "rural general acute care hospital." However, a "rural general acute care hospital" shall not be required by the department to provide surgery and anesthesia services. A "rural general acute care hospital" shall meet either of the following conditions:

(1) The hospital meets criteria for designation within peer group six or eight, as defined in the report entitled Hospital Peer Grouping for Efficiency Comparison, dated December 20, 1982.

(2) The hospital meets the criteria for designation within peer group five or seven, as defined in the report entitled Hospital Peer Grouping for Efficiency Comparison, dated December 20, 1982, and has no more than 76 acute care beds and is located in a census dwelling place of 15,000 or less population according to the 1980 federal census.

(b) "Acute psychiatric hospital" means a health facility having a duly constituted governing body with overall administrative and professional responsibility and an organized medical staff that provides 24-hour inpatient care for persons with mental health disorders or other patients referred to in Division 5 (commencing with Section 5000) or Division 6 (commencing with Section 6000) of the Welfare and Institutions Code, including the following basic services: medical, nursing, rehabilitative, pharmacy, and dietary services.

(c) (1) "Skilled nursing facility" means a health facility that provides skilled nursing care and supportive care to patients whose primary need is for availability of skilled nursing care on an extended basis.

(2) "Skilled nursing facility" includes a "small house skilled nursing facility (SHSNF)," as defined in Section 1323.5.

(d) "Intermediate care facility" means a health facility that provides inpatient care to ambulatory or nonambulatory patients who have recurring need for skilled nursing

supervision and need supportive care, but who do not require availability of continuous skilled nursing care.

(e) "Intermediate care facility/developmentally disabled habilitative" means a facility with a capacity of 4 to 15 beds that provides 24-hour personal care, habilitation, developmental, and supportive health services to 15 or fewer persons with developmental disabilities who have intermittent recurring needs for nursing services, but have been certified by a physician and surgeon as not requiring availability of continuous skilled nursing care.

(f) "Special hospital" means a health facility having a duly constituted governing body with overall administrative and professional responsibility and an organized medical or dental staff that provides inpatient or outpatient care in dentistry or maternity.

(g) "Intermediate care facility/developmentally disabled" means a facility that provides 24-hour personal care, habilitation, developmental, and supportive health services to persons with developmental disabilities whose primary need is for developmental services and who have a recurring but intermittent need for skilled nursing services.

(h) "Intermediate care facility/developmentally disabled-nursing" means a facility with a capacity of 4 to 15 beds that provides 24-hour personal care, developmental services, and nursing supervision for persons with developmental disabilities who have intermittent recurring needs for skilled nursing care but have been certified by a physician and surgeon as not requiring continuous skilled nursing care. The facility shall serve medically fragile persons with developmental disabilities or who demonstrate significant developmental delay that may lead to a developmental disability if not treated.

(i) (1) "Congregate living health facility" means a residential home with a capacity, except as provided in paragraph (4), of no more than 18 beds, that provides inpatient care, including the following basic services: medical supervision, 24-hour skilled nursing and supportive care, pharmacy, dietary, social, recreational, and at least one type of service specified in paragraph (2). The primary need of congregate living health facility residents shall be for availability of skilled nursing care on a recurring, intermittent, extended, or continuous basis. This care is generally less intense than that provided in general acute care hospitals but more intense than that provided in skilled nursing facilities.

(2) Congregate living health facilities shall provide one or more of the following services:

(A) Services for persons who are mentally alert, persons with physical disabilities, who may be ventilator dependent.

(B) Services for persons who have a diagnosis of terminal illness, a diagnosis of a life-threatening illness, or both. Terminal illness means the individual has a life expectancy of six months or less as stated in writing by his or her attending physician and surgeon. A "life-threatening illness" means the individual has an illness that can lead to a possibility of a termination of life within five years or less as stated in writing by his or her attending physician and surgeon.

(C) Services for persons who are catastrophically and severely disabled. A person who is catastrophically and severely disabled means a person whose origin of disability was acquired through trauma or nondegenerative neurologic illness, for whom it has been determined that active rehabilitation would be beneficial and to whom these services are being provided. Services offered by a congregate living health facility to a person who is catastrophically disabled shall include, but not be limited to, speech, physical, and occupational therapy.

(3) A congregate living health facility license shall specify which of the types of persons described in paragraph (2) to whom a facility is licensed to provide services.

(4) (A) A facility operated by a city and county for the purposes of delivering services under this section may have a capacity of 59 beds.

(B) A congregate living health facility not operated by a city and county servicing persons who are terminally ill, persons who have been diagnosed with a life-threatening illness, or both, that is located in a county with a population of 500,000 or more persons, or located in a county of the 16th class pursuant to Section 28020 of the Government Code, may have not more than 25 beds for the purpose of serving persons who are terminally ill.

(5) A congregate living health facility shall have a noninstitutional, homelike environment.

(j) (1) "Correctional treatment center" means a health facility operated by the Department of Corrections and Rehabilitation, the Department of Corrections and Rehabilitation, Division of Juvenile Facilities, or a county, city, or city and county law enforcement agency that, as determined by the department, provides inpatient health services to that portion of the inmate population who do not require a general acute care level of basic services. This definition shall not apply to those areas of a law enforcement facility that houses inmates or wards who may be receiving outpatient services and are housed separately for reasons of improved access to health care, security, and protection. The health services provided by a correctional treatment center shall include, but are not limited to, all of the following basic services: physician and surgeon, psychiatrist, psychologist, nursing, pharmacy, and dietary. A correctional treatment center may provide the following services: laboratory, radiology, perinatal, and any other services approved by the department.

(2) Outpatient surgical care with anesthesia may be provided, if the correctional treatment center meets the same requirements as a surgical clinic licensed pursuant to Section 1204, with the exception of the requirement that patients remain less than 24 hours.

(3) Correctional treatment centers shall maintain written service agreements with general acute care hospitals to provide for those inmate physical health needs that cannot be met by the correctional treatment center.

(4) Physician and surgeon services shall be readily available in a correctional treatment center on a 24-hour basis.

(5) It is not the intent of the Legislature to have a correctional treatment center supplant the general acute care hospitals at the California Medical Facility, the California Men's Colony, and the California Institution for Men. This subdivision shall not be construed to prohibit the Department of Corrections and Rehabilitation from obtaining a correctional treatment center license at these sites.

(k) "Nursing facility" means a health facility licensed pursuant to this chapter that is certified to participate as a provider of care either as a skilled nursing facility in the federal Medicare Program under Title XVIII of the federal Social Security Act (42 U.S.C. Sec. 1395 et seq.) or as a nursing facility in the federal Medicaid Program under Title XIX of the federal Social Security Act (42 U.S.C. Sec. 1396 et seq.), or as both.

(l) Regulations defining a correctional treatment center described in subdivision (j) that is operated by a county, city, or city and county, the Department of Corrections and Rehabilitation, or the Department of Corrections and Rehabilitation, Division of Juvenile Facilities, shall not become effective prior to, or, if effective, shall be inoperative until January 1, 1996, and until that time these correctional facilities are exempt from any licensing requirements.

(m) "Intermediate care facility/developmentally disabled-continuous nursing (ICF/DD-CN)" means a homelike facility with a capacity of four to eight, inclusive, beds that provides 24-hour personal care, developmental services, and nursing supervision for persons with developmental disabilities who have continuous needs for skilled nursing care and have been certified by a physician and surgeon as warranting continuous skilled nursing care. The facility shall serve medically fragile persons who have developmental disabilities or demonstrate significant developmental delay that may lead to a developmental disability if not treated. ICF/DD-CN facilities shall be subject to licensure under this chapter upon adoption of licensing regulations in accordance with Section 1275.3. A facility providing continuous skilled nursing services to persons with developmental disabilities pursuant to Section 14132.20 or 14495.10 of the Welfare and Institutions Code shall apply for licensure under this subdivision within 90 days after the regulations become effective, and may continue to operate pursuant to those sections until its licensure application is either approved or denied.

(n) "Hospice facility" means a health facility licensed pursuant to this chapter with a capacity of no more than 24 beds that provides hospice services. Hospice services include, but are not limited to, routine care, continuous care, inpatient respite care, and inpatient hospice care as defined in subdivision (d) of Section 1339.40, and is operated by a provider of hospice services that is licensed pursuant to Section 1751 and certified as a hospice pursuant to Part 418 of Title 42 of the Code of Federal Regulations.
(Amended by Stats. 2015, Ch. 483, Sec. 1. (AB 1211) Effective October 4, 2015.)
1250.02.
Article 9 (commencing with Section 70901) of Chapter 1 of Division 5 of Title 22 of the California Code of Regulations, as adopted to implement the requirements of Section 2 of Chapter 67 of the Statutes of 1988, shall apply to a rural general acute care hospital as defined in Section 1250. Any reference in those provisions to the Office of Statewide Health Planning and Development shall instead refer to the department. Any reference in those provisions to a small and rural hospital shall instead refer to a rural general acute care hospital. The department may adopt regulations to implement or administer this action.
(Added by Stats. 1993, Ch. 931, Sec. 3. Effective January 1, 1994.)
1250.03.
A rural general acute care hospital that does not provide surgical and anesthesia services shall maintain written transfer agreements with one or more general acute care hospitals that provide surgical and anesthesia services.
(Added by renumbering Section 1250.1 (as added by Stats. 1993, Ch. 931) by Stats. 1994, Ch. 146, Sec. 94. Effective January 1, 1995.)
1250.05.
(a) All general acute care hospitals licensed under this chapter shall maintain a medical records system, based upon current standards for medical record retrieval and storage, that organizes all medical records for each patient under a unique identifier.
(b) This section shall not require electronic records or require that all portions of patients' records be stored in a single location.
(c) In addition, all general acute care hospitals shall have the ability to identify the location of all portions of a patient's medical record that are maintained under the general acute care hospital's license.
(d) All general acute care hospitals, including those holding a consolidated general acute care license pursuant to Section 1250.8, shall develop and implement policies and procedures to ensure that relevant portions of patients' medical records can be made available within a reasonable period of time to respond to the request of a treating physician, other authorized medical professionals, authorized representatives of the department, or any other person authorized by law to make such a request, taking into consideration the physical location of the records and hours of operation of the facility where those records are located, as well as the best interests of the patients.
(Added by Stats. 1998, Ch. 310, Sec. 12. Effective August 19, 1998.)
1250.06.
A licensed general acute care hospital, as defined pursuant to subdivision (a) of Section 1250, or an acute psychiatric hospital, as defined pursuant to subdivision (b) of Section 1250, shall adopt policies and procedures regarding the responsibility for ensuring proper methods of repackaging and labeling of bulk cleaning agents, solvents, chemicals, and nondrug hazardous substances used throughout the hospital. The hospital is not required to consult a pharmacist regarding the repackaging and labeling of these substances, except for areas where sterile compounding is performed.
(Added by Stats. 2014, Ch. 319, Sec. 4. (SB 1039) Effective January 1, 2015.)

1250.1.
(a) The department shall adopt regulations that define all of the following bed classifications for health facilities:
(1) General acute care.
(2) Skilled nursing.
(3) Intermediate care-developmental disabilities.
(4) Intermediate care—other.
(5) Acute psychiatric.
(6) Specialized care, with respect to special hospitals only.
(7) Chemical dependency recovery.
(8) Intermediate care facility/developmentally disabled habilitative.
(9) Intermediate care facility/developmentally disabled nursing.
(10) Congregate living health facility.
(11) Pediatric day health and respite care facility, as defined in Section 1760.2.
(12) Correctional treatment center. For correctional treatment centers that provide psychiatric and psychological services provided by county mental health agencies in local detention facilities, the State Department of State Hospitals shall adopt regulations specifying acute and nonacute levels of 24-hour care. Licensed inpatient beds in a correctional treatment center shall be used only for the purpose of providing health services.
(13) Hospice facility.
(b) Except as provided in Section 1253.1, beds classified as intermediate care beds, on September 27, 1978, shall be reclassified by the department as intermediate care—other. This reclassification shall not constitute a "project" within the meaning of Section 127170 and shall not be subject to any requirement for a certificate of need under Chapter 1 (commencing with Section 127125) of Part 2 of Division 107, and regulations of the department governing intermediate care prior to the effective date shall continue to be applicable to the intermediate care—other classification unless and until amended or repealed by the department.
(Amended by Stats. 2012, Ch. 673, Sec. 3. (SB 135) Effective January 1, 2013.)
1250.2.
(a) (1) As defined in Section 1250, "health facility" includes a "psychiatric health facility," defined to mean a health facility, licensed by the State Department of Health Care Services, that provides 24-hour inpatient care for people with mental health disorders or other persons described in Division 5 (commencing with Section 5000) or Division 6 (commencing with Section 6000) of the Welfare and Institutions Code. This care shall include, but not be limited to, the following basic services: psychiatry, clinical psychology, psychiatric nursing, social work, rehabilitation, drug administration, and appropriate food services for those persons whose physical health needs can be met in an affiliated hospital or in outpatient settings.
(2) It is the intent of the Legislature that the psychiatric health facility shall provide a distinct type of service to psychiatric patients in a 24-hour acute inpatient setting. The State Department of Health Care Services shall require regular utilization reviews of admission and discharge criteria and lengths of stay in order to ensure that these patients are moved to less restrictive levels of care as soon as appropriate.
(b) (1) The State Department of Health Care Services may issue a special permit to a psychiatric health facility for it to provide structured outpatient services (commonly referred to as SOPS) consisting of morning, afternoon, or full daytime organized programs, not exceeding 10 hours, for acute daytime care for patients admitted to the facility. This subdivision shall not be construed as requiring a psychiatric health facility to apply for a special permit to provide these alternative levels of care.
(2) The Legislature recognizes that, with access to structured outpatient services, as an alternative to 24-hour inpatient care, certain patients would be provided with effective intervention and less restrictive levels of care. The Legislature further recognizes that, for certain patients, the less restrictive levels of care eliminate the need for inpatient care, enable earlier discharge from inpatient care by providing a continuum of care with effective aftercare services, or reduce or prevent the need for a subsequent readmission to inpatient care.
(c) Any reference in any statute to Section 1250 of the Health and Safety Code shall be deemed and construed to also be a reference to this section.
(d) Notwithstanding any other law, and to the extent consistent with federal law, a psychiatric health facility shall be eligible to participate in the medicare program under Title XVIII of the federal Social Security Act (42 U.S.C. Sec. 1395 et seq.), and the medicaid program under Title XIX of the federal Social Security Act (42 U.S.C. Sec. 1396 et seq.), if all of the following conditions are met:
(1) The facility is a licensed facility.
(2) The facility is in compliance with all related statutes and regulations enforced by the State Department of Health Care Services, including regulations contained in Chapter 9 (commencing with Section 77001) of Division 5 of Title 22 of the California Code of Regulations.
(3) The facility meets the definitions and requirements contained in subdivisions (e) and (f) of Section 1861 of the federal Social Security Act (42 U.S.C. Sec. 1395x(e) and (f)), including the approval process specified in Section 1861(e)(7)(B) of the federal Social Security Act (42 U.S.C. Sec. 1395x(e)(7)(B)), which requires that the state agency responsible for licensing hospitals has ensured that the facility meets licensing requirements.
(4) The facility meets the conditions of participation for hospitals pursuant to Part 482 of Title 42 of the Code of Federal Regulations.
(Amended by Stats. 2014, Ch. 144, Sec. 26. (AB 1847) Effective January 1, 2015.)
1250.3.

(a) As defined in Section 1250, "health facility" includes the following type: "Chemical dependency recovery hospital" means a health facility that provides 24-hour inpatient care for persons who have a dependency on alcohol or other drugs, or both alcohol and other drugs. This care shall include, but not be limited to, the following basic services: patient counseling, group therapy, physical conditioning, family therapy, outpatient services, and dietetic services. Each facility shall have a medical director who is a physician and surgeon licensed to practice in this state.

(b) The Legislature finds and declares that problems related to the inappropriate use of alcohol or other drugs, or both alcohol and other drugs, are widespread and adversely affect the general welfare of the people of the State of California. It is the intent of the Legislature that the chemical dependency recovery hospital will provide an innovative inpatient treatment program for persons who have a dependency on alcohol or drugs, or both alcohol and other drugs. The Legislature further finds and declares that significant cost reductions can be achieved by chemical dependency recovery hospitals when both of the following conditions exist:

(1) Architectural requirements established by the department encourage a flexible and open construction approach that significantly reduces capital construction costs.

(2) Programs are designed to provide comprehensive inpatient treatment while permitting substantial flexibility in the use of qualified personnel to meet the specific needs of the patients of the facility.

(c) Beds classified as chemical dependency recovery beds in a general acute care hospital or acute psychiatric hospital or a freestanding facility that is owned or leased by the general acute care hospital or the acute psychiatric hospital, that is located on the same premises or adjacent premises thereof, not to exceed a 15-mile radius within the same health facility planning area, as defined January 1, 1981, by the Office of Statewide Health Planning and Development, and that is under the administrative control of the general acute care hospital or the acute psychiatric hospital, shall be used exclusively for alcohol or other drug dependency treatment, or both alcohol and other drug dependency treatment. No general acute care hospital or acute psychiatric hospital or a freestanding facility, as defined in this subdivision, shall, without fulfilling the requirements of the licensing laws and health planning laws, convert beds classified as chemical dependency recovery beds to any other bed classification or provide new chemical dependency recovery beds by increasing bed capacity.

(d) (1) Chemical dependency recovery services may be provided as a supplemental service in existing general acute care beds and acute psychiatric beds in a general acute care hospital or in existing acute psychiatric beds in an acute psychiatric hospital or in existing beds in a freestanding facility, as defined in subdivision (c). When providing chemical dependency recovery services as a supplemental service, the general acute care hospital, acute psychiatric hospital, or freestanding facility, as defined in subdivision (c), shall provide the supplemental services in a distinct part of the hospital or freestanding facility, if the distinct part satisfies the criteria established by law and regulation for approval as a chemical dependency recovery supplemental service.

(2) For purposes of this subdivision, "distinct part" means an identifiable unit of a hospital or a freestanding facility, as defined in subdivision (c), accommodating beds, and related services, including, but not limited to, contiguous rooms, a wing, a floor, or a building that is approved by the department for a specific purpose. Notwithstanding any other provisions of this subdivision, an acute psychiatric hospital that provides all of the basic services specified in subdivision (b) of Section 1250 may, subject to the approval of the department, have all of its licensed acute psychiatric beds approved for chemical dependency recovery services. Chemical dependency recovery services provided pursuant to this subdivision shall not require a separate license or reclassification of beds under the health planning laws.

(e) If the chemical dependency recovery hospital is not a supplemental service of a general acute care hospital, it shall have agreements with one or more general acute care hospitals providing for 24-hour emergency service and pharmacy, laboratory, and any other services that the department may require.

(f) Any reference in any statute to Section 1250 shall be deemed and construed to also be a reference to this section.
(Amended by Stats. 2006, Ch. 538, Sec. 349. Effective January 1, 2007.)
1250.4.

(a) As used in this section:

(1) "Department" means the Department of Corrections or the Department of the Youth Authority.

(2) "Communicable, contagious, or infectious disease" means any disease that is capable of being transmitted from person to person with or without contact and as established by the State Department of Health Services pursuant to Section 120130, and Section 2500 et seq. of Title 17 of the California Code of Regulations.

(3) "Inmate or ward" means any person incarcerated within the jurisdiction of the Department of Corrections or the Department of the Youth Authority, with the exception of a person on parole.

(4) "Institution" means any state prison, camp, center, office, or other facility under the jurisdiction of the Department of Corrections or the Department of the Youth Authority.

(5) "Medical director," "chief of medical services," or "chief medical officer" means the medical officer, acting medical officer, medical director, or the physician designated by the department to act in that capacity, who is responsible for directing the medical treatment programs and medical services for all health services and services supporting the health services provided in the institution.

(b) Each health care facility in the Department of Corrections and in the Department of the Youth Authority shall have a medical director in charge of the health care services of that facility who shall be a physician and surgeon licensed to practice in California and who shall be appointed by the directors of the departments. The medical director shall direct the medical treatment programs for all health services and services supporting the health services provided in the facility.

(c) The medical director, chief of medical services, chief medical officer, or the physician designated by the department to act in that capacity, shall use every available means to ascertain the existence of, and to immediately investigate, all reported or suspected cases of any communicable, contagious, or infectious disease and to ascertain the source or sources of the infections and prevent the spread of the disease. In carrying out these investigations, the medical director, chief of medical services, chief medical officer, or the physician designated by the department to act in that capacity, is hereby invested with full powers of inspection, examination, and quarantine or isolation of all inmates or wards known to be, or reasonably suspected to be, infected with a communicable, contagious, or infectious disease.

(d) The medical director, chief of medical services, chief medical officer, or the physician designated by the department to act in that capacity, shall order an inmate or ward to receive an examination or test, or may order an inmate or ward to receive treatment if the medical director, chief of medical services, chief medical officer, or the physician designated by the department to act in that capacity, has reasonable suspicion that the inmate or ward has, has had, or has been exposed to a communicable, contagious, or infectious disease and the medical director, chief of medical services, chief medical officer, or the physician designated by the department to act in that capacity, has reasonable grounds to believe that it is necessary for the preservation and protection of staff and inmates or wards.

(e) Notwithstanding Section 2600 or 2601 of the Penal Code, or any other provision of law, any inmate or ward who refuses to submit to an examination, test, or treatment for any communicable, contagious, or infectious disease or who refuses treatment for any communicable, contagious, or infectious disease, or who, after notice, violates, or refuses or neglects to conform to any rule, order, guideline, or regulation prescribed by the department with regard to communicable disease control shall be tested involuntarily and may be treated involuntarily. This inmate or ward shall be subject to disciplinary action as described in Title 15 of the California Code of Regulations.

(f) This section shall not apply to HIV or AIDS. Testing, treatment, counseling, prevention, education, or other procedures dealing with HIV and AIDS shall be conducted as prescribed in Title 8 (commencing with Section 7500) of Part 3 of the Penal Code.

(g) This section shall not apply to tuberculosis. Tuberculosis shall be addressed as prescribed in Title 8.7 (commencing with Section 7570) of the Penal Code.
(Amended by Stats. 1996, Ch. 1023, Sec. 152. Effective September 29, 1996.)
1250.5.

"Council" means the Advisory Health Council.
(Added by Stats. 1973, Ch. 1202.)
1250.6.

Any requirement placed upon, or reference to, a corporation in this chapter, shall also apply to a limited liability company.
(Added by Stats. 2001, Ch. 685, Sec. 2. Effective January 1, 2002.)
1250.7.

(a) (1) With respect to each hospital designated by the department as a critical access hospital, and certified as such by the Secretary of the United States Department of Health and Human Services under the federal Medicare Rural Hospital Flexibility Program, the department may develop criteria to waive any requirements of Division 5 (commencing with Section 70001) of Title 22 of the California Code of Regulations that are in conflict with the federal requirements for designation in the federal program, if the department finds that it is in the public interest to do so, and the department determines that the waiver would not negatively affect the quality of patient care.

(2) The criteria established pursuant to this subdivision shall not be considered regulations within the meaning of Section 11342 of the Government Code, and shall not be subject to adoption as regulations pursuant to Chapter 3.5 (commencing with Section 11340) of Part 1 of Division 3 of Title 2 of the Government Code.

(b) Nothing in this section shall be construed to mean that a critical access hospital is not a general acute care hospital. Every hospital designated by the department as a critical access hospital and certified as such by the United States Department of Health and Human Services shall be deemed to be a general acute care hospital, as defined in subdivision (a) of Section 1250, even if the department waives regulatory requirements otherwise applicable to general acute care hospitals pursuant to this section.
(Added by Stats. 2002, Ch. 752, Sec. 2. Effective January 1, 2003.)
1250.8.

(a) Notwithstanding subdivision (a) of Section 127170, the department, upon application of a general acute care hospital that meets all the criteria of subdivision (b), and other applicable requirements of licensure, shall issue a single consolidated license to a general acute care hospital that includes more than one physical plant maintained and operated on separate premises or that has multiple licenses for a single health facility on the same premises. A single consolidated license shall not be issued where the separate freestanding physical plant is a skilled nursing facility or an intermediate care facility, whether or not the location of the skilled nursing facility or intermediate care facility is contiguous to the general acute care hospital unless the hospital is exempt from the requirements of subdivision (b) of Section 1254, or the facility is part of the physical structure licensed to provide acute care.

(b) The issuance of a single consolidated license shall be based on the following criteria:
(1) There is a single governing body for all the facilities maintained and operated by the licensee.

(2) There is a single administration for all the facilities maintained and operated by the licensee.

(3) There is a single medical staff for all the facilities maintained and operated by the licensee, with a single set of bylaws, rules, and regulations, which prescribe a single committee structure.

(4) Except as provided otherwise in this paragraph, the physical plants maintained and operated by the licensee which are to be covered by the single consolidated license are located not more than 15 miles apart. If an applicant provides evidence satisfactory to the department that it can comply with all requirements of licensure and provide quality care and adequate administrative and professional supervision, the director may issue a single consolidated license to a general acute care hospital that operates two or more physical plants located more than 15 miles apart under any of the following circumstances:

(A) One or more of the physical plants is located in a rural area, as defined by regulations of the director.

(B) One or more of the physical plants provides only outpatient services, as defined by the department.

(C) If Section 14105.986 of the Welfare and Institutions Code is implemented and the applicant meets all of the following criteria:

(i) The applicant is a nonprofit corporation.

(ii) The applicant is a children's hospital listed in Section 10727 of the Welfare and Institutions Code.

(iii) The applicant is affiliated with a major university medical school and located adjacent thereto.

(iv) The applicant operates a regional tertiary care facility.

(v) One of the physical plants is located in a county that has a consolidated and county government structure.

(vi) One of the physical plants is located in a county having a population between 1,000,000 and 2,000,000.

(vii) The applicant is located in a city with a population between 50,000 and 100,000.

(c) In issuing the single consolidated license, the state department shall specify the location of each supplemental service and the location of the number and category of beds provided by the licensee. The single consolidated license shall be renewed annually.

(d) To the extent required by Chapter 1 (commencing with Section127125) of Part 2 of Division 107, a general acute care hospital that has been issued a single consolidated license:

(1) Shall not transfer from one facility to another a special service described in Section 1255 without first obtaining a certificate of need.

(2) Shall not transfer, in whole or in part, from one facility to another, a supplemental service, as defined in regulations of the director pursuant to this chapter, without first obtaining a certificate of need, unless the licensee, 30 days prior to the relocation, notifies the Office of Statewide Health Planning and Development, the applicable health systems agency, and the state department of the licensee's intent to relocate the supplemental service, and includes with this notice a cost estimate, certified by a person qualified by experience or training to render the estimates, which estimates that the cost of the transfer will not exceed the capital expenditure threshold established by the Office of Statewide Health Planning and Development pursuant to Section 127170.

(3) Shall not transfer beds from one facility to another facility, without first obtaining a certificate of need unless, 30 days prior to the relocation, the licensee notifies the Office of Statewide Health Planning and Development, the applicable health systems agency, and the state department of the licensee's intent to relocate health facility beds, and includes with this notice both of the following:

(A) A cost estimate, certified by a person qualified by experience or training to render the estimates, which estimates that the cost of the relocation will not exceed the capital expenditure threshold established by the Office of Statewide Health Planning and Development pursuant to Section 127170.

(B) The identification of the number, classification, and location of the health facility beds in the transferor facility and the proposed number, classification, and location of the health facility beds in the transferee facility.

Except as otherwise permitted in Chapter 1 (commencing with Section 127125) of Part 2 of Division 107, or as authorized in an approved certificate of need pursuant to that chapter, health facility beds transferred pursuant to this section shall be used in the transferee facility in the same bed classification as defined in Section 1250.1, as the beds were classified in the transferor facility.

Health facility beds transferred pursuant to this section shall not be transferred back to the transferor facility for two years from the date of the transfer, regardless of cost, without first obtaining a certificate of need pursuant to Chapter 1 (commencing with Section 127125) of Part 2 of Division 107.

(e) Transfers pursuant to subdivision (d) shall satisfy all applicable requirements of licensure and shall be subject to the written approval, if required, of the state department. The state department may adopt regulations that are necessary to implement this section. These regulations may include a requirement that each facility of a health facility subject to a single consolidated license have an onsite full-time or part-time administrator.

(f) As used in this section, "facility" means a physical plant operated or maintained by a health facility subject to a single, consolidated license issued pursuant to this section.

(g) For purposes of selective provider contracts negotiated under the Medi-Cal program, the treatment of a health facility with a single consolidated license issued pursuant to this section shall be subject to negotiation between the health facility and the California Medical Assistance Commission. A general acute care hospital that is issued a single consolidated license pursuant to this section may, at its option, be enrolled in the Medi-

Cal program as a single business address or as separate business addresses for one or more of the facilities subject to the single consolidated license. Irrespective of whether the general acute care hospital is enrolled at one or more business addresses, the department may require the hospital to file separate cost reports for each facility pursuant to Section 14170 of the Welfare and Institutions Code.

(h) For purposes of the Annual Report of Hospitals required by regulations adopted by the state department pursuant to this part, the state department and the Office of Statewide Health Planning and Development may require reporting of bed and service utilization data separately by each facility of a general acute care hospital issued a single consolidated license pursuant to this section.

(i) The amendments made to this section during the 1985–86 Regular Session of the Legislature pertaining to the issuance of a single consolidated license to a general acute care hospital in the case where the separate physical plant is a skilled nursing facility or intermediate care facility shall not apply to the following facilities:

(1) A facility that obtained a certificate of need after August 1, 1984, and prior to February 14, 1985, as described in this subdivision. The certificate of need shall be for the construction of a skilled nursing facility or intermediate care facility that is the same facility for which the hospital applies for a single consolidated license, pursuant to subdivision (a).

(2) A facility for which a single consolidated license has been issued pursuant to subdivision (a), as described in this subdivision, prior to the effective date of the amendments made to this section during the 1985–86 Regular Session of the Legislature.

A facility that has been issued a single consolidated license pursuant to subdivision (a), as described in this subdivision, shall be granted renewal licenses based upon the same criteria used for the initial consolidated license.

(j) If the state department issues a single consolidated license pursuant to this section, the state department may take any action authorized by this chapter, including, but not limited to, any action specified in Article 5 (commencing with Section 1294), with respect to a facility, or a service provided in a facility, that is included in the consolidated license.

(k) The eligibility for participation in the Medi-Cal program (Chapter 7 (commencing with Section 14000) of Part 3 of Division 9 of the Welfare and Institutions Code) of a facility that is included in a consolidated license issued pursuant to this section, provides outpatient services, and is located more than 15 miles from the health facility issued the consolidated license shall be subject to a determination of eligibility by the state department. This subdivision shall not apply to a facility that is located in a rural area and is included in a consolidated license issued pursuant to subparagraphs (A), (B), and (C) of paragraph (4) of subdivision (b). Regardless of whether a facility has received or not received a determination of eligibility pursuant to this subdivision, this subdivision shall not affect the ability of a licensed professional, providing services covered by the Medi-Cal program to a person eligible for Medi-Cal in a facility subject to a determination of eligibility pursuant to this subdivision, to bill the Medi-Cal program for those services provided in accordance with applicable regulations.

(l) Notwithstanding any other provision of law, the director may issue a single consolidated license for a general acute care hospital to Children's Hospital Oakland and San Ramon Regional Medical Center.

(m) Notwithstanding any other provision of law, the director may issue a single consolidated license for a general acute care hospital to Children's Hospital Oakland and the John Muir Medical Center, Concord Campus.

(n) (1) To the extent permitted by federal law, payments made to Children's Hospital Oakland pursuant to Section 14166.11 of the Welfare and Institutions Code shall be adjusted as follows:

(A) The number of Medi-Cal payment days and net revenues calculated for the John Muir Medical Center, Concord Campus under the consolidated license shall not be used for eligibility purposes for the private hospital disproportionate share hospital replacement funds for Children's Hospital Oakland.

(B) The number of Medi-Cal payment days calculated for hospital beds located at John Muir Medical Center, Concord Campus that are included in the consolidated license beginning in the 2007–08 fiscal year shall only be used for purposes of calculating disproportionate share hospital payments authorized under Section 14166.11 of the Welfare and Institutions Code at Children's Hospital Oakland to the extent that the inclusion of those days does not exceed the total Medi-Cal payment days used to calculate Children's Hospital Oakland payments for the 2006–07 fiscal year disproportionate share replacement.

(2) This subdivision shall become inoperative in the event that the two facilities covered under the consolidated license described in subdivision (a) are located within a 15-mile radius of each other.

(Amended by Stats. 2008, Ch. 179, Sec. 136. Effective January 1, 2009.)

1250.11.

The State Department of Public Health shall develop written guidelines and regulations as necessary to minimize the risk of transmission of blood-borne infectious diseases from health care worker to patient, from patient to patient, and from patient to health care worker. In so doing, the department shall consider the recommendations made by the federal Centers for Disease Control and Prevention for preventing transmission of HIV and Hepatitis B. The department shall also take into account existing regulations of the department as well as standards, guidelines, and regulations pursuant to the California Occupational Safety and Health Act of 1973 (Part 1 (commencing with Section 6300) of Division 5 of the Labor Code) regarding infection control to prevent infection or disease as a result of the transmission of blood-borne pathogens. In so doing, the department shall consult with the Medical Board of California, the Dental Board of California, and the

Board of Registered Nursing as well as associations representing health care professions, associations of licensed health facilities, organizations that advocate on behalf of those infected with HIV, and organizations representing consumers of health care. The department shall complete its review of the need for guidelines and regulations by January 1, 1993.

(Amended by Stats. 2017, Ch. 561, Sec. 100. (AB 1516) Effective January 1, 2018.)

1251.

"License" means a basic permit to operate a health facility with an authorized number and classification of beds. A license shall not be transferable.

(Amended by Stats. 1976, Ch. 854.)

1251.3.

A health facility licensed as a general acute care hospital, providing alcohol recovery services, may convert its licensure category to an acute psychiatric hospital and it may reclassify all of its general acute care beds to acute psychiatric without first obtaining a certificate of need pursuant to Section 127170 if all of the following conditions are met:

(a) The health facility notifies, in writing, the State Department and the Office of Statewide Health Planning and Development on or before September 3, 1982.

(b) The project would reclassify all of the facility's general acute care beds to acute psychiatric.

(c) The total licensed capacity of the facility to be converted does not exceed 31 beds.

(Amended by Stats. 1996, Ch. 1023, Sec. 155. Effective September 29, 1996.)

1251.4.

(a) Notwithstanding any other law, upon application of the Department of Corrections and Rehabilitation, the department shall change the license category of a general acute care hospital licensed to the Department of Corrections and Rehabilitation to a correctional treatment center license. No licensing inspection is required for this change of license category.

(b) Notwithstanding any other law, upon application of the Department of Corrections and Rehabilitation, the department shall change the license category of a general acute care hospital or any other licensed health facility located on the grounds of a prison to a correctional treatment center license regardless of the location of the buildings included in those licenses. No licensing inspection is required for this change of license category.

(Added by Stats. 2014, Ch. 26, Sec. 10. (AB 1468) Effective June 20, 2014.)

1251.5.

A "special permit" is a permit issued in addition to a license, authorizing a health facility to offer one or more of the special services specified in Section 1255 when the state department has determined that the health facility has met the standards for quality of care established by state department pursuant to Article 3 (commencing with Section 1275).

(Added by Stats. 1973, Ch. 1202.)

1252.

(a) "Special service" means a functional division, department, or unit of a health facility that is organized, staffed, and equipped to provide a specific type or types of patient care and that has been identified by regulations of the state department and for which the state department has established special standards for quality of care. "Special service" does not include a functional division, department, or unit of a nursing facility, as defined in subdivision (k) of Section 1250, that is organized, staffed, and equipped to provide inpatient physical therapy services, occupational therapy services, or speech pathology and audiology services to residents of the facility if these services are provided solely to meet the federal Centers for Medicare and Medicaid Services certification requirements. "Special service" includes physical therapy services, occupational therapy services, or speech pathology and audiology services provided by a nursing facility, as defined in subdivision (k) of Section 1250, to outpatients.

(b) This section does not limit the department's ability to evaluate compliance with the therapy requirements for nursing facilities and skilled nursing facilities established in Title 22 of the California Code of Regulations during investigations or inspections, including, but not limited to, inspections conducted pursuant to Section 1422, or to limit the department's ability to enforce the therapy requirements.

(Amended by Stats. 2014, Ch. 288, Sec. 1. (AB 1974) Effective January 1, 2015.)

1253.

(a) No person, firm, partnership, association, corporation, or political subdivision of the state, or other governmental agency within the state shall operate, establish, manage, conduct, or maintain a health facility in this state, without first obtaining a license therefor as provided in this chapter, nor provide, after July 1, 1974, special services without approval of the state department. However, any health facility offering any special service on the effective date of this section shall be approved by the state department to continue those services until the state department evaluates the quality of those services and takes permitted action.

(b) This section shall not apply to a receiver appointed by the court to temporarily operate a long-term health care facility pursuant to Article 8 (commencing with Section 1325).

(Amended by Stats. 2000, Ch. 451, Sec. 3. Effective January 1, 2001.)

1253.1.

(a) Any skilled nursing facility or intermediate care facility that on the effective date of this section is providing care for the developmentally disabled may utilize beds designated for that purpose to provide intermediate care for the developmentally disabled without obtaining a certificate of need, a change in licensure category, or a change in bed classification pursuant to subdivision (c) of Section 1250.1, provided the facility meets and continues to meet the following criteria:

(1) The facility was surveyed on or before July 18, 1977, by the State Department of Health for certification under the federal ICF/MR program pursuant to Section 449.13 of Title 42 of the Code of Federal Regulations, and the beds designated for intermediate care for the developmentally disabled were certified by the state department, either before or after that date, to meet the standards set forth in Section 449.13 of Title 42 of the Code of Federal Regulations.

(2) Not less than 95 percent of the beds so certified for intermediate care for the developmentally disabled are utilized exclusively for provision of care to residents with a developmental disability, as defined in subdivision (a) of Section 4512 of the Welfare and Institutions Code. Nothing in this paragraph shall require continuous bed occupancy, but a bed certified for intermediate care for the developmentally disabled shall be deemed to be converted to another use if occupied by a resident who is not developmentally disabled.

(3) On and after the effective date of regulations implementing this section, no change of ownership has occurred with respect to the facility requiring issuance of a new license, except a change occurring because of a decrease in the number of partners of a licensed partnership or a reorganization of the governing structure of a licensee in which there is no change in the relative ownership interests.

(b) Any facility receiving an exemption under subdivision (a) shall, with respect to beds designated for intermediate care for the developmentally disabled, be subject to regulations of the state department applicable to that level of care, rather than the level of care for which the beds are licensed. The state department shall indicate on the license of any facility receiving an exemption pursuant to subdivision (a) that the licensee has been determined by the state department to meet the criteria of subdivision (a).

(c) The licensee of any facility receiving an exemption under this section shall notify the state department not less than 30 days prior to taking action that will cause the facility to cease meeting the criteria specified in paragraph (2) or (3) of subdivision (a).

(d) Upon a change of ownership of the facility or change in ownership interests not meeting the criterion for continued exemption specified in paragraph (3) of subdivision (a), the applicant for relicensure shall elect as follows:

(1) To reclassify all skilled nursing beds that have been exempted under this section to the intermediate care-developmental disabilities classification, or to continue the skilled nursing classification with respect to skilled nursing beds that have received the exemption.

(2) To reclassify intermediate care beds that have been exempted under this section to the intermediate care-developmental disabilities classification, or to reclassify intermediate care beds that have received the exemption to the intermediate care-other classification.

Reclassification of beds pursuant to this subdivision shall not constitute a "project" within the meaning of Section 127170 and shall not be subject to any requirement for a certificate of need under Chapter 1 (commencing with Section 127125) of Part 2 of Division 107.

(Amended by Stats. 1996, Ch. 1023, Sec. 155.5. Effective September 29, 1996.)

1253.5.

(a) The State Department of Public Health, upon issuance and renewal of a license for a general acute care hospital as defined in subdivision (a) of Section 1250, an acute psychiatric hospital as defined in subdivision (b) of Section 1250, or a special hospital as defined in subdivision (f) of Section 1250, shall separately identify on the license each supplemental service, including the address of where each outpatient service is provided and the type of services provided at each outpatient location.

(b) On or before July 1, 2010, the department shall post and make available on its Web site a listing of all outpatient services of licensed hospitals identified on the hospital's license as a supplemental service pursuant to subdivision (a). The listing shall include the name and physical address of where the outpatient service is provided. The department's Web site shall include a disclaimer that the information contained in the listing is limited to the outpatient service information reported to the department by licensed hospitals.

(c) The department shall work with stakeholders to review, streamline, and revise the initial and renewal license application form prescribed and furnished by the department to any person, firm, association, partnership, or corporation desiring a license, a change in licensed beds or services, or renewing a license for a hospital, acute psychiatric hospital, or special hospital.

(Added by Stats. 2008, Ch. 396, Sec. 1. Effective January 1, 2009.)

1253.6.

(a) This section shall govern applications by general acute care hospitals for supplemental services approval for outpatient clinic services.

(b) Upon receipt of an initial application by a licensed general acute care hospital to add a new or modify an existing outpatient service as a supplemental service, the department shall, within 30 days of receipt of the initial application, review the entire application, determine whether the application is missing information or has insufficient information, and, on the basis of this determination, provide the hospital with guidance on how to provide the missing information.

(c) Upon determination by the department that an application for an outpatient clinic service as a supplemental service is complete pursuant to subdivision (b), the department shall investigate the facts set forth in the application and, if the department finds that the statements contained in the application are true, that the establishment of the operation of the supplemental service are in conformity with the intent and purpose of this chapter, and that the applicant is in compliance with this chapter and the rules and regulations of the department, the department shall approve the additional or modified outpatient clinic service, add it to the hospital license, and issue a new license. However, if the department determines in the course of the investigation that additional information is needed to determine whether the statements contained in the application are true or that the establishment or the continued operation of the supplemental service are in conformity with the intent and purpose of this chapter, or that the applicant is in compliance with this chapter and the rules and regulations of the department, the applicant shall provide the additional information to the department upon request. If the department finds that the statements contained in the application are not true, or that the establishment of the outpatient service as a supplemental service is not in conformity with the intent and purpose of this chapter, or if the applicant fails to provide any additional information to the department within 30 days of the request, the department shall deny the outpatient clinic services application. The department shall either grant or deny the application for the outpatient clinic service as a supplemental service within 100 days of the filing of a completed application.

(d) If a licensed general acute care hospital has previously been approved for an outpatient clinic service within 30 days after receipt of a completed application for an additional outpatient clinic service, the department shall approve the additional or modified outpatient clinic service, add it to the hospital license, and issue a new license, unless the applicant does not meet the requirements of this section. Notwithstanding any other law, the department shall not be required to conduct an onsite inspection prior to approval of an outpatient clinic service pursuant to this section. However, nothing shall preclude the department from conducting an onsite inspection at any time, or denying an application, in accordance with subdivision (c). If the department determines that the applicant does not meet the requirements of this section, the department shall provide the hospital, in writing, the particular basis for this determination.

(e) A completed application for purposes of this section shall include all of the following:

(1) The appropriate forms, fees, and documentation, as determined by the department.

(2) A description of the type of outpatient clinic service to be operated, the character and scope of the service to be provided, and a complete description of the building, its location and proximity to the main hospital building, facilities, equipment, apparatus, and appliances to be furnished and used in the operation of the outpatient clinic service and evidence satisfactory to the department that the hospital owns and will operate the outpatient clinic service that is the subject of the application.

(3) Written policies and procedures governing the operation of the outpatient clinic service and its reporting relationship to the applicant.

(4) Evidence of the hospital's compliance with applicable building standards and possession of a fire clearance for the outpatient clinic service space.

(f) The outpatient clinic service that is the subject of the application shall be limited to providing nonemergency primary health care services in a clinical environment to patients who remain in the outpatient clinic for less than 24 hours.

(g) For purposes of this section "outpatient clinic services" shall have the same meaning as the services that may be provided by a primary care clinic in accordance with subdivision (a) of Section 1204. Nothing in this section shall be interpreted to mean that supplemental outpatient services established by a general acute care hospital pursuant to this section shall be considered primary care clinics for licensing, regulatory, or enforcement purposes.

(Added by Stats. 2009, Ch. 543, Sec. 2. (AB 1544) Effective January 1, 2010.)

1253.7.

(a) For purposes of this chapter, "observation services" means outpatient services provided by a general acute care hospital and that have been ordered by a provider, to those patients who have unstable or uncertain conditions potentially serious enough to warrant close observation, but not so serious as to warrant inpatient admission to the hospital. Observation services may include the use of a bed, monitoring by nursing and other staff, and any other services that are reasonable and necessary to safely evaluate a patient's condition or determine the need for a possible inpatient admission to the hospital.

(b) When a patient in an inpatient unit of a hospital or in an observation unit, as defined in subdivision (c), is receiving observation services, or following a change in a patient's status from inpatient to observation, the patient shall receive written notice, as soon as practicable, that he or she is on observation status. The notice shall state that while on observation status, the patient's care is being provided on an outpatient basis, which may affect his or her health care coverage reimbursement.

(c) For purposes of this chapter, "observation unit" means an area in which observation services are provided in a setting outside of any inpatient unit and that is not part of an emergency department of a general acute care hospital. A hospital may establish one or more observation units that shall be marked with signage identifying the observation unit area as an outpatient area. The signage shall use the term "outpatient" in the title of the designated area to indicate clearly to all patients and family members that the observation services provided in the center are not inpatient services. Identifying an observation unit by a name or term other than that used in this subdivision does not exempt the general acute care hospital from compliance with the requirements of this section.

(d) Notwithstanding subdivisions (d) and (e) of Section 1275, an observation unit shall comply with the same licensed nurse-to-patient ratios as supplemental emergency services. This subdivision is not intended to alter or amend the effect of any regulation adopted pursuant to Section 1276.4 as of the effective date of the act that added this subdivision.

(Added by Stats. 2016, Ch. 723, Sec. 1. (SB 1076) Effective January 1, 2017.)

1254.

(a) Except as provided in subdivision (e), the state department shall inspect and license health facilities. The state department shall license health facilities to provide their respective basic services specified in Section 1250. Except as provided in Section 1253,

the state department shall inspect and approve a general acute care hospital to provide special services as specified in Section 1255. The state department shall develop and adopt regulations to implement the provisions contained in this section.

(b) Upon approval, the state department shall issue a separate license for the provision of the basic services enumerated in subdivision (c) or (d) of Section 1250 whenever these basic services are to be provided by an acute care hospital, as defined in subdivision (a), (b), or (f) of that section, where the services enumerated in subdivision (c) or (d) of Section 1250 are to be provided in any separate freestanding facility, whether or not the location of the separate freestanding facility is contiguous to the acute care hospital. The same requirement shall apply to any new freestanding facility constructed for the purpose of providing basic services, as defined in subdivision (c) or (d) of Section 1250, by any acute care hospital on or after January 1, 1984.

(c) (1) Those beds licensed to an acute care hospital which, prior to January 1, 1984, were separate freestanding beds and were not part of the physical structure licensed to provide acute care, and which beds were licensed to provide those services enumerated in subdivision (c) or (d) of Section 1250, are exempt from the requirements of subdivision (b).

(2) All beds licensed to an acute care hospital and located within the physical structure in which acute care is provided are exempt from the requirements of subdivision (b) irrespective of the date of original licensure of the beds, or the licensed category of the beds.

(3) All beds licensed to an acute care hospital owned and operated by the State of California or any other public agency are exempt from the requirements of subdivision (b).

(4) All beds licensed to an acute care hospital in a rural area as defined by Chapter 1010, of the Statutes of 1982, are exempt from the requirements of subdivision (b), except where there is a freestanding skilled nursing facility or intermediate care facility which has experienced an occupancy rate of 95 percent or less during the past 12 months within a 25-mile radius or which may be reached within 30 minutes using a motor vehicle.

(5) All beds licensed to an acute care hospital which meet the criteria for designation within peer group six or eight, as defined in the report entitled Hospital Peer Grouping for Efficiency Comparison, dated December 20, 1982, and published by the California Health Facilities Commission, and all beds in hospitals which have fewer than 76 licensed acute care beds and which are located in a census designation place of 15,000 or less population, are exempt from the requirements of subdivision (b), except where there is a freestanding skilled nursing facility or intermediate care facility which has experienced an occupancy rate of 95 percent or less during the past 12 months within a 25-mile radius or which may be reached within 30 minutes using a motor vehicle.

(6) All beds licensed to an acute care hospital which has had a certificate of need approved by a health systems agency on or before July 1, 1983, are exempt from the requirements of subdivision (b).

(7) All beds licensed to an acute care hospital are exempt from the requirements of subdivision (b), if reimbursement from the Medi-Cal program for beds licensed for the provision of services enumerated in subdivision (c) or (d) of Section 1250 and not otherwise exempt does not exceed the reimbursement which would be received if the beds were in a separately licensed facility.

(d) Except as provided in Section 1253, the state department shall inspect and approve a general acute care hospital to provide special services as specified in Section 1255. The state department shall develop and adopt regulations to implement subdivisions (a) to (d), inclusive, of this section.

(e) The State Department of Health Care Services shall inspect and license psychiatric health facilities. The State Department of Health Care Services shall license psychiatric health facilities to provide their basic services specified in Section 1250.2. The State Department of Health Care Services shall develop, adopt, or amend regulations to implement this subdivision.

(Amended by Stats. 2013, Ch. 23, Sec. 8. (AB 82) Effective June 27, 2013.)

1254.1.

(a) The State Department of Health Care Services shall license psychiatric health facilities to provide their basic services specified in Section 1250.

(b) Any reference in any statute to Section 1254 shall be deemed and construed to also be a reference to this section.

(Amended by Stats. 2013, Ch. 23, Sec. 9. (AB 82) Effective June 27, 2013.)

1254.2.

(a) The state department, in addition to the licensing duties imposed by Section 1254, shall license chemical dependency recovery hospitals to provide the basic services specified in subdivision (a) of Section 1250.3.

(b) Any reference in any statute to Section 1254 shall be deemed and construed to also be a reference to this section.

(Added by Stats. 1980, Ch. 707.)

1254.4.

(a) A general acute care hospital shall adopt a policy for providing family or next of kin with a reasonably brief period of accommodation, as described in subdivision (b), from the time that a patient is declared dead by reason of irreversible cessation of all functions of the entire brain, including the brain stem, in accordance with Section 7180, through discontinuation of cardiopulmonary support for the patient. During this reasonably brief period of accommodation, a hospital is required to continue only previously ordered cardiopulmonary support. No other medical intervention is required.

(b) For purposes of this section, a "reasonably brief period" means an amount of time afforded to gather family or next of kin at the patient's bedside.

(c) (1) A hospital subject to this section shall provide the patient's legally recognized health care decisionmaker, if any, or the patient's family or next of kin, if available, with a written statement of the policy described in subdivision (a), upon request, but no later than shortly after the treating physician has determined that the potential for brain death is imminent.

(2) If the patient's legally recognized health care decisionmaker, family, or next of kin voices any special religious or cultural practices and concerns of the patient or the patient's family surrounding the issue of death by reason of irreversible cessation of all functions of the entire brain of the patient, the hospital shall make reasonable efforts to accommodate those religious and cultural practices and concerns.

(d) For purposes of this section, in determining what is reasonable, a hospital shall consider the needs of other patients and prospective patients in urgent need of care.

(e) There shall be no private right of action to sue pursuant to this section.

(Added by Stats. 2008, Ch. 465, Sec. 1. Effective January 1, 2009.)

1254.5.

(a) The Legislature finds and declares that the disease of eating disorders is not simply medical or psychiatric, but involves biological, sociological, psychological, family, medical, and spiritual components. In addition, the Legislature finds and declares that the treatment of eating disorders is multifaceted, and like the treatment of chemical dependency, does not fall neatly into either the traditional medical or psychiatric milieu.

(b) The inpatient treatment of eating disorders shall be provided only in state licensed hospitals, which may be general acute care hospitals as defined in subdivision (a) of Section 1250, acute psychiatric hospitals as defined in subdivision (b) of Section 1250, or any other licensed health facility designated by the State Department of Public Health.

(c) "Eating disorders," for the purposes of this section, shall have the meaning of the term as defined in the Diagnostic and Statistical Manual of Mental Disorders, as published by the American Psychiatric Association.

(Amended by Stats. 2015, Ch. 435, Sec. 1. (AB 614) Effective January 1, 2016.)

1254.6.

(a) A hospital shall provide, free of charge, information and instructional materials regarding sudden infant death syndrome, as described in Section 1596.847, explaining the medical effects upon infants and young children and emphasizing measures that may reduce the risk.

(b) The information and materials described in subdivision (a) shall be provided to parents or guardians of each newborn, upon discharge from the hospital. In the event of home birth attended by a licensed midwife, the midwife shall provide the information and instructional materials to the parents or guardians of the newborn.

(c) To the maximum extent practicable, the materials provided to parents or guardians of each newborn shall substantially reflect the information contained in materials approved by the state department for public circulation. The state department shall make available to hospitals, free of charge, information in camera-ready typesetting format. Nothing in this section prohibits a hospital from obtaining free and suitable information from any other public or private agency.

(Added by Stats. 1997, Ch. 263, Sec. 2. Effective January 1, 1998.)

1254.7.

(a) It is the intent of the Legislature that pain be assessed and treated promptly, effectively, and for as long as pain persists.

(b) A health facility licensed pursuant to this chapter shall, as a condition of licensure, include pain as an item to be assessed. The health facility shall ensure that pain assessment is performed in a consistent manner that is appropriate to the patient. The pain assessment shall be noted in the patient's chart.

(Amended by Stats. 2017, Ch. 615, Sec. 2. (AB 1048) Effective January 1, 2018.)

1255.

(a) In addition to the basic services offered under the license, a general acute care hospital may be approved in accordance with subdivision (c) of Section 1277 to offer special services, including, but not limited to, the following:

(1) Radiation therapy department.

(2) Burn center.

(3) Emergency center.

(4) Hemodialysis center (or unit).

(5) Psychiatric.

(6) Intensive care newborn nursery.

(7) Cardiac surgery.

(8) Cardiac catheterization laboratory.

(9) Renal transplant.

(10) Other special services as the department may prescribe by regulation.

(b) A general acute care hospital that exclusively provides acute medical rehabilitation center services may be approved in accordance with subdivision (b) of Section 1277 to offer special services not requiring surgical facilities.

(c) The department shall adopt standards for special services and other regulations as may be necessary to implement this section.

(d) (1) For cardiac catheterization laboratory service, the department shall, at a minimum, adopt standards and regulations that specify that only diagnostic services, and what diagnostic services, may be offered by a general acute care hospital or a multispecialty clinic as defined in subdivision (I) of Section 1206 that is approved to provide cardiac catheterization laboratory service but is not also approved to provide cardiac surgery services, together with the conditions under which the cardiac catheterization laboratory service may be offered.

(2) Except as provided in paragraph (3), a cardiac catheterization laboratory service shall be located in a general acute care hospital that is either licensed to perform cardiovascular procedures requiring extracorporeal coronary artery bypass that meets all of the applicable licensing requirements relating to staff, equipment, and space for service, or shall, at a minimum, have a licensed intensive care service and coronary care service and maintain a written agreement for the transfer of patients to a general acute care hospital that is licensed for cardiac surgery or shall be located in a multispecialty clinic as defined in subdivision (I) of Section 1206. The transfer agreement shall include protocols that will minimize the need for duplicative cardiac catheterizations at the hospital in which the cardiac surgery is to be performed.

(3) Commencing March 1, 2013, a general acute care hospital that has applied for program flexibility on or before July 1, 2012, to expand cardiac catheterization laboratory services may utilize cardiac catheterization space that is in conformance with applicable building code standards, including those promulgated by the Office of Statewide Health Planning and Development, provided that all of the following conditions are met:

(A) The expanded laboratory space is located in the building so that the space is connected to the general acute care hospital by an enclosed all-weather passageway that is accessible by staff and patients who are accompanied by staff.

(B) The service performs cardiac catheterization services on no more than 25 percent of the hospital's inpatients who need cardiac catheterizations.

(C) The service complies with the same policies and procedures approved by hospital medical staff for cardiac catheterization laboratories that are located within the general acute care hospital, and the same standards and regulations prescribed by the department for cardiac catheterization laboratories located inside general acute care hospitals, including, but not limited to, appropriate nurse-to-patient ratios under Section 1276.4, and with all standards and regulations prescribed by the Office of Statewide Health Planning and Development. Emergency regulations allowing a general acute care hospital to operate a cardiac catheterization laboratory service shall be adopted by the department and by the Office of Statewide Health Planning and Development by February 28, 2013.

(D) Emergency regulations implementing this paragraph have been adopted by the department and by the Office of Statewide Health Planning and Development by February 28, 2013.

(E) This paragraph shall not apply to more than two general acute care hospitals.

(4) After March 1, 2014, an acute care hospital may only operate a cardiac catheterization laboratory service pursuant to paragraph (3) if the department and the Office of Statewide Health Planning and Development have adopted regulations in accordance with the requirements of Chapter 3.5 (commencing with Section 11340) of Part 1 of Division 3 of Title 2 of the Government Code that provide adequate protection to patient health and safety including, but not limited to, building standards contained in Part 2.5 (commencing with Section 18901) of Division 13.

(5) Notwithstanding Section 129885, cardiac catheterization laboratory services expanded in accordance with paragraph (3) shall be subject to all applicable building standards. The Office of Statewide Health Planning and Development shall review the services for compliance with the OSHPD 3 requirements of the most recent version of the California Building Standards Code.

(e) For purposes of this section, "multispecialty clinic," as defined in subdivision (I) of Section 1206, includes an entity in which the multispecialty clinic holds at least a 50-percent general partner interest and maintains responsibility for the management of the service, if all of the following requirements are met:

(1) The multispecialty clinic existed as of March 1, 1983.

(2) Prior to March 1, 1985, the multispecialty clinic did not offer cardiac catheterization services, dynamic multiplane imaging, or other types of coronary or similar angiography.

(3) The multispecialty clinic creates only one entity that operates its service at one site.

(4) These entities shall have the equipment and procedures necessary for the stabilization of patients in emergency situations prior to transfer and patient transfer arrangements in emergency situations that shall be in accordance with the standards established by the Emergency Medical Services Authority, including the availability of comprehensive care and the qualifications of any general acute care hospital expected to provide emergency treatment.

(f) Except as provided in this section and in Sections 100921 and 100922, under no circumstances shall cardiac catheterizations be performed outside of a general acute care hospital or a multispecialty clinic, as defined in subdivision (I) of Section 1206, that qualifies for this definition as of March 1, 1983.

(Amended by Stats. 2015, Ch. 303, Sec. 246. (AB 731) Effective January 1, 2016.)

1255.1.

(a) Any hospital that provides emergency medical services under Section 1255 shall, as soon as possible, but not later than 90 days prior to a planned reduction or elimination of the level of emergency medical services, provide notice of the intended change to the state department, the local government entity in charge of the provision of health services, and all health care service plans or other entities under contract with the hospital to provide services to enrollees of the plan or other entity.

(b) In addition to the notice required by subdivision (a), the hospital shall, within the time limits specified in subdivision (a), provide public notice of the intended change in a manner that is likely to reach a significant number of residents of the community serviced by that facility.

(c) A hospital shall not be subject to this section or Section 1255.2 if the state department does either of the following:

(1) Determines that the use of resources to keep the emergency center open substantially threatens the stability of the hospital as a whole.

(2) Cites the emergency center for unsafe staffing practices.

(Added by Stats. 1998, Ch. 995, Sec. 1. Effective January 1, 1999.)

1255.2.

A health facility implementing a downgrade or change shall make reasonable efforts to ensure that the community served by its facility is informed of the downgrade or closure. Reasonable efforts may include, but not be limited to, advertising the change in terms likely to be understood by a layperson, soliciting media coverage regarding the change, informing patients of the facility of the impending change, and notifying contracting health care service plans as required in Section 1255.1.

(Added by Stats. 1998, Ch. 995, Sec. 2. Effective January 1, 1999.)

1255.25.

(a) (1) Not less than 30 days prior to closing a health facility, as defined in subdivision (a) or (b) of Section 1250, or eliminating a supplemental service, as defined in Section 70067 of Chapter 1 of Division 5 of Title 22 of the California Code of Regulations, the facility shall provide public notice of the proposed closure or elimination of the supplemental service, including a notice posted at the entrance to all affected facilities and a notice to the department and the board of supervisors of the county in which the health facility is located.

(2) Not less than 30 days prior to relocating the provision of supplemental services to a different campus, a health facility, as defined in subdivision (a) or (b) of Section 1250, shall provide public notice of the proposed relocation of supplemental services, including a notice posted at the entrance to all affected facilities and notice to the department and the board of supervisors of the county in which the health facility is located.

(b) The notice required by paragraph (1) or (2) of subdivision (a) shall include all of the following:

(1) A description of the proposed closure, elimination, or relocation. The description shall be limited to publicly available data, including the number of beds eliminated, if any, the probable decrease in the number of personnel, and a summary of any service that is being eliminated, if applicable.

(2) A description of the three nearest available comparable services in the community. If the health facility closing these services serves Medi-Cal or Medicare patients, this health facility shall specify if the providers of the nearest available comparable services serve these patients.

(3) A telephone number and address for each of the following, where interested parties may offer comments:

(A) The health facility.

(B) The parent entity, if any, or contracted company, if any, that acts as the corporate administrator of the health facility.

(C) The chief executive officer.

(c) Notwithstanding subdivisions (a) and (b), this section shall not apply to county facilities subject to Section 1442.5.

(Added by Stats. 2008, Ch. 459, Sec. 2. Effective January 1, 2009.)

1255.3.

On or before June 30, 1999, with the state department as the lead agency, the state department and the Emergency Medical Services Authority, in consultation with hospitals and other health care providers and local emergency medical services agencies, shall designate signage requirements for a health facility holding a special permit for a standby emergency medical service located in an urban area. The signage shall not include the word "emergency" and shall reflect the type of emergency services provided by the facility, and be easily understood by the average person. The facility shall not post signs, distribute literature, or advertise that emergency services are available at the facility. Nothing in this section shall be construed to mean that a facility is no longer providing emergency services for purposes of billing or reimbursement. A small and rural hospital, as defined in Section 124840, is not subject to the requirements of this section.

(Added by Stats. 1998, Ch. 995, Sec. 3. Effective January 1, 1999.)

1255.5.

For purposes of Section 1255, the following definitions apply:

(a) "Cardiac catheterization" includes an intravascular insertion of a catheter into the heart for the primary definition and diagnosis of an anatomic cardiac lesion. For the purposes of this definition, the insertion of a Swan-Ganz thermodilution cardiac output catheter, a venous line, and a temporary pacemaking electrode catheter are excluded.

(b) "Cardiac surgery" means surgery on the heart or great vessels requiring a thoracotomy and extracorporeal circulation.

(c) "Cardiovascular surgery service" means a program of a general acute care hospital which has the capability of performing cardiac catheterizations and cardiac surgery as defined in this section. Under no circumstances shall there exist in a general acute care hospital a cardiac surgery service without a cardiac catheterization laboratory service.

(d) "Cardiac catheterization laboratory service" means a program of a general acute care hospital which has the capability of performing cardiac catheterization. Cardiac catheterization laboratory service does not include pediatric cardiac catheterization laboratory service.

(e) "Pediatric cardiac surgery service" means a program of a general acute care hospital which has the capability of performing cardiac catheterization and cardiac surgery, as defined in this section, for the diagnosis and treatment of congenital defects in children. Cardiac catheterization for pediatric patients shall be performed only in a general acute care hospital that has the capability to perform cardiac surgery on pediatric patients.

(f) "Intensive care newborn nursery services" means the provision of comprehensive and intensive care for all contingencies of the newborn infant, including intensive, intermediate, and continuing care. Policies, procedures, and space requirements for intensive, intermediate, and continuing care services shall be based upon the standards and recommendations of the American Academy of Pediatrics Guidelines for Perinatal Care, 1983.

(Amended by Stats. 1998, Ch. 775, Sec. 2. Effective January 1, 1999.)

1255.6.

During cardiovascular surgery, a perfusionist, as defined by Chapter 5.67 (commencing with Section 2590) of Division 2 of the Business and Professions Code, shall operate the extracorporeal equipment under the immediate supervision of the cardiovascular surgeon or anesthesiologist. The determination of the qualifications and competence of a perfusionist, and the awarding of appropriate privileges, shall be the responsibility of the general acute care hospital or its medical staff.

(Added by Stats. 1998, Ch. 775, Sec. 3. Effective January 1, 1999.)

1255.7.

(a) (1) For purposes of this section, "safe-surrender site" means either of the following:

(A) A location designated by the board of supervisors of a county or by a local fire agency, upon the approval of the appropriate local governing body of the agency, to be responsible for accepting physical custody of a minor child who is 72 hours old or younger from a parent or individual who has lawful custody of the child and who surrenders the child pursuant to Section 271.5 of the Penal Code. Before designating a location as a safe-surrender site pursuant to this subdivision, the designating entity shall consult with the governing body of a city, if the site is within the city limits, and with representatives of a fire department and a child welfare agency that may provide services to a child who is surrendered at the site, if that location is selected.

(B) A location within a public or private hospital that is designated by that hospital to be responsible for accepting physical custody of a minor child who is 72 hours old or younger from a parent or individual who has lawful custody of the child and who surrenders the child pursuant to Section 271.5 of the Penal Code.

(2) For purposes of this section, "parent" means a birth parent of a minor child who is 72 hours old or younger.

(3) For purposes of this section, "personnel" means a person who is an officer or employee of a safe-surrender site or who has staff privileges at the site.

(4) A hospital and a safe-surrender site designated by the county board of supervisors or by a local fire agency, upon the approval of the appropriate local governing body of the agency, shall post a sign displaying a statewide logo that has been adopted by the State Department of Social Services that notifies the public of the location where a minor child 72 hours old or younger may be safely surrendered pursuant to this section.

(b) Personnel on duty at a safe-surrender site shall accept physical custody of a minor child 72 hours old or younger pursuant to this section if a parent or other individual having lawful custody of the child voluntarily surrenders physical custody of the child to personnel who are on duty at the safe-surrender site. Safe-surrender site personnel shall ensure that a qualified person does all of the following:

(1) Places a coded, confidential ankle bracelet on the child.

(2) Provides, or makes a good faith effort to provide, to the parent or other individual surrendering the child a copy of a unique, coded, confidential ankle bracelet identification in order to facilitate reclaiming the child pursuant to subdivision (f). However, possession of the ankle bracelet identification, in and of itself, does not establish parentage or a right to custody of the child.

(3) Provides, or makes a good faith effort to provide, to the parent or other individual surrendering the child a medical information questionnaire, which may be declined, voluntarily filled out and returned at the time the child is surrendered, or later filled out and mailed in the envelope provided for this purpose. This medical information questionnaire shall not require identifying information about the child or the parent or individual surrendering the child, other than the identification code provided in the ankle bracelet placed on the child. Every questionnaire provided pursuant to this section shall begin with the following notice in no less than 12-point type:

NOTICE: THE BABY YOU HAVE BROUGHT IN TODAY MAY HAVE SERIOUS MEDICAL NEEDS IN THE FUTURE THAT WE DON'T KNOW ABOUT TODAY. SOME ILLNESSES, INCLUDING CANCER, ARE BEST TREATED WHEN WE KNOW ABOUT FAMILY MEDICAL HISTORIES. IN ADDITION, SOMETIMES RELATIVES ARE NEEDED FOR LIFE-SAVING TREATMENTS. TO MAKE SURE THIS BABY WILL HAVE A HEALTHY FUTURE, YOUR ASSISTANCE IN COMPLETING THIS QUESTIONNAIRE FULLY IS ESSENTIAL. THANK YOU.

(c) Personnel of a safe-surrender site that has physical custody of a minor child pursuant to this section shall ensure that a medical screening examination and any necessary medical care is provided to the minor child. Notwithstanding any other provision of law, the consent of the parent or other relative shall not be required to provide that care to the minor child.

(d) (1) As soon as possible, but in no event later than 48 hours after the physical custody of a child has been accepted pursuant to this section, personnel of the safe-surrender site that has physical custody of the child shall notify child protective services or a county agency providing child welfare services pursuant to Section 16501 of the Welfare and Institutions Code, that the safe-surrender site has physical custody of the child pursuant to this section. In addition, medical information pertinent to the child's health, including, but not limited to, information obtained pursuant to the medical information questionnaire described in paragraph (3) of subdivision (b) that has been received by or is in the possession of the safe-surrender site shall be provided to that child protective services or county agency.

(2) Any personal identifying information that pertains to a parent or individual who surrenders a child that is obtained pursuant to the medical information questionnaire is confidential and shall be exempt from disclosure by the child protective services or county agency under the California Public Records Act (Chapter 3.5 (commencing with Section 6250) of Division 7 of Title 1 of the Government Code). Personal identifying information that pertains to a parent or individual who surrenders a child shall be redacted from any

medical information provided to child protective services or the county agency providing child welfare services.
(e) Child protective services or the county agency providing child welfare services pursuant to Section 16501 of the Welfare and Institutions Code shall assume temporary custody of the child pursuant to Section 300 of the Welfare and Institutions Code immediately upon receipt of notice under subdivision (d). Child protective services or the county agency providing child welfare services pursuant to Section 16501 of the Welfare and Institutions Code shall immediately investigate the circumstances of the case and file a petition pursuant to Section 311 of the Welfare and Institutions Code. Child protective services or the county agency providing child welfare services pursuant to Section 16501 of the Welfare and Institutions Code shall immediately notify the State Department of Social Services of each child to whom this subdivision applies upon taking temporary custody of the child pursuant to Section 300 of the Welfare and Institutions Code. As soon as possible, but no later than 24 hours after temporary custody is assumed, child protective services or the county agency providing child welfare services pursuant to Section 16501 of the Welfare and Institutions Code shall report all known identifying information concerning the child, except personal identifying information pertaining to the parent or individual who surrendered the child, to the California Missing Children Clearinghouse and to the National Crime Information Center.
(f) If, prior to the filing of a petition under subdivision (e), a parent or individual who has voluntarily surrendered a child pursuant to this section requests that the safe-surrender site that has physical custody of the child pursuant to this section return the child and the safe-surrender site still has custody of the child, personnel of the safe-surrender site shall either return the child to the parent or individual or contact a child protective agency if any personnel at the safe-surrender site knows or reasonably suspects that the child has been the victim of child abuse or neglect. The voluntary surrender of a child pursuant to this section is not in and of itself a sufficient basis for reporting child abuse or neglect. The terms "child abuse," "child protective agency," "mandated reporter," "neglect," and "reasonably suspects" shall be given the same meanings as in Article 2.5 (commencing with Section 11164) of Title 1 of Part 4 of the Penal Code.
(g) Subsequent to the filing of a petition under subdivision (e), if within 14 days of the voluntary surrender described in this section, the parent or individual who surrendered custody returns to claim physical custody of the child, the child welfare agency shall verify the identity of the parent or individual, conduct an assessment of his or her circumstances and ability to parent, and request that the juvenile court dismiss the petition for dependency and order the release of the child, if the child welfare agency determines that none of the conditions described in subdivisions (a) to (d), inclusive, of Section 319 of the Welfare and Institutions Code currently exist.
(h) A safe-surrender site, or the personnel of a safe-surrender site, shall not have liability of any kind for a surrendered child prior to taking actual physical custody of the child. A safe-surrender site, or personnel of the safe-surrender site, that accepts custody of a surrendered child pursuant to this section shall not be subject to civil, criminal, or administrative liability for accepting the child and caring for the child in the good faith belief that action is required or authorized by this section, including, but not limited to, instances where the child is older than 72 hours or the parent or individual surrendering the child did not have lawful physical custody of the child. A safe-surrender site, or the personnel of a safe-surrender site, shall not be subject to civil, criminal, or administrative liability for a surrendered child prior to the time that the site or its personnel know, or should know, that the child has been surrendered. This subdivision does not confer immunity from liability for personal injury or wrongful death, including, but not limited to, injury resulting from medical malpractice.
(i) (1) In order to encourage assistance to persons who voluntarily surrender physical custody of a child pursuant to this section or Section 271.5 of the Penal Code, no person who, without compensation and in good faith, provides assistance for the purpose of effecting the safe surrender of a minor 72 hours old or younger shall be civilly liable for injury to or death of the minor child as a result of his or her acts or omissions. This immunity does not apply to an act or omission constituting gross negligence, recklessness, or willful misconduct.
(2) For purposes of this section, "assistance" means transporting the minor child to the safe-surrender site as a person with lawful custody, or transporting or accompanying the parent or person with lawful custody at the request of that parent or person to effect the safe surrender, or performing any other act in good faith for the purpose of effecting the safe surrender of the minor.
(j) For purposes of this section, "lawful custody" means physical custody of a minor 72 hours old or younger accepted by a person from a parent of the minor, who the person believes in good faith is the parent of the minor, with the specific intent and promise of effecting the safe surrender of the minor.
(k) Any identifying information that pertains to a parent or individual who surrenders a child pursuant to this section, that is obtained as a result of the questionnaire described in paragraph (3) of subdivision (b) or in any other manner, is confidential, shall be exempt from disclosure under the California Public Records Act (Chapter 3.5 (commencing with Section 6250) of Division 7 of Title 1 of the Government Code), and shall not be disclosed by any personnel of a safe-surrender site that accepts custody of a child pursuant to this section.
(Amended by Stats. 2010, Ch. 567, Sec. 1. (AB 1048) Effective January 1, 2011.)
1255.8.
(a) For purposes of this section, the following terms have the following meanings:
(1) "Colonized" means that a pathogen is present on the patient's body, but is not causing any signs or symptoms of an infection.
(2) "Committee" means the Healthcare Associated Infection Advisory Committee established pursuant to Section 1288.5.
(3) "Health facility" means a facility as defined in subdivision (a) of Section 1250.
(4) "Health-care-associated infection," "health-facility-acquired infection," or "HAI" means a health-care-associated infection as defined by the National Healthcare Safety Network of the federal Centers for Disease Control and Prevention, unless the department adopts a definition consistent with the recommendations of the committee or its successor.
(5) "MRSA" means Methicillin-resistant Staphylococcus aureus.
(b) (1) Each patient who is admitted to a health facility shall be tested for MRSA in the following cases, within 24 hours of admission:
(A) The patient is scheduled for inpatient surgery and has a documented medical condition making the patient susceptible to infection, based either upon federal Centers for Disease Control and Prevention findings or the recommendations of the committee or its successor.
(B) It has been documented that the patient has been previously discharged from a general acute care hospital within 30 days prior to the current hospital admission.
(C) The patient will be admitted to an intensive care unit or burn unit of the hospital.
(D) The patient receives inpatient dialysis treatment.
(E) The patient is being transferred from a skilled nursing facility.
(2) The department may interpret this subdivision to take into account the recommendations of the federal Centers for Disease Control and Prevention, or recommendations of the committee or its successor.
(3) If a patient tests positive for MRSA, the attending physician shall inform the patient or the patient's representative immediately or as soon as practically possible.
(4) A patient who tests positive for MRSA infection shall, prior to discharge, receive oral and written instruction regarding aftercare and precautions to prevent the spread of the infection to others.
(c) Commencing January 1, 2011, a patient tested in accordance with subdivision (b) and who shows evidence of increased risk of invasive MRSA shall again be tested for MRSA immediately prior to discharge from the facility. This subdivision shall not apply to a patient who has tested positive for MRSA infection or colonization upon entering the facility.
(d) A patient who is tested pursuant to subdivision (c) and who tests positive for MRSA infection shall receive oral and written instructions regarding aftercare and precautions to prevent the spread of the infection to others.
(e) The infection control policy required pursuant to Section 70739 of Title 22 of the California Code of Regulations, at a minimum, shall include all of the following:
(1) Procedures to reduce health care associated infections.
(2) Regular disinfection of all restrooms, countertops, furniture, televisions, telephones, bedding, office equipment, and surfaces in patient rooms, nursing stations, and storage units.
(3) Regular removal of accumulations of bodily fluids and intravenous substances, and cleaning and disinfection of all movable medical equipment, including point-of-care testing devices such as glucometers, and transportable medical devices.
(4) Regular cleaning and disinfection of all surfaces in common areas in the facility such as elevators, meeting rooms, and lounges.
(f) Each facility shall designate an infection control officer who, in conjunction with the hospital infection control committee, shall ensure implementation of the testing and reporting provisions of this section and other hospital infection control efforts. The reports shall be presented to the appropriate committee within the facility for review. The name of the infection control officer shall be made publicly available, upon request.
(g) The department shall establish a health care acquired infection program pursuant to this section.
(Added by Stats. 2008, Ch. 296, Sec. 3. Effective January 1, 2009.)
1256.
(a) The use of the name or title "hospital" by any person or persons to identify or represent a facility for the diagnosis, care, and treatment of human illness other than a facility subject to or specifically exempted from the licensure provisions of this chapter is prohibited. Notwithstanding any other provisions of the laws of this state, the name or title "hospital" shall not be used by any sanitarium, nursing home, convalescent home, or maternity home, unless preceded by some qualifying descriptive word such as convalescent, geriatric, rehabilitation, or nursing.
(b) This section shall not prohibit the use of the word "hospital" to identify or represent an approved pediatric supplemental service of a general acute care hospital that is either of the following:
(1) A children's hospital as defined by Section 10727 of the Welfare and Institutions Code.
(2) A University of California children's hospital as defined by Section 10728 of the Welfare and Institutions Code.
(Amended by Stats. 2001, Ch. 290, Sec. 1. Effective January 1, 2002.)
1256.01.
(a) The Elective Percutaneous Coronary Intervention (PCI) Program is hereby established in the department. The purpose of the program is to allow the department to certify general acute care hospitals that are licensed to provide urgent and emergent cardiac catheterization laboratory service in California, and that meet the requirements of this section, to perform scheduled, elective percutaneous transluminal coronary angioplasty and stent placement for eligible patients.
(b) For purposes of this section, the following terms have the following meanings:

(1) "Certified hospital" means an eligible hospital that is certified by the department to participate in the Elective Percutaneous Coronary Intervention (PCI) Program established by this section.

(2) "Elective Percutaneous Coronary Intervention (elective PCI)" means scheduled percutaneous transluminal coronary angioplasty and stent placement. Elective PCI does not include urgent or emergent PCI that is scheduled on an ad hoc basis.

(3) "Eligible hospital" means a general acute care hospital that has an approved cardiac catheterization laboratory, does not have onsite cardiac surgery, and is in substantial compliance with all applicable state and federal licensing laws and regulations.

(4) "Interventionalist" means a licensed cardiologist who meets the requirements for performing elective PCI.

(c) To participate in the Elective PCI Program, an eligible hospital shall obtain certification from the department and shall meet all of the following requirements:

(1) Demonstrate that it complies with the recommendations of the Society for Cardiovascular Angiography and Interventions (SCAI), the American College of Cardiology Foundation, and the American Heart Association, for performance of PCI without onsite cardiac surgery, as those recommendations may evolve over time.

(2) Provide evidence showing the full support from hospital administration in fulfilling the necessary institutional requirements, including, but not limited to, appropriate support services such as respiratory care and blood banking.

(3) Participate in, and provide timely submission of data to, the American College of Cardiology-National Cardiovascular Data Registry.

(4) Confer rights to transfer the data submitted pursuant to paragraph (3) to the Office of Statewide Health Planning and Development.

(5) Any additional requirements the department deems necessary to protect patient safety or ensure quality of care.

(d) An eligible hospital shall submit an application to the department pursuant to Section 1265 to obtain certification to participate in the Elective PCI Program. The application shall include sufficient information to demonstrate compliance with the standards set forth in this section, and shall also include the effective date for initiating elective PCI service, the general service area, a description of the population to be served, a description of the services to be provided, a description of backup emergency services, the availability of comprehensive care, and the qualifications of the eligible hospital. The department may require that additional information be submitted with the application. Failure to submit any required criteria or additional information shall disqualify the applicant from the application process and from consideration for participation in the program. The department may deny an Elective PCI Program applicant pursuant to Article 2 (commencing with Section 1265).

(e) An eligible hospital that, as of December 31, 2014, was participating in the Elective Percutaneous Coronary Intervention Pilot Program established under Chapter 295 of the Statutes of 2008, as amended by Chapter 202 of the Statutes of 2013, may continue to perform elective PCI and shall be considered a certified hospital until January 1, 2016. On and after January 1, 2016, a hospital described in this subdivision shall not be considered a certified hospital unless the hospital has obtained a certification under this section.

(f) The Office of Statewide Health Planning and Development shall, using the data transferred pursuant to paragraph (4) of subdivision (c), annually develop and make available to the public a report regarding each certified hospital's performance on mortality, stroke rate, and emergency coronary artery bypass graft rate.

(g) The department may establish an advisory oversight committee composed of two interventionalists from certified hospitals, two interventionalists from general acute care hospitals that are not certified hospitals, and a representative of the department, for the purpose of analyzing the report issued under subdivision (f) and making recommendations for changing the data to be included in future reports issued under subdivision (f).

(h) If at any time a certified hospital fails to meet the criteria set forth in this section for being a certified hospital or fails to safeguard patient safety, as determined by the department, the department may suspend or revoke, pursuant to Section 70309 of Title 22 of the California Code of Regulations, the certification issued to that hospital under this section. A hospital whose certification is revoked pursuant to this subdivision may request an appeal with the department and is not precluded from reapplying for certification under this section.

(i) The department may charge certified hospitals a supplemental licensing fee, the amount of which shall not exceed the reasonable cost to the department of overseeing the program.

(j) The department may contract with a professional entity with medical program knowledge to meet the requirements of this section.

(Added by Stats. 2014, Ch. 368, Sec. 1. (SB 906) Effective January 1, 2015.)

1256.1.

A general acute care hospital shall not hold itself out directly or indirectly by any sign, brochure, or advertisement as providing any service or services that require a supplemental or special service unless that general acute care hospital has first obtained a supplemental or special service approval from the State Department of Public Health to operate that service.

(Amended by Stats. 2017, Ch. 561, Sec. 101. (AB 1516) Effective January 1, 2018.)

1256.2.

(a) (1) No general acute care hospital may promulgate policies or implement practices that determine differing standards of obstetrical care based upon a patient's source of payment or ability to pay for medical services.

(2) Each hospital holding an obstetrical services permit shall provide the licensing and certification division of the department with a written policy statement reflecting

paragraph (1) and shall post written notices of this policy in the obstetrical admitting areas of the hospital by July 1, 1999. Notices posted pursuant to this section shall be posted in the predominant language or languages spoken in the hospital's service area.

(b) It shall constitute unprofessional conduct within the meaning of the Medical Practice Act, Chapter 5 (commencing with Section 2000) of Division 2 of the Business and Professions Code, for a physician or surgeon to deny, or threaten to withhold pain management services from a woman in active labor, based upon that patient's source of payment, or ability to pay for medical services.

(Added by Stats. 1998, Ch. 652, Sec. 2. Effective January 1, 1999.)

1257.

The state department may delegate to local health departments the authority to verify compliance with the licensing and approval provisions of this chapter, to provide consultation, and to recommend disciplinary action by the department against those licensed or approved under the provisions of this chapter. In exercising the authority so delegated, the local health department shall conform to the requirements of this chapter and to the rules and regulations of the state department. Payment to the local health departments for services performed pursuant to this section shall be in accordance with a budget submitted by the local health department and approved by the state department. Such expenditures shall not exceed amounts appropriated by the Legislature for the purpose of such inspection and enforcement.

(Added by Stats. 1973, Ch. 1202.)

1257.5.

(a) All registered nurses, certified nurse assistants, licensed vocational nurses, and physicians working in skilled nursing facilities, as defined in subdivision (c) of Section 1250, or congregate living health facilities, as defined in subdivision (i) of Section 1250, shall participate in a training program, to be prescribed by the department, that focuses on preventing and eliminating discrimination based on sexual orientation and gender identity.

(b) The department may incorporate the training prescribed in subdivision (a) into any existing training program that is designed to prevent or eliminate discrimination in senior care facilities.

(c) The department may charge each licensee who is subject to subdivision (a) a fee associated with determining compliance. The fee shall not exceed the department's costs for the enforcement of this section.

(d) "Sexual orientation" and "gender identity" have the same meanings as those terms are used in Section 422.56 of the Penal Code.

(Added by Stats. 2008, Ch. 550, Sec. 2. Effective January 1, 2009.)

1257.7.

(a) After July 1, 2010, all hospitals licensed pursuant to subdivisions (a), (b), and (f) of Section 1250 shall conduct, not less than annually, a security and safety assessment and, using the assessment, develop and annually update based on the assessment, a security plan with measures to protect personnel, patients, and visitors from aggressive or violent behavior. The security and safety assessment shall examine trends of aggressive or violent behavior at the facility. These hospitals shall track incidents of aggressive or violent behavior as part of the quality assessment and improvement program and for the purposes of developing a security plan to deter and manage further aggressive or violent acts of a similar nature. The plan may include, but shall not be limited to, security considerations relating to all of the following:

(1) Physical layout.

(2) Staffing.

(3) Security personnel availability.

(4) Policy and training related to appropriate responses to violent acts.

(5) Efforts to cooperate with local law enforcement regarding violent acts in the facility.

In developing this plan, the hospital shall consider guidelines or standards on violence in health care facilities issued by the department, the Division of Occupational Safety and Health, and the federal Occupational Safety and Health Administration. As part of the security plan, a hospital shall adopt security policies including, but not limited to, personnel training policies designed to protect personnel, patients, and visitors from aggressive or violent behavior. In developing the plan and the assessment, the hospital shall consult with affected employees, including the recognized collective bargaining agent or agents, if any, and members of the hospital medical staff organized pursuant to Section 2282 of the Business and Professions Code. This consultation may occur through hospital committees.

(b) The individual or members of a hospital committee responsible for developing the security plan shall be familiar with all of the following:

(1) The role of security in hospital operations.

(2) Hospital organization.

(3) Protective measures, including alarms and access control.

(4) The handling of disturbed patients, visitors, and employees.

(5) Identification of aggressive and violent predicting factors.

(6) Hospital safety and emergency preparedness.

(7) The rudiments of documenting and reporting crimes, including, by way of example, not disturbing a crime scene.

(c) The hospital shall have sufficient personnel to provide security pursuant to the security plan developed pursuant to subdivision (a). Persons regularly assigned to provide security in a hospital setting shall be trained regarding the role of security in hospital operations, including the identification of aggressive and violent predicting factors and management of violent disturbances.

(d) Any act of assault, as defined in Section 240 of the Penal Code, or battery, as defined in Section 242 of the Penal Code, that results in injury or involves the use of a firearm or

other dangerous weapon, against any on-duty hospital personnel shall be reported to the local law enforcement agency within 72 hours of the incident. Any other act of assault, as defined in Section 240 of the Penal Code, or battery, as defined in Section 242 of the Penal Code, against any on-duty hospital personnel may be reported to the local law enforcement agency within 72 hours of the incident. No health facility or employee of a health facility who reports a known or suspected instance of assault or battery pursuant to this section shall be civilly or criminally liable for any report required by this section. No health facility or employee of a health facility who reports a known or suspected instance of assault or battery that is authorized, but not required, by this section, shall be civilly or criminally liable for the report authorized by this section unless it can be proven that a false report was made and the health facility or its employee knew that the report was false or was made with reckless disregard of the truth or falsity of the report, and any health facility or employee of a health facility who makes a report known to be false or with reckless disregard of the truth or falsity of the report shall be liable for any damages caused. Any individual knowingly interfering with or obstructing the lawful reporting process shall be guilty of a misdemeanor. "Dangerous weapon," as used in this section, means any weapon the possession or concealed carrying of which is prohibited by any provision listed in Section 16590 of the Penal Code.
(Amended by Stats. 2010, Ch. 178, Sec. 36. (SB 1115) Effective January 1, 2011. Operative January 1, 2012, by Sec. 107 of Ch. 178.)
1257.8.
(a) All hospital employees regularly assigned to the emergency department shall receive, by July 1, 1995, and thereafter, on a continuing basis as provided for in the security plan developed pursuant to Section 1257.7, security education and training relating to the following topics:
(1) General safety measures.
(2) Personal safety measures.
(3) The assault cycle.
(4) Aggression and violence predicting factors.
(5) Obtaining patient history from a patient with violent behavior.
(6) Characteristics of aggressive and violent patients and victims.
(7) Verbal and physical maneuvers to diffuse and avoid violent behavior.
(8) Strategies to avoid physical harm.
(9) Restraining techniques.
(10) Appropriate use of medications as chemical restraints.
(11) Any resources available to employees for coping with incidents of violence, including, by way of example, critical incident stress debriefing or employee assistance programs.
(b) As provided in the security plan developed pursuant to Section 1257.7, members of the medical staff of each hospital and all other practitioners, including, but not limited to, nurse practitioners, physician assistants, and other personnel, who are regularly assigned to the emergency department or other departments identified in the security plan shall receive the same training as that provided to hospital employees or, at a minimum, training determined to be sufficient pursuant to the security plan.
(c) Temporary personnel shall be oriented as required pursuant to the security plan. This section shall not be construed to preempt state law or regulations generally affecting temporary personnel in hospitals.
(Added by Stats. 1993, Ch. 936, Sec. 3. Effective January 1, 1994.)
1257.9.
(a) (1) The department shall recommend training for general acute care hospitals, as defined in subdivision (a) of Section 1250, and special hospitals, as defined in subdivision (f) of Section 1250, that is intended to improve breast-feeding rates among mothers and infants. This recommended training should be designed for general acute care hospitals that provide maternity care and have exclusive patient breast-feeding rates in the lowest 25 percent, according to the data published yearly by the State Department of Public Health, when ranked from highest to lowest rates. The training offered shall include a minimum of eight hours of training provided to appropriate administrative and supervisory staff on hospital policies and recommendations that promote exclusive breast-feeding. Hospitals that meet the minimum criteria for exclusive breast-feeding rates prescribed in the most current Healthy People Guidelines of the United States Department of Health and Human Services shall be excluded from the training requirements recommended by this paragraph.
(2) The department shall notify the hospital director or other person in charge of a hospital to which paragraph (1) applies, that the eight-hour model training course developed pursuant to subdivision (b) of Section 123360, is available, upon request, to the hospital.
(b) The recommendations provided for in this section are advisory only. Nothing in this section shall require a hospital to comply with the training recommended by this section. Section 1290 shall not apply to this section, nor shall meeting the recommendations of this section be a condition of licensure.
(Added by Stats. 2007, Ch. 460, Sec. 2. Effective January 1, 2008.)
1258.
No health facility which permits sterilization operations for contraceptive purposes to be performed therein, nor the medical staff of such health facility, shall require the individual upon whom such a sterilization operation is to be performed to meet any special nonmedical qualifications, which are not imposed on individuals seeking other types of operations in the health facility. Such prohibited nonmedical qualifications shall include, but not be limited to, age, marital status, and number of natural children.
Nothing in this section shall prohibit requirements relating to the physical or mental condition of the individual or affect the right of the attending physician to counsel or advise his patient as to whether or not sterilization is appropriate. This section shall not affect existing law with respect to individuals below the age of majority.
(Added by Stats. 1974, Ch. 755.)
1259.
(a) (1) The Legislature finds and declares that California is becoming a land of people whose languages and cultures give the state a global quality. The Legislature further finds and declares that access to basic health care services is the right of every resident of the state, and that access to information regarding basic health care services is an essential element of that right.
(2) Therefore, it is the intent of the Legislature that when language or communication barriers exist between patients and the staff of any general acute care hospital, arrangements shall be made for interpreters or bilingual professional staff to ensure adequate and speedy communication between patients and staff.
(b) As used in this section:
(1) "Interpreter" means a person fluent in English and in the necessary second language, who can accurately speak, read, and readily interpret the necessary second language, or a person who can accurately sign and read sign language. Interpreters shall have the ability to translate the names of body parts and to describe competently symptoms and injuries in both languages. Interpreters may include members of the medical or professional staff.
(2) "Language or communication barriers" means:
(A) With respect to spoken language, barriers that are experienced by individuals who are limited-English-speaking or non-English-speaking individuals who speak the same primary language and who comprise at least 5 percent of the population of the geographical area served by the hospital or of the actual patient population of the hospital. In cases of dispute, the State Department of Public Health shall determine, based on objective data, whether the 5 percent population standard applies to a given hospital.
(B) With respect to sign language, barriers that are experienced by individuals who are deaf and whose primary language is sign language.
(c) To ensure access to health care information and services for limited-English-speaking or non-English-speaking residents and deaf residents, licensed general acute care hospitals shall:
(1) Review existing policies regarding interpreters for patients with limited-English proficiency and for patients who are deaf, including the availability of staff to act as interpreters.
(2) (A) (i) Adopt and review annually a policy for providing language assistance services to patients with language or communication barriers. The policy shall include procedures for providing, to the extent possible, as determined by the hospital, the use of an interpreter whenever a language or communication barrier exists, except when the patient, after being informed of the availability of the interpreter service, chooses to use a family member or friend who volunteers to interpret. The procedures shall be designed to maximize efficient use of interpreters and minimize delays in providing interpreters to patients. The procedures shall ensure, to the extent possible, as determined by the hospital, that interpreters are available, either on the premises or accessible by telephone, 24 hours a day.
(ii) The hospital shall, on or before July 1, 2016, and every January 1 thereafter, make the updated policy and a notice of availability of language assistance services available to the public on its Internet Web site. The notice shall be in English and in the other languages most commonly spoken in the hospital's service area. For purposes of this paragraph, the hospital shall make the notice available in the language of individuals who meet the definition of having a language barrier pursuant to subparagraph (A) of paragraph (2) of subdivision (b); however, a hospital is not required to make the notice available in more than five languages other than English.
(B) (i) The hospital shall, on or before July 1, 2016, and every January 1 thereafter, transmit to the department a copy of the updated policy and shall include a description of its efforts to ensure adequate and speedy communication between patients with language or communication barriers and staff.
(ii) The department shall make the updated policy available to the public on its Internet Web site.
(3) Develop, and post in conspicuous locations, notices that advise patients and their families of the availability of interpreters, the procedure for obtaining an interpreter, and the telephone numbers where complaints may be filed concerning interpreter service problems, including, but not limited to, a TDD number for the deaf or hard of hearing. The notices shall be posted, at a minimum, in the emergency room, the admitting area, the entrance, and in outpatient areas. Notices shall inform patients that interpreter services are available upon request, shall list the languages for which interpreter services are available, shall instruct patients to direct complaints regarding interpreter services to the department, and shall provide the local address and telephone number of the department, including, but not limited to, a TDD number for the deaf or hard of hearing.
(4) Identify and record a patient's primary language and dialect on one or more of the following: patient medical chart, hospital bracelet, bedside notice, or nursing card.
(5) Prepare and maintain as needed a list of interpreters who have been identified as proficient in sign language and in the languages of the population of the geographical area serviced who have the ability to translate the names of body parts, injuries, and symptoms.
(6) Notify employees of the hospital's commitment to provide interpreters to all patients who request them.
(7) Review all standardized written forms, waivers, documents, and informational materials available to patients upon admission to determine which to translate into languages other than English.

(8) Consider providing its nonbilingual staff with standardized picture and phrase sheets for use in routine communications with patients who have language or communication barriers.

(9) Consider developing community liaison groups to enable the hospital and the limited-English-speaking and deaf communities to ensure the adequacy of the interpreter services.

(d) Noncompliance with this section shall be reportable to licensing authorities.

(e) Section 1290 does not apply to this section.

(Amended by Stats. 2017, Ch. 561, Sec. 102. (AB 1516) Effective January 1, 2018.)

1259.5.

By January 1, 1995, each general acute care hospital, acute psychiatric hospital, special hospital, psychiatric health facility, and chemical dependency recovery hospital shall establish written policies and procedures to screen patients routinely for the purpose of detecting spousal or partner abuse. The policies shall include guidelines on all of the following:

(a) Identifying, through routine screening, spousal or partner abuse among patients.

(b) Documenting patient injuries or illnesses attributable to spousal or partner abuse.

(c) Educating appropriate hospital staff about the criteria for identifying, and the procedures for handling, patients whose injuries or illnesses are attributable to spousal or partner abuse.

(d) Advising patients exhibiting signs of spousal or partner abuse of crisis intervention services that are available either through the hospital facility or through community-based crisis intervention and counseling services.

(e) Providing to patients who exhibit signs of spousal or partner abuse information on domestic violence and a referral list, to be updated periodically, of private and public community agencies that provide, or arrange for, evaluation of and care for persons experiencing spousal or partner abuse, including, but not limited to, hot lines, local battered women's shelters, legal services, and information about temporary restraining orders.

(Amended by Stats. 1994, Ch. 146, Sec. 95. Effective January 1, 1995.)

1260.

(a) Except as provided in subdivision (b), any member of the board of directors of a nonprofit corporation that is subject to Section 5914 of the Corporations Code, who negotiates the terms and conditions of a sale or transfer of assets, as described in Section 5914 of the Corporations Code, is prohibited from receiving, directly or indirectly, any salary, compensation, payment, or other form of remuneration from the for-profit corporation or entity or mutual benefit corporation following the close of the sale or other transfer of assets. This prohibition shall not apply to any reimbursement or payment made to a member of the board of directors, who is a physician or other health care provider, for direct patient care services provided to patients covered by a health insurer, health care service plan, employer, or other entity that provides health care coverage, and that is owned, operated, or affiliated with the purchasing for-profit corporation or entity, provided that the amounts payable for the services rendered are no greater than the amounts payable to other physicians or health care providers providing the same or similar services.

For the purpose of this section, "direct patient care services" mean health care services provided directly to a patient, and do not include services provided through an intermediary. Further, in order to qualify for the exemption in this subdivision, the direct patient care services must be health care services that are regularly provided by other physicians or other health care providers in the community who are also receiving reimbursements or payments from the same health insurer, health care service plan, employer, or other entity that is owned or operated by, or affiliated with, the purchasing for-profit corporation or entity.

(b) After a period of two years following the close of the sale or other transfer of assets, a person who was a member of the board of directors of the nonprofit corporation who is prohibited from receiving any remuneration from the for-profit corporation or entity or mutual benefit corporation under subdivision (a) may enter into usual and customary business transactions with the for-profit corporation or entity or mutual benefit corporation so long as the following facts are established:

(1) Prior to authorizing or approving the transaction, the representative of the for-profit corporation or entity or mutual benefit corporation considered and in good faith determined after reasonable investigation under the circumstances that the corporation could not have obtained a more advantageous arrangement with reasonable effort under the circumstances.

(2) The for-profit corporation or entity or mutual benefit corporation, in fact could not have obtained a more advantageous arrangement with reasonable effort under the circumstances.

(c) Any person who is a member of management of the nonprofit corporation and who presents information or opinions to the board regarding the sale or other transfer of assets as described in subdivision (a) that are relied upon, or considered by, any of the board members in making decisions regarding the sale or transfer, may make a written affirmative declaration that he or she will not work for, or receive any form of remuneration from, the for-profit corporation or entity or the mutual benefit corporation in the future.

(d) In making any decision regarding the sale or other transfer of the nonprofit corporation's assets, as described in Section 5914 of the Corporations Code, the board of the nonprofit corporation is prohibited from substantially relying on any information presented by any person to whom subdivision (c) applies who has not made a written affirmative declaration pursuant to subdivision (c). This subdivision shall not apply to any person whose only role in the sale or transfer is to provide to the nonprofit corporation

exclusively factual information about the nonprofit corporation, community, financial status, or other similar data.

(e) In performing those duties of a director set forth in subdivision (d), the board of directors may contract with independent counsel, accountants, financial analysts, or other professionals whom the board believes to be reliable and competent in the matters presented, to review and evaluate information and advice presented by an employee who has not signed an affirmative declaration pursuant to subdivision (c). Any director who substantially relies on information and advice presented by such an independent professional shall be deemed to have not violated subdivision (d).

(Added by Stats. 1997, Ch. 890, Sec. 1. Effective October 12, 1997.)

1260.1.

(a) Except as provided in subdivision (b), any member of the board of directors of a nonprofit corporation that is subject to Section 5920 of the Corporations Code, who negotiates the terms and conditions of a sale or transfer of assets, as described in Section 5920 of the Corporations Code, is prohibited from receiving, directly or indirectly, any salary, compensation, payment, or other form of remuneration from the purchasing public benefit corporation or entity following the close of the sale or other transfer of assets. This prohibition shall not apply to any reimbursement or payment made to a member of the board of directors, who is a physician or other health care provider, for direct patient care services provided to patients covered by a health insurer, health care service plan, employer, or other entity that provides health care coverage, and that is owned, operated, or affiliated with the purchasing public benefit corporation or entity, provided that the amounts payable for the services rendered are no greater than the amounts payable to other physicians or health care providers providing the same or similar services.

For the purpose of this section, "direct patient care services" means health care services provided directly to a patient, and does not include services provided through an intermediary. Further, in order to qualify for the exemption in this subdivision, the direct patient care services must be health care services that are regularly provided by other physicians or other health care providers in the community who are also receiving reimbursements or payments from the same health insurer, health care service plan, employer, or other entity that is owned or operated by, or affiliated with, the purchasing public benefit corporation or entity.

(b) After a period of two years following the close of the sale or other transfer of assets, a person who was a member of the board of directors of the selling nonprofit corporation who is prohibited from receiving any remuneration from the purchasing public benefit corporation or entity under subdivision (a) may enter into usual and customary business transactions with the purchasing public benefit corporation or entity so long as the following facts are established:

(1) Prior to authorizing or approving the transaction, the representative of the purchasing public benefit corporation or entity considered and in good faith determined after reasonable investigation under the circumstances that the purchasing public benefit corporation could not have obtained a more advantageous arrangement with reasonable effort under the circumstances.

(2) The purchasing public benefit corporation or entity, in fact, could not have obtained a more advantageous arrangement with reasonable effort under the circumstances.

(c) Any person who is a member of management of the selling nonprofit corporation and who presents information or opinions to the board regarding the sale or other transfer of assets as described in subdivision (a) that are relied upon, or considered by, any of the board members in making decisions regarding the sale or transfer, may make a written affirmative declaration that he or she will not work for, or receive any form of remuneration from, the purchasing public benefit corporation or entity in the future.

(d) In making any decision regarding the sale or other transfer of the nonprofit corporation's assets, as described in Section 5920 of the Corporations Code, the board of the selling nonprofit corporation is prohibited from substantially relying on any information presented by any person to whom subdivision (c) applies who has not made a written affirmative declaration pursuant to subdivision (c). This subdivision shall not apply to any person whose only role in the sale or transfer is to provide to the selling nonprofit corporation exclusively factual information about the selling nonprofit corporation, community, financial status, or other similar data.

(e) In performing those duties of a director set forth in subdivision (d), the board of directors may contract with independent counsel, accountants, financial analysts, or other professionals whom the board believes to be reliable and competent in the matters presented, to review and evaluate information and advice presented by an employee who has not signed an affirmative declaration pursuant to subdivision (c). Any director who substantially relies on information and advice presented by the independent professional shall be deemed to have not violated subdivision (d).

(Added by Stats. 1999, Ch. 850, Sec. 12. Effective January 1, 2000.)

1261.

(a) A health facility shall allow a patient's domestic partner, the children of the patient's domestic partner, and the domestic partner of the patient's parent or child to visit, unless one of the following is met:

(1) No visitors are allowed.

(2) The facility reasonably determines that the presence of a particular visitor would endanger the health or safety of a patient, member of the health facility staff, or other visitor to the health facility, or would significantly disrupt the operations of a facility.

(3) The patient has indicated to health facility staff that the patient does not want this person to visit.

(b) This section may not be construed to prohibit a health facility from otherwise establishing reasonable restrictions upon visitation, including restrictions upon the hours of visitation and number of visitors.
(c) For purposes of this section, "domestic partner" has the same meaning as that term is used in Section 297 of the Family Code.
(Added by Stats. 1999, Ch. 588, Sec. 4. Effective January 1, 2000.)
1261.3.
(a) Notwithstanding any other provision of law, for a patient aged 50 years or older, a registered nurse or licensed pharmacist may administer in a skilled nursing facility, as defined in subdivision (c) of Section 1250, influenza and pneumococcal immunizations pursuant to standing orders and without patient-specific orders if all of the following criteria are met:
(1) The skilled nursing facility medical director, as defined in Section 72305 of Title 22 of the California Code of Regulations, has approved the immunization standing orders established by the facility.
(2) The standing orders meet the recommendations of the Advisory Committee on Immunization Practices (ACIP) of the federal Centers for Disease Control and Prevention.
(b) Nothing in this section amends, alters, or restricts the scope of registered nurse practice including, but not limited to, the scope of practice set forth in Article 2 (commencing with Section 2725) of Chapter 6 of Division 2 of the Business and Professions Code, the implementing regulations, and interpretative bulletins or practice advisories issued by the Board of Registered Nursing.
(Added by Stats. 2005, Ch. 58, Sec. 1. Effective January 1, 2006.)
1261.5.
(a) The number of oral dosage form or suppository form drugs provided by a pharmacy to a health facility licensed pursuant to subdivision (c) or (d), or both subdivisions (c) and (d), of Section 1250 of this code for storage in a secured emergency supplies container, pursuant to Section 4119 of the Business and Professions Code, shall be limited to 48. The State Department of Public Health may limit the number of doses of each drug available to not more than 16 doses of any separate drug dosage form in each emergency supply.
(b) Not more than four of the 48 oral form or suppository form drugs secured for storage in the emergency supplies container shall be psychotherapeutic drugs, except that the department may grant a program flexibility request to the facility to increase the number of psychotherapeutic drugs in the emergency supplies container to not more than 10 if the facility can demonstrate the necessity for an increased number of drugs based on the needs of the patient population at the facility. In addition, the four oral form or suppository form psychotherapeutic drug limit shall not apply to a special treatment program service unit distinct part, as defined in Section 1276.9. The department shall limit the number of doses of psychotherapeutic drugs available to not more than four doses in each emergency supply. Nothing in this section shall alter or diminish informed consent requirements, including, but not limited to, the requirements of Section 1418.9.
(c) Any limitations established pursuant to subdivisions (a) and (b) on the number and quantity of oral dosage or suppository form drugs provided by a pharmacy to a health facility licensed pursuant to subdivision (c) or (d), or both subdivisions (c) and (d), of Section 1250 for storage in a secured emergency supplies container shall not apply to an automated drug delivery system, as defined in Section 1261.6, when a pharmacist controls access to the drugs.
(Amended by Stats. 2010, Ch. 328, Sec. 111. (SB 1330) Effective January 1, 2011.)
1261.6.
(a) (1) For purposes of this section and Section 1261.5, an "automated drug delivery system" means a mechanical system that performs operations or activities, other than compounding or administration, relative to the storage, dispensing, or distribution of drugs. An automated drug delivery system shall collect, control, and maintain all transaction information to accurately track the movement of drugs into and out of the system for security, accuracy, and accountability.
(2) For purposes of this section, "facility" means a health facility licensed pursuant to subdivision (c), (d), or (k) of Section 1250 that has an automated drug delivery system provided by a pharmacy.
(3) For purposes of this section, "pharmacy services" means the provision of both routine and emergency drugs and biologicals to meet the needs of the patient, as prescribed by a physician.
(b) Transaction information shall be made readily available in a written format for review and inspection by individuals authorized by law. These records shall be maintained in the facility for a minimum of three years.
(c) Individualized and specific access to automated drug delivery systems shall be limited to facility and contract personnel authorized by law to administer drugs.
(d) (1) The facility and the pharmacy shall develop and implement written policies and procedures to ensure safety, accuracy, accountability, security, patient confidentiality, and maintenance of the quality, potency, and purity of stored drugs. Policies and procedures shall define access to the automated drug delivery system and limits to access to equipment and drugs.
(2) All policies and procedures shall be maintained at the pharmacy operating the automated drug delivery system and the location where the automated drug delivery system is being used.
(e) When used as an emergency pharmaceutical supplies container, drugs removed from the automated drug delivery system shall be limited to the following:
(1) A new drug order given by a prescriber for a patient of the facility for administration prior to the next scheduled delivery from the pharmacy, or 72 hours, whichever is less. The drugs shall be retrieved only upon authorization by a pharmacist and after the pharmacist has reviewed the prescriber's order and the patient's profile for potential contraindications and adverse drug reactions.
(2) Drugs that a prescriber has ordered for a patient on an as-needed basis, if the utilization and retrieval of those drugs are subject to ongoing review by a pharmacist.
(3) Drugs designed by the patient care policy committee or pharmaceutical service committee of the facility as emergency drugs or acute onset drugs. These drugs may be retrieved from an automated drug delivery system pursuant to the order of a prescriber for emergency or immediate administration to a patient of the facility. Within 48 hours after retrieval under this paragraph, the case shall be reviewed by a pharmacist.
(f) When used to provide pharmacy services pursuant to Section 4119.1 of the Business and Professions Code, the automated drug delivery system shall be subject to all of the following requirements:
(1) Drugs removed from the automated drug delivery system for administration to a patient shall be in properly labeled units of administration containers or packages.
(2) A pharmacist shall review and approve all orders prior to a drug being removed from the automated drug delivery system for administration to a patient. The pharmacist shall review the prescriber's order and the patient's profile for potential contraindications and adverse drug reactions.
(3) The pharmacy providing services to the facility pursuant to Section 4119.1 of the Business and Professions Code shall control access to the drugs stored in the automated drug delivery system.
(4) Access to the automated drug delivery system shall be controlled and tracked using an identification or password system or biosensor.
(5) The automated drug delivery system shall make a complete and accurate record of all transactions that will include all users accessing the system and all drugs added to, or removed from, the system.
(6) After the pharmacist reviews the prescriber's order, access by licensed personnel to the automated drug delivery system shall be limited only to drugs ordered by the prescriber and reviewed by the pharmacist and that are specific to the patient. When the prescriber's order requires a dosage variation of the same drug, licensed personnel shall have access to the drug ordered for that scheduled time of administration.
(7) (A) Systems that allow licensed personnel to have access to multiple drugs and are not patient specific in their design, shall be allowed under this subdivision if those systems have electronic and mechanical safeguards in place to ensure that the drugs delivered to the patient are specific to that patient. Each facility using such an automated drug system shall notify the department in writing prior to the utilization of the system. The notification submitted to the department pursuant to this paragraph shall include, but is not limited to, information regarding system design, personnel with system access, and policies and procedures covering staff training, storage, and security, and the facility's administration of these types of systems.
(B) As part of its routine oversight of these facilities, the department shall review a facility's medication training, storage, and security, and its administration procedures related to its use of an automated drug delivery system to ensure that adequate staff training and safeguards are in place to make sure that the drugs delivered are appropriate for the patient. If the department determines that a facility is not in compliance with this section, the department may revoke its authorization to use automated drug delivery systems granted under subparagraph (A).
(g) The stocking of an automated drug delivery system shall be performed by a pharmacist. If the automated drug delivery system utilizes removable pockets, cards, drawers, similar technology, or unit of use or single dose containers as defined by the United States Pharmacopoeia, the stocking system may be done outside of the facility and be delivered to the facility if all of the following conditions are met:
(1) The task of placing drugs into the removable pockets, cards, drawers, or unit of use or single dose containers is performed by a pharmacist, or by an intern pharmacist or a pharmacy technician working under the direct supervision of a pharmacist.
(2) The removable pockets, cards, drawers, or unit of use or single dose containers are transported between the pharmacy and the facility in a secure tamper-evident container.
(3) The facility, in conjunction with the pharmacy, has developed policies and procedures to ensure that the removable pockets, cards, drawers, or unit of use or single dose containers are properly placed into the automated drug delivery system.
(h) Review of the drugs contained within, and the operation and maintenance of, the automated drug delivery system shall be done in accordance with law and shall be the responsibility of the pharmacy. The review shall be conducted on a monthly basis by a pharmacist and shall include a physical inspection of the drugs in the automated drug delivery system, an inspection of the automated drug delivery system machine for cleanliness, and a review of all transaction records in order to verify the security and accountability of the system.
(i) Drugs dispensed from an automated drug delivery system that meets the requirements of this section shall not be subject to the labeling requirements of Section 4076 of the Business and Professions Code or Section 111480 of this code if the drugs to be placed into the automated drug delivery system are in unit dose packaging or unit of use and if the information required by Section 4076 of the Business and Professions Code and Section 111480 of this code is readily available at the time of drug administration. For purposes of this section, unit dose packaging includes blister pack cards.
(j) This section shall become inoperative on July 1, 2019, and, as of January 1, 2020, is repealed.
(Amended by Stats. 2018, Ch. 666, Sec. 10. (SB 1447) Effective January 1, 2019. Section operative July 1, 2019. Repealed as of January 1, 2020, by its own provisions. See later operative version added by Stats. 2018, Ch. 666.)

1261.6.

(a) (1) For purposes of this section and Section 1261.5, an "automated drug delivery system" means a mechanical system that performs operations or activities, other than compounding or administration, relative to the storage, dispensing, or distribution of drugs. An automated drug delivery system shall collect, control, and maintain all transaction information to accurately track the movement of drugs into and out of the system for security, accuracy, and accountability.

(2) For purposes of this section, "facility" means a health facility licensed pursuant to subdivision (c), (d), or (k) of Section 1250 that has an automated drug delivery system provided by a pharmacy.

(3) For purposes of this section, "pharmacy services" means the provision of both routine and emergency drugs and biologicals to meet the needs of the patient, as prescribed by a physician.

(b) Transaction information shall be made readily available in a written format for review and inspection by individuals authorized by law. These records shall be maintained in the facility for a minimum of three years.

(c) Individualized and specific access to automated drug delivery systems shall be limited to facility and contract personnel authorized by law to administer drugs.

(d) (1) The facility and the pharmacy shall develop and implement written policies and procedures to ensure safety, accuracy, accountability, security, patient confidentiality, and maintenance of the quality, potency, and purity of stored drugs. Policies and procedures shall define access to the automated drug delivery system and limits to access to equipment and drugs.

(2) All policies and procedures shall be maintained at the pharmacy operating the automated drug delivery system and the location where the automated drug delivery system is being used.

(e) When used as an emergency pharmaceutical supplies container, drugs removed from the automated drug delivery system shall be limited to the following:

(1) A new drug order given by a prescriber for a patient of the facility for administration prior to the next scheduled delivery from the pharmacy, or 72 hours, whichever is less. The drugs shall be retrieved only upon authorization by a pharmacist and after the pharmacist has reviewed the prescriber's order and the patient's profile for potential contraindications and adverse drug reactions.

(2) Drugs that a prescriber has ordered for a patient on an as-needed basis, if the utilization and retrieval of those drugs are subject to ongoing review by a pharmacist.

(3) Drugs designed by the patient care policy committee or pharmaceutical service committee of the facility as emergency drugs or acute onset drugs. These drugs may be retrieved from an automated drug delivery system pursuant to the order of a prescriber for emergency or immediate administration to a patient of the facility. Within 48 hours after retrieval under this paragraph, the case shall be reviewed by a pharmacist.

(f) When used to provide pharmacy services pursuant to Section 4017.3 of, and Article 25 (commencing with Section 4427) of Chapter 9 of Division 2 of, the Business and Professions Code, the automated drug delivery system shall be subject to all of the following requirements:

(1) Drugs removed from the automated drug delivery system for administration to a patient shall be in properly labeled units of administration containers or packages.

(2) A pharmacist shall review and approve all orders prior to a drug being removed from the automated drug delivery system for administration to a patient. The pharmacist shall review the prescriber's order and the patient's profile for potential contraindications and adverse drug reactions.

(3) The pharmacy providing services to the facility pursuant to Article 25 (commencing with Section 4427) of Chapter 9 of Division 2 of the Business and Professions Code shall control access to the drugs stored in the automated drug delivery system.

(4) Access to the automated drug delivery system shall be controlled and tracked using an identification or password system or biosensor.

(5) The automated drug delivery system shall make a complete and accurate record of all transactions that will include all users accessing the system and all drugs added to, or removed from, the system.

(6) After the pharmacist reviews the prescriber's order, access by licensed personnel to the automated drug delivery system shall be limited only to drugs ordered by the prescriber and reviewed by the pharmacist and that are specific to the patient. When the prescriber's order requires a dosage variation of the same drug, licensed personnel shall have access to the drug ordered for that scheduled time of administration.

(7) (A) Systems that allow licensed personnel to have access to multiple drugs and are not patient specific in their design, shall be allowed under this subdivision if those systems have electronic and mechanical safeguards in place to ensure that the drugs delivered to the patient are specific to that patient. Each facility using such an automated drug delivery system shall notify the department in writing prior to the utilization of the system. The notification submitted to the department pursuant to this paragraph shall include, but is not limited to, information regarding system design, personnel with system access, and policies and procedures covering staff training, storage, and security, and the facility's administration of these types of systems.

(B) As part of its routine oversight of these facilities, the department shall review a facility's medication training, storage, and security, and its administration procedures related to its use of an automated drug delivery system to ensure that adequate staff training and safeguards are in place to make sure that the drugs delivered are appropriate for the patient. If the department determines that a facility is not in compliance with this section, the department may revoke its authorization to use automated drug delivery systems granted under subparagraph (A).

(g) The stocking of an automated drug delivery system shall be performed by a pharmacist. If the automated drug delivery system utilizes removable pockets, cards, drawers, similar technology, or unit of use or single dose containers as defined by the United States Pharmacopoeia, the stocking system may be done outside of the facility and be delivered to the facility if all of the following conditions are met:

(1) The task of placing drugs into the removable pockets, cards, drawers, or unit of use or single dose containers is performed by a pharmacist, or by an intern pharmacist or a pharmacy technician working under the direct supervision of a pharmacist.

(2) The removable pockets, cards, drawers, or unit of use or single dose containers are transported between the pharmacy and the facility in a secure tamper-evident container.

(3) The facility, in conjunction with the pharmacy, has developed policies and procedures to ensure that the removable pockets, cards, drawers, or unit of use or single dose containers are properly placed into the automated drug delivery system.

(h) Review of the drugs contained within, and the operation and maintenance of, the automated drug delivery system shall be done in accordance with law and shall be the responsibility of the pharmacy. The review shall be conducted on a monthly basis by a pharmacist and shall include a physical inspection of the drugs in the automated drug delivery system, an inspection of the automated drug delivery system machine for cleanliness, and a review of all transaction records in order to verify the security and accountability of the system.

(i) Drugs dispensed from an automated drug delivery system that meets the requirements of this section shall not be subject to the labeling requirements of Section 4076 of the Business and Professions Code or Section 111480 of this code if the drugs to be placed into the automated drug delivery system are in unit dose packaging or unit of use and if the information required by Section 4076 of the Business and Professions Code and Section 111480 of this code is readily available at the time of drug administration. For purposes of this section, unit dose packaging includes blister pack cards.

(j) This section shall become operative on July 1, 2019.

(Repealed and added by Stats. 2018, Ch. 666, Sec. 11. (SB 1447) Effective January 1, 2019. Section operative July 1, 2019, by its own provisions.)

1262.

(a) When a mental health patient is being discharged from one of the facilities specified in subdivision (c), the patient and the patient's conservator, guardian, or other legally authorized representative shall be given a written aftercare plan prior to the patient's discharge from the facility. The written aftercare plan shall include, to the extent known, all of the following components:

(1) The nature of the illness and followup required.

(2) Medications including side effects and dosage schedules. If the patient was given an informed consent form with his or her medications, the form shall satisfy the requirement for information on side effects of the medications.

(3) Expected course of recovery.

(4) Recommendations regarding treatment that are relevant to the patient's care.

(5) Referrals to providers of medical and mental health services.

(6) Other relevant information.

(b) The patient shall be advised by facility personnel that he or she may designate another person to receive a copy of the aftercare plan. A copy of the aftercare plan shall be given to any person designated by the patient.

(c) Subdivision (a) applies to all of the following facilities:

(1) A state mental hospital.

(2) A general acute care hospital as described in subdivision (a) of Section 1250.

(3) An acute psychiatric hospital as described in subdivision (b) of Section 1250.

(4) A psychiatric health facility as described in Section 1250.2.

(5) A mental health rehabilitation center as described in Section 5675 of the Welfare and Institutions Code.

(6) A skilled nursing facility with a special treatment program, as described in Section 51335 and Sections 72443 to 72475, inclusive, of Title 22 of the California Code of Regulations.

(d) For purposes of this section, "mental health patient" means a person who is admitted to the facility primarily for the diagnosis or treatment of a mental disorder. (Amended by Stats. 1998, Ch. 346, Sec. 1. Effective January 1, 1999.)

1262.4.

(a) No hospital, as defined in subdivisions (a), (b), and (f) of Section 1250, may cause the transfer of homeless patients from one county to another county for the purpose of receiving supportive services from a social services agency, health care service provider, or nonprofit social services provider within the other county, without prior notification to, and authorization from, the social services agency, health care service provider, or nonprofit social services provider.

(b) For purposes of this section, "homeless patient" means an individual who lacks a fixed and regular nighttime residence, or who has a primary nighttime residence that is a supervised publicly or privately operated shelter designed to provide temporary living accommodations, or who is residing in a public or private place that was not designed to provide temporary living accommodations or to be used as a sleeping accommodation for human beings.

(Amended by Stats. 2007, Ch. 130, Sec. 152. Effective January 1, 2008.)

1262.5.

(a) Each hospital shall have a written discharge planning policy and process.

(b) The policy required by subdivision (a) shall require that appropriate arrangements for posthospital care, including, but not limited to, care at home, in a skilled nursing or intermediate care facility, or from a hospice, are made prior to discharge for those patients who are likely to suffer adverse health consequences upon discharge if there is no adequate discharge planning. If the hospital determines that the patient and family members or interested persons need to be counseled to prepare them for posthospital care, the hospital shall provide for that counseling.

(c) As part of the discharge planning process, the hospital shall provide each patient who has been admitted to the hospital as an inpatient with an opportunity to identify one family caregiver who may assist in posthospital care, and shall record this information in the patient's medical chart.

(1) In the event that the patient is unconscious or otherwise incapacitated upon admittance to the hospital, the hospital shall provide the patient or patient's legal guardian with an opportunity to designate a caregiver within a specified time period, at the discretion of the attending physician, following the patient's recovery of consciousness or capacity. The hospital shall promptly document the attempt in the patient's medical record.

(2) In the event that the patient or legal guardian declines to designate a caregiver pursuant to this section, the hospital shall promptly document this declination in the patient's medical record, when appropriate.

(d) The policy required by subdivision (a) shall require that the patient's designated family caregiver be notified of the patient's discharge or transfer to another facility as soon as possible and, in any event, upon issuance of a discharge order by the patient's attending physician. If the hospital is unable to contact the designated caregiver, the lack of contact shall not interfere with, delay, or otherwise affect the medical care provided to the patient or an appropriate discharge of the patient. The hospital shall promptly document the attempted notification in the patient's medical record.

(e) The process required by subdivision (a) shall require that the patient and family caregiver be informed of the continuing health care requirements following discharge from the hospital. The right to information regarding continuing health care requirements following discharge shall also apply to the person who has legal responsibility to make decisions regarding medical care on behalf of the patient, if the patient is unable to make those decisions for himself or herself. The hospital shall provide an opportunity for the patient and his or her designated family caregiver to engage in the discharge planning process, which shall include providing information and, when appropriate, instruction regarding the posthospital care needs of the patient. This information shall include, but is not limited to, education and counseling about the patient's medications, including dosing and proper use of medication delivery devices, when applicable. The information shall be provided in a culturally competent manner and in a language that is comprehensible to the patient and caregiver, consistent with the requirements of state and federal law, and shall include an opportunity for the caregiver to ask questions about the posthospital care needs of the patient.

(f) (1) A transfer summary shall accompany the patient upon transfer to a skilled nursing or intermediate care facility or to the distinct part-skilled nursing or intermediate care service unit of the hospital. The transfer summary shall include essential information relative to the patient's diagnosis, hospital course, pain treatment and management, medications, treatments, dietary requirement, rehabilitation potential, known allergies, and treatment plan, and shall be signed by the physician.

(2) A copy of the transfer summary shall be given to the patient and the patient's legal representative, if any, prior to transfer to a skilled nursing or intermediate care facility.

(g) A hospital shall establish and implement a written policy to ensure that each patient receives, at the time of discharge, information regarding each medication dispensed, pursuant to Section 4074 of the Business and Professions Code.

(h) A hospital shall provide every patient anticipated to be in need of long-term care at the time of discharge with contact information for at least one public or nonprofit agency or organization dedicated to providing information or referral services relating to community-based long-term care options in the patient's county of residence and appropriate to the needs and characteristics of the patient. At a minimum, this information shall include contact information for the area agency on aging serving the patient's county of residence, local independent living centers, or other information appropriate to the needs and characteristics of the patient.

(i) A contract between a general acute care hospital and a health care service plan that is issued, amended, renewed, or delivered on or after January 1, 2002, shall not contain a provision that prohibits or restricts any health care facility's compliance with the requirements of this section.

(j) Discharge planning policies adopted by a hospital in accordance with this section shall ensure that planning is appropriate to the condition of the patient being discharged from the hospital and to the discharge destination and meets the needs and acuity of patients.

(k) This section does not require a hospital to do any of the following:

(1) Adopt a policy that would delay discharge or transfer of a patient.

(2) Disclose information if the patient has not provided consent that meets the standards required by state and federal laws governing the privacy and security of protected health information.

(3) Comply with the requirements of this section in an area of the hospital where clinical care is provided, unless medically indicated.

(l) This section does not supersede or modify any privacy and information security requirements and protections in federal and state law regarding protected health information or personally identifiable information, including, but not limited to, the federal Health Insurance Portability and Accountability Act of 1996 (42 U.S.C. Sec. 300gg).

(m) For the purposes of this section, "family caregiver" means a relative, friend, or neighbor who provides assistance related to an underlying physical or mental disability but who is unpaid for those services.

(n) (1) Each hospital, as defined in subdivisions (a), (b), and (f) of Section 1250, shall include within its hospital discharge policy a written homeless patient discharge planning policy and process.

(2) The policy shall require a hospital to inquire about a patient's housing status during the discharge planning process. Housing status may not be used to discriminate against a patient or prevent medically necessary care or hospital admission.

(3) The policy shall require an individual discharge plan for a homeless patient that helps prepare the homeless patient for return to the community by connecting him or her with available community resources, treatment, shelter, and other supportive services. The discharge planning shall be guided by the best interests of the homeless patient, his or her physical and mental condition, and the homeless patient's preferences for placement. The homeless patient shall be informed of available placement options.

(4) Unless the homeless patient is being transferred to another licensed health facility, the policy shall require the hospital to identify a postdischarge destination for the homeless patient as follows, with priority given to identifying a sheltered destination with supportive services:

(A) A social services agency, nonprofit social services provider, or governmental service provider that has agreed to accept the homeless patient, if he or she has agreed to the placement. Notwithstanding paragraph (2) of subdivision (k) and subdivision (l), the hospital shall provide potential receiving agencies or providers written or electronic information about the homeless patient's known posthospital health and behavioral health care needs and shall document the name of the person at the agency or provider who agreed to accept the homeless patient.

(B) The homeless patient's residence. In the case of a homeless patient, "residence" for the purposes of this subparagraph means the location identified to the hospital by the homeless patient as his or her principal dwelling place.

(C) An alternative destination, as indicated by the homeless patient pursuant to the discharge planning process described in paragraph (3). The hospital shall document the destination indicated by the homeless patient or his or her representative.

(5) The policy shall require that information regarding discharge or transfer be provided to the homeless patient in a culturally competent manner and in a language that is understood by the homeless patient.

(o) The hospital shall document all of the following prior to discharging a homeless patient:

(1) The treating physician has determined the homeless patient's clinical stability for discharge, including, but not limited to, an assessment as to whether the patient is alert and oriented to person, place, and time, and the physician or designee has communicated postdischarge medical needs to the homeless patient.

(2) The homeless patient has been offered a meal, unless medically indicated otherwise.

(3) If the homeless patient's clothing is inadequate, the hospital shall offer the homeless patient weather-appropriate clothing.

(4) The homeless patient has been referred to a source of followup care, if medically necessary.

(5) The homeless patient has been provided with a prescription, if needed, and, for a hospital with an onsite pharmacy licensed and staffed to dispense outpatient medication, an appropriate supply of all necessary medication, if available.

(6) The homeless patient has been offered or referred to screening for infectious disease common to the region, as determined by the local health department.

(7) The homeless patient has been offered vaccinations appropriate to the homeless patient's presenting medical condition.

(8) The treating physician has provided a medical screening examination and evaluation. If the treating physician determines that the results of the medical screening examination and evaluation indicate that followup behavioral health care is needed, the homeless patient shall be treated or referred to an appropriate provider. The hospital shall make a good faith effort to contact one of the following, if applicable:

(A) The homeless patient's health plan, if the homeless patient is enrolled in a health plan.

(B) The homeless patient's primary care provider, if the patient has identified one.

(C) Another appropriate provider, including, but not limited to, the coordinated entry system.

(9) The homeless patient has been screened for, and provided assistance to enroll in, any affordable health insurance coverage for which he or she is eligible.

(10) The hospital has offered the homeless patient transportation after discharge to the destination identified in paragraph (4) of subdivision (n), if that destination is within a maximum travel time of 30 minutes or a maximum travel distance of 30 miles of the hospital. This requirement shall not be construed to prevent a hospital from offering transportation to a more distant destination.

(p) A hospital shall develop a written plan for coordinating services and referrals for homeless patients with the county behavioral health agency, health care and social services agencies in the region, health care providers, and nonprofit social services providers, as available, to assist with ensuring appropriate homeless patient discharge. The plan shall be updated annually and shall include all of the following:

(1) A list of local homeless shelters, including their hours of operation, admission procedures and requirements, client population served, and general scope of medical and behavioral health services available.

(2) The hospital's procedures for homeless patient discharge referrals to shelter, medical care, and behavioral health care.

(3) The contact information for the homeless shelter's intake coordinator.

(4) Training protocols for discharge planning staff.

(q) Each hospital shall maintain a log of homeless patients discharged and the destinations to which they were released after discharge pursuant to paragraph (10) of subdivision (o), if any. The hospital shall maintain evidence of completion of the homeless patient discharge protocol in the log or in the patient's medical record.

(r) For purposes of this section, "homeless patient" has the same meaning as provided in Section 1262.4.

(s) It is the intent of the Legislature that nothing in this section shall be construed to preempt, limit, prohibit, or otherwise affect, the adoption, implementation, or enforcement of local ordinances, codes, regulations, or orders related to the homeless patient discharge processes, except to the extent that any such provision of law is inconsistent with the provisions of this section, and then only to the extent of the inconsistency. A local ordinance, code, regulation, or order is not deemed inconsistent with this section if it affords greater protection to homeless patients than the requirements set forth in this section. Where local ordinances, codes, regulations, or orders duplicate or supplement this section, this section shall be construed as providing alternative remedies and shall not be construed to preempt the field.

(t) Nothing in this section alters the health and social service obligations described in Section 17000 of the Welfare and Institutions Code.

(u) Subdivisions (n) to (t), inclusive, do not apply to the state hospitals under the jurisdiction of the State Department of State Hospitals, as specified in Sections 4100 and 7200 of the Welfare and Institutions Code.

(v) This section shall become operative on July 1, 2019.

(Repealed and added by Stats. 2018, Ch. 981, Sec. 2. (SB 1152) Effective January 1, 2019. Section operative July 1, 2019, by its own provisions.)

1262.6.

(a) Each hospital shall provide each patient, upon admission or as soon thereafter as reasonably practical, written information regarding the patient's right to the following:

(1) To be informed of continuing health care requirements following discharge from the hospital.

(2) To be informed that, if the patient so authorizes, that a friend or family member may be provided information about the patient's continuing health care requirements following discharge from the hospital.

(3) Participate actively in decisions regarding medical care. To the extent permitted by law, participation shall include the right to refuse treatment.

(4) Appropriate pain assessment and treatment consistent with Sections 124960 and 124961.

(b) A hospital may include the information required by this section with other notices to the patient regarding patient rights. If a hospital chooses to include this information along with existing notices to the patient regarding patient rights, this information shall be provided when the hospital exhausts its existing inventory of written materials and prints new written materials.

(Added by Stats. 2001, Ch. 691, Sec. 3. Effective January 1, 2002.)

1262.7.

(a) A skilled nursing facility, as defined in subdivision (c) of Section 1250, shall admit a patient only upon a physician's order and only if the facility is able to provide necessary care for the patient.

(b) The administrator or designee of a skilled nursing facility shall be responsible for screening patients for admission to the facility to ensure that the facility admits only those patients for whom it can provide necessary care. The administrator, or his or her designee, shall conduct preadmission personal interviews as appropriate with the patient's physician, the patient, the patient's next of kin or sponsor, or the representative of the facility from which the patient is being transferred. A telephone interview may be conducted when a personal interview is not feasible.

(Added by Stats. 2001, Ch. 691, Sec. 4. Effective January 1, 2002.)

1262.8.

(a) A noncontracting hospital shall not bill a patient who is an enrollee of a health care service plan for poststabilization care, except for applicable copayments, coinsurance, and deductibles, unless one of the following conditions are met:

(1) The patient or the patient's spouse or legal guardian refuses to consent, pursuant to subdivision (f), for the patient to be transferred to the contracting hospital as requested and arranged for by the patient's health care service plan.

(2) The hospital is unable to obtain the name and contact information of the patient's health care service plan as provided in subdivision (c).

(b) If a patient with an emergency medical condition, as defined by Section 1317.1, is covered by a health care service plan that requires prior authorization for poststabilization care, a noncontracting hospital, except as provided in subdivision (n), shall, prior to providing poststabilization care, do all of the following once the emergency medical condition has been stabilized, as defined by Section 1317.1:

(1) Seek to obtain the name and contact information of the patient's health care service plan. The hospital shall document its attempt to ascertain this information in the patient's medical record, which shall include requesting the patient's health care service plan member card or asking the patient, or a family member or other person accompanying the patient, if he or she can identify the patient's health care service plan, or any other means known to the hospital for accurately identifying the patient's health care service plan.

(2) Contact the patient's health care service plan, or the health plan's contracting medical provider, for authorization to provide poststabilization care, if identification of the plan was obtained pursuant to paragraph (1).

(A) The hospital shall make the contact described in this subparagraph by either following the instructions on the patient's health care service plan member card or using the contact information provided by the patient's health care service plan pursuant to subdivision (j) or (k).

(B) A representative of the hospital shall not be required to make more than one telephone call to the health care service plan, or its contracting medical provider, provided that in all cases the health care service plan, or its contracting medical provider, shall be able to reach a representative of the hospital upon returning the call, should the plan, or its contracting medical provider, need to call back. The representative of the hospital who makes the telephone call may be, but is not required to be, a physician and surgeon.

(3) Upon request of the patient's health care service plan, or the health plan's contracting medical provider, provide to the plan, or its contracting medical provider, the treating physician and surgeon's diagnosis and any other relevant information reasonably necessary for the health care service plan or the plan's contracting medical provider to make a decision to authorize poststabilization care or to assume management of the patient's care by prompt transfer.

(c) A noncontracting hospital that is not able to obtain the name and contact information of the patient's health care service plan pursuant to subdivision (b) is not subject to the requirements of this section.

(d) (1) A health care service plan, or its contracting medical provider, that is contacted by a noncontracting hospital pursuant to paragraph (2) of subdivision (b), shall, within 30 minutes from the time the noncontracting hospital makes the initial contact, do either of the following:

(A) Authorize poststabilization care.

(B) Inform the noncontracting hospital that it will arrange for the prompt transfer of the enrollee to another hospital.

(2) If the health care service plan, or its contracting medical provider, does not notify the noncontracting hospital of its decision pursuant to paragraph (1) within 30 minutes, the poststabilization care shall be deemed authorized, and the health care service plan, or its contracting medical provider, shall pay charges for the care, in accordance with the Knox-Keene Health Care Service Plan Act of 1975 (Chapter 2.2 (commencing with Section 1340) of Division 2) and any regulation adopted thereunder.

(3) If the health care service plan, or its contracting medical provider, notified the noncontracting hospital that it would assume management of the patient's care by prompt transfer, but either the health care service plan or its contracting medical provider fails to transfer the patient within a reasonable time, the poststabilization care shall be deemed authorized, and the health care service plan, or its contracting medical provider, shall pay charges, in accordance with the Knox-Keene Health Care Service Plan Act of 1975 (Chapter 2.2 (commencing with Section 1340) of Division 2 of the Health and Safety Code) and any regulation adopted thereunder, for the care until the enrollee is transferred.

(4) If the health care service plan, or its contracting medical provider, provides authorization to the noncontracting hospital for specified poststabilization care and services, the health care service plan, or its contracting medical provider, shall be responsible to pay for that authorized care.

(e) If a health care service plan, or its contracting medical provider, decides to assume management of the patient's care by prompt transfer, the health care service plan, or its contracting medical provider, shall do all of the following:

(1) Arrange and pay the reasonable charges associated with the transfer of the patient.

(2) Pay for all of the immediately required medically necessary care rendered to the patient prior to the transfer in order to maintain the patient's clinical stability.

(3) Be responsible for making all arrangements for the patient's transfer, including, but not limited to, finding a contracted facility available for the transfer of the patient.

(f) (1) If the patient, or the patient's spouse or legal guardian refuses to consent to the patient's transfer under subdivision (e), the noncontracting hospital shall promptly provide a written notice to the patient or the patient's spouse or legal guardian indicating that the patient will be financially responsible for any further poststabilization care provided by the hospital.

(2) For patients whose primary language is one of the Medi-Cal threshold languages, the notice shall be delivered to them in their primary language.

(3) The Department of Managed Health Care shall translate the notice required by this subdivision in all Medi-Cal threshold languages and make the translations available to the hospitals subject to this section.

(4) The written notice provided pursuant to this subdivision shall include the following statement:

THIS NOTICE MUST BE PROVIDED TO YOU UNDER CALIFORNIA LAW

"You have received emergency care at a hospital that is not a part of your health plan's provider network. Under state law, emergency care must be paid by your health plan no matter where you get that care. The doctor who is caring for you has decided that you may be safely moved to another hospital for the additional care you need. Because you no longer need emergency care, your health plan has not authorized further care at this hospital. Your health plan has arranged for you to be moved to a hospital that is in your health plan's provider network.

If you agree to be moved, your health plan will pay for your care at that hospital. You will only have to pay for your deductible, copayments, or coinsurance for care. You will not have to pay for your deductible, copayments, or coinsurance for transportation costs to another hospital that is covered by your health plan.

IF YOU CHOOSE TO STAY AT THIS HOSPITAL FOR YOUR ADDITIONAL CARE, YOU WILL HAVE TO PAY THE FULL COST OF CARE NOW THAT YOU NO LONGER NEED EMERGENCY CARE. This cost may include the cost of the doctor or doctors, the hospital, and any laboratory, radiology, or other services that you receive.

If you do not think you can be safely moved, talk to the doctor about your concerns. If you would like additional help, you may contact:

Your health plan member services department. Look on your health plan member card for that phone number. You can file a grievance with your plan.

The HMO Helpline at 888-HMO-2219. The HMO Helpline is available 24 hours a day, 7 days a week. The HMO Helpline can work with your health plan to address your concerns, but you may still have to pay the full cost of care at this hospital if you stay."

(5) The hospital shall give one copy of the written notice required by this subdivision to the patient, or the patient's spouse or legal guardian, for signature and may retain a copy in the patient's medical record.

(6) The hospital shall ensure prompt delivery of the notice to the patient or his or her spouse or legal guardian. The hospital shall obtain signed acceptance of the written notice required by this subdivision, and signed acceptance of any other documents the hospital requires for any further poststabilization care, from the patient or the patient's spouse or legal guardian, and shall provide the health care service plan, or its contracting medical provider, with confirmation of the patient's, or his or her spouse or legal guardian's, receipt of the written notice.

(7) If the noncontracting hospital fails to meet the requirements of this subdivision, the hospital shall not bill the patient or the patient's health care service plan, or its contracting medical provider, for poststabilization care provided to the patient.

(8) If the patient, or the patient's spouse or legal guardian, refuses to sign the notice, the noncontracting hospital shall document in the patient's medical record that the notice was provided and signature was refused. Upon the patient's refusal to sign, the patient shall assume financial responsibility for any further poststabilization care provided by the hospital.

(9) The Department of Managed Health Care may, by regulation, modify the wording of the notice required under this subdivision for clarity, readability, and accuracy of the information provided.

(10) The Department of Managed Health Care may, in conjunction with consumer groups, health care service plans, and hospitals, modify the wording of the notice to include language regarding Medicare beneficiaries, if appropriate under Medicare rules. The initial modification shall not be subject to the Administrative Procedure Act (Chapter 3.5 (commencing with Section 11340, et. seq.) of Part 1 of Division 3 of Title 2 of the Government Code).

(g) If poststabilization care has been authorized by the health care service plan, the noncontracting hospital shall request the patient's medical record from the patient's health care service plan or its contracting medical provider.

(h) The health care service plan, or its contracting medical provider, shall, upon conferring with the noncontracting hospital, transmit any appropriate portion of the patient's medical record, if the records are in the plan's possession, via facsimile transmission or electronic mail, whichever method is requested by the noncontracting hospital's representative or the noncontracting physician and surgeon. The health care service plan, or its contracting medical provider, shall transmit the patient's medical record in a manner that complies with all legal requirements to protect the patient's privacy.

(i) A health care service plan, or its contracting medical provider, that requires prior authorization for poststabilization care shall provide 24-hour access for patients and providers, including noncontracting hospitals, to obtain timely authorization for medically necessary poststabilization care.

(j) A health care service plan shall provide all noncontracting hospitals in the state with specific contact information needed to make the contact required by this section. The contact information provided to hospitals shall be updated as necessary, but no less than once a year.

(k) In addition to meeting the requirements of subdivision (j), a health care service plan shall provide the contact information described in subdivision (j) to the Department of Managed Health Care. The contact information provided pursuant to this subdivision shall be updated as necessary, but no less than once a year. The receiving department shall post this contact information on its Internet Web site no later than January 1 of each calendar year.

(l) This section shall only apply to a noncontracting hospital.

(m) For purposes of this section, the following definitions shall apply:

(1) "Health care service plan" means a health care service plan licensed pursuant to Chapter 2.2 (commencing with Section 1340) of Division 2 that covers hospital, medical, or surgical expenses.

(2) "Noncontracting hospital" means a general acute care hospital, as defined in subdivision (a) of Section 1250 or an acute psychiatric hospital, as defined in subdivision (b) of Section 1250, that does not have a written contract with the patient's health care service plan to provide health care services to the patient.

(3) "Poststabilization care" means medically necessary care provided after an emergency medical condition has been stabilized, as defined by subdivision (j) of Section 1317.1.

(4) "Contracting medical provider" means a medical group, independent practice association, or any other similar organization that, pursuant to a signed written contract, has agreed to accept responsibility for provision or reimbursement of a noncontracting hospital for emergency and poststabilization services provided to a health plan's enrollees.

(n) Subdivisions (b) to (h), inclusive, shall not apply to minor treatment procedures, if all of the following apply:

(1) The procedure is provided in the treatment area of the emergency department.

(2) The procedure concludes the treatment of the presenting emergency medical condition of a patient and is related to that condition, even though the treatment may not resolve the underlying medical condition.

(3) The procedure is performed according to accepted standards of practice.

(4) The procedure would result in the direct discharge or release of the patient from the emergency department following this care.

(o) Nothing in this section is intended to prevent a health care service plan or its contracting medical provider from assuming management of the patient's care at any time after the initial provision of poststabilization care by the noncontracting hospital before the patient has been discharged. Upon the request of the health care service plan or its contracting medical provider, the noncontracting hospital shall provide the health care service plan or its contracting medical provider with any information specified in paragraph (3) of subdivision (b).

(p) Nothing in this section shall authorize a provider of health care services to bill a Medi-Cal beneficiary enrolled in a Medi-Cal managed care plan or otherwise alter the provisions of subdivision (a) of Section 14019.3 of the Welfare and Institutions Code. (Repealed and added by Stats. 2008, Ch. 603, Sec. 2. Effective January 1, 2009.)

1263.

(a) This section shall be known and may be cited as the Dementia Training Standards Act of 2001.

(b) (1) Any certified nurse assistant employed by a skilled nursing facility or intermediate care facility shall have completed at least two hours of initial dementia-specific training as part of the facility's orientation program. The training shall be completed within the first 40 hours of employment.

(2) The facility shall develop a dementia-specific training component within the existing orientation program, to be implemented no later than July 1, 2002.

(3) The facility's modified orientation program shall be reviewed by the department in a phasein schedule that begins no later than July 1, 2002, and is completed no later than July 1, 2005.

(c) Any certified nursing assistant employed by a skilled nursing facility or intermediate care facility shall participate in a minimum of five hours of dementia-specific in-service training per year, as part of the facility's in-service training.

(d) Freestanding and hospital-based pediatric skilled nursing facilities with exclusively pediatric occupancy shall be exempt from the requirements set forth in this section. (Added by Stats. 2001, Ch. 339, Sec. 1. Effective January 1, 2002.)

1264.

(a) Any health facility licensed under Section 1250 that provides prenatal screening ultrasound to detect congenital heart defects shall require that the ultrasound be performed by a sonographer who is nationally certified in obstetrical ultrasound by the American Registry for Diagnostic Medical Sonography (ARDMS), nationally certified in cardiac sonography by Cardiovascular Credentialing International (CCI), or credentialed in sonography by the American Registry of Radiologic Technologists (ARRT).

(b) For purposes of this section, the following shall apply:

(1) A sonographer is also known as an "ultrasound technologist" or "sonologist."

(2) "Sonographer" means any nonphysician who is qualified by national certification or academic or clinical experience to perform diagnostic medical ultrasound, with a subspecialty in obstetrical ultrasound.

(c) (1) Any sonographer who is certified as required in subdivision (a) or otherwise meets the requirements of this section, shall, in performing a prenatal ultrasound to detect congenital heart defects, perform the work under the supervision of a licensed physician and surgeon.

(2) For purposes of this section, licensed physician and surgeon means any physician and surgeon, licensed pursuant to Chapter 5 (commencing with Section 2000) of Division 2 of the Business and Professions Code.

(d) Any person with a minimum of two years of full-time work experience in this state as a sonographer in prenatal ultrasound and has obtained, or is in the process of obtaining, 30 continuing medical education credits over a three-year period in ultrasound shall be deemed to be in compliance with the requirements of this section.

(e) A health facility shall develop policies and procedures to implement the requirements of this section.

(f) This section and policies and procedures adopted pursuant to this section shall not prohibit any physician and surgeon licensed pursuant to Chapter 5 (commencing with Section 2000) of Division 2 of the Business and Professions Code from performing a prenatal ultrasound nor in any other way limit the ability of a licensed physician and surgeon to practice medicine in a manner consistent with that license.

(g) This section and policies and procedures adopted pursuant to this section shall not apply to any physician and surgeon, sonologist, certified nurse-midwife, or nurse practitioner who performs limited prenatal ultrasounds for the purpose of obtaining an amniotic fluid index, fetal position, a biophysical profile or dating a pregnancy prior to 20 weeks gestation.

(h) Article 4 (commencing with Section 1235) and any other provision relating to criminal sanctions for violations of this chapter shall not apply to any person who violates this section or any regulation adopted pursuant to this section.

(i) This section shall become operative on July 1, 2006. (Added by Stats. 2004, Ch. 770, Sec. 2. Effective January 1, 2005. Section operative July 1, 2006, by its own provisions.)

ARTICLE 2. Administration [1265 - 1272]

(Article 2 added by Stats. 1973, Ch. 1202.)

1265.

Any person, political subdivision of the state, or governmental agency desiring a license for a health facility, approval for a special service under this chapter, or approval to manage a health facility currently licensed as a health facility, as defined in subdivision (a), (b), (c), (d), or (f) of Section 1250, that has not filed an application for a license to operate that facility shall file with the department a verified application on forms prescribed and furnished by the department, containing all of the following:

(a) The name of the applicant and, if an individual, whether the applicant has attained the age of 18 years.

(b) The type of facility or health facility.

(c) The location thereof.

(d) The name of the person in charge thereof.

(e) Evidence satisfactory to the department that the applicant is of reputable and responsible character. If the applicant is a firm, association, organization, partnership, business trust, corporation, or company, like evidence shall be submitted as to the members or shareholders thereof, and the person in charge of the health facility for which application for license is made. If the applicant is a political subdivision of the state or other governmental agency, like evidence shall be submitted as to the person in charge of the health facility for which application for license is made.

(f) Evidence satisfactory to the department of the ability of the applicant to comply with this chapter and of rules and regulations promulgated under this chapter by the department.

(g) Evidence satisfactory to the department that the applicant to operate a skilled nursing facility or intermediate care facility possesses financial resources sufficient to operate the facility for a period of at least 45 days. A management company shall not be required to submit this information.

(h) Each applicant for a license to operate a skilled nursing facility or intermediate care facility shall disclose to the department evidence of the right to possession of the facility at the time the application is granted, which may be satisfied by the submission of a copy of applicable portions of a lease agreement or deed of trust. The names and addresses of any persons or organizations listed as owner of record in the real estate, including the buildings and the grounds appurtenant to the buildings, shall be disclosed to the department.

(i) Any other information as may be required by the department for the proper administration and enforcement of this chapter.

(j) Upon submission of an application to the department by an intermediate care facility/developmentally disabled habilitative or an intermediate care facility/developmentally disabled-nursing, the application shall include a statement of need signed by the chairperson of the area board pursuant to Chapter 4 (commencing with Section 4570) of Division 4.5 of the Welfare and Institutions Code. In the event the area board has not provided the statement of need within 30 days of receipt of the request from the applicant, the department may process the application for license without the statement.

(k) The information required pursuant to this section, other than individuals' social security numbers, shall be made available to the public upon request, and shall be included in the department's public file regarding the facility.

(l) With respect to a facility licensed as a health facility, as defined in subdivision (a), (b), or (f) of Section 1250, for purposes of this section, "manage" means to assume operational control of the facility.

(Amended by Stats. 2005, Ch. 507, Sec. 1. Effective January 1, 2006.)

1265.1.

(a) An application for licensure under this chapter may be denied by the state department if the applicant for a license has been convicted of a crime, as defined in Section 1265.2, or on the ground of knowingly making a false statement of fact required to be revealed in an application for such licensure.

(b) If the applicant is a firm, partnership, association, or corporation, the conviction of any officer, director, shareholder with a beneficial ownership interest in the applicant exceeding 10 percent, or the person in charge of the health facility may serve as the basis for denial of the license by the state department. If the applicant is a political subdivision of the state or other governmental agency, the conviction of such a crime by the person in charge of the health facility may serve as the basis for denial of the license by the state department.

(c) The record of conviction or a certified copy thereof certified by the clerk of the court or by the judge in whose court the conviction is had, shall be conclusive evidence thereof.

(Added by Stats. 1980, Ch. 708.)

1265.2.

A "crime," within the meaning of this chapter, means a violation of a law or regulation which is substantially related to the qualifications or duties of the applicant or licensee or which is substantially related to the functions of the business for which the license was, or is to be, issued.

A "conviction," within the meaning of this chapter, means a plea or verdict of guilty or a conviction following a plea of nolo contendere. Any action which the state department is permitted to take following the establishment of a conviction may be taken when the time for appeal has elapsed, or the judgment of conviction has been affirmed on appeal or when an order granting probation is made suspending the imposition of sentence, notwithstanding a subsequent order pursuant to the provisions of Section 1203.4 of the Penal Code permitting such person to withdraw his plea of guilty and to enter a plea of not guilty, or setting aside the verdict of guilty, or dismissing the accusation, information, or indictment.

Evidence of conviction of a misdemeanor following a plea of nolo contendere pursuant to the provisions of Section 1290 shall not be admissible in any hearing conducted under Section 1269 or 1295.

No application for licensure shall be denied nor shall a license be suspended or revoked solely on the basis of the conviction of a crime if the director determines that the person has been rehabilitated in accordance with standards for rehabilitation developed by the director. The director shall take into account all competent evidence of rehabilitation furnished by the applicant or licensee.

(Amended by Stats. 1980, Ch. 1285.)

1265.3.

(a) For any individual or entity that seeks approval to operate or manage a health facility licensed pursuant to subdivision (a), (b), or (f) of Section 1250 and is subject to Section 1265, the department shall consider the following:

(1) To determine whether the applicant is of reputable and responsible character, the department shall consider any available information that the applicant has demonstrated a pattern and practice of violations of state or federal laws and regulations. The department shall give particular consideration to those violations that affect the applicant's ability to deliver safe patient care.

(2) To determine whether the applicant has the ability to comply with this chapter and the rules and regulations adopted under this chapter, the department shall consider evidence that shall include all of the following:

(A) If any, prior history of operating in this state any other facility licensed pursuant to Section 1250, and the applicant's history of substantial compliance with the requirements imposed under that license, applicable federal laws and regulations, and requirements governing the operators of those facilities.

(B) If any, prior history of operating in any other state any facility authorized to receive Medicare Program reimbursement or Medicaid Program reimbursement, and the applicant's history of substantial compliance with that state's requirements, and applicable federal laws, regulations, and requirements.

(C) If any, prior history of providing health services as a licensed health professional or an individual or entity contracting with a health care service plan or insurer, and the applicant's history of substantial compliance with state requirements, and applicable federal law, regulations, and requirements.

(b) The department may also require the entity described in subdivision (a) to furnish other information or documents for the proper administration and enforcement of the licensing laws.

(Added by Stats. 2005, Ch. 507, Sec. 2. Effective January 1, 2006.)

1265.4.

(a) A licensed health facility, as defined in subdivision (a), (b), (c), (d), (f), or (k) of Section 1250, shall employ a full-time, part-time, or consulting dietitian. A health facility that employs a registered dietitian less than full time, shall also employ a full-time dietetic services supervisor who meets the requirements of subdivision (b) to supervise dietetic service operations. The dietetic services supervisor shall receive frequently scheduled consultation from a qualified dietitian.

(b) The dietetic services supervisor shall have completed at least one of the following educational requirements:

(1) A baccalaureate degree with major studies in food and nutrition, dietetics, or food management and has one year of experience in the dietetic service of a licensed health facility.

(2) A graduate of a dietetic technician training program approved by the American Dietetic Association, accredited by the Commission on Accreditation for Dietetics Education, or currently registered by the Commission on Dietetic Registration.

(3) A graduate of a dietetic assistant training program approved by the American Dietetic Association.

(4) Is a graduate of a dietetic services training program approved by the Dietary Managers Association and is a certified dietary manager credentialed by the Certifying Board of the Dietary Managers Association, maintains this certification, and has received at least six hours of in-service training on the specific California dietary service requirements contained in Title 22 of the California Code of Regulations prior to assuming full-time duties as a dietetic services supervisor at the health facility.

(5) Is a graduate of a college degree program with major studies in food and nutrition, dietetics, food management, culinary arts, or hotel and restaurant management and is a certified dietary manager credentialed by the Certifying Board of the Dietary Managers Association, maintains this certification, and has received at least six hours of in-service training on the specific California dietary service requirements contained in Title 22 of the California Code of Regulations prior to assuming full-time duties as a dietetic services supervisor at the health facility.

(6) A graduate of a state approved program that provides 90 or more hours of classroom instruction in dietetic service supervision, or 90 hours or more of combined classroom instruction and instructor led interactive Web-based instruction in dietetic service supervision.

(7) Received training experience in food service supervision and management in the military equivalent in content to paragraph (2), (3), or (6).

(c) Pursuant to Section 1276, the State Department of Public Health may grant a program flexibility request to the facility to modify the requirements in subdivision (b) for any individual who has at least five years experience prior to January 1, 2009, as a dietetic services supervisor in a health facility specified in subdivision (a) to allow that individual to function as a dietetic services supervisor for a period not to exceed 18 months, as long as the individual is enrolled in a program that meets the requirements listed in subdivision (b). The department may extend the program flexibility request for a period not to exceed six months if the individual can demonstrate to the department that the coursework could not otherwise be completed within the original 18-month period. Program flexibility requests shall be submitted not later than December 31, 2009. (Added by Stats. 2008, Ch. 225, Sec. 1. Effective January 1, 2009.)

1265.5.

(a) (1) Prior to the initial licensure or renewal of a license of any person or persons to operate or manage an intermediate care facility/developmentally disabled habilitative, an intermediate care facility/developmentally disabled-nursing, an intermediate care facility/developmentally disabled-continuous nursing, or an intermediate care facility/developmentally disabled, other than an intermediate care facility/developmentally disabled operated by the state, that secures criminal record clearances for its employees through a method other than as specified in this section or upon the hiring of direct care staff by any of these facilities, the department shall secure from the Department of Justice criminal offender record information to determine whether the applicant, facility administrator or manager, any direct care staff, or any other adult living in the same location, has ever been convicted of a crime other than a minor traffic violation.

(2) (A) The criminal record clearance shall require the applicant to submit electronic fingerprint images and related information of the facility administrator or manager, and any direct care staff, or any other adult living in the same location, to the Department of Justice. Applicants shall be responsible for any cost associated with capturing or transmitting the fingerprint images and related information.

(B) The criminal record clearance shall be completed prior to direct staff contact with residents of the facility. A criminal record clearance shall be complete when the department has obtained the person's criminal record information from the Department of Justice and has determined that he or she is not disqualified from engaging in the activity for which clearance is required.

(3) (A) The Licensing and Certification Program shall issue an All Facilities Letter (AFL) to facility licensees when it determines that both of the following criteria have been met for a period of 30 days:

(i) The program receives, within three business days, 95 percent of its total responses indicating no evidence of recorded criminal information from the Department of Justice.

(ii) The program processes 95 percent of its total responses requiring disqualification in accordance with subdivision (b), with notices mailed to the facility no later than 45 days after the date that the criminal offender record information report is received from the Department of Justice.

(B) After the AFL is issued, facilities shall not allow newly hired facility administrators, managers, direct care staff, or any other adult living in the same location to have direct contact with clients or residents of the facility prior to completion of the criminal record clearance. A criminal record clearance shall be complete when the department has obtained the person's criminal offender record information search response from the Department of Justice and has determined that the person is not disqualified from engaging in the activity for which clearance is required.

(C) An applicant or certificate holder who may be disqualified on the basis of a criminal conviction shall provide the department with a certified copy of the judgment of each conviction. In addition, the individual may, during a period of two years after the department receives the criminal record report, provide the department with evidence of good character and rehabilitation in accordance with subdivision (c). Upon receipt of a new application for certification of the individual, the department may receive and consider the evidence during the two-year period without requiring additional fingerprint imaging to clear the individual.

(D) The department's Licensing and Certification Program shall explore and implement methods for maximizing its efficiency in processing criminal record clearances within the requirements of law, including a streamlined clearance process for persons that have been disqualified on the basis of criminal convictions that do not require automatic denial pursuant to subdivision (b).

(4) An applicant and any other person specified in this subdivision, as part of the background clearance process, shall provide information as to whether or not the person has any prior criminal convictions, has had any arrests within the past 12-month period, or has any active arrests, and shall certify that, to the best of his or her knowledge, the information provided is true. This requirement is not intended to duplicate existing requirements for individuals who are required to submit fingerprint images as part of a criminal background clearance process. Every applicant shall provide information on any prior administrative action taken against him or her by any federal, state, or local governmental agency and shall certify that, to the best of his or her knowledge, the information provided is true. An applicant or other person required to provide information pursuant to this section that knowingly or willfully makes false statements, representations, or omissions may be subject to administrative action, including, but not limited to, denial of his or her application or exemption or revocation of any exemption previously granted.

(b) (1) The application for licensure or renewal shall be denied if the criminal record indicates that the person seeking initial licensure or renewal of a license referred to in subdivision (a) has been convicted of a violation or attempted violation of any one or more of the following Penal Code provisions: Section 187, subdivision (a) of Section 192, Section 203, 205, 206, 207, 209, 210, 210.5, 211, 220, 222, 243.4, 245, 261, 262, or 264.1, Sections 265 to 267, inclusive, Section 273a, 273d, 273.5, or 285, subdivisions (c), (d), (f), and (g) of Section 286, Section 288, subdivisions (c), (d), (f), and (g) of Section 287 or of former Section 288a, Section 288.5, 289, 289.5, 368, 451, 459, 470, 475, 484, or 484b, Sections 484d to 484j, inclusive, Section 487, subdivision (a) of Section 487a, or Section 488, 496, 503, 518, or 666, unless any of the following applies:

(A) The person was convicted of a felony and has obtained a certificate of rehabilitation under Chapter 3.5 (commencing with Section 4852.01) of Title 6 of Part 3 of the Penal Code and the information or accusation against the person has been dismissed pursuant to Section 1203.4 of the Penal Code with regard to that felony.

(B) The person was convicted of a misdemeanor and the information or accusation against the person has been dismissed pursuant to Section 1203.4 or 1203.4a of the Penal Code.

(C) The person was convicted of a felony or a misdemeanor, but has previously disclosed the fact of each conviction to the department and the department has made a determination in accordance with law that the conviction does not disqualify the person.

(2) The application for licensure or renewal shall be denied if the criminal record of the person includes a conviction in another state for an offense that, if committed or attempted in this state, would have been punishable as one or more of the offenses set forth in paragraph (1), unless evidence of rehabilitation comparable to the dismissal of a misdemeanor or a certificate of rehabilitation as set forth in subparagraph (A) or (B) of paragraph (1) is provided to the department.

(c) If the criminal record of a person described in subdivision (a) indicates any conviction other than a minor traffic violation or other than a conviction listed in subdivision (b), the department may deny the application for licensure or renewal. In determining whether or not to deny the application for licensure or renewal pursuant to this subdivision, the department shall take into consideration the following factors as evidence of good character and rehabilitation:

(1) The nature and seriousness of the offense under consideration and its relationship to their employment duties and responsibilities.

(2) Activities since conviction, including employment or participation in therapy or education, that would indicate changed behavior.

(3) The time that has elapsed since the commission of the conduct or offense referred to in paragraph (1) or (2) and the number of offenses.

(4) The extent to which the person has complied with any terms of parole, probation, restitution, or any other sanction lawfully imposed against the person.

(5) Any rehabilitation evidence, including character references, submitted by the person.

(6) Employment history and current employer recommendations.

(7) Circumstances surrounding the commission of the offense that would demonstrate the unlikelihood of repetition.

(8) The granting by the Governor of a full and unconditional pardon.

(9) A certificate of rehabilitation from a superior court.

(d) Nothing in this section shall be construed to require a criminal record check of a person receiving services in an intermediate care facility/developmentally disabled habilitative, intermediate care facility/developmentally disabled-nursing, intermediate care facility/developmentally disabled-continuous nursing, or intermediate care facility/developmentally disabled.

(e) For purposes of this section, "direct care staff" means all facility staff who are trained and experienced in the care of persons with developmental disabilities and who directly provide program and nursing services to clients. Administrative and licensed personnel shall be considered direct care staff when directly providing program and nursing services to clients. Persons employed as consultants and acting as direct care staff shall be subject to the same requirements for a criminal record clearance as other direct care staff. However, the employing facility shall not be required to pay any costs associated with that criminal record clearance.

(f) Upon the employment of any person specified in subdivision (a), and prior to any contact with clients or residents, the facility shall ensure that electronic fingerprint images are submitted to the Department of Justice for the purpose of obtaining a criminal record check.

(g) The department shall develop procedures to ensure that any licensee, direct care staff, or certificate holder for whom a criminal record has been obtained pursuant to this section or Section 1338.5 or 1736 shall not be required to obtain multiple criminal record clearances.

(h) In addition to the persons who are not required to obtain multiple criminal record clearances pursuant to subdivision (g), a person shall not be required to obtain a separate criminal record clearance if the person meets all of the following criteria:

(1) The person is employed as a consultant and acts as direct care staff.

(2) The person is a registered nurse, licensed vocational nurse, physical therapist, occupational therapist, or speech-language pathologist.

(3) The person has obtained a criminal record clearance as a prerequisite to holding a license or certificate to provide direct care services.

(4) The person has a license or certificate to provide direct care service that is in good standing with the appropriate licensing or certification board.

(5) The person is providing time-limited specialized clinical care or services.

(6) The person is not left alone with the client.

(i) If, at any time, the department determines that it does not meet the standards specified in clauses (i) and (ii) of subparagraph (A) of paragraph (3) of subdivision (a), for a period of 90 consecutive days, the requirements in paragraph (3) of subdivision (a) shall be suspended until the department determines that it has met those standards for a period of 90 consecutive days.

(j) During any period of time in which paragraph (3) of subdivision (a) is inoperative, facilities may allow newly hired facility administrators, managers, direct care staff, or any other adult living in the same location to have direct contact with clients or residents of the facility after those persons have submitted live-scan fingerprint images to the Department of Justice, and the department shall issue an AFL advising of this change in the statutory requirement.

(k) Notwithstanding any other provision of law, the department is authorized to provide an individual with a copy of his or her state or federal level criminal offender record information search response as provided to that department by the Department of Justice if the department has denied a criminal background clearance based on this information and the individual makes a written request to the department for a copy specifying an address to which it is to be sent. The state or federal level criminal offender record information search response shall not be modified or altered from its form or content as provided by the Department of Justice and shall be provided to the address specified by the individual in his or her written request. The department shall retain a copy of the individual's written request and the response and date provided.
(Amended by Stats. 2018, Ch. 423, Sec. 32. (SB 1494) Effective January 1, 2019.)
1265.6.
Notwithstanding any other provision of law, a registered nurse within his or her scope of practice may require direct care staff in an intermediate care facility/developmentally disabled habilitative or an intermediate care facility/developmentally disabled-nursing to administer blood glucose testing for a person with developmental disabilities who resides at the facility and who has diabetes, if all of the following criteria are met:
(a) The blood glucose testing is specifically ordered by a physician. The results of the testing shall be reported to a registered nurse as specified in the physician's order.
(b) Prior to performing the blood glucose testing, the direct care staff shall be trained by the registered nurse to perform the testing and shall demonstrate proficiency in performing the testing while under the immediate supervision of the registered nurse.
(c) Training of direct care staff to perform blood glucose testing shall include, but not be limited to, an overview of the basic disease process of type I and type II diabetes, recognition of the signs and symptoms of hypoglycemia and hyperglycemia, the role of nutrition management in diabetes, diabetes and blood sugar control, long-term complications of diabetes, specific instruction in utilizing and the use of a specific over-the-counter glucose monitoring device that is approved by the FDA, including the cleaning and maintaining the accuracy of the client-specific glucose monitoring device, proper infection control practices related to the use of the device, including the handling and disposal of infectious waste, and recording accurate records of blood glucose readings in the client medical record. Records of blood glucose readings shall be reviewed by the facility registered nurse at least monthly.
(d) A signed written statement shall be prepared by the registered nurse that includes a certification of the direct care staff's competence to perform the testing and that identifies the clients residing at the facility for whom the certification is applicable. This certification shall be placed and maintained in the direct care staff's training record.
(e) The certification of competence to perform the blood glucose testing shall be procedure and client specific, and shall not be transferred between clients residing at the facility or other facilities.
(f) The registered nurse shall be responsible for monitoring and implementing the direct care staff blood glucose testing. At least once every three months, the registered nurse shall observe and confirm the direct care staff person's proficiency in performing the approved testing and shall update the certification. The proficiency determination shall include a determination by the registered nurse that the direct care staff remains proficient in demonstrating the specified method for cleaning and recalibration of the glucose monitoring device.
(g) A registered nurse shall provide continuing in-service education on the management of diabetes and the use of blood glucose monitoring devices not less than once per year and include documentation of the content of the training and the staff who were in attendance.
(h) A facility shall develop a written policy and procedure governing blood glucose testing for clients residing at the facility that shall include procedures for the training and competency assessment of direct care staff as required by this section.
(i) A facility shall have received a certificate of waiver pursuant to subdivision (n) of Section 483.460 of Title 42 of the Code of Federal Regulations prior to the implementation of blood glucose testing and shall retain a copy of the CLIA waiver for inspection by the department.
(Amended by Stats. 2007, Ch. 130, Sec. 154. Effective January 1, 2008.)
1265.7.
(a) (1) The state department shall adopt regulations for the licensure of congregate living health facilities. The regulations shall include minimum standards of adequacy, safety, and sanitation of the physical plant and equipment, minimum standards for staffing with duly qualified personnel, and training of the staff, and minimum standards for providing the services offered.
(2) Regulations for facilities approved to provide services for persons who may be ventilator dependent shall ensure that residents of these facilities are assured appropriate supportive health services in the most normal, least restrictive physical and rehabilitative environment appropriate to individual resident needs.
(3) Regulations for facilities approved to provide services for persons who are terminally ill, who have a diagnosis of a life-threatening illness, who are catastrophically and severely disabled, or any combination of those persons, shall ensure that residents of these facilities receive supportive health services, based on individual resident acuity levels in the most normal, least restrictive physical environment for individual resident needs.
(b) Pending adoption of the regulations pursuant to paragraphs (2) and (3) of subdivision (a), an entity shall be licensed as a congregate living health facility serving persons who are terminally ill, persons who are catastrophically and severely disabled, persons who are mentally alert but physically disabled, or any combination of these

persons, by the state department beginning July 1, 1988, if it meets the requirements identified in subdivision (i) of Section 1250 and in Section 1267.13.
(Amended by Stats. 1992, Ch. 494, Sec. 1. Effective January 1, 1993.)
1265.8.
In addition to the requirements of this chapter, any person, political subdivision of the state, or governmental agency desiring a license for a health facility shall file with the state department a verified statement that it has complied with the requirements of Chapter 1 (commencing with Section 15000) of Division 12.5, and it has received approval pursuant to that chapter. The state department shall not issue any license until such requirement has been met.
(Added by Stats. 1973, Ch. 1202.)
1265.9.
(a) On and after July 1, 2015, any acute psychiatric hospital that submits a completed application and is operated by the State Department of State Hospitals may be approved by the State Department of Public Health to offer, as a supplemental service, an Enhanced Treatment Program (ETP) that meets the requirements of this section, Section 4144 of the Welfare and Institutions Code, and applicable regulations.
(b) This section shall remain in effect for each pilot ETP until January 1 of the fifth calendar year after each pilot ETP site has admitted its first patient, and is repealed as of January 1 of the fifth calendar year after each pilot ETP site has admitted its first patient, unless a later enacted statute extending the program is enacted prior to those dates. The State Department of State Hospitals shall post a declaration on its Internet Web site when the condition for repealing this section is met stating that this section is repealed.
(c) (1) Prior to the admission of the first patient into the last pilot ETP, the State Department of Public Health may adopt emergency regulations in accordance with the Administrative Procedure Act (Chapter 3.5 (commencing with Section 11340) of Part 1 of Division 3 of Title 2 of the Government Code) to implement this section. The adoption of an emergency regulation under this paragraph is deemed to address an emergency, for purposes of Sections 11346.1 and 11349.6 of the Government Code, and the State Department of Public Health is hereby exempted for this purpose from the requirements of subdivision (b) of Section 11346.1 of the Government Code.
(2) As an alternative to paragraph (1) and notwithstanding the rulemaking provisions of Administrative Procedures Act (Chapter 3.5 (commencing with Section 11340) of Part 1 of Division 3 of Title 2 of the Government Code), the director of the State Department of Public Health may implement this section, in whole or in part, by means of an all facility letter or other similar instruction.
(d) An ETP shall meet all of the following requirements:
(1) Maintain a staff-to-patient ratio of one to five.
(2) Limit each room to one patient.
(3) Each patient room shall allow visual access by staff 24 hours per day.
(4) Each patient room shall have a toilet and sink in the room.
(5) Each patient room door shall have the capacity to be locked externally. The door may be locked when clinically indicated and determined to be the least restrictive treatment environment for the patient's care and treatment pursuant to Section 4144 of the Welfare and Institutions Code, but shall not be considered seclusion, as defined by subdivision (e) of Section 1180.1, for purposes of Division 1.5 (commencing with Section 1180).
(6) Provide emergency egress for ETP patients.
(7) In the event seclusion or restraints, as defined by Section 1180.1, are used in an ETP, all state licensing and regulations shall be followed.
(8) A full-time independent patients' rights advocate who provides patients' rights advocacy services shall be assigned to each ETP.
(e) The ETPs shall adopt and implement policies and procedures necessary to encourage patient improvement, recovery, and a return to a standard treatment environment, and to create identifiable facility requirements and bench marks. The policies and procedures shall also provide all of the following:
(1) Criteria and process for admission into an ETP pursuant to Section 4144 of the Welfare and Institutions Code.
(2) Clinical assessment and review focused on behavior, history, high risk of most dangerous behavior, and clinical need for patients to receive treatment in an ETP as the least restrictive treatment environment.
(3) A process for identifying an ETP along a continuum of care that will best meet the patient's needs, including least restrictive treatment environment.
(4) A process for creating and implementing a treatment plan with regular clinical review and reevaluation of placement back into a standard treatment environment and discharge and reintegration planning as specified in subdivision (e) of Section 4144 of the Welfare and Institutions Code.
(f) Patients who have been admitted to an ETP shall have the same rights guaranteed to patients not in an ETP with the exception set forth in paragraph (5) of subdivision (d).
(g) For purposes of paragraph (1) of subdivision (d), "staff" means licensed nurses and psychiatric technicians providing direct patient care.
(Added by Stats. 2014, Ch. 718, Sec. 2. (AB 1340) Effective January 1, 2015. Repealed on date prescribed by its own provisions.)
1265.10.
(a) A licensed health facility, as defined in subdivision (a), (b), (c), (d), (f), or (k) of Section 1250, shall make available wholesome, plant-based meals of such variety as to meet the needs of patients in accordance with their physicians' orders.
(b) Notwithstanding any other law, including, but not limited to, Section 1290, a violation of this section shall not constitute a crime.
(c) For the purposes of this section, "plant-based meals" shall mean entire meals that contain no animal products or byproducts, including meat, poultry, fish, dairy, or eggs.

(Added by Stats. 2018, Ch. 512, Sec. 2. (SB 1138) Effective January 1, 2019.)

1266.

(a) The Licensing and Certification Division shall be supported entirely by federal funds and special funds by no earlier than the beginning of the 2009–10 fiscal year unless otherwise specified in statute, or unless funds are specifically appropriated from the General Fund in the annual Budget Act or other enacted legislation. For the 2007–08 fiscal year, General Fund support shall be provided to offset licensing and certification fees in an amount of not less than two million seven hundred eighty-two thousand dollars ($2,782,000).

(b) (1) The Licensing and Certification Program fees for the 2006–07 fiscal year shall be as follows:

Type of Facility	Fee	
General Acute Care Hospitals	$134.10	per bed
Acute Psychiatric Hospitals	$134.10	per bed
Special Hospitals	$134.10	per bed
Chemical Dependency Recovery Hospitals	$123.52	per bed
Skilled Nursing Facilities	$202.96	per bed
Intermediate Care Facilities	$202.96	per bed
Intermediate Care Facilities- Developmentally Disabled	$592.29	per bed
Intermediate Care Facilities- Developmentally Disabled-Habilitative	$1,000.00	per facility
Intermediate Care Facilities- Developmentally Disabled-Nursing	$1,000.00	per facility
Home Health Agencies	$2,700.00	per facility
Referral Agencies	$5,537.71	per facility
Adult Day Health Centers	$4,650.02	per facility
Congregate Living Health Facilities	$202.96	per bed
Psychology Clinics	$600.00	per facility
Primary Clinics- Community and Free	$600.00	per facility
Specialty Clinics- Rehab Clinics (For profit)	$2,974.43	per facility
(Nonprofit)	$500.00	per facility
Specialty Clinics- Surgical and Chronic	$1,500.00	per facility
Dialysis Clinics	$1,500.00	per facility
Pediatric Day Health/Respite Care	$142.43	per bed
Alternative Birthing Centers	$2,437.86	per facility
Hospice	$1,000.00	per provider
Correctional Treatment Centers	$590.39	per bed

(2) (A) In the first year of licensure for intermediate care facility/developmentally disabled-continuous nursing (ICF/DD-CN) facilities, the licensure fee for those facilities shall be equivalent to the licensure fee for intermediate care facility/developmentally disabled-nursing facilities during the same year. Thereafter, the licensure fee for ICF/DD-CN facilities shall be established pursuant to the same procedures described in this section.

(B) In the first year of licensure for hospice facilities, the licensure fee shall be equivalent to the licensure fee for congregate living health facilities during the same year. Thereafter, the licensure fee for hospice facilities shall be established pursuant to the same procedures described in this section.

(c) Commencing in the 2015–16 fiscal year, the fees for skilled nursing facilities shall be increased so as to generate four hundred thousand dollars ($400,000) for the California Department of Aging's Long-Term Care Ombudsman Program for its work related to investigating complaints made against skilled nursing facilities and increasing visits to those facilities.

(d) Commencing February 1, 2007, and every February 1 thereafter, the department shall publish a list of estimated fees pursuant to this section. The calculation of estimated fees and the publication of the report and list of estimated fees shall not be subject to the rulemaking requirements of Chapter 3.5 (commencing with Section 11340) of Part 1 of Division 3 of Title 2 of the Government Code.

(e) Notwithstanding Section 10231.5 of the Government Code, by February 1 of each year, the department shall prepare the following reports and shall make those reports, and the list of estimated fees required to be published pursuant to subdivision (d), available to the public by submitting them to the Legislature and posting them on the department's Internet Web site:

(1) A report of all costs for activities of the Licensing and Certification Program. At a minimum, this report shall include a narrative of all baseline adjustments and their calculations, a description of how each category of facility was calculated, descriptions of assumptions used in any calculations, and shall recommend Licensing and Certification Program fees in accordance with the following:

(A) Projected workload and costs shall be grouped for each fee category, including workload costs for facility categories that have been established by statute and for which licensing regulations and procedures are under development.

(B) Cost estimates, and the estimated fees, shall be based on the appropriation amounts in the Governor's proposed budget for the next fiscal year, with and without policy adjustments to the fee methodology.

(C) The allocation of program, operational, and administrative overhead, and indirect costs to fee categories shall be based on generally accepted cost allocation methods. Significant items of costs shall be directly charged to fee categories if the expenses can be reasonably identified to the fee category that caused them. Indirect and overhead costs shall be allocated to all fee categories using a generally accepted cost allocation method.

(D) The amount of federal funds and General Fund moneys to be received in the budget year shall be estimated and allocated to each fee category based upon an appropriate metric.

(E) The fee for each category shall be determined by dividing the aggregate state share of all costs for the Licensing and Certification Program by the appropriate metric for the category of licensure. Amounts actually received for new licensure applications, including change of ownership applications, and late payment penalties, pursuant to Section 1266.5, during each fiscal year shall be calculated and 95 percent shall be applied to the appropriate fee categories in determining Licensing and Certification Program fees for the second fiscal year following receipt of those funds. The remaining 5 percent shall be retained in the fund as a reserve until appropriated.

(2) (A) A staffing and systems analysis to ensure efficient and effective utilization of fees collected, proper allocation of departmental resources to licensing and certification activities, survey schedules, complaint investigations, enforcement and appeal activities, data collection and dissemination, surveyor training, and policy development.

(B) The analysis under this paragraph shall be made available to interested persons and shall include all of the following:

(i) The number of surveyors and administrative support personnel devoted to the licensing and certification of health care facilities.

(ii) The percentage of time devoted to licensing and certification activities for the various types of health facilities.

(iii) The number of facilities receiving full surveys and the frequency and number of followup visits.

(iv) The number and timeliness of complaint investigations, including data on the department's compliance with the requirements of paragraphs (3), (4), and (5) of subdivision (a) of Section 1420.

(v) Data on deficiencies and citations issued, and numbers of citation review conferences and arbitration hearings.

(vi) Other applicable activities of the licensing and certification division.

(3) The annual program fee report described in subdivision (d) of Section 1416.36.

(f) The reports required pursuant to subdivision (e) shall be submitted in compliance with Section 9795 of the Government Code.

(g) Commencing in the 2018–19 fiscal year, the department may assess a supplemental license fee on facilities located in the County of Los Angeles for all facility types set forth in this section. This supplemental license fee shall be in addition to the license fees set forth in subdivision (d). The department shall calculate the supplemental license fee based upon the difference between the estimated costs of regulating facility types licensed in the County of Los Angeles, including, but not limited to, the costs associated with the department's contract for licensing and certification activities with the County of Los Angeles and the costs of the department conducting the licensing and certification activities for facilities located in the County of Los Angeles. The supplemental license fees shall be used to cover the costs to administer and enforce state licensure standards and other federal compliance activities for facilities located in the County of Los Angeles, as described in the annual report. The supplemental license fee shall be based upon the fee methodology published in the annual report described in subdivision (d).

(h) (1) The department shall adjust the list of estimated fees published pursuant to subdivision (d) if the annual Budget Act or other enacted legislation includes an appropriation that differs from those proposed in the Governor's proposed budget for that fiscal year.

(2) The department shall publish a final fee list, with an explanation of any adjustment, by the issuance of an all facilities letter, by posting the list on the department's Internet Web site, and by including the final fee list as part of the licensing application package, within 14 days of the enactment of the annual Budget Act. The adjustment of fees and the publication of the final fee list shall not be subject to the rulemaking requirements of Chapter 3.5 (commencing with Section 11340) of Part 1 of Division 3 of Title 2 of the Government Code.

(i) (1) Fees shall not be assessed or collected pursuant to this section from any state department, authority, bureau, commission, or officer, unless federal financial participation would become available by doing so and an appropriation is included in the annual Budget Act for that state department, authority, bureau, commission, or officer for this purpose. Fees shall not be assessed or collected pursuant to this section from any clinic that is certified only by the federal government and is exempt from licensure under Section 1206, unless federal financial participation would become available by doing so.

(2) For the 2006–07 state fiscal year, a fee shall not be assessed or collected pursuant to this section from any general acute care hospital owned by a health care district with 100 beds or less.

(j) The Licensing and Certification Program may change annual license expiration renewal dates to provide for efficiencies in operational processes or to provide for sufficient cashflow to pay for expenditures. If an annual license expiration date is changed, the renewal fee shall be prorated accordingly. Facilities shall be provided with a 60-day notice of any change in their annual license renewal date.

(k) Commencing with the 2018–19 November Program estimate, the Licensing and Certification Program shall evaluate the feasibility of reducing investigation timelines based on experience with implementing paragraphs (3), (4), and (5) of subdivision (a) of Section 1420.

(Amended by Stats. 2018, Ch. 34, Sec. 5. (AB 1810) Effective June 27, 2018.)

1266.1.

(a) Each new or renewal application for a license for a psychiatric health facility shall be accompanied by a fee credited to the State Department of Health Care Services for its costs incurred in the review of psychiatric health facility programs, in connection with the licensing of these facilities. The amount of the fees shall be determined and collected by the State Department of Health Care Services, but the total amount of the fees collected shall not exceed the actual costs of licensure and review of psychiatric health facility programs, including, but not limited to, the costs of processing the application, inspection costs, and other related costs.

(b) New or renewal licensure application fees for psychiatric health facilities shall be collected by the State Department of Health Care Services.

(c) The annual fees shall be waived for any psychiatric health facility conducted, maintained, or operated by this state or any state department, authority, bureau, commission, or officer, or by the Regents of the University of California, or by a local hospital district, city, county, or city and county.

(d) If additional private psychiatric health facilities seek new licensure on or after January 1, 1991, the State Department of Health Care Services may increase the fees for all private psychiatric health facilities with more than nine beds sufficient to accommodate the increased level of workload and costs.

(e) (1) Any licensee desiring to obtain a special permit to offer and provide structured outpatient services shall file an application with the State Department of Health Care Services.

(2) The application for a special permit, if any, shall be submitted with each new or renewal application for a license for a psychiatric health facility, and shall be accompanied by a reasonable fee, as determined by the State Department of Health Care Services, not to exceed the actual costs of administration related to the special permit. An application for a special permit submitted by a psychiatric health facility operated by a public entity shall be exempt from the fee required pursuant to this section for the issuance of the special permit.

(3) The State Department of Health Care Services shall not issue a special permit unless the applicant furnishes all of the following:

(A) Its annual licensing fee required pursuant to subdivision (a).

(B) A completed application submitted on forms furnished by the department.

(C) A written agreement ensuring that the facility will have additional staffing for the services to be provided under the special permit, that the additional staffing will meet the same professional standards as required by regulation for inpatient services, and that a coordinator of these services will be appointed.

(D) Any other information or documentation as may be required by the department for its proper and efficient administration and enforcement of special permit services.

(4) The provision of structured outpatient services pursuant to a special permit may be as an alternative to admission to inpatient services, as aftercare services following discharge from inpatient care, or as both.

(Amended by Stats. 2013, Ch. 23, Sec. 10. (AB 82) Effective June 27, 2013.)

1266.5.

(a) Whenever any entity required to pay fees pursuant to Section 1266 continues to operate beyond its license expiration date, without the Licensing and Certification Program renewal fees first having been paid as required by this division, those fees are delinquent.

(b) A late payment penalty shall be added to any delinquent fees due with an application for license renewal made later than midnight of the license expiration date. The late payment penalty shall be computed as follows:

(1) For a delinquency period of 30 days or less, the penalty shall be 10 percent of the fee.

(2) For a delinquency period of more than 30 days to and including 60 days, the penalty shall be 20 percent of the fee.

(3) For a delinquency period of more than 60 days, the penalty shall be 60 percent of the fee.

(c) The department may, upon written notification to the licensee, offset any moneys owed to the licensee by the Medi-Cal program or any other payment program administered by the department, to recoup the license renewal fee and any associated late payment penalties.

(d) No license may be renewed without payment of the Licensing and Certification Program fee plus any late payment penalty.

(Added by Stats. 2006, Ch. 74, Sec. 7. Effective July 12, 2006.)

1266.7.

The annual Licensing and Certification Program fee for a congregate living health facility shall be set in accordance with Section 1266.

(Added by Stats. 2006, Ch. 74, Sec. 8. Effective July 12, 2006.)

1266.9.

There is hereby created in the State Treasury the State Department of Public Health Licensing and Certification Program Fund. The revenue collected in accordance with Section 1266 shall be deposited in the State Department of Public Health Licensing and Certification Program Fund and shall be available for expenditure, upon appropriation by the Legislature, to support the department's Licensing and Certification Program's operation. Interest earned on the moneys in the fund shall be deposited as revenue into the fund to support the department's Licensing and Certification Program's operation.

(Amended by Stats. 2007, Ch. 483, Sec. 15. Effective January 1, 2008.)

1266.10.

The amount of three million two hundred four thousand three hundred seventy dollars ($3,204,370) is appropriated from the General Fund to the State Department of Health Services, for a loan for use to support the operations of the Licensing and Certification Program. Repayment of this loan shall be made with proceeds from fees collected pursuant to Section 1266, in three equal annual installments of one million sixty-eight thousand one hundred twenty-three dollars ($1,068,123), commencing on July 1, 2007, or upon the enactment of the Budget Act of 2007, whichever is later.

(Added by Stats. 2006, Ch. 74, Sec. 10. Effective July 12, 2006.)

1266.12.

(a) The annual Licensing and Certification Program fee for a skilled nursing facility, intermediate care facility, general acute care hospital, acute psychiatric hospital, special hospital, chemical dependency recovery hospital, correctional treatment center, intermediate care facility/developmentally disabled, intermediate care facility/developmentally disabled nursing, and intermediate care facility/developmentally disabled habilitative shall be set in accordance with Section 1266.

(b) Commencing January 1, 2007, the department shall give priority in conducting initial licensing surveys to each intermediate care facility/developmentally disabled, intermediate care facility/developmentally disabled habilitative, and intermediate care facility/developmentally disabled nursing. Upon successful completion of licensure, and upon notification by the facility that it is ready for an initial certification survey, the department shall schedule and initiate a certification survey within 60 days.

(Added by Stats. 2006, Ch. 74, Sec. 11. Effective July 12, 2006.)

1267.

(a) (1) Each license issued pursuant to this chapter shall expire 12 months from the date of its issuance and each special permit shall expire on the expiration date of the license. Application for renewal of a license or special permit accompanied by the necessary fee shall be filed with the state department not less than 30 days prior to the expiration date. Failure to make a timely renewal shall result in expiration of the license or special permit.

(2) Notwithstanding paragraph (1), the license of a facility operated by a receiver appointed pursuant to Article 8 (commencing with Section 1325) shall not expire during the period of the receivership, and for 30 days thereafter.

(b) A renewal license or special permit may be issued for a period not to exceed two years if the holder of the license or special permit has been found in substantial compliance with any statutory requirements, regulations, or standards during the preceding license period. However, for a health facility specified in subdivision (a) or (b) of Section 1250, a renewal license or special permit may be issued for a period not to exceed three years, if the holder of the license or special permit has been found in substantial compliance with statutory requirements, regulations, or standards during the preceding license period.

(c) Notwithstanding the length of the period for which a renewal license is issued, a license fee shall be due and payable annually.

(Amended by Stats. 2000, Ch. 451, Sec. 5. Effective January 1, 2001.)

1267.5.

(a) (1) Each applicant for a license to operate a skilled nursing facility or intermediate care facility shall disclose to the state department the name and business address of each general partner if the applicant is a partnership, or each director and officer if the applicant is a corporation, and each person having a beneficial ownership interest of 5 percent or more in the applicant corporation or partnership.

(2) If any person described in paragraph (1) has served or currently serves as an administrator, general partner, trustee or trust applicant, sole proprietor of any applicant or licensee who is a sole proprietorship, executor, or corporate officer or director of, or has held a beneficial ownership interest of 5 percent or more in, any other skilled nursing facility or intermediate care facility or in any community care facility licensed pursuant to Chapter 3 (commencing with Section 1500) of this division, the applicant shall disclose the relationship to the state department, including the name and current or last address of the health facility or community care facility and the date the relationship commenced and, if applicable, the date it was terminated.

(3) (A) If the facility is operated by, or proposed to be operated in whole or part under, a management contract, the names and addresses of any person or organization, or both, having an ownership or control interest of 5 percent or more in the management company shall be disclosed to the state department. This provision shall not apply if the management company has submitted an application for licensure with the state department and has complied with paragraph (1).

(B) If the management company is a subsidiary of one or more other organizations, the information shall include the names and addresses of the parent organizations of the management company and the names and addresses of any officer or director of the parent organizations. The failure to comply with this subparagraph may result in action to revoke or deny a license. However, once the information that is required under this subparagraph is provided, the action to revoke the license shall terminate.

(4) If the applicant or licensee is a subsidiary of one or more other organizations, the information shall include the names and addresses of the parent organizations of the subsidiary and the names and addresses of any officer or director of the parent organizations.

(5) The information required by this subdivision shall be provided to the state department upon initial application for licensure, and any change in the information shall be provided to the state department within 30 calendar days of that change.

(6) Except as provided in subparagraph (B) of paragraph (3), the failure to comply with this section may result in action to revoke or deny a license.

(7) The information required by this section shall be made available to the public upon request, shall be included in the public file of the facility, and by July 1, 2002, shall be included in the department's automated certification licensing administration information management system.

(b) On and after January 1, 1990, no person may acquire a beneficial interest of 5 percent or more in any corporation or partnership licensed to operate a skilled nursing facility or intermediate care facility, or in any management company under contract with a licensee of a skilled nursing facility or intermediate care facility, nor may any person become an officer or director of, or general partner in, a corporation, partnership, or management company of this type without the prior written approval of the state department. Each application for departmental approval pursuant to this subdivision shall include the information specified in subdivision (a) as regards the person for whom the application is made.

The state department shall approve or disapprove the application within 30 days after receipt thereof, unless the state department, with just cause, extends the application review period beyond 30 days.

(c) The state department may deny approval of a license application or of an application for approval under subdivision (b) if a person named in the application, as required by this section, was an officer, director, general partner, or owner of a 5-percent or greater beneficial interest in a licensee of, or in a management company under contract with a licensee of, a skilled nursing facility, intermediate care facility, community care facility, or residential care facility for the elderly at a time when one or more violations of law were committed therein that resulted in suspension or revocation of its license, or at a time when a court-ordered receiver was appointed pursuant to Section 1327, or at a time when a final Medi-Cal decertification action was taken under federal law. However, the prior suspension, revocation, or court-ordered receivership of a license shall not be grounds for denial of the application if the applicant shows to the satisfaction of the state department (1) that the person in question took every reasonably available action to prevent the violation or violations that resulted in the disciplinary action and (2) that he or she took every reasonably available action to correct the violation or violations once he or she knew, or with the exercise of reasonable diligence should have known of, the violation or violations.

(d) No application shall be denied pursuant to this section until the state department first (1) provides the applicant with notice in writing of grounds for the proposed denial of application, and (2) affords the applicant an opportunity to submit additional documentary evidence in opposition to the proposed denial.

(e) Nothing in this section shall cause any individual to be personally liable for any civil penalty assessed pursuant to Chapter 2.4 (commencing with Section 1417) or create any new criminal or civil liability contrary to general laws limiting that liability.

(f) This section shall not apply to a bank, trust company, financial institution, title insurer, controlled escrow company, or underwritten title company to which a license is issued in a fiduciary capacity.

(g) As used in this section, "person" has the same meaning as specified in Section 19.

(h) This section shall not apply to the directors of a nonprofit corporation exempt from taxation under Section 23701d of the Revenue and Taxation Code that operates a skilled nursing facility or intermediate care facility in conjunction with a licensed residential facility, where the directors serve without financial compensation and are not compensated by the nonprofit corporation in any other capacity.
(Amended by Stats. 2001, Ch. 685, Sec. 4. Effective January 1, 2002.)
1267.7.
The State Department of Health Services and the State Department of Developmental Services shall jointly develop and implement licensing and Medi-Cal regulations appropriate to intermediate care facility/developmentally disabled-habilitative facilities. These regulations shall ensure that residents of these facilities are assured appropriate developmental and supportive health services in the most normal, least restrictive physical and programmatic environments appropriate to individual resident needs. Regulations adopted pursuant to this section shall include provision for maximum utilization of generic community resources in the provision of services to residents and participation of the residents in community activities.
(Repealed and added by Stats. 1987, Ch. 1456, Sec. 2.5.)
1267.75.
(a) A licensee of an intermediate care facility/developmentally disabled habilitative, as defined in subdivision (e) of Section 1250, or of an intermediate care facility/developmentally disabled, as defined in subdivision (g) of Section 1250, for no more than six residents, except for the larger facilities provided for in paragraph (1) of subdivision (k), may install and utilize delayed egress devices of the time delay type in combination with secured perimeters in accordance with the provisions of this section.

(b) For purposes of this section, the following definitions shall apply:

(1) "Delayed egress device" means a device that precludes the use of exits for a predetermined period of time. These devices shall not delay any resident's departure from the facility for longer than 30 seconds.

(2) "Secured perimeters" means fences that meet the requirements prescribed by this section.

(c) Only individuals meeting all of the following conditions may be admitted to or reside in a facility described in subdivision (a) utilizing delayed egress devices of the time delay type in combination with secured perimeters:

(1) The person shall have a developmental disability as defined in Section 4512 of the Welfare and Institutions Code.

(2) The person shall be receiving services and case management from a regional center under the Lanterman Developmental Disabilities Services Act (Division 4.5 (commencing with Section 4500) of the Welfare and Institutions Code).

(3) (A) The person shall be 14 years of age or older.

(B) Notwithstanding subparagraph (A), a child who is at least 10 years of age and less than 14 years of age may be placed in a licensed facility described in subdivision (a) using delayed egress devices of the time delay type in combination with secured perimeters only if both of the following occur:

(i) A comprehensive assessment is conducted and an individual program plan meeting is convened to determine the services and supports needed for the child to receive services in a less restrictive, unlocked residential setting in California, and the regional center requests assistance from the State Department of Developmental Services' statewide specialized resource service to identify options to serve the child in a less restrictive, unlocked residential setting in California.

(ii) The regional center requests placement of the child in a facility described in subdivision (a) using delayed egress devices of the time delay type in combination with secured perimeters on the basis that the placement is necessary to prevent out-of-state placement or placement in a more restrictive, locked residential setting such as a developmental center, institution for mental disease, or psychiatric facility, and the State Department of Developmental Services approves the request.

(4) (A) An interdisciplinary team, through the individual program plan (IPP) process pursuant to Section 4646.5 of the Welfare and Institutions Code, shall have determined that the person lacks hazard awareness or impulse control and, for his or her safety and security, requires the level of supervision afforded by a facility equipped with delayed egress devices of the time delay type in combination with secured perimeters and that, but for this placement, the person would be at risk of admission to, or would have no option but to remain in, a more restrictive placement. The individual program planning team shall convene every 90 days after admission to determine and document the continued appropriateness of the current placement and progress in implementing the transition plan.

(B) The clients' rights advocate for the regional center shall be notified of the proposed admission and the individual program plan meeting and may participate in the individual program plan meeting, unless the consumer objects on his or her own behalf.

(d) The licensee shall be subject to all applicable fire and building codes, regulations, and standards, and shall receive approval by the county or city fire department, the local fire prevention district, or the State Fire Marshal for the installed devices and secured perimeters.

(e) The licensee shall provide staff training regarding the use and operation of the delayed egress devices of the time delay type and secured perimeters, protection of residents' personal rights, lack of hazard awareness and impulse control behavior, and emergency evacuation procedures.

(f) The licensee shall revise its facility plan of operation. These revisions shall first be approved by the State Department of Developmental Services. The plan of operation shall not be approved by the State Department of Public Health unless the licensee provides certification that the plan was approved by the State Department of Developmental Services. The plan shall include, but not be limited to, all of the following:

(1) A description of how the facility is to be equipped with secured perimeters that are consistent with regulations adopted by the State Fire Marshal pursuant to Section 13143.6.

(2) A description of how the facility will provide training for staff.

(3) A description of how the facility will ensure the protection of the residents' personal rights consistent with Sections 4502, 4503, and 4504 of the Welfare and Institutions Code, and any applicable personal rights provided in Title 22 of the California Code of Regulations.

(4) A description of how the facility will manage residents' lack of hazard awareness and impulse control behavior, which shall emphasize positive behavioral supports and techniques that are alternatives to physical, chemical, or mechanical restraints, or seclusion.

(5) A description of the facility's emergency evacuation procedures.

(6) A description of how the facility will comply with applicable health and safety standards.

(g) Delayed egress devices of the time delay type in combination with secured perimeters shall not substitute for adequate staff.

(h) Emergency fire and earthquake drills shall be conducted on each shift in accordance with existing licensing requirements, and shall include all facility staff providing resident care and supervision on each shift.

(i) Interior and exterior space shall be available on the facility premises to permit clients to move freely and safely.

(j) For the purposes of using secured perimeters, the licensee shall not be required to obtain a waiver or exception to a regulation that would otherwise prohibit the locking of a perimeter fence or gate.

(k) Except as provided in subdivision (k) of Section 4684.81 of the Welfare and Institutions Code, the state shall not authorize or fund more than a combined total of 150 beds statewide in facilities with secured perimeters under this section and under Section 1531.15. The department shall notify the appropriate fiscal and policy committees of the Legislature through the January and May budget estimates prior to authorizing an increase above a combined total of 100 beds statewide in facilities with secured perimeters under this section and under Section 1531.15.

(1) A minimum of 50 beds shall be available within programs designed for individuals who are designated incompetent to stand trial pursuant to Section 1370.1 of the Penal Code. These beds shall be within facilities that are exclusively used to provide care for individuals who are placed and participating in forensic competency training pursuant to Section 1370.1 of the Penal Code, except as provided in paragraph (2). No more than half of these facilities may have more than six beds and no facility may have more than 15 beds.

(2) When, in the joint determination of the regional center and the facility administrator, an individual would be most appropriately served in a specific program, regardless of whether the facility meets the criteria established in paragraph (1), individuals who are not similarly designated may be placed in the same facility. That placement may occur only when the individual's planning team determines that the placement and the facility plan of operation meet the individual's needs and that placement is not incompatible with the needs and safety of other facility residents.

(l) This section shall become operative only upon the filing of emergency regulations by the State Department of Developmental Services. These regulations shall be developed with stakeholders, including the State Department of Public Health, consumer advocates, and regional centers. The regulations shall establish program standards for homes that include delayed egress devices of the time delay type in combination with secured perimeters, including requirements and timelines for the completion and updating of a comprehensive assessment of the consumer's needs, including the identification through the individual program plan process of the services and supports needed to transition the consumer to a less restrictive living arrangement, and a timeline for identifying or developing those services and supports. The regulations shall establish a statewide limit on the total number of beds in homes with delayed egress devices of the time delay type in combination with secured perimeters. The adoption of these regulations shall be deemed to be an emergency and necessary for the immediate preservation of the public peace, health and safety, or general welfare.

(m) This section shall not apply to developmental centers and state-operated community facilities.

(Amended by Stats. 2015, Ch. 23, Sec. 2. (SB 82) Effective June 24, 2015. Note: Pursuant to provisions in subd. (l) (formerly in subd. (k)), this section, as added by Stats. 2012, Ch. 25, became operative on June 13, 2013.)

1267.8.

(a) An intermediate care facility/developmentally disabled habilitative or an intermediate care facility/developmentally disabled—nursing or a congregate living health facility shall meet the same fire safety standards adopted by the State Fire Marshal pursuant to Sections 13113, 13113.5, 13143, and 13143.6 that apply to community care facilities, as defined in Section 1502, of similar size and with residents of similar age and ambulatory status. No other state or local regulations relating to fire safety shall apply to these facilities and the requirements specified in this section shall be uniformly enforced by state and local fire authorities.

(b) An intermediate care facility/developmentally disabled habilitative or an intermediate care facility/developmentally disabled—nursing or a congregate living health facility shall meet the same seismic safety requirements applied to community care facilities of similar size with residents of similar age and ambulatory status. No additional requirements relating to seismic safety shall apply to such facilities.

(c) Whether or not unrelated persons are living together, an intermediate care facility/developmentally disabled habilitative which serves six or fewer persons or an intermediate care facility/developmentally disabled—nursing which serves six or fewer persons or a congregate living health facility shall be considered a residential use of property for the purposes of this article. In addition, the residents and operators of the facility shall be considered a family for the purposes of any law or zoning ordinance that is related to the residential use of property pursuant to this article.

(d) For the purposes of all local ordinances, an intermediate care facility/developmentally disabled habilitative that serves six or fewer persons or an intermediate care facility/developmentally disabled—nursing that serves six or fewer persons or a congregate living health facility shall not be included within the definition of a boarding house, rooming house, institution or home for the care of minors, the aged, or persons with mental health disorders, foster care home, guest home, rest home, community residence, or other similar term that implies that the intermediate care facility/developmentally disabled habilitative or intermediate care facility/developmentally disabled—nursing or a congregate living health facility is a business run for profit or differs in any other way from a single-family residence.

(e) This section does not forbid a city, county, or other local public entity from placing restrictions on building heights, setback, lot dimensions, or placement of signs of an intermediate care facility/developmentally disabled habilitative that serves six or fewer persons or an intermediate care facility/developmentally disabled—nursing that serves six or fewer persons or a congregate living health facility as long as those restrictions are identical to those applied to other single-family residences.

(f) This section does not forbid the application to an intermediate care facility/developmentally disabled habilitative or an intermediate care facility/developmentally disabled—nursing or a congregate living health facility of any local ordinance that deals with health and safety, building standards, environmental impact standards, or any other matter within the jurisdiction of a local public entity, as long as that ordinance does not distinguish intermediate care facility/developmentally disabled habilitative that serves six or fewer persons or an intermediate care facility/developmentally disabled—nursing or a congregate living health facility from other single-family dwellings and that the ordinance does not distinguish residents of the intermediate care facility/developmentally disabled habilitative or intermediate care facility/developmentally disabled—nursing that serves six or fewer persons or a congregate living health facility from persons who reside in other single-family dwellings.

(g) No conditional use permit, zoning variance, or other zoning clearance shall be required of an intermediate care facility/developmentally disabled habilitative that serves six or fewer persons or an intermediate care facility/developmentally disabled—nursing that serves six or fewer persons or a congregate living health facility that is not required of a single-family residence in the same zone.

(h) Use of a single-family dwelling for purposes of an intermediate care facility/developmentally disabled habilitative serving six or fewer persons or an intermediate care facility/developmentally disabled—nursing that serves six or fewer persons or a congregate living health facility shall not constitute a change of occupancy for purposes of Part 1.5 (commencing with Section 17910) of Division 13 or local building codes. However, nothing in this section supersedes Section 13143 to the extent these provisions are applicable to intermediate care facility/developmentally disabled habilitative providing care for six or fewer residents or an intermediate care facility/developmentally disabled—nursing serving six or fewer persons or a congregate living health facility.

(Amended by Stats. 2014, Ch. 144, Sec. 27. (AB 1847) Effective January 1, 2015.)

1267.9.

(a) The Legislature hereby declares it to be the policy of the state to prevent overconcentrations of intermediate care facilities/development ally disabled habilitative, intermediate care facilities/developmentally disabled-nursing, congregate living health facilities, or pediatric day health and respite care facilities, as defined in Section 1760.2, which impair the integrity of residential neighborhoods. Therefore, the director shall deny an application for a new intermediate care facility/developmentally disabled habilitative license, a new intermediate care facility/developmentally disabled-nursing license, a congregate living health facility, or a pediatric day health and respite care facility license if the director determines that the location is in such proximity to an existing intermediate care facility/developmentally disabled habilitative, an intermediate care facility/developmentally disabled-nursing, a congregate living health facility, or a pediatric day health and respite care facility as would result in overconcentration.

(b) As used in this section, "overconcentration" means that if a new license is issued, either of the following will occur:

(1) There will be intermediate care facilities/developmentally disabled habilitative, intermediate care facilities/developmentally disabled-nursing, residential care facilities, as defined in Section 1502, or pediatric day health and respite care facilities which are separated by a distance of less than 300 feet, as measured from any point upon the outside walls of the structures housing the facilities.

(2) There will be congregate living health facilities serving persons who are terminally ill, diagnosed with a life-threatening illness, or catastrophically and severely disabled, as defined in Section 1250, which are separated by a distance of less than 1,000 feet, as measured from any point upon the outside walls of the structures housing the facilities. Based on special local needs and conditions, the director may approve a separation distance of less than 300 feet or 1,000 feet, whichever is applicable, with the approval of the city or county in which the proposed facility will be located.

(c) At least 45 days prior to approving any application for a new intermediate care facility/developmentally disabled habilitative, a new intermediate care facility/developmentally disabled-nursing, a congregate living health facility, or a pediatric day health and respite care facility, the director shall notify, in writing, the city or county planning authority in which the facility will be located, of the proposed location of the facility.

(d) Any city or county may request denial of the license applied for on the basis of overconcentration of intermediate care facilities/developmentally disabled habilitative, intermediate care facilities/developmentally disabled-nursing, a congregate living health facility, or a pediatric day health and respite care facility.

(e) Nothing in this section authorizes the director, on the basis of overconcentration, to refuse to renew an intermediate care facility/development ally disabled habilitative license, an intermediate care facility/developmental ly disabled-nursing license, a congregate living health facility license, or a pediatric day health and respite care facility license, or to refuse to grant a license upon a change of ownership of an existing intermediate care facility/developmentally disabled habilitative, intermediate care facility/developmentally disabled-nursing, a congregate living health facility, or a pediatric day health and respite care facility where there is no change in the location of the facility.

(f) Foster family homes and residential care facilities for the elderly shall not be considered in determining overconcentration of intermediate care facilities/developmentally disabled-habilitative, intermediate care facilities/developmentally disabled-nursing, residential care facilities, as defined in Section 1502, congregate living health facilities, or pediatric day health and respite care facilities.

(Amended by Stats. 1990, Ch. 1227, Sec. 5. Effective September 24, 1990.)

1267.11.

Each intermediate care facility/developmentally disabled-habilitative shall designate direct care staff persons to supervise the direct care services to clients for at least 56 hours per week. The hours of these supervisory staff persons shall be applied against the total number of direct care hours required in regulations developed by the department pursuant to Section 1267.7. These supervisory staff persons shall, at a minimum, meet one of the following criteria:

(a) Possession of a valid vocational nurse or psychiatric technician license issued by the Board of Vocational Nurse and Psychiatric Technician Examiners.

(b) Completion of at least 30 college or university units in education, social services, behavioral sciences, health sciences, or related fields, and six months experience providing direct services to developmentally disabled persons.

(c) Eighteen months experience providing direct services to developmentally disabled persons while under the supervision of a person who meets the requirements of a mental retardation professional as defined in regulations promulgated pursuant to Section 1267.7.

(Added by Stats. 1987, Ch. 1456, Sec. 2.7.)

1267.12.

No person shall be admitted, or accepted for care, or discharged, by a congregate living health facility except upon the order of a physician and surgeon. Admission criteria shall be subject to review and approval by the state department. All persons admitted or accepted for care by the congregate living health facility shall remain under the care of a physician and surgeon who shall see the resident at least every 30 calendar days or more frequently if required by the resident's medical condition.

(Added by Stats. 1988, Ch. 1478, Sec. 8. Effective September 28, 1988.)

1267.13.

Pursuant to paragraph (3) of subdivision (a) and subdivision (b) of Section 1265.7, this section shall be effective until the adoption of permanent regulations. Notwithstanding, the state department has authority to make reasonable accommodation for exceptions to the standards in this section, providing the health, safety, and quality of patient care is not compromised. No exceptions shall be made for building standards. Prior written approval communicating the terms and conditions under which the exception is granted shall be required. Applicants shall request the exception in writing accompanied by detailed, supporting documentation.

Congregate living health facilities serving persons who are terminally ill, persons who are catastrophically and severely disabled, persons who are mentally alert but physically disabled, or any combination of these persons, shall conform to the following:

(a) Facilities shall obtain and maintain a valid fire clearance from the appropriate authority having jurisdiction over the facility, based on compliance with state regulations concerning fire and life safety, as adopted by the State Fire Marshal.

(b) The State Fire Marshal, with the advice of the State Board of Fire Services, shall adopt regulations on or before January 1, 1991, following a public hearing, establishing minimum requirements for the protection of life and property for congregate living health facilities serving terminally ill persons, catastrophically and severely disabled persons, persons who are mentally alert but physically disabled, or any combination of these persons. These minimum requirements shall recognize the residential and noninstitutional setting of congregate living health facilities serving terminally ill persons, catastrophically and severely disabled persons, persons who are mentally alert but physically disabled, or any combination of these persons.

(c) Facilities shall be in a homelike residential setting. Living accommodations and grounds shall be related to the facility's function and clientele. Facilities shall provide sufficient space for comfortable living accommodations and privacy for residents, staff, and others who may reside in the facility.

(d) Common rooms, including, but not limited to, living rooms, dining rooms, and dens or other recreation or activity rooms, shall be provided and shall have sufficient space, separation, or both to promote and facilitate the program of activities and to prevent these activities from interfering with other functions. Accommodations shall ensure adequate space for residents to have visitors and for privacy during visits, if desired.

(e) Resident bedrooms shall have adequate space to allow easy passage throughout; permit comfortable usage of furnishings; promote ease of nursing care; and accommodate use of assistive devices, including, but not limited to, wheelchairs, walkers, and patient lifts, when needed.

(f) No room commonly used for other purposes, including, but not limited to, a hall, stairway, attic, garage, storage area, shed, or similar detached building, shall be used as a sleeping room for any resident.

(g) No resident bedroom shall be used as a passageway to another room, bath, or toilet.

(h) Not more than two residents shall share a bedroom.

(i) Equipment and supplies necessary for personal care and maintenance of adequate hygiene shall be readily available to all residents.

(j) Toilets and bathrooms shall be conveniently located. At least one toilet and washbasin shall be provided per six residents. At least one bathtub or shower shall be provided per 10 residents. Individual privacy shall be provided in all toilet, bath and shower areas. Separate toilet, washbasin, and bathtub or shower accommodations shall be provided for staff.

(k) Sufficient room shall be available throughout the facility to accommodate and serve all persons in comfort and safety. The premises shall be maintained in good repair and shall provide a safe, clean, and healthful environment.

(l) Facilities shall have equipment and supplies appropriate to meet the routine and specialized needs of all residents.

(m) All persons shall be protected from hazards throughout the premises:

(1) Stairways, inclines, ramps, open porches, and other areas of potential hazard to residents with poor balance or eyesight shall be made inaccessible unless well lighted and equipped with sturdy hand railings.

(2) Night lights shall be maintained in hallways and passages to nonprivate bathrooms.

(3) All indoor and outdoor passageways and stairways shall be kept free of obstructions.

(4) Fireplaces, woodstoves, and open-faced heaters shall be adequately screened.

(5) Facilities shall assure the inaccessibility of fishponds, wading pools, hot tubs, swimming pools, or similar bodies of water or other areas of potential hazard when not in active use.

(n) Facilities serving persons who are terminally ill, catastrophically and severely disabled, mentally alert but physically disabled, or any combination of these persons, shall, in addition to the requirements of this chapter and until specific regulations governing their operation are filed, conform to regulations contained in Chapter 3 of Division 5 of Title 22 of the California Code of Regulations of April 1, 1988, with the exception of the following sections or portions of sections: 72007, 72053, 72073, subdivision (a) of Section 72077, 72097, 72099, 72103, 72203, subdivision (a) of Section 72205, 72301, 72305, subdivision (a) of Section 72325, 72327, 72329, 72331, 72337, subdivisions (b), (g), and (h) of Section 72351, 72353, subdivision (a) of Section 72367, 72373, subdivision (b) of Section 72375, 72401, 72403, 72405, 72407, 72409, 72411, 72413, 72415, 72417, 72419, 72421, 72423, 72425, 72427, 72429, 72431, 72433, 72435, 72437, 72439, 72441, 72443, 72445, 72447, 72449, 72451, 72453, 72455, 72457, 72459, 72461, 72463, 72465, 72467, 72469, 72471, 72473, 72475, 72503, paragraph (2) of subdivision (a) of Section 72513, 72520, 72535, 72555, 72557, subdivisions (a) and (b) of Section 72601, subdivision (d) of Section 72607, subdivisions (a) and (d) of Section 72609, 72611, 72615, 72617, 72629, 72631, 72633, 72635, subdivisions (b), (c), and (d) of Section 72639, 72641, and 72665.

(o) (1) Facilities serving persons who are terminally ill, catastrophically and severely disabled, mentally alert but physically disabled, or any combination of these persons, shall have an administrator who is responsible for the day-to-day operation of the facility. The administrator may be either a licensed registered nurse, a nursing home administrator, or the licensee. The administrator shall be present at the facility a sufficient number of hours to ensure the smooth operation of the facility. If the administrator is also the registered nurse fulfilling the duties specified in paragraph (2), the administrator shall not be responsible for more than one facility. In all other circumstances, the administrator shall not be responsible for more than three facilities with an aggregate total of 75 beds and these facilities shall be within one hour's surface travel time of each other.

(2) (A) For each congregate living health facility of more than six beds serving persons who are terminally ill, catastrophically and severely disabled, mentally alert but physically disabled, or any combination of these persons, there shall be, at a minimum, a registered nurse or licensed vocational nurse awake and on duty at all times. A registered nurse shall be awake and on duty eight hours a day, five days a week.

(B) For each congregate living health facility of six or fewer beds serving persons who are terminally ill, catastrophically and severely disabled, mentally alert but physically disabled, or any combination of these persons, a registered nurse shall visit each patient at least twice a week for approximately two hours, or more as patient care requires.

(C) For all congregate living health facilities serving persons who are terminally ill, catastrophically and severely disabled, mentally alert but physically disabled, or any combination of these persons, a registered nurse shall be available for consultation and able to come into the facility within 30 minutes, if necessary, when no registered nurse is on duty. In addition, certified nurse assistants, or persons with similar training and experience as determined by the department, shall be awake and on duty in the facility in at least the following ratios: facilities with six beds or less, one per shift; facilities with 7 to 12 beds, two per shift; facilities with 13 to 25 beds, three per day and evening shifts and two per nocturnal shift. No nursing services personnel shall be assigned housekeeping or dietary duties.

(3) Notwithstanding the provisions of this subdivision, the facility shall provide appropriately qualified staff in sufficient numbers to meet patient care needs.

(4) Nursing service personnel shall be employed and on duty in at least the number and with the qualifications determined by the department to provide the necessary nursing services for patients admitted for care. The department may require a facility to provide additional professional, administrative, or supportive personnel whenever the state department determines through a written evaluation, that additional personnel are needed to provide for the health and safety of patients.

(5) All staff members shall receive orientation regarding care appropriate for the patients' diagnoses and individual resident needs. Orientation shall include a minimum of 16 hours during the first 40 hours of employment.

(6) Nothing in this chapter shall prevent the use of volunteers; however, volunteers shall not be used as substitutes for the personnel required in the above sections. Volunteers providing patient care services shall:

(A) Be provided clearly defined roles and written job descriptions.

(B) Receive orientation and training equivalent to that provided paid staff.

(C) Possess education and experience equal to that required of paid staff performing similar functions.

(D) Conform to the facility's policies and procedures.

(E) Receive periodic performance evaluations.

(p) The interim standards prescribed by this section shall become inoperative upon the filing of the regulations with the Secretary of State.

(Amended by Stats. 1993, Ch. 1020, Sec. 1. Effective January 1, 1994.)

1267.15.

(a) Congregate living health facilities shall be freestanding, but this does not preclude their location on the premises of a hospital. Congregate living health facilities shall be separately licensed.

(b) Notwithstanding subdivision (a), multiple congregate living health facilities may exist in one multifloor building if all of the following requirements are satisfied:

(1) Each facility meets other applicable building standards not related to multiple floors.

(2) Each facility is separated by a wall, floor, or other permanent partition but may share an elevator, stairs, or stairwell, and need not be freestanding.

(3) Proposals to develop proximate congregate living health facilities are supported by the county health department and the board of supervisors in the county in which the facilities are to be located.

(4) The congregate living health facilities are proposed for one of the following locations:

(A) McClellan Air Force Base Building No. 522, located at 3201 James Way, McClellan, California.

(B) McClellan Air Force Base Building No. 523, located at 3207 James Way, McClellan, California.

(C) McClellan Air Force Base Building No. 524, located at 5621 Dudley Blvd., McClellan, California.

(D) McClellan Air Force Base Building No. 525, located at 5327 Dudley Blvd., McClellan, California.

(Amended by Stats. 2013, Ch. 722, Sec. 3. (SB 534) Effective January 1, 2014.)

1267.16.

(a) A congregate living health facility which serves six or fewer persons shall be considered a residential use of property for purposes of any zoning ordinance or law related to the residential use of property. This article does not forbid any city, county, or local public entity from placing restrictions on building heights, setback, lot dimensions, or placement of signs of a congregate living health facility as long as these restrictions are identical to those applied to single-family residences.

(b) This article does not forbid the application to a congregate living health facility of any local ordinance which deals with health and safety, building standards, environmental impact standards, or any other matter within the jurisdiction of a local public entity, except as provided in subdivisions (a) and (b) of Section 1267.9 and this section.

(c) Any congregate living health facility of more than six beds for persons who are terminally ill and any congregate living health facility of more than six beds for persons who are catastrophically and severely disabled shall be subject to the conditional use permit requirements of the city or county in which it is located unless those requirements are waived by the city or county. However, any facility that, on the effective date of this section, is performing the functions of a congregate living health facility for persons who are terminally ill and that is subsequently licensed as a congregate living health facility within 18 months of the effective date of this section shall not be subject to the conditional use permit requirements of the city or county in which it is located, unless the number of beds is increased.

(Amended by Stats. 1989, Ch. 1393, Sec. 7. Effective October 2, 1989.)

1267.17.

Each congregate living health facility shall conspicuously post the license, or a true copy thereof in a location accessible to public view.

(Added by Stats. 1988, Ch. 1478, Sec. 12. Effective September 28, 1988.)

1267.19.

Congregate living health facilities shall not be subject to architectural plan review by the Office of Statewide Health Planning and Development. As part of the application for licensure, the prospective licensee shall submit evidence of compliance with local building code requirements. In addition, the physical environment shall be adequate to provide for the level of care and service required by the residents of the facility, as determined by the department.

(Amended by Stats. 2006, Ch. 538, Sec. 350. Effective January 1, 2007.)

1268.

(a) Upon the filing of the application for licensure or for a special permit for special services and full compliance with this chapter and the rules and regulations of the state

department, the state department shall issue to the applicant the license or special permit applied for. A license shall not be issued or renewed for beds permanently converted to other than patient use and that do not meet construction and operational requirements. However, if the director finds that the applicant is not in compliance with the laws or regulations of this part, the director shall deny the applicant a license or a special permit for special services. Additionally, the director shall not issue a license covering a project within the meaning of Section 127170 for which there is no valid, subsisting, and unexpired certificate of need issued pursuant to Chapter 1 (commencing with Section 127125) of Part 2 of Division 107.

(b) As a condition of licensure, the director shall require evidence that the applicant have a written policy relating to the dissemination of the following information to patients:

(1) A summary of current state laws requiring child passenger restraint systems to be used when transporting children in motor vehicles.

(2) A listing of child passenger restraint system programs located within the county, as required by Section 27360 or 27362 of the Vehicle Code.

(3) Information describing the risks of death or serious injury associated with the failure to utilize a child passenger restraint system.

A hospital may satisfy the requirements of this paragraph by reproducing for distribution materials specified in Section 27366 of the Vehicle Code, describing the risks of injury or death as a result of the failure to utilize passenger restraints for infants and children, as provided, without charge, by the Department of the California Highway Patrol. A hospital that does not have these materials, but demonstrates that it has made a written request to the Department of the California Highway Patrol for the materials, is in compliance with this paragraph.

(c) The conversion of a general acute care hospital or special hospital to a general acute care hospital that exclusively provides acute medical rehabilitation center services shall not require a certificate of need, as required by Section 127170, if the health facility is rendering the services specified in subdivision (f) of Section 1250 on January 1, 1979.

(Amended (as amended by Stats. 1995, Ch. 512) by Stats. 1996, Ch. 1023, Sec. 157. Effective September 29, 1996.)

1268.5.

(a) Notwithstanding the provisions of Section 1268 requiring full compliance with this chapter and the rules and regulations of the state department as a condition to the issuance of a license or special permit, the state department may issue a provisional license to a health facility except for a health facility defined in subdivisions (a) and (b) of Section 1250, if:

(1) The facility and the applicant for licensure substantially meet the standards specified by this chapter and regulations adopted pursuant to this chapter.

(2) No violation of this chapter or regulations adopted pursuant to this chapter exists in the facility which jeopardizes the health or safety of patients.

(3) The applicant has adopted a plan for correction of any existing violations which is satisfactory to the state department.

(b) A provisional license issued under this section shall expire not later than six months after the date of issuance, or at an earlier time as determined by the state department at the time of issuance, and may not be renewed. At the end of the provisional license period under this section or Section 1437 the state department shall assess the facility's full compliance with licensure requirements. The state department may extend a provisional license for a period of no longer than six months from the time of the extension for one of the following purposes:

(1) Requiring the facility's full compliance with a plan of correction, which includes time frames, as specified by the state department.

(2) Allowing the provisional licensee to comply with Section 1336.2.

(3) Providing for a change of ownership.

(4) Instituting a receivership of the facility.

The length of the extension period shall be determined by the state department at the time of the issuance of the extension.

(c) The department shall not apply less stringent criteria when issuing a provisional license pursuant to this section than it applies when issuing a license pursuant to Section 1268.

It is the intent of the Legislature in enacting this section to additionally provide for continuity of reimbursement under the Medi-Cal Act, Chapter 7 (commencing with Section 14000) of Part 3 of Division 9 of the Welfare and Institutions Code, whenever ownership of a skilled nursing facility or intermediate care facility is transferred.

(Amended by Stats. 1989, Ch. 811, Sec. 1.)

1268.6.

(a) Commencing October 1, 2011, as a requirement of initial licensure of an intermediate care facility/developmentally disabled-habilitative or an intermediate care facility/developmentally disabled-nursing, the applicant or designee of the applicant shall attend a sixteen-hour orientation program approved by the State Department of Developmental Services.

(b) The sixteen-hour orientation program shall contain both of the following:

(1) Eight hours of the orientation program shall outline the role, requirements, and regulations of each of the following:

(A) The scope of responsibility for operation including regulatory requirements and statutes governing the facility type.

(B) Local planning.

(C) Regional center and other community support services.

(D) All federal and state agencies responsible for licensing and certification, and data collection.

(E) Government and private agencies responsible for ensuring the rights of the developmentally disabled.

(2) Eight hours of the orientation program shall outline the statutory and regulatory requirements related to business management. The program shall include, but need not be limited to, all of the following:

(A) Cost reporting.

(B) General accounting principles.

(C) The State Department of Health Care Services' audit process.

(D) The regional center vendorization process.

(c) The orientation shall be conducted by relevant community services and provider organizations. Organizations conducting the orientation class shall be responsible for keeping a record of all attendees and shall provide the department with the information within 15 working days or upon request. Instructors of the orientation shall have knowledge or experience in the subject area to be taught, and shall meet any of the following criteria:

(1) Possession of a four-year college degree relevant to the course or courses to be taught.

(2) Be a health professional with a valid and current license to practice in California.

(3) Have at least two years experience in California as an administrator of a long-term health care facility that provides services to persons with developmental disabilities within the last eight years.

(d) If the licensee can demonstrate to the satisfaction of the department that the licensee, or a representative of the licensee, has taken the orientation program any year prior to opening a new facility, the licensee shall not be required to repeat the program to open the facility.

(e) This section shall become operative on October 1, 2011.

(Repealed (in Sec. 1) and added by Stats. 2010, Ch. 473, Sec. 2. (AB 2675) Effective January 1, 2011. Section operative October 1, 2011, by its own provisions.)

1269.

Immediately upon the denial of any application for a license or for a special permit for special services, the state department shall notify the applicant in writing. Within 20 days after the state department mails the notice, the applicant may present his written petition for a hearing to the state department. Upon receipt by the state department of the petition in proper form, such petition shall be set for hearing. The proceedings shall be conducted in accordance with Chapter 5 (commencing with Section 11500) of Part 1 of Division 3 of Title 2 of the Government Code, and the state department has all the powers granted therein.

(Added by Stats. 1973, Ch. 1202.)

1270.

The provisions of this chapter do not apply to the following institutions:

(a) Any facility conducted by and for the adherents of any well-recognized church or religious denomination for the purpose of providing facilities for the care or treatment of the sick who depend upon prayer or spiritual means for healing in the practice of the religion of that church or denomination.

(b) Hotels or other similar places that furnish only board and room, or either, to their guests.

(c) Any house or institution supplying board and room only, or room only, or board only; provided, that no resident thereof requires any element of medical care as determined by the department.

For the purpose of this subdivision "medical care" means those services required to be provided by health professionals in accordance with the provisions of Division 2 (commencing with Section 500) of the Business and Professions Code. In addition, medical services means those services provided by health facilities as defined in Sections 1250, 1250.2, and 1250.3 which includes nursing care to patients whose primary need is for the availability of licensed nursing care on an extended, continuous, intermittent, or part-time basis.

(d) Any facility as defined in Section 1502.

(Amended by Stats. 1988, Ch. 1478, Sec. 14. Effective September 28, 1988.)

1271.

(a) The Legislature finds and declares that uniform orientation and training are fundamental to ensuring a high level of competency of state personnel charged with enforcing state law regulating the licensure, certification, and inspection of long-term health care facilities.

(b) The state department shall develop, adopt, and implement comprehensive continuing orientation and in-service training programs. The comprehensive programs shall, at a minimum, include, but not be limited to, both of the following:

(1) An orientation program consisting of instruction in basic enforcement, inspection, investigation, and survey skills and techniques, patients' rights and safety, health facility, clinic, and agency licensing regulations, and supervised on-the-job training in long-term health care facilities.

(2) Ongoing in-service training to maintain continuing competency in existing and new inspection, investigation, and enforcement skills, patient care modalities, and to assure statewide uniform interpretation and application of long-term health care facility licensing regulations.

(c) The state department shall establish and maintain a program review function responsible for inspecting, monitoring, evaluating, and providing consultative support and assistance to licensing and certification field offices. The program review shall ensure that the licensing and certification field offices implement, enforce, and interpret applicable state statutes, licensing regulations, certification standards, and departmental policies and procedures in an effective and uniform manner statewide.

(Added by Stats. 1985, Ch. 11, Sec. 3. Effective March 6, 1985.)

1271.1.

(a) A health facility may place up to 50 percent of its licensed bed capacity in voluntary suspension for a period not exceeding three years, upon submitting written notification to the state department and to the Office of Statewide Health Planning and Development. However, this section does not authorize a health facility to deactivate all beds utilized for the provision of a basic service or to deactivate all beds utilized for a special service or other supplemental service for which the health facility holds a special permit or licensure approval. Prior to the expiration of the voluntary suspension, the health facility may request an extension, that may be granted by the director if the director finds, after consultation with the Director of the Office of Statewide Health Planning and Development, that there is no identified need for additional beds (of the category suspended) in the service area of the health facility. If during a period of voluntary suspension under this section the statewide Health Facilities and Services Plan identifies a need for additional beds (of the category suspended) in the health facility's service area, the Director of the Office of Statewide Health Planning and Development may require the health facility to terminate the voluntary suspension and exercise one of the following options, at the discretion of the health facility: (1) place some or all of the suspended beds in operation, in accordance with the identified need, within one year following his or her order, or (2) alternatively have the beds deemed permanently converted to other than patient use within the meaning of Section 1268.

(b) A health facility may remove all or any portion of its voluntarily suspended bed capacity from voluntary suspension by request to the state department, which request shall be granted unless the areas housing the suspended beds fail to meet currently applicable operational requirements or fail to meet construction requirements for the health facility in effect at the time the request for suspension of the beds was received by the state department.

(c) While health facility beds are in suspension pursuant to subdivision (a), the beds shall not be deemed to be permanently converted to other than patient use, for purposes of Section 1268. The requirements of this section shall not apply to any temporary deactivation of beds necessitated by the work of construction or other activities required with respect to a project for which a certificate of need or certificate of exemption has been granted pursuant to Chapter 1 (commencing with Section 127125) of Part 2 of Division 107. Nothing in this section shall in any way limit or affect the authority of a health facility to use a portion of its beds in one bed classification in another bed classification as permitted by subdivision (a) of Section 127170, including the use of general acute care beds as skilled nursing beds; provided, however, that when beds in a particular classification are suspended pursuant to this section, the remainder of the health facility's beds in the same classification may not be used so as to result in elimination of all beds utilized for provision of a basic service or utilized for provision of a special service or other supplemental service for which the health facility holds a special permit or licensure approval.

(Amended by Stats. 1996, Ch. 1023, Sec. 158. Effective September 29, 1996.)

1271.15.

(a) Notwithstanding any provision of law to the contrary, including, but not limited to, Section 1271.1, a health facility may do any of the following:

(1) (A) It may place all or a portion of its licensed bed capacity in voluntary suspension for the purposes of using the facility to operate a licensed mental health rehabilitation center pursuant to Section 5675 of the Welfare and Institutions Code after submitting written notification to the State Department of Health Services and to the Office of Statewide Health Planning and Development. During the period of voluntary suspense, the facility shall remain under the jurisdiction of the office. The office shall enforce both the mental health rehabilitation center requirements and the health facility requirements of the California Building Standards Code.

(B) A mental health rehabilitation center operating under this paragraph may remove all or any portion of its voluntarily suspended bed capacity from voluntary suspension by submitting a request to the State Department of Health Services.

(C) The department shall grant the request under subparagraph (B) to remove bed capacity from voluntary suspension and to reinstatement of the health facility bed capacity, unless the facility fails to meet currently applicable operational requirements for a health facility.

(b) This section authorizes the voluntary suspension of bed capacity or surrender of a license by a health facility only for the purpose of converting the facility for use as a licensed mental health rehabilitation center pursuant to Section 5675 of the Welfare and Institutions Code.

(Added by Stats. 2004, Ch. 509, Sec. 1. Effective January 1, 2005.)

1272.

(a) If a general acute care hospital or an acute psychiatric hospital submits a written application to the department's centralized applications unit, the department shall do both of the following:

(1) Complete its evaluation and approve or deny the application within 100 days of receiving it, including completing any activities pursuant to paragraph (2).

(2) Once the written application is approved, the district office of the department shall, within 30 business days from the date of approval, complete any additional review, including an onsite visit, if applicable, and submit its findings to the department. If the hospital's application is approved, the department shall add it to the hospital's license and issue a new or revised license on the 31st business day following approval of the written application.

(b) Notwithstanding subdivision (a), if a general acute care hospital or an acute psychiatric hospital submits a written application to expand a service that it currently provides and that is currently approved by the department, the department shall, within 30 business days of receipt of the completed application, approve the expansion, add it to the hospital license, and issue a revised license, unless the hospital is out of compliance with existing laws governing the service to be expanded. A service approved pursuant to this subdivision shall remain licensed for not more than 18 months, unless the department approves the license for a longer period. The department shall not be required to conduct an onsite inspection of the service to approve the expansion. This subdivision does not preclude the department from conducting an onsite inspection of a hospital at any time or denying an application in accordance with this subdivision.

(c) A general acute care hospital or an acute psychiatric hospital that receives a license to modify, add, or expand a service or program pursuant to this section shall comply with all laws related to that service or program.

(d) The department shall develop a centralized applications advice program to assist hospitals in identifying and completing the correct paperwork and other requirements necessary to modify, add, or expand a service or program.

(e) On or before December 31, 2019, the department shall develop an automated application system to process applications submitted pursuant to this section. (Amended by Stats. 2019, Ch. 38, Sec. 13. (SB 78) Effective June 27, 2019.)

(Article 2.5 repealed and added by Stats. 1985, Ch. 11, Sec. 4.)

1273.

Members of the committee shall serve without compensation, but shall receive the current per diem, subsistence, and travel reimbursement paid to state managers, supervisors, and confidential employees for expenses incurred in the performance of their duties. (Repealed and added by Stats. 1985, Ch. 11, Sec. 4. Effective March 6, 1985.)

1274.

The committee shall meet on call of the director but no less than one time per year. (Amended by Stats. 1986, Ch. 1351, Sec. 2.)

(Article 3 added by Stats. 1973, Ch. 1202.)

1275.

(a) (1) The department shall adopt, amend, or repeal, in accordance with Chapter 3.5 (commencing with Section 11340) of Part 1 of Division 3 of Title 2 of the Government Code and Chapter 4 (commencing with Section 18935) of Part 2.5 of Division 13, any reasonable rules and regulations as may be necessary or proper to carry out the purposes and intent of this chapter and to enable the state department to exercise the powers and perform the duties conferred upon it by this chapter, not inconsistent with any other law including, but not limited to, the California Building Standards Law, Part 2.5 (commencing with Section 18901) of Division 13.

(2) All regulations in effect on December 31, 1973, which were adopted by the State Board of Public Health, the State Department of Public Health, the State Department of Mental Hygiene, or the State Department of Health relating to licensed health facilities shall remain in full force and effect until altered, amended, or repealed by the director or pursuant to Section 25 or other provisions of law.

(b) Notwithstanding this section or any other law, the Office of Statewide Health Planning and Development shall adopt and enforce regulations prescribing building standards for the adequacy and safety of health facility physical plants.

(c) The building standards adopted by the State Fire Marshal, and the Office of Statewide Health Planning and Development pursuant to subdivision (b), for the adequacy and safety of freestanding physical plants housing outpatient services of a health facility licensed under subdivision (a) or (b) of Section 1250 shall not be more restrictive or comprehensive than the comparable building standards established, or otherwise made applicable, by the State Fire Marshal and the Office of Statewide Health Planning and Development to clinics and other facilities licensed pursuant to Chapter 1 (commencing with Section 1200).

(d) Except as provided in subdivision (f), the licensing standards adopted by the department under subdivision (a) for outpatient services located in a freestanding physical plant of a health facility licensed under subdivision (a) or (b) of Section 1250 shall not be more restrictive or comprehensive than the comparable licensing standards applied by the department to clinics and other facilities licensed under Chapter 1 (commencing with Section 1200).

(e) Except as provided in subdivision (f), the state agencies specified in subdivisions (c) and (d) shall not enforce any standard applicable to outpatient services located in a freestanding physical plant of a health facility licensed pursuant to subdivision (a) or (b) of Section 1250, to the extent that the standard is more restrictive or comprehensive than the comparable licensing standards applied to clinics and other facilities licensed under Chapter 1 (commencing with Section 1200).

(f) All health care professionals providing services in settings authorized by this section shall be members of the organized medical staff of the health facility to the extent medical staff membership would be required for the provision of the services within the health facility. All services shall be provided under the respective responsibilities of the governing body and medical staff of the health facility.

(g) (1) Notwithstanding any other law, the department may, without taking regulatory action pursuant to Chapter 3.5 (commencing with Section 11340) of Part 1 of Division 3 of Title 2 of the Government Code, update references in the California Code of Regulations to health care standards of practice adopted by a recognized state or national association when the state or national association and its outdated standards are already named in the California Code of Regulations. When updating these references, the department shall:

(A) Post notice of the department's proposed adoption of the state or national association's health care standards of practice on its Internet Web site for at least 45 days. The notice shall include the name of the state or national association, the title of the health care standards of practice, and the version of the updated health care standards of practice to be adopted.

(B) Notify stakeholders that the proposed standards have been posted on the department's Internet Web site by issuing a mailing to the most recent stakeholder list on file with the department's Office of Regulations.

(C) Submit to the Office of Administrative Law the notice required pursuant to this paragraph. The office shall publish in the California Regulatory Notice Register any notice received pursuant to this subparagraph.

(D) Accept public comment for at least 30 days after the conclusion of the 45-day posting period specified in subparagraph (A).

(2) If a member of the public requests a public hearing during the public comment period, a hearing shall be held and comments shall be considered prior to the adoption of the state or national association's health care standards of practice.

(3) If no member of the public requests a public hearing, the department shall consider any comments received during the public comment period prior to the adoption of the health care standards.

(4) Written responses to public comments shall not be required. If public comments are submitted in opposition to the adoption of the proposed standards, or the state or national association named in the California Code of Regulations no longer exists, the department shall seek adoption of the standards using the regulatory process specified in Chapter 3.5 (commencing with Section 11340) of Part 1 of Division 3 of Title 2 of the Government Code. A state or national association named in the California Code of Regulations that has changed its name does not constitute an association that no longer exists.

(5) If no opposition is received by the department, the department shall update its Internet Web site to notify the public that the standard has been adopted and the effective date of that standard.

(h) For purposes of this section, "freestanding physical plant" means any building which is not physically attached to a building in which inpatient services are provided. (Amended by Stats. 2015, Ch. 435, Sec. 2. (AB 614) Effective January 1, 2016.)

1275.1.

(a) Notwithstanding any rules or regulations governing other health facilities, the regulations developed by the State Department of Health Care Services, or a predecessor, for psychiatric health facilities shall prevail. The regulations applying to psychiatric health facilities shall prescribe standards of adequacy, safety, and sanitation of the physical plant, of staffing with duly qualified licensed personnel, and of services based on the needs of the persons served thereby.

(b) The regulations shall include standards appropriate for two levels of disorder:

(1) Involuntary ambulatory psychiatric patients.

(2) Voluntary ambulatory psychiatric patients.

For purposes of this subdivision, "ambulatory patients" shall include, but not be limited to, deaf, blind, and physically handicapped persons. Disoriented persons who are not bedridden or confined to a wheelchair shall also be considered as ambulatory patients.

(c) The regulations shall not require, but may permit building and services requirements for hospitals which are only applicable to physical health care needs of patients that can be met in an affiliated hospital or in outpatient settings including, but not limited to, such requirements as surgical, dietary, laboratory, laundry, central supply, radiologic, and pharmacy.

(d) The regulations shall include provisions for an "open planning" architectural concept.

(e) The regulations shall exempt from seismic requirements all structures of Type V and of one-story construction.

(f) Standards for involuntary patients shall include provisions to allow for restraint and seclusion of patients. These standards shall provide for adequate safeguards for patient safety and protection of patient rights.

(g) The regulations shall provide for the retention by the psychiatric health facility of a consultant pharmacist, who shall supervise and review pharmaceutical services within the facility and perform any other services, including prevention of the unlawful diversion of controlled substances subject to abuse, as the State Department of Health Care Services may by regulation require. Regulations adopted pursuant to this subdivision shall take into consideration the varying bed sizes of psychiatric health facilities. (Amended by Stats. 2013, Ch. 23, Sec. 11. (AB 82) Effective June 27, 2013.)

1275.2.

(a) Notwithstanding any rules or regulations governing other health facilities, the regulations adopted by the state department for chemical dependency recovery hospitals shall prevail. The regulations applying to chemical dependency recovery hospitals shall prescribe standards of adequacy, safety, and sanitation of the physical plant, of staffing with duly qualified personnel, and of services based on the needs of the persons served thereby.

(b) The regulations shall include provisions for an "open planning" architectural concept.

(c) Notwithstanding the provisions of Chapter 1 (commencing with Section 15000) of Division 12.5, the regulations shall exempt from seismic requirements all freestanding structures of a chemical dependency recovery hospital. Chemical dependency recovery services provided as a supplemental service in general acute care beds or general acute psychiatric beds shall not be exempt from seismic requirements.

(d) Regulations shall be developed pursuant to this section and presented for adoption at a public hearing within 180 days of the effective date of this section.

(e) In order to assist in the rapid development of regulations for chemical dependency recovery hospitals, the director of the state department, not later than 30 days after the effective date of this section, shall convene an advisory committee composed of two representatives of the State Department of Health Care Services, one representative of the Office of Statewide Health Planning and Development, two persons with experience operating facilities with alcohol or medicinal drug dependency programs, and any other persons having a professional or personal nonfinancial interest in development of such regulations. The members of such advisory committee who are not state officers or employees shall pay their own expenses related to participation on the committee. The committee shall meet at the call of the director until such time as the proposed regulations are presented for adoption at public hearing.
(Amended by Stats. 2013, Ch. 22, Sec. 14. (AB 75) Effective June 27, 2013. Operative July 1, 2013, by Sec. 110 of Ch. 22.)
1275.3.
(a) The State Department of Public Health and the State Department of Developmental Services shall jointly develop and implement licensing regulations appropriate for an intermediate care facility/developmentally disabled-nursing and an intermediate care facility/developmentally disabled-continuous nursing.
(b) The regulations adopted pursuant to subdivision (a) shall ensure that residents of an intermediate care facility/developmentally disabled-nursing and an intermediate care facility/developmentally disabled-continuous nursing receive appropriate medical and nursing services, and developmental program services in a normalized, least restrictive physical and programmatic environment appropriate to individual resident need.
In addition, the regulations shall do all of the following:
(1) Include provisions for the completion of a clinical and developmental assessment of placement needs, including medical and other needs, and the degree to which they are being met, of clients placed in an intermediate care facility/developmentally disabled-nursing and an intermediate care facility/developmentally disabled-continuous nursing and for the monitoring of these needs at regular intervals.
(2) Provide for maximum utilization of generic community resources by clients residing in a facility.
(3) Require the State Department of Developmental Services to review and approve an applicant's facility program plan as a prerequisite to the licensing and certification process.
(4) Require that the physician providing the certification that placement in the intermediate care facility/developmentally disabled-nursing or intermediate care facility/developmentally disabled-continuous nursing is needed, consult with the physician who is the physician of record at the time the person's proposed placement is being considered by the interdisciplinary team.
(c) Regulations developed pursuant to this section shall include licensing fee schedules appropriate to facilities which will encourage their development.
(d) Until the departments adopt regulations pursuant to this section relating to services by an intermediate care facility/developmentally disabled-nursing, the licensed intermediate care facility/developmentally disabled-nursing shall comply with federal certification standards for intermediate care facilities for individuals with intellectual disabilities, as specified in Sections 483.400 to 483.480, inclusive, of Title 42 of the Code of Federal Regulations, in effect immediately preceding January 1, 2018.
(e) This section shall not supersede the authority of the State Fire Marshal pursuant to Sections 13113, 13113.5, 13143, and 13143.6 to the extent that these sections are applicable to community care facilities.
(Amended by Stats. 2018, Ch. 34, Sec. 6. (AB 1810) Effective June 27, 2018.)
1275.4.
(a) On or before January 1, 2017, each skilled nursing facility, as defined in subdivision (c) of Section 1250, shall adopt and implement an antimicrobial stewardship policy that is consistent with antimicrobial stewardship guidelines developed by the federal Centers for Disease Control and Prevention, the federal Centers for Medicare and Medicaid Services, the Society for Healthcare Epidemiology of America, or similar recognized professional organizations.
(b) All skilled nursing facilities, as defined in subdivision (c) of Section 1250, shall comply with this section. Failure to comply with the requirements of this section may subject the facility to the enforcement actions set forth in Section 1423.
(Added by Stats. 2015, Ch. 764, Sec. 2. (SB 361) Effective October 10, 2015.)
1275.5.
(a) The regulations relating to the licensing of hospitals, heretofore adopted by the State Department of Public Health pursuant to former Chapter 2 (commencing with Section 1400) of Division 2, and in effect immediately prior to July 1, 1973, shall remain in effect and shall be fully enforceable with respect to any hospital required to be licensed by this chapter, unless and until the regulations are readopted, amended, or repealed by the director.
(b) The regulations relating to private institutions receiving or caring for persons with mental health disorders, persons with developmental disabilities, and persons who lack legal competence to make decisions heretofore adopted by the Department of Mental Hygiene pursuant to Chapter 1 (commencing with Section 7000) of Division 7 of the Welfare and Institutions Code, and in effect immediately prior to July 1, 1973, shall remain in effect and shall be fully enforceable with respect to any facility, establishment, or institution for the reception and care of persons with mental health disorders, persons with developmental disabilities, and persons who lack legal competence to make decisions required to be licensed by the provisions of this chapter unless and until those regulations are readopted, amended, or repealed by the director.

(c) (1) All regulations relating to the licensing of psychiatric health facilities heretofore adopted by the State Department of Health Services, pursuant to authority now vested in the State Department of Health Care Services by Section 4080 of the Welfare and Institutions Code, and in effect immediately preceding September 20, 1988, shall remain in effect and shall be fully enforceable by the State Department of Health Care Services with respect to any facility or program required to be licensed as a psychiatric health facility, unless and until readopted, amended, or repealed by the Director of Health Care Services.
(2) The State Department of Health Care Services shall succeed to and be vested with all duties, powers, purposes, functions, responsibilities, and jurisdiction as they relate to licensing psychiatric health facilities.
(Amended by Stats. 2014, Ch. 144, Sec. 28. (AB 1847) Effective January 1, 2015.)
1275.6.
(a) A health facility licensed pursuant to subdivision (a) or (b) of Section 1250 may provide in any alternative setting health care services and programs which may be provided by any other provider of health care outside of a hospital building or which are not otherwise specifically prohibited by this chapter. In addition, the state department and the Office of Statewide Health Planning and Development shall adopt and enforce standards which permit the ability of a health facility licensed pursuant to subdivision (a) or (b) of Section 1250 to use its space for alternative purposes.
(b) In adopting regulations implementing this section, and in reviewing an application or other request by a health facility licensed pursuant to subdivision (a) or (b) of Section 1250, pursuant to Section 1265, and subdivision (b) of Section 1276, relating to services provided in alternative settings, the state department may adopt or impose reasonable standards and conditions which promote and protect patient health, safety, security, and quality of health care.
(c) Pending the adoption of regulations referred to in subdivision (b), the state department may condition approval of the alternative service or alternative setting on reasonable standards consistent with this section and subdivisions (d) and (e) of Section 1275. The state department and the Office of Statewide Health Planning and Development may adopt these standards by mutual agreement with a health facility proposing a service and may, after consultation with appropriate professional and trade associations, establish guidelines for hospitals wishing to institute an alternative service or to provide a service in an alternative setting. Services provided outside of a hospital building under this section shall be subject to the licensing standards, if any, that are applicable to the same or similar service provided by nonhospital providers outside of a hospital building. The intent of this subdivision is to assure timely introduction of safe and efficacious innovations in health care services by providing a mechanism for the temporary implementation and evaluation of standards for alternative services and settings and to facilitate the adoption of appropriate regulations by the state department.
(d) All health care professionals providing services in settings authorized by this section shall be members of the organized medical staff of the health facility to the extent medical staff membership would be required for the provision of the services within the health facility. All services shall be provided under the respective responsibilities of the governing body and medical staff of the health facility. Nothing in this section shall be construed to repeal or otherwise affect Section 2400 of the Business and Professions Code, or to exempt services provided under this section from licensing standards, if any, established by or otherwise applicable to, the same or similar service provided by nonhospital providers outside of a hospital building.
(e) For purposes of this section, "hospital building" shall have the same meaning as that term is defined in Section 15026.
(Added by Stats. 1987, Ch. 1171, Sec. 2.)
1275.7.
(a) The Legislature makes the following findings and declarations:
(1) The theft of newborn babies from hospitals is a serious societal problem that must be addressed.
(2) There is no statutory requirement that hospitals offering maternity services establish policies and procedures that protect newborns and their parents from physical harm and emotional distress resulting from baby thefts.
(3) Societal change has popularized a more open and natural birthing process, which, unfortunately, increases the risk of thefts of newborns from hospitals and other health facilities offering maternity services.
(4) Baby thefts detrimentally affect the emotional and physical health of newborns and their families.
(5) It is the intent of the Legislature in enacting this chapter to take reasonable steps toward reducing baby thefts.
(b) On or before July 1, 1991, the state department shall adopt regulations requiring any hospital or other health facility offering maternity services to establish written policies and procedures designed to promote the protection of babies and the reduction of baby thefts from hospitals or other health facilities offering maternity services. Those hospitals and facilities shall establish the policies and procedures no later than 60 days after the regulations become effective.
(c) The state department shall review the policies and procedures established by the hospitals and other health facilities, as required by subdivision (b), to determine compliance with the regulations adopted by the state department, pursuant to subdivision (b).
(d) Hospitals and other health facilities offering maternity services shall periodically review their policies and procedures established pursuant to this section. The review need not occur more frequently than every two years.
(Added by Stats. 1990, Ch. 768, Sec. 1.)

1275.8.

(a) On or before January 1, 2020, each general acute care hospital, as defined in subdivision (a) of Section 1250, and acute psychiatric hospital, as defined in subdivision (b) of Section 1250, shall adopt and implement a linen laundry processing policy that is consistent and in accordance with the most recent infection control guidelines and standards developed by the following:

(1) The federal Centers for Disease Control and Prevention.

(2) The federal Centers for Medicare and Medicaid Services.

(b) A general acute care hospital and an acute psychiatric hospital that uses a medical laundry service provider shall comply with the requirements of subdivision (a).

(Added by Stats. 2018, Ch. 587, Sec. 2. (AB 2679) Effective January 1, 2019.)

1276.

(a) The building standards published in the State Building Standards Code by the Office of Statewide Health Planning and Development, and the regulations adopted by the state department shall, as applicable, prescribe standards of adequacy, safety, and sanitation of the physical plant, of staffing with duly qualified licensed personnel, and of services, based on the type of health facility and the needs of the persons served thereby.

(b) These regulations shall permit program flexibility by the use of alternate concepts, methods, procedures, techniques, equipment, personnel qualifications, bulk purchasing of pharmaceuticals, or conducting of pilot projects as long as statutory requirements are met and the use has the prior written approval of the department or the office, as applicable. The approval of the department or the office shall provide for the terms and conditions under which the exception is granted. A written request plus supporting evidence shall be submitted by the applicant or licensee to the department or office regarding the exception, as applicable.

(c) While it is the intent of the Legislature that health facilities shall maintain continuous, ongoing compliance with the licensing rules and regulations, it is the further intent of the Legislature that the state department expeditiously review and approve, if appropriate, applications for program flexibility. The Legislature recognizes that health care technology, practice, pharmaceutical procurement systems, and personnel qualifications and availability are changing rapidly. Therefore, requests for program flexibility require expeditious consideration.

(d) The state department shall, on or before April 1, 1989, develop a standardized form and format for requests by health facilities for program flexibility. Health facilities shall thereafter apply to the state department for program flexibility in the prescribed manner. After the state department receives a complete application requesting program flexibility, it shall have 60 days within which to approve, approve with conditions or modifications, or deny the application. Denials and approvals with conditions or modifications shall be accompanied by an analysis and a detailed justification for any conditions or modifications imposed. Summary denials to meet the 60-day timeframe shall not be permitted.

(e) Notwithstanding any other provision of law or regulation, the State Department of Health Services shall provide flexibility in its pharmaceutical services requirements to permit any state department that operates state facilities subject to these provisions to establish a single statewide formulary or to procure pharmaceuticals through a departmentwide or multidepartment bulk purchasing arrangement. It is the intent of the Legislature that consolidation of these activities be permitted in order to allow the more cost-effective use and procurement of pharmaceuticals for the benefit of patients and residents of state facilities.

(Amended by Stats. 2005, Ch. 80, Sec. 1. Effective July 19, 2005.)

1276.05.

(a) The Office of Statewide Health Planning and Development shall allow any general acute care hospital facility that needs to relocate services on an interim basis as part of its approval plan for compliance with Article 8 (commencing with Section 130000) or Article 9 (commencing with Section 130050) in the Alfred E. Alquist Hospital Facilities Seismic Safety Act of 1983 (Chapter 1 (commencing with Section 129675) of Part 7 of Division 107) flexibility in achieving compliance with, or in substantial satisfaction of the objectives of, building standards adopted pursuant to Section 1276 with regard to the use of interim space for the provision of hospital services, or both, on a case-by-case basis so long as public safety is not compromised.

(b) The state department shall allow any facility to which subdivision (a) applies flexibility in achieving compliance with, or in substantial satisfaction of, the objectives of licensing standards, or both, with regard to the use of interim space for the provision of hospital services, or both, on a case-by-case basis so long as public safety is not compromised.

(c) Hospital licensees, upon application for program flexibility under this section, shall provide public notice of the proposed interim use of space that houses at least one of the eight basic services that are required in a general acute care hospital in a manner that is likely to reach a substantial number of residents of the community served by the facility and employees of the facility.

(d) No request shall be approved under this section for a waiver of any primary structural system, fire and life safety requirements, or any requirement with respect to accessibility for persons with disabilities.

(e) In approving any request pursuant to this section for flexibility, the office shall consider public comments.

(f) The state department shall establish a unit with two statewide liaisons for the purposes of the Alfred E. Alquist Hospital Facilities Seismic Safety Act of 1983 (Chapter 1 (commencing with Section 129675) of Part 7 of Division 107), to do all of the following:

(1) Serve as a central resource for hospital representatives on licensing issues relative to Article 8 or Article 9 in the Alfred E. Alquist Hospital Facilities Seismic Safety Act of 1983 and provide licensing information to the public, upon request.

(2) Serve as liaison with the Office of Statewide Health Planning and Development, the State Fire Marshal, the Seismic Safety Commission, and other entities as necessary on hospital operational issues with respect to Article 8 or Article 9 in the Alfred E. Alquist Hospital Facilities Seismic Safety Act of 1983.

(3) Ensure statewide compliance with respect to licensing issues relative to hospital buildings that are required to meet standards established by Article 8 or Article 9 in the Alfred E. Alquist Hospital Facilities Seismic Safety Act of 1983.

(4) Process requests for program flexibility under subdivision (a).

(5) Accept and consider public comments on requests for flexibility.

(g) Each compliance plan, in providing for an interim use of space in which flexibility is requested, shall identify the duration of time proposed for the interim use of the space. Upon any amendment of a hospital's approved compliance plan, any hospital for which a flexibility plan has been approved pursuant to subdivision (a) shall provide a copy of the amended plan to the State Department of Health Services within 30 days.

(Amended by Stats. 2001, Ch. 228, Sec. 1. Effective September 4, 2001.)

1276.1.

In setting personnel standards for licensed health facilities pursuant to Section 1276, the department may set such standards itself or may adopt them by reference to named standard-setting organizations. If the department adopts standards for a category of health personnel by reference to a specified organization, the department shall either:

(a) List in the regulation the education, training, experience, examinations, or other requirements set by the specified organization; or

(b) Retain on file and available for public inspection a listing of the education, training, experience, examinations, or other requirements set by the specified organization; or

(c) Have direct statutory authority or requirement to use the standards of the specified organization.

(Added by Stats. 1978, Ch. 1106.)

1276.2.

Standards and regulations adopted by the state department pursuant to Section 1276 shall not require the use of a registered nurse for the performance of any service or staffing of any position in freestanding skilled nursing facilities that may lawfully be performed or staffed by a licensed vocational nurse pursuant to the Vocational Nursing Practice Act (Chapter 6.5 (commencing with Section 2840) of Division 2 of the Business and Professions Code) and applicable federal regulations, when a facility is unable to obtain a registered nurse, except that a licensed vocational nurse employed in accordance with this section shall be a permanent employee of the facility. The facility shall make a good faith effort to obtain a registered nurse prior to determining that it is unable to obtain a registered nurse for the relevant shift, and this effort shall be noted in the facility's records. The facility shall make provision for a registered nurse to be available for consultation and professional assistance during the hours in which a licensed vocational nurse is used as provided by this section. The facility shall maintain a record of the identity and phone number of the registered nurse that is to be available for consultation and professional assistance, as required by this section. If the substitution of a licensed vocational nurse for a registered nurse occurs more often than seven days per month, the facility shall obtain program flexibility approval from the state department pursuant to subdivision (b) of Section 1276. Nothing in this section shall permit a licensed vocational nurse to act as director of nurses pursuant to the Vocational Nursing Practice Act. This section applies to staffing for the evening and night shifts only, except that if the level of care is determined by the state department to be inadequate, the state department may require the facility to provide additional staffing.

This section shall not apply to the Medi-Cal regulations adopted pursuant to Sections 14114 and 14132.25 of the Welfare and Institutions Code.

(Added by Stats. 1994, Ch. 645, Sec. 1. Effective January 1, 1995.)

1276.3.

(a) The Legislature finds and declares that the citizens of California are in danger of being injured and killed in the state's surgical suites and procedural rooms in licensed health facilities, because of the many intense heat sources present in an oxygen-rich environment. It is the intent of the Legislature that this section promote maximum fire and panic safety standards in surgical suites and procedural rooms in licensed health facilities, and other areas that pose a danger due to the presence of oxygen, in California.

(b) (1) The state department, shall promote safety by requiring that licensed health facilities that have surgical suites and procedural rooms provide information and training in fire and panic safety in oxygen rich environments, including equipment, safety, and emergency plans, as part of an orientation for new employees, and ongoing inservice training.

(2) The licensed health facilities described in paragraph (1) shall use the fire safety guidelines in oxygen rich environments published by the Association of Operating Room Nurses or any other nationally recognized body or organization, and approved by the state department.

(c) The licensed health facilities described in paragraph (1) of subdivision (b) shall determine the modality of training and the number of hours of training required.

(Added by Stats. 1992, Ch. 992, Sec. 1. Effective January 1, 1993.)

1276.4.

(a) By January 1, 2002, the State Department of Public Health shall adopt regulations that establish minimum, specific, and numerical licensed nurse-to-patient ratios by licensed nurse classification and by hospital unit for all health facilities licensed pursuant to subdivision (a), (b), or (f) of Section 1250. The State Department of Public Health shall adopt these regulations in accordance with the department's licensing and certification regulations as stated in Sections 70053.2, 70215, and 70217 of Title 22 of the California Code of Regulations, and the professional and vocational regulations in

Section 1443.5 of Title 16 of the California Code of Regulations. The department shall review these regulations five years after adoption and shall report to the Legislature regarding any proposed changes. Flexibility shall be considered by the department for rural general acute care hospitals in response to their special needs. As used in this subdivision, "hospital unit" means a critical care unit, burn unit, labor and delivery room, postanesthesia service area, emergency department, operating room, pediatric unit, step-down/intermediate care unit, specialty care unit, telemetry unit, general medical care unit, subacute care unit, and transitional inpatient care unit. The regulation addressing the emergency department shall distinguish between regularly scheduled core staff licensed nurses and additional licensed nurses required to care for critical care patients in the emergency department.

(b) These ratios shall constitute the minimum number of registered and licensed nurses that shall be allocated. Additional staff shall be assigned in accordance with a documented patient classification system for determining nursing care requirements, including the severity of the illness, the need for specialized equipment and technology, the complexity of clinical judgment needed to design, implement, and evaluate the patient care plan and the ability for self-care, and the licensure of the personnel required for care.

(c) "Critical care unit" as used in this section means a unit that is established to safeguard and protect patients whose severity of medical conditions requires continuous monitoring, and complex intervention by licensed nurses.

(d) All health facilities licensed under subdivision (a), (b), or (f) of Section 1250 shall adopt written policies and procedures for training and orientation of nursing staff.

(e) No registered nurse shall be assigned to a nursing unit or clinical area unless that nurse has first received orientation in that clinical area sufficient to provide competent care to patients in that area, and has demonstrated current competence in providing care in that area.

(f) The written policies and procedures for orientation of nursing staff shall require that all temporary personnel shall receive orientation and be subject to competency validation consistent with Sections 70016.1 and 70214 of Title 22 of the California Code of Regulations.

(g) Requests for waivers to this section that do not jeopardize the health, safety, and well-being of patients affected and that are needed for increased operational efficiency may be granted by the department to rural general acute care hospitals meeting the criteria set forth in Section 70059.1 of Title 22 of the California Code of Regulations.

(h) In case of conflict between this section and any provision or regulation defining the scope of nursing practice, the scope of practice provisions shall control.

(i) The regulations adopted by the department shall augment and not replace existing nurse-to-patient ratios that exist in regulation or law for the intensive care units, the neonatal intensive care units, or the operating room.

(j) The regulations adopted by the department shall not replace existing licensed staff-to-patient ratios for hospitals operated by the State Department of State Hospitals.

(k) The regulations adopted by the department for health facilities licensed under subdivision (b) of Section 1250 that are not operated by the State Department of State Hospitals shall take into account the special needs of the patients served in the psychiatric units.

(l) The department may take into consideration the unique nature of the University of California teaching hospitals as educational institutions when establishing licensed nurse-to-patient ratios. The department shall coordinate with the Board of Registered Nursing to ensure that staffing ratios are consistent with the Board of Registered Nursing approved nursing education requirements. This includes nursing clinical experience incidental to a work-study program rendered in a University of California clinical facility approved by the Board of Registered Nursing provided there will be sufficient direct care registered nurse preceptors available to ensure safe patient care.

(Amended by Stats. 2012, Ch. 24, Sec. 11. (AB 1470) Effective June 27, 2012.)

1276.5.

(a) The department shall adopt regulations setting forth the minimum number of equivalent nursing hours per patient required in skilled nursing and intermediate care facilities, subject to the specific requirements of Section 14110.7 of the Welfare and Institutions Code. However, notwithstanding Section 14110.7 or any other law, commencing January 1, 2000, the minimum number of actual nursing hours per patient required in a skilled nursing facility shall be 3.2 hours, except as provided in Section 1276.9.

(b) (1) For the purposes of this section, "nursing hours" means the number of hours of work performed per patient day by aides, nursing assistants, or orderlies plus two times the number of hours worked per patient day by registered nurses and licensed vocational nurses (except directors of nursing in facilities of 60 or larger capacity) and, in the distinct part of facilities and freestanding facilities providing care for persons with developmental disabilities or mental health disorders by licensed psychiatric technicians who perform direct nursing services for patients in skilled nursing and intermediate care facilities, except when the skilled nursing and intermediate care facility is licensed as a part of a state-owned hospital or developmental center, and except that nursing hours for skilled nursing facilities means the actual hours of work, without doubling the hours performed per patient day by registered nurses and licensed vocational nurses.

(2) Concurrent with implementation of the first year of rates established under the Medi-Cal Long Term Care Reimbursement Act of 1990 (Article 3.8 (commencing with Section 14126) of Chapter 7 of Part 3 of Division 9 of the Welfare and Institutions Code), for the purposes of this section, "nursing hours" means the number of hours of work performed per patient day by aides, nursing assistants, registered nurses, and licensed vocational nurses (except directors of nursing in facilities of 60 or larger capacity) and, in the distinct part of facilities and freestanding facilities providing care for persons with developmental disabilities or mental health disorders, by licensed psychiatric technicians who performed direct nursing services for patients in skilled nursing and intermediate care facilities, except when the skilled nursing and intermediate care facility is licensed as a part of a state-owned hospital or developmental center.

(c) Notwithstanding Section 1276, the department shall require the utilization of a registered nurse at all times if the department determines that the services of a skilled nursing and intermediate care facility require the utilization of a registered nurse.

(d) (1) Except as otherwise provided by law, the administrator of an intermediate care facility/developmentally disabled, intermediate care facility/developmentally disabled habilitative, or an intermediate care facility/developmentally disabled—nursing shall be either a licensed nursing home administrator or a qualified intellectual disability professional as defined in Section 483.430 of Title 42 of the Code of Federal Regulations.

(2) To qualify as an administrator for an intermediate care facility for the developmentally disabled, a qualified intellectual disability professional shall complete at least six months of administrative training or demonstrate six months of experience in an administrative capacity in a licensed health facility, as defined in Section 1250, excluding those facilities specified in subdivisions (e), (h), and (i).

(Amended by Stats. 2017, Ch. 52, Sec. 2. (SB 97) Effective July 10, 2017.)

1276.6.

Each facility shall certify, under penalty of perjury and to the best of their knowledge, on a form provided by the department, that funds received pursuant to increasing the staffing ratio to 3.2, as provided for in Section 1276.5, were expended for this purpose. The facility shall return the form to the department within 30 days of receipt by the facility.

(Added by Stats. 2000, Ch. 93, Sec. 6. Effective July 7, 2000.)

1276.65.

(a) For purposes of this section, the following definitions shall apply:

(1) "Direct care service hours" means the actual hours of work performed per patient day by a direct caregiver, as defined in paragraph (2). Until final regulations are promulgated to implement this section as amended by the act that added this paragraph, the department shall recognize the hours performed by direct caregivers, to the same extent as those hours are recognized by the department pursuant to Section 1276.5 on July 1, 2017.

(2) "Direct caregiver" means a registered nurse, as referred to in Section 2732 of the Business and Professions Code, a licensed vocational nurse, as referred to in Section 2864 of the Business and Professions Code, a psychiatric technician, as referred to in Section 4516 of the Business and Professions Code, and a certified nurse assistant, or a nursing assistant participating in an approved training program, as defined in Section 1337, while performing nursing services as described in Sections 72309, 72311, and 72315 of Title 22 of the California Code of Regulations, as those sections read on July 1, 2017.

(3) "Skilled nursing facility" means a skilled nursing facility as defined in subdivision (c) of Section 1250.

(b) A person employed to provide services such as food preparation, housekeeping, laundry, or maintenance services shall not provide nursing care to residents and shall not be counted in determining ratios under this section.

(c) (1) (A) Notwithstanding any other law, the department shall develop regulations that become effective August 1, 2003, that establish staff-to-patient ratios for direct caregivers working in a skilled nursing facility.

(B) Effective July 1, 2018, skilled nursing facilities, except those skilled nursing facilities that are a distinct part of a general acute care facility or a state-owned hospital or developmental center, shall have a minimum number of direct care services hours of 3.5 per patient day, except as set forth in Section 1276.9.

(C) Skilled nursing facilities shall have a minimum of 2.4 hours per patient day for certified nurse assistants in order to meet the requirements in subparagraph (B).

(D) The department shall repeal and amend existing regulations and adopt emergency regulations to implement the amendments made by the act that added this subparagraph. The department shall consult stakeholders prior to promulgation of regulations and shall provide a 90-day notice to stakeholders prior to adopting regulations. The adoption of these regulations shall be deemed to be an emergency and necessary for the immediate preservation of the public peace, health and safety, or general welfare.

(2) The department, in developing staff-to-patient ratios for direct caregivers and licensed nurses required by this section, shall convert the existing requirement under Section 1276.5 of this code and Section 14110.7 of the Welfare and Institutions Code for direct care service hours per patient day of care and shall verify that no less care is given than is required pursuant to Section 1276.5 of this code and Section 14110.7 of the Welfare and Institutions Code. Further, the department shall develop the ratios in a manner that minimizes additional state costs, maximizes resident quality of care, and takes into account the length of the shift worked. In developing the regulations, the department shall develop a procedure for facilities to apply for a waiver that addresses individual patient needs except that in no instance shall the minimum staff-to-patient ratios be less than the 3.5 direct care service hours per patient day required pursuant to subparagraph (B) of paragraph (1).

(d) The direct care service hour requirements to be developed pursuant to this section shall be minimum standards only. Skilled nursing facilities shall employ and schedule additional staff as needed to ensure quality resident care based on the needs of individual residents and to ensure compliance with all relevant state and federal staffing requirements.

(e) No later than January 1, 2006, and every five years thereafter, the department shall consult with consumers, consumer advocates, recognized collective bargaining agents, and providers to determine the sufficiency of the staffing standards provided in this section and may adopt regulations to increase the minimum staffing ratios to adequate levels.

(f) In a manner pursuant to federal requirements, every skilled nursing facility shall post information about staffing levels that includes the current number of licensed and unlicensed nursing staff directly responsible for resident care in the facility. This posting shall include staffing requirements developed pursuant to this section.

(g) (1) Notwithstanding any other law, the department shall inspect for compliance with this section during state and federal periodic inspections, including, but not limited to, those inspections required under Section 1422. This inspection requirement shall not limit the department's authority in other circumstances to cite for violations of this section or to inspect for compliance with this section.

(2) A violation of the regulations developed pursuant to this section may constitute a class "B," "A," or "AA" violation pursuant to the standards set forth in Section 1424. The department shall set a timeline for phase-in of penalties pursuant to this section through all-facility letters or other similar instructions.

(h) The requirements of this section are in addition to any requirement set forth in Section 1276.5 of this code and Section 14110.7 of the Welfare and Institutions Code.

(i) Implementation of the staffing standard developed pursuant to requirements set forth in this section shall be contingent on an appropriation in the annual Budget Act and continued federal approval of the Skilled Nursing Facility Quality Assurance Fee pursuant to Article 7.6 (commencing with Section 1324.20).

(j) In implementing this section, the department may contract as necessary, on a bid or nonbid basis, for professional consulting services from nationally recognized higher education and research institutions, or other qualified individuals and entities not associated with a skilled nursing facility, with demonstrated expertise in long-term care. This subdivision establishes an accelerated process for issuing contracts pursuant to this section and contracts entered into pursuant to this section shall be exempt from the requirements of Chapter 1 (commencing with Section 10100) and Chapter 2 (commencing with Section 10290) of Part 2 of Division 2 of the Public Contract Code.

(k) This section shall not apply to facilities defined in Section 1276.9.

(l) The department shall adopt emergency regulations or all-facility letters, or other similar instructions, to create a waiver of the direct care service hour requirements established in this section for skilled nursing facilities by July 1, 2018, to address a shortage of available and appropriate health care professionals and direct caregivers. Waivers granted pursuant to these provisions shall be reviewed annually and either renewed or revoked. The adoption of these regulations shall be deemed to be an emergency and necessary for the immediate preservation of the public peace, health and safety, or general welfare.

(m) The department shall evaluate the impact of the changes made to this section by the act that added this subdivision regarding patient quality of care and shall work with other state departments, as necessary, to evaluate the workforce available to meet these requirements, including an evaluation of the effectiveness of the minimum requirements of 2.4 hours per patient day for certified nursing assistants specified in subparagraph (C) of paragraph (1) of subdivision (c). The department may contract with a vendor for purposes of conducting this evaluation.

(Amended by Stats. 2017, Ch. 52, Sec. 3. (SB 97) Effective July 10, 2017.)

1276.7.

(a) (1) On or before May 1, 2001, the department shall determine the need, and provide subsequent recommendations, for any increase in the minimum number of nursing hours per patient day in skilled nursing facilities. The department shall analyze the relationship between staffing levels and quality of care in skilled nursing facilities. The analysis shall include, but not be limited to, all of the following:

(A) A determination of average staffing levels in this state.

(B) A review of facility expenditures on nursing staff, including salary, wages, and benefits.

(C) A review of other states' staffing requirements as relevant to this state.

(D) A review of available research and reports on the issue of staffing levels and quality of care.

(E) The number of Medi-Cal beds in a facility.

(F) The corporate status of the facility.

(G) Information on compliance with both state and federal standards.

(H) Work force availability trends.

(2) The department shall prepare a report on its analysis and recommendations and submit this report to the Legislature, including its recommendations for any staffing increases and proposed timeframes and costs for implementing any increase.

(b) It is the intent of the Legislature to establish sufficient staffing levels required to provide quality skilled nursing care. It is further the intent of the Legislature to increase the minimum number of direct care nursing hours per patient day in skilled nursing facilities to 3.5 hours by 2004 or to whatever staffing levels the department determines are required to provide California nursing home residents with a safe environment and quality skilled nursing care.

(Added by Stats. 2000, Ch. 451, Sec. 7. Effective January 1, 2001.)

1276.8.

Notwithstanding any other provision of law, including, but not limited to, Section 1276, the following shall apply:

(a) As used in this code, "respiratory care practitioner," "respiratory therapist," "respiratory therapy technician," and "inhalation therapist" mean a respiratory care practitioner certified under the Respiratory Care Practice Act (Chapter 8.3 (commencing with Section 3700) of Division 2 of the Business and Professions Code).

(b) The definition of respiratory care services, respiratory therapy, inhalation therapy, or the scope of practice of respiratory care, shall be as described in Section 3702 of the Business and Professions Code.

(c) Respiratory care may be performed in hospitals, ambulatory or in-home care, and other settings where respiratory care is performed under the supervision of a medical director in accordance with the prescription of a physician and surgeon. Respiratory care may also be provided during the transportation of a patient, and under any circumstances where an emergency necessitates respiratory care.

(d) In addition to other licensed health care practitioners authorized to administer respiratory care, a certified respiratory care practitioner may accept, transcribe, and implement the written and verbal orders of a physician and surgeon pertaining to the practice of respiratory care.

(Amended by Stats. 2006, Ch. 538, Sec. 351. Effective January 1, 2007.)

1276.9.

(a) A special treatment program service unit distinct part shall have a minimum 2.3 nursing hours per patient per day.

(b) For purposes of this section, "special treatment program service unit distinct part" means an identifiable and physically separate unit of a skilled nursing facility or an entire skilled nursing facility that provides therapeutic programs to an identified population group of persons with mental health disorders.

(c) For purposes of this section, "nursing hours" means the number of hours of work performed per patient day by aides, nursing assistants, or orderlies, plus two times the number of hours worked per patient day by registered nurses and licensed vocational nurses (except directors of nursing in facilities of 60 or larger capacity), and, in the distinct part of facilities and freestanding facilities providing care for persons with developmental disabilities or mental health disorders, by licensed psychiatric technicians who perform direct nursing services for patients in skilled nursing and intermediate care facilities, except when the skilled nursing and intermediate care facility is licensed as a part of a state hospital.

(d) A special treatment program service unit distinct part shall also have an overall average weekly staffing level of 3.2 hours per patient per day, calculated without regard to the doubling of nursing hours, as described in paragraph (1) of subdivision (b) of Section 1276.5, for the special treatment program service unit distinct part.

(e) The calculation of the overall staffing levels in these facilities for the special treatment program service unit distinct part shall include staff from all of the following categories:

(1) Certified nurse assistants.

(2) Licensed vocational nurses.

(3) Registered nurses.

(4) Licensed psychiatric technicians.

(5) Psychiatrists.

(6) Psychologists.

(7) Social workers.

(8) Program staff who provide rehabilitation, counseling, or other therapeutic services.

(Amended by Stats. 2014, Ch. 144, Sec. 30. (AB 1847) Effective January 1, 2015.)

1277.

(a) No license shall be issued by the department unless it finds that the premises, the management, the bylaws, rules and regulations, the equipment, the staffing, both professional and nonprofessional, and the standards of care and services are adequate and appropriate, and that the health facility is operated in the manner required by this chapter and by the rules and regulations adopted hereunder.

(b) (1) Notwithstanding any provision of Part 2 (commencing with Section 5600) of Division 5 of, or Division 7 (commencing with Section 7100) of, the Welfare and Institutions Code or any other law to the contrary, except Sections 2072 and 2073 of the Business and Professions Code, the licensure requirements for professional personnel, including, but not limited to, physicians and surgeons, dentists, podiatrists, psychologists, marriage and family therapists, pharmacists, registered nurses, clinical social workers, and professional clinical counselors in the state and other governmental health facilities licensed by the department shall not be less than for those professional personnel in health facilities under private ownership.

(2) Persons employed as psychologists and clinical social workers, while continuing in their employment in the same class as of January 1, 1979, in the same state or other governmental health facility licensed by the department, including those persons on authorized leave, but not including intermittent personnel, shall be exempt from the requirements of paragraph (1).

(3) The requirements of paragraph (1) may be waived by the department solely for persons in the professions of psychology, marriage and family therapy, clinical social work, or professional clinical counseling who are gaining qualifying experience for licensure in such profession in this state. A waiver granted pursuant to this paragraph shall not exceed four years from commencement of the employment in this state, at which time licensure shall have been obtained or the employment shall be terminated, except that an extension of a waiver of licensure may be granted for one additional year, based on extenuating circumstances determined by the department pursuant to subdivision (e). For persons employed as psychologists, clinical social workers, marriage and family therapists, or professional clinical counselors less than full time, an extension of a waiver of licensure may be granted for additional years proportional to the extent of part-time employment, as long as the person is employed without interruption in service, but in no case shall the waiver of licensure exceed six years in the case of clinical social workers,

marriage and family therapists, or professional clinical counselors, or five years in the case of psychologists.

(4) The durational limitation upon waivers pursuant to paragraph (3) shall not apply to any of the following:

(A) Active candidates for a doctoral degree in social work, social welfare, or social science, who are enrolled at an accredited university, college, or professional school, but these limitations shall apply following completion of this training.

(B) Active candidates for a doctoral degree in marriage and family therapy who are enrolled at a school, college, or university, specified in subdivision (b) of Section 4980.36 of, or subdivision (b) of Section 4980.37 of, the Business and Professions Code, but the limitations shall apply following completion of the training.

(C) Active candidates for a doctoral degree in professional clinical counseling who are enrolled at a school, college, or university, specified in subdivision (b) of Section 4999.32 of, or subdivision (b) of Section 4999.33 of, the Business and Professions Code, but the limitations shall apply following the completion of the training.

(5) A waiver pursuant to paragraph (3) shall be granted only to the extent necessary to qualify for licensure, except that personnel recruited for employment from outside this state and whose experience is sufficient to gain admission to a licensing examination shall nevertheless have one year from the date of their employment in California to become licensed, at which time licensure shall have been obtained or the employment shall be terminated, provided that the employee shall take the licensure examination at the earliest possible date after the date of his or her employment. If the employee does not pass the examination at that time, he or she shall have a second opportunity to pass the next possible examination, subject to the one-year limit.

(c) A special permit shall be issued by the department when it finds that the staff, both professional and nonprofessional, and the standards of care and services are adequate and appropriate, and that the special services unit is operated in the manner required in this chapter and by the rules and regulations adopted hereunder.

(d) The department shall apply the same standards to state and other governmental health facilities that it licenses as it applies to health facilities in private ownership, including standards specifying the level of training and supervision of all unlicensed practitioners. Except for psychologists, the department may grant an extension of a waiver of licensure for personnel recruited from outside this state for one additional year, based upon extenuating circumstances as determined by the department pursuant to subdivision (e).

(e) The department shall grant a request for an extension of a waiver based on extenuating circumstances, pursuant to subdivision (b) or (d), if any of the following circumstances exist:

(1) The person requesting the extension has experienced a recent catastrophic event that may impair the person's ability to qualify for and pass the license examination. Those events may include, but are not limited to, significant hardship caused by a natural disaster, serious and prolonged illness of the person, serious and prolonged illness or death of a child, spouse, or parent, or other stressful circumstances.

(2) The person requesting the extension has difficulty speaking or writing the English language, or other cultural and ethnic factors exist that substantially impair the person's ability to qualify for and pass the license examination.

(3) The person requesting the extension has experienced other personal hardship that the department, in its discretion, determines to warrant the extension.

(Amended by Stats. 2017, Ch. 151, Sec. 1. (AB 1456) Effective July 31, 2017.)

1278.

Any officer, employee, or agent of the state department may, upon presentation of proper identification, enter and inspect any building or premises at any reasonable time to secure compliance with, or to prevent a violation of, any provision of this chapter.

(Added by Stats. 1973, Ch. 1202.)

1278.5.

(a) The Legislature finds and declares that it is the public policy of the State of California to encourage patients, nurses, members of the medical staff, and other health care workers to notify government entities of suspected unsafe patient care and conditions. The Legislature encourages this reporting in order to protect patients and in order to assist those accreditation and government entities charged with ensuring that health care is safe. The Legislature finds and declares that whistleblower protections apply primarily to issues relating to the care, services, and conditions of a facility and are not intended to conflict with existing provisions in state and federal law relating to employee and employer relations.

(b) (1) No health facility shall discriminate or retaliate, in any manner, against any patient, employee, member of the medical staff, or any other health care worker of the health facility because that person has done either of the following:

(A) Presented a grievance, complaint, or report to the facility, to an entity or agency responsible for accrediting or evaluating the facility, or the medical staff of the facility, or to any other governmental entity.

(B) Has initiated, participated, or cooperated in an investigation or administrative proceeding related to the quality of care, services, or conditions at the facility that is carried out by an entity or agency responsible for accrediting or evaluating the facility or its medical staff, or governmental entity.

(2) No entity that owns or operates a health facility, or that owns or operates any other health facility, shall discriminate or retaliate against any person because that person has taken any actions pursuant to this subdivision.

(3) A violation of this section shall be subject to a civil penalty of not more than twenty-five thousand dollars ($25,000). The civil penalty shall be assessed and recovered

through the same administrative process set forth in Chapter 2.4 (commencing with Section 1417) for long-term health care facilities.

(c) Any type of discriminatory treatment of a patient by whom, or upon whose behalf, a grievance or complaint has been submitted, directly or indirectly, to a governmental entity or received by a health facility administrator within 180 days of the filing of the grievance or complaint, shall raise a rebuttable presumption that the action was taken by the health facility in retaliation for the filing of the grievance or complaint.

(d) (1) There shall be a rebuttable presumption that discriminatory action was taken by the health facility, or by the entity that owns or operates that health facility, or that owns or operates any other health facility, in retaliation against an employee, member of the medical staff, or any other health care worker of the facility, if responsible staff at the facility or the entity that owns or operates the facility had knowledge of the actions, participation, or cooperation of the person responsible for any acts described in paragraph (1) of subdivision (b), and the discriminatory action occurs within 120 days of the filing of the grievance or complaint by the employee, member of the medical staff or any other health care worker of the facility.

(2) For purposes of this section, discriminatory treatment of an employee, member of the medical staff, or any other health care worker includes, but is not limited to, discharge, demotion, suspension, or any unfavorable changes in, or breach of, the terms or conditions of a contract, employment, or privileges of the employee, member of the medical staff, or any other health care worker of the health care facility, or the threat of any of these actions.

(e) The presumptions in subdivisions (c) and (d) shall be presumptions affecting the burden of producing evidence as provided in Section 603 of the Evidence Code.

(f) Any person who willfully violates this section is guilty of a misdemeanor punishable by a fine of not more than seventy-five thousand dollars ($75,000), in addition to the civil penalty provided in paragraph (3) of subdivision (b).

(g) An employee who has been discriminated against in employment pursuant to this section shall be entitled to reinstatement, reimbursement for lost wages and work benefits caused by the acts of the employer, and the legal costs associated with pursuing the case, or to any remedy deemed warranted by the court pursuant to this chapter or any other applicable provision of statutory or common law. A health care worker who has been discriminated against pursuant to this section shall be entitled to reimbursement for lost income and the legal costs associated with pursuing the case, or to any remedy deemed warranted by the court pursuant to this chapter or other applicable provision of statutory or common law. A member of the medical staff who has been discriminated against pursuant to this section shall be entitled to reinstatement, reimbursement for lost income resulting from any change in the terms or conditions of his or her privileges caused by the acts of the facility or the entity that owns or operates a health facility or any other health facility that is owned or operated by that entity, and the legal costs associated with pursuing the case, or to any remedy deemed warranted by the court pursuant to this chapter or any other applicable provision of statutory or common law.

(h) The medical staff of the health facility may petition the court for an injunction to protect a peer review committee from being required to comply with evidentiary demands on a pending peer review hearing from the member of the medical staff who has filed an action pursuant to this section, if the evidentiary demands from the complainant would impede the peer review process or endanger the health and safety of patients of the health facility during the peer review process. Prior to granting an injunction, the court shall conduct an in camera review of the evidence sought to be discovered to determine if a peer review hearing, as authorized in Section 805 and Sections 809 to 809.5, inclusive, of the Business and Professions Code, would be impeded. If it is determined that the peer review hearing will be impeded, the injunction shall be granted until the peer review hearing is completed. Nothing in this section shall preclude the court, on motion of its own or by a party, from issuing an injunction or other order under this subdivision in the interest of justice for the duration of the peer review process to protect the person from irreparable harm.

(i) For purposes of this section, "health facility" means any facility defined under this chapter, including, but not limited to, the facility's administrative personnel, employees, boards, and committees of the board, and medical staff.

(j) This section shall not apply to an inmate of a correctional facility or juvenile facility of the Department of Corrections and Rehabilitation, or to an inmate housed in a local detention facility including a county jail or a juvenile hall, juvenile camp, or other juvenile detention facility.

(k) This section shall not apply to a health facility that is a long-term health care facility, as defined in Section 1418. A health facility that is a long-term health care facility shall remain subject to Section 1432.

(l) Nothing in this section shall be construed to limit the ability of the medical staff to carry out its legitimate peer review activities in accordance with Sections 809 to 809.5, inclusive, of the Business and Professions Code.

(m) Nothing in this section abrogates or limits any other theory of liability or remedy otherwise available at law.

(Amended by Stats. 2017, Ch. 275, Sec. 1. (AB 1102) Effective January 1, 2018.)

1279.

(a) Every health facility for which a license or special permit has been issued shall be periodically inspected by the department, or by another governmental entity under contract with the department. The frequency of inspections shall vary, depending upon the type and complexity of the health facility or special service to be inspected, unless otherwise specified by state or federal law or regulation. The inspection shall include participation by the California Medical Association consistent with the manner in which it participated in inspections, as provided in Section 1282 prior to September 15, 1992.

(b) Except as provided in subdivision (c), inspections shall be conducted no less than once every two years and as often as necessary to ensure the quality of care being provided.

(c) For a health facility specified in subdivision (a), (b), or (f) of Section 1250, inspections shall be conducted no less than once every three years, and as often as necessary to ensure the quality of care being provided.

(d) During the inspection, the representative or representatives shall offer such advice and assistance to the health facility as they deem appropriate.

(e) For acute care hospitals of 100 beds or more, the inspection team shall include at least a physician, registered nurse, and persons experienced in hospital administration and sanitary inspections. During the inspection, the team shall offer advice and assistance to the hospital as it deems appropriate.

(f) The department shall ensure that a periodic inspection conducted pursuant to this section is not announced in advance of the date of inspection. An inspection may be conducted jointly with inspections by entities specified in Section 1282. However, if the department conducts an inspection jointly with an entity specified in Section 1282 that provides notice in advance of the periodic inspection, the department shall conduct an additional periodic inspection that is not announced or noticed to the health facility.

(g) Notwithstanding any other provision of law, the department shall inspect for compliance with provisions of state law and regulations during a state periodic inspection or at the same time as a federal periodic inspection, including, but not limited to, an inspection required under this section. If the department inspects for compliance with state law and regulations at the same time as a federal periodic inspection, the inspection shall be done consistent with the guidance of the federal Centers for Medicare and Medicaid Services for the federal portion of the inspection.

(h) The department shall emphasize consistency across the state and its district offices when conducting licensing and certification surveys and complaint investigations, including the selection of state or federal enforcement remedies in accordance with Section 1423. The department may issue federal deficiencies and recommend federal enforcement actions in those circumstances where they provide more rigorous enforcement action.

(Amended by Stats. 2008, Ch. 758, Sec. 2. Effective September 30, 2008.)
1279.1.

(a) A health facility licensed pursuant to subdivision (a), (b), or (f) of Section 1250 shall report an adverse event to the department no later than five days after the adverse event has been detected, or, if that event is an ongoing urgent or emergent threat to the welfare, health, or safety of patients, personnel, or visitors, not later than 24 hours after the adverse event has been detected. Disclosure of individually identifiable patient information shall be consistent with applicable law.

(b) For purposes of this section, "adverse event" includes any of the following:

(1) Surgical events, including the following:

(A) Surgery performed on a wrong body part that is inconsistent with the documented informed consent for that patient. A reportable event under this subparagraph does not include a situation requiring prompt action that occurs in the course of surgery or a situation that is so urgent as to preclude obtaining informed consent.

(B) Surgery performed on the wrong patient.

(C) The wrong surgical procedure performed on a patient, which is a surgical procedure performed on a patient that is inconsistent with the documented informed consent for that patient. A reportable event under this subparagraph does not include a situation requiring prompt action that occurs in the course of surgery, or a situation that is so urgent as to preclude the obtaining of informed consent.

(D) Retention of a foreign object in a patient after surgery or other procedure, excluding objects intentionally implanted as part of a planned intervention and objects present prior to surgery that are intentionally retained.

(E) Death during or up to 24 hours after induction of anesthesia after surgery of a normal, healthy patient who has no organic, physiologic, biochemical, or psychiatric disturbance and for whom the pathologic processes for which the operation is to be performed are localized and do not entail a systemic disturbance.

(2) Product or device events, including the following:

(A) Patient death or serious disability associated with the use of a contaminated drug, device, or biologic provided by the health facility when the contamination is the result of generally detectable contaminants in the drug, device, or biologic, regardless of the source of the contamination or the product.

(B) Patient death or serious disability associated with the use or function of a device in patient care in which the device is used or functions other than as intended. For purposes of this subparagraph, "device" includes, but is not limited to, a catheter, drain, or other specialized tube, infusion pump, or ventilator.

(C) Patient death or serious disability associated with intravascular air embolism that occurs while being cared for in a facility, excluding deaths associated with neurosurgical procedures known to present a high risk of intravascular air embolism.

(3) Patient protection events, including the following:

(A) An infant discharged to the wrong person.

(B) Patient death or serious disability associated with patient disappearance for more than four hours, excluding events involving adults who have competency or decisionmaking capacity.

(C) A patient suicide or attempted suicide resulting in serious disability while being cared for in a health facility due to patient actions after admission to the health facility, excluding deaths resulting from self-inflicted injuries that were the reason for admission to the health facility.

(4) Care management events, including the following:

(A) A patient death or serious disability associated with a medication error, including, but not limited to, an error involving the wrong drug, the wrong dose, the wrong patient, the wrong time, the wrong rate, the wrong preparation, or the wrong route of administration, excluding reasonable differences in clinical judgment on drug selection and dose.

(B) A patient death or serious disability associated with a hemolytic reaction due to the administration of ABO-incompatible blood or blood products.

(C) Maternal death or serious disability associated with labor or delivery in a low-risk pregnancy while being cared for in a facility, including events that occur within 42 days postdelivery and excluding deaths from pulmonary or amniotic fluid embolism, acute fatty liver of pregnancy, or cardiomyopathy.

(D) Patient death or serious disability directly related to hypoglycemia, the onset of which occurs while the patient is being cared for in a health facility.

(E) Death or serious disability, including kernicterus, associated with failure to identify and treat hyperbilirubinemia in neonates during the first 28 days of life. For purposes of this subparagraph, "hyperbilirubinemia" means bilirubin levels greater than 30 milligrams per deciliter.

(F) A Stage 3 or 4 ulcer, acquired after admission to a health facility, excluding progression from Stage 2 to Stage 3 if Stage 2 was recognized upon admission.

(G) A patient death or serious disability due to spinal manipulative therapy performed at the health facility.

(5) Environmental events, including the following:

(A) A patient death or serious disability associated with an electric shock while being cared for in a health facility, excluding events involving planned treatments, such as electric countershock.

(B) Any incident in which a line designated for oxygen or other gas to be delivered to a patient contains the wrong gas or is contaminated by a toxic substance.

(C) A patient death or serious disability associated with a burn incurred from any source while being cared for in a health facility.

(D) A patient death associated with a fall while being cared for in a health facility.

(E) A patient death or serious disability associated with the use of restraints or bedrails while being cared for in a health facility.

(6) Criminal events, including the following:

(A) Any instance of care ordered by or provided by someone impersonating a physician, nurse, pharmacist, or other licensed health care provider.

(B) The abduction of a patient of any age.

(C) The sexual assault on a patient within or on the grounds of a health facility.

(D) The death or significant injury of a patient or staff member resulting from a physical assault that occurs within or on the grounds of a facility.

(7) An adverse event or series of adverse events that cause the death or serious disability of a patient, personnel, or visitor.

(c) The facility shall inform the patient or the party responsible for the patient of the adverse event by the time the report is made.

(d) "Serious disability" means a physical or mental impairment that substantially limits one or more of the major life activities of an individual, or the loss of bodily function, if the impairment or loss lasts more than seven days or is still present at the time of discharge from an inpatient health care facility, or the loss of a body part.

(e) Nothing in this section shall be interpreted to change or otherwise affect hospital reporting requirements regarding reportable diseases or unusual occurrences, as provided in Section 70737 of Title 22 of the California Code of Regulations. The department shall review Section 70737 of Title 22 of the California Code of Regulations requiring hospitals to report "unusual occurrences" and consider amending the section to enhance the clarity and specificity of this hospital reporting requirement.

(Amended by Stats. 2007, Ch. 130, Sec. 156. Effective January 1, 2008.)
1279.2.

(a) (1) In any case in which the department receives a report from a facility pursuant to Section 1279.1, or a written or oral complaint involving a health facility licensed pursuant to subdivision (a), (b), or (f) of Section 1250, that indicates an ongoing threat of imminent danger of death or serious bodily harm, the department shall make an onsite inspection or investigation within 48 hours or two business days, whichever is greater, of the receipt of the report or complaint and shall complete that investigation within 45 days.

(2) Until the department has determined by onsite inspection that the adverse event has been resolved, the department shall, not less than once a year, conduct an unannounced inspection of any health facility that has reported an adverse event pursuant to Section 1279.1.

(b) In any case in which the department is able to determine from the information available to it that there is no threat of imminent danger of death or serious bodily harm to that patient or other patients, the department shall complete an investigation of the report within 45 days.

(c) If the department does not meet the timeframes established in subdivision (a), the department shall document the extenuating circumstances explaining why it could not meet the timeframes. The department shall provide written notice to the facility and the complainant, if any, of the basis for the extenuating circumstances and the anticipated completion date.

(d) The department shall notify the complainant and licensee in writing of the department's determination as a result of an inspection or report.

(e) For purposes of this section, "complaint" means any oral or written notice to the department, other than a report from the health facility, of an alleged violation of applicable requirements of state or federal law or an allegation of facts that might constitute a violation of applicable requirements of state or federal law.

(f) The costs of administering and implementing this section shall be paid from funds derived from existing licensing fees paid by general acute care hospitals, acute psychiatric hospitals, and special hospitals.

(g) In enforcing this section and Sections 1279 and 1279.1, the department shall take into account the special circumstances of small and rural hospitals, as defined in Section 124840, in order to protect the quality of patient care in those hospitals.

(h) In preparing the staffing and systems analysis required pursuant to Section 1266, the department shall also report regarding the number and timeliness of investigations of adverse events initiated in response to reports of adverse events.

(Amended by Stats. 2015, Ch. 18, Sec. 6. (SB 75) Effective June 24, 2015.)

1279.3.

(a) By January 1, 2015, the department shall provide information regarding reports of substantiated adverse events pursuant to Section 1279.1 and the outcomes of inspections and investigations conducted pursuant to Section 1279.1, on the department's Internet Web site and in written form in a manner that is readily accessible to consumers in all parts of California, and that protects patient confidentiality.

(b) By January 1, 2009, and until January 1, 2015, the department shall make information regarding reports of substantiated adverse events pursuant to Section 1279.1, and outcomes of inspections and investigations conducted pursuant to Section 1279.1, readily accessible to consumers throughout California. The department shall also compile and make available, to entities deemed appropriate by the department, data regarding these reports of substantiated adverse events pursuant to Section 1279.1 and outcomes of inspections and investigations conducted pursuant to Section 1279.1, in order that these entities may post this data on their Internet Web sites. Entities deemed appropriate by the department shall enter into a memorandum of understanding with the department that requires the inclusion of all data and all hospital information provided by the department. These entities may include universities, consumer organizations, or health care quality organizations.

(c) The information required pursuant to this section shall include, but not be limited to, information regarding each substantiated adverse event, as defined in Section 1279.1, reported to the department, and may include compliance information history. The names of the health care professionals and health care workers shall not be included in the information released by the department to the public.

(Added by Stats. 2006, Ch. 647, Sec. 3. Effective January 1, 2007. Operative July 1, 2007, by Sec. 5 of Ch. 647.)

1279.6.

(a) A health facility, as defined in subdivision (a), (b), (c), or (f) of Section 1250, shall develop, implement, and comply with a patient safety plan for the purpose of improving the health and safety of patients and reducing preventable patient safety events. The patient safety plan shall be developed by the facility, in consultation with the facility's various health care professionals.

(b) The patient safety plan required pursuant to subdivision (a) shall, at a minimum, provide for the establishment of all of the following:

(1) A patient safety committee or equivalent committee in composition and function. The committee shall be composed of the facility's various health care professionals, including, but not limited to, physicians, nurses, pharmacists, and administrators. The committee shall do all of the following:

(A) Review and approve the patient safety plan.

(B) Receive and review reports of patient safety events as defined in subdivision (c).

(C) Monitor implementation of corrective actions for patient safety events.

(D) Make recommendations to eliminate future patient safety events.

(E) Review and revise the patient safety plan, at least once a year, but more often if necessary, to evaluate and update the plan, and to incorporate advancements in patient safety practices.

(2) A reporting system for patient safety events that allows anyone involved, including, but not limited to, health care practitioners, facility employees, patients, and visitors, to make a report of a patient safety event to the health facility.

(3) A process for a team of facility staff to conduct analyses, including, but not limited to, root cause analyses of patient safety events. The team shall be composed of the facility's various categories of health care professionals, with the appropriate competencies to conduct the required analyses.

(4) A reporting process that supports and encourages a culture of safety and reporting patient safety events.

(5) A process for providing ongoing patient safety training for facility personnel and health care practitioners.

(c) For the purposes of this section, patient safety events shall be defined by the patient safety plan and shall include, but not be limited to, all adverse events or potential adverse events as described in Section 1279.1 that are determined to be preventable, and health-care-associated infections (HAI), as defined in the federal Centers for Disease Control and Prevention's National Healthcare Safety Network, or its successor, unless the department accepts the recommendation of the Healthcare Associated Infection Advisory Committee, or its successor, that are determined to be preventable.

(Added by Stats. 2008, Ch. 294, Sec. 2. Effective January 1, 2009.)

1279.7.

(a) A health facility, as defined in subdivision (a), (b), (c), or (f) of Section 1250, shall implement a facilitywide hand hygiene program.

(b) Commencing January 1, 2017, a health facility, as defined in subdivision (a), (b), (c), or (f) of Section 1250, is prohibited from using an epidural connector that would fit into a connector other than the type it was intended for, unless an emergency or urgent situation exists and the prohibition would impair the ability to provide health care.

(c) Commencing January 1, 2016, a health facility, as defined in subdivision (a), (b), (c), or (f) of Section 1250, is prohibited from using an intravenous connector that would fit into a connector other than the type it was intended for, unless an emergency or urgent situation exists and the prohibition would impair the ability to provide health care.

(d) Commencing July 1, 2016, a health facility, as defined in subdivision (a), (b), (c), or (f) of Section 1250, is prohibited from using an enteral feeding connector that would fit into a connector other than the type it was intended for, unless an emergency or urgent situation exists and the prohibition would impair the ability to provide health care.

(e) The Advanced Medical Technology Association shall, on January 1 of each year until the standards are developed, provide the Legislature with a report on the progress of the International Organization for Standardization in developing new design standards for connectors for intravenous, epidural, or enteral applications.

(f) A health facility that is required to develop a patient safety plan pursuant to Section 1279.6 shall include in the patient safety plan measures to prevent adverse events associated with misconnecting intravenous, enteral feeding, and epidural lines. This subdivision shall become inoperative as to epidural connectors upon the operative date of subdivision (b), and as to intravenous connectors upon the operative date of subdivision (c), and as to enteral feeding connectors upon the operative date of subdivision (d).

(Amended by Stats. 2016, Ch. 86, Sec. 174. (SB 1171) Effective January 1, 2017.)

1279.8.

(a) Every health facility, as defined in subdivision (c), (d), (e), (g), (h), (i), or (m) of Section 1250, shall, for the purpose of addressing issues that arise when a patient is missing from the facility, develop and comply with an absentee notification plan as part of the written plans and procedures that are required pursuant to federal or state law. The plan shall include and be limited to the following: a requirement that an administrator of the facility, or his or her designee, inform the patient's authorized representative when that patient is missing from the facility and the circumstances in which an administrator of the facility, or his or her designee, shall notify local law enforcement when a patient is missing from the facility.

(b) This section shall not apply to state hospitals under the jurisdiction of the State Department of State Hospitals when the executive director of the state hospital, or his or her designee, determines that informing the patient's authorized representative that a patient is missing will create a risk to the safety and security of the state hospital.

(Added by Stats. 2013, Ch. 674, Sec. 1. (AB 620) Effective January 1, 2014.)

1280.

(a) The state department may provide consulting services upon request to any health facility to assist in the identification or correction of deficiencies or the upgrading of the quality of care provided by the health facility.

(b) The state department shall notify the health facility of all deficiencies in its compliance with this chapter and the rules and regulations adopted hereunder, and the health facility shall agree with the state department upon a plan of correction that shall give the health facility a reasonable time to correct these deficiencies. If at the end of the allotted time, as revealed by inspection, the health facility has failed to correct the deficiencies, the director may take action to revoke or suspend the license.

(c) (1) In addition to subdivision (a), if the health facility is licensed under subdivision (a), (b), or (f) of Section 1250, and if the facility fails to implement a plan of correction that has been agreed upon by both the facility and the state department within a reasonable time, the state department may order implementation of the plan of correction previously agreed upon by the facility and the state department. If the facility and the state department fail to agree upon a plan of correction within a reasonable time and if the deficiency poses an immediate and substantial hazard to the health or safety of patients, then the director may take action to order implementation of a plan of correction devised by the state department. The order shall be in writing and shall contain a statement of the reasons for the order. If the facility does not agree that the deficiency poses an immediate and substantial hazard to the health or safety of patients or if the facility believes that the plan of correction will not correct the hazard, or if the facility proposes a more efficient or effective means of remedying the deficiency, the facility may, within 10 days of receiving the plan of correction from the department, appeal the order to the director. The director shall review information provided by the facility, the department, and other affected parties and within a reasonable time render a decision in writing that shall include a statement of reasons for the order. During the period which the director is reviewing the appeal, the order to implement the plan of correction shall be stayed. The opportunity for appeal provided pursuant to this subdivision shall not be deemed to be an adjudicative hearing and is not required to comply with Section 100171.

(2) If any condition within a health facility licensed under subdivision (a), (b), or (f) of Section 1250 poses an immediate and substantial hazard to the health or safety of patients, the state department may order either of the following until the hazardous condition is corrected:

(A) Reduction in the number of patients.

(B) Closure of the unit or units within the facility that pose the risk. If the unit to be closed is an emergency room in a designated facility, as defined in Section 1797.67, the state department shall notify and coordinate with the local emergency medical services agency.

(3) The facility may appeal an order pursuant to paragraph (2) by appealing to the superior court of the county in which the facility is located.

(4) Paragraph (2) shall not apply to a deficiency for which the facility was cited prior to January 1, 1994.

(d) Reports on the results of each inspection of a health facility shall be prepared by the inspector or inspector team and shall be kept on file in the state department along with

the plan of correction and health facility comments. The inspection report may include a recommendation for reinspection. Inspection reports of an intermediate care facility/developmentally disabled habilitative or an intermediate care facility/developmentally disabled—nursing shall be provided by the state department to the appropriate regional center pursuant to Chapter 5 (commencing with Section 4620) of Division 4.5 of the Welfare and Institutions Code.
(e) All inspection reports and lists of deficiencies shall be open to public inspection when the state department has received verification that the health facility has received the report from the state department. All plans of correction shall be open to public inspection upon receipt by the state department.
(f) In no event shall the act of providing a plan of correction, the content of the plan of correction, or the execution of a plan of correction, be used in any legal action or administrative proceeding as an admission within the meaning of Sections 1220 to 1227, inclusive, of the Evidence Code against the health facility, its licensee, or its personnel.
(Amended by Stats. 1997, Ch. 220, Sec. 10. Effective August 4, 1997.)
1280.1.
(a) Subject to subdivision (d), prior to the effective date of regulations adopted to implement Section 1280.3, if a licensee of a health facility licensed under subdivision (a), (b), or (f) of Section 1250 receives a notice of deficiency constituting an immediate jeopardy to the health or safety of a patient and is required to submit a plan of correction, the department may assess the licensee an administrative penalty in an amount not to exceed twenty-five thousand dollars ($25,000) per violation.
(b) If the licensee disputes a determination by the department regarding the alleged deficiency or the alleged failure to correct a deficiency, or regarding the reasonableness of the proposed deadline for correction or the amount of the penalty, the licensee may, within 10 days, request a hearing pursuant to Section 131071. Penalties shall be paid when appeals have been exhausted and the department's position has been upheld.
(c) For purposes of this section "immediate jeopardy" means a situation in which the licensee's noncompliance with one or more requirements of licensure has caused, or is likely to cause, serious injury or death to the patient.
(d) This section shall apply only to incidents occurring on or after January 1, 2007. With respect to incidents occurring on or after January 1, 2009, the amount of the administrative penalties assessed under subdivision (a) shall be up to one hundred thousand dollars ($100,000) per violation. With respect to incidents occurring on or after January 1, 2009, the amount of the administrative penalties assessed under subdivision (a) shall be up to fifty thousand dollars ($50,000) for the first administrative penalty, up to seventy-five thousand dollars ($75,000) for the second subsequent administrative penalty, and up to one hundred thousand dollars ($100,000) for the third and every subsequent violation. An administrative penalty issued after three years from the date of the last issued immediate jeopardy violation shall be considered a first administrative penalty so long as the facility has not received additional immediate jeopardy violations and is found by the department to be in substantial compliance with all state and federal licensing laws and regulations. The department shall have full discretion to consider all factors when determining the amount of an administrative penalty pursuant to this section.
(e) No new regulations are required or authorized for implementation of this section.
(f) This section shall become inoperative on the effective date of regulations promulgated by the department pursuant to Section 1280.3.
(g) In enforcing this section, the department shall take into consideration the special circumstances of small and rural hospitals, as defined in Section 124840, in order to protect access to quality care in those hospitals.
(Amended by Stats. 2008, Ch. 605, Sec. 1. Effective January 1, 2009. Inoperative on date prescribed in subd. (f).)
1280.2.
(a) No deficiency cited pursuant to paragraph (2) of subdivision (b) of Section 1280 or Section 1280.1 shall be for the failure of a facility to meet the requirements of the California Building Standards Code if, as of January 1, 1994, the hospital building was approved under Chapter 12.5 (commencing with Section 15000) of Division 12.5, or if the hospital building was exempt from that approval under any other provision of law in effect on that date.
(b) It is the intent of the Legislature that neither the amendments made to Section 1280 by the act that added this section, nor Section 1280.1 shall be construed to require the retrofitting of hospital buildings built prior to January 1, 1994, to meet seismic standards in effect on that date.
(Added by Stats. 1993, Ch. 1152, Sec. 3. Effective January 1, 1994.)
1280.3.
(a) Commencing on the effective date of the regulations adopted pursuant to this section, the director may assess an administrative penalty against a licensee of a health facility licensed under subdivision (a), (b), or (f) of Section 1250 for a deficiency constituting an immediate jeopardy violation as determined by the department up to a maximum of seventy-five thousand dollars ($75,000) for the first administrative penalty, up to one hundred thousand dollars ($100,000) for the second subsequent administrative penalty, and up to one hundred twenty-five thousand dollars ($125,000) for the third and every subsequent violation. An administrative penalty issued after three years from the date of the last issued immediate jeopardy violation shall be considered a first administrative penalty so long as the facility has not received additional immediate jeopardy violations and is found by the department to be in substantial compliance with all state and federal licensing laws and regulations. The department shall have full discretion to consider all factors when determining the amount of an administrative penalty pursuant to this section.
(b) Except as provided in subdivision (c), for a violation of this chapter or the rules and regulations promulgated thereunder that does not constitute a violation of subdivision (a), the department may assess an administrative penalty in an amount of up to twenty-five thousand dollars ($25,000) per violation. This subdivision shall also apply to violation of regulations set forth in Article 3 (commencing with Section 127400) of Chapter 2 of Part 2 of Division 107 or the rules and regulations promulgated thereunder.
The department shall promulgate regulations establishing the criteria to assess an administrative penalty against a health facility licensed pursuant to subdivisions (a), (b), or (f) of Section 1250. The criteria shall include, but need not be limited to, the following:
(1) The patient's physical and mental condition.
(2) The probability and severity of the risk that the violation presents to the patient.
(3) The actual financial harm to patients, if any.
(4) The nature, scope, and severity of the violation.
(5) The facility's history of compliance with related state and federal statutes and regulations.
(6) Factors beyond the facility's control that restrict the facility's ability to comply with this chapter or the rules and regulations promulgated thereunder.
(7) The demonstrated willfulness of the violation.
(8) The extent to which the facility detected the violation and took steps to immediately correct the violation and prevent the violation from recurring.
(c) The department shall not assess an administrative penalty for minor violations.
(d) The regulations shall not change the definition of immediate jeopardy as established in this section.
(e) The regulations shall apply only to incidents occurring on or after the effective date of the regulations.
(f) If the licensee disputes a determination by the department regarding the alleged deficiency or alleged failure to correct a deficiency, or regarding the reasonableness of the proposed deadline for correction or the amount of the penalty, the licensee may, within 10 working days, request a hearing pursuant to Section 131071. Penalties shall be paid when all appeals have been exhausted and the department's position has been upheld.
(g) For purposes of this section, "immediate jeopardy" means a situation in which the licensee's noncompliance with one or more requirements of licensure has caused, or is likely to cause, serious injury or death to the patient.
(h) In enforcing subdivision (a) the department shall take into consideration the special circumstances of small and rural hospitals, as defined in Section 124840, in order to protect access to quality care in those hospitals.
(Amended by Stats. 2008, Ch. 605, Sec. 3. Effective January 1, 2009.)
1280.4.
(a) If a licensee of a health facility licensed under subdivision (a), (b), or (f) of Section 1250 fails to report an adverse event pursuant to Section 1279.1, the department may assess the licensee a civil penalty in an amount not to exceed one hundred dollars ($100) for each day that the adverse event is not reported following the initial five-day period or 24-hour period, as applicable, pursuant to subdivision (a) of Section 1279.1.
(b) If a licensee of a health facility licensed under subdivision (a) or (b) of Section 1250 is required to, and fails to, immediately report an incident under subdivision (a) of Section 4427.5 of the Welfare and Institutions Code, the department may assess the licensee a civil penalty in the amount not to exceed one hundred dollars ($100) for each day that the incident was not reported to law enforcement.
(c) If a licensee disputes a determination by the department regarding an alleged failure to report as described in this section, the licensee may, within 10 days, request a hearing pursuant to Section 131071. Penalties shall be paid when appeals pursuant to those provisions have been exhausted.
(Amended by Stats. 2013, Ch. 724, Sec. 1. (SB 651) Effective January 1, 2014.)
1280.5.
The state department shall accept, consider, and resolve written appeals by a licensee or health facility administrator of findings made upon the inspection of a health facility.
(Added by Stats. 1988, Ch. 595, Sec. 1.)
1280.6.
In assessing an administrative penalty pursuant to Section 1280.1 or Section 1280.3 against a licensee of a health facility licensed under subdivision (a) of Section 1250 owned by a nonprofit corporation that shares an identical board of directors with a nonprofit health care service plan licensed pursuant to Chapter 2.2 (commencing with Section 1340), the director shall consider whether the deficiency arises from an incident that is the subject of investigation of, or has resulted in a fine to, the health care service plan by the Department of Managed Health Care. If the deficiency results from the same incident, the director shall limit the administrative penalty to take into consideration the penalty imposed by the Department of Managed Health Care.
(Added by Stats. 2006, Ch. 895, Sec. 5.5. Effective January 1, 2007.)
1280.15.
(a) A clinic, health facility, home health agency, or hospice licensed pursuant to Section 1204, 1250, 1725, or 1745 shall prevent unlawful or unauthorized access to, and use or disclosure of, patients' medical information, as defined in Section 56.05 of the Civil Code and consistent with Section 1280.18. For purposes of this section, internal paper records, electronic mail, or facsimile transmissions inadvertently misdirected within the same facility or health care system within the course of coordinating care or delivering services shall not constitute unauthorized access to, or use or disclosure of, a patient's medical information. The department, after investigation, may assess an administrative penalty for a violation of this section of up to twenty-five thousand dollars ($25,000) per patient whose medical information was unlawfully or without authorization accessed, used,

or disclosed, and up to seventeen thousand five hundred dollars ($17,500) per subsequent occurrence of unlawful or unauthorized access, use, or disclosure of that patient's medical information. For purposes of the investigation, the department shall consider the clinic's, health facility's, agency's, or hospice's history of compliance with this section and other related state and federal statutes and regulations, the extent to which the facility detected violations and took preventative action to immediately correct and prevent past violations from recurring, and factors outside its control that restricted the facility's ability to comply with this section. The department shall have full discretion to consider all factors when determining whether to investigate and the amount of an administrative penalty, if any, pursuant to this section.

(b) (1) A clinic, health facility, home health agency, or hospice to which subdivision (a) applies shall report any unlawful or unauthorized access to, or use or disclosure of, a patient's medical information to the department no later than 15 business days after the unlawful or unauthorized access, use, or disclosure has been detected by the clinic, health facility, home health agency, or hospice.

(2) Subject to subdivision (c), a clinic, health facility, home health agency, or hospice shall also report any unlawful or unauthorized access to, or use or disclosure of, a patient's medical information to the affected patient or the patient's representative at the last known address, or by an alternative means or at an alternative location as specified by the patient or the patient's representative in writing pursuant to Section 164.522(b) of Title 45 of the Code of Federal Regulations, no later than 15 business days after the unlawful or unauthorized access, use, or disclosure has been detected by the clinic, health facility, home health agency, or hospice. Notice may be provided by email only if the patient has previously agreed in writing to electronic notice by email.

(c) (1) A clinic, health facility, home health agency, or hospice shall delay the reporting, as required pursuant to paragraph (2) of subdivision (b), of any unlawful or unauthorized access to, or use or disclosure of, a patient's medical information beyond 15 business days if a law enforcement agency or official provides the clinic, health facility, home health agency, or hospice with a written or oral statement that compliance with the reporting requirements of paragraph (2) of subdivision (b) would likely impede the law enforcement agency's investigation that relates to the unlawful or unauthorized access to, and use or disclosure of, a patient's medical information and specifies a date upon which the delay shall end, not to exceed 60 days after a written request is made, or 30 days after an oral request is made. A law enforcement agency or official may request an extension of a delay based upon a written declaration that there exists a bona fide, ongoing, significant criminal investigation of serious wrongdoing relating to the unlawful or unauthorized access to, and use or disclosure of, a patient's medical information, that notification of patients will undermine the law enforcement agency's investigation, and that specifies a date upon which the delay shall end, not to exceed 60 days after the end of the original delay period.

(2) If the statement of the law enforcement agency or official is made orally, then the clinic, health facility, home health agency, or hospice shall do both of the following:

(A) Document the oral statement, including, but not limited to, the identity of the law enforcement agency or official making the oral statement and the date upon which the oral statement was made.

(B) Limit the delay in reporting the unlawful or unauthorized access to, or use or disclosure of, the patient's medical information to the date specified in the oral statement, not to exceed 30 calendar days from the date that the oral statement is made, unless a written statement that complies with the requirements of this subdivision is received during that time.

(3) A clinic, health facility, home health agency, or hospice shall submit a report that is delayed pursuant to this subdivision not later than 15 business days after the date designated as the end of the delay.

(d) If a clinic, health facility, home health agency, or hospice to which subdivision (a) applies violates subdivision (b), the department may assess the licensee a penalty in the amount of one hundred dollars ($100) for each day that the unlawful or unauthorized access, use, or disclosure is not reported to the department or the affected patient, following the initial 15-day period specified in subdivision (b). However, the total combined penalty assessed by the department under subdivision (a) and this subdivision shall not exceed two hundred fifty thousand dollars ($250,000) per reported event. For enforcement purposes, it shall be presumed that the facility did not notify the affected patient if the notification was not documented. This presumption may be rebutted by a licensee only if the licensee demonstrates, by a preponderance of the evidence, that the notification was made.

(e) In enforcing subdivisions (a) and (d), the department shall take into consideration the special circumstances of small and rural hospitals, as defined in Section 124840, and primary care clinics, as defined in subdivision (a) of Section 1204, in order to protect access to quality care in those hospitals and clinics. When assessing a penalty on a skilled nursing facility or other facility subject to Section 1423, 1424, 1424.1, or 1424.5, the department shall issue only the higher of either a penalty for the violation of this section or a penalty for violation of Section 1423, 1424, 1424.1, or 1424.5, not both.

(f) All penalties collected by the department pursuant to this section, Sections 1280.1, 1280.3, and 1280.4, shall be deposited into the Internal Departmental Quality Improvement Account, which is hereby created within the Special Deposit Fund under Section 16370 of the Government Code. Upon appropriation by the Legislature, moneys in the account shall be expended for internal quality improvement activities in the Licensing and Certification Program.

(g) If the licensee disputes a determination by the department regarding a failure to prevent or failure to timely report unlawful or unauthorized access to, or use or disclosure of, patients' medical information, or the imposition of a penalty under this section, the licensee may, within 10 days of receipt of the penalty assessment, request a hearing pursuant to Section 131071. Penalties shall be paid when appeals have been exhausted and the penalty has been upheld.

(h) In lieu of disputing the determination of the department regarding a failure to prevent or failure to timely report unlawful or unauthorized access to, or use or disclosure of, patients' medical information, transmit to the department 75 percent of the total amount of the administrative penalty, for each violation, within 30 business days of receipt of the administrative penalty.

(i) For purposes of this section, the following definitions shall apply:

(1) "Reported event" means all breaches included in any single report that is made pursuant to subdivision (b), regardless of the number of breach events contained in the report.

(2) "Unauthorized" means the inappropriate access, review, or viewing of patient medical information without a direct need for medical diagnosis, treatment, or other lawful use as permitted by the Confidentiality of Medical Information Act (Part 2.6 (commencing with Section 56) of Division 1 of the Civil Code) or any other statute or regulation governing the lawful access, use, or disclosure of medical information.

(Amended by Stats. 2014, Ch. 412, Sec. 1. (AB 1755) Effective January 1, 2015.)

1280.16.

For purposes of Sections 1280.17, 1280.18, 1280.19, and 1280.20, the following definitions apply:

(a) "Department" means the State Department of Public Health.

(b) "Director" means the State Public Health Officer.

(c) "Medical information" means the term as defined in Section 56.05 of the Civil Code.

(d) "Provider of health care" means the term as defined in Sections 56.05 and 56.06 of the Civil Code.

(e) "Unauthorized access" means the inappropriate review or viewing of patient medical information without a direct need for diagnosis, treatment, or other lawful use as permitted by the Confidentiality of Medical Information Act (Part 2.6 (commencing with Section 56) of Division 1 of the Civil Code) or by other statutes or regulations governing the lawful access, use, or disclosure of medical information.

(Added by renumbering Section 130201 by Stats. 2014, Ch. 31, Sec. 24. (SB 857) Effective June 20, 2014.)

1280.17.

(a) (1) The department may assess an administrative fine against any person or any provider of health care, whether licensed or unlicensed, for any violation of Section 1280.18 of this code or Part 2.6 (commencing with Section 56) of Division 1 of the Civil Code in an amount as provided in Section 56.36 of the Civil Code. Proceedings against any person or entity for a violation of this section shall be held in accordance with administrative adjudication provisions of Chapter 4.5 (commencing with Section 11400) and Chapter 5 (commencing with Section 11500) of Part 1 of Division 3 of Title 2 of the Government Code.

(2) Paragraph (1) shall not apply to a clinic, health facility, agency, or hospice licensed pursuant to Section 1204, 1250, 1725, or 1745.

(b) The department shall adopt, amend, or repeal, in accordance with the provisions of Chapter 3.5 (commencing with Section 11340) of Part 1 of Division 3 of Title 2 of the Government Code, rules and regulations as may be reasonable and proper to carry out the purposes and intent of Sections 1280.18, 1280.19, and 1280.20, and to enable the authority to exercise the powers and perform the duties conferred upon it by those sections not inconsistent with any other provision of law.

(Added by renumbering Section 130202 by Stats. 2014, Ch. 31, Sec. 25. (SB 857) Effective June 20, 2014.)

1280.18.

(a) Every provider of health care shall establish and implement appropriate administrative, technical, and physical safeguards to protect the privacy of a patient's medical information. Every provider of health care shall reasonably safeguard confidential medical information from any unauthorized access or unlawful access, use, or disclosure.

(b) In exercising its duties pursuant to Section 1280.17, the department shall consider the provider's capability, complexity, size, and history of compliance with this section and other related state and federal statutes and regulations, the extent to which the provider detected violations and took steps to immediately correct and prevent past violations from reoccurring, and factors beyond the provider's immediate control that restricted the facility's ability to comply with this section.

(c) The department may conduct joint investigations of individuals and health facilities for violations of this section and Section 1280.15, respectively.

(Added by renumbering Section 130203 by Stats. 2014, Ch. 31, Sec. 26. (SB 857) Effective June 20, 2014.)

1280.19.

The Internal Health Information Integrity Quality Improvement Account is hereby created in the State Treasury. All administrative fines assessed by the department pursuant to Section 56.36 of the Civil Code shall be deposited in the Internal Health Information Integrity Quality Improvement Account. Notwithstanding Section 16305.7 of the Government Code, all interest earned on the moneys deposited in the account shall be retained in the account. Upon appropriation by the Legislature, money in the account shall be used for the purpose of supporting quality improvement activities in the department.

(Added by renumbering Section 130204 by Stats. 2014, Ch. 31, Sec. 27. (SB 857) Effective June 20, 2014.)

1280.20.

Notwithstanding any other law, the director may send a recommendation for further investigation of, or discipline for, a potential violation of the licensee's relevant licensing authority. The recommendation shall include all documentary evidence collected by the director in evaluating whether or not to make that recommendation. The recommendation and accompanying evidence shall be deemed in the nature of an investigative communication and be protected by Section 6254 of the Government Code. The licensing authority of the provider of health care shall review all evidence submitted by the director and may take action for further investigation or discipline of the licensee.
(Added by renumbering Section 130205 by Stats. 2014, Ch. 31, Sec. 28. (SB 857) Effective June 20, 2014.)

1281.
All public and private general acute care hospitals either shall comply with the standards for the examination and treatment of victims of sexual assault and attempted sexual assault, including child molestation, and the collection and preservation of evidence therefrom, specified in Section 13823.11 of the Penal Code, and the protocol and guidelines therefor established pursuant to Section 13823.5 of the Penal Code, or they shall adopt a protocol for the immediate referral of these victims to a local hospital that so complies, and shall notify local law enforcement agencies, the district attorney, and local victim assistance agencies of the adoption of the referral protocol.
(Added by Stats. 1985, Ch. 812, Sec. 1.)

1282.
(a) The state department shall have the authority to contract for outside personnel to perform inspections of health facilities as the need arises. The state department, when feasible, shall contract with nonprofit, professional organizations which have demonstrated the ability to carry out the provisions of this chapter. The organizations shall include, but not be limited to, the California Medical Association Committee on Medical Staff Surveys and participants in the Consolidated Hospital Survey Program. Quality of care inspections have been performed in recent years by the California Medical Association Committee on Staff Surveys and other organizations which have combined their efforts in the Consolidated Hospital Survey Program. It is the intent of the Legislature that these organizations or comparable organizations shall continue to perform these inspections by contract when sufficient manpower is available from the organizations to do so, unless the state department demonstrates that the inspections fail to assure compliance with the quality of care standards set by this chapter.
(b) If, pursuant to this section, the state department contracts with the Joint Commission on Accreditation of Hospitals to perform all or any part of a quality of care inspection for a health facility specified in subdivision (a) of Section 1250, and if that health facility contracts with the Joint Commission on Accreditation of Hospitals to perform an accreditation inspection and survey at the same time as the quality of care inspection, the health facility shall transmit to the state department, within 30 days of receipt, a copy of the final accreditation report of the Joint Commission on the Accreditation of Hospitals. However, if the Joint Commission on Accreditation of Hospitals conducts an accreditation inspection and survey at a health facility at a time other than the time at which, pursuant to this section, it participates in a quality of care inspection at that facility, then the health facility shall not be required to transmit a copy of the final accreditation report to the state department.
(Amended by Stats. 1983, Ch. 992, Sec. 3.)

1283.
(a) No health facility shall surrender the physical custody of a minor under 16 years of age to any person unless such surrender is authorized in writing by the child's parent, the person having legal custody of the child, or the caregiver of the child who is a relative of the child and who may authorize medical care and dental care under Section 6550 of the Family Code.
(b) A health facility shall report to the State Department of Health Services, on forms supplied by the department, the name and address of any person and, in the case of a person acting as an agent for an organization, the name and address of the organization, into whose physical custody a minor under the age of 16 is surrendered, other than a parent, relative by blood or marriage, or person having legal custody. This report shall be transmitted to the department within 48 hours of the surrendering of custody. No report to the department is required if a minor under the age of 16 is transferred to another health facility for further care or if this minor comes within Section 300, 601, or 602 of the Welfare and Institutions Code and is released to an agent of a public welfare, probation, or law enforcement agency.
(Amended by Stats. 1996, Ch. 563, Sec. 4. Effective January 1, 1997.)

1284.
A licensed inpatient mental health facility shall be subject to the provisions of Section 5622 of the Welfare and Institutions Code.
(Amended by Stats. 1987, Ch. 835, Sec. 1.)

1285.
(a) No patient shall be detained in a health facility solely for the nonpayment of a bill.
(b) For the purposes of this section, "detained" means the intentional confinement of a patient in a health facility without authorization of the patient or any other person who may be authorized to provide consent to care on behalf of the patient.
(c) Any person who is detained in a health facility solely for the nonpayment of a bill has a cause of action against the health facility for the detention, which may be brought by that person or that person's parent, guardian, conservator, or other legal representative. The cause of action may be brought against the health facility, proprietor, lessee or their agents, or against any person, corporation, association, or directors thereof. Any person who has been detained in a health facility, solely for the nonpayment of a bill, who has brought an action for the detention, may recover general and punitive damages, court

costs, and reasonable attorney's fees actually incurred and any other relief which the court in its discretion may allow.
(d) Violation of subdivision (a) is a misdemeanor punishable as prescribed in Section 1290.
(Amended by Stats. 1981, Ch. 714.)

1286.
(a) Smoking a tobacco product shall be prohibited in patient care areas, waiting rooms, and visiting rooms of a health facility, except those areas specifically designated as smoking areas, and in patient rooms as specified in subdivision (b).
(b) Smoking a tobacco product shall not be permitted in a patient room unless all persons assigned to the room have requested a room where smoking is permitted. In the event that the health facility occupancy has reached capacity, the health facility shall have reasonable time to reassign patients to appropriate rooms.
(c) Clearly legible signs shall either:
(1) State that smoking is unlawful and be conspicuously posted by, or on behalf of, the owner or manager of the health facility, in all areas of a health facility where smoking is unlawful, or
(2) Identify "smoking permitted" areas, and be posted by, or on behalf of, the owner or manager of the health facility, only in areas of the health facility where smoking is lawfully permitted.
If "smoking permitted" signs are posted, there shall also be conspicuously posted, near all major entrances, clearly legible signs stating that smoking is unlawful except in areas designated "smoking permitted."
(d) No signs pertaining to smoking are required to be posted in patient rooms.
(e) This section shall not apply to skilled nursing facilities, intermediate care facilities, and intermediate care facilities for the developmentally disabled.
(f) For purposes of this section, "smoking" has the same meaning as in subdivision (c) of Section 22950.5 of the Business and Professions Code.
(g) For purposes of this section, "tobacco product" means a product or device as defined in subdivision (d) of Section 22950.5 of the Business and Professions Code.
(Amended by Stats. 2016, 2nd Ex. Sess., Ch. 7, Sec. 12. (SB 5 2x) Effective June 9, 2016.)

1288.
(a) Except as provided in subdivision (b), the licensee of each skilled nursing or intermediate care facility shall notify, in writing, all patients for whom the facility's services are not reimbursed pursuant to the provisions of Chapter 7 (commencing with Section 14000) of Part 3 of Division 9 of the Welfare and Institutions Code, or such patient's responsible agent, of any scheduled room rate increase at least 30 calendar days in advance of the increase.
(b) The licensee need not delay rate increases in order to provide the notice prescribed by subdivision (a) during any period when such delay would result in a loss to the facility of Medi-Cal reimbursement revenues available to it under Chapter 7 (commencing with Section 14000) of Part 3 of Division 9 of the Welfare and Institutions Code due to increases in allowable Medi-Cal reimbursement rates (1) implemented by emergency regulation or (2) made retroactive. In such cases, the licensee shall provide the notice as many days in advance as is possible without loss of Medi-Cal revenues or, if not possible without Medi-Cal revenue losses, at the time of effectuating the rate increase. Nothing contained in this subdivision shall be construed as authorizing retroactive room rate increases for facility services to patients that are not reimbursed under Chapter 7 (commencing with Section 14000) of Part 3 of Division 9 of the Welfare and Institutions Code.
(Added by Stats. 1980, Ch. 891.)

1288.4.
A health facility licensed under subdivision (a), (b), or (f) of Section 1250 shall post conspicuously, in a prominent location within the premises and accessible to public view, a notice providing the telephone number of the state department's regional licensing office where complaints regarding the facility may be reported. The state department shall inform the health facility of the telephone number to be included in the notice.
(Added by Stats. 1993, Ch. 1152, Sec. 4. Effective January 1, 1994.)

1289.
(a) No owner, employee, agent, or consultant of a long-term health care facility, as defined in Section 1418, or member of his or her immediate family, or representative of a public agency or organization operating within the long-term health care facility with state, county, or city authority, or member of his or her immediate family, shall purchase or receive any item or property with a fair market value of more than one hundred dollars ($100) from a resident in the long-term health care facility, unless the purchase or receipt is made or conducted in the presence of a representative of the Office of the State Long-Term Care Ombudsman, as defined in subdivision (c) of Section 9701 of the Welfare and Institutions Code. The role of the ombudsman is to witness the transaction and to question the resident and others as appropriate, about the transaction. The ombudsman may submit written comments pertaining to the transaction into the health records of the resident. The Office of the State Long-Term Care Ombudsman shall establish guidelines concerning activities of ombudsmen pursuant to this section. Additionally, the transaction described in this subdivision shall be recorded by the facility in the health records of the resident. The record of the transaction shall include the name and address of the purchaser, date and location of the transaction, description of property sold, and purchase price. The instrument shall include signatures of the resident, the purchaser, and the witnessing ombudsman.
(b) Any owner, employee, agent, or consultant of a long-term health care facility, or member of his or her immediate family, or representative of a public agency or

organization operating within the long-term health care facility with state, county, or city authority, or member of his or her immediate family, who violates subdivision (a) shall be required to return the item or property he or she purchased to the person from whom it was purchased, if he or she still possesses it. If the employee no longer possesses the item or property, he or she shall pay the person who sold the item or property the fair market value at the time he or she would otherwise be required to return the property.

(c) Craft items, which are those items made by residents of a long-term health care facility, are exempt from the provisions of this section.

(d) Any violation of this section shall be subject to a civil penalty not to exceed one thousand dollars ($1,000) which shall be enforced by the Department of Aging. The Department of Aging may bring a cause of action in a court of competent jurisdiction to enforce the provisions of this subdivision.

(e) Notwithstanding Section 1290, any person who violates this section is guilty of an infraction and shall be punished by a fine of not more than one hundred dollars ($100). (Added by Stats. 1984, Ch. 1182, Sec. 1.)

1289.3.

(a) A long-term health care facility, as defined in Section 1418, which fails to make reasonable efforts to safeguard patient property shall reimburse a patient for or replace stolen or lost patient property at its then current value. The facility shall be presumed to have made reasonable efforts to safeguard patient property if the facility has shown clear and convincing evidence of its efforts to meet each of the requirements specified in Section 1289.4. The presumption shall be a rebuttable presumption, and the resident or the resident's representative may pursue this matter in any court of competent jurisdiction.

(b) A citation shall be issued if the long-term health care facility has no program in place or if the facility has not shown clear and convincing evidence of its efforts to meet all of the requirements set forth in Section 1289.4. The department shall issue a deficiency in the event that the manner in which the policies have been implemented is inadequate or the individual facility situation warrants additional theft and loss protections.

(c) The department shall not determine that a long-term health care facility's program is inadequate based solely on the occasional occurrence of theft or loss in a facility. (Added by Stats. 1987, Ch. 1235, Sec. 2.)

1289.4.

A theft and loss program shall be implemented by the long-term health care facilities within 90 days after January 1, 1988. The program shall include all of the following:

(a) Establishment and posting of the facility's policy regarding theft and investigative procedures.

(b) Orientation to the policies and procedures for all employees within 90 days of employment.

(c) Documentation of lost and stolen patient property with a value of twenty-five dollars ($25) or more and, upon request, the documented theft and loss record for the past 12 months shall be made available to the State Department of Public Health, the county health department or law enforcement agencies, and to the office of the State Long-Term Care Ombudsman in response to a specific complaint. The documentation shall include, but not be limited to, the following:

(1) A description of the article.

(2) Its estimated value.

(3) The date and time the theft or loss was discovered.

(4) If determinable, the date and time the loss or theft occurred.

(5) The action taken.

(d) A written patient personal property inventory is established upon admission and retained during the resident's stay in the long-term health care facility. A copy of the written inventory shall be provided to the resident or the person acting on the resident's behalf. Subsequent items brought into or removed from the facility shall be added to or deleted from the personal property inventory by the facility at the written request of the resident, the resident's family, a responsible party, or a person acting on behalf of a resident. The facility shall not be liable for items which have not been requested to be included in the inventory or for items which have been deleted from the inventory. A copy of a current inventory shall be made available upon request to the resident, responsible party, or other authorized representative. The resident, resident's family, or a responsible party may list those items that are not subject to addition or deletion from the inventory, such as personal clothing or laundry, that are subject to frequent removal from the facility.

(e) Inventory and surrender of the resident's personal effects and valuables upon discharge to the resident or authorized representative in exchange for a signed receipt.

(f) Inventory and surrender of personal effects and valuables following the death of a resident to the authorized representative in exchange for a signed receipt. Immediate notice to the public administrator of the county upon the death of a resident without known next of kin as provided in Section 7600.5 of the Probate Code.

(g) Documentation, at least semiannually, of the facility's efforts to control theft and loss, including the review of theft and loss documentation and investigative procedures and results of the investigation by the administrator and, when feasible, the resident council.

(h) Establishment of a method of marking, to the extent feasible, personal property items for identification purposes upon admission and, as added to the property inventory list, including engraving of dentures and tagging of other prosthetic devices.

(i) Reports to the local law enforcement agency within 36 hours when the administrator of the facility has reason to believe patient property with a then-current value of one hundred dollars ($100) or more has been stolen. Copies of those reports for the preceding 12 months shall be made available to the State Department of Public Health and law enforcement agencies.

(j) Maintenance of a secured area for patients' property which is available for safekeeping of patient property upon the request of the patient or the patient's responsible party. Provide a lock for the resident's bedside drawer or cabinet upon request of and at the expense of the resident, the resident's family, or authorized representative. The facility administrator shall have access to the locked areas upon request.

(k) A copy of this section and Sections 1289.3 and 1289.5 is provided by a facility to all of the residents and their responsible parties, and, available upon request, to all of the facility's prospective residents and their responsible parties.

(l) Notification to all current residents and all new residents, upon admission, of the facility's policies and procedures relating to the facility's theft and loss prevention program. (Amended by Stats. 2010, Ch. 328, Sec. 112. (SB 1330) Effective January 1, 2011.)

1289.5.

No provision of a contract of admission, which includes all documents which a resident or his or her representative is required to sign at the time of, or as a condition of, admission to a long-term health care facility, shall require or imply a lesser standard of responsibility for the personal property of residents than is required by law. (Added by Stats. 1987, Ch. 1235, Sec. 4.)

ARTICLE 3.5. Hospital Infectious Disease Control Program [1288.45 - 1288.95]

(Article 3.5 added by Stats. 2006, Ch. 526, Sec. 2.)

1288.45.

For purposes of this article, the following definitions shall apply:

(a) "Advisory committee" or "HAI-AC" means the Healthcare Associated Infection Advisory Committee established pursuant to Section 1288.5.

(b) "Health-care-associated infection," "health facility acquired infection," or "HAI" means an infection defined by the National Health and Safety Network of the federal Centers for Disease Control and Prevention, unless the department adopts a definition consistent with the recommendations of the advisory committee or its successor.

(c) "Hospital" means a general acute care hospital as defined pursuant to subdivision (a) of Section 1250.

(d) "Infection prevention professional" means a registered nurse, medical technologist, or other salaried employee or consultant who, within two years of appointment, will meet the education and experience requirements for certification established by the national Certification Board for Infection Control and Epidemiology (CBIC), but does not include a physician who is appointed or receives a stipend as the infection prevention and control committee chairperson or hospital epidemiologist.

(e) "MRSA" means methicillin-resistant Staphylococcus aureus.

(f) "National Healthcare Safety Network" or "NHSN" means a secure, Internet-based system developed and managed by the federal Centers for Disease Control and Prevention (CDC) to collect, analyze, and report risk-adjusted HAI data related to the incidence of HAI and the process measures implemented to prevent these infections.

(g) "Program" means the health care infection surveillance, prevention, and control program within the department. (Added by Stats. 2008, Ch. 294, Sec. 4. Effective January 1, 2009.)

1288.5.

(a) By July 1, 2007, the department shall appoint a Healthcare Associated Infection Advisory Committee (HAI-AC) that shall make recommendations related to methods of reporting cases of hospital acquired infections occurring in general acute care hospitals, and shall make recommendations on the use of national guidelines and the public reporting of process measures for preventing the spread of HAI that are reported to the department pursuant to subdivision (b) of Section 1288.8.

(b) The advisory committee shall include persons with expertise in the surveillance, prevention, and control of hospital-acquired infections, including department staff, local health department officials, health care infection control professionals, hospital administration professionals, health care providers, health care consumers, physicians with expertise in infectious disease and hospital epidemiology, and integrated health care systems experts or representatives.

(c) The advisory committee shall meet at least every quarter and shall serve without compensation, but shall be reimbursed for travel-related expenses that include transportation, lodging, and meals at the state per diem reimbursement rate.

(d) In addition to the responsibilities enumerated in subdivision (a), the advisory committee shall do all of the following:

(1) Review and evaluate federal and state legislation, regulations, and accreditation standards and communicate to the department how hospital infection prevention and control programs will be impacted.

(2) In accordance with subdivision (a) of Section 1288.6, recommend a method by which the number of infection prevention professionals would be assessed in each hospital.

(3) Recommend an educational curriculum by which health facility evaluator nurses and department consultants would be trained to survey for hospital infection surveillance, prevention, and control programs.

(4) Recommend a method by which hospitals are audited to determine the validity and reliability of data submitted to the NHSN and the department.

(5) Recommend a standardized method by which an HAI occurring after hospital discharge would be identified.

(6) Recommend a method by which risk-adjusted HAI data would be reported to the public, the Legislature, and the Governor.

(7) Recommend a standardized method by which department health facility evaluator nurses and consultants would evaluate health care workers for compliance with infection

prevention procedures including, but not limited to, hand hygiene and environmental sanitation procedures.

(8) Recommend a method by which all hospital infection prevention professionals would be trained to use the NHSN HAI surveillance reporting system.

(Amended by Stats. 2008, Ch. 294, Sec. 5. Effective January 1, 2009.)

1288.55.

(a) (1) Each health facility, as defined in paragraph (3) of subdivision (a) of Section 1255.8, shall quarterly report all cases of health-care-associated MRSA bloodstream infection, health-care-associated clostridium difficile infection, and health-care-associated Vancomycin-resistant enterococcal bloodstream infection, and the number of inpatient days.

(2) Each health facility shall report quarterly to the department all central line associated bloodstream infections and the total central line days.

(3) Each health facility shall report quarterly to the department all health-care-associated surgical site infections of deep or organ space surgical sites, health-care-associated infections of orthopedic surgical sites, cardiac surgical sites, and gastrointestinal surgical sites designated as clean and clean-contaminated, and the number of surgeries involving deep or organ space, and orthopedic, cardiac, and gastrointestinal surgeries designated clean and clean-contaminated.

(b) The department's licensing and certification program shall do all of the following:

(1) Commencing January 1, 2011, post on the department's Web site information regarding the incidence rate of health-care-acquired central line associated bloodstream infections acquired at each health facility in California, including information on the number of inpatient days.

(2) Commencing January 1, 2012, post on the department's Web site information regarding the incidence rate of deep or organ space surgical site infections, orthopedic, cardiac, and gastrointestinal surgical procedures designated as clean and clean-contaminated, acquired at each health facility in California, including information on the number of inpatient days.

(3) No later than January 1, 2011, post on the department's Web site information regarding the incidence rate of health-care-associated MRSA bloodstream infection, health-care-associated clostridium difficile infection, and health-care-associated Vancomycin-resistant enterococcal bloodstream infection, at each health facility in California, including information on the number of inpatient days.

(c) Any information reported publicly as required under this section shall meet all of the following requirements:

(1) The department shall follow a risk adjustment process that is consistent with the federal Centers for Disease Control and Prevention's National Healthcare Safety Network (NHSN), or its successor, risk adjustment, and use its definitions, unless the department adopts, by regulation, a fair and equitable risk adjustment process that is consistent with the recommendations of the Healthcare Associated Infection Advisory Committee (HAI-AC), established pursuant to Section 1288.5, or its successor.

(2) For purposes of reporting, as required in subdivisions (a) and (b), an infection shall be reported using the NHSN definitions unless the department accepts the recommendation of the HAI-AC or its successor.

(3) If the federal Centers for Disease Control and Prevention do not use a public reporting model for specific health-care-acquired infections, then the department shall base its public reporting of incidence rate on the number of inpatient days for infection reporting, or the number of specified device days for relevant device-related infections, and the number of specified surgeries conducted for surgical site infection reporting, unless the department adopts a public reporting model that is consistent with recommendations of the HAI-AC or its successor.

(d) Health facilities that report data pursuant to the system shall report this data to the NHSN and the department, as appropriate.

(Added by Stats. 2008, Ch. 296, Sec. 4. Effective January 1, 2009.)

1288.6.

(a) (1) Each general acute care hospital, in collaboration with infection prevention and control professionals, and with the participation of senior health care facility leadership shall, as a component of its strategic plan, at least once every three years, prepare a written report that examines the hospital's existing resources and evaluates the quality and effectiveness of the hospital's infection surveillance and prevention program.

(2) The report shall evaluate and include information on all of the following:

(A) The risk and cost of the number of invasive patient procedures performed at the hospital.

(B) The number of intensive care beds.

(C) The number of emergency department visits to the hospital.

(D) The number of outpatient visits by departments.

(E) The number of licensed beds.

(F) Employee health and occupational health measures implemented at the hospital.

(G) Changing demographics of the community being served by the hospital.

(H) An estimate of the need and recommendations for additional resources for infection prevention and control programs necessary to address the findings of the plan.

(3) The report shall be updated annually, and shall be revised at regular intervals, if necessary, to accommodate technological advances and new information and findings contained in the triennial strategic plan with respect to improving disease surveillance and the prevention of HAI.

(b) Each general acute care hospital that uses central venous catheters (CVCs) shall implement policies and procedures to prevent occurrences of health care associated infection, as recommended by the Centers for Disease Control and Prevention intravascular bloodstream infection guidelines or other evidence-based national guidelines, as recommended by the advisory committee. A general acute care hospital that uses CVCs shall internally report CVC associated blood stream infection rates in intensive care units, utilizing device days to calculate the rate for each type of intensive care unit, to the appropriate medical staff committee of the hospital on a regular basis.

(Added by Stats. 2006, Ch. 526, Sec. 2. Effective January 1, 2007.)

1288.7.

By July 1, 2007, the department shall require that each general acute care hospital, in accordance with the Centers for Disease Control guidelines, take all of the following actions:

(a) Annually offer onsite influenza vaccinations, if available, to all hospital employees at no cost to the employee. Each general acute care hospital shall require its employees to be vaccinated, or if the employee elects not to be vaccinated, to declare in writing that he or she has declined the vaccination.

(b) Institute respiratory hygiene and cough etiquette protocols, develop and implement procedures for the isolation of patients with influenza, and adopt a seasonal influenza plan.

(c) Revise an existing or develop a new disaster plan that includes a pandemic influenza component. The plan shall also document any actual or recommended collaboration with local, regional, and state public health agencies or officials in the event of an influenza pandemic.

(Added by Stats. 2006, Ch. 526, Sec. 2. Effective January 1, 2007.)

1288.8.

(a) By January 1, 2008, the department shall take all of the following actions to protect against HAI in general acute care hospitals statewide:

(1) Implement an HAI surveillance and prevention program designed to assess the department's resource needs, educate health facility evaluator nurses in HAI, and educate department staff on methods of implementing recommendations for disease prevention.

(2) Revise existing and adopt new administrative regulations, as necessary, to incorporate current federal Centers for Disease Control and Prevention (CDC) guidelines and standards for HAI prevention.

(3) Require that general acute care hospitals develop a process for evaluating the judicious use of antibiotics, the results of which shall be monitored jointly by appropriate representatives and committees involved in quality improvement activities.

(b) On and after January 1, 2008, each general acute care hospital shall implement and annually report to the department on its implementation of infection surveillance and infection prevention process measures that have been recommended by the federal Centers for Disease Control and Prevention Healthcare Infection Control Practices Advisory Committee, as suitable for a mandatory public reporting program. Initially, these process measures shall include the CDC guidelines for central line insertion practices, surgical antimicrobial prophylaxis, and influenza vaccination of patients and healthcare personnel. In consultation with the advisory committee, the department shall make this information public no later than six months after receiving the data.

(c) The advisory committee shall make recommendations for phasing in the implementation and public reporting of additional process measures and outcome measures by January 1, 2008, and, in doing so, shall consider the measures recommended by the CDC.

(d) Each general acute care hospital shall also submit data on implemented process measures to the National Healthcare Safety Network of the CDC, or to any other scientifically valid national HAI reporting system based upon the recommendation of the federal Centers for Disease Control and Prevention Healthcare Infection Control Practices Advisory Committee or to another scientifically valid reporting database, as determined by the department based on the recommendations of the HAI-AC. Hospitals shall utilize the federal Centers for Disease Control and Prevention definitions and methodology for surveillance of HAI. Hospitals participating in the California Hospital Assessment and Reporting Task Force (CHART) shall publicly report those HAI measures as agreed to by all CHART hospitals.

(e) In addition to the requirements in subdivision (a), the department shall establish an infection surveillance, prevention, and control program to do all of the following:

(1) Designate infection prevention professionals to serve as consultants to the licensing and certification program.

(2) Provide education and training to department health facility evaluator nurses and consultants to effectively survey hospitals for compliance with infection surveillance, prevention, and control recommendations, as well as state and federal statutes and regulations.

(3) By January 1, 2011, in consultation with the HAI-AC, develop a scientifically valid statewide electronic reporting system or utilize an existing scientifically valid database system capable of receiving electronically transmitted reports from hospitals related to HAI.

(4) Provide current infection prevention and control information to the public on the Internet.

(5) Beginning January 1, 2011, provide to the Governor, the Legislature, and the Chairs of the Senate Committee on Health and Assembly Committee on Health, and post on the department's Web site, an annual report of publicly reported HAI infection information received and reported pursuant to this article.

(Amended by Stats. 2008, Ch. 294, Sec. 6. Effective January 1, 2009.)

1288.85.

Each general acute care hospital, as defined in subdivision (a) of Section 1250, shall do all of the following by July 1, 2015:

(a) Adopt and implement an antimicrobial stewardship policy in accordance with guidelines established by the federal government and professional organizations. This policy shall include a process to evaluate the judicious use of antibiotics in accordance with paragraph (3) of subdivision (a) of Section 1288.8.

(b) Develop a physician supervised multidisciplinary antimicrobial stewardship committee, subcommittee, or workgroup.

(c) Appoint to the physician supervised multidisciplinary antimicrobial stewardship committee, subcommittee, or workgroup, at least one physician or pharmacist who is knowledgeable about the subject of antimicrobial stewardship through prior training or attendance at continuing education programs, including programs offered by the federal Centers for Disease Control and Prevention, the Society for Healthcare Epidemiology of America, or similar recognized professional organizations.

(d) Report antimicrobial stewardship program activities to each appropriate hospital committee undertaking clinical quality improvement activities.

(Added by Stats. 2014, Ch. 843, Sec. 1. (SB 1311) Effective January 1, 2015.)

1288.9.

By January 1, 2009, the department shall do all of the following:

(a) Require each general acute care hospital to develop, implement, and periodically evaluate compliance with policies and procedures to prevent secondary surgical site infections (SSI). The results of this evaluation shall be monitored by the infection prevention committee and reported to the surgical committee of the hospital.

(b) Require each general acute care hospital to develop policies and procedures to implement the current Centers for Disease Control and Prevention guidelines and Institute for Healthcare Improvement (IHI) process measures designed to prevent ventilator associated pneumonia.

(c) During surveys, evaluate the facility's compliance with existing policies and procedures to prevent HAI, including any externally or internally reported HAI process and outcome measures.

(Added by Stats. 2006, Ch. 526, Sec. 2. Effective January 1, 2007.)

1288.95.

(a) No later than January 1, 2010, a physician designated as a hospital epidemiologist or infection surveillance, prevention, and control committee chairperson shall participate in a continuing medical education (CME) training program offered by the federal Centers for Disease Control and Prevention (CDC) and the Society for Healthcare Epidemiologists of America, or other recognized professional organization. The CME program shall be specific to infection surveillance, prevention, and control. Documentation of attendance shall be placed in the physician's credentialing file.

(b) Beginning January 2010, all staff and contract physicians and all other licensed independent contractors, including, but not limited to, nurse practitioners and physician assistants, shall be trained in methods to prevent transmission of HAI, including, but not limited to, MRSA and Clostridium difficile infection.

(c) By January 2010, all permanent and temporary hospital employees and contractual staff, including students, shall be trained in hospital-specific infection prevention and control policies, including, but not limited to, hand hygiene, facility-specific isolation procedures, patient hygiene, and environmental sanitation procedures. The training shall be given annually and when new policies have been adopted by the infection surveillance, prevention, and control committee.

(d) Environmental services staff shall be trained by the hospital and shall be observed for compliance with hospital sanitation measures. The training shall be given at the start of employment, when new prevention measures have been adopted, and annually thereafter. Cultures of the environment may be randomly obtained by the hospital to determine compliance with hospital sanitation procedures.

(Added by Stats. 2008, Ch. 294, Sec. 7. Effective January 1, 2009.)

ARTICLE 4. Offenses [1290 - 1293.2]

(Article 4 added by Stats. 1973, Ch. 1202.)

1290.

(a) Except as provided in subdivision (b) or (c), any person who violates this chapter or Section 127050 or 128600, or who willfully or repeatedly violates any rule or regulation adopted under this chapter or Section 127050 or 128600 is guilty of a misdemeanor and upon conviction thereof shall be punished by a fine not to exceed one thousand dollars ($1,000) or by imprisonment in the county jail for a period not to exceed 180 days, or by both the fine and imprisonment.

(b) Any person who violates Section 1286 is guilty of an infraction and shall be punished by a fine of not more than one hundred dollars ($100).

(c) Any person who willfully or repeatedly violates this chapter or Chapter 2.4 (commencing with Section 1417), excluding Sections 1425 and 1432, or any rule or regulation adopted under this chapter, relating to the operation or maintenance of a long-term health care facility as defined in Section 1418, is guilty of a misdemeanor and upon conviction thereof shall be punished by a fine not to exceed two thousand five hundred dollars ($2,500) or by imprisonment in the county jail for a period not to exceed 180 days, or by both.

In determining the punishment to be imposed upon a conviction under this subdivision, the court shall consider all relevant facts, including, but not limited to, the following:

(1) Whether the violation exposed the patient to the risk of death or serious physical harm.

(2) Whether the violation had a direct or immediate relationship to the health, safety, or security of the patient.

(3) Evidence, if any, of willfulness.

(4) The number of repeated violations.

(5) The presence or absence of good faith efforts by the defendant to prevent the violation.

(d) For the purposes of this section, "willfully" or "willful" means the person doing an act or omitting to do an act intends the act or omission, and knows the relevant circumstances connected therewith.

(Amended by Stats. 1995, Ch. 415, Sec. 2. Effective January 1, 1996.)

1291.

The director may bring an action to enjoin the violation or threatened violation of Section 1253 in the superior court in and for the county in which the violation occurred or is about to occur. Any proceeding under this section shall conform to the requirements of Chapter 3 (commencing with Section 525) of Title 7 of Part 2 of the Code of Civil Procedure, except that the director shall not be required to allege facts necessary to show or tending to show lack of adequate remedy at law or irreparable damage or loss. Upon a finding by the director that the violations threaten the health or safety of patients in, or served by, a health facility, the health officer of any county or city health department which has been delegated inspection authority as defined in Section 1257 may bring an action to enjoin the violation, threatened violation, or continued violation by any health facility which is located in an area which is under his or her local health jurisdiction. Prior to bringing an action to enjoin the violation, the department shall ensure, to the extent feasible, that written notice of the proposed action is provided to each patient or the party responsible for each patient, each patient's physician and appropriate agencies which may be able to assist in, or facilitate, the placement of the patient in a licensed facility.

With respect to any and all actions brought pursuant to this section alleging the actual violation of Section 1253, the court shall, if it finds the allegations to be true, issue its order enjoining the facility from continuance of the violation.

(Amended by Stats. 1987, Ch. 233, Sec. 1.)

1292.

Any action brought by the director against a health facility shall not abate by reason of a sale or other transfer of ownership of the health facility which is a party to the action except with express written consent of the director.

(Repealed and added by Stats. 1973, Ch. 1202.)

1293.

The district attorney of every county shall, upon application by the state department or its authorized representative, institute and conduct the prosecution of any action for violation within his county of any provisions of this chapter.

(Added by Stats. 1973, Ch. 1202.)

1293.2.

It is a misdemeanor for any person to do any of the following:

(a) Willfully prevent, interfere with, or attempt to impede in any way the work of any duly authorized representative of the state department in the lawful enforcement of this chapter.

(b) Willfully prevent or attempt to prevent the representative from examining any relevant books or records in the conduct of his or her official duties under this chapter.

(c) Willfully prevent or interfere with the representative in the preserving of evidence of any violation of this chapter or of the rules and regulations adopted under this chapter.

(d) For purposes of this section, "willfully" means the person doing an act or omitting to do an act, intends the act or omission and knows the relevant circumstances connected therewith.

(Added by Stats. 1985, Ch. 700, Sec. 6.)

ARTICLE 5. Suspension and Revocation [1294 - 1300]

(Article 5 added by Stats. 1973, Ch. 1202.)

1294.

The state department may suspend or revoke any license or special permit issued under the provisions of this chapter upon any of the following grounds and in the manner provided in this chapter:

(a) Violation by the licensee or holder of a special permit of any of the provisions of this chapter or of the rules and regulations promulgated under this chapter.

(b) Violation by a facility certified as a skilled nursing facility under Title XVIII of the Social Security Act or as a nursing facility under Title XIX of the Social Security Act, or as both, of any federal statutes or regulations applicable to its operation.

(c) Aiding, abetting, or permitting the violation of any provision of this chapter or of the rules and regulations promulgated under this chapter.

(d) Conduct inimical to the public health, morals, welfare, or safety of the people of the State of California in the maintenance and operation of the premises or services for which a license or special permit is issued.

(e) The conviction of a licensee, or other person mentioned in subdivision (b) of Section 1265.1, at any time during licensure, of a crime as defined in Section 1265.2.

(Amended by Stats. 2000, Ch. 451, Sec. 7.5. Effective January 1, 2001.)

1294.5.

The department may suspend or revoke any license or special permit issued under the provisions of this chapter if the licensee or holder of a special permit willfully fails to comply with the provisions of the regulations contained in Article 6 (commencing with Section 14190), Chapter 7, Part 3, Division 9, of the Welfare and Institutions Code and regulations promulgated thereunder.

(Added by Stats. 1975, Ch. 220.)

1295.

Proceedings for the suspension, revocation, or denial of licenses or special permits under this chapter shall be conducted in accordance with Section 100171. In the event of conflict between this chapter and Section 100171, Section 100171 shall prevail.

(Amended by Stats. 1997, Ch. 220, Sec. 12. Effective August 4, 1997.)

1296.

The director may temporarily suspend any license or special permit prior to any hearing, when in his or her opinion the action is necessary to protect the public welfare. The director shall notify the licensee or holder of a special permit of the temporary suspension and the effective date thereof and at the same time shall serve the provider with an accusation. Upon receipt of a notice of defense by the licensee or holder of a special permit, the director shall within 15 days set the matter for hearing, which shall be held as soon as possible but not later than 30 days after receipt of the notice. The temporary suspension shall remain in effect until the hearing is completed and the director has made a final determination on the merits. However, the temporary suspension shall be deemed vacated if the director fails to make a final determination on the merits within 60 days after the original hearing has been completed.

If the provisions of this chapter or the rules or regulations promulgated by the director are violated by a licensee or holder of a special permit which is a group, corporation, or other association, the director may suspend the license or special permit of such organization or may suspend the license or special permit as to any individual person within the organization who is responsible for the violation.
(Amended by Stats. 1987, Ch. 1425, Sec. 1.)

1297.
The withdrawal of an application for a license or a special permit after it has been filed with the state department shall not, unless the state department consents in writing to such withdrawal, deprive the state department of its authority to institute or continue a proceeding against the applicant for the denial of the license or a special permit upon any ground provided by law or to enter an order denying the license or special permit upon any such ground.

The suspension, expiration, or forfeiture by operation of law of a license or a special permit issued by the state department, or its suspension, forfeiture, or cancellation by order of the state department or by order of a court of law, or its surrender without the written consent of the state department, shall not deprive the state department of its authority to institute or continue a disciplinary proceeding against the licensee or holder of a special permit upon any ground provided by law or to enter an order suspending or revoking the license or special permit or otherwise taking disciplinary action against the licensee or holder of a special permit on any such ground.
(Added by Stats. 1973, Ch. 1202.)

1298.
(a) (1) No person, firm, partnership, association, corporation, political subdivision of the state, or other governmental agency within the state shall continue to operate, conduct, or maintain an existing health facility without having applied for and obtained a license or a special permit as provided for in this chapter.
(2) This subdivision shall not apply to a receiver appointed by the court to temporarily operate a long-term health care facility pursuant to Article 8 (commencing with Section 1325).
(b) Any license or special permit revoked pursuant to this chapter may be reinstated pursuant to Section 11522 of the Government Code.
(Amended by Stats. 2000, Ch. 451, Sec. 8. Effective January 1, 2001.)

1300.
(a) Any licensee or holder of a special permit may, with the approval of the state department, surrender his or her license or special permit for suspension or cancellation by the state department. Any license or special permit suspended or canceled pursuant to this section may be reinstated by the state department on receipt of an application showing compliance with the requirements of Section 1265.
(b) Before approving a downgrade or closure of emergency services pursuant to subdivision (a), the state department shall receive a copy of the impact evaluation of the county to determine impacts, including, but not limited to, an impact evaluation of the downgrade or closure upon the community, including community access to emergency care, and how that downgrade or closure will affect emergency services provided by other entities. Development of the impact evaluation shall incorporate at least one public hearing. The county in which the proposed downgrade or closure will occur shall ensure the completion of the impact evaluation, and shall notify the state department of results of an impact evaluation within three days of the completion of that evaluation. The county may designate the local emergency medical services agency as the appropriate agency to conduct the impact evaluation. The impact evaluation and hearing shall be completed within 60 days of the county receiving notification of intent to downgrade or close emergency services. The county or designated local emergency medical services agency shall ensure that all hospital and prehospital health care providers in the geographic area impacted by the service closure or change are consulted with, and that local emergency service agencies and planning or zoning authorities are notified, prior to completing an impact evaluation as required by this section. This subdivision shall be implemented on and after the date that the county in which the proposed downgrade or closure will occur, or its designated local emergency medical services agency, has developed a policy specifying the criteria it will consider in conducting an impact evaluation, as required by subdivision (c).
(c) The Emergency Medical Services Authority shall develop guidelines for development of impact evaluation policies. On or before June 30, 1999, each county or its designated local emergency medical services agency shall develop a policy specifying the criteria it will consider in conducting an impact evaluation pursuant to subdivision (b). Each county or its designated local emergency medical services agency shall submit its impact evaluation policy to the state department and the Emergency Medical Services Authority within three days of completion of the policy. The Emergency Medical Services Authority shall provide technical assistance upon request to a county or its designated local emergency medical services agency.

(Amended by Stats. 1999, Ch. 83, Sec. 95. Effective January 1, 2000.)

ARTICLE 6. Malpractice Actions [1305 - 1308]
(Article 6 added by Stats. 1973, Ch. 1202.)

1305.
(a) Every insurer providing professional liability insurance to a health facility licensed pursuant to this chapter and every health facility or associated group of health facilities licensed pursuant to this chapter under common ownership which are self insured shall report periodically, but in no event less than once each year, to the state department any final judgment over three thousand dollars ($3,000) rendered against such health facility during the preceding year in, or any settlement over three thousand dollars ($3,000) during the preceding year of, a claim or action for damages for personal injuries caused by an error, omission, or negligence in the performance of its professional services, or by the performance of its professional services without consent.
(b) In the event that there are no final judgments or settlements in excess of three thousand dollars ($3,000) during the year such fact shall also be reported to the department.
(Added by Stats. 1973, Ch. 1202.)

1306.
Notwithstanding any other provision of law, no insurer shall enter into a settlement exceeding three thousand dollars ($3,000) to settle a claim or action referred to in Section 1305 without the written consent of the insured, except that this prohibition shall not void any settlement entered into without such written consent.

The requirement of written consent can only be waived by both the insured and the insurer.

The provisions of this section shall only apply to a settlement on a policy of insurance executed or renewed on or after January 1, 1971.
(Added by Stats. 1973, Ch. 1202.)

1307.
The state department shall keep a record of all reports made pursuant to Section 1305.
(Amended by Stats. 1992, Ch. 713, Sec. 18. Effective September 15, 1992.)

1308.
The state department shall notify every health facility licensed pursuant to this chapter and every insurer providing professional liability insurance to such health facilities of the provisions of this article.
(Added by Stats. 1973, Ch. 1202.)

ARTICLE 6.5. Release of Sex Offender to Long-Term Health Care Facility [1312- 1312.]
(Article 6.5 added by Stats. 2005, Ch. 466, Sec. 1.)

1312.
Before a person who is required to register as a sex offender under Section 290 of the Penal Code is released into a long-term health care facility, as defined in Section 1418, the Department of Corrections and Rehabilitation, the State Department of State Hospitals, or any other official in charge of the place of confinement, shall notify the facility, in writing, that the sex offender is being released to reside at the facility.
(Amended by Stats. 2012, Ch. 24, Sec. 12. (AB 1470) Effective June 27, 2012.)

ARTICLE 7. Other Services [1315 - 1323.1]
(Article 7 added by Stats. 1973, Ch. 1202.)

1315.
Dental services, as defined in the Dental Practice Act, may be provided patients in health facilities licensed under this chapter. Such services shall be provided by persons licensed by the State of California pursuant to Section 1611 of the Business and Professions Code. However, this section shall not limit or restrict the right of a licensed physician and surgeon to perform any acts authorized under the Medical Practice Act.
(Repealed and added by Stats. 1973, Ch. 1202.)

1316.
(a) The rules of a health facility shall include provisions for use of the facility by, and staff privileges for, duly licensed podiatrists within the scope of their respective licensure, subject to rules and regulations governing such use or privileges established by the health facility. Such rules and regulations shall not discriminate on the basis of whether the staff member holds a M. D., D.O., or D.P.M. degree, within the scope of their respective licensure. Each health facility shall establish a staff comprised of physicians and surgeons, podiatrists, or any combination thereof, which shall regulate the admission, conduct suspension, or termination of the staff appointment of the podiatrists while using the facilities. No classification of health facilities by the state department, nor any other classification of health facilities based on quality of service or otherwise, by any person, body, or governmental agency of this state or any subdivision thereof shall be affected by a health facility's provision for use of its facilities by duly licensed podiatrists, nor shall any such classification be affected by the subjection of the podiatrists, to the rules and regulations of a staff comprising podiatrists, physicians and surgeons, or any combination thereof, which govern the podiatrists' use of the facilities. No classification of health facilities by any governmental agency of this state or any subdivision thereof pursuant to present law or laws passed hereinafter for the purposes of ascertaining eligibility for compensation, reimbursement, or other benefit for treatment of patients shall be affected by a health facility's provision for use of its facilities by duly licensed podiatrists, nor shall any such classification be affected by the subjection of the podiatrists and dentists to the rules and regulations of a staff comprising podiatrists, physicians and surgeons, or any combination thereof, which govern the podiatrists' use of the facilities.
With regard to the practice of podiatry in health facilities throughout this state, medical staff status shall include and provide for the right to pursue and practice full clinical and

surgical privileges for holders of M.D., D.O., and D. P.M. degrees within the scope of their respective licensure. Such rights and privileges shall be limited or restricted only upon the basis of an individual practitioner's demonstrated competence. Such competence shall be determined by health facility rules, regulations, and procedures which are necessary and are applied in good faith, equally and in a nondiscriminatory manner, to all practitioners regardless of whether they hold a M.D., D.O., or D.P.M. degree.

Nothing in this section shall be construed to require a health facility to offer a specific health service or services not otherwise offered. If a health service is offered, the facility shall not discriminate between persons holding M.D. , D.O., or D.P.M. degrees who are authorized by law to perform such services.

This subdivision shall not prohibit a health facility which is a clinical teaching facility owned or operated by a university operating a school of medicine from requiring that a podiatrist have a faculty teaching appointment as a condition for eligibility for staff privileges for that facility.

(b) The rules of a health facility which include provisions for use of the facility by, and staff privileges for, medical staff shall not discriminate on the basis of whether the staff member holds a M.D., D.O., or D.P.M. degree, within the scope of their respective licensure. The health facility staff processing, reviewing, evaluating, and determining qualifications for staff privileges for medical staff shall include, if possible, staff members that hold M.D., D.O., and D.P.M. degrees.

(c) Any violation by a health facility of the provisions of this section may be enjoined in an action brought in the name of the people of the State of California by the district attorney of the county in which the health facility is located, upon receipt of a complaint by an aggrieved physician and surgeon or podiatrist.

(Amended by Stats. 1977, Ch. 1214.)

1316.5.

(a) (1) Each health facility owned and operated by the state offering care or services within the scope of practice of a psychologist shall establish rules and medical staff bylaws that include provisions for medical staff membership and clinical privileges for clinical psychologists within the scope of their licensure as psychologists, subject to the rules and medical staff bylaws governing medical staff membership or privileges as the facility shall establish. The rules and regulations shall not discriminate on the basis of whether the staff member holds an M.D., D.O., D.D.S., D.P.M., or doctoral degree in psychology within the scope of the member's respective licensure. Each of these health facilities owned and operated by the state shall establish a staff comprised of physicians and surgeons, dentists, podiatrists, psychologists, or any combination thereof, that shall regulate the admission, conduct, suspension, or termination of the staff appointment of psychologists employed by the health facility.

(2) With regard to the practice of psychology in health facilities owned and operated by the state offering care or services within the scope of practice of a psychologist, medical staff status shall include and provide for the right to pursue and practice full clinical privileges for holders of a doctoral degree of psychology within the scope of their respective licensure. These rights and privileges shall be limited or restricted only upon the basis of an individual practitioner's demonstrated competence. Competence shall be determined by health facility rules and medical staff bylaws that are necessary and are applied in good faith, equally and in a nondiscriminatory manner, to all practitioners, regardless of whether they hold an M.D., D.O., D.D.S., D.P.M., or doctoral degree in psychology.

(3) Nothing in this subdivision shall be construed to require a health facility owned and operated by the state to offer a specific health service or services not otherwise offered. If a health service is offered in such a health facility that includes provisions for medical staff membership and clinical privileges for clinical psychologists, the facility shall not discriminate between persons holding an M.D., D.O., D.D.S., D.P.M., or doctoral degree in psychology who are authorized by law to perform the service within the scope of the person's respective licensure.

(4) The rules and medical staff bylaws of a health facility owned and operated by the state that include provisions for medical staff membership and clinical privileges for medical staff and duly licensed clinical psychologists shall not discriminate on the basis of whether the staff member holds an M.D., D.O., D.D.S., D.P.M., or doctoral degree in psychology within the scope of the member's respective licensure. The health facility staff of these health facilities who process, review, evaluate, and determine qualifications for staff privileges for medical staff shall include, if possible, staff members who are clinical psychologists.

(b) (1) The rules of a health facility not owned or operated by this state may enable the appointment of clinical psychologists on the terms and conditions that the facility shall establish. In these health facilities, clinical psychologists may hold membership and serve on committees of the medical staff and carry professional responsibilities consistent with the scope of their licensure and their competence, subject to the rules of the health facility.

(2) Nothing in this subdivision shall be construed to require a health facility not owned or operated by this state to offer a specific health service or services not otherwise offered. If a health service is offered by a health facility with both licensed physicians and surgeons and clinical psychologists on the medical staff, which both licensed physicians and surgeons and clinical psychologists are authorized by law to perform, the service may be performed by either, without discrimination.

(3) This subdivision shall not prohibit a health facility that is a clinical teaching facility owned or operated by a university operating a school of medicine from requiring that a clinical psychologist have a faculty teaching appointment as a condition for eligibility for staff privileges at that facility.

(4) In any health facility that is not owned or operated by this state that provides staff privileges to clinical psychologists, the health facility staff who process, review, evaluate, and determine qualifications for staff privileges for medical staff shall include, if possible, staff members who are clinical psychologists.

(c) No classification of health facilities by the department, nor any other classification of health facilities based on quality of service or otherwise, by any person, body, or governmental agency of this state or any subdivision thereof shall be affected by a health facility's provision for use of its facilities by duly licensed clinical psychologists, nor shall any classification of these facilities be affected by the subjection of the psychologists to the rules and regulations of the organized professional staff. No classification of health facilities by any governmental agency of this state or any subdivision thereof pursuant to any law, whether enacted prior or subsequent to the effective date of this section, for the purposes of ascertaining eligibility for compensation, reimbursement, or other benefit for treatment of patients shall be affected by a health facility's provision for use of its facilities by duly licensed clinical psychologists, nor shall any classification of these facilities be affected by the subjection of the psychologists to the rules and regulations of the organized professional staff which govern the psychologists' use of the facilities.

(d) "Clinical psychologist," as used in this section, means a psychologist licensed by this state who meets both of the following requirements:

(1) Possesses an earned doctorate degree in psychology from an educational institution meeting the criteria of subdivision (b) of Section 2914 of the Business and Professions Code.

(2) Has not less than two years clinical experience in a multidisciplinary facility licensed or operated by this or another state or by the United States to provide health care, or, is listed in the latest edition of the National Register of Health Service Providers in Psychology, as adopted by the Council for the National Register of Health Service Providers in Psychology.

(e) Nothing in this section is intended to expand the scope of licensure of clinical psychologists. Notwithstanding the Ralph C. Dills Act (Chapter 10.3 (commencing with Section 3512) of Division 4 of Title 1 of the Government Code), the Public Employment Relations Board is precluded from creating any additional bargaining units for the purpose of exclusive representation of state psychologist employees that might result because of medical staff membership and/or privilege changes for psychologists due to the enactment of provisions by Assembly Bill No. 3141 of the 1995–96 Regular Session.

(Amended by Stats. 2012, Ch. 24, Sec. 13. (AB 1470) Effective June 27, 2012.)

1316.6.

Notwithstanding any other provision of this chapter, the exercise of privileges in any health facility may be limited, restricted, or revoked for the violation of such health facility's rules, regulations, or procedures which are applied, in good faith, in a nondiscriminatory manner to all practitioners in such health facility exercising such privileges or entitled to exercise such privileges.

(Added by Stats. 1978, Ch. 116.)

1317.

(a) Emergency services and care shall be provided to any person requesting the services or care, or for whom services or care is requested, for any condition in which the person is in danger of loss of life, or serious injury or illness, at any health facility licensed under this chapter that maintains and operates an emergency department to provide emergency services to the public when the health facility has appropriate facilities and qualified personnel available to provide the services or care.

(b) In no event shall the provision of emergency services and care be based upon, or affected by, the person's ethnicity, citizenship, age, preexisting medical condition, insurance status, economic status, ability to pay for medical services, or any other characteristic listed or defined in subdivision (b) or (e) of Section 51 of the Civil Code, except to the extent that a circumstance such as age, sex, preexisting medical condition, or physical or mental disability is medically significant to the provision of appropriate medical care to the patient.

(c) Neither the health facility, its employees, nor any physician and surgeon, dentist, clinical psychologist, or podiatrist shall be liable in any action arising out of a refusal to render emergency services or care if the refusal is based on the determination, exercising reasonable care, that the person is not suffering from an emergency medical condition, or that the health facility does not have the appropriate facilities or qualified personnel available to render those services.

(d) Emergency services and care shall be rendered without first questioning the patient or any other person as to his or her ability to pay therefor. However, the patient or his or her legally responsible relative or guardian shall execute an agreement to pay therefor or otherwise supply insurance or credit information promptly after the services are rendered.

(e) If a health facility subject to this chapter does not maintain an emergency department, its employees shall nevertheless exercise reasonable care to determine whether an emergency exists and shall direct the persons seeking emergency care to a nearby facility that can render the needed services, and shall assist the persons seeking emergency care in obtaining the services, including transportation services, in every way reasonable under the circumstances.

(f) A general acute care hospital or acute psychiatric hospital shall not require a person who voluntarily seeks care to be in custody pursuant to Section 5150 of the Welfare and Institutions Code as a condition of accepting a transfer of that person after his or her written consent for treatment and transfer is documented or in the absence of evidence of probable cause for detention, as defined in Section 5150.05 of the Welfare and Institutions Code.

(g) An act or omission of a rescue team established by a health facility licensed under this chapter, or operated by the federal or state government, a county, or by the Regents of the University of California, done or omitted while attempting to resuscitate a person who is in immediate danger of loss of life shall not impose any liability upon the health facility, the officers, members of the staff, nurses, or employees of the health facility, including, but not limited to, the members of the rescue team, or upon the federal or state government or a county, if good faith is exercised.

(h) "Rescue team," as used in this section, means a special group of physicians and surgeons, nurses, and employees of a health facility who have been trained in cardiopulmonary resuscitation and have been designated by the health facility to attempt, in cases of emergency, to resuscitate persons who are in immediate danger of loss of life.

(i) This section does not relieve a health facility of any duty otherwise imposed by law upon the health facility for the designation and training of members of a rescue team or for the provision or maintenance of equipment to be used by a rescue team.

(Amended by Stats. 2018, Ch. 831, Sec. 1. (AB 2983) Effective January 1, 2019.)

1317.1.

Unless the context otherwise requires, the following definitions shall control the construction of this article and Section 1371.4:

(a) (1) "Emergency services and care" means medical screening, examination, and evaluation by a physician and surgeon, or, to the extent permitted by applicable law, by other appropriate licensed persons under the supervision of a physician and surgeon, to determine if an emergency medical condition or active labor exists and, if it does, the care, treatment, and surgery, if within the scope of that person's license, necessary to relieve or eliminate the emergency medical condition, within the capability of the facility.

(2) (A) "Emergency services and care" also means an additional screening, examination, and evaluation by a physician, or other personnel to the extent permitted by applicable law and within the scope of their licensure and clinical privileges, to determine if a psychiatric emergency medical condition exists, and the care and treatment necessary to relieve or eliminate the psychiatric emergency medical condition, within the capability of the facility.

(B) The care and treatment necessary to relieve or eliminate a psychiatric emergency medical condition may include admission or transfer to a psychiatric unit within a general acute care hospital, as defined in subdivision (a) of Section 1250, or to an acute psychiatric hospital, as defined in subdivision (b) of Section 1250, pursuant to subdivision (k). Nothing in this subparagraph shall be construed to permit a transfer that is in conflict with the Lanterman-Petris-Short Act (Part 1 (commencing with Section 5000) of Division 5 of the Welfare and Institutions Code).

(C) For the purposes of Section 1371.4, emergency services and care as defined in subparagraph (A) shall not apply to Medi-Cal managed care plan contracts entered into with the State Department of Health Care Services pursuant to Chapter 7 (commencing with Section 14000), Chapter 8 (commencing with Section 14200), and Chapter 8.75 (commencing with Section 14590) of Part 3 of Division 9 of the Welfare and Institutions Code, to the extent that those services are excluded from coverage under those contracts.

(D) This paragraph does not expand, restrict, or otherwise affect the scope of licensure or clinical privileges for clinical psychologists or other medical personnel.

(b) "Emergency medical condition" means a medical condition manifesting itself by acute symptoms of sufficient severity (including severe pain) such that the absence of immediate medical attention could reasonably be expected to result in any of the following:

(1) Placing the patient's health in serious jeopardy.

(2) Serious impairment to bodily functions.

(3) Serious dysfunction of any bodily organ or part.

(c) "Active labor" means a labor at a time at which either of the following would occur:

(1) There is inadequate time to effect safe transfer to another hospital prior to delivery.

(2) A transfer may pose a threat to the health and safety of the patient or the unborn child.

(d) "Hospital" means all hospitals with an emergency department licensed by the state department.

(e) "State department" means the State Department of Public Health.

(f) "Medical hazard" means a material deterioration in medical condition in, or jeopardy to, a patient's medical condition or expected chances for recovery.

(g) "Board" means the Medical Board of California.

(h) "Within the capability of the facility" means those capabilities that the hospital is required to have as a condition of its emergency medical services permit and services specified on Services Inventory Form 7041 filed by the hospital with the Office of Statewide Health Planning and Development.

(i) "Consultation" means the rendering of an opinion or advice, prescribing treatment, or the rendering of a decision regarding hospitalization or transfer by telephone or other means of communication. When determined to be medically necessary, jointly by the treating physician and surgeon, or by other appropriate licensed persons acting within their scope of licensure, under the supervision of a physician and surgeon, and the consulting physician and surgeon, "consultation" includes review of the patient's medical record, examination, and treatment of the patient in person by a consulting physician and surgeon, or by other appropriate licensed persons acting within their scope of licensure under the supervision of a consulting physician and surgeon, who is qualified to give an opinion or render the necessary treatment in order to stabilize the patient. A request for consultation shall be made by the treating physician and surgeon, or by other appropriate licensed persons acting within their scope of licensure under the supervision of a treating physician and surgeon, provided the request is made with the contemporaneous approval of the treating physician and surgeon. The treating physician and surgeon may request to communicate directly with the consulting physician and surgeon, and when determined to

be medically necessary, jointly by the treating physician and surgeon and the consulting physician and surgeon, the consulting physician and surgeon shall examine and treat the patient in person. The consulting physician and surgeon is ultimately responsible for providing the necessary consultation to the patient, regardless of who makes the in-person appearance.

(j) A patient is "stabilized" or "stabilization" has occurred when, in the opinion of the treating physician and surgeon, or other appropriate licensed persons acting within their scope of licensure under the supervision of a treating physician and surgeon, the patient's medical condition is such that, within reasonable medical probability, no material deterioration of the patient's condition is likely to result from, or occur during, the release or transfer of the patient as provided for in Section 1317.2, Section 1317.2a, or other pertinent statute.

(k) (1) "Psychiatric emergency medical condition" means a mental disorder that manifests itself by acute symptoms of sufficient severity that it renders the patient as being either of the following:

(A) An immediate danger to himself or herself or to others.

(B) Immediately unable to provide for, or utilize, food, shelter, or clothing, due to the mental disorder.

(2) This subdivision does not expand, restrict, or otherwise affect the scope of licensure or clinical privileges for clinical psychologists or medical personnel.

(l) This section shall not be construed to expand the scope of licensure for licensed persons providing services pursuant to this section.

(Amended (as amended by Stats. 2009, Ch. 423) by Stats. 2011, Ch. 333, Sec. 2. (SB 233) Effective January 1, 2012.)

1317.2.

A person needing emergency services and care shall not be transferred from a hospital to another hospital for any nonmedical reason (such as the person's inability to pay for any emergency service or care) unless each of the following conditions are met:

(a) The person is examined and evaluated by a physician and surgeon, including, if necessary, consultation, prior to transfer.

(b) The person has been provided with emergency services and care so that it can be determined, within reasonable medical probability, that the transfer or delay caused by the transfer will not create a medical hazard to the person.

(c) A physician and surgeon at the transferring hospital has notified and has obtained the consent to the transfer by a physician and surgeon at the receiving hospital and confirmation by the receiving hospital that the person meets the hospital's admissions criteria relating to appropriate bed, personnel, and equipment necessary to treat the person.

(d) The transferring hospital provides for appropriate personnel and equipment that a reasonable and prudent physician and surgeon in the same or similar locality exercising ordinary care would use to effect the transfer.

(e) All of the person's pertinent medical records and copies of all the appropriate diagnostic test results that are reasonably available are transferred with the person.

(f) The records transferred with the person include a "Transfer Summary" signed by the transferring physician and surgeon that contains relevant transfer information. The form of the "Transfer Summary" shall, at a minimum, contain the person's name, address, sex, race, age, insurance status, and medical condition; the name and address of the transferring physician and surgeon or emergency department personnel authorizing the transfer; the time and date the person was first presented at the transferring hospital; the name of the physician and surgeon at the receiving hospital consenting to the transfer and the time and date of the consent; the time and date of the transfer; the reason for the transfer; and the declaration of the signor that the signor is assured, within reasonable medical probability, that the transfer creates no medical hazard to the patient. Neither the transferring physician and surgeon nor transferring hospital shall be required to duplicate, in the "Transfer Summary," information contained in medical records transferred with the person.

(g) The transfer conforms with regulations established by the state department. These regulations may prescribe minimum protocols for patient transfers.

(h) The patient shall be asked if there is a preferred contact person to be notified and, prior to the transfer, the hospital shall make a reasonable attempt to contact that person and alert him or her about the proposed transfer, in accordance with subdivision (b) of Section 56.1007 of the Civil Code. If the patient is not able to respond, the hospital shall make a reasonable effort to ascertain the identity of the preferred contact person or the next of kin and alert him or her about the transfer, in accordance with subdivision (b) of Section 56.1007 of the Civil Code. The hospital shall document in the patient's medical record any attempts to contact a preferred contact person or next of kin.

(i) This section shall not apply to a transfer of a patient for medical reasons.

(j) This section shall not prohibit the transfer or discharge of a patient when the patient or the patient's representative requests a transfer or discharge and gives informed consent to the transfer or discharge against medical advice.

(Amended by Stats. 2013, Ch. 711, Sec. 1. (AB 974) Effective January 1, 2014.)

1317.2a.

(a) A hospital which has a legal obligation, whether imposed by statute or by contract, to the extent of that contractual obligation, to any third-party payor, including, but not limited to, a health maintenance organization, health care service plan, nonprofit hospital service plan, insurer, or preferred provider organization, a county, or an employer to provide care for a patient under the circumstances specified in Section 1317.2 shall receive that patient to the extent required by the applicable statute or by the terms of the contract, or, when the hospital is unable to accept a patient for whom it has a legal obligation to provide care whose transfer will not create a medical hazard as specified in Section 1317.2, it shall make appropriate arrangements for the patient's care.

(b) A county hospital shall accept a patient whose transfer will not create a medical hazard as specified in Section 1317.2 and who is determined by the county to be eligible to receive health care services required under Part 5 (commencing with Section 17000) of Division 9 of the Welfare and Institutions Code, unless the hospital does not have appropriate bed capacity, medical personnel, or equipment required to provide care to the patient in accordance with accepted medical practice. When a county hospital is unable to accept a patient whose transfer will not create a medical hazard as specified in Section 1317.2, it shall make appropriate arrangements for the patient's care. The obligation to make appropriate arrangements as set forth in this subdivision does not mandate a level of service or payment, modify the county's obligations under Part 5 (commencing with Section 17000) of Division 9 of the Welfare and Institutions Code, create a cause of action, or limit a county's flexibility to manage county health systems within available resources. However, the county's flexibility shall not diminish a county's responsibilities under Part 5 (commencing with Section 17000) of Division 9 of the Welfare and Institutions Code or the requirements contained in Chapter 2.5 (commencing with Section 1440).

(c) The receiving hospital shall provide personnel and equipment reasonably required in the exercise of good medical practice for the care of the transferred patient.

(d) Any third-party payor, including, but not limited to, a health maintenance organization, health care service plan, nonprofit hospital service plan, insurer, or preferred provider organization, or employer which has a statutory or contractual obligation to provide or indemnify emergency medical services on behalf of a patient shall be liable, to the extent of the contractual obligation to the patient, for the reasonable charges of the transferring hospital and the treating physicians for the emergency services provided pursuant to this article, except that the patient shall be responsible for uncovered services, or any deductible or copayment obligation. Notwithstanding this section, the liability of a third-party payor which has contracted with health care providers for the provision of these emergency services shall be set by the terms of that contract. Notwithstanding this section, the liability of a third-party payor that is licensed by the Insurance Commissioner or the Director of the Department of Managed Health Care and has a contractual obligation to provide or indemnify emergency medical services under a contract which covers a subscriber or an enrollee shall be determined in accordance with the terms of that contract and shall remain under the sole jurisdiction of that licensing agency.

(e) A hospital which has a legal obligation to provide care for a patient as specified by subdivision (a) of Section 1317.2a to the extent of its legal obligation, imposed by statute or by contract to the extent of that contractual obligation, which does not accept transfers of, or make other appropriate arrangements for, medically stable patients in violation of this article or regulations adopted pursuant thereto shall be liable for the reasonable charges of the transferring hospital and treating physicians for providing services and care which should have been provided by the receiving hospital.

(f) Subdivisions (d) and (e) do not apply to county obligations under Section 17000 of the Welfare and Institutions Code.

(g) Nothing in this section shall be interpreted to require a hospital to make arrangements for the care of a patient for whom the hospital does not have a legal obligation to provide care.

(Amended by Stats. 2000, Ch. 857, Sec. 17. Effective January 1, 2001.)

1317.3.

(a) As a condition of licensure, each hospital shall adopt, in consultation with the medical staff, policies and transfer protocols consistent with this article and regulations adopted hereunder.

(b) As a condition of licensure, each hospital shall adopt a policy prohibiting discrimination in the provision of emergency services and care based on ethnicity, citizenship, age, preexisting medical condition, insurance status, economic status, ability to pay for medical services, or any characteristic listed or defined in subdivision (b) or (e) of Section 51 of the Civil Code, except to the extent that a circumstance such as age, sex, preexisting medical condition, or physical or mental disability is medically significant to the provision of appropriate medical care to the patient. Transfer by a hospital of a patient who requires evaluation for involuntary psychiatric treatment, as determined by the receiving hospital or other receiving health facility, based upon the decision of a professional person duly authorized by law to make that decision, shall not constitute discrimination for the purposes of this section, if the transferring hospital has not been designated as an evaluation facility by a county pursuant to Section 5150 of the Welfare and Institutions Code, and if the transfer is in compliance with Section 1317.2.

(c) As a condition of licensure, each hospital shall require that physicians and surgeons who serve on an "on-call" basis to the hospital's emergency room cannot refuse to respond to a call on the basis of the patient's ethnicity, citizenship, age, preexisting medical condition, insurance status, economic status, ability to pay for medical services, or any characteristic listed or defined in subdivision (b) or (e) of Section 51 of the Civil Code, except to the extent that a circumstance such as age, sex, preexisting medical condition, or physical or mental disability is medically significant to the provision of appropriate medical care to the patient. If a contract between a physician and surgeon and hospital for the provision of emergency room coverage presently prevents the hospital from imposing those conditions, the conditions shall be included in the contract as soon as is legally permissible. Nothing in this section shall be construed as requiring that any physician serve on an "on-call" basis.

(d) As a condition of licensure, all hospitals shall inform all persons presented to an emergency room or their representatives if any are present and the person is unable to understand verbal or written communication, both orally and in writing, of the reasons for the transfer or refusal to provide emergency services and care and of the person's right to emergency services and care prior to transfer or discharge without regard to ability to pay. Nothing in this subdivision requires notification of the reasons for the transfer in advance of the transfer where a person is unaccompanied and the hospital has made a reasonable effort to locate a representative, and because of the person's physical or mental condition, notification is not possible. All hospitals shall prominently post a sign in their emergency rooms informing the public of their rights. Both the posted sign and written communication concerning the transfer or refusal to provide emergency services and care shall give the address of the department as the government agency to contact in the event the person wishes to complain about the hospital's conduct.

(e) If a hospital does not timely adopt the policies and protocols required in this article, the hospital, in addition to denial or revocation of any of its licenses, shall be subject to a fine not to exceed one thousand dollars ($1,000) each day after expiration of 60 days' written notice from the state department that the hospital's policies or protocols required by this article are inadequate unless the delay is excused by the state department upon a showing of good and sufficient cause by the hospital. The notice shall include a detailed statement of the state department's reasons for its determination and suggested changes to the hospital's protocols which would be acceptable to the state department.

(f) Each hospital's policies and protocols required in or under this article shall be submitted for approval to the state department by December 31, 1988.

(Amended by Stats. 2007, Ch. 568, Sec. 38. Effective January 1, 2008.)

1317.4.

(a) All hospitals shall maintain records of each transfer made or received, including the "Memorandum of Transfer" described in subdivision (f) of Section 1317.2, for a period of three years.

(b) All hospitals making or receiving transfers shall file with the state department annual reports on forms prescribed by the department which shall describe the aggregate number of transfers made and received according to the person's insurance status and reasons for transfers.

(c) The receiving hospital, and all physicians, other licensed emergency room health personnel, and certified prehospital emergency personnel at the receiving hospital who know of apparent violations of this article or the regulations adopted hereunder shall, and the corresponding personnel at the transferring hospital and the transferring hospital may, report the apparent violations to the state department on a form prescribed by the state department within one week following its occurrence. The state department shall promptly send a copy of the form to the hospital administrator and appropriate medical staff committee of the transferring hospital and the local emergency medical services agency, unless the state department concludes that the complaint does not allege facts requiring further investigation, or is otherwise unmeritorious, or the state department concludes, based upon the circumstances of the case, that its investigation of the allegations would be impeded by disclosure of the form. When two or more persons required to report jointly have knowledge of an apparent violation, a single report may be made by a member of the team selected by mutual agreement in accordance with hospital protocols. Any individual, required to report by this section, who disagrees with the proposed joint report has a right and duty to separately report.

A failure to report under this subdivision shall not constitute a violation within the meaning of Section 1290 or 1317.6.

(d) No hospital, government agency, or person shall retaliate against, penalize, institute a civil action against, or recover monetary relief from, or otherwise cause any injury to a physician or other personnel for reporting in good faith an apparent violation of this article or the regulations adopted hereunder to the state department, hospital, medical staff, or any other interested party or government agency.

(e) No hospital, government agency, or person shall retaliate against, penalize, institute a civil action against, or recover monetary relief from, or otherwise cause any injury to a physician who refused to transfer a patient when the physician determines, within reasonable medical probability, that the transfer or delay caused by the transfer will create a medical hazard to the person.

(f) Any person who violates subdivision (d) or (e) of Section 1317.4 is subject to a civil money penalty of no more than ten thousand dollars ($10,000) per violation. The remedy specified in this section shall be in addition to any other remedy provided by law.

(g) The state department shall on an annual basis publish and provide to the Legislature a statistical summary by county on the extent of economic transfers of emergency patients, the frequency of medically hazardous transfers, the insurance status of the patient populations being transferred and all violations finally determined by the state department describing the nature of the violations, hospitals involved, and the action taken by the state department in response. These summaries shall not reveal the identity of individual persons transferred.

(h) Proceedings by the state department to impose a fine under Section 1317.3 or 1317.6, and proceedings by the board to impose a fine under Section 1317.6, shall be conducted as follows:

(1) If a hospital desires to contest a proposed fine, the hospital shall within 15 business days after service of the notice of proposed fine notify the director in writing of its intention to contest the proposed fine. If requested by the hospital, the director or the director's designee, shall hold, within 30 business days, an informal conference, at the conclusion of which he or she may affirm, modify, or dismiss the proposed fine. If the director or the director's designee affirms, modifies, or dismisses the proposed fine, he or she shall state with particularity in writing his or her reasons for that action, and shall immediately transmit a copy thereof to the hospital. If the hospital desires to contest a determination made after the informal conference, the hospital shall inform the director in

writing within 15 business days after it receives the decision by the director or director's designee. The hospital shall not be required to request an informal conference to contest a proposed fine, as specified in this section. If the hospital fails to notify the director in writing that it intends to protest the proposed fine within the times specified in this subdivision, the proposed fine shall be deemed a final order of the state department and shall not be subject to further administrative review.
(2) If a hospital notifies the director that it intends to contest a proposed fine, the director shall immediately notify the Attorney General. Upon notification, the Attorney General shall promptly take all appropriate action to enforce the proposed fine in a court of competent jurisdiction for the county in which the hospital is located.
(3) A judicial action to enforce a proposed fine shall be filed by the Attorney General after a hospital notifies the director of its intent to contest the proposed fine. If a judicial proceeding is prosecuted under the provisions of this section, the state department shall have the burden of establishing by a preponderance of the evidence that the alleged facts supporting the proposed fine occurred, that the alleged facts constituted a violation for which a fine may be assessed under Section 1317.3, 1317.4, or 1317.6, and the proposed fine is appropriate. The state department shall also have the burden of establishing by a preponderance of the evidence that the assessment of the proposed fine should be upheld. If a hospital timely notifies the state department of its decision to contest a proposed fine, the fine shall not be due and payable unless and until the judicial proceeding is terminated in favor of the state department.
(4) Action brought under the provisions of this section shall be set for trial at the earliest possible date and shall take precedence on the court calendar over all other cases except matters to which equal or superior precedence is specifically granted by law. Times for responsive pleading and for hearing any such proceeding shall be set by the judge of the court with the object of securing a decision as to subject matters at the earliest possible time.
(5) If the proposed fine is dismissed or reduced, the state department shall take action immediately to ensure that the public records reflect in a prominent manner that the proposed fine was dismissed or reduced.
(6) In lieu of a judicial proceeding, the state department and the hospital may jointly elect to submit the matter to binding arbitration, in which case, the department shall initiate arbitration proceedings. The parties shall agree upon an arbitrator designated by the American Arbitration Association in accordance with the Association's established rules and procedures. The arbitration hearing shall be set within 45 days of the parties' joint election, but in no event less than 28 days from the date of selection of an arbitrator. The arbitration hearing may be continued up to 15 days if necessary at the arbitrator's discretion. The decision of arbitrator shall be based upon substantive law and shall be binding on all parties, subject to judicial review. This review shall be limited to whether there was substantial evidence to support the decision of the arbitrator.
(7) Proceedings by the board to impose a fine under Section 1317.6 shall be conducted in accordance with Chapter 5 (commencing with Section 11500) of Part 1 of Division 3 of Title 2 of the Government Code.
(Added by Stats. 1987, Ch. 1240, Sec. 7.)
1317.4a.
(a) Notwithstanding subdivision (j) of Section 1317.1, a patient may be transferred for admission to a psychiatric unit within a general acute care hospital, as defined in subdivision (a) of Section 1250, or an acute psychiatric hospital, as defined in subdivision (b) of Section 1250, for care and treatment that is solely necessary to relieve or eliminate a psychiatric emergency medical condition, as defined in subdivision (k) of Section 1317.1, provided that, in the opinion of the treating provider, the patient's psychiatric emergency medical condition is such that, within reasonable medical probability, no material deterioration of the patient's psychiatric emergency medical condition is likely to result from, or occur during, a transfer of the patient. A provider shall notify the patient's health care service plan, or the health plan's contracting medical provider of the need for the transfer if identification of the plan is obtained pursuant to paragraph (1) of subdivision (b).
(b) A hospital that transfers a patient pursuant to subdivision (a) shall do both of the following:
(1) Seek to obtain the name and contact information of the patient's health care service plan. The hospital shall document its attempt to ascertain this information in the patient's medical record. The hospital's attempt to ascertain the information shall include requesting the patient's health care service plan member card, asking the patient, the patient's family member, or other person accompanying the patient if he or she can identify the patient's health care service plan, or using other means known to the hospital to accurately identify the patient's health care service plan.
(2) Notify the patient's health care service plan or the health plan's contracting medical provider of the transfer, provided that the identification of the plan was obtained pursuant to paragraph (1). The hospital shall provide the plan or its contracting medical provider with the name of the patient, the patient's member identification number, if known, the location and contact information, including a telephone number, for the location where the patient will be admitted, and the preliminary diagnosis.
(c) (1) A hospital shall make the notification described in paragraph (2) of subdivision (b) by either following the instructions on the patient's health care service plan member card or by using the contact information provided by the patient's health care service plan. A health care service plan shall provide all noncontracting hospitals in the state to which one of its members would be transferred pursuant to paragraph (1) of subdivision (b) with specific contact information needed to make the contact required by this section. The contact information provided to hospitals shall be updated as necessary, but no less than once a year.
(2) A hospital making the transfer pursuant to subdivision (a) shall not be required to make more than one telephone call to the health care service plan, or its contracting medical provider, provided that in all cases the health care service plan, or its contracting medical provider, shall be able to reach a representative of the provider upon returning the call, should the plan, or its contracting medical provider, need to call back. The representative of the hospital who makes the telephone call may be, but is not required to be, a physician and surgeon.
(d) If a transfer made pursuant to subdivision (a) is made to a facility that does not have a contract with the patient's health care service plan, the plan may subsequently require and make provision for the transfer of the patient receiving services pursuant to this section and subdivision (a) of Section 1317.1 from the noncontracting facility to a general acute care hospital, as defined in subdivision (a) of Section 1250, or an acute psychiatric hospital, as defined in subdivision (b) of Section 1250, that has a contract with the plan or its delegated payer, provided that in the opinion of the treating provider the patient's psychiatric emergency medical condition is such that, within reasonable medical probability, no material deterioration of the patient's psychiatric emergency medical condition is likely to result from, or occur during, the transfer of the patient.
(e) Upon admission, the hospital to which the patient was transferred shall notify the health care service plan of the transfer, provided that the facility has the name and contact information of the patient's health care service plan. The facility shall not be required to make more than one telephone call to the health care service plan, or its contracting medical provider, provided that in all cases the health care service plan, or its contracting medical provider, shall be able to reach a representative of the facility upon returning the call, should the plan, or its contracting medical provider, need to call back. The representative of the facility who makes the telephone call may be, but is not required to be, a physician and surgeon.
(f) Nothing in this subdivision shall be construed to require providers to seek authorization to provide emergency services and care, as defined in paragraph (2) of subdivision (a) of Section 1317.1, to a patient who has a psychiatric emergency medical condition, as defined in subdivision (k) of Section 1317.1, that is not otherwise required by law.
(Added by Stats. 2009, Ch. 423, Sec. 2. (AB 235) Effective January 1, 2010.)
1317.5.
(a) All alleged violations of this article and the regulations adopted hereunder shall be investigated by the state department. The state department, with the agreement of the local EMS agency, may refer violations of this article to the local EMS agency for investigation. The investigation shall be conducted pursuant to procedures established by the state department and shall be completed no later than 60 days after the report of apparent violation is received by the state department.
(b) At the conclusion of its investigation, the state department or the local EMS agency shall refer any alleged violation by a physician to the Medical Board of California unless it is determined that the complaint is without a reasonable basis.
(Amended (as added by Stats. 1987, Ch. 1240) by Stats. 1989, Ch. 886, Sec. 93.)
1317.6.
(a) Hospitals found by the state department to have committed or to be responsible for a violation of this article or the regulations adopted pursuant thereto shall be subject to a civil penalty by the state department in an amount not to exceed twenty-five thousand dollars ($25,000) for each hospital violation. In determining the amount of the fine for a hospital violation, the state department shall take into account all of the following:
(1) Whether the violation was knowing or unintentional.
(2) Whether the violation resulted or was reasonably likely to result in a medical hazard to the patient.
(3) The frequency or gravity of the violation.
(4) Other civil fines which have been imposed as a result of the violation under Section 1395 of Title 42 of the United States Code.
(b) Notwithstanding this section, the director shall refer any alleged violation by a hospital owned and operated by a health care service plan involving a plan member or enrollee to the Department of Managed Health Care unless the director determines the complaint is without reasonable basis. The Department of Managed Health Care shall have sole authority and responsibility to enforce this article with respect to violations involving hospitals owned and operated by health care service plans in their treatment of plan members or enrollees.
(c) Physicians and surgeons found by the board to have committed, or to be responsible for, a violation of this article or the regulations adopted pursuant thereto shall be subject to any and all penalties which the board may lawfully impose and may be subject to a civil penalty by the board in an amount not to exceed five thousand dollars ($5,000) for each violation. A civil penalty imposed under this subdivision shall not duplicate federal fines, and the board shall credit any federal fine against a civil penalty imposed under this subdivision.
(d) The board may impose fines when it finds any of the following:
(1) The violation was knowing or willful.
(2) The violation was reasonably likely to result in a medical hazard.
(3) There are repeated violations.
(e) It is the intent of the Legislature that the state department has primary responsibility for regulating the conduct of hospital emergency departments and that fines imposed under this section should not be duplicated by additional fines imposed by the federal government as a result of the conduct which constituted a violation of this section. To effectuate the Legislature's intent, the Governor shall inform the Secretary of the federal Department of Health and Human Services of the enactment of this section and request the federal department to credit any penalty assessed under this section against any

subsequent civil monetary penalty assessed pursuant to Section 1395dd of Title 42 of the United States Code for the same violation.

(f) There shall be a cumulative maximum limit of thirty thousand dollars ($30,000) in fines assessed against hospitals under this article and under Section 1395dd of Title 42 of the United States Code for the same circumstances. To effectuate this cumulative maximum limit, the state department shall do both of the following:

(1) As to state fines assessed prior to the final conclusion, including judicial review, if available, of an action against a hospital by the federal Department of Health and Human Services under Section 1395dd of Title 42 of the United States Code (for the same circumstances finally deemed to have been a violation of this article or the regulations adopted hereunder, because of the state department action authorized by this article), remit and return to the hospital within 30 days after conclusion of the federal action, that portion of the state fine necessary to assure that the cumulative maximum limit is not exceeded.

(2) Immediately credit against state fines assessed after the final conclusion, including judicial review, if available, of an action against a hospital by the federal Department of Health and Human Services under Section 1395dd of Title 42 of the United States Code, which results in a fine against a hospital (for the same circumstances finally deemed to have been a violation of this article or the regulations adopted hereunder, because of the state department action authorized by this article), the amount of the federal fine, necessary to assure the cumulative maximum limit is not exceeded.

(g) Any hospital found by the state department pursuant to procedures established by the state department to have committed a violation of this article or the regulations adopted hereunder may have its emergency medical service permit revoked or suspended by the state department.

(h) Any administrative or medical personnel who knowingly and intentionally violates any provision of this article, may be charged by the local district attorney with a misdemeanor.

(i) Notification of each violation found by the state department of the provisions of this article or the regulations adopted hereunder shall be sent by the state department to the Joint Commission for the Accreditation of Hospitals, the state emergency medical services authority, and local emergency medical services agencies.

(j) Any person who suffers personal harm and any medical facility which suffers a financial loss as a result of a violation of this article or the regulations adopted hereunder may recover, in a civil action against the transferring or receiving hospital, damages, reasonable attorney's fees, and other appropriate relief. Transferring and receiving hospitals from which inappropriate transfers of persons are made or refused in violation of this article and the regulations adopted hereunder shall be liable for the reasonable charges of the receiving or transferring hospital for providing the services and care which should have been provided. Any person potentially harmed by a violation of this article or the regulations adopted hereunder, or the local district attorney or the Attorney General, may bring a civil action against the responsible hospital or administrative or medical personnel, to enjoin the violation, and if the injunction issues, the court shall award reasonable attorney's fees. The provisions of this subdivision are in addition to other civil remedies and do not limit the availability of the other remedies.

(k) The civil remedies established by this section do not apply to violations of any requirements established by any county or county agency.

(Amended by Stats. 2000, Ch. 857, Sec. 18. Effective January 1, 2001.)

1317.7.

This article does not preempt any county or any other governmental agency acting within its authority from regulating emergency care or patient transfers, including the imposition of more specific duties, consistent with the requirements of this article and its implementing regulations. Any inconsistent requirements imposed by the Medi-Cal program shall preempt this article with respect to Medi-Cal beneficiaries. To the extent hospitals and physicians enter into contractual relationships with county or other governmental agencies which impose more stringent transfer requirements, those contractual agreements shall control.

(Amended (as added by Stats. 1987, Ch. 1240) by Stats. 1988, Ch. 888, Sec. 4. Effective September 14, 1988.)

1317.8.

If any provision of this article is declared unlawful or unconstitutional in any judicial action, the remaining provisions of this chapter shall remain in effect.

(Added by Stats. 1987, Ch. 1240, Sec. 11.)

1317.9a.

(a) This article shall not be construed as altering or repealing Section 2400 of the Business and Professions Code.

(b) Nothing in Sections 1317 et seq. and 1798.170 et seq. shall prevent a physician from exercising his or her professional judgment in conflict with any state or local regulation adopted pursuant to Section 1317 et seq. or 1798.170 et seq., so long as the judgment conforms with Sections 1317, 1317.1, and, except for subdivision (g), Section 1317.2, and acting in compliance with the state or local regulation would be contrary to the best interests of the patient.

(Added by Stats. 1987, Ch. 1240, Sec. 13.)

1317.10.

Notwithstanding Sections 1317 and 1317.2, Stanford Hospital and Clinics and Lucile Packard Children's Hospital at Stanford shall be treated as a single licensed facility for purposes of providing emergency services and care to patients with conditions related to active labor presenting to the emergency department at Stanford Hospital and Clinics if all of the following conditions are met:

(a) The two hospitals have entered into an agreement in which Lucile Packard Children's Hospital at Stanford accepts and provides emergency services and care to all patients who are in active labor presenting to the emergency department at Stanford Hospital and Clinics, without regard to insurance status, financial status, or other nonclinical factors.

(b) A physician and surgeon, qualified emergency department registered nurse, or other appropriately licensed personnel under the supervision of a physician and surgeon determines, prior to the transfer, that the patient has signs or symptoms, or both, suggestive of active labor, the patient can be safely transferred from the emergency department at Stanford Hospital and Clinics to the labor and delivery department of Lucile Packard Children's Hospital at Stanford, and the patient does not have a condition, illness, or injury more appropriately treated in the emergency department.

(c) The patient has the right to refuse the transfer.

(d) Each hospital has a prepared plan to promptly transport the patient with an employee escort who has specialized training in transporting women in labor.

(Added by Stats. 2012, Ch. 18, Sec. 2. (SB 630) Effective June 15, 2012.)

1318.

(a) The director shall require as a condition precedent to the issuance, or renewal, of any license for a health facility, if the licensee handles or will handle any money of patients within the health facility, that the applicant for the license or the renewal of the license file or have on file with the state department a bond executed by an admitted surety insurer in a sum to be fixed by the state department based upon the magnitude of the operations of the applicant, but which sum shall not be less than one thousand dollars ($1,000), running to the State of California and conditioned upon the licensee's faithful and honest handling of the money of patients within the health facility.

(b) Every person injured as a result of any improper or unlawful handling of the money of a patient of a health facility may bring an action in a proper court on the bond required to be posted by the licensee pursuant to this section for the amount of damage the person suffered as a result thereof to the extent covered by the bond.

(c) The failure of any licensee under this section to maintain on file with the state department a bond in the amount prescribed by the director or who embezzles any patient's trust funds shall constitute cause for the revocation of the license.

(d) The provisions of this section shall not apply if the licensee handles less than twenty-five dollars ($25) per patient and less than five hundred dollars ($500) for all patients in any month.

(e) The director may exempt licensed health facilities of the types specified in subdivisions (a), (b), (c), and (f) of Section 1250 from the requirements of this section. However, the exemption from the bond purchase requirements of this section shall not affect the financial liability of such health facilities.

(Amended by Stats. 1982, Ch. 517, Sec. 266.)

1319.

The rules of a health facility may include provisions that require every member of the medical staff to have professional liability insurance as a condition to being on the medical staff of the health facility.

(Added by Stats. 1974, Ch. 889.)

1320.

A skilled nursing facility or intermediate care facility shall not require patients to purchase drugs, or rent or purchase medical supplies or equipment, from any particular pharmacy or other source.

This section shall not preclude a skilled nursing facility or intermediate care facility from requiring that the patient's pharmacy or other source comply with the facility's policies and procedures reasonably necessary for the care of the patient or policies and procedures required to meet the intent of state or federal regulations. Nothing in this section shall preclude a skilled nursing facility or intermediate care facility from requiring that controlled substances which are periodically counted by the facility on at least a daily basis be dispensed by the patient's pharmacy in containers suitable for that purpose.

(Added by Stats. 1980, Ch. 785.)

1321.

No health facility shall advertise or represent in any way that it provides occupational therapy services unless such services are provided under the administrative control of the health facility by an occupational therapist or occupational therapy assistant within the meaning of Section 2570 of the Business and Professions Code.

(Added by Stats. 1977, Ch. 836.)

1322.

A hospital which contracts with an insurer, nonprofit hospital service plan, or health care service plan shall not determine or condition medical staff membership or clinical privileges upon the basis of a physician and surgeon's or podiatrist's participation or nonparticipation in a contract with that insurer, hospital service plan, or health care service plan.

(Amended by Stats. 1992, Ch. 981, Sec. 3. Effective January 1, 1993.)

1323.

(a) A health facility, as defined by subdivisions (c) to (g), inclusive, of Section 1250, which has a significant beneficial interest in an ancillary health service provider or which knows that an ancillary health service provider has a significant beneficial interest in the health facility shall disclose that interest in writing to the patients of the health facility, or their representatives, and advise the patients, or their representatives, that they may choose to have another ancillary health service provider provide any supplies or services ordered by a member of the medical staff of the health facility.

(b) If supplies or services are provided on an outpatient basis by an ancillary health service provider which is not on the same site as, or which is not on a site which is adjacent to, a health facility, as defined by subdivision (a) or (b) of Section 1250, which has a significant beneficial interest in the ancillary health service provider, or if the ancillary health service provider has a significant beneficial interest in the health facility, the ancillary health service provider shall disclose that interest in writing to the customers of the ancillary health service provider, or their representatives, and advise the customers, or their representatives, that they may choose to have another ancillary health service provider provide any supplies or services ordered by a member of the medical staff of the health facility.

(c) A health facility, as defined by Section 1250, shall not charge, bill, or otherwise solicit payment from a patient on behalf of, or refer a patient to, another health facility in which the health facility has a significant beneficial interest unless the health facility first discloses in writing to the patient, or his or her representative, that the patient may choose to have another health facility provide any supplies or services ordered by a member of the medical staff of the health facility.

(d) (1) Except as provided in paragraph (2), "significant beneficial interest" means any financial interest that is equal to or greater than the lesser of the following:

(A) Five percent of the whole.

(B) Five thousand dollars ($5,000).

(2) "Significant beneficial interest" does not include any of the following interests:

(A) A lease agreement between a health facility, ancillary health service provider, another health facility, or a parent corporation of the health facility, or any combination thereof.

(B) Any financial interest held by a health facility or ancillary health service provider in the stock of a publicly held health facility or ancillary health service provider, or any parent corporation of a health facility or ancillary health service provider, if that financial interest does not exceed 5 percent of any class of equity securities of the health facility, ancillary health service provider, or parent corporation.

(C) An ownership interest in a health facility or ancillary health service provider if more than three-fourths of the patients of the health facility or ancillary health service provider are members of a prepaid group practice health care service plan, as defined by Section 1345.

(e) (1) "Ancillary health service provider" includes, but is not limited to, providers of pharmaceutical, laboratory, optometry, prosthetic, or orthopedic supplies or services, suppliers of durable medical equipment, home-health service providers, and providers of mental health or substance abuse services.

(2) As used in subdivision (b), "adjacent" means real property located within a 400-yard radius of the boundaries of the site on which the health facility is located.

(f) Neither a health facility nor an ancillary health service provider is required to make any disclosures required by this section to any patients or customers, or their representatives, if the patients or customers are enrolled in organizations or entities which provide or arrange for the provision of health care services in exchange for a prepaid capitation payment or premium.

(Added by Stats. 1985, Ch. 952, Sec. 1.)

1323.1.

(a) A general acute care hospital shall notify each patient scheduled for a service in a hospital-based outpatient clinic when that service is available in another location that is not hospital-based. The notification shall be in substantially the following form:
The location where you are being scheduled to receive services is a hospital-based clinic, and, therefore, may have higher costs. The same service may be available at another location within our health system that is not hospital-based, which may cost less. Check with the [insert name of office] at [insert telephone number] for another location within our health system, or check with your health insurance company, for more information about other locations that may cost less.

(b) For purposes of this section, a "hospital-based outpatient clinic" means a department of a provider, as defined in Section 413.65(a)(2) of Title 42 of the Code of Federal Regulations, that is not located on the campus of that provider.

(c) This section shall not apply to a general acute care hospital operated by a nonprofit corporation under common control with a nonprofit health care service plan licensed pursuant to the Knox-Keene Health Care Service Plan Act of 1975 (Chapter 2.2 (commencing with Section 1340) of Division 2) that exclusively contracts with no more than two medical groups in the state to provide and arrange for medical services for the enrollees of the health care service plan, so long as the cost-sharing design does not vary based on whether the care is provided in a hospital-based clinic or a medical office building.

(Added by Stats. 2016, Ch. 501, Sec. 1. (SB 1365) Effective January 1, 2017.)

ARTICLE 7.2. Small House Skilled Nursing Facilities [1323.5 - 1323.6]

(Article 7.2 added by Stats. 2012, Ch. 671, Sec. 2.)

1323.5.

(a) (1) The Small House Skilled Nursing Facilities Pilot Program (SHSNF PP) is hereby established within the department. The purpose of the pilot program is to allow the department to authorize the development and operation of up to 10 small house skilled nursing facilities that are licensed to provide skilled nursing care and supportive care to patients in small, homelike, residential settings that incorporate emerging patient-centered health care concepts. The long-range goal of the pilot program is to evaluate the models developed under the pilot program to determine if each model improves patient satisfaction and clinical outcomes in a cost-effective manner. The models developed shall also be eligible for certification for participation in the federal Medicare Program under Title XVIII of the federal Social Security Act (42 U.S.C. Sec. 1395 et seq.) as skilled nursing facilities or in the federal Medicaid Program under Title XIX of the federal Social Security Act (42 U.S.C. Sec. 1396 et seq.), as nursing facilities, or as both.

(2) For purposes of the pilot program, the department shall permit the formulation of standards for long-term care that may extend beyond, or vary from, traditional long-term health care facility models, including, but not limited to, facility layout and design consistent with newly adopted revisions to the California Building Standards Code, nursing care levels, staffing levels, infection control, sanitation, dietary services, and other personal care and habilitation provisions that may be more flexible than those currently required in California for skilled nursing facilities and continuous nursing facilities.

(3) The department shall establish criteria to measure the benefits and successes of this type of long-term care facility, as a whole, and to compare the results achieved by each model variant. The department shall evaluate and analyze the emerging concepts in long-term skilled nursing care developed pursuant to the pilot program for purposes of considering future regulatory modification.

(b) Facilities that are eligible for participation in the pilot program shall have all of the following characteristics:

(1) To the extent permitted under federal law, each home shall consist of a homelike, rather than institutional, environment, including the following characteristics:

(A) The home shall be accessible to disabled persons, and shall be designed as a house, an apartment, or a distinct area within an existing skilled nursing facility that meets the standards described in paragraph (2) of subdivision (a) that is similar to housing available within the surrounding community, and that includes shared areas that would only be commonly shared in a private home or apartment.

(B) The home shall not, to the extent practicable, contain institutional features. These include, but are not limited to, nursing stations, medication carts, room numbers, and wall-mounted licenses or certificates that could appropriately be accessed through other means.

(C) (i) The home shall include resident rooms that accommodate not more than two residents per room. Facilities are encouraged to include private, single-occupancy bedrooms that are shared only at the request of a resident to accommodate a spouse, partner, family member, or friend, and that contain a full private and accessible bathroom.
(ii) Double-occupancy rooms shall contain a full private and accessible bathroom, and each resident's bedroom area shall be visually separated from the other by a full height wall or a permanently installed sliding door, folding door, or partition. Walls, doors, or partitions used to separate resident bedroom areas shall provide visual and acoustic separation. A door leading to each resident's bedroom area in addition to the corridor door is not required, unless needed to achieve visual or acoustic separation.
(iii) Each resident shall have direct use of, and access to, an exterior window at all times.

(D) The home shall contain a living area where residents and staff may socialize, dine, and prepare food together that provides, at a minimum, a living room seating area, and a dining area large enough to accommodate all residents and at least two staff members. The home shall contain a full kitchen open to the living and dining rooms that may be utilized by residents that shall provide for separation in accordance with the California Building Standards Code.

(E) The home shall contain ample natural light.

(F) The home shall have built-in safety features to allow all areas of the facility to be accessible to residents during the majority of the day and night.

(G) The home shall provide access to secured outdoor space.

(H) The home shall endeavor to create an aging-in-place environment where long-stay residents may form permanent homes with each other.

(I) The home shall prepare, cook, and serve meals on a daily basis for residents in the home. Nothing in this subparagraph shall prohibit a home from utilizing outside resources in a manner approved by the department.

(c) As used in this article, the following definitions apply:

(1) "Pilot facility" means a Small House Skilled Nursing Facility (SHSNF) participating in the Small House Skilled Nursing Facilities Pilot Program (SHSNF PP) established by this article.

(2) "Small house skilled nursing facility" (SHSNF) means a health facility that provides skilled nursing care and supportive care in a small, homelike, residential setting in an apartment, cottage, house, or similar residential unit, to patients whose primary need is for the availability of skilled nursing care on an extended basis. A SHSNF may consist of a group or cluster of such residential homes, each home having 12 or fewer beds, or a distinct area within an existing skilled nursing facility that otherwise meets the definition of a SHSNF, is physically separate and distinguishable from the remainder of the skilled nursing facility, and has a distinct entry with no through traffic of staff, residents, or visitors not affiliated with the SHSNF. A SHSNF may also be a distinct part of a general acute care hospital or an acute psychiatric hospital, pursuant to subdivision (c) of Section 1418. Regardless of location, all SHSNFs shall meet all standards.

(3) "Home" means an apartment, cottage, house, or other similar residential unit that serves 12 or fewer residents.

(4) "Supportive care" includes the provision of socialization, activity aide services, and homemaker services.

(5) "Homemaker services" means food preparation, housekeeping, laundry, and maintenance services.

(6) "Versatile worker" means a certified nursing assistant who provides personal care, socialization, activity aide services, meal preparation services, and laundry and housekeeping services.

(d) Each pilot facility shall be subject to all licensing enforcement provisions to which other skilled nursing facilities are subject, including, but not limited to, Section 1424.5, Article 7.6 (commencing with Section 1324.20), and Article 8 (commencing with Section 1325).

(e) Unless otherwise operating on an existing skilled nursing facility license, each pilot facility shall be subject to the Licensing and Certification program fee for skilled nursing facilities pursuant to Section 1266.

(f) Each pilot facility shall receive a peer group weighted average Medi-Cal reimbursement rate as calculated by the State Department of Health Care Services.

(g) (1) Each pilot facility shall provide for consistent staff assignments and self-managed work teams of direct care staff, including staff working as versatile workers. Licensed nursing staff shall direct the versatile workers in all activities delegated under the licensed nurses' scope of practice. A versatile worker may be supervised by nonclinical staff when performing nonclinical duties, at the discretion of the facility.

(2) (A) The pilot facility shall provide training for all staff involved in the operation of the home, to be completed prior to initial operation of the home, concerning the philosophy, operations, and skills required to implement and maintain self-directed care, self-managed work teams, a noninstitutional approach to long-term care, safety and emergency skills, food handling and safety, and other elements necessary for the successful operation of the home. Versatile workers and other staff interacting with residents in the homes shall demonstrate proficiency in these areas as well as the facility's policies and procedures, conflict resolution, and self-directed care principles.

(B) Replacement staff shall undergo the training described in subparagraph (A) within two weeks of commencing employment with the pilot facility.

(h) A facility may be licensed by the department as a pilot facility pursuant to this article if the facility meets both of the following requirements:

(1) The facility has been determined by the department to comply with all provisions necessary to be certified to participate as a provider of care either as a skilled nursing facility in the federal Medicare Program under Title XVIII of the federal Social Security Act (42 U.S.C. Sec. 1395 et seq.) or as a nursing facility in the federal Medicaid Program under Title XIX of the federal Social Security Act (42 U.S.C. Sec. 1396 et seq.), or as both.

(2) The facility has been determined by the department and the Office of Statewide Health Planning and Development (OSHPD) to fully comply with all pilot program requirements required under the provisions of this article, including payment of the licensing fee for a skilled nursing facility pursuant to Section 1266.

(i) In developing standards for this pilot program, the department shall, together with OSHPD and the Office of the State Long-Term Care Ombudsman, consult long-term care providers, health care advocacy organizations, health care employee organizations, consumer advocates, elder care advocates, and others identified as having a vested interest in long-term health care.

(j) The department shall issue one or more all-facility letters that provide the standards to be used by providers accepted into the pilot program for the development and operation of all pilot facilities.

(k) The department shall have authority to waive any standard for skilled nursing facilities established elsewhere in this chapter, Chapter 2.4 (commencing with Section 1417), and any regulations adopted thereunder, if the health, safety, and quality of patient care is not adversely affected. Prior written approval communicating the terms and conditions under which the waiver is granted shall be required. Applicants shall request the waiver in writing, accompanied by detailed, supporting documentation.

(l) (1) Consistent with this article, the department shall invite all eligible providers to submit an application to participate in the SHSNF PP at specified intervals over the first two years of the pilot program. The applications shall include sufficient information to demonstrate the provider's experience in establishing and operating one or more care facilities offering the level of care to be furnished by pilot facilities, including the name and location of each facility currently or previously licensed to the provider, whether within California or in another state.

(2) The department may require that additional information and documents be submitted with, or subsequently in support of, the application. Failure to provide any required information or documentation shall disqualify the applicant from the application process and from consideration for participation in the pilot program. The department may select providers for participation in the SHSNF PP based on the applicant's ability to meet or exceed the criteria described in this article.

(m) If, at any time, a pilot facility fails to meet the criteria set forth in this article for being a pilot facility, or fails to safeguard patient health, safety, welfare, and security as determined by the department, the department shall remove that pilot facility from participation in the pilot program.

(n) The costs of the creation, administration, and evaluation of the pilot program shall be borne by the facilities participating in the pilot project.

(o) Each pilot facility shall provide any reports to the department that the department deems necessary for modifications to the pilot program, the guidance or regulations governing the pilot facilities, and any other information the pilot facilities deem relevant in evaluating the success of the pilot program in delivering improved patient care. The department may inspect a participating pilot facility at any time.

(p) The department shall prepare and submit a report to the Legislature on the results of the SHSNF PP. The department may prepare the evaluation, analysis, and report itself, or may do so under contract. The report shall be submitted to the Legislature at least 24 months prior to the termination of the pilot program, and shall include an evaluation of the pilot program's cost, safety, and quality of care.

(q) This section and the pilot program shall not be construed to limit providers not participating in the pilot from pursuing approval for similar practices through program flexibility or similar existing process allowed by law.

(Amended by Stats. 2018, Ch. 115, Sec. 1. (SB 1280) Effective January 1, 2019. Repealed as of January 1, 2026, pursuant to Section 1323.6.)

1323.6.

This article shall remain in effect only until January 1, 2026, and as of that date is repealed, unless a later enacted statute, that is enacted before January 1, 2026, deletes or extends that date.

(Amended by Stats. 2018, Ch. 115, Sec. 2. (SB 1280) Effective January 1, 2019. Repealed as of January 1, 2026, by its own provisions. Note: Repeal affects Article 7.2, commencing with Section 1323.5.)

ARTICLE 7.5. Intermediate Care Facilities' Quality Assurance Fees [1324 - 1324.14]

(Article 7.5 added by Stats. 2003, Ch. 230, Sec. 5.)

1324.

For purposes of this article, the following definitions shall apply:

(a) (1) "Gross receipts" means gross receipts paid as compensation for services provided to residents of a designated intermediate care facility.

(2) "Gross receipts" does not mean charitable contributions.

(3) For state and local government owned facilities, "gross receipts" shall include any contributions from government sources or General Fund expenditures for the care of residents of a designated intermediate care facility.

(b) "Eligible facility" means a designated intermediate care facility that has paid the fee as described in Section 1324.2, for a particular state fiscal year.

(c) "Designated intermediate care facility" or "facility" means a facility as defined in subdivision (e), (g), or (h) of Section 1250.

(Added by Stats. 2003, Ch. 230, Sec. 5. Effective August 11, 2003. Conditionally inoperative as provided in Section 1324.12.)

1324.2.

(a) As a condition for participation in the Medi-Cal program, there shall be imposed each state fiscal year upon the entire gross receipts of a designated intermediate care facility a quality assurance fee, as calculated in accordance with subdivision (b).

(b) The quality assurance fee to be paid pursuant to subdivision (c) of Section 1324.4 shall be an amount determined each quarter of the state fiscal year by multiplying the facility's gross receipts in the preceding quarter by 6 percent. For reporting purposes, the quality assurance fee is considered to be on a cash basis of accounting.

(Added by Stats. 2003, Ch. 230, Sec. 5. Effective August 11, 2003. Conditionally inoperative as provided in Section 1324.12.)

1324.4.

(a) On or before August 31 of each year, each designated intermediate care facility subject to Section 1324.2 shall report to the department, in a prescribed form, the facility's gross receipts for the preceding state fiscal year.

(b) On or before the last day of each calendar quarter, each designated intermediate care facility shall file a report with the department, in a prescribed form, showing the facility's gross receipts for the preceding quarter.

(c) A newly licensed care facility, as defined by the department, shall be exempt from the requirements of subdivision (a) for its year of operation, but shall complete all requirements of subdivision (b) for any portion of the quarter in which it commences operations.

(d) The quality assurance fee, as calculated pursuant to subdivision (b) of Section 1324.2, shall be paid to the department on or before the last day of the quarter following the quarter for which the fee is imposed.

(e) The payment of the quality assurance fee a designated intermediate care facility shall be reported as an allowable cost for Medi-Cal reimbursement purposes.

(f) The department shall make retrospective adjustments, as necessary, to the amounts calculated pursuant to subdivision (b) of Section 1324.2 in order to assure that the facility's aggregate quality assurance fee for any particular state fiscal year does not exceed 6 percent of the facility's aggregate annual gross receipts for that year.

(Added by Stats. 2003, Ch. 230, Sec. 5. Effective August 11, 2003. Conditionally inoperative as provided in Section 1324.12.)

1324.6.

(a) The Director of Health Services, or his or her designee, shall administer this article.

(b) The director may adopt regulations as are necessary to implement this article. These regulations may be adopted as emergency regulations in accordance with the rulemaking provisions of the Administrative Procedure Act (Chapter 3.5 (commencing with Section 11340) of Part 1 of Division 3 of Title 2 of the Government Code). For purposes of this article, the adoption of regulations shall be deemed an emergency and necessary for the immediate preservation of the public peace, health and safety, or general welfare. The regulations shall include, but not be limited to, any regulations necessary for either of the following purposes:

(1) The administration of this article, including the proper imposition and collection of the quality assurance fee.

(2) The development of any forms necessary to obtain required information from facilities subject to the quality assurance fee.

(c) As an alternative to subdivision (b), and notwithstanding Chapter 3.5 (commencing with Section 11340) of Part 1 of Division 3 of Title 2 of the Government Code, the director may implement this article by means of a provider bulletin, or other similar instructions, without taking regulatory action.

(Added by Stats. 2003, Ch. 230, Sec. 5. Effective August 11, 2003. Conditionally inoperative as provided in Section 1324.12.)

1324.8.

(a) The quality assurance fee assessed and collected pursuant to this article shall be deposited in the General Fund.

(b) Notwithstanding subdivision (a), commencing August 1, 2013, the quality assurance fee assessed and collected pursuant to this article shall be deposited in the Long-Term Care Quality Assurance Fund established pursuant to Section 1324.9.

(Amended by Stats. 2012, Ch. 23, Sec. 15. (AB 1467) Effective June 27, 2012. Section conditionally inoperative as provided in Section 1324.12.)

1324.9.

(a) The Long-Term Care Quality Assurance Fund is hereby created in the State Treasury. Notwithstanding Section 13340 of the Government Code, moneys in the fund shall be continuously appropriated, without regard to fiscal year, to the State Department of Health Care Services for the purposes of this article and Article 7.6 (commencing with Section 1324.20). Notwithstanding Section 16305.7 of the Government Code, the fund shall contain all interest and dividends earned on moneys in the fund.

(b) Notwithstanding any other law, beginning August 1, 2013, all revenues received by the State Department of Health Care Services categorized by the State Department of Health Care Services as long-term care quality assurance fees shall be deposited into the Long-Term Care Quality Assurance Fund. Revenue that shall be deposited into this fund shall include quality assurance fees imposed pursuant to this article and quality assurance fees imposed pursuant to Article 7.6 (commencing with Section 1324.20).

(c) Notwithstanding any other law, the Controller may use the funds in the Long-Term Care Quality Assurance Fund for cashflow loans to the General Fund as provided in Sections 16310 and 16381 of the Government Code.

(Amended by Stats. 2016, Ch. 30, Sec. 3. (SB 833) Effective June 27, 2016. Conditionally inoperative as provided in Section 1324.12.)

1324.10.

In addition to the rate of payment that an eligible facility would otherwise receive for intermediate care facility services provided to Medi-Cal beneficiaries, an eligible facility shall receive quarterly supplemental Medi-Cal reimbursement, in an amount determined by the department.

The supplemental Medi-Cal reimbursement provided by this section shall be paid to support the facility's quality improvement efforts and shall be distributed under a payment methodology based on intermediate care services provided to Medi-Cal patients at the eligible facility, either on a per diem basis, or on any other federally permissible basis. (Added by Stats. 2003, Ch. 230, Sec. 5. Effective August 11, 2003. Conditionally inoperative as provided in Section 1324.12.)

1324.12.

(a) (1) The department shall seek approval from the federal Centers for Medicare and Medicaid Services for the implementation of this article.

(2) If after seeking federal approval, federal approval is not obtained, this article shall not be implemented.

(3) The Director of Health Services may alter the methodology specified in this article to the extent necessary to meet the requirements of federal law or regulations, or to obtain federal approval.

(b) If there is a final judicial determination by any court of appellate jurisdiction or a final determination by the Administrator of the federal Center for Medicare and Medicaid Services that the supplemental reimbursement provided by this article shall be made to any facility not described in this article, this article shall immediately become inoperative. (Added by Stats. 2003, Ch. 230, Sec. 5. Effective August 11, 2003. Note: Implementation and termination provisions affect Article 7.5, comprising Sections 1324 to 1324.14.)

1324.14.

In implementing this article, the department may utilize the services of the Medi-Cal fiscal intermediary through a change order to the fiscal intermediary contract to administer this program, consistent with the requirements of Sections 14104.6, 14104.7, 14104.8, and 14104.9 of the Welfare and Institutions Code.

(Added by Stats. 2003, Ch. 230, Sec. 5. Effective August 11, 2003. Conditionally inoperative as provided in Section 1324.12.)

ARTICLE 7.6. Skilled Nursing Facility Quality Assurance Fee [1324.20 - 1324.30]

(Article 7.6 added by Stats. 2004, Ch. 875, Sec. 1.)

1324.20.

For purposes of this article, the following definitions shall apply:

(a) (1) "Continuing care retirement community" means a provider of a continuum of services, including independent living services, assisted living services as defined in paragraph (5) of subdivision (a) of Section 1771, and skilled nursing care, on a single campus, that is subject to Section 1791, or a provider of such a continuum of services on a single campus that has not received a Letter of Exemption pursuant to subdivision (d) of Section 1771.3.

(2) Notwithstanding paragraph (1), beginning with the 2010–11 rate year and for every rate year thereafter, the term "continuing care retirement community" shall have the definition contained in paragraph (11) of subdivision (c) of Section 1771.

(b) "Department," unless otherwise specified, means the State Department of Health Care Services.

(c) (1) "Exempt facility" means a skilled nursing facility that is part of a continuing care retirement community, a skilled nursing facility operated by the state or another public entity, a unit that provides pediatric subacute services in a skilled nursing facility, a skilled nursing facility that is certified by the department for a special treatment program and is an institution for mental disease as defined in Section 1396d(i) of Title 42 of the United States Code, or a skilled nursing facility that is a distinct part of a facility that is licensed as a general acute care hospital.

(2) Notwithstanding paragraph (1), beginning with the 2010–11 rate year and for every rate year thereafter, the term "exempt facility" shall mean a skilled nursing facility that is part of a continuing care retirement community, as defined in paragraph (2) of subdivision (a), a skilled nursing facility operated by the state or another public entity, a unit that provides pediatric subacute services in a skilled nursing facility, a skilled nursing facility that is certified by the department for a special treatment program and is an institution for mental disease as defined in Section 1396d(i) of Title 42 of the United

States Code, or a skilled nursing facility that is a distinct part of a facility that is licensed as a general acute care hospital.

(3) Notwithstanding paragraph (1), beginning with the 2010–11 rate year and every rate year thereafter, a multilevel facility, as described in paragraph (1) of subdivision (a), shall not be exempt from the quality assurance fee requirements pursuant to this article, unless it meets the definition of a continuing care retirement community in paragraph (11) of subdivision (c) of Section 1771.

(4) (A) Notwithstanding paragraph (1), beginning with the 2011–12 rate year, and every rate year thereafter, a unit that provides freestanding pediatric subacute care services in a skilled nursing facility, as described in paragraph (1) of subdivision (c), shall not be exempt from the quality assurance fee requirements pursuant to this article.

(B) For the purposes of this article, "freestanding pediatric subacute care unit" has the same meaning as defined in Section 51215.8 of Title 22 of the California Code of Regulations.

(d) (1) "Net revenue" means gross resident revenue for routine nursing services and ancillary services provided to all residents by a skilled nursing facility, less Medicare revenue for routine and ancillary services, including Medicare revenue for services provided to residents covered under a Medicare managed care plan, less payer discounts and applicable contractual allowances as permitted under federal law and regulation.

(2) Notwithstanding paragraph (1), for the 2009–10, 2010–11, and 2011–12 rate years, and each rate year thereafter, "net revenue" means gross resident revenue for routine nursing services and ancillary services provided to all residents by a skilled nursing facility, including Medicare revenue for routine and ancillary services and Medicare revenue for services provided to residents covered under a Medicare managed care plan, less payer discounts and applicable contractual allowances as permitted under federal law and regulation. To implement this paragraph, the department shall request federal approval pursuant to Section 1324.27.

(3) "Net revenue" does not mean charitable contributions and bad debt.

(e) "Payer discounts and contractual allowances" means the difference between the facility's resident charges for routine or ancillary services and the actual amount paid.

(f) "Skilled nursing facility" means a licensed facility as defined in subdivision (c) of Section 1250.

(Amended by Stats. 2012, Ch. 34, Sec. 12. (SB 1009) Effective June 27, 2012. See operational conditions in Section 1324.28. Inoperative after July 31, 2020. Repealed as of January 1, 2021, pursuant to Section 1324.30.)

1324.21.

(a) For facilities licensed under subdivision (c) of Section 1250, there shall be imposed each fiscal year a uniform quality assurance fee per resident day. The uniform quality assurance fee shall be based upon the entire net revenue of all skilled nursing facilities subject to the fee, except an exempt facility, as defined in Section 1324.20, calculated in accordance with subdivision (b).

(b) The amount of the uniform quality assurance fee to be assessed per resident day shall be determined based on the aggregate net revenue of skilled nursing facilities subject to the fee, in accordance with the methodology outlined in the request for federal approval required by Section 1324.27 and in regulations, provider bulletins, or other similar instructions. The uniform quality assurance fee shall be calculated as follows:

(1) (A) For the rate year 2004–05, the net revenue shall be projected for all skilled nursing facilities subject to the fee. The projection of net revenue shall be based on prior rate-year data. Once determined, the aggregate projected net revenue for all facilities shall be multiplied by 2.7 percent, as determined under the approved methodology, and then divided by the projected total resident days of all providers subject to the fee.

(B) Notwithstanding subparagraph (A), the Director of Health Care Services may increase the amount of the fee up to 3 percent of the aggregate projected net revenue if necessary for the implementation of Article 3.8 (commencing with Section 14126) of Chapter 7 of Part 3 of Division 9 of the Welfare and Institutions Code.

(2) (A) For the rate year 2005–06 and subsequent rate years through and including the 2009–10 rate year, the net revenue shall be projected for all skilled nursing facilities subject to the uniform quality assurance fee. The projection of net revenue shall be based on the prior rate year's data. Once determined, the aggregate projected net revenue for all facilities shall be multiplied by 6 percent, as determined under the approved methodology, and then divided by the projected total resident days of all providers subject to the fee. The amounts so determined shall be subject to the provisions of subdivision (d).

(B) For the 2010–11 rate year and subsequent rate years, the net revenue shall be projected for all skilled nursing facilities subject to the uniform quality assurance fee. The projection of net revenue shall be based on the prior year's data trended forward, using historical increases in net revenues. Once determined, the aggregate projected net revenue for all facilities shall be multiplied by 6 percent, as determined under the approved methodology, and then divided by the projected total resident days of all providers subject to the fee. The amounts so determined shall be subject to subdivision (d).

(c) The director may assess and collect a nonuniform fee consistent with the methodology approved pursuant to Section 1324.27.

(d) In no case shall the fees collected annually pursuant to this article, taken together with applicable licensing fees, exceed the amounts allowable under federal law.

(e) If there is a delay in the implementation of this article for any reason, including a delay in the approval of the quality assurance fee and methodology by the federal Centers for Medicare and Medicaid Services, in the 2004–05 rate year or in any other rate year, all of the following shall apply:

(1) Any facility subject to the fee may be assessed the amount the facility will be required to pay to the department, but shall not be required to pay the fee until the methodology is approved and Medi-Cal rates are increased in accordance with paragraph (2) of subdivision (a) of Section 1324.28 and the increased rates are paid to facilities.

(2) The department may retroactively increase and make payment of rates to facilities.

(3) Facilities that have been assessed a fee by the department shall pay the fee assessed within 60 days of the date rates are increased in accordance with paragraph (2) of subdivision (a) of Section 1324.28 and paid to facilities.

(4) The department shall accept a facility's payment notwithstanding that the payment is submitted in a subsequent fiscal year than the fiscal year in which the fee is assessed.

(Amended by Stats. 2010, Ch. 717, Sec. 4. (SB 853) Effective October 19, 2010. See operational conditions in Section 1324.28. Inoperative after July 31, 2020. Repealed as of January 1, 2021, pursuant to Section 1324.30.)

1324.22.

(a) The quality assurance fee, as calculated pursuant to Section 1324.21, shall be paid by the provider to the department for deposit in the State Treasury on a monthly basis on or before the last day of the month following the month for which the fee is imposed, except as provided in subdivision (e) of Section 1324.21.

(b) On or before the last day of each calendar quarter, each skilled nursing facility shall file a report with the department, in a prescribed form, showing the facility's total resident days for the preceding quarter and payments made. If it is determined that a lesser amount was paid to the department, the facility shall pay the amount owed in the preceding quarter to the department with the report. Any amount determined to have been paid in excess to the department during the previous quarter shall be credited to the amount owed in the following quarter.

(c) On or before August 31 of each year, each skilled nursing facility subject to an assessment pursuant to Section 1324.21 shall report to the department, in a prescribed form, the facility's total resident days and total payments made for the preceding state fiscal year. If it is determined that a lesser amount was paid to the department during the previous year, the facility shall pay the amount owed to the department with the report.

(d) (1) A newly licensed skilled nursing facility shall complete all requirements of subdivision (a) for any portion of the year in which it commences operations and of subdivision (b) for any portion of the quarter in which it commences operations.

(2) For purposes of this subdivision, "newly licensed skilled nursing facility" means a location that has not been previously licensed as a skilled nursing facility.

(e) (1) When a skilled nursing facility fails to pay all or part of the quality assurance fee within 60 days of the date that payment is due, the department may deduct the unpaid assessment and interest owed from any Medi-Cal reimbursement payments to the facility until the full amount is recovered. Any deduction shall be made only after written notice to the facility and may be taken over a period of time taking into account the financial condition of the facility.

(2) In addition to the provisions of paragraph (1), any unpaid quality assurance fee assessed by this article shall constitute a debt due to the state and may be collected pursuant to Section 12419.5 of the Government Code.

(f) Notwithstanding any other provision of law, the department shall continue to assess and collect the quality assurance fee, including any previously unpaid quality assurance fee, from each skilled nursing facility, irrespective of any changes in ownership or ownership interest or control or the transfer of any portion of the assets of the facility to another owner.

(g) During the time period in which a temporary manager is appointed to a facility pursuant to Section 1325.5 or during which a receiver is appointed by a court pursuant to Section 1327, the State Department of Public Health shall not be responsible for any unpaid quality assurance fee assessed prior to the time period of the temporary manager or receiver. Nothing in this subdivision shall affect the responsibility of the facility to make all payments of unpaid or current quality assurance fees, as required by this section and Section 1324.21.

(h) If all or any part of the quality assurance fee remains unpaid, the department may take either or both of the following actions:

(1) Assess a penalty equal to 50 percent of the unpaid fee amount for unpaid fees assessed during the 2004–05 to 2009–10, inclusive, rate years, and up to 50 percent of the unpaid fee amount for unpaid fees assessed during the 2010–11 rate year and any subsequent rate year.

(2) (A) Delay license renewal.

(B) Beginning with the 2010–11 rate year, the department may recommend to the State Department of Public Health that license renewal be delayed until the full amount of the quality assurance fee, penalties, and interest is recovered.

(i) In accordance with the provisions of the Medicaid State Plan, the payment of the quality assurance fee shall be considered as an allowable cost for Medi-Cal reimbursement purposes.

(j) The assessment process pursuant to this section shall become operative not later than 60 days from receipt of federal approval of the quality assurance fee, unless extended by the department. The department may assess fees and collect payment in accordance with subdivision (e) of Section 1324.21 in order to provide retroactive payments for any rate increase authorized under this article.

(k) The amendments made to subdivision (d) and the addition of subdivision (f) by the act that added this subdivision shall not be construed as substantive changes, but are merely clarifying existing law.

(l) (1) Notwithstanding any other provision of law, for the 2011–12 rate year, the department may waive the actions provided under subdivision (h), or may allow a freestanding pediatric subacute care facility to delay payments for up to six months, to ensure the facility has the financial stability required to pay the fee.

(2) For the purposes of this article, "freestanding pediatric subacute care facility" has the same meaning as defined in Section 51215.8 of Title 22 of the California Code of Regulations.

(Amended by Stats. 2011, 1st Ex. Sess., Ch. 4, Sec. 2. (AB 19 1x) Effective June 29, 2011. See operational conditions in Section 1324.28. Inoperative after July 31, 2020. Repealed as of January 1, 2021, pursuant to Section 1324.30.)

1324.23.

(a) The Director of Health Care Services, or his or her designee, shall administer this article.

(b) The director may adopt regulations as are necessary to implement this article. These regulations may be adopted as emergency regulations in accordance with the rulemaking provisions of the Administrative Procedure Act (Chapter 3.5 (commencing with Section 11340) of Part 1 of Division 3 of Title 2 of the Government Code). For purposes of this article, the adoption of regulations shall be deemed an emergency and necessary for the immediate preservation of the public peace, health and safety, or general welfare. The regulations shall include, but need not be limited to, any regulations necessary for any of the following purposes:

(1) The administration of this article, including the proper imposition and collection of the quality assurance fee not to exceed amounts reasonably necessary for purposes of this article.

(2) The development of any forms necessary to obtain required information from facilities subject to the quality assurance fee.

(3) To provide details, definitions, formulas, and other requirements.

(c) As an alternative to subdivision (b), and notwithstanding the rulemaking provisions of Chapter 3.5 (commencing with Section 11340) of Part 1 of Division 3 of Title 2 of the Government Code, the director may implement this article, in whole or in part, by means of a provider bulletin or other similar instructions, without taking regulatory action, provided that no such bulletin or other similar instructions shall remain in effect after July 31, 2020. It is the intent of the Legislature that the regulations adopted pursuant to subdivision (b) shall be adopted on or before July 31, 2020.

(Amended by Stats. 2015, Ch. 17, Sec. 1. (AB 119) Effective June 24, 2015. See operational conditions in Section 1324.28. Inoperative after July 31, 2020. Repealed as of January 1, 2021, pursuant to Section 1324.30.)

1324.24.

(a) The quality assurance fee assessed and collected pursuant to this article shall be deposited in the State Treasury.

(b) Notwithstanding subdivision (a), commencing August 1, 2013, the quality assurance fee assessed and collected pursuant to this article shall be deposited in the Long-Term Care Quality Assurance Fund established pursuant to Section 1324.9.

(Amended by Stats. 2012, Ch. 23, Sec. 17. (AB 1467) Effective June 27, 2012. See operational conditions in Section 1324.28. Inoperative after July 31, 2020. Repealed as of January 1, 2021, pursuant to Section 1324.30.)

1324.25.

The funds assessed pursuant to this article shall be available to enhance federal financial participation in the Medi-Cal program or to provide additional reimbursement to, and to support facility quality improvement efforts in, licensed skilled nursing facilities.

(Added by Stats. 2004, Ch. 875, Sec. 1. Effective September 29, 2004. See operational conditions in Section 1324.28. Inoperative after July 31, 2020. Repealed as of January 1, 2021, pursuant to Section 1324.30.)

1324.26.

In implementing this article, the department may utilize the services of the Medi-Cal fiscal intermediary through a change order to the fiscal intermediary contract to administer this program, consistent with the requirements of Sections 14104.6, 14104.7, 14104.8, and 14104.9 of the Welfare and Institutions Code.

(Added by Stats. 2004, Ch. 875, Sec. 1. Effective September 29, 2004. See operational conditions in Section 1324.28. Inoperative after July 31, 2020. Repealed as of January 1, 2021, pursuant to Section 1324.30.)

1324.27.

(a) (1) The department shall request approval from the federal Centers for Medicare and Medicaid Services for the implementation of this article. In making this request, the department shall seek specific approval from the federal Centers for Medicare and Medicaid Services to exempt facilities identified in subdivision (c) of Section 1324.20, including the submission of a request for waiver of broad-based requirement, waiver of uniform fee requirement, or both, pursuant to paragraphs (1) and (2) of subdivision (e) of Section 433.68 of Title 42 of the Code of Federal Regulations.

(2) The director may alter the methodology specified in this article, to the extent necessary to meet the requirements of federal law or regulations or to obtain federal approval. The Director of Health Care Services may also add new categories of exempt facilities or apply a nonuniform fee to the skilled nursing facilities subject to the fee in order to meet requirements of federal law or regulations. The Director of Health Care Services may apply a zero fee to one or more exempt categories of facilities, if necessary to obtain federal approval.

(3) If after seeking federal approval, federal approval is not obtained, this article shall not be implemented.

(b) The department shall make retrospective adjustments, as necessary, to the amounts calculated pursuant to Section 1324.21 in order to assure that the aggregate quality assurance fee for any particular state fiscal year does not exceed 6 percent of the aggregate annual net revenue of facilities subject to the fee.

(Amended by Stats. 2012, Ch. 631, Sec. 2. (AB 1489) Effective September 27, 2012. See operational conditions in Section 1324.28. Inoperative after July 31, 2020. Repealed as of January 1, 2021, pursuant to Section 1324.30.)

1324.28.

(a) This article shall be implemented as long as both of the following conditions are met:
(1) The state receives federal approval of the quality assurance fee from the federal Centers for Medicare and Medicaid Services.
(2) Legislation is enacted in the 2004 legislative session making an appropriation from the General Fund and from the Federal Trust Fund to fund a rate increase for skilled nursing facilities, as defined under subdivision (c) of Section 1250, for the 2004–05 rate year in an amount consistent with the Medi-Cal rates that specific facilities would have received under the rate methodology in effect as of July 31, 2004, plus the proportional costs as projected by Medi-Cal for new state or federal mandates.
(b) This article shall remain operative only as long as all of the following conditions are met:
(1) The federal Centers for Medicare and Medicaid Services continues to allow the use of the provider assessment provided in this article.
(2) The Medi-Cal Long-Term Care Reimbursement Act, Article 3.8 (commencing with Section 14126) of Chapter 7 of Part 3 of Division 9 of the Welfare and Institutions Code, as added during the 2003–04 Regular Session by the act adding this section, is enacted and implemented on or before July 31, 2005, or as extended as provided in that article, and remains in effect thereafter.
(3) The state has continued its maintenance of effort for the level of state funding of nursing facility reimbursement for the 2005–06 rate year, and for every subsequent rate year continuing through the 2011–12 rate year, in an amount not less than the amount that specific facilities would have received under the rate methodology in effect on July 31, 2004, plus Medi-Cal's projected proportional costs for new state or federal mandates, not including the quality assurance fee.
(4) The full amount of the quality assurance fee assessed and collected pursuant to this article remains available for the purposes specified in Section 1324.25 and for related purposes.
(c) If all of the conditions in subdivision (a) are met, this article is implemented, and subsequently, any one of the conditions in subdivision (b) is not met, on and after the date that the department makes that determination, this article shall not be implemented, notwithstanding that the condition or conditions subsequently may be met.
(d) Notwithstanding subdivisions (a), (b), and (c), in the event of a final judicial determination made by any state or federal court that is not appealed, or by a court of appellate jurisdiction that is not further appealed, in any action by any party, or a final determination by the administrator of the federal Centers for Medicare and Medicaid Services, that federal financial participation is not available with respect to any payment made under the methodology implemented pursuant to this article because the methodology is invalid, unlawful, or contrary to any provision of federal law or regulations, or of state law, this section shall become inoperative.
(Amended by Stats. 2010, Ch. 717, Sec. 8. (SB 853) Effective October 19, 2010. Conditionally inoperative as provided in subd. (d). Inoperative after July 31, 2020. Repealed as of January 1, 2021, pursuant to Section 1324.30. Note: Operational conditions in subds. (a), (b), and (c) apply to Article 7.6, commencing with Section 1324.20.)

1324.29.

(a) The quality assurance fee shall cease to be assessed after July 31, 2020.
(b) Notwithstanding subdivision (a) and Section 1324.30, the department's authority and obligation to collect all quality assurance fees and penalties, including interest, shall continue in effect and shall not cease until the date that all amounts are paid or recovered in full.
(c) This section shall remain operative until the date that all fees and penalties, including interest, have been recovered pursuant to subdivision (b), and as of that date is repealed.
(Amended by Stats. 2015, Ch. 17, Sec. 2. (AB 119) Effective June 24, 2015. See operational conditions in Section 1324.28. Repealed as of date prescribed by its own provisions.)

1324.30.

This article shall become inoperative after July 31, 2020, and, as of January 1, 2021, is repealed, unless a later enacted statute, that becomes operative on or before January 1, 2021, deletes or extends the dates on which it becomes inoperative and is repealed.
(Amended by Stats. 2015, Ch. 17, Sec. 3. (AB 119) Effective June 24, 2015. Repealed as of January 1, 2021, by its own provisions. Note: Termination clause affects Article 7.6, commencing with Section 1324.20 (except Section 1324.29).)

ARTICLE 8. Management of Long-Term Health Care Facilities [1325 - 1335]
(Article 8 added by Stats. 1982, Ch. 1456, Sec. 2.)

1325.

The Legislature finds and declares that the transfer trauma which accompanies the abrupt and involuntary transfer of patients from one nursing home to another should be avoided when reasonable alternatives exist.

It is the intent of the Legislature in enacting this article to provide an alternative by establishing a system whereby the State Department of Health Services may apply for a court order appointing a receiver to temporarily operate a long-term health care facility. The receivership is not intended to punish a licensee or to replace attempts to secure cooperative action to protect the patients' health and security. The receivership is intended to protect the patients in the absence of other reasonably available alternatives.

The receiver may be appointed when a long-term health care facility is found to be in such condition that continued operation by the licensee, or his or her representative, presents a substantial probability or imminent danger of serious physical harm or death to the patients.

The receiver shall assume the operation of such a facility in order to either bring it into compliance with law and return it to the original licensee in accordance with standards set forth in this article, or facilitate a transfer of ownership to a new licensee. The receiver shall assure the orderly transfer of patients should the facility ultimately close.
(Amended by Stats. 1990, Ch. 1385, Sec. 1. Effective September 28, 1990.)

1325.5.

(a) It is the intent of the Legislature in enacting this section to empower the state department to take quick, effective action to protect the health and safety of residents of long-term health care facilities and to minimize the effects of transfer trauma that accompany the abrupt transfer of elderly and disabled residents.
(b) For purposes of this section, "temporary manager" means the person, corporation, or other entity, appointed temporarily by the state department as a substitute facility manager or administrator with authority to hire, terminate, or reassign staff, obligate facility funds, alter facility procedures, and manage the facility to correct deficiencies identified in the facility's operation.
(c) The director may appoint a temporary manager when any of the following circumstances exist:
(1) The residents of the long-term health care facility are in immediate danger of death or permanent injury by virtue of the failure of the facility to comply with federal or state requirements applicable to the operation of the facility.
(2) As a result of the change in the status of the license or operation of a long-term health care facility, the facility is required to comply with Section 1336.2, the facility fails to comply with Section 1336.2, and the state department has determined that the facility is unwilling or unable to meet the requirements of Section 1336.2.
(d) Upon appointment, the temporary manager shall take all necessary steps and make best efforts to eliminate immediate danger of death or permanent injury to residents or complete transfer of residents to alternative placements pursuant to Section 1336.2.
(e) (1) The appointment of a temporary manager shall become effective immediately and shall continue until any of the following events occurs:
(A) The temporary manager notifies the department, and the department verifies, that the facility meets state and, if applicable, federal standards for operation, and will be able to continue to maintain compliance with those standards after the termination of temporary management.
(B) A receiver is appointed under this article.
(C) The department approves a new management company.
(D) A new operator is licensed.
(E) The state department closes the facility, through an orderly transfer of the residents.
(F) A hearing or court order ends the temporary manager appointment.
(G) The appointment is terminated by the department or the temporary manager.
(2) The appointment of a temporary manager shall authorize the temporary manager to act pursuant to this section. The appointment shall be made pursuant to an agreement between the temporary manager and the state department that outlines the circumstances under which the temporary manager may expend funds. The temporary manager shall make no long-term capital investments to the facility without the permission of the state department. The state department shall provide the licensee and administrator with a statement of allegations at the time of appointment. Within 48 hours, the department shall provide the licensee and the administrator with a formal statement of cause and concerns. The statement of cause and concerns shall specify the factual and legal basis for the imposition of the temporary manager and shall be supported by the declaration of the director or the director's authorized designee. The statement of cause and concerns shall notify the licensee of the licensee's right to petition the Office of Administrative Hearings for a hearing to contest the appointment of the temporary manager and shall provide the licensee with a form and appropriate information for the licensee's use in requesting a hearing.
(f) (1) The licensee of a long-term health care facility may contest the appointment of the temporary manager by filing a petition for an order to terminate the appointment of the temporary manager with the Office of Administrative Hearings, within 60 days from the date of mailing of the statement of cause and concerns. On the same day as the petition is filed with the Office of Administrative Hearings, the licensee shall deliver a copy of the petition to the office of the director.
(2) Upon receipt of a petition of hearing, the Office of Administrative Hearings shall set a hearing date and time within five business days of the receipt of the petition. The office shall promptly notify the licensee and the state department of the date, time, and place of the hearing. The office shall assign the case to an administrative law judge. At the hearing, relevant evidence may be presented pursuant to Section 11513 of the Government Code. The administrative law judge shall issue a written decision on the petition within five business days of the conclusion of the hearing. The five-day time periods for holding the hearing and rendering a decision may be extended by the agreement of the parties.
(3) The administrative law judge shall uphold the appointment of the temporary manager if the state department proves, by a preponderance of the evidence, that the circumstances specified in subdivision (c) applied to the facility at the time of the appointment. The administrative law judge shall order the termination of the temporary manager if the burden of proof is not satisfied.
(g) The decision of the administrative law judge is subject to judicial review as provided in Section 1094.5 of the Code of Civil Procedure by the superior court sitting in the

county where the facility is located. This review may be requested by the licensee of the facility or the state department by filing a petition seeking relief from the order. The petition may also request the issuance of temporary injunctive relief pending the decision on the petition. The superior court shall hold a hearing within five business days of the filing of the petition and shall issue a decision on the petition within five days of the hearing. The state department may be represented by legal counsel within the state department for purposes of court proceedings authorized under this section.

(h) If the licensee of the long-term health care facility does not protest the appointment, it shall continue in accordance with subdivision (e).

(i) (1) If the licensee of the long-term health care facility petitions the Office of Administrative Hearings pursuant to subdivision (f), the appointment of the temporary manager by the director pursuant to this section shall continue until it is terminated by the administrative law judge or by the superior court, or it shall continue for 30 days from the date the administrative law judge or the superior court upholds the appointment of the temporary manager, whichever is earlier.

(2) At any time during the appointment of the temporary manager, the director may request an extension of the appointment by filing a petition for hearing with the Office of Administrative Hearings and serving a copy of the petition on the licensee. The office shall proceed as specified in paragraph (2) of subdivision (f). The administrative law judge may extend the appointment of the temporary manager as follows:

(A) Upon a showing by the state department that the conditions specified in subdivision (c) continue to exist, an additional 60 days.

(B) Upon a finding that the state department is seeking a receiver, until the state department has secured the services of a receiver pursuant to this article.

(3) The licensee or the state department may request review of the administrative law judge's decision on the extension as provided in subdivision (g).

(j) The temporary manager appointed pursuant to this section shall meet the following qualifications:

(1) Be qualified to oversee correction of deficiencies on the basis of experience and education.

(2) Not have been found guilty of misconduct by any licensing board.

(3) Have no financial ownership interest in the facility and have no member of his or her immediate family who has a financial ownership interest in the facility.

(4) Not currently serve, or within the past two years have served, as a member of the staff of the facility.

(5) Be acceptable to the facility.

(k) Payment of the temporary manager's salary or fee shall comply with the following requirements:

(1) Shall be paid directly by the facility while the temporary manager is assigned to that facility.

(2) Shall be equivalent to the sum of the following:

(A) The prevailing salary or fee paid by licensees for positions of the same type in the facility's geographic area.

(B) Additional costs that reasonably would have been incurred by the licensee if the licensee had been in an employment relationship.

(C) Any other reasonable costs incurred by the appointed temporary manager in furnishing services pursuant to this section.

(3) May exceed the amount specified in paragraph (2) if the department is otherwise unable to attract a qualified temporary manager.

(l) The state department may use funds from the Health Facilities Citation Penalties Account, pursuant to Section 1417.2, to operate the facility after all other facility revenues are exhausted.

(m) The state department shall adopt regulations for the administration of this section on or before December 31, 2001.

(Amended by Stats. 2001, Ch. 685, Sec. 7. Effective January 1, 2002.)

1326.

As used in this article, "long-term health care facility" means any skilled nursing facility, intermediate care facility, intermediate care facility/developmentally disabled, intermediate care facility/developmentally disabled habilitative, intermediate care facility/developmentally disabled-nursing, intermediate care facility/developmentally disabled-continuous nursing, or congregate living health facility licensed pursuant to this chapter.

(Amended by Stats. 2009, 4th Ex. Sess., Ch. 5, Sec. 7. Effective July 28, 2009.)

1327.

(a) Whenever circumstances exist indicating that continued management of a long-term health care facility by the current licensee would present a substantial probability or imminent danger of serious physical harm or death to the patients, or there exists in the facility a condition in substantial violation of this chapter or the rules and regulations adopted pursuant to this chapter, or the facility exhibits a pattern or practice of habitual violation of this chapter or the rules and regulations adopted pursuant thereto, or the facility is closing or intends to terminate operation as a licensed long-term health care facility and adequate arrangements for relocation of residents have not been made at least 30 days prior to the closing or termination, the director may petition the superior court for the county in which the long-term health care facility is located for an order appointing a receiver to temporarily operate the long-term health care facility in accordance with this article.

The petition shall allege the facts upon which the action is based and shall be supported by an affidavit of the director. A copy of the petition and affidavits, together with an order to appear and show cause why temporary authority to operate the long-term health care facility should not be vested in a receiver pursuant to this article, shall be delivered to the licensee, administrator, or a responsible person at the facility to the attention of the licensee and administrator. The order shall specify a hearing date, which shall be not less than five, nor more than 10, days following delivery of the petition and order upon the licensee, except that the court may shorten or lengthen the time upon a showing of just cause.

(b) If the director files a petition pursuant to subdivision (a) for appointment of a receiver to operate a long-term health care facility, in accordance with Section 564 of the Code of Civil Procedure, the director may also petition the court, in accordance with Section 527 of the Code of Civil Procedure, for an order appointing a temporary receiver. A temporary receiver appointed by the court pursuant to this subdivision shall serve until the court has made a final determination on the petition for appointment of a receiver filed pursuant to subdivision (a). A receiver appointed pursuant to this subdivision shall have the same powers and duties as a receiver would have if appointed pursuant to subdivision (a).

At the time of the hearing, the state department shall advise the licensee of the name of the proposed receiver. The receiver shall be a licensed nursing home administrator or other responsible person or entity, as determined by the court, from a list of qualified receivers established by the state department, with input from providers of long-term care and consumer representatives. The department shall consult with the Board of Nursing Home Administrators, in order to screen potential receivers who are licensed by the board, and to determine if they are administrators in good standing. Persons appearing on the list shall have experience in the delivery of health care services, and, if feasible, shall have experience with the operation of a long-term health care facility. The receivers shall have sufficient background and experience in management and finances to ensure compliance with orders issued by the court. The owner, licensee, or administrator shall not be appointed as the receiver unless authorized by the court.

If at the conclusion of the hearing, which may include oral testimony and cross-examination at the option of any party, the court determines that adequate grounds exist for the appointment of a receiver and that there is no other reasonably available remedy to protect the patients, the court may issue an order appointing a receiver to temporarily operate the long-term health care facility and enjoining the licensee from interfering with the receiver in the conduct of his or her duties. The court shall in any such proceedings make written findings of fact and conclusions of law, and shall require an appropriate bond to be filed by the receiver and paid for by the licensee. The bond shall be in an amount necessary to protect the licensee in the event of any failure on the part of the receiver to act in a reasonable manner. The bond requirement may be waived by the licensee.

The court may permit the licensee to participate in the continued operation of the facility during the pendency of any receivership ordered pursuant to this section and shall issue an order detailing the nature and scope of participation.

Failure of the licensee to appear at the hearing on the petition shall constitute an admission of all factual allegations contained in the petition for purposes of these proceedings only.

The licensee shall receive notice and a copy of the application each time the receiver applies to the court or the state department for instructions regarding his or her duties under the provisions of this article, when an accounting pursuant to Section 1330 is submitted, and when a report pursuant to Section 1332 or other report is submitted. The licensee shall have an opportunity to present objections or otherwise participate in any such proceeding.

(c) (1) The director may petition the superior court pursuant to this section for the county in which any health facility, as defined in subdivision (e), (g), or (h) of Section 1250, providing long-term care for persons with developmental disabilities is located, for an order appointing a temporary receiver to operate the facility for a maximum of 120 days in accordance with this article.

(2) The state department may provide onsite technical assistance to the receiver appointed pursuant to this subdivision, if requested by the receiver, to continue operation of the facility. The technical assistance may include, but need not be limited to, technical assistance regarding any of the following:

(A) Staff training and personnel management.

(B) Rate adjustment applications and appeals.

(C) Administrative practices and procedures.

(D) Fiscal management.

(E) Licensing regulations and review procedures.

(3) The state department shall notify the State Department of Developmental Services and the appropriate regional center, or centers, of the receivership action.

(4) When the director has determined that the facility specified in paragraph (1) presents a risk of abruptly closing, but the director determines that the situation does not require the filing of a petition with the court for an order appointing a receiver, the director may provide onsite technical assistance as specified in paragraph (2) to the operator of the facility if the operator requests the assistance.

(Amended by Stats. 1994, Ch. 1275, Sec. 56. Effective January 1, 1995.)

1327.1.

The state department shall investigate within 30 days of receipt of a complaint alleging that circumstances permitting a petition for receivership under Section 1327 exist in a long-term health care facility. The result of the investigation shall be documented by the state department in the facility file.

(Added by Stats. 1990, Ch. 940, Sec. 2.)

1327.2.

In the event that the state department proceeds with a receivership petition, the state department shall hold an informational meeting in the affected community for residents, family members, and interested parties.

(Added by Stats. 1990, Ch. 940, Sec. 3.)

1327.3.

Subdivision (b) of Section 1327 shall not be construed to prohibit the state department from including on its list of qualified receivers a consortium of community agencies that includes one or more licensed nursing home administrators, as long as the consortium is established as a legal entity.

The court may approve receivership arrangements where more than one individual shares receivership duties, as long as one licensed nursing home administrator or other responsible person or entity is the legally appointed receiver.

(Added by Stats. 1990, Ch. 940, Sec. 4.)

1327.5.

No person shall impede the operation of a receivership created under Section 1327. There shall be an automatic stay for a 60-day period subsequent to the appointment of a receiver, of any action that would interfere with the functioning of the facility, including, but not limited to, cancellation of insurance policies executed by the licensees, termination of utility services, attachments or set-offs of resident trust funds and working capital accounts and repossession of equipment in the facility.

(Added by Stats. 1987, Ch. 666, Sec. 1.5.)

1328.

(a) Notwithstanding any other provision of law, the receiver shall be liable only for damages resulting from gross negligence in the operation of the facility or intentional tortious acts.

(b) Notwithstanding any other provision of law, the State of California shall be liable only for damages resulting from negligence of the receiver in the operation of the facility.

(c) The licensee shall not be liable for any occurrences during the receivership except to the extent that the occurrences are the result of the licensee's conduct.

(Added by Stats. 1982, Ch. 1456, Sec. 2.)

1329.

(a) When a receiver is appointed, the licensee may, at the discretion of the court, be divested of possession and control of the facility in favor of the receiver. The receiver appointed pursuant to this article:

(1) May exercise those powers and shall perform those duties ordered by the court, in addition to other duties provided by statute.

(2) Shall operate the facility in a manner which assures safety and adequate health care for the residents.

(3) Shall have the same rights to possession of the building in which the facility is located, and of all goods and fixtures in the building at the time the petition for receivership is filed, as the licensee and administrator would have had if the receiver had not been appointed.

(4) May use the funds, building, fixtures, furnishings, and any accompanying consumable goods in the provision of care and services to residents and to any other persons receiving services from the facility at the time the petition for receivership was filed.

(5) Shall take title to all revenue coming to the facility in the name of the receiver who shall use it for the following purposes in descending order of priority:

(A) To pay wages to staff. The receiver shall have full power to hire, direct, manage, and discharge employees of the facility, subject to any contractual rights they may have. The receiver shall pay employees at the same rate of compensation, including benefits, that the employees would have received from the licensee.

(B) To preserve patient funds. The receiver shall be entitled to, and shall take, possession of all property or assets of residents which are in the possession of the licensee or operator of the facility. The receiver shall preserve all property, assets, and records of residents of which the receiver takes possession.

(C) To contract for outside services as may be needed for the operation of the long-term health care facility. Any contract for outside services in excess of three thousand dollars ($3,000) shall be approved by the court.

(D) To pay commercial creditors of the long-term health care facility. Except as provided in Section 1329.5, the receiver shall honor all leases, mortgages, and secured transactions affecting the building in which the facility is located and all goods and fixtures in the building of which the receiver has taken possession, but only to the extent of payments which, in the case of a rental agreement, are for the use of the property during the period of receivership, or which, in the case of a purchase agreement, come due during the period of receivership.

(E) To receive a salary, as approved by the court.

(F) To do all things necessary and proper to maintain and operate the facility in accordance with sound fiscal policies. The receiver shall take action as is reasonably necessary to protect or conserve the assets or property of which the receiver takes possession and may use such assets or property only in the performance of the powers and duties set out in this section and by order of the court.

(G) To ask the court for direction in the treatment of debts incurred prior to the appointment, where the licensee's debts appear extraordinary, of questionable validity, or unrelated to the normal and expected maintenance and operation of the facility, or where payment of the debts will interfere with the purposes of receivership.

(b) A person who is served with notice of an order of the court appointing a receiver and of the receiver's name and address shall be liable to pay the receiver, rather than the licensee, for any goods or services provided by the long-term health care facility after the date of the order. The receiver shall give a receipt for each payment and shall keep a copy of each receipt on file. The receiver shall deposit amounts received in a special account and shall use this account for all disbursements. Payment to the receiver pursuant to this subdivision shall discharge the obligation to the extent of the payment and shall not thereafter be the basis of a claim by the licensee or any other person. A resident may not be discharged nor may any contract or rights be forfeited or impaired, nor may any forfeiture be effected or liability increased, by reason of an omission to pay the licensee, operator, or other person a sum paid to the receiver pursuant to this subdivision.

(c) Nothing contained in this section shall be construed to suspend, during the temporary management by the receiver, any obligation of the licensee for payment of local, state, or federal taxes. No licensee may be held liable for acts or omissions of the receiver during the term of the temporary management.

(d) Upon petition of the receiver, the court may order immediate payment to the receiver for past services which have been rendered and billed, and the court may also order a sum not to exceed one month's advance payment to the receiver of any sums that will become payable under the Medi-Cal program.

(Amended by Stats. 1990, Ch. 1385, Sec. 3. Effective September 28, 1990.)

1329.5.

(a) A receiver may not be required to honor any lease, mortgage, or secured transaction entered into by the licensee of the facility and another party if the court finds that the agreement between the parties was entered into for a collusive, fraudulent purpose or that the agreement is unrelated to the operation of the facility.

Any lease, mortgage, or secured transaction or any agreement unrelated to the operation of the facility which the receiver is permitted to dishonor pursuant to this subdivision shall only be subject to nonpayment by the receiver for the duration of the receivership, and the dishonoring of the lease, mortgage, security interest, or other agreement, to this extent, by the receiver shall not relieve the owner or operator of the facility from any liability for the full amount due under the lease, mortgage, security interest, or other agreement.

(b) If the receiver is in possession of real estate or goods subject to a lease, mortgage, or security interest which the receiver is permitted to avoid pursuant to subdivision (a), and if the real estate or goods are necessary for the continued operation of the facility, the receiver may apply to the court to set a reasonable rent, price, or rate of interest to be paid by the receiver during the duration of the receivership. The court shall hold a hearing on this application within 15 days. The receiver shall send notice of the application to any known owner of the property involved at least 10 days prior to the hearing.

Payment by the receiver of the amount determined by the court to be reasonable is a defense to any action against the receiver for payment or possession of the goods or real estate, subject to the lease or mortgage, which is brought by any person who received the notice required by this subdivision. However, payment by the receiver of the amount determined by the court to be reasonable shall not relieve the owner or operator of the facility from any liability for the difference between the amount paid by the receiver and the amount due under the original lease, mortgage, or security interest.

(Amended by Stats. 1987, Ch. 1425, Sec. 3.)

1330.

A monthly accounting shall be made by the receiver to the state department of all moneys received and expended by the receiver on or before the 15th day of the following month or as ordered by the court, and the remainder of income over expenses for such month shall be returned to the licensee. A copy of the accounting shall be provided to the licensee. The licensee or owner of the long-term health care facility may petition the court for a determination as to the reasonableness of any expenditure made pursuant to paragraph (5) of subdivision (a) of Section 1329.

(Added by Stats. 1982, Ch. 1456, Sec. 2.)

1331.

(a) The receiver shall be appointed for an initial period of not more than six months. The initial six-month period may be extended for additional periods not exceeding six months, as determined by the court pursuant to this section. At the end of four months, the receiver shall report to the court on its assessment of the probability that the long-term health care facility will meet state standards for operation by the end of the initial six-month period and will continue to maintain compliance with those standards after termination of the receiver's management. If it appears that the facility cannot be brought into compliance with state standards within the initial six-month period, the court shall take appropriate action as follows:

(1) Extend the receiver's management for an additional six months if there is a substantial likelihood that the facility will meet state standards within that period and will maintain compliance with the standards after termination of the receiver's management. The receiver shall report to the court in writing upon the facility's progress at the end of six weeks of any extension ordered pursuant to this paragraph.

(2) Order the director to revoke or temporarily suspend, or both, the license pursuant to Section 1296 and extend the receiver's management for the period necessary to transfer patients in accordance with the transfer plan, but for not more than six months from the date of initial appointment of a receiver, or 14 days, whichever is greater. An extension of an additional six months may be granted if deemed necessary by the court.

(b) If it appears at the end of six weeks of an extension ordered pursuant to paragraph (1) of subdivision (a) that the facility cannot be brought into compliance with state standards for operation or that it will not maintain compliance with those standards after the receiver's management is terminated, the court shall take appropriate action as specified in paragraph (2) of subdivision (a).

(c) In evaluating the probability that a long-term health care facility will maintain compliance with state standards of operation after the termination of receiver management ordered by the court, the court shall consider at least the following factors:

(1) The duration, frequency, and severity of past violations in the facility.

(2) History of compliance in other long-term health care facilities operated by the proposed licensee.

(3) Efforts by the licensee to prevent and correct past violations.

(4) The financial ability of the licensee to operate in compliance with state standards.

(5) The recommendations and reports of the receiver.

(d) Management of a long-term health care facility operated by a receiver pursuant to this article shall not be returned to the licensee, to any person related to the licensee, or to any person who served as a member of the facility's staff or who was employed by the licensee prior to the appointment of the receiver unless both of the following conditions are met:

(1) The department believes that it would be in the best interests of the residents of the facility, requests that the court return the operation of the facility to the former licensee, and provides clear and convincing evidence to the court that it is in the best interests of the facility's residents to take that action.

(2) The court finds that the licensee has fully cooperated with the department in the appointment and ongoing activities of a receiver appointed pursuant to this section, and, if applicable, any temporary manager appointed pursuant to Section 1325.5.

(e) The owner of the facility may at any time sell, lease, or close the facility, subject to the following provisions:

(1) If the owner closes the facility, or the sale or lease results in the closure of the facility, the court shall determine if a transfer plan is necessary. If the court so determines, the court shall adopt and implement a transfer plan of not more than 30 days.

(2) If the licensee proposes to sell or lease the facility and the facility will continue to operate as a long-term health care facility, the court and the state department shall reevaluate any proposed transfer plan. If the court and the state department determine that the sale or lease of the facility will result in compliance with licensing standards, the transfer plan and the receivership shall, subject to those conditions that the court may impose and enforce, be terminated upon the effective date of the sale or lease.

(Amended by Stats. 2001, Ch. 685, Sec. 8. Effective January 1, 2002.)

1332.

The salary of the receiver shall be set by the court commensurate with long-term health care facility industry standards, giving due consideration to the difficulty of the duties undertaken, and shall be paid from the revenue coming to the facility. If the revenue is insufficient to pay the salary in addition to other expenses of the operating facility, the receiver's salary shall be paid from the General Fund.

(Amended by Stats. 1987, Ch. 666, Sec. 4.)

1333.

(a) To the extent state funds are advanced for the salary of the receiver or for other expenses in connection with the receivership, as limited by subdivision (d) of Section 1329, the state shall be reimbursed from the revenues accruing to the facility or to the licensee or an entity related to the licensee. Any reimbursement received by the state shall be redeposited in the account from which the state funds were advanced. If the revenues are insufficient to reimburse the state, the unreimbursed amount shall constitute a lien upon the assets of the facility or the proceeds from the sale thereof. The lien shall not attach to the interests of a lessor, unless the lessor is operating the facility.

(b) For purposes of this section, "entity related to the licensee" means an entity, other than a natural person, of which the licensee is a subsidiary or an entity in which any person who was obligated to disclose information under Section 1267.5 possesses an interest that would also require disclosure pursuant to Section 1267.5.

(Amended by Stats. 2000, Ch. 451, Sec. 12. Effective January 1, 2001.)

1334.

(a) Nothing in this article shall impair the right of the owner of a long-term health care facility to dispose of his or her property interests in the facility, but any facility operated by a receiver pursuant to this article shall remain subject to such administration until terminated by the court. The termination shall be promptly effectuated, provided that the interests of the patients have been safeguarded as determined by the court.

(b) Nothing in this article shall limit the power of the court to appoint a receiver under any other applicable provision of law or to order any other remedy available under law.

(Added by Stats. 1982, Ch. 1456, Sec. 2.)

1335.

The state department shall adopt regulations for the administration of this article. Nothing in this article shall impair the authority of the state department to temporarily suspend licenses under Section 1296 or to reach a voluntary agreement with the licensee for alternate management of a long-term health care facility. Nothing in this article shall authorize the state department to interfere in any labor dispute.

(Added by Stats. 1982, Ch. 1456, Sec. 2.)

ARTICLE 8.5. Long-Term Care Facility Advance Notification Requirements [1336 - 1336.4]

(Article 8.5 added by Stats. 1983, Ch. 799, Sec. 1.)

1336.

(a) Notwithstanding any other law, a long-term health care facility shall give written notice to the affected residents or to the guardians of the affected residents at least 60 days prior to any change in the status of the license or in the operation of the facility resulting in the inability of the facility to care for its residents.

(b) If residents' placement problems are encountered that cannot be satisfactorily resolved within this 60-day period, the State Department of Public Health and the health facility shall agree on an extension which shall not exceed an additional 60 days.

(c) The facility shall provide an appropriate team of professional staff to assist residents and families in obtaining alternative placement. The facility shall hold a community meeting for residents and their families no later than 30 days after providing the written notice pursuant to subdivision (a). The facility shall provide notice of the meeting to residents and their families and to local health authorities. The facility shall also provide notice of the community meeting to the State Department of Public Health as part of the proposed relocation plan submitted to the department pursuant to paragraph (1) of subdivision (g) of Section 1336.2.

(d) This section shall not apply to actions initiated by the State Department of Public Health to suspend or revoke the license.

(Amended by Stats. 2017, Ch. 185, Sec. 1. (AB 275) Effective January 1, 2018.)

1336.1.

(a) After notifying its affected residents, the facility shall, in response to inquiries made by prospective residents or their representatives, include notification of the change in the status of the license or the operation of the facility.

(b) The facility shall give written notification to the office of the State Long-Term Care Ombudsman of the change in the status of the license or the operation of the facility, including a voluntary closure and the planned date of closure, at least 60 days prior to any change in the status of the license or the operation of the facility.

(c) The facility shall give written notification to the State Department of Health Care Services and any health plan of an affected resident of the change in the status of the license or the operation of the facility, including a voluntary closure and the planned date of closure, at least 60 days prior to any change in the status of the license or the operation of the facility. This notification shall also include the names of residents that are covered by Medi-Cal or by the specific health plan.

(Amended by Stats. 2017, Ch. 185, Sec. 2. (AB 275) Effective January 1, 2018.)

1336.2.

(a) Before residents are transferred due to any change in the status of the license or operation of a facility, including a facility closure or voluntary or involuntary termination of a facility's Medi-Cal or Medicare certification, the facility shall take reasonable steps to transfer affected residents safely and minimize possible transfer trauma by, at a minimum, doing all of the following:

(1) Be responsible for ensuring that the resident's attending physician or the facility medical director, if the resident does not have an attending physician, completes the medical assessment of the resident's condition and susceptibility to adverse health consequences, including psychosocial effects, prior to written notice of transfer being given to the resident. The assessment shall not be considered complete unless it provides, in accordance with these assessments, recommendations for counseling, followup visits, and other recommended services, by designated health professionals, and for preventing or ameliorating potential adverse health consequences in the event of transfer.

(2) Be responsible for ensuring that a licensed marriage and family therapist, a licensed clinical social worker, a licensed psychologist, a licensed psychiatrist, or a licensed professional clinical counselor and the facility nursing staff complete an assessment of the social and physical functioning of the resident based on the relevant portions of the minimum data set, as described in Section 14110.15 of the Welfare and Institutions Code, before written notice of transfer is given to the resident. The assessment shall not be considered complete unless it provides recommendations for preventing or ameliorating potential adverse health consequences in the event of transfer. The assessment may be amended because of a change in the resident's health care needs. The assessment shall also include a recommendation for the type of facility that would best meet the resident's needs.

(3) (A) Be responsible for evaluating the relocation needs of the resident including proximity to the resident's representative and determine the most appropriate and available type of future care and services for the resident before written notice of transfer is given to the resident or the resident's representative. The health facility shall discuss the evaluation and medical assessment with the resident or the resident's representative and make the evaluation and assessment part of the medical records for transfer.

(B) If the resident or resident's representative chooses to make a transfer prior to completion of assessments, the facility shall inform the resident or the resident's representative, in writing, of the importance of obtaining the assessments and followup consultation.

(4) At least 60 days in advance of the transfer, inform the resident or the resident's representative of alternative facilities that are available and adequate to meet resident and family needs.

(5) Arrange for appropriate future medical care and services, unless the resident or resident's representative has otherwise made these arrangements. This requirement does not obligate a facility to pay for future care and services.

(b) The facility shall provide an appropriate team of professional staff to perform the services required in subdivision (a).

(c) The facility shall also give written notice to affected residents or their representatives, advising them of the requirements in subdivision (a) at least 60 days in advance of transfer. If a facility is required to give written notice pursuant to Section 1336, then the notice shall advise the affected resident or resident's representative of the requirements in subdivision (a). If the transfer is made pursuant to subdivision (g), the notice shall include notification to the resident or resident's representative that the transfer plan is available to the resident or resident's representative free of charge upon request.

(d) In the event of a temporary suspension of a facility's license pursuant to Section 1296, the 60-day notice requirement in subdivision (c) shall not apply, but the facility shall provide the relocation services required in subdivision (a) unless the State Department of Public Health provides the services pursuant to subdivision (f).

(e) The State Department of Public Health may make available assistance for the placement of hard-to-place residents based on its determination of the benefit and necessity of that assistance. A hard-to-place resident is a resident whose level of care, physical malady, or behavioral management needs are substantially beyond the norm.

(f) The State Department of Public Health may provide, or arrange for the provision of, necessary relocation services at a facility, including medical assessments, counseling, and placement of residents, if it determines that these services are needed promptly to prevent adverse health consequences to residents, and the facility refuses, or does not have adequate staffing, to provide the services. In these cases, the facility or the licensee shall reimburse the State Department of Public Health for the cost of providing the relocation services. The State Department of Public Health's participation shall not relieve the facility of any responsibility under this section. If the State Department of Public Health does not provide or arrange for the provision of the necessary relocation services, and the facility refuses to provide the relocation services required in subdivision (a), then the State Department of Public Health shall request that the Attorney General's office or the local district attorney's office seek injunctive relief and damages in the same manner as provided for in Chapter 5 (commencing with Section 17200) of Part 2 of Division 7 of the Business and Professions Code.

(g) (1) If 10 or more residents are likely to be transferred due to any voluntary or involuntary change in the status of the license or operation of a facility, including a facility closure or voluntary or involuntary termination of a facility's Medi-Cal or Medicare certification, the facility shall submit a proposed relocation plan for the affected residents to the State Department of Public Health for approval at least 30 days prior to the written transfer notification given to any resident or resident's representative. The proposed relocation plan shall provide for implementation of the relocation services in subdivision (a) and shall describe the availability of beds in the area for residents to be transferred, the proposed discharge process, and the staffing available to assist in the transfers. The proposed relocation plan shall also include, but not be limited to, all of the following information:

(A) The number of residents affected by the proposed closure.

(B) The number of residents who do not have a legal representative and do not have the capacity to make decisions for themselves as described in Section 1418.8.

(C) Attestation that each resident will undergo a medical assessment pursuant to paragraph (1) of subdivision (a) before being relocated.

(D) The availability of alternative skilled nursing facility beds or other available long-term care beds within the community.

(E) The reason for the proposed closure.

(F) The actions the facility is taking to transfer affected residents safely and minimize possible transfer trauma.

(2) The proposed relocation plan shall become effective upon the date the State Department of Public Health grants its approval. The State Department of Public Health shall base its approval of a proposed relocation plan on the standards specified in this section, including, but not limited to, its determination that the plan provides adequate protections to minimize transfer trauma for residents. The State Department of Public Health shall promptly either approve or reject the proposed relocation plan within 14 working days of receipt from the facility. If the State Department of Public Health rejects the proposed relocation plan, the facility may resubmit amended proposed relocation plans, each of which the State Department of Public Health shall promptly either approve or reject within 14 working days of receipt from the facility. Until one proposed relocation plan has been approved by the State Department of Public Health, and until the facility complies with the requirements in subdivision (a), the facility may not issue a notice of transfer. The facility shall submit the proposed relocation plan to the local long-term care ombudsperson at the same time the plan is submitted to the State Department of Public Health.

(h) The resident shall have the right to remain in the facility for up to 60 days after the approved written notice of the facility's intent to transfer the resident if an appropriate placement based on the relocation assessment and relocation recommendations has not been made. The facility shall be required to maintain an appropriate level of staffing in order to ensure the well-being of all the residents as they continue to reside in the facility. The State Department of Public Health shall monitor the facility's staging of transfers, and, if it determines that the facility's staging of placements is causing a detrimental impact on those residents being transferred, then the State Department of Public Health shall limit the number of residents being transferred per day until it determines when it is safe to increase the numbers.

(i) Nothing in this section shall be construed to prohibit a facility from withdrawing a closure date or resident notification prior to any resident being relocated.

(Amended by Stats. 2017, Ch. 185, Sec. 3. (AB 275) Effective January 1, 2018.)
1336.3.

(a) In the event of an emergency, such as earthquake, fire, or flood that threatens the safety or welfare of the residents in a facility, the facility shall do all of the following:

(1) Notify, as soon as possible, family members, guardians of residents, the State Department of Public Health, and the ombudsperson for that facility of the emergency and the steps that the facility plans to take for the welfare of the residents.

(2) Provide the services set forth in subdivision (a) of Section 1336.2 if further relocation of a resident is necessary.

(3) Undertake prompt medical assessment of, and provide counseling as needed to, residents whose further relocation is not necessary but who have suffered or may suffer adverse health consequences due to the emergency or sudden transfer.

(b) (1) Each facility shall adopt a written emergency preparedness plan and shall make that plan available to the State Department of Public Health upon request. The plan shall comply with the requirements in this section and the State Department of Public Health's Contingency Plan for Licensed Facilities. The facility, as part of its emergency preparedness planning, shall seek to enter into reciprocal or other agreements with nearby facilities and hospitals to provide temporary care for residents in the event of an emergency. The facility shall report to the State Department of Public Health the name of any facility or hospital that fails or refuses to enter into such agreements and the stated reason for that failure or refusal.

(2) Section 1336.2 does not apply in the event of transfers made pursuant to an emergency preparedness plan. In any event, however, the facility shall provide the notice and services described in subdivisions (a) to (c), inclusive, of Section 1336.2.

(Amended by Stats. 2018, Ch. 92, Sec. 130. (SB 1289) Effective January 1, 2019.)
1336.4.

Failure to comply with the requirements in Sections 1336 to 1336.3, inclusive, shall be subject to issuance of citations and imposition of civil penalties pursuant to Chapter 2.4 (commencing with Section 1417), and Sections 72701 and following of the California Administrative Code.

(Added by Stats. 1987, Ch. 1251, Sec. 3.)

ARTICLE 9. Training Programs in Skilled Nursing and Intermediate Care Facilities [1337 - 1338.5]

(Article 9 added by Stats. 1978, Ch. 351.)
1337.

(a) The Legislature finds that the quality of patient care in skilled nursing and intermediate care facilities is dependent upon the competence of the personnel who staff its facilities. The Legislature further finds that direct patient care in skilled nursing and intermediate care facilities is currently rendered largely by certified nurse assistants. To assure the availability of trained personnel in skilled nursing and intermediate care facilities, the Legislature intends that all such facilities in this state participate in approved training programs established under this article. This article shall not apply to intermediate care facilities/developmentally disabled habilitative, intermediate care facility/developmentally disabled-nursing, and intermediate care facility/developmentally disabled-continuous nursing which have staff training programs approved by the State Department of Developmental Services, general acute care hospitals, acute psychiatric hospitals, or special hospitals.

(b) The requirement that certified nurse assistants obtain a criminal record clearance upon certification and biannually thereafter shall apply regardless of the setting in which the certified nurse assistant is employed.

(c) The department shall develop procedures to ensure that certified nurse assistants employed by intermediate care facilities for the developmentally disabled/habilitative and intermediate care facilities for the developmentally disabled/nursing shall not be required to obtain multiple criminal record clearances.

(d) For the purpose of this article:

(1) "Nurse assistant" means any unlicensed aide, assistant, or orderly, who performs nursing services directed at the safety, comfort, personal hygiene, or protection of patients in a skilled nursing or intermediate care facility.

(2) "Approved training program" means a program for the training of nurse assistants that meets the criteria established and approved under this chapter.

(3) "Certified nurse assistant" means any person who holds himself or herself out as a certified nurse assistant and who, for compensation, performs basic patient care services directed at the safety, comfort, personal hygiene, and protection of patients, and is certified as having completed the requirements of this article. These services shall not include any services which may only be performed by a licensed person and otherwise shall be performed under the supervision of a registered nurse, as defined in Section 2725 of the Business and Professions Code, or a licensed vocational nurse, as defined in Section 2859 of the Business and Professions Code.

(4) "State department" means the State Department of Public Health.

(Amended by Stats. 2009, 4th Ex. Sess., Ch. 5, Sec. 8. Effective July 28, 2009.)
1337.1.

A skilled nursing facility or intermediate care facility shall adopt an approved training program that meets standards established by the department. The approved training program shall consist of at least all of the following:

(a) An orientation program to be given to newly employed nurse assistants prior to providing direct patient care in skilled nursing facility or intermediate care facilities.

(b) (1) A precertification training program consisting of at least 60 classroom hours of training on basic nursing skills, patient safety and rights, the social and psychological problems of patients, and resident abuse prevention, recognition, and reporting pursuant to subdivision (e). The 60 classroom hours of training may be conducted within a skilled nursing facility or intermediate care facility or in an educational institution or agency. A skilled nursing facility or intermediate care facility may conduct the 60 classroom hours of training in an online or distance learning course format, as approved by the department.

(2) In addition to the 60 classroom hours of training required under paragraph (1), the precertification training program shall consist of at least 100 hours of supervised and on-the-job training clinical practice. The 100 hours may consist of normal employment as a nurse assistant under the supervision of either the director of nurse training or a licensed nurse qualified to provide nurse assistant training who has no other assigned duties while providing the training.

(3) At least two hours of the 60 hours of classroom training shall address the special needs of persons with developmental and mental disorders, including intellectual disability, cerebral palsy, epilepsy, dementia, Parkinson's disease, and mental illness. At least two hours of the 60 hours of classroom training shall address the special needs of persons with Alzheimer's disease and related dementias.

(4) At least four hours of the 100 hours of supervised clinical training shall address the special needs of persons with developmental and mental disorders, including intellectual disability, cerebral palsy, epilepsy, Alzheimer's disease and related dementias, and Parkinson's disease.

(5) In a precertification training program subject to this subdivision, credit shall be given for the training received in an approved precertification training program adopted by another skilled nursing facility or intermediate care facility.

(6) This subdivision shall not apply to a skilled nursing facility or intermediate care facility that demonstrates to the department that it employs only nurse assistants with a valid certification.

(c) Continuing in-service training to ensure continuing competency in existing and new nursing skills.

(d) Each facility shall consider including training regarding the characteristics and method of assessment and treatment of acquired immune deficiency syndrome (AIDS).

(e) (1) The approved training program shall include, within the 60 hours of classroom training, a minimum of six hours of instruction on preventing, recognizing, and reporting instances of resident abuse utilizing those courses developed pursuant to Section 13823.93 of the Penal Code, and a minimum of one hour of instruction on preventing, recognizing, and reporting residents' rights violations.

(2) A minimum of four hours of instruction on preventing, recognizing, and reporting instances of resident abuse, including instruction on preventing, recognizing, and reporting residents' rights violations, shall be included within the total minimum hours of continuing education or in-service training required and in effect for certified nurse assistants.

(Amended by Stats. 2018, Ch. 769, Sec. 2. (AB 2850) Effective January 1, 2019.)

1337.15.

(a) A person who provides instruction or training, at a skilled nursing facility or intermediate care facility or in an educational institution, as part of a certified nurse assistant precertification training program described in Section 1337.1 or 1337.3 may be any licensed vocational nurse or registered nurse with no less than two years of nursing experience, of which no less than one year is in providing care and services to chronically ill or elderly patients in an acute care hospital, skilled nursing facility, intermediate care facility, home care, hospice care, or other long-term care setting.

(b) Notwithstanding any other law, a person described in subdivision (a) shall not be required to hold a teaching credential to provide instruction as part of a certified nurse assistant precertification training program described in Section 1337.1 or 1337.3.

(Added by Stats. 2018, Ch. 769, Sec. 3. (AB 2850) Effective January 1, 2019.)

1337.16.

(a) An online or distance learning nurse assistant training program shall comply with all of the following requirements:

(1) Provide online instruction in which the trainees and the approved instructor are online at the same or similar times and which allows them to use real-time collaborative software that combines audio, video, file sharing, or any other forms of approved interaction and communication.

(2) Require the use of a personal identification number or personal identification information that confirms the identity of the trainees and instructors, including, but not limited to, having trainees sign an affidavit attesting under penalty of perjury to their identity while completing the program.

(3) Provide safeguards to protect personal information.

(4) Include policies and procedures to ensure that instructors are accessible to trainees outside of the normal instruction times.

(5) Include policies and procedures for equipment failures, student absences, and completing assignments past original deadlines.

(6) Provide a clear explanation on its Internet Web site of all technology requirements to participate and complete the program.

(7) Provide the department with statistics about the performance of trainees in the program, including, but not limited to, exam pass rate and the rate at which trainees repeat each module of the program, and any other information requested by the department regarding trainee participation in and completion of the program.

(b) In addition to the requirements set forth in subdivision (a), an online or distance learning nurse assistant training program shall meet the same standards as a traditional, classroom-based program, and comply with any other standard established by the department for online or distance learning nurse assistant training programs. Notwithstanding any other law, the department may, without taking any regulatory actions pursuant to Chapter 3.5 (commencing with Section 11340) of Part 1 of Division 3 of Title 2 of the Government Code, implement, interpret, or make specific this section by means of an All Facilities Letter (AFL) or similar instruction.

(c) As a condition of approval by the department, an online or distance learning nurse assistant training program shall provide the department with access rights to the program for the purposes of verifying that program complies with all requirements and allowing the department to monitor online or distance learning sessions.

(Added by Stats. 2018, Ch. 769, Sec. 4. (AB 2850) Effective January 1, 2019.)

1337.2.

(a) An applicant for certification as a certified nurse assistant shall comply with each of the following:

(1) Be at least 16 years of age.

(2) Have successfully completed a training program approved by the department, which includes an examination to test the applicant's knowledge and skills related to basic patient care services.

(3) Obtain a criminal record clearance pursuant to Section 1338.5.

(b) (1) No later than July 1, 2019, the department shall require the applicant to provide either the individual taxpayer identification number or social security number for purposes of applying for a certificate or the renewal of a certificate.

(2) If the department utilizes a national examination to issue a certificate, and if a reciprocity agreement or comity exists between the State of California and the state requesting release of the individual taxpayer identification number or social security number, any deputy, agent, clerk, officer, or employee of the department may release an individual's taxpayer identification number or social security number to an examination or certifying entity, only for the purpose of verification of certification or examination status.

(3) The individual taxpayer identification or the social security number shall serve to establish the identification of persons affected by state tax laws and for purposes of establishing compliance with subsection (a) of Section 666 of Title 42 of the United States Code, Section 60.15 of Title 45 of the Code of Federal Regulations, Section 17520 of the Family Code, and Section 11105 of the Penal Code, and to that end, the information furnished pursuant to this section shall be used exclusively for those purposes.

(4) The department shall not do either of the following:

(A) Require an applicant to disclose citizenship status or immigration status for purposes of the application or renewal of a certificate.

(B) Deny licensure to an otherwise qualified and eligible applicant based solely on his or her citizenship status or immigration status.

(c) The state department may establish procedures for issuing certificates which recognize certification programs in other states and countries.

(d) Upon written application, criminal record clearance pursuant to Section 1338.5, and documentation of passing an appropriate competency examination, the state department may issue a certificate to any applicant who possesses a valid state license as either a licensed vocational nurse or a registered nurse issued by any other state or foreign country, and who, in the opinion of the state department, has the qualifications specified in this article.

(e) Upon written application, criminal record clearance pursuant to Section 1338.5, and documentation of passing an appropriate examination, the state department may issue a certificate to any applicant who has completed the fundamentals of nursing courses in a school for registered nurses, approved by the Board of Registered Nursing, or in a school for licensed vocational nurses, approved by the Board of Vocational Nurse and Psychiatric Technician Examiners, which are substantially equivalent to the certification training program specified in this article.

(f) Every person certified as a nurse assistant under this article may be known as a "certified nurse assistant" and may place the letters CNA after his or her name when working in a licensed health facility. An individual working independently, providing personal care services, may not advertise or represent himself or herself as a certified nurse assistant.

(g) Any person holding a nurse assistant certificate issued by the state department prior to January 1, 1988, may continue to hold himself or herself out as a certified nurse assistant until January 1, 1991. Thereafter, it shall be unlawful for any person not certified under this article to hold himself or herself out to be a certified nurse assistant. Any person willfully making any false representation as being a certified nurse assistant is guilty of a misdemeanor.

(h) Any person who violates this article is guilty of a misdemeanor and, upon a conviction thereof, shall be punished by imprisonment in the county jail for not more than 180 days, or by a fine of not less than twenty dollars ($20) nor more than one thousand dollars ($1,000), or by both such fine and imprisonment.

(Amended by Stats. 2018, Ch. 838, Sec. 8. (SB 695) Effective January 1, 2019.)

1337.3.

(a) The department shall prepare and maintain a list of approved training programs for nurse assistant certification. The list shall include training programs conducted by skilled nursing facilities or intermediate care facilities, as well as local agencies and education programs. In addition, the list shall include information on whether a training center is currently training nurse assistants, their competency test pass rates, and the number of nurse assistants they have trained. Clinical portions of the training programs may be obtained as on-the-job training, supervised by a qualified director of staff development or licensed nurse.

(b) It shall be the duty of the department to inspect a representative sample of training programs. The department shall protect consumers and students in any training program against fraud, misrepresentation, or other practices that may result in improper or excessive payment of funds paid for training programs. In evaluating a training center's training program, the department shall examine each training center's trainees' competency test passage rate, and require each program to maintain an average 60 percent test score passage rate to maintain its participation in the program. The average test score passage rate shall be calculated over a two-year period. If the department determines that a training program is not complying with regulations or is not meeting the competency passage rate requirements, notice thereof in writing shall be immediately given to the program. If the program has not been brought into compliance within a reasonable time, the program may be removed from the approved list and notice thereof in writing given to it. Programs removed under this article shall be afforded an opportunity to request reinstatement of program approval at any time. The department's district offices shall inspect facility-based centers as part of their annual survey.

(c) Notwithstanding Section 1337.1, the approved training program shall consist of at least the following:

(1) A 16-hour orientation program to be given to newly employed nurse assistants prior to providing direct patient care, and consistent with federal training requirements for facilities participating in the Medicare or Medicaid programs.

(2) (A) A precertification training program consisting of at least 60 classroom hours of training on basic nursing skills, patient safety and rights, the social and psychological problems of patients, and elder abuse recognition and reporting pursuant to subdivision (e) of Section 1337.1. The 60 classroom hours of training may be conducted within a skilled nursing facility, an intermediate care facility, or an educational institution or agency. A health facility, educational institution, or local agency may conduct the 60 classroom hours of training in an online or distance learning course format, as approved by the department.

(B) In addition to the 60 classroom hours of training required under subparagraph (A), the precertification program shall also consist of 100 hours of supervised and on-the-job training clinical practice. The 100 hours may consist of normal employment as a nurse assistant under the supervision of either the director of staff development or a licensed nurse qualified to provide nurse assistant training who has no other assigned duties while providing the training.

(3) At least two hours of the 60 hours of classroom training and at least four hours of the 100 hours of the supervised clinical training shall address the special needs of persons with developmental and mental disorders, including intellectual disability, Alzheimer's disease, cerebral palsy, epilepsy, dementia, Parkinson's disease, and mental illness.

(d) The department, in consultation with the State Department of Education and other appropriate organizations, shall develop criteria for approving training programs, that includes program content for orientation, training, inservice and the examination for testing knowledge and skills related to basic patient care services and shall develop a plan that identifies and encourages career ladder opportunities for certified nurse assistants. This group shall also recommend, and the department shall adopt, regulation changes necessary to provide for patient care when facilities utilize noncertified nurse assistants who are performing direct patient care. The requirements of this subdivision shall be established by January 1, 1989.

(e) On or before January 1, 2004, the department, in consultation with the State Department of Education, the American Red Cross, and other appropriate organizations, shall do the following:

(1) Review the current examination for approved training programs for certified nurse assistants to ensure the accurate assessment of whether a nurse assistant has obtained the required knowledge and skills related to basic patient care services.

(2) Develop a plan that identifies and encourages career ladder opportunities for certified nurse assistants, including the application of on-the-job postcertification hours to educational credits.

(f) A skilled nursing facility or intermediate care facility shall determine the number of specific clinical hours within each module identified by the department required to meet the requirements of subdivision (d), subject to subdivisions (b) and (c). The facility shall consider the specific hours recommended by the state department when adopting the precertification training program required by this chapter.

(g) This article shall not apply to a program conducted by any church or denomination for the purpose of training the adherents of the church or denomination in the care of the sick in accordance with its religious tenets.

(h) The Chancellor of the California Community Colleges shall provide to the department a standard process for approval of college credit. The department shall make this information available to all training programs in the state.

(i) An online or distance learning nurse assistant training program shall meet the same standards as a traditional, classroom-based program.

(j) An online nurse assistant training program shall contract with a licensed skilled nursing facility or intermediate care facility for the purpose of coordinating and completing the clinical portion of the nurse assistant training program.

(Amended by Stats. 2018, Ch. 769, Sec. 5. (AB 2850) Effective January 1, 2019.)

1337.4.

Every skilled nursing or intermediate care facility shall designate a licensed nurse as a director of staff development who shall be responsible for the management of the approved training program.

(Amended by Stats. 1988, Ch. 825, Sec. 3.)

1337.5.

(a) Approved training programs shall be conducted during the normal working hours of the nurse assistant unless the nurse assistant receives at least the normal hourly wage for any additional time spent in the training program.

(b) On or after September 1, 1978, only the following persons may be employed by a skilled nursing facility or intermediate care facility as a nurse assistant:

(1) A certified nurse assistant.

(2) A nurse assistant hired on a temporary basis who has been employed less than a maximum total of three months in skilled nursing facilities or intermediate care facilities, including the current period of employment.

(3) A nurse assistant who, within three months of the date of employment, is enrolled in an approved certification training program which requires completion not more than six months from the date of employment; provided, that the employing facility may apply to the state department for an extension of the deadline under this paragraph for enrollment in a certification training program if the facility has a contract to obtain the training from

an educational institution, approved by the facility, which operates on a semester basis and cannot enroll nursing assistant students except at semester intervals; and the delayed enrollment will not postpone completion of certification training beyond nine months from the date of employment.

(Added by renumbering Section 1337.9 by Stats. 1987, Ch. 1177, Sec. 11.)

1337.6.

(a) Certificates issued under this article shall be renewed every two years and renewal shall be conditional upon the occurrence of all of the following:

(1) The certificate holder submitting documentation of completion of 48 hours of in-service training every two years obtained through an approved training program or taught by a director of staff development for a licensed skilled nursing or intermediate care facility that has been approved by the department, or by individuals or programs approved by the department. At least 12 of the 48 hours of in-service training shall be completed in each of the two years. Twenty-four of the 48 hours of in-service training may be obtained through an online computer training program approved by the Licensing and Certification Division of the department.

(2) (A) A vendor of online programs for continuing education shall ensure that each online course contains all of the following:

(i) An interactive portion where the participants receive feedback, through online communication, based on input from the participant.

(ii) Required use of a personal identification number or personal identification information to confirm the identity of the participant.

(iii) A final screen displaying a printable statement, to be signed by the participant, certifying that the identified participant completed the course. The vendor shall obtain a copy of the final screen statement with the original signature of the participant prior to the issuance of a certificate of completion. The signed statement of completion shall be maintained by the vendor for a period of three years and shall be made available to the department upon demand.

(B) The department may approve online programs for continuing education that do not meet the requirements of subparagraph (A) if the vendor demonstrates to the department's satisfaction that, through advanced technology, the course and the course delivery meet the other requirements of this section.

(3) The certificate holder obtaining a criminal record clearance.

(b) Certificates issued under this article shall expire on the certificate holder's birthday.

(c) To renew an unexpired certificate, the certificate holder shall, on or before the certificate expiration date, apply for renewal on a form provided by the department and submit documentation of the required in-service training.

(d) The department shall give written notice to a certificate holder 90 days in advance of the renewal date and, 90 days in advance of the expiration of the fourth year that a renewal application has not been submitted, and shall give written notice informing the certificate holder, in general terms, of the provisions of this article. Nonreceipt of the renewal notice does not relieve the certificate holder of the obligation to make a timely renewal. Failure to make a timely renewal shall result in expiration of the certificate.

(e) Except as otherwise provided in this article, an expired certificate may be renewed at any time within two years after its expiration on the filing of an application for renewal on a form prescribed by the department and documentation of the required in-service education.

Renewal under this article shall be effective on the date on which the application is filed. If so renewed, the certificate shall continue in effect until the date provided for in this article, when it shall expire if it is not again renewed.

(f) If a certified nurse assistant applies for renewal more than two years after the expiration, the certified nurse assistant shall complete an approved 75-hour competency evaluation training program and competency evaluation program. A suspended certificate is subject to expiration and shall be renewed as provided in this article, but this renewal does not entitle the certificate holder, while the certificate remains suspended, and, until it is reinstated, to engage in the certified activity, or in any other activity or conduct in violation of the order or judgment by which the certificate was suspended.

(g) A revoked certificate is subject to expiration as provided in this article, but it cannot be renewed.

(h) Except as provided in subdivision (i), a certificate that is not renewed within four years after its expiration cannot be renewed, restored, reissued, or reinstated except upon completion of a certification program unless deemed otherwise by the department if both of the following conditions are met:

(1) No fact, circumstance, or condition exists that, if the certificate was issued, would justify its revocation or suspension.

(2) The person takes and passes any examination that may be required of an applicant for a new certificate at that time, that shall be given by an approved provider of a certification training program.

(i) A certified nurse assistant whose certificate has expired after two years may have his or her certificate renewed if he or she completes 75 hours in an approved competency evaluation training program, passes a competency test, and obtains a criminal background clearance prior to the renewal. The department shall develop a training program for these previously certified individuals.

(j) Certificate holders shall notify the department within 60 days of any change of address. Any notice sent by the department shall be effective if mailed to the current address filed with the department.

(k) Certificate holders that have been certified as both nurse assistants pursuant to this article and home health aides pursuant to Chapter 8 (commencing with Section 1725) of Division 2 shall renew their certificates at the same time on one application.

(Amended by Stats. 2006, Ch. 74, Sec. 12. Effective July 12, 2006.)

1337.8.
(a) The state department shall investigate complaints concerning misconduct by certified nurse assistants and may take disciplinary action pursuant to Section 1337.9.
(b) The state department shall maintain a registry that includes the certification status of all certified nurse assistants, including the status of any proposed or completed disciplinary actions.
(c) Long-term health care facilities, as defined in Section 1418, that hire certified nursing assistants shall consult the state department's registry prior to hiring these individuals or placing them in direct contact with patients.
(Repealed and added by Stats. 1994, Ch. 1246, Sec. 6. Effective January 1, 1995.)
1337.9.
(a) The Legislature finds and declares all of the following:
(1) Recidivism is reduced when criminal offenders are given the opportunity to secure employment and engage in a trade, occupation, or profession.
(2) It is in the interest of public safety to assist in the rehabilitation of criminal offenders by removing impediments and restrictions upon the offenders' ability to obtain employment or engage in a trade, occupation, or profession based solely upon the existence of a criminal record.
(3) It is the intent of the Legislature that the state department, in determining eligibility under this section, have discretion to consider a conviction, but that the conviction not operate as an automatic bar to certification.
(b) The state department may deny an application for, initiate an action to suspend or revoke a certificate for, or deny a training and examination application for, a nurse assistant for any of the following:
(1) Unprofessional conduct, including, but not limited to, incompetence, gross negligence, unless due to circumstances beyond the nurse assistant's control, physical, mental, or verbal abuse of patients, or misappropriation of property of patients or others.
(2) Conviction of a crime substantially related to the qualifications, functions, and duties of a certified nurse assistant if the state department determines that the applicant or certificate holder has not adequately demonstrated that he or she has been rehabilitated and will present a threat to the health, safety, or welfare of patients.
(3) Conviction for, or use of, any controlled substance as defined in Division 10 (commencing with Section 11000), or any dangerous drug, as defined in Section 4022 of the Business and Professions Code, or alcoholic beverages, to an extent or in a manner dangerous or injurious to the certified nurse assistant, any other person, or the public, to the extent that this use would impair the ability to conduct, with safety to the public, the practice authorized by a certificate.
(4) Procuring a certified nurse assistant certificate by fraud or misrepresentation or mistake.
(5) Making or giving any false statement or information in conjunction with the application for issuance of a nurse assistant certificate or training and examination application.
(6) Impersonating any applicant, or acting as proxy for an applicant, in any examination required under this article for the issuance of a certificate.
(7) Impersonating another certified nurse assistant, a licensed vocational nurse, or a registered nurse, or permitting or allowing another person to use a certificate for the purpose of providing nursing services.
(8) Violating or attempting to violate, directly or indirectly, or assisting in or abetting the violating of, or conspiring to violate any provision or term of, this article.
(c) In determining whether or not to deny the application for licensure or renewal pursuant to paragraph (2) of subdivision (b), the department shall take into consideration the following factors as evidence of good character and rehabilitation:
(1) The nature and seriousness of the conduct or crime under consideration and its relationship to their employment duties and responsibilities.
(2) Activities since conviction, including employment or participation in therapy or education, that would indicate changed behavior.
(3) The period of time that has elapsed since the commission of the conduct or offense referred to in paragraph (1) or (2) and the number of offenses.
(4) The extent to which the person has complied with any terms of parole, probation, restitution, or any other sanction lawfully imposed against the person.
(5) Any rehabilitation evidence, including character references, submitted by the person.
(6) Employment history and current employer recommendations.
(7) Circumstances surrounding the commission of the offense that would demonstrate the unlikelihood of repetition.
(8) An order from a superior court pursuant to Section 1203.4, 1203.4a, or 1203.41 of the Penal Code.
(9) The granting by the Governor of a full and unconditional pardon.
(10) A certificate of rehabilitation from a superior court.
(d) When the state department determines that a certificate shall be suspended, the state department shall specify the period of actual suspension. The state department may stay the suspension and place the certificate holder on probation with specified conditions for a period not to exceed two years. If the state department determines that probation is the appropriate action, the certificate holder shall be notified that in lieu of the state department proceeding with a formal action to suspend the certification and in lieu of an appeal pursuant to subdivision (g), the certificate holder may request to enter into a diversion program agreement. A diversion program agreement shall specify terms and conditions related to matters, including, but not limited to, work performance, rehabilitation, training, counseling, progress reports, and treatment programs. If a certificate holder successfully completes a diversion program, no action shall be taken upon the allegations that were the basis for the diversion agreement. Upon failure of the certificate holder to comply with the terms and conditions of an agreement, the state department may proceed with a formal action to suspend or revoke the certification.
(e) A plea or verdict of guilty, or a conviction following a plea of nolo contendere shall be deemed a conviction within the meaning of this article. The state department may deny an application or deny, suspend, or revoke a certification based on a conviction as provided in this article when the judgment of conviction is entered or when an order granting probation is made suspending the imposition of sentence.
(f) Upon determination to deny an application or deny, revoke, or suspend a certificate, the state department shall notify the applicant or certificate holder in writing by certified mail of all of the following:
(1) The reasons for the determination.
(2) The applicant's or certificate holder's right to appeal the determination.
(g) (1) Upon written notification that the state department has determined that an application shall be denied or a certificate shall be denied, suspended, or revoked, the applicant or certificate holder may request an administrative hearing by submitting a written request to the state department within 20 business days of receipt of the written notification. Upon receipt of a written request, the state department shall hold an administrative hearing pursuant to the procedures specified in Section 100171, except where those procedures are inconsistent with this section.
(2) A hearing under this section shall be conducted within 60 days of the receipt of the written request of the applicant or certificate holder submitted pursuant to paragraph (1) by a hearing officer or administrative law judge designated by the director at a location, other than the work facility, convenient to the applicant or certificate holder unless the applicant or certificate holder agrees to an extension. The hearing shall be tape recorded and a written decision shall be sent by certified mail to the applicant or certificate holder within 30 calendar days of the hearing. Except as specified in subdivision (h), the effective date of an action to revoke or suspend a certificate shall be specified in the written decision, or if no administrative hearing is timely requested, the effective date shall be 21 business days from written notification of the department's determination to revoke or suspend.
(h) The state department may revoke or suspend a certificate prior to any hearing when immediate action is necessary in the judgment of the director to protect the public welfare. Notice of this action, including a statement of the necessity of immediate action to protect the public welfare, shall be sent in accordance with subdivision (d). If the certificate holder requests an administrative hearing pursuant to subdivision (g), the state department shall hold the administrative hearing as soon as possible but not later than 30 calendar days from receipt of the request for a hearing. A written hearing decision upholding or setting aside the action shall be sent by certified mail to the certificate holder within 30 calendar days of the hearing.
(i) Upon the expiration of the term of suspension, he or she shall be reinstated by the state department and shall be entitled to resume practice unless it is established to the satisfaction of the state department that the person has practiced as a certified nurse assistant in this state during the term of suspension. In this event, the state department shall revoke the person's certificate.
(j) Upon a determination to deny an application or deny, revoke, or suspend a certificate, the state department shall notify the employer of the applicant and certificate holder in writing of that determination, and whether the determination is final, or whether a hearing is pending relating to this determination. If a licensee or facility is required to deny employment or terminate employment of the employee based upon notice from the state that the employee is determined to be unsuitable for employment under this section, the licensee or facility shall not incur criminal, civil, unemployment insurance, workers' compensation, or administrative liability as a result of that denial or termination.
(Amended by Stats. 2014, Ch. 847, Sec. 1. (SB 1384) Effective January 1, 2015.)
1338.
(a) The state department shall, through the Medi-Cal program, provide rate adjustments to skilled nursing or intermediate care facilities for the portion of additional costs attributable to the requirements of Sections 1337.1, 1337. 3, and 1337.5 with respect to Medi-Cal patients. The portion of such additional costs attributable to Medi-Cal shall be the same as the ratio of Medi-Cal patients to total patients in the facility. Such rate adjustments shall also include provisions for an increase in wages for nurse assistants who receive certificates pursuant to Section 1337.3 and a continuing wage differential between certified and uncertified nurse assistants thereafter.
(b) On and after September 1, 1978, the rate adjustments specified in subdivision (a) shall not be paid to any skilled nursing facility or intermediate care facility which has not received approval of the state department for an approved training program that meets the standards and requirements of Section 1337.1, unless the facility has had an application for such approval on file with the state department on or before August 1, 1978, which has not been approved or rejected. However, payment of such rate adjustments to facilities with applications on file with the state department on or before August 1, 1978, which have not received action by the state department, shall cease upon rejection of the application.
Within one week after the effective date of this article the state department shall notify all skilled nursing facilities or intermediate care facilities, which have not filed an application with the state department for approval of an approved training program, of the requirements of this subdivision.
(c) Facilities granted an exemption by the state department prior to the effective date of this section pursuant to subsection (i) of Section 51510 or subsection (h) of Section 51511 of Title 22 of the California Administrative Code shall be entitled to continuance of such exemption unless and until the facility ceases to meet any of the eligibility criteria which are specified in such regulations on the effective date of this section.

(Added by Stats. 1978, Ch. 351.)

1338.1.

The state department shall assign sufficient qualified employees to supervise and evaluate training programs required by this article.

(Added by Stats. 1978, Ch. 351.)

1338.2.

(a) The state department shall convene a work group to develop recommendations to the department on ways to expand the availability of training programs and certified nurse assistants available for hire in the state. The work group shall investigate, but not be limited to investigating, all of the following:

(1) Work-based learning programs for students in the regional occupational programs in the state.

(2) Utilization of apprenticeships.

(3) Promotional programs for training centers and certified nurse assistant jobs.

(4) Utilization of expanded data resources.

(b) The recommendations required by subdivision (a) shall be submitted by the work group to the state department on or before July 1, 2001.

(c) The work group shall consist of, but not be limited to, all of the following:

(1) A representative from the State Department of Education.

(2) Nurse-Assistant training center representatives.

(3) A director of staff development for a long-term health care facility.

(4) A publisher of nurse assistant training and competency curricula.

(5) An industry representative.

(6) A currently certified nurse assistant.

(7) A consumer representative.

(8) A labor union representative.

(9) A representative of the American Red Cross.

(10) The Chancellor of the California Community Colleges.

(11) A representative from the Office of Statewide Health Planning and Development.

(12) A registered nurse and a licensed vocational nurse, both of whom are currently providing long-term care nursing services.

(Added by Stats. 1999, Ch. 719, Sec. 5. Effective January 1, 2000.)

1338.3.

The State Director of Health Services may adopt emergency regulations pursuant to Chapter 3.5 (commencing with Section 11340) of Part 1 of Division 3 of Title 3 of the Government Code to implement this article. The adoption of the regulations shall be deemed to be an emergency and necessary for the immediate preservation of the public peace, health, or safety. Notwithstanding Chapter 3.5 (commencing with Section 11340) of Part 1 of Division 3 of Title 2 of the Government Code, emergency regulations adopted by the State Department of Health Services in order to implement this article shall not be subject to the review and approval of the Office of Administrative Law. These regulations shall become effective immediately upon filing with the Secretary of State.

(Repealed and added by Stats. 1987, Ch. 1177, Sec. 13.)

1338.5.

(a) (1) (A) A criminal record clearance shall be conducted for all nurse assistants by the submission of fingerprint images and related information to the state department for processing at the Department of Justice. The licensing and certification program shall issue an All Facilities Letter (AFL) to facility licensees when both of the following criteria are met:

(i) The program receives, within three business days, 95 percent of its total responses indicating no evidence of recorded criminal information from the Department of Justice.

(ii) The program processes 95 percent of its total responses requiring disqualification in accordance with subparagraph (C) of paragraph (2) of subdivision (a) of Section 1337.9, as that section read on January 1, 2014, no later than 45 days after the date that the report is received from the Department of Justice.

(B) After the AFL is issued, licensees shall not allow nurse assistant trainees or newly hired nurse assistants to have direct contact with clients or residents of the facility prior to completion of the criminal record clearance. A criminal record clearance shall be complete when the department has obtained the person's criminal offender record information search response information from the Department of Justice and has determined that the person is not disqualified from engaging in the activity for which clearance is required. Notwithstanding any other provision of law, the department may, without taking regulatory action pursuant to Chapter 3.5 (commencing with Section 11340) of Part 1 of Division 3 of Title 2 of the Government Code, implement, interpret, or make specific this paragraph by means of an AFL or similar instruction. The fee to cover the processing costs of the Department of Justice, not including the costs associated with capturing or transmitting the fingerprint images and related information, shall not exceed thirty-two dollars ($32) per submission.

(C) An applicant or certificate holder who may be disqualified on the basis of a criminal conviction shall provide the department with a certified copy of the judgment of each conviction. In addition, the individual may, during a period of two years after the department receives the criminal record report, provide the department with evidence of good character and rehabilitation in accordance with subdivision (c) of Section 1337.9. Upon receipt of a new application for certification of the individual, the department may receive and consider the evidence during the two-year period without requiring additional fingerprint imaging to clear the individual.

(D) The department's Licensing and Certification Program shall explore and implement methods for maximizing its efficiency in processing criminal record clearances within the requirements of law, including a streamlined clearance process for persons who have been disqualified on the basis of criminal convictions.

(2) (A) Upon enrollment in a training program for nurse assistant certification, and prior to direct contact with residents, a candidate for training shall submit a training and examination application and the fingerprint cards to the state department to receive a criminal record review through the Department of Justice. Submission of the fingerprints to the Federal Bureau of Investigation shall be at the discretion of the state department.

(B) An applicant and any other person specified in this subdivision, as part of the background clearance process, shall provide information as to whether or not the person has any prior criminal convictions, has had any arrests within the past 12-month period, or has any active arrests, and shall certify that, to the best of his or her knowledge, the information provided is true. This requirement is not intended to duplicate existing requirements for individuals who are required to submit fingerprint images as part of a criminal background clearance process. Every applicant shall provide information on any prior administrative action taken against him or her by any federal, state, or local government agency and shall certify that, to the best of his or her knowledge, the information provided is true. An applicant or other person required to provide information pursuant to this section that knowingly or willfully makes false statements, representations, or omissions may be subject to administrative action, including, but not limited to, denial of his or her application or exemption or revocation of any exemption previously granted.

(3) Each health facility that operates and is used as a clinical skills site for certification training, and each health facility, prior to hiring a nurse assistant applicant certified in another state or country, shall arrange for and pay the cost of the fingerprint live scan service and the Department of Justice processing costs for each applicant. Health facilities may not pass these costs through to nurse assistant applicants unless allowed by federal law enacted subsequent to the effective date of this paragraph.

(b) The use of fingerprint live scan technology implemented by the Department of Justice by the year 1999 shall be used by the Department of Justice to generate timely and accurate positive fingerprint identification prior to nurse assistant certification and prior to direct contact with residents by the nurse assistant applicant. The department shall explore options to work with private and governmental agencies to ensure that licensees have adequate access to electronic transmission sites, including requiring the department to maintain a contract for electronic transmission services in each of the district offices where facilities have indicated problems with timely access to electronic transmission sites or consistent delays of more than three business days in obtaining appointments for electronic transmission services through a private entity, government agency, or law enforcement agency.

(c) The state department shall develop procedures to ensure that any licensee, direct care staff, or certificate holder for whom a criminal record has been obtained pursuant to this section or Section 1265.5 or 1736 shall not be required to obtain multiple criminal record clearances.

(d) If the department is experiencing a delay in processing the renewal of the certified nursing assistant's certification at the time of the expiration of the certified nursing assistant's certification, the department may extend the expiration of the certified nursing assistant's certification for six months.

(e) If, at any time, the department determines that it does not meet the standards specified in clauses (i) and (ii) of subparagraph (A) of paragraph (1) of subdivision (a), for a period of 90 consecutive days, the requirements in paragraph (1) of subdivision (a) shall be inoperative until the department can demonstrate it has met those standards for a period of 90 consecutive days.

(f) During any time in which the requirements of paragraph (1) of subdivision (a) are inoperative, facilities may allow newly hired nurse assistants to have direct contact with clients or residents of the facility after those persons have submitted live scan fingerprint images to the Department of Justice, and the department shall issue an AFL advising facilities of this change in the statutory requirements.

(g) Notwithstanding any other law, the department is authorized to provide an individual with a copy of his or her state or federal level criminal offender record information search response as provided to that department by the Department of Justice if the department has denied a criminal background clearance based on this information and the individual makes a written request to the department for a copy specifying an address to which it is to be sent. The state or federal level criminal offender record information search response shall not be modified or altered from its form or content as provided by the Department of Justice and shall be provided to the address specified by the individual in their written request. The department shall retain a copy of the individual's written request and the response and date provided.

(Amended by Stats. 2014, Ch. 847, Sec. 2. (SB 1384) Effective January 1, 2015.)

ARTICLE 10. Primary Health Service Hospitals [1339 - 1339.25]

(Article 10 added by Stats. 1978, Ch. 1332.)

1339.

The Legislature hereby finds and declares that:

(a) In many areas, small, rural general acute care hospitals are experiencing financial difficulties brought upon partially because of governmental regulations and underutilization of acute care beds.

(b) Closure of such facilities, in most cases, would represent a direct threat to the health and well-being of both the resident and tourist populations served by these facilities.

(c) Availability and accessibility to primary and preventive health care services could be greatly improved through coordination with existing resources in the area.

(d) Because of the special attributes of the small, rural general acute care hospital, such as longevity, focus of community support, critical geographic location, and availability of services, such facilities could serve as the major focal point for the promotion of health and the delivery of health care services within the rural community.

(e) There is a lack of systematic study and evaluation of the economics of efficiently operating small rural hospitals and the ways in which these hospitals might more effectively meet the health needs of their communities.
(Amended by Stats. 1982, Ch. 1010, Sec. 1.)
1339.3.
It is, therefore, the intent of the Legislature to designate certain general acute care hospitals as primary health service hospitals, which will facilitate the diversification of the small rural hospital. The designation shall apply only to those general acute care hospitals that meet the criteria set forth in this article and which are designated by the state department.
(Repealed and added by Stats. 1982, Ch. 1010, Sec. 3.)
1339.5.
As used in this article, unless otherwise indicated:
(a) "Health systems agency" means a health systems agency established pursuant to Public Law 93-641.
(b) "Primary care mid-level health practitioner" means a physician assistant certified pursuant to Chapter 7.7 (commencing with Section 3500) of Division 2 of the Business and Professions Code and also means a registered nurse who meets the standards for a nurse practitioner adopted pursuant to Article 8 (commencing with Section 2834) of Chapter 6 of Division 2 of the Business and Professions Code, and also means a nurse midwife certified pursuant to Article 2.5 (commencing with Section 2746) of Chapter 6 of Division 2 of the Business and Professions Code.
(c) "Swing bed" means beds licensed for general acute care pursuant to Section 1250.1 that may, subject to this article, be used as skilled nursing beds, as classified in Section 1250.1. Swing beds shall retain the general acute care bed classification, for the purposes of Chapter 1 (commencing with Section 127125) of Part 2 of Division 107.
(Amended by Stats. 1996, Ch. 1023, Sec. 159. Effective September 29, 1996.)
1339.7.
The state department shall administer the program authorized in this article. In administering the program, the state department shall do all of the following:
(a) Verify hospital eligibility, pursuant to Section 1339.9, and designate those hospitals as primary health service hospitals.
(b) Establish criteria for the health service plans pursuant to Section 1339.15.
(c) Review a general acute care hospital's health service plan based upon recommendations of the local health systems agency, input from local public meetings, recommendations of the medical advisory panel, as appropriate, and the adequacy of the plan in meeting the criteria established pursuant to this section. The state department shall approve, deny, or defer the plan in whole or in part and shall notify the hospital of its findings, in writing, within 120 days after receipt of the plan. The plan shall be deemed approved if the hospital has not received notification from the state department within the 120-day period.
(d) Negotiate and grant exceptions to the licensure requirements for general acute care hospitals that are necessary to serve the purposes of this article when the granting of such exceptions do not jeopardize the health and welfare of the patients. Exceptions that are granted shall be consistent with the primary health service hospital's plan and any amendments thereto.
(e) Convene an advisory panel to review the medical-surgical and obstetrical services proposed as part of the primary hospital service plan and make recommendations to the state department on the medical appropriateness of those services according to the primary health service hospital's proposed plan. The panel shall include, but not be limited to, a rural hospital administrator, a rural family practice physician and surgeon, a rural hospital nurse administrator, an internist, a primary care mid-level practitioner, and a physician and surgeon from a hospital which serves as a referral center for rural hospitals.
(f) Issue evidence of primary health service hospital designation and evidence of the number of acute care beds approved as swing beds pursuant to paragraph (4) of subdivision (b) of Section 1339.15.
(g) Monitor the performance of the primary health service hospital to assure compliance with such hospital's plan and licensure requirements from which such hospitals are not exempt.
(h) Immediately upon the denial of a primary health service hospital's health service plan, or a portion thereof, notify the hospital in writing. Within 20 days after the state department mails the notice, the hospital may present a written petition for a hearing to the state department. Upon receipt by the state department of the petition in proper form, the petition shall be set for hearing. The proceedings shall be conducted in accordance with Chapter 5 (commencing with Section 11500) of Part 1 of Division 3 of Title 2 of the Government Code, and the state department has all the powers granted therein.
(i) Compile and make available to health systems agencies and primary health service hospitals, information regarding state and federal funding programs for which the primary health service hospital may be eligible, the procedures necessary to apply for funding, and a description of how such requests may be incorporated into a primary health service hospital's plan and opportunities for diversification of services, the requirements and feasibility, and the procedures for development of such services.
(j) On behalf of primary health service hospitals, seek appropriate federal waivers consistent with the intent of this act.
(k) Contract with one or more health systems agencies to perform the functions specified in subdivision (c) of Section 1339.11.
(l) Develop or assist hospitals submitting a primary health service plan pursuant to Section 1339.15 to develop the following:

(1) Alternative methods of filing claims which reduce administrative costs.
(2) Alternative methods of Medi-Cal payment to hospitals.
(3) Other methods of filing claims which reduce administrative costs.
(4) Simplified and abbreviated procedures required by the department of Medi-Cal costs reports.
(5) An abbreviated medical and social review process and other control processes.
(m) Provide technical assistance to primary health service hospitals in development of their health service plan.
(Amended by Stats. 1982, Ch. 1010, Sec. 5.)
1339.8.
The Office of Statewide Health Planning and Development shall review and approve the number of swing beds that may be designated pursuant to paragraph (4) of subdivision (b) of Section 1339.15, based upon community need and projected utilization and issue a certificate of need pursuant to the review and approval. Except as provided herein, a primary health service hospital shall be subject to the requirements pertaining to approval of projects, as defined in Section 127170, that are set forth in Chapter 1 (commencing with Section 127125) of Part 2 of Division 107.
(Amended by Stats. 1996, Ch. 1023, Sec. 160. Effective September 29, 1996.)
1339.9.
In order to be eligible for designation as a primary health service hospital, a hospital shall be licensed pursuant to subdivision (a) of Section 1250 and meet one of the following criteria:
(a) Be located outside of a standard metropolitan statistical area, be located at least 15 miles from another licensed acute care hospital, and have 60 or fewer acute care beds.
(b) Be located at least 20 miles from any other licensed acute care hospital and have 60 or fewer acute care beds.
(c) Be the only licensed acute care hospital in the county and have fewer than 100 acute care beds.
(Repealed and added by Stats. 1982, Ch. 1010, Sec. 9.)
1339.10.
(a) The department may request and maintain employment information for nurse assistants and direct care staff of intermediate care facilities/developmentally disabled, other than state-operated intermediate care facilities/developmentally disabled that secure criminal record clearances for employees through another method, intermediate care facilities/developmentally disabled-habilitative, or intermediate care facilities/developmentally disabled-nursing.
(b) Within five working days of receipt of a criminal record or information from the Department of Justice pursuant to Section 1338.5, the department shall notify the licensee and applicant of any criminal convictions.
(c) The department shall conduct a feasibility study to assess the additional technology requirements necessary to include previous and current employment information on its registry and to make that information available to potential employers. The department shall report to the Legislature by July 1, 2000, as to the results of the study.
(Added by renumbering Section 1339.9 (as added by Stats. 1998, Ch. 716, Sec. 1) by Stats. 2015, Ch. 303, Sec. 248. (AB 731) Effective January 1, 2016.)
1339.11.
Health systems agencies shall do all of the following:
(a) Verify information in the health service plan received from hospitals in their respective health service area.
(b) Within 45 days make a recommendation, including findings, to the state department regarding the need for, and ability of the hospital to implement its health services plan for hospitals in their respective health service area.
(c) Upon contracting with the state department, provide technical assistance to primary health service hospitals in the preparation of health services pursuant to Section 1339.15.
(d) In the event a health systems agency is unable to perform the functions, the state department shall perform those functions.
(Repealed and added by Stats. 1982, Ch. 1010, Sec. 11.)
1339.13.
Any primary health service hospital, or any group thereof, may submit a health service plan to the state department when a public meeting, which satisfies the following criteria, has been conducted in the community by the hospital with respect to such hospital's health service plan for the community, or when more than one hospital is involved, in the communities for which the hospitals propose to provide primary health service hospital services:
(a) The plan is made available for public review at least two weeks prior to the public meeting.
(b) Notices announcing the public meeting are posted in publicly visible places in the community and at the hospital at least 10 days prior to the public meeting.
(c) A public notice is published in a newspaper of general circulation not less than 10 or more than 20 days prior to the public meeting.
(Repealed and added by Stats. 1982, Ch. 1010, Sec. 13.)
1339.15.
A primary health service hospital may request waivers pursuant to subdivision (d) of Section 1339.7, and Section 1339.25, authorization for swing beds pursuant to Section 1339.8 and seek the benefits pursuant to subdivision (l) of Section 1339.7 by submitting a health service plan. The health service plan shall be submitted to the state department and the health systems agency and shall contain the following as appropriate and dependent on the needs of the community:
(a) A description of the hospital's current capabilities with emphasis on the following:

(1) Primary and preventive care services including life saving services.

(2) Community access to health services.

(3) Cost effectiveness.

(b) Additionally, and as appropriate, the plan shall include:

(1) A description of any services to be deleted from those authorized by license at the time the plan is submitted with a description of the impact the deletion of this service will have on the community.

(2) A description of any services to be added to those authorized by license at the time the plan is submitted, including evidence of market feasibility, methods and schedule for plan implementation, evidence of community and medical staff support of the plan, and evidence of coordination with other health providers and services in the community.

(3) Requests for waivers or exemptions which do not jeopardize the health, safety, and well-being of patients affected, and which are needed for increased operational efficiency or to implement the health service plan.

(4) Identification of the number of acute care beds in the hospital, if any, requested for use as swing beds, depending upon community need and projected utilization, including a description of the way in which medical care will be provided to those patients and a description of how the facility will provide for the transfer of long-term care patients when the need for acute care beds develops.

(Repealed and added by Stats. 1982, Ch. 1010, Sec. 15.)

1339.17.

A primary health service hospital may amend its health service plan. Such amendments shall be subject to the provisions of subdivision (c) of Section 1337.7 and Section 1339.13. Amendments shall not be made to such plan solely for the purpose of circumventing sanctions administered for noncompliance with such hospital's health service plan.

(Amended by Stats. 1982, Ch. 1010, Sec. 16.)

1339.19.

The primary health service hospital shall operate under the following requirements:

(a) The primary health service hospital shall be subject to the regulations contained in Division 5 (commencing with Section 70001) of Title 22 of the California Administrative Code that are not waived as a result of the health service plan or subsequent amendments to such plan.

(b) Services offered by the primary health service hospital shall be limited in scope according to its license or authorized by an approved health service plan, and any subsequent amendments thereto.

(c) All or a portion of the health service plan shall be implemented, based upon an agreed timetable between the state department and the hospital, and to the extent that state and federal requirements are waived.

(d) The hospital shall remain in compliance with its plan in accordance with subdivision (c).

(Amended by Stats. 1983, Ch. 1285, Sec. 5.)

1339.21.

(a) In accordance with the procedures prescribed in subdivision (h) of Section 1339.7, the state department shall terminate a hospital's health service plan or its designation as a primary health service hospital, or both, when it finds that the hospital is not in compliance with Section 1339.19 or the welfare or safety of the patients served by the facility is adversely affected, or both.

(b) A primary health service hospital may terminate its designation or health service plan, or both, after giving a 30-day notice to the state department.

(c) Upon termination from the project, as prescribed by this section, the hospital shall revert to the same status it held immediately preceding its designation or approval of its plan, or both.

(Amended by Stats. 1982, Ch. 1010, Sec. 19.)

1339.25.

Implementation of this article shall be consistent with federal rules and regulations in effect on January 1, 1979, and as adopted on or after such date. In keeping with the intent in enacting this article and to the extent permitted by federal law, each department within the Health and Welfare Agency may waive requirements, provide exemptions to the enforcement of statutes upon which the requirements were based, allow flexible enforcement of regulations and policies, and make resources available which are necessary for the administration of this article, including technical assistance to primary health service hospitals in developing their health service plans.

(Amended by Stats. 1982, Ch. 1010, Sec. 21.)

ARTICLE 10.5. Special Hospital: Hospice [1339.30 - 1339.36]

(Article 10.5 added by Stats. 1989, Ch. 1, Sec. 2.)

1339.30.

A Special Hospital: Hospice Pilot Project is hereby created. This pilot project shall be established and administered by the department, and shall consist of up to three pilot projects, one of which shall be located in San Diego. The department shall license facilities that are part of the pilot project for the duration of the pilot project as a special hospital: hospice. No person or entity shall be licensed as a special hospital: hospice unless that person or entity is participating in this pilot project.

The purpose of the pilot project is to determine the need of hospice patients for acute inpatient hospital care.

This article shall not preclude the provision of appropriate hospice services in other settings.

The pilot project does not constitute an approved project as defined in subdivision (b) of Section 128130.

(Amended by Stats. 1996, Ch. 1023, Sec. 161. Effective September 29, 1996.)

1339.31.

For the purposes of this article, the following definitions shall apply:

(a) "Hospice" means a specialized form of multidisciplinary health care which is designed to provide palliative care, alleviate the physical, emotional, social and spiritual discomforts of an individual who is experiencing the last phases of life due to the existence of a terminal disease, and to provide supportive care for the primary care giver and the family of the hospice patient, and which meets all of the following criteria:

(1) Considers the patient and the patient's family, in addition to the patient, as the unit of care.

(2) Utilizes a multidisciplinary team to assess the physical, medical, psychological, social, and spiritual needs of the patient and the patient's family.

(3) Requires the multidisciplinary team to develop an overall plan of care and to provide coordinated care, which emphasizes supportive services such as home care, pain control, and limited inpatient services. Limited inpatient services are intended to ensure both continuity of care and appropriateness of services for those patients who cannot be managed at home because of acute complications or the temporary absence of a capable primary care giver.

(4) Provides for the palliative medical treatment of pain and symptoms associated with a terminal illness but does not provide for efforts to cure disease.

(5) Provides for bereavement following death to assist the family to cope with social and emotional needs associated with the death of the patient.

(6) Actively utilizes volunteers in the delivery of hospice services.

(7) To the extent appropriate, based on the medical needs of the patient, provides services in the patient's home or primary place of residence.

(b) "Palliative care" means interventions that focus primarily on reduction or abatement of pain and other disease-related symptoms, rather than treatment aimed at investigation and intervention for the purpose of cure or prolongation of life.

(c) "Primary care giver" means the individual who is identified as the primary person charged with responsibility for the care of the hospice patient who agrees to accept that responsibility. The individual designated may be a family member, a friend or an individual hired by the hospice patient but shall be an individual who is actually available to provide 24-hour coverage for care of the hospice patient. However, it shall not be necessary that the individual reside in the hospice patient's home.

(d) "Primary place of residence" means the patient's long-term residence and includes the patient's home, a friend's home, a congregate living health facility, a hospice residential care facility, or a skilled nursing facility if the patient resides there on a permanent full-time basis.

(e) "Special hospital: hospice" means a health facility which is a component part of a hospice, as defined in subdivision (a), and which provides general inpatient care, as defined in federal Medicare program regulations adopted pursuant to Section 1861(dd)(2) and Section 1814(a)(7) of the federal Social Security Act.

(f) "Terminal illness" means a medical condition resulting in a life expectancy of the patient of six months, or less.

(Added by Stats. 1989, Ch. 1, Sec. 2. Effective January 13, 1989.)

1339.32.

A special hospital: hospice shall be deemed to provide acute palliative care. All patients receiving inpatient care in a Special Hospital: Hospice Project shall be admitted by, and under the supervision of, a physician member of the organized medical staff.

(Amended by Stats. 1996, Ch. 413, Sec. 1. Effective January 1, 1997.)

1339.33.

Notwithstanding any other provisions of law, in order to be licensed as a special hospital: hospice, each project facility shall meet the requirements of Sections 70101 to 70137, inclusive, 70201 to 70219, inclusive, 70241 to 70279, inclusive, 70701 to 70707, inclusive, and 70708 to 70765, inclusive, of Title 22 of the California Code of Regulations; Sections 2-1001A to 2-1015A, inclusive, Section 2-1018A, Sections 2-1020A to 2-1024A, inclusive, Sections 2-1026A to 2-1028A, inclusive, Section 2-1040A, Section 2-1044A, and Section 2-1051A of Title 24 of the California Code of Regulations. In addition to complying with these regulations in Titles 22 and 24 of the California Code of Regulations, each facility shall meet, for the duration of the project, the hospice standards used by the Medicare program (42 C.F.R., Part 418, Sections 418.1 to 418.405, inclusive) the Medi-Cal program (subdivision (e) of Sections 51003 to 51543, inclusive, of Title 22, California Code of Regulations), and the Joint Commission on the Accreditation of Healthcare Organizations' "Hospice Standards Manual."

Each facility licensed as a special hospital: hospice shall maintain a transfer agreement with a general acute care hospital.

(Amended by Stats. 1996, Ch. 413, Sec. 2. Effective January 1, 1997.)

1339.34.

(a) Each facility that is part of the project shall report to the Legislature at the end of each year of operation on all of the following factors:

(1) Acuity levels of patients using the project facilities; relative cost-effectiveness of these facilities.

(2) Quality of care in the facilities.

(3) Utilization of the facilities.

(4) Staffing requirements of the facilities.

(b) Reports shall be submitted to the Legislature no later than three months after the close of the 12-month period for which the report is made. However, the Legislature may approve requests to extend this deadline that are submitted no later than 30 days prior to the deadline and that state the reason for the delay and corrective measures that have been taken to avoid future delays. No report deadline will be extended for more than three months beyond the original report date.

(Amended by Stats. 1996, Ch. 413, Sec. 3. Effective January 1, 1997.)

1339.35.

The project shall commence on January 1, 1990. However, the State Department of Health Services may establish an earlier commencement date for any one of the facilities if that facility has been licensed as a special hospital: hospice prior to January 1, 1990.
(Amended by Stats. 1996, Ch. 413, Sec. 4. Effective January 1, 1997.)

1339.36.

The fee for each new or renewal application for a license for a Special Hospital: Hospice Pilot Project facility shall be the annual fee as set forth for general acute care hospitals in subdivision (a) of Section 1266. If the annual fees do not cover the necessary costs which the Division of Licensure and Certification expends to manage this pilot project, the facilities shall be assessed an annual pro rata share of the excess costs.
(Added by Stats. 1989, Ch. 1, Sec. 2. Effective January 13, 1989.)

ARTICLE 10.6. Hospice Licensing [1339.40 - 1339.44]

(Article 10.6 added by Stats. 2012, Ch. 673, Sec. 5.)

1339.40.

For the purposes of this article, the following definitions apply:
(a) "Bereavement services" has the same meaning as defined in subdivision (a) of Section 1746.
(b) "Hospice care" means a specialized form of interdisciplinary health care that is designed to provide palliative care, alleviate the physical, emotional, social, and spiritual discomforts of an individual who is experiencing the last phases of life due to the existence of a terminal disease, and provide supportive care to the primary caregiver and the family of the hospice patient, and that meets all of the following criteria:
(1) Considers the patient and the patient's family, in addition to the patient, as the unit of care.
(2) Utilizes an interdisciplinary team to assess the physical, medical, psychological, social, and spiritual needs of the patient and the patient's family.
(3) Requires the interdisciplinary team to develop an overall plan of care and to provide coordinated care that emphasizes supportive services, including, but not limited to, home care, pain control, and limited inpatient services. Limited inpatient services are intended to ensure both continuity of care and appropriateness of services for those patients who cannot be managed at home because of acute complications or the temporary absence of a capable primary caregiver.
(4) Provides for the palliative medical treatment of pain and other symptoms associated with a terminal disease, but does not provide for efforts to cure the disease.
(5) Provides for bereavement services following death to assist the family in coping with social and emotional needs associated with the death of the patient.
(6) Actively utilizes volunteers in the delivery of hospice services.
(7) To the extent appropriate, based on the medical needs of the patient, provides services in the patient's home or primary place of residence.
(c) "Hospice facility" means a health facility as defined in subdivision (n) of Section 1250.
(d) "Inpatient hospice care" means hospice care that is provided to patients in a hospice facility, including routine, continuous and inpatient care directly as specified in Section 418.110 of Title 42 of the Code of Federal Regulations, and may include short-term inpatient respite care as specified in Section 418.108 of Title 42 of the Code of Federal Regulations.
(e) "Interdisciplinary team" has the same meaning as defined in subdivision (g) of Section 1746.
(f) "Medical direction" has the same meaning as defined in subdivision (h) of Section 1746.
(g) "Palliative care" has the same meaning as defined in subdivision (j) of Section 1746.
(h) "Plan of care" has the same meaning as defined in subdivision (l) of Section 1746.
(i) "Skilled nursing services" has the same meaning as defined in subdivision (n) of Section 1746.
(j) "Social services/counseling services" has the same meaning as defined in subdivision (o) of Section 1746.
(k) "Terminal disease" or "terminal illness" has the same meaning as defined in subdivision (p) of Section 1746.
(l) "Volunteer services" has the same meaning as defined in subdivision (q) of Section 1746.
(Amended by Stats. 2013, Ch. 289, Sec. 1. (SB 816) Effective January 1, 2014.)

1339.41.

(a) A person, governmental agency, or political subdivision of the state shall not be licensed as a hospice facility under this chapter unless the person or entity is a provider of hospice services licensed pursuant to Section 1751 and is certified as a hospice facility under Part 418 of Title 42 of the Code of Federal Regulations.
(b) A hospice provider that intends to provide inpatient hospice care in the hospice provider's own facility shall submit an application and fee for licensure as a hospice facility under this chapter. Notwithstanding the maximum period for a provisional license under subdivision (b) of Section 1268.5, the department may issue a provisional license to a hospice facility for a period of up to one year.
(c) A verified application for a new license completed on forms furnished by the department shall be submitted to the department upon the occurrence of either of the following:
(1) Establishment of a hospice facility.
(2) Change of ownership.
(d) The licensee shall submit to the department a verified application for a corrected license completed on forms furnished by the department upon the occurrence of any of the following:

(1) Construction of new or replacement hospice facility.
(2) Increase in licensed bed capacity.
(3) Change of name of facility.
(4) Change of licensed category.
(5) Change of location of facility.
(6) Change in bed classification.
(e) (1) A hospice facility that participates in the Medicare and Medicaid programs may obtain initial certification from a federal Centers for Medicare and Medicaid Services (CMS) approved accreditation organization.
(2) If the CMS-approved accreditation organization conducts certification inspections, the hospice facility shall transmit to the department, within 30 days of receipt, a copy of the final accreditation report of the accreditation organization.
(f) A hospice facility shall be separately licensed, irrespective of the location of the facility.
(g) (1) The licensee shall notify the department in writing of any changes in the information provided pursuant to subdivision (d) within 10 days of these changes. This notice shall include information and documentation regarding the changes.
(2) Each licensee shall notify the department within 10 days in writing of any change of the mailing address of the licensee. This notice shall include the new mailing address of the licensee.
(3) When a change in the principal officer of a corporate licensee, including the chairman, president, or general manager occurs, the licensee shall notify the department of this change within 10 days in writing. This notice shall include the name and business address of the officer.
(4) Any decrease in licensed bed capacity of the facility shall require notification by letter to the department and shall result in the issuance of a corrected license.
(Amended by Stats. 2013, Ch. 76, Sec. 107. (AB 383) Effective January 1, 2014.)

1339.42.

(a) No private or public organization, including, but not limited to, any partnership, corporation, or political subdivision of the state, or other governmental agency within the state, shall do any of the following without a license issued pursuant to this chapter:
(1) Represent itself to be a hospice facility by its name or advertisement, soliciting, or any other presentments to the public, or in the context of services within the scope of this chapter imply that it is licensed to provide those services or to make any reference to employee bonding in relation to those services.
(2) Use the words "hospice facility," "hospice home," "hospice-facility," or any combination of those terms, within its name.
(3) Use words to imply that it is licensed as a hospice facility to provide those services.
(b) A hospice facility licensee shall obtain criminal background checks for its employees, volunteers, and contractors in accordance with federal Medicare conditions of participation (42 C.F.R. Part 418 et seq.) and as may be required in accordance with state law. The hospice facility licensee shall pay the costs of obtaining a criminal background check.
(Added by Stats. 2012, Ch. 673, Sec. 5. (SB 135) Effective January 1, 2013.)

1339.43.

(a) A hospice facility shall provide a home-like environment that is comfortable and accommodating to both the patient and patient's visitors.
(b) Building standards for hospice facilities adopted pursuant to this chapter relating to fire and panic safety, and other regulations for hospice facilities adopted pursuant to this chapter, shall apply uniformly throughout the state. No city, county, city and county, including a charter city or charter county, or fire protection district shall adopt or enforce any ordinance or local rule or regulation relating to fire and panic safety in buildings or structures subject to this section that is inconsistent with the rules and regulations for hospice facilities adopted pursuant to this chapter.
(c) The hospice facility shall meet the fire protection standards set forth in the federal Medicare conditions of participation (42 C.F.R. Part 418 et seq.).
(d) A hospice facility may operate as a freestanding health facility.
(1) Until the Office of the State Fire Marshal, in consultation with the Office of Statewide Health Planning and Development, develops and adopts building standards for hospice facilities, a freestanding hospice facility shall meet applicable building standards and requirements relating to the physical environment of the facility as specified in Section 418.110 of Title 42 of the Code of Federal Regulations. The building standards developed shall, at a minimum, maintain the requirements specified in that section.
(2) A freestanding hospice facility shall be under the jurisdiction of the local building department. As part of the license application, the prospective licensee shall submit evidence of compliance with applicable building standards for hospice facilities.
(3) The physical environment of the hospice facility shall be adequate to provide the level of care and service required by the residents of the facility as determined by the department.
(e) A hospice facility may be located within the physical plant of another health facility.
(1) Notwithstanding subdivision (d) and paragraphs (8) and (9) of subdivision (b) of Section 129725, a hospice facility located within the physical plant of another licensed health facility that is under the jurisdiction of the Office of Statewide Health Planning and Development, shall meet the building standards for that category of health facility within which the hospice facility is located, and plans shall be submitted to the office for review of any new construction or renovation of these hospice facilities. As part of the license application, the prospective licensee shall submit evidence of compliance with the building codes enforced by the Office of Statewide Health Planning and Development.
(2) The physical environment of the facility shall be adequate to provide the level of care and service required by the residents of the facility as determined by the department.

(3) In the event the space used by the hospice facility reverts back to the facility with which the hospice facility shared the space, the building standards applicable to the former shared space, as identified by date of enactment of the standards, shall not change due solely to the reversion.

(4) A hospice facility that provides inpatient hospice care and is located within, adjacent to or physically connected to another health facility shall provide all of the following:

(A) A designated nursing station.

(B) Adequate space for the preparation of drugs with lockable, secure storage that is accessible only by authorized personnel.

(C) Signage that shall clearly demarcate the hospice facility area from the facility with which the hospice facility shares space.

(D) Doors for every exit and entrance to the hospice facility.

(E) Contiguous beds within the designated area set aside for the hospice facility.

(f) If a freestanding hospice facility is located on the site of or is physically connected to a health facility that is under the jurisdiction of the Office of Statewide Health Planning and Development or both, the hospice facility shall submit plans for any new construction or renovation of the hospice facility to the office for plan review and approval. The Office of Statewide Health Planning and Development shall review the hospice facility plans to identify any impacts to the health facility under the office's jurisdiction that may compromise the health facility's continued compliance with applicable laws and regulations.
(Amended by Stats. 2013, Ch. 289, Sec. 2. (SB 816) Effective January 1, 2014.)

1339.44.

(a) A hospice facility shall provide, or make provision for, all of the following services and requirements:

(1) (A) Medical direction and adequate staff. Minimum staffing standards that require at least one registered nurse to be on duty 24 hours per day and a maximum of six patients assigned at any given time per direct caregiver.

(B) For purposes of this section, any additional direct caregiver necessary beyond the registered nurse required pursuant to paragraph (1) may include a registered nurse, as described in Section 2732 of the Business and Professions Code, a licensed vocational nurse, as described in Section 2864 of the Business and Professions Code, and a certified nurse assistant.

(2) Skilled nursing services.

(3) Palliative care.

(4) Social services and counseling services.

(5) Bereavement services.

(6) Volunteer services.

(7) Dietary services.

(8) Pharmaceutical services.

(9) Physical therapy, occupational therapy, and speech-language therapy.

(10) Patient rights.

(11) Disaster preparedness. Disaster preparedness plans for both internal and external disasters shall protect hospice patients, employees, and visitors, and reflect coordination with local agencies that are responsible for disaster preparedness and emergency response.

(12) An adequate, safe, and sanitary physical environment.

(13) Housekeeping services.

(14) Patient medical records.

(15) Other administrative requirements.

(b) The department may adopt regulations that establish standards for the provision of the services in subdivision (a) and any additional qualifications and requirements for licensure above the requirements of this article.

(c) A hospice patient has a right to be informed of his or her rights, and the hospice facility shall protect and promote the exercise of these rights. The hospice facility shall comply with the patients' rights regulation in Section 418.52 of Title 42 of the Code of Federal Regulations unless the department adopts regulations establishing alternative standards pursuant to Section 1250.1. In addition, the hospice facility shall provide each patient with all of the following:

(1) Information at admission to a hospice facility pursuant to Chapter 3.9 (commencing with Section 1599).

(2) Full information regarding his or her health status and options for end-of-life care.

(3) Care that reflects individual preferences regarding end-of-life care, including the right to refuse any treatment or procedure.

(4) Treatment with consideration, respect, and full recognition of dignity and individuality, including privacy in treatment and care of personal needs.

(5) Right to visitors of the patient's choosing, at any time the patient chooses, and privacy for those visits.

(d) The hospice facility shall continue to provide services to family and friends after the patient's stay in the hospice facility in accordance with the patient's plan of care. These services may be provided by the hospice services program that operates the hospice facility.

(e) The hospice facility shall demonstrate the ability to meet licensing requirements and shall be fully responsible for meeting all licensing requirements, regardless of whether those requirements are met through direct provision by the facility or under contract with another entity. The hospice facility's reliance on contractors to meet the licensing requirements does not exempt the hospice facility from any requirements or in any way alter the hospice facility's responsibilities. When a health facility provides services under contract to a hospice facility, nothing shall preclude the department from holding the health facility responsible for violations of the law, if the department determines that the facts also constitute a separate violation for the health facility providing services under contract.

(f) The hospice facility shall provide inpatient hospice care in compliance with Section 418.3 and Sections 418.52 to 418.116, inclusive, of Title 42 of the Code of Federal Regulations until the department adopts regulations establishing alternative standards pursuant to Section 1250.1.
(Added by Stats. 2012, Ch. 673, Sec. 5. (SB 135) Effective January 1, 2013.)

ARTICLE 11. Payers' Bill of Rights [1339.50 - 1339.59]

(Article 11 added by Stats. 2003, Ch. 582, Sec. 6.)

1339.50.

This article shall be known and may be cited as the Payers' Bill of Rights.
(Added by Stats. 2003, Ch. 582, Sec. 6. Effective January 1, 2004.)

1339.51.

(a) (1) Beginning July 1, 2004, a hospital, as defined in paragraph (2) of subdivision (b), shall make a written or electronic copy of its charge description master available, either by posting an electronic copy of the charge description master on the hospital's Internet Web site, or by making one written or electronic copy available at the hospital location.

(2) A small and rural hospital, as defined in Section 124840, shall be exempt from paragraph (1).

(b) For purposes of this article, the following definitions shall apply:

(1) "Charge description master" means a uniform schedule of charges represented by the hospital as its gross billed charge for a given service or item, regardless of payer type.

(2) "Hospital" means a hospital, as defined in subdivision (a), (b), or (f) of Section 1250, that uses a charge description master.

(3) "Office" means the Office of Statewide Health Planning and Development.

(c) The hospital shall post a clear and conspicuous notice in its emergency department, if any, in its admissions office, and in its billing office that informs patients that the hospital's charge description master is available in the manner described in subdivision (a).

(d) Any information about charges provided pursuant to subdivision (a) shall include information about where to obtain information regarding hospital quality, including hospital outcome studies available from the office and hospital survey information available from the Joint Commission for Accreditation of Healthcare Organizations.
(Added by Stats. 2003, Ch. 582, Sec. 6. Effective January 1, 2004.)

1339.52.

A hospital may not condition acceptance of a contract with a health care service plan or health insurer upon the health care service plan or health insurer waiving any provision of this article.
(Added by Stats. 2003, Ch. 582, Sec. 6. Effective January 1, 2004.)

1339.54.

Any person may file a claim with the department alleging a violation of this article. The department shall investigate and inform the complaining person of its determination whether a violation has occurred and what action it will take.
(Added by Stats. 2003, Ch. 582, Sec. 6. Effective January 1, 2004.)

1339.55.

(a) Beginning July 1, 2004, each hospital shall file a copy of its charge description master annually with the office, in a format determined by the office.

(b) Each hospital shall calculate an estimate of the percentage increase in the hospital's gross revenue due to any price increase for charges for patient services during the 12-month period beginning with the effective date of the charge description master filed with the office. Each hospital shall file the calculation and supporting documentation with the office, in a form prescribed by the office, at the time that the charge description master is filed. The office may compile and publish this information on its Internet Web site.
(Added by Stats. 2003, Ch. 582, Sec. 6. Effective January 1, 2004.)

1339.56.

(a) Each hospital shall compile a list of 25 common outpatient procedures and shall submit annually to the office a list of its average charges for those procedures, in a method determined by the office. The office may develop a uniform reporting form for the purposes of this subdivision and may require hospitals to file this completed form with the office. The office shall publish this information on its Internet Web site.

(b) The office shall establish a list of the 25 most commonly performed inpatient procedures in California hospitals, as grouped by Medicare diagnostic-related group. The office shall develop a list of each hospital's average charges for those procedures, if applicable, and shall update the list at least annually. The office shall publish this information on its Internet Web site.

(c) Each hospital shall provide a copy of the lists described in subdivisions (a) and (b) to any person upon request.
(Amended by Stats. 2005, Ch. 532, Sec. 1. Effective January 1, 2006.)

1339.58.

Any information provided by the office on its Internet Web site pursuant to Section 1339.56 or 1339.57 may inform persons where quality of care information about hospitals may be obtained, including hospital outcome studies available from the office and hospital survey information available from the Joint Commission for Accreditation of Healthcare Organizations.
(Added by Stats. 2003, Ch. 582, Sec. 6. Effective January 1, 2004.)

1339.585.

Upon the request of a person without health coverage, a hospital shall provide the person with a written estimate of the amount the hospital will require the person to pay for the

health care services, procedures, and supplies that are reasonably expected to be provided to the person by the hospital, based upon an average length of stay and services provided for the person's diagnosis. The hospital may provide this estimate during normal business office hours. In addition to the estimate, the hospital shall provide information about its financial assistance and charity care policies and contact information for a hospital employee or office from which the person may obtain further information about these policies. If requested, the hospital shall also provide the person with an application form for financial assistance or charity care. This section shall not apply to emergency services provided to a person pursuant to Section 1317.
(Added by Stats. 2005, Ch. 532, Sec. 3. Effective January 1, 2006.)

1339.59.

(a) A hospital shall be in violation of this article if it knowingly or negligently fails to comply with the requirements of this article.

(b) A hospital that does not file with the office the information required by this article may be liable for civil penalties as specified in Section 128770.
(Amended by Stats. 2005, Ch. 532, Sec. 4. Effective January 1, 2006.)

CHAPTER 2.05. Minimization of Medication-Related Errors [1339.63-1339.63.]

(Chapter 2.05 added by Stats. 2000, Ch. 816, Sec. 1.)

1339.63.

(a) (1) As a condition of licensure under this division, every general acute care hospital, as defined in subdivision (a) of Section 1250, special hospital, as defined in subdivision (f) of Section 1250, and surgical clinic, as defined in paragraph (1) of subdivision (b) of Section 1204, shall adopt a formal plan to eliminate or substantially reduce medication-related errors. With the exception of small and rural hospitals, as defined in Section 124840, this plan shall include technology implementation, such as, but not limited to, computerized physician order entry or other technology that, based upon independent, expert scientific advice and data, has been shown effective in eliminating or substantially reducing medication-related errors.

(2) Each facility's plan shall be provided to the State Department of Health Services no later than January 1, 2002. Within 90 days after submitting a plan, the department shall either approve the plan, or return it to the facility with comments and suggestions for improvement. The facility shall revise and resubmit the plan within 90 days after receiving it from the department. The department shall provide final written approval within 90 days after resubmission, but in no event later than January 1, 2003. The plan shall be implemented on or before January 1, 2005.

(b) Any of the following facilities that is in the process of constructing a new structure or retrofitting an existing structure for the purposes of complying with seismic safety requirements shall be exempt from implementing a plan by January 1, 2005:

(1) General acute care hospitals, as defined in subdivision (a) of Section 1250.

(2) Special hospitals, as defined in subdivision (f) of Section 1250.

(3) Surgical clinics, as defined in paragraph (1) of subdivision (b) of Section 1204.

(c) The implementation date for facilities that are in the process of constructing a new structure or retrofitting an existing structure is six months after the date of completion of all retrofitting or new construction. The exemption and new implementation date specified in subdivision (b) and this subdivision apply to those facilities that have construction plans and financing for projects in place no later than July 1, 2002.

(d) For purposes of this chapter, a "medication-related error" means any preventable medication-related event that adversely affects a patient in a facility listed in subdivision (a), and that is related to professional practice, or health care products, procedures, and systems, including, but not limited to, prescribing, prescription order communications, product labeling, packaging and nomenclature, compounding, dispensing, distribution, administration, education, monitoring, and use.

(e) Each facility's plan shall do the following:

(1) Evaluate, assess, and include a method to address each of the procedures and systems listed under subdivision (d) to identify weaknesses or deficiencies that could contribute to errors in the administration of medication.

(2) Include an annual review to assess the effectiveness of the implementation of each of the procedures and systems listed under subdivision (d).

(3) Be modified as warranted when weaknesses or deficiencies are noted to achieve the reduction of medication errors.

(4) Describe the technology to be implemented and how it is expected to reduce medication-related errors as described in paragraph (1) of subdivision (a).

(5) Include a system or process to proactively identify actual or potential medication-related errors. The system or process shall include concurrent and retrospective review of clinical care.

(6) Include a multidisciplinary process, including health care professionals responsible for pharmaceuticals, nursing, medical, and administration, to regularly analyze all identified actual or potential medication-related errors and describe how the analysis will be utilized to change current procedures and systems to reduce medication-related errors.

(7) Include a process to incorporate external medication-related error alerts to modify current processes and systems as appropriate. Failure to meet this criterion shall not cause disapproval of the initial plan submitted.

(f) Beginning January 1, 2005, the department shall monitor the implementation of each facility's plan upon licensure visits.

(g) The department may work with the facility's health care community to present an annual symposium to recognize the best practices for each of the procedures and systems listed under subdivision (d).
(Amended by Stats. 2003, Ch. 62, Sec. 177. Effective January 1, 2004.)

CHAPTER 2.1. Establishment of County Departments Pertaining to Out-of-Home Care Facilities [1339.70- 1339.70.]

(Chapter 2.1 added by Stats. 1978, Ch. 275.)

1339.70.

Notwithstanding any other provision of law, a county may by ordinance establish a department of the county which may combine in the department any or all of the functions specified in this section or related functions. The duties of the department shall be specified in the county ordinance establishing the department. Such duties may include the following:

(a) The performance of any function which is authorized by Section 1257 to be delegated to local health departments, to the extent delegated by the state department to the department established pursuant to this section. For purposes of this section and Section 1257, a department established pursuant to this section shall be deemed to be a local health department.

(b) The performance of any function which is authorized by Section 1511 to be delegated by the state department to a county, to the extent delegated by the state department to the department authorized by this section.

(c) The performance of any function in connection with, or related to, the certification of health facilities or community care facilities for participation in programs conducted pursuant to Title XVIII, Title XIX, or other provisions of the federal Social Security Act.

(d) The performance of any information and referral activities which are authorized by law to be performed by a county or any of its departments or officers in connection with health facilities or community care facilities.

(e) The performance of any function authorized by law to be performed by a county or any of its officers or departments in connection with the sanitation, maintenance, occupancy, or other aspects of the physical plant or environmental management of or concerning any health facility or community care facility. For purposes of this section, the department authorized by this section shall be deemed to be a county health department under the control of a county health officer with respect to any provision of law authorizing the performance of any function concerning any health facility or community care facility by a local health department or health officer.

(f) The determination of the suitability for county use, placements, or referrals of particular health facilities or community care facilities.

This section shall not be construed as authorizing the performance of any activity by any county which the county would not otherwise be authorized to perform. This section shall not operate as an independent grant of authority for the performance of any function by a county, but shall permit the consolidation in an existing or new county department of any or all functions which counties are authorized to perform in connection with the matters specified in this section.

For purposes of this section, "health facility" means a health facility as defined in Section 1250, and "community care facility" means a community care facility as defined in Section 1502.
(Added by renumbering Section 1339.50 by Stats. 1985, Ch. 106, Sec. 79.)

CHAPTER 2.15. Hospital and Other Provider Requirements for Dissemination of Information Relating to Reproductive Health Services [1339.80 - 1339.81]

(Chapter 2.15 added by Stats. 2000, Ch. 347, Sec. 1.)

1339.80.

Hospitals and other providers are not required to post, send, deliver, or otherwise provide the statement described in paragraph (1) of subdivision (b) of Section 1363.02, paragraph (1) of subdivision (b) of Section 10604.1 of the Insurance Code, or paragraph (1) of subdivision (b) of Section 14016.8 of the Welfare and Institutions Code.
(Added by Stats. 2000, Ch. 347, Sec. 1. Effective January 1, 2001.)

1339.81.

For purposes of this chapter, "provider" means any professional person, organization, health facility, or other person or institution licensed by the state to deliver or furnish health care services.
(Added by Stats. 2000, Ch. 347, Sec. 1. Effective January 1, 2001.)

CHAPTER 2.2. Health Care Service Plans [1340 - 1399.864]

(Chapter 2.2 added by Stats. 1975, Ch. 941.)

ARTICLE 1. General [1340 - 1345.5]

(Article 1 added by Stats. 1975, Ch. 941.)

1340.

This chapter shall be known and may be cited as the Knox-Keene Health Care Service Plan Act of 1975.

(Added by Stats. 1975, Ch. 941.)

1341.

(a) There is in state government, in the California Health and Human Services Agency, a Department of Managed Health Care that has charge of the execution of the laws of this state relating to health care service plans and the health care service plan business including, but not limited to, those laws directing the department to ensure that health care service plans provide enrollees with access to quality health care services and protect and promote the interests of enrollees.

(b) The chief officer of the Department of Managed Health Care is the Director of the Department of Managed Health Care. The director shall be appointed by the Governor and shall hold office at the pleasure of the Governor. The director shall receive an annual salary as fixed in the Government Code. Within 15 days from the time of the director's appointment, the director shall take and subscribe to the constitutional oath of office and file it in the office of the Secretary of State.

(c) The director shall be responsible for the performance of all duties, the exercise of all powers and jurisdiction, and the assumption and discharge of all responsibilities vested by law in the department. The director has and may exercise all powers necessary or convenient for the administration and enforcement of, among other laws, the laws described in subdivision (a).

(Amended by Stats. 2011, Ch. 552, Sec. 2. (AB 922) Effective January 1, 2012.)

1341.1.

The director shall have his or her principal office in the City of Sacramento, and may establish branch offices in the City and County of San Francisco, in the City of Los Angeles, and in the City of San Diego. The director shall from time to time obtain the necessary furniture, stationery, fuel, light, and other proper conveniences for the transaction of the business of the Department of Managed Health Care.

(Amended by Stats. 2000, Ch. 857, Sec. 20. Effective January 1, 2001.)

1341.2.

In accordance with the laws governing the state civil service, the director shall employ and, with the approval of the Department of Finance, fix the compensation of such personnel as the director needs to discharge properly the duties imposed upon the director by law, including, but not limited to, a chief deputy, a public information officer, a chief enforcement counsel, and legal counsel to act as the attorney for the director in actions or proceedings brought by or against the director under or pursuant to any provision of any law under the director's jurisdiction, or in which the director joins or intervenes as to a matter within the director's jurisdiction, as a friend of the court or otherwise, and stenographic reporters to take and transcribe the testimony in any formal hearing or investigation before the director or before a person authorized by the director. The personnel of the Department of Managed Health Care shall perform such duties as the director assigns to them. Such employees as the director designates by rule or order shall, within 15 days after their appointments, take and subscribe to the constitutional oath of office and file it in the office of the Secretary of State.

(Amended by Stats. 2000, Ch. 857, Sec. 21. Effective January 1, 2001.)

1341.3.

The director shall adopt a seal bearing the inscription: "Director, Department of Managed Health Care, State of California." The seal shall be affixed to or imprinted on all orders and certificates issued by him or her and such other instruments as he or she directs. All courts shall take judicial notice of this seal.

(Amended by Stats. 2000, Ch. 857, Sec. 22. Effective January 1, 2001.)

1341.4.

(a) In order to effectively support the Department of Managed Health Care in the administration of this law, there is hereby established in the State Treasury, the Managed Care Fund. The administration of the Department of Managed Health Care shall be supported from the Managed Care Fund.

(b) In any fiscal year, the Managed Care Fund shall maintain not more than a prudent 5 percent reserve unless otherwise determined by the Department of Finance.

(Amended by Stats. 2007, Ch. 577, Sec. 6. Effective October 13, 2007.)

1341.45.

(a) There is hereby created in the State Treasury the Managed Care Administrative Fines and Penalties Fund.

(b) The fines and administrative penalties collected pursuant to this chapter, on and after September 30, 2008, shall be deposited into the Managed Care Administrative Fines and Penalties Fund.

(c) The fines and administrative penalties deposited into the Managed Care Administrative Fines and Penalties Fund shall be transferred by the department, beginning September 1, 2009, and annually thereafter, as follows:

(1) The first one million dollars ($1,000,000) shall be transferred to the Medically Underserved Account for Physicians within the Health Professions Education Fund and shall, upon appropriation by the Legislature, be used for the purposes of the Steven M. Thompson Physician Corps Loan Repayment Program, as specified in Article 5 (commencing with Section 128550) or Chapter 5 of Part 3 of Division 107 and, notwithstanding Section 128555, shall not be used to provide funding for the Physician Volunteer Program.

(2) Any amount over the first one million dollars ($1,000,000), including accrued interest, in the fund shall be transferred to the Health Care Services Plan Fines and Penalties Fund created pursuant to Section 15893 of the Welfare and Institutions Code and, notwithstanding Section 13340 of the Government Code, shall be continuously appropriated for the purposes specified in Section 15894 of the Welfare and Institutions Code.

(d) Notwithstanding subdivision (b) of Section 1356 and Section 1356.1, the fines and administrative penalties authorized pursuant to this chapter shall not be used to reduce the assessments imposed on health care service plans pursuant to Section 1356.

(e) The amendments made to this section by the act adding this subdivision shall become operative on July 1, 2014.

(f) The amendments made to this section by the act adding this subdivision shall become operative on July 1, 2017.

(Amended by Stats. 2017, Ch. 52, Sec. 4. (SB 97) Effective July 10, 2017. Amended version operative from July 1, 2017, by subdivision (f).)

1341.5.

(a) The director, as a general rule, shall publish or make available for public inspection any information filed with or obtained by the department, unless the director finds that this availability or publication is contrary to law. No provision of this chapter authorizes the director or any of the director's assistants, clerks, or deputies to disclose any information withheld from public inspection except among themselves or when necessary or appropriate in a proceeding or investigation under this chapter or to other federal or state regulatory agencies. No provision of this chapter either creates or derogates from any privilege that exists at common law or otherwise when documentary or other evidence is sought under a subpoena directed to the director or any of his or her assistants, clerks, or deputies.

(b) It is unlawful for the director or any of his or her assistants, clerks, or deputies to use for personal benefit any information that is filed with or obtained by the director and that is not then generally available to the public.

(Added by Stats. 1999, Ch. 525, Sec. 27. Effective January 1, 2000. Operative July 1, 2000, or sooner, by Sec. 214 of Ch. 525.)

1341.6.

(a) The Attorney General shall render to the director opinions upon all questions of law, relating to the construction or interpretation of any law under the director's jurisdiction or arising in the administration thereof, that may be submitted to the Attorney General by the director and upon the director's request shall act as the attorney for the director in actions and proceedings brought by or against the director under or pursuant to any provision of any law under the director's jurisdiction.

(b) Sections 11041, 11042, and 11043 of the Government Code do not apply to the Director of the Department of Managed Health Care.

(Amended by Stats. 2000, Ch. 857, Sec. 23. Effective January 1, 2001.)

1341.7.

(a) Neither the director nor any of the director's assistants, clerks, or deputies shall be interested as a director, officer, shareholder, member other than a member of an organization formed for religious purposes, partner, agent, or employee of any person who, during the period of the official's or employee's association with the Department of Managed Health Care, was licensed or applied for a license as a health care service plan under this chapter.

(b) Nothing contained in subdivision (a) shall prohibit the holdings or purchasing of any securities by the director, an assistant, clerk, or deputy in accordance with rules which shall be adopted for the purpose of protecting the public interest and avoiding conflicts of interest.

(c) Nothing in this section shall prohibit or preclude the director or any of the director's assistants, clerks, or deputies or any employee of the Department of Managed Health Care from obtaining health care services as a subscriber or an enrollee from a plan licensed under this chapter, subject to any rules that may be adopted hereunder or pursuant to proper authority.

(Amended by Stats. 2000, Ch. 857, Sec. 24. Effective January 1, 2001.)

1341.8.

The director shall have the powers of a head of a department pursuant to Chapter 2 (commencing with Section 11150) of Part 1 of Division 3 of Title 2 of the Government Code. The director may make the agreements that he or she deems necessary or appropriate in exercising his or her powers.

(Added by Stats. 1999, Ch. 525, Sec. 30. Effective January 1, 2000. Operative July 1, 2000, or sooner, by Sec. 214 of Ch. 525.)

1341.9.

The director and department succeed to, and are vested with, all duties, powers, purposes, responsibilities, and jurisdiction of the Commissioner of Corporations and the Department of Corporations as they relate to the Department of Corporations' Health Plan Program, health care service plans, and the health care service plan business, including those powers and duties specified in this chapter. Nothing in this section abrogates, limits, diminishes, or otherwise restricts the duties, powers, purposes, responsibilities, and jurisdictions of the Commissioner of Corporations and the Department of Corporations under the Investment Program, the Financial Services Program, and the other laws in which jurisdiction is vested in the Commissioner of Corporations and the Department of Corporations.

(Added by Stats. 1999, Ch. 525, Sec. 31. Effective January 1, 2000. Operative July 1, 2000, or sooner, by Sec. 214 of Ch. 525.)

1341.10.

The department may use the unexpended balance of funds available for use in connection with the performance of the functions of the Department of Corporations to which the department succeeds pursuant to Section 1341.9.

(Added by Stats. 1999, Ch. 525, Sec. 32. Effective January 1, 2000. Operative July 1, 2000, or sooner, by Sec. 214 of Ch. 525.)

1341.11.

All officers and employees of the Department of Corporations who, on the operative date of this section, are performing any duty, power, purpose, responsibility, or jurisdiction to which the department succeeds, who are serving in the state civil service, other than as temporary employees, and engaged in the performance of a function vested by the department by Section 1341.9, shall be transferred to the department. The status, positions, and rights of those persons shall not be affected by the transfer and shall be retained by those persons as officers and employees of the department, pursuant to the State Civil Service Act (Part 2 (commencing with Section 18500) of Division 5 of Title 2 of the Government Code), except as to positions exempted from civil service.
(Added by Stats. 1999, Ch. 525, Sec. 33. Effective January 1, 2000. Operative July 1, 2000, or sooner, by Sec. 214 of Ch. 525.)

1341.12.

The department shall have possession and control of all records, papers, offices, equipment, supplies, moneys, funds, appropriations, licenses, permits, agreements, contracts, claims, judgments, land, and other property, real or personal, connected with the administration of, or held for the benefit or use of, the Department of Corporations for the performance of the functions transferred to the department by Section 1341.9.
(Added by Stats. 1999, Ch. 525, Sec. 34. Effective January 1, 2000. Operative July 1, 2000, or sooner, by Sec. 214 of Ch. 525.)

1341.13.

All officers or employees of the department employed after the operative date of this section shall be appointed by the director.
(Added by Stats. 1999, Ch. 525, Sec. 35. Effective January 1, 2000. Operative July 1, 2000, or sooner, by Sec. 214 of Ch. 525.)

1341.14.

(a) Any regulation, order, or other action, adopted, prescribed, taken, or performed by the Department of Corporations or by an officer of the Department of Corporations in the administration of a program or the performance of a duty, responsibility, or authorization transferred to the department by Section 1341.9 shall remain in effect and shall be deemed to be a regulation, order, or action of the department.
(b) No suit, action, or other proceeding lawfully commenced by or against the Department of Corporations or any other officer of the state, in relation to the administration of any program or the discharge of any duty, responsibility, or authorization transferred to the department by Section 1341.9 shall abate by reason of the transfer of the program, duty, responsibility, or authorization.
(Added by Stats. 1999, Ch. 525, Sec. 36. Effective January 1, 2000. Operative July 1, 2000, or sooner, by Sec. 214 of Ch. 525.)

1342.

It is the intent and purpose of the Legislature to promote the delivery and the quality of health and medical care to the people of the State of California who enroll in, or subscribe for the services rendered by, a health care service plan or specialized health care service plan by accomplishing all of the following:
(a) Ensuring the continued role of the professional as the determiner of the patient's health needs which fosters the traditional relationship of trust and confidence between the patient and the professional.
(b) Ensuring that subscribers and enrollees are educated and informed of the benefits and services available in order to enable a rational consumer choice in the marketplace.
(c) Prosecuting malefactors who make fraudulent solicitations or who use deceptive methods, misrepresentations, or practices which are inimical to the general purpose of enabling a rational choice for the consumer public.
(d) Helping to ensure the best possible health care for the public at the lowest possible cost by transferring the financial risk of health care from patients to providers.
(e) Promoting effective representation of the interests of subscribers and enrollees.
(f) Ensuring the financial stability thereof by means of proper regulatory procedures.
(g) Ensuring that subscribers and enrollees receive available and accessible health and medical services rendered in a manner providing continuity of care.
(h) Ensuring that subscribers and enrollees have their grievances expeditiously and thoroughly reviewed by the department.
(Amended by Stats. 2002, Ch. 797, Sec. 2. Effective January 1, 2003.)

1342.4.

(a) The Department of Managed Health Care and the Department of Insurance shall maintain a joint senior level working group to ensure clarity for health care consumers about who enforces their patient rights and consistency in the regulations of these departments.
(b) The joint working group shall undertake a review and examination of the Health and Safety Code, the Insurance Code, and the Welfare and Institutions Code as they apply to the Department of Managed Health Care and the Department of Insurance to ensure consistency in consumer protection.
(c) The joint working group shall review and examine all of the following processes in each department:
(1) Grievance and consumer complaint processes, including, but not limited to, outreach, standard complaints, including coverage and medical necessity complaints, independent medical review, and information developed for consumer use.
(2) The processes used to ensure enforcement of the law, including, but not limited to, the medical survey and audit process in the Health and Safety Code and market conduct exams in the Insurance Code.
(3) The processes for regulating the timely payment of claims.
(d) The joint working group shall report its findings to the Insurance Commissioner and the Director of the Department of Managed Health Care for review and approval. The

commissioner and the director shall submit the approved final report under signature to the Legislature by January 1 of every year for five years.
(Added by Stats. 2002, Ch. 793, Sec. 1. Effective January 1, 2003.)

1342.5.

The director shall consult with the Insurance Commissioner prior to adopting any regulations applicable to health care service plans subject to this chapter and other entities governed by the Insurance Code for the specific purpose of ensuring, to the extent practical, that there is consistency of regulations applicable to these plans and entities by the Insurance Commissioner and the Director of the Department of Managed Health Care.
(Amended by Stats. 2007, Ch. 577, Sec. 8. Effective October 13, 2007.)

1342.6.

It is the intent of the Legislature to ensure that the citizens of this state receive high-quality health care coverage in the most efficient and cost-effective manner possible. In furtherance of this intent, the Legislature finds and declares that it is in the public interest to promote various types of contracts between public or private payers of health care coverage, and institutional or professional providers of health care services. This intent has been demonstrated by the recent enactment of Chapters 328, 329, and 1594 of the Statutes of 1982, authorizing various types of contracts to be entered into between public or private payers of health care coverage, and institutional or professional providers of health care services. The Legislature further finds and declares that individual providers, whether institutional or professional, and individual purchasers, have not proven to be efficient-sized bargaining units for these contracts, and that the formation of groups and combinations of institutional and professional providers and combinations of purchasing groups for the purpose of creating efficient-sized contracting units represents a meaningful addition to the health care marketplace. The Legislature further finds and declares that negotiations between purchasers or payers of health services, and health care service plans governed by the provisions of this chapter, or through a person or entity acting for, or on behalf of, a purchaser or payer of health services, or a health care service plan, are in furtherance of the public's interest in obtaining quality health care services in the most efficient and cost-effective manner possible. It is the intent of the Legislature, therefore, that the formation of groups and combinations of providers and purchasing groups for the purpose of creating efficient-sized contracting units be recognized as the creation of a new product within the health care marketplace, and be subject, therefore, only to those antitrust prohibitions applicable to the conduct of other presumptively legitimate enterprises.
This section does not change existing antitrust law as it relates to any agreement or arrangement to exclude from any of the above-described groups or combinations, any person who is lawfully qualified to perform the services to be performed by the members of the group or combination, where the ground for the exclusion is failure to possess the same license or certification as is possessed by the members of the group or combination.
(Added by Stats. 1985, Ch. 1592, Sec. 2.)

1342.7.

(a) The Legislature finds that in enacting Sections 1367.215, 1367.25, 1367.45, 1367.51, and 1374.72, it did not intend to limit the department's authority to regulate the provision of medically necessary prescription drug benefits by a health care service plan to the extent that the plan provides coverage for those benefits.
(b) (1) Nothing in this chapter shall preclude a plan from filing relevant information with the department pursuant to Section 1352 to seek the approval of a copayment, deductible, limitation, or exclusion to a plan's prescription drug benefits. If the department approves an exclusion to a plan's prescription drug benefits, the exclusion shall not be subject to review through the independent medical review process pursuant to Section 1374.30 on the grounds of medical necessity. The department shall retain its role in assessing whether issues are related to coverage or medical necessity pursuant to paragraph (2) of subdivision (d) of Section 1374.30.
(2) A plan seeking approval of a copayment or deductible may file an amendment pursuant to Section 1352.1. A plan seeking approval of a limitation or exclusion shall file a material modification pursuant to subdivision (b) of Section 1352.
(c) Nothing in this chapter shall prohibit a plan from charging a subscriber or enrollee a copayment or deductible for a prescription drug benefit or from setting forth by contract, a limitation or an exclusion from, coverage of prescription drug benefits, if the copayment, deductible, limitation, or exclusion is reported to, and found unobjectionable by, the director and disclosed to the subscriber or enrollee pursuant to the provisions of Section 1363.
(d) The department in developing standards for the approval of a copayment, deductible, limitation, or exclusion to a plan's prescription drug benefits, shall consider alternative benefit designs, including, but not limited to, the following:
(1) Different out-of-pocket costs for consumers, including copayments and deductibles.
(2) Different limitations, including caps on benefits.
(3) Use of exclusions from coverage of prescription drugs to treat various conditions, including the effect of the exclusions on the plan's ability to provide basic health care services, the amount of subscriber or enrollee premiums, and the amount of out-of-pocket costs for an enrollee.
(4) Different packages negotiated between purchasers and plans.
(5) Different tiered pharmacy benefits, including the use of generic prescription drugs.
(6) Current and past practices.
(e) The department shall develop a regulation outlining the standards to be used in reviewing a plan's request for approval of its proposed copayment, deductible, limitation, or exclusion on its prescription drug benefits.

(f) Nothing in subdivision (b) or (c) shall permit a plan to limit prescription drug benefits provided in a manner that is inconsistent with Sections 1367.215, 1367.25, 1367.45, 1367.51, and 1374.72.

(g) Nothing in this section shall be construed to require or authorize a plan that contracts with the State Department of Health Services to provide services to Medi-Cal beneficiaries or with the Managed Risk Medical Insurance Board to provide services to enrollees of the Healthy Families Program to provide coverage for prescription drugs that are not required pursuant to those programs or contracts, or to limit or exclude any prescription drugs that are required by those programs or contracts.

(h) Nothing in this section shall be construed as prohibiting or otherwise affecting a plan contract that does not cover outpatient prescription drugs except for coverage for limited classes of prescription drugs because they are integral to treatments covered as basic health care services, including, but not limited to, immunosuppressives, in order to allow for transplants of bodily organs.

(i) The department shall periodically review its regulations developed pursuant to this section.

(j) This section shall become operative on January 2, 2003, and shall only apply to contracts issued, amended, or renewed on or after that date.

(Amended by Stats. 2012, Ch. 728, Sec. 81. (SB 71) Effective January 1, 2013.)

1342.71.

(a) The Legislature hereby finds and declares all of the following:

(1) The federal Patient Protection and Affordable Care Act, its implementing regulations and guidance, and related state law prohibit discrimination based on a person's expected length of life, present or predicted disability, degree of medical dependency, quality of life, or other health conditions, including benefit designs that have the effect of discouraging the enrollment of individuals with significant health needs.

(2) The Legislature intends to build on the existing state and federal law to ensure that health coverage benefit designs do not have an unreasonable discriminatory impact on chronically ill individuals, and to ensure affordability of outpatient prescription drugs.

(3) Assignment of all or most prescription medications that treat a specific medical condition to the highest cost tiers of a formulary may effectively discourage enrollment by chronically ill individuals, and may result in lower adherence to a prescription drug treatment regimen.

(b) A nongrandfathered health care service plan contract that is offered, amended, or renewed on or after January 1, 2017, shall comply with this section. The cost-sharing limits established by this section apply only to outpatient prescription drugs covered by the contract that constitute essential health benefits, as defined in Section 1367.005.

(c) A health care service plan contract that provides coverage for outpatient prescription drugs shall cover medically necessary prescription drugs, including nonformulary drugs determined to be medically necessary consistent with this chapter.

(d) (1) Consistent with federal law and guidance, the formulary or formularies for outpatient prescription drugs maintained by the health care service plan shall not discourage the enrollment of individuals with health conditions and shall not reduce the generosity of the benefit for enrollees with a particular condition in a manner that is not based on a clinical indication or reasonable medical management practices. Section 1342.7 and any regulations adopted pursuant to that section shall be interpreted in a manner that is consistent with this section.

(2) For combination antiretroviral drug treatments that are medically necessary for the treatment of AIDS/HIV, a health care service plan contract shall cover a single-tablet drug regimen that is as effective as a multitablet regimen unless, consistent with clinical guidelines and peer-reviewed scientific and medical literature, the multitablet regimen is clinically equally or more effective and more likely to result in adherence to a drug regimen.

(e) A health care service plan contract shall ensure that the placement of prescription drugs on formulary tiers is based on clinically indicated, reasonable medical management practices.

(f) (1) This section shall not be construed to require a health care service plan to impose cost sharing.

(2) This section shall not be construed to require cost sharing for prescription drugs that state or federal law otherwise requires to be provided without cost sharing.

(3) A plan's prescription drug benefit shall provide that if the pharmacy's retail price for a prescription drug is less than the applicable copayment or coinsurance amount, the enrollee shall not be required to pay more than the retail price. The payment rendered shall constitute the applicable cost sharing and shall apply to the deductible, if any, and also to the maximum out-of-pocket limit in the same manner as if the enrollee had purchased the prescription medication by paying the cost-sharing amount.

(g) In the provision of outpatient prescription drug coverage, a health care service plan may utilize formulary, prior authorization, step therapy, or other reasonable medical management practices consistent with this chapter.

(h) This section does not apply to a health care service plan contract with the State Department of Health Care Services.

(Amended (as amended by Stats. 2016, Ch. 86, Sec. 175) by Stats. 2018, Ch. 787, Sec. 1. (SB 1021) Effective January 1, 2019.)

1342.72.

(a) For combination antiretroviral drug treatments that are medically necessary for the prevention of AIDS/HIV, a health care service plan shall not have utilization management policies or procedures, including a standard of care, which rely on a multitablet drug regimen instead of a single-tablet drug regimen unless, consistent with clinical guidelines and peer-reviewed scientific and medical literature, the multitablet regimen is clinically

equally or more effective and equally or more likely to result in adherence to a drug regimen.

(b) This section does not apply to a health care service plan contract with the State Department of Health Care Services.

(c) This section shall remain in effect only until January 1, 2023, and as of that date is repealed, unless a later enacted statute that is enacted before January 1, 2023, deletes or extends that date.

(Added by Stats. 2018, Ch. 787, Sec. 3. (SB 1021) Effective January 1, 2019. Repealed as of January 1, 2023, by its own provisions.)

1342.73.

(a) (1) With respect to an individual or group health care service plan contract subject to Section 1367.006, the copayment, coinsurance, or any other form of cost sharing for a covered outpatient prescription drug for an individual prescription for a supply of up to 30 days shall not exceed two hundred fifty dollars ($250), except as provided in paragraphs (2) and (3).

(2) With respect to products with actuarial value at, or equivalent to, the bronze level, cost sharing for a covered outpatient prescription drug for an individual prescription for a supply of up to 30 days shall not exceed five hundred dollars ($500), except as provided in paragraph (3).

(3) For a health care service plan contract that is a "high deductible health plan" under the definition set forth in Section 223(c)(2) of Title 26 of the United States Code, paragraphs (1) and (2) of this subdivision shall apply only once an enrollee's deductible has been satisfied for the year.

(4) For a nongrandfathered individual or small group health care service plan contract, the annual deductible for outpatient drugs, if any, shall not exceed twice the amount specified in paragraph (1) or (2), respectively.

(5) For purposes of paragraphs (1) and (2), "any other form of cost sharing" shall not include a deductible.

(b) (1) If a health care service plan contract for a nongrandfathered individual or small group product maintains a drug formulary grouped into tiers that includes a fourth tier, a health care service plan contract shall use the following definitions for each tier of the drug formulary:

(A) Tier one shall consist of most generic drugs and low-cost preferred brand name drugs.

(B) Tier two shall consist of nonpreferred generic drugs, preferred brand name drugs, and any other drugs recommended by the health care service plan's pharmacy and therapeutics committee based on safety, efficacy, and cost.

(C) Tier three shall consist of nonpreferred brand name drugs or drugs that are recommended by the health care service plan's pharmacy and therapeutics committee based on safety, efficacy, and cost, or that generally have a preferred and often less costly therapeutic alternative at a lower tier.

(D) Tier four shall consist of drugs that are biologics, drugs that the Food and Drug Administration of the United States Department of Health and Human Services or the manufacturer requires to be distributed through a specialty pharmacy, drugs that require the enrollee to have special training or clinical monitoring for self-administration, or drugs that cost the health plan more than six hundred dollars ($600) net of rebates for a one-month supply.

(2) In placing specific drugs on specific tiers, or choosing to place a drug on the formulary, the health care service plan shall take into account the other provisions of this section and this chapter.

(3) A health care service plan contract may maintain a drug formulary with fewer than four tiers. A health care service plan contract shall not maintain a drug formulary with more than four tiers.

(4) This section shall not be construed to limit a health care service plan from placing any drug in a lower tier.

(c) This section does not apply to a health care service plan contract with the State Department of Health Care Services.

(d) This section shall remain in effect only until January 1, 2024, and as of that date is repealed, unless a later enacted statute that is enacted before January 1, 2024, deletes or extends that date.

(Added by Stats. 2018, Ch. 787, Sec. 4. (SB 1021) Effective January 1, 2019. Repealed as of January 1, 2024, by its own provisions.)

1342.8.

The State Department of Health Services and the department shall coordinate, to the extent feasible, audits or surveys of physician offices required by this chapter and by the managed care program under the Medi-Cal Act (Chapter 7 (commencing with Section 14000) of Part 3 of Division 9 of the Welfare and Institutions Code) and for any physician office auditing required by this chapter.

(Added by Stats. 1998, Ch. 647, Sec. 2. Effective January 1, 1999.)

1343.

(a) This chapter shall apply to health care service plans and specialized health care service plan contracts as defined in subdivisions (f) and (o) of Section 1345.

(b) The director may by the adoption of rules or the issuance of orders deemed necessary and appropriate, either unconditionally or upon specified terms and conditions or for specified periods, exempt from this chapter any class of persons or plan contracts if the director finds the action to be in the public interest and not detrimental to the protection of subscribers, enrollees, or persons regulated under this chapter, and that the regulation of the persons or plan contracts is not essential to the purposes of this chapter.

(c) The director, upon request of the Director of Health Care Services, shall exempt from this chapter any county-operated pilot program contracting with the State Department of Health Care Services pursuant to Article 7 (commencing with Section 14490) of Chapter 8 of Part 3 of Division 9 of the Welfare and Institutions Code. The director may exempt noncounty-operated pilot programs upon request of the Director of Health Care Services. Those exemptions may be subject to conditions the Director of Health Care Services deems appropriate.

(d) Upon the request of the Director of Health Care Services, the director may exempt from this chapter any mental health plan contractor or any capitated rate contract under Chapter 8.9 (commencing with Section 14700) of Part 3 of Division 9 of the Welfare and Institutions Code. Those exemptions may be subject to conditions the Director of Health Care Services deems appropriate.

(e) This chapter shall not apply to:

(1) A person organized and operating pursuant to a certificate issued by the Insurance Commissioner unless the entity is directly providing the health care service through those entity-owned or contracting health facilities and providers, in which case this chapter shall apply to the insurer's plan and to the insurer.

(2) A plan directly operated by a bona fide public or private institution of higher learning which directly provides health care services only to its students, faculty, staff, administration, and their respective dependents.

(3) A person who does all of the following:

(A) Promises to provide care for life or for more than one year in return for a transfer of consideration from, or on behalf of, a person 60 years of age or older.

(B) Has obtained a written license pursuant to Chapter 2 (commencing with Section 1250) or Chapter 3.2 (commencing with Section 1569).

(C) Has obtained a certificate of authority from the State Department of Social Services.

(4) The Major Risk Medical Insurance Board when engaging in activities under Chapter 8 (commencing with Section 10700) of Part 2 of Division 2 of the Insurance Code, Part 6.3 (commencing with Section 12695) of Division 2 of the Insurance Code, and Part 6.5 (commencing with Section 12700) of Division 2 of the Insurance Code.

(5) The California Small Group Reinsurance Fund.

(Amended by Stats. 2012, Ch. 34, Sec. 13. (SB 1009) Effective June 27, 2012. Operative July 1, 2012, by Sec. 254 of Ch. 34.)

1343.1.

This chapter shall not apply to any program developed under the authority of Chapter 8.75 (commencing with Section 14591) of Part 3 of Division 9 of the Welfare and Institutions Code.

(Amended by Stats. 2011, Ch. 367, Sec. 2. (AB 574) Effective January 1, 2012.)

1343.5.

In any proceeding under this chapter, the burden of proving an exemption or an exception from a definition is upon the person claiming it.

(Added by Stats. 1978, Ch. 778.)

1344.

(a) The director may from time to time adopt, amend, and rescind any rules, forms, and orders that are necessary to carry out the provisions of this chapter, including rules governing applications and reports, and defining any terms, whether or not used in this chapter, insofar as the definitions are not inconsistent with the provisions of this chapter. For the purpose of rules and forms, the director may classify persons and matters within the director's jurisdiction, and may prescribe different requirements for different classes. The director may waive any requirement of any rule or form in situations where in the director's discretion that requirement is not necessary in the public interest or for the protection of the public, subscribers, enrollees, or persons or plans subject to this chapter. The director may adopt rules consistent with federal regulations and statutes to regulate health care coverage supplementing Medicare.

(b) The director may, by regulation, modify the wording of any notice required by this chapter for purposes of clarity, readability, and accuracy, except that a modification shall not change the substantive meaning of the notice.

(c) The director may honor requests from interested parties for interpretive opinions.

(d) No provision of this chapter imposing any liability applies to any act done or omitted in good faith in conformity with any rule, form, order, or written interpretive opinion of the director, or any opinion of the Attorney General, notwithstanding that the rule, form, order, or written interpretive opinion may later be amended or rescinded or be determined by judicial or other authority to be invalid for any reason.

(Amended by Stats. 2009, Ch. 298, Sec. 3. (AB 1540) Effective January 1, 2010.)

1345.

As used in this chapter:

(a) "Advertisement" means any written or printed communication or any communication by means of recorded telephone messages or by radio, television, or similar communications media, published in connection with the offer or sale of plan contracts.

(b) "Basic health care services" means all of the following:

(1) Physician services, including consultation and referral.

(2) Hospital inpatient services and ambulatory care services.

(3) Diagnostic laboratory and diagnostic and therapeutic radiologic services.

(4) Home health services.

(5) Preventive health services.

(6) Emergency health care services, including ambulance and ambulance transport services and out-of-area coverage. "Basic health care services" includes ambulance and ambulance transport services provided through the "911" emergency response system.

(7) Hospice care pursuant to Section 1368.2.

(c) "Enrollee" means a person who is enrolled in a plan and who is a recipient of services from the plan.

(d) "Evidence of coverage" means any certificate, agreement, contract, brochure, or letter of entitlement issued to a subscriber or enrollee setting forth the coverage to which the subscriber or enrollee is entitled.

(e) "Group contract" means a contract which by its terms limits the eligibility of subscribers and enrollees to a specified group.

(f) "Health care service plan" or "specialized health care service plan" means either of the following:

(1) Any person who undertakes to arrange for the provision of health care services to subscribers or enrollees, or to pay for or to reimburse any part of the cost for those services, in return for a prepaid or periodic charge paid by or on behalf of the subscribers or enrollees.

(2) Any person, whether located within or outside of this state, who solicits or contracts with a subscriber or enrollee in this state to pay for or reimburse any part of the cost of, or who undertakes to arrange or arranges for, the provision of health care services that are to be provided wholly or in part in a foreign country in return for a prepaid or periodic charge paid by or on behalf of the subscriber or enrollee.

(g) "License" means, and "licensed" refers to, a license as a plan pursuant to Section 1353.

(h) "Out-of-area coverage," for purposes of paragraph (6) of subdivision (b), means coverage while an enrollee is anywhere outside the service area of the plan, and shall also include coverage for urgently needed services to prevent serious deterioration of an enrollee's health resulting from unforeseen illness or injury for which treatment cannot be delayed until the enrollee returns to the plan's service area.

(i) "Provider" means any professional person, organization, health facility, or other person or institution licensed by the state to deliver or furnish health care services.

(j) "Person" means any person, individual, firm, association, organization, partnership, business trust, foundation, labor organization, corporation, limited liability company, public agency, or political subdivision of the state.

(k) "Service area" means a geographical area designated by the plan within which a plan shall provide health care services.

(l) "Solicitation" means any presentation or advertising conducted by, or on behalf of, a plan, where information regarding the plan, or services offered and charges therefor, is disseminated for the purpose of inducing persons to subscribe to, or enroll in, the plan.

(m) "Solicitor" means any person who engages in the acts defined in subdivision (l).

(n) "Solicitor firm" means any person, other than a plan, who through one or more solicitors engages in the acts defined in subdivision (l).

(o) "Specialized health care service plan contract" means a contract for health care services in a single specialized area of health care, including dental care, for subscribers or enrollees, or which pays for or which reimburses any part of the cost for those services, in return for a prepaid or periodic charge paid by or on behalf of the subscribers or enrollees.

(p) "Subscriber" means the person who is responsible for payment to a plan or whose employment or other status, except for family dependency, is the basis for eligibility for membership in the plan.

(q) Unless the context indicates otherwise, "plan" refers to health care service plans and specialized health care service plans.

(r) "Plan contract" means a contract between a plan and its subscribers or enrollees or a person contracting on their behalf pursuant to which health care services, including basic health care services, are furnished; and unless the context otherwise indicates it includes specialized health care service plan contracts; and unless the context otherwise indicates it includes group contracts.

(s) All references in this chapter to financial statements, assets, liabilities, and other accounting items mean those financial statements and accounting items prepared or determined in accordance with generally accepted accounting principles, and fairly presenting the matters which they purport to present, subject to any specific requirement imposed by this chapter or by the director.

(Amended by Stats. 2002, Ch. 760, Sec. 1. Effective January 1, 2003.)

1345.5.

(a) "Minimum essential coverage" means any of the following:

(1) Coverage under any of the following government-sponsored programs:

(A) The Medicare program under Part A or Part C of Title XVIII of the federal Social Security Act.

(B) Full scope coverage under the Medi-Cal program, including the Medi-Cal Access Program and Medi-Cal for Pregnant Women, and other full scope health coverage programs administered and determined to be minimum essential coverage by the State Department of Health Care Services.

(C) The Medicaid program under Title XIX of the federal Social Security Act.

(D) The CHIP program under Title XXI of the federal Social Security Act or under a qualified CHIP look-alike program, as defined in Section 2107(g) of the federal Social Security Act.

(E) Medical coverage under Chapter 55 of Title 10 of the United States Code, including coverage under the TRICARE program.

(F) A health care program under Chapter 17 or Chapter 18 of Title 38 of the United States Code.

(G) A health plan under Section 2504(e) of Title 22 of the United States Code, relating to Peace Corps volunteers.

(H) The Nonappropriated Fund health benefits program of the Department of Defense, established under Section 349 of the National Defense Authorization Act for Fiscal Year 1995.

(I) Refugee Medical Assistance, supported by the Administration for Children and Families, which is authorized under Section 412(e)(7)(A) of The Immigration and Nationality Act.

(J) A successor program to one of the above programs, as determined by the department or, pursuant to subparagraph (B), by the State Department of Health Care Services.

(2) The University of California Student Health Insurance Plan and the University of California Voluntary Dependent Plan.

(3) Coverage under an eligible employer-sponsored plan, including grandfathered plans and policies. "Eligible employer-sponsored plan" means a group health plan offered in connection with employment to an employee or related individuals, including a governmental plan within the meaning of Section 2791(d)(8) of the federal Public Health Service Act (42 U.S.C. Sec. 201 et seq.) or any other plan, group health care service plan contract, or group health insurance policy offered in the small or large group market within the state.

(4) Coverage under an individual health care service plan contract or individual health insurance policy, including grandfathered contracts and policies, or student health coverage that substantially meets all the requirements of Title I of the Affordable Care Act pertaining to nongrandfathered, individual health insurance coverage.

(5) Any other health benefits coverage similar in form and substance to the benefits described in this subdivision that is determined by the department to constitute minimum essential coverage pursuant to this section.

(b) "Minimum essential coverage" does not include health coverage as follows:

(1) Coverage of the following excepted benefits:

(A) Coverage only for accident or disability income insurance, or a combination of the two.

(B) Coverage issued as a supplement to liability insurance.

(C) Liability insurance, including general liability insurance and automobile liability insurance.

(D) Workers' compensation or similar insurance.

(E) Automobile medical payment insurance.

(F) Credit-only insurance.

(G) Coverage for onsite medical clinics.

(H) Other similar health coverage, under which benefits for medical care are secondary or incidental to other health benefits.

(2) Coverage of the following excepted benefits, if offered separately:

(A) Limited scope dental or vision benefits, or benefits limited to any other single specialized area of health care.

(B) Benefits for long-term care, nursing home care, home health care, community-based care, or any combination thereof.

(C) Other similar, limited benefits.

(3) Coverage of the following excepted benefits if offered as independent, noncoordinated benefits.

(A) Coverage only for a specified disease or illness.

(B) Hospital indemnity or other fixed indemnity insurance.

(4) Coverage of the following excepted benefits if offered as a separate contract for health care coverage:

(A) Medicare supplemental health insurance, as defined under Section 1395ss(g)(1) of Title 42 of the United States Code.

(B) Coverage supplemental to the coverage provided under Chapter 55 (commencing with Section 1071) of Title 10 of the United States Code.

(c) Notwithstanding Chapter 3.5 (commencing with Section 11340) of Part 1 of Division 3 of Title 2 of the Government Code, the department, or the State Department of Health Care Services, may implement, interpret, or make specific this section by means of guidance or instructions, without taking regulatory action.

(Added by Stats. 2019, Ch. 38, Sec. 14. (SB 78) Effective June 27, 2019.)

ARTICLE 2. Administration [1346 - 1348.96]

(Article 2 added by Stats. 1975, Ch. 941.)

1346.

(a) The director shall administer and enforce this chapter and shall have the following powers:

(1) Recommend and propose the enactment of any legislation necessary to protect and promote the interests of the public, subscribers, enrollees, and providers of health care services in health care service plans in the State of California.

(2) Provide information to federal and state legislative committees and executive agencies concerning plans.

(3) Assist, advise, and cooperate with federal, state, and local agencies and officials to protect and promote the interests of plans, subscribers, enrollees, and the public.

(4) Study, investigate, research, and analyze matters affecting the interests of plans, subscribers, enrollees, and the public.

(5) Hold public hearings, subpoena witnesses, take testimony, compel the production of books, papers, documents, and other evidence, and call upon other state agencies for information to implement the purposes, and enforce this chapter.

(6) Conduct audits and examinations of the books and records of plans and other persons subject to this chapter, and may prescribe by rule or order, but is not limited to, the following:

(A) The form and contents of financial statements required under this chapter.

(B) The circumstances under which consolidated statements shall be filed.

(C) The circumstances under which financial statements shall be audited by independent certified public accountants or public accountants.

(7) Conduct necessary onsite medical surveys of the health delivery system of each plan.

(8) Propose, develop, conduct, and assist in educational programs for the public, subscribers, enrollees, and licensees.

(9) Promote and establish standards of ethical conduct for the administration of plans and undertake activities to encourage responsibility in the promotion and sale of plan contracts and the enrollment of subscribers or enrollees in the plans.

(10) Advise the Governor on all matters affecting the interests of plans, subscribers, enrollees, and the public.

(11) Determine that investments of a plan's assets necessary to meet the requirements of Section 1376 are acceptable. For those purposes, reinvestment in the plan and investment in any obligations set forth in Article 3 (commencing with Section 1170) of, and Article 4 (commencing with Section 1190) of, Chapter 2 of Part 2 of Division 1 of the Insurance Code shall be considered acceptable. All other assets shall be invested in a prudent manner.

(b) The powers enumerated in subdivision (a) shall not limit, diminish, or otherwise restrict the other powers of the director specifically set forth in this chapter and other laws.

(Amended by Stats. 1999, Ch. 525, Sec. 43. Effective January 1, 2000. Operative July 1, 2000, or sooner, by Sec. 214 of Ch. 525.)

1346.1.

The department shall maintain a database indicating for each county, the names of the health care service plans that operate in that particular county.

(Added by Stats. 2003, Ch. 80, Sec. 1. Effective January 1, 2004.)

1346.2.

The director shall, in coordination with the Insurance Commissioner, review the Internet portal developed by the United States Secretary of Health and Human Services under subdivision (a) of Section 1103 of the federal Patient Protection and Affordable Care Act (Public Law 111-148) and paragraph (5) of subdivision (c) of Section 1311 of that act, and any enhancements to that portal expected to be implemented by the secretary on or before January 1, 2015. The review shall examine whether the Internet portal provides sufficient information regarding all health benefit products offered by health care service plans and health insurers in the individual and small employer markets in California to facilitate fair and affirmative marketing of all individual and small employer products, particularly outside the California Health Benefit Exchange created under Title 22 (commencing with Section 100500) of the Government Code. If the director and the Insurance Commissioner jointly determine that the Internet portal does not adequately achieve those purposes, they shall jointly develop and maintain an electronic clearinghouse to achieve those purposes. In performing this function, the director and the Insurance Commissioner shall routinely monitor individual and small employer benefit filings with, and complaints submitted by individuals and small employers to, their respective departments, and shall use any other available means to maintain the clearinghouse.

(Added by Stats. 2010, Ch. 659, Sec. 3. (SB 900) Effective January 1, 2011.)

1346.4.

(a) The Legislature finds and declares all of the following:

(1) That millions of Californians are insured under health care service plans regulated by the Knox-Keene Health Care Service Plan Act of 1975, and that more Californians each year are insuring themselves under these health plans.

(2) That greater awareness of the rights and protections afforded by the Knox-Keene Health Care Service Plan Act of 1975 will further the act's goal of providing access to quality health care.

(3) That the public, Knox-Keene providers, and those seeking to form health care service plans under the act will benefit from having the text of the act available to them, affording a greater understanding of what the act does and making it easier for providers to comply with its provisions.

(b) The director shall annually publish this chapter and make it available for sale to the public.

(Amended by Stats. 1999, Ch. 525, Sec. 44. Effective January 1, 2000. Operative July 1, 2000, or sooner, by Sec. 214 of Ch. 525.)

1346.5.

If the director determines that an entity purporting to be a health care service plan exempt from the provisions of Section 740 of the Insurance Code is not a health care service plan, the director shall inform the Department of Insurance of that finding. However, if the director determines that an entity is a health care service plan, the director shall prepare and maintain for public inspection a list of those persons or entities described in subdivision (a) of Section 740 of the Insurance Code, which are not subject to the jurisdiction of another agency of this or another state or the federal government and which the director knows to be operating in the state. There shall be no liability of any kind on the part of the state, the director, and employees of the Department of Managed Health Care for the accuracy of the list or for any comments made with respect to it. Additionally, any solicitor or solicitor firm who advertises or solicits health care service plan coverage in this state described in subdivision (a) of Section 740 of the Insurance Code, which is provided by any person or entity described in subdivision (c) of that section, and where such coverage does not meet all pertinent requirements specified in the Insurance Code, and which is not provided or completely underwritten, insured or otherwise fully covered by a health care service plan, shall advise and disclose to any purchaser, prospective purchaser, covered person or entity, all financial and operational information relative to the content and scope of the plan and, specifically, as to the lack of plan coverage.

(Amended by Stats. 2000, Ch. 857, Sec. 28. Effective January 1, 2001.)

1347.15.

(a) There is hereby established in the Department of Managed Health Care the Financial Solvency Standards Board composed of eight members. The members shall consist of the director, or the director's designee, and seven members appointed by the director. The seven members appointed by the director may be, but are not necessarily limited to, individuals with training and experience in the following subject areas or fields: medical and health care economics; accountancy, with experience in integrated or affiliated health care delivery systems; excess loss insurance underwriting in the medical, hospital, and health plan business; actuarial studies in the area of health care delivery systems; management and administration in integrated or affiliated health care delivery systems; investment banking; and information technology in integrated or affiliated health care delivery systems. The members appointed by the director shall be appointed for a term of three years, but may be removed or reappointed by the director before the expiration of the term.

(b) The purpose of the board is to do all of the following:

(1) Advise the director on matters of financial solvency affecting the delivery of health care services.

(2) Develop and recommend to the director financial solvency requirements and standards relating to plan operations, plan-affiliate operations and transactions, plan-provider contractual relationships, and provider-affiliate operations and transactions.

(3) Periodically monitor and report on the implementation and results of the financial solvency requirements and standards.

(c) Financial solvency requirements and standards recommended to the director by the board may, after a period of review and comment not to exceed 45 days, be noticed for adoption as regulations as proposed or modified under the rulemaking provisions of the Administrative Procedure Act (Chapter 3.5 (commencing with Section 11340) of Part 1 of Division 3 of Title 2 of the Government Code). During the director's 45-day review and comment period, the director, in consultation with the board, may postpone the adoption of the requirements and standards pending further review and comment. Nothing in this subdivision prohibits the director from adopting regulations, including emergency regulations, under the rulemaking provisions of the Administrative Procedure Act.

(d) The board shall meet at least quarterly and at the call of the chair. In order to preserve the independence of the board, the director shall not serve as chair. The members of the board may establish their own rules and procedures. All members shall serve without compensation, but shall be reimbursed from department funds for expenses actually and necessarily incurred in the performance of their duties.

(e) For purposes of this section, "board" means the Financial Solvency Standards Board. (Amended by Stats. 2007, Ch. 577, Sec. 10. Effective October 13, 2007.)

1347.5.

(a) A health care service plan providing individual coverage in the Exchange shall cooperate with requests from the Exchange to collaborate in the development of, and participate in the implementation of, the Medi-Cal program's premium and cost-sharing payments under Sections 14102 and 14148.65 of the Welfare and Institutions Code for eligible Exchange enrollees.

(b) A health care service plan providing individual coverage in the Exchange shall not charge, bill, ask, or require an enrollee receiving benefits under Section 14102 or 14148.65 of the Welfare and Institutions Code to make any premium or cost-sharing payments for any services that are subject to premium or cost-sharing payments by the State Department of Health Care Services under Section 14102 or 14148.65 of the Welfare and Institutions Code.

(c) For purposes of this section, "Exchange" means the California Health Benefit Exchange established pursuant to Title 22 (commencing with Section 100500) of the Government Code.

(Amended by Stats. 2015, Ch. 303, Sec. 249. (AB 731) Effective January 1, 2016.)

1348.

(a) Every health care service plan licensed to do business in this state shall establish an antifraud plan. The purpose of the antifraud plan shall be to organize and implement an antifraud strategy to identify and reduce costs to the plans, providers, subscribers, enrollees, and others caused by fraudulent activities, and to protect consumers in the delivery of health care services through the timely detection, investigation, and prosecution of suspected fraud. The antifraud plan elements shall include, but not be limited to, all of the following: the designation of, or a contract with, individuals with specific investigative expertise in the management of fraud investigations; training of plan personnel and contractors concerning the detection of health care fraud; the plan's procedure for managing incidents of suspected fraud; and the internal procedure for referring suspected fraud to the appropriate government agency.

(b) Every plan shall submit its antifraud plan to the department no later than July 1, 1999. Any changes shall be filed with the department pursuant to Section 1352. The submission shall describe the manner in which the plan is complying with subdivision (a), and the name and telephone number of the contact person to whom inquiries concerning the antifraud plan may be directed.

(c) Every health care service plan that establishes an antifraud plan pursuant to subdivision (a) shall provide to the director an annual written report describing the plan's efforts to deter, detect, and investigate fraud, and to report cases of fraud to a law enforcement agency. For those cases that are reported to law enforcement agencies by the plan, this report shall include the number of cases prosecuted to the extent known by the plan. This report may also include recommendations by the plan to improve efforts to combat health care fraud.

(d) Nothing in this section shall be construed to limit the director's authority to implement this section in accordance with Section 1344.

(e) For purposes of this section, "fraud" includes, but is not limited to, knowingly making or causing to be made any false or fraudulent claim for payment of a health care benefit.

(f) Nothing in this section shall be construed to limit any civil, criminal, or administrative liability under any other provision of law.

(Amended by Stats. 1999, Ch. 525, Sec. 48. Effective January 1, 2000. Operative July 1, 2000, or sooner, by Sec. 214 of Ch. 525.)

1348.5.

A health care service plan shall comply with the provisions of Section 56.107 of the Civil Code to the extent required by that section. To the extent this chapter conflicts with Section 56.107 of the Civil Code, the provisions of Section 56.107 of the Civil Code shall control.

(Added by Stats. 2013, Ch. 444, Sec. 10. (SB 138) Effective January 1, 2014.)

1348.6.

(a) No contract between a health care service plan and a physician, physician group, or other licensed health care practitioner shall contain any incentive plan that includes specific payment made directly, in any type or form, to a physician, physician group, or other licensed health care practitioner as an inducement to deny, reduce, limit, or delay specific, medically necessary, and appropriate services provided with respect to a specific enrollee or groups of enrollees with similar medical conditions.

(b) Nothing in this section shall be construed to prohibit contracts that contain incentive plans that involve general payments, such as capitation payments, or shared-risk arrangements that are not tied to specific medical decisions involving specific enrollees or groups of enrollees with similar medical conditions. The payments rendered or to be rendered to physicians, physician groups, or other licensed health care practitioners under these arrangements shall be deemed confidential information in accordance with subdivision (d) of Section 1351.

(Added by Stats. 1996, Ch. 1014, Sec. 2. Effective January 1, 1997.)

1348.8.

(a) A health care service plan that provides, operates, or contracts for telephone medical advice services to its enrollees and subscribers shall do all of the following:

(1) Ensure that the in-state or out-of-state telephone medical advice service complies with the requirements of Chapter 15 (commencing with Section 4999) of Division 2 of the Business and Professions Code.

(2) Ensure that the staff providing telephone medical advice services for the in-state or out-of-state telephone medical advice service are licensed as follows:

(A) For full service health care service plans, the staff hold a valid California license as a registered nurse or a valid license in the state within which they provide telephone medical advice services as a physician and surgeon or physician assistant, and are operating in compliance with the laws governing their respective scopes of practice.

(B) (i) For specialized health care service plans providing, operating, or contracting with a telephone medical advice service in California, the staff shall be appropriately licensed, registered, or certified as a dentist pursuant to Chapter 4 (commencing with Section 1600) of Division 2 of the Business and Professions Code, as a dental hygienist pursuant to Article 7 (commencing with Section 1740) of Chapter 4 of Division 2 of the Business and Professions Code, as a physician and surgeon pursuant to Chapter 5 (commencing with Section 2000) of Division 2 of the Business and Professions Code or the Osteopathic Initiative Act, as a registered nurse pursuant to Chapter 6 (commencing with Section 2700) of Division 2 of the Business and Professions Code, as a psychologist pursuant to Chapter 6.6 (commencing with Section 2900) of Division 2 of the Business and Professions Code, as an optometrist pursuant to Chapter 7 (commencing with Section 3000) of Division 2 of the Business and Professions Code, as a marriage and family therapist pursuant to Chapter 13 (commencing with Section 4980) of Division 2 of the Business and Professions Code, as a licensed clinical social worker pursuant to Chapter 14 (commencing with Section 4991) of Division 2 of the Business and Professions Code, as a professional clinical counselor pursuant to Chapter 16 (commencing with Section 4999.10) of Division 2 of the Business and Professions Code, or as a chiropractor pursuant to the Chiropractic Initiative Act, and operating in compliance with the laws governing their respective scopes of practice.

(ii) For specialized health care service plans providing, operating, or contracting with an out-of-state telephone medical advice service, the staff shall be health care professionals, as identified in clause (i), who are licensed, registered, or certified in the state within which they are providing the telephone medical advice services and are operating in compliance with the laws governing their respective scopes of practice. All registered nurses providing telephone medical advice services to both in-state and out-of-state business entities registered pursuant to this chapter shall be licensed pursuant to Chapter 6 (commencing with Section 2700) of Division 2 of the Business and Professions Code.

(3) Ensure that every full service health care service plan provides for a physician and surgeon who is available on an on-call basis at all times the service is advertised to be available to enrollees and subscribers.

(4) Ensure that staff members handling enrollee or subscriber calls, who are not licensed, certified, or registered as required by paragraph (2), do not provide telephone medical advice. Those staff members may ask questions on behalf of a staff member who is licensed, certified, or registered as required by paragraph (2), in order to help ascertain the condition of an enrollee or subscriber so that the enrollee or subscriber can be referred to licensed staff. However, under no circumstances shall those staff members use the answers to those questions in an attempt to assess, evaluate, advise, or make any decision regarding the condition of an enrollee or subscriber or determine when an enrollee or subscriber needs to be seen by a licensed medical professional.

(5) Ensure that no staff member uses a title or designation when speaking to an enrollee or subscriber that may cause a reasonable person to believe that the staff member is a licensed, certified, or registered professional described in Section 4999.2 of the Business and Professions Code unless the staff member is a licensed, certified, or registered professional.

(6) Ensure that the in-state or out-of-state telephone medical advice service designates an agent for service of process in California and files this designation with the director.

(7) Require that the in-state or out-of-state telephone medical advice service makes and maintains records for a period of five years after the telephone medical advice services are provided, including, but not limited to, oral or written transcripts of all medical advice conversations with the health care service plan's enrollees or subscribers in California and copies of all complaints. If the records of telephone medical advice services are kept out of state, the health care service plan shall, upon the request of the director, provide the records to the director within 10 days of the request.

(8) Ensure that the telephone medical advice services are provided consistent with good professional practice.

(b) The director shall forward to the Department of Consumer Affairs, within 30 days of the end of each calendar quarter, data regarding complaints filed with the department concerning telephone medical advice services.

(c) For purposes of this section, "telephone medical advice" means a telephonic communication between a patient and a health care professional in which the health care professional's primary function is to provide to the patient a telephonic response to the patient's questions regarding his or her or a family member's medical care or treatment. "Telephone medical advice" includes assessment, evaluation, or advice provided to patients or their family members.

(Amended by Stats. 2016, Ch. 799, Sec. 42. (SB 1039) Effective January 1, 2017.)

1348.9.

(a) On or before July 1, 2003, the director shall adopt regulations to establish the Consumer Participation Program, which shall allow for the director to award reasonable advocacy and witness fees to any person or organization that demonstrates that the person or organization represents the interests of consumers and has made a substantial contribution on behalf of consumers to the adoption of any regulation or to an order or decision made by the director if the order or decision has the potential to impact a significant number of enrollees.

(b) The regulations adopted by the director shall include specifications for eligibility of participation, rates of compensation, and procedures for seeking compensation. The regulations shall require that the person or organization demonstrate a record of advocacy on behalf of health care consumers in administrative or legislative proceedings in order to determine whether the person or organization represents the interests of consumers.

(c) This section shall apply to all proceedings of the department, but shall not apply to resolution of individual grievances, complaints, or cases.

(d) Fees awarded pursuant to this section may not exceed three hundred fifty thousand dollars ($350,000) each fiscal year.

(e) The fees awarded pursuant to this section shall be considered costs and expenses pursuant to Section 1356 and shall be paid from the assessment made under that section. Notwithstanding the provisions of this subdivision, the amount of the assessment shall not be increased to pay the fees awarded under this section.

(f) The department shall report to the appropriate policy and fiscal committees of the Legislature before March 1, 2004, and annually thereafter, the following information:

(1) The amount of reasonable advocacy and witness fees awarded each fiscal year.

(2) The individuals or organization to whom advocacy and witness fees were awarded pursuant to this section.

(3) The orders, decisions, and regulations pursuant to which the advocacy and witness fees were awarded.

(g) This section shall remain in effect only until January 1, 2024, and as of that date is repealed, unless a later enacted statute, that is enacted before January 1, 2024, deletes or extends that date.

(Amended by Stats. 2017, Ch. 52, Sec. 5. (SB 97) Effective July 10, 2017. Repealed as of January 1, 2024, by its own provisions.)

1348.95.

Commencing March 1, 2013, and at least annually thereafter, every health care service plan, not including a health care service plan offering specialized health care service plan contracts, shall provide to the department, in a form and manner determined by the department in consultation with the Department of Insurance, the number of enrollees, by product type, as of December 31 of the prior year, that receive health care coverage under a health care service plan contract that covers individuals, small groups, large groups, or administrative services only business lines. Health care service plans shall include the enrollment data in specific product types as determined by the department, including, but not limited to, HMO, point-of-service, PPO, grandfathered, and Medi-Cal managed care. The department shall publicly report the data provided by each health care service plan pursuant to this section, including, but not limited to, posting the data on the Department's Internet Web site. The department shall consult with the Department of Insurance to ensure that the data reported is comparable and consistent, does not duplicate existing reporting requirements, and utilizes existing reporting formats.

(Added by Stats. 2012, Ch. 852, Sec. 1. (AB 1083) Effective January 1, 2013.)

1348.96.

Any data submitted by a health care service plan to the United States Secretary of Health and Human Services, or his or her designee, for purposes of the risk adjustment program described in Section 1343 of the federal Patient Protection and Affordable Care Act (42

U.S.C. Sec. 18063) shall be concurrently submitted to the department in the same format. The department shall use the information to monitor federal implementation of risk adjustment in the state and to ensure that health care service plans are in compliance with federal requirements related to risk adjustment.

(Added by Stats. 2013, 1st Ex. Sess., Ch. 2, Sec. 1. (SB 2 1x) Effective September 30, 2013.)

ARTICLE 3. Licensing and Fees [1349 - 1356.2]

(Article 3 added by Stats. 1975, Ch. 941.)

1349.

It is unlawful for any person to engage in business as a plan in this state or to receive advance or periodic consideration in connection with a plan from or on behalf of persons in this state unless such person has first secured from the director a license, then in effect, as a plan or unless such person is exempted by the provisions of Section 1343 or a rule adopted thereunder. A person licensed pursuant to this chapter need not be licensed pursuant to the Insurance Code to operate a health care service plan or specialized health care service plan unless the plan is operated by an insurer, in which case the insurer shall also be licensed by the Insurance Commissioner.

(Amended by Stats. 1999, Ch. 525, Sec. 49. Effective January 1, 2000. Operative July 1, 2000, or sooner, by Sec. 214 of Ch. 525.)

1349.1.

A health care service plan which satisfies both of the following criteria is exempt from Section 1349:

(a) Provides only emergency ambulance services or advanced life support services, as defined by Section 1797.52, or both.

(b) Is operated by the State of California, any city, county, city and county, public district, or public authority.

(Added by Stats. 1986, Ch. 502, Sec. 1.)

1349.2.

(a) A health care service plan, including a self-insured reimbursement plan that pays for or reimburses any part of the cost of health care services, operated by any city, county, city and county, public entity, political subdivision, or public joint labor management trust that satisfies all of the following criteria is exempt from this chapter:

(1) Provides services or reimbursement only to employees, retirees, and the dependents of those employees and retirees, of any participating city, county, city and county, public entity, or political subdivision, but not to the general public.

(2) Provides funding for the program.

(3) Provides that providers are reimbursed solely on a fee-for-service basis, so that providers are not at risk in contracting arrangements.

(4) Complies with Section 1378 and, to the extent that a plan contracts directly with providers for health care services, complies with Section 1379.

(5) Does not reduce or change current benefits except in accordance with collective bargaining agreements, or as otherwise authorized by the governing body in the case of unrepresented employees, and provides, pays for, or reimburses at least part of the cost of all basic health care services as defined in subdivision (b) of Section 1345. Plans covering only a single specialized health care service, including dental, vision, or mental health services, shall not be required to cover all basic health care services.

(6) Refrains from any conduct that constitutes fraud or dishonest dealing or unfair competition, as defined by Section 17200 of the Business and Professions Code, and notifies enrollees of their right to file complaints with the director regarding any violation of this exemption.

(7) Maintains a fiscally sound operation and makes adequate provision against the risk of insolvency so that enrollees are not at risk, individually or collectively, as evidenced by audited financial statements submitted to the director as of the end of the plan's fiscal year, within 180 days after the close of that fiscal year. The financial statements shall be accompanied by a report, certificate, or opinion of an independent certified public accountant. The financial statements shall be prepared in accordance with generally accepted accounting principles. The audit shall be conducted in accordance with generally accepted auditing standards. However, audits of public entities or political subdivisions shall be conducted in accordance with governmental auditing standards. Upon request, the governing body of the plan shall provide copies thereof, without charge, to any enrollee or recognized and participating employee organization.

(8) Submits with the annual financial statements required under paragraph (7), a declaration, which shall conform to Section 2015.5 of the Code of Civil Procedure, executed by a plan official authorized by the governing body of the plan, that the plan complies with this subdivision.

(b) The director's responsibilities under this section shall be limited to enforcing compliance with this section. Nothing in this section shall impair or impede the director's enforcement authority or the remedies available under this chapter, including, but not limited to, the termination of the plan's exemption under this section.

(c) A public joint labor management trust is a trust maintained by one or more participating cities, counties, cities and counties, public entities, or political subdivisions that appoint management representatives, and one or more recognized and participating employee organizations representing the employees of one or more of the cities, counties, cities and counties, public entities, or political subdivisions that appoint labor representatives, in which the management representatives and the labor representatives have equal voting power in the operation of the trust.

(d) A public joint labor management trust shall not be deemed to provide services or reimbursement to the general public if, in addition to providing services or reimbursement to the persons described in paragraph (1) of subdivision (a), it provides services or reimbursement only to employees, retirees, and dependents of those employees and retirees, of the recognized and participating employee organizations or of the trust.

(e) Nothing in this section shall be construed to prohibit a recognized and participating employee organization from filing a complaint with the director regarding a violation of this section.

(Amended by Stats. 1999, Ch. 525, Sec. 50. Effective January 1, 2000. Operative July 1, 2000, or sooner, by Sec. 214 of Ch. 525.)

1350.

(a) Consistent with federal law, a sponsor of a prescription drug plan authorized by the federal Medicare Prescription Drug, Improvement, and Modernization Act of 2003 (P.L. 108-173) shall hold a valid license as a health care service plan issued by the department or as a life and disability insurer by the Department of Insurance.

(b) An entity that is licensed as a health care service plan and that operates a prescription drug plan shall be subject to the provisions of this chapter, unless preempted by federal law.

(Added by Stats. 2005, Ch. 230, Sec. 1. Effective September 6, 2005.)

1351.

Each application for licensure as a health care service plan or specialized health care service plan under this chapter shall be verified by an authorized representative of the applicant, and shall be in a form prescribed by the department. This application shall be accompanied by the fee prescribed by subdivision (a) of Section 1356 and shall set forth or be accompanied by each and all of the following:

(a) The basic organizational documents of the applicant; such as, the articles of incorporation, articles of association, partnership agreement, trust agreement, or other applicable documents and all amendments thereto.

(b) A copy of the bylaws, rules and regulations, or similar documents regulating the conduct of the internal affairs of the applicant.

(c) A list of the names, addresses, and official positions of the persons who are to be responsible for the conduct of the affairs of the applicant, which shall include among others, all members of the board of directors, board of trustees, executive committee, or other governing board or committee, the principal officers, each shareholder with over 5-percent interest in the case of a corporation, and all partners or members in the case of a partnership or association, and each person who has loaned funds to the applicant for the operation of its business.

(d) A copy of any contract made, or to be made, between the applicant and any provider of health care services, or persons listed in subdivision (c), or any other person or organization agreeing to perform an administrative function or service for the plan. The director by rule may identify contracts excluded from this requirement and make provision for the submission of form contracts. The payment rendered or to be rendered to such provider of health care services shall be deemed confidential information that shall not be divulged by the director, except that such payment may be disclosed and become a public record in any legislative, administrative, or judicial proceeding or inquiry. The plan shall also submit the name and address of each physician employed by or contracting with the plan, together with his or her license number.

(e) A statement describing the plan, its method of providing for health care services and its physical facilities. If applicable, this statement shall include the health care delivery capabilities of the plan including the number of full-time and part-time primary physicians, the number of full-time and part-time and specialties of all nonprimary physicians; the numbers and types of licensed or state-certified health care support staff, the number of hospital beds contracted for, and the arrangements and the methods by which health care services will be provided. For purposes of this subdivision, primary physicians include general and family practitioners, internists, pediatricians, obstetricians, and gynecologists.

(f) A copy of the forms of evidence of coverage and of the disclosure forms or material which are to be issued to subscribers or enrollees of the plan.

(g) A copy of the form of the individual contract which is to be issued to individual subscribers and the form of group contract which is to be issued to any employers, unions, trustees, or other organizations.

(h) Financial statements accompanied by a report, certificate, or opinion of an independent certified public accountant. However, financial statements from public entities or political subdivisions of the state need not include a report, certificate, or opinion by an independent certified public accountant if the financial statement complies with such requirements as may be established by regulation of the director.

(i) A description of the proposed method of marketing the plan and a copy of any contract made with any person to solicit on behalf of the plan or a copy of the form of agreement used and a list of the contracting parties.

(j) A power of attorney duly executed by any applicant, not domiciled in this state, appointing the director the true and lawful attorney in fact of such applicant in this state for the purposes of service of all lawful process in any legal action or proceeding against the plan on a cause of action arising in this state.

(k) A statement describing the service area or areas to be served, including the service location for each provider rendering professional services on behalf of the plan and the location of any other plan facilities where required by the director.

(l) A description of enrollee-subscriber grievance procedures to be utilized as required by this chapter, and a copy of the form specified by subdivision (c) of Section 1368.

(m) A description of the procedures and programs for internal review of the quality of health care pursuant to the requirements set forth in this chapter.

(n) A description of the mechanism by which enrollees and subscribers will be afforded an opportunity to express their views on matters relating to the policy and operation of the plan.

(o) Evidence of adequate insurance coverage or self-insurance to respond to claims for damages arising out of the furnishing of health care services.

(p) Evidence of adequate insurance coverage or self-insurance to protect against losses of facilities where required by the director.

(q) If required by the director by rule pursuant to Section 1376, a fidelity bond or a surety bond in the amount prescribed.

(r) Evidence of adequate workmen's compensation insurance coverage to protect against claims arising out of work-related injuries that might be brought by the employees and staff of a plan against the plan.

(s) All relevant information known to the applicant concerning whether the plan, its management company, or any other affiliate of the plan, or any controlling person, officer, director, or other person occupying a principal management or supervisory position in the plan, management company, or other affiliate, has any of the following:

(1) Any history of noncompliance with applicable state or federal laws, regulations, or requirements related to providing, or arranging to provide for, health care services or benefits in this state or any other state.

(2) Any history of noncompliance with applicable state or federal laws, regulations, or requirements related to providing, or arranging to provide for, health care services or benefits authorized for reimbursement under the federal Medicare or Medicaid Program.

(3) Any history of noncompliance with applicable state or federal laws, regulations, or requirements related to providing, or arranging for the provision of, health care services as a licensed health professional or an individual or entity contracting with a health care service plan or insurer in this state or any other state.

(t) Such other information as the director may reasonably require.

(Amended by Stats. 2006, Ch. 758, Sec. 2. Effective January 1, 2007.)

1351.1.

In addition to the requirements of Section 1351 and upon request of the director, each application shall be accompanied by authorization for disclosure to the director of financial records of each health care service plan or specialized health care service plan licensed under this chapter pursuant to Section 7473 of the Government Code. For the purpose of this chapter, the authorization for disclosure shall also include the financial records of any association, partnership or corporation controlling, controlled by or otherwise affiliated with a health care service plan or specialized health care service plan.

(Amended by Stats. 1999, Ch. 525, Sec. 52. Effective January 1, 2000. Operative July 1, 2000, or sooner, by Sec. 214 of Ch. 525.)

1351.2.

(a) If a prepaid health plan operating lawfully under the laws of Mexico elects to operate a health care service plan in this state, the prepaid health plan shall apply for licensure as a health care service plan under this chapter by filing an application for licensure in the form prescribed by the department and verified by an authorized representative of the applicant. The prepaid health plan shall be subject to the provisions of this chapter, and the rules adopted by the director thereunder, as determined by the director to be applicable. The application shall be accompanied by the fee prescribed by subdivision (a) of Section 1356 and shall demonstrate compliance with the following requirements:

(1) The prepaid health plan is constituted and operating lawfully under the laws of Mexico and, if required by Mexican law, is authorized as an Insurance Institution Specializing in Health by the Mexican Insurance Commission. If the Mexican Insurance Commission determines that the prepaid health plan is not required to be authorized as an Insurance Institution Specializing in Health under the laws of Mexico, the applicant shall obtain written verification from the Mexican Insurance Commission stating that the applicant is not required to be authorized as an Insurance Institution Specializing in Health in Mexico. A Mexican prepaid health plan that is not required to be an Insurance Institution Specializing in Health shall obtain written verification from the Mexican Ministry of Health that the prepaid health plan and its provider network are operating in full compliance of Mexican law.

(2) The prepaid health plan offers and sells in this state only employer-sponsored group plan contracts exclusively for the benefit of Mexican nationals legally employed in the County of San Diego or the County of Imperial, and for the benefit of their dependents regardless of nationality, that pay for, reimburse the cost of, or arrange for the provision or delivery of health care services that are to be provided or delivered wholly in Mexico, except for the provision or delivery of those health care services set forth in paragraph (4).

(3) Solicitation of plan contracts in this state is made only through insurance brokers and agents licensed in this state or a third-party administrator licensed in this state, each of which is authorized to offer and sell plan group contracts.

(4) Group contracts provide, through a contract of insurance between the prepaid health plan and an insurer admitted in this state, for the reimbursement of emergency and urgent care services provided out of area as required by subdivision (h) of Section 1345.

(5) All advertising, solicitation material, disclosure statements, evidences of coverage, and contracts are in compliance with the appropriate provisions of this chapter and the rules or orders of the director. The director shall require that each of these documents contain a legend in 10-point type, in both English and Spanish, declaring that the health care service plan contract provided by the prepaid health plan may be limited as to benefits, rights, and remedies under state and federal law.

(6) All funds received by the prepaid health plan from a subscriber are deposited in an account of a bank organized under the laws of this state or in an account of a national bank located in this state.

(7) The prepaid health plan maintains a tangible net equity as required by this chapter and the rules of the director, as calculated under United States generally accepted accounting principles, in the amount of a least one million dollars ($1,000,000). In lieu of

an amount in excess of the minimum tangible net equity of one million dollars ($1,000,000), the prepaid health plan may demonstrate a reasonable acceptable alternative reimbursement arrangement that the director may in his or her discretion accept. The prepaid health plan shall also maintain a fidelity bond and a surety bond as required by Section 1376 and the rules of the director.

(8) The prepaid health plan agrees to make all of its books and records, including the books and records of health care providers in Mexico, available to the director in the form and at the time and place requested by the director. Books and records shall be made available to the director no later than 24 hours from the date of the request.

(9) The prepaid health plan files a consent to service of process with the director and agrees to be subject to the laws of this state and the United States in any investigation, examination, dispute, or other matter arising from the advertising, solicitation, or offer and sale of a plan contract, or the management or provision of health care services in this state or throughout the United States. The prepaid health plan shall agree to notify the director, immediately and in no case later than one business day, if it is subject to any investigation, examination, or administrative or legal action relating to the prepaid health plan or the operations of the prepaid health plan initiated by the government of Mexico or the government of any state of Mexico against the prepaid health plan or any officer, director, security holder, or contractor owning 10 percent or more of the securities of the prepaid health plan. The prepaid health plan shall agree that in the event of conflict of laws in any action arising out of the license, the laws of California and the United States shall apply.

(10) The prepaid health plan agrees that disputes arising from the group contracts involving group contractholders and providers of health care services in the United States shall be subject to the jurisdiction of the courts of this state and the United States.

(11) The prepaid health plan shall employ or designate a medical director who holds an unrestricted license to practice medicine in this state issued pursuant to Section 2050 of the Business and Professions Code or pursuant to the Osteopathic Act for health care services set forth in paragraph (4). For health care services that are to be provided or delivered wholly in Mexico, the prepaid health plan may employ or designate a medical director operating under the laws of Mexico.

(b) The prepaid health plan shall pay the application processing fee and other fees and assessments set forth in Section 1356. The director, by order, may designate provisions of this chapter and rules adopted thereunder that need not be applied to a prepaid health plan licensed under the laws of Mexico when consistent with the intent and purpose of this chapter, and in the public interest.

(c) If the plan ceases to operate legally in Mexico, the director shall immediately deliver written notice to the health care service plan that it is not in compliance with the provisions of this section. If this occurs, a health care service plan shall do all of the following:

(1) Provide the director with written proof that the prepaid health plan has complied with the laws of Mexico not later than 45 days after the date the written notice is received by the health care service plan.

(2) If, by the 45th day, the health care service plan is unable to provide written confirmation that it is in full compliance with Mexican law, the director shall notify the health care service plan in writing that it is prohibited from accepting any new enrollees or subscribers. The health care service plan shall be given an additional 180 days to comply with Mexican law or to become a licensed health care service plan.

(3) If, at the end of the 180-day notice period in paragraph (2), the health care service plan has not complied with the laws of Mexico or California, the director shall issue an order that the health care service plan cease and desist operations in California.
(Amended (as amended by Stats. 2004, Ch. 491, Sec. 1) by Stats. 2007, Ch. 196, Sec. 1. Effective January 1, 2008.)
1351.3.
On and after January 1, 2007, the department, in considering an application for an initial license for any entity under this chapter, shall consider any information provided concerning whether the plan, its management company, or any other affiliate of the plan, or any controlling person, officer, director, or other person occupying a principal management or supervisory position in the plan, management company, or affiliate has any history of noncompliance, as described in subdivision (s) of Section 1351, and any other relevant information concerning misconduct.
(Added by Stats. 2006, Ch. 758, Sec. 3. Effective January 1, 2007.)
1352.
(a) A licensed plan shall, within 30 days after any change in the information contained in its application, other than financial or statistical information, file an amendment thereto in the manner the director may by rule prescribe setting forth the changed information. However, the addition of any association, partnership, or corporation in a controlling, controlled, or affiliated status relative to the plan shall necessitate filing, within a 30-day period of an authorization for disclosure to the director of financial records of the person pursuant to Section 7473 of the Government Code.
(b) Prior to a material modification of its plan or operations, a plan shall give notice thereof to the director, who shall, within 20 business days or such additional time as the plan may specify, by order approve, disapprove, suspend, or postpone the effectiveness of the change, subject to Section 1354.
(c) A plan shall, within five days, give written notice to the director in the form as by rule may be prescribed, of a change in the officers, directors, partners, controlling shareholders, principal creditors, or persons occupying similar positions or performing similar functions, of the plan and of a management company of the plan, and of a parent company of the plan or management company. The director may by rule define the positions, duties, and relationships which are referred to in this subdivision.

(d) The fee for filing a notice of material modification pursuant to subdivision (b) shall be the actual cost to the director of processing the notice, including overhead, but shall not exceed seven hundred fifty dollars ($750).
(Amended by Stats. 2007, Ch. 577, Sec. 11. Effective October 13, 2007.)
1352.1.
(a) Except as provided in subdivision (b), no plan shall enter into any new or modified plan contract or publish or distribute, or allow to be published or distributed on its behalf, any disclosure form or evidence of coverage, unless (1) a true copy thereof has first been filed with the director, at least 30 days prior to any such use, or any shorter period as the director by rule or order may allow, and (2) the director by notice has not found the plan contract, disclosure form, or evidence of coverage, wholly or in part, to be untrue, misleading, deceptive, or otherwise not in compliance with this chapter or the rules thereunder, and specified the deficiencies, within at least 30 days or any shorter time as the director by rule or order may allow.
(b) Except as provided in subdivision (c), a licensed plan which has been continuously licensed under this chapter for the preceding 18 months and which has had group contracts in effect at all times during that period may enter a new or modified group contract or may publish or distribute, or allow to be published or distributed on its behalf, any group disclosure form or evidence of coverage without having filed the same for the director's prior approval, if the plan and the materials comply with each of the following conditions:
(1) The contract, disclosure form, or evidence of coverage, or any material provision thereof, has not been previously disapproved by the director by written notice to the plan and the plan reasonably believes that the contract, disclosure form, and evidence of coverage do not violate any requirements of this chapter or the rules thereunder.
(2) The plan files the contract and any related disclosure form and evidence of coverage with the director not later than 10 business days after entering the contract, or within any additional period as the director by rule or order may provide.
(3) If the person or group entering into the contract with the plan is not an employee welfare benefit plan, as defined in the Employee Retirement Income Security Act of 1974 (29 U.S.C. Sec. 1001 et seq.), the person or group is not organized solely or principally for the purpose of providing health benefits to members of the group.
(c) The director by order may require a plan which has entered any group contract or published or distributed, or allowed to be published or distributed on its behalf, any disclosure form or evidence of coverage in violation of this chapter or the rules thereunder to comply with subdivision (a) prior to entering group contracts, or a specified class of group contracts, and prior to publishing or distributing, or allowing to be published or distributed on its behalf, related disclosure forms and evidences of coverage. An order issued pursuant to this subdivision shall be effective for 12 months from its issuance, and may be renewed by order if the contracts, disclosure forms, or evidences of coverage submitted under this subdivision indicate difficulties of voluntary compliance with the applicable provisions of this chapter and the rules thereunder.
(d) A licensed plan or other person regulated under this chapter may, within 30 days after receipt of any notice or order under this section, file a written request for a hearing with the director.
(Amended by Stats. 1999, Ch. 525, Sec. 55. Effective January 1, 2000. Operative July 1, 2000, or sooner, by Sec. 214 of Ch. 525.)
1353.
The director shall issue a license to any person filing an application pursuant to this article, if the director, upon due consideration of the application and of the information obtained in any investigation, including, if necessary, an onsite inspection, determines that the applicant has satisfied the provisions of this chapter and that, in the judgment of the director, a disciplinary action pursuant to Section 1386 would not be warranted against such applicant. Otherwise, the director shall deny the application.
(Amended by Stats. 1999, Ch. 525, Sec. 56. Effective January 1, 2000. Operative July 1, 2000, or sooner, by Sec. 214 of Ch. 525.)
1354.
Upon denial of application for licensure, or the issuance of an order pursuant to Section 1352 disapproving, suspending, or postponing a material modification, the director shall notify the applicant in writing, stating the reason for the denial and that the applicant has the right to a hearing if the applicant makes written request within 30 days after the date of mailing of the notice of denial. Service of the notice required by this subdivision may be made by certified mail addressed to the applicant at the latest address filed by the applicant in writing with the department.
(Amended by Stats. 1999, Ch. 525, Sec. 57. Effective January 1, 2000. Operative July 1, 2000, or sooner, by Sec. 214 of Ch. 525.)
1355.
Every plan's license issued under this chapter shall remain in effect until revoked or suspended by the director, except that every transitional license shall expire on September 30, 1978, unless such expiration date is extended by the director.
(Amended by Stats. 1999, Ch. 525, Sec. 58. Effective January 1, 2000. Operative July 1, 2000, or sooner, by Sec. 214 of Ch. 525.)
1356.
(a) Each plan applying for licensure under this chapter shall reimburse the director for the actual cost of processing the application, including overhead, up to an amount not to exceed twenty-five thousand dollars ($25,000). The cost shall be billed not more frequently than monthly and shall be remitted by the applicant to the director within 30 days of the date of billing. The director shall not issue a license to an applicant prior to receiving payment in full from that applicant for all amounts charged pursuant to this subdivision.

(b) (1) In addition to other fees and reimbursements required to be paid under this chapter, each licensed plan shall pay to the director an amount as estimated by the director for the ensuing fiscal year, as a reimbursement of its share of all costs and expenses, including, but not limited to, costs and expenses associated with routine financial examinations, grievances, and complaints including maintaining a toll-free telephone number for consumer grievances and complaints, investigation and enforcement, medical surveys and reports, and overhead reasonably incurred in the administration of this chapter and not otherwise recovered by the director under this chapter or from the Managed Care Fund. The amount may be paid in two equal installments. The first installment shall be paid on or before August 1 of each year, and the second installment shall be paid on or before December 15 of each year.

(2) The amount paid by each plan shall be ten thousand dollars ($10,000) plus an amount up to, but not exceeding, an amount computed in accordance with paragraph (3).

(3) (A) In addition to the amount specified in paragraph (2), all plans, except specialized plans, shall pay 65 percent of the total amount of the department's costs and expenses for the ensuing fiscal year as estimated by the director. The amount per plan shall be calculated on a per enrollee basis as specified in paragraph (4).

(B) In addition to the amount specified in paragraph (2), all specialized plans shall pay 35 percent of the total amount of the department's costs and expenses for the ensuing fiscal year as estimated by the director. The amount per plan shall be calculated on a per enrollee basis as specified in paragraph (4).

(4) The amount paid by each plan shall be for each enrollee enrolled in its plan in this state as of the preceding March 31, and shall be fixed by the director by notice to all licensed plans on or before June 15 of each year. A plan that is unable to report the number of enrollees enrolled in the plan because it does not collect that data, shall provide the director with an estimate of the number of enrollees enrolled in the plan and the method used for determining the estimate. The director may, upon giving written notice to the plan, revise the estimate if the director determines that the method used for determining the estimate was not reasonable.

(5) In determining the amount assessed, the director shall consider all appropriations from the Managed Care Fund for the support of this chapter and all reimbursements provided for in this chapter.

(c) Each licensed plan shall also pay two thousand dollars ($2,000), plus an amount up to, but not exceeding, forty-eight hundredths of one cent ($0.0048), for each enrollee for the purpose of reimbursing its share of all costs and expenses, including overhead, reasonably anticipated to be incurred by the department in administering Sections 1394.7 and 1394.8 during the current fiscal year. The amount charged shall be remitted within 30 days of the date of billing.

(d) In no case shall the reimbursement, payment, or other fee authorized by this section exceed the cost, including overhead, reasonably incurred in the administration of this chapter.

(e) For the purpose of calculating the assessment under this section, an enrollee who is enrolled in one plan and who receives health care services under arrangements made by another plan or plans, whether pursuant to a contract, agreement, or otherwise, shall be considered to be enrolled in each of the plans.

(f) On and after January 1, 2009, no refunds or reductions of the amounts assessed shall be allowed if any miscalculated assessment is based on a plan's overestimate of enrollment.

(Amended by Stats. 2008, Ch. 607, Sec. 2. Effective September 30, 2008.)

1356.1.

Notwithstanding subdivision (f) of Section 1356, as amended by Section 2.5 of Chapter 722 of the Statutes of 1991, and subdivision (d) of Section 1356, as amended by Section 3 of Chapter 722 of the Statutes of 1991, if the director determines that the charges and assessments set forth in this chapter for any year are in excess of the amount necessary, or are insufficient, to meet the expenses of administration of this chapter, for that year, the assessments and charges for the following year shall be adjusted on a pro rata basis in accordance with the percentage of the excess or insufficiency as related to the actual charges and assessments for the year for which the excess or insufficiency occurred, in order to recover the actual costs of administration.

(Amended by Stats. 1999, Ch. 525, Sec. 60. Effective January 1, 2000. Operative July 1, 2000, or sooner, by Sec. 214 of Ch. 525.)

1356.2.

The director, by notice to all licensed health care service plans on or before October 15, 2010, may require health care service plans to pay an additional assessment to provide the department with sufficient revenues to support costs and expenses of the department as set forth in subdivision (b) of Section 1341.4 and Section 1356 for the 2010–11 fiscal year. The assessment paid pursuant to this section shall be separate and independent of the assessment imposed pursuant to subdivision (b) of Section 1356 and shall not be aggregated with the assessment imposed pursuant to subdivision (b) of Section 1356 for the purposes of limitation or otherwise. The assessment paid pursuant to this section shall not be subject to the limitations imposed on assessments pursuant to Section 1356.1. In imposing an assessment pursuant to this section, the director shall levy on each health care service plan an amount determined by the director using the categories of plans in the schedules set forth in subdivision (b) of Section 1356. The assessments imposed pursuant to this section shall be paid in full by December 1, 2010. On and after July 1, 2011, and until August 31, 2015, the director may raise the assessment limit described in subdivision (b) of Section 1356 to incorporate the annual expenditure levels set forth in this section.

(Added by Stats. 2010, Ch. 717, Sec. 11. (SB 853) Effective October 19, 2010.)

ARTICLE 3.1. Small Employer Group Access to Contracts for Health Care Services [1357 - 1357.19]

(Article 3.1 added by Stats. 1992, Ch. 1128, Sec. 5.)

1357.

As used in this article:

(a) "Dependent" means the spouse or child of an eligible employee, subject to applicable terms of the health care plan contract covering the employee, and includes dependents of guaranteed association members if the association elects to include dependents under its health coverage at the same time it determines its membership composition pursuant to subdivision (o).

(b) "Eligible employee" means either of the following:

(1) Any permanent employee who is actively engaged on a full-time basis in the conduct of the business of the small employer with a normal workweek of at least 30 hours, at the small employer's regular places of business, who has met any statutorily authorized applicable waiting period requirements. The term does not include sole proprietors or the spouses of those sole proprietors, partners of a partnership or the spouses of those partners, or employees who work on a part-time, temporary, or substitute basis. It includes any eligible employee, as defined in this paragraph, who obtains coverage through a guaranteed association. Employees of employers purchasing through a guaranteed association are eligible employees if they would otherwise meet the definition except for the number of persons employed by the employer. Permanent employees who work at least 20 hours but not more than 29 hours are eligible employees if all four of the following apply:

(A) They otherwise meet the definition of an eligible employee except for the number of hours worked.

(B) The employer offers the employees health coverage under a health benefit plan.

(C) All similarly situated individuals are offered coverage under the health benefit plan.

(D) The employee shall have worked at least 20 hours per normal workweek for at least 50 percent of the weeks in the previous calendar quarter. The health care service plan may request any necessary information to document the hours and time period in question, including, but not limited to, payroll records and employee wage and tax filings.

(2) Any member of a guaranteed association as defined in subdivision (o).

(c) "In force business" means an existing health benefit plan contract issued by the plan to a small employer.

(d) "Late enrollee" means an eligible employee or dependent who has declined enrollment in a health benefit plan offered by a small employer at the time of the initial enrollment period provided under the terms of the health benefit plan and who subsequently requests enrollment in a health benefit plan of that small employer, provided that the initial enrollment period shall be a period of at least 30 days. It also means any member of an association that is a guaranteed association as well as any other person eligible to purchase through the guaranteed association when that person has failed to purchase coverage during the initial enrollment period provided under the terms of the guaranteed association's plan contract and who subsequently requests enrollment in the plan, provided that the initial enrollment period shall be a period of at least 30 days. However, an eligible employee, any other person eligible for coverage through a guaranteed association pursuant to subdivision (o), or an eligible dependent shall not be considered a late enrollee if any of the following is applicable:

(1) The individual meets all of the following requirements:

(A) He or she was covered under another employer health benefit plan, the Healthy Families Program, the Access for Infants and Mothers (AIM) Program, or the Medi-Cal program at the time the individual was eligible to enroll.

(B) He or she certified at the time of the initial enrollment that coverage under another employer health benefit plan, the Healthy Families Program, the AIM Program, or the Medi-Cal program was the reason for declining enrollment, provided that, if the individual was covered under another employer health plan, the individual was given the opportunity to make the certification required by this subdivision and was notified that failure to do so could result in later treatment as a late enrollee.

(C) He or she has lost or will lose coverage under another employer health benefit plan as a result of termination of employment of the individual or of a person through whom the individual was covered as a dependent, change in employment status of the individual or of a person through whom the individual was covered as a dependent, termination of the other plan's coverage, cessation of an employer's contribution toward an employee or dependent's coverage, death of the person through whom the individual was covered as a dependent, legal separation, or divorce; or he or she has lost or will lose coverage under the Healthy Families Program, the AIM Program, or the Medi-Cal program.

(D) He or she requests enrollment within 30 days after termination of coverage or employer contribution toward coverage provided under another employer health benefit plan, or requests enrollment within 60 days after termination of Medi-Cal program coverage, AIM Program coverage, or Healthy Families Program coverage.

(2) The employer offers multiple health benefit plans and the employee elects a different plan during an open enrollment period.

(3) A court has ordered that coverage be provided for a spouse or minor child under a covered employee's health benefit plan.

(4) (A) In the case of an eligible employee, as defined in paragraph (1) of subdivision (b), the plan cannot produce a written statement from the employer stating that the individual or the person through whom the individual was eligible to be covered as a dependent, prior to declining coverage, was provided with, and signed, acknowledgment of an explicit written notice in boldface type specifying that failure to elect coverage during the initial enrollment period permits the plan to impose, at the time of the individual's later decision to elect coverage, an exclusion from coverage for a period of

12 months as well as a six-month preexisting condition exclusion, unless the individual meets the criteria specified in paragraph (1), (2), or (3).

(B) In the case of an association member who did not purchase coverage through a guaranteed association, the plan cannot produce a written statement from the association stating that the association sent a written notice in boldface type to all potentially eligible association members at their last known address prior to the initial enrollment period informing members that failure to elect coverage during the initial enrollment period permits the plan to impose, at the time of the member's later decision to elect coverage, an exclusion from coverage for a period of 12 months as well as a six-month preexisting condition exclusion unless the member can demonstrate that he or she meets the requirements of subparagraphs (A), (C), and (D) of paragraph (1) or meets the requirements of paragraph (2) or (3).

(C) In the case of an employer or person who is not a member of an association, was eligible to purchase coverage through a guaranteed association, and did not do so, and would not be eligible to purchase guaranteed coverage unless purchased through a guaranteed association, the employer or person can demonstrate that he or she meets the requirements of subparagraphs (A), (C), and (D) of paragraph (1), or meets the requirements of paragraph (2) or (3), or that he or she recently had a change in status that would make him or her eligible and that application for enrollment was made within 30 days of the change.

(5) The individual is an employee or dependent who meets the criteria described in paragraph (1) and was under a COBRA continuation provision and the coverage under that provision has been exhausted. For purposes of this section, the definition of "COBRA" set forth in subdivision (e) of Section 1373.621 shall apply.

(6) The individual is a dependent of an enrolled eligible employee who has lost or will lose his or her coverage under the Healthy Families Program, the AIM Program, or the Medi-Cal program and requests enrollment within 60 days after termination of that coverage.

(7) The individual is an eligible employee who previously declined coverage under an employer health benefit plan and who has subsequently acquired a dependent who would be eligible for coverage as a dependent of the employee through marriage, birth, adoption, or placement for adoption, and who enrolls for coverage under that employer health benefit plan on his or her behalf and on behalf of his or her dependent within 30 days following the date of marriage, birth, adoption, or placement for adoption, in which case the effective date of coverage shall be the first day of the month following the date the completed request for enrollment is received in the case of marriage, or the date of birth, or the date of adoption or placement for adoption, whichever applies. Notice of the special enrollment rights contained in this paragraph shall be provided by the employer to an employee at or before the time the employee is offered an opportunity to enroll in plan coverage.

(8) The individual is an eligible employee who has declined coverage for himself or herself or his or her dependents during a previous enrollment period because his or her dependents were covered by another employer health benefit plan at the time of the previous enrollment period. That individual may enroll himself or herself or his or her dependents for plan coverage during a special open enrollment opportunity if his or her dependents have lost or will lose coverage under that other employer health benefit plan. The special open enrollment opportunity shall be requested by the employee not more than 30 days after the date that the other health coverage is exhausted or terminated. Upon enrollment, coverage shall be effective not later than the first day of the first calendar month beginning after the date the request for enrollment is received. Notice of the special enrollment rights contained in this paragraph shall be provided by the employer to an employee at or before the time the employee is offered an opportunity to enroll in plan coverage.

(e) "New business" means a health care service plan contract issued to a small employer that is not the plan's in force business.

(f) "Preexisting condition provision" means a contract provision that excludes coverage for charges or expenses incurred during a specified period following the employee's effective date of coverage, as to a condition for which medical advice, diagnosis, care, or treatment was recommended or received during a specified period immediately preceding the effective date of coverage.

(g) "Creditable coverage" means:

(1) Any individual or group policy, contract, or program that is written or administered by a disability insurer, health care service plan, fraternal benefits society, self-insured employer plan, or any other entity, in this state or elsewhere, and that arranges or provides medical, hospital, and surgical coverage not designed to supplement private or governmental plans. The term includes continuation or conversion coverage but does not include accident only, credit, coverage for onsite medical clinics, disability income, Medicare supplement, long-term care, dental, vision, coverage issued as a supplement to liability insurance, insurance arising out of a workers' compensation or similar law, automobile medical payment insurance, or insurance under which benefits are payable with or without regard to fault and that is statutorily required to be contained in any liability insurance policy or equivalent self-insurance.

(2) The Medicare Program pursuant to Title XVIII of the federal Social Security Act (42 U.S.C. Sec. 1395 et seq.).

(3) The Medicaid program pursuant to Title XIX of the federal Social Security Act (42 U.S.C. Sec. 1396 et seq.).

(4) Any other publicly sponsored program, provided in this state or elsewhere, of medical, hospital, and surgical care.

(5) Chapter 55 (commencing with Section 1071) of Title 10 of the United States Code (Civilian Health and Medical Program of the Uniformed Services (CHAMPUS)).

(6) A medical care program of the Indian Health Service or of a tribal organization.

(7) A state health benefits risk pool.

(8) A health plan offered under Chapter 89 (commencing with Section 8901) of Title 5 of the United States Code (Federal Employees Health Benefits Program (FEHBP)).

(9) A public health plan as defined in federal regulations authorized by Section 2701(c)(1)(I) of the federal Public Health Service Act, as amended by Public Law 104-191, the federal Health Insurance Portability and Accountability Act of 1996.

(10) A health benefit plan under Section 5(e) of the federal Peace Corps Act (22 U.S.C. Sec. 2504(e)).

(11) Any other creditable coverage as defined by subdivision (c) of Section 2701 of Title XXVII of the federal Public Health Service Act (42 U.S.C. Sec. 300gg-3(c)).

(h) "Rating period" means the period for which premium rates established by a plan are in effect and shall be no less than six months.

(i) "Risk adjusted employee risk rate" means the rate determined for an eligible employee of a small employer in a particular risk category after applying the risk adjustment factor.

(j) "Risk adjustment factor" means the percentage adjustment to be applied equally to each standard employee risk rate for a particular small employer, based upon any expected deviations from standard cost of services. The factor may not be more than 110 percent or less than 90 percent.

(k) "Risk category" means the following characteristics of an eligible employee: age, geographic region, and family composition of the employee, plus the health benefit plan selected by the small employer.

(1) No more than the following age categories may be used in determining premium rates:

Under 30
30–39
40–49
50–54
55–59
60–64
65 and over.

However, for the 65 years of age and over category, separate premium rates may be specified depending upon whether coverage under the plan contract will be primary or secondary to benefits provided by the Medicare Program pursuant to Title XVIII of the federal Social Security Act (42 U.S.C. Sec. 1395 et seq.).

(2) Small employer health care service plans shall base rates to small employers using no more than the following family size categories:

(A) Single.

(B) Married couple.

(C) One adult and child or children.

(D) Married couple and child or children.

(3) (A) In determining rates for small employers, a plan that operates statewide shall use no more than nine geographic regions in the state, have no region smaller than an area in which the first three digits of all its ZIP Codes are in common within a county, and divide no county into more than two regions. Plans shall be deemed to be operating statewide if their coverage area includes 90 percent or more of the state's population. Geographic regions established pursuant to this section shall, as a group, cover the entire state, and the area encompassed in a geographic region shall be separate and distinct from areas encompassed in other geographic regions. Geographic regions may be noncontiguous.

(B) (i) In determining rates for small employers, a plan that does not operate statewide shall use no more than the number of geographic regions in the state that is determined by the following formula: the population, as determined in the last federal census, of all counties that are included in their entirety in a plan's service area divided by the total population of the state, as determined in the last federal census, multiplied by nine. The resulting number shall be rounded to the nearest whole integer. No region may be smaller than an area in which the first three digits of all its ZIP Codes are in common within a county and no county may be divided into more than two regions. The area encompassed in a geographic region shall be separate and distinct from areas encompassed in other geographic regions. Geographic regions may be noncontiguous. A plan shall not have less than one geographic area.

(ii) If the formula in clause (i) results in a plan that operates in more than one county having only one geographic region, then the formula in clause (i) shall not apply and the plan may have two geographic regions, provided that no county is divided into more than one region.

This section does not require a plan to establish a new service area or to offer health coverage on a statewide basis, outside of the plan's existing service area.

(l) "Small employer" means either of the following:

(1) Any person, firm, proprietary or nonprofit corporation, partnership, public agency, or association that is actively engaged in business or service, that, on at least 50 percent of its working days during the preceding calendar quarter or preceding calendar year, employed at least two, but no more than 50, eligible employees, the majority of whom were employed within this state, that was not formed primarily for purposes of buying health care service plan contracts, and in which a bona fide employer-employee relationship exists. In determining whether to apply the calendar quarter or calendar year test, a health care service plan shall use the test that ensures eligibility if only one test would establish eligibility. However, for purposes of subdivisions (a), (b), and (c) of Section 1357.03, the definition shall include employers with at least two eligible employees. In determining the number of eligible employees, companies that are affiliated companies and that are eligible to file a combined tax return for purposes of state taxation shall be considered one employer. Subsequent to the issuance of a health care

service plan contract to a small employer pursuant to this article, and for the purpose of determining eligibility, the size of a small employer shall be determined annually. Except as otherwise specifically provided in this article, provisions of this article that apply to a small employer shall continue to apply until the plan contract anniversary following the date the employer no longer meets the requirements of this definition. It includes any small employer as defined in this paragraph who purchases coverage through a guaranteed association, any employer purchasing coverage for employees through a guaranteed association, and any small employer as defined in this paragraph who purchases coverage through any arrangement.

(2) Any guaranteed association, as defined in subdivision (n), that purchases health coverage for members of the association.

(m) "Standard employee risk rate" means the rate applicable to an eligible employee in a particular risk category in a small employer group.

(n) "Guaranteed association" means a nonprofit organization comprised of a group of individuals or employers who associate based solely on participation in a specified profession or industry, accepting for membership any individual or employer meeting its membership criteria, and that (1) includes one or more small employers as defined in paragraph (1) of subdivision (l), (2) does not condition membership directly or indirectly on the health or claims history of any person, (3) uses membership dues solely for and in consideration of the membership and membership benefits, except that the amount of the dues shall not depend on whether the member applies for or purchases insurance offered to the association, (4) is organized and maintained in good faith for purposes unrelated to insurance, (5) has been in active existence on January 1, 1992, and for at least five years prior to that date, (6) has included health insurance as a membership benefit for at least five years prior to January 1, 1992, (7) has a constitution and bylaws, or other analogous governing documents that provide for election of the governing board of the association by its members, (8) offers any plan contract that is purchased to all individual members and employer members in this state, (9) includes any member choosing to enroll in the plan contracts offered to the association provided that the member has agreed to make the required premium payments, and (10) covers at least 1,000 persons with the health care service plan with which it contracts. The requirement of 1,000 persons may be met if component chapters of a statewide association contracting separately with the same carrier cover at least 1,000 persons in the aggregate.

This subdivision applies regardless of whether a contract issued by a plan is with an association, or a trust formed for or sponsored by an association, to administer benefits for association members.

For purposes of this subdivision, an association formed by a merger of two or more associations after January 1, 1992, and otherwise meeting the criteria of this subdivision shall be deemed to have been in active existence on January 1, 1992, if its predecessor organizations had been in active existence on January 1, 1992, and for at least five years prior to that date and otherwise met the criteria of this subdivision.

(o) "Members of a guaranteed association" means any individual or employer meeting the association's membership criteria if that person is a member of the association and chooses to purchase health coverage through the association. At the association's discretion, it also may include employees of association members, association staff, retired members, retired employees of members, and surviving spouses and dependents of deceased members. However, if an association chooses to include these persons as members of the guaranteed association, the association shall make that election in advance of purchasing a plan contract. Health care service plans may require an association to adhere to the membership composition it selects for up to 12 months.

(p) "Affiliation period" means a period that, under the terms of the health care service plan contract, is required to elapse before health care services under the contract become effective.

(Amended by Stats. 2018, Ch. 700, Sec. 1. (SB 1375) Effective January 1, 2019.)

1357.01.

Every health care service plan offering plan contracts to small employer groups shall in addition to complying with the provisions of this chapter and the rules adopted thereunder comply with the provisions of this article.

(Added by Stats. 1992, Ch. 1128, Sec. 5. Effective January 1, 1993. Operative July 1, 1993, by Sec. 15 of Ch. 1128.)

1357.02.

(a) A health care service plan providing or arranging for the provision of basic health care services to small employers shall be subject to this article if either of the following conditions are met:

(1) Any portion of the premium is paid by a small employer, or any covered individual is reimbursed, whether through wage adjustments or otherwise, by a small employer for any portion of the premium.

(2) The plan contract is treated by the small employer or any of the covered individuals as part of a plan or program for the purposes of Section 106 or 162 of the Internal Revenue Code.

(b) This article shall not apply to health plan contracts for coverage of Medicare services pursuant to contracts with the United States government, Medicare supplement, Medi-Cal contracts with the State Department of Health Services, long-term care coverage, or specialized health plan contracts.

(Amended by Stats. 1993, Ch. 1146, Sec. 1.2. Effective October 11, 1993.)

1357.025.

Nothing in this article shall be construed to preclude the application of this chapter to either of the following:

(a) An association, trust, or other organization acting as a "health care service plan" as defined under Section 1345.

(b) An association, trust, or other organization or person presenting information regarding a health care service plan to persons who may be interested in subscribing or enrolling in the plan.

(Added by Stats. 1993, Ch. 1146, Sec. 1.4. Effective October 11, 1993.)

1357.03.

(a) (1) Upon the effective date of this article, a plan shall fairly and affirmatively offer, market, and sell all of the plan's health care service plan contracts that are sold to small employers or to associations that include small employers to all small employers in each service area in which the plan provides or arranges for the provision of health care services.

(2) Each plan shall make available to each small employer all small employer health care service plan contracts that the plan offers and sells to small employers or to associations that include small employers in this state.

(3) No plan or solicitor shall induce or otherwise encourage a small employer to separate or otherwise exclude an eligible employee from a health care service plan contract that is provided in connection with the employee's employment or membership in a guaranteed association.

(4) A plan contracting to participate in the voluntary purchasing pool for small employers provided for under Article 4 (commencing with Section 10730) of Chapter 8 of Part 2 of Division 2 of the Insurance Code shall be deemed in compliance with the requirements of paragraph (1) for a contract offered through the voluntary purchasing pool established under Article 4 (commencing with Section 10730) of Chapter 8 of Part 2 of Division 2 of the Insurance Code in those geographic regions in which plans participate in the pool, if the contract is offered exclusively through the pool.

(5) (A) A plan shall be deemed to meet the requirements of paragraphs (1) and (2) with respect to a plan contract that qualifies as a grandfathered health plan under Section 1251 of PPACA if all of the following requirements are met:

(i) The plan offers to renew the plan contract, unless the plan withdraws the plan contract from the small employer market pursuant to subdivision (e) of Section 1357.11.

(ii) The plan provides appropriate notice of the grandfathered status of the contract in any materials provided to an enrollee of the contract describing the benefits provided under the contract, as required under PPACA.

(iii) The plan makes no changes to the benefits covered under the plan contract other than those required by a state or federal law, regulation, rule, or guidance and those permitted to be made to a grandfathered health plan under PPACA.

(B) For purposes of this paragraph, "PPACA" means the federal Patient Protection and Affordable Care Act (Public Law 111-148), as amended by the federal Health Care and Education Reconciliation Act of 2010 (Public Law 111-152), and any rules, regulations, or guidance issued thereunder. For purposes of this paragraph, a "grandfathered health plan" shall have the meaning set forth in Section 1251 of PPACA.

(b) Every plan shall file with the director the reasonable employee participation requirements and employer contribution requirements that will be applied in offering its plan contracts. Participation requirements shall be applied uniformly among all small employer groups, except that a plan may vary application of minimum employee participation requirements by the size of the small employer group and whether the employer contributes 100 percent of the eligible employee's premium. Employer contribution requirements shall not vary by employer size. A health care service plan shall not establish a participation requirement that (1) requires a person who meets the definition of a dependent in subdivision (a) of Section 1357 to enroll as a dependent if he or she is otherwise eligible for coverage and wishes to enroll as an eligible employee and (2) allows a plan to reject an otherwise eligible small employer because of the number of persons that waive coverage due to coverage through another employer. Members of an association eligible for health coverage under subdivision (o) of Section 1357, but not electing any health coverage through the association, shall not be counted as eligible employees for purposes of determining whether the guaranteed association meets a plan's reasonable participation standards.

(c) The plan shall not reject an application from a small employer for a health care service plan contract if all of the following are met:

(1) The small employer, as defined by paragraph (1) of subdivision (l) of Section 1357, offers health benefits to 100 percent of its eligible employees, as defined by paragraph (1) of subdivision (b) of Section 1357. Employees who waive coverage on the grounds that they have other group coverage shall not be counted as eligible employees.

(2) The small employer agrees to make the required premium payments.

(3) The small employer agrees to inform the small employers' employees of the availability of coverage and the provision that those not electing coverage must wait one year to obtain coverage through the group if they later decide they would like to have coverage.

(4) The employees and their dependents who are to be covered by the plan contract work or reside in the service area in which the plan provides or otherwise arranges for the provision of health care services.

(d) No plan or solicitor shall, directly or indirectly, engage in the following activities:

(1) Encourage or direct small employers to refrain from filing an application for coverage with a plan because of the health status, claims experience, industry, occupation of the small employer, or geographic location provided that it is within the plan's approved service area.

(2) Encourage or direct small employers to seek coverage from another plan or the voluntary purchasing pool established under Article 4 (commencing with Section 10730) of Chapter 8 of Part 2 of Division 2 of the Insurance Code because of the health status, claims experience, industry, occupation of the small employer, or geographic location provided that it is within the plan's approved service area.

(e) A plan shall not, directly or indirectly, enter into any contract, agreement, or arrangement with a solicitor that provides for or results in the compensation paid to a solicitor for the sale of a health care service plan contract to be varied because of the health status, claims experience, industry, occupation, or geographic location of the small employer. This subdivision does not apply to a compensation arrangement that provides compensation to a solicitor on the basis of percentage of premium, provided that the percentage shall not vary because of the health status, claims experience, industry, occupation, or geographic area of the small employer.

(f) A policy or contract that covers two or more employees shall not establish rules for eligibility, including continued eligibility, of an individual, or dependent of an individual, to enroll under the terms of the plan based on any of the following health status-related factors:

(1) Health status.

(2) Medical condition, including physical and mental illnesses.

(3) Claims experience.

(4) Receipt of health care.

(5) Medical history.

(6) Genetic information.

(7) Evidence of insurability, including conditions arising out of acts of domestic violence.

(8) Disability.

(g) A plan shall comply with the requirements of Section 1374.3.

(Amended by Stats. 2010, Ch. 661, Sec. 1. (SB 1163) Effective January 1, 2011.)

1357.035.

(a) Between July 26, 1993, and October 24, 1993, as well as 60 days prior to the expiration of an existing plan contract that expires prior to July 1, 1994, or, for plan contracts expiring after July 1, 1994, 60 days prior to July 1, 1994, an association that meets the definition of guaranteed association, as set forth in Section 1357, except for the requirement that 1,000 persons be covered, shall be entitled to purchase small employer health coverage as if the association were a guaranteed association, except that the coverage shall be guaranteed only for those members of an association, as defined in Section 1357, (1) who were receiving coverage or had successfully applied for coverage through the association as of June 30, 1993, (2) who were receiving coverage through the association as of December 31, 1992, and whose coverage lapsed at any time thereafter because the employment through which coverage was received ended or an employer's contribution to health coverage ended, or (3) who were covered at any time between June 30, 1993, and July 1, 1994, under a contract that was in force on June 30, 1993.

(b) An association obtaining health coverage for its members pursuant to this section shall otherwise be afforded all the rights of a guaranteed association under this chapter including, but not limited to, guaranteed renewability of coverage.

(c) No later than August 25, 1993, plans that, at any time during the 1993 calendar year have provided coverage to associations that would be eligible for coverage under this section shall notify those associations of their rights under this section. Ninety days prior to the expiration of a plan contract that expires prior to July 1, 1994, or, for plan contracts expiring after July 1, 1994, 90 days prior to July 1, 1994, health plans that have in force coverage with an association that would be eligible for coverage under this section shall notify the association of its rights under this section.

(Amended by Stats. 1993, Ch. 1146, Sec. 2.5. Effective October 11, 1993.)

1357.04.

(a) After a small employer submits a completed application form for a plan contract, the plan shall, within 30 days, notify the employer of the employer's actual premium charges for that plan contract established in accordance with Section 1357.12. The employer shall have 30 days in which to exercise the right to buy coverage at the quoted premium charges.

(b) When a small employer submits a premium payment, based on the quoted premium charges, and that payment is delivered or postmarked, whichever occurs earlier, within the first 15 days of the month, coverage under the plan contract shall become effective no later than the first day of the following month. When that payment is neither delivered nor postmarked until after the 15th day of a month, coverage shall become effective no later than the first day of the second month following delivery or postmark of the payment.

(c) During the first 30 days after the effective date of the plan contract, the small employer shall have the option of changing coverage to a different plan contract offered by the same health care service plan. If a small employer notifies the plan of the change within the first 15 days of a month, coverage under the new plan contract shall become effective no later than the first day of the following month. If a small employer notifies the plan of the change after the 15th day of a month, coverage under the new plan contract shall become effective no later than the first day of the second month following notification.

(Amended by Stats. 1993, Ch. 113, Sec. 2.5. Effective July 13, 1993.)

1357.05.

Except in the case of a late enrollee, or for satisfaction of a preexisting condition clause in the case of initial coverage of an eligible employee, a plan may not exclude any eligible employee or dependent who would otherwise be entitled to health care services on the basis of an actual or expected health condition of that employee or dependent. No plan contract may limit or exclude coverage for a specific eligible employee or dependent by type of illness, treatment, medical condition, or accident, except for preexisting conditions as permitted by Section 1357.06.

(Amended by Stats. 1995, Ch. 668, Sec. 2. Effective January 1, 1996.)

1357.06.

(a) (1) Preexisting condition provisions of a plan contract shall not exclude coverage for a period beyond six months following the individual's effective date of coverage and may only relate to conditions for which medical advice, diagnosis, care, or treatment, including prescription drugs, was recommended or received from a licensed health practitioner during the six months immediately preceding the effective date of coverage.

(2) Notwithstanding paragraph (1), a plan contract offered to a small employer shall not impose any preexisting condition provision upon any child under 19 years of age.

(b) A plan that does not utilize a preexisting condition provision may impose a waiting or affiliation period, not to exceed 60 days, before the coverage issued subject to this article shall become effective. During the waiting or affiliation period no premiums shall be charged to the enrollee or the subscriber.

(c) In determining whether a preexisting condition provision or a waiting or affiliation period applies to any person, a plan shall credit the time the person was covered under creditable coverage, provided the person becomes eligible for coverage under the succeeding plan contract within 62 days of termination of prior coverage, exclusive of any waiting or affiliation period, and applies for coverage with the succeeding plan contract within the applicable enrollment period. A plan shall also credit any time an eligible employee must wait before enrolling in the plan, including any affiliation or employer-imposed waiting or affiliation period. However, if a person's employment has ended, the availability of health coverage offered through employment or sponsored by an employer has terminated, or an employer's contribution toward health coverage has terminated, a plan shall credit the time the person was covered under creditable coverage if the person becomes eligible for health coverage offered through employment or sponsored by an employer within 180 days, exclusive of any waiting or affiliation period, and applies for coverage under the succeeding plan contract within the applicable enrollment period.

(d) In addition to the preexisting condition exclusions authorized by subdivision (a) and the waiting or affiliation period authorized by subdivision (b), health plans providing coverage to a guaranteed association may impose on employers or individuals purchasing coverage who would not be eligible for guaranteed coverage if they were not purchasing through the association a waiting or affiliation period, not to exceed 60 days, before the coverage issued subject to this article shall become effective. During the waiting or affiliation period, no premiums shall be charged to the enrollee or the subscriber.

(e) An individual's period of creditable coverage shall be certified pursuant to subdivision (e) of Section 2701 of Title XXVII of the federal Public Health Services Act (42 U.S.C. Sec. 300gg(e)).

(f) A health care service plan issuing group coverage may not impose a preexisting condition exclusion to a condition relating to benefits for pregnancy or maternity care.

(Amended by Stats. 2010, Ch. 656, Sec. 1. (AB 2244) Effective January 1, 2011.)

1357.07.

No plan contract may exclude late enrollees from coverage for more than 12 months from the date of the late enrollees application for coverage. No premium shall be charged to the late enrollee until the exclusion period has ended.

(Added by Stats. 1992, Ch. 1128, Sec. 5. Effective January 1, 1993. Operative July 1, 1993, by Sec. 15 of Ch. 1128.)

1357.08.

All health care service plan contracts offered to a small employer shall provide to subscribers and enrollees at least all of the basic health care services included in subdivision (b) of Section 1345, and in Section 1300.67 of the California Code of Regulations.

(Added by Stats. 1992, Ch. 1128, Sec. 5. Effective January 1, 1993. Operative July 1, 1993, by Sec. 15 of Ch. 1128.)

1357.09.

No plan shall be required to offer a health care service plan contract or accept applications for the contract pursuant to this article in the case of any of the following:

(a) To a small employer, if the small employer is not physically located in a plan's approved service areas, or if an eligible employee and dependents who are to be covered by the plan contract do not work or reside within a plan's approved service areas.

(b) (1) Within a specific service area or portion of a service area, if a plan reasonably anticipates and demonstrates to the satisfaction of the director that it will not have sufficient health care delivery resources to assure that health care services will be available and accessible to the eligible employee and dependents of the employee because of its obligations to existing enrollees.

(2) A plan that cannot offer a health care service plan contract to small employers because it is lacking in sufficient health care delivery resources within a service area or a portion of a service area may not offer a contract in the area in which the plan is not offering coverage to small employers to new employer groups with more than 50 eligible employees until the plan notifies the director that it has the ability to deliver services to small employer groups, and certifies to the director that from the date of the notice it will enroll all small employer groups requesting coverage in that area from the plan unless the plan has met the requirements of subdivision (d).

(3) Nothing in this article shall be construed to limit the director's authority to develop and implement a plan of rehabilitation for a health care service plan whose financial viability or organizational and administrative capacity has become impaired.

(c) Offer coverage to a small employer or an eligible employee as defined under paragraph (2) of subdivision (b) of Section 1357 that, within 12 months of application for coverage, disenrolled from a plan contract offered by the plan.

(d) (1) The director approves the plan's certification that the number of eligible employees and dependents enrolled under contracts issued during the current calendar year equals or exceeds either of the following:

(A) In the case of a plan that administers any self-funded health coverage arrangements in California, 10 percent of the total enrollment of the plan in California as of December 31 of the preceding year.

(B) In the case of a plan that does not administer any self-funded health coverage arrangements in California, 8 percent of the total enrollment of the plan in California as of December 31 of the preceding year. If that certification is approved, the plan shall not offer any health care service plan contract to any small employers during the remainder of the current year.

(2) If a health care service plan treats an affiliate or subsidiary as a separate carrier for the purpose of this article because one health care service plan is qualified under the federal Health Maintenance Organization Act (42 U.S.C. Sec. 300e et seq.) and does not offer coverage to small employers, while the affiliate or subsidiary offers a plan contract that is not qualified under the federal Health Maintenance Organization Act (42 U.S.C. Sec. 300e et seq.) and offers plan contracts to small employers, the health care service plan offering coverage to small employers shall enroll new eligible employees and dependents, equal to the applicable percentage of the total enrollment of both the health care service plan qualified under the federal Health Maintenance Organization Act (42 U.S.C. Sec. 300e et seq.) and its affiliate or subsidiary.

(3) (A) The certified statement filed pursuant to this subdivision shall state the following:
(i) Whether the plan administers any self-funded health coverage arrangements in California.
(ii) The plan's total enrollment as of December 31 of the preceding year.
(iii) The number of eligible employees and dependents enrolled under contracts issued to small employer groups during the current calendar year.
(B) The director shall, within 45 days, approve or disapprove the certified statement. If the certified statement is disapproved, the plan shall continue to issue coverage as required by Section 1357.03 and be subject to disciplinary action as set forth in Article 7 (commencing with Section 1386).

(e) A health care service plan that, as of December 31 of the prior year, had a total enrollment of fewer than 100,000 and 50 percent or more of the plan's total enrollment have premiums paid by the Medi-Cal program.

(f) A social health maintenance organization, as described in subdivision (a) of Section 2355 of the federal Deficit Reduction Act of 1984 (P.L. 98-369), that, as of December 31 of the prior year, had a total enrollment of fewer than 100,000 and has 50 percent or more of the organization's total enrollment premiums paid by the Medi-Cal program or Medicare programs, or by a combination of Medi-Cal and Medicare. In no event shall this exemption be based upon enrollment in Medicare supplement contracts, as described in Article 3.5 (commencing with Section 1358).
(Amended by Stats. 2006, Ch. 538, Sec. 353. Effective January 1, 2007.)

1357.10.
The director may require a plan to discontinue the offering of contracts or acceptance of applications from any small employer or group with more than 50 employees upon a determination by the director that the plan does not have sufficient financial viability, or organizational and administrative capacity to assure the delivery of health care services to its enrollees. In determining whether the conditions of this section have been met, the director shall consider, but not be limited to, the plan's compliance with the requirements of Section 1367, Article 6 (commencing with Section 1375), and the rules adopted thereunder.
(Amended by Stats. 1999, Ch. 525, Sec. 63. Effective January 1, 2000. Operative July 1, 2000, or sooner, by Sec. 214 of Ch. 525.)

1357.12.
Premiums for contracts offered or delivered by plans on or after the effective date of this article shall be subject to the following requirements:
(a) (1) The premium for new business shall be determined for an eligible employee in a particular risk category after applying a risk adjustment factor to the plan's standard employee risk rates. The risk adjusted employee risk rate may not be more than 120 percent or less than 80 percent of the plan's applicable standard employee risk rate until July 1, 1996. Effective July 1, 1996, this factor may not be more than 110 percent or less than 90 percent.
(2) The premium charged a small employer for new business shall be equal to the sum of the risk adjusted employee risk rates.
(3) The standard employee risk rates applied to a small employer for new business shall be in effect for no less than six months.
(b) (1) The premium for in force business shall be determined for an eligible employee in a particular risk category after applying a risk adjustment factor to the plan's standard employee risk rates. The risk adjusted employee risk rates may not be more than 120 percent or less than 80 percent of the plan's applicable standard employee risk rate until July 1, 1996. Effective July 1, 1996, this factor may not be more than 110 percent or less than 90 percent. The factor effective July 1, 1996, shall apply to in force business at the earlier of either the time of renewal or July 1, 1997. The risk adjustment factor applied to a small employer may not increase by more than 10 percentage points from the risk adjustment factor applied in the prior rating period. The risk adjustment factor for a small employer may not be modified more frequently than every 12 months.
(2) The premium charged a small employer for in force business shall be equal to the sum of the risk adjusted employee risk rates. The standard employee risk rates shall be in effect for no less than six months.
(3) For a contract that a plan has discontinued offering, the risk adjustment factor applied to the standard employee risk rates for the first rating period of the new contract that the small employer elects to purchase shall be no greater than the risk adjustment factor applied in the prior rating period to the discontinued contract. However, the risk adjusted employee risk rate may not be more than 120 percent or less than 80 percent of the plan's applicable standard employee risk rate until July 1, 1996. Effective July 1, 1996, this factor may not be more than 110 percent or less than 90 percent. The factor effective July 1, 1996, shall apply to in force business at the earlier of either the time of renewal or July 1, 1997. The risk adjustment factor for a small employer may not be modified more frequently than every 12 months.
(c) (1) For any small employer, a plan may, with the consent of the small employer, establish composite employee and dependent rates for either new business or renewal of in force business. The composite rates shall be determined as the average of the risk adjusted employee risk rates for the small employer, as determined in accordance with the requirements of subdivisions (a) and (b). The sum of the composite rates so determined shall be equal to the sum of the risk adjusted employee risk rates for the small employer.
(2) The composite rates shall be used for all employees and dependents covered throughout a rating period of no less than six months nor more than 12 months, except that a plan may reserve the right to redetermine the composite rates if the enrollment under the contract changes by more than a specified percentage during the rating period. Any redetermination of the composite rates shall be based on the same risk adjusted employee risk rates used to determine the initial composite rates for the rating period. If a plan reserves the right to redetermine the rates and the enrollment changes more than the specified percentage, the plan shall redetermine the composite rates if the redetermined rates would result in a lower premium for the small employer. A plan reserving the right to redetermine the composite rates based upon a change in enrollment shall use the same specified percentage to measure that change with respect to all small employers electing composite rates.
(Amended by Stats. 1996, Ch. 50, Sec. 1. Effective May 24, 1996.)

1357.13.
Plans shall apply standard employee risk rates consistently with respect to all small employers.
(Added by Stats. 1992, Ch. 1128, Sec. 5. Effective January 1, 1993. Operative July 1, 1993, by Sec. 15 of Ch. 1128.)

1357.14.
In connection with the offering for sale of any plan contract to a small employer, each plan shall make a reasonable disclosure, as part of its solicitation and sales materials, of the following:
(a) The extent to which premium rates for a specified small employer are established or adjusted in part based upon the actual or expected variation in service costs or actual or expected variation in health condition of the employees and dependents of the small employer.
(b) The provisions concerning the plan's right to change premium rates and the factors other than provision of services experience that affect changes in premium rates.
(c) Provisions relating to the guaranteed issue and renewal of contracts.
(d) Provisions relating to the effect of any preexisting condition provision.
(e) Provisions relating to the small employer's right to apply for any contract written, issued, or administered by the plan at the time of application for a new health care service plan contract, or at the time of renewal of a health care service plan contract.
(f) The availability, upon request, of a listing of all the plan's contracts and benefit plan designs offered to small employers, including the rates for each contract.
(g) At the time it offers a contract to a small employer, each plan shall provide the small employer with a statement of all of its plan contracts offered to small employers, including the rates for each plan contract, in the service area in which the employer's employees and eligible dependents who are to be covered by the plan contract work or reside. For purposes of this subdivision, plans that are affiliated plans or that are eligible to file a consolidated income tax return shall be treated as one health plan.
(h) Each plan shall do all of the following:
(1) Prepare a brochure that summarizes all of its plan contracts offered to small employers and to make this summary available to any small employer and to solicitors upon request. The summary shall include for each contract information on benefits provided, a generic description of the manner in which services are provided, such as how access to providers is limited, benefit limitations, required copayments and deductibles, standard employee risk rates, an explanation of the manner in which creditable coverage is calculated if a preexisting condition or affiliation period is imposed, and a phone number that can be called for more detailed benefit information. Plans are required to keep the information contained in the brochure accurate and up to date and, upon updating the brochure, send copies to solicitors and solicitor firms with whom the plan contracts to solicit enrollments or subscriptions.
(2) For each contract, prepare a more detailed evidence of coverage and make it available to small employers, solicitors, and solicitor firms upon request. The evidence of coverage shall contain all information that a prudent buyer would need to be aware of in making contract selections.
(3) Provide to small employers and solicitors, upon request, for any given small employer the sum of the standard employee risk rates and the sum of the risk adjusted employee risk rates. When requesting this information, small employers, solicitors, and solicitor firms shall provide the plan with the information the plan needs to determine the small employer's risk adjusted employee risk rate.
(4) Provide copies of the current summary brochure to all solicitors and solicitor firms contracting with the plan to solicit enrollments or subscriptions from small employers. For purposes of this subdivision, plans that are affiliated plans or that are eligible to file a consolidated income tax return shall be treated as one health plan.

(i) Every solicitor or solicitor firm contracting with one or more plans to solicit enrollments or subscriptions from small employers shall do all of the following:

(1) When providing information on contracts to a small employer but making no specific recommendations on particular plan contracts:

(A) Advise the small employer of the plan's obligation to sell to any small employer any plan contract it offers to small employers and provide them, upon request, with the actual rates that would be charged to that employer for a given contract.

(B) Notify the small employer that the solicitor or solicitor firm will procure rate and benefit information for the small employer on any plan contract offered by a plan whose contract the solicitor sells.

(C) Notify the small employer that upon request the solicitor or solicitor firm will provide the small employer with the summary brochure required under paragraph (1) of subdivision (h) for any plan contract offered by a plan with whom the solicitor or solicitor firm has contracted with to solicit enrollments or subscriptions.

(2) When recommending a particular benefit plan design or designs, advise the small employer that, upon request, the agent will provide the small employer with the brochure required by paragraph (1) of subdivision (h) containing the benefit plan design or designs being recommended by the agent or broker.

(3) Prior to filing an application for a small employer for a particular contract:

(A) For each of the plan contracts offered by the plan whose contract the solicitor or solicitor firm is offering, provide the small employer with the benefit summary required in paragraph (1) of subdivision (h) and the sum of the standard employee risk rates for that particular employer.

(B) Notify the small employer that, upon request, the solicitor or solicitor firm will provide the small employer with an evidence of coverage brochure for each contract the plan offers.

(C) Notify the small employer that, from July 1, 1993, to July 1, 1996, actual rates may be 20 percent higher or lower than the sum of the standard employee risk rates, and from July 1, 1996, and thereafter, actual rates may be 10 percent higher or lower than the sum of the standard employee risk rates, depending on how the plan assesses the risk of the small employer's group.

(D) Notify the small employer that, upon request, the solicitor or solicitor firm will submit information to the plan to ascertain the small employer's sum of the risk adjusted employee risk rate for any contract the plan offers.

(E) Obtain a signed statement from the small employer acknowledging that the small employer has received the disclosures required by this section.

(Amended by Stats. 1997, Ch. 336, Sec. 5. Effective August 21, 1997.)

1357.15.

(a) At least 20 business days prior to renewing or amending a plan contract subject to this article which will be in force on the operative date of this article, a plan shall file a notice of material modification with the director in accordance with the provisions of Section 1352. The notice of material modification shall include a statement certifying that the plan is in compliance with subdivision (j) of Section 1357 and Section 1357.12. The certified statement shall set forth the standard employee risk rate for each risk category and the highest and lowest risk adjustment factors that will be used in setting the rates at which the contract will be renewed or amended. Any action by the director, as permitted under Section 1352, to disapprove, suspend or postpone the plan's use of a plan contract shall be in writing, specifying the reasons that the plan contract does not comply with the requirements of this chapter.

(b) At least 20 business days prior to offering a plan contract subject to this article, all plans shall file a notice of material modification with the director in accordance with the provisions of Section 1352. The notice of material modification shall include a statement certifying that the plan is in compliance with subdivision (j) of Section 1357 and Section 1357.12. The certified statement shall set forth the standard employee risk rate for each risk category and the highest and lowest risk adjustment factors that will be used in setting the rates at which the contract will be offered. Plans that will be offering to a small employer plan contracts approved by the director prior to the effective date of this article shall file a notice of material modification in accordance with this subdivision. Any action by the director, as permitted under Section 1352, to disapprove, suspend or postpone the plan's use of a plan contract shall be in writing, specifying the reasons that the plan contract does not comply with the requirements of this chapter.

(c) Prior to making any changes in the risk categories, risk adjustment factors or standard employee risk rates filed with the director pursuant to subdivision (a) or (b), the plan shall file as an amendment a statement setting forth the changes and certifying that the plan is in compliance with subdivision (j) of Section 1357 and Section 1357.12. A plan may commence offering plan contracts utilizing the changed risk categories set forth in the certified statement on the 31st day from the date of the filing, or at an earlier time determined by the director, unless the director disapproves the amendment by written notice, stating the reasons therefor. If only the standard employee risk rate is being changed, and not the risk categories or risk adjustment factors, a plan may commence offering plan contracts utilizing the changed standard employee risk rate upon filing the certified statement unless the director disapproves the amendment by written notice.

(d) Periodic changes to the standard employee risk rate that a plan proposes to implement over the course of up to 12 consecutive months may be filed in conjunction with the certified statement filed under subdivision (a), (b), or (c).

(e) Each plan shall maintain at its principal place of business all of the information required to be filed with the director pursuant to this section.

(f) Each plan shall make available to the director, on request, the risk adjustment factor used in determining the rate for any particular small employer.

(g) Nothing in this section shall be construed to limit the director's authority to enforce the rating practices set forth in this article.

(Amended by Stats. 1999, Ch. 525, Sec. 65. Effective January 1, 2000. Operative July 1, 2000, or sooner, by Sec. 214 of Ch. 525.)

1357.16.

(a) Health care service plans may enter into contractual agreements with qualified associations, as defined in subdivision (b), under which these qualified associations may assume responsibility for performing specific administrative services, as defined in this section, for qualified association members. Health care service plans that enter into agreements with qualified associations for assumption of administrative services shall establish uniform definitions for the administrative services that may be provided by a qualified association or its third-party administrator. The health care service plan shall permit all qualified associations to assume one or more of these functions when the health care service plan determines the qualified association demonstrates the administrative capacity to assume these functions.

For the purposes of this section, administrative services provided by qualified associations or their third-party administrators shall be services pertaining to eligibility determination, enrollment, premium collection, sales, or claims administration on a per-claim basis that would otherwise be provided directly by the health care service plan or through a third-party administrator on a commission basis or an agent or solicitor workforce on a commission basis.

Each health care service plan that enters into an agreement with any qualified association for the provision of administrative services shall offer all qualified associations with which it contracts the same premium discounts for performing those services the health care service plan has permitted the qualified association or its third-party administrator to assume. The health care service plan shall apply these uniform discounts to the health care service plan's risk adjusted employee risk rates after the health plan has determined the qualified association's risk adjusted employee risk rates pursuant to Section 1357.12. The health care service plan shall report to the Department of Managed Health Care its schedule of discount for each administrative service.

In no instance may a health care service plan provide discounts to qualified associations that are in any way intended to, or materially result in, a reduction in premium charges to the qualified association due to the health status of the membership of the qualified association. In addition to any other remedies available to the director to enforce this chapter, the director may declare a contract between a health care service plan and a qualified association for administrative services pursuant to this section null and void if the director determines any discounts provided to the qualified association are intended to, or materially result in, a reduction in premium charges to the qualified association due to the health status of the membership of the qualified association.

(b) For the purposes of this section, a qualified association is a nonprofit corporation comprised of a group of individuals or employers who associate based solely on participation in a specified profession or industry, that conforms to all of the following requirements:

(1) It accepts for membership any individual or small employer meeting its membership criteria.

(2) It does not condition membership directly or indirectly on the health or claims history of any person.

(3) It uses membership dues solely for and in consideration of the membership and membership benefits, except that the amount of the dues shall not depend on whether the member applies for or purchases insurance offered by the association.

(4) It is organized and maintained in good faith for purposes unrelated to insurance.

(5) It existed on January 1, 1972, and has been in continuous existence since that date.

(6) It has a constitution and bylaws or other analogous governing documents that provide for election of the governing board of the association by its members.

(7) It offered, marketed, or sold health coverage to its members for 20 continuous years prior to January 1, 1993.

(8) It agrees to offer only to association members any plan contract.

(9) It agrees to include any member choosing to enroll in the plan contract offered by the association, provided that the member agrees to make required premium payments.

(10) It complies with all provisions of this article.

(11) It had at least 10,000 enrollees covered by association sponsored plans immediately prior to enactment of Chapter 1128 of the Statutes of 1992.

(12) It applies any administrative cost at an equal rate to all members purchasing coverage through the qualified association.

(c) A qualified association shall comply with Section 1357.52.

(Amended by Stats. 2012, Ch. 728, Sec. 82. (SB 71) Effective January 1, 2013.)

1357.17.

The director may issue regulations that are necessary to carry out the purposes of this article. Prior to the public comment period required on the regulations under the Administrative Procedure Act, the director shall provide the Insurance Commissioner with a copy of the proposed regulations. The Insurance Commissioner shall have 30 days to notify the director in writing of any comments on the regulations. The Insurance Commissioner's comments shall be included in the public notice issued on the regulations. Any rules and regulations adopted pursuant to this article may be adopted as emergency regulations in accordance with the Administrative Procedure Act (Chapter 3.5 (commencing with Section 11340) of Part 1 of Division 3 of Title 2 of the Government Code). Until December 31, 1994, the adoption of these regulations shall be deemed an emergency and necessary for the immediate preservation of the public peace, health and safety or general welfare.

(Amended by Stats. 1999, Ch. 525, Sec. 67. Effective January 1, 2000. Operative July 1, 2000, or sooner, by Sec. 214 of Ch. 525.)

1357.19.

This article shall not apply to a health care service plan contract that is subject to Article 3.16 (commencing with Section 1357.500) or Article 3.17 (commencing with Section 1357.600), except as otherwise provided in those articles.

(Added by Stats. 2012, Ch. 852, Sec. 2. (AB 1083) Effective January 1, 2013.)

ARTICLE 3.15. Preexisting Condition Provisions [1357.50 - 1357.55]

(Article 3.15 repealed (in Sec. 5) and added by Stats. 2012, Ch. 852, Sec. 4.)

1357.50.

(a) For purposes of this article, the following definitions shall apply:

(1) "Health benefit plan" means a health care service plan contract that provides medical, hospital, and surgical benefits. The term does not include coverage of Medicare services pursuant to contracts with the United States government, Medicare supplement coverage, or coverage under a specialized health care service plan contract.

(2) "Preexisting condition provision" means a contract provision that excludes coverage for charges or expenses incurred during a specified period following the enrollee's effective date of coverage, as to a condition for which medical advice, diagnosis, care, or treatment was recommended or received during a specified period immediately preceding the effective date of coverage.

(3) "Creditable coverage" means:

(A) Any individual or group policy, contract, or program that is written or administered by a health insurer, nonprofit hospital service plan, health care service plan, fraternal benefits society, self-insured employer plan, or any other entity, in this state or elsewhere, and that arranges or provides medical, hospital and surgical coverage not designed to supplement other private or governmental plans. The term includes continuation or conversion coverage but does not include accident only, credit, coverage for onsite medical clinics, disability income, Medicare supplement, long-term care insurance, dental, vision, coverage issued as a supplement to liability insurance, insurance arising out of a workers' compensation or similar law, automobile medical payment insurance, or insurance under which benefits are payable with or without regard to fault and that is statutorily required to be contained in any liability insurance policy or equivalent self-insurance.

(B) The Medicare Program pursuant to Title XVIII of the federal Social Security Act (42 U.S.C. Sec. 1395 et seq.).

(C) The Medicaid Program pursuant to Title XIX of the federal Social Security Act (42 U.S.C. Sec. 1396 et seq.).

(D) Any other publicly sponsored program, provided in this state or elsewhere, of medical, hospital, and surgical care.

(E) 10 U.S.C. Chapter 55 (commencing with Section 1071) (Civilian Health and Medical Program of the Uniformed Services (CHAMPUS)).

(F) A medical care program of the Indian Health Service or of a tribal organization.

(G) A health plan offered under 5 U.S.C. Chapter 89 (commencing with Section 8901) (Federal Employees Health Benefits Program (FEHBP)).

(H) A public health plan as defined in federal regulations authorized by Section 2701(c)(1)(I) of the Public Health Service Act, as amended by Public Law 104-191, the Health Insurance Portability and Accountability Act of 1996.

(I) A health benefit plan under Section 5(e) of the Peace Corps Act (22 U.S.C. Sec. 2504(e)).

(J) Any other creditable coverage as defined by subsection (c) of Section 2704 of Title XXVII of the federal Public Health Service Act (42 U.S.C. Sec. 300gg-3(c)).

(4) "Waivered condition provision" means a contract provision that excludes coverage for charges or expenses incurred during a specified period of time for one or more specific, identified, medical conditions.

(5) "Affiliation period" means a period that, under the terms of the health benefit plan, must expire before health care services under the plan become effective.

(6) "Waiting period" means a period that is required to pass with respect to an employee before the employee is eligible to be covered for benefits under the terms of the plan.

(7) "Grandfathered health benefit plan" means a health benefit plan that is a grandfathered health plan, as defined in Section 1251 of PPACA.

(8) "Nongrandfathered health benefit plan" means a health benefit plan that is not a grandfathered health plan as defined in Section 1251 of PPACA.

(9) "PPACA" means the federal Patient Protection and Affordable Care Act (Public Law 111-148), as amended by the federal Health Care and Education Reconciliation Act of 2010 (Public Law 111-152), and any rules, regulations, or guidance issued pursuant to that law.

(Repealed (in Sec. 5) and added by Stats. 2012, Ch. 852, Sec. 4. (AB 1083) Effective January 1, 2013. Section operative January 1, 2014, pursuant to Section 1357.55.)

1357.51.

(a) A health benefit plan for group coverage shall not impose any preexisting condition provision or waivered condition provision upon any enrollee.

(b) (1) A nongrandfathered health benefit plan for individual coverage shall not impose any preexisting condition provision or waivered condition provision upon any enrollee.

(2) A grandfathered health benefit plan for individual coverage shall not exclude coverage on the basis of a waivered condition provision or preexisting condition provision for a period greater than 12 months following the enrollee's effective date of coverage, nor limit or exclude coverage for a specific enrollee by type of illness, treatment, medical condition, or accident, except for satisfaction of a preexisting condition provision or waivered condition provision pursuant to this article. Waivered condition provisions or preexisting condition provisions contained in individual grandfathered health benefit plans

may relate only to conditions for which medical advice, diagnosis, care, or treatment, including use of prescription drugs, was recommended or received from a licensed health practitioner during the 12 months immediately preceding the effective date of coverage.

(3) If Section 5000A of the Internal Revenue Code, as added by Section 1501 of PPACA, is repealed or amended to no longer apply to the individual market, as defined in Section 2791 of the Public Health Service Act (42 U.S.C. Sec. 300gg-91), paragraph (1) shall become inoperative 12 months after the date of that repeal or amendment and thereafter paragraph (2) shall apply also to nongrandfathered health benefit plans for individual coverage.

(4) In determining whether a preexisting condition provision or a waivered condition provision applies to an individual under this subdivision, a plan shall credit the time the individual was covered under creditable coverage, provided that the individual becomes eligible for coverage under the succeeding plan contract within 62 days of termination of prior coverage and applies for coverage under the succeeding plan within the applicable enrollment period.

(c) A health benefit plan for group or individual coverage shall not impose any waiting or affiliation period.

(Amended by Stats. 2014, Ch. 195, Sec. 2. (SB 1034) Effective January 1, 2015. Section operative January 1, 2014, pursuant to Section 1357.55.)

1357.52.

A health benefit plan for group coverage shall not establish rules for eligibility, including continued eligibility, of an individual, or dependent of an individual, to enroll under the terms of the plan based on any of the following health status-related factors:

(a) Health status.

(b) Medical condition, including physical and mental illnesses.

(c) Claims experience.

(d) Receipt of health care.

(e) Medical history.

(f) Genetic information.

(g) Evidence of insurability, including conditions arising out of acts of domestic violence.

(h) Disability.

(i) Any other health status-related factor as determined by any federal regulations, rules, or guidance issued pursuant to Section 2705 of the Public Health Service Act.

(Repealed (in Sec. 5) and added by Stats. 2012, Ch. 852, Sec. 4. (AB 1083) Effective January 1, 2013. Section operative January 1, 2014, pursuant to Section 1357.55.)

1357.55.

This article shall become operative on January 1, 2014.

(Repealed (in Sec. 5) and added by Stats. 2012, Ch. 852, Sec. 4. (AB 1083) Effective January 1, 2013. Note: This section prescribes a delayed operative date (January 1, 2014) for new Article 3.15, commencing with Section 1357.50.)

ARTICLE 3.16. Nongrandfathered Small Employer Plans [1357.500 - 1357.516]

(Article 3.16 added by Stats. 2012, Ch. 852, Sec. 3.)

1357.500.

As used in this article, the following definitions shall apply:

(a) "Child" means a child described in Section 22775 of the Government Code and subdivisions (n) to (p), inclusive, of Section 599.500 of Title 2 of the California Code of Regulations.

(b) "Dependent" means the spouse or registered domestic partner, or child, of an eligible employee, subject to applicable terms of the health care service plan contract covering the employee, and includes dependents of guaranteed association members if the association elects to include dependents under its health coverage at the same time it determines its membership composition pursuant to subdivision (m).

(c) "Eligible employee" means either of the following:

(1) Any permanent employee who is actively engaged on a full-time basis in the conduct of the business of the small employer with a normal workweek of an average of 30 hours per week over the course of a month, at the small employer's regular places of business, who has met any statutorily authorized applicable waiting period requirements. The term does not include sole proprietors or the spouses of those sole proprietors, partners of a partnership or the spouses of those partners, or employees who work on a part-time, temporary, or substitute basis. It includes any eligible employee, as defined in this paragraph, who obtains coverage through a guaranteed association. Employees of employers purchasing through a guaranteed association are eligible employees if they would otherwise meet the definition except for the number of persons employed by the employer. Permanent employees who work at least 20 hours but not more than 29 hours are eligible employees if all four of the following apply:

(A) They otherwise meet the definition of an eligible employee except for the number of hours worked.

(B) The employer offers the employees health coverage under a health benefit plan.

(C) All similarly situated individuals are offered coverage under the health benefit plan.

(D) The employee shall have worked at least 20 hours per normal workweek for at least 50 percent of the weeks in the previous calendar quarter. The health care service plan may request any necessary information to document the hours and time period in question, including, but not limited to, payroll records and employee wage and tax filings.

(2) Any member of a guaranteed association as defined in subdivision (m).

(d) "Exchange" means the California Health Benefit Exchange created by Section 100500 of the Government Code.

(e) "In force business" means an existing health benefit plan contract issued by the plan to a small employer.

(f) "Late enrollee" means an eligible employee or dependent who has declined enrollment in a health benefit plan offered by a small employer at the time of the initial enrollment period provided under the terms of the health benefit plan consistent with the periods provided pursuant to Section 1357.503 and who subsequently requests enrollment in a health benefit plan of that small employer, except where the employee or dependent qualifies for a special enrollment period provided pursuant to Section 1357.503. It also means any member of an association that is a guaranteed association as well as any other person eligible to purchase through the guaranteed association when that person has failed to purchase coverage during the initial enrollment period provided under the terms of the guaranteed association's plan contract consistent with the periods provided pursuant to Section 1357.503 and who subsequently requests enrollment in the plan, except where that member or person qualifies for a special enrollment period provided pursuant to Section 1357.503.

(g) "New business" means a health care service plan contract issued to a small employer that is not the plan's in force business.

(h) "Preexisting condition provision" means a contract provision that excludes coverage for charges or expenses incurred during a specified period following the enrollee's effective date of coverage, as to a condition for which medical advice, diagnosis, care, or treatment was recommended or received during a specified period immediately preceding the effective date of coverage. No health care service plan shall limit or exclude coverage for any individual based on a preexisting condition whether or not any medical advice, diagnosis, care, or treatment was recommended or received before that date.

(i) "Creditable coverage" means:

(1) Any individual or group policy, contract, or program that is written or administered by a disability insurer, health care service plan, fraternal benefits society, self-insured employer plan, or any other entity, in this state or elsewhere, and that arranges or provides medical, hospital, and surgical coverage not designed to supplement other private or governmental plans. The term includes continuation or conversion coverage but does not include accident only, credit, coverage for onsite medical clinics, disability income, Medicare supplement, long-term care, dental, vision, coverage issued as a supplement to liability insurance, insurance arising out of a workers' compensation or similar law, automobile medical payment insurance, or insurance under which benefits are payable with or without regard to fault and that is statutorily required to be contained in any liability insurance policy or equivalent self-insurance.

(2) The Medicare Program pursuant to Title XVIII of the federal Social Security Act (42 U.S.C. Sec. 1395 et seq.).

(3) The Medicaid program pursuant to Title XIX of the federal Social Security Act (42 U.S.C. Sec. 1396 et seq.).

(4) Any other publicly sponsored program, provided in this state or elsewhere, of medical, hospital, and surgical care.

(5) Chapter 55 (commencing with Section 1071) of Title 10 of the United States Code (Civilian Health and Medical Program of the Uniformed Services (CHAMPUS)).

(6) A medical care program of the Indian Health Service or of a tribal organization.

(7) A health plan offered under Chapter 89 (commencing with Section 8901) of Title 5 of the United States Code (Federal Employees Health Benefits Program (FEHBP)).

(8) A public health plan as defined in federal regulations authorized by Section 2701(c)(1)(I) of the federal Public Health Service Act, as amended by Public Law 104-191, the federal Health Insurance Portability and Accountability Act of 1996.

(9) A health benefit plan under Section 5(e) of the federal Peace Corps Act (22 U.S.C. Sec. 2504(e)).

(10) Any other creditable coverage as defined by subsection (c) of Section 2704 of Title XXVII of the federal Public Health Service Act (42 U.S.C. Sec. 300gg-3(c)).

(j) "Rating period" means the period for which premium rates established by a plan are in effect and shall be no less than 12 months from the date of issuance or renewal of the plan contract.

(k) (1) "Small employer" means any of the following:

(A) For plan years commencing on or after January 1, 2014, and on or before December 31, 2015, any person, firm, proprietary or nonprofit corporation, partnership, public agency, or association that is actively engaged in business or service, that, on at least 50 percent of its working days during the preceding calendar quarter or preceding calendar year, employed at least one, but no more than 50, eligible employees, the majority of whom were employed within this state, that was not formed primarily for purposes of buying health care service plan contracts, and in which a bona fide employer-employee relationship exists. For plan years commencing on or after January 1, 2016, any person, firm, proprietary or nonprofit corporation, partnership, public agency, or association that is actively engaged in business or service, that, on at least 50 percent of its working days during the preceding calendar quarter or preceding calendar year, employed at least one, but no more than 100, employees, the majority of whom were employed within this state, that was not formed primarily for purposes of buying health care service plan contracts, and in which a bona fide employer-employee relationship exists. In determining whether to apply the calendar quarter or calendar year test, a health care service plan shall use the test that ensures eligibility if only one test would establish eligibility. In determining the number of employees or eligible employees, companies that are affiliated companies and that are eligible to file a combined tax return for purposes of state taxation shall be considered one employer. Subsequent to the issuance of a health care service plan contract to a small employer pursuant to this article, and for the purpose of determining eligibility, the size of a small employer shall be determined annually. Except as otherwise specifically provided in this article, provisions of this article that apply to a small employer shall continue to apply until the plan contract anniversary following the date the employer no longer meets the requirements of this definition. It includes any small employer as defined in this paragraph who purchases coverage through a guaranteed association, any employer purchasing coverage for employees through a guaranteed association, and any small employer as defined in this paragraph who purchases coverage through any arrangement.

(B) Any guaranteed association, as defined in subdivision (l), that purchases health coverage for members of the association.

(2) For plan years commencing on or after January 1, 2019, for purposes of determining whether an employer has one employee, sole proprietors and their spouses, and partners of a partnership and their spouses, are not employees.

(3) For plan years commencing on or after January 1, 2016, the definition of small employer, for purposes of determining employer eligibility in the small employer market, shall be determined using the method for counting full-time employees and full-time equivalent employees set forth in Section 4980H(c)(2) of the Internal Revenue Code.

(l) "Guaranteed association" means a nonprofit organization comprised of a group of individuals or employers who associate based solely on participation in a specified profession or industry, accepting for membership any individual or employer meeting its membership criteria, and that (1) includes one or more small employers as defined in subparagraph (A) of paragraph (1) of subdivision (k), (2) does not condition membership directly or indirectly on the health or claims history of any person, (3) uses membership dues solely for and in consideration of the membership and membership benefits, except that the amount of the dues shall not depend on whether the member applies for or purchases insurance offered to the association, (4) is organized and maintained in good faith for purposes unrelated to insurance, (5) has been in active existence on January 1, 1992, and for at least five years prior to that date, (6) has included health insurance as a membership benefit for at least five years prior to January 1, 1992, (7) has a constitution and bylaws, or other analogous governing documents that provide for election of the governing board of the association by its members, (8) offers any plan contract that is purchased to all individual members and employer members in this state, (9) includes any member choosing to enroll in the plan contracts offered to the association provided that the member has agreed to make the required premium payments, and (10) covers at least 1,000 persons with the health care service plan with which it contracts. The requirement of 1,000 persons may be met if component chapters of a statewide association contracting separately with the same carrier cover at least 1,000 persons in the aggregate.

This subdivision applies regardless of whether a contract issued by a plan is with an association, or a trust formed for or sponsored by an association, to administer benefits for association members.

For purposes of this subdivision, an association formed by a merger of two or more associations after January 1, 1992, and otherwise meeting the criteria of this subdivision shall be deemed to have been in active existence on January 1, 1992, if its predecessor organizations had been in active existence on January 1, 1992, and for at least five years prior to that date and otherwise met the criteria of this subdivision.

(m) "Members of a guaranteed association" means any individual or employer meeting the association's membership criteria if that person is a member of the association and chooses to purchase health coverage through the association. At the association's discretion, it also may include employees of association members, association staff, retired members, retired employees of members, and surviving spouses and dependents of deceased members. However, if an association chooses to include these persons as members of the guaranteed association, the association shall make that election in advance of purchasing a plan contract. Health care service plans may require an association to adhere to the membership composition it selects for up to 12 months.

(n) "Affiliation period" means a period that, under the terms of the health care service plan contract, must expire before health care services under the contract become effective.

(o) "Grandfathered health plan" has the meaning set forth in Section 1251 of PPACA.

(p) "Nongrandfathered small employer health care service plan contract" means a small employer health care service plan contract that is not a grandfathered health plan.

(q) "Plan year" has the meaning set forth in Section 144.103 of Title 45 of the Code of Federal Regulations.

(r) "PPACA" means the federal Patient Protection and Affordable Care Act (Public Law 111-148), as amended by the federal Health Care and Education Reconciliation Act of 2010 (Public Law 111-152), and any rules, regulations, or guidance issued thereunder.

(s) "Small employer health care service plan contract" means a health care service plan contract issued to a small employer.

(t) "Waiting period" means a period that is required to pass with respect to an employee before the employee is eligible to be covered for benefits under the terms of the contract.

(u) "Registered domestic partner" means a person who has established a domestic partnership as described in Section 297 of the Family Code.

(v) "Family" means the subscriber and his or her dependent or dependents.

(w) "Health benefit plan" means a health care service plan contract that provides medical, hospital, and surgical benefits for the covered eligible employees of a small employer and their dependents. The term does not include coverage of Medicare services pursuant to contracts with the United States government, Medicare supplement coverage, or coverage under a specialized health care service plan contract.

(Amended by Stats. 2018, Ch. 700, Sec. 2. (SB 1375) Effective January 1, 2019.)

1357.501.

This article shall apply only to nongrandfathered small employer health care service plan contracts and only with respect to plan years beginning on or after January 1, 2014.

(Added by Stats. 2012, Ch. 852, Sec. 3. (AB 1083) Effective January 1, 2013.)

1357.502.

(a) A health care service plan providing or arranging for the provision of essential health benefits, as defined by the state pursuant to Section 1302 of PPACA, to small employers shall be subject to this article if either of the following conditions is met:

(1) Any portion of the premium is paid by a small employer, or any covered individual is reimbursed, whether through wage adjustments or otherwise, by a small employer for any portion of the premium.

(2) The plan contract is treated by the small employer or any of the covered individuals as part of a plan or program for the purposes of Section 106 or 162 of the Internal Revenue Code.

(b) This article shall not apply to health care service plan contracts for coverage of Medicare services pursuant to contracts with the United States government, Medicare supplement, Medi-Cal contracts with the State Department of Health Care Services, long-term care coverage, or specialized health care service plan contracts.

(Added by Stats. 2012, Ch. 852, Sec. 3. (AB 1083) Effective January 1, 2013.)

1357.502.5.

Nothing in this article shall be construed to preclude the application of this chapter to either of the following:

(a) An association, trust, or other organization acting as a "health care service plan" as defined under Section 1345.

(b) An association, trust, or other organization or person presenting information regarding a health care service plan to persons who may be interested in subscribing or enrolling in the plan.

(Added by Stats. 2012, Ch. 852, Sec. 3. (AB 1083) Effective January 1, 2013.)

1357.503.

(a) (1) Each plan shall fairly and affirmatively offer, market, and sell all of the plan's small employer health care service plan contracts to all small employers in each service area in which the plan provides or arranges for the provision of health care services.

(2) Each plan shall make available to each small employer all small employer health care service plan contracts that the plan offers and sells to small employers or to associations that include small employers in this state. Health coverage through an association that is not related to employment shall be considered individual coverage. The status of each distinct member of an association shall determine whether that member's association coverage is individual, small group, or large group health coverage.

(3) A plan that offers qualified health plans through the Exchange shall be deemed to be in compliance with paragraphs (1) and (2) with respect to small employer health care service plan contracts offered through the Exchange in those geographic regions in which the plan offers plan contracts through the Exchange.

(b) A plan shall provide enrollment periods consistent with PPACA and described in Section 155.725 of Title 45 of the Code of Federal Regulations. Each plan shall provide special enrollment periods consistent with the special enrollment periods described in Section 1399.849, to the extent permitted by PPACA, except for both of the following:

(1) The special enrollment period described in paragraph (3) of subdivision (c) of Section 1399.849.

(2) The triggering events identified in paragraphs (d)(3) and (d)(6) of Section 155.420 of Title 45 of the Code of Federal Regulations with respect to plan contracts offered through the Exchange.

(c) No plan or solicitor shall induce or otherwise encourage a small employer to separate or otherwise exclude an eligible employee from a health care service plan contract that is provided in connection with employee's employment or membership in a guaranteed association.

(d) Every plan shall file with the director the reasonable employee participation requirements and employer contribution requirements that will be applied in offering its plan contracts. Participation requirements shall be applied uniformly among all small employer groups, except that a plan may vary application of minimum employee participation requirements by the size of the small employer group and whether the employer contributes 100 percent of the eligible employee's premium. Employer contribution requirements shall not vary by employer size. A health care service plan shall not establish a participation requirement that (1) requires a person who meets the definition of a dependent in Section 1357.500 to enroll as a dependent if he or she is otherwise eligible for coverage and wishes to enroll as an eligible employee and (2) allows a plan to reject an otherwise eligible small employer because of the number of persons that waive coverage due to coverage through another employer. Members of an association eligible for health coverage under subdivision (m) of Section 1357.500, but not electing any health coverage through the association, shall not be counted as eligible employees for purposes of determining whether the guaranteed association meets a plan's reasonable participation standards.

(e) The plan shall not reject an application from a small employer for a small employer health care service plan contract if all of the following conditions are met:

(1) The small employer offers health benefits to 100 percent of its eligible employees. Employees who waive coverage on the grounds that they have other group coverage shall not be counted as eligible employees.

(2) The small employer agrees to make the required premium payments.

(3) The small employer agrees to inform the small employer's employees of the availability of coverage and the provision that those not electing coverage must wait until the next open enrollment or a special enrollment period to obtain coverage through the group if they later decide they would like to have coverage.

(4) The employees and their dependents who are to be covered by the plan contract work or reside in the service area in which the plan provides or otherwise arranges for the provision of health care services.

(f) A plan or solicitor shall not, directly or indirectly, engage in the following activities:

(1) Encourage or direct small employers to refrain from filing an application for coverage with a plan because of the health status, claims experience, industry, occupation of the small employer, or geographic location provided that it is within the plan's approved service area.

(2) Encourage or direct small employers to seek coverage from another plan because of the health status, claims experience, industry, occupation of the small employer, or geographic location provided that it is within the plan's approved service area.

(3) Employ marketing practices or benefit designs that will have the effect of discouraging the enrollment of individuals with significant health needs or discriminate based on an individual's race, color, national origin, present or predicted disability, age, sex, gender identity, sexual orientation, expected length of life, degree of medical dependency, quality of life, or other health conditions.

(g) A plan shall not, directly or indirectly, enter into any contract, agreement, or arrangement with a solicitor that provides for or results in the compensation paid to a solicitor for the sale of a health care service plan contract to be varied because of the health status, claims experience, industry, occupation, or geographic location of the small employer. This subdivision does not apply to a compensation arrangement that provides compensation to a solicitor on the basis of percentage of premium, provided that the percentage shall not vary because of the health status, claims experience, industry, occupation, or geographic area of the small employer.

(h) (1) A policy or contract that covers a small employer, as defined in Section 1304(b) of PPACA and in Section 1357.500, shall not establish rules for eligibility, including continued eligibility, of an individual, or dependent of an individual, to enroll under the terms of the policy or contract based on any of the following health status-related factors:

(A) Health status.

(B) Medical condition, including physical and mental illnesses.

(C) Claims experience.

(D) Receipt of health care.

(E) Medical history.

(F) Genetic information.

(G) Evidence of insurability, including conditions arising out of acts of domestic violence.

(H) Disability.

(I) Any other health status-related factor as determined by any federal regulations, rules, or guidance issued pursuant to Section 2705 of the federal Public Health Service Act.

(2) Notwithstanding Section 1389.1, a health care service plan shall not require an eligible employee or dependent to fill out a health assessment or medical questionnaire prior to enrollment under a small employer health care service plan contract. A health care service plan shall not acquire or request information that relates to a health status-related factor from the applicant or his or her dependent or any other source prior to enrollment of the individual.

(i) (1) A health care service plan shall consider as a single risk pool for rating purposes in the small employer market the claims experience of all enrollees in all nongrandfathered small employer health benefit plans offered by the health care service plan in this state, whether offered as health care service plan contracts or health insurance policies, including those insureds and enrollees who enroll in coverage through the Exchange and insureds and enrollees covered by the health care service plan outside of the Exchange.

(2) At least each calendar year, and no more frequently than each calendar quarter, a health care service plan shall establish an index rate for the small employer market in the state based on the total combined claims costs for providing essential health benefits, as defined pursuant to Section 1302 of PPACA and Section 1367.005, within the single risk pool required under paragraph (1). The index rate shall be adjusted on a marketwide basis based on the total expected marketwide payments and charges under the risk adjustment program established for the state pursuant to Section 1343 of PPACA and Exchange user fees, as described in subdivision (d) of Section 156.80 of Title 45 of the Code of Federal Regulations. The premium rate for all of the nongrandfathered small employer health benefit plans within the single risk pool required under paragraph (1) shall use the applicable marketwide adjusted index rate, subject only to the adjustments permitted under paragraph (3).

(3) A health care service plan may vary premium rates for a particular nongrandfathered small employer health care service plan contract from its index rate based only on the following actuarially justified plan-specific factors:

(A) The actuarial value and cost-sharing design of the plan contract.

(B) The plan contract's provider network, delivery system characteristics, and utilization management practices.

(C) The benefits provided under the plan contract that are in addition to the essential health benefits, as defined pursuant to Section 1302 of PPACA. These additional benefits shall be pooled with similar benefits within the single risk pool required under paragraph (1) and the claims experience from those benefits shall be utilized to determine rate variations for plan contracts that offer those benefits in addition to essential health benefits.

(D) With respect to catastrophic plans, as described in subsection (e) of Section 1302 of PPACA, the expected impact of the specific eligibility categories for those plans.

(E) Administrative costs, excluding any user fees required by the Exchange.

(j) A plan shall comply with the requirements of Section 1374.3.

(k) (1) Except as provided in paragraph (2), if Section 2702 of the federal Public Health Service Act (42 U.S.C. Sec. 300gg-1), as added by Section 1201 of PPACA, is repealed, this section shall become inoperative 12 months after the repeal date, in which case health care service plans subject to this section shall instead be governed by Section

1357.03 to the extent permitted by federal law, and all references in this article to this section shall instead refer to Section 1357.03 except for purposes of paragraph (2).
(2) Subdivision (b) shall remain operative with respect to health care service plan contracts offered through the Exchange.
(Amended by Stats. 2018, Ch. 700, Sec. 3. (SB 1375) Effective January 1, 2019. Conditionally inoperative as prescribed by its own provisions.)
1357.503.035.
(a) For plan contracts subject to this article, an association that meets the definition of a guaranteed association, as set forth in Section 1357.500, except for the requirement that 1,000 persons be covered, shall be entitled to purchase small employer health coverage as if the association were a guaranteed association, except that the coverage shall be guaranteed only for those members of an association, as defined in subdivision (m) of Section 1357.500, (1) who were receiving coverage or had successfully applied for coverage through the association as of June 30, 1993, (2) who were receiving coverage through the association as of December 31, 1992, and whose coverage lapsed at any time thereafter because the employment through which coverage was received ended or an employer's contribution to health coverage ended, or (3) who were covered at any time between June 30, 1993, and July 1, 1994, under a contract that was in force on June 30, 1993.
(b) An association obtaining health coverage for its members pursuant to this section shall otherwise be afforded all the rights of a guaranteed association under this chapter, including, but not limited to, guaranteed renewability of coverage.
(Added by Stats. 2012, Ch. 852, Sec. 3. (AB 1083) Effective January 1, 2013.)
1357.504.
(a) With respect to small employer health care service plan contracts offered outside the Exchange, after a small employer submits a completed application form for a plan contract, the health care service plan shall, within 30 days, notify the employer of the employer's actual premium charges for that plan contract established in accordance with Section 1357.512. The employer shall have 30 days in which to exercise the right to buy coverage at the quoted premium charges.
(b) Except as provided in subdivision (c), when a small employer submits a premium payment, based on the quoted premium charges, and that payment is delivered or postmarked, whichever occurs earlier, within the first 15 days of the month, coverage under the plan contract shall become effective no later than the first day of the following month. When that payment is neither delivered nor postmarked until after the 15th day of a month, coverage shall become effective no later than the first day of the second month following delivery or postmark of the payment.
(c) (1) With respect to a small employer health care service plan contract offered through the Exchange, a plan shall apply coverage effective dates consistent with those required under Section 155.720 of Title 45 of the Code of Federal Regulations and of subdivision (e) of Section 1399.849.
(2) With respect to a small employer health care service plan contract offered outside the Exchange for which an individual applies during a special enrollment period described in subdivision (b) of Section 1357.503, the following provisions shall apply:
(A) Coverage under the plan contract shall become effective no later than the first day of the first calendar month beginning after the date the plan receives the request for special enrollment.
(B) Notwithstanding subparagraph (A), in the case of a birth, adoption, or placement for adoption, coverage under the plan contract shall become effective on the date of birth, adoption, or placement for adoption.
(d) During the first 30 days after the effective date of the plan contract, the small employer shall have the option of changing coverage to a different plan contract offered by the same health care service plan. If a small employer notifies the plan of the change within the first 15 days of a month, coverage under the new plan contract shall become effective no later than the first day of the following month. If a small employer notifies the plan of the change after the 15th day of a month, coverage under the new plan contract shall become effective no later than the first day of the second month following notification.
(e) All eligible employees and dependents listed on a small employer's completed application shall be covered on the effective date of the health benefit plan.
(Amended by Stats. 2015, Ch. 303, Sec. 250. (AB 731) Effective January 1, 2016.)
1357.506.
A small employer health care service plan contract shall not impose a preexisting condition provision or a waiting or affiliation period upon any individual.
(Repealed and added by Stats. 2014, Ch. 195, Sec. 4. (SB 1034) Effective January 1, 2015.)
1357.507.
Nothing in this article shall be construed as prohibiting a health care service plan from restricting enrollment of late enrollees to open enrollment periods provided under Section 1357.503 as authorized under Section 2702 of the federal Public Health Service Act.
(Added by Stats. 2012, Ch. 852, Sec. 3. (AB 1083) Effective January 1, 2013.)
1357.508.
A small employer health care service plan contract shall provide to subscribers and enrollees at least all of the essential health benefits as defined by the state pursuant to Section 1302 of PPACA.
(Added by Stats. 2012, Ch. 852, Sec. 3. (AB 1083) Effective January 1, 2013.)
1357.509.
(a) To the extent permitted by PPACA, a plan shall not be required to offer a health care service plan contract or accept applications for the contract pursuant to this article in the case of any of the following:

(1) To a small employer, if the eligible employees and dependents who are to be covered by the plan contract do not live, work, or reside within a plan's approved service areas.
(2) (A) Within a specific service area or portion of a service area, if a plan reasonably anticipates and demonstrates to the satisfaction of the director all of the following:
(i) It will not have sufficient health care delivery resources to ensure that health care services will be available and accessible to the eligible employee and dependents of the employee because of its obligations to existing enrollees.
(ii) It is applying this subparagraph uniformly to all employers without regard to the claims experience of those employers, and their employees and dependents, or any health status-related factor relating to those employees and dependents.
(iii) The action is not unreasonable or clearly inconsistent with the intent of this chapter.
(B) A plan that cannot offer a health care service plan contract to small employers because it is lacking in sufficient health care delivery resources within a service area or a portion of a service area pursuant to subparagraph (A) may not offer a contract in the area in which the plan is not offering coverage to small employers to new employer groups until the later of the following dates:
(i) The 181st day after the date that coverage is denied pursuant to this paragraph.
(ii) The date the plan notifies the director that it has the ability to deliver services to small employer groups, and certifies to the director that from the date of the notice it will enroll all small employer groups requesting coverage in that area from the plan.
(C) Subparagraph (B) shall not limit the plan's ability to renew coverage already in force or relieve the plan of the responsibility to renew that coverage as described in Section 1365.
(D) Coverage offered within a service area after the period specified in subparagraph (B) shall be subject to the requirements of this section.
(b) (1) A health care service plan may decline to offer a health care service plan contract to a small employer if the plan demonstrates to the satisfaction of the director both of the following:
(A) It does not have the financial reserves necessary to underwrite additional coverage. In determining whether this subparagraph has been satisfied, the director shall consider, but not be limited to, the plan's compliance with the requirements of Section 1367, Article 6 (commencing with Section 1375), and the rules adopted thereunder.
(B) It is applying this paragraph uniformly to all employers without regard to the claims experience of those employers and their employees and dependents or any health status-related factor relating to those employees and dependents.
(2) A plan that denies coverage to a small employer under paragraph (1) shall not offer coverage in the group market before the later of the following dates:
(A) The 181st day after the date that coverage is denied pursuant to paragraph (1).
(B) The date the plan demonstrates to the satisfaction of the director that the plan has sufficient financial reserves necessary to underwrite additional coverage.
(3) Paragraph (2) shall not limit the plan's ability to renew coverage already in force or relieve the plan of the responsibility to renew that coverage as described in Section 1365.
(4) Coverage offered within a service area after the period specified in paragraph (2) shall be subject to the requirements of this section.
(c) Nothing in this article shall be construed to limit the director's authority to develop and implement a plan of rehabilitation for a health care service plan whose financial viability or organizational and administrative capacity has become impaired, to the extent permitted by PPACA.
(Amended by Stats. 2013, 1st Ex. Sess., Ch. 2, Sec. 6. (SB 2 1x) Effective September 30, 2013.)
1357.510.
The director may require a plan to discontinue the offering of contracts or acceptance of applications from any small employer or group upon a determination by the director that the plan does not have sufficient financial viability, or organizational and administrative capacity to ensure the delivery of health care services to its enrollees. In determining whether the conditions of this section have been met, the director shall consider, but not be limited to, the plan's compliance with the requirements of Section 1367, Article 6 (commencing with Section 1375), and the rules adopted thereunder.
(Added by Stats. 2012, Ch. 852, Sec. 3. (AB 1083) Effective January 1, 2013.)
1357.512.
(a) The premium rate for a small employer health care service plan contract issued, amended, or renewed on or after January 1, 2014, shall vary with respect to the particular coverage involved only by the following:
(1) Age, pursuant to the age bands established by the United States Secretary of Health and Human Services and the age rating curve established by the Centers for Medicare and Medicaid Services pursuant to Section 2701(a)(3) of the federal Public Health Service Act (42 U.S.C. Sec. 300gg(a)(3)). Rates based on age shall be determined using the individual's age as of the date of the contract issuance or renewal, as applicable, and shall not vary by more than three to one for like individuals of different age who are 21 years of age or older as described in federal regulations adopted pursuant to Section 2701(a)(3) of the federal Public Health Service Act (42 U.S.C. Sec. 300gg(a)(3)).
(2) (A) Geographic region. The geographic regions for purposes of rating shall be the following:
(i) Region 1 shall consist of the Counties of Alpine, Amador, Butte, Calaveras, Colusa, Del Norte, Glenn, Humboldt, Lake, Lassen, Mendocino, Modoc, Nevada, Plumas, Shasta, Sierra, Siskiyou, Sutter, Tehama, Trinity, Tuolumne, and Yuba.
(ii) Region 2 shall consist of the Counties of Marin, Napa, Solano, and Sonoma.
(iii) Region 3 shall consist of the Counties of El Dorado, Placer, Sacramento, and Yolo.
(iv) Region 4 shall consist of the City and County of San Francisco.
(v) Region 5 shall consist of the County of Contra Costa.

(vi) Region 6 shall consist of the County of Alameda.

(vii) Region 7 shall consist of the County of Santa Clara.

(viii) Region 8 shall consist of the County of San Mateo.

(ix) Region 9 shall consist of the Counties of Monterey, San Benito, and Santa Cruz.

(x) Region 10 shall consist of the Counties of Mariposa, Merced, San Joaquin, Stanislaus, and Tulare.

(xi) Region 11 shall consist of the Counties of Fresno, Kings, and Madera.

(xii) Region 12 shall consist of the Counties of San Luis Obispo, Santa Barbara, and Ventura.

(xiii) Region 13 shall consist of the Counties of Imperial, Inyo, and Mono.

(xiv) Region 14 shall consist of the County of Kern.

(xv) Region 15 shall consist of the ZIP Codes in the County of Los Angeles starting with 906 to 912, inclusive, 915, 917, 918, and 935.

(xvi) Region 16 shall consist of the ZIP Codes in the County of Los Angeles other than those identified in clause (xv).

(xvii) Region 17 shall consist of the Counties of Riverside and San Bernardino.

(xviii) Region 18 shall consist of the County of Orange.

(xix) Region 19 shall consist of the County of San Diego.

(B) No later than June 1, 2017, the department, in collaboration with the Exchange and the Department of Insurance, shall review the geographic rating regions specified in this paragraph and the impacts of those regions on the health care coverage market in California, and submit a report to the appropriate policy committees of the Legislature. The requirement for submitting a report under this subparagraph is inoperative June 1, 2021, pursuant to Section 10231.5 of the Government Code.

(3) Whether the contract covers an individual or family, as described in PPACA.

(b) The rate for a health care service plan contract subject to this section shall not vary by any factor not described in this section.

(c) The total premium charged to a small employer pursuant to this section shall be determined by summing the premiums of covered employees and dependents in accordance with Section 147.102(c)(1) of Title 45 of the Code of Federal Regulations.

(d) The rating period for rates subject to this section shall be no less than 12 months from the date of issuance or renewal of the plan contract.

(e) If Section 2701 of the federal Public Health Service Act (42 U.S.C. Sec. 300gg), as added by Section 1201 of PPACA, is repealed, this section shall become inoperative 12 months after the repeal date, in which case rates for health care service plan contracts subject to this section shall instead be subject to Section 1357.12, to the extent permitted by federal law, and all references to this section shall be deemed to be references to Section 1357.12.

(Amended by Stats. 2013, 1st Ex. Sess., Ch. 2, Sec. 7. (SB 2 1x) Effective September 30, 2013. Conditionally inoperative as prescribed by its own provisions.)

1357.514.

In connection with the offering for sale of a small employer health care service plan contract subject to this article, each plan shall make a reasonable disclosure, as part of its solicitation and sales materials, of the following:

(a) The provisions concerning the plan's right to change premium rates and the factors other than provision of services experience that affect changes in premium rates. The plan shall disclose that claims experience cannot be used.

(b) Provisions relating to the guaranteed issue and renewal of contracts.

(c) A statement that no preexisting condition provisions shall be allowed.

(d) Provisions relating to the small employer's right to apply for any small employer health care service plan contract written, issued, or administered by the plan at the time of application for a new health care service plan contract, or at the time of renewal of a health care service plan contract, consistent with the requirements of PPACA.

(e) The availability, upon request, of a listing of all the plan's contracts and benefit plan designs offered, both inside and outside the Exchange, to small employers, including the rates for each contract.

(f) At the time it offers a contract to a small employer, each plan shall provide the small employer with a statement of all of its small employer health care service plan contracts, including the rates for each plan contract, in the service area in which the employer's employees and eligible dependents who are to be covered by the plan contract work or reside. For purposes of this subdivision, plans that are affiliated plans or that are eligible to file a consolidated income tax return shall be treated as one health plan.

(g) Each plan shall do all of the following:

(1) Prepare a brochure that summarizes all of its plan contracts offered to small employers and to make this summary available to any small employer and to solicitors upon request. The summary shall include for each contract information on benefits provided, a generic description of the manner in which services are provided, such as how access to providers is limited, benefit limitations, required copayments and deductibles, and a telephone number that can be called for more detailed benefit information. Plans are required to keep the information contained in the brochure accurate and up to date and, upon updating the brochure, send copies to solicitors and solicitor firms with whom the plan contracts to solicit enrollments or subscriptions.

(2) For each contract, prepare a more detailed evidence of coverage and make it available to small employers, solicitors, and solicitor firms upon request. The evidence of coverage shall contain all information that a prudent buyer would need to be aware of in making contract selections.

(3) Provide copies of the current summary brochure to all solicitors and solicitor firms contracting with the plan to solicit enrollments or subscriptions from small employers. For purposes of this subdivision, plans that are affiliated plans or that are eligible to file a consolidated income tax return shall be treated as one health plan.

(h) Every solicitor or solicitor firm contracting with one or more plans to solicit enrollments or subscriptions from small employers shall do all of the following:

(1) When providing information on contracts to a small employer but making no specific recommendations on particular plan contracts:

(A) Advise the small employer of the plan's obligation to sell to any small employer any small employer health care service plan contract, consistent with PPACA, and provide the small employer, upon request, with the actual rates that would be charged to that employer for a given contract.

(B) Notify the small employer that the solicitor or solicitor firm will procure rate and benefit information for the small employer on any plan contract offered by a plan whose contract the solicitor sells.

(C) Notify the small employer that upon request the solicitor or solicitor firm will provide the small employer with the summary brochure required under paragraph (1) of subdivision (g) for any plan contract offered by a plan with which the solicitor or solicitor firm has contracted to solicit enrollments or subscriptions.

(D) Notify the small employer of the availability of coverage and the availability of tax credits for certain employers consistent with PPACA and state law, including any rules, regulations, or guidance issued in connection therewith.

(2) When recommending a particular benefit plan design or designs, advise the small employer that, upon request, the agent will provide the small employer with the brochure required by paragraph (1) of subdivision (g) containing the benefit plan design or designs being recommended by the agent or broker.

(3) Prior to filing an application for a small employer for a particular contract:

(A) For each of the plan contracts offered by the plan whose contract the solicitor or solicitor firm is offering, provide the small employer with the benefit summary required in paragraph (1) of subdivision (g) and the premium for that particular employer.

(B) Notify the small employer that, upon request, the solicitor or solicitor firm will provide the small employer with an evidence of coverage brochure for each contract the plan offers.

(C) Obtain a signed statement from the small employer acknowledging that the small employer has received the disclosures required by this section.

(Amended by Stats. 2014, Ch. 195, Sec. 5. (SB 1034) Effective January 1, 2015.)

1357.515.

(a) At least 20 business days prior to renewing or amending a plan contract subject to this article which will be in force on the operative date of this article, a plan shall file a notice of material modification with the director in accordance with the provisions of Section 1352. The notice of material modification shall include a statement certifying that the plan is in compliance with Section 1357.512. Any action by the director, as permitted under Section 1352, to disapprove, suspend, or postpone the plan's use of a plan contract shall be in writing, specifying the reasons that the plan contract does not comply with the requirements of this chapter.

(b) At least 20 business days prior to offering a plan contract subject to this article, all plans shall file a notice of material modification with the director in accordance with the provisions of Section 1352. The notice of material modification shall include a statement certifying that the plan is in compliance with Section 1357.512. Plans that will be offering to a small employer plan contracts approved by the director prior to the effective date of this article shall file a notice of material modification in accordance with this subdivision. Any action by the director, as permitted under Section 1352, to disapprove, suspend, or postpone the plan's use of a plan contract shall be in writing, specifying the reasons that the plan contract does not comply with the requirements of this chapter.

(c) Each plan shall maintain at its principal place of business all of the information required to be filed with the director pursuant to this section.

(d) Nothing in this section shall be construed to limit the director's authority to enforce the rating practices set forth in this article.

(Added by Stats. 2012, Ch. 852, Sec. 3. (AB 1083) Effective January 1, 2013.)

1357.516.

(a) Health care service plans may enter into contractual agreements with qualified associations, as defined in subdivision (b), under which these qualified associations may assume responsibility for performing specific administrative services, as defined in this section, for qualified association members. Health care service plans that enter into agreements with qualified associations for assumption of administrative services shall establish uniform definitions for the administrative services that may be provided by a qualified association or its third-party administrator. The health care service plan shall permit all qualified associations to assume one or more of these functions when the health care service plan determines the qualified association demonstrates the administrative capacity to assume these functions.

For the purposes of this section, administrative services provided by qualified associations or their third-party administrators shall be services pertaining to eligibility determination, enrollment, premium collection, sales, or claims administration on a per-claim basis that would otherwise be provided directly by the health care service plan or through a third-party administrator on a commission basis or an agent or solicitor workforce on a commission basis. Each health care service plan that enters into an agreement with any qualified association for the provision of administrative services shall offer all qualified associations with which it contracts the same premium discounts for performing those services the health care service plan has permitted the qualified association or its third-party administrator to assume. The health care service plan shall report to the department its schedule of discounts for each administrative service.

In no instance may a health care service plan provide discounts to qualified associations that are in any way intended to, or materially result in, a reduction in premium charges to the qualified association due to the health status of the membership of the qualified association. In addition to any other remedies available to the director to enforce this chapter, the director may declare a contract between a health care service plan and a qualified association for administrative services pursuant to this section null and void if the director determines any discounts provided to the qualified association are intended to, or materially result in, a reduction in premium charges to the qualified association due to the health status of the membership of the qualified association.

(b) For the purposes of this section, a qualified association is a nonprofit corporation comprised of a group of individuals or employers who associate based solely on participation in a specified profession or industry that conforms to all of the following requirements:

(1) It accepts for membership any individual or small employer meeting its membership criteria.

(2) It does not condition membership directly or indirectly on the health or claims history of any person.

(3) It uses membership dues solely for and in consideration of the membership and membership benefits, except that the amount of the dues shall not depend on whether the member applies for or purchases insurance offered by the association.

(4) It is organized and maintained in good faith for purposes unrelated to insurance.

(5) It existed on January 1, 1972, and has been in continuous existence since that date.

(6) It has a constitution and bylaws or other analogous governing documents that provide for election of the governing board of the association by its members.

(7) It offered, marketed, or sold health coverage to its members for 20 continuous years prior to January 1, 1993.

(8) It agrees to offer only to association members any plan contract.

(9) It agrees to include any member choosing to enroll in the plan contract offered by the association, provided that the member agrees to make required premium payments.

(10) It complies with all provisions of this article.

(11) It had at least 10,000 enrollees covered by association sponsored plans immediately prior to enactment of Chapter 1128 of the Statutes of 1992.

(12) It applies any administrative cost at an equal rate to all members purchasing coverage through the qualified association.

(c) A qualified association shall comply with Section 1357.52.

(Added by Stats. 2012, Ch. 852, Sec. 3. (AB 1083) Effective January 1, 2013.)

ARTICLE 3.17. Grandfathered Small Employer Plans [1357.600 - 1357.618]
(Article 3.17 added by Stats. 2012, Ch. 852, Sec. 6.)
1357.600.

As used in this article, the following definitions shall apply:

(a) "Dependent" means the spouse or registered domestic partner, or child, of an eligible employee, subject to applicable terms of the health care service plan contract covering the employee, and includes dependents of guaranteed association members if the association elects to include dependents under its health coverage at the same time it determines its membership composition pursuant to subdivision (n).

(b) "Eligible employee" means either of the following:

(1) Any permanent employee who is actively engaged on a full-time basis in the conduct of the business of the small employer with a normal workweek of an average of 30 hours per week over the course of a month, at the small employer's regular places of business, who has met any statutorily authorized applicable waiting period requirements. The term does not include sole proprietors or the spouses of those sole proprietors, partners of a partnership or the spouses of those partners, or employees who work on a part-time, temporary, or substitute basis. It includes any eligible employee, as defined in this paragraph, who obtains coverage through a guaranteed association. Employees of employers purchasing through a guaranteed association are eligible employees if they would otherwise meet the definition except for the number of persons employed by the employer. Permanent employees who work at least 20 hours but not more than 29 hours are eligible employees if all four of the following apply:

(A) They otherwise meet the definition of an eligible employee except for the number of hours worked.

(B) The employer offers the employees health coverage under a health benefit plan.

(C) All similarly situated individuals are offered coverage under the health benefit plan.

(D) The employee shall have worked at least 20 hours per normal workweek for at least 50 percent of the weeks in the previous calendar quarter. The health care service plan may request any necessary information to document the hours and time period in question, including, but not limited to, payroll records and employee wage and tax filings.

(2) Any member of a guaranteed association as defined in subdivision (n).

(c) "In force business" means an existing health benefit plan contract issued by the plan to a small employer.

(d) "Late enrollee" means an eligible employee or dependent who has declined enrollment in a health benefit plan offered by a small employer at the time of the initial enrollment period provided under the terms of the health benefit plan and who subsequently requests enrollment in a health benefit plan of that small employer, provided that the initial enrollment period shall be a period of at least 30 days. It also means any member of an association that is a guaranteed association as well as any other person eligible to purchase through the guaranteed association when that person has failed to purchase coverage during the initial enrollment period provided under the terms of the guaranteed association's plan contract and who subsequently requests enrollment in the plan, provided that the initial enrollment period shall be a period of at least 30 days. However, an eligible employee, any other person eligible for coverage through a guaranteed association pursuant to subdivision (n), or an eligible dependent shall not be considered a late enrollee if any of the following is applicable:

(1) The individual meets all of the following requirements:

(A) He or she was covered under another employer health benefit plan, the Healthy Families Program, the Access for Infants and Mothers (AIM) Program, the Medi-Cal program, or coverage through the California Health Benefit Exchange at the time the individual was eligible to enroll.

(B) He or she certified at the time of the initial enrollment that coverage under another employer health benefit plan, the Healthy Families Program, the AIM Program, the Medi-Cal program, or coverage through the California Health Benefit Exchange was the reason for declining enrollment, provided that, if the individual was covered under another employer health benefit plan, including a plan offered through the California Health Benefit Exchange, the individual was given the opportunity to make the certification required by this subdivision and was notified that failure to do so could result in later treatment as a late enrollee.

(C) He or she has lost or will lose coverage under another employer health benefit plan as a result of termination of employment of the individual or of a person through whom the individual was covered as a dependent, change in employment status of the individual or of a person through whom the individual was covered as a dependent, termination of the other plan's coverage, cessation of an employer's contribution toward an employee's or dependent's coverage, death of the person through whom the individual was covered as a dependent, legal separation, or divorce; or he or she has lost or will lose coverage under the Healthy Families Program, the AIM Program, the Medi-Cal program, or coverage through the California Health Benefit Exchange.

(D) He or she requests enrollment within 30 days after termination of coverage or employer contribution toward coverage provided under another employer health benefit plan, or requests enrollment within 60 days after termination of Medi-Cal program coverage, AIM Program coverage, Healthy Families Program coverage, or coverage through the California Health Benefit Exchange.

(2) The employer offers multiple health benefit plans and the employee elects a different plan during an open enrollment period.

(3) A court has ordered that coverage be provided for a spouse or minor child under a covered employee's health benefit plan.

(4) (A) In the case of an eligible employee, as defined in paragraph (1) of subdivision (b), the plan cannot produce a written statement from the employer stating that the individual or the person through whom the individual was eligible to be covered as a dependent, prior to declining coverage, was provided with, and signed, acknowledgment of an explicit written notice in boldface type specifying that failure to elect coverage during the initial enrollment period permits the plan to impose, at the time of the individual's later decision to elect coverage, an exclusion from eligibility for coverage until the next open enrollment period, unless the individual meets the criteria specified in paragraph (1), (2), or (3). This exclusion from eligibility for coverage shall not be considered a waiting period in violation of Section 1357.51 or 1357.607.

(B) In the case of an association member who did not purchase coverage through a guaranteed association, the plan cannot produce a written statement from the association stating that the association sent a written notice in boldface type to all potentially eligible association members at their last known address prior to the initial enrollment period informing members that failure to elect coverage during the initial enrollment period permits the plan to impose, at the time of the member's later decision to elect coverage, an exclusion from eligibility for coverage until the next open enrollment period, unless the individual meets the requirements of subparagraphs (A), (C), and (D) of paragraph (1) or meets the requirements of paragraph (2) or (3). This exclusion from eligibility for coverage shall not be considered a waiting period in violation of Section 1357.51 or 1357.607.

(C) In the case of an employer or person who is not a member of an association, was eligible to purchase coverage through a guaranteed association, and did not do so, and would not be eligible to purchase guaranteed coverage unless purchased through a guaranteed association, the employer or person can demonstrate that he or she meets the requirements of subparagraphs (A), (C), and (D) of paragraph (1), or meets the requirements of paragraph (2) or (3), or that he or she recently had a change in status that would make him or her eligible and that application for enrollment was made within 30 days of the change.

(5) The individual is an employee or dependent who meets the criteria described in paragraph (1) and was under a COBRA continuation provision and the coverage under that provision has been exhausted. For purposes of this section, the definition of "COBRA" set forth in subdivision (e) of Section 1373.621 shall apply.

(6) The individual is a dependent of an enrolled eligible employee who has lost or will lose his or her coverage under the Healthy Families Program, the AIM Program, the Medi-Cal program, or a health benefit plan offered through the California Health Benefit Exchange and requests enrollment within 60 days after termination of that coverage.

(7) The individual is an eligible employee who previously declined coverage under an employer health benefit plan, including a plan offered through the California Health Benefit Exchange, and who has subsequently acquired a dependent who would be eligible for coverage as a dependent of the employee through marriage, birth, adoption, or placement for adoption, and who enrolls for coverage under that employer health benefit plan on his or her behalf and on behalf of his or her dependent within 30 days following the date of marriage, birth, adoption, or placement for adoption, in which case the effective date of coverage shall be the first day of the month following the date the completed request for enrollment is received in the case of marriage, or the date of birth, or the date of adoption or placement for adoption, whichever applies. Notice of the special enrollment rights contained in this paragraph shall be provided by the employer to an employee at or before the time the employee is offered an opportunity to enroll in plan coverage.

(8) The individual is an eligible employee who has declined coverage for himself or herself or his or her dependents during a previous enrollment period because his or her dependents were covered by another employer health benefit plan, including a plan offered through the California Health Benefit Exchange, at the time of the previous enrollment period. That individual may enroll himself or herself or his or her dependents for plan coverage during a special open enrollment opportunity if his or her dependents have lost or will lose coverage under that other employer health benefit plan. The special open enrollment opportunity shall be requested by the employee not more than 30 days after the date that the other health coverage is exhausted or terminated. Upon enrollment, coverage shall be effective not later than the first day of the first calendar month beginning after the date the request for enrollment is received. Notice of the special enrollment rights contained in this paragraph shall be provided by the employer to an employee at or before the time the employee is offered an opportunity to enroll in plan coverage.

(e) "Preexisting condition provision" means a contract provision that excludes coverage for charges or expenses incurred during a specified period following the enrollee's effective date of coverage, as to a condition for which medical advice, diagnosis, care, or treatment was recommended or received during a specified period immediately preceding the effective date of coverage. A health care service plan shall not limit or exclude coverage for any individual based on a preexisting condition whether or not any medical advice, diagnosis, care, or treatment was recommended or received before that date.

(f) "Creditable coverage" means:

(1) Any individual or group policy, contract, or program that is written or administered by a disability insurer, health care service plan, fraternal benefits society, self-insured employer plan, or any other entity, in this state or elsewhere, and that arranges or provides medical, hospital, and surgical coverage not designed to supplement other private or governmental plans. The term includes continuation or conversion coverage but does not include accident only, credit, coverage for onsite medical clinics, disability income, Medicare supplement, long-term care, dental, vision, coverage issued as a supplement to liability insurance, insurance arising out of a workers' compensation or similar law, automobile medical payment insurance, or insurance under which benefits are payable with or without regard to fault and that is statutorily required to be contained in any liability insurance policy or equivalent self-insurance.

(2) The Medicare Program pursuant to Title XVIII of the federal Social Security Act (42 U.S.C. Sec. 1395 et seq.).

(3) The Medicaid program pursuant to Title XIX of the federal Social Security Act (42 U.S.C. Sec. 1396 et seq.).

(4) Any other publicly sponsored program, provided in this state or elsewhere, of medical, hospital, and surgical care.

(5) Chapter 55 (commencing with Section 1071) of Title 10 of the United States Code (Civilian Health and Medical Program of the Uniformed Services (CHAMPUS)).

(6) A medical care program of the Indian Health Service or of a tribal organization.

(7) A health plan offered under Chapter 89 (commencing with Section 8901) of Title 5 of the United States Code (Federal Employees Health Benefits Program (FEHBP)).

(8) A public health plan as defined in federal regulations authorized by Section 2701(c)(1)(I) of the federal Public Health Service Act, as amended by Public Law 104-191, the federal Health Insurance Portability and Accountability Act of 1996.

(9) A health benefit plan under Section 5(e) of the federal Peace Corps Act (22 U.S.C. Sec. 2504(e)).

(10) Any other creditable coverage as defined by subsection (c) of Section 2704 of Title XXVII of the federal Public Health Service Act (42 U.S.C. Sec. 300gg-3(c)).

(g) "Rating period" means the period for which premium rates established by a plan are in effect and shall be no less than 12 months from the date of issuance or renewal of the health care service plan contract.

(h) "Risk adjusted employee risk rate" means the rate determined for an eligible employee of a small employer in a particular risk category after applying the risk adjustment factor.

(i) "Risk adjustment factor" means the percentage adjustment to be applied equally to each standard employee risk rate for a particular small employer, based upon any expected deviations from standard cost of services. This factor may not be more than 110 percent or less than 90 percent.

(j) "Risk category" means the following characteristics of an eligible employee: age, geographic region, and family composition of the employee, plus the health benefit plan selected by the small employer.

(1) No more than the following age categories may be used in determining premium rates:
Under 30
30–39
40–49
50–54
55–59
60–64
65 and over.
However, for the 65 years of age and over category, separate premium rates may be specified depending upon whether coverage under the plan contract will be primary or secondary to benefits provided by the Medicare Program pursuant to Title XVIII of the federal Social Security Act (42 U.S.C. Sec. 1395 et seq.).

(2) Small employer health care service plans shall base rates to small employers using no more than the following family size categories:
(A) Single.

(B) Married couple or registered domestic partners.

(C) One adult and child or children.

(D) Married couple or registered domestic partners and child or children.

(3) (A) In determining rates for small employers, a plan that operates statewide shall use no more than nine geographic regions in the state, have no region smaller than an area in which the first three digits of all its ZIP Codes are in common within a county, and divide no county into more than two regions. Plans shall be deemed to be operating statewide if their coverage area includes 90 percent or more of the state's population. Geographic regions established pursuant to this section shall, as a group, cover the entire state, and the area encompassed in a geographic region shall be separate and distinct from areas encompassed in other geographic regions. Geographic regions may be noncontiguous.

(B) (i) In determining rates for small employers, a plan that does not operate statewide shall use no more than the number of geographic regions in the state that is determined by the following formula: the population, as determined in the last federal census, of all counties that are included in their entirety in a plan's service area divided by the total population of the state, as determined in the last federal census, multiplied by nine. The resulting number shall be rounded to the nearest whole integer. A region shall not be smaller than an area in which the first three digits of all its ZIP Codes are in common within a county and no county may be divided into more than two regions. The area encompassed in a geographic region shall be separate and distinct from areas encompassed in other geographic regions. Geographic regions may be noncontiguous. A plan shall not have less than one geographic area.

(ii) If the formula in clause (i) results in a plan that operates in more than one county having only one geographic region, then the formula in clause (i) shall not apply and the plan may have two geographic regions, provided that no county is divided into more than one region.

This section does not require a plan to establish a new service area or to offer health coverage on a statewide basis, outside of the plan's existing service area.

(k) (1) "Small employer" means any of the following:

(A) For plan years commencing on or after January 1, 2014, and on or before December 31, 2015, any person, firm, proprietary or nonprofit corporation, partnership, public agency, or association that is actively engaged in business or service, that, on at least 50 percent of its working days during the preceding calendar quarter or preceding calendar year, employed at least one, but no more than 50, eligible employees, the majority of whom were employed within this state, that was not formed primarily for purposes of buying health care service plan contracts, and in which a bona fide employer-employee relationship exists. For plan years commencing on or after January 1, 2016, any person, firm, proprietary or nonprofit corporation, partnership, public agency, or association that is actively engaged in business or service, that, on at least 50 percent of its working days during the preceding calendar quarter or preceding calendar year, employed at least one, but no more than 100, eligible employees, the majority of whom were employed within this state, that was not formed primarily for purposes of buying health care service plan contracts, and in which a bona fide employer-employee relationship exists. In determining whether to apply the calendar quarter or calendar year test, a health care service plan shall use the test that ensures eligibility if only one test would establish eligibility. In determining the number of eligible employees, companies that are affiliated companies and that are eligible to file a combined tax return for purposes of state taxation shall be considered one employer. Subsequent to the issuance of a health care service plan contract to a small employer pursuant to this article, and for the purpose of determining eligibility, the size of a small employer shall be determined annually. Except as otherwise specifically provided in this article, provisions of this article that apply to a small employer shall continue to apply until the plan contract anniversary following the date the employer no longer meets the requirements of this definition. It includes any small employer as defined in this subparagraph who purchases coverage through a guaranteed association, any employer purchasing coverage for employees through a guaranteed association, and any small employer as defined in this paragraph who purchases coverage through any arrangement.

(B) Any guaranteed association, as defined in subdivision (m), that purchases health coverage for members of the association.

(2) For plan years commencing on or after January 1, 2019, for purposes of determining whether an employer has one employee, sole proprietors and their spouses, and partners of a partnership and their spouses, are not employees.

(l) "Standard employee risk rate" means the rate applicable to an eligible employee in a particular risk category in a small employer group.

(m) "Guaranteed association" means a nonprofit organization comprised of a group of individuals or employers who associate based solely on participation in a specified profession or industry, accepting for membership any individual or employer meeting its membership criteria, and that (1) includes one or more small employers as defined in subparagraph (A) of paragraph (1) of subdivision (k), (2) does not condition membership directly or indirectly on the health or claims history of any person, (3) uses membership dues solely for and in consideration of the membership and membership benefits, except that the amount of the dues shall not depend on whether the member applies for or purchases insurance offered to the association, (4) is organized and maintained in good faith for purposes unrelated to insurance, (5) has been in active existence on January 1, 1992, and for at least five years prior to that date, (6) has included health insurance as a membership benefit for at least five years prior to January 1, 1992, (7) has a constitution and bylaws, or other analogous governing documents that provide for election of the governing board of the association by its members, (8) offers any plan contract that is purchased to all individual members and employer members in this state, (9) includes any member choosing to enroll in the plan contracts offered to the association provided that the member has agreed to make the required premium payments, and (10) covers at least 1,000 persons with the health care service plan with which it contracts. The requirement of 1,000 persons may be met if component chapters of a statewide association contracting separately with the same carrier cover at least 1,000 persons in the aggregate.

This subdivision applies regardless of whether a contract issued by a plan is with an association, or a trust formed for or sponsored by an association, to administer benefits for association members.

For purposes of this subdivision, an association formed by a merger of two or more associations after January 1, 1992, and otherwise meeting the criteria of this subdivision shall be deemed to have been in active existence on January 1, 1992, if its predecessor organizations had been in active existence on January 1, 1992, and for at least five years prior to that date and otherwise met the criteria of this subdivision.

(n) "Members of a guaranteed association" means any individual or employer meeting the association's membership criteria if that person is a member of the association and chooses to purchase health coverage through the association. At the association's discretion, it also may include employees of association members, association staff, retired members, retired employees of members, and surviving spouses and dependents of deceased members. However, if an association chooses to include these persons as members of the guaranteed association, the association shall make that election in advance of purchasing a plan contract. Health care service plans may require an association to adhere to the membership composition it selects for up to 12 months.

(o) "Affiliation period" means a period that, under the terms of the health care service plan contract, must expire before health care services under the contract become effective.

(p) "Grandfathered small employer health care service plan contract" means a small employer health care service plan contract that constitutes a grandfathered health plan.

(q) "Grandfathered health plan" has the meaning set forth in Section 1251 of PPACA.

(r) "Nongrandfathered small employer health care service plan contract" means a small employer health care service plan contract that is not a grandfathered health plan.

(s) "Plan year" has the meaning set forth in Section 144.103 of Title 45 of the Code of Federal Regulations.

(t) "PPACA" means the federal Patient Protection and Affordable Care Act (Public Law 111-148), as amended by the federal Health Care and Education Reconciliation Act of 2010 (Public Law 111-152), and any rules, regulations, or guidance issued thereunder.

(u) "Registered domestic partner" means a person who has established a domestic partnership as described in Section 297 of the Family Code.

(v) "Small employer health care service plan contract" means a health care service plan contract issued to a small employer.

(w) "Waiting period" means a period that is required to pass with respect to an employee before the employee is eligible to be covered for benefits under the terms of the contract.
(Amended by Stats. 2018, Ch. 700, Sec. 4. (SB 1375) Effective January 1, 2019.)
1357.601.

This article shall apply only to grandfathered small group health care service plan contracts and only with respect to plan years commencing on or after January 1, 2014.
(Added by Stats. 2012, Ch. 852, Sec. 6. (AB 1083) Effective January 1, 2013.)
1357.602.

(a) A health care service plan providing or arranging for the provision of basic health care services to small employers shall be subject to this article if either of the following conditions are met:

(1) Any portion of the premium is paid by a small employer, or any covered individual is reimbursed, whether through wage adjustments or otherwise, by a small employer for any portion of the premium.

(2) The plan contract is treated by the small employer or any of the covered individuals as part of a plan or program for the purposes of Section 106 or 162 of the Internal Revenue Code.

(b) This article shall not apply to health care service plan contracts for coverage of Medicare services pursuant to contracts with the United States government, Medicare supplement, Medi-Cal contracts with the State Department of Health Care Services, long-term care coverage, or specialized health care service plan contracts.
(Added by Stats. 2012, Ch. 852, Sec. 6. (AB 1083) Effective January 1, 2013.)
1357.603.

Nothing in this article shall be construed to preclude the application of this chapter to either of the following:

(a) An association, trust, or other organization acting as a "health care service plan" as defined under Section 1345.

(b) An association, trust, or other organization or person presenting information regarding a health care service plan to persons who may be interested in subscribing or enrolling in the plan.
(Added by Stats. 2012, Ch. 852, Sec. 6. (AB 1083) Effective January 1, 2013.)
1357.604.

(a) (1) A plan shall fairly and affirmatively renew a grandfathered health plan contract with a small employer.

(2) Each plan shall make available to each small employer all nongrandfathered small employer health care service plan contracts that the plan offers and sells to small employers or to associations that include small employers in this state consistent with Article 3.1 (commencing with Section 1357).

(3) No plan or solicitor shall induce or otherwise encourage a small employer to separate or otherwise exclude an eligible employee from a health care service plan contract that is provided in connection with the employee's employment or membership in a guaranteed association.

(b) Every plan shall file with the director the reasonable employee participation requirements and employer contribution requirements that will be applied in renewing its grandfathered health care service plan contracts. Participation requirements shall be applied uniformly among all small employer groups, except that a plan may vary application of minimum employee participation requirements by the size of the small employer group and whether the employer contributes 100 percent of the eligible employee's premium. Employer contribution requirements shall not vary by employer size. A health care service plan shall not establish a participation requirement that (1) requires a person who meets the definition of a dependent in subdivision (a) of Section 1357.600 to enroll as a dependent if he or she is otherwise eligible for coverage and wishes to enroll as an eligible employee and (2) allows a plan to reject an otherwise eligible small employer because of the number of persons that waive coverage due to coverage through another employer. Members of an association eligible for health coverage under subdivision (n) of Section 1357.600, but not electing any health coverage through the association, shall not be counted as eligible employees for purposes of determining whether the guaranteed association meets a plan's reasonable participation standards.

(c) No plan or solicitor shall, directly or indirectly, engage in the following activities:

(1) Encourage or direct small employers to refrain from filing an application for coverage or renewal of coverage with a plan because of the health status, claims experience, industry, occupation of the small employer, or geographic location provided that it is within the plan's approved service area.

(2) Encourage or direct small employers to seek coverage from another plan, or coverage offered through the California Health Benefit Exchange, because of the health status, claims experience, industry, occupation of the small employer, or geographic location provided that it is within the plan's approved service area.

(d) A plan shall not, directly or indirectly, enter into any contract, agreement, or arrangement with a solicitor that provides for or results in the compensation paid to a solicitor for the sale of a health care service plan contract to be varied because of the health status, claims experience, industry, occupation, or geographic location of the small employer. This subdivision does not apply to a compensation arrangement that provides compensation to a solicitor on the basis of percentage of premium, provided that the percentage shall not vary because of the health status, claims experience, industry, occupation, or geographic area of the small employer or small employer's employees.

(e) A policy or contract that covers a small employer, as defined in Section 1304(b) of PPACA and in subdivision (k) of Section 1357.600 shall not establish rules for eligibility, including continued eligibility, of an individual, or dependent of an individual, to enroll under the terms of the plan based on any of the following health status-related factors:

(1) Health status.

(2) Medical condition, including physical and mental illnesses.

(3) Claims experience.

(4) Receipt of health care.

(5) Medical history.

(6) Genetic information.

(7) Evidence of insurability, including conditions arising out of acts of domestic violence.

(8) Disability.

(9) Any other health status-related factor as determined by any federal regulations, rules, or guidance issued pursuant to Section 2705 of the federal Public Health Service Act.

(f) A plan shall comply with the requirements of Section 1374.3.
(Added by Stats. 2012, Ch. 852, Sec. 6. (AB 1083) Effective January 1, 2013.)
1357.606.

(a) For plan contracts expiring after July 1, 1994, 60 days prior to July 1, 1994, an association that meets the definition of a guaranteed association, as set forth in Section 1357.600, except for the requirement that 1,000 persons be covered, shall be entitled to renew grandfathered small employer health care service plan contracts as if the association were a guaranteed association, except that the coverage shall be guaranteed only for those members of an association, as defined in Section 1357.600, (1) who were receiving coverage or had successfully applied for coverage through the association as of June 30, 1993, (2) who were receiving coverage through the association as of December 31, 1992, and whose coverage lapsed at any time thereafter because the employment through which coverage was received ended or an employer's contribution to health coverage ended, or (3) who were covered at any time between June 30, 1993, and July 1, 1994, under a contract that was in force on June 30, 1993.

(b) An association obtaining health coverage for its members pursuant to this section shall otherwise be afforded all the rights of a guaranteed association under this chapter, including, but not limited to, guaranteed renewability of coverage.
(Added by Stats. 2012, Ch. 852, Sec. 6. (AB 1083) Effective January 1, 2013.)
1357.607.

A small employer health care service plan contract shall not impose a preexisting condition provision or a waiting or affiliation period upon any individual.
(Repealed and added by Stats. 2014, Ch. 195, Sec. 8. (SB 1034) Effective January 1, 2015.)
1357.608.

Nothing in this article shall be construed as prohibiting a health care service plan from restricting enrollment of late enrollees to open enrollment periods consistent with federal law.
(Added by Stats. 2012, Ch. 852, Sec. 6. (AB 1083) Effective January 1, 2013.)
1357.609.

All grandfathered small employer health care service plan contracts shall provide to subscribers and enrollees at least all of the basic health care services included in subdivision (b) of Section 1345, and in Section 1300.67 of the California Code of Regulations.

(Added by Stats. 2012, Ch. 852, Sec. 6. (AB 1083) Effective January 1, 2013.)

1357.610.

(a) No plan shall be required by the provisions of this article:

(1) To offer coverage under a small employer's health care service plan contract to an otherwise eligible employee or dependent, when the eligible employee or dependent does not work or reside within the plan's approved service area, except as provided in Chapter 7 (commencing with Section 3750) of Part 1 of Division 9 of the Family Code.

(2) To offer coverage under a small employer's health care service plan contract to an eligible employee, as defined in paragraph (2) of subdivision (b) of Section 1357.600, who within 12 months of application for coverage terminated from a small employer health care service plan contract offered by the plan.

(b) Nothing in this article shall be construed to limit the director's authority to develop and implement a plan of rehabilitation for a health care service plan whose financial viability or organizational and administrative capacity has become impaired.

(Added by Stats. 2012, Ch. 852, Sec. 6. (AB 1083) Effective January 1, 2013.)

1357.611.

(a) The director may require a plan to discontinue the renewal of grandfathered small employer health care service plan contracts or the offering or acceptance of applications from any group upon a determination by the director that the plan does not have sufficient financial viability, or organizational and administrative capacity to ensure the delivery of health care services to its enrollees. In determining whether the conditions of this section have been met, the director shall consider, but not be limited to, the plan's compliance with the requirements of Section 1367, Article 6 (commencing with Section 1375), and the rules adopted thereunder.

(b) Nothing in this article shall be construed to limit the director's authority to develop and implement a plan of rehabilitation for a health care service plan whose financial viability or organizational and administrative capacity has become impaired.

(Added by Stats. 2012, Ch. 852, Sec. 6. (AB 1083) Effective January 1, 2013.)

1357.612.

Premiums for grandfathered contracts renewed by plans on or after January 1, 2014, shall be subject to the following requirements:

(a) (1) The premium for in force business shall be determined for an eligible employee in a particular risk category after applying a risk adjustment factor to the plan's standard employee risk rates. The risk adjusted employee risk rates may not be more than 110 percent or less than 90 percent. The risk adjustment factor applied to a small employer may not increase by more than 10 percentage points from the risk adjustment factor applied in the prior rating period. The risk adjustment factor for a small employer may not be modified more frequently than every 12 months.

(2) The premium charged a small employer for in force business shall be equal to the sum of the risk adjusted employee risk rates. The standard employee risk rates shall be in effect for no less than 12 months.

(b) (1) For any small employer, a plan may, with the consent of the small employer, establish composite employee and dependent rates for renewal of in force business. The composite rates shall be determined as the average of the risk adjusted employee risk rates for the small employer, as determined in accordance with the requirements of subdivision (a). The sum of the composite rates so determined shall be equal to the sum of the risk adjusted employee risk rates for the small employer.

(2) The composite rates shall be used for all employees and dependents covered throughout a rating period of 12 months, except that a plan may reserve the right to redetermine the composite rates if the enrollment under the contract changes by more than a specified percentage during the rating period. Any redetermination of the composite rates shall be based on the same risk adjusted employee risk rates used to determine the initial composite rates for the rating period. If a plan reserves the right to redetermine the rates and the enrollment changes more than the specified percentage, the plan shall redetermine the composite rates if the redetermined rates would result in a lower premium for the small employer. A plan reserving the right to redetermine the composite rates based upon a change in enrollment shall use the same specified percentage to measure that change with respect to all small employers electing composite rates.

(Added by Stats. 2012, Ch. 852, Sec. 6. (AB 1083) Effective January 1, 2013.)

1357.613.

Plans shall apply standard employee risk rates consistently with respect to all small employers.

(Added by Stats. 2012, Ch. 852, Sec. 6. (AB 1083) Effective January 1, 2013.)

1357.614.

In connection with the renewal of a grandfathered small employer health care service plan contract, each plan shall make a reasonable disclosure, as part of its solicitation and sales materials, of the following:

(a) The extent to which premium rates for a specified small employer are established or adjusted in part based upon the actual or expected variation in service costs of the employees and dependents of the small employer.

(b) The provisions concerning the plan's right to change premium rates and the factors other than provision of services experience that affect changes in premium rates.

(c) Provisions relating to the guaranteed issue and renewal of contracts.

(d) Provisions relating to the effect of any waiting or affiliation provision.

(e) Provisions relating to the small employer's right to apply for any nongrandfathered small employer health care service plan contract written, issued, or administered by the plan at the time of application for a new health care service plan contract, or at the time of renewal of a health care service plan contract, consistent with the requirements of PPACA.

(f) The availability, upon request, of a listing of all the plan's nongrandfathered small employer health care service plan contracts and benefit plan designs offered, both inside and outside the California Health Benefit Exchange, including the rates for each contract.

(g) At the time it renews a grandfathered small employer health care service plan contract, each plan shall provide the small employer with a statement of all of its nongrandfathered small employer health care service plan contracts, including the rates for each plan contract, in the service area in which the employer's employees and eligible dependents who are to be covered by the plan contract work or reside. For purposes of this subdivision, plans that are affiliated plans or that are eligible to file a consolidated income tax return shall be treated as one health plan.

(h) Each plan shall do all of the following:

(1) Prepare a brochure that summarizes all of its small employer health care service plan contracts and to make this summary available to any small employer and to solicitors upon request. The summary shall include for each contract information on benefits provided, a generic description of the manner in which services are provided, such as how access to providers is limited, benefit limitations, required copayments and deductibles, standard employee risk rates, and a telephone number that can be called for more detailed benefit information. Plans are required to keep the information contained in the brochure accurate and up to date and, upon updating the brochure, send copies to solicitors and solicitor firms with which the plan contracts to solicit enrollments or subscriptions.

(2) For each contract, prepare a more detailed evidence of coverage and make it available to small employers, solicitors, and solicitor firms upon request. The evidence of coverage shall contain all information that a prudent buyer would need to be aware of in making contract selections.

(3) Provide to small employers and solicitors, upon request, for any given small employer the sum of the standard employee risk rates and the sum of the risk adjusted employee risk rates. When requesting this information, small employers, solicitors, and solicitor firms shall provide the plan with the information the plan needs to determine the small employer's risk adjusted employee risk rate.

(4) Provide copies of the current summary brochure to all solicitors and solicitor firms contracting with the plan to solicit enrollments or subscriptions from small employers. For purposes of this subdivision, plans that are affiliated plans or that are eligible to file a consolidated income tax return shall be treated as one health plan.

(Amended by Stats. 2014, Ch. 195, Sec. 9. (SB 1034) Effective January 1, 2015.)

1357.615.

(a) At least 20 business days prior to renewing or amending a small employer health care service plan contract subject to this article, a plan shall file a notice of material modification with the director in accordance with the provisions of Section 1352. The notice of material modification shall include a statement certifying that the plan is in compliance with subdivision (i) of Section 1357.600 and Section 1357.612. The certified statement shall set forth the standard employee risk rate for each risk category and the highest and lowest risk adjustment factors that will be used in setting the rates at which the contract will be renewed or amended. Any action by the director, as permitted under Section 1352, to disapprove, suspend, or postpone the plan's use of a plan contract shall be in writing, specifying the reasons that the plan contract does not comply with the requirements of this chapter.

(b) Prior to making any changes in the risk categories, risk adjustment factors or standard employee risk rates filed with the director pursuant to subdivision (a), the plan shall file as an amendment a statement setting forth the changes and certifying that the plan is in compliance with subdivision (i) of Section 1357.600 and Section 1357.612. A plan may commence utilizing the changed risk categories set forth in the certified statement on the 31st day from the date of the filing, or at an earlier time determined by the director, unless the director disapproves the amendment by written notice, stating the reasons therefor. If only the standard employee risk rate is being changed, and not the risk categories or risk adjustment factors, a plan may commence utilizing the changed standard employee risk rate upon filing the certified statement unless the director disapproves the amendment by written notice.

(c) Periodic changes to the standard employee risk rate that a plan proposes to implement over the course of up to 12 consecutive months may be filed in conjunction with the certified statement filed under subdivision (a) or (b).

(d) Each plan shall maintain at its principal place of business all of the information required to be filed with the director pursuant to this section.

(e) Each plan shall make available to the director, on request, the risk adjustment factor used in determining the rate for any particular small employer.

(f) Nothing in this section shall be construed to limit the director's authority to enforce the rating practices set forth in this article.

(Added by Stats. 2012, Ch. 852, Sec. 6. (AB 1083) Effective January 1, 2013.)

1357.616.

(a) Health care service plans may enter into contractual agreements with qualified associations, as defined in subdivision (b), under which these qualified associations may assume responsibility for performing specific administrative services, as defined in this section, for qualified association members. Health care service plans that enter into agreements with qualified associations for assumption of administrative services shall establish uniform definitions for the administrative services that may be provided by a qualified association or its third-party administrator. The health care service plan shall permit all qualified associations to assume one or more of these functions when the health care service plan determines the qualified association demonstrates the administrative capacity to assume these functions.

For the purposes of this section, administrative services provided by qualified associations or their third-party administrators shall be services pertaining to eligibility determination, enrollment, premium collection, sales, or claims administration on a per-claim basis that would otherwise be provided directly by the health care service plan or through a third-party administrator on a commission basis or an agent or solicitor workforce on a commission basis.

Each health care service plan that enters into an agreement with any qualified association for the provision of administrative services shall offer all qualified associations with which it contracts the same premium discounts for performing those services the health care service plan has permitted the qualified association or its third-party administrator to assume. The health care service plan shall apply these uniform discounts to the health care service plan's risk adjusted employee risk rates after the health plan has determined the qualified association's risk adjusted employee risk rates pursuant to Section 1357.612. The health care service plan shall report to the department its schedule of discounts for each administrative service.

In no instance may a health care service plan provide discounts to qualified associations that are in any way intended to, or materially result in, a reduction in premium charges to the qualified association due to the health status of the membership of the qualified association. In addition to any other remedies available to the director to enforce this chapter, the director may declare a contract between a health care service plan and a qualified association for administrative services pursuant to this section null and void if the director determines any discounts provided to the qualified association are intended to, or materially result in, a reduction in premium charges to the qualified association due to the health status of the membership of the qualified association.

(b) For the purposes of this section, a qualified association is a nonprofit corporation comprised of a group of individuals or employers who associate based solely on participation in a specified profession or industry, that conforms to all of the following requirements:

(1) It accepts for membership any individual or small employer meeting its membership criteria.

(2) It does not condition membership directly or indirectly on the health or claims history of any person.

(3) It uses membership dues solely for and in consideration of the membership and membership benefits, except that the amount of the dues shall not depend on whether the member applies for or purchases insurance offered by the association.

(4) It is organized and maintained in good faith for purposes unrelated to insurance.

(5) It existed on January 1, 1972, and has been in continuous existence since that date.

(6) It has a constitution and bylaws or other analogous governing documents that provide for election of the governing board of the association by its members.

(7) It offered, marketed, or sold health coverage to its members for 20 continuous years prior to January 1, 1993.

(8) It agrees to offer only to association members any plan contract.

(9) It agrees to include any member choosing to enroll in the plan contract offered by the association, provided that the member agrees to make required premium payments.

(10) It complies with all provisions of this article.

(11) It had at least 10,000 enrollees covered by association sponsored plans immediately prior to enactment of Chapter 1128 of the Statutes of 1992.

(12) It applies any administrative cost at an equal rate to all members purchasing coverage through the qualified association.

(c) A qualified association shall comply with Section 1357.52.

(Added by Stats. 2012, Ch. 852, Sec. 6. (AB 1083) Effective January 1, 2013.)

1357.618.

(a) The department may adopt emergency regulations implementing this article no later than August 31, 2013. The department may readopt any emergency regulation authorized by this section that is the same as or substantially equivalent to an emergency regulation previously adopted under this section.

(b) The initial adoption of emergency regulations implementing this section and the one readoption of emergency regulations authorized by this section shall be deemed an emergency and necessary for the immediate preservation of the public peace, health, safety, or general welfare. The initial emergency regulations and the one readoption of emergency regulations authorized by this section shall be submitted to the Office of Administrative Law for filing with the Secretary of State and each shall remain in effect for no more than 180 days, by which time final regulations may be adopted.

(Added by Stats. 2012, Ch. 852, Sec. 6. (AB 1083) Effective January 1, 2013.)

ARTICLE 3.5. Additional Requirements for Medicare Supplement Contracts [1358.1 - 1358.24]

(Article 3.5 repealed and added by Stats. 2000, Ch. 706, Sec. 2.)

1358.1.

Every health care service plan that offers any contract that primarily or solely supplements Medicare or that is advertised or represented as a supplement to Medicare, shall, in addition to complying with this chapter and rules of the director, comply with this article. The basic health care services required to be provided pursuant to Sections 1345 and 1367 shall not be included in Medicare supplement contracts subject to this article, to the extent that California is required to disallow coverage for these health care services under the federal Medicare supplement standardization requirements set forth in Section 1882 of the federal Social Security Act (42 U.S.C.A. Sec. 1395ss).

(Repealed and added by Stats. 2000, Ch. 706, Sec. 2. Effective January 1, 2001.)

1358.2.

The purpose of this article is to provide for the reasonable standardization of coverage and simplification of terms and benefits of Medicare supplement contracts, to facilitate public understanding and comparison of those contracts, to eliminate provisions contained in those contracts that may be misleading or confusing in connection with the purchase of the contracts or with the settlement of claims, and to provide for full disclosures in the sale of Medicare supplement contracts to persons eligible for Medicare.

(Repealed and added by Stats. 2000, Ch. 706, Sec. 2. Effective January 1, 2001.)

1358.3.

(a) Except as otherwise provided in this section or in Sections 1358.7, 1358.12, 1358.13, 1358.16, and 1358.21, this article shall apply to all group and individual Medicare supplement contracts advertised, solicited, or issued for delivery in this state on or after January 1, 2001.

(b) This article shall not apply to a contract of one or more employers or labor organizations, or of the trustees of a fund established by one or more employers or labor organizations, or combination thereof, for employees or former employees, or a combination thereof, or for members or former members, or a combination thereof, of the labor organizations.

(c) This article shall not apply to Medicare supplement policies or certificates subject to Article 6 (commencing with Section 10192.1) of Chapter 1 of Part 1 of Division 2 of the Insurance Code.

(Repealed and added by Stats. 2000, Ch. 706, Sec. 2. Effective January 1, 2001.)

1358.4.

The following definitions apply for the purposes of this article:

(a) "Applicant" means:

(1) An individual enrollee who seeks to contract for health coverage, in the case of an individual Medicare supplement contract.

(2) An enrollee who seeks to obtain health coverage through a group, in the case of a group Medicare supplement contract.

(b) "Bankruptcy" means that situation in which a Medicare Advantage organization that is not an issuer has filed, or has had filed against it, a petition for declaration of bankruptcy and has ceased doing business in the state.

(c) "Continuous period of creditable coverage" means the period during which an individual was covered by creditable coverage, if during the period of the coverage the individual had no breaks in coverage greater than 63 days.

(d) (1) "Creditable coverage" means, with respect to an individual, coverage of the individual provided under any of the following:

(A) Any individual or group contract, policy, certificate, or program that is written or administered by a health care service plan, health insurer, fraternal benefits society, self-insured employer plan, or any other entity, in this state or elsewhere, and that arranges or provides medical, hospital, and surgical coverage not designed to supplement other private or governmental plans. The term includes continuation or conversion coverage.

(B) Part A or B of Title XVIII of the federal Social Security Act (42 U.S.C. Sec. 1395c et seq.) (Medicare).

(C) Title XIX of the federal Social Security Act (42 U.S.C. Sec. 1396 et seq.) (Medicaid), other than coverage consisting solely of benefits under Section 1928 of that act.

(D) Chapter 55 of Title 10 of the United States Code (CHAMPUS).

(E) A medical care program of the Indian Health Service or of a tribal organization.

(F) A state health benefits risk pool.

(G) A health plan offered under Chapter 89 of Title 5 of the United States Code (Federal Employees Health Benefits Program).

(H) A public health plan as defined in federal regulations authorized by Section 2701(c)(1)(I) of the federal Public Health Service Act, as amended by Public Law 104-191, the federal Health Insurance Portability and Accountability Act of 1996.

(I) A health benefit plan under Section 5(e) of the federal Peace Corps Act (22 U.S.C. Sec. 2504(e)).

(J) Any other publicly sponsored program, provided in this state or elsewhere, of medical, hospital, and surgical care.

(K) Any other creditable coverage as defined by subsection (c) of Section 2701 of Title XXVII of the federal Public Health Service Act (42 U.S.C. Sec. 300gg(c)).

(2) "Creditable coverage" shall not include one or more, or any combination of, the following:

(A) Coverage for accident-only or disability income insurance, or any combination thereof.

(B) Coverage issued as a supplement to liability insurance.

(C) Liability insurance, including general liability insurance and automobile liability insurance.

(D) Workers' compensation or similar insurance.

(E) Automobile medical payment insurance.

(F) Credit-only insurance.

(G) Coverage for onsite medical clinics.

(H) Other similar insurance coverage, specified in federal regulations, under which benefits for medical care are secondary or incidental to other insurance benefits.

(3) "Creditable coverage" shall not include the following benefits if they are provided under a separate policy, certificate, or contract or are otherwise not an integral part of the plan:

(A) Limited scope dental or vision benefits.

(B) Benefits for long-term care, nursing home care, home health care, community-based care, or any combination thereof.

(C) Other similar, limited benefits as are specified in federal regulations.

(4) "Creditable coverage" shall not include the following benefits if offered as independent, noncoordinated benefits:

(A) Coverage only for a specified disease or illness.

(B) Hospital indemnity or other fixed indemnity insurance.

(5) "Creditable coverage" shall not include the following if offered as a separate policy, certificate, or contract:

(A) Medicare supplemental health insurance as defined under Section 1882(g)(1) of the federal Social Security Act.

(B) Coverage supplemental to the coverage provided under Chapter 55 of Title 10 of the United States Code.

(C) Similar supplemental coverage provided to coverage under a group health plan.

(e) "Employee welfare benefit plan" means a plan, fund, or program of employee benefits as defined in Section 1002 of Title 29 of the United States Code (Employee Retirement Income Security Act).

(f) "Insolvency" means when an issuer, licensed to transact the business of a health care service plan in this state, has had a final order of liquidation entered against it with a finding of insolvency by a court of competent jurisdiction in the issuer's state of domicile.

(g) "Issuer" means a health care service plan delivering, or issuing for delivery, Medicare supplement contracts in this state, but does not include entities subject to Article 6 (commencing with Section 10192.1) of Chapter 1 of Part 2 of Division 2 of the Insurance Code.

(h) "Medicare" means the federal Health Insurance for the Aged Act, Title XVIII of the Social Security Amendments of 1965, as amended.

(i) "Medicare Advantage Plan" means a plan of coverage for health benefits under Medicare Part C and includes:

(1) Coordinated care plans that provide health care services, including, but not limited to, health care service plans (with or without a point-of-service option), plans offered by provider-sponsored organizations, and preferred provider organizations plans.

(2) Medical savings account plans coupled with a contribution into a Medicare Advantage medical savings account.

(3) Medicare Advantage private fee-for-service plans.

(j) "Medicare supplement contract" means a group or individual plan contract of hospital and medical service associations or health care service plans, other than a contract issued pursuant to a contract under Section 1876 of the federal Social Security Act (42 U.S.C. Sec. 1395mm) or an issued contract under a demonstration project specified in Section 1395ss(g)(1) of Title 42 of the United States Code, that is advertised, marketed, or designed primarily as a supplement to reimbursements under Medicare for the hospital, medical, or surgical expenses of persons eligible for Medicare. "Contract" means "Medicare supplement contract," unless the context requires otherwise. "Medicare supplement contract" does not include a Medicare Advantage plan established under Medicare Part C, an outpatient prescription drug plan established under Medicare Part D, or a health care prepayment plan that provides benefits pursuant to an agreement under subparagraph (A) of paragraph (1) of subsection (a) of Section 1833 of the federal Social Security Act.

(k) "1990 standardized Medicare supplement benefit plan," "1990 standardized benefit plan," or "1990 plan" means a group or individual Medicare supplement contract issued on or after July 21, 1992, and with an effective date prior to June 1, 2010, and includes Medicare supplement contracts renewed on or after that date that are not replaced by the issuer at the request of the enrollee or subscriber.

(l) "2010 standardized Medicare supplement benefit plan," "2010 standardized benefit plan," or "2010 plan" means a group or individual Medicare supplement contract issued with an effective date on or after June 1, 2010.

(m) "Secretary" means the Secretary of the United States Department of Health and Human Services.

(Amended by Stats. 2010, Ch. 328, Sec. 116. (SB 1330) Effective January 1, 2011.)
1358.5.

(a) A contract shall not be advertised, solicited, or issued for delivery as a Medicare supplement contract unless the contract contains definitions or terms that conform to the requirements of this section.

(1) (A) "Accident," "accidental injury," or "accidental means" shall be defined to employ "result" language and shall not include words that establish an accidental means test or use words such as "external, violent, visible wounds" or other similar words of description or characterization.

(B) The definition shall not be more restrictive than the following: "injury or injuries for which benefits are provided means accidental bodily injury sustained by the covered person that is the direct result of an accident, independent of disease or bodily infirmity or any other cause, and occurs while coverage is in force."

(C) The definition may provide that injuries shall not include injuries for which benefits are provided or available under any workers' compensation, employer's liability, or similar law, unless prohibited by law.

(2) "Benefit period" or "Medicare benefit period" shall not be defined more restrictively than as defined in the Medicare program.

(3) "Convalescent nursing home," "extended care facility," or "skilled nursing facility" shall not be defined more restrictively than as defined in the Medicare program.

(4) "Health care expenses" means for purposes of Section 1358.14, expenses of health care service plans associated with the delivery of health care services, which expenses are analogous to incurred losses of insurers.

(5) "Hospital" may be defined in relation to its status, facilities, and available services or to reflect its accreditation by the Joint Commission on Accreditation of Hospitals, but not more restrictively than as defined in the Medicare Program.

(6) "Medicare" shall be defined in the contract. "Medicare" may be substantially defined as "The Health Insurance for the Aged Act, Title XVIII of the Social Security Amendments of 1965, as amended," or "Title I, Part I of Public Law 89-97, as enacted by the 89th Congress and popularly known as the Health Insurance for the Aged Act, as amended," or words of similar import.

(7) "Medicare eligible expenses" shall mean expenses of the kinds covered by Medicare Parts A and B, to the extent recognized as reasonable and medically necessary by Medicare.

(8) "Physician" shall not be defined more restrictively than as defined in the Medicare Program.

(9) (A) "Sickness" shall not be defined more restrictively than as follows: "sickness means illness or disease of an insured person that first manifests itself after the effective date of insurance and while the insurance is in force."

(B) The definition may be further modified to exclude sicknesses or diseases for which benefits are provided under any workers' compensation, occupational disease, employer's liability, or similar law.

(b) Nothing in this section shall be construed as prohibiting any contract, by definitions or express provisions, from limiting or restricting any or all of the benefits provided under the contract, except in-area and out-of-area emergency services, to those health care services that are delivered by issuer, employed, owned, or contracting providers, and provider facilities, so long as the contract complies with the provisions of Sections 1358.14 and 1367 and with Section 1300.67 of Title 28 of the California Code of Regulations.

(c) Nothing in this section shall be construed as prohibiting any contract that limits or restricts any or all of the benefits provided under the contract in the manner contemplated in subdivision (b) from limiting its obligation to deliver services, and disclaiming any liability from any delay or failure to provide those services (1) in the event of a major disaster or epidemic or (2) in the event of circumstances not reasonably within the control of the issuer, such as the partial or total destruction of facilities, war, riot, civil insurrection, disability of a significant part of its health personnel, or similar circumstances so long as the provisions comply with the provisions of subdivision (h) of Section 1367.

(Amended by Stats. 2005, Ch. 206, Sec. 2. Effective January 1, 2006.)
1358.6.

(a) (1) Except for permitted preexisting condition clauses as described in Sections 1358.7, 1358.8, and 1358.81, a contract shall not be advertised, solicited, or issued for delivery as a Medicare supplement contract if the contract contains definitions, limitations, exclusions, conditions, reductions, or other provisions that are more restrictive or limiting than that term as officially used in Medicare, except as expressly authorized by this article.

(2) No issuer may advertise, solicit, or issue for delivery any Medicare supplement contract with hospital or medical coverage if the contract contains any of the prohibited provisions described in subdivision (b).

(b) The following provisions shall be deemed to be unfair, unreasonable, and inconsistent with the objectives of this chapter and shall not be contained in any Medicare supplement contract:

(1) Any waiver, exclusion, limitation, or reduction based on or relating to a preexisting disease or physical condition, unless that waiver, exclusion, limitation, or reduction (A) applies only to coverage for specified services rendered not more than six months from the effective date of coverage, (B) is based on or relates only to a preexisting disease or physical condition defined no more restrictively than a condition for which medical advice was given or treatment was recommended by or received from a physician within six months before the effective date of coverage, (C) does not apply to any coverage under any group contract, and (D) is approved in advance by the director. Any limitations with respect to a preexisting condition shall appear as a separate paragraph of the contract and be labeled "Preexisting Condition Limitations."

(2) Except with respect to a group contract subject to, and in compliance with, Section 1399.62, any provision denying coverage, after termination of the contract, for services provided continuously beginning while the contract was in effect, during the continuous total disability of the subscriber or enrollee, except that the coverage may be limited to a reasonable period of time not less than the duration of the contract benefit period, if any, and may be limited to the maximum benefits provided under the contract.

(c) A Medicare supplement contract in force shall not contain benefits that duplicate benefits provided by Medicare.

(d) (1) Subject to paragraphs (4) and (5) of subdivision (a) of Section 1358.8, a Medicare supplement contract with benefits for outpatient prescription drugs that was issued prior to January 1, 2006, shall be renewed for current enrollees and subscribers, at their option, who do not enroll in Medicare Part D.

(2) A Medicare supplement contract with benefits for outpatient prescription drugs shall not be issued on and after January 1, 2006.

(3) On and after January 1, 2006, a Medicare supplement contract with benefits for outpatient prescription drugs shall not be renewed after the enrollee or subscriber enrolls in Medicare Part D unless both of the following conditions exist:

(A) The contract is modified to eliminate outpatient prescription drug coverage for outpatient prescription drug expenses incurred after the effective date of the individual's coverage under a Medicare Part D plan.

(B) The premium is adjusted to reflect the elimination of outpatient prescription drug coverage at the time of enrollment in Medicare Part D, accounting for any claims paid if applicable.

(Amended by Stats. 2009, Ch. 10, Sec. 2. Effective July 2, 2009.)
1358.7.

A contract shall not be advertised, solicited, or issued for delivery as a Medicare supplement contract prior to January 1, 2001, unless it meets or exceeds requirements applicable pursuant to this code that were in effect prior to that date.
(Repealed and added by Stats. 2000, Ch. 706, Sec. 2. Effective January 1, 2001.)
1358.8.
The following standards are applicable to all Medicare supplement contracts advertised, solicited, or issued for delivery on or after January 1, 2001, and with an effective date prior to June 1, 2010. A contract shall not be advertised, solicited, or issued for delivery as a Medicare supplement contract unless it complies with these benefit standards.
(a) The following general standards apply to Medicare supplement contracts and are in addition to all other requirements of this article:
(1) A Medicare supplement contract shall not exclude or limit benefits for losses incurred more than six months from the effective date of coverage because it involved a preexisting condition. The contract shall not define a preexisting condition more restrictively than a condition for which medical advice was given or treatment was recommended by or received from a physician within six months before the effective date of coverage.
(2) A Medicare supplement contract shall not indemnify against losses resulting from sickness on a different basis than losses resulting from accidents.
(3) A Medicare supplement contract shall provide that benefits designed to cover cost-sharing amounts under Medicare will be changed automatically to coincide with any changes in the applicable Medicare deductible, copayment, or coinsurance amounts. Prepaid or periodic charges may be modified to correspond with those changes.
(4) A Medicare supplement contract shall not provide for termination of coverage of a spouse solely because of the occurrence of an event specified for termination of coverage of the covered person, other than the nonpayment of the prepaid or periodic charge.
(5) Each Medicare supplement contract shall be guaranteed renewable.
(A) The issuer shall not cancel or nonrenew the contract solely on the ground of health status of the individual.
(B) The issuer shall not cancel or nonrenew the contract for any reason other than nonpayment of the prepaid or periodic charge or misrepresentation of the risk by the applicant that is shown by the plan to be material to the acceptance for coverage. The contestability period for Medicare supplement contracts shall be two years.
(C) If a group Medicare supplement contract is terminated by the subscriber and is not replaced as provided under subparagraph (E), the issuer shall offer enrollees an individual Medicare supplement contract that, at the option of the enrollee, either provides for continuation of the benefits contained in the terminated contract or provides for benefits that otherwise meet the requirements of this subsection.
(D) If an individual is an enrollee in a group Medicare supplement contract and the individual membership in the group is terminated, the issuer shall either offer the enrollee the conversion opportunity described in subparagraph (C) or, at the option of the subscriber, shall offer the enrollee continuation of coverage under the group contract.
(E) If a group Medicare supplement contract is replaced by another group Medicare supplement contract purchased by the same subscriber, the issuer of the replacement contract shall offer coverage to all persons covered under the old group contract on its date of termination. Coverage under the new contract shall not result in any exclusion for preexisting conditions that would have been covered under the group contract being replaced.
(F) If a Medicare supplement contract eliminates an outpatient prescription drug benefit as a result of requirements imposed by the Medicare Prescription Drug, Improvement, and Modernization Act of 2003 (Public Law 108-173), the contract as modified as a result of that act shall be deemed to satisfy the guaranteed renewal requirements of this paragraph.
(6) Termination of a Medicare supplement contract shall be without prejudice to any continuous loss that commenced while the contract was in force, but the extension of benefits beyond the period during which the contract was in force may be predicated upon the continuous total disability of the covered person, limited to the duration of the contract benefit period, if any, or to payment of the maximum benefits. Receipt of Medicare Part D benefits shall not be considered in determining a continuous loss.
(7) (A) (i) A Medicare supplement contract shall provide that benefits and prepaid or periodic charges under the contract shall be suspended at the request of the enrollee for the period, not to exceed 24 months, in which the enrollee has applied for and is determined to be entitled to medical assistance under Title XIX of the federal Social Security Act, but only if the enrollee notifies the issuer of the contract within 90 days after the date the individual becomes entitled to assistance.
If suspension occurs and if the enrollee loses entitlement to medical assistance, the contract shall be automatically reinstituted (effective as of the date of termination of entitlement) as of the termination of entitlement if the enrollee provides notice of loss of entitlement within 90 days after the date of loss and pays the prepaid or periodic charge attributable to the period, effective as of the date of termination of entitlement. Upon receipt of timely notice, the issuer shall return directly to the enrollee that portion of the prepaid or periodic charge attributable to the period the enrollee was entitled to medical assistance, subject to adjustment for paid claims.
(ii) A Medicare supplement contract shall provide that benefits and premiums under the contract shall be suspended at the request of the enrollee or subscriber for any period that may be provided by federal regulation if the enrollee or subscriber is entitled to benefits under Section 226(b) of the Social Security Act and is covered under a group health plan, as defined in Section 1862(b)(1)(A)(v) of the Social Security Act. If suspension occurs and the enrollee or subscriber loses coverage under the group health plan, the contract shall be automatically reinstituted, effective as of the date of loss of

coverage if the enrollee or subscriber provides notice within 90 days of the date of the loss of coverage.
(B) Reinstitution of coverages:
(i) Shall not provide for any waiting period with respect to treatment of preexisting conditions.
(ii) Shall provide for resumption of coverage that is substantially equivalent to coverage in effect before the date of suspension. If the suspended Medicare supplement contract provided coverage for outpatient prescription drugs, reinstitution of the contract for a Medicare Part D enrollee shall not include coverage for outpatient prescription drugs but shall otherwise provide coverage that is substantially equivalent to the coverage in effect before the date of suspension.
(iii) Shall provide for classification of prepaid or periodic charges on terms at least as favorable to the enrollee as the prepaid or periodic charge classification terms that would have applied to the enrollee had the coverage not been suspended.
(8) If an issuer makes a written offer to the Medicare supplement enrollee or subscriber of one or more of its plan contracts, to exchange during a specified period from his or her 1990 standardized plan, as described in Section 1358.9, to a 2010 standardized plan, as described in Section 1358.91, the offer and subsequent exchange shall comply with the following requirements:
(A) An issuer need not provide justification to the director if the enrollee or subscriber replaces a 1990 standardized plan contract with an issue age rated 2010 standardized plan contract at the enrollee or subscriber's original issue age and duration. If an enrollee or subscriber's plan contract to be replaced is priced on an issue age rate schedule at the time of that offer, the rate charged to the enrollee or subscriber for the new exchanged plan shall recognize the plan contract reserve buildup, due to the prefunding inherent in the use of an issue age rate basis, for the benefit of the enrollee or subscriber. The method proposed to be used by an issuer shall be filed with the director.
(B) The rating class of the new plan contract shall be the class closest to the enrollee or subscriber's class of the replaced coverage.
(C) An issuer may not apply new preexisting condition limitations or a new incontestability period to the new plan contract for those benefits contained in the exchanged 1990 standardized plan contract of the enrollee or subscriber, but may apply preexisting condition limitations of no more than six months to any added benefits contained in the new 2010 standardized plan contract not contained in the exchanged plan contract. This subparagraph shall not apply to an applicant who is guaranteed issue under Section 1358.11 or 1358.12.
(D) The new plan contract shall be offered to all enrollees or subscribers within a given plan, except where the offer or issue would be in violation of state or federal law.
(9) A Medicare supplement contract shall not be limited to coverage for a single disease or affliction.
(10) A Medicare supplement contract shall provide an examination period of 30 days after the receipt of the contract by the applicant for purposes of review, during which time the applicant may return the contract as described in subdivision (e) of Section 1358.17.
(11) A Medicare supplement contract shall additionally meet any other minimum benefit standards as established by the director.
(12) Within 30 days prior to the effective date of any Medicare benefit changes, an issuer shall file with the director, and notify its subscribers and enrollees of, modifications it has made to Medicare supplement contracts.
(A) The notice shall include a description of revisions to the Medicare Program and a description of each modification made to the coverage provided under the Medicare supplement contract.
(B) The notice shall inform each subscriber and enrollee as to when any adjustment in the prepaid or periodic charges will be made due to changes in Medicare benefits.
(C) The notice of benefit modifications and any adjustments to the prepaid or periodic charges shall be in outline form and in clear and simple terms so as to facilitate comprehension. The notice shall not contain or be accompanied by any solicitation.
(13) No modifications to existing Medicare supplement coverage shall be made at the time of, or in connection with, the notice requirements of this article except to the extent necessary to eliminate duplication of Medicare benefits and any modifications necessary under the contract to provide indexed benefit adjustment.
(b) With respect to the standards for basic (core) benefits for benefit plans A to J, inclusive, every issuer shall make available a contract including only the following basic "core" package of benefits to each prospective applicant. This "core" package of benefits shall be referred to as standardized Medicare supplement benefit plan "A". An issuer may make available to prospective applicants any of the other Medicare supplement benefit plans in addition to the basic core package, but not in lieu of that package.
(1) Coverage of Part A Medicare eligible expenses for hospitalization to the extent not covered by Medicare from the 61st day to the 90th day, inclusive, in any Medicare benefit period.
(2) Coverage of Part A Medicare eligible expenses incurred for hospitalization to the extent not covered by Medicare for each Medicare lifetime inpatient reserve day used.
(3) Upon exhaustion of the Medicare hospital inpatient coverage including the lifetime reserve days, coverage of 100 percent of the Medicare Part A eligible expenses for hospitalization paid at the applicable prospective payment system rate or other appropriate Medicare standard of payment, subject to a lifetime maximum benefit of an additional 365 days. The provider shall accept the issuer's payment as payment in full and may not bill the enrollee or subscriber for any balance.
(4) Coverage under Medicare Parts A and B for the reasonable cost of the first three pints of blood, or equivalent quantities of packed red blood cells, as defined under federal regulations, unless replaced in accordance with federal regulations.

(5) Coverage for the coinsurance amount, or in the case of hospital outpatient services, the copayment amount, of Medicare eligible expenses under Part B regardless of hospital confinement, subject to the Medicare Part B deductible.

(c) The following additional benefits shall be included in Medicare supplement benefit plans B to J, inclusive, only as provided by Section 1358.9.

(1) With respect to the Medicare Part A deductible, coverage for all of the Medicare Part A inpatient hospital deductible amount per benefit period.

(2) With respect to skilled nursing facility care, coverage for the actual billed charges up to the coinsurance amount from the 21st day to the 100th day, inclusive, in a Medicare benefit period for posthospital skilled nursing facility care eligible under Medicare Part A.

(3) With respect to the Medicare Part B deductible, coverage for all of the Medicare Part B deductible amount per calendar year regardless of hospital confinement.

(4) With respect to 80 percent of the Medicare Part B excess charges, coverage for 80 percent of the difference between the actual Medicare Part B charge as billed, not to exceed any charge limitation established by the Medicare Program or state law, and the Medicare-approved Part B charge.

(5) With respect to 100 percent of the Medicare Part B excess charges, coverage for all of the difference between the actual Medicare Part B charge as billed, not to exceed any charge limitation established by the Medicare Program or state law, and the Medicare-approved Part B charge.

(6) With respect to the basic outpatient prescription drug benefit, coverage for 50 percent of outpatient prescription drug charges, after a two-hundred-fifty-dollar ($250) calendar year deductible, to a maximum of one thousand two hundred fifty dollars ($1,250) in benefits received by the insured per calendar year, to the extent not covered by Medicare. On and after January 1, 2006, no Medicare supplement contract may be sold or issued if it includes a prescription drug benefit.

(7) With respect to the extended outpatient prescription drug benefit, coverage for 50 percent of outpatient prescription drug charges, after a two-hundred-fifty-dollar ($250) calendar year deductible, to a maximum of three thousand dollars ($3,000) in benefits received by the insured per calendar year, to the extent not covered by Medicare. On and after January 1, 2006, no Medicare supplement contract may be sold or issued if it includes a prescription drug benefit.

(8) With respect to medically necessary emergency care in a foreign country, coverage to the extent not covered by Medicare for 80 percent of the billed charges for Medicare-eligible expenses for medically necessary emergency hospital, physician, and medical care received in a foreign country, which care would have been covered by Medicare if provided in the United States and which care began during the first 60 consecutive days of each trip outside the United States, subject to a calendar year deductible of two hundred fifty dollars ($250), and a lifetime maximum benefit of fifty thousand dollars ($50,000). For purposes of this benefit, "emergency care" shall mean care needed immediately because of an injury or an illness of sudden and unexpected onset.

(9) With respect to the preventive medical care benefit, coverage for the following preventive health services:

(A) An annual clinical preventive medical history and physical examination that may include tests and services from subparagraph (B) and patient education to address preventive health care measures.

(B) The following screening tests or preventive services that are not covered by Medicare, the selection and frequency of which are determined to be medically appropriate by the attending physician:

(i) Fecal occult blood test.

(ii) Mammogram.

(C) Influenza vaccine administered at any appropriate time during the year. Reimbursement shall be for the actual charges up to 100 percent of the Medicare-approved amount for each service, as if Medicare were to cover the service as identified in American Medical Association Current Procedural Terminology (AMACPT) codes, to a maximum of one hundred twenty dollars ($120) annually under this benefit. This benefit shall not include payment for any procedure covered by Medicare.

(10) With respect to the at-home recovery benefit, coverage for services to provide short-term, at-home assistance with activities of daily living for those recovering from an illness, injury, or surgery.

(A) For purposes of this benefit, the following definitions shall apply:

(i) "Activities of daily living" include, but are not limited to, bathing, dressing, personal hygiene, transferring, eating, ambulating, assistance with drugs that are normally self-administered, and changing bandages or other dressings.

(ii) "Care provider" means a duly qualified or licensed home health aide or homemaker, or a personal care aide or nurse provided through a licensed home health care agency or referred by a licensed referral agency or licensed nurses registry.

(iii) "Home" shall mean any place used by the insured as a place of residence, provided that the place would qualify as a residence for home health care services covered by Medicare. A hospital or skilled nursing facility shall not be considered the insured's place of residence.

(iv) "At-home recovery visit" means the period of a visit required to provide at-home recovery care, without any limit on the duration of the visit, except that each consecutive four hours in a 24-hour period of services provided by a care provider is one visit.

(B) With respect to coverage requirements and limitations, the following shall apply:

(i) At-home recovery services provided shall be primarily services that assist in activities of daily living.

(ii) The covered person's attending physician shall certify that the specific type and frequency of at-home recovery services are necessary because of a condition for which a home care plan of treatment was approved by Medicare.

(iii) Coverage is limited to the following:

(I) No more than the number and type of at-home recovery visits certified as necessary by the covered person's attending physician. The total number of at-home recovery visits shall not exceed the number of Medicare-approved home health care visits under a Medicare-approved home care plan of treatment.

(II) The actual charges for each visit up to a maximum reimbursement of forty dollars ($40) per visit.

(III) One thousand six hundred dollars ($1,600) per calendar year.

(IV) Seven visits in any one week.

(V) Care furnished on a visiting basis in the insured's home.

(VI) Services provided by a care provider as defined in subparagraph (A).

(VII) At-home recovery visits while the covered person is covered under the contract and not otherwise excluded.

(VIII) At-home recovery visits received during the period the covered person is receiving Medicare-approved home care services or no more than eight weeks after the service date of the last Medicare-approved home health care visit.

(C) Coverage is excluded for the following:

(i) Home care visits paid for by Medicare or other government programs.

(ii) Care provided by family members, unpaid volunteers, or providers who are not care providers.

(d) The standardized Medicare supplement benefit plan "K" shall consist of the following benefits:

(1) Coverage of 100 percent of the Medicare Part A hospital coinsurance amount for each day used from the 61st to the 90th day, inclusive, in any Medicare benefit period.

(2) Coverage of 100 percent of the Medicare Part A hospital coinsurance amount for each Medicare lifetime inpatient reserve day used from the 91st to the 150th day, inclusive, in any Medicare benefit period.

(3) Upon exhaustion of the Medicare hospital inpatient coverage, including the lifetime reserve days, coverage of 100 percent of the Medicare Part A eligible expenses for hospitalization paid at the applicable prospective payment system rate, or other appropriate Medicare standard of payment, subject to a lifetime maximum benefit of an additional 365 days. The provider shall accept the issuer's payment for this benefit as payment in full and shall not bill the enrollee or subscriber for any balance.

(4) With respect to the Medicare Part A deductible, coverage for 50 percent of the Medicare Part A inpatient hospital deductible amount per benefit period until the out-of-pocket limitation described in paragraph (10) is met.

(5) With respect to skilled nursing facility care, coverage for 50 percent of the coinsurance amount for each day used from the 21st day to the 100th day, inclusive, in a Medicare benefit period for posthospital skilled nursing facility care eligible under Medicare Part A until the out-of-pocket limitation described in paragraph (10) is met.

(6) With respect to hospice care, coverage for 50 percent of cost sharing for all Medicare Part A eligible expenses and respite care until the out-of-pocket limitation described in paragraph (10) is met.

(7) Coverage for 50 percent, under Medicare Part A or B, of the reasonable cost of the first three pints of blood or equivalent quantities of packed red blood cells, as defined under federal regulations, unless replaced in accordance with federal regulations, until the out-of-pocket limitation described in paragraph (10) is met.

(8) Except for coverage provided in paragraph (9), coverage for 50 percent of the cost sharing otherwise applicable under Medicare Part B after the enrollee or subscriber pays the Part B deductible, until the out-of-pocket limitation is met as described in paragraph (10).

(9) Coverage of 100 percent of the cost sharing for Medicare Part B preventive services, after the enrollee or subscriber pays the Medicare Part B deductible.

(10) Coverage of 100 percent of all cost sharing under Medicare Parts A and B for the balance of the calendar year after the individual has reached the out-of-pocket limitation on annual expenditures under Medicare Parts A and B of four thousand dollars ($4,000) in 2006, indexed each year by the appropriate inflation adjustment specified by the secretary.

(e) The standardized Medicare supplement benefit plan "L" shall consist of the following benefits:

(1) The benefits described in paragraphs (1), (2), (3), and (9) of subdivision (d).

(2) With respect to the Medicare Part A deductible, coverage for 75 percent of the Medicare Part A inpatient hospital deductible amount per benefit period until the out-of-pocket limitation described in paragraph (8) is met.

(3) With respect to skilled nursing facility care, coverage for 75 percent of the coinsurance amount for each day used from the 21st day to the 100th day, inclusive, in a Medicare benefit period for posthospital skilled nursing facility care eligible under Medicare Part A until the out-of-pocket limitation described in paragraph (8) is met.

(4) With respect to hospice care, coverage for 75 percent of cost sharing for all Medicare Part A eligible expenses and respite care until the out-of-pocket limitation described in paragraph (8) is met.

(5) Coverage for 75 percent, under Medicare Part A or B, of the reasonable cost of the first three pints of blood or equivalent quantities of packed red blood cells, as defined under federal regulations, unless replaced in accordance with federal regulations, until the out-of-pocket limitation described in paragraph (8) is met.

(6) Except for coverage provided in paragraph (7), coverage for 75 percent of the cost sharing otherwise applicable under Medicare Part B after the enrollee or subscriber pays the Part B deductible until the out-of-pocket limitation described in paragraph (8) is met.

(7) Coverage for 100 percent of the cost sharing for Medicare Part B preventive services after the enrollee or subscriber pays the Part B deductible.

(8) Coverage of 100 percent of the cost sharing for Medicare Parts A and B for the balance of the calendar year after the individual has reached the out-of-pocket limitation on annual expenditures under Medicare Parts A and B of two thousand dollars ($2,000) in 2006, indexed each year by the appropriate inflation adjustment specified by the secretary.

(f) A contract shall not contain any provision delaying the effective date of coverage beyond the first day of the month following the date of receipt by the issuer of the applicant's properly completed application, except that the effective date of coverage may be delayed until the 65th birthday of an applicant who is to become eligible for Medicare by reason of age if the application is received any time during the three months immediately preceding the applicant's 65th birthday.

(Amended by Stats. 2009, Ch. 10, Sec. 3. Effective July 2, 2009.)

1358.81.

The following standards are applicable to all Medicare supplement contracts delivered or issued for delivery in this state with an effective date on or after June 1, 2010. No contract may be advertised, solicited, delivered, or issued for delivery in this state as a Medicare supplement contract unless it complies with these benefit standards. No issuer may offer any 1990 standardized Medicare supplement contract for sale with an effective date on or after June 1, 2010. Benefit standards applicable to Medicare supplement contracts issued with an effective date before June 1, 2010, remain subject to the requirements of Section 1358.8.

(a) The following general standards apply to Medicare supplement contracts and are in addition to all other requirements of this article.

(1) A Medicare supplement contract shall not exclude or limit benefits for losses incurred more than six months from the effective date of coverage because it involved a preexisting condition. The contract shall not define a preexisting condition more restrictively than a condition for which medical advice was given or treatment was recommended by, or received from, a physician within six months before the effective date of coverage.

(2) A Medicare supplement contract shall not indemnify against losses resulting from sickness on a different basis than losses resulting from accidents.

(3) A Medicare supplement contract shall provide that benefits designed to cover cost-sharing amounts under Medicare will be changed automatically to coincide with any changes in the applicable Medicare deductible, copayment, or coinsurance amounts. Prepaid or periodic charges may be modified to correspond with those changes.

(4) A Medicare supplement contract shall not provide for termination of coverage of a spouse solely because of the occurrence of an event specified for termination of coverage of the enrollee or subscriber, other than the nonpayment of prepaid or periodic charges.

(5) Each Medicare supplement contract shall be guaranteed renewable.

(A) The issuer shall not cancel or nonrenew the contract solely on the ground of health status of the individual.

(B) The issuer shall not cancel or nonrenew the contract for any reason other than nonpayment of prepaid or periodic charges or misrepresentation of the risk by the applicant that is shown by the plan to be material to the acceptance for coverage. The contestability period for Medicare supplement contracts shall be two years.

(C) If the Medicare supplement contract is terminated by the group contractholder and is not replaced as provided under subparagraph (E), the issuer shall offer enrollees or subscribers an individual Medicare supplement contract which, at the option of the enrollee or subscriber, does one of the following:

(i) Provides for continuation of the benefits contained in the group contract.

(ii) Provides for benefits that otherwise meet the requirements of one of the standardized contracts defined in this article.

(D) If an individual is an enrollee or subscriber in a group Medicare supplement contract and the individual terminates membership in the group, the issuer shall do one of the following:

(i) Offer the enrollee or subscriber the conversion opportunity described in subparagraph (C).

(ii) At the option of the group contractholder, offer the enrollee or subscriber continuation of coverage under the group contract.

(E) (i) If a group Medicare supplement contract is replaced by another group Medicare supplement contract purchased by the same group contractholder, the issuer of the replacement contract shall offer coverage to all persons covered under the old group contract on its date of termination. Coverage under the new contract shall not result in any exclusion for preexisting conditions that would have been covered under the group contract being replaced.

(ii) If a Medicare supplement contract replaces another Medicare supplement contract that has been in force for six months or more, the replacing issuer shall not impose an exclusion or limitation based on a preexisting condition. If the original coverage has been in force for less than six months, the replacing issuer shall waive any time period applicable to preexisting conditions, waiting periods, elimination periods, or probationary periods in the new contract to the extent the time was spent under the original coverage.

(6) Termination of a Medicare supplement contract shall be without prejudice to any continuous loss that commenced while the contract was in force, but the extension of benefits beyond the period during which the contract was in force may be predicated upon the continuous total disability of the enrollee or subscriber, limited to the duration of the contract benefit period, if any, or payment of the maximum benefits. Receipt of Medicare Part D benefits shall not be considered in determining a continuous loss.

(7) (A) (i) A Medicare supplement contract shall provide that benefits and prepaid or periodic charges under the contract shall be suspended at the request of the enrollee or subscriber for the period, not to exceed 24 months, in which the enrollee or subscriber

has applied for, and is determined to be entitled to, medical assistance under Medi-Cal under Title XIX of the federal Social Security Act, but only if the enrollee or subscriber notifies the issuer of the contract within 90 days after the date the individual becomes entitled to assistance. Upon receipt of timely notice, the insurer shall return directly to the enrollee or subscriber that portion of the prepaid or periodic charge attributable to the period of Medi-Cal eligibility, subject to adjustment for paid claims.

(ii) If suspension occurs and if the enrollee or subscriber loses entitlement to medical assistance under Medi-Cal, the Medicare supplement contract shall be automatically reinstituted (effective as of the date of termination of entitlement) as of the termination of entitlement if the enrollee or subscriber provides notice of loss of entitlement within 90 days after the date of loss and pays the prepaid or periodic charge attributable to the period, effective as of the date of termination of entitlement or equivalent coverage shall be provided if the prior contract is no longer available.

(iii) Each Medicare supplement contract shall provide that benefits and prepaid or periodic charges under the contract shall be suspended (for any period that may be provided by federal regulation) at the request of the enrollee or subscriber if the enrollee or subscriber is entitled to benefits under Section 226(b) of the Social Security Act and is covered under a group health plan (as defined in Section 1862(b)(1)(A)(v) of the Social Security Act). If suspension occurs and if the enrollee or subscriber loses coverage under the group health plan, the contract shall be automatically reinstituted (effective as of the date of loss of coverage) if the enrollee or subscriber provides notice of loss of coverage within 90 days after the date of the loss and pays the applicable prepaid or periodic charge.

(B) Reinstitution of coverages shall comply with all of the following requirements:

(i) Not provide for any waiting period with respect to treatment of preexisting conditions.

(ii) Provide for resumption of coverage that is substantially equivalent to coverage in effect before the date of suspension.

(iii) Provide for classification of prepaid or periodic charges on terms at least as favorable to the enrollee or subscriber as the classification of the prepaid or periodic charge that would have applied to the enrollee or subscriber had the coverage not been suspended.

(8) A Medicare supplement contract shall not be limited to coverage for a single disease or affliction.

(9) A Medicare supplement contract shall provide an examination period of 30 days after the receipt of the contract by the applicant for purposes of review, during which time the applicant may return the contract as described in subdivision (e) of Section 1358.17.

(10) A Medicare supplement contract shall additionally meet any other minimum benefit standards as established by the director.

(11) Within 30 days prior to the effective date of any Medicare benefit changes, an issuer shall file with the director, and notify its subscribers and enrollees of, modifications it has made to Medicare supplement contracts.

(A) The notice shall include a description of revisions to the Medicare Program and a description of each modification made to the coverage provided under the Medicare supplement contract.

(B) The notice shall inform each subscriber and enrollee as to when any adjustment in the prepaid or periodic charges will be made due to changes in Medicare benefits.

(C) The notice of benefit modifications and any adjustments to the prepaid or periodic charges shall be in outline form and in clear and simple terms so as to facilitate comprehension. The notice shall not contain or be accompanied by any solicitation.

(12) No modifications to existing Medicare supplement coverage shall be made at the time of, or in connection with, the notice requirements of this article except to the extent necessary to eliminate duplication of Medicare benefits and any modifications necessary under the contract to provide indexed benefit adjustment.

(b) With respect to the standards for basic (core) benefits for benefit plans A, B, C, D, F, high deductible F, G, M, and N, every issuer of Medicare supplement benefit plans shall make available a contract including only the following basic "core" package of benefits to each prospective enrollee or subscriber. An issuer may make available to prospective enrollees or subscribers any of the other Medicare supplement benefit plans in addition to the basic core package, but not in lieu of that package.

(1) Coverage of Part A Medicare eligible expenses for hospitalization to the extent not covered by Medicare from the 61st day through the 90th day, inclusive, in any Medicare benefit period.

(2) Coverage of Part A Medicare eligible expenses incurred for hospitalization to the extent not covered by Medicare for each Medicare lifetime inpatient reserve day used.

(3) Upon exhaustion of the Medicare hospital inpatient coverage, including the lifetime reserve days, coverage of 100 percent of the Medicare Part A eligible expenses for hospitalization paid at the applicable prospective payment system (PPS) rate, or other appropriate Medicare standard of payment, subject to a lifetime maximum benefit of an additional 365 days. The provider shall accept the issuer's payment as payment in full and may not bill the insured for any balance.

(4) Coverage under Medicare Parts A and B for the reasonable cost of the first three pints of blood or equivalent quantities of packed red blood cells, as defined under federal regulations, unless replaced in accordance with federal regulations.

(5) Coverage for the coinsurance amount, or in the case of hospital outpatient department services paid under a prospective payment system, the copayment amount, of Medicare eligible expenses under Part B regardless of hospital confinement, subject to the Medicare Part B deductible.

(6) Coverage of cost sharing for all Part A Medicare eligible hospice care and respite care expenses.

(c) The following additional benefits shall be included in Medicare supplement benefit plans B, C, D, F, high deductible F, G, M, and N, consistent with the plan type and benefits for each plan as provided in Section 1358.91:

(1) With respect to the Medicare Part A deductible, coverage for 100 percent of the Medicare Part A inpatient hospital deductible amount per benefit period.

(2) With respect to the Medicare Part A deductible, coverage for 50 percent of the Medicare Part A inpatient hospital deductible amount per benefit period.

(3) With respect to skilled nursing facility care, coverage for the actual billed charges up to the coinsurance amount from the 21st day through the 100th day in a Medicare benefit period for posthospital skilled nursing facility care eligible under Medicare Part A.

(4) With respect to the Medicare Part B deductible, coverage for 100 percent of the Medicare Part B deductible amount per calendar year regardless of hospital confinement.

(5) With respect to 100 percent of the Medicare Part B excess charges, coverage for all of the difference between the actual Medicare Part B charges as billed, not to exceed any charge limitation established by the Medicare program or state law, and the Medicare-approved Part B charge.

(6) With respect to medically necessary emergency care in a foreign country, coverage to the extent not covered by Medicare for 80 percent of the billed charges for Medicare-eligible expenses for medically necessary emergency hospital, physician, and medical care received in a foreign country, which care would have been covered by Medicare if provided in the United States and which care began during the first 60 consecutive days of each trip outside the United States, subject to a calendar year deductible of two hundred fifty dollars ($250), and a lifetime maximum benefit of fifty thousand dollars ($50,000). For purposes of this benefit, "emergency care" shall mean care needed immediately because of an injury or an illness of sudden and unexpected onset. (Added by Stats. 2009, Ch. 10, Sec. 4. Effective July 2, 2009.)

1358.9.

The following standards are applicable to all Medicare supplement contracts delivered or issued for delivery in this state on or after July 21, 1992, and with an effective date prior to June 1, 2010.

(a) An issuer shall make available to each prospective enrollee a contract form containing only the basic (core) benefits, as defined in subdivision (b) of Section 1358.8.

(b) No groups, packages, or combinations of Medicare supplement benefits other than those listed in this section shall be offered for sale in this state, except as may be permitted by subdivision (f) and by Section 1358.10.

(c) Benefit plans shall be uniform in structure, language, designation and format to the standard benefit plans A to L, inclusive, listed in subdivision (e), and shall conform to the definitions in Section 1358.4. Each benefit shall be structured in accordance with the format provided in subdivisions (b), (c), (d), and (e) of Section 1358.8 and list the benefits in the order listed in subdivision (e). For purposes of this section, "structure, language, and format" means style, arrangement, and overall content of a benefit.

(d) An issuer may use, in addition to the benefit plan designations required in subdivision (c), other designations to the extent permitted by law.

(e) With respect to the makeup of benefit plans, the following shall apply:

(1) Standardized Medicare supplement benefit plan A shall be limited to the basic (core) benefit common to all benefit plans, as defined in subdivision (b) of Section 1358.8.

(2) Standardized Medicare supplement benefit plan B shall include only the following: the core benefit, plus the Medicare Part A deductible as defined in paragraph (1) of subdivision (c) of Section 1358.8.

(3) Standardized Medicare supplement benefit plan C shall include only the following: the core benefit, plus the Medicare Part A deductible, skilled nursing facility care, Medicare Part B deductible, and medically necessary emergency care in a foreign country as defined in paragraphs (1), (2), (3), and (8) of subdivision (c) of Section 1358.8, respectively.

(4) Standardized Medicare supplement benefit plan D shall include only the following: the core benefit, plus the Medicare Part A deductible, skilled nursing facility care, medically necessary emergency care in a foreign country, and the at-home recovery benefit as defined in paragraphs (1), (2), (8), and (10) of subdivision (c) of Section 1358.8, respectively.

(5) Standardized Medicare supplement benefit plan E shall include only the following: the core benefit, plus the Medicare Part A deductible, skilled nursing facility care, medically necessary emergency care in a foreign country, and preventive medical care as defined in paragraphs (1), (2), (8), and (9) of subdivision (c) of Section 1358.8, respectively.

(6) Standardized Medicare supplement benefit plan F shall include only the following: the core benefit, plus the Medicare Part A deductible, the skilled nursing facility care, the Medicare Part B deductible, 100 percent of the Medicare Part B excess charges, and medically necessary emergency care in a foreign country as defined in paragraphs (1), (2), (3), (5), and (8) of subdivision (c) of Section 1358.8, respectively.

(7) Standardized Medicare supplement benefit high deductible plan F shall include only the following: 100 percent of covered expenses following the payment of the annual high deductible plan F deductible. The covered expenses include the core benefit, plus the Medicare Part A deductible, skilled nursing facility care, the Medicare Part B deductible, 100 percent of the Medicare Part B excess charges, and medically necessary emergency care in a foreign country as defined in paragraphs (1), (2), (3), (5), and (8) of subdivision (c) of Section 1358.8, respectively. The annual high deductible plan F deductible shall consist of out-of-pocket expenses, other than premiums, for services covered by the Medicare supplement plan F policy, and shall be in addition to any other specific benefit deductibles. The annual high deductible Plan F deductible shall be one thousand five hundred dollars ($1,500) for 1998 and 1999, and shall be based on the calendar year, as adjusted annually thereafter by the secretary to reflect the change in

the Consumer Price Index for all urban consumers for the 12-month period ending with August of the preceding year, and rounded to the nearest multiple of ten dollars ($10).

(8) Standardized Medicare supplement benefit plan G shall include only the following: the core benefit, plus the Medicare Part A deductible, skilled nursing facility care, 80 percent of the Medicare Part B excess charges, medically necessary emergency care in a foreign country, and the at-home recovery benefit as defined in paragraphs (1), (2), (4), (8), and (10) of subdivision (c) of Section 1358.8, respectively.

(9) Standardized Medicare supplement benefit plan H shall consist of only the following: the core benefit, plus the Medicare Part A deductible, skilled nursing facility care, basic outpatient prescription drug benefit, and medically necessary emergency care in a foreign country as defined in paragraphs (1), (2), (6), and (8) of subdivision (c) of Section 1358.8, respectively. The outpatient prescription drug benefit shall not be included in a Medicare supplement contract sold on or after January 1, 2006.

(10) Standardized Medicare supplement benefit plan I shall consist of only the following: the core benefit, plus the Medicare Part A deductible, skilled nursing facility care, 100 percent of the Medicare Part B excess charges, basic outpatient prescription drug benefit, medically necessary emergency care in a foreign country, and at-home recovery benefit as defined in paragraphs (1), (2), (5), (6), (8), and (10) of subdivision (c) of Section 1358.8, respectively. The outpatient prescription drug benefit shall not be included in a Medicare supplement contract sold on or after January 1, 2006.

(11) Standardized Medicare supplement benefit plan J shall consist of only the following: the core benefit, plus the Medicare Part A deductible, skilled nursing facility care, Medicare Part B deductible, 100 percent of the Medicare Part B excess charges, extended outpatient prescription drug benefit, medically necessary emergency care in a foreign country, preventive medical care, and at-home recovery benefit as defined in paragraphs (1), (2), (3), (5), (7), (8), (9), and (10) of subdivision (c) of Section 1358.8, respectively. The outpatient prescription drug benefit shall not be included in a Medicare supplement contract sold on or after January 1, 2006.

(12) Standardized Medicare supplement benefit high deductible plan J shall consist of only the following: 100 percent of covered expenses following the payment of the annual high deductible plan J deductible. The covered expenses include the core benefit, plus the Medicare Part A deductible, skilled nursing facility care, Medicare Part B deductible, 100 percent of the Medicare Part B excess charges, extended outpatient prescription drug benefit, medically necessary emergency care in a foreign country, preventive medical care benefit, and at-home recovery benefit as defined in paragraphs (1), (2), (3), (5), (7), (8), (9), and (10) of subdivision (c) of Section 1358.8, respectively. The annual high deductible plan J deductible shall consist of out-of-pocket expenses, other than premiums, for services covered by the Medicare supplement plan J policy, and shall be in addition to any other specific benefit deductibles. The annual deductible shall be one thousand five hundred dollars ($1,500) for 1998 and 1999, and shall be based on a calendar year, as adjusted annually thereafter by the secretary to reflect the change in the Consumer Price Index for all urban consumers for the 12-month period ending with August of the preceding year, and rounded to the nearest multiple of ten dollars ($10). The outpatient prescription drug benefit shall not be included in a Medicare supplement contract sold on or after January 1, 2006.

(13) Standardized Medicare supplement benefit plan K shall consist of only those benefits described in subdivision (d) of Section 1358.8.

(14) Standardized Medicare supplement benefit plan L shall consist of only those benefits described in subdivision (e) of Section 1358.8.

(f) An issuer may, with the prior approval of the director, offer contracts with new or innovative benefits in addition to the benefits provided in a contract that otherwise complies with the applicable standards. The new or innovative benefits may include benefits that are appropriate to Medicare supplement contracts, that are not otherwise available and that are cost-effective and offered in a manner that is consistent with the goal of simplification of Medicare supplement contracts. On and after January 1, 2006, the innovative benefit shall not include an outpatient prescription drug benefit. (Amended by Stats. 2009, Ch. 10, Sec. 5. Effective July 2, 2009.)

1358.91.

The following standards are applicable to all Medicare supplement contracts delivered or issued for delivery in this state with an effective date on or after June 1, 2010. No contract may be advertised, solicited, delivered, or issued for delivery in this state as a Medicare supplement contract unless it complies with these benefit plan standards. Benefit plan standards applicable to Medicare supplement contracts issued with an effective date before June 1, 2010, remain subject to the requirements of Section 1358.9.

(a) (1) An issuer shall make available to each prospective enrollee and subscriber a contract containing only the basic (core) benefits, as defined in subdivision (b) of Section 1358.81.

(2) If an issuer makes available any of the additional benefits described in subdivision (c) of Section 1358.81, or offers standardized benefit plan K or L, as described in paragraphs (8) and (9) of subdivision (e), then the issuer shall make available to each prospective enrollee and subscriber, in addition to a contract with only the basic (core) benefits as described in paragraph (1), a contract containing either standardized benefit plan C, as described in paragraph (3) of subdivision (e), or standardized benefit plan F, as described in paragraph (5) of subdivision (e).

(b) No groups, packages or combinations of Medicare supplement benefits other than those listed in this section shall be offered for sale in this state, except as may be permitted in subdivision (f) and by Section 1358.10.

(c) Benefit plans shall be uniform in structure, language, designation, and format to the standard benefit plans listed in subdivision (e) and conform to the definitions in Section

1358.4. Each benefit shall be structured in accordance with the format provided in subdivisions (b) and (c) of Section 1358.81; or, in the case of plan K or L, in paragraph (8) or (9) of subdivision (e) of Section 1358.91 and list the benefits in the order shown in subdivision (e). For purposes of this section, "structure, language, and format" means style, arrangement, and overall content of a benefit.

(d) In addition to the benefit plan designations required in subdivision (c), an issuer may use other designations to the extent permitted by law.

(e) With respect to the makeup of 2010 standardized benefit plans, the following shall apply:

(1) Standardized Medicare supplement benefit plan A shall include only the following: the basic (core) benefits as defined in subdivision (b) of Section 1358.81.

(2) Standardized Medicare supplement benefit plan B shall include only the following: the basic (core) benefit as defined in subdivision (b) of Section 1358.81, plus 100 percent of the Medicare Part A deductible as defined in paragraph (1) of subdivision (c) of Section 1358.81.

(3) Standardized Medicare supplement benefit plan C shall include only the following: the basic (core) benefit as defined in subdivision (b) of Section 1358.81, plus 100 percent of the Medicare Part A deductible, skilled nursing facility care, 100 percent of the Medicare Part B deductible, and medically necessary emergency care in a foreign country, as defined in paragraphs (1), (3), (4), and (6) of subdivision (c) of Section 1358.81, respectively.

(4) Standardized Medicare supplement benefit plan D shall include only the following: the basic (core) benefit, as defined in subdivision (b) of Section 1358.81, plus 100 percent of the Medicare Part A deductible, skilled nursing facility care, and medically necessary emergency care in a foreign country, as defined in paragraphs (1), (3), and (6) of subdivision (c) of Section 1358.81, respectively.

(5) Standardized Medicare supplement benefit plan F shall include only the following: the basic (core) benefit as defined in subdivision (b) of Section 1358.81, plus 100 percent of the Medicare Part A deductible, skilled nursing facility care, 100 percent of the Medicare Part B deductible, 100 percent of the Medicare Part B excess charges, and medically necessary emergency care in a foreign country, as defined in paragraphs (1), (3), (4), (5), and (6) of subdivision (c) of Section 1358.81, respectively.

(6) Standardized Medicare supplement benefit high deductible plan F shall include only the following: 100 percent of covered expenses following the payment of the annual deductible set forth in subparagraph (B).

(A) The basic (core) benefit as defined in subdivision (b) of Section 1358.81, plus 100 percent of the Medicare Part A deductible, skilled nursing facility care, 100 percent of the Medicare Part B deductible, 100 percent of the Medicare Part B excess charges, and medically necessary emergency care in a foreign country, as defined in paragraphs (1), (3), (4), (5), and (6) of subdivision (c) of Section 1358.81, respectively.

(B) The annual deductible in high deductible plan F shall consist of out-of-pocket expenses, other than premiums, for services covered by plan F, and shall be in addition to any other specific benefit deductibles. The basis for the deductible shall be one thousand five hundred dollars ($1,500) and shall be adjusted annually from 1999 by the Secretary of the United States Department of Health and Human Services to reflect the change in the Consumer Price Index for all urban consumers for the 12-month period ending with August of the preceding year, and rounded to the nearest multiple of ten dollars ($10).

(7) (A) Standardized Medicare supplement benefit plan G shall include only the following: the basic (core) benefit as defined in subdivision (b) of Section 1358.81, plus 100 percent of the Medicare Part A deductible, skilled nursing facility care, 100 percent of the Medicare Part B excess charges, and medically necessary emergency care in a foreign country, as defined in paragraphs (1), (3), (5), and (6) of subdivision (c) of Section 1358.81, respectively.

(B) Effective January 1, 2020, the standardized benefit plans described in paragraph (4) of subdivision (a) of Section 1358.92 (redesignated high deductible plan G) may be offered to any individual who was eligible for Medicare prior to January 1, 2020.

(8) Standardized Medicare supplement benefit plan K shall include only the following:

(A) Coverage of 100 percent of the Part A hospital coinsurance amount for each day used from the 61st through the 90th day in any Medicare benefit period.

(B) Coverage of 100 percent of the Part A hospital coinsurance amount for each Medicare lifetime inpatient reserve day used from the 91st through the 150th day in any Medicare benefit period.

(C) Upon exhaustion of the Medicare hospital inpatient coverage, including the lifetime reserve days, coverage of 100 percent of the Medicare Part A eligible expenses for hospitalization paid at the applicable prospective payment system (PPS) rate, or other appropriate Medicare standard of payment, subject to a lifetime maximum benefit of an additional 365 days. The provider shall accept the issuer's payment as payment in full and may not bill the insured for any balance.

(D) Coverage for 50 percent of the Medicare Part A inpatient hospital deductible amount per benefit period until the out-of-pocket limitation is met as described in subparagraph (J).

(E) Coverage for 50 percent of the coinsurance amount for each day used from the 21st day through the 100th day in a Medicare benefit period for posthospital skilled nursing facility care eligible under Medicare Part A until the out-of-pocket limitation is met as described in subparagraph (J).

(F) Coverage for 50 percent of cost sharing for all Part A Medicare eligible expenses and respite care until the out-of-pocket limitation is met as described in subparagraph (J).

(G) Coverage for 50 percent, under Medicare Part A or B, of the reasonable cost of the first three pints of blood, or equivalent quantities of packed red blood cells, as defined

under federal regulations, unless replaced in accordance with federal regulations until the out-of-pocket limitation is met as described in subparagraph (J).

(H) Except for coverage provided in subparagraph (I), coverage for 50 percent of the cost sharing otherwise applicable under Medicare Part B after the enrollee or subscriber pays the Part B deductible until the out-of-pocket limitation is met as described in subparagraph (J).

(I) Coverage of 100 percent of the cost sharing for Medicare Part B preventive services after the enrollee or subscriber pays the Part B deductible.

(J) Coverage of 100 percent of all cost sharing under Medicare Parts A and B for the balance of the calendar year after the individual has reached the out-of-pocket limitation on annual expenditures under Medicare Parts A and B of four thousand dollars ($4,000) in 2006, indexed each year by the appropriate inflation adjustment specified by the Secretary of the United States Department of Health and Human Services.

(9) Standardized Medicare supplement benefit plan L shall include only the following:

(A) The benefits described in subparagraphs (A), (B), (C), and (I) of paragraph (8).

(B) The benefits described in subparagraphs (D), (E), (F), (G), and (H) of paragraph (8), but substituting 75 percent for 50 percent.

(C) The benefit described in subparagraph (J) of paragraph (8), but substituting two thousand dollars ($2,000) for four thousand dollars ($4,000).

(10) Standardized Medicare supplement benefit plan M shall include only the following: the basic (core) benefit as defined in subdivision (b) of Section 1358.81, plus 50 percent of the Medicare Part A deductible, skilled nursing facility care, and medically necessary emergency care in a foreign country, as defined in paragraphs (2), (3), and (6) of subdivision (c) of Section 1358.81, respectively.

(11) Standardized Medicare supplement benefit plan N shall include only the following: the basic (core) benefit as defined in subdivision (b) of Section 1358.81, plus 100 percent of the Medicare Part A deductible, skilled nursing facility care, and medically necessary emergency care in a foreign country, as defined in paragraphs (1), (3), and (6) of subdivision (c) of Section 1358.81, respectively, with copayments in the following amounts:

(A) The lesser of twenty dollars ($20) or the Medicare Part B coinsurance or copayment for each covered health care provider office visit, including visits to medical specialists.

(B) The lesser of fifty dollars ($50) or the Medicare Part B coinsurance or copayment for each covered emergency room visit; however, this copayment shall be waived if the enrollee or subscriber is admitted to any hospital and the emergency visit is subsequently covered as a Medicare Part A expense.

(f) An issuer may, with the prior approval of the director, offer contracts with new or innovative benefits, in addition to the standardized benefits provided in a contract that otherwise complies with the applicable standards. The new or innovative benefits shall include only benefits that are appropriate to Medicare supplement contracts, are new or innovative, are not otherwise available, and are cost effective. Approval of new or innovative benefits shall not adversely impact the goal of Medicare supplement simplification. New or innovative benefits shall not include an outpatient prescription drug benefit. New or innovative benefits shall not be used to change or reduce benefits, including a change of any cost-sharing provision, in any standardized plan.
(Amended by Stats. 2019, Ch. 157, Sec. 1. (SB 784) Effective July 30, 2019.)
1358.92.
The following standards are applicable to all Medicare supplement policies or certificates delivered or issued for delivery in this state to individuals newly eligible for Medicare on or after January 1, 2020. No policy or certificate that provides coverage of the Medicare Part B deductible may be advertised, solicited, delivered or issued for delivery in the state as a Medicare supplement policy or certificate to individuals newly eligible for Medicare on or after January 1, 2020. All policies must comply with the following benefit standards. Benefit plan standards applicable to Medicare supplement policies and certificates issued to individuals eligible for Medicare before January 1, 2020, remain subject to the requirements of Section 1358.91 or 1358.9, as applicable.

(a) The standards and requirements of Section 1358.91 shall apply to all Medicare supplement policies or certificates delivered or issued for delivery to individuals newly eligible for Medicare on or after January 1, 2020, with the following exceptions:

(1) Standardized Medicare supplement benefit plan C is redesignated as plan D and shall provide the benefits described in paragraph (3) of subdivision (e) of Section 1358.91 but shall not provide coverage for 100 percent, or any portion, of the Medicare Part B deductible.

(2) Standardized Medicare supplement benefit plan F is redesignated as plan G and shall provide the benefits described in paragraph (5) of subdivision (e) of Section 1358.91, but shall not provide coverage for 100 percent, or any portion, of the Medicare Part B deductible.

(3) Standardized Medicare supplement benefit plans C, F, and high deductible plan F may not be offered to individuals newly eligible for Medicare on or after January 1, 2020.

(4) Standardized Medicare supplement benefit high deductible plan F is redesignated as high deductible plan G and shall provide the benefits described for standardized Medicare supplement benefit high deductible plan F in paragraph (6) of subdivision (e) of Section 1358.91, but shall not provide coverage for 100 percent, or any portion, of the Medicare Part B deductible. The Medicare Part B deductible paid by the beneficiary shall be considered an out-of-pocket expense in meeting the annual deductible under high deductible plan G.

(5) The reference to standardized Medicare supplement benefit plan C or F in paragraph (2) of subdivision (a) of Section 1358.91 shall, for purposes of this section, be deemed a reference to standardized Medicare supplement benefit plan D or G, respectively.

(b) This section shall apply only to individuals who are newly eligible for Medicare on or after January 1, 2020. For purposes of this section, "newly eligible Medicare beneficiary" means an individual who satisfies one of the following:

(1) The individual has attained 65 years of age on or after January 1, 2020.

(2) The individual is entitled to benefits under Medicare Part A pursuant to Section 226(b) or 226A of the Social Security Act, or is deemed eligible for benefits under Section 226(a) of the Social Security Act, on or after January 1, 2020.

(c) For purposes of subdivision (e) of Section 1358.12, in the case of an individual newly eligible for Medicare on or after January 1, 2020, any reference to standardized Medicare supplement benefit plan C, plan F, or high deductible plan F shall be deemed to be a reference to standardized Medicare supplement benefit plan D, plan G, or high deductible plan G, respectively, that meet the requirements of subdivision (a).

(d) On or after January 1, 2020, the standardized Medicare supplement benefit plans described in paragraph (4) of subdivision (a) may be offered to any individual who was eligible for Medicare prior to January 1, 2020, in addition to the standardized Medicare supplement benefit plans described in subdivision (e) of Section 1358.91.

(Added by Stats. 2019, Ch. 157, Sec. 2. (SB 784) Effective July 30, 2019.)

1358.10.

(a) (1) This section shall apply to Medicare Select contracts, as defined in this section.

(2) A contract shall not be advertised as a Medicare Select contract unless it meets the requirements of this section.

(b) For the purposes of this section:

(1) "Complaint" means any dissatisfaction expressed by an individual concerning a Medicare Select issuer or its network providers.

(2) "Grievance" means dissatisfaction expressed in writing by an individual covered by a Medicare Select contract with the administration, claims practices, or provision of services concerning a Medicare Select issuer or its network providers.

(3) "Medicare Select issuer" means an issuer offering, or seeking to offer, a Medicare Select contract.

(4) "Medicare Select contract" means a Medicare supplement contract that contains restricted network provisions.

(5) "Network provider" means a provider of health care, or a group of providers of health care, which has entered into a written agreement with the issuer to provide benefits covered under a Medicare Select contract. "Provider network" means a grouping of network providers.

(6) "Restricted network provision" means any provision which conditions the payment of benefits, in whole or in part, on the use of network providers.

(7) "Service area" means the geographic area approved by the director within which an issuer is authorized to offer a Medicare Select contract.

(c) The director may authorize an issuer to offer a Medicare Select contract pursuant to Section 4358 of the federal Omnibus Budget Reconciliation Act (OBRA) of 1990 if the director finds that the issuer's Medicare Select contracts are in compliance with this chapter and if the director finds that the issuer has satisfied all of the requirements of this section.

(d) A Medicare Select issuer shall not issue a Medicare Select contract in this state until its plan of operation has been approved by the director.

(e) A Medicare Select issuer shall file a proposed plan of operation with the director in a format prescribed by the director. The plan of operation shall contain at least the following information:

(1) Evidence that all covered services that are subject to restricted network provisions are available and accessible through network providers, including a demonstration of all of the following:

(A) That services can be provided by network providers with reasonable promptness with respect to geographic location, hours of operation, and afterhour care. The hours of operation and availability of afterhour care shall reflect usual practice in the local area. Geographic availability shall reflect the usual travel times within the community.

(B) That the number of network providers in the service area is sufficient, with respect to current and expected enrollees, as to either of the following:

(i) To deliver adequately all services that are subject to a restricted network provision.

(ii) To make appropriate referrals.

(C) There are written agreements with network providers describing specific responsibilities.

(D) Emergency care is available 24 hours per day and seven days per week.

(E) In the case of covered services that are subject to a restricted network provision and are provided on a prepaid basis, that there are written agreements with network providers prohibiting the providers from billing or otherwise seeking reimbursement from or recourse against any individual covered under a Medicare Select contract.

This subparagraph shall not apply to supplemental charges or coinsurance amounts as stated in the Medicare Select contract.

(2) A statement or map providing a clear description of the service area.

(3) A description of the grievance procedure to be utilized.

(4) A description of the quality assurance program, including all of the following:

(A) The formal organizational structure.

(B) The written criteria for selection, retention, and removal of network providers.

(C) The procedures for evaluating quality of care provided by network providers, and the process to initiate corrective action when warranted.

(5) A list and description, by specialty, of the network providers.

(6) Copies of the written information proposed to be used by the issuer to comply with subdivision (i).

(7) Any other information requested by the director.

(f) (1) A Medicare Select issuer shall file any proposed changes to the plan of operation, except for changes to the list of network providers, with the director prior to implementing the changes. Changes shall be considered approved by the director after 30 days unless specifically disapproved.

(2) An updated list of network providers shall be filed with the director at least quarterly.

(g) A Medicare Select contract shall not restrict payment for covered services provided by nonnetwork providers if:

(1) The services are for symptoms requiring emergency care or are immediately required for an unforeseen illness, injury, or condition.

(2) It is not reasonable to obtain services through a network provider.

(h) A Medicare Select contract shall provide payment for full coverage under the contract for covered services that are not available through network providers.

(i) A Medicare Select issuer shall make full and fair disclosure in writing of the provisions, restrictions, and limitations of the Medicare Select contract to each applicant. This disclosure shall include at least the following:

(1) An outline of coverage sufficient to permit the applicant to compare the coverage and charges of the Medicare Select contract with both of the following:

(A) Other Medicare supplement contracts offered by the issuer.

(B) Other Medicare Select contracts.

(2) A description, including address, telephone number, and hours of operation, of the network providers, including primary care physicians, specialty physicians, hospitals, and other providers.

(3) A description of the restricted network provisions, including payments for coinsurance and deductibles when providers other than network providers are utilized. The description shall inform the applicant that expenses incurred when using out-of-network providers are excluded from the out-of-pocket annual limit in benefit plans K and L, unless the contract provides otherwise.

(4) A description of coverage for emergency and urgently needed care and other out-of-service area coverage.

(5) A description of limitations on referrals to restricted network providers and to other providers.

(6) A description of the enrollee's rights to purchase any other Medicare supplement contract otherwise offered by the issuer.

(7) A description of the Medicare Select issuer's quality assurance program and grievance procedure.

(j) Prior to the sale of a Medicare Select contract, a Medicare Select issuer shall obtain from the applicant a signed and dated form stating that the applicant has received the information provided pursuant to subdivision (i) and that the applicant understands the restrictions of the Medicare Select contract.

(k) A Medicare Select issuer shall have and use procedures for hearing complaints and resolving written grievances from the enrollees. The procedures shall be aimed at mutual agreement for settlement and may include arbitration procedures.

(1) The grievance procedure shall be described in the contract and in the outline of coverage.

(2) At the time the contract is issued, the issuer shall provide detailed information to the enrollee describing how a grievance may be registered with the issuer.

(3) Grievances shall be considered in a timely manner and shall be transmitted to appropriate decisionmakers who have authority to fully investigate the issue and take corrective action.

(4) If a grievance is found to be valid, corrective action shall be taken promptly.

(5) All concerned parties shall be notified about the results of a grievance.

(6) The issuer shall report no later than each March 31st to the director regarding its grievance procedure. The report shall be in a format prescribed by the director and shall contain the number of grievances filed in the past year and a summary of the subject, nature, and resolution of those grievances.

(l) At the time of initial purchase, a Medicare Select issuer shall make available to each applicant for a Medicare Select contract the opportunity to purchase any Medicare supplement contract otherwise offered by the issuer.

(m) (1) At the request of an enrollee under a Medicare Select contract, a Medicare Select issuer shall make available to the enrollee the opportunity to purchase a Medicare supplement contract offered by the issuer that has comparable or lesser benefits and that does not contain a restricted network provision, if a Medicare supplement contract of that nature is offered by the issuer. The issuer shall make the contracts available without regard to the health status of the enrollee and without requiring evidence of insurability after the Medicare Select contract has been in force for six months.

(2) For the purposes of this subdivision, a Medicare supplement contract will be considered to have comparable or lesser benefits unless it contains one or more significant benefits not included in the Medicare Select contract being replaced. For the purposes of this paragraph, a significant benefit means coverage for the Medicare Part A deductible, coverage for at-home recovery services, or coverage for Medicare Part B excess charges.

(n) Medicare Select contracts shall provide for continuation of coverage in the event the secretary determines that Medicare Select contracts issued pursuant to this section should be discontinued due to either the failure of the Medicare Select program to be reauthorized under law or its substantial amendment.

(1) Each Medicare Select issuer shall make available to each enrollee covered by a Medicare Select contract the opportunity to purchase any Medicare supplement contract offered by the issuer that has comparable or lesser benefits and that does not contain a restricted provider network provision, if a Medicare supplement contract of that nature is offered by the issuer. The issuer shall make the contracts available without regard to the

health status of the enrollee and without requiring evidence of insurability after the Medicare Select contract has been in force for six months.

(2) For the purposes of this subdivision, a Medicare supplement contract will be considered to have comparable or lesser benefits unless it contains one or more significant benefits not included in the Medicare Select contract being replaced. For the purposes of this paragraph, a significant benefit means coverage for the Medicare Part A deductible, coverage for at-home recovery services, or coverage for Medicare Part B excess charges.

(o) An issuer offering Medicare Select contracts shall comply with reasonable requests for data made by state or federal agencies, including the United States Department of Health and Human Services, for the purpose of evaluating the Medicare Select program. An issuer shall not issue a Medicare Select contract in this state until the contract has been approved by the director.

(Amended by Stats. 2005, Ch. 206, Sec. 6. Effective January 1, 2006.)

1358.11.

(a) (1) An issuer shall not deny or condition the offering or effectiveness of any Medicare supplement contract available for sale in this state, nor discriminate in the pricing of a contract because of the health status, claims experience, receipt of health care, or medital condition of an applicant in the case of an application for a contract that is submitted prior to or during the six-month period beginning with the first day of the first month in which an individual is both 65 years of age or older and is enrolled for benefits under Medicare Part B. Each Medicare supplement contract currently available from an issuer shall be made available to all applicants who qualify under this subdivision and who are 65 years of age or older.

(2) (A) An issuer shall make available Medicare supplement benefit plans A, B, C, and F, if currently available, to an applicant who qualifies under this subdivision who is 64 years of age or younger and who does not have end-stage renal disease. An issuer shall also make available to those applicants Medicare supplement benefit plan K or L, if currently available, or Medicare supplement benefit plan M or N, if currently available. The selection between Medicare supplement benefit plan K or L and the selection between Medicare supplement benefit plan M or N shall be made at the issuer's discretion.

(B) For contracts sold or issued on or after January 1, 2020, to newly eligible Medicare beneficiaries, as defined in subdivision (b) of Section 1358.92, an issuer shall make available Medicare supplement benefit plans A, B, D, and G, if currently available, to applicants who qualify under this subdivision who are 64 years of age or younger and who do not have end-stage renal disease. An issuer shall also make available to those applicants Medicare supplement benefit plan K or L, if currently available, or Medicare supplement benefit plan M or N, if currently available. The selection between Medicare supplement benefit plan K or L and the selection between Medicare supplement benefit plan M or N shall be made at the issuer's discretion.

(3) This section and Section 1358.12 do not prohibit an issuer in determining subscriber rates from treating applicants who are under 65 years of age and are eligible for Medicare Part B as a separate risk classification.

(b) (1) If an applicant qualifies under subdivision (a) and submits an application during the time period referenced in subdivision (a) and, as of the date of application, has had a continuous period of creditable coverage of at least six months, the issuer shall not exclude benefits based on a preexisting condition.

(2) If the applicant qualifies under subdivision (a) and submits an application during the time period referenced in subdivision (a) and, as of the date of application, has had a continuous period of creditable coverage that is less than six months, the issuer shall reduce the period of any preexisting condition exclusion by the aggregate of the period of creditable coverage applicable to the applicant as of the enrollment date. The manner of the reduction under this subdivision shall be as specified by the director.

(c) Except as provided in subdivision (b) and Section 1358.23, subdivision (a) shall not be construed as preventing the exclusion of benefits under a contract, during the first six months, based on a preexisting condition for which the enrollee received treatment or was otherwise diagnosed during the six months before the coverage became effective.

(d) An individual enrolled in Medicare by reason of disability shall be entitled to open enrollment described in this section for six months after the date of their enrollment in Medicare Part B, or if notified retroactively of their eligibility for Medicare, for six months following notice of eligibility. Sales during the open enrollment period shall not be discouraged by any means, including the altering of the commission structure.

(e) (1) An individual enrolled in Medicare Part B is entitled to open enrollment described in this section for six months following:

(A) Receipt of a notice of termination or, if no notice is received, the effective date of termination from any employer-sponsored health plan including an employer-sponsored retiree health plan.

(B) Receipt of a notice of loss of eligibility due to the divorce or death of a spouse or, if no notice is received, the effective date of loss of eligibility due to the divorce or death of a spouse, from any employer-sponsored health plan including an employer-sponsored retiree health plan.

(C) Termination of health care services for a military retiree or the retiree's Medicare eligible spouse or dependent as a result of a military base closure or loss of access to health care services because the base no longer offers services or because the individual relocates.

(2) For purposes of this subdivision, "employer-sponsored retiree health plan" includes any coverage for medical expenses, including coverage under the Consolidated Omnibus Budget Reconciliation Act of 1985 (COBRA) and the California Continuation Benefits Replacement Act (Cal-COBRA), that is directly or indirectly sponsored or established by an employer for employees or retirees, their spouses, dependents, or other included covered persons.

(f) An individual enrolled in Medicare Part B is entitled to open enrollment described in this section if the individual was covered under a policy, certificate, or contract providing Medicare supplement coverage but that coverage terminated because the individual established residence at a location not served by the issuer.

(g) (1) An individual whose coverage was terminated by a Medicare Advantage plan shall be entitled to an additional 60-day open enrollment period to be added on to and run consecutively after any open enrollment period authorized by federal law or regulation, for any and all Medicare supplement coverage available on a guaranteed basis under state and federal law or regulations for persons terminated by their Medicare Advantage plan.

(2) Health plans that terminate Medicare enrollees shall notify those enrollees in the termination notice of the additional open enrollment period authorized by this subdivision. Health plan notices shall inform enrollees of the opportunity to secure advice and assistance from the HICAP in their area, along with the toll-free telephone number for HICAP.

(h) (1) An individual shall be entitled to an annual open enrollment period lasting 30 days or more, commencing with the individual's birthday, during which time that person may purchase any Medicare supplement coverage that offers benefits equal to or lesser than those provided by the previous coverage. During this open enrollment period, no issuer that falls under this provision shall deny or condition the issuance or effectiveness of Medicare supplement coverage, nor discriminate in the pricing of coverage, because of health status, claims experience, receipt of health care, or medical condition of the individual if, at the time of the open enrollment period, the individual is covered under another Medicare supplement policy, certificate, or contract. An issuer that offers Medicare supplement contracts shall notify an enrollee of their rights under this subdivision at least 30 and no more than 60 days before the beginning of the open enrollment period.

(2) For purposes of this subdivision, the following provisions shall apply:

(A) A 1990 standardized Medicare supplement benefit plan A shall be deemed to offer benefits equal to those provided by a 2010 standardized Medicare supplement benefit plan A.

(B) A 1990 standardized Medicare supplement benefit plan B shall be deemed to offer benefits equal to those provided by a 2010 standardized Medicare supplement benefit plan B.

(C) A 1990 standardized Medicare supplement benefit plan C shall be deemed to offer benefits equal to those provided by a 2010 standardized Medicare supplement benefit plan C.

(D) A 1990 standardized Medicare supplement benefit plan D shall be deemed to offer benefits equal to those provided by a 2010 standardized Medicare supplement benefit plan D.

(E) A 1990 standardized Medicare supplement benefit plan E shall be deemed to offer benefits equal to those provided by a 2010 standardized Medicare benefit plan D.

(F) (i) A 1990 standardized Medicare supplement benefit plan F shall be deemed to offer benefits equal to those provided by a 2010 standardized Medicare benefit plan F.

(ii) A 1990 standardized Medicare supplement benefit high deductible plan F shall be deemed to offer benefits equal to those provided by a 2010 standardized Medicare supplement benefit high deductible plan F.

(G) A 1990 standardized Medicare supplement benefit plan G shall be deemed to offer benefits equal to those provided by a 2010 standardized Medicare supplement benefit plan G.

(H) A 1990 standardized Medicare supplement benefit plan H shall be deemed to offer benefits equal to those provided by a 2010 standardized Medicare supplement benefit plan D.

(I) A 1990 standardized Medicare supplement benefit plan I shall be deemed to offer benefits equal to those provided by a 2010 standardized Medicare supplement benefit plan G.

(J) (i) A 1990 standardized Medicare supplement benefit plan J shall be deemed to offer benefits equal to those provided by a 2010 standardized Medicare supplement benefit plan F.

(ii) A 1990 standardized Medicare supplement benefit high deductible plan J shall be deemed to offer benefits equal to those provided by a 2010 standardized Medicare supplement benefit high deductible plan F.

(K) A 1990 standardized Medicare supplement benefit plan K shall be deemed to offer benefits equal to those provided by a 2010 standardized Medicare supplement benefit plan K.

(L) A 1990 standardized Medicare supplement benefit plan L shall be deemed to offer benefits equal to those provided by a 2010 standardized Medicare supplement benefit plan L.

(i) An individual enrolled in Medicare Part B is entitled to open enrollment described in this section upon being notified that, because of an increase in the individual's income or assets, they meet one of the following requirements:

(1) They are no longer eligible for Medi-Cal benefits.

(2) They are only eligible for Medi-Cal benefits with a share of cost and certifies at the time of application that they have not met the share of cost.

(Amended by Stats. 2019, Ch. 157, Sec. 3. (SB 784) Effective July 30, 2019.)

1358.12.

(a) (1) With respect to the guaranteed issue of a Medicare supplement contract, eligible persons are those individuals described in subdivision (b) who seek to enroll under the contract during the period specified in subdivision (c), and who submit evidence of the date of termination or disenrollment or enrollment in Medicare Part D with the application for a Medicare supplement contract.

(2) With respect to eligible persons, an issuer shall not take any of the following actions:

(A) Deny or condition the issuance or effectiveness of a Medicare supplement contract described in subdivision (e) that is offered and is available for issuance to new enrollees by the issuer.

(B) Discriminate in the pricing of that Medicare supplement contract because of health status, claims experience, receipt of health care, or medical condition.

(C) Impose an exclusion of benefits based on a preexisting condition under that Medicare supplement contract.

(b) An eligible person is an individual described in any of the following paragraphs:

(1) The individual is enrolled under an employee welfare benefit plan that provides health benefits that supplement the benefits under Medicare and either of the following applies:

(A) The plan either terminates or ceases to provide all of those supplemental health benefits to the individual.

(B) The employer no longer provides the individual with insurance that covers all of the payment for the 20-percent coinsurance.

(2) The individual is enrolled with a Medicare Advantage organization under a Medicare Advantage plan under Medicare Part C, and any of the following circumstances apply:

(A) The certification of the organization or plan has been terminated.

(B) The organization has terminated or otherwise discontinued providing the plan in the area in which the individual resides.

(C) The individual is no longer eligible to elect the plan because of a change in the individual's place of residence or other change in circumstances specified by the secretary. Those changes in circumstances shall not include termination of the individual's enrollment on the basis described in Section 1851(g)(3)(B) of the federal Social Security Act where the individual has not paid premiums on a timely basis or has engaged in disruptive behavior as specified in standards under Section 1856 of the federal Social Security Act, or the plan is terminated for all individuals within a residence area.

(D) (i) The Medicare Advantage plan in which the individual is enrolled reduces any of its benefits or increases the amount of cost sharing or premium or discontinues for other than good cause relating to quality of care, its relationship or contract under the plan with a provider who is currently furnishing services to the individual. An individual shall be eligible under this subparagraph for a Medicare supplement contract issued by the same issuer through which the individual was enrolled at the time the reduction, increase, or discontinuance described above occurs or, commencing January 1, 2007, for one issued by a subsidiary of the parent company of that issuer or by a network that contracts with the parent company of that issuer. If no Medicare supplement contract is available to the individual from the same issuer, a subsidiary of the parent company of the issuer, or a network that contracts with the parent company of the issuer, the individual shall be eligible for a Medicare supplement contract pursuant to paragraph (1) of subdivision (e) issued by any issuer, if the Medicare Advantage plan in which the individual is enrolled does any of the following:

(I) Increases the premium by 15 percent or more.

(II) Increases physician, hospital, or drug copayments by 15 percent or more.

(III) Reduces any benefits under the plan.

(IV) Discontinues, for other than good cause relating to quality of care, its relationship or contract under the plan with a provider who is currently furnishing services to the individual.

(ii) Enrollment in a Medicare supplement contract from an issuer unaffiliated with the issuer of the Medicare Advantage plan in which the individual is enrolled shall be permitted only during the annual election period for a Medicare Advantage plan, except where the Medicare Advantage plan has discontinued its relationship with a provider currently furnishing services to the individual. Nothing in this section shall be construed to authorize an individual to enroll in a group Medicare supplement policy if the individual does not meet the eligibility requirements for the group.

(E) The individual demonstrates, in accordance with guidelines established by the secretary, either of the following:

(i) The organization offering the plan substantially violated a material provision of the organization's contract under this article in relation to the individual, including the failure to provide on a timely basis medically necessary care for which benefits are available under the plan or the failure to provide the covered care in accordance with applicable quality standards.

(ii) The organization, or agent or other entity acting on the organization's behalf, materially misrepresented the plan's provisions in marketing the plan to the individual.

(F) The individual meets other exceptional conditions as the secretary may provide.

(3) The individual is 65 years of age or older, is enrolled with a Program of All-Inclusive Care for the Elderly (PACE) provider under Section 1894 of the federal Social Security Act, and circumstances similar to those described in paragraph (2) exist that would permit discontinuance of the individual's enrollment with the provider, if the individual were enrolled in a Medicare Advantage plan.

(4) The individual meets both of the following conditions:

(A) The individual is enrolled with any of the following:

(i) An eligible organization under a contract under Section 1876 of the federal Social Security Act (Medicare cost).

(ii) A similar organization operating under demonstration project authority, effective for periods before April 1, 1999.

(iii) An organization under an agreement under Section 1833(a)(1)(A) of the federal Social Security Act (health care prepayment plan).

(iv) An organization under a Medicare Select policy.

(B) The enrollment ceases under the same circumstances that would permit discontinuance of an individual's election of coverage under paragraph (2) or (3).

(5) The individual is enrolled under a Medicare supplement contract, and the enrollment ceases because of any of the following circumstances:

(A) The insolvency of the issuer or bankruptcy of the nonissuer organization, or other involuntary termination of coverage or enrollment under the contract.

(B) The issuer of the contract substantially violated a material provision of the contract.

(C) The issuer, or an agent or other entity acting on the issuer's behalf, materially misrepresented the contract's provisions in marketing the contract to the individual.

(6) The individual meets both of the following conditions:

(A) The individual was enrolled under a Medicare supplement contract and terminates enrollment and subsequently enrolls, for the first time, with any Medicare Advantage organization under a Medicare Advantage plan under Medicare Part C, any eligible organization under a contract under Section 1876 of the federal Social Security Act (Medicare cost), any similar organization operating under demonstration project authority, any PACE provider under Section 1894 of the federal Social Security Act, or a Medicare Select policy.

(B) The subsequent enrollment under subparagraph (A) is terminated by the individual during any period within the first 12 months of the subsequent enrollment (during which the enrollee is permitted to terminate the subsequent enrollment under Section 1851(e) of the federal Social Security Act).

(7) The individual upon first becoming eligible for benefits under Medicare Part A at 65 years of age, enrolls in a Medicare Advantage plan under Medicare Part C or with a PACE provider under Section 1894 of the federal Social Security Act, and disenrolls from the plan or program not later than 12 months after the effective date of enrollment.

(8) The individual while enrolled under a Medicare supplement contract that covers outpatient prescription drugs enrolls in a Medicare Part D plan during the initial enrollment period, terminates enrollment in the Medicare supplement contract, and submits evidence of enrollment in Medicare Part D along with the application for a contract described in paragraph (4) of subdivision (e).

(c) (1) In the case of an individual described in paragraph (1) of subdivision (b), the guaranteed issue period begins on the later of the following two dates and ends on the date that is 63 days after the date the applicable coverage terminated:

(A) The date the individual receives a notice of termination or cessation of all supplemental health benefits or, if no notice is received, the date of the notice denying a claim because of a termination or cessation of benefits.

(B) The date that the applicable coverage terminates or ceases.

(2) In the case of an individual described in paragraphs (2), (3), (4), (6), and (7) of subdivision (b) whose enrollment is terminated involuntarily, the guaranteed issue period begins on the date that the individual receives a notice of termination and ends 63 days after the date the applicable coverage is terminated.

(3) In the case of an individual described in subparagraph (A) of paragraph (5) of subdivision (b), the guaranteed issue period begins on the earlier of the following two dates and ends on the date that is 63 days after the date the coverage is terminated:

(A) The date that the individual receives a notice of termination, a notice of the issuer's bankruptcy or insolvency, or other similar notice if any.

(B) The date that the applicable coverage is terminated.

(4) In the case of an individual described in paragraph (2), (3), (6), or (7) of, or in subparagraph (B) or (C) of paragraph (5) of, subdivision (b) who disenrolls voluntarily, the guaranteed issue period begins on the date that is 60 days before the effective date of the disenrollment and ends on the date that is 63 days after the effective date of the disenrollment.

(5) In the case of an individual described in paragraph (8) of subdivision (b), the guaranteed issue period begins on the date the individual receives notice pursuant to Section 1882(v)(2)(B) of the federal Social Security Act from the Medicare supplement issuer during the 60-day period immediately preceding the initial enrollment period for Medicare Part D and ends on the date that is 63 days after the effective date of the individual's coverage under Medicare Part D.

(6) In the case of an individual described in subdivision (b) who is not included in this subdivision, the guaranteed issue period begins on the effective date of disenrollment and ends on the date that is 63 days after the effective date of disenrollment.

(d) (1) In the case of an individual described in paragraph (6) of subdivision (b), or deemed to be so described pursuant to this paragraph, whose enrollment with an organization or provider described in subparagraph (A) of paragraph (6) of subdivision (b) is involuntarily terminated within the first 12 months of enrollment and who, without an intervening enrollment, enrolls with another such organization or provider, the subsequent enrollment shall be deemed to be an initial enrollment described in paragraph (6) of subdivision (b).

(2) In the case of an individual described in paragraph (7) of subdivision (b), or deemed to be so described pursuant to this paragraph, whose enrollment with a plan or in a program described in paragraph (7) of subdivision (b) is involuntarily terminated within the first 12 months of enrollment and who, without an intervening enrollment, enrolls in another such plan or program, the subsequent enrollment shall be deemed to be an initial enrollment described in paragraph (7) of subdivision (b).

(3) For purposes of paragraphs (6) and (7) of subdivision (b), an enrollment of an individual with an organization or provider described in subparagraph (A) of paragraph (6) of subdivision (b), or with a plan or in a program described in paragraph (7) of subdivision (b), shall not be deemed to be an initial enrollment under this paragraph after

the two-year period beginning on the date on which the individual first enrolled with such an organization, provider, plan, or program.

(e) (1) Under paragraphs (1), (2), (3), (4), and (5) of subdivision (b), an eligible individual is entitled to a Medicare supplement contract that has a benefit package classified as Plan A, B, C, F (including a high deductible Plan F), K, L, M, or N offered by any issuer.

(2) (A) Under paragraph (6) of subdivision (b), an eligible individual is entitled to the same Medicare supplement contract in which he or she was most recently enrolled, if available from the same issuer. If that contract is not available, the eligible individual is entitled to a Medicare supplement contract that has a benefit package classified as Plan A, B, C, F (including a high deductible Plan F), K, L, M, or N offered by any issuer.

(B) On and after January 1, 2006, an eligible individual described in this paragraph who was most recently enrolled in a Medicare supplement contract with an outpatient prescription drug benefit, is entitled to a Medicare supplement contract that is available from the same issuer but without an outpatient prescription drug benefit or, at the election of the individual, has a benefit package classified as a Plan A, B, C, F (including high deductible Plan F), K, L, M, or N that is offered by any issuer.

(3) Under paragraph (7) of subdivision (b), an eligible individual is entitled to any Medicare supplement contract offered by any issuer.

(4) Under paragraph (8) of subdivision (b), an eligible individual is entitled to a Medicare supplement contract that has a benefit package classified as Plan A, B, C, F (including a high deductible Plan F), K, L, M, or N and that is offered and is available for issuance to a new enrollee by the same issuer that issued the individual's Medicare supplement contract with outpatient prescription drug coverage.

(f) (1) At the time of an event described in subdivision (b) by which an individual loses coverage or benefits due to the termination of a contract or agreement, policy, or plan, the organization that terminates the contract or agreement, the issuer terminating the policy or contract, or the administrator of the plan being terminated, respectively, shall notify the individual of his or her rights under this section and of the obligations of issuers of Medicare supplement contracts under subdivision (a). The notice shall be communicated contemporaneously with the notification of termination.

(2) At the time of an event described in subdivision (b) by which an individual ceases enrollment under a contract or agreement, policy, or plan, the organization that offers the contract or agreement, regardless of the basis for the cessation of enrollment, the issuer offering the policy or contract, or the administrator of the plan, respectively, shall notify the individual of his or her rights under this section, and of the obligations of issuers of Medicare supplement contracts under subdivision (a). The notice shall be communicated within 10 working days of the date the issuer received notification of disenrollment.

(g) An issuer shall refund any unearned premium that an enrollee or subscriber paid in advance and shall terminate coverage upon the request of an enrollee or subscriber.

(Amended by Stats. 2011, Ch. 270, Sec. 2. (AB 151) Effective January 1, 2012.)

1358.13.

(a) An issuer shall comply with Section 1882(c)(3) of the federal Social Security Act (as enacted by Section 4081(b)(2)(C) of the federal Omnibus Budget Reconciliation Act of 1987 (OBRA), Public Law 100-203) by doing all of the following:

(1) Accepting a notice from a Medicare Administrative Contractor, formerly known as a fiscal intermediary or carrier, on dually assigned claims submitted by participating physicians and suppliers as a claim for benefits in place of any other claim form otherwise required and making a payment determination on the basis of the information contained in that notice.

(2) Notifying the participating physician or supplier and the beneficiary of the payment determination.

(3) Paying the participating physician or supplier directly.

(4) Furnishing, at the time of enrollment, each enrollee with a card listing the contract name, number, and a central mailing address to which notices respecting coverage from a Medicare Administrative Contractor may be sent.

(5) Paying user fees established under Section 1395u(h)(3)(B) of Title 42 of the United States Code, for claim notices that are transmitted electronically or otherwise.

(6) Providing to the secretary, at least annually, a central mailing address to which all claims may be sent by Medicare Administrative Contractors.

(b) Compliance with the requirements set forth in subdivision (a) shall be certified on the Medicare supplement insurance experience reporting form provided by the director.

(Amended by Stats. 2009, Ch. 10, Sec. 9. Effective July 2, 2009.)

1358.14.

(a) (1) (A) With respect to loss ratio standards, a Medicare supplement contract shall not be advertised, solicited, or issued for delivery unless the contract can be expected, as estimated for the entire period for which prepaid or periodic charges are computed to provide coverage, to return to subscribers and enrollees in the form of aggregate benefits under the contract, not including anticipated refunds or credits provided under the contract, at least 75 percent of the aggregate amount of charges earned in the case of group contracts, or at least 65 percent of the aggregate amount of charges earned in the case of individual contracts, on the basis of incurred claims or costs of health care services experience and earned prepaid or periodic charges for that period and in accordance with accepted actuarial principles and practices.

(B) Loss ratio standards shall be calculated on the basis of incurred health care expenses where coverage is provided by a health care service plan on a service rather than reimbursement basis, and earned prepaid or periodic charges shall be calculated for the period and in accordance with accepted actuarial principles and practices. Incurred health care expenses where coverage is provided by a health care service plan shall not include any of the following:

(i) Home office and overhead costs.

(ii) Advertising costs.

(iii) Commissions and other acquisition costs.

(iv) Taxes.

(v) Capital costs.

(vi) Administrative costs.

(vii) Claims processing costs.

(2) All filings of rates and rating schedules shall demonstrate that expected claims in relation to prepaid or periodic charges comply with the requirements of this section when combined with actual experience to date. Filings of rate revisions shall also demonstrate that the anticipated loss ratio over the entire future period for which the revised rates are computed to provide coverage can be expected to meet the appropriate loss ratio standards.

(3) For purposes of applying paragraph (1) of subdivision (a) and paragraph (3) of subdivision (d) of Section 1358.15 only, contracts issued as a result of solicitations of individuals through the mail or by mass media advertising, including both print and broadcast advertising, shall be deemed to be individual contracts.

(b) (1) With respect to refund or credit calculations, an issuer shall collect and file with the director by May 31 of each year the data contained in the applicable reporting form required by the director (NAIC Appendix A) for each type of coverage in a standard Medicare supplement benefit plan.

(2) If on the basis of the experience as reported the benchmark ratio since inception (ratio 1) exceeds the adjusted experience ratio since inception (ratio 3), then a refund or credit calculation is required. The refund calculation shall be done on a statewide basis for each type of contract offered by the issuer. For purposes of the refund or credit calculation, experience on contracts issued within the reporting year shall be excluded.

(3) For the purposes of this section, with respect to contracts advertised, solicited, or issued for delivery prior to January 1, 2001, the issuer shall make the refund or credit calculation separately for all individual contracts, including all group contracts subject to an individual loss ratio standard when issued, combined and all other group contracts combined for experience after January 1, 2001. The first report pursuant to paragraph (1) shall be due by May 31, 2003.

(4) A refund or credit shall be made only when the benchmark loss ratio exceeds the adjusted experience loss ratio and the amount to be refunded or credited exceeds ten dollars ($10). The refund shall include interest from the end of the calendar year to the date of the refund or credit at a rate specified by the secretary, but in no event shall it be less than the average rate of interest for 13-week Treasury notes. A refund or credit against prepaid or periodic charges due shall be made by September 30 following the experience year upon which the refund or credit is based.

(c) An issuer of Medicare supplement contracts shall file annually its prepaid or periodic charges and supporting documentation including ratios of incurred losses to earned prepaid or periodic charges by contract duration for approval by the director in accordance with the filing requirements and procedures prescribed by the director. The supporting documentation shall also demonstrate in accordance with actuarial standards of practice using reasonable assumptions that the appropriate loss ratio standards can be expected to be met over the entire period for which charges are computed. The demonstration shall exclude active life reserves. An expected third-year loss ratio that is greater than or equal to the applicable percentage shall be demonstrated for contracts in force less than three years.

As soon as practicable, but prior to the effective date of enhancements in Medicare benefits, every issuer of Medicare supplement contracts shall file with the director, in accordance with applicable filing procedures, all of the following:

(1) (A) Appropriate prepaid or periodic charge adjustments necessary to produce loss ratios as anticipated for the current charge for the applicable contracts. The supporting documents necessary to justify the adjustment shall accompany the filing.

(B) An issuer shall make prepaid or periodic charge adjustments necessary to produce an expected loss ratio under the contract to conform to minimum loss ratio standards for Medicare supplement contracts and that are expected to result in a loss ratio at least as great as that originally anticipated in the rates used to produce current charges by the issuer for the Medicare supplement contracts. No charge adjustment that would modify the loss ratio experience under the contract other than the adjustments described in this section shall be made with respect to a contract at any time other than upon its renewal date or anniversary date.

(C) If an issuer fails to make prepaid or periodic charge adjustments acceptable to the director, the director may order charge adjustments, refunds, or credits deemed necessary to achieve the loss ratio required by this section.

(2) Any appropriate contract amendments needed to accomplish the Medicare supplement contract modifications necessary to eliminate benefit duplications with Medicare. The contract amendments shall provide a clear description of the Medicare supplement benefits provided by the contract.

(d) (1) The director may conduct a public hearing to gather information concerning a request by an issuer for an increase in a rate for a contract form issued before or after the effective date of January 1, 2001, if the experience of the form for the previous reporting period is not in compliance with the applicable loss ratio standard. The determination of compliance is made without consideration of any refund or credit for the reporting period. Public notice of the hearing shall be furnished in a manner deemed appropriate by the director.

(2) The director may conduct a public hearing to gather information if the experience of the form filed under paragraph (1) of subdivision (b) for the previous reporting period is not in compliance with the applicable loss ratio standard.

The determination of compliance is made without consideration of any refund or credit for the reporting period. Public notice of the hearing shall be furnished in a manner deemed appropriate by the director.
(Amended by Stats. 2005, Ch. 206, Sec. 10. Effective January 1, 2006.)
1358.145.
(a) The calculation of actual or expected loss ratios shall be pursuant to the formula in subdivision (a) of Section 1358.14, and pursuant to definitions, procedures, and other provisions as may be deemed by the director, with due consideration of the circumstances of the particular issuer, to be fair, reasonable, and consistent with the objectives of this chapter.
(b) Each issuer shall submit to the department a copy of the calculations for the actual or expected loss ratio as required by Section 1358.14. The calculations shall include the following data: the actual loss ratio for the entire period in which the contract has been in force, as well as for the immediate past three years and for each year in which the contract has been in force, the scale of prepaid or periodic charges for the loss ratio calculation period, a description of all assumptions, the formula used to calculate gross prepaid or periodic charges, the expected level of earned prepaid or periodic charges in the loss ratio calculation period, and the expected level of incurred claims for reimbursement, including paid claims and incurred but not paid claims, in the loss ratio calculation period. The calculations shall be accompanied by an actuarial certification, consisting of a signed declaration of an actuary who is a member in good standing of the American Academy of Actuaries in which the actuary states that the assumptions used in calculating the expected loss ratio are appropriate and reasonable, taking into account that the calculations are in accordance with the provisions of subdivision (a) and the provisions referred to therein. In addition, the director may require the issuer to submit actuarial certification, as described above, by one or more unaffiliated actuaries acceptable to the director.
(c) Notwithstanding the calculations required by subdivision (b), contracts shall be deemed to comply with the loss ratio standards if, and shall be deemed not to comply with the loss standards unless: (1) for the most recent year, the ratio of the incurred losses to earned prepaid charges for contracts that have been in force for three years or more is greater than or equal to the applicable percentages contained in this section; and (2) the expected losses in relation to charges over the entire period for which the contract is rated comply with the requirements of this section. An expected third-year loss ratio that is greater than or equal to the applicable percentage shall be demonstrated for contracts in force less than three years.
(Added by Stats. 2000, Ch. 706, Sec. 2. Effective January 1, 2001.)
1358.146.
The following format shall be used for reporting loss ratio experience:

MEDICARE SUPPLEMENT HEALTH CARE SERVICE PLAN CONTRACT EXPERIENCE EXHIBIT

For the year ended December 31, 20__.
For the State of California.

Of the _____ health care service plan.
Address (City, State, and Zip Code) _____
Person Completing this Exhibit _____
To be filed by June 30th following the filing under Section 1358.14 of the Health and Safety Code.

		Costs for Health Care Services	
	Prepaid or		Percentage
	Periodic		of Prepaid
	Charges		or Periodic
Classification	Earned	Amount	Charges Earned

Experience on
Individual Plan
Contracts

1. _____ Contracts issued
_____ through 20__

_____ Reporting State
_____ Nationwide

2. _____ Contracts issued
_____ after 20__

_____ Reporting State
_____ Nationwide

Experience on Group
Plan Contracts

1. _____ Contracts Issued
_____ through 20__

_____ Reporting State
_____ Nationwide

2. _____ Contracts Issued
_____ after 20__

_____ Reporting State
_____ Nationwide

The undersigned officer hereby certifies that the company named above has complied with the requirements contained in the federal Omnibus Budget Reconciliation Act of 1987, Section 4081.
Signature
Title and name (please type)

INSTRUCTIONS FOR COMPLETING MEDICARE SUPPLEMENT HEALTH CARE SERVICE PLAN CONTRACT EXPERIENCE EXHIBIT

1. Experience on plan contracts issued more than three years prior to the reporting year should be shown separately as indicated on the form. For example, for the reporting year ended 12/31/88 (filed on June 30, 1989), experience on plan contracts issued in 1985 and prior should be shown separately from that of plan contracts issued in 1986 and later. For group coverage, the year of issue should be based on when the contract was issued if available; otherwise use the master plan contract year of issue.
2. Allocation of reserves on a state-by-state basis should be on sound actuarial principles and be consistent from year to year.
3. Membership or plan contract fees, if any, constitute, and should be included with, prepaid or periodic charges earned. Earned prepaid or periodic charges may be shown on an annual basis net of loadings for nonannual modes.
4. Mass marketing group coverage subject to individual loss ratio standards should be included with individual plan contracts.
5. Any dividends paid to subscribers should be included with costs for health care.
6. Neither costs for health care services nor earned prepaid or periodic charges should be adjusted for changes in plan contract (additional) reserves.

DEFINITIONS

For purposes of this form:
1. "Costs for health care services" means payment for health care services plus the increase in claim reserves. Claim reserves include only those unpaid liabilities for claims that have already been incurred. Costs for health care services in this exhibit do not include plan contract additional reserves.
(Added by Stats. 2000, Ch. 706, Sec. 2. Effective January 1, 2001.)
1358.15.
(a) An issuer shall not advertise, solicit, or issue for delivery a Medicare supplement contract to a resident of this state unless the contract has been filed with and approved by the director in accordance with filing requirements and procedures prescribed by the director. Until January 1, 2001, or 90 days after approval of Medicare supplement contracts submitted for approval pursuant to this section, whichever is later, issuers may continue to offer and market previously approved Medicare supplement contracts.
(b) An issuer shall file any riders or amendments to contract forms to delete outpatient prescription drug benefits, as required by the Medicare Prescription Drug, Improvement, and Modernization Act of 2003 (P.L. 108-173), only in the state where the contract was issued.
(c) An issuer shall not use or change prepaid or periodic charges for a Medicare supplement contract unless the charges and supporting documentation have been filed with and approved by the director in accordance with the filing requirements and procedures prescribed by the director.
(d) (1) Except as provided in paragraph (2), an issuer shall not file for approval more than one contract of each type for each standard Medicare supplement benefit plan.

(2) An issuer may offer, with the approval of the director, up to four additional contracts of the same type for the same standard Medicare supplement benefit plan, one for each of the following cases:

(A) The inclusion of new or innovative benefits.

(B) The addition of either direct response or agent marketing methods.

(C) The addition of either guaranteed issue or underwritten coverage.

(D) The offering of coverage to individuals eligible for Medicare by reason of disability.

(3) For the purposes of this section, a "type" means an individual contract, a group contract, an individual Medicare Select contract, or a group Medicare Select contract.

(e) (1) Except as provided in subdivision (a), an issuer shall continue to make available for purchase any contract issued after January 1, 2001, that has been approved by the director. A contract shall not be considered to be available for purchase unless the issuer has actively offered it for sale in the previous 12 months.

(A) An issuer may discontinue the availability of a contract if the issuer provides to the director in writing its decision at least 30 days prior to discontinuing the availability of the form of the contract. After receipt of the notice by the director, the issuer shall no longer offer for sale the contract in this state.

(B) An issuer that discontinues the availability of a contract pursuant to subparagraph (A) shall not file for approval a new contract of the same type for the same standard Medicare supplement benefit plan as the discontinued contract for a period of five years after the issuer provides notice to the director of the discontinuance. The period of discontinuance may be reduced if the director determines that a shorter period is appropriate.

(2) The sale or other transfer of Medicare supplement business to another issuer shall be considered a discontinuance for the purposes of this section.

(3) A change in the rating structure or methodology shall be considered a discontinuance under paragraph (1) unless the issuer complies with the following requirements:

(A) The issuer provides an actuarial memorandum, in a form and manner prescribed by the director, describing the manner in which the revised rating methodology and resultant rates differ from the existing rating methodology and existing rates.

(B) The issuer does not subsequently put into effect a change of rates or rating factors that would cause the percentage differential between the discontinued and subsequent rates as described in the actuarial memorandum to change. The director may approve a change to the differential that is in the public interest.

(f) (1) Except as provided in paragraph (2), the experience of all contracts of the same type in a standard Medicare supplement benefit plan shall be combined for purposes of the refund or credit calculation prescribed in Section 1358.14.

(2) Contracts assumed under an assumption reinsurance agreement shall not be combined with the experience of other contracts for purposes of the refund or credit calculation.

(g) A Medicare supplement contract shall be deemed not to be fair, just, or consistent with the objectives of this chapter at all times, and shall not be advertised, solicited, or issued for delivery at any time, except during that period of time, if any, beginning with the date of receipt by the plan of notification by the director that the provisions of the contract are deemed to be fair, just, and consistent with the objectives of this chapter, and ending with the earlier to occur of the events indicated in subdivision (h).

(h) The period of time indicated in subdivision (g) shall terminate at the earlier to occur of (1) receipt by the plan of written revocation by the director of the immediate past notification referred to in subdivision (g) specifying the basis for the revocation, (2) the last day of the prepaid or periodic charge calculation period, that in no event may exceed one year, or (3) June 30, of the next succeeding calendar year.

(i) An issuer shall secure the director's review of a contract subject to this article by submitting, not less than 30 days prior to any proposed advertising or other use of the contract not already protected by a currently effective notice under subdivision (g), the following for the director's review:

(1) A copy of the contract.

(2) A copy of the disclosure form.

(3) A representation that the contract complies with the provisions of this chapter and the rules adopted thereunder.

(4) A completed copy of the "Medicare Supplement Health Care Service Plan Contract Experience Exhibit" set forth in Section 1358.145.

(5) A copy of the calculations for the actual or expected loss ratio.

(6) Supporting data used in calculating the actual or expected loss ratio as indicated in Section 1358.14.

(7) An actuarial certification, as specified in Section 1358.14, of the loss ratio computations.

(8) If required by the director, actuarial certification, as specified in Section 1358.14, of the loss ratio computations by one or more unaffiliated actuaries acceptable to the director.

(9) An undertaking by the issuer to notify the subscribers in writing within 60 days of decertification, if the contract is identified as a certified contract at the time of sale and later decertified.

(10) A signed statement of the president of the issuer or other officer of the issuer designated by that person attesting that the information submitted for review is accurate and complete and does not misrepresent any material fact.

(j) An issuer that submits information pursuant to subdivision (i) shall provide any additional information as may be requested by the director to enable the director to conclude that the contract complies with the provisions of this chapter and rules adopted thereunder.

(k) For the purposes of this section, the term "decertified," as applied to a contract, means that the director by written notice has found that the contract no longer complies with the provisions of this chapter and the rules adopted thereunder and has revoked the prior authorization to display on the contract the emblem indicating certification.

(l) Benefits designed to cover cost-sharing amounts under Medicare will be changed automatically to coincide with any changes in the applicable Medicare deductible amount and copayment percentage factors and the amount of prepaid charges may be modified, as indicated in paragraph (6) of subdivision (a) of Section 1300.67.4 of Title 28 of the California Code of Regulations, to correspond with those changes.

(Amended by Stats. 2005, Ch. 206, Sec. 11. Effective January 1, 2006.)

1358.16.

(a) An issuer or other entity may provide a commission or other compensation to a solicitor or other representative for the sale of a Medicare supplement contract only if the first year commission or other first year compensation is no more than 200 percent of the commission or other compensation paid for selling or servicing the contract in the second year or period.

(b) The commission or other compensation provided in subsequent renewal years shall be the same as that provided in the second year or period and shall be provided for no fewer than five renewal years.

(c) No issuer shall provide compensation to a solicitor or solicitor firm, and no solicitor or solicitor firm shall receive compensation, greater than the renewal compensation payable by the replacing issuer on renewal contracts if an existing contract is replaced.

(d) For purposes of this section, "commission" or "compensation" includes pecuniary or nonpecuniary remuneration of any kind relating to the sale or renewal of the contract, including, but not limited to, bonuses, gifts, prizes, awards, and finders' fees.

(Amended by Stats. 2005, Ch. 206, Sec. 12. Effective January 1, 2006.)

1358.17.

(a) (1) Medicare supplement contracts shall include a renewal or continuation provision. The language or specifications of the provision shall be consistent with subdivision (a) of Section 1365 and the rules adopted thereunder. The provision shall be appropriately captioned and shall appear on the first page of the contract, and shall include any reservation by the issuer of the right to change prepaid or periodic charges and any automatic renewal increases based on the enrollee's age.

(2) The contract shall contain the provisions required to be set forth by Section 1300.67.4 of Title 28 of the California Code of Regulations.

(b) (1) Except for contract amendments by which the issuer effectuates a request made in writing by the enrollee, exercises a specifically reserved right under a Medicare supplement contract, or is required to reduce or eliminate benefits to avoid duplication of Medicare benefits, all amendments to a Medicare supplement contract after the date of issue or upon reinstatement or renewal that reduce or eliminate benefits or coverage in the contract shall require a signed acceptance by the subscriber. After the date of contract issue, any amendment that increases benefits or coverage with a concomitant increase in prepaid or periodic charges during the contract term shall be agreed to in writing signed by the subscriber, unless the benefits are required by the minimum standards for Medicare supplement contracts, or if the increased benefits or coverage is required by law. If a separate additional charge is made for benefits provided in connection with contract amendments, the charge shall be set forth in the contract.

(2) An issuer shall not in any way reduce or eliminate any benefit or coverage under a Medicare supplement contract at any time after the date of entering the contract, including dates of reinstatement or renewal, unless and until the change is voluntarily agreed to in writing signed by the subscriber or enrollee, or is required to reduce or eliminate benefits to avoid duplication of Medicare benefits. The issuer shall not increase benefits or coverage with a concomitant increase in prepaid or periodic charges during the term of the contract unless and until the change is voluntarily agreed to in writing signed by the subscriber or enrollee or unless the increased benefits or coverage is required by law or regulation.

(c) Medicare supplement contracts shall not provide for the payment of benefits based on standards described as "usual and customary," "reasonable and customary," or words of similar import.

(d) If a Medicare supplement contract contains any limitations with respect to preexisting conditions, those limitations shall appear as a separate paragraph of the contract and be labeled as "Preexisting Condition Limitations."

(e) (1) Medicare supplement contracts shall have a notice prominently printed in no less than 10-point uppercase type, on the cover page of the contract or attached thereto stating that the applicant shall have the right to return the contract within 30 days of its receipt via regular mail, and to have any charges refunded in a timely manner if, after examination of the contract, the covered person is not satisfied for any reason. The return shall void the contract from the beginning, and the parties shall be in the same position as if no contract had been issued.

(2) For purposes of this section, a timely manner shall be no later than 30 days after the issuer receives the returned contract.

(3) If the issuer fails to refund all prepaid or periodic charges paid in a timely manner, then the applicant shall receive interest on the paid charges at the legal rate of interest on judgments as provided in Section 685.010 of the Code of Civil Procedure. The interest shall be paid from the date the issuer received the returned contract.

(f) (1) Issuers of health care service plan contracts that provide hospital or medical expense coverage on an expense incurred or indemnity basis to persons eligible for Medicare shall provide to those applicants a guide to health insurance for people with Medicare in the form developed jointly by the National Association of Insurance Commissioners and the Centers for Medicare and Medicaid Services and in a type size no smaller than 12-point type. Delivery of the guide shall be made whether or not the contracts are advertised, solicited, or issued for delivery as Medicare supplement contracts as defined in this article. Except in the case of direct response issuers, delivery of the guide shall be made to the applicant at the time of application, and acknowledgment of receipt of the guide shall be obtained by the issuer. Direct response issuers shall deliver the guide to the applicant upon request, but not later than at the time the contract is delivered.

(2) For the purposes of this section, "form" means the language, format, type size, type proportional spacing, bold character, and line spacing.

(g) As soon as practicable, but no later than 30 days prior to the annual effective date of any Medicare benefit changes, an issuer shall notify its enrollees and subscribers of modifications it has made to Medicare supplement contracts in a format acceptable to the director. The notice shall include both of the following:

(1) A description of revisions to the Medicare Program and a description of each modification made to the coverage provided under the Medicare supplement contract.

(2) Inform each enrollee as to when any adjustment in prepaid or periodic charges is to be made due to changes in Medicare.

(h) The notice of benefit modifications and any adjustments of prepaid or periodic charges shall be in outline form and in clear and simple terms so as to facilitate comprehension.

(i) The notices shall not contain or be accompanied by any solicitation.

(j) (1) Issuers shall provide an outline of coverage to all applicants at the time application is presented to the prospective applicant and, except for direct response policies, shall obtain an acknowledgment of receipt of the outline from the applicant. If an outline of coverage is provided at the time of application and the Medicare supplement contract is issued on a basis which would require revision of the outline, a substitute outline of coverage properly describing the contract shall accompany the contract when it is delivered and contain the following statement, in no less than 12-point type, immediately above the company name:

"NOTICE: Read this outline of coverage carefully. It is not identical to the outline of coverage provided upon application and the coverage originally applied for has not been issued."

(2) The outline of coverage provided to applicants pursuant to this section consists of four parts: a cover page, information about prepaid or periodic charges, disclosure pages, and charts displaying the features of each benefit plan offered by the issuer. The outline of coverage shall be in the language and format prescribed below in no less than 12-point type. All Medicare supplement plans authorized by federal law shall be shown on the cover page, and the plans that are offered by the issuer shall be prominently identified. Information about prepaid or periodic charges for plans that are offered shall be shown on the cover page or immediately following the cover page and shall be prominently displayed. The charge and mode shall be stated for all plans that are offered to the prospective applicant. All possible charges for the prospective applicant shall be illustrated.

(3) (A) The following shall only apply to contracts sold for effective dates prior to June 1, 2010:

(i) The outline of coverage shall include the items, and in the same order, specified in the chart set forth in Section 17 of the Model Regulation to implement the NAIC Medicare Supplement Insurance Minimum Standards Model Act, as adopted by the National Association of Insurance Commissioners in 2004.

(ii) The cover page shall contain the 14-plan (A-L) charts. The plans offered by the issuer shall be clearly identified. Innovative benefits shall be explained in a manner approved by the director.

(B) The following shall only apply to policies sold for effective dates on or after June 1, 2010:

(i) The outline of coverage shall include the items, and in the same order specified in the chart set forth in Section 17 of the Model Regulation to implement the NAIC Medicare Supplement Insurance Minimum Standards Model Act, as adopted by the National Association of Insurance Commissioners in 2008.

(ii) The cover page shall contain all Medicare supplement benefit plan charts A to D, inclusive, F, high deductible F, G, and K to N, inclusive. The plans offered by the issuer shall be clearly identified. Innovative benefits shall be explained in a manner approved by the director.

The text shall read: "Medicare supplement contracts can be sold in only standard plans. This chart shows the benefits included in each plan. Every insurance company must offer Plan A. Some plans may not be available. Plans E, H, I, and J are no longer available for sale. [This sentence shall not appear after June 1, 2011.]"

(4) The disclosure pages shall be in the language and format described below in no less than 12-point type.

INFORMATION ABOUT PREPAID OR PERIODIC CHARGES

[Insert plan's name] can only raise your charges if it raises the charge for all contracts like yours in this state. [If the charge is based on the increasing age of the enrollee, include information specifying when charges will change.]

DISCLOSURES

Use this outline to compare benefits and charges among policies.

[The following additional language shall be included under "DISCLOSURES" for contracts with effective dates on or after June 1, 2010, but shall not appear after June 1, 2011.] This outline shows benefits and premiums of policies sold for effective dates on or after June 1, 2010. Policies sold for effective dates prior to June 1, 2010, have different benefits and premiums. Plans E, H, I, and J are no longer available for sale.

READ YOUR POLICY VERY CAREFULLY

This is only an outline describing the most important features of your Medicare supplement plan contract. This is not the plan contract and only the actual contract provisions will control. You must read the contract itself to understand all of the rights and duties of both you and [insert the health care service plan's name].

RIGHT TO RETURN POLICY

If you find that you are not satisfied with your contract, you may return it to [insert plan's address]. If you send the contract back to us within 30 days after you receive it, we will treat the contract as if it had never been issued and return all of your payments.

POLICY REPLACEMENT

If you are replacing other health coverage, do NOT cancel it until you have actually received your new contract and are sure you want to keep it.

NOTICE

This contract may not fully cover all of your medical costs. Neither [insert the health care service plan's name] nor its agents are connected with Medicare.

This outline of coverage does not give all the details of Medicare coverage. Contact your local social security office or consult "The Medicare Handbook" for further details and limitations applicable to Medicare.

COMPLETE ANSWERS ARE VERY IMPORTANT

When you fill out the application for the new contract, be sure to answer truthfully and completely all questions about your medical and health history. The company may cancel your contract and refuse to pay any claims if you leave out or falsify important medical information. [If the contract is guaranteed issue, this paragraph need not appear.] Review the application carefully before you sign it. Be certain that all information has been properly recorded. [The charts displaying the features of each benefit plan offered by the issuer shall use the uniform format and language shown in the charts set forth in Section 17 of the Model Regulation to Implement the NAIC Medicare Supplement Insurance Minimum Standards Model Act, as most recently adopted by the National Association of Insurance Commissioners. No more than four benefit plans may be shown on one chart. For purposes of illustration, charts for each benefit plan are set forth below. An issuer may use additional benefit plan designations on these charts.]

[Include an explanation of any innovative benefits on the cover page and in the chart, in a manner approved by the director.]

(k) Notwithstanding Section 1300.63.2 of Title 28 of the California Code of Regulations, no issuer shall combine the evidence of coverage and disclosure form into a single document relating to a contract that supplements Medicare, or is advertised or represented as a supplement to Medicare, with hospital or medical coverage.

(l) The director may adopt regulations to implement this article, including, but not limited to, regulations that specify the required information to be contained in the outline of coverage provided to applicants pursuant to this section, including the format of tables, charts, and other information.

(m) (1) Any health care service plan contract, other than a Medicare supplement contract, a contract issued pursuant to a contract under Section 1876 of the federal Social Security Act (42 U.S.C. Sec. 1395 et seq.), a disability income policy, or any other contract identified in subdivision (b) of Section 1358.3, issued for delivery in this state to persons eligible for Medicare, shall notify enrollees under the contract that the contract is not a Medicare supplement contract. The notice shall either be printed or attached to the first page of the outline of coverage delivered to enrollees under the contract, or if no outline of coverage is delivered, to the first page of the contract delivered to enrollees. The notice shall be in no less than 12-point type and shall contain the following language: "THIS CONTRACT IS NOT A MEDICARE SUPPLEMENT. If you are eligible for Medicare, review the Guide to Health Insurance for People with Medicare available from the company."

(2) Applications provided to persons eligible for Medicare for the health insurance contracts described in paragraph (1) shall disclose the extent to which the contract duplicates Medicare in a manner required by the director. The disclosure statement shall be provided as a part of, or together with, the application for the contract.

(n) A Medicare supplement contract that does not cover custodial care shall, on the cover page of the outline of coverages, contain the following statement in uppercase type: "THIS POLICY DOES NOT COVER CUSTODIAL CARE IN A SKILLED NURSING CARE FACILITY."

(o) An issuer shall comply with all notice requirements of the Medicare Prescription Drug, Improvement, and Modernization Act of 2003 (P.L. 108-173).

(Amended by Stats. 2009, Ch. 10, Sec. 10. Effective July 2, 2009.)

1358.18.

In the interest of full and fair disclosure, and to ensure the availability of necessary consumer information to potential subscribers or enrollees not possessing a special knowledge of Medicare, health care service plans, or Medicare supplement contracts, an issuer shall comply with the following provisions:

(a) Application forms shall include the following questions designed to elicit information as to whether, as of the date of the application, the applicant currently has Medicare supplement, Medicare Advantage, Medi-Cal coverage, or another health insurance policy or certificate or plan contract in force or whether a Medicare supplement contract is intended to replace any other disability policy or certificate, or plan contract, presently in force. A supplementary application or other form to be signed by the applicant and solicitor containing those questions and statements may be used.

"(Statements)

(1) You do not need more than one Medicare supplement policy or contract.

(2) If you purchase this contract, you may want to evaluate your existing health coverage and decide if you need multiple coverages.

(3) You may be eligible for benefits under Medi-Cal or Medicaid and may not need a Medicare supplement contract.

(4) If, after purchasing this contract, you become eligible for Medi-Cal, the benefits and premiums under your Medicare supplement contract can be suspended, if requested, during your entitlement to benefits under Medi-Cal or Medicaid for 24 months. You must request this suspension within 90 days of becoming eligible for Medi-Cal or Medicaid. If you are no longer entitled to Medi-Cal or Medicaid, your suspended Medicare supplement contract or, if that is no longer available, a substantially equivalent contract, will be reinstituted if requested within 90 days of losing your Medi-Cal or Medicaid eligibility. If the Medicare supplement contract provided coverage for outpatient prescription drugs and you enrolled in Medicare Part D while your contract was suspended, the reinstituted contract will not have outpatient prescription drug coverage, but will otherwise be substantially equivalent to your coverage before the date of the suspension.

(5) If you are eligible for, and have enrolled in, a Medicare supplement contract by reason of disability and you later become covered by an employer or union-based group health plan, the benefits and premiums under your Medicare supplement contract can be suspended, if requested, while you are covered under the employer or union-based group health plan. If you suspend your Medicare supplement contract under these circumstances and later lose your employer or union-based group health plan, your suspended Medicare supplement contract or, if that is no longer available, a substantially equivalent contract, will be reinstituted if requested within 90 days of losing your employer or union-based group health plan. If the Medicare supplement contract provided coverage for outpatient prescription drugs and you enrolled in Medicare Part D while your contract was suspended, the reinstituted contract will not have outpatient prescription drug coverage, but will otherwise be substantially equivalent to your coverage before the date of the suspension.

(6) Counseling services are available in this state to provide advice concerning your purchase of Medicare supplement coverage and concerning medical assistance through the Medi-Cal or Medicaid Program, including benefits as a qualified Medicare beneficiary (QMB) and a specified low-income Medicare beneficiary (SLMB). Information regarding counseling services may be obtained from the California Department of Aging.
(Questions)

If you lost or are losing other health insurance coverage and received a notice from your prior insurer saying you were eligible for guaranteed issue of a Medicare supplement insurance contract or that you had certain rights to buy such a contract, you may be guaranteed acceptance in one or more of our Medicare supplement plans. Please include a copy of the notice from your prior insurer with your application. PLEASE ANSWER ALL QUESTIONS.
[Please mark Yes or No below with an "X."]
To the best of your knowledge,
(1) (a) Did you turn 65 years of age in the last 6 months?
Yes_____ No_____
(b) Did you enroll in Medicare Part B in the last 6 months?
Yes_____ No_____
(c) If yes, what is the effective date?_____
(2) Are you covered for medical assistance through California's Medi-Cal program?
NOTE TO APPLICANT: If you have a share of cost under the Medi-Cal program, please answer NO to this question.
Yes_____ No_____
If yes,
(a) Will Medi-Cal pay your premiums for this Medicare supplement contract?
Yes_____ No_____
(b) Do you receive benefits from Medi-Cal OTHER THAN payments toward your Medicare Part B premium?
Yes_____ No_____
(3) (a) If you had coverage from any Medicare plan other than original Medicare within the past 63 days (for example, a Medicare Advantage plan or a Medicare HMO or PPO), fill in your start and end dates below. If you are still covered under this plan, leave "END" blank.
START __/__/__ END __/__/__
(b) If you are still covered under the Medicare plan, do you intend to replace your current coverage with this new Medicare supplement contract?
Yes_____ No_____
(c) Was this your first time in this type of Medicare plan?
Yes_____ No_____
(d) Did you drop a Medicare supplement contract to enroll in the Medicare plan?
Yes_____ No_____
(4) (a) Do you have another Medicare supplement policy or certificate or contract in force?
Yes_____ No_____
(b) If so, with what company, and what plan do you have? [optional for Direct Mailers]
Yes_____ No_____
(c) If so, do you intend to replace your current Medicare supplement policy or certificate or contract with this contract?
Yes_____ No_____
(5) Have you had coverage under any other health insurance within the past 63 days? (For example, an employer, union, or individual plan)
Yes_____ No_____
(a) If so, with what companies and what kind of policy?
_____

_____
_____
_____
(b) What are your dates of coverage under the other policy?
START __/__/__ END __/__/__
(If you are still covered under the other policy, leave "END" blank)."
(b) Solicitors shall list any other health insurance policies or plan contracts they have sold to the applicant as follows:
(1) List policies and contracts sold that are still in force.
(2) List policies and contracts sold in the past five years that are no longer in force.
(c) An issuer issuing Medicare supplement contracts without a solicitor or solicitor firm (a direct response issuer) shall return to the applicant, upon delivery of the contract, a copy of the application or supplemental forms, signed by the applicant and acknowledged by the issuer.
(d) Upon determining that a sale will involve replacement of Medicare supplement coverage, an issuer, other than a direct response issuer, or its agent, shall furnish the applicant, prior to issuance for delivery of the Medicare supplement contract, a notice regarding replacement of Medicare supplement coverage. One copy of the notice signed by the applicant and the agent, except where the coverage is sold without an agent, shall be provided to the applicant and an additional signed copy shall be retained by the issuer. A direct response issuer shall deliver to the applicant at the time of the issuance of the contract the notice regarding replacement of Medicare supplement coverage.
(e) The notice required by subdivision (d) for an issuer shall be provided in substantially the following form in no less than 12-point type:

NOTICE TO APPLICANT REGARDING REPLACEMENT OF MEDICARE SUPPLEMENT COVERAGE OR MEDICARE ADVANTAGE

(Company name and address)

SAVE THIS NOTICE! IT MAY BE IMPORTANT TO YOU IN THE FUTURE
According to [your application] [information you have furnished], you intend to lapse or otherwise terminate an existing Medicare supplement policy or contract or Medicare Advantage plan and replace it with a contract to be issued by [Plan Name]. Your contract to be issued by [Plan Name] will provide 30 days within which you may decide without cost whether you desire to keep the contract. You should review this new coverage carefully. Compare it with all accident and sickness coverage you now have. Terminate your present policy or contract only if, after due consideration, you find that purchase of this Medicare supplement coverage is a wise decision.
STATEMENT TO APPLICANT BY PLAN, SOLICITOR, SOLICITOR FIRM, OR OTHER REPRESENTATIVE:
(1) I have reviewed your current medical or health coverage. To the best of my knowledge, the replacement of coverage involved in this transaction does not duplicate coverage or, if applicable, Medicare Advantage coverage because you intend to terminate your existing Medicare supplement coverage or leave your Medicare Advantage plan. The replacement contract is being purchased for the following reason (check one):
___ Additional benefits.
___ No change in benefits, but lower premiums or charges.
___ Fewer benefits and lower premiums or charges.
___ Plan has outpatient prescription drug coverage and applicant is enrolled in Medicare Part D.
___ Disenrollment from a Medicare Advantage plan. Reasons for disenrollment:
___ Other. (please specify) _____.
(2) If the issuer of the Medicare supplement contract being applied for does not impose, or is otherwise prohibited from imposing, preexisting condition limitations, please skip to statement 3 below. Health conditions that you may presently have (preexisting conditions) may not be immediately or fully covered under the new contract. This could result in denial or delay of a claim for benefits under the new contract, whereas a similar claim might have been payable under your present contract.
(3) State law provides that your replacement Medicare supplement contract may not contain new preexisting conditions, waiting periods, elimination periods, or probationary periods. The plan will waive any time periods applicable to preexisting conditions, waiting periods, elimination periods, or probationary periods in the new coverage for similar benefits to the extent that time was spent (depleted) under the original contract.
(4) If you still wish to terminate your present policy or contract and replace it with new coverage, be certain to truthfully and completely answer any and all questions on the application concerning your medical and health history. Failure to include all material medical information on an application requesting that information may provide a basis for the plan to deny any future claims and to refund your prepaid or periodic payment as though your contract had never been in force. After the application has been completed and before you sign it, review it carefully to be certain that all information has been properly recorded.
(5) Do not cancel your present Medicare supplement coverage until you have received your new contract and are sure you want to keep it.

```
┌─────────────────────────────────────────────────┐
│ (Signature of Solicitor, Solicitor Firm, or Other Representative) │
│ [Typed Name and Address of Plan, Solicitor, or Solicitor Firm] │
│                                                   │
│ ─────────────────────────────────────────────── │
│                                                   │
│ (Applicant's Signature)                           │
│                                                   │
│ ─────────────────────────────────────────────── │
│                                                   │
│ (Date)                                            │
└─────────────────────────────────────────────────┘
```

(f) The application form or other consumer information for persons eligible for Medicare and used by an issuer shall contain, as an attachment, a Medicare supplement buyer's guide in the form approved by the director. The application or other consumer information, containing, as an attachment, the buyer's guide, shall be mailed or delivered to each applicant applying for that coverage at or before the time of application and, to establish compliance with this subdivision, the issuer shall obtain an acknowledgment of receipt of the attached buyer's guide from each applicant. An issuer shall not make use of or otherwise disseminate any buyer's guide that does not accurately outline current Medicare supplement benefits. An issuer shall not be required to provide more than one copy of the buyer's guide to any applicant.

(g) An issuer may comply with the requirement of this section in the case of group contracts by causing the subscriber (1) to disseminate copies of the disclosure form containing as an attachment the buyer's guide to all persons eligible under the group contract at the time those persons are offered the Medicare supplement plan, and (2) collecting and forwarding to the issuer an acknowledgment of receipt of the disclosure form containing, as an attachment, the buyer's guide from each enrollee.

(h) An issuer shall not require, request, or obtain health information as part of the application process for an applicant who is eligible for guaranteed issuance of, or open enrollment for, any Medicare supplement coverage pursuant to Section 1358.11 or 1358.12, except for purposes of paragraph (1) or (2) of subdivision (a) of Section 1358.11 when the applicant is first enrolled in Medicare Part B. The application form shall include a clear and conspicuous statement that the applicant is not required to provide health information during a period where guaranteed issue or open enrollment applies, as specified in Section 1358.11 or 1358.12, except for purposes of paragraph (1) or (2) of subdivision (a) of Section 1358.11 when the applicant is first enrolled in Medicare Part B, and shall inform the applicant of those periods of guaranteed issuance of Medicare supplement coverage. This subdivision does not prohibit an issuer from requiring proof of eligibility for a guaranteed issuance of Medicare supplement coverage.
(Amended by Stats. 2016, Ch. 86, Sec. 176. (SB 1171) Effective January 1, 2017.)

1358.19.

An issuer shall provide a copy of any Medicare supplement advertisement intended for use in this state whether through written, radio, or television medium to the director for review or approval.
(Repealed and added by Stats. 2000, Ch. 706, Sec. 2. Effective January 1, 2001.)

1358.20.

(a) An issuer, directly or through solicitors or other representatives, shall do each of the following:
(1) Establish marketing procedures to ensure that any comparison of Medicare supplement coverage by its solicitors or other representatives will be fair and accurate.
(2) Establish marketing procedures to ensure that excessive coverage is not sold or issued.
(3) Display prominently by type, stamp, or other appropriate means, on the first page of the outline of coverage and contract, the following:
"Notice to buyer: This Medicare supplement contract may not cover all of your medical expenses."
(4) Inquire and otherwise make every reasonable effort to identify whether a prospective applicant for a Medicare supplement contract already has health care coverage and the types and amounts of that coverage.
(5) Provide, on the application form for Medicare supplement contracts, a statement that reads as follows: "A rate guide is available that compares the policies sold by different insurers. You can obtain a copy of this rate guide by calling the Department of Managed Health Care's consumer toll-free telephone number (1-888-HMO-2219), by calling the Health Insurance Counseling and Advocacy Program (HICAP) toll-free telephone number (1-800-434-0222), or by accessing the Department of Managed Health Care's Internet Web site (www.dmhc.ca.gov)."
(6) Establish auditable procedures for verifying compliance with this subdivision.
(b) In addition to the practices prohibited by this code or any other law, the following acts and practices are prohibited:
(1) Twisting, which means knowingly making any misleading representation or incomplete or fraudulent comparison of any coverages or issuers for the purpose of inducing or tending to induce, any person to lapse, forfeit, surrender, terminate, retain, pledge, assign, borrow on, or convert any coverage or to take out coverage with another plan or insurer.
(2) High pressure tactics, which means employing any method of marketing having the effect of or tending to induce the purchase of coverage through force, fright, threat, whether explicit or implied, or undue pressure to purchase or recommend the purchase of coverage.

(3) Cold lead advertising, which means making use directly or indirectly of any method of marketing that fails to disclose in a conspicuous manner that a purpose of the method of marketing is the solicitation of coverage and that contact will be made by a health care service plan or its representative.
(c) The terms "Medicare supplement," "Medigap," "Medicare Wrap-Around" and words of similar import shall not be used unless the contract is issued in compliance with this article.
(Amended by Stats. 2009, Ch. 10, Sec. 12. Effective July 2, 2009.)

1358.21.

(a) In recommending the purchase or replacement of any Medicare supplement coverage, an issuer or its representative shall make reasonable efforts to determine the appropriateness of a recommended purchase or replacement.
(b) Any sale of a Medicare supplement contract that will provide an individual more than one Medicare supplement policy or certificate, or contract, is prohibited.
(c) An issuer shall not issue a Medicare supplement contract to an individual enrolled in Medicare Part C unless the effective date of the coverage is after the termination date of the individual's coverage under Medicare Part C.
(Amended by Stats. 2005, Ch. 206, Sec. 16. Effective January 1, 2006.)

1358.22.

(a) On or before March 1 of each year, an issuer shall report the following information for every individual resident of this state for which the issuer has in force more than one Medicare supplement contract:
(1) Contract number.
(2) Date of issuance.
(b) The items set forth above shall be grouped by enrollee.
(Added by Stats. 2000, Ch. 706, Sec. 2. Effective January 1, 2001.)

1358.225.

(a) Every issuer shall, by June 30 of each year, file with the director a list of its Medicare supplement contracts offered or issued or outstanding in this state as of the end of the previous calendar year.
(b) The list shall identify the filing issuer by name and address, shall identify each type of contract it offers by name and form number, if one is used, and shall differentiate between contracts filed with and approved by the director in years prior to the previous calendar year, and those filed and approved in the previous calendar year.
(c) The list shall specifically identify all of the following:
(1) Contracts that are issued and outstanding in this state but are no longer offered for sale.
(2) Contracts that, for any reason, were not filed and approved by the director.
(3) Contracts for which the director's approval was withdrawn within the previous calendar year.
(d) The director shall, on or before the first day of September of each year provide the secretary with a list identifying each contract by name and address and the information required to be submitted by this section.
(Added by Stats. 2000, Ch. 706, Sec. 2. Effective January 1, 2001.)

1358.23.

(a) If a Medicare supplement contract replaces another Medicare supplement policy or certificate, or contract, the replacing issuer shall waive any time periods applicable to preexisting conditions, waiting periods, elimination periods, and probationary periods in the new Medicare supplement contract for similar benefits to the extent that time was spent under the original policy or certificate, or contract.
(b) If a Medicare supplement contract replaces another Medicare supplement policy or certificate, or contract, that has been in effect for at least six months, the replacing contract shall not provide any time period applicable to preexisting conditions, waiting periods, elimination periods and probationary periods for benefits similar to those contained in the original policy or certificate, or contract.
(Added by Stats. 2000, Ch. 706, Sec. 2. Effective January 1, 2001.)

1358.24.

This section applies to all contracts that become effective on or after May 21, 2009.
(a) In addition to the requirements set forth under Sections 1365.5 and 1374.7, an issuer of a Medicare supplement contract shall adhere to the requirements imposed by the federal Genetic Information Nondiscrimination Act of 2008 (Public Law 110-233), as follows:
(1) The issuer shall not deny or condition the issuance or effectiveness of the contract, including the imposition of any exclusion of benefits under the contract based on a preexisting condition, on the basis of the genetic information with respect to that individual or a family member of the individual.
(2) The issuer shall not discriminate in the pricing of the contract, including the adjustment of prepaid or periodic charges, of an individual on the basis of the genetic information with respect to that individual or a family member of the individual.
(b) Nothing in subdivision (a) shall be construed to limit the ability of an issuer, to the extent otherwise permitted by law, to do any of the following:
(1) Deny or condition the issuance or effectiveness of the contract or increase the prepaid or periodic charge for a group based on the manifestation of a disease or disorder of an enrollee, subscriber, or applicant.
(2) Increase the prepaid or periodic charge for any contract issued to an individual based on the manifestation of a disease or disorder of an individual who is covered under the contract. For purposes of this paragraph, the manifestation of a disease or disorder in one individual shall not also be used as genetic information about other group members and to further increase the prepaid or periodic charge for the group.

(c) An issuer of a Medicare supplement contract shall not request or require an individual or a family member of that individual to undergo a genetic test.

(d) Subdivision (c) shall not be construed to preclude an issuer of a Medicare supplement contract from obtaining and using the results of a genetic test in making a determination regarding payment, as defined for the purposes of applying the regulations promulgated under Part C of Title XI and Section 264 of the Health Insurance Portability and Accountability Act of 1996, as may be revised from time to time, and consistent with subdivision (a).

(e) For purposes of carrying out subdivision (d), an issuer of a Medicare supplement contract may request only the minimum amount of information necessary to accomplish the intended purpose.

(f) An issuer of a Medicare supplement contract shall not request, require, seek, or purchase genetic information for underwriting purposes.

(g) An issuer of a Medicare supplement contract shall not request, require, seek, or purchase genetic information with respect to any individual or a family member of that individual prior to the individual's enrollment under the contract in connection with that enrollment.

(h) If an issuer of a Medicare supplement contract obtains genetic information incidental to the requesting, requiring, or purchasing of other information concerning any individual or a family member of that individual, the request, requirement, or purchase shall not be considered a violation of subdivision (g) if the request, requirement, or purchase is not in violation of subdivision (f). However, the issuer shall not use any genetic information obtained under this section for any prohibited purpose described in this section or in Sections 1365.5 and 1374.7.

(i) For the purposes of this section, the following definitions shall apply:

(1) "Issuer of a Medicare supplement contract" includes a third-party administrator, or other person acting for or on behalf of an issuer.

(2) "Family member" means, with respect to an individual, any other individual who is a first-degree, second-degree, third-degree, or fourth-degree relative of the individual.

(3) "Genetic information" means, with respect to any individual, information about the individual's genetic tests, the genetic tests of family members of the individual, and the manifestation of a disease or disorder in family members of the individual. The term includes, with respect to any individual, any request for, or receipt of, genetic services, or participation in clinical research which includes genetic services, by the individual or any family member of the individual. Any reference to genetic information concerning an individual or family member of an individual who is a pregnant woman, includes genetic information of any fetus carried by that pregnant woman, or with respect to an individual or family member utilizing reproductive technology, includes genetic information of any embryo legally held by an individual or family member. The term "genetic information" does not include information about the sex or age of any individual.

(4) "Genetic services" means a genetic test, genetic education, genetic counseling, including obtaining, interpreting, or assessing genetic information.

(5) "Genetic test" means an analysis of human DNA, RNA, chromosomes, proteins, or metabolites, that detect genotypes, mutations, or chromosomal changes. The term "genetic test" does not mean an analysis of proteins or metabolites that does not detect genotypes, mutations, or chromosomal changes; or an analysis of proteins or metabolites that is directly related to a manifested disease, disorder, or pathological condition that could reasonably be detected by a health care professional with appropriate training and expertise in the field of medicine involved.

(6) "Underwriting purposes" includes all of the following:

(A) Rules for, or determination of, eligibility, including enrollment and continued eligibility, for benefits under the contract.

(B) The computation of prepaid or periodic charges or contribution amounts under the contract.

(C) The application of any preexisting condition exclusion under the contract.

(D) Other activities related to the creation, renewal, or replacement of a contract of health insurance or health benefits.

(Added by Stats. 2009, Ch. 10, Sec. 13. Effective July 2, 2009.)

ARTICLE 4. Solicitation and Enrollment [1359 - 1366.6]

(Article 4 added by Stats. 1975, Ch. 941.)

1359.

(a) The director may require that solicitors and solicitor firms, and principal persons engaged in the supervision of solicitation for plans of solicitor firms, meet such reasonable and appropriate standards with respect to training, experience, and other qualifications as the director finds necessary and appropriate in the public interest or for the protection of subscribers, enrollees, and plans. For such purposes, the director may do the following:

(1) Appropriately classify such persons and individuals.

(2) Specify that all or any portion of such standards shall be applicable to any such class.

(3) Require individuals in any such class to pass examinations prescribed in accordance with such rules.

(b) The director may prescribe by rule reasonable fees and charges to defray the costs of carrying out this section, including, but not limited to, fees for any examination administered by the director or under his or her direction.

(Amended by Stats. 1999, Ch. 525, Sec. 85. Effective January 1, 2000. Operative July 1, 2000, or sooner, by Sec. 214 of Ch. 525.)

1360.

(a) No plan, solicitor, solicitor firm, or representative shall use or permit the use of any advertising or solicitation which is untrue or misleading, or any form of evidence of coverage which is deceptive. For purposes of this article:

(1) A written or printed statement or item of information shall be deemed untrue if it does not conform to fact in any respect which is, or may be significant to an enrollee or subscriber, or potential enrollee or subscriber in a plan.

(2) A written or printed statement or item of information shall be deemed misleading whether or not it may be literally true, if, in the total context in which the statement is made or such item of information is communicated, such statement or item of information may be understood by a person not possessing special knowledge regarding health care coverage, as indicating any benefit or advantage, or the absence of any exclusion, limitation, or disadvantage of possible significance to an enrollee, or potential enrollee or subscriber, in a plan, and such is not the case.

(3) An evidence of coverage shall be deemed to be deceptive if the evidence of coverage taken as a whole and with consideration given to typography and format, as well as language, shall be such as to cause a reasonable person, not possessing special knowledge of plans, and evidence of coverage therefor to expect benefits, service charges, or other advantages which the evidence of coverage does not provide or which the plan issuing such coverage or evidence of coverage does not regularly make available to enrollees or subscribers covered under such evidence of coverage.

(b) No plan, or solicitor, or representative shall use or permit the use of any verbal statement which is untrue, misleading, or deceptive or make any representations about coverage offered by the plan or its cost that does not conform to fact. All verbal statements are to be held to the same standards as those for printed matter provided in subdivision (a).

(Added by Stats. 1975, Ch. 941.)

1360.1.

It is unlawful for any person, including a plan, subject to this chapter to represent or imply in any manner that the person or plan has been sponsored, recommended, or approved, or that the person's or plan's abilities or qualifications have in any respect been passed upon, by the director. Nothing in this section prohibits a statement (other than in a paid advertisement) that a person or plan holds a license under this chapter, if such statement is true and if the effect of such licensing is not misrepresented.

(Amended by Stats. 1999, Ch. 525, Sec. 86. Effective January 1, 2000. Operative July 1, 2000, or sooner, by Sec. 214 of Ch. 525.)

1360.5.

(a) For purposes of this section, "Exchange" means the California Health Benefit Exchange established pursuant to Section 100500 of the Government Code.

(b) It is an unfair business practice for a solicitor or solicitor firm to hold himself, herself, or itself out as representing, constituting, or otherwise providing services on behalf of the Exchange unless the solicitor or solicitor firm has a valid agreement with the Exchange to engage in those activities.

(c) It is an unfair business practice for a health care service plan to hold itself out as representing, constituting, or otherwise providing services on behalf of the Exchange unless the plan has a valid agreement with the Exchange to engage in those activities.

(Added by Stats. 2012, Ch. 876, Sec. 2. (AB 1761) Effective January 1, 2013.)

1361.

(a) Except as provided in subdivision (b), no plan shall publish or distribute, or allow to be published or distributed on its behalf, any advertisement not subject to Section 1352.1 unless (1) a true copy thereof has first been filed with the director, at least 30 days prior to any such use, or any shorter period as the director by rule or order may allow, and (2) the director by notice has not found the advertisement, wholly or in part, to be untrue, misleading, deceptive, or otherwise not in compliance with this chapter or the rules thereunder, and specified the deficiencies, within the 30 days or any shorter time as the director by rule or order may allow.

(b) Except as provided in subdivision (c), a licensed plan which has been continuously licensed under this chapter for the preceding 18 months may publish or distribute or allow to be published or distributed on its behalf an advertisement not subject to Section 1352.1 without having filed the same for the director's prior approval, if the plan and the material comply with each of the following conditions:

(1) The advertisement or a material provision thereof has not been previously disapproved by the director by written notice to the plan and the plan reasonably believes that the advertisement does not violate any requirement of this chapter or the rules thereunder.

(2) The plan files a true copy of each new or materially revised advertisement, used by it or by any person acting on behalf of the plan, with the director not later than 10 business days after publication or distribution of the advertisement or within such additional period as the director may allow by rule or order.

(c) If the director finds that any advertisement of a plan has materially failed to comply with this chapter or the rules thereunder, the director may, by order, require the plan to publish in the same or similar medium, an approved correction or retraction of any untrue, misleading, or deceptive statement contained in the advertising, and may prohibit the plan from publishing or distributing, or allowing to be published or distributed on its behalf the advertisement or any new materially revised advertisement without first having filed a copy thereof with the director, 30 days prior to the publication or distribution thereof, or any shorter period specified in the order. An order issued under this subdivision shall be effective for 12 months from its issuance, and may be renewed by order if the advertisements submitted under this subdivision indicate difficulties of voluntary compliance with the applicable provisions of this chapter and the rules thereunder.

(d) A licensed plan or other person regulated under this chapter may, within 30 days after receipt of any notice or order under this section, file a written request for a hearing with the director.

(e) The director by rule or order may classify plans and advertisements and exempt certain classes, wholly or in part, either unconditionally or upon specified terms and conditions or for specified periods, from the application of subdivisions (a) and (b). (Amended by Stats. 1999, Ch. 525, Sec. 87. Effective January 1, 2000. Operative July 1, 2000, or sooner, by Sec. 214 of Ch. 525.)

1361.1.

(a) It is an unfair business practice for a solicitor, solicitor firm, or representative of a health care service plan to sell, solicit, or negotiate the purchase of health care coverage products by any of the following methods:

(1) The use of a marketing technique known as cold lead advertising when marketing a Medicare product. As used in this section, "cold lead advertising" means making use directly or indirectly of a method of marketing that fails to disclose in a conspicuous manner that a purpose of the marketing is health care service plan sales solicitation and that contact will be made by a solicitor, solicitor firm, or representative of a health care service plan.

(2) The use of an appointment that was made to discuss a particular Medicare product or to solicit the sale of a particular Medicare product in order to solicit the sale of another Medicare product or other health care coverage products, unless the consumer specifically agrees in advance of the appointment to discuss that other Medicare product or other types of health care coverage products during the same appointment.

(b) As used in this section, "Medicare product" includes Medicare Parts A, B, C, and D, and Medicare supplement plans.

(Amended by Stats. 2009, Ch. 140, Sec. 97. (AB 1164) Effective January 1, 2010.)

1362.

As used in Sections 1363 and 1364:

(a) "Benefits and coverage" means the health care services available under a plan contract.

(b) "Exception" means any provision in a plan contract whereby coverage for a specified hazard or condition is entirely eliminated.

(c) "Reduction" means any provision in a plan contract which reduces the amount of a plan benefit to some amount or period less than would be otherwise payable for medically authorized expenses or services had such a reduction not been used.

(d) "Limitation" means any provision other than an exception or a reduction which restricts coverage under the plan.

(e) "Presenting for examination or sale" means either (1) publication and dissemination of any brochure, mailer, advertisement, or form which constitutes a presentation of the provisions of the plan and which provides a plan enrollment or application form, or (2) consultations or discussions between prospective plan members or their contract agents and solicitors or representatives of a plan, when such consultations or discussions include presentation of formal, organized information about the plan which is intended to influence or inform the prospective member or contract holder, such as brochures, summaries, charts, slides, or other modes of information.

(f) "Disclosure form" means the disclosure form, material, or information required pursuant to Section 1363.

(g) For the purposes of Sections 1363 and 1364, where the definition of the term "hospital" in the plan contract omits care in any "health facility" defined pursuant to subdivision (a) or (b) of Section 1250 of this code, the omitted coverage shall constitute a limitation; and where the definition of the term "nursing home" in the plan omits care in any "health facility" defined pursuant to subdivision (c) or (d) of Section 1250 of this code, the omitted coverage shall constitute a limitation.

(Added by Stats. 1975, Ch. 941.)

1363.

(a) The director shall require the use by each plan of disclosure forms or materials containing information regarding the benefits, services, and terms of the plan contract as the director may require, so as to afford the public, subscribers, and enrollees with a full and fair disclosure of the provisions of the plan in readily understood language and in a clearly organized manner. The director may require that the materials be presented in a reasonably uniform manner so as to facilitate comparisons between plan contracts of the same or other types of plans. Nothing contained in this chapter shall preclude the director from permitting the disclosure form to be included with the evidence of coverage or plan contract.

The disclosure form shall provide for at least the following information, in concise and specific terms, relative to the plan, together with additional information as may be required by the director, in connection with the plan or plan contract:

(1) The principal benefits and coverage of the plan, including coverage for acute care and subacute care.

(2) The exceptions, reductions, and limitations that apply to the plan.

(3) The full premium cost of the plan.

(4) Any copayment, coinsurance, or deductible requirements that may be incurred by the member or the member's family in obtaining coverage under the plan.

(5) The terms under which the plan may be renewed by the plan member, including any reservation by the plan of any right to change premiums.

(6) A statement that the disclosure form is a summary only, and that the plan contract itself should be consulted to determine governing contractual provisions. The first page of the disclosure form shall contain a notice that conforms with all of the following conditions:

(A) (i) States that the evidence of coverage discloses the terms and conditions of coverage.

(ii) States, with respect to individual plan contracts, small group plan contracts, and any other group plan contracts for which health care services are not negotiated, that the

applicant has a right to view the evidence of coverage prior to enrollment, and, if the evidence of coverage is not combined with the disclosure form, the notice shall specify where the evidence of coverage can be obtained prior to enrollment.

(B) Includes a statement that the disclosure and the evidence of coverage should be read completely and carefully and that individuals with special health care needs should read carefully those sections that apply to them.

(C) Includes the plan's telephone number or numbers that may be used by an applicant to receive additional information about the benefits of the plan or a statement where the telephone number or numbers are located in the disclosure form.

(D) For individual contracts, and small group plan contracts as defined in Article 3.1 (commencing with Section 1357), the disclosure form shall state where the health plan benefits and coverage matrix is located.

(E) Is printed in type no smaller than that used for the remainder of the disclosure form and is displayed prominently on the page.

(7) A statement as to when benefits shall cease in the event of nonpayment of the prepaid or periodic charge and the effect of nonpayment upon an enrollee who is hospitalized or undergoing treatment for an ongoing condition.

(8) To the extent that the plan permits a free choice of provider to its subscribers and enrollees, the statement shall disclose the nature and extent of choice permitted and the financial liability that is, or may be, incurred by the subscriber, enrollee, or a third party by reason of the exercise of that choice.

(9) A summary of the provisions required by subdivision (g) of Section 1373, if applicable.

(10) If the plan utilizes arbitration to settle disputes, a statement of that fact.

(11) A summary of, and a notice of the availability of, the process the plan uses to authorize, modify, or deny health care services under the benefits provided by the plan, pursuant to Sections 1363.5 and 1367.01.

(12) A description of any limitations on the patient's choice of primary care physician, specialty care physician, or nonphysician health care practitioner, based on service area and limitations on the patient's choice of acute care hospital care, subacute or transitional inpatient care, or skilled nursing facility.

(13) General authorization requirements for referral by a primary care physician to a specialty care physician or a nonphysician health care practitioner.

(14) Conditions and procedures for disenrollment.

(15) A description as to how an enrollee may request continuity of care as required by Section 1373.96 and request a second opinion pursuant to Section 1383.15.

(16) Information concerning the right of an enrollee to request an independent review in accordance with Article 5.55 (commencing with Section 1374.30).

(17) A notice as required by Section 1364.5.

(b) (1) As of July 1, 1999, the director shall require each plan offering a contract to an individual or small group to provide with the disclosure form for individual and small group plan contracts a uniform health plan benefits and coverage matrix containing the plan's major provisions in order to facilitate comparisons between plan contracts. The uniform matrix shall include the following category descriptions together with the corresponding copayments and limitations in the following sequence:

(A) Deductibles.

(B) Lifetime maximums.

(C) Professional services.

(D) Outpatient services.

(E) Hospitalization services.

(F) Emergency health coverage.

(G) Ambulance services.

(H) Prescription drug coverage.

(I) Durable medical equipment.

(J) Mental health services.

(K) Chemical dependency services.

(L) Home health services.

(M) Other.

(2) The following statement shall be placed at the top of the matrix in all capital letters in at least 10-point boldface type:

THIS MATRIX IS INTENDED TO BE USED TO HELP YOU COMPARE COVERAGE BENEFITS AND IS A SUMMARY ONLY. THE EVIDENCE OF COVERAGE AND PLAN CONTRACT SHOULD BE CONSULTED FOR A DETAILED DESCRIPTION OF COVERAGE BENEFITS AND LIMITATIONS.

(3) (A) A health care service plan contract subject to Section 2715 of the federal Public Health Service Act (42 U.S.C. Sec. 300gg-15), shall satisfy the requirements of this subdivision by providing the uniform summary of benefits and coverage required under Section 2715 of the federal Public Health Service Act (42 U.S.C. Sec. 300gg-15) and any rules or regulations issued thereunder. A health care service plan that issues the uniform summary of benefits referenced in this paragraph shall do both of the following:

(i) Ensure that all applicable benefit disclosure requirements specified in this chapter and in Title 28 of the California Code of Regulations are met in other health plan documents provided to enrollees under the provisions of this chapter.

(ii) Consistent with applicable law, advise applicants and enrollees, in a prominent place in the plan documents referenced in subdivision (a), that enrollees are not financially responsible in payment of emergency care services, in any amount that the health care service plan is obligated to pay, beyond the enrollee's copayments, coinsurance, and deductibles as provided in the enrollee's health care service plan contract.

(B) Commencing October 1, 2016, the uniform summary of benefits and coverage referenced in this paragraph shall constitute a vital document for the purposes of Section

1367.04. Not later than July 1, 2016, the department shall develop written translations of the template uniform summary of benefits and coverage for all language groups identified by the State Department of Health Care Services in all plan letters as of August 27, 2014, for translation services pursuant to Section 14029.91 of the Welfare and Institutions Code, except for any language group for which the United States Department of Labor has already prepared a written translation. Not later than July 1, 2016, the department shall make available on its Internet Web site written translations of the template uniform summary of benefits and coverage developed by the department, and written translations prepared by the United States Department of Labor, if available, for any language group to which this subparagraph applies.

(C) Subdivision (c) shall not apply to a health care service plan contract subject to subparagraph (A).

(4) A health care service plan may satisfy the requirements of this subdivision for the dental services offered under a contract subject to Section 1363.04 by providing the uniform benefit disclosure benefits and coverage disclosure matrix consistent with the requirements of that section.

(c) Nothing in this section shall prevent a plan from using appropriate footnotes or disclaimers to reasonably and fairly describe coverage arrangements in order to clarify any part of the matrix that may be unclear.

(d) All plans, solicitors, and representatives of a plan shall, when presenting any plan contract for examination or sale to an individual prospective plan member, provide the individual with a properly completed disclosure form, as prescribed by the director pursuant to this section for each plan so examined or sold.

(e) In the case of group contracts, the completed disclosure form and evidence of coverage shall be presented to the contractholder upon delivery of the completed health care service plan agreement.

(f) Group contractholders shall disseminate copies of the completed disclosure form to all persons eligible to be a subscriber under the group contract at the time those persons are offered the plan. If the individual group members are offered a choice of plans, separate disclosure forms shall be supplied for each plan available. Each group contractholder shall also disseminate or cause to be disseminated copies of the evidence of coverage to all applicants, upon request, prior to enrollment and to all subscribers enrolled under the group contract.

(g) In the case of conflicts between the group contract and the evidence of coverage, the provisions of the evidence of coverage shall be binding upon the plan notwithstanding any provisions in the group contract that may be less favorable to subscribers or enrollees.

(h) In addition to the other disclosures required by this section, every health care service plan and any agent or employee of the plan shall, when presenting a plan for examination or sale to any individual purchaser or the representative of a group consisting of 25 or fewer individuals, disclose in writing the ratio of premium costs to health services paid for plan contracts with individuals and with groups of the same or similar size for the plan's preceding fiscal year. A plan may report that information by geographic area, provided the plan identifies the geographic area and reports information applicable to that geographic area.

(i) Subdivision (b) shall not apply to any coverage provided by a plan for the Medi-Cal program or the Medicare Program pursuant to Title XVIII and Title XIX of the federal Social Security Act.

(Amended by Stats. 2018, Ch. 933, Sec. 1. (SB 1008) Effective January 1, 2019.)

1363.01.

(a) Every plan that covers prescription drug benefits shall provide notice in the evidence of coverage and disclosure form to enrollees regarding whether the plan uses a formulary. The notice shall be in language that is easily understood and in a format that is easy to understand. The notice shall include an explanation of what a formulary is, how the plan determines which prescription drugs are included or excluded, and how often the plan reviews the contents of the formulary.

(b) Every plan that covers prescription drug benefits shall provide to members of the public, upon request, information regarding whether a specific drug or drugs are on the plan's formulary. Notice of the opportunity to secure this information from the plan, including the plan's telephone number for making a request of this nature and the Internet Web site where the formulary is posted under Section 1367.205, shall be included in the evidence of coverage and disclosure form to enrollees.

(c) Every plan shall notify enrollees, and members of the public who request formulary information, that the presence of a drug on the plan's formulary does not guarantee that an enrollee will be prescribed that drug by his or her prescribing provider for a particular medical condition.

(Amended by Stats. 2014, Ch. 575, Sec. 2. (SB 1052) Effective January 1, 2015.)

1363.02.

(a) The Legislature finds and declares that the right of every patient to receive basic information necessary to give full and informed consent is a fundamental tenet of good public health policy and has long been the established law of this state. Some hospitals and other providers do not provide a full range of reproductive health services and may prohibit or otherwise not promote sterilization, infertility treatments, abortion, or contraceptive services, including emergency contraception. It is the intent of the Legislature that every patient be given full and complete information about the health care services available to allow patients to make well informed health care decisions.

(b) On or before July 1, 2001, a health care service plan that covers hospital, medical, and surgical benefits shall do both of the following:

(1) Include the following statement, in at least 12-point boldface type, at the beginning of each provider directory:

"Some hospitals and other providers do not provide one or more of the following services that may be covered under your plan contract and that you or your family member might need: family planning; contraceptive services, including emergency contraception; sterilization, including tubal ligation at the time of labor and delivery; infertility treatments; or abortion. You should obtain more information before you enroll. Call your prospective doctor, medical group, independent practice association, or clinic, or call the health plan at (insert the health plan's membership services number or other appropriate number that individuals can call for assistance) to ensure that you can obtain the health care services that you need."

(2) Place the statement described in paragraph (1) in a prominent location on any provider directory posted on the health plan's website, if any, and include this statement in a conspicuous place in the plan's evidence of coverage and disclosure forms.

(c) A health care service plan shall not be required to provide the statement described in paragraph (1) of subdivision (b) in a service area in which none of the hospitals, health facilities, clinics, medical groups, or independent practice associations with which it contracts limit or restrict any of the reproductive services described in the statement.

(d) This section shall not apply to specialized health care service plans or Medicare supplement plans.

(Added by Stats. 2000, Ch. 347, Sec. 2. Effective January 1, 2001.)

1363.03.

(a) Every health care service plan that covers prescription drug benefits and that issues a card to enrollees for claims processing purposes shall issue to each of its enrollees a uniform card containing uniform prescription drug information. The uniform prescription drug information card shall, at a minimum, include the following information:

(1) The name or logo of the benefit administrator or health care service plan issuing the card, which shall be displayed on the front side of the card.

(2) The enrollee's identification number, or the subscriber's identification number when the enrollee is a dependent who accesses services using the subscriber's identification number, which shall be displayed on the front side of the card.

(3) A telephone number that pharmacy providers may call for assistance.

(4) Information required by the benefit administrator or health care service plan that is necessary to commence processing the pharmacy claim, except as provided for in paragraph (5).

(5) A health care service plan shall not be required to print any of the following information on a member card:

(A) Any number that is the same for all of its members, provided that the health care service plan provides this number to the pharmacy on an annual basis.

(B) Any information that may result in fraudulent use of the card.

(C) Any information that is otherwise prohibited from being included on the card.

(b) Beginning July 1, 2002, the new uniform prescription drug information card required by subdivision (a) shall be issued by a health care service plan to an enrollee upon enrollment or upon any change in the enrollee's coverage that impacts the data content or format of the card.

(c) Nothing in this section requires a health care service plan to issue a separate card for prescription drug coverage if the plan issues a card for health care coverage in general and the card is able to accommodate the information required by subdivision (a).

(d) This bill shall not apply to a nonprofit health care service plan with at least 3.5 million enrollees that owns or operates its own pharmacies and that provides health care services to enrollees in a specific geographic area through a mutually exclusive contract with a single medical group.

(e) "Card" as used in this section includes other technology that performs substantially the same function as a card.

(f) For purposes of this section, if a health care service plan delegates responsibility for issuing the uniform prescription drug information card to a contractor or agent, then the contract between the health care service plan and its contractor or agent shall require compliance with this section.

(Added by Stats. 2001, Ch. 622, Sec. 1. Effective January 1, 2002.)

1363.04.

(a) For plan years on and after January 1, 2021, or 12 months after regulations are adopted under subdivision (f), whichever occurs later, a health care service plan that issues, sells, renews, or offers a contract that covers dental services in this state, in addition to any other applicable disclosure requirements, shall utilize a uniform benefits and coverage disclosure matrix, which shall be developed by the department, in conjunction with the Department of Insurance, and in consultation with stakeholders. At a minimum, the benefits and coverage disclosure matrix shall require the health care service plan to make available all of the following information relating to covered dental services, together with the corresponding copayments or coinsurance and limitations:

(1) The annual overall plan deductible.

(2) The annual benefit limit.

(3) Coverage for the following categories:

(A) Preventive and diagnostic services.

(B) Basic services.

(C) Major services.

(D) Orthodontia services.

(4) Dental plan reimbursement levels and estimated enrollee cost share for services.

(5) Waiting periods.

(6) Examples to illustrate coverage and estimated enrollee costs of commonly used benefits. The examples shall include at least one service from each of the following categories listed in paragraph (3):

(A) Preventive and diagnostic services.

(B) Basic services.

(C) Major services.

(b) All plans, solicitors, and representatives of a plan that issue, sell, renew, or offer a health care plan contract that covers dental services shall, when presenting any plan contract for examination or sale to an individual prospective plan member, make available to the individual a properly completed benefits and coverage disclosure matrix, as prescribed by the director pursuant to this section for each dental plan examined or sold.

(c) In the case of group contracts for dental services, the completed benefits and coverage disclosure matrix and evidence of coverage shall be made available to the contractholder upon delivery of the completed health care service plan agreement.

(d) Group contractholders shall make available the completed benefits and coverage disclosure matrix to all persons eligible to be a subscriber under the group contract at the time those persons are offered the dental plan. If the individual group members are offered a choice of dental plans, separate matrices shall be made available for each dental plan offered. Each group contractholder shall also make available copies of the evidence of coverage to all applicants, upon request, prior to enrollment and to all subscribers enrolled under the group contract.

(e) The health care service plan offering a dental product in the individual, small, or large group market shall make available the benefits and coverage disclosure matrix to all individuals newly enrolling for coverage, experiencing a special enrollment event, and renewing coverage, and shall make available the benefits and coverage disclosure matrix to all other enrollees upon request.

(f) (1) The department shall adopt emergency regulations pursuant to Chapter 3.5 (commencing with Section 11340) of Part 1 of Division 3 of Title 2 of the Government Code to implement this section. The department shall consult with the Department of Insurance in adopting the emergency regulations, as appropriate. The adoption of regulations pursuant to this section shall be deemed to be an emergency and necessary for the immediate preservation of the public peace, health, or safety.

(2) Notwithstanding Chapter 3.5 (commencing with Section 11340) of Part 1 of Division 3 of Title 2 of the Government Code, emergency regulations adopted pursuant to this section shall not be subject to the review and approval of the Office of Administrative Law. The regulations shall become effective immediately upon filing with the Secretary of State. The regulations shall not remain in effect more than 120 days unless the adopting agency complies with all of the provisions of Chapter 3.5 (commencing with Section 11340) as required by subdivision (c) of Section 11346.1 of the Government Code.

(g) This section does not apply to Medi-Cal dental managed care contracts authorized under Chapter 7 (commencing with Section 14000) and Chapter 8 (commencing with Section 14200) of Part 3 of Division 9 of the Welfare and Institutions Code.

(Added by Stats. 2018, Ch. 933, Sec. 2. (SB 1008) Effective January 1, 2019.)

1363.05.

(a) For every plan contract that provides or supplements Medicare benefits, a plan shall include within its disclosure form the following statement in at least 12-point type:

"For additional information concerning covered benefits, contact the Health Insurance Counseling and Advocacy Program (HICAP) or your agent. HICAP provides health insurance counseling for California senior citizens. Call the HICAP toll-free telephone number, 1-800-434-0222, for a referral to your local HICAP office. HICAP is a service provided free of charge by the State of California."

(b) For every plan contract that provides or supplements Medicare benefits, a plan shall modify its disclosure forms to comply with subdivision (a) no later than January 1, 1998.

(c) Every health care service plan that provides or supplements Medicare benefits shall notify those current enrollees who enrolled prior to the modification of disclosure forms to include the disclosure statement required by subdivision (a) of the availability of the HICAP program. That notification shall include the same language as is required by subdivision (a). That notification may be by free standing document and shall be made no later than January 1, 1998.

(Added by Stats. 1996, Ch. 1113, Sec. 1. Effective January 1, 1997.)

1363.06.

(a) The Department of Managed Health Care and the Department of Insurance shall compile information as required by this section and Section 10127.14 of the Insurance Code into two comparative benefit matrices. The first matrix shall compare benefit packages offered pursuant to Section 1373.62 and Section 10127.15 of the Insurance Code. The second matrix shall compare benefit packages offered pursuant to Sections 1366.35, 1373.6, and 1399.804 and Sections 10785, 10901.2, and 12682.1 of the Insurance Code.

(b) The comparative benefit matrix shall include:

(1) Benefit information submitted by health care service plans pursuant to subdivision (d) and by health insurers pursuant to Section 10127.14 of the Insurance Code.

(2) The following statements in at least 12-point type at the top of the matrix:

(A) "This benefit summary is intended to help you compare coverage and benefits and is a summary only. For a more detailed description of coverage, benefits, and limitations, please contact the health care service plan or health insurer."

(B) "The comparative benefit summary is updated annually, or more often if necessary to be accurate."

(C) "The most current version of this comparative benefit summary is available on (address of the plan's or insurer's Internet Web site)."

This subparagraph applies only to those plans or insurers that maintain an Internet Web site.

(3) The telephone number or numbers that may be used by an applicant to contact either the department or the Department of Insurance, as appropriate, for further assistance.

(c) The Department of Managed Health Care and the Department of Insurance shall jointly prepare two standardized templates for use by health care service plans and health insurers in submitting the information required pursuant to subdivision (d) and subdivision (d) of Section 10127.14 of the Insurance Code. The templates shall be exempt from the provisions of Chapter 3.5 (commencing with Section 11340) of Part 1 of Division 3 of Title 2 of the Government Code.

(d) Health care service plans, except specialized health care service plans, shall submit the following to the department by January 31, 2003, and annually thereafter:

(1) A summary explanation of the following for each product described in subdivision (a).

(A) Eligibility requirements.

(B) The full premium cost of each benefit package in the service area in which the individual and eligible dependents work or reside.

(C) When and under what circumstances benefits cease.

(D) The terms under which coverage may be renewed.

(E) Other coverage that may be available if benefits under the described benefit package cease.

(F) The circumstances under which choice in the selection of physicians and providers is permitted.

(G) Lifetime and annual maximums.

(H) Deductibles.

(2) A summary explanation of coverage for the following, together with the corresponding copayments and limitations, for each product described in subdivision (a):

(A) Professional services.

(B) Outpatient services.

(C) Hospitalization services.

(D) Emergency health coverage.

(E) Ambulance services.

(F) Prescription drug coverage.

(G) Durable medical equipment.

(H) Mental health services.

(I) Residential treatment.

(J) Chemical dependency services.

(K) Home health services.

(L) Custodial care and skilled nursing facilities.

(3) The telephone number or numbers that may be used by an applicant to access a health care service plan customer service representative and to request additional information about the plan contract.

(4) Any other information specified by the department in the template.

(e) Each health care service plan shall provide the department with updates to the information required by subdivision (d) at least annually, or more often if necessary to maintain the accuracy of the information.

(f) The department and the Department of Insurance shall make the comparative benefit matrices available on their respective Internet Web sites and to the health care service plans and health insurers for dissemination as required by Section 1373.6 and Section 12682.1 of the Insurance Code, after confirming the accuracy of the description of the matrices with the health care service plans and health insurers.

(g) As used in this section and Section 1363.07, "benefit matrix" shall have the same meaning as benefit summary.

(h) (1) This section shall be inoperative on January 1, 2014.

(2) If Section 5000A of the Internal Revenue Code, as added by Section 1501 of PPACA, is repealed or amended to no longer apply to the individual market, as defined in Section 2791 of the federal Public Health Service Act (42 U.S.C. Sec. 300gg-91), this section shall become operative on the date of that repeal or amendment.

(3) For purposes of this subdivision, "PPACA" means the federal Patient Protection and Affordable Care Act (Public Law 111-148), as amended by the federal Health Care Education and Reconciliation Act of 2010 (Public Law 111-152), and any rules, regulations, or guidance issued pursuant to that law.

(Amended by Stats. 2013, Ch. 441, Sec. 1. (AB 1180) Effective October 1, 2013. Inoperative, by its own provisions, on January 1, 2014, subject to condition for resuming operation.)

1363.07.

(a) Each health care service plan shall send copies of the comparative benefit matrix prepared pursuant to Section 1363.06 on an annual basis, or more frequently as the matrix is updated by the department and the Department of Insurance, to solicitors and solicitor firms and employers with whom the plan contracts.

(b) Each health care service plan shall require its representatives and solicitors and soliciting firms with which it contracts, to provide a copy of the comparative benefit matrix to individuals when presenting any benefit package for examination or sale.

(c) Each health care service plan that maintains an Internet Web site shall make a downloadable copy of the comparative benefit matrix described in Section 1363.06 available through a link on its site to the Internet Web sites of the department and the Department of Insurance.

(d) (1) This section shall be inoperative on January 1, 2014.

(2) If Section 5000A of the Internal Revenue Code, as added by Section 1501 of PPACA, is repealed or amended to no longer apply to the individual market, as defined in Section 2791 of the federal Public Health Service Act (42 U.S.C. Sec. 300gg-91), this section shall become operative on the date of that repeal or amendment.

(3) For purposes of this subdivision, "PPACA" means the federal Patient Protection and Affordable Care Act (Public Law 111-148), as amended by the federal Health Care

Education and Reconciliation Act of 2010 (Public Law 111-152), and any rules, regulations, or guidance issued pursuant to that law.

(Amended by Stats. 2013, Ch. 441, Sec. 2. (AB 1180) Effective October 1, 2013. Inoperative, by its own provisions, on January 1, 2014, subject to condition for resuming operation.)

1363.1.

Any health care service plan that includes terms that require binding arbitration to settle disputes and that restrict, or provide for a waiver of, the right to a jury trial shall include, in clear and understandable language, a disclosure that meets all of the following conditions:

(a) The disclosure shall clearly state whether the plan uses binding arbitration to settle disputes, including specifically whether the plan uses binding arbitration to settle claims of medical malpractice.

(b) The disclosure shall appear as a separate article in the agreement issued to the employer group or individual subscriber and shall be prominently displayed on the enrollment form signed by each subscriber or enrollee.

(c) The disclosure shall clearly state whether the subscriber or enrollee is waiving his or her right to a jury trial for medical malpractice, other disputes relating to the delivery of service under the plan, or both, and shall be substantially expressed in the wording provided in subdivision (a) of Section 1295 of the Code of Civil Procedure.

(d) In any contract or enrollment agreement for a health care service plan, the disclosure required by this section shall be displayed immediately before the signature line provided for the representative of the group contracting with a health care service plan and immediately before the signature line provided for the individual enrolling in the health care service plan.

(Added by Stats. 1994, Ch. 653, Sec. 3. Effective January 1, 1995.)

1363.2.

On or before July 1, 1999, the disclosure form required pursuant to Section 1363 shall also contain a statement that enrollees are encouraged to use appropriately the "911" emergency response system, in areas where the system is established and operating, when they have an emergency medical condition that requires an emergency response.

(Added by Stats. 1998, Ch. 979, Sec. 2. Effective January 1, 1999.)

1363.5.

(a) A plan shall disclose or provide for the disclosure to the director and to network providers the process the plan, its contracting provider groups, or any entity with which the plan contracts for services that include utilization review or utilization management functions, uses to authorize, modify, or deny health care services under the benefits provided by the plan, including coverage for subacute care, transitional inpatient care, or care provided in skilled nursing facilities. A plan shall also disclose those processes to enrollees or persons designated by an enrollee, or to any other person or organization, upon request. The disclosure to the director shall include the policies, procedures, and the description of the process that are filed with the director pursuant to subdivision (b) of Section 1367.01.

(b) The criteria or guidelines used by plans, or any entities with which plans contract for services that include utilization review or utilization management functions, to determine whether to authorize, modify, or deny health care services shall:

(1) Be developed with involvement from actively practicing health care providers.

(2) Be consistent with sound clinical principles and processes.

(3) Be evaluated, and updated if necessary, at least annually.

(4) If used as the basis of a decision to modify, delay, or deny services in a specified case under review, be disclosed to the provider and the enrollee in that specified case.

(5) Be available to the public upon request. A plan shall only be required to disclose the criteria or guidelines for the specific procedures or conditions requested. A plan may charge reasonable fees to cover administrative expenses related to disclosing criteria or guidelines pursuant to this paragraph, limited to copying and postage costs. The plan may also make the criteria or guidelines available through electronic communication means.

(c) The disclosure required by paragraph (5) of subdivision (b) shall be accompanied by the following notice: "The materials provided to you are guidelines used by this plan to authorize, modify, or deny care for persons with similar illnesses or conditions. Specific care and treatment may vary depending on individual need and the benefits covered under your contract."

(Amended by Stats. 2000, Ch. 1067, Sec. 6. Effective January 1, 2001.)

1364.

Where the director finds it necessary in the interest of full and fair disclosure, all advertising and other consumer information disseminated by a plan for the purpose of influencing persons to become members of a plan shall contain such supplemental disclosure information as the director may require.

(Amended by Stats. 1999, Ch. 525, Sec. 90. Effective January 1, 2000. Operative July 1, 2000, or sooner, by Sec. 214 of Ch. 525.)

1364.1.

Within 30 days of receiving the notice required by Section 1255.1, a health care service plan shall notify, or provide for the notification of, enrollees who have selected a medical group or independent practice association that uses a hospital that will reduce or eliminate its emergency services. The plan may require that its contracting medical groups and independent practice associations that use the hospital provide this notice. The notice shall include a list of alternate hospitals that may be used by enrollees for emergency services.

(Added by Stats. 1998, Ch. 995, Sec. 5. Effective January 1, 1999.)

1364.5.

(a) On or before July 1, 2001, every health care service plan shall file with the director a copy of their policies and procedures to protect the security of patient medical information to ensure compliance with the Confidentiality of Information Act (Part 2.6 (commencing with Section 56) of Division 1 of the Civil Code). Any amendment to the policies and procedures shall be filed in accordance with Section 1352.

(b) On and after July 1, 2001, every health care service plan shall, upon request, provide to enrollees and subscribers a written statement that describes how the contracting organization or health care service plan maintains the confidentiality of medical information obtained by and in the possession of the contracting organization or the health care service plan.

(c) The statement required by subdivision (b) shall be in at least 12-point type and meet the following requirements:

(1) The statement shall describe how the contracting organization or health care service plan protects the confidentiality of medical information pursuant to this article and inform patients or enrollees and subscribers that any disclosure of medical information beyond the provisions of the law is prohibited.

(2) The statement shall describe the types of medical information that may be collected and the type of sources that may be used to collect the information, the purposes for which the contracting organization or plan will obtain medical information from other health care providers.

(3) The statement shall describe the circumstances under which medical information may be disclosed without prior authorization, pursuant to Section 56.10 of the Civil Code.

(4) The statement shall describe how patients or enrollees and subscribers may obtain access to medical information created by and in the possession of the contracting organization or health care service plan, including copies of medical information.

(d) On and after July 1, 2001, every health care service plan shall include in its evidence of coverage or disclosure form the following notice, in 12-point type:

A STATEMENT DESCRIBING (NAME OR PLAN OR "OUR") POLICIES AND PROCEDURES FOR PRESERVING THE CONFIDENTIALITY OF MEDICAL RECORDS IS AVAILABLE AND WILL BE FURNISHED TO YOU UPON REQUEST.

(Amended by Stats. 2000, Ch. 1067, Sec. 7. Effective January 1, 2001.)

1365.

(a) An enrollment or a subscription shall not be canceled or not renewed except for the following reasons:

(1) (A) Except as otherwise specified in subparagraph (C), for nonpayment of the required premiums by the individual, employer, or contractholder if the individual, employer, or contractholder has been duly notified and billed for the charge and at least a 30-day grace period has elapsed since the date of notification or, if longer, the period of time required for notice and any other requirements pursuant to Section 2703, 2712, or 2742 of the federal Public Health Service Act (42 U.S.C. Secs. 300gg-2, 300gg-12, and 300gg-42) and any subsequent rules or regulations has elapsed.

(B) Pursuant to subparagraph (A), a health care service plan shall continue to provide coverage as required by the individual's, employer's, or contractholder's health care service plan contract during the 30-day period described in subparagraph (A).

(C) (i) For nonpayment of the required premiums by an individual who receives advance payments of the premium tax credit authorized by Section 36B of the Internal Revenue Code or advanced premium assistance subsidy authorized by Section 100800 of the Government Code, or both, if the individual has been duly notified and billed for the charge and a grace period of three consecutive months has elapsed since the last day of paid coverage.

(ii) During the first month of the three-month grace period described in clause (i), a health care service plan shall continue to do both of the following:

(I) Collect advance payments of the federal premium tax credit or state advanced premium assistance subsidy, or both, on behalf of the enrollee.

(II) Provide coverage as required by the individual's health care service plan contract.

(iii) If the individual exhausts the three-month grace period described in clause (i) without paying all outstanding premiums due, the health care service plan shall return both of the following:

(I) Advance payments of the premium tax credit paid on behalf of the individual for the second and third months of the three-month grace period described in clause (i), pursuant to Section 156.270(e)(2) of Title 45 of the Code of Federal Regulations.

(II) The advanced premium assistance subsidy paid on behalf of the individual for the second and third months of the three-month grace period described in clause (i), pursuant to subdivision (a) of Section 100805 of the Government Code.

(iv) A health care service plan shall comply with all federal and state laws and regulations relating to cancellations, terminations, or nonrenewals of coverage due to nonpayment of premiums by individuals who receive advance payments of the federal premium tax credit or state advanced premium assistance subsidy. For a health care service plan contract issued, amended, or renewed on or after January 1, 2020, all requirements applicable to cancellations, terminations, or nonrenewals of coverage due to nonpayment of premiums by individuals who receive advance payments of premium tax credit authorized by Section 36B of the Internal Revenue Code shall apply to cancellations, terminations, or nonrenewals of coverage due to nonpayment of premiums by individuals who receive advanced premium assistance subsidy authorized by Section 100800 of the Government Code.

(2) The plan demonstrates fraud or an intentional misrepresentation of material fact under the terms of the health care service plan contract by the individual contractholder or employer.

(3) In the case of an individual health care service plan contract, the individual subscriber no longer resides, lives, or works in the plan's service area, but only if the coverage is

terminated uniformly without regard to any health status-related factor of covered individuals.

(4) In the case of a group health care service plan contract, violation of a material contract provision relating to employer contribution or group participation rates by the contractholder or employer.

(5) If the plan ceases to provide or arrange for the provision of health benefits for new health care service plan contracts in the individual or group market, or all markets, in this state, provided, however, that the following conditions are satisfied:

(A) Notice of the decision to cease new or existing health benefit plans in the state is provided to the director, the individual or group contractholder or employer, and the enrollees covered under those contracts, at least 180 days prior to discontinuation of those contracts.

(B) Health benefit plans shall not be canceled for 180 days after the date of the notice required under subparagraph (A) and, for that business of a plan that remains in force, any plan that ceases to offer for sale new health benefit plans shall continue to be governed by this section with respect to business conducted under this section.

(C) Except as authorized under subdivision (b) of Section 1357.09 and Section 1357.10, a plan that ceases to write new health benefit plans in the individual or group market, or all markets, in this state shall be prohibited from offering for sale health benefit plans in that market or markets in this state for a period of five years from the date of the discontinuation of the last coverage not so renewed.

(6) If the plan withdraws a health benefit plan from the market, provided that all of the following conditions are satisfied:

(A) The plan notifies all affected subscribers, contractholders, employers, and enrollees and the director at least 90 days prior to the discontinuation of the plan.

(B) The plan makes available to the individual or group contractholder or employer all health benefit plans that it makes available to new individual or group business, respectively.

(C) In exercising the option to discontinue a health benefit plan under this paragraph and in offering the option of coverage under subparagraph (B), the plan acts uniformly without regard to the claims experience of the individual or contractholder or employer, or any health status-related factor relating to enrollees or potential enrollees.

(D) For small employer health care service plan contracts offered under Article 3.1 (commencing with Section 1357), the premium for the new plan contract complies with the renewal increase requirements set forth in Section 1357.12. This subparagraph shall not apply after December 31, 2013.

(7) In the case of a group health benefit plan, if an individual or employer ceases to be a member of a guaranteed association, as defined in subdivision (n) of Section 1357, but only if that coverage is terminated under this paragraph uniformly without regard to any health status-related factor relating to any enrollee.

(b) (1) An enrollee or subscriber who alleges that an enrollment or subscription has been or will be improperly canceled, rescinded, or not renewed may request a review by the director pursuant to Section 1368.

(2) If the director determines that a proper complaint exists, the director shall notify the plan and the enrollee or subscriber who requested the review.

(3) If, after review, the director determines that the cancellation, rescission, or failure to renew is contrary to existing law, the director shall order the plan to reinstate the enrollee or subscriber. Within 15 days after receipt of that order, the health care service plan shall request a hearing or reinstate the enrollee or subscriber.

(4) If an enrollee or subscriber requests a review of the health care service plan's determination to cancel or rescind or failure to renew the enrollee's or subscriber's health care service plan contract pursuant to this section, the health care service plan shall continue to provide coverage to the enrollee or subscriber under the terms of the contract until a final determination of the enrollee's or subscriber's request for review has been made by the director. This paragraph shall not apply if the health care service plan cancels or does not renew the enrollee's or subscriber's health care service plan contract for nonpayment of premiums pursuant to paragraph (1) of subdivision (a).

(5) A reinstatement pursuant to this subdivision shall be retroactive to the time of cancellation, rescission, or failure to renew and the plan shall be liable for the expenses incurred by the subscriber or enrollee for covered health care services from the date of cancellation, rescission, or nonrenewal to and including the date of reinstatement. The health care service plan shall reimburse the enrollee or subscriber for any expenses incurred pursuant to this paragraph within 30 days of receipt of the completed claim.

(c) This section shall not abrogate any preexisting contracts entered into prior to the effective date of this chapter between a subscriber or enrollee and a health care service plan or a specialized health care service plan, including, but not limited to, the financial liability of the plan, except that each plan shall, if directed to do so by the director, exercise its authority, if any, under those preexisting contracts to conform them to existing law.

(d) As used in this section, "health benefit plan" means any individual or group insurance policy or health care service plan contract that provides medical, hospital, and surgical benefits. The term does not include accident only, credit, or disability income coverage, coverage of Medicare services pursuant to contracts with the United States government, Medicare supplement coverage, long-term care insurance, dental or vision coverage, coverage issued as a supplement to liability insurance, insurance arising out of workers' compensation law or similar law, automobile medical payment insurance, or insurance under which benefits are payable with or without regard to fault and that is statutorily required to be contained in any liability insurance policy or equivalent self-insurance.

(e) On or before July 1, 2011, the director may issue guidance to health care service plans regarding compliance with this section and that guidance shall not be subject to the

Administrative Procedure Act (Chapter 3.5 (commencing with Section 11340) of Part 1 of Division 3 of Title 2 of the Government Code). Any guidance issued pursuant to this subdivision shall only be effective through December 31, 2013, or until the director adopts and effects regulations pursuant to the Administrative Procedure Act, whichever occurs first.

(Amended by Stats. 2019, Ch. 38, Sec. 15. (SB 78) Effective June 27, 2019.)

1365.5.

(a) No health care service plan or specialized health care service plan shall refuse to enter into any contract or shall cancel or decline to renew or reinstate any contract because of the race, color, national origin, ancestry, religion, sex, marital status, sexual orientation, or age of any contracting party, prospective contracting party, or person reasonably expected to benefit from that contract as a subscriber, enrollee, member, or otherwise.

(b) The terms of any contract shall not be modified, and the benefits or coverage of any contract shall not be subject to any limitations, exceptions, exclusions, reductions, copayments, coinsurance, deductibles, reservations, or premium, price, or charge differentials, or other modifications because of the race, color, national origin, ancestry, religion, sex, marital status, sexual orientation, or age of any contracting party, potential contracting party, or person reasonably expected to benefit from that contract as a subscriber, enrollee, member, or otherwise; except that premium, price, or charge differentials because of the age of any individual when based on objective, valid, and up-to-date statistical and actuarial data are not prohibited.

(c) It shall be deemed a violation of subdivision (a) for any health care service plan to utilize marital status, living arrangements, occupation, sex, beneficiary designation, ZIP Codes or other territorial classification, or any combination thereof for the purpose of establishing sexual orientation. Nothing in this section shall be construed to alter in any manner the existing law prohibiting health care service plans from conducting tests for the presence of human immunodeficiency virus or evidence thereof.

(d) This section shall not be construed to limit the authority of the director to adopt or enforce regulations prohibiting discrimination because of sex, marital status, or sexual orientation.

(e) "Sex" as used in this section shall have the same meaning as "gender," as defined in Section 422.56 of the Penal Code.

(f) The changes made to this section by the act adding this subdivision shall only apply to contracts issued, amended, or renewed on or after January 1, 2011.

(Amended by Stats. 2009, Ch. 365, Sec. 1. (AB 119) Effective January 1, 2010.)

1366.

(a) No plan may use in its name, any of the words "insurance," "casualty," "surety," "mutual," or any other words descriptive of the insurance, casualty, or surety business or use any name similar to the name or description of any insurance or surety corporation doing business in this state unless such plan controls or is controlled by an entity licensed as an insurer pursuant to the provisions of the Insurance Code and the plan employs a name related to that of such controlled or controlling entity.

(b) Section 2415 of the Business and Professions Code, pertaining to fictitious names, shall not apply to plans, except specialized health care service plans.

(c) No plan or solicitor firm may adopt a name style that is deceptive, or one that could cause the public to believe the plan is affiliated with, or recommended by any governmental or private entity unless such affiliation or endorsement exists.

(Amended by Stats. 1980, Ch. 1313.)

1366.1.

(a) The department shall adopt regulations on or before July 1, 2003, that establish an extended geographic accessibility standard for access to health care providers served by a health care service plan in counties with a population of 500,000 or less, and that, as of January 1, 2002, have two or fewer health care service plans providing coverage to the entire county in the commercial market.

(b) This section shall not apply to specialized health care service plans or health care service plan contracts that provide benefits to enrollees through any of the following:

(1) Preferred provider contracting arrangements.

(2) The Medi-Cal program.

(3) The Healthy Families program.

(c) (1) At least 30 days before a health care service plan files for modification of its license with the department in order to withdraw from a county with a population of 500,000 or less, or a portion of that county, the health care service plan shall hold a public meeting in the county or portion of the county from which it intends to withdraw, and shall do all of the following:

(A) Provide notice announcing the public meeting at least 30 days prior to the public meeting to all affected enrollees, health care providers, advocates, public officials, and other interested parties.

(B) Provide notice announcing the public meeting at least 30 days prior to the public meeting in a newspaper of general circulation within the affected county or portion of the affected county.

(C) At the public meeting, allow testimony, which may be limited to a certain length of time by the health care service plan, of all interested parties.

(D) Send a summary of the comments received at the public meeting to the department.

(E) Send a summary of the comments received at the public meeting to the Centers for Medicare and Medicaid Services if the modification would affect Medicare beneficiaries.

(F) File with the department for review, no less than 30 days prior to the date of mailing or publication, the notices required under subparagraphs (A) and (B).

(2) A representative of the department shall attend the public meeting.

(Added by Stats. 2002, Ch. 549, Sec. 1. Effective January 1, 2003. See somewhat similar section added by Stats. 2002, Ch. 928, which prevails to the extent of any conflicting provisions.)

1366.1.

(a) The department shall adopt regulations on or before July 1, 2003, that establish an extended geographic accessibility standard for access to health care providers served by a health care service plan in counties with a population of 500,000 or less, and that, as of January 1, 2002, have two or fewer health care service plans providing coverage to the entire county in the commercial market.

(b) This section shall not apply to specialized health care service plans or health care service plan contracts that provide benefits to enrollees through any of the following:

(1) Preferred provider contracting arrangements.

(2) The Medi-Cal program.

(3) The Healthy Families Program.

(4) The federal Medicare program.

(c) At least 30 days before a health care service plan files a notice of material modification of its license with the department to withdraw from a county with a population of 500,000 or less, the health care service plan shall hold a public meeting in the county from which it is intending to withdraw, and shall do all of the following:

(1) Provide notice announcing the public meeting at least 30 days prior to the public meeting to all affected enrollees, health care providers with which it contracts, the members of the board of supervisors of the affected county, the members of the city councils of cities in the affected county, and members of the Legislature who represent the affected county.

(2) Provide notice announcing the public meeting at least 15 days prior to the public meeting in a newspaper of general circulation within the affected county.

(3) At the public meeting, allow testimony, which may be limited to a certain length of time by the health care service plan, of all interested parties.

(4) File with the department for review, no less than 30 days prior to the date of mailing or publication, the notices required under paragraphs (1) and (2).

(d) The department may require a health care service plan that has filed to withdraw from a portion of a county with a population of less than 500,000, to hold a hearing for affected enrollees.

(e) A representative of the department shall attend the public meeting described in this section.

(Added by Stats. 2002, Ch. 928, Sec. 1. Effective January 1, 2003. See somewhat similar section added by Stats. 2002, Ch. 549.)

1366.2.

(a) A full health care service plan shall make available to a group subscriber, upon request, the termination date of all major health care provider contracts that are for services in the geographic area for which the group subscriber has secured coverage and that include a specified termination date.

(b) For purposes of this section, the following terms have the following meanings:

(1) "Enrollee" means a person who is enrolled in a health care service plan and who is a recipient of services from the plan.

(2) "Full health care service plan" means a plan that meets the definition set forth in subdivision (f) of Section 1345, and that has a total enrolled membership exceeding 499,999 enrollees.

(3) "Hospital" means a general acute care hospital.

(4) "Major health care provider contract" means a contract between a full service plan and provider group or hospital covering more than 25,000 of that plan's enrollees. "Major health care provider contract" does not mean a provider contract between a specialized health care service plan and a provider group or hospital.

(5) "Provider group" means a medical group, independent practice association, or other similar group of providers with a total enrolled membership exceeding 99,999 enrollees.

(Added by Stats. 2004, Ch. 411, Sec. 1. Effective September 9, 2004.)

1366.3.

(a) On and after January 1, 2005, a health care service plan issuing individual plan contracts that ceases to offer individual coverage in this state shall offer coverage to the subscribers who had been covered by those contracts at the time of withdrawal under the same terms and conditions as provided in paragraph (3) of subdivision (a), paragraphs (2) to (4), inclusive, of subdivision (b), subdivisions (c) to (e), inclusive, and subdivision (h) of Section 1373.6.

(b) A health care service plan that ceases to offer individual coverage in a service area shall offer the coverage required by subdivision (a) to subscribers who had been covered by those contracts at the time of withdrawal, if the plan continues to offer group coverage in that service area. This subdivision shall not apply to coverage provided pursuant to a preferred provider organization.

(c) The department may adopt regulations to implement this section.

(d) This section shall not apply when a plan participating in Medi-Cal, Healthy Families, Access for Infants and Mothers, or any other contract between the plan and a government entity no longer contracts with the government entity to provide health coverage in the state, or a specified area of the state, nor shall this section apply when a plan ceases entirely to market, offer, and issue any and all forms of coverage in any part of this state after the effective date of this section.

(e) (1) On and after January 1, 2014, and except as provided in paragraph (2), the reference to Section 1373.6 in subdivision (a) shall not apply to any health plan contracts.

(2) If Section 5000A of the Internal Revenue Code, as added by Section 1501 of the federal Patient Protection and Affordable Care Act (Public Law 111-148), as amended by the federal Health Care and Education Reconciliation Act of 2010 (Public Law 111-152), is repealed or amended to no longer apply to the individual market, as defined in Section 2791 of the federal Public Health Service Act (42 U.S.C. Section 300gg-91), paragraph (1) shall become inoperative on the date of that repeal or amendment.

(Amended by Stats. 2013, Ch. 441, Sec. 3. (AB 1180) Effective October 1, 2013.)

1366.4.

(a) A medical group, physician, or independent practice association that contracts with a health care service plan may enter into contracts with licensed nonphysician providers to provide services, as defined in Section 1300.67(a)(1) of Title 28 of the California Code of Regulations, to plan enrollees covered by the contract between the plan and the group, physician, or association.

(b) The licensed nonphysician provider described in subdivision (a) that contracts with a medical group, physician, or independent practice association may directly bill, if direct billing is otherwise permitted by law, a health care service plan for covered services pursuant to a contract with the health care service plan that specifies direct billing. Direct billing pursuant to this subdivision is permitted only to the extent that the same services are not billed for by the medical group, physician, or independent practice association.

(c) A health care service plan may require the nonphysician provider to complete an appropriate credentialing process.

(d) Every health care service plan may either list licensed nonphysician providers that contract with medical groups, physicians, and independent practice associations pursuant to subdivision (b) in any listing or directory of plan health care providers that is provided to enrollees or to the public, or may include a notification in the plan's evidence of coverage or provider list that the health care service plan has contracts with nonphysician providers, pursuant to subdivision (b), and may list the types of contracted nonphysician providers. The notification may inform an enrollee that he or she may obtain a list of the nonphysician providers by contacting his or her primary or specialist medical group. The listing may indicate whether licensed nonphysician providers may be accessed directly by enrollees.

(e) Nothing in this section shall be construed to authorize, or otherwise require the director to approve, a risk-sharing arrangement between a plan and a provider.

(Amended by Stats. 2009, Ch. 298, Sec. 4. (AB 1540) Effective January 1, 2010.)

1366.6.

(a) For purposes of this section, the following definitions shall apply:

(1) "Exchange" means the California Health Benefit Exchange established in Title 22 (commencing with Section 100500) of the Government Code.

(2) "Federal act" means the federal Patient Protection and Affordable Care Act (Public Law 111-148), as amended by the federal Health Care and Education Reconciliation Act of 2010 (Public Law 111-152), and any amendments to, or regulations or guidance issued under, those acts.

(3) "Qualified health plan" has the same meaning as that term is defined in Section 1301 of the federal act.

(4) "Small employer" has the same meaning as that term is defined in Section 1357.500.

(b) (1) Health care service plans participating in the individual market of the Exchange shall fairly and affirmatively offer, market, and sell in the individual market of the Exchange at least one product within each of the five levels of coverage contained in subsections (d) and (e) of Section 1302 of the federal act. Health care service plans participating in the Small Business Health Options Program (SHOP Program) of the Exchange, established pursuant to subdivision (m) of Section 100504 of the Government Code, shall fairly and affirmatively offer, market, and sell in the SHOP Program at least one product within each of the four levels of coverage contained in subsection (d) of Section 1302 of the federal act.

(2) The board established under Section 100500 of the Government Code may require plans to sell additional products within each of the levels of coverage identified in paragraph (1).

(3) This subdivision shall not apply to a plan that solely offers supplemental coverage in the Exchange under paragraph (10) of subdivision (a) of Section 100504 of the Government Code.

(4) This subdivision shall not apply to a bridge plan product that meets the requirements of Section 100504.5 of the Government Code to the extent approved by the appropriate federal agency.

(c) (1) Health care service plans participating in the Exchange that sell any products outside the Exchange shall do both of the following:

(A) Fairly and affirmatively offer, market, and sell all products made available to individuals in the Exchange to individuals purchasing coverage outside the Exchange.

(B) Fairly and affirmatively offer, market, and sell all products made available to small employers in the Exchange to small employers purchasing coverage outside the Exchange.

(2) For purposes of this subdivision, "product" does not include contracts entered into pursuant to Part 6.2 (commencing with Section 12693) of Division 2 of the Insurance Code between the Managed Risk Medical Insurance Board and health care service plans for enrolled Healthy Families beneficiaries or to contracts entered into pursuant to Chapter 7 (commencing with Section 14000) of, or Chapter 8 (commencing with Section 14200) of, Part 3 of Division 9 of the Welfare and Institutions Code between the State Department of Health Care Services and health care service plans for enrolled Medi-Cal beneficiaries, or for contracts with bridge plan products that meet the requirements of Section 100504.5 of the Government Code.

(d) (1) Commencing January 1, 2014, a health care service plan shall, with respect to individual plan contracts that cover hospital, medical, or surgical benefits, only sell the five levels of coverage contained in subsections (d) and (e) of Section 1302 of the federal act, except that a health care service plan that does not participate in the Exchange shall, with respect to individual plan contracts that cover hospital, medical, or surgical benefits, only sell the four levels of coverage contained in subsection (d) of Section 1302 of the federal act.

(2) Commencing January 1, 2014, a health care service plan shall, with respect to small employer plan contracts that cover hospital, medical, or surgical expenses, only sell the four levels of coverage contained in subsection (d) of Section 1302 of the federal act.

(e) Commencing January 1, 2014, a health care service plan that does not participate in the Exchange shall, with respect to individual or small employer plan contracts that cover hospital, medical, or surgical benefits, offer at least one standardized product that has been designated by the Exchange in each of the four levels of coverage contained in subsection (d) of Section 1302 of the federal act. This subdivision shall only apply if the board of the Exchange exercises its authority under subdivision (c) of Section 100504 of the Government Code. Nothing in this subdivision shall require a plan that does not participate in the Exchange to offer standardized products in the small employer market if the plan only sells products in the individual market. Nothing in this subdivision shall require a plan that does not participate in the Exchange to offer standardized products in the individual market if the plan only sells products in the small employer market. This subdivision shall not be construed to prohibit the plan from offering other products provided that it complies with subdivision (d).

(f) For purposes of this section, a bridge plan product shall mean an individual health benefit plan, as defined in subdivision (f) of Section 1399.845, that is offered by a health care service plan licensed under this chapter that contracts with the Exchange pursuant to Title 22 (commencing with Section 100500) of the Government Code.

(g) This section shall become inoperative on the October 1 that is five years after the date that federal approval of the bridge plan option occurs, and, as of the second January 1 thereafter, is repealed, unless a later enacted statute that is enacted before that date deletes or extends the dates on which it becomes inoperative and is repealed.

(Amended (as amended by Stats. 2013, 1st Ex. Sess., Ch. 5, Sec. 8) by Stats. 2014, Ch. 572, Sec. 5. (SB 959) Effective January 1, 2015. Conditionally inoperative, on date prescribed by its own provisions. Repealed, by its own provisions, on second January 1 after inoperative date. See later operative version, as amended by Sec. 6 of Stats. 2014, Ch. 572.)

1366.6.

(a) For purposes of this section, the following definitions shall apply:

(1) "Exchange" means the California Health Benefit Exchange established in Title 22 (commencing with Section 100500) of the Government Code.

(2) "Federal act" means the federal Patient Protection and Affordable Care Act (Public Law 111-148), as amended by the federal Health Care and Education Reconciliation Act of 2010 (Public Law 111-152), and any amendments to, or regulations or guidance issued under, those acts.

(3) "Qualified health plan" has the same meaning as that term is defined in Section 1301 of the federal act.

(4) "Small employer" has the same meaning as that term is defined in Section 1357.500.

(b) (1) Health care service plans participating in the individual market of the Exchange shall fairly and affirmatively offer, market, and sell in the individual market of the Exchange at least one product within each of the five levels of coverage contained in subsections (d) and (e) of Section 1302 of the federal act. Health care service plans participating in the Small Business Health Options Program (SHOP Program) of the Exchange, established pursuant to subdivision (m) of Section 100504 of the Government Code, shall fairly and affirmatively offer, market, and sell in the SHOP Program at least one product within each of the four levels of coverage contained in subsection (d) of Section 1302 of the federal act.

(2) The board established under Section 100500 of the Government Code may require plans to sell additional products within each of the levels of coverage identified in paragraph (1).

(3) This subdivision shall not apply to a plan that solely offers supplemental coverage in the Exchange under paragraph (10) of subdivision (a) of Section 100504 of the Government Code.

(c) (1) Health care service plans participating in the Exchange that sell any products outside the Exchange shall do both of the following:

(A) Fairly and affirmatively offer, market, and sell all products made available to individuals in the Exchange to individuals purchasing coverage outside the Exchange.

(B) Fairly and affirmatively offer, market, and sell all products made available to small employers in the Exchange to small employers purchasing coverage outside the Exchange.

(2) For purposes of this subdivision, "product" does not include contracts entered into pursuant to Part 6.2 (commencing with Section 12693) of Division 2 of the Insurance Code between the Managed Risk Medical Insurance Board and health care service plans for enrolled Healthy Families beneficiaries or to contracts entered into pursuant to Chapter 7 (commencing with Section 14000) of, or Chapter 8 (commencing with Section 14200) of, Part 3 of Division 9 of the Welfare and Institutions Code between the State Department of Health Care Services and health care service plans for enrolled Medi-Cal beneficiaries.

(d) (1) Commencing January 1, 2014, a health care service plan shall, with respect to individual plan contracts that cover hospital, medical, or surgical benefits, only sell the five levels of coverage contained in subsections (d) and (e) of Section 1302 of the federal act, except that a health care service plan that does not participate in the Exchange shall, with respect to individual plan contracts that cover hospital, medical, or surgical benefits,

only sell the four levels of coverage contained in subsection (d) of Section 1302 of the federal act.

(2) Commencing January 1, 2014, a health care service plan shall, with respect to small employer plan contracts that cover hospital, medical, or surgical expenses, only sell the four levels of coverage contained in subsection (d) of Section 1302 of the federal act.

(e) Commencing January 1, 2014, a health care service plan that does not participate in the Exchange shall, with respect to individual or small employer plan contracts that cover hospital, medical, or surgical benefits, offer at least one standardized product that has been designated by the Exchange in each of the four levels of coverage contained in subdivision (d) of Section 1302 of the federal act. This subdivision shall only apply if the board of the Exchange exercises its authority under subdivision (c) of Section 100504 of the Government Code. Nothing in this subdivision shall require a plan that does not participate in the Exchange to offer standardized products in the small employer market if the plan only sells products in the individual market. Nothing in this subdivision shall require a plan that does not participate in the Exchange to offer standardized products in the individual market if the plan only sells products in the small employer market. This subdivision shall not be construed to prohibit the plan from offering other products provided that it complies with subdivision (d).

(f) This section shall become operative only if Section 8 of the act that added this section becomes inoperative pursuant to subdivision (g) of that Section 8.

(Amended (as added by Stats. 2013, 1st Ex. Sess., Ch. 5, Sec. 9) by Stats. 2014, Ch. 572, Sec. 6. (SB 959) Effective January 1, 2015. Section conditionally operative by its own provisions.)

ARTICLE 4.5. California Cobra Program [1366.20 - 1366.29]

(Article 4.5 added by Stats. 1997, Ch. 665, Sec. 1.)

1366.20.

(a) This article shall be known as the California Continuation Benefits Replacement Act, or "Cal-COBRA."

(b) It is the intent of the Legislature that continued access to health insurance coverage is provided to employees, and their dependents, of employers with 2 to 19 eligible employees who are not currently offered continuation coverage under the Consolidated Omnibus Budget Reconciliation Act of 1985.

(c) It is the intent of the Legislature that any federal assistance that is or may become available to qualified beneficiaries under this article be effectively and promptly implemented by the department.

(d) The director, in consultation with the Insurance Commissioner, may adopt emergency regulations to implement this article in accordance with Chapter 3.5 (commencing with Section 11340) of Part 1 of Division 3 of Title 2 of the Government Code by making a finding of emergency and demonstrating the need for immediate action in the event that any federal assistance is or becomes available to qualified beneficiaries under this article. The adoption of these regulations shall be considered by the Office of Administrative Law to be necessary to avoid serious harm to the public peace, health, safety, or general welfare. Any regulations adopted pursuant to this subdivision shall be substantially similar to those adopted by the Insurance Commissioner under subdivision (d) of Section 10128.50 of the Insurance Code.

(Amended by Stats. 2009, Ch. 3, Sec. 1. Effective May 12, 2009.)

1366.21.

The definitions contained in this section govern the construction of this article.

(a) "Continuation coverage" means extended coverage under the group benefit plan in which an eligible employee or eligible dependent is currently enrolled, or, in the case of a termination of the group benefit plan or an employer open enrollment period, extended coverage under the group benefit plan currently offered by the employer.

(b) "Group benefit plan" means any health care service plan contract provided pursuant to Article 3.1 (commencing with Section 1357) to an employer with 2 to 19 eligible employees, as defined in Section 1357, as well as a specialized health care service plan contract provided to an employer with 2 to 19 eligible employees, as defined in Section 1357.

(c) (1) "Qualified beneficiary" means any individual who, on the day before the qualifying event, is an enrollee in a group benefit plan offered by a health care service plan pursuant to Article 3.1 (commencing with Section 1357) and has a qualifying event, as defined in subdivision (d).

(2) "Qualified beneficiary eligible for premium assistance under ARRA" means a qualified beneficiary, as defined in paragraph (1), who (A) was or is eligible for continuation coverage as a result of the involuntary termination of the covered employee's employment during the period specified in subparagraph (A) of paragraph (3) of subdivision (a) of Section 3001 of ARRA, (B) elects continuation coverage, and (C) meets the definition of "qualified beneficiary" set forth in paragraph (3) of Section 1167 of Title 29 of the United States Code, as used in subparagraph (E) of paragraph (10) of subdivision (a) of Section 3001 of ARRA or any subsequent rules or regulations issued pursuant to that law.

(3) "ARRA" means Title III of Division B of the federal American Recovery and Reinvestment Act of 2009 or any amendment to that federal law extending federal premium assistance to qualified beneficiaries.

(d) "Qualifying event" means any of the following events that, but for the election of continuation coverage under this article, would result in a loss of coverage under the group benefit plan to a qualified beneficiary:

(1) The death of the covered employee.

(2) The termination of employment or reduction in hours of the covered employee's employment, except that termination for gross misconduct does not constitute a qualifying event.

(3) The divorce or legal separation of the covered employee from the covered employee's spouse.

(4) The loss of dependent status by a dependent enrolled in the group benefit plan.

(5) With respect to a covered dependent only, the covered employee's entitlement to benefits under Title XVIII of the United States Social Security Act (Medicare).

(e) "Employer" means any employer that meets the definition of "small employer" as set forth in Section 1357 and (1) employed 2 to 19 eligible employees on at least 50 percent of its working days during the preceding calendar year, or, if the employer was not in business during any part of the preceding calendar year, employed 2 to 19 eligible employees on at least 50 percent of its working days during the preceding calendar quarter, (2) has contracted for health care coverage through a group benefit plan offered by a health care service plan, and (3) is not subject to Section 4980B of the United States Internal Revenue Code or Chapter 18 of the Employee Retirement Income Security Act, 29 U.S.C. Section 1161 et seq.

(f) "Core coverage" means coverage of basic health care services, as defined in subdivision (b) of Section 1345, and other hospital, medical, or surgical benefits provided by the group benefit plan that a qualified beneficiary was receiving immediately prior to the qualifying event, other than noncore coverage.

(g) "Noncore coverage" means coverage for vision and dental care.

(Amended by Stats. 2010, Ch. 24, Sec. 1. (SB 838) Effective June 3, 2010.)

1366.22.

The continuation coverage requirements of this article do not apply to the following individuals:

(a) Individuals who are entitled to Medicare benefits or become entitled to Medicare benefits pursuant to Title XVIII of the United States Social Security Act, as amended or superseded. Entitlement to Medicare Part A only constitutes entitlement to benefits under Medicare.

(b) Individuals who have other hospital, medical, or surgical coverage or who are covered or become covered under another group benefit plan, including a self-insured employee welfare benefit plan, that provides coverage for individuals and that does not impose any exclusion or limitation with respect to any preexisting condition of the individual, other than a preexisting condition limitation or exclusion that does not apply to or is satisfied by the qualified beneficiary pursuant to Sections 1357 and 1357.06. A group conversion option under any group benefit plan shall not be considered as an arrangement under which an individual is or becomes covered.

(c) Individuals who are covered, become covered, or are eligible for federal COBRA coverage pursuant to Section 4980B of the United States Internal Revenue Code or Chapter 18 of the Employee Retirement Income Security Act, 29 U.S.C. Section 1161 et seq.

(d) Individuals who are covered, become covered, or are eligible for coverage pursuant to Chapter 6A of the Public Health Service Act, 42 U.S.C. Section 300bb-1 et seq.

(e) Qualified beneficiaries who fail to meet the requirements of subdivision (b) of Section 1366.24 or subdivision (h) of Section 1366.25 regarding notification of a qualifying event or election of continuation coverage within the specified time limits.

(f) Except as provided in Section 3001 of ARRA, qualified beneficiaries who fail to submit the correct premium amount required by subdivision (b) of Section 1366.24 and Section 1366.26, in accordance with the terms and conditions of the plan contract, or fail to satisfy other terms and conditions of the plan contract.

(Amended by Stats. 2010, Ch. 24, Sec. 2. (SB 838) Effective June 3, 2010.)

1366.23.

(a) Every health care service plan, including a specialized health care service plan contract, that provides coverage under a group benefit plan to an employer, as defined in Section 1366.21, shall offer continuation coverage, pursuant to this section, to a qualified beneficiary under the contract upon a qualifying event without evidence of insurability. The qualified beneficiary shall, upon election, be able to continue his or her coverage under the group benefit plan, subject to the contract's terms and conditions, and subject to the requirements of this article. Except as otherwise provided in this article, continuation coverage shall be provided under the same terms and conditions that apply to similarly situated individuals under the group benefit plan.

(b) Every health care service plan shall also offer the continuation coverage to a qualified beneficiary who (1) elects continuation coverage under a group benefit plan, as defined in this article or in Section 10128.51 of the Insurance Code, but whose continuation coverage is terminated pursuant to subdivision (b) of Section 1366.27, prior to any other termination date specified in Section 1366.27, or (2) who elects coverage through the health care service plan during any employer open enrollment, and the employer has contracted with the health care service plan to provide coverage to the employer's active employees. This continuation coverage shall be provided only for the balance of the period that the qualified beneficiary would have remained covered under the prior group benefit plan had the employer not terminated the group contract with the previous health care service plan or insurer.

(c) Every health care service plan or specialized health care service plan shall offer a qualified beneficiary the ability to elect the same core, noncore, or core and noncore coverage that the qualified beneficiary had immediately prior to the qualifying event.

(d) Any child who is born to a former employee who is a qualified beneficiary who has elected continuation coverage pursuant to this article or a child who is placed for adoption with a former employee who is a qualified beneficiary who has elected continuation coverage pursuant to this article during the period of continuation coverage provided by this article shall be considered a qualified beneficiary entitled to receive benefits pursuant to this article for the remainder of the period that the former employee is covered pursuant to this article, if the child is enrolled under a group benefit plan as a

dependent of that former employee who is a qualified beneficiary within 30 days of the child's birth or placement for adoption.

(e) An individual who becomes a qualified beneficiary pursuant to this article shall continue to receive coverage pursuant to this article until continuation coverage is terminated at the qualified beneficiary's election or pursuant to Section 1366.27, whichever comes first, even if the employer that sponsored the group benefit plan that is continued subsequently becomes subject to Section 4980B of the United States Internal Revenue Code or Chapter 18 of the Employee Retirement Income Security Act, 29 U.S.C. Sec. 1161 et seq.

(f) A qualified beneficiary electing coverage pursuant to this section shall be considered part of the group contract and treated as similarly situated employees for contract purposes, unless otherwise specified in this article.

(Amended by Stats. 1998, Ch. 107, Sec. 8. Effective July 6, 1998.)

1366.24.

(a) Every health care service plan evidence of coverage, provided for group benefit plans subject to this article, that is issued, amended, or renewed on or after January 1, 1999, shall disclose to covered employees of group benefit plans subject to this article the ability to continue coverage pursuant to this article, as required by this section.

(b) This disclosure shall state that all enrollees who are eligible to be qualified beneficiaries, as defined in subdivision (c) of Section 1366.21, shall be required, as a condition of receiving benefits pursuant to this article, to notify, in writing, the health care service plan, or the employer if the employer contracts to perform the administrative services as provided for in Section 1366.25, of all qualifying events as specified in paragraphs (1), (3), (4), and (5) of subdivision (d) of Section 1366.21 within 60 days of the date of the qualifying event. This disclosure shall inform enrollees that failure to make the notification to the health care service plan, or to the employer when under contract to provide the administrative services, within the required 60 days will disqualify the qualified beneficiary from receiving continuation coverage pursuant to this article. The disclosure shall further state that a qualified beneficiary who wishes to continue coverage under the group benefit plan pursuant to this article must request the continuation in writing and deliver the written request, by first-class mail, or other reliable means of delivery, including personal delivery, express mail, or private courier company, to the health care service plan, or to the employer if the plan has contracted with the employer for administrative services pursuant to subdivision (d) of Section 1366.25, within the 60-day period following the later of (1) the date that the enrollee's coverage under the group benefit plan terminated or will terminate by reason of a qualifying event, or (2) the date the enrollee was sent notice pursuant to subdivision (e) of Section 1366.25 of the ability to continue coverage under the group benefit plan. The disclosure required by this section shall also state that a qualified beneficiary electing continuation shall pay to the health care service plan, in accordance with the terms and conditions of the plan contract, which shall be set forth in the notice to the qualified beneficiary pursuant to subdivision (d) of Section 1366.25, the amount of the required premium payment, as set forth in Section 1366.26. The disclosure shall further require that the qualified beneficiary's first premium payment required to establish premium payment be delivered by first-class mail, certified mail, or other reliable means of delivery, including personal delivery, express mail, or private courier company, to the health care service plan, or to the employer if the employer has contracted with the plan to perform the administrative services pursuant to subdivision (d) of Section 1366.25, within 45 days of the date the qualified beneficiary provided written notice to the health care service plan or the employer, if the employer has contracted to perform the administrative services, of the election to continue coverage in order for coverage to be continued under this article. This disclosure shall also state that the first premium payment must equal an amount sufficient to pay any required premiums and all premiums due, and that failure to submit the correct premium amount within the 45-day period will disqualify the qualified beneficiary from receiving continuation coverage pursuant to this article.

(c) The disclosure required by this section shall also describe separately how qualified beneficiaries whose continuation coverage terminates under a prior group benefit plan pursuant to subdivision (b) of Section 1366.27 may continue their coverage for the balance of the period that the qualified beneficiary would have remained covered under the prior group benefit plan, including the requirements for election and payment. The disclosure shall clearly state that continuation coverage shall terminate if the qualified beneficiary fails to comply with the requirements pertaining to enrollment in, and payment of premiums to, the new group benefit plan within 30 days of receiving notice of the termination of the prior group benefit plan.

(d) Prior to August 1, 1998, every health care service plan shall provide to all covered employees of employers subject to this article a written notice containing the disclosures required by this section, or shall provide to all covered employees of employers subject to this section a new or amended evidence of coverage that includes the disclosures required by this section. Any specialized health care service plan that, in the ordinary course of business, maintains only the addresses of employer group purchasers of benefits and does not maintain addresses of covered employees, may comply with the notice requirements of this section through the provision of the notices to its employer group purchasers of benefits.

(e) Every plan disclosure form issued, amended, or renewed on and after January 1, 1999, for a group benefit plan subject to this article shall provide a notice that, under state law, an enrollee may be entitled to continuation of group coverage and that additional information regarding eligibility for this coverage may be found in the plan's evidence of coverage.

(f) Every disclosure issued, amended, or renewed on and after July 1, 2006, for a group benefit plan subject to this article shall include the following notice:

"Please examine your options carefully before declining this coverage. You should be aware that companies selling individual health insurance typically require a review of your medical history that could result in a higher premium or you could be denied coverage entirely."

(Amended by Stats. 2005, Ch. 526, Sec. 2. Effective January 1, 2006.)

1366.25.

(a) Every group contract between a health care service plan and an employer subject to this article that is issued, amended, or renewed on or after July 1, 1998, shall require the employer to notify the plan, in writing, of any employee who has had a qualifying event, as defined in paragraph (2) of subdivision (d) of Section 1366.21, within 30 days of the qualifying event. The group contract shall also require the employer to notify the plan, in writing, within 30 days of the date, when the employer becomes subject to Section 4980B of the United States Internal Revenue Code or Chapter 18 of the Employee Retirement Income Security Act, 29 U.S.C. Sec. 1161 et seq.

(b) Every group contract between a plan and an employer subject to this article that is issued, amended, or renewed on or after July 1, 1998, shall require the employer to notify qualified beneficiaries currently receiving continuation coverage, whose continuation coverage will terminate under one group benefit plan prior to the end of the period the qualified beneficiary would have remained covered, as specified in Section 1366.27, of the qualified beneficiary's ability to continue coverage under a new group benefit plan for the balance of the period the qualified beneficiary would have remained covered under the prior group benefit plan. This notice shall be provided either 30 days prior to the termination or when all enrolled employees are notified, whichever is later.

Every health care service plan and specialized health care service plan shall provide to the employer replacing a health care service plan contract issued by the plan, or to the employer's agent or broker representative, within 15 days of any written request, information in possession of the plan reasonably required to administer the notification requirements of this subdivision and subdivision (c).

(c) Notwithstanding subdivision (a), the group contract between the health care service plan and the employer shall require the employer to notify the successor plan in writing of the qualified beneficiaries currently receiving continuation coverage so that the successor plan, or contracting employer or administrator, may provide those qualified beneficiaries with the necessary premium information, enrollment forms, and instructions consistent with the disclosure required by subdivision (c) of Section 1366.24 and subdivision (e) of this section to allow the qualified beneficiary to continue coverage. This information shall be sent to all qualified beneficiaries who are enrolled in the plan and those qualified beneficiaries who have been notified, pursuant to Section 1366.24, of their ability to continue their coverage and may still elect coverage within the specified 60-day period. This information shall be sent to the qualified beneficiary's last known address, as provided to the employer by the health care service plan or disability insurer currently providing continuation coverage to the qualified beneficiary. The successor plan shall not be obligated to provide this information to qualified beneficiaries if the employer or prior plan or insurer fails to comply with this section.

(d) A health care service plan may contract with an employer, or an administrator, to perform the administrative obligations of the plan as required by this article, including required notifications and collecting and forwarding premiums to the health care service plan. Except for the requirements of subdivisions (a), (b), and (c), this subdivision shall not be construed to permit a plan to require an employer to perform the administrative obligations of the plan as required by this article as a condition of the issuance or renewal of coverage.

(e) Every health care service plan, or employer or administrator that contracts to perform the notice and administrative services pursuant to this section, shall, within 14 days of receiving a notice of a qualifying event, provide to the qualified beneficiary the necessary benefits information, premium information, enrollment forms, and disclosures consistent with the notice requirements contained in subdivisions (b) and (c) of Section 1366.24 to allow the qualified beneficiary to formally elect continuation coverage. This information shall be sent to the qualified beneficiary's last known address.

(f) Every health care service plan, or employer or administrator that contracts to perform the notice and administrative services pursuant to this section, shall, during the 180-day period ending on the date that continuation coverage is terminated pursuant to paragraphs (1), (3), and (5) of subdivision (a) of Section 1366.27, notify a qualified beneficiary who has elected continuation coverage pursuant to this article of the date that his or her coverage will terminate, and shall notify the qualified beneficiary of any conversion coverage available to that qualified beneficiary. This requirement shall not apply when the continuation coverage is terminated because the group contract between the plan and the employer is being terminated.

(g) (1) A health care service plan shall provide to a qualified beneficiary who has a qualifying event during the period specified in subparagraph (A) of paragraph (3) of subdivision (a) of Section 3001 of ARRA, a written notice containing information on the availability of premium assistance under ARRA. This notice shall be sent to the qualified beneficiary's last known address. The notice shall include clear and easily understandable language to inform the qualified beneficiary that changes in federal law provide a new opportunity to elect continuation coverage with a 65-percent premium subsidy and shall include all of the following:

(A) The amount of the premium the person will pay. For qualified beneficiaries who had a qualifying event between September 1, 2008, and May 12, 2009, inclusive, if a health care service plan is unable to provide the correct premium amount in the notice, the notice may contain the last known premium amount and an opportunity for the qualified beneficiary to request, through a toll-free telephone number, the correct premium that would apply to the beneficiary.

(B) Enrollment forms and any other information required to be included pursuant to subdivision (e) to allow the qualified beneficiary to elect continuation coverage. This information shall not be included in notices sent to qualified beneficiaries currently enrolled in continuation coverage.

(C) A description of the option to enroll in different coverage as provided in subparagraph (B) of paragraph (1) of subdivision (a) of Section 3001 of ARRA. This description shall advise the qualified beneficiary to contact the covered employee's former employer for prior approval to choose this option.

(D) The eligibility requirements for premium assistance in the amount of 65 percent of the premium under Section 3001 of ARRA.

(E) The duration of premium assistance available under ARRA.

(F) A statement that a qualified beneficiary eligible for premium assistance under ARRA may elect continuation coverage no later than 60 days of the date of the notice.

(G) A statement that a qualified beneficiary eligible for premium assistance under ARRA who rejected or discontinued continuation coverage prior to receiving the notice required by this subdivision has the right to withdraw that rejection and elect continuation coverage with the premium assistance.

(H) A statement that reads as follows:

"IF YOU ARE HAVING ANY DIFFICULTIES READING OR UNDERSTANDING THIS NOTICE, PLEASE CONTACT [name of health plan] at [insert appropriate telephone number]."

(2) With respect to qualified beneficiaries who had a qualifying event between September 1, 2008, and May 12, 2009, inclusive, the notice described in this subdivision shall be provided by the later of May 26, 2009, or seven business days after the date the plan receives notice of the qualifying event.

(3) With respect to qualified beneficiaries who had or have a qualifying event between May 13, 2009, and the later date specified in subparagraph (A) of paragraph (3) of subdivision (a) of Section 3001 of ARRA, inclusive, the notice described in this subdivision shall be provided within the period of time specified in subdivision (e).

(4) Nothing in this section shall be construed to require a health care service plan to provide the plan's evidence of coverage as a part of the notice required by this subdivision, and nothing in this section shall be construed to require a health care service plan to amend its existing evidence of coverage to comply with the changes made to this section by the enactment of Assembly Bill 23 of the 2009–10 Regular Session or by the act amending this section during the second year of the 2009–10 Regular Session.

(5) The requirement under this subdivision to provide a written notice to a qualified beneficiary and the requirement under paragraph (1) of subdivision (h) to provide a new opportunity to a qualified beneficiary to elect continuation coverage shall be deemed satisfied if a health care service plan previously provided a written notice and additional election opportunity under Section 3001 of ARRA to that qualified beneficiary prior to the effective date of the act adding this paragraph.

(h) (1) Notwithstanding any other provision of law, a qualified beneficiary eligible for premium assistance under ARRA may elect continuation coverage no later than 60 days after the date of the notice required by subdivision (g).

(2) For a qualified beneficiary who elects to continue coverage pursuant to this subdivision, the period beginning on the date of the qualifying event and ending on the effective date of the continuation coverage shall be disregarded for purposes of calculating a break in coverage in determining whether a preexisting condition provision applies under subdivision (c) of Section 1357.06 or subdivision (e) of Section 1357.51.

(3) For a qualified beneficiary who had a qualifying event between September 1, 2008, and February 16, 2009, inclusive, and who elects continuation coverage pursuant to paragraph (1), the continuation coverage shall commence on the first day of the month following the election.

(4) For a qualified beneficiary who had a qualifying event between February 17, 2009, and May 12, 2009, inclusive, and who elects continuation coverage pursuant to paragraph (1), the effective date of the continuation coverage shall be either of the following, at the option of the beneficiary, provided that the beneficiary pays the applicable premiums:

(A) The date of the qualifying event.

(B) The first day of the month following the election.

(5) Notwithstanding any other provision of law, a qualified beneficiary who is eligible for the special election opportunity described in paragraph (17) of subdivision (a) of Section 3001 of ARRA may elect continuation coverage no later than 60 days after the date of the notice required under subdivision (j). For a qualified beneficiary who elects coverage pursuant to this paragraph, the continuation coverage shall be effective as of the first day of the first period of coverage after the date of termination of employment, except, if federal law permits, coverage shall take effect on the first day of the month following the election. However, for purposes of calculating the duration of continuation coverage pursuant to Section 1366.27, the period of that coverage shall be determined as though the qualifying event was a reduction of hours of the employee.

(6) Notwithstanding any other provision of law, a qualified beneficiary who is eligible for any other special election opportunity under ARRA may elect continuation coverage no later than 60 days after the date of the special election notice required under ARRA.

(i) A health care service plan shall provide a qualified beneficiary eligible for premium assistance under ARRA written notice of the extension of that premium assistance as required under Section 3001 of ARRA.

(j) A health care service plan, or an administrator or employer if administrative obligations have been assumed by those entities pursuant to subdivision (d), shall give the qualified beneficiaries described in subparagraph (C) of paragraph (17) of subdivision (a) of Section 3001 of ARRA the written notice required by that paragraph by implementing the following procedures:

(1) The health care service plan shall, within 14 days of the effective date of the act adding this subdivision, send a notice to employers currently contracting with the health care service plan for a group benefit plan subject to this article. The notice shall do all of the following:

(A) Advise the employer that employees whose employment is terminated on or after March 2, 2010, who were previously enrolled in any group health care service plan or health insurance policy offered by the employer may be entitled to special health coverage rights, including a subsidy paid by the federal government for a portion of the premium.

(B) Ask the employer to provide the health care service plan with the name, address, and date of termination of employment for any employee whose employment is terminated on or after March 2, 2010, and who was at any time covered by any health care service plan or health insurance policy offered to their employees on or after September 1, 2008.

(C) Provide employers with a format and instructions for submitting the information to the health care service plan, or their administrator or employer who has assumed administrative obligations pursuant to subdivision (d), by telephone, fax, electronic mail, or mail.

(2) Within 14 days of receipt of the information specified in paragraph (1) from the employer, the health care service plan shall send the written notice specified in paragraph (17) of subdivision (a) of Section 3001 of ARRA to those individuals.

(3) If an individual contacts his or her health care service plan and indicates that he or she experienced a qualifying event that entitles him or her to the special election period described in paragraph (17) of subdivision (a) of Section 3001 of ARRA or any other special election provision of ARRA, the plan shall provide the individual with the written notice required under paragraph (17) of subdivision (a) of Section 3001 of ARRA or any other applicable provision of ARRA, regardless of whether the plan receives information from the individual's previous employer regarding that individual pursuant to Section 24100. The plan shall review the individual's application for coverage under this special election notice to determine if the individual qualifies for the special election period and the premium assistance under ARRA. The plan shall comply with paragraph (5) if the individual does not qualify for either the special election period or premium assistance under ARRA.

(4) The requirement under this subdivision to provide the written notice described in paragraph (17) of subdivision (a) of Section 3001 of ARRA to a qualified beneficiary and the requirement under paragraph (5) of subdivision (h) to provide a new opportunity to a qualified beneficiary to elect continuation coverage shall be deemed satisfied if a health care service plan previously provided the written notice and additional election opportunity described in paragraph (17) of subdivision (a) of Section 3001 of ARRA to that qualified beneficiary prior to the effective date of the act adding this paragraph.

(5) If an individual does not qualify for either a special election period or the premium assistance under ARRA, the health care service plan shall provide a written notice to that individual that shall include information on the right to appeal as set forth in Section 3001 of ARRA.

(6) A health care service plan shall provide information on its publicly accessible Internet Web site regarding the premium assistance made available under ARRA and any special election period provided under that law. A plan may fulfill this requirement by linking or otherwise directing consumers to the information regarding COBRA continuation coverage premium assistance located on the Internet Web site of the United States Department of Labor. The information required by this paragraph shall be located in a section of the plan's Internet Web site that is readily accessible to consumers, such as the Web site's Frequently Asked Questions section.

(k) For purposes of implementing federal premium assistance for continuation coverage, the department may designate a model notice or notices that may be used by health care service plans. Use of the model notice or notices shall not require prior approval of the department. Any model notice or notices designated by the department for purposes of this subdivision shall not be subject to the Administrative Procedure Act (Chapter 3.5 (commencing with Section 11340) of Part 1 of Division 3 of Title 2 of the Government Code).

(l) Notwithstanding any other provision of law, a qualified beneficiary eligible for premium assistance under ARRA may elect to enroll in different coverage subject to the criteria provided under subparagraph (B) of paragraph (1) of subdivision (a) of Section 3001 of ARRA.

(m) A qualified beneficiary enrolled in continuation coverage as of February 17, 2009, who is eligible for premium assistance under ARRA may request application of the premium assistance as of March 1, 2009, or later, consistent with ARRA.

(n) A health care service plan that receives an election notice from a qualified beneficiary eligible for premium assistance under ARRA, pursuant to subdivision (h), shall be considered a person entitled to reimbursement, as defined in Section 6432(b)(3) of the Internal Revenue Code, as amended by paragraph (12) of subdivision (a) of Section 3001 of ARRA.

(o) (1) For purposes of compliance with ARRA, in the absence of guidance from, or if specifically required for state-only continuation coverage by, the United States Department of Labor, the Internal Revenue Service, or the Centers for Medicare and Medicaid Services, a health care service plan may request verification of the involuntary termination of a covered employee's employment from the covered employee's former employer or the qualified beneficiary seeking premium assistance under ARRA.

(2) A health care service plan that requests verification pursuant to paragraph (1) directly from a covered employee's former employer shall do so by providing a written notice to the employer. This written notice shall be sent by mail or facsimile to the covered employee's former employer within seven business days from the date the plan

receives the qualified beneficiary's election notice pursuant to subdivision (h). Within 10 calendar days of receipt of written notice required by this paragraph, the former employer shall furnish to the health care service plan written verification as to whether the covered employee's employment was involuntarily terminated.

(3) A qualified beneficiary requesting premium assistance under ARRA may furnish to the health care service plan a written document or other information from the covered employee's former employer indicating that the covered employee's employment was involuntarily terminated. This document or information shall be deemed sufficient by the health care service plan to establish that the covered employee's employment was involuntarily terminated for purposes of ARRA, unless the plan makes a reasonable and timely determination that the documents or information provided by the qualified beneficiary are legally insufficient to establish involuntary termination of employment.

(4) If a health care service plan requests verification pursuant to this subdivision and cannot verify involuntary termination of employment within 14 business days from the date the employer receives the verification request or from the date the plan receives documentation or other information from the qualified beneficiary pursuant to paragraph (3), the health care service plan shall either provide continuation coverage with the federal premium assistance to the qualified beneficiary or send the qualified beneficiary a denial letter which shall include notice of his or her right to appeal that determination pursuant to ARRA.

(5) No person shall intentionally delay verification of involuntary termination of employment under this subdivision.

(p) The provision of information and forms related to the premium assistance available pursuant to ARRA to individuals by a health care service plan shall not be considered a violation of this chapter provided that the plan complies with all of the requirements of this article.

(Amended by Stats. 2010, Ch. 24, Sec. 3. (SB 838) Effective June 3, 2010.)

1366.26.

A qualified beneficiary electing continuation coverage shall pay to the health care service plan, on or before the due date of each payment but not more frequently than on a monthly basis, not more than 110 percent of the applicable rate charged for a covered employee or, in the case of dependent coverage, not more than 110 percent of the applicable rate charged to a similarly situated individual under the group benefit plan being continued under the group contract. In the case of a qualified beneficiary who is determined to be disabled pursuant to Title II or Title XVI of the United States Social Security Act, the qualified beneficiary shall be required to pay to the health care service plan an amount no greater than 150 percent of the group rate after the first 18 months of continuation coverage provided pursuant to this section. In no case shall a health care service plan charge an employer an additional fee for administering Cal-COBRA other than those incorporated in the risk adjusted employee risk rate as provided for in subdivision (i) of Section 1357.

(Amended by Stats. 1998, Ch. 107, Sec. 10. Effective July 6, 1998.)

1366.27.

(a) The continuation coverage provided pursuant to this article shall terminate at the first to occur of the following:

(1) In the case of a qualified beneficiary who is eligible for continuation coverage pursuant to paragraph (2) of subdivision (d) of Section 1366.21, the date 36 months after the date the qualified beneficiary's benefits under the contract would otherwise have terminated because of a qualifying event.

(2) Except as provided in Section 3001 of ARRA, the end of the period for which premium payments were made, if the qualified beneficiary ceases to make payments or fails to make timely payments of a required premium, in accordance with the terms and conditions of the plan contract. In the case of nonpayment of premiums, reinstatement shall be governed by the terms and conditions of the plan contract and by Section 3001 of ARRA, if applicable.

(3) In the case of a qualified beneficiary who is eligible for continuation coverage pursuant to paragraph (1), (3), (4), or (5) of subdivision (d) of Section 1366.21, the date 36 months after the date the qualified beneficiary's benefits under the contract would otherwise have terminated by reason of a qualifying event.

(4) The requirements of this article no longer apply to the qualified beneficiary pursuant to the provisions of Section 1366.22.

(5) In the case of a qualified beneficiary who is eligible for continuation coverage pursuant to paragraph (2) of subdivision (d) of Section 1366.21, and determined, under Title II or Title XVI of the Social Security Act, to be disabled at any time during the first 60 days of continuation coverage, and the spouse or dependent who has elected coverage pursuant to this article, the date 36 months after the date the qualified beneficiary's benefits under the contract would otherwise have terminated because of a qualifying event. The qualified beneficiary shall notify the plan, or the employer or administrator that contracts to perform administrative services, of the social security determination within 60 days of the date of the determination letter and prior to the end of the original 36-month continuation coverage period in order to be eligible for coverage pursuant to this subdivision. If the qualified beneficiary is no longer disabled under Title II or Title XVI of the Social Security Act, the benefits provided in this paragraph shall terminate on the later of the date provided by paragraph (1), or the month that begins more than 31 days after the date of the final determination under Title II or Title XVI of the United States Social Security Act that the qualified beneficiary is no longer disabled. A qualified beneficiary eligible for 36 months of continuation coverage as a result of a disability shall notify the plan, or the employer or administrator that contracts to perform the notice and administrative services, within 30 days of a determination that the qualified beneficiary is no longer disabled.

(6) In the case of a qualified beneficiary who is initially eligible for and elects continuation coverage pursuant to paragraph (2) of subdivision (d) of Section 1366.21, but who has another qualifying event, as described in paragraph (1), (3), (4), or (5) of subdivision (d) of Section 1366.21, within 36 months of the date of the first qualifying event, and the qualified beneficiary has notified the plan, or the employer or administrator under contract to provide administrative services, of the second qualifying event within 60 days of the date of the second qualifying event, the date 36 months after the date of the first qualifying event.

(7) The employer, or any successor employer or purchaser of the employer, ceases to provide any group benefit plan to his or her employees.

(8) The qualified beneficiary moves out of the plan's service area or the qualified beneficiary commits fraud or deception in the use of plan services.

(b) If the group contract between the plan and the employer is terminated prior to the date the qualified beneficiary's continuation coverage would terminate pursuant to this section, coverage under the prior plan shall terminate and the qualified beneficiary may elect continuation coverage under the subsequent group benefit plan, if any, pursuant to the requirements of subdivision (b) of Section 1366.23 and subdivision (c) of Section 1366.24.

(c) The amendments made to this section by Assembly Bill 1401 of the 2001–02 Regular Session shall apply to individuals who begin receiving continuation coverage under this article on or after January 1, 2003.

(Amended by Stats. 2010, Ch. 24, Sec. 4. (SB 838) Effective June 3, 2010.)

1366.28.

A health care service plan subject to this article shall not be obligated to provide continuation coverage to a qualified beneficiary pursuant to this article if an enrollee fails to make the notification required by Section 1366.24, or if the employer of the enrollee fails to comply with Section 1366.25.

(Added by Stats. 1997, Ch. 665, Sec. 1. Effective January 1, 1998.)

1366.29.

(a) A health care service plan shall offer an enrollee who has exhausted continuation coverage under COBRA the opportunity to continue coverage for up to 36 months from the date the enrollee's continuation coverage began, if the enrollee is entitled to less than 36 months of continuation coverage under COBRA. The health care service plan shall offer coverage pursuant to the terms of this article, including the rate limitations contained in Section 1366.26.

(b) Notification of the coverage available under this section shall be included in the notice of the pending termination of COBRA coverage that is required to be provided to COBRA beneficiaries and that is required to be provided under Section 1366.24.

(c) For purposes of this section, "COBRA" means Section 4980B of Title 26 of the United States Code, Sections 1161 et seq. of Title 29 of the United States Code, and Section 300bb of Title 42 of the United States Code.

(d) This section shall not apply to specialized health care service plans providing noncore coverage, as defined in subdivision (g) of Section 1366.21.

(e) This section shall become operative on September 1, 2003, and shall apply to individuals who begin receiving COBRA coverage on or after January 1, 2003.

(Added by Stats. 2002, Ch. 794, Sec. 4. Effective January 1, 2003. Section operative September 1, 2003, by its own provisions.)

ARTICLE 4.6. Coverage for Federally Eligible Defined Individuals [1366.35 - 1366.50]

(Article 4.6 added by Stats. 2000, Ch. 810, Sec. 1.)

1366.35.

(a) A health care service plan providing coverage for hospital, medical, or surgical benefits under an individual health care service plan contract may not, with respect to a federally eligible defined individual desiring to enroll in individual health insurance coverage, decline to offer coverage to, or deny enrollment of, the individual or impose any preexisting condition exclusion with respect to the coverage.

(b) For purposes of this section, "federally eligible defined individual" means an individual who, as of the date on which the individual seeks coverage under this section, meets all of the following conditions:

(1) Has had 18 or more months of creditable coverage, and whose most recent prior creditable coverage was under a group health plan, a federal governmental plan maintained for federal employees, or a governmental plan or church plan as defined in the federal Employee Retirement Income Security Act of 1974 (29 U.S.C. Sec. 1002).

(2) Is not eligible for coverage under a group health plan, Medicare, or Medi-Cal, and does not have other health insurance coverage.

(3) Was not terminated from his or her most recent creditable coverage due to nonpayment of premiums or fraud.

(4) If offered continuation coverage under COBRA or Cal-COBRA, has elected and exhausted that coverage.

(c) Every health care service plan shall comply with applicable federal statutes and regulations regarding the provision of coverage to federally eligible defined individuals, including any relevant application periods.

(d) A health care service plan shall offer the following health benefit plan contracts under this section that are designed for, made generally available to, are actively marketed to, and enroll, individuals: (1) either the two most popular products as defined in Section 300gg-41(c)(2) of Title 42 of the United States Code and Section 148.120(c)(2) of Title 45 of the Code of Federal Regulations or (2) the two most representative products as defined in Section 300gg-41(c)(3) of the United States Code and Section 148.120(c)(3) of Title 45 of the Code of Federal Regulations, as determined by the plan in compliance with federal law. A health care service plan that offers only one health benefit plan

contract to individuals, excluding health benefit plans offered to Medi-Cal or Medicare beneficiaries, shall be deemed to be in compliance with this article if it offers that health benefit plan contract to federally eligible defined individuals in a manner consistent with this article.

(e) (1) In the case of a health care service plan that offers health insurance coverage in the individual market through a network plan, the plan may do both of the following:

(A) Limit the individuals who may be enrolled under that coverage to those who live, reside, or work within the service area for the network plan.

(B) Within the service area of the plan, deny coverage to individuals if the plan has demonstrated to the director that the plan will not have the capacity to deliver services adequately to additional individual enrollees because of its obligations to existing group contractholders and enrollees and individual enrollees, and that the plan is applying this paragraph uniformly to individuals without regard to any health status-related factor of the individuals and without regard to whether the individuals are federally eligible defined individuals.

(2) A health care service plan, upon denying health insurance coverage in any service area in accordance with subparagraph (B) of paragraph (1), may not offer coverage in the individual market within that service area for a period of 180 days after the coverage is denied.

(f) (1) A health care service plan may deny health insurance coverage in the individual market to a federally eligible defined individual if the plan has demonstrated to the director both of the following:

(A) The plan does not have the financial reserves necessary to underwrite additional coverage.

(B) The plan is applying this subdivision uniformly to all individuals in the individual market and without regard to any health status-related factor of the individuals and without regard to whether the individuals are federally eligible defined individuals.

(2) A health care service plan, upon denying individual health insurance coverage in any service area in accordance with paragraph (1), may not offer that coverage in the individual market within that service area for a period of 180 days after the date the coverage is denied or until the issuer has demonstrated to the director that the plan has sufficient financial reserves to underwrite additional coverage, whichever is later.

(g) The requirement pursuant to federal law to furnish a certificate of creditable coverage shall apply to health insurance coverage offered by a health care service plan in the individual market in the same manner as it applies to a health care service plan in connection with a group health benefit plan.

(h) A health care service plan shall compensate a life agent or fire and casualty broker-agent whose activities result in the enrollment of federally eligible defined individuals in the same manner and consistent with the renewal commission amounts as the plan compensates life agents or fire and casualty broker-agents for other enrollees who are not federally eligible defined individuals and who are purchasing the same individual health benefit plan contract.

(i) Every health care service plan shall disclose as part of its COBRA or Cal-COBRA disclosure and enrollment documents, an explanation of the availability of guaranteed access to coverage under the Health Insurance Portability and Accountability Act of 1996, including the necessity to enroll in and exhaust COBRA or Cal-COBRA benefits in order to become a federally eligible defined individual.

(j) No health care service plan may request documentation as to whether or not a person is a federally eligible defined individual other than is permitted under applicable federal law or regulations.

(k) This section shall not apply to coverage defined as excepted benefits pursuant to Section 300gg(c) of Title 42 of the United States Code.

(l) This section shall apply to health care service plan contracts offered, delivered, amended, or renewed on or after January 1, 2001.

(m) (1) This section shall be inoperative on January 1, 2014.

(2) If Section 5000A of the Internal Revenue Code, as added by Section 1501 of PPACA, is repealed or amended to no longer apply to the individual market, as defined in Section 2791 of the federal Public Health Service Act (42 U.S.C. Section 300gg-91), this section shall become operative on the date of that repeal or amendment.

(3) For purposes of this subdivision, "PPACA" means the federal Patient Protection and Affordable Care Act (Public Law 111-148), as amended by the federal Health Care Education and Reconciliation Act of 2010 (Public Law 111-152), and any rules, regulations, or guidance issued pursuant to that law.

(Amended by Stats. 2013, Ch. 441, Sec. 4. (AB 1180) Effective October 1, 2013. Inoperative, by its own provisions, on January 1, 2014, subject to condition for resuming operation.)

1366.50.

(a) On and after January 1, 2014, a health care service plan providing individual or group health care coverage shall provide to enrollees or subscribers who cease to be enrolled in coverage a notice informing them that they may be eligible for reduced-cost coverage through the California Health Benefit Exchange established under Title 22 (commencing with Section 100500) of the Government Code or no-cost coverage through Medi-Cal. The notice shall include information on obtaining coverage pursuant to those programs, shall be in no less than 12-point type, and shall be developed by the department, no later than July 1, 2013, in consultation with the Department of Insurance and the California Health Benefit Exchange.

(b) The notice described in subdivision (a) may be incorporated into or sent simultaneously with and in the same manner as any other notices sent by the health care service plan.

(c) This section shall not apply with respect to a specialized health care service plan contract or a Medicare supplemental plan contract.

(Added by Stats. 2012, Ch. 851, Sec. 3. (AB 792) Effective January 1, 2013.)

ARTICLE 5. Standards [1367 - 1374.195]

(Article 5 added by Stats. 1975, Ch. 941.)

1367.

A health care service plan and, if applicable, a specialized health care service plan shall meet the following requirements:

(a) Facilities located in this state including, but not limited to, clinics, hospitals, and skilled nursing facilities to be utilized by the plan shall be licensed by the State Department of Public Health, where licensure is required by law. Facilities not located in this state shall conform to all licensing and other requirements of the jurisdiction in which they are located.

(b) Personnel employed by or under contract to the plan shall be licensed or certified by their respective board or agency, where licensure or certification is required by law.

(c) Equipment required to be licensed or registered by law shall be so licensed or registered, and the operating personnel for that equipment shall be licensed or certified as required by law.

(d) The plan shall furnish services in a manner providing continuity of care and ready referral of patients to other providers at times as may be appropriate consistent with good professional practice.

(e) (1) All services shall be readily available at reasonable times to each enrollee consistent with good professional practice. To the extent feasible, the plan shall make all services readily accessible to all enrollees consistent with Section 1367.03.

(2) To the extent that telehealth services are appropriately provided through telehealth, as defined in subdivision (a) of Section 2290.5 of the Business and Professions Code, these services shall be considered in determining compliance with Section 1300.67.2 of Title 28 of the California Code of Regulations.

(3) The plan shall make all services accessible and appropriate consistent with Section 1367.04.

(f) The plan shall employ and utilize allied health manpower for the furnishing of services to the extent permitted by law and consistent with good medical practice.

(g) The plan shall have the organizational and administrative capacity to provide services to subscribers and enrollees. The plan shall be able to demonstrate to the department that medical decisions are rendered by qualified medical providers, unhindered by fiscal and administrative management.

(h) (1) Contracts with subscribers and enrollees, including group contracts, and contracts with providers, and other persons furnishing services, equipment, or facilities to or in connection with the plan, shall be fair, reasonable, and consistent with the objectives of this chapter. All contracts with providers shall contain provisions requiring a fast, fair, and cost-effective dispute resolution mechanism under which providers may submit disputes to the plan, and requiring the plan to inform its providers upon contracting with the plan, or upon change to these provisions, of the procedures for processing and resolving disputes, including the location and telephone number where information regarding disputes may be submitted.

(2) A health care service plan shall ensure that a dispute resolution mechanism is accessible to noncontracting providers for the purpose of resolving billing and claims disputes.

(3) On and after January 1, 2002, a health care service plan shall annually submit a report to the department regarding its dispute resolution mechanism. The report shall include information on the number of providers who utilized the dispute resolution mechanism and a summary of the disposition of those disputes.

(i) A health care service plan contract shall provide to subscribers and enrollees all of the basic health care services included in subdivision (b) of Section 1345, except that the director may, for good cause, by rule or order exempt a plan contract or any class of plan contracts from that requirement. The director shall by rule define the scope of each basic health care service that health care service plans are required to provide as a minimum for licensure under this chapter. Nothing in this chapter shall prohibit a health care service plan from charging subscribers or enrollees a copayment or a deductible for a basic health care service consistent with Section 1367.006 or 1367.007, provided that the copayments, deductibles, or other cost sharing are reported to the director and set forth to the subscriber or enrollee pursuant to the disclosure provisions of Section 1363. Nothing in this chapter shall prohibit a health care service plan from setting forth, by contract, limitations on maximum coverage of basic health care services, provided that the limitations are reported to, and held unobjectionable by, the director and set forth to the subscriber or enrollee pursuant to the disclosure provisions of Section 1363.

(j) A health care service plan shall not require registration under the federal Controlled Substances Act (21 U.S.C. Sec. 801 et seq.) as a condition for participation by an optometrist certified to use therapeutic pharmaceutical agents pursuant to Section 3041.3 of the Business and Professions Code.

Nothing in this section shall be construed to permit the director to establish the rates charged subscribers and enrollees for contractual health care services.

The director's enforcement of Article 3.1 (commencing with Section 1357) shall not be deemed to establish the rates charged subscribers and enrollees for contractual health care services.

The obligation of the plan to comply with this chapter shall not be waived when the plan delegates any services that it is required to perform to its medical groups, independent practice associations, or other contracting entities.

(Amended by Stats. 2013, Ch. 316, Sec. 2. (SB 639) Effective January 1, 2014.)

1367.001.

(a) To the extent required by federal law, every health care service plan that issues, sells, renews, or offers contracts for health care coverage in this state shall comply with the requirements of Section 2711 of the federal Public Health Service Act (42 U.S.C. Sec. 300gg-11) and any rules or regulations issued under that section, in addition to any state laws or regulations that do not prevent the application of those requirements.

(b) Nothing in this section shall be construed to apply to a health care service plan contract or insurance policy issued, sold, renewed, or offered for health care services or coverage provided in the Medi-Cal program (Chapter 7 (commencing with Section 14000) of Part 3 of Division 9 of the Welfare and Institutions Code), the Healthy Families Program (Part 6.2 (commencing with Section 12693) of Division 2 of the Insurance Code), the Access for Infants and Mothers Program (Part 6.3 (commencing with Section 12695) of Division 2 of the Insurance Code), the California Major Risk Medical Insurance Program (Part 6.5 (commencing with Section 12700) of Division 2 of the Insurance Code), or the Federal Temporary High Risk Insurance Pool (Part 6.6 (commencing with Section 12739.5) of Division 2 of the Insurance Code), to the extent consistent with the federal Patient Protection and Affordable Care Act (Public Law 111-148).

(Added by Stats. 2011, Ch. 644, Sec. 1. (SB 51) Effective January 1, 2012.)

1367.002.

To the extent required by federal law, a group or individual health care service plan contract issued, amended, renewed, or delivered on or after September 23, 2010, shall comply with Section 2713 of the federal Public Health Service Act (42 U.S.C. Sec. 300gg-13), as added by Section 1001 of the federal Patient Protection and Affordable Care Act (P.L. 111-148), and any rules or regulations issued under that section.

(Amended by Stats. 2011, Ch. 296, Sec. 141. (AB 1023) Effective January 1, 2012.)

1367.003.

(a) A health care service plan that issues, sells, renews, or offers health care service plan contracts for health care coverage in this state, including a grandfathered health plan, but not including specialized health care service plan contracts that provide only dental or vision services, shall provide an annual rebate to each enrollee under that coverage, on a pro rata basis, if the ratio of the amount of premium revenue expended by the health care service plan on the costs for reimbursement for clinical services provided to enrollees under that coverage and for activities that improve health care quality to the total amount of premium revenue, excluding federal and state taxes and licensing or regulatory fees and after accounting for payments or receipts for risk adjustment, risk corridors, and reinsurance, is less than the following:

(1) With respect to a health care service plan offering coverage in the large group market, 85 percent.

(2) With respect to a health care service plan offering coverage in the small group market or in the individual market, 80 percent.

(b) A health care service plan that issues, sells, renews, or offers health care service plan contracts for health care coverage in this state, including a grandfathered health plan, shall comply with the following minimum medical loss ratios:

(1) With respect to a health care service plan offering coverage in the large group market, 85 percent.

(2) With respect to a health care service plan offering coverage in the small group market or in the individual market, 80 percent.

(c) (1) The total amount of an annual rebate required under this section shall be calculated in an amount equal to the product of the following:

(A) The amount by which the percentage described in paragraph (1) or (2) of subdivision (a) exceeds the ratio described in paragraph (1) or (2) of subdivision (a).

(B) The total amount of premium revenue, excluding federal and state taxes and licensing or regulatory fees and after accounting for payments or receipts for risk adjustment, risk corridors, and reinsurance.

(2) A health care service plan shall provide a rebate owing to an enrollee no later than September 30 of the calendar year following the year for which the ratio described in subdivision (a) was calculated.

(d) The director may adopt regulations in accordance with the Administrative Procedure Act (Chapter 3.5 (commencing with Section 11340) of Part 1 of Division 3 of Title 2 of the Government Code) that are necessary to implement the medical loss ratio as described under Section 2718 of the federal Public Health Service Act (42 U.S.C. Sec. 300gg-18), and any federal rules or regulations issued under that section.

(e) The requirements of this section shall be implemented as described in Section 2791 of the federal Public Health Service Act (42 U.S.C. Sec. 300gg-91) and the requirements of Section 2718 of the federal Public Health Service Act (42 U.S.C. Sec. 300gg-18) and any rules or regulations issued under those sections as in effect on January 1, 2017.

(f) This section does not apply to provisions of this chapter pertaining to financial statements, assets, liabilities, and other accounting items to which subdivision (s) of Section 1345 applies.

(g) This section does not apply to a health care service plan contract or insurance policy issued, sold, renewed, or offered for health care services or coverage provided in the Medi-Cal program (Chapter 7 (commencing with Section 14000) of Part 3 of Division 9 of the Welfare and Institutions Code).

(Amended by Stats. 2018, Ch. 678, Sec. 1. (AB 2499) Effective January 1, 2019.)

1367.004.

(a) A health care service plan that issues, sells, renews, or offers a contract covering dental services shall file a report with the department by July 31 of each year, which shall be known as the MLR annual report. The MLR annual report shall be organized by market and product type and shall contain the same information required in the 2013 federal Medical Loss Ratio (MLR) Annual Reporting Form (CMS-10418). The department shall post a health care service plan's MLR annual report on its Internet Web site within 45 days after receiving the report.

(b) The MLR reporting year shall be for the calendar year during which dental coverage is provided by the plan. As applicable, all terms used in the MLR annual report shall have the same meaning as used in the federal Public Health Service Act (42 U.S.C. Sec. 300gg-18), Part 158 (commencing with Section 158.101) of Title 45 of the Code of Federal Regulations, and Section 1367.003.

(c) If the director decides to conduct a financial examination, as described in Section 1382, because the director finds it necessary to verify the health care service plan's representations in the MLR annual report, the department shall provide the health care service plan with a notification 30 days before the commencement of the financial examination.

(d) The health care service plan shall have 30 days from the date of notification to electronically submit to the department all requested records, books, and papers specified in subdivision (a) of Section 1381. The director may extend the time for a health care service plan to comply with this subdivision upon a finding of good cause.

(e) The department shall make available to the public all of the data provided to the department pursuant to this section.

(f) This section does not apply to a health care service plan contract issued, sold, renewed, or offered for health care services or coverage provided in the Medi-Cal program (Chapter 7 (commencing with Section 14000) and Chapter 8 (commencing with Section 14200) of Part 3 of Division 9 of the Welfare and Institutions Code), the Medi-Cal Access Program (Chapter 2 (commencing with Section 15810) of Part 3.3 of Division 9 of the Welfare and Institutions Code), or the California Major Risk Medical Insurance Program (Chapter 4 (commencing with Section 15870) of Part 3.3 of Division 9 of the Welfare and Institutions Code), to the extent consistent with the federal Patient Protection and Affordable Care Act (Public Law 111-148).

(g) The department may issue guidance to specialized health care service plans subject to this section regarding compliance with this section. The guidance shall not be subject to the rulemaking provisions of the Administrative Procedure Act (Chapter 3.5 (commencing with Section 11340) of Part 1 of Division 3 of Title 2 of the Government Code), and shall be effective only until the department adopts regulations pursuant to that act. The department shall consult with the Department of Insurance in issuing the guidance specified in this section.

(Amended by Stats. 2018, Ch. 933, Sec. 3. (SB 1008) Effective January 1, 2019.)

1367.005.

(a) An individual or small group health care service plan contract issued, amended, or renewed on or after January 1, 2017, shall, at a minimum, include coverage for essential health benefits pursuant to PPACA and as outlined in this section. For purposes of this section, "essential health benefits" means all of the following:

(1) Health benefits within the categories identified in Section 1302(b) of PPACA: ambulatory patient services, emergency services, hospitalization, maternity and newborn care, mental health and substance use disorder services, including behavioral health treatment, prescription drugs, rehabilitative and habilitative services and devices, laboratory services, preventive and wellness services and chronic disease management, and pediatric services, including oral and vision care.

(2) (A) The health benefits covered by the Kaiser Foundation Health Plan Small Group HMO 30 plan (federal health product identification number 40513CA035) as this plan was offered during the first quarter of 2014, as follows, regardless of whether the benefits are specifically referenced in the evidence of coverage or plan contract for that plan:

(i) Medically necessary basic health care services, as defined in subdivision (b) of Section 1345 and in Section 1300.67 of Title 28 of the California Code of Regulations.

(ii) The health benefits mandated to be covered by the plan pursuant to statutes enacted before December 31, 2011, as described in the following sections: Sections 1367.002, 1367.06, and 1367.35 (preventive services for children); Section 1367.25 (prescription drug coverage for contraceptives); Section 1367.45 (AIDS vaccine); Section 1367.46 (HIV testing); Section 1367.51 (diabetes); Section 1367.54 (alpha-fetoprotein testing); Section 1367.6 (breast cancer screening); Section 1367.61 (prosthetics for laryngectomy); Section 1367.62 (maternity hospital stay); Section 1367.63 (reconstructive surgery); Section 1367.635 (mastectomies); Section 1367.64 (prostate cancer); Section 1367.65 (mammography); Section 1367.66 (cervical cancer); Section 1367.665 (cancer screening tests); Section 1367.67 (osteoporosis); Section 1367.68 (surgical procedures for jaw bones); Section 1367.71 (anesthesia for dental); Section 1367.9 (conditions attributable to diethylstilbestrol); Section 1368.2 (hospice care); Section 1370.6 (cancer clinical trials); Section 1371.5 (emergency response ambulance or ambulance transport services); subdivision (b) of Section 1373 (sterilization operations or procedures); Section 1373.4 (inpatient hospital and ambulatory maternity); Section 1374.56 (phenylketonuria); Section 1374.17 (organ transplants for HIV); Section 1374.72 (mental health parity); and Section 1374.73 (autism/behavioral health treatment).

(iii) Any other benefits mandated to be covered by the plan pursuant to statutes enacted before December 31, 2011, as described in those statutes.

(iv) The health benefits covered by the plan that are not otherwise required to be covered under this chapter, to the extent required pursuant to Sections 1367.18, 1367.21, 1367.215, 1367.22, 1367.24, and 1367.25, and Section 1300.67.24 of Title 28 of the California Code of Regulations.

(v) Any other health benefits covered by the plan that are not otherwise required to be covered under this chapter.

(B) If there are any conflicts or omissions in the plan identified in subparagraph (A) as compared with the requirements for health benefits under this chapter that were enacted prior to December 31, 2011, the requirements of this chapter shall be controlling, except as otherwise specified in this section.

(C) Notwithstanding subparagraph (B) or any other provision of this section, the home health services benefits covered under the plan identified in subparagraph (A) shall be deemed to not be in conflict with this chapter.

(D) For purposes of this section, the Paul Wellstone and Pete Domenici Mental Health Parity and Addiction Equity Act of 2008 (Public Law 110-343) shall apply to a contract subject to this section. Coverage of mental health and substance use disorder services pursuant to this paragraph, along with any scope and duration limits imposed on the benefits, shall be in compliance with the Paul Wellstone and Pete Domenici Mental Health Parity and Addiction Equity Act of 2008 (Public Law 110-343), and all rules, regulations, or guidance issued pursuant to Section 2726 of the federal Public Health Service Act (42 U.S.C. Sec. 300gg-26).

(3) With respect to habilitative services, in addition to any habilitative services and devices identified in paragraph (2), coverage shall also be provided as required by federal rules, regulations, and guidance issued pursuant to Section 1302(b) of PPACA. Habilitative services and devices shall be covered under the same terms and conditions applied to rehabilitative services and devices under the plan contract. Limits on habilitative and rehabilitative services and devices shall not be combined.

(4) With respect to pediatric vision care, the same health benefits for pediatric vision care covered under the Federal Employees Dental and Vision Insurance Program vision plan with the largest national enrollment as of the first quarter of 2014. The pediatric vision care benefits covered pursuant to this paragraph shall be in addition to, and shall not replace, any vision services covered under the plan identified in paragraph (2).

(5) With respect to pediatric oral care, the same health benefits for pediatric oral care covered under the dental benefit received by children under the Medi-Cal program as of 2014, including the provision of medically necessary orthodontic care provided pursuant to the federal Children's Health Insurance Program Reauthorization Act of 2009. The pediatric oral care benefits covered pursuant to this paragraph shall be in addition to, and shall not replace, any dental or orthodontic services covered under the plan identified in paragraph (2).

(b) Treatment limitations imposed on health benefits described in this section shall be no greater than the treatment limitations imposed by the corresponding plans identified in subdivision (a), subject to the requirements set forth in paragraph (2) of subdivision (a).

(c) Except as provided in subdivision (d), nothing in this section shall be construed to permit a health care service plan to make substitutions for the benefits required to be covered under this section, regardless of whether those substitutions are actuarially equivalent.

(d) To the extent permitted under Section 1302 of PPACA and any rules, regulations, or guidance issued pursuant to that section, and to the extent that substitution would not create an obligation for the state to defray costs for any individual, a plan may substitute its prescription drug formulary for the formulary provided under the plan identified in subdivision (a) as long as the coverage for prescription drugs complies with the sections referenced in clauses (ii) and (iv) of subparagraph (A) of paragraph (2) of subdivision (a) that apply to prescription drugs.

(e) A health care service plan, or its agent, solicitor, or representative, shall not issue, deliver, renew, offer, market, represent, or sell any product, contract, or discount arrangement as compliant with the essential health benefits requirement in federal law, unless it meets all of the requirements of this section.

(f) This section applies regardless of whether the plan contract is offered inside or outside the California Health Benefit Exchange created by Section 100500 of the Government Code.

(g) This section shall not be construed to exempt a plan or a plan contract from meeting other applicable requirements of law.

(h) This section shall not be construed to prohibit a plan contract from covering additional benefits, including, but not limited to, spiritual care services that are tax deductible under Section 213 of the Internal Revenue Code.

(i) Subdivision (a) does not apply to any of the following:

(1) A specialized health care service plan contract.

(2) A Medicare supplement plan.

(3) A plan contract that qualifies as a grandfathered health plan under Section 1251 of PPACA or any rules, regulations, or guidance issued pursuant to that section.

(j) This section shall not be implemented in a manner that conflicts with a requirement of PPACA.

(k) This section shall be implemented only to the extent essential health benefits are required pursuant to PPACA.

(l) An essential health benefit is required to be provided under this section only to the extent that federal law does not require the state to defray the costs of the benefit.

(m) This section does not obligate the state to incur costs for the coverage of benefits that are not essential health benefits as defined in this section.

(n) A plan is not required to cover, under this section, changes to health benefits that are the result of statutes enacted on or after December 31, 2011.

(o) (1) The department may adopt emergency regulations implementing this section. The department may, on a one-time basis, readopt any emergency regulation authorized by this section that is the same as, or substantially equivalent to, an emergency regulation previously adopted under this section.

(2) The initial adoption of emergency regulations implementing this section and the readoption of emergency regulations authorized by this subdivision shall be deemed an

emergency and necessary for the immediate preservation of the public peace, health, safety, or general welfare. The initial emergency regulations and the readoption of emergency regulations authorized by this section shall be submitted to the Office of Administrative Law for filing with the Secretary of State and each shall remain in effect for no more than 180 days, by which time final regulations may be adopted.

(3) The initial adoption of emergency regulations implementing this section made during the 2015–16 Regular Session of the Legislature and the readoption of emergency regulations authorized by this subdivision shall be deemed an emergency and necessary for the immediate preservation of the public peace, health, safety, or general welfare. The initial emergency regulations and the readoption of emergency regulations authorized by this section shall be submitted to the Office of Administrative Law for filing with the Secretary of State and each shall remain in effect for no more than 180 days, by which time final regulations may be adopted.

(4) The director shall consult with the Insurance Commissioner to ensure consistency and uniformity in the development of regulations under this subdivision.

(5) This subdivision shall become inoperative on July 1, 2018.

(p) For purposes of this section, the following definitions apply:

(1) "Habilitative services" means health care services and devices that help a person keep, learn, or improve skills and functioning for daily living. Examples include therapy for a child who is not walking or talking at the expected age. These services may include physical and occupational therapy, speech-language pathology, and other services for people with disabilities in a variety of inpatient or outpatient settings, or both. Habilitative services shall be covered under the same terms and conditions applied to rehabilitative services under the plan contract.

(2) (A) "Health benefits," unless otherwise required to be defined pursuant to federal rules, regulations, or guidance issued pursuant to Section 1302(b) of PPACA, means health care items or services for the diagnosis, cure, mitigation, treatment, or prevention of illness, injury, disease, or a health condition, including a behavioral health condition.

(B) "Health benefits" does not mean any cost-sharing requirements such as copayments, coinsurance, or deductibles.

(3) "PPACA" means the federal Patient Protection and Affordable Care Act (Public Law 111-148), as amended by the federal Health Care and Education Reconciliation Act of 2010 (Public Law 111-152), and any rules, regulations, or guidance issued thereunder.

(4) "Small group health care service plan contract" means a group health care service plan contract issued to a small employer, as defined in Section 1357.500.

(Amended (as added by Stats. 2015, Ch. 648, Sec. 2) by Stats. 2016, Ch. 86, Sec. 177. (SB 1171) Effective January 1, 2017.)

1367.006.

(a) This section shall apply to nongrandfathered individual and group health care service plan contracts that provide coverage for essential health benefits, as defined in Section 1367.005, and that are issued, amended, or renewed on or after January 1, 2015.

(b) (1) For nongrandfathered health care service plan contracts in the individual or small group markets, a health care service plan contract, except a specialized health care service plan contract, that is issued, amended, or renewed on or after January 1, 2015, shall provide for a limit on annual out-of-pocket expenses for all covered benefits that meet the definition of essential health benefits in Section 1367.005, including out-of-network emergency care consistent with Section 1371.4.

(2) For nongrandfathered health care service plan contracts in the large group market, a health care service plan contract, except a specialized health care service plan contract, that is issued, amended, or renewed on or after January 1, 2015, shall provide for a limit on annual out-of-pocket expenses for covered benefits, including out-of-network emergency care consistent with Section 1371.4. This limit shall only apply to essential health benefits, as defined in Section 1367.005, that are covered under the plan to the extent that this provision does not conflict with federal law or guidance on out-of-pocket maximums for nongrandfathered health care service plan contracts in the large group market.

(c) (1) The limit described in subdivision (b) shall not exceed the limit described in Section 1302(c) of PPACA, and any subsequent rules, regulations, or guidance issued under that section.

(2) The limit described in subdivision (b) shall result in a total maximum out-of-pocket limit for all covered essential health benefits equal to the dollar amounts in effect under Section 223(c)(2)(A)(ii) of the Internal Revenue Code of 1986 with the dollar amounts adjusted as specified in Section 1302(c)(1)(B) of PPACA.

(3) For family coverage, an individual within a family shall not have a maximum out-of-pocket limit that is greater than the maximum out-of-pocket limit for individual coverage for that product.

(d) Nothing in this section shall be construed to affect the reduction in cost sharing for eligible enrollees described in Section 1402 of PPACA, and any subsequent rules, regulations, or guidance issued under that section.

(e) If an essential health benefit is offered or provided by a specialized health care service plan, the total annual out-of-pocket maximum for all covered essential benefits shall not exceed the limit in subdivision (b). This section shall not apply to a specialized health care service plan that does not offer an essential health benefit as defined in Section 1367.005.

(f) The maximum out-of-pocket limit shall apply to any copayment, coinsurance, deductible, and any other form of cost sharing for all covered benefits that meet the definition of essential health benefits in Section 1367.005.

(g) (1) (A) Except as provided in paragraph (2), if a health care service plan contract for family coverage includes a deductible, an individual within a family shall not have a

deductible that is greater than the deductible limit for individual coverage for that product.

(B) Except as provided in paragraph (2), if a large group market health care service plan contract for family coverage that is issued, amended, or renewed on or after January 1, 2017, includes a deductible, an individual within a family shall not have a deductible that is more than the deductible limit for individual coverage for that product.

(2) (A) If a health care service plan contract for family coverage includes a deductible and is a high deductible health plan under the definition set forth in Section 223(c)(2) of Title 26 of the United States Code, the plan contract shall include a deductible for each individual covered by the plan that is equal to either the amount set forth in Section 223(c)(2)(A)(i)(II) of Title 26 of the United States Code or the deductible for individual coverage under the plan contract, whichever is greater.

(B) If a large group market health care service plan contract for family coverage that is issued, amended, or renewed on or after January 1, 2017, includes a deductible and is a high deductible health plan under the definition set forth in Section 223(c)(2) of Title 26 of the United States Code, the plan contract shall include a deductible for each individual covered by the plan that is equal to either the amount set forth in Section 223(c)(2)(A)(i)(II) of Title 26 of the United States Code or the deductible for individual coverage under the plan contract, whichever is greater.

(h) For nongrandfathered health plan contracts in the group market, "plan year" has the meaning set forth in Section 144.103 of Title 45 of the Code of Federal Regulations. For nongrandfathered health plan contracts sold in the individual market, "plan year" means the calendar year.

(i) "PPACA" means the federal Patient Protection and Affordable Care Act (Public Law 111-148), as amended by the federal Health Care and Education Reconciliation Act of 2010 (Public Law 111-152), and any rules, regulations, or guidance issued thereunder. (Amended by Stats. 2015, Ch. 641, Sec. 1. (AB 1305) Effective January 1, 2016.)

1367.007.

(a) (1) For a small employer health care service plan contract offered, sold, or renewed on or after January 1, 2014, the deductible under the plan shall not exceed:

(A) Two thousand dollars ($2,000) in the case of a plan contract covering a single individual.

(B) Four thousand dollars ($4,000) in the case of any other plan contract.

(2) The dollar amounts in this section shall be indexed consistent with Section 1302(c)(4) of PPACA and any federal rules or guidance pursuant to that section.

(3) The limitation in this subdivision shall be applied in a manner that does not affect the actuarial value of any small employer health care service plan contract.

(4) For small group products at the bronze level of coverage, as defined in Section 1367.008, the department may permit plans to offer a higher deductible in order to meet the actuarial value requirement of the bronze level. In making this determination, the department shall consider affordability of cost sharing for enrollees and shall also consider whether enrollees may be deterred from seeking appropriate care because of higher cost sharing.

(b) Nothing in this section shall be construed to allow a plan contract to have a deductible that applies to preventive services as defined in Section 1367.002.

(c) "PPACA" means the federal Patient Protection and Affordable Care Act (Public Law 111-148), as amended by the federal Health Care and Education Reconciliation Act of 2010 (Public Law 111-152), and any rules, regulations, or guidance issued thereunder. (Amended by Stats. 2015, Ch. 641, Sec. 2. (AB 1305) Effective January 1, 2016.)

1367.008.

(a) Levels of coverage for the nongrandfathered individual market are defined as follows:

(1) Bronze level: A health care service plan contract in the bronze level shall provide a level of coverage that is actuarially equivalent to 60 percent of the full actuarial value of the benefits provided under the plan contract.

(2) Silver level: A health care service plan contract in the silver level shall provide a level of coverage that is actuarially equivalent to 70 percent of the full actuarial value of the benefits provided under the plan contract.

(3) Gold level: A health care service plan contract in the gold level shall provide a level of coverage that is actuarially equivalent to 80 percent of the full actuarial value of the benefits provided under the plan contract.

(4) Platinum level: A health care service plan contract in the platinum level shall provide a level of coverage that is actuarially equivalent to 90 percent of the full actuarial value of the benefits provided under the plan contract.

(b) Actuarial value for nongrandfathered individual health care service plan contracts shall be determined in accordance with the following:

(1) Actuarial value shall not vary by more than plus or minus 2 percent.

(2) Actuarial value shall be determined on the basis of essential health benefits as defined in Section 1367.005 and as provided to a standard, nonelderly population. For this purpose, a standard population shall not include those receiving coverage through the Medi-Cal or Medicare programs.

(3) The department may use the actuarial value methodology developed consistent with Section 1302(d) of PPACA.

(4) The actuarial value for pediatric dental benefits, whether offered by a full service plan or a specialized plan, shall be consistent with federal law and guidance applicable to the plan type.

(5) The department, in consultation with the Department of Insurance and the Exchange, shall consider whether to exercise state-level flexibility with respect to the actuarial value calculator in order to take into account the unique characteristics of the California health care coverage market, including the prevalence of health care service plans, total cost of

care paid for by the plan, price of care, patterns of service utilization, and relevant demographic factors.

(c) (1) A catastrophic plan is a health care service plan contract that provides no benefits for any plan year until the enrollee has incurred cost-sharing expenses in an amount equal to the annual limit on out-of-pocket costs as specified in Section 1367.006 except that it shall provide coverage for at least three primary care visits. A carrier that is not participating in the Exchange shall not offer, market, or sell a catastrophic plan in the individual market.

(2) A catastrophic plan may be offered only in the individual market and only if consistent with this paragraph. Catastrophic plans may be offered only if either of the following apply:

(A) The individual purchasing the plan has not yet attained 30 years of age before the beginning of the plan year.

(B) The individual has a certificate of exemption from Section 5000(A) of the Internal Revenue Code because the individual is not offered affordable coverage or because the individual faces hardship.

(d) "PPACA" means the federal Patient Protection and Affordable Care Act (Public Law 111-148), as amended by the federal Health Care and Education Reconciliation Act of 2010 (Public Law 111-152), and any rules, regulations, or guidance issued thereunder. (Added by Stats. 2013, Ch. 316, Sec. 6. (SB 639) Effective January 1, 2014.)

1367.0085.

Notwithstanding paragraph (1) of subdivision (b) of Section 1367.008 and paragraph (1) of subdivision (b) of Section 1367.009, the actuarial value for a nongrandfathered bronze level high deductible health plan, as defined in Section 223(c)(2) of Title 26 of the United States Code, may range from plus 4 percent to minus 2 percent. (Added by Stats. 2019, Ch. 38, Sec. 16. (SB 78) Effective June 27, 2019.)

1367.009.

(a) Levels of coverage for the nongrandfathered small group market are defined as follows:

(1) Bronze level: A health care service plan contract in the bronze level shall provide a level of coverage that is actuarially equivalent to 60 percent of the full actuarial value of the benefits provided under the plan contract.

(2) Silver level: A health care service plan contract in the silver level shall provide a level of coverage that is actuarially equivalent to 70 percent of the full actuarial value of the benefits provided under the plan contract.

(3) Gold level: A health care service plan contract in the gold level shall provide a level of coverage that is actuarially equivalent to 80 percent of the full actuarial value of the benefits provided under the plan contract.

(4) Platinum level: A health care service plan contract in the platinum level shall provide a level of coverage that is actuarially equivalent to 90 percent of the full actuarial value of the benefits provided under the plan contract.

(b) Actuarial value for nongrandfathered small employer health care service plan contracts shall be determined in accordance with the following:

(1) Actuarial value shall not vary by more than plus or minus 2 percent.

(2) Actuarial value shall be determined on the basis of essential health benefits as defined in Section 1367.005 and as provided to a standard, nonelderly population. For this purpose, a standard population shall not include those receiving coverage through the Medi-Cal or Medicare programs.

(3) The department may use the actuarial value methodology developed consistent with Section 1302(d) of PPACA.

(4) The actuarial value for pediatric dental benefits, whether offered by a full service plan or a specialized plan, shall be consistent with federal law and guidance applicable to the plan type.

(5) The department, in consultation with the Department of Insurance and the Exchange, shall consider whether to exercise state-level flexibility with respect to the actuarial value calculator in order to take into account the unique characteristics of the California health care coverage market, including the prevalence of health care service plans, total cost of care paid for by the plan, price of care, patterns of service utilization, and relevant demographic factors.

(6) Employer contributions toward health reimbursement accounts and health savings accounts shall count toward the actuarial value of the product in the manner specified in federal rules and guidance.

(c) "PPACA" means the federal Patient Protection and Affordable Care Act (Public Law 111-148), as amended by the federal Health Care and Education Reconciliation Act of 2010 (Public Law 111-152), and any rules, regulations, or guidance issued thereunder. (Added by Stats. 2013, Ch. 316, Sec. 7. (SB 639) Effective January 1, 2014.)

1367.01.

(a) A health care service plan and any entity with which it contracts for services that include utilization review or utilization management functions, that prospectively, retrospectively, or concurrently reviews and approves, modifies, delays, or denies, based in whole or in part on medical necessity, requests by providers prior to, retrospectively, or concurrent with the provision of health care services to enrollees, or that delegates these functions to medical groups or independent practice associations or to other contracting providers, shall comply with this section.

(b) A health care service plan that is subject to this section shall have written policies and procedures establishing the process by which the plan prospectively, retrospectively, or concurrently reviews and approves, modifies, delays, or denies, based in whole or in part on medical necessity, requests by providers of health care services for plan enrollees. These policies and procedures shall ensure that decisions based on the medical necessity of proposed health care services are consistent with criteria or guidelines that are

supported by clinical principles and processes. These criteria and guidelines shall be developed pursuant to Section 1363.5. These policies and procedures, and a description of the process by which the plan reviews and approves, modifies, delays, or denies requests by providers prior to, retrospectively, or concurrent with the provision of health care services to enrollees, shall be filed with the director for review and approval, and shall be disclosed by the plan to providers and enrollees upon request, and by the plan to the public upon request.

(c) A health care service plan subject to this section, except a plan that meets the requirements of Section 1351.2, shall employ or designate a medical director who holds an unrestricted license to practice medicine in this state issued pursuant to Section 2050 of the Business and Professions Code or pursuant to the Osteopathic Act, or, if the plan is a specialized health care service plan, a clinical director with California licensure in a clinical area appropriate to the type of care provided by the specialized health care service plan. The medical director or clinical director shall ensure that the process by which the plan reviews and approves, modifies, or denies, based in whole or in part on medical necessity, requests by providers prior to, retrospectively, or concurrent with the provision of health care services to enrollees, complies with the requirements of this section.

(d) If health plan personnel, or individuals under contract to the plan to review requests by providers, approve the provider's request, pursuant to subdivision (b), the decision shall be communicated to the provider pursuant to subdivision (h).

(e) No individual, other than a licensed physician or a licensed health care professional who is competent to evaluate the specific clinical issues involved in the health care services requested by the provider, may deny or modify requests for authorization of health care services for an enrollee for reasons of medical necessity. The decision of the physician or other health care professional shall be communicated to the provider and the enrollee pursuant to subdivision (h).

(f) The criteria or guidelines used by the health care service plan to determine whether to approve, modify, or deny requests by providers prior to, retrospectively, or concurrent with, the provision of health care services to enrollees shall be consistent with clinical principles and processes. These criteria and guidelines shall be developed pursuant to the requirements of Section 1363.5.

(g) If the health care service plan requests medical information from providers in order to determine whether to approve, modify, or deny requests for authorization, the plan shall request only the information reasonably necessary to make the determination.

(h) In determining whether to approve, modify, or deny requests by providers prior to, retrospectively, or concurrent with the provision of health care services to enrollees, based in whole or in part on medical necessity, a health care service plan subject to this section shall meet the following requirements:

(1) Decisions to approve, modify, or deny, based on medical necessity, requests by providers prior to, or concurrent with the provision of health care services to enrollees that do not meet the requirements for the time period for review required by paragraph (2), shall be made in a timely fashion appropriate for the nature of the enrollee's condition, not to exceed five business days from the plan's receipt of the information reasonably necessary and requested by the plan to make the determination. In cases where the review is retrospective, the decision shall be communicated to the individual who received services, or to the individual's designee, within 30 days of the receipt of information that is reasonably necessary to make this determination, and shall be communicated to the provider in a manner that is consistent with current law. For purposes of this section, retrospective reviews shall be for care rendered on or after January 1, 2000.

(2) When the enrollee's condition is such that the enrollee faces an imminent and serious threat to his or her health, including, but not limited to, the potential loss of life, limb, or other major bodily function, or the normal timeframe for the decisionmaking process, as described in paragraph (1), would be detrimental to the enrollee's life or health or could jeopardize the enrollee's ability to regain maximum function, decisions to approve, modify, or deny requests by providers prior to, or concurrent with, the provision of health care services to enrollees, shall be made in a timely fashion appropriate for the nature of the enrollee's condition, not to exceed 72 hours or, if shorter, the period of time required under Section 2719 of the federal Public Health Service Act (42 U.S.C. Sec. 300gg-19) and any subsequent rules or regulations issued thereunder, after the plan's receipt of the information reasonably necessary and requested by the plan to make the determination. Nothing in this section shall be construed to alter the requirements of subdivision (b) of Section 1371.4. Notwithstanding Section 1371.4, the requirements of this division shall be applicable to all health plans and other entities conducting utilization review or utilization management.

(3) Decisions to approve, modify, or deny requests by providers for authorization prior to, or concurrent with, the provision of health care services to enrollees shall be communicated to the requesting provider within 24 hours of the decision. Except for concurrent review decisions pertaining to care that is underway, which shall be communicated to the enrollee's treating provider within 24 hours, decisions resulting in denial, delay, or modification of all or part of the requested health care service shall be communicated to the enrollee in writing within two business days of the decision. In the case of concurrent review, care shall not be discontinued until the enrollee's treating provider has been notified of the plan's decision and a care plan has been agreed upon by the treating provider that is appropriate for the medical needs of that patient.

(4) Communications regarding decisions to approve requests by providers prior to, retrospectively, or concurrent with the provision of health care services to enrollees shall specify the specific health care service approved. Responses regarding decisions to deny, delay, or modify health care services requested by providers prior to, retrospectively, or

concurrent with the provision of health care services to enrollees shall be communicated to the enrollee in writing, and to providers initially by telephone or facsimile, except with regard to decisions rendered retrospectively, and then in writing, and shall include a clear and concise explanation of the reasons for the plan's decision, a description of the criteria or guidelines used, and the clinical reasons for the decisions regarding medical necessity. Any written communication to a physician or other health care provider of a denial, delay, or modification of a request shall include the name and telephone number of the health care professional responsible for the denial, delay, or modification. The telephone number provided shall be a direct number or an extension, to allow the physician or health care provider easily to contact the professional responsible for the denial, delay, or modification. Responses shall also include information as to how the enrollee may file a grievance with the plan pursuant to Section 1368, and in the case of Medi-Cal enrollees, shall explain how to request an administrative hearing and aid paid pending under Sections 51014.1 and 51014.2 of Title 22 of the California Code of Regulations.

(5) If the health care service plan cannot make a decision to approve, modify, or deny the request for authorization within the timeframes specified in paragraph (1) or (2) because the plan is not in receipt of all of the information reasonably necessary and requested, or because the plan requires consultation by an expert reviewer, or because the plan has asked that an additional examination or test be performed upon the enrollee, provided the examination or test is reasonable and consistent with good medical practice, the plan shall, immediately upon the expiration of the timeframe specified in paragraph (1) or (2) or as soon as the plan becomes aware that it will not meet the timeframe, whichever occurs first, notify the provider and the enrollee, in writing, that the plan cannot make a decision to approve, modify, or deny the request for authorization within the required timeframe, and specify the information requested but not received, or the expert reviewer to be consulted, or the additional examinations or tests required. The plan shall also notify the provider and enrollee of the anticipated date on which a decision may be rendered. Upon receipt of all information reasonably necessary and requested by the plan, the plan shall approve, modify, or deny the request for authorization within the timeframes specified in paragraph (1) or (2), whichever applies.

(6) If the director determines that a health care service plan has failed to meet any of the timeframes in this section, or has failed to meet any other requirement of this section, the director may assess, by order, administrative penalties for each failure. A proceeding for the issuance of an order assessing administrative penalties shall be subject to appropriate notice to, and an opportunity for a hearing with regard to, the person affected, in accordance with subdivision (a) of Section 1397. The administrative penalties shall not be deemed an exclusive remedy for the director. These penalties shall be paid to the Managed Care Administrative Fines and Penalties Fund and shall be used for the purposes specified in Section 1341.45.

(i) A health care service plan subject to this section shall maintain telephone access for providers to request authorization for health care services.

(j) A health care service plan subject to this section that reviews requests by providers prior to, retrospectively, or concurrent with, the provision of health care services to enrollees shall establish, as part of the quality assurance program required by Section 1370, a process by which the plan's compliance with this section is assessed and evaluated. The process shall include provisions for evaluation of complaints, assessment of trends, implementation of actions to correct identified problems, mechanisms to communicate actions and results to the appropriate health plan employees and contracting providers, and provisions for evaluation of any corrective action plan and measurements of performance.

(k) The director shall review a health care service plan's compliance with this section as part of its periodic onsite medical survey of each plan undertaken pursuant to Section 1380, and shall include a discussion of compliance with this section as part of its report issued pursuant to that section.

(l) This section shall not apply to decisions made for the care or treatment of the sick who depend upon prayer or spiritual means for healing in the practice of religion as set forth in subdivision (a) of Section 1270.

(m) Nothing in this section shall cause a health care service plan to be defined as a health care provider for purposes of any provision of law, including, but not limited to, Section 6146 of the Business and Professions Code, Sections 3333.1 and 3333.2 of the Civil Code, and Sections 340.5, 364, 425.13, 667.7, and 1295 of the Code of Civil Procedure.

(Amended by Stats. 2010, Ch. 658, Sec. 5. (AB 2470) Effective January 1, 2011.)
1367.010.
(a) (1) A nongrandfathered health care service plan, except a health care service plan offering a specialized health care service plan contract, that offers, amends, or renews a large group health care service plan contract shall not market, offer, amend, or renew a large group plan contract that provides a minimum value of less than 60 percent.

(2) This section shall not apply to limited wraparound coverage, consistent with Section 146.145(b) of Title 45 of the Code of Federal Regulations.

(b) For purposes of this section, a plan shall provide a minimum value of at least 60 percent, as described in Section 36B(c)(2)(C) of the federal Internal Revenue Code and any regulation or guidance adopted under that section.

(c) The following definitions apply for purposes of this section:

(1) "Large group health care service plan contract" means a group health care service plan contract other than a contract issued to a "small employer," as defined in Section 1357, 1357.500, or 1357.600.

(2) "Plan year" has the meaning set forth in Section 144.103 of Title 45 of the Code of Federal Regulations.

(Added by Stats. 2015, Ch. 617, Sec. 2. (AB 248) Effective January 1, 2016.)
1367.012.
(a) (1) A small employer health care service plan contract in effect on December 31, 2013, and still in effect as of the effective date of this section, that does not qualify as a grandfathered health plan under Section 1251 of PPACA may be renewed until January 1, 2015, and may continue to be in force until December 31, 2015, subject to applicable federal law, and any other requirements imposed by this chapter.

(2) A small employer health care service plan contract described in paragraph (1) may continue to be in force after December 31, 2015, if the contract is amended to comply with all of the provisions listed in subdivision (e) by January 1, 2016, and complies with all other applicable provisions of law.

(b) (1) If a health care service plan offers for renewal a small employer health care service plan contract pursuant to paragraph (1) of subdivision (a), the health care service plan shall provide notice to the group contractholder regarding the option to renew coverage pursuant to subdivision (a) using the relevant notice attached to the guidance entitled "Insurance Standards Bulletin Series – Extension of Transition Policy through October 1, 2016," issued by the United States Department of Health and Human Services, Centers for Medicare and Medicaid Services on March 5, 2014.

(2) A health care service plan shall include the following notice with the notice issued pursuant to paragraph (1):

"New health care coverage options are available in California. You currently have health care coverage that is not required to comply with many new laws. A new health care service plan contract may be more affordable and/or offer more comprehensive benefits. New plans may also have limits on deductibles and out-of-pocket costs, while your existing plan may have no such limits.

You have the option to remain with your current coverage for one more year or switch to new coverage that complies with the new laws. Covered California, the state's new health insurance marketplace, offers small employers health insurance from a number of companies through its Small Business Health Options Program (SHOP). Federal tax credits are available through the SHOP to those small employers that qualify. Talk to Covered California (1-877-453-9198), your plan representative, or your insurance agent to discuss your options."

(3) A health care service plan shall include with the notices issued pursuant to paragraphs (1) and (2), the premium, cost sharing, and benefits associated with the plan's standard benefit designs approved consistent with subdivision (c) of Section 100504 of the Government Code for the geographic region of the small employer.

(4) A health care service plan that offers for renewal a small employer health care service plan contract pursuant to paragraph (1) of subdivision (a) shall offer renewal to all employers whose health care service plan contract with that health care service plan was in effect on December 31, 2013.

(c) (1) A small employer health care service plan contract in effect on December 31, 2013, and still in effect as of the effective date of this section, that does not qualify as a grandfathered health plan under Section 1251 of PPACA that is renewed on or before January 1, 2015, and that continues to be in force until no later than December 31, 2015, is exempt from the following provisions:

(A) Paragraphs (1) and (2) of subdivision (a) of, and subdivisions (e) and (i) of, Section 1357.503.

(B) Section 1357.512.

(C) Sections 1367.005 and 1357.508.

(D) Section 1367.0065.

(E) Section 1367.006.

(F) Section 1367.007.

(G) Section 1367.009.

(2) Notwithstanding paragraphs (1) and (2) of subdivision (a) of, and subdivision (e) of, Section 1357.503, a small employer health care service plan contract subject to this section shall only be offered, marketed, and sold to an employer whose health care service plan contract with that health care service plan was in effect on December 31, 2013.

(d) A small employer health care service plan contract described in paragraph (1) of subdivision (a) shall be subject to Sections 1357.12 and 1357.13, and shall continue to be subject to Article 3.16 (commencing with Section 1357.500), except as provided in subdivision (c), and to all otherwise applicable provisions of this chapter.

(e) No later than January 1, 2016, a small employer health care service plan contract described in paragraph (1) of subdivision (a) may be amended to comply with all of the following:

(1) Paragraphs (1) and (2) of subdivision (a) of, and subdivisions (e) and (i) of, Section 1357.503.

(2) Section 1357.512.

(3) Sections 1357.508 and 1367.005.

(4) Section 1367.006.

(5) Section 1367.007.

(6) Section 1367.009.

(f) This section shall be implemented only to the extent permitted by PPACA.

(g) For purposes of this section, the following definitions shall apply:

(1) "PPACA" means the federal Patient Protection and Affordable Care Act (Public Law 111-148), as amended by the federal Health Care and Education Reconciliation Act of 2010 (Public Law 111-152), and any rules, regulations, or guidance issued pursuant to that law.

(2) "Small employer health care service plan contract" means a group health care service plan contract, other than a specialized health care service plan contract, issued to a small employer, as defined in subdivision (s) of Section 1357.500.
(Added by Stats. 2014, Ch. 84, Sec. 1. (SB 1446) Effective July 7, 2014.)
1367.015.
In addition to complying with subdivision (h) of Section 1367.01, in determining whether to approve, modify, or deny requests by providers prior to, retrospectively, or concurrent with the provision of health care services to enrollees, based in whole or in part on medical necessity, a health care service plan subject to Section 1367.01 shall not base decisions to deny requests by providers for authorization for mental health services or to deny claim reimbursement for mental health services on either of the following:
(a) Whether admission was voluntary or involuntary.
(b) The method of transportation to the health facility.
(Added by Stats. 2008, Ch. 722, Sec. 1. Effective January 1, 2009.)

1367.02.

(a) On or before July 1, 1999, for purposes of public disclosure, every health care service plan shall file with the department a description of any policies and procedures related to economic profiling utilized by the plan and its medical groups and individual practice associations. The filing shall describe how these policies and procedures are used in utilization review, peer review, incentive and penalty programs, and in provider retention and termination decisions. The filing shall also indicate in what manner, if any, the economic profiling system being used takes into consideration risk adjustments that reflect case mix, type and severity of patient illness, age of patients, and other enrollee characteristics that may account for higher or lower than expected costs or utilization of services. The filing shall also indicate how the economic profiling activities avoid being in conflict with subdivision (g) of Section 1367, which requires each plan to demonstrate that medical decisions are rendered by qualified medical providers, unhindered by fiscal and administrative management. Any changes to the policies and procedures shall be filed with the director pursuant to Section 1352. Nothing in this section shall be construed to restrict or impair the department, in its discretion, from utilizing the information filed pursuant to this section for purposes of ensuring compliance with this chapter.
(b) The director shall make each plan's filing available to the public upon request. The director shall not publicly disclose any information submitted pursuant to this section that is determined by the director to be confidential pursuant to state law.
(c) Each plan that uses economic profiling shall, upon request, provide a copy of economic profiling information related to an individual provider, contracting medical group, or individual practice association to the profiled individual, group, or association. In addition, each plan shall require as a condition of contract that its medical groups and individual practice associations that maintain economic profiles of individual providers shall, upon request, provide a copy of individual economic profiling information to the individual providers who are profiled. The economic profiling information provided pursuant to this section shall be provided upon request until 60 days after the date upon which the contract between the plan and the individual provider, medical group, or individual practice association terminates, or until 60 days after the date the contract between the medical group or individual practice association and the individual provider terminates, whichever is applicable.
(d) For the purposes of this article, "economic profiling" shall mean any evaluation of a particular physician, provider, medical group, or individual practice association based in whole or in part on the economic costs or utilization of services associated with medical care provided or authorized by the physician, provider, medical group, or individual practice association.
(Amended by Stats. 1999, Ch. 525, Sec. 95. Effective January 1, 2000. Operative July 1, 2000, or sooner, by Sec. 214 of Ch. 525.)

1367.03.

(a) Not later than January 1, 2004, the department shall develop and adopt regulations to ensure that enrollees have access to needed health care services in a timely manner. In developing these regulations, the department shall develop indicators of timeliness of access to care and, in so doing, shall consider the following as indicators of timeliness of access to care:
(1) Waiting times for appointments with physicians, including primary care and specialty physicians.
(2) Timeliness of care in an episode of illness, including the timeliness of referrals and obtaining other services, if needed.
(3) Waiting time to speak to a physician, registered nurse, or other qualified health professional acting within his or her scope of practice who is trained to screen or triage an enrollee who may need care.
(b) In developing these standards for timeliness of access, the department shall consider the following:
(1) Clinical appropriateness.
(2) The nature of the specialty.
(3) The urgency of care.
(4) The requirements of other provisions of law, including Section 1367.01 governing utilization review, that may affect timeliness of access.
(c) The department may adopt standards other than the time elapsed between the time an enrollee seeks health care and obtains care. If the department chooses a standard other than the time elapsed between the time an enrollee first seeks health care and obtains it, the department shall demonstrate why that standard is more appropriate. In developing these standards, the department shall consider the nature of the plan network.
(d) The department shall review and adopt standards, as needed, concerning the availability of primary care physicians, specialty physicians, hospital care, and other health care, so that consumers have timely access to care. In so doing, the department shall consider the nature of physician practices, including individual and group practices as well as the nature of the plan network. The department shall also consider various circumstances affecting the delivery of care, including urgent care, care provided on the same day, and requests for specific providers. If the department finds that health care service plans and health care providers have difficulty meeting these standards, the department may make recommendations to the Assembly Committee on Health and the Senate Committee on Insurance of the Legislature pursuant to subdivision (i).
(e) In developing standards under subdivision (a), the department shall consider requirements under federal law, requirements under other state programs, standards adopted by other states, nationally recognized accrediting organizations, and professional associations. The department shall further consider the needs of rural areas, specifically those in which health facilities are more than 30 miles apart and any requirements imposed by the State Department of Health Care Services on health care service plans that contract with the State Department of Health Care Services to provide Medi-Cal managed care.
(f) (1) Contracts between health care service plans and health care providers shall ensure compliance with the standards developed under this section. These contracts shall require reporting by health care providers to health care service plans and by health care service plans to the department to ensure compliance with the standards.
(2) Health care service plans shall report annually to the department on compliance with the standards in a manner specified by the department. The reported information shall allow consumers to compare the performance of plans and their contracting providers in complying with the standards, as well as changes in the compliance of plans with these standards.
(3) The department may develop standardized methodologies for reporting that shall be used by health care service plans to demonstrate compliance with this section and any regulations adopted pursuant to it. The methodologies shall be sufficient to determine compliance with the standards developed under this section for different networks of providers if a health care service plan uses a different network for Medi-Cal managed care products than for other products or if a health care service plan uses a different network for individual market products than for small group market products. The development and adoption of these methodologies shall not be subject to the Administrative Procedure Act (Chapter 3.5 (commencing with Section 11340) of Part 1 of Division 3 of Title 2 of the Government Code) until January 1, 2020. The department shall consult with stakeholders in developing standardized methodologies under this paragraph.
(g) (1) When evaluating compliance with the standards, the department shall focus more upon patterns of noncompliance rather than isolated episodes of noncompliance.
(2) The director may investigate and take enforcement action against plans regarding noncompliance with the requirements of this section. Where substantial harm to an enrollee has occurred as a result of plan noncompliance, the director may, by order, assess administrative penalties subject to appropriate notice of, and the opportunity for, a hearing in accordance with Section 1397. The plan may provide to the director, and the director may consider, information regarding the plan's overall compliance with the requirements of this section. The administrative penalties shall not be deemed an exclusive remedy available to the director. These penalties shall be paid to the Managed Care Administrative Fines and Penalties Fund and shall be used for the purposes specified in Section 1341.45. The director shall periodically evaluate grievances to determine if any audit, investigative, or enforcement actions should be undertaken by the department.
(3) The director may, after appropriate notice and opportunity for hearing in accordance with Section 1397, by order, assess administrative penalties if the director determines that a health care service plan has knowingly committed, or has performed with a frequency that indicates a general business practice, either of the following:
(A) Repeated failure to act promptly and reasonably to assure timely access to care consistent with this chapter.
(B) Repeated failure to act promptly and reasonably to require contracting providers to assure timely access that the plan is required to perform under this chapter and that have been delegated by the plan to the contracting provider when the obligation of the plan to the enrollee or subscriber is reasonably clear.
(C) The administrative penalties available to the director pursuant to this section are not exclusive, and may be sought and employed in any combination with civil, criminal, and other administrative remedies deemed warranted by the director to enforce this chapter.
(4) The administrative penalties shall be paid to the Managed Care Administrative Fines and Penalties Fund and shall be used for the purposes specified in Section 1341.45.
(h) The department shall work with the patient advocate to assure that the quality of care report card incorporates information provided pursuant to subdivision (f) regarding the degree to which health care service plans and health care providers comply with the requirements for timely access to care.
(i) The department shall annually review information regarding compliance with the standards developed under this section and shall make recommendations for changes that further protect enrollees. Commencing no later than December 1, 2015, and annually thereafter, the department shall post its final findings from the review on its Internet Web site.
(j) The department shall post on its Internet Web site any waivers or alternative standards that the department approves under this section on or after January 1, 2015.
(Amended by Stats. 2014, Ch. 573, Sec. 1. (SB 964) Effective January 1, 2015.)
1367.031.

(a) A health care service plan contract that is issued, renewed, or amended on or after July 1, 2017, shall provide information to an enrollee regarding the standards for timely access to care adopted pursuant to Section 1367.03 and the information required by this section, including information related to receipt of interpreter services in a timely manner, no less than annually.

(b) A health care service plan at a minimum shall provide information regarding appointment wait times for urgent care, nonurgent primary care, nonurgent specialty care, and telephone screening established pursuant to Section 1367.03 to enrollees and contracting providers. The information shall also include notice of the availability of interpreter services at the time of the appointment pursuant to Section 1367.04. A health care service plan may indicate that exceptions to appointment wait times may apply if the department has found exceptions to be permissible.

(c) The information required to be provided pursuant to this section shall be provided to an enrollee with individual coverage upon initial enrollment and annually thereafter upon renewal, and to enrollees and subscribers with group coverage upon initial enrollment and annually thereafter upon renewal. A health care service plan may include this information with other materials sent to the enrollee. The information shall also be provided in the following manner:

(1) In a separate section of the evidence of coverage titled "Timely Access to Care."
(2) At least annually, in or with newsletters, outreach, or other materials that are routinely disseminated to the plan's enrollees.
(3) Commencing January 1, 2018, in a separate section of the provider directory published and maintained by the health care service plan pursuant to Section 1367.27. The separate section shall be titled "Timely Access to Care."
(4) On the Internet Web site published and maintained by the health care service plan, in a manner that allows enrollees and prospective enrollees to easily locate the information.

(d) (1) A health care service plan shall provide the information required by this section to contracting providers on no less than an annual basis.
(2) A health care service plan shall also inform a contracting provider of all of the following:
(A) Information about a health care service plan's obligation under California law to provide or arrange for timely access to care.
(B) How a contracting provider or enrollee can contact the health care service plan to obtain assistance if a patient is unable to obtain a timely referral to an appropriate provider.
(C) The toll-free telephone number for the Department of Managed Health Care where providers and enrollees can file a complaint if they are unable to obtain a timely referral to an appropriate provider.
(3) A health care service plan may comply with this subdivision by including the information with an existing communication with a contracting provider.

(e) This section shall apply to Medi-Cal managed care plan contracts entered into with the State Department of Health Care Services pursuant to Chapter 7 (commencing with Section 14000) or Chapter 8 (commencing with Section 14200) of Part 3 of Division 9 of the Welfare and Institutions Code.
(Added by Stats. 2016, Ch. 500, Sec. 1. (SB 1135) Effective January 1, 2017.)
1367.035.

(a) As part of the reports submitted to the department pursuant to subdivision (f) of Section 1367.03 and regulations adopted pursuant to that section, a health care service plan shall submit to the department, in a manner specified by the department, data regarding network adequacy, including, but not limited to, the following:
(1) Provider office location.
(2) Area of specialty.
(3) Hospitals where providers have admitting privileges, if any.
(4) Providers with open practices.
(5) The number of patients assigned to a primary care provider or, for providers who do not have assigned enrollees, information that demonstrates the capacity of primary care providers to be accessible and available to enrollees.
(6) Grievances regarding network adequacy and timely access that the health care service plan received during the preceding calendar year.

(b) A health care service plan that uses a network for its Medi-Cal managed care product line that is different from the network used for its other product lines shall submit the data required under subdivision (a) for its Medi-Cal managed care product line separately from the data submitted for its other product lines.

(c) A health care service plan that uses a network for its individual market product line that is different from the network used for its small group market product line shall submit the data required under subdivision (a) for its individual market product line separate from the data submitted for its small group market product line.

(d) The department shall review the data submitted pursuant to this section for compliance with this chapter.

(e) In submitting data under this section, a health care service plan that provides services to Medi-Cal beneficiaries pursuant to Chapter 7 (commencing with Section 14000) or Chapter 8 (commencing with Section 14200) of Part 3 of Division 9 of the Welfare and Institutions Code shall provide the same data to the State Department of Health Care Services pursuant to Section 14456.3 of the Welfare and Institutions Code.

(f) In developing the format and requirements for reports, data, or other information provided by plans pursuant to subdivision (a), the department shall not create duplicate reporting requirements, but, instead, shall take into consideration all existing relevant reports, data, or other information provided by plans to the department. This subdivision does not limit the authority of the department to request additional information from the plan as deemed necessary to carry out and complete any enforcement action initiated under this chapter.

(g) If the department requests additional information or data to be reported pursuant to subdivision (a), which is different or in addition to the information required to be reported in paragraphs (1) to (6), inclusive, of subdivision (a), the department shall provide health care service plans notice of that change by November 1 of the year prior to the change.

(h) A health care service plan may include in the provider contract provisions requiring compliance with the reporting requirements of Section 1367.03 and this section.
(Amended by Stats. 2015, Ch. 303, Sec. 253. (AB 731) Effective January 1, 2016.)
1367.04.

(a) Not later than January 1, 2006, the department shall develop and adopt regulations establishing standards and requirements to provide health care service plan enrollees with appropriate access to language assistance in obtaining health care services.

(b) In developing the regulations, the department shall require every health care service plan and specialized health care service plan to assess the linguistic needs of the enrollee population, excluding Medi-Cal enrollees, and to provide for translation and interpretation for medical services, as indicated. A health care service plan that participates in the Healthy Families Program may assess the Healthy Families Program enrollee population separately from the remainder of its enrollee population for purposes of subparagraph (A) of paragraph (1). A health care service plan that chooses to separate its Healthy Families Program enrollment from the remainder of its enrollee population shall treat the Healthy Families Program population separately for purposes of determining whether subparagraph (A) of paragraph (1) is applicable, and shall also treat the Healthy Families Program population separately for purposes of applying the percentage and numerical thresholds in subparagraph (A) of paragraph (1). The regulations shall include the following:

(1) Requirements for the translation of vital documents that include the following:
(A) A requirement that all vital documents, as defined pursuant to subparagraph (B), be translated into an indicated language, as follows:
(i) A health care service plan with an enrollment of 1,000,000 or more shall translate vital documents into the top two languages other than English as determined by the needs assessment as required by this subdivision and any additional languages when 0.75 percent or 15,000 of the enrollee population, whichever number is less, excluding Medi-Cal enrollment and treating Healthy Families Program enrollment separately indicates in the needs assessment as required by this subdivision a preference for written materials in that language.
(ii) A health care service plan with an enrollment of 300,000 or more but less than 1,000,000 shall translate vital documents into the top one language other than English as determined by the needs assessment as required by this subdivision and any additional languages when 1 percent or 6,000 of the enrollee population, whichever number is less, excluding Medi-Cal enrollment and treating Healthy Families Program enrollment separately indicates in the needs assessment as required by this subdivision a preference for written materials in that language.
(iii) A health care service plan with an enrollment of less than 300,000 shall translate vital documents into a language other than English when 3,000 or more or 5 percent of the enrollee population, whichever number is less, excluding Medi-Cal enrollment and treating Healthy Families Program enrollment separately indicates in the needs assessment as required by this subdivision a preference for written materials in that language.
(B) Specification of vital documents produced by the plan that are required to be translated. The specification of vital documents shall not exceed that of the United States Department of Health and Human Services (HHS) Office for Civil Rights (OCR) Policy Guidance (65 Federal Register 52762 (August 30, 2000)), but shall include all of the following:
(i) Applications.
(ii) Consent forms.
(iii) Letters containing important information regarding eligibility and participation criteria.
(iv) Notices pertaining to the denial, reduction, modification, or termination of services and benefits, and the right to file a grievance or appeal.
(v) Notices advising limited-English-proficient persons of the availability of free language assistance and other outreach materials that are provided to enrollees.
(vi) Translated documents shall not include a health care service plan's explanation of benefits or similar claim processing information that is sent to enrollees, unless the document requires a response by the enrollee.
(C) (i) For those documents described in subparagraph (B) that are not standardized but contain enrollee specific information, health care service plans shall not be required to translate the documents into the threshold languages identified by the needs assessment as required by this subdivision, but rather shall include with the documents a written notice of the availability of interpretation services in the threshold languages identified by the needs assessment as required by this subdivision. A health care service plan subject to the requirements in Section 1367.042 shall also include with the documents a written notice of the availability of interpretation services in the top 15 languages spoken by limited-English-proficient (LEP) individuals in California as determined by the State Department of Health Care Services.
(ii) Upon request, the enrollee shall receive a written translation of the documents described in clause (i). The health care service plan shall have up to, but not to exceed, 21 days to comply with the enrollee's request for a written translation. If an enrollee requests a translated document, all timeframes and deadline requirements related to the document that apply to the health care service plan and enrollees under the provisions of this chapter and under any regulations adopted pursuant to this chapter shall begin to run upon the health care service plan's issuance of the translated document.

(iii) For grievances that require expedited plan review and response in accordance with subdivision (b) of Section 1368.01, the health care service plan may satisfy this requirement by providing notice of the availability and access to oral interpretation services.

(D) A requirement that health care service plans advise limited-English-proficient enrollees of the availability of interpreter services.

(2) Standards to ensure the quality and accuracy of the written translations and that a translated document meets the same standards required for the English language version of the document. The English language documents shall determine the rights and obligations of the parties, and the translated documents shall be admissible in evidence only if there is a dispute regarding a substantial difference in the material terms and conditions of the English language document and the translated document.

(3) Requirements for surveying the language preferences and needs assessments of health care service plan enrollees within one year of the effective date of the regulations that permit health care service plans to utilize various survey methods, including, but not limited to, the use of existing enrollment and renewal processes, subscriber newsletters, or other mailings. Health care service plans shall update the needs assessment, demographic profile, and language translation requirements every three years.

(4) Requirements for individual enrollee access to interpretation services that include the following:

(A) A requirement that an interpreter meets, at a minimum, all of the following qualifications:

(i) Demonstrated proficiency in both English and the target language.

(ii) Knowledge in both English and the target language of health care terminology and concepts relevant to health care delivery systems.

(iii) Adheres to generally accepted interpreter ethics principles, including client confidentiality.

(B) A requirement that the enrollee with limited English proficiency shall not be required to provide his or her own interpreter or rely on a staff member who does not meet the qualifications described in subparagraph (A) to communicate directly with the limited-English-proficient enrollee.

(C) A requirement that the enrollee with limited English proficiency shall not be required to rely on an adult or minor child accompanying the enrollee to interpret or facilitate communication except under either of the following circumstances:

(i) In an emergency, as described in Section 1317.1, if a qualified interpreter is not immediately available for the enrollee with limited English proficiency.

(ii) If the individual with limited English proficiency specifically requests that the accompanying adult interpret or facilitate communication, the accompanying adult agrees to provide that assistance, and reliance on that accompanying adult for that assistance is appropriate under the circumstances.

(5) Standards to ensure the quality and timeliness of oral interpretation services provided by health care service plans.

(c) In developing the regulations, standards, and requirements, the department shall consider the following:

(1) Publications and standards issued by federal agencies, such as the Culturally and Linguistically Appropriate Services (CLAS) in Health Care issued by the United States Department of Health and Human Services Office of Minority Health in December 2000, and the United States Department of Health and Human Services (HHS) Office for Civil Rights (OCR) Policy Guidance (65 Federal Register 52762 (August 30, 2000)).

(2) Other cultural and linguistic requirements under state programs, such as Medi-Cal Managed Care Policy Letters, cultural and linguistic requirements imposed by the State Department of Health Care Services on health care service plans that contract to provide Medi-Cal managed care services, and cultural and linguistic requirements imposed by the Managed Risk Medical Insurance Board on health care service plans that contract to provide services in the Healthy Families Program.

(3) Standards adopted by other states pertaining to language assistance requirements for health care service plans.

(4) Standards established by California or nationally recognized accrediting, certifying, or licensing organizations and medical and health care interpreter professional associations regarding interpretation services.

(5) Publications, guidelines, reports, and recommendations issued by state agencies or advisory committees, such as the report card to the public on the comparative performance of plans and reports on cultural and linguistic services issued by the Office of Patient Advocate and the report to the Legislature from the Task Force on Culturally and Linguistically Competent Physicians and Dentists established by former Section 852 of the Business and Professions Code.

(6) Examples of best practices relating to language assistance services by health care providers and health care service plans, including existing practices.

(7) Information gathered from complaints to the HMO Helpline and consumer assistance centers regarding language assistance services.

(8) The cost of compliance and the availability of translation and interpretation services and professionals.

(9) Flexibility to accommodate variations in plan networks and method of service delivery. The department shall allow for health care service plan flexibility in determining compliance with the standards for oral and written interpretation services.

(d) The department shall work to ensure that the biennial reports required by this section, and the data collected for those reports, are consistent with reports required by government-sponsored programs and do not require duplicative or conflicting data collection or reporting.

(e) The department shall seek public input from a wide range of interested parties through advisory bodies established by the director.

(f) A contract between a health care service plan and a health care provider shall require compliance with the standards developed under this section. In furtherance of this section, the contract shall require providers to cooperate with the plan by providing any information necessary to assess compliance.

(g) The department shall report biennially to the Legislature and advisory bodies established by the director regarding plan compliance with the standards, including results of compliance audits made in conjunction with other audits and reviews. The reported information shall also be included in the publication required under subparagraph (B) of paragraph (1) of subdivision (b) of Section 136000. The department shall also utilize the reported information to make recommendations for changes that further enhance standards pursuant to this section. The department may also delay or otherwise phase-in implementation of standards and requirements in recognition of costs and availability of translation and interpretation services and professionals.

(h) (1) Except for contracts with the State Department of Health Care Services Medi-Cal program, the standards developed under this section shall be considered the minimum required for compliance.

(2) The regulations shall provide that a health plan is in compliance if the plan is required to meet the same or similar standards by the Medi-Cal program, either by contract or state law, if the standards provide as much access to cultural and linguistic services as the standards established by this section for an equal or higher number of enrollees and therefore meet or exceed the standards of the regulations established pursuant to this section, and the department determines that the health care service plan is in compliance with the standards required by the Medi-Cal program. To meet this requirement, the department shall not be required to perform individual audits. The department shall, to the extent feasible, rely on audits, reports, or other oversight and enforcement methods used by the State Department of Health Care Services.

(3) The determination pursuant to paragraph (2) shall only apply to the enrollees covered by the Medi-Cal program standards. A health care service plan subject to paragraph (2) shall comply with the standards established by this section with regard to enrollees not covered by the Medi-Cal program.

(i) This section does not prohibit a government purchaser from including in their contracts additional translation or interpretation requirements, to meet linguistic or cultural needs, beyond those set forth pursuant to this section.

(Amended by Stats. 2018, Ch. 92, Sec. 131. (SB 1289) Effective January 1, 2019.)

1367.041.

(a) A health care service plan that advertises or markets products in the individual or small group health care service plan markets, or allows any other person or business to market or advertise on its behalf in the individual or small group health care service plan markets, in a non-English language that does not meet the requirements set forth in Sections 1367.04 and 1367.07, shall provide the following documents in the same non-English language:

(1) Welcome letters or notices of initial coverage, if provided.

(2) Applications for enrollment and any information pertinent to eligibility or participation.

(3) Notices advising limited-English-proficient persons of the availability of no-cost translation and interpretation services.

(4) Notices pertaining to the right and instructions on how an enrollee may file a grievance.

(5) The uniform summary of benefits and coverage required pursuant to subparagraph (A) of paragraph (3) of subdivision (b) of Section 1363.

(b) A health care service plan shall use a trained and qualified translator for all written translations of marketing and advertising materials relating to health care service plan products, and for all of the documents specified in subdivision (a).

(c) This section shall not apply to a specialized health care service plan that does not offer an essential health benefit as defined in Section 1367.005.

(Added by Stats. 2013, Ch. 447, Sec. 1. (SB 353) Effective January 1, 2014.)

1367.042.

(a) A health care service plan shall notify enrollees and members of the public of all of the following information:

(1) The availability of language assistance services, including oral interpretation and translated written materials, free of charge and in a timely manner pursuant to Section 1367.04, and how to access these services. This information shall be available in the top 15 languages spoken by limited-English-proficient individuals in California as determined by the State Department of Health Care Services.

(2) The availability of appropriate auxiliary aids and services, including qualified interpreters for individuals with disabilities and information in alternate formats, free of charge and in a timely manner, when those aids and services are necessary to ensure an equal opportunity to participate for individuals with disabilities.

(3) The health plan does not discriminate on the basis of race, color, national origin, ancestry, religion, sex, marital status, gender, gender identity, sexual orientation, age, or disability.

(4) The availability of the grievance procedure described in Section 1368, how to file a grievance, including the name of the plan representative and the telephone number, address, and email address of the plan representative who may be contacted about the grievance, and how to submit the grievance to the department for review after completing the grievance process or participating in the process for at least 30 days.

(5) How to file a discrimination complaint with the United States Department of Health and Human Services Office for Civil Rights if there is a concern of discrimination based on race, color, national origin, age, disability, or sex.

(b) The information required to be provided pursuant to this section shall be provided to an enrollee with individual coverage upon initial enrollment and annually thereafter upon renewal, and to enrollees and subscribers with group coverage upon initial enrollment and annually thereafter upon renewal. A health care service plan may include this information with other materials sent to the enrollee. The information shall also be provided in the following manner:

(1) In a conspicuously visible location in the evidence of coverage.

(2) At least annually, in or with newsletters, outreach, or other materials that are routinely disseminated to the plan's enrollees.

(3) On the Internet Web site published and maintained by the health care service plan, in a manner that allows enrollees, prospective enrollees, and members of the public to easily locate the information.

(c) (1) A specialized health care plan that is not a covered entity, as defined in Section 92.4 of Title 45 of the Code of Federal Regulations, subject to Section 1557 of the federal Patient Protection and Affordable Care Act (42 U.S.C. Sec. 18116) may request an exemption from the requirements under this section.

(2) The department shall not grant an exemption under this subdivision to a specialized health care service plan that arranges for mental health benefits, except for employee assistance program plans.

(3) The department shall provide information on its Internet Web site about any exemptions granted under this subdivision.

(d) This section does not apply to Medi-Cal managed care plan contracts entered into with the State Department of Health Care Services pursuant to Chapter 7 (commencing with Section 14000) or Chapter 8 (commencing with Section 14200) of Part 3 of Division 9 of the Welfare and Institutions Code.

(Amended by Stats. 2018, Ch. 92, Sec. 132. (SB 1289) Effective January 1, 2019.)

1367.05.

(a) Nothing in this chapter shall prohibit a health care service plan from entering into a contract with a dental college approved by the Board of Dental Examiners of California under which the dental college provides for or arranges for the provision of dental care to enrollees of the plan through the practice of dentistry by either of the following:

(1) Bona fide students of dentistry or dental hygiene operating under subdivision (b) of Section 1626 of the Business and Professions Code.

(2) Bona fide clinicians or instructors operating under subdivision (c) of Section 1626 of the Business and Professions Code.

(b) A plan that contracts with a dental college for the delivery of dental care pursuant to subdivision (a) shall disclose to enrollees in the disclosure form and the evidence of coverage, or the combined evidence of coverage and disclosure form, and, if the plan provides a listing of providers to the enrollees, in the listing of providers, that the dental care provided by the dental college will be provided by students of dentistry or dental hygiene and clinicians or instructors of the dental college.

(Added by Stats. 1996, Ch. 492, Sec. 7. Effective January 1, 1997.)

1367.06.

(a) A health care service plan contract, except a specialized health care service plan contract, that is issued, amended, delivered, or renewed on or after January 1, 2005, that covers outpatient prescription drug benefits shall include coverage for inhaler spacers when medically necessary for the management and treatment of pediatric asthma.

(b) If a subscriber has coverage for outpatient prescription drugs, a health care service plan contract, except a specialized health care service plan contract, that is issued, amended, delivered, or renewed on or after January 1, 2005, shall include coverage for the following equipment and supplies when medically necessary for the management and treatment of pediatric asthma:

(1) Nebulizers, including face masks and tubing.

(2) Peak flow meters.

(c) The quantity of the equipment and supplies required to be covered pursuant to subdivisions (a) and (b) may be limited by the health care service plan if the limitations do not inhibit appropriate compliance with treatment as prescribed by the enrollee's physician and surgeon. A health care service plan shall provide for an expeditious process for approving additional or replacement inhaler spacers, nebulizers, and peak flow meters when medically necessary for an enrollee to maintain compliance with his or her treatment regimen. The process required by Section 1367.24 may be used to satisfy the requirements of this section for an inhaler spacer.

(d) Education for pediatric asthma, including education to enable an enrollee to properly use the device identified in subdivisions (a) and (b), shall be consistent with current professional medical practice.

(e) The coverage required by this section shall be provided under the same general terms and conditions, including copayments and deductibles, applicable to all other benefits provided by the plan.

(f) A health care service plan shall disclose the benefits under this section in its evidence of coverage and disclosure forms.

(g) A health care service plan may not reduce or eliminate coverage as a result of the requirements of this section.

(h) Nothing in this section shall be construed to deny or restrict in any way the department's authority to ensure plan compliance with this chapter, if a plan provides coverage for prescription drugs.

(Added by Stats. 2004, Ch. 711, Sec. 1. Effective January 1, 2005.)

1367.07.

Within one year after a health care service plan's assessment pursuant to subdivision (b) of Section 1367.04, the health care service plan shall report to the department, in a format specified by the department, regarding internal policies and procedures related to cultural appropriateness in each of the following contexts:

(a) Collection of data regarding the enrollee population pursuant to the health care service plan's assessment conducted in accordance with subdivision (b) of Section 1367.04.

(b) Education of health care service plan staff who have routine contact with enrollees regarding the diverse needs of the enrollee population.

(c) Recruitment and retention efforts that encourage workforce diversity.

(d) Evaluation of the health care service plan's programs and services with respect to the plan's enrollee population, using processes such as an analysis of complaints and satisfaction survey results.

(e) The periodic provision of information regarding the ethnic diversity of the plan's enrollee population and any related strategies to plan providers. Plans may use existing means of communication.

(f) The periodic provision of educational information to plan enrollees on the plan's services and programs. Plans may use existing means of communication.

(Amended by Stats. 2008, Ch. 179, Sec. 139. Effective January 1, 2009.)

1367.08.

A health care service plan shall annually disclose to the governing board of a public agency that is the subscriber of a group contract, the name and address of, and amount paid to, any agent, broker, or individual to whom the plan paid fees or commissions related to the public agency's group contract. As part of this disclosure, the health care service plan shall include the name, address, and amounts paid to the specific agents, brokers, or individuals involved in transactions with the public agency. The compensation disclosure required by this section is in addition to any other compensation disclosure requirements that exist under law.

(Added by Stats. 2008, Ch. 331, Sec. 1. Effective January 1, 2009.)

1367.09.

(a) An enrollee with coverage for Medicare benefits who is discharged from an acute care hospital shall be allowed to return to a skilled nursing facility in which the enrollee resided prior to hospitalization, or the skilled nursing unit of a continuing care retirement community or multilevel facility in which the enrollee is a resident for continuing treatment related to the acute care hospital stay, if all of the following conditions are met:

(1) The enrollee is a resident of a continuing care retirement community, as defined in paragraph (10) of subdivision (a) of Section 1771, or is a resident of a multilevel facility, as defined in paragraph (9) of subdivision (d) of Section 15432 of the Government Code, or has resided for at least 60 days in a skilled nursing facility, as defined in Section 1250, that serves the needs of special populations, including religious and cultural groups.

(2) The primary care physician, and the treating physician if appropriate, in consultation with the patient, determines that the medical care needs of the enrollee, including continuity of care, can be met in the skilled nursing facility, or the skilled nursing unit of the continuing care retirement community, or multilevel facility. If a determination not to return the patient to the facility is made, the physician shall document reasons in the patient's medical record and share that written explanation with the patient.

(3) The skilled nursing facility, continuing care retirement facility, or multilevel facility is within the service area and agrees to abide by the plan's standards and terms and conditions related to the following:

(A) Utilization review, quality assurance, peer review, and access to health care services.

(B) Management and administrative procedures, including data and financial reporting that may be required by the plan.

(C) Licensing and certification as required by Section 1367.

(D) Appropriate certification of the facility by the Health Care Financing Administration or other federal and state agencies.

(4) (A) The skilled nursing facility, multilevel facility, or continuing care retirement community agrees to accept reimbursement from the health care service plan for covered services at either of the following rates:

(i) The rate applicable to similar skilled nursing coverage for facilities participating in the plan.

(ii) Upon mutual agreement, at a rate negotiated in good faith by the health care service plan or designated agent on an individual, per enrollee, contractual basis.

(B) Reimbursement shall not necessarily be based on actual costs and may be comparable to similar skilled nursing facility reimbursement methods available for other plan contracted facilities available to the individual member.

(b) The health care service plan, or designated agent, shall be required to reimburse the skilled nursing facility, continuing care retirement facility, or multilevel facility at the rate agreed to in paragraph (4) of subdivision (a).

(c) No skilled nursing facility, multilevel facility, or continuing care retirement community shall collect, or attempt to collect, or maintain any action of law, against a subscriber or enrollee to collect reimbursement owed by the health care service plan for health care services provided pursuant to this section, or for any amount in excess of the payment amount that the facility has agreed to accept in its agreement with the health care service plan.

(d) Reimbursement by the health care service plan or designated agent shall be for those services included in the Medicare risk contract between the health care service plan and enrollee.

(e) Nothing in this section requires a skilled nursing facility, continuing care retirement facility, or multilevel facility to accept as a skilled nursing unit patient anyone other than a resident of the facility.

(f) This section shall apply to a health care service plan contract that is issued, amended, or renewed on or after January 1, 1999.

(Added by Stats. 1998, Ch. 124, Sec. 2. Effective January 1, 1999.)

1367.1.

Subdivision (i) of Section 1367 shall apply to transitionally licensed plans only insofar as it relates to contracts entered into, amended, delivered, or renewed in this state on or after October 1, 1977.

(Added by Stats. 1977, Ch. 818.)

1367.2.

(a) On and after January 1, 1990, every health care service plan that covers hospital, medical, or surgical expenses on a group basis shall offer coverage for the treatment of alcoholism under such terms and conditions as may be agreed upon between the group subscriber and the health care service plan. Every plan shall communicate the availability of such coverage to all group subscribers and to all prospective group subscribers with whom they are negotiating.

(b) If the group subscriber or policyholder agrees to such coverage or to coverage for treatment of chemical dependency, or nicotine use, the treatment may take place in facilities licensed to provide alcoholism or chemical dependency services under Chapter 2 (commencing with Section 1250) of Division 2.

(Amended by Stats. 1989, Ch. 688, Sec. 1.)

1367.3.

(a) Every health care service plan that covers hospital, medical, or surgical expenses on a group basis shall offer benefits for the comprehensive preventive care of children. This section shall apply to children 17 and 18 years of age, except as provided in subparagraph (D) of paragraph (2) of subdivision (b). Every plan shall communicate the availability of these benefits to all group contractholders and to all prospective group contractholders with whom they are negotiating. This section shall apply to a plan that, by rule or order of the director, has been exempted from subdivision (i) of Section 1367, insofar as that section and the rules thereunder relate to the provision of the preventive health care services described herein.

(b) For purposes of this section, benefits for the comprehensive preventive care of children shall comply with both of the following:

(1) Be consistent with both of the following:

(A) The most recent Recommendations for Preventive Pediatric Health Care, as adopted by the American Academy of Pediatrics.

(B) The most current version of the Recommended Childhood Immunization Schedule/United States, jointly adopted by the American Academy of Pediatrics, the Advisory Committee on Immunization Practices, and the American Academy of Family Physicians, unless the State Department of Public Health determines, within 45 days of the published date of the schedule, that the schedule is not consistent with the purposes of this section.

(2) Provide for the following:

(A) Periodic health evaluations.

(B) Immunizations.

(C) Laboratory services in connection with periodic health evaluations.

(D) Screening for blood lead levels in children of any age who are at risk for lead poisoning, as determined by a physician and surgeon affiliated with the plan, if the screening is prescribed by a health care provider affiliated with the plan.

(c) For purposes of this section, a health care provider is any of the following:

(1) A person licensed to practice medicine pursuant to Article 3 (commencing with Section 2050) of Chapter 5 of Division 2 of the Business and Professions Code.

(2) A nurse practitioner licensed to practice pursuant to Article 8 (commencing with Section 2834) of Chapter 6 of Division 2 of the Business and Professions Code.

(3) A physician assistant licensed to practice pursuant to Article 3 (commencing with Section 3513) of Chapter 7.7 of Division 2 of the Business and Professions Code.

(Amended by Stats. 2017, Ch. 507, Sec. 1. (AB 1316) Effective January 1, 2018.)

1367.35.

(a) On and after January 1, 1993, every health care service plan that covers hospital, medical, or surgical expenses on a group basis shall provide benefits for the comprehensive preventive care of children 16 years of age or younger under terms and conditions agreed upon between the group subscriber and the plan. Every plan shall communicate the availability of these benefits to all group contractholders and to all prospective group contractholders with whom they are negotiating. This section shall apply to each plan that, by rule or order of the director, has been exempted from subdivision (i) of Section 1367, insofar as that section and the rules thereunder relate to the provision of the preventive health care services described in this section.

(b) For purposes of this section, benefits for the comprehensive preventive care of children shall comply with both of the following:

(1) Be consistent with both of the following:

(A) The Recommendations for Preventive Pediatric Health Care, as adopted by the American Academy of Pediatrics in September of 1987.

(B) The most current version of the Recommended Childhood Immunization Schedule/United States, jointly adopted by the American Academy of Pediatrics, the Advisory Committee on Immunization Practices, and the American Academy of Family Physicians, unless the State Department of Health Services determines, within 45 days of the published date of the schedule, that the schedule is not consistent with the purposes of this section.

(2) Provide for all of the following:

(A) Periodic health evaluations.

(B) Immunizations.

(C) Laboratory services in connection with periodic health evaluations.

(Amended by Stats. 1999, Ch. 525, Sec. 97. Effective January 1, 2000. Operative July 1, 2000, or sooner, by Sec. 214 of Ch. 525.)

1367.36.

(a) A risk-based contract between a health care service plan and a physician or physician group that is issued, amended, delivered, or renewed in this state on or after January 1, 2001, shall not include a provision that requires a physician or a physician group to assume financial risk for the acquisition costs of required immunizations for children as a condition of accepting the risk-based contract. A physician or physician group shall not be required to assume financial risk for immunizations that are not part of the current contract.

(b) Beginning January 1, 2001, with respect to immunizations for children that are not part of the current contract between a health care service plan and a physician or a physician group, the health care service plan shall reimburse a physician or physician group at the lowest of the following, until the contract is renegotiated: (1) the physician's actual acquisition cost, (2) the "average wholesale price" as published in the Drug Topics Red Book, or (3) the lowest acquisition cost through sources made available to the physician by the health care service plan. Reimbursements shall be made within 45 days of receipt by the plan of documents from the physician demonstrating that the immunizations were performed, consistent with Section 1371 or through an alternative funding mechanism mutually agreed to by the health care service plan and the physician or physician group. The alternative funding mechanism shall be based on reimbursements consistent with this subdivision.

(c) Physicians and physician groups may assume financial risk for providing required immunizations, if the immunizations have experiential data that has been negotiated and agreed upon by the health care service plan and the physician risk-bearing organization. However, a health care service plan shall not require a physician risk-bearing organization to accept financial risk or impose additional risk on a physician risk-bearing organization in violation of subdivision (a).

(d) A health care service plan shall not include the acquisition costs associated with required immunizations for children in the capitation rate of a physician who is individually capitated.

(Added by Stats. 2000, Ch. 845, Sec. 1. Effective January 1, 2001.)

1367.4.

No plan issuing, providing, or administering any contract of individual or group coverage providing medical, surgical, or dental expense benefits applied for and issued on or after January 1, 1986, shall refuse to cover, or refuse to continue to cover, or limit the amount, extent, or kind of coverage available to an individual, or charge a different rate for the same coverage solely because of blindness or partial blindness.

"Blindness or partial blindness" means central visual acuity of not more than 20/200 in the better eye, after correction, or visual acuity greater than 20/200 but with a limitation in the fields of vision so that the widest diameter of the visual field subtends an angle no greater than 20 degrees, certified by a licensed physician and surgeon who specializes in diseases of the eye or a licensed optometrist.

(Added by Stats. 1985, Ch. 971, Sec. 1.)

1367.41.

(a) Commencing January 1, 2017, a health care service plan shall maintain a pharmacy and therapeutics committee that shall be responsible for developing, maintaining, and overseeing any drug formulary list. If the plan delegates responsibility for the formulary to any entity, the obligation of the plan to comply with this chapter shall not be waived.

(b) The pharmacy and therapeutics committee board membership shall conform with both of the following:

(1) Represent a sufficient number of clinical specialties to adequately meet the needs of enrollees.

(2) Consist of a majority of individuals who are practicing physicians, practicing pharmacists, and other practicing health professionals who are licensed to prescribe drugs.

(c) Members of the board shall abstain from voting on any issue in which the member has a conflict of interest with respect to the issuer or a pharmaceutical manufacturer.

(d) At least 20 percent of the board membership shall not have a conflict of interest with respect to the issuer or any pharmaceutical manufacturer.

(e) The pharmacy and therapeutics committee shall meet at least quarterly and shall maintain written documentation of the rationale for its decisions regarding the development of, or revisions to, the formulary drug list.

(f) The pharmacy and therapeutics committee shall do all of the following:

(1) Develop and document procedures to ensure appropriate drug review and inclusion.

(2) Base clinical decisions on the strength of the scientific evidence and standards of practice, including assessing peer-reviewed medical literature, pharmacoeconomic studies, outcomes research data, and other related information.

(3) Consider the therapeutic advantages of drugs in terms of safety and efficacy when selecting formulary drugs.

(4) Review policies that guide exceptions and other utilization management processes, including drug utilization review, quantity limits, and therapeutic interchange.

(5) Evaluate and analyze treatment protocols and procedures related to the plan's formulary at least annually.

(6) Review and approve all clinical prior authorization criteria, step therapy protocols, and quantity limit restrictions applied to each covered drug.

(7) Review new United States Food and Drug Administration-approved drugs and new uses for existing drugs.

(8) Ensure that the plan's formulary drug list or lists cover a range of drugs across a broad distribution of therapeutic categories and classes and recommended drug treatment regimens that treat all disease states and do not discourage enrollment by any group of enrollees.

(9) Ensure that the plan's formulary drug list or lists provide appropriate access to drugs that are included in broadly accepted treatment guidelines and that are indicative of general best practices at the time.

(g) This section shall be interpreted consistent with federal guidance issued under paragraph (3) of subdivision (a) of Section 156.122 of Title 45 of the Code of Federal Regulations. This section shall apply to the individual, small group, and large group markets.

(Added by Stats. 2015, Ch. 619, Sec. 3. (AB 339) Effective January 1, 2016.)

1367.42.

(a) For plan years commencing on or after January 1, 2017, a plan that provides essential health benefits shall allow an enrollee to access prescription drug benefits at an in-network retail pharmacy unless the prescription drug is subject to restricted distribution by the United States Food and Drug Administration or requires special handling, provider coordination, or patient education that cannot be provided by a retail pharmacy.

(b) A nongrandfathered individual or small group health plan contract may charge an enrollee a different cost sharing for obtaining a covered drug at a retail pharmacy, but all cost sharing shall count toward the plan's annual limitation on cost sharing consistent with Section 1367.006.

(Added by Stats. 2015, Ch. 619, Sec. 4. (AB 339) Effective January 1, 2016.)

1367.43.

Commencing January 1, 2019, a health care service plan shall prorate an enrollee's cost sharing for a partial fill of a prescription dispensed pursuant to Section 4052.10 of the Business and Professions Code. This section shall only apply to oral, solid dosage forms of prescription drugs.

(Added by Stats. 2017, Ch. 615, Sec. 3. (AB 1048) Effective January 1, 2018.)

1367.45.

(a) Every individual or group health care service plan contract that is issued, amended, or renewed on or after January 1, 2002, that covers hospital, medical, or surgery expenses shall provide coverage for a vaccine for acquired immune deficiency syndrome (AIDS) that is approved for marketing by the federal Food and Drug Administration and that is recommended by the United States Public Health Service.

(b) This section may not be construed to require a health care service plan to provide coverage for any clinical trials relating to an AIDS vaccine or for any AIDS vaccine that has been approved by the federal Food and Drug Administration in the form of an investigational new drug application.

(c) A health care service plan that contracts directly with an individual provider or provider organization may not delegate the risk adjusted treatment cost of providing services under this section unless the requirements of Section 1375.5 are met.

(d) Nothing in this section is to be construed in any manner to limit or impede a health care service plan's power or responsibility to negotiate the most cost-effective price for vaccine purchases.

(e) Nothing in this section shall be construed to deny or restrict in any way the department's authority to ensure plan compliance with this chapter when a plan provides coverage for prescription drugs.

(Amended by Stats. 2002, Ch. 791, Sec. 5. Effective January 1, 2003.)

1367.46.

Every individual or group health care service plan contract that is issued, amended, or renewed on or after January 1, 2009, that covers hospital, medical, or surgery expenses shall provide coverage for human immunodeficiency virus (HIV) testing, regardless of whether the testing is related to a primary diagnosis.

(Added by Stats. 2008, Ch. 631, Sec. 1. Effective January 1, 2009.)

1367.47.

(a) The maximum amount a health care service plan may require an enrollee to pay at the point of sale for a covered prescription drug is the lesser of the following:

(1) The applicable cost-sharing amount for the prescription drug.

(2) The retail price.

(b) A health care service plan shall not require a pharmacist or pharmacy to charge or collect from an enrollee a cost-sharing amount that exceeds the total retail price for the prescription drug.

(c) The payment rendered shall constitute the applicable cost sharing and shall apply to the deductible, if any, and also to the maximum out-of-pocket limit in the same manner as if the enrollee had purchased the prescription drug by paying the cost-sharing amount.

(Added by Stats. 2018, Ch. 770, Sec. 2. (AB 2863) Effective January 1, 2019.)

1367.49.

(a) A contract issued, amended, renewed, or delivered on or after January 1, 2015, by or on behalf of a health care service plan and a provider or supplier shall not contain any provision that restricts the ability of the health care service plan to furnish consumers or purchasers information concerning any of the following:

(1) The cost range of a procedure or a full course of treatment, including, but not limited to, facility, professional, and diagnostic services, prescription drugs, durable medical equipment, and other items and services related to the treatment.

(2) The quality of services performed by the provider or supplier.

(b) Any contractual provision inconsistent with this section shall be void and unenforceable.

(c) A health care service plan shall provide the provider or supplier an advance opportunity of 30 days to review the methodology and data developed and compiled by the health care service plan, and used pursuant to subdivision (a), before cost or quality information is provided to consumers or purchasers, including material revisions or additions of new information. At the time the health care service plan provides a provider or supplier with the opportunity to review the methodology and data, it shall also notify the provider or supplier in writing of their opportunity to provide an Internet Web site link pursuant to subdivision (f).

(d) If the information proposed to be furnished to enrollees and subscribers on the quality of services performed by a provider or supplier is data that the plan has developed and compiled, the plan shall utilize appropriate risk adjustment factors to account for different characteristics of the population, such as case mix, severity of patient's condition, comorbidities, outlier episodes, and other factors to account for differences in the use of health care resources among providers and suppliers.

(e) Any Internet Web site owned or controlled by a health care service plan, or operated by another person or entity under contract with or on behalf of a health care service plan, that displays the information developed and compiled by the health care service plan as referenced by this section shall prominently post the following statement:

"Individual facilities or health care providers may disagree with the methodology used to define the cost ranges, the cost data, or quality measures. Many factors may influence cost or quality, including, but not limited to, the cost of uninsured and charity care, the type and severity of procedures, the case mix of a facility, special services such as trauma centers, burn units, medical and other educational programs, research, transplant services, technology, payer mix, and other factors affecting individual facilities and health care providers."

A health care service plan and a provider or supplier shall not be precluded from mutually agreeing in writing to an alternative method of conveying this statement.

(f) If a provider or supplier chooses to provide an Internet Web site link where a response to the health care service plan's posting may be found, it shall do so in a timely manner in order to satisfy the requirements of this section. If a provider or supplier chooses to provide a response, a plan shall post, in an easily identified manner, a prominent link to the provider's or supplier's Internet Web site where a response to the plan's posting may be found. A health care service plan and a provider or supplier shall not be precluded from mutually agreeing in writing to an alternative method to convey a provider's or supplier's response.

(g) For the purposes of this section, the following definitions shall apply:

(1) "Consumers" means enrollees or subscribers of the health care service plan or beneficiaries of a self-funded health coverage arrangement administered by the health care service plan or other persons entitled to access services through a network established by the health care service plan.

(2) "Provider" has the same meaning as that term is defined in Section 1367.50.

(3) "Purchasers" means the sponsors of a self-funded health coverage arrangement administered by the health care service plan.

(4) "Supplier" has the same meaning as that term is defined in Section 1367.50.

(h) Section 1390 shall not apply for purposes of this section.

(Amended by Stats. 2014, Ch. 83, Sec. 1. (SB 1340) Effective January 1, 2015.)

1367.5.

No health care service plan contract that is issued, amended, renewed, or delivered on and after January 1, 2002, shall contain a provision that prohibits or restricts any health facilities' compliance with the requirements of Section 1262.5.

(Added by Stats. 2001, Ch. 691, Sec. 5. Effective January 1, 2002.)

1367.50.

(a) No contract in existence or issued, amended, or renewed on or after January 1, 2013, between a health care service plan and a provider or a supplier shall prohibit, condition, or in any way restrict the disclosure of claims data related to health care services provided to an enrollee or subscriber of the health care service plan or beneficiaries of any self-funded health coverage arrangement administered by the health care service plan, to a qualified entity, as defined in Section 1395kk(e)(2) of Title 42 of the United States Code. All disclosures of data made under this section shall comply with all applicable state and federal laws for the protection of the privacy and security of the data, including, but not limited to, the federal Health Insurance Portability and Accountability Act of 1996 (Public Law 104-191) and the federal Health Information Technology for Economic and Clinical Health Act, Title XIII of the federal American Recovery and Reinvestment Act of 2009 (Public Law 111-5), and implementing regulations.

(b) For purposes of this section, the following definitions apply:

(1) "PPACA" means the federal Patient Protection and Affordable Care Act (Public Law 111-148), as amended by the federal Health Care and Education Reconciliation Act of 2010 (Public Law 111-152).

(2) "Provider" means a hospital, a skilled nursing facility, a comprehensive outpatient rehabilitation facility, a home health agency, a hospice, a clinic, or a rehabilitation agency.

(3) "Supplier" means a physician and surgeon or other health care practitioner, or an entity that furnishes health care services other than a provider.

(Added by Stats. 2012, Ch. 869, Sec. 2. (SB 1196) Effective January 1, 2013.)

1367.51.

(a) Every health care service plan contract, except a specialized health care service plan contract, that is issued, amended, delivered, or renewed on or after January 1, 2000, and that covers hospital, medical, or surgical expenses shall include coverage for the following equipment and supplies for the management and treatment of insulin-using diabetes, non-insulin-using diabetes, and gestational diabetes as medically necessary, even if the items are available without a prescription:

(1) Blood glucose monitors and blood glucose testing strips.

(2) Blood glucose monitors designed to assist the visually impaired.

(3) Insulin pumps and all related necessary supplies.

(4) Ketone urine testing strips.

(5) Lancets and lancet puncture devices.

(6) Pen delivery systems for the administration of insulin.

(7) Podiatric devices to prevent or treat diabetes-related complications.

(8) Insulin syringes.

(9) Visual aids, excluding eyewear, to assist the visually impaired with proper dosing of insulin.

(b) Every health care service plan contract, except a specialized health care service plan contract, that is issued, amended, delivered, or renewed on or after January 1, 2000, that covers prescription benefits shall include coverage for the following prescription items if the items are determined to be medically necessary:

(1) Insulin.

(2) Prescriptive medications for the treatment of diabetes.

(3) Glucagon.

(c) The copayments and deductibles for the benefits specified in subdivisions (a) and (b) shall not exceed those established for similar benefits within the given plan.

(d) Every plan shall provide coverage for diabetes outpatient self-management training, education, and medical nutrition therapy necessary to enable an enrollee to properly use the equipment, supplies, and medications set forth in subdivisions (a) and (b), and additional diabetes outpatient self-management training, education, and medical nutrition therapy upon the direction or prescription of those services by the enrollee's participating physician. If a plan delegates outpatient self-management training to contracting providers, the plan shall require contracting providers to ensure that diabetes outpatient self-management training, education, and medical nutrition therapy are provided by appropriately licensed or registered health care professionals.

(e) The diabetes outpatient self-management training, education, and medical nutrition therapy services identified in subdivision (d) shall be provided by appropriately licensed or registered health care professionals as prescribed by a participating health care professional legally authorized to prescribe the service. These benefits shall include, but not be limited to, instruction that will enable diabetic patients and their families to gain an understanding of the diabetic disease process, and the daily management of diabetic therapy, in order to thereby avoid frequent hospitalizations and complications.

(f) The copayments for the benefits specified in subdivision (d) shall not exceed those established for physician office visits by the plan.

(g) Every health care service plan governed by this section shall disclose the benefits covered pursuant to this section in the plan's evidence of coverage and disclosure forms.

(h) A health care service plan may not reduce or eliminate coverage as a result of the requirements of this section.

(i) Nothing in this section shall be construed to deny or restrict in any way the department's authority to ensure plan compliance with this chapter when a plan provides coverage for prescription drugs.

(Amended by Stats. 2002, Ch. 791, Sec. 6. Effective January 1, 2003.)

1367.54.

(a) Every group health care service plan contract that provides maternity benefits, except for a specialized health care service plan contract, that is issued, amended, renewed, or delivered on or after January 1, 1999, and every individual health care service plan contract of a type and form first offered for sale on or after January 1, 1999, that provides maternity benefits, except a specialized health care service plan contract, shall provide coverage for participation in the California Prenatal Screening Program, which is a statewide prenatal testing program administered by the State Department of Public Health, pursuant to Section 124977. Notwithstanding any other provision of law, a health care service plan that provides maternity benefits shall not require participation in the statewide prenatal testing program administered by the State Department of Public Health as a prerequisite to eligibility for, or receipt of, any other service.

(b) Coverage required by this section shall not be subject to copayment, coinsurance, deductible, or any other form of cost sharing.

(c) Reimbursement for services covered pursuant to this section shall be paid at the amount set pursuant to Section 124977 and regulations adopted thereunder.

(Amended by Stats. 2015, Ch. 18, Sec. 7. (SB 75) Effective June 24, 2015.)

1367.6.

(a) Every health care service plan contract, except a specialized health care service plan contract, that is issued, amended, delivered, or renewed on or after January 1, 2000, shall provide coverage for screening for, diagnosis of, and treatment for, breast cancer.

(b) No health care service plan contract shall deny enrollment or coverage to an individual solely due to a family history of breast cancer, or who has had one or more diagnostic procedures for breast disease but has not developed or been diagnosed with breast cancer.

(c) Every health care service plan contract shall cover screening and diagnosis of breast cancer, consistent with generally accepted medical practice and scientific evidence, upon the referral of the enrollee's participating physician.

(d) Treatment for breast cancer under this section shall include coverage for prosthetic devices or reconstructive surgery to restore and achieve symmetry for the patient incident to a mastectomy. Coverage for prosthetic devices and reconstructive surgery shall be subject to the copayment, or deductible and coinsurance conditions, that are applicable to the mastectomy and all other terms and conditions applicable to other benefits.

(e) As used in this section, "mastectomy" means the removal of all or part of the breast for medically necessary reasons, as determined by a licensed physician and surgeon. Partial removal of a breast includes, but is not limited to, lumpectomy, which includes surgical removal of the tumor with clear margins.

(f) As used in this section, "prosthetic devices" means the provision of initial and subsequent devices pursuant to an order of the patient's physician and surgeon.

(Amended by Stats. 2012, Ch. 449, Sec. 2. (SB 255) Effective January 1, 2013.)

1367.61.

Every health care service plan contract which provides for the surgical procedure known as a laryngectomy and which is issued, amended, delivered, or renewed in this state on or after January 1, 1993, shall include coverage for prosthetic devices to restore a method of speaking for the patient incident to the laryngectomy.

Coverage for prosthetic devices shall be subject to the deductible and coinsurance conditions applied to the laryngectomy and all other terms and conditions applicable to other benefits. As used in this section, "laryngectomy" means the removal of all or part of the larynx for medically necessary reasons, as determined by a licensed physician and surgeon.

Any provision in any contract issued, amended, delivered, or renewed in this state on or after January 1, 1993, which is in conflict with this section shall be of no force or effect. As used in this section, "prosthetic devices" means and includes the provision of initial and subsequent prosthetic devices, including installation accessories, pursuant to an order of the patient's physician and surgeon. "Prosthetic devices" does not include electronic voice producing machines.

(Added by Stats. 1992, Ch. 808, Sec. 1. Effective January 1, 1993.)

1367.62.

(a) No health care service plan contract that is issued, amended, renewed, or delivered on or after the effective date of the act adding this section, that provides maternity coverage, shall do any of the following:

(1) Restrict benefits for inpatient hospital care to a time period less than 48 hours following a normal vaginal delivery and less than 96 hours following a delivery by caesarean section. However, coverage for inpatient hospital care may be for a time period less than 48 or 96 hours if both of the following conditions are met:

(A) The decision to discharge the mother and newborn before the 48- or 96-hour time period is made by the treating physicians in consultation with the mother.

(B) The contract covers a postdischarge followup visit for the mother and newborn within 48 hours of discharge, when prescribed by the treating physician. The visit shall be provided by a licensed health care provider whose scope of practice includes postpartum care and newborn care. The visit shall include, at a minimum, parent education, assistance and training in breast or bottle feeding, and the performance of any necessary maternal or neonatal physical assessments. The treating physician shall disclose to the mother the availability of a postdischarge visit, including an in-home visit, physician office visit, or plan facility visit. The treating physician, in consultation with the mother, shall determine whether the postdischarge visit shall occur at home, the plan's facility, or the treating physician's office after assessment of certain factors. These factors shall include, but not be limited to, the transportation needs of the family, and environmental and social risks.

(2) Reduce or limit the reimbursement of the attending provider for providing care to an individual enrollee in accordance with the coverage requirements.

(3) Provide monetary or other incentives to an attending provider to induce the provider to provide care to an individual enrollee in a manner inconsistent with the coverage requirements.

(4) Deny a mother or her newborn eligibility, or continued eligibility, to enroll or to renew coverage solely to avoid the coverage requirements.

(5) Provide monetary payments or rebates to a mother to encourage her to accept less than the minimum coverage requirements.

(6) Restrict inpatient benefits for the second day of hospital care in a manner that is less than favorable to the mother or her newborn than those provided during the preceding portion of the hospital stay.

(7) Require the treating physician to obtain authorization from the health care service plan prior to prescribing any services covered by this section.

(b) (1) Every health care service plan shall include notice of the coverage specified in subdivision (a) in the plan's evidence of coverage for evidences of coverage issued on or after January 1, 1998, and except as specified in paragraph (2), shall provide additional written notice of this coverage during the course of the enrollee's prenatal care. The contract may require the treating physician or the enrollee's medical group to provide this additional written notice of coverage during the course of the enrollee's prenatal care.

(2) Health care service plans that issue contracts that provide for coverage of the type commonly referred to as "preferred provider organizations" shall provide additional written notice to all females between the ages of 10 and 50 who are covered by those contracts of the coverage under subdivision (a) within 60 days of the effective date of this act. The plan shall provide additional written notice of the coverage specified in subdivision (a) during the course of prenatal care if both of the following conditions are met:

(A) The plan previously notified subscribers that hospital stays for delivery would be inconsistent with the requirement in subparagraph (A) of paragraph (1) of subdivision (a).

(B) The plan received notice, whether by receipt of a claim, a request for preauthorization for pregnancy-related services, or other actual notice that the enrollee is pregnant.

(c) Nothing in this section shall be construed to prohibit a plan from negotiating the level and type of reimbursement with a provider for care provided in accordance with this section.

(Amended by Stats. 1997, Ch. 798, Sec. 1. Effective October 9, 1997.)

1367.625.

(a) By July 1, 2019, a health care service plan shall develop a maternal mental health program designed to promote quality and cost-effective outcomes. The program shall be developed consistent with sound clinical principles and processes. The program guidelines and criteria shall be made available upon request to medical providers, including a contracting obstetric provider.

(b) For the purposes of this section, the following terms have the following meanings:

(1) "Contracting obstetric provider" means an individual who is certified or licensed pursuant to Division 2 (commencing with Section 500) of the Business and Professions Code, or an initiative act referred to in that division, and who is contracted with the enrollee's health care service plan to provide services under the enrollee's plan contract.

(2) "Maternal mental health" means a mental health condition that occurs during pregnancy or during the postpartum period and includes, but is not limited to, postpartum depression.

(c) This section shall not apply to specialized health care service plans, except specialized behavioral health-only plans offering professional mental health services.

(Added by Stats. 2018, Ch. 755, Sec. 1. (AB 2193) Effective January 1, 2019.)

1367.63.

(a) Every health care service plan contract, except a specialized health care service plan contract, that is issued, amended, renewed, or delivered in this state on or after July 1, 1999, shall cover reconstructive surgery, as defined in subdivision (c), that is necessary to achieve the purposes specified in subparagraph (A) or (B) of paragraph (1) of subdivision (c). Nothing in this section shall be construed to require a plan to provide coverage for cosmetic surgery, as defined in subdivision (d).

(b) No individual, other than a licensed physician competent to evaluate the specific clinical issues involved in the care requested, may deny initial requests for authorization of coverage for treatment pursuant to this section. For a treatment authorization request submitted by a podiatrist or an oral and maxillofacial surgeon, the request may be reviewed by a similarly licensed individual, competent to evaluate the specific clinical issues involved in the care requested.

(c) (1) "Reconstructive surgery" means surgery performed to correct or repair abnormal structures of the body caused by congenital defects, developmental abnormalities, trauma, infection, tumors, or disease to do either of the following:

(A) To improve function.

(B) To create a normal appearance, to the extent possible.

(2) As of July 1, 2010, "reconstructive surgery" shall include medically necessary dental or orthodontic services that are an integral part of reconstructive surgery, as defined in paragraph (1), for cleft palate procedures.

(3) For purposes of this section, "cleft palate" means a condition that may include cleft palate, cleft lip, or other craniofacial anomalies associated with cleft palate.

(d) "Cosmetic surgery" means surgery that is performed to alter or reshape normal structures of the body in order to improve appearance.

(e) In interpreting the definition of reconstructive surgery, a health care service plan may utilize prior authorization and utilization review that may include, but need not be limited to, any of the following:

(1) Denial of the proposed surgery if there is another more appropriate surgical procedure that will be approved for the enrollee.

(2) Denial of the proposed surgery or surgeries if the procedure or procedures, in accordance with the standard of care as practiced by physicians specializing in reconstructive surgery, offer only a minimal improvement in the appearance of the enrollee.

(3) Denial of payment for procedures performed without prior authorization.

(4) For services provided under the Medi-Cal program (Chapter 7 (commencing with Section 14000) of Part 3 of Division 9 of the Welfare and Institutions Code), denial of the proposed surgery if the procedure offers only a minimal improvement in the appearance of the enrollee, as may be defined in any regulations that may be promulgated by the State Department of Health Care Services.

(f) As applied to services described in paragraph (2) of subdivision (c) only, this section shall not apply to Medi-Cal managed care plans that contract with the State Department of Health Care Services pursuant to Chapter 7 (commencing with Section 14000) of, Chapter 8 (commencing with Section 14200) of, or Chapter 8.75 (commencing with Section 14591) of, Part 3 of Division 9 of the Welfare and Institutions Code, where such contracts do not provide coverage for California Children's Services (CCS) or dental services.

(Amended by Stats. 2011, Ch. 367, Sec. 3. (AB 574) Effective January 1, 2012.)

1367.635.

(a) Every health care service plan contract that is issued, amended, renewed, or delivered on or after January 1, 1999, that provides coverage for surgical procedures known as mastectomies and lymph node dissections, shall do all of the following:

(1) Allow the length of a hospital stay associated with those procedures to be determined by the attending physician and surgeon in consultation with the patient, postsurgery, consistent with sound clinical principles and processes. No health care service plan shall require a treating physician and surgeon to receive prior approval from the plan in determining the length of hospital stay following those procedures.

(2) Cover prosthetic devices or reconstructive surgery, including devices or surgery to restore and achieve symmetry for the patient incident to the mastectomy. Coverage for prosthetic devices and reconstructive surgery shall be subject to the deductible and coinsurance conditions applicable to other benefits.

(3) Cover all complications from a mastectomy, including lymphedema.

(b) As used in this section, all of the following definitions apply:

(1) "Coverage for prosthetic devices or reconstructive surgery" means any initial and subsequent reconstructive surgeries or prosthetic devices, and followup care deemed necessary by the attending physician and surgeon.

(2) "Prosthetic devices" means and includes the provision of initial and subsequent prosthetic devices pursuant to an order of the patient's physician and surgeon.

(3) "Mastectomy" means the removal of all or part of the breast for medically necessary reasons, as determined by a licensed physician and surgeon. Partial removal of a breast includes, but is not limited to, lumpectomy, which includes surgical removal of the tumor with clear margins.

(4) "To restore and achieve symmetry" means that, in addition to coverage of prosthetic devices and reconstructive surgery for the diseased breast on which the mastectomy was performed, prosthetic devices and reconstructive surgery for a healthy breast is also covered if, in the opinion of the attending physician and surgeon, this surgery is necessary to achieve normal symmetrical appearance.

(c) No individual, other than a licensed physician and surgeon competent to evaluate the specific clinical issues involved in the care requested, may deny requests for authorization of health care services pursuant to this section.

(d) No health care service plan shall do any of the following in providing the coverage described in subdivision (a):

(1) Reduce or limit the reimbursement of the attending provider for providing care to an individual enrollee or subscriber in accordance with the coverage requirements.

(2) Provide monetary or other incentives to an attending provider to induce the provider to provide care to an individual enrollee or subscriber in a manner inconsistent with the coverage requirements.

(3) Provide monetary payments or rebates to an individual enrollee or subscriber to encourage acceptance of less than the coverage requirements.

(e) On or after July 1, 1999, every health care service plan shall include notice of the coverage required by this section in the plan's evidence of coverage.

(f) Nothing in this section shall be construed to limit retrospective utilization review and quality assurance activities by the plan.

(Amended by Stats. 2012, Ch. 449, Sec. 3. (SB 255) Effective January 1, 2013.)

1367.64.

(a) Every individual or group health care service plan contract, except for a specialized health care service plan contract, that is issued, amended, or renewed on or after January 1, 1999, shall be deemed to provide coverage for the screening and diagnosis of prostate cancer, including, but not limited to, prostate-specific antigen testing and digital rectal examinations, when medically necessary and consistent with good professional practice.

(b) Nothing in this section shall be construed to establish a new mandated benefit or to prevent application of deductible or copayment provisions in a policy or plan, nor shall this section be construed to require that a policy or plan be extended to cover any other procedures under an individual or a group health care service plan contract. Nothing in this section shall be construed to authorize an enrollee to receive the services required to be covered by this section if those services are furnished by a nonparticipating provider, unless the enrollee is referred to that provider by a participating physician or nurse practitioner providing care.

(Added by Stats. 1998, Ch. 839, Sec. 1. Effective January 1, 1999.)

1367.65.

(a) On or after January 1, 2000, each health care service plan contract, except a specialized health care service plan contract, that is issued, amended, delivered, or renewed shall be deemed to provide coverage for mammography for screening or diagnostic purposes upon referral by a participating nurse practitioner, participating certified nurse-midwife, participating physician assistant, or participating physician, providing care to the patient and operating within the scope of practice provided under existing law.

(b) This section does not prevent application of copayment or deductible provisions in a plan, nor shall this section be construed to require that a plan be extended to cover any other procedures under an individual or a group health care service plan contract. This section does not authorize a plan enrollee to receive the services required to be covered by this section if those services are furnished by a nonparticipating provider, unless the plan enrollee is referred to that provider by a participating physician, nurse practitioner, or certified nurse-midwife providing care.

(Amended by Stats. 2013, Ch. 76, Sec. 108. (AB 383) Effective January 1, 2014.)

1367.656.

(a) Notwithstanding any other law, an individual or group health care service plan contract issued, amended, or renewed on or after January 1, 2015, that provides coverage for prescribed, orally administered anticancer medications used to kill or slow the growth of cancerous cells shall comply with all of the following:

(1) Notwithstanding any deductible, the total amount of copayments and coinsurance an enrollee is required to pay shall not exceed two hundred fifty dollars ($250) for an individual prescription of up to a 30-day supply of a prescribed orally administered anticancer medication covered by the contract.

(2) For a health care service plan contract that meets the definition of a "high deductible health plan" set forth in Section 223(c)(2) of Title 26 of the United States Code, paragraph (1) shall only apply once an enrollee's deductible has been satisfied for the year.

(3) Paragraph (1) shall not apply to any coverage under a health care service plan contract for the Medicare Program pursuant to Title XVIII of the federal Social Security Act (42 U.S.C. Sec. 1395 et seq.).

(4) A prescription for an orally administered anticancer medication shall be provided consistent with the appropriate standard of care for that medication.

(b) This section shall remain in effect only until January 1, 2024, and as of that date is repealed.

(Amended by Stats. 2018, Ch. 427, Sec. 1. (AB 1860) Effective January 1, 2019. Repealed as of January 1 2024, by its own provisions.)

1367.66.

Every individual or group health care service plan contract, except for a specialized health care service plan, that is issued, amended, or renewed on or after January 1, 2002, and that includes coverage for treatment or surgery of cervical cancer shall also be deemed to provide coverage for an annual cervical cancer screening test upon the referral of the patient's physician and surgeon, a nurse practitioner, or a certified nurse midwife, providing care to the patient and operating within the scope of practice otherwise permitted for the licensee.

The coverage for an annual cervical cancer screening test provided pursuant to this section shall include the conventional Pap test, a human papillomavirus screening test that is approved by the federal Food and Drug Administration, and the option of any cervical cancer screening test approved by the federal Food and Drug Administration, upon the referral of the patient's health care provider.

Nothing in this section shall be construed to establish a new mandated benefit or to prevent application of deductible or copayment provisions in an existing plan contract. The Legislature intends in this section to provide that cervical cancer screening services are deemed to be covered if the plan contract includes coverage for cervical cancer treatment or surgery.

(Amended by Stats. 2010, Ch. 328, Sec. 119. (SB 1330) Effective January 1, 2011.)

1367.665.

Every individual or group health care service plan contract, except for a specialized health care service plan contract, that is issued, amended, delivered, or renewed on or after July 1, 2000, shall be deemed to provide coverage for all generally medically accepted cancer screening tests, subject to all terms and conditions that would otherwise apply.

(Added by Stats. 1999, Ch. 543, Sec. 1. Effective January 1, 2000.)

1367.67.

Every health care service plan contract that provides hospital, medical, or surgical coverage, that is issued, amended, delivered, or renewed in this state on or after January 1, 1994, shall be deemed to include coverage for services related to diagnosis, treatment, and appropriate management of osteoporosis. The services may include, but need not be limited to, all Food and Drug Administration approved technologies, including bone mass measurement technologies as deemed medically appropriate.

(Added by Stats. 1993, Ch. 1208, Sec. 2. Effective January 1, 1994.)

1367.68.

(a) Any provision in a health care service plan contract entered into, amended, or renewed in this state on or after July 1, 1995, that excludes coverage for any surgical procedure for any condition directly affecting the upper or lower jawbone, or associated bone joints, shall have no force or effect as to any enrollee if that provision results in any failure to provide medically-necessary basic health care services to the enrollee pursuant to the plan's definition of medical necessity.

(b) For purposes of this section, "plan contract" means every plan contract, except a specialized health care service plan contract, that covers hospital, medical, or surgical expenses.

(c) Nothing in this section shall be construed to prohibit a plan from excluding coverage for dental services provided that any exclusion does not result in any failure to provide medically-necessary basic health care services.

(Added by Stats. 1994, Ch. 1282, Sec. 1. Effective January 1, 1995.)

1367.69.

(a) On or after January 1, 1995, every health care service plan contract that provides hospital, medical, or surgical coverage, that is issued, amended, delivered, or renewed in this state, shall include obstetrician-gynecologists as eligible primary care physicians, provided they meet the plan's eligibility criteria for all specialists seeking primary care physician status.

(b) For purposes of this section, the term "primary care physician" means a physician, as defined in Section 14254 of the Welfare and Institutions Code, who has the responsibility for providing initial and primary care to patients, for maintaining the continuity of patient care, and for initiating referral for specialist care. This means providing care for the majority of health care problems, including, but not limited to, preventive services, acute and chronic conditions, and psychosocial issues.

(Added by Stats. 1994, Ch. 759, Sec. 2. Effective January 1, 1995.)

1367.695.

(a) The Legislature finds and declares that the unique, private, and personal relationship between women patients and their obstetricians and gynecologists warrants direct access to obstetrical and gynecological physician services.

(b) Commencing January 1, 1999, every health care service plan contract issued, amended, renewed, or delivered in this state, except a specialized health care service plan, shall allow an enrollee the option to seek obstetrical and gynecological physician services directly from a participating obstetrician and gynecologist or directly from a participating family practice physician and surgeon designated by the plan as providing obstetrical and gynecological services.

(c) In implementing this section, a health care service plan may establish reasonable provisions governing utilization protocols and the use of obstetricians and gynecologists, or family practice physicians and surgeons, as provided for in subdivision (b), participating in the plan network, medical group, or independent practice association, provided that these provisions shall be consistent with the intent of this section and shall be those customarily applied to other physicians and surgeons, such as primary care physicians and surgeons, to whom the enrollee has direct access, and shall not be more restrictive for the provision of obstetrical and gynecological physician services. An enrollee shall not be required to obtain prior approval from another physician, another provider, or the health care service plan prior to obtaining direct access to obstetrical and gynecological physician services, but the plan may establish reasonable requirements for the participating obstetrician and gynecologist or family practice physician and surgeon, as provided for in subdivision (b), to communicate with the enrollee's primary care physician and surgeon regarding the enrollee's condition, treatment, and any need for followup care.

(d) This section shall not be construed to diminish the provisions of Section 1367.69.

(e) The Department of Managed Health Care shall report to the Legislature, on or before January 1, 2000, on the implementation of this section.

(Amended by Stats. 2000, Ch. 857, Sec. 33. Effective January 1, 2001.)

1367.7.

On and after January 1, 1980, every health care service plan contract that covers hospital, medical, or surgical expenses on a group basis, and which offers maternity coverage in such groups, shall also offer coverage for prenatal diagnosis of genetic disorders of the fetus by means of diagnostic procedures in cases of high-risk pregnancy. Every health care service plan shall communicate the availability of such coverage to all group contract holders and to all groups with whom they are negotiating.

(Added by Stats. 1979, Ch. 629.)

1367.71.

(a) Every health care service plan contract, other than a specialized health care service plan contract, that is issued, amended, renewed, or delivered on or after January 1, 2000, shall be deemed to cover general anesthesia and associated facility charges for dental procedures rendered in a hospital or surgery center setting, when the clinical status or underlying medical condition of the patient requires dental procedures that ordinarily would not require general anesthesia to be rendered in a hospital or surgery center setting. The health care service plan may require prior authorization of general anesthesia and associated charges required for dental care procedures in the same manner that prior authorization is required for other covered diseases or conditions.

(b) This section shall apply only to general anesthesia and associated facility charges for only the following enrollees, and only if the enrollees meet the criteria in subdivision (a):

(1) Enrollees who are under seven years of age.

(2) Enrollees who are developmentally disabled, regardless of age.

(3) Enrollees whose health is compromised and for whom general anesthesia is medically necessary, regardless of age.

(c) Nothing in this section shall require the health care service plan to cover any charges for the dental procedure itself, including, but not limited to, the professional fee of the dentist. Coverage for anesthesia and associated facility charges pursuant to this section shall be subject to all other terms and conditions of the plan that apply generally to other benefits.

(d) Nothing in this section shall be construed to allow a health care service plan to deny coverage for basic health care services, as defined in Section 1345.

(e) A health care service plan may include coverage specified in subdivision (a) at any time prior to January 1, 2000.

(Added by Stats. 1998, Ch. 790, Sec. 1. Effective January 1, 1999.)

1367.8.

No plan issuing, providing, or administering any individual or group health care service plan entered into, amended, or issued on or after January 1, 1981, shall refuse to cover, or refuse to continue to cover, or limit the amount, extent or kind of coverage available to an individual, or charge a different rate for the same coverage solely because of a physical or mental impairment, except where the refusal, limitation or rate differential is based on sound actuarial principles applied to actual experience, or, if insufficient actual experience is available, then to sound underwriting practices.

This section shall not apply to a health maintenance organization qualified pursuant to Title XIII of the federal Public Health Service Act if such organization gives public notice 30 days in advance, in a newspaper of general circulation published in the area served by the health maintenance organization, of its open enrollment period required by such act.

(Added by Stats. 1980, Ch. 352.)

1367.9.

No health care service plan contract which covers hospital, medical, or surgical expenses shall be issued, amended, delivered, or renewed in this state on or after January 1, 1981, if it contains any exclusion, reduction, or other limitations, as to coverage, deductibles, or coinsurance or copayment provisions applicable solely to conditions attributable to diethylstilbestrol or exposure to diethylstilbestrol.

Any provision in any contract issued, amended, delivered, or renewed in this state on or after January 1, 1981, which is in conflict with this section shall be of no force or effect.

(Added by renumbering Section 1367.8 (as added by Stats. 1980, Ch. 776) by Stats. 1981, Ch. 714.)

1367.10.

(a) Every health care service plan shall include within its disclosure form and within its evidence of coverage a statement clearly describing how participation in the plan may affect the choice of physician, hospital, or other health care providers, the basic method of reimbursement, including the scope and general methods of payment made to its contracting providers of health care services, and whether financial bonuses or any other incentives are used. The disclosure form and evidence of coverage shall indicate that if an enrollee wishes to know more about these issues, the enrollee may request additional information from the health care service plan, the enrollee's provider, or the provider's medical group or independent practice association regarding the information required pursuant to subdivision (b).

(b) If a plan, medical group, independent practice association, or participating health care provider uses or receives financial bonuses or any other incentives, the plan, medical group, independent practice association, or health care provider shall provide a written summary to any person who requests it that includes all of the following:

(1) A general description of the bonus and any other incentive arrangements used in its compensation agreements. Nothing in this section shall be construed to require disclosure of trade secrets or commercial or financial information that is privileged or confidential, such as payment rates, as determined by the director, pursuant to state law.

(2) A description regarding whether, and in what manner, the bonuses and any other incentives are related to a provider's use of referral services.

(c) The statements and written information provided pursuant to subdivisions (a) and (b) shall be communicated in clear and simple language that enables consumers to evaluate and compare health care service plans.

(d) The plan shall clearly inform prospective enrollees that participation in that plan will affect the person's choice of provider by placing the following statement in a conspicuous place on all material required to be given to prospective enrollees including promotional and descriptive material, disclosure forms, and certificates and evidences of coverage: PLEASE READ THE FOLLOWING INFORMATION SO YOU WILL KNOW FROM WHOM OR WHAT GROUP OF PROVIDERS HEALTH CARE MAY BE OBTAINED

It is not the intent of this section to require that the names of individual health care providers be enumerated to prospective enrollees.

If the health care service plan provides a list of providers to patients or contracting providers, the plan shall include within the provider listing a notification that enrollees may contact the plan in order to obtain a list of the facilities with which the health care service plan is contracting for subacute care and/or transitional inpatient care.

(Amended by Stats. 1999, Ch. 525, Sec. 99. Effective January 1, 2000. Operative July 1, 2000, or sooner, by Sec. 214 of Ch. 525.)

1367.11.

(a) Every health care service plan issued, amended, or renewed on or after January 1, 1987, that offers coverage for medical transportation services, shall contain a provision providing for direct reimbursement to any provider of covered medical transportation services if the provider has not received payment for those services from any other source.

(b) Subdivision (a) shall not apply to any transaction between a provider of medical transportation services and a health care service plan if the parties have entered into a contract providing for direct payment.

(c) For purposes of this subdivision, "direct reimbursement" means the following: The enrollee shall file a claim for the medical transportation service with the plan; the plan shall pay the medical transportation provider directly; and the medical transportation provider shall not demand payment from the enrollee until having received payment from the plan, at which time the medical transportation provider may demand payment from the enrollee for any unpaid portion of the provider's fee.

(Added by Stats. 1986, Ch. 930, Sec. 1.)

1367.12.

No health care service plan that administers Medicare coverage and federal employee programs may require that more than one form be submitted per claim in order to receive payment or reimbursement under any or all of those policies or programs.

(Added by Stats. 1987, Ch. 1191, Sec. 1.)

1367.15.

(a) This section shall apply to individual health care service plan contracts and plan contracts sold to employer groups with fewer than two eligible employees as defined in subdivision (b) of Section 1357 covering hospital, medical, or surgical expenses, which is issued, amended, delivered, or renewed on or after January 1, 1994.

(b) As used in this section, "block of business" means individual plan contracts or plan contracts sold to employer groups with fewer than two eligible employees as defined in subdivision (b) of Section 1357, with distinct benefits, services, and terms. A "closed block of business" means a block of business for which a health care service plan ceases to actively offer or sell new plan contracts.

(c) No block of business shall be closed by a health care service plan unless (1) the plan permits an enrollee to receive health care services from any block of business that is not closed and that provides comparable benefits, services, and terms, with no additional underwriting requirement, or (2) the plan pools the experience of the closed block of business with all appropriate blocks of business that are not closed for the purpose of determining the premium rate of any plan contract within the closed block, with no rate penalty or surcharge beyond that which reflects the experience of the combined pool.

(d) A block of business shall be presumed closed if either of the following is applicable:

(1) There has been an overall reduction in that block of 12 percent in the number of in force plan contracts for a period of 12 months.

(2) That block has less than 1,000 enrollees in this state. This presumption shall not apply to a block of business initiated within the previous 24 months, but notification of that block shall be provided to the director pursuant to subdivision (e).

The fact that a block of business does not meet one of the presumptions set forth in this subdivision shall not preclude a determination that it is closed as defined in subdivision (b).

(e) A health care service plan shall notify the director in writing within 30 days of its decision to close a block of business or, in the absence of an actual decision to close a block of business, within 30 days of its determination that a block of business is within the presumption set forth in subdivision (d). When the plan decides to close a block, the written notice shall fully disclose all information necessary to demonstrate compliance with the requirements of subdivision (c). When the plan determines that a block is within the presumption, the written notice shall fully disclose all information necessary to demonstrate that the presumption is applicable. In the case of either notice, the plan shall provide additional information within 15 days after any request of the director.

(f) A health care service plan shall preserve for a period of not less than five years in an identified location and readily accessible for review by the director all books and records relating to any action taken by a plan pursuant to subdivision (c).

(g) No health care service plan shall offer or sell any contract, or provide misleading information about the active or closed status of a block of business, for the purpose of evading this section.

(h) A health care service plan shall bring any blocks of business closed prior to the effective date of this section into compliance with the terms of this section no later than December 31, 1994.

(i) This section shall not apply to health care service plan contracts providing small employer health coverage to individuals or employer groups with fewer than two eligible employees if that coverage is provided pursuant to Article 3.1 (commencing with Section 1357) and, with specific reference to coverage for individuals or employer groups with fewer than two eligible employees, is approved by the director pursuant to Section 1357.15, provided a plan electing to sell coverage pursuant to this subdivision shall do so until such time as the plan ceases to market coverage to small employers and complies with paragraph (5) of subdivision (a) of Section 1365.

(j) This section shall not apply to coverage of Medicare services pursuant to contracts with the United States government, Medicare supplement, dental, vision, or conversion coverage.

(Amended by Stats. 2010, Ch. 658, Sec. 6. (AB 2470) Effective January 1, 2011.)

1367.18.

(a) Every health care service plan, except a specialized health care service plan, that covers hospital, medical, or surgical expenses on a group basis shall offer coverage for orthotic and prosthetic devices and services under the terms and conditions that may be agreed upon between the group subscriber and the plan. Every plan shall communicate the availability of that coverage to all group contractholders and to all prospective group contractholders with whom they are negotiating. Any coverage for prosthetic devices shall include original and replacement devices, as prescribed by a physician and surgeon or doctor of podiatric medicine acting within the scope of his or her license. Any coverage for orthotic devices shall provide for coverage when the device, including original and replacement devices, is prescribed by a physician and surgeon or doctor of podiatric medicine acting within the scope of his or her license, or is ordered by a licensed health care provider acting within the scope of his or her license. Every plan shall have the right to conduct a utilization review to determine medical necessity prior to authorizing these services.

(b) Notwithstanding subdivision (a), on and after July 1, 2007, the amount of the benefit for orthotic and prosthetic devices and services shall be no less than the annual and lifetime benefit maximums applicable to the basic health care services required to be provided under Section 1367. If the contract does not include any annual or lifetime benefit maximums applicable to basic health care services, the amount of the benefit for orthotic and prosthetic devices and services shall not be subject to an annual or lifetime maximum benefit level. Any copayment, coinsurance, deductible, and maximum out-of-pocket amount applied to the benefit for orthotic and prosthetic devices and services shall be no more than the most common amounts applied to the basic health care services required to be provided under Section 1367.

(Amended by Stats. 2006, Ch. 756, Sec. 1. Effective January 1, 2007.)

1367.19.

On and after January 1, 1991, every health care service plan, except a specialized health care service plan, that covers hospital, medical, or surgical expenses on a group basis shall offer coverage as an option for special footwear needed by persons who suffer from foot disfigurement under such terms and conditions as may be agreed upon between the group contract holder and the plan.

As used in this section, foot disfigurement shall include, but not be limited to, disfigurement from cerebral palsy, arthritis, polio, spinabifida, diabetes, and foot disfigurement caused by accident or developmental disability.

(Added by Stats. 1990, Ch. 1680, Sec. 1.)

1367.20.

Every health care service plan that provides prescription drug benefits and maintains one or more drug formularies shall provide to members of the public, upon request, a copy of the most current list of prescription drugs on the formulary of the plan by major therapeutic category, with an indication of whether any drugs on the list are preferred over other listed drugs. If the health care service plan maintains more than one formulary, the plan shall notify the requester that a choice of formulary lists is available.

(Added by Stats. 1998, Ch. 69, Sec. 1. Effective January 1, 1999.)

1367.205.

(a) In addition to the list required to be provided under Section 1367.20, a health care service plan that provides prescription drug benefits and maintains one or more drug formularies shall do all of the following:

(1) Post the formulary or formularies for each product offered by the plan on the plan's Internet Web site in a manner that is accessible and searchable by potential enrollees, enrollees, providers, the general public, the department, and federal agencies as required by federal law or regulations.

(2) Update the formularies posted pursuant to paragraph (1) with any change to those formularies on a monthly basis.

(3) No later than six months after the date that a standard formulary template is developed under subdivision (b), use that template to display the formulary or formularies for each product offered by the plan.

(b) (1) By January 1, 2017, the department and the Department of Insurance shall jointly, and with input from interested parties from at least one public meeting, develop a standard formulary template for purposes of paragraph (3) of subdivision (a). In developing the template, the department and Department of Insurance shall take into consideration existing requirements for reporting of formulary information established by the federal Centers for Medicare and Medicaid Services. To the extent feasible, in developing the template, the department and the Department of Insurance shall evaluate a way to include on the template, in addition to the information required to be included under paragraph (2), cost-sharing information for drugs subject to coinsurance.

(2) The standard formulary template shall include the notification described in subdivision (c) of Section 1363.01, and as applied to a particular formulary for a product offered by a plan, shall do all of the following:

(A) Include information on cost-sharing tiers and utilization controls, including prior authorization or step therapy requirements, for each drug covered by the product.

(B) Indicate any drugs on the formulary that are preferred over other drugs on the formulary.

(C) Include information to educate enrollees about the differences between drugs administered or provided under a health care service plan's medical benefit and drugs prescribed under a health care service plan's prescription drug benefit and about how to obtain coverage information regarding drugs that are not covered under the plan's prescription drug benefit.

(D) Include information to educate enrollees that health care service plans that provide prescription drug benefits are required to have a method for enrollees to obtain prescription drugs not listed in the health plan drug formulary if the drugs are deemed medically necessary by a clinician pursuant to Section 1367.24.

(E) Include information on which medications are covered, including both generic and brand name.

(F) Include information on what tier of the plan's drug formulary each medication is in.

(c) For purposes of this section, "formulary" means the complete list of drugs preferred for use and eligible for coverage under a health care service plan product and includes the drugs covered under the pharmacy benefit of the product.

(Amended by Stats. 2015, Ch. 619, Sec. 5. (AB 339) Effective January 1, 2016.)

1367.21.

(a) No health care service plan contract which covers prescription drug benefits shall be issued, amended, delivered, or renewed in this state if the plan limits or excludes coverage for a drug on the basis that the drug is prescribed for a use that is different from the use for which that drug has been approved for marketing by the federal Food and Drug Administration (FDA), provided that all of the following conditions have been met:

(1) The drug is approved by the FDA.

(2) (A) The drug is prescribed by a participating licensed health care professional for the treatment of a life-threatening condition; or

(B) The drug is prescribed by a participating licensed health care professional for the treatment of a chronic and seriously debilitating condition, the drug is medically necessary to treat that condition, and the drug is on the plan formulary. If the drug is not on the plan formulary, the participating subscriber's request shall be considered pursuant to the process required by Section 1367.24.

(3) The drug has been recognized for treatment of that condition by any of the following:

(A) The American Hospital Formulary Service's Drug Information.

(B) One of the following compendia, if recognized by the federal Centers for Medicare and Medicaid Services as part of an anticancer chemotherapeutic regimen:

(i) The Elsevier Gold Standard's Clinical Pharmacology.

(ii) The National Comprehensive Cancer Network Drug and Biologics Compendium.

(iii) The Thomson Micromedex DrugDex.

(C) Two articles from major peer reviewed medical journals that present data supporting the proposed off-label use or uses as generally safe and effective unless there is clear and convincing contradictory evidence presented in a major peer reviewed medical journal.

(b) It shall be the responsibility of the participating prescriber to submit to the plan documentation supporting compliance with the requirements of subdivision (a), if requested by the plan.

(c) Any coverage required by this section shall also include medically necessary services associated with the administration of a drug, subject to the conditions of the contract.

(d) For purposes of this section, "life-threatening" means either or both of the following:

(1) Diseases or conditions where the likelihood of death is high unless the course of the disease is interrupted.

(2) Diseases or conditions with potentially fatal outcomes, where the end point of clinical intervention is survival.

(e) For purposes of this section, "chronic and seriously debilitating" means diseases or conditions that require ongoing treatment to maintain remission or prevent deterioration and cause significant long-term morbidity.

(f) The provision of drugs and services when required by this section shall not, in itself, give rise to liability on the part of the plan.

(g) Nothing in this section shall be construed to prohibit the use of a formulary, copayment, technology assessment panel, or similar mechanism as a means for appropriately controlling the utilization of a drug that is prescribed for a use that is different from the use for which that drug has been approved for marketing by the FDA.

(h) If a plan denies coverage pursuant to this section on the basis that its use is experimental or investigational, that decision is subject to review under Section 1370.4.

(i) Health care service plan contracts for the delivery of Medi-Cal services under the Waxman-Duffy Prepaid Health Plan Act (Chapter 8 (commencing with Section 14200) of Part 3 of Division 9 of the Welfare and Institutions Code) are exempt from the requirements of this section.

(Amended by Stats. 2009, Ch. 479, Sec. 1. (AB 830) Effective January 1, 2010.)

1367.215.

(a) Every health care service plan contract that covers prescription drug benefits shall provide coverage for appropriately prescribed pain management medications for terminally ill patients when medically necessary. The plan shall approve or deny the request by the provider for authorization of coverage for an enrollee who has been determined to be terminally ill in a timely fashion, appropriate for the nature of the enrollee's condition, not to exceed 72 hours of the plan's receipt of the information requested by the plan to make the decision. If the request is denied or if additional information is required, the plan shall contact the provider within one working day of the determination, with an explanation of the reason for the denial or the need for additional information. The requested treatment shall be deemed authorized as of the expiration of the applicable timeframe. The provider shall contact the plan within one business day of proceeding with the deemed authorized treatment, to do all of the following:

(1) Confirm that the timeframe has expired.

(2) Provide enrollee identification.

(3) Notify the plan of the provider or providers performing the treatment.

(4) Notify the plan of the facility or location where the treatment was rendered.

(b) This section does not apply to coverage for any drug that is prescribed for a use that is different from the use for which that drug has been approved for marketing by the federal Food and Drug Administration. Coverage for different-use drugs is subject to Section 1367.21.

(c) Nothing in this section shall be construed to deny or restrict in any way the department's authority to ensure plan compliance with this chapter when a plan provides coverage for prescription drugs.

(Amended by Stats. 2002, Ch. 791, Sec. 2. Effective January 1, 2003.)

1367.22.

(a) A health care service plan contract, issued, amended, or renewed on or after July 1, 1999, that covers prescription drug benefits shall not limit or exclude coverage for a drug for an enrollee if the drug previously had been approved for coverage by the plan for a medical condition of the enrollee and the plan's prescribing provider continues to prescribe the drug for the medical condition, provided that the drug is appropriately prescribed and is considered safe and effective for treating the enrollee's medical condition. Nothing in this section shall preclude the prescribing provider from prescribing another drug covered by the plan that is medically appropriate for the enrollee, nor shall anything in this section be construed to prohibit generic drug substitutions as authorized by Section 4073 of the Business and Professions Code. For purposes of this section, a prescribing provider shall include a provider authorized to write a prescription, pursuant to subdivision (a) of Section 4059 of the Business and Professions Code, to treat a medical condition of an enrollee.

(b) This section does not apply to coverage for any drug that is prescribed for a use that is different from the use for which that drug has been approved for marketing by the federal Food and Drug Administration. Coverage for different-use drugs is subject to Section 1367.21.

(c) This section shall not be construed to restrict or impair the application of any other provision of this chapter, including, but not limited to, Section 1367, which includes among its requirements that plans furnish services in a manner providing continuity of care and demonstrate that medical decisions are rendered by qualified medical providers unhindered by fiscal and administrative management.

(d) This section does not prohibit a health care service plan from charging a subscriber or enrollee a copayment or a deductible for prescription drug benefits or from setting forth, by contract, limitations on maximum coverage of prescription drug benefits, provided that the copayments, deductibles, or limitations are reported to, and held unobjectionable by, the director and set forth to the subscriber or enrollee pursuant to the disclosure provisions of Section 1363.

(Amended by Stats. 2002, Ch. 760, Sec. 2. Effective January 1, 2003.)

1367.23.

(a) On and after January 1, 1994, every group health care service plan contract, which is issued, amended, or renewed, shall include a provision requiring the health care service plan to notify the group contractholders in writing of the cancellation of the plan contract and shall include in their contract with group contractholders a provision requiring the group contractholder to mail promptly to each subscriber a legible, true copy of any notice of cancellation of the plan contract which may be received from the plan and to provide promptly to the plan proof of that mailing and the date thereof.

(b) The notice of cancellation from the group contractholder to the subscriber required by subdivision (a) shall include information regarding the conversion rights of persons covered under the plan contract upon termination of the plan contract. This information shall be in clear and easily understandable language.
(Added by Stats. 1993, Ch. 1154, Sec. 1. Effective January 1, 1994.)

1367.24.

(a) Every health care service plan that provides prescription drug benefits shall maintain an expeditious process by which prescribing providers may obtain authorization for a medically necessary nonformulary prescription drug. On or before July 1, 1999, every health care service plan that provides prescription drug benefits shall file with the department a description of its process, including timelines, for responding to authorization requests for nonformulary drugs. Any changes to this process shall be filed with the department pursuant to Section 1352. Each plan shall provide a written description of its most current process, including timelines, to its prescribing providers. For purposes of this section, a prescribing provider shall include a provider authorized to write a prescription, pursuant to subdivision (a) of Section 4040 of the Business and Professions Code, to treat a medical condition of an enrollee.

(b) Any plan that disapproves a request made pursuant to subdivision (a) by a prescribing provider to obtain authorization for a nonformulary drug shall provide the reasons for the disapproval in a notice provided to the enrollee. The notice shall indicate that the enrollee may file a grievance with the plan if the enrollee objects to the disapproval, including any alternative drug or treatment offered by the plan. The notice shall comply with subdivision (b) of Section 1368.02. Any health plan that is required to maintain an external exception request review process pursuant to subdivision (k) shall indicate in the notice required under this subdivision that the enrollee may file a grievance seeking an external exception request review.

(c) The process described in subdivision (a) by which prescribing providers may obtain authorization for medically necessary nonformulary drugs shall not apply to a nonformulary drug that has been prescribed for an enrollee in conformance with the provisions of Section 1367.22.

(d) The process described in subdivision (a) by which enrollees may obtain medically necessary nonformulary drugs, including specified timelines for responding to prescribing provider authorization requests, shall be described in evidence of coverage and disclosure forms, as required by subdivision (a) of Section 1363, issued on or after July 1, 1999.

(e) Every health care service plan that provides prescription drug benefits shall maintain, as part of its books and records under Section 1381, all of the following information, which shall be made available to the director upon request:

(1) The complete drug formulary or formularies of the plan, if the plan maintains a formulary, including a list of the prescription drugs on the formulary of the plan by major therapeutic category with an indication of whether any drugs are preferred over other drugs.

(2) Records developed by the pharmacy and therapeutic committee of the plan, or by others responsible for developing, modifying, and overseeing formularies, including medical groups, individual practice associations, and contracting pharmaceutical benefit management companies, used to guide the drugs prescribed for the enrollees of the plan, that fully describe the reasoning behind formulary decisions.

(3) Any plan arrangements with prescribing providers, medical groups, individual practice associations, pharmacists, contracting pharmaceutical benefit management companies, or other entities that are associated with activities of the plan to encourage formulary compliance or otherwise manage prescription drug benefits.

(f) If a plan provides prescription drug benefits, the department shall, as part of its periodic onsite medical survey of each plan undertaken pursuant to Section 1380, review the performance of the plan in providing those benefits, including, but not limited to, a review of the procedures and information maintained pursuant to this section, and describe the performance of the plan as part of its report issued pursuant to Section 1380.

(g) The director shall not publicly disclose any information reviewed pursuant to this section that is determined by the director to be confidential pursuant to state law.

(h) For purposes of this section, "authorization" means approval by the health care service plan to provide payment for the prescription drug.

(i) Nonformulary prescription drugs shall include any drug for which an enrollee's copayment or out-of-pocket costs are different than the copayment for a formulary prescription drug, except as otherwise provided by law or regulation or in cases in which the drug has been excluded in the plan contract pursuant to Section 1342.7.

(j) Nothing in this section shall be construed to restrict or impair the application of any other provision of this chapter, including, but not limited to, Section 1367, which includes among its requirements that a health care service plan furnish services in a manner providing continuity of care and demonstrate that medical decisions are rendered by qualified medical providers unhindered by fiscal and administrative management.

(k) For any individual, small group, or large health plan contracts, a health care service plan's process described in subdivision (a) shall comply with the request for exception and external exception request review processes described in subdivision (c) of Section 156.122 of Title 45 of the Code of Federal Regulations. This subdivision shall not apply to Medi-Cal managed care health care service plan contracts as described in subdivision (l).

(l) "Medi-Cal managed care health care service plan contract" means any entity that enters into a contract with the State Department of Health Care Services pursuant to Chapter 7 (commencing with Section 14000), Chapter 8 (commencing with Section 14200), or Chapter 8.75 (commencing with Section 14591) of Part 3 of Division 9 of the Welfare and Institutions Code.

(m) Nothing in this section shall be construed to affect an enrollee's or subscriber's eligibility to submit a grievance to the department for review under Section 1368 or to apply to the department for an independent medical review under Section 1370.4, or Article 5.55 (commencing with Section 1374.30) of this chapter.
(Amended by Stats. 2015, Ch. 654, Sec. 1. (SB 282) Effective January 1, 2016.)

1367.241.

(a) Notwithstanding any other law, on and after January 1, 2013, a health care service plan that provides coverage for prescription drugs shall accept only the prior authorization form developed pursuant to subdivision (c), or an electronic prior authorization process described in subdivision (e), when requiring prior authorization for prescription drugs. This section does not apply in the event that a physician or physician group has been delegated the financial risk for prescription drugs by a health care service plan and does not use a prior authorization process. This section does not apply to a health care service plan, or to its affiliated providers, if the health care service plan owns and operates its pharmacies and does not use a prior authorization process for prescription drugs.

(b) If a health care service plan or a contracted physician group fails to respond within 72 hours for nonurgent requests, and within 24 hours if exigent circumstances exist, upon receipt of a completed prior authorization request from a prescribing provider, the prior authorization request shall be deemed to have been granted. The requirements of this subdivision shall not apply to contracts entered into pursuant to Chapter 7 (commencing with Section 14000), Chapter 8 (commencing with Section 14200), or Chapter 8.75 (commencing with Section 14591) of Part 3 of Division 9 of the Welfare and Institutions Code. Medi-Cal managed care health care service plans that contract under those chapters shall not be required to maintain an external exception request review as provided in Section 156.122 of Title 45 of the Code of Federal Regulations.

(c) On or before January 1, 2017, the department and the Department of Insurance shall jointly develop a uniform prior authorization form. Notwithstanding any other law, on and after July 1, 2017, or six months after the form is completed pursuant to this section, whichever is later, every prescribing provider shall use that uniform prior authorization form, or an electronic prior authorization process described in subdivision (e), to request prior authorization for coverage of prescription drugs and every health care service plan shall accept that form or electronic process as sufficient to request prior authorization for prescription drugs.

(d) The prior authorization form developed pursuant to subdivision (c) shall meet the following criteria:

(1) The form shall not exceed two pages.

(2) The form shall be made electronically available by the department and the health care service plan.

(3) The completed form may also be electronically submitted from the prescribing provider to the health care service plan.

(4) The department and the Department of Insurance shall develop the form with input from interested parties from at least one public meeting.

(5) The department and the Department of Insurance, in development of the standardized form, shall take into consideration the following:

(A) Existing prior authorization forms established by the federal Centers for Medicare and Medicaid Services and the State Department of Health Care Services.

(B) National standards pertaining to electronic prior authorization.

(e) A prescribing provider may use an electronic prior authorization system utilizing the standardized form described in subdivision (c) or an electronic process developed specifically for transmitting prior authorization information that meets the National Council for Prescription Drug Programs' SCRIPT standard for electronic prior authorization transactions.

(f) Subdivision (a) does not apply if any of the following occurs:

(1) A contracted physician group is delegated the financial risk for prescription drugs by a health care service plan.

(2) A contracted physician group uses its own internal prior authorization process rather than the health care service plan's prior authorization process for plan enrollees.

(3) A contracted physician group is delegated a utilization management function by the health care service plan concerning any prescription drug, regardless of the delegation of financial risk.

(g) For prescription drugs, prior authorization requirements described in subdivisions (c) and (e) apply regardless of how that benefit is classified under the terms of the health plan's group or individual contract.

(h) For purposes of this section:

(1) "Prescribing provider" shall include a provider authorized to write a prescription, pursuant to subdivision (a) of Section 4040 of the Business and Professions Code, to treat a medical condition of an enrollee.

(2) "Exigent circumstances" exist when an enrollee is suffering from a health condition that may seriously jeopardize the enrollee's life, health, or ability to regain maximum function or when an enrollee is undergoing a current course of treatment using a nonformulary drug.

(3) "Completed prior authorization request" means a completed uniform prior authorization form developed pursuant to subdivision (c), or a completed request submitted using an electronic prior authorization system described in subdivision (e), or, for contracted physician groups described in subdivision (f), the process used by the contracted physician group.
(Amended by Stats. 2015, Ch. 654, Sec. 2. (SB 282) Effective January 1, 2016.)

1367.243.

(a) (1) A health care service plan that reports rate information pursuant to Section 1385.03 or 1385.045 shall report the information described in paragraph (2) to the department no later than October 1 of each year, beginning October 1, 2018.

(2) For all covered prescription drugs, including generic drugs, brand name drugs, and specialty drugs dispensed at a plan pharmacy, network pharmacy, or mail order pharmacy for outpatient use, all of the following shall be reported:

(A) The 25 most frequently prescribed drugs.

(B) The 25 most costly drugs by total annual plan spending.

(C) The 25 drugs with the highest year-over-year increase in total annual plan spending.

(b) The department shall compile the information reported pursuant to subdivision (a) into a report for the public and legislators that demonstrates the overall impact of drug costs on health care premiums. The data in the report shall be aggregated and shall not reveal information specific to individual health care service plans.

(c) For the purposes of this section, a "specialty drug" is one that exceeds the threshold for a specialty drug under the Medicare Part D program (Medicare Prescription Drug, Improvement, and Modernization Act of 2003 (Public Law 108-173)).

(d) By January 1 of each year, beginning January 1, 2019, the department shall publish on its Internet Web site the report required pursuant to subdivision (b).

(e) After the report required in subdivision (b) is released, the department shall include the report as part of the public meeting required pursuant to subdivision (b) of Section 1385.045.

(f) Except for the report required pursuant to subdivision (b), the department shall keep confidential all of the information provided to the department pursuant to this section, and the information shall be protected from public disclosure.

(Added by Stats. 2017, Ch. 603, Sec. 1. (SB 17) Effective January 1, 2018.)

1367.244.

(a) A request for an exception to a health care service plan's step therapy process for prescription drugs may be submitted in the same manner as a request for prior authorization for prescription drugs pursuant to Section 1367.241, and shall be treated in the same manner, and shall be responded to by the health care service plan in the same manner, as a request for prior authorization for prescription drugs.

(b) The department and the Department of Insurance shall include a provision for step therapy exception requests in the uniform prior authorization form developed pursuant to subdivision (c) of Section 1367.241.

(Added by Stats. 2015, Ch. 621, Sec. 1. (AB 374) Effective January 1, 2016.)

1367.25.

(a) A group health care service plan contract, except for a specialized health care service plan contract, that is issued, amended, renewed, or delivered on or after January 1, 2000, to December 31, 2015, inclusive, and an individual health care service plan contract that is amended, renewed, or delivered on or after January 1, 2000, to December 31, 2015, inclusive, except for a specialized health care service plan contract, shall provide coverage for the following, under general terms and conditions applicable to all benefits:

(1) A health care service plan contract that provides coverage for outpatient prescription drug benefits shall include coverage for a variety of federal Food and Drug Administration (FDA)-approved prescription contraceptive methods designated by the plan. In the event the patient's participating provider, acting within his or her scope of practice, determines that none of the methods designated by the plan is medically appropriate for the patient's medical or personal history, the plan shall also provide coverage for another FDA-approved, medically appropriate prescription contraceptive method prescribed by the patient's provider.

(2) Benefits for an enrollee under this subdivision shall be the same for an enrollee's covered spouse and covered nonspouse dependents.

(b) (1) A health care service plan contract, except for a specialized health care service plan contract, that is issued, amended, renewed, or delivered on or after January 1, 2016, shall provide coverage for all of the following services and contraceptive methods for women:

(A) Except as provided in subparagraphs (B) and (C) of paragraph (2), all FDA-approved contraceptive drugs, devices, and other products for women, including all FDA-approved contraceptive drugs, devices, and products available over the counter, as prescribed by the enrollee's provider.

(B) Voluntary sterilization procedures.

(C) Patient education and counseling on contraception.

(D) Followup services related to the drugs, devices, products, and procedures covered under this subdivision, including, but not limited to, management of side effects, counseling for continued adherence, and device insertion and removal.

(2) (A) Except for a grandfathered health plan, a health care service plan subject to this subdivision shall not impose a deductible, coinsurance, copayment, or any other cost-sharing requirement on the coverage provided pursuant to this subdivision. Cost sharing shall not be imposed on any Medi-Cal beneficiary.

(B) If the FDA has approved one or more therapeutic equivalents of a contraceptive drug, device, or product, a health care service plan is not required to cover all of those therapeutically equivalent versions in accordance with this subdivision, as long as at least one is covered without cost sharing in accordance with this subdivision.

(C) If a covered therapeutic equivalent of a drug, device, or product is not available, or is deemed medically inadvisable by the enrollee's provider, a health care service plan shall provide coverage, subject to a plan's utilization management procedures, for the prescribed contraceptive drug, device, or product without cost sharing. Any request by a contracting provider shall be responded to by the health care service plan in compliance with the Knox-Keene Health Care Service Plan Act of 1975, as set forth in this chapter and, as applicable, with the plan's Medi-Cal managed care contract.

(3) Except as otherwise authorized under this section, a health care service plan shall not impose any restrictions or delays on the coverage required under this subdivision.

(4) Benefits for an enrollee under this subdivision shall be the same for an enrollee's covered spouse and covered nonspouse dependents.

(5) For purposes of paragraphs (2) and (3) of this subdivision, and subdivision (d), "health care service plan" shall include Medi-Cal managed care plans that contract with the State Department of Health Care Services pursuant to Chapter 7 (commencing with Section 14000) and Chapter 8 (commencing with Section 14200) of Part 3 of Division 9 of the Welfare and Institutions Code.

(c) Notwithstanding any other provision of this section, a religious employer may request a health care service plan contract without coverage for FDA-approved contraceptive methods that are contrary to the religious employer's religious tenets. If so requested, a health care service plan contract shall be provided without coverage for contraceptive methods.

(1) For purposes of this section, a "religious employer" is an entity for which each of the following is true:

(A) The inculcation of religious values is the purpose of the entity.

(B) The entity primarily employs persons who share the religious tenets of the entity.

(C) The entity serves primarily persons who share the religious tenets of the entity.

(D) The entity is a nonprofit organization as described in Section 6033(a)(3)(A)(i) or (iii) of the Internal Revenue Code of 1986, as amended.

(2) Every religious employer that invokes the exemption provided under this section shall provide written notice to prospective enrollees prior to enrollment with the plan, listing the contraceptive health care services the employer refuses to cover for religious reasons.

(d) (1) Every health care service plan contract that is issued, amended, renewed, or delivered on or after January 1, 2017, shall cover up to a 12-month supply of FDA-approved, self-administered hormonal contraceptives when dispensed or furnished at one time for an enrollee by a provider, pharmacist, or at a location licensed or otherwise authorized to dispense drugs or supplies.

(2) Nothing in this subdivision shall be construed to require a health care service plan contract to cover contraceptives provided by an out-of-network provider, pharmacy, or location licensed or otherwise authorized to dispense drugs or supplies, except as may be otherwise authorized by state or federal law or by the plan's policies governing out-of-network coverage.

(3) Nothing in this subdivision shall be construed to require a provider to prescribe, furnish, or dispense 12 months of self-administered hormonal contraceptives at one time.

(4) A health care service plan subject to this subdivision, in the absence of clinical contraindications, shall not impose utilization controls or other forms of medical management limiting the supply of FDA-approved, self-administered hormonal contraceptives that may be dispensed or furnished by a provider or pharmacist, or at a location licensed or otherwise authorized to dispense drugs or supplies to an amount that is less than a 12-month supply.

(e) This section shall not be construed to exclude coverage for contraceptive supplies as prescribed by a provider, acting within his or her scope of practice, for reasons other than contraceptive purposes, such as decreasing the risk of ovarian cancer or eliminating symptoms of menopause, or for contraception that is necessary to preserve the life or health of an enrollee.

(f) This section shall not be construed to deny or restrict in any way the department's authority to ensure plan compliance with this chapter when a plan provides coverage for contraceptive drugs, devices, and products.

(g) This section shall not be construed to require an individual or group health care service plan contract to cover experimental or investigational treatments.

(h) For purposes of this section, the following definitions apply:

(1) "Grandfathered health plan" has the meaning set forth in Section 1251 of PPACA.

(2) "PPACA" means the federal Patient Protection and Affordable Care Act (Public Law 111-148), as amended by the federal Health Care and Education Reconciliation Act of 2010 (Public Law 111-152), and any rules, regulations, or guidance issued thereunder.

(3) With respect to health care service plan contracts issued, amended, or renewed on or after January 1, 2016, "provider" means an individual who is certified or licensed pursuant to Division 2 (commencing with Section 500) of the Business and Professions Code, or an initiative act referred to in that division, or Division 2.5 (commencing with Section 1797) of this code.

(Amended by Stats. 2016, Ch. 499, Sec. 3. (SB 999) Effective January 1, 2017.)

1367.27.

(a) Commencing July 1, 2016, a health care service plan shall publish and maintain a provider directory or directories with information on contracting providers that deliver health care services to the plan's enrollees, including those that accept new patients. A provider directory shall not list or include information on a provider that is not currently under contract with the plan.

(b) A health care service plan shall provide the directory or directories for the specific network offered for each product using a consistent method of network and product naming, numbering, or other classification method that ensures the public, enrollees, potential enrollees, the department, and other state or federal agencies can easily identify the networks and plan products in which a provider participates. By July 31, 2017, or 12 months after the date provider directory standards are developed under subdivision (k), whichever occurs later, a health care service plan shall use the naming, numbering, or classification method developed by the department pursuant to subdivision (k).

(c) (1) An online provider directory or directories shall be available on the plan's Internet Web site to the public, potential enrollees, enrollees, and providers without any restrictions or limitations. The directory or directories shall be accessible without any requirement that an individual seeking the directory information demonstrate coverage with the plan, indicate interest in obtaining coverage with the plan, provide a member identification or policy number, provide any other identifying information, or create or access an account.

(2) The online provider directory or directories shall be accessible on the plan's public Internet Web site through an identifiable link or tab and in a manner that is accessible and searchable by enrollees, potential enrollees, the public, and providers. By July 31, 2017, or 12 months after the date provider directory standards are developed under subdivision (k), whichever occurs later, the plan's public Internet Web site shall allow provider searches by, at a minimum, name, practice address, city, ZIP Code, California license number, National Provider Identifier number, admitting privileges to an identified hospital, product, tier, provider language or languages, provider group, hospital name, facility name, or clinic name, as appropriate.

(d) (1) A health care service plan shall allow enrollees, potential enrollees, providers, and members of the public to request a printed copy of the provider directory or directories by contacting the plan through the plan's toll-free telephone number, electronically, or in writing. A printed copy of the provider directory or directories shall include the information required in subdivisions (h) and (i). The printed copy of the provider directory or directories shall be provided to the requester by mail postmarked no later than five business days following the date of the request and may be limited to the geographic region in which the requester resides or works or intends to reside or work.

(2) A health care service plan shall update its printed provider directory or directories at least quarterly, or more frequently, if required by federal law.

(e) (1) The plan shall update the online provider directory or directories, at least weekly, or more frequently, if required by federal law, when informed of and upon confirmation by the plan of any of the following:

(A) A contracting provider is no longer accepting new patients for that product, or an individual provider within a provider group is no longer accepting new patients.

(B) A provider is no longer under contract for a particular plan product.

(C) A provider's practice location or other information required under subdivision (h) or (i) has changed.

(D) Upon completion of the investigation described in subdivision (o), a change is necessary based on an enrollee complaint that a provider was not accepting new patients, was otherwise not available, or whose contact information was listed incorrectly.

(E) Any other information that affects the content or accuracy of the provider directory or directories.

(2) Upon confirmation of any of the following, the plan shall delete a provider from the directory or directories when:

(A) A provider has retired or otherwise has ceased to practice.

(B) A provider or provider group is no longer under contract with the plan for any reason.

(C) The contracting provider group has informed the plan that the provider is no longer associated with the provider group and is no longer under contract with the plan.

(f) The provider directory or directories shall include both an email address and a telephone number for members of the public and providers to notify the plan if the provider directory information appears to be inaccurate. This information shall be disclosed prominently in the directory or directories and on the plan's Internet Web site.

(g) The provider directory or directories shall include the following disclosures informing enrollees that they are entitled to both of the following:

(1) Language interpreter services, at no cost to the enrollee, including how to obtain interpretation services in accordance with Section 1367.04.

(2) Full and equal access to covered services, including enrollees with disabilities as required under the federal Americans with Disabilities Act of 1990 and Section 504 of the Rehabilitation Act of 1973.

(h) A full service health care service plan and a specialized mental health plan shall include all of the following information in the provider directory or directories:

(1) The provider's name, practice location or locations, and contact information.

(2) Type of practitioner.

(3) National Provider Identifier number.

(4) California license number and type of license.

(5) The area of specialty, including board certification, if any.

(6) The provider's office email address, if available.

(7) The name of each affiliated provider group currently under contract with the plan through which the provider sees enrollees.

(8) A listing for each of the following providers that are under contract with the plan:

(A) For physicians and surgeons, the provider group, and admitting privileges, if any, at hospitals contracted with the plan.

(B) Nurse practitioners, physician assistants, psychologists, acupuncturists, optometrists, podiatrists, chiropractors, licensed clinical social workers, marriage and family therapists, professional clinical counselors, qualified autism service providers, as defined in Section 1374.73, nurse midwives, and dentists.

(C) For federally qualified health centers or primary care clinics, the name of the federally qualified health center or clinic.

(D) For any provider described in subparagraph (A) or (B) who is employed by a federally qualified health center or primary care clinic, and to the extent their services may be accessed and are covered through the contract with the plan, the name of the provider, and the name of the federally qualified health center or clinic.

(E) Facilities, including, but not limited to, general acute care hospitals, skilled nursing facilities, urgent care clinics, ambulatory surgery centers, inpatient hospice, residential care facilities, and inpatient rehabilitation facilities.

(F) Pharmacies, clinical laboratories, imaging centers, and other facilities providing contracted health care services.

(9) The provider directory or directories may note that authorization or referral may be required to access some providers.

(10) Non-English language, if any, spoken by a health care provider or other medical professional as well as non-English language spoken by a qualified medical interpreter, in accordance with Section 1367.04, if any, on the provider's staff.

(11) Identification of providers who no longer accept new patients for some or all of the plan's products.

(12) The network tier to which the provider is assigned, if the provider is not in the lowest tier, as applicable. Nothing in this section shall be construed to require the use of network tiers other than contract and noncontracting tiers.

(13) All other information necessary to conduct a search pursuant to paragraph (2) of subdivision (c).

(i) A vision, dental, or other specialized health care service plan, except for a specialized mental health plan, shall include all of the following information for each provider directory or directories used by the plan for its networks:

(1) The provider's name, practice location or locations, and contact information.

(2) Type of practitioner.

(3) National Provider Identifier number.

(4) California license number and type of license, if applicable.

(5) The area of specialty, including board certification, or other accreditation, if any.

(6) The provider's office email address, if available.

(7) The name of each affiliated provider group or specialty plan practice group currently under contract with the plan through which the provider sees enrollees.

(8) The names of each allied health care professional to the extent there is a direct contract for those services covered through a contract with the plan.

(9) The non-English language, if any, spoken by a health care provider or other medical professional as well as non-English language spoken by a qualified medical interpreter, in accordance with Section 1367.04, if any, on the provider's staff.

(10) Identification of providers who no longer accept new patients for some or all of the plan's products.

(11) All other applicable information necessary to conduct a provider search pursuant to paragraph (2) of subdivision (c).

(j) (1) The contract between the plan and a provider shall include a requirement that the provider inform the plan within five business days when either of the following occurs:

(A) The provider is not accepting new patients.

(B) If the provider had previously not accepted new patients, the provider is currently accepting new patients.

(2) If a provider who is not accepting new patients is contacted by an enrollee or potential enrollee seeking to become a new patient, the provider shall direct the enrollee or potential enrollee to both the plan for additional assistance in finding a provider and to the department to report any inaccuracy with the plan's directory or directories.

(3) If an enrollee or potential enrollee informs a plan of a possible inaccuracy in the provider directory or directories, the plan shall promptly investigate, and, if necessary, undertake corrective action within 30 business days to ensure the accuracy of the directory or directories.

(k) (1) On or before December 31, 2016, the department shall develop uniform provider directory standards to permit consistency in accordance with subdivision (b) and paragraph (2) of subdivision (c) and development of a multiplan directory by another entity. Those standards shall not be subject to the Administrative Procedure Act (Chapter 3.5 (commencing with Section 11340) of Part 1 of Division 3 of Title 2 of the Government Code), until January 1, 2021. No more than two revisions of those standards shall be exempt from the Administrative Procedure Act (Chapter 3.5 (commencing with Section 11340) of Part 1 of Division 3 of Title 2 of the Government Code) pursuant to this subdivision.

(2) In developing the standards under this subdivision, the department shall seek input from interested parties throughout the process of developing the standards and shall hold at least one public meeting. The department shall take into consideration any requirements for provider directories established by the federal Centers for Medicare and Medicaid Services and the State Department of Health Care Services.

(3) By July 31, 2017, or 12 months after the date provider directory standards are developed under this subdivision, whichever occurs later, a plan shall use the standards developed by the department for each product offered by the plan.

(l) (1) A plan shall take appropriate steps to ensure the accuracy of the information concerning each provider listed in the plan's provider directory or directories in accordance with this section, and shall, at least annually, review and update the entire provider directory or directories for each product offered. Each calendar year the plan shall notify all contracted providers described in subdivisions (h) and (i) as follows:

(A) For individual providers who are not affiliated with a provider group described in subparagraph (A) or (B) of paragraph (8) of subdivision (h) and providers described in subdivision (i), the plan shall notify each provider at least once every six months.

(B) For all other providers described in subdivision (h) who are not subject to the requirements of subparagraph (A), the plan shall notify its contracted providers to ensure that all of the providers are contacted by the plan at least once annually.

(2) The notification shall include all of the following:

(A) The information the plan has in its directory or directories regarding the provider or provider group, including a list of networks and plan products that include the contracted provider or provider group.

(B) A statement that the failure to respond to the notification may result in a delay of payment or reimbursement of a claim pursuant to subdivision (p).

(C) Instructions on how the provider or provider group can update the information in the provider directory or directories using the online interface developed pursuant to subdivision (m).

(3) The plan shall require an affirmative response from the provider or provider group acknowledging that the notification was received. The provider or provider group shall confirm that the information in the provider directory or directories is current and accurate or update the information required to be in the directory or directories pursuant to this section, including whether or not the provider or provider group is accepting new patients for each plan product.

(4) If the plan does not receive an affirmative response and confirmation from the provider that the information is current and accurate or, as an alternative, updates any information required to be in the directory or directories pursuant to this section, within 30 business days, the plan shall take no more than 15 business days to verify whether the provider's information is correct or requires updates. The plan shall document the receipt and outcome of each attempt to verify the information. If the plan is unable to verify whether the provider's information is correct or requires updates, the plan shall notify the provider 10 business days in advance of removal that the provider will be removed from the provider directory or directories. The provider shall be removed from the provider directory or directories at the next required update of the provider directory or directories after the 10-business-day notice period. A provider shall not be removed from the provider directory or directories if he or she responds before the end of the 10-business-day notice period.

(5) General acute care hospitals shall be exempt from the requirements in paragraphs (3) and (4).

(m) A plan shall establish policies and procedures with regard to the regular updating of its provider directory or directories, including the weekly, quarterly, and annual updates required pursuant to this section, or more frequently, if required by federal law or guidance.

(1) The policies and procedures described under this subdivision shall be submitted by a plan annually to the department for approval and in a format described by the department pursuant to Section 1367.035.

(2) Every health care service plan shall ensure processes are in place to allow providers to promptly verify or submit changes to the information required to be in the directory or directories pursuant to this section. Those processes shall, at a minimum, include an online interface for providers to submit verification or changes electronically and shall generate an acknowledgment of receipt from the health care service plan. Providers shall verify or submit changes to information required to be in the directory or directories pursuant to this section using the process required by the health care service plan.

(3) The plan shall establish and maintain a process for enrollees, potential enrollees, other providers, and the public to identify and report possible inaccurate, incomplete, or misleading information currently listed in the plan's provider directory or directories. This process shall, at a minimum, include a telephone number and a dedicated email address at which the plan will accept these reports, as well as a hyperlink on the plan's provider directory Internet Web site linking to a form where the information can be reported directly to the plan through its Internet Web site.

(n) (1) This section does not prohibit a plan from requiring its provider groups or contracting specialized health care service plans to provide information to the plan that is required by the plan to satisfy the requirements of this section for each of the providers that contract with the provider group or contracting specialized health care service plan. This responsibility shall be specifically documented in a written contract between the plan and the provider group or contracting specialized health care service plan.

(2) If a plan requires its contracting provider groups or contracting specialized health care service plans to provide the plan with information described in paragraph (1), the plan shall continue to retain responsibility for ensuring that the requirements of this section are satisfied.

(3) A provider group may terminate a contract with a provider for a pattern or repeated failure of the provider to update the information required to be in the directory or directories pursuant to this section.

(4) A provider group is not subject to the payment delay described in subdivision (p) if all of the following occurs:

(A) A provider does not respond to the provider group's attempt to verify the provider's information. As used in this paragraph, "verify" means to contact the provider in writing, electronically, and by telephone to confirm whether the provider's information is correct or requires updates.

(B) The provider group documents its efforts to verify the provider's information.

(C) The provider group reports to the plan that the provider should be deleted from the provider group in the plan directory or directories.

(5) Section 1375.7, known as the Health Care Providers' Bill of Rights, applies to any material change to a provider contract pursuant to this section.

(o) (1) Whenever a health care service plan receives a report indicating that information listed in its provider directory or directories is inaccurate, the plan shall promptly investigate the reported inaccuracy and, no later than 30 business days following receipt of the report, either verify the accuracy of the information or update the information in its provider directory or directories, as applicable.

(2) When investigating a report regarding its provider directory or directories, the plan shall, at a minimum, do the following:

(A) Contact the affected provider no later than five business days following receipt of the report.

(B) Document the receipt and outcome of each report. The documentation shall include the provider's name, location, and a description of the plan's investigation, the outcome of the investigation, and any changes or updates made to its provider directory or directories.

(C) If changes to a plan's provider directory or directories are required as a result of the plan's investigation, the changes to the online provider directory or directories shall be made no later than the next scheduled weekly update, or the update immediately following that update, or sooner if required by federal law or regulations. For printed provider directories, the change shall be made no later than the next required update, or sooner if required by federal law or regulations.

(p) (1) Notwithstanding Sections 1371 and 1371.35, a plan may delay payment or reimbursement owed to a provider or provider group as specified in subparagraph (A) or (B), if the provider or provider group fails to respond to the plan's attempts to verify the provider's or provider group's information as required under subdivision (l). The plan shall not delay payment unless it has attempted to verify the provider's or provider group's information. As used in this subdivision, "verify" means to contact the provider or provider group in writing, electronically, and by telephone to confirm whether the provider's or provider group's information is correct or requires updates. A plan may seek to delay payment or reimbursement owed to a provider or provider group only after the 10-business day notice period described in paragraph (4) of subdivision (l) has lapsed.

(A) For a provider or provider group that receives compensation on a capitated or prepaid basis, the plan may delay no more than 50 percent of the next scheduled capitation payment for up to one calendar month.

(B) For any claims payment made to a provider or provider group, the plan may delay the claims payment for up to one calendar month beginning on the first day of the following month.

(2) A plan shall notify the provider or provider group 10 business days before it seeks to delay payment or reimbursement to a provider or provider group pursuant to this subdivision. If the plan delays a payment or reimbursement pursuant to this subdivision, the plan shall reimburse the full amount of any payment or reimbursement subject to delay to the provider or provider group according to either of the following timelines, as applicable:

(A) No later than three business days following the date on which the plan receives the information required to be submitted by the provider or provider group pursuant to subdivision (l).

(B) At the end of the one-calendar month delay described in subparagraph (A) or (B) of paragraph (1), as applicable, if the provider or provider group fails to provide the information required to be submitted to the plan pursuant to subdivision (l).

(3) A plan may terminate a contract for a pattern or repeated failure of the provider or provider group to alert the plan to a change in the information required to be in the directory or directories pursuant to this section.

(4) A plan that delays payment or reimbursement under this subdivision shall document each instance a payment or reimbursement was delayed and report this information to the department in a format described by the department pursuant to Section 1367.035. This information shall be submitted along with the policies and procedures required to be submitted annually to the department pursuant to paragraph (1) of subdivision (m).

(5) With respect to plans with Medi-Cal managed care contracts with the State Department of Health Care Services pursuant to Chapter 7 (commencing with Section 14000), Chapter 8 (commencing with Section 14200), or Chapter 8.75 (commencing with Section 14591) of the Welfare and Institutions Code, this subdivision shall be implemented only to the extent consistent with federal law and guidance.

(q) In circumstances where the department finds that an enrollee reasonably relied upon materially inaccurate, incomplete, or misleading information contained in a health plan's provider directory or directories, the department may require the health plan to provide coverage for all covered health care services provided to the enrollee and to reimburse the enrollee for any amount beyond what the enrollee would have paid, had the services been delivered by an in-network provider under the enrollee's plan contract. Prior to requiring reimbursement in these circumstances, the department shall conclude that the services received by the enrollee were covered services under the enrollee's plan contract. In those circumstances, the fact that the services were rendered or delivered by a noncontracting or out-of-plan provider shall not be used as a basis to deny reimbursement to the enrollee.

(r) Whenever a plan determines as a result of this section that there has been a 10 percent change in the network for a product in a region, the plan shall file an amendment to the plan application with the department consistent with subdivision (f) of Section 1300.52 of Title 28 of the California Code of Regulations.

(s) This section applies to plans with Medi-Cal managed care contracts with the State Department of Health Care Services pursuant to Chapter 7 (commencing with Section 14000), Chapter 8 (commencing with Section 14200), or Chapter 8.75 (commencing with Section 14591) of the Welfare and Institutions Code to the extent consistent with federal law and guidance and state law guidance issued after January 1, 2016. Notwithstanding any other provision to the contrary in a plan contract with the State Department of Health Care Services, and to the extent consistent with federal law and guidance and state guidance issued after January 1, 2016, a Medi-Cal managed care plan that complies with the requirements of this section shall not be required to distribute a printed provider directory or directories, except as required by paragraph (1) of subdivision (d).

(t) A health plan that contracts with multiple employer welfare agreements regulated pursuant to Article 4.7 (commencing with Section 742.20) of Chapter 1 of Part 2 of Division 1 of the Insurance Code shall meet the requirements of this section.

(u) This section shall not be construed to alter a provider's obligation to provide health care services to an enrollee pursuant to the provider's contract with the plan.

(v) As part of the department's routine examination of the fiscal and administrative affairs of a health care service plan pursuant to Section 1382, the department shall include a review of the health care service plan's compliance with subdivision (p).

(w) For purposes of this section, "provider group" means a medical group, independent practice association, or other similar group of providers.

(Amended by Stats. 2016, Ch. 86, Sec. 178. (SB 1171) Effective January 1, 2017.)

1367.29.

(a) On and after July 1, 2011, in accordance with subdivision (b), a health care service plan that provides coverage for professional mental health services, including a specialized health care service plan that provides coverage for professional mental health services, shall issue an identification card to an enrollee in order to assist the enrollee with accessing health benefits coverage information, including, but not limited to, in-network provider access information, and claims processing purposes. The identification card, at a minimum, shall include all of the following information:

(1) The name of the health care service plan issuing the identification card.

(2) The enrollee's identification number.

(3) A telephone number that enrollees or providers may call for assistance with health benefits coverage information, in-network provider access information, and claims processing information, and if assessment services are provided by the health care service plan, access to assessment services for the purpose of referral to an appropriate level of care or an appropriate health care provider.

(4) The health care service plan's Internet Web site address.

(b) The identification card required by this section shall be issued by a health care service plan or a specialized health care service plan to an enrollee upon enrollment or upon a change in the enrollee's coverage that impacts the data content or format of the card.

(c) This section does not require a health care service plan to issue a separate identification card for professional mental health services coverage if the plan issues a card for health care coverage in general and the card provides the information required by this section.

(d) If a health care service plan or a specialized health care service plan, as described in subdivision (a), delegates responsibility for issuing the identification card to a contractor or an agent, the contractor or agent shall be required to comply with this section.

(e) This section does not prohibit a health care service plan or a specialized health care service plan from meeting the standards of the Workgroup for Electronic Data Interchange (WEDI) or other national uniform standards with respect to identification cards, and a health care service plan shall be deemed compliant with this section if the plan conforms with these standards, as long as the minimum requirements described in subdivision (a) have been met.

(f) For the purposes of this section, "identification card" includes other technology that performs substantially the same function as an identification card.

(g) (1) This section shall not apply to Medicare supplement insurance, employee assistance programs, CHAMPUS supplement insurance, or TRI-CARE supplement insurance, or to hospital indemnity, accident-only, and specified disease insurance. This section shall also not apply to specialized health care service plans, except behavioral health-only plans.

(2) Notwithstanding paragraph (1), this section shall not apply to a behavioral health-only plan that provides coverage for professional mental health services pursuant to a contract with a health care service plan or insurer if that plan or insurer issues an identification card to its subscribers or insureds pursuant to this section or Section 10123.198 of the Insurance Code.

(Amended by Stats. 2018, Ch. 687, Sec. 1. (SB 910) Effective January 1, 2019.)

1367.30.

Notwithstanding any other provision of law, every group health care service plan contract marketed, issued, or delivered to a resident of this state, regardless of the situs of the contract or the subscriber, shall be subject to Section 1374.58.

(Added by Stats. 2011, Ch. 722, Sec. 1. (SB 757) Effective January 1, 2012.)

1367.31.

(a) Every health care service plan contract issued, amended, renewed, or delivered on or after January 1, 2017, shall be prohibited from requiring an enrollee to receive a referral prior to receiving coverage or services for reproductive and sexual health care.

(b) (1) For the purposes of this section, "reproductive and sexual health care services" are all reproductive and sexual health services described in Sections 6925, 6926, 6927, and 6928 of the Family Code, or Section 121020 of the Health and Safety Code, obtained by a patient.

(2) For the purposes of this section, "reproductive and sexual health care services" do not include the services subject to a health care service plan's referral procedures as required by subdivisions (a) and (b) of Section 1374.16.

(3) This section applies whether or not the patient is a minor.

(c) In implementing this section, a health care service plan may establish reasonable provisions governing utilization protocols for obtaining reproductive and sexual health care services, as provided for in subdivision (a), from health care providers participating in, or contracting with, the plan network, medical group, or independent practice association, provided that these provisions shall be consistent with the intent of this

section and shall be those customarily applied to other health care providers, such as primary care physicians and surgeons, to whom the enrollee has direct access, and shall not be more restrictive for the provision of reproductive and sexual health care services. An enrollee shall not be required to obtain prior approval from another physician, another provider, or the health care service plan prior to obtaining direct access to reproductive and sexual health care services. A health care service plan may establish reasonable provisions governing communication with the enrollee's primary care physician and surgeon regarding the enrollee's condition, treatment, and any need for followup care.

(d) This section shall not apply to a health care service plan contract that does not require enrollees to obtain a referral from their primary care physician prior to seeking covered health care services from a specialist.

(e) A health care service plan shall not impose utilization protocols related to contraceptive drugs, supplies, and devices beyond the provisions outlined in Section 1367.25 of this code or Section 14132 of the Welfare and Institutions Code.

(f) This section shall not apply to specialized health care service plan contracts or any health care service plan that is governed by Section 14131 of the Welfare and Institutions Code.

(Added by Stats. 2016, Ch. 495, Sec. 3. (AB 1954) Effective January 1, 2017.)

1368.

(a) Every plan shall do all of the following:

(1) Establish and maintain a grievance system approved by the department under which enrollees may submit their grievances to the plan. Each system shall provide reasonable procedures in accordance with department regulations that shall ensure adequate consideration of enrollee grievances and rectification when appropriate.

(2) Inform its subscribers and enrollees upon enrollment in the plan and annually thereafter of the procedure for processing and resolving grievances. The information shall include the location and telephone number where grievances may be submitted.

(3) Provide forms for grievances to be given to subscribers and enrollees who wish to register written grievances. The forms used by plans licensed pursuant to Section 1353 shall be approved by the director in advance as to format.

(4) (A) Provide for a written acknowledgment within five calendar days of the receipt of a grievance, except as noted in subparagraph (B). The acknowledgment shall advise the complainant of the following:

(i) That the grievance has been received.

(ii) The date of receipt.

(iii) The name of the plan representative and the telephone number and address of the plan representative who may be contacted about the grievance.

(B) (i) Grievances received by telephone, by facsimile, by email, or online through the plan's Internet Web site pursuant to Section 1368.015, that are not coverage disputes, disputed health care services involving medical necessity, or experimental or investigational treatment and that are resolved by the next business day following receipt are exempt from the requirements of subparagraph (A) and paragraph (5). The plan shall maintain a log of all these grievances. The log shall be periodically reviewed by the plan and shall include the following information for each complaint:

(I) The date of the call.

(II) The name of the complainant.

(III) The complainant's member identification number.

(IV) The nature of the grievance.

(V) The nature of the resolution.

(VI) The name of the plan representative who took the call and resolved the grievance.

(ii) For health plan contracts in the individual, small group, or large group markets, a health care service plan's response to grievances subject to Section 1367.24 shall also comply with subdivision (c) of Section 156.122 of Title 45 of the Code of Federal Regulations. This paragraph shall not apply to Medi-Cal managed care health care service plan contracts or any entity that enters into a contract with the State Department of Health Care Services pursuant to Chapter 7 (commencing with Section 14000), Chapter 8 (commencing with Section 14200), or Chapter 8.75 (commencing with Section 14591) of Part 3 of Division 9 of the Welfare and Institutions Code.

(5) Provide subscribers and enrollees with written responses to grievances, with a clear and concise explanation of the reasons for the plan's response. For grievances involving the delay, denial, or modification of health care services, the plan response shall describe the criteria used and the clinical reasons for its decision, including all criteria and clinical reasons related to medical necessity. If a plan, or one of its contracting providers, issues a decision delaying, denying, or modifying health care services based in whole or in part on a finding that the proposed health care services are not a covered benefit under the contract that applies to the enrollee, the decision shall clearly specify the provisions in the contract that exclude that coverage.

(6) For grievances involving the cancellation, rescission, or nonrenewal of a health care service plan contract, the health care service plan shall continue to provide coverage to the enrollee or subscriber under the terms of the health care service plan contract until a final determination of the enrollee's or subscriber's request for review has been made by the health care service plan or the director pursuant to Section 1365 and this section. This paragraph shall not apply if the health care service plan cancels or fails to renew the enrollee's or subscriber's health care service plan contract for nonpayment of premiums pursuant to paragraph (1) of subdivision (a) of Section 1365.

(7) Keep in its files all copies of grievances, and the responses thereto, for a period of five years.

(b) (1) (A) After either completing the grievance process described in subdivision (a), or participating in the process for at least 30 days, a subscriber or enrollee may submit the grievance to the department for review. In any case determined by the department to be a case involving an imminent and serious threat to the health of the patient, including, but not limited to, severe pain, the potential loss of life, limb, or major bodily function, cancellations, rescissions, or the nonrenewal of a health care service plan contract, or in any other case where the department determines that an earlier review is warranted, a subscriber or enrollee shall not be required to complete the grievance process or to participate in the process for at least 30 days before submitting a grievance to the department for review.

(B) A grievance may be submitted to the department for review and resolution prior to any arbitration.

(C) Notwithstanding subparagraphs (A) and (B), the department may refer any grievance that does not pertain to compliance with this chapter to the State Department of Public Health, the California Department of Aging, the federal Health Care Financing Administration, or any other appropriate governmental entity for investigation and resolution.

(2) If the subscriber or enrollee is a minor, or is incompetent or incapacitated, the parent, guardian, conservator, relative, or other designee of the subscriber or enrollee, as appropriate, may submit the grievance to the department as the agent of the subscriber or enrollee. Further, a provider may join with, or otherwise assist, a subscriber or enrollee, or the agent, to submit the grievance to the department. In addition, following submission of the grievance to the department, the subscriber or enrollee, or the agent, may authorize the provider to assist, including advocating on behalf of the subscriber or enrollee. For purposes of this section, a "relative" includes the parent, stepparent, spouse, adult son or daughter, grandparent, brother, sister, uncle, or aunt of the subscriber or enrollee.

(3) The department shall review the written documents submitted with the subscriber's or the enrollee's request for review, or submitted by the agent on behalf of the subscriber or enrollee. The department may ask for additional information, and may hold an informal meeting with the involved parties, including providers who have joined in submitting the grievance or who are otherwise assisting or advocating on behalf of the subscriber or enrollee. If after reviewing the record, the department concludes that the grievance, in whole or in part, is eligible for review under the independent medical review system established pursuant to Article 5.55 (commencing with Section 1374.30), the department shall immediately notify the subscriber or enrollee, or agent, of that option and shall, if requested orally or in writing, assist the subscriber or enrollee in participating in the independent medical review system.

(4) If after reviewing the record of a grievance, the department concludes that a health care service eligible for coverage and payment under a health care service plan contract has been delayed, denied, or modified by a plan, or by one of its contracting providers, in whole or in part due to a determination that the service is not medically necessary, and that determination was not communicated to the enrollee in writing along with a notice of the enrollee's potential right to participate in the independent medical review system, as required by this chapter, the director shall, by order, assess administrative penalties. A proceeding for the issuance of an order assessing administrative penalties shall be subject to appropriate notice of, and the opportunity for, a hearing with regard to the person affected in accordance with Section 1397. The administrative penalties shall not be deemed an exclusive remedy available to the director. These penalties shall be paid to the Managed Care Administrative Fines and Penalties Fund and shall be used for the purposes specified in Section 1341.45.

(5) The department shall send a written notice of the final disposition of the grievance, and the reasons therefor, to the subscriber or enrollee, the agent, to any provider that has joined with or is otherwise assisting the subscriber or enrollee, and to the plan, within 30 calendar days of receipt of the request for review unless the director, in his or her discretion, determines that additional time is reasonably necessary to fully and fairly evaluate the relevant grievance. In any case not eligible for the independent medical review system established pursuant to Article 5.55 (commencing with Section 1374.30), the department's written notice shall include, at a minimum, the following:

(A) A summary of its findings and the reasons why the department found the plan to be, or not to be, in compliance with any applicable laws, regulations, or orders of the director.

(B) A discussion of the department's contact with any medical provider, or any other independent expert relied on by the department, along with a summary of the views and qualifications of that provider or expert.

(C) If the enrollee's grievance is sustained in whole or in part, information about any corrective action taken.

(6) In any department review of a grievance involving a disputed health care service, as defined in subdivision (b) of Section 1374.30, that is not eligible for the independent medical review system established pursuant to Article 5.55 (commencing with Section 1374.30), in which the department finds that the plan has delayed, denied, or modified health care services that are medically necessary, based on the specific medical circumstances of the enrollee, and those services are a covered benefit under the terms and conditions of the health care service plan contract, the department's written notice shall do either of the following:

(A) Order the plan to promptly offer and provide those health care services to the enrollee.

(B) Order the plan to promptly reimburse the enrollee for any reasonable costs associated with urgent care or emergency services, or other extraordinary and compelling health care services, when the department finds that the enrollee's decision to secure those services outside of the plan network was reasonable under the circumstances. The department's order shall be binding on the plan.

(7) Distribution of the written notice shall not be deemed a waiver of any exemption or privilege under existing law, including, but not limited to, Section 6254.5 of the Government Code, for any information in connection with and including the written notice, nor shall any person employed or in any way retained by the department be required to testify as to that information or notice.

(8) The director shall establish and maintain a system of aging of grievances that are pending and unresolved for 30 days or more that shall include a brief explanation of the reasons each grievance is pending and unresolved for 30 days or more.

(9) A subscriber or enrollee, or the agent acting on behalf of a subscriber or enrollee, may also request voluntary mediation with the plan prior to exercising the right to submit a grievance to the department. The use of mediation services shall not preclude the right to submit a grievance to the department upon completion of mediation. In order to initiate mediation, the subscriber or enrollee, or the agent acting on behalf of the subscriber or enrollee, and the plan shall voluntarily agree to mediation. Expenses for mediation shall be borne equally by both sides. The department shall have no administrative or enforcement responsibilities in connection with the voluntary mediation process authorized by this paragraph.

(c) The plan's grievance system shall include a system of aging of grievances that are pending and unresolved for 30 days or more. The plan shall provide a quarterly report to the director of grievances pending and unresolved for 30 or more days with separate categories of grievances for Medicare enrollees and Medi-Cal enrollees. The plan shall include with the report a brief explanation of the reasons each grievance is pending and unresolved for 30 days or more. The plan may include the following statement in the quarterly report that is made available to the public by the director:

"Under Medicare and Medi-Cal law, Medicare enrollees and Medi-Cal enrollees each have separate avenues of appeal that are not available to other enrollees. Therefore, grievances pending and unresolved may reflect enrollees pursuing their Medicare or Medi-Cal appeal rights."

If requested by a plan, the director shall include this statement in a written report made available to the public and prepared by the director that describes or compares grievances that are pending and unresolved with the plan for 30 days or more. Additionally, the director shall, if requested by a plan, append to that written report a brief explanation, provided in writing by the plan, of the reasons why grievances described in that written report are pending and unresolved for 30 days or more. The director shall not be required to include a statement or append a brief explanation to a written report that the director is required to prepare under this chapter, including Sections 1380 and 1397.5.

(d) Subject to subparagraph (C) of paragraph (1) of subdivision (b), the grievance or resolution procedures authorized by this section shall be in addition to any other procedures that may be available to any person, and failure to pursue, exhaust, or engage in the procedures described in this section shall not preclude the use of any other remedy provided by law.

(e) Nothing in this section shall be construed to allow the submission to the department of any provider grievance under this section. However, as part of a provider's duty to advocate for medically appropriate health care for his or her patients pursuant to Sections 510 and 2056 of the Business and Professions Code, nothing in this subdivision shall be construed to prohibit a provider from contacting and informing the department about any concerns he or she has regarding compliance with or enforcement of this chapter.

(f) To the extent required by Section 2719 of the federal Public Health Service Act (42 U.S.C. Sec. 300gg-19) and any subsequent rules or regulations, there shall be an independent external review pursuant to the standards required by the United States Secretary of Health and Human Services of a health care service plan's cancellation, rescission, or nonrenewal of an enrollee's or subscriber's coverage.

(Amended by Stats. 2015, Ch. 654, Sec. 3. (SB 282) Effective January 1, 2016.)

1368.01.

(a) The grievance system shall require the plan to resolve grievances within 30 days, except as provided in subdivision (c).

(b) The grievance system shall include a requirement for expedited plan review of grievances for cases involving an imminent and serious threat to the health of the patient, including, but not limited to, severe pain, potential loss of life, limb, or major bodily function. When the plan has notice of a case requiring expedited review, the grievance system shall require the plan to immediately inform enrollees and subscribers in writing of their right to notify the department of the grievance. The grievance system shall also require the plan to provide enrollees, subscribers, and the department with a written statement on the disposition or pending status of the grievance no later than three days from receipt of the grievance, except as provided in subdivision (c). Paragraph (4) of subdivision (a) of Section 1368 shall not apply to grievances handled pursuant to this section.

(c) A health care service plan contract in the individual, small group, or large group markets that provides coverage for outpatient prescription drugs shall comply with subdivision (c) of Section 156.122 of Title 45 of the Code of Federal Regulations. This subdivision shall not apply to Medi-Cal managed care health care service plan contracts or any entity that enters into a contract with the State Department of Health Care Services pursuant to Chapter 7 (commencing with Section 14000), Chapter 8 (commencing with Section 14200), or Chapter 8.75 (commencing with Section 14591) of Part 3 of Division 9 of the Welfare and Institutions Code.

(Amended by Stats. 2015, Ch. 654, Sec. 4. (SB 282) Effective January 1, 2016.)

1368.015.

(a) Effective July 1, 2003, every plan with an Internet Web site shall provide an online form through its Internet Web site that subscribers or enrollees can use to file with the plan a grievance, as described in Section 1368, online.

(b) The Internet Web site shall have an easily accessible online grievance submission procedure that shall be accessible through a hyperlink on the Internet Web site's home page or member services portal clearly identified as "GRIEVANCE FORM." All information submitted through this process shall be processed through a secure server.

(c) The online grievance submission process shall be approved by the Department of Managed Health Care and shall meet the following requirements:

(1) It shall utilize an online grievance form in HTML format that allows the user to enter required information directly into the form.

(2) It shall allow the subscriber or enrollee to preview the grievance that will be submitted, including the opportunity to edit the form prior to submittal.

(3) It shall include a current hyperlink to the California Department of Managed Health Care Internet Web site, and shall include a statement in a legible font that is clearly distinguishable from other content on the page and is in a legible size and type, containing the following language:

"The California Department of Managed Health Care is responsible for regulating health care service plans. If you have a grievance against your health plan, you should first telephone your health plan at (insert health plan's telephone number) and use your health plan's grievance process before contacting the department. Utilizing this grievance procedure does not prohibit any potential legal rights or remedies that may be available to you. If you need help with a grievance involving an emergency, a grievance that has not been satisfactorily resolved by your health plan, or a grievance that has remained unresolved for more than 30 days, you may call the department for assistance. You may also be eligible for an Independent Medical Review (IMR). If you are eligible for IMR, the IMR process will provide an impartial review of medical decisions made by a health plan related to the medical necessity of a proposed service or treatment, coverage decisions for treatments that are experimental or investigational in nature and payment disputes for emergency or urgent medical services. The department also has a toll-free telephone number (1-888-HMO-2219) and a TDD line (1-877-688-9891) for the hearing and speech impaired. The department's Internet Web site http://www.hmohelp.ca.gov has complaint forms, IMR application forms and instructions online."

The plan shall update the URL, hyperlink, and telephone numbers in this statement as necessary.

(d) A plan that utilizes a hardware system that does not have the minimum system requirements to support the software necessary to meet the requirements of this section is exempt from these requirements until January 1, 2006.

(e) For purposes of this section, the following terms shall have the following meanings:

(1) "Homepage" means the first page or welcome page of an Internet Web site that serves as a starting point for navigation of the Internet Web site.

(2) "HTML" means Hypertext Markup Language, the authoring language used to create documents on the World Wide Web, which defines the structure and layout of a Web document.

(3) "Hyperlink" means a special HTML code that allows text or graphics to serve as a link that, when clicked on, takes a user to another place in the same document, to another document, or to another Internet Web site or Web page.

(4) "Member services portal" means the first page or welcome page of an Internet Web site that can be reached directly by the Internet Web site's homepage and that serves as a starting point for a navigation of member services available on the Internet Web site.

(5) "Secure server" means an Internet connection to an Internet Web site that encrypts and decrypts transmissions, protecting them against third-party tampering and allowing for the secure transfer of data.

(6) "URL" or "Uniform Resource Locator" means the address of an Internet Web site or the location of a resource on the World Wide Web that allows a browser to locate and retrieve the Internet Web site or the resource.

(7) "Internet Web site" means a site or location on the World Wide Web.

(f) (1) Every health care service plan, except a plan that primarily serves Medi-Cal or Healthy Families Program enrollees, shall maintain an Internet Web site. For a health care service plan that provides coverage for professional mental health services, the Internet Web site shall include, but not be limited to, providing information to subscribers, enrollees, and providers that will assist subscribers and enrollees in accessing mental health services as well as the information described in Section 1368.016.

(2) The provision in paragraph (1) that requires compliance with Section 1368.016 shall not apply to a health care service plan that contracts with a specialized health care service plan, insurer, or other entity to cover professional mental health services for its enrollees, provided that the health care service plan provides a link on its Internet Web site to an Internet Web site operated by the specialized health care service plan, insurer, or other entity with which it contracts, and that plan, insurer, or other entity complies with Section 1368.016.

(Amended by Stats. 2009, Ch. 575, Sec. 2. (SB 296) Effective January 1, 2010.)
1368.016.

(a) A health care service plan that provides coverage for professional mental health services, including a specialized health care service plan that provides coverage for professional mental health services, shall, pursuant to subdivision (f) of Section 1368.015, include on its Internet Web site, or provide a link to, the following information:

(1) A telephone number that the enrollee or provider can call, during normal business hours, for assistance obtaining mental health benefits coverage information, including the extent to which benefits have been exhausted, in-network provider access information, and claims processing information.

(2) A link to prescription drug formularies posted pursuant to Section 1367.205, or instructions on how to obtain the formulary, as described in Section 1367.20.

(3) A detailed summary that describes the process by which the plan reviews and authorizes or approves, modifies, or denies requests for health care services as described in Sections 1363.5 and 1367.01.

(4) Lists of providers or instructions on how to obtain the provider list, as required by Section 1367.27.

(5) A detailed summary of the enrollee grievance process as described in Sections 1368 and 1368.015.

(6) A detailed description of how an enrollee may request continuity of care pursuant to subdivisions (a) and (b) of Section 1373.95.

(7) Information concerning the right, and applicable procedure, of an enrollee to request an independent medical review pursuant to Section 1374.30.

(b) Any modified material described in subdivision (a) shall be updated at least quarterly.

(c) The information described in subdivision (a) may be made available through a secured Internet Web site that is only accessible to enrollees.

(d) The material described in subdivision (a) shall also be made available to enrollees in hard copy upon request.

(e) This article does not preclude a health care service plan from including additional information on its Internet Web site for applicants, enrollees or subscribers, or providers, including, but not limited to, the cost of procedures or services by health care providers in a plan's network.

(f) The department shall include on the department's Internet Web site a link to the Internet Web site of each health care service plan and specialized health care service plan described in subdivision (a).

(g) This section shall not apply to Medicare supplement insurance, employee assistance programs, CHAMPUS supplement insurance, or TRI-CARE supplement insurance, or to hospital indemnity, accident-only, and specified disease insurance. This section shall also not apply to specialized health care service plans, except behavioral health-only plans.

(h) This section shall not apply to a health care service plan that contracts with a specialized health care service plan, insurer, or other entity to cover professional mental health services for its enrollees, provided that the health care service plan provides a link on its Internet Web site to an Internet Web site operated by the specialized health care service plan, insurer, or other entity with which it contracts, and that plan, insurer, or other entity complies with this section or Section 10123.199 of the Insurance Code.

(Amended by Stats. 2018, Ch. 687, Sec. 2. (SB 910) Effective January 1, 2019.)
1368.02.

(a) The director shall establish and maintain a toll-free telephone number for the purpose of receiving complaints regarding health care service plans regulated by the director.

(b) Every health care service plan shall publish the department's toll-free telephone number, the department's TDD line for the hearing and speech impaired, the plan's telephone number, and the department's Internet Web site address, on every plan contract, on every evidence of coverage, on copies of plan grievance procedures, on plan complaint forms, and on all written notices to enrollees required under the grievance process of the plan, including any written communications to an enrollee that offer the enrollee the opportunity to participate in the grievance process of the plan and on all written responses to grievances. The department's telephone number, the department's TDD line, the plan's telephone number, and the department's Internet Web site address shall be displayed by the plan in each of these documents in 12-point boldface type in the following regular type statement:

"The California Department of Managed Health Care is responsible for regulating health care service plans. If you have a grievance against your health plan, you should first telephone your health plan at (insert health plan's telephone number) and use your health plan's grievance process before contacting the department. Utilizing this grievance procedure does not prohibit any potential legal rights or remedies that may be available to you. If you need help with a grievance involving an emergency, a grievance that has not been satisfactorily resolved by your health plan, or a grievance that has remained unresolved for more than 30 days, you may call the department for assistance. You may also be eligible for an Independent Medical Review (IMR). If you are eligible for IMR, the IMR process will provide an impartial review of medical decisions made by a health plan related to the medical necessity of a proposed service or treatment, coverage decisions for treatments that are experimental or investigational in nature and payment disputes for emergency or urgent medical services. The department also has a toll-free telephone number (1-888-HMO-2219) and a TDD line (1-877-688-9891) for the hearing and speech impaired. The department's Internet Web site http://www.hmohelp.ca.gov has complaint forms, IMR application forms and instructions online."

(Amended by Stats. 2011, Ch. 552, Sec. 3. (AB 922) Effective January 1, 2012.)
1368.03.

(a) The department may require enrollees and subscribers to participate in a plan's grievance process for up to 30 days before pursuing a grievance through the department or the independent medical review system. However, the department may not impose this waiting period for expedited review cases covered by subdivision (b) of Section 1368.01 or in any other case where the department determines that an earlier review is warranted.

(b) Notwithstanding subdivision (a), the department may refer any grievance issue that does not pertain to compliance with this chapter to the State Department of Health Services, the California Department of Aging, the federal Health Care Financing Administration, or any other appropriate governmental entity for investigation and resolution.

(c) This section shall become operative on January 1, 2001, and then only if Assembly Bill 55 of the 1999–2000 Regular Session is enacted.

(Repealed (in Sec. 4) and added by Stats. 1999, Ch. 542, Sec. 5. Effective January 1, 2000. Section operative January 1, 2001, by its own provisions.)

1368.04.

(a) The director shall investigate and take enforcement action against plans regarding grievances reviewed and found by the department to involve noncompliance with the requirements of this chapter, including grievances that have been reviewed pursuant to the independent medical review system established pursuant to Article 5.55 (commencing with Section 1374.30). Where substantial harm to an enrollee has occurred as a result of plan noncompliance, the director shall, by order, assess administrative penalties subject to appropriate notice of, and the opportunity for, a hearing with regard to the person affected in accordance with Section 1397. The administrative penalties shall not be deemed an exclusive remedy available to the director. These penalties shall be paid to the Managed Care Administrative Fines and Penalties Fund and shall be used for the purposes specified in Section 1341.45. The director shall periodically evaluate grievances to determine if any audit, investigative, or enforcement actions should be undertaken by the department.

(b) The director may, after appropriate notice and opportunity for hearing in accordance with Section 1397, by order, assess administrative penalties if the director determines that a health care service plan has knowingly committed, or has performed with a frequency that indicates a general business practice, either of the following:

(1) Repeated failure to act promptly and reasonably to investigate and resolve grievances in accordance with Section 1368.01.

(2) Repeated failure to act promptly and reasonably to resolve grievances when the obligation of the plan to the enrollee or subscriber is reasonably clear.

(c) The administrative penalties available to the director pursuant to this section are not exclusive, and may be sought and employed in any combination with civil, criminal, and other administrative remedies deemed warranted by the director to enforce this chapter.

(d) The administrative penalties authorized pursuant to this section shall be paid to the Managed Care Administrative Fines and Penalties Fund and shall be used for the purposes specified in Section 1341.45.

(Amended by Stats. 2008, Ch. 607, Sec. 6. Effective September 30, 2008.)

1368.05.

(a) (1) By enacting this section, which was originally enacted by Assembly Bill 922 (Chapter 552 of the Statutes of 2011), the Legislature recognizes that, because of the enactment of federal health care reform on March 23, 2010, and the implementation of various provisions by January 1, 2014, and the ongoing complexities of health care reform, it is appropriate to transfer the direct consumer assistance activities that were newly conferred on the Office of Patient Advocate to the Department of Managed Health Care, and the Legislature recognizes that these new duties are necessary to be carried out by the department in partnership with community-based consumer assistance organizations for the purposes of serving California's health care consumers.

(2) In addition to maintaining the toll-free telephone number for the purpose of receiving complaints regarding health care service plans as required in Section 1368.02, the department and its contractors shall carry out these new responsibilities, which include assisting consumers in navigating private and public health care coverage and assisting consumers in determining the regulator that regulates the health care coverage of a particular consumer. In order to further assist in implementing health care reform, the department and its contractors shall also receive and respond to inquiries, complaints, and requests for assistance and education concerning health care coverage available in California.

(b) (1) The department shall annually contract with community-based organizations in furtherance of providing assistance to consumers as described in subdivision (a), as authorized by and in accordance with Section 19130 of the Government Code.

(2) These organizations shall be community-based nonprofit consumer assistance programs that shall include in their mission the assistance of, and duty to, health care consumers.

(3) Contracting consumer assistance organizations shall have experience in assisting consumers in navigating the local health care system, advising consumers regarding their health care coverage options, assisting consumers with problems in accessing health care services, and serving consumers with special needs, including, but not limited to, consumers with limited-English language proficiency, consumers requiring culturally competent services, low-income consumers, consumers with disabilities, consumers with low literacy rates, and consumers with multiple health conditions, including behavioral health. The organizations shall also have experience with, and the capacity for, collecting and reporting data regarding the consumers they assist, including demographic data, source of coverage, regulator, type of problem or issue, and resolution of complaints.

(Amended by Stats. 2015, Ch. 303, Sec. 256. (AB 731) Effective January 1, 2016.)

1368.1.

(a) A plan that denies coverage to an enrollee with a terminal illness, which for the purposes of this section refers to an incurable or irreversible condition that has a high probability of causing death within one year or less, for treatment, services, or supplies deemed experimental, as recommended by a participating plan provider, shall provide to the enrollee within five business days all of the following information:

(1) A statement setting forth the specific medical and scientific reasons for denying coverage.

(2) A description of alternative treatment, services, or supplies covered by the plan, if any. Compliance with this subdivision by a plan shall not be construed to mean that the plan is engaging in the unlawful practice of medicine.

(3) Copies of the plan's grievance procedures or complaint form, or both. The complaint form shall provide an opportunity for the enrollee to request a conference as part of the plan's grievance system provided under Section 1368.

(b) Upon receiving a complaint form requesting a conference pursuant to paragraph (3) of subdivision (a), the plan shall provide the enrollee, within 30 calendar days, an opportunity to attend a conference, to review the information provided to the enrollee pursuant to paragraphs (1) and (2) of subdivision (a), conducted by a plan representative having authority to determine the disposition of the complaint. The plan shall allow attendance, in person, at the conference, by an enrollee, a designee of the enrollee, or both, or, if the enrollee is a minor or incompetent, the parent, guardian, or conservator of the enrollee, as appropriate. However, the conference required by this subdivision shall be held within five business days if the treating participating physician determines, after consultation with the health plan medical director or his or her designee, based on standard medical practice, that the effectiveness of either the proposed treatment, services, or supplies or any alternative treatment, services, or supplies covered by the plan, would be materially reduced if not provided at the earliest possible date.

(c) Nothing in this section shall limit the responsibilities, rights, or authority provided in Sections 1370 and 1370.1.

(Added by Stats. 1994, Ch. 582, Sec. 1. Effective January 1, 1995.)

1368.2.

(a) On and after January 1, 2002, every group health care service plan contract, except a specialized health care service plan contract, which is issued, amended, or renewed, shall include a provision for hospice care.

(b) The hospice care shall at a minimum be equivalent to hospice care provided by the federal Medicare program pursuant to Title XVIII of the Social Security Act.

(c) The hospice care provided under this section is not required to include preliminary services set forth in subdivision (d) of Section 1749. However, an enrollee who receives those preliminary services shall remain eligible for coverage of curative treatment by a health care service plan during the course of preliminary services and prior to the election of hospice services.

(d) The following are applicable to this section and to paragraph (7) of subdivision (b) of Section 1345:

(1) The definitions in Section 1746, except for subdivisions (o) and (p) of that section.

(2) The "federal regulations" which means the regulations adopted for hospice care under Title XVIII of the Social Security Act in Title 42 of the Code of Federal Regulations, Chapter IV, Part 418, except Subparts A, B, G, and H, and any amendments or successor provisions thereto.

(e) The director no later than January 1, 2001, shall adopt regulations to implement this section. The regulations shall meet all of the following requirements:

(1) Be consistent with all material elements of the federal regulations that are not by their terms applicable only to eligible Medicare beneficiaries. If there is a conflict between a federal regulation and any state regulation, other than those adopted pursuant to this section, the director shall adopt the regulation that is most favorable for plan subscribers, members or enrollees to receive hospice care.

(2) Be consistent with any other applicable federal or state laws.

(3) Be consistent with the definitions of Section 1746, except for subdivisions (o) and (p) of that section.

(f) This section is not applicable to the subscribers, members, or enrollees of a health care service plan who elect to receive hospice care under the Medicare program.

(Amended by Stats. 2005, Ch. 77, Sec. 30. Effective January 1, 2006.)

1368.5.

(a) Every health care service plan that offers coverage for a service that is within the scope of practice of a duly licensed pharmacist may pay or reimburse the cost of the service performed by a pharmacist for the plan if the pharmacist otherwise provides services for the plan.

(b) Payment or reimbursement may be made pursuant to this section for a service performed by a duly licensed pharmacist only when all of the following conditions are met:

(1) The service performed is within the lawful scope of practice of the pharmacist.

(2) The coverage otherwise provides reimbursement for identical services performed by other licensed health care providers.

(c) Nothing in this section shall require the plan to pay a claim to more than one provider for duplicate service or be interpreted to limit physician reimbursement.

(Added by Stats. 1996, Ch. 527, Sec. 1. Effective January 1, 1997.)

1368.6.

(a) Effective January 1, 2020, there is established a pilot project to assess the impact of health care service plan and pharmacy benefit manager prohibitions on the dispensing of certain amounts of prescription drugs by network retail pharmacies. The provisions of subdivision (b) shall apply to pharmacy providers located in the Counties of Riverside and Sonoma.

(b) Pursuant to the pilot project, a health care service plan shall not prohibit, or permit any delegated pharmacy benefit manager to prohibit, a pharmacy provider from dispensing a particular amount of a prescribed medication if the plan or pharmacy benefit manager allows that amount to be dispensed through a pharmacy owned or controlled by the plan or pharmacy benefit manager, unless the prescription drug is subject to restricted distribution by the federal Food and Drug Administration or requires special handling, provider coordination, or patient education that cannot be provided by a retail pharmacy.

(c) This section shall not be construed to prohibit a health care service plan or pharmacy benefit manager from requiring the same reimbursement and terms and conditions for a pharmacy network provider as for a pharmacy owned or controlled by the health care service plan or pharmacy benefit manager.

(d) This section shall not be construed to prohibit differential cost sharing designed to encourage or discourage the use of mail-order pharmacy services or preferred pharmacies.

(e) On or before July 1, 2020, health care service plans subject to this section shall report annually to the Department of Managed Health Care information and data relating to changes, if any, to costs and utilization of prescription drugs attributable to the prohibition of contract terms in subdivision (b). The department shall solicit and receive any additional information relevant to changes in costs or utilization attributable to the pilot project from other interested stakeholders. The department shall summarize data received pursuant to this subdivision and provide the summary to the Governor and health policy committees of the Legislature on or before December 31, 2022.

(f) This section shall remain in effect only until January 1, 2023, and as of that date is repealed.

(Added by Stats. 2018, Ch. 905, Sec. 3. (AB 315) Effective January 1, 2019. Repealed as of January 1, 2023, by its own provisions.)

1368.7.

(a) A health care service plan shall provide an enrollee who has been displaced by a state of emergency, as declared by the Governor pursuant to Section 8625 of the Government Code, access to medically necessary health care services.

(b) Within 48 hours of a declaration by the Governor of a state of emergency that displaces or has the immediate potential to displace enrollees, a health care service plan operating in the county or counties included in the declaration shall file with the department a notification describing whether the plan has experienced or expects to experience any disruption to the operation of the plan, explaining how the plan is communicating with potentially impacted enrollees, and summarizing the actions the plan has taken or is in the process of taking to ensure that the health care needs of enrollees are met. This may require the plan to take actions, including, but not limited to, the following:

(1) Relax time limits for prior authorization, precertification, or referrals.

(2) Extend filing deadlines for claims.

(3) Suspend prescription refill limitations and allow an impacted enrollee to refill his or her prescriptions at an out-of-network pharmacy.

(4) Authorize an enrollee to replace medical equipment or supplies.

(5) Allow an enrollee to access an appropriate out-of-network provider if an in-network provider is unavailable due to the state of emergency or if the enrollee is out of the area due to displacement.

(6) Have a toll-free telephone number that an affected enrollee may call for answers to questions, including questions about the loss of health insurance identification cards, access to prescription refills, or how to access health care.

(c) This section shall not be construed to limit the Governor's authority under the California Emergency Services Act (Chapter 7 (commencing with Section 8550) of Division 1 of Title 2 of the Government Code), or the director's authority under any provision of this chapter.

(Added by Stats. 2018, Ch. 196, Sec. 1. (AB 2941) Effective January 1, 2019.)

1369.

Every plan shall establish procedures to permit subscribers and enrollees to participate in establishing the public policy of the plan. For purposes of this section, public policy means acts performed by a plan or its employees and staff to assure the comfort, dignity, and convenience of patients who rely on the plan's facilities to provide health care services to them, their families, and the public.

(Amended by Stats. 2005, Ch. 45, Sec. 1. Effective January 1, 2006.)

1370.

Every plan shall establish procedures in accordance with department regulations for continuously reviewing the quality of care, performance of medical personnel, utilization of services and facilities, and costs. Notwithstanding any other provision of law, there shall be no monetary liability on the part of, and no cause of action for damages shall arise against, any person who participates in plan or provider quality of care or utilization reviews by peer review committees which are composed chiefly of physicians and surgeons or dentists, psychologists, or optometrists, or any of the above, for any act performed during the reviews if the person acts without malice, has made a reasonable effort to obtain the facts of the matter, and believes that the action taken is warranted by the facts, and neither the proceedings nor the records of the reviews shall be subject to discovery, nor shall any person in attendance at the reviews be required to testify as to what transpired thereat. Disclosure of the proceedings or records to the governing body of a plan or to any person or entity designated by the plan to review activities of the plan or provider committees shall not alter the status of the records or of the proceedings as privileged communications.

The above prohibition relating to discovery or testimony shall not apply to the statements made by any person in attendance at a review who is a party to an action or proceeding the subject matter of which was reviewed, or to any person requesting hospital staff privileges, or in any action against an insurance carrier alleging bad faith by the carrier in refusing to accept a settlement offer within the policy limits, or to the director in conducting surveys pursuant to Section 1380.

This section shall not be construed to confer immunity from liability on any health care service plan. In any case in which, but for the enactment of the preceding provisions of this section, a cause of action would arise against a health care service plan, the cause of action shall exist notwithstanding the provisions of this section.

(Amended by Stats. 1999, Ch. 525, Sec. 105. Effective January 1, 2000. Operative July 1, 2000, or sooner, by Sec. 214 of Ch. 525.)

1370.1.

Nothing in this article shall be construed to prevent a plan from utilizing subcommittees to participate in peer review activities, nor to prevent a plan from delegating the responsibilities required by Section 1370, as it determines to be appropriate, to subcommittees including subcommittees composed of a majority of nonphysician health care providers licensed pursuant to the Business and Professions Code, so long as the plan controls the scope of authority delegated and may revoke all or part of this authority at any time. Persons who participate in the subcommittees shall be entitled to the same immunity from monetary liability and actions for civil damages as persons who participate in plan or provider peer review committees pursuant to Section 1370.

(Amended by Stats. 1988, Ch. 828, Sec. 2.)

1370.2.

Upon an appeal to the plan of a contested claim, the plan shall refer the claim to the medical director or other appropriately licensed health care provider. This health care provider or the medical director shall review the appeal and, if he or she determines that he or she is competent to evaluate the specific clinical issues presented in the claim, shall make a determination on the appealed claim. If the health care provider or medical director determines that he or she is not competent to evaluate the specific clinical issues of the appealed claim, prior to making a determination, he or she shall consult with an appropriately licensed health care provider who is competent to evaluate the specific clinical issues presented in the claim. For the purposes of this section, "competent to evaluate the specific clinical issues" means that the reviewer has education, training, and relevant expertise that is pertinent for evaluating the specific clinical issues that serve as the basis of the contested claim. The requirements of this section shall apply to claims that are contested on the basis of a clinical issue, the necessity for treatment, or the type of treatment proposed or utilized. The plan shall determine whether or not to use an appropriate specialist provider in the review of contested claims.

(Added by Stats. 1994, Ch. 614, Sec. 2. Effective January 1, 1995.)

1370.4.

(a) Every health care service plan shall provide an external, independent review process to examine the plan's coverage decisions regarding experimental or investigational therapies for individual enrollees who meet all of the following criteria:

(1) (A) The enrollee has a life-threatening or seriously debilitating condition.

(B) For purposes of this section, "life-threatening" means either or both of the following:

(i) Diseases or conditions where the likelihood of death is high unless the course of the disease is interrupted.

(ii) Diseases or conditions with potentially fatal outcomes, where the end point of clinical intervention is survival.

(C) For purposes of this section, "seriously debilitating" means diseases or conditions that cause major irreversible morbidity.

(2) The enrollee's physician certifies that the enrollee has a condition, as defined in paragraph (1), for which standard therapies have not been effective in improving the condition of the enrollee, for which standard therapies would not be medically appropriate for the enrollee, or for which there is no more beneficial standard therapy covered by the plan than the therapy proposed pursuant to paragraph (3).

(3) Either (A) the enrollee's physician, who is under contract with or employed by the plan, has recommended a drug, device, procedure, or other therapy that the physician certifies in writing is likely to be more beneficial to the enrollee than any available standard therapies, or (B) the enrollee, or the enrollee's physician who is a licensed, board-certified or board-eligible physician qualified to practice in the area of practice appropriate to treat the enrollee's condition, has requested a therapy that, based on two documents from the medical and scientific evidence, as defined in subdivision (d), is likely to be more beneficial for the enrollee than any available standard therapy. The physician certification pursuant to this subdivision shall include a statement of the evidence relied upon by the physician in certifying his or her recommendation. Nothing in this subdivision shall be construed to require the plan to pay for the services of a nonparticipating physician provided pursuant to this subdivision, that are not otherwise covered pursuant to the plan contact.

(4) The enrollee has been denied coverage by the plan for a drug, device, procedure, or other therapy recommended or requested pursuant to paragraph (3).

(5) The specific drug, device, procedure, or other therapy recommended pursuant to paragraph (3) would be a covered service, except for the plan's determination that the therapy is experimental or investigational.

(b) The plan's decision to delay, deny, or modify experimental or investigational therapies shall be subject to the independent medical review process under Article 5.55 (commencing with Section 1374.30) except that, in lieu of the information specified in subdivision (b) of Section 1374.33, an independent medical reviewer shall base his or her determination on relevant medical and scientific evidence, including, but not limited to, the medical and scientific evidence defined in subdivision (d).

(c) The independent medical review process shall also meet the following criteria:

(1) The plan shall notify eligible enrollees in writing of the opportunity to request the external independent review within five business days of the decision to deny coverage.

(2) If the enrollee's physician determines that the proposed therapy would be significantly less effective if not promptly initiated, the analyses and recommendations of the experts on the panel shall be rendered within seven days of the request for expedited review. At the request of the expert, the deadline shall be extended by up to three days for a delay in providing the documents required. The timeframes specified in this paragraph shall be in addition to any otherwise applicable timeframes contained in subdivision (c) of Section 1374.33.

(3) Each expert's analysis and recommendation shall be in written form and state the reasons the requested therapy is or is not likely to be more beneficial for the enrollee

than any available standard therapy, and the reasons that the expert recommends that the therapy should or should not be provided by the plan, citing the enrollee's specific medical condition, the relevant documents provided, and the relevant medical and scientific evidence, including, but not limited to, the medical and scientific evidence as defined in subdivision (d), to support the expert's recommendation.

(4) Coverage for the services required under this section shall be provided subject to the terms and conditions generally applicable to other benefits under the plan contract.

(d) For the purposes of subdivision (b), "medical and scientific evidence" means the following sources:

(1) Peer-reviewed scientific studies published in or accepted for publication by medical journals that meet nationally recognized requirements for scientific manuscripts and that submit most of their published articles for review by experts who are not part of the editorial staff.

(2) Peer-reviewed literature, biomedical compendia, and other medical literature that meet the criteria of the National Institutes of Health's National Library of Medicine for indexing in Index Medicus, Excerpta Medicus (EMBASE), Medline, and MEDLARS database of Health Services Technology Assessment Research (HSTAR).

(3) Medical journals recognized by the Secretary of Health and Human Services, under Section 1861(t)(2) of the Social Security Act.

(4) Either of the following reference compendia:

(A) The American Hospital Formulary Service's Drug Information.

(B) The American Dental Association Accepted Dental Therapeutics.

(5) Any of the following reference compendia, if recognized by the federal Centers for Medicare and Medicaid Services as part of an anticancer chemotherapeutic regimen:

(A) The Elsevier Gold Standard's Clinical Pharmacology.

(B) The National Comprehensive Cancer Network Drug and Biologics Compendium.

(C) The Thomson Micromedex DrugDex.

(6) Findings, studies, or research conducted by or under the auspices of federal government agencies and nationally recognized federal research institutes, including the Federal Agency for Health Care Policy and Research, National Institutes of Health, National Cancer Institute, National Academy of Sciences, Health Care Financing Administration, Congressional Office of Technology Assessment, and any national board recognized by the National Institutes of Health for the purpose of evaluating the medical value of health services.

(7) Peer-reviewed abstracts accepted for presentation at major medical association meetings.

(e) The independent review process established by this section shall be required on and after January 1, 2001.

(Amended by Stats. 2009, Ch. 479, Sec. 2. (AB 830) Effective January 1, 2010.)
1370.6.

(a) For an enrollee diagnosed with cancer and accepted into a phase I, phase II, phase III, or phase IV clinical trial for cancer, every health care service plan contract, except a specialized health care service plan contract, that is issued, amended, delivered, or renewed in this state, shall provide coverage for all routine patient care costs related to the clinical trial if the enrollee's treating physician, who is providing covered health care services to the enrollee under the enrollee's health benefit plan contract, recommends participation in the clinical trial after determining that participation in the clinical trial has a meaningful potential to benefit the enrollee. For purposes of this section, a clinical trial's endpoints shall not be defined exclusively to test toxicity, but shall have a therapeutic intent.

(b) (1) "Routine patient care costs" means the costs associated with the provision of health care services, including drugs, items, devices, and services that would otherwise be covered under the plan or contract if those drugs, items, devices, and services were not provided in connection with an approved clinical trial program, including:

(A) Health care services typically provided absent a clinical trial.

(B) Health care services required solely for the provision of the investigational drug, item, device, or service.

(C) Health care services required for the clinically appropriate monitoring of the investigational item or service.

(D) Health care services provided for the prevention of complications arising from the provision of the investigational drug, item, device, or service.

(E) Health care services needed for the reasonable and necessary care arising from the provision of the investigational drug, item, device, or service, including the diagnosis or treatment of the complications.

(2) For purposes of this section, "routine patient care costs" does not include the costs associated with the provision of any of the following:

(A) Drugs or devices that have not been approved by the federal Food and Drug Administration and that are associated with the clinical trial.

(B) Services other than health care services, such as travel, housing, companion expenses, and other nonclinical expenses, that an enrollee may require as a result of the treatment being provided for purposes of the clinical trial.

(C) Any item or service that is provided solely to satisfy data collection and analysis needs and that is not used in the clinical management of the patient.

(D) Health care services that, except for the fact that they are being provided in a clinical trial, are otherwise specifically excluded from coverage under the enrollee's health plan.

(E) Health care services customarily provided by the research sponsors free of charge for any enrollee in the trial.

(3) Nothing in this section shall require a health care service plan contracting with the State Department of Health Services for the purpose of providing Medi-Cal benefits to enrolled beneficiaries or contracting with the Managed Risk Medical Insurance Board for

the purposes of providing benefits under the Healthy Families Program, the Access for Infants and Mothers Program, or the California Major Risk Medical Insurance Program, to be responsible for reimbursement of services excluded from their contract because another entity is responsible by statute or otherwise for reimbursement of the service provider.

(c) The treatment shall be provided in a clinical trial that either:

(1) Involves a drug that is exempt under federal regulations from a new drug application.

(2) Is approved by one of the following:

(A) One of the National Institutes of Health.

(B) The federal Food and Drug Administration, in the form of an investigational new drug application.

(C) The United States Department of Defense.

(D) The United States Veterans' Administration.

(d) In the case of health care services provided by a participating provider, the payment rate shall be at the agreed-upon rate. In the case of a nonparticipating provider, the payment shall be at the negotiated rate the plan would otherwise pay to a participating provider for the same services, less any applicable copayments and deductibles.

(e) Nothing in this section shall be construed to prohibit a health care service plan from restricting coverage for clinical trials to participating hospitals and physicians in California unless the protocol for the clinical trial is not provided for at a California hospital or by a California physician.

(f) The provision of services when required by this section shall not, in itself, give rise to liability on the part of the health care service plan.

(g) Nothing in this section shall be construed to limit, prohibit, or modify an enrollee's rights to the independent review process available under Section 1370.4 or to the Independent Medical Review System available under Article 5.55 (commencing with Section 1374.30).

(h) Nothing in this section shall be construed to otherwise limit or modify any existing requirements under the provisions of this chapter or to prevent application of copayment or deductible provisions in a plan.

(i) Copayments and deductibles applied to services delivered in a clinical trial shall be the same as those applied to the same services if not delivered in a clinical trial.

(Added by Stats. 2001, Ch. 172, Sec. 1. Effective January 1, 2002.)
1371.

(a) (1) A health care service plan, including a specialized health care service plan, shall reimburse claims or a portion of a claim, whether in state or out of state, as soon as practicable, but no later than 30 working days after receipt of the claim by the health care service plan, or if the health care service plan is a health maintenance organization, 45 working days after receipt of the claim by the health care service plan, unless the claim or portion thereof is contested by the plan, in which case the claimant shall be notified, in writing, that the claim is contested or denied, within 30 working days after receipt of the claim by the health care service plan, or if the health care service plan is a health maintenance organization, 45 working days after receipt of the claim by the health care service plan. The notice that a claim is being contested shall identify the portion of the claim that is contested and the specific reasons for contesting the claim.

(2) If an uncontested claim is not reimbursed by delivery to the claimants' address of record within the respective 30 or 45 working days after receipt, interest shall accrue at the rate of 15 percent per annum beginning with the first calendar day after the 30- or 45-working-day period. A health care service plan shall automatically include in its payment of the claim all interest that has accrued pursuant to this section without requiring the claimant to submit a request for the interest amount. A plan failing to comply with this requirement shall pay the claimant a ten dollar ($10) fee.

(3) For the purposes of this section, a claim, or portion thereof, is reasonably contested if the plan has not received the completed claim and all information necessary to determine payer liability for the claim, or has not been granted reasonable access to information concerning provider services. Information necessary to determine payer liability for the claim includes, but is not limited to, reports of investigations concerning fraud and misrepresentation, and necessary consents, releases, and assignments, a claim on appeal, or other information necessary for the plan to determine the medical necessity for the health care services provided.

(4) If a claim or portion thereof is contested on the basis that the plan has not received all information necessary to determine payer liability for the claim or portion thereof and notice has been provided pursuant to this section, the plan shall have 30 working days or, if the health care service plan is a health maintenance organization, 45 working days after receipt of this additional information to complete reconsideration of the claim. If a plan has received all of the information necessary to determine payer liability for a contested claim and has not reimbursed a claim it has determined to be payable within 30 working days of the receipt of that information, or if the plan is a health maintenance organization, within 45 working days of receipt of that information, interest shall accrue and be payable at a rate of 15 percent per annum beginning with the first calendar day after the 30- or 45-working-day period.

(b) Notwithstanding any other law, a specialized health care service plan that undertakes solely to arrange for the provision of vision care services may use a statistically reliable method to investigate suspected fraud and to recover overpayments made as a result of fraud only if the specialized health care service plan complies with this subdivision.

(1) A specialized health care service plan's statistically reliable method, and how the specialized health care service plan intends to utilize that method to determine recovery of overpayments made as a result of fraud, shall be submitted to, and approved by, the department as elements of the specialized health care service plan's antifraud plan established and approved pursuant to Section 1348. The specialized health care service

plan's utilization of a statistically reliable method shall help protect and promote the interests of enrollees and shall help ensure a stable health care delivery system. The statistically reliable method shall be consistent with direction provided by the International Standards for the Professional Practice of Internal Auditing and the guidance provided by the International Professional Practices Framework guide, which are both produced by the Institute of Internal Auditors.

(2) Pursuant to its antifraud plan established and approved pursuant to Section 1348, a specialized health care service plan shall provide a written notice of suspected fraud to a provider that includes, at a minimum, all of the following:

(A) A clear description of the specialized health care service plan's statistically reliable methodology. The description shall include information that ensures that the sample size used to calculate the repayment amount is consistent with the professional guidance provided in the 2009 edition of the American Institute of Certified Public Accountants' Audit Sampling Considerations of Circular A-133 Compliance Audits.

(B) A clear description of the universe of claims from which the statistical random sample was drawn and, if different, the universe of claims upon which the statistical analysis was applied to generate the recovery amount.

(C) A clear explanation of how the specialized health care service plan's statistically reliable methodology was utilized in the specialized health care service plan's findings of suspected fraud.

(D) Notice that a provider may dispute the specialized health care service plan's findings within 45 working days from the date of receipt of the notice of suspected fraud.

(E) The following information for each of the claims in the statistical sample that was utilized in the specialized health care service plan's findings:

(i) The claim number.

(ii) The name of the patient.

(iii) The date of service.

(iv) The date of payment.

(v) A clear explanation of the basis upon which the specialized health care service plan suspects the claim is fraudulent.

(3) A specialized health care service plan that undertakes solely to arrange for the provision of vision care services may use a statistically reliable method to recover overpayments made as a result of suspected fraud only if the universe of claims upon which the statistical analysis is performed consists only of those claims made between 365 days from the date of payment of the earliest in time claim and the date of payment of the latest in time claim. Notice shall be mailed to the provider no later than 60 days following the date of payment of the latest in time claim.

(4) If the provider contests the specialized health care service plan's notice of suspected fraud, the provider, within 45 working days of the date of receipt of the notice of suspected fraud, shall send written notice to the specialized health care service plan stating the basis upon which the provider believes that the claims are not fraudulent. The specialized health care service plan shall receive and process this contested notice of suspected fraud as a provider dispute pursuant to subdivision (a) of this section, paragraph (1) of subdivision (h) of Section 1367, and the regulations promulgated thereunder.

(5) A specialized health care service plan may offset the amount the specialized health care service plan disclosed as overpaid to the provider in an uncontested notice of suspected fraud against the provider's current claim submissions only if all of the following requirements are met:

(A) The provider fails to reimburse the specialized health care service plan within 45 working days from the date of receipt by the provider of the notice of suspected fraud.

(B) The specialized health care service plan sends written notice to the provider no less than 10 working days prior to withholding current claim payments in which the specialized health care service plan, at a minimum, states its intent to withhold current claim payments and identifies the claim payments that the specialized health care service plan intends to withhold.

(C) The withheld claim payments do not exceed the amount asserted by the specialized health care service plan to be owed to the specialized health care service plan in its notice of suspected fraud.

(6) This section does not limit or remove a specialized health care service plan's obligation to comply with its antifraud plan established pursuant to Section 1348, or to limit or remove the specialized health care service plan's obligation to comply with the requirements for claims subject to subdivision (a).

(7) This subdivision does not limit or remove a specialized health care service plan's ability to recover overpayments as long as recovery is consistent with applicable law, including subdivision (a) and the regulations promulgated thereunder.

(8) This subdivision does not apply to claims submitted by a physician and surgeon for medical or surgical services that are outside the scope of practice of an optometrist pursuant to the Optometry Practice Act (Chapter 7 (commencing with Section 3000) of Division 2 of the Business and Professions Code).

(c) The obligation of a specialized health care service plan to comply with this section is not waived when the specialized health care service plan requires its medical groups, independent practice associations, or other contracting entities to pay claims for covered services.

(Amended by Stats. 2018, Ch. 525, Sec. 1. (AB 1092) Effective January 1, 2019.)
1371.1.

(a) (1) Whenever a health care service plan, including a specialized health care service plan, determines that in reimbursing a claim for provider services an institutional or professional provider has been overpaid, and then notifies the provider in writing through a separate notice identifying the overpayment and the amount of the overpayment, the provider shall reimburse the health care service plan within 30 working days of receipt by the provider of the notice of overpayment unless the overpayment or portion thereof is contested by the provider in which case the health care service plan shall be notified, in writing, within 30 working days. The notice that an overpayment is being contested shall identify the portion of the overpayment that is contested and the specific reasons for contesting the overpayment.

(2) If the provider does not make reimbursement for an uncontested overpayment within 30 working days after receipt, interest shall accrue at the rate of 10 percent per annum beginning with the first calendar day after the 30-working-day period.

(3) A prorated cost-sharing payment, or any portion thereof, made to a pharmacist for the dispensing of a partial fill pursuant to Section 4052.10 of the Business and Professions Code shall not be considered to be an overpayment pursuant to this section.

(b) (1) This subdivision shall only apply to a health care service plan contract covering dental services or a specialized health care service plan contract covering dental services pursuant to this chapter.

(2) The health care service plan's notice of overpayment shall inform the provider how to access the plan's dispute resolution mechanism offered pursuant to subdivision (h) of Section 1367. The notice shall include the name and address to which the dispute should be submitted and a statement that Section 1371.1 of the Health and Safety Code requires a provider to reimburse the plan for an overpayment within 30 working days of receipt by the provider of the notice of overpayment unless the provider contests the overpayment within 30 working days. The notice shall also include information clearly identifying the claim, the name of the patient, the date of service, and a clear explanation of the basis upon which the plan or the plan's capitated provider believes the amount paid on the claim was in excess of the amount due, including interest and penalties on the claim. The notice shall also include a statement that if the provider does not make reimbursement of an uncontested overpayment within 30 working days after receipt of the notice, interest shall accrue at a rate of 10 percent per annum.

(Amended by Stats. 2017, Ch. 615, Sec. 4. (AB 1048) Effective January 1, 2018.)
1371.2.

No health care service plan, including a specialized health care service plan, shall request reimbursement for overpayment or reduce the level of payment to a provider based solely on the allegation that the provider has entered into a contract with any other licensed health care service plan for participation in a benefit plan that has been approved by the director.

(Amended by Stats. 2002, Ch. 760, Sec. 3. Effective January 1, 2003.)
1371.22.

If a contract between a health care service plan and a provider requires that the provider accept, as payment from the plan, the lowest payment rate charged by the provider to any patient or third party, this contract provision shall not be deemed to apply to, or take into consideration, any cash payments made to the provider by individual patients who do not have any private or public form of health care coverage for the service rendered by the provider, as described in subdivision (c) of Section 657 of the Business and Professions Code. This section shall apply to a provider contract that is issued, amended, or renewed on or after the effective date of this section.

(Added by Stats. 1998, Ch. 20, Sec. 2. Effective April 14, 1998.)
1371.25.

A plan, any entity contracting with a plan, and providers are each responsible for their own acts or omissions, and are not liable for the acts or omissions of, or the costs of defending, others. Any provision to the contrary in a contract with providers is void and unenforceable. Nothing in this section shall preclude a finding of liability on the part of a plan, any entity contracting with a plan, or a provider, based on the doctrines of equitable indemnity, comparative negligence, contribution, or other statutory or common law bases for liability.

(Added by Stats. 1995, Ch. 774, Sec. 2. Effective January 1, 1996.)
1371.3.

On and after January 1, 1994, every group health care service plan that provides hospital, medical, or surgical expense benefits for plan members and their dependents shall authorize and permit assignment of the enrollee's or subscriber's right to any reimbursement for health care services covered under the plan contract to the State Department of Health Services when health care services are provided to a Medi-Cal beneficiary. This section, however, shall not apply to a Medi-Cal beneficiary for health care services provided pursuant to a contract with the State Department of Health Services under Chapter 7 (commencing with Section 14000) or Chapter 8 (commencing with Section 14200) of Part 3 of Division 9 of the Welfare and Institutions Code.

(Added by Stats. 1993, Ch. 744, Sec. 1. Effective January 1, 1994.)
1371.30.

(a) (1) By September 1, 2017, the department shall establish an independent dispute resolution process for the purpose of processing and resolving a claim dispute between a health care service plan and a noncontracting individual health professional for services subject to subdivision (a) of Section 1371.9.

(2) Prior to initiating the independent dispute resolution process, the parties shall complete the plan's internal process.

(3) If either the noncontracting individual health professional or the plan appeals a claim to the department's independent dispute resolution process, the other party shall participate in the appeal process as described in this section.

(b) (1) The department shall establish uniform written procedures for the submission, receipt, processing, and resolution of claim payment disputes pursuant to this section and any other guidelines for implementing this section.

(2) The department shall establish reasonable and necessary fees for the purpose of administering this section, to be paid by both parties.

(3) In establishing the independent dispute resolution process, the department shall permit the bundling of claims submitted to the same plan or the same delegated entity for the same or similar services by the same noncontracting individual health professional.

(4) The department shall permit a physician group, independent practice association, or other entity authorized to act on behalf of a noncontracting individual health professional to initiate and participate in the independent dispute resolution process.

(5) In deciding the dispute, the independent organization shall base its decision regarding the appropriate reimbursement on all relevant information.

(c) (1) The department may contract with one or more independent organizations to conduct the proceedings. The independent organization handling a dispute shall be independent of either party to the dispute.

(2) The department shall establish conflict-of-interest standards, consistent with the purposes of this section, that an organization shall meet in order to qualify to administer the independent dispute resolution program. The conflict-of-interest standards shall be consistent with the standards pursuant to subdivisions (c) and (d) of Section 1374.32.

(3) The department may contract with the same independent organization or organizations as the Department of Insurance.

(4) The department shall provide, upon the request of an interested person, a copy of all nonproprietary information, as determined by the director, filed with the department by an independent organization seeking to contract with the department to administer the independent dispute resolution process pursuant to this section. The department may charge a nominal fee to cover the costs of providing a copy of the information pursuant to this paragraph.

(5) The independent organization retained to conduct proceedings shall be deemed to be consultants for purposes of Section 43.98 of the Civil Code.

(6) Contracts entered into pursuant to the authority in this subdivision shall be exempt from Part 2 (commencing with Section 10100) of Division 2 of the Public Contract Code, Section 19130 of the Government Code, and Chapter 6 (commencing with Section 14825) of Part 5.5 of Division 3 of the Government Code and shall be exempt from the review or approval of any division of the Department of General Services.

(d) The decision obtained through the department's independent dispute resolution process shall be binding on both parties. The plan shall implement the decision obtained through the independent dispute resolution process. If dissatisfied, either party may pursue any right, remedy, or penalty established under any other applicable law.

(e) This section shall not apply to a Medi-Cal managed health care service plan or any entity that enters into a contract with the State Department of Health Care Services pursuant to Chapter 7 (commencing with Section 14000), Chapter 8 (commencing with Section 14200), and Chapter 8.75 (commencing with Section 14591) of Part 3 of Division 9 of the Welfare and Institutions Code.

(f) If a health care service plan delegates payment functions to a contracted entity, including, but not limited to, a medical group or independent practice association, then the delegated entity shall comply with this section.

(g) This section shall not apply to emergency services and care, as defined in Section 1317.1.

(h) The definitions in subdivision (f) of Section 1371.9 shall apply for purposes of this section.

(i) This section shall not be construed to alter a health care service plan's obligations pursuant to Sections 1371 and 1371.4.

(j) Notwithstanding Chapter 3.5 (commencing with Section 11340) of Part 1 of Division 3 of Title 2 of the Government Code, the department may implement, interpret, or make specific this section by means of all-plan letters or similar instructions, without taking regulatory action, until the time regulations are adopted.

(k) By January 1, 2019, the department shall provide a report to the Governor, the President pro Tempore of the Senate, the Speaker of the Assembly, and the Senate and Assembly Committees on Health of the data and information provided in the independent dispute resolution process in a manner and format specified by the Legislature.

(Added by Stats. 2016, Ch. 492, Sec. 1. (AB 72) Effective January 1, 2017.)

1371.31.

(a) (1) For services rendered subject to Section 1371.9, effective July 1, 2017, unless otherwise agreed to by the noncontracting individual health professional and the plan, the plan shall reimburse the greater of the average contracted rate or 125 percent of the amount Medicare reimburses on a fee-for-service basis for the same or similar services in the general geographic region in which the services were rendered. For the purposes of this section, "average contracted rate" means the average of the contracted commercial rates paid by the health plan or delegated entity for the same or similar services in the geographic region. This subdivision does not apply to subdivision (c) of Section 1371.9 or subdivision (b) of this section.

(2) (A) By July 1, 2017, each health care service plan and its delegated entities shall provide to the department all of the following:

(i) Data listing its average contracted rates for the plan for services most frequently subject to Section 1371.9 in each geographic region in which the services are rendered for the calendar year 2015.

(ii) Its methodology for determining the average contracted rate for the plan for services subject to Section 1371.9. The methodology to determine an average contracted rate shall ensure that the plan includes the highest and lowest contracted rates for the calendar year 2015.

(iii) The policies and procedures used to determine the average contracted rates under this subdivision.

(B) For each calendar year after the plan's initial submission of the average contracted rate as specified in subparagraph (A) and until the standardized methodology under paragraph (3) is specified, a health care service plan and the plan's delegated entities shall adjust the rate initially established pursuant to this subdivision by the Consumer Price Index for Medical Care Services, as published by the United States Bureau of Labor Statistics.

(3) (A) By January 1, 2019, the department shall specify a methodology that plans and delegated entities shall use to determine the average contracted rates for services most frequently subject to Section 1371.9. This methodology shall take into account, at a minimum, information from the independent dispute resolution process, the specialty of the individual health professional, and the geographic region in which the services are rendered. The methodology to determine an average contracted rate shall ensure that the plan includes the highest and lowest contracted rates.

(B) Health care service plans and delegated entities shall provide to the department the policies and procedures used to determine the average contracted rates in compliance with subparagraph (A).

(C) If, based on the health care service plan's model, a health care service plan does not pay a statistically significant number or dollar amount of claims for services covered under Section 1371.9, the health care service plan shall demonstrate to the department that it has access to a statistically credible database reflecting rates paid to noncontracting individual health professionals for services provided in a geographic region and shall use that database to determine an average contracted rate required pursuant to paragraph (1).

(D) The department shall review the information filed pursuant to this subdivision as part of its examination of fiscal and administrative affairs pursuant to Section 1382.

(E) The average contracted rate data submitted pursuant to this section shall be confidential and not subject to disclosure under the California Public Records Act (Chapter 3.5 (commencing with Section 6250) of Division 7 of Title 1 of the Government Code).

(F) In developing the standardized methodology under this subdivision, the department shall consult with interested parties throughout the process of developing the standards, including the Department of Insurance, representatives of health plans, insurers, health care providers, hospitals, consumer advocates, and other stakeholders it deems appropriate. The department shall hold the first stakeholder meeting no later than July 1, 2017.

(4) A health care service plan shall include in its reports submitted to the department pursuant to Section 1367.035 and regulations adopted pursuant to that section, in a manner specified by the department, the number of payments made to noncontracting individual health professionals for services at a contracting health facility and subject to Section 1371.9, as well as other data sufficient to determine the proportion of noncontracting individual health professionals to contracting individual health professionals at contracting health facilities, as defined in subdivision (f) of Section 1371.9. The department shall include a summary of this information in its January 1, 2019, report required pursuant to subdivision (k) of Section 1371.30 and its findings regarding the impact of the act that added this section on health care service plan contracting and network adequacy.

(5) A health care service plan that provides services subject to Section 1371.9 shall meet the network adequacy requirements set forth in this chapter, including, but not limited to, subdivisions (d) and (e) of Section 1367 of this code and in Exhibits (H) and (I) of subdivision (d) of Section 1300.51 of, and Sections 1300.67.2 and 1300.67.2.1 of, Title 28 of the California Code of Regulations, including, but not limited to, inpatient hospital services and specialist physician services, and if necessary, the department may adopt additional regulations related to those services. This section shall not be construed to limit the director's authority under this chapter.

(6) For purposes of this section for Medicare fee-for-service reimbursement, geographic regions shall be the geographic regions specified for physician reimbursement for Medicare fee-for-service by the United States Department of Health and Human Services.

(7) A health care service plan shall authorize and permit assignment of the enrollee's right, if any, to any reimbursement for health care services covered under the plan contract to a noncontracting individual health professional who furnishes the health care services rendered subject to Section 1371.9. Lack of assignment pursuant to this paragraph shall not be construed to limit the applicability of this section, Section 1371.30, or Section 1371.9.

(8) A noncontracting individual health professional, health care service plan, or health care service plan's delegated entity who disputes the claim reimbursement under this section shall utilize the independent dispute resolution process described in Section 1371.30.

(b) If nonemergency services are provided by a noncontracting individual health professional consistent with subdivision (c) of Section 1371.9 to an enrollee who has voluntarily chosen to use his or her out-of-network benefit for services covered by a plan that includes coverage for out-of-network benefits, unless otherwise agreed to by the plan and the noncontracting individual health professional, the amount paid by the health care service plan shall be the amount set forth in the enrollee's evidence of coverage. This payment is not subject to the independent dispute resolution process described in Section 1371.30.

(c) If a health care service plan delegates the responsibility for payment of claims to a contracted entity, including, but not limited to, a medical group or independent practice association, then the entity to which that responsibility is delegated shall comply with the requirements of this section.

(d) (1) A payment made by the health care service plan to the noncontracting health care professional for nonemergency services as required by Section 1371.9 and this section, in addition to the applicable cost sharing owed by the enrollee, shall constitute payment in full for nonemergency services rendered unless either party uses the independent dispute resolution process or other lawful means pursuant to Section 1371.30.

(2) Notwithstanding any other law, the amounts paid by a plan for services under this section shall not constitute the prevailing or customary charges, the usual fees to the general public, or other charges for other payers for an individual health professional.

(3) This subdivision shall not preclude the use of the independent dispute resolution process pursuant to Section 1371.30.

(e) This section shall not apply to a Medi-Cal managed health care service plan or any other entity that enters into a contract with the State Department of Health Care Services pursuant to Chapter 7 (commencing with Section 14000), Chapter 8 (commencing with Section 14200), and Chapter 8.75 (commencing with Section 14591) of Part 3 of Division 9 of the Welfare and Institutions Code.

(f) This section shall not apply to emergency services and care, as defined in Section 1317.1.

(g) The definitions in subdivision (f) of Section 1371.9 shall apply for purposes of this section.

(h) This section shall not be construed to alter a health care service plan's obligations pursuant to Sections 1371 and 1371.4.

(Added by Stats. 2016, Ch. 492, Sec. 2. (AB 72) Effective January 1, 2017.)

1371.35.

(a) A health care service plan, including a specialized health care service plan, shall reimburse each complete claim, or portion thereof, whether in state or out of state, as soon as practical, but no later than 30 working days after receipt of the complete claim by the health care service plan, or if the health care service plan is a health maintenance organization, 45 working days after receipt of the complete claim by the health care service plan. However, a plan may contest or deny a claim, or portion thereof, by notifying the claimant, in writing, that the claim is contested or denied, within 30 working days after receipt of the claim by the health care service plan, or if the health care service plan is a health maintenance organization, 45 working days after receipt of the claim by the health care service plan. The notice that a claim, or portion thereof, is contested shall identify the portion of the claim that is contested, by revenue code, and the specific information needed from the provider to reconsider the claim. The notice that a claim, or portion thereof, is denied shall identify the portion of the claim that is denied, by revenue code, and the specific reasons for the denial. A plan may delay payment of an uncontested portion of a complete claim for reconsideration of a contested portion of that claim so long as the plan pays those charges specified in subdivision (b).

(b) If a complete claim, or portion thereof, that is neither contested nor denied, is not reimbursed by delivery to the claimant's address of record within the respective 30 or 45 working days after receipt, the plan shall pay the greater of fifteen dollars ($15) per year or interest at the rate of 15 percent per annum beginning with the first calendar day after the 30- or 45-working-day period. A health care service plan shall automatically include the fifteen dollars ($15) per year or interest due in the payment made to the claimant, without requiring a request therefor.

(c) For the purposes of this section, a claim, or portion thereof, is reasonably contested if the plan has not received the completed claim. A paper claim from an institutional provider shall be deemed complete upon submission of a legible emergency department report and a completed UB 92 or other format adopted by the National Uniform Billing Committee, and reasonable relevant information requested by the plan within 30 working days of receipt of the claim. An electronic claim from an institutional provider shall be deemed complete upon submission of an electronic equivalent to the UB 92 or other format adopted by the National Uniform Billing Committee, and reasonable relevant information requested by the plan within 30 working days of receipt of the claim. However, if the plan requests a copy of the emergency department report within the 30 working days after receipt of the electronic claim from the institutional provider, the plan may also request additional reasonable relevant information within 30 working days of receipt of the emergency department report, at which time the claim shall be deemed complete. A claim from a professional provider shall be deemed complete upon submission of a completed HCFA 1500 or its electronic equivalent or other format adopted by the National Uniform Billing Committee, and reasonable relevant information requested by the plan within 30 working days of receipt of the claim. The provider shall provide the plan reasonable relevant information within 10 working days of receipt of a written request that is clear and specific regarding the information sought. If, as a result of reviewing the reasonable relevant information, the plan requires further information, the plan shall have an additional 15 working days after receipt of the reasonable relevant information to request the further information, notwithstanding any time limit to the contrary in this section, at which time the claim shall be deemed complete.

(d) This section shall not apply to claims about which there is evidence of fraud and misrepresentation, to eligibility determinations, or in instances where the plan has not been granted reasonable access to information under the provider's control. A plan shall specify, in a written notice sent to the provider within the respective 30- or 45-working days of receipt of the claim, which, if any, of these exceptions applies to a claim.

(e) If a claim or portion thereof is contested on the basis that the plan has not received information reasonably necessary to determine payer liability for the claim or portion thereof, then the plan shall have 30 working days or, if the health care service plan is a health maintenance organization, 45 working days after receipt of this additional information to complete reconsideration of the claim. If a claim, or portion thereof, undergoing reconsideration is not reimbursed by delivery to the claimant's address of record within the respective 30 or 45 working days after receipt of the additional information, the plan shall pay the greater of fifteen dollars ($15) per year or interest at

the rate of 15 percent per annum beginning with the first calendar day after the 30- or 45-working-day period. A health care service plan shall automatically include the fifteen dollars ($15) per year or interest due in the payment made to the claimant, without requiring a request therefor.

(f) The obligation of the plan to comply with this section shall not be deemed to be waived when the plan requires its medical groups, independent practice associations, or other contracting entities to pay claims for covered services. This section shall not be construed to prevent a plan from assigning, by a written contract, the responsibility to pay interest and late charges pursuant to this section to medical groups, independent practice associations, or other entities.

(g) A plan shall not delay payment on a claim from a physician or other provider to await the submission of a claim from a hospital or other provider, without citing specific rationale as to why the delay was necessary and providing a monthly update regarding the status of the claim and the plan's actions to resolve the claim, to the provider that submitted the claim.

(h) A health care service plan shall not request or require that a provider waive its rights pursuant to this section.

(i) This section shall not apply to capitated payments.

(j) This section shall apply only to claims for services rendered to a patient who was provided emergency services and care as defined in Section 1317.1 in the United States on or after September 1, 1999.

(k) This section shall not be construed to affect the rights or obligations of any person pursuant to Section 1371.

(l) This section shall not be construed to affect a written agreement, if any, of a provider to submit bills within a specified time period.

(Amended by Stats. 2000, Ch. 827, Sec. 4. Effective January 1, 2001.)

1371.36.

(a) A health care service plan shall not deny payment of a claim on the basis that the plan, medical group, independent practice association, or other contracting entity did not provide authorization for health care services that were provided in a licensed acute care hospital and that were related to services that were previously authorized, if all of the following conditions are met:

(1) It was medically necessary to provide the services at the time.

(2) The services were provided after the plan's normal business hours.

(3) The plan does not maintain a system that provides for the availability of a plan representative or an alternative means of contact through an electronic system, including voicemail or electronic mail, whereby the plan can respond to a request for authorization within 30 minutes of the time that a request was made.

(b) This section shall not apply to investigational or experimental therapies, or other noncovered services.

(Added by Stats. 2000, Ch. 827, Sec. 5. Effective January 1, 2001.)

1371.37.

(a) A health care service plan is prohibited from engaging in an unfair payment pattern, as defined in this section.

(b) Consistent with subdivision (a) of Section 1371.39, the director may investigate a health care service plan to determine whether it has engaged in an unfair payment pattern.

(c) An "unfair payment pattern," as used in this section, means any of the following:

(1) Engaging in a demonstrable and unjust pattern, as defined by the department, of reviewing or processing complete and accurate claims that results in payment delays.

(2) Engaging in a demonstrable and unjust pattern, as defined by the department, of reducing the amount of payment or denying complete and accurate claims.

(3) Failing on a repeated basis to pay the uncontested portions of a claim within the timeframes specified in Section 1371, 1371.1, or 1371.35.

(4) Failing on a repeated basis to automatically include the interest due on claims pursuant to Section 1371.

(d) (1) Upon a final determination by the director that a health care service plan has engaged in an unfair payment pattern, the director may:

(A) Impose monetary penalties as permitted under this chapter.

(B) Require the health care service plan for a period of three years from the date of the director's determination, or for a shorter period prescribed by the director, to pay complete and accurate claims from the provider within a shorter period of time than that required by Section 1371. The provisions of this subparagraph shall not become operative until January 1, 2002.

(C) Include a claim for costs incurred by the department in any administrative or judicial action, including investigative expenses and the cost to monitor compliance by the plan.

(2) For any overpayment made by a health care service plan while subject to the provisions of paragraph (1), the provider shall remain liable to the plan for repayment pursuant to Section 1371.1.

(e) The enforcement remedies provided in this section are not exclusive and shall not limit or preclude the use of any otherwise available criminal, civil, or administrative remedy.

(f) The penalties set forth in this section shall not preclude, suspend, affect, or impact any other duty, right, responsibility, or obligation under a statute or under a contract between a health care service plan and a provider.

(g) A health care service plan may not delegate any statutory liability under this section.

(h) For the purposes of this section, "complete and accurate claim" has the same meaning as that provided in the regulations adopted by the department pursuant to subdivision (a) of Section 1371.38.

(i) On or before December 31, 2001, the department shall report to the Legislature and the Governor information regarding the development of the definition of "unjust pattern" as used in this section. This report shall include, but not be limited to, a description of the process used and a list of the parties involved in the department's development of this definition as well as recommendations for statutory adoption.

(j) The department shall make available upon request and on its website, information regarding actions taken pursuant to this section, including a description of the activities that were the basis for the action.

(Added by Stats. 2000, Ch. 827, Sec. 6. Effective January 1, 2001.)

1371.38.

(a) The department shall, on or before July 1, 2001, adopt regulations that ensure that plans have adopted a dispute resolution mechanism pursuant to subdivision (h) of Section 1367. The regulations shall require that any dispute resolution mechanism of a plan is fair, fast, and cost-effective for contracting and non-contracting providers and define the term "complete and accurate claim, including attachments and supplemental information or documentation."

(b) On or before December 31, 2001, the department shall report to the Governor and the Legislature its recommendations for any additional statutory requirements relating to plan and provider dispute resolution mechanisms.

(Added by Stats. 2000, Ch. 827, Sec. 7. Effective January 1, 2001.)

1371.39.

(a) Providers may report to the department through the toll-free provider line, email address, or another method designated by the department, instances in which the provider believes a plan is engaging in an unfair payment pattern.

(b) Plans may report to the department through the toll-free provider line, email address, or another method designated by the department, instances in which the plan believes a provider is engaging in an unfair billing pattern.

(c) "Unfair billing pattern" means engaging in a demonstrable and unjust pattern of unbundling of claims, upcoding of claims, or other demonstrable and unjustified billing patterns, as defined by the department.

(d) On or before July 1, 2019, and at least annually thereafter, the department shall review complaints filed pursuant to subdivision (a). If the review of complaint data indicates a possible unfair payment pattern, the department may conduct an audit or an enforcement action pursuant to subdivision (s) of Section 1300.71 of Title 28 of the California Code of Regulations.

(Amended by Stats. 2018, Ch. 303, Sec. 1. (AB 2674) Effective January 1, 2019.)

1371.4.

(a) A health care service plan that covers hospital, medical, or surgical expenses, or its contracting medical providers, shall provide 24-hour access for enrollees and providers, including, but not limited to, noncontracting hospitals, to obtain timely authorization for medically necessary care, for circumstances where the enrollee has received emergency services and care is stabilized, but the treating provider believes that the enrollee may not be discharged safely. A physician and surgeon shall be available for consultation and for resolving disputed requests for authorizations. A health care service plan that does not require prior authorization as a prerequisite for payment for necessary medical care following stabilization of an emergency medical condition or active labor need not satisfy the requirements of this subdivision.

(b) A health care service plan, or its contracting medical providers, shall reimburse providers for emergency services and care provided to its enrollees, until the care results in stabilization of the enrollee, except as provided in subdivision (c). As long as federal or state law requires that emergency services and care be provided without first questioning the patient's ability to pay, a health care service plan shall not require a provider to obtain authorization prior to the provision of emergency services and care necessary to stabilize the enrollee's emergency medical condition.

(c) Payment for emergency services and care may be denied only if the health care service plan, or its contracting medical providers, reasonably determines that the emergency services and care were never performed; provided that a health care service plan, or its contracting medical providers, may deny reimbursement to a provider for a medical screening examination in cases when the plan enrollee did not require emergency services and care and the enrollee reasonably should have known that an emergency did not exist. A health care service plan may require prior authorization as a prerequisite for payment for necessary medical care following stabilization of an emergency medical condition.

(d) If there is a disagreement between the health care service plan and the provider regarding the need for necessary medical care, following stabilization of the enrollee, the plan shall assume responsibility for the care of the patient either by having medical personnel contracting with the plan personally take over the care of the patient within a reasonable amount of time after the disagreement, or by having another general acute care hospital under contract with the plan agree to accept the transfer of the patient as provided in Section 1317.2, Section 1317.2a, or other pertinent statute. However, this requirement shall not apply to necessary medical care provided in hospitals outside the service area of the health care service plan. If the health care service plan fails to satisfy the requirements of this subdivision, further necessary care shall be deemed to have been authorized by the plan. Payment for this care may not be denied.

(e) A health care service plan may delegate the responsibilities enumerated in this section to the plan's contracting medical providers.

(f) Subdivisions (b), (c), (d), (g), and (h) shall not apply with respect to a nonprofit health care service plan that has 3,500,000 enrollees and maintains a prior authorization system that includes the availability by telephone within 30 minutes of a practicing emergency department physician.

(g) The Department of Managed Health Care shall adopt by July 1, 1995, on an emergency basis, regulations governing instances when an enrollee requires medical care following stabilization of an emergency medical condition, including appropriate timeframes for a health care service plan to respond to requests for treatment authorization.

(h) The Department of Managed Health Care shall adopt, by July 1, 1999, on an emergency basis, regulations governing instances when an enrollee in the opinion of the treating provider requires necessary medical care following stabilization of an emergency medical condition, including appropriate timeframes for a health care service plan to respond to a request for treatment authorization from a treating provider who has a contract with a plan.

(i) The definitions set forth in Section 1317.1 shall control the construction of this section.

(j) (1) A health care service plan that is contacted by a hospital pursuant to Section 1262.8 shall, within 30 minutes of the time the hospital makes the initial telephone call requesting information, either authorize poststabilization care or inform the hospital that it will arrange for the prompt transfer of the enrollee to another hospital.

(2) A health care service plan that is contacted by a hospital pursuant to Section 1262.8 shall reimburse the hospital for poststabilization care rendered to the enrollee if any of the following occur:

(A) The health care service plan authorizes the hospital to provide poststabilization care.

(B) The health care service plan does not respond to the hospital's initial contact or does not make a decision regarding whether to authorize poststabilization care or to promptly transfer the enrollee within the timeframe set forth in paragraph (1).

(C) There is an unreasonable delay in the transfer of the enrollee, and the noncontracting physician and surgeon determines that the enrollee requires poststabilization care.

(3) A health care service plan shall not require a hospital representative or a noncontracting physician and surgeon to make more than one telephone call pursuant to Section 1262.8 to the number provided in advance by the health care service plan. The representative of the hospital that makes the telephone call may be, but is not required to be, a physician and surgeon.

(4) An enrollee who is billed by a hospital in violation of Section 1262.8 may report receipt of the bill to the health care service plan and the department. The department shall forward that report to the State Department of Public Health.

(5) For purposes of this section, "poststabilization care" means medically necessary care provided after an emergency medical condition has been stabilized.

(Amended by Stats. 2008, Ch. 603, Sec. 4. Effective January 1, 2009.)

1371.5.

(a) No health care service plan that provides basic health care services shall require prior authorization or refuse to pay for any ambulance or ambulance transport services, referred to in paragraph (6) of subdivision (b) of Section 1345, provided to an enrollee as a result of a "911" emergency response system request for assistance if either of the following conditions apply:

(1) The request was made for an emergency medical condition and ambulance transport services were required.

(2) An enrollee reasonably believed that the medical condition was an emergency medical condition and reasonably believed that the condition required ambulance transport services.

(b) As used in this section, "emergency medical condition" has the same meaning as in Section 1317.1.

(c) The determination as to whether an enrollee reasonably believed that the medical condition was an emergency medical condition that required an emergency response shall not be based solely upon a retrospective analysis of the level of care eventually provided to, or a final discharge of, the person who received emergency assistance.

(d) A health care service plan shall not be required to pay for any ambulance or ambulance transport services if the health care service plan determines that the ambulance or ambulance transport services were never performed, an emergency condition did not exist, or upon findings of fraud, incorrect billings, the provision of services that were not covered under the member's current benefit plan, or membership that was invalid at the time services were delivered for the pending emergency claim.

(Added by Stats. 1998, Ch. 979, Sec. 3. Effective January 1, 1999.)

1371.8.

A health care service plan that authorizes a specific type of treatment by a provider shall not rescind or modify this authorization after the provider renders the health care service in good faith and pursuant to the authorization for any reason, including, but not limited to, the plan's subsequent rescission, cancellation, or modification of the enrollee's or subscriber's contract or the plan's subsequent determination that it did not make an accurate determination of the enrollee's or subscriber's eligibility. This section shall not be construed to expand or alter the benefits available to the enrollee or subscriber under a plan. The Legislature finds and declares that by adopting the amendments made to this section by Assembly Bill 1324 of the 2007–08 Regular Session it does not intend to instruct a court as to whether or not the amendments are existing law.

(Amended by Stats. 2007, Ch. 702, Sec. 1. Effective January 1, 2008.)

1371.9.

(a) (1) Except as provided in subdivision (c), a health care service plan contract issued, amended, or renewed on or after July 1, 2017, shall provide that if an enrollee receives covered services from a contracting health facility at which, or as a result of which, the enrollee receives services provided by a noncontracting individual health professional, the enrollee shall pay no more than the same cost sharing that the enrollee would pay for the

same covered services received from a contracting individual health professional. This amount shall be referred to as the "in-network cost-sharing amount."
(2) An enrollee shall not owe the noncontracting individual health professional more than the in-network cost-sharing amount for services subject to this section. At the time of payment by the plan to the noncontracting individual health professional, the plan shall inform the enrollee and the noncontracting individual health professional of the in-network cost-sharing amount owed by the enrollee.
(3) A noncontracting individual health professional shall not bill or collect any amount from the enrollee for services subject to this section except for the in-network cost-sharing amount. Any communication from the noncontracting individual health professional to the enrollee prior to the receipt of information about the in-network cost-sharing amount pursuant to paragraph (2) shall include a notice in 12-point bold type stating that the communication is not a bill and informing the enrollee that the enrollee shall not pay until he or she is informed by his or her health care service plan of any applicable cost sharing.
(4) (A) If the noncontracting individual health professional has received more than the in-network cost-sharing amount from the enrollee for services subject to this section, the noncontracting individual health professional shall refund any overpayment to the enrollee within 30 calendar days after receiving payment from the enrollee.
(B) If the noncontracting individual health professional does not refund any overpayment to the enrollee within 30 calendar days after being informed of the enrollee's in-network cost-sharing amount, interest shall accrue at the rate of 15 percent per annum beginning with the date payment was received from the enrollee.
(C) A noncontracting individual health professional shall automatically include in his or her refund to the enrollee all interest that has accrued pursuant to this section without requiring the enrollee to submit a request for the interest amount.
(b) Except for services subject to subdivision (c), the following shall apply:
(1) Any cost sharing paid by the enrollee for the services subject to this section shall count toward the limit on annual out-of-pocket expenses established under Section 1367.006.
(2) Cost sharing arising from services subject to this section shall be counted toward any deductible in the same manner as cost sharing would be attributed to a contracting individual health professional.
(3) The cost sharing paid by the enrollee pursuant to this section shall satisfy the enrollee's obligation to pay cost sharing for the health service and shall constitute "applicable cost sharing owed by the enrollee."
(c) For services subject to this section, if an enrollee has a health care service plan that includes coverage for out-of-network benefits, a noncontracting individual health professional may bill or collect from the enrollee the out-of-network cost sharing, if applicable, only when the enrollee consents in writing and that written consent demonstrates satisfaction of all the following criteria:
(1) At least 24 hours in advance of care, the enrollee shall consent in writing to receive services from the identified noncontracting individual health professional.
(2) The consent shall be obtained by the noncontracting individual health professional in a document that is separate from the document used to obtain the consent for any other part of the care or procedure. The consent shall not be obtained by the facility or any representative of the facility. The consent shall not be obtained at the time of admission or at any time when the enrollee is being prepared for surgery or any other procedure.
(3) At the time consent is provided, the noncontracting individual health professional shall give the enrollee a written estimate of the enrollee's total out-of-pocket cost of care. The written estimate shall be based on the professional's billed charges for the service to be provided. The noncontracting individual health professional shall not attempt to collect more than the estimated amount without receiving separate written consent from the enrollee or the enrollee's authorized representative, unless circumstances arise during delivery of services that were unforeseeable at the time the estimate was given that would require the provider to change the estimate.
(4) The consent shall advise the enrollee that he or she may elect to seek care from a contracted provider or may contact the enrollee's health care service plan in order to arrange to receive the health service from a contracted provider for lower out-of-pocket costs.
(5) The consent and estimate shall be provided to the enrollee in the language spoken by the enrollee, if the language is a Medi-Cal threshold language, as defined in subdivision (d) of Section 128552.
(6) The consent shall also advise the enrollee that any costs incurred as a result of the enrollee's use of the out-of-network benefit shall be in addition to in-network cost-sharing amounts and may not count toward the annual out-of-pocket maximum on in-network benefits or a deductible, if any, for in-network benefits.
(d) A noncontracting individual health professional who fails to comply with the requirements of subdivision (c) has not obtained written consent for purposes of this section. Under those circumstances, subdivisions (a) and (b) shall apply and subdivision (c) shall not apply.
(e) (1) A noncontracting individual health professional may advance to collections only the in-network cost-sharing amount, as determined by the plan pursuant to subdivision (a) or the out-of-network cost-sharing amount owed pursuant to subdivision (c), that the enrollee has failed to pay.
(2) The noncontracting individual health professional, or any entity acting on his or her behalf, including any assignee of the debt, shall not report adverse information to a consumer credit reporting agency or commence civil action against the enrollee for a minimum of 150 days after the initial billing regarding amounts owed by the enrollee under subdivision (a) or (c).
(3) With respect to an enrollee, the noncontracting individual health professional, or any entity acting on his or her behalf, including any assignee of the debt, shall not use wage garnishments or liens on primary residences as a means of collecting unpaid bills under this section.
(f) For purposes of this section and Sections 1371.30 and 1371.31, the following definitions shall apply:
(1) "Contracting health facility" means a health facility that is contracted with the enrollee's health care service plan to provide services under the enrollee's plan contract. A contracting health care facility includes, but is not limited to, the following providers:
(A) A licensed hospital.
(B) An ambulatory surgery or other outpatient setting, as described in subdivision (a), (d), (e), (g), or (h) of Section 1248.1.
(C) A laboratory.
(D) A radiology or imaging center.
(2) "Cost sharing" includes any copayment, coinsurance, or deductible, or any other form of cost sharing paid by the enrollee other than premium or share of premium.
(3) "Individual health professional" means a physician and surgeon or other professional who is licensed by this state to deliver or furnish health care services. For this purpose, an "individual health professional" shall not include a dentist, licensed pursuant to the Dental Practice Act (Chapter 4 (commencing with Section 1600) of Division 2 of the Business and Professions Code).
(4) "In-network cost-sharing amount" means an amount no more than the same cost sharing the enrollee would pay for the same covered service received from a contracting health professional. The in-network cost-sharing amount with respect to an enrollee with coinsurance shall be based on the amount paid by the plan pursuant to paragraph (1) of subdivision (a) of Section 1371.31.
(5) "Noncontracting individual health professional" means a physician and surgeon or other professional who is licensed by the state to deliver or furnish health care services and who is not contracted with the enrollee's health care service product. For this purpose, a "noncontracting individual health professional" shall not include a dentist, licensed pursuant to the Dental Practice Act (Chapter 4 (commencing with Section 1600) of Division 2 of the Business and Professions Code). Application of this definition is not precluded by a noncontracting individual health professional's affiliation with a group.
(g) This section shall not be construed to require a health care service plan to cover services not required by law or by the terms and conditions of the health care service plan contract.
(h) This section shall not be construed to exempt a plan or provider from the requirements under Section 1371.4 or 1373.96, nor abrogate the holding in Prospect Medical Group, Inc. v. Northridge Emergency Medical Group (2009) 45 Cal.4th 497.
(i) If a health care service plan delegates payment functions to a contracted entity, including, but not limited to, a medical group or independent practice association, the delegated entity shall comply with this section.
(j) This section shall not apply to a Medi-Cal managed health care service plan or any other entity that enters into a contract with the State Department of Health Care Services pursuant to Chapter 7 (commencing with Section 14000), Chapter 8 (commencing with Section 14200), and Chapter 8.75 (commencing with Section 14591) of Part 3 of Division 9 of the Welfare and Institutions Code.
(k) This section shall not apply to emergency services and care, as defined in Section 1317.1.
(Added by Stats. 2016, Ch. 492, Sec. 3. (AB 72) Effective January 1, 2017.)

1372.

Subject to the applicable provisions of this chapter, a plan may offer one or more plan contracts or specialized health care service plan contracts, except that a specialized health care service plan contract shall not offer one or more basic health care services except as may be permitted by rule or order of the director. Advertising, disclosure forms, contract forms, and evidences of coverage for more than one type of plan contract or specialized health care service plan contract, or both, may not be used except as authorized by the director pursuant to this chapter.
(Amended by Stats. 1999, Ch. 525, Sec. 108. Effective January 1, 2000. Operative July 1, 2000, or sooner, by Sec. 214 of Ch. 525.)

1373.

(a) (1) A plan contract may not provide an exception for other coverage if the other coverage is entitlement to Medi-Cal benefits under Chapter 7 (commencing with Section 14000) or Chapter 8 (commencing with Section 14200) of Part 3 of Division 9 of the Welfare and Institutions Code, or Medicaid benefits under Subchapter 19 (commencing with Section 1396) of Chapter 7 of Title 42 of the United States Code.
(2) Each plan contract shall be interpreted not to provide an exception for the Medi-Cal or Medicaid benefits.
(3) A plan contract shall not provide an exemption for enrollment because of an applicant's entitlement to Medi-Cal benefits under Chapter 7 (commencing with Section 14000) or Chapter 8 (commencing with Section 14200) of Part 3 of Division 9 of the Welfare and Institutions Code, or Medicaid benefits under Subchapter 19 (commencing with Section 1396) of Chapter 7 of Title 42 of the United States Code.
(4) A plan contract may not provide that the benefits payable thereunder are subject to reduction if the individual insured has entitlement to the Medi-Cal or Medicaid benefits.
(b) (1) A plan contract that provides coverage, whether by specific benefit or by the effect of general wording, for sterilization operations or procedures shall not impose any disclaimer, restriction on, or limitation of, coverage relative to the covered individual's reason for sterilization.

(2) As used in this section, "sterilization operations or procedures" shall have the same meaning as that specified in Section 10120 of the Insurance Code.

(c) Every plan contract that provides coverage to the spouse or dependents of the subscriber or spouse shall grant immediate accident and sickness coverage, from and after the moment of birth, to each newborn infant of any subscriber or spouse covered and to each minor child placed for adoption from and after the date on which the adoptive child's birth parent or other appropriate legal authority signs a written document, including, but not limited to, a health facility minor release report, a medical authorization form, or a relinquishment form, granting the subscriber or spouse the right to control health care for the adoptive child or, absent this written document, on the date there exists evidence of the subscriber's or spouse's right to control the health care of the child placed for adoption. No plan may be entered into or amended if it contains any disclaimer, waiver, or other limitation of coverage relative to the coverage or insurability of newborn infants of, or children placed for adoption with, a subscriber or spouse covered as required by this subdivision.

(d) (1) Every plan contract that provides that coverage of a dependent child of a subscriber shall terminate upon attainment of the limiting age for dependent children specified in the plan, shall also provide that attainment of the limiting age shall not operate to terminate the coverage of the child while the child is and continues to meet both of the following criteria:

(A) Incapable of self-sustaining employment by reason of a physically or mentally disabling injury, illness, or condition.

(B) Chiefly dependent upon the subscriber for support and maintenance.

(2) The plan shall notify the subscriber that the dependent child's coverage will terminate upon attainment of the limiting age unless the subscriber submits proof of the criteria described in subparagraphs (A) and (B) of paragraph (1) to the plan within 60 days of the date of receipt of the notification. The plan shall send this notification to the subscriber at least 90 days prior to the date the child attains the limiting age. Upon receipt of a request by the subscriber for continued coverage of the child and proof of the criteria described in subparagraphs (A) and (B) of paragraph (1), the plan shall determine whether the child meets that criteria before the child attains the limiting age. If the plan fails to make the determination by that date, it shall continue coverage of the child pending its determination.

(3) The plan may subsequently request information about a dependent child whose coverage is continued beyond the limiting age under this subdivision but not more frequently than annually after the two-year period following the child's attainment of the limiting age.

(4) If the subscriber changes carriers to another plan or to a health insurer, the new plan or insurer shall continue to provide coverage for the dependent child. The new plan or insurer may request information about the dependent child initially and not more frequently than annually thereafter to determine if the child continues to satisfy the criteria in subparagraphs (A) and (B) of paragraph (1). The subscriber shall submit the information requested by the new plan or insurer within 60 days of receiving the request.

(5) (A) Except as set forth in subparagraph (B), under no circumstances shall the limiting age be less than 26 years of age with respect to plan years beginning on or after September 23, 2010.

(B) For plan years beginning before January 1, 2014, a group health care service plan contract that qualifies as a grandfathered health plan under Section 1251 of the federal Patient Protection and Affordable Care Act (Public Law 111-148) and that makes available dependent coverage of children may exclude from coverage an adult child who has not attained 26 years of age only if the adult child is eligible to enroll in an eligible employer-sponsored health plan, as defined in Section 5000A(f)(2) of the Internal Revenue Code, other than a group health plan of a parent.

(C) (i) With respect to a child (I) whose coverage under a group or individual plan contract ended, or who was denied or not eligible for coverage under a group or individual plan contract, because under the terms of the contract the availability of dependent coverage of children ended before the attainment of 26 years of age, and (II) who becomes eligible for that coverage by reason of the application of this paragraph, the health care service plan shall give the child an opportunity to enroll that shall continue for at least 30 days. This opportunity and the notice described in clause (ii) shall be provided not later than the first day of the first plan year beginning on or after September 23, 2010, consistent with the federal Patient Protection and Affordable Care Act (Public Law 111-148), as amended by the federal Health Care and Education Reconciliation Act of 2010 (Public Law 111-152), and any additional federal guidance or regulations issued by the United States Secretary of Health and Human Services.

(ii) The health care service plan shall provide written notice stating that a dependent described in clause (i) who has not attained 26 years of age is eligible to enroll in the plan for coverage. This notice may be provided to the dependent's parent on behalf of the dependent. If the notice is included with other enrollment materials for a group plan, the notice shall be prominent.

(iii) In the case of an individual who enrolls under this subparagraph, coverage shall take effect no later than the first day of the first plan year beginning on or after September 23, 2010.

(iv) A dependent enrolling in a group health plan for coverage pursuant to this subparagraph shall be treated as a special enrollee as provided under the rules of Section 146.117(d) of Title 45 of the Code of Federal Regulations. The health care service plan shall offer the recipient of the notice all of the benefit packages available to similarly situated individuals who did not lose coverage by reason of cessation of dependent status. Any difference in benefits or cost-sharing requirements shall constitute a different benefit package. A dependent enrolling in a group health plan for coverage

pursuant to this subparagraph shall not be required to pay more for coverage than similarly situated individuals who did not lose coverage by reason of cessation of dependent status.

(D) Nothing in this section shall require a health care service plan to make coverage available for a child of a child receiving dependent coverage. Nothing in this section shall be construed to modify the definition of "dependent" as used in the Revenue and Taxation Code with respect to the tax treatment of the cost of coverage.

(e) A plan contract that provides coverage, whether by specific benefit or by the effect of general wording, for both an employee and one or more covered persons dependent upon the employee and provides for an extension of the coverage for any period following a termination of employment of the employee shall also provide that this extension of coverage shall apply to dependents upon the same terms and conditions precedent as applied to the covered employee, for the same period of time, subject to payment of premiums, if any, as required by the terms of the policy and subject to any applicable collective bargaining agreement.

(f) A group contract shall not discriminate against handicapped persons or against groups containing handicapped persons. Nothing in this subdivision shall preclude reasonable provisions in a plan contract against liability for services or reimbursement of the handicap condition or conditions relating thereto, as may be allowed by rules of the director.

(g) Every group contract shall set forth the terms and conditions under which subscribers and enrollees may remain in the plan in the event the group ceases to exist, the group contract is terminated, or an individual subscriber leaves the group, or the enrollees' eligibility status changes.

(h) (1) A health care service plan or specialized health care service plan may provide for coverage of, or for payment for, professional mental health services, or vision care services, or for the exclusion of these services. If the terms and conditions include coverage for services provided in a general acute care hospital or an acute psychiatric hospital as defined in Section 1250 and do not restrict or modify the choice of providers, the coverage shall extend to care provided by a psychiatric health facility as defined in Section 1250.2 operating pursuant to licensure by the State Department of Health Care Services. A health care service plan that offers outpatient mental health services but does not cover these services in all of its group contracts shall communicate to prospective group contractholders as to the availability of outpatient coverage for the treatment of mental or nervous disorders.

(2) No plan shall prohibit the member from selecting any psychologist who is licensed pursuant to the Psychology Licensing Law (Chapter 6.6 (commencing with Section 2900) of Division 2 of the Business and Professions Code), any optometrist who is the holder of a certificate issued pursuant to Chapter 7 (commencing with Section 3000) of Division 2 of the Business and Professions Code or, upon referral by a physician and surgeon licensed pursuant to the Medical Practice Act (Chapter 5 (commencing with Section 2000) of Division 2 of the Business and Professions Code), (A) any marriage and family therapist who is the holder of a license under Section 4980.50 of the Business and Professions Code, (B) any licensed clinical social worker who is the holder of a license under Section 4996 of the Business and Professions Code, (C) any registered nurse licensed pursuant to Chapter 6 (commencing with Section 2700) of Division 2 of the Business and Professions Code, who possesses a master's degree in psychiatric-mental health nursing and is listed as a psychiatric-mental health nurse by the Board of Registered Nursing, (D) any advanced practice registered nurse certified as a clinical nurse specialist pursuant to Article 9 (commencing with Section 2838) of Chapter 6 of Division 2 of the Business and Professions Code who participates in expert clinical practice in the specialty of psychiatric-mental health nursing, to perform the particular services covered under the terms of the plan, and the certificate holder is expressly authorized by law to perform these services, or (E) any professional clinical counselor who is the holder of a license under Chapter 16 (commencing with Section 4999.10) of Division 2 of the Business and Professions Code.

(3) Nothing in this section shall be construed to allow any certificate holder or licensee enumerated in this section to perform professional mental health services beyond his or her field or fields of competence as established by his or her education, training, and experience.

(4) For the purposes of this section:

(A) "Marriage and family therapist" means a licensed marriage and family therapist who has received specific instruction in assessment, diagnosis, prognosis, and counseling, and psychotherapeutic treatment of premarital, marriage, family, and child relationship dysfunctions, which is equivalent to the instruction required for licensure on January 1, 1981.

(B) "Professional clinical counselor" means a licensed professional clinical counselor who has received specific instruction in assessment, diagnosis, prognosis, counseling, and psychotherapeutic treatment of mental and emotional disorders, which is equivalent to the instruction required for licensure on January 1, 2012.

(5) Nothing in this section shall be construed to allow a member to select and obtain mental health or psychological or vision care services from a certificate holder or licenseholder who is not directly affiliated with or under contract to the health care service plan or specialized health care service plan to which the member belongs. All health care service plans and individual practice associations that offer mental health benefits shall make reasonable efforts to make available to their members the services of licensed psychologists. However, a failure of a plan or association to comply with the requirements of the preceding sentence shall not constitute a misdemeanor.

(6) As used in this subdivision, "individual practice association" means an entity as defined in subsection (5) of Section 1307 of the federal Public Health Service Act (42 U.S.C. Sec. 300e-1(5)).

(7) Health care service plan coverage for professional mental health services may include community residential treatment services that are alternatives to inpatient care and that are directly affiliated with the plan or to which enrollees are referred by providers affiliated with the plan.

(i) If the plan utilizes arbitration to settle disputes, the plan contracts shall set forth the type of disputes subject to arbitration, the process to be utilized, and how it is to be initiated.

(j) A plan contract that provides benefits that accrue after a certain time of confinement in a health care facility shall specify what constitutes a day of confinement or the number of consecutive hours of confinement that are requisite to the commencement of benefits.

(k) If a plan provides coverage for a dependent child who is over 26 years of age and enrolled as a full-time student at a secondary or postsecondary educational institution, the following shall apply:

(1) Any break in the school calendar shall not disqualify the dependent child from coverage.

(2) If the dependent child takes a medical leave of absence, and the nature of the dependent child's injury, illness, or condition would render the dependent child incapable of self-sustaining employment, the provisions of subdivision (d) shall apply if the dependent child is chiefly dependent on the subscriber for support and maintenance.

(3) (A) If the dependent child takes a medical leave of absence from school, but the nature of the dependent child's injury, illness, or condition does not meet the requirements of paragraph (2), the dependent child's coverage shall not terminate for a period not to exceed 12 months or until the date on which the coverage is scheduled to terminate pursuant to the terms and conditions of the plan, whichever comes first. The period of coverage under this paragraph shall commence on the first day of the medical leave of absence from the school or on the date the physician and surgeon determines the illness prevented the dependent child from attending school, whichever comes first. Any break in the school calendar shall not disqualify the dependent child from coverage under this paragraph.

(B) Documentation or certification of the medical necessity for a leave of absence from school shall be submitted to the plan at least 30 days prior to the medical leave of absence from the school, if the medical reason for the absence and the absence are foreseeable, or 30 days after the start date of the medical leave of absence from school and shall be considered prima facie evidence of entitlement to coverage under this paragraph.

(4) This subdivision shall not apply to a specialized health care service plan or to a Medicare supplement plan.

(Amended by Stats. 2013, Ch. 23, Sec. 14. (AB 82) Effective June 27, 2013.)
1373.1.

Every group plan entered into, amended, or renewed on or after January 1, 1977, which provides hospital, medical, or surgical expense benefits for employees or subscribers and their dependents, and which contains provisions granting the employee or subscriber the right to convert the coverage in the event of termination of employment or membership, shall include in such conversion provisions the same conversion rights and conditions to a covered dependent spouse of the employee or subscriber in the event the covered dependent spouse ceases to be a qualified family member by reason of termination of marriage or death of the employee or subscriber. Such conversion rights shall not require a physical examination or a statement of health.

(Added by Stats. 1976, Ch. 1173.)
1373.2.

Every group health care service plan entered into, amended, or renewed on or after January 1, 1976, which provides hospital, medical, or surgical expense benefits for employees or subscribers and their dependents and which contains provisions granting the employee or subscriber the right to convert the coverage in the event of termination of employment or membership, shall include in such conversion provisions the same conversion rights and conditions to a covered dependent spouse of the employee or subscriber in the event the covered dependent spouse ceases to be a qualified family member by reason of termination of marriage.

(Added by Stats. 1976, Ch. 1079.)
1373.3.

An enrollee shall not be prohibited from selecting as a primary care physician any available primary care physician who contracts with the plan in the service area where the enrollee lives or works. This section shall apply to any plan contract issued, amended, renewed, or delivered on or after January 1, 1996.

(Added by Stats. 1995, Ch. 515, Sec. 2. Effective January 1, 1996.)
1373.4.

(a) No health care service plan contract that is issued, amended, renewed, or delivered on or after July 1, 2003, that provides maternity coverage shall do either of the following:

(1) Contain a copayment or deductible for inpatient hospital maternity services that exceeds the most common amount of the copayment or deductible contained in the contract for inpatient services provided for other covered medical conditions.

(2) Contain a copayment or deductible for ambulatory care maternity services that exceeds the most common amount of the copayment or deductible contained in the contract for ambulatory care services provided for other covered medical conditions.

(b) No health care service plan that provides maternity benefits for a person covered continuously from conception shall be issued, amended, delivered, or renewed in this state if it contains any exclusion, reduction, or other limitations as to coverage,

deductibles, or coinsurance provisions as to involuntary complications of pregnancy, unless the provisions apply generally to all benefits paid under the plan.

(c) If the pregnancy is interrupted, the maternity deductible charged for prenatal care and delivery shall be based on the value of the medical services received, providing it is never more than two-thirds of the plan's maternity deductible.

(d) For purposes of this section, involuntary complications of pregnancy shall include, but not be limited to, puerperal infection, eclampsia, cesarean section delivery, ectopic pregnancy, and toxemia.

(e) This section shall not permit copayments or deductibles in the Medi-Cal program that are not otherwise authorized under state or federal law.

(f) This section shall become operative on July 1, 2003.

(Repealed (in Sec. 2) and added by Stats. 2002, Ch. 880, Sec. 3. Effective January 1, 2003. Section operative July 1, 2003, by its own provisions.)
1373.5.

When spouses are both employed as employees, and both have enrolled themselves and their eligible family members under a group health care service plan provided by their respective employers, and each spouse is covered as an employee under the terms of the same master contract, each spouse may claim on his or her behalf, or on behalf of his or her enrolled dependents, the combined maximum contractual benefits to which an employee is entitled under the terms of the master contract, not to exceed in the aggregate 100 percent of the charge for the covered expense or service.

This section shall apply to every group plan entered into, delivered, amended, or renewed in this state on or after January 1, 1978.

(Amended by Stats. 2016, Ch. 50, Sec. 52. (SB 1005) Effective January 1, 2017.)
1373.6.

This section does not apply to a specialized health care service plan contract or to a plan contract that primarily or solely supplements Medicare. The director may adopt rules consistent with federal law to govern the discontinuance and replacement of plan contracts that primarily or solely supplement Medicare.

(a) (1) Every group contract entered into, amended, or renewed on or after September 1, 2003, that provides hospital, medical, or surgical expense benefits for employees or members shall provide that an employee or member whose coverage under the group contract has been terminated by the employer shall be entitled to convert to nongroup membership, without evidence of insurability, subject to the terms and conditions of this section.

(2) If the health care service plan provides coverage under an individual health care service plan contract, other than conversion coverage under this section, it shall offer one of the two plans that it is required to offer to a federally eligible defined individual pursuant to Section 1366.35. The plan shall provide this coverage at the same rate established under Section 1399.805 for a federally eligible defined individual. A health care service plan that is federally qualified under the federal Health Maintenance Organization Act (42 U.S.C. Sec. 300e et seq.) may charge a rate for the coverage that is consistent with the provisions of that act.

(3) If the health care service plan does not provide coverage under an individual health care service plan contract, it shall offer a health benefit plan contract that is the same as a health benefit contract offered to a federally eligible defined individual pursuant to Section 1366.35. The health care service plan may offer either the most popular health maintenance organization model plan or the most popular preferred provider organization plan, each of which has the greatest number of enrolled individuals for its type of plan as of January 1 of the prior year, as reported by plans that provide coverage under an individual health care service plan contract to the department or the Department of Insurance by January 31, 2003, and annually thereafter. A health care service plan subject to this paragraph shall provide this coverage with the same cost-sharing terms and at the same premium as a health care service plan providing coverage to that individual under an individual health care service plan contract pursuant to Section 1399.805. The health care service plan shall file the health benefit plan it will offer, including the premium it will charge and the cost-sharing terms of the plan, with the Department of Managed Health Care.

(b) A conversion contract shall not be required to be made available to an employee or member if termination of his or her coverage under the group contract occurred for any of the following reasons:

(1) The group contract terminated or an employer's participation terminated and the group contract is replaced by similar coverage under another group contract within 15 days of the date of termination of the group coverage or the subscriber's participation.

(2) The employee or member failed to pay amounts due the health care service plan.

(3) The employee or member was terminated by the health care service plan from the plan for good cause.

(4) The employee or member knowingly furnished incorrect information or otherwise improperly obtained the benefits of the plan.

(5) The employer's hospital, medical, or surgical expense benefit program is self-insured.

(c) A conversion contract is not required to be issued to any person if any of the following facts are present:

(1) The person is covered by or is eligible for benefits under Title XVIII of the United States Social Security Act.

(2) The person is covered by or is eligible for hospital, medical, or surgical benefits under any arrangement of coverage for individuals in a group, whether insured or self-insured.

(3) The person is covered for similar benefits by an individual policy or contract.

(4) The person has not been continuously covered during the three-month period immediately preceding that person's termination of coverage.

(d) Benefits of a conversion contract shall meet the requirements for benefits under this chapter.
(e) Unless waived in writing by the plan, written application and first premium payment for the conversion contract shall be made not later than 63 days after termination from the group. A conversion contract shall be issued by the plan which shall be effective on the day following the termination of coverage under the group contract if the written application and the first premium payment for the conversion contract are made to the plan not later than 63 days after the termination of coverage, unless these requirements are waived in writing by the plan.
(f) The conversion contract shall cover the employee or member and his or her dependents who were covered under the group contract on the date of their termination from the group.
(g) A notification of the availability of the conversion coverage shall be included in each evidence of coverage. However, it shall be the sole responsibility of the employer to notify its employees of the availability, terms, and conditions of the conversion coverage which responsibility shall be satisfied by notification within 15 days of termination of group coverage. Group coverage shall not be deemed terminated until the expiration of any continuation of the group coverage. For purposes of this subdivision, the employer shall not be deemed the agent of the plan for purposes of notification of the availability, terms, and conditions of conversion coverage.
(h) As used in this section, "hospital, medical, or surgical benefits under state or federal law" do not include benefits under Chapter 7 (commencing with Section 14000) or Chapter 8 (commencing with Section 14200) of Part 3 of Division 9 of the Welfare and Institutions Code, or Title XIX of the United States Social Security Act.
(i) Every group contract entered into, amended, or renewed before September 1, 2003, shall be subject to the provisions of this section as it read prior to its amendment by Assembly Bill 1401 of the 2001–02 Regular Session.
(j) (1) On and after January 1, 2014, and except as provided in paragraph (2), this section shall apply only to individual grandfathered health plan contracts previously issued pursuant to this section to federally eligible defined individuals.
(2) If Section 5000A of the Internal Revenue Code, as added by Section 1501 of PPACA, is repealed or amended to no longer apply to the individual market, as defined in Section 2791 of the federal Public Health Service Act (42 U.S.C. Section 300gg-91), paragraph (1) shall become inoperative on the date of that repeal or amendment.
(3) For purposes of this subdivision, the following definitions apply:
(A) "Grandfathered health plan" has the same meaning as that term is defined in Section 1251 of PPACA.
(B) "PPACA" means the federal Patient Protection and Affordable Care Act (Public Law 111-148), as amended by the federal Health Care Education and Reconciliation Act of 2010 (Public Law 111-152), and any rules, regulations, or guidance issued pursuant to that law.
(Amended by Stats. 2013, Ch. 441, Sec. 5. (AB 1180) Effective October 1, 2013.)
1373.620.
(a) (1) At least 60 days prior to the plan renewal date, a health care service plan that does not otherwise issue individual health care service plan contracts shall issue the notice described in paragraph (2) to any subscriber enrolled in an individual health benefit plan contract issued pursuant to Section 1373.6 that is not a grandfathered health plan.
(2) The notice shall be in at least 12-point type and shall include all of the following:
(A) Notice that, as of the renewal date, the individual plan contract will not be renewed.
(B) The availability of individual health coverage through Covered California, including at least all of the following:
(i) That, beginning on January 1, 2014, individuals seeking coverage may not be denied coverage based on health status.
(ii) That the premium rates for coverage offered by a health care service plan or a health insurer cannot be based on an individual's health status.
(iii) That individuals obtaining coverage through Covered California may, depending upon income, be eligible for premium subsidies and cost-sharing subsidies.
(iv) That individuals seeking coverage must obtain this coverage during an open or special enrollment period, and a description of the open and special enrollment periods that may apply.
(b) (1) At least 60 days prior to the plan renewal date, a health care service plan that issues individual health care service plan contracts shall issue the notice described in paragraph (2) to a subscriber enrolled in an individual health benefit plan contract issued pursuant to Section 1366.35 or 1373.6 that is not a grandfathered health plan.
(2) The notice shall be in at least 12-point type and shall include all of the following:
(A) Notice that, as of the renewal date, the individual plan contract will not be renewed.
(B) Information regarding the individual health plan contract that the health plan will issue as of January 1, 2014, which the health plan has reasonably concluded is the most comparable to the individual's current plan. The notice shall include information on premiums for the possible replacement plan and instructions that the individual can continue their coverage by paying the premium stated by the due date.
(C) Notice of the availability of other individual health coverage through Covered California, including at least all of the following:
(i) That, beginning on January 1, 2014, individuals seeking coverage may not be denied coverage based on health status.
(ii) That the premium rates for coverage offered by a health care service plan or a health insurer cannot be based on an individual's health status.
(iii) That individuals obtaining coverage through Covered California may, depending upon income, be eligible for premium subsidies and cost-sharing subsidies.
(iv) That individuals seeking coverage must obtain this coverage during an open or special enrollment period, and a description of the open and special enrollment periods that may apply.
(c) No later than September 1, 2013, the department, in consultation with the Department of Insurance, shall adopt uniform model notices that health plans shall use to comply with subdivisions (a) and (b) and Sections 1366.50, 1373.622, and 1399.861. Use of the model notices shall not require prior approval by the department. The model notices adopted by the department for purposes of this section shall not be subject to the Administrative Procedure Act (Chapter 3.5 (commencing with Section 11340) of Part 1 of Division 3 of Title 2 of the Government Code). The director may modify the wording of these model notices specifically for the purposes of clarity, readability, and accuracy.
(d) The notices required in this section are vital documents, pursuant to clause (iii) of subparagraph (B) of paragraph (1) of subdivision (b) of Section 1367.04, and shall be subject to the applicable requirements of that section.
(e) For purposes of this section, the following definitions shall apply:
(1) "Covered California" means the California Health Benefit Exchange established pursuant to Section 100500 of the Government Code.
(2) "Grandfathered health plan" has the same meaning as that term is defined in Section 1251 of PPACA.
(3) "PPACA" means the federal Patient Protection and Affordable Care Act (Public Law 111-148), as amended by the federal Health Care and Education Reconciliation Act of 2010 (Public Law 111-152), and any rules, regulations, or guidance issued pursuant to that law.
(Added by Stats. 2013, Ch. 441, Sec. 6. (AB 1180) Effective October 1, 2013.)
1373.621.
(a) Except for a specialized health care service plan, every health care service plan contract that is issued, amended, delivered, or renewed in this state on or after January 1, 1999, that provides hospital, medical, or surgical expense coverage under an employer-sponsored group plan for an employer subject to COBRA, as defined in subdivision (e), or an employer group for which the plan is required to offer Cal-COBRA coverage, as defined in subdivision (f), including a carrier providing replacement coverage under Section 1399.63, shall further offer the former employee the opportunity to continue benefits as required under subdivision (b), and shall further offer the former spouse of an employee or former employee the opportunity to continue benefits as required under subdivision (c).
(b) (1) In the event a former employee who worked for the employer for at least five years prior to the date of termination of employment and who is 60 years of age or older on the date employment ends is entitled to and so elects to continue benefits under COBRA or Cal-COBRA for himself or herself and for any spouse, the employee or spouse may further continue benefits beyond the date coverage under COBRA or Cal-COBRA ends, as set forth in paragraph (2). Except as otherwise specified, continuation coverage shall be under the same benefit terms and conditions as if the continuation coverage under COBRA or Cal-COBRA had remained in force. For the employee or spouse, continuation coverage following the end of COBRA or Cal-COBRA is subject to payment of premiums to the health care service plan. Individuals ineligible for COBRA or Cal-COBRA, or who are eligible but have not elected or exhausted continuation coverage under federal COBRA or Cal-COBRA, are not entitled to continuation coverage under this section. Premiums for continuation coverage under this section shall be billed by, and remitted to, the health care service plan in accordance with subdivision (d). Failure to pay the requisite premiums may result in termination of the continuation coverage in accordance with the applicable provisions in the plan's group subscriber agreement with the former employer.
(2) The employer shall notify the former employee or spouse or both, or the former spouse of the employee or former employee, of the availability of the continuation benefits under this section in accordance with Section 2800.2 of the Labor Code. To continue health care coverage pursuant to this section, the individual shall elect to do so by notifying the plan in writing within 30 calendar days prior to the date continuation coverage under COBRA or Cal-COBRA is scheduled to end. Every health care service plan and specialized health care service plan shall provide to the employer replacing a health care service plan contract issued by the plan, or to the employer's agent or broker representative, within 15 days of any written request, information in possession of the plan reasonably required to administer the requirements of Section 2800.2 of the Labor Code.
(3) The continuation coverage shall end automatically on the earlier of (A) the date the individual reaches age 65, (B) the date the individual is covered under any group health plan not maintained by the employer or any other health plan, regardless of whether that coverage is less valuable, (C) the date the individual becomes entitled to Medicare under Title XVIII of the Social Security Act, (D) for a spouse, five years from the date on which continuation coverage under COBRA or Cal-COBRA was scheduled to end for the spouse, or (E) the date on which the employer terminates its group subscriber agreement with the health care service plan and ceases to provide coverage for any active employees through that plan, in which case the health care service plan shall notify the former employee or spouse or both of the right to a conversion plan in accordance with Section 1373.6.
(c) (1) If a former spouse of an employee or former employee was covered as a qualified beneficiary under COBRA or Cal-COBRA, the former spouse may further continue benefits beyond the date coverage under COBRA or Cal-COBRA ends, as set forth in paragraph (2) of subdivision (b). Except as otherwise specified in this section, continuation coverage shall be under the same benefit terms and conditions as if the continuation coverage under COBRA or Cal-COBRA had remained in force. Continuation coverage following the

end of COBRA or Cal-COBRA is subject to payment of premiums to the health care service plan. Premiums for continuation coverage under this section shall be billed by, and remitted to, the health care service plan in accordance with subdivision (d). Failure to pay the requisite premiums may result in termination of the continuation coverage in accordance with the applicable provisions in the plan's group subscriber agreement with the employer or former employer.

(2) The continuation coverage for the former spouse shall end automatically on the earlier of (A) the date the individual reaches 65 years of age, (B) the date the individual is covered under any group health plan not maintained by the employer or any other health plan, regardless of whether that coverage is less valuable, (C) the date the individual becomes entitled to Medicare under Title XVIII of the Social Security Act, (D) five years from the date on which continuation coverage under COBRA or Cal-COBRA was scheduled to end for the former spouse, or (E) the date on which the employer or former employer terminates its group subscriber agreement with the health care service plan and ceases to provide coverage for any active employees through that plan.

(d) (1) If the premium charged to the employer for a specific employee or dependent eligible under this section is adjusted for the age of the specific employee, or eligible dependent, on other than a composite basis, the rate for continuation coverage under this section shall not exceed 102 percent of the premium charged by the plan to the employer for an employee of the same age as the former employee electing continuation coverage in the case of an individual who was eligible for COBRA, and 110 percent in the case of an individual who was eligible for Cal-COBRA. If the coverage continued is that of a former spouse, the premium charged shall not exceed 102 percent of the premium charged by the plan to the employer for an employee of the same age as the former spouse selecting continuation coverage in the case of an individual who was eligible for COBRA, and 110 percent in the case of an individual who was eligible for Cal-COBRA.

(2) If the premium charged to the employer for a specific employee or dependent eligible under this section is not adjusted for age of the specific employee, or eligible dependent, then the rate for continuation coverage under this section shall not exceed 213 percent of the applicable current group rate. For purposes of this section, the "applicable current group rate" means the total premiums charged by the health care service plan for coverage for the group, divided by the relevant number of covered persons.

(3) However, in computing the premiums charged to the specific employer group, the health care service plan shall not include consideration of the specific medical care expenditures for beneficiaries receiving continuation coverage pursuant to this section.

(e) For purposes of this section, "COBRA" means Section 4980B of Title 26 of the United States Code, Section 1161 et seq. of Title 29 of the United States Code, and Section 300bb of Title 42 of the United States Code, as added by the Consolidated Omnibus Budget Reconciliation Act of 1985 (Public Law 99-272), and as amended.

(f) For purposes of this section, "Cal-COBRA" means the continuation coverage that must be offered pursuant to Article 4.5 (commencing with Section 1366.20), or Article 1.7 (commencing with Section 10128.50) of Chapter 1 of Part 2 of Division 2 of the Insurance Code.

(g) For the purposes of this section, "former spouse" means either an individual who is divorced from an employee or former employee or an individual who was married to an employee or former employee at the time of the death of the employee or former employee.

(h) Every plan evidence of coverage that is issued, amended, or renewed after July 1, 1999, shall contain a description of the provisions and eligibility requirements for the continuation coverage offered pursuant to this section.

(i) This section does not apply to any individual who is not eligible for its continuation coverage prior to January 1, 2005.

(Amended by Stats. 2013, Ch. 441, Sec. 7. (AB 1180) Effective October 1, 2013.)

1373.622.

(a) (1) After the termination of the pilot program under Section 1373.62, a health care service plan shall continue to provide coverage under the same terms and conditions specified in Section 1376.62 as it existed on January 1, 2007, including the terms of the standard benefit plan and the subscriber payment amount, to each individual who was terminated from the program pursuant to subdivision (f) of Section 12725 of the Insurance Code during the term of the pilot program and who enrolled or applied to enroll in a standard benefit plan within 63 days of termination. The State Department of Health Care Services shall continue to pay the amount described in Section 1376.62 for each of those individuals. A health care service plan shall not be required to offer the coverage described in Section 1373.62 after the termination of the pilot program to individuals not already enrolled in the program.

(2) Notwithstanding paragraph (1) of this subdivision or Section 1373.62 as it existed on January 1, 2007, the following rules shall apply:

(A) (i) A health care service plan shall not be obligated to provide coverage to any individual pursuant to this section on or after January 1, 2014.

(ii) The State Department of Health Care Services shall not be obligated to provide any payment to any health care service plan under this section for (I) health care expenses incurred on or after January 1, 2014, or (II) the standard monthly administrative fee, as defined in Section 1373.62 as it existed on January 1, 2007, for any month after December 2013.

(B) Each health care service plan providing coverage pursuant to this section shall, on or before October 1, 2013, send a notice to each individual enrolled in a standard benefit plan that is in at least 12-point type and with, at minimum, the following information:

(i) Notice as to whether or not the plan will terminate as of January 1, 2014.

(ii) The availability of individual health coverage, including through Covered California, including at least all of the following:

(I) That, beginning on January 1, 2014, individuals seeking coverage may not be denied coverage based on health status.

(II) That the premium rates for coverage offered by a health care service plan or a health insurer cannot be based on an individual's health status.

(III) That individuals obtaining coverage through Covered California may, depending upon income, be eligible for premium subsidies and cost-sharing subsidies.

(IV) That individuals seeking coverage must obtain this coverage during an open or special enrollment period, and a description of the open and special enrollment periods that may apply.

(C) As a condition of receiving payment for a reporting period pursuant to this section, a health care service plan shall provide the State Department of Health Care Services with a complete, final annual reconciliation report by the earlier of December 31, 2014, or an earlier date as prescribed by Section 1373.62, as it existed on January 1, 2007, for that reporting period. To the extent that it receives a complete, final reconciliation report for a reporting period by the date required pursuant to this subparagraph, the State Department of Health Care Services shall complete reconciliation with the health care service plan for that reporting period within 18 months after receiving the report.

(b) If the state fails to expend, pursuant to this section, sufficient funds for the state's contribution amount to any health care service plan, the health care service plan may increase the monthly payments that its subscribers are required to pay for any standard benefit plan to the amount that the State Department of Health Care Services would charge without a state subsidy for the same plan issued to the same individual within the program.

(c) Notwithstanding Chapter 3.5 (commencing with Section 11340) of Part 1 of Division 3 of Title 2 of the Government Code, the State Department of Health Care Services may implement, interpret, or make specific this section by means of all-county letters, plan letters, plan or provider bulletins, or similar instructions, without taking regulatory action.

(Amended by Stats. 2015, Ch. 18, Sec. 8. (SB 75) Effective June 24, 2015.)

1373.65.

(a) At least 75 days before the termination date of its contract with a provider group or a general acute care hospital, the health care service plan shall submit an enrollee block transfer filing to the department that includes the written notice the plan proposes to send to affected enrollees. The plan may not send this notice to enrollees until the department has reviewed and approved its content. If the department does not respond within seven days of the date of its receipt of the filing, the notice shall be deemed approved.

(b) At least 60 days before the termination date of a contract between a health care service plan and a provider group or a general acute care hospital, the plan shall send the written notice described in subdivision (a) by United States mail to enrollees who are assigned to the terminated provider group or hospital. A plan that is unable to comply with the timeframe because of exigent circumstances shall apply to the department for a waiver. The plan is excused from complying with this requirement only if its waiver application is granted by the department or the department does not respond within seven days of the date of its receipt of the waiver application. If the terminated provider is a hospital and the plan assigns enrollees to a provider group with exclusive admitting privileges to the hospital, the plan shall send the written notice to each enrollee who is a member of the provider group and who resides within a 15-mile radius of the terminated hospital. If the plan operates as a preferred provider organization or assigns members to a provider group with admitting privileges to hospitals in the same geographic area as the terminated hospital, the plan shall send the written notice to all enrollees who reside within a 15-mile radius of the terminated hospital.

(c) The health care service plan shall send enrollees of a preferred provider organization the written notice required by subdivision (b) only if the terminated provider is a general acute care hospital.

(d) If an individual provider terminates his or her contract or employment with a provider group that contracts with a health care service plan, the plan may require that the provider group send the notice required by subdivision (b).

(e) If, after sending the notice required by subdivision (b), a health care service plan reaches an agreement with a terminated provider to renew or enter into a new contract or to not terminate their contract, the plan shall offer each affected enrollee the option to return to that provider. If an affected enrollee does not exercise this option, the plan shall reassign the enrollee to another provider.

(f) A health care service plan and a provider shall include in all written, printed, or electronic communications sent to an enrollee that concern the contract termination or block transfer, the following statement in not less than 8-point type: "If you have been receiving care from a health care provider, you may have a right to keep your provider for a designated time period. Please contact your HMO's customer service department, and if you have further questions, you are encouraged to contact the Department of Managed Health Care, which protects HMO consumers, by telephone at its toll-free number, 1-888-HMO-2219, or at a TDD number for the deaf or hard of hearing at 1-877-688-9891, or online at www.hmohelp.ca.gov."

(g) For purposes of this section, "provider group" means a medical group, independent practice association, or any other similar organization.

(Amended by Stats. 2016, Ch. 94, Sec. 17. (AB 1709) Effective January 1, 2017.)

1373.7.

A health care service plan contract, which is written or issued for delivery outside of California and which provides benefits for California residents that are within the scope of psychological practice, shall not be deemed to prohibit persons covered under the contract from selecting a psychologist licensed in California to perform the services in

California which are within the terms of the contract even though the psychologist is not licensed in the state where the contract is written or issued for delivery.
(Added by Stats. 1981, Ch. 558.)
1373.8.
A health care service plan contract where the plan is licensed to do business in this state and the plan provides coverage that includes California residents, but that may be written or issued for delivery outside of California, and where benefits are provided within the scope of practice of a licensed clinical social worker, a registered nurse licensed pursuant to Chapter 6 (commencing with Section 2700) of Division 2 of the Business and Professions Code who possesses a master's degree in psychiatric-mental health nursing and is listed as a psychiatric-mental health nurse by the Board of Registered Nursing, an advanced practice registered nurse who is certified as a clinical nurse specialist pursuant to Article 9 (commencing with Section 2838) of Chapter 6 of Division 2 of the Business and Professions Code who participates in expert clinical practice in the specialty of psychiatric-mental health nursing, a marriage and family therapist who is the holder of a license under Section 4980.50 of the Business and Professions Code, or a professional clinical counselor who is the holder of a license under Chapter 16 (commencing with Section 4999.10) of Division 2 of the Business and Professions Code shall not be deemed to prohibit persons covered under the contract from selecting those licensed persons in California to perform the services in California that are within the terms of the contract even though the licensees are not licensed in the state where the contract is written or issued for delivery.
It is the intent of the Legislature in amending this section in the 1984 portion of the 1983–84 Legislative Session that persons covered by the contract and those providers of health care specified in this section who are licensed in California should be entitled to the benefits provided by the plan for services of those providers rendered to those persons.
(Amended by Stats. 2011, Ch. 381, Sec. 31. (SB 146) Effective January 1, 2012.)
1373.9.
(a) Except in the case of a specialized health care service plan, a health care service plan which negotiates and enters into a contract with professional providers to provide services at alternative rates of payment of the type described in Sections 10133 and 11512 of the Insurance Code, shall give reasonable consideration to timely written proposals for affiliation by licensed or certified professional providers.
(b) For the purposes of this section, the following definitions are applicable:
(1) "Reasonable consideration" means consideration in good faith of the terms of proposals for affiliation prior to the time that contracts for alternative rates of payment are entered into or renewed. A plan may specify the terms and conditions of affiliation to assure cost efficiency, qualification of providers, appropriate utilization of services, accessibility, convenience to persons who would receive the provider's services, and consistency with the plan's basic method of operation, but shall not exclude providers because of their category of license.
(2) "Professional provider" means a holder of a certificate or license under Division 2 (commencing with Section 500) of the Business and Professions Code, or any initiative act referred to therein, except for those certified or licensed pursuant to Article 3 of Chapter 5 (commencing with Section 2050) or Chapter 11 (commencing with Section 4800), who may, within the scope of their licenses, perform the services of a specific plan benefit defined in the health care service plan's contracts with its enrollees.
(c) A plan which has an affiliation with an institutional provider or with professional providers is not required by this section to give consideration to affiliation with professional providers who hold the same category of license or certificate and propose to serve a geographic area served adequately by the affiliated providers that provide their professional services as employees or agents of that institutional or professional provider, or contract with that institutional or professional provider to provide professional services.
(Added by Stats. 1984, Ch. 977, Sec. 1.)
1373.95.
(a) (1) A health care service plan, other than a specialized health care service plan that offers professional mental health services on an employer-sponsored group basis, shall file a written continuity of care policy as a material modification with the department before March 31, 2004.
(2) A health care service plan shall include all of the following in its written continuity of care policy:
(A) A description of the plan's process for the block transfer of enrollees from a terminated provider group or hospital to a new provider group or hospital.
(B) A description of the manner in which the plan facilitates the completion of covered services pursuant to Section 1373.96.
(C) A template of the notice the plan proposes to send to enrollees describing its policy and informing enrollees of their right to completion of covered services.
(D) A description of the plan's process to review an enrollee's request for the completion of covered services.
(E) A provision ensuring that reasonable consideration is given to the potential clinical effect on an enrollee's treatment caused by a change of provider.
(3) If approved by the department, the provisions of the written continuity of care policy shall replace all prior continuity of care policies. The plan shall file a revision of the policy with the department if it makes a material change to it.
(b) (1) The provisions of this subdivision apply to a specialized health care service plan that offers professional mental health services on an employer-sponsored group basis.
(2) The plan shall file with the department a written policy describing the manner in which it facilitates the continuity of care for a new enrollee who has been receiving services from

a nonparticipating mental health provider for an acute, serious, or chronic mental health condition when his or her employer changed health plans. The written policy shall allow the new enrollee a reasonable transition period to continue his or her course of treatment with the nonparticipating mental health provider prior to transferring to a participating provider and shall include the provision of mental health services on a timely, appropriate, and medically necessary basis from the nonparticipating provider. The policy may provide that the length of the transition period take into account on a case-by-case basis, the severity of the enrollee's condition and the amount of time reasonably necessary to effect a safe transfer. The policy shall ensure that reasonable consideration is given to the potential clinical effect of a change of provider on the enrollee's treatment for the condition. The policy shall describe the plan's process to review an enrollee's request to continue his or her course of treatment with a nonparticipating mental health provider. Nothing in this paragraph shall be construed to require the plan to accept a nonparticipating mental health provider onto its panel for treatment of other enrollees. For purposes of the continuing treatment of the transferring enrollee, the plan may require the nonparticipating mental health provider, as a condition of the right conferred under this section, to enter into its standard mental health provider contract.
(3) A plan may require a nonparticipating mental health provider whose services are continued pursuant to the written policy, to agree in writing to the same contractual terms and conditions that are imposed upon the plan's participating providers, including location within the plan's service area, reimbursement methodologies, and rates of payment. If the plan determines that an enrollee's health care treatment should temporarily continue with his or her existing provider or nonparticipating mental health provider, the plan shall not be liable for actions resulting solely from the negligence, malpractice, or other tortious or wrongful acts arising out of the provisions of services by the existing provider or a nonparticipating mental health provider.
(4) The written policy shall not apply to an enrollee who is offered an out-of-network option or to an enrollee who had the option to continue with his or her previous specialized health care service plan that offers professional mental health services on an employer-sponsored group basis or mental health provider and instead voluntarily chose to change health plans.
(5) This subdivision shall not apply to a specialized health care service plan that offers professional mental health services on an employer-sponsored group basis if it includes out-of-network coverage that allows the enrollee to obtain services from his or her existing mental health provider or nonparticipating mental health provider.
(c) The health care service plan, including a specialized health care service plan that offers professional mental health services on an employer-sponsored group basis, shall provide to all new enrollees notice of its written continuity of care policy and information regarding the process for an enrollee to request a review under the policy and shall provide, upon request, a copy of the written policy to an enrollee.
(d) Nothing in this section shall require a health care service plan or a specialized health care service plan that offers professional mental health services on an employer-sponsored group basis to cover services or provide benefits that are not otherwise covered under the terms and conditions of the plan contract.
(e) The following definitions apply for the purposes of this section:
(1) "Hospital" means a general acute care hospital.
(2) "Nonparticipating mental health provider" means a psychiatrist, licensed psychologist, licensed marriage and family therapist, licensed social worker, or licensed professional clinical counselor who does not contract with the specialized health care service plan that offers professional mental health services on an employer-sponsored group basis.
(3) "Provider group" means a medical group, independent practice association, or any other similar organization.
(Amended by Stats. 2011, Ch. 381, Sec. 32. (SB 146) Effective January 1, 2012.)
1373.96.
(a) A health care service plan shall, at the request of an enrollee, provide for the completion of covered services as set forth in this section by a terminated provider or by a nonparticipating provider.
(b) (1) The completion of covered services shall be provided by a terminated provider to an enrollee who, at the time of the contract's termination, was receiving services from that provider for one of the conditions described in subdivision (c).
(2) The completion of covered services shall be provided by a nonparticipating provider to a newly covered enrollee who, at the time his or her coverage became effective, was receiving services from that provider for one of the conditions described in subdivision (c).
(c) The health care service plan shall provide for the completion of covered services for the following conditions:
(1) An acute condition. An acute condition is a medical condition that involves a sudden onset of symptoms due to an illness, injury, or other medical problem that requires prompt medical attention and that has a limited duration. Completion of covered services shall be provided for the duration of the acute condition.
(2) A serious chronic condition. A serious chronic condition is a medical condition due to a disease, illness, or other medical problem or medical disorder that is serious in nature and that persists without full cure or worsens over an extended period of time or requires ongoing treatment to maintain remission or prevent deterioration. Completion of covered services shall be provided for a period of time necessary to complete a course of treatment and to arrange for a safe transfer to another provider, as determined by the health care service plan in consultation with the enrollee and the terminated provider or nonparticipating provider and consistent with good professional practice. Completion of covered services under this paragraph shall not exceed 12 months from the contract

termination date or 12 months from the effective date of coverage for a newly covered enrollee.

(3) A pregnancy. A pregnancy is the three trimesters of pregnancy and the immediate postpartum period. Completion of covered services shall be provided for the duration of the pregnancy.

(4) A terminal illness. A terminal illness is an incurable or irreversible condition that has a high probability of causing death within one year or less. Completion of covered services shall be provided for the duration of a terminal illness, which may exceed 12 months from the contract termination date or 12 months from the effective date of coverage for a new enrollee.

(5) The care of a newborn child between birth and age 36 months. Completion of covered services under this paragraph shall not exceed 12 months from the contract termination date or 12 months from the effective date of coverage for a newly covered enrollee.

(6) Performance of a surgery or other procedure that is authorized by the plan as part of a documented course of treatment and has been recommended and documented by the provider to occur within 180 days of the contract's termination date or within 180 days of the effective date of coverage for a newly covered enrollee.

(d) (1) The plan may require the terminated provider whose services are continued beyond the contract termination date pursuant to this section to agree in writing to be subject to the same contractual terms and conditions that were imposed upon the provider before termination, including, but not limited to, credentialing, hospital privileging, utilization review, peer review, and quality assurance requirements. If the terminated provider does not agree to comply or does not comply with these contractual terms and conditions, the plan is not required to continue the provider's services beyond the contract termination date.

(2) Unless otherwise agreed upon by the terminated provider and the plan or by the individual provider and the provider group, the services rendered pursuant to this section shall be compensated at rates and methods of payment similar to those used by the plan or the provider group for currently contracting providers providing similar services who are not capitated and who are practicing in the same or a similar geographic area as the terminated provider. Neither the plan nor the provider group is required to continue the services of a terminated provider if the provider does not accept the payment rates provided for in this paragraph.

(e) (1) The plan may require a nonparticipating provider whose services are continued pursuant to this section for a newly covered enrollee to agree in writing to be subject to the same contractual terms and conditions that are imposed upon currently contracting providers providing similar services who are not capitated and who are practicing in the same or a similar geographic area as the nonparticipating provider, including, but not limited to, credentialing, hospital privileging, utilization review, peer review, and quality assurance requirements. If the nonparticipating provider does not agree to comply or does not comply with these contractual terms and conditions, the plan is not required to continue the provider's services.

(2) Unless otherwise agreed upon by the nonparticipating provider and the plan or by the nonparticipating provider and the provider group, the services rendered pursuant to this section shall be compensated at rates and methods of payment similar to those used by the plan or the provider group for currently contracting providers providing similar services who are not capitated and who are practicing in the same or a similar geographic area as the nonparticipating provider. Neither the plan nor the provider group is required to continue the services of a nonparticipating provider if the provider does not accept the payment rates provided for in this paragraph.

(f) The amount of, and the requirement for payment of, copayments, deductibles, or other cost-sharing components during the period of completion of covered services with a terminated provider or a nonparticipating provider are the same as would be paid by the enrollee if receiving care from a provider currently contracting with or employed by the plan.

(g) If a plan delegates the responsibility of complying with this section to a provider group, the plan shall ensure that the requirements of this section are met.

(h) This section does not require a plan to provide for completion of covered services by a provider whose contract with the plan or provider group has been terminated or not renewed for reasons relating to a medical disciplinary cause or reason, as defined in paragraph (6) of subdivision (a) of Section 805 of the Business and Professions Code, or fraud or other criminal activity.

(i) This section does not require a plan to cover services or provide benefits that are not otherwise covered under the terms and conditions of the plan contract. Except as provided in subdivision (l), this section does not apply to a newly covered enrollee covered under an individual subscriber agreement who is undergoing a course of treatment on the effective date of his or her coverage for a condition described in subdivision (c).

(j) Except as provided in subdivision (l), this section does not apply to a newly covered enrollee who is offered an out-of-network option or to a newly covered enrollee who had the option to continue with his or her previous health plan or provider and instead voluntarily chose to change health plans.

(k) The provisions contained in this section are in addition to any other responsibilities of a health care service plan to provide continuity of care pursuant to this chapter. This section does not preclude a plan from providing continuity of care beyond the requirements of this section.

(l) (1) A health care service plan shall, at the request of a newly covered enrollee under an individual health care service plan contract, arrange for the completion of covered services as set forth in this section by a nonparticipating provider for one of the

conditions described in subdivision (c) if the newly covered enrollee meets both of the following:

(A) The newly covered enrollee's prior coverage was terminated under paragraph (5) or (6) of subdivision (a) of Section 1365 or subdivision (d) or (e) of Section 10273.6 of the Insurance Code, which includes circumstances when a health benefit plan is withdrawn from any portion of a market.

(B) At the time his or her coverage became effective, the newly covered enrollee was receiving services from that provider for one of the conditions described in subdivision (c).

(2) The completion of covered services required to be provided under this subdivision apply to services rendered to the newly covered enrollee on and after the effective date of his or her new coverage.

(3) A violation of this subdivision does not constitute a crime under Section 1390.

(m) Notice as to the process by which an enrollee may request completion of covered services pursuant to this section shall be provided in every disclosure form as required under Section 1363 and in any evidence of coverage issued after January 1, 2018. A plan shall provide a written copy of this information to its contracting providers and provider groups. A plan shall also provide a copy to its enrollees upon request. Notice as to the availability of the right to request completion of covered services shall be part of, accompany, or be sent simultaneously with any termination of coverage notice sent in the circumstances described in subdivision (l).

(n) The following definitions apply for the purposes of this section:

(1) "Individual provider" means a person who is a licentiate, as defined in Section 805 of the Business and Professions Code, or a person licensed under Chapter 2 (commencing with Section 1000) of Division 2 of the Business and Professions Code.

(2) "Nonparticipating provider" means a provider who is not contracted with the enrollee's health care service plan to provide services under the enrollee's plan contract.

(3) "Provider" shall have the same meaning as set forth in subdivision (i) of Section 1345.

(4) "Provider group" means a medical group, independent practice association, or any other similar organization.

(Amended by Stats. 2018, Ch. 92, Sec. 133. (SB 1289) Effective January 1, 2019.)

1373.10.

(a) On and after January 1, 1985, every health care service plan, that is not a health maintenance organization or is not a plan that enters exclusively into specialized health care service plan contracts, as defined by subdivision (n) of Section 1345, which provides coverage for hospital, medical, or surgical expenses, shall offer coverage to group contract holders for expenses incurred as a result of treatment by holders of certificates under Section 4938 of the Business and Professions Code, under such terms and conditions as may be agreed upon between the health care service plan and the group contract holder.

A health care service plan is not required to offer the coverage provided by this section as part of any contract covering employees of a public entity.

(b) For the purposes of this section, "health maintenance organization" or "HMO" means a public or private organization, organized under the laws of this state, which does all of the following:

(1) Provides or otherwise makes available to enrolled participants health care services, including at least the following basic health care services: usual physician services, hospitalization, laboratory, X-ray, emergency and preventive services, and out-of-area coverage.

(2) Is compensated, except for copayments, for the provision of basic health care services listed in paragraph (1) to enrolled participants on a predetermined periodic rate basis.

(3) Provides physician services primarily directly through physicians who are either employees or partners of the organization, or through arrangements with individual physicians or one or more groups of physicians, organized on a group practice or individual practice basis.

(Added by renumbering Section 1373.4 (as amended by Stats. 1985, Ch. 84) by Stats. 1986, Ch. 718, Sec. 3.)

1373.11.

A health care service plan that offers or provides one or more podiatry services, as defined in Section 2472 of the Business and Professions Code, as a specific podiatric plan benefit shall not refuse to give reasonable consideration to affiliation with podiatrists for the provision of service solely on the basis that they are podiatrists.

(Added by renumbering Section 1373.7 (as added by Stats. 1984, Ch. 163) by Stats. 1986, Ch. 718, Sec. 4.)

1373.12.

A health care service plan which offers or provides one or more chiropractic services, as defined in Section 7 of the Chiropractic Initiative Act, as a specific chiropractic plan benefit, when those services are not provided pursuant to a contract as described in subdivision (a) of Section 1373.9, shall not refuse to give reasonable consideration to affiliation with chiropractors for provision of services solely on the basis that they are chiropractors. Section 1390 shall not apply to this section.

(Added by Stats. 1991, Ch. 1224, Sec. 1.)

1373.13.

(a) It is the intent of the Legislature that all persons licensed in this state to engage in the practice of dentistry shall be accorded equal professional status and privileges, without regard to the degree earned.

(b) Notwithstanding any other provision of law, no health care service plan shall discriminate, with respect to the provision of, or contracts for, professional services, against a licensed dentist solely on the basis of the educational degree held by the dentist.

(Added by Stats. 1991, Ch. 729, Sec. 2.)

1373.14.

Except for a preexisting condition, any health care service plan, except a specialized health care service plan, which provides coverage on a group or individual basis for long-term care facility services or home-based care shall not exclude persons covered by the plan from receiving these benefits, if they are diagnosed as having any significant destruction of brain tissue with resultant loss of brain function, including, but not limited to, progressive, degenerative, and dementing illnesses, including, but not limited to, Alzheimer's disease, from the coverage offered for long-term care facility services or home-based care.

For purposes of this section, where a particular disease can be determined only with an autopsy, "diagnosed" means clinical diagnosis not dependent on pathological confirmation, but employing nationally accepted criteria.

(Amended by Stats. 1988, Ch. 1049, Sec. 1.)

1373.18.

Whenever any health care service plan, except a specialized health care service plan, negotiates and enters into a contract with providers to provide services at alternative rates of payment of the type described in Sections 10133 and 11512 of the Insurance Code, and enrollee copayments are to be based upon a percentage of the fee for services to be rendered, the amount of the enrollee copayment shall be calculated exclusively from the negotiated alternative rate for the service rendered. No health care service plan or provider, negotiating and entering into a contract pursuant to this section, shall charge or collect copayment amounts greater than those calculated in accordance with this section. This section shall become operative on January 1, 1993.

(Added by Stats. 1991, Ch. 827, Sec. 1. Section operative January 1, 1993, by its own provisions.)

1373.19.

Any health care service plan that includes a term that requires the parties to submit to binding arbitration shall, for those cases or disputes for which the total amount of damages claimed is two hundred thousand dollars ($200,000) or less, provide for selection by the parties of a single neutral arbitrator who shall have no jurisdiction to award more than two hundred thousand dollars ($200,000). This provision shall not be subject to waiver, except that nothing in this section shall prevent the parties to an arbitration from agreeing in writing, after a case or dispute has arisen and a request for arbitration has been submitted, to use a tripartite arbitration panel that includes two party-appointed arbitrators or a panel of three neutral arbitrators, or another multiple arbitrator system mutually agreeable to the parties. The agreement shall clearly indicate, in boldface type, that "A case or dispute subject to binding arbitration has arisen between the parties and we mutually agree to waive the requirement that cases or disputes for which the total amount of damages claimed is two hundred thousand dollars ($200,000) or less be adjudicated by a single neutral arbitrator." If the parties agree to waive the requirement to use a single neutral arbitrator, the enrollee or subscriber shall have three business days to rescind the agreement. If the agreement is also signed by counsel of the enrollee or subscriber, the agreement shall be immediately binding and may not be rescinded. If the parties are unable to agree on the selection of a neutral arbitrator, and the plan does not use a professional dispute resolution organization independent of the plan that has a procedure for a rapid selection or default appointment of a neutral arbitrator, the method provided in Section 1281.6 of the Code of Civil Procedure may be utilized.

(Amended by Stats. 1996, Ch. 1093, Sec. 1. Effective January 1, 1997.)

1373.20.

(a) If a plan uses arbitration to settle disputes with enrollees or subscribers, and does not use a professional dispute resolution organization independent of the plan that has a procedure for a rapid selection, or default appointment, of neutral arbitrators, the following requirements shall be met by the plan with respect to the arbitration of the disputes and shall not be subject to waiver:

(1) If the party seeking arbitration and the plan against which arbitration is sought, in cases or disputes requiring a single neutral arbitrator, are unable to select a neutral arbitrator within 30 days after service of a written demand requesting the designation, it shall be conclusively presumed that the agreed method of selection has failed and the method provided in Section 1281.6 of the Code of Civil Procedure may be utilized.

(2) In cases or disputes in which the parties have agreed to use a tripartite arbitration panel consisting of two party arbitrators and one neutral arbitrator, and the party arbitrators are unable to agree on the designation of a neutral arbitrator within 30 days after service of a written demand requesting the designation, it shall be conclusively presumed that the agreed method of selection has failed and the method provided in Section 1281.6 of the Code of Civil Procedure may be utilized.

(b) If a court reviewing a petition filed pursuant to Section 1373.19 or subdivision (a) finds that a party has engaged in dilatory conduct intended to cause delay in proceeding under the arbitration agreement, the court, by order, may award reasonable costs, including attorney fees, incurred in connection with the filing of the petition.

(c) If a plan uses arbitration to settle disputes with enrollees or subscribers, the following requirements shall be met with respect to extreme hardship cases:

(1) The plan contract shall contain a provision for the assumption of all or a portion of an enrollee's or subscriber's share of the fees and expenses of the neutral arbitrator in cases of extreme hardship.

(2) The plan shall disclose this provision to subscribers in any evidence of coverage issued or amended after August 1, 1997.

(3) The plan shall provide enrollees, upon request, with an application for relief under this subdivision, or information on how to obtain an application from the professional dispute resolution organization that will administer the arbitration process. If the plan uses a professional dispute resolution organization independent of the plan, the provision for assumption of the arbitration fees in cases of extreme hardship shall be established and administered by the dispute resolution organization.

(4) Approval or denial of the application shall be determined by either (A) a professional dispute resolution organization independent of the plan if the plan uses a professional dispute resolution organization, or (B) a neutral arbitrator who is not assigned to hear the underlying dispute, who has been selected pursuant to paragraph (1) of subdivision (a), and whose fees and expenses are paid for by the plan.

(Added by Stats. 1996, Ch. 1093, Sec. 2. Effective January 1, 1997.)

1373.21.

(a) If a health care service plan uses arbitration to settle disputes with enrollees or subscribers, it shall require that an arbitration award be accompanied by a written decision to the parties that indicates the prevailing party, the amount of any award and other relevant terms of the award, and the reasons for the award rendered.

(b) A copy of any modified written decision, including the amount of the award and other relevant terms of the award, the reasons for the award rendered, the name of the arbitrator or arbitrators, but excluding the names of the enrollee, the plan, witnesses, attorneys, providers, health plan employees, and health facilities, shall be provided to the department on a quarterly basis. The department shall make these modified decisions available to the public upon request.

(c) Subdivision (b) shall not preclude the department from requesting and securing from any plan copies of complete arbitration decisions issued pursuant to subdivision (a) for the purposes of administering this chapter.

(d) If the department receives a request for information about an arbitration decision obtained by the department pursuant to subdivision (b) or (c), the department shall not release information identifying a person or entity whose name has been or should have been removed from the arbitration decision pursuant to subdivision (b).

(e) Nothing in this section shall be construed to preclude the department, or any plan or person, from disclosing information contained in an arbitration decision if the disclosure is otherwise permitted by law.

(Added by Stats. 1998, Ch. 838, Sec. 1. Effective January 1, 1999.)

1374.

If a health care service plan entered into, amended, or renewed in this state on or after the effective date of this section provides in any manner for coverage for an employee and a covered spouse dependent on such employee, the plan shall not provide for coverage under conditions less favorable for employees than coverage provided for covered spouses dependent upon the employees.

(Added by Stats. 1976, Ch. 59.)

1374.3.

Notwithstanding any other provision of this chapter or of a health care service plan contract, every health care service plan shall comply with the requirements of Chapter 7 (commencing with Section 3750) of Part 1 of Division 9 of the Family Code and Section 14124.94 of the Welfare and Institutions Code.

(Amended by Stats. 1996, Ch. 1062, Sec. 18. Effective January 1, 1997.)

1374.5.

A health care service plan, which is issued, renewed, or amended on or after January 1, 1988, which includes mental health services coverage in nongroup contracts may not include a lifetime waiver for that coverage with respect to any applicant. The lifetime waiver of coverage provision shall be deemed unenforceable.

(Added by Stats. 1987, Ch. 1163, Sec. 1.)

1374.51.

No plan may utilize any information regarding whether an enrollee's psychiatric inpatient admission was made on a voluntary or involuntary basis for the purpose of determining eligibility for claim reimbursement.

(Added by Stats. 2001, Ch. 506, Sec. 3. Effective January 1, 2002.)

1374.55.

(a) On and after January 1, 1990, every health care service plan contract that is issued, amended, or renewed that covers hospital, medical, or surgical expenses on a group basis, where the plan is not a health maintenance organization as defined in Section 1373.10, shall offer coverage for the treatment of infertility, except in vitro fertilization, under those terms and conditions as may be agreed upon between the group subscriber and the plan. Every plan shall communicate the availability of that coverage to all group contractholders and to all prospective group contractholders with whom they are negotiating.

(b) For purposes of this section, "infertility" means either (1) the presence of a demonstrated condition recognized by a licensed physician and surgeon as a cause of infertility, or (2) the inability to conceive a pregnancy or to carry a pregnancy to a live birth after a year or more of regular sexual relations without contraception. "Treatment for infertility" means procedures consistent with established medical practices in the treatment of infertility by licensed physicians and surgeons including, but not limited to, diagnosis, diagnostic tests, medication, surgery, and gamete intrafallopian transfer. "In vitro fertilization" means the laboratory medical procedures involving the actual in vitro fertilization process.

(c) On and after January 1, 1990, every health care service plan that is a health maintenance organization, as defined in Section 1373.10, and that issues, renews, or amends a health care service plan contract that provides group coverage for hospital, medical, or surgical expenses shall offer the coverage specified in subdivision (a),

according to the terms and conditions that may be agreed upon between the group subscriber and the plan to group contractholders with at least 20 employees to whom the plan is offered. The plan shall communicate the availability of the coverage to those group contractholders and prospective group contractholders with whom the plan is negotiating.
(d) This section shall not be construed to deny or restrict in any way any existing right or benefit to coverage and treatment of infertility under an existing law, plan, or policy.
(e) This section shall not be construed to require any employer that is a religious organization to offer coverage for forms of treatment of infertility in a manner inconsistent with the religious organization's religious and ethical principles.
(f) (1) This section shall not be construed to require any plan, which is a subsidiary of an entity whose owner or corporate member is a religious organization, to offer coverage for treatment of infertility in a manner inconsistent with that religious organization's religious and ethical principles.
(2) For purposes of this subdivision, "subsidiary" of a specified corporation means a corporation more than 45 percent of the voting power of which is owned directly, or indirectly through one or more subsidiaries, by the specified corporation.
(g) Consistent with Section 1365.5, coverage for the treatment of infertility shall be offered and, if purchased, provided without discrimination on the basis of age, ancestry, color, disability, domestic partner status, gender, gender expression, gender identity, genetic information, marital status, national origin, race, religion, sex, or sexual orientation. Nothing in this subdivision shall be construed to interfere with the clinical judgment of a physician and surgeon.
(Amended by Stats. 2013, Ch. 644, Sec. 1. (AB 460) Effective January 1, 2014.)

1374.56.

(a) On and after July 1, 2000, every health care service plan contract, except a specialized health care service plan contract, issued, amended, delivered, or renewed in this state that provides coverage for hospital, medical, or surgical expenses shall provide coverage for the testing and treatment of phenylketonuria (PKU) under the terms and conditions of the plan contract.
(b) Coverage for treatment of phenylketonuria (PKU) shall include those formulas and special food products that are part of a diet prescribed by a licensed physician and managed by a health care professional in consultation with a physician who specializes in the treatment of metabolic disease and who participates in or is authorized by the plan, provided that the diet is deemed medically necessary to avert the development of serious physical or mental disabilities or to promote normal development or function as a consequence of phenylketonuria (PKU).
(c) Coverage pursuant to this section is not required except to the extent that the cost of the necessary formulas and special food products exceeds the cost of a normal diet.
(d) For purposes of this section, the following definitions shall apply:
(1) "Formula" means an enteral product or enteral products for use at home that are prescribed by a physician or nurse practitioner, or ordered by a registered dietician upon referral by a health care provider authorized to prescribe dietary treatments, as medically necessary for the treatment of phenylketonuria (PKU).
(2) "Special food product" means a food product that is both of the following:
(A) Prescribed by a physician or nurse practitioner for the treatment of phenylketonuria (PKU) and is consistent with the recommendations and best practices of qualified health professionals with expertise germane to, and experience in the treatment and care of, phenylketonuria (PKU). It does not include a food that is naturally low in protein, but may include a food product that is specially formulated to have less than one gram of protein per serving.
(B) Used in place of normal food products, such as grocery store foods, used by the general population.
(Added by Stats. 1999, Ch. 541, Sec. 1. Effective January 1, 2000.)

1374.57.

(a) No group health care service plan that provides hospital, medical, or surgical expense benefits for employees or subscribers and their dependents shall exclude a dependent child from eligibility or benefits solely because the dependent child does not reside with the employee or subscriber.
(b) A health care service plan that provides hospital, medical, or surgical expense benefits for employees or subscribers and their dependents shall enroll, upon application by the employer or group administrator, a dependent child of the noncustodial parent when the parent is the employee or subscriber, at any time the noncustodial or custodial parent makes an application for enrollment to the employer or group administrator when a court order for medical support exists. Except as provided in Section 1374.3, the application to the employer or group administrator shall be made within 90 days of the issuance of the court order. In the case of children who are eligible for medicaid, the State Department of Health Services or the district attorney in whose jurisdiction the child resides may make that application.
(c) This section shall not be construed to require that a health care service plan enroll a dependent who resides outside the plan's geographic service area, except as provided in Section 1374.3.
(d) Notwithstanding any other provision of this section, all health care service plans shall comply with the standards set forth in Section 1374.3.
(Amended by Stats. 1994, Ch. 147, Sec. 9. Effective July 11, 1994.)

1374.58.

(a) A group health care service plan that provides hospital, medical, or surgical expense benefits shall provide equal coverage to employers or guaranteed associations, as defined in Section 1357, for the registered domestic partner of an employee or subscriber to the same extent, and subject to the same terms and conditions, as provided to a spouse of the employee or subscriber, and shall inform employers and guaranteed associations of this coverage. A plan shall not offer or provide coverage for a registered domestic partner that is not equal to the coverage provided to the spouse of an employee or subscriber, and shall not discriminate in coverage between spouses or domestic partners of a different sex and spouses or domestic partners of the same sex. The prohibitions and requirements imposed by this section are in addition to any other prohibitions and requirements imposed by law.
(b) If an employer or guaranteed association has purchased coverage for spouses and registered domestic partners pursuant to subdivision (a), a health care service plan that provides hospital, medical, or surgical expense benefits for employees or subscribers and their spouses shall enroll, upon application by the employer or group administrator, a registered domestic partner of an employee or subscriber in accordance with the terms and conditions of the group contract that apply generally to all spouses under the plan, including coordination of benefits.
(c) For purposes of this section, the term "domestic partner" shall have the same meaning as that term is used in Section 297 of the Family Code.
(d) (1) A health care service plan may require that the employee or subscriber verify the status of the domestic partnership by providing to the plan a copy of a valid Declaration of Domestic Partnership filed with the Secretary of State pursuant to Section 298 of the Family Code or an equivalent document issued by a local agency of this state, another state, or a local agency of another state under which the partnership was created. The plan may also require that the employee or subscriber notify the plan upon the termination of the domestic partnership.
(2) Notwithstanding paragraph (1), a health care service plan may require the information described in that paragraph only if it also requests from the employee or subscriber whose spouse is provided coverage, verification of marital status and notification of dissolution of the marriage.
(e) Nothing in this section shall be construed to expand the requirements of Section 4980B of Title 26 of the United States Code, Section 1161, and following, of Title 29 of the United States Code, or Section 300bb-1, and following, of Title 42 of the United States Code, as added by the Consolidated Omnibus Budget Reconciliation Act of 1985 (Public Law 99-272), and as those provisions may be later amended.
(f) A plan subject to this section that is issued, amended, delivered, or renewed in this state on or after January 2, 2005, shall be deemed to provide coverage for registered domestic partners that is equal to the coverage provided to a spouse of an employee or subscriber.
(Amended by Stats. 2011, Ch. 722, Sec. 2. (SB 757) Effective January 1, 2012.)

1374.7.

(a) No plan shall refuse to enroll any person or accept any person as a subscriber or renew any person as a subscriber after appropriate application on the basis of a person's genetic characteristics that may, under some circumstances, be associated with disability in that person or that person's offspring. No plan shall require a higher rate or charge, or offer or provide different terms, conditions, or benefits, on the basis of a person's genetic characteristics that may, under some circumstances, be associated with disability in that person or that person's offspring.
(b) No plan shall seek information about a person's genetic characteristics for any nontherapeutic purpose.
(c) No discrimination shall be made in the fees or commissions of a solicitor or solicitor firm for an enrollment or a subscription or the renewal of an enrollment or subscription of any person on the basis of a person's genetic characteristics that may, under some circumstances, be associated with disability in that person or that person's offspring.
(d) "Genetic characteristics" as used in this section means either of the following:
(1) Any scientifically or medically identifiable gene or chromosome, or combination or alteration thereof, that is known to be a cause of a disease or disorder in a person or his or her offspring, or that is determined to be associated with a statistically increased risk of development of a disease or disorder, and that is presently not associated with any symptoms of any disease or disorder.
(2) Inherited characteristics that may derive from the individual or family member, that are known to be a cause of a disease or disorder in a person or his or her offspring, or that are determined to be associated with a statistically increased risk of development of a disease or disorder, and that are presently not associated with any symptoms of any disease or disorder.
(Amended by Stats. 1999, Ch. 311, Sec. 3. Effective January 1, 2000.)

1374.75.

(a) No health care service plan shall deny, refuse to enroll, refuse to renew, cancel, restrict, or otherwise terminate, exclude, or limit coverage, or charge a different rate for the same coverage, on the basis that the applicant or covered person is, has been, or may be a victim of domestic violence.
(b) Nothing in this section shall prevent a health care service plan from underwriting coverage on the basis of the medical condition of an individual so long as the consideration of the condition (1) does not take into account whether such an individual's medical condition was caused by an act of domestic violence, (2) is the same with respect to an applicant or enrollee who is not the subject of domestic violence as with an applicant or enrollee who is the subject of domestic violence, and (3) does not violate any other act, regulation, or rule of law. The fact that an individual is, has been, or may be the subject of domestic violence shall not be considered a medical condition.
(c) As used in this section, "domestic violence" means domestic violence, as defined in Section 6211 of the Family Code.
(Added by Stats. 1995, Ch. 603, Sec. 1. Effective January 1, 1996.)

1374.8.

(a) A health care service plan shall not release any information to an employer that would directly or indirectly indicate to the employer that an employee is receiving or has received services from a health care provider covered by the plan unless authorized to do so by the employee. An insurer that has, pursuant to an agreement, assumed the responsibility to pay compensation pursuant to Article 3 (commencing with Section 3750) of Chapter 4 of Part 1 of Division 4 of the Labor Code, shall not be considered an employer for the purposes of this section.

(b) Nothing in this section prohibits a health care service plan from releasing relevant information described in this section for the purposes set forth in Chapter 12 (commencing with Section 1871) of Part 2 of Division 1 of the Insurance Code.

(c) Nothing in this section prohibits a health care service plan from releasing relevant information described in this section for the purposes set forth in Section 1385.10.

(Amended by Stats. 2014, Ch. 577, Sec. 1. (SB 1182) Effective January 1, 2015.)

1374.9.

For violations of Section 1374.7, the director may, after appropriate notice and opportunity for hearing, by order, levy administrative penalties as follows:

(a) Any health care service plan that violates Section 1374.7, or that violates any rule or order adopted or issued pursuant to this section, is liable for administrative penalties of not less than two thousand five hundred dollars ($2,500) for each first violation, and of not less than five thousand dollars ($5,000) nor more than ten thousand dollars ($10,000) for each second violation, and of not less than fifteen thousand dollars ($15,000) and not more than one hundred thousand dollars ($100,000) for each subsequent violation.

(b) The administrative penalties shall be paid to the Managed Care Administrative Fines and Penalties Fund and shall be used for the purposes specified in Section 1341.45.

(c) The administrative penalties available to the director pursuant to this section are not exclusive, and may be sought and employed in any combination with civil, criminal, and other administrative remedies deemed advisable by the director to enforce the provisions of this chapter.

(Amended by Stats. 2008, Ch. 607, Sec. 7. Effective September 30, 2008.)

1374.10.

(a) Every health care service plan that covers hospital, medical or surgical expenses and which is not qualified as a health maintenance organization under Title XIII of the federal Public Health Service Act (42 U.S.C. Sec. 300e, et seq.) shall make available and offer to include in every group contract entered into on or after January 1, 1979, benefits for home health care as set forth in this section provided by a licensed home health agency subject to the right of the subscriber group to reject the benefits or to select any alternative level of benefits as may be offered by the health care service plan.

In rural areas where there are no licensed home health agencies or in which the supply of home health agency services does not meet the needs of the community, the services of visiting nurses, if available, shall be offered under the health care service plan subject to the terms and conditions set forth in subdivision (b).

(b) As used in this section:

(1) "Home health care" means the continued care and treatment of a covered person who is under the direct care and supervision of a physician but only if (i) continued hospitalization would have been required if home health care were not provided, (ii) the home health treatment plan is established and approved by a physician within 14 days after an inpatient hospital confinement has ended and such treatment plan is for the same or related condition for which the covered person was hospitalized, and (iii) home health care commences within 14 days after the hospital confinement has ended. "Home health services" consist of, but shall not be limited to, the following: (i) part-time or intermittent skilled nursing services provided by a registered nurse or licensed vocational nurse; (ii) part-time or intermittent home health aide services which provide supportive services in the home under the supervision of a registered nurse or a physical, speech or occupational therapist; (iii) physical, occupational or speech therapy; and (iv) medical supplies, drugs and medicines prescribed by a physician and related pharmaceutical services, and laboratory services to the extent such charges or costs would have been covered under the plan if the covered person had remained in the hospital.

(2) "Home health agency" means a public or private agency or organization licensed by the State Department of Health Services in accordance with the provisions of Chapter 8 (commencing with Section 1725) of Division 2 of the Health and Safety Code.

(c) The plan may contain a limitation on the number of home health visits for which benefits are payable, but the number of such visits shall not be less than 100 in any calendar year or in any continuous 12-month period for each person covered under the plan. Except for a home health aide, each visit by a representative of a home health agency shall be considered as one home health care visit. A visit of four hours or less by a home health aide shall be considered as one home health visit.

(d) Home health benefits in this section shall be subject to all other provisions of this chapter. In addition, such benefits may be subject to an annual deductible of not more than fifty dollars ($50) for each person covered under a plan, and may be subject to a coinsurance provision which provides coverage of not less than 80 percent of the reasonable charges for such services.

(e) Nothing in this section shall preclude a plan offering other health care benefits provided in the home.

(f) Nothing in this section shall relieve any plan from providing all basic health care services as required by subdivision (i) of Section 1367 except that a plan subject to this section may fulfill that requirement with respect to home health services in connection with any particular group contract by providing benefits for home health care as set forth in this section if the subscriber group has not rejected such benefits.

(Added by Stats. 1978, Ch. 1130.)

1374.11.

No health care service plan shall deny a claim for hospital, medical, surgical, dental, or optometric services for the sole reason that the individual served was confined in a city or county jail or was a juvenile detained in any facility, if such individual is otherwise entitled to reimbursement for such services under such contract and incurs expense for the services so provided during confinement. This provision shall apply to any health care service plan contract entered into or renewed on or after July 1, 1980, whether or not such contract contains any provision terminating benefits under such plan upon an individual's confinement in a city or county jail or juvenile detention facility.

(Added by Stats. 1980, Ch. 90.)

1374.12.

No health care service plan contract issued, entered into, or renewed on or after July 1, 1984, shall be deemed to contain any provision restricting the liability of the plan with respect to expenses solely because the expenses were incurred while the member was in a state hospital, if the policy, contract, or agreement would have paid for the services but for the fact that they were provided in a state hospital. Nothing in this section shall be deemed to require a plan to pay a state hospital for covered expenses incurred by a member at a rate or charge higher than the plan would pay for such services to a hospital with which the plan has entered a contract providing for alternative rates of payment or limiting payments for services secured by members.

(Added by Stats. 1983, Ch. 796, Sec. 1. Effective September 14, 1983.)

1374.13.

(a) For the purposes of this section, the definitions in subdivision (a) of Section 2290.5 of the Business and Professions Code shall apply.

(b) It is the intent of the Legislature to recognize the practice of telehealth as a legitimate means by which an individual may receive health care services from a health care provider without in-person contact with the health care provider.

(c) No health care service plan shall require that in-person contact occur between a health care provider and a patient before payment is made for the covered services appropriately provided through telehealth, subject to the terms and conditions of the contract entered into between the enrollee or subscriber and the health care service plan, and between the health care service plan and its participating providers or provider groups.

(d) No health care service plan shall limit the type of setting where services are provided for the patient or by the health care provider before payment is made for the covered services appropriately provided through telehealth, subject to the terms and conditions of the contract entered into between the enrollee or subscriber and the health care service plan, and between the health care service plan and its participating providers or provider groups.

(e) The requirements of this section shall also apply to health care service plan and Medi-Cal managed care plan contracts with the State Department of Health Care Services pursuant to Chapter 7 (commencing with Section 14000) or Chapter 8 (commencing with Section 14200) of Part 3 of Division 9 of the Welfare and Institutions Code.

(f) Notwithstanding any other provision, this section shall not be interpreted to authorize a health care service plan to require the use of telehealth when the health care provider has determined that it is not appropriate.

(Amended by Stats. 2012, Ch. 782, Sec. 6. (AB 1733) Effective January 1, 2013.)

1374.15.

Any health care service plan shall, upon request by any public entity or political subdivision of the state with whom it has entered into a contract, disclose within a reasonable time period, not to exceed 60 calendar days, the method and data used in calculating the rates of payment for the contract.

(Added by Stats. 1991, Ch. 898, Sec. 2.)

1374.16.

(a) Every health care service plan, except a specialized health care service plan, shall establish and implement a procedure by which an enrollee may receive a standing referral to a specialist. The procedure shall provide for a standing referral to a specialist if the primary care physician determines in consultation with the specialist, if any, and the plan medical director or his or her designee, that an enrollee needs continuing care from a specialist. The referral shall be made pursuant to a treatment plan approved by the health care service plan in consultation with the primary care physician, the specialist, and the enrollee, if a treatment plan is deemed necessary to describe the course of the care. A treatment plan may be deemed to be not necessary provided that a current standing referral to a specialist is approved by the plan or its contracting provider, medical group, or independent practice association. The treatment plan may limit the number of visits to the specialist, limit the period of time that the visits are authorized, or require that the specialist provide the primary care physician with regular reports on the health care provided to the enrollee.

(b) Every health care service plan, except a specialized health care service plan, shall establish and implement a procedure by which an enrollee with a condition or disease that requires specialized medical care over a prolonged period of time and is life-threatening, degenerative, or disabling may receive a referral to a specialist or specialty care center that has expertise in treating the condition or disease for the purpose of having the specialist coordinate the enrollee's health care. The referral shall be made if the primary care physician, in consultation with the specialist or specialty care center if any, and the plan medical director or his or her designee determines that this specialized medical care is medically necessary for the enrollee. The referral shall be made pursuant to a treatment plan approved by the health care service plan in consultation with the primary care physician, specialist or specialty care center, and enrollee, if a treatment plan is deemed necessary to describe the course of care. A treatment plan may be deemed to be not necessary provided that the appropriate referral to a specialist or specialty care center is approved by the plan or its contracting provider, medical group, or independent practice association. After the referral is made, the specialist shall be authorized to provide health care services that are within the specialist's area of expertise and training to the enrollee in the same manner as the enrollee's primary care physician, subject to the terms of the treatment plan.

(c) The determinations described in subdivisions (a) and (b) shall be made within three business days of the date the request for the determination is made by the enrollee or the enrollee's primary care physician and all appropriate medical records and other items of information necessary to make the determination are provided. Once a determination is made, the referral shall be made within four business days of the date the proposed treatment plan, if any, is submitted to the plan medical director or his or her designee.

(d) Subdivisions (a) and (b) do not require a health care service plan to refer to a specialist who, or to a specialty care center that, is not employed by or under contract with the health care service plan to provide health care services to its enrollees, unless there is no specialist within the plan network that is appropriate to provide treatment to the enrollee, as determined by the primary care physician in consultation with the plan medical director as documented in the treatment plan developed pursuant to subdivision (a) or (b).

(e) For the purposes of this section, "specialty care center" means a center that is accredited or designated by an agency of the state or federal government or by a voluntary national health organization as having special expertise in treating the life-threatening disease or condition or degenerative and disabling disease or condition for which it is accredited or designated.

(f) As used in this section, a "standing referral" means a referral by a primary care physician to a specialist for more than one visit to the specialist, as indicated in the treatment plan, if any, without the primary care physician having to provide a specific referral for each visit.

(g) This section shall become operative on (1) January 1, 2004, or (2) the date of adoption of an accreditation or designation by an agency of the state or federal government or by a voluntary national health organization of an HIV or AIDS specialist, whichever date is earlier.

(Repealed (in Sec. 1) and added by Stats. 2000, Ch. 426, Sec. 2. Effective January 1, 2001. Section operative January 1, 2004, or sooner, by its own provisions.)

1374.17.

(a) A health care service plan shall not deny coverage that is otherwise available under the plan contract for the costs of solid organ or other tissue transplantation services based upon the enrollee or subscriber being infected with the human immunodeficiency virus.

(b) Notwithstanding any other provision of law, in the provision of benefits required by this section, a health care service plan may utilize case management, network providers, utilization review techniques, prior authorization, copayments, or other cost sharing, subject to the terms and conditions of the plan contract and consistent with sound clinical processes and guidelines.

(Added by Stats. 2005, Ch. 419, Sec. 1. Effective January 1, 2006.)

1374.19.

(a) This section shall only apply to a health care service plan covering dental services or a specialized health care service plan contract covering dental service pursuant to this chapter.

(b) For purposes of this section, the following terms have the following meanings:

(1) "Coordination of benefits" means the method by which a health care service plan covering dental services or a specialized health care service plan contract, covering dental services, and one or more other health care service plans, specialized health care service plans, or disability insurers, covering dental services, pay their respective reimbursements for dental benefits when an enrollee is covered by multiple health care service plans or specialized health care services plan contracts, or a combination thereof, or a combination of health care service plans or specialized health care service plan contracts and disability insurers.

(2) "Primary dental benefit plan" means a health care service plan or specialized health care service plan contract regulated pursuant to this chapter or a dental insurance policy issued by a disability insurer regulated pursuant to Part 2 (commencing with Section 10110) of Division 2 of the Insurance Code that provides an enrollee or insured with primary dental coverage.

(3) "Secondary dental benefit plan" means a health care service plan or specialized health care service plan contract regulated pursuant to this chapter or a dental insurance policy issued by a disability insurer regulated pursuant to Part 2 (commencing with Section 10110) of Division 2 of the Insurance Code that provides an enrollee or insured with secondary dental coverage.

(c) A health care service plan covering dental services or a specialized health care service plan issuing a specialized health care service plan contract covering dental services shall declare its coordination of benefits policy prominently in its evidence of coverage or contract with both enrollee and subscriber.

(d) When a primary dental benefit plan is coordinating its benefits with one or more secondary dental benefits plans, it shall pay the maximum amount required by its contract with the enrollee or subscriber.

(e) A health care service plan covering dental services or a specialized health care service plan contract covering dental services, when acting as a secondary dental benefit plan, shall pay the lesser of either the amount that it would have paid in the absence of any other dental benefit coverage, or the enrollee's total out-of-pocket cost payable under the primary dental benefit plan for benefits covered under the secondary plan.

(f) Nothing in this section is intended to conflict with or modify the way in which a health care service plan covering dental services or a specialized health care service plan covering dental services determines which dental benefit plan is primary and which is secondary in coordinating benefits with another plan or insurer pursuant to existing state law or regulation.

(Added by Stats. 2007, Ch. 164, Sec. 2. Effective January 1, 2008.)

1374.195.

(a) With respect to a contract between a health care service plan or specialized health care service plan and a dentist to provide covered dental services to enrollees of the plan, the contract shall not require a dentist to accept an amount set by the plan as payment for dental care services provided to an enrollee that are not covered services under the enrollee's plan contract. This subdivision shall only apply to provider contracts issued, amended, or renewed on or after January 1, 2011.

(b) A provider shall not charge more for dental services that are not covered services under a plan contract than his or her usual and customary rate for those services. The department shall not be required to enforce this subdivision.

(c) The evidence of coverage and disclosure form, or combined evidence of coverage and disclosure form, for every health care service plan contract covering dental services, or specialized health care service plan contract covering dental services, that is issued, amended, or renewed on or after July 1, 2011, shall include the following statement:

IMPORTANT: If you opt to receive dental services that are not covered services under this plan, a participating dental provider may charge you his or her usual and customary rate for those services. Prior to providing a patient with dental services that are not a covered benefit, the dentist should provide to the patient a treatment plan that includes each anticipated service to be provided and the estimated cost of each service. If you would like more information about dental coverage options, you may call member services at [insert appropriate telephone number] or your insurance broker. To fully understand your coverage, you may wish to carefully review this evidence of coverage document.

(d) For purposes of this section, "covered services" or "covered dental services" means dental care services for which the plan is obligated to pay pursuant to an enrollee's plan contract, or for which the plan would be obligated to pay pursuant to an enrollee's plan contract but for the application of contractual limitations such as deductibles, copayments, coinsurance, waiting periods, annual or lifetime maximums, frequency limitations, or alternative benefit payments.

(Added by Stats. 2010, Ch. 673, Sec. 1. (AB 2275) Effective January 1, 2011.)

ARTICLE 5.5. Health Care Service Plan Coverage Contract Changes [1374.20 - 1374.29]

(Heading of Article 5.5 amended by Stats. 2002, Ch. 336, Sec. 2.)

1374.20.

(a) No group health care service plan shall change the premium rates or applicable copayments or coinsurances or deductibles for the length of the contract, except as specified in subdivision (b), during any of the following time periods:

(1) After the group contractholder has delivered written notice of acceptance of the contract.

(2) After the start of the employer's annual open enrollment period.

(3) After the receipt of payment of the premium for the first month of coverage in accordance with the contract effective date.

(b) Changes to the premium rates or applicable copayments or coinsurances or deductibles of a contract shall, subject to the plan meeting the requirements of this article, be allowed in any of the following circumstances:

(1) When authorized or required in the group contract.

(2) When the contract was agreed to under a preliminary agreement that states that it is subject to execution of a definitive agreement.

(3) When the plan and contractholder mutually agree in writing.

(Added by Stats. 2002, Ch. 336, Sec. 4. Effective January 1, 2003.)

1374.21.

(a) (1) A change in premium rates or changes in coverage stated in a group health care service plan contract shall not become effective unless the plan has delivered in writing a notice indicating the change or changes at least 60 days prior to the contract renewal effective date.

(2) The notice delivered pursuant to paragraph (1) for large group health plans shall also include the following information:

(A) Whether the rate proposed to be in effect is greater than the average rate increase for individual market products negotiated by the California Health Benefit Exchange for the most recent calendar year for which the rates are final.

(B) Whether the rate proposed to be in effect is greater than the average rate increase negotiated by the Board of Administration of the Public Employees' Retirement System for the most recent calendar year for which the rates are final.

(C) Whether the rate change includes any portion of the excise tax paid by the health plan.

(b) A health care service plan that declines to offer coverage to or denies enrollment for a large group applying for coverage shall, at the time of the denial of coverage, provide the applicant with the specific reason or reasons for the decision in writing, in clear, easily understandable language.

(c) (1) For small group health care service plan contracts, if the department determines that a rate is unreasonable or not justified consistent with Article 6.2 (commencing with Section 1385.01), the plan shall notify the contractholder of this determination. This notification may be included in the notice required in subdivision (a).

(2) The notification to the contractholder shall be developed by the department and shall include the following statements in 14-point type:

(A) The Department of Managed Health Care has determined that the rate for this product is unreasonable or not justified after reviewing information submitted to it by the plan.

(B) The contractholder has the option to obtain other coverage from this plan or another plan, or to keep this coverage.

(C) Small business purchasers may want to contact Covered California at www.coveredca.com for help in understanding available options.

(3) In developing the notification, the department shall take into consideration that this notice is required to be provided to a small group applicant pursuant to subdivision (g) of Section 1385.03.

(4) The development of the notification required under this subdivision shall not be subject to the Administrative Procedure Act (Chapter 3.5 (commencing with Section 11340) of Part 1 of Division 3 of Title 2 of the Government Code).

(5) The plan may include in the notification to the contractholder the Internet Web site address at which the plan's final justification for implementing an increase that has been determined to be unreasonable by the director may be found pursuant to Section 154.230 of Title 45 of the Code of Federal Regulations.

(6) The notice shall also be provided to the solicitor for the contractholder, if any, so that the solicitor may assist the purchaser in finding other coverage.

(Amended by Stats. 2016, Ch. 498, Sec. 1. (SB 908) Effective January 1, 2017.)

1374.22.

(a) The written notice described in subdivision (a) of Section 1374.21 shall be delivered by mail at the last known address at least 60 days prior to the renewal effective date to the group contract holder.

(b) The written notice shall state in italics and in 12-point type the actual dollar amount and the specific percentage of the premium rate increase. Further, the notice shall describe in plain understandable English and highlighted in italics any changes in the plan design or change in benefits with reduction in benefits, waivers, exclusions, or conditions.

(c) The written notice shall specify in a minimum of 10-point bold typeface the reason or reasons for premium rate changes, plan design, or plan benefit changes.

(Amended by Stats. 2010, Ch. 661, Sec. 3. (SB 1163) Effective January 1, 2011.)

1374.23.

Notwithstanding subdivision (a) of Section 1374.22, if the plan does not guarantee either premium rates or plan design or benefits for any specified time period greater than 180 days, it shall deliver the written notice by mail to the group contract holder at least 30 days prior to the group contract renewal effective date.

(Added by Stats. 1990, Ch. 949, Sec. 1.)

1374.24.

There shall be no liability on the part of, and no cause of action of any nature shall arise against, any health care service plan required to provide the notice or its authorized representatives, or agents, for any statement made, unless shown to have been made with malice in fact, by any of them in (a) any written notice or in any other oral or written communication specifying the reasons for the notice, (b) any communication providing information pertaining to that notice, or (c) evidence submitted at any court proceeding or informal inquiry in which that notice is at issue.

(Added by Stats. 1990, Ch. 949, Sec. 1.)

1374.25.

Proof of mailing a notice and the reason therefor to the appropriate entity or individual at the most current policy or plan address shall be sufficient proof of the notice required by this chapter.

(Added by Stats. 1990, Ch. 949, Sec. 1.)

1374.255.

(a) This section shall apply to grandfathered health care service plan contracts and nongrandfathered health care service plan contracts in the individual or small group markets that are issued, amended, or renewed on or after January 1, 2017.

(b) Notwithstanding paragraph (1) of subdivision (b) of Section 1374.20, a health care service plan contract shall not change the cost-sharing design during the plan year, except when required by state or federal law.

(c) For purposes of this section, the following definitions shall apply:

(1) "Cost sharing" includes any copayment, coinsurance, deductible, or any other form of cost sharing by the enrollee other than the premium or share of premium.

(2) "Plan year" has the meaning set forth in Section 144.103 of Title 45 of the Code of Federal Regulations. For nongrandfathered health care service plan contracts in the individual market, "plan year" means the calendar year.

(3) "Cost-sharing design" means the amount or proportion of cost sharing applied to a covered benefit.

(Added by Stats. 2016, Ch. 192, Sec. 1. (SB 923) Effective January 1, 2017.)

1374.26.

The director may, as required by this article, or from time to time as conditions warrant, pursuant to Chapter 3.5 (commencing with Section 11340) of Part 1 of Division 3 of Title 2 of the Government Code, adopt reasonable regulations, and amendments and additions thereto, as are necessary to administer this article.

(Amended by Stats. 1999, Ch. 525, Sec. 112. Effective January 1, 2000. Operative July 1, 2000, or sooner, by Sec. 214 of Ch. 525.)

1374.27.

The director may levy administrative penalties and may suspend or revoke the license or licenses issued to any health care service plan, after notice and hearing, to have violated this article or a regulation adopted pursuant to the authority of this article. Notice of hearing shall be accomplished and a hearing conducted in accordance with Chapter 5

(commencing with Section 11500) of Part 1 of Division 3 of Title 2 of the Government Code, and the director shall have all of the powers granted therein.

The remedies available to the director pursuant to this article are not exclusive, and may be sought and employed in any combination with other remedies deemed advisable by the director to enforce the provisions of this article.

(Amended by Stats. 1999, Ch. 525, Sec. 113. Effective January 1, 2000. Operative July 1, 2000, or sooner, by Sec. 214 of Ch. 525.)

1374.28.

In addition to any other penalty provided by law or the availability of any administrative procedure, if a health care service plan, after notice and hearing, is found to have violated this article, or regulations adopted pursuant to this article, or knowingly permits any person to do so, the director may suspend the authority of the plan to transact business.

(Amended by Stats. 1999, Ch. 525, Sec. 114. Effective January 1, 2000. Operative July 1, 2000, or sooner, by Sec. 214 of Ch. 525.)

1374.29.

The purpose of this article is to promote the public interest, to prevent unfair and unlawful health care business practices, and to promote adequate consumer and employer advance notice of changes in the cost of health coverage in order to allow for comparative shopping and to reduce the cost of health coverage.

(Added by renumbering Section 1374.20 by Stats. 2002, Ch. 336, Sec. 3. Effective January 1, 2003.)

ARTICLE 5.55. Appeals Seeking Independent Medical Reviews [1374.30 - 1374.36]

(Article 5.55 added by Stats. 1999, Ch. 533, Sec. 1.)

1374.30.

(a) Commencing January 1, 2001, there is hereby established in the department the Independent Medical Review System.

(b) For the purposes of this chapter, "disputed health care service" means any health care service eligible for coverage and payment under a health care service plan contract that has been denied, modified, or delayed by a decision of the plan, or by one of its contracting providers, in whole or in part due to a finding that the service is not medically necessary. A decision regarding a disputed health care service relates to the practice of medicine and is not a coverage decision. A disputed health care service does not include services provided by a specialized health care service plan, except to the extent that the service (1) involves the practice of medicine, or (2) is provided pursuant to a contract with a health care service plan that covers hospital, medical, or surgical benefits. If a plan, or one of its contracting providers, issues a decision denying, modifying, or delaying health care services, based in whole or in part on a finding that the proposed health care services are not a covered benefit under the contract that applies to the enrollee, the statement of decision shall clearly specify the provision in the contract that excludes that coverage.

(c) For the purposes of this chapter, "coverage decision" means the approval or denial of health care services by a plan, or by one of its contracting entities, substantially based on a finding that the provision of a particular service is included or excluded as a covered benefit under the terms and conditions of the health care service plan contract. A "coverage decision" does not encompass a plan or contracting provider decision regarding a disputed health care service.

(d) (1) All enrollee grievances involving a disputed health care service are eligible for review under the Independent Medical Review System if the requirements of this article are met. If the department finds that an enrollee grievance involving a disputed health care service does not meet the requirements of this article for review under the Independent Medical Review System, the enrollee request for review shall be treated as a request for the department to review the grievance pursuant to subdivision (b) of Section 1368. All other enrollee grievances, including grievances involving coverage decisions, remain eligible for review by the department pursuant to subdivision (b) of Section 1368.

(2) In any case in which an enrollee or provider asserts that a decision to deny, modify, or delay health care services was based, in whole or in part, on consideration of medical necessity, the department shall have the final authority to determine whether the grievance is more properly resolved pursuant to an independent medical review as provided under this article or pursuant to subdivision (b) of Section 1368.

(3) The department shall be the final arbiter when there is a question as to whether an enrollee grievance is a disputed health care service or a coverage decision. The department shall establish a process to complete an initial screening of an enrollee grievance. If there appears to be any medical necessity issue, the grievance shall be resolved pursuant to an independent medical review as provided under this article or pursuant to subdivision (b) of Section 1368.

(e) Every health care service plan contract that is issued, amended, renewed, or delivered in this state on or after January 1, 2000, shall provide an enrollee with the opportunity to seek an independent medical review whenever health care services have been denied, modified, or delayed by the plan, or by one of its contracting providers, if the decision was based in whole or in part on a finding that the proposed health care services are not medically necessary. For purposes of this article, an enrollee may designate an agent to act on his or her behalf, as described in paragraph (2) of subdivision (b) of Section 1368. The provider may join with or otherwise assist the enrollee in seeking an independent medical review, and may advocate on behalf of the enrollee.

(f) Medi-Cal beneficiaries enrolled in a health care service plan shall not be excluded from participation. Medicare beneficiaries enrolled in a health care service plan shall not be excluded unless expressly preempted by federal law. Reviews of cases for Medi-Cal

enrollees shall be conducted in accordance with statutes and regulations for the Medi-Cal program.
(g) The department may seek to integrate the quality of care and consumer protection provisions, including remedies, of the Independent Medical Review System with related dispute resolution procedures of other health care agency programs, including the Medicare and Medi-Cal programs, in a way that minimizes the potential for duplication, conflict, and added costs. Nothing in this subdivision shall be construed to limit any rights conferred upon enrollees under this chapter.
(h) The independent medical review process authorized by this article is in addition to any other procedures or remedies that may be available.
(i) Every health care service plan shall prominently display in every plan member handbook or relevant informational brochure, in every plan contract, on enrollee evidence of coverage forms, on copies of plan procedures for resolving grievances, on letters of denials issued by either the plan or its contracting organization, on the grievance forms required under Section 1368, and on all written responses to grievances, information concerning the right of an enrollee to request an independent medical review in cases where the enrollee believes that health care services have been improperly denied, modified, or delayed by the plan, or by one of its contracting providers.
(j) An enrollee may apply to the department for an independent medical review when all of the following conditions are met:
(1) (A) The enrollee's provider has recommended a health care service as medically necessary, or
(B) The enrollee has received urgent care or emergency services that a provider determined was medically necessary, or
(C) The enrollee, in the absence of a provider recommendation under subparagraph (A) or the receipt of urgent care or emergency services by a provider under subparagraph (B), has been seen by an in-plan provider for the diagnosis or treatment of the medical condition for which the enrollee seeks independent review. The plan shall expedite access to an in-plan provider upon request of an enrollee. The in-plan provider need not recommend the disputed health care service as a condition for the enrollee to be eligible for an independent review.
For purposes of this article, the enrollee's provider may be an out-of-plan provider. However, the plan shall have no liability for payment of services provided by an out-of-plan provider, except as provided pursuant to subdivision (c) of Section 1374.34.
(2) The disputed health care service has been denied, modified, or delayed by the plan, or by one of its contracting providers, based in whole or in part on a decision that the health care service is not medically necessary.
(3) The enrollee has filed a grievance with the plan or its contracting provider pursuant to Section 1368, and the disputed decision is upheld or the grievance remains unresolved after 30 days. The enrollee shall not be required to participate in the plan's grievance process for more than 30 days. In the case of a grievance that requires expedited review pursuant to Section 1368.01, the enrollee shall not be required to participate in the plan's grievance process for more than three days.
(k) An enrollee may apply to the department for an independent medical review of a decision to deny, modify, or delay health care services, based in whole or in part on a finding that the disputed health care services are not medically necessary, within six months of any of the qualifying periods or events under subdivision (j). The director may extend the application deadline beyond six months if the circumstances of a case warrant the extension.
(l) The enrollee shall pay no application or processing fees of any kind.
(m) As part of its notification to the enrollee regarding a disposition of the enrollee's grievance that denies, modifies, or delays health care services, the plan shall provide the enrollee with a one- or two-page application form approved by the department, and an addressed envelope, which the enrollee may return to initiate an independent medical review. The plan shall include on the form any information required by the department to facilitate the completion of the independent medical review, such as the enrollee's diagnosis or condition, the nature of the disputed health care service sought by the enrollee, a means to identify the enrollee's case, and any other material information. The form shall also include the following:
(1) Notice that a decision not to participate in the independent medical review process may cause the enrollee to forfeit any statutory right to pursue legal action against the plan regarding the disputed health care service.
(2) A statement indicating the enrollee's consent to obtain any necessary medical records from the plan, any of its contracting providers, and any out-of-plan provider the enrollee may have consulted on the matter, to be signed by the enrollee.
(3) Notice of the enrollee's right to provide information or documentation, either directly or through the enrollee's provider, regarding any of the following:
(A) A provider recommendation indicating that the disputed health care service is medically necessary for the enrollee's medical condition.
(B) Medical information or justification that a disputed health care service, on an urgent care or emergency basis, was medically necessary for the enrollee's medical condition.
(C) Reasonable information supporting the enrollee's position that the disputed health care service is or was medically necessary for the enrollee's medical condition, including all information provided to the enrollee by the plan or any of its contracting providers, still in the possession of the enrollee, concerning a plan or provider decision regarding disputed health care services, and a copy of any materials the enrollee submitted to the plan, still in the possession of the enrollee, in support of the grievance, as well as any additional material that the enrollee believes is relevant.
(4) A section designed to collect information on the enrollee's ethnicity, race, and primary language spoken that includes both of the following:
(A) A statement of intent indicating that the information is used for statistics only, in order to ensure that all enrollees get the best care possible.
(B) A statement indicating that providing this information is optional and will not affect the independent medical review process in any way.
(n) Upon notice from the department that the health care service plan's enrollee has applied for an independent medical review, the plan or its contracting providers shall provide to the independent medical review organization designated by the department a copy of all of the following documents within three business days of the plan's receipt of the department's notice of a request by an enrollee for an independent review:
(1) (A) A copy of all of the enrollee's medical records in the possession of the plan or its contracting providers relevant to each of the following:
(i) The enrollee's medical condition.
(ii) The health care services being provided by the plan and its contracting providers for the condition.
(iii) The disputed health care services requested by the enrollee for the condition.
(B) Any newly developed or discovered relevant medical records in the possession of the plan or its contracting providers after the initial documents are provided to the independent medical review organization shall be forwarded immediately to the independent medical review organization. The plan shall concurrently provide a copy of medical records required by this subparagraph to the enrollee or the enrollee's provider, if authorized by the enrollee, unless the offer of medical records is declined or otherwise prohibited by law. The confidentiality of all medical record information shall be maintained pursuant to applicable state and federal laws.
(2) A copy of all information provided to the enrollee by the plan and any of its contracting providers concerning plan and provider decisions regarding the enrollee's condition and care, and a copy of any materials the enrollee or the enrollee's provider submitted to the plan and to the plan's contracting providers in support of the enrollee's request for disputed health care services. This documentation shall include the written response to the enrollee's grievance, required by paragraph (4) of subdivision (a) of Section 1368. The confidentiality of any enrollee medical information shall be maintained pursuant to applicable state and federal laws.
(3) A copy of any other relevant documents or information used by the plan or its contracting providers in determining whether disputed health care services should have been provided, and any statements by the plan and its contracting providers explaining the reasons for the decision to deny, modify, or delay disputed health care services on the basis of medical necessity. The plan shall concurrently provide a copy of documents required by this paragraph, except for any information found by the director to be legally privileged information, to the enrollee and the enrollee's provider. The department and the independent medical review organization shall maintain the confidentiality of any information found by the director to be the proprietary information of the plan.
(o) This section shall become operative on July 1, 2015.
(Repealed (in Sec. 1) and added by Stats. 2012, Ch. 872, Sec. 2. (SB 1410) Effective January 1, 2013. Section operative July 1, 2015, by its own provisions.)

1374.31.

(a) If there is an imminent and serious threat to the health of the enrollee, as specified in subdivision (c) of Section 1374.33, all necessary information and documents shall be delivered to an independent medical review organization within 24 hours of approval of the request for review. In reviewing a request for review, the department may waive the requirement that the enrollee follow the plan's grievance process in extraordinary and compelling cases, where the director finds that the enrollee has acted reasonably.
(b) The department shall expeditiously review requests and immediately notify the enrollee in writing as to whether the request for an independent medical review has been approved, in whole or in part, and, if not approved, the reasons therefor. The plan shall promptly issue a notification to the enrollee, after submitting all of the required material to the independent medical review organization, that includes an annotated list of documents submitted and offer the enrollee the opportunity to request copies of those documents from the plan. The department shall promptly approve enrollee requests whenever the enrollee's plan has agreed that the case is eligible for an independent medical review. The department shall not refer coverage decisions for independent review. To the extent an enrollee request for independent review is not approved by the department, the enrollee request shall be treated as an immediate request for the department to review the grievance pursuant to subdivision (b) of Section 1368.
(c) An independent medical review organization, specified in Section 1374.32, shall conduct the review in accordance with Section 1374.33 and any regulations or orders of the director adopted pursuant thereto. The organization's review shall be limited to an examination of the medical necessity of the disputed health care services and shall not include any consideration of coverage decisions or other contractual issues.
(Added by Stats. 1999, Ch. 533, Sec. 1. Effective January 1, 2000.)

1374.32.

(a) The department shall contract with one or more independent medical review organizations in the state to conduct reviews for purposes of this article. The independent medical review organizations shall be independent of any health care service plan doing business in this state. The director may establish additional requirements, including conflict-of-interest standards, consistent with the purposes of this article, that an organization shall be required to meet in order to qualify for participation in the Independent Medical Review System and to assist the department in carrying out its responsibilities.
(b) The independent medical review organizations and the medical professionals retained to conduct reviews shall be deemed to be medical consultants for purposes of Section 43.98 of the Civil Code.

(c) The independent medical review organization, any experts it designates to conduct a review, or any officer, director, or employee of the independent medical review organization shall not have any material professional, familial, or financial affiliation, as determined by the director, with any of the following:

(1) The plan.

(2) Any officer, director, or employee of the plan.

(3) A physician, the physician's medical group, or the independent practice association involved in the health care service in dispute.

(4) The facility or institution at which either the proposed health care service, or the alternative service, if any, recommended by the plan, would be provided.

(5) The development or manufacture of the principal drug, device, procedure, or other therapy proposed by the enrollee whose treatment is under review, or the alternative therapy, if any, recommended by the plan.

(6) The enrollee or the enrollee's immediate family.

(d) In order to contract with the department for purposes of this article, an independent medical review organization shall meet all of the following requirements:

(1) The organization shall not be an affiliate or a subsidiary of, nor in any way be owned or controlled by, a health plan or a trade association of health plans. A board member, director, officer, or employee of the independent medical review organization shall not serve as a board member, director, or employee of a health care service plan. A board member, director, or officer of a health plan or a trade association of health plans shall not serve as a board member, director, officer, or employee of an independent medical review organization.

(2) The organization shall submit to the department the following information upon initial application to contract for purposes of this article and, except as otherwise provided, annually thereafter upon any change to any of the following information:

(A) The names of all stockholders and owners of more than 5 percent of any stock or options, if a publicly held organization.

(B) The names of all holders of bonds or notes in excess of one hundred thousand dollars ($100,000), if any.

(C) The names of all corporations and organizations that the independent medical review organization controls or is affiliated with, and the nature and extent of any ownership or control, including the affiliated organization's type of business.

(D) The names and biographical sketches of all directors, officers, and executives of the independent medical review organization, as well as a statement regarding any past or present relationships the directors, officers, and executives may have with any health care service plan, disability insurer, managed care organization, provider group, or board or committee of a plan, managed care organization, or provider group.

(E) (i) The percentage of revenue the independent medical review organization receives from expert reviews, including, but not limited to, external medical reviews, quality assurance reviews, and utilization reviews.

(ii) The names of any health care service plan or provider group for which the independent medical review organization provides review services, including, but not limited to, utilization review, quality assurance review, and external medical review. Any change in this information shall be reported to the department within five business days of the change.

(F) A description of the review process including, but not limited to, the method of selecting expert reviewers and matching the expert reviewers to specific cases.

(G) A description of the system the independent medical review organization uses to identify and recruit medical professionals to review treatment and treatment recommendation decisions, the number of medical professionals credentialed, and the types of cases and areas of expertise that the medical professionals are credentialed to review.

(H) A description of how the independent medical review organization ensures compliance with the conflict-of-interest provisions of this section.

(3) The organization shall demonstrate that it has a quality assurance mechanism in place that does the following:

(A) Ensures that the medical professionals retained are appropriately credentialed and privileged.

(B) Ensures that the reviews provided by the medical professionals are timely, clear, and credible, and that reviews are monitored for quality on an ongoing basis.

(C) Ensures that the method of selecting medical professionals for individual cases achieves a fair and impartial panel of medical professionals who are qualified to render recommendations regarding the clinical conditions and the medical necessity of treatments or therapies in question.

(D) Ensures the confidentiality of medical records and the review materials, consistent with the requirements of this section and applicable state and federal law.

(E) Ensures the independence of the medical professionals retained to perform the reviews through conflict-of-interest policies and prohibitions, and ensures adequate screening for conflicts of interest, pursuant to paragraph (5).

(4) Medical professionals selected by independent medical review organizations to review medical treatment decisions shall be physicians or other appropriate providers who meet the following minimum requirements:

(A) The medical professional shall be a clinician expert in the treatment of the enrollee's medical condition and knowledgeable about the proposed treatment through recent or current actual clinical experience treating patients with the same or a similar medical condition as the enrollee.

(B) Notwithstanding any other provision of law, the medical professional shall hold a nonrestricted license in any state of the United States, and for physicians, a current certification by a recognized American medical specialty board in the area or areas

appropriate to the condition or treatment under review. The independent medical review organization shall give preference to the use of a physician licensed in California as the reviewer, except when training and experience with the issue under review reasonably requires the use of an out-of-state reviewer.

(C) The medical professional shall have no history of disciplinary action or sanctions, including, but not limited to, loss of staff privileges or participation restrictions, taken or pending by any hospital, government, or regulatory body.

(5) Neither the expert reviewer, nor the independent medical review organization, shall have any material professional, material familial, or material financial affiliation with any of the following:

(A) The plan or a provider group of the plan, except that an academic medical center under contract to the plan to provide services to enrollees may qualify as an independent medical review organization provided it will not provide the service and provided the center is not the developer or manufacturer of the proposed treatment.

(B) Any officer, director, or management employee of the plan.

(C) The physician, the physician's medical group, or the independent practice association (IPA) proposing the treatment.

(D) The institution at which the treatment would be provided.

(E) The development or manufacture of the treatment proposed for the enrollee whose condition is under review.

(F) The enrollee or the enrollee's immediate family.

(6) For purposes of this section, the following terms shall have the following meanings:

(A) "Material familial affiliation" means any relationship as a spouse, child, parent, sibling, spouse's parent, or child's spouse.

(B) "Material professional affiliation" means any physician-patient relationship, any partnership or employment relationship, a shareholder or similar ownership interest in a professional corporation, or any independent contractor arrangement that constitutes a material financial affiliation with any expert or any officer or director of the independent medical review organization. "Material professional affiliation" does not include affiliations that are limited to staff privileges at a health facility.

(C) "Material financial affiliation" means any financial interest of more than 5 percent of total annual revenue or total annual income of an independent medical review organization or individual to which this subdivision applies. "Material financial affiliation" does not include payment by the plan to the independent medical review organization for the services required by this section, nor does "material financial affiliation" include an expert's participation as a contracting plan provider where the expert is affiliated with an academic medical center or a National Cancer Institute-designated clinical cancer research center.

(e) The department shall provide, upon the request of any interested person, a copy of all nonproprietary information, as determined by the director, filed with it by an independent medical review organization seeking to contract under this article. The department may charge a nominal fee to the interested person for photocopying the requested information.

(f) This section shall become operative on July 1, 2015.

(Repealed (in Sec. 3) and added by Stats. 2012, Ch. 872, Sec. 4. (SB 1410) Effective January 1, 2013. Section operative July 1, 2015, by its own provisions.)

1374.33.

(a) Upon receipt of information and documents related to a case, the medical professional reviewer or reviewers selected to conduct the review by the independent medical review organization shall promptly review all pertinent medical records of the enrollee, provider reports, as well as any other information submitted to the organization as authorized by the department or requested from any of the parties to the dispute by the reviewers. If reviewers request information from any of the parties, a copy of the request and the response shall be provided to all of the parties. The reviewer or reviewers shall also review relevant information related to the criteria set forth in subdivision (b).

(b) Following its review, the reviewer or reviewers shall determine whether the disputed health care service was medically necessary based on the specific medical needs of the enrollee and any of the following:

(1) Peer-reviewed scientific and medical evidence regarding the effectiveness of the disputed service.

(2) Nationally recognized professional standards.

(3) Expert opinion.

(4) Generally accepted standards of medical practice.

(5) Treatments that are likely to provide a benefit to a patient for conditions for which other treatments are not clinically efficacious.

(c) The organization shall complete its review and make its determination in writing, and in layperson's terms to the maximum extent practicable, within 30 days of the receipt of the application for review and supporting documentation, or within less time as prescribed by the director. If the disputed health care service has not been provided and the enrollee's provider or the department certifies in writing that an imminent and serious threat to the health of the enrollee may exist, including, but not limited to, serious pain, the potential loss of life, limb, or major bodily function, or the immediate and serious deterioration of the health of the enrollee, the analyses and determinations of the reviewers shall be expedited and rendered within three days of the receipt of the information. Subject to the approval of the department, the deadlines for analyses and determinations involving both regular and expedited reviews may be extended by the director for up to three days in extraordinary circumstances or for good cause.

(d) The medical professionals' analyses and determinations shall state whether the disputed health care service is medically necessary. Each analysis shall cite the enrollee's medical condition, the relevant documents in the record, and the relevant findings associated with the provisions of subdivision (b) to support the determination. If more than one medical professional reviews the case, the recommendation of the majority shall prevail. If the medical professionals reviewing the case are evenly split as to whether the disputed health care service should be provided, the decision shall be in favor of providing the service.

(e) The independent medical review organization shall provide the director, the plan, the enrollee, and the enrollee's provider with the analyses and determinations of the medical professionals reviewing the case, and a description of the qualifications of the medical professionals. The independent medical review organization shall keep the names of the reviewers confidential in all communications with entities or individuals outside the independent medical review organization, except in cases where the reviewer is called to testify and in response to court orders. If more than one medical professional reviewed the case and the result was differing determinations, the independent medical review organization shall provide each of the separate reviewer's analyses and determinations.

(f) The director shall immediately adopt the determination of the independent medical review organization, and shall promptly issue a written decision to the parties that shall be binding on the plan.

(g) After removing the names of the parties, including, but not limited to, the enrollee, all medical providers, the plan, and any of the plan's employees or contractors, director decisions adopting a determination of an independent medical review organization shall be made available by the department to the public in a searchable database on the department's Internet Web site, after considering applicable laws governing disclosure of public records, confidentiality, and personal privacy.

(h) (1) Information regarding each director decision provided by the database referenced in subdivision (g) shall include all of the following:

(A) Enrollee demographic profile information, including age and gender.

(B) The enrollee diagnosis and disputed health care service.

(C) Whether the independent medical review was for medically necessary services pursuant to this article or for experimental or investigational therapies pursuant to Section 1370.4.

(D) Whether the independent medical review was standard or expedited.

(E) Length of time from the receipt by the independent medical review organization of the application for review and supporting documentation to the rendering of a determination by the independent medical review organization in writing.

(F) Length of time from receipt by the department of the independent medical review application to the issuance of the director's determination in writing to the parties that is binding on the health care service plan.

(G) Credentials and qualifications of the reviewer or reviewers.

(H) The nature of the statutory criteria set forth in subdivision (b) that the reviewer or reviewers used to make the case decision.

(I) The final result of the determination.

(J) The year the determination was made.

(K) A detailed case summary that includes the specific standards, criteria, and medical and scientific evidence, if any, that led to the case decision.

(2) The database referenced in subdivision (g) shall be accompanied by all of the following:

(A) The annual rate of independent medical review among the total enrolled population.

(B) The annual rate of independent medical review cases by health care service plan.

(C) The number, type, and resolution of independent medical review cases by health care service plan.

(D) The number, type, and resolution of independent medical review cases by ethnicity, race, and primary language spoken.

(i) This section shall become operative on July 1, 2015.

(Repealed (in Sec. 5) and added by Stats. 2012, Ch. 872, Sec. 6. (SB 1410) Effective January 1, 2013. Section operative July 1, 2015, by its own provisions.)

1374.34.

(a) Upon receiving the decision adopted by the director pursuant to Section 1374.33 that a disputed health care service is medically necessary, the plan shall promptly implement the decision. In the case of reimbursement for services already rendered, the plan shall reimburse the provider or enrollee, whichever applies, within five working days. In the case of services not yet rendered, the plan shall authorize the services within five working days of receipt of the written decision from the director, or sooner if appropriate for the nature of the enrollee's medical condition, and shall inform the enrollee and provider of the authorization in accordance with the requirements of paragraph (3) of subdivision (h) of Section 1367.01.

(b) A plan shall not engage in any conduct that has the effect of prolonging the independent review process. The engaging in that conduct or the failure of the plan to promptly implement the decision is a violation of this chapter and, in addition to any other fines, penalties, and other remedies available to the director under this chapter, the plan shall be subject to an administrative penalty of not less than five thousand dollars ($5,000) for each day that the decision is not implemented. The administrative penalties shall be paid to the Managed Care Administrative Fines and Penalties Fund and shall be used for the purposes specified in Section 1341.45.

(c) The director shall require the plan to promptly reimburse the enrollee for any reasonable costs associated with those services when the director finds that the disputed health care services were a covered benefit under the terms and conditions of the health care service plan contract, and the services are found by the independent medical review organization to have been medically necessary pursuant to Section 1374.33, and either the enrollee's decision to secure the services outside of the plan provider network was

reasonable under the emergency or urgent medical circumstances, or the health care service plan contract does not require or provide prior authorization before the health care services are provided to the enrollee.

(d) In addition to requiring plan compliance regarding subdivisions (a), (b), and (c) the director shall review individual cases submitted for independent medical review to determine whether any enforcement actions, including penalties, may be appropriate. In particular, where substantial harm, as defined in Section 3428 of the Civil Code, to an enrollee has already occurred because of the decision of a plan, or one of its contracting providers, to delay, deny, or modify covered health care services that an independent medical review determines to be medically necessary pursuant to Section 1374.33, the director shall impose penalties.

(e) Pursuant to Section 1368.04, the director shall perform an annual audit of independent medical review cases for the dual purposes of education and the opportunity to determine if any investigative or enforcement actions should be undertaken by the department, particularly if a plan repeatedly fails to act promptly and reasonably to resolve grievances associated with a delay, denial, or modification of medically necessary health care services when the obligation of the plan to provide those health care services to enrollees or subscribers is reasonably clear.

(f) A plan's provision of prescription drugs to a Medi-Cal beneficiary pursuant to paragraph (5) of subdivision (b) of Section 14105.33 of the Welfare and Institutions Code and in accordance with the State Department of Health Care Services coverage policies shall not be a ground for an enforcement action. Nothing in this article is intended to limit a plan's responsibility to provide medically necessary health care services pursuant to this chapter.

(Amended by Stats. 2014, Ch. 40, Sec. 1. (SB 870) Effective June 20, 2014.)

1374.35.

(a) After considering the results of a competitive bidding process and any other relevant information on program costs, the director shall establish a reasonable, per-case reimbursement schedule to pay the costs of independent medical review organization reviews, which may vary depending on the type of medical condition under review and on other relevant factors.

(b) The costs of the independent medical review system for enrollees shall be borne by health care service plans pursuant to an assessment fee system established by the director. In determining the amount to be assessed, the director shall consider all appropriations available for the support of this chapter, and existing fees paid to the department. The director may adjust fees upward or downward, on a schedule set by the department, to address shortages or overpayments, and to reflect utilization of the independent review process.

(Added by Stats. 1999, Ch. 533, Sec. 1. Effective January 1, 2000.)

1374.36.

(a) The director shall submit to the Legislature by March 1, 2002, a report on the initial implementation of this article. The report shall include a description of assessments imposed on plans to implement this article, increased staffing and other resources attributable to these new responsibilities, and any redirection of existing staff and resources to carry out these responsibilities. A single copy of the report shall be made available at no cost to members of the public upon request. The department may recover the cost of additional copies that are requested.

(b) This section shall become operative on January 1, 2001, and then only if Assembly Bill 55 of the 1999–2000 Regular Session is enacted.

(Added by Stats. 1999, Ch. 542, Sec. 11. Effective January 1, 2000. Section operative January 1, 2001, by its own provisions.)

ARTICLE 5.6. Point-of-Service Health Care Service Plan Contracts [1374.60 - 1374.76]

(Article 5.6 added by Stats. 1993, Ch. 987, Sec. 3.)

1374.60.

For purpose of this article, the following definitions shall apply:

(a) A "point-of-service plan contract" means any plan contract offered by a health care service plan whereby the health care service plan assumes financial risk for both "in-network coverage or services" and "out-of-network coverage or services." The term "point-of-service plan contract" shall not apply to a plan contract where the out-of-network coverage or service is underwritten by an insurance company admitted in this state or is provided by a self-insured employer and is offered in conjunction with in-network coverage or services provided pursuant to a health care service plan contract.

(b) "Out-of-network coverage or services" means health care services received either from (1) providers who are not employed by, under contract with, or otherwise affiliated with the health care service plan, except for health care services received from these providers in an emergency or when referred or authorized by the plan under procedures specifically reviewed and approved by the director or (2) providers who are employed by, under contract with, or otherwise affiliated with a health care service plan in instances when the "in-network coverage or services" requirements for care set forth in the health care service plan's approved evidence of coverage are not met.

(c) "In-network coverage or services" means all of the following:

(1) All the health care services provided or offered under the requirements of this chapter that are received from a provider employed by, under contract with, or otherwise affiliated with the health care service plan and in accordance with the procedures set forth in the plan's approved evidence of coverage.

(2) Health care services received from a provider not affiliated with the health care service plan when the plan arranges for the enrollee to receive services from that provider.

(3) Out-of-area emergency care provided in accordance with the procedures set by the health care service plan to be followed in securing these services.
(Amended by Stats. 1999, Ch. 525, Sec. 115. Effective January 1, 2000. Operative July 1, 2000, or sooner, by Sec. 214 of Ch. 525.)

1374.62.

A point-of-service plan contract, in which any risk for out-of-network coverage or services is transferred from a health care service plan through reinsurance, shall be subject to this article.
(Added by Stats. 1993, Ch. 987, Sec. 3. Effective January 1, 1994.)

1374.64.

(a) Only a plan that has been licensed under this chapter and in operation in this state for a period of five years or more, or a plan licensed under this chapter and operating in this state for a period of five or more years under a combination of (1) licensure under this chapter and (2) pursuant to a certificate of authority issued by the Department of Insurance may offer a point-of-service contract. A specialized health care service plan shall not offer a point-of-service plan contract unless this plan was formerly registered under the Knox-Mills Health Plan Act (Article 2.5 (commencing with Section 12530) of Chapter 6 of Part 2 of Division 3 of Title 2 of the Government Code), as repealed by Chapter 941 of the Statutes of 1975, and offered point-of-service plan contracts previously approved by the director on July 1, 1976, and on September 1, 1993.
(b) A plan may offer a point-of-service plan contract only if the director has not found the plan to be in violation of any requirements, including administrative capacity, under this chapter or the rules adopted thereunder and the plan meets, at a minimum, the following financial criteria:
(1) The minimum financial criteria for a plan that maintains a minimum net worth of at least five million dollars ($5,000,000) shall be:
(A) (i) Initial tangible net equity so that the plan is not required to file monthly reports with the director as required by Section 1300.84.3(d)(1)(G) of Title 28 of the California Code of Regulations and then have and maintain adjusted tangible net equity to be determined pursuant to either of the following:
(I) In the case of a plan that is required to have and maintain a tangible net equity as required by Section 1300.76(a)(1) or (2) of Title 28 of the California Code of Regulations, multiply 130 percent times the sum resulting from the addition of the plan's tangible net equity required by Section 1300.76(a)(1) or (2) of Title 28 of the California Code of Regulations and the number that equals 10 percent of the plan's annualized health care expenditures for out-of-network services for point-of-service enrollees.
(II) In the case of a plan that is required to have and maintain a tangible net equity as required by Section 1300.76(a)(3) of Title 28 of the California Code of Regulations, recalculate the plan's tangible net equity under Section 1300.76(a)(3) of Title 28 of the California Code of Regulations excluding the plan's annualized health care expenditures for out-of-network services for point-of-service enrollees, add together the number resulting from this recalculation and the number that equals 10 percent of the plan's annualized health care expenditures for out-of-network services for point-of-service enrollees, and multiply this sum times 130 percent, provided that the product of this multiplication must exceed 130 percent of the tangible net equity required by Section 1300.76(a)(3) of Title 28 of the California Code of Regulations so that the plan is not required to file monthly reports to the director as required by Section 1300.84.3(d)(1)(G) of Title 28 of the California Code of Regulations.
(ii) The failure of a plan offering a point-of-service plan contract under this article to maintain adjusted tangible net equity as determined by this subdivision shall require the filing of monthly reports with the director pursuant to Section 1300.84.3(d) of Title 28 of the California Code of Regulations, in addition to any other requirements that may be imposed by the director on a plan under this article and chapter.
(iii) The calculation of tangible net equity under any report to be filed by a plan offering a point-of-service plan contract under this article and required of a plan pursuant to Section 1384, and the regulations adopted thereunder, shall be on the basis of adjusted tangible net equity as determined under this subdivision.
(B) Demonstrates adequate working capital, including (i) a current ratio (current assets divided by current liabilities) of at least 1:1, after excluding obligations of officers, directors, owners, or affiliates, or (ii) evidence that the plan is now meeting its obligations on a timely basis and has been doing so for at least the preceding two years. Short-term obligations of affiliates for goods or services arising in the normal course of business that are payable on the same terms as equivalent transactions with nonaffiliates shall not be excluded. For purposes of this subdivision, an obligation is considered short term if the repayment schedule is 30 days or fewer.
(C) Demonstrates a trend of positive earnings over the previous eight fiscal quarters.
(2) The minimum financial criteria for a plan that maintains a minimum net worth of at least one million five hundred thousand dollars ($1,500,000) but less than five million dollars ($5,000,000) shall be:
(A) (i) Initial tangible net equity so that the plan is not required to file monthly reports with the director as required by Section 1300.84.3(d)(1)(G) of Title 28 of the California Code of Regulations and then have and maintain adjusted tangible net equity to be determined pursuant to either of the following:
(I) In the case of a plan that is required to have and maintain a tangible net equity as required by Section 1300.76(a)(1) or (2) of Title 28 of the California Code of Regulations, multiply 130 percent times the sum resulting from the addition of the plan's tangible net equity required by Section 1300.76(a)(1) or (2) of Title 28 of the California Code of Regulations and the number that equals 10 percent of the plan's annualized health care expenditures for out-of-network services for point-of-service enrollees.
(II) In the case of a plan that is required to have and maintain a tangible net equity as required by Section 1300.76(a)(3) of Title 28 of the California Code of Regulations, recalculate the plan's tangible net equity under Section 1300.76(a)(3) excluding the plan's annualized health care expenditures for out-of-network services for point-of-service enrollees, add together the number resulting from this recalculation and the number that equals 10 percent of the plan's annualized health care expenditures for out-of-network services for point-of-service enrollees, and multiply this sum times 130 percent, provided that the product of this multiplication must exceed 130 percent of the tangible net equity required by Section 1300.76(a)(3) of Title 28 of the California Code of Regulations so that the plan is not required to file monthly reports to the director as required by Section 1300.84.3(d)(1)(G) of Title 28 of the California Code of Regulations.
(ii) The failure of a plan offering a point-of-service plan contract under this article to maintain adjusted tangible net equity as determined by this subdivision shall require the filing of monthly reports with the director pursuant to Section 1300.84.3(d) of Title 28 of the California Code of Regulations, in addition to any other requirements that may be imposed by the director on a plan under this article and chapter.
(iii) The calculation of tangible net equity under any report to be filed by a plan offering a point-of-service plan contract under this article and required of a plan pursuant to Section 1384, and the regulations adopted thereunder, shall be on the basis of adjusted tangible net equity as determined under this subdivision.
(B) Demonstrates adequate working capital, including (i) a current ratio (current assets divided by current liabilities) of at least 1:1, after excluding obligations of officers, directors, owners, or affiliates or (ii) evidence that the plan is now meeting its obligations on a timely basis and has been doing so for at least the preceding two years. Short-term obligations of affiliates for goods or services arising in the normal course of business that are payable on the same terms as equivalent transactions with nonaffiliates shall not be excluded. For purposes of this subdivision, an obligation is considered short term if the repayment schedule is 30 days or fewer.
(C) Demonstrates a trend of positive earnings over the previous eight fiscal quarters.
(D) Demonstrates to the director that it has obtained insurance for the cost of providing any point-of-service enrollee with out-of-network covered health care services, the aggregate value of which exceeds five thousand dollars ($5,000) in any year. This insurance shall obligate the insurer to continue to provide care for the period in which a premium was paid in the event a plan becomes insolvent. Where a plan cannot obtain insurance as required by this subparagraph, then a plan may demonstrate to the director that it has made other arrangements, acceptable to the director, for the cost of providing enrollees out-of-network health care services; but in this case the expenditure for total out-of-network costs for all enrollees in all point-of-service contracts shall be limited to a percentage, acceptable to the director, not to exceed 15 percent of total health care expenditures for all its enrollees.
(c) Within 30 days of the close of each month a plan offering point-of-service plan contracts under paragraph (2) of subdivision (b) shall file with the director a monthly financial report consisting of a balance sheet and statement of operations of the plan, which need not be certified, and a calculation of the adjusted tangible net equity required under subparagraph (A). The financial statements shall be prepared on a basis consistent with the financial statements furnished by the plan pursuant to Section 1300.84.2 of Title 28 of the California Code of Regulations. A plan shall also make special reports to the director as the director may from time to time require. Each report to be filed by a plan pursuant to this subdivision shall be verified by a principal officer of the plan as set forth in Section 1300.84.2(e) of Title 28 of the California Code of Regulations.
(d) If it appears to the director that a plan does not have sufficient financial viability, or organizational and administrative capacity to ensure the delivery of health care services to its enrollees, the director may, by written order, direct the plan to discontinue the offering of a point-of-service plan contract. The order shall be effective immediately.
(Amended by Stats. 2009, Ch. 298, Sec. 5. (AB 1540) Effective January 1, 2010.)

1374.65.

Point-of-service plan contracts shall:
(a) Provide incentives, including financial incentives, for enrollees to use in-network coverage or services.
(b) Only offer coverage or services obtained out-of-network if it also provides coverage or services on an in-network basis.
(c) Shall not consider the following to be out-of-network coverage or services:
(1) Health care services received from a provider not affiliated with the health care service plan when the plan arranges for the enrollee to receive services from that provider.
(2) Out-of-area emergency care provided in accordance with the procedures set by the health care service plan to be followed in securing these services.
(Added by Stats. 1993, Ch. 987, Sec. 3. Effective January 1, 1994.)

1374.66.

Any health care service plan that offers a point-of-service plan contract may do all of the following:
(a) Limit or exclude coverage for specific types of services or conditions when obtained out-of-plan.
(b) Include annual out-of-pocket limits, copayments, and annual and lifetime maximum benefit limits for out-of-network coverage or services that are different or separate from any amounts or limits applied to in-network coverage or services, and may impose a deductible on coverage for out-of-network coverage or services.
(c) To the extent permitted under this chapter, may limit the groups to which a point-of-service plan contract is offered, and may adopt nondiscriminatory renewal guidelines under which one or more point-of-service plan contracts would be replaced with other

than point-of-service plan contracts. If a point-of-service plan contract is sold to a group, then the group shall offer it to all members of that group who are eligible for coverage by the health care service plan.

(d) Treat as out-of-network services those services that an enrollee obtains from a provider affiliated with the plan, but not in accordance with the authorization procedures set forth in the health care service plan's approved evidence of coverage.

(e) Contracts between health care service plans and medical providers, for the purpose of providing medical services under point-of-service contracts, may include risk-sharing arrangements for out-of-network services, but only if the risk sharing arrangements meet all of the following conditions:

(1) The contracting medical provider agrees to participate in risk-sharing arrangements applicable to out-of-network services.

(2) If the medical provider is reimbursed on a capitated or prepaid basis, the contract shall clearly disclose the capitation or prepayment amount to be paid to the medical provider for in-network services received by enrollees under point-of-service contracts.

(3) Any capitation or prepayment amounts paid to the medical provider shall not place the medical provider directly at risk for or directly transfer liability for out-of-network services received by enrollees under point-of-service contracts.

(4) The risk-sharing arrangements for out-of-network services may provide a bonus or incentive to the medical provider to attempt to reduce the utilization of out-of-network services, but shall not place the medical provider at risk for any amounts in excess of the amounts used by the plan to budget for or fund the risk-sharing pool for out-of-network services.

(5) The contract between the medical provider and the plan shall clearly disclose the mathematical method by which funding for the risk-sharing arrangement is established, the mathematical method by which and the extent to which payments for out-of-network services are debited against the risk-sharing funds, and the method by which the risk-sharing arrangement is reconciled on no less than an annual basis.

(6) The contract is approved by the director.

(Amended by Stats. 1999, Ch. 525, Sec. 117. Effective January 1, 2000. Operative July 1, 2000, or sooner, by Sec. 214 of Ch. 525.)

1374.67.

A health care service plan offering a point-of-service plan contract is subject to the following limitations:

(a) A health care service plan shall limit its offering of point-of-service plan contracts so that no more than 50 percent of the plan's total premium revenue in any fiscal quarter is earned from point-of-service plan contracts.

(b) A health care service plan offering a point-of-service plan contract shall not expend in any fiscal-year quarter more than 20 percent of its total health care expenditures for all its enrollees for out-of-network services for point-of-service enrollees.

(c) If the amount specified in subdivision (a) or (b) is exceeded by 2 percent in any quarter, the health care service plan shall come into compliance with subdivisions (a) and (b) by the end of the next following quarter. If compliance with the amount specified in subdivisions (a) and (b) is not demonstrated in the health care service plan's next quarterly report, the director may prohibit the health care service plan from offering a point-of-service plan contract to new groups, or may require the health care service plan to amend one or more of its point-of-service contracts at the time of renewal to delete some or all of the out-of-network coverage or services as may be necessary for the plan to demonstrate compliance to the director's satisfaction.

(d) The limitation imposed by this section shall not apply to a plan which in substantial part indemnified subscribers and enrollees pursuant to contracts issued under such plan's former registration under the Knox-Mills Health Plan Act in 1975 and as of that date, and on September 1, 1993, was offering point-of-service plan contracts previously approved by the director.

(Amended by Stats. 1999, Ch. 525, Sec. 118. Effective January 1, 2000. Operative July 1, 2000, or sooner, by Sec. 214 of Ch. 525.)

1374.68.

A health care service plan that offers a point-of-service plan contract shall do all of the following:

(a) Deposit with the director or, at the discretion of the director, with any organization or trustee acceptable to the director through which a custodial or controlled account is maintained, cash, securities, or any combination of these, which is acceptable to the director, that at all times have a fair market value equal to the greater of either one of the following:

(1) Two hundred thousand dollars ($200,000).

(2) One hundred twenty percent of the plan's current monthly claims payable plus incurred but not reported balance for coverage out-of-network coverage or services provided under point-of-service contracts.

(b) Track out-of-network point-of-service utilization separately from in-network utilization.

(c) Record point-of-service utilization in a manner that will permit utilization and cost reporting as the director may require.

(d) Demonstrate to the satisfaction of the director that the health care service plan has the fiscal, administrative, and marketing capacity to control its point-of-service plan contract enrollment, utilization, and costs so as not to jeopardize the financial viability or organizational and administrative capacity of the health care service plan.

(e) Maintain the deposit required under subdivision (a) in a manner agreed to by the director, subject to subdivision (a) of Section 1377 and any regulations adopted thereunder.

(f) Any deposit made pursuant to this section shall be a credit against any deposit required by subdivision (a) of Section 1377.

(Amended by Stats. 1999, Ch. 525, Sec. 119. Effective January 1, 2000. Operative July 1, 2000, or sooner, by Sec. 214 of Ch. 525.)

1374.69.

At least 20 business days prior to offering a point-of-service plan contract, a health care service plan shall file a notice of material modification in accordance with Section 1352. The notice of material modification shall include, but not be limited to, provisions specifying how the health care service plan shall accomplish all of the following:

(a) Design the benefit levels and conditions of coverage for in-network coverage and services and out-of-network point-of-service utilization.

(b) Provide or arrange for the provision of adequate systems to do all of the following:

(1) Process and pay claims for all out-of-network coverage and services.

(2) Generate accurate financial and utilization data and reports on a timely basis, so that it and any authorized regulatory agency can evaluate the health care service plan's experience with point-of-service plan contracts and monitor compliance with point-of-service plan contract projections established by the health care service plan and regulatory requirements.

(3) Track and monitor the quality of health care obtained out-of-network by plan enrollees to the extent reasonable and possible.

(4) Respond promptly to enrollee grievances and complaints, written or oral, including those regarding services obtained out-of-network.

(5) Meet the requirements for a point-of-service plan contract set forth in this section and any additional requirements that may be required by the director.

(c) Comply initially and on an ongoing basis with the requirements of this article.

(d) This section shall become operative July 1, 1995.

(Amended by Stats. 1999, Ch. 525, Sec. 120. Effective January 1, 2000. Operative July 1, 2000, or sooner, by Sec. 214 of Ch. 525.)

1374.71.

No plan formerly registered under the Knox-Mills Health Plan Act (Article 2.5 (commencing with Section 12530) of Chapter 6 of Part 2 of Division 3 of Title 2 of the Government Code) in 1975 shall be required to file a notice of material modification under Section 1374.69 or 1374.70 for any point-of-service plan contract previously approved by the director under this chapter and offered by plan on or before September 1, 1993.

(Amended by Stats. 1999, Ch. 525, Sec. 121. Effective January 1, 2000. Operative July 1, 2000, or sooner, by Sec. 214 of Ch. 525.)

1374.72.

(a) Every health care service plan contract issued, amended, or renewed on or after July 1, 2000, that provides hospital, medical, or surgical coverage shall provide coverage for the diagnosis and medically necessary treatment of severe mental illnesses of a person of any age, and of serious emotional disturbances of a child, as specified in subdivisions (d) and (e), under the same terms and conditions applied to other medical conditions as specified in subdivision (c).

(b) These benefits shall include the following:

(1) Outpatient services.

(2) Inpatient hospital services.

(3) Partial hospital services.

(4) Prescription drugs, if the plan contract includes coverage for prescription drugs.

(c) The terms and conditions applied to the benefits required by this section, that shall be applied equally to all benefits under the plan contract, shall include, but not be limited to, the following:

(1) Maximum lifetime benefits.

(2) Copayments.

(3) Individual and family deductibles.

(d) For the purposes of this section, "severe mental illnesses" shall include:

(1) Schizophrenia.

(2) Schizoaffective disorder.

(3) Bipolar disorder (manic-depressive illness).

(4) Major depressive disorders.

(5) Panic disorder.

(6) Obsessive-compulsive disorder.

(7) Pervasive developmental disorder or autism.

(8) Anorexia nervosa.

(9) Bulimia nervosa.

(e) For the purposes of this section, a child suffering from, "serious emotional disturbances of a child" shall be defined as a child who (1) has one or more mental disorders as identified in the most recent edition of the Diagnostic and Statistical Manual of Mental Disorders, other than a primary substance use disorder or developmental disorder, that result in behavior inappropriate to the child's age according to expected developmental norms, and (2) who meets the criteria in paragraph (2) of subdivision (a) of Section 5600.3 of the Welfare and Institutions Code.

(f) This section shall not apply to contracts entered into pursuant to Chapter 7 (commencing with Section 14000) or Chapter 8 (commencing with Section 14200) of Division 9 of Part 3 of the Welfare and Institutions Code, between the State Department of Health Services and a health care service plan for enrolled Medi-Cal beneficiaries.

(g) (1) For the purpose of compliance with this section, a plan may provide coverage for all or part of the mental health services required by this section through a separate specialized health care service plan or mental health plan, and shall not be required to obtain an additional or specialized license for this purpose.

(2) A plan shall provide the mental health coverage required by this section in its entire service area and in emergency situations as may be required by applicable laws and regulations. For purposes of this section, health care service plan contracts that provide

benefits to enrollees through preferred provider contracting arrangements are not precluded from requiring enrollees who reside or work in geographic areas served by specialized health care service plans or mental health plans to secure all or part of their mental health services within those geographic areas served by specialized health care service plans or mental health plans.

(3) Notwithstanding any other provision of law, in the provision of benefits required by this section, a health care service plan may utilize case management, network providers, utilization review techniques, prior authorization, copayments, or other cost sharing.

(h) Nothing in this section shall be construed to deny or restrict in any way the department's authority to ensure plan compliance with this chapter when a plan provides coverage for prescription drugs.

(Amended by Stats. 2002, Ch. 791, Sec. 7. Effective January 1, 2003.)

1374.73.

(a) (1) Every health care service plan contract that provides hospital, medical, or surgical coverage shall also provide coverage for behavioral health treatment for pervasive developmental disorder or autism no later than July 1, 2012. The coverage shall be provided in the same manner and shall be subject to the same requirements as provided in Section 1374.72.

(2) Notwithstanding paragraph (1), as of the date that proposed final rulemaking for essential health benefits is issued, this section does not require any benefits to be provided that exceed the essential health benefits that all health plans will be required by federal regulations to provide under Section 1302(b) of the federal Patient Protection and Affordable Care Act (Public Law 111-148), as amended by the federal Health Care and Education Reconciliation Act of 2010 (Public Law 111-152).

(3) This section shall not affect services for which an individual is eligible pursuant to Division 4.5 (commencing with Section 4500) of the Welfare and Institutions Code or Title 14 (commencing with Section 95000) of the Government Code.

(4) This section shall not affect or reduce any obligation to provide services under an individualized education program, as defined in Section 56032 of the Education Code, or an individual service plan, as described in Section 5600.4 of the Welfare and Institutions Code, or under the federal Individuals with Disabilities Education Act (20 U.S.C. Sec. 1400 et seq.) and its implementing regulations.

(b) Every health care service plan subject to this section shall maintain an adequate network that includes qualified autism service providers who supervise or employ qualified autism service professionals or paraprofessionals who provide and administer behavioral health treatment. A health care service plan is not prevented from selectively contracting with providers within these requirements.

(c) For the purposes of this section, the following definitions shall apply:

(1) "Behavioral health treatment" means professional services and treatment programs, including applied behavior analysis and evidence-based behavior intervention programs, that develop or restore, to the maximum extent practicable, the functioning of an individual with pervasive developmental disorder or autism and that meet all of the following criteria:

(A) The treatment is prescribed by a physician and surgeon licensed pursuant to Chapter 5 (commencing with Section 2000) of, or is developed by a psychologist licensed pursuant to Chapter 6.6 (commencing with Section 2900) of, Division 2 of the Business and Professions Code.

(B) The treatment is provided under a treatment plan prescribed by a qualified autism service provider and is administered by one of the following:

(i) A qualified autism service provider.

(ii) A qualified autism service professional supervised by the qualified autism service provider.

(iii) A qualified autism service paraprofessional supervised by a qualified autism service provider or qualified autism service professional.

(C) The treatment plan has measurable goals over a specific timeline that is developed and approved by the qualified autism service provider for the specific patient being treated. The treatment plan shall be reviewed no less than once every six months by the qualified autism service provider and modified whenever appropriate, and shall be consistent with Section 4686.2 of the Welfare and Institutions Code pursuant to which the qualified autism service provider does all of the following:

(i) Describes the patient's behavioral health impairments or developmental challenges that are to be treated.

(ii) Designs an intervention plan that includes the service type, number of hours, and parent participation needed to achieve the plan's goal and objectives, and the frequency at which the patient's progress is evaluated and reported.

(iii) Provides intervention plans that utilize evidence-based practices, with demonstrated clinical efficacy in treating pervasive developmental disorder or autism.

(iv) Discontinues intensive behavioral intervention services when the treatment goals and objectives are achieved or no longer appropriate.

(D) The treatment plan is not used for purposes of providing or for the reimbursement of respite, day care, or educational services and is not used to reimburse a parent for participating in the treatment program. The treatment plan shall be made available to the health care service plan upon request.

(2) "Pervasive developmental disorder or autism" shall have the same meaning and interpretation as used in Section 1374.72.

(3) "Qualified autism service provider" means either of the following:

(A) A person who is certified by a national entity, such as the Behavior Analyst Certification Board, with a certification that is accredited by the National Commission for Certifying Agencies, and who designs, supervises, or provides treatment for pervasive

developmental disorder or autism, provided the services are within the experience and competence of the person who is nationally certified.

(B) A person licensed as a physician and surgeon, physical therapist, occupational therapist, psychologist, marriage and family therapist, educational psychologist, clinical social worker, professional clinical counselor, speech-language pathologist, or audiologist pursuant to Division 2 (commencing with Section 500) of the Business and Professions Code, who designs, supervises, or provides treatment for pervasive developmental disorder or autism, provided the services are within the experience and competence of the licensee.

(4) "Qualified autism service professional" means an individual who meets all of the following criteria:

(A) Provides behavioral health treatment, which may include clinical case management and case supervision under the direction and supervision of a qualified autism service provider.

(B) Is supervised by a qualified autism service provider.

(C) Provides treatment pursuant to a treatment plan developed and approved by the qualified autism service provider.

(D) Is a behavioral service provider who meets the education and experience qualifications described in Section 54342 of Title 17 of the California Code of Regulations for an Associate Behavior Analyst, Behavior Analyst, Behavior Management Assistant, Behavior Management Consultant, or Behavior Management Program.

(E) Has training and experience in providing services for pervasive developmental disorder or autism pursuant to Division 4.5 (commencing with Section 4500) of the Welfare and Institutions Code or Title 14 (commencing with Section 95000) of the Government Code.

(F) Is employed by the qualified autism service provider or an entity or group that employs qualified autism service providers responsible for the autism treatment plan.

(5) "Qualified autism service paraprofessional" means an unlicensed and uncertified individual who meets all of the following criteria:

(A) Is supervised by a qualified autism service provider or qualified autism service professional at a level of clinical supervision that meets professionally recognized standards of practice.

(B) Provides treatment and implements services pursuant to a treatment plan developed and approved by the qualified autism service provider.

(C) Meets the education and training qualifications described in Section 54342 of Title 17 of the California Code of Regulations.

(D) Has adequate education, training, and experience, as certified by a qualified autism service provider or an entity or group that employs qualified autism service providers.

(E) Is employed by the qualified autism service provider or an entity or group that employs qualified autism service providers responsible for the autism treatment plan.

(d) This section shall not apply to the following:

(1) A specialized health care service plan that does not deliver mental health or behavioral health services to enrollees.

(2) A health care service plan contract in the Medi-Cal program (Chapter 7 (commencing with Section 14000) of Part 3 of Division 9 of the Welfare and Institutions Code).

(e) This section does not limit the obligation to provide services under Section 1374.72.

(f) As provided in Section 1374.72 and in paragraph (1) of subdivision (a), in the provision of benefits required by this section, a health care service plan may utilize case management, network providers, utilization review techniques, prior authorization, copayments, or other cost sharing.

(Amended by Stats. 2017, Ch. 385, Sec. 1. (AB 1074) Effective January 1, 2018.)

1374.74.

(a) The department, in consultation with the Department of Insurance, shall convene an Autism Advisory Task Force by February 1, 2012, in collaboration with other agencies, departments, advocates, autism experts, health plan and health insurer representatives, and other entities and stakeholders that it deems appropriate. The Autism Advisory Task Force shall develop recommendations regarding behavioral health treatment that is medically necessary for the treatment of individuals with autism or pervasive developmental disorder. The Autism Advisory Task Force shall address all of the following:

(1) Interventions that have been scientifically validated and have demonstrated clinical efficacy.

(2) Interventions that have measurable treatment outcomes.

(3) Patient selection, monitoring, and duration of therapy.

(4) Qualifications, training, and supervision of providers.

(5) Adequate networks of providers.

(b) The Autism Advisory Task Force shall also develop recommendations regarding the education, training, and experience requirements that unlicensed individuals providing autism services shall meet in order to secure a license from the state.

(c) The department shall submit a report of the Autism Advisory Task Force to the Governor, the President pro Tempore of the Senate, the Speaker of the Assembly, and the Senate and Assembly Committees on Health by December 31, 2012, on which date the task force shall cease to exist.

(Amended by Stats. 2012, Ch. 162, Sec. 82. (SB 1171) Effective January 1, 2013.)

1374.76.

(a) No later than January 1, 2015, a large group health care service plan contract shall provide all covered mental health and substance use disorder benefits in compliance with the Paul Wellstone and Pete Domenici Mental Health Parity and Addiction Equity Act of 2008 (Public Law 110-343) and all rules, regulations, and guidance issued pursuant to Section 2726 of the federal Public Health Service Act (42 U.S.C. Sec. 300gg-26).

(b) No later than January 1, 2015, an individual or small group health care service plan contract shall provide all covered mental health and substance use disorder benefits in compliance with the Paul Wellstone and Pete Domenici Mental Health Parity and Addiction Equity Act of 2008 (Public Law 110-343), all rules, regulations, and guidance issued pursuant to Section 2726 of the federal Public Health Service Act (42 U.S.C. Sec. 300gg-26), and Section 1367.005.

(c) Until January 1, 2016, the director may issue guidance to health care service plans regarding compliance with this section. This guidance shall not be subject to the Administrative Procedure Act (Chapter 3.5 (commencing with Section 11340) of Part 1 of Division 3 of Title 2 of the Government Code). Any guidance issued pursuant to this subdivision shall be effective only until the director adopts regulations pursuant to the Administrative Procedure Act. The department shall consult with the Department of Insurance in issuing guidance under this subdivision.

(Added by Stats. 2014, Ch. 31, Sec. 8. (SB 857) Effective June 20, 2014.)

ARTICLE 6. Operation and Renewal Requirements and Procedures [1375.1 - 1385]

(Article 6 added by Stats. 1975, Ch. 941.)

1375.1.

(a) Every plan shall have and shall demonstrate to the director that it has all of the following:

(1) A fiscally sound operation and adequate provision against the risk of insolvency.

(2) Assumed full financial risk on a prospective basis for the provision of covered health care services, except that a plan may obtain insurance or make other arrangements for the cost of providing to any subscriber or enrollee covered health care services, the aggregate value of which exceeds five thousand dollars ($5,000) in any year, for the cost of covered health care services provided to its members other than through the plan because medical necessity required their provision before they could be secured through the plan, and for not more than 90 percent of the amount by which its costs for any of its fiscal years exceed 115 percent of its income for that fiscal year.

(3) A procedure for prompt payment or denial of provider and subscriber or enrollee claims, including those telehealth services, as defined in subdivision (a) of Section 2290.5 of the Business and Professions Code, covered by the plan. Except as provided in Section 1371, a procedure meeting the requirements of Subchapter G of the regulations (29 C.F.R. Part 2560) under Public Law 93-406 (88 Stats. 829-1035, 29 U.S.C. Secs. 1001 et seq.) shall satisfy this requirement.

(b) In determining whether the conditions of this section have been met, the director shall consider, but not be limited to, the following:

(1) The financial soundness of the plan's arrangements for health care services and the schedule of rates and charges used by the plan.

(2) The adequacy of working capital.

(3) Agreements with providers for the provision of health care services.

(c) For the purposes of this section, "covered health care services" means health care services provided under all plan contracts.

(Amended by Stats. 2012, Ch. 782, Sec. 7. (AB 1733) Effective January 1, 2013.)

1375.2.

On and after October 1, 1977, every plan operating under a transitional license shall have a fiscally sound operation.

(Added by Stats. 1977, Ch. 818.)

1375.3.

(a) A health care service plan shall meet and confer with the director and his or her designated representatives at least 10 business days prior to filing a petition commencing a case for bankruptcy under Title 11 of the United States Code, except under extraordinary circumstances. If extraordinary circumstances preclude a meet and confer with the director within the 10-day time period prior to the filing of a petition for bankruptcy, the plan shall meet and confer with the department at least 24 hours prior to filing the petition. A plan shall notify the department concurrently upon filing the petition. These meetings shall be deemed confidential.

(b) At the director's request, a plan shall provide within the time period specified by the department, information to assist in ensuring continuity of care and uninterrupted access to health care services for plan subscribers and enrollees. The information may include, but is not limited to, the following:

(1) A list of all providers with which the plan contracts and material information regarding the contracts including, but not limited to, the grounds for termination of the contract and the term remaining on the contract.

(2) A list of employer groups who subscribe with the plan.

(3) A list of the enrollees of the plan.

(4) A list of enrollees undergoing current treatment and a description of the authorized treatment for the enrollee.

(5) A list of all brokers and agents involved in the negotiation of subscriber contracts.

(6) A list of all enrollees who contract as individual subscribers for coverage by the plan.

(c) Notwithstanding subdivision (a), nothing in this section shall preclude the director from exercising powers and duties authorized under this chapter.

(Added by Stats. 2002, Ch. 928, Sec. 2. Effective January 1, 2003.)

1375.4.

(a) Every contract between a health care service plan and a risk-bearing organization that is issued, amended, renewed, or delivered in this state on or after July 1, 2000, shall include provisions concerning the following, as to the risk-bearing organization's administrative and financial capacity, which shall be effective as of January 1, 2001:

(1) A requirement that the risk-bearing organization furnish financial information to the health care service plan or the plan's designated agent and meet any other financial requirements that assist the health care service plan in maintaining the financial viability of its arrangements for the provision of health care services in a manner that does not adversely affect the integrity of the contract negotiation process.

(2) A requirement that the health care service plan disclose information to the risk-bearing organization that enables the risk-bearing organization to be informed regarding the financial risk assumed under the contract.

(3) A requirement that the health care service plans provide payments of all risk arrangements, excluding capitation, within 180 days after close of the fiscal year.

(b) In accordance with subdivision (a) of Section 1344, the director shall adopt regulations on or before June 30, 2000, to implement this section which shall, at a minimum, provide for the following:

(1) (A) A process for reviewing or grading risk-bearing organizations based on the following criteria:

(i) The risk-bearing organization meets criterion 1 if it reimburses, contests, or denies claims for health care services it has provided, arranged, or for which it is otherwise financially responsible in accordance with the timeframes and other requirements described in Section 1371 and in accordance with any other applicable state and federal laws and regulations.

(ii) The risk-bearing organization meets criterion 2 if it estimates its liability for incurred but not reported claims pursuant to a method that has not been held objectionable by the director, records the estimate at least quarterly as an accrual in its books and records, and appropriately reflects this accrual in its financial statements.

(iii) The risk-bearing organization meets criterion 3 if it maintains at all times a positive tangible net equity, as defined in subdivision (e) of Section 1300.76 of Title 28 of the California Code of Regulations.

(iv) The risk-bearing organization meets criterion 4 if it maintains at all times a positive level of working capital (excess of current assets over current liabilities).

(B) A risk-bearing organization may reduce its liabilities for purposes of calculating tangible net equity, pursuant to clause (iii) of subparagraph (A), and working capital, pursuant to clause (iv) of subparagraph (A), by the amount of any liabilities the payment of which is guaranteed by a sponsoring organization pursuant to a qualified guarantee. A sponsoring organization is one that has a tangible net equity of a level to be established by the director that is in excess of all amounts that it has guaranteed to any person or entity. A qualified guarantee is one that meets all of the following:

(i) It is approved by a board resolution of the sponsoring organization.

(ii) The sponsoring organization agrees to submit audited annual financial statements to the plan within 120 days of the end of the sponsoring organization's fiscal year.

(iii) The guarantee is unconditional except for a maximum monetary limit.

(iv) The guarantee is not limited in duration with respect to liabilities arising during the term of the guarantee.

(v) The guarantee provides for six months' advance notice to the plan prior to its cancellation.

(2) The information required from risk-bearing organizations to assist in reviewing or grading these risk-bearing organizations, including balance sheets, claims reports, and designated annual, quarterly, or monthly financial statements prepared in accordance with generally accepted accounting principles, to be used in a manner, and to the extent necessary, provided to a single external party as approved by the director to the extent that it does not adversely affect the integrity of the contract negotiation process between the health care service plan and the risk-bearing organizations.

(3) Audits to be conducted in accordance with generally accepted auditing standards and in a manner that avoids duplication of review of the risk-bearing organization.

(4) A process for corrective action plans, as mutually agreed upon by the health care service plan and the risk-bearing organization and as approved by the director, for cases where the review or grading indicates deficiencies that need to be corrected by the risk-bearing organization, and contingency plans to ensure the delivery of health care services if the corrective action fails. The corrective action plan shall be approved by the director and standardized, to the extent possible, to meet the needs of the director and all health care service plans contracting with the risk-bearing organization. If the health care service plan and the risk-bearing organization are unable to determine a mutually agreeable corrective action plan, the director shall determine the corrective action plan.

(5) The disclosure of information by health care service plans to the risk-bearing organization that enables the risk-bearing organization to be informed regarding the risk assumed under the contract, including:

(A) Enrollee information monthly.

(B) Risk arrangement information, information pertaining to any pharmacy risk assumed under the contract, information regarding incentive payments, and information on income and expenses assigned to the risk-bearing organization quarterly.

(6) Periodic reports from each health care service plan to the director that include information concerning the risk-bearing organizations and the type and amount of financial risk assumed by them, and, if deemed necessary and appropriate by the director, a registration process for the risk-bearing organizations.

(7) The confidentiality of financial and other records to be produced, disclosed, or otherwise made available, unless as otherwise determined by the director.

(c) The failure by a health care service plan to comply with the contractual requirements pursuant to this section shall constitute grounds for disciplinary action. The director shall, as appropriate, within 60 days after receipt of documented violation from a risk-bearing organization, investigate and take enforcement action against a health care service plan that fails to comply with these requirements and shall periodically evaluate contracts between health care service plans and risk-bearing organizations to determine if any audit, evaluation, or enforcement actions should be undertaken by the department.

(d) The Financial Solvency Standards Board established in Section 1347.15 shall study and report to the director on or before January 1, 2001, regarding all of the following:

(1) The feasibility of requiring that there be in force insurance coverage commensurate with the financial risk assumed by the risk-bearing organization to protect against financial losses.

(2) The appropriateness of different risk-bearing arrangements between health care service plans and risk-bearing organizations.

(3) The appropriateness of the four criteria specified in paragraph (1) of subdivision (b).

(e) This section shall not apply to specialized health care service plans.

(f) For purposes of this section, "provider organization" means a medical group, independent practice association, or other entity that delivers, furnishes, or otherwise arranges for or provides health care services, but does not include an individual or a plan.

(g) (1) For purposes of this section, a "risk-bearing organization" means a professional medical corporation, other form of corporation controlled by physicians and surgeons, a medical partnership, a medical foundation exempt from licensure pursuant to subdivision (l) of Section 1206, or another lawfully organized group of physicians that delivers, furnishes, or otherwise arranges for or provides health care services, but does not include an individual or a health care service plan, and that does all of the following:

(A) Contracts directly with a health care service plan or arranges for health care services for the health care service plan's enrollees.

(B) Receives compensation for those services on any capitated or fixed periodic payment basis.

(C) Is responsible for the processing and payment of claims made by providers for services rendered by those providers on behalf of a health care service plan that are covered under the capitation or fixed periodic payment made by the plan to the risk-bearing organization. Nothing in this subparagraph in any way limits, alters, or abrogates any responsibility of a health care service plan under existing law.

(2) Notwithstanding paragraph (1), risk-bearing organizations shall not be deemed to include a provider organization that meets either of the following requirements:

(A) The health care service plan files with the department consolidated financial statements that include the provider organization.

(B) The health care service plan is the only health care service plan with which the provider organization contracts for arranging or providing health care services and, during the previous and current fiscal years, the provider organization's maximum potential expenses for providing or arranging for health care services did not exceed 115 percent of its maximum potential revenue for providing or arranging for those services.

(h) For purposes of this section, "claims" include, but are not limited to, contractual obligations to pay capitation or payments on a managed hospital payment basis.

(Amended by Stats. 2009, Ch. 298, Sec. 6. (AB 1540) Effective January 1, 2010.)

1375.5.

No contract between a risk-bearing organization and a health care service plan that is issued, amended, delivered, or renewed in this state on or after July 1, 2000, shall include any provision that requires the risk-bearing organization to be at financial risk for the provision of health care services, unless the provision has first been negotiated and agreed to between the health care service plan and the risk-bearing organization.

This section shall not prevent a risk-bearing organization from accepting the financial risk pursuant to a contract that meets the requirements of Section 1375.4.

(Amended by Stats. 2002, Ch. 798, Sec. 1. Effective January 1, 2003.)

1375.6.

No contract between a risk-bearing organization and a health care service plan that is issued, amended, delivered, or renewed in this state on or after July 1, 2000, shall include any provision that requires a provider to accept rates or methods of payment specified in contracts with health care service plan affiliates or nonaffiliates unless the provision has been first negotiated and agreed to between the health care service plan and the risk-bearing organization.

(Added by Stats. 1999, Ch. 529, Sec. 5. Effective January 1, 2000.)

1375.7.

(a) This section shall be known and may be cited as the Health Care Providers' Bill of Rights.

(b) No contract issued, amended, or renewed on or after January 1, 2003, between a plan and a health care provider for the provision of health care services to a plan enrollee or subscriber shall contain any of the following terms:

(1) (A) Authority for the plan to change a material term of the contract, unless the change has first been negotiated and agreed to by the provider and the plan or the change is necessary to comply with state or federal law or regulations or any accreditation requirements of a private sector accreditation organization. If a change is made by amending a manual, policy, or procedure document referenced in the contract, the plan shall provide 45 business days' notice to the provider, and the provider has the right to negotiate and agree to the change. If the plan and the provider cannot agree to the change to a manual, policy, or procedure document, the provider has the right to terminate the contract prior to the implementation of the change. In any event, the plan shall provide at least 45 business days' notice of its intent to change a material term, unless a change in state or federal law or regulations or any accreditation requirements of a private sector accreditation organization requires a shorter timeframe for compliance. However, if the parties mutually agree, the 45-business day notice requirement may be waived. Nothing in this subparagraph limits the ability of the parties to mutually agree to the proposed change at any time after the provider has received notice of the proposed change.

(B) If a contract between a provider and a plan provides benefits to enrollees or subscribers through a preferred provider arrangement, the contract may contain provisions permitting a material change to the contract by the plan if the plan provides at least 45 business days' notice to the provider of the change and the provider has the right to terminate the contract prior to the implementation of the change.

(C) If a contract between a noninstitutional provider and a plan provides benefits to enrollees or subscribers covered under the Medi-Cal or Healthy Families Program and compensates the provider on a fee-for-service basis, the contract may contain provisions permitting a material change to the contract by the plan, if the following requirements are met:

(i) The plan gives the provider a minimum of 90 business days' notice of its intent to change a material term of the contract.

(ii) The plan clearly gives the provider the right to exercise his or her intent to negotiate and agree to the change within 30 business days of the provider's receipt of the notice described in clause (i).

(iii) The plan clearly gives the provider the right to terminate the contract within 90 business days from the date of the provider's receipt of the notice described in clause (i) if the provider does not exercise the right to negotiate the change or no agreement is reached, as described in clause (ii).

(iv) The material change becomes effective 90 business days from the date of the notice described in clause (i) if the provider does not exercise his or her right to negotiate the change, as described in clause (ii), or to terminate the contract, as described in clause (iii).

(2) A provision that requires a health care provider to accept additional patients beyond the contracted number or in the absence of a number if, in the reasonable professional judgment of the provider, accepting additional patients would endanger patients' access to, or continuity of, care.

(3) A requirement to comply with quality improvement or utilization management programs or procedures of a plan, unless the requirement is fully disclosed to the health care provider at least 15 business days prior to the provider executing the contract. However, the plan may make a change to the quality improvement or utilization management programs or procedures at any time if the change is necessary to comply with state or federal law or regulations or any accreditation requirements of a private sector accreditation organization. A change to the quality improvement or utilization management programs or procedures shall be made pursuant to paragraph (1).

(4) A provision that waives or conflicts with any provision of this chapter. A provision in the contract that allows the plan to provide professional liability or other coverage or to assume the cost of defending the provider in an action relating to professional liability or other action is not in conflict with, or in violation of, this chapter.

(5) A requirement to permit access to patient information in violation of federal or state laws concerning the confidentiality of patient information.

(c) With respect to a health care service plan contract covering dental services or a specialized health care service plan contract covering dental services, all of the following shall apply:

(1) If a material change is made to the health care service plan's rules, guidelines, policies, or procedures concerning dental provider contracting or coverage of or payment for dental services, the plan shall provide at least 45 business days' written notice to the dentists contracting with the health care service plan to provide services under the plan's individual or group plan contracts, including specialized health care service plan contracts, unless a change in state or federal law or regulations or any accreditation requirements of a private sector accreditation organization requires a shorter timeframe for compliance. For purposes of this paragraph, written notice shall include notice by electronic mail or facsimile transmission. This paragraph shall apply in addition to the other applicable requirements imposed under this section, except that it shall not apply where notice of the proposed change is required to be provided pursuant to subparagraph (C) of paragraph (1) of subdivision (b).

(2) For purposes of paragraph (1), a material change made to a health care service plan's rules, guidelines, policies, or procedures concerning dental provider contracting or coverage of or payment for dental services is a change to the system by which the plan adjudicates and pays claims for treatment that would reasonably be expected to cause delays or disruptions in processing claims or making eligibility determinations, or a change to the general coverage or general policies of the plan that affect rates and fees paid to providers.

(3) A plan that automatically renews a contract with a dental provider shall annually make available to the provider, within 60 days following a request by the provider, either online, via email, or in paper form, a copy of its current contract and a summary of the changes described in paragraph (1) of subdivision (b) that have been made since the contract was issued or last renewed.

(4) This subdivision shall not apply to a health care service plan that exclusively contracts with no more than two medical groups in the state to provide or arrange for the provision of professional medical services to the enrollees of the plan.

(d) (1) When a contracting agent sells, leases, or transfers a health provider's contract to a payor, the rights and obligations of the provider shall be governed by the underlying contract between the health care provider and the contracting agent.

(2) For purposes of this subdivision, the following terms shall have the following meanings:

(A) "Contracting agent" has the meaning set forth in paragraph (2) of subdivision (d) of Section 1395.6.

(B) "Payor" has the meaning set forth in paragraph (3) of subdivision (d) of Section 1395.6.

(e) Any contract provision that violates subdivision (b), (c), or (d) shall be void, unlawful, and unenforceable.

(f) The department shall compile the information submitted by plans pursuant to subdivision (h) of Section 1367 into a report and submit the report to the Governor and the Legislature by March 15 of each calendar year.

(g) Nothing in this section shall be construed or applied as setting the rate of payment to be included in contracts between plans and health care providers.

(h) For purposes of this section the following definitions apply:

(1) "Health care provider" means any professional person, medical group, independent practice association, organization, health care facility, or other person or institution licensed or authorized by the state to deliver or furnish health services.

(2) "Material" means a provision in a contract to which a reasonable person would attach importance in determining the action to be taken upon the provision.

(Amended by Stats. 2012, Ch. 447, Sec. 1. (AB 2252) Effective January 1, 2013.)

1375.8.

(a) The Legislature finds the following:

(1) Because of the nature and cost of certain medical items, the financial risk of these items is better retained by the health care service plan than by a health care service provider.

(2) Allowing a health care service provider to take the financial risk for the items described in this section only if the provider specifically requests in writing to assume that risk, will assist in maintaining patient access to health care service providers.

(b) (1) Notwithstanding Section 1375.5, no health care service plan contract that is issued, amended, delivered, or renewed in this state on or after July 1, 2003, shall require or allow a health care service provider to assume or be at any financial risk for any item described in subparagraphs (A) to (F), inclusive, of paragraph (2) when covered under the applicable plan contract and administered in the office of a physician and surgeon or prescribed by a physician and surgeon for self-administration by the patient. "Self-administration," for the purposes of this section, means an injectable medication that can be safely given intramuscularly, or in the muscle, or subcutaneously, or under the skin, by the patient or his or her family member.

(2) The items described in subparagraphs (A) to (F), inclusive, shall, instead, be reimbursed on a fee-for-service basis at the negotiated contract rate or through an alternate funding mechanism mutually agreed to by the health care service plan and the health care service provider, subject to any applicable copayment or deductible, by the health care service plan.

(A) Injectable chemotherapeutic medications and injectable adjunct pharmaceutical therapies for side effects.

(B) Injectable medications or blood products used for hemophilia.

(C) Injectable medications related to transplant services.

(D) Adult vaccines.

(E) Self-injectable medications.

(F) Other injectable medication or medication in an implantable dosage form costing more than two hundred fifty dollars ($250) per dose.

(3) Notwithstanding the provisions of paragraphs (1) and (2), a health care service provider may assume financial risk for the items described in subparagraphs (A) to (F), inclusive, of paragraph (2) after making the request in writing at the time of negotiating an initial contract or renewing a contract with a health care service plan. No health care service plan may request or require that as a condition of the contract agreement a health care service provider shall request to assume the financial risk for any of those items.

(c) The following definitions apply for the purposes of this section:

(1) "Financial risk" means any contractual financial agreement between a health care service provider and a health care service plan for services rendered to a patient or enrollee if the reimbursement from a health care service plan is other than a fee for service rate structure. "Financial risk" includes, but is not limited to, capitation payments, case rates, and risk pools.

(2) "Health care service provider" means an individual, partnership, group, or corporation lawfully licensed or organized under Division 2 (commencing with Section 500) of the Business and Professions Code, unless specifically exempt from those provisions, or licensed under Section 1204 or exempt from licensure under Section 1206 that delivers, furnishes, or otherwise arranges for or provides health care services. "Health care service provider" does not include a health facility as defined in Section 1250, a hospice, a surgical center, or a home infusion provider.

(d) This section shall not preclude any payment by a health care service plan to a health care service provider for the performance of any services related to quality measures and programs.

(e) This section shall not apply to a contract that is between a health care service plan and a health care service provider or a provider organization that meets either of the requirements set forth in paragraph (2) of subdivision (g) of Section 1375.4 or to a contract between licensed health care service plans or to a contract between a health care service plan and a health care service plan with waivers.

(Added by Stats. 2002, Ch. 798, Sec. 2. Effective January 1, 2003.)

1375.9.

(a) A health care service plan shall ensure that there is at least one full-time equivalent primary care physician for every 2,000 enrollees of the plan. The number of enrollees per primary care physician may be increased by up to 1,000 additional enrollees for each full-time equivalent nonphysician medical practitioner supervised by that primary care physician.

(b) This section shall not require a primary care physician to accept an assignment of enrollees by a health care service plan without his or her approval, or that would be contrary to paragraph (2) of subdivision (b) of Section 1375.7.

(c) This section does not modify subdivision (e) of Section 2836.1 of the Business and Professions Code or subdivision (b) of Section 3516 of the Business and Professions Code.

(d) For purposes of this section, a primary care provider includes a "nonphysician medical practitioner," which is defined as a physician assistant performing services under the supervision of a primary care physician in compliance with Chapter 7.7 (commencing with Section 3500) of Division 2 of the Business and Professions Code or a nurse practitioner performing services in collaboration with a physician pursuant to Chapter 6 (commencing with Section 2700) of Division 2 of the Business and Professions Code.

(Amended by Stats. 2018, Ch. 152, Sec. 1. (SB 997) Effective January 1, 2019.)

1376.

(a) No plan shall conduct any activity regulated by this chapter in contravention of such rules and regulations as the director may prescribe as necessary or appropriate in the public interest or for the protection of plans, subscribers, and enrollees to provide safeguards with respect to the financial responsibility of plans. Such rules and regulations may require a minimum capital or net worth, limitations on indebtedness, procedures for the handling of funds or assets, including segregation of funds, assets and net worth, the maintenance of appropriate insurance and a fidelity bond and the maintenance of a surety bond in an amount not exceeding fifty thousand dollars ($50,000).

(b) The surety bond referred to in subdivision (a) shall be conditioned upon compliance by the licensee with the provisions of this chapter and the rules and regulations adopted pursuant to this chapter and orders issued under this chapter. Every surety bond shall provide that no suit may be maintained to enforce any liability thereon unless brought within two years after the act upon which such suit is based.

(c) For purposes of computing any minimum capital requirement which may be prescribed by the rules and regulations of the director under subdivision (a), any operating cost assistance or direct loan made to a plan by the United States Department of Health and Human Services pursuant to Public Law 93-222, as amended, may be treated as a subordinated loan, notwithstanding any express terms thereof to the contrary.

(d) Each solicitor and solicitor firm shall handle funds received for the account of plans, subscribers, or groups in accordance with such rules as the director may adopt pursuant to this subdivision.

(e) The director may, by regulation, designate requirements of this section or regulations adopted pursuant to this section, from which public entities and political subdivisions of the state shall be exempt.

(Amended by Stats. 1999, Ch. 525, Sec. 123. Effective January 1, 2000. Operative July 1, 2000, or sooner, by Sec. 214 of Ch. 525.)

1376.1.

The deposit requirements of Section 1300.76.1 of Title 28 of the California Code of Regulations shall not apply to any plan operated by a county, or city and county, if both of the following apply:

(a) All of the evidence of indebtedness of the county, or city and county, has been rated "A" or better by Moody's Investors Service, Inc. or Standard & Poor's Corporation, based on a rating conducted during the immediately preceding 12 months.

(b) The county, or city and county, has cash or cash equivalents in an amount equal to fifty million dollars ($50,000,000) or more, based on its audited financial statements for the immediately preceding fiscal year. For purposes of this subdivision, the term "equivalents" shall have the same meaning as in Section 1300.77 of Title 28 of the California Code of Regulations.

(Amended by Stats. 2009, Ch. 298, Sec. 7. (AB 1540) Effective January 1, 2010.)

1377.

(a) Every plan which reimburses providers of health care services that do not contract in writing with the plan to provide health care services, or which reimburses its subscribers or enrollees for costs incurred in having received health care services from providers that do not contract in writing with the plan, in an amount which exceeds 10 percent of its total costs for health care services for the immediately preceding six months, shall comply with the requirements set forth in either paragraph (1) or (2):

(1) (A) Place with the director, or with any organization or trustee acceptable to the director through which a custodial or controlled account is maintained, a noncontracting provider insolvency deposit consisting of cash or securities that are acceptable to the director that at all times have a fair market value in an amount at least equal to 120 percent of the sum of the following:

(i) All claims for noncontracting provider services received for reimbursement, but not yet processed.

(ii) All claims for noncontracting provider services denied for reimbursement during the previous 45 days.

(iii) All claims for noncontracting provider services approved for reimbursement, but not yet paid.

(iv) An estimate of claims for noncontracting provider services incurred, but not reported.

(B) Each plan licensed pursuant to this chapter prior to January 1, 1991, shall, upon that date, make a deposit of 50 percent of the amount required by subparagraph (A), and shall maintain additional cash or cash equivalents as defined by rule of the director, in the amount of 50 percent of the amount required by subparagraph (A), and shall make a deposit of 100 percent of the amount required by subparagraph (A) by January 1, 1992.

(C) The amount of the deposit shall be reasonably estimated as of the first day of the month and maintained for the remainder of the month.

(D) The deposit required by this paragraph is in addition to the deposit that may be required by rule of the director and is an allowable asset of the plan in the determination of tangible net equity as defined in subdivision (b) of Section 1300.76 of Title 28 of the California Code of Regulations. All income from the deposit shall be an asset of the plan and may be withdrawn by the plan at any time.

(E) A health care service plan that has made a deposit may withdraw that deposit or any part of the deposit if (i) a substitute deposit of cash or securities of equal amount and value is made, (ii) the fair market value exceeds the amount of the required deposit, or (iii) the required deposit under this paragraph is reduced or eliminated. Deposits, substitutions, or withdrawals may be made only with the prior written approval of the director, but approval shall not be required for the withdrawal of earned income.

(F) The deposit required under this section is in trust and may be used only as provided by this section. The director or, if a receiver has been appointed, the receiver shall use the deposit of an insolvent health care service plan, as defined in Sections 1394.7 and 1394.8, for payment of covered claims for services rendered by noncontracting providers under circumstances covered by the plan. All claims determined by the director or receiver, in his or her discretion, to be eligible for reimbursement under this section shall be paid on a pro rata basis based on assets available from the deposit to pay the ultimate liability for incurred expenditures. Partial distribution may be made pending final distribution. Any amount of the deposit remaining shall be paid into the liquidation or receivership of the health care service plan. The director may also use the deposit of an insolvent health care service plan for payment of any administrative costs associated with the administration of this section. The department, the director, and any employee of the department shall not be liable, as provided by Section 820.2 of the Government Code, for an injury resulting from an exercise of discretion pursuant to this section. Nothing in this section shall be construed to provide immunity for the acts of a receiver, except when the director is acting as a receiver.

(G) The director may, by regulation, prescribe the time, manner, and form for filing claims.

(H) The director may permit a plan to meet a portion of this requirement by a deposit of tangible assets acceptable to the director, the fair market value of which shall be determined on at least an annual basis by the director. The plan shall bear the cost of any appraisal or valuations required hereunder by the director.

(2) Maintain adequate insurance, or a guaranty arrangement approved in writing by the director, to pay for any loss to providers, subscribers, or enrollees claiming reimbursement due to the insolvency of the plan.

(b) Whenever the reimbursements described in this section exceed 10 percent of the plan's total costs for health care services over the immediately preceding six months, the plan shall file a written report with the director containing the information necessary to determine compliance with subdivision (a) no later than 30 business days from the first day of the month. Upon an adequate showing by the plan that the requirements of this section should be waived or reduced, the director may waive or reduce these requirements to an amount as the director deems sufficient to protect subscribers and enrollees of the plan consistent with the intent and purpose of this chapter.

(c) Every plan which reimburses providers of health care service on a fee-for-services basis; or which directly reimburses its subscribers or enrollees, to an extent exceeding 10 percent of its total payments for health care services, shall estimate and record in the books of account a liability for incurred and unreported claims. Upon a determination by the director that the estimate is inadequate, the director may require the plan to increase its estimate of incurred and unreported claims. Every plan shall promptly report to the director whenever these reimbursables exceed 10 percent of its total expenditures for health care services.

As used herein, the term "fee-for-services" refers to the situation where the amount of reimbursement paid by the plan to providers of service is determined by the amount and type of service rendered by the provider of service.

(d) In the event an insolvent plan covered by this section fails to pay a noncontracting provider sums for covered services owed, the provider shall first look to the uncovered expenditures insolvency deposit or the insurance or guaranty arrangement maintained by the plan for payment. When a plan becomes insolvent, in no event shall a noncontracting provider, or agent, trustee, or assignee thereof, attempt to collect from the subscriber or enrollee sums owed for covered services by the plan or maintain any action at law against a subscriber or enrollee to collect sums owed by the plan for covered services without having first attempted to obtain reimbursement from the plan.

(Amended by Stats. 2009, Ch. 298, Sec. 8. (AB 1540) Effective January 1, 2010.)

1378.

No plan shall expend for administrative costs in any fiscal year an excessive amount of the aggregate dues, fees and other periodic payments received by the plan for providing health care services to its subscribers or enrollees. The term "administrative costs," as used herein, includes costs incurred in connection with the solicitation of subscribers or enrollees for the plan.

This section shall not preclude a plan from expending additional sums of money for administrative costs provided such money is not derived from revenue obtained from subscribers or enrollees of the plan.

(Added by Stats. 1975, Ch. 941.)

1379.

(a) Every contract between a plan and a provider of health care services shall be in writing, and shall set forth that in the event the plan fails to pay for health care services as set forth in the subscriber contract, the subscriber or enrollee shall not be liable to the provider for any sums owed by the plan.

(b) In the event that the contract has not been reduced to writing as required by this chapter or that the contract fails to contain the required prohibition, the contracting provider shall not collect or attempt to collect from the subscriber or enrollee sums owed by the plan.

(c) No contracting provider, or agent, trustee or assignee thereof, may maintain any action at law against a subscriber or enrollee to collect sums owed by the plan.

(Added by Stats. 1975, Ch. 941.)

1379.5.

(a) On and after July 1, 2008, every contract between a plan and a health care provider who provides health care services in Mexico to an enrollee of the plan shall require the health care provider knowing of, or in attendance on, a case or suspected case of any disease or condition listed in subdivision (j) of Section 2500 of Title 17 of the California Code of Regulations to report the case to the health officer of the jurisdiction in California where the patient in the case resides, or if the patient resides in Mexico and is employed in California, the contract shall require a health care provider to report the case to the health officer of the jurisdiction where the patient in the case is employed. The contract provision shall require the health care provider to make the report in accordance with subdivision (d) of Section 2500 of Title 17 of the California Code of Regulations, except that for reports in cases where the patient resides in Mexico the contract shall require the report to be made to the health officer of the jurisdiction where the patient is employed.

(b) For purposes of this section, the terms "case," "health care provider," "health officer," "in attendance," and "suspected case" shall have the same meanings as set forth in subdivision (a) of Section 2500 of Title 17 of the California Code of Regulations.

(c) A plan's obligations under this section shall be limited to the following:

(1) Ensuring that the contracts executed by providers who provide health care services in Mexico satisfy the requirements set forth in subdivision (a).

(2) Giving the following written notice to the provider at the time the signed contract is delivered:

"This contract contains specific requirements regarding reporting of actual or suspected diseases or conditions to California health officers."

(Added by Stats. 2007, Ch. 385, Sec. 1. Effective January 1, 2008.)

1380.

(a) The department shall conduct periodically an onsite medical survey of the health delivery system of each plan. The survey shall include a review of the procedures for obtaining health services, the procedures for regulating utilization, peer review mechanisms, internal procedures for assuring quality of care, and the overall performance of the plan in providing health care benefits and meeting the health needs of the subscribers and enrollees.

(b) The survey shall be conducted by a panel of qualified health professionals experienced in evaluating the delivery of prepaid health care. The department shall be authorized to contract with professional organizations or outside personnel to conduct medical surveys and these contracts shall be on a noncompetitive bid basis and shall be exempt from Chapter 2 (commencing with Section 10290) of Part 2 of Division 2 of the Public Contract Code. These organizations or personnel shall have demonstrated the ability to objectively evaluate the delivery of health care by plans or health maintenance organizations.

(c) Surveys performed pursuant to this section shall be conducted as often as deemed necessary by the director to assure the protection of subscribers and enrollees, but not less frequently than once every three years. Nothing in this section shall be construed to require the survey team to visit each clinic, hospital office, or facility of the plan. To avoid duplication, the director shall employ, but is not bound by, the following:

(1) For hospital-based health care service plans, to the extent necessary to satisfy the requirements of this section, the findings of inspections conducted pursuant to Section 1279.

(2) For health care service plans contracting with the State Department of Health Services pursuant to the Waxman-Duffy Prepaid Health Plan Act, the findings of reviews conducted pursuant to Section 14456 of the Welfare and Institutions Code.

(3) To the extent feasible, reviews of providers conducted by professional standards review organizations, and surveys and audits conducted by other governmental entities.

(d) Nothing in this section shall be construed to require the medical survey team to review peer review proceedings and records conducted and compiled under Section 1370 or medical records. However, the director shall be authorized to require onsite review of these peer review proceedings and records or medical records where necessary to determine that quality health care is being delivered to subscribers and enrollees. Where medical record review is authorized, the survey team shall insure that the confidentiality of physician-patient relationship is safeguarded in accordance with existing law and neither the survey team nor the director or the director's staff may be compelled to disclose this information except in accordance with the physician-patient relationship. The director shall ensure that the confidentiality of the peer review proceedings and records is maintained. The disclosure of the peer review proceedings and records to the director or the medical survey team shall not alter the status of the proceedings or records as privileged and confidential communications pursuant to Sections 1370 and 1370.1.

(e) The procedures and standards utilized by the survey team shall be made available to the plans prior to the conducting of medical surveys.

(f) During the survey the members of the survey team shall examine the complaint files kept by the plan pursuant to Section 1368. The survey report issued pursuant to subdivision (i) shall include a discussion of the plan's record for handling complaints.

(g) During the survey the members of the survey team shall offer such advice and assistance to the plan as deemed appropriate.

(h) (1) Survey results shall be publicly reported by the director as quickly as possible but no later than 180 days following the completion of the survey unless the director determines, in his or her discretion, that additional time is reasonably necessary to fully and fairly report the survey results. The director shall provide the plan with an overview of survey findings and notify the plan of deficiencies found by the survey team at least 90 days prior to the release of the public report.

(2) Reports on all surveys, deficiencies, and correction plans shall be open to public inspection except that no surveys, deficiencies, or correction plans shall be made public unless the plan has had an opportunity to review the report and file a response within 45 days of the date that the department provided the report to the plan. After reviewing the plan's response, the director shall issue a final report that excludes any survey information and legal findings and conclusions determined by the director to be in error, describes compliance efforts, identifies deficiencies that have been corrected by the plan by the time of the director's receipt of the plan's 45-day response, and describes remedial actions for deficiencies requiring longer periods to the remedy required by the director or proposed by the plan.

(3) The final report shall not include a description of "acceptable" or of "compliance" for any uncorrected deficiency.

(4) Upon making the final report available to the public, a single copy of a summary of the final report's findings shall be made available free of charge by the department to members of the public, upon request. Additional copies of the summary may be provided at the department's cost. The summary shall include a discussion of compliance efforts, corrected deficiencies, and proposed remedial actions.

(5) If requested by the plan, the director shall append the plan's response to the final report issued pursuant to paragraph (2), and shall append to the summary issued pursuant to paragraph (4) a brief statement provided by the plan summarizing its response to the report. The plan may modify its response or statement at any time and provide modified copies to the department for public distribution no later than 10 days from the date of notification from the department that the final report will be made available to the public. The plan may file an addendum to its response or statement at any time after the final report has been made available to the public. The addendum to the response or statement shall also be made available to the public.

(6) Any information determined by the director to be confidential pursuant to statutes relating to the disclosure of records, including the California Public Records Act (Chapter 3.5 (commencing with Section 6250) of Division 7 of Title 1 of the Government Code), shall not be made public.

(i) (1) The director shall give the plan a reasonable time to correct deficiencies. Failure on the part of the plan to comply to the director's satisfaction shall constitute cause for disciplinary action against the plan.

(2) No later than 18 months following release of the final report required by subdivision (h), the department shall conduct a follow-up review to determine and report on the status of the plan's efforts to correct deficiencies. The department's follow-up report shall identify any deficiencies reported pursuant to subdivision (h) that have not been corrected to the satisfaction of the director.

(3) If requested by the plan, the director shall append the plan's response to the follow-up report issued pursuant to paragraph (2). The plan may modify its response at any time and provide modified copies to the department for public distribution no later than 10 days from the date of notification from the department that the follow-up report will be made available to the public. The plan may file an addendum to its response at any time after the follow-up report has been made available to the public. The addendum to the response or statement shall also be made available to the public.

(j) The director shall provide to the plan and to the executive officer of the Board of Dental Examiners a copy of information relating to the quality of care of any licensed dental provider contained in any report described in subdivisions (h) and (i) that, in the judgment of the director, indicates clearly excessive treatment, incompetent treatment, grossly negligent treatment, repeated negligent acts, or unnecessary treatment. Any confidential information provided by the director shall not be made public pursuant to this subdivision. Notwithstanding any other provision of law, the disclosure of this information to the plan and to the executive officer shall not operate as a waiver of confidentiality. There shall be no liability on the part of, and no cause of action of any nature shall arise against, the State of California, the Department of Managed Health Care, the Director of the Department of Managed Health Care, the Board of Dental Examiners, or any officer, agent, employee, consultant, or contractor of the state or the department or the board for the release of any false or unauthorized information pursuant to this section, unless the release of that information is made with knowledge and malice.

(k) Nothing in this section shall be construed as affecting the director's authority pursuant to Article 7 (commencing with Section 1386) or Article 8 (commencing with Section 1390) of this chapter.

(Amended by Stats. 2000, Ch. 857, Sec. 41. Effective January 1, 2001.)

1380.1.

(a) The Legislature finds and declares as follows:

(1) Multiple medical quality audits of health care providers, as many as 25 for some physician offices, increase costs for health care providers and health plans, and thus ultimately increase costs for the purchaser and the consumer, and result in the direction of limited health care resources to administrative costs instead of to patient care.

(2) Streamlining the multiple medical quality audits required by health care service plans and insurers is vital to increasing the resources directed to patient care.

(3) Few legislative proposals affecting health care services have the potential of benefiting all of the affected parties, including health plans, health care providers, purchasers, and consumers, through a reduction in administrative costs but without negatively affecting patient care.

(b) The Advisory Committee on Managed Care shall recommend to the director standards for a uniform medical quality audit system, which shall include a single periodic medical

quality audit. The director shall publish proposed regulations in that regard on or before January 1, 2002.

(c) In developing those standards, the Advisory Committee on Managed Care shall seek comment from a broad and balanced range of interested parties.

(d) The recommendations shall include all of the following:

(1) Standards that will serve as the basis of the single periodic medical quality audit necessary to meet the criteria of this section.

(2) Standards that will not be covered by the single periodic medical quality audit and that may be audited directly by health care service plans.

(3) A list of those private sector accreditation organizations, if any, that have or can develop systems comparable to the recommended system, and the capability and expertise to accredit, audit, or credential providers.

(e) (1) The director may approve private sector accreditation organizations as qualified organizations to perform the single periodic medical quality audits.

(2) Audits shall be conducted at least annually.

(f) The single medical quality audit shall not prevent licensed health care service plans from developing performance criteria or conducting separate audits for governmental or regulatory purposes, purchasers, or to address consumer complaints and grievances, management changes, or plan initiatives to improve or monitor quality.

(Repealed and added by Stats. 2000, Ch. 856, Sec. 2. Effective January 1, 2001.)

1380.3.

The department shall coordinate the surveys conducted pursuant to Section 1380 with the State Department of Health Care Services, to the extent possible, in order to allow for simultaneous oversight of Medi-Cal managed care plans by both departments, provided that this coordination does not result in a delay of the surveys required under Section 1380 or in the failure of the department to conduct those surveys.

(Repealed and added by Stats. 2014, Ch. 573, Sec. 4. (SB 964) Effective January 1, 2015.)

1381.

(a) All records, books, and papers of a plan, management company, solicitor, solicitor firm, and any provider or subcontractor providing health care or other services to a plan, management company, solicitor, or solicitor firm shall be open to inspection during normal business hours by the director.

(b) To the extent feasible, all such records, books, and papers described in subdivision (a) shall be located in this state. In examining such records outside this state, the director shall consider the cost to the plan, consistent with the effectiveness of the director's examination, and may upon reasonable notice require that such records, books and papers, or a specified portion thereof, be made available for examination in this state, or that a true and accurate copy of such records, books and papers, or a specified portion thereof, be furnished to the director.

(Amended by Stats. 1999, Ch. 525, Sec. 128. Effective January 1, 2000. Operative July 1, 2000, or sooner, by Sec. 214 of Ch. 525.)

1382.

(a) The director shall conduct an examination of the fiscal and administrative affairs of any health care service plan, and each person with whom the plan has made arrangements for administrative, management, or financial services, as often as deemed necessary to protect the interest of subscribers or enrollees, but not less frequently than once every five years.

(b) The expense of conducting any additional or nonroutine examinations pursuant to this section, and the expense of conducting any additional or nonroutine medical surveys pursuant to Section 1380 shall be charged against the plan being examined or surveyed. The amount shall include the actual salaries or compensation paid to the persons making the examination or survey, the expenses incurred in the course thereof, and overhead costs in connection therewith as fixed by the director. In determining the cost of examinations or surveys, the director may use the estimated average hourly cost for all persons performing examinations or surveys of plans for the fiscal year. The amount charged shall be remitted by the plan to the director. If recovery of these costs cannot be made from the plan, these costs may be added to, but subject to the limitation of, the assessment provided for in subdivision (b) of Section 1356.

(c) Reports of all examinations shall be open to public inspection, except that no examination shall be made public, unless the plan has had an opportunity to review the examination report and file a statement or response within 45 days of the date that the department provided the report to the plan. After reviewing the plan's response, the director shall issue a final report that excludes any survey information, legal findings, or conclusions determined by the director to be in error, describes compliance efforts, identifies deficiencies that have been corrected by the plan on or before the time the director receives the plan's response, and describes remedial actions for deficiencies requiring longer periods for the remedy required by the director or proposed by the plan.

(d) If requested in writing by the plan, the director shall append the plan's response to the final report issued pursuant to subdivision (c). The plan may modify its response or statement at any time and provide modified copies to the department for public distribution not later than 10 days from the date of notification from the department that the final report will be made available to the public. The addendum to the response or statement shall also be made available to the public.

(e) Notwithstanding subdivision (c), any health care service plan that contracts with the State Department of Health Services to provide service to Medi-Cal beneficiaries pursuant to Chapter 8 (commencing with Section 14200) of Part 3 of Division 9 of the Welfare and Institutions Code may make a written request to the director to permit the State Department of Health Services to review its examination report.

(f) Upon receipt of the written request described in subdivision (e), the director may, consistent with Section 6254.5 of the Government Code, permit the State Department of Health Services to review the plan's examination report.

(g) Nothing in this section shall be construed as affecting the director's authority pursuant to Article 7 (commencing with Section 1386) or Article 8 (commencing with Section 1390).

(Amended by Stats. 1999, Ch. 525, Sec. 129. Effective January 1, 2000. Operative July 1, 2000, or sooner, by Sec. 214 of Ch. 525.)

1383.

Every plan that is a health maintenance organization qualified under Section 1310(d) of Title XIII of the federal Public Health Service Act, shall provide the department with a copy of the reports the plan files annually with the United States Department of Health, Education, and Welfare pursuant to Title XIII of the federal Public Health Service Act.

(Repealed and added by Stats. 1979, Ch. 1083.)

1383.1.

(a) On or before July 1, 1997, every health care service plan shall file with the department a written policy, which is not subject to approval or disapproval by the department, describing the manner in which the plan determines if a second medical opinion is medically necessary and appropriate. Notice of the policy and information regarding the manner in which an enrollee may receive a second medical opinion shall be provided to all enrollees in the plan's evidence of coverage. The written policy shall describe the manner in which requests for a second medical opinion are reviewed by the plan.

(b) This section shall not apply to any health care service plan contract authorized under Article 5.6 (commencing with Section 1374.60).

(c) Nothing in this section shall require a health care service plan to cover services or provide benefits that are not otherwise covered under the terms and conditions of the plan contract, nor to provide services through providers who are not under contract with the plan.

(Amended by Stats. 1998, Ch. 215, Sec. 2. Effective January 1, 1999.)

1383.15.

(a) When requested by an enrollee or participating health professional who is treating an enrollee, a health care service plan shall provide or authorize a second opinion by an appropriately qualified health care professional. Reasons for a second opinion to be provided or authorized shall include, but are not limited to, the following:

(1) If the enrollee questions the reasonableness or necessity of recommended surgical procedures.

(2) If the enrollee questions a diagnosis or plan of care for a condition that threatens loss of life, loss of limb, loss of bodily function, or substantial impairment, including, but not limited to, a serious chronic condition.

(3) If the clinical indications are not clear or are complex and confusing, a diagnosis is in doubt due to conflicting test results, or the treating health professional is unable to diagnose the condition, and the enrollee requests an additional diagnosis.

(4) If the treatment plan in progress is not improving the medical condition of the enrollee within an appropriate period of time given the diagnosis and plan of care, and the enrollee requests a second opinion regarding the diagnosis or continuance of the treatment.

(5) If the enrollee has attempted to follow the plan of care or consulted with the initial provider concerning serious concerns about the diagnosis or plan of care.

(b) For purposes of this section, an appropriately qualified health care professional is a primary care physician or specialist who is acting within his or her scope of practice and who possesses a clinical background, including training and expertise, related to the particular illness, disease, condition or conditions associated with the request for a second opinion. For purposes of a specialized health care service plan, an appropriately qualified health care professional is a licensed health care provider who is acting within his or her scope of practice and who possesses a clinical background, including training and expertise, related to the particular illness, disease, condition or conditions associated with the request for a second opinion.

(c) If an enrollee or participating health professional who is treating an enrollee requests a second opinion pursuant to this section, an authorization or denial shall be provided in an expeditious manner. When the enrollee's condition is such that the enrollee faces an imminent and serious threat to his or her health, including, but not limited to, the potential loss of life, limb, or other major bodily function, or lack of timeliness that would be detrimental to the enrollee's ability to regain maximum function, the second opinion shall be authorized or denied in a timely fashion appropriate for the nature of the enrollee's condition, not to exceed 72 hours after the plan's receipt of the request, whenever possible. Each plan shall file with the Department of Managed Health Care timelines for responding to requests for second opinions for cases involving emergency needs, urgent care, and other requests by July 1, 2000, and within 30 days of any amendment to the timelines. The timelines shall be made available to the public upon request.

(d) If a health care service plan approves a request by an enrollee for a second opinion, the enrollee shall be responsible only for the costs of applicable copayments that the plan requires for similar referrals.

(e) If the enrollee is requesting a second opinion about care from his or her primary care physician, the second opinion shall be provided by an appropriately qualified health care professional of the enrollee's choice within the same physician organization.

(f) If the enrollee is requesting a second opinion about care from a specialist, the second opinion shall be provided by any provider of the enrollee's choice from any independent practice association or medical group within the network of the same or equivalent specialty. If the specialist is not within the same physician organization, the plan shall incur the cost or negotiate the fee arrangements of that second opinion, beyond the applicable copayments which shall be paid by the enrollee. If not authorized by the plan, additional medical opinions not within the original physician organization shall be the responsibility of the enrollee.

(g) If there is no participating plan provider within the network who meets the standard specified in subdivision (b), then the plan shall authorize a second opinion by an appropriately qualified health professional outside of the plan's provider network. In approving a second opinion either inside or outside of the plan's provider network, the plan shall take into account the ability of the enrollee to travel to the provider.

(h) The health care service plan shall require the second opinion health professional to provide the enrollee and the initial health professional with a consultation report, including any recommended procedures or tests that the second opinion health professional believes appropriate. Nothing in this section shall be construed to prevent the plan from authorizing, based on its independent determination, additional medical opinions concerning the medical condition of an enrollee.

(i) If the health care service plan denies a request by an enrollee for a second opinion, it shall notify the enrollee in writing of the reasons for the denial and shall inform the enrollee of the right to file a grievance with the plan. The notice shall comply with subdivision (b) of Section 1368.02.

(j) Unless authorized by the plan, in order for services to be covered the enrollee shall obtain services only from a provider who is participating in, or under contract with, the plan pursuant to the specific contract under which the enrollee is entitled to health care services. The plan may limit referrals to its network of providers if there is a participating plan provider who meets the standard specified in subdivision (b).

(k) This section shall not apply to health care service plan contracts that provide benefits to enrollees through preferred provider contracting arrangements if, subject to all other terms and conditions of the contract that apply generally to all other benefits, access to and coverage for second opinions are not limited.

(Amended by Stats. 2001, Ch. 328, Sec. 3. Effective January 1, 2002.)

1384.

(a) Within 90 days after receipt of a request from the director, a plan or other person subject to this chapter shall submit to the director an audit report containing audited financial statements covering the 12-calendar months next preceding the month of receipt of the request, or another period as the director may require.

(b) On or before 105 days after the date of a notice of surrender or order of revocation, a plan shall file with the director a closing audit report containing audited financial statements. The reporting period for the closing audit report shall be the 12-month period preceding the date of the notice of surrender or order of revocation, or for another period as the director may specify. This report shall include other relevant information as specified by rule of the director. The director shall not consent to a surrender and an order of revocation shall not be considered final until the closing audit report has been filed with the director and all concerns raised by the director therefrom have been resolved by the plan, as determined by the director. For good cause, the director may waive the requirement of a closing audit report.

(c) Except as otherwise provided in this subdivision, each plan shall submit financial statements prepared as of the close of its fiscal year within 120 days after the close of the fiscal year. The financial statements referred to in this subdivision and in subdivisions (a) and (b) of this section shall be accompanied by a report, certificate, or opinion of an independent certified public accountant or independent public accountant. The audits shall be conducted in accordance with generally accepted auditing standards and the rules and regulations of the director. However, financial statements from public entities or political subdivisions of the state whose audits are conducted by a county grand jury shall be submitted within 180 days after the close of the fiscal year and need not include a report, certificate, or opinion by an independent certified public accountant or an independent public accountant, and the audit shall be conducted in accordance with governmental auditing standards.

(d) A plan, solicitor, or solicitor firm shall make any special reports to the director as the director may from time to time require.

(e) For good cause and upon written request, the director may extend the time for compliance with subdivisions (a), (b), and (h) of this section.

(f) A plan, solicitor, or solicitor firm shall, when requested by the director, for good cause, submit its unaudited financial statement, prepared in accordance with generally accepted accounting principles and consisting of at least a balance sheet and statement of income as of the date and for the period specified by the director. The director may require the submission of these reports on a monthly or other periodic basis.

(g) If the report, certificate, or opinion of the independent accountant referred to in subdivision (c) is in any way qualified, the director may require the plan to take any action as the director deems appropriate to permit an independent accountant to remove the qualification from the report, certificate, or opinion.

(h) The director may reject any financial statement, report, certificate, or opinion filed pursuant to this section by notifying the plan, solicitor, or solicitor firm required to make this filing of its rejection and the cause thereof. Within 30 days after the receipt of the notice, the person shall correct the deficiency, and the failure so to do shall be deemed a violation of this chapter. The director shall retain a copy of all filings so rejected.

(i) The director may make rules and regulations specifying the form and content of the reports and financial statements referred to in this section, and may require that these reports and financial statements be verified by the plan or other person subject to this chapter in a manner as the director may prescribe.

(Amended by Stats. 1999, Ch. 525, Sec. 130. Effective January 1, 2000. Operative July 1, 2000, or sooner, by Sec. 214 of Ch. 525.)

1385.

Each plan, solicitor firm, and solicitor shall keep and maintain current such books of account and other records as the director may by rule require for the purposes of this chapter. Every plan shall require all providers who contract with the plan to report to the plan in writing all surcharge and copayment moneys paid by subscribers and enrollees directly to such providers, unless the director expressly approves otherwise.

(Amended by Stats. 1999, Ch. 525, Sec. 131. Effective January 1, 2000. Operative July 1, 2000, or sooner, by Sec. 214 of Ch. 525.)

ARTICLE 6.1. Pharmacy Benefit Management Services [1385.001 - 1385.007]

(Article 6.1 added by Stats. 2018, Ch. 905, Sec. 4.)

1385.001.

For the purposes of this article, "pharmacy benefit manager" means a person, business, or other entity that, pursuant to a contract with a health care service plan, manages the prescription drug coverage provided by the health care service plan, including, but not limited to, the processing and payment of claims for prescription drugs, the performance of drug utilization review, the processing of drug prior authorization requests, the adjudication of appeals or grievances related to prescription drug coverage, contracting with network pharmacies, and controlling the cost of covered prescription drugs. This definition shall not include a health care service plan licensed under this chapter or any individual employee of a health care service plan or its contracted provider, as defined in subdivision (i) of Section 1345, performing the services described in this section.

(Added by Stats. 2018, Ch. 905, Sec. 4. (AB 315) Effective January 1, 2019. Operative on January 1, 2020, pursuant to Section 1385.002.)

1385.002.

(a) Except as specified in Section 1385.007, the requirements of this article shall become operative on January 1, 2020.

(b) Notwithstanding subdivision (a), the department has the authority to enforce the provisions of this article, including the authority to adopt, amend, or repeal any rules and regulations, not inconsistent with the laws of this state, as may be necessary for the protection of the public and to implement this article, including, but not limited to, the director's enforcement authority under this chapter.

(c) Notwithstanding subdivision (a) and Chapter 3.5 (commencing with Section 11340) of Part 1 of Division 3 of Title 2 of the Government Code, the department may implement, interpret, or make specific this article by means of all-plan letters or similar instructions to plans and pharmacy benefit managers, without taking regulatory action, until such time as regulations are adopted.

(d) The department may contract with a consultant or consultants with expertise in this subject area to assist the department in developing guidance or instructions described in subdivision (c), or the report required pursuant to Section 1385.007. The department's contract with a consultant shall include conflict-of-interest provisions to prohibit a person from participating in any report in which the person knows or has reason to know he or she has a material financial interest, including, but not limited to, a person who has a consulting or other agreement with a person or organization that would be affected by the results of the report.

(e) Contracts entered into pursuant to the authority in this article shall be exempt from Chapter 6 (commencing with Section 14825) of Part 5.5 of Division 3 of Title 2 of the Government Code, Section 19130 of the Government Code, and Part 2 (commencing with Section 10100) of Division 2 of the Public Contract Code, and shall be exempt from the review or approval of any division of the Department of General Services.

(Added by Stats. 2018, Ch. 905, Sec. 4. (AB 315) Effective January 1, 2019.)

1385.003.

(a) A health care service plan shall disclose to a contracted pharmacy provider or its contracting agent the prescription drug information contained in subdivision (a) of Section 1363.03, including, but not limited to, the telephone number pharmacy providers may call for assistance and information necessary to process a pharmacy claim.

(b) A health care service plan shall not include in a contract with a pharmacy provider or its contracting agent a provision that prohibits the provider from informing a patient of a less costly alternative to a prescribed medication.

(Added by Stats. 2018, Ch. 905, Sec. 4. (AB 315) Effective January 1, 2019. Operative on January 1, 2020, pursuant to Section 1385.002.)

1385.004.

(a) A health care service plan that contracts with a pharmacy benefit manager for management of any or all of its prescription drug coverage shall require the pharmacy benefit manager to do all of the following:

(1) Comply with the provisions of Section 1385.003.

(2) Register with the department pursuant to the requirements of this article.

(3) Exercise good faith and fair dealing in the performance of its contractual duties to a health care service plan.

(4) Comply with the requirements of Chapter 9.5 (commencing with Section 4430) of Division 2 of the Business and Professions Code, as applicable.

(5) Inform all pharmacists under contract with or subject to contracts with the pharmacy benefit manager of the pharmacist's rights to submit complaints to the department under Section 1371.39 and of the pharmacist's rights as a provider under Section 1375.7.

(b) A pharmacy benefit manager shall notify a health care service plan in writing of any activity, policy, or practice of the pharmacy benefit manager that directly or indirectly presents a conflict of interest that interferes with the discharge of the pharmacy benefit manager's duty to the health care service plan to exercise good faith and fair dealing in the performance of its contractual duties pursuant to subdivision (a).

(Added by Stats. 2018, Ch. 905, Sec. 4. (AB 315) Effective January 1, 2019. Operative on January 1, 2020, pursuant to Section 1385.002.)

1385.005.

(a) A pharmacy benefit manager required to register with the department pursuant to Section 1385.004 shall complete an application for registration with the department that shall include, but not be limited to, all of the information required by subdivision (c).

(b) A pharmacy benefit manager registration obtained pursuant to this section is not transferable.

(c) The department shall develop an application form for pharmacy benefit manager registration. The application form for a pharmacy benefit manager registration shall require the pharmacy benefit manager to submit the following information to the department:

(1) The name of the pharmacy benefit manager.

(2) The address and contact telephone number for the pharmacy benefit manager.

(3) The name and address of the pharmacy benefit manager's agent for service of process in the state.

(4) The name and address of each person beneficially interested in the pharmacy benefit manager.

(5) The name and address of each person with management or control over the pharmacy benefit manager.

(d) If the applicant is a partnership or other unincorporated association, a limited liability company, or a corporation, and the number of partners, members, or stockholders, as the case may be, exceeds five, the application shall so state, and shall further state the name, address, usual occupation, and professional qualifications of each of the five partners, members, or stockholders who own the five largest interests in the applicant entity. Upon request by the department, the applicant shall furnish the department with the name, address, usual occupation, and professional qualifications of partners, members, or stockholders not named in the application, or shall refer the department to an appropriate source for that information.

(e) The application shall contain a statement to the effect that the applicant has not been convicted of a felony and has not violated any of the provisions of this article. If the applicant cannot make this statement, the application shall contain a statement of the violation, if any, or shall describe the reasons that prevent the applicant from being able to comply with the requirements with respect to the statement.

(f) The department may set a fee for a registration required by this article. The application fee shall not exceed the reasonable costs of the department in carrying out its duties under this article.

(g) Within 30 days of a change in any of the information disclosed to the department on an application for a registration, the pharmacy benefit manager shall notify the department of that change in writing.

(h) For purposes of this section, "person beneficially interested" with respect to a pharmacy benefit manager means and includes the following:

(1) If the applicant is a partnership or other unincorporated association, each partner or member.

(2) If the applicant is a corporation, each of its officers, directors, and stockholders, provided that a natural person shall not be deemed to be beneficially interested in a nonprofit corporation.

(3) If the applicant is a limited liability company, each officer, manager, or member.

(Added by Stats. 2018, Ch. 905, Sec. 4. (AB 315) Effective January 1, 2019. Operative on January 1, 2020, pursuant to Section 1385.002.)

1385.006.

The failure by a health care service plan to comply with the contractual requirements pursuant to this article shall constitute grounds for disciplinary action. The director shall, as appropriate, investigate and take enforcement action against a health care service plan that fails to comply with these requirements and shall periodically evaluate contracts between health care service plans and pharmacy benefit managers to determine if any audit, evaluation, or enforcement actions should be undertaken by the department.

(Added by Stats. 2018, Ch. 905, Sec. 4. (AB 315) Effective January 1, 2019. Operative on January 1, 2020, pursuant to Section 1385.002.)

1385.007.

(a) By July 1, 2019, the department, in collaboration with other agencies, departments, advocates, experts, health care service plan representatives, and other entities and stakeholders that it deems appropriate, shall convene a Task Force on Pharmacy Benefit Management Reporting to determine what information related to pharmaceutical costs, if any, the department should require to be reported by health care service plans or their contracted pharmacy benefit managers, in addition to reporting required by Section 1367.243. The task force shall consider inclusion of information including, but not limited to, the following:

(1) Wholesale acquisition costs of pharmaceuticals.

(2) Rebates obtained by the health care service plan or the pharmacy benefit manager from pharmaceutical manufacturers.

(3) Payments to network pharmacies.

(4) Exclusivity arrangements between health care service plans or contracted pharmacy benefit managers with pharmaceutical manufacturers.

(b) The task force shall consider the results of information reporting pursuant to Section 1367.243 and Chapter 9 (commencing with Section 127675) of Part 2 of Division 107 in determining what information should be reported pursuant to subdivision (a).

(c) The department shall submit a report of the Task Force on Pharmacy Benefit Management Reporting to the President pro Tempore of the Senate, the Speaker of the Assembly, and the Senate and Assembly Committees on Health, with the recommendations of the task force no later than February 1, 2020, on which date the task force shall cease to exist.

(d) This section shall become inoperative on February 1, 2020, and, as of January 1, 2021, is repealed.

(Added by Stats. 2018, Ch. 905, Sec. 4. (AB 315) Effective January 1, 2019. Section inoperative February 1, 2020. Repealed as of January 1, 2021, by its own provisions.)

ARTICLE 6.2. Review of Rate Increases [1385.01 - 1385.13]

(Article 6.2 added by Stats. 2010, Ch. 661, Sec. 4.)

1385.01.

For purposes of this article, the following definitions shall apply:

(a) "Large group health care service plan contract" means a group health care service plan contract other than a contract issued to a small employer, as defined in Section 1357, 1357.500, or 1357.600.

(b) "Small group health care service plan contract" means a group health care service plan contract issued to a small employer, as defined in Section 1357, 1357.500, or 1357.600.

(c) "PPACA" means Section 2794 of the federal Public Health Service Act (42 U.S.C. Sec. 300gg-94), as amended by the federal Patient Protection and Affordable Care Act (Public Law (111-148)), and any subsequent rules, regulations, or guidance issued under that section.

(d) "Unreasonable rate increase" has the same meaning as that term is defined in PPACA.

(Amended by Stats. 2012, Ch. 852, Sec. 7. (AB 1083) Effective January 1, 2013.)

1385.02.

This article shall apply to health care service plan contracts offered in the individual or group market in California. However, this article shall not apply to a specialized health care service plan contract; a Medicare supplement contract subject to Article 3.5 (commencing with Section 1358.1); a health care service plan contract offered in the Medi-Cal program (Chapter 7 (commencing with Section 14000) of Part 3 of Division 9 of the Welfare and Institutions Code); a health care service plan contract offered in the Healthy Families Program (Part 6.2 (commencing with Section 12693) of Division 2 of the Insurance Code), the Access for Infants and Mothers Program (Part 6.3 (commencing with Section 12695) of Division 2 of the Insurance Code), the California Major Risk Medical Insurance Program (Part 6.5 (commencing with Section 12700) of Division 2 of the Insurance Code), or the Federal Temporary High Risk Pool (Part 6.6 (commencing with Section 12739.5) of Division 2 of the Insurance Code); a health care service plan conversion contract offered pursuant to Section 1373.6; or a health care service plan contract offered to a federally eligible defined individual under Article 4.6 (commencing with Section 1366.35) or Article 10.5 (commencing with Section 1399.801).

(Added by Stats. 2010, Ch. 661, Sec. 4. (SB 1163) Effective January 1, 2011.)

1385.03.

(a) All health care service plans shall file with the department all required rate information for grandfathered individual and grandfathered and nongrandfathered small group health care service plan contracts at least 120 days prior to implementing any rate change. All health care service plans shall file with the department all required rate information for nongrandfathered individual health care service plan contracts on the earlier of the following dates:

(1) One hundred days before October 15 of the preceding policy year.

(2) The date specified in the federal guidance issued pursuant to Section 154.220(b) of Title 45 of the Code of Federal Regulations.

(b) A plan shall disclose to the department all of the following for each individual and small group rate filing:

(1) Company name and contact information.

(2) Number of plan contract forms covered by the filing.

(3) Plan contract form numbers covered by the filing.

(4) Product type, such as a preferred provider organization or health maintenance organization.

(5) Segment type.

(6) Type of plan involved, such as for profit or not for profit.

(7) Whether the products are opened or closed.

(8) Enrollment in each plan contract and rating form.

(9) Enrollee months in each plan contract form.

(10) Annual rate.

(11) Total earned premiums in each plan contract form.

(12) Total incurred claims in each plan contract form.

(13) Average rate increase initially requested.

(14) Review category: initial filing for new product, filing for existing product, or resubmission.

(15) Average rate of increase.

(16) Effective date of rate increase.

(17) Number of subscribers or enrollees affected by each plan contract form.

(18) The plan's overall annual medical trend factor assumptions in each rate filing for all benefits and by aggregate benefit category, including hospital inpatient, hospital outpatient, physician services, prescription drugs and other ancillary services, laboratory, and radiology. A plan may provide aggregated additional data that demonstrates or reasonably estimates year-to-year cost increases in specific benefit categories in the geographic regions listed in Sections 1357.512 and 1399.855. A health plan that

exclusively contracts with no more than two medical groups in the state to provide or arrange for professional medical services for the enrollees of the plan shall instead disclose the amount of its actual trend experience for the prior contract year by aggregate benefit category, using benefit categories that are, to the maximum extent possible, the same or similar to those used by other plans.

(19) The amount of the projected trend attributable to the use of services, price inflation, or fees and risk for annual plan contract trends by aggregate benefit category, such as hospital inpatient, hospital outpatient, physician services, prescription drugs and other ancillary services, laboratory, and radiology. A health plan that exclusively contracts with no more than two medical groups in the state to provide or arrange for professional medical services for the enrollees of the plan shall instead disclose the amount of its actual trend experience for the prior contract year by aggregate benefit category, using benefit categories that are, to the maximum extent possible, the same or similar to those used by other plans.

(20) A comparison of claims cost and rate of changes over time.

(21) Any changes in enrollee cost sharing over the prior year associated with the submitted rate filing.

(22) Any changes in enrollee benefits over the prior year associated with the submitted rate filing.

(23) The certification described in subdivision (b) of Section 1385.06.

(24) Any changes in administrative costs.

(25) Any other information required for rate review under PPACA.

(c) A health care service plan subject to subdivision (a) shall also disclose the following aggregate data for all rate filings submitted under this section in the individual and small group health plan markets:

(1) Number and percentage of rate filings reviewed by the following:

(A) Plan year.

(B) Segment type.

(C) Product type.

(D) Number of subscribers.

(E) Number of covered lives affected.

(2) The plan's average rate increase by the following categories:

(A) Plan year.

(B) Segment type.

(C) Product type.

(3) Any cost containment and quality improvement efforts since the plan's last rate filing for the same category of health benefit plan. To the extent possible, the plan shall describe any significant new health care cost containment and quality improvement efforts and provide an estimate of potential savings together with an estimated cost or savings for the projection period.

(d) The department may require all health care service plans to submit all rate filings to the National Association of Insurance Commissioners' System for Electronic Rate and Form Filing (SERFF). Submission of the required rate filings to SERFF shall be deemed to be filing with the department for purposes of compliance with this section.

(e) A plan shall submit any other information required under PPACA. A plan shall also submit any other information required pursuant to any regulation adopted by the department to comply with this article.

(f) (1) A plan shall respond to the department's request for any additional information necessary for the department to complete its review of the plan's rate filing for individual and small group health care service plan contracts under this article within five business days of the department's request or as otherwise required by the department.

(2) Except as provided in paragraph (3), the department shall determine whether a plan's rate increase for individual and small group health care service plan contracts is unreasonable or not justified no later than 60 days following receipt of all the information the department requires to makes its determination.

(3) For all nongrandfathered individual health care service plan contracts, the department shall issue a determination that the plan's rate increase is unreasonable or not justified no later than 15 days before October 15 of the preceding policy year. If a health care service plan fails to provide all the information the department requires in order for the department to make its determination, the department may determine that a plan's rate increase is unreasonable or not justified.

(g) If the department determines that a plan's rate increase for individual or small group health care service plan contracts is unreasonable or not justified consistent with this article, the health care service plan shall provide notice of that determination to any individual or small group applicant. The notice provided to an individual applicant shall be consistent with the notice described in subdivision (c) of Section 1389.25. The notice provided to a small group applicant shall be consistent with the notice described in subdivision (c) of Section 1374.21.

(h) For purposes of this section, "policy year" has the same meaning as set forth in subdivision (g) of Section 1399.845.

(Amended by Stats. 2017, Ch. 468, Sec. 2. (AB 156) Effective January 1, 2018.)

1385.04.

(a) For large group health care service plan contracts, all health plans shall file with the department at least 60 days prior to implementing any rate change all required rate information for unreasonable rate increases. This filing shall be concurrent with the written notice described in subdivision (a) of Section 1374.21.

(b) For large group rate filings, health plans shall submit all information that is required by PPACA. A plan shall also submit any other information required pursuant to any regulation adopted by the department to comply with this article.

(c) A health care service plan subject to subdivision (a) shall also disclose the following aggregate data for all rate filings submitted under this section in the large group health plan market:

(1) Number and percentage of rate filings reviewed by the following:

(A) Plan year.

(B) Segment type.

(C) Product type.

(D) Number of subscribers.

(E) Number of covered lives affected.

(2) The plan's average rate increase by the following categories:

(A) Plan year.

(B) Segment type.

(C) Product type.

(3) Any cost containment and quality improvement efforts since the plan's last rate filing for the same category of health benefit plan. To the extent possible, the plan shall describe any significant new health care cost containment and quality improvement efforts and provide an estimate of potential savings together with an estimated cost or savings for the projection period.

(d) The department may require all health care service plans to submit all rate filings to the National Association of Insurance Commissioners' System for Electronic Rate and Form Filing (SERFF). Submission of the required rate filings to SERFF shall be deemed to be filing with the department for purposes of compliance with this section.

(Added by Stats. 2010, Ch. 661, Sec. 4. (SB 1163) Effective January 1, 2011.)

1385.045.

(a) For large group health care service plan contracts, each health plan shall file with the department the weighted average rate increase for all large group benefit designs during the 12-month period ending January 1 of the following calendar year. The average shall be weighted by the number of enrollees in each large group benefit design in the plan's large group market and adjusted to the most commonly sold large group benefit design by enrollment during the 12-month period. For the purposes of this section, the large group benefit design includes, but is not limited to, benefits such as basic health care services and prescription drugs. The large group benefit design shall not include cost sharing, including, but not limited to, deductibles, copays, and coinsurance.

(b) (1) A plan shall also submit any other information required pursuant to any regulation adopted by the department to comply with this article.

(2) The department shall conduct an annual public meeting regarding large group rates within four months of posting the aggregate information described in this section in order to permit a public discussion of the reasons for the changes in the rates, benefits, and cost sharing in the large group market. The meeting shall be held in either the Los Angeles area or the San Francisco Bay area.

(c) A health care service plan subject to subdivision (a) shall also disclose the following for the aggregate rate information for the large group market submitted under this section:

(1) For rates effective during the 12-month period ending January 1 of the following year, number and percentage of rate changes reviewed by the following:

(A) Plan year.

(B) Segment type, including whether the rate is community rated, in whole or in part.

(C) Product type.

(D) Number of enrollees.

(E) The number of products sold that have materially different benefits, cost sharing, or other elements of benefit design.

(2) For rates effective during the 12-month period ending January 1 of the following year, any factors affecting the base rate, and the actuarial basis for those factors, including all of the following:

(A) Geographic region.

(B) Age, including age rating factors.

(C) Occupation.

(D) Industry.

(E) Health status factors, including, but not limited to, experience and utilization.

(F) Employee, and employee and dependents, including a description of the family composition used.

(G) Enrollees' share of premiums.

(H) Enrollees' cost sharing, including cost sharing for prescription drugs.

(I) Covered benefits in addition to basic health care services, as defined in Section 1345, and other benefits mandated under this article.

(J) Which market segment, if any, is fully experience rated and which market segment, if any, is in part experience rated and in part community rated.

(K) Any other factor that affects the rate that is not otherwise specified.

(3) (A) The plan's overall annual medical trend factor assumptions for all benefits and by aggregate benefit category, including hospital inpatient, hospital outpatient, physician services, prescription drugs and other ancillary services, laboratory, and radiology for the applicable 12-month period ending January 1 of the following year. A health plan that exclusively contracts with no more than two medical groups in the state to provide or arrange for professional medical services for the enrollees of the plan shall instead disclose the amount of its actual trend experience for the prior contract year by aggregate benefit category, using benefit categories, to the maximum extent possible, that are the same as, or similar to, those used by other plans.

(B) The amount of the projected trend separately attributable to the use of services, price inflation, and fees and risk for annual plan contract trends by aggregate benefit category, including hospital inpatient, hospital outpatient, physician services, prescription drugs and other ancillary services, laboratory, and radiology. A health plan that exclusively contracts with no more than two medical groups in the state to provide or arrange for professional medical services for the enrollees of the plan shall instead disclose the amount of its actual trend experience for the prior contract year by aggregate benefit category, using benefit categories that are, to the maximum extent possible, the same or similar to those used by other plans.

(C) A comparison of the aggregate per enrollee per month costs and rate of changes over the last five years for each of the following:

(i) Premiums.

(ii) Claims costs, if any.

(iii) Administrative expenses.

(iv) Taxes and fees.

(D) Any changes in enrollee cost sharing over the prior year associated with the submitted rate information, including both of the following:

(i) Actual copays, coinsurance, deductibles, annual out of pocket maximums, and any other cost sharing by the benefit categories determined by the department.

(ii) Any aggregate changes in enrollee cost sharing over the prior years as measured by the weighted average actuarial value, weighted by the number of enrollees.

(E) Any changes in enrollee benefits over the prior year, including a description of benefits added or eliminated, as well as any aggregate changes, as measured as a percentage of the aggregate claims costs, listed by the categories determined by the department.

(F) Any cost containment and quality improvement efforts since the plan's prior year's information pursuant to this section for the same category of health benefit plan. To the extent possible, the plan shall describe any significant new health care cost containment and quality improvement efforts and provide an estimate of potential savings together with an estimated cost or savings for the projection period.

(G) The number of products covered by the information that incurred the excise tax paid by the health plan.

(4) (A) For covered prescription generic drugs excluding specialty generic drugs, prescription brand name drugs excluding specialty drugs, and prescription brand name and generic specialty drugs dispensed at a plan pharmacy, network pharmacy, or mail order pharmacy for outpatient use, all of the following shall be disclosed:

(i) The percentage of the premium attributable to prescription drug costs for the prior year for each category of prescription drugs as defined in this subparagraph.

(ii) The year-over-year increase, as a percentage, in per-member, per-month total health plan spending for each category of prescription drugs as defined in this subparagraph.

(iii) The year-over-year increase in per-member, per-month costs for drug prices compared to other components of the health care premium.

(iv) The specialty tier formulary list.

(B) The plan shall include the percentage of the premium attributable to prescription drugs administered in a doctor's office that are covered under the medical benefit as separate from the pharmacy benefit, if available.

(C) (i) The plan shall include information on its use of a pharmacy benefit manager, if any, including which components of the prescription drug coverage described in subparagraphs (A) and (B) are managed by the pharmacy benefit manager.

(ii) The plan shall also include the name or names of the pharmacy benefit manager, or managers if the plan uses more than one.

(d) The information required pursuant to this section shall be submitted to the department on or before October 1, 2018, and on or before October 1 annually thereafter. Information submitted pursuant to this section is subject to Section 1385.07.

(e) For the purposes of this section, a "specialty drug" is one that exceeds the threshold for a specialty drug under the Medicare Part D program (Medicare Prescription Drug, Improvement, and Modernization Act of 2003 (Public Law 108-173)).

(Amended by Stats. 2017, Ch. 603, Sec. 2. (SB 17) Effective January 1, 2018.)

1385.05.

Notwithstanding any provision in a contract between a health care service plan and a provider, the department may request from a health care service plan any information required under this article or PPACA.

(Added by Stats. 2010, Ch. 661, Sec. 4. (SB 1163) Effective January 1, 2011.)

1385.06.

(a) A filing submitted under this article shall be actuarially sound.

(b) (1) The plan shall contract with an independent actuary or actuaries consistent with this section.

(2) A filing submitted under this article shall include a certification by an independent actuary or actuarial firm that the rate increase is reasonable or unreasonable and, if unreasonable, that the justification for the increase is based on accurate and sound actuarial assumptions and methodologies. Unless PPACA requires a certification of actuarial soundness for each large group contract, a filing submitted under Section 1385.04 shall include a certification by an independent actuary, as described in this section, that the aggregate or average rate increase is based on accurate and sound actuarial assumptions and methodologies.

(3) The actuary or actuarial firm acting under paragraph (2) shall not be an affiliate or a subsidiary of, nor in any way owned or controlled by, a health care service plan or a trade association of health care service plans. A board member, director, officer, or employee of the actuary or actuarial firm shall not serve as a board member, director, or employee of a health care service plan. A board member, director, or officer of a health care service plan or a trade association of health care service plans shall not serve as a board member, director, officer, or employee of the actuary or actuarial firm.

(c) Nothing in this article shall be construed to permit the director to establish the rates charged subscribers and enrollees for covered health care services.

(Added by Stats. 2010, Ch. 661, Sec. 4. (SB 1163) Effective January 1, 2011.)

1385.07.

(a) Notwithstanding Chapter 3.5 (commencing with Section 6250) of Division 7 of Title 1 of the Government Code, all information submitted under this article shall be made publicly available by the department except as provided in subdivision (b).

(b) (1) The contracted rates between a health care service plan and a provider shall be deemed confidential information that shall not be made public by the department and are exempt from disclosure under the California Public Records Act (Chapter 3.5 (commencing with Section 6250) of Division 7 of Title 1 of the Government Code). The contracted rates between a health care service plan and a provider shall not be disclosed by a health care service plan to a large group purchaser that receives information pursuant to Section 1385.10.

(2) The contracted rates between a health care service plan and a large group shall be deemed confidential information that shall not be made public by the department and are exempt from disclosure under the California Public Records Act (Chapter 3.5 (commencing with Section 6250) of Division 7 of Title 1 of the Government Code). Information provided to a large group purchaser pursuant to Section 1385.10 shall be deemed confidential information that shall not be made public by the department and shall be exempt from disclosure under the California Public Records Act (Chapter 3.5 (commencing with Section 6250) of Division 7 of Title 1 of the Government Code).

(c) All information submitted to the department under this article shall be submitted electronically in order to facilitate review by the department and the public.

(d) In addition, the department and the health care service plan shall, at a minimum, make the following information readily available to the public on their Internet Web sites, in plain language and in a manner and format specified by the department, except as provided in subdivision (b). For individual and small group health care service plan contracts, the information shall be made public for 120 days prior to the implementation of the rate increase. For large group health care service plan contracts, the information shall be made public for 60 days prior to the implementation of the rate increase. The information shall include:

(1) Justifications for any unreasonable rate increases, including all information and supporting documentation as to why the rate increase is justified.

(2) A plan's overall annual medical trend factor assumptions in each rate filing for all benefits.

(3) A health plan's actual costs, by aggregate benefit category to include hospital inpatient, hospital outpatient, physician services, prescription drugs and other ancillary services, laboratory, and radiology.

(4) The amount of the projected trend attributable to the use of services, price inflation, or fees and risk for annual plan contract trends by aggregate benefit category, such as hospital inpatient, hospital outpatient, physician services, prescription drugs and other ancillary services, laboratory, and radiology. A health plan that exclusively contracts with no more than two medical groups in the state to provide or arrange for professional medical services for the enrollees of the plan shall instead disclose the amount of its actual trend experience for the prior contract year by aggregate benefit category, using benefit categories that are, to the maximum extent possible, the same or similar to those used by other plans.

(Amended by Stats. 2016, Ch. 498, Sec. 3. (SB 908) Effective January 1, 2017.)

1385.08.

(a) On or before July 1, 2012, the director may issue guidance to health care service plans regarding compliance with this article. This guidance shall not be subject to the Administrative Procedure Act (Chapter 3.5 (commencing with Section 11340) of Part 1 of Division 3 of Title 2 of the Government Code).

(b) The department shall consult with the Department of Insurance in issuing guidance under subdivision (a), in adopting necessary regulations, in posting information on its Internet Web site under this article, and in taking any other action for the purpose of implementing this article.

(Added by Stats. 2010, Ch. 661, Sec. 4. (SB 1163) Effective January 1, 2011.)

1385.10.

(a) (1) A health care service plan shall annually provide claims data at no charge to a large group purchaser if the large group purchaser requests the information and otherwise meets the requirements of this section.

(2) The health care service plan shall provide claims data that a qualified statistician has determined are deidentified so that the claims data do not identify or do not provide a reasonable basis from which to identify an individual. If the statistician is unable to determine that the data has been deidentified, then the data that cannot be deidentified shall not be provided by the health care service plan to the large group purchaser. A health care service plan may provide the claims data in an aggregated form as necessary to comply with subdivisions (e) and (f).

(b) (1) As an alternative to providing claims data required pursuant to subdivision (a), the plan shall provide, at no charge to a large group purchaser, all of the following:

(A) Deidentified data sufficient for the large group purchaser to calculate the cost of obtaining similar services from other health plans and evaluate cost-effectiveness by service and disease category.

(B) Deidentified aggregated patient-level data on demographics, prescribing, encounters, inpatient services, outpatient services, and any other data that is comparable to what is required of the health plan to comply with risk adjustment, reinsurance, or risk corridors pursuant to the federal Patient Protection and Affordable Care Act (Public Law 111-148),

as amended by the federal Health Care and Education Reconciliation Act of 2010 (Public Law 111-152), and any rules, regulations, or guidance issued thereunder.

(C) Deidentified aggregated patient-level data used to experience rate the large group, including diagnostic and procedure coding and costs assigned to each service that the plan has available.

(2) The health care service plan shall obtain a formal determination from a qualified statistician that the data provided pursuant to this subdivision have been deidentified so that the data do not identify or do not provide a reasonable basis from which to identify an individual. If the statistician is unable to determine that the data has been deidentified, the health care service plan shall not provide the data that cannot be deidentified to the large group purchaser. The statistician shall document the formal determination in writing and shall, upon request, provide the protocol used for deidentification to the department.

(c) Data provided pursuant to this section shall only be provided to a large group purchaser that meets both of the following conditions:

(1) Is able to demonstrate its ability to comply with state and federal privacy laws.

(2) Is a large group purchaser that is either an employer with an enrollment of greater than 1,000 covered lives and at least 500 covered lives enrolled with the health care service plan providing the information or a multiemployer trust with an enrollment of greater than 500 covered lives and at least 250 covered lives enrolled with the health care service plan providing the information.

(d) Nothing in this section shall be construed to prohibit a plan and purchaser from negotiating the release of additional information not described in this section.

(e) All disclosures of data to the large group purchaser made pursuant to this section shall comply with the federal Health Insurance Portability and Accountability Act of 1996 (Public Law 104-191) and the federal Health Information Technology for Economic and Clinical Health Act, Title XIII of the federal American Recovery and Reinvestment Act of 2009 (Public Law 111-5), and implementing regulations.

(f) All disclosures of data to the large group purchaser made pursuant to this section shall comply with the Confidentiality of Medical Information Act (Chapter 1 (commencing with Section 56) of Part 2.6 of Division 1 of the Civil Code).

(Added by Stats. 2014, Ch. 577, Sec. 3. (SB 1182) Effective January 1, 2015.)

1385.11.

(a) Whenever it appears to the department that any person has engaged, or is about to engage, in any act or practice constituting a violation of this article, including the filing of inaccurate or unjustified rates or inaccurate or unjustified rate information, the department may review the rate filing to ensure compliance with the law.

(b) The department may review other filings.

(c) The department shall accept and post to its Internet Web site any public comment on a rate increase submitted to the department during the applicable period described in subdivision (d) of Section 1385.07.

(d) The department shall report to the Legislature at least quarterly on all unreasonable rate filings.

(e) The department shall post on its Internet Web site any changes submitted by the plan to the proposed rate increase, including any documentation submitted by the plan supporting those changes.

(f) If the director makes a decision that an unreasonable rate increase is not justified or that a rate filing contains inaccurate information, the department shall post that decision on its Internet Web site.

(g) Nothing in this article shall be construed to impair or impede the department's authority to administer or enforce any other provision of this chapter.

(Amended by Stats. 2016, Ch. 498, Sec. 4. (SB 908) Effective January 1, 2017.)

1385.13.

The department shall do all of the following in a manner consistent with applicable federal laws, rules, and regulations:

(a) Provide data to the United States Secretary of Health and Human Services on health care service plan rate trends in premium rating areas.

(b) Commencing with the creation of the Exchange, provide to the Exchange such information as may be necessary to allow compliance with federal law, rules, regulations, and guidance.

(Added by Stats. 2010, Ch. 661, Sec. 4. (SB 1163) Effective January 1, 2011.)

ARTICLE 7. Discipline [1386 - 1389]

(Article 7 added by Stats. 1975, Ch. 941.)

1386.

(a) The director may, after appropriate notice and opportunity for a hearing, by order suspend or revoke any license issued under this chapter to a health care service plan or assess administrative penalties if the director determines that the licensee has committed any of the acts or omissions constituting grounds for disciplinary action.

(b) The following acts or omissions constitute grounds for disciplinary action by the director:

(1) The plan is operating at variance with the basic organizational documents as filed pursuant to Section 1351 or 1352, or with its published plan, or in any manner contrary to that described in, and reasonably inferred from, the plan as contained in its application for licensure and annual report, or any modification thereof, unless amendments allowing the variation have been submitted to, and approved by, the director.

(2) The plan has issued, or permits others to use, evidence of coverage or uses a schedule of charges for health care services that do not comply with those published in the latest evidence of coverage found unobjectionable by the director.

(3) The plan does not provide basic health care services to its enrollees and subscribers as set forth in the evidence of coverage. This subdivision shall not apply to specialized health care service plan contracts.

(4) The plan is no longer able to meet the standards set forth in Article 5 (commencing with Section 1367).

(5) The continued operation of the plan will constitute a substantial risk to its subscribers and enrollees.

(6) The plan has violated or attempted to violate, or conspired to violate, directly or indirectly, or assisted in or abetted a violation or conspiracy to violate any provision of this chapter, any rule or regulation adopted by the director pursuant to this chapter, or any order issued by the director pursuant to this chapter.

(7) The plan has engaged in any conduct that constitutes fraud or dishonest dealing or unfair competition, as defined by Section 17200 of the Business and Professions Code.

(8) The plan has permitted, or aided or abetted any violation by an employee or contractor who is a holder of any certificate, license, permit, registration, or exemption issued pursuant to the Business and Professions Code or this code that would constitute grounds for discipline against the certificate, license, permit, registration, or exemption.

(9) The plan has aided or abetted or permitted the commission of any illegal act.

(10) The engagement of a person as an officer, director, employee, associate, or provider of the plan contrary to the provisions of an order issued by the director pursuant to subdivision (c) of this section or subdivision (d) of Section 1388.

(11) The engagement of a person as a solicitor or supervisor of solicitation contrary to the provisions of an order issued by the director pursuant to Section 1388.

(12) The plan, its management company, or any other affiliate of the plan, or any controlling person, officer, director, or other person occupying a principal management or supervisory position in the plan, management company, or affiliate, has been convicted of or pleaded nolo contendere to a crime, or committed any act involving dishonesty, fraud, or deceit, which crime or act is substantially related to the qualifications, functions, or duties of a person engaged in business in accordance with this chapter. The director may revoke or deny a license hereunder irrespective of a subsequent order under the provisions of Section 1203.4 of the Penal Code.

(13) The plan violates Section 510, 2056, or 2056.1 of the Business and Professions Code or Section 1375.7.

(14) The plan has been subject to a final disciplinary action taken by this state, another state, an agency of the federal government, or another country for any act or omission that would constitute a violation of this chapter.

(15) The plan violates the Confidentiality of Medical Information Act (Part 2.6 (commencing with Section 56) of Division 1 of the Civil Code).

(16) The plan violates Section 806 of the Military and Veterans Code.

(17) The plan violates Section 1262.8.

(c) (1) The director may prohibit any person from serving as an officer, director, employee, associate, or provider of any plan or solicitor firm, or of any management company of any plan, or as a solicitor, if either of the following applies:

(A) The prohibition is in the public interest and the person has committed, caused, participated in, or had knowledge of a violation of this chapter by a plan, management company, or solicitor firm.

(B) The person was an officer, director, employee, associate, or provider of a plan or of a management company or solicitor firm of any plan whose license has been suspended or revoked pursuant to this section and the person had knowledge of, or participated in, any of the prohibited acts for which the license was suspended or revoked.

(2) A proceeding for the issuance of an order under this subdivision may be included with a proceeding against a plan under this section or may constitute a separate proceeding, subject in either case to subdivision (d).

(d) A proceeding under this section shall be subject to appropriate notice to, and the opportunity for a hearing with regard to, the person affected in accordance with subdivision (a) of Section 1397.

(Amended by Stats. 2008, Ch. 603, Sec. 5. Effective January 1, 2009.)

1387.

(a) Any person who violates any provision of this chapter, or who violates any rule or order adopted or issued pursuant to this chapter, shall be liable for a civil penalty not to exceed two thousand five hundred dollars ($2,500) for each violation, which shall be assessed and recovered in a civil action brought in the name of the people of the State of California by the director in any court of competent jurisdiction.

(b) As applied to the civil penalties for acts in violation of this chapter, the remedies provided by this section and by other sections of this chapter are not exclusive, and may be sought and employed in any combination to enforce this chapter.

(c) No action shall be maintained to enforce any liability created under subdivision (a), unless brought before the expiration of four years after the act or transaction constituting the violation.

(Amended by Stats. 1999, Ch. 525, Sec. 133. Effective January 1, 2000. Operative July 1, 2000, or sooner, by Sec. 214 of Ch. 525.)

1388.

(a) The director may, after appropriate notice and opportunity for hearing, by order, censure a person acting as a solicitor or solicitor firm, or suspend for a period not exceeding 24 months or bar a person from operating as a solicitor or solicitor firm, or assess administrative penalties against a person acting as a solicitor or solicitor firm if the director determines that the person has committed any of the acts or omissions constituting grounds for disciplinary action.

(b) The following acts or omissions constitute grounds for disciplinary action by the director:

(1) The continued operation of the solicitor or solicitor firm in a manner that may constitute a substantial risk to a plan or subscribers and enrollees.

(2) The solicitor or solicitor firm has violated or attempted to violate, or conspired to violate, directly or indirectly, or assisted in or abetted a violation or conspiracy to violate any provision of this chapter, any rule or regulation adopted by the director pursuant to the chapter, or any order issued by the director pursuant to this chapter.

(3) The solicitor or solicitor firm has engaged in any conduct that constitutes fraud or dishonest dealing or unfair competition, as defined by Section 17200 of the Business and Professions Code.

(4) The engagement of a person as an officer, director, employee, or associate of the solicitor firm contrary to the provisions of an order issued by the director pursuant to subdivision (d) of this section or subdivision (c) of Section 1386.

(5) The solicitor or solicitor firm, or its management company, or any other affiliate of the solicitor firm, or any controlling person, officer, director, or other person occupying a principal management or supervisory position in that solicitor firm, management company, or affiliate, has been convicted or pleaded nolo contendere to a crime, or committed any act involving dishonesty, fraud, or deceit, which crime or act is substantially related to the qualifications, functions, or duties of a person engaged in business in accordance with the provisions of this chapter. The director may issue an order hereunder irrespective of a subsequent order under the provisions of Section 1203.4 of the Penal Code.

(c) The director shall notify plans of any order issued pursuant to subdivision (a) which suspends or bars a person from engaging in operations as a solicitor or solicitor firm. It shall be unlawful for any plan, after receipt of notice of the order, to receive any new subscribers or enrollees through that person or to otherwise utilize any solicitation services of that person in violation thereof.

(d) (1) The director may prohibit any person from serving as an officer, director, employee, or associate of any plan or solicitor firm, or as a solicitor, if that person was an officer, director, employee, or associate of a solicitor firm that has been the subject of an order of suspension or bar from engaging in operations as a solicitor firm pursuant to this section and that person had knowledge of, or participated in, any of the prohibited acts for which the order was issued.

(2) A proceeding for the issuance of an order under this subdivision may be included with a proceeding against a solicitor firm under this section or may constitute a separate proceeding, subject in either case to subdivision (e).

(e) A proceeding for the issuance of an order under this section shall be subject to appropriate notice to, and the opportunity for a hearing with regard to, the person affected in accordance with subdivision (a) of Section 1397.

(Amended by Stats. 1999, Ch. 525, Sec. 134. Effective January 1, 2000. Operative July 1, 2000, or sooner, by Sec. 214 of Ch. 525.)

1389.

(a) A person whose license has been revoked, or suspended for more than one year, may petition the director to reinstate the license as provided by Section 11522 of the Government Code. No petition may be considered if the petitioner is under criminal sentence for a violation of this chapter, or any offense which would constitute grounds for discipline, or denial of licensure under this chapter, including any period of probation or parole.

(b) A person who is barred, or suspended for more than one year, from acting as a solicitor or solicitor firm pursuant to Section 1388, or who is subject to an order, pursuant to subdivision (c) of Section 1386 or subdivision (d) of Section 1388, which by its terms is effective for more than one year, may petition the director to reduce by order such penalty in a manner generally consistent with the provisions of Section 11522 of the Government Code. No petition may be considered if the petitioner is under criminal sentence for a violation of this chapter, or any offense which would constitute grounds for discipline under this chapter, including any period of probation or parole.

(c) The petition for restoration shall be in the form prescribed by the director and the director may condition the granting of such petition upon such additional information and undertakings as the director may require in order to determine whether such person, if restored, would engage in business in full compliance with the objectives and provisions of this chapter and the rules and regulations adopted by the director pursuant to this chapter.

(d) The director may, by rule, prescribe a fee not to exceed five hundred dollars ($500) for the filing of a petition for restoration pursuant to this section. In addition, the director may condition the granting of such a petition to a plan upon payment of the assessment due and unpaid pursuant to subdivision (b) of Section 1356 as of the 15th day of December occurring within the preceding 12-calendar months and, if the plan's suspension or revocation was in effect for more than 12 months, upon the filing of a new plan application and the payment of the fee prescribed by subdivision (a) of Section 1356.

(Amended by Stats. 1999, Ch. 525, Sec. 135. Effective January 1, 2000. Operative July 1, 2000, or sooner, by Sec. 214 of Ch. 525.)

ARTICLE 7.5. Underwriting Practices [1389.1 - 1389.8]

(Article 7.5 added by Stats. 1993, Ch. 1210, Sec. 3.)

1389.1.

(a) The director shall not approve any plan contract unless the director finds that the application conforms to both of the following requirements:

(1) All applications for coverage which include health-related questions shall contain clear and unambiguous questions designed to ascertain the health condition or history of the applicant.

(2) The application questions related to an applicant's health shall be based on medical information that is reasonable and necessary for medical underwriting purposes. The application shall include a prominently displayed notice that shall read:

"California law prohibits an HIV test from being required or used by health care service plans as a condition of obtaining coverage."

(b) Nothing in this section shall authorize the director to establish or require a single or standard application form for application questions.

(Amended by Stats. 1999, Ch. 525, Sec. 136. Effective January 1, 2000. Operative July 1, 2000, or sooner, by Sec. 214 of Ch. 525.)

1389.2.

At the request of the director, a health care service plan shall provide a written statement of the actuarial basis for any medical underwriting decision on any application form, or contract issued or delivered to, or denied a resident of this state.

(Amended by Stats. 1999, Ch. 525, Sec. 137. Effective January 1, 2000. Operative July 1, 2000, or sooner, by Sec. 214 of Ch. 525.)

1389.21.

(a) A health care service plan shall not rescind a plan contract, or limit any provisions of a plan contract, once an enrollee is covered under the contract unless the plan can demonstrate that the enrollee has performed an act or practice constituting fraud or made an intentional misrepresentation of material fact as prohibited by the terms of the contract.

(b) If a plan intends to rescind a plan contract pursuant to subdivision (a), the plan shall send a notice to the enrollee or subscriber via regular certified mail at least 30 days prior to the effective date of the rescission explaining the reasons for the intended rescission and notifying the enrollee or subscriber of his or her right to appeal that decision to the director pursuant to subdivision (b) of Section 1365.

(c) Notwithstanding subdivision (a), Section 1365 or any other provision of law, after 24 months following the issuance of a health care service plan contract, a plan shall not rescind the plan contract for any reason, and shall not cancel the plan contract, limit any of the provisions of the plan contract, or raise premiums on the plan contract due to any omissions, misrepresentations, or inaccuracies in the application form, whether willful or not. Nothing in this subdivision shall be construed to alter existing law that otherwise applies to a health care service plan within the first 24 months following the issuance of a health care service plan contract.

(Amended by Stats. 2010, Ch. 658, Sec. 8. (AB 2470) Effective January 1, 2011.)

1389.25.

(a) (1) This section shall apply only to a full service health care service plan offering health coverage in the individual market in California and shall not apply to a specialized health care service plan, a health care service plan contract in the Medi-Cal program (Chapter 7 (commencing with Section 14000) of Part 3 of Division 9 of the Welfare and Institutions Code), a health care service plan conversion contract offered pursuant to Section 1373.6, a health care service plan contract in the Healthy Families Program (Part 6.2 (commencing with Section 12693) of Division 2 of the Insurance Code), or a health care service plan contract offered to a federally eligible defined individual under Article 4.6 (commencing with Section 1366.35).

(2) A local initiative, as defined in subdivision (w) of Section 53810 of Title 22 of the California Code of Regulations, that is awarded a contract by the State Department of Health Care Services pursuant to subdivision (b) of Section 53800 of Title 22 of the California Code of Regulations, shall not be subject to this section unless the plan offers coverage in the individual market to persons not covered by Medi-Cal or the Healthy Families Program.

(b) (1) No change in the premium rate or coverage for an individual plan contract shall become effective unless the plan has provided a written notice of the change at least 10 days prior to the start of the annual enrollment period applicable to the contract or 60 days prior to the effective date of the contract renewal, whichever occurs earlier in the calendar year.

(2) The written notice required pursuant to paragraph (1) shall be provided to the individual contractholder at his or her last address known to the plan. The notice shall state in italics and in 12-point type the actual dollar amount of the premium rate increase and the specific percentage by which the current premium will be increased. The notice shall describe in plain, understandable English any changes in the plan design or any changes in benefits, including a reduction in benefits or changes to waivers, exclusions, or conditions, and highlight this information by printing it in italics. The notice shall specify in a minimum of 10-point bold typeface, the reason for a premium rate change or a change to the plan design or benefits.

(c) (1) If the department determines that a rate is unreasonable or not justified consistent with Article 6.2 (commencing with Section 1385.01), the plan shall notify the contractholder of this determination. This notification may be included in the notice required in subdivision (b). The notification to the contractholder shall be developed by the department. The development of the notification required under this subdivision shall not be subject to the Administrative Procedure Act (Chapter 3.5 (commencing with Section 11340) of Part 1 of Division 3 of Title 2 of the Government Code).

(2) The notification to the contractholder shall include the following statements in 14-point type:

(A) The Department of Managed Health Care has determined that the rate for this product is unreasonable or not justified after reviewing information submitted to it by the plan.

(B) During the open enrollment period, the contractholder has the option to obtain other coverage from this plan or another plan, or to keep this coverage.

(C) The contractholder may want to contact Covered California at www.coveredca.com for help in understanding available options.

(D) Many Californians are eligible for financial assistance from Covered California to help pay for coverage.

(3) The plan may include in the notification to the contractholder the Internet Web site address at which the plan's final justification for implementing an increase that has been determined to be unreasonable by the director may be found pursuant to Section 154.230 of Title 45 of the Code of Federal Regulations.

(4) The notice shall also be provided to the solicitor for the contractholder, if any, so that the solicitor may assist the purchaser in finding other coverage.

(5) In developing the notification, the department shall take into consideration that this notice is required to be provided to an individual applicant pursuant to subdivision (g) of Section 1385.03.

(d) If a plan rejects a dependent of a subscriber applying to be added to the subscriber's individual grandfathered health plan, rejects an applicant for a Medicare supplement plan contract due to the applicant having end-stage renal disease, or offers an individual grandfathered health plan to an applicant at a rate that is higher than the standard rate, the plan shall inform the applicant about the California Major Risk Medical Insurance Program (MRMIP) (Chapter 4 (commencing with Section 15870) of Part 3.3 of Division 9 of the Welfare and Institutions Code) and about the new coverage options and the potential for subsidized coverage through Covered California. The plan shall direct persons seeking more information to MRMIP, Covered California, plan or policy representatives, insurance agents, or an entity paid by Covered California to assist with health coverage enrollment, such as a navigator or an assister.

(e) A notice provided pursuant to this section is a private and confidential communication and, at the time of application, the plan shall give the individual applicant the opportunity to designate the address for receipt of the written notice in order to protect the confidentiality of any personal or privileged information.

(f) For purposes of this section, the following definitions shall apply:

(1) "Covered California" means the California Health Benefit Exchange established pursuant to Section 100500 of the Government Code.

(2) "Grandfathered health plan" has the same meaning as that term is defined in Section 1251 of PPACA.

(3) "PPACA" means the federal Patient Protection and Affordable Care Act (Public Law 111-148), as amended by the federal Health Care and Education Reconciliation Act of 2010 (Public Law 111-152), and any rules, regulations, or guidance issued pursuant to that law.

(Amended by Stats. 2016, Ch. 498, Sec. 5. (SB 908) Effective January 1, 2017.)

1389.3.

No health care service plan shall engage in the practice of postclaims underwriting. For purposes of this section, "postclaims underwriting" means the rescinding, canceling, or limiting of a plan contract due to the plan's failure to complete medical underwriting and resolve all reasonable questions arising from written information submitted on or with an application before issuing the plan contract. This section shall not limit a plan's remedies described in subdivision (a) of Section 1389.21.

(Amended by Stats. 2010, Ch. 658, Sec. 9. (AB 2470) Effective January 1, 2011.)

1389.4.

(a) A full service health care service plan that issues, renews, or amends individual health plan contracts shall be subject to this section.

(b) A health care service plan subject to this section shall have written policies, procedures, or underwriting guidelines establishing the criteria and process whereby the plan makes its decision to provide or to deny coverage to individuals applying for coverage and sets the rate for that coverage. These guidelines, policies, or procedures shall ensure that the plan rating and underwriting criteria comply with Sections 1365.5 and 1389.1 and all other applicable provisions of state and federal law.

(c) On or before June 1, 2006, and annually thereafter, every health care service plan shall file with the department a general description of the criteria, policies, procedures, or guidelines the plan uses for rating and underwriting decisions related to individual health plan contracts, which means automatic declinable health conditions, health conditions that may lead to a coverage decline, height and weight standards, health history, health care utilization, lifestyle, or behavior that might result in a decline for coverage or severely limit the plan products for which they would be eligible. A plan may comply with this section by submitting to the department underwriting materials or resource guides provided to plan solicitors or solicitor firms, provided that those materials include the information required to be submitted by this section.

(d) Commencing January 1, 2011, the director shall post on the department's Internet Web site, in a manner accessible and understandable to consumers, general, noncompany specific information about rating and underwriting criteria and practices in the individual market and information about the California Major Risk Medical Insurance Program (Part 6.5 (commencing with Section 12700) of Division 2 of the Insurance Code) and the federal temporary high risk pool established pursuant to Part 6.6 (commencing with Section 12739.5) of Division 2 of the Insurance Code. The director shall develop the information for the Internet Web site in consultation with the Department of Insurance to enhance the consistency of information provided to consumers. Information about individual health coverage shall also include the following notification: "Please examine your options carefully before declining group coverage or continuation coverage, such as COBRA, that may be available to you. You should be aware that companies selling individual health insurance typically require a review of your medical history that could result in a higher premium or you could be denied coverage entirely."

(e) This section does not authorize public disclosure of company specific rating and underwriting criteria and practices submitted to the director.

(f) This section does not apply to a closed block of business, as defined in Section 1367.15.

(g) (1) This section shall become inoperative on November 1, 2013, or the 91st calendar day following the adjournment of the 2013–14 First Extraordinary Session, whichever date is later.

(2) If Section 5000A of the Internal Revenue Code, as added by Section 1501 of PPACA, is repealed or amended to no longer apply to the individual market, as defined in Section 2791 of the federal Public Health Service Act (42 U.S.C. Sec. 300gg-91), this section shall become operative 12 months after the date of that repeal or amendment.
(Amended (as amended by Stats. 2013, 1st Ex. Sess., Ch. 2, Sec. 9) by Stats. 2015, Ch. 303, Sec. 261. (AB 731) Effective January 1, 2016. Inoperative, by its own provisions, on November 1, 2013, subject to condition for resuming operation. See later operative version, as amended by Sec. 262 of Stats. 2015, Ch. 303.)
1389.4.

(a) A full service health care service plan that renews individual grandfathered health benefit plans shall be subject to this section.

(b) A health care service plan subject to this section shall have written policies, procedures, or underwriting guidelines establishing the criteria and process whereby the plan makes its decision to provide or to deny coverage to dependents applying for an individual grandfathered health plan and sets the rate for that coverage. These guidelines, policies, or procedures shall ensure that the plan rating and underwriting criteria comply with Sections 1365.5 and 1389.1 and all other applicable provisions of state and federal law.

(c) On or before the June 1 next following the operative date of this section, and annually thereafter, every health care service plan shall file with the department a general description of the criteria, policies, procedures, or guidelines the plan uses for rating and underwriting decisions related to individual grandfathered health plans, which means automatic declinable health conditions, health conditions that may lead to a coverage decline, height and weight standards, health history, health care utilization, lifestyle, or behavior that might result in a decline for coverage or severely limit the plan products for which they would be eligible. A plan may comply with this section by submitting to the department underwriting materials or resource guides provided to plan solicitors or solicitor firms, provided that those materials include the information required to be submitted by this section.

(d) This section does not authorize public disclosure of company specific rating and underwriting criteria and practices submitted to the director.

(e) For purposes of this section, the following definitions shall apply:

(1) "PPACA" means the federal Patient Protection and Affordable Care Act (Public Law 111-148), as amended by the federal Health Care and Education Reconciliation Act of 2010 (Public Law 111-152), and any rules, regulations, or guidance issued pursuant to that law.

(2) "Grandfathered health plan" has the same meaning as that term is defined in Section 1251 of PPACA.

(f) (1) This section shall become operative on November 1, 2013, or the 91st calendar day following the adjournment of the 2013–14 First Extraordinary Session, whichever date is later.

(2) If Section 5000A of the Internal Revenue Code, as added by Section 1501 of PPACA, is repealed or amended to no longer apply to the individual market, as defined in Section 2791 of the federal Public Health Service Act (42 U.S.C. Sec. 300gg-91), this section shall become inoperative 12 months after the date of that repeal or amendment.
(Amended (as added by Stats. 2013, 1st Ex. Sess., Ch. 2, Sec. 10) by Stats. 2015, Ch. 303, Sec. 262. (AB 731) Effective January 1, 2016. Conditionally inoperative as prescribed by its own provisions. Upon inoperation, see the previous version, as amended by Sec. 261 of Stats. 2015, Ch. 303, which would resume operation.)
1389.5.

(a) This section applies to a health care service plan that provides coverage under an individual plan contract that is issued, amended, delivered, or renewed on or after January 1, 2007.

(b) At least once each year, the health care service plan shall permit an individual who has been covered for at least 18 months under an individual plan contract to transfer, without medical underwriting, to any other individual plan contract offered by that same health care service plan that provides equal or lesser benefits, as determined by the plan. "Without medical underwriting" means that the health care service plan shall not decline to offer coverage to, or deny enrollment of, the individual or impose any preexisting condition exclusion on the individual who transfers to another individual plan contract pursuant to this section.

(c) The plan shall establish, for the purposes of subdivision (b), a ranking of the individual plan contracts it offers to individual purchasers and post the ranking on its Internet Web site or make the ranking available upon request. The plan shall update the ranking whenever a new benefit design for individual purchasers is approved.

(d) The plan shall notify in writing all enrollees of the right to transfer to another individual plan contract pursuant to this section, at a minimum, when the plan changes the enrollee's premium rate. Posting this information on the plan's Internet Web site shall not constitute notice for purposes of this subdivision. The notice shall adequately inform enrollees of the transfer rights provided under this section, including information on the process to obtain details about the individual plan contracts available to that enrollee and advising that the enrollee may be unable to return to his or her current individual plan contract if the enrollee transfers to another individual plan contract.

(e) The requirements of this section do not apply to the following:

(1) A federally eligible defined individual, as defined in subdivision (c) of Section 1399.801, who is enrolled in an individual health benefit plan contract offered pursuant to Section 1366.35.

(2) An individual offered conversion coverage pursuant to Section 1373.6.

(3) Individual coverage under a specialized health care service plan contract.

(4) An individual enrolled in the Medi-Cal program pursuant to Chapter 7 (commencing with Section 14000) of Division 9 of Part 3 of the Welfare and Institutions Code.

(5) An individual enrolled in the Access for Infants and Mothers Program pursuant to Part 6.3 (commencing with Section 12695) of Division 2 of the Insurance Code.

(6) An individual enrolled in the Healthy Families Program pursuant to Part 6.2 (commencing with Section 12693) of Division 2 of the Insurance Code.

(f) It is the intent of the Legislature that individuals shall have more choice in their health coverage when health care service plans guarantee the right of an individual to transfer to another product based on the plan's own ranking system. The Legislature does not intend for the department to review or verify the plan's ranking for actuarial or other purposes.

(g) (1) This section shall become inoperative January 1, 2014, or the 91st calendar day following the adjournment of the 2013–14 First Extraordinary Session, whichever date is later.

(2) If Section 5000A of the Internal Revenue Code, as added by Section 1501 of PPACA, is repealed or amended to no longer apply to the individual market, as defined in Section 2791 of the federal Public Health Service Act (42 U.S.C. Sec. 300gg-91), this section shall become operative 12 months after the date of that repeal or amendment.
(Amended by Stats. 2015, Ch. 303, Sec. 263. (AB 731) Effective January 1, 2016. Inoperative, by its own provisions, on January 1, 2014, subject to condition for resuming operation.)
1389.6.

Compensation of a person or entity employed by, or contracted with, a health care service plan shall not be based on, or related in any way to, the number of contracts that the person or entity has caused or recommended to be rescinded, canceled, or limited, or the resulting cost savings to the health plan. A health care service plan shall not set performance goals or quotas, or provide compensation to any person or entity employed by, or contracted with, the health care service plan, based on the number of persons whose coverage is rescinded or any financial savings to the health care service plan associated with rescission of coverage.
(Added by Stats. 2008, Ch. 188, Sec. 1. Effective January 1, 2009.)
1389.7.

(a) Every health care service plan that offers, issues, or renews individual plan contracts shall offer to any individual, who was covered under an individual plan contract that was rescinded, a new individual plan contract, without medical underwriting, that provides equal benefits. A health care service plan may also permit an individual, who was covered under an individual plan contract that was rescinded, to remain covered under that individual plan contract, with a revised premium rate that reflects the number of persons remaining on the plan contract.

(b) "Without medical underwriting" means that the health care service plan shall not decline to offer coverage to, or deny enrollment of, the individual or impose any preexisting condition exclusion on the individual who is issued a new individual plan contract or remains covered under an individual plan contract pursuant to this section.

(c) If a new individual plan contract is issued, the plan may revise the premium rate to reflect only the number of persons covered on the new individual plan contract.

(d) Notwithstanding subdivisions (a) and (b), if an individual was subject to a preexisting condition provision or a waiting or an affiliation period under the individual plan contract that was rescinded, the health care service plan may apply the same preexisting condition provision or waiting or affiliation period in the new individual plan contract. The time period in the new individual plan contract for the preexisting condition provision or waiting or affiliation period shall not be longer than the one in the individual plan contract that was rescinded and the health care service plan shall credit any time that the individual was covered under the rescinded individual plan contract.

(e) The plan shall notify in writing all enrollees of the right to coverage under an individual plan contract pursuant to this section, at a minimum, when the plan rescinds the individual plan contract. The notice shall adequately inform enrollees of the right to coverage provided under this section.

(f) The plan shall provide 60 days for enrollees to accept the offered new individual plan contract and this contract shall be effective as of the effective date of the original plan contract and there shall be no lapse in coverage.

(g) This section does not apply to any individual whose information in the application for coverage and related communications led to the rescission.

(h) (1) This section shall become inoperative on January 1, 2014, or the 91st calendar day following the adjournment of the 2013–14 First Extraordinary Session, whichever date is later.

(2) If Section 5000A of the Internal Revenue Code, as added by Section 1501 of PPACA, is repealed or amended to no longer apply to the individual market, as defined in Section 2791 of the federal Public Health Service Act (42 U.S.C. Sec. 300gg-91), this section shall become operative 12 months after the date of that repeal or amendment.
(Amended (as amended by Stats. 2013, 1st Ex. Sess., Ch. 2, Sec. 12) by Stats. 2015, Ch. 303, Sec. 264. (AB 731) Effective January 1, 2016. Inoperative, by its own provisions, on January 1, 2014, subject to condition for resuming operation. See later operative version, as amended by Sec. 265 of Stats. 2015, Ch. 303.)
1389.7.

(a) Every health care service plan that offers, issues, or renews individual plan contracts shall offer to any individual, who was covered by the plan under an individual plan contract that was rescinded, a new individual plan contract that provides the most equivalent benefits.

(b) A health care service plan that offers, issues, or renews individual plan contracts inside or outside the California Health Benefit Exchange may also permit an individual, who was covered by the plan under an individual plan contract that was rescinded, to remain covered under that individual plan contract, with a revised premium rate that reflects the number of persons remaining on the individual plan contract consistent with Section 1399.855.

(c) The plan shall notify in writing all enrollees of the right to coverage under an individual plan contract pursuant to this section, at a minimum, when the plan rescinds the individual plan contract. The notice shall adequately inform enrollees of the right to coverage provided under this section.

(d) The plan shall provide 60 days for enrollees to accept the offered new individual plan contract under subdivision (a), and this contract shall be effective as of the effective date of the original plan contract and there shall be no lapse in coverage.

(e) This section does not apply to any individual whose information in the application for coverage and related communications led to the rescission.

(f) This section applies notwithstanding subdivision (a) or (d) of Section 1399.849.

(g) (1) This section shall become operative on January 1, 2014, or the 91st calendar day following the adjournment of the 2013–14 First Extraordinary Session, whichever date is later.

(2) If Section 5000A of the Internal Revenue Code, as added by Section 1501 of PPACA, is repealed or amended to no longer apply to the individual market, as defined in Section 2791 of the federal Public Health Service Act (42 U.S.C. Sec. 300gg-91), this section shall become inoperative 12 months after the date of that repeal or amendment.

(Amended (as added by Stats. 2013, 1st Ex. Sess., Ch. 2, Sec. 13) by Stats. 2015, Ch. 303, Sec. 265. (AB 731) Effective January 1, 2016. Conditionally inoperative as prescribed by its own provisions. Upon inoperation, see the previous version, as amended by Sec. 264 of Stats. 2015, Ch. 303, which would resume operation.)

1389.8.

(a) Notwithstanding any other provision of law, an agent, broker, solicitor, solicitor firm, or representative who assists an applicant in submitting an application to a health care service plan has the duty to assist the applicant in providing answers to health questions accurately and completely.

(b) An agent, broker, solicitor, solicitor firm, or representative who assists an applicant in submitting an application to a health care service plan shall attest on the written application to both of the following:

(1) That to the best of his or her knowledge, the information on the application is complete and accurate.

(2) That he or she explained to the applicant, in easy-to-understand language, the risk to the applicant of providing inaccurate information and that the applicant understood the explanation.

(c) If, in an attestation required by subdivision (b), a declarant willfully states as true any material fact he or she knows to be false, that person shall, in addition to any applicable penalties or remedies available under current law, be subject to a civil penalty of up to ten thousand dollars ($10,000). Any public prosecutor may bring a civil action to impose that civil penalty. These penalties shall be paid to the Managed Care Fund.

(d) A health care service plan application shall include a statement advising declarants of the civil penalty authorized under this section.

(Added by Stats. 2008, Ch. 604, Sec. 2. Effective January 1, 2009.)

ARTICLE 8. Other Enforcement Procedures [1390 - 1394.3]

(Article 8 added by Stats. 1975, Ch. 941.)

1390.

Any person who willfully violates any provision of this chapter or of any rule or order thereunder shall upon conviction be fined not more than ten thousand dollars ($10,000) or imprisoned pursuant to subdivision (h) of Section 1170 of the Penal Code, or in a county jail for not more than one year, or be punished by both such fine and imprisonment, but no person may be imprisoned for the violation of any rule or order if it is proven that such person had no knowledge of the rule or order.

(Amended by Stats. 2011, Ch. 15, Sec. 138. (AB 109) Effective April 4, 2011. Operative October 1, 2011, by Sec. 636 of Ch. 15, as amended by Stats. 2011, Ch. 39, Sec. 68.)

1391.

(a) (1) The director may issue an order directing a plan, solicitor firm, or any representative thereof, a solicitor, or any other person to cease and desist from engaging in any act or practice in violation of the provisions of this chapter, any rule adopted pursuant to this chapter, or any order issued by the director pursuant to this chapter.

(2) If the plan, solicitor firm, or any representative thereof, or solicitor, or any other person fails to file a written request for a hearing within 30 days from the date of service of the order, the order shall be deemed a final order of the director and shall not be subject to review by any court or agency, notwithstanding subdivision (b) of Section 1397.

(b) If a timely request for a hearing is made by a licensed plan, the request shall automatically stay the effect of the order only to the extent that the order requires the cessation of operation of the plan or prohibits acceptance of new members by the plan or both. However, no automatic stay shall be issued if any examination or inspection of the plan performed by the director discloses, or reports or documents submitted to the director by the plan on their face show, that the plan is in violation of any fiscal requirement of this chapter or in violation of any requirement of Section 1384 or 1385. In the event of an automatic stay, only that portion of the order requiring cessation of operation or prohibiting enrollment shall be stayed and all other portions of the order shall remain effective. If a hearing is held, and a finding is made that the health or safety of the members and potential members of the plan might be adversely affected by its

continued operation, the stay shall be terminated. This finding shall be made, if at all, not later than 30 days after the date of the hearing.

(c) If a timely request for a hearing is made by an unlicensed plan, the director may stay the effect of the order to the extent that the order requires the cessation of operation of the plan or prohibits acceptance of new members by the plan, for that period and subject to those conditions that the director may require, upon a determination by the director that the action would be in the public interest.

(Amended by Stats. 1999, Ch. 525, Sec. 138. Effective January 1, 2000. Operative July 1, 2000, or sooner, by Sec. 214 of Ch. 525.)

1391.5.

(a) If, after examination or investigation, the director has reasonable grounds to believe that irreparable loss and injury to the plan's enrollee or enrollees occurred or may occur as a result of any act or practice unless the director acts immediately, the director may, by written order, addressed to that person, order the discontinuance of the unsafe or injurious act or practice. The order shall become effective immediately, but shall not become final except in accordance with this section.

(b) No order issued pursuant to this section shall become final except after notice to the affected person of the director's intention to make the order final and of the reasons for the finding. The director shall also notify that person that upon receiving a request for hearing by the plan, the matter shall be set for hearing to commence with 15 business days after receipt of the request, unless that person consents to have the hearing commence at a later date.

(c) If no hearing is requested within 15 days after the mailing or service of the required notice, and none is ordered by the director, the order shall become final on the 15th day without a hearing and shall not be subject to review by any court or agency notwithstanding subdivision (b) of Section 1397.

(d) If a hearing is requested or ordered, it shall be held in accordance with the provisions of the Administrative Procedure Act (Chapter 5 (commencing with Section 11500) of Part 1 of Division 3 of Title 2 of the Government Code), and the director shall have all of the powers granted under that act.

(e) If, upon conclusion of the hearing, it appears to the director that the affected person has conducted business in an unsafe or injurious manner, the director shall make the order of discontinuance final.

(f) For purposes of this section, "person" includes any plan, solicitor firm, or any representative thereof, a solicitor, or any other person defined in subdivision (j) of Section 1345.

(Amended by Stats. 2000, Ch. 857, Sec. 44. Effective January 1, 2001.)

1392.

(a) (1) Whenever it appears to the director that any person has engaged, or is about to engage, in any act or practice constituting a violation of any provision of this chapter, any rule adopted pursuant to this chapter, or any order issued pursuant to this chapter, the director may bring an action in superior court, or the director may request the Attorney General to bring an action to enjoin these acts or practices or to enforce compliance with this chapter, any rule or regulation adopted by the director pursuant to this chapter, or any order issued by the director pursuant to this chapter, or to obtain any other equitable relief.

(2) If the director determines that it is in the public interest, the director may include in any action authorized by paragraph (1) a claim for any ancillary or equitable relief and the court shall have jurisdiction to award this additional relief.

(3) Upon a proper showing, a permanent or preliminary injunction, restraining order, writ of mandate, or other relief shall be granted, and a receiver, monitor, conservator, or other designated fiduciary or officer of the court may be appointed for the defendant or the defendant's assets.

(b) A receiver, monitor, conservator, or other designated fiduciary, or officer of the court appointed by the superior court pursuant to this section may, with the approval of the court, exercise any or all of the powers of the defendant's officers, directors, partners, or trustees, or any other person who exercises similar powers and performs similar duties, including the filing of a petition for bankruptcy. No action at law or in equity may be maintained by any party against the director, or a receiver, monitor, conservator, or other designated fiduciary or officer of the court by reason of their exercising these powers or performing these duties pursuant to the order of, or with the approval of, the superior court.

(Amended by Stats. 1999, Ch. 525, Sec. 140. Effective January 1, 2000. Operative July 1, 2000, or sooner, by Sec. 214 of Ch. 525.)

1393.

(a) The superior court of the county in which is located the principal office of the plan in this state shall, upon the filing by the director of a verified application showing any of the conditions enumerated in Section 1386 to exist, issue its order vesting title to all of the assets of the plan, wherever situated, in the director or the director's successor in office, in his or her official capacity as such, and direct the director to take possession of all of its books, records, property, real and personal, and assets, and to conduct, as conservator, the business or portion of the business of the person as may seem appropriate to the director, and enjoining the person and its officers, directors, agents, servants, and employees from the transaction of its business or disposition of its property until the further order of the court.

(b) Whenever it appears to the director that irreparable loss and injury to the property and business of the plan or to the plan's enrollees has occurred or may occur unless the director acts immediately, the director, without notice and before applying to the court for any order, may take possession of the property, business, books, records, and accounts of the plan, and of the offices and premises occupied by it for the transaction of its business, and retain possession until returned to the plan or until further order of the director or subject to an order of the court. Any person having possession of and refusing to deliver any of the books, records, or assets of a plan against which a seizure order has been issued by the director, shall be guilty of a misdemeanor and punishable by a fine not exceeding ten thousand dollars ($10,000) or imprisonment not exceeding one year, or both the fine and imprisonment. Whenever the director has taken possession of any plan pursuant to this subdivision, the owners, officers, and directors of the plan may apply to the superior court in the county in which the principal office of the plan is located, within 10 days after the taking, to enjoin further proceedings. The court, after citing the director to show cause why further proceedings should not be enjoined, and after a hearing and a determination of the facts upon the merits, may do any of the following:

(1) Dismiss the application after confirming the director's authority to take possession of all of the plan's books, records, property, real and personal, and assets, and to conduct, as conservator, the business or portion of the business as the director may deem appropriate, and enjoining the owners, officers, and directors, and their agents and employees, from the transaction of plan business or disposition of plan property until the further order of the court.

(2) Enjoin the director from further proceedings and direct the director to surrender the property and business to the plan.

(3) Make any further order as may be just.

(c) If any facts occur that would entitle the director to take possession of the property, business, and assets of the plan, the director may appoint a conservator over the plan and require any bond of the conservator as the director deems proper. The conservator, under the direction of the director, shall take possession of the property, business, and assets of the plan pending further disposition of its business. The conservator shall retain possession until the property, business, and assets of the plan are returned to the plan, or until further order of the director, except that the conservator shall be able to pay necessary costs of the ongoing operation without formal order of the director. Whenever the director has taken possession of any plan pursuant to subdivision (b), the director shall, within 10 days after the taking, apply to the superior court in the county in which the principal office of the plan is located for an order confirming the director's appointment of the conservator. The order may be given after a hearing upon notice that the court prescribes.

(d) (1) Subject to the other provisions of this section, a conservator, while in possession of the property, business, and assets of a plan, has the same powers and rights, and is subject to the same duties and obligations, as the director under the same circumstances, and during this time, the rights of a plan and of all persons with respect to the plan are the same as if the director had taken possession of the property, business, and assets of the plan, for the purpose of carrying out the conservatorship.

(2) Subject to the other provisions of this section, a conservator, while in possession of the property, business, and assets of a plan, shall have all of the rights, powers, and privileges of the plan, and its officers and directors, for the purpose of carrying out the conservatorship. All expenses of any conservatorship shall be paid from the assets of the plan, and shall be a lien on the plan which shall be prior to any other lien.

(3) No action at law or in equity may be maintained by any party against the director or a conservator by reason of their exercising or performing the privileges, powers, rights, duties, and obligations pursuant to the order, or with the approval, of the superior court.

(e) Upon appointing a conservator, the director shall cause to be made and completed, at the earliest possible date, an examination of the affairs of the plan as shall be necessary to inform the director as to the plan's financial condition.

(f) If the director becomes satisfied that it may be done safely and in the public interest, the director may terminate the conservatorship and permit the plan for which the conservator was appointed to resume its business under the direction of its board of directors, subject to any terms, conditions, restrictions, and limitations the director prescribes.

(Amended by Stats. 1999, Ch. 525, Sec. 141. Effective January 1, 2000. Operative July 1, 2000, or sooner, by Sec. 214 of Ch. 525.)

1393.5.

(a) A person who violates Section 1349, or any person who directly or indirectly participates in the direction of the management or policies of the person in violation of Section 1349, including, but not limited to, any officer, director, partner, or other person occupying a principal management or supervisory position, shall be liable for civil penalties as follows:

(1) A sum not more than two thousand five hundred dollars ($2,500), and (2) a sum not exceeding five hundred dollars ($500) for each subscriber under an individual or group plan contract which was entered into or renewed while such person was in violation of Section 1349.

(b) The penalty specified in paragraph (2) of subdivision (a) shall be imposed only if one or more of the following occurs:

(1) The solicitation of the entry into or renewal of such contract, or of any subscription or enrollment thereunder, included the use by the plan or a representative of the plan of any advertising, evidence of coverage, or disclosure form which was untrue, misleading, or deceptive.

(2) The contract is not in compliance with this chapter, or the rules adopted pursuant to this chapter.

(3) The plan does not have a financially sound operation and adequate provision against the risk of insolvency.

(4) The plan has operated in violation of the provisions of subdivision (a), (b), (c), (d), or (e) of Section 1367.

(5) The plan has not complied with the provisions of Section 1379.

(c) The civil penalty may be assessed and recovered only in a civil action. The cause of action may be brought in the name of the people of the State of California by the Attorney General or the director, as determined by the director.

(Amended by Stats. 1999, Ch. 525, Sec. 142. Effective January 1, 2000. Operative July 1, 2000, or sooner, by Sec. 214 of Ch. 525.)

1393.6.

For violations of Article 3.1 (commencing with Section 1357), Article 3.15 (commencing with Section 1357.50), Article 3.16 (commencing with Section 1357.500), and Article 3.17 (commencing with Section 1357.600), the director may, after appropriate notice and opportunity for hearing, by order levy administrative penalties as follows:

(a) Any person, solicitor, or solicitor firm, other than a health care service plan, who willfully violates any provision of this chapter, or who willfully violates any rule or order adopted or issued pursuant to this chapter, is liable for administrative penalties of not less than two hundred fifty dollars ($250) for each first violation, and of not less than one thousand dollars ($1,000) and not more than two thousand five hundred dollars ($2,500) for each subsequent violation.

(b) Any health care service plan that willfully violates any provision of this chapter, or that willfully violates any rule or order adopted or issued pursuant to this chapter, is liable for administrative penalties of not less than two thousand five hundred dollars ($2,500) for each first violation, and of not less than five thousand dollars ($5,000) nor more than ten thousand dollars ($10,000) for each second violation, and of not less than fifteen thousand dollars ($15,000) and not more than one hundred thousand dollars ($100,000) for each subsequent violation.

(c) The administrative penalties shall be paid to the Managed Care Administrative Fines and Penalties Fund and shall be used for the purposes specified in Section 1341.45.

(d) The administrative penalties available to the director pursuant to this section are not exclusive, and may be sought and employed in any combination with civil, criminal, and other administrative remedies deemed advisable by the director to enforce the provisions of this chapter.

(Amended by Stats. 2012, Ch. 852, Sec. 8. (AB 1083) Effective January 1, 2013.)

1394.

The civil, criminal, and administrative remedies available to the director pursuant to this article are not exclusive, and may be sought and employed in any combination deemed advisable by the director to enforce the provisions of this chapter.

(Amended by Stats. 1999, Ch. 525, Sec. 144. Effective January 1, 2000. Operative July 1, 2000, or sooner, by Sec. 214 of Ch. 525.)

1394.1.

Notwithstanding any other provision of law, the director may file a verified complaint for involuntary dissolution of a health care service plan on any one or more of the grounds specified in subdivision (b) of Section 1386. The complaint shall be filed in the superior court of the county where the principal executive office of the health care service plan is located or, if the principal executive office of the health care service plan is not located in this state, or the health care service plan has no such office, the County of Sacramento.

(Amended by Stats. 1999, Ch. 525, Sec. 145. Effective January 1, 2000. Operative July 1, 2000, or sooner, by Sec. 214 of Ch. 525.)

1394.2.

Notwithstanding any other provision of law, in any involuntary dissolution of a health care service plan as provided for in Section 1394.1, or other insolvency proceeding involving a health care service plan, the following expenses and claims have priority in the following order:

(a) First, administrative expenses allowed by the superior court and any fees and charges assessed against the estate of the dissolved health care service plan in conjunction with the dissolution of the estate.

(b) Second, taxes due the State of California.

(c) Third, claims having preference by the laws of the United States and by the laws of this state.

(d) Fourth, claims of health care service plan subscribers and enrollees for reimbursement for services rendered by noncontracting providers. Upon proper showing, the superior court may make an order relieving subscribers and enrollees from liability or stay any proceeding to secure payment for any services rendered by a noncontracting provider upon payment, in whole or in part, of the claim or claims of those noncontracting providers.

(e) Fifth, claims of health care service plan group contract holders for reimbursement for services rendered by noncontracting providers to subscribers and enrollees under the group contract.

(f) Sixth, any and all claims, including all officers' and directors' claims for indemnity, arising against the estate of the dissolved health care service plan.

(Added by Stats. 1985, Ch. 908, Sec. 6.)

1394.3.

Except as provided for in Section 1394.1, and 1394.2, the involuntary dissolution of a health care service plan shall be in accordance with either of the following:

(a) Chapter 18 (commencing with Section 1800) of Division 1 of Title 1 of the Corporations Code, if the plan is incorporated under the General Corporation Law.

(b) Chapter 15 (commencing with Section 8510) of Part 3 of Division 2 of Title 1 of the Corporations Code if the plan is incorporated under the Nonprofit Corporation Law.

(Amended by Stats. 1999, Ch. 525, Sec. 146. Effective January 1, 2000. Operative July 1, 2000, or sooner, by Sec. 214 of Ch. 525.)

ARTICLE 8.5. Service of Process [1394.5 - 1394.8]

(Article 8.5 added by Stats. 1989, Ch. 845, Sec. 4.)

1394.5.
When any person, including any nonresident of this state, engages in conduct prohibited or made actionable by this chapter or any rule, regulation, or order adopted hereunder, whether or not the person has filed a power of attorney under subdivision (j) of Section 1351, and personal jurisdiction over the person cannot otherwise be obtained in this state, that conduct shall be considered equivalent to the appointment of the director or the director's successor in office to be the attorney in fact to receive any lawful process in any noncriminal suit, action, or proceeding against the person or the person's successor, executor, or administrator which arises out of that conduct and which is brought under this chapter or any rule, regulation, or order adopted hereunder, with the same force and validity as if personally served. Service may be made by leaving a copy of the process in the office of the director, but it is not effective unless the plaintiff or petitioner, who may be the director in a suit, action, or proceeding instituted by him or her, forthwith sends notice of the service and a copy of the process by registered or certified mail to the defendant or respondent at his or her last known address or takes other steps which are reasonably calculated to give actual notice, and in a court action, an affidavit of compliance with this section is filed in the case on or before the return day of the process, if any, or within such further time as the court allows. In the case of administrative orders issued by the director, the affidavit of compliance need not be filed with the administrative tribunal unless the respondent requests a hearing.
(Amended by Stats. 1999, Ch. 525, Sec. 147. Effective January 1, 2000. Operative July 1, 2000, or sooner, by Sec. 214 of Ch. 525.)
1394.7.
(a) As used in this section the following definitions shall apply:
(1) "Health care service plan" means any plan as defined in Section 1345, but this section does not apply to specialized health care service contracts.
(2) "Carrier" means a health care service plan, an insurer issuing group disability coverage which covers hospital, medical, or surgical expenses, a nonprofit hospital service plan, or any other entity responsible for either the payment of benefits or the provision of hospital, medical, and surgical benefits under a group contract.
(3) "Insolvency" means that the director has determined that the health care service plan is not financially able to provide health care services to its enrollees and (A) the director has taken an action pursuant to Section 1386, 1391, or 1399, or (B) an order requested by the director or the Attorney General has been issued by the superior court under Section 1392, 1393, or 1394.1.
(b) In the event of the insolvency of a health care service plan and upon order of the director, any health care service plan which the director determines to have sufficient health care delivery resources and sufficient financial and administrative capacity and that participated in the enrollment process with the insolvent health care service plan at the last regular open enrollment period of a group shall offer enrollees of the group in the insolvent health care service plan a 30-day enrollment period commencing upon the date specified by the director. Each health care service plan shall offer enrollees of the group in the insolvent health care service plan the same coverages and rates that it offered to enrollees of the group at the last regular open enrollment period of the group. Coverage shall be effective upon receipt by the successor plan of an application for enrollment by or on behalf of a subscriber or enrollee of the insolvent plan. The director shall send a notice of the insolvency of a health care service plan to the Insurance Commissioner.
(c) If no other carrier had been offered to groups enrolled in the insolvent health care service plan, or if the director determines that the other carriers do not include a sufficient number of health care service plans that have adequate health care delivery resources or the financial or administrative capacity to assure that health care services will be available and accessible to all of the group enrollees of the insolvent health care service plan, then the director shall allocate equitably the insolvent health care service plan's group contracts for the groups, except for Medi-Cal contracts made pursuant to Section 14200 of the Welfare and Institutions Code, among all health care service plans which operate within at least a portion of the service area of the insolvent health care service plan, taking into consideration the health care delivery resources and the financial and administrative capacity of each health care service plan. The director shall also have the authority to allocate equitably enrollees, except Medi-Cal enrollees, if he or she has been unable to successfully place them through the open enrollment procedure in subdivision (b). The director shall make every reasonable effort to allocate enrollees within 30 days of the insolvency of the plan, but not later than 45 days after insolvency. Each health care service plan to which a group or groups are so allocated shall offer the group or groups the health care service plan's coverage which is most similar to each group's coverage with the insolvent health care service plan, as determined by the director, at rates determined in accordance with the successor health care service plan's existing rating methodology. Coverage shall be effective upon the date specified by the director. Further, except to the extent benefits for any condition would have been reduced or excluded under the insolvent health care service plan's contract or policy, no provision in a successor health care service plan's contract of coverage that would operate to reduce or exclude benefits on the basis that the condition giving rise to benefits preexisted on the effective date of the enrollee's assignment to the succeeding health care service plan shall be applied with respect to those enrollees validly covered under the insolvent health care service plan's contract or policy on the date of the assignment. The State Department of Health Services shall have the authority to allocate Medi-Cal enrollees to other carriers with valid Medi-Cal contracts, which operate within the same service area of an insolvent Medi-Cal contractor and that have sufficient capacity to absorb the Medi-Cal enrollees allocated to them.
(d) The director shall also allocate equitably the insolvent health care service plan's nongroup enrollees among all health care service plans which operate within at least a portion of the service area of the insolvent health care service plan, taking into consideration the health care delivery resources or the financial and administrative capacity of each health care service plan. Each health care service plan to which nongroup enrollees are allocated shall offer the nongroup enrollees the health care service plan's most similar coverage for individual or conversion coverage, as determined by the director, taking into consideration his or her type of coverage in the insolvent health care service plan, at rates determined in accordance with the successor health care service plan's existing rating methodology. Coverage shall be effective upon the date specified by the director. Further, except to the extent benefits for any condition would have been reduced or excluded under the insolvent health care service plan's contract or policy, no provision in a successor health care service plan's contract of coverage that would operate to reduce or exclude benefits on the basis that the condition giving rise to benefits preexisted on the effective date of the enrollee's assignment to the succeeding health care service plan shall be applied with respect to those enrollees validly covered under the insolvent health care service plan's contract or policy on the date of the assignment. Successor health care service plans which do not offer direct nongroup enrollment may aggregate all allocated nongroup enrollees into one group for rating and coverage purposes.
(e) Contracting providers shall continue to provide services to enrollees of an insolvent plan until the effective date of an enrollee's coverage in a successor plan selected pursuant to either open enrollment or the allocation process but in no event for the period exceeding that required by their contract or 45 days in the case of allocation, whichever is greater; or for a period exceeding that required by their contract or 30 days in the case of open enrollment, whichever is greater.
(f) The failure to comply with an order under this section shall constitute a violation of this section.
(Amended by Stats. 1999, Ch. 525, Sec. 148. Effective January 1, 2000. Operative July 1, 2000, or sooner, by Sec. 214 of Ch. 525.)
1394.8.
(a) As used in this section:
(1) "Carrier" means a specialized health care service plan, and any of the following entities which offer coverage comparable to the coverages offered by a specialized health care service plan: an insurer issuing group disability coverage; a nonprofit hospital service plan; or any other entity responsible for either the payment of benefits for or the provisions of services under a group contract.
(2) "Insolvency" means that the director has determined that the specialized health care service plan is not financially able to provide specialized health care services to its enrollees and (A) the director has taken an action pursuant to Section 1386, 1391, 1399, or (B) an order requested by the director or the Attorney General has been issued by the superior court under Sections 1392, 1393, or 1394.1.
(3) "Specialized health care service plan" means any plan authorized to issue only specialized health care service plan contracts as defined in Section 1345.
(b) In the event of the insolvency of a specialized health care service plan and upon order of the director, any specialized health care service plan which the director determines to have sufficient health care delivery resources and sufficient financial and administrative capacity and that participated in the enrollment process with the insolvent specialized health care service plan at the last regular open enrollment period of a group for the same type of specialized health care services shall offer enrollees of the group in the insolvent specialized health care service plan a 30-day enrollment period commencing upon the date specified by the director. Each specialized health care service plan shall offer enrollees of the group in the insolvent specialized health care service plan the same specialized coverage and rates that it offered to the enrollees of the group at its last regular open enrollment period. Coverage shall be effective upon receipt by the successor plan of an application for enrollment by or on behalf of a subscriber or enrollee of the insolvent plan. The director shall send a notice of the insolvency of a specialized health care service plan to the Insurance Commissioner.
(c) If no other carrier for the same type of specialized health care services had been offered to some groups enrolled in the insolvent specialized health care service plan, or if the director determines that the other carriers do not include a sufficient number of specified health care service plans which have adequate health care delivery resources or the financial and administrative capacity to assure that the specialized health care services will be available and accessible to all of the group enrollees of the insolvent specialized health care service plan, then the director shall allocate equitably the insolvent specialized health care service plan's group contracts for the groups among all specialized health care service plans which offer the same type of specialized health care services as the insolvent plan and which operate within at least a portion of the service area of the insolvent specialized health care service plan, taking into consideration the health care delivery resources and the financial and administrative capacity of each specialized health care service plan. The director shall also have the authority to allocate equitable enrollees if he or she has been unable to successfully place them through the open enrollment procedure in subdivision (b). The director shall make every reasonable effort to allocate enrollees within 30 days of the insolvency of the plan, but not later than 45 days after insolvency. Each specialized health care service plan to which a group or groups is so allocated shall offer such group or groups the specialized health care service plan's coverage which is most similar to each group's coverage with the insolvent specialized health care service plan as determined by the director, at rates determined in accordance with the successor specialized health care service plan's existing rating methodology. Coverage shall be effective on a date specified by the director. Further, except to the extent benefits for any condition would have been reduced or excluded under the insolvent specialized health care service plan's contract or policy, no provision

in a successor specialized health care service plan's contract of coverage which would operate to reduce or exclude benefits on the basis that the condition giving rise to benefits preexisted on the effective date of the enrollee's assignment to the succeeding plan shall be applied with respect to those enrollees validly covered under the insolvent specialized health care service plan's contract or policy on the date of the assignment.

(d) The director shall also allocate equitably the insolvent specialized health care service plan's nongroup enrollees among all specialized health care services which offer the same type of specialized health care services as the insolvent plan and which operate within at least a portion of the insolvent specialized health care service plan's service area, taking into consideration the health care delivery resources and the financial and administrative capacity of each specialized health care service plan. Each specialized health care service plan to which nongroup enrollees are allocated shall offer the nongroup enrollees the health care service plan's most similar coverage for individual or conversion coverage, as determined by the director, taking into consideration his or her type of coverage in the insolvent specialized health care service plan at rates determined in accordance with the successor specialized health care service plan's existing rating methodology. Coverage shall be effective on the date specified by the director. Further, except to the extent benefits for any condition would have been reduced or excluded under the insolvent specialized health care service plan's contract or policy, no provision in a successor specialized health care service plan's contract of coverage which would operate to reduce or exclude benefits on the basis that the condition giving rise to benefits preexisted on the effective date of the enrollee's assignment to the succeeding plan shall be applied with respect to those enrollees validly covered under the insolvent specialized health care service plan's contract or policy on the date of the assignment. Successor specialized health care service plans which do not offer direct nongroup enrollment may aggregate all allocated nongroup enrollees into one group for rating and coverage purposes.

(e) Contracting providers shall continue to provide services to enrollees of an insolvent plan until the effective date of an enrollee's coverage in a successor plan selected pursuant to either open enrollment or the allocation process but in no event for the period exceeding that required by their contract or 45 days in the case of allocation, whichever is greater; or for a period exceeding that required by their contract or 30 days in the case of open enrollment, whichever is greater.

(f) Failure to comply with an order pursuant to this section shall constitute a violation of this section.

(Amended by Stats. 1999, Ch. 525, Sec. 149. Effective January 1, 2000. Operative July 1, 2000, or sooner, by Sec. 214 of Ch. 525.)

ARTICLE 9. Miscellaneous [1395 - 1399.5]

(Article 9 added by Stats. 1975, Ch. 941.)

1395.

(a) Notwithstanding Article 6 (commencing with Section 650) of Chapter 1 of Division 2 of the Business and Professions Code, any health care service plan or specialized health care service plan may, except as limited by this subdivision, solicit or advertise with regard to the cost of subscription or enrollment, facilities and services rendered, provided, however, Article 5 (commencing with Section 600) of Chapter 1 of Division 2 of the Business and Professions Code remains in effect. Any price advertisement shall be exact, without the use of such phrases as "as low as," "and up," "lowest prices" or words or phrases of similar import. Any advertisement that refers to services, or costs for the services, and that uses words of comparison must be based on verifiable data substantiating the comparison. Any health care service plan or specialized health care service plan so advertising shall be prepared to provide information sufficient to establish the accuracy of the comparison. Price advertising shall not be fraudulent, deceitful, or misleading, nor contain any offers of discounts, premiums, gifts, or bait of similar nature. In connection with price advertising, the price for each product or service shall be clearly identifiable. The price advertised for products shall include charges for any related professional services, including dispensing and fitting services, unless the advertisement specifically and clearly indicates otherwise.

(b) Plans licensed under this chapter shall not be deemed to be engaged in the practice of a profession, and may employ, or contract with, any professional licensed pursuant to Division 2 (commencing with Section 500) of the Business and Professions Code to deliver professional services. Employment by or a contract with a plan as a provider of professional services shall not constitute a ground for disciplinary action against a health professional licensed pursuant to Division 2 (commencing with Section 500) of the Business and Professions Code by a licensing agency regulating a particular health care profession.

(c) A health care service plan licensed under this chapter may directly own, and may directly operate through its professional employees or contracted licensed professionals, offices and subsidiary corporations, including pharmacies that satisfy the requirements of subdivision (d) of Section 4080.5 of the Business and Professions Code, as are necessary to provide health care services to the plan's subscribers and enrollees.

(d) A professional licensed pursuant to the provisions of Division 2 (commencing with Section 500) of the Business and Professions Code who is employed by, or under contract to, a plan may not own or control offices or branch offices beyond those expressly permitted by the provisions of the Business and Professions Code.

(e) Nothing in this chapter shall be construed to repeal, abolish, or diminish the effect of Section 129450 of the Health and Safety Code.

(f) Except as specifically provided in this chapter, nothing in this chapter shall be construed to limit the effect of the laws governing professional corporations, as they appear in applicable provisions of the Business and Professions Code, upon specialized health care service plans.

(g) No representative of a participating health, dental, or vision plan or its subcontractor representative shall in any manner use false or misleading claims to misrepresent itself, the plan, the subcontractor, or the Healthy Families or Medi-Cal program while engaging in application assistance activities that are subject to this section. Notwithstanding any other provision of this chapter, any representative of the health, dental, or vision care plan or of the health, dental, or vision care plan's subcontractor who violates any of the provisions of Section 12693.325 of the Insurance Code shall only be subject to a fine of five hundred dollars ($500) for each of those violations.

(h) A health care service plan shall comply with Section 12693.325 of the Insurance Code and Section 14409 of the Welfare and Institutions Code. In addition to any other disciplinary powers provided by this chapter, if a health care service plan violates any of the provisions of Section 12693.325 of the Insurance Code, the department may prohibit the health care service plan from providing application assistance and contacting applicants pursuant to Section 12693.325 of the Insurance Code.

(Amended by Stats. 2001, Ch. 171, Sec. 2. Effective August 10, 2001.)

1395.5.

(a) Except as provided in subdivisions (b) and (c), no contract that is issued, amended, renewed, or delivered on or after January 1, 1999, between a health care service plan, including a specialized health care service plan, and a provider shall contain provisions that prohibit, restrict, or limit the health care provider from advertising.

(b) Nothing in this section shall be construed to prohibit plans from establishing reasonable guidelines in connection with the activities regulated pursuant to this chapter, including those to prevent advertising that is, in whole or in part, untrue, misleading, deceptive, or otherwise inconsistent with this chapter or the rules and regulations promulgated thereunder. For advertisements mentioning a provider's participation in a plan, nothing in this section shall be construed to prohibit plans from requiring each advertisement to contain a disclaimer to the effect that the provider's services may be covered for some, but not all, plan contracts, or that plan contracts may cover some, but not all, provider services.

(c) Nothing in this section is intended to prohibit provisions or agreements intended to protect service marks, trademarks, trade secrets, or other confidential information or property. If a health care provider participates on a provider panel or network as a result of a direct contractual arrangement with a health care service plan that, in turn, has entered into a direct contractual arrangement with another person or entity, pursuant to which enrollees, subscribers, insureds, and other beneficiaries of that other person or entity may receive covered services from the health care provider, then nothing in this section is intended to prohibit reasonable provisions or agreements in the direct contractual arrangement between the health care provider and the health care service plan that protect the name or trade name of the other person or entity or require that the health care provider obtain the consent of the health care service plan prior to the use of the name or trade name of the other person or entity in any advertising by the health care provider.

(d) Nothing in this section shall be construed to impair or impede the authority of the director to regulate advertising, disclosure, or solicitation pursuant to this chapter.

(Amended by Stats. 1999, Ch. 525, Sec. 150. Effective January 1, 2000. Operative July 1, 2000, or sooner, by Sec. 214 of Ch. 525.)

1395.6.

(a) In order to prevent the improper selling, leasing, or transferring of a health care provider's contract, it is the intent of the Legislature that every arrangement that results in a payor paying a health care provider a reduced rate for health care services based on the health care provider's participation in a network or panel shall be disclosed to the provider in advance and that the payor shall actively encourage beneficiaries to use the network, unless the health care provider agrees to provide discounts without that active encouragement.

(b) Beginning July 1, 2000, every contracting agent that sells, leases, assigns, transfers, or conveys its list of contracted health care providers and their contracted reimbursement rates to a payor, as defined in subparagraph (A) of paragraph (3) of subdivision (d), or another contracting agent shall, upon entering or renewing a provider contract, do all of the following:

(1) Disclose to the provider whether the list of contracted providers may be sold, leased, transferred, or conveyed to other payors or other contracting agents, and specify whether those payors or contracting agents include workers' compensation insurers or automobile insurers.

(2) Disclose what specific practices, if any, payors utilize to actively encourage a payor's beneficiaries to use the list of contracted providers when obtaining medical care that entitles a payor to claim a contracted rate. For purposes of this paragraph, a payor is deemed to have actively encouraged its beneficiaries to use the list of contracted providers if one of the following occurs:

(A) The payor's contract with subscribers or insureds offers beneficiaries direct financial incentives to use the list of contracted providers when obtaining medical care. "Financial incentives" means reduced copayments, reduced deductibles, premium discounts directly attributable to the use of a provider panel, or financial penalties directly attributable to the nonuse of a provider panel.

(B) The payor provides information to its beneficiaries, who are parties to the contract, or, in the case of workers' compensation insurance, the employer, advising them of the existence of the list of contracted providers through the use of a variety of advertising or marketing approaches that supply the names, addresses, and telephone numbers of contracted providers to beneficiaries in advance of their selection of a health care provider, which approaches may include, but are not limited to, the use of provider directories, or the use of toll-free telephone numbers or Internet web site addresses supplied directly to every beneficiary. However, internet web site addresses alone shall not be deemed to satisfy the requirements of this subparagraph. Nothing in this subparagraph shall prevent contracting agents or payors from providing only listings of providers located within a reasonable geographic range of a beneficiary.

(3) Disclose whether payors to which the list of contracted providers may be sold, leased, transferred, or conveyed may be permitted to pay a provider's contracted rate without actively encouraging the payors' beneficiaries to use the list of contracted providers when obtaining medical care. Nothing in this subdivision shall be construed to require a payor to actively encourage the payor's beneficiaries to use the list of contracted providers when obtaining medical care in the case of an emergency.

(4) Disclose, upon the initial signing of a contract, and within 30 calendar days of receipt of a written request from a provider or provider panel, a payor summary of all payors currently eligible to claim a provider's contracted rate due to the provider's and payor's respective written agreement with any contracting agent.

(5) Allow providers, upon the initial signing, renewal, or amendment of a provider contract, to decline to be included in any list of contracted providers that is sold, leased, transferred, or conveyed to payors that do not actively encourage the payors' beneficiaries to use the list of contracted providers when obtaining medical care as described in paragraph (2). Each provider's election under this paragraph shall be binding on the contracting agent with which the provider has the contract and any contracting agent that buys, leases, or otherwise obtains the list of contracted providers. A provider shall not be excluded from any list of contracted providers that is sold, leased, transferred, or conveyed to payors that actively encourage the payors' beneficiaries to use the list of contracted providers when obtaining medical care, based upon the provider's refusal to be included on any list of contracted providers that is sold, leased, transferred, or conveyed to payors that do not actively encourage the payors' beneficiaries to use the list of contracted providers when obtaining medical care.

(6) Nothing in this subdivision shall be construed to impose requirements or regulations upon payors, as defined in subparagraph (A) of paragraph (3) of subdivision (d).

(c) Beginning July 1, 2000, a payor, as defined in subparagraph (B) of paragraph (3) of subdivision (d), shall do all of the following:

(1) Provide an explanation of benefits or explanation of review that identifies the name of the network that has a written agreement signed by the provider whereby the payor is entitled, directly or indirectly, to pay a preferred rate for the services rendered.

(2) Demonstrate that it is entitled to pay a contracted rate within 30 business days of receipt of a written request from a provider who has received a claim payment from the payor. The failure of a payor to make the demonstration within 30 business days shall render the payor responsible for the amount that the payor would have been required to pay pursuant to the applicable health care service plan contract, including a specialized health care service plan contract, covering the beneficiary, which amount shall be due and payable within 10 business days of receipt of written notice from the provider, and shall bar the payor from taking any future discounts from that provider without the provider's express written consent until the payor can demonstrate to the provider that it is entitled to pay a contracted rate as provided in this paragraph. A payor shall be deemed to have demonstrated that it is entitled to pay a contracted rate if it complies with either of the following:

(A) Discloses the name of the network that has a written agreement with the provider whereby the provider agrees to accept discounted rates, and describes the specific practices the payor utilizes to comply with paragraph (2) of subdivision (b).

(B) Identifies the provider's written agreement with a contracting agent whereby the provider agrees to be included on lists of contracted providers sold, leased, transferred, or conveyed to payors that do not actively encourage beneficiaries to use the list of contracted providers pursuant to paragraph (5) of subdivision (b).

(d) For the purposes of this section, the following terms have the following meanings:

(1) "Beneficiary" means:

(A) For workers' compensation insurance, an employee seeking health care services for a work-related injury.

(B) For automobile insurance, those persons covered under the medical payments portion of the insurance contract.

(C) For group or individual health services covered through a health care service plan contract, including a specialized health care service plan contract, or a policy of disability insurance that covers hospital, medical, or surgical benefits, a subscriber, an enrollee, a policyholder, or an insured.

(2) "Contracting agent" means a health care service plan, including a specialized health care service plan, while engaged, for monetary or other consideration, in the act of selling, leasing, transferring, assigning, or conveying, a provider or provider panel to payors to provide health care services to beneficiaries.

(3) (A) For the purposes of subdivision (b), "payor" means a health care service plan, including a specialized health care service plan, an insurer licensed under the Insurance Code to provide disability insurance that covers hospital, medical, or surgical benefits, automobile insurance, workers' compensation insurance, or a self-insured employer that is responsible to pay for health care services provided to beneficiaries.

(B) For the purposes of subdivision (c), "payor" means only a health care service plan, including a specialized health care service plan that has purchased, leased, or otherwise obtained the use of a provider or provider panel to provide health care services to beneficiaries pursuant to a contract that authorizes payment at discounted rates.

(4) "Payor summary" means a written summary that includes the payor's name and the type of plan, including, but not limited to, a group health plan, an automobile insurance plan, and a workers' compensation insurance plan.

(5) "Provider" means any of the following:

(A) Any person licensed or certified pursuant to Division 2 (commencing with Section 500) of the Business and Professions Code.

(B) Any person licensed pursuant to the Chiropractic Initiative Act or the Osteopathic Initiative Act.

(C) Any person licensed pursuant to Chapter 2.5 (commencing with Section 1440) of Division 2.

(D) A clinic, health dispensary, or health facility licensed pursuant to Division 2 (commencing with Section 1200).

(E) Any entity exempt from licensure pursuant to Section 1206.

(e) This section shall become operative on July 1, 2000.

(Amended by Stats. 2000, Ch. 1069, Sec. 2. Effective January 1, 2001.)

1395.7.

(a) A staff-model dental health care service plan that arranges for or establishes credit extended by a third party shall establish and comply with policies and procedures that ensure that its dentists, employees, and agents, and employees or agents of its dentists, comply with Section 654.3 of the Business and Professions Code.

(b) A staff-model dental health care service plan that arranges for or establishes credit extended by a third party shall establish and comply with policies and procedures that ensure that, within 15 business days of an enrollee's request, the plan refunds to a lender any payment received through that credit for treatment that has not been rendered or costs that have not been incurred.

(c) A staff-model dental health care service plan that directly extends credit or establishes a payment plan shall, at a minimum, establish and comply with policies and procedures that ensure that, within 15 business days of an enrollee's request, the plan refunds to the enrollee any payment received through that credit or payment plan for treatment that has not been rendered or costs that have not been incurred.

(d) For purposes of this section, the following definitions shall apply:

(1) "Staff-model dental health care service plan" means a specialized health care service plan that contracts to provide coverage for dental care services and that retains dentists as employees to care for its enrollees.

(2) "Enrollee" includes, but is not limited to, an enrollee's parent or other legal representative.

(Added by Stats. 2009, Ch. 418, Sec. 2. (AB 171) Effective January 1, 2010.)

1396.

It is unlawful for any person willfully to make any untrue statement of material fact in any application, notice, amendment, report, or other submission filed with the director under this chapter or the regulations adopted thereunder, or willfully to omit to state in any application, notice, or report any material fact which is required to be stated therein.

(Amended by Stats. 1999, Ch. 525, Sec. 151. Effective January 1, 2000. Operative July 1, 2000, or sooner, by Sec. 214 of Ch. 525.)

1396.5.

A nonprofit hospital corporation which substantially indemnified subscribers and enrollees and was operating in 1965 under Chapter 11A (commencing with Section 11490) of Part 2 of Division 2 of the Insurance Code and which is regulated under the Knox-Keene Health Care Service Plan Act shall enjoy the privileges under the act which would have been available to it had it been registered under the Knox-Mills Health Plan Act and applied for a license under the Knox-Keene Health Care Service Plan Act in 1976.

(Added by Stats. 1990, Ch. 1043, Sec. 10.)

1397.

(a) Whenever reference is made in this chapter to a hearing before or by the director, the hearing shall be held in accordance with the Administrative Procedure Act (Chapter 5 (commencing with Section 11500) of Part 1 of Division 3 of Title 2 of the Government Code), and the director shall have all of the powers granted under that act.

(b) Every final order, decision, license, or other official act of the director under this chapter is subject to judicial review in accordance with the law.

(Amended by Stats. 1999, Ch. 525, Sec. 152. Effective January 1, 2000. Operative July 1, 2000, or sooner, by Sec. 214 of Ch. 525.)

1397.5.

(a) The director shall make and file annually with the Department of Managed Health Care as a public record, an aggregate summary of grievances against plans filed with the director by enrollees or subscribers. This summary shall include at least all of the following information:

(1) The total number of grievances filed.

(2) The types of grievances.

(b) The summary set forth in subdivision (a) shall include the following disclaimer: THIS INFORMATION IS PROVIDED FOR STATISTICAL PURPOSES ONLY. THE DIRECTOR OF THE DEPARTMENT OF MANAGED CARE HAS NEITHER INVESTIGATED NOR DETERMINED WHETHER THE GRIEVANCES COMPILED WITHIN THIS SUMMARY ARE REASONABLE OR VALID.

(c) Nothing in this section shall require or authorize the disclosure of grievances filed with or received by the director and made confidential pursuant to any other provision of law including, but not limited to, the California Public Records Act (Chapter 3.5 (commencing with Section 6250) of Division 7 of Title 1 of the Government Code) and the Information Practices Act of 1977 (Chapter 1 (commencing with Section 1798) of Title 1.8 of Part 4 of Division 3 of the Civil Code). Nothing in this section shall affect any other provision of law including, but not limited to, the California Public Records Act and the Information Practices Act of 1977.

(Amended by Stats. 2000, Ch. 857, Sec. 46. Effective January 1, 2001.)

1397.6.

The director may contract with necessary medical consultants to assist with the health care program. These contracts shall be on a noncompetitive bid basis and shall be exempt from Chapter 2 (commencing with Section 10290) of Part 2 of Division 2 of the Public Contract Code.

(Amended by Stats. 1999, Ch. 525, Sec. 154. Effective January 1, 2000. Operative July 1, 2000, or sooner, by Sec. 214 of Ch. 525.)

1398.5.

All references to the Knox-Mills Health Plan Act (Article 2.5 (commencing with Section 12530) of Chapter 6 of Part 2 of Division 3 of the Government Code), which was repealed by Chapter 941 of the Statutes of 1975, shall be deemed to be references to the Knox-Keene Health Care Service Plan Act of 1975.

(Added by Stats. 1976, Ch. 490.)

1399.

(a) Surrender of a license as a health plan becomes effective 30 days after receipt of an application to surrender the license or within a shorter period of time as the director may determine, unless a revocation or suspension proceeding is pending when the application is filed or a proceeding to revoke or suspend or to impose conditions upon the surrender is instituted within 30 days after the application is filed. If this proceeding is pending or instituted, surrender becomes effective at the time and upon the conditions as the director by order determines.

(b) If the director finds that any plan is no longer in existence, or has ceased to do business or has failed to initiate business activity as a licensee within six months after licensure, or cannot be located after reasonable search, the director may by order summarily revoke the license of the plan.

(c) The director may summarily suspend or revoke the license of a plan upon (1) failure to pay any fee required by this chapter within 15 days after notice by the director that the fee is due and unpaid, (2) failure to file any amendment or report required under this chapter within 15 days after notice by the director that the report is due, (3) failure to maintain any bond or insurance pursuant to Section 1376, (4) failure to maintain a deposit, insurance, or guaranty arrangement pursuant to Section 1377, or (5) failure to maintain a deposit pursuant to Section 1300.76.1 of Title 28 of the California Code of Regulations.

(Amended by Stats. 2009, Ch. 298, Sec. 9. (AB 1540) Effective January 1, 2010.)

1399.1.

(a) All orders and other actions taken by the Commissioner of Corporations pursuant to the authority contained in subdivision (c) of Section 1350 on or before September 30, 1977, and all administrative or judicial decisions or orders relating to the same and all conditions imposed upon the same remain in effect against a plan holding a transitional license.

(b) The Knox-Mills Health Plan Act as in effect prior to its repeal continues to govern all suits, actions, prosecutions or proceedings which are pending or which may be initiated under subdivision (c) of Section 1350 on the basis of facts or circumstances occurring on or before September 30, 1977.

(Amended by Stats. 1999, Ch. 525, Sec. 157. Effective January 1, 2000. Operative July 1, 2000, or sooner, by Sec. 214 of Ch. 525.)

1399.3.

(a) A material change made by a health care service plan, as defined in subdivision (f) of Section 1345, to the terms and conditions of a contract between the health care service plan and a solicitor shall not become effective until the health care service plan has delivered to the solicitor, at least 45 days prior to the effective date of the change, written or electronic notice indicating the change or changes to the contract. For purposes of this section, a "material change" is a change made to a provision of the contract affecting any of the following:

(1) Commissions, bonuses, and incentives paid to the solicitor.

(2) Right of survivorship.

(3) Indemnification of the solicitor by the health care service plan.

(4) Errors and omissions coverage requirements for the solicitor.

(b) Subdivision (a) shall not apply under either of the following circumstances:

(1) The change to the contract is mutually agreed upon by the health care service plan and the solicitor.

(2) The change to the contract is required by state or federal law.

(Added by Stats. 2015, Ch. 482, Sec. 1. (AB 1163) Effective January 1, 2016.)

1399.5.

It is the intent of the Legislature that the provisions of this chapter shall be applicable to any private or public entity or political subdivision which, in return for a prepaid or periodic charge paid by or on behalf of a subscriber or enrollee, provides, administers or otherwise arranges for the provision of health care services, as defined in this chapter, unless such entity is exempted from the provisions of this chapter by, or pursuant to, Section 1343.

(Amended by Stats. 1980, Ch. 628.)

ARTICLE 9.5. Claims Reviewers [1399.55 - 1399.57]

(Article 9.5 added by Stats. 1992, Ch. 544, Sec. 1.)

1399.55.

Health care service plans shall, upon rejecting a claim from a health care provider or a patient, and upon their demand, disclose the specific rationale used in determining why the claim was rejected. Nothing in this section is intended to expand or restrict the ability of a health care provider or a patient from having health care coverage approved in advance of services.

(Added by Stats. 1992, Ch. 544, Sec. 1. Effective January 1, 1993.)

1399.56.

Compensation of a person retained by a health care service plan to review claims for health care services shall not be based on either of the following:

(a) A percentage of the amount by which a claim is reduced for payment.

(b) The number of claims or the cost of services for which the person has denied authorization or payment.

(Amended by Stats. 1995, Ch. 787, Sec. 2. Effective January 1, 1996.)

1399.57.

This article does not apply to services or benefits provided pursuant to Medi-Cal, including services or benefits provided under Chapters 7 (commencing with Section 14000) and 8 (commencing with Section 14200) of Part 3 of Division 9 of the Welfare and Institutions Code.

(Added by Stats. 1992, Ch. 544, Sec. 1. Effective January 1, 1993.)

ARTICLE 10. Discontinuance and Replacement of Group Health Care Service Plan Contracts [1399.60 - 1399.64]

(Article 10 added by Stats. 1977, Ch. 64.)

1399.60.

The provisions of this article shall apply to all group health care service contracts issued in this state pursuant to this chapter.

(Added by Stats. 1977, Ch. 64.)

1399.61.

In this article, unless the context otherwise requires:

(a) "Carrier" shall mean the health care service plan or other entity responsible for the payment of benefits or provision of services under a group contract.

(b) "Dependent" shall have the meaning set forth in a contract.

(c) "Discontinuance" shall mean the termination of the contract between the entire employer unit under a contract and the health care service plan, and does not refer to the termination of any agreement between any individual member under a contract and the health care service plan.

(d) "Employee" shall mean all agents, employees, and members of unions or associations to whom benefits are provided under a contract.

(e) "Extension of benefits" shall mean the continuation of coverage under a particular benefit provided under a contract following discontinuance with respect to an employee or dependent who is totally disabled on the date of discontinuance.

(f) "Contract" shall mean any group health care service plan or contract subject to the provisions of this article.

(g) "Contractholder" shall mean the entity to which a contract is issued.

(h) "Dues" shall mean the consideration payable to the carrier.

(i) "Replacement coverage" shall mean the benefits provided by a succeeding carrier.

(j) "Totally disabled" shall have the meaning set forth in a contract.

(Amended by Stats. 1983, Ch. 126, Sec. 1.)

1399.62.

(a) Every contract containing hospital, medical, or surgical expense benefits or service benefits shall contain a reasonable extension of such benefits upon discontinuance of the contract with respect to employees or dependents who are totally disabled while enrolled under the contract on or after the date this article becomes applicable to such contract and who continue to be totally disabled at the date of discontinuance of the contract.

(b) Every contract providing hospital, medical or surgical expense benefits or service benefits shall be deemed to include a reasonable extension of such benefits upon discontinuance of the contract if it provides benefits for covered services directly relating to the condition causing total disability existing at the time dues payments cease for the employee or dependent and incurred during a period of not less than 12 months thereafter, which period shall not be interrupted by discontinuance of the contract. That extension of benefits may be terminated at such time as the employee or dependent is no longer totally disabled or at such time as a succeeding carrier may elect to provide replacement coverage to that employee or dependent without limitation as to the disabling condition.

(c) The services provided during any extension of benefits may be subject to all limitations or restrictions contained in the contract.

(Amended by Stats. 1983, Ch. 888, Sec. 1.)

1399.63.

(a) Any carrier providing replacement coverage with respect to hospital, medical or surgical expense or service benefits within a period of 60 days from the date of discontinuance of a prior contract or policy providing such hospital, medical or surgical expense or service benefits shall immediately cover all employees and dependents who were validly covered under the previous contract or policy at the date of discontinuance, including all former employees entitled to continuation coverage under Section 1373.621, who are within the definitions of eligibility under the succeeding carrier's contract and who would otherwise be eligible for coverage under the succeeding carrier's contract, regardless of any provisions of the contract relating to active full-time employment or hospital confinement or pregnancy. However, with respect to employees or dependents who are totally disabled on the date of discontinuance of the prior carrier's contract or policy and entitled to an extension of benefits pursuant to subdivision (b) of Section 1399.62, or pursuant to subdivision (d) of Section 10128.2 of the Insurance Code, the succeeding carrier is not required to provide benefits for services or expenses directly related to any conditions which caused the total disability.

(b) Except as otherwise provided in subdivision (a), until an employee or dependent entitled to coverage under a succeeding carrier's contract pursuant to subdivision (a) of this section qualifies for full benefits by meeting all effective date requirements of the succeeding carrier's contract, the level of benefits shall not be lower than the benefits provided under the prior carrier's contract or policy reduced by the amount of benefits paid by the prior carrier. Such employee or dependent shall continue to be covered by the succeeding carrier until the earlier of the following dates:

(1) The date coverage would terminate for an employee or dependent in accordance with the provisions of the succeeding carrier's contract, or

(2) In the case of an employee or dependent who was totally disabled on the date of discontinuance of the prior carrier's contract or policy and entitled to an extension of benefits pursuant to subdivision (d) of Section 10128.2 of the Insurance Code or subdivision (b) of Section 1399. 62, the date the period of extension of benefits terminates or, if the prior carrier's contract or policy is not subject to this article, the date to which benefits would have been extended had the prior carrier's contract or policy been subject to this article.

(c) Except as otherwise provided in this section, and except to the extent that benefits for the condition would have been reduced or excluded under the prior carrier's contract or policy, no provision in a succeeding carrier's contract of replacement coverage which would operate to reduce or exclude benefits on the basis that the condition giving rise to benefits preexisted the effective date of the succeeding carrier's contract shall be applied with respect to those employees, former employees entitled to continuation coverage under Section 1373.621, and dependents validly covered under the prior carrier's contract or policy on the date of discontinuance.

(d) In a situation where a determination of the prior carrier's benefit is required by the succeeding carrier, at the succeeding carrier's request, the prior carrier shall furnish a statement of benefits available or pertinent information, sufficient to permit verification of the benefit determination by the succeeding carrier.

(e) For purposes of subdivision (a), a succeeding carrier's coverage shall not exclude any dependent child who was covered by the previous carrier solely because the plan member does not provide the primary support for that dependent child.

(f) Except to the extent that benefits for the condition would have been reduced or excluded under the prior carrier's contract or policy, no provision in the succeeding carrier's contract, where an employee changes carriers due to a change in employment or other circumstances, that would operate to reduce or exclude benefits for the following congenital craniofacial anomalies: cleft lip and palate (as defined in ICD-9-CM Diagnosis Code 749, International Classification of Diseases, 9th Revision, Clinical Modification, Volume 1, Second Edition, September, 1980), acrocephalosyndactyly (as defined in ICD-9-CM Diagnosis Code 755.55, cranio only), and other congenital musculoskeletal anomalies (as defined in ICD-9-CM Diagnosis Code 756.0), on the basis that the condition giving rise to benefits preexisted the effective date of the succeeding carrier's contract, shall be applied to those employees, former employees entitled to continuation coverage under Section 1373.621, and dependents validly covered under the prior carrier's contract or policy on the date the prior contract or policy terminated when payment or services had been commenced by the previous carrier. That succeeding coverage shall otherwise be subject to all other provisions of the contract between the insured and the succeeding carrier. Nothing in this subdivision shall be construed to limit or otherwise affect any obligation of a succeeding carrier to provide benefits for a condition not specified in this subdivision, where expressly or impliedly required by other provisions of this chapter; this subdivision is not intended to affect the construction of the language of any other provision of this chapter.

(Amended by Stats. 1995, Ch. 489, Sec. 2. Effective January 1, 1996.)

1399.64.

This article shall apply to all contracts issued, delivered, amended, or renewed in this state after January 1, 1977. A policy subject to the provisions of this article which is issued, delivered, amended as to benefits, or renewed in this state on or after the effective date of amendments to this article made at the 1977–1978 Regular Session of the Legislature shall be construed to be in compliance with the provisions of this article and such amendments to this article.

(Added by Stats. 1977, Ch. 64.)

ARTICLE 10.2. Mergers and Acquisitions of Health Care Service Plans [1399.65 - 1399.66]

(Article 10.2 added by Stats. 2018, Ch. 292, Sec. 1.)

1399.65.

(a) (1) A health care service plan that intends to merge or consolidate with, or enter into an agreement resulting in its purchase, acquisition, or control by, any entity, including another health care service plan or a health insurer licensed under the Insurance Code, shall give notice to, and secure prior approval from, the director.

(2) The transactions or agreements described in paragraph (1) may not be completed until the director approves the transaction or agreement.

(3) A health care service plan described in paragraph (1) shall meet all of the requirements of this chapter. The health care service plan shall file all the information necessary for the director to make the determination to approve, conditionally approve, or disapprove the transaction or agreement described in paragraph (1), including, but not limited to, a complete description of the proposed transaction or agreement, any modified exhibits for plan licensure pursuant to Section 1351, any approvals by federal or other state agencies required for the transaction or agreement, and any supporting documentation required by the director.

(4) The director may conditionally approve the transaction or agreement, contingent upon the health care service plan's agreement to fulfill one or more conditions to benefit subscribers and enrollees of the health care service plan, provide for a stable health care delivery system, and impose other conditions specific to the transaction or agreement in furtherance of this chapter. The director shall engage stakeholders in determining the measures for improvement. For a major transaction or agreement, the director shall

obtain an independent analysis of the impact of the transaction or agreement on subscribers and enrollees, the stability of the health care delivery system, and other relevant provisions of this chapter. For any other transaction or agreement, the director may obtain an independent analysis consistent with this paragraph.

(5) If an entity involved in the transaction or agreement is a nonprofit corporation described in Section 5046 of the Corporations Code, the health care service plan shall file all the information required by Article 11 (commencing with Section 1399.70).

(b) In addition to any grounds for disapproval as a result of information provided by a health care service plan pursuant to paragraph (3) of subdivision (a), the director may disapprove the transaction or agreement if the director finds the transaction or agreement would substantially lessen competition in health care service plan products or create a monopoly in this state, including, but not limited to, health coverage products for a specific line of business. In making this finding, the director may obtain an opinion from a consultant or consultants with the expertise to assess the competitive impact of the transaction or agreement.

(c) Prior to approving, conditionally approving, or disapproving a major transaction or agreement, the department shall hold a public meeting on the proposed transaction or agreement. For any other transaction or agreement, the department may hold a public meeting on the proposed transaction or agreement. The public meeting shall be conducted pursuant to the Bagley-Keene Open Meeting Act (Article 9 (commencing with Section 11120) of Chapter 1 of Part 1 of Division 3 of Title 2 of the Government Code). The meeting shall permit the parties to the proposed transaction and members of the public to provide written and verbal comments regarding the proposed transaction. If a substantive change in the proposed transaction or agreement is submitted to the director after the initial public meeting, the director may conduct an additional public meeting to hear comments from interested parties with respect to that change. The director shall consider the testimony and comments received at the public meeting in making the determination to approve, conditionally approve, or disapprove the transaction or agreement.

(d) If the director determines a material amount of assets of a health care service plan is subject to purchase, acquisition, or control, the director shall prepare a statement describing the proposed transaction or agreement subject to subdivision (a) and make it available to the public. The statement shall be made available before the public meeting.

(e) This section does not limit the authority of the director to enforce any other provision of this chapter.

(f) For purposes of this section, "entity" means a health care service plan, an individual, a corporation, a limited liability company, a partnership, an association, a joint stock company, a business trust, an unincorporated organization, any similar entity, or any combination thereof acting in concert.

(g) (1) For purposes of this section, "major transaction or agreement" means a transaction or agreement that meets any of the following criteria:

(A) Affects a significant number of enrollees.

(B) Involves a material amount of assets.

(C) Adversely affects either the subscribers or enrollees or the stability of the health care delivery system because of the entity's market position, including, but not limited to, the entity's market exit from a market segment or the entity's dominance of a market segment.

(2) The director shall, upon request, make available to the public his or her determination of whether a transaction or agreement meets the criteria set forth in this subdivision.

(Added by Stats. 2018, Ch. 292, Sec. 1. (AB 595) Effective January 1, 2019.)

1399.66.

(a) Notwithstanding subdivision (d) of Section 1352, a health care service plan that files a material modification that is a transaction or agreement described in subdivision (a) of Section 1399.65 shall be subject to the same fees required by subdivision (a) of Section 1356.

(b) (1) In addition to paying the fees described in subdivision (a), the health care service plan shall reimburse the director for the reasonable costs of all of the following:

(A) The independent analysis described in paragraph (4) of subdivision (a) of Section 1399.65.

(B) The opinion described in subdivision (b) of Section 1399.65.

(C) The public meeting described in subdivision (c)

(D) The statement described in subdivision (d) of Section 1399.65.

(2) The reimbursement required by this subdivision shall be irrespective of the director's approval, conditional approval, or disapproval of the transaction or agreement described in subdivision (a) of Section 1399.65.

(3) If a transaction described in subdivision (a) of Section 1399.65 involves two health care service plans, the director shall determine whether the reimbursement requirements of this subdivision apply to one or both of the plans.

(Added by Stats. 2018, Ch. 292, Sec. 1. (AB 595) Effective January 1, 2019.)

ARTICLE 11. Nonprofit Plans [1399.70 - 1399.76]

(Article 11 added by Stats. 1995, Ch. 792, Sec. 1.)

1399.70.

(a) In addition to the information required by subdivision (a) of Section 1399.73, a nonprofit health care service plan submitting an application to the director to restructure or convert its activities pursuant to this article shall submit to the director a copy of all of its original and amended articles of incorporation and bylaws, as well as a report summarizing the activities undertaken by the plan to meet its nonprofit obligations as directed by the director.

(b) The report required by this section shall include a summary of the following:

(1) The nature of public benefit or charitable activities undertaken by the plan.

(2) The expenditures incurred by the plan on these public benefit or charitable activities.

(3) The plan's procedure for avoiding conflicts of interest involving public benefit or charitable activities and a summary of any conflicts that have occurred and the manner in which they were resolved.

(c) The report required by this section shall also include a written plan that specifies on a projected basis the information required by subdivision (b) for the immediately following fiscal year.

(d) When requested by the director, the plan shall promptly supplement the report to include any additional information as the director deems necessary to ascertain whether the plan's assets are appropriately being used by the plan to meet its nonprofit obligations.

(e) For purposes of this article, a "nonprofit health care service plan" includes a plan formed under or subject to Part 2 (commencing with Section 5110) or Part 3 (commencing with Section 7110) of Division 2 of the Corporations Code.

(Amended by Stats. 1999, Ch. 525, Sec. 158. Effective January 1, 2000. Operative July 1, 2000, or sooner, by Sec. 214 of Ch. 525.)

1399.71.

(a) Any nonprofit health care service plan that intends to restructure its activities as defined in subdivision (d) shall, prior to restructuring, secure approval from the director.

(b) Every nonprofit health care service plan that applies to the department to restructure its activities shall submit for approval by the department a public benefit program that identifies activities to be undertaken by the nonprofit health care service plan following restructuring to continue to meet its nonprofit public benefit obligations. The program shall include all information required pursuant to subdivisions (b) and (c) of Section 1399.70.

(c) The director shall apply the requirements of Section 1399.72 to the public benefit program submitted for approval as part of a restructuring proposal submitted pursuant to subdivision (b) of this section. The set-aside requirement in paragraph (1) of subdivision (c) of Section 1399.72 shall apply only to the fair value of the portion of the nonprofit health care service plan involved in the restructuring, as determined by the director.

(d) (1) For the purposes of this section, a "restructuring" or "restructure" by a nonprofit health care service plan means the sale, lease, conveyance, exchange, transfer, or other similar disposition of a substantial amount of a nonprofit health care service plan's assets, as determined by the director, to a business or entity carried on for profit. Nothing in this section shall be construed to prohibit the director from consolidating actions taken by a plan for the purpose of treating the consolidated actions as a restructuring or restructure of the plan.

(2) For the purposes of this section, a "restructuring" or "restructure" by a nonprofit health care service plan shall not include any sales or purchases undertaken in the normal and ordinary course of plan business. The director may request information from the plan to verify that transactions qualify as occurring in the normal and ordinary course of plan business, and are not subject to the requirements of subdivision (e).

(e) Notwithstanding that a transaction or consolidated transactions involve a substantial amount of a nonprofit health care service plan's assets and are not in the normal and ordinary course of plan business, a "restructuring" or "restructure" by a nonprofit health care service plan shall not include any of the following transactions:

(1) Investments in a wholly owned subsidiary of the nonprofit health care service plan in which all of the following occur:

(A) Any profit from the investment will not inure to the benefit of any individual.

(B) The investment is fundamentally consistent with and advances the public benefit, charitable, or mutual benefit purpose of the plan.

(C) The investment does not adversely impact the plan's ability to fulfill its public benefit, charitable, or mutual benefit purposes.

(D) No officer or director of the plan has any financial interest constituting a conflict of interest in the investments.

(E) The investment results in the provision of services, goods, or insurance to or for the benefit of the plan or its members, enrollees, or groups.

(2) Sales or purchases of plan assets, including interests in wholly owned subsidiaries and in joint ventures, partnerships, and other investments in for-profit entities, in which all of the following occur:

(A) Any profit from the sale will not inure to the benefit of any individual.

(B) The sale or purchase is fundamentally consistent with and advances the public benefit, charitable, or mutual benefit purposes of the plan.

(C) The plan receives all proceeds from the sale.

(D) No officer or director of the plan has any financial interest constituting a conflict of interest in the sale or purchase.

(E) The transaction is conducted at arm's length and for fair market value.

(F) The sale or purchase does not adversely impact the plan's ability to fulfill its public benefit, charitable, or mutual benefit purposes.

(3) Investments in or joint ventures and partnerships with a for-profit entity in which all of the following occur:

(A) Any profit will not inure to the benefit of any individual.

(B) The mission or purpose of the investment, joint venture, or partnership is fundamentally consistent with the public benefit, charitable, or mutual benefit purposes of the plan.

(C) No officer or director of the plan has any financial interest constituting a conflict of interest in the investment, joint venture, or partnership.

(D) The transaction is conducted at arm's length and for fair market value.

(E) The investment, joint venture, or partnership furthers the plan's ability to fulfill its public benefit, charitable, or mutual benefit purposes.

(F) The investment, joint venture, or partnership results in the provision of services, goods, or insurance to or for the benefit of the plan or its members, enrollees, or groups. The sharing of profits or earnings upon a reasonable and equitable basis reflecting the contribution of other participants to the investment, joint venture, or partnership or the success thereof shall not constitute private inurement.

(f) All transactions subject to the exemptions listed in subdivision (e) may not be executed by the plan without the written prior approval of the director. In the application for material modification seeking approval, the plan shall demonstrate that the proposed transaction meets all of the relevant conditions for exemption required by subdivision (e).

(g) Prior to issuing a decision to approve an application for a material modification involving a transaction that is exempt pursuant to subdivision (e), the director shall issue a public notice of the filing of the application and may seek public review and comment on the director's determination that the transaction is exempt under subdivision (e).

(h) The director may approve or deny the material modification request, or approve the request with conditions necessary to satisfy the requirements of this section, taking into consideration any public comments submitted to the director.

(Amended by Stats. 1999, Ch. 525, Sec. 159. Effective January 1, 2000. Operative July 1, 2000, or sooner, by Sec. 214 of Ch. 525.)

1399.72.

(a) Any health care service plan that intends to convert from nonprofit to for-profit status, as defined in subdivision (b), shall, prior to the conversion, secure approval from the director.

(b) For the purposes of this section, a "conversion" or "convert" by a nonprofit health care service plan means the transformation of the plan from nonprofit to for-profit status, as determined by the director.

(c) Prior to approving a conversion, the director shall find that the conversion proposal meets all of the following charitable trust requirements:

(1) The fair market value of the nonprofit plan is set aside for appropriate charitable purposes. In determining fair market value, the director shall consider, but not be bound by, any market-based information available concerning the plan.

(2) The set-aside shall be dedicated and transferred to one or more existing or new tax-exempt charitable organizations operating pursuant to Section 501(c)(3) (26 U.S.C.A. Sec. 501(c)(3)) of the federal Internal Revenue Code. The director shall consider requiring that a portion of the set-aside include equity ownership in the plan. Further, the director may authorize the use of a federal Internal Revenue Code Section 501(c)(4) organization (26 U.S.C.A. Sec. 501(c)(4)) if, in the director's view, it is necessary to ensure effective management and monetization of equity ownership in the plan and if the plan agrees that the Section 501(c)(4) organization will be limited exclusively to these functions, that funds generated by the monetization shall be transferred to the Section 501(c)(3) organization except to the extent necessary to fund the level of activity of the Section 501(c)(4) organization as may be necessary to preserve the organization's tax status, that no funds or other resources controlled by the Section 501(c)(4) organization shall be expended for campaign contributions, lobbying, or other political activities, and that the Section 501(c)(4) organization shall comply with reporting requirements that are applicable to Section 501(c)(3) organizations, and that the 501(c)(4) organization shall be subject to any other requirements imposed upon 501(c)(3) organizations that the director determines to be appropriate.

(3) Each 501(c)(3) or 501(c)(4) organization receiving a set-aside, its directors and officers, and its assets including any plan stock, shall be independent of any influence or control by the health care service plan and its directors, officers, subsidiaries, or affiliates.

(4) The charitable mission and grant-making functions of the charitable organization receiving any set-aside shall be dedicated to serving the health care needs of the people of California.

(5) Every 501(c)(3) or 501(c)(4) organization that receives a set-aside under this section shall have in place procedures and policies to prohibit conflicts of interest, including those associated with grant-making activities that may benefit the plan, including the directors, officers, subsidiaries, or affiliates of the plan.

(6) Every 501(c)(3) or 501(c)(4) organization that receives a set-aside under this section shall demonstrate that its directors and officers have sufficient experience and judgment to administer grant-making and other charitable activities to serve the state's health care needs.

(7) Every 501(c)(3) or 501(c)(4) organization that receives a set-aside under this section shall provide the director and the Attorney General with an annual report that includes a detailed description of its grant-making and other charitable activities related to its use of the set-aside received from the health care service plan. The annual report shall be made available by the director and the Attorney General for public inspection, notwithstanding the California Public Records Act (Chapter 3.5 (commencing with Section 6250) of Division 7 of Title 1 of the Government Code). Each organization shall submit the annual report for its immediately preceding fiscal year within 120 days after the close of that fiscal year. When requested by the director or the Attorney General, the organization shall promptly supplement the report to include any additional information that the director or the Attorney General deems necessary to ascertain compliance with this article.

(8) The plan has satisfied the requirements of this chapter, and a disciplinary action pursuant to Section 1386 is not warranted against the plan.

(d) The plan shall not file any forms or documents required by the Secretary of State in connection with any conversion or restructuring until the plan has received an order of the director approving the conversion or restructuring, or unless authorized to do so by the director.

(Amended by Stats. 1999, Ch. 525, Sec. 160. Effective January 1, 2000. Operative July 1, 2000, or sooner, by Sec. 214 of Ch. 525.)

1399.73.

(a) An application for a conversion or restructuring shall contain the information the director may require, by rule or order.

(b) The director shall charge a health care service plan an application filing fee. The fee for filing an application shall be the actual cost of processing the application, including the overhead costs. The filing fee shall include the costs of undertaking the activities described in subdivisions (c), (d), and (e) of Section 1399.74.

(c) The director may contract with experts or consultants to assist the director in reviewing the application. Contract costs shall not exceed an amount that is reasonable and necessary to review the application. Any contract entered into under this subdivision shall be on a noncompetitive bid basis and shall be exempt from Chapter 2 (commencing with Section 10290) of Part 2 of Division 2 of the Public Contract Code. The applicant shall promptly pay the director, upon request, for all contract costs.

(Amended by Stats. 1999, Ch. 525, Sec. 161. Effective January 1, 2000. Operative July 1, 2000, or sooner, by Sec. 214 of Ch. 525.)

1399.74.

(a) By July 1, 1996, the director shall adopt regulations, on an emergency basis, that specify the application procedures and requirements for the restructuring or conversion of nonprofit health care service plans. This subdivision shall not be construed to limit or otherwise restrict the director's authority to adopt regulations under Section 1344, including, but not limited to, any additional regulations to implement this article.

(b) Upon receiving an application to restructure or convert, the director shall publish a notice in one or more newspapers of general circulation in the plan's service area describing the name of the applicant, the nature of the application, and the date of receipt of the application. The notice shall indicate that the director will be soliciting public comments and will hold a public hearing on the application. The director shall require the plan to publish a written notice concerning the application pursuant to conditions imposed by rule or order.

(c) Any applications, reports, plans, or other documents under this article shall be public records, subject to the California Public Records Act (Chapter 3.5 (commencing with Section 6250) of Division 7 of Title 1 of the Government Code) and regulations adopted by the director thereunder. The director shall provide the public with prompt and reasonable access to public records relating to the restructuring and conversion of health care service plans. Access to public records covered by this section shall be made available no later than one month prior to any solicitation for public comments or public hearing scheduled pursuant to this article.

(d) Prior to approving any conversion or restructuring, the director shall solicit public comments in written form and shall hold at least one public hearing concerning the plan's proposal to comply with the set- aside and other conditions required under this article.

(e) The director may disapprove any application to restructure or convert if the application does not meet the requirements of this chapter or of the Nonprofit Corporation Law (Div. 2 (commencing with Sec. 5000), Title 1, Corp. C.), including any requirements imposed by rule or order of the director.

(Amended by Stats. 1999, Ch. 525, Sec. 162. Effective January 1, 2000. Operative July 1, 2000, or sooner, by Sec. 214 of Ch. 525.)

1399.75.

(a) This article shall apply to the restructuring or conversion of nonprofit mutual benefit health care service plans to the extent these plans have held or currently hold assets subject to a charitable trust obligation, as determined by the director.

(b) Nonprofit mutual benefit health care service plans that do not have, or have only a partial, charitable trust obligation, and that intend to convert or restructure their activities shall, prior to the conversion or restructuring, secure approval from the director.

(c) Prior to approving a mutual benefit health care service plan restructuring or conversion under subdivision (b), the director shall find that the plan has complied with its noncharitable obligations including, but not limited to, any obligations set forth in its articles of incorporation regarding the dedication and distribution of assets.

(d) The director, in carrying out the department's responsibilities under subdivision (c), may apply, to the extent appropriate in each case as determined by the director, the beneficiary protections authorized in this act, including, but not limited to, protections concerning the fair market value of assets, the avoidance of conflicts of interest, and the avoidance of undue influence or control, with respect to a mutual benefit plan's proposed disposition of assets.

(e) Nothing in this section shall be construed to limit the director's, Attorney General's, or a court's authority under existing law to impose charitable trust obligations upon any or all of the assets of a mutual benefit corporation or otherwise treat a mutual benefit corporation in the same manner as a public benefit corporation.

(Amended by Stats. 1999, Ch. 525, Sec. 163. Effective January 1, 2000. Operative July 1, 2000, or sooner, by Sec. 214 of Ch. 525.)

1399.76.

This article shall not apply to a nonprofit health care service plan restructure or conversion that has been submitted as a material modification to the department for review and approval prior to May 16, 1995.

(Added by Stats. 1995, Ch. 792, Sec. 1. Effective January 1, 1996.)

ARTICLE 11.1. Consumer Operated and Oriented Plans [1399.80 - 1399.88]
(Article 11.1 added by Stats. 2012, Ch. 859, Sec. 2.)

1399.80.

For purposes of this article, the following definitions shall apply:

(a) "Consumer operated and oriented plan" means a nonprofit member organization or nonprofit member corporation that has been established consistent with the requirements of Section 1322 of PPACA and Subpart F (commencing with Section 156.500) of Part 156 of Subchapter B of Subtitle A of Title 45 of the Code of Federal Regulations and remains in full compliance with those requirements. A consumer operated and oriented plan shall also be known as a "CO-OP."

(b) "Formation board" means the initial board of directors of a CO-OP before it has begun accepting enrollment and had an election by the members of the CO-OP to the board of directors.

(c) "Member" includes all individuals, including dependents, 18 years of age or older covered under health care service plan contracts issued by the CO-OP health care service plan.

(d) "Operational board" means the board of directors elected by the members of the CO-OP after it has begun accepting enrollment under its health care service plan contracts.

(e) "PPACA" means the federal Patient Protection and Affordable Care Act (Public Law 111-148), as amended by the Health Care and Education Reconciliation Act of 2010 (Public Law 111-152), and any rules or regulations issued thereunder.

(f) "Nonprofit member organization" or "nonprofit member corporation" means a nonprofit public benefit corporation organized under Part 2 (commencing with Section 5110) of Division 2 of Title 1 of the Corporations Code, a nonprofit mutual benefit corporation organized under Part 3 (commencing with Section 7110) of Division 2 of Title 1 of the Corporations Code, or a similar entity organized under applicable provisions of the Corporations Code, or in the case of a foreign corporation, a nonprofit public benefit corporation, a mutual benefit corporation, or a similar entity organized under nonprofit laws in a state other than California.

(g) "Solvency loan" means a loan provided by the federal Centers for Medicare and Medicaid Services to a nonprofit member organization or nonprofit member corporation seeking to become licensed as a CO-OP health care service plan, to be used to assist in meeting the state's fiscal soundness and solvency requirements.

(h) "Start-up loan" means a loan provided by the federal Centers for Medicare and Medicaid Services to a nonprofit member organization or nonprofit member corporation seeking to become licensed as a CO-OP health care service plan, to be used for allowed expenses associated with establishing a CO-OP, as further specified by PPACA.

(Added by Stats. 2012, Ch. 859, Sec. 2. (AB 1846) Effective January 1, 2013.)

1399.81.

The director shall have the authority to issue a license to act as a health care service plan to a CO-OP that has been organized as a nonprofit member organization or nonprofit member corporation under the laws of this state. The director may also issue a license to act as a health care service plan to a foreign CO-OP that has been organized as a nonprofit member organization or nonprofit member corporation under the laws of another state, provided that the entity meets the requirements governing CO-OPs under PPACA and this article. A CO-OP seeking or maintaining a license pursuant to this article shall be subject to the same fees that are imposed on other health care service plans pursuant to Article 3 (commencing with Section 1349).

(Added by Stats. 2012, Ch. 859, Sec. 2. (AB 1846) Effective January 1, 2013.)

1399.83.

(a) A domestic or foreign CO-OP licensed as a health care service plan pursuant to this article shall be subject to all of the provisions of this chapter and all applicable rules and regulations of the director, including, but not limited to, the general provisions governing the issuance of a license in Article 3 (commencing with Section 1349), the operation and renewal provisions in Article 6 (commencing with Section 1375), and the financial responsibility requirements in Article 9 (commencing with Section 1300.75) of Chapter 2 of Division 1 of Title 28 of the California Code of Regulations.

(b) In compliance with Section 1322(c)(5) of PPACA (42 U.S.C. Sec. 18042(c)(5)), and any rules or regulations issued under that section, a domestic or foreign CO-OP licensed as a health care service plan shall be subject to any state laws that do not prevent the application of requirements under PPACA.

(Added by Stats. 2012, Ch. 859, Sec. 2. (AB 1846) Effective January 1, 2013.)

1399.84.

The director may request any documentation relating to a CO-OP's start-up loan or solvency loan.

(Added by Stats. 2012, Ch. 859, Sec. 2. (AB 1846) Effective January 1, 2013.)

1399.86.

(a) A CO-OP shall be subject at all times to the prohibitions in PPACA against converting or selling to a for-profit or nonconsumer-operated entity at any time after receiving a solvency loan.

(b) A CO-OP shall do all of the following, in addition to any other requirements imposed under Section 156.515 of Title 45 of the Code of Federal Regulations:

(1) Implement policies and procedures to foster and ensure member control of the organization. For purposes of this paragraph, a CO-OP shall meet the following requirements:

(A) The CO-OP shall have governing documents that incorporate governing rules that ensure that the directors of the operational board are elected by a majority vote of a quorum of the CO-OP members.

(B) All members of the CO-OP shall be eligible to vote for each director on the CO-OP's operational board.

(C) Each member of the CO-OP shall have one vote in the election of each director of the CO-OP's operational board.

(D) The first elected directors of the CO-OP's operational board shall be elected no later than one year after the effective date on which the CO-OP provides coverage to its first member; the entire operational board shall be elected no later than two years after the same date.

(E) Elections of the directors on the CO-OP's operational board shall be contested so that the total number of candidates for vacant positions on the operational board exceeds the number of vacant positions, except in cases where a seat is vacated midterm due to death, resignation, or removal.

(F) A majority of the voting directors on the operational board shall be members of the CO-OP.

(2) Have an operational board of directors that meets the following requirements:

(A) Each director shall have one vote unless he or she is a nonvoting director.

(B) Positions on the board of directors may be designated for individuals with specialized expertise, experience, or affiliation (for example, providers, employers, including small business consortia, and unions); however, those positions shall not constitute a majority of the operational board even if the individuals in those positions are also members of the CO-OP.

(C) (i) No representative of any federal, state, or local government, or of any political subdivision or instrumentality thereof, and no representative of any organization described in Section 156.510(b)(1)(i) of Title 45 of the Code of Federal Regulations may serve as staff of the CO-OP or on the CO-OP's formation board or operational board.

(ii) No board member or staff of the CO-OP shall enter into an agreement or transaction that would jeopardize member control as required by Section 156.515 of Title 45 of the Code of Federal Regulations. A board member or staff of the CO-OP shall only enter in arm's length transactions as described in Section 156.510(b)(2)(ii) of Title 45 of the Code of Federal Regulations.

(3) Have governing documents that incorporate ethics, conflict of interest, and disclosure standards. These standards shall protect against health care coverage industry involvement and interference. In addition, these standards shall ensure that each director acts in the sole interest of the CO-OP, its members, and its local geographic community, as appropriate, and acts consistently with the terms of the CO-OP's governance documents and applicable state and federal law. At a minimum, these standards shall include the following:

(A) A mechanism to identify potential ethical or other conflicts of interest.

(B) A duty on the CO-OP's executive officers and directors to publicly disclose all potential conflicts of interest pursuant to the same standards required for state boards or commissions.

(C) A process to determine the extent to which a conflict exists.

(D) A process to address any conflict of interest.

(E) A process to be followed in the event a director or executive officer of the CO-OP violates the standards described in this paragraph.

(Added by Stats. 2012, Ch. 859, Sec. 2. (AB 1846) Effective January 1, 2013.)

1399.88.

In addition to any applicable requirements in this chapter for maintaining a license, a CO-OP is required at all times to be in full compliance with the requirements of PPACA governing CO-OPs. The department may request the federal government's certification that a CO-OP is in compliance with the requirements of PPACA governing CO-OPs, as well as the status of the CO-OP's compliance with its obligations under any loan or loan modification agreement.

(Added by Stats. 2012, Ch. 859, Sec. 2. (AB 1846) Effective January 1, 2013.)

ARTICLE 11.5. Individual Access to Contracts for Health Care Services [1399.801 - 1399.818]

(Heading of Article 11.5 renumbered from Article 10.5 by Stats. 2001, Ch. 159, Sec. 126.)

1399.801.

As used in this article:

(a) "Creditable coverage" means:

(1) Any individual or group policy, contract, or program that is written or administered by a disability insurer, health care service plan, fraternal benefits society, self-insured employer plan, or any other entity, in this state or elsewhere, and that arranges or provides medical, hospital, and surgical coverage not designed to supplement other plans. The term includes continuation or conversion coverage but does not include accident only, credit, disability income, Medicare supplement, long-term care, dental, vision, coverage issued as a supplement to liability insurance, insurance arising out of a workers' compensation or similar law, automobile medical payment insurance, or insurance under which benefits are payable with or without regard to fault and that is statutorily required to be contained in any liability insurance policy or equivalent self-insurance.

(2) The federal Medicare program pursuant to Title XVIII of the Social Security Act.

(3) The medicaid program pursuant to Title XIX of the Social Security Act.

(4) Any other publicly sponsored program, provided in this state or elsewhere, of medical, hospital, and surgical care.

(5) 10 U.S.C.A. Chapter 55 (commencing with Section 1071) (CHAMPUS).

(6) A medical care program of the Indian Health Service or of a tribal organization.

(7) A state health benefits risk pool.

(8) A health plan offered under 5 U.S.C.A. Chapter 89 (commencing with Section 8901) (FEHBP).

(9) A public health plan as defined in federal regulations authorized by Section 2701(c)(1)(I) of the Public Health Service Act, as amended by Public Law 104-191, the Health Insurance Portability and Accountability Act of 1996.

(10) A health benefit plan under 22 U.S.C.A. 2504(e) of the Peace Corps Act.

(b) "Dependent" means the spouse or child of an eligible individual or other individual applying for coverage, subject to applicable terms of the health care plan contract covering the eligible person.

(c) "Federally eligible defined individual" means an individual who as of the date on which the individual seeks coverage under this part, (1) has 18 or more months of creditable coverage, and whose most recent prior creditable coverage was under a group health plan, a federal governmental plan maintained for federal employees, or a governmental plan or church plan as defined in the federal Employee Retirement Income Security Act of 1974 (29 U.S.C. Sec. 1002), (2) is not eligible for coverage under a group health plan, Medicare, or Medi-Cal, and has no other health insurance coverage, (3) was not terminated from his or her most recent creditable coverage due to nonpayment of premiums or fraud, and (4) if offered continuation coverage under COBRA or Cal-COBRA, had elected and exhausted this coverage.

(d) "In force business" means an existing health benefit plan contract issued by the plan to a federally eligible defined individual.

(e) "New business" means a health care service plan contract issued to an eligible individual that is not the plan's in force business.

(f) "Preexisting condition provision" means a contract provision that excludes coverage for charges and expenses incurred during a specified period following the eligible individual's effective date, as to a condition for which medical advice, diagnosis, and care of treatment was recommended or received during a specified period immediately preceding the effective date of coverage.

(Added by Stats. 2000, Ch. 810, Sec. 2. Effective January 1, 2001.)

1399.802.

(a) Every health care service plan offering plan contracts to individuals shall, in addition to complying with the provisions of this chapter and the rules adopted thereunder, comply with the provisions of this article.

(b) For the purposes of determining eligibility for small employer coverage, a sole proprietor and the sole proprietor's spouse are not employees with respect to a sole proprietorship that consists only of the sole proprietor and the sole proprietor's spouse. A partner and a partner's spouse are not employees of a partnership that consists solely of partners and their spouses. Employer group health care service plans shall not be issued, marketed, or sold to a sole proprietorship or partnership without employees directly or indirectly through any arrangement. Only individual health care service plans shall be sold to any entity without employees.

(Amended by Stats. 2018, Ch. 700, Sec. 5. (SB 1375) Effective January 1, 2019.)

1399.803.

Nothing in this article shall be construed to preclude the application of this chapter to either of the following: (a) an association, trust, or other organization acting as a health care service plan as defined under Section 1345, or (b) an association, trust, multiple employer welfare arrangement, or other organization or person presenting information regarding a health care service plan to persons who may be interested in subscribing or enrolling in the plan.

(Added by Stats. 2000, Ch. 810, Sec. 2. Effective January 1, 2001.)

1399.804.

(a) Commencing January 1, 2001, a plan shall fairly and affirmatively offer, market, and sell the health care service plan contracts described in subdivision (d) of Section 1366.35 that are sold to individuals or to associations that include individuals to all federally eligible defined individuals in each service area in which the plan provides or arranges for the provision of health care services. Each plan shall make available to each federally eligible defined individual the identified health care service plan contracts which the plan offers and sells to individuals or to associations that include individuals.

(b) The plan may not reject an application from a federally eligible defined individual for a health care service plan contract under the following circumstances:

(1) The federally eligible defined individual as defined by subdivision (c) of Section 1399.801 agrees to make the required premium payments.

(2) The federally eligible defined individual, and his or her dependents who are to be covered by the plan contract, work or reside in the service area in which the plan provides or otherwise arranges for the provision of health care services.

(c) No plan or solicitor shall, directly or indirectly, encourage or direct federally eligible defined individuals to refrain from filing an application for coverage with a plan because of health status, claims experience, industry, occupation, receipt of health care, genetic information, evidence of insurability, including conditions arising out of acts of domestic violence, disability, or geographic location provided that it is within the plan's approved service area.

(d) No plan shall, directly or indirectly, enter into any contract, agreement, or arrangement with a solicitor that provides for or results in the compensation paid to a solicitor for the sale of a health care service plan contract to be varied because of health status, claims experience, industry, occupation, receipt of health care, genetic information, evidence of insurability, including conditions arising out of acts of domestic violence, disability, or geographic location of the individual.

(e) Each plan shall comply with the requirements of Section 1374.3.

(Added by Stats. 2000, Ch. 810, Sec. 2. Effective January 1, 2001.)

1399.805.

(a) (1) After the federally eligible defined individual submits a completed application form for a plan contract, the plan shall, within 30 days, notify the individual of the individual's actual premium charges for that plan contract, unless the plan has provided notice of the premium charge prior to the application being filed. In no case shall the premium charged for any health care service plan contract identified in subdivision (d) of Section 1366.35 exceed the following amounts:

(A) For health care service plan contracts that offer services through a preferred provider arrangement, the average premium paid by a subscriber of the Major Risk Medical Insurance Program who is of the same age and resides in the same geographic area as the federally eligible defined individual. However, for a federally eligible defined individual who is between the ages of 60 and 64 years, inclusive, the premium shall not exceed the average premium paid by a subscriber of the Major Risk Medical Insurance Program who is 59 years of age and resides in the same geographic area as the federally eligible defined individual.

(B) For health care service plan contracts identified in subdivision (d) of Section 1366.35 that do not offer services through a preferred provider arrangement, 170 percent of the standard premium charged to an individual who is of the same age and resides in the same geographic area as the federally eligible defined individual. However, for a federally eligible defined individual who is between the ages of 60 and 64 years, inclusive, the premium shall not exceed 170 percent of the standard premium charged to an individual who is 59 years of age and resides in the same geographic area as the federally eligible defined individual. The individual shall have 30 days in which to exercise the right to buy coverage at the quoted premium rates.

(2) A plan may adjust the premium based on family size, not to exceed the following amounts:

(A) For health care service plans that offer services through a preferred provider arrangement, the average of the Major Risk Medical Insurance Program rate for families of the same size that reside in the same geographic area as the federally eligible defined individual.

(B) For health care service plans identified in subdivision (d) of Section 1366.35 that do not offer services through a preferred provider arrangement, 170 percent of the standard premium charged to a family that is of the same size and resides in the same geographic area as the federally eligible defined individual.

(3) This subdivision shall become inoperative on January 1, 2014. This subdivision shall become operative on January 1, 2020.

(b) (1) After the federally eligible defined individual submits a completed application form for a plan contract, the plan shall, within 30 days, notify the individual of the individual's actual premium charges for that plan contract, unless the plan has provided notice of the premium charge prior to the application being filed. In no case shall the premium charged for any health care service plan contract identified in subdivision (d) of Section 1366.35 exceed the following amounts:

(A) With respect to the rate charged for coverage provided in 2014, the rate charged in 2013 for that coverage multiplied by 1.09.

(B) With respect to the rate charged for coverage provided in 2015 and each subsequent year, the rate charged in the prior year multiplied by a factor of one plus the percentage change in the statewide average premium for the second lowest cost silver plan offered on the Exchange. The Exchange shall determine the percentage change in the statewide average premium for the second lowest cost silver plan by subtracting clause (i) from clause (ii) and dividing the result by clause (i).

(i) The average of the premiums charged in the year prior to the applicable year for the second lowest cost silver plan in all 19 rating regions, with the premium for each region weighted based on the region's relative share of the Exchange's total individual enrollment according to the latest data available to the Exchange.

(ii) The average of the premiums to be charged in the applicable year for the second lowest cost silver plan in all 19 rating regions, with the premium for each region weighted based on the region's relative share of the Exchange's total individual enrollment according to the latest data available to the Exchange.

(C) The Exchange shall determine the percentage change in the statewide average premium no later than 30 days after the Exchange's rates for individual coverage for the applicable year have been finalized.

(2) For purposes of this subdivision, "Exchange" means the California Health Benefit Exchange established pursuant to Section 100500 of the Government Code.

(3) This subdivision shall become operative on January 1, 2014. This subdivision shall become inoperative on January 1, 2020.

(c) When a federally eligible defined individual submits a premium payment, based on the quoted premium charges, and that payment is delivered or postmarked, whichever occurs earlier, within the first 15 days of the month, coverage shall begin no later than the first day of the following month. When that payment is neither delivered or postmarked until after the 15th day of a month, coverage shall become effective no later than the first day of the second month following delivery or postmark of the payment.

(d) During the first 30 days after the effective date of the plan contract, the individual shall have the option of changing coverage to a different plan contract offered by the same health care service plan. If the individual notified the plan of the change within the first 15 days of a month, coverage under the new plan contract shall become effective no later than the first day of the following month. If an enrolled individual notified the plan of the change after the 15th day of a month, coverage under the new plan contract shall become effective no later than the first day of the second month following notification.

(e) (1) On and after January 1, 2014, and except as provided in paragraph (2), this section shall apply only to individual grandfathered health plan contracts previously issued pursuant to this section to federally eligible defined individuals.

(2) If Section 5000A of the Internal Revenue Code, as added by Section 1501 of PPACA, is repealed or amended to no longer apply to the individual market, as defined in Section 2791 of the federal Public Health Service Act (42 U.S.C. Section 300gg-91), paragraph (1) shall become inoperative on the date of that repeal or amendment and this section shall apply to health care service plan contracts issued, amended, or renewed on or after that date.

(3) For purposes of this subdivision, the following definitions apply:

(A) "Grandfathered health plan" has the same meaning as that term is defined in Section 1251 of PPACA.

(B) "PPACA" means the federal Patient Protection and Affordable Care Act (Public Law 111-148), as amended by the federal Health Care Education and Reconciliation Act of 2010 (Public Law 111-152), and any rules, regulations, or guidance issued pursuant to that law.

(Amended by Stats. 2013, Ch. 441, Sec. 9. (AB 1180) Effective October 1, 2013.)

1399.806.

A plan may not exclude any federally eligible defined individual, or his or her dependents, who would otherwise be entitled to health care services on the basis of an actual or expected health condition of that individual or dependent. No plan contract may limit or exclude coverage for a specific federally eligible defined individual, or his or her dependents, by type of illness, treatment, medical condition, or accident.

(Added by Stats. 2000, Ch. 810, Sec. 2. Effective January 1, 2001.)

1399.809.

The director may require a plan to discontinue the offering of contracts or the acceptance of applications from any individual upon a determination by the director that the plan does not have sufficient financial viability, organization, and administrative capacity to assure the delivery of health care services to its enrollees. In determining whether the conditions of this section have been met, the director shall consider, but not be limited to, the plan's compliance with the requirements of Section 1367, Article 6 (commencing with Section 1375), and the rules adopted thereunder.

(Added by Stats. 2000, Ch. 810, Sec. 2. Effective January 1, 2001.)

1399.810.

All health care service plan contracts offered to a federally eligible defined individual shall be renewable with respect to the individual and dependents at the option of the contractholder except in cases of:

(a) Nonpayment of the required premiums.

(b) Fraud or misrepresentation by the contractholder.

(c) The plan ceases to provide or arrange for the provision of health care services for individual health care service plan contracts in this state, provided, however, that the following conditions are satisfied:

(1) Notice of the decision to cease new or existing individual health benefit plans in this state is provided to the director and to the contractholder.

(2) Individual health care service plan contracts subject to this chapter shall not be canceled for 180 days after the date of the notice required under paragraph (1) and for that business of a plan that remains in force, any plan that ceases to offer for sale new individual health care service plan contracts shall continue to be governed by this article with respect to business conducted under this article.

(3) A plan that ceases to write new individual business in this state after January 1, 2001, shall be prohibited from offering for sale new individual health care service plan contracts in this state for a period of three years from the date of the notice to the director.

(d) When the plan withdraws a health care service plan contract from the individual market, provided that the plan makes available to eligible individuals all plan contracts that it makes available to new individual business, and provided that the premium for the new plan contract complies with the renewal increase requirements set forth in Section 1399.811.

(e) (1) On and after January 1, 2014, and except as provided in paragraph (2), this section shall apply only to individual grandfathered health plan contracts previously issued pursuant to this section to federally eligible defined individuals.

(2) If Section 5000A of the Internal Revenue Code, as added by Section 1501 of PPACA, is repealed or amended to no longer apply to the individual market, as defined in Section 2791 of the federal Public Health Service Act (42 U.S.C. Section 300gg-91), paragraph (1) shall become inoperative on the date of that repeal or amendment and this section shall apply to health care service plan contracts issued, amended, or renewed on or after that date.

(3) For purposes of this subdivision, the following definitions apply:

(A) "Grandfathered health plan" has the same meaning as that term is defined in Section 1251 of PPACA.

(B) "PPACA" means the federal Patient Protection and Affordable Care Act (Public Law 111-148), as amended by the federal Health Care Education and Reconciliation Act of 2010 (Public Law 111-152), and any rules, regulations, or guidance issued pursuant to that law.

(Amended by Stats. 2013, Ch. 441, Sec. 10. (AB 1180) Effective October 1, 2013.)

1399.811.

(a) (1) Premiums for contracts offered, delivered, amended, or renewed by plans on or after January 1, 2001, shall be subject to the following requirements:

(A) The premium for new business for a federally eligible defined individual shall not exceed the following amounts:

(i) For health care service plan contracts identified in subdivision (d) of Section 1366.35 that offer services through a preferred provider arrangement, the average premium paid by a subscriber of the Major Risk Medical Insurance Program who is of the same age and resides in the same geographic area as the federally eligible defined individual. However, for federally eligible defined individuals who are between the ages of 60 to 64 years, inclusive, the premium shall not exceed the average premium paid by a subscriber of the Major Risk Medical Insurance Program who is 59 years of age and resides in the same geographic area as the federally eligible defined individual.

(ii) For health care service plan contracts identified in subdivision (d) of Section 1366.35 that do not offer services through a preferred provider arrangement, 170 percent of the standard premium charged to an individual who is of the same age and resides in the same geographic area as the federally eligible defined individual. However, for federally eligible defined individuals who are between the ages of 60 to 64 years, inclusive, the premium shall not exceed 170 percent of the standard premium charged to an individual who is 59 years of age and resides in the same geographic area as the federally eligible defined individual.

(B) The premium for in force business for a federally eligible defined individual shall not exceed the following amounts:

(i) For health care service plan contracts identified in subdivision (d) of Section 1366.35 that offer services through a preferred provider arrangement, the average premium paid by a subscriber of the Major Risk Medical Insurance Program who is of the same age and resides in the same geographic area as the federally eligible defined individual. However, for federally eligible defined individuals who are between the ages of 60 and 64 years, inclusive, the premium shall not exceed the average premium paid by a subscriber of the Major Risk Medical Insurance Program who is 59 years of age and resides in the same geographic area as the federally eligible defined individual.

(ii) For health care service plan contracts identified in subdivision (d) of Section 1366.35 that do not offer services through a preferred provider arrangement, 170 percent of the standard premium charged to an individual who is of the same age and resides in the same geographic area as the federally eligible defined individual. However, for federally eligible defined individuals who are between the ages of 60 and 64 years, inclusive, the premium shall not exceed 170 percent of the standard premium charged to an individual who is 59 years of age and resides in the same geographic area as the federally eligible defined individual. The premium effective on January 1, 2001, shall apply to in force business at the earlier of either the time of renewal or July 1, 2001.

(2) This subdivision shall become inoperative on January 1, 2014. This subdivision shall become operative on January 1, 2020.

(b) (1) Premiums for contracts offered, delivered, amended, or renewed by plans on or after January 1, 2014, shall be subject to the following requirements:

(A) With respect to the rate charged for coverage provided in 2014, the rate charged in 2013 for that coverage multiplied by 1.09.

(B) With respect to the rate charged for coverage provided in 2015 and each subsequent year, the rate charged in the prior year multiplied by a factor of one plus the percentage change in the statewide average premium for the second lowest cost silver plan offered on the Exchange. The Exchange shall determine the percentage change in the statewide average premium for the second lowest cost silver plan by subtracting clause (i) from clause (ii) and dividing the result by clause (i).

(i) The average of the premiums charged in the year prior to the applicable year for the second lowest cost silver plan in all 19 rating regions, with the premium for each region weighted based on the region's relative share of the Exchange's total individual enrollment according to the latest data available to the Exchange.

(ii) The average of the premiums to be charged in the applicable year for the second lowest cost silver plan in all 19 rating regions, with the premium for each region weighted based on the region's relative share of the Exchange's total individual enrollment according to the latest data available to the Exchange.

(C) The Exchange shall determine the percentage change in the statewide average premium no later than 30 days after the Exchange's rates for individual coverage for the applicable year have been finalized.

(2) For purposes of this subdivision, "Exchange" means the California Health Benefit Exchange established pursuant to Section 100500 of the Government Code.

(3) This subdivision shall become operative on January 1, 2014. This subdivision shall become inoperative on January 1, 2020.

(c) The premium applied to a federally eligible defined individual may not increase by more than the following amounts:

(1) For health care service plan contracts identified in subdivision (d) of Section 1366.35 that offer services through a preferred provider arrangement, the average increase in the premiums charged to a subscriber of the Major Risk Medical Insurance Program who is of the same age and resides in the same geographic area as the federally eligible defined individual.

(2) For health care service plan contracts identified in subdivision (d) of Section 1366.35 that do not offer services through a preferred provider arrangement, the increase in premiums charged to a nonfederally eligible defined individual who is of the same age and resides in the same geographic area as the federally eligible defined individual. The premium for an eligible individual may not be modified more frequently than every 12 months.

(3) For a contract that a plan has discontinued offering, the premium applied to the first rating period of the new contract that the federally eligible defined individual elects to purchase shall be no greater than the premium applied in the prior rating period to the discontinued contract.

(d) (1) On and after January 1, 2014, and except as provided in paragraph (2), this section shall apply only to individual grandfathered health plan contracts previously issued pursuant to this section to federally eligible defined individuals.

(2) If Section 5000A of the Internal Revenue Code, as added by Section 1501 of PPACA, is repealed or amended to no longer apply to the individual market, as defined in Section 2791 of the federal Public Health Service Act (42 U.S.C. Section 300gg-91), paragraph (1) shall become inoperative on the date of that repeal or amendment and this section shall apply to health care service plan contracts issued, amended, or renewed on or after that date.

(3) For purposes of this subdivision, the following definitions apply:

(A) "Grandfathered health plan" has the same meaning as that term is defined in Section 1251 of PPACA.

(B) "PPACA" means the federal Patient Protection and Affordable Care Act (Public Law 111-148), as amended by the federal Health Care Education and Reconciliation Act of 2010 (Public Law 111-152), and any rules, regulations, or guidance issued pursuant to that law.

(Amended by Stats. 2013, Ch. 441, Sec. 11. (AB 1180) Effective October 1, 2013.)
1399.812.

Plans shall apply premiums consistently with respect to all federally eligible defined individuals who apply for coverage.

(Added by Stats. 2000, Ch. 810, Sec. 2. Effective January 1, 2001.)
1399.813.

In connection with the offering for sale of any plan contract to an individual, each plan shall make a reasonable disclosure, as part of its solicitation and sales materials, of all individual contracts.

(Added by Stats. 2000, Ch. 810, Sec. 2. Effective January 1, 2001.)
1399.814.

Nothing in this article shall be construed to require a health benefit plan to offer a contract to an individual if the plan does not otherwise offer contracts to individuals.
(Added by Stats. 2000, Ch. 810, Sec. 2. Effective January 1, 2001.)
1399.815.

(a) At least 20 business days prior to renewing or amending a plan contract subject to this article, or at least 20 business days prior to the initial offering of a plan contract subject to this article, a plan shall file a notice of an amendment with the director in accordance with the provisions of Section 1352. The notice of an amendment shall include a statement certifying that the plan is in compliance with subdivision (a) of Section 1399.805 and with Section 1399.811. Any action by the director, as permitted under Section 1352, to disapprove, suspend, or postpone the plan's use of a plan contract shall be in writing, specifying the reasons the plan contract does not comply with the requirements of this chapter.

(b) Prior to making any changes in the premium, the plan shall file an amendment in accordance with the provisions of Section 1352, and shall include a statement certifying the plan is in compliance with subdivision (a) of Section 1399.805 and with Section 1399.811. All other changes to a plan contract previously filed with the director pursuant to subdivision (a) shall be filed as an amendment in accordance with the provisions of Section 1352, unless the change otherwise would require the filing of a material modification.

(c) (1) On and after January 1, 2014, and except as provided in paragraph (2), this section shall apply only to individual grandfathered health plan contracts previously issued pursuant to this section to federally eligible defined individuals.

(2) If Section 5000A of the Internal Revenue Code, as added by Section 1501 of PPACA, is repealed or amended to no longer apply to the individual market, as defined in Section 2791 of the federal Public Health Service Act (42 U.S.C. Section 300gg-91), paragraph (1) shall become inoperative on the date of that repeal or amendment and this section shall apply to plan contracts issued, amended, or renewed on or after that date.

(3) For purposes of this subdivision, the following definitions apply:

(A) "Grandfathered health plan" has the same meaning as that term is defined in Section 1251 of PPACA.

(B) "PPACA" means the federal Patient Protection and Affordable Care Act (Public Law 111-148), as amended by the federal Health Care Education and Reconciliation Act of 2010 (Public Law 111-152), and any rules, regulations, or guidance issued pursuant to that law.

(Amended by Stats. 2013, Ch. 441, Sec. 12. (AB 1180) Effective October 1, 2013.)
1399.817.

The director may issue regulations that are necessary to carry out the purposes of this article. Any rules and regulations adopted pursuant to this article may be adopted as emergency regulations in accordance with Chapter 3.5 (commencing with Section 11340) of Part 1 of Division 3 of Title 2 of the Government Code. Until December 31, 2001, the adoption of these regulations shall be deemed an emergency and necessary for the immediate preservation of the public peace, health and safety, or general welfare. The regulations shall be enforced by the director.

(Added by Stats. 2000, Ch. 810, Sec. 2. Effective January 1, 2001.)
1399.818.

This article shall apply to health care service plan contracts offered, delivered, amended, or renewed on or after January 1, 2001.

(Added by Stats. 2000, Ch. 810, Sec. 2. Effective January 1, 2001.)

ARTICLE 11.7. Child Access to Health Care Coverage [1399.825 - 1399.836]
(Heading of Article 11.7 amended by Stats. 2013, 1st Ex. Sess., Ch. 2, Sec. 15.)
1399.825.

As used in this article:

(a) "Child" means any individual under 19 years of age.

(b) "Individual grandfathered plan coverage" means health care coverage in which an individual was enrolled on March 23, 2010, consistent with Section 1251 of PPACA and any rules or regulations adopted pursuant to that law.

(c) "Initial open enrollment period" means the open enrollment period beginning on January 1, 2011, and ending 60 days thereafter.

(d) "Late enrollee" means a child without coverage who did not enroll in a health care service plan contract during an open enrollment period because of any of the following:

(1) The child lost dependent coverage due to termination or change in employment status of the child or the person through whom the child was covered; cessation of an

employer's contribution toward an employee or dependent's coverage; death of the person through whom the child was covered as a dependent; legal separation; divorce; loss of coverage under the Healthy Families Program, the Access for Infants and Mothers Program, or the Medi-Cal program; or adoption of the child.

(2) The child became a resident of California during a month that was not the child's birth month.

(3) The child is born as a resident of California and did not enroll in the month of birth.

(4) The child is mandated to be covered pursuant to a valid state or federal court order.

(e) "Open enrollment period" means the annual open enrollment period, subsequent to the initial open enrollment period, applicable to each individual child that is the month of the child's birth date.

(f) "PPACA" means the federal Patient Protection and Affordable Care Act (Public Law 111-148), as amended by the Health Care and Education Reconciliation Act of 2010 (Public Law 111-152), and any subsequent rules or regulations issued pursuant to that law.

(g) "Preexisting condition exclusion" means, with respect to coverage, a limitation or exclusion of benefits relating to a condition based on the fact that the condition was present before the date of enrollment of the coverage, whether or not any medical advice, diagnosis, care, or treatment was recommended or received before that date.

(h) "Responsible party for a child" means an adult having custody of the child or with responsibility for the financial needs of the child, including the responsibility to provide health care coverage.

(i) "Standard risk rate" means the lowest rate that can be offered for a child with the same benefit plan, effective date, age, geographic region, and family status.

(Added by Stats. 2010, Ch. 656, Sec. 3. (AB 2244) Effective January 1, 2011. Inoperative, pursuant to Section 1399.836, on January 1, 2014, subject to condition for resuming operation.)

1399.826.

(a) (1) During each open enrollment period, every health care service plan offering plan contracts in the individual market, other than individual grandfathered plan coverage, shall offer to the responsible party for a child coverage for the child that does not exclude or limit coverage due to any preexisting condition of the child.

(b) A health care service plan offering coverage in the individual market shall not reject an application for a health care service plan contract from a child or filed on behalf of a child by the responsible party during an open enrollment period or from a late enrollee during a period no longer than 63 days from the qualifying event listed in subdivision (d) of Section 1399.825.

(c) Except to the extent permitted by federal law, rules, regulations, or guidance issued by the relevant federal agency, a health care service plan shall not condition the issuance or offering of individual coverage on any of the following factors:

(1) Health status.

(2) Medical condition, including physical and mental illnesses.

(3) Claims experience.

(4) Receipt of health care.

(5) Medical history.

(6) Genetic information.

(7) Evidence of insurability, including conditions arising out of acts of domestic violence.

(8) Disability.

(9) Any other health status-related factor as determined by department.

This subdivision shall not apply to a contract providing individual grandfathered plan coverage.

(d) When a responsible party for a child submits a premium payment, based on the quoted premium charges, and that payment is delivered or postmarked, whichever occurs earlier, within the first 15 days of the month, coverage under the plan contract shall become effective no later than the first day of the following month. When that payment is neither delivered nor postmarked until after the 15th day of the month, coverage shall become effective no later than the first day of the second month following delivery or postmark of the payment.

(e) A health care service plan offering coverage in the individual market shall not reject the request of a responsible party for a child to include that child as a dependent on an existing health care service plan contract that includes dependent coverage during an open enrollment period.

(f) Nothing in this article shall be construed to prohibit a health care service plan offering coverage in the individual market from establishing rules for eligibility for coverage and offering coverage pursuant to those rules for children and individuals based on factors otherwise authorized under federal and state law for health plan contracts in addition to those offered on a guaranteed issue basis during an open enrollment period to children or late enrollees pursuant to this article. However, a health care service plan, other than a plan providing individual grandfathered plan coverage, shall not impose a preexisting condition provision on coverage, including dependent coverage, offered to a child.

(g) Nothing in this article shall be construed to require a plan to establish a new service area or to offer health coverage on a statewide basis, outside of the plan's existing service area.

(h) Nothing in this article shall be construed to prevent a health care service plan from offering coverage to a family member of an enrollee in grandfathered health plan coverage consistent with Section 1251 of PPACA.

(Added by Stats. 2010, Ch. 656, Sec. 3. (AB 2244) Effective January 1, 2011. Inoperative, pursuant to Section 1399.836, on January 1, 2014, subject to condition for resuming operation.)

1399.827.

This article shall not apply to health care service plan contracts for coverage of Medicare services pursuant to contracts with the United States government, Medicare supplement contracts, Medi-Cal contracts with the State Department of Health Care Services, plan contracts offered under the Healthy Families Program, long-term care coverage, or specialized health care service plan contracts.

(Added by Stats. 2010, Ch. 656, Sec. 3. (AB 2244) Effective January 1, 2011. Inoperative, pursuant to Section 1399.836, on January 1, 2014, subject to condition for resuming operation.)

1399.828.

(a) Upon the effective date of this article, a health care service plan shall fairly and affirmatively offer, market, and sell all of the plan's health care service plan contracts that are offered and sold to a child or the responsible party for a child in each service area in which the plan provides or arranges for the provision of health care services during any open enrollment period, to late enrollees, and during any other period in which state or federal law, rules, regulations, or guidance expressly provide that a health care service plan shall not condition offer or acceptance of coverage on any preexisting condition.

(b) No health care service plan or solicitor shall, directly or indirectly, engage in the following activities:

(1) Encourage or direct a child or responsible party for a child to refrain from filing an application for coverage with a plan because of the health status, claims experience, industry, occupation, or geographic location, provided that the location is within the plan's approved service area, of the child.

(2) Encourage or direct a child or responsible party for a child to seek coverage from another plan because of the health status, claims experience, industry, occupation, or geographic location, provided that the location is within the plan's approved service area, of the child.

(c) A health care service plan shall not, directly or indirectly, enter into any contract, agreement, or arrangement with a solicitor that provides for or results in the compensation paid to a solicitor for the sale of a health care service plan contract to be varied because of the health status, claims experience, industry, occupation, or geographic location of the child. This subdivision does not apply to a compensation arrangement that provides compensation to a solicitor on the basis of percentage of premium, provided that the percentage shall not vary because of the health status, claims experience, industry, occupation, or geographic area of the child.

(Added by Stats. 2010, Ch. 656, Sec. 3. (AB 2244) Effective January 1, 2011. Inoperative, pursuant to Section 1399.836, on January 1, 2014, subject to condition for resuming operation.)

1399.829.

(a) A health care service plan may use the following characteristics of an eligible child for purposes of establishing the rate of the plan contract for that child, where consistent with federal regulations under PPACA: age, geographic region, and family composition, plus the health care service plan contract selected by the child or the responsible party for the child.

(b) From the effective date of this article to December 31, 2013, inclusive, rates for a child applying for coverage shall be subject to the following limitations:

(1) During any open enrollment period or for late enrollees, the rate for any child due to health status shall not be more than two times the standard risk rate for a child.

(2) The rate for a child shall be subject to a 20-percent surcharge above the highest allowable rate on a child applying for coverage who is not a late enrollee and who failed to maintain coverage with any health care service plan or health insurer for the 90-day period prior to the date of the child's application. The surcharge shall apply for the 12-month period following the effective date of the child's coverage.

(3) If expressly permitted under PPACA and any rules, regulations, or guidance issued pursuant to that act, a health care service plan may rate a child based on health status during any period other than an open enrollment period if the child is not a late enrollee.

(4) If expressly permitted under PPACA and any rules, regulations, or guidance issued pursuant to that act, a health care service plan may condition an offer or acceptance of coverage on any preexisting condition or other health status-related factor for a period other than an open enrollment period and for a child who is not a late enrollee.

(c) For any individual health care service plan contract issued, sold, or renewed prior to December 31, 2013, the health plan shall provide to a child or responsible party for a child a notice that states the following:

"Please consider your options carefully before failing to maintain or renewing coverage for a child for whom you are responsible. If you attempt to obtain new individual coverage for that child, the premium for the same coverage may be higher than the premium you pay now."

(d) A child who applied for coverage between September 23, 2010, and the end of the initial open enrollment period shall be deemed to have maintained coverage during that period.

(e) Effective January 1, 2014, except for individual grandfathered health plan coverage, the rate for any child shall be identical to the standard risk rate.

(f) Health care service plans shall not require documentation from applicants relating to their coverage history.

(g) (1) On and after the operative date of the act adding this subdivision, and until January 1, 2014, a health care service plan shall provide the model notice, as provided in paragraph (3), to all applicants for coverage under this article and to all enrollees, or the responsible party for an enrollee, renewing coverage under this article that contains the following information:

(A) Information about the open enrollment period provided under Section 1399.849.

(B) An explanation that obtaining coverage during the open enrollment period described in Section 1399.849 will not affect the effective dates of coverage for coverage purchased pursuant to this article unless the applicant cancels that coverage.

(C) An explanation that coverage purchased pursuant to this article shall be effective as required under subdivision (d) of Section 1399.826 and that such coverage shall not prevent an applicant from obtaining new coverage during the open enrollment period described in Section 1399.849.

(D) Information about the Medi-Cal program, information about the Healthy Families Program if the Healthy Families Program is accepting enrollment, and information about subsidies available through the California Health Benefit Exchange.

(2) The notice described in paragraph (1) shall be in plain language and 14-point type.

(3) The department shall adopt a uniform model notice to be used by health care service plans in order to comply with this subdivision, and shall consult with the Department of Insurance in adopting that uniform model notice. Use of the model notice shall not require prior approval of the department. The model notice adopted by the department for purposes of this section shall not be subject to the Administrative Procedure Act (Chapter 3.5 (commencing with Section 11340) of Part 1 of Division 3 of Title 2 of the Government Code).

(Amended by Stats. 2013, 1st Ex. Sess., Ch. 2, Sec. 16. (SB 2 1x) Effective September 30, 2013. Inoperative, pursuant to Section 1399.836, on January 1, 2014, subject to condition for resuming operation.)

1399.832.

No health care service plan shall be required to offer a health care service plan contract or accept applications for the contract pursuant to this article in the case of any of the following:

(a) To a child, if the child who is to be covered by the plan contract does not work or reside within the plan's approved service areas.

(b) (1) Within a specific service area or portion of a service area, if the plan reasonably anticipates and demonstrates to the satisfaction of the director that it will not have sufficient health care delivery resources to ensure that health care services will be available and accessible to the child because of its obligations to existing enrollees.

(2) A health care service plan that cannot offer a health care service plan contract to individuals or children because it is lacking in sufficient health care delivery resources within a service area or a portion of a service area may not offer a contract in the area in which the plan is not offering coverage to individuals to new employer groups until the plan notifies the director that it has the ability to deliver services to individuals, and certifies to the director that from the date of the notice it will enroll all individuals requesting coverage in that area from the plan.

(3) Nothing in this article shall be construed to limit the director's authority to develop and implement a plan of rehabilitation for a health care service plan whose financial viability or organizational and administrative capacity has become impaired.

(Added by Stats. 2010, Ch. 656, Sec. 3. (AB 2244) Effective January 1, 2011. Inoperative, pursuant to Section 1399.836, on January 1, 2014, subject to condition for resuming operation.)

1399.833.

The director may require a health care service plan to discontinue the offering of contracts or acceptance of applications from any individual or child or responsible party for a child upon a determination by the director that the plan does not have sufficient financial viability or organizational and administrative capacity to ensure the delivery of health care services to its enrollees. In determining whether the conditions of this section have been met, the director shall consider, but not be limited to, the plan's compliance with the requirements of Section 1367, Article 6 (commencing with Section 1375.1), and the rules adopted under those provisions.

(Added by Stats. 2010, Ch. 656, Sec. 3. (AB 2244) Effective January 1, 2011. Inoperative, pursuant to Section 1399.836, on January 1, 2014, subject to condition for resuming operation.)

1399.834.

(a) All health care service plan contracts offered to a child or on behalf of a child to a responsible party for a child shall conform to the requirements of Sections 1365, 1366.3, and 1373.6, and shall be renewable at the option of the enrollee or responsible party for a child on behalf of the enrollee except as permitted to be canceled, rescinded, or not renewed pursuant to Section 1365.

(b) Any plan that ceases to offer for sale new individual health care service plan contracts pursuant to Section 1365 shall continue to be governed by this article with respect to business conducted under this article.

(c) Except as authorized under Section 1399.833, a plan that, as of the effective date of this article, does not write new health care service plan contracts for children in this state or that, after the effective date of this article, ceases to write new health care service plan contracts for children in this state shall be prohibited from offering for sale new individual health care service plan contracts in this state for a period of five years from the date of notice to the director.

(Amended by Stats. 2011, Ch. 296, Sec. 143. (AB 1023) Effective January 1, 2012. Inoperative, pursuant to Section 1399.836, on January 1, 2014, subject to condition for resuming operation.)

1399.835.

On or before July 1, 2011, the director may issue guidance to health plans regarding compliance with this article and that guidance shall not be subject to the Administrative Procedure Act (Chapter 3.5 (commencing with Section 11340) of Part 1 of Division 3 of Title 2 of the Government Code). The guidance shall only be effective until the director

and the Insurance Commissioner adopt joint regulations pursuant to the Administrative Procedure Act.

(Amended by Stats. 2011, Ch. 296, Sec. 144. (AB 1023) Effective January 1, 2012. Inoperative, pursuant to Section 1399.836, on January 1, 2014, subject to condition for resuming operation.)

1399.836.

(a) This article shall become inoperative on January 1, 2014, or the 91st calendar day following the adjournment of the 2013–14 First Extraordinary Session, whichever date is later.

(b) If Section 5000A of the Internal Revenue Code, as added by Section 1501 of PPACA, is repealed or amended to no longer apply to the individual market, as defined in Section 2791 of the federal Public Health Service Act (42 U.S.C. Sec. 300gg-91), this article shall become operative 12 months after the date of that repeal or amendment.

(Amended by Stats. 2015, Ch. 303, Sec. 266. (AB 731) Effective January 1, 2016. Note: This section provides for Article 11.7 (commencing with Section 1399.825) to become inoperative on January 1, 2014, and to resume operation later under certain conditions.)

ARTICLE 11.8. Individual Access to Health Care Coverage [1399.845 - 1399.864]

(Article 11.8 added by Stats. 2013, 1st Ex. Sess., Ch. 2, Sec. 18.)

1399.845.

For purposes of this article, the following definitions shall apply:

(a) "Child" means a child described in Section 22775 of the Government Code and subdivisions (n) to (p), inclusive, of Section 599.500 of Title 2 of the California Code of Regulations.

(b) "Dependent" means the spouse or registered domestic partner, or child, of an individual, subject to applicable terms of the health benefit plan.

(c) "Exchange" means the California Health Benefit Exchange created by Section 100500 of the Government Code.

(d) "Family" means the subscriber and his or her dependent or dependents.

(e) "Grandfathered health plan" has the same meaning as that term is defined in Section 1251 of PPACA.

(f) "Health benefit plan" means any individual or group health care service plan contract that provides medical, hospital, and surgical benefits. The term does not include a specialized health care service plan contract, a health care service plan contract provided in the Medi-Cal program (Chapter 7 (commencing with Section 14000) of Part 3 of Division 9 of the Welfare and Institutions Code), the Healthy Families Program (Part 6.2 (commencing with Section 12693) of Division 2 of the Insurance Code), the Access for Infants and Mothers Program (Part 6.3 (commencing with Section 12695) of Division 2 of the Insurance Code), or the program under Part 6.4 (commencing with Section 12699.50) of Division 2 of the Insurance Code, or Medicare supplement coverage, to the extent consistent with PPACA.

(g) "Policy year" means the period from January 1 to December 31, inclusive.

(h) "PPACA" means the federal Patient Protection and Affordable Care Act (Public Law 111-148), as amended by the federal Health Care and Education Reconciliation Act of 2010 (Public Law 111-152), and any rules, regulations, or guidance issued pursuant to that law.

(i) "Preexisting condition provision" means a contract provision that excludes coverage for charges or expenses incurred during a specified period following the enrollee's effective date of coverage, as to a condition for which medical advice, diagnosis, care, or treatment was recommended or received during a specified period immediately preceding the effective date of coverage.

(j) "Rating period" means the calendar year for which premium rates are in effect pursuant to subdivision (d) of Section 1399.855.

(k) "Registered domestic partner" means a person who has established a domestic partnership as described in Section 297 of the Family Code.

(Added by Stats. 2013, 1st Ex. Sess., Ch. 2, Sec. 18. (SB 2 1x) Effective September 30, 2013.)

1399.846.

For the purposes of determining eligibility for small employer coverage, a sole proprietor and the sole proprietor's spouse are not employees with respect to a sole proprietorship that consists only of the sole proprietor and the sole proprietor's spouse. A partner and a partner's spouse are not employees of a partnership that consists solely of partners and their spouses. Employer group health care service plans shall not be issued, marketed, or sold to a sole proprietorship or partnership without employees directly or indirectly through any arrangement. Only individual health care service plans shall be sold to any entity without employees.

(Added by Stats. 2018, Ch. 700, Sec. 6. (SB 1375) Effective January 1, 2019.)

1399.847.

Except as provided in Sections 1399.858 and 1399.861, the provisions of this article shall only apply with respect to nongrandfathered individual health benefit plans offered by a health care service plan, and shall apply in addition to the other provisions of this chapter and the rules adopted thereunder.

(Added by Stats. 2013, 1st Ex. Sess., Ch. 2, Sec. 18. (SB 2 1x) Effective September 30, 2013.)

1399.849.

(a) (1) On and after October 1, 2013, a plan shall fairly and affirmatively offer, market, and sell all of the plan's health benefit plans that are sold in the individual market for policy years on or after January 1, 2014, to all individuals and dependents in each service area in which the plan provides or arranges for the provision of health care services. A plan shall limit enrollment in individual health benefit plans to open enrollment periods, annual enrollment periods, and special enrollment periods as provided in subdivisions (c) and (d).

(2) A plan shall allow the subscriber of an individual health benefit plan to add a dependent to the subscriber's plan at the option of the subscriber, consistent with the open enrollment, annual enrollment, and special enrollment period requirements in this section.

(b) An individual health benefit plan issued, amended, or renewed on or after January 1, 2014, shall not impose any preexisting condition provision upon any individual.

(c) (1) With respect to individual health benefit plans offered outside of the Exchange, a plan shall provide an initial open enrollment period from October 1, 2013, to March 31, 2014, inclusive, an annual enrollment period for the policy year beginning on January 1, 2015, from November 15, 2014, to February 15, 2015, inclusive, annual enrollment periods for policy years beginning on or after January 1, 2016, to December 31, 2018, inclusive, from November 1, of the preceding calendar year, to January 31 of the benefit year, inclusive, and annual enrollment periods for policy years beginning on or after January 1, 2019, from October 15, of the preceding calendar year, to January 15 of the benefit year, inclusive.

(2) With respect to individual health benefit plans offered through the Exchange, a plan shall provide an annual enrollment period for the policy years beginning on January 1, 2016, to December 31, 2018, inclusive, from November 1, of the preceding calendar year, to January 31 of the benefit year, inclusive, and annual enrollment periods for policy years beginning on or after January 1, 2019, from November 1 to December 15 of the preceding calendar year, inclusive.

(3) With respect to individual health benefit plans offered through the Exchange, for policy years beginning on or after January 1, 2019, a plan shall provide a special enrollment period for all individuals selecting an individual health benefit plan through the Exchange from October 15 to October 31 of the preceding calendar year, inclusive, and from December 16, of the preceding calendar year, to January 15 of the benefit year, inclusive. An application for a health benefit plan submitted during these two special enrollment periods shall be treated the same as an application submitted during the annual open enrollment period. The effective date of coverage for plan selections made between October 15 and October 31, inclusive, shall be January 1 of the benefit year, and for plan selections made from December 16 to January 15, inclusive, shall be no later than February 1 of the benefit year.

(4) Pursuant to Section 147.104(b)(2) of Title 45 of the Code of Federal Regulations, for individuals enrolled in noncalendar year individual health plan contracts, a plan shall also provide a limited open enrollment period beginning on the date that is 30 calendar days prior to the date the policy year ends in 2014.

(d) (1) Subject to paragraph (2), commencing January 1, 2014, a plan shall allow an individual to enroll in or change individual health benefit plans as a result of the following triggering events:

(A) The individual or the individual's dependent loses minimum essential coverage. For purposes of this paragraph, the following definitions shall apply:

(i) "Minimum essential coverage" has the same meaning as that term is defined in Section 1345.5 or subsection (f) of Section 5000A of the Internal Revenue Code (26 U.S.C. Sec. 5000A).

(ii) "Loss of minimum essential coverage" includes, but is not limited to, loss of that coverage due to the circumstances described in Section 54.9801-6(a)(3)(i) to (iii), inclusive, of Title 26 of the Code of Federal Regulations and the circumstances described in Section 1163 of Title 29 of the United States Code. "Loss of minimum essential coverage" also includes loss of that coverage for a reason that is not due to the fault of the individual.

(iii) "Loss of minimum essential coverage" does not include loss of that coverage due to the individual's failure to pay premiums on a timely basis or situations allowing for a rescission, subject to clause (ii) and Sections 1389.7 and 1389.21.

(B) The individual gains a dependent or becomes a dependent.

(C) The individual is mandated to be covered as a dependent pursuant to a valid state or federal court order.

(D) The individual has been released from incarceration.

(E) The individual's health coverage issuer substantially violated a material provision of the health coverage contract.

(F) The individual gains access to new health benefit plans as a result of a permanent move.

(G) The individual was receiving services from a contracting provider under another health benefit plan, as defined in Section 1399.845 of this code or Section 10965 of the Insurance Code, for one of the conditions described in subdivision (c) of Section 1373.96 of this code and that provider is no longer participating in the health benefit plan.

(H) The individual demonstrates to the Exchange, with respect to health benefit plans offered through the Exchange, or to the department, with respect to health benefit plans offered outside the Exchange, that the individual did not enroll in a health benefit plan during the immediately preceding enrollment period available to the individual because the individual was misinformed that the individual was covered under minimum essential coverage.

(I) The individual is a member of the reserve forces of the United States military returning from active duty or a member of the California National Guard returning from active duty service under Title 32 of the United States Code.

(J) With respect to individual health benefit plans offered through the Exchange, in addition to the triggering events listed in this paragraph, any other events listed in Section 155.420(d) of Title 45 of the Code of Federal Regulations.

(2) With respect to individual health benefit plans offered outside the Exchange, an individual shall have 60 days from the date of a triggering event identified in paragraph (1) to apply for coverage from a health care service plan subject to this section. With respect to individual health benefit plans offered through the Exchange, an individual shall have 60 days from the date of a triggering event identified in paragraph (1) to select a plan offered through the Exchange, unless a longer period is provided in Part 155 (commencing with Section 155.10) of Subchapter B of Subtitle A of Title 45 of the Code of Federal Regulations.

(e) With respect to individual health benefit plans offered through the Exchange, the effective date of coverage required pursuant to this section shall be consistent with the dates specified in Section 155.410 or 155.420 of Title 45 of the Code of Federal Regulations, as applicable. A dependent who is a registered domestic partner pursuant to Section 297 of the Family Code shall have the same effective date of coverage as a spouse.

(f) With respect to individual health benefit plans offered outside the Exchange, the following provisions shall apply:

(1) After an individual submits a completed application form for a plan contract, the health care service plan shall, within 30 days, notify the individual of the individual's actual premium charges for that plan established in accordance with Section 1399.855. The individual shall have 30 days in which to exercise the right to buy coverage at the quoted premium charges.

(2) With respect to an individual health benefit plan for which an individual applies during the initial open enrollment period described in paragraph (1) of subdivision (c), when the subscriber submits a premium payment, based on the quoted premium charges, and that payment is delivered or postmarked, whichever occurs earlier, by December 15, 2013, coverage under the individual health benefit plan shall become effective no later than January 1, 2014. When that payment is delivered or postmarked within the first 15 days of any subsequent month, coverage shall become effective no later than the first day of the following month. When that payment is delivered or postmarked between December 16, 2013, to December 31, 2013, inclusive, or after the 15th day of any subsequent month, coverage shall become effective no later than the first day of the second month following delivery or postmark of the payment.

(3) With respect to an individual health benefit plan for which an individual applies during the annual open enrollment period described in paragraph (1) of subdivision (c), when the individual submits a premium payment, based on the quoted premium charges, and that payment is delivered or postmarked, whichever occurs later, by December 15 of the preceding calendar year, coverage shall become effective on January 1 of the benefit year. When that payment is delivered or postmarked within the first 15 days of any subsequent month, coverage shall become effective no later than the first day of the following month. When that payment is delivered or postmarked between December 16 to December 31, inclusive, or after the 15th day of any subsequent month, coverage shall become effective no later than the first day of the second month following delivery or postmark of the payment.

(4) With respect to an individual health benefit plan for which an individual applies during a special enrollment period described in subdivision (d), the following provisions shall apply:

(A) When the individual submits a premium payment, based on the quoted premium charges, and that payment is delivered or postmarked, whichever occurs earlier, within the first 15 days of the month, coverage under the plan shall become effective no later than the first day of the following month. When the premium payment is neither delivered nor postmarked until after the 15th day of the month, coverage shall become effective no later than the first day of the second month following delivery or postmark of the payment.

(B) Notwithstanding subparagraph (A), in the case of a birth, adoption, or placement for adoption, the coverage shall be effective on the date of birth, adoption, or placement for adoption.

(C) Notwithstanding subparagraph (A), in the case of marriage or becoming a registered domestic partner or in the case where a qualified individual loses minimum essential coverage, the coverage effective date shall be the first day of the month following the date the plan receives the request for special enrollment.

(g) (1) A health care service plan shall not establish rules for eligibility, including continued eligibility, of any individual to enroll under the terms of an individual health benefit plan based on any of the following factors:

(A) Health status.

(B) Medical condition, including physical and mental illnesses.

(C) Claims experience.

(D) Receipt of health care.

(E) Medical history.

(F) Genetic information.

(G) Evidence of insurability, including conditions arising out of acts of domestic violence.

(H) Disability.

(I) Any other health status-related factor as determined by any federal regulations, rules, or guidance issued pursuant to Section 2705 of the federal Public Health Service Act (Public Law 78-410).

(2) Notwithstanding Section 1389.1, a health care service plan shall not require an individual applicant or the applicant's dependent to fill out a health assessment or medical questionnaire prior to enrollment under an individual health benefit plan. A health care service plan shall not acquire or request information that relates to a health status-related factor from the applicant or the applicant's dependent or any other source prior to enrollment of the individual.

(h) (1) A health care service plan shall consider as a single risk pool for rating purposes in the individual market the claims experience of all insureds and all enrollees in all nongrandfathered individual health benefit plans offered by that health care service plan in this state, whether offered as health care service plan contracts or individual health insurance policies, including those insureds and enrollees who enroll in individual coverage through the Exchange and insureds and enrollees who enroll in individual coverage outside of the Exchange. Student health insurance coverage, as that coverage is defined in Section 147.145(a) of Title 45 of the Code of Federal Regulations, shall not be included in a health care service plan's single risk pool for individual coverage.

(2) Each calendar year, a health care service plan shall establish an index rate for the individual market in the state based on the total combined claims costs for providing essential health benefits, as defined pursuant to Section 1302 of PPACA, within the single risk pool required under paragraph (1). The index rate shall be adjusted on a marketwide basis based on the total expected marketwide payments and charges under the risk adjustment program established for the state pursuant to Section 1343 of PPACA and Exchange user fees, as described in subdivision (d) of Section 156.80 of Title 45 of the Code of Federal Regulations. The premium rate for all of the health benefit plans in the individual market within the single risk pool required under paragraph (1) shall use the applicable marketwide adjusted index rate, subject only to the adjustments permitted under paragraph (3).

(3) A health care service plan may vary premium rates for a particular health benefit plan from its index rate based only on the following actuarially justified plan-specific factors:

(A) The actuarial value and cost-sharing design of the health benefit plan.

(B) The health benefit plan's provider network, delivery system characteristics, and utilization management practices.

(C) The benefits provided under the health benefit plan that are in addition to the essential health benefits, as defined pursuant to Section 1302 of PPACA and Section 1367.005. These additional benefits shall be pooled with similar benefits within the single risk pool required under paragraph (1) and the claims experience from those benefits shall be utilized to determine rate variations for plans that offer those benefits in addition to essential health benefits.

(D) With respect to catastrophic plans, as described in subsection (e) of Section 1302 of PPACA, the expected impact of the specific eligibility categories for those plans.

(E) Administrative costs, excluding user fees required by the Exchange.

(i) This section shall only apply with respect to individual health benefit plans for policy years on or after January 1, 2014.

(j) This section shall not apply to a grandfathered health plan.

(k) If Section 5000A of the Internal Revenue Code, as added by Section 1501 of PPACA, is repealed or amended to no longer apply to the individual market, as defined in Section 2791 of the federal Public Health Service Act (42 U.S.C. Sec. 300gg-91), subdivisions (a), (b), and (g) shall become inoperative 12 months after that repeal or amendment. (Amended by Stats. 2019, Ch. 38, Sec. 17. (SB 78) Effective June 27, 2019.)

1399.851.

(a) Commencing October 1, 2013, a health care service plan or solicitor shall not, directly or indirectly, engage in the following activities:

(1) Encourage or direct an individual to refrain from filing an application for individual coverage with a plan because of the health status, claims experience, industry, occupation, or geographic location, provided that the location is within the plan's approved service area, of the individual.

(2) Encourage or direct an individual to seek individual coverage from another plan or health insurer or the California Health Benefit Exchange because of the health status, claims experience, industry, occupation, or geographic location, provided that the location is within the plan's approved service area, of the individual.

(3) Employ marketing practices or benefit designs that will have the effect of discouraging the enrollment of individuals with significant health needs or discriminate based on an individual's race, color, national origin, present or predicted disability, age, sex, gender identity, sexual orientation, expected length of life, degree of medical dependency, quality of life, or other health conditions.

(b) Commencing October 1, 2013, a health care service plan shall not, directly or indirectly, enter into any contract, agreement, or arrangement with a solicitor that provides for or results in the compensation paid to a solicitor for the sale of an individual health benefit plan to be varied because of the health status, claims experience, industry, occupation, or geographic location of the individual. This subdivision does not apply to a compensation arrangement that provides compensation to a solicitor on the basis of percentage of premium, provided that the percentage shall not vary because of the health status, claims experience, industry, occupation, or geographic area of the individual.

(c) This section shall only apply with respect to individual health benefit plans for policy years on or after January 1, 2014.

(Added by Stats. 2013, 1st Ex. Sess., Ch. 2, Sec. 18. (SB 2 1x) Effective September 30, 2013.)

1399.853.

(a) An individual health benefit plan shall be renewable at the option of the enrollee except as permitted to be canceled, rescinded, or not renewed pursuant to Section 1365 and Section 155.430(b) of Title 45 of the Code of Federal Regulations.

(b) Any plan that ceases to offer for sale new individual health benefit plans pursuant to Section 1365 shall continue to be governed by this article with respect to business conducted under this article.

(Added by Stats. 2013, 1st Ex. Sess., Ch. 2, Sec. 18. (SB 2 1x) Effective September 30, 2013.)

1399.855.

(a) With respect to individual health benefit plans for policy years on or after January 1, 2014, a health care service plan may use only the following characteristics of an individual, and any dependent thereof, for purposes of establishing the rate of the individual health benefit plan covering the individual and the eligible dependents thereof, along with the health benefit plan selected by the individual:

(1) Age, pursuant to the age bands established by the United States Secretary of Health and Human Services and the age rating curve established by the federal Centers for Medicare and Medicaid Services pursuant to Section 2701(a)(3) of the federal Public Health Service Act (42 U.S.C. Sec. 300gg(a)(3)). Rates based on age shall be determined using the individual's age as of the date of the health benefit plan contract issuance or renewal, as applicable, and shall not vary by more than three to one for like individuals of different age who are 21 years of age or older as described in federal regulations adopted pursuant to Section 2701(a)(3) of the federal Public Health Service Act (42 U.S.C. Sec. 300gg(a)(3)).

(2) (A) Geographic region. The geographic regions for purposes of rating shall be the following:

(i) Region 1 shall consist of the Counties of Alpine, Amador, Butte, Calaveras, Colusa, Del Norte, Glenn, Humboldt, Lake, Lassen, Mendocino, Modoc, Nevada, Plumas, Shasta, Sierra, Siskiyou, Sutter, Tehama, Trinity, Tuolumne, and Yuba.

(ii) Region 2 shall consist of the Counties of Marin, Napa, Solano, and Sonoma.

(iii) Region 3 shall consist of the Counties of El Dorado, Placer, Sacramento, and Yolo.

(iv) Region 4 shall consist of the City and County of San Francisco.

(v) Region 5 shall consist of the County of Contra Costa.

(vi) Region 6 shall consist of the County of Alameda.

(vii) Region 7 shall consist of the County of Santa Clara.

(viii) Region 8 shall consist of the County of San Mateo.

(ix) Region 9 shall consist of the Counties of Monterey, San Benito, and Santa Cruz.

(x) Region 10 shall consist of the Counties of Mariposa, Merced, San Joaquin, Stanislaus, and Tulare.

(xi) Region 11 shall consist of the Counties of Fresno, Kings, and Madera.

(xii) Region 12 shall consist of the Counties of San Luis Obispo, Santa Barbara, and Ventura.

(xiii) Region 13 shall consist of the Counties of Imperial, Inyo, and Mono.

(xiv) Region 14 shall consist of the County of Kern.

(xv) Region 15 shall consist of the ZIP Codes in the County of Los Angeles starting with 906 to 912, inclusive, 915, 917, 918, and 935.

(xvi) Region 16 shall consist of the ZIP Codes in the County of Los Angeles other than those identified in clause (xv).

(xvii) Region 17 shall consist of the Counties of Riverside and San Bernardino.

(xviii) Region 18 shall consist of the County of Orange.

(xix) Region 19 shall consist of the County of San Diego.

(B) No later than June 1, 2017, the department, in collaboration with the Exchange and the Department of Insurance, shall review the geographic rating regions specified in this paragraph and the impacts of those regions on the health care coverage market in California, and make a report to the appropriate policy committees of the Legislature.

(3) Whether the plan covers an individual or family, as described in PPACA.

(b) The rate for a health benefit plan subject to this section shall not vary by any factor not described in this section.

(c) With respect to family coverage under an individual health benefit plan, the rating variation permitted under paragraph (1) of subdivision (a) shall be applied based on the portion of the premium attributable to each family member covered under the plan. The total premium for family coverage shall be determined by summing the premiums for each individual family member. In determining the total premium for family members, premiums for no more than the three oldest family members who are under 21 years of age shall be taken into account.

(d) The rating period for rates subject to this section shall be from January 1 to December 31, inclusive.

(e) This section does not apply to an individual health benefit plan that is a grandfathered health plan.

(f) The requirement for submitting a report imposed under subparagraph (B) of paragraph (2) of subdivision (a) is inoperative on June 1, 2021, pursuant to Section 10231.5 of the Government Code.

(g) If Section 5000A of the Internal Revenue Code, as added by Section 1501 of PPACA, is repealed or amended to no longer apply to the individual market, as defined in Section 2791 of the federal Public Health Service Act (42 U.S.C. Sec. 300gg-91), this section shall become inoperative 12 months after the date of that repeal or amendment. (Amended by Stats. 2015, Ch. 303, Sec. 267. (AB 731) Effective January 1, 2016. Conditionally inoperative as prescribed by its own provisions.)

1399.857.

(a) A health care service plan shall not be required to offer an individual health benefit plan or accept applications for the plan pursuant to Section 1399.849 in the case of any of the following:

(1) To an individual who does not live or reside within the plan's approved service areas.

(2) (A) Within a specific service area or portion of a service area, if the plan reasonably anticipates and demonstrates to the satisfaction of the director both of the following:

(i) It will not have sufficient health care delivery resources to ensure that health care services will be available and accessible to the individual because of its obligations to existing enrollees.

(ii) It is applying this subparagraph uniformly to all individuals without regard to the claims experience of those individuals or any health status-related factor relating to those individuals.

(B) A health care service plan that cannot offer an individual health benefit plan to individuals because it is lacking in sufficient health care delivery resources within a service area or a portion of a service area pursuant to subparagraph (A) shall not offer a health benefit plan in that area to individuals until the later of the following dates:

(i) The 181st day after the date coverage is denied pursuant to this paragraph.

(ii) The date the plan notifies the director that it has the ability to deliver services to individuals, and certifies to the director that from the date of the notice it will enroll all individuals requesting coverage in that area from the plan.

(C) Subparagraph (B) shall not limit the plan's ability to renew coverage already in force or relieve the plan of the responsibility to renew that coverage as described in Section 1365.

(D) Coverage offered within a service area after the period specified in subparagraph (B) shall be subject to this section.

(b) (1) A health care service plan may decline to offer an individual health benefit plan to an individual if the plan demonstrates to the satisfaction of the director both of the following:

(A) It does not have the financial reserves necessary to underwrite additional coverage. In determining whether this subparagraph has been satisfied, the director shall consider, but not be limited to, the plan's compliance with the requirements of Section 1367, Article 6 (commencing with Section 1375), and the rules adopted thereunder.

(B) It is applying this subdivision uniformly to all individuals without regard to the claims experience of those individuals or any health status-related factor relating to those individuals.

(2) A plan that denies coverage to an individual under paragraph (1) shall not offer coverage before the later of the following dates:

(A) The 181st day after the date that coverage is denied pursuant to this subdivision.

(B) The date the plan demonstrates to the satisfaction of the director that the plan has sufficient financial reserves necessary to underwrite additional coverage.

(3) Paragraph (2) shall not limit the plan's ability to renew coverage already in force or relieve the plan of the responsibility to renew that coverage as described in Section 1365.

(4) Coverage offered within a service area after the period specified in paragraph (2) shall be subject to this section.

(c) Nothing in this article shall be construed to limit the director's authority to develop and implement a plan of rehabilitation for a health care service plan whose financial viability or organizational and administrative capacity has become impaired, to the extent permitted by PPACA.

(d) This section shall not apply to an individual health benefit plan that is a grandfathered health plan.

(Added by Stats. 2013, 1st Ex. Sess., Ch. 2, Sec. 18. (SB 2 1x) Effective September 30, 2013.)

1399.858.

The director may require a plan to discontinue the offering of contracts or acceptance of applications from any individual, or responsible party for an individual, upon a determination by the director that the plan does not have sufficient financial viability, or organizational and administrative capacity to ensure the delivery of health care services to its enrollees. In determining whether the conditions of this section have been met, the director shall consider, but not be limited to, the plan's compliance with the requirements of Section 1367, Article 6 (commencing with Section 1375), and the rules adopted thereunder.

(Added by Stats. 2013, 1st Ex. Sess., Ch. 2, Sec. 18. (SB 2 1x) Effective September 30, 2013.)

1399.859.

(a) A health care service plan that receives an application for an individual health benefit plan outside the Exchange during the initial open enrollment period, an annual enrollment period, or a special enrollment period described in Section 1399.849 shall inform the applicant that he or she may be eligible for lower cost coverage through the Exchange and shall inform the applicant of the applicable enrollment period provided through the Exchange described in Section 1399.849.

(b) On or before October 1, 2013, and annually every October 1 thereafter, a health care service plan shall issue a notice to a subscriber enrolled in an individual health benefit plan offered outside the Exchange. The notice shall inform the subscriber that he or she may be eligible for lower cost coverage through the Exchange and shall inform the subscriber of the applicable open enrollment period and special enrollment periods provided through the Exchange described in Section 1399.849.

(c) This section shall not apply where the individual health benefit plan described in subdivision (a) or (b) is a grandfathered health plan.

(Amended by Stats. 2017, Ch. 468, Sec. 4. (AB 156) Effective January 1, 2018.)

1399.861.

(a) On or before October 1, 2013, and annually every October 1 thereafter, a health care service plan shall issue the following notice to all subscribers enrolled in an individual health benefit plan that is a grandfathered health plan:

New improved health insurance options are available in California. You currently have health insurance that is not required to follow many of the new laws. For example, your plan may not provide preventive health services without you having to pay any cost sharing (copayments or coinsurance). Also, your current plan may be allowed to increase your rates based on your health status while new plans and policies cannot. You have the option to remain in your current plan or switch to a new plan. Under the new rules, a health plan cannot deny your application based on any health conditions you may have. For more information about your options, please contact Covered California at _____, your plan representative or insurance agent, or an entity paid by Covered California to assist with health coverage enrollment such as a navigator or an assister.

(b) Commencing October 1, 2013, a health care service plan shall include the notice described in subdivision (a) in any renewal material of the individual grandfathered health plan and in any application for dependent coverage under the individual grandfathered health plan.

(c) A health care service plan shall not advertise or market an individual health benefit plan that is a grandfathered health plan for purposes of enrolling a dependent of a subscriber into the plan for policy years on or after January 1, 2014. Nothing in this subdivision shall be construed to prohibit an individual enrolled in an individual grandfathered health plan from adding a dependent to that plan to the extent permitted by PPACA.

(Amended by Stats. 2014, Ch. 31, Sec. 9. (SB 857) Effective June 20, 2014.)

1399.862.

Except as otherwise provided in this article, this article shall only be implemented to the extent that it meets or exceeds the requirements set forth in PPACA.

(Added by Stats. 2013, 1st Ex. Sess., Ch. 2, Sec. 18. (SB 2 1x) Effective September 30, 2013.)

1399.863.

(a) The department may adopt emergency regulations implementing this article no later than December 31, 2014. The department may readopt any emergency regulation authorized by this section that is the same as or substantially equivalent to an emergency regulation previously adopted under this section.

(b) The initial adoption of emergency regulations implementing this article and the one readoption of emergency regulations authorized by this section shall be deemed an emergency and necessary for the immediate preservation of the public peace, health, safety, or general welfare. Initial emergency regulations and the one readoption of emergency regulations authorized by this section shall be exempt from review by the Office of Administrative Law. The initial emergency regulations and the one readoption of emergency regulations authorized by this section shall be submitted to the Office of Administrative Law for filing with the Secretary of State and each shall remain in effect for no more than one year, by which time final regulations may be adopted. The department shall consult with the Insurance Commissioner prior to adopting any regulations pursuant to this section for the specific purpose of ensuring, to the extent practical, that there is consistency of regulations applicable to entities regulated by the department and those regulated by the Insurance Commissioner.

(Added by Stats. 2013, 1st Ex. Sess., Ch. 2, Sec. 18. (SB 2 1x) Effective September 30, 2013.)

1399.864.

(a) For purposes of this article, a bridge plan product shall mean an individual health benefit plan, as defined in subdivision (f) of Section 1399.845, that is offered by a health care service plan licensed under this chapter that contracts with the Exchange pursuant to Title 22 (commencing with Section 100500) of the Government Code.

(b) Until December 31, 2014, a health care service plan that contracts with the California Health Benefit Exchange to offer a qualified bridge plan product pursuant to Section 100504 of the Government Code shall do all of the following:

(1) As of the effective date of this section, if the health care service plan has not been approved by the director to offer individual health benefit plans pursuant to this chapter, the plan shall file a material modification pursuant to Section 1352 to expand its license to include individual health benefit plans.

(2) As of the effective date of this section, if the health care service plan has been approved by the director to offer individual health benefit plans pursuant to this chapter, the plan shall, pursuant to Section 1352, file an amendment to expand its license to include a bridge plan product as an individual health benefit plan.

(c) During the time the health care service plan's material modification or amendment is pending approval by the director, the health care service plan shall be deemed to comply with subdivision (b) of Section 100507 of the Government Code.

(d) A health care service plan shall maintain a medical loss ratio of 85 percent for the bridge plan product. A health care service plan shall utilize, to the extent possible, the same methodology for calculating the medical loss ratio for the bridge plan product that is used for calculating the health care service plan medical loss ratio pursuant to Section 1367.003 and shall report its medical loss ratio for the bridge plan product to the department as provided in Section 1367.003.

(e) Notwithstanding subdivision (a) of Section 1399.849, a health care service plan selling a bridge plan product shall not be required to fairly and affirmatively offer, market, and sell the health care service plan's bridge plan product except to individuals eligible for the bridge plan product pursuant to the State Department of Health Care Services and the Medi-Cal managed care plan's contract entered into pursuant to Section 14005.70 of the Welfare and Institutions Code, provided the health care service plan meets the requirements of subdivision (b) of Section 14005.70 of the Welfare and Institutions Code.

(f) Notwithstanding subdivision (c) of Section 1399.849, a health care service plan selling a bridge plan product shall provide an initial open enrollment period of six months, and an annual enrollment period and a special enrollment period consistent with the annual enrollment and special enrollment periods of the Exchange.

(g) This section shall become inoperative on the October 1 that is five years after the date that federal approval of the bridge plan option occurs, and, as of the second January 1 thereafter, is repealed, unless a later enacted statute that is enacted before that date deletes or extends the dates on which it becomes inoperative and is repealed.

(Added by Stats. 2013, 1st Ex. Sess., Ch. 5, Sec. 10. (SB 3 1x) Effective September 30, 2013. Conditionally inoperative, on date prescribed by its own provisions. Repealed, by its own provisions, on second January 1 after inoperative date.)

CHAPTER 2.25. Disease Management [1399.900 - 1399.904]

(Heading of Chapter 2.25 renumbered from Chapter 2.5 (as added by Stats. 2000, Ch. 1065) by Stats. 2002, Ch. 664, Sec. 129.)

1399.900.

(a) For the purposes of this chapter, "disease management organization" means an entity that provides disease management programs and services and that contracts with any of the following:

(1) A health care service plan.

(2) A contractor of a health care service plan.

(3) An employer.

(4) A publicly financed health care program.

(5) A government agency.

(b) A disease management organization shall not include an entity whose primary purpose is to market specific products or services to enrollees of a health care service plan.

(c) No medical group, individual licensed pursuant to Division 2 (commencing with Section 500) of the Business and Professions Code, or health facility as defined in Section 1250, that provides disease management programs and services incidental to their primary professional practices, shall be considered a disease management organization.

(Added by Stats. 2000, Ch. 1065, Sec. 2. Effective January 1, 2001.)

1399.901.

For the purposes of this chapter, "disease management programs and services" means services administered to patients in order to improve their overall health and to prevent clinical exacerbations and complications utilizing cost-effective, evidence-based, or consensus-based practice guidelines and patient self-management strategies. Disease management programs and services shall contain all of the following:

(a) A population identification process.

(b) Evidence-based or consensus-based clinical practice guidelines, risk identification, and matching of interventions with clinical need.

(c) Patient self-management and disease education.

(d) Process and outcomes measurement, evaluation, management, and reporting.

(Added by Stats. 2000, Ch. 1065, Sec. 2. Effective January 1, 2001.)

1399.902.

(a) Every disease management organization shall obtain physician authorization prior to the time that the disease management organization, its employees, or independent contractors do either of the following:

(1) Provide home health care services utilized in the treatment of a patient.

(2) Dispense, administer, or prescribe a prescription medication.

(b) For purposes of this section, a valid prescription written by a treating physician shall constitute authorization to dispense a prescription medication.

(c) Home health care followup visits made solely for patient assessment, monitoring, or education are not subject to the physician authorization requirement in subdivision (a).

(d) Nothing in this section, in the absence of authorization granted by any other law, shall be construed to authorize the activities described in paragraphs (1) and (2) of subdivision (a).

(Added by Stats. 2000, Ch. 1065, Sec. 2. Effective January 1, 2001.)

1399.903.

A disease management organization may receive medical information as provided in paragraph (17) of subdivision (c) of Section 56.10 of the Civil Code. However, a disease management organization shall be subject to the other provisions of the Confidentiality of Medical Information Act (Part 2.6 (commencing with Section 56) of Division 1 of the Civil Code), including, but not limited to, subdivisions (d) and (e) of Section 56.10 of, and Section 56.36 of, the Civil Code.

(Added by Stats. 2000, Ch. 1065, Sec. 2. Effective January 1, 2001.)

1399.904.

A disease management organization shall not use medical information obtained pursuant to Section 1399.903 to solicit or to offer for sale to a health care service plan enrollee any products or services in the provision of disease management services to the enrollee. However, an enrollee may elect to use a disease management organization to obtain information about health care products and services and, pursuant to that election by the enrollee, the disease management organization may offer to the enrollee health care products or services that are directly related to the enrollee's condition.

(Added by Stats. 2000, Ch. 1065, Sec. 2. Effective January 1, 2001.)

CHAPTER 2.3. Referral Agencies [1400 - 1413]

(Chapter 2.3 added by Stats. 1973, Ch. 924.)

ARTICLE 1. General Provisions [1400 - 1409.3]

(Article 1 added by Stats. 1973, Ch. 924.)

1400.

(a) It is unlawful for any person, association, or corporation to establish, conduct or maintain a referral agency or to refer any person for remuneration to any extended care, skilled nursing home or intermediate care facility or a distinct part of a facility providing extended care, skilled nursing home care, or intermediate care, without first having obtained a written license therefor as provided in this chapter from the director or from an inspection service approved by the director pursuant to Section 1257.

(b) It is unlawful for any person, association, or corporation to establish, conduct, or maintain a referral agency or to refer any person for remuneration to any person or agency outside a long-term health care facility, as defined in Section 1418, for professional services for which the long-term health care facility does not employ a qualified professional person to furnish a specific service, including, but not limited to, laboratory, diagnostic, or therapy services, unless the long-term health care facility complies with current federal and state laws regarding the provision of these services and all of the following conditions are met:

(1) The services will be provided in accordance with professional standards applicable to the provision of these services in a long-term health care facility.

(2) The long-term health care facility assumes responsibility for timeliness of the services.

(3) Services are provided or obtained only when ordered by the attending physician and a notation is made in the resident's medical chart reflecting that the service has been provided to the resident.

(Amended by Stats. 2004, Ch. 661, Sec. 1. Effective January 1, 2005.)

1401.

As used in this chapter "referral agency" means a private, profit or nonprofit agency which is engaged in the business of referring persons for remuneration to any extended care, skilled nursing home or intermediate care facility or a distinct part of a facility providing extended care, skilled nursing home care, or intermediate care.

(Added by Stats. 1973, Ch. 924.)

1403.

Each application for a license or renewal of license under this chapter shall be accompanied by an annual Licensing and Certification Program fee set in accordance with Section 1266. Each license shall expire 12 months from its date of issuance and application for renewal accompanied by the fee shall be filed with the director not later than 30 days prior to the date of expiration.

(Amended by Stats. 2006, Ch. 74, Sec. 15. Effective July 12, 2006.)

1404.

No licensee under this chapter shall have a direct or indirect financial interest in any medical facility doing business with the licensee.

(Added by Stats. 1973, Ch. 924.)

1404.5.

A license application shall be submitted to the department whenever any of the following circumstances occur:

(a) Change of ownership of the referral agency.

(b) Change of name of the referral agency.

(c) Change of location of the referral agency.

(Added by Stats. 1985, Ch. 700, Sec. 10.)

1405.

Any person, partnership, firm, corporation or association desiring to obtain a license shall file with the department an application on forms furnished by the department. The application shall contain all of the following:

(a) Name of applicant, and if an individual, whether the applicant has attained the age of 18 years.

(b) Name of referral agency.

(c) The location of the referral agency.

(d) The business or occupation engaged in by each applicant, and by each partner, officer and director, for at least two years immediately preceding the filing of the application. In addition, each such person shall submit a statement setting forth whether he or she has previously engaged in the operation of a referral agency, whether he or she has been involved in, or the subject of, a refusal or revocation of a referral agency license, and whether he or she has been convicted of a crime other than a minor traffic offense.

(e) If the applicant is a corporation, the name and principal business address of each officer and director of the corporation; and for nonpublic corporations, the name and business address of each stockholder owning 10 percent or more of the stock and the name and business address of any corporation member who has responsibility in the operation of the facility.

(f) If the applicant is a partnership, the name and principal business address of each partner.

(g) Evidence of the right to occupy the premises where the referral agency is to be located.

(h) A copy of the partnership agreement of the Articles of Incorporation, if applicable.

(i) A copy of the current organization chart.

(j) A schedule of fees to be charged and collected by the referral agency, and a statement of the method by which each fee is to be computed or determined.

(k) A declaration that the licensee will not have any financial interest in any health facility doing business with the referral agency.

(l) Evidence satisfactory to the department that the applicant demonstrates reputable and responsible character and the capability to comply with this chapter.

(Repealed and added by Stats. 1985, Ch. 700, Sec. 12.)

1406.

This chapter shall not apply to any local public agency performing referral services without cost to recipients of public social services when otherwise authorized by law.

(Added by Stats. 1985, Ch. 700, Sec. 13.)

1407.

(a) Any licensee desiring to voluntarily surrender his or her license for cancellation or temporary suspension shall notify the department in writing as soon as possible and, in all cases, at least 30 days prior to the effective date of cancellation or temporary suspension of the license.

(b) Any license placed in temporary suspension pursuant to this section may be reinstated by the department within 12 months of the date of the voluntary suspension on receipt of an application and evidence showing compliance with licensing requirements.

(Added by Stats. 1985, Ch. 700, Sec. 14.)

1408.

(a) Upon verification of compliance with this chapter and with the approval of the department, the department shall issue the license to the applicant.

(b) If the applicant is not in compliance with this chapter, the department shall deny the applicant a license. Immediately upon the denial of any license, the department shall notify the applicant in writing. Within 20 days of receipt of the department's notice, the applicant may present his or her written petition for a hearing to the department. The proceedings shall be conducted in accordance with Section 100171.

(Amended by Stats. 1997, Ch. 220, Sec. 14. Effective August 4, 1997.)

1409.

Separate licenses shall be required for referral agencies which are maintained on separate, noncontiguous premises.

(Added by Stats. 1985, Ch. 700, Sec. 16.)

1409.1.

The license or true copy thereof shall be conspicuously posted in a prominent location accessible to public view.

(Added by Stats. 1985, Ch. 700, Sec. 17.)

1409.2.

Licenses issued pursuant to this article are not transferable.

(Added by Stats. 1985, Ch. 700, Sec. 18.)

1409.3.

(a) The licensee shall notify the department within 10 days in writing when a change of stockholder owning 10 percent or more of the nonpublic corporate stock occurs. The writing shall include the name and principal mailing addresses of the new stockholder.

(b) When a change of agency manager occurs, the department shall be notified in writing within 10 days by the licensee. The notification shall include the name of the new agency manager.

(c) Each licensee shall notify the department within 10 days in writing of any change of the mailing address of the licensee. The writing shall include the new mailing address of the licensee.

(d) When a change in the principal officer of a corporate licensee, chairperson, president, or general manager, occurs the department shall be notified within 10 days in writing by the licensee. The writing shall include the name and principal business address of the officer.

(Added by Stats. 1985, Ch. 700, Sec. 19.)

ARTICLE 2. Penalties [1410 - 1413]

(Article 2 added by Stats. 1973, Ch. 924.)

1410.

The department may suspend or revoke licenses issued under this chapter for violation of any provisions of this chapter or rules and regulations promulgated hereunder. In addition, the department shall assess a civil penalty in the amount of fees received by a licensee as a result of a violation of any provisions of this chapter or rules and regulations promulgated hereunder. Proceedings to suspend or revoke a license shall be conducted pursuant to Section 100171.

(Amended by Stats. 1997, Ch. 220, Sec. 15. Effective August 4, 1997.)

1411.

A violation of the provisions of this chapter or rules and regulations promulgated hereunder by a person licensed pursuant to Division 2 (commencing with Section 500) or a person certificated or licensed pursuant to Chapter 17 (commencing with Section 9000) of Division 3 of, the Business and Professions Code may be grounds for suspension or revocation of the person's license under such division.

(Added by Stats. 1973, Ch. 924.)

1412.

Any person, association or corporation referring persons without a license in violation of Section 1400 shall be liable for a civil penalty in the amount of the remuneration illegally recieved, which shall be assessed and recovered in a civil action brought in the name of the people of the State of California by the Attorney General in any court of competent jurisdiction.

(Added by Stats. 1973, Ch. 924.)

1413.

Civil penalties collected pursuant to this article shall be used to administer the provisions of this chapter.

(Added by Stats. 1973, Ch. 924.)

CHAPTER 2.35. Nursing Home Administrator Program [1416 - 1416.86]

(Chapter 2.35 added by Stats. 2001, Ch. 687, Sec. 5.)

ARTICLE 1. General Provisions [1416 - 1416.6]

(Article 1 added by Stats. 2001, Ch. 687, Sec. 5.)

1416.

This chapter shall be known and may be cited as the Nursing Home Administrators' Act.

(Added by Stats. 2001, Ch. 687, Sec. 5. Effective January 1, 2002.)

1416.1.

There is hereby established in the State Department of Health Services a Nursing Home Administrator Program (NHAP), which shall license and regulate nursing home administrators.

(Added by Stats. 2001, Ch. 687, Sec. 5. Effective January 1, 2002.)

1416.2.

(a) The following definitions shall apply to this chapter:

(1) "Department" means the State Department of Health Services.

(2) "NHAP" or "program" means the Nursing Home Administrator Program.

(3) "State" means California, unless applied to the different parts of the United States. In this latter case, "state" includes the District of Columbia and the territories.

(4) "Nursing home" means any institution, facility, place, building, or agency, or portion thereof, licensed as a skilled nursing facility, intermediate care facility, or intermediate care facility/developmentally disabled, as defined in Chapter 2 (commencing with Section 1250). "Nursing home" also means an intermediate care facility/developmentally disabled habilitative, intermediate care facility/developmentally disabled-nursing, or congregate living health facility, as defined in Chapter 2 (commencing with Section 1250), if a licensed nursing home administrator is charged with the general administration of the facility.

(5) "Nursing home administrator" means an individual educated and trained within the field of nursing home administration who carries out the policies of the licensee of a nursing home and is licensed in accordance with this chapter. The nursing home administrator is charged with the general administration of a nursing home, regardless of whether he or she has an ownership interest and whether the administrator's function or duties are shared with one or more other individuals.

(6) "Administrator-in-Training Program" or "AIT Program" means a program that is approved by the NHAP in which qualified persons participate under the coordination, supervision, and teaching of a preceptor, as described in Section 1416.57, who has obtained approval from the NHAP.

(b) Nothing in this section shall be construed to allow the program to have jurisdiction over an administrator of an intermediate care facility/developmentally disabled-nursing or an intermediate care facility/developmentally disabled habilitative, if the administrator of the facility is not using licensure under this chapter to qualify as an administrator in accordance with subdivision (d) of Section 1276.5.

(c) Nothing in this section shall be construed to define an intermediate care facility/developmentally disabled-nursing or an intermediate care facility/developmentally disabled habilitative as a nursing home for purposes other than the licensure of nursing home administrators under this chapter.

(Added by Stats. 2001, Ch. 687, Sec. 5. Effective January 1, 2002.)

1416.4.

The program shall adopt rules and regulations that are reasonably necessary to carry out this chapter. The rules and regulations shall be adopted, amended, and repealed in accordance with Chapter 3.5 (commencing with Section 11340) of Part 1 of Division 3 of Title 2 of the Government Code. To the extent that the regulations governing the nursing home administrator program that are in effect prior to January 1, 2002, are not in conflict with this chapter, they shall remain in effect until new regulations are implemented for purposes of this chapter.

(Added by Stats. 2001, Ch. 687, Sec. 5. Effective January 1, 2002.)

1416.6.

(a) It shall be a misdemeanor for any person to act or serve in the capacity of a nursing home administrator, unless he or she is the holder of an active nursing home administrator's license issued in accordance with this chapter. Persons carrying out functions and duties delegated by a licensed nursing home administrator shall not be acting in violation of this chapter.

(b) (1) This chapter shall not apply to any person who serves as an acting administrator as provided in this subdivision when a licensed administrator is not available because of death, illness, or any other reason.

(2) A person who is acting as an administrator shall notify the program in writing within five days of acting in this capacity and provide factual information and specific circumstances necessitating the use of an acting administrator.

(3) No person shall act as an administrator for more than 10 days unless arrangements have been made for part-time supervision of his or her activities by a nursing home administrator who holds a license or provisional license under this chapter. Supervision shall include at least 8 hours per week of direct onsite supervision by the licensed administrator. The program shall be notified in writing of the nature of this arrangement. No person shall act as an administrator for more than two months without the written approval of the program. The program shall not approve a person to act as an administrator for more than six months.

(4) If the acting administrator is an administrator in training, then the supervision required by paragraph (3) may be counted towards the total hours of supervised training required by subdivision (f) of Section 1416.57.

(c) Notwithstanding subdivision (b), an individual acting as an administrator for more than 10 days must have management experience in a health facility.

(Added by Stats. 2001, Ch. 687, Sec. 5. Effective January 1, 2002.)

(Article 2 added by Stats. 2001, Ch. 687, Sec. 5.)

1416.10.

In conformity with the requirements of Section 1908(c) of the Social Security Act (42 U.S.C. Sec. 1396g(c)), the program shall have all of the following powers and duties:

(a) To develop, impose, and enforce standards that shall be met by individuals in order to receive a license as a nursing home administrator. At a minimum, the standards shall be designed to ensure that nursing home administrators shall be individuals who have not committed acts or crimes constituting grounds for denial of licensure and who are qualified by training or experience in the field of institutional administration to serve as nursing home administrators.

(b) To develop and apply procedures, including examinations and investigations, for determining whether an individual meets the standards.

(c) To issue licenses to individuals who have been determined to meet the standards, and to revoke or suspend licenses where grounds exist for those actions.

(d) To establish and carry out procedures designed to ensure that individuals licensed as nursing home administrators will, during any period that they serve as an administrator, comply with the required standards.

(e) To receive, investigate, and take appropriate action with respect to any charge or complaint filed with the program alleging that an individual licensed as a nursing home administrator has failed to comply with the required standards.

(f) To conduct studies of the administration of nursing homes within the state, with a view to the improvement of the standards imposed for the licensing of nursing home administrators, and of procedures and methods for the enforcement of standards with respect to administrators of nursing homes who have been licensed under this chapter.

(g) To receive and administer all funds and grants as are made available to the program in order to carry out the purposes of this chapter.

(h) To encourage qualified educational institutions and other qualified organizations to establish, provide, and conduct training and instruction programs and courses that will enable all otherwise qualified individuals to attain the qualifications necessary to meet the standards set by the program for licensed nursing home administrators, and to enable licensed nursing home administrators to meet the continuing education requirements for the renewal of their licenses.

(i) To consult with and seek the recommendations of the appropriate statewide professional societies, associations, institutional organizations, and educational institutions in the development of educational programs.

(j) To give due consideration to the recommendations of the National Advisory Council on Nursing Home Administration, in accordance with the provisions of subdivision (f) of Section 1908 of Title XIX of the Social Security Act (42 U.S.C. Sec. 1396g(f)).
(Added by Stats. 2001, Ch. 687, Sec. 5. Effective January 1, 2002.)

1416.12.

The following enforcement actions taken by the department against a facility and the name of the licensed administrator of the facility shall be reported to the program.

(a) Temporary suspension orders.

(b) Final decertification from the Medi-Cal or Medicare programs based on failure to meet certification requirements.

(c) Service of an accusation to revoke a facility's license.

(d) All class "AA" citations and three class "A" citations issued to a facility with the same administrator within a one-calendar year period. The department shall notify the program in the event that citations are overturned or modified in citation review conference, through binding arbitration, or on appeal.
(Added by Stats. 2001, Ch. 687, Sec. 5. Effective January 1, 2002.)

(Article 3 added by Stats. 2001, Ch. 687, Sec. 5.)

1416.20.

(a) The nursing home administrator licensing examination shall cover the broad aspects of nursing home administration.

(b) Unless otherwise provided in this article, every applicant for an initial license as a nursing home administrator shall pass a nursing home administrator licensing examination, which shall consist of a state and national examination. The state examination shall be held at least four times a year, at a time and place determined by the program. The national examination is computer-based and shall be scheduled by the applicant after the applicant is notified by the program of his or her eligibility to take the examination.

(c) If an applicant for licensure under this article, submits an endorsement certificate from another state indicating that he or she scored at least 75 percent on the national examination, the applicant shall be required to take only the California state part of the licensing examination. If the applicant scored less than 75 percent on the national examination, he or she shall take both the state and national examination.
(Added by Stats. 2001, Ch. 687, Sec. 5. Effective January 1, 2002.)

1416.22.

(a) To qualify for the licensing examination, an applicant must be at least 18 years of age, be a citizen of the United States or a legal resident, be of reputable and responsible character, demonstrate an ability to comply with this chapter, and comply with at least one of the following requirements:

(1) Have a master's degree in nursing home administration or a related health administration field. The master's program in which the degree was obtained must have included an internship or residency of at least 480 hours in a skilled nursing facility or intermediate care facility.

(2) (A) With regard to applicants who have a current valid license as a nursing home administrator in another state and apply for licensure in this state, meet the minimum education requirements that existed in this state at the time the applicant was originally licensed in the other state.

(B) The minimum education requirements that have existed in California are as follows:

Prior to 7/1/73	None
From 7/1/73 to 6/30/74	30 semester units
From 7/1/74 to 6/30/75	45 semester units
From 7/1/75 to 6/30/80	60 semester units
From 7/1/80 to present	Baccalaureate degree

(3) A doctorate degree in medicine, a current valid license as a physician and surgeon, and the completion of a program-approved AIT Program of at least 1,000 hours.

(4) A baccalaureate degree, and the completion of a program-approved AIT Program of at least 1,000 hours.

(5) Ten years of recent full-time work experience, and a current license, as a licensed registered nurse, and the completion of a program-approved AIT Program of at least 1,000 hours. At least the most recent five years of the 10 years of work experience shall be in a supervisory or director of nursing position.

(6) Ten years of full-time work experience in any department of a skilled nursing facility, an intermediate care facility, or an intermediate care facility developmentally/disabled with at least 60 semester units (or 90 quarter units) of college or university courses, and the completion of a program-approved AIT Program of at least 1,000 hours. At least the most recent five years of the 10 years of work experience shall be in a position as a department manager.

(7) Ten years of full-time hospital administration experience in an acute care hospital with at least 60 semester units (or 90 quarter units) of college or university courses, and the completion of a program-approved AIT Program of at least 1,000 hours. At least the most recent five years of the 10 years of work experience shall be in a supervisory position.

(b) An applicant for the licensing examination may obtain from the department a waiver of the education requirements in subdivision (a) if they meet the requirements of Section 1416.23.

(c) If the applicant and the preceptor provide compelling evidence that previous work experience of the applicant directly relates to nursing home administrator duties, the program may accept a waiver exception to a portion of the AIT Program that requires 1,000 hours. An applicant seeking a waiver of the educational requirements pursuant to Section 1416.23 shall not be eligible for a waiver under this subdivision.

(d) The applicant shall submit an official transcript that evidences the completion of required college and university courses, degrees, or both. An applicant who applies for the licensing examination on the basis of work experience shall submit a declaration signed under penalty of perjury, verifying his or her work experience. This declaration shall be signed by a licensed nursing home administrator, physician and surgeon, chief of staff, director of nurses, or registered nurse who can attest to the applicant's work experience.
(Amended by Stats. 2008, Ch. 397, Sec. 1. Effective January 1, 2009.)

1416.23.

(a) Upon request of an applicant who is a member of a church or religious denomination, recognized by the Internal Revenue Service under Section 501(c)(3) of the Internal Revenue Code, that owns and operates a faith-based skilled nursing facility in California, and whose teachings historically prohibit the acquisition of the formal education that would otherwise be required to qualify for the AIT Program and the licensing examination, that applicant may seek an educational waiver. That applicant shall be required to possess at least an accredited high school diploma or proof of successfully passing a General Educational Development (GED) test of the American Council on Education or the California High School Proficiency Examination, as well as 10 years of full-time work experience in business, health, or rehabilitation fields, with at least five of the 10 years of work experience in business, health, or rehabilitation management or administration.

(b) The department may review the applicant's church's or religious denomination's Internal Revenue Code 501(c)(3) application, including attachments, the Internal Revenue Service's Letter of Determination of tax-exempt status to the church or religious denomination, and the church's or religious denomination's bylaws, constitution, or member orientation information to confirm an applicant's eligibility for the educational waiver. The applicant's church or religious denomination shall provide the foregoing information to the department for its review and processing of the educational waiver application. The department shall accept notarized copies of these documents.

(c) If the educational requirements are waived, the applicant successfully completes the program-approved 1,000 hour AIT Program, and is successful in passing the national and state licensing examinations, the applicant may only serve as a nursing home administrator in a facility that is owned and operated by the applicant's church or religious denomination.
(Added by Stats. 2008, Ch. 397, Sec. 2. Effective January 1, 2009.)

1416.24.

(a) An application for a nursing home administrator license shall be submitted to the program on a form provided by the program, with the appropriate nonrefundable fee for any required examination, the application, and licensure. The application shall contain information the program deems necessary to determine the applicant's qualifications and a statement whether the individual has been convicted of any crime other than a minor traffic violation. Each applicant shall meet the current requirements for any required examination and licensure. Applicants for licensure shall submit evidence of electronic transmission of fingerprints or fingerprint cards to the program.

(b) A completed application package, together with the examination application, and licensure fees must be received by the program at least 30 days prior to the examination date.

(c) (1) The withdrawal of an application for a license after it has been filed with the department shall not, unless the department consents in writing to the withdrawal, deprive the department of its authority to institute or continue a proceeding against the applicant for the denial of the license upon any ground provided by law or to enter an order denying the license upon that ground.

(2) The suspension, expiration, or forfeiture by operation of law of a license issued by the department, the suspension, forfeiture, or cancellation by order of the department or a court of law of a license, or the surrender without the written consent of the department of a license, shall not deprive the department of its authority to institute or continue a disciplinary proceeding against the licensee upon any ground provided by law or to enter an order suspending or revoking the license or otherwise taking disciplinary action against the licensee on any grounds.

(d) An application that is submitted to the program is valid for only one year after the date of receipt. An applicant who fails to meet all requirements for licensure, including successfully passing the national and state examinations during that one-year period, shall be required to submit another application and appropriate application and examination fees to the program before attempting further examinations.

(e) The program may extend the one-year period described in subdivision (d) upon a showing of good cause. For purposes of this subdivision, good causes shall include, but shall not be limited to, delays in the processing of the application, or delays in applying for and taking the examination caused by illness, accident, or other extenuating circumstances.

(f) An applicant shall submit documentation and evidence to the program of his or her eligibility for licensure.

(g) At the time of the examination, the applicant shall read and sign the Examination Security Agreement and comply with its terms.

(Added by Stats. 2001, Ch. 687, Sec. 5. Effective January 1, 2002.)

1416.26.

(a) As part of the application process for a nursing home administrator license, an applicant shall electronically submit fingerprint images and related information, for a criminal offender record information search, to the Department of Justice and the Federal Bureau of Investigation, through the Department of Justice. The applicant shall provide proof of electronic transmission of his or her fingerprint images and related information to the Department of Justice and the Federal Bureau of Investigation. Upon receipt of the fingerprint images and related information, the Department of Justice shall notify the department with a state or federal level criminal offender record information search response. If no state or federal level criminal record information has been recorded, the Department of Justice shall provide the department with a statement of that fact.

(b) This criminal record clearance shall be completed prior to issuing a license. Applicants shall be responsible for any costs associated with the criminal record clearance. The fee to cover the processing costs of the Department of Justice, not including the costs associated with capturing or transmitting the fingerprint images and related information, shall not exceed thirty-two dollars ($32) for a state level criminal offender record information search, and shall not exceed twenty-four dollars ($24) for a federal level criminal offender record information search.

(Amended by Stats. 2006, Ch. 902, Sec. 3. Effective January 1, 2007.)

1416.28.

(a) Notwithstanding any other law, the program shall at the time of application, issuance, or renewal of a nursing home administrator license require that the applicant or licensee provide his or her federal employer identification number or his or her social security number.

(b) Any applicant or licensee failing to provide his or her federal identification number or social security number shall be reported by the program to the Franchise Tax Board and, if failing to provide after notification pursuant to paragraph (1) of subdivision (b) of Section 19528 of the Revenue and Taxation Code, shall be subject to the penalty provided in paragraph (2) of subdivision (b) of Section 19528 of the Revenue and Taxation Code.

(c) In addition to the penalty specified in subdivision (b), the program may not process any application, original license, or renewal of a license unless the applicant or licensee provides his or her federal employer identification number or social security number where requested on the application.

(d) The program shall, upon request of the Franchise Tax Board, furnish to the Franchise Tax Board the following information with respect to every licensee:

(1) Name.

(2) Address or addresses of record.

(3) Federal employer identification number or social security number.

(4) Type of license.

(5) Effective date of license or renewal.

(6) Expiration date of license.

(7) Whether license is active or inactive, if known.

(8) Whether license is new or a renewal.

(e) The reports required under this section shall be filed on magnetic media or in other machine-readable form, according to standards furnished by the Franchise Tax Board.

(f) The program shall provide to the Franchise Tax Board the information required by this section at a time that the Franchise Tax Board may require.

(g) Notwithstanding Chapter 3.5 (commencing with Section 6250) of Division 7 of Title 1 of the Government Code, the social security number and federal employer identification number furnished pursuant to this section shall not be deemed to be a public record and shall not be open to the public for inspection.

(h) Any deputy, agent, clerk, officer, or employee of the program described in this chapter, any former officer or employee, or other individual who in the course of his or her employment or duty has or has had access to the information required to be furnished under this chapter, may not disclose or make known in any manner that information, except as provided in this section to the Franchise Tax Board or as provided in subdivision (j).

(i) It is the intent of the Legislature in enacting this section to utilize the social security account number or federal employer identification number for the purpose of establishing the identification of persons affected by state tax laws and for purposes of compliance with Section 17520 of the Family Code and, to that end, the information furnished pursuant to this section shall be used exclusively for those purposes.

(j) If the program utilizes a national examination to issue a license, and if a reciprocity agreement or comity exists between California and the state requesting release of the social security number, any deputy, agent, clerk, officer, or employee of the program described in this chapter may release a social security number to an examination or licensing entity, only for the purpose of verification of licensure or examination status.

(Added by Stats. 2001, Ch. 687, Sec. 5. Effective January 1, 2002.)

1416.30.

(a) The program shall require compliance with any judgment or order for support prior to issuance or renewal of a license.

(b) Each applicant for the issuance or renewal of a nursing home administrator license, who is not in compliance with a judgment or order for support shall be subject to Section 11350.6 of the Welfare and Institutions Code.

(c) "Compliance with a judgment or order of support" has the same meaning as specified in paragraph (4) of subdivision (a) of Section 11350.6 of the Welfare and Institutions Code.

(Added by Stats. 2001, Ch. 687, Sec. 5. Effective January 1, 2002.)

1416.32.

(a) Prior to admission to the licensing examination, the applicant shall read and sign an examination security agreement and comply with its terms.

(b) The program may deny, suspend, revoke, or otherwise restrict the license of an applicant or a licensee for any of the following acts:

(1) Having or attempting to have an impersonator take the examination on one's behalf.

(2) Impersonating or attempting to impersonate another to take the examination on that person's behalf.

(3) Communicating or attempting to communicate about the examination content with another examinee or with any person other than the examination staff. This includes divulging the content of specific written examination items to examination preparation providers.

(4) Copying questions or making notes of examination materials or revealing the content of the examination to others who are preparing to take the NHAP examination or who are preparing others to take such examination.

(5) Obstructing or attempting to obstruct the administration of the examination in any way.

(c) It is a misdemeanor for any person to engage in any conduct that subverts or attempts to subvert any licensing examination or the administration of an examination, including, but not limited to, the following conduct:

(1) Conduct that violates the security of the examination materials, removing from the examination room any examination materials without authorization, the unauthorized reproduction by any means of any portion of the actual licensing examination, aiding by any means the unauthorized reproduction of any portion of the actual licensing examination, paying or using professional or paid examination-takers for the purpose of reconstructing any portion of the licensing examination, obtaining examination questions or other examination material, except by specific authorization either before, during, or after an examination, using or purporting to use any examination questions or materials that were improperly removed or taken from any examination for the purpose of instructing or preparing any applicant for examination, or selling, distributing, buying, receiving, or having unauthorized possession of any portion of a future, current, or previously administered licensing examination.

(2) Communicating with any other candidate during the administration of a licensing examination, copying answers from another examinee or permitting one's answers to be copied by another examinee, having in one's possession during the administration of the licensing examination any books, equipment, notes, written or printed materials, or data of any kind, other than the examination materials distributed, or otherwise authorized to be in one's possession during the examination, or impersonating any examinee or having an impersonator take the licensing examination on one's behalf.

(d) Nothing in this section shall preclude prosecution under the authority provided for in any other provision of law.

(e) In addition to any other penalties, a person found guilty of violating this section, shall be liable for the actual damages sustained by the agency administering the examination not to exceed ten thousand dollars ($10,000) and the costs of litigation.

(f) The proceedings under this section shall be governed by Chapter 3 (commencing with Section 525) of Title 7 of Part 2 of the Code of Civil Procedure.

(g) The remedy provided for by this section shall be in addition to, and not a limitation on, the authority provided for in any other provision of law.

(Added by Stats. 2001, Ch. 687, Sec. 5. Effective January 1, 2002.)

1416.34.

(a) (1) In order to have a passing score on either the national or state examination, an examinee shall earn a score of at least 75 percent.

(2) An applicant who fails to pass either the national or state examination shall retake the entire national or state examination.

(3) An applicant who fails to pass either the state or national examination after three attempts shall receive additional training as outlined by the program from a program-approved preceptor, prior to participating in another examination.

(b) The examination shall be administered and evaluated by either of the following:

(1) The department.

(2) A contractor or vendor pursuant to a written agreement with the program or department.

(c) The results of the examination shall be provided to each applicant in a timely manner, not to exceed 90 days from the date of the examination.

(d) The program shall issue a license to an applicant who successfully passes the required examination and has satisfied all other requirements for licensure.

(e) A license shall be effective for a period of two years from the date of issuance.

(f) The program shall issue a provisional license to candidates who meet the provisional licensure requirements established by this chapter.

(g) The program shall replace a lost, damaged, or destroyed license certificate upon receipt of a written request from a licensee and payment of the duplicate license fee. A licensee shall complete a request for a duplicate license on the required program form, and then submit it to the program.

(h) A licensee shall inform the program of the licensee's current home address, mailing address, and if employed by a nursing facility, the name and address of that employer. A licensee shall report a change in any of this information to the program within 30 calendar days. Failure of the licensee to provide timely notice to the program may result in a citation penalty. A licensee shall provide to the program an address to be included in the public files.

(i) A licensee shall display his or her license and show to anyone upon request in order to inform patients or the public as to the identity of the regulatory agency that they may contact if they have questions or complaints regarding the licensee.

(Added by Stats. 2001, Ch. 687, Sec. 5. Effective January 1, 2002.)

1416.36.

(a) The fees prescribed by this chapter are as follows:

(1) The application fee for reviewing an applicant's eligibility to take the examination shall be twenty-five dollars ($25).

(2) The application fee for persons applying for reciprocity consideration licensure under Section 1416.40 shall be fifty dollars ($50).

(3) The application fee for persons applying for the AIT Program shall be one hundred dollars ($100).

(4) The examination fees shall be:

(A) Two hundred seventy-five dollars ($275) for an automated national examination.

(B) Two hundred ten dollars ($210) for an automated state examination or one hundred forty dollars ($140) for a written state examination.

(5) The fee for an initial license shall be one hundred ninety dollars ($190).

(6) The renewal fee for an active or inactive license shall be one hundred ninety dollars ($190).

(7) The delinquency fee shall be fifty dollars ($50).

(8) The duplicate license fee shall be twenty-five dollars ($25).

(9) The fee for a provisional license shall be two hundred fifty dollars ($250).

(10) The fee for endorsement of credentials to the licensing authority of another state shall be twenty-five dollars ($25).

(11) The preceptor certification fee shall be fifty dollars ($50) for each three-year period.

(12) The biennial fee for approval of a continuing education provider shall be one hundred fifty dollars ($150).

(13) The biennial fee for approval of a continuing education course shall be not more than fifteen dollars ($15).

(b) (1) If the revenue projected to be collected is less than the projected costs for the budget year, the department may propose that fees be adjusted to an amount sufficient to cover the reasonable regulatory costs to the department. Notwithstanding Section 10231.5 of the Government Code, commencing February 1, 2013, and every February 1 thereafter, the department shall publish a list of proposed adjustments to fees pursuant to this section. The department shall make this list available to the public by submitting it to the appropriate policy and fiscal committees of the Legislature and by posting it on the department's Internet Web site.

(2) The list described in paragraph (1) shall be submitted in compliance with Section 9795 of the Government Code.

(c) (1) The department shall, within 30 days of the enactment of the annual Budget Act each year, publish a list of actual numerical fee charges as adjusted pursuant to this section. The final fee list, with an explanation of any adjustment, shall be published by both of the following means:

(A) On the department's Internet Web site.

(B) In the initial licensing application package, by including a reference to the link to the department's Internet Web site address as described in subparagraph (A).

(2) (A) This adjustment of fees and the publication of the fee list shall not be subject to the requirements of Chapter 3.5 (commencing with Section 11340) of Part 1 of Division 3 of Title 2 of the Government Code.

(d) (1) Notwithstanding Section 10231.5 of the Government Code, by February 1 of each year, the department shall prepare a report containing the following information, and shall make this report available to the public by submitting it to the appropriate policy and fiscal committees of the Legislature and by posting it on the department's Internet Web site, as required by Section 1266:

(A) Estimates of costs to implement activities required by this chapter and estimated fee revenue.

(B) Recommended adjustments to fees based on projected workload and costs.

(C) An analysis containing the following information for the current fiscal year and each of the previous four fiscal years:

(i) The number of persons applying for a nursing home administrator's license, the number of nursing home administrator licenses approved or denied, and the number of nursing home administrator licenses renewed.

(ii) The number of applicants taking the nursing home administrator exam and the number of applicants who pass or fail the exam.

(iii) The number of persons applying for, accepted into, and completing the AIT Program.

(iv) The number, source, and disposition of complaints made against persons in the AIT Program and licensed nursing home administrators, including the length of time between receipt of the complaint and completion of the investigation.

(v) The number and type of final administrative, remedial, or disciplinary actions taken against licensed nursing home administrators.

(vi) A listing of the names and nature of violations for individual licensed nursing home administrators, including final administrative, remedial, or disciplinary actions taken.

(vii) The number of appeals, informal conferences, or hearings filed by nursing home administrators or held, the length of time between the request being filed and the final determination of the appeal, and the number of administrative, remedial, or disciplinary actions taken.

(2) The report required to be submitted pursuant to paragraph (1) shall be submitted in compliance with Section 9795 of the Government Code.

(Amended by Stats. 2012, Ch. 672, Sec. 3. (AB 1710) Effective January 1, 2013.)

1416.38.

Within 10 days after the beginning of every month, all fees collected by the program for the month preceding, under this chapter, shall be paid into the State Department of Public Health Licensing and Certification Program Fund established by Section 1266.9, to defray the expenses of the program and in carrying out and enforcing the provisions of this chapter.

(Amended by Stats. 2012, Ch. 672, Sec. 4. (AB 1710) Effective January 1, 2013.)

1416.40.

(a) For purposes of this chapter, "reciprocity applicant" means any applicant who holds a current license as a nursing home administrator in another state has been licensed and in good standing, has passed the national examination, and the applicant is otherwise qualified.

(b) An applicant who holds a current valid license as a nursing home administrator in another state may be issued a one-year provisional license as a reciprocity applicant pursuant to this section. The provisional license authorizes the holder to work in this state at a licensed nursing facility during the one-year licensure period.

(c) The applicant shall obtain an application form from the program, complete the form accurately, and, under penalty of perjury, certify the experience, education, and criminal record history information supplied in the application. The applicant shall submit the application to the program, along with any supporting documents to substantiate the application and the applicable provisional, examination, and licensure fees.

(d) The provisional license may be granted to a reciprocity applicant who complies with all of the following informational requirements:

(1) Provides a statement of health consistent with an ability to perform the duties of a nursing home administrator.

(2) Discloses the fact of and the circumstances surrounding any of the following:

(A) Conviction of any criminal law violation of any country, state, or municipality, except minor traffic violations. The applicant shall submit appropriate criminal record information for purposes of this subparagraph.

(B) Any discipline affecting nursing home administrator licensure in any state.

(C) Any pending investigations or disciplinary actions concerning, or surrender of, nursing home administrator licensure in any state. The applicant shall submit an endorsement certificate to verify state licensure and substantiate if he or she has no pending investigation, disciplinary action, or surrender under this subparagraph.

(3) Submits official transcripts as evidence of completed college or university courses and degrees.

(4) Provides satisfactory evidence of current or recent employment experience within the last five years as a licensed nursing home administrator.

(5) Submits proof that the applicant is at least 18 years of age.

(e) The reciprocity applicant who holds a provisional license as authorized by this section shall be required to pass the state examination. If the provisional licensee, fails to pass the state examination within the one-year provisional licensure period, the provisional license shall expire and no further reciprocity accommodations shall be allowed. The

provisional license may not be renewed or extended. At the expiration of the provisional license the applicant may seek licensure in this state through standard procedures.
(Added by Stats. 2001, Ch. 687, Sec. 5. Effective January 1, 2002.)

1416.42.
(a) Except for provisional licenses issued pursuant to Section 1416.40, each license issued pursuant to this chapter shall expire 24 months from the date of issuance.
(b) To renew an unexpired license the licensee shall, at least 30 days prior to the expiration of the license, submit an application for renewal on a form provided by the program, accompanied by the renewal fee. An applicant may request either an active license or an inactive license. If an applicant requests an active license, he or she shall submit proof of completion of the required hours of program-approved continuing education.
(c) A delinquency fee is payable for license renewals not received by the program one day after the license expires.
(d) A license which has expired may be reinstated within three years following the date of expiration. The licensee shall apply for reinstatement on a form provided by the program and submit the completed form together with the current fee for license renewal. If the licensee requests an active license, he or she shall furnish proof of completion of the required hours of continuing education. The reinstatement shall be effective on the date that the completed application, including required fees, is submitted and approved.
(Added by Stats. 2001, Ch. 687, Sec. 5. Effective January 1, 2002.)

1416.44.
(a) Notwithstanding any other provision of law, a licensee who permitted his or her license to expire while serving in any branch of the armed services of the United States during a period of war, as defined in subdivision (e), may, upon application, reinstate his or her license without examination or penalty if the following conditions are met:
(1) His or her license was valid at the time he or she entered the armed services.
(2) The application for reinstatement is made while serving in the armed services, not later than one year from the date of discharge from active service or return to inactive military status, or within three years following the license date of expiration whichever is the most recent time period.
(3) The application for reinstatement is accompanied by an affidavit showing the date of entrance into the service, whether still in the service or date of discharge, and the renewal fee for the current renewal period in which the application is filed is paid.
(4) The application for reinstatement indicates no criminal convictions while absent from the profession.
(b) If application for reinstatement is filed more than one year after discharge or return to inactive status, the applicant, in the discretion of the licensing program, may be required to pass an examination and pay additional fees.
(c) Unless otherwise specifically provided by law, any licensee who, either part time or full time, practices in this state the nursing home administrator profession shall be required to maintain his or her license in good standing even though he or she is in military service.
(d) For the purposes in this section, time spent by a licensee in receiving treatment or hospitalization in any veterans' facility during which he or she is prevented from practicing his or her profession or vocation shall be excluded in determining the periods specified in paragraph (2) of subdivision (a).
(e) As used in this section, "war" means any of the following circumstances:
(1) Whenever Congress has declared war and peace has not formally been restored.
(2) Whenever the United States is engaged in active military operations against any foreign power, whether or not war has been formally declared.
(3) Whenever the United States is assisting the United Nations, in actions involving the use of armed force, to restore international peace and security.
(Added by Stats. 2001, Ch. 687, Sec. 5. Effective January 1, 2002.)

1416.45.
A licensee may not engage in licensed activity while his or her license is suspended or revoked, or after it has expired.
(Added by Stats. 2001, Ch. 687, Sec. 5. Effective January 1, 2002.)

1416.46.
(a) A revoked license may not be renewed.
(b) A licensee whose license has been revoked may petition the program for reinstatement after a period of not less than one year has elapsed from the effective date of the decision or from the date of the denial of a similar petition. The petitioner shall be afforded an opportunity to present either oral or written argument before the program. The program shall decide the petition and the decision shall include the reasons therefor, and any terms and conditions that the program reasonably deems appropriate to impose as a condition of reinstatement.
(Added by Stats. 2001, Ch. 687, Sec. 5. Effective January 1, 2002.)

1416.48.
A licensee who does not intend to engage in activity requiring nursing home administrator licensure may file a request to place his or her license in inactive status. An inactive license is subject to all requirements for renewal, including payment of fees, but completion of continuing education is not required to renew an inactive license. However, proof of completion of 40 continuing education credits during the last two years shall be submitted together with an application for reinstatement of an active license.
(Added by Stats. 2001, Ch. 687, Sec. 5. Effective January 1, 2002.)

1416.50.
(a) For purposes of this chapter, "continuing education" means any course of study offered by an educational institution, association, professional society, or organization for the purpose of providing continuing education for nursing home administrators.

(b) This section shall govern the continuing education requirements needed by a nursing home administrator to renew his or her nursing home administrator license.
(c) In order to renew a license, the applicant shall provide evidence satisfactory to the program that he or she has completed 40 hours of program-approved continuing education courses, of which at least 10 total hours shall be specifically in the area of aging or patient care.
(d) The continuing education courses to be approved for credit toward the continuing education requirements may include the following subject areas offered by accredited colleges, universities, community colleges, or a training entity approved by the department.
(1) Resident care.
(2) Personnel management.
(3) Financial management.
(4) Environmental management.
(5) Regulatory management.
(6) Organizational management.
(7) Patient care and aging.
(e) No continuing education credit shall be allowed for courses failed according to the institution's grading determination.
(f) If the program finds that programs of training and instruction conducted within the state are not sufficient in number or content to enable nursing home administrators to meet requirements established by law and this chapter, the program may approve courses conducted within and without this state as sufficient to meet educational requirements established by law and this chapter. For the purposes of this subdivision, the program shall have the authority to receive funds in a manner consistent with the requirements of the federal government.
(Added by Stats. 2001, Ch. 687, Sec. 5. Effective January 1, 2002.)

ARTICLE 4. Training [1416.55 - 1416.57]
(Article 4 added by Stats. 2001, Ch. 687, Sec. 5.)

1416.55.
(a) An Administrator-in-Training Program (AIT Program) shall be developed by the NHAP, in consultation with representatives from the long-term care industry and advocacy groups. The AIT Program shall include, but not be limited to, all of the following areas of instruction:
(1) Orientation.
(2) Administration and business office.
(3) State and federal regulations governing long-term care facilities.
(4) Residents' rights and abuse prevention.
(5) Staffing requirements and workforce retention.
(6) Nursing services.
(7) Resident activities.
(8) Resident care.
(9) Social services.
(10) Dietary management.
(11) Environmental care, including housekeeping, laundry, and maintenance.
(12) Financial management.
(13) General management.
(14) Government regulations.
(15) Legal management.
(16) Personnel management and training.
(17) Consultants and contracts.
(18) Medical records.
(19) Public relations and marketing.
(b) A person who seeks to satisfy requirements for admission to licensure examinations through participation in an AIT Program shall first receive approval to begin the AIT Program. An applicant shall successfully complete the AIT Program in a program-approved facility under the coordination, supervision, and teaching of a preceptor who has obtained certification from the program and continues to meet the qualifications set forth in the rules and regulations of the program.
(c) In order to be eligible for the AIT Program, an applicant shall submit an application package on forms provided by the NHAP, and pay the applicable fees established by this chapter. The applicant shall be at least 18 years of age.
(d) In addition to the requirements in subdivision (c), the applicant shall meet one or a combination of the following requirements to be eligible for the AIT Program:
(1) A doctorate degree in medicine and a current valid license as a physician and surgeon.
(2) A baccalaureate degree.
(3) Ten years of full-time work experience and a current valid license as a registered nurse. At least the most recent five years of the 10 years of work experience shall be in a supervisory or director of nursing position.
(4) Ten years of full-time work experience in any department of a skilled nursing facility, an intermediate care facility, or an intermediate care facility/developmentally disabled with at least 60 semester units (or 90 quarter units) of college or university courses. At least the most recent five years of the 10 years of work experience shall be in a position as a department manager.
(5) Ten years of full-time hospital administration experience in an acute care hospital with at least 60 semester units (or 90 quarter units) of college or university courses. At least the most recent five years of the 10 years of work experience shall be in a supervisory position.

(e) An applicant for the AIT Program may obtain from the department a waiver of the education requirements in subdivision (d) if he or she meets the requirements of Section 1416.23.

(f) The applicant shall submit an official transcript that evidences the completion of required college or university courses, degrees, or both. An applicant who is a member of a recognized church or religious denomination whose teachings historically prohibit the acquisition of the formal education that would otherwise be required to qualify the applicant for the AIT Program may request a written waiver of the education requirements from the department.

(g) An applicant who qualifies for the AIT Program on the basis of work experience shall submit a declaration signed under penalty of perjury verifying his or her work experience. This declaration shall be signed by a licensed nursing home administrator, physician and surgeon, chief of staff, director of nurses, or registered nurse who can attest to the applicant's work experience.

(Amended by Stats. 2008, Ch. 397, Sec. 3. Effective January 1, 2009.)

1416.57.

(a) An individual may, upon compliance with the requirements of this section, be approved by the program to be a preceptor who is authorized to provide a training program in which the preceptor coordinates, supervises, and teaches persons seeking to meet specified requirements to qualify for the licensing examination under this chapter. The approval obtained under this section shall be effective for a period of two years, after which the preceptor is required to renew his or her preceptor status and attend a preceptor training course provided by the program.

(b) In order to qualify to be a preceptor, a person shall meet all of the following conditions:

(1) Be a current active California licensed nursing home administrator.

(2) Have no pending disciplinary actions.

(3) Have served for at least two years as the designated administrator of a California licensed nursing home or for at least four years as the designated assistant administrator of a California licensed nursing home.

(4) Have gained experience in all administrative functions of a nursing home.

(c) The applicant seeking approval to be a preceptor shall submit an application form provided by the program that requires the applicant's name, address, birth date, the states and dates of issuance of all professional licenses, including those as a nursing home administrator, and any other information required by the program.

(d) At the time of application, for purposes of substantiating that the conditions specified in subdivision (b) have been met, the applicant shall provide satisfactory evidence of his or her education, experience, and knowledge that qualifies him or her to supervise the training of an AIT Program participant and verification that the facilities at which the applicant has had direct management control as an administrator had a continuous operating history, free from major deficiencies, during the period of the applicant's administration.

(e) An applicant shall not be approved as a preceptor until the applicant attends a preceptor's training seminar provided or approved by the program.

(f) (1) For purposes of this section, "AIT" means Administrator-in-Training.

(2) The following requirements shall apply to a preceptor approved pursuant to this section:

(A) The preceptor shall provide a directly supervised training program that will include a minimum of 20 hours per week and a maximum of 60 hours per week and be available at least by telephone at all other times. There shall be regular personal contact between the preceptor and the AIT during the training program. For purposes of this subparagraph, "a directly supervised training program" means supervision by a preceptor of an AIT during the performance of duties authorized by this section. The preceptor shall be available during the AIT's performance of those duties.

(B) The preceptor shall be the designated administrator of the facility where the training is conducted.

(C) The preceptor may not supervise more than two AIT trainees during the same time period.

(D) The preceptor shall inform the NHAP of any significant training program changes dealing with his or her specific AIT.

(E) The preceptor shall rate the AIT's training performance and complete an AIT evaluation report at the end of the AIT's training.

(F) The preceptor shall be evaluated by the program based on the examination success and failure history of his or her AIT trainees and the program may revoke or suspend preceptor certificates as appropriate.

(Added by Stats. 2001, Ch. 687, Sec. 5. Effective January 1, 2002.)

ARTICLE 5. Enforcement [1416.60 - 1416.86]

(Article 5 added by Stats. 2001, Ch. 687, Sec. 5.)

1416.60.

Each licensee shall, within 30 days, after each appointment as the designated administrator of a nursing home and after any termination of that appointment, notify the program. Each notification shall include the name of the administrator, the nursing home administrator number assigned, the name and address of the facility or facilities involved, and the date of the appointment or termination. All information provided pursuant to this section shall be public information.

(Added by Stats. 2001, Ch. 687, Sec. 5. Effective January 1, 2002.)

1416.62.

The program shall maintain a current list of nursing home administrators who have been placed on probation or had their licenses suspended or revoked within the last three years. The program shall provide the current list of these administrators to licensed

nursing homes and the department district offices every six months. The current list shall also be available to the general public upon request.

(Added by Stats. 2001, Ch. 687, Sec. 5. Effective January 1, 2002.)

1416.64.

(a) The program shall maintain a record of enforcement actions reported to the program, pursuant to Section 1416.12. The program shall routinely review the citation logs and files of nursing home administrators whose facilities have received citations from the department to determine if remedial or disciplinary action against the administrator is warranted based on the administrator's involvement or culpability in the citations. Regardless of the facility's performance record, the program may initiate disciplinary action against an administrator who violates any statute or regulation governing licensed nursing home administrators.

(b) Following receipt of reports on temporary suspension orders, service of an accusation for facility license revocations, or final decertification of a facility from participation in the Medi-Cal or Medicare programs, due to failure to meet certification standards, the program shall make a determination as to whether the evidence available warrants remedial or disciplinary action against the administrator or constitutes grounds for denial, suspension, or revocation pursuant to Section 1416.76.

(c) If the program determines that action against the administrator is not warranted, the program shall document in the file the reasons and specific circumstances for not taking remedial or disciplinary action against the administrator's license.

(d) The program shall consider all of the following prior to making a determination to initiate disciplinary action:

(1) Any information provided to the program by the administrator pursuant to this section.

(2) Whether the administrator was in fact the designated administrator of the facility when the violation occurred, or the designated administrator of the facility during the period of time the citation covered.

(3) Whether the administrator should have or could have prevented the violation or violations that occurred.

(e) Prior to making a final determination to initiate action against an administrator, the program shall notify the administrator that the program is considering action and provide the administrator with an opportunity to show just cause why remedial or disciplinary action should not be initiated.

(f) If the program determines that grounds for remedial or disciplinary action exist, the program may initiate either or both of the following actions, as warranted:

(1) Remedial action, including, but not limited to, a conference with the administrator, a letter of warning, or both.

(2) Disciplinary action, including, but not limited to, citations, fines, formal letters of reprimand, probation, denial, suspension, revocation of the administrator's license, or any combination of these actions.

(Added by Stats. 2001, Ch. 687, Sec. 5. Effective January 1, 2002.)

1416.66.

(a) The program shall develop and make available a form that may be utilized at the nursing home administrator's option to provide the program with relevant information, documentation, and background on any actions reported to the program pursuant Section 1416.12.

(b) Any reports received pursuant to Section 1416.12 shall remain in the administrator's file for five years, unless the program is notified that the action has been modified or overturned. Any modification of an action shall be noted and documented in the administrator's file.

(Added by Stats. 2001, Ch. 687, Sec. 5. Effective January 1, 2002.)

1416.68.

(a) It is the responsibility of the nursing home administrator as the managing officer of the facility to plan, organize, direct, and control the day-to-day functions of a facility and to maintain the facility's compliance with applicable laws, rules, and regulations.

(b) The administrator shall be vested with adequate authority to comply with the laws, rules, and regulations relating to the management of the facility.

(c) No licensee shall be cited for any violation caused by any person licensed pursuant to the Medical Practice Act (Chapter 5 (commencing with Section 2000) of Division 2 of the Business and Professions Code) if the person is independent of, and not connected with, the facility and the licensee shows that he or she has exercised reasonable care and diligence in notifying these persons of their duties to the patients in the nursing facility.

(d) The delegation of any authority by a licensee shall not diminish the responsibilities of that licensee.

(Added by Stats. 2001, Ch. 687, Sec. 5. Effective January 1, 2002.)

1416.69.

(a) Within 24 hours after the nursing home administrator acquires actual knowledge or credible information that any of the events specified in subdivision (b) has occurred, the nursing home administrator shall notify the department's district office for licensing and certification of that knowledge or information. This notification may be in written form if it is provided by telephone facsimile or overnight mail, or by telephone with a written confirmation within five calendar days. The information provided pursuant to this subdivision may not be released to the public by the department unless its release is needed to justify an action taken by the department or it otherwise becomes a matter of public record. A violation of this section may result in a citation.

(b) All of the following occurrences shall require notification pursuant to this section as long as the administrator has actual knowledge of the occurrence:

(1) The licensee of a facility receives notice that a judgment lien has been levied against the facility or any of the assets of the facility or the licensee.

(2) A financial institution refuses to honor a check or other instrument issued by the licensee to its employees for a regular payroll.

(3) The supplies, including food items and other perishables, on hand in the facility fall below the minimum specified by any applicable statute or regulation.

(4) The financial resources of the licensee fall below the amount needed to operate the facility for a period of at least 45 days based on the current occupancy of the facility.

(5) The licensee fails to make timely payment of any premiums required to maintain required insurance policies or bonds in effect, or any tax lien levied by any government agency.

(Added by Stats. 2001, Ch. 687, Sec. 5. Effective January 1, 2002.)

1416.70.

(a) The program shall establish a system for the issuance of citations to licensees, examinees, or participants of any program activity offered or approved by the program. The citations may contain an order of abatement, an order to pay an administrative fine assessed by the program chief, or both, where the licensee, examinee, or participant is in violation of any state or federal statute or regulation governing licensed nursing home administrators.

(b) The system shall contain all of the following provisions:

(1) Citations shall be in writing and shall describe with particularity the nature of the violation, including specific reference to the provision of law determined to have been violated.

(2) Where appropriate, the citation shall contain an order of abatement fixing reasonable time for abatement of the violation.

(3) (A) Administrative fines assessed by the program shall be separate from and shall not preclude the levying of any other fines or any civil or criminal penalty.

(B) In no event shall the administrative fine assessed by the program be less than fifty dollars ($50) or exceed two thousand five hundred dollars ($2,500) for each violation. The total assessment shall not exceed ten thousand dollars ($10,000) for each investigation or for counts involving fraudulent billings submitted to insurance companies, Medi-Cal, or Medicare programs.

(4) In assessing a fine, the program shall give due consideration to the appropriateness of the amount of the fine with respect to factors such as the gravity of the violation, the good faith effort of the licensee, examinee, or participant, the unprofessional conduct, including, but not limited to, incompetence and negligence in the performance of the duties and responsibilities of an administrator, the extent to which the cited person has mitigated or attempted to mitigate any damage or injury caused by his or her violation, whether the violation was related to patient care, the history of any previous violations, and other matters as may be appropriate.

(5) A citation or fine assessment issued pursuant to a citation shall inform the licensee, examinee, or participant that if he or she desires a hearing to contest the finding of a violation, the hearing shall be requested by written notice to the program within 30 days after the date of issuance of the citation or assessment. A licensee may, in lieu of contesting a citation pursuant to this section, transmit to the state department 75 percent of the amount specified in the citation for each violation within 15 business days after the issuance of the citation.

(6) Failure of a licensee, examinee, or participant to pay a fine within 30 days of the date of the assessment, unless the citation is being appealed, may result in further disciplinary action being taken by the program. Where a citation is not contested and a fine is not paid, the full amount of the assessed fine, along with any accrued penalty interest, shall be added to the fee for renewal of the license. A license shall not be renewed without payment of the renewal fee, fine, and accrued interest penalty. A citation may be issued without the assessment of an administrative fine.

(c) Assessment of administrative fines may be limited to only particular violations of the applicable licensing act. Notwithstanding any other provisions of law, where a fine is paid to satisfy an assessment based on the finding of a violation, payment of the fine shall be represented as satisfactory resolution of the matter for purposes of public disclosures. Administrative fines collected pursuant to this section shall be deposited in the State Department of Public Health Licensing and Certification Program Fund established by Section 1266.9.

(Amended by Stats. 2012, Ch. 672, Sec. 5. (AB 1710) Effective January 1, 2013.)

1416.72.

(a) The program may issue a citation to any person who holds a license from the program and who violates any statute or regulation governing licensed nursing home administrators.

(b) Any licensee served with a citation may contest the citation by appeal to the program within 30 days of service of the citation. Appeals shall be conducted pursuant to Section 100171.

(c) In addition to requesting a hearing before an administrative law judge, the licensee may, within 10 days after service of the citation, notify the department in writing of his or her request for an informal conference with the department regarding the violations cited in the citation. At the time of requesting an informal conference, the licensee shall inform the department whether he or she shall be represented at the informal conference by legal counsel. Failure to notify the department of legal representation shall not result in forfeiture of the right to have legal counsel present. Unless the request for an informal hearing is made within the 10-day period, the licensee's right to an informal hearing is deemed waived.

(d) The department shall hold an informal conference with the licensee and, if applicable, his or her legal counsel or authorized representatives. At the conclusion of the informal conference the department may affirm, modify, or dismiss the citation, including any administrative fine levied, or order of abatement issued.

(e) The licensee does not waive his or her request for a hearing to contest a citation by requesting an informal conference. If the citation is dismissed after the informal conference, the request for a hearing on the matter of the citation shall be deemed to be withdrawn. If the citation, including any administrative fine levied or order of abatement, is modified or affirmed, the citation shall be upheld and the licensee shall, within 15 working days from the date the citation review conference decision was rendered, notify the director or the director's designee that he or she wishes to appeal the decision through the procedures set forth in Section 100171.

(Added by Stats. 2001, Ch. 687, Sec. 5. Effective January 1, 2002.)

1416.74.

(a) The time allowed for abatement of violation shall begin the first day after the order of abatement has been served or received. If a licensee who has been issued an order of abatement is unable to complete the correction within the time set forth in the citation because of conditions beyond his or her control after the exercise of reasonable diligence, the licensee may request from the program an extension of time in which to complete the correction. The request shall be in writing and made within the time set for abatement.

(b) An order of abatement shall either be personally served upon the licensee or mailed by certified mail, return receipt requested.

(c) When an order of abatement is not contested, or if the order is appealed and the licensee does not prevail, failure to abate the violation cited within the time specified in the citation shall constitute a violation and failure to comply with the order of abatement. Where a licensee has failed to correct a violation within the time specified in the citation the department shall assess the licensee a civil penalty in the amount of fifty dollars ($50) for each day that the violation continues beyond the date specified in the citation. If the licensee disputes a determination by the department regarding alleged failure to correct a violation or regarding the reasonableness of the proposed deadline for correction, the licensee may request an informal conference to contest the determination.

(d) Any unpaid administrative fine shall begin accruing a 7-percent interest penalty on the unpaid balance due. This interest shall continue to accrue until the administrative fine and interest are paid in full.

(Added by Stats. 2001, Ch. 687, Sec. 5. Effective January 1, 2002.)

1416.75.

The program may deny, or may suspend or revoke, a license upon any of the following grounds:

(a) Gross negligence.

(b) Incompetence.

(c) The conviction of any crime involving dishonesty or which is substantially related to the qualifications, functions, or duties of a nursing home administrator. A conviction following a plea of nolo contendere is deemed to be a conviction within the meaning of this section.

(d) Using fraud or deception in applying for a license or in taking the examination provided for in this chapter.

(e) Treating or attempting to treat any physical or mental condition without being currently licensed to do so.

(f) Violating Section 650 of the Business and Professions Code, any provision of this chapter, or any rule or regulation of the program adopted pursuant to this chapter.

(g) Lack of any qualification requirement for the license.

(h) Failure to report under Section 1416.60 to the program, without just cause.

(Added by Stats. 2001, Ch. 687, Sec. 5. Effective January 1, 2002.)

1416.76.

(a) The program may deny a nursing home administrator applicant or licensee, a license, based on one of the following grounds:

(1) Conviction of a crime. A conviction within the meaning of this section means a plea or verdict of guilty or a conviction following a plea of nolo contendere. The program may take action following the establishment of a conviction after the time for appeal has elapsed, or the judgment of conviction has been affirmed on appeal, or when an order granting probation is made suspending the imposition of sentence, irrespective of a subsequent order under Section 1203.4 of the Penal Code.

(2) Commits any act involving dishonesty, fraud, or deceit with the intent to substantially benefit himself or herself or another, or substantially injure another.

(3) Commits any act which, if done by a licentiate, would be grounds for suspension or revocation of license. The program may deny a license pursuant to this subdivision only if the crime or act is substantially related to the qualifications, functions, or duties of a nursing home administrator.

(b) Notwithstanding any other provision of this chapter, no person shall be denied a license solely on the basis that he or she has been convicted of a felony if he or she has obtained a certificate of rehabilitation under Section 4852.01 of the Penal Code, or that he or she has been convicted of a misdemeanor and has met all applicable requirements of the criteria of rehabilitation developed by the program pursuant to subdivision (f).

(c) The program may deny a nursing home administrator license on the ground that the applicant knowingly made a false statement of fact required to be revealed in the application for the license.

(d) The program may suspend or revoke a license on the ground that the applicant or licensee has been convicted of a crime, as defined in paragraph (1) of subdivision (a), if the crime is substantially related to the qualifications, functions, or duties of a nursing home administrator.

(e) The program shall develop criteria to use to determine whether a crime or act is substantially related to the qualifications, functions, or duties of a nursing home administrator, and shall use the criteria when considering the denial, suspension, or revocation of a license.

(f) The program shall develop criteria to be used by the program to evaluate the rehabilitation of a person when considering the denial, suspension, or revocation of a license under this section.

(g) The program shall take into account all competent evidence of rehabilitation furnished by the applicant or licensee pursuant to the evaluation process set forth in subdivision (f).

(Added by Stats. 2001, Ch. 687, Sec. 5. Effective January 1, 2002.)

1416.77.

The program may deny, or may suspend or revoke, a nursing home administrator license or participation in specific training program areas under this chapter upon any of the following grounds:

(a) Misappropriation of funds or property of the facility, the patients, or of others.

(b) Using fraud, deception, or misrepresentation in applying for the AIT Program, the examination for licensure, or any other program functions provided for in this chapter.

(c) Procuring a nursing home license by fraud, deception, or misrepresentation.

(d) Impersonating any applicant or acting as a proxy for an applicant in an examination.

(e) Impersonating any licensed nursing home administrator.

(f) Treating or attempting to treat any physical or mental condition without having a valid license to do so.

(g) Violating Section 650 of the Business and Professions Code, any provisions of this chapter, or any rule or regulation of the program adopted pursuant to this chapter.

(h) Lack of any qualification requirement for a license, participation in the AIT Program or preceptor program.

(i) A pattern of failure to report changes under Section 1416.60 to the program without just cause.

(j) Failure to comply with this chapter or the laws, rules, and regulations relating to health facilities.

(k) The commission of any dishonest, corrupt, or fraudulent act or any act of physical or mental, including sexual, abuse of any person in connection with the administration of, or any patient in, a nursing home.

(l) Violation by the licensee of any of the provisions of this chapter or of the rules and regulations promulgated under this chapter.

(m) Aiding, abetting, or conspiring with another person to violate provisions of this chapter or of the rules and regulations promulgated under this chapter.

(n) Violation of the examination security agreement.

(Added by Stats. 2001, Ch. 687, Sec. 5. Effective January 1, 2002.)

1416.78.

(a) The program may place a nursing home administrator license on probation in lieu of formal action to suspend or revoke the license if the department determines that probation is the appropriate action. Upon successful completion of the probation period, the license shall be restored to regular status.

(b) The probationary license shall be based upon an agreement entered into between the licensee and the program that specifies terms and conditions of licensure during the probationary period. The terms and conditions shall be related to matters, including, but not limited to, work performance, rehabilitation, training, counseling, progress reports, and treatment programs.

(c) The term of the probationary license shall not exceed two years. If the licensee successfully completes the term of probation, as determined by the department, no further action shall be taken upon the allegations that were the basis for the probationary license. If the licensee fails to comply with the terms and conditions of the probationary license agreement, the department may proceed with a formal action to suspend or revoke the license.

(Added by Stats. 2001, Ch. 687, Sec. 5. Effective January 1, 2002.)

1416.80.

Upon the determination to deny application for licensure for grounds specified in Section 1416.77, the program shall immediately notify the applicant in writing by certified mail. A petition for an administrative hearing must be received by the program within 20 business days of receipt of notification. Upon receipt, the department shall set the matter for administrative hearing, pursuant to procedures specified in Section 100171.

(Added by Stats. 2001, Ch. 687, Sec. 5. Effective January 1, 2002.)

1416.82.

(a) Proceedings to suspend or revoke licensure for grounds specified in Section 1416.77 shall be conducted in accordance with Section 100171. In the event of conflict between this chapter and Section 100171, Section 100171 shall prevail.

(b) (1) The program may temporarily suspend any license prior to any hearing if the action is necessary to protect the public welfare. The program shall notify the licensee of the temporary suspension and the effective date. Upon receipt of a notice of defense by the licensee, the department shall set the matter within 15 days. The administrative hearing conducted in accordance with Section 100171 shall be held as soon as possible but not later than 30 days after receipt of the notice. The temporary suspension shall remain in effect until the hearing is completed and the department has made a final determination on the merits. However, the temporary suspension shall be deemed vacated if the department fails to make a final determination on the merits of the action within 60 days after the original hearing has been completed. If the provisions of this chapter or the rules or regulations promulgated by the director are violated by a licensee, the director may suspend the license for the violation.

(2) If the program determines that the temporary suspension shall become an actual suspension, the department shall specify the period of the suspension, not to exceed two

years. The program may determine that the suspension shall be stayed, and place the licensee on probation for a period that shall not exceed two years.

(c) The program may suspend or revoke a license prior to any hearing when immediate action is necessary in the judgment of the director to protect the public welfare. Proceedings for immediate revocation shall be conducted in accordance with Section 100171. The department shall set the matter for hearing within 15 days and hold the administrative hearing as soon as possible but not later than 30 calendar days from receipt of the request for a hearing. A written hearing decision upholding or setting aside the action shall be sent by certified mail to the licenseholder within 30 calendar days of the hearing.

(Added by Stats. 2001, Ch. 687, Sec. 5. Effective January 1, 2002.)

1416.84.

Whenever any person has engaged, or is about to engage, in any acts or practices that constitute, or will constitute, a violation of this chapter, the superior court in and for the county in which those acts or practices take place, or are about to take place, may issue an injunction or other appropriate order, restraining the conduct, on application of the program, to the Attorney General, or the district attorney.

(Added by Stats. 2001, Ch. 687, Sec. 5. Effective January 1, 2002.)

1416.86.

If any provision of this chapter, or the application thereof to any person or circumstance, is held invalid, that invalidity shall not affect other provisions or applications of this chapter that can be given effect without the invalid provision or application, and to this end the provisions of this chapter are declared to be severable.

(Added by Stats. 2001, Ch. 687, Sec. 5. Effective January 1, 2002.)

CHAPTER 2.4. Quality of Long-Term Health Facilities [1417 - 1439.8]

(Chapter 2.4 added by Stats. 1973, Ch. 1057.)

1417.

This chapter shall be known and may be cited as the Long-Term Care, Health, Safety, and Security Act of 1973.

(Added by Stats. 1973, Ch. 1057.)

1417.1.

It is the intent of the Legislature in enacting this chapter to establish (1) a citation system for the imposition of prompt and effective civil sanctions against long-term health care facilities in violation of the laws and regulations of this state, and the federal laws and regulations as applicable to nursing facilities as defined in subdivision (k) of Section 1250, relating to patient care; (2) an inspection and reporting system to ensure that long-term health care facilities are in compliance with state statutes and regulations pertaining to patient care; and (3) a provisional licensing mechanism to ensure that full-term licenses are issued only to those long-term health care facilities that meet state standards relating to patient care.

(Amended by Stats. 1992, Ch. 1163, Sec. 2. Effective January 1, 1993. Amendatory changes are conditionally inoperative as prescribed by Sec. 8 of Ch. 1163.)

1417.15.

(a) (1) If one or more of the following remedies is actually imposed for violation of state or federal requirements, the long-term health care facility shall post a notice of the imposed remedy or remedies, in the form specified in subdivision (c), on all doors providing ingress to or egress from the facility, except as specified in paragraph (2):

(A) License suspension.

(B) Termination of certification for Medicare or Medi-Cal.

(C) Denial of payment by Medicare or Medi-Cal for all otherwise eligible residents.

(D) Denial of payment by Medicare or Medi-Cal for otherwise eligible incoming residents.

(E) Ban on admission of any type.

(2) For purposes of this subdivision, a distinct part nursing facility shall only be required to post the notice on all main doors providing ingress to or egress from the distinct part, and not on all of the doors providing ingress to or egress from the facility. An intermediate care facility/developmentally disabled habilitative and an intermediate care facility/developmentally disabled-nursing shall post this notice on the inside of all doors providing ingress to or egress from the facility.

(b) A violation of the requirement of subdivision (a) shall be issued and enforced in the manner of a class "B" violation.

(c) The form of the notice established pursuant to subdivision (a) shall be entitled "Notice of Violation Remedies." Each notice shall list the remedy or remedies imposed, as set forth in subdivision (a), and shall include the date the remedy was imposed. The notice shall be typeset on white bond paper, 8 $1/2$ x 11 inches in size, in boldface black type in a 16-point sans serif type font. A facility may remove the notice on or after the date on which the sanction is lifted.

(Amended by Stats. 2001, Ch. 685, Sec. 11. Effective January 1, 2002.)

1417.2.

(a) Notwithstanding Section 1428, moneys collected as a result of state and federal civil penalties imposed under this chapter or federal law shall be deposited into accounts that are hereby established in the Special Deposit Fund created pursuant to Section 16370 of the Government Code. These accounts are titled the State Health Facilities Citation Penalties Account, into which moneys derived from civil penalties for violations of state law shall be deposited, and the Federal Health Facilities Citation Penalties Account, into which moneys derived from civil penalties for violations of federal law shall be deposited. Moneys from these accounts shall be used, notwithstanding Section 16370 of the Government Code, upon appropriation by the Legislature, in accordance with state and federal law for the protection of health or property of residents of long-term health care facilities, including, but not limited to, the following:

(1) Relocation expenses incurred by the department, in the event of a facility closure.

(2) Maintenance of facility operation pending correction of deficiencies or closure, such as temporary management or receivership, in the event that the revenues of the facility are insufficient.

(3) Reimbursing residents for personal funds lost. In the event that the loss is a result of the actions of a long-term health care facility or its employees, the revenues of the facility shall first be used.

(4) The costs associated with informational meetings required under Section 1327.2.

(5) Support for the Long-Term Care Ombudsman Program established pursuant to Chapter 11 (commencing with Section 9700) of Division 8.5 of the Welfare and Institutions Code in an amount appropriated from the State Health Facilities Citation Penalties Account for this purpose in the annual Budget Act.

(b) Notwithstanding subdivision (a), the balance in the State Health Facilities Citation Penalties Account shall not, at any time, exceed ten million dollars ($10,000,000).

(c) Moneys from the Federal Health Facilities Citation Penalties Account, in the amount not to exceed one hundred thirty thousand dollars ($130,000), may also be used, notwithstanding Section 16370 of the Government Code, upon appropriation by the Legislature, in accordance with state and federal law for the improvement of quality of care and quality of life for long-term health care facilities residents pursuant to Section 1417.3.

(d) The department shall post on its Internet Web site, and shall update on a quarterly basis, all of the following regarding the funds in the State Health Facilities Citation Penalties Account and the Federal Health Facilities Citation Penalties Account:

(1) The specific sources of funds deposited into the account.

(2) The amount of funds in the account that have not been allocated.

(3) A detailed description of how funds in the account have been allocated and expended, including, but not limited to, the names of persons or entities that received the funds, the amount of salaries paid to temporary managers, and a description of equipment purchased with the funds. However, the description shall not include the names of residents.

(Amended by Stats. 2011, Ch. 8, Sec. 2. (SB 72) Effective March 24, 2011.)

1417.3.

The department shall promote quality of care and quality of life for residents, clients, and patients in long-term health care facility services through specific activities that include, but are not limited to, all of the following:

(a) Research and evaluation of innovative facility resident care models.

(b) (1) Provision of statewide training on effective facility practices.

(2) Training also shall include topics related to the provision of quality of care and quality of life for facility residents. The topics for training shall be identified by the department through a periodic survey. The curriculum for the training provided under this paragraph shall be developed in consultation with representatives from provider associations, consumer associations, and others, as deemed appropriate by the state department.

(c) The establishment of separate units to respond to facility requests for technical assistance regarding licensing and certification requirements, compliance with federal and state standards, and related operational issues.

(d) State employees providing technical assistance to facilities pursuant to this section are only required to report violations they discover during the provision of the assistance to the appropriate district office if the violations constitute an immediate and serious threat to the health and welfare of, or have resulted in actual harm to, patients, residents, or clients of the facility.

(e) The state department shall measure facility satisfaction and the effectiveness of the technical assistance provided pursuant to subdivision (c).

(f) No person employed in the technical assistance or training units under subdivisions (b) and (c) shall also participate in the licensing, surveying, or direct regulation of facilities.

(g) This section shall not diminish the department's ongoing survey and enforcement process.

(Amended by Stats. 2001, Ch. 685, Sec. 12. Effective January 1, 2002.)

1417.4.

(a) There is hereby established in the state department the Quality Awards Program for nursing homes.

(b) The department shall establish criteria under the program, after consultation with stakeholder groups, for recognizing all skilled nursing facilities that provide exemplary care to residents.

(c) (1) Monetary awards shall be made to Quality Awards Program recipients that serve high proportions of Medi-Cal residents to the extent funds are appropriated each year in the annual Budget Act.

(2) Monetary awards presented under this section and paid for by funds appropriated from the General Fund shall be used for staff bonuses and distributed in accordance with criteria established by the department.

(3) Monetary awards presented under this section and paid for from funds from the Federal Citation Penalty Account shall be used to fund innovative facility grants to improve the quality of care and quality of life for residents in skilled nursing facilities, or to fund innovative efforts to increase employee recruitment, or retention, or both, subject to federal approval.

(d) The department shall establish criteria for selecting facilities to receive the quality awards, in consultation with senior advocacy organizations, employee labor organizations representing facility employees, nursing home industry representatives, and other interested parties as deemed appropriate by the department. The criteria established pursuant to this subdivision shall not be considered regulations within the meaning of Section 11342 of the Government Code, and shall not be subject to adoption as regulations pursuant to Chapter 3.5 (commencing with Section 11340) of Part 1 of Division 3 of Title 2 of the Government Code.

(e) The department shall publish an annual listing of the Quality Awards Program recipients with the dollar amount awarded, if applicable. The department shall also publish an annual listing of the Quality Awards Program recipients that receive innovative facility grants with the purpose of the grant and the grant amount.

(f) All of the funds available for the programs described in this section shall be disbursed to qualified facilities by January 1, 2002, and January 1 of each year thereafter.

(Amended by Stats. 2001, Ch. 171, Sec. 2.3. Effective August 10, 2001.)

1418.

As used in this chapter:

(a) "Long-term health care facility" means any facility licensed pursuant to Chapter 2 (commencing with Section 1250) that is any of the following:

(1) Skilled nursing facility.

(2) Intermediate care facility.

(3) Intermediate care facility/developmentally disabled.

(4) Intermediate care facility/developmentally disabled habilitative.

(5) Intermediate care facility/developmentally disabled-nursing.

(6) Congregate living health facility.

(7) Nursing facility.

(8) Intermediate care facility/developmentally disabled-continuous nursing.

(b) "Long-term health care facility" also includes a pediatric day health and respite care facility licensed pursuant to Chapter 8.6 (commencing with Section 1760).

(c) "Long-term health care facility" does not include a general acute care hospital or an acute psychiatric hospital, except for that distinct part of the hospital that provides skilled nursing facility, intermediate care facility, intermediate care facility/developmentally disabled, or pediatric day health and respite care facility services.

(d) "Licensee" means the holder of a license issued under Chapter 2 (commencing with Section 1250) or Chapter 8.6 (commencing with Section 1760) for a long-term health care facility.

(Amended by Stats. 2013, Ch. 724, Sec. 2. (SB 651) Effective January 1, 2014.)

1418.1.

(a) Any person receiving respite care services shall be permitted to bring medications to the skilled nursing facility or intermediate care facility if the contents have been examined and positively identified upon the patient's admission to the facility by the patient's personal physician and surgeon or a pharmacist retained by the facility.

(b) A skilled nursing facility or intermediate care facility providing respite care services shall not be required to afford a person receiving respite care services a bedhold when the person is transferred to a general acute care hospital, as defined in Section 1250.

(c) A skilled nursing facility or intermediate care facility providing respite care services shall permit the personal physician and surgeon of a person receiving respite care services to issue advance orders for care and treatment for a period not to exceed 90 days from the date of admission of the person, based on the person's medical history, diagnosis, and physical assessment conducted upon admission. The skilled nursing facility or intermediate care facility may readmit the person for respite care services on the basis of the advance orders for care and treatment, unless the personal physician and surgeon of the person indicates that there has been a significant change in the person's medical condition. These advance orders shall only be used by the skilled nursing or intermediate care facility during periods in which the person is receiving respite care services.

(d) A skilled nursing facility or intermediate care facility providing respite care services may implement an abbreviated resident assessment and care planning procedure for persons admitted for respite care services consistent with the facility's obligation to protect the health and safety of residents and the general public. The abbreviated resident assessment and care planning procedure shall address the necessary care services required by the person admitted for respite care during the length of the respite care stay. The abbreviated resident assessment and care planning procedure documents do not have to be updated with every readmission of the same person to the facility for respite care services, unless the personal physician and surgeon of the person indicates that there has been a significant change in the person's medical condition.

(e) As used in this section, "respite care services" means service provided to frail elderly or functionally impaired persons in a licensed skilled nursing facility or intermediate care facility, as defined in Section 1250, on a temporary or periodic basis to relieve persons who are providing their care at home.

(f) As used in this section, "temporary or periodic" means a period of time not to exceed 15 consecutive days or a total of 45 days in any one year.

(g) No more than 10 percent of a skilled nursing or intermediate care facility's total licensed bed capacity may be used during any one calendar year for the provision of respite care services as defined in this section. A facility may exceed this limit with the prior written approval of the State Department of Health Services.

(Added by Stats. 1990, Ch. 1329, Sec. 4. Effective September 26, 1990.)

1418.2.

(a) Every facility licensed pursuant to subdivisions (c), (d), (e), and (g) of Section 1250 and every skilled nursing facility licensed separately under subdivision (a) of Section 1250 shall establish and maintain a resident council. Each council shall include the residents of the health facility, and may include family members of residents, advocates, or ombudsman groups interested in residents of health facilities, and personnel of the health facility. Family members of residents shall be invited to meetings of resident councils.

The council shall meet at regularly scheduled intervals, maintain written minutes, including names of council members present, and have minutes available for review by the state department upon its request. Facility policies on resident councils shall in no way limit the right of residents to meet independently with outside persons or facility personnel as determined solely by the residents of the facility.

Written minutes of regularly scheduled council meetings may include recommendations from the council to the licensee of the health facility which shall be provided to the licensee. The licensee shall provide evidence of review and action on these recommendations to the state department upon its request.

(b) Any health facility which fails to establish a resident council as prescribed in subdivision (a) shall be subject to the provisions of Section 1280.

(c) The state department shall, by regulation, specify those circumstances under which a health facility may be exempted from the provisions of subdivisions (a) and (b), including, but not limited to, the following:

(1) A resident population consisting of a majority of patients with progressively disabling disorders defined in Section 1250.4.

(2) Facilities with no more than six residents which provide alternate means for residents to actively share in planning and enhancing of life in the facility.

(3) Other circumstances as determined by the state department.

(Amended by Stats. 1986, Ch. 1351, Sec. 3.)

1418.21.

(a) A skilled nursing facility that has been certified for purposes of Medicare or Medicaid shall post the overall facility rating information determined by the federal Centers for Medicare and Medicaid Services (CMS) in accordance with the following requirements:

(1) The information shall be posted in at least the following locations in the facility:

(A) An area accessible and visible to members of the public.

(B) An area used for employee breaks.

(C) An area used by residents for communal functions, such as dining, resident council meetings, or activities.

(2) The information shall be posted on white or light-colored paper that includes all of the following, in the following order:

(A) The full name of the facility, in a clear and easily readable font of at least 28 point.

(B) The full address of the facility in a clear and easily readable font of at least 20 point.

(C) The most recent overall star rating given by CMS to that facility, except that a facility shall have seven business days from the date when it receives a different rating from CMS to include the updated rating in the posting. The star rating shall be aligned in the center of the page. The star rating shall be expressed as the number that reflects the number of stars given to the facility by CMS. The number shall be in a clear and easily readable font of at least two inches print.

(D) Directly below the star symbols shall be the following text in a clear and easily readable font of at least 28 point:

"The above number is out of 5 stars."

(E) Directly below the text described in subparagraph (D) shall be the following text in a clear and easily readable font of at least 14 point:

"This facility is reviewed annually and has been licensed by the State of California and certified by the federal Centers for Medicare and Medicaid Services (CMS). CMS rates facilities that are certified to accept Medicare or Medicaid. CMS gave the above rating to this facility. A detailed explanation of this rating is maintained at this facility and will be made available upon request. This information can also be accessed online at the Nursing Home Compare Internet Web site at http://www.medicare.gov/NHcompare. Like any information, the Five-Star Quality Rating System has strengths and limits. The criteria upon which the rating is determined may not represent all of the aspects of care that may be important to you. You are encouraged to discuss the rating with facility staff. The Five-Star Quality Rating System was created to help consumers, their families, and caregivers compare nursing homes more easily and help identify areas about which you may want to ask questions. Nursing home ratings are assigned based on ratings given to health inspections, staffing, and quality measures. Some areas are assigned a greater weight than other areas. These ratings are combined to calculate the overall rating posted here."

(F) Directly below the text described in subparagraph (E), the following text shall appear in a clear and easily readable font of at least 14 point:

"State licensing information on skilled nursing facilities is available on the State Department of Public Health's Internet Web site at: www.cdph.ca.gov, under Programs, Licensing and Certification, Health Facilities Consumer Information System."

(3) For the purposes of this section, "a detailed explanation of this rating" shall include, but shall not be limited to, a printout of the information explaining the Five-Star Quality Rating System that is available on the CMS Nursing Home Compare Internet Web site. This information shall be maintained at the facility and shall be made available upon request.

(4) The requirements of this section shall be in addition to any other posting or inspection report availability requirements.

(b) Violation of this section shall constitute a class B violation, as defined in subdivision (e) of Section 1424 and, notwithstanding Section 1290, shall not constitute a crime. Fines from a violation of this section shall be deposited into the State Health Facilities Citation Penalties Account, created pursuant to Section 1417.2.

(c) This section shall be operative on January 1, 2011.

(Amended by Stats. 2010, Ch. 328, Sec. 120. (SB 1330) Effective January 1, 2011.)

1418.3.

(a) Each licensed skilled nursing facility shall, when requested by a member of a patient's family, allow the family to meet privately with a family member who is a resident in the facility.

(b) "Family member" for the purposes of this section means an immediate family member or family member designated and documented on the patient's record at the time of admission to the facility.

(Added by Stats. 1987, Ch. 1125, Sec. 1.)

1418.4.

(a) No licensed skilled nursing facility or intermediate care facility may prohibit the formation of a family council, and, when requested by a member of the resident's family or the resident's representative, the family council shall be allowed to meet in a common meeting room of the facility at least once a month during mutually agreed upon hours.

(b) Facility policies on family councils shall in no way limit the right of residents, family members, and family council members to meet independently with outside persons, including members of nonprofit or government organizations or with facility personnel during nonworking hours.

(c) "Family council" for the purpose of this section means a meeting of family members, friends, or representatives of two or more residents to confer in private without facility staff.

(d) Family councils shall also be provided adequate space on a prominent bulletin board or other posting area for the display of meeting notices, minutes, newsletters, or other information pertaining to the operation or interest of the family council.

(e) Staff or visitors may attend family council meetings, at the group's invitation.

(f) The facility shall provide a designated staff person who shall be responsible for providing assistance and responding to written requests that result from family council meetings.

(g) The facility shall consider the views and act upon the grievances and recommendations of a family council concerning proposed policy and operational decisions affecting resident care and life in the facility.

(h) The facility shall respond in writing to written requests or concerns of the family council, within 10 working days.

(i) When a family council exists, the facility shall include notice of the family council meetings in at least a quarterly mailing, and shall inform family members or representatives of new residents who are identified on the admissions agreement, during the admissions process, or in the resident's records, of the existence of the family council. The notice shall include the time, place, and date of meetings, and the person to contact regarding involvement in the family council.

(j) No facility shall willfully interfere with the formation, maintenance, or promotion of a family council. For the purposes of this subdivision, willful interference shall include, but not be limited to, discrimination or retaliation in any way against an individual as a result of his or her participation in a family council, or the willful scheduling of facility events in conflict with a previously scheduled family council meeting.

(k) (1) Violation of the provisions of this section shall constitute a violation of the residents' rights.

(2) Violation of the provisions of this section shall constitute a class "B" violation, as defined in Section 1424.

(Amended by Stats. 2000, Ch. 448, Sec. 1. Effective January 1, 2001.)

1418.5.

No regulation adopted with respect to skilled nursing facilities or intermediate care facilities shall prohibit patients in the facility from storing nonprescription or topical ophthalmic medications at their bedside unless contraindicated by the patient's attending physician or the facility.

(Amended by Stats. 1982, Ch. 408, Sec. 1.)

1418.6.

No long-term health care facility shall accept or retain any patient for whom it cannot provide adequate care.

(Added by Stats. 1985, Ch. 11, Sec. 7. Effective March 6, 1985.)

1418.7.

(a) Long-term health care facilities, as defined in Section 1418, shall develop and implement policies and procedures designed to reduce theft and loss.

(b) The facility program shall include all of the following:

(1) Establishment and posting of the facility's theft and loss policies.

(2) Orientation of employees to those policies.

(3) Documentation of theft and loss of property with a value of twenty-five dollars ($25) or more.

(4) Inventory of patient's personal property upon admission.

(5) Inventory of and surrender of patient's personal property upon death or discharge.

(6) Regular review of the effectiveness of the policies and procedures.

(7) Marking of patient's personal property, including dentures and prosthetic and orthopedic devices.

(8) Reports to local law enforcement of stolen property with a value of one hundred dollars ($100) or more.

(9) Methods for securing personal property.

(10) Notification of residents and families of the facility's policies.

(c) The policies and procedures developed by the facilities pursuant to this section shall be in accordance with Section 1289.4, as added by Assembly Bill 2047 of the 1987–88 Regular Session of the Legislature, if that bill is enacted and becomes effective.

(d) If a facility has shown clear and convincing evidence of its efforts to comply with the requirements of this section, no citation shall be issued as a result of the occasional occurrence of theft and loss in a facility.

(Added by Stats. 1987, Ch. 1226, Sec. 1.)

1418.8.

(a) If the attending physician and surgeon of a resident in a skilled nursing facility or intermediate care facility prescribes or orders a medical intervention that requires that informed consent be obtained prior to administration of the medical intervention, but is unable to obtain informed consent because the physician and surgeon determines that the resident lacks capacity to make decisions concerning his or her health care and that there is no person with legal authority to make those decisions on behalf of the resident, the physician and surgeon shall inform the skilled nursing facility or intermediate care facility.

(b) For purposes of subdivision (a), a resident lacks capacity to make a decision regarding his or her health care if the resident is unable to understand the nature and consequences of the proposed medical intervention, including its risks and benefits, or is unable to express a preference regarding the intervention. To make the determination regarding capacity, the physician shall interview the patient, review the patient's medical records, and consult with skilled nursing or intermediate care facility staff, as appropriate, and family members and friends of the resident, if any have been identified.

(c) For purposes of subdivision (a), a person with legal authority to make medical treatment decisions on behalf of a patient is a person designated under a valid Durable Power of Attorney for Health Care, a guardian, a conservator, or next of kin. To determine the existence of a person with legal authority, the physician shall interview the patient, review the medical records of the patient, and consult with skilled nursing or intermediate care facility staff, as appropriate, and with family members and friends of the resident, if any have been identified.

(d) The attending physician and the skilled nursing facility or intermediate care facility may initiate a medical intervention that requires informed consent pursuant to subdivision (e) in accordance with acceptable standards of practice.

(e) Where a resident of a skilled nursing facility or intermediate care facility has been prescribed a medical intervention by a physician and surgeon that requires informed consent and the physician has determined that the resident lacks capacity to make health care decisions and there is no person with legal authority to make those decisions on behalf of the resident, the facility shall, except as provided in subdivision (h), conduct an interdisciplinary team review of the prescribed medical intervention prior to the administration of the medical intervention. The interdisciplinary team shall oversee the care of the resident utilizing a team approach to assessment and care planning, and shall include the resident's attending physician, a registered professional nurse with responsibility for the resident, other appropriate staff in disciplines as determined by the resident's needs, and, where practicable, a patient representative, in accordance with applicable federal and state requirements. The review shall include all of the following:

(1) A review of the physician's assessment of the resident's condition.

(2) The reason for the proposed use of the medical intervention.

(3) A discussion of the desires of the patient, where known. To determine the desires of the resident, the interdisciplinary team shall interview the patient, review the patient's medical records, and consult with family members or friends, if any have been identified.

(4) The type of medical intervention to be used in the resident's care, including its probable frequency and duration.

(5) The probable impact on the resident's condition, with and without the use of the medical intervention.

(6) Reasonable alternative medical interventions considered or utilized and reasons for their discontinuance or inappropriateness.

(f) A patient representative may include a family member or friend of the resident who is unable to take full responsibility for the health care decisions of the resident, but who has agreed to serve on the interdisciplinary team, or other person authorized by state or federal law.

(g) The interdisciplinary team shall periodically evaluate the use of the prescribed medical intervention at least quarterly or upon a significant change in the resident's medical condition.

(h) In case of an emergency, after obtaining a physician and surgeon's order as necessary, a skilled nursing or intermediate care facility may administer a medical intervention that requires informed consent prior to the facility convening an interdisciplinary team review. If the emergency results in the application of physical or chemical restraints, the interdisciplinary team shall meet within one week of the emergency for an evaluation of the medical intervention.

(i) Physicians and surgeons and skilled nursing facilities and intermediate care facilities shall not be required to obtain a court order pursuant to Section 3201 of the Probate Code prior to administering a medical intervention which requires informed consent if the requirements of this section are met.

(j) Nothing in this section shall in any way affect the right of a resident of a skilled nursing facility or intermediate care facility for whom medical intervention has been prescribed, ordered, or administered pursuant to this section to seek appropriate judicial relief to review the decision to provide the medical intervention.

(k) No physician or other health care provider, whose action under this section is in accordance with reasonable medical standards, is subject to administrative sanction if the physician or health care provider believes in good faith that the action is consistent with this section and the desires of the resident, or if unknown, the best interests of the resident.

(l) The determinations required to be made pursuant to subdivisions (a), (e), and (g), and the basis for those determinations shall be documented in the patient's medical record and shall be made available to the patient's representative for review.

(Amended by Stats. 2006, Ch. 538, Sec. 355. Effective January 1, 2007.)

1418.81.

(a) In order to assure the provision of quality patient care and as part of the planning for that quality patient care, commencing at the time of admission, a skilled nursing facility, as defined in subdivision (c) of Section 1250, shall include in a resident's care assessment the resident's projected length of stay and the resident's discharge potential. The assessment shall include whether the resident has expressed or indicated a preference to return to the community and whether the resident has social support, such as family, that may help to facilitate and sustain return to the community. The assessment shall be recorded with the relevant portions of the minimum data set, as described in Section 14110.15 of the Welfare and Institutions Code. The plan of care shall reflect, if applicable, the care ordered by the attending physician needed to assist the resident in achieving the resident's preference of return to the community.

(b) The skilled nursing facility shall evaluate the resident's discharge potential at least quarterly or upon a significant change in the resident's medical condition.

(c) The interdisciplinary team shall oversee the care of the resident utilizing a team approach to assessment and care planning and shall include the resident's attending physician, a registered professional nurse with responsibility for the resident, other appropriate staff in disciplines as determined by the resident's needs, and, where practicable, a resident's representative, in accordance with applicable federal and state requirements.

(d) If return to the community is part of the care plan, the facility shall provide to the resident or responsible party and document in the care plan the information concerning services and resources in the community. That information may include information concerning:

(1) In-home supportive services provided by a public authority or other legally recognized entity, if any.

(2) Services provided by the Area Agency on Aging, if any.

(3) Resources available through an independent living center.

(4) Other resources or services in the community available to support return to the community.

(e) If the resident is otherwise eligible, a skilled nursing facility shall make, to the extent services are available in the community, a reasonable attempt to assist a resident who has a preference for return to the community and who has been determined to be able to do so by the attending physician, to obtain assistance within existing programs, including appropriate case management services, in order to facilitate return to the community. The targeted case management services provided by entities other than the skilled nursing facility shall be intended to facilitate and sustain return to the community.

(f) Costs to skilled nursing facilities to comply with this section shall be allowable for Medi-Cal reimbursement purposes pursuant to Section 1324.25, but shall not be considered a new state mandate under Section 14126.023 of the Welfare and Institutions Code.

(Added by Stats. 2004, Ch. 875, Sec. 2. Effective September 29, 2004.)

1418.9.

(a) If the attending physician and surgeon of a resident in a skilled nursing facility prescribes, orders, or increases an order for an antipsychotic medication for the resident, the physician and surgeon shall do both of the following:

(1) Obtain the informed consent of the resident for purposes of prescribing, ordering, or increasing an order for the medication.

(2) Seek the consent of the resident to notify the resident's interested family member, as designated in the medical record. If the resident consents to the notice, the physician and surgeon shall make reasonable attempts, either personally or through a designee, to notify the interested family member, as designated in the medical record, within 48 hours of the prescription, order, or increase of an order.

(b) Notification of an interested family member is not required under paragraph (2) of subdivision (a) if any of the following circumstances exist:

(1) There is no interested family member designated in the medical record.

(2) The resident has been diagnosed as terminally ill by his or her physician and surgeon and is receiving hospice services from a licensed, certified hospice agency in the facility.

(3) The resident has not consented to the notification.

(c) As used in this section, the following definitions shall apply:

(1) "Resident" means a patient of a skilled nursing facility who has the capacity to consent to make decisions concerning his or her health care, including medications.

(2) "Designee" means a person who has agreed with the physician and surgeon to provide the notice required by this section.

(3) "Antipsychotic medication" means a medication approved by the United States Food and Drug Administration for the treatment of psychosis.

(4) "Increase of an order" means an increase of the dosage of the medication above the dosage range stated in a prior consent from the resident.

(d) This section shall not be construed to require consent from an interested family member for an attending physician and surgeon of a resident to prescribe, order, or increase an order for antipsychotic medication.

(Added by Stats. 2000, Ch. 46, Sec. 1. Effective January 1, 2001.)

1418.91.

(a) A long-term health care facility shall report all incidents of alleged abuse or suspected abuse of a resident of the facility to the department immediately, or within 24 hours.

(b) A failure to comply with the requirements of this section shall be a class "B" violation.

(c) For purposes of this section, "abuse" shall mean any of the conduct described in subdivisions (a) and (b) of Section 15610.07 of the Welfare and Institutions Code.

(d) This section shall not change any reporting requirements under Section 15630 of the Welfare and Institutions Code, or as otherwise specified in the Elder Abuse and Dependent Adult Civil Protection Act, Chapter 11 (commencing with Section 15600) of Part 3 of Division 9 of the Welfare and Institutions Code.

(Added by Stats. 2000, Ch. 451, Sec. 17. Effective January 1, 2001.)

1419.

(a) The department shall establish a centralized consumer response unit within the Licensing and Certification Division of the department to respond to consumer inquiries and complaints.

(b) Upon receipt of consumer inquiries, the unit shall offer assistance to consumers in resolving concerns about the quality of care and the quality of life in long-term health care facilities.

This assistance may include, but shall not be limited to, all of the following:

(1) Offering to provide to consumers education and information about state licensing and federal certification standards, resident rights, name and address of facilities, referral to other entities as appropriate, and facility compliance history.

(2) Offering to participate in telephone conference calls between consumers and providers to resolve concerns within the scope of the authority of the department. If the inquiry or concern is determined to warrant an onsite investigation, the inquiry or concern shall be considered a complaint and handled pursuant to the complaint investigation process set forth in Section 1420.

(3) Initiating onsite investigations in response to oral or written complaints made pursuant to this section if the unit determines that there is a reasonable basis to believe that the allegations in the complaints describe one or more violations of state law by a long-term care facility.

(c) Nothing in subdivision (a) or (b) shall preclude the department from taking any or all enforcement actions available under state or federal law.

(d) Any person may request an inspection of any long-term health care facility in accordance with this chapter by giving to the department oral or written notice of an alleged violation of applicable requirements of state law. Any written notice may be signed by the complainant setting forth with reasonable particularity the matters complained of. Oral notice may be made by telephone or personal visit. Any oral complaint shall be reduced to writing by the department. The substance of the complaint shall be provided to the licensee no earlier than at the commencement of the inspection.

(e) Neither the substance of the complaint provided the licensee nor any copy of the complaint or record published, released, or otherwise made available to the licensee shall disclose the name of any individual complainant or other person mentioned in the complaint, except the name or names of any duly authorized officer, employee, or agent of the state department conducting the investigation or inspection pursuant to this chapter, unless the complainant specifically requests the release of the name or names or the matter results in a judicial proceeding.

(Amended by Stats. 2001, Ch. 680, Sec. 3. Effective January 1, 2002.)

1420.

(a) (1) Upon receipt of a written or oral complaint, the state department shall assign an inspector to make a preliminary review of the complaint and shall notify the complainant within two working days of the receipt of the complaint of the name of the inspector. Unless the state department determines that the complaint is willfully intended to harass a licensee or is without any reasonable basis, it shall make an onsite inspection or investigation within 10 working days of the receipt of the complaint. In any case in which the complaint involves a threat of imminent danger of death or serious bodily harm, the state department shall make an onsite inspection or investigation within 24 hours of the receipt of the complaint. In any event, the complainant shall be promptly informed of the state department's proposed course of action and of the opportunity to accompany the inspector on the inspection or investigation of the facility. Upon the request of either the complainant or the state department, the complainant or his or her representative, or both, may be allowed to accompany the inspector to the site of the alleged violations during his or her tour of the facility, unless the inspector determines that the privacy of any patient would be violated thereby.

(2) When conducting an onsite inspection or investigation pursuant to this section, the state department shall collect and evaluate all available evidence and may issue a citation based upon, but not limited to, all of the following:

(A) Observed conditions.

(B) Statements of witnesses.

(C) Facility records.

(3) (A) For a complaint that involves a threat of imminent danger of death or serious bodily harm that is received on or after July 1, 2016, the state department shall complete an investigation of the complaint within 90 days of receipt of the complaint. At the completion of the complaint investigation, the state department shall notify the complainant and licensee in writing of the state department's determination as a result of the inspection or investigation.

(B) The time period described in subparagraph (A) may be extended up to an additional 60 days if the investigation cannot be completed due to extenuating circumstances. The state department shall document these circumstances in its final determination and notify the facility and the complainant in writing of the basis for the extension and the estimated completion date.

(4) (A) For a complaint that does not involve a threat of imminent danger of death or serious bodily harm pursuant to paragraph (3) and that is received on or after July 1,

2017, and prior to July 1, 2018, the state department shall complete an investigation of the complaint within 90 days of receipt of the complaint. At the completion of the complaint investigation, the state department shall notify the complainant and licensee in writing of the state department's determination as a result of the inspection or investigation.

(B) The time period described in subparagraph (A) may be extended up to an additional 90 days if the investigation cannot be completed due to extenuating circumstances. The state department shall document these circumstances in its final determination and notify the facility and the complainant in writing of the basis for the extension and the estimated completion date.

(5) (A) For a complaint that is received on or after July 1, 2018, the state department shall complete an investigation of the complaint within 60 days of receipt of the complaint. At the completion of the complaint investigation, the state department shall notify the complainant and licensee in writing of the state department's determination as a result of the inspection or investigation.

(B) The time period described in subparagraph (A) may be extended up to an additional 60 days if the investigation cannot be completed due to extenuating circumstances. The state department shall document these circumstances in its final determination and notify the facility and the complainant in writing of the basis for the extension and the estimated completion date.

(b) Upon being notified of the state department's determination as a result of the inspection or investigation, a complainant who is dissatisfied with the state department's determination, regarding a matter which would pose a threat to the health, safety, security, welfare, or rights of a resident, shall be notified by the state department of the right to an informal conference, as set forth in this section. The complainant may, within five business days after receipt of the notice, notify the director in writing of his or her request for an informal conference. The informal conference shall be held with the designee of the director for the county in which the long-term health care facility which is the subject of the complaint is located. The long-term health care facility may participate as a party in this informal conference. The director's designee shall notify the complainant and licensee of his or her determination within 10 working days after the informal conference and shall apprise the complainant and licensee in writing of the appeal rights provided in subdivision (c).

(c) If the complainant is dissatisfied with the determination of the director's designee in the county in which the facility is located, the complainant may, within 15 days after receipt of this determination, notify in writing the Deputy Director of the Licensing and Certification Division of the state department, who shall assign the request to a representative of the Complainant Appeals Unit for review of the facts that led to both determinations. As a part of the Complainant Appeals Unit's independent investigation, and at the request of the complainant, the representative shall interview the complainant in the district office where the complaint was initially referred. Based upon this review, the Deputy Director of the Licensing and Certification Division of the state department shall make his or her own determination and notify the complainant and the facility within 30 days.

(d) Any citation issued as a result of a conference or review provided for in subdivision (b) or (c) shall be issued and served upon the facility within 30 days of the final determination. Service shall be effected either personally or by registered or certified mail. A copy of the citation shall also be sent to each complainant by registered or certified mail.

(e) A miniexit conference shall be held with the administrator or his or her representative upon leaving the facility at the completion of the investigation to inform him or her of the status of the investigation. The state department shall also state the items of noncompliance and compliance found as a result of a complaint and those items found to be in compliance, provided the disclosure maintains the anonymity of the complainant. In any matter in which there is a reasonable probability that the identity of the complainant will not remain anonymous, the state department shall also notify the facility that it is unlawful to discriminate or seek retaliation against a resident, employee, or complainant.

(f) Any citation issued as a result of the complaint investigation provided for in paragraph (3), (4), or (5) of subdivision (a), and in compliance with Section 1423, shall be issued and served upon the facility within 30 days of the completion of the complaint investigation.

(g) For purposes of this section, "complaint" means any oral or written notice to the state department, other than a report from the facility of an alleged violation of applicable requirements of state or federal law or any alleged facts that might constitute such a violation.

(h) Nothing in this section shall be interpreted to diminish the state department's authority and obligation to investigate any alleged violation of applicable requirements of state or federal law, or any alleged facts that might constitute a violation of applicable requirements of state or federal law, and to enforce applicable requirements of law.

(Amended by Stats. 2015, Ch. 18, Sec. 9. (SB 75) Effective June 24, 2015.)

1421.

(a) Any duly authorized officer, employee, or agent of the state department may enter and inspect any long-term health care facility, including, but not limited to, interviewing residents and reviewing records, at any time to enforce any provision of this chapter.

(b) Patients shall be treated with consideration, respect, and full recognition of dignity during the course of the investigation or inspection.

(c) Inspections conducted pursuant to complaints filed with the state department shall be conducted in such a manner as to ensure maximum effectiveness while respecting the rights of patients in the facility. No advance notice shall be given of any inspection conducted pursuant to this chapter unless previously and specifically authorized by the director or required by federal law.

(d) Any public employee giving any advance notice in violation of this section shall be deemed to be in violation of subdivision (t) of Section 19572 of the Government Code and shall be suspended from all duties without pay for a period determined by the director.

(e) Except as otherwise specified by law, any duly authorized officer, employee, or agent of the state department shall not limit the scope of practice of registered nurses acting under Section 2725 of the Business and Professions Code. Further, these agents shall not prohibit the performing of functions by registered nurses when those nurses are performing under standardized procedures, where their activity is consistent with the scope of nursing practice, as set forth in Section 2725 of the Business and Professions Code.

(Amended by Stats. 1986, Ch. 1351, Sec. 4.)

1421.1.

(a) Within 24 hours of the occurrence of any of the events specified in subdivision (b), the licensee of a skilled nursing facility shall notify the department of the occurrence. This notification may be in written form if it is provided by telephone facsimile or overnight mail, or by telephone with a written confirmation within five calendar days. The information provided pursuant to this subdivision may not be released to the public by the department unless its release is needed to justify an action taken by the department or it otherwise becomes a matter of public record. A violation of this section is a class "B" violation.

(b) All of the following occurrences shall require notification pursuant to this section:

(1) The licensee of a facility receives notice that a judgment lien has been levied against the facility or any of the assets of the facility or the licensee.

(2) A financial institution refuses to honor a check or other instrument issued by the licensee to its employees for a regular payroll.

(3) The supplies, including food items and other perishables, on hand in the facility fall below the minimum specified by any applicable statute or regulation.

(4) The financial resources of the licensee fall below the amount needed to operate the facility for a period of at least 45 days based on the current occupancy of the facility. The determination that financial resources have fallen below the amount needed to operate the facility shall be based upon the current number of occupied beds in the facility multiplied by the current daily Medi-Cal reimbursement rate multiplied by 45 days.

(5) The licensee fails to make timely payment of any premiums required to maintain required insurance policies or bonds in effect, or any tax lien levied by any government agency.

(Amended by Stats. 2001, Ch. 685, Sec. 14. Effective January 1, 2002.)

1421.5.

(a) (1) Within 24 hours of the filing of a bankruptcy petition under Title 11 of the United States Code or any other laws of the United States, by any person or entity holding a controlling interest in a long-term health care facility, the licensee of the long-term health care facility shall provide written notification to the department of the filing of the petition and the location of the court in which the petition was filed. The written notification may be provided to the department by telephone facsimile or overnight mail.

(2) Within 24 hours of the appointment of a trustee by the bankruptcy court, the long-term health care facility shall provide written notification to the department of the name, address, and telephone number of the trustee. The written notification may be provided to the department by telephone facsimile or overnight mail.

(3) The department shall provide written notification to the trustee of the requirements of operating a licensed long-term health care facility within three days of being notified of the appointment of the trustee. The contents of this written notice may be provided to the trustee by telephone facsimile or overnight mail and shall include, but not be limited to, all of the following:

(A) The trustee is required to manage and operate the long-term health care facility according to the requirements of state law, in the same manner that the owner or possessor of the facility would be required to manage and operate the facility, including, but not limited to, complying with Article 8.5 (commencing with Section 1336) of Chapter 2, Chapter 3.9 (commencing with Section 1599), and Sections 72527, 73523, and 76525 of Title 22 of the California Code of Regulations.

(B) The transfer of patients pursuant to the liquidation of a licensed long-term health care facility presents a compelling public health and safety risk, and the trustee will not be exempted from complying with applicable state law for any reason.

(b) (1) As mandated by subdivision (b) of Section 959 of Title 28 of the United States Code, an individual appointed as a trustee in a bankruptcy proceeding described in this section that involves any person or entity holding a controlling interest in a long-term health care facility shall comply with all state licensing and federal certification requirements applicable to the long-term health care facility, including, but not limited to, those governing patient rights, transfer or discharge, and facility closure. The transfer of patients pursuant to the liquidation of a licensed long-term health care facility presents a compelling public health and safety risk, and a trustee shall not be exempted from complying with applicable state law for any reason.

(2) If a trustee fails to comply with the state licensing requirements applicable to a long-term health care facility, the department shall report the trustee's actions to the bankruptcy court and intervene as appropriate to ensure continued facility compliance with those requirements.

(Added by Stats. 1998, Ch. 474, Sec. 1. Effective January 1, 1999.)

1422.

(a) The Legislature finds and declares that it is the public policy of this state to ensure that long-term health care facilities provide the highest level of care possible. The Legislature further finds that inspections are the most effective means of furthering this policy. It is not the intent of the Legislature by the amendment of subdivision (b) enacted by Chapter 1595 of the Statutes of 1982 to reduce in any way the resources available to the state department for inspections, but rather to provide the state department with the greatest flexibility to concentrate its resources where they can be most effective. It is the intent of the Legislature to create a survey process that includes state-based survey components and that determines compliance with federal and California requirements for certified long-term health care facilities. It is the further intent of the Legislature to execute this inspection in the form of a single survey process, to the extent that this is possible and permitted under federal law. The inability of the state to conduct a single survey in no way exempts the state from the requirement under this section that state-based components be inspected in long-term health care facilities as required by law.

(b) (1) (A) Notwithstanding Section 1279 or any other provision of law, without providing notice of these inspections, the department, in addition to any inspections conducted pursuant to complaints filed pursuant to Section 1419, shall conduct inspections annually, except with regard to those facilities which have no class "AA," class "A," or class "B" violations in the past 12 months. The state department shall also conduct inspections as may be necessary to ensure the health, safety, and security of patients in long-term health care facilities. Every facility shall be inspected at least once every two years. The department shall vary the cycle in which inspections of long-term health care facilities are conducted to reduce the predictability of the inspections.

(B) Inspections and investigations of long-term health care facilities that are certified by the Medicare Program or the Medicaid Program shall determine compliance with federal standards and California statutes and regulations to the extent that California statutes and regulations provide greater protection to residents, or are more precise than federal standards, as determined by the department. Notwithstanding any other provision of law, the department may, without taking regulatory action pursuant to Chapter 3.5 (commencing with Section 11340) of Part 1 of Division 3 of Title 2 of the Government Code, implement, interpret, or make specific this paragraph by means of an All Facilities Letter (AFL) or similar instruction. Prior to issuing an AFL or similar instruction, the department shall consult with interested parties and shall inform the appropriate committees of the Legislature. The department shall also post the AFL or similar instruction on its Web site so that any person may observe which California laws and regulations provide greater protection to its residents or are more precise than federal standards. Nothing in this subdivision is intended to change existing statutory or regulatory requirements governing the care provided to long-term health care facility residents.

(C) In order to ensure maximum effectiveness of inspections conducted pursuant to this article, the department shall identify all state law standards for the staffing and operation of long-term health care facilities. Costs of the additional survey and inspection activities required by Chapter 895 of the Statutes of 2006 shall be included as Licensing and Certification Program activities for the purposes of calculating fees in accordance with Section 1266.

(2) The state department shall submit to the federal Department of Health and Human Services on or before July 1, 1985, for review and approval, a request to implement a three-year pilot program designed to lessen the predictability of the long-term health care facility inspection process. Two components of the pilot program shall be (A) the elimination of the present practice of entering into a one-year certification agreement, and (B) the conduct of segmented inspections of a sample of facilities with poor inspection records, as defined by the state department. At the conclusion of the pilot project, an analysis of both components shall be conducted by the state department to determine effectiveness in reducing inspection predictability and the respective cost benefits. Implementation of this pilot project is contingent upon federal approval.

(c) Except as otherwise provided in subdivision (b), the state department shall conduct unannounced direct patient care inspections at least annually to inspect physician and surgeon services, nursing services, pharmacy services, dietary services, and activity programs of all the long-term health care facilities. Facilities evidencing repeated serious problems in complying with this chapter or a history of poor performance, or both, shall be subject to periodic unannounced direct patient care inspections during the inspection year. The direct patient care inspections shall assist the state department in the prioritization of its efforts to correct facility deficiencies.

(d) All long-term health care facilities shall report to the state department any changes in the nursing home administrator or the director of nursing services within 10 calendar days of the changes.

(e) Within 90 days after the receipt of notice of a change in the nursing home administrator or the director of nursing services, the state department may conduct an abbreviated inspection of the long-term health care facilities.

(f) If a change in a nursing home administrator occurs and the Board of Nursing Home Administrators notifies the state department that the new administrator is on probation or has had his or her license suspended within the previous three years, the state department shall conduct an abbreviated survey of the long-term health care facility employing that administrator within 90 days of notification.

(Amended by Stats. 2007, Ch. 188, Sec. 13. Effective August 24, 2007.)

1422.1.

(a) Notwithstanding Section 1422, the State Department of Public Health shall conduct, when feasible, annual licensing inspections of licensed long-term health care facilities providing special treatment programs for the mentally disordered, concurrently with inspections conducted by the State Department of Health Care Services for the purposes of approving the special treatment program.

(b) The State Department of Public Health survey teams conducting inspections pursuant to this section shall include at least one licensed mental health professional if the inspections are not done concurrently pursuant to subdivision (a).

(c) Survey team members shall receive training specific to the mental health treatment needs of mentally disordered residents served in these facilities.

(Amended by Stats. 2012, Ch. 34, Sec. 15. (SB 1009) Effective June 27, 2012.)

1422.5.

(a) The department shall develop and establish a consumer information service system to provide updated and accurate information to the general public and consumers regarding long-term care facilities in their communities. The consumer information service system shall include, but need not be limited to, all of the following elements:

(1) An on-line inquiry system accessible through a statewide toll-free telephone number and the Internet.

(2) Long-term health care facility profiles, with data on services provided, a history of all citations and complaints for the last two full survey cycles, and ownership information. The profile for each facility shall include, but not be limited to, all of the following:

(A) The name, address, and telephone number of the facility.

(B) The number of units or beds in the facility.

(C) Whether the facility accepts Medicare or Medi-Cal patients.

(D) Whether the facility has a special care unit or program for people with Alzheimer's disease and other dementias, and whether the facility participates in the voluntary disclosure program for special care units.

(E) Whether the facility is a for-profit or not-for-profit provider.

(3) Information regarding substantiated complaints shall include the action taken and the date of action.

(4) Information regarding the state citations assessed shall include the status of the state citation, including the facility's plan or correction, and information as to whether an appeal has been filed.

(5) Any appeal resolution pertaining to a citation or complaint shall be updated on the file in a timely manner.

(b) Where feasible, the department shall interface the consumer information service system with its Automated Certification and Licensure Information Management System.

(c) It is the intent of the Legislature that the department, in developing and establishing the system pursuant to subdivision (a), maximize the use of available federal funds.

(d) (1) Notwithstanding the consumer information service system established pursuant to subdivision (a), by January 1, 2002, the state department shall develop a method whereby information is provided to the public and consumers on long-term health care facilities. The information provided shall include, but not be limited to, all of the following elements:

(A) Substantiated complaints, including the action taken and the date of the action.

(B) State citations assessed, including the status of any citation and whether an appeal has been filed.

(C) State actions, including license suspensions, revocations, and receiverships.

(D) Federal enforcement sanctions imposed, including any denial of payment, temporary management, termination, or civil money penalty of five hundred dollars ($500) or more.

(E) Any information or data beneficial to the public and consumers.

(2) This subdivision shall become inoperative on July 1, 2003.

(e) In implementing this section, the department shall ensure the confidentiality of personal and identifying information of residents and employees and shall not disclose this information through the consumer information service system developed pursuant to this section.

(Amended by Stats. 2001, Ch. 685, Sec. 16. Effective January 1, 2002.)

1422.6.

Each skilled nursing facility and intermediate care facility shall post a copy of the notice required pursuant to Section 9718 of the Welfare and Institutions Code in a conspicuous location in at least four areas of the facility, as follows:

(a) One location that is accessible to members of the public.

(b) One location that is used for employee breaks.

(c) One location that is next to a telephone designated for resident use.

(d) One location that is used for communal functions for residents, such as for dining or resident council meetings and activities.

(Added by Stats. 2000, Ch. 451, Sec. 22. Effective January 1, 2001.)

1422.7.

The state department shall provide the office, as defined in subdivision (c) of Section 9701 of the Welfare and Institutions Code, with copies of inspection reports for long-term health care facilities upon request. The state department shall provide the office with copies of all class "AA," "A," and "B" citations issued.

(Added by Stats. 1984, Ch. 1632, Sec. 3.)

1423.

(a) If upon inspection or investigation the director determines that any nursing facility is in violation of any state or federal law or regulation relating to the operation or maintenance of the facility, or determines that any other long-term health care facility is in violation of any statutory provision or regulation relating to the operation or maintenance of the facility, the director shall promptly, but not later than 24 hours, excluding Saturday, Sunday, and holidays, after the director determines or has reasonable cause to determine that an alleged violation has occurred, issue a notice to correct the violation and of intent to issue a citation to the licensee. Before completing the investigation and making the final determination whether to issue a citation, the department shall hold an exit

conference with the licensee to identify the potential for issuing a citation for any violation, discuss investigative findings, and allow the licensee to provide the department with additional information related to the violation. The department shall consider this additional information, in conjunction with information from the inspection or investigation, in determining whether to issue a citation, or whether other action would be appropriate. If the department determines that the violation warrants the issuing of a citation and an exit conference has been completed it shall either:

(1) Recommend the imposition of a federal enforcement remedy or remedies on a nursing facility in accordance with federal law; or

(2) Issue a citation pursuant to state licensing laws, and if the facility is a nursing facility, may recommend the imposition of a federal enforcement remedy.

A state citation shall be served upon the licensee within 30 days after completion of the investigation. Service shall be effected either personally or by registered or certified mail. A copy of the citation shall also be sent to each complainant. Each citation shall be in writing and shall describe with particularity the nature of the violation, including a reference to the statutory provision, standard, rule, or regulation alleged to have been violated, the particular place or area of the facility in which it occurred, as well as the amount of any proposed assessment of a civil penalty. The name of any patient jeopardized by the alleged violation shall not be specified in the citation in order to protect the privacy of the patient. However, at the time the licensee is served with the citation, the licensee shall also be served with a written list of each of the names of the patients alleged to have been jeopardized by the violation, that shall not be subject to disclosure as a public record. The citation shall fix the earliest feasible time for the elimination of the condition constituting the alleged violation, when appropriate.

(b) Where no harm to patients, residents, or guests has occurred, a single incident, event, or occurrence shall result in no more than one citation for each statute or regulation violated.

(c) No citation shall be issued for a violation that has been reported by the licensee to the state department, or its designee, as an "unusual occurrence," if all of the following conditions are met:

(1) The violation has not caused harm to any patient, resident, or guest, or significantly contributed thereto.

(2) The licensee has promptly taken reasonable measures to correct the violation and to prevent a recurrence.

(3) The unusual occurrence report was the first source of information reported to the state department, or its designee, regarding the violation.

(Amended by Stats. 2015, Ch. 18, Sec. 10. (SB 75) Effective June 24, 2015.)

1423.5.

(a) The state department shall centrally review federal deficiencies and supporting documentation that may require the termination of certification for a nursing facility. The state department shall develop a standardized methodology for conducting the central review of these deficiencies. The standardized methodology shall assess all of the following:

(1) The extent to which the survey team followed established survey protocols.

(2) The thoroughness of the investigation or review.

(3) The quality of documentation.

(4) The consistency in interpreting federal requirements.

(b) The state department shall develop a system for tracking patterns and a quality assurance process for preventing, detecting, and correcting inconsistent or poor quality survey practices.

(c) (1) On or before December 1 of each year, the state department shall provide to the Legislature a summary of federal and state enforcement actions taken against nursing facilities during the previous state fiscal year.

(2) The report summarizing federal and state enforcement actions required under this subdivision shall be combined with the report required under Section 1438 into a single report. The time period for each report shall cover the previous state fiscal year.

(Amended by Stats. 2001, Ch. 685, Sec. 17. Effective January 1, 2002.)

1424.

Citations issued pursuant to this chapter shall be classified according to the nature of the violation and shall indicate the classification on the face thereof.

(a) In determining the amount of the civil penalty, all relevant facts shall be considered, including, but not limited to, the following:

(1) The probability and severity of the risk that the violation presents to the patient's or resident's mental and physical condition.

(2) The patient's or resident's medical condition.

(3) The patient's or resident's mental condition and his or her history of mental disability or disorder.

(4) The good faith efforts exercised by the facility to prevent the violation from occurring.

(5) The licensee's history of compliance with regulations.

(b) Relevant facts considered by the department in determining the amount of the civil penalty shall be documented by the department on an attachment to the citation and available in the public record. This requirement shall not preclude the department or a facility from introducing facts not listed on the citation to support or challenge the amount of the civil penalty in any proceeding set forth in Section 1428.

(c) Class "AA" violations are violations that meet the criteria for a class "A" violation and that the state department determines to have been a direct proximate cause of death of a patient or resident of a long-term health care facility. Except as provided in Section 1424.5, a class "AA" citation is subject to a civil penalty in the amount of not less than five thousand dollars ($5,000) and not exceeding twenty-five thousand dollars ($25,000) for each citation. In any action to enforce a citation issued under this subdivision, the state department shall prove all of the following:

(1) The violation was a direct proximate cause of death of a patient or resident.

(2) The death resulted from an occurrence of a nature that the regulation was designed to prevent.

(3) The patient or resident suffering the death was among the class of persons for whose protection the regulation was adopted.

If the state department meets this burden of proof, the licensee shall have the burden of proving that the licensee did what might reasonably be expected of a long-term health care facility licensee, acting under similar circumstances, to comply with the regulation. If the licensee sustains this burden, then the citation shall be dismissed.

Except as provided in Section 1424.5, for each class "AA" citation within a 12-month period that has become final, the state department shall consider the suspension or revocation of the facility's license in accordance with Section 1294. For a third or subsequent class "AA" citation in a facility within that 12-month period that has been sustained, the state department shall commence action to suspend or revoke the facility's license in accordance with Section 1294.

(d) Class "A" violations are violations which the state department determines present either (1) imminent danger that death or serious harm to the patients or residents of the long-term health care facility would result therefrom, or (2) substantial probability that death or serious physical harm to patients or residents of the long-term health care facility would result therefrom. A physical condition or one or more practices, means, methods, or operations in use in a long-term health care facility may constitute a class "A" violation. The condition or practice constituting a class "A" violation shall be abated or eliminated immediately, unless a fixed period of time, as determined by the state department, is required for correction. Except as provided in Section 1424.5, a class "A" citation is subject to a civil penalty in an amount not less than one thousand dollars ($1,000) and not exceeding ten thousand dollars ($10,000) for each and every citation. If the state department establishes that a violation occurred, the licensee shall have the burden of proving that the licensee did what might reasonably be expected of a long-term health care facility licensee, acting under similar circumstances, to comply with the regulation. If the licensee sustains this burden, then the citation shall be dismissed.

(e) Except as provided in paragraph (4) of subdivision (a) of Section 1424.5, class "B" violations are violations that the state department determines have a direct or immediate relationship to the health, safety, or security of long-term health care facility patients or residents, other than class "AA" or "A" violations. Unless otherwise determined by the state department to be a class "A" violation pursuant to this chapter and rules and regulations adopted pursuant thereto, any violation of a patient's rights as set forth in Sections 72527 and 73523 of Title 22 of the California Code of Regulations, that is determined by the state department to cause or under circumstances likely to cause significant humiliation, indignity, anxiety, or other emotional trauma to a patient is a class "B" violation. A class "B" citation is subject to a civil penalty in an amount not less than one hundred dollars ($100) and not exceeding one thousand dollars ($1,000) for each and every citation. A class "B" citation shall specify the time within which the violation is required to be corrected. If the state department establishes that a violation occurred, the licensee shall have the burden of proving that the licensee did what might reasonably be expected of a long-term health care facility licensee, acting under similar circumstances, to comply with the regulation. If the licensee sustains this burden, then the citation shall be dismissed.

In the event of any citation under this paragraph, if the state department establishes that a violation occurred, the licensee shall have the burden of proving that the licensee did what might reasonably be expected of a long-term health care facility licensee, acting under similar circumstances, to comply with the regulation. If the licensee sustains this burden, then the citation shall be dismissed.

(f) (1) Any willful material falsification or willful material omission in the health record of a patient of a long-term health care facility is a violation.

(2) "Willful material falsification," as used in this section, means any entry in the patient health care record pertaining to the administration of medication, or treatments ordered for the patient, or pertaining to services for the prevention or treatment of decubitus ulcers or contractures, or pertaining to tests and measurements of vital signs, or notations of input and output of fluids, that was made with the knowledge that the records falsely reflect the condition of the resident or the care or services provided.

(3) "Willful material omission," as used in this section, means the willful failure to record any untoward event that has affected the health, safety, or security of the specific patient, and that was omitted with the knowledge that the records falsely reflect the condition of the resident or the care or services provided.

(g) Except as provided in subdivision (a) of Section 1424.5, a violation of subdivision (f) may result in a civil penalty not to exceed ten thousand dollars ($10,000), as specified in paragraphs (1) to (3), inclusive.

(1) The willful material falsification or willful material omission is subject to a civil penalty of not less than two thousand five hundred dollars ($2,500) or more than ten thousand dollars ($10,000) in instances where the health care record is relied upon by a health care professional to the detriment of a patient by affecting the administration of medications or treatments, the issuance of orders, or the development of plans of care. In all other cases, violations of this subdivision are subject to a civil penalty not exceeding two thousand five hundred dollars ($2,500).

(2) Where the penalty assessed is one thousand dollars ($1,000) or less, the violation shall be issued and enforced, except as provided in this subdivision, in the same manner as a class "B" violation, and shall include the right of appeal as specified in Section 1428. Where the assessed penalty is in excess of one thousand dollars ($1,000), or for skilled

nursing facilities or intermediate care facilities as specified in paragraphs (1) and (2) of subdivision (a) of Section 1418, in excess of two thousand dollars ($2,000), the violation shall be issued and enforced, except as provided in this subdivision, in the same manner as a class "A" violation, and shall include the right of appeal as specified in Section 1428. Nothing in this section shall be construed as a change in previous law enacted by Chapter 11 of the Statutes of 1985 relative to this paragraph, but merely as a clarification of existing law.

(3) Nothing in this subdivision shall preclude the state department from issuing a class "A" or class "B" citation for any violation that meets the requirements for that citation, regardless of whether the violation also constitutes a violation of this subdivision. However, no single act, omission, or occurrence may be cited both as a class "A" or class "B" violation and as a violation of this subdivision.

(h) Where the licensee has failed to post the notices as required by Section 9718 of the Welfare and Institutions Code in the manner required under Section 1422.6, the state department shall assess the licensee a civil penalty in the amount of one hundred dollars ($100) for each day the failure to post the notices continues. Where the total penalty assessed is less than two thousand dollars ($2,000), the violation shall be issued and enforced in the same manner as a class "B" violation, and shall include the right of appeal as specified in Section 1428. Where the assessed penalty is equal to or in excess of two thousand dollars ($2,000), the violation shall be issued and enforced in the same manner as a class "A" violation and shall include the right of appeal as specified in Section 1428. Any fines collected pursuant to this subdivision shall be used to fund the costs incurred by the California Department of Aging in producing and posting the posters.

(i) The director shall prescribe procedures for the issuance of a notice of violation with respect to violations having only a minimal relationship to patient safety or health.

(j) The department shall provide a copy of all citations issued under this section to the affected residents whose treatment was the basis for the issuance of the citation, to the affected residents' designated family member or representative of each of the residents, and to the complainant if the citation was issued as a result of a complaint.

(k) Nothing in this section is intended to change existing statutory or regulatory requirements governing the ability of a licensee to contest a citation pursuant to Section 1428.

(l) The department shall ensure that district office activities performed under Sections 1419 to 1424, inclusive, are consistent with the requirements of these sections and all applicable laws and regulations. To ensure the integrity of these activities, the department shall establish a statewide process for the collection of postsurvey evaluations from affected facilities.

(Amended (as amended by Stats. 2011, 1st Ex. Sess., Ch. 4, Sec. 6) by Stats. 2011, Ch. 729, Sec. 3. (AB 641) Effective January 1, 2012.)

1424.1.

(a) On and after the effective date of this section, no citation shall be issued or sustained under this chapter for a violation of any regulation discovered and recorded by a facility if all of the following conditions have been met:

(1) The facility maintains an ongoing quality assurance and patient care audit program, which includes maintenance of a quality assurance log which is made available to the state department at the commencement of each inspection and investigation. The facility shall retain this log for the current year and the preceding three years.

(2) The violation was not willful and resulted in no actual harm to any patient or guest.

(3) The violation was first discovered by the licensee and was promptly and accurately recorded in the quality assurance log prior to discovery by the state department.

(4) Promptly upon discovery, the facility implemented remedial action satisfactory to the state department to correct the violation and prevent a recurrence. If the state department determines that remedial action voluntarily undertaken by the facility is unsatisfactory, the state department shall allow the facility reasonable time to augment the remedial action before the condition shall be deemed to be a violation.

(b) Except as otherwise provided in this section, a quality assurance log which meets the criteria of this section shall not be discoverable or admissible in any action against the licensee. The quality assurance log shall be discoverable pursuant to a motion to produce under Chapter 14 (commencing with Section 2031.010) of Title 4 of Part 4 of the Code of Civil Procedure and admissible only for purposes of impeachment. However, the court, in a motion pursuant to Section 2025.420 of the Code of Civil Procedure, or at trial or other proceeding, may limit access to those entries which would be admissible for impeachment purposes.

(c) The quality assurance log shall be made available upon request to any of the following:

(1) Full-time state employees of the Office of the State Long-Term Care Ombudsman.

(2) Ombudsman coordinators, as defined in Section 9701 of the Welfare and Institutions Code.

(3) Ombudsmen qualified by medical training as defined in Section 9701 of the Welfare and Institutions Code, with the approval of either the State Long-Term Care Ombudsman or ombudsman coordinator.

The licensee may make the quality assurance log available, in the licensee's discretion, to any representative of the Office of the State Long-Term Care Ombudsman, as defined in Section 9701 of the Welfare and Institutions Code, without liability for the disclosure. Each representative of the Office of the State Long-Term Care Ombudsman who has been provided access to a facility's quality assurance log pursuant to this section shall maintain all disclosures in confidence.

(Amended by Stats. 2005, Ch. 294, Sec. 22. Effective January 1, 2006.)

1424.5.

(a) In lieu of the fines specified in subdivisions (c), (d), (e), and (g) of Section 1424, fines imposed on skilled nursing facilities or intermediate care facilities, as specified in paragraphs (1) and (2) of subdivision (a) of Section 1418, shall be as follows:
(1) A class "AA" citation is subject to a civil penalty in an amount not less than twenty-five thousand dollars ($25,000) and not exceeding one hundred thousand dollars ($100,000) for each and every citation. For a second or subsequent class "AA" citation in a skilled nursing facility or intermediate care facility within a 24-month period, the state department shall commence action to suspend or revoke the facility's license in accordance with Section 1294.
(2) A class "A" citation is subject to a civil penalty in an amount not less than two thousand dollars ($2,000) and not exceeding twenty thousand dollars ($20,000) for each and every citation.
(3) Any "willful material falsification" or "willful material omission," as those terms are defined in subdivision (f) of Section 1424, in the health record of a resident is subject to a civil penalty in an amount not less than two thousand dollars ($2,000) and not exceeding twenty thousand dollars ($20,000) for each and every citation.
(4) A class "B" citation is subject to a civil penalty in an amount not less than one hundred dollars ($100) and not exceeding two thousand dollars ($2,000) for each and every citation. Class "B" violations are violations that the state department determines have a direct or immediate relationship to the health, safety, or security of long-term health care facility patients or residents, other than class "AA" or "A" violations. Unless otherwise determined by the state department to be a class "A" violation pursuant to this chapter and rules and regulations adopted pursuant thereto, any violation of a patient's rights as set forth in Sections 72527 and 73523 of Title 22 of the California Code of Regulations, that is determined by the state department to cause, or under circumstances to be likely to cause, significant humiliation, indignity, anxiety, or other emotional trauma to a patient is a class "B" violation. A class "B" citation shall specify the time within which the violation is required to be corrected. If the state department establishes that a violation occurred, the licensee shall have the burden of proving that the licensee did what might reasonably be expected of a long-term health care facility licensee, acting under similar circumstances, to comply with the regulation. If the licensee sustains this burden, then the citation shall be dismissed.
(b) A licensee may, in lieu of contesting a class "AA" or class "A" citation pursuant to Section 1428, transmit to the state department, the minimum amount specified by law, or 65 percent of the amount specified in the citation, whichever is greater, for each violation, within 30 business days after the issuance of the citation.
(Amended (as amended by Stats. 2011, 1st Ex. Sess., Ch. 4, Sec. 7) by Stats. 2011, Ch. 729, Sec. 4. (AB 641) Effective January 1, 2012.)
1424.6.
Failure by a developmental center to report incidents as required under subdivision (a) of Section 4427.5 of the Welfare and Institutions Code shall be deemed a class B violation if the incident occurs in a distinct part long-term health care facility, and shall be subject to the penalties specified in Section 1424.5 for distinct part skilled nursing facilities or distinct part intermediate care facilities, or Section 1424 for other distinct part long-term health care facilities.
(Added by Stats. 2013, Ch. 724, Sec. 3. (SB 651) Effective January 1, 2014.)
1425.
Where a licensee has failed to correct a violation within the time specified in the citation, the state department shall assess the licensee a civil penalty in the amount of fifty dollars ($50) for each day that such deficiency continues beyond the date specified for correction. If the licensee disputes a determination by the state department regarding alleged failure to correct a violation or regarding the reasonableness of the proposed deadline for correction, the licensee may request an informal conference and contest such determination.
(Amended by Stats. 1980, Ch. 1082.)
1426.
After consultation with industry, professional, and consumer groups affected thereby, but not later than three months after the effective date of this chapter, the director shall publish proposed regulations setting forth the criteria and, where feasible, the specific acts that constitute class "A" and "B" violations under this chapter. Not later than six months after the effective date of this chapter, the director shall adopt regulations setting forth criteria and, where feasible, specific acts constituting class "A" and "B" violations. The regulations shall be adopted as prescribed in Chapter 4.5 (commencing with Section 11371) of Part 1 of Division 3 of Title 2 of the Government Code, except that such regulations shall not be adopted as emergency regulations pursuant to subdivision (b) of Section 11421 of the Government Code and shall not mandate a quality of care or new procedures which were not required on January 1, 1974, without providing additional reimbursement if the change in quality of care or the new procedures entail substantial new costs.
For purposes of this section, "new costs" shall not include costs which are the direct or indirect consequence of meeting the requirements of the citation system established under this chapter.
(Added by Stats. 1973, Ch. 1057.)
1427.
(a) When the administration of medications, treatments, or other care is not recorded, as required by law, in the health care record for a patient of a long-term health care facility, it shall be presumed that the required medication, treatment, or care has not been provided.
(b) The presumption established by this section may be rebutted by a licensee only upon a showing of a preponderance of the evidence.
(c) This presumption applies to any action against any long-term health care facility which is filed by the state department pursuant to this chapter or Chapter 2 (commencing with Section 1250). In any other action against a long-term health care facility, the court may apply the presumption when the interests of justice requires.
(Repealed and added by Stats. 1985, Ch. 11, Sec. 11. Effective March 6, 1985.)
1428.
(a) If the licensee desires to contest a citation or the proposed assessment of a civil penalty therefor, the licensee shall use the processes described in subdivisions (b) and (c) for classes "AA," "A," or "B" citations.
(b) If a licensee intends to contest a class "AA" or a class "A" citation, the licensee shall inform the director in writing, within 15 business days of the service of the citation of the licensee's intent to adjudicate the validity of the citation in the superior court in the county in which the long-term health care facility is located. In order to perfect a judicial appeal of a contested citation, a licensee shall file a civil action in the superior court in the county in which the long-term health care facility is located. The action shall be filed no later than 90 calendar days after a licensee notifies the director that he or she intends to contest the citation, and served not later than 90 days after filing. Notwithstanding any other provision of law, a licensee prosecuting a judicial appeal shall file and serve a case management statement pursuant to Rule 212 of the California Rules of Court within six months after the department files its answer in the appeal. Notwithstanding subdivision (d), the court shall dismiss the appeal upon motion of the department if the case management statement is not filed by the licensee within the period specified. The court may affirm, modify, or dismiss the citation, the level of the citation, or the amount of the proposed assessment of the civil penalty.
(c) If a licensee desires to contest a class "B" citation, the licensee shall, within 15 working days after service of the citation, notify the director or the director's designee that he or she wishes to appeal the citation through the procedures set forth in Section 100171 or elects to submit the matter to binding arbitration in accordance with subdivision (d). The administrative law judge may affirm, modify, or dismiss the citation or the proposed assessment of a civil penalty. The licensee may choose to have his or her appeal heard by the administrative law judge or submit the matter to binding arbitration by notifying the director in writing within 15 business days of the service of the citation.
(d) If a licensee is dissatisfied with the decision of the administrative law judge, the licensee may, in lieu of seeking judicial review of the decision as provided in Section 1094.5 of the Code of Civil Procedure, elect to submit the matter to binding arbitration by filing, within 60 days of its receipt of the decision, a request for arbitration with the American Arbitration Association. The parties shall agree upon an arbitrator designated from the American Arbitration Association in accordance with the association's established rules and procedures. The arbitration hearing shall be set within 45 days of the election to arbitrate, but in no event less than 28 days from the date of selection of an arbitrator. The arbitration hearing may be continued up to 15 additional days if necessary at the arbitrator's discretion. Except as otherwise specifically provided in this subdivision, the arbitration hearing shall be conducted in accordance with the American Arbitration Association's established rules and procedures. The arbitrator shall determine whether the licensee violated the regulation or regulations cited by the department, and whether the citation meets the criteria established in Sections 1423 and 1424. If the arbitrator determines that the licensee has violated the regulation or regulations cited by the department, and that the class of the citation should be upheld, the proposed assessment of a civil penalty shall be affirmed, subject to the limitations established in Section 1424. The licensee and the department shall each bear its respective portion of the cost of arbitration. A resident, or his or her designated representative, or both, may make an oral or written statement regarding the citation, at any arbitration hearing to which the matter has been submitted.
(e) If an appeal is prosecuted under this section, including an appeal taken in accordance with Section 100171, the department shall have the burden of establishing by a preponderance of the evidence that (1) the alleged violation did occur, (2) the alleged violation met the criteria for the class of citation alleged, and (3) the assessed penalty was appropriate. The department shall also have the burden of establishing by a preponderance of the evidence that the assessment of a civil penalty should be upheld. If a licensee appeals a contested citation or the assessment of a civil penalty, no civil penalty shall be due and payable unless and until the appeal is terminated in favor of the department.
(f) In assessing the civil penalty for a violation, all relevant facts shall be considered, including, but not limited to, all of the following:
(1) The probability and severity of the risk which the violation presents to the patient's or resident's mental and physical condition.
(2) The patient's or resident's medical condition.
(3) The patient's or resident's mental condition and his or her history of mental disability.
(4) The good faith efforts exercised by the facility to prevent the violation from occurring.
(5) The licensee's history of compliance with regulations.
(g) Except as otherwise provided in this subdivision, an assessment of civil penalties for a class "A" or class "B" violation shall be trebled and collected for a second and subsequent violation for which a citation of the same class was issued within any 12-month period. Trebling shall occur only if the first citation issued within the 12-month period was issued in the same class, a civil penalty was assessed, and a plan of correction was submitted for the previous same-class violation occurring within the period, without regard to whether the action to enforce the previous citation has become final. However, the increment to the civil penalty required by this subdivision shall not be due and payable unless and until the previous action has terminated in favor of the department.

If the class "B" citation is issued for a patient's rights violation, as defined in subdivision (e) of Section 1424, it shall not be trebled unless the department determines the violation has a direct or immediate relationship to the health, safety, security, or welfare of long-term health care facility residents.

(h) The director shall prescribe procedures for the issuance of a notice of violation with respect to violations having only a minimal relationship to safety or health.

(i) Actions brought under this chapter shall be set for trial at the earliest possible date and shall take precedence on the court calendar over all other cases except matters to which equal or superior precedence is specifically granted by law. Times for responsive pleading and for hearing the proceeding shall be set by the judge of the court with the object of securing a decision as to subject matters at the earliest possible time.

(j) If the citation is dismissed, the department shall take action immediately to ensure that the public records reflect in a prominent manner that the citation was dismissed.

(k) Penalties paid on violations under this chapter shall be applied against the department's accounts to offset any costs incurred by the state pursuant to this chapter. Any costs or penalties assessed pursuant to this chapter shall be paid within 30 days of the date the decision becomes final. If a facility does not comply with this requirement, the state department shall withhold any payment under the Medi-Cal program until the debt is satisfied. No payment shall be withheld if the department determines that it would cause undue hardship to the facility or to patients or residents of the facility.

(l) The amendments made to subdivisions (a) and (c) of this section by Chapter 84 of the Statutes of 1988, to extend the number of days allowed for the provision of notification to the director, do not affect the right, that is also contained in those amendments, to request judicial relief from these time limits.

(m) If a licensee exercises its right to a citation review conference prior to January 1, 2012, the citation review conference and all notices, reviews, and appeals thereof shall be conducted pursuant to this section as it read on December 31, 2011.
(Amended by Stats. 2011, Ch. 729, Sec. 5. (AB 641) Effective January 1, 2012.)
1428.1.
Except as provided in subdivision (b) of Section 1424.5, a licensee may, in lieu of contesting a citation pursuant to Section 1428, transmit to the state department the minimum amount specified by law, or 65 percent of the amount specified in the citation, whichever is greater, for each violation within 15 business days after the issuance of the citation.
(Amended by Stats. 2001, Ch. 685, Sec. 19. Effective January 1, 2002.)
1428.2.
In the case of a class "A" or class "AA" citation issued to a long-term health care facility which is appealed, the citation shall expire and have no further legal effect, if the Attorney General has not filed an action in the court of competent jurisdiction, within one year from the date the facility notifies the State Department of Public Health of its intent to contest the citation in court.
(Amended by Stats. 2011, Ch. 729, Sec. 6. (AB 641) Effective January 1, 2012.)
1429.
(a) Each class "AA" and class "A" citation specified in subdivisions (c) and (d) of Section 1424 that is issued, or a copy or copies thereof, shall be prominently posted for 120 days. The citation or copy shall be posted in a place or places in plain view of the patients or residents in the long-term health care facility, persons visiting those patients or residents, and persons who inquire about placement in the facility.

(1) The citation shall be posted in at least the following locations in the facility:

(A) An area accessible and visible to members of the public.

(B) An area used for employee breaks.

(C) An area used by residents for communal functions, such as dining, resident council meetings, or activities.

(2) The citation, along with a cover sheet, shall be posted on a white or light-colored sheet of paper, at least $8\frac{1}{2}$ by 11 inches in size, that includes all of the following information:

(A) The full name of the facility, in a clear and easily readable font in at least 28-point type.

(B) The full address of the facility, in a clear and easily readable font in at least 20-point type.

(C) Whether the citation is class "AA" or class "A."

(3) The facility may post the plan of correction.

(4) The facility may post a statement disputing the citation or a statement showing the appeal status, or both.

(5) The facility may remove and discontinue the posting required by this section if the citation is withdrawn or dismissed by the department.

(b) Each class "B" citation specified in subdivision (e) of Section 1424 that is issued pursuant to this section and that has become final, or a copy or copies thereof, shall be retained by the licensee at the facility cited until the violation is corrected to the satisfaction of the department. Each citation shall be made promptly available by the licensee for inspection or examination by any member of the public who so requests. In addition, every licensee shall post in a place or places in plain view of the patient or resident in the long-term health care facility, persons visiting those patients or residents, and persons who inquire about placement in the facility, a prominent notice informing those persons that copies of all final uncorrected citations issued by the department to the facility will be made promptly available by the licensee for inspection by any person who so requests.

(c) A violation of this section shall constitute a class "B" violation, and shall be subject to a civil penalty in the amount of one thousand dollars ($1,000), as provided in subdivision (e) of Section 1424. Notwithstanding Section 1290, a violation of this section shall not constitute a crime. Fines imposed pursuant to this section shall be deposited into the State Health Facilities Citation Penalties Account, created pursuant to Section 1417.2.
(Amended by Stats. 2011, Ch. 729, Sec. 7. (AB 641) Effective January 1, 2012.)
1429.1.
(a) If a long-term health care facility licensed as a skilled nursing facility or an intermediate care facility, as defined in paragraphs (1) and (2) of subdivision (a) of Section 1418, has one or more of the following remedies actually imposed for violation of state or federal requirements, the facility shall provide written notification of the action to each resident, the resident's responsible party and legal representative, and all applicants for admission to the facility:

(1) Termination of the facility's provider agreement to participate in the Medicare program, medicaid program, or both programs.

(2) Denial of Medicare or medicaid payment for new admissions to the facility.

(3) Denial by the Health Care Financing Administration of Medicare or medicaid payment for all individuals in the facility.

(4) A ban on admissions, of any type.

(b) A violation of the requirements of this section shall be a class "B" violation.
(Added by Stats. 2000, Ch. 451, Sec. 28. Effective January 1, 2001.)
1430.
(a) Except where the state department has taken action and the violations have been corrected to its satisfaction, a licensee who commits a class "A" or "B" violation may be enjoined from permitting the violation to continue or may be sued for civil damages within a court of competent jurisdiction. An action for injunction or civil damages, or both, may be prosecuted by the Attorney General in the name of the people of the State of California upon his or her own complaint or upon the complaint of a board, officer, person, corporation, or association, or by a person acting for the interests of itself, its members, or the general public. The amount of civil damages that may be recovered in an action brought pursuant to this section may not exceed the maximum amount of civil penalties that could be assessed on account of the violation or violations.

(b) A current or former resident or patient of a skilled nursing facility, as defined in subdivision (c) of Section 1250, or intermediate care facility, as defined in subdivision (d) of Section 1250, may bring a civil action against the licensee of a facility who violates any rights of the resident or patient as set forth in the Patients Bill of Rights in Section 72527 of Title 22 of the California Code of Regulations, or any other right provided for by federal or state law or regulation. The suit shall be brought in a court of competent jurisdiction. The licensee shall be liable for the acts of the licensee's employees. The licensee shall be liable for up to five hundred dollars ($500), and for costs and attorney fees, and may be enjoined from permitting the violation to continue. An agreement by a resident or patient of a skilled nursing facility or intermediate care facility to waive his or her rights to sue pursuant to this subdivision shall be void as contrary to public policy.

(c) The remedies specified in this section shall be in addition to any other remedy provided by law.
(Amended by Stats. 2004, Ch. 270, Sec. 2. Effective January 1, 2005.)
1431.
It is a misdemeanor for any person to do any of the following:

(a) Willfully prevent, interfere with, or attempt to impede in any way the work of any duly authorized representative of the state department in the lawful enforcement of any provision of this chapter.

(b) Willfully prevent or attempt to prevent any such representative from examining any relevant books or records in the conduct of his official duties under this chapter.

(c) Willfully prevent or interfere with any such representative in the preserving of evidence of any violation of any of the provisions of this chapter or of the rules and regulations promulgated under this chapter.
(Added by Stats. 1973, Ch. 1057.)
1432.
(a) No licensee shall discriminate or retaliate in any manner against any complainant, or any patient or employee in its long-term health care facility, on the basis or for the reason that the complainant, patient, employee, or any other person has presented a grievance or complaint, or has initiated or cooperated in any investigation or proceeding of any governmental entity relating to care, services, or conditions at that facility. A licensee who violates this section is subject to a civil penalty of no more than ten thousand dollars ($10,000), to be assessed by the director and collected in the manner provided in Section 1430.

(b) Any attempt to expel a patient from a long-term health care facility, or any type of discriminatory treatment of a patient by whom, or upon whose behalf, a grievance or complaint has been submitted, directly or indirectly, to any governmental entity or received by a long-term health care facility administrator or any proceeding instituted under or related to this chapter within 180 days of the filing of the complaint or the institution of the action, shall raise a rebuttable presumption that the action was taken by the licensee in retaliation for the filing of the complaint.

(c) Any attempt to terminate the employment, or other discriminatory treatment, of any employee who has presented a grievance or complaint or has initiated, participated, or cooperated in any investigation or proceeding of any governmental entity as specified in subdivision (a), and where the facility or licensee had knowledge of the employee's initiation, participation, or cooperation, shall raise a rebuttable presumption that the action was taken by the licensee in retaliation if it occurs within 120 days of the filing of the grievance or complaint, or the institution of the action.

(d) Presumptions provided for in subdivisions (b) and (c) shall be presumptions affecting the burden of producing evidence as provided in Section 603 of the Evidence Code.

(e) Where the civil penalty assessed is one thousand dollars ($1,000) or less, the violation shall be issued and enforced in the same manner as a class "B" violation, except in no case shall the penalty be trebled. Where the civil penalty assessed is in excess of one thousand dollars ($1,000), the violation shall be issued and enforced in the same manner as a class "A" violation, except in no case shall the penalty be trebled.

(f) Any person who willfully violates this section is guilty of an infraction punishable by a fine of not more than ten thousand dollars ($10,000).

(g) A licensee who violates this section is subject to a civil penalty or a criminal fine, but not both.

(h) Each long-term health care facility shall prominently post in a facility location accessible to staff, patients, and visitors written notice of the right to request an inspection pursuant to Section 1419, the procedure for doing so, including the right to remain anonymous, and the prohibition against retaliation.

(i) For purposes of this section, "complainant" means any person who has filed a complaint, as defined in Section 1420.

(Amended by Stats. 2001, Ch. 685, Sec. 20. Effective January 1, 2002.)

1432.1.

No licensee shall be cited for any violation caused by any person licensed pursuant to the Medical Practice Act (Chapter 5 (commencing with Section 2000) of Division 2 of the Business and Professions Code) if the person is independent of, and not connected with, the licensee and the licensee shows that he or she has exercised reasonable care and diligence in notifying these persons of their duty to the patients in the licensee's long-term health care facility.

(Added by Stats. 1984, Ch. 1631, Sec. 6.)

1433.

The remedies provided by this chapter are cumulative, and shall not be construed as restricting any remedy, provisional or otherwise, provided by law for the benefit of any party, and no judgment under this chapter shall preclude any party from obtaining additional relief based upon the same facts.

(Added by Stats. 1973, Ch. 1057.)

1434.

Commencing in 1974, the state department shall, on or before February 1 of each year, notify all public agencies which refer patients to long-term health care facilities of all of the long-term health care facilities in the area found upon inspection within the previous 12-month period to be without class "A" or "B" violations. Public agencies shall give priority to such long-term health care facilities in referring publicly assisted patients. No public agency shall refer patients to long-term health care facilities with any uncorrected class "A" violations or five or more uncorrected class "B" violations, except those long-term health care facilities which the director may exempt because of a lack of facilities of the same type in the area sufficient to satisfy the demand for services provided by such type of facilities.

(Added by Stats. 1973, Ch. 1057.)

1436.

On or before July 1, 1974, the state department shall provide for additional and ongoing training for inspectors charged with implementation of this chapter in investigative techniques and standards relating to the quality of care provided by long-term health care facilities. The investigative-technique element of such training shall be adopted after consultation with the Department of Justice and such investigative training may, but need not, be provided through a contract with the Department of Justice.

(Added by Stats. 1973, Ch. 1057.)

1437.

If a health facility, or an applicant for a license has not been previously licensed pursuant to Chapter 2 (commencing with Section 1250), the state department may only provisionally license the facility as provided in this section. A provisional license to operate a health facility shall terminate six months from the date of issuance. Within 30 days of the termination of a provisional license, the state department shall give the facility a full and complete inspection, and, if the facility meets all applicable requirements for licensure, a regular license shall be issued. If the health facility does not meet the requirements for licensure but has made substantial progress towards meeting the requirements, as determined by the state department, the initial provisional license shall be renewed for six months. If the state department determines that there has not been substantial progress towards meeting licensure requirements at the time of the first full inspection provided by this section, or, if the state department determines upon its inspection made within 30 days of the termination of a renewed provisional license that there is lack of full compliance with the requirements, no further license shall be issued. If an applicant for a provisional license to operate a health facility has been denied provisional licensing by the state department, he or she may contest the denial by filing a request for a hearing pursuant to Section 100171.

The department shall not apply less stringent criteria when granting a provisional license pursuant to this section than it applies when granting a permanent license.

General acute care hospitals and acute psychiatric hospitals are exempt from this section.

(Amended by Stats. 1997, Ch. 220, Sec. 17. Effective August 4, 1997.)

1437.5.

(a) If a facility is certified to participate in the federal Medicare program as a skilled nursing facility under Title XVIII of the Social Security Act, in the medicaid program as a nursing facility under Title XIX of the Social Security Act, or in both and any of the following occurs, the state department may rescind its regular license to operate and issue a provisional license under Section 1437:

(1) The facility's provider agreement is terminated, by the federal government or the department.

(2) A temporary manager is appointed, under federal law, to operate it.

(3) Payment becomes due on a federal civil money penalty of seven thousand dollars ($7,000) per day, or greater, imposed on it.

(4) A federal civil monetary penalty of any amount is imposed and has continued for a period of 30 days or more.

(5) A federal civil monetary penalty of any amount is imposed and has accrued in an amount equal to, or greater than, thirty-five thousand dollars ($35,000).

(b) The state department may not take action pursuant to subdivision (a) until a final administrative decision is issued if the facility has requested a hearing pursuant to federal law, until a facility has waived its right to a hearing under federal law, or until the time for requesting a hearing under federal law has expired and a hearing request was not received by federal authorities.

(c) If a receiver or temporary manager is appointed to operate a skilled nursing facility or an intermediate care facility, pursuant to paragraphs (1) and (2) of subdivision (a) of Section 1418, pursuant to state law, or as otherwise specified in regulations adopted by the department, the state department may rescind its regular license to operate and issue a provisional license under this section.

(d) (1) A provisional license issued pursuant to this section shall terminate six months from the date of issuance unless extended by the department.

(2) At least 30 days prior to the termination of a provisional license, the department shall give the facility a full and complete inspection. If, at the time of the inspection, it is determined that the facility meets all applicable requirements for licensure, a regular license shall be restored. If, at the time of the inspection, it is determined that the facility does not meet the requirements for licensure, but the facility has made substantial progress towards meeting the requirements, as determined by the department, the provisional license shall be renewed for six months. If, at the time of the first inspection, the department determines that there has not been substantial progress towards meeting the requirements for licensure, or, if at any subsequent inspection the department determines that there has not been substantial progress towards meeting requirements identified at the most recent previous inspection, a regular license shall not be issued.

(e) The facility may request a hearing in writing within 10 days of the receipt of notice from the department denying a regular license under this section. The provisional license shall remain in effect during the pendency of the hearing. The hearing shall be held in accordance with Section 100171. The hearing officer shall uphold the denial of a regular license if the department proves, by a preponderance of the evidence, that the licensee did not meet the requirements for licensure.

(Amended by Stats. 2001, Ch. 685, Sec. 21. Effective January 1, 2002.)

1438.

The state department shall review the effectiveness of the enforcement system in maintaining the quality of care provided by long-term health care facilities and shall submit a report thereon to the Legislature on enforcement activities, on or before December 1, 2001, and annually thereafter, together with any recommendations of the state department for additional legislation which it deems necessary to improve the effectiveness of the enforcement system or to enhance the quality of care provided by long-term health care facilities. This report shall be combined with the report required under Section 1423.5 into a single report. The time period for each report shall cover the previous state fiscal year.

(Amended by Stats. 2001, Ch. 685, Sec. 22. Effective January 1, 2002.)

1439.

Any writing received, owned, used, or retained by the state department in connection with the provisions of this chapter is a public record within the meaning of subdivision (d) of Section 6252 of the Government Code, and, as such, is open to public inspection pursuant to the provision of Sections 6253, 6256, 6257, and 6258 of the Government Code. However, the names of any persons contained in such records, except the names of duly authorized officers, employees, or agents of the state department conducting an investigation or inspection in response to a complaint filed pursuant to this chapter, shall not be open to public inspection and copies of such records provided for public inspection shall have such names deleted.

(Added by Stats. 1973, Ch. 1057.)

1439.2.

Every long-term health care facility shall provide an activity program to the residents of the facility to meet the needs and interests of the residents and to encourage self-care and resumption of normal activities, in accordance with a patient activity plan developed by the facility including, but not limited to, self-help skills, such as personal hygiene, care of personal effects and living environment, nutrition, management of bedside medications of nonprescription drugs, management of petty funds for personal use, and cooperative relations with peers and staff to help keep them closer to the reality of their environment. The patient activity plan of each individual shall be reviewed and approved in writing at least quarterly by the attending physician as not being in conflict with the patient's treatment plan.

(Added by Stats. 1984, Ch. 1029, Sec. 1.)

1439.5.

(a) The state department shall undertake the immediate development, implementation, and maintenance of an automated information system. The automated information system shall be developed to ensure both of the following:

(1) The most effective operation of this chapter and Chapter 2 (commencing with Section 1250), including, but not limited to, all of the following:

(A) Gathering data necessary to maximize enforcement and monitoring capabilities.

(B) Increasing accessibility of facility information.

(C) Identifying any trends of substandard care.

(D) Providing management information.

(2) The provision of information to the general public pursuant to subdivision (b). The state department shall take all necessary action to obtain maximum federal funding assistance to develop, implement, and maintain an automated information system.

(b) The state department shall develop a consumer information system, pursuant to Section 1422.5, to provide information to the general public and long-term health care services consumers regarding long-term health care facilities in this state. The state department shall utilize, to the extent possible, the information provided by its automated information system. Prior to implementation, the consumer information system shall be presented to the Health Care Advisory Committee for its review and comments. (Added by Stats. 1985, Ch. 11, Sec. 14. Effective March 6, 1985.)

1439.6.

(a) Except as provided in subdivision (b), if a resident is notified in writing of a facility-initiated transfer or discharge from a long-term health care facility, the facility shall also send a copy of the notice to the local long-term care ombudsman at the same time notice is provided to the resident or the resident's representative.

(b) If a resident is subject to a facility-initiated transfer to a general acute care hospital on an emergency basis, the facility shall provide a copy of the notice to the ombudsman as soon as practicable.

(c) The copy of the notice shall be sent by fax machine or email, as may be directed by the local long-term care ombudsman, unless the facility does not have fax or email capability, in which case the copy of the notice shall be sent by first-class mail, postage prepaid. A facility's failure to timely send a copy of the notice shall constitute a class B violation, as defined in subdivision (e) of Section 1424.

(d) For the purposes of this section, a "facility-initiated transfer or discharge" is a transfer or discharge that is initiated by the facility and not by the resident, whether or not the resident agrees to the facility's decision.

(Added by Stats. 2017, Ch. 274, Sec. 1. (AB 940) Effective January 1, 2018.)

1439.7.

Notwithstanding Section 14124.7 of the Welfare and Institutions Code, a long-term health care facility participating as a provider under the Medi-Cal program may transfer or seek to evict a resident, within 90 days of admission, if all of the following conditions are met:

(a) The facility requests specific information regarding the assets and liabilities of a prospective private-pay resident prior to acceptance of the resident into the facility.

(b) The facility relies on the information provided pursuant to subdivision (a) in deciding to admit the resident.

(c) The facility promptly and diligently investigates the representation regarding the resident's assets and liabilities, and discovers that the resident's financial assets and liabilities are materially different than represented.

(d) The 90-day limit on transfer or eviction shall not apply if, in fact, the resident fraudulently misrepresented his or her assets and liabilities so that if the material facts were known at the time by the facility the resident would not have been admitted, and the facility could not have discovered the misrepresentation with the exercise of reasonable diligence.

(e) In no event, shall the facility take action to transfer or evict a resident under subdivision (d) unless the action is initiated within 18 months of the date of admission.

(f) A facility shall promptly notify the state department and the Office of the Long-Term Care Ombudsman as defined in subdivision (c) of Section 9701 of the Welfare and Institutions Code, prior to taking action to transfer or evict a resident under this section. (Added by Stats. 1985, Ch. 11, Sec. 15. Effective March 6, 1985.)

1439.8.

Every long-term health care facility shall reveal to applicants for admission, or their designated representatives, orally and in writing, and prior to admission, whether the facility participates in the Medi-Cal program, and the circumstances under which the law permits a Medi-Cal recipient to be transferred involuntarily. (Added by Stats. 1985, Ch. 11, Sec. 16. Effective March 6, 1985.)

CHAPTER 2.45. Lesbian, Gay, Bisexual, and Transgender Long-Term Care Facility Residents' Bill of Rights [1439.50 - 1439.54]

(Chapter 2.45 added by Stats. 2017, Ch. 483, Sec. 3.)

1439.50.

For the purposes of this chapter, the following definitions shall apply:

(a) "Gender expression" has the same meaning as defined in Section 51 of the Civil Code.

(b) "Gender identity" means a person's identity based on the individual's stated gender identity, without regard to whether the self-identified gender accords with the individual's physical appearance, surgical history, genitalia, legal sex, sex assigned at birth, or name and sex, as it appears in medical records, and without regard to any contrary statement by any other person, including a family member, conservator, or legal representative. An individual who lacks the present ability to communicate his or her gender identity shall retain the gender identity most recently expressed by that individual.

(c) "Gender-nonconforming" means a person whose gender expression does not conform to stereotypical expectations of how a man or woman should appear or act.

(d) "LGBT" means lesbian, gay, bisexual, or transgender.

(e) "Long-term care facility" or "facility" includes facilities listed in Section 1418 of this code and subdivision (b) of Section 9701 of the Welfare and Institutions Code.

(f) "Long-term care facility staff" or "facility staff" means all individuals employed by or contracted directly with the facility.

(g) "Resident" means a resident or patient of a long-term care facility.

(h) "Transgender" means a person whose gender identity differs from the person's assigned or presumed sex at birth.

(i) "Transition" means to undergo a process by which a person changes physical sex characteristics or gender expression to match the person's inner sense of being male or female. This process may include, among other things, a name change, a change in preferred pronouns, and a change in social gender expression, as indicated by hairstyle, clothing, and restroom use. Transition may or may not include hormone use and surgery. (Added by Stats. 2017, Ch. 483, Sec. 3. (SB 219) Effective January 1, 2018.)

1439.51.

(a) Except as provided in subdivision (b), it shall be unlawful for a long-term care facility or facility staff to take any of the following actions wholly or partially on the basis of a person's actual or perceived sexual orientation, gender identity, gender expression, or human immunodeficiency virus (HIV) status:

(1) Deny admission to a long-term care facility, transfer or refuse to transfer a resident within a facility or to another facility, or discharge or evict a resident from a facility.

(2) Deny a request by residents to share a room.

(3) Where rooms are assigned by gender, assigning, reassigning, or refusing to assign a room to a transgender resident other than in accordance with the transgender resident's gender identity, unless at the transgender resident's request.

(4) Prohibit a resident from using, or harass a resident who seeks to use or does use, a restroom available to other persons of the same gender identity, regardless of whether the resident is making a gender transition or appears to be gender-nonconforming. Harassment includes, but is not limited to, requiring a resident to show identity documents in order to gain entrance to a restroom available to other persons of the same gender identity.

(5) Willfully and repeatedly fail to use a resident's preferred name or pronouns after being clearly informed of the preferred name or pronouns.

(6) Deny a resident the right to wear or be dressed in clothing, accessories, or cosmetics that are permitted for any other resident.

(7) Restrict a resident's right to associate with other residents or with visitors, including the right to consensual sexual relations, unless the restriction is uniformly applied to all residents in a nondiscriminatory manner. This section does not preclude a facility from banning or restricting sexual relations, as long as the ban or restriction is applied uniformly and in a nondiscriminatory manner.

(8) Deny or restrict medical or nonmedical care that is appropriate to a resident's organs and bodily needs, or provide medical or nonmedical care in a manner that, to a similarly situated reasonable person, unduly demeans the resident's dignity or causes avoidable discomfort.

(b) This section shall not apply to the extent that it is incompatible with any professionally reasonable clinical judgment.

(c) Each facility shall post the following notice alongside its current nondiscrimination policy in all places and on all materials where that policy is posted:

"[Name of facility] does not discriminate and does not permit discrimination, including, but not limited to, bullying, abuse, or harassment, on the basis of actual or perceived sexual orientation, gender identity, gender expression, or HIV status, or based on association with another individual on account of that individual's actual or perceived sexual orientation, gender identity, gender expression, or HIV status. You may file a complaint with the Office of the State Long-Term Care Ombudsman [provide contact information] if you believe that you have experienced this kind of discrimination." (Added by Stats. 2017, Ch. 483, Sec. 3. (SB 219) Effective January 1, 2018.)

1439.52.

A facility shall employ procedures for recordkeeping, including, but not limited to, records generated at the time of admission, that include the gender identity, correct name, as indicated by the resident, and pronoun of each resident, as indicated by the resident. (Added by Stats. 2017, Ch. 483, Sec. 3. (SB 219) Effective January 1, 2018.)

1439.53.

(a) Long-term care facilities shall protect personally identifiable information regarding residents' sexual orientation, whether a resident is transgender, a resident's transition history, and HIV status from unauthorized disclosure, as required by the federal Health Insurance Portability and Accountability Act of 1996 (42 U.S.C. Sec. 300gg), if applicable, the Confidentiality of Medical Information Act (Part 2.6 (commencing with Section 56) of Division 1 of the Civil Code), if applicable, regulations promulgated thereunder, if applicable, and any other applicable provision of federal or state law. A facility shall take any steps reasonably necessary to minimize the likelihood of inadvertent or incidental disclosure of that information to other residents, visitors, or facility staff, except to the minimum extent necessary for facility staff to perform their duties.

(b) Long-term care facility staff not directly involved in providing direct care to a resident, including, but not limited to, a transgender or gender-nonconforming resident, shall not be present during physical examination or the provision of personal care to that resident if the resident is partially or fully unclothed without the express permission of that resident, or his or her legally authorized representative or responsible party. A facility shall use doors, curtains, screens, or other effective visual barriers to provide bodily privacy for all residents, including, but not limited to, transgender or gender-nonconforming residents, whenever they are partially or fully unclothed. In addition, all residents, including, but not limited to, LGBT residents, shall be informed of and have the right to refuse to be examined, observed, or treated by any facility staff when the primary purpose is educational or informational rather than therapeutic, or for resident appraisal or reappraisal, and that refusal shall not diminish the resident's access to care for the primary purpose of diagnosis or treatment.

(Added by Stats. 2017, Ch. 483, Sec. 3. (SB 219) Effective January 1, 2018.)
1439.54.
A violation of this chapter shall be treated as a violation under Chapter 2 (commencing with Section 1250), Chapter 2.4 (commencing with Section 1417), or Chapter 3.2 (commencing with Section 1569).
(Added by Stats. 2017, Ch. 483, Sec. 3. (SB 219) Effective January 1, 2018.)

CHAPTER 2.5. County Medical Facilities [1440 - 1498]

(Chapter 2.5 added by Stats. 1961, Ch. 1993.)

ARTICLE 1. Administration [1440 - 1462]

(Article 1 added by Stats. 1961, Ch. 1993.)

1440.
As used in this chapter the term "board" means the board of supervisors of a county.
(Added by Stats. 1961, Ch. 1993.)

1441.
The board of supervisors in each county may establish and maintain a county hospital, prescribe rules for the government and management thereof, appoint a county physician and other necessary officers and employees thereof, who shall hold office during the pleasure of the board and authorize said hospital to be a member of and maintain membership in any local, state or national group or association organized and operated for the promotion of the public health and welfare or the advancement of the efficiency of hospital administration and in connection therewith to use tax funds for the payment of dues and fees.
(Added by Stats. 1961, Ch. 1993.)

1441.5.
(a) A member of a county hospital's medical or allied health professional staff who is an officer of the board of supervisors, or of a board or commission appointed by the board of supervisors for the operation of a county hospital shall not be deemed to be "financially interested," for purposes of Section 1090 of the Government Code, in any of the contracts set forth in subdivision (b) made by any county body or board of which the officer is a member if all of the following conditions are satisfied:
(1) The officer abstains from any participation in the making of the contract.
(2) The officer's relationship to the contract is disclosed to the body or board and noted in its official records.
(3) If the requirements of paragraphs (1) and (2) are satisfied, the body or board does both of the following, without any participation by the officer:
(A) Finds that the contract is fair to the county hospital and in its best interest.
(B) Authorizes the contract in good faith.
(b) Subdivision (a) shall apply to the following contracts:
(1) A contract between the county hospital and the officer for the officer to provide professional services to the hospital's patients, employees, or medical staff members and their respective dependents, provided that similar contracts exist with other staff members and the amounts payable under the contract are no greater than the amounts payable under similar contracts covering the same or similar services.
(2) A contract to provide services to covered persons between the county hospital and any insurance company, health care service plan, employer, or other entity which provides health care coverage, and which also has a contract with the officer to provide professional services to its covered persons.
(3) A contract in which the county hospital and the officer are both parties if other members of the county hospital's medical or allied health professional staff are also parties, directly or through their professional corporations or other practice entities, provided the officer is offered terms no more favorable than those offered any other party who is a member of the county hospital's medical or allied health professional staff.
(c) This section does not permit an otherwise prohibited individual to be a member of the board of supervisors or any committee or commission thereof. Nothing in this section shall authorize a contract that would otherwise be prohibited by Section 2400 of the Business and Professions Code.
(d) For purposes of this section, a contract entered into by a professional corporation or other practice entity in which the officer has an interest shall be deemed the same as a contract entered into by the officer directly.
(Added by Stats. 1996, Ch. 447, Sec. 2. Effective January 1, 1997.)
1442.5.
(a) Prior to (1) closing , (2) eliminating or reducing the level of medical services provided by, or (3) the leasing, selling, or transfer of management of, a county facility, the board shall provide public notice, including notice posted at the entrance to all county health care facilities, of public hearings to be held by the board prior to its decision to proceed. The notice shall be posted not less than 14 days prior to the public hearings. The notice shall contain a list of the proposed reductions or changes, by facility and service. The notice shall include the amount and type of each proposed change, the expected savings, and the number of persons affected.
(b) Notwithstanding the board's closing of, the elimination of or reduction in the level of services provided by, or the leasing, selling, or transfer of management of, a county facility subsequent to January 1, 1975, the county shall fulfill its duty to provide care to all indigent people, either directly through county facilities or indirectly through alternative means.
(1) Where the county duty is fulfilled by a contractual arrangement with a private facility or individual, the facility or individual shall assume the county's full obligation to provide care to those who cannot afford it, and make their services available to Medi-Cal and Medicare recipients.
(2) Where the county duty is fulfilled by alternative means, the facility or individual providing services shall be in compliance with Sections 441.18 and 1277.
(3) The board shall designate an agency to provide a 24-hour information service that can give eligible people immediate information on the available services and access to them, and an agency to receive and respond to complaints from people eligible for services under this chapter. The designated agency may be the agency that operates the facility. This subdivision applies only in instances in which there is (1) a closing of, (2) an elimination or reduction in the level of services provided by, or (3) the leasing, selling, or transfer of, a county facility.
(4) The board shall arrange for all facilities or individuals contracting to provide services to indigent people to be listed in the local telephone directory under county listings, and shall specify therein that the facilities or individuals fulfill the obligations of county facilities.
(5) Section 25371 of the Government Code does not relieve the county of the obligation to comply with this section.
(Amended by Stats. 1999, Ch. 83, Sec. 101. Effective January 1, 2000.)
1443.
The board may provide for transporting the needy sick to and from hospitals to which they may be sent by authority of the board, and may provide for transporting indigents to other counties or states when such indigents will thereby cease to become public charges, or when friends or relatives of such indigents agree to assume the cost and expense of the care and maintenance of such indigents, or when such indigents are legally public charges in the places to which they are so transported.
(Added by Stats. 1961, Ch. 1993.)
1444.
The board of supervisors in each county or city and county, having a population of one million or more, may purchase ambulances, establish and maintain an ambulance service, and prescribe rules for the government and management thereof. In any county where such a service has been established, any person who has been injured in an accident or is ill and in need of immediate transportation to a hospital may be taken to any available hospital. If he is indigent and unable to pay for the service, the cost shall be a proper charge against the county. If he is not indigent, he shall reimburse the county for the cost of transportation, which shall be in accordance with a schedule to be adopted by the board, and in no case less than the actual cost.
(Added by Stats. 1961, Ch. 1993.)
1444.6.
If a county hospital requests an ambulance to transfer a mental health patient who is unstable and has a history of being assaultive to another facility, notwithstanding any other provision of law, the director of the hospital or a designee shall inform the ambulance personnel of the instability and potential assaultiveness of the mental health patient. The county hospital shall establish procedures as are necessary to assure that the notification required by this section is given in appropriate cases and to assure that these notifications are documented.
(Added by Stats. 1987, Ch. 928, Sec. 1.)
1445.
Under such limitations and restrictions as are prescribed by law, and in addition to jurisdiction and powers otherwise conferred, the boards of supervisors in each county may provide for the care and maintenance of the indigent sick or dependent poor of the county, and may provide medical and dental care and health services and supplies to persons in need thereof who are unable to provide the same for themselves, and for these purposes may levy the necessary taxes. Each county may, insofar as it is able to do so, provide the means to meet promptly and adequately the health needs of the indigent sick, the aged, and the poor, for the better prevention of serious illness and incapacity, to the end that such persons will not become public charges at the greater expense of those resources set aside for the public health and welfare.
(Added by Stats. 1961, Ch. 1993.)
1446.
Except as otherwise provided in this chapter, a person, in order to be eligible for care, shall be a resident of the state and county wherein care is furnished as defined in Chapter 2 (commencing with Section 17100) of Part 5 of Division 9 of the Welfare and Institutions Code.
(Amended by Stats. 1974, Ch. 545.)
1447.
Notwithstanding any other provisions of the Welfare and Institutions Code, the county which is responsible for the payment of public assistance to any person or group of persons under Chapter 2 (commencing with Section 11200), Chapter 3 (commencing with Section 12000), or Chapter 4 (commencing with Section 12500) of Part 3 of Division 9 of that code, and the needy relative in the case of aid to needy children, shall provide the necessary hospital or medical care, or both, if otherwise qualified for that care. If a recipient of public assistance moves from one county to another county within this state to make his or her home, the county to which the recipient removes shall become responsible for providing medical or hospital care or both upon notification by the first county that the recipient has moved to the second county for the purpose of making his or her home in that county, provided that the recipient is otherwise qualified for the care, except that he or she need not meet the residence qualifications set forth in Section 17105 of the Welfare and Institutions Code.
(Amended by Stats. 1985, Ch. 106, Sec. 81.)
1451.

(a) Except as otherwise provided in this section, the board shall not let the care, maintenance, or attendance of the indigent sick or dependent poor by contract to any person.

(b) The board may secure for the indigent sick, and other persons admissible to the county hospital, at an agreed rate, hospital service, or any portion thereof, from any public or private hospital, clinic, rest home, sanitarium, or other suitable facility, or from any corporation formed under Section 9201 of the Corporations Code or under Chapter 11A (commencing with Section 11491) of Part 2 of Division 2 of the Insurance Code that operates in the state, in the following cases:

(1) Cases of unusual difficulty.

(2) Cases that require treatment, or hospital services, or the use of facilities not immediately available in the county hospital.

(3) Cases requiring emergency care or continued treatment after the emergency has ceased to exist.

(c) As used in this section, "hospital service" includes medical, surgical, radiological, laboratory, nursing service, convalescent care, and the furnishing of the necessary professional personnel, equipment, and facilities to manage the needs of patients on a continuing basis in accordance with accepted medical standards, with a staff of professional nursing personnel who are assigned and available under a clear and definite responsibility to the institution rendering the service for the provision of services to the patients, and any other care, service, or supplies that may be necessary for the treatment of the sick or injured.

(d) The county may also contract with licensed boarding homes for 24-hour care for dependent children under the age of 18 years when suitable facilities are not otherwise available in any institution or establishment maintained and operated by the county.

(e) The county may also contract for medical treatment of persons admissible to the county hospital with any licensed physician and surgeon, or a corporation operating under Section 9201 of the Corporations Code.

(f) The county may also contract for health care services when the board determines that the hospital services or any portion thereof rendered by the county hospital should be coordinated with those provided by any other source.

(Amended by Stats. 2006, Ch. 538, Sec. 356. Effective January 1, 2007.)

1451.5.

The board may authorize payment for care provided, on or after January 1, 1962, to an indigent resident of the county in a hospital or medical facility located in another state, where that care is provided in an emergency or can be secured at a lesser expense than would be the case were the person to be transported to a comparable facility in this State.

(Added by Stats. 1963, Ch. 2167.)

1452.

The board of supervisors of counties of the 20th class and 40th to 58th class, inclusive, in connection with the administration of a county hospital may establish in the county treasury a special fund to be known as the "Hospital Trust Fund," into which may be placed deposits made voluntarily by patients entering such hospital.

At the time of any patient's dismissal from a county hospital, there shall be refunded to him, upon the order of the business manager or other person designated by the board of supervisors, such portion of the deposit made voluntarily by the patient at the time of his entrance into the hospital as was unneeded for his care while confined therein. The portion earned by the hospital shall be transferred to the hospital fund in the county treasury.

Upon presentation of an order for refund under this section, the county auditor shall draw his warrant on the Hospital Trust Fund, and the county treasurer shall pay the amount due thereon.

If no refund is made within 30 days after the patient's discharge, the patient may file a claim against the county pursuant to Article 1 of Chapter 4 of Division 3 of Title 3 of the Government Code.

(Added by Stats. 1961, Ch. 1993.)

1453.

The board of supervisors of any county in connection with the administration of any county hospital may establish in the county treasury a special fund to be known as the "patients' personal deposit fund." When such fund is established, any patient in the hospital may request the superintendent thereof to deposit in the fund any moneys belonging to the patient. Upon any such request by any patient any moneys belonging to the patient shall be deposited in the name of that patient in the patients' personal deposit fund, except that if a guardian or conservator of the estate is appointed for the patient, then the guardian or conservator shall have the right to demand and receive such moneys or to withdraw either in whole or in part the moneys theretofore deposited in the fund in the name of the patient. Any of the funds belonging to a patient deposited in the patients' personal deposit fund may be used for the purchase of personal incidentals for the patient or otherwise used for the personal needs and benefits of the patient upon his request. At the time of the discharge from the hospital of any patient there shall be refunded to him upon the order of the superintendent the balance of any moneys standing to the credit of the patient in the fund.

Prior to the time of the discharge of any patient, upon the demand of the patient there shall be refunded to him upon the order of the superintendent the whole or any portion of the balance of any moneys standing to the credit of the patient in the fund. Upon such demand of the patient, or upon the discharge of the patient from the hospital, or upon the demand of the guardian or conservator of the estate of the patient, the superintendent shall order the refund to the patient or the payment to such guardian or conservator as hereinbefore provided.

(Amended by Stats. 1979, Ch. 730.)

1454.

In any county where a county hospital has been established, any expectant mother who is unable to pay for her necessary care shall be admitted to the county hospital, and the cost of her maintenance and care shall be a proper charge against and shall be paid by the county of her residence.

(Added by Stats. 1961, Ch. 1993.)

1455.

The board shall appoint a suitable graduate, or graduates, in medicine to attend such indigent sick or dependent poor in the county hospitals and almshouses.

(Added by Stats. 1961, Ch. 1993.)

1456.

(a) In the interest of public health and safety the board of supervisors of any county which maintains a county hospital may by ordinance establish a hospital and safety commission. The commission shall be advisory to the board of supervisors.

(b) The commission shall exercise such powers and perform such duties relating to the administration of the county hospital as shall be prescribed by the ordinance. The commission shall further exercise such powers and perform such duties as shall be prescribed by the ordinance and which may include the following:

1. To promote safety among all county officers and employees and to develop a program of accident prevention.

2. To investigate all industrial, vehicular and all other accidents to county personnel and county equipment, including privately owned equipment operated by county personnel under contract with the county.

3. To hold hearings in the course of such investigation and to report to the board of supervisors upon all accidents reported to and investigated by the commission.

4. To recommend to the board of supervisors safety rules and regulations promoting the health and safety of all county officers and employees and agents in the prosecution of their office or employment and their use of all equipment in the course of their duties as such officers, employees, and agents.

(c) The commission shall be appointed by the board of supervisors. No person holding any elective office shall be appointed to the commission. Members of the commission shall be residents of the county. Members shall be appointed in the manner prescribed by the ordinance and shall serve for such term as is prescribed therein; subject, however, to the power of the board of supervisors to remove any member of the commission at any time by three-fifths vote of the board.

(d) The members of the commission shall serve with or without compensation as prescribed by the ordinance.

(e) Members of the commission may, when and if so provided in the ordinance, receive actual and necessary expenses in traveling from their place of residence to the place of meeting of the commission, and return, and such expenses shall be a proper charge upon the county; provided, however, that in no event shall any charge be made upon the county for any expense incurred by any member for any meal eaten at any meeting of the commission.

(f) Meetings of the commission shall be held in accord with the provisions of Chapter 9 (commencing with Section 54950) of Part 1 of Division 2 of Title 5 of the Government Code.

(g) The provisions of Section 54954 of the Government Code notwithstanding, any meeting of the commission shall be held only in a public building of the county and within the county in which such commission is established.

(h) The ordinance establishing the commission shall specifically prescribe the following:

(1) The name of the commission;

(2) The functions and duties thereof;

(3) Number of members, method of appointment and term of members;

(4) A statement of whether or not payment of compensation to members of the commission is authorized and, if authorized, a statement of the amount of such compensation and the maximum number of meetings of the commission in any one calendar month for which such compensation may be paid;

(5) A statement of whether or not traveling expenses are authorized and, if authorized, a statement of the rate which will be allowed for mileage.

(6) Subject to the limitations prescribed by this section, such ordinance may contain such additional provisions as the board of supervisors may deem expedient for the proper administration of the affairs of the commission.

(i) Any ordinance of any county establishing a hospital or a safety commission enacted prior to the effective date of this section is hereby validated, provided that the provisions of the ordinance substantially comply with the limitations and authorizations set forth in this section; provided expressly, however, that any such hospital or safety commission created by ordinance enacted prior to the effective date of this section shall cease to exist at the close of the 60th day following the effective date of this section, and no hospital or safety commission established by any such ordinance, or established in any other manner whatever, shall continue to exist or function thereafter in any county unless and until such hospital or safety commission is established by ordinance under the provisions of this section.

(Amended by Stats. 1976, Ch. 799.)

1457.

(a) The State Department of Health Services, with the advice of the State Department of Social Services, shall prescribe the records to be kept by county hospitals of persons received into or discharged from these institutions, including, but not limited to, records for the admission and processing of county hospital patients.

(b) The records shall be preserved and maintained pursuant to regulations adopted by the department, or at the request of the county physician or other person in charge of the county hospital, the board of supervisors of the county may authorize the destruction of any record, paper or document prescribed by the department following compliance with the conditions prescribed in Section 26205 of the Government Code.

(c) (1) Notwithstanding any other provision of law, those records of a hospital, or any other county medical facility, subject to this chapter that reveal the rates of payment for health care services rendered by or purchased by the hospital or other medical facility, or the deliberative processes, discussions, communications, or any other portion or aspect of the negotiations leading to those payment rates, shall not be considered public records subject to disclosure pursuant to the California Public Records Act, Chapter 3.5 (commencing with Section 6250) of Division 7 of Title 1 of the Government Code, nor shall they be subject to public disclosure pursuant to any other law requiring the disclosure of records, for a period of three years following execution of a related contract establishing rates of payment.

(2) Notwithstanding paragraph (1), public disclosure or nondisclosure of records relating to any matters or activities connected with selective provider contracts entered into pursuant to Article 2.6 (commencing with Section 14081) of Chapter 7 of Part 3 of Division 9 of the Welfare and Institutions Code shall be determined pursuant to Article 2.6 (commencing with Section 14081) of Chapter 7 of Part 3 of Division 9 of the Welfare and Institutions Code and subdivision (q) of Section 6254 of the Government Code, and other applicable provisions of Chapter 3.5 (commencing with Section 6250) of Division 7 of Title 1 of the Government Code.

(Amended by Stats. 1995, Ch. 138, Sec. 1. Effective January 1, 1996.)

1458.

The board may provide a farm in connection with the county hospital or almshouse and may make regulations for working the same.

(Added by Stats. 1965, Ch. 1784.)

1459.

No county hospital which permits sterilization operations for contraceptive purposes to be performed therein, nor the medical staff of such hospital, shall require the individual upon whom such a sterilization operation is to be performed to meet any special nonmedical qualifications, which are not imposed on individuals seeking other types of operations in the hospital. Such prohibited nonmedical qualifications shall include, but not be limited to, age, marital status, and number of natural children.

Nothing in this section shall prohibit requirements relating to the physical or mental condition of the individual or affect the right of the attending physician to counsel or advise his patient as to whether or not sterilization is appropriate. This section shall not affect existing law with respect to individuals below the age of majority.

(Added by Stats. 1972, Ch. 1425.)

1460.

(a) Upon a determination and establishment of the need to recruit and retain registered nurses, licensed vocational nurses, X-ray technicians, laboratory technologists, and other health care professionals, the board of supervisors of a county may establish nursing or health care professional scholarships. For purposes of this section, "health care professional" shall not include a physician and surgeon.

(b) The board of supervisors, or a designee of the board, shall administer the scholarship program for students participating in a nurse or health care professional training program and shall adopt such rules and regulations as are reasonably necessary to carry out the provisions of this section.

(c) Scholarships made pursuant to this section, shall be repayable to the board of supervisors or canceled under the following conditions:

(1) A graduate nurse or health care professional who maintains employment in a county-operated health facility for less than one year after becoming licensed shall repay the scholarship in addition to accrued interest charges. The scholarships shall be repayable to the board of supervisors under the terms specified in the agreement.

(2) The total amount of the scholarship and all accrued interest shall be canceled for a graduate nurse or graduate health care professional who maintains employment in a county-operated facility for more than a year from the date of licensure and may be canceled under any other conditions established by rules and regulations adopted by the board of supervisors. For the purposes of this section, one year of employment in a county-operated health facility shall be deemed to have lapsed one year from the date the licensed nurse or health care professional presents proof, in writing, to the board of supervisors, or designee of the board, that he or she is licensed and is employed in a county-operated health facility.

(d) In addition to the principal amount of the scholarship, interest shall accrue on the principal at a rate to be established by the board of supervisors. Interest shall accrue from the date the scholarship is made until it is repaid unless the scholarship is canceled pursuant to paragraph (2) of subdivision (c).

(Amended by Stats. 1989, Ch. 326, Sec. 3.)

1461.

Notwithstanding any other provisions of law, the board of directors of any hospital subject to this chapter may order that any hearings on the reports of hospital medical audit or quality assurance committees be held in closed session. An applicant or medical staff member whose staff privileges are the direct subject of a hearing may request a public hearing. Deliberations of the board of directors in connection with matters pertaining to these hearings may be held in closed session.

(Added by Stats. 1993, Ch. 1137, Sec. 21. Effective January 1, 1994. Operative April 1, 1994, by Sec. 23 of Ch. 1137.)

1462.

(a) Except as provided in this section or Section 1461, all of the sessions of the board of directors of any hospital subject to this chapter, whether regular or special, shall be open to the public.

(b) The board of directors may order that a meeting held solely for the purpose of discussion or deliberation, or both, of reports involving hospital trade secrets to be held in closed session. Except as provided in this subdivision, the closed session shall meet all applicable requirements of Chapter 9 (commencing with Section 54950) of Division 2 of Title 5 of the Government Code.

(c) "Hospital trade secrets," as used in this section, means a "trade secret," as defined in subdivision (d) of Section 3426.1 of the Civil Code, and which meets both of the following:

(1) Is necessary to initiate a new hospital service or program or add a hospital facility.

(2) Would, if prematurely disclosed, create a substantial probability of depriving the hospital of substantial economic benefit.

(d) The exemption provided in subdivision (b) to the general open meeting requirements for a meeting of the board of directors, shall not apply to a meeting where there is action taken, as defined in Section 54952.6 of the Government Code.

(e) Nothing in this section shall be construed to permit the board of directors to order a closed meeting for the purposes of discussing or deliberating, or to permit the discussion or deliberation in any closed meeting of, any proposals regarding:

(1) The sale, conversion, contract for management, or leasing of any county hospital or the assets thereof, to any for-profit or not-for-profit entity, agency, association, organization, governmental body, person, partnership, corporation, or other district.

(2) The conversion of any county hospital to any other form of ownership by the county.

(3) The dissolution of the county hospital.

(Added by Stats. 1995, Ch. 529, Sec. 13. Effective October 4, 1995.)

ARTICLE 2. Liability for Cost of Care [1473 - 1475]

(Article 2 added by Stats. 1961, Ch. 1993.)

1473.

The board of supervisors in each county may fix the rates to be charged patients admitted to any county hospital and may direct any county officer to collect the amounts due the county for hospitalization and medical care. In fixing and collecting hospital charges the board may exercise all the powers conferred by Chapter 5 (commencing with Section 17400) of Part 5 of Division 9 of the Welfare and Institutions Code. The board, or such county officer as it may authorize or designate, may adjust or compromise hospital charges for any of the following reasons:

(a) The patient, his estate, or legally responsible relatives are unable to pay the charges.

(b) Collection of the charges is barred by the statute of limitations or is otherwise legally uncollectible.

(c) The cost of administering a collection procedure would exceed the amount of revenue which might reasonably be anticipated would be recovered.

(d) Neither the patient nor his legally responsible relatives can be located.

The amendments to this section enacted by the Legislature at the 1973–74 Regular Session shall not be construed to require that any county adopt standards of indigency or requirements of reimbursement more stringent than those in use by such county immediately prior to the effective date of such amendments.

For the purposes of this chapter responsible relative is defined in Section 17300 of the Welfare and Institutions Code.

(Amended by Stats. 1976, Ch. 162.)

1474.

In collecting charges for care rendered under this chapter, the board may exercise all powers provided in Chapter 5 (commencing with Section 17400) of Part 5 of Division 9 of the Welfare and Institutions Code, as enacted and as it may be amended thereafter.

(Amended by Stats. 1974, Ch. 545.)

1475.

Unless there exists a reciprocal agreement relating to the expense of medical care and treatment, it shall be the duty of every county to pay for the expense of treatment of its indigent residents furnished by the county hospital of any other county. As a condition of liability, the county providing such medical and hospital care shall, not more than ten (10) days after admission, give notice to the county of residence.

(Added by Stats. 1961, Ch. 1993.)

ARTICLE 4. Victims of Sexual Offenses [1491 - 1492]

(Article 4 added by Stats. 1976, Ch. 750.)

1491.

In addition to any examination performed without charge to a victim of rape or other sexual assault pursuant to Section 13823.95 of the Penal Code, a county hospital shall, without charge, provide the victim of rape, or other sexual assault, with testing for venereal disease and pregnancy.

(Amended by Stats. 1988, Ch. 1575, Sec. 2.)

1492.

A county hospital shall provide persons examined or treated in connection with rape or other sexual assaults with information regarding assistance which may be provided pursuant to Article 1 (commencing with Section 13959) of Chapter 5 of Part 4 of Division 3 of Title 2 of the Government Code, together with forms made available by the California Victim Compensation Board for filing of claims thereunder.

(Amended by Stats. 2016, Ch. 31, Sec. 160. (SB 836) Effective June 27, 2016.)

ARTICLE 5. Continuing Education [1496 - 1498]

(Article 5 added by Stats. 1979, Ch. 613.)

1496.

As used in this article:

(a) "Continuing education program" means educational programs designed to increase the knowledge and skills of health workers.

(b) "Licensed health worker" means any person who works in a health profession that requires licensure under the laws of California.

(c) "Non-county-employed health worker" means any person employed in a health facility, other than a county-operated health facility, in a county in which a continuing education program is offered or is to be offered.

(d) "Nonlicensed health worker" means any person who performs duties in a health facility and who is not required to be licensed to perform such duties under the laws of California.

(Added by Stats. 1979, Ch. 613.)

1496.5.

Any county may conduct continuing education programs for non-county-employed licensed health workers or non-county-employed nonlicensed health workers as prescribed in this article.

(Added by Stats. 1979, Ch. 613.)

1497.

(a) Any county health facility, including, but not limited to, hospitals, mental health facilities, and other public health facilities, may utilize its county staff personnel to conduct continuing education programs for non-county-employed licensed health workers or non-county-employed nonlicensed health workers.

(b) A county may contract with a community college, college, university, hospital, or other health facility for purposes of conducting continuing education programs pursuant to this article.

(Added by Stats. 1979, Ch. 613.)

1497.5.

(a) Any county conducting continuing educational programs pursuant to this article shall charge and collect fees sufficient to defray the cost of such instruction and training. Such fees may be reduced to the extent of any federal funds obtained by the county for the purpose of providing such instruction and training.

(b) Any fees collected pursuant to this section shall be placed in a continuing education program fund of the county. The revenue in such a fund shall be used for the sole purpose of supporting and continually upgrading such continuing educational programs.

(Added by Stats. 1979, Ch. 613.)

1498.

Any county conducting a continuing education program pursuant to this article shall maintain individual records of attendance and the number of continuing education units earned by participants, if any, in such program. Copies of such information shall be made available upon request and at the cost of reproduction to participants in such program.

(Added by Stats. 1979, Ch. 613.)

CHAPTER 2.6. Use of Administrative Action for Licensure [1499- 1499.]

(Chapter 2.6 added by Stats. 2006, Ch. 902, Sec. 4.)

1499.

(a) Any person or entity licensed or certificated under Chapter 1 (commencing with Section 1200), Chapter 2 (commencing with Section 1250), Chapter 2.3 (commencing with Section 1400), Chapter 2.35 (commencing with Section 1416), Chapter 3.3 (commencing with Section 1570), Chapter 8 (commencing with Section 1725), Chapter 8.3 (commencing with Section 1743), Chapter 8.5 (commencing with Section 1745), or Chapter 8.6 (commencing with Section 1760) of this code, or under Section 1247.6 of the Business and Professions Code, shall, in addition to all other requirements, disclose as part of the application for the license or certificate any revocation or other final administrative action taken against a license, certificate, registration, or other approval to engage in a profession, vocation, or occupation, or a license or other permission to operate a facility or institution.

(b) The department may consider, in determining whether to grant or deny the license or certification, any final revocation or other final administrative action taken against a license, certificate, registration, or other permission to engage in a profession, vocation, or occupation or a license or other permission to operate a facility or institution.

(c) An applicant and any other person specified in this subdivision, as part of the background clearance process, shall provide information as to whether or not the person has any prior criminal convictions, has had any arrests within the past 12-month period, or has any active arrests, and shall certify that, to the best of his or her knowledge, the information provided is true. This requirement is not intended to duplicate existing requirements for individuals who are required to submit fingerprint images as part of a criminal background clearance process. Every applicant shall provide information on any prior administrative action taken against him or her by any federal, state, or local government agency and shall certify that, to the best of his or her knowledge, the information provided is true. An applicant or other person required to provide information pursuant to this section that knowingly or willfully makes false statements, representations, or omissions may be subject to administrative action, including, but not limited to, denial of his or her application or exemption or revocation of any exemption previously granted.

(Amended by Stats. 2010, Ch. 328, Sec. 122. (SB 1330) Effective January 1, 2011.)

CHAPTER 3. California Community Care Facilities Act [1500 - 1567.87]

(Chapter 3 repealed and added by Stats. 1973, Ch. 1203.)

ARTICLE 1. General Provisions [1500 - 1518]

(Article 1 added by Stats. 1973, Ch. 1203.)

1500.

This chapter shall be known and may be cited as the California Community Care Facilities Act.

(Repealed and added by Stats. 1973, Ch. 1203.)

1501.

(a) The Legislature hereby finds and declares that there is an urgent need to establish a coordinated and comprehensive statewide service system of quality community care for mentally ill, developmentally and physically disabled, and children and adults who require care or services by a facility or organization issued a license or special permit pursuant to this chapter.

(b) Therefore, the Legislature declares it is the intent of the state to develop policies and programs designed to: (1) insure a level of care and services in the community which is equal to or better than that provided by the state hospitals; (2) assure that all people who require them are provided with the appropriate range of social rehabilitative, habilitative and treatment services, including residential and nonresidential programs tailored to their needs; (3) protect the legal and human rights of a person in or receiving services from a community care facility; (4) insure continuity of care between the medical-health elements and the supportive care-rehabilitation elements of California's health systems; (5) insure that facilities providing community care are adequate, safe and sanitary; (6) assure that rehabilitative and treatment services are provided at a reasonable cost; (7) assure that state payments for community care services are based on a flexible rate schedule varying according to type and cost of care and services provided; (8) encourage the utilization of personnel from state hospitals and the development of training programs to improve the quality of staff in community care facilities; and (9) insure the quality of community care facilities by evaluating the care and services provided and furnishing incentives to upgrade their quality.

(Amended by Stats. 1974, Ch. 497.)

1501.1.

(a) It is the policy of the state to facilitate the proper placement of every child in residential care facilities where the placement is in the best interests of the child. A county may require placement or licensing agencies, or both placement and licensing agencies, to actively seek out-of-home care facilities capable of meeting the varied needs of the child. Therefore, in placing children in out-of-home care, particular attention should be given to the individual child's needs, the ability of the facility to meet those needs, the needs of other children in the facility, the licensing requirements of the facility as determined by the licensing agency, and the impact of the placement on the family reunification plan.

(b) Pursuant to this section, children with varying designations and varying needs, including, on and after January 1, 2012, nonminor dependents, as defined in subdivision (v) of Section 11400 of the Welfare and Institutions Code, except as provided by statute, may be placed in the same facility provided the facility is licensed, complies with all licensing requirements relevant to the protection of the child, and has a special permit, if necessary, to meet the needs of each child so placed. A facility may not require, as a condition of placement, that a child be identified as an individual with exceptional needs as defined by Section 56026 of the Education Code.

(c) Neither the requirement for any license nor any regulation shall restrict the implementation of the provisions of this section. Implementation of this section does not obviate the requirement for a facility to be licensed by the department.

(d) Pursuant to this section, children with varying designations and varying needs, including, on and after January 1, 2012, nonminor dependents, as defined in subdivision (v) of Section 11400 of the Welfare and Institutions Code, except as provided by statute, may be placed in the same licensed foster family home or with a foster family agency for subsequent placement in a certified family home or with a resource family. Children, including nonminor dependents, with developmental disabilities, mental disorders, or physical disabilities may be placed in licensed foster family homes or certified family homes or with resource families, provided that an appraisal of the child's or nonminor dependent's needs and the ability of the receiving home to meet those needs is made jointly by the placement agency and the licensee in the case of licensed foster family homes or the placement agency and the foster family agency in the case of certified family homes or resource families, and is followed by written confirmation prior to placement. The appraisal shall confirm that the placement poses no threat to any child in the home.

(e) (1) For purposes of this chapter, the placing of children by foster family agencies shall be referred to as "subsequent placement" to distinguish the activity from the placing by public agencies.

(2) For purposes of this chapter, and unless otherwise specified, references to a "child" shall include a "nonminor dependent" and "nonminor former dependent or ward" as those terms are defined in subdivision (v) and paragraph (1) of subdivision (aa) of Section 11400 of the Welfare and Institutions Code.

(Amended by Stats. 2016, Ch. 612, Sec. 14. (AB 1997) Effective January 1, 2017.)

1502.

As used in this chapter:

(a) "Community care facility" means any facility, place, or building that is maintained and operated to provide nonmedical residential care, day treatment, adult day care, or foster family agency services for children, adults, or children and adults, including, but not limited to, the physically handicapped, mentally impaired, incompetent persons, and abused or neglected children, and includes the following:

(1) "Residential facility" means any family home, group care facility, or similar facility determined by the department, for 24-hour nonmedical care of persons in need of personal services, supervision, or assistance essential for sustaining the activities of daily living or for the protection of the individual.

(2) "Adult day program" means any community-based facility or program that provides care to persons 18 years of age or older in need of personal services, supervision, or assistance essential for sustaining the activities of daily living or for the protection of these individuals on less than a 24-hour basis.

(3) "Therapeutic day services facility" means any facility that provides nonmedical care, counseling, educational or vocational support, or social rehabilitation services on less than a 24-hour basis to persons under 18 years of age who would otherwise be placed in foster care or who are returning to families from foster care. Program standards for these facilities shall be developed by the department, pursuant to Section 1530, in consultation with therapeutic day services and foster care providers.

(4) "Foster family agency" means any public agency or private organization, organized and operated on a nonprofit basis, engaged in any of the following:

(A) Recruiting, certifying, approving, and training of, and providing professional support to, foster parents and resource families.

(B) Coordinating with county placing agencies to find homes for foster children in need of care.

(C) Providing services and supports to licensed or certified foster parents, county-approved resource families, and children to the extent authorized by state and federal law.

(5) "Foster family home" means any residential facility providing 24-hour care for six or fewer foster children that is owned, leased, or rented and is the residence of the foster parent or parents, including their family, in whose care the foster children have been placed. The placement may be by a public or private child placement agency or by a court order, or by voluntary placement by a parent, parents, or guardian. It also means a foster family home described in Section 1505.2.

(6) "Small family home" means any residential facility, in the licensee's family residence, that provides 24-hour care for six or fewer foster children who have mental disorders or developmental or physical disabilities and who require special care and supervision as a result of their disabilities. A small family home may accept children with special health care needs, pursuant to subdivision (a) of Section 17710 of the Welfare and Institutions Code. In addition to placing children with special health care needs, the department may approve placement of children without special health care needs, up to the licensed capacity.

(7) "Social rehabilitation facility" means any residential facility that provides social rehabilitation services for no longer than 18 months in a group setting to adults recovering from mental illness who temporarily need assistance, guidance, or counseling. Program components shall be subject to program standards pursuant to Article 1 (commencing with Section 5670) of Chapter 2.5 of Part 2 of Division 5 of the Welfare and Institutions Code.

(8) "Community treatment facility" means any residential facility that provides mental health treatment services to children in a group setting and that has the capacity to provide secure containment. Program components shall be subject to program standards developed and enforced by the State Department of Health Care Services pursuant to Section 4094 of the Welfare and Institutions Code.

Nothing in this section shall be construed to prohibit or discourage placement of persons who have mental or physical disabilities into any category of community care facility that meets the needs of the individual placed, if the placement is consistent with the licensing regulations of the department.

(9) "Full-service adoption agency" means any licensed entity engaged in the business of providing adoption services, that does all of the following:

(A) Assumes care, custody, and control of a child through relinquishment of the child to the agency or involuntary termination of parental rights to the child.

(B) Assesses the birth parents, prospective adoptive parents, or child.

(C) Places children for adoption.

(D) Supervises adoptive placements.

Private full-service adoption agencies shall be organized and operated on a nonprofit basis. As a condition of licensure to provide intercountry adoption services, a full-service adoption agency shall be accredited and in good standing according to Part 96 (commencing with Section 96.1) of Title 22 of the Code of Federal Regulations, or supervised by an accredited primary provider, or acting as an exempted provider, in compliance with Subpart F (commencing with Section 96.29) of Part 96 of Title 22 of the Code of Federal Regulations.

(10) "Noncustodial adoption agency" means any licensed entity engaged in the business of providing adoption services, that does all of the following:

(A) Assesses the prospective adoptive parents.

(B) Cooperatively matches children freed for adoption, who are under the care, custody, and control of a licensed adoption agency, for adoption, with assessed and approved adoptive applicants.

(C) Cooperatively supervises adoption placements with a full-service adoptive agency, but does not disrupt a placement or remove a child from a placement.

Private noncustodial adoption agencies shall be organized and operated on a nonprofit basis. As a condition of licensure to provide intercountry adoption services, a noncustodial adoption agency shall be accredited and in good standing according to Part 96 (commencing with Section 96.1) of Title 22 of the Code of Federal Regulations, or supervised by an accredited primary provider, or acting as an exempted provider, in compliance with Subpart F (commencing with Section 96.29) of Part 96 of Title 22 of the Code of Federal Regulations.

(11) "Transitional shelter care facility" means any group care facility that provides for 24-hour nonmedical care of persons in need of personal services, supervision, or assistance essential for sustaining the activities of daily living or for the protection of the individual. Program components shall be subject to program standards developed by the State Department of Social Services pursuant to Section 1502.3.

(12) "Transitional housing placement provider" means an organization licensed by the department pursuant to Section 1559.110 to provide transitional housing to foster children who are at least 16 years of age to promote their transition to adulthood. A transitional housing placement provider shall be privately operated and organized on a nonprofit basis.

(13) "Group home" means a residential facility that provides 24-hour care and supervision to children, delivered at least in part by staff employed by the licensee in a structured environment. The care and supervision provided by a group home shall be nonmedical, except as otherwise permitted by law.

(14) "Runaway and homeless youth shelter" means a group home licensed by the department to operate a program pursuant to Section 1502.35 to provide voluntary, short-term, shelter and personal services to runaway youth or homeless youth, as defined in paragraph (2) of subdivision (a) of Section 1502.35.

(15) "Enhanced behavioral supports home" means a facility certified by the State Department of Developmental Services pursuant to Article 3.6 (commencing with Section 4684.80) of Chapter 6 of Division 4.5 of the Welfare and Institutions Code, and licensed by the State Department of Social Services as an adult residential facility or a group home that provides 24-hour nonmedical care to individuals with developmental disabilities who require enhanced behavioral supports, staffing, and supervision in a homelike setting. An enhanced behavioral supports home shall have a maximum capacity of four consumers, shall conform to Section 441.530(a)(1) of Title 42 of the Code of Federal Regulations, and shall be eligible for federal Medicaid home- and community-based services funding.

(16) "Community crisis home" means a facility certified by the State Department of Developmental Services pursuant to Article 8 (commencing with Section 4698) of Chapter 6 of Division 4.5 of the Welfare and Institutions Code, and licensed by the State Department of Social Services pursuant to Article 9.7 (commencing with Section 1567.80), as an adult residential facility, providing 24-hour nonmedical care to individuals with developmental disabilities receiving regional center service, in need of crisis intervention services, and who would otherwise be at risk of admission to the acute crisis center at Fairview Developmental Center, Sonoma Developmental Center, an acute general hospital, acute psychiatric hospital, an institution for mental disease, as described in Part 5 (commencing with Section 5900) of Division 5 of the Welfare and Institutions Code, or an out-of-state placement. A community crisis home shall have a maximum capacity of eight consumers, as defined in subdivision (a) of Section 1567.80, shall conform to Section 441.530(a)(1) of Title 42 of the Code of Federal Regulations, and shall be eligible for federal Medicaid home- and community-based services funding.

(17) "Crisis nursery" means a facility licensed by the department to operate a program pursuant to Section 1516 to provide short-term care and supervision for children under six years of age who are voluntarily placed for temporary care by a parent or legal guardian due to a family crisis or stressful situation.

(18) "Short-term residential therapeutic program" means a residential facility operated by a public agency or private organization and licensed by the department pursuant to Section 1562.01 that provides an integrated program of specialized and intensive care and supervision, services and supports, treatment, and short-term, 24-hour care and supervision to children. The care and supervision provided by a short-term residential therapeutic program shall be nonmedical, except as otherwise permitted by law. Private short-term residential therapeutic programs shall be organized and operated on a nonprofit basis. A short-term residential therapeutic program may be operated as a children's crisis residential program.

(19) "Private alternative boarding school" means a group home licensed by the department to operate a program pursuant to Section 1502.2 to provide youth with 24-hour residential care and supervision, which, in addition to providing educational services to youth, provides, or holds itself out as providing, behavioral-based services to youth with social, emotional, or behavioral issues. The care and supervision provided by a private alternative boarding school shall be nonmedical, except as otherwise permitted by law.

(20) "Private alternative outdoor program" means a group home licensed by the department to operate a program pursuant to Section 1502.21 to provide youth with 24-hour residential care and supervision, which provides, or holds itself out as providing, behavioral-based services in an outdoor living setting to youth with social, emotional, or behavioral issues. The care and supervision provided by a private alternative outdoor program shall be nonmedical, except as otherwise permitted by law.

(21) "Children's crisis residential program" means a facility licensed by the department as a short-term residential therapeutic program pursuant to Section 1562.02 and approved by the State Department of Health Care Services, or a county mental health plan to which the State Department of Health Care Services has delegated approval authority, to operate a children's crisis residential mental health program approval

pursuant to Section 11462.011 of the Welfare and Institutions Code, to serve children experiencing mental health crises as an alternative to psychiatric hospitalization.

(b) "Department" or "state department" means the State Department of Social Services.

(c) "Director" means the Director of Social Services.

(Amended by Stats. 2017, Ch. 731, Sec. 1.5. (SB 612) Effective January 1, 2018.)

1502.2.

(a) Commencing January 1, 2018, the department shall license private alternative boarding schools, as defined in paragraph (19) of subdivision (a) of Section 1502, as a group home pursuant to this chapter. A licensed private alternative boarding school shall comply with all provisions of this chapter that are applicable to group homes, unless otherwise indicated, and with this section.

(b) A licensed private alternative boarding school shall comply with all of the following:

(1) It shall be owned and operated on a nonprofit basis by a private nonprofit corporation or a nonprofit organization.

(2) It shall prepare and maintain a current written plan of operation, as defined by the department.

(3) It shall offer 24-hour, nonmedical care and supervision to youth who voluntarily consent to being admitted to the program and who are voluntarily admitted by his or her parent or legal guardian.

(4) (A) It shall not admit a child younger than 12 years of age.

(B) It shall not admit a youth who has been assessed by a licensed mental health professional as seriously emotionally disturbed, unless the youth does not require care in a licensed health facility and the State Department of Health Care Services has certified the facility as a program that meets the standards to provide mental health treatment services for a child having a serious emotional disturbance, as set forth in Section 4096.5 of the Welfare and Institutions Code.

(5) It shall provide each prospective youth and his or her parent or legal guardian with an accurate written description of the programs and services to be provided. If it advertises or promotes special care, programming, or environments for persons with behavioral, emotional, or social challenges, the written description shall include how its programs and services are intended to achieve the advertised or promoted claims.

(6) It shall ensure that all individuals providing behavioral-based services to youth at the facility are licensed or certified by the appropriate agency, department, or accrediting body, as specified by the department in regulation.

(7) It shall not use secure containment or manual or mechanical restraints.

(8) If it offers access to, or holds itself out as offering access to, mental health services, it shall ensure that those services are provided by a licensed mental health provider.

(9) If it advertises or includes in its marketing materials reference to providing alcohol or substance abuse treatment, it shall ensure that the treatment is provided by a licensed or certified alcoholism or drug abuse recovery or treatment facility.

(c) A private alternative boarding school shall submit a staff training plan to the department as part of its plan of operation. In addition to the training required of group home staff, the staff training plan shall include, but not be limited to, training in all of the following subject areas:

(1) Youth rights, as described in subdivision (d).

(2) Physical and psychosocial needs of youth.

(3) Appropriate responses to emergencies, including an emergency intervention plan.

(4) Cultural competency and sensitivity in issues relating to the lesbian, gay, bisexual, and transgender communities.

(5) Laws pertaining to residential care facilities for youth.

(d) (1) A youth admitted to a licensed private alternative boarding school shall be accorded the following rights and any other rights adopted by the department in regulations, a list of which shall be publicly posted and accessible to youth. The personal rights enumerated in Section 84072 of Title 22 of the California Code of Regulations shall not apply.

(A) To be accorded dignity in his or her personal relationships with staff, youth, and other persons.

(B) To live in a safe, healthy, and comfortable environment where he or she is treated with respect.

(C) To be free from physical, sexual, emotional, or other abuse, or corporal punishment.

(D) To be granted a reasonable level of personal privacy in accommodations, personal care and assistance, and visits.

(E) To confidential care of his or her records and personal information, and to approve release of those records before release, except as otherwise authorized or required by law.

(F) To care, supervision, and services that meet his or her individual needs and that are delivered by staff who are sufficient in numbers, qualifications, and competency to meet his or her needs and ensure his or her safety.

(G) To be served food and beverages of the quality and in the quantity necessary to meet his or her nutritional and physical needs.

(H) (i) To present grievances and recommend changes in policies, procedures, and services to the facility's staff, management, and governing authority, or any other person without restraint, coercion, discrimination, reprisal, or other retaliatory actions.

(ii) To have the licensee take prompt actions to respond to grievances presented pursuant to clause (i).

(I) To be able to contact parents or legal guardians, including visits and scheduled and unscheduled private telephone conversations, written correspondence, and electronic communications, unless prohibited by court order.

(J) To be fully informed, as evidenced by the youth's written acknowledgment, before, or at the time of, admission at the facility, of all the rules governing the youth's conduct and responsibilities.

(K) To receive in the admission agreement information that details the planned programs and services for the youth.

(L) To have his or her parents or legal guardians remove him or her from the facility.

(M) To consent to have visitors or telephone calls during reasonable hours, privately and without prior notice, if the visitors or telephone calls do not disrupt planned activities and are not prohibited by court order or by the youth's parent or legal guardian.

(N) To be free of corporal punishment, physical restraints of any kind, and deprivation of basic necessities, including education, as a punishment, deterrent, or incentive.

(O) To have caregivers who have received instruction on cultural competency and sensitivity relating to, and best practices for, providing adequate care to lesbian, gay, bisexual, and transgender youth in out-of-home care.

(P) To be free from acts that seek to change his or her sexual orientation, including efforts to change his or her gender expressions, or to eliminate or reduce sexual or romantic attractions or feelings toward individuals of the same sex.

(Q) To have fair and equal access to all available services, placement, care, treatment, and benefits and to not be subjected to discrimination or harassment on the basis of actual or perceived race, ethnic group identification, ancestry, national origin, color, religion, sex, sexual orientation, gender identity, mental or physical disability, or HIV status.

(R) To be free from abusive, humiliating, degrading, or traumatizing actions.

(2) Paragraph (1) shall not be interpreted to require a licensed private alternative boarding school to take any action that would impair the health or safety of youth in the facility.

(e) (1) A licensed private alternative boarding school is not an eligible placement option pursuant to Section 319, 361.2, 450, or 727 of the Welfare and Institutions Code.

(2) A licensed private alternative boarding school shall not be eligible for a rate pursuant to Section 11462 of the Welfare and Institutions Code.

(f) This section does not apply to any facility operated, licensed, or certified by the Department of Corrections and Rehabilitation and its Division of Juvenile Justice, the California Conservation Corps, the Military Department, or any other governmental entity or to a boarding school that solely focuses on academics.

(g) (1) On or before January 1, 2018, the department shall adopt regulations to implement this section, in consultation with interested parties, including representatives of private alternative boarding schools, former residents of private alternative boarding schools, and advocates for youth. Until regulations are adopted and become effective pursuant to the Administrative Procedure Act (Chapter 3.5 (commencing with Section 11340) of Part 1 of Division 3 of Title 2 of the Government Code), a private alternative boarding school shall be governed by the regulations applicable to group homes in Chapter 5 (commencing with Section 84000) of Division 6 of Title 22 of the California Code of Regulations.

(2) The department may adopt emergency regulations to implement this section. The adoption, amendment, repeal, or readoption of a regulation authorized by this section is deemed to address an emergency, for purposes of Sections 11346.1 and 11349.6 of the Government Code, and the department is hereby exempted for this purpose from the requirements of subdivision (b) of Section 11346.1 of the Government Code.

(h) A private alternative boarding school operating before January 1, 2018, shall comply with licensing requirements on or before July 1, 2018.

(i) For the purpose of this section, "youth" means a person who is 12 to 17 years of age, inclusive, or a person who is 18 years of age if he or she is completing high school or its equivalent.

(Amended by Stats. 2017, Ch. 561, Sec. 104. (AB 1516) Effective January 1, 2018.)

1502.21.

(a) Commencing January 1, 2019, the department shall license private alternative outdoor programs, as defined in paragraph (20) of subdivision (a) of Section 1502, as a group home pursuant to this chapter. A private alternative outdoor program shall comply with the provisions of this chapter that are applicable to group homes, unless otherwise indicated, and with this section.

(b) A licensed private alternative outdoor program shall comply with all of the following:

(1) It shall be owned and operated on a nonprofit basis by a private nonprofit corporation or a nonprofit organization.

(2) It shall prepare and maintain a current, written plan of operation, as defined by the department.

(3) It shall offer 24-hour, nonmedical care and supervision to youth who voluntarily consent to being admitted to the program and who are voluntarily admitted by his or her parent or legal guardian.

(4) It shall have a ratio of one staff person to every four youths.

(5) (A) It shall not admit a child who is younger than 12 years of age.

(B) It shall not admit a youth who has been assessed by a licensed mental health professional as seriously emotionally disturbed, unless the youth does not require care in a licensed health facility and the State Department of Health Care Services has certified the program as a program that meets the standards to provide mental health treatment services for a child having a serious emotional disturbance, as set forth in Section 4096.5 of the Welfare and Institutions Code.

(6) It shall provide each prospective youth and his or her parent or legal guardian with an accurate written description of the programs and services to be provided. If it advertises or promotes special care, programming, or environments for persons with behavioral,

emotional, or social challenges, the written description shall include how its programs and services are intended to achieve the advertised or promoted claims.

(7) It shall ensure that all individuals providing behavioral-based services to youth in the program are licensed or certified by the appropriate agency, department, or accrediting body, as specified by the department in regulation.

(8) It shall not use secure containment or manual or mechanical restraints.

(9) If it offers access to, or holds itself out as offering access to, mental health services, it shall ensure that those services are provided by a licensed mental health provider.

(10) If it advertises or includes in its marketing materials reference to providing alcohol or substance abuse treatment, it shall ensure that the treatment is provided by a licensed or certified alcoholism or drug abuse recovery or treatment facility.

(c) (1) In addition to the training required of group home staff by department regulations, a staff member of a licensed private alternative outdoor program who supervises youth shall receive an additional number of hours of initial and annual training, to be determined by the department in regulations developed in consultation with stakeholders.

(2) A private alternative outdoor program shall submit a staff training plan to the department as part of its plan of operation. The staff training plan shall provide for the number of additional initial and annual training hours required by paragraph (1) and shall include, but not be limited to, training in all of the following subject areas:

(A) Youth rights, as described in subdivision (d).

(B) Physical and psychosocial needs of youth.

(C) Appropriate responses to emergencies, including an emergency intervention plan.

(D) Cultural competency and sensitivity in issues relating to the lesbian, gay, bisexual, and transgender communities.

(E) Laws pertaining to residential care facilities for youth.

(F) Low-impact camping.

(G) Navigation skills.

(H) Water, food, and shelter procurement.

(I) Recognition of poisonous plants.

(J) Wilderness first aid.

(K) Health issues related to acclimation and exposure.

(L) Report writing and log maintenance.

(d) (1) A youth admitted to a licensed private alternative outdoor program shall be accorded the following rights and any other rights adopted by the department by regulation, a list of which shall be publicly posted and accessible to youth. The personal rights enumerated in Section 84072 of Title 22 of the California Code of Regulations shall not apply.

(A) To be accorded dignity in his or her personal relationships with staff, youth, and other persons.

(B) To live in a safe, healthy, and comfortable environment where he or she is treated with respect.

(C) To be free from physical, sexual, emotional, or other abuse, or corporal punishment.

(D) To be granted a reasonable level of personal privacy in accommodations, personal care and assistance, and visits.

(E) To confidential care of his or her records and personal information, and to approve release of those records before release, except as otherwise authorized or required by law.

(F) To care, supervision, and services that meet his or her individual needs and that are delivered by staff who are sufficient in numbers, qualifications, and competency to meet his or her needs and ensure his or her safety.

(G) To be served food and beverages of the quality and in the quantity necessary to meet his or her nutritional and physical needs.

(H) (i) To present grievances and recommend changes in policies, procedures, and services to the program's staff, management, and governing authority, or any other person without restraint, coercion, discrimination, reprisal, or other retaliatory actions.

(ii) To have the licensee take prompt actions to respond to grievances presented pursuant to clause (i).

(I) To be able to contact parents or legal guardians, including visits and scheduled and unscheduled private telephone conversations, written correspondence, and electronic communications, unless prohibited by court order.

(J) To be fully informed, as evidenced by the youth's written acknowledgment, before, or at the time of, admission in the program, of all the rules governing the youth's conduct and responsibilities.

(K) To receive in the admission agreement information that details the planned programs and services for the youth.

(L) To have his or her parents or legal guardians remove him or her from the program.

(M) To consent to have visitors or telephone calls during reasonable hours, privately and without prior notice, provided the visitors or telephone calls do not disrupt planned activities and are not prohibited by court order or by the youth's parent or legal guardian.

(N) To be free of corporal punishment, physical restraints of any kind, and deprivation of basic necessities, including education, as a punishment, deterrent, or incentive.

(O) To have caregivers who have received instruction on cultural competency and sensitivity relating to, and best practices for, providing adequate care to lesbian, gay, bisexual, and transgender youth in out-of-home care.

(P) To be free from acts that seek to change his or her sexual orientation, including efforts to change his or her gender expressions, or to eliminate or reduce sexual or romantic attractions or feelings toward individuals of the same sex.

(Q) To have fair and equal access to all available services, placement, care, treatment, and benefits and to not be subjected to discrimination or harassment on the basis of actual or perceived race, ethnic group identification, ancestry, national origin, color, religion, sex, sexual orientation, gender identity, mental or physical disability, or HIV status.

(R) To be free from abusive, humiliating, degrading, or traumatizing actions.

(2) Paragraph (1) shall not be interpreted to require a licensed private alternative outdoor program to take any action that would impair the health or safety of youth in the program.

(e) (1) A licensed private alternative outdoor program is not an eligible placement option pursuant to Section 319, 361.2, 450, or 727 of the Welfare and Institutions Code.

(2) A licensed private alternative outdoor program shall not be eligible for a rate pursuant to Section 11462 of the Welfare and Institutions Code.

(f) This section does not apply to programs operated, licensed, or certified by the Department of Corrections and Rehabilitation and its Division of Juvenile Justice, the California Conservation Corps, or the Military Department, programs operated by any governmental entity, any organized camp as defined in Section 18897, outdoor activities for youth designed to be primarily recreational, including, but not limited to, activities organized by Outward Bound, Boy Scouts, Girl Scouts, Camp Fire, or other similar organizations, or any camp exclusively serving children with a medical diagnosis for a physical condition or illness, including, but not limited to, cancer, muscular dystrophy, or burn injuries.

(g) (1) On or before January 1, 2019, the department shall adopt regulations to implement this section in consultation with interested parties, including representatives of private alternative outdoor programs, former participants in private alternative outdoor programs, and advocates for youth. Regulations adopted pursuant to this section shall be contained in the regulations applicable to group homes in Chapter 5 (commencing with Section 84000) of Division 6 of Title 22 of the California Code of Regulations.

(2) The department may adopt emergency regulations to implement this section. The adoption, amendment, repeal, or readoption of a regulation authorized by this section is deemed to address an emergency, for purposes of Sections 11346.1 and 11349.6 of the Government Code, and the department is hereby exempted for this purpose from the requirements of subdivision (b) of Section 11346.1 of the Government Code.

(h) A private alternative outdoor program operating before January 1, 2019, shall comply with licensing requirements on or before July 1, 2019.

(i) For the purpose of this section, "youth" means a person who is 12 to 17 years of age, inclusive, or a person who is 18 years of age if he or she is completing high school or its equivalent.

(Amended by Stats. 2017, Ch. 561, Sec. 105. (AB 1516) Effective January 1, 2018.)

1502.3.

For purposes of this chapter, a "community care facility," pursuant to Section 1502, includes a transitional shelter care facility. A "transitional shelter care facility" means a short-term residential care program that meets all of the following requirements:

(a) It is owned by the county, and operated by the county or by a private nonprofit organization under contract to the county.

(b) It is a group care facility that provides for 24-hour nonmedical care of children who are in need of personal services, supervision, or assistance that is essential for sustaining the activities of daily living, or for the protection of the individual on a short-term basis. As used in this section, "short-term" means up to 90 days from the date of admission.

(c) It is for the sole purpose of providing care for children who have been removed from their homes as a result of abuse or neglect, or both; for children who have been adjudged wards of the court; and, for children who are seriously emotionally disturbed children. For purposes of this subdivision, "abuse or neglect" means the same as defined in Section 300 of the Welfare and Institutions Code. For purposes of this subdivision, "wards of the court" means the same as defined in Section 602 of the Welfare and Institutions Code. For purposes of this subdivision, "seriously emotionally disturbed children" means the same as defined in subdivision (a) of Section 5600.3 of the Welfare and Institutions Code.

(d) It primarily serves children who have previously been placed in a community care facility and are awaiting placement in a different community care facility that is appropriate to their needs. Children residing in transitional shelter care facilities may include children who are very difficult to place in appropriate community care facilities because of factors which may be present in combination, including: threatening, aggressive, suicide, runaway or destructive behaviors and behaviors as defined in Section 5600.3 of the Welfare and Institutions Code.

(e) Based upon an agreement with the county, the licensee shall agree to accept, for placement into its transitional shelter care program, all children referred by the county.

(f) The licensee shall not discharge any child without the permission of the county, except when a child:

(1) Commits an unlawful act and the child must be detained in a juvenile institution.

(2) Requires either of the following:

(A) Physical health care in an acute care hospital.

(B) Mental health services in an acute psychiatric hospital.

(g) The licensee shall provide a program that is designed to be flexible enough to care for a highly variable population size and shall allow for the special needs of sibling groups.

(Amended by Stats. 2017, Ch. 732, Sec. 4. (AB 404) Effective January 1, 2018.)

1502.35.

(a) The department shall license a runaway and homeless youth shelter as a group home pursuant to this chapter. A runaway and homeless youth shelter shall meet all of the following requirements:

(1) The shelter shall offer short-term, 24-hour, nonmedical care and supervision and personal services to youth who voluntarily enter the shelter. As used in this paragraph, "short-term" means no more than 21 consecutive days from the date of admission.

(2) The shelter shall serve homeless youth and runaway youth.

(A) "Homeless youth" means a youth 12 to 17 years of age, inclusive, or 18 years of age if the youth is completing high school or its equivalent, who is in need of services and without a place of shelter.

(B) "Runaway youth"means a youth 12 to 17 years of age, inclusive, or 18 years of age if the youth is completing high school or its equivalent, who absents himself or herself from home or place of legal residence without the permission of his or her family, legal guardian, or foster parent.

(3) The shelter shall have a maximum capacity of 25 youths.

(4) The shelter shall have a ratio of one staff person to every eight youths. For purposes of this paragraph, a volunteer may be counted in the staff-to-youth ratio if the volunteer has satisfied the same training requirements as a paid shelter staff member and other requirements set forth in regulations, and a paid shelter staff member is present during the time the volunteer is on duty.

(5) Bunk beds may be permitted in the shelter, but shall not consist of more than two tiers.

(6) The shelter shall be owned and operated on a nonprofit basis by a private nonprofit corporation, a nonprofit organization, or a public agency.

(b) Shelter staff shall, prior to admission to the shelter, determine if a youth poses a threat to himself or herself or others in the shelter. A youth may not be admitted into the shelter if it is determined that the youth poses such a threat.

(c) An assessment shall not be required for admission, but shelter staff shall assess youth served within 72 hours of admission to the shelter.

(d) Shelter staff shall assist youth served in obtaining emergency health-related services.

(e) The shelter shall establish procedures to assist youth in securing long-term stability that includes all of the following:

(1) Reconnecting the youth with his or her family, legal guardian, or nonrelative extended family members when possible to do so.

(2) Coordinating with appropriate individuals, local government agencies, or organizations to help foster youth secure a suitable foster care placement.

(f) The shelter shall ensure all homeless youth and runaway youth have fair and equal access to services, care, and treatment provided by the shelter, and are not subjected to discrimination or harassment on the basis of actual or perceived race, ethnic group identification, ancestry, national origin, color, religion, sex, sexual orientation, gender identity, mental or physical disability, or HIV status.

(g) Prior to employment or interaction with youth at a runaway and homeless youth shelter, all persons specified in subdivision (b) of Section 1522 shall complete a criminal record review pursuant to Section 1522 and a Child Abuse Central Index check pursuant to Section 1522.1.

(h) A runaway and homeless youth shelter shall collect and maintain all of the following information in a monthly report, in a format specified by the department, and make the report available to the department upon request:

(1) Total number of youth served per month.

(2) Age of each youth served.

(3) Length of stay of each youth served.

(4) Number of times a youth accesses the shelter and services at the shelter.

(i) Notwithstanding Section 1522.43, the department shall not require a runaway and homeless youth shelter to maintain a needs and services plan, as defined in Section 84001 of Title 22 of the California Code of Regulations, for a youth served. Nothing in this subdivision precludes the department from requiring a runaway and homeless youth shelter to maintain an assessment, as defined by the department, for youths served.

(j) The department may license a shelter pursuant to this section if the shelter is operating in two physical locations on or before January 1, 2013, with only one physical location providing overnight residential care, and the shelter meets the requirements of this section. If a shelter described in this subdivision is licensed pursuant to this section, the department shall permit the shelter to retain its two physical locations and issue a license for each physical location.

(k) A runaway and homeless youth shelter is not an eligible placement option pursuant to Sections 319, 361.2, 450, and 727 of the Welfare and Institutions Code.

(l) A runaway and homeless youth shelter's program shall not be eligible for a rate pursuant to Section 11462 of the Welfare and Institutions Code. This does not preclude a runaway and homeless youth shelter from receiving reimbursement for providing services to a foster youth as may be provided at the discretion of a county.

(m) On or before December 1, 2014, the department shall adopt regulations to implement this section, in consultation with interested parties, including representatives of provider organizations that serve homeless or runaway youth. The regulations developed pursuant to this subdivision shall be contained in the regulations for group homes found in Chapter 5 (commencing with Section 84000) of Division 6 of Title 22 of the California Code of Regulations.

(n) Notwithstanding the Administrative Procedure Act (Chapter 3.5 (commencing with Section 11340) of Part 1 of Division 3 of Title 2 of the Government Code), the department may implement the applicable provisions of this section by publishing information releases or similar instructions from the director until the regulations adopted by the department pursuant to subdivision (l) become effective.

(Added by Stats. 2013, Ch. 485, Sec. 2. (AB 346) Effective January 1, 2014.)

1502.4.

(a) A licensed short-term residential therapeutic program, as defined in paragraph (18) of subdivision (a) of Section 1502, may only accept for placement a child who does not require inpatient care in a licensed health facility and who has been assessed pursuant to Section 11462.01 of the Welfare and Institutions Code as meeting the applicable criteria for placement in a short-term residential therapeutic program.

(b) For the purposes of this chapter, the following definitions shall apply:

(1) "Health facility" has the meaning set forth in Section 1250.

(2) "Seriously emotionally disturbed" has the same meaning as that term is used in subdivision (a) of Section 5600.3 of the Welfare and Institutions Code.

(c) The department shall not evaluate, nor have any responsibility or liability with regard to the evaluation of, the mental health treatment services provided pursuant to this section.

(d) This section shall become operative on January 1, 2017.

(Amended (as added by Stats. 2015, Ch. 773, Sec. 8) by Stats. 2016, Ch. 612, Sec. 16. (AB 1997) Effective January 1, 2017.)

1502.45.

(a) (1) Notwithstanding Section 1502.4, a community care facility licensed as a group home for children pursuant to this chapter may only accept for placement, and provide care and supervision to, a child assessed as seriously emotionally disturbed as long as the child does not need inpatient care in a licensed health facility, as defined in Section 1250.

(2) For the purpose of this section, the following definitions shall apply:

(A) "Health facility" has the meaning set forth in Section 1250.

(B) "Seriously emotionally disturbed" has the same meaning as that term is used in subdivision (a) of Section 5600.3 of the Welfare and Institutions Code.

(b) If a child described in subdivision (a) is placed into a group home program classified at rate classification level 13 or rate classification level 14 pursuant to Section 11462.015 of the Welfare and Institutions Code, the licensee shall meet both of the following requirements:

(1) The licensee shall agree to accept, for placement into its group home program, only children who have been assessed as seriously emotionally disturbed by either of the following:

(A) An interagency placement committee, as described in Section 4096.1 of the Welfare and Institutions Code or by a licensed mental health professional, as defined in subdivision (g) of Section 4096 of the Welfare and Institutions Code.

(B) A licensed mental health professional, as defined in subdivision (g) of Section 4096 of the Welfare and Institutions Code, if the child is privately placed or only county funded.

(2) The program is certified by the State Department of Health Care Services, pursuant to Section 4096.55 of the Welfare and Institutions Code, as a program that provides mental health treatment services for seriously emotionally disturbed children.

(c) The department shall not evaluate, or have any responsibility or liability with regard to the evaluation of, the mental health treatment services provided pursuant to this section.

(Amended by Stats. 2018, Ch. 910, Sec. 2. (AB 1930) Effective January 1, 2019.)

1502.5.

Notwithstanding Section 1502, residential care facilities for the elderly, as defined in Section 1569.2, shall not be considered community care facilities and shall be subject only to the California Residential Care Facilities for the Elderly Act (Chapter 3.2 (commencing with Section 1569)).

(Amended by Stats. 1989, Ch. 1360, Sec. 83.)

1502.6.

The department shall deny a private adoption agency a license, or revoke an existing private adoption agency license, unless the applicant or licensee demonstrates that it currently and continuously employs either an executive director or a supervisor who has had at least five years of full-time social work employment in the field of child welfare as described in Chapter 5 (commencing with Section 16500) of Part 4 of Division 9 of the Welfare and Institutions Code or Division 13 (commencing with Section 8500) of the Family Code, two years of which shall have been spent performing adoption social work services in either the department or a licensed California adoption agency.

(Amended by Stats. 1999, Ch. 83, Sec. 102. Effective January 1, 2000.)

1502.7.

(a) On or before July 1, 2012, the department, in consultation with representatives of the Legislature, the County Welfare Directors Association, the Chief Probation Officers of California, the California Youth Connection, the Judicial Council, former foster youth, child advocacy organizations, dependency counsel for children, juvenile justice advocacy organizations, foster caregiver organizations, labor organizations, and representatives of tribes, shall revise regulations regarding health and safety standards for licensing foster family homes and community care facilities in which nonminor dependents, as defined in subdivision (v) of Section 11400 of the Welfare and Institutions Code, of the juvenile court are placed under the responsibility of the county welfare or probation department or an Indian tribe that entered into an agreement pursuant to Section 10553.1 of the Welfare and Institutions Code.

(b) The regulations shall recognize the status of nonminor dependents as legal adults. At a minimum, the regulations shall provide both of the following:

(1) That nonminors described in subdivision (a) shall have the greatest amount of freedom that will safely prepare them for self-sufficiency.

(2) That nonminors described in subdivision (a) in a community care facility shall not be subject to criminal background clearances pursuant to Sections 1522 and 1522.1, for the purposes of facility licensing.

(c) Notwithstanding the Administrative Procedure Act. Chapter 3.5 (commencing with Section 11340) of Part 1 of Division 3 of Title 2 of the Government Code, the department shall, in consultation with the stakeholders listed in subdivision (a), prepare for implementation of the applicable provisions of this section by publishing all-county letters or similar instructions from the director by October 1, 2011, to be effective January 1, 2012. Emergency regulations to implement this section may be adopted by the director in accordance with the Administrative Procedure Act. The initial adoption of the emergency regulations and one readoption of the initial regulations shall be deemed to be an emergency and necessary for the immediate preservation of the public peace, health, safety, or general welfare. Initial emergency regulations and the first readoption of those emergency regulations shall be exempt from review by the Office of Administrative Law. The emergency regulations authorized by this section shall be submitted to the Office of Administrative Law for filing with the Secretary of State and shall remain in effect for no more than 180 days.

(Added by Stats. 2010, Ch. 559, Sec. 4. (AB 12) Effective January 1, 2011.)

1502.8.

The department shall adopt regulations consistent with paragraph (24) of subdivision (a) of Section 16001.9 of the Welfare and Institutions Code.

(Added by Stats. 2015, Ch. 805, Sec. 1. (SB 731) Effective January 1, 2016.)

1503.

As used in this chapter, "license" means a basic permit to operate a community care facility.

A license shall not be transferable.

(Repealed and added by Stats. 1973, Ch. 1203.)

1503.2.

Every facility licensed or certified pursuant to this chapter shall have one or more carbon monoxide detectors in the facility that meet the standards established in Chapter 8 (commencing with Section 13260) of Part 2 of Division 12. The department shall account for the presence of these detectors during inspections.

(Added by Stats. 2014, Ch. 503, Sec. 1. (AB 2386) Effective January 1, 2015.)

1503.5.

(a) A facility shall be deemed to be an "unlicensed community care facility" and "maintained and operated to provide nonmedical care" if it is unlicensed and not exempt from licensure and any one of the following conditions is satisfied:

(1) The facility is providing care or supervision, as defined by this chapter or the rules and regulations adopted pursuant to this chapter.

(2) The facility is held out as or represented as providing care or supervision, as defined by this chapter or the rules and regulations adopted pursuant to this chapter.

(3) The facility accepts or retains residents who demonstrate the need for care or supervision, as defined by this chapter or the rules and regulations adopted pursuant to this chapter.

(4) The facility represents itself as a licensed community care facility.

(5) The facility is performing any of the functions of a foster family agency or holding itself out as a foster family agency.

(6) The facility is performing any of the functions of an adoption agency or holding itself out as performing any of the functions of an adoption agency as specified in paragraph (9) of subdivision (a) of Section 1502 or subdivision (b) of Section 8900.5 of the Family Code.

(b) No unlicensed community care facility, as defined in subdivision (a), shall operate in this state.

(c) Upon discovery of an unlicensed community care facility, the department shall refer residents to the appropriate local or state ombudsman, or placement, adult protective services, or child protective services agency if either of the following conditions exist:

(1) There is an immediate threat to the clients' health and safety.

(2) The facility will not cooperate with the licensing agency to apply for a license, meet licensing standards, and obtain a valid license.

(Amended by Stats. 2007, Ch. 583, Sec. 12. Effective January 1, 2008.)

1504.

As used in this chapter, "special permit" means a permit issued by the state department authorizing a community care facility to offer specialized services as designated by the director in regulations.

A special permit shall not be transferable.

(Amended by Stats. 1980, Ch. 1285.)

1504.5.

(a) (1) This chapter does not apply to any independent living arrangement or supportive housing, described in paragraph (2) of subdivision (c), for individuals with disabilities who are receiving community living support services, as described in paragraph (1) of subdivision (c).

(2) This section does not affect the provisions of Section 1503.5 or 1505.

(3) Community living support services described in paragraph (1) of subdivision (c) do not constitute care or supervision.

(b) (1) The Legislature finds and declares that there is an urgent need to increase the access to supportive housing, as described in paragraph (2) of subdivision (c), and to foster community living support services, as described in paragraph (1) of subdivision (c), as an effective and cost-efficient method of serving persons with disabilities who wish to live independently.

(2) It is the intent of the Legislature that persons with disabilities be permitted to do both of the following:

(A) Receive one or more community living support services in the least restrictive setting possible, such as in a person's private home or supportive housing residence.

(B) Voluntarily choose to receive support services in obtaining and maintaining supportive housing.

(3) It is the intent of the Legislature that community living support services, as described in paragraph (1) of subdivision (c), enable persons with disabilities to live more independently in the community for long periods of time.

(c) (1) "Community living support services," for purposes of this section, are voluntary and chosen by persons with disabilities in accordance with their preferences and goals for independent living. "Community living support services" may include, but are not limited to, any of the following:

(A) Supports that are designed to develop and improve independent living and problemsolving skills.

(B) Education and training in meal planning and shopping, budgeting and managing finances, medication self-management, transportation, vocational and educational development, and the appropriate use of community resources and leisure activities.

(C) Assistance with arrangements to meet the individual's basic needs such as financial benefits, food, clothing, household goods, and housing, and locating and scheduling for appropriate medical, dental, and vision benefits and care.

(2) "Supportive housing," for purposes of this section, is rental housing that has all of the following characteristics:

(A) It is affordable to people with disabilities.

(B) It is independent housing in which each tenant meets all of the following conditions:

(i) Holds a lease or rental agreement in his or her own name and is responsible for paying his or her own rent.

(ii) Has his or her own room or apartment and is individually responsible for arranging any shared tenancy.

(C) It is permanent, wherein each tenant may stay as long as he or she pays his or her share of rent and complies with the terms of his or her lease.

(D) It is tenancy housing under which supportive housing providers are required to comply with applicable state and federal laws governing the landlord-tenant relationship.

(E) Participation in services or any particular type of service is not required as a condition of tenancy.

(d) Counties may contract with agencies or individuals to assist persons with disabilities in securing their own homes and to provide persons with disabilities with the supports needed to live in their own homes, including supportive housing.

(e) For purposes of this section and notwithstanding any other provision of law, an individual with disabilities may contract for the provision of any of the community support services specified in paragraph (1) of subdivision (c) in the individual's own home including supportive housing, as part of that individual's service, care, or independent living plan, only through a government funded program or a private health or disability insurance plan.

(f) An individual's receipt of community living support services as defined in paragraph (1) of subdivision (c) shall not be construed to mean that the individual requires care or supervision or is receiving care or supervision.

(Added by Stats. 2002, Ch. 428, Sec. 1. Effective January 1, 2003.)

1505.

This chapter does not apply to any of the following:

(a) Any health facility, as defined by Section 1250.

(b) Any clinic, as defined by Section 1202.

(c) Any juvenile placement facility approved by the Department of Corrections and Rehabilitation, Division of Juvenile Justice, or any juvenile hall operated by a county.

(d) Any place in which a juvenile is judicially placed pursuant to subdivision (a) of Section 727 of the Welfare and Institutions Code.

(e) Any child day care facility, as defined in Section 1596.750.

(f) (1) Any facility conducted by and for the adherents of any well-recognized church or religious denomination for the purpose of providing facilities for the care or treatment of the sick who depend solely upon prayer or spiritual means for healing in the practice of the religion of the church or denomination.

(2) A private alternative boarding school or private alternative outdoor program, as defined in subdivision (a) of Section 1502, that uses prayer or spiritual means as a component of its programming or services in addition to behavioral-based services is subject to licensure under this chapter.

(g) Any school dormitory or similar facility determined by the department, except a private alternative boarding school or private alternative outdoor program, as defined in subdivision (a) of Section 1502.

(h) Any house, institution, hotel, homeless shelter, or other similar place that supplies board and room only, or room only, or board only, provided that no resident thereof requires any element of care, as determined by the department.

(i) Recovery houses or other similar facilities providing group living arrangements for adults recovering from alcoholism or drug addiction where the facility provides no care or supervision.

(j) Any alcoholism or drug abuse recovery or treatment facility as defined in Section 11834.02.

(k) Any arrangement for the receiving and care of persons by a relative or any arrangement for the receiving and care of persons from only one family by a close friend of the parent, guardian, or conservator, if the arrangement is not for financial profit and occurs only occasionally and irregularly, as defined by regulations of the department. For purposes of this chapter, arrangements for the receiving and care of persons by a relative shall include relatives of the child for the purpose of keeping sibling groups together.

(l) (1) Any home of a relative caregiver of children who are placed by a juvenile court, supervised by the county welfare or probation department, and the placement of whom is

approved according to subdivision (d) of Section 309 of the Welfare and Institutions Code.
(2) Any home of a nonrelative extended family member, as described in Section 362.7 of the Welfare and Institutions Code, providing care to children who are placed by a juvenile court, supervised by the county welfare or probation department, and the placement of whom is approved according to subdivision (d) of Section 309 of the Welfare and Institutions Code.
(3) On and after January 1, 2012, any supervised independent living placement for nonminor dependents, as defined in subdivision (w) of Section 11400 of the Welfare and Institutions Code, who are placed by the juvenile court, supervised by the county welfare department, probation department, Indian tribe, consortium of tribes, or tribal organization that entered into an agreement pursuant to Section 10553.1 of the Welfare and Institutions Code, and whose placement is approved pursuant to subdivision (k) of Section 11400 of the Welfare and Institutions Code.
(4) A Transitional Housing Program-Plus, as defined in subdivision (s) of Section 11400 of the Welfare and Institutions Code, that serves only eligible former foster youth over 18 years of age who have exited from the foster care system on or after their 18th birthday, and that has obtained certification from the applicable county in accordance with subdivision (c) of Section 16522 of the Welfare and Institutions Code.
(m) Any supported living arrangement for individuals with developmental disabilities, as defined in Section 4689 of the Welfare and Institutions Code.
(n) (1) Any family home agency, family home, or family teaching home, as defined in Section 4689.1 of the Welfare and Institutions Code, that is vendored by the State Department of Developmental Services and that does any of the following:
(A) As a family home approved by a family home agency, provides 24-hour care for one or two adults with developmental disabilities in the residence of the family home provider or providers and the family home provider or providers' family, and the provider is not licensed by the State Department of Social Services or the State Department of Public Health or certified by a licensee of the State Department of Social Services or the State Department of Public Health.
(B) As a family teaching home approved by a family home agency, provides 24-hour care for a maximum of three adults with developmental disabilities in independent residences, whether contiguous or attached, and the provider is not licensed by the State Department of Social Services or the State Department of Public Health or certified by a licensee of the State Department of Social Services or the State Department of Public Health.
(C) As a family home agency, engages in recruiting, approving, and providing support to family homes.
(2) This subdivision does not establish by implication either a family home agency or family home licensing category.
(o) Any facility in which only Indian children who are eligible under the federal Indian Child Welfare Act (Chapter 21 (commencing with Section 1901) of Title 25 of the United States Code) are placed and that is one of the following:
(1) An extended family member of the Indian child, as defined in Section 1903 of Title 25 of the United States Code.
(2) A foster home that is licensed, approved, or specified by the Indian child's tribe pursuant to Section 1915 of Title 25 of the United States Code.
(p) (1) (A) Any housing occupied by elderly or disabled persons, or both, that is initially approved and operated under a regulatory agreement pursuant to Section 202 of Public Law 86-372 (12 U.S.C. Sec. 1701q), or Section 811 of Public Law 101-625 (42 U.S.C. Sec. 8013), or whose mortgage is insured pursuant to Section 236 of Public Law 90-448 (12 U.S.C. Sec. 1715z), or that receives mortgage assistance pursuant to Section 221d(3) of Public Law 87-70 (12 U.S.C. Sec. 1715l), where supportive services are made available to residents at their option, as long as the project owner or operator does not contract for or provide the supportive services.
(B) Any housing that qualifies for a low-income housing credit pursuant to Section 252 of Public Law 99-514 (26 U.S.C. Sec. 42) or that is subject to the requirements for rental dwellings for low-income families pursuant to Section 8 of Public Law 93-383 (42 U.S.C. Sec. 1437f), and that is occupied by elderly or disabled persons, or both, where supportive services are made available to residents at their option, as long as the project owner or operator does not contract for or provide the supportive services.
(2) The project owner or operator to which paragraph (1) applies may coordinate, or help residents gain access to, the supportive services, either directly, or through a service coordinator.
(q) A resource family, as defined in Section 16519.5 of the Welfare and Institutions Code, that has been approved by a county child welfare department or probation department.
(r) A home approved by a licensed private adoption agency pursuant to Section 8704.5 of the Family Code, for the placement of a nondependent child who is relinquished for adoption to the adoption agency.
(s) An occasional short-term babysitter, as described in Section 362.04 of the Welfare and Institutions Code.
(t) An alternative caregiver, except as specified in Section 16501.02 of the Welfare and Institutions Code.
(u) Except as specified in subdivision (b) of Section 16501.01 of the Welfare and Institutions Code, a respite care provider certified by a county.
(v) Any similar facility determined by the department.
(Amended by Stats. 2018, Ch. 910, Sec. 3. (AB 1930) Effective January 1, 2019.)
1505.2.
A licensing agency may authorize a foster family home to provide 24-hour care for up to eight foster children, for the purpose of placing siblings or half siblings together in foster care. This authorization may be granted only if all of the following conditions are met:
(A) The foster family home is not a specialized foster care home as defined in subdivision (i) of Section 17710 of the Welfare and Institutions Code.
(B) The home is sufficient in size to accommodate the needs of all children in the home.
(C) For each child to be placed, the child's placement social worker has determined that the child's needs will be met and has documented that determination.
The licensing agency may authorize a foster family home to provide 24-hour care for more than eight children only if the foster family home specializes in the care of sibling groups, that placement is solely for the purpose of placing together one sibling group that exceeds eight children, and all of the above listed conditions are met.
(Added by Stats. 1997, Ch. 793, Sec. 9. Effective January 1, 1998.)
1505.5.
(a) The director shall adopt regulations authorizing residential facilities, as defined in Section 1502, to fill unused capacity on a short-term, time-limited basis to provide temporary respite care for persons who are frail and elderly, adults with functional impairments, and persons with mental health disorders who need 24-hour supervision and who are being cared for by a caretaker or caretakers. The regulations shall address provisions for liability coverage and the level of facility responsibility for routine medical care and medication management, and may require screening of persons to determine the level of care required, a physical history completed by the person's personal physician, and other alternative admission criteria to protect the health and safety of persons applying for respite care. The regulations shall permit these facilities to charge a fee for services provided, which shall include, but not be limited to, supervision, room, leisure activities, and meals.
(b) No facility shall accept persons in need of care beyond the level of care for which that facility is licensed.
(Amended by Stats. 2014, Ch. 144, Sec. 31. (AB 1847) Effective January 1, 2015.)
1506.
(a) (1) A foster family agency may use only a certified family home or a resource family that has been certified or approved by that agency or, pursuant to Section 1506.5, a licensed foster family home or a county-approved resource family approved for this use by the county.
(2) A home selected and certified or approved for the reception and care of children by a foster family agency is not subject to Section 1508. A certified family home or a resource family of a foster family agency shall not be licensed as a residential facility.
(3) A child with a developmental disability who is placed in a certified family home or with a resource family by a foster family agency that is operating under agreement with the regional center responsible for that child may remain in the certified family home or with the resource family after 18 years of age. The determination regarding whether and how long he or she may remain as a resident after 18 years of age shall be made through the agreement of all parties involved, including the resident, the certified parent or resource family, the foster family agency social worker, the resident's regional center case manager, and the resident's parent, legal guardian, or conservator, as appropriate. This determination shall include a needs and service plan that contains an assessment of the child's needs to ensure continued compatibility with the other children in placement. The needs and service plan shall be completed no more than six months prior to the child's 18th birthday. The assessment shall be documented and maintained in the child's file with the foster family agency.
(4) (A) A certified family home or resource family of a foster family agency may be concurrently certified as a host family pursuant to Section 1559.110 if the home is certified by the same private, nonprofit organization licensed to operate as a transitional housing placement provider and foster family agency.
(B) Notwithstanding subdivision (c) of Section 1559.110, a host family certified pursuant to subparagraph (A) shall comply with the laws applicable to a certified family home or resource family, as determined by the department, for each participant placed with the host family.
(b) (1) A foster family agency shall certify to the department that the certified family home has met the department's licensing standards. A foster family agency may require a certified family home to meet additional standards or be compatible with its treatment approach.
(2) The foster family agency shall issue a certificate of approval to the certified family home upon its determination that it has met the standards established by the department and before the placement of any child in the home. The certificate shall be valid for a period not to exceed one year. The annual recertification shall require a certified family home to complete at least eight hours of structured applicable training or continuing education. At least one hour of training during the first six months following initial certification shall be dedicated to meeting the requirements of paragraph (1) of subdivision (b) of Section 11174.1 of the Penal Code.
(3) If the agency determines that the home no longer meets the standards, it shall notify the department and the local placing agency.
(4) This subdivision shall apply to foster family agencies only until December 31, 2019, in accordance with Section 1517.
(c) As used in this chapter, "certified family home" means an individual or family certified by a licensed foster family agency and issued a certificate of approval by that agency as meeting licensing standards, and used exclusively by that foster family agency for placements.
(d) (1) A foster family agency shall not accept applications to certify foster homes and shall instead approve resource families pursuant to Section 1517.
(2) (A) A foster family agency that chooses not to approve resource families shall not recruit any new applicants, but may continue to coordinate with county placing agencies

to find homes for foster children with its existing certified family homes, as authorized by the department.

(B) No later than July 1, 2017, a foster family agency described in subparagraph (A) shall, in addition to the notification required in paragraph (4) of subdivision (f) of Section 1517, notify its certified family homes that, in order to care for foster children after December 31, 2019, a certified family is required to submit an application for resource family approval to the county in which the home is located or to a foster family agency that approves resource families and shall complete the approval process no later than December 31, 2019.

(e) (1) Social work personnel for a foster family agency shall have a master's degree or higher from an accredited or state-approved graduate school in social work or social welfare, or equivalent education and experience, as determined by the department.

(2) Persons who possess a master's degree or higher from an accredited or state-approved graduate school in any of the following areas, or equivalent education and experience, as determined by the department, shall be considered to be qualified to perform social work activities in a foster family agency:

(A) Marriage, family, and child counseling.

(B) Child psychology.

(C) Child development.

(D) Counseling psychology.

(E) Social psychology.

(F) Clinical psychology.

(G) Educational psychology, consistent with the scope of practice as described in Section 4989.14 of the Business and Professions Code.

(H) Education, with emphasis on counseling.

(I) An area that includes the core content areas required for licensure as a Licensed Professional Clinical Counselor, as specified in Sections 4999.32 and 4999.33 of the Business and Professions Code.

(J) A subject area that is functionally equivalent to those listed in subparagraphs (A) to (I), inclusive, as set forth by the department.

(f) (1) In addition to the degree specifications in subdivision (e), all of the following coursework and field practice or experience, as defined in departmental regulations, shall be required of all new hires for the position of social work personnel effective January 1, 1995:

(A) At least three semester units of field practice at the master's level or six months' full-time equivalent experience in a public or private social service agency setting.

(B) At least nine semester units of coursework related to human development or human behavior, or, within the first year of employment, experience working with children and families as a major responsibility of the position under the supervision of a supervising social worker.

(C) At least three semester units in working with minority populations or six months of experience in working with minority populations or training in cultural competency and working with minority populations within the first six months of employment as a condition of employment.

(D) At least three semester units in child welfare or at least six months of experience in a public or private child welfare social services setting for a nonsupervisory social worker. A supervising social worker shall have two years' experience in a public or private child welfare social services setting.

(2) (A) Persons who do not meet the requirements specified in subdivision (e) or this subdivision may apply for an exception as provided for in subdivisions (h) and (i).

(B) Exceptions granted by the department prior to January 1, 1995, shall remain in effect.

(3) (A) Persons who are hired as social work personnel on or after January 1, 1995, who do not meet the requirements listed in this subdivision shall be required to successfully meet those requirements in order to be employed as social work personnel in a foster family agency.

(B) Employees who were hired prior to January 1, 1995, shall not be required to meet the requirements of this subdivision in order to remain employed as social work personnel in a foster family agency.

(4) Coursework and field practice or experience completed to fulfill the degree requirements of subdivision (e) may be used to satisfy the requirements of this subdivision.

(g) In addition to the degree specifications in subdivision (e) and the coursework and field practice or experience described in subdivision (f), social work personnel shall meet core competencies to participate in the assessment and evaluation of an applicant or resource family, as determined by the department in written directives or regulations adopted pursuant to Section 16519.5 of the Welfare and Institutions Code.

(h) Individuals seeking an exception to the requirements of subdivision (e) or (f) based on completion of equivalent education and experience shall apply to the department by the process established by the department.

(i) The department shall complete the process for the exception to minimum education and experience requirements described in subdivisions (e) and (f) within 30 days of receiving the exception application of social work personnel or supervising social worker qualifications from the foster family agency.

(j) For purposes of this section, "social work personnel" means supervising social workers and nonsupervisory social workers.

(Amended by Stats. 2017, Ch. 731, Sec. 2. (SB 612) Effective January 1, 2018.)

1506.1.

(a) A foster family agency shall prepare and maintain a current, written plan of operation as required by the department.

(b) (1) A foster family agency shall have national accreditation from an entity identified by the department pursuant to the process described in paragraph (8) of subdivision (b) of Section 11463 of the Welfare and Institutions Code.

(2) The following applies to a foster family agency licensed before January 1, 2017:

(A) The foster family agency shall have until December 31, 2018, to obtain accreditation.

(B) The foster family agency shall submit documentation of accreditation or application for accreditation to the department in a time and manner as determined by the department.

(C) The foster family agency shall provide documentation to the department reporting its accreditation status as of January 1, 2018, and July 1, 2018, in a time and manner as determined by the department.

(3) The following applies to a foster family agency licensed on or after January 1, 2017:

(A) The foster family agency shall have up to 24 months from the date of licensure to obtain accreditation.

(B) The foster family agency applicant shall submit documentation of accreditation or application for accreditation with its application for licensure.

(C) The foster family agency shall provide documentation to the department reporting its accreditation status at 12 months and at 18 months after the date of licensure.

(4) This subdivision does not preclude the department from requesting additional information from the foster family agency regarding its accreditation status.

(5) The department may revoke a foster family agency's license pursuant to Article 5 (commencing with Section 1550) for failure to obtain accreditation within the timeframes specified in this subdivision.

(6) The department may extend the date by which to comply with paragraph (2), as applicable, for up to one year upon the request of a foster family agency that has been vendored as a service provider by a regional center for persons with development disabilities. In determining whether to extend the date, the department shall consult with any county placement agency that places children with the foster family agency, the vendorizing regional center, and the State Department of Developmental Services.

(c) On and after January 1, 2017, a foster family agency's plan of operation shall include a program statement. The program statement shall contain a description of all of the following:

(1) The core services and supports, as set forth in paragraph (5) of subdivision (b) of Section 11463 of the Welfare and Institutions Code, and as prescribed by the department, to be offered to children and their families, as appropriate or as necessary.

(2) The treatment practices that will be used in serving children and families.

(3) The procedures for the development, implementation, and periodic updating of the needs and services plan for children placed with the foster family agency or served by the foster family agency, consistent with the case plans as developed by the county placing agency, that support the reasonable and prudent parent standard, as defined in Section 362.05 of the Welfare and Institutions Code, and procedures for collaborating with the child and family team as described in paragraph (4) of subdivision (a) of Section 16501 of the Welfare and Institutions Code, that includes, but is not limited to, a description of the services to be provided to meet the treatment needs of children assessed.

(4) (A) How the foster family agency will comply with the resource family approval standards and requirements, as set forth in Section 1517.

(B) A foster family agency that chooses not to approve resource families pursuant to Section 1517 shall describe in the program statement the transition plan for its certified family homes to obtain resource family approval prior to December 31, 2019.

(5) The population or populations to be served.

(6) The ability to support the differing needs of children and their families.

(7) The plan for the supervision, evaluation, and training of staff. The training plan shall be appropriate to meet the needs of children, and it shall be consistent with the training provided to resource families as set forth in Section 16519.5 of the Welfare and Institutions Code.

(8) The ability to provide or arrange for treatment services to meet the individual needs of children placed in certified family homes or with resource families, as specified in Section 11402 of the Welfare and Institutions Code.

(9) The plan for the training, supervision, and support of resource families to meet the appropriate needs of children, consistent with the training requirements set forth in Section 16519.5 of the Welfare and Institutions Code. To the extent possible, the foster family agency training plan for resource families shall be consistent with the training requirements set forth by the county child welfare placing agency.

(10) The agency or agencies that the foster family agency has partnered with, either formally or informally, to provide additional supports and services to families and children during care and postpermanency.

(11) The plan for participation in child and family teams and supporting the participation of the agency's resource families in those teams, as appropriate.

(12) Any other information that may be prescribed by the department for the proper administration of this section.

(d) In addition to the rules and regulations adopted pursuant to this chapter, a county licensed to operate a foster family agency shall describe, in the plan of operation, its conflict-of-interest mitigation plan, on and after January 1, 2017, as set forth in subdivision (g) of Section 11462.02 of the Welfare and Institutions Code.

(e) (1) (A) (i) A foster family agency applicant shall submit an application to the department that includes a letter of recommendation in support of its program from a county placing agency.

(ii) The letter of recommendation shall include a statement that the county placing agency reviewed the applicant's program statement.

(iii) If the letter of recommendation is not from the county in which the facility is located, the foster family agency applicant shall include with its application a statement that it provided the county in which the facility is located an opportunity for that county to review the program statement and notified that county that the facility has received a letter of recommendation from another county.

(B) If the application does not contain a letter of recommendation as described in subparagraph (A), then the department shall cease review of the application. This paragraph does not constitute a denial of the application for purposes of Section 1526 or any other law.

(C) A new letter of recommendation is not required when a foster family agency moves locations.

(2) A foster family agency shall submit a copy of its program statement to all county placing agencies with which placements are coordinated or for which services are provided, including the county in which the facility is located, for optional review when the foster family agency updates its program statement.

(f) The department shall have the authority to inspect a foster family agency pursuant to the system of governmental monitoring and oversight developed by the department on and after January 1, 2017, pursuant to subdivision (c) of Section 11463 of the Welfare and Institutions Code.

(Amended by Stats. 2017, Ch. 732, Sec. 6. (AB 404) Effective January 1, 2018.)

1506.3.

A foster family agency shall employ one full-time social work supervisor for every eight social workers or fraction thereof in the agency.

(Amended by Stats. 2016, Ch. 612, Sec. 19. (AB 1997) Effective January 1, 2017.)

1506.5.

(a) Foster family agencies shall not use foster family homes licensed by a county or resource families approved by a county without the approval of the licensing or approving county. When approval is granted, a written agreement between the foster family agency and the county shall specify the nature of administrative control and case management responsibility and the nature and number of the children to be served in the home.

(b) Before a foster family agency may use a licensed foster family home it shall review and, with the exception of a new fingerprint clearance, qualify the home in accordance with Section 1506.

(c) When approval is granted pursuant to subdivision (a), and for the duration of the agreement permitting the foster family agency use of the licensed foster family home or county-approved resource family, no child shall be placed in that home except through the foster family agency.

(d) Nothing in this section shall transfer or eliminate the responsibility of the placing agency for the care, custody, or control of the child. Nothing in this section shall relieve a foster family agency of its responsibilities for or on behalf of a child placed with it.

(e) (1) If an application to a foster family agency for a certificate of approval indicates, or the department determines during the application review process, that the applicant previously was issued a license under this chapter or under Chapter 1 (commencing with Section 1200), Chapter 2 (commencing with Section 1250), Chapter 3.01 (commencing with Section 1568.01), Chapter 3.2 (commencing with Section 1569), Chapter 3.4 (commencing with Section 1596.70), Chapter 3.5 (commencing with Section 1596.90), or Chapter 3.6 (commencing with Section 1597.30) and the prior license was revoked within the preceding two years, the foster family agency shall cease any further review of the application until two years have elapsed from the date of the revocation.

(2) If an application to a foster family agency for a certificate of approval indicates, or the department determines during the application review process, that the applicant previously was issued a certificate of approval by a foster family agency that was revoked by the department pursuant to subdivision (b) of Section 1534 within the preceding two years, the foster family agency shall cease any further review of the application until two years have elapsed from the date of the revocation.

(3) If an application to a foster family agency for a certificate of approval indicates, or the department determines during the application review process, that the applicant was excluded from a facility licensed by the department or from a certified family home pursuant to Section 1558, 1568.092, 1569.58, or 1596.8897, the foster family agency shall cease any further review of the application unless the excluded person has been reinstated pursuant to Section 11522 of the Government Code by the department.

(4) The cessation of review shall not constitute a denial of the application for purposes of subdivision (b) of Section 1534 or any other law.

(f) (1) If an application to a foster family agency for a certificate of approval indicates, or the department determines during the application review process, that the applicant had previously applied for a license under any of the chapters listed in paragraph (1) of subdivision (e) and the application was denied within the last year, the foster family agency shall cease further review of the application as follows:

(A) When the applicant petitioned for a hearing, the foster family agency shall cease further review of the application until one year has elapsed from the effective date of the decision and order of the department upholding a denial.

(B) When the department informed the applicant of his or her right to petition for a hearing and the applicant did not petition for a hearing, the foster family agency shall cease further review of the application until one year has elapsed from the date of the notification of the denial and the right to petition for a hearing.

(2) The foster family agency may continue to review the application if the department has determined that the reasons for the denial of the application were due to circumstances and a condition that either have been corrected or are no longer in existence.

(3) The cessation of review shall not constitute a denial of the application for purposes of subdivision (b) of Section 1534 or any other law.

(g) (1) If an application to a foster family agency for a certificate of approval indicates, or the department determines during the application review process, that the applicant had previously applied for a certificate of approval with a foster family agency and the department ordered the foster family agency to deny the application pursuant to subdivision (b) of Section 1534, the foster family agency shall cease further review of the application as follows:

(A) In cases where the applicant petitioned for a hearing, the foster family agency shall cease further review of the application until one year has elapsed from the effective date of the decision and order of the department upholding a denial.

(B) In cases where the department informed the applicant of his or her right to petition for a hearing and the applicant did not petition for a hearing, the foster family agency shall cease further review of the application until one year has elapsed from the date of the notification of the denial and the right to petition for a hearing.

(2) The foster family agency may continue to review the application if the department has determined that the reasons for the denial of the application were due to circumstances and conditions that either have been corrected or are no longer in existence.

(3) The cessation of review shall not constitute a denial of the application for purposes of subdivision (b) of Section 1534 or any other law.

(h) Subdivisions (e), (f), and (g) shall apply only to certified family home applications received on or before December 31, 2016, in accordance with Section 1517.

(Amended by Stats. 2016, Ch. 612, Sec. 20. (AB 1997) Effective January 1, 2017.)

1506.6.

(a) It is the intent of the Legislature that public and private efforts to recruit foster parents not be competitive and that the total number of foster parents be increased.

(b) A foster family agency shall not certify a family home that is licensed by the department or a county. A licensed foster family home shall forfeit its license, pursuant to subdivision (b) of Section 1524, concurrent with final certification by the foster family agency. The department or a county shall not license a family home that is certified by a foster family agency. A certified family home shall forfeit its certificate concurrent with final licensing by the department or a county.

(c) (1) A licensed foster family home shall forfeit its license, pursuant to subdivision (b) of Section 1524, concurrent with resource family approval by a foster family agency or a county.

(2) A certified family home shall forfeit its certificate of approval concurrent with resource family approval by a foster family agency, pursuant to subdivision (f) of Section 1517, or a county.

(3) A resource family approved pursuant to Section 1517 shall forfeit its approval concurrent with resource family approval by another foster family agency or a county.

(Amended by Stats. 2016, Ch. 612, Sec. 21. (AB 1997) Effective January 1, 2017.)

1506.7.

(a) A foster family agency shall require the owner or operator of a family home applying for certification to sign an application that shall contain, but shall not be limited to, the following information:

(1) Whether the applicant has been certified, and by which foster family agency.

(2) Whether the applicant has been decertified, and by which foster family agency.

(3) Whether a placement hold has been placed on the applicant by a foster family agency, and by which foster family agency.

(4) Whether the applicant has been a foster home licensed by a county or by the state and, if so, by which county or state, or whether the applicant has been approved for relative placement by a county and, if so, by which county.

(b) (1) The application form signed by the owner or operator of the family home applying for certification shall contain notice to the applicant for certification that the foster family agency is required to check references of all foster family agencies that have previously certified the applicant and of all state or county licensing offices that have licensed the applicant as a foster parent, and that the signing of the application constitutes the authorization of the applicant for the foster family agency to conduct its check of references.

(2) The application form signed by the owner or operator of the family home applying for certification shall be signed with a declaration by the applicant that the information submitted is true, correct, and contains no material omissions of fact to the best knowledge and belief of the applicant. Any person who declares as true any material matter pursuant to this section that he or she knows to be false is guilty of a misdemeanor. The application shall include a statement that submitting false information is a violation of law punishable by incarceration, a fine, or both incarceration and a fine.

(c) This section shall apply only to certified family home applications received on or before December 31, 2016, in accordance with Section 1517.

(Amended by Stats. 2016, Ch. 612, Sec. 22. (AB 1997) Effective January 1, 2017.)

1506.8.

(a) Before certifying a family home, a foster family agency shall contact any foster family agencies by whom an applicant has been previously certified and any state or county licensing offices that have licensed the applicant as a foster parent, and shall conduct a reference check as to the applicant.

(b) This section shall apply only to certified family home applications received on or before December 31, 2016, in accordance with Section 1517.

(Amended by Stats. 2016, Ch. 612, Sec. 23. (AB 1997) Effective January 1, 2017.)

1506.9.

(a) No person shall incur civil liability as a result of providing the department with any of the following:

(1) The foster family agency providing to the department a log of family homes certified and decertified.

(2) The foster family agency notifying the department of its determination to decertify a certified family home due to any of the following actions by the certified family parent:

(A) Violating licensing rules and regulations.

(B) Aiding, abetting, or permitting the violation of licensing rules and regulations.

(C) Conducting oneself in a way that is inimical to the health, morals, welfare, or safety of a child placed in that certified family home.

(D) Being convicted of a crime while a certified family parent.

(E) Knowingly allowing any child to have illegal drugs or alcohol.

(F) Committing an act of child abuse or neglect or an act of violence against another person.

(b) Neither the department, a foster family agency, or a county shall incur civil liability for providing a county or a foster family agency with information if the communication is for the purpose of aiding in the evaluation of an application for certification of a family home by a foster family agency or for licensure as a foster home or approval of a relative placement by a county or by the department.

(Added by Stats. 2004, Ch. 643, Sec. 4. Effective January 1, 2005.)

1507.

(a) Notwithstanding any other provision of law, incidental medical services may be provided in a community care facility. If the medical services constitute a substantial component of the services provided by the community care facility as defined by the director in regulations, the medical services component shall be approved as set forth in Chapter 1 (commencing with Section 1200) or Chapter 2 (commencing with Section 1250).

(b) Notwithstanding any other provision of law, if the requirements of subdivision (c) are met, the department shall permit incidental medical services to be provided in community care facilities for adults by facility staff who are not licensed health care professionals but who are trained by a licensed health care professional and supervised according to the client's individualized health care plan prepared pursuant to subdivision (c). Incidental medical services provided by trained facility staff for the following conditions shall be limited as follows:

(1) Colostomy and ileostomy: changing bags and cleaning stoma.

(2) Urinary catheter: emptying bags in day care facilities; emptying and changing bags in residential facilities.

(3) Gastrostomy: feeding, hydration, cleaning stoma, and adding medication per physician's or nurse practitioner's orders for the routine medication of patients with chronic, stable conditions.

(c) Facility staff may provide incidental medical services if the following conditions have been met:

(1) For regional center clients the following shall apply:

(A) An individualized health care plan, which may be part of a client's individual program plan, shall be prepared for each client by a health care team that shall include the client or his or her designee if the client is not able to participate in planning his or her health care, the client's primary care physician or nurse practitioner or other health care professional designated by the physician or nurse practitioner, the licensee or licensee's designee, any involved social worker or regional center worker, and any health care professional designated to monitor the client's individualized health care plan.

(B) The client's individualized health care plan shall be reassessed at least every 12 months or more frequently as determined by the client's physician or nurse practitioner during the time the client receives incidental medical services in the facility.

(C) The client's regional center, primary care physician or nurse practitioner, or other health care professional designated by the physician or nurse practitioner shall identify the health care professional who shall be responsible for training facility staff in the provision of incidental medical services.

(D) Facility staff shall be trained by the identified health care professional practicing within his or her scope of practice who shall monitor, according to the individualized health care plan, the staff's ability to provide incidental medical services and who shall review, correct, or update facility staff training as the health care professional deems necessary.

(E) The regional center or placing agency shall evaluate, monitor, and have responsibility for oversight of the incidental medical services provided in the facility by facility staff. However, nothing in this section shall preclude the department from taking an administrative action against a licensee or facility staff member for failure or refusal to carry out, or negligence in carrying out, his or her duties in providing these incidental medical services.

(2) For persons who are not regional center clients, the following shall apply:

(A) An individualized health care plan shall be prepared that includes the physician's or nurse practitioner's order for services to be provided during the time the client is in the day care facility. The plan shall be prepared by a team that includes the client or his or her designee if the client is not able to participate in planning his or her care, the client's social worker, conservator, or legal guardian, as appropriate, a licensed health care professional, and the licensee or the licensee's designee.

(B) The client's individualized health care plan shall be reassessed at least every 12 months or more frequently as determined by the client's physician or nurse practitioner during the time the client receives incidental medical services in the facility.

(C) A licensed health care professional practicing within his or her scope of practice shall train the staff of the facility on procedures for caring for clients who require incidental medical services and shall periodically review, correct, or update facility staff training as the health care professional deems necessary.

(d) Facilities providing incidental medical services shall remain in substantial compliance with all other applicable regulations of the department.

(e) The department shall adopt emergency regulations for community care facilities for adults by February 1, 1997, to do all of the following:

(1) Specify incidental medical services that may be provided. These incidental medical services shall include, but need not be limited to, any of the following: gastrostomy, colostomy, ileostomy, and urinary catheters.

(2) Specify the conditions under which incidental medical services may be provided.

(3) Specify the medical services that, due to the level of care required, are prohibited services.

(f) The department shall consult with the State Department of Developmental Services, the State Department of Health Care Services, the Association of Regional Center Agencies, and provider associations in the development of the regulations required by subdivision (e).

(Amended by Stats. 2012, Ch. 34, Sec. 18. (SB 1009) Effective June 27, 2012.)

1507.1.

(a) An adult community care facility may permit incidental medical services to be provided through a home health agency licensed pursuant to Chapter 8 (commencing with Section 1725) when all of the following conditions are met:

(1) The facility, in the judgment of the department, has the ability to provide the supporting care and supervision appropriate to meet the needs of the client receiving care from a home health agency.

(2) The home health agency has been advised of the regulations pertaining to adult community care facilities and the requirements related to incidental medical services being provided in the facility.

(3) There is evidence of an agreed-upon protocol between the home health agency and the adult community care facility. The protocol shall address areas of responsibility of the home health agency and the adult community care facility and the need for communication and the sharing of client information related to the home health care plan. Client information may be shared between the home health agency and the adult community care facility relative to the client's medical condition and the care and treatment provided to the client by the home health agency, including, but not limited to, medical information defined by the Confidentiality of Medical Information Act, Part 2.6 (commencing with Section 56) of Division 1 of the Civil Code.

(4) There is ongoing communication between the home health agency and the adult community care facility about the services provided to the client by the home health agency and the frequency and duration of care to be provided.

(b) Nothing in this section is intended to expand the scope of care and supervision for an adult community care facility, as prescribed by this chapter.

(c) Nothing in this section shall require any care or supervision to be provided by the adult community care facility beyond that which is permitted in this chapter.

(d) The department shall not be responsible for the evaluation of medical services provided to the client of the adult community care facility by the home health agency.

(e) Any regulations, policies, or procedures related to sharing client information and development of protocols, established by the department pursuant to this section, shall be developed in consultation with the State Department of Health Services and persons representing home health agencies and adult community care facilities.

(Added by Stats. 1998, Ch. 831, Sec. 1. Effective January 1, 1999.)

1507.15.

Every community care facility that provides adult residential care or offers an adult day program shall, for the purpose of addressing issues that arise when an adult resident or an adult day program participant is missing from the facility, develop and comply with an absentee notification plan for each resident or participant. The plan shall be part of the written Needs and Services Plan. The plan shall include and be limited to the following: a requirement that an administrator of the facility, or his or her designee, inform the resident's or participant's authorized representative when that resident or participant is missing from the facility and the circumstances in which an administrator of the facility, or his or her designee, shall notify local law enforcement when a resident or participant is missing from the facility.

(Added by Stats. 2013, Ch. 674, Sec. 2. (AB 620) Effective January 1, 2014.)

1507.2.

Notwithstanding any other provision of this chapter, a child with special health care needs, as defined in subdivision (a) of Section 17710 of the Welfare and Institutions Code, may be accepted in a specialized foster care home, as defined in subdivision (i) of Section 17710 of the Welfare and Institutions Code, or retained beyond the age of 18, in accordance with Part 5.5 (commencing with Section 17700) of Division 9 of the Welfare and Institutions Code, relating to children with special health care needs. If the facility accepts a child with special health care needs, or retains a child with special health care needs beyond 18 years of age, the facility shall maintain all documents required as evidence of compliance with Part 5.5 (commencing with Section 17700) of Division 9 of the Welfare and Institutions Code in the files of the facility that are available for inspection by the foster family agency or licensing agency.

(Amended by Stats. 2017, Ch. 732, Sec. 7. (AB 404) Effective January 1, 2018.)

1507.25.

(a) (1) Notwithstanding any other law, a person described in paragraph (2), who is not a licensed health care professional, but who is trained to administer injections by a licensed health care professional practicing within his or her scope of practice, may administer emergency medical assistance and injections for severe diabetic hypoglycemia and anaphylactic shock to a foster child in placement.

(2) The following individuals shall be authorized to administer emergency medical assistance and injections in accordance with this subdivision:

(A) A relative caregiver.

(B) A nonrelative extended family member.

(C) A foster family home parent.

(D) A member of a resource family, as defined in subdivision (c) of Section 16519.5 of the Welfare and Institutions Code.

(E) A small family home parent.

(F) A certified parent of a foster family agency.

(G) A designated substitute caregiver of a foster family home, a certified family home, or resource family.

(H) A staff member of a small family home or a group home who provides direct care and supervision to children and youth residing in the small family home or group home.

(I) A staff member of a short-term residential therapeutic program, including a children's crisis residential program, who provides direct care and supervision to children and youth residing in the facility.

(J) A staff member of a transitional shelter care facility or a temporary shelter care facility who provides direct care and supervision to children and youth residing in the facility.

(3) The licensed health care professional shall periodically review, correct, or update training provided pursuant to this section as he or she deems necessary and appropriate.

(b) (1) Notwithstanding any other law, a person described in paragraph (2), who is not a licensed health care professional, but who is trained to administer injections by a licensed health care professional practicing within his or her scope of practice, may administer subcutaneous injections of other medications, including insulin, as prescribed by the child's physician, to a foster child in placement.

(2) The following individuals shall be authorized to give prescribed injections, including insulin, in accordance with this subdivision:

(A) A relative caregiver.

(B) A nonrelative extended family member.

(C) A foster family home parent.

(D) A member of a resource family, as defined in subdivision (c) of Section 16519.5 of the Welfare and Institutions Code.

(E) A small family home parent.

(F) A certified parent of a foster family agency.

(G) In the absence of a foster parent, a designated substitute caregiver in a foster family home, a certified family home, or resource family.

(H) A direct care staff member of a short-term residential therapeutic program, including a children's crisis residential program, who provides direct care and supervision to children and youth residing in the facility.

(3) The licensed health care professional shall periodically review, correct, or update training provided pursuant to this section as he or she deems necessary and appropriate.

(c) For purposes of this section, administration of an insulin injection shall include all necessary supportive activities related to the preparation and administration of the injection, including glucose testing and monitoring.

(d) Notwithstanding Part 5.5 (commencing with Section 17700) of Division 9 of, and particularly subdivision (g) of Section 17710 of, the Welfare and Institutions Code, a child's need to receive injections pursuant to this section shall not be the sole basis for determining that the child has a medical condition requiring specialized in-home health care.

(e) This section does not supersede the requirements of Section 369.5 of the Welfare and Institutions Code, with respect to the administration of psychotropic medication to a dependent child of the court.

(Amended by Stats. 2018, Ch. 910, Sec. 4. (AB 1930) Effective January 1, 2019.)

1507.3.

(a) Notwithstanding Section 1566.45 or any other provision of law, a residential facility that provides care to adults may obtain a waiver from the department for the purpose of allowing a resident who has been diagnosed as terminally ill by his or her physician and surgeon to remain in the facility, or allowing a person who has been diagnosed as terminally ill by his or her physician and surgeon to become a resident of the facility if that person is already receiving hospice services and would continue to receive hospice services without disruption if he or she became a resident, when all of the following conditions are met:

(1) The facility agrees to retain the terminally ill resident, or accept as a resident the terminally ill person, and to seek a waiver on behalf of the individual, provided the individual has requested the waiver and is capable of deciding to obtain hospice services.

(2) The terminally ill resident, or the terminally ill person to be accepted as a resident, has obtained the services of a hospice certified in accordance with federal medicare conditions of participation and licensed pursuant to Chapter 8 (commencing with Section 1725) or Chapter 8.5 (commencing with Section 1745).

(3) The facility, in the judgment of the department, has the ability to provide care and supervision appropriate to meet the needs of the terminally ill resident, or the terminally ill person to be accepted as a resident, and is in substantial compliance with regulations governing the operation of residential facilities that provide care to adults.

(4) The hospice has agreed to design and provide for care, services, and necessary medical intervention related to the terminal illness as necessary to supplement the care and supervision provided by the facility.

(5) An agreement has been executed between the facility and the hospice regarding the care plan for the terminally ill resident, or the terminally ill person to be accepted as a resident. The care plan shall designate the primary caregiver, identify other caregivers, and outline the tasks the facility is responsible for performing and the approximate frequency with which they shall be performed. The care plan shall specifically limit the facility's role for care and supervision to those tasks authorized for a residential facility under this chapter.

(6) The facility has obtained the agreement of those residents who share the same room with the terminally ill resident, or any resident who will share a room with the terminally ill person to be accepted as a resident, to allow the hospice caregivers into their residence.

(b) At any time that the licensed hospice, the facility, or the terminally ill resident determines that the resident's condition has changed so that continued residence in the facility will pose a threat to the health and safety of the terminally ill resident or any other resident, the facility may initiate procedures for a transfer.

(c) A facility that has obtained a hospice waiver from the department pursuant to this section, or an Adult Residential Facility for Persons with Special Health Care Needs (ARFPSHN) licensed pursuant to Article 9 (commencing with Section 1567.50), need not call emergency response services at the time of a life-threatening emergency if the hospice agency is notified instead and all of the following conditions are met:

(1) The resident is receiving hospice services from a licensed hospice agency.

(2) The resident has completed an advance directive, as defined in Section 4605 of the Probate Code, requesting to forego resuscitative measures.

(3) The facility has documented that facility staff have received training from the hospice agency on the expected course of the resident's illness and the symptoms of impending death.

(d) Nothing in this section is intended to expand the scope of care and supervision for a residential facility, as defined in this chapter, that provides care to adults nor shall a facility be required to alter or extend its license in order to retain a terminally ill resident, or allow a terminally ill person to become a resident of the facility, as authorized by this section.

(e) Nothing in this section shall require any care or supervision to be provided by the residential facility beyond that which is permitted in this chapter.

(f) Nothing in this section is intended to expand the scope of life care contracts or the contractual obligation of continuing care retirement communities as defined in Section 1771.

(g) The department shall not be responsible for the evaluation of medical services provided to the resident by the hospice and shall have no liability for the independent acts of the hospice.

(h) The department, in consultation with the State Fire Marshal, shall develop and expedite implementation of regulations related to residents who have been diagnosed as terminally ill who remain in the facility and who are nonambulatory that ensure resident safety but also provide flexibility to allow residents to remain in the least restrictive environment.

(i) Nothing in this section shall be construed to relieve a licensed residential facility that provides care to adults of its responsibility to do both of the following:

(1) Notify the fire authority having jurisdiction of the presence of a bedridden resident in the facility as required pursuant to subdivision (e) of Section 1566.45.

(2) Obtain and maintain a fire clearance from the fire authority having jurisdiction.

(j) The requirement in paragraph (1) of subdivision (a) to obtain a waiver, and the requirement in paragraph (1) of subdivision (i) shall not apply to a facility licensed as an ARFPSHN pursuant to Article 9 (commencing with Section 1567.50).

(Amended by Stats. 2010, Ch. 211, Sec. 1. (AB 2629) Effective January 1, 2011.)

1507.5.

(a) In-home medical care and home and community-based services, as described in subdivisions (t) and (u) of Section 14132 of the Welfare and Institutions Code, may, when deemed medically appropriate by the State Department of Health Services, be provided by a licensed home health agency to children with special medical needs, as defined by the State Department of Health Services, in foster family homes. For children described in this section, these medical services shall not be considered as a substantial component of the services provided by the licensee for the purposes of Section 1507. To be eligible under this section for placement in a foster home, a child shall be receiving medical supervision and medical case management by an agent designated by the State Department of Health Services.

(b) No more than two children eligible for services under this section may be placed in a single licensed foster family home at one time.

(c) The State Department of Social Services and its agents shall not evaluate or have any responsibility or liability for the evaluation of the medical services described in this section.

(Amended by Stats. 1989, Ch. 1175, Sec. 2.)

1507.6.

(a) Mental health services, as deemed necessary by the placing agency, may be provided to children in a group home. Except for the physical safety and direct care and supervision of children so placed, the State Department of Social Services and its agents shall not evaluate or have responsibility or liability for the evaluation of mental health services provided in those homes. Supervision of mental health treatment services provided to a child in a group home shall be a case management responsibility of the placing agency.

(b) (1) Psychotropic medications shall be used only in accordance with the written directions of the physician prescribing the medication and as authorized by the juvenile court pursuant to Section 369.5 or 739.5 of the Welfare and Institutions Code.

(2) The facility shall maintain in a child's records all of the following information:

(A) A copy of any court order authorizing the psychotropic medication for the child.

(B) A separate log for each psychotropic medication prescribed for the child, showing all of the following:

(i) The name of the medication.

(ii) The date of the prescription.

(iii) The quantity of medication and number of refills initially prescribed.

(iv) When applicable, any additional refills prescribed.

(v) The required dosage and directions for use as specified in writing by the physician prescribing the medication, including any changes directed by the physician.

(vi) The date and time of each dose taken by the child.

(3) This subdivision does not apply to a runaway and homeless youth shelter, as defined in Section 1502.

(4) The requirements regarding juvenile court authorization, as described in paragraph (1), and maintaining a copy of any court order, as described in subparagraph (A) of paragraph (2), shall only apply to private alternative boarding schools and private alternative outdoor programs, as defined in Section 1502, as otherwise required by applicable law.

(Amended by Stats. 2016, Ch. 864, Sec. 6. (SB 524) Effective January 1, 2017.)

1508.

No person, firm, partnership, association, or corporation within the state and no state or local public agency shall operate, establish, manage, conduct, or maintain a community care facility in this state, without a current valid license therefor as provided in this chapter.

No person, firm, partnership, association, or corporation within the state and no state or local public agency shall provide specialized services within a community care facility in this state, without a current valid special permit therefor as provided in this chapter.

Except for a juvenile hall operated by a county, or a public recreation program, this section applies to community care facilities directly operated by a state or local public agency. Each community care facility operated by a state or local public agency shall comply with the standards established by the director for community care facilities.

As used in this chapter, "local public agency" means a city, county, special district, school district, community college district, chartered city, or chartered city and county.

(Amended by Stats. 1986, Ch. 1016, Sec. 2.)

1509.

The state department shall inspect and license community care facilities, except as otherwise provided in Section 1508. The state department shall inspect and issue a special permit to a community care facility to provide specialized services.

(Amended by Stats. 1980, Ch. 1285.)

1509.5.

(a) The department and the licensing agencies with which it contracts for licensing shall review and make a final determination within 60 days of an applicant's submission of a complete application on all applications for a license to operate a community care facility if the applicant possesses a current valid license to operate a community care facility at another site. Applicants shall note on the application, or in a cover letter to the application, that they possess a current valid license at another site, and the number of that license.

(b) The department shall request a fire safety clearance from the appropriate fire marshal within five days of receipt of an application described in subdivision (a). The applicant shall be responsible for requesting and obtaining the required criminal record clearances.

(c) If the department for any reason is unable to comply with subdivision (a), it shall, within 60 days of receipt of the application described in subdivision (a), grant a provisional license to the applicant to operate for a period not to exceed six months, except as provided in subdivision (d). While the provisional license is in effect, the department shall continue its investigation and make a final determination on the application before the provisional license expires. The provisional license shall be granted, provided the department knows of no life safety risks, the criminal records clearances, if applicable, are complete, and the fire safety clearance is complete. The director may extend the term of a provisional license for an additional six months at the time of the application, if the director determines that more than six months will be required to achieve full compliance with licensing standards due to circumstances beyond the control of the applicant, and if all other requirements for a license have been met.

(d) If the department does not issue a provisional license pursuant to subdivision (c), the department shall issue a notice to the applicant identifying whether the provisional license has not been issued due to the existence of a life safety risk, lack of a fire safety clearance, lack of a criminal records clearance, failure to complete the application, or any combination of these reasons. If a life safety risk is identified, the risk preventing the issuance of the provisional license shall be clearly explained. If a lack of the fire safety clearance is identified, the notice shall include the dates on which the department requested the clearance and the current status of that request, and the fire marshal's name and telephone number to whom a fire safety clearance request was sent. The department shall identify the names of individuals for whom criminal records clearances are lacking. If failure to complete the application is identified, the notice shall list all of the forms or attachments that are missing or incorrect. This notice shall be sent to the applicant no later than 60 days after the applicant filed the application. If the reasons identified in the notice are corrected, the department shall issue the provisional license within five days after the corrections are made.

(e) The department shall, immediately after January 1, 1993, develop expedited procedures necessary to implement subdivisions (a), (b), (c), and (d).

(f) The department shall, immediately after January 1, 1993, develop an appeal procedure for applicants under this section for both denial of licenses and delay in processing applications.

(Added by Stats. 1992, Ch. 570, Sec. 1. Effective January 1, 1993.)

1510.

The state department may provide consulting services upon request to any community care facility to assist in the identification or correction of deficiencies and in the upgrading of the quality of care provided by such community care facility.

(Repealed and added by Stats. 1973, Ch. 1203.)

1511.

The state department may contract for state, county, or other public agencies to assume specified licensing, approval, or consultation responsibilities. In exercising the authority so delegated, such agencies shall conform to the requirements of this chapter and to the rules, regulations, and standards of the state department. The state department shall reimburse agencies for services performed pursuant to this section, and such payments shall not exceed actual cost.

If any grants-in-aid are made by the federal government for the support of any inspection or consultation service approved by the state department, the amount of the federal grant shall first be applied to defer the cost of the service before state reimbursement is made.

(Repealed and added by Stats. 1973, Ch. 1203.)

1512.

Each residential community care facility shall state, on its client information form or admission agreement, and on its patient's rights form, the facility's policy concerning family visits and other communication with resident clients and shall, except as otherwise provided in this section, promptly post notice of its visiting policy at a location in the facility that is accessible to residents and families. The requirement that a facility post notice of the facility's visiting policy does not apply to any facility serving six or fewer clients.

The community care facility's policy concerning family visits and communication shall be designed to encourage regular family involvement with the resident client and shall provide ample opportunities for family participation in activities at the facility.

(Amended by Stats. 1987, Ch. 1022, Sec. 5.)

1512.5.

(a) No residential facility may prohibit the formation of a family council, and, when requested by a member of the resident's family or the resident's responsible party, the family council shall be allowed to meet in a common meeting room of the facility during mutually agreed upon hours.

(b) Facility policies on family councils shall in no way limit the right of residents and family members to meet independently with outside persons, including members of nonprofit or government organizations or with facility personnel during nonworking hours.

(c) "Family council" for the purpose of this section means a meeting of family members, friends, responsible parties, or agents as defined in Section 14110.8 of the Welfare and Institutions Code of two or more patients to confer in private without facility staff.

(d) Family councils shall also be provided adequate space on a prominent bulletin board or other posting area for the display of meeting notices, minutes, and newsletters.

(Added by Stats. 1989, Ch. 466, Sec. 1.)

1513.

No license or special permit issued pursuant to the provisions of this chapter shall have any property value for sale or exchange purposes and no person, including any owner, agent, or broker, shall sell or exchange any license or special permit for any commercial purpose.

(Amended by Stats. 1980, Ch. 1285.)

1514.

(a) Each residential care facility licensed under this chapter shall reveal its license number in all advertisements, publications, or announcements made with the intent to attract clients or residents.

(b) Advertisements, publications, or announcements subject to the requirements of subdivision (a) shall include, but are not limited to, those contained in the following:

(1) Newspaper or magazine.

(2) Consumer report.

(3) Announcement of intent to commence business.

(4) Telephone directory yellow pages.

(5) Professional or service directory.

(6) Radio or television commercial.

(Added by Stats. 1989, Ch. 458, Sec. 2.)

1515.

(a) The department shall authorize county welfare departments to undertake comprehensive recruitment programs, including but not limited to media advertising, public awareness campaigns and public speaking engagements to ensure an adequate number of foster homes are available to meet the child welfare placement needs in each county.

(b) In counties in which the county has contracted with the state to license foster parents, if the county undertakes a recruitment program, it shall be done by the placement agency. The state shall not be required to perform any acts in connection with a recruitment program.

(c) The recruitment of potential foster parents shall include diligent efforts to recruit individuals who reflect the ethnic, racial, and cultural diversity of foster children.

(Amended by Stats. 2014, Ch. 772, Sec. 5. (SB 1460) Effective January 1, 2015.)

1516.

(a) A crisis nursery, as defined in paragraph (17) of subdivision (a) of Section 1502, shall be licensed by the department to operate a crisis residential overnight program. Notwithstanding Section 1596.80, a crisis nursery may also provide crisis day services.

(b) A crisis nursery shall be organized and operated on a nonprofit basis by either a private nonprofit corporation or a nonprofit public benefit corporation.

(c) A facility licensed on or before January 1, 2004, as a group home for children under six years of age with a licensed capacity greater than 14 children, but less than 21 children, that provides crisis nursery services shall be allowed to retain its capacity if issued a crisis nursery license until there is a change in the licensee's program, location, or client population.

(d) Each crisis nursery shall collect and maintain information, in a format specified by the department, indicating the total number of children placed in the program, the length of stay for each child, the reasons given for the use of the crisis nursery, and the age of each child. This information shall be made available to the department upon request.

(e) Notwithstanding Section 1596.80, a crisis nursery may provide crisis day services for children under six years of age at the same site that it is providing crisis residential overnight services.

(1) A child shall not receive crisis day services at a crisis nursery for more than 30 calendar days, maximum of 12 hours per day, or a total of 360 hours, in a six-month period unless the department issues an exception to allow a child to receive additional crisis day services in a six-month period.

(2) The department, upon receipt of an exception request pursuant to paragraph (1) and supporting documentation as required by the department, shall respond within five working days to approve or deny the request.

(3) No more than two exceptions, in seven-calendar day or 84-hour increments, may be granted per child in a six-month period.

(f) A crisis nursery license shall be issued for a specific capacity determined by the department.

(1) (A) The maximum licensed capacity for crisis day services shall be based on 35 square feet of indoor activity space per child. Bedrooms, bathrooms, halls, offices, isolation areas, food-preparation areas, and storage places shall not be included in the calculation of indoor activity space. Floor area under tables, desks, chairs, and other equipment intended for use as part of children's activities shall be included in the calculation of indoor space.

(B) There shall be at least 75 square feet per child of outdoor activity space based on the total licensed capacity. Swimming pools, adjacent pool decking, and natural or man-made hazards shall not be included in the calculation of outdoor activity space.

(2) Except as provided in subdivision (c), the maximum licensed capacity for a crisis residential overnight program shall be 14 children.

(3) A child who has been voluntarily placed in a crisis residential overnight program shall be included in the licensed capacity for crisis day services.

(g) Exceptions to group home licensing regulations pursuant to subdivision (c) of Section 84200 of Title 22 of the California Code of Regulations, in effect on August 1, 2004, for county-operated or county-contracted emergency shelter care facilities that care for children under six years of age for no more than 30 days, shall be contained in regulations for crisis nurseries.

(h) For purposes of this section, the following definitions shall apply:

(1) "Crisis day services" means temporary, nonmedical care and supervision for children under six years of age who are voluntarily placed by a parent or legal guardian due to a family crisis or stressful situation for less than 24 hours per day. Crisis day services shall be provided during a time period defined by the crisis nursery in its plan of operation, but not to exceed a period of 14 hours per day. The plan of operation shall assure sleeping arrangements are available for children there after 7 p.m. A child may not receive crisis day services at a crisis nursery for more than 30 calendar days, or a total of 360 hours, in a six-month period unless the department issues an exception.

(2) "Crisis residential overnight program" means short-term, 24-hour nonmedical residential care and supervision, including overnight, for children under six years of age who are voluntarily placed by a parent or legal guardian due to a family crisis or stressful situation for no more than 30 days.

(3) "Voluntarily placed" means a child, who is not receiving Aid to Families with Dependent Children-Foster Care, placed by a parent or legal guardian who retains physical custody of, and remains responsible for, the care of his or her children who are placed for temporary emergency care. "Voluntarily placed" does not include placement of a child who has been removed from the care and custody of his or her parent or legal guardian and placed in foster care by a child welfare services agency.

(Amended by Stats. 2014, Ch. 735, Sec. 2. (AB 2228) Effective January 1, 2015.)

1517.

(a) (1) Pursuant to subdivision (a) of Section 16519.5 of the Welfare and Institutions Code, the State Department of Social Services shall implement a unified, family friendly, and child-centered resource family approval process to replace the existing multiple processes for licensing foster family homes, certifying foster homes by licensed foster family agencies, approving relatives and nonrelative extended family members as foster care providers, and approving guardians and adoptive families.

(2) For purposes of this chapter, a "resource family" means an individual or family that has successfully met both the home environment assessment and the permanency assessment criteria, as set forth in Section 16519.5 of the Welfare and Institutions Code, necessary for providing care for a child placed by a public or private child placement agency by court order, or voluntarily placed by a parent or legal guardian.

(3) There is no fundamental right to approval as a resource family.

(4) (A) A resource family shall be considered eligible to provide foster care for children in out-of-home placement and shall be considered approved for adoption and guardianship.

(B) Notwithstanding subparagraph (A), a foster family agency may approve a resource family to care for a specific child, as specified in the written directives or regulations adopted pursuant to Section 16519.5 of the Welfare and Institutions Code.

(5) For purposes of this chapter, "resource family approval" means that the applicant or resource family successfully meets the home environment assessment and permanency assessment standards adopted pursuant to subdivision (d) of Section 16519.5 of the Welfare and Institutions Code. This approval is in lieu of a certificate of approval issued by a licensed foster family agency pursuant to subdivision (b) of Section 1506.

(6) Approval of a resource family does not guarantee an initial, continued, or adoptive placement of a child with a resource family. Approval of a resource family does not guarantee the establishment of a legal guardianship of a child with a resource family.

(7) (A) Notwithstanding paragraphs (1) to (6), inclusive, a foster family agency shall cease any further review of an application if the applicant has had a previous application denial within the preceding year by the department or county, or if the applicant has had a previous rescission, revocation, or exemption denial or exemption rescission by the department or county within the preceding two years.

(B) If an individual was excluded from a resource family home or facility licensed by the department, a foster family agency shall cease review of the individual's application unless the excluded individual has been reinstated pursuant to subdivision (g) of Section 16519.6 of the Welfare and Institutions Code or Section 1569.53, subdivision (h) of Section 1558, subdivision (h) of Section 1569.58, or subdivision (h) of Section 1596.8897 of this code.

(C) The cessation of review shall not constitute a denial of the application for purposes of this section, Section 16519.5 of the Welfare and Institutions Code, or any other law.

(D) For purposes of this section, the date of a previous denial, rescission, revocation, exemption denial or exemption rescission, or exclusion shall be either of the following:

(i) The effective date of a final decision or order upholding a notice of action or exclusion order.

(ii) The date on the notice of the decision to deny, rescind, revoke, or exclude if the notice was not appealed or otherwise constitutes a final decision.

(8) A resource family shall meet the approval standards set forth in Section 16519.5 of the Welfare and Institutions Code, comply with the written directives or regulations adopted pursuant to Section 16519.5 of the Welfare and Institutions Code, and comply with other applicable federal and state laws in order to maintain approval.

(9) A resource family may be approved by a county child welfare department or probation department pursuant to Section 16519.5 of the Welfare and Institutions Code or by a foster family agency pursuant to this section.

(10) A resource family shall not be licensed to operate a residential facility, as defined in Section 1502, a residential care facility for the elderly, as defined in Section 1569.2, or a residential care facility for persons with chronic life-threatening illnesses, as defined in Section 1568.01, on the same premises used as the residence of the resource family.

(11) (A) An applicant who withdraws an application prior to its approval or denial may resubmit the application within 12 months of the withdrawal.

(B) Nothing in this paragraph shall preclude a foster family agency from requiring an applicant to complete an application activity, even if that activity was previously completed.

(b) (1) A foster family agency that approves resource families shall comply with the provisions of this section.

(2) Notwithstanding any other law, a foster family agency shall require its applicants and resource families to meet the resource family approval standards set forth in Section 16519.5 of the Welfare and Institutions Code, the written directives or regulations adopted thereto, and other applicable laws prior to approval and in order to maintain approval.

(3) A foster family agency shall be responsible for all of the following:

(A) Complying with the applicable provisions of this chapter, the regulations for foster family agencies, the resource family approval standards and requirements set forth in Article 2 (commencing with Section 16519.5) of Chapter 5 of Part 4 of Division 9 of the Welfare and Institutions Code, and the applicable written directives or regulations adopted thereto by the department.

(B) Implementing the requirements for the resource family approval and utilizing standardized documentation established by the department.

(C) Ensuring staff have the education, experience, and core competencies necessary to participate in the assessment and evaluation of an applicant or resource family.

(D) Taking the following actions, as applicable:

(i) (I) Approving or denying resource family applications, including preparing a written report that evaluates the applicant's capacity to foster, adopt, or provide legal guardianship of a child based on all of the information gathered through the resource family application and assessment processes.

(II) The applicant's preference to provide a specific level of permanency, including adoption, guardianship, or, in the case of a relative, placement with a fit and willing relative, shall not be a basis to deny an application.

(ii) Rescinding approvals of resource families.

(E) Providing to the department a log of resource families that were approved or had approval rescinded during the month by the 10th day of the following month.

(F) (i) Updating resource family approval annually and as necessary to address any changes that have occurred in the resource family's circumstances, including, but not limited to, moving to a new home location or commencing operation of a family day care home, as defined in Section 1596.78.

(ii) A foster family agency shall conduct an announced inspection of a resource family home during the annual update, and as necessary to address any changes specified in clause (i), to ensure that the resource family is conforming to all applicable laws and the written directives or regulations adopted pursuant to Section 16519.5 of the Welfare and Institutions Code.

(G) Monitoring resource families through all of the following:

(i) Ensuring that social workers who identify a condition in the home that may not meet the resource family approval standards while in the course of a routine visit to children subsequently placed with a resource family take appropriate action as needed.

(ii) Requiring resource families to meet the approval standards set forth in Section 16519.5 of the Welfare and Institutions Code and to comply with the written directives or regulations adopted thereto, other applicable laws, and corrective action plans as necessary to correct identified deficiencies. If corrective action is not completed as specified in the plan, the foster family agency or the department may rescind the approval of the resource family or take other administrative action in accordance with applicable law or the written directives or regulations adopted pursuant to Section 16519.5 of the Welfare and Institutions Code.

(iii) Requiring resource families to report to the foster family agency any incidents, as specified in the written directives or regulations adopted pursuant to Section 16519.5 of the Welfare and Institutions Code.

(iv) Inspecting resource family homes as often as necessary to ensure the quality of care provided.

(H) Performing corrective action as required by the department.

(I) Submitting information and data that the department determines is necessary to study, monitor, and prepare the report specified in paragraph (6) of subdivision (f) of Section 16519.5 of the Welfare and Institutions Code.

(J) (i) Ensuring applicants and resource families meet the training requirements, and, if applicable, the specialized training requirements set forth in Section 16519.5 of the Welfare and Institutions Code.

(ii) Nothing in this section shall preclude a foster family agency from requiring training in excess of the requirements in this section.

(4) A foster family agency may cooperatively match a child who is under the care, custody, and control of a county with a resource family for initial placement.

(c) In addition to subdivision (f) of Section 16519.5 of the Welfare and Institutions Code, the State Department of Social Services shall be responsible for all of the following:

(1) Requiring foster family agencies to monitor resource families, including, but not limited to, inspecting resource family homes, developing and monitoring resource family corrective action plans to correct identified deficiencies, and rescinding resource family approval if compliance with a corrective action plan is not achieved.

(2) Investigating all complaints regarding a resource family approved by a foster family agency and taking any action it deems necessary. This shall include investigating any incidents reported about a resource family indicating that the approval standard is not being maintained. Complaint investigations shall be conducted in accordance with the written directives or regulations adopted pursuant to Section 16519.5 of the Welfare and Institutions Code. A foster family agency shall not conduct an internal investigation regarding an incident report or complaint against a resource family that interferes with an investigation being conducted by the department.

(3) Rescinding approvals of a resource family approved by a foster family agency.

(4) Excluding a resource family parent or applicant or other individual from presence in any resource family home or licensed community care facility consistent with the established standard, from being a member of the board of directors, an executive director, or an officer of a licensed community care facility, or prohibiting a licensed community care facility from employing the resource family parent or other individual, if appropriate.

(5) Issuing a temporary suspension order that suspends the resource family approval prior to a hearing, when urgent action is needed to protect a child from physical or mental abuse, abandonment, or any other substantial threat to health or safety.

(6) Providing a resource family parent, applicant, excluded individual, or individual who is the subject of a criminal record exemption denial or rescission with due process pursuant to this chapter and subdivisions (g) to (n), inclusive, of Section 16519.6 of the Welfare and Institutions Code if the department has ordered a foster family agency to deny a resource family application or rescind the approval of a resource family, has excluded an individual, has denied or rescinded a criminal record exemption, or has taken other administrative action.

(d) (1) The department may enter and inspect the home of a resource family approved by a foster family agency to secure compliance with the resource family approval standards, investigate a complaint or incident, or ensure the quality of care provided.

(2) Upon a finding of noncompliance, the department may require a foster family agency to deny a resource family application, rescind the approval of a resource family, or take other action the department may deem necessary for the protection of a child placed with the resource family.

(A) If the department requires a foster family agency to deny an application, rescind the approval of a resource family, or take another action, the department shall serve an order of denial or rescission, or another order, that notifies the resource family or applicant and foster family agency of the basis of the department's action and of the resource family's or applicant's right to a hearing.

(B) (i) Except as otherwise specified in this section, a hearing conducted pursuant to this section shall be conducted in accordance with Section 1551.

(ii) Notwithstanding the time for hearings set forth in this chapter, a hearing conducted pursuant to this section shall be held within the timelines specified in subdivisions (f) to (h), inclusive, of Section 16519.6 of the Welfare and Institutions Code.

(iii) Consistent with subdivision (h) of Section 16519.6 of the Welfare and Institutions Code and notwithstanding Section 1550.5, proceedings regarding the temporary suspension of a resource family approval shall not include an interim hearing.

(C) The department's order of the application denial, rescission of the approval, or another action shall remain in effect until the hearing is completed and the department has made a final determination on the merits.

(D) A foster family agency's failure to comply with the department's order to deny an application or rescind the approval of a resource family, or another order, by placing or retaining a child in care shall be grounds for disciplining the foster family agency pursuant to Section 1550.

(e) Nothing in this section or in Article 2 (commencing with Section 16519.5) of Chapter 5 of Part 4 of Division 9 of the Welfare and Institutions Code limits the authority of the department to inspect, evaluate, investigate a complaint or incident, or initiate a disciplinary action against a foster family agency pursuant to this chapter or to take any action it may deem necessary for the health and safety of children placed with the foster family agency.

(f) (1) The applicable certification and oversight processes shall continue to be administered for foster homes certified by a foster family agency prior to January 1, 2017, or as specified in paragraph (2), until the certification is revoked or forfeited by operation of law pursuant to this subdivision.

(2) Notwithstanding paragraph (3), a foster family agency shall approve or deny all certified family home applications received on or before December 31, 2016, in accordance with this chapter.

(3) On and after January 1, 2017, a foster family agency shall not accept applications to certify foster homes and shall approve resource families in lieu of certifying foster homes.

(4) No later than July 1, 2019, each foster family agency shall provide the following information to its certified family homes:

(A) A detailed description of the resource family approval program.

(B) Notification that, in order to care for a foster child, resource family approval is required by December 31, 2020.

(C) Notification that a certificate of approval shall be forfeited by operation of law, as specified in paragraph (8).

(5) The following shall apply to all certified family homes:

(A) A certified family home with an approved adoptive home study, completed prior to January 1, 2018, shall be deemed to be a resource family.

(B) A certified family home that had a child in placement at any time between January 1, 2017, and December 31, 2017, inclusive, may be approved as a resource family on the date of successful completion of a family evaluation pursuant to Section 16519.5 of the Welfare and Institutions Code.

(C) A certified family home that provided county-authorized respite services at any time between January 1, 2017, and December 31, 2017, inclusive, may be approved as a resource family on the date of successful completion of a family evaluation pursuant to Section 16519.5 of the Welfare and Institutions Code.

(6) A foster family agency may provide supportive services to all certified family homes with a child in placement to assist with the resource family transition and to minimize placement disruptions.

(7) An individual who is approved as a resource family pursuant to subparagraph (B) or (C) of paragraph (5) shall be fingerprinted pursuant to Section 8712 of the Family Code upon filing an application for adoption.

(8) All certificates of approval for certified family homes shall be forfeited by operation of law on December 31, 2020, except as provided in this paragraph:

(A) All certified family homes that did not have a child in placement or did not provide county-authorized respite services at any time between January 1, 2017, and December 31, 2017, inclusive, shall forfeit the certificate of approval by operation of law on January 1, 2018.

(B) For certified family homes with a pending resource family application on December 31, 2020, the certificate of approval shall be forfeited by operation of law upon approval as a resource family. If approval is denied, forfeiture by operation of law shall occur on the date of completion of any proceedings required by law to ensure due process.

(C) A certificate of approval shall be forfeited by operation of law upon approval as a resource family.

(g) A foster family agency may obtain any arrest or conviction records or reports from any law enforcement agency as necessary to the performance of its duties, as provided in this section.

(h) A foster family agency may review and discuss with an applicant the data contained in the statewide child welfare database, and provided to the foster family agency by a county, that is pertinent to conducting a family evaluation, as specified in the written directives or regulations adopted pursuant to Section 16519.5 of the Welfare and Institutions Code.

(Amended by Stats. 2018, Ch. 935, Sec. 1.5. (SB 1083) Effective January 1, 2019.)

1517.1.

(a) (1) Pursuant to subdivision (a) of Section 16519.5 of the Welfare and Institutions Code, the State Department of Social Services shall implement a unified, family friendly, and child-centered resource family approval process to replace the existing multiple processes for licensing foster family homes, certifying foster homes by licensed foster family agencies, approving relatives and nonrelative extended family members as foster care providers, and approving guardians and adoptive families.

(2) For purposes of this section, a "resource family" means an individual or family that has successfully met both the home environment assessment and the permanency assessment criteria, as set forth in Section 16519.5 of the Welfare and Institutions Code, necessary for providing care for a child placed by a public or private child placement agency by court order, or voluntarily placed by a parent or legal guardian.

(b) (1) The applicable licensure and oversight processes shall continue to be administered for foster family homes licensed prior to January 1, 2017, or as specified in paragraph (2), until the license is revoked or forfeited by operation of law pursuant to this section or Section 1524.

(2) The department shall approve or deny all foster family home license applications received on or before December 31, 2016, in accordance with this chapter.

(3) On and after January 1, 2017, the department shall not accept applications to license foster family homes.

(4) The following shall apply to all foster family homes:

(A) A foster family home with an approved adoptive home study, completed prior to January 1, 2018, shall be deemed to be a resource family.

(B) A certified family home that had a child in placement at any time between January 1, 2017, and December 31, 2017, inclusive, may be approved as a resource family on the date of successful completion of a family evaluation pursuant to Section 16519.5 of the Welfare and Institutions Code.

(C) A foster family home that provided county-authorized respite services at any time between January 1, 2017, and December 31, 2017, inclusive, may be approved as a resource family on the date of successful completion of a family evaluation pursuant to Section 16519.5 of the Welfare and Institutions Code.

(5) An individual who is approved as a resource family pursuant to subparagraph (B) or (C) of paragraph (4) shall be fingerprinted pursuant to Section 8712 of the Family Code upon filing an application for adoption.

(6) All foster family home licenses shall be forfeited by operation of law on December 31, 2020, except as provided in this paragraph or Section 1524.

(A) All licensed foster family homes that did not have a child in placement or did not provide county-authorized respite services at any time between January 1, 2017, and December 31, 2017, inclusive, shall forfeit the license by operation of law on January 1, 2018.

(B) For foster family home licensees who have pending resource family applications on December 31, 2020, the foster family home license shall be forfeited by operation of law upon approval as a resource family. If approval is denied, forfeiture by operation of law shall occur on the date of completion of any proceedings required by law to ensure due process.

(C) A foster family home license shall be forfeited by operation of law upon approval as a resource family.

(Amended by Stats. 2018, Ch. 935, Sec. 2.5. (SB 1083) Effective January 1, 2019.)

1517.2.

(a) The application form signed by a resource family applicant of a foster family agency shall be signed with a declaration by the applicant that the information submitted is true, correct, and contains no material omissions of fact to the best knowledge and belief of the applicant. Any person who willfully and knowingly, with the intent to deceive, makes a false statement or fails to disclose a material fact in his or her application is guilty of a misdemeanor.

(b) Before approving a resource family, a foster family agency shall conduct a reference check of the applicant by contacting all of the following:

(1) Any foster family agencies that have certified the applicant.

(2) Any state or county licensing offices that have licensed the applicant as a foster family home.

(3) Any counties that have approved the applicant as a relative or nonrelative extended family member.

(4) Any foster family agencies or counties that have approved the applicant as a resource family.

(5) Any state licensing offices that have licensed the applicant as a community care facility, child day care center, or family child care home.

(c) The department, a county, or a foster family agency may request information from, or divulge information to, the department, a county, or a foster family agency regarding a prospective resource family for the purpose of conducting, and as necessary to conduct, a reference check to determine whether it is safe and appropriate to approve an applicant to be a resource family.

(Added by Stats. 2016, Ch. 612, Sec. 27. (AB 1997) Effective January 1, 2017.)

1517.3.

(a) A person shall not incur civil liability as a result of providing the department with either of the following:

(1) A foster family agency's log of resource families that have been approved or have had approval rescinded.

(2) Notification of a foster family agency's determination to rescind the approval of a resource family due to any of the following actions by a resource family parent:

(A) Violation of Section 16519.5, the written directives or regulations adopted pursuant to Section 16519.5, or any other applicable law.

(B) Aiding, abetting, or permitting the violation of Section 16519.5, the written directives or regulations adopted pursuant to Section 16519.5, or any other applicable law.

(C) Conduct that poses a risk or threat to the health and safety, protection, or well-being of a child, or the people of the State of California.

(D) Conviction at any time before or during his or her approval of a crime described in Section 1522.

(E) Knowingly allowing a child to have illegal drugs, alcohol, or any tobacco product, as defined in subdivision (d) of Section 22950.5 of the Business and Professions Code.

(F) Committing an act of child abuse or neglect or an act of violence against another person.

(b) The department, a county, or a foster family agency shall not incur civil liability for providing each other with information if the communication is for the purpose of aiding in the evaluation of an application for approval of a resource family by a foster family agency.

(Added by Stats. 2016, Ch. 612, Sec. 28. (AB 1997) Effective January 1, 2017.)

1517.4.

(a) (1) A foster family agency shall place a resource family on inactive status upon notification by the resource family in accordance with this section and the written directives or regulations adopted by the department pursuant to Section 16519.5 of the Welfare and Institutions Code.

(2) For purposes of this section, and notwithstanding Section 1517 of this code or Section 16519.5 of the Welfare and Institutions Code, "inactive status" means a period of time during which a resource family is not eligible to provide foster care for a child and is not subject to an approval update.

(b) The written directives or regulations adopted by the department pursuant to Section 16519.5 of the Welfare and Institutions Code shall include, but not be limited to, all of the following:

(1) The method by which a resource family shall notify a foster family agency of the following:

(A) A request to be placed on inactive status.

(B) A request to end inactive status.

(2) The actions to be taken by a foster family agency to end an inactive status.

(3) Any time limitations on inactive status.

(4) The circumstances under which a foster family agency shall conduct inspections of the home of a resource family during a period of inactive status.

(c) Nothing in this section or in Article 2 (commencing with Section 16519.5) of Chapter 5 of Part 4 of Division 9 of the Welfare and Institutions Code limits the authority of the department to enter and inspect the home of a resource family on inactive status in order to investigate a complaint or incident or to ensure unauthorized care and supervision is not being provided to a child.

(d) A resource family shall maintain all approval standards required by Section 1517 upon ending inactive status.

(e) This section does not limit the authority of the department to institute or continue an administrative action against a resource family or any individual residing or regularly present in the home of a resource family during a period of inactive status.

(Added by Stats. 2017, Ch. 732, Sec. 11. (AB 404) Effective January 1, 2018.)

1517.5.

(a) A resource family currently approved by a foster family agency pursuant to this section or Section 1517 may be approved by a subsequent foster family agency upon the successful completion of activities, as specified by the department, which shall include, but not be limited to, all of the following:

(1) The resource family shall complete the following activities:

(A) Submit an application for resource family approval to the second foster family agency.

(B) Notwithstanding paragraph (1) of subdivision (h) of Section 1522, comply with the criminal record clearance requirements set forth in Section 16519.5 of the Welfare and Institutions Code as part of an approval update with the subsequent foster family agency, including the submission of fingerprints pursuant to Section 8712 of the Family Code.

(C) Cooperate with the subsequent foster family agency in conducting an approval update, as specified in the written directives or regulations adopted by the department pursuant to Section 16519.5 of the Welfare and Institutions Code.

(2) The subsequent foster family agency shall complete all of the following activities:

(A) Conduct a background check of the resource family and all adults residing or regularly present in the home in accordance with Section 1517 and as specified in the written directives or regulations adopted by the department pursuant to Section 16519.5 of the Welfare and Institutions Code.

(B) Conduct a reference check pursuant to Section 1517.2.

(C) Complete an approval update for the resource family as specified in the written directives or regulations adopted by the department pursuant to Section 16519.5 of the Welfare and Institutions Code.

(i) The subsequent foster family agency shall request a copy of the written report completed pursuant to Section 1517 and any updates to the written report regarding the resource family from the current foster family agency.

(ii) The current foster family agency shall forward a copy of the written report completed pursuant to Section 1517 and any updates to the written report regarding the resource family to the subsequent foster family agency within 20 business days of receipt of the request.

(b) A resource family currently approved by a county pursuant to Section 16519.5 of the Welfare and Institutions Code may be approved by a subsequent foster family agency upon the successful completion of activities, as specified by the department, which shall include, but not be limited to, all of the following:

(1) The resource family shall complete all of the following activities:

(A) Submit an application for resource family approval to the subsequent foster family agency.

(B) Notwithstanding paragraph (1) of subdivision (h) of Section 1522, comply with the criminal record clearance requirements set forth in Section 16519.5 of the Welfare and Institutions Code as part of an approval update with the subsequent foster family agency, including the submission of fingerprints pursuant to Section 8712 of the Family Code.

(C) Cooperate with the subsequent foster family agency in conducting an approval update, as specified in the written directives or regulations adopted by the department pursuant to Section 16519.5 of the Welfare and Institutions Code.

(2) The subsequent foster family agency shall complete all of the following activities:

(A) Conduct a background check of the resource family and all adults residing or regularly present in the home in accordance with Section 1517 and as specified in the written directives or regulations adopted by the department pursuant to Section 16519.5 of the Welfare and Institutions Code.

(B) Conduct a reference check pursuant to Section 1517.2.

(C) Complete an approval update for the resource family, as specified in the written directives or regulations adopted by the department pursuant to Section 16519.5 of the Welfare and Institutions Code.

(i) The subsequent foster family agency shall request a copy of the written report completed pursuant to Section 16519.5 of the Welfare and Institutions Code and any updates to the written report regarding the resource family from the county.

(ii) The county shall forward a copy of the written report and any updates to the written report completed pursuant to Section 16519.5 of the Welfare and Institutions Code regarding the resource family to the subsequent foster family agency within 20 business days of receipt of the request.

(c) Resource family approval by a current foster family agency or a county shall be forfeited by operation of law upon approval as a resource family by a subsequent foster family agency in accordance with this section.

(d) A resource family approved pursuant to this section shall comply with the written directives or regulations adopted pursuant to Section 16519.5 of the Welfare and Institutions Code and comply with other applicable federal and state laws in order to maintain approval.

(e) For purposes of this section, the following definitions shall apply:

(1) "Current foster family agency" means a foster family agency by which a resource family is currently approved pursuant to this section or Section 1517.

(2) "Subsequent foster family agency" means a foster family agency to which a resource family has submitted an application for resource family approval pursuant to this section.

(3) "County" means a county child welfare or probation department by which a resource family is currently approved pursuant to Section 16519.5 of the Welfare and Institutions Code.

(Amended by Stats. 2018, Ch. 910, Sec. 7. (AB 1930) Effective January 1, 2019.)

1518.

(a) Nothing in this chapter shall authorize the imposition of rent regulations or controls for licensed community care facilities.

(b) Licensed community care facilities shall not be subject to controls on rent imposed by any state or local agency or other local government or entity.

(Added by Stats. 1981, Ch. 386.)

ARTICLE 2. Administration [1520 - 1526.8]

(Article 2 added by Stats. 1973, Ch. 1203.)

1520.

Any person desiring issuance of a license for a community care facility or a special permit for specialized services under this chapter shall file with the department, pursuant to regulations, an application on forms furnished by the department, which shall include, but not be limited to:

(a) Evidence satisfactory to the department of the ability of the applicant to comply with this chapter and of rules and regulations promulgated under this chapter by the department.

(b) Evidence satisfactory to the department that the applicant is of reputable and responsible character. The evidence shall include, but not be limited to, a criminal record clearance pursuant to Section 1522, employment history, and character references. If the applicant is a firm, association, organization, partnership, business trust, corporation, or company, like evidence shall be submitted as to the members or shareholders thereof, and the person in charge of the community care facility for which application for issuance of license or special permit is made.

(c) Evidence satisfactory to the department that the applicant has sufficient financial resources to maintain the standards of service required by regulations adopted pursuant to this chapter.

(d) Disclosure of the applicant's prior or present service as an administrator, general partner, corporate officer, or director of, or as a person who has held or holds a beneficial ownership of 10 percent or more in, any community care facility or in any facility licensed pursuant to Chapter 1 (commencing with Section 1200) or Chapter 2 (commencing with Section 1250).

(e) Disclosure of any revocation or other disciplinary action taken, or in the process of being taken, against a license held or previously held by the entities specified in subdivision (d).

(f) Disclosure of any revocation, rescission, or other disciplinary action taken, or in the process of being taken, against a certificate of approval held by the applicant pursuant to this chapter or Article 2 (commencing with Section 16519.5) of Chapter 5 of Part 4 of Division 9 of the Welfare and Institutions Code.

(g) A signed statement that the person desiring issuance of a license or special permit has read and understood the community care facility licensure statute and regulations that pertain to the applicant's category of licensure.

(h) Any other information that may be required by the department for the proper administration and enforcement of this chapter.

(i) In implementing this section, the department shall give due consideration to the functions of each separate licensing category.

(j) Failure of the applicant to cooperate with the licensing agency in the completion of the application shall result in the denial of the application. Failure to cooperate means that

the information described in this section and in regulations of the department has not been provided, or not provided in the form requested by the licensing agency, or both.

(Amended by Stats. 2017, Ch. 732, Sec. 13. (AB 404) Effective January 1, 2018.)

1520.1.

In addition to Section 1520, applicants for a group home or short-term residential therapeutic program license shall meet the following requirements:

(a) (1) During the first 12 months of operation, the facility shall operate with a provisional license. After eight months of operation, the department shall conduct a comprehensive review of the facility for compliance with all applicable laws and regulations and help develop a plan of correction with the provisional licensee, if appropriate. By the end of the 12th month of operation, the department shall determine if the permanent license should be issued.

(2) If the department determines that the group home or short-term residential therapeutic program is in substantial compliance with licensing standards, notwithstanding Section 1525.5, the department may extend the provisional license for up to an additional six months for either of the following reasons:

(A) The group home or short-term residential therapeutic program requires additional time to be in full compliance with licensing standards.

(B) After 12 months of operation, the group home or short-term residential therapeutic program is not operating at 50 percent of its licensed capacity.

(3) By no later than the first business day of the 17th month of operation, the department shall conduct an additional review of a facility for which a provisional license is extended pursuant to paragraph (2), in order to determine whether a permanent license should be issued.

(4) The department may deny a group home or short-term residential therapeutic program license application at any time during the term of the provisional license to protect the health and safety of clients. If the department denies the application, the group home or short-term residential therapeutic program shall cease operation immediately. Continued operation of the facility after the department denies the application or the provisional license expires shall constitute unlicensed operation.

(5) When the department notifies a city or county planning authority pursuant to subdivision (c) of Section 1520.5, the department shall briefly describe the provisional licensing process and the timelines provided for under that process, as well as provide the name, address, and telephone number of the district office licensing the facility where a complaint or comment about the group home's or short-term residential therapeutic program's operation may be filed.

(b) (1) After the production of the booklet provided for in paragraph (2), every member of the group home's board of directors or governing body and every member of a short-term residential therapeutic program's board of directors or governing body shall, prior to becoming a member of the board of directors or governing body sign a statement that he or she understands his or her legal duties and obligations as a member of the board of directors or governing body and that the group home's or short-term residential therapeutic program's operation is governed by laws and regulations that are enforced by the department, as set forth in the booklet. The applicant, provisional licensee, and licensee shall have this statement available for inspection by the department. For members of the board of directors or governing body when the booklet is produced, the licensee shall obtain this statement by the next scheduled meeting of the board of directors or governing body. Compliance with this paragraph shall be a condition of licensure.

(2) The department shall distribute to every group home provider and short-term residential therapeutic program provider, respectively, detailed information designed to educate members of the group home provider's or short-term residential therapeutic program provider's board of directors or governing body of their roles and responsibilities as members of a public benefit corporation under the laws of this state. The information shall be included in a booklet, may be revised as deemed necessary by the department, and shall include, but not be limited to, all of the following:

(A) The financial responsibilities of a member of the board of directors or governing body.

(B) Disclosure requirements for self-dealing transactions.

(C) Legal requirements pertaining to articles of incorporation, bylaws, length of member terms, voting procedures, board or governing body meetings, quorums, minutes of meetings, and, as provided for in subdivision (f), member duties.

(D) A general overview of the laws and regulations governing the group home's or short-term residential therapeutic program's operation that are enforced by the department.

(c) All financial records submitted by a facility to the department, or that are submitted as part of an audit of the facility, including, but not limited to, employee timecards and timesheets, shall be signed and dated by the employee and by the group home representative or short-term residential therapeutic program representative who is responsible for ensuring the accuracy of the information contained in the record, or when a time clock is used, the payroll register shall be signed and dated, and those financial records shall contain an affirmative statement that the signatories understand that the information contained in the document is correct to the best of their knowledge and that submission of false or misleading information may be prosecuted as a crime.

(d) An applicant, provisional licensee, or licensee shall maintain, submit, and sign financial documents to verify the legitimacy and accuracy of these documents. These documents include, but are not limited to, the group home or short-term residential therapeutic program application, any financial documents and plans of corrections submitted to the department, and timesheets.

(e) (1) It is the intent of the Legislature that a group home or short-term residential therapeutic program have either representatives on its board of directors, as listed in paragraph (2), or a community advisory board, that meets at least annually.

(2) The representatives on the board of directors or the community advisory board members should consist of at least the following persons:

(A) A member of the facility's board of directors.

(B) Members of the community where the facility is located.

(C) Neighbors of the facility.

(D) Current or former clients of the facility.

(E) A representative from a local law enforcement or other city or county representative.

(f) Each group home or short-term residential therapeutic program provider shall schedule and conduct quarterly meetings of its board of directors or governing body. During these quarterly meetings, the board of directors or governing body shall review and discuss licensing reports, financial and program audit reports of its group home or short-term residential therapeutic program operations, special incident reports, and any administrative action against the licensee or its employees. The minutes shall reflect the board's or governing body's discussion of these documents and the group home's or short-term residential therapeutic program's operation. The licensee shall make available the minutes of group home's or short-term residential therapeutic program's board of directors or governing body meetings to the department.

(Amended by Stats. 2016, Ch. 612, Sec. 29. (AB 1997) Effective January 1, 2017.)

1520.11.

(a) A corporation that applies for licensure with the department shall list the facilities that any member of the board of directors, an executive director, or any officer has been licensed to operate, been employed in, or served as a member of the board of directors, the executive director, or an officer.

(b) The department shall not issue a provisional license or license to any corporate applicant that has a member of the board of directors, an executive director, or an officer, who is not eligible for licensure pursuant to Section 1520.3 or Section 1558.1.

(c) The department may revoke the license of any corporate licensee that has a member of the board of directors, an executive director, or an officer, who is not eligible for licensure pursuant to Section 1520.3 or Section 1558.1.

(d) Prior to instituting an administrative action pursuant to either subdivision (b) or (c), the department shall notify the applicant or licensee of the person's ineligibility to be a member of the board of directors, an executive director, or an officer of the applicant or licensee. The licensee shall remove the person from that position within 15 days or, if the person has client contact, he or she shall be removed immediately upon notification.

(Added by Stats. 1998, Ch. 311, Sec. 13. Effective August 19, 1998.)

1520.2.

(a) Every licensed community care facility, at the request of a majority of its residents, shall assist its residents in establishing and maintaining a resident-oriented facility council. The council shall be composed of residents of the facility and may include family members of residents of the facility. The council may, among other things, make recommendations to facility administrators to improve the quality of daily living in the facility and may negotiate to protect residents' rights with facility administrators.

(b) A violation of subdivision (a) shall not be subject to the provisions of Section 1540 but shall be subject to the provisions of Section 1534 and any other provisions of this chapter.

(c) This section shall not apply to a community care facility as defined in paragraphs (3), (5), and (6) of subdivision (a) of Section 1502, or to a community care facility licensed to provide care for six or fewer individuals.

(Added by Stats. 1984, Ch. 1272, Sec. 1.)

1520.3.

(a) (1) If an application for a license or special permit indicates, or the department determines during the application review process, that the applicant previously was issued a license under this chapter or under Chapter 1 (commencing with Section 1200), Chapter 2 (commencing with Section 1250), Chapter 3.01 (commencing with Section 1568.01), Chapter 3.2 (commencing with Section 1569), Chapter 3.3 (commencing with Section 1570), Chapter 3.4 (commencing with Section 1596.70), Chapter 3.5 (commencing with Section 1596.90), or Chapter 3.6 (commencing with Section 1597.30), or that the applicant previously was approved as a resource family under Article 2 (commencing with Section 16519.5) of Chapter 5 of Part 4 of Division 9 of the Welfare and Institutions Code, and the prior license was revoked or prior approval was rescinded within the preceding two years, the department shall cease any further review of the application until two years shall have elapsed from the date of the revocation or rescission. The cessation of review shall not constitute a denial of the application for purposes of Section 1526 or any other provision of law.

(2) If an application for a license or special permit indicates, or the department determines during the application review process, that the applicant previously was issued a certificate of approval by a foster family agency that was revoked or rescinded by the department pursuant to subdivision (c) of Section 1517 or subdivision (b) of Section 1534 within the preceding two years, the department shall cease any further review of the application until two years shall have elapsed from the date of the revocation or rescission.

(3) If an application for a license or special permit indicates, or the department determines during the application review process, that the applicant was excluded from a facility licensed by the department, a certified family home or resource family home of a foster family agency pursuant to Section 1558, 1568.092, 1569.58, or 1596.8897, or a resource family home of a county pursuant to Section 16519.6 of the Welfare and Institutions Code, the department shall cease any further review of the application unless the excluded individual has been reinstated by the department pursuant to Section 11522 of the Government Code or Section 16519.6 of the Welfare and Institutions Code, as applicable.

(b) If an application for a license or special permit indicates, or the department determines during the application review process, that the applicant had previously applied for a license under any of the chapters listed in paragraph (1) of subdivision (a) or for resource family approval pursuant to Article 2 (commencing with Section 16519.5) of Chapter 5 of Part 5 of Division 9 of the Welfare and Institutions Code and the application was denied within the last year, the department shall cease further review of the application as follows:

(1) In cases in which the applicant petitioned for a hearing, the department shall cease further review of the application until one year has elapsed from the effective date of the decision and order of the department upholding a denial.

(2) In cases in which the department or county informed the applicant of his or her right to petition for a hearing and the applicant did not petition for a hearing, the department shall cease further review of the application until one year has elapsed from the date of the notification of the denial and the right to petition for a hearing.

(3) The department may continue to review the application if it has determined that the reasons for the denial of the application were due to circumstances and conditions which either have been corrected or are no longer in existence.

(c) If an application for a license or special permit indicates, or the department determines during the application review process, that the applicant had previously applied for a certificate of approval with a foster family agency and the department ordered the foster family agency to deny the application pursuant to subdivision (c) of Section 1517 or subdivision (b) of Section 1534, the department shall cease further review of the application as follows:

(1) In cases in which the applicant petitioned for a hearing, the department shall cease further review of the application until one year has elapsed from the effective date of the decision and order of the department upholding a denial.

(2) In cases in which the department informed the applicant of his or her right to petition for a hearing and the applicant did not petition for a hearing, the department shall cease further review of the application until one year has elapsed from the date of the notification of the denial and the right to petition for a hearing.

(3) The department may continue to review the application if it has determined that the reasons for the denial of the application were due to circumstances and conditions that either have been corrected or are no longer in existence.

(d) The cessation of review shall not constitute a denial of the application for purposes of Section 1526 or any other law.

(Amended by Stats. 2017, Ch. 732, Sec. 14. (AB 404) Effective January 1, 2018.)

1520.5.

(a) The Legislature hereby declares it to be the policy of the state to prevent overconcentrations of residential facilities that impair the integrity of residential neighborhoods. Therefore, the department shall deny an application for a new residential facility license if the department determines that the location is in a proximity to an existing residential facility that would result in overconcentration.

(b) As used in this section, "overconcentration" means that if a new license is issued, there will be residential facilities that are separated by a distance of 300 feet or less, as measured from any point upon the outside walls of the structures housing those facilities. Based on special local needs and conditions, the department may approve a separation distance of less than 300 feet with the approval of the city or county in which the proposed facility will be located.

(c) At least 45 days prior to approving any application for a new residential facility, the department, or county licensing agency, shall notify, in writing, the planning agency of the city, if the facility is to be located in the city, or the planning agency of the county, if the facility is to be located in an unincorporated area, of the proposed location of the facility.

(d) Any city or county may request denial of the license applied for on the basis of overconcentration of residential facilities.

(e) Nothing in this section authorizes the department, on the basis of overconcentration, to refuse to grant a license upon a change of ownership of an existing residential facility when there is no change in the location of the facility.

(f) Foster family homes and residential facilities for the elderly shall not be considered in determining overconcentration of residential facilities, and license applications for those facilities shall not be denied upon the basis of overconcentration.

(g) Transitional shelter care facilities and temporary shelter care facilities shall not be considered in determining overconcentration of residential facilities, and license applications for those facilities shall not be denied upon the basis of overconcentration.

(Amended by Stats. 2015, Ch. 773, Sec. 15. (AB 403) Effective January 1, 2016.)

1520.7.

(a) Every community care facility that is licensed or has a special permit for specialized services pursuant to Section 1525 shall provide a copy of the disaster and mass casualty plan required pursuant to Section 80023 of Title 22 of the California Code of Regulations to any fire department, law enforcement agency, or civil defense or other disaster authority in the area or community in which the facility is located, upon request by the fire department, law enforcement agency, or civil defense or other disaster authority. Section 1540 shall not apply to this section.

(b) The department is not required to monitor compliance with this section as part of its regulatory monitoring functions.

(Added by Stats. 2007, Ch. 18, Sec. 1. Effective January 1, 2008.)

1521.

Any person desiring a license for a community care facility under the provisions of this chapter which is required by other code provisions or rules or regulations of the state department pursuant to other code provisions to have a medical director, organized medical staff, or resident medical staff or to provide professional nursing services by a

registered nurse or supervision of nursing services by a licensed registered nurse, a graduate nurse, a licensed vocational nurse, or a certified psychiatric technician shall comply with the health planning requirements contained in Part 1.5 (commencing with Section 437) of Division 1.
All other community care facilities shall be exempt from the health planning requirements contained in Part 1.5 (commencing with Section 437) of Division 1.
(Amended by Stats. 1974, Ch. 497.)
1521.5.
(a) The county welfare director shall, prior to the issuance of any foster family home license, ensure that the county licensing staff, or the placement staff, conducts one or more in-home interviews with the prospective foster parent sufficient to collect information on caregiver qualifications that may be used by the placement agency to evaluate the ability, willingness, and readiness of the prospective foster parent to meet the varying needs of children. The inability of a prospective foster parent to meet the varying needs of children shall not, in and of itself, preclude a prospective foster parent from obtaining a foster family home license.
(b) All in-home interviews required by this section shall be on an in-person basis.
(c) If the in-home interview is conducted by the licensing agency, it shall be a part of the licensing record, and shall be shared with the placement agency pursuant to subdivision (e) of Section 1798.24 of the Civil Code.
(d) The in-home interview required by this section shall be completed no later than 120 days following notification by the licensing agency.
(e) No license shall be issued unless an in-home interview has been conducted as required by this section.
(Amended by Stats. 2002, Ch. 918, Sec. 1. Effective January 1, 2003.)
1521.6.
(a) The Legislature recognizes the importance of ensuring that prospective foster family homes meet specified health and safety requirements. Moreover, the Legislature acknowledges that there is a further need to evaluate a licensed foster parent's ability, readiness, and willingness to meet the varying needs of children, including hard-to-place children, in order to ensure competent placement resources. Therefore, it is the intent of the Legislature that the State Department of Social Services, in consultation with county placement agencies, foster care providers, and other interested parties, develop and implement through regulations, a comprehensive home study process that integrates the decision outcome of the home study developed pursuant to Section 16518 of the Welfare and Institutions Code, as a criteria for placement.
(b) This section shall become inoperative on the date the regulations adopted pursuant to this section are filed with the Secretary of State.
(Amended by Stats. 2001, Ch. 653, Sec. 4. Effective October 10, 2001. Inoperative on date prescribed by its own provisions.)
1522.
The Legislature recognizes the need to generate timely and accurate positive fingerprint identification of applicants as a condition of issuing licenses, permits, or certificates of approval for persons to operate or provide direct care services in a community care facility, foster family home, or a certified family home or resource family of a licensed foster family agency. Therefore, the Legislature supports the use of the fingerprint live-scan technology, as identified in the long-range plan of the Department of Justice for fully automating the processing of fingerprints and other data by the year 1999, otherwise known as the California Crime Information Intelligence System (CAL-CII), to be used for applicant fingerprints. It is the intent of the Legislature in enacting this section to require the fingerprints of those individuals whose contact with community care clients may pose a risk to the clients' health and safety. An individual shall be required to obtain either a criminal record clearance or a criminal record exemption from the State Department of Social Services before the individual's initial presence in a community care facility or certified family home.
(a) (1) Before and, as applicable, subsequent to issuing a license or special permit to a person to operate or manage a community care facility, the State Department of Social Services shall secure from an appropriate law enforcement agency a criminal record to determine whether the applicant or any other person specified in subdivision (b) has been convicted of a crime other than a minor traffic violation or arrested for any crime specified in Section 290 of the Penal Code, or for violating Section 245, 273ab, or 273.5 of the Penal Code, subdivision (b) of Section 273a of the Penal Code, or, prior to January 1, 1994, paragraph (2) of Section 273a of the Penal Code, or for any crime for which the department is prohibited from granting a criminal record exemption pursuant to subdivision (g).
(2) The criminal history information shall include the full criminal record, if any, of those persons, and subsequent arrest information pursuant to Section 11105.2 of the Penal Code.
(3) The following shall apply to the criminal record information:
(A) If the State Department of Social Services finds that the applicant, or any other person specified in subdivision (b), has been convicted of a crime other than a minor traffic violation, the application shall be denied, unless the department grants an exemption pursuant to subdivision (g).
(B) If the State Department of Social Services finds that the applicant, or any other person specified in subdivision (b), is awaiting trial for a crime other than a minor traffic violation, the State Department of Social Services may cease processing the criminal record information until the conclusion of the trial.
(C) If no criminal record information has been recorded, the Department of Justice shall provide the applicant and the State Department of Social Services with a statement of that fact.
(D) If the State Department of Social Services finds, after licensure, that the licensee, or any other person specified in paragraph (1) of subdivision (b), has been convicted of a crime other than a minor traffic violation, the license may be revoked, unless the department grants an exemption pursuant to subdivision (g).
(E) An applicant and any other person specified in subdivision (b) shall submit fingerprint images and related information to the Department of Justice for the purpose of searching the criminal records of the Federal Bureau of Investigation, in addition to the criminal records search required by this subdivision. If an applicant and all other persons described in subdivision (b) meet all of the conditions for licensure, except receipt of the Federal Bureau of Investigation's criminal offender record information search response for the applicant or any of the persons described in subdivision (b), the department may issue a license if the applicant and each person described in subdivision (b) has signed and submitted a statement that the person has never been convicted of a crime in the United States, other than a traffic infraction, as prescribed in paragraph (1) of subdivision (a) of Section 42001 of the Vehicle Code. If, after licensure, or the issuance of a certificate of approval of a certified family home by a foster family agency, the department determines that the licensee or any other person specified in subdivision (b) has a criminal record, the department may revoke the license, or require a foster family agency to revoke the certificate of approval, pursuant to Section 1550. The department may also suspend the license or require a foster family agency to suspend the certificate of approval pending an administrative hearing pursuant to Section 1550.5.
(F) The State Department of Social Services shall develop procedures to provide the individual's state and federal criminal history information with the written notification of the individual's exemption denial or revocation based on the criminal record. Receipt of the criminal history information shall be optional on the part of the individual, as set forth in the agency's procedures. The procedure shall protect the confidentiality and privacy of the individual's record, and the criminal history information shall not be made available to the employer.
(G) Notwithstanding any other law, the department is authorized to provide an individual with a copy of the individual's state or federal level criminal offender record information search response as provided to that department by the Department of Justice if the department has denied a criminal background clearance based on this information and the individual makes a written request to the department for a copy specifying an address to which it is to be sent. The state or federal level criminal offender record information search response shall not be modified or altered from its form or content as provided by the Department of Justice and shall be provided to the address specified by the individual in the individual's written request. The department shall retain a copy of the individual's written request and the response and date provided.
(b) (1) In addition to the applicant, this section shall be applicable to criminal record clearances and exemptions for the following persons:
(A) Adults responsible for administration or direct supervision of staff.
(B) Any adult, other than a client, residing in the facility, certified family home, or resource family home.
(C) Any person who provides client assistance in dressing, grooming, bathing, or personal hygiene. Any nurse assistant or home health aide meeting the requirements of Section 1338.5 or 1736.6, respectively, who is not employed, retained, or contracted by the licensee, and who has been certified or recertified on or after July 1, 1998, shall be deemed to meet the criminal record clearance requirements of this section. A certified nurse assistant and certified home health aide who will be providing client assistance and who falls under this exemption shall provide one copy of their current certification, prior to providing care, to the community care facility. The facility shall maintain the copy of the certification on file as long as care is being provided by the certified nurse assistant or certified home health aide at the facility or in a certified family home or resource family home of a foster family agency. This paragraph does not restrict the right of the department to exclude a certified nurse assistant or certified home health aide from a licensed community care facility or certified family home or resource family home of a foster family agency pursuant to Section 1558.
(D) Any staff person, volunteer, or employee who has contact with the clients.
(E) If the applicant is a firm, partnership, association, or corporation, the chief executive officer or other person serving in like capacity.
(F) Additional officers of the governing body of the applicant, or other persons with a financial interest in the applicant, as determined necessary by the department by regulation. The criteria used in the development of these regulations shall be based on the person's capability to exercise substantial influence over the operation of the facility.
(2) The following persons are exempt from the requirements applicable under paragraph (1):
(A) A medical professional, as defined in department regulations, who holds a valid license or certification from the person's governing California medical care regulatory entity and who is not employed, retained, or contracted by the licensee if all of the following apply:
(i) The criminal record of the person has been cleared as a condition of licensure or certification by the person's governing California medical care regulatory entity.
(ii) The person is providing time-limited specialized clinical care or services.
(iii) The person is providing care or services within the person's scope of practice.
(iv) The person is not a community care facility licensee or an employee of the facility.
(B) A third-party repair person or similar retained contractor if all of the following apply:
(i) The person is hired for a defined, time-limited job.
(ii) The person is not left alone with clients.
(iii) When clients are present in the room in which the repair person or contractor is working, a staff person who has a criminal record clearance or exemption is also present.

(C) Employees of a licensed home health agency and other members of licensed hospice interdisciplinary teams who have a contract with a client or resident of the facility, certified family home, or resource family home and are in the facility, certified family home, or resource family home at the request of that client or resident's legal decisionmaker. The exemption does not apply to a person who is a community care facility licensee or an employee of the facility.

(D) Clergy and other spiritual caregivers who are performing services in common areas of the community care facility, certified family home, or resource family home or who are advising an individual client at the request of, or with the permission of, the client or legal decisionmaker, are exempt from fingerprint and criminal background check requirements imposed by community care licensing. This exemption does not apply to a person who is a community care licensee or employee of the facility.

(E) Members of fraternal, service, or similar organizations who conduct group activities for clients if all of the following apply:

(i) Members are not left alone with clients.

(ii) Members do not transport clients off the facility, certified family home, or resource family home premises.

(iii) The same organization does not conduct group activities for clients more often than defined by the department's regulations.

(3) In addition to the exemptions in paragraph (2), the following persons in foster family homes, resource family homes, certified family homes, and small family homes are exempt from the requirements applicable under paragraph (1):

(A) Adult friends and family of the foster parent, who come into the home to visit for a length of time no longer than defined by the department in regulations, provided that the adult friends and family of the foster parent are not left alone with the foster children. However, the foster parent, acting as a reasonable and prudent parent, as defined in paragraph (2) of subdivision (a) of Section 362.04 of the Welfare and Institutions Code, may allow adult friends and family to provide short-term care to the foster child and act as an appropriate occasional short-term babysitter for the child.

(B) Parents of a foster child's friend when the foster child is visiting the friend's home and the friend, foster parent, or both are also present. However, the foster parent, acting as a reasonable and prudent parent, may allow the parent of the foster child's friend to act as an appropriate, occasional short-term babysitter for the child without the friend being present.

(C) Individuals who are engaged by a foster parent to provide short-term care to the child for periods not to exceed 24 hours. Caregivers shall use a reasonable and prudent parent standard in selecting appropriate individuals to act as appropriate occasional short-term babysitters.

(4) In addition to the exemptions specified in paragraph (2), the following persons in adult day care and adult day support centers are exempt from the requirements applicable under paragraph (1):

(A) Unless contraindicated by the client's individualized program plan (IPP) or needs and service plan, a spouse, significant other, relative, or close friend of a client, or an attendant or a facilitator for a client with a developmental disability if the attendant or facilitator is not employed, retained, or contracted by the licensee. This exemption applies only if the person is visiting the client or providing direct care and supervision to the client.

(B) A volunteer if all of the following apply:

(i) The volunteer is supervised by the licensee or a facility employee with a criminal record clearance or exemption.

(ii) The volunteer is never left alone with clients.

(iii) The volunteer does not provide any client assistance with dressing, grooming, bathing, or personal hygiene other than washing of hands.

(5) (A) In addition to the exemptions specified in paragraph (2), the following persons in adult residential and social rehabilitation facilities, unless contraindicated by the client's individualized program plan (IPP) or needs and services plan, are exempt from the requirements applicable under paragraph (1): a spouse, significant other, relative, or close friend of a client, or an attendant or a facilitator for a client with a developmental disability if the attendant or facilitator is not employed, retained, or contracted by the licensee. This exemption applies only if the person is visiting the client or providing direct care and supervision to that client.

(B) This subdivision does not prevent a licensee from requiring a criminal record clearance of any individual exempt from the requirements of this section, provided that the individual has client contact.

(6) Any person similar to those described in this subdivision, as defined by the department in regulations.

(c) (1) Subsequent to initial licensure, a person specified in subdivision (b) who is not exempted from fingerprinting shall obtain either a criminal record clearance or an exemption from disqualification pursuant to subdivision (g) from the State Department of Social Services prior to employment, residence, or initial presence in the facility. A person specified in subdivision (b) who is not exempt from fingerprinting shall be fingerprinted and shall sign a declaration under penalty of perjury regarding any prior criminal convictions. The licensee shall submit fingerprint images and related information to the Department of Justice and the Federal Bureau of Investigation, through the Department of Justice, for a state and federal level criminal offender record information search, or comply with paragraph (1) of subdivision (h). These fingerprint images and related information shall be sent by electronic transmission in a manner approved by the State Department of Social Services and the Department of Justice for the purpose of obtaining a permanent set of fingerprints, and shall be submitted to the Department of Justice by the licensee. A licensee's failure to prohibit the employment, residence, or initial presence

of a person specified in subdivision (b) who is not exempt from fingerprinting and who has not received either a criminal record clearance or an exemption from disqualification pursuant to subdivision (g) or to comply with paragraph (1) of subdivision (h), as required in this section, shall result in the citation of a deficiency and the immediate assessment of civil penalties in the amount of one hundred dollars ($100) per violation per day for a maximum of five days, unless the violation is a second or subsequent violation within a 12-month period in which case the civil penalties shall be in the amount of one hundred dollars ($100) per violation for a maximum of 30 days, and shall be grounds for disciplining the licensee pursuant to Section 1550. The department may assess civil penalties for continued violations as permitted by Section 1548. The fingerprint images and related information shall then be submitted to the Department of Justice for processing. Upon request of the licensee, who shall enclose a self-addressed stamped postcard for this purpose, the Department of Justice shall verify receipt of the fingerprints.

(2) Within 14 calendar days of the receipt of the fingerprint images, the Department of Justice shall notify the State Department of Social Services of the criminal record information, as provided in subdivision (a). If no criminal record information has been recorded, the Department of Justice shall provide the licensee and the State Department of Social Services with a statement of that fact within 14 calendar days of receipt of the fingerprint images. Documentation of the individual's clearance or exemption from disqualification shall be maintained by the licensee and be available for inspection. If new fingerprint images are required for processing, the Department of Justice shall, within 14 calendar days from the date of receipt of the fingerprints, notify the licensee that the fingerprints were illegible, the Department of Justice shall notify the State Department of Social Services, as required by Section 1522.04, and shall also notify the licensee by mail, within 14 days of electronic transmission of the fingerprints to the Department of Justice, if the person has no criminal history recorded. A violation of the regulations adopted pursuant to Section 1522.04 shall result in the citation of a deficiency and an immediate assessment of civil penalties in the amount of one hundred dollars ($100) per violation per day for a maximum of five days, unless the violation is a second or subsequent violation within a 12-month period in which case the civil penalties shall be in the amount of one hundred dollars ($100) per violation for a maximum of 30 days, and shall be grounds for disciplining the licensee pursuant to Section 1550. The department may assess civil penalties for continued violations as permitted by Section 1548.

(3) Except for persons specified in subdivision (b) who are exempt from fingerprinting, the licensee shall endeavor to ascertain the previous employment history of persons required to be fingerprinted. If it is determined by the State Department of Social Services, on the basis of the fingerprint images and related information submitted to the Department of Justice, that subsequent to obtaining a criminal record clearance or exemption from disqualification pursuant to subdivision (g), the person has been convicted of, or is awaiting trial for, a sex offense against a minor, or has been convicted for an offense specified in Section 243.4, 273a, 273ab, 273d, 273g, or 368 of the Penal Code, or a felony, the State Department of Social Services shall notify the licensee to act immediately to terminate the person's employment, remove the person from the community care facility, or bar the person from entering the community care facility. The State Department of Social Services may subsequently grant an exemption from disqualification pursuant to subdivision (g). If the conviction or arrest was for another crime, except a minor traffic violation, the licensee shall, upon notification by the State Department of Social Services, act immediately to either (A) terminate the person's employment, remove the person from the community care facility, or bar the person from entering the community care facility; or (B) seek an exemption from disqualification pursuant to subdivision (g). The State Department of Social Services shall determine if the person shall be allowed to remain in the facility until a decision on the exemption from disqualification is rendered. A licensee's failure to comply with the department's prohibition of employment, contact with clients, or presence in the facility as required by this paragraph shall result in a citation of deficiency and an immediate assessment of civil penalties in the amount of one hundred dollars ($100) per violation per day and shall be grounds for disciplining the licensee pursuant to Section 1550.

(4) The department may issue an exemption from disqualification on its own motion pursuant to subdivision (g) if the person's criminal history indicates that the person is of good character based on the age, seriousness, and frequency of the conviction or convictions. The department, in consultation with interested parties, shall develop regulations to establish the criteria to grant an exemption from disqualification pursuant to this paragraph.

(5) Concurrently with notifying the licensee pursuant to paragraph (3), the department shall notify the affected individual of the right to seek an exemption from disqualification pursuant to subdivision (g). The individual may seek an exemption from disqualification only if the licensee terminates the person's employment or removes the person from the facility after receiving notice from the department pursuant to paragraph (3).

(d) (1) Before and, as applicable, subsequent to issuing a license or certificate of approval to any person or persons to operate a foster family home, certified family home as described in Section 1506, or resource family pursuant to Section 1517 of this code or Section 16519.5 of the Welfare and Institutions Code, the State Department of Social Services or other approving authority shall secure California and Federal Bureau of Investigation criminal history information to determine whether the applicant or any person specified in subdivision (b) who is not exempt from fingerprinting has ever been convicted of a crime other than a minor traffic violation or arrested for any crime specified in subdivision (c) of Section 290 of the Penal Code, for violating Section 245, 273ab, or 273.5, subdivision (b) of Section 273a or, prior to January 1, 1994, paragraph (2) of Section 273a, of the Penal Code, or for any crime for which the department is prohibited

from granting a criminal record exemption pursuant to subdivision (g). The State Department of Social Services or other approving authority shall not issue a license or certificate of approval to any foster family home, certified family home, or resource family applicant who has not obtained both a California and Federal Bureau of Investigation criminal record clearance or exemption from disqualification pursuant to subdivision (g).
(2) The criminal history information shall include the full criminal record, if any, of those persons.
(3) Neither the Department of Justice nor the State Department of Social Services may charge a fee for the fingerprinting of an applicant for a license, special permit, or certificate of approval described in this subdivision. The record, if any, shall be taken into consideration when evaluating a prospective applicant.
(4) The following shall apply to the criminal record information:
(A) If the applicant or other persons specified in subdivision (b) who are not exempt from fingerprinting have convictions that would make the applicant's home unfit as a foster family home, a certified family home, or resource family, the license, special permit, certificate of approval, or presence shall be denied.
(B) If the State Department of Social Services finds that the applicant, or any person specified in subdivision (b) who is not exempt from fingerprinting is awaiting trial for a crime other than a minor traffic violation, the State Department of Social Services or other approving authority may cease processing the criminal record information until the conclusion of the trial.
(C) For purposes of this subdivision, a criminal record clearance provided under Section 8712 of the Family Code may be used by the department or other approving authority.
(D) To the same extent required for federal funding, a person specified in subdivision (b) who is not exempt from fingerprinting shall submit a set of fingerprint images and related information to the Department of Justice and the Federal Bureau of Investigation, through the Department of Justice, for a state and federal level criminal offender record information search, in addition to the criminal records search required by subdivision (a).
(5) Any person specified in this subdivision shall, as a part of the application, be fingerprinted and sign a declaration under penalty of perjury regarding any prior criminal convictions or arrests for any crime against a child, spousal or cohabitant abuse, or any crime for which the department cannot grant an exemption if the person was convicted and shall submit these fingerprints to the licensing agency or other approving authority.
(6) (A) Subsequent to initial licensure, certification, or approval, a person specified in subdivision (b) who is not exempt from fingerprinting shall obtain both a California and Federal Bureau of Investigation criminal record clearance, or an exemption from disqualification pursuant to subdivision (g), prior to employment, residence, or initial presence in the foster family home, certified family home, or resource family home. A foster family home licensee or foster family agency shall submit fingerprint images and related information of persons specified in subdivision (b) who are not exempt from fingerprinting to the Department of Justice and the Federal Bureau of Investigation, through the Department of Justice, for a state and federal level criminal offender record information search, or to comply with paragraph (1) of subdivision (h). A foster family home licensee's or a foster family agency's failure to either prohibit the employment, residence, or initial presence of a person specified in subdivision (b) who is not exempt from fingerprinting and who has not received either a criminal record clearance or an exemption from disqualification pursuant to subdivision (g), or comply with paragraph (1) of subdivision (h), as required in this section, shall result in a citation of a deficiency, and the immediate civil penalties of one hundred dollars ($100) per violation per day for a maximum of five days, unless the violation is a second or subsequent violation within a 12-month period in which case the civil penalties shall be in the amount of one hundred dollars ($100) per violation for a maximum of 30 days, and shall be grounds for disciplining the licensee pursuant to Section 1550. A violation of the regulation adopted pursuant to Section 1522.04 shall result in the citation of a deficiency and an immediate assessment of civil penalties in the amount of one hundred dollars ($100) per violation per day for a maximum of five days, unless the violation is a second or subsequent violation within a 12-month period in which case the civil penalties shall be in the amount of one hundred dollars ($100) per violation for a maximum of 30 days, and shall be grounds for disciplining the foster family home licensee or the foster family agency pursuant to Section 1550. The State Department of Social Services may assess penalties for continued violations, as permitted by Section 1548. The fingerprint images shall then be submitted to the Department of Justice for processing.
(B) Upon request of the licensee, who shall enclose a self-addressed envelope for this purpose, the Department of Justice shall verify receipt of the fingerprints. Within five working days of the receipt of the criminal record or information regarding criminal convictions from the Department of Justice, the department shall notify the applicant of any criminal arrests or convictions. If no arrests or convictions are recorded, the Department of Justice shall provide the foster family home licensee or the foster family agency with a statement of that fact concurrent with providing the information to the State Department of Social Services.
(7) If the State Department of Social Services or other approving authority finds that the applicant, or any other person specified in subdivision (b) who is not exempt from fingerprinting, has been convicted of a crime other than a minor traffic violation, the application or presence shall be denied, unless the department grants an exemption from disqualification pursuant to subdivision (g).
(8) If the State Department of Social Services or other approving authority finds, after licensure or the granting of the certificate of approval, that the licensee, certified foster parent, resource family, or any other person specified in subdivision (b) who is not exempt from fingerprinting, has been convicted of a crime other than a minor traffic violation, the license or certificate of approval may be revoked or rescinded by the department or the foster family agency, whichever is applicable, unless the department grants an exemption from disqualification pursuant to subdivision (g). A licensee's failure to comply with the department's prohibition of employment, contact with clients, or presence in the facility as required by paragraph (3) of subdivision (c) shall be grounds for disciplining the licensee pursuant to Section 1550.
(e) (1) The State Department of Social Services shall not use a record of arrest to deny, revoke, rescind, or terminate any application, license, certificate of approval, employment, or residence unless the department investigates the incident and secures evidence, whether or not related to the incident of arrest, that is admissible in an administrative hearing to establish conduct by the person that may pose a risk to the health and safety of any person who is or may become a client.
(2) The department shall not issue a criminal record clearance to a person who has been arrested for any crime specified in Section 290 of the Penal Code, or for violating Section 245, 273ab, or 273.5, or subdivision (b) of Section 273a, of the Penal Code, or, prior to January 1, 1994, paragraph (2) of Section 273a of the Penal Code, or for any crime for which the department is prohibited from granting a criminal record exemption pursuant to subdivision (g), prior to the completion of an investigation pursuant to paragraph (1).
(3) The State Department of Social Services is authorized to obtain any arrest or conviction records or reports from any law enforcement agency as necessary to the performance of its duties to inspect, license, and investigate community care facilities and individuals associated with a community care facility.
(f) (1) For purposes of this section or any other provision of this chapter, a conviction means a plea or verdict of guilty or a conviction following a plea of nolo contendere. Any action that the State Department of Social Services is permitted to take following the establishment of a conviction may be taken when the time for appeal has elapsed, when the judgment of conviction has been affirmed on appeal, or when an order granting probation is made suspending the imposition of sentence, notwithstanding a subsequent order pursuant to Sections 1203.4 and 1203.4a of the Penal Code permitting the person to withdraw a plea of guilty and to enter a plea of not guilty, or setting aside the verdict of guilty, or dismissing the accusation, information, or indictment. For purposes of this section or any other provision of this chapter, the record of a conviction, or a copy thereof certified by the clerk of the court or by a judge of the court in which the conviction occurred, shall be conclusive evidence of the conviction. For purposes of this section or any other provision of this chapter, the arrest disposition report certified by the Department of Justice, or documents admissible in a criminal action pursuant to Section 969b of the Penal Code, shall be prima facie evidence of the conviction, notwithstanding any other law prohibiting the admission of these documents in a civil or administrative action.
(2) For purposes of this section or any other provision of this chapter, the department shall consider criminal convictions from another state or federal court as if the criminal offense was committed in this state.
(g) (1) Except as otherwise provided in this subdivision with respect to a foster care provider applicant, including a relative caregiver, nonrelative extended family member, or resource family, after review of the record, the department may grant an exemption from disqualification for a license or special permit as specified in paragraph (4) of subdivision (a), or for a license, special permit, or certificate of approval as specified in paragraphs (4), (7), and (8) of subdivision (d), or for employment, residence, or presence in a community care facility as specified in paragraphs (3), (4), and (5) of subdivision (c), if the department has substantial and convincing evidence to support a reasonable belief that the applicant and the person convicted of the crime, if other than the applicant, are of good character as to justify issuance of the license or special permit or granting an exemption for purposes of subdivision (c). Except as otherwise provided in this subdivision, an exemption shall not be granted pursuant to this subdivision if the conviction was for any of the following offenses:
(A) (i) An offense specified in Section 220, 243.4, or 264.1, subdivision (a) of Section 273a, or, prior to January 1, 1994, paragraph (1) of Section 273a, Section 273ab, 273d, 288, or 289, subdivision (c) of Section 290, or Section 368, of the Penal Code, or was a conviction of another crime against an individual specified in subdivision (c) of Section 667.5 of the Penal Code.
(ii) Notwithstanding clause (i), the department may grant an exemption regarding the conviction for an offense described in paragraph (1), (2), (7), or (8) of subdivision (c) of Section 667.5 of the Penal Code, if the employee or prospective employee has been rehabilitated as provided in Section 4852.03 of the Penal Code, has maintained the conduct required in Section 4852.05 of the Penal Code for at least 10 years, and has the recommendation of the district attorney representing the employee's county of residence, or if the employee or prospective employee has received a certificate of rehabilitation pursuant to Chapter 3.5 (commencing with Section 4852.01) of Title 6 of Part 3 of the Penal Code.
(B) A felony offense specified in Section 729 of the Business and Professions Code or Section 206 or 215, subdivision (a) of Section 347, subdivision (b) of Section 417, or subdivision (a) of Section 451 of the Penal Code.
(2) (A) For a foster care provider applicant, a resource family applicant, or a prospective respite care provider, as described in Section 16501.01 of the Welfare and Institutions Code, an exemption shall not be granted if that applicant, or any individual subject to the background check requirements of this section pursuant to foster care provider applicant, resource family approval, or respite care provider standards, has a conviction for any of the following offenses:
(i) An offense specified in Section 220, 243.4, or 264.1, subdivision (a) of Section 273a, or, prior to January 1, 1994, paragraph (1) of Section 273a, Section 273ab, 273d, 288, or 289, subdivision (c) of Section 290, or Section 368, of the Penal Code, or was a

conviction of another crime against an individual specified in subdivision (c) of Section 667.5 of the Penal Code.

(ii) A felony offense specified in Section 729 of the Business and Professions Code or Section 206 or 215, subdivision (a) of Section 347, subdivision (b) of Section 417, or subdivision (a) of Section 451 of the Penal Code.

(iii) Under no circumstances shall an exemption be granted pursuant to this subdivision to any foster care provider applicant if that applicant, or any other person specified in subdivision (b) in those homes, has a felony conviction for either of the following offenses:

(I) A felony conviction for child abuse or neglect, spousal abuse, crimes against a child, including child pornography, or for a crime involving violence, including rape, sexual assault, or homicide, but not including other physical assault and battery. For purposes of this subparagraph, a crime involving violence means a violent crime specified in clause (i) of subparagraph (A), or clause (ii) of this subparagraph.

(II) A felony conviction, within the last five years, for physical assault, battery, or a drug- or alcohol-related offense.

(III) This clause shall not apply to licenses or approvals wherein a caregiver was granted an exemption to a criminal conviction described in clause (i) prior to the enactment of this clause.

(IV) This clause shall remain operative only to the extent that compliance with its provisions is required by federal law as a condition for receiving funding under Title IV-E of the federal Social Security Act (42 U.S.C. Sec. 670 et seq.).

(B) The department or other approving entity may grant an exemption from disqualification to a foster care provider, resource family applicant, or any individual subject to the background check requirements of this section pursuant to foster care provider applicant, resource family approval, or respite care provider standards, if the department or other approving entity has substantial and convincing evidence to support a reasonable belief that the applicant or the person convicted of the crime, if other than the applicant, is of present good character necessary to justify the granting of an exemption and the conviction is for one of the following offenses:

(i) (I) Any misdemeanor conviction within the last five years that is not otherwise prohibited by subparagraph (A).

(II) Notwithstanding subparagraph (A), a misdemeanor conviction for statutory rape, as defined in Section 261.5 of the Penal Code, a misdemeanor conviction for indecent exposure, as defined in Section 314 of the Penal Code, or a misdemeanor conviction for financial abuse against an elder, as defined in Section 368 of the Penal Code, shall be eligible for the consideration of an exemption as set forth in subparagraph (C).

(ii) Any felony conviction within the last seven years that is not otherwise prohibited by subparagraph (A).

(C) When granting an exemption for a crime listed in subparagraph (B), the department or other approving entity shall consider all reasonably available information, including, but not limited to, the following:

(i) The nature of the crime or crimes.

(ii) The period of time since the crime was committed.

(iii) The number of offenses.

(iv) Circumstances surrounding the commission of the crime indicating the likelihood of future criminal activity.

(v) Activities since conviction, including employment, participation in therapy, education, or treatment.

(vi) Whether the person convicted has successfully completed probation or parole, obtained a certificate of rehabilitation, or been granted a pardon by the Governor.

(vii) Any character references or other evidence submitted by the applicant.

(viii) Whether the person convicted demonstrated honesty and truthfulness concerning the crime or crimes during the application and approval process and made reasonable efforts to assist the department in obtaining records and documents concerning the crime or crimes.

(D) (i) The department or other approving entity shall grant an exemption from disqualification to a foster care provider applicant, resource family applicant, or any person subject to the background check requirements of this section pursuant to foster care provider applicant, resource family approval, or respite care provider standards, who has been convicted of an offense not listed in subparagraph (A) or (B), if the individual's state and federal criminal history information received from the Department of Justice independently supports a reasonable belief that the applicant or the person convicted of the crime, if other than the applicant, is of present good character necessary to justify the granting of an exemption.

(ii) Notwithstanding the fact that an individual meets the criteria described in clause (i), the department or other approving entity, at its discretion, as necessary to protect the health and safety of a child, may evaluate a person described in clause (i), for purposes of making an exemption decision, pursuant to the criteria described in subparagraphs (B) and (C).

(E) This paragraph shall not apply to licenses or approvals for which a caregiver was granted an exemption for a criminal conviction prior to January 1, 2018.

(3) The department shall not prohibit a person from being employed or having contact with clients in a facility, certified family home, or resource family home on the basis of a denied criminal record exemption request or arrest information unless the department complies with the requirements of Section 1558 of this code or Section 16519.6 of the Welfare and Institutions Code, as applicable.

(h) (1) For purposes of compliance with this section, the department may permit an individual to transfer a current criminal record clearance, as defined in subdivision (a), from one facility to another, as long as the criminal record clearance has been processed

through a state licensing district office, and is being transferred to another facility licensed by a state licensing district office. The request shall be in writing to the State Department of Social Services, and shall include a copy of the person's driver's license or valid identification card issued by the Department of Motor Vehicles, or a valid photo identification issued by another state or the United States government if the person is not a California resident. Upon request of the licensee, who shall enclose a self-addressed envelope for this purpose, the State Department of Social Services shall verify whether the individual has a clearance that can be transferred.

(2) The State Department of Social Services shall hold criminal record clearances in its active files for a minimum of three years after an employee is no longer employed at a licensed facility in order for the criminal record clearance to be transferred.

(3) A criminal record clearance or exemption processed by the department, a county office with clearance and exemption authority pursuant to Section 16519.5 of the Welfare and Institutions Code, or a county office with department-delegated licensing authority shall be accepted by the department or county upon notification of transfer.

(4) With respect to notifications issued by the Department of Justice pursuant to Section 11105.2 of the Penal Code and Section 1522.1 concerning an individual whose criminal record clearance was originally processed by the department, a county office with clearance and exemption authority pursuant to Section 16519.5 of the Welfare and Institutions Code, or a county office with department-delegated licensing authority, all of the following shall apply:

(A) The Department of Justice shall process a request from the department or a county to receive the notice only if all of the following conditions are met:

(i) The request shall be submitted to the Department of Justice by the agency to be substituted to receive the notification.

(ii) The request shall be for the same applicant type as the type for which the original clearance was obtained.

(iii) The request shall contain all prescribed data elements and format protocols pursuant to a written agreement between the department and the Department of Justice.

(B) (i) On or before January 7, 2005, the department shall notify the Department of Justice of all county offices that have department-delegated licensing authority.

(ii) The department shall notify the Department of Justice within 15 calendar days of the date on which a new county office receives department-delegated licensing authority or a county's delegated licensing authority is rescinded.

(C) The Department of Justice shall charge the department, a county office with department-delegated licensing authority, or a county child welfare agency with criminal record clearance and exemption authority, a fee for each time a request to substitute the recipient agency is received for purposes of this paragraph. This fee shall not exceed the cost of providing the service.

(i) The full criminal record obtained for purposes of this section may be used by the department or by a licensed adoption agency as a clearance required for adoption purposes.

(j) If a licensee or facility is required by law to deny employment or to terminate employment of any employee based on written notification from the department that the employee has a prior criminal conviction or is determined unsuitable for employment under Section 1558, the licensee or facility shall not incur civil liability or unemployment insurance liability as a result of that denial or termination.

(k) The State Department of Social Services may charge a reasonable fee for the costs of processing electronic fingerprint images and related information.

(Amended by Stats. 2019, Ch. 27, Sec. 8. (SB 80) Effective June 27, 2019.)

1522.01.

(a) Any person required to be registered as a sex offender under Section 290 of the Penal Code shall disclose this fact to the licensee of a community care facility before becoming a client of that facility. A community care facility client who fails to disclose to the licensee his or her status as a registered sex offender shall be guilty of a misdemeanor punishable pursuant to subdivision (a) of Section 1540. The community care facility licensee shall not be liable if the client who is required to register as a sex offender fails to disclose this fact to the community care facility licensee. However, this immunity does not apply if the community care facility licensee knew that the client was required to register as a sex offender.

(b) Any person or persons operating, pursuant to this chapter, a community care facility that accepts as a client an individual who is required to be registered as a sex offender under Section 290 of the Penal Code shall confirm or deny whether any client of the facility is a registered sex offender in response to any person who inquires whether any client of the facility is a registered sex offender and who meets any of the following criteria:

(1) The person is the parent, family member, or guardian of a child residing within a one-mile radius of the facility.

(2) The person occupies a personal residence within a one-mile radius of the facility.

(3) The person operates a business within a one-mile radius of the facility.

(4) The person is currently a client within the facility or a family member of a client within the facility.

(5) The person is applying for placement in the facility, or placement of a family member in the facility.

(6) The person is arranging for a client to be placed in the facility.

(7) The person is a law enforcement officer.

If the community care facility licensee indicates a client is a registered sex offender, the interested person may describe physical characteristics of a client and the facility shall disclose that client's name upon request, if the physical description matches the client. The facility shall also advise the interested person that information about registered sex offenders is available to the public via the Internet Web site maintained by the Department of Justice pursuant to Section 290.46 of the Penal Code.

(c) Any person who uses information disclosed pursuant to this section to commit a felony shall be punished, in addition and consecutive to, any other punishment, by a five-year term of imprisonment pursuant to subdivision (h) of Section 1170 of the Penal Code.

(d) Any person who uses information disclosed pursuant to this section to commit a misdemeanor shall be subject to, in addition to any other penalty or fine imposed, a fine of not less than five hundred dollars ($500) and not more than one thousand dollars ($1,000).

(e) Except as authorized under another provision of law, or to protect a child, use of any of the information disclosed pursuant to this section for the purpose of applying for, obtaining, or denying any of the following, is prohibited:

(1) Health insurance.

(2) Insurance.

(3) Loans.

(4) Credit.

(5) Employment.

(6) Education, scholarships, or fellowships.

(7) Benefits, privileges, or services provided by any business establishment.

(8) Housing or accommodations.

(f) Any use of information disclosed pursuant to this section for purposes other than those provided by subdivisions (a) and (b) shall make the user liable for the actual damages, and any amount that may be determined by a jury or a court sitting without a jury, not exceeding three times the amount of actual damage, and not less than two hundred fifty dollars ($250), and attorney's fees, exemplary damages, or a civil penalty not exceeding twenty-five thousand dollars ($25,000).

(g) Whenever there is reasonable cause to believe that any person or group of persons is engaged in a pattern or practice of misuse of the information disclosed pursuant to this section, the Attorney General, any district attorney, or city attorney, or any person aggrieved by the misuse of that information is authorized to bring a civil action in the appropriate court requesting preventive relief, including an application for a permanent or temporary injunction, restraining order, or other order against the person or group of persons responsible for the pattern or practice of misuse. The foregoing remedies shall be independent of any other remedies or procedures that may be available to an aggrieved party under other provisions of law, including Part 2 (commencing with Section 43) of Division 1 of the Civil Code.

(h) The civil and criminal penalty moneys collected pursuant to this section shall be transferred to the Community Care Licensing Division of the State Department of Social Services, upon appropriation by the Legislature.

(Amended by Stats. 2011, Ch. 15, Sec. 139. (AB 109) Effective April 4, 2011. Operative October 1, 2011, by Sec. 636 of Ch. 15, as amended by Stats. 2011, Ch. 39, Sec. 68.)

1522.02.

(a) The department may adopt regulations to create substitute employee registries for persons working at more than one facility licensed pursuant to this chapter, Chapter 3.01 (commencing with Section 1568.01), Chapter 3.2 (commencing with Section 1569), Chapter 3.4 (commencing with Section 1569.70), Chapter 3.5 (commencing with Section 1596.90), or Chapter 3.6 (commencing with Section 1597.30), in order to permit these registries to submit fingerprint cards, and child abuse index information for child care registries so that these facilities have available cleared care staff.

(b) The department may operate a substitute child care employee registry pilot program for the purposes of subdivision (a) and may charge participating registry facilities an administrative fee. The pilot program is subject to all of the following:

(1) The pilot program shall be limited to screening employees for facilities licensed as child care facilities.

(2) Registries shall not hire any child care worker for employment at a child care facility who requires an exemption from the criminal background clearance requirements of law.

(3) The department shall only guarantee the authenticity of criminal background and child abuse index information that registries provide to child care facilities. Any other information provided by registries may be verified by child care facility operators.

(4) The department may limit the operation of the pilot program to the Counties of Alameda, Contra Costa, Monterey, San Benito, San Francisco, San Luis Obispo, Santa Barbara, Santa Clara, Santa Cruz, San Mateo, and Ventura.

(Amended by Stats. 2002, Ch. 669, Sec. 2. Effective January 1, 2003.)

1522.03.

The Department of Justice may charge a fee sufficient to cover its cost in providing services in accordance with Section 1522 to comply with the 14-day requirement for provision to the department of the criminal record information, as contained in subdivision (c) of Section 1522.

(Amended by Stats. 1998, Ch. 311, Sec. 16. Effective August 19, 1998.)

1522.04.

(a) The Legislature recognizes the need to generate timely and accurate positive fingerprint identification of applicants as a condition of issuing licenses, permits, or certificates of approval for persons to operate or provide direct care services in a community care facility, or a residential care facility, child day care facility, or foster family agency, licensed by the department pursuant to this chapter, Chapter 3.01 (commencing with Section 1568.01), Chapter 3.2 (commencing with Section 1569), Chapter 3.4 (commencing with Section 1596.70), Chapter 3.5 (commencing with Section 1596.90), or Chapter 3.6 (commencing with Section 1597.30), or certified family home. Therefore, the Legislature supports the use of the fingerprint live-scan technology, as identified in the long-range plan of the Department of Justice, for fully automating the processing of

fingerprints and other data by the year 1999, otherwise known as the California Crime Information Intelligence System (CAL-CII) to be used for applicant fingerprints. Therefore, when live-scan technology is operational, individuals shall be required to obtain either a criminal record clearance from the Department of Justice or a criminal record exemption from the State Department of Social Services, before their initial presence in a community care facility. The regulations shall also cover the submission of fingerprint information to the Federal Bureau of Investigation.

(b) Upon implementation of an electronic fingerprinting system with terminals located statewide and managed by the Department of Justice, the Department of Justice shall ascertain the criminal history information required pursuant to subdivision (a) of Section 1522.04. If the Department of Justice cannot ascertain the information required pursuant to that subdivision within three working days, the Department of Justice shall notify the State Department of Social Services, or county licensing agencies, either by telephone and by subsequent confirmation in writing by first-class mail, or by electronic or facsimile transmission. At its discretion, the Department of Justice may forward one copy of the fingerprint cards to any other bureau of investigation it may deem necessary in order to verify any record of previous arrests or convictions of the fingerprinted individual.

(c) For purposes of this section, live-scan technology is operational when the Department of Justice and the district offices of the Community Care Licensing Division of the department live-scan sites are operational and the department is receiving 95 percent of its total responses indicating either no evidence of recorded criminal information or evidence of recorded criminal information from the Department of Justice within three business days.

(Amended by Stats. 2000, Ch. 819, Sec. 3. Effective January 1, 2001.)

1522.06.

(a) Individuals who are volunteer candidates for mentoring children in foster care settings, as defined by the department, in private alternative boarding schools, or in private alternative outdoor programs, shall be subject to a criminal background investigation prior to having unsupervised contact with the children. The criminal background check shall be initiated and conducted pursuant to either Sections 1522 and 1522.1 or Section 1596.603, as applicable. Sections 1522 and 1522.1 may be utilized by a county social services agency in cooperation with, or as a component of, a licensed foster family agency.

(b) (1) The Department of Justice shall not charge a processing fee with respect to any individual to whom subdivision (a) applies for a state-level criminal offender record information search pursuant to Section 1522.

(2) The State Department of Social Services shall not charge a fee for the cost of a criminal background investigation under Section 1522 with respect to any individual to whom subdivision (a) applies.

(Amended by Stats. 2016, Ch. 864, Sec. 7. (SB 524) Effective January 1, 2017.)

1522.07.

(a) Notwithstanding subdivision (d) of Section 1522, foster family agencies shall submit fingerprints of their certified foster parent applicants to the Department of Justice using a card provided by the State Department of Social Services for that purpose.

(b) Within 30 calendar days of the receipt of the fingerprints, the Department of Justice shall notify the State Department of Social Services of the criminal record information, as provided in subdivision (a) of Section 1522. If no criminal record information has been recorded, the Department of Justice shall provide the foster family agency and the State Department of Social Services with a statement of that fact within 15 calendar days of receipt of the fingerprints. If new fingerprints are required for processing, the Department of Justice shall, within 15 calendar days from the date of receipt of the fingerprints, notify the licensee that the fingerprints were illegible.

(Added by Stats. 1991, Ch. 1200, Sec. 5. Effective October 14, 1991.)

1522.08.

(a) In order to protect the health and safety of persons receiving care or services from individuals or facilities licensed by the state or from individuals certified or approved by a foster family agency, the following information may be shared:

(1) The California Department of Aging, State Department of Public Health, State Department of Health Care Services, State Department of Social Services, and the Emergency Medical Services Authority may share information with respect to applicants, licensees, certificate holders, or individuals who have been the subject of any administrative action resulting in the denial, suspension, probation, revocation, or rescission of a license, permit, or certificate of approval, or in the exclusion of any person from a facility, certified family home, or resource family home who is subject to a background check, as otherwise provided by law.

(2) The State Department of Social Services and county child welfare agencies may share information with respect to applicants, licensees, certificate holders, or individuals who have been the subject of any administrative action resulting in the denial, suspension, probation, revocation, or rescission of a license, permit, or certificate of approval, or in the exclusion of any person from a facility, certified family home, or resource family home who is subject to a background check, as otherwise provided by law.

(b) The State Department of Social Services shall maintain a centralized system for the monitoring and tracking of final administrative actions, to be used by the California Department of Aging, State Department of Public Health, State Department of Health Care Services, State Department of Social Services, the Emergency Medical Services Authority, and county child welfare agencies as a part of the background check process. The State Department of Social Services may charge a fee to departments under the jurisdiction of the California Health and Human Services Agency and to county child welfare agencies sufficient to cover the cost of providing those departments with the final administrative action specified in subdivision (a). To the extent that additional funds are needed for this purpose, implementation of this subdivision shall be contingent upon a specific appropriation provided for this purpose in the annual Budget Act.

(c) The State Department of Social Services, in consultation with the other departments under the jurisdiction of the California Health and Human Services Agency, may adopt regulations to implement this section.

(d) For the purposes of this section and Section 1499, "administrative action" means any proceeding initiated by the California Department of Aging, State Department of Public Health, State Department of Health Care Services, State Department of Social Services, Emergency Medical Services Authority, and county child welfare agencies to determine the rights and duties of an applicant, licensee, certificate holder, or other individual or entity over which the department has jurisdiction. "Administrative action" may include, but is not limited to, action involving the denial of an application for, or the suspension, revocation, or rescission of, any license, special permit, certificate of approval, administrator certificate, criminal record clearance, exemption, or exclusion.

(Amended (as amended by Stats. 2014, Ch. 222, Sec. 1) by Stats. 2017, Ch. 732, Sec. 18. (AB 404) Effective January 1, 2018.)

1522.09.

(a) The department shall, no later than July 1, 2017, develop a notice that does all of the following:

(1) Contains the telephone number to make a complaint regarding a community care facility or child care facility.

(2) Includes information about the prohibition of impeding mandated reports.

(3) Includes information about the option to make a confidential complaint.

(b) The notice developed pursuant to subdivision (a) shall be posted conspicuously in a prominent area in all foster family agencies.

(Added by Stats. 2016, Ch. 850, Sec. 1. (AB 1001) Effective January 1, 2017.)

1522.1.

(a) Prior to granting a license to, or otherwise approving, any individual to care for or reside with children, the department shall check the Child Abuse Central Index pursuant to paragraph (4) of subdivision (b) of Section 11170 of the Penal Code. The Department of Justice shall maintain and continually update an index of reports of child abuse by providers and shall inform the department of subsequent reports received from the Child Abuse Central Index pursuant to Section 11170 of the Penal Code and the criminal history. The department shall investigate any reports received from the Child Abuse Central Index. The investigation shall include, but not be limited to, the review of the investigation report and file prepared by the child protective agency which investigated the child abuse report. Licensure or approval shall not be denied based upon a report from the Child Abuse Central Index unless child abuse or severe neglect is substantiated.

(b) For any application received on or after January 1, 2008, if any prospective foster parent, or adoptive parent, or any person 18 years of age or older residing in their household, has lived in another state in the preceding five years, the licensing agency or licensed adoption agency shall check that state's child abuse and neglect registry, in addition to checking the Child Abuse Central Index as provided for in subdivision (a). The department, in consultation with the County Welfare Directors Association, shall develop and promulgate the process and criteria to be used to review and consider other states' findings of child abuse or neglect.

(c) If any person in the household is 18 years of age or older and has lived in another state in the preceding five years, the department or its designated representative shall check the other state's child abuse and neglect registry to the same extent required for federal funding, in addition to checking the Child Abuse Central Index as provided for in subdivision (a), prior to granting a license to, or otherwise approving, any foster family home, certified family home, resource family, or person for whom an adoption home study is conducted or who has filed to adopt.

(Amended by Stats. 2017, Ch. 732, Sec. 19. (AB 404) Effective January 1, 2018.)

1522.2.

If a local law enforcement agency, a probation officer, or a local department or agency that provides social services becomes aware that an employee of a community treatment facility, a day treatment facility, a group home, a short-term residential therapeutic program, or a foster family agency has been arrested for child abuse, as defined in Section 11165.6 of the Penal Code, after determining that the potential for abuse is present and that the employee is free to return to the facility where children are present, the local law enforcement agency, probation officer, or local department or agency shall notify the licensee of the charge of abuse.

(Amended by Stats. 2016, Ch. 612, Sec. 30. (AB 1997) Effective January 1, 2017.)

1522.4.

(a) In addition to any other requirements of this chapter and except for foster family homes, small family homes, and certified family homes and resource families of foster family agencies, all of the following apply to any community care facility providing 24-hour care for children:

(1) The facility shall have one or more facility managers. "Facility manager," as used in this section, means a person on the premises with the authority and responsibility necessary to manage and control the day-to-day operation of a community care facility and supervise the clients. The facility manager, licensee, and administrator, or any combination thereof, may be the same person provided he or she meets all applicable requirements. If the administrator is also the facility manager for the same facility, this person shall be limited to the administration and management of only one facility.

(2) The facility manager shall have at least one year of experience working with the client group served, or equivalent education or experience, as determined by the department.

(3) A facility manager shall be at the facility at all times when one or more clients are present. To ensure adequate supervision of clients when clients are at the facility outside of their normal schedule, a current telephone number where the facility manager can be reached shall be provided to the clients, licensing agency, school, and any other agency or person as the department determines is necessary. The facility manager shall instruct these agencies and individuals to notify him or her when clients will be returning to the facility outside of the normal hours.

(4) The Legislature intends to upgrade the quality of care in licensed facilities. For the purposes of Sections 1533 and 1534, the licensed facility shall be inspected and evaluated for quality of care at least once each year, without advance notice and as often as necessary, without advance notice, to ensure the quality of care being provided. Paragraphs (1), (2), and (3) shall apply only to new facilities licensed for six or fewer children which apply for a license after January 1, 1985, and all other new facilities licensed for seven or more children which apply for a license after January 1, 1988. Existing facilities licensed for seven or more children shall comply by January 1, 1989.

(b) An employee of the state or county employed in the administration of this chapter or employed in a position that is in any way concerned with facilities licensed under this chapter shall not hold a license or have a direct or indirect financial interest in a facility described in subdivision (a).

The department, by regulation, shall make the determination pursuant to the purposes of this section and chapter, as to what employment is in the administration of this chapter or in any way concerned with facilities licensed under this chapter and what financial interest is direct or indirect.

This subdivision does not prohibit the state or county from securing a license for, or operating, a facility that is otherwise required to be licensed under this chapter.

(c) (1) No group home, short-term residential therapeutic program, or foster family agency licensee, or employee, member of the board of directors, or officer of a group home, short-term residential therapeutic program, or foster family agency licensee, shall offer gifts or other remuneration of any type to any employee of the State Department of Social Services or placement agency that exceeds the monetary limits for gifts to employees of the State of California pursuant to Title 9 (commencing with Section 81000) of the Government Code and regulations adopted thereunder by the Fair Political Practices Commission.

(2) No employee of the department or a placement agency shall accept any gift or other remuneration of any type from a group home, short-term residential therapeutic program, or foster family agency licensee or employee, member of the board of directors, or officer of a group home, short-term residential therapeutic program, or foster family agency licensee that exceeds the monetary limits for gifts to employees of the State of California in Title 9 (commencing with Section 81000) of the Government Code and regulations adopted thereunder by the Fair Political Practices Commission.

(3) Violation of this subdivision is punishable as a misdemeanor.

(Amended by Stats. 2017, Ch. 732, Sec. 20. (AB 404) Effective January 1, 2018.)

1522.41.

(a) (1) The department, in consultation and collaboration with county placement officials, group home provider organizations, the Director of Health Care Services, and the Director of Developmental Services, shall develop and establish an administrator certification training program to ensure that administrators of group home facilities have appropriate training to provide the care and services for which a license or certificate is issued.

(2) The department shall develop and establish an administrator certification training program to ensure that administrators of short-term residential therapeutic program facilities have appropriate training to provide the care and services for which a license or certificate is issued.

(b) (1) In addition to any other requirements or qualifications required by the department, an administrator of a group home or short-term residential therapeutic program shall successfully complete a specified department-approved training certification program, pursuant to subdivision (c), prior to employment.

(2) In those cases when the individual is both the licensee and the administrator of a facility, the individual shall comply with all of the licensee and administrator requirements of this section.

(3) Failure to comply with this section shall constitute cause for revocation of the license of the facility.

(4) The licensee shall notify the department within 10 days of any change in administrators.

(c) (1) The administrator certification programs for group homes shall require a minimum of 40 hours of classroom instruction that provides training on a uniform core of knowledge in each of the following areas:

(A) Laws, regulations, and policies and procedural standards that impact the operations of the type of facility for which the applicant will be an administrator.

(B) Business operations.

(C) Management and supervision of staff.

(D) Psychosocial and educational needs of the facility residents, including, but not limited to, the information described in subdivision (d) of Section 16501.4 of the Welfare and Institutions Code.

(E) Community and support services.

(F) Physical needs of facility residents.

(G) Assistance with self-administration, storage, misuse, and interaction of medication used by facility residents.

(H) Resident admission, retention, and assessment procedures, including the right of a foster child to have fair and equal access to all available services, placement, care, treatment, and benefits, and to not be subjected to discrimination or harassment on the basis of actual or perceived race, ethnic group identification, ancestry, national origin, color, religion, sex, sexual orientation, gender identity, mental or physical disability, or HIV status.

(I) Instruction on cultural competency and sensitivity and related best practices for providing adequate care for children across diverse ethnic and racial backgrounds, as well as children identifying as lesbian, gay, bisexual, or transgender.

(J) Nonviolent emergency intervention and reporting requirements.

(K) Basic instruction on the existing laws and procedures regarding the safety of foster youth at school and the ensuring of a harassment- and violence-free school environment contained in Article 3.6 (commencing with Section 32228) of Chapter 2 of Part 19 of Division 1 of Title 1 of the Education Code.

(L) The information described in subdivision (i) of Section 16521.5 of the Welfare and Institutions Code. The program may use the curriculum created pursuant to subdivision (h), and described in subdivision (i), of Section 16521.5 of the Welfare and Institutions Code.

(2) The administrator certification programs for short-term residential therapeutic programs shall require a minimum of 40 hours of classroom instruction that provides training on a uniform core of knowledge in each of the following areas:

(A) Laws, regulations, and policies and procedural standards that impact the operations of the type of facility for which the applicant will be an administrator.

(B) Business operations and management and supervision of staff, including staff training.

(C) Physical and psychosocial needs of the children, including behavior management, de-escalation techniques, and trauma informed crisis management planning.

(D) Permanence, well-being, and educational needs of the children.

(E) Community and support services, including accessing local behavioral and mental health supports and interventions, substance use disorder treatments, and culturally relevant services, as appropriate.

(F) Understanding the requirements and best practices regarding psychotropic medications, including, but not limited to, court authorization, uses, benefits, side effects, interactions, assistance with self-administration, misuse, documentation, storage, and metabolic monitoring of children prescribed psychotropic medications.

(G) Admission, retention, and assessment procedures, including the right of a foster child to have fair and equal access to all available services, placement, care, treatment, and benefits, and to not be subjected to discrimination or harassment on the basis of actual or perceived race, ethnic group identification, ancestry, national origin, color, religion, sex, sexual orientation, gender identity, mental or physical disability, or HIV status.

(H) The federal Indian Child Welfare Act (25 U.S.C. Sec. 1901 et seq.), its historical significance, the rights of children covered by the act, and the best interests of Indian children as including culturally appropriate, child-centered practices that respect Native American history, culture, retention of tribal membership, and connection to the tribal community and traditions.

(I) Instruction on cultural competency and sensitivity and related best practices for providing adequate care for children across diverse ethnic and racial backgrounds, as well as children identifying as lesbian, gay, bisexual, or transgender.

(J) Nonviolent emergency intervention and reporting requirements.

(K) Basic instruction on the existing laws and procedures regarding the safety of foster youth at school and the ensuring of a harassment- and violence-free school environment contained in Article 3.6 (commencing with Section 32228) of Chapter 2 of Part 19 of Division 1 of Title 1 of the Education Code.

(L) The information described in subdivision (i) of Section 16521.5 of the Welfare and Institutions Code. The program may use the curriculum created pursuant to subdivision (h), and described in subdivision (i), of Section 16521.5 of the Welfare and Institutions Code.

(d) Administrators who possess a valid group home license, issued by the department, are exempt from completing an approved initial certification training program and taking a written test, provided the individual completes 12 hours of classroom instruction in the following uniform core of knowledge areas:

(1) Laws, regulations, and policies and procedural standards that impact the operations of a short-term residential therapeutic program.

(2) (A) Authorization, uses, benefits, side effects, interactions, assistance with self-administration, misuse, documentation, and storage of medications.

(B) Metabolic monitoring of children prescribed psychotropic medications.

(3) Admission, retention, and assessment procedures, including the right of a foster child to have fair and equal access to all available services, placement, care, treatment, and benefits, and to not be subjected to discrimination or harassment on the basis of actual or perceived race, ethnic group identification, ancestry, national origin, color, religion, sex, sexual orientation, gender identity, mental or physical disability, or HIV status.

(4) The federal Indian Child Welfare Act (25 U.S.C. Sec. 1901 et seq.), its historical significance, the rights of children covered by the act, and the best interests of Indian children as including culturally appropriate, child-centered practices that respect Native American history, culture, retention of tribal membership, and connection to the tribal community and traditions.

(5) Instruction on cultural competency and sensitivity and related best practices for providing adequate care for children across diverse ethnic and racial backgrounds, as well as children identifying as lesbian, gay, bisexual, or transgender.

(6) Physical and psychosocial needs of children, including behavior management, deescalation techniques, and trauma informed crisis management planning.

(e) Individuals applying for administrator certification under this section shall successfully complete an approved administrator certification training program, pass a written test administered by the department within 60 days of completing the program, and submit to the department the documentation required by subdivision (f) within 30 days after being notified of having passed the test. The department may extend these time deadlines for good cause. The department shall notify the applicant of his or her test results within 30 days of administering the test.

(f) The department shall not begin the process of issuing a certificate until receipt of all of the following:

(1) A certificate of completion of the administrator training required pursuant to this chapter.

(2) The fee required for issuance of the certificate. A fee of one hundred dollars ($100) shall be charged by the department to cover the costs of processing the application for certification.

(3) Documentation from the applicant that he or she has passed the written test.

(4) Submission of fingerprints pursuant to Section 1522. The department may waive the submission for those persons who have a current clearance on file.

(5) That person is at least 21 years of age.

(g) It shall be unlawful for any person not certified under this section to hold himself or herself out as a certified administrator of a group home or short-term residential therapeutic program. Any person willfully making any false representation as being a certified administrator or facility manager is guilty of a misdemeanor.

(h) (1) Certificates issued under this section shall be renewed every two years and renewal shall be conditional upon the certificate holder submitting documentation of completion of 40 hours of continuing education related to the core of knowledge specified in subdivision (c). No more than one-half of the required 40 hours of continuing education necessary to renew the certificate may be satisfied through online courses. All other continuing education hours shall be completed in a classroom setting. For purposes of this section, an individual who is a group home or short-term residential therapeutic program administrator and who is required to complete the continuing education hours required by the regulations of the State Department of Developmental Services, and approved by the regional center, may have up to 24 of the required continuing education course hours credited toward the 40-hour continuing education requirement of this section. The department shall accept for certification, community college course hours approved by the regional centers.

(2) Every administrator of a group home or short-term residential therapeutic program shall complete the continuing education requirements of this subdivision.

(3) Certificates issued under this section shall expire every two years on the anniversary date of the initial issuance of the certificate, except that any administrator receiving his or her initial certification on or after July 1, 1999, shall make an irrevocable election to have his or her recertification date for any subsequent recertification either on the date two years from the date of issuance of the certificate or on the individual's birthday during the second calendar year following certification. The department shall send a renewal notice to the certificate holder 90 days prior to the expiration date of the certificate. If the certificate is not renewed prior to its expiration date, reinstatement shall only be permitted after the certificate holder has paid a delinquency fee equal to three times the renewal fee and has provided evidence of completion of the continuing education required.

(4) To renew a certificate, the certificate holder shall, on or before the certificate expiration date, request renewal by submitting to the department documentation of completion of the required continuing education courses and pay the renewal fee of one hundred dollars ($100), irrespective of receipt of the department's notification of the renewal. A renewal request postmarked on or before the expiration of the certificate shall be proof of compliance with this paragraph.

(5) A suspended or revoked certificate shall be subject to expiration as provided for in this section. If reinstatement of the certificate is approved by the department, the certificate holder, as a condition precedent to reinstatement, shall submit proof of compliance with paragraphs (1) and (2) of this subdivision, and shall pay a fee in an amount equal to the renewal fee, plus the delinquency fee, if any, accrued at the time of its revocation or suspension. Delinquency fees, if any, accrued subsequent to the time of its revocation or suspension and prior to an order for reinstatement, shall be waived for a period of 12 months to allow the individual sufficient time to complete the required continuing education units and to submit the required documentation. Individuals whose certificates will expire within 90 days after the order for reinstatement may be granted a three-month extension to renew their certificates during which time the delinquency fees shall not accrue.

(6) A certificate that is not renewed within four years after its expiration shall not be renewed, restored, reissued, or reinstated except upon completion of a certification training program, passing any test that may be required of an applicant for a new certificate at that time, and paying the appropriate fees provided for in this section.

(7) A fee of twenty-five dollars ($25) shall be charged for the reissuance of a lost certificate.

(8) A certificate holder shall inform the department of his or her employment status and change of mailing address within 30 days of any change.

(i) Unless otherwise ordered by the department, the certificate shall be considered forfeited under either of the following conditions:

(1) The department has revoked any license held by the administrator after the department issued the certificate.

(2) The department has issued an exclusion order against the administrator pursuant to Section 1558, 1568.092, 1569.58, or 1596.8897, after the department issued the certificate, and the administrator did not appeal the exclusion order or, after the appeal, the department issued a decision and order that upheld the exclusion order.

(j) (1) The department, in consultation and collaboration with county placement officials, provider organizations, the State Department of Health Care Services, and the State Department of Developmental Services, shall establish, by regulation, the program content, the testing instrument, the process for approving administrator certification training programs, and criteria to be used in authorizing individuals, organizations, or educational institutions to conduct certification training programs and continuing education courses. The department may also grant continuing education hours for continuing courses offered by accredited educational institutions that are consistent with the requirements in this section. The department may deny vendor approval to any agency or person in any of the following circumstances:

(A) The applicant has not provided the department with evidence satisfactory to the department of the ability of the applicant to satisfy the requirements of vendorization set out in the regulations adopted by the department.

(B) The applicant person or agency has a conflict of interest in that the person or agency places its clients in group homes or short-term residential therapeutic programs.

(C) The applicant public or private agency has a conflict of interest in that the agency is mandated to place clients in group homes or short-term residential therapeutic programs and to pay directly for the services. The department may deny vendorization to this type of agency only as long as there are other vendor programs available to conduct the certification training programs and conduct education courses.

(2) The department may authorize vendors to conduct the administrator's certification training program pursuant to this section. The department shall conduct the written test pursuant to regulations adopted by the department.

(3) The department shall prepare and maintain an updated list of approved training vendors.

(4) The department may inspect administrator certification training programs and continuing education courses, including online courses, at no charge to the department, to determine if content and teaching methods comply with regulations. If the department determines that any vendor is not complying with the requirements of this section, the department shall take appropriate action to bring the program into compliance, which may include removing the vendor from the approved list.

(5) The department shall establish reasonable procedures and timeframes not to exceed 30 days for the approval of vendor training programs.

(6) The department may charge a reasonable fee, not to exceed one hundred fifty dollars ($150) every two years, to certification program vendors for review and approval of the initial 40-hour training program pursuant to subdivision (c). The department may also charge the vendor a fee, not to exceed one hundred dollars ($100) every two years, for the review and approval of the continuing education courses needed for recertification pursuant to this subdivision.

(7) (A) A vendor of online programs for continuing education shall ensure that each online course contains all of the following:

(i) An interactive portion in which the participant receives feedback, through online communication, based on input from the participant.

(ii) Required use of a personal identification number or personal identification information to confirm the identity of the participant.

(iii) A final screen displaying a printable statement, to be signed by the participant, certifying that the identified participant completed the course. The vendor shall obtain a copy of the final screen statement with the original signature of the participant prior to the issuance of a certificate of completion. The signed statement of completion shall be maintained by the vendor for a period of three years and be available to the department upon demand. Any person who certifies as true any material matter pursuant to this clause that he or she knows to be false is guilty of a misdemeanor.

(B) Nothing in this subdivision shall prohibit the department from approving online programs for continuing education that do not meet the requirements of subparagraph (A) if the vendor demonstrates to the department's satisfaction that, through advanced technology, the course and the course delivery meet the requirements of this section.

(k) The department shall establish a registry for holders of certificates that shall include, at a minimum, information on employment status and criminal record clearance.

(l) Notwithstanding any law to the contrary, vendors approved by the department who exclusively provide either initial or continuing education courses for certification of administrators of a group home or short-term residential therapeutic program as defined by regulations of the department, an adult residential facility as defined by regulations of the department, or a residential care facility for the elderly as defined in subdivision (k) of Section 1569.2, shall be regulated solely by the department pursuant to this chapter. No other state or local governmental entity shall be responsible for regulating the activity of those vendors.

(Amended by Stats. 2017, Ch. 24, Sec. 7. (SB 89) Effective June 27, 2017.)
1522.42.

(a) The department, in consultation and collaboration with county placement officials, provider organizations, the State Department of Health Care Services, and the State Department of Developmental Services, shall adopt regulations that establish standardized training and continuing education curricula for facility managers and direct child care workers in group homes.

(b) The regulations required by subdivision (a) shall specify the date by which new and current employees shall be required to meet the standardized training and continuing education requirements. For persons employed as child care staff and facility managers on the effective date of the regulations, the department shall provide adequate time for these persons to comply with the regulatory requirements.

(Amended by Stats. 2012, Ch. 34, Sec. 21. (SB 1009) Effective June 27, 2012.)
1522.43.

(a) (1) For the duties the department imposes on a group home administrator or short-term residential therapeutic program administrator in this chapter and in regulations adopted by the department, every group home and short-term residential therapeutic program shall state in its plan of operation, the number of hours per week that the administrator shall spend completing those duties and how the group home administrator or short-term residential therapeutic program administrator shall accomplish those duties, including use of support personnel.

(2) For initial applicants, the information in paragraph (1) shall be contained in the plan of operation submitted to the department in the application.

(3) For current licensees, the licensee shall submit an amended plan of operation that contains the information required by paragraph (1) within six months of the effective date of this section. For changes in the group home administrator duties imposed by the department in this chapter or in regulations, a current licensee shall have six months after the effective date of those duties to submit an amended plan of operation to reflect the new administrator duties.

(b) (1) The department may review a group home's or short-term residential therapeutic program's plan of operation to determine if the plan of operation is sufficient to ensure that the facility will operate in compliance with applicable licensing laws and regulations. As part of the review, the department may request that a peer review panel review the plan of operation for a group home as prescribed in paragraph (2), or for a short-term residential therapeutic program as prescribed in paragraph (3).

(2) The peer review panel shall consist of two representatives from the department, including one from the unit that governs programs and one from the unit that governs licensing, a qualified group home administrator, an experienced group home provider in good standing, and a member or members from the placement agency or agencies that place children in group homes, and may also include the local county behavioral health department, as appropriate.

(3) The peer review panel shall consist of two representatives from the department, including one from the unit that governs programs and one from the unit that governs licensing, a qualified short-term residential therapeutic program administrator, a short-term residential therapeutic program provider in good standing, and a member or members from the placement agency or agencies that place children in short-term residential therapeutic programs, and may also include the local county behavioral health department, as appropriate.

(c) A group home or short-term residential therapeutic program shall develop a daily schedule of activities for the children at the facility. The facility shall have this schedule available for inspection by the department. The activities in which the children are scheduled to participate shall be designed to meet the needs of the individual child, and shall be based on that child's needs and services plan.

(d) The department shall establish a process, no later than January 1, 2017, for convening the peer review panel as set forth in subdivision (b) for review of the plans of operation for short-term residential therapeutic programs, and shall develop this process in consultation with the County Welfare Directors Association of California, Chief Probation Officers of California, County Behavioral Health Directors Association of California, and stakeholders.

(Amended by Stats. 2016, Ch. 612, Sec. 33. (AB 1997) Effective January 1, 2017.)
1522.44.

(a) It is the policy of the state that caregivers of children in foster care possess knowledge and skills relating to the reasonable and prudent parent standard, as defined in subdivision (c) of Section 362.05 of the Welfare and Institutions Code.

(b) Except for licensed foster family homes, certified family homes, and resource families approved by a foster family agency, each licensed community care facility that provides care and supervision to children and operates with staff shall designate at least one onsite staff member to apply the reasonable and prudent parent standard to decisions involving the participation of a child who is placed in the facility in age or developmentally appropriate activities in accordance with the requirements of Section 362.05 of the Welfare and Institutions Code, Section 671(a)(10) of Title 42 of the United States Code, and the regulations adopted by the department pursuant to this chapter.

(c) A licensed and certified foster parent, resource family, or facility staff member, as described in subdivision (b), shall receive training related to the reasonable and prudent parent standard that is consistent with Section 671(a)(24) of Title 42 of the United States Code. This training shall include knowledge and skills relating to the reasonable and prudent parent standard for the participation of the child in age or developmentally appropriate activities, including knowledge and skills relating to the developmental stages of the cognitive, emotional, physical, and behavioral capacities of a child, and knowledge and skills relating to applying the standard to decisions such as whether to allow the child to engage in extracurricular, enrichment, cultural, and social activities, including sports, field trips, and overnight activities lasting one or more days, and to decisions involving the signing of permission slips and arranging of transportation for the child to and from extracurricular, enrichment, and social activities.

(d) This section does not apply to a runaway and homeless youth shelter, a private alternative boarding school, or a private alternative outdoor program, as those terms are defined, respectively, in subdivision (a) of Section 1502.

(Amended by Stats. 2016, Ch. 864, Sec. 8.5. (SB 524) Effective January 1, 2017.)
1522.5.

The State Department of Social Services, in processing fingerprint clearances, shall give expeditious treatment to employees of, and applicants for employment with, community care facilities, as defined in Section 1502, which provide services to children, and child day care facilities, as defined in Section 1596.750.

(Added by Stats. 1986, Ch. 927, Sec. 3. Effective September 22, 1986.)

1523.1.

(a) (1) An application fee adjusted by facility and capacity shall be charged by the department for the issuance of a license. After initial licensure, a fee shall be charged by the department annually on each anniversary of the effective date of the license. The fees are for the purpose of financing the activities specified in this chapter. Fees shall be assessed as follows, subject to paragraph (2):

Fee Schedule			
Facility Type	Capacity	Initial Application	Annual
Foster Family and Adoption Agencies		$3,025	$1,513
	1–15	$182	$91
	16–30	$303	$152
	31–60	$605	$303
	61–75	$758	$378
	76–90	$908	$454
	91–120	$1,210	$605
Adult Day Programs	121+	$1,513	$757
	1–3	$454	$454
	4–6	$908	$454
	7–15	$1,363	$681
	16–30	$1,815	$908
Other Community Care Facilities	31–49	$2,270	$1,135
	50–74	$2,725	$1,363
	75–100	$3,180	$1,590
	101–150	$3,634	$1,817
	151–200	$4,237	$2,119
	201–250	$4,840	$2,420
	251–300	$5,445	$2,723
	301–350	$6,050	$3,025
	351–400	$6,655	$3,328
	401–500	$7,865	$3,933
	501–600	$9,075	$4,538
	601–700	$10,285	$5,143
	701+	$12,100	$6,050

(2) (A) The Legislature finds that all revenues generated by fees for licenses computed under this section and used for the purposes for which they were imposed are not subject to Article XIII B of the California Constitution.

(B) The department, at least every five years, shall analyze initial application fees and annual fees issued by it to ensure the appropriate fee amounts are charged. The department shall recommend to the Legislature that fees established by the Legislature be adjusted as necessary to ensure that the amounts are appropriate.

(b) (1) In addition to fees set forth in subdivision (a), the department shall charge the following fees:

(A) A fee that represents 50 percent of an established application fee when an existing licensee moves the facility to a new physical address.

(B) A fee that represents 50 percent of the established application fee when a corporate licensee changes who has the authority to select a majority of the board of directors.

(C) A fee of twenty-five dollars ($25) when an existing licensee seeks to either increase or decrease the licensed capacity of the facility.

(D) An orientation fee of fifty dollars ($50) for attendance by any individual at a department-sponsored orientation session.

(E) A probation monitoring fee equal to the current annual fee, in addition to the current annual fee for that category and capacity for each year a license has been placed on probation as a result of a stipulation or decision and order pursuant to the administrative adjudication procedures of the Administrative Procedure Act (Chapter 4.5 (commencing with Section 11400) and Chapter 5 (commencing with Section 11500) of Part 1 of Division 3 of Title 2 of the Government Code).

(F) A late fee that represents an additional 50 percent of the established current annual fee when any licensee fails to pay the current annual licensing fee on or before the due date as indicated by postmark on the payment.

(G) A fee to cover any costs incurred by the department for processing payments including, but not limited to, bounced check charges, charges for credit and debit transactions, and postage due charges.

(H) A plan of correction fee of two hundred dollars ($200) when any licensee does not implement a plan of correction on or prior to the date specified in the plan.

(I) Additional fees established by the department by regulation for private alternative boarding schools and private alternative outdoor programs, as necessary to regulate those licensees.

(2) Foster family homes and resource families approved by a foster family agency shall be exempt from the fees imposed pursuant to this subdivision.

(3) (A) Foster family agencies shall be annually assessed eighty-eight dollars ($88) for each certified family home and resource family certified or approved by the agency.

(B) A foster family agency shall not be annually assessed the fee described in subparagraph (A) for a resource family placed on inactive status in accordance with Section 1517.4 if the period of inactivity exceeds one year.

(4) A local jurisdiction shall not impose a business license, fee, or tax for the privilege of operating a facility licensed under this chapter that serves six or fewer persons.

(c) (1) The revenues collected from licensing fees pursuant to this section shall be utilized by the department for the purpose of ensuring the health and safety of all individuals provided care and supervision by licensees and to support activities of the licensing program, including, but not limited to, monitoring facilities for compliance with licensing laws and regulations pursuant to this chapter, and other administrative activities in support of the licensing program, when appropriated for these purposes. The revenues collected shall be used in addition to any other funds appropriated in the Budget Act in support of the licensing program. The department shall adjust the fees collected pursuant to this section as necessary to ensure that they do not exceed the costs described in this paragraph.

(2) The department shall not utilize any portion of these revenues sooner than 30 days after notification in writing of the purpose and use of this revenue, as approved by the Director of Finance, to the Chairperson of the Joint Legislative Budget Committee, and the chairpersons of the committee in each house that considers appropriations for each fiscal year. The department shall submit a budget change proposal to justify any positions or any other related support costs on an ongoing basis.

(d) A facility may use a bona fide business check to pay the license fee required under this section.

(e) The failure of an applicant or licensee to pay all applicable and accrued fees and civil penalties shall constitute grounds for denial or forfeiture of a license.

(Amended by Stats. 2017, Ch. 732, Sec. 21. (AB 404) Effective January 1, 2018.)

1523.2.

(a) Beginning with the 1996–97 fiscal year, there is hereby created in the State Treasury the Technical Assistance Fund, from which money, upon appropriation by the Legislature in the Budget Act, shall be expended by the department to fund administrative and other activities in support of the licensing program.

(b) In each fiscal year, fees collected by the department pursuant to Sections 1523.1, 1568.05, 1569.185, and 1596.803 shall be deposited into the Technical Assistance Fund created pursuant to subdivision (a) and shall be expended by the department for the purpose of ensuring the health and safety of all individuals provided care and supervision by licensees and to support activities of the licensing program, including, but not limited to, monitoring facilities for compliance with applicable laws and regulations.

(c) Notwithstanding any other provision of law, revenues received by the department from payment of civil penalties imposed on licensed facilities pursuant to Sections 1522, 1536, 1547, 1548, 1568.0821, 1568.0822, 1568.09, 1569.17, 1569.485, and 1569.49 shall be deposited into the Technical Assistance Fund created pursuant to subdivision (a), and may be expended by the department for the technical assistance, training, and education of licensees.

(Amended by Stats. 2014, Ch. 29, Sec. 6. (SB 855) Effective June 20, 2014.)

1523.5.

Transitional shelter care facilities, as defined in Section 1502.3, shall be exempt from the fees imposed pursuant to subdivision (a) of Section 1523.1.

(Amended by Stats. 2017, Ch. 732, Sec. 22. (AB 404) Effective January 1, 2018.)

1524.

A license shall be forfeited by operation of law when one of the following occurs:

(a) The licensee sells or otherwise transfers the facility or facility property, except when change of ownership applies to transferring of stock when the facility is owned by a corporation, and when the transfer of stock does not constitute a majority change of ownership.

(b) The licensee surrenders the license to the department.

(c) (1) The licensee moves a facility from one location to another. The department shall develop regulations to ensure that the facilities are not charged a full licensing fee and do not have to complete the entire application process when applying for a license for the new location.

(2) This subdivision shall not apply to a licensed foster family or a home certified by a licensed foster family agency. When a foster family home licensee or certified home parent moves to a new location, the existing license or certification may be transferred to the new location. All caregivers to whom this paragraph applies shall be required to meet all applicable licensing laws and regulations at the new location.

(d) The licensee is convicted of an offense for which the department is prohibited from granting a criminal record exemption pursuant to paragraph (1) of subdivision (g) of Section 1522.

(e) The licensee dies. If an adult relative notifies the department of his or her desire to continue operation of the facility and submits an application, the department shall expedite the application. The department shall promulgate regulations for expediting applications submitted pursuant to this subdivision.

(f) The licensee abandons the facility.

(g) When the certification issued by the State Department of Developmental Services to a licensee of an Adult Residential Facility for Persons with Special Health Care Needs, licensed pursuant to Article 9 (commencing with Section 1567.50), is rescinded.

(h) When the certification issued by the State Department of Developmental Services to a licensee of an enhanced behavioral supports home, licensed pursuant to Article 9.5 (commencing with Section 1567.61), is rescinded.

(i) When the certificate of program approval issued by the State Department of Developmental Services, pursuant to Article 8 (commencing with Section 4698) of Chapter 6 of Division 4.5 of the Welfare and Institutions Code, to a licensee of a community crisis home, licensed pursuant to Article 9.7 (commencing with Section 1567.80), is rescinded.

(j) A group home license issued to a county shall be forfeited by operation of law when the county receives a license to operate a temporary shelter care facility in accordance with Section 1530.8.

(k) A temporary shelter care facility license issued to a private, nonprofit organization under contract with a county shall be forfeited by operation of law upon termination of the contract in accordance with Section 1530.8.

(l) A foster family home license is forfeited by operation of law, as provided in Section 1517.1 of this code or Section 16519.5 of the Welfare and Institutions Code.

(Amended by Stats. 2018, Ch. 910, Sec. 9. (AB 1930) Effective January 1, 2019.)

1524.01.

A resource family approval shall be forfeited by operation of law when one of the following occurs:

(a) The resource family surrenders the approval to the licensed foster family agency.

(b) The resource family is convicted of an offense for which the department is prohibited from granting a criminal record exemption pursuant to paragraph (2) of subdivision (g) of Section 1522.

(c) The sole resource family parent dies.

(d) The resource family abandons the approved home.

(e) The resource family fails to cooperate with an annual update, as described in subparagraph (F) of paragraph (3) of subdivision (b) of Section 1517, within 30 days of the date of written notice by the licensed foster family agency.

(f) A resource family approval is forfeited by operation of law as provided in Section 1517.5 of this code or Section 16519.58 of the Welfare and Institutions Code.

(Added by Stats. 2018, Ch. 910, Sec. 10. (AB 1930) Effective January 1, 2019.)

1524.1.

(a) Notwithstanding Section 1524, in the event of a sale of a licensed community care facility, except foster family homes and small family homes, where the sale will result in a new license being issued, the sale and transfer of property and business shall be subject to both of the following:

(1) The licensee shall provide written notice to the department and to each resident or client or his or her legal representative of the licensee's intent to sell the facility at least 60 days prior to the transfer of property or business, or at the time that a bona fide offer is made, whichever period is longer.

(2) The licensee shall, prior to entering into an admission agreement, inform all residents/clients, or their legal representatives, admitted to the facility after notification to the department, of the licensee's intent to sell the property or business.

(b) Except as provided in subdivision (e), the property and business shall not be transferred until the buyer qualifies for a license or provisional license pursuant to this chapter.

(1) The seller shall notify, in writing, a prospective buyer of the necessity to obtain a license, as required by this chapter, if the buyer's intent is to continue operating the facility as a community care facility. The seller shall send a copy of this written notice to the licensing agency.

(2) The prospective buyer shall submit an application for a license, as specified in Section 1520, within five days of the acceptance of the offer by the seller.

(c) No transfer of the property or business shall be permitted until 60 days have elapsed from the date when notice has been provided to the department pursuant to paragraph (1) of subdivision (a).

(d) The department shall give priority to applications for licensure that are submitted pursuant to this section in order to ensure timely transfer of the property and business. The department shall make a decision within 60 days after a complete application is submitted on whether to issue a license pursuant to Section 1520.

(e) If the parties involved in the transfer of the property and business fully comply with this section, then the transfer may be completed and the buyer shall not be considered to be operating an unlicensed facility while the department makes a final determination on the application for licensure.

(Added by Stats. 1992, Ch. 873, Sec. 1. Effective January 1, 1993.)

1524.5.

(a) In addition to any other requirements of this chapter, any community care facility providing residential care for six or fewer persons, except family homes certified by foster family agencies, foster family homes, and small family homes, shall provide a procedure approved by the licensing agency for immediate response to incidents and complaints. This procedure shall include a method of assuring that the owner, licensee, or person designated by the owner or licensee is notified of the incident, that the owner, licensee, or person designated by the owner or licensee has personally investigated the matter, and that the person making the complaint or reporting the incident has received a written response of action taken or a reason why no action needs to be taken.

(b) In order to assure the opportunity for complaints to be made directly to the owner, licensee, or person designated by the owner or licensee, and to provide the opportunity for the owner, licensee, or person designated by the owner or licensee to meet residents and learn of problems in the neighborhood, any facility, except family homes certified by foster family agencies, foster family homes, and small family homes, shall establish a fixed time on a weekly basis when the owner, licensee, or person designated by the owner or licensee will be present.

(c) Facilities shall establish procedures to comply with the requirements of this section on or before July 1, 1996.

(Amended by Stats. 1995, Ch. 706, Sec. 1. Effective January 1, 1996.)

1524.6.

(a) In addition to any other requirement of this chapter, any group home or short-term residential therapeutic program, as defined by regulations of the department, providing care for any number of persons, that is not already subject to the requirements of Section 1524.5, shall provide a procedure approved by the licensing agency for immediate response to incidents and complaints, as defined by regulations of the department. This procedure shall include a method of ensuring that the owner, licensee, or person designated by the owner or licensee is notified of the incident or complaint, that the owner, licensee, or person designated by the owner or licensee has personally investigated the matter, and that the person making the complaint or reporting the incident has received a written response, within 30 days of receiving the complaint, of action taken, or a reason why no action needs to be taken.

(b) In order to ensure the opportunity for complaints to be made directly to the owner, licensee, or person designated by the owner or licensee, and to provide the opportunity for the owner, licensee, or person designated by the owner or licensee to meet neighborhood residents and learn of problems in the neighborhood, any group home or short-term residential therapeutic program shall establish a fixed time on a periodic basis when the owner, licensee, or person designated by the owner or licensee will be present. At this fixed time, information shall be provided to neighborhood residents of the complaint procedure pursuant to Section 1538.

(c) Facilities shall establish procedures to comply with the requirements of this section on or before July 1, 2005.

(d) This section shall not apply to family homes certified by foster family agencies, foster family homes, and small family homes. It is not the intent of the Legislature that this section be applied in a way that is contrary to the child's best interests.

(Amended by Stats. 2016, Ch. 612, Sec. 36. (AB 1997) Effective January 1, 2017.)

1524.7.

The State Department of Social Services shall provide to residential care facilities a form, which the residential care facility shall attach to each resident admission agreement, notifying the resident that he or she is entitled to obtain services and equipment from the telephone company. The form shall include the following information:

"Any hearing or speech impaired, or otherwise disabled resident of any residential care facility is entitled to equipment and service by the telephone company, pursuant to Section 2881 of the Public Utilities Code, to improve the quality of their telecommunications. Any resident who has a declaration from a licensed professional or a state or federal agency pursuant to Section 2881 of the Public Utilities Code that he or she is hearing or speech impaired, or otherwise disabled should contact the local telephone company and ask for assistance in obtaining this equipment and service."

This section shall not be construed to require, in any way, the licensee to provide a separate telephone line for any resident.

(Added by Stats. 1996, Ch. 448, Sec. 1. Effective January 1, 1997.)

1525.

Upon the filing of the application for issuance of a license or for a special permit and substantial compliance with the provisions of this chapter and the rules and regulations of the department, the director shall issue to the applicant the license or special permit. If the director finds that the applicant is not in compliance with the laws or regulations of this chapter, the director shall deny the applicant a license or special permit.

(Amended by Stats. 1992, Ch. 1315, Sec. 4. Effective January 1, 1993.)

1525.25.

(a) It is the intent of the Legislature to provide for proper case management and orderly transition in placement when family home licensing or family home certification changes occur. Placing, licensing, and foster family agencies shall be advised in a timely manner that a licensed foster family home or certified home intends to change its licensing or certification status.

(b) Upon receiving notification that a licensed foster family home is forfeiting its license, the county shall evaluate the needs of any child still placed in the home and determine whether the child requires the level of care to be provided when the home has been certified by a foster family agency. Any child not requiring that level of care shall be moved to a home that provides the appropriate level of care.

(Added by Stats. 1991, Ch. 1200, Sec. 6. Effective October 14, 1991.)

1525.3.

Prior to the issuance of any new license or special permit pursuant to this chapter, the applicant shall attend an orientation given by the department. The orientation given by the department shall outline all of the following:

(a) The rules and regulations of the department applicable to a community care facility.

(b) The scope of operation of a community care facility.

(c) The responsibility entailed in operating a community care facility.

(Added by Stats. 1989, Ch. 606, Sec. 4.)

1525.5.

(a) The department may issue provisional licenses to operate community care facilities for facilities that it determines are in substantial compliance with this chapter and the rules and regulations adopted pursuant to this chapter, provided that no life safety risks are involved, as determined by the department. In determining whether any life safety risks are involved, the department shall require completion of all applicable fire clearances and criminal record clearances as otherwise required by the department's rules and regulations. The provisional license shall expire six months from the date of issuance, or at any earlier time as the department may determine, and may not be renewed. However, the department may extend the term of a provisional license for an additional six months at time of application, if it is determined that more than six months will be required to achieve full compliance with licensing standards due to circumstances beyond the control of the applicant, provided all other requirements for a license have been met.

(b) This section shall not apply to foster family homes.

(Amended by Stats. 2016, Ch. 612, Sec. 37. (AB 1997) Effective January 1, 2017.)

1526.

Immediately upon the denial of any application for a license or for a special permit, the state department shall notify the applicant in writing. Within 15 days after the state department mails the notice, the applicant may present his written petition for a hearing to the state department. Upon receipt by the state department of the petition in proper form, such petition shall be set for hearing. The proceedings shall be conducted in accordance with Chapter 5 (commencing with Section 11500) of Part 1 of Division 3 of Title 2 of the Government Code, and the state department has all the powers granted therein.

(Amended by Stats. 1976, Ch. 597.)

1526.5.

(a) Within 90 days after a facility accepts its first client for placement following the issuance of a license or special permit pursuant to Section 1525, the department shall inspect the facility. The licensee shall, within five business days after accepting its first client for placement, notify the department that the facility has commenced operating. Foster family homes are exempt from the provisions of this subdivision.

(b) The inspection required by subdivision (a) shall be conducted to evaluate compliance with rules and regulations and to assess the facility's continuing ability to meet regulatory requirements. The department may take appropriate remedial action as authorized by this chapter.

(Amended by Stats. 2006, Ch. 902, Sec. 7. Effective January 1, 2007.)

1526.75.

(a) It is the intent of the Legislature to maintain quality resources for children needing placement away from their families. If, during a periodic inspection or an inspection pursuant to Section 1526.5, a facility is found out of compliance with one or more of the licensing standards of the department, the department shall, unless an ongoing investigation precludes it, advise the provider of the noncompliance as soon as possible. The provider shall be given the opportunity to correct the deficiency.

(b) The department shall implement a procedure whereby citations for noncompliance may be appealed and reviewed.

(c) Nothing in this section shall preclude the department from taking any action it may deem necessary to ensure the safety of children and adults placed in any facility.

(Added by Stats. 1987, Ch. 1212, Sec. 2.)

1526.8.

(a) It is the intent of the Legislature that the department develop modified staffing levels and requirements for crisis nurseries, provided that the health, safety, and well-being of the children in care are protected and maintained.

(1) All caregivers shall be certified in pediatric cardiopulmonary resuscitation (CPR) and pediatric first aid. Certification shall be demonstrated by current and valid pediatric CPR and pediatric first aid cards issued by the American Red Cross, the American Heart Association, by a training program that has been approved by the Emergency Medical Services Authority pursuant to Section 1797.191, or from an accredited college or university.

(2) The licensee shall develop, maintain, and implement a written staff training plan for the orientation, continuing education, on-the-job training and development, supervision, and evaluation of all lead caregivers, caregivers, and volunteers. The licensee shall incorporate the training plan in the crisis nursery plan of operation.

(3) The licensee shall designate at least one lead caregiver to be present at the crisis nursery at all times when children are present. The lead caregiver shall have one of the following education and experience qualifications:

(A) Completion of 12 postsecondary semester units or equivalent quarter units, with a passing grade, as determined by the institution, in classes with a focus on early childhood education, child development, or child health at an accredited college or university, as determined by the department, and six months of work experience in a licensed group home, licensed infant care center, or comparable group child care program or family day care. At least three semester units, or equivalent quarter units, or equivalent experience shall include coursework or experience in the care of infants.

(B) A current and valid Child Development Associate (CDA) credential, with the appropriate age level endorsement issued by the CDA National Credentialing Program, and at least six months of on-the-job training or work experience in a licensed child care center or comparable group child care program.

(C) A current and valid Child Development Associate Teacher Permit issued by the California Commission on Teacher Credentialing pursuant to Sections 80105 to 80116, inclusive, of Title 5 of the California Code of Regulations.

(4) Lead caregivers shall have a minimum of 24 hours of training and orientation before working with children. One year experience in a supervisory position in a child care or group care facility may substitute for 16 hours of training and orientation. The written staff training plan shall require the lead caregiver to receive and document a minimum of 20 hours of annual training directly related to the functions of his or her position.

(5) Caregiver staff shall complete a minimum of 24 hours of initial training within the first 90 days of employment. Eight hours of training shall be completed before the caregiver staff are responsible for children, left alone with children, and counted in the staff-to-child ratios described in subdivision (c). A maximum of four hours of training may be satisfied by job shadowing.

(b) The department shall allow the use of fully trained and qualified volunteers as caregivers in a crisis nursery, subject to the following conditions:

(1) Volunteers shall be fingerprinted for the purpose of conducting a criminal record review as specified in subdivision (b) of Section 1522.

(2) Volunteers shall complete a child abuse central index check as specified in Section 1522.1.

(3) Volunteers shall be in good physical health and be tested for tuberculosis not more than one year prior to, or seven days after, initial presence in the facility.

(4) Volunteers shall complete a minimum of 16 hours of training as specified in paragraphs (5) and (6).

(5) Prior to assuming the duties and responsibilities of a crisis caregiver or being counted in the staff-to-child ratio, volunteers shall complete at least five hours of initial training divided as follows:

(A) Two hours of crisis nursery job shadowing.

(B) One hour of review of community care licensing regulations.

(C) Two hours of review of the crisis nursery program, including the facility mission statement, goals and objectives, child guidance techniques, and special needs of the client population they serve.

(6) Within 90 days, volunteers who are included in the staff-to-child ratios shall do both of the following:

(A) Acquire a certification in pediatric first aid and pediatric cardiopulmonary resuscitation.

(B) Complete at least 11 hours of training covering child care health and safety issues, trauma informed care, the importance of family and sibling relationships, temperaments of children, self-regulation skills and techniques, and program child guidance techniques.

(7) Volunteers who meet the requirements of paragraphs (1), (2), and (3), but who have not completed the training specified in paragraph (4), (5), or (6) may assist a fully trained and qualified staff person in performing child care duties. However, these volunteers shall not be left alone with children, shall always be under the direct supervision and observation of a fully trained and qualified staff person, and shall not be counted in meeting the minimum staff-to-child ratio requirements.

(c) The department shall allow the use of fully trained and qualified volunteers to be counted in the staff-to-child ratio in a crisis nursery subject to the following conditions:

(1) The volunteers have fulfilled the requirements in paragraphs (1) to (6), inclusive, of subdivision (b).

(2) There shall be at least one fully qualified and employed staff person on site at all times.

(3) (A) There shall be at least one employed staff person or volunteer caregiver for each group of six children, or fraction thereof, who are 18 months of age or older, and one

employed staff person or volunteer caregiver for each group of three children, or fraction thereof, who are under 18 months of age from 7 a.m. to 7 p.m.

(B) There shall be at least one employed staff person or volunteer caregiver for each group of six children, or fraction thereof, who are 18 months of age or older, and one employed staff person or volunteer caregiver for each group of four children, or fraction thereof, who are under 18 months of age from 7 p.m. to 7 a.m.

(C) There shall be at least one employed staff person present for every volunteer caregiver used by the crisis nursery for the purpose of meeting the minimum caregiver staffing requirements.

(D) The crisis nursery's plan of operation shall address how it will deal with unexpected circumstances related to staffing and ensure that additional caregivers are available when needed.

(d) There shall be at least one staff person or volunteer caregiver awake at all times from 7 p.m. to 7 a.m.

(e) (1) When a child has a health condition that requires prescription medication, the licensee shall ensure that the caregiver does all of the following:

(A) Assists children with the taking of the medication as needed.

(B) Ensures that instructions are followed as outlined by the appropriate medical professional.

(C) Stores the medication in accordance with the label instructions in the original container with the original unaltered label in a locked and safe area that is not accessible to children.

(D) Administers the medication as directed on the label and prescribed by the physician in writing.

(i) The licensee shall obtain, in writing, approval and instructions from the child's authorized representative for administration of the prescription medication for the child. This documentation shall be kept in the child's record.

(ii) The licensee shall not administer prescription medication to a child in accordance with instructions from the child's authorized representative if the authorized representative's instructions conflict with the physician's written instructions or the label directions as prescribed by the child's physician.

(2) Nonprescription medications may be administered without approval or instructions from the child's physician if all of the following conditions are met:

(A) Nonprescription medications shall be administered in accordance with the product label directions on the nonprescription medication container or containers.

(B) (i) For each nonprescription medication, the licensee shall obtain, in writing, approval and instructions from the child's authorized representative for administration of the nonprescription medication to the child. This documentation shall be kept in the child's record.

(ii) The licensee shall not administer nonprescription medication to a child in accordance with instructions from the child's authorized representative if the authorized representative's instructions conflict with the product label directions on the nonprescription medication container or containers.

(3) The licensee shall develop and implement a written plan to record the administration of the prescription and nonprescription medications and to inform the child's authorized representative daily, for crisis day services, and upon discharge for overnight care, when the medications have been given.

(4) When no longer needed by the child, or when the child is removed or discharged from the crisis nursery, all medications shall be returned to the child's authorized representative or disposed of after an attempt to reach the authorized representative.

(Amended by Stats. 2014, Ch. 735, Sec. 3. (AB 2228) Effective January 1, 2015.)

ARTICLE 2.5. Foster Home and Small Family Home Insurance Fund [1527 - 1527.8]

(Article 2.5 added by Stats. 1986, Ch. 1330, Sec. 3.)

1527.

As used in this article:

(a) "Aircraft" includes, but is not limited to, any airplane, glider, or hot air balloon.

(b) "Bodily injury" means any bodily injury, sickness, or disease sustained by any person including death at any time resulting therefrom.

(c) "Foster child" means a person under 19 years of age who has been placed in the care and supervision of licensed foster parents or, on and after January 1, 2019, a resource family, as defined in Section 16519.5 of the Welfare and Institutions Code.

(d) "Foster parent" means the person, and including his or her spouse if the spouse is a resident of the same household, providing care, custody, and control of a foster child in a licensed foster family home or licensed small family home, as defined in Section 1502, or, on and after January 1, 2019, a resource family, as defined in Section 16519.5 of the Welfare and Institutions Code.

(e) "Occurrence" means an accident, including continuous or repeated exposure to conditions, which results in bodily injury or personal injury neither expected nor intended by the foster parent. Multiple incidents of a general course of conduct shall be considered one occurrence, regardless of the period of time during which the acts transpired.

(f) "Motor vehicle" means an automobile, motorcycle, moped, midget automobile, including the type commonly referred to as a kart, go-kart, speedmobile, or by a comparable name whether commercially built or otherwise, trailer or semitrailer designed for travel on public roads, including any machinery or apparatus attached thereto, or snowmobile.

(g) "Personal injury" means any injury to the feelings or reputation of any person or organization arising out of libel, slander, defamation, or disparagement, wrongful eviction, or entry.

(h) "Property damage" means any physical injury to, or destruction of, tangible property, including the loss of use thereof at any time resulting therefrom.

(i) "Watercraft" includes, but is not limited to, any boat, ship, raft, or canoe, whether motorized or not.

(Amended by Stats. 2018, Ch. 910, Sec. 11. (AB 1930) Effective January 1, 2019.)

1527.1.

There is hereby established the Foster Family Home and Small Family Home Insurance Fund within the State Department of Social Services. The fund shall consist of all moneys appropriated by the Legislature. The department may contract with another state agency to set up and operate the fund and perform other administrative functions that may be necessary to carry out the intentions of this article. The purpose of the fund is to pay, on behalf of foster family homes and small family homes, as defined in Section 1502, and, on or after January 1, 2019, resource families, as defined in Section 16519.5 of the Welfare and Institutions Code, claims of foster children, their parents, guardians, or guardians ad litem resulting from occurrences peculiar to the foster care relationship and the provision of foster care services. The fund may sue and be sued.

(Amended by Stats. 2018, Ch. 910, Sec. 12. (AB 1930) Effective January 1, 2019.)

1527.2.

The fund, subject to this article, shall pay, on behalf of foster family homes, small family homes, and, on and after January 1, 2019, resource families, any claims of foster children, their parents, guardians, or guardians ad litem for damages arising from, and peculiar to, the foster care relationship and the provision of foster care services, or shall reimburse foster family homes, small family homes, and resource families for those damages.

(Amended by Stats. 2018, Ch. 910, Sec. 13. (AB 1930) Effective January 1, 2019.)

1527.3.

The fund shall not be liable for any of the following:

(a) Any loss arising out of a dishonest, fraudulent, criminal, or intentional act of a foster parent.

(b) Any occurrence that does not arise from the foster-care relationship.

(c) Any bodily injury arising out of the operation or use of any motor vehicle, aircraft, or watercraft owned or operated by, or rented or loaned to, any foster parent.

(d) Any loss arising out of licentious, immoral, or sexual behavior on the part of a foster parent intended to lead to, or culminating in, any sexual act.

(e) Any allegation of alienation of affection against a foster parent.

(f) Any loss or damage arising out of occurrences prior to October 1, 1986.

(g) Exemplary damages.

(h) Any liability of a foster parent that is uninsured due solely to the foster parent's failure to obtain insurance specified in Section 676.7 of the Insurance Code. Nothing in this subdivision shall be construed to expand the liability of the fund with respect to insured foster parents.

(Amended by Stats. 2013, Ch. 494, Sec. 2. (SB 522) Effective January 1, 2014.)

1527.35.

The fund shall not be liable for any loss arising out of the dishonest, fraudulent, criminal, or intentional act of any person if the date of the loss is prior to July 1, 2013.

(Added by Stats. 2013, Ch. 494, Sec. 3. (SB 522) Effective January 1, 2014.)

1527.4.

Notwithstanding any other provision of this article, the fund shall not be liable for damages in excess of three hundred thousand dollars ($300,000) for any single foster family home, small family home, or, on and after January 1, 2019, resource family for all claims arising due to one or more occurrences during any consecutive 12-month period. The fund shall be liable only once for damages arising from one occurrence.

(Amended by Stats. 2018, Ch. 910, Sec. 14. (AB 1930) Effective January 1, 2019.)

1527.5.

The fund shall be liable, if a claim is approved, to pay on behalf of each licensed foster family home, small family home, or, on or after January 1, 2019, resource family, all sums which the foster family home, small family home, or resource family is obligated to pay as a result of a valid claim of bodily injury or personal injury arising out of the activities of a foster parent or foster parents, which occurs while the foster child resides in the foster family home, small family home, or resource family. Claims specified in this section of a foster child or a parent, guardian, or guardian ad litem of a foster child shall be the sole responsibility of the fund.

(Amended by Stats. 2018, Ch. 910, Sec. 15. (AB 1930) Effective January 1, 2019.)

1527.6.

(a) A claim against the fund shall be filed with the fund in accordance with claims procedures and on forms prescribed by the State Department of Social Services or its designated contract agency.

(b) A claim against the fund filed by a foster parent or a third party shall be submitted to the fund within the applicable period of limitations for the appropriate civil action underlying the claim, subject to subdivision (a) of Section 352 of the Code of Civil Procedure as that section applies to a minor. If a claim is not submitted to the fund within the applicable time, there shall be no recourse against the fund.

(c) (1) The department shall approve or reject a claim within 180 days after it is presented.

(2) The department or an agency designated pursuant to Section 1527.1 shall notify a claimant of the decision to approve or reject a claim within 15 days of the decision.

(d) (1) A person shall not bring a civil action against a foster parent for which the fund is liable unless that person has first filed a claim against the fund and the claim has been rejected, or the claim has been filed, approved, and paid, and damages in excess of the payment are claimed.

(2) An applicable statute of limitations for a cause of action that arises out of the same occurrence for which a claim has been filed with the fund shall be tolled from the date the claim against the fund has been filed until the date the department, or an agency designated pursuant to Section 1527.1, has notified the person that the department has either rejected or approved the claim.
(Amended by Stats. 2012, Ch. 642, Sec. 1. (AB 2019) Effective January 1, 2013.)
1527.7.
All processing of decisions and reports, payment of claims, and other administrative actions relating to the fund shall be conducted by the State Department of Social Services or its designated contract agency.
(Added by Stats. 1986, Ch. 1330, Sec. 3. Effective September 29, 1986.)
1527.8.
The fund established pursuant to Section 1527.1 shall be maintained at an adequate level to meet anticipated liabilities.
(Amended by Stats. 2012, Ch. 642, Sec. 2. (AB 2019) Effective January 1, 2013.)

ARTICLE 2.7. Foster Parent Training [1529.1 - 1529.2]
(Article 2.7 added by Stats. 1988, Ch. 1142, Sec. 7.)
1529.1.
It is the intent of the Legislature that persons desiring to become, or to continue being, foster parents shall receive training in order to assist them in being effective substitute caregivers and to enhance the safety and growth of children placed with them. There is a need to develop a basic curriculum, a program for continuing education, and specialized training for parents caring for children with unique needs.
(Added by Stats. 1988, Ch. 1142, Sec. 7. Effective September 22, 1988.)
1529.2.
(a) It is the intent of the Legislature that all foster parents have the necessary knowledge, skills, and abilities to support the safety, permanency, and well-being of children in foster care. Initial and ongoing preparation and training of foster parents should support the foster parent's role in parenting vulnerable children, youth, and young adults, including supporting the children's connection with their families. Their training should be ongoing in order to provide foster parents with information on new practices and requirements and other helpful topics within the child welfare and probation systems and may be offered in a classroom setting, online, or individually.
(b) A licensed or certified foster parent shall complete a minimum of eight training hours annually, a portion of which shall be from one or more of the following topics, as prescribed by the department, pursuant to subdivision (a):
(1) Age-appropriate child and adolescent development.
(2) Health issues in foster care, including, but not limited to, the authorization, uses, risks, benefits, assistance with self-administration, oversight, and monitoring of psychotropic or other medications, and trauma, mental health, and substance use disorder treatments for children in foster care under the jurisdiction of the juvenile court, including how to access those treatments. Health issues in foster care, including, but not limited to, the authorization, uses, risks, benefits, assistance with self-administration, oversight, and monitoring of psychotropic or other medications, and trauma, mental health, and substance use disorder treatments for children in foster care under the jurisdiction of the juvenile court, including how to access those treatments, as the information is also described in subdivision (d) of Section 16501.4 of the Welfare and Institutions Code.
(3) Positive discipline and the importance of self-esteem.
(4) Preparation of children and youth for a successful transition to adulthood.
(5) The right of a foster child to have fair and equal access to all available services, placement, care, treatment, and benefits, and to not be subjected to discrimination or harassment on the basis of actual or perceived race, ethnic group identification, ancestry, national origin, color, religion, sex, sexual orientation, gender identity, mental or physical disability, or HIV status.
(6) Instruction on cultural competency and sensitivity and related best practices for providing adequate care for children across diverse ethnic and racial backgrounds, as well as children identifying as lesbian, gay, bisexual, or transgender.
(7) The information described in subdivision (i) of Section 16521.5 of the Welfare and Institutions Code. The program may use the curriculum created pursuant to subdivision (h), and described in subdivision (i), of Section 16521.5 of the Welfare and Institutions Code.
(c) In addition to any training required by this section, a foster parent may be required to receive specialized training, as relevant, for the purpose of preparing the foster parent to meet the needs of a particular child in care. This training may include, but is not limited to, the following:
(1) Understanding how to use best practices for providing care and supervision to commercially sexually exploited children.
(2) Understanding cultural needs of children, including, but not limited to, cultural competency and sensitivity and related best practices for providing adequate care to children across diverse ethnic and racial backgrounds, as well as children identifying as lesbian, gay, bisexual, or transgender.
(3) Understanding the requirements and best practices regarding psychotropic medications, including, but not limited to, court authorization, benefits, uses, side effects, interactions, assistance with self-administration, misuse, documentation, storage, and metabolic monitoring of children prescribed psychotropic medications.
(4) Understanding the federal Indian Child Welfare Act (25 U.S.C. Sec. 1901 et seq.), its historical significance, the rights of children covered by the act, and the best interests of Indian children, including the role of the caregiver in supporting culturally appropriate,

child-centered practices that respect Native American history, culture, retention of tribal membership, and connection to the tribal community and traditions.
(5) Understanding how to use best practices for providing care and supervision to nonminor dependents.
(6) Understanding how to use best practices for providing care and supervision to children with special health care needs.
(d) No child shall be placed with a foster parent unless each foster parent in the home meets the requirements of this section.
(e) (1) Upon the request of the licensed or certified foster parent for a hardship waiver from the annual training requirement or a request for an extension of the deadline, the county may, at its option, on a case-by-case basis, waive the training requirement or extend any established deadline for a period not to exceed one year, if the training requirement presents a severe and unavoidable obstacle to continuing as a foster parent.
(2) Obstacles for which a county may grant a hardship waiver or extension are:
(A) Lack of access to training due to the cost or travel required or lack of child care to participate in the training, when online resources are not available.
(B) Family emergency.
(3) Before a waiver or extension may be granted, the licensed or certified foster parent should explore the opportunity of receiving training online or by video or written materials.
(f) (1) Foster parent training may be obtained through sources that include, but are not necessarily limited to, community colleges, counties, hospitals, foster parent associations, the California State Foster Parent Association's conference, online resources, adult schools, and certified foster parent instructors.
(2) In addition to the foster parent training provided by community colleges, foster family agencies shall provide a program of training for their certified foster families.
(g) (1) Training certificates shall be submitted to the appropriate licensing or foster family agency.
(2) Upon completion, a licensed or certified parent shall submit a certificate of completion for the annual training requirements.
(h) Nothing in this section shall preclude a county or a foster family agency from requiring foster parent training in excess of the requirements in this section.
(i) (1) Notwithstanding any other law, contracts or grants awarded for purposes of this section shall be exempt from the personal services contracting requirements of Article 4 (commencing with Section 19130) of Chapter 5 of Part 2 of Division 5 of Title 2 of the Government Code.
(2) Notwithstanding any other law, contracts or grants awarded for purposes of this section shall be exempt from the Public Contract Code and the State Contracting Manual, and shall not be subject to the approval of the Department of General Services.
(j) This section shall become operative on January 1, 2017.
(k) This section shall remain in effect only until January 1, 2020, and as of that date is repealed, unless a later enacted statute that is enacted before January 1, 2020, deletes or extends that date.
(Amended by Stats. 2017, Ch. 732, Sec. 23. (AB 404) Effective January 1, 2018. Repealed as of January 1, 2020, by its own provisions.)

ARTICLE 3. Regulations [1530 - 1539]
(Article 3 added by Stats. 1973, Ch. 1203.)
1530.
The state department shall adopt, amend, or repeal, in accordance with Chapter 4.5 (commencing with Section 11371) of Part 1 of Division 3 of Title 2 of the Government Code, such reasonable rules, regulations, and standards as may be necessary or proper to carry out the purposes and intent of this chapter and to enable the state department to exercise the powers and perform the duties conferred upon it by this chapter, not inconsistent with any of the provisions of any statute of this state.
Such regulations shall designate separate categories of licensure under which community care facilities shall be licensed pursuant to this chapter, which shall include a separate license category for residential care facilities for the elderly. Such regulations shall also designate the specialized services which community care facilities may be approved to provide pursuant to this chapter.
(Amended by Stats. 1978, Ch. 288.)
1530.1.
(a) The department shall adopt regulations, in consultation with providers, consumers, and other interested parties, to combine adult day care and adult day support centers licensing categories into one category, which shall be designated adult day programs.
(b) The consolidated regulations shall take into account the diversity of consumers and their caregivers, and the role of licensing in promoting consumer choice, health and safety, independence, and inclusion in the community.
(c) The department shall also take into account the diversity of existing programs designed to meet unique consumer needs, including, but not limited to, programs serving elders with cognitive or physical impairments, non-facility-based programs serving persons with developmental disabilities, respite-only programs, and other programs serving a unique population.
(Added by Stats. 2002, Ch. 773, Sec. 5. Effective January 1, 2003.)
1530.3.
The director shall report to the Legislature during the 2007–08 budget hearings on the progress of the department's children's residential regulation review workgroup. The report shall include all of the following:
(a) A summary of the activities of the workgroup up to the date of the report.
(b) The timeline for completion of the workgroup's activities.

(c) Any recommendations being considered for statutory, regulatory, and policy changes, and any workplan for the implementation of those recommendations.
(Added by Stats. 2006, Ch. 388, Sec. 2. Effective January 1, 2007.)
1530.5.
(a) The department, in establishing regulations, including provisions for periodic inspections, under this chapter for foster family homes and certified family homes of foster family agencies, shall consider these homes as private residences, and shall establish regulations for these foster family homes and certified family homes of foster family agencies as an entirely separate regulation package from regulations for all other community care facilities. Certified family homes of foster family agencies and foster family homes shall not be subject to civil penalties pursuant to this chapter, except for penalties imposed pursuant to Sections 1522 and 1547. The department, in adopting and amending regulations for these foster family homes and certified family homes of foster family agencies, shall consult with foster parent and foster family agency organizations in order to ensure compliance with the requirement of this section.
(b) This section shall not apply to small family homes or foster family agencies as defined in Section 1502.
(Amended by Stats. 2012, Ch. 663, Sec. 3. (SB 1319) Effective January 1, 2013.)
1530.6.
(a) Notwithstanding any other law, persons licensed or approved pursuant to this chapter to provide residential foster care to a child either placed with them pursuant to order of the juvenile court or voluntarily placed with them by the person or persons having legal custody of the child, may give the same legal consent for that child as a parent except for the following:
(1) Marriage.
(2) Entry into the Armed Forces.
(3) Medical and dental treatment, except that consent may be given for ordinary medical and dental treatment for the child, including, but not limited to, immunizations, physical examinations, and X-rays.
(4) Educational decisions that are required to be made by a child's educational rights holder.
(5) If the child is voluntarily placed by the parent or parents, those items as are agreed to in writing by the parties to the placement.
(b) To this effect, the department shall prescribe rules and regulations to carry out the intent of this section.
(c) This section does not apply to any situation in which a juvenile court order expressly reserves the right to consent to those activities to the court.
(Amended by Stats. 2017, Ch. 732, Sec. 24. (AB 404) Effective January 1, 2018.)
1530.7.
(a) A licensed children's residential facility shall maintain a smoke-free environment in the facility.
(b) A person who is licensed, certified, or approved pursuant to this chapter to provide residential care in a foster family home, certified family home, or resource family home shall not smoke a tobacco product or permit any other person to smoke a tobacco product inside the home, and, when the child is present, on the outdoor grounds of the home.
(c) A person who is licensed, certified, or approved pursuant to this chapter to provide residential foster care shall not smoke a tobacco product in any motor vehicle that is regularly used to transport a child.
(d) For purposes of this section, "smoke" has the same meaning as in subdivision (c) of Section 22950.5 of the Business and Professions Code.
(e) For purposes of this section, "tobacco product" means a product or device as defined in subdivision (d) of Section 22950.5 of the Business and Professions Code.
(Amended by Stats. 2017, Ch. 732, Sec. 25. (AB 404) Effective January 1, 2018.)
1530.8.
(a) (1) The department shall adopt regulations for community care facilities licensed as group homes, and for temporary shelter care facilities as defined in subdivision (c), that care for dependent children, children placed by a regional center, or voluntary placements, who are younger than six years of age. The department shall adopt regulations that apply to short-term residential therapeutic programs that care for children younger than six years of age. The regulations shall include the standards set forth in subdivision (c) of Section 11467.1 of the Welfare and Institutions Code.
(2) The department shall adopt regulations under this section that apply to minor parent programs serving children younger than six years of age who reside in a group home with a minor parent who is the primary caregiver of the child. The department shall adopt regulations under this section that apply to short-term residential therapeutic programs that provide minor parent programs serving children younger than six years of age.
(3) To the extent that the department determines they are necessary, the department shall adopt regulations under this section that apply to group homes or short-term residential therapeutic programs that care for dependent children who are 6 to 12 years of age, inclusive. In order to determine whether such regulations are necessary, and what any resulting standards should include, the department shall consult with interested parties that include, but are not limited to, representatives of current and former foster youth, advocates for children in foster care, county welfare and mental health directors, chief probation officers, representatives of care providers, experts in child development, and representatives of the Legislature. The standards may provide normative guidelines differentiated by the needs specific to children in varying age ranges that fall between 6 and 12 years of age, inclusive. Prior to adopting regulations, the department shall submit for public comment, by July 1, 2017, any proposed regulations.

(b) The regulations shall include physical environment standards, including staffing and health and safety requirements, that meet or exceed state child care standards under Title 5 and Title 22 of the California Code of Regulations.
(c) For purposes of this section, a "temporary shelter care facility" means any residential facility that meets all of the following requirements:
(1) It is owned and operated by the county or on behalf of a county by a private, nonprofit agency.
(2) It is a 24-hour facility that provides no more than 10 calendar days of residential care and supervision for children who have been removed from their homes as a result of abuse or neglect, as defined in Section 300 of the Welfare and Institutions Code, or both.
(d) (1) The department may license a temporary shelter care facility pursuant to this chapter on or after January 1, 2016. A temporary shelter care license may be issued only to a county operating a licensed group home, or to an agency on behalf of a county, as of January 1, 2016.
(2) The department shall consult with counties that operate these shelters as licensed group homes to develop a transition plan for the development of temporary shelter care facilities to address the unique circumstances and needs of the populations they serve, while remaining consistent with the principles of the act that added this subdivision.
(3) These transition plans shall describe circumstances under which children will be admitted for a period in excess of 24 hours and reflect necessary staffing levels or staffing transitions.
(e) (1) A group home license issued to a county will be forfeited by operation of law upon receipt of a license to operate a temporary shelter care facility as described in Section 11462.022 of the Welfare and Institutions Code.
(2) Nothing in this subdivision shall preclude a county from applying for and being licensed as a short-term residential therapeutic program pursuant to Section 1562.01 or a runaway and homeless youth shelter pursuant to Section 1502.35, or a foster family agency as authorized by subdivision (b) of Section 11462.02 of the Welfare and Institutions Code.
(Amended by Stats. 2017, Ch. 732, Sec. 26. (AB 404) Effective January 1, 2018.)
1530.9.
(a) The department shall, with the advice and assistance of the State Department of Health Care Services, counties, parent and children's advocacy groups, and group home providers, adopt regulations for the licensing of licensed community treatment facilities at the earliest possible date.
(b) The regulations adopted pursuant to this section shall specify requirements for facility operation and maintenance.
(c) Program certification and standards enforcement shall be the responsibility of the State Department of Health Care Services, pursuant to Section 4094 of the Welfare and Institutions Code. The State Department of Social Services shall not issue a community treatment facility license unless the applicant has obtained certification of compliance from the State Department of Health Care Services.
(Amended by Stats. 2012, Ch. 34, Sec. 22. (SB 1009) Effective June 27, 2012.)
1530.91.
(a) Except as provided in subdivision (b) any care provider that provides foster care for children pursuant to this chapter shall provide each schoolage child and his or her authorized representative, as defined in regulations adopted by the department, who is placed in foster care, with an age and developmentally appropriate orientation that includes an explanation of the rights of the child, as specified in Section 16001.9 of the Welfare and Institutions Code, and addresses the child's questions and concerns.
(b) Any facility licensed to provide foster care for six or more children pursuant to this chapter shall post a listing of a foster child's rights specified in Section 16001.9 of the Welfare and Institutions Code. The office of the State Foster Care Ombudsperson shall design posters and provide the posters to each facility subject to this subdivision. The posters shall include the telephone number of the State Foster Care Ombudsperson.
(Added by Stats. 2001, Ch. 683, Sec. 1.5. Effective January 1, 2002.)
1531.
The regulations for a license shall prescribe standards of safety and sanitation for the physical plant and standards for basic personal care, supervision, and services based upon the category of licensure.
The regulations for a special permit shall prescribe standards for the quality of specialized services, including, but not limited to, staffing with duly qualified personnel which take into account the age, physical and mental capabilities, and the needs of the persons to be served.
The state department's regulations shall allow for the development of new and innovative community programs.
(Added by Stats. 1973, Ch. 1203.)
1531.1.
(a) A residential facility licensed as an adult residential facility, group home, short-term residential therapeutic program, small family home, foster family home, or a family home certified by a foster family agency may install and utilize delayed egress devices of the time delay type.
(b) As used in this section, "delayed egress device" means a device that precludes the use of exits for a predetermined period of time. These devices shall not delay any resident's departure from the facility for longer than 30 seconds.
(c) Within the 30 seconds of delay, facility staff may attempt to redirect a resident who attempts to leave the facility.
(d) Any person accepted by a residential facility or family home certified by a foster family agency utilizing delayed egress devices shall meet all of the following conditions:

(1) The person shall have a developmental disability as defined in Section 4512 of the Welfare and Institutions Code.

(2) The person shall be receiving services and case management from a regional center under the Lanterman Developmental Disabilities Services Act (Division 4.5 (commencing with Section 4500) of the Welfare and Institutions Code).

(3) An interdisciplinary team, through the individual program plan (IPP) process pursuant to Section 4646.5 of the Welfare and Institutions Code, shall have determined that the person lacks hazard awareness or impulse control and requires the level of supervision afforded by a facility equipped with delayed egress devices, and that but for this placement, the person would be at risk of admission to, or would have no option but to remain in, a more restrictive state hospital or state developmental center placement.

(e) The facility shall be subject to all fire and building codes, regulations, and standards applicable to residential care facilities for the elderly utilizing delayed egress devices, and shall receive approval by the county or city fire department, the local fire prevention district, or the State Fire Marshal for the installed delayed egress devices.

(f) The facility shall provide staff training regarding the use and operation of the egress control devices utilized by the facility, protection of residents' personal rights, lack of hazard awareness and impulse control behavior, and emergency evacuation procedures.

(g) The facility shall develop a plan of operation approved by the State Department of Social Services that includes a description of how the facility is to be equipped with egress control devices that are consistent with regulations adopted by the State Fire Marshal pursuant to Section 13143.

(h) The plan shall include, but shall not be limited to, all of the following:

(1) A description of how the facility will provide training for staff regarding the use and operation of the egress control devices utilized by the facility.

(2) A description of how the facility will ensure the protection of the residents' personal rights consistent with Sections 4502, 4503, and 4504 of the Welfare and Institutions Code.

(3) A description of how the facility will manage the person's lack of hazard awareness and impulse control behavior.

(4) A description of the facility's emergency evacuation procedures.

(i) Delayed egress devices shall not substitute for adequate staff. Except for facilities operating in accordance with Section 1531.15, the capacity of the facility shall not exceed six residents.

(j) Emergency fire and earthquake drills shall be conducted at least once every three months on each shift, and shall include all facility staff providing resident care and supervision on each shift.

(Amended by Stats. 2017, Ch. 561, Sec. 108. (AB 1516) Effective January 1, 2018.)

1531.15.

(a) A licensee of an adult residential facility, short-term residential therapeutic program, or group home for no more than six residents, except for the larger facilities provided for in paragraph (1) of subdivision (k), that is utilizing delayed egress devices pursuant to Section 1531.1, may install and utilize secured perimeters in accordance with the provisions of this section.

(b) As used in this section, "secured perimeters" means fences that meet the requirements prescribed by this section.

(c) Only individuals meeting all of the following conditions may be admitted to or reside in a facility described in subdivision (a) utilizing secured perimeters:

(1) The person shall have a developmental disability as defined in Section 4512 of the Welfare and Institutions Code.

(2) The person shall be receiving services and case management from a regional center under the Lanterman Developmental Disabilities Services Act (Division 4.5 (commencing with Section 4500) of the Welfare and Institutions Code).

(3) (A) The person shall be 14 years of age or older, except as specified in subparagraph (B).

(B) Notwithstanding subparagraph (A), a child who is at least 10 years of age and less than 14 years of age may be placed in a licensed group home described in subdivision (a) using secured perimeters only if both of the following occur:

(i) A comprehensive assessment is conducted and an individual program plan meeting is convened to determine the services and supports needed for the child to receive services in a less restrictive, unlocked residential setting in California, and the regional center requests assistance from the State Department of Developmental Services' statewide specialized resource service to identify options to serve the child in a less restrictive, unlocked residential setting in California.

(ii) The regional center requests placement of the child in a licensed group home described in subdivision (a) using secured perimeters on the basis that the placement is necessary to prevent out-of-state placement or placement in a more restrictive, locked residential setting such as a developmental center, institution for mental disease or psychiatric facility, and the State Department of Developmental Services approves the request.

(4) The person is not a foster child under the jurisdiction of the juvenile court pursuant to Section 300, 450, 601, or 602 of the Welfare and Institutions Code.

(5) (A) An interdisciplinary team, through the individual program plan (IPP) process pursuant to Section 4646.5 of the Welfare and Institutions Code, shall have determined the person lacks hazard awareness or impulse control and, for his or her safety and security, requires the level of supervision afforded by a facility equipped with secured perimeters, and, but for this placement, the person would be at risk of admission to, or would have no option but to remain in, a more restrictive placement. The individual program planning team shall convene every 90 days after admission to determine and

document the continued appropriateness of the current placement and progress in implementing the transition plan.

(B) The clients' rights advocate for the regional center shall be notified of the proposed admission and the individual program plan meeting and may participate in the individual program plan meeting unless the consumer objects on his or her own behalf.

(d) The licensee shall be subject to all applicable fire and building codes, regulations, and standards, and shall receive approval by the county or city fire department, the local fire prevention district, or the State Fire Marshal for the installed secured perimeters.

(e) The licensee shall provide staff training regarding the use and operation of the secured perimeters, protection of residents' personal rights, lack of hazard awareness and impulse control behavior, and emergency evacuation procedures.

(f) The licensee shall revise its facility plan of operation. These revisions shall first be approved by the State Department of Developmental Services. The plan of operation shall not be approved by the State Department of Social Services unless the licensee provides certification that the plan was approved by the State Department of Developmental Services. The plan shall include, but not be limited to, all of the following:

(1) A description of how the facility is to be equipped with secured perimeters that are consistent with regulations adopted by the State Fire Marshal pursuant to Section 13143.6.

(2) A description of how the facility will provide training for staff.

(3) A description of how the facility will ensure the protection of the residents' personal rights consistent with Sections 4502, 4503, and 4504 of the Welfare and Institutions Code, and any applicable personal rights provided in Title 22 of the California Code of Regulations.

(4) A description of how the facility will manage residents' lack of hazard awareness and impulse control behavior, which shall emphasize positive behavioral supports and techniques that are alternatives to physical, chemical, or mechanical restraints, or seclusion.

(5) A description of the facility's emergency evacuation procedures.

(6) A description of how the facility will comply with applicable health and safety standards.

(g) Secured perimeters shall not substitute for adequate staff.

(h) Emergency fire and earthquake drills shall be conducted on each shift in accordance with existing licensing requirements, and shall include all facility staff providing resident care and supervision on each shift.

(i) Interior and exterior space shall be available on the facility premises to permit clients to move freely and safely.

(j) For the purpose of using secured perimeters, the licensee shall not be required to obtain a waiver or exception to a regulation that would otherwise prohibit the locking of a perimeter fence or gate.

(k) Except as provided in subdivision (k) of Section 4684.81 of the Welfare and Institutions Code, the state shall not authorize or fund more than a combined total of 150 beds statewide in facilities with secured perimeters under this section and under Section 1267.75. The department shall notify the appropriate fiscal and policy committees of the Legislature through the January and May budget estimates prior to authorizing an increase above a combined total of 100 beds statewide in facilities with secured perimeters under this section and under Section 1267.75.

(1) A minimum of 50 beds shall be available within programs designed for individuals who are designated incompetent to stand trial pursuant to Section 1370.1 of the Penal Code. These beds shall be within facilities that are exclusively used to provide care for individuals who are placed and participating in forensic competency training pursuant to Section 1370.1 of the Penal Code, except as provided in paragraph (2). No more than half of these facilities may have more than six beds and no facility may have more than 15 beds.

(2) When, in the joint determination of the regional center and the facility administrator, an individual would be most appropriately served in a specific program, regardless of whether the facility meets the criteria established in paragraph (1), individuals who are not similarly designated may be placed in the same facility. That placement may occur only when the individual's planning team determines that the placement and the facility plan of operation meet the individual's needs and that placement is not incompatible with the needs and safety of other facility residents.

(l) This section shall become operative only upon the publication in Title 17 of the California Code of Regulations of emergency regulations filed by the State Department of Developmental Services. These regulations shall be developed with stakeholders, including the State Department of Social Services, consumer advocates, and regional centers. The regulations shall establish program standards for homes that include secured perimeters, including requirements and timelines for the completion and updating of a comprehensive assessment of each consumer's needs, including the identification through the individual program plan process of the services and supports needed to transition the consumer to a less restrictive living arrangement, and a timeline for identifying or developing those services and supports. The regulations shall establish a statewide limit on the total number of beds in homes with secured perimeters. The adoption of these regulations shall be deemed to be an emergency and necessary for the immediate preservation of the public peace, health and safety, or general welfare. (Amended by Stats. 2016, Ch. 612, Sec. 41. (AB 1997) Effective January 1, 2017. Section conditionally operative as prescribed by its own provisions.)

1531.18.

A prospective applicant for licensure shall be notified at the time of the initial request for information regarding application for licensure that, prior to obtaining licensure, the facility shall secure and maintain a fire clearance approval from the local fire enforcing

agency or the State Fire Marshal, whichever has primary fire protection jurisdiction. The prospective applicant shall be notified of the provisions of Section 13235, relating to the fire safety clearance application. The prospective applicant for licensure shall be notified that the fire clearance shall be in accordance with state and local fire safety regulations. (Added by renumbering Section 1531.2 (as added by Stats. 1989, Ch. 993, Sec. 2) by Stats. 2015, Ch. 303, Sec. 271. (AB 731) Effective January 1, 2016.)
1531.2.
(a) Upon the filing by the department of emergency regulations with the Secretary of State, an adult day program, as defined in Division 6 of Title 22 of the California Code of Regulations, or Section 1502, that provides care and supervision for adults with Alzheimer's disease and other dementias may install for the safety and security of these persons secured perimeter fences or egress control devices of the time-delay type on exit doors if they meet all of the requirements for additional safeguards required by those regulations. The initial adoption of new emergency regulations on and after January 1, 1999, shall be deemed to be an emergency and necessary for the immediate preservation of the public peace, health and safety, or general welfare.
(b) As used in this section, "egress control device" means a device that precludes the use of exits for a predetermined period of time. An egress control device shall not delay any client's departure from the facility for longer than 30 seconds. Facility staff may attempt to redirect a client who attempts to leave the facility.
(c) A facility that installs an egress control device pursuant to this section shall meet all of the following requirements:
(1) The facility shall be subject to all fire and building codes, regulations, and standards applicable to adult day programs using egress control devices or secured perimeter fences and before using an egress control device shall receive a fire clearance from the fire authority having jurisdiction for the egress control devices.
(2) The facility shall require any client entering the facility to provide documentation of a diagnosis by a physician of Alzheimer's disease or other dementias, if such a diagnosis has been made. For purposes of this section, Alzheimer's disease shall include dementia and related disorders that increase the tendency to wander, decrease hazard awareness, and decrease the ability to communicate.
(3) The facility shall provide staff training regarding the use and operation of the egress control devices used by the facility, the protection of clients' personal rights, wandering behavior and acceptable methods of redirection, and emergency evacuation procedures for persons with dementia.
(4) All admissions to the facility shall continue to be voluntary on the part of the client or with the lawful consent of the client's conservator or a person who has the authority to act on behalf of the client. Persons who have the authority to act on behalf of a client may include the client's spouse, relative or relatives, or designated care giver or care givers.
(5) Any client entering a facility pursuant to this section who does not have a conservator or does not have a person with the authority to act on his or her behalf shall sign a statement of voluntary entry. The facility shall retain the original statement in the client's file at the facility.
(6) The use of egress control devices or secured perimeter fences shall not substitute for adequate staff. Staffing ratios shall at all times meet the requirements of applicable regulations.
(7) Emergency fire and earthquake drills shall be conducted at least once every three months, or more frequently as required by a county or city fire department or local fire prevention district. The drills shall include all facility staff and volunteers providing client care and supervision.
(8) The facility shall develop a plan of operation approved by the department that includes a description of how the facility is to be equipped with egress control devices that are consistent with regulations adopted by the State Fire Marshal pursuant to Section 13143. The plan shall include, but not be limited to, all of the following:
(A) A description of how the facility will provide training to staff regarding the use and operation of the egress control device utilized by the facility.
(B) A description of how the facility will ensure the protection of the residents' personal rights consistent with Sections 4502, 4503, and 4504 of the Welfare and Institutions Code.
(C) A description of the facility's emergency evacuation procedures for persons with Alzheimer's disease and other dementias.
(d) This section does not require an adult day program to use secured perimeters or egress control devices in providing care for persons with Alzheimer's disease or other dementias.
(e) The department shall adopt regulations to implement this section in accordance with those provisions of the Administrative Procedure Act contained in Chapter 3.5 (commencing with Section 11340) of Part 1 of Division 3 of Title 2 of the Government Code.
(f) The State Fire Marshal may also adopt regulations to implement this section.
(Amended (as added by Stats. 1998, Ch. 729) by Stats. 2002, Ch. 773, Sec. 6. Effective January 1, 2003.)
1531.3.
The State Fire Marshal shall establish separate fire and panic safety standards and criteria for the evaluation of each category of license described in subdivision (a) of Section 1502. The State Fire Marshal shall take into consideration the characteristics of the persons served by each facility in establishing these standards and criteria.
(Added by Stats. 1992, Ch. 1288, Sec. 1. Effective January 1, 1993.)
1531.4.

On and after January 1, 1999, no security window bars may be installed or maintained on any community care facility unless the security window bars meet current state and local requirements, as applicable, for security window bars and safety release devices.
(Added by Stats. 1998, Ch. 343, Sec. 1. Effective January 1, 1999.)
1531.5.
(a) The State Department of Social Services shall not deny a license for a foster family home solely on the basis that the applicant is a parent who has administered corporal punishment not constituting child abuse, or will continue to administer such corporal punishment, to his or her own children.
(b) Nothing in this section shall be construed to prevent the state department from denying a license for a foster care home where the applicant has been found by the state department to have engaged in child abuse.
(c) As used in this section, "child abuse" means a situation in which a child suffers from any one or more of the following:
(1) Serious physical injury inflicted upon the child by other than accidental means.
(2) Harm by reason of intentional neglect or malnutrition or sexual abuse.
(3) Going without necessary and basic physical care.
(4) Willful mental injury, negligent treatment, or maltreatment of a child under the age of 18 by a person who is responsible for the child's welfare under circumstances which indicate that the child's health or welfare is harmed or threatened thereby, as determined in accordance with regulations prescribed by the Director of Social Services.
(5) Any condition which results in the violation of the rights of physical, mental, or moral welfare of a child or jeopardizes the child's present or future health, opportunity for normal development, or capacity for independence.
(d) Nothing in this section shall be construed to permit a foster parent to administer any corporal punishment to a foster child.
(Added by Stats. 1983, Ch. 521, Sec. 1.)
1531.6.
(a) Each group home, transitional shelter care facility, and short-term residential therapeutic program, as defined in Section 1502, and each temporary shelter care facility as defined in subdivision (c) of Section 1530.8, shall develop protocols that dictate the circumstances under which law enforcement may be contacted in response to the conduct of a child residing at the facility.
(b) The protocols shall, at a minimum, do all of the following:
(1) Employ trauma-informed and evidence-based deescalation and intervention techniques when staff is responding to the behavior of a child residing in the facility.
(2) Require staff to undergo annual training on the facility's protocols developed pursuant to this section.
(3) Specify that contacting law enforcement shall only be used as a last resort once all other deescalation and intervention techniques have been exhausted, and only upon approval of a staff supervisor.
(4) Address contacting law enforcement in an emergency situation if there is an immediate risk of serious harm to a child or others.
(5) Identify and describe collaborative relationships with community-based service organizations that provide culturally relevant and trauma-informed services to youth served by the facility to prevent, or as an alternative to, arrest, detention, and incarceration for system-impacted youth.
(c) This section does not prohibit a facility or a facility employee from contacting law enforcement in an instance in which the facility or a facility employee is required by law to report an incident, which includes, but is not limited to, mandated reporting of child abuse, or if the child is missing or has run away.
(d) Each group home, transitional shelter care facility, short-term residential therapeutic program, and temporary shelter care facility shall include the protocols developed pursuant to this section in its emergency intervention plan and its plan of operation.
(e) This section shall become inoperative on July 1, 2023, and, as of January 1, 2024, is repealed.
(Added by Stats. 2018, Ch. 35, Sec. 6. (AB 1811) Effective June 27, 2018. Inoperative July 1, 2023. Repealed as of January 1, 2024, by its own provisions.)
1532.
The Committee on Community Care Facilities of the State Social Services Advisory Board shall advise the director regarding regulations, policy, and administrative practices pertaining to community care facilities. The committee shall review proposed regulations for community care facilities, and submit its written comments to the director prior to the adoption of these regulations.
The committee shall be solely advisory in character and shall not be delegated any administrative authority or responsibility. Committee members shall be selected from concerned interests, including representatives of professional associations, providers and employees of care and services, and consumers of community care facility services.
(Amended by Stats. 1984, Ch. 1143, Sec. 3.)
1533.
(a) Except as otherwise provided in this section, any duly authorized officer, employee, or agent of the State Department of Social Services may, upon presentation of proper identification, enter and inspect any place providing personal care, supervision, and services at any time, with or without advance notice, to secure compliance with, or to prevent a violation of, any provision of this chapter.
(b) (1) Foster family homes that are considered private residences for the purposes of Section 1530.5 shall not be subject to inspection by the department or its officers without advance notice, except in response to a complaint, a plan of correction, or as set forth in Section 1534. The complaint inspection shall not constitute an inspection as required by Section 1534. Announced inspections of foster family homes required by Section 1534

shall be made during normal business hours, unless the serious nature of a complaint requires otherwise.

(2) As used in this subdivision, "normal business hours" means from 8 a.m. to 5 p.m., inclusive, of each day from Monday to Friday, inclusive, other than state holidays. (Amended by Stats. 2014, Ch. 29, Sec. 7. (SB 855) Effective June 20, 2014.)

1534.

(a) (1) (A) Except for foster family homes, every licensed community care facility shall be subject to unannounced inspections by the department.

(B) Foster family homes shall be subject to announced inspections by the department, except that a foster family home shall be subject to unannounced inspections in response to a complaint, a plan of correction, or under any of the circumstances set forth in subparagraph (B) of paragraph (2).

(2) (A) The department may inspect these facilities as often as necessary to ensure the quality of care provided.

(B) The department shall conduct an annual unannounced inspection of a facility under any of the following circumstances:

(i) When a license is on probation.

(ii) When the terms of agreement in a facility compliance plan require an annual inspection.

(iii) When an accusation against a licensee is pending.

(iv) When a facility requires an annual inspection as a condition of receiving federal financial participation.

(v) In order to verify that a person who has been ordered out of a facility by the department is no longer at the facility.

(C) On and after January 1, 2017, and until January 1, 2018, the following shall apply:

(i) Except for foster family homes, the department shall conduct annual unannounced inspections of no less than 30 percent of every licensed community care facility not subject to an inspection under subparagraph (B).

(ii) The department shall conduct annual announced inspections of no less than 30 percent of foster family homes not subject to an inspection under subparagraph (B).

(iii) These inspections shall be conducted based on a random sampling methodology developed by the department.

(iv) The department shall inspect a licensed community care facility at least once every three years.

(D) On and after January 1, 2018, and until January 1, 2019, the following shall apply:

(i) The department shall conduct annual unannounced inspections of no less than 20 percent of adult residential facilities, adult day programs, social rehabilitation facilities, enhanced behavioral support homes for adults, and community crisis homes, as defined in Section 1502, which are not subject to an inspection under subparagraph (B).

(ii) These inspections shall be conducted based on a random sampling methodology developed by the department.

(iii) The department shall inspect an adult residential facility, adult day program, social rehabilitation facility, enhanced behavioral support home for adults, and community crisis home, as defined in Section 1502, at least once every two years.

(E) On and after January 1, 2019, the department shall conduct annual unannounced inspections of all adult residential facilities, adult day programs, social rehabilitation facilities, enhanced behavioral support homes for adults, and community crisis homes, as defined in Section 1502, and adult residential facilities for persons with special health care needs, as defined in Section 4684.50 of the Welfare and Institutions Code.

(F) On and after January 1, 2018, all of the following shall apply:

(i) Except for foster family homes, the department shall conduct annual unannounced inspections of no less than 20 percent of residential care facilities for children, as defined in Section 1502, including enhanced behavioral support homes for children, transitional housing placement providers, and foster family agencies not subject to an inspection under subparagraph (B).

(ii) The department shall conduct annual announced inspections of no less than 20 percent of foster family homes, as defined in Section 1502, not subject to an inspection under subparagraph (B).

(iii) The inspections in clauses (i) and (ii) shall be conducted based on a random sampling methodology developed by the department.

(iv) The department shall conduct unannounced inspections of residential care facilities for children, as defined in Section 1502, including enhanced behavioral support homes for children, transitional housing placement providers, and foster family agencies, and announced inspections of foster family homes, at least once every two years.

(3) In order to facilitate direct contact with group home or short-term residential therapeutic program clients, the department may interview children who are clients of group homes or short-term residential therapeutic programs at any public agency or private agency at which the client may be found, including, but not limited to, a juvenile hall, recreation or vocational program, or a public or nonpublic school. The department shall respect the rights of the child while conducting the interview, including informing the child that he or she has the right not to be interviewed and the right to have another adult present during the interview.

(4) The department shall notify the community care facility in writing of all deficiencies in its compliance with the provisions of this chapter and the rules and regulations adopted pursuant to this chapter, and shall set a reasonable length of time for compliance by the facility.

(5) Reports on the results of each inspection, evaluation, or consultation shall be kept on file in the department, and all inspection reports, consultation reports, lists of deficiencies, and plans of correction shall be open to public inspection.

(b) (1) This section does not limit the authority of the department to inspect or evaluate a licensed foster family agency, a certified family home, or any aspect of a program in which a licensed community care facility is certifying compliance with licensing requirements.

(2) (A) A foster family agency shall conduct an announced inspection of a certified family home during the annual recertification described in Section 1506 in order to ensure that the certified family home meets all applicable licensing standards. A foster family agency may inspect a certified family home as often as necessary to ensure the quality of care provided.

(B) In addition to the inspections required pursuant to subparagraph (A), a foster family agency shall conduct an unannounced inspection of a certified family home under any of the following circumstances:

(i) When a certified family home is on probation.

(ii) When the terms of the agreement in a facility compliance plan require an annual inspection.

(iii) When an accusation against a certified family home is pending.

(iv) When a certified family home requires an annual inspection as a condition of receiving federal financial participation.

(v) In order to verify that a person who has been ordered out of a certified family home by the department is no longer at the home.

(3) Upon a finding of noncompliance by the department, the department may require a foster family agency to deny or revoke the certificate of approval of a certified family home, or take other action the department may deem necessary for the protection of a child placed with the certified family home. The certified parent or prospective foster parent shall be afforded the due process provided pursuant to this chapter.

(4) If the department requires a foster family agency to deny or revoke the certificate of approval, the department shall serve an order of denial or revocation upon the certified or prospective foster parent and foster family agency that shall notify the certified or prospective foster parent of the basis of the department's action and of the certified or prospective foster parent's right to a hearing.

(5) Within 15 days after the department serves an order of denial or revocation, the certified or prospective foster parent may file a written appeal of the department's decision with the department. The department's action shall be final if the certified or prospective foster parent does not file a written appeal within 15 days after the department serves the denial or revocation order.

(6) The department's order of the denial or revocation of the certificate of approval shall remain in effect until the hearing is completed and the director has made a final determination on the merits.

(7) A certified or prospective foster parent who files a written appeal of the department's order with the department pursuant to this section shall, as part of the written request, provide his or her current mailing address. The certified or prospective foster parent shall subsequently notify the department in writing of any change in mailing address, until the hearing process has been completed or terminated.

(8) Hearings held pursuant to this section shall be conducted in accordance with Chapter 5 (commencing with Section 11500) of Part 1 of Division 3 of Title 2 of the Government Code. In all proceedings conducted in accordance with this section, the standard of proof shall be by a preponderance of the evidence.

(9) The department may institute or continue a disciplinary proceeding against a certified or prospective foster parent upon any ground provided by this section or Section 1550, enter an order denying or revoking the certificate of approval, or otherwise take disciplinary action against the certified or prospective foster parent, notwithstanding any resignation, withdrawal of application, forfeiture, surrender of the certificate of approval, or denial or revocation of the certificate of approval by the foster family agency.

(10) A foster family agency's failure to comply with the department's order to deny or revoke the certificate of approval by placing or retaining children in care shall be grounds for disciplining the licensee pursuant to Section 1550.

(c) This section shall become operative on January 1, 2017.

(Amended by Stats. 2018, Ch. 910, Sec. 16. (AB 1930) Effective January 1, 2019.)

1534.1.

(a) The department shall ensure that the licensee's plan of correction is verifiable and measurable. The plan of correction shall specify what evidence is acceptable to establish that a deficiency has been corrected. This evidence shall be included in the department's facility file.

(b) The department shall specify in its licensing report all violations that, if not corrected, will have a direct and immediate risk to the health, safety, or personal rights of clients in care.

(c) The department shall complete all complaint investigations and place a note of final conclusion in the department's facility file, consistent with the confidentiality provisions in subdivision (c) of Section 1538, regardless of whether the licensee voluntarily surrendered the license.

(Added by Stats. 2008, Ch. 291, Sec. 5. Effective September 25, 2008.)

1534.5.

The state department shall provide the office, as defined in subdivision (c) of Section 9701 of the Welfare and Institutions Code, with copies of inspection reports for community care facilities upon request.

(Added by Stats. 1984, Ch. 1632, Sec. 4.)

1535.

(a) On or before January 1, 1986, the state department shall publish a comprehensive consumer guideline brochure to assist persons in the evaluation and selection of a licensed community care facility. The department shall develop the brochure for publication with the advice and assistance of the Advisory Committee on Community Care Facilities, the State Department of Aging, and the State Department of Health Care Services.

(b) The consumer guideline brochure shall include, but not be limited to, guidelines highlighting resident health and safety issues to be considered in the selection of a community care facility, locations of the licensing offices of the State Department of Social Services where facility records may be reviewed, types of local organizations which may have additional information on specific facilities, and a list of recommended inquiries to be made in the selection of a community care facility.

(c) Upon publication, the consumer guideline brochures shall be distributed to statewide community care facility resident advocacy groups, statewide consumer advocacy groups, state and local ombudsmen, and all licensed community care facilities. The brochure shall be made available on request to all other interested persons.

(Amended by Stats. 2013, Ch. 22, Sec. 16. (AB 75) Effective June 27, 2013. Operative July 1, 2013, by Sec. 110 of Ch. 22.)

1536.

(a) (1) At least annually, the department shall publish and make available to interested persons a list or lists covering all licensed community care facilities and the services for which each facility has been licensed or issued a special permit.

(2) For a group home, transitional housing placement provider, community treatment facility, runaway and homeless youth shelter, temporary shelter care facility, transitional shelter care facility, or short-term residential therapeutic program, the list shall include both of the following:

(A) The number of licensing complaints, types of complaint, and outcomes of complaints, including citations, fines, exclusion orders, license suspensions, revocations, and surrenders.

(B) The number, types, and outcomes of law enforcement contacts made by the facility staff or children, as reported pursuant to subdivision (a) of Section 1538.7.

(3) This subdivision does not apply to foster family homes or the certified family homes or resource families of foster family agencies.

(b) Subject to subdivision (c), to protect the personal privacy of foster family homes and the certified family homes and resource families of foster family agencies, and to preserve the security and confidentiality of the placements in the homes, the names, addresses, and other identifying information of facilities licensed as foster family homes and certified family homes and resource families of foster family agencies shall be considered personal information for purposes of the Information Practices Act of 1977 (Chapter 1 (commencing with Section 1798) of Title 1.8 of Part 4 of Division 3 of the Civil Code). This information shall not be disclosed by any state or local agency pursuant to the California Public Records Act (Chapter 3.5 (commencing with Section 6250) of Division 7 of Title 1 of the Government Code), except as necessary for administering the licensing program, facilitating the placement of children in these facilities, and providing names and addresses, upon request, only to bona fide professional foster parent organizations and to professional organizations educating foster parents, including the Foster and Kinship Care Education Program of the California Community Colleges.

(c) (1) Notwithstanding subdivision (b), the department, a county, or a foster family agency may request information from, or divulge information to, the department, a county, or a foster family agency, regarding a prospective certified parent, foster parent, or relative caregiver for the purpose of, and as necessary to, conduct a reference check to determine whether it is safe and appropriate to license, certify, or approve an applicant to be a certified parent, foster parent, or relative caregiver.

(2) This subdivision shall apply only to applications received on or before December 31, 2016, in accordance with Section 1517 or 1517.1 of this code or Section 16519.5 of the Welfare and Institutions Code.

(d) The department may issue a citation and, after the issuance of that citation, may assess a civil penalty of fifty dollars ($50) per day for each instance of a foster family agency's failure to provide the department with a log of certified and decertified homes or a log of resource families that were approved or had approval rescinded during the month by the 10th day of the following month.

(e) The Legislature encourages the department, when funds are available for this purpose, to develop a database that would include all of the following information:

(1) Monthly reports by a foster family agency regarding certified family homes and resource families.

(2) A log of certified and decertified family homes, approved resource families, and resource families for which approval was rescinded, provided by a foster family agency to the department.

(3) Notification by a foster family agency to the department informing the department of a foster family agency's determination to decertify a certified family home or rescind the approval of a resource family due to any of the following actions by the certified family parent or resource family:

(A) Violating licensing rules and regulations.

(B) Aiding, abetting, or permitting the violation of licensing rules and regulations.

(C) Conducting oneself in a way that is inimical to the health, morals, welfare, or safety of a child placed in that certified family home, or for a resource family, engaging in conduct that poses a risk or threat to the health and safety, protection, or well-being of a child or nonminor dependent.

(D) Being convicted of a crime while a certified family parent or resource family.

(E) Knowingly allowing any child to have illegal drugs or alcohol.

(F) Committing an act of child abuse or neglect or an act of violence against another person.

(f) At least annually, the department shall post on its Internet Web site a statewide summary of the information gathered pursuant to Sections 1538.8 and 1538.9. The summary shall include only deidentified and aggregate information that does not violate the confidentiality of a child's identity and records.

(Amended by Stats. 2017, Ch. 732, Sec. 27. (AB 404) Effective January 1, 2018.)

1536.1.

(a) "Placement agency" means a county probation department, county welfare department, county social service department, county mental health department, county public guardian, general acute care hospital discharge planner or coordinator, conservator pursuant to Part 3 (commencing with Section 1800) of Division 4 of the Probate Code, conservator pursuant to Chapter 3 (commencing with Section 5350) of Part 1 of Division 5 of the Welfare and Institutions Code, and regional center for persons with developmental disabilities, that is engaged in finding homes or other places for placement of persons of any age for temporary or permanent care.

(b) A placement agency shall place individuals only in licensed community care facilities, facilities that are exempt from licensing under Section 1505 or if the facility satisfies subdivision (c) of Section 362 of the Welfare and Institutions Code, or with a foster family agency.

(c) No employee of a placement agency shall place, refer, or recommend placement of a person in a facility operating without a license, unless the facility is exempt from licensing under Section 1505 or unless the facility satisfies subdivision (c) of Section 362 of the Welfare and Institutions Code. Violation of this subdivision is a misdemeanor.

(d) Any employee of a placement agency who knows, or reasonably suspects, that a facility that is not exempt from licensing is operating without a license shall report the name and address of the facility to the department. Failure to report as required by this subdivision is a misdemeanor.

(e) The department shall investigate any report filed under subdivision (d). If the department has probable cause to believe that the facility that is the subject of the report is operating without a license, the department shall investigate the facility within 10 days after receipt of the report.

(f) A placement agency shall notify the appropriate licensing agency of known or suspected incidents that would jeopardize the health or safety of residents in a community care facility. Reportable incidents include, but are not limited to, all of the following:

(1) Incidents of physical or sexual abuse.

(2) A violation of personal rights.

(3) A situation in which a facility is unclean, unsafe, unsanitary, or in poor condition.

(4) A situation in which a facility has insufficient personnel or incompetent personnel on duty.

(5) A situation in which residents experience mental or verbal abuse.

(6) A situation in which residents are inadequately supervised.

(7) Incidents of abuse, neglect, or exploitation of a nonminor dependent, as defined in subdivision (v) of Section 11400 of the Welfare and Institutions Code, by a licensed caregiver while the nonminor is in a foster care placement.

(Amended by Stats. 2011, Ch. 459, Sec. 3. (AB 212) Effective October 4, 2011.)

1536.2.

(a) When a placement agency has placed a child with a foster family agency for subsequent placement in a certified family home or with a resource family, the foster family agency shall ensure placement of the child in a home that best meets the needs of the child.

(b) A home that best meets the needs of the child shall satisfy all of the following criteria:

(1) The child's caregiver is able to meet the health, safety, and well-being needs of the child.

(2) The child's caregiver is permitted to maintain the least restrictive and most family-like environment that serves the needs of the child.

(3) The child is permitted to engage in reasonable, age-appropriate, day-to-day activities that promote the most family-like environment for the foster child.

(4) The foster child's caregiver shall use a reasonable and prudent parent standard, as defined in paragraph (2) of subdivision (a) of Section 362.04 of the Welfare and Institutions Code, to determine activities that are age-appropriate and meet the needs of the child. Nothing in this section shall be construed to permit a child's caregiver to permit the child to engage in activities that carry an unreasonable risk of harm, or subject the child to abuse or neglect.

(Amended by Stats. 2017, Ch. 732, Sec. 28. (AB 404) Effective January 1, 2018.)

1536.3.

A public agency social worker shall, in determining whether to refer an individual to an adult residential care facility, take into account the compatibility of the individual with the other residents in light of any medical diagnoses or behavioral problems.

(Added by Stats. 1994, Ch. 1258, Sec. 2. Effective January 1, 1995.)

1537.

The director shall have the authority to contract for personal services as required in order to perform inspections of, or consultation with, community care facilities.

(Added by Stats. 1973, Ch. 1203.)

1538.

(a) Any person may request an inspection of any community care facility, or certified family home or resource family of a foster family agency, in accordance with this chapter by transmitting to the state department notice of an alleged violation of applicable requirements prescribed by statutes or regulations of this state, including, but not limited to, a denial of access of any person authorized to enter the facility pursuant to Section

9701 of the Welfare and Institutions Code. A complaint may be made either orally or in writing.

(b) The substance of the complaint shall be provided to the licensee, or certified family home or resource family and foster family agency, no earlier than at the time of the inspection. Unless the complainant specifically requests otherwise, neither the substance of the complaint provided to the licensee, or certified family home or resource family and foster family agency, nor any copy of the complaint or any record published, released, or otherwise made available to the licensee, or certified family home or resource family and foster family agency, shall disclose the name of any person mentioned in the complaint except the name of any duly authorized officer, employee, or agent of the state department conducting the investigation or inspection pursuant to this chapter.

(c) (1) Upon receipt of a complaint, other than a complaint alleging denial of a statutory right of access to a community care facility, or certified family home or resource family of a foster family agency, the state department shall make a preliminary review and, unless the state department determines that the complaint is willfully intended to harass a licensee, certified family home, or resource family, or is without any reasonable basis, it shall make an onsite inspection of the community care facility, certified family home, or resource family home within 10 days after receiving the complaint, except where a visit would adversely affect the licensing investigation or the investigation of other agencies. In either event, the complainant shall be promptly informed of the state department's proposed course of action.

(2) If the department determines that the complaint is intended to harass, is without a reasonable basis, or, after a site inspection, is unfounded, then the complaint and any documents related to it shall be marked confidential and shall not be disclosed to the public. If the complaint investigation included a site visit, the licensee, or certified family home or resource family and foster family agency, shall be notified in writing within 30 days of the dismissal that the complaint has been dismissed.

(d) Upon receipt of a complaint alleging denial of a statutory right of access to a community care facility, or certified family home or resource family home of a foster family agency, the department shall review the complaint. The complainant shall be notified promptly of the department's proposed course of action.

(e) The department shall commence performance of complaint inspections of certified family homes upon the employment of sufficient personnel to carry out this function, and by no later than June 30, 1999. Upon implementation, the department shall notify all licensed foster family agencies.

(f) Upon receipt of a complaint concerning the care of a client in an Adult Residential Facility for Persons with Special Health Care Needs licensed pursuant to Article 9 (commencing with Section 1567.50), the department shall notify the appropriate regional center and the State Department of Developmental Services for the purposes of investigating the complaint.

(g) Upon receipt of a complaint concerning the vendorization of an Adult Residential Facility for Persons with Special Health Care Needs, the department shall notify the State Department of Developmental Services for purposes of investigating the complaint.
(Amended by Stats. 2017, Ch. 732, Sec. 29. (AB 404) Effective January 1, 2018.)
1538.2.
The director shall establish an automated license information system on licensees and former licensees of licensed community care facilities. The system shall maintain a record of any information that may be pertinent, as determined by the director, for licensure under this chapter and Chapter 3.6 (commencing with Section 1597.30). This information may include, but is not limited to, the licensees' addresses, telephone numbers, violations of any laws related to the care of clients in a community care facility, licenses, revocation of any licenses and, to the extent permitted by federal law, social security numbers.
(Amended by Stats. 2004, Ch. 833, Sec. 3. Effective January 1, 2005.)
1538.3.
A county may develop a cooperative agreement with the department to access disclosable, public record information from an automated system, other than the system described in Section 1538.2, concerning substantiated complaints for all group home or short-term residential therapeutic programs, as defined by regulations of the department, located within that county. Access to the database may be accomplished through a secure online transaction protocol.
(Amended by Stats. 2016, Ch. 612, Sec. 44. (AB 1997) Effective January 1, 2017.)
1538.5.
(a) (1) Not less than 30 days prior to the anniversary of the effective date of a residential community care facility license, except licensed foster family homes, the department may transmit a copy to the board members of the licensed facility, parents, legal guardians, conservators, clients' rights advocates, or placement agencies, as designated in each resident's placement agreement, of all inspection reports given to the facility by the department during the past year as a result of a substantiated complaint regarding a violation of this chapter relating to resident abuse and neglect, food, sanitation, incidental medical care, and residential supervision. During that one-year period the copy of the notices transmitted and the proof of the transmittal shall be open for public inspection.
(2) The department may transmit copies of the inspection reports referred to in paragraph (1) concerning a group home or short-term residential therapeutic program, as defined by regulations of the department, to the county in which the group home or short-term residential therapeutic program is located, if requested by that county.
(3) A group home or short-term residential therapeutic program shall maintain, at the facility, a copy of all licensing reports for the past three years that would be accessible to the public through the department, for inspection by placement officials, current and prospective facility clients, and these clients' family members who visit the facility.

(b) The facility operator, at the expense of the facility, shall transmit a copy of all substantiated complaints, by certified mail, to those persons described pursuant to paragraph (1) of subdivision (a) in the following cases:
(1) In the case of a substantiated complaint relating to resident physical or sexual abuse, the facility shall have three days from the date the facility receives the licensing report from the department to comply.
(2) In the case in which a facility has received three or more substantiated complaints relating to the same violation during the past 12 months, the facility shall have five days from the date the facility receives the licensing report to comply.
(c) A residential facility shall retain a copy of the notices transmitted pursuant to subdivision (b) and proof of their transmittal by certified mail for a period of one year after their transmittal.
(d) If a residential facility to which this section applies fails to comply with this section, as determined by the department, the department shall initiate civil penalty action against the facility in accordance with this article and the related rules and regulations.
(e) Not less than 30 days prior to the anniversary of the effective date of the license of any group home or short-term residential therapeutic program, as defined by regulations of the department, at the request of the county in which the group home or short-term residential therapeutic program is located, a group home or short-term residential therapeutic program shall transmit to the county a copy of all incident reports prepared by the group home or short-term residential therapeutic program and transmitted to a placement agency, as described in subdivision (f) of Section 1536.1, in a county other than the county in which the group home or short-term residential therapeutic program is located that involved a response by local law enforcement or emergency services personnel, including runaway incidents. The county shall designate an official for the receipt of the incident reports and shall notify the group home or short-term residential therapeutic program of the designation. Prior to transmitting copies of incident reports to the county, the group home or short-term residential therapeutic program shall redact the name of any child referenced in the incident reports, and other identifying information regarding any child referenced in the reports. The county may review the incident reports to ensure that the group home or short-term residential therapeutic program has taken appropriate action to ensure the health and safety of the residents of the facility.
(f) The department shall notify the residential community care facility of its obligation when it is required to comply with this section.
(Amended by Stats. 2016, Ch. 612, Sec. 45. (AB 1997) Effective January 1, 2017.)
1538.55.
(a) The licensee of an Adult Residential Facility for Persons with Special Health Care Needs (ARFPSHN), licensed pursuant to Article 9 (commencing with Section 1567.50), shall report to the department's Community Care Licensing Division, within the department's next working day and to the regional center with whom the ARFPSHN contracts, and the State Department of Developmental Services, within 24 hours upon the occurrence of any of the following events:
(1) The death of any client from any cause.
(2) The use of an automated external defibrillator.
(3) Any injury to any client that requires medical treatment.
(4) Any unusual incident that threatens the physical or emotional health or safety of any client.
(5) Any suspected physical or psychological abuse of any client.
(6) Epidemic outbreaks.
(7) Poisonings.
(8) Catastrophes.
(9) Fires or explosions that occur in or on the premises.
(b) The licensee additionally shall submit a written report to the department's Community Care Licensing Division, the regional center with whom the ARFPSHN contracts, and the State Department of Developmental Services within seven days following any event set forth in subdivision (a), and shall include the following:
(1) Client's name, age, sex, and date of admission.
(2) The date and nature of event.
(3) The attending physician's name, findings, and treatment, if any.
(4) The disposition of the case.
(c) The department's Community Care Licensing Division shall notify the State Department of Developmental Services upon its findings of any deficiencies or of possible actions to exclude, pursuant to Section 1558, any individual from an ARFPSHN.
(Added by Stats. 2005, Ch. 558, Sec. 3. Effective January 1, 2006.)
1538.6.
(a) When the department periodically reviews the record of substantiated complaints against each group home or short-term residential therapeutic program, pursuant to its oversight role as prescribed by Section 1534, to determine whether the nature, number, and severity of incidents upon which complaints were based constitute a basis for concern as to whether the provider is capable of effectively and efficiently operating the program, and if the department determines that there is cause for concern, it may contact the county in which a group home or short-term residential therapeutic program is located and placement agencies in other counties using the group home or short-term residential therapeutic program, and request their recommendations as to what action, if any, the department should take with regard to the provider's status as a licensed group home or short-term residential therapeutic program provider.
(b) It is the intent of the Legislature that the department make every effort to communicate with the county in which a group home or short-term residential therapeutic program is located when the department has concerns about group homes or short-term residential therapeutic programs within that county.

(Amended by Stats. 2016, Ch. 612, Sec. 46. (AB 1997) Effective January 1, 2017.)
1538.7.

(a) A group home, transitional housing placement provider, community treatment facility, runaway and homeless youth shelter, temporary shelter care facility, transitional shelter care facility, or short-term residential therapeutic program shall report to the department's Community Care Licensing Division upon the occurrence of any incident concerning a child in the facility involving contact with law enforcement. At least every six months, the facility shall provide a followup report for each incident, including the type of incident, whether the incident involved an alleged violation of any crime described in Section 602 of the Welfare and Institutions Code by a child residing in the facility; whether staff, children, or both were involved; the gender, race, ethnicity, and age of children involved; and the outcomes, including arrests, removals of children from placement, or termination or suspension of staff.

(b) (1) If the department determines that, based on the licensed capacity, a facility has reported, pursuant to subdivision (a), a greater than average number of law enforcement contacts involving an alleged violation of any crime described in Section 602 of the Welfare and Institutions Code by a child residing in the facility, the department shall inspect the facility at least once a year.

(2) An inspection conducted pursuant to paragraph (1) does not constitute an unannounced inspection required pursuant to Section 1534.

(c) If an inspection is required pursuant to subdivision (b), the Community Care Licensing Division shall provide the report to the department's Children and Family Services Division and to any other public agency that has certified the facility's program or any component of the facility's program including, but not limited to, the State Department of Health Care Services, which certifies group homes or approves short-term residential therapeutic programs pursuant to Section 4096.5 of the Welfare and Institutions Code.
(Amended by Stats. 2017, Ch. 732, Sec. 30. (AB 404) Effective January 1, 2018.)
1538.75.

(a) (1) The department shall allocate funds appropriated for the purpose of providing training and community-based, culturally relevant, trauma-informed services in order to reduce the frequency of law enforcement involvement and delinquency petitions arising from incidents at group homes and other facilities licensed to provide residential care to dependent children. For county departments participating in the program, participation shall be at the county's option.

(2) The department's allocation of the funds shall include, at a minimum, both of the following:

(A) Consultation with stakeholders to establish a methodology to identify facilities in need of training and to establish a methodology for defining areas of highest need for services for youth. The department shall involve stakeholders from rural areas and counties with fewer than 1,000,000 residents.

(B) Identification of highest areas of need by county based on youth living in areas with the highest rate of crossover and dual status youth as described in subdivision (a) of Section 241.1 of the Welfare and Institutions Code, youth placed in probation-supervised foster care placements and foster youth placed in juvenile hall, and youth living in congregate care facilities specified in Sections 1536 and 1538.7, with excessive licensing complaints and excessive calls to law enforcement.

(b) (1) Eligible lead agencies include county child welfare departments, county behavioral health departments, county public health departments, or private nonprofit community-based agencies with experience providing social and mental health services to youth and families. For county departments participating in the program, participation shall be at the county's option.

(2) A group home, transitional shelter care facility, short-term residential therapeutic program, as defined in Section 1502, and temporary shelter care facility, as defined in subdivision (c) of Section 1530.8, is ineligible to receive funds as specified in this section.

(c) (1) By March 1, 2019, the department shall allocate the funds appropriated to it for these purposes in the annual Budget Act to lead agencies that submit a three-year plan via a request for proposal developed by the department. Funds awarded but not expended during any year shall remain eligible for expenditure by a selected lead agency in the following year. Up to 10 percent of funds awarded may be allocated to the lead agency for the coordination and administration of the program.

(2) (A) A prospective lead agency shall indicate its interest in participating in the program by submitting a three-year plan by February 1 of the first year, and shall submit any plan modifications by February 1 of each subsequent year.

(B) The plan shall designate the lead agency and the community-based organization or organizations that will provide services, including program descriptions and the targeted geographic areas in most need of services. The plan shall provide evidence of all of the following:

(i) Braided or matching county funds of at least 25 percent.

(ii) A memorandum of understanding (MOU) with local law enforcement assuring law enforcement participation in the training and diversion protocols. A plan that does not include a direct MOU with law enforcement may be considered, but plans that include the MOU will have priority for funding.

(iii) Direct coordination of services with identified facilities and collaboration regarding the integration of services with the facility program.

(iv) Youth educational and well-being outcome measures developed in coordination with the department.

(C) The lead agency shall allocate no less than 90 percent of the funds awarded to one or more community-based service providers to provide direct services as described in this section.

(D) If the lead agency is also a community-based organization, the lead agency may directly administer services under this section.

(3) Funding provided to a county pursuant to this section shall supplement, and not supplant, county funding expended for purposes described in subdivision (a) as of the 2016–17 fiscal year.

(4) The department shall issue guidance to eligible lead agencies regarding fund and plan requirements by October 1 of each year in order to ensure maximum utilization of federal funding opportunities, and may periodically revise that guidance following consultation with county agencies, other state departments, advocates for children and youth, and other stakeholders.

(d) (1) For the purposes of this section, community-based, culturally relevant, trauma-informed services include, but are not limited to, mentoring, educational enrichment, college and career prep, arts, recreation, cultural and ethnic studies, cultural healing practices, permanency services, and self-awareness and health programming, which shall be provided as alternatives to arrest, detention, and incarceration for system-impacted youth living in areas with the highest rates of foster youth arrests and crossover youth.

(2) The services described in paragraph (1) shall be provided by nongovernmental organizations that are easily accessible to residents of the congregate care facilities.

(e) The department shall use five hundred thousand dollars ($500,000) of the funds appropriated to it in the annual Budget Act for purposes of this section to contract with one or more community-based organizations for training purposes pursuant to subdivision (a). The department shall seek federal matching funds to maximize funding for this purpose. The department shall consider the allocation of funds as specified in subdivision (c) when contracting for training purposes.

(1) Training and technical assistance to professionals interacting with youth shall include all of the following:

(A) Adolescent development principles.

(B) Deescalation techniques.

(C) Culturally relevant and trauma-informed interventions.

(2) Training shall be provided to group home, shelter, and short-term residential treatment program staff, and the responding local law enforcement serving youth living in the facilities or areas identified in paragraph (2) of subdivision (a).

(f) The department shall contract with a research firm or university to measure youth outcomes and justice system measures over a three-year period beginning July 1, 2019.

(1) Youth outcome measures may include, but are not limited to, exits to families from congregate care, improvement in the youths' health and well-being, school and community stability, educational attainment, and employment opportunities, as described in Section 11467 of the Welfare and Institutions Code.

(2) Justice system measures may include, but are not limited to, frequency of law enforcement responses to facilities for low-level offenses, number of charges filed resulting from law enforcement responses, number of hearings resulting from law enforcement responses, days youth spend in detention, youth placement in congregate care, school and placement disruptions, and facility staff turnover.

(3) The department shall seek any necessary federal approvals to obtain federal financial participation for the training and evaluation pursuant to this section, including any approvals necessary to obtain enhanced federal financial participation, as applicable.

(g) The department shall adopt regulations as required to implement the provisions of this section. Notwithstanding the rulemaking provisions of the Administrative Procedure Act (Chapter 3.5 (commencing with Section 11340) of Part 1 of Division 3 of Title 2 of the Government Code), the department may implement and administer this section through all-county letters or similar written instructions until regulations are adopted.

(h) Notwithstanding any other law, contracts or grants awarded for purposes of this section shall be exempt from the personal services contracting requirements of Article 4 (commencing with Section 19130) of Chapter 5 of Part 2 of Division 5 of Title 2 of the Government Code.

(i) Notwithstanding any other law, contracts or grants awarded for purposes of this section shall be exempt from the Public Contract Code and the State Contracting Manual, and shall not be subject to the approval of the Department of General Services.

(j) This section shall become inoperative on July 1, 2023, and, as of January 1, 2024, is repealed.
(Added by Stats. 2018, Ch. 35, Sec. 7. (AB 1811) Effective June 27, 2018. Inoperative July 1, 2023. Repealed as of January 1, 2024, by its own provisions.)
1538.8.

(a) (1) In order to review and evaluate the use of psychotropic medications in group homes and short-term residential therapeutic programs, the department shall compile, to the extent feasible and not otherwise prohibited by law and based on information received from the State Department of Health Care Services, at least annually, information concerning each group home and short-term residential therapeutic program, including, but not limited to, the child welfare psychotropic medication measures developed by the department and the following Healthcare Effectiveness Data and Information Set (HEDIS) measures related to psychotropic medications:

(A) Follow-Up Care for Children Prescribed Attention Deficit Hyperactivity Disorder Medication (HEDIS ADD), which measures the number of children 6 to 12 years of age, inclusive, who have a visit with a provider with prescribing authority within 30 days of the new prescription.

(B) Use of Multiple Concurrent Antipsychotics in Children and Adolescents (HEDIS APC), which does both of the following:

(i) Measures the number of children receiving an antipsychotic medication for at least 60 out of 90 days and the number of children who additionally receive a second antipsychotic medication that overlaps with the first.

(ii) Reports a total rate and age stratifications including 6 to 11 years of age, inclusive, and 12 to 17 years of age, inclusive.

(C) Use of First-Line Psychosocial Care for Children and Adolescents on Antipsychotics (HEDIS APP), which measures whether a child has received psychosocial services 90 days before through 30 days after receiving a new prescription for an antipsychotic medication.

(D) Metabolic Monitoring for Children and Adolescents on Antipsychotics (HEDIS APM), which does both of the following:

(i) Measures testing for glucose or HbA1c and lipid or cholesterol of a child who has received at least two different antipsychotic prescriptions on different days.

(ii) Reports a total rate and age stratifications including 6 to 11 years of age, inclusive, and 12 to 17 years of age, inclusive.

(2) The department shall post the list of data to be collected pursuant to this subdivision on the department's Internet Web site.

(b) The data in subdivision (a) concerning psychotropic medication, mental health services, and placement shall be drawn from existing data maintained by the State Department of Health Care Services and the State Department of Social Services and shared pursuant to a data sharing agreement meeting the requirements of all applicable state and federal laws and regulations.

(c) This section does not apply to a runaway and homeless youth shelter, a private alternative boarding school, or a private alternative outdoor program, as those terms are defined, respectively, in Section 1502.

(Amended by Stats. 2016, Ch. 864, Sec. 10.5. (SB 524) Effective January 1, 2017.)
1538.9.

(a) (1) (A) The department shall consult with the State Department of Health Care Services and stakeholders to establish a methodology for identifying those group homes providing care under the AFDC-FC program pursuant to Sections 11460 and 11462 of the Welfare and Institutions Code that have levels of psychotropic drug utilization warranting additional review. The methodology shall be adopted on or before July 1, 2016.

(B) Every three years after adopting the methodology developed under subparagraph (A), or earlier if needed, the department shall consult with the State Department of Health Care Services and stakeholders and revise the methodology, if necessary.

(2) If the department, applying the methodology described in paragraph (1), determines that a facility appears to have levels of psychotropic drug utilization warranting additional review, it shall inspect the facility at least once a year.

(3) The inspection of the facility shall include, but not be limited to, a review of the following:

(A) Plan of operation, policies, procedures, and practices.

(B) Child-to-staff ratios.

(C) Staff qualifications and training.

(D) Implementation of children's needs and services plan.

(E) Availability of psychosocial and other alternative treatments to the use of psychotropic medications.

(F) Other factors that the department determines contribute to levels of psychotropic drug utilization that warrant additional review.

(G) Confidential interviews of children residing in the facility at the time of the inspection.

(4) The inspection of the facility may include, but is not limited to, the following:

(A) Confidential interviews of children who resided in the facility within the last six months.

(B) Confidential discussions with physicians identified as prescribing the medications.

(b) Following an inspection conducted pursuant to this section, the department, as it deems appropriate, may do either or both of the following:

(1) Share relevant information and observations with county placing agencies, social workers, probation officers, the court, dependency counsel, or the Medical Board of California, as applicable.

(2) Share relevant information and observations with the facility and require the facility to submit a plan, within 30 days of receiving the information and observations from the department, to address any identified risks within the control of the facility related to psychotropic medication. The department shall approve the plan and verify implementation of the plan to determine whether those risks have been remedied.

(c) (1) Notwithstanding the rulemaking provisions of the Administrative Procedure Act (Chapter 3.5 (commencing with Section 11340) of Part 1 of Division 3 of Title 2 of the Government Code), until emergency regulations are filed with the Secretary of State, the department may implement this section through all-county letters or similar instructions.

(2) On or before January 1, 2017, the department shall adopt regulations to implement this section. The initial adoption, amendment, or repeal of a regulation authorized by this subdivision is deemed to address an emergency, for purposes of Sections 11346.1 and 11349.6 of the Government Code, and the department is hereby exempted for that purpose from the requirements of subdivision (b) of Section 11346.1 of the Government Code. After the initial adoption, amendment, or repeal of an emergency regulation pursuant to this section, the department may twice request approval from the Office of Administrative Law to readopt the regulation as an emergency regulation pursuant to Section 11346.1 of the Government Code. The department shall adopt final regulations on or before January 1, 2018.

(d) Nothing in this section does any of the following:

(1) Replaces or alters other requirements for responding to complaints and making inspections or visits to group homes, including, but not limited to, those set forth in Sections 1534 and 1538.

(2) Prevents or precludes the department from taking any other action permitted under any other law, including any regulation adopted pursuant to this chapter.

(e) The methodology developed pursuant to this section shall apply to short-term residential therapeutic programs, as defined in Section 1502, in a manner determined by the department.

(f) This section does not apply to a runaway and homeless youth shelter, a private alternative boarding school, or a private alternative outdoor program, as those terms are defined, respectively, in Section 1502.

(Amended by Stats. 2016, Ch. 864, Sec. 11.5. (SB 524) Effective January 1, 2017.)
1539.

No licensee, or officer or employee of the licensee, shall discriminate or retaliate in any manner, including, but not limited to, eviction or threat of eviction, against any person receiving the services of the licensee's community care facility, or against any employee of the licensee's facility, on the basis, or for the reason that, the person or employee or any other person has initiated or participated in the filing of a complaint, grievance, or a request for inspection with the department pursuant to this chapter or has initiated or participated in the filing of a complaint, grievance, or request for investigation with the appropriate local or state ombudsman.

(Amended by Stats. 2013, Ch. 295, Sec. 1. (AB 581) Effective January 1, 2014.)

ARTICLE 4. Offenses [1540 - 1549]

(Article 4 added by Stats. 1973, Ch. 1203.)
1540.

(a) Any person who violates this chapter, or who willfully or repeatedly violates any rule or regulation promulgated under this chapter, is guilty of a misdemeanor and upon conviction thereof shall be punished by a fine not to exceed one thousand dollars ($1,000) or by imprisonment in the county jail for a period not to exceed 180 days, or by both such fine and imprisonment.

(b) Operation of a community care facility without a license shall be subject to a summons to appear in court.

(Amended by Stats. 1985, Ch. 1415, Sec. 2.)
1540.1.

Upon a finding by the licensing authority that a facility is in operation without a license, a peace officer, as defined in Chapter 4.5 (commencing with Section 830) of Title 3 of Part 2 of the Penal Code, may enforce Section 1503.5, or Section 1508, or both sections by utilizing the procedures set forth in Chapter 5 (commencing with Section 853.5) of Title 3 of Part 2 of the Penal Code. A facility violating Section 1503.5 or 1508, or both, is guilty of an infraction punishable by a fine of two hundred dollars ($200) for each day of violation. Upon a determination that a community care facility is in violation of Section 1503.5 or 1508, or both, and after a citation has been issued, the peace officer shall immediately notify the licensing authority in the department.

(Amended by Stats. 1987, Ch. 856, Sec. 1.)
1540.2.

Any person who, without lawful authorization from a duly authorized officer, employee, or agent of the department, informs an owner, operator, employee, agent, or resident of a community care facility, of an impending and unannounced site visit to that facility by personnel of the department is guilty of a misdemeanor and upon conviction thereof shall be punished by a fine not to exceed one thousand dollars ($1,000), by imprisonment in the county jail for a period not to exceed 180 days, or by both a fine and imprisonment.

(Amended by Stats. 1991, Ch. 888, Sec. 2.)
1541.

The director may bring an action to enjoin the violation or threatened violation of Section 1503.5 or 1508, or both, in the superior court in and for the county in which the violation occurred or is about to occur. Any proceeding under the provisions of this section shall conform to the requirements of Chapter 3 (commencing with Section 525) of Title 7 of Part 2 of the Code of Civil Procedure, except that the director shall not be required to allege facts necessary to show or tending to show lack of adequate remedy at law or irreparable damage or loss. Upon a finding by the director that the violations threaten the health or safety of persons in, or served by, a community care facility, the agency contracted with pursuant to Section 1511 may bring an action to enjoin the violation, threatened violation, or continued violation by any community care facility which is located in an area for which it is responsible pursuant to the terms of the contract.

With respect to any and all actions brought pursuant to this section alleging actual violation of Section 1503.5 or 1508, or both, the court shall, if it finds the allegations to be true, issue its order enjoining the community care facility from continuance of the violation.

(Amended by Stats. 1985, Ch. 1415, Sec. 4.)
1542.

Any action brought by the director against a community care facility shall not abate by reason of a sale or other transfer of ownership of the community care facility which is a party to the action except with express written consent of the director.

(Added by Stats. 1973, Ch. 1203.)
1543.

Notwithstanding any other provision of this chapter, the district attorney of every county, and city attorneys in those cities which have city attorneys who have jurisdiction to prosecute misdemeanors pursuant to Section 72193 of the Government Code, shall, upon their own initiative or upon application by the state department or its authorized representative, institute and conduct the prosecution of any action for violation within his or her county of any provisions of this chapter.

(Amended by Stats. 2002, Ch. 784, Sec. 513. Effective January 1, 2003.)
1546.

An emergency client contingency account may be established within the Technical Assistance Fund to which not more than 50 percent of each penalty assessed pursuant to

Section 1548 is deposited for use by the Community Care Licensing Division of the department, at the discretion of the director, for the care and relocation of clients when a facility's license is revoked or temporarily suspended. The money in the account shall cover costs, including, but not limited to, transportation expenses, expenses incurred in notifying family members, and any other costs directly associated with providing continuous care and supervision to the clients. The department may seek the opinion of stakeholders and local governmental agencies in developing policies for emergency client care and supervision.

(Repealed and added by Stats. 2014, Ch. 29, Sec. 10. (SB 855) Effective June 20, 2014.)

1546.1.

(a) (1) It is the intent of the Legislature in enacting this section to authorize the department to take quick, effective action to protect the health and safety of clients of community care facilities and to minimize the effects of transfer trauma that accompany the abrupt transfer of clients by appointing a temporary manager to assume the operation of a facility that is found to be in a condition in which continued operation by the licensee or his or her representative presents a substantial probability of imminent danger of serious physical harm or death to the clients.

(2) A temporary manager appointed pursuant to this section shall assume the operation of the facility in order to bring it into compliance with the law, facilitate a transfer of ownership to a new licensee, or ensure the orderly transfer of clients should the facility be required to close. Upon a final decision and order of revocation of the license or a forfeiture by operation of law, the department shall immediately issue a provisional license to the appointed temporary manager. Notwithstanding the applicable sections of this code governing the revocation of a provisional license, the provisional license issued to a temporary manager shall automatically expire upon the termination of the temporary manager. The temporary manager shall possess the provisional license solely for purposes of carrying out the responsibilities authorized by this section and the duties set forth in the written agreement between the department and the temporary manager. The temporary manager does not have the right to appeal the expiration of the provisional license.

(b) For purposes of this section, "temporary manager" means the person, corporation, or other entity appointed temporarily by the department as a substitute facility licensee or administrator with authority to hire, terminate, reassign staff, obligate facility funds, alter facility procedures, and manage the facility to correct deficiencies identified in the facility's operation. The temporary manager has the final authority to direct the care and supervision activities of any person associated with the facility, including superseding the authority of the licensee and the administrator.

(c) The director may appoint a temporary manager when it is determined that it is necessary to temporarily suspend any license of a community care facility pursuant to Section 1550.5 and any of the following circumstances exist:

(1) The immediate relocation of the clients is not feasible based on transfer trauma, lack of alternate placements, or other emergency considerations for the health and safety of the clients.

(2) The licensee is unwilling or unable to comply with the requirements of Section 1556 for the safe and orderly relocation of clients when ordered to do so by the department.

(d) (1) Upon appointment, the temporary manager shall complete its application for a license to operate a community care facility and take all necessary steps and make best efforts to eliminate any substantial threat to the health and safety to clients or complete the transfer of clients to alternative placements pursuant to Section 1556. For purposes of a provisional license issued to a temporary manager, the licensee's existing fire safety clearance shall serve as the fire safety clearance for the temporary manager's provisional license.

(2) A person shall not impede the operation of a temporary manager. The temporary manager's access to, or possession of, the property shall not be interfered with during the term of the temporary manager appointment. There shall be an automatic stay for a 60-day period subsequent to the appointment of a temporary manager of any action that would interfere with the functioning of the facility, including, but not limited to, termination of utility services, attachments or setoffs of client trust funds, and repossession of equipment in the facility.

(e) (1) The appointment of a temporary manager shall be immediately effective and shall continue for a period not to exceed 60 days unless otherwise extended in accordance with paragraph (2) of subdivision (h) at the discretion of the department or otherwise terminated earlier by any of the following events:

(A) The temporary manager notifies the department, and the department verifies, that the facility meets state and, if applicable, federal standards for operation, and will be able to continue to maintain compliance with those standards after the termination of the appointment of the temporary manager.

(B) The department approves a new temporary manager.

(C) A new operator is licensed.

(D) The department closes the facility.

(E) A hearing or court order ends the temporary manager appointment, including the appointment of a receiver under Section 1546.2.

(F) The appointment is terminated by the department or the temporary manager.

(2) The appointment of a temporary manager shall authorize the temporary manager to act pursuant to this section. The appointment shall be made pursuant to a written agreement between the temporary manager and the department that outlines the circumstances under which the temporary manager may expend funds. The department shall provide the licensee and administrator with a copy of the accusation to appoint a temporary manager at the time of appointment. The accusation shall notify the licensee of

the licensee's right to petition the Office of Administrative Hearings for a hearing to contest the appointment of the temporary manager as described in subdivision (f) and shall provide the licensee with a form and appropriate information for the licensee's use in requesting a hearing.

(3) The director may rescind the appointment of a temporary manager and appoint a new temporary manager at any time that the director determines the temporary manager is not adhering to the conditions of the appointment.

(f) (1) The licensee of a community care facility may contest the appointment of the temporary manager by filing a petition for an order to terminate the appointment of the temporary manager with the Office of Administrative Hearings within 15 days from the date of mailing of the accusation to appoint a temporary manager under subdivision (e). On the same day the petition is filed with the Office of Administrative Hearings, the licensee shall serve a copy of the petition to the office of the director.

(2) Upon receipt of a petition under paragraph (1), the Office of Administrative Hearings shall set a hearing date and time within 10 business days of the receipt of the petition. The office shall promptly notify the licensee and the department of the date, time, and place of the hearing. The office shall assign the case to an administrative law judge. At the hearing, relevant evidence may be presented pursuant to Section 11513 of the Government Code. The administrative law judge shall issue a written decision on the petition within 10 business days of the conclusion of the hearing. The 10-day time period for holding the hearing and for rendering a decision may be extended by the written agreement of the parties.

(3) The administrative law judge shall uphold the appointment of the temporary manager if the department proves, by a preponderance of the evidence, that the circumstances specified in subdivision (c) applied to the facility at the time of the appointment. The administrative law judge shall order the termination of the temporary manager if the burden of proof is not satisfied.

(4) The decision of the administrative law judge is subject to judicial review as provided in Section 1094.5 of the Code of Civil Procedure by the superior court of the county where the facility is located. This review may be requested by the licensee of the facility or the department by filing a petition seeking relief from the order. The petition may also request the issuance of temporary injunctive relief pending the decision on the petition. The superior court shall hold a hearing within 10 business days of the filing of the petition and shall issue a decision on the petition within 10 days of the hearing. The department may be represented by legal counsel within the department for purposes of court proceedings authorized under this section.

(g) If the licensee of the community care facility does not protest the appointment or does not prevail at either the administrative hearing under paragraph (2) of subdivision (f) or the superior court hearing under paragraph (4) of subdivision (f), the temporary manager shall continue in accordance with subdivision (e).

(h) (1) If the licensee of the community care facility petitions the Office of Administrative Hearings pursuant to subdivision (f), the appointment of the temporary manager by the director pursuant to this section shall continue until it is terminated by the administrative law judge or by the superior court, or it shall continue until the conditions of subdivision (e) are satisfied, whichever is earlier.

(2) At any time during the appointment of the temporary manager, the director may request an extension of the appointment by filing a petition for hearing with the Office of Administrative Hearings and serving a copy of the petition on the licensee. The office shall proceed as specified in paragraph (2) of subdivision (f). The administrative law judge may extend the appointment of the temporary manager an additional 60 days upon a showing by the department that the conditions specified in subdivision (c) continue to exist.

(3) The licensee or the department may request review of the administrative law judge's decision on the extension as provided in paragraph (4) of subdivision (f).

(i) The temporary manager appointed pursuant to this section shall meet the following qualifications:

(1) Be qualified to oversee correction of deficiencies on the basis of experience and education.

(2) Not be the subject of any pending actions by the department or any other state agency nor have ever been excluded from a department licensed facility or had a license or certification suspended or revoked by an administrative action by the department or any other state agency.

(3) Not have a financial ownership interest in the facility and not have a member of his or her immediate family who has a financial ownership interest in the facility.

(4) Not currently serve, or within the past two years have served, as a member of the staff of the facility.

(j) Payment of the costs of the temporary manager shall comply with the following requirements:

(1) Upon agreement with the licensee, the costs of the temporary manager and any other expenses in connection with the temporary management shall be paid directly by the facility while the temporary manager is assigned to that facility. Failure of the licensee to agree to the payment of those costs may result in the payment of the costs by the department and subsequent required reimbursement to the department by the licensee pursuant to this section.

(2) Direct costs of the temporary manager shall be equivalent to the sum of the following:

(A) The prevailing fee paid by licensees for positions of the same type in the facility's geographic area.

(B) Additional costs that reasonably would have been incurred by the licensee if the licensee and the temporary manager had been in an employment relationship.

(C) Any other reasonable costs incurred by the temporary manager in furnishing services pursuant to this section.

(3) Direct costs may exceed the amount specified in paragraph (2) if the department is otherwise unable to attract a qualified temporary manager.

(k) (1) The responsibilities of the temporary manager may include, but are not limited to, the following:

(A) Paying wages to staff. The temporary manager shall have the full power to hire, direct, manage, and discharge employees of the facility, subject to any contractual rights they may have. The temporary manager shall pay employees at the same rate of compensation, including benefits, that the employees would have received from the licensee or wages necessary to provide adequate staff for the protection of clients and compliance with the law.

(B) Preserving client funds. The temporary manager shall be entitled to, and shall take possession of, all property or assets of clients that are in the possession of the licensee or administrator of the facility. The temporary manager shall preserve all property, assets, and records of clients of which the temporary manager takes possession.

(C) Contracting for outside services as may be needed for the operation of the facility. Any contract for outside services in excess of five thousand dollars ($5,000) shall be approved by the director.

(D) Paying commercial creditors of the facility to the extent required to operate the facility. The temporary manager shall honor all leases, mortgages, and secured transactions affecting the building in which the facility is located and all goods and fixtures in the building, but only to the extent of payments that, in the case of a rental agreement, are for the use of the property during the period of the temporary management, or that, in the case of a purchase agreement, come due during the period of the temporary management.

(E) Doing all things necessary and proper to maintain and operate the facility in accordance with sound fiscal policies. The temporary manager shall take action as is reasonably necessary to protect or conserve the assets or property of which the temporary manager takes possession and may use those assets or property only in the performance of the powers and duties set out in this section.

(2) Expenditures by the temporary manager in excess of five thousand dollars ($5,000) shall be approved by the director. Total encumbrances and expenditures by the temporary manager for the duration of the temporary management shall not exceed the sum of forty-nine thousand nine hundred ninety-nine dollars ($49,999) unless approved by the director in writing.

(3) The temporary manager shall make no capital improvements to the facility in excess of five thousand dollars ($5,000) without the approval of the director.

(l) (1) To the extent department funds are advanced for the costs of the temporary manager or for other expenses in connection with the temporary management, the department shall be reimbursed from the revenues accruing to the facility or to the licensee or an entity related to the licensee. Any reimbursement received by the department shall be redeposited in the account from which the department funds were advanced. If the revenues are insufficient to reimburse the department, the unreimbursed amount shall constitute grounds for a monetary judgment in civil court and a subsequent lien upon the assets of the facility or the proceeds from the sale thereof. Pursuant to Chapter 2 (commencing with Section 697.010) of Division 2 of Title 9 of Part 2 of the Code of Civil Procedure, a lien against the personal assets of the facility or an entity related to the licensee based on the monetary judgment obtained shall be filed with the Secretary of State on the forms required for a notice of judgment lien. A lien against the real property of the facility or an entity related to the licensee based on the monetary judgment obtained shall be recorded with the county recorder of the county where the facility of the licensee is located or where the real property of the entity related to the licensee is located. The lien shall not attach to the interests of a lessor, unless the lessor is operating the facility. The authority to place a lien against the personal and real property of the licensee for the reimbursement of any state funds expended pursuant to this section shall be given judgment creditor priority.

(2) For purposes of this section, "entity related to the licensee" means an entity, other than a natural person, of which the licensee is a subsidiary or an entity in which a person who was obligated to disclose information under Section 1520 possesses an interest that would also require disclosure pursuant to Section 1520.

(m) Appointment of a temporary manager under this section does not relieve the licensee of any responsibility for the care and supervision of clients under this chapter. The licensee, even if the license is deemed surrendered or the facility abandoned, shall be required to reimburse the department for all costs associated with operation of the facility during the period the temporary manager is in place that are not accounted for by using facility revenues or for the relocation of clients handled by the department if the licensee fails to comply with the relocation requirements of Section 1556 when required by the department to do so. If the licensee fails to reimburse the department under this section, then the department, along with using its own remedies available under this chapter, may request that the Attorney General's office, the city attorney's office, or the local district attorney's office seek any available criminal, civil, or administrative remedy, including, but not limited to, injunctive relief, restitution, and damages in the same manner as provided for in Chapter 5 (commencing with Section 17200) of Part 2 of Division 7 of the Business and Professions Code.

(n) The department may use funds from the emergency client contingency account pursuant to Section 1546 when needed to supplement the operation of the facility or the transfer of clients under the control of the temporary manager appointed under this section if facility revenues are unavailable or exhausted when needed. Pursuant to subdivision (l), the licensee shall be required to reimburse the department for any funds used from the emergency client contingency account during the period of control of the temporary manager and any incurred costs of collection.

(o) This section does not apply to a residential facility that serves six or fewer persons and is also the principal residence of the licensee.

(p) Notwithstanding any other provision of law, the temporary manager shall be liable only for damages resulting from gross negligence in the operation of the facility or intentional tortious acts.

(q) All governmental immunities otherwise applicable to the state shall also apply to the state in the use of a temporary manager in the operation of a facility pursuant to this section.

(r) A licensee shall not be liable for any occurrences during the temporary management under this section except to the extent that the occurrences are the result of the licensee's conduct.

(s) The department may adopt regulations for the administration of this section. (Amended by Stats. 2015, Ch. 303, Sec. 273. (AB 731) Effective January 1, 2016.)

1546.2.

(a) It is the intent of the Legislature in enacting this section to authorize the department to take quick, effective action to protect the health and safety of residents of community care facilities and to minimize the effects of transfer trauma that accompany the abrupt transfer of clients through a system whereby the department may apply for a court order appointing a receiver to temporarily operate a community care facility. The receivership is not intended to punish a licensee or to replace attempts to secure cooperative action to protect the clients' health and safety. The receivership is intended to protect the clients in the absence of other reasonably available alternatives. The receiver shall assume the operation of the facility in order to bring it into compliance with law, facilitate a transfer of ownership to a new licensee, or ensure the orderly transfer of clients should the facility be required to close.

(b) (1) Whenever circumstances exist indicating that continued management of a community care facility by the current licensee would present a substantial probability or imminent danger of serious physical harm or death to the clients, or the facility is closing or intends to terminate operation as a community care facility and adequate arrangements for the relocation of clients have not been made at least 30 days prior to the closing or termination, the director may petition the superior court for the county in which the community care facility is located for an order appointing a receiver to temporarily operate the community care facility in accordance with this section.

(2) The petition shall allege the facts upon which the action is based and shall be supported by an affidavit of the director. A copy of the petition and affidavit, together with an order to appear and show cause why temporary authority to operate the community care facility should not be vested in a receiver pursuant to this section, shall be delivered to the licensee, administrator, or a responsible person at the facility to the attention of the licensee and administrator. The order shall specify a hearing date, which shall be not less than 10, nor more than 15, days following delivery of the petition and order upon the licensee, except that the court may shorten or lengthen the time upon a showing of just cause.

(c) (1) If the director files a petition pursuant to subdivision (b) for appointment of a receiver to operate a community care facility, in accordance with Section 564 of the Code of Civil Procedure, the director may also petition the court, in accordance with Section 527 of the Code of Civil Procedure, for an order appointing a temporary receiver. A temporary receiver appointed by the court pursuant to this subdivision shall serve until the court has made a final determination on the petition for appointment of a receiver filed pursuant to subdivision (b). A receiver appointed pursuant to this subdivision shall have the same powers and duties as a receiver would have if appointed pursuant to subdivision (b). Upon the director filing a petition for a receiver, the receiver shall complete its application for a provisional license to operate a community care facility. For purposes of a provisional license issued to a receiver, the licensee's existing fire safety clearance shall serve as the fire safety clearance for the receiver's provisional license.

(2) At the time of the hearing, the department shall advise the licensee of the name of the proposed receiver. The receiver shall be a certified community care facility administrator or other responsible person or entity, as determined by the court, from a list of qualified receivers established by the department, and, if need be, with input from providers of residential care and consumer representatives. Persons appearing on the list shall have experience in the delivery of care services to clients of community care facilities, and, if feasible, shall have experience with the operation of a community care facility, shall not be the subject of any pending actions by the department or any other state agency, and shall not have ever been excluded from a department licensed facility nor have had a license or certification suspended or revoked by an administrative action by the department or any other state agency. The receivers shall have sufficient background and experience in management and finances to ensure compliance with orders issued by the court. The owner, licensee, or administrator shall not be appointed as the receiver unless authorized by the court.

(3) If at the conclusion of the hearing, which may include oral testimony and cross-examination at the option of any party, the court determines that adequate grounds exist for the appointment of a receiver and that there is no other reasonably available remedy to protect the clients, the court may issue an order appointing a receiver to temporarily operate the community care facility and enjoining the licensee from interfering with the receiver in the conduct of his or her duties. In these proceedings, the court shall make written findings of fact and conclusions of law and shall require an appropriate bond to be filed by the receiver and paid for by the licensee. The bond shall be in an amount necessary to protect the licensee in the event of any failure on the part of the receiver to act in a reasonable manner. The bond requirement may be waived by the licensee.

(4) The court may permit the licensee to participate in the continued operation of the facility during the pendency of any receivership ordered pursuant to this section and shall issue an order detailing the nature and scope of participation.

(5) Failure of the licensee to appear at the hearing on the petition shall constitute an admission of all factual allegations contained in the petition for purposes of these proceedings only.

(6) The licensee shall receive notice and a copy of the application each time the receiver applies to the court or the department for instructions regarding his or her duties under this section, when an accounting pursuant to subdivision (i) is submitted, and when any other report otherwise required under this section is submitted. The licensee shall have an opportunity to present objections or otherwise participate in those proceedings.

(d) A person shall not impede the operation of a receivership created under this section. The receiver's access to, or possession of, the property shall not be interfered with during the term of the receivership. There shall be an automatic stay for a 60-day period subsequent to the appointment of a receiver of any action that would interfere with the functioning of the facility, including, but not limited to, cancellation of insurance policies executed by the licensees, termination of utility services, attachments or setoffs of client trust funds and working capital accounts, and repossession of equipment in the facility.

(e) When a receiver is appointed, the licensee may, at the discretion of the court, be divested of possession and control of the facility in favor of the receiver. If the court divests the licensee of possession and control of the facility in favor of the receiver, the department shall immediately issue a provisional license to the receiver. Notwithstanding the applicable sections of this code governing the revocation of a provisional license, the provisional license issued to a receiver shall automatically expire upon the termination of the receivership. The receiver shall possess the provisional license solely for purposes of carrying out the responsibilities authorized by this section and the duties ordered by the court. The receiver shall have no right to appeal the expiration of the provisional license.

(f) A receiver appointed pursuant to this section:

(1) May exercise those powers and shall perform those duties ordered by the court, in addition to other duties provided by statute.

(2) Shall operate the facility in a manner that ensures the safety and adequate care for the clients.

(3) Shall have the same rights to possession of the building in which the facility is located, and of all goods and fixtures in the building at the time the petition for receivership is filed, as the licensee and administrator would have had if the receiver had not been appointed.

(4) May use the funds, building, fixtures, furnishings, and any accompanying consumable goods in the provision of care and services to clients and to any other persons receiving services from the facility at the time the petition for receivership was filed.

(5) Shall take title to all revenue coming to the facility in the name of the receiver who shall use it for the following purposes in descending order of priority:

(A) To pay wages to staff. The receiver shall have full power to hire, direct, manage, and discharge employees of the facility, subject to any contractual rights they may have. The receiver shall pay employees at the same rate of compensation, including benefits, that the employees would have received from the licensee or wages necessary to provide adequate staff for the protection of the clients and compliance with the law.

(B) To preserve client funds. The receiver shall be entitled to, and shall take, possession of all property or assets of clients that are in the possession of the licensee or operator of the facility. The receiver shall preserve all property, assets, and records of clients of which the receiver takes possession.

(C) To contract for outside services as may be needed for the operation of the community care facility. Any contract for outside services in excess of five thousand dollars ($5,000) shall be approved by the court.

(D) To pay commercial creditors of the facility to the extent required to operate the facility. Except as provided in subdivision (h), the receiver shall honor all leases, mortgages, and secured transactions affecting the building in which the facility is located and all goods and fixtures in the building of which the receiver has taken possession, but only to the extent of payments which, in the case of a rental agreement, are for the use of the property during the period of receivership, or which, in the case of a purchase agreement, come due during the period of receivership.

(E) To receive a salary, as approved by the court.

(F) To do all things necessary and proper to maintain and operate the facility in accordance with sound fiscal policies. The receiver shall take action as is reasonably necessary to protect or conserve the assets or property of which the receiver takes possession and may use those assets or property only in the performance of the powers and duties set out in this section and by order of the court.

(G) To ask the court for direction in the treatment of debts incurred prior to the appointment, if the licensee's debts appear extraordinary, of questionable validity, or unrelated to the normal and expected maintenance and operation of the facility, or if payment of the debts will interfere with the purposes of receivership.

(g) (1) A person who is served with notice of an order of the court appointing a receiver and of the receiver's name and address shall be liable to pay the receiver, rather than the licensee, for any goods or services provided by the community care facility after the date of the order. The receiver shall give a receipt for each payment and shall keep a copy of each receipt on file. The receiver shall deposit amounts received in a special account and shall use this account for all disbursements. Payment to the receiver pursuant to this subdivision shall discharge the obligation to the extent of the payment and shall not thereafter be the basis of a claim by the licensee or any other person. A client shall not be evicted nor may any contract or rights be forfeited or impaired, nor may any forfeiture

be effected or liability increased, by reason of an omission to pay the licensee, operator, or other person a sum paid to the receiver pursuant to this subdivision.

(2) This section shall not be construed to suspend, during the temporary management by the receiver, any obligation of the licensee for payment of local, state, or federal taxes. A licensee shall not be held liable for acts or omissions of the receiver during the term of the temporary management.

(3) Upon petition of the receiver, the court may order immediate payment to the receiver for past services that have been rendered and billed, and the court may also order a sum not to exceed one month's advance payment to the receiver of any sums that may become payable under the Medi-Cal program.

(h) (1) A receiver shall not be required to honor a lease, mortgage, or secured transaction entered into by the licensee of the facility and another party if the court finds that the agreement between the parties was entered into for a collusive, fraudulent purpose or that the agreement is unrelated to the operation of the facility.

(2) A lease, mortgage, or secured transaction or an agreement unrelated to the operation of the facility that the receiver is permitted to dishonor pursuant to this subdivision shall only be subject to nonpayment by the receiver for the duration of the receivership, and the dishonoring of the lease, mortgage, security interest, or other agreement, to this extent, by the receiver shall not relieve the owner or operator of the facility from any liability for the full amount due under the lease, mortgage, security interest, or other agreement.

(3) If the receiver is in possession of real estate or goods subject to a lease, mortgage, or security interest that the receiver is permitted to dishonor pursuant to paragraph (1), and if the real estate or goods are necessary for the continued operation of the facility, the receiver may apply to the court to set a reasonable rent, price, or rate of interest to be paid by the receiver during the duration of the receivership. The court shall hold a hearing on this application within 15 days. The receiver shall send notice of the application to any known owner of the property involved at least 10 days prior to the hearing.

(4) Payment by the receiver of the amount determined by the court to be reasonable is a defense to any action against the receiver for payment or possession of the goods or real estate, subject to the lease or mortgage, which is brought by any person who received the notice required by this subdivision. However, payment by the receiver of the amount determined by the court to be reasonable shall not relieve the owner or operator of the facility from any liability for the difference between the amount paid by the receiver and the amount due under the original lease, mortgage, or security interest.

(i) A monthly accounting shall be made by the receiver to the department of all moneys received and expended by the receiver on or before the 15th day of the following month or as ordered by the court, and the remainder of income over expenses for that month shall be returned to the licensee. A copy of the accounting shall be provided to the licensee. The licensee or owner of the community care facility may petition the court for a determination as to the reasonableness of any expenditure made pursuant to paragraph (5) of subdivision (f).

(j) (1) The receiver shall be appointed for an initial period of not more than three months. The initial three-month period may be extended for additional periods not exceeding three months, as determined by the court pursuant to this section. At the end of one month, the receiver shall report to the court on its assessment of the probability that the community care facility will meet state standards for operation by the end of the initial three-month period and will continue to maintain compliance with those standards after termination of the receiver's management. If it appears that the facility cannot be brought into compliance with state standards within the initial three-month period, the court shall take appropriate action as follows:

(A) Extend the receiver's management for an additional three months if there is a substantial likelihood that the facility will meet state standards within that period and will maintain compliance with the standards after termination of the receiver's management. The receiver shall report to the court in writing upon the facility's progress at the end of six weeks of any extension ordered pursuant to this paragraph.

(B) Order the director to revoke or temporarily suspend, or both, the license pursuant to Article 5 (commencing with Section 1550) and extend the receiver's management for the period necessary to transfer clients in accordance with the transfer plan, but for not more than three months from the date of initial appointment of a receiver, or 14 days, whichever is greater. An extension of an additional three months may be granted if deemed necessary by the court.

(2) If it appears at the end of six weeks of an extension ordered pursuant to subparagraph (A) of paragraph (1) that the facility cannot be brought into compliance with state standards for operation or that it will not maintain compliance with those standards after the receiver's management is terminated, the court shall take appropriate action as specified in subparagraph (B) of paragraph (1).

(3) In evaluating the probability that a community care facility will maintain compliance with state standards of operation after the termination of receiver management ordered by the court, the court shall consider at least the following factors:

(A) The duration, frequency, and severity of past violations in the facility.

(B) History of compliance in other care facilities operated by the proposed licensee.

(C) Efforts by the licensee to prevent and correct past violations.

(D) The financial ability of the licensee to operate in compliance with state standards.

(E) The recommendations and reports of the receiver.

(4) Management of a community care facility operated by a receiver pursuant to this section shall not be returned to the licensee, to any person related to the licensee, or to any person who served as a member of the facility's staff or who was employed by the

licensee prior to the appointment of the receiver unless both of the following conditions are met:
(A) The department believes that it would be in the best interests of the clients of the facility, requests that the court return the operation of the facility to the former licensee, and provides clear and convincing evidence to the court that it is in the best interests of the facility's clients to take that action.
(B) The court finds that the licensee has fully cooperated with the department in the appointment and ongoing activities of a receiver appointed pursuant to this section, and, if applicable, any temporary manager appointed pursuant to Section 1546.1.
(5) The owner of the facility may at any time sell, lease, or close the facility, subject to the following provisions:
(A) If the owner closes the facility, or the sale or lease results in the closure of the facility, the court shall determine if a transfer plan is necessary. If the court so determines, the court shall adopt and implement a transfer plan consistent with the provisions of Section 1556.
(B) If the licensee proposes to sell or lease the facility and the facility will continue to operate as a community care facility, the court and the department shall reevaluate any proposed transfer plan. If the court and the department determine that the sale or lease of the facility will result in compliance with licensing standards, the transfer plan and the receivership shall, subject to those conditions that the court may impose and enforce, be terminated upon the effective date of the sale or lease.
(k) (1) The salary of the receiver shall be set by the court commensurate with community care facility industry standards, giving due consideration to the difficulty of the duties undertaken, and shall be paid from the revenue coming to the facility. If the revenue is insufficient to pay the salary in addition to other expenses of operating the facility, the receiver's salary shall be paid from the emergency client contingency account as provided in Section 1546. State advances of funds in excess of five thousand dollars ($5,000) shall be approved by the director. Total advances for encumbrances and expenditures shall not exceed the sum of forty-nine thousand nine hundred ninety-nine dollars ($49,999) unless approved by the director in writing.
(2) To the extent state funds are advanced for the salary of the receiver or for other expenses in connection with the receivership, as limited by subdivision (g), the state shall be reimbursed from the revenues accruing to the facility or to the licensee or an entity related to the licensee. Any reimbursement received by the state shall be redeposited in the account from which the state funds were advanced. If the revenues are insufficient to reimburse the state, the unreimbursed amount shall constitute grounds for a monetary judgment in civil court and a subsequent lien upon the assets of the facility or the proceeds from the sale thereof. Pursuant to Chapter 2 (commencing with Section 697.010) of Division 2 of Title 9 of Part 2 of the Code of Civil Procedure, a lien against the personal assets of the facility or an entity related to the licensee based on the monetary judgment obtained shall be filed with the Secretary of State on the forms required for a notice of judgment lien. A lien against the real property of the facility or an entity related to the licensee based on the monetary judgment obtained shall be recorded with the county recorder of the county where the facility of the licensee is located or where the real property of the entity related to the licensee is located. The lien shall not attach to the interests of a lessor, unless the lessor is operating the facility. The authority to place a lien against the personal and real property of the licensee for the reimbursement of any state funds expended pursuant to this section shall be given judgment creditor priority.
(3) For purposes of this subdivision, "entity related to the licensee" means an entity, other than a natural person, of which the licensee is a subsidiary or an entity in which any person who was obligated to disclose information under Section 1520 possesses an interest that would also require disclosure pursuant to Section 1520.
(l) (1) This section does not impair the right of the owner of a community care facility to dispose of his or her property interests in the facility, but any facility operated by a receiver pursuant to this section shall remain subject to that administration until terminated by the court. The termination shall be promptly effectuated, provided that the interests of the clients have been safeguarded as determined by the court.
(2) This section does not limit the power of the court to appoint a receiver under any other applicable provision of law or to order any other remedy available under law.
(m) (1) Notwithstanding any other provision of law, the receiver shall be liable only for damages resulting from gross negligence in the operation of the facility or intentional tortious acts.
(2) All governmental immunities otherwise applicable to the State of California shall also apply in the use of a receiver in the operation of a facility pursuant to this section.
(3) The licensee shall not be liable for any occurrences during the receivership except to the extent that the occurrences are the result of the licensee's conduct.
(n) The department may adopt regulations for the administration of this section. This section does not impair the authority of the department to temporarily suspend licenses under Section 1550.5 or to reach a voluntary agreement with the licensee for alternate management of a community care facility including the use of a temporary manager under Section 1546.1. This section does not authorize the department to interfere in a labor dispute.
(o) This section does not apply to a residential facility that serves six or fewer persons and is also the principal residence of the licensee.
(p) This section does not apply to a licensee that has obtained a certificate of authority to offer continuing care contracts, as defined in paragraph (8) of subdivision (c) of Section 1771.
(Amended by Stats. 2015, Ch. 303, Sec. 274. (AB 731) Effective January 1, 2016.)
1547.
(a) Notwithstanding any other provision of this chapter, any person who violates Section 1503.5 or 1508, or both, may be assessed by the department an immediate civil penalty in the amount of two hundred dollars ($200) per day of the violation.
(b) The civil penalty authorized in subdivision (a) shall be imposed if an unlicensed facility is operated and the operator refuses to seek licensure or the operator seeks licensure and the licensure application is denied and the operator continues to operate the unlicensed facility, unless other remedies available to the department, including criminal prosecution, are deemed more effective by the department.
(c) An operator may appeal the assessment to the director. The department shall adopt regulations setting forth the appeal procedure.
(Amended by Stats. 1990, Ch. 1488, Sec. 1.)
1548.
(a) In addition to the suspension, temporary suspension, or revocation of a license issued under this chapter, the department shall levy civil penalties as follows:
(b) (1) The amount of the civil penalty shall be one hundred dollars ($100) per day for each violation of this chapter if an agency or facility fails to correct a deficiency after being provided a specified length of time to correct that deficiency.
(A) If a licensee or a licensee's representative submits evidence to the department that the licensee has corrected a deficiency, and the department, after reviewing that evidence, has determined that the deficiency has been corrected, the civil penalty shall cease as of the day the department received that evidence.
(B) If the department deems it necessary, the department shall inspect the facility within five working days after the department receives evidence pursuant to subparagraph (A) to confirm that the deficiency has been corrected.
(C) If the department determines that the deficiency has not been corrected, the civil penalty shall continue to accrue from the date of the original citation.
(D) If the department is able to verify that the deficiency was corrected prior to the date on which the department received the evidence pursuant to subparagraph (A), the civil penalty shall cease as of that earlier date.
(2) (A) If the department issues a notification of deficiency to an agency or facility for a repeat violation of a violation specified in paragraph (1), the department shall assess an immediate civil penalty of two hundred fifty dollars ($250) per repeat violation and one hundred dollars ($100) for each day the repeat violation continues after citation. The notification of deficiency shall state the manner in which the deficiency constitutes a repeat violation and shall be submitted to a supervisor for review and approval.
(B) For purposes of this section, "repeat violation" means a violation within 12 months of a prior violation of a statutory or regulatory provision designated by the same combination of letters or numerals, or both letters and numerals.
(C) Notwithstanding subparagraphs (A) and (B), the department, in its sole discretion, may reduce the civil penalty for the cited repeat violation to the level of the underlying violation, as applicable, if it determines that the cited repeat violation is not substantially similar to the original violation.
(3) If the nature or seriousness of the violation or the frequency of the violation warrants a higher penalty or an immediate civil penalty assessment, or both, as provided in this chapter, a correction of the deficiency shall not impact the imposition of a civil penalty.
(c) The department shall assess an immediate civil penalty of five hundred dollars ($500) per violation and one hundred dollars ($100) for each day the violation continues after citation for any of the following serious violations:
(1) Any violation that the department determines resulted in the injury or illness of a person in care.
(2) (A) Fire clearance violations, including, but not limited to, overcapacity, ambulatory status, inoperable smoke alarms, and inoperable fire alarm systems. The civil penalty shall not be assessed if the licensee has done either of the following:
(i) Requested the appropriate fire clearance based on ambulatory, nonambulatory, or bedridden status, and the decision is pending.
(ii) Initiated eviction proceedings.
(B) A licensee denied a clearance for bedridden residents may appeal to the fire authority, and, if that appeal is denied, may subsequently appeal to the Office of the State Fire Marshal, and shall not be assessed an immediate civil penalty until the final appeal is decided, or after 60 days has passed from the date of the citation, whichever is earlier.
(3) Absence of supervision, as required by statute or regulation.
(4) Accessible bodies of water, when prohibited in this chapter or regulations adopted pursuant to this chapter.
(5) Accessible firearms, ammunition, or both.
(6) Refused entry to a facility or any part of a facility in violation of Section 1533, 1534, or 1538.
(7) The presence of a person subject to a department Order of Exclusion on the premises.
(d) If the department issues a notification of deficiency to an agency or facility for a repeat violation specified in subdivision (c), the department shall assess an immediate civil penalty of one thousand dollars ($1,000) per repeat violation and one hundred dollars ($100) for each day the repeat violation continues after citation. The notification of deficiency shall state the manner in which the deficiency constitutes a repeat violation and shall be submitted to a supervisor for review and approval.
(e) (1) For a violation that the department determines resulted in the death of a resident at an adult residential facility, social rehabilitation facility, enhanced behavioral supports home licensed as an adult residential facility, adult residential facility for persons with special health care needs, or community crisis home, the civil penalty shall be fifteen thousand dollars ($15,000).

(2) For a violation that the department determines resulted in the death of a person receiving care at an adult day program, the civil penalty shall be assessed as follows:
(A) Seven thousand five hundred dollars ($7,500) for a facility licensed to care for 50 or fewer persons.
(B) Ten thousand dollars ($10,000) for a facility licensed to care for 51 or more persons.
(3) For a violation that the department determines resulted in the death of a person receiving care at a therapeutic day services facility, community treatment facility, transitional shelter care facility, transitional housing placement provider, small family home, crisis nursery, group home, enhanced behavioral supports home licensed as a group home, or short-term residential therapeutic program, the civil penalty shall be assessed as follows:
(A) Seven thousand five hundred dollars ($7,500) for a facility licensed to care for 40 or fewer children.
(B) Ten thousand dollars ($10,000) for a facility licensed to care for 41 to 100, inclusive, children.
(C) Fifteen thousand dollars ($15,000) for a facility licensed to care for more than 100 children.
(4) For a violation that the department determines resulted in the death of a youth receiving care at a runaway and homeless youth shelter licensed as a group home, the civil penalty shall be five thousand dollars ($5,000).
(5) For a violation that the department determines resulted in the death of a child receiving care through a foster family agency, the civil penalty shall be seven thousand five hundred dollars ($7,500).
(6) For a violation that the department determines resulted in the death of an individual receiving care or services through a full-service or noncustodial adoption agency, the civil penalty shall be seven thousand five hundred dollars ($7,500).
(f) (1) (A) For a violation that the department determines constitutes physical abuse, as defined in Section 15610.63 of the Welfare and Institutions Code, or resulted in serious bodily injury, as defined in Section 243 of the Penal Code, to a resident at an adult residential facility, social rehabilitation facility, enhanced behavioral supports home licensed as an adult residential facility, adult residential facility for persons with special health care needs, or community crisis home, the civil penalty shall be ten thousand dollars ($10,000).
(B) For a violation that the department determines constitutes physical abuse, as defined in Section 15610.63 of the Welfare and Institutions Code, or resulted in serious bodily injury, as defined in Section 243 of the Penal Code, to a person receiving care at an adult day program, the civil penalty shall be assessed as follows:
(i) Two thousand five hundred dollars ($2,500) for a facility licensed to care for 50 or fewer persons.
(ii) Five thousand dollars ($5,000) for a facility licensed to care for 51 or more persons.
(C) For a violation that the department determines constitutes physical abuse, as defined in paragraph (2), or resulted in serious bodily injury, as defined in Section 243 of the Penal Code, to a person receiving care at a therapeutic day services facility, community treatment facility, transitional shelter care facility, transitional housing placement provider, small family home, crisis nursery, group home, enhanced behavioral supports home licensed as a group home, or short-term residential therapeutic program, the civil penalty shall be assessed as follows:
(i) Two thousand five hundred dollars ($2,500) for a facility licensed to care for 40 or fewer children.
(ii) Five thousand dollars ($5,000) for a facility licensed to care for 41 to 100, inclusive, children.
(iii) Ten thousand dollars ($10,000) for a facility licensed to care for more than 100 children.
(D) For a violation that the department determines constitutes physical abuse, as defined in paragraph (2), or resulted in serious bodily injury, as defined in Section 243 of the Penal Code, to a youth receiving care at a runaway and homeless youth shelter licensed as a group home, the civil penalty shall be one thousand dollars ($1,000).
(E) For a violation that the department determines constitutes physical abuse, as defined in paragraph (2), or resulted in serious bodily injury, as defined in Section 243 of the Penal Code, to a child receiving care through a foster family agency, the civil penalty shall be two thousand five hundred dollars ($2,500).
(F) For a violation that the department determines constitutes physical abuse, as defined in paragraph (2), or resulted in serious bodily injury, as defined in Section 243 of the Penal Code, to an individual receiving care or services through a full-service or noncustodial adoption agency, the civil penalty shall be two thousand five hundred dollars ($2,500).
(2) For purposes of subparagraphs (C), (D), (E), and (F) of paragraph (1), "physical abuse" includes physical injury inflicted upon a child by another person by other than accidental means, sexual abuse as defined in Section 11165.1 of the Penal Code, neglect as defined in Section 11165.2 of the Penal Code, or unlawful corporal punishment or injury as defined in Section 11165.4 of the Penal Code when the person responsible for the child's welfare is a licensee, administrator, or employee of any facility licensed to care for children.
(g) (1) Before the assessment of a civil penalty pursuant to subdivision (e) or (f), the decision shall be approved by the program administrator of the Community Care Licensing Division.
(2) (A) The department shall reduce the amount of a civil penalty due pursuant to subdivision (e) or (f) by the amount of the civil penalty already assessed for the underlying violation.

(B) If the amount of the civil penalty that the department has already assessed for the underlying violation exceeds the amount of the penalty pursuant to subdivision (e) or (f), the larger amount shall prevail and be due and payable as already assessed by the department.
(h) (1) A notification of a deficiency written by a representative of the department shall include a factual description of the nature of the deficiency fully stating the manner in which the licensee failed to comply with the specified statute or regulation, and, if applicable, the particular place or area of the facility in which the deficiency occurred. The department shall make a good faith effort to work with the licensee to determine the cause of the deficiency and ways to prevent any repeat violations.
(2) The department shall adopt regulations setting forth the appeal procedures for deficiencies.
(i) (1) A licensee shall have the right to submit to the department a written request for a formal review of a civil penalty assessed pursuant to subdivision (e) or (f) within 15 business days of receipt of the notice of a civil penalty assessment and shall provide all available supporting documentation at that time. The review shall be conducted by the deputy director of the Community Care Licensing Division. The licensee may submit additional supporting documentation that was unavailable at the time of submitting the request for review within the first 30 business days after submitting the request for review. If the department requires additional information from the licensee, that information shall be requested within the first 30 business days after receiving the request for review. The licensee shall provide this additional information within 30 business days of receiving the request from the department. If the deputy director determines that the civil penalty was not assessed, or the finding of deficiency was not made, in accordance with applicable statutes or regulations of the department, he or she may amend or dismiss the civil penalty or finding of deficiency. The licensee shall be notified in writing of the deputy director's decision within 60 business days of the date when all necessary information has been provided to the department by the licensee.
(2) Upon exhausting the review described in paragraph (1), a licensee may further appeal that decision to an administrative law judge. Proceedings shall be conducted in accordance with Chapter 5 (commencing with Section 11500) of Part 1 of Division 3 of Title 2 of the Government Code, and the department shall have all the powers granted by those provisions. In all proceedings conducted in accordance with this section, the standard of proof shall be by a preponderance of the evidence.
(3) If, in addition to an assessment of civil penalties, the department elects to file an administrative action to suspend or revoke the facility license that includes violations relating to the assessment of the civil penalties, the department review of the pending appeal shall cease and the assessment of the civil penalties shall be heard as part of the administrative action process.
(4) Civil penalties shall be due and payable when administrative appeals have been exhausted. Unless payment arrangements have been made that are acceptable to the department, a civil penalty not paid within 30 days shall be subject to late fees, as specified by the department in regulation.
(j) (1) A licensee shall have the right to submit to the department a written request for a formal review of any other civil penalty or deficiency not described in subdivision (i) within 15 business days of receipt of the notice of a civil penalty assessment or a finding of a deficiency, and shall provide all available supporting documentation at that time. The review shall be conducted by a regional manager of the Community Care Licensing Division. The licensee may submit additional supporting documentation that was unavailable at the time of submitting the request for review within the first 30 business days after submitting the request for review. If the department requires additional information from the licensee, that information shall be requested within the first 30 business days after receiving the request for review. The licensee shall provide this additional information within 30 business days of receiving the request from the department. If the regional manager determines that the civil penalty was not assessed, or the finding of the deficiency was not made, in accordance with applicable statutes or regulations of the department, he or she may amend or dismiss the civil penalty or finding of deficiency. The licensee shall be notified in writing of the regional manager's decision within 60 business days of the date when all necessary information has been provided to the department by the licensee.
(2) Upon exhausting the review described in paragraph (1), the licensee may further appeal that decision to the program administrator of the Community Care Licensing Division within 15 business days of receipt of notice of the regional manager's decision. The licensee may submit additional supporting documentation that was unavailable at the time of appeal to the program administrator within the first 30 business days after requesting that appeal. If the department requires additional information from the licensee, that information shall be requested within the first 30 business days after receiving the request for the appeal. The licensee shall provide this additional information within 30 business days of receiving the request from the department. If the program administrator determines that the civil penalty was not assessed, or the finding of the deficiency was not made, in accordance with applicable statutes or regulations of the department, he or she may amend or dismiss the civil penalty or finding of deficiency. The licensee shall be notified in writing of the program administrator's decision within 60 business days of the date when all necessary information has been provided to the department by the licensee. The program administrator's decision is considered final and concludes the licensee's administrative appeal rights regarding the appeal conducted pursuant to this paragraph.
(3) Civil penalties shall be due and payable when administrative appeals have been exhausted. Unless payment arrangements have been made that are acceptable to the

department, a civil penalty not paid within 30 days shall be subject to late fees, as specified by the department in regulation.
(k) The department shall adopt regulations implementing this section.
(l) The department shall, by January 1, 2016, amend its regulations to reflect the changes to this section made by Section 2 of Chapter 813 of the Statutes of 2014.
(m) As provided in Section 11466.31 of the Welfare and Institutions Code, the department may offset civil penalties owed by a group home or short-term residential therapeutic program against moneys to be paid by a county for the care of minors after the group home or short-term residential therapeutic program has exhausted its appeal of the civil penalty assessment. The department shall provide the group home or short-term residential therapeutic program a reasonable opportunity to pay the civil penalty before instituting the offset provision.
(n) Notwithstanding the Administrative Procedure Act (Chapter 3.5 (commencing with Section 11340) of Part 1 of Division 3 of Title 2 of the Government Code), the department may implement and administer the changes made by the act that added this subdivision through all-county letters or similar written instructions until regulations are adopted pursuant to the Administrative Procedure Act.
(o) This section shall become operative on July 1, 2017.
(Repealed (in Sec. 1.5) and added by Stats. 2016, Ch. 823, Sec. 2.5. (AB 2231) Effective January 1, 2017. Section operative July 1, 2017, by its own provisions.)
1548.1.
The Legislature finds and declares that the current civil penalty structure for facilities licensed by the State Department of Social Services is insufficient to ensure the health and safety of those in care. It is the intent of the Legislature to comprehensively increase these penalties for all facilities in subsequent legislation, with particular emphasis on penalties for violations that result in serious injury or death.
(Added by Stats. 2014, Ch. 29, Sec. 13. (SB 855) Effective June 20, 2014.)
1549.
The civil, criminal, and administrative remedies available to the department pursuant to this article are not exclusive, and may be sought and employed in any combination deemed advisable by the department to enforce this chapter.
(Added by Stats. 1985, Ch. 1415, Sec. 6.)
ARTICLE 5. Suspension and Revocation [1550 - 1557.5]
(Article 5 added by Stats. 1973, Ch. 1203.)
1550.
The department may deny an application for, or suspend or revoke, any license, or any special permit, certificate of approval, or administrator certificate, issued under this chapter upon any of the following grounds and in the manner provided in this chapter, or may deny a transfer of a license pursuant to paragraph (2) of subdivision (b) of Section 1524 for any of the following grounds:
(a) Violation of this chapter or of the rules and regulations promulgated under this chapter by the licensee or holder of a special permit or certificate.
(b) Aiding, abetting, or permitting the violation of this chapter or of the rules and regulations promulgated under this chapter.
(c) Conduct which is inimical to the health, morals, welfare, or safety of either the people of this state or an individual in, or receiving services from, the facility or certified family home.
(d) The conviction of a licensee, holder of a special permit or certificate, or other person mentioned in Section 1522, at any time before or during licensure, of a crime as defined in Section 1522.
(e) The licensee of any facility, the holder of a special permit or certificate, or the person providing direct care or supervision knowingly allows any child to have illegal drugs or alcohol.
(f) Engaging in acts of financial malfeasance concerning the operation of a facility or certified family home, including, but not limited to, improper use or embezzlement of client moneys and property or fraudulent appropriation for personal gain of facility moneys and property, or willful or negligent failure to provide services.
(Amended by Stats. 2014, Ch. 29, Sec. 14. (SB 855) Effective June 20, 2014.)
1550.5.
The director may temporarily suspend any license prior to any hearing when, in the opinion of the director, the action is urgent to protect residents or clients of the facility from physical or mental abuse, abandonment, or any other substantial threat to health or safety. The director shall serve the licensee with the temporary suspension order, a copy of available discovery and other relevant evidence in the possession of the department, including, but not limited to, affidavits, declarations, and any other evidence upon which the director relied in issuing the temporary suspension order, the names of the department's witnesses, and the effective date of the temporary suspension and at the same time shall serve the licensee with an accusation.
(a) (1) The department shall notify the licensee, upon service of an order of temporary license suspension, of the licensee's right to an interim hearing on the order. The department shall also provide the licensee with a form and appropriate information for the licensee's use in requesting an interim hearing. The department shall also notify the licensee, upon service, of the licensee's independent right to seek review of the order by the superior court pursuant to Section 1085 of the Code of Civil Procedure.
(2) (A) The licensee may request an interim hearing by mailing or delivering a written request to the Office of Administrative Hearings. The licensee shall mail or deliver the request to the address or location specified on the request form served with the order. The licensee shall mail or deliver the request within five days after service of the order. Upon receipt of a timely request for an interim hearing, the Office of Administrative Hearings shall set a hearing date and time which shall be within 10 working days of the office's receipt of the request. The Office of Administrative Hearings shall promptly notify the licensee of the date, time, and place of the hearing. The licensee's request for an interim hearing shall not stay the operation of the order.
(B) Nothing in this section precludes a licensee from proceeding directly to a full evidentiary hearing or from seeking review of the temporary suspension order by the superior court without first requesting an interim hearing. Nothing in this section requires resolution of the interim hearing prior to review of the temporary suspension order by the superior court. The relief that may be ordered is a stay of the temporary suspension order.
(3) (A) An interim hearing shall be held before an administrative law judge of the Office of Administrative Hearings. The interim hearing shall be held at the regional office of the Office of Administrative Hearings having jurisdiction over the location of the facility.
(B) For purposes of the interim hearing conducted pursuant to this section, the licensee and department shall, at a minimum, have the following rights:
(i) To be represented by counsel.
(ii) To have a record made of the proceedings, copies of which may be obtained by the licensee upon payment of reasonable charges associated with the record.
(iii) To present written evidence in the form of relevant declarations, affidavits, and documents. No later than five working days prior to the interim hearing, the department and the respondent shall serve the opposing party, by overnight delivery or facsimile transmission, with any additional available pertinent discovery that the department or respondent will present at the hearing and that was not provided to the licensee at the time the temporary suspension order was issued. The additional discovery shall include, but not be limited to, affidavits, declarations, and the names of witnesses who will testify at the full evidentiary hearing. The department and the respondent shall have a continuing obligation to exchange discovery as described in this section, up to and including the day of the interim hearing. There shall be no oral testimony at the interim hearing.
(iv) In lieu of an affidavit by an alleged victim named in the accusation, the department and the respondent shall be permitted, at the discretion of the administrative law judge, to introduce at the interim hearing hearsay evidence as to any statement made by the alleged victim as if the alleged victim executed an affidavit. In deciding whether the hearsay statement should be admitted as evidence in the interim hearing, the administrative law judge shall consider the circumstances that would indicate the trustworthiness of the statement.
(v) To present oral argument.
(C) Consistent with the standards of proof applicable to a preliminary injunction entered under Section 527 of the Code of Civil Procedure, the administrative law judge shall vacate the temporary suspension order where, in the exercise of discretion, the administrative law judge concludes both of the following:
(i) There is a reasonable probability that the licensee will prevail in the underlying action.
(ii) The likelihood of physical or mental abuse, abandonment, or other substantial threat to the health or safety of residents or clients in not sustaining the order does not outweigh the likelihood of injury to the licensee in sustaining the order.
(D) The interim hearing shall be reported or recorded pursuant to subdivision (d) of Section 11512 of the Government Code.
(4) The administrative law judge shall issue a verbal interim decision at the conclusion of the interim hearing which sustains or vacates the order. The administrative law judge shall issue a written interim decision within five working days following the conclusion of the interim hearing. The written interim decision shall include findings of fact and a conclusion articulating the connection between the evidence produced at the hearing and the decision reached.
(5) The interim decision shall be subject to review only pursuant to Section 1094.5 of the Code of Civil Procedure. The department or the licensee may file a petition for that review. A petition for review under Section 1094.5 of the Code of Civil Procedure shall be heard by the court within 10 days of its filing and the court shall issue its judgment on the petition within 10 days of the conclusion of the hearing.
(6) The department may proceed with the accusation as otherwise provided by this section and Section 1551 notwithstanding an interim decision by the administrative law judge that vacates the order of temporary license suspension.
(b) Upon receipt of a notice of defense to the accusation by the licensee, the director shall, within 15 days, set the matter for a full evidentiary hearing, and the hearing shall be held as soon as possible but not later than 30 days after receipt of the notice. The temporary suspension shall remain in effect until the time the hearing is completed and the director has made a final determination on the merits, unless it is earlier vacated by interim decision of the administrative law judge or a superior court judge. However, the temporary suspension shall be deemed vacated if the director fails to make a final determination on the merits within 30 days after the original hearing has been completed.
(Amended by Stats. 1997, Ch. 728, Sec. 1. Effective January 1, 1998.)
1550.7.
(a) The department shall conduct an unannounced visit to a facility within 30 days after the effective date of a temporary suspension of a license in order to ensure that the facility is nonoperational, unless the department previously has verified that the facility is nonoperational.
(b) The department shall conduct an unannounced visit to a facility within 30 days after the effective date of a revocation of a license, in order to ensure that the facility is nonoperational, unless the department previously has verified that the facility is nonoperational.
(Added by Stats. 2008, Ch. 291, Sec. 8. Effective September 25, 2008.)
1551.

(a) Proceedings for the suspension, revocation, or denial of a license, registration, special permit, certificate of approval, or any administrator certificate under this chapter, or denial of transfer of a license pursuant to paragraph (2) of subdivision (c) of Section 1524, shall be conducted in accordance with Chapter 5 (commencing with Section 11500) of Part 1 of Division 3 of Title 2 of the Government Code, and the department shall have all the powers granted by those provisions. In the event of conflict between this chapter and the Government Code, the Government Code shall prevail.

(b) In all proceedings conducted in accordance with this section, the standard of proof to be applied shall be by the preponderance of the evidence.

(c) If the license, special permit, certificate of approval, or administrator certificate is not temporarily suspended pursuant to Section 1550, the hearing shall be held within 90 calendar days after receipt of the notice of defense, unless a continuance of the hearing is granted by the department or the administrative law judge. When the matter has been set for hearing only the administrative law judge may grant a continuance of the hearing. The administrative law judge may, but need not, grant a continuance of the hearing only upon finding the existence of one or more of the following:

(1) The death or incapacitating illness of a party, a representative or attorney of a party, a witness to an essential fact, or of the parent, child, or member of the household of such person, when it is not feasible to substitute another representative, attorney, or witness because of the proximity of the hearing date.

(2) Lack of notice of hearing as provided in Section 11509 of the Government Code.

(3) A material change in the status of the case where a change in the parties or pleadings requires postponement, or an executed settlement or stipulated findings of fact obviate the need for hearing. A partial amendment of the pleadings shall not be good cause for continuance to the extent that the unamended portion of the pleadings is ready to be heard.

(4) A stipulation for continuance signed by all parties or their authorized representatives, including, but not limited to, a representative, which is communicated with the request for continuance to the administrative law judge no later than 25 business days before the hearing.

(5) The substitution of the representative or attorney of a party upon showing that the substitution is required.

(6) The unavailability of a party, representative, or attorney of a party, or witness to an essential fact due to a conflicting and required appearance in a judicial matter if when the hearing date was set, the person did not know and could neither anticipate nor at any time avoid the conflict, and the conflict with request for continuance is immediately communicated to the administrative law judge.

(7) The unavailability of a party, a representative or attorney of a party, or a material witness due to an unavoidable emergency.

(8) Failure by a party to comply with a timely discovery request if the continuance request is made by the party who requested the discovery.

(Amended by Stats. 2014, Ch. 29, Sec. 15. (SB 855) Effective June 20, 2014.)

1551.1.

(a) The administrative law judge conducting a hearing under this article may permit the testimony of a child witness, or a similarly vulnerable witness, including a witness who is developmentally disabled, to be taken outside the presence of the respondent or respondents if all of the following conditions exist:

(1) The administrative law judge determines that taking the witness's testimony outside the presence of the respondent or respondents is necessary to ensure truthful testimony.

(2) The witness is likely to be intimidated by the presence of the respondent or respondents.

(3) The witness is afraid to testify in front of the respondent or respondents.

(b) If the testimony of the witness is taken outside of the presence of the respondent or respondents, the department shall provide for the use of one-way closed-circuit television so the respondent or respondents can observe the testimony of the witness. Nothing in this section shall limit a respondent's right of cross-examination.

(c) The administrative law judge conducting a hearing under this section may clear the hearing room of any persons who are not a party to the action in order to protect any witness from intimidation or other harm, taking into account the rights of all persons.

(Added by Stats. 1994, Ch. 1267, Sec. 3. Effective January 1, 1995.)

1551.15.

(a) In any administrative proceeding conducted pursuant to this article in which a child or other minor is the victim in an allegation of inappropriate sexual conduct, evidence of specific instances of the victim's sexual conduct with individuals other than the alleged perpetrator is subject to all of the following limitations:

(1) The evidence is not discoverable unless it is to be offered at an administrative proceeding to attack the credibility of the victim, as provided for in subdivision (b). This paragraph is intended only to limit the scope of discovery and is not intended to affect the methods of discovery authorized by statute.

(2) The evidence is not admissible at the administrative proceeding unless offered to attack the credibility of the victim, as provided for in subdivision (b).

(3) Reputation or opinion evidence regarding the sexual behavior of the victim is not admissible for any purpose.

(b) Evidence of specific instances of a victim's sexual conduct with individuals other than the alleged perpetrator is presumed inadmissible absent an offer of proof establishing its relevance and reliability and that its probative value is not substantially outweighed by the probability that its admission will create substantial danger of undue prejudice or confuse the issues.

(c) As used in this section, "victim" means a person who claims to have been subjected to inappropriate sexual conduct by an alleged perpetrator, including, but not limited to, a person who is an adult at the time of hearing, but was under 18 years of age at the time of the alleged inappropriate sexual conduct.

(Added by Stats. 2018, Ch. 910, Sec. 17. (AB 1930) Effective January 1, 2019.)

1551.2.

(a) (1) An out-of-court statement made by a minor under 12 years of age who is the subject or victim of an allegation at issue is admissible evidence at an administrative hearing conducted pursuant to this article. The out-of-court statement may be used to support a finding of fact unless an objection is timely made and the objecting party establishes that the statement is unreliable because it was the product of fraud, deceit, or undue influence. However, the out-of-court statement may not be the sole basis for the finding of fact, unless the adjudicator finds that the time, content, and circumstances of the statement provide sufficient indicia of reliability.

(2) The proponent of the statement shall give reasonable notice to all parties of the intended introduction of the statement at the hearing.

(3) For purposes of this subdivision, an objection is timely if it identifies with reasonable specificity the disputed out-of-court statement and it gives the proponent of the evidence a reasonable period of time to prepare a response to the objection prior to the hearing.

(b) This section shall not be construed to limit the right of any party to the administrative hearing to subpoena a witness whose statement is admitted as evidence or to introduce admissible evidence relevant to the weight of the hearsay evidence or the credibility of the hearsay declarant.

(Added by Stats. 2002, Ch. 707, Sec. 1. Effective January 1, 2003.)

1551.3.

Notwithstanding Sections 11425.10 and 11425.20 of the Government Code, a proceeding conducted pursuant to Section 1534, 1551, or 1558 against a foster family home, certified family home, or resource family of a foster family agency shall be confidential and not open to the public in order to preserve the confidential information of a child or foster parent consistent with the confidentiality requirements in Section 1536 of this code, Section 11167.5 of the Penal Code, and Sections 827, 10850, and 16519.55 of the Welfare and Institutions Code. Notwithstanding this requirement, an administrative law judge may admit those persons deemed to have a direct and legitimate interest in a particular case or the work of the court on a case-by-case basis and with any admonishments, limitations, or protective orders that may be necessary to preserve the confidential nature of the proceedings.

(Amended by Stats. 2018, Ch. 910, Sec. 18. (AB 1930) Effective January 1, 2019.)

1551.5.

In addition to the witness fees and mileage provided by Section 11450.40 of the Government Code, the department may pay actual, necessary, and reasonable expenses in an amount not to exceed the per diem allowance payable to a nonrepresented state employee on travel status. The department may pay witness expenses in advance of the hearing.

(Amended by Stats. 1995, Ch. 938, Sec. 60. Effective January 1, 1996. Operative July 1, 1997, by Sec. 98 of Ch. 938.)

1553.

The withdrawal of an application for a license or a special permit after it has been filed with the state department shall not, unless the state department consents in writing to such withdrawal, deprive the state department of its authority to institute or continue a proceeding against the applicant for the denial of the license or a special permit upon any ground provided by law or to enter an order denying the license or special permit upon any such ground.

The suspension, expiration, or forfeiture by operation of law of a license or a special permit issued by the state department, or its suspension, forfeiture, or cancellation by order of the state department or by order of a court of law, or its surrender without the written consent of the state department, shall not deprive the state department of its authority to institute or continue a disciplinary proceeding against the licensee or holder of a special permit upon any ground provided by law or to enter an order suspending or revoking the license or special permit or otherwise taking disciplinary action against the licensee or holder of a special permit on any such ground.

(Added by Stats. 1973, Ch. 1203.)

1554.

Any license, registration, or special permit suspended pursuant to this chapter, and any special permit revoked pursuant to this chapter, may be reinstated pursuant to the provisions of Section 11522 of the Government Code.

(Amended by Stats. 1980, Ch. 1285.)

1555.

Whenever a license, registration, or special permit issued under this chapter for a community care facility is suspended, revoked, temporarily suspended, forfeited, canceled, or expires, the department shall provide written notice of that occurrence within 10 days to the local director of social services and the probation officer of the county in which the community care facility is located.

(Added by Stats. 1984, Ch. 821, Sec. 1.)

1556.

(a) If the director determines that it is necessary to temporarily suspend any license or special permit of a community care facility in order to protect the residents or clients of the facility from physical or mental abuse, abandonment, or any other substantial threat to health or safety, the department shall make every effort to minimize transfer trauma for the residents or clients.

(b) The department shall contact any local agency that may have assessment, placement, protective, or advocacy responsibility for the residents or clients of a facility after a decision is made to temporarily suspend the license or special permit of the facility and prior to its implementation. The department shall work together with these agencies and the licensee, if the director determines it to be appropriate, to locate alternative placement sites, and to contact relatives or other persons responsible for the care of these residents or clients, provide onsite evaluation of the residents or clients, and assist in the transfer of the residents or clients.

(c) In any case where the department alleges that a client or resident has a health condition or health conditions which cannot be cared for within the limits of the license or special permit, or requires inpatient care in a health facility licensed pursuant to Chapter 2 (commencing with Section 1250), the department shall do all of the following:

(1) Consult with appropriate medical personnel about when the client or resident should be removed from the facility and how transfer trauma can be minimized.

(2) If the department temporarily suspends the license or special permit of a facility, use medical personnel deemed appropriate by the department to provide onsite evaluation of the clients or residents.

(3) If the department does not suspend the license or special permit of a facility, order the licensee to remove only those clients or residents who have health conditions which cannot be cared for within the limits of the license or special permit or require inpatient care in a health facility licensed pursuant to Chapter 2 (commencing with Section 1250), as determined by the department, if the department determines that other clients or residents are not in physical danger.

(d) In any case where the department orders the temporary suspension of a licensee or orders the licensee, or holder of a special permit, to remove a client or resident who has a health condition or health conditions which cannot be cared for within the limits of the license or special permit or requires inpatient care in a health facility licensed pursuant to Chapter 2 (commencing with Section 1250), the department may require the licensee or holder of a special permit to do all of the following:

(1) Prepare and submit to the department a written plan for the safe and orderly relocation of the client or resident, in a form acceptable to the department.

(2) Comply with all terms and conditions of the approved relocation plan.

(3) Provide any other information as may be required by the department for the proper administration and enforcement of this section.

(Amended by Stats. 2014, Ch. 29, Sec. 16. (SB 855) Effective June 20, 2014.)
1556.5.

(a) If the department, as a condition of licensure, requires the chief executive officer or other authorized member of the board of directors and the administrator of a foster family agency to attend an orientation given by the licensing agency that outlines the applicable rules and regulations for operation of a foster family agency, that orientation shall include, but not be limited to, a description of policies, procedures, or practices that violate paragraph (1) or (2) of subdivision (i) of Section 11166 of the Penal Code.

(b) If the department requires, as part of an application for licensure for a foster family agency, a written plan of operation, that plan of operation shall include a written plan establishing policies, procedures, or practices to ensure that the foster family agency does not violate paragraph (1) or (2) of subdivision (i) of Section 11166 of the Penal Code.

(c) For purposes of this section, a foster family agency is defined in paragraph (4) of subdivision (a) of Section 1502.

(Added by Stats. 2016, Ch. 850, Sec. 2. (AB 1001) Effective January 1, 2017.)
1557.5.

Each facility required to be licensed pursuant to this chapter shall keep a current record of clients in the facility, including the client's name and ambulatory status, and the name, address, and telephone number of the client's physician and of any person or agency responsible for the care of the client. The facility shall protect the privacy and confidentiality of this information.

(Added by Stats. 1985, Ch. 869, Sec. 3. See similar Section 1557.5 added by Stats. 1985, Ch. 1096.)
1557.5.

Each facility required to be licensed shall keep a current record of all of the following:

(a) Clients in the facility, including each client's name and ambulatory status.

(b) The name, address, and telephone number of each client's physician.

(c) The name, address, and telephone number of any person or agency responsible for the care of a client.

The facility shall respect the privacy and confidentiality of this information.

(Added by Stats. 1985, Ch. 1096, Sec. 2.)

ARTICLE 5.5. Employee Actions [1558 - 1558.3]

(Article 5.5 added by Stats. 1989, Ch. 825, Sec. 1.)

1558.

(a) The department may prohibit any person from being a member of the board of directors, an executive director, or an officer of a licensee, or a licensee from employing, or continuing the employment of, or allowing in a licensed facility or certified family home, or allowing contact with clients of a licensed facility or certified family home by, any employee, prospective employee, or person who is not a client who has:

(1) Violated, or aided or permitted the violation by any other person of, any provisions of this chapter or of any rules or regulations promulgated under this chapter.

(2) Engaged in conduct that is inimical to the health, morals, welfare, or safety of either the people of this state or an individual in, or receiving services from, the facility or certified family home.

(3) Been denied an exemption to work or to be present in a facility or certified family home, when that person has been convicted of a crime, as defined in Section 1522.

(4) Engaged in any other conduct that would constitute a basis for disciplining a licensee or certified family home.

(5) Engaged in acts of financial malfeasance concerning the operation of a facility or certified family home, including, but not limited to, improper use or embezzlement of client moneys and property or fraudulent appropriation for personal gain of facility moneys and property, or willful or negligent failure to provide services.

(b) The excluded person, the facility or certified family home, and the licensee shall be given written notice of the basis of the department's action and of the excluded person's right to an appeal. The notice shall be served either by personal service or by registered mail. Within 15 days after the department serves the notice, the excluded person may file with the department a written appeal of the exclusion order. If the excluded person fails to file a written appeal within the prescribed time, the department's action shall be final.

(c) (1) The department may require the immediate removal of a member of the board of directors, an executive director, or an officer of a licensee or exclusion of an employee, prospective employee, or person who is not a client from a facility or certified family home pending a final decision of the matter, when, in the opinion of the director, the action is necessary to protect residents or clients from physical or mental abuse, abandonment, or any other substantial threat to their health or safety.

(2) If the department requires the immediate removal of a member of the board of directors, an executive director, or an officer of a licensee or exclusion of an employee, prospective employee, or person who is not a client from a facility or certified family home, the department shall serve an order of immediate exclusion upon the excluded person that shall notify the excluded person of the basis of the department's action and of the excluded person's right to a hearing.

(3) Within 15 days after the department serves an order of immediate exclusion, the excluded person may file a written appeal of the exclusion with the department. The department's action shall be final if the excluded person does not appeal the exclusion within the prescribed time. The department shall do both of the following upon receipt of a written appeal:

(A) Within 30 days of receipt of the appeal, serve an accusation upon the excluded person.

(B) Within 60 days of receipt of a notice of defense pursuant to Section 11506 of the Government Code by the excluded person to conduct a hearing on the accusation.

(4) An order of immediate exclusion of the excluded person from the facility or certified family home shall remain in effect until the hearing is completed and the director has made a final determination on the merits. However, the order of immediate exclusion shall be deemed vacated if the director fails to make a final determination on the merits within 60 days after the original hearing has been completed.

(d) An excluded person who files a written appeal with the department pursuant to this section shall, as part of the written request, provide his or her current mailing address. The excluded person shall subsequently notify the department in writing of any change in mailing address, until the hearing process has been completed or terminated.

(e) Hearings held pursuant to this section shall be conducted in accordance with Chapter 5 (commencing with Section 11500) of Division 3 of Title 2 of the Government Code. The standard of proof shall be the preponderance of the evidence and the burden of proof shall be on the department.

(f) The department may institute or continue a disciplinary proceeding against a member of the board of directors, an executive director, or an officer of a licensee or an employee, prospective employee, or person who is not a client upon any ground provided by this section. The department may enter an order prohibiting any person from being a member of the board of directors, an executive director, or an officer of a licensee or prohibiting the excluded person's employment or presence in the facility or certified family home, or otherwise take disciplinary action against the excluded person, notwithstanding any resignation, withdrawal of employment application, or change of duties by the excluded person, or any discharge, failure to hire, or reassignment of the excluded person by the licensee or that the excluded person no longer has contact with clients at the facility or certified family home.

(g) A licensee's or certified family home's failure to comply with the department's exclusion order after being notified of the order shall be grounds for disciplining the licensee pursuant to Section 1550.

(h) (1) (A) In cases in which the excluded person appealed the exclusion order, the person shall be prohibited from working in any facility or being licensed to operate any facility licensed by the department or from being a certified foster parent for the remainder of the excluded person's life, unless otherwise ordered by the department.

(B) The excluded individual may petition for reinstatement one year after the effective date of the decision and order of the department upholding the exclusion order pursuant to Section 11522 of the Government Code. The department shall provide the excluded person with a copy of Section 11522 of the Government Code with the decision and order.

(2) (A) In cases in which the department informed the excluded person of his or her right to appeal the exclusion order and the excluded person did not appeal the exclusion order, the person shall be prohibited from working in any facility or being licensed to operate any facility licensed by the department or a certified foster parent for the remainder of the excluded person's life, unless otherwise ordered by the department.

(B) The excluded individual may petition for reinstatement after one year has elapsed from the date of the notification of the exclusion order pursuant to Section 11522 of the Government Code. The department shall provide the excluded person with a copy of Section 11522 of the Government Code with the exclusion order.

(i) Notwithstanding paragraph (2) of subdivision (a) or subdivision (c) of Section 1550, the department shall take reasonable action, including, but not limited to, prohibiting a person from being a member of the board of directors, an executive director, or an officer of a licensee of a licensed facility or certified family home, or denying an application for, or suspending or revoking, a license, special permit, certificate of approval, or administrator certificate, issued under this chapter, or denying a transfer of a license pursuant to paragraph (2) of subdivision (c) of Section 1524, upon a finding of a violation of subdivision (i) of Section 11166 of the Penal Code.

(j) For purposes of this section, exclusion from a licensed foster family home or certified family home shall include exclusion from a resource family, as defined in Section 1517 of this code and Section 16519.5 of the Welfare and Institutions Code.

(Amended by Stats. 2018, Ch. 910, Sec. 19. (AB 1930) Effective January 1, 2019.)

1558.1.

(a) (1) If the department determines that a person was issued a license under this chapter, Chapter 1 (commencing with Section 1200), Chapter 2 (commencing with Section 1250), Chapter 3.01 (commencing with Section 1568.01), Chapter 3.2 (commencing with Section 1569), Chapter 3.3 (commencing with Section 1570), Chapter 3.4 (commencing with Section 1596.70), Chapter 3.5 (commencing with Section 1596.90), or Chapter 3.6 (commencing with Section 1597.30), or that the applicant previously was approved as a resource family under Article 2 (commencing with Section 16519.5) of Chapter 5 of Part 4 of Division 9 of the Welfare and Institutions Code, and the prior license was revoked or prior approval was rescinded within the preceding two years, the department shall exclude the person from, and remove the person from the position of a member of the board of directors, an executive director, or an officer of a licensee of, any facility licensed by the department pursuant to the chapter.

(2) If the department determines that a person previously was issued a certificate of approval by a foster family agency that was revoked or rescinded by the department pursuant to subdivision (c) of Section 1517 or subdivision (b) of Section 1534 within the preceding two years, the department shall exclude the person from, and remove the person from the position of a member of the board of directors, an executive director, or an officer of a licensee of, any facility licensed by the department pursuant to this chapter.

(b) If the department determines that the person had previously applied for a license under this chapter, Chapter 1 (commencing with Section 1200), Chapter 2 (commencing with Section 1250), Chapter 3.01 (commencing with Section 1568.01), Chapter 3.2 (commencing with Section 1569), Chapter 3.3 (commencing with Section 1570), Chapter 3.4 (commencing with Section 1596.70), Chapter 3.5 (commencing with Section 1596.90), or Chapter 3.6 (commencing with Section 1597.30), and the application was denied within the last year, the department shall exclude the person from, and remove the person from the position of a member of the board of directors, an executive director, or an officer of a licensee of, any facility licensed by the department pursuant to this chapter and as follows:

(1) In cases in which the applicant petitioned for a hearing, the department shall exclude the person from, and remove the person from the position of a member of the board of directors, an executive director, or an officer of a licensee of, any facility licensed by the department pursuant to this chapter until one year has elapsed from the effective date of the decision and order of the department upholding a denial.

(2) In cases in which the department or county informed the applicant of his or her right to petition for a hearing and the applicant did not petition for a hearing, the department shall exclude the person from, and remove the person from the position of a member of the board of directors, an executive director, or an officer of a licensee of, any facility licensed by the department pursuant to this chapter until one year has elapsed from the date of the notification of the denial and the right to petition for a hearing.

(c) If the department determines that the person had previously applied for a certificate of approval with a foster family agency, and the department ordered the foster family agency to deny the application pursuant to subdivision (c) of Section 1517 or subdivision (b) of Section 1534, the department shall exclude the person from, and remove the person from the position of a member of the board of directors, an executive director, or an officer of a licensee of, any facility licensed by the department pursuant to this chapter and as follows:

(1) In cases in which the applicant petitioned for a hearing, the department shall exclude the person from, and remove the person from the position of a member of the board of directors, an executive director, or an officer of a licensee of, any facility licensed by the department pursuant to this chapter until one year has elapsed from the effective date of the decision and order of the department upholding a denial.

(2) In cases in which the department informed the applicant of his or her right to petition for a hearing and the applicant did not petition for a hearing, the department shall exclude the person from, and remove the person from the position of a member of the board of directors, an executive director, or an officer of a licensee of, any facility licensed by the department pursuant to this chapter until one year has elapsed from the date of the notification of the denial and the right to petition for a hearing.

(d) Exclusion or removal of an individual pursuant to this section shall not be considered an order of exclusion for purposes of Section 1558 of this code, Section 16519.6 of the Welfare and Institutions Code, or any other law.

(e) The department may determine not to exclude the person from, or remove the person from the position of a member of the board of directors, an executive director, or an officer of a licensee of, any facility licensed by the department pursuant to this chapter if it has determined that the reasons for the denial of the application or revocation of the facility license or certificate of approval, or the denial or rescission of resource family approval, were due to circumstances and conditions that either have been corrected or are no longer in existence.

(f) For purposes of this section, exclusion from a licensed facility shall include exclusion from a resource family, as defined in Section 1517 of this code and Section 16519.5 of the Welfare and Institutions Code. The exclusion of a resource family or an applicant for

resource family approval pursuant to this section shall only be imposed as set forth in the written directives or regulations adopted pursuant to Section 16519.5 of the Welfare and Institutions Code.

(Amended by Stats. 2018, Ch. 910, Sec. 20. (AB 1930) Effective January 1, 2019.)

1558.3.

The department shall conduct an unannounced visit to a facility within 30 days after the department serves an order of immediate exclusion from the facility upon the licensee or a person subject to immediate removal or exclusion from the facility pursuant to paragraph (3) of subdivision (c) of Section 1522 and subdivision (c) of Section 1558 and in order to ensure that the excluded person is not within the facility, unless the department previously has verified that the excluded person is not within the facility.

(Added by Stats. 2008, Ch. 291, Sec. 9. Effective September 25, 2008.)

ARTICLE 5.7. Transitional Housing Placement Program [1559.110-1559.110.]

(Heading of Article 5.7 amended by Stats. 2017, Ch. 731, Sec. 3.)

1559.110.

(a) (1) The State Department of Social Services shall license transitional housing placement providers pursuant to this chapter.

(2) A transitional housing placement provider may operate either of the following programs, as described in Section 16522.1 of the Welfare and Institutions Code:

(A) A Transitional Housing Placement program for participants who are minor foster children.

(B) A Transitional Housing Placement program for participants who are nonminor dependents.

(3) Prior to licensure, a transitional housing placement provider shall obtain program certification from the applicable county, in accordance with Section 16522.1 of the Welfare and Institutions Code. For purposes of this paragraph, "applicable county" means the county where the administrative office or subadministrative office of a transitional housing placement provider is located, or a primary placing county.

(b) Transitional housing placement providers shall provide supervised transitional housing services to foster children who are at least 16 years of age.

(c) Transitional housing placement providers shall certify that housing units are adequate, safe, and sanitary.

(d) Transitional housing units shall include any of the following:

(1) A host family certified by a transitional housing placement provider with whom a participant lives in an apartment, single-family dwelling, or condominium owned, rented, or leased by the host family.

(2) A staffed site in which a participant lives in an apartment, single-family dwelling, or condominium owned, rented, or leased by a transitional housing placement provider either with an adult employee of the provider who provides supervision or in a building in which one or more adult employees of the provider reside and provide supervision.

(3) A remote site in which a participant lives independently in an apartment, single-family dwelling, or condominium owned, rented, or leased by a transitional housing placement provider under the supervision of the provider if the department provides approval. The remote site shall only be available to nonminor dependents.

(e) (1) A transitional housing placement provider may cosign a lease with a nonminor dependent as specified by the department.

(2) A participant shall not be permitted to solely sign a rental or lease agreement.

(f) A transitional housing placement provider's plan of operation shall include a program statement. The program statement shall contain a description of the core services and supports, as set forth in paragraph (5) of subdivision (b) of Section 11463 of the Welfare and Institutions Code, and as prescribed by the department, to be offered to participants, as appropriate or as necessary.

(g) (1) The department shall adopt regulations to govern transitional housing placement providers licensed pursuant to this section.

(2) The regulations shall be age appropriate and recognize that nonminor dependents who are about to exit from the foster care system should be subject to fewer restrictions than those who are foster children. At a minimum, the regulations shall provide for all of the following:

(A) Require programs that serve both minor foster children and nonminor dependents to have separate rules and program design, as appropriate, for these two groups of youth.

(B) Allow nonminor dependents to have the greatest amount of freedom possible in order to prepare them for their transition to adulthood, in accordance with paragraph (1) of subdivision (b) of Section 1502.7.

(C) Maintain a program staffing ratio for minor foster children of case manager to participant not to exceed 1 to 12, inclusive.

(D) Maintain a program staffing ratio for nonminor dependents of case manager to participant not to exceed a shared average caseload of 1 to 12, inclusive, with a designated lead case manager assigned to each youth.

(E) Allow a nonminor dependent participant to share a bedroom in a transitional housing unit with any of the following persons:

(i) Another participant as approved by the provider.

(ii) A participant in Transitional Housing Program-Plus, as defined in subdivision (s) of Section 11400 of the Welfare and Institutions Code, as approved by the provider.

(iii) A nonparticipant roommate as approved by the provider on a case-by-case basis, as specified by the department.

(iv) The participant's children.

(v) Any other person as specified by the department.

(F) Allow a minor participant to share a bedroom in a transitional housing unit with any of the following persons:

(i) Another participant as approved by the provider.

(ii) A participant in Transitional Housing Program-Plus, as defined in subdivision (s) of Section 11400 of the Welfare and Institutions Code, as approved by the provider.

(iii) The participant's children.

(iv) A nonparticipant roommate as approved by the provider on a case-by-case basis, as specified by the department.

(v) Any other person as specified by the department.

(G) Any adult who is not a participant, including participants in Transitional Housing Program-Plus, as defined in subdivision (s) of Section 11400 of the Welfare and Institutions Code, and who resides with a participant shall obtain a criminal record clearance or exemption in accordance with Section 1522.

(h) (1) A program manager for a Transitional Housing Placement program for nonminor dependents shall have a master's degree or higher from an accredited or state-approved graduate school, or equivalent education and experience, as determined by the department.

(2) Persons who possess a master's degree or higher from an accredited or state-approved graduate school in any of the following areas, or equivalent education and experience, as determined by the department, shall be considered to be qualified to perform program manager activities in a Transitional Housing Placement program for nonminor dependents:

(A) Marriage, family, and child counseling.

(B) Child psychology.

(C) Child development.

(D) Counseling psychology.

(E) Social psychology.

(F) Clinical psychology.

(G) Educational psychology.

(H) Education, with emphasis on counseling.

(I) Social work or social welfare.

(J) An area that includes the counseling or psychotherapy content required for licensure as a Licensed Professional Clinical Counselor, as specified in Sections 4999.32 and 4999.33 of the Business and Professions Code.

(K) A subject area that is functionally equivalent to those listed in subparagraphs (A) to (J), inclusive, as set forth by the department.

(i) (1) (A) In addition to the degree specifications in subdivision (h), a program manager for a Transitional Housing Placement program for nonminor dependents shall have a minimum of two years' experience in a public or private child welfare social services setting or specific experience working with transition age youth who are 16 to 24 years of age, inclusive.

(B) Documentation of the completed education and experience requirements shall be maintained in the personnel file.

(C) A transitional housing placement provider may request an exception, as specified in subdivision (j), for a person who does not meet the requirements specified in this subdivision or subdivision (h).

(D) Persons who were hired as program managers prior to January 1, 2018, shall not be required to meet the requirements of this subdivision in order to remain employed as program managers.

(j) (1) A transitional housing placement provider shall apply to the department, using the process established by the department, to request an exception to the requirements of subdivision (h) or (i) based on completion of equivalent education and experience.

(2) The department may grant exceptions to the requirements described in subdivisions (h) and (i) if the person to whom the exception would apply has a baccalaureate degree from an accredited or state-approved college or university.

(3) The department shall approve or deny exceptions to the requirements described in subdivisions (h) and (i) within 30 days of receiving the exception request from the provider.

(k) (1) A case manager for a Transitional Housing Placement program for nonminor dependents shall meet either of the following requirements:

(A) A minimum of a baccalaureate degree in any of the areas specified in paragraph (2) of subdivision (h).

(B) A minimum of a baccalaureate degree in an area not specified in paragraph (2) of subdivision (h) and a minimum of two years' experience in a public or private child welfare social services setting, or specific experience working with transition age youth who are 16 to 24 years of age, inclusive.

(2) Documentation of the completed education and experience requirements shall be maintained in the personnel file.

(3) Persons who were hired as case managers prior to January 1, 2018, shall not be required to meet the requirements of this subdivision in order to remain employed as a case manager.

(4) A transitional housing placement provider shall apply to the department, using the process established by the department, to request an exception to the requirements of subparagraph (A) or (B) of paragraph (1) based on completion of equivalent education and experience shall apply to the department using the process established by the department.

(Amended by Stats. 2017, Ch. 731, Sec. 4. (SB 612) Effective January 1, 2018.)

ARTICLE 6. Other Provisions [1560 - 1564]

(Article 6 added by Stats. 1973, Ch. 1203.)

1560.

(a) The director shall require as a condition precedent to the issuance of any license or special permit for a community care facility, if the licensee or holder of a special permit

handles or will handle any money of a person within the community care facility, that the applicant for the license or special permit file or have on file with the state department a bond issued by a surety company admitted to do business in this state in a sum to be fixed by the state department based upon the magnitude of the operations of the applicant, but which sum shall not be less than one thousand dollars ($1,000), running to the State of California and conditioned upon his or her faithful and honest handling of the money of persons within the facility.

(b) The failure of any licensee under this chapter to maintain on file with the state department a bond in the amount prescribed by the director or who embezzles the trust funds of a person in the facility shall constitute cause for the revocation of the license.

(c) The provisions of this section shall not apply if the licensee meets both of the following requirements:

(1) The licensee operates a community care facility which is licensed to care for children including, but not limited to, a foster family home.

(2) The licensee handles moneys of persons within the community care facility in amounts less than fifty dollars ($50) per person and less than five hundred dollars ($500) for all persons in any month.

(Amended by Stats. 1992, Ch. 1315, Sec. 9. Effective January 1, 1993.)

1561.

The director may grant a partial or total variance from the bonding requirements of Section 1560 for any community care facility if he finds that compliance with them is so onerous that a community care facility will cease to operate, and if he also finds that money of the persons received or cared for in the community care facility has been, or will be, deposited in a bank in this state, in a trust company authorized to transact a trust business in this state, or in a savings and loan association in this state, upon condition that such money may not be withdrawn except on authorization of the guardian or conservator of such person.

(Added by Stats. 1973, Ch. 1203.)

1562.

(a) The department shall ensure that operators and staffs of community care facilities have appropriate training to provide the care and services for which a license or certificate is issued. The section shall not apply to a facility licensed as an Adult Residential Facility for Persons with Special Health Care Needs pursuant to Article 9 (commencing with Section 1567.50).

(b) It is the intent of the Legislature that children in foster care reside in the least restrictive, family-based settings that can meet their needs, and that group homes and short-term residential therapeutic programs will be used only for short-term, specialized, and intensive treatment purposes that are consistent with a case plan that is determined by a child's best interests. Accordingly, the Legislature encourages the department to adopt policies, practices, and guidance that ensure that the education, qualification, and training requirements for child care staff in group homes and short-term residential therapeutic programs are consistent with the intended role of group homes and short-term residential therapeutic programs to provide short-term, specialized, and intensive treatment, with a particular focus on crisis intervention, behavioral stabilization, and other treatment-related goals, as well as the connections between those efforts and work toward permanency for children.

(c) (1) Each person employed as a facility manager or staff member of a group home or short-term residential therapeutic program, as defined in paragraphs (13) and (18) of subdivision (a) of Section 1502, who provides direct care and supervision to children and youth residing in the group home or short-term residential therapeutic program shall be at least 21 years of age.

(2) Paragraph (1) shall not apply to a facility manager or staff member employed at the group home before October 1, 2014.

(3) For purposes of this subdivision, "group home" does not include a runaway and homeless youth shelter.

(Amended by Stats. 2016, Ch. 612, Sec. 51. (AB 1997) Effective January 1, 2017.)

1562.01.

(a) The department shall license short-term residential therapeutic programs, as defined in paragraph (18) of subdivision (a) of Section 1502, pursuant to this chapter. A short-term residential therapeutic program shall comply with all requirements of this chapter that are applicable to group homes and to the requirements of this section.

(b) (1) A short-term residential therapeutic program shall have national accreditation from an entity identified by the department pursuant to the process described in paragraph (6) of subdivision (b) of Section 11462 of the Welfare and Institutions Code.

(2) A short-term residential therapeutic program applicant shall submit documentation of accreditation or application for accreditation with its application for licensure.

(3) A short-term residential therapeutic program shall have up to 24 months from the date of licensure to obtain accreditation.

(4) A short-term residential therapeutic program shall provide documentation to the department reporting its accreditation status at 12 months and at 18 months after the date of licensure.

(5) This subdivision does not preclude the department from requesting additional information from the short-term residential therapeutic program regarding its accreditation status.

(6) The department may revoke a short-term residential therapeutic program's license pursuant to Article 5 (commencing with Section 1550) for failure to obtain accreditation within the timeframes specified in this subdivision.

(c) (1) A short-term residential therapeutic program shall have up to 12 months from the date of licensure to obtain in good standing a mental health program approval that includes a Medi-Cal mental health certification, as set forth in Sections 4096.5 and 11462.01 of the Welfare and Institutions Code.

(2) A short-term residential therapeutic program shall maintain the program approval described in paragraph (1) in good standing during its licensure.

(3) The department shall track the number of licensed short-term residential therapeutic programs that were unable to obtain a mental health program approval and provide that information to the Legislature annually as part of the State Budget process.

(d) (1) A short-term residential therapeutic program shall prepare and maintain a current, written plan of operation as required by the department.

(2) The plan of operation shall include, but not be limited to, all of the following:

(A) A statement of purposes and goals.

(B) A plan for the supervision, evaluation, and training of staff. The training plan shall be appropriate to meet the needs of staff and children.

(C) A program statement that includes all of the following:

(i) Description of the short-term residential therapeutic program's ability to support the differing needs of children and their families with short-term, specialized, and intensive treatment.

(ii) Description of the core services, as set forth in paragraph (1) of subdivision (b) of Section 11462 of the Welfare and Institutions Code, to be offered to children and their families, as appropriate or necessary.

(iii) Procedures for the development, implementation, and periodic updating of the needs and services plan for children served by the short-term residential therapeutic program and procedures for collaborating with the child and family team described in paragraph (4) of subdivision (a) of Section 16501 of the Welfare and Institutions Code, that include, but are not limited to, a description of the services to be provided to meet the treatment needs of the child as assessed, pursuant to subdivision (d) or (e) of Section 11462.01 of the Welfare and Institutions Code, the anticipated duration of the treatment, and the timeframe and plan for transitioning the child to a less restrictive family environment.

(iv) A description of the population or populations to be served.

(v) A description of compliance with the mental health program approval requirement in subdivision (c). A short-term residential therapeutic program that has not satisfied the requirement in subdivision (c) shall demonstrate the ability to meet the mental health service needs of children.

(vi) (I) A description of how the short-term residential therapeutic program, in accordance with the child's case plan and the child and family team recommendations, will provide for, arrange for the provision of, or assist in, both of the following:

(ia) Identification of home-based family settings for a child who no longer needs the level of care and supervision provided by a short-term residential therapeutic program.

(ib) Continuity of care, services, and treatment as a child moves from his or her short-term residential therapeutic program placement to home-based family care or to a permanent living situation through reunification, adoption, or guardianship.

(II) This clause shall not be interpreted to supersede the placement and care responsibility vested in the county child welfare agency or probation department.

(vii) Any other information that may be prescribed by the department for the proper administration of this section.

(e) In addition to the rules and regulations adopted pursuant to this chapter, a county licensed to operate a short-term residential therapeutic program shall describe, in the plan of operation, its conflict of interest mitigation plan, as set forth in subdivision (g) of Section 11462.02 of the Welfare and Institutions Code.

(f) (1) (A) (i) A short-term residential therapeutic program applicant shall submit an application to the department that includes a letter of recommendation in support of its program from a county placing agency.

(ii) The letter of recommendation shall include a statement that the county placing agency reviewed a copy of the applicant's program statement.

(iii) If the letter of recommendation is not from the county in which the facility is located, the short-term residential therapeutic program applicant shall include, with its application, a statement that it provided the county in which the facility is located an opportunity for that county to review the program statement and notified that county that the facility has received a letter of recommendation from another county.

(B) If the application does not contain a letter of recommendation as described in subparagraph (A), then the department shall cease review of the application. Nothing in this paragraph shall constitute a denial of the application for purposes of Section 1526 or any other law.

(C) A new letter of recommendation is not required when a short-term residential therapeutic program moves locations.

(2) A short-term residential therapeutic program shall submit a copy of its program statement to all county placing agencies from which the short-term residential therapeutic program accepts placements, including the county in which the facility is located, for optional review when the short-term residential therapeutic program updates its program statement.

(g) (1) The department shall adopt regulations to establish requirements for the education, qualification, and training of facility managers and staff who provide care and supervision to children or who have regular, direct contact with children in the course of their responsibilities in short-term residential therapeutic programs consistent with the intended role of these facilities to provide short-term, specialized, and intensive treatment.

(2) Requirements shall include, but not be limited to, all of the following:

(A) Staff classifications.

(B) Specification of the date by which employees shall be required to meet the education and qualification requirements.

(C) Any other requirements that may be prescribed by the department for the proper administration of this section.

(h) The department shall adopt regulations to specify training requirements for staff who provide care and supervision to children or who have regular, direct contact with children in the course of their responsibilities. These requirements shall include the following:

(1) Timeframes for completion of training, including the following:

(A) Training that shall be completed prior to unsupervised care of children.

(B) Training to be completed within the first 180 days of employment.

(C) Training to be completed annually.

(2) Topics to be covered in the training shall include, but are not limited to, the following:

(A) Child and adolescent development, including sexual orientation, gender identity, and gender expression.

(B) The effects of trauma, including grief and loss, and child abuse and neglect on child development and behavior and methods to behaviorally support children impacted by that trauma or child abuse and neglect.

(C) The rights of a child in foster care, including the right to have fair and equal access to all available services, placement, care, treatment, and benefits, and to not be subjected to discrimination or harassment on the basis of actual or perceived race, ethnic group identification, ancestry, national origin, color, religion, sex, sexual orientation, gender identity, mental or physical disability, or HIV status.

(D) Positive discipline and the importance of self-esteem.

(E) Core practice model.

(F) An overview of the child welfare and probation systems.

(G) Reasonable and prudent parent standard.

(H) Instruction on cultural competency and sensitivity and related best practices for providing adequate care for children across diverse ethnic and racial backgrounds, as well as children identifying as lesbian, gay, bisexual, or transgender.

(I) Awareness and identification of commercial sexual exploitation and best practices for providing care and supervision to commercially sexually exploited children.

(J) The federal Indian Child Welfare Act (25 U.S.C. Sec. 1901 et seq.), its historical significance, the rights of children covered by the act, and the best interests of Indian children, including the role of the caregiver in supporting culturally appropriate, child-centered practices that respect Native American history, culture, retention of tribal membership, and connection to the tribal community and traditions.

(K) Permanence, well-being, and educational needs of children.

(L) Basic instruction on existing laws and procedures regarding the safety of foster youth at school; and ensuring a harassment and violence free school environment pursuant to Article 3.6 (commencing with Section 32228) of Chapter 2 of Part 19 of Division 1 of Title 1 of the Education Code.

(M) Best practices for providing care and supervision to nonminor dependents.

(N) Health issues in foster care.

(O) Physical and psychosocial needs of children, including behavior management, deescalation techniques, and trauma-informed crisis management planning.

(i) (1) Each person employed as a facility manager or staff member of a short-term residential therapeutic program, who provides direct care and supervision to children and youth residing in the short-term residential therapeutic program shall be at least 21 years of age.

(2) This subdivision shall not apply to a facility manager or staff member employed, before October 1, 2014, at a short-term residential therapeutic program that was operating under a group home license prior to January 1, 2017.

(j) Notwithstanding any other section of this chapter, the department may establish requirements for licensed group homes that are transitioning to short-term residential therapeutic programs, which may include, but not be limited to, requirements related to application and plan of operation.

(k) A short-term residential therapeutic program shall have a qualified and certified administrator, as set forth in Section 1522.41.

(l) The department shall have the authority to inspect a short-term residential therapeutic program pursuant to the system of governmental monitoring and oversight developed by the department pursuant to subdivision (c) of Section 11462 of the Welfare and Institutions Code.

(Amended by Stats. 2017, Ch. 732, Sec. 33. (AB 404) Effective January 1, 2018.)

1562.02.

(a) The department may license a short-term residential therapeutic program operating as a children's crisis residential program pursuant to this chapter. A children's crisis residential program shall meet all of the following requirements:

(1) If the program serves children who are not experiencing mental health crises, have an identifiable and physically separate unit for those children who are experiencing mental health crises. The separate unit shall be indicated on the short-term residential therapeutic program's license.

(2) Obtain and have in good standing a mental health program approval that includes a Medi-Cal mental health certification, as described in Section 11462.01 of the Welfare and Institutions Code, and a children's crisis residential mental health program approval, as described in Section 11462.011 of the Welfare and Institutions Code, both of which are issued by the State Department of Health Care Services, or a county mental health plan to which the department has delegated approval authority. The short-term residential therapeutic program shall obtain a mental health program approval before operating as a children's crisis residential program. The department may revoke a program's license pursuant to Section 1550 for a program's failure to maintain the mental health program approval.

(3) Comply with all applicable licensing standards for a short-term residential therapeutic program, unless the department specifies otherwise in regulations that comply with applicable statutory requirements related to licensure.

(b) Contingent upon an appropriation in the annual Budget Act for these purposes, the department shall begin implementation of this section no later than July 1, 2018, and shall commence the licensing process for children's crisis residential programs no later than January 1, 2019.

(Added by Stats. 2017, Ch. 704, Sec. 3. (AB 501) Effective January 1, 2018.)

1562.03.

(a) The department shall establish regulations for short-term residential therapeutic programs that are operated as children's crisis residential programs. At a minimum, the regulations shall include all of the following:

(1) Therapeutic programming shall be provided seven days a week, including weekends and holidays, with sufficient mental health professional and paraprofessional staff, as required by the facility's children's crisis residential mental health program approval in accordance with the standards and procedures established pursuant to Section 11462.011 of the Welfare and Institutions Code, to maintain an appropriate treatment setting and services, based on individual children's needs.

(2) The program shall be staffed with sufficient personnel to accept children 24 hours per day, seven days a week and to admit children, at a minimum, from 7 a.m. to 11 p.m., seven days a week, 365 days per year. The program shall be sufficiently staffed to discharge children, as appropriate, seven days a week, 365 days per year.

(3) Facilities shall be limited to fewer than 16 beds, with at least 50 percent of those beds in single-occupancy rooms.

(4) Facilities shall include ample physical space for accommodating individuals who provide daily emotional and physical supports to each child and for integrating family members into the day-to-day care of the youth.

(5) The program shall collaborate with each child's existing mental health team, if applicable, child and family team, if applicable, and other formal and natural supports within 24 hours of intake and throughout the course of care and treatment as appropriate.

(6) The program shall create and assist with the implementation of a plan for transitioning each admitted child from the program to his or her home and community, including the establishment of a mental health or child and family team if there is not one already.

(b) The program shall annually provide the department with all of the following data as it pertains to children in foster care and children not in foster care in conjunction with its application for licensure renewal:

(1) Age and gender of clients served.

(2) Duration of stay.

(3) Professional classification of staff and contracted staff.

(4) Type of placement the client was discharged to.

(Added by Stats. 2017, Ch. 704, Sec. 4. (AB 501) Effective January 1, 2018.)

1562.3.

(a) The Director of Social Services, in consultation with the Director of Health Care Services and the Director of Developmental Services, shall establish a training program to ensure that licensees, operators, and staffs of adult residential care facilities, as defined in paragraph (1) of subdivision (a) of Section 1502, have appropriate training to provide the care and services for which a license or certificate is issued. The training program shall be developed in consultation with provider organizations.

(b) (1) An administrator of an adult residential care facility, as defined in paragraph (1) of subdivision (a) of Section 1502, shall successfully complete a department-approved certification program pursuant to subdivision (c) prior to employment.

(2) In those cases where the individual is both the licensee and the administrator of a facility, the individual shall comply with both the licensee and administrator requirements of this section.

(3) Failure to comply with this section shall constitute cause for revocation of the license of the facility.

(4) The licensee shall notify the department within 30 days of any change in administrators.

(c) (1) The administrator certification program shall require a minimum of 35 hours of classroom instruction that provides training on a uniform core of knowledge in each of the following areas:

(A) Laws, regulations, and policies and procedural standards that impact the operations of the type of facility for which the applicant will be an administrator.

(B) Business operations.

(C) Management and supervision of staff.

(D) Psychosocial needs of the facility residents.

(E) Community and support services.

(F) Physical needs for facility residents.

(G) Use, misuse, and interaction of medication commonly used by facility residents.

(H) Resident admission, retention, and assessment procedures.

(I) Nonviolent crisis intervention for administrators.

(J) Cultural competency and sensitivity in issues relating to the underserved aging lesbian, gay, bisexual, and transgender community.

(2) The requirement for 35 hours of classroom instruction pursuant to this subdivision shall not apply to persons who were employed as administrators prior to July 1, 1996. A person holding the position of administrator of an adult residential facility on June 30, 1996, shall file a completed application for certification with the department on or before April 1, 1998. In order to be exempt from the 35-hour training program and the test

component, the application shall include documentation showing proof of continuous employment as the administrator of an adult residential facility between, at a minimum, June 30, 1994, and June 30, 1996. An administrator of an adult residential facility who became certified as a result of passing the department-administered challenge test, that was offered between October 1, 1996, and December 23, 1996, shall be deemed to have fulfilled the requirements of this paragraph.

(3) Unless an extension is granted to the applicant by the department, an applicant for an administrator's certificate shall, within 60 days of the applicant's completion of classroom instruction, pass the written test provided in this section.

(d) The department shall not begin the process of issuing a certificate until receipt of all of the following:

(1) A certificate of completion of the administrator training required pursuant to this chapter.

(2) The fee required for issuance of the certificate. A fee of one hundred dollars ($100) shall be charged by the department to cover the costs of processing the application for certification.

(3) Documentation from the applicant that he or she has passed the written test.

(4) Submission of fingerprints. The department and the Department of Justice shall expedite the criminal record clearance for holders of certificates of completion. The department may waive the submission for those persons who have a current clearance on file.

(e) It shall be unlawful for any person not certified under this section to hold himself or herself out as a certified administrator of an adult residential facility. A person willfully making any false representation as being a certified administrator is guilty of a misdemeanor.

(f) (1) Certificates issued under this section shall be renewed every two years and renewal shall be conditional upon the certificate holder submitting documentation of completion of 40 hours of continuing education related to the core of knowledge specified in subdivision (c). No more than one-half of the required 40 hours of continuing education necessary to renew the certificate may be satisfied through online courses. All other continuing education hours shall be completed in a classroom setting. For purposes of this section, an individual who is an adult residential facility administrator and who is required to complete the continuing education hours required by the regulations of the State Department of Developmental Services, and approved by the regional center, shall be permitted to have up to 24 of the required continuing education course hours credited toward the 40-hour continuing education requirement of this section. Community college course hours approved by the regional centers shall be accepted by the department for certification.

(2) Every licensee and administrator of an adult residential facility is required to complete the continuing education requirements of this subdivision.

(3) Certificates issued under this section shall expire every two years, on the anniversary date of the initial issuance of the certificate, except that any administrator receiving his or her initial certification on or after January 1, 1999, shall make an irrevocable election to have his or her recertification date for any subsequent recertification either on the date two years from the date of issuance of the certificate or on the individual's birthday during the second calendar year following certification. The department shall send a renewal notice to the certificate holder 90 days prior to the expiration date of the certificate. If the certificate is not renewed prior to its expiration date, reinstatement shall only be permitted after the certificate holder has paid a delinquency fee equal to three times the renewal fee and has provided evidence of completion of the continuing education required.

(4) To renew a certificate, the certificate holder shall, on or before the certificate expiration date, request renewal by submitting to the department documentation of completion of the required continuing education courses and pay the renewal fee of one hundred dollars ($100), irrespective of receipt of the department's notification of the renewal. A renewal request postmarked on or before the expiration of the certificate is proof of compliance with this paragraph.

(5) A suspended or revoked certificate is subject to expiration as provided for in this section. If reinstatement of the certificate is approved by the department, the certificate holder, as a condition precedent to reinstatement, shall submit proof of compliance with paragraphs (1) and (2) and shall pay a fee in an amount equal to the renewal fee, plus the delinquency fee, if any, accrued at the time of its revocation or suspension. Delinquency fees, if any, accrued subsequent to the time of its revocation or suspension and prior to an order for reinstatement, shall be waived for one year to allow the individual sufficient time to complete the required continuing education units and to submit the required documentation. Individuals whose certificates will expire within 90 days after the order for reinstatement may be granted a three-month extension to renew their certificates during which time the delinquency fees shall not accrue.

(6) A certificate that is not renewed within four years after its expiration shall not be renewed, restored, reissued, or reinstated except upon completion of a certification training program, passing any test that may be required of an applicant for a new certificate at that time, and paying the appropriate fees provided for in this section.

(7) A fee of twenty-five dollars ($25) shall be charged for the reissuance of a lost certificate.

(8) A certificate holder shall inform the department of his or her employment status within 30 days of any change.

(g) The certificate shall be considered forfeited under the following conditions:

(1) The administrator has had a license revoked, suspended, or denied as authorized under Section 1550.

(2) The administrator has been denied employment, residence, or presence in a facility based on action resulting from an administrative hearing pursuant to Section 1522 or 1558.

(h) (1) The department, in consultation with the State Department of Health Care Services and the State Department of Developmental Services, shall establish, by regulation, the program content, the testing instrument, the process for approving certification training programs, and criteria to be used in authorizing individuals, organizations, or educational institutions to conduct certification training programs and continuing education courses. These regulations shall be developed in consultation with provider organizations, and shall be made available at least six months prior to the deadline required for certification. The department may deny vendor approval to any agency or person in any of the following circumstances:

(A) The applicant has not provided the department with evidence satisfactory to the department of the ability of the applicant to satisfy the requirements of vendorization set out in the regulations adopted by the department pursuant to subdivision (i).

(B) The applicant person or agency has a conflict of interest in that the person or agency places its clients in adult residential facilities.

(C) The applicant public or private agency has a conflict of interest in that the agency is mandated to place clients in adult residential facilities and to pay directly for the services. The department may deny vendorization to this type of agency only as long as there are other vendor programs available to conduct the certification training programs and conduct education courses.

(2) The department may authorize vendors to conduct the administrator's certification training program pursuant to provisions set forth in this section. The department shall conduct the written test pursuant to regulations adopted by the department.

(3) The department shall prepare and maintain an updated list of approved training vendors.

(4) The department may inspect certification training programs and continuing education courses, including online courses, at no charge to the department, to determine if content and teaching methods comply with regulations. If the department determines that any vendor is not complying with the intent of this section, the department shall take appropriate action to bring the program into compliance, which may include removing the vendor from the approved list.

(5) The department shall establish reasonable procedures and timeframes not to exceed 30 days for the approval of vendor training programs.

(6) The department may charge a reasonable fee, not to exceed one hundred fifty dollars ($150) every two years to certification program vendors for review and approval of the initial 35-hour training program pursuant to subdivision (c). The department may also charge the vendor a fee not to exceed one hundred dollars ($100) every two years for the review and approval of the continuing education courses needed for recertification pursuant to this subdivision.

(7) (A) A vendor of online programs for continuing education shall ensure that each online course contains all of the following:

(i) An interactive portion in which the participant receives feedback, through online communication, based on input from the participant.

(ii) Required use of a personal identification number or personal identification information to confirm the identity of the participant.

(iii) A final screen displaying a printable statement, to be signed by the participant, certifying that the identified participant completed the course. The vendor shall obtain a copy of the final screen statement with the original signature of the participant prior to the issuance of a certificate of completion. The signed statement of completion shall be maintained by the vendor for a period of three years and be available to the department upon demand. Any person who certifies as true any material matter pursuant to this clause that he or she knows to be false is guilty of a misdemeanor.

(B) This subdivision shall not prohibit the department from approving online programs for continuing education that do not meet the requirements of subparagraph (A) if the vendor demonstrates to the department's satisfaction that, through advanced technology, the course and the course delivery meet the requirements of this section.

(i) The department shall establish a registry for holders of certificates that shall include, at a minimum, information on employment status and criminal record clearance.
(Amended by Stats. 2014, Ch. 71, Sec. 86. (SB 1304) Effective January 1, 2015.)
1562.35.
Notwithstanding any law to the contrary, including, but not limited to Section 1562.3, vendors approved by the department who exclusively provide either initial or continuing education courses for certification of administrators of an adult residential facility as defined by the department, a group home facility as defined by the department, a short-term residential therapeutic program as defined by the department, or a residential care facility for the elderly as defined in subdivision (k) of Section 1569.2, shall be regulated solely by the department pursuant to this chapter. No other state or local governmental entity shall be responsible for regulating the activity of those vendors.
(Amended by Stats. 2016, Ch. 612, Sec. 53. (AB 1997) Effective January 1, 2017.)
1562.4.
Any person who becomes an administrator of an adult residential facility, as defined in paragraph (1) of subdivision (a) of Section 1502, on or after July 1, 1996, shall, at a minimum, fulfill all of the following requirements:
(a) Be at least 21 years of age.
(b) Provide documentation of having successfully completed a certification program approved by the department and successfully passing the state examination.

(c) Have a high school diploma or pass a general educational development test as described in Article 3 (commencing with Section 51420) of Chapter 3 of Part 28 of the Education Code.
(d) Obtain a criminal record clearance as provided for in Sections 1522 and 1522.03.
(Amended by Stats. 2005, Ch. 558, Sec. 6. Effective January 1, 2006.)
1562.5.
(a) The director shall ensure that, within six months after obtaining licensure, an administrator of an adult residential facility and a program director of a social rehabilitation facility shall receive four hours of training on the needs of residents who may be infected with the human immunodeficiency virus (HIV), and on basic information about tuberculosis. Administrators and program directors shall attend update training sessions every two years after satisfactorily completing the initial training to ensure that information received on HIV and tuberculosis remains current. The training shall consist of three hours on HIV and one hour on tuberculosis.
(b) The training shall consist of all of the following:
(1) Universal blood and body fluid precautions.
(2) Basic AIDS and HIV information, including modes of transmission.
(3) Legal protections for persons with HIV or AIDS.
(4) Referral information to local government, community-based, and other organizations that provide social, support, or health services and social services to people with HIV or AIDS.
(5) Information about the residential care needs of people living with HIV or AIDS, including nutritional needs.
(6) Recognition of the signs and symptoms of tuberculosis.
(7) Tuberculosis testing requirements for staff, volunteers, and residents.
(8) Tuberculosis prevention.
(9) Tuberculosis treatment.
(c) The department shall ensure compliance with this section. In the event of noncompliance, the director shall develop and implement a plan of correction requiring that the training take place within six months of the violation.
(d) All administrators of adult residential and program directors of social rehabilitation facilities licensed on or before January 1, 1994, shall complete the training by December 31, 1994, and every two years thereafter. Newly employed administrators and program directors shall complete training within six months after commencing employment.
(e) Eligible providers of training and study courses shall be limited to any of the following:
(1) County and city health departments.
(2) American Lung Association affiliates.
(3) Any agency with a contract to provide HIV, AIDS, or tuberculosis education with either the State Department of Health Services, or the federal Centers for Disease Control.
(4) The California Association of AIDS Agencies.
(5) Any providers approved by the State Department of Social Services for training of personnel employed in residential care facilities for the elderly, adult residential facilities, or residential care facilities for the chronically ill.
(f) Providers shall use HIV, AIDS, and tuberculosis materials produced, approved, or distributed by any of the following:
(1) The federal Centers for Disease Control.
(2) The American Lung Association.
(3) The University of California.
(4) The California Association of AIDS Agencies.
(5) The California AIDS Clearinghouse.
(6) County and city health departments.
(g) In the event that an administrator or program director demonstrates to the department a significant difficulty in accessing training, the administrators and program directors of these facilities shall have the option of fulfilling these training requirements through a study course consisting of written and/or video educational materials.
(h) Successful completion of the training or study course by administrators and program directors and the biannual update described in this section shall be verified with the department during the annual review of the facility pursuant to subdivision (a) of Section 1534. Trained administrators and program directors shall disseminate the HIV, AIDS, and tuberculosis materials to facility personnel.
(Amended by Stats. 1994, Ch. 146, Sec. 101. Effective January 1, 1995.)
1562.6.
(a) The administrator of an adult residential care facility that provides services for residents who have mental illness shall ensure that a written intake assessment is prepared by a licensed mental health professional prior to acceptance of the client. This assessment may be provided by a student intern if the work is supervised by a properly licensed mental health professional. Facility administrators may utilize placement agencies, including, but not limited to, county clinics for referrals and assessments.
(b) Within 30 days after an inspection of an adult residential care facility the State Department of Social Services shall provide the licensee with a copy of the licensing report verifying compliance or noncompliance by the facility with applicable licensing provisions. This report shall not include confidential client information, and copies of reports within the last 24 months shall be provided by the facility to the public upon request.
(Added by Stats. 1996, Ch. 828, Sec. 2. Effective January 1, 1997.)
1563.
(a) The department shall ensure that licensing personnel at the department have appropriate training to properly carry out this chapter.

(b) The department shall institute a staff development and training program to develop among departmental staff the knowledge and understanding necessary to successfully carry out this chapter. Specifically, the program shall do all of the following:

(1) Provide staff with 36 hours of training per year that reflects the needs of persons served by community care facilities. This training shall, where appropriate, include specialized instruction in the needs of foster children, persons with mental disorders, or developmental or physical disabilities, or other groups served by specialized community care facilities.

(2) Give priority to applications for employment from persons with experience as care providers to persons served by community care facilities.

(3) Provide new staff with comprehensive training within the first six months of employment. This comprehensive training shall, at a minimum, include the following core areas: administrative action process, client populations, conducting facility visits, cultural awareness, documentation skills, facility operations, human relation skills, interviewing techniques, investigation processes, and regulation administration.

(c) In addition to the requirements in subdivision (b), group home, short-term residential therapeutic program, and foster family agency licensing personnel shall receive a minimum of 24 hours of training per year to increase their understanding of children in group homes, short-term residential therapeutic programs, certified homes, and foster family homes. The training shall cover, but not be limited to, all of the following topics:

(1) The types and characteristics of emotionally troubled children.

(2) The high-risk behaviors they exhibit.

(3) The biological, psychological, interpersonal, and social contributors to these behaviors.

(4) The range of management and treatment interventions utilized for these children, including, but not limited to, nonviolent, emergency intervention techniques.

(5) The right of a foster child to have fair and equal access to all available services, placement, care, treatment, and benefits, and to not be subjected to discrimination or harassment on the basis of actual or perceived race, ethnic group identification, ancestry, national origin, color, religion, sex, sexual orientation, gender identity, mental or physical disability, or HIV status.

(d) The training described in subdivisions (b) and (c) may include the following topics:

(1) An overview of the child protective and probation systems.

(2) The effects of trauma, including grief and loss, and child abuse or neglect on child development and behavior, and methods to behaviorally support children impacted by that trauma or child abuse and neglect.

(3) Positive discipline and the importance of self-esteem.

(4) Health issues in foster care, including, but not limited to, the authorization, uses, risks, benefits, assistance with self-administration, oversight, and monitoring of psychotropic medications, and trauma, mental health, and substance use disorder treatments for children in foster care under the jurisdiction of the juvenile court, including how to access those treatments.

(5) Accessing the services and supports available to foster children to address educational needs, physical, mental, and behavioral health, substance use disorders, and culturally relevant services.

(6) Instruction on cultural competency and sensitivity and related best practices for, providing adequate care for children across diverse ethnic and racial backgrounds, as well as for children identifying as lesbian, gay, bisexual, and transgender.

(7) Understanding how to use best practices for providing care and supervision to commercially sexually exploited children.

(8) Understanding the federal Indian Child Welfare Act (25 U.S.C. Sec. 1901 et seq.), its historical significance, the rights of children covered by the act, and the best interests of Indian children, including the role of the caregiver in supporting culturally appropriate, child-centered practices that respect Native American history, culture, retention of tribal membership, and connection to the tribal community and traditions.

(9) Understanding how to use best practices for providing care and supervision to nonminor dependents.

(10) Understanding how to use best practices for providing care and supervision to children with special health care needs.

(11) Basic instruction on existing laws and procedures regarding the safety of foster youth at school; and ensuring a harassment and violence free school environment pursuant to Article 3.6 (commencing with Section 32228) of Chapter 2 of Part 19 of Division 1 of Title 1 of the Education Code.

(12) Permanence, well-being, and educational needs of children.

(13) Child and adolescent development, including sexual orientation, gender identity, and gender expression.

(14) The role of foster parents, including working cooperatively with the child welfare or probation agency, the child's family, and other service providers implementing the case plan.

(15) A foster parent's responsibility to act as a reasonable and prudent parent, and to provide a family setting that promotes normal childhood experiences that serve the needs of the child.

(16) Physical and psychosocial needs of children, including behavior management, deescalation techniques, and trauma informed crisis management planning.

(Amended by Stats. 2016, Ch. 612, Sec. 54. (AB 1997) Effective January 1, 2017.)

1564.

(a) No individual who has ever been convicted of a sex offense against a minor shall reside in a community care facility that is within one mile of an elementary school.

(b) Any community care facility which is located within one mile of an elementary school shall obtain from each individual who is a resident of the facility on the effective date of this section a signed statement that the resident or applicant for residence has never been convicted of a sex offense against a minor.

(c) If on January 1, 1983, a person who has been convicted of a sex offense against a minor is residing in a community care facility that is within one mile of a school, the operator shall notify the appropriate placement agency. Continued residence in the facility shall extend no longer than six months.

(d) Prior to placement in a community care facility which is located within one mile of an elementary school, the placement agency shall obtain, from the client to be placed, a signed statement that he or she has never been convicted of a sex offense against a minor. Any placement agent who knowingly places a person who has been convicted of a sex offense against a minor in a facility which is located within one mile of an elementary school shall be guilty of a misdemeanor.

Where there is no placement agency involved, the community care facility shall obtain from any applicant a signed statement that he or she has never been convicted of a sex offense against a minor.

(e) Any resident or applicant for residence who makes a false statement as to a conviction for a prior sex offense against a minor is guilty of a misdemeanor.

(f) For purposes of this section, "sex offense" means any one or more of the following offenses:

(1) Any offense defined in Section 220, 261, 261.5, 266, 266e, 266f, 266i, 266j, 267, 273f as it pertains to houses of prostitution, 273g, 285, 286, 287, 288, 289, 290, 311, 311.2, 311.4, 313.1, 318, subdivision (a) or (d) of Section 647, 647a, 650 $\frac{1}{2}$ as it relates to lewd or lascivious behavior, 653f, or 653m, or former Section 288a of, the Penal Code.

(2) Any offense defined in subdivision (5) of former Section 647 of the Penal Code repealed by Chapter 560 of the Statutes of 1961, or any offense defined in subdivision (2) of former Section 311 of the Penal Code repealed by Chapter 2147 of the Statutes of 1961, if the offense defined in such sections was committed prior to September 15, 1961.

(3) Any offense defined in Section 314 of the Penal Code committed on or after September 15, 1961.

(4) Any offense defined in subdivision (1) of former Section 311 of the Penal Code repealed by Chapter 2147 of the Statutes of 1961 committed on or after September 7, 1955, and prior to September 15, 1961.

(5) Any offense involving lewd and lascivious conduct under Section 272 of the Penal Code committed on or after September 15, 1961.

(6) Any offense involving lewd and lascivious conduct under former Section 702 of the Welfare and Institutions Code repealed by Chapter 1616 of the Statutes of 1961, if such offense was committed prior to September 15, 1961.

(7) Any offense defined in Section 286 or 288a of the Penal Code prior to the effective date of the amendment of either section enacted at the 1975–76 Regular Session of the Legislature committed prior to the effective date of the amendment.

(8) Any attempt or conspiracy to commit any of the above-mentioned offenses.

(9) Any federal sex offense or any sex offense committed or attempted in any other state which, if committed or attempted in this state, would have been punishable as one or more of the above-mentioned offenses.

(g) This section shall not apply to residential care facilities for the elderly or to any person receiving community supervision and treatment pursuant to Title 15 (commencing with Section 1600) of Part 2 of the Penal Code.

(Amended by Stats. 2018, Ch. 423, Sec. 33. (SB 1494) Effective January 1, 2019.)

ARTICLE 7. Local Regulation [1566 - 1566.8]
(Article 7 added by Stats. 1978, Ch. 891.)

1566.

The Legislature hereby declares that it is the policy of this state that each county and city shall permit and encourage the development of sufficient numbers and types of residential care facilities as are commensurate with local need.

The provisions of this article shall apply equally to any chartered city, general law city, county, city and county, district, and any other local public entity.

For the purposes of this article, "six or fewer persons" does not include the licensee or members of the licensee's family or persons employed as facility staff.

(Added by Stats. 1978, Ch. 891.)

1566.1.

Any person licensed under the provisions of this chapter who operates, or proposes to operate a residential facility, the department or other public agency authorized to license such a facility, or any public or private agency which uses or may use the services of the facility to place its clients, may invoke the provisions of this article.

This section shall not be construed to prohibit any interested party from bringing suit to invoke the provisions of this article.

(Added by Stats. 1978, Ch. 891.)

1566.2.

A residential facility, which serves six or fewer persons shall not be subject to any business taxes, local registration fees, use permit fees, or other fees to which other family dwellings of the same type in the same zone are not likewise subject. Nothing in this section shall be construed to forbid the imposition of local property taxes, fees for water service and garbage collection, fees for inspections not prohibited by Section 1566.3, local bond assessments, and other fees, charges, and assessments to which other family dwellings of the same type in the same zone are likewise subject. Neither the State Fire Marshal nor any local public entity shall charge any fee for enforcing fire inspection regulations pursuant to state law or regulation or local ordinance, with respect to residential facilities that serve six or fewer persons, except for fees authorized pursuant to Section 13235.

For purposes of this section, "family dwellings," includes, but is not limited to, single-family dwellings, units in multifamily dwellings, including units in duplexes and units in apartment dwellings, mobilehomes, including mobilehomes located in mobilehome parks, units in cooperatives, units in condominiums, units in townhouses, and units in planned unit developments.

(Amended by Stats. 2009, 4th Ex. Sess., Ch. 12, Sec. 13. Effective July 28, 2009.)

1566.25.

If a county of residence agrees to pay a placement county the costs of providing services to a minor pursuant to subdivision (a) of Section 740 of the Welfare and Institutions Code, all of the following shall apply:

(a) The county of residence shall agree to pay the placement county the actual costs of providing services to a child placed in a community care facility outside his or her county of residence by a placement agency, as defined in Section 1536.1, that are incurred by the probation department, social services department, health department, or mental health department of the placement county for which the placement county is not otherwise reimbursed.

(b) Claims made by the county of placement to the county of residency pursuant to subdivision (a) shall include documentation and shall be paid within 30 days of submission of these claims.

(c) For the purposes of this section, the county from where the child was placed in the community care facility shall be considered the county of residency.

(Added by Stats. 1992, Ch. 1153, Sec. 4. Effective January 1, 1993.)

1566.3.

(a) Whether or not unrelated persons are living together, a residential facility that serves six or fewer persons shall be considered a residential use of property for the purposes of this article. In addition, the residents and operators of such a facility shall be considered a family for the purposes of any law or zoning ordinance that relates to the residential use of property pursuant to this article.

(b) For the purpose of all local ordinances, a residential facility that serves six or fewer persons shall not be included within the definition of a boarding house, rooming house, institution or home for the care of minors, the aged, or persons with mental health disorders, foster care home, guest home, rest home, community residence, or other similar term that implies that the residential facility is a business run for profit or differs in any other way from a family dwelling.

(c) This section shall not be construed to prohibit a city, county, or other local public entity from placing restrictions on building heights, setback, lot dimensions, or placement of signs of a residential facility that serves six or fewer persons as long as those restrictions are identical to those applied to other family dwellings of the same type in the same zone.

(d) This section shall not be construed to prohibit the application to a residential care facility of any local ordinance that deals with health and safety, building standards, environmental impact standards, or any other matter within the jurisdiction of a local public entity if the ordinance does not distinguish residential care facilities that serve six or fewer persons from other family dwellings of the same type in the same zone and if the ordinance does not distinguish residents of the residential care facilities from persons who reside in other family dwellings of the same type in the same zone. Nothing in this section shall be construed to limit the ability of a local public entity to fully enforce a local ordinance, including, but not limited to, the imposition of fines and other penalties associated with violations of local ordinances covered by this section.

(e) No conditional use permit, zoning variance, or other zoning clearance shall be required of a residential facility that serves six or fewer persons that is not required of a family dwelling of the same type in the same zone.

(f) Use of a family dwelling for purposes of a residential facility serving six or fewer persons shall not constitute a change of occupancy for purposes of Part 1.5 (commencing with Section 17910) of Division 13 or local building codes. However, nothing in this section is intended to supersede Section 13143 or 13143.6, to the extent such sections are applicable to residential facilities providing care for six or fewer residents.

(g) For the purposes of this section, "family dwelling," includes, but is not limited to, single-family dwellings, units in multifamily dwellings, including units in duplexes and units in apartment dwellings, mobilehomes, including mobilehomes located in mobilehome parks, units in cooperatives, units in condominiums, units in townhouses, and units in planned unit developments.

(Amended by Stats. 2014, Ch. 144, Sec. 32. (AB 1847) Effective January 1, 2015.)

1566.4.

No fire inspection clearance or other permit, license, clearance, or similar authorization shall be denied to a residential facility because of a failure to comply with local ordinances from which such facilities are exempt under Section 1566.3, provided that the applicant otherwise qualifies for such fire clearance, license, permit, or similar authorization.

(Added by Stats. 1978, Ch. 891.)

1566.45.

(a) (1) For purposes of this section, "bedridden" means requiring assistance in turning and repositioning in bed or being unable to independently transfer to and from bed, except in a facility with appropriate and sufficient care staff, mechanical devices, if necessary, and safety precautions, as determined by the director in regulations.

(2) In developing the regulations for child residential facilities, the department shall take into consideration the size and weight of the child.

(3) For purposes of this section, the status of being bedridden shall not include a temporary illness or recovery from surgery that persists for 14 days or less.

(4) The determination of the bedridden status of persons with developmental disabilities shall be made by the Director of Social Services or his or her designated representative, in consultation with the Director of Developmental Services or his or her designated representative, after consulting the resident's individual safety plan. The determination of the bedridden status of all other persons with disabilities who are not developmentally disabled shall be made by the Director of Social Services, or his or her designated representative.

(b) No client shall be admitted to or retained in a residential facility if he or she requires 24-hour skilled nursing care, except for a facility licensed as an Adult Residential Facility for Persons with Special Health Care Needs pursuant to Article 9 (commencing with Section 1567.50).

(c) A bedridden person may be admitted to, and remain in, a residential facility that secures and maintains an appropriate fire clearance. A fire clearance shall be issued to a facility in which one or more bedridden persons reside if either of the following conditions are met:

(1) The fire safety requirements are met. Clients who are unable to independently transfer to and from bed, but who do not need assistance to turn or reposition in bed, shall be considered nonambulatory for purposes of this paragraph.

(2) Alternative methods of protection are approved.

(d) Notwithstanding paragraph (3) of subdivision (a), a bedridden client may be retained in a residential facility in excess of 14 days if all of the following requirements are satisfied:

(1) The facility notifies the department in writing that the person is recovering from a temporary illness or surgery.

(2) The facility submits to the department, with the notification required in paragraph (1), a physician and surgeon's written statement to the effect that the client's illness or recovery is of a temporary nature. The statement shall contain an estimated date upon which the illness or recovery is expected to end or upon which the client is expected to no longer be confined to bed.

(3) The department determines that the client's health and safety is adequately protected in the facility and that transfer to a higher level of care is not necessary.

(4) This subdivision does not expand the scope of care and supervision of a residential facility.

(e) Notwithstanding the length of stay of a bedridden client, every residential facility admitting or retaining a bedridden client shall, within 48 hours of the client's admission or retention in the facility, notify the fire authority having jurisdiction over the bedridden client's location of the estimated length of time the client will retain his or her bedridden status in the facility.

(f) (1) The department and the Office of the State Fire Marshal, in consultation with the State Department of Developmental Services, shall each promulgate regulations that meet all of the following conditions:

(A) Are consistent with this section.

(B) Are applicable to facilities regulated under this chapter, consistent with the regulatory requirements of the California Building Standards Code for fire and life safety for the respective occupancy classifications into which the State Department of Social Services' community care licensing classifications fall.

(C) Permit clients to remain in homelike settings.

(2) At a minimum, these regulations shall do both of the following with regard to a residential care facility that provides care for six or fewer clients, at least one of whom is bedridden:

(A) Clarify the fire and life safety requirements for a fire clearance for the facility.

(B) Identify procedures for requesting the approval of alternative means of providing equivalent levels of fire and life safety protection. Either the facility, the client or client's representative, or local fire official may request from the Office of the State Fire Marshal a written opinion concerning the interpretation of the regulations promulgated by the State Fire Marshal pursuant to this section for a particular factual dispute. The State Fire Marshal shall issue the written opinion within 45 days following the request.

(g) For facilities that care for six or fewer clients, a local fire official shall not impose fire safety requirements stricter than the fire safety regulations promulgated for the particular type of facility by the Office of the State Fire Marshal or the local fire safety requirements imposed on any other single family dwelling, whichever is more strict.

(h) This section and regulations promulgated thereunder shall be interpreted in a manner that provides flexibility to allow bedridden persons to avoid institutionalization and be admitted to, and safely remain in, community-based residential care facilities.

(Amended by Stats. 2010, Ch. 211, Sec. 2. (AB 2629) Effective January 1, 2011.)

1566.5.

For the purposes of any contract, deed, or covenant for the transfer of real property executed on or after January 1, 1979, a residential facility which serves six or fewer persons shall be considered a residential use of property and a use of property by a single family, notwithstanding any disclaimers to the contrary.

(Added by Stats. 1978, Ch. 891.)

1566.6.

The department shall annually prepare, with a quarterly update commencing July 1, 1979, specifying newly licensed facilities, a list or lists of all licensed community care facilities in the state, other than foster family homes, which shall include the information required by Section 1536 and shall additionally specify as to each such facility the licensed capacity of the facility and whether it is licensed by the state department or by another public agency

pursuant to Section 1511. Compliance with this section shall also constitute compliance with Section 1536.
(Amended by Stats. 1984, Ch. 1615, Sec. 7.)
1566.7.
The department shall notify affected placement agencies and the Office of the State Long-Term Care Ombudsman, as defined in subdivision (c) of Section 9701 of the Welfare and Institutions Code, whenever the department substantiates that a violation has occurred, which poses a serious threat to the health and safety of any resident when the violation results in the assessment of any penalty or causes an accusation to be filed for the revocation of a license. If the violation is appealed by the facility within 15 business days, the department shall only notify placement agencies of the violation when the appeal has been exhausted. If the appeal process has not been completed within 60 days, the placement agency shall be notified with a notation which indicates that the case is still under appeal. The notice to each placement agency shall be updated monthly for the following 24-month period and shall include the name and location of the facility, the amount of the fine, the nature of the violation, the corrective action taken, the status of the revocation, and the resolution of the complaint. At any time during which a facility is found to have one or more of the following serious deficiencies, the director shall provide an immediate notice of not to exceed five working days to the placement agency:
(a) Discovery that an employee of the facility has a criminal record which would affect the facility's compliance with Section 1522.
(b) Discovery that a serious incident that resulted in physical or emotional trauma of a resident has occurred in a facility.
(Amended by Stats. 2016, Ch. 823, Sec. 3. (AB 2231) Effective January 1, 2017.)
1566.75.
(a) By January 1, 2006, the department's Community Care Licensing Division shall enter into memoranda of understanding with up to 10 local mental health departments that volunteer to participate. Each memorandum of understanding shall outline a formal protocol to address shared responsibilities, monitoring responsibilities, facility closures, training, and a process for mediation of disputes between the local mental health authority and the department's local licensing office relating to adult residential facilities and social rehabilitation facilities.
(b) On or before January 31, 2006, the department shall transmit a copy of each memorandum of understanding that has been signed to the Legislature.
(Added by Stats. 2004, Ch. 660, Sec. 1. Effective January 1, 2005.)
1566.8.
Notwithstanding any other provision of law, if according to the rules and regulations of a mobilehome park, the park is designated as a family park or a section of a mixed mobilehome park is designated as a family section, no rule, regulation, rental agreement, or any other provision in existence on the effective date of this section shall, directly or indirectly, prohibit a person from operating in any mobilehome in a family park or designated family section, a licensed foster family home.
(Added by Stats. 1987, Ch. 1092, Sec. 3. Effective September 24, 1987.)

ARTICLE 8. Community Care Facilities for Wards of the Juvenile Court [1567 - 1567.8]

(Article 8 added by Stats. 1978, Ch. 889.)
1567.
It is the intent of the Legislature that each county be encouraged to provide, in the county, a number and variety of licensed community care facilities, as defined in Sections 1502 and 1503 of the Health and Safety Code, commensurate to the needs of minors adjudged wards of the juvenile court pursuant to Section 601 or 602 of the Welfare and Institutions Code, hereinafter in this article referred to as wards of the juvenile court, who are residents of the county.
(Added by Stats. 1978, Ch. 889.)
1567.1.
It is further the intent of the Legislature that, where city or county zoning restrictions unreasonably impair the ability of a county to serve the needs of its residents who are wards of the juvenile court, the removal of these restrictions is hereby encouraged and is a matter of high state interest.
(Added by Stats. 1978, Ch. 889.)
1567.2.
As used in this article, the term "wards of the juvenile court" shall include minors who have been found by the juvenile court to be described by Section 601 or 602 of the Welfare and Institutions Code, as well as minors who are described by Section 601 or 602 of the Welfare and Institutions Code who have been diverted from formal juvenile court proceedings. It is further the intent of the Legislature to encourage that wards of the juvenile court be placed in licensed community care facilities within their county of residence, unless an individual ward has identifiable needs requiring specialized care which cannot be provided in a local facility, or unless the needs of the individual ward dictate physical separation from his family.
(Added by Stats. 1978, Ch. 889.)
1567.3.
(a) No licensed community care facility may receive a ward of the juvenile court as described in Section 602 of the Welfare and Institutions Code until the probation officer of the county in which the community care facility is located has received notice, in writing, by fax, or electronically transmitted, of the placement, as prescribed in Section 740 of the Welfare and Institutions Code, including the name of the ward, the juvenile record of the ward, including any known prior offenses or gang affiliation, and the ward's county of residence, from the probation officer of the county making the placement, or, in the case of a ward of the Department of Corrections and Rehabilitation, Division of Juvenile

Facilities, the parole officer in charge of the case. The licensed community care facility shall maintain a copy of this notice on file as evidence of compliance with this section.
(b) (1) The probation officer of a county making an out-of-county placement of a ward of the juvenile court as described in Section 602 of the Welfare and Institutions Code shall notify the probation officer of the county in which the community care facility is located at least 24 hours prior to receipt of the ward by the licensed community care facility. If the ward is received on a weekend or holiday, notification shall be made by the end of the next business day.
(2) A probation officer of a county making an out-of-county placement of a ward of the juvenile court who makes a notification pursuant to paragraph (1) shall also send, at that time, a copy of the notification to the community care facility where the ward is being placed.
(Amended by Stats. 2009, Ch. 46, Sec. 3. (SB 352) Effective January 1, 2010.)
1567.4.
The State Department of Social Services shall provide, at cost, quarterly to each county and to each city, upon the request of the county or city, and to the chief probation officer of each county and city and county, a roster of all community care facilities licensed as small family homes, short-term residential therapeutic programs, or group homes located in the county, which provide services to wards of the juvenile court, including information as to whether each facility is licensed by the state or the county, the type of facility, and the licensed bed capacity of each such facility. Information concerning the facility shall be limited to that available through the computer system of the State Department of Social Services.
(Amended by Stats. 2016, Ch. 612, Sec. 55. (AB 1997) Effective January 1, 2017.)
1567.7.
This article shall not apply to existing community care facilities for wards of the juvenile court which have received city or county zoning approval prior to the effective date of this article.
(Added by Stats. 1978, Ch. 889.)
1567.8.
A community care facility for wards of the juvenile court, which serves six or fewer persons shall not be subject to any business taxes, local registration fees, use permit fees, or other fees to which other single family dwellings are not likewise subject. Nothing in this section shall be construed to forbid the imposition of local property taxes, fees for water service and garbage collection, fees for inspections not prohibited by Section 1567.9, local bond assessments, and other fees, charges, and assessments to which other single family dwellings are likewise subject. Neither the State Fire Marshal nor any local public entity shall charge any fee for enforcing fire inspection regulations pursuant to state law or regulation or local ordinance, with respect to community care facilities for wards of the juvenile court which serve six or fewer persons.
(Added by Stats. 1978, Ch. 889.)

ARTICLE 9. Adult Residential Facilities for Persons with Special Health Care Needs: Licensing [1567.50- 1567.50.]

(Article 9 added by Stats. 2005, Ch. 558, Sec. 7.)
1567.50.
(a) Notwithstanding that a community care facility means a place that provides nonmedical care under subdivision (a) of Section 1502, pursuant to Article 3.5 (commencing with Section 4684.50) of Chapter 6 of Division 4.5 of the Welfare and Institutions Code, the department shall jointly implement with the State Department of Developmental Services a licensing program to provide special health care and intensive support services to adults in homelike community settings.
(b) The State Department of Social Services may license, subject to the following conditions, an Adult Residential Facility for Persons with Special Health Care Needs to provide 24-hour services to up to five adults with developmental disabilities who have special health care and intensive support needs, as defined in subdivisions (f) and (g) of Section 4684.50 of the Welfare and Institutions Code.
(1) The State Department of Developmental Services shall be responsible for granting the certificate of program approval for an Adult Residential Facility for Persons with Special Health Care Needs (ARFPSHN). The State Department of Social Services shall not issue a license unless the applicant has obtained a certification of program approval from the State Department of Developmental Services.
(2) The State Department of Social Services shall ensure that the ARFPSHN meets the administration requirements under Article 2 (commencing with Section 1520) including, but not limited to, requirements relating to fingerprinting and criminal records under Section 1522.
(3) The State Department of Social Services shall administer employee actions under Article 5.5 (commencing with Section 1558).
(4) The regional center shall monitor and enforce compliance of the program and health and safety requirements, including monitoring and evaluating the quality of care and intensive support services. The State Department of Developmental Services shall ensure that the regional center performs these functions.
(5) The State Department of Developmental Services may decertify any ARFPSHN that does not comply with program requirements. When the State Department of Developmental Services determines that urgent action is necessary to protect clients of the ARFPSHN from physical or mental abuse, abandonment, or any other substantial threat to their health and safety, the State Department of Developmental Services may request the regional center or centers to remove the clients from the ARFPSHN or direct the regional center or centers to obtain alternative services for the consumers within 24 hours.

(6) The State Department of Social Services may initiate proceedings for temporary suspension of the license pursuant to Section 1550.5.

(7) The State Department of Developmental Services, upon its decertification, shall inform the State Department of Social Services of the licensee's decertification, with its recommendation concerning revocation of the license, for which the State Department of Social Services may initiate proceedings pursuant to Section 1550.

(8) The State Department of Developmental Services and the regional centers shall provide the State Department of Social Services all available documentation and evidentiary support necessary for any enforcement proceedings to suspend the license pursuant to Section 1550.5, to revoke or deny a license pursuant to Section 1551, or to exclude an individual pursuant to Section 1558.

(9) The State Department of Social Services Community Care Licensing Division shall enter into a memorandum of understanding with the State Department of Developmental Services to outline a formal protocol to address shared responsibilities, including monitoring responsibilities, complaint investigations, administrative actions, and closures.

(10) The licensee shall provide documentation that, in addition to the administrator requirements set forth under paragraph (4) of subdivision (a) of Section 4684.63 of the Welfare and Institutions Code, the administrator, prior to employment, has completed a minimum of 35 hours of initial training in the general laws, regulations and policies and procedural standards applicable to facilities licensed by the State Department of Social Services under Article 2 (commencing with Section 1520). Thereafter, the licensee shall provide documentation every two years that the administrator has completed 40 hours of continuing education in the general laws, regulations and policies and procedural standards applicable to adult residential facilities. The training specified in this section shall be provided by a vendor approved by the State Department of Social Services and the cost of the training shall be borne by the administrator or licensee.

(c) This article shall only be implemented to the extent that funds are made available through an appropriation in the annual Budget Act.

(Amended by Stats. 2010, Ch. 717, Sec. 13. (SB 853) Effective October 19, 2010.)

ARTICLE 9.5. Enhanced Behavioral Supports Homes [1567.61 - 1567.70]
(Article 9.5 added by Stats. 2014, Ch. 30, Sec. 6.)

1567.61.
As used in this article the following terms apply:

(a) "Consumer" or "client" means an individual who has been determined by a regional center to meet the eligibility criteria of Section 4512 of the Welfare and Institutions Code and applicable regulations and for whom the regional center has accepted responsibility.

(b) "Individual behavior supports plan" means the plan that identifies and documents the behavior and intensive support and service needs of a consumer and details the strategies to be employed and services to be provided to address those needs, and includes the entity responsible for providing those services and timelines for when each identified individual behavior support will commence.

(c) "Individual behavior supports team" means those individuals who develop, monitor, and revise the individual behavior supports plan for consumers residing in an enhanced behavioral supports home, pursuant to subdivision (d) of Section 4684.80 of the Welfare and Institutions Code.

(Added by Stats. 2014, Ch. 30, Sec. 6. (SB 856) Effective June 20, 2014. Repealed as of January 1, 2021, pursuant to Section 1567.70.)

1567.62.
(a) Each enhanced behavioral supports home shall be licensed as an adult residential facility or a group home and certified by the State Department of Developmental Services.

(b) A certificate of program approval issued by the State Department of Developmental Services shall be a condition of licensure for the enhanced behavioral supports home by the State Department of Social Services.

(c) An enhanced behavioral supports home shall not be licensed by the State Department of Social Services until the certificate of program approval, granted by the State Department of Developmental Services, has been received.

(d) Placements of dual agency clients into enhanced behavioral supports homes that are licensed as group homes shall be subject to the limitations on the duration of the placement set forth in Sections 319.2 and 319.3 of, and subparagraphs (A) and (B) of paragraph (9) of subdivision (e) of Section 361.2 of, the Welfare and Institutions Code.

(e) For the purpose of this article, dual agency clients are foster children in temporary custody of the child welfare agency under Section 319 of the Welfare and Institutions Code or under the jurisdiction of the juvenile court pursuant to Section 300, 450, 601, or 602 of the Welfare and Institutions Code who are also either a consumer of regional center services, or who are receiving services under the California Early Intervention Services Act (Title 14 (commencing with Section 95000) of the Government Code), but who are under three years of age and have not yet been determined to have a developmental disability.

(f) The State Department of Social Services is not responsible for any of the following:

(1) Developing and approving a consumer's individual behavior supports plan in conjunction with the consumer's individual behavior supports team.

(2) (A) Oversight of any services that may be provided by a licensed health professional or licensed mental health professional to a consumer.

(B) Services provided by a licensed health or licensed mental health professional means services that may only be provided under the authority of the licensed health service provider's or licensed mental health service provider's professional license.

(g) Subdivision (f) does not limit the State Department of Social Services' ability to enforce Chapter 3 (commencing with Section 1500), and applicable regulations.

(Amended by Stats. 2019, Ch. 28, Sec. 2. (SB 81) Effective June 27, 2019. Repealed as of January 1, 2021, pursuant to Section 1567.70.)

1567.63.
The license applicant shall submit a facility program plan to the State Department of Developmental Services for approval and submit the approved plan to the State Department of Social Services as part of the facility plan of operation. The plan of operation shall be approved by the State Department of Social Services prior to licensure. (Added by Stats. 2014, Ch. 30, Sec. 6. (SB 856) Effective June 20, 2014. Repealed as of January 1, 2021, pursuant to Section 1567.70.)

1567.64.
The State Department of Social Services shall adopt regulations to address, at a minimum, staffing structure, staff qualifications, and training. Training requirements shall include a minimum of 16 hours of emergency intervention training. "Emergency intervention training" means the techniques the licensee will use to prevent injury to, and maintain safety for, consumers who are a danger to themselves or others and shall emphasize positive behavioral supports and techniques that are alternatives to physical restraints.

(Added by Stats. 2014, Ch. 30, Sec. 6. (SB 856) Effective June 20, 2014. Repealed as of January 1, 2021, pursuant to Section 1567.70.)

1567.65.
If the State Department of Social Services determines that urgent action is necessary to protect a consumer residing in an enhanced behavioral supports home from physical or mental abuse, abandonment, or any other substantial threat to their health and safety, the State Department of Social Services shall notify the State Department of Developmental Services. The State Department of Developmental Services may request that the regional center or centers take action within 24 hours, which may include, as appropriate, the removal of a consumer from the enhanced behavioral supports home or obtaining alternative or additional services. When possible, an individual program plan (IPP) meeting shall be convened to determine the appropriate action pursuant to this section. In any case, an IPP meeting shall be convened within 30 days following an action pursuant to this section.

(Added by Stats. 2014, Ch. 30, Sec. 6. (SB 856) Effective June 20, 2014. Repealed as of January 1, 2021, pursuant to Section 1567.70.)

1567.66.
An enhanced behavioral supports home employing secured perimeters shall comply with Section 1531.15 and applicable regulations.

(Added by Stats. 2014, Ch. 30, Sec. 6. (SB 856) Effective June 20, 2014. Repealed as of January 1, 2021, pursuant to Section 1567.70.)

1567.67.
(a) The State Department of Social Services shall revoke the enhanced behavioral supports home's facility license if the State Department of Developmental Services has decertified an enhanced behavioral supports home program certification pursuant to Article 3.6 (commencing with Section 4684.80) of Chapter 6 of Division 4.5 of the Welfare and Institutions Code.

(b) The State Department of Developmental Services and regional centers shall, for purposes of assisting in licensing, provide the State Department of Social Services with all available documentation and evidentiary support that was submitted to the State Department of Developmental Services in connection with certification by an applicant for licensure under this article.

(Added by Stats. 2014, Ch. 30, Sec. 6. (SB 856) Effective June 20, 2014. Repealed as of January 1, 2021, pursuant to Section 1567.70.)

1567.68.
(a) A license shall not be issued pursuant to this article before emergency regulations for this article filed by the State Department of Developmental Services have been published.

(b) Emergency regulations to implement this article may be adopted by the director of the State Department of Social Services in accordance with the Administrative Procedure Act (Chapter 3.5 (commencing with Section 11340) of Part 1 of Division 3 of Title 2 of the Government Code). These regulations shall be developed in consultation with system stakeholders. The initial adoption of the emergency regulations and one readoption of the initial regulations shall be deemed to be an emergency and necessary for the immediate preservation of the public peace, health, safety, or general welfare. Initial emergency regulations and the first readoption of those emergency regulations shall be exempt from review by the Office of Administrative Law. The emergency regulations authorized by this section shall be submitted to the Office of Administrative Law for filing with the Secretary of State and shall remain in effect for no more than 180 days.

(c) The adoption, initial amendment, repeal, or readoption of a regulation authorized by this section is deemed to be an emergency and necessary for the immediate preservation of the public peace, health, safety, or general welfare for purposes of Sections 11346.1 and 11349.6 of the Government Code, and the State Department of Social Services is hereby exempted from the requirement that it describe specific facts showing the need for immediate action. A certificate of compliance for these implementing regulations shall be filed within 24 months following the adoption of the first emergency regulations filed pursuant to this section. The emergency regulations may be readopted and remain in effect until approval of the certificate of compliance.

(Added by Stats. 2014, Ch. 30, Sec. 6. (SB 856) Effective June 20, 2014. Repealed as of January 1, 2021, pursuant to Section 1567.70.)

1567.69.
This article does not interfere with the authority of the State Department of Social Services to temporarily suspend or revoke the license of an enhanced behavioral supports home pursuant to Section 1550.

(Amended by Stats. 2015, Ch. 303, Sec. 277. (AB 731) Effective January 1, 2016. Repealed as of January 1, 2021, pursuant to Section 1567.70.)

1567.70.

This article shall remain in effect only until January 1, 2021, and as of that date is repealed, unless a later enacted statute, that is enacted before January 1, 2021, deletes or extends that date.

(Amended by Stats. 2019, Ch. 28, Sec. 3. (SB 81) Effective June 27, 2019. Repealed as of January 1, 2021, by its own provisions. Note: Repeal affects Article 9.5, commencing with Section 1567.61.)

ARTICLE 9.7. Community Crisis Home Licensure [1567.80 - 1567.87]
(Article 9.7 added by Stats. 2014, Ch. 30, Sec. 7.)
1567.80.

For the purposes of this article, the following definitions apply:

(a) "Consumer" or "client" means an individual who has been determined by a regional center to meet the eligibility criteria of Section 4512 of the Welfare and Institutions Code and applicable regulations, and for whom the regional center has accepted responsibility.

(b) "Individual behavior support plan" means the plan that identifies and documents the behavioral and intensive support and service needs of a consumer and details the strategies to be employed, and services to be provided, to address those needs, and includes the entity responsible for providing those services and timelines for when each identified individual behavioral support will commence.

(Added by Stats. 2014, Ch. 30, Sec. 7. (SB 856) Effective June 20, 2014.)
1567.81.

(a) (1) Each community crisis home shall be licensed as an adult residential facility or a group home, pursuant to this article, and certified by the State Department of Developmental Services, pursuant to Article 8 (commencing with Section 4698) of Chapter 6 of Division 4.5 of the Welfare and Institutions Code.

(2) Notwithstanding whether a community crisis home is licensed for more than six consumers, subdivisions (a) and (b) of Section 1524.5 shall apply.

(b) A certificate of program approval issued by the State Department of Developmental Services, pursuant to Article 8 (commencing with Section 4698) of Chapter 6 of Division 4.5 of the Welfare and Institutions Code, shall be a condition of licensure for the community crisis home by the State Department of Social Services.

(c) A community crisis home shall not be licensed by the State Department of Social Services until the certificate of program approval, issued by the State Department of Developmental Services, has been received.

(d) Placements of dual agency clients into community crisis homes that are licensed as group homes shall be subject to the placement duration limitations described in Sections 319.2 and 319.3 of, and subparagraphs (A) and (B) of paragraph (9) of subdivision (e) of Section 361.2 of, the Welfare and Institutions Code.

(e) For the purpose of this article, dual agency clients are foster children in temporary custody of the child welfare agency under Section 319 of the Welfare and Institutions Code or under the jurisdiction of the juvenile court pursuant to Section 300, 450, 601, or 602 of the Welfare and Institutions Code who are also either a consumer of regional center services, or who are receiving services under the California Early Intervention Services Act (Title 14 (commencing with Section 95000) of the Government Code), but who are under three years of age and have not yet been determined to have a developmental disability.

(f) The State Department of Social Services shall not be responsible for any of the following:

(1) Developing and approving a consumer's individual behavior support plan in conjunction with the consumer's individual behavior support team.

(2) Oversight of any services that may be provided by a licensed health or licensed mental health professional to a consumer. "Services provided by a licensed health or licensed mental health professional" means services that may only be provided under the authority of the licensed health or licensed mental health service provider's professional license.

(g) Subdivision (f) does not limit the State Department of Social Services' ability to enforce this chapter and applicable regulations.

(Amended by Stats. 2019, Ch. 28, Sec. 4. (SB 81) Effective June 27, 2019.)
1567.82.

The State Department of Social Services' regulations shall address at least both of the following:

(a) Staffing structure, staff qualifications, and training.

(b) Training requirements shall include a minimum of 16 hours of emergency intervention training. "Emergency intervention training" shall include the techniques the licensee will use to prevent injury and maintain safety regarding consumers who are a danger to self or others and shall emphasize positive behavioral supports and techniques that are alternatives to physical restraints.

(Added by Stats. 2014, Ch. 30, Sec. 7. (SB 856) Effective June 20, 2014.)
1567.83.

(a) When the State Department of Social Services determines that urgent action is necessary to protect consumers residing in a community crisis home from physical or mental abuse, abandonment, or any other substantial threat to their health and safety, the State Department of Social Services shall notify the State Department of Developmental Services. The State Department of Developmental Services may request that the regional center or centers take action within 24 hours, which may include, as appropriate, the removal of a consumer from the community crisis home or obtaining alternative or additional services. When possible, an individual program plan (IPP) meeting shall be convened to determine the appropriate action pursuant to this section. In any case, an IPP meeting shall be convened within 30 days following an action pursuant to this section.

(b) Nothing in this article shall interfere with the authority of the State Department of Social Services to temporarily suspend or revoke the license of a community crisis home pursuant to Section 1550.

(Added by Stats. 2014, Ch. 30, Sec. 7. (SB 856) Effective June 20, 2014.)
1567.84.

The licensee shall submit the facility program plan approved by the State Department of Developmental Services, pursuant to Section 4698 of the Welfare and Institutions Code, to the State Department of Social Services as part of the facility plan of operation. The plan of operation shall be approved by the State Department of Social Services prior to licensure.

(Added by Stats. 2014, Ch. 30, Sec. 7. (SB 856) Effective June 20, 2014.)
1567.85.

If applicable, a community crisis home shall be in compliance with Section 1531.15 and the applicable regulations.

(Added by Stats. 2014, Ch. 30, Sec. 7. (SB 856) Effective June 20, 2014.)
1567.86.

(a) The State Department of Social Services shall revoke the community crisis home's facility license if the State Department of Developmental Services has rescinded a community crisis home's certificate of program approval.

(b) The State Department of Developmental Services and regional centers shall provide the State Department of Social Services all available documentation and evidentiary support necessary for the licensing and administration of community crisis homes and enforcement of this article and the applicable regulations.

(Added by Stats. 2014, Ch. 30, Sec. 7. (SB 856) Effective June 20, 2014.)
1567.87.

(a) A license shall not be issued pursuant to this article until the publication in Title 17 of the California Code of Regulations of emergency regulations filed by the State Department of Developmental Services pursuant to Section 4698.1 of the Welfare and Institutions Code.

(b) Emergency regulations to implement this article may be adopted by the Director of Social Services in accordance with the Administrative Procedure Act (Chapter 3.5 (commencing with Section 11340) of Part 1 of Division 3 of Title 2 of the Government Code). These emergency regulations shall be developed in consultation with system stakeholders. The initial adoption of the emergency regulations and one readoption of the initial regulations shall be deemed to be an emergency and necessary for the immediate preservation of the public peace, health and safety, or general welfare. Initial emergency regulations and the first readoption of those emergency regulations shall be exempt from review by the Office of Administrative Law. The emergency regulations authorized by this section shall be submitted to the Office of Administrative Law for filing with the Secretary of State and shall remain in effect for no more than 180 days.

(c) The adoption, amendment, repeal, or readoption of a regulation authorized by this section is deemed to be an emergency and necessary for the immediate preservation of the public peace, health and safety, or general welfare for purposes of Sections 11346.1 and 11349.6 of the Government Code, and the State Department of Social Services is hereby exempted from the requirement that it describe specific facts showing the need for immediate action. A certificate of compliance for these implementing regulations shall be filed within 24 months following the adoption of the first emergency regulations filed pursuant to this section. The emergency regulations may be readopted and remain in effect until approval of the certificate of compliance.

(Added by Stats. 2014, Ch. 30, Sec. 7. (SB 856) Effective June 20, 2014.)

CHAPTER 3.01. Residential Care Facilities for Persons With Chronic Life-Threatening Illness [1568.01 - 1568.094]

(Chapter 3.01 added by Stats. 1990, Ch. 1333, Sec. 1.5.)
1568.01.

For purposes of this chapter, the following definitions shall apply:

(a) "Activities of daily living" means housework, meals, laundry, taking medication, money management, appropriate transportation, correspondence, telephoning, dressing, feeding, toileting, bathing, grooming, mobility, and related tasks.

(b) "Care and supervision" means ongoing assistance with activities of daily living without which a resident's physical health, mental health, safety, or welfare would be endangered.

(c) "Chronic, life-threatening illness" means HIV disease or AIDS.

(d) "Department" means the State Department of Social Services.

(e) "Director" means the Director of Social Services.

(f) "Family dwelling" includes, but is not limited to, single-family dwellings, units in multifamily dwellings, including units in duplexes and units in apartment dwellings, mobilehomes, including mobilehomes located in mobilehome parks, units in cooperatives, units in condominiums, units in townhouses, and units in planned unit developments.

(g) "Family unit" means at least one parent or guardian and one or more of that parent or guardian's children. For purposes of this chapter, each family unit shall include at least one adult with HIV disease or AIDS, at least one child with HIV or AIDS, or both.

(h) "Fund" means the Residential Care Facilities for Persons with Chronic Life-Threatening Illness Fund created by subdivision (c) of Section 1568.05.

(i) "Placement agency" means any state agency, county agency, or private agency which receives public funds, in part, to identify housing options for persons with chronic, life-threatening illness and refers these persons to housing.

(j) "Residential care facility" means a residential care facility for persons with chronic, life-threatening illness who are 18 years of age or older or are emancipated minors, and for family units.
(k) "Six or fewer persons" does not include the licensee or members of the licensee's family or persons employed as facility staff.
(l) "Terminal disease" or "terminal illness" means a medical condition resulting from a prognosis of a life expectancy of one year or less, if the disease follows its normal course.
(Amended by Stats. 2004, Ch. 121, Sec. 1. Effective January 1, 2005.)

1568.02.

(a) (1) The department shall license residential care facilities for persons with chronic, life-threatening illness under a separate category.
(2) A residential care facility for persons with chronic, life-threatening illness may allow a person who has been diagnosed by his or her physician or surgeon as terminally ill, as defined in subdivision (l) of Section 1568.01, to become a resident of the facility if the person receives hospice services from a hospice certified in accordance with federal Medicare conditions of participation and is licensed pursuant to Chapter 8 (commencing with Section 1725) or Chapter 8.5 (commencing with Section 1745).
(b) The licensee of every facility required to be licensed pursuant to this chapter shall provide the following basic services for each resident:
(1) Room and board. No more than two residents shall share a bedroom, except that the director, in his or her discretion, may waive this limitation.
(2) Access to adequate common areas, including recreation areas and shared kitchen space with adequate refrigerator space for the storage of medications.
(3) Consultation with a nutritionist, including consultation on cultural dietary needs.
(4) Personal care services, as needed, including, but not limited to, activities of daily living. A facility may have a written agreement with another agency to provide personal care services, except that the facility shall be responsible for meeting the personal care needs of each resident.
(5) Access to case management for social services. A facility may have a written agreement with another agency to provide case management.
(6) Development, implementation, and monitoring of an individual services plan. All health services components of the plan shall be developed and monitored in coordination with the home health agency or hospice agency and shall reflect the elements of the resident's plan of treatment developed by the home health agency or hospice agency.
(7) Intake and discharge procedures, including referral to outplacement resources.
(8) Access to psychosocial support services.
(9) Access to community-based and county services system.
(10) Access to a social and emotional support network of the resident's own choosing, within the context of reasonable visitation rules established by the facility.
(11) Access to intermittent home health care services in accordance with paragraph (1) of subdivision (c).
(12) Access to substance abuse services in accordance with paragraph (3) of subdivision (c).
(13) Adequate securable storage space for personal items.
(c) The licensee of every facility required to be licensed pursuant to this chapter shall demonstrate, at the time of application, all of the following:
(1) Written agreement with a licensed home health agency or hospice agency. Resident information may be shared between the home health agency or hospice agency and the residential care facility for a person with a chronic, life-threatening illness relative to the resident's medical condition and the care and treatment provided to the resident by the home health agency or hospice agency, including, but not limited to, medical information, as defined by the Confidentiality of Medical Information Act, Part 2.6 (commencing with Section 56) of Division 1 of the Civil Code. Any regulations, policies, or procedures related to sharing resident information and development of protocols, established by the department pursuant to this section, shall be developed in consultation with the State Department of Health Care Services and persons representing home health agencies, hospice agencies, and residential care facilities for persons with chronic, life-threatening illness.
(2) Written agreement with a psychosocial services agency, unless the services are provided by the facility's professional staff.
(3) Written agreement with a substance abuse agency, unless the services are provided by the facility's professional staff.
(4) Ability to provide linguistic services for residents who do not speak English.
(5) Ability to provide culturally appropriate services.
(6) Ability to reasonably accommodate residents with physical disabilities, including, but not limited to, residents with motor impairments, physical access to areas of the facility used by residents, and access to interpreters for deaf or hard-of-hearing residents.
(7) Written nondiscrimination policy, which shall be posted in a conspicuous place in the facility.
(8) Written policy on drug and alcohol use, including, but not limited to, a prohibition on the use of illegal substances.
(d) A facility licensed pursuant to this chapter that intends to serve a specific population, such as women, family units, minority and ethnic populations, or homosexual men or women, shall demonstrate, at the time of application, the ability and resources to provide services that are appropriate to the targeted population.
(e) A facility licensed pursuant to this chapter shall not house more than 25 residents, except that the director may authorize a facility to house up to 50 residents.
(f) If the administrator is responsible for more than two facilities, the facility manager shall meet the qualifications of both the administrator and the facility manager, as described in Sections 87864 and 87864.1 of Title 22 of the California Code of Regulations.
(g) Each licensee shall employ additional personnel as necessary to meet the needs of the residents and comply with the requirements of this chapter and the regulations adopted by the department pursuant to this chapter. On-call personnel shall be able to be on the facility premises within 30 minutes of the receipt of a telephone call.
(Amended by Stats. 2016, Ch. 94, Sec. 18. (AB 1709) Effective January 1, 2017.)

1568.021.

(a) If the applicant for a license for a residential care facility handles or will handle any money of a resident of the facility, the applicant or licensee shall file or have on file with the department a bond issued by a surety company admitted to do business in this state in a sum to be fixed by the department based upon the magnitude of the operations of the applicant or licensee, but which sum shall not be less than one thousand dollars ($1,000), running to the State of California and conditioned upon his or her faithful and honest handling of the money of residents of the facility.
(b) The failure of any licensee under this chapter to maintain on file with the department a bond in the amount prescribed by the department or the embezzlement by a licensee of trust funds of a resident of the facility shall constitute cause for the revocation of the license.
(c) This section shall not apply if the licensee handles moneys of residents of the facility in amounts less than fifty dollars ($50) per person and less than five hundred dollars ($500) for all persons in any month.
(d) The director may grant a partial or total variance from the requirements of this section if the director finds that compliance with them is so onerous that a residential care facility will cease to operate, and if the director also finds that money of the residents received or cared for in the facility has been, or will be, deposited in a bank in this state, in a trust company authorized to transact a trust business in this state, or in a savings and loan association in this state, upon condition that the money may not be withdrawn except on authorization of the person or a representative who is legally authorized to make financial decisions on behalf of the person.
(Amended by Stats. 1992, Ch. 1315, Sec. 11. Effective January 1, 1993.)

1568.03.

(a) No person, firm, partnership, association, or corporation within the state and no state or local public agency shall operate, establish, manage, conduct, or maintain a residential care facility in this state without first obtaining and maintaining a valid license therefor, as provided in this chapter.
(b) A facility may accept or retain residents requiring varying levels of care. However, a facility shall not accept or retain residents who require a higher level of care than the facility is authorized to provide. Persons who require 24-hour skilled nursing intervention shall not be appropriate for a residential care facility.
(c) This chapter shall not apply to the following:
(1) Any health facility, as defined in Section 1250.
(2) Any clinic, as defined in Section 1200.
(3) Any arrangement for the receiving and care of persons with chronic, life-threatening illness by a relative, guardian or conservator, significant other, or close friend; or any arrangement for the receiving and care of persons with chronic, life-threatening illness from only one family as respite for the relative, guardian or conservator, significant other, or close friend, if the arrangement is not for financial profit and occurs only occasionally and irregularly, as defined by regulations of the department.
(4) (A) Any house, institution, hotel, foster home, shared housing project, or other similar facility that is limited to providing any of the following: housing, meals, transportation, housekeeping, recreational and social activities, the enforcement of house rules, counseling on activities of daily living, and service referrals, as long as both of the following conditions are met:
(i) After any referral, all residents thereof independently obtain care and supervision and medical services without the assistance of the facility or of any person or entity with an organizational or financial connection with that facility.
(ii) No resident thereof has an unmet need for care and supervision or protective supervision. A memorandum of understanding between the facility and any service agency to which it refers residents does not necessarily itself constitute an agreement for care and supervision of the resident.
(B) In determining the applicability of this paragraph, the department shall determine the residents' need for care and supervision, if any, and shall identify the persons or entities providing or assisting in the provision of care and supervision. This paragraph shall apply only if the department determines that the care and supervision needs of all residents are being independently met.
(5) (A) (i) Any housing occupied by elderly or disabled persons, or both, that is approved and operated pursuant to Section 202 of Public Law 86-372 (12 U.S.C. Sec. 1701q), or Section 811 of Public Law 101-625 (42 U.S.C. Sec. 8013), or whose mortgage is insured pursuant to Section 236 of Public Law 90-448 (12 U.S.C. Sec. 1715z), or that receives mortgage assistance pursuant to Section 221d (3) of Public Law 87-70 (12 U.S.C. Sec. 1751l), where supportive services are made available to residents at their option, as long as the project owner or operator does not contract for or provide the supportive services.
(ii) Any housing that qualifies for a low-income housing credit pursuant to Section 252 of Public Law 99-514 (26 U.S.C. Sec. 42) or that is subject to the requirements for rental dwellings for low-income families pursuant to Section 8 of Public Law 93-383 (42 U.S.C. Sec. 1437f), and that is occupied by elderly or disabled persons, or both, where supportive services are made available to residents at their option, as long as the project owner or operator does not contract for or provide the supportive services.
(B) The project owner or operator to which subparagraph (A) applies may coordinate, or help residents gain access to, the supportive services, either directly or through a service coordinator.

(6) Any similar facility determined by the director.

(d) A holder of a residential care facility license may hold or obtain an additional license or a child day care facility license, as long as the services required by each license are provided at separate locations or distinctly separate sections of the building.

(e) The director may bring an action to enjoin the violation or threatened violation of this section in the superior court in and for the county in which the violation occurred or is about to occur. Any proceeding under this section shall conform to the requirements of Chapter 3 (commencing with Section 525) of Title 7 of Part 2 of the Code of Civil Procedure, except that the director shall not be required to allege facts necessary to show or tending to show lack of adequate remedy at law or irreparable damage or loss. The court shall, if it finds the allegations to be true, issue its order enjoining continuance of the violation.

(Amended by Stats. 2010, Ch. 328, Sec. 123. (SB 1330) Effective January 1, 2011.)

1568.04.

Any person desiring issuance of a license for a residential care facility under this chapter shall file with the department, pursuant to regulations adopted by the department, an application. The application shall be provided on a form furnished by the department, and shall include, but not be limited to, all of the following:

(a) Evidence satisfactory to the department of all of the following:

(1) The ability of the applicant to comply with this chapter and of rules and regulations adopted pursuant to this chapter by the department.

(2) The applicant has sufficient financial resources to maintain the standards of service required by regulations adopted pursuant to this chapter.

(3) Following the department's adoption of regulations specifying the levels of care to be provided under this chapter, the applicant's ability to meet regulatory requirements for the level of care the facility intends to provide.

(4) Compliance or ability to comply with Section 1568.02.

(b) Disclosure of the applicant's prior or present service as an administrator, general partner, corporate officer or director of, or as a person who has held or holds a beneficial ownership of 10 percent or more in, any residential care facility or in any clinic or facility licensed pursuant to Chapter 1 (commencing with Section 1200), Chapter 2 (commencing with Section 1250), or Chapter 3 (commencing with Section 1500).

(c) Disclosure of any revocation or other disciplinary action taken, or in the process of being taken, against a license held or previously held by the entities specified in subdivision (b).

(d) Any other information as may be required by the department for the proper administration and enforcement of this chapter.

(e) A signed statement that the person desiring issuance of a license has read this chapter and the regulations adopted pursuant to this chapter and understands the statute and regulations applicable to a residential care facility.

(Amended by Stats. 1992, Ch. 1315, Sec. 12. Effective January 1, 1993.)

1568.041.

(a) The department shall designate at least one person in each region to be responsible for all activities pertaining to license application as well as prescribed monitoring of licensees. In those regions which have a concentration of licensees, the department shall make every effort to identify at least one person in each district office whose sole responsibility will be for facilities licensed pursuant to this chapter.

(b) The department shall ensure that those personnel identified in subdivision (a) receive periodic training regarding the most recent developments in the HIV epidemic and the care and supervision of people with HIV disease.

(Added by Stats. 1993, Ch. 1215, Sec. 4. Effective January 1, 1994.)

1568.042.

(a) A corporation that applies for licensure with the department shall list the facilities that any member of the board of directors, the executive director, or an officer has been licensed to operate, been employed in, or served as a member of the board of directors, the executive director, or an officer.

(b) The department shall not issue a provisional license or license to any corporate applicant that has a member of the board of directors, an executive director, or an officer who is not eligible for licensure pursuant to subdivision (f) of Section 1568.065 and Section 1568.093.

(c) The department may revoke the license of any corporate licensee that has a member of the board of directors, an executive director, or an officer who is not eligible for licensure pursuant to subdivision (f) of Section 1568.065 and Section 1568.093.

(d) Prior to instituting an administrative action pursuant to either subdivision (b) or (c), the department shall notify the applicant or licensee of the person's ineligibility to be a member of the board of directors, an executive director, or an officer of the applicant or licensee, and shall give the applicant or licensee 15 days to remove the person from that position.

(Added by Stats. 1998, Ch. 311, Sec. 31. Effective August 19, 1998.)

1568.043.

A residential care facility for persons with chronic, life-threatening illness shall have one or more carbon monoxide detectors in the facility that meet the standards established on Chapter 8 (commencing with Section 13260) of Part 2 of Division 12. The department shall account for the presence of these detectors during inspections.

(Added by Stats. 2014, Ch. 503, Sec. 2. (AB 2386) Effective January 1, 2015.)

1568.05.

(a) (1) An application fee adjusted by facility and capacity, shall be charged by the department for a license to operate a residential care facility for persons with chronic life-threatening illness. After initial licensure, a fee shall be charged by the department annually, on each anniversary of the effective date of the license. The fees are for the purpose of financing the activities specified in this chapter. Fees shall be assessed as follows, subject to paragraph (2):

Fee Schedule		
Capacity	Initial Application	Annual
1–6	$605	$303 plus $11 per bed
7–15	$758	$378 plus $11 per bed
16–25	$908	$454 plus $11 per bed
26+	$1,060	$530 plus $11 per bed

(2) (A) The Legislature finds that all revenues generated by fees for licenses computed under this section and used for the purposes for which they were imposed are not subject to Article XIII B of the California Constitution.

(B) The department, at least every five years, shall analyze initial application fees and annual fees issued by it to ensure the appropriate fee amounts are charged. The department shall recommend to the Legislature that fees established by the Legislature be adjusted as necessary to ensure that the amounts are appropriate.

(b) (1) In addition to fees set forth in subdivision (a), the department shall charge the following fees:

(A) A fee that represents 50 percent of an established application fee when an existing licensee moves the facility to a new physical address.

(B) A fee that represents 50 percent of the established application fee when a corporate licensee changes who has the authority to select a majority of the board of directors.

(C) A fee of twenty-five dollars ($25) when an existing licensee seeks to either increase or decrease the licensed capacity of the facility.

(D) An orientation fee of fifty dollars ($50) for attendance by any individual at a department-sponsored orientation session.

(E) A probation monitoring fee equal to the current annual fee, in addition to the current annual fee for that category and capacity for each year a license has been placed on probation as a result of a stipulation or decision and order pursuant to the administrative adjudication procedures of the Administrative Procedure Act (Chapter 4.5 (commencing with Section 11400) and Chapter 5 (commencing with Section 11500) of Part 1 of Division 3 of Title 2 of the Government Code).

(F) A late fee that represents an additional 50 percent of the current established annual fee when any licensee fails to pay the current annual licensing fee on or before the due date as indicated by postmark on the payment.

(G) A fee to cover any costs incurred by the department for processing payments including, but not limited to, bounced check charges, charges for credit and debit transactions, and postage due charges.

(H) A plan of correction fee of two hundred dollars ($200) when any licensee does not implement a plan of correction on or prior to the date specified in the plan.

(2) No local governmental entity shall impose any business license, fee, or tax for the privilege of operating a facility licensed under this chapter which serves six or fewer persons.

(c) All fees collected pursuant to subdivisions (a) and (b) shall be deposited in the Technical Assistance Fund.

(d) The revenues collected from licensing fees pursuant to this section shall be utilized by the department for the purpose of ensuring the health and safety of all individuals provided care and supervision by licensees and to support activities of the licensing program, including, but not limited to, monitoring facilities for compliance with licensing laws and regulations pursuant to this chapter, and other administrative activities in support of the licensing program, when appropriated for these purposes. The revenues collected shall be used in addition to any other funds appropriated in the Budget Act in support of the licensing program. The department shall adjust the fees collected pursuant to this section as necessary to ensure that they do not exceed the costs described in this subdivision.

(e) The department shall not utilize any portion of the revenues collected pursuant to this section sooner than 30 days after notification in writing of the purpose and use of this revenue, as approved by the Director of Finance, to the Chairperson of the Joint Legislative Budget Committee, and the chairpersons of the committee in each house that considers appropriations for each fiscal year. The department shall submit a budget change proposal to justify any positions or any other related support costs on an ongoing basis.

(f) Fees established pursuant to this section shall not be effective unless licensing fees are established for all adult residential facilities licensed by the department.

(g) A residential care facility may use a bona fide business check to pay the license fee required under this section.

(h) The failure of an applicant for licensure or a licensee to pay all applicable and accrued fees and civil penalties shall constitute grounds for denial or forfeiture of a license.

(Amended by Stats. 2014, Ch. 29, Sec. 19. (SB 855) Effective June 20, 2014.)

1568.06.

(a) Upon initial application for licensure, residential care facilities shall be provided a printed copy of all applicable regulations for the operation of these facilities by the department, without charge. The department shall provide all licensees with copies of proposed changes in regulations applicable to residential care facilities prior to public hearings on those proposed changes, and copies of all adopted changes in regulations applicable to residential care facilities immediately upon their adoption.

(b) As a requirement for licensure, an applicant shall attend an orientation given by the department which outlines the applicable rules and regulations and the scope and responsibility for operation of a residential care facility. The orientation shall include information on relevant community services.

(Amended by Stats. 1993, Ch. 1215, Sec. 5. Effective January 1, 1994.)

1568.061.

A license shall be forfeited by operation of law prior to its expiration date when any of the following occurs:

(a) The licensee sells or otherwise transfers the facility or the real property on which the facility is located, except when change of ownership applies to transferring of stock when the facility is owned by a corporation and when the transfer of stock does not constitute a majority change in ownership.

(b) The licensee surrenders the license to the department.

(c) The licensee moves a facility from one location to another. The department shall develop regulations to ensure that a licensee is not charged a full licensing fee and is not required to complete the entire application process when applying for a license for the new location.

(d) The licensee is convicted of an offense specified in Section 220, 243.4, or 264.1, or paragraph (1) of Section 273a, Section 273d, 288, or 289 of the Penal Code, or is convicted of another crime specified in subdivision (c) of Section 667.5 of the Penal Code.

(e) The licensee dies. When a licensee dies, the continued operation shall be subject to the requirements of Section 1568.064.

(Amended by Stats. 1992, Ch. 1315, Sec. 14. Effective January 1, 1993.)

1568.062.

(a) Upon the filing of the application for issuance of a license and substantial compliance with this chapter and the rules and regulations of the department adopted pursuant to this chapter, the director shall issue to the applicant the license to operate a residential care facility. If the director finds that the applicant is not in compliance with this chapter or the regulations adopted pursuant to this chapter, the director shall deny the applicant a license.

(b) The director may issue provisional licenses to operate residential care facilities for any facility which the director determines is in substantial compliance with this chapter and the rules and regulations adopted pursuant to this chapter, provided that no life safety risks are involved, as determined by the director. In determining whether any life safety risks are involved, the director shall require completion of all applicable fire clearances and criminal record clearances as otherwise required by the department's rules and regulations. A provisional license issued pursuant to this subdivision shall expire six months from the date of issuance, or at an earlier time as the director may determine, and may not be renewed. However, the director may extend the term of a provisional license for an additional six months at the time of application, if it is determined that more than six months will be required to achieve full compliance with licensing standards due to circumstances beyond the control of the applicant, and if all other requirements for a license have been met.

(Amended by Stats. 1992, Ch. 1315, Sec. 15. Effective January 1, 1993.)

1568.063.

Immediately upon the denial of any application for a license, the department shall notify the applicant in writing. Within 15 days after the department mails the notice of denial, the applicant may present his or her written petition for a hearing to the department. Upon receipt by the department of the petition in proper form, the petition shall be set for hearing.

(Amended by Stats. 1991, Ch. 832, Sec. 7.)

1568.064.

(a) When a licensee dies, an adult relative who has control of the property may continue operation of the facility if the following conditions are met:

(1) The department receives notification of the death during the next normal workday and is informed of the relative's intent to continue operating the facility as a residential care facility for persons with chronic, life-threatening illnesses.

(2) The relative files application, within five days of the date of death, shows evidence satisfactory to the department that he or she has the ability to operate the facility, submits his or her fingerprint card, and provides evidence of the licensee's death.

(b) The department shall make a decision within 60 days after the application is submitted on whether to issue a provisional license pursuant to Section 1568.062. A provisional license shall be granted only if the department is satisfied that the conditions specified in subdivision (a) have been met and that the health and safety of the residents of the facility will not be jeopardized.

(c) If the relative complies with subdivision (a), he or she shall not be considered to be operating an unlicensed facility while the department decides whether to grant the provisional license.

(Added by Stats. 1990, Ch. 1333, Sec. 1.5.)

1568.065.

(a) Proceedings for the suspension, revocation, or denial of a license under this chapter shall be conducted in accordance with Chapter 5 (commencing with Section 11500) of Part 1 of Division 3 of Title 2 of the Government Code, and the department shall have all those powers granted by the provisions. In the event of conflict between this chapter and those provisions of the Government Code, this chapter shall prevail.

(b) In all proceedings conducted in accordance with this section, the standard of proof to be applied shall be by the preponderance of the evidence.

(c) If the license is not temporarily suspended pursuant to Section 1568.082, the hearing shall be held within 90 calendar days after receipt of the notice of defense, unless a continuance of the hearing is granted by the department or the administrative law judge. When the matter has been set for hearing, only the administrative law judge may grant a continuance of the hearing. The administrative law judge may, but need not, grant a continuance of the hearing, only upon finding the existence of any of the following:

(1) The death or incapacitating illness of a party, a representative or attorney of a party, a witness to an essential fact, or of the parent, child, or member of the household of that person, when it is not feasible to substitute another representative, attorney, or witness because of the proximity of the hearing date.

(2) Lack of notice of hearing as provided in Section 11509 of the Government Code.

(3) A material change in the status of the case where a change in the parties or pleadings requires postponement, or an executed settlement or stipulated findings of fact obviate the need for hearing. A partial amendment of the pleadings shall not be good cause for continuance to the extent that the unamended portion of the pleadings is ready to be heard.

(4) A stipulation for continuance signed by all parties or their authorized representatives, including, but not limited to, a representative, which is communicated with the request for continuance to the administrative law judge no later than 25 business days before the hearing.

(5) The substitution of the representative or attorney of a party upon showing that the substitution is required.

(6) The unavailability of a party, representative, or attorney of a party, or witness to an essential fact due to a conflicting and required appearance in a judicial matter if when the hearing date was set, the person did not know and could neither anticipate nor at any time avoid the conflict, and the conflict with request for continuance is immediately communicated to the administrative law judge.

(7) The unavailability of a party, a representative or attorney of a party, or a material witness due to an unavoidable emergency.

(8) Failure by a party to comply with a timely discovery request if the continuance request is made by the party who requested the discovery.

(d) In addition to the witness fees and mileage provided by Section 11450.40 of the Government Code, the department may pay actual, necessary, and reasonable expenses in an amount not to exceed the per diem allowance payable to a nonrepresented state employee on travel status. The department may pay witness expenses pursuant to this section in advance of the hearing.

(e) (1) The withdrawal of an application for a license or a special permit after it has been filed with the department shall not deprive the department of its authority to institute or continue a proceeding against the applicant for the denial of the license or a special permit upon any ground provided by law or to enter an order denying the license or special permit upon any ground provided by law.

(2) The suspension, expiration, or forfeiture by operation of law of a license issued by the department, or its suspension, forfeiture, or cancellation by order of the department or by order of a court of law, or its surrender, shall not deprive the department of its authority to institute or continue a disciplinary proceeding against the licensee upon any ground provided by law or to enter an order suspending or revoking the license or otherwise taking disciplinary action against the licensee on any ground provided by law.

(f) (1) If an application for a license indicates, or the department determines during the application review process, that the applicant previously was issued a license under this chapter or under Chapter 1 (commencing with Section 1200), Chapter 2 (commencing with Section 1250), Chapter 3 (commencing with Section 1500), Chapter 3.3 (commencing with Section 1569), Chapter 3.4 (commencing with Section 1596.70), Chapter 3.5 (commencing with Section 1596.90), or Chapter 3.6 (commencing with Section 1597.30) and the prior license was revoked within the preceding two years, the department shall cease any further review of the application until two years shall have elapsed from the date of the revocation.

(2) If an application for a license or special permit indicates, or the department determines during the application review process, that the applicant previously was issued a certificate of approval by a foster family agency that was revoked by the department pursuant to subdivision (b) of Section 1534 within the preceding two years, the department shall cease any further review of the application until two years have elapsed from the date of the revocation.

(3) If an application for a license or special permit indicates, or the department determines during the application review process, that the applicant was excluded from a facility licensed by the department pursuant to Section 1558, 1568.092, 1569.58, or 1596.8897, the department shall cease any further review of the application unless the excluded individual has been reinstated pursuant to Section 11522 of the Government Code by the department.

(4) If an application for a license indicates, or the department determines during the application review process, that the applicant had previously applied for a license under any of the chapters listed in paragraph (1) and the application was denied within the last year, the department shall cease further review of the application as follows:

(A) In cases where the applicant petitioned for a hearing, the department shall cease further review of the application until one year has elapsed from the effective date of the decision and order of the department upholding a denial.

(B) In cases where the department informed the applicant of his or her right to petition for a hearing and the applicant did not petition for a hearing, the department shall cease further review of the application until one year has elapsed from the date of the notification of the denial and the right to petition for a hearing.

(C) The department may continue to review the application if it has determined that the reasons for the denial of the application were due to circumstances and conditions which either have been corrected or are no longer in existence.

(5) If an application for a license or special permit indicates, or the department determines during the application review process, that the applicant had previously applied for a certificate of approval with a foster family agency and the department ordered the foster family agency to deny the application pursuant to subdivision (b) of Section 1534, the department shall cease further review of the application as follows:

(A) In cases where the applicant petitioned for a hearing, the department shall cease further review of the application until one year has elapsed from the effective date of the decision and order of the department upholding a denial.

(B) In cases where the department informed the applicant of his or her right to petition for a hearing and the applicant did not petition for a hearing, the department shall cease further review of the application until one year has elapsed from the date of the notification of the denial and the right to petition for a hearing.

(C) The department may continue to review the application if it has determined that the reasons for the denial of the application were due to circumstances and conditions that either have been corrected or are no longer in existence.

(6) The cessation of review shall not constitute a denial of the application for purposes of Section 1568.062 or any other law.

(Amended by Stats. 1997, Ch. 617, Sec. 7. Effective January 1, 1998.)

1568.0651.

(a) The administrative law judge conducting a hearing under this article may permit the testimony of a child witness, or a similarly vulnerable witness, including a witness who is developmentally disabled, to be taken outside the presence of the respondent or respondents if all of the following conditions exist:

(1) The administrative law judge determines that taking the witness's testimony outside the presence of the respondent or respondents is necessary to ensure truthful testimony.

(2) The witness is likely to be intimidated by the presence of the respondent or respondents.

(3) The witness is afraid to testify in front of the respondent or respondents.

(b) If the testimony of the witness is taken outside of the presence of the respondent or respondents, the department shall provide for the use of one-way closed-circuit television so the respondent or respondents can observe the testimony of the witness. Nothing in this section shall limit a respondent's right of cross-examination.

(c) The administrative law judge conducting a hearing under this section may clear the hearing room of any persons who are not a party to the action in order to protect any witness from intimidation or other harm, taking into account the rights of all persons.

(Added by Stats. 1994, Ch. 1267, Sec. 4. Effective January 1, 1995.)

1568.0652.

(a) (1) An out-of-court statement made by a minor under 12 years of age who is the subject or victim of an allegation at issue is admissible evidence at an administrative hearing conducted pursuant to this article. The out-of-court statement may be used to support a finding of fact unless an objection is timely made and the objecting party establishes that the statement is unreliable because it was the product of fraud, deceit, or undue influence. However, the out-of-court statement may not be the sole basis for the finding of fact, unless the adjudicator finds that the time, content, and circumstances of the statement provide sufficient indicia of reliability.

(2) The proponent of the statement shall give reasonable notice to all parties of the intended introduction of the statement at the hearing.

(3) For purposes of this subdivision, an objection is timely if it identifies with reasonable specificity the disputed out-of-court statement and it gives the proponent of the evidence a reasonable period of time to prepare a response to the objection prior to the hearing.

(b) This section shall not be construed to limit the right of any party to the administrative hearing to subpoena a witness whose statement is admitted as evidence or to introduce admissible evidence relevant to the weight of the hearsay evidence or the credibility of the hearsay declarant.

(Added by Stats. 2002, Ch. 707, Sec. 2. Effective January 1, 2003.)

1568.067.

(a) No license issued pursuant to this chapter shall have any property value for sale or exchange purposes and no person, including any owner, agent, or broker, shall sell or exchange any license for any commercial purpose.

(b) (1) Each residential care facility licensed under this chapter shall reveal its license number in all advertisements, publications, or announcements made with the intent to attract clients or residents.

(2) Advertisements, publications, or announcements subject to the requirements of paragraph (1) shall include, but not be limited to, those contained in a newspaper or magazine, consumer report, announcement of intent to commence business, telephone directory yellow pages, professional or service directory, or radio or television commercial.

(Added by Stats. 1991, Ch. 832, Sec. 10.)

1568.068.

(a) Notwithstanding Section 1568.061, in the event of a sale of a licensed residential care for persons with chronic, life-threatening illness facility where the sale will result in a new license being issued, the sale and transfer of property and business shall be subject to both of the following:

(1) The licensee shall provide written notice to the department and to each resident or his or her legal representative of the licensee's intent to sell the facility at least 60 days prior to the transfer of property or business, or at the time that a bona fide offer is made, whichever period is longer.

(2) The licensee shall, prior to entering into an admission agreement, inform all residents, or their legal representatives, admitted to the facility after notification to the department, of the licensee's intent to sell the property or business.

(b) Except as provided in subdivision (e), the property and business shall not be transferred until the buyer qualifies for a license or provisional license pursuant to this chapter.

(1) The seller shall notify, in writing, a prospective buyer of the necessity to obtain a license, as required by this chapter, if the buyer's intent is to continue operating the facility as a residential care facility for the chronically ill. The seller shall send a copy of this written notice to the licensing agency.

(2) The prospective buyer shall submit an application for a license, as specified in Section 1568.04, within five days of the acceptance of the offer by the seller.

(c) No transfer of the property or business shall be permitted until 60 days have elapsed from the date when notice has been provided to the department pursuant to paragraph (1) of subdivision (a).

(d) The department shall give priority to applications for licensure that are submitted pursuant to this section in order to ensure timely transfer of the property and business. The department shall make a decision within 60 days after a complete application is submitted on whether to issue a license pursuant to Section 1568.04.

(e) If the parties involved in the transfer of the property and business fully comply with this section, then the transfer may be completed and the buyer shall not be considered to be operating an unlicensed facility while the department makes a final determination on the application for licensure.

(Added by Stats. 1992, Ch. 873, Sec. 2. Effective January 1, 1993.)

1568.07.

(a) (1) Within 90 days after a facility accepts its first resident for placement following its initial licensure, the department shall conduct an unannounced inspection of the facility to evaluate compliance with rules and regulations and to assess the facility's continuing ability to meet regulatory requirements. The licensee shall notify the department, within five business days after accepting its first resident for placement, that the facility has commenced operating.

(2) The department may take appropriate remedial action as provided for in this chapter.

(b) (1) Every licensed residential care facility shall be periodically inspected and evaluated for quality of care by a representative or representatives designated by the director. Unannounced inspections shall be conducted at least annually and as often as necessary to ensure the quality of care being provided.

(2) During each licensing inspection the department shall determine if the facility meets regulatory standards, including, but not limited to, providing residents with the appropriate level of care based on the facility's license, providing adequate staffing and services, updated resident records and assessments, and compliance with basic health and safety standards.

(3) If the department determines that a resident requires a higher level of care than the facility is authorized to provide, the department may initiate a professional level of care assessment by an assessor approved by the department. An assessment shall be conducted in consultation with the resident, the resident's physician and surgeon, and the resident's case manager, and shall reflect the desires of the resident, the resident's physician and surgeon, and the resident's case manager. The assessment also shall recognize that certain illnesses are episodic in nature and that the resident's need for a higher level of care may be temporary.

(4) The department shall notify the residential care facility in writing of all deficiencies in its compliance with this chapter and the rules and regulations adopted pursuant to this chapter, and shall set a reasonable length of time for compliance by the facility.

(5) Reports on the results of each inspection or consultation shall be kept on file in the department, and all inspection reports, consultation reports, lists of deficiencies, and plans of correction shall be open to public inspection.

(c) Any duly authorized officer, employee, or agent of the department may, upon presentation of proper identification, enter and inspect any place providing personal care, supervision, and services, at any time, with or without advance notice, to secure compliance with, or to prevent a violation of, this chapter.

(d) A licensee, or officer or employee of the licensee, shall not discriminate or retaliate in any manner, including, but not limited to, eviction or threat of eviction, against any person receiving the services of the licensee's facility, or against any employee of the licensee's facility, on the basis, or for the reason, that the person or employee or any other person initiated or participated in the filing of a complaint, grievance, or a request for inspection with the department pursuant to this chapter or initiated or participated in the filing of a complaint, grievance, or request for investigation with the appropriate local or state ombudsman.

(e) A person who, without lawful authorization from a duly authorized officer, employee, or agent of the department, informs an owner, operator, employee, agent, or resident of a residential care facility, of an impending or proposed inspection of that facility by personnel of the department, is guilty of a misdemeanor and upon conviction thereof shall be punished by a fine not to exceed one thousand dollars ($1,000), by imprisonment in the county jail for a period not to exceed 180 days, or by both a fine and imprisonment.

(Amended by Stats. 2015, Ch. 303, Sec. 278. (AB 731) Effective January 1, 2016.)

1568.071.

(a) Any person may request an inspection of any residential care facility in accordance with this chapter by transmitting to the department notice of an alleged violation of applicable requirements prescribed by statutes or regulations of this state.

(b) The substance of the complaint shall be provided to the licensee no earlier than at the time of the inspection. Unless the complainant specifically requests otherwise, neither the substance of the complaint provided the licensee nor any copy of the complaint or any record published, released, or otherwise made available to the licensee shall disclose the name of any person mentioned in the complaint except the name of any duly authorized officer, employee, or agent of the department conducting the investigation or inspection pursuant to this chapter.

(c) Upon receipt of a complaint, other than a complaint alleging denial of a statutory right of access to a residential care facility, the department shall make a preliminary review and, unless the department determines that the complaint is willfully intended to harass a licensee or is without any reasonable basis, it shall make an onsite inspection within 10 days after receiving the complaint except where the visit would adversely affect the licensing investigation or the investigation of other agencies, including, but not limited to, law enforcement agencies. In either event, the complainant shall be promptly informed of the department's proposed course of action.

(d) Upon receipt of a complaint alleging denial of a statutory right of access to a residential facility, the department shall review the complaint. The complainant shall be notified promptly of the department's proposed course of action.
(Added by Stats. 1990, Ch. 1333, Sec. 1.5.)
1568.0715.

(a) The department shall ensure that the licensee's plan of correction is verifiable and measurable. The plan of correction shall specify what evidence is acceptable to establish that a deficiency has been corrected. This evidence shall be included in the department's facility file.

(b) The department shall specify in its licensing report all violations that, if not corrected, will have a direct and immediate risk to the health, safety, or personal rights of residents in care.

(c) The department shall complete all complaint investigations and place a note of final conclusion in the department's facility file, regardless of whether the licensee voluntarily surrendered the license.
(Added by Stats. 2008, Ch. 291, Sec. 10. Effective September 25, 2008.)
1568.072.

(a) The department shall adopt, amend, and repeal, in accordance with Chapter 3.5 (commencing with Section 11340) of Part 1 of Division 3 of Title 2 of the Government Code, any reasonable rules, regulations, and standards as may be necessary or proper to carry out the purposes and intent of this chapter and to enable the department to exercise the powers and perform the duties conferred upon it by this chapter, not inconsistent with state law.

(b) Regulations for a license shall prescribe standards of safety and sanitation, for the physical plant, as well as for the basic care and supervision, personal care, and services to be provided by a facility.

(c) Regulations shall specify the application and licensing process, the range of services, alternative methods for providing those services, the appraisal and assessment process, and facility staffing and training requirements.

(d) Regulations shall allow for the development of new and innovative community programs.
(Amended by Stats. 1991, Ch. 832, Sec. 12.)
1568.073.

(a) (1) The department may order the licensee to remove a resident who has a health condition which cannot be cared for within the limits of the license or requires inpatient care in a health facility as determined by the department pursuant to Section 1568.07.
(2) When the department determines that the resident's mental or physical condition requires immediate transfer from the facility in order to protect the health and safety of the resident, the department may order the licensee to remove the resident after the department consults with a physician or other medical professional about the transfer and ways in which transfer trauma can be minimized.

(b) (1) When the department determines that a resident has a health condition which cannot be cared for within the limits of the license or requires inpatient care in a health facility, the department shall give notice to the resident, his or her legal representative when appropriate, his or her physician when applicable, his or her case manager when applicable, and the licensee. The notice shall specify a deadline for submitting a written plan for relocation and inform the resident of his or her right for a review and determination. The resident, or his or her legal representative, shall have three working days to inform the licensee of the request for review. The licensee shall forward the request to the department within two working days of receipt. Failure or refusal by the licensee to submit the request to the department may subject the licensee to the civil penalties as specified in Section 1568.0822. The department shall not refuse to consider the request if the licensee fails or refuses to submit the request to the department.
(2) The review and determination shall be completed within 30 days from the date that the resident was initially informed of the need to relocate. If the determination is made that the resident must relocate, the notice shall include a plan for transfer including ways to minimize transfer trauma for the resident.
(3) The department may require the licensee to prepare and submit to the department a written plan for relocation, to comply with the terms and conditions of the approved plan, and to provide other information as necessary for the enforcement of this section.

(c) The provisions allowing for a resident's right to a review prior to transfer as provided in subdivision (b) neither negates the department's authority and responsibility to require

an immediate transfer according to paragraph (2) of subdivision (a) when the department finds and provides evidence that the resident must be relocated in order to protect the health and safety of the resident, nor implies any right to a fair hearing pursuant to Chapter 7 (commencing with Section 10950) of Part 2 of Division 9 of the Welfare and Institutions Code.

(d) The department shall specify by regulation the process for making relocation decisions and for appealing and reviewing those decisions pursuant to this section.
(Added by Stats. 1990, Ch. 1333, Sec. 1.5.)
1568.075.
On and after January 1, 1999, no security window bars may be installed or maintained on any residential care facility unless the security window bars meet current state and local requirements, as applicable, for security window bars and safety release devices.
(Added by Stats. 1998, Ch. 343, Sec. 2. Effective January 1, 1999.)
1568.08.
Each facility required to be licensed under this chapter shall keep a current record of all of the following:

(a) Residents in the facility, including each resident's name and ambulatory status.

(b) The name and telephone number of each resident's physician and surgeon.

(c) The name, address, and telephone number of any person or agency responsible for the care of a resident.

(d) Updated resident file records, including, but not limited to, the current physician and surgeon report, residential appraisal, level of services required and documentation of any health related services provided to residents.
The facility shall respect the privacy and confidentiality of this information.
(Added by Stats. 1990, Ch. 1333, Sec. 1.5.)
1568.081.

(a) A placement agency shall place individuals only in licensed residential care facilities or facilities which are exempt from licensure under subdivision (c) of Section 1568.03.

(b) No employee of a placement agency shall place, refer, or recommend placement of a person in a facility operating without a license, unless the facility is exempt from licensure under subdivision (c) of Section 1568.03. Violation of this subdivision is a misdemeanor.

(c) Any employee of a placement agency who knows, or reasonably suspects that a facility, which is not exempt from licensure under this chapter, is operating without a license shall report the name and address of the facility to the department. Failure to report as required by this subdivision is a misdemeanor.

(d) The department shall investigate any report filed under subdivision (c). If the department has probable cause to believe that the facility which is the subject of the report is operating without a license, the department shall investigate the facility within 10 days after receipt of the report.

(e) A placement agency shall notify the department of any known or suspected incidents which would jeopardize the health or safety of residents in a residential care facility. Reportable incidents include, but are not limited to, all of the following:
(1) Incidents of physical abuse.
(2) Any violation of personal rights.
(3) Any situation in which a facility is unclean, unsafe, unsanitary, or in poor condition.
(4) Any situation in which a facility has insufficient personnel or incompetent personnel on duty.
(5) Any situation in which residents experience mental or verbal abuse.
(6) Any situation in which a facility is suspected of accepting or retaining residents who require a higher level of care than the facility is authorized to provide.
(Added by Stats. 1990, Ch. 1333, Sec. 1.5.)
1568.082.

(a) The department may suspend or revoke any license issued under this chapter upon any of the following grounds and in the manner provided in this chapter:
(1) Violation by the licensee of this chapter or of the rules and regulations adopted pursuant to this chapter.
(2) Aiding, abetting, or permitting the violation of this chapter or of the rules and regulations adopted pursuant to this chapter.
(3) Conduct which is inimical to the health, welfare, or safety of either an individual in or receiving services from the facility or the people of the State of California.
(4) The provision of services beyond the level the facility is authorized to provide, or accepting or retaining residents who require services of a higher level than the facility is authorized to provide.
(5) Engaging in acts of financial malfeasance concerning the operation of a facility, including, but not limited to, improper use or embezzlement of client moneys and property or fraudulent appropriation for personal gain of facility moneys and property, or willful or negligent failure to provide services.

(b) The director may temporarily suspend any license, prior to any hearing when, in the opinion of the director, the action is necessary to protect residents of the facility from physical or mental abuse, abandonment, or any other substantial threat to health or safety. The director shall notify the licensee of the temporary suspension and the effective date of the temporary suspension, and at the same time shall serve the provider with an accusation. Upon receipt of a notice of defense to the accusation by the licensee, the director shall, within 15 days, set the matter for hearing, and the hearing shall be held as soon as possible, but not later than 30 days after receipt of the notice. The temporary suspension shall remain in effect until the time the hearing is completed and the director has made a final determination on the merits. However, the temporary suspension shall be deemed vacated if the director fails to make a final determination on the merits within 30 days after the original hearing has been completed.

(c) In any case where the department orders the licensee to remove a resident who has a health condition or health conditions which cannot be cared for within the limits of the license or special permit or requires inpatient care in a health facility licensed pursuant to Chapter 2 (commencing with Section 1250), the licensee shall do all of the following:
(1) Prepare and submit to the department a written plan for relocation of the client or resident, in a form acceptable to the department.
(2) Comply with all terms and conditions of the approved relocation plan.
(3) Provide any other information as may be required by the department for the proper administration and enforcement of this section.
(Amended by Stats. 1998, Ch. 311, Sec. 32. Effective August 19, 1998.)
1568.0821.
(a) Notwithstanding any other provision of this chapter, any person who violates Section 1568.03 shall be assessed by the department an immediate civil penalty in the amount of one hundred dollars ($100) per resident for each day of the violation.
(b) The civil penalty authorized in subdivision (a) shall be two hundred dollars ($200) per resident for each day of the violation if an unlicensed facility is operated and the operator refuses to seek licensure or the operator seeks licensure and the license application is denied and the operator continues to operate the unlicensed facility.
(c) An operator may appeal the assessment to the director. The department shall adopt regulations setting forth the appeal procedure.
(Amended by Stats. 2000, Ch. 819, Sec. 4. Effective January 1, 2001.)
1568.0822.
(a) In addition to the suspension, temporary suspension, or revocation of a license issued under this chapter, the department shall levy civil penalties as follows:
(b) (1) The amount of the civil penalty shall be one hundred dollars ($100) per day for each violation of this chapter if a facility fails to correct a deficiency after being provided a specified length of time to correct that deficiency.
(A) If a licensee or a licensee's representative submits evidence to the department that the licensee has corrected a deficiency, and the department, after reviewing that evidence, has determined that the deficiency has been corrected, the civil penalty shall cease as of the day the department received that evidence.
(B) If the department deems it necessary, the department shall inspect the facility within five working days after the department receives evidence pursuant to subparagraph (A) to confirm that the deficiency has been corrected.
(C) If the department determines that the deficiency has not been corrected, the civil penalty shall continue to accrue from the date of the original citation.
(D) If the department is able to verify that the deficiency was corrected prior to the date on which the department received the evidence pursuant to subparagraph (A), the civil penalty shall cease as of that earlier date.
(2) (A) If the department issues a notification of deficiency to a facility for a repeat violation of a violation specified in paragraph (1), the department shall assess an immediate civil penalty of two hundred fifty dollars ($250) per repeat violation and one hundred dollars ($100) for each day the repeat violation continues after citation. The notification of deficiency shall state the manner in which the deficiency constitutes a repeat violation and shall be submitted to a supervisor for review and approval.
(B) For purposes of this section, "repeat violation" means a violation within 12 months of a prior violation of a statutory or regulatory provision designated by the same combination of letters or numerals, or both letters and numerals.
(C) Notwithstanding subparagraphs (A) and (B), the department, in its sole discretion, may reduce the civil penalty for the cited repeat violation to the level of the underlying violation, as applicable, if it determines that the cited repeat violation is not substantially similar to the original violation.
(3) If the nature or seriousness of the violation or the frequency of the violation warrants a higher penalty or an immediate civil penalty assessment, or both, as provided in this chapter, a correction of the deficiency shall not impact the imposition of a civil penalty.
(c) The department shall assess an immediate civil penalty of five hundred dollars ($500) per violation and one hundred dollars ($100) for each day the violation continues after citation for any of the following serious violations:
(1) Any violation that the department determines resulted in the injury or illness of a resident.
(2) (A) Fire clearance violations, including, but not limited to, overcapacity, ambulatory status, inoperable smoke alarms, and inoperable fire alarm systems. The civil penalty shall not be assessed if the licensee has done either of the following:
(i) Requested the appropriate fire clearance based on ambulatory, nonambulatory, or bedridden status, and the decision is pending.
(ii) Initiated eviction proceedings.
(B) A licensee denied a clearance for bedridden residents may appeal to the fire authority, and, if that appeal is denied, may subsequently appeal to the Office of the State Fire Marshal, and shall not be assessed an immediate civil penalty until the final appeal is decided, or after 60 days has passed from the date of the citation, whichever is earlier.
(3) Absence of supervision, as required by statute and regulation.
(4) Accessible bodies of water, when prohibited in this chapter or regulations adopted pursuant to this chapter.
(5) Accessible firearms, ammunition, or both.
(6) Refused entry to a facility or any part of a facility in violation of Section 1568.07 or 1568.071.
(7) The presence of a person subject to a department Order of Exclusion on the premises.
(d) If the department issues a notification of deficiency to a facility for a repeat violation of a violation specified in subdivision (c), the department shall assess an immediate civil penalty of one thousand dollars ($1,000) per repeat violation and one hundred dollars ($100) for each day the repeat violation continues after citation. The notification of deficiency shall state the manner in which the deficiency constitutes a repeat violation and shall be submitted to a supervisor for review and approval.
(e) For a violation that the department determines resulted in the death of a resident, the civil penalty shall be fifteen thousand dollars ($15,000).
(f) For a violation that the department determines constitutes physical abuse, as defined in Section 15610.63 of the Welfare and Institutions Code, or resulted in serious bodily injury, as defined in Section 243 of the Penal Code, to a resident, the civil penalty shall be ten thousand dollars ($10,000).
(g) (1) Before the assessment of a civil penalty pursuant to subdivision (e) or (f), the decision shall be approved by the program administrator of the Community Care Licensing Division.
(2) (A) The department shall reduce the amount of a civil penalty due pursuant to subdivision (e) or (f) by the amount of the civil penalty already assessed for the underlying violation.
(B) If the amount of the civil penalty that the department has already assessed for the underlying violation exceeds the amount of the penalty pursuant to subdivision (e) or (f), the larger amount shall prevail and be due and payable as already assessed by the department.
(h) (1) A notification of a deficiency written by a representative of the department shall include a factual description of the nature of the deficiency fully stating the manner in which the licensee failed to comply with the specified statute or regulation, and, if applicable, the particular place or area in which the deficiency occurred. The department shall make a good faith effort to work with the licensee to determine the cause of the deficiency and ways to prevent any repeat violations.
(2) The department shall adopt regulations setting forth appeal procedures for deficiencies.
(i) (1) A licensee shall have the right to submit to the department a written request for a formal review of a civil penalty assessed pursuant to subdivision (e) or (f) within 15 business days of receipt of the notice of a civil penalty assessment and shall provide all available supporting documentation at that time. The review shall be conducted by the deputy director of the Community Care Licensing Division. The licensee may submit additional supporting documentation that was unavailable at the time of submitting the request for review within the first 30 business days after submitting the request for review. If the department requires additional information from the licensee, that information shall be requested within the first 30 business days after receiving the request for review. The licensee shall provide this additional information within 30 business days of receiving the request from the department. If the deputy director determines that the civil penalty was not assessed, or the finding of deficiency that resulted in the assessment of the civil penalty was not made, in accordance with applicable statutes or regulations of the department, he or she may amend or dismiss the civil penalty or finding of deficiency. The licensee shall be notified in writing of the deputy director's decision within 60 business days of the date when all necessary information has been provided to the department by the licensee.
(2) Upon exhausting the review described in paragraph (1), a licensee may further appeal that decision to an administrative law judge. Proceedings shall be conducted in accordance with Chapter 5 (commencing with Section 11500) of Part 1 of Division 3 of Title 2 of the Government Code, and the department shall have all the powers granted by those provisions. In all proceedings conducted in accordance with this section, the standard of proof shall be by a preponderance of the evidence.
(3) If, in addition to an assessment of civil penalties, the department elects to file an administrative action to suspend or revoke the facility license that includes violations relating to the assessment of the civil penalties, the department review of the pending appeal shall cease and the assessment of the civil penalties shall be heard as part of the administrative action process.
(4) Civil penalties shall be due and payable when administrative appeals have been exhausted. Unless payment arrangements have been made that are acceptable to the department, a civil penalty not paid within 30 days shall be subject to late fees, as specified by the department in regulation.
(j) (1) A licensee shall have the right to submit to the department a written request for a formal review of any other civil penalty or deficiency not described in subdivision (i) within 15 business days of receipt of the notice of a civil penalty assessment or a finding of a deficiency, and shall provide all available supporting documentation at that time. The review shall be conducted by a regional manager of the Community Care Licensing Division. The licensee may submit additional supporting documentation that was unavailable at the time of submitting the request for review within the first 30 business days after submitting the request for review. If the department requires additional information from the licensee, that information shall be requested within the first 30 business days after receiving the request for review. The licensee shall provide this additional information within 30 business days of receiving the request from the department. If the regional manager determines that the civil penalty was not assessed, or the finding of the deficiency was not made, in accordance with applicable statutes or regulations of the department, he or she may amend or dismiss the civil penalty or finding of deficiency. The licensee shall be notified in writing of the regional manager's decision within 60 business days of the date when all necessary information has been provided to the department by the licensee.
(2) Upon exhausting the review described in paragraph (1), the licensee may further appeal that decision to the program administrator of the Community Care Licensing Division within 15 business days of receipt of notice of the regional manager's decision.

The licensee may submit additional supporting documentation that was unavailable at the time of appeal to the program administrator within the first 30 business days after requesting that appeal. If the department requires additional information from the licensee, that information shall be requested within the first 30 business days after receiving the request for the appeal. The licensee shall provide this additional information within 30 business days of receiving the request from the department. If the program administrator determines that the civil penalty was not assessed, or the finding of the deficiency was not made, in accordance with applicable statutes or regulations of the department, he or she may amend or dismiss the civil penalty or finding of deficiency. The licensee shall be notified in writing of the program administrator's decision within 60 business days of the date when all necessary information has been provided to the department by the licensee. The program administrator's decision is considered final and concludes the licensee's administrative appeal rights regarding the appeal conducted pursuant to this paragraph.

(3) Civil penalties shall be due and payable when administrative appeals have been exhausted. Unless payment arrangements have been made that are acceptable to the department, a civil penalty not paid within 30 days shall be subject to late fees, as specified by the department in regulation.

(k) The department shall adopt regulations implementing this section.

(l) The department shall, by January 1, 2016, amend its regulations to reflect the changes to this section made by Section 4 of Chapter 813 of the Statutes of 2014.

(m) Notwithstanding the Administrative Procedure Act (Chapter 3.5 (commencing with Section 11340) of Part 1 of Division 3 of Title 2 of the Government Code), the department may implement and administer the changes made by the act that added this subdivision through all-county letters or similar written instructions until regulations are adopted pursuant to the Administrative Procedure Act.

(n) This section shall become operative on July 1, 2017.

(Repealed (in Sec. 4) and added by Stats. 2016, Ch. 823, Sec. 5. (AB 2231) Effective January 1, 2017. Section operative July 1, 2017, by its own provisions.)
1568.0823.

(a) Any person who violates this chapter, or who willfully or repeatedly violates any rule or regulation adopted under this chapter, is guilty of a misdemeanor and upon conviction thereof shall be punished by a fine not to exceed one thousand dollars ($1,000), or by imprisonment in the county jail for a period not to exceed 180 days, or by both fine and imprisonment.

(b) Operation of a residential care facility without a license shall be subject to a summons to appear in court.

(c) Notwithstanding any other provision of this chapter, the district attorney of every county, and the city attorneys in those cities which have city attorneys who have jurisdiction to prosecute misdemeanors pursuant to Section 72193 of the Government Code, shall, upon their own initiative or upon application by the department or its authorized representative, institute and conduct the prosecution of any action for violation within his or her county of this chapter.

(Amended (as added by Stats. 1991, Ch. 832) by Stats. 2002, Ch. 784, Sec. 514. Effective January 1, 2003.)
1568.0824.

A person who, without lawful authorization from a duly authorized officer, employee, or agent of the department, informs an owner, operator, employee, agent, or resident of a residential care facility for persons with a chronic, life-threatening illness of an impending and unannounced site visit to that facility by personnel of the department, is guilty of a misdemeanor and upon conviction thereof shall be punished by a fine not to exceed one thousand dollars ($1,000), by imprisonment in the county jail for a period not to exceed 180 days, or by both a fine and imprisonment.

(Added by renumbering Section 1568.0823 (as added by Stats. 1991, Ch. 888, Sec. 3) by Stats. 2015, Ch. 303, Sec. 279. (AB 731) Effective January 1, 2016.)
1568.0825.

(a) The department shall conduct an unannounced visit to a facility within 30 days after the effective date of a temporary suspension of a license in order to ensure that the facility is nonoperational, unless the department previously has verified that the facility is nonoperational.

(b) The department shall conduct an unannounced visit to a facility within 30 days after the effective date of a revocation of a license in order to ensure that the facility is nonoperational, unless the department previously has verified that the facility is nonoperational.

(Added by Stats. 2008, Ch. 291, Sec. 12. Effective September 25, 2008.)
1568.083.

(a) The department, State Fire Marshal, or local fire officials shall not make a de facto determination of a resident's ambulatory or nonambulatory status based on a resident's placement in the facility. Interpretation of regulations related to fire safety in residential care facilities shall be made to provide flexibility to allow residents to remain in the least restrictive environment.

(b) This chapter shall not preempt the application of any local zoning requirements to residential care facility, except as provided for in Section 1568.0831.

(Added by Stats. 1990, Ch. 1333, Sec. 1.5.)
1568.0831.

(a) (1) Whether or not unrelated persons are living together, a residential care facility that serves six or fewer persons shall be considered a residential use of property for the purposes of this chapter. In addition, the residents and operators of the facility shall be considered a family for the purposes of any law or zoning ordinance that relates to the residential use of property pursuant to this chapter.

(2) For the purpose of all local ordinances, a residential care facility that serves six or fewer persons shall not be included within the definition of a boarding house, rooming house, institution, guest home, rest home, community residence, or other similar term that implies that the residential care facility is a business run for profit or differs in any other way from a family dwelling.

(3) This section shall not be construed to prohibit a city, county, or other local public entity from placing restrictions on building heights, setback, lot dimensions, or placement of signs of a residential care facility that serves six or fewer persons as long as the restrictions are identical to those applied to other family dwellings of the same type in the same zone.

(4) This section shall not be construed to prohibit the application to a residential care facility of any local ordinance that deals with health and safety, building standards, environmental impact standards, or any other matter within the jurisdiction of a local public entity if the ordinance does not distinguish residential care facilities that serve six or fewer persons from other family dwellings of the same type in the same zone and if the ordinance does not distinguish residents of residential care facilities from persons who reside in other family dwellings of the same type in the same zone.

(5) No conditional use permit, zoning variance, or other zoning clearance shall be required of a residential care facility that serves six or fewer persons that is not required of a family dwelling of the same type in the same zone.

(6) Use of a family dwelling for purposes of a residential care facility serving six or fewer persons shall not constitute a change of occupancy for purposes of Part 1.5 (commencing with Section 17910) of Division 13 or local building codes. However, nothing in this section is intended to supersede Section 13143 or 13143.6, to the extent these sections are applicable to residential care facilities serving six or fewer persons.

(b) No fire inspection clearance or other permit, license, clearance, or similar authorization shall be denied to a residential care facility because of a failure to comply with local ordinances from which the facilities are exempt under subdivision (a), provided that the applicant otherwise qualifies for the fire clearance, license, permit, or similar authorization.

(c) For the purposes of any contract, deed, or covenant for the transfer of real property executed on or after January 1, 1979, a residential care facility that serves six or fewer persons shall be considered a residential use of property and a use of property by a single family, notwithstanding any disclaimers to the contrary.

(d) Nothing in this chapter shall authorize the imposition of rent regulations or controls for licensed residential care facilities.

(e) Licensed residential care facilities shall not be subject to controls on rent imposed by any state or local agency or other local government or entity.

(Amended by Stats. 2014, Ch. 144, Sec. 33. (AB 1847) Effective January 1, 2015.)
1568.0832.

(a) (1) For purposes of this section, "bedridden" means requiring assistance in turning and repositioning in bed or being unable to independently transfer to and from bed, except in a facility with appropriate and sufficient care staff, mechanical devices, if necessary, and safety precautions, as determined by the director in regulations.

(2) For purposes of this section, the status of being bedridden shall not include a temporary illness or recovery from surgery that persists for 14 days or less.

(3) The determination of the bedridden status of persons with developmental disabilities shall be made by the Director of Social Services or his or her designated representative, in consultation with the Director of Developmental Services or his or her designated representative, after consulting the resident's individual safety plan. The determination of the bedridden status of all other persons with disabilities who are not developmentally disabled shall be made by the Director of Social Services, or his or her designated representative.

(b) A bedridden person may be admitted to, and remain in, a residential facility that secures and maintains an appropriate fire clearance. A fire clearance shall be issued to a facility in which one or more bedridden persons reside if either of the following conditions are met:

(1) The fire safety requirements are met. Residents who are unable to independently transfer to and from bed, but who do not need assistance to turn or reposition in bed, shall be considered nonambulatory for purposes of this paragraph.

(2) Alternative methods of protection are approved.

(c) Notwithstanding paragraph (2) of subdivision (a), a bedridden resident may be retained in a residential care facility in excess of 14 days if all of the following conditions are met:

(1) The facility notifies the department in writing that the person is recovering from a temporary illness or surgery.

(2) The facility submits to the department, with the notification required in paragraph (1), a physician and surgeon's written statement to the effect that the resident's illness or recovery is of a temporary nature. The statement shall contain an estimated date upon which the illness or recovery is expected to end or upon which the resident is expected to no longer be confined to bed.

(3) The department determines that the resident's health and safety is adequately protected in the facility and that transfer to a higher level of care is not necessary.

(4) This subdivision does not expand the scope of care and supervision of a residential care facility.

(d) Notwithstanding the length of stay of a bedridden resident, every residential facility admitting or retaining a bedridden resident shall, within 48 hours of the resident's admission or retention in the facility, notify the fire authority having jurisdiction over the bedridden resident's location of the estimated length of time the resident will retain his or her bedridden status in the facility.

(e) (1) The department and the Office of the State Fire Marshal, in consultation with the State Department of Developmental Services, shall each promulgate regulations that meet all of the following conditions:

(A) Are consistent with this section.

(B) Are applicable to facilities regulated under this chapter, consistent with the regulatory requirements of the California Building Standards Code for fire and life safety for the respective occupancy classifications into which the State Department of Social Services' community care licensing classifications fall.

(C) Permit residents to remain in homelike settings.

(2) At a minimum, these regulations shall do both of the following with regard to a residential care facility that provides care for six or fewer residents, at least one of whom is bedridden:

(A) Clarify the fire and life safety requirements for a fire clearance for the facility.

(B) Identify procedures for requesting the approval of alternative means of providing equivalent levels of fire and life safety protection. Either the facility, the resident or resident's representative, or local fire official may request from the Office of the State Fire Marshal a written opinion concerning the interpretation of the regulations promulgated by the State Fire Marshal pursuant to this section for a particular factual dispute. The State Fire Marshal shall issue the written opinion within 45 days following the request.

(f) For facilities that care for six or fewer residents, a local fire official shall not impose fire safety requirements stricter than the fire safety regulations promulgated for the particular type of facility by the Office of the State Fire Marshal or the local fire safety requirements imposed on any other single family dwelling, whichever is more strict.

(g) This section and any regulations promulgated thereunder shall be interpreted in a manner that provides flexibility to allow bedridden persons to avoid institutionalization and be admitted to, and safely remain in, community-based residential care facilities. (Amended by Stats. 2010, Ch. 211, Sec. 3. (AB 2629) Effective January 1, 2011.)

1568.09.

It is the intent of the Legislature in enacting this section to require the electronic fingerprint images of those individuals whose contact with residents of residential care facilities for persons with a chronic, life-threatening illness may pose a risk to the residents' health and safety.

It is the intent of the Legislature, in enacting this section, to require the electronic fingerprint images of those individuals whose contact with community care clients may pose a risk to the clients' health and safety. An individual shall be required to obtain either a criminal record clearance or a criminal record exemption from the State Department of Social Services before his or her initial presence in a residential care facility for persons with a chronic, life-threatening illness.

(a) (1) Before and, as applicable, subsequent to issuing a license to a person or persons to operate or manage a residential care facility, the department shall secure from an appropriate law enforcement agency a criminal record to determine whether the applicant or any other person specified in subdivision (b) has ever been convicted of a crime other than a minor traffic violation or arrested for any crime specified in subdivision (c) of Section 290 of the Penal Code, or for violating Section 245, 273ab, or 273.5, subdivision (b) of Section 273a, or, prior to January 1, 1994, paragraph (2) of Section 273a, of the Penal Code, or for any crime for which the department is prohibited from granting a criminal record exemption pursuant to subdivision (f).

(2) The criminal history information shall include the full criminal record, if any, of those persons, and subsequent arrest information pursuant to Section 11105.2 of the Penal Code.

(3) The following shall apply to the criminal record information:

(A) If the State Department of Social Services finds that the applicant or another person specified in subdivision (b), has been convicted of a crime, other than a minor traffic violation, the application shall be denied, unless the director grants an exemption pursuant to subdivision (f).

(B) If the State Department of Social Services finds that the applicant, or another person specified in subdivision (b), is awaiting trial for a crime other than a minor traffic violation, the State Department of Social Services may cease processing the criminal record information until the conclusion of the trial.

(C) If no criminal record information has been recorded, the Department of Justice shall provide the applicant and the State Department of Social Services with a statement of that fact.

(D) If the State Department of Social Services finds after licensure that the licensee, or any other person specified in paragraph (2) of subdivision (b), has been convicted of a crime other than a minor traffic violation, the license may be revoked, unless the director grants an exemption pursuant to subdivision (f).

(E) An applicant and any other person specified in subdivision (b) shall submit fingerprint images and related information to the Department of Justice and the Federal Bureau of Investigation, through the Department of Justice, for a state and federal level criminal offender record information search, in addition to the search required by this subdivision. If an applicant meets all other conditions for licensure, except receipt of the Federal Bureau of Investigation's criminal history information for the applicant and persons listed in subdivision (b), the department may issue a license if the applicant and each person described by subdivision (b) has signed and submitted a statement that he or she has never been convicted of a crime in the United States, other than a traffic infraction as defined in paragraph (1) of subdivision (a) of Section 42001 of the Vehicle Code. If, after licensure, the department determines that the licensee or person specified in subdivision (b) has a criminal record, the license may be revoked pursuant to subdivision (a) of Section 1568.082. The department may also suspend the license pending an administrative hearing pursuant to subdivision (b) of Section 1568.082.

(b) In addition to the applicant, this section shall be applicable to criminal record clearances and exemptions for the following persons:

(1) Adults responsible for administration or direct supervision of staff of the facility.

(2) A person, other than a resident, residing in the facility.

(3) A person who provides resident assistance in dressing, grooming, bathing, or personal hygiene. A nurse assistant or home health aide meeting the requirements of Section 1338.5 or 1736.6, respectively, who is not employed, retained, or contracted by the licensee, and who has been certified or recertified on or after July 1, 1998, shall be deemed to meet the criminal record clearance requirements of this section. A certified nurse assistant and certified home health aide who will be providing client assistance and who falls under this exemption shall provide one copy of his or her current certification, prior to providing care, to the residential care facility for persons with a chronic, life-threatening illness. The facility shall maintain the copy of the certification on file as long as care is being provided by the certified nurse assistant or certified home health aide at the facility. This paragraph does not restrict the right of the department to exclude a certified nurse assistant or certified home health aide from a licensed residential care facility for persons with a chronic, life-threatening illness pursuant to Section 1568.092.

(4) (A) A staff person, volunteer, or employee who has contact with the residents.

(B) A volunteer shall be exempt from the requirements of this subdivision if he or she is a relative, significant other, or close friend of a client receiving care in the facility and the volunteer does not provide direct care and supervision of residents. A volunteer who provides direct care and supervision shall be exempt if the volunteer is a resident's spouse, significant other, close friend, or family member and provides direct care and supervision to that resident only at the request of the resident. The department may define in regulations persons similar to those described in this subparagraph who may be exempt from the requirements of this subdivision.

(5) If the applicant is a firm, partnership, association, or corporation, the chief executive officer or other person serving in that capacity.

(6) Additional officers of the governing body of the applicant, or other persons with a financial interest in the applicant, as determined necessary by the department by regulation. The criteria used in the development of these regulations shall be based on the person's capability to exercise substantial influence over the operation of the facility.

(c) (1) (A) Subsequent to initial licensure, a person specified in subdivision (b) and not exempted from fingerprinting shall obtain either a criminal record clearance or an exemption from disqualification, pursuant to subdivision (f), from the State Department of Social Services prior to employment, residence, or initial presence in the facility. A person specified in subdivision (b) who is not exempt from fingerprinting shall be fingerprinted and shall sign a declaration under penalty of perjury regarding any prior criminal convictions. The licensee shall submit fingerprint images and related information to the Department of Justice and the Federal Bureau of Investigation, through the Department of Justice, for a state and federal level criminal offender record information search, or to comply with paragraph (1) of subdivision (g), prior to the person's employment, residence, or initial presence in the residential care facility.

(B) These fingerprint images and related information shall be electronically submitted to the Department of Justice in a manner approved by the State Department of Social Services and the Department of Justice, for the purpose of obtaining a permanent set of fingerprints. A licensee's failure to submit fingerprint images and related information to the Department of Justice, or to comply with paragraph (1) of subdivision (g), as required in this section, shall result in the citation of a deficiency and an immediate assessment of civil penalties in the amount of one hundred dollars ($100) per violation per day for a maximum of five days, unless the violation is a second or subsequent violation within a 12-month period in which case the civil penalties shall be in the amount of one hundred dollars ($100) per violation for a maximum of 30 days, and shall be grounds for disciplining the licensee pursuant to Section 1568.082. The State Department of Social Services may assess civil penalties for continued violations as allowed in Section 1568.0822. The fingerprint images and related information shall then be submitted to the Department of Justice for processing. The licensee shall maintain and make available for inspection documentation of the individual's clearance or exemption.

(2) A violation of the regulations adopted pursuant to Section 1522.04 shall result in the citation of a deficiency and an immediate assessment of civil penalties in the amount of one hundred dollars ($100) per violation per day for a maximum of five days, unless the violation is a second or subsequent violation within a 12-month period in which case the civil penalties shall be in the amount of one hundred dollars ($100) per violation for a maximum of 30 days, and shall be grounds for disciplining the licensee pursuant to Section 1568.082. The department may assess civil penalties for continued violations as permitted by Section 1568.0822.

(3) Within 14 calendar days of the receipt of the fingerprint images, the Department of Justice shall notify the State Department of Social Services of the criminal record information, as provided for in this subdivision. If no criminal record information has been recorded, the Department of Justice shall provide the licensee and the State Department of Social Services with a statement of that fact within 14 calendar days of receipt of the fingerprint images. If new fingerprint images are required for processing, the Department of Justice shall, within 14 calendar days from the date of receipt of the fingerprint images, notify the licensee that the fingerprint images were illegible. The Department of Justice shall notify the department, as required by Section 1522.04, and shall notify the licensee by mail within 14 days of electronic transmission of the fingerprint images to the Department of Justice, if the person has no criminal history record.

(4) Except for persons specified in paragraph (2) of subdivision (b), the licensee shall endeavor to ascertain the previous employment history of persons required to be fingerprinted under this subdivision. If it is determined by the State Department of Social

Services, on the basis of the fingerprint images submitted to the Department of Justice, that the person has been convicted of a sex offense against a minor, an offense specified in Section 243.4, 273a, 273ab, 273d, 273g, or 368 of the Penal Code, or a felony, the department shall notify the licensee to act immediately to terminate the person's employment, remove the person from the residential care facility, or bar the person from entering the residential care facility. The department may subsequently grant an exemption pursuant to subdivision (f). If the conviction was for another crime, except a minor traffic violation, the licensee shall, upon notification by the department, act immediately to either (A) terminate the person's employment, remove the person from the residential care facility, or bar the person from entering the residential care facility; or (B) seek an exemption pursuant to subdivision (f). The department shall determine if the person shall be allowed to remain in the facility until a decision on the exemption is rendered. A licensee's failure to comply with the department's prohibition of employment, contact with clients, or presence in the facility as required by this paragraph shall result in a citation of deficiency and an immediate assessment of civil penalties by the department against the licensee, in the amount of one hundred dollars ($100) per violation per day for a maximum of five days, unless the violation is a second or subsequent violation within a 12-month period in which case the civil penalties shall be in the amount of one hundred dollars ($100) per violation for a maximum of 30 days, and shall be grounds for disciplining the licensee pursuant to Section 1568.082.
(5) The department may issue an exemption on its own motion pursuant to subdivision (f) if the person's criminal history indicates that the person is of good character based on the age, seriousness, and frequency of the conviction or convictions. The department, in consultation with interested parties, shall develop regulations to establish the criteria to grant an exemption pursuant to this paragraph.
(6) Concurrently with notifying the licensee pursuant to paragraph (4), the department shall notify the affected individual of his or her right to seek an exemption pursuant to subdivision (f). The individual may seek an exemption only if the licensee terminates the person's employment or removes the person from the facility after receiving notice from the department pursuant to paragraph (4).
(d) (1) For purposes of this section or any other provision of this chapter, a conviction means a plea or verdict of guilty or a conviction following a plea of nolo contendere. An action that the department is permitted to take following the establishment of a conviction may be taken when the time for appeal has elapsed, when the judgment of conviction has been affirmed on appeal, or when an order granting probation is made suspending the imposition of the sentence, notwithstanding a subsequent order pursuant to Sections 1203.4 and 1203.4a of the Penal Code permitting that person to withdraw his or her plea of guilty and to enter a plea of not guilty, setting aside the verdict of guilty, or dismissing the accusation, information, or indictment. For purposes of this chapter, the record of a conviction, or a copy thereof certified by the clerk of the court or by a judge of the court in which the conviction occurred, shall be conclusive evidence of the conviction. For purposes of this section or any other provision of this chapter, the arrest disposition report certified by the Department of Justice, or documents admissible in a criminal action pursuant to Section 969b of the Penal Code, shall be prima facie evidence of the conviction, notwithstanding any other provision of law prohibiting the admission of these documents in a civil or administrative action.
(2) For purposes of this section or any other provision of this chapter, the department shall consider criminal convictions from another state or federal court as if the criminal offense was committed in this state.
(e) (1) The State Department of Social Services shall not use a record of arrest to deny, revoke, or terminate any application, license, employment, or residence unless the department investigates the incident and secures evidence, whether or not related to the incident of arrest, that is admissible in an administrative hearing to establish conduct by the person that may pose a risk to the health and safety of any person who is or may become a client.
(2) The department shall not issue a criminal record clearance to a person who has been arrested for any crime specified in Section 290 of the Penal Code, for violating Section 245, 273ab, or 273.5, or subdivision (b) of Section 273a, of the Penal Code, or, prior to January 1, 1994, paragraph (2) of Section 273a of the Penal Code, or for any crime for which the department is prohibited from granting a criminal record exemption pursuant to subdivision (f), prior to the department's completion of an investigation pursuant to paragraph (1).
(3) The State Department of Social Services is authorized to obtain arrest or conviction records or reports from a law enforcement agency as necessary to the performance of its duties to inspect, license, and investigate community care facilities and individuals associated with a community care facility.
(f) (1) After review of the record, the director may grant an exemption from disqualification for a license as specified in paragraphs (1) and (4) of subdivision (a), or for employment, residence, or presence in a residential care facility as specified in paragraphs (4), (5), and (6) of subdivision (c) if the director has substantial and convincing evidence to support a reasonable belief that the applicant and the person convicted of the crime, if other than the applicant, are of such good character as to justify issuance of the license or special permit or granting an exemption for purposes of subdivision (c). However, an exemption shall not be granted pursuant to this subdivision if the conviction was for any of the following offenses:
(A) An offense specified in Section 220, 243.4, or 264.1, subdivision (a) of Section 273a, or, prior to January 1, 1994, paragraph (1) of Section 273a, Section 273ab, 273d, 288, or 289, subdivision (c) of Section 290, or Section 368, of the Penal Code, or was a conviction of another crime against an individual specified in subdivision (c) of Section 667.5 of the Penal Code.
(B) A felony offense specified in Section 729 of the Business and Professions Code or Section 206 or 215, subdivision (a) of Section 347, subdivision (b) of Section 417, or subdivision (a) of Section 451 of the Penal Code.
(2) The department shall not prohibit a person from being employed or having contact with clients in a facility on the basis of a denied criminal record exemption request or arrest information unless the department complies with Section 1568.092.
(g) (1) For purposes of compliance with this section, the department may permit an individual to transfer a current criminal record clearance, as defined in subdivision (a), from one facility to another, as long as the criminal record clearance has been processed through a state licensing district office, and is being transferred to another facility licensed by a state licensing district office. The request shall be in writing to the department, and shall include a copy of the person's driver's license or valid identification card issued by the Department of Motor Vehicles, or a valid photo identification issued by another state or the United States government if the person is not a California resident. Upon request of the licensee, who shall enclose a self-addressed stamped envelope for this purpose, the department shall verify whether the individual has a clearance that can be transferred.
(2) The State Department of Social Services shall hold criminal record clearances in its active files for a minimum of two years after an employee is no longer employed at a licensed facility in order for the criminal record clearance to be transferred.
(h) If a licensee or facility is required by law to deny employment or to terminate employment of any employee based on written notification from the state department that the employee has a prior criminal conviction or is determined unsuitable for employment under Section 1568.092, the licensee or facility shall not incur civil liability or unemployment insurance liability as a result of that denial or termination.
(i) (1) The Department of Justice shall charge a fee sufficient to cover its cost in providing services to comply with the 14-day requirement contained in subdivision (c) for provision to the department of criminal record information.
(2) Paragraph (1) shall cease to be implemented when the department adopts emergency regulations pursuant to Section 1522.04, and shall become inoperative when permanent regulations are adopted under that section.
(j) Notwithstanding any other law, the department may provide an individual with a copy of his or her state or federal level criminal offender record information search response as provided to that department by the Department of Justice if the department has denied a criminal background clearance based on this information and the individual makes a written request to the department for a copy specifying an address to which it is to be sent. The state or federal level criminal offender record information search response shall not be modified or altered from its form or content as provided by the Department of Justice and shall be provided to the address specified by the individual in his or her written request. The department shall retain a copy of the individual's written request and the response and date provided.
(Amended by Stats. 2014, Ch. 824, Sec. 2. (AB 2632) Effective January 1, 2015.)
1568.092.
(a) The department may prohibit any person from being a member of the board of directors, an executive director, or an officer of a licensee or a licensee from employing, or continuing the employment of, or allowing in a licensed facility, or allowing contact with clients of a licensed facility by, any employee, prospective employee, or person who is not a client who has:
(1) Violated, aided, or permitted the violation by any other person of this chapter or of any rules or regulations adopted under this chapter.
(2) Engaged in conduct that is inimical to the health, welfare, or safety of either an individual, in or receiving services from the facility, or the people of the State of California.
(3) Been denied an exemption to work or to be present in a facility, when that person has been convicted of a crime as defined in Section 1568.09.
(4) Engaged in any other conduct that would constitute a basis for disciplining a licensee.
(5) Engaged in acts of financial malfeasance concerning the operation of a facility, including, but not limited to, improper use or embezzlement of client moneys and property or fraudulent appropriation for personal gain of facility moneys and property, or willful or negligent failure to provide services.
(b) The excluded person, the facility, and the licensee shall be given written notice of the basis of the action of the department and of the right to an appeal of the excluded person. The notice shall be served either by personal service or by registered mail. Within 15 days after the department serves the notice, the excluded person may file with the department a written appeal of the exclusion order. If the excluded person fails to file a written appeal within the prescribed time, the action of the department shall be final.
(c) (1) The department may require the immediate removal of an executive director, a board member, or an officer of a licensee or exclusion of an employee, prospective employee, or person who is not a client from a facility pending a final decision of the matter when, in the opinion of the director, the action is necessary to protect residents or clients from physical or mental abuse, abandonment, or any other substantial threat to their health or safety.
(2) If the department requires the immediate removal of a member of the board of directors, an executive director, or an officer of a licensee or exclusion of an employee, prospective employee, or person who is not a client from a facility, the department shall serve an order of immediate exclusion upon the excluded person that shall notify the excluded person of the basis of the department's action and of the excluded person's right to a hearing.
(3) Within 15 days after the department serves an order of immediate exclusion, the excluded person may file a written appeal of the exclusion with the department. The department's action shall be final if the excluded person does not appeal the exclusion

within the prescribed time. The department shall do the following upon receipt of a written appeal:

(A) Within 30 days of receipt of the appeal, serve an accusation upon the excluded person.

(B) Within 60 days of receipt of a notice of defense by the excluded person pursuant to Section 11506 of the Government Code, conduct a hearing on the accusation.

(4) An order of immediate exclusion of the excluded person from the facility shall remain in effect until the hearing is completed and the department has made a final determination on the merits. However, the order of immediate exclusion shall be deemed vacated if the department fails to make a final determination on the merits within 60 days after the original hearing has been completed.

(d) An excluded person who files a written appeal of the exclusion order with the department pursuant to this section shall, as part of the written request, provide his or her current mailing address. The excluded person shall subsequently notify the department in writing of any change in mailing address, until the hearing process has been completed or terminated.

(e) Hearings held pursuant to this section shall be conducted in accordance with Chapter 5 (commencing with Section 11500) of Division 3 of Title 2 of the Government Code. The standard of proof shall be the preponderance of the evidence and the burden of proof shall be on the department.

(f) The department may institute or continue a disciplinary proceeding against a member of the board of directors, an executive director, or an officer of a licensee or an employee, prospective employee, or person who is not a client upon any ground provided by this section. The department may enter an order prohibiting any person from being a member of the board of directors, an executive director, or an officer of a licensee or prohibiting the excluded person's employment or presence in the facility, or otherwise take disciplinary action against the excluded person, notwithstanding any resignation, withdrawal of employment application, or change of duties by the excluded person, or any discharge, failure to hire, or reassignment of the excluded person by the licensee or that the excluded person no longer has contact with clients at the facility.

(g) A licensee's failure to comply with the department's exclusion order after being notified of the order shall be grounds for disciplining the licensee pursuant to Section 1568.082.

(h) (1) (A) In cases in which the excluded person appealed the exclusion order and there is a decision and order of the department upholding the exclusion order, the person shall be prohibited from working in any facility or being licensed to operate any facility licensed by the department or from being a certified foster parent or resource family for the remainder of the excluded person's life, unless otherwise ordered by the department.

(B) The excluded individual may petition for reinstatement one year after the effective date of the decision and order of the department upholding the exclusion order pursuant to Section 11522 of the Government Code. The department shall provide the excluded person with a copy of Section 11522 of the Government Code with the decision and order.

(2) (A) In cases in which the department informed the excluded person of his or her right to appeal the exclusion order and the excluded person did not appeal the exclusion order, the person shall be prohibited from working in any facility or being licensed to operate any facility licensed by the department or a certified foster parent or resource family for the remainder of the excluded person's life, unless otherwise ordered by the department.

(B) The excluded individual may petition for reinstatement after one year has elapsed from the date of the notification of the exclusion order pursuant to Section 11522 of the Government Code. The department shall provide the excluded person with a copy of Section 11522 of the Government Code with the exclusion order.

(Amended by Stats. 2017, Ch. 732, Sec. 34. (AB 404) Effective January 1, 2018.)

1568.093.

(a) (1) If the department determines that a person was issued a license under this chapter or under Chapter 1 (commencing with Section 1200), Chapter 2 (commencing with Section 1250), Chapter 3.01 (commencing with Section 1568.01), Chapter 3.2 (commencing with Section 1569), Chapter 3.4 (commencing with Section 1596.70), Chapter 3.5 (commencing with Section 1596.90), or Chapter 3.6 (commencing with Section 1597.30) and the prior license was revoked within the preceding two years, the department shall exclude the person from, and remove him or her as, a member of the board of directors, an executive director, or an officer of a licensee of, any facility licensed by the department pursuant to the chapter.

(2) If the department determines that a person previously was issued a certificate of approval by a foster family agency which was revoked by the department pursuant to subdivision (b) of Section 1534 within the preceding two years, the department shall exclude the person from, and remove him or her as, a member of the board of directors, an executive director, or an officer of a licensee of, any facility licensed by the department pursuant to this chapter.

(b) If the department determines that the person had previously applied for a license under any of the chapters listed in paragraph (1) of subdivision (a) and the application was denied within the last year, the department shall exclude the person from, and remove him or her as, a member of the board of directors, an executive director, or an officer of a licensee of, any facility licensed by the department pursuant to this chapter and as follows:

(1) In cases where the applicant petitioned for a hearing, the department shall exclude the person from, and remove him or her as, a member of the board of directors, an executive director, or an officer of a licensee of, any facility licensed by the department

pursuant to this chapter until one year has elapsed from the effective date of the decision and order of the department upholding a denial.

(2) In cases where the department informed the applicant of his or her right to petition for a hearing and the applicant did not petition for a hearing, the department shall exclude the person from, and remove him or her as, a member of the board of directors, an executive director, or an officer of a licensee of, any facility licensed by the department pursuant to this chapter until one year has elapsed from the date of the notification of the denial and the right to petition for a hearing.

(c) If the department determines that the person had previously applied for a certificate of approval with a foster family agency and the department ordered the foster family agency to deny the application pursuant to subdivision (b) of Section 1534, the department shall exclude the person from, and remove him or her as, a member of the board of directors, an executive director, or an officer of a licensee of, any facility licensed by the department pursuant to this chapter and as follows:

(1) In cases where the applicant petitioned for a hearing, the department shall exclude the person from, and remove him or her as, a member of the board of directors, an executive director, or an officer of a licensee of, any facility licensed by the department pursuant to this chapter until one year has elapsed from the effective date of the decision and order of the department upholding a denial.

(2) In cases where the department informed the applicant of his or her right to petition for a hearing and the applicant did not petition for a hearing, the department shall exclude the person from, and remove him or her as, a member of the board of directors, an executive director, or an officer of a licensee of, any facility licensed by the department pursuant to this chapter until one year has elapsed from the date of the notification of the denial and the right to petition for a hearing.

(d) Exclusion or removal of an individual pursuant to this section shall not be considered an order of exclusion for purposes of Section 1568.092 or any other law.

(e) The department may determine not to exclude the person from, and remove from being a member of the board of directors, an executive director, or officer of a licensee of, any facility licensed by the department pursuant to this chapter if it has determined that the reasons for the denial of the application or revocation of the facility license or certificate of approval were due to circumstances and conditions that either have been corrected or are no longer in existence.

(Amended by Stats. 1998, Ch. 311, Sec. 35. Effective August 19, 1998.)

1568.094.

The department shall conduct an unannounced visit to a facility within 30 days after the department serves an order of immediate exclusion from the facility upon the licensee or a person subject to immediate removal or exclusion from the facility pursuant to paragraph (4) of subdivision (c) of Section 1568.09 and subdivision (c) of Section 1568.092 in order to ensure that the excluded person is not within the facility, unless the department previously has verified that the excluded person is not within the facility.

(Added by Stats. 2008, Ch. 291, Sec. 13. Effective September 25, 2008.)

CHAPTER 3.1. Alzheimer's Day Care-Resource Centers Act [1568.15 - 1568.17]

(Heading of Chapter 3.1 renumbered from Chapter 3.3 (as amended by Stats. 1987, Ch. 947) by Stats. 1988, Ch. 160, Sec. 90.)

1568.15.

The Secretary of California Health and Human Services shall be responsible for the oversight and coordination of programs serving people living with Alzheimer's disease and related disorders and their families. This responsibility shall include, but not be limited to:

(a) State level support and assistance to all programs within the Health and Human Services Agency and member departments developed for this target population.

(b) Establishment of the Alzheimer's Disease and Related Disorders Advisory Committee pursuant to Section 1568.17.

(c) Review of the recommendations contained in the 1987 California Alzheimer's Disease Task Force Report and subsequent state plans, in consultation with appropriate state departments and the Alzheimer's Disease and Related Disorders Advisory Committee.

(Amended by Stats. 2008, Ch. 339, Sec. 2. Effective January 1, 2009.)

1568.17.

(a) The California Health and Human Services Agency shall establish an Alzheimer's Disease and Related Disorders Advisory Committee consisting of 14 members selected as follows:

(1) One representing the field of academic medical research.

(2) One representing the field of social research.

(3) One representing the field of mental health.

(4) One representing the Alzheimer's day care resource centers.

(5) One representing the Alzheimer's disease diagnostic and treatment centers.

(6) Two representing families of persons suffering from Alzheimer's disease or related disorders.

(7) Two representing organizations providing services to Alzheimer's disease patients.

(8) One representing a consumer organization representing persons with Alzheimer's disease.

(9) One representing a member of the State Bar who is familiar with the legal issues confronting Alzheimer's disease victims and their families.

(10) Two people who have been diagnosed with Alzheimer's disease to serve one-year terms.

(11) The Secretary of California Health and Human Services or his or her designee.

(b) Members shall serve at the pleasure of the Secretary of California Health and Human Services. The agency secretary may establish fixed terms for advisory committee membership. For purposes of continuity, those terms shall be staggered.

(c) Members shall serve without compensation, but shall receive reimbursement for travel and other necessary expenses actually incurred in the performance of their official duties.

(d) The Alzheimer's Disease and Related Disorders Advisory Committee shall do all of the following:

(1) Provide ongoing advice and assistance to the administration and the Legislature as to the program needs and priorities of the target population.

(2) Provide planning support to the administration and the Legislature by updating recommendations of the 1987 California Alzheimer's Disease Task Force Report and regularly reviewing and updating recommendations as needed.

(3) Appoint a chairperson and vice chairperson.

(4) Meet quarterly.

(e) The Alzheimer's Disease and Related Disorders Advisory Committee shall do all of the following when making policy and plan recommendations:

(1) Consult with a broad range of stakeholders, including, but not limited to, people diagnosed with Alzheimer's disease, family caregivers, community-based and institutional providers, Alzheimer's disease researchers and academicians, formal caregivers, the Alzheimer's Association, the California Commission on Aging, and other state entities.

(2) Consider the recommendations of other state plans, including, but not limited to, the Olmstead Plan, the Long-Range Strategic Plan on Aging, and the California Department of Aging's State Plan on Aging.

(3) Consider cultural and linguistic factors that impact persons with Alzheimer's disease and their families who are from diverse populations.

(4) Review current state policies and practices concerning care and treatment related to Alzheimer's disease and other dementia disorders, and develop recommendations concerning all of the following issues:

(A) Community-based support for California's diverse people with Alzheimer's disease and their family members.

(B) Choices for care and residence for persons with Alzheimer's disease and their families.

(C) An integrated public health care management approach to Alzheimer's disease in health care settings that makes full use of dementia care practices.

(D) The dementia competence of health care professionals.

(E) Early identification and intervention through increasing public awareness of Alzheimer's disease.

(f) All meetings of the advisory committee, and any subcommittees thereof, shall be open to the public and adequate notice shall be provided in accordance with Article 9 (commencing with Section 11120) of Chapter 1 of Part 1 of Division 3 of Title 2 of the Government Code.

(Amended by Stats. 2008, Ch. 339, Sec. 3. Effective January 1, 2009.)

CHAPTER 3.2. Residential Care Facilities for the Elderly [1569 - 1569.889]

(Heading of Chapter 3.2 renumbered from Chapter 3.3 (as added by Stats. 1985, Ch. 1127) by Stats. 1988, Ch. 160, Sec. 91.)

ARTICLE 1. General Provisions [1569 - 1569.5]

(Article 1 added by Stats. 1985, Ch. 1127, Sec. 3.)

1569.

This chapter shall be known and may be cited as the California Residential Care Facilities for the Elderly Act.

(Added by Stats. 1985, Ch. 1127, Sec. 3.)

1569.1.

The Legislature hereby finds and declares:

(a) The Legislature has taken steps in recent years to develop a continuum of long-term social and health support services for older persons in the community that provide a range of options for long-term care and residential care facilities for the elderly are central in that continuum.

(b) These efforts require a reevaluation of residential care for the elderly outside the constraints of the Community Care Facilities Act.

(c) The Community Care Facilities Act was enacted in 1973 with the primary purpose of ensuring that residents of state hospitals would have access to safe, alternative community-based housing.

(d) Since that time, due to shortages in affordable housing and a greater demand for residences for the elderly providing some care and supervision, a growing number of elderly persons with health and social care needs now reside in community care facilities that may or may not be designed to meet their needs.

(e) Progress in the field of gerontology has provided new insights and information as to the types of services required to allow older persons to remain as independent as possible while residing in a residential care facility for the elderly.

(f) The fluctuating health and social status of older persons demands a system of residential care that can respond to these needs by making available multilevels of service within the facility, thus reducing the need for residents with fluctuating conditions to move between medical and nonmedical facilities.

(g) Residential care facilities for the elderly which are not primarily medically oriented represent a humane approach to meeting the housing, social and service needs of older persons, and can provide a homelike environment for older persons with a variety of care needs.

(h) It is, therefore, the intent of the Legislature to require that residential care facilities for the elderly be licensed as a separate category within the existing licensing structure of the State Department of Social Services.

(Added by Stats. 1985, Ch. 1127, Sec. 3.)

1569.2.

As used in this chapter:

(a) "Administrator" means the individual designated by the licensee to act on behalf of the licensee in the overall management of the facility. The licensee, if an individual, and the administrator may be one and the same person.

(b) "Beneficial ownership interest" means an ownership interest through the possession of stock, equity in capital, or any interest in the profits of the applicant or licensee, or through the possession of such an interest in other entities that directly or indirectly hold an interest in the applicant or licensee. The percentage of beneficial ownership in the applicant or licensee that is held by any other entity is determined by multiplying the other entities' percentage of ownership interest at each level.

(c) "Care and supervision" means the facility assumes responsibility for, or provides or promises to provide in the future, ongoing assistance with activities of daily living without which the resident's physical health, mental health, safety, or welfare would be endangered. Assistance includes assistance with taking medications, money management, or personal care.

(d) "Chain" means a group of two or more licensees that are controlled, as defined in this section, by the same persons or entities.

(e) "Control" means the ability to direct the operation or management of the applicant or licensee and includes the ability to exercise control through intermediary or subsidiary entities.

(f) "Department" means the State Department of Social Services.

(g) "Director" means the Director of Social Services.

(h) "Health-related services" mean services that shall be directly provided by an appropriate skilled professional, including a registered nurse, licensed vocational nurse, physical therapist, or occupational therapist.

(i) "Instrumental activities of daily living" means any of the following: housework, meals, laundry, taking of medication, money management, appropriate transportation, correspondence, telephoning, and related tasks.

(j) "License" means a basic permit to operate a residential care facility for the elderly.

(k) "Parent organization" means an organization in control of another organization either directly or through one or more intermediaries.

(l) "Personal activities of daily living" means any of the following: dressing, feeding, toileting, bathing, grooming, and mobility and associated tasks.

(m) "Personal care" means assistance with personal activities of daily living, to help provide for and maintain physical and psychosocial comfort.

(n) "Protective supervision" means observing and assisting confused residents, including persons with dementia, to safeguard them against injury.

(o) (1) "Residential care facility for the elderly" means a housing arrangement chosen voluntarily by persons 60 years of age or over, or their authorized representative, where varying levels and intensities of care and supervision, protective supervision, or personal care are provided, based upon their varying needs, as determined in order to be admitted and to remain in the facility. Persons under 60 years of age with compatible needs may be allowed to be admitted or retained in a residential care facility for the elderly as specified in Section 1569.316.

(2) This subdivision shall be operative only until the enactment of legislation implementing the three levels of care in residential care facilities for the elderly pursuant to Section 1569.70.

(p) (1) "Residential care facility for the elderly" means a housing arrangement chosen voluntarily by persons 60 years of age or over, or their authorized representative, where varying levels and intensities of care and supervision, protective supervision, personal care, or health-related services are provided, based upon their varying needs, as determined in order to be admitted and to remain in the facility. Persons under 60 years of age with compatible needs may be allowed to be admitted or retained in a residential care facility for the elderly as specified in Section 1569.316.

(2) This subdivision shall become operative upon the enactment of legislation implementing the three levels of care in residential care facilities for the elderly pursuant to Section 1569.70.

(q) "Sundowning" means a condition in which persons with cognitive impairment experience recurring confusion, disorientation, and increasing levels of agitation that coincide with the onset of late afternoon and early evening.

(r) "Supportive services" means resources available to the resident in the community that help to maintain their functional ability and meet their needs as identified in the individual resident assessment. Supportive services may include any of the following: medical, dental, and other health care services; transportation; recreational and leisure activities; social services; and counseling services.

(Amended by Stats. 2016, Ch. 86, Sec. 179. (SB 1171) Effective January 1, 2017.)

1569.3.

The license of any facility licensed as a residential facility for the elderly under the California Community Care Facilities Act provided for in Chapter 3 (commencing with Section 1500) on January 1, 1986, shall automatically be transferred for the unexpired term of the license to licensure as a residential care facility for the elderly under this chapter.

(Amended by Stats. 2005, Ch. 423, Sec. 3. Effective January 1, 2006.)

1569.5.

(a) The director shall adopt regulations authorizing residential care facilities for the elderly, as defined in Section 1569.2, to fill unused capacity on a short-term, time-limited basis to provide temporary respite care for persons who are frail and elderly, adults who have functional impairments, or persons with mental health disorders who need 24-hour supervision and who are being cared for by a caretaker or caretakers. The regulations shall address provisions for liability coverage and the level of facility responsibility for routine medical care and medication management, and may require screening of persons to determine the level of care required, a physical history completed by the person's personal physician, and other alternative admission criteria to protect the health and safety of persons applying for respite care. The regulations shall permit these facilities to charge a fee for the services provided, which shall include, but not be limited to, supervision, room, leisure activities, and meals.

(b) No facility shall accept persons in need of care beyond the level of care for which that facility is licensed.

(Amended by Stats. 2014, Ch. 144, Sec. 34. (AB 1847) Effective January 1, 2015.)

ARTICLE 2. Licensing [1569.10 - 1569.24]

(Article 2 added by Stats. 1985, Ch. 1127, Sec. 3.)

1569.10.

No person, firm, partnership, association, or corporation within the state and no state or local public agency shall operate, establish, manage, conduct, or maintain a residential facility for the elderly in this state without a current valid license or current valid special permit therefor, as provided in this chapter.

(Amended by Stats. 1987, Ch. 1069, Sec. 4.)

1569.11.

The department shall inspect and license residential care facilities for the elderly. A license is not transferable.

(Added by Stats. 1985, Ch. 1127, Sec. 3.)

1569.12.

The department may provide consulting services upon request to any residential care facility for the elderly to assist in the identification or correction of deficiencies and in the upgrading of the quality of care provided by the facility.

(Added by Stats. 1985, Ch. 1127, Sec. 3.)

1569.13.

(a) The department may contract for state, county, or other public agencies to assume specified licensing, approval, or consultation responsibilities. In exercising the authority so delegated, these agencies shall conform to the requirements of this chapter and to the rules, regulations, and standards of the department. The department shall reimburse agencies for services performed pursuant to this section, and the payments shall not exceed actual cost.

If any grants-in-aid are made by the federal government for the support of any inspection or consultation service approved by the department, the amount of the federal grant shall first be applied to defer the cost of the service before state reimbursement is made.

(b) The department may contract with any county for the purposes of having the county assume the responsibility within the county for the licensing and regulation of residential care facilities for the elderly serving six or fewer persons. Prior to the department contracting with any county for the licensing and regulation of residential care facilities for the elderly serving six or fewer persons, the department shall develop uniform standards which specify and delineate the responsibilities of contracting counties and the department. The department shall reimburse the county for the services performed, not to exceed the actual cost, out of the funds allocated to the department for the licensing and regulation of those facilities. The county shall conform to the requirements of this chapter and to the rules, regulations, and standards of the department.

(Amended by Stats. 1989, Ch. 488, Sec. 1.)

1569.14.

No license issued pursuant to this chapter shall have any property value for sale or exchange purposes and no person, including any owner, agent, or broker, shall sell or exchange any license for any commercial purpose.

(Added by Stats. 1985, Ch. 1127, Sec. 3.)

1569.145.

This chapter shall not apply to any of the following:

(a) A health facility, as defined by Section 1250.

(b) A clinic, as defined by Section 1200.

(c) A facility conducted by and for the adherents of a well-recognized church or religious denomination for the purpose of providing facilities for the care or treatment of the sick who depend upon prayer or spiritual means for healing in the practice of the religion of that church or denomination.

(d) A house, institution, hotel, congregate housing project for the elderly, or other similar place that is limited to providing one or more of the following: housing, meals, transportation, housekeeping, or recreational and social activities; or that have residents independently accessing supportive services, provided, however, that no resident thereof requires an element of care and supervision or protective supervision as determined by the director. This subdivision shall not include a home or residence that is described in subdivision (f).

(e) Recovery houses or other similar facilities providing group living arrangements for persons recovering from alcoholism or drug addiction where the facility provides no care or supervision.

(f) (1) An arrangement for the care and supervision of a person or persons by a family member.

(2) An arrangement for the care and supervision of a person or persons from only one family by a close friend, whose friendship preexisted the contact between the provider and the recipient, and both of the following are met:

(A) The care and supervision is provided in a home or residence chosen by the recipient.

(B) The arrangement is not of a business nature and occurs only as long as the needs of the recipient for care and supervision are adequately met.

(g) (1) (A) Any housing occupied by elderly or disabled persons, or both, that is approved and operated pursuant to Section 202 of Public Law 86-372 (12 U.S.C. Sec. 1701q), or Section 811 of Public Law 101-625 (42 U.S.C. Sec. 8013), or whose mortgage is insured pursuant to Section 236 of Public Law 90-448 (12 U.S.C. Sec. 1715z), or that receives mortgage assistance pursuant to Section 221d(3) of Public Law 87-70 (12 U.S.C. Sec. 1715l), where supportive services are made available to residents at their option, as long as the project owner or operator does not contract for or provide the supportive services.

(B) Any housing that qualifies for a low-income housing credit pursuant to Section 252 of Public Law 99-514 (26 U.S.C. Sec. 42) or that is subject to the requirements for rental dwellings for low-income families pursuant to Section 8 of Public Law 93-383 (42 U.S.C. Sec. 1437f), and that is occupied by elderly or disabled persons, or both, where supportive services are made available to residents at their option, as long as the project owner or operator does not contract for or provide the supportive services.

(2) The project owner or operator to which paragraph (1) applies may coordinate, or help residents gain access to, the supportive services, either directly, or through a service coordinator.

(h) A similar facility determined by the director.

(i) For purposes of this section, "family member" means a spouse, by marriage or otherwise, child or stepchild, by natural birth or by adoption, parent, brother, sister, half brother, half sister, parent-in-law, brother-in-law, sister-in-law, nephew, niece, aunt, uncle, first cousin, or a person denoted by the prefix "grand" or "great," or the spouse of one of these persons.

(j) A person shall not be exempted from this chapter's licensure requirements if he or she has been appointed as conservator of the person, estate of the person, or both, if the person is receiving care and supervision from the conservator as regulated by this chapter, unless the conservator is otherwise exempted under other provisions of this section.

(Amended by Stats. 2009, Ch. 82, Sec. 3. (AB 123) Effective January 1, 2010.)

1569.147.

(a) Nothing in this chapter authorizes the imposition of rent regulations or controls for licensed residential care facilities for the elderly.

(b) Licensed residential care facilities for the elderly are not subject to controls on rent imposed by any state or local agency or other local government entity.

(Added by Stats. 1985, Ch. 1127, Sec. 3.)

1569.149.

A prospective applicant for licensure shall be notified at the time of the initial request for information regarding application for licensure that, prior to obtaining licensure, the facility shall secure and maintain a fire clearance approval from the local fire enforcing agency, as defined in Section 13244, or the State Fire Marshal, whichever has primary fire protection jurisdiction. The prospective applicant shall be notified of the provisions of Section 13235, relating to the fire safety clearance application. The prospective applicant for licensure shall be notified that the fire clearance shall be in accordance with state and local fire safety regulations.

(Added by Stats. 1989, Ch. 993, Sec. 3.)

1569.15.

(a) Any person seeking a license for a residential care facility for the elderly under this chapter shall file with the department, pursuant to regulations, an application on forms furnished by the department, that shall include, but not be limited to, all of the following:

(1) Evidence satisfactory to the department of the ability of the applicant to comply with this chapter and of rules and regulations adopted under this chapter by the department.

(2) Evidence satisfactory to the department that the applicant is of reputable and responsible character. The evidence shall include, but not be limited to, a criminal record clearance pursuant to Section 1569.17, employment history, and character references. If the applicant is a firm, association, organization, partnership, business trust, corporation, or company, like evidence shall be submitted as to the individuals or entities holding a beneficial ownership interest of 10 percent or more, and the person who has operational control of the residential care facility for the elderly for which the application for issuance of license or special permit is made. Notwithstanding anything in this section, an applicant or licensee is not required to disclose the names of investors in a publicly traded company or investment fund if those investors are silent investors who do not have influence or control over operations of the company, fund, or facility.

(3) If applicable, the following information:

(A) Whether it is a for-profit or not-for-profit provider.

(B) The name, address, license number, and licensing agency name of other health, residential, or community care facilities owned, managed, or operated by the same applicant or by any parent organization of the applicant.

(C) The name and business address of any person or entity that controls, as defined in Section 1569.2, the applicant.

(D) If part of a chain, as defined in Section 1569.2, a diagram indicating the relationship between the applicant and the persons or entities that are part of the chain, including those that are controlled by the same parties, and in a separate list, the name, address, and license number, if applicable, for each person or entity in the diagram.

(E) The name and address of any persons, organizations, or entities that own the real property on which the facility seeking licensure and the licensed facilities described in subparagraph (B) are located.

(F) The name and address of any management company serving the facility and the same information required of applicants in subparagraphs (C) and (D) for the management company.

(4) Evidence satisfactory to the department that the applicant has sufficient financial resources to maintain the standards of service required by regulations adopted pursuant to this chapter.

(5) The name of the person with operational control of the applicant, such as the chief executive officer, general partner, owner or like party, and state that person's prior or present service as an administrator, chief executive officer, general partner, director like role of, or as a person who has held or holds a beneficial ownership interest of 10 percent or more in, any residential care facility for the elderly, in any facility licensed pursuant to Chapter 1 (commencing with Section 1200), Chapter 2 (commencing with Section 1250), or Chapter 3 (commencing with Section 1500), or a similarly licensed facility in California or any other state within the past 10 years.

(6) The following information regarding the applicant and each individual or entity identified pursuant to paragraph (5):

(A) Any revocation, suspension, probation, exclusion order, or other similar administrative disciplinary action that was filed and sustained in California or any other state, or in the process of being adjudicated, against a facility associated with a person identified pursuant to paragraph (5) or by any authority responsible for the licensing of health, residential, or community care facilities within the past 10 years.

(B) Copies of final findings, orders, or both, issued by any health, residential, or community care licensing agency or any court relevant to the actions described in subparagraph (A).

(C) Any petition for bankruptcy relief filed within five years of the date of application involving operation or closure of a health, residential, or community care facility licensed in California or any other state, the court, date, and case number of the filing, and whether a discharge was granted. If a discharge was not granted, the applicant shall provide copies of any court findings supporting denial of discharge.

(7) Any other information as may be required by the department for the proper administration and enforcement of this chapter.

(8) Following the implementation of Article 7 (commencing with Section 1569.70), evidence satisfactory to the department of the applicant's ability to meet regulatory requirements for the level of care the facility intends to provide.

(9) Evidence satisfactory to the department of adequate knowledge of supportive services and other community supports that may be necessary to meet the needs of elderly residents.

(10) A signed statement that the person desiring issuance of a license has read and understood the residential care facility for the elderly statute and regulations.

(11) Designation by the applicant of the individual who shall be the administrator of the facility, including, if the applicant is an individual, whether or not the applicant shall also be the administrator.

(12) Evidence of the right of possession of the facility prior to the time the license is granted, which may be satisfied by the submission of a copy of the entire lease agreement or deed.

(13) Evidence of successfully completing a certified prelicensure education program pursuant to Section 1569.23.

(14) For any facility that promotes or advertises or plans to promote or advertise special care, special programming, or special environments for persons with dementia, disclosure to the department of the special features of the facility in its plan of operation.

(b) The department shall cross-check all applicant information disclosed pursuant to paragraph (5) of subdivision (a), if electronically available, with the State Department of Public Health to determine if the applicant has a prior history of operating, holding a position in, or having ownership in, any entity specified in paragraph (5) of subdivision (a).

(c) Failure of the applicant to cooperate with the licensing agency in the completion of the application may result in the denial of the application. Failure to cooperate means that the information described in this section and in the regulations of the department has not been provided, or has not been provided in the form requested by the licensing agency, or both.

(d) The information required by this section shall be provided to the department upon initial application for licensure, and any change in the information shall be provided to the department within 30 calendar days of that change unless a shorter timeframe is required by the department. A licensee of multiple facilities may provide a single notice of changes to the department on behalf of all licensed facilities within the chain. Information pertaining to facilities operated in other states may be updated on an annual basis, except for the following information:

(1) Information specified in paragraph (6) of subdivision (a) shall be updated within 30 calendar days of the change.

(2) Information specified in subparagraph (B) of paragraph (3) of subdivision (a) shall be updated within six months after the change.

(e) An applicant or licensee shall maintain an email address of record with the department. The applicant or licensee shall provide written notification to the department of the email address and of any change to the email address within 10 business days of the change.

(f) (1) The department may deny an application for licensure or may subsequently revoke a license under this chapter if the applicant knowingly withheld material information or made a false statement of material fact with regard to information that was required by the application for licensure.

(2) The department may deny an application for licensure or may subsequently revoke a license under this chapter if the applicant did not disclose administrative disciplinary actions on the application as required by paragraph (6) of subdivision (a).

(3) In addition to the remedies provided under this chapter, the department may, subsequent to licensure, assess a civil penalty of one thousand dollars ($1,000) for a material violation of this section.

(Amended by Stats. 2015, Ch. 628, Sec. 2. (AB 601) Effective January 1, 2016.)

1569.150.

(a) The department and the licensing agencies with which it contracts for licensing shall review and make a final determination within 60 days of an applicant's submission of a complete application on all applications for a license to operate a residential care facility for the elderly if the applicant possesses a current valid license to operate a residential care facility for the elderly at another site. Applicants shall note on the application, or in a cover letter to the application, that they possess a current valid license at another site, and the number of that license.

(b) The department shall request a fire safety clearance from the appropriate fire marshal within five days of receipt of an application described in subdivision (a). The applicant shall be responsible for requesting and obtaining the required criminal record clearances.

(c) If the department for any reason is unable to comply with subdivision (a), it shall, within 60 days of receipt of the application described in subdivision (a), grant a provisional license to the applicant to operate for a period not to exceed six months, except as provided in subdivision (d). While the provisional license is in effect, the department shall continue its investigation and make a final determination on the application before the provisional license expires. The provisional license shall be granted, provided the department knows of no life safety risks, the criminal records clearances, if applicable, are complete, and the fire safety clearance is complete. The director may extend the term of a provisional license for an additional six months at the time of the application, if the director determines that more than six months will be required to achieve full compliance with licensing standards due to circumstances beyond the control of the applicant, and if all other requirements for a license have been met.

(d) If the department does not issue a provisional license pursuant to subdivision (c), the department shall issue a notice to the applicant identifying whether the provisional license has not been issued due to the existence of a life safety risk, lack of a fire safety clearance, lack of a criminal records clearance, failure to complete the application, or any combination of these reasons. If a life safety risk is identified, the risk preventing the issuance of the provisional license shall be clearly explained. If a lack of the fire safety clearance is identified, the notice shall include the dates on which the department requested the clearance and the current status of that request, and the fire marshal's name and telephone number to whom a fire safety clearance request was sent. The department shall identify the names of individuals for whom criminal records clearances are lacking. If failure to complete the application is identified, the notice shall list all of the forms or attachments that are missing or incorrect. This notice shall be sent to the applicant no later than 60 days after the applicant filed the application. If the reasons identified in the notice are corrected, the department shall issue the provisional license within five days after the corrections are made.

(e) The department shall, immediately after January 1, 1993, develop expedited procedures necessary to implement subdivisions (a), (b), (c), and (d).

(f) The department shall, immediately after January 1, 1993, develop an appeal procedure for applicants under this section for both denial of licenses and delay in processing applications.

(Added by Stats. 1992, Ch. 570, Sec. 2. Effective January 1, 1993.)

1569.151.

Upon receipt of an application to operate a residential care facility for the elderly from an applicant who is also applying or intends to apply for a permit to sell deposit subscriptions on life care contracts pursuant to Chapter 10 (commencing with Section 1770), the department shall review the application for licensure to determine the applicant's ability and intent to meet all statutory and regulatory requirements for a residential care facility for the elderly.

Upon determination that the applicant has provided satisfactory evidence of ability and intent, the department shall issue a preliminary approval for licensure, for purposes of the applicant obtaining a permit to sell deposit subscriptions for life care contracts. Preliminary approval does not guarantee that a license will be issued by the department.

(Added by Stats. 1986, Ch. 844, Sec. 2.5.)

1569.1515.

(a) A corporation that applies for licensure with the department shall list the facilities that any member of the board of directors, the executive director, or an officer has been licensed to operate, been employed in, or served as a member of the board of directors, the executive director, or an officer.

(b) The department shall not issue a provisional license or license to any corporate applicant that has a member of the board of directors, the executive director, or an officer who is not eligible for licensure pursuant to Sections 1569.16 and 1569.59.

(c) The department may revoke the license of any corporate licensee that has a member of the board of directors, the executive director, or an officer who is not eligible for licensure pursuant to Sections 1569.16 and 1569.59.

(d) Prior to instituting an administrative action pursuant to either subdivision (b) or (c), the department shall notify the applicant or licensee of the person's ineligibility to be a member of the board of directors, an executive director, or an officer of the applicant or

licensee, and shall give the applicant or licensee 15 days to remove the person from that position.
(Added by Stats. 1998, Ch. 311, Sec. 36. Effective August 19, 1998.)
1569.152.
(a) A residential care facility for the elderly, as defined in Section 1569.2, which fails to make reasonable efforts to safeguard resident property shall reimburse a resident for or replace stolen or lost resident property at its then current value. The facility shall be presumed to have made reasonable efforts to safeguard resident property if the facility has shown clear and convincing evidence of its efforts to meet each of the requirements specified in Section 1569.153. The presumption shall be a rebuttable presumption, and the resident or the resident's representative may pursue this matter in any court of competent jurisdiction.
(b) A civil penalty shall be levied if the residential care facility for the elderly has no program in place or if the facility has not shown clear and convincing evidence of its efforts to meet all of the requirements set forth in Section 1569.153. The State Department of Social Services shall issue a deficiency in the event that the manner in which the policies have been implemented is inadequate or the individual facility situation warrants additional theft and loss protections.
(c) The department shall not determine that a facility's program is inadequate based solely on the occasional occurrence of theft or loss in a facility.
(Added by Stats. 1988, Ch. 750, Sec. 2.)
1569.153.
A theft and loss program shall be implemented by the residential care facilities for the elderly within 90 days after January 1, 1989. The program shall include all of the following:
(a) Establishment and posting of the facility's policy regarding theft and investigative procedures.
(b) Orientation to the policies and procedures for all employees within 90 days of employment.
(c) Documentation of lost and stolen resident property with a value of twenty-five dollars ($25) or more within 72 hours of the discovery of the loss or theft and, upon request, the documented theft and loss record for the past 12 months shall be made available to the State Department of Social Services, law enforcement agencies and to the office of the State Long-Term Care Ombudsman in response to a specific complaint. The documentation shall include, but not be limited to, the following:
(1) A description of the article.
(2) Its estimated value.
(3) The date and time the theft or loss was discovered.
(4) If determinable, the date and time the loss or theft occurred.
(5) The action taken.
(d) A written resident personal property inventory is established upon admission and retained during the resident's stay in the residential care facility for the elderly. Inventories shall be written in ink, witnessed by the facility and the resident or resident's representative, and dated. A copy of the written inventory shall be provided to the resident or the person acting on the resident's behalf. All additions to an inventory shall be made in ink, and shall be witnessed by the facility and the resident or resident's representative, and dated. Subsequent items brought into or removed from the facility shall be added to or deleted from the personal property inventory by the facility at the written request of the resident, the resident's family, a responsible party, or a person acting on behalf of a resident. The facility shall not be liable for items which have not been requested to be included in the inventory or for items which have been deleted from the inventory. A copy of a current inventory shall be made available upon request to the resident, responsible party, or other authorized representative. The resident, resident's family, or a responsible party may list those items which are not subject to addition or deletion from the inventory, such as personal clothing or laundry, which are subject to frequent removal from the facility.
(e) Inventory and surrender of the resident's personal effects and valuables upon discharge to the resident or authorized representative in exchange for a signed receipt.
(f) Inventory and surrender of personal effects and valuables following the death of a resident to the authorized representative in exchange for a signed receipt. Immediate written notice to the public administrator of the county upon the death of a resident whose heirs are unable or unwilling to claim the property as specified in Chapter 20 (commencing with Section 1140) of Division 3 of the Probate Code.
(g) Documentation, at least semiannually, of the facility's efforts to control theft and loss, including the review of theft and loss documentation and investigative procedures and results of the investigation by the administrator and, when feasible, the resident council.
(h) Establishment of a method of marking, to the extent feasible, personal property items for identification purposes upon admission and, as added to the property inventory list, including engraving of dentures and tagging of other prosthetic devices.
(i) Reports to the local law enforcement agency within 36 hours when the administrator of the facility has reason to believe resident property with a then current value of one hundred dollars ($100) or more has been stolen. Copies of those reports for the preceding 12 months shall be made available to the State Department of Social Services and law enforcement agencies.
(j) Maintenance of a secured area for residents' property which is available for safekeeping of resident property upon the request of the resident or the resident's responsible party. Provide a lock for the resident's bedside drawer or cabinet upon request of and at the expense of the resident, the resident's family, or authorized representative. The facility administrator shall have access to the locked areas upon request.

(k) A copy of this section and Sections 1569.152 and 1569.154 is provided by a facility to all of the residents and their responsible parties, and, available upon request, to all of the facility's prospective residents and their responsible parties.
(l) Notification to all current residents and all new residents, upon admission, of the facility's policies and procedures relating to the facility's theft and loss prevention program.
(m) Only those residential units in which there are no unrelated residents and where the unit can be secured by the resident or residents are exempt from the requirements of this section.
(Added by Stats. 1988, Ch. 750, Sec. 3.)
1569.154.
No provision of a contract of admission, which includes all documents which a resident or his or her representative is required to sign at the time of, or as a condition of, admission to a residential care facility for the elderly, shall require or imply a lesser standard of responsibility for the personal property of residents than is required by law.
(Added by Stats. 1988, Ch. 750, Sec. 4.)
1569.155.
Upon initial licensure, residential care facilities for the elderly shall be provided a printed copy of all applicable regulations by the department, without charge. All licensees shall subscribe to the appropriate regulation subscription service and are responsible for keeping current on changes in regulatory requirements.
(Added by Stats. 1985, Ch. 1127, Sec. 3.)
1569.156.
(a) A residential care facility for the elderly shall do all of the following:
(1) Not condition the provision of care or otherwise discriminate based on whether or not an individual has executed an advance directive, consistent with applicable laws and regulations.
(2) Provide education to staff on issues concerning advance directives.
(3) Provide written information, upon admission, about the right to make decisions concerning medical care, including the right to accept or refuse medical or surgical treatment and the right, under state law, to formulate advance directives.
(4) Provide written information about policies of the facility regarding the implementation of the rights described in paragraph (3).
(b) For purposes of this section, "advance directive" means an "advance health care directive," as defined in Section 4605 of the Probate Code, or some other form of instruction recognized under state law specifically addressing the provision of health care.
(Amended by Stats. 1999, Ch. 658, Sec. 2. Effective January 1, 2000. Operative July 1, 2000, by Sec. 43 of Ch. 658.)
1569.157.
(a) Every licensed residential care facility for the elderly, at the request of two or more residents, shall assist the residents in establishing and maintaining a single resident council at the facility. The resident council shall be composed of residents of the facility. Family members, resident representatives, advocates, long-term care ombudsman program representatives, facility staff, or others may participate in resident council meetings and activities at the invitation of the resident council.
(b) A resident council may, among other things, make recommendations to facility administrators to improve the quality of daily living and care in the facility and to promote and protect residents' rights.
(c) If a resident council submits written concerns or recommendations, the facility shall respond in writing regarding any action or inaction taken in response to those concerns or recommendations within 14 calendar days.
(d) Facility policies on resident councils shall not limit the right of residents to meet independently with outside persons or facility personnel.
(e) Each resident council member shall be informed by the facility of his or her right to be interviewed as part of the regulatory inspection process.
(f) Facilities shall promote resident councils as follows:
(1) If a facility has a resident council, the facility shall inform new residents of the existence of the resident council. The facility shall also provide information on the time, place, and dates of resident council meetings and the resident representative to contact regarding involvement in the resident council.
(2) If a facility has a resident council and a licensed capacity of 16 or more, the facility shall appoint a designated staff liaison to assist the resident council, make a room available for resident council meetings, and post meeting information in a central location readily accessible to residents, relatives, and resident representatives.
(3) If a facility does not have a resident council, upon admission, the facility shall provide written information on the resident's right to form a resident council to the resident and the resident representative, as indicated in the admissions agreement.
(4) Upon request, and with the permission of the resident council, the facility shall share the name and contact information of the designated representative of the resident council with the long-term care ombudsman program.
(g) A facility shall not willfully interfere with the formation, maintenance, or promotion of a resident council, or its participation in the regulatory inspection process. For the purposes of this subdivision, willful interference shall include, but not be limited to, discrimination or retaliation in any way against an individual as a result of his or her participation in a resident council, refusal to publicize resident council meetings or provide appropriate space for either meetings or a bulletin board, or failure to respond to written requests by the resident council in a timely manner.
(h) The text of this section with the heading "Rights of Resident Councils" shall be posted in a prominent place at the facility accessible to residents, family members, and resident representatives.

(i) A violation of this section shall not be subject to the provisions of Section 1569.40. A violation of this section shall constitute a violation of resident rights. A facility that violates this section shall be subject to a daily civil penalty of two hundred fifty dollars ($250) until the violation is corrected. A violation shall be deemed to have been corrected on the date the facility submits documentation of the correction to the department if the correction is verified by the department.
(Amended by Stats. 2014, Ch. 177, Sec. 1. (AB 1572) Effective January 1, 2015.)
1569.158.
(a) A residential care facility for the elderly shall not prohibit the formation of a family council. When requested by a member of the resident's family or the resident representative, a family council shall be allowed to meet in a common meeting room of the facility during mutually agreed upon hours.
(b) Facility policies on family councils shall in no way limit the right of residents and participants in a family council to meet independently with outside persons, including members of nonprofit or government organizations or with facility personnel during nonworking hours.
(c) "Family council" for the purpose of this section means a meeting of family members, friends, representatives, or agents as defined in Section 14110.8 of the Welfare and Institutions Code of two or more residents to confer in private without facility staff.
(d) Family councils shall be provided adequate space on a prominent bulletin board or other posting area for the display of meeting notices, minutes, information, and newsletters.
(e) Facility personnel or visitors may attend a family council meeting only at the family council's invitation.
(f) If a family council submits written concerns or recommendations, the facility shall respond in writing regarding any action or inaction taken in response to the concerns or recommendations within 14 calendar days.
(g) (1) If a facility has a family council, the facility shall include notice of the family council and its meetings to family members and resident representatives in routine mailings and shall inform family members and resident representatives of new and current residents who are identified on the admissions agreement during the admissions process or in the resident's records, of the existence of the family council, the time and place of meetings of the family council, and the name of the family council representative.
(2) If a facility does not have a family council, the facility shall provide, upon admission of a new resident, written information to the resident's family or resident representative of their right to form a family council.
(3) Upon request, and with the permission of the family council, the facility shall share the name and contact information of the designated representative of the family council with the long-term care ombudsman program.
(h) If a facility has a family council and a licensed capacity of 16 or more, the facility shall appoint a designated staff liaison who shall be responsible for providing assistance to the family council and responding to written requests that result from family council meetings.
(i) A facility shall not willfully interfere with the formation, maintenance, or promotion of a family council, or its participation in the regulatory inspection process. For the purposes of this subdivision, willful interference shall include, but shall not be limited to, discrimination or retaliation in any way against an individual as a result of his or her participation in a family council, refusal to publicize family council meetings or provide appropriate space for meetings or postings as required under this section, or failure to respond to written requests by a family council in a timely manner.
(j) A violation of this section shall not be subject to the provisions of Section 1569.40. A violation of this section shall constitute a violation of resident rights. A facility that violates this section shall be subject to a daily civil penalty of two hundred fifty dollars ($250) until the violation is corrected. A violation shall be deemed to have been corrected on the date the facility submits documentation of the correction to the department if the correction is verified by the department.
(Amended by Stats. 2014, Ch. 177, Sec. 2. (AB 1572) Effective January 1, 2015.)
1569.159.
The State Department of Social Services shall provide to residential care facilities for the elderly a form, which the residential care facility for the elderly shall attach to each resident admission agreement, notifying the resident that he or she is entitled to obtain services and equipment from the telephone company. The form shall include the following information:
"Any hearing or speech impaired, or otherwise disabled resident of any residential care facility for the elderly is entitled to equipment and service by the telephone company, pursuant to Section 2881 of the Public Utilities Code, to improve the quality of their telecommunications. Any resident who has a declaration from a licensed professional, or a state or federal agency pursuant to Section 2881 of the Public Utilities Code, that he or she is hearing or speech impaired, or otherwise disabled should contact the local telephone company and ask for assistance in obtaining this equipment and service."
This section shall not be construed to require, in any way, the licensee to provide a separate telephone line for any resident.
(Added by Stats. 1996, Ch. 448, Sec. 2. Effective January 1, 1997.)
1569.16.
(a) (1) If an application for a license indicates, or the department determines during the application review process, that the applicant previously was issued a license under this chapter or under Chapter 1 (commencing with Section 1200), Chapter 2 (commencing with Section 1250), Chapter 3 (commencing with Section 1500), Chapter 3.01 (commencing with Section 1568.01), Chapter 3.4 (commencing with Section 1596.70), Chapter 3.5 (commencing with Section 1596.90), or Chapter 3.6 (commencing with Section 1597.30) and the prior license was revoked within the preceding two years, the department shall cease any further review of the application until two years have elapsed from the date of the revocation. All residential care facilities for the elderly are exempt from the health planning requirements contained in Part 2 (commencing with Section 127125) of Division 107.
(2) If an application for a license or special permit indicates, or the department determines during the application review process, that the applicant previously was issued a certificate of approval by a foster family agency that was revoked by the department pursuant to subdivision (b) of Section 1534 within the preceding two years, the department shall cease any further review of the application until two years shall have elapsed from the date of the revocation.
(3) If an application for a license or special permit indicates, or the department determines during the application review process, that the applicant was excluded from a facility licensed by the department pursuant to Section 1558, 1568.092, 1569.58, or 1596.8897, the department shall cease any further review of the application unless the excluded individual has been reinstated pursuant to Section 11522 of the Government Code by the department.
(b) If an application for a license or special permit indicates, or the department determines during the application review process, that the applicant had previously applied for a license under any of the chapters listed in paragraph (1) of subdivision (a) and the application was denied within the last year, the department shall, except as provided in Section 1569.22, cease further review of the application until one year has elapsed from the date of the denial letter. In those circumstances where denials are appealed and upheld at an administrative hearing, review of the application shall cease for one year from the date of the decision and order being rendered by the department. The cessation of review shall not constitute a denial of the application. If there are coapplicants and the department denies a license due to concerns pertaining solely to one of the coapplicants, any other coapplicant may withdraw its application, and with the department's written consent pursuant to Section 1569.52, shall not be deemed to have a license application denied.
(c) If an application for a license or special permit indicates, or the department determines during the application review process, that the applicant had previously applied for a certificate of approval with a foster family agency and the department ordered the foster family agency to deny the application pursuant to subdivision (b) of Section 1534, the department shall cease further review of the application as follows:
(1) In cases where the applicant petitioned for a hearing, the department shall cease further review of the application until one year has elapsed from the effective date of the decision and order of the department upholding a denial.
(2) In cases where the department informed the applicant of his or her right to petition for a hearing and the applicant did not petition for a hearing, the department shall cease further review of the application until one year has elapsed from the date of the notification of the denial and the right to petition for a hearing.
(3) The department may continue to review the application if it has determined that the reasons for the denial of the application were due to circumstances and conditions that either have been corrected or are no longer in existence.
(d) The cessation of review shall not constitute a denial of the application for purposes of Section 1526 or any other law.
(Amended by Stats. 2015, Ch. 628, Sec. 3. (AB 601) Effective January 1, 2016.)
1569.17.
The Legislature recognizes the need to generate timely and accurate positive fingerprint identification of applicants as a condition of issuing licenses, permits, or certificates of approval for persons to operate or provide direct care services in a residential care facility for the elderly. It is the intent of the Legislature in enacting this section to require the fingerprints of those individuals whose contact with clients of residential care facilities for the elderly may pose a risk to the clients' health and safety. An individual shall be required to obtain either a criminal record clearance or a criminal record exemption from the State Department of Social Services before his or her initial presence in a residential care facility for the elderly.
(a) (1) Before and, as applicable, subsequent to issuing a license to any person or persons to operate or manage a residential care facility for the elderly, the department shall secure from an appropriate law enforcement agency a criminal record to determine whether the applicant or any other person specified in subdivision (b) has ever been convicted of a crime other than a minor traffic violation or arrested for any crime specified in subdivision (c) of Section 290 of the Penal Code, or for violating Section 245, 273ab, or 273.5, subdivision (b) of Section 273a, or, prior to January 1, 1994, paragraph (2) of Section 273a, of the Penal Code, or for any crime for which the department is prohibited from granting a criminal record exemption pursuant to subdivision (f).
(2) The criminal history information shall include the full criminal record, if any, of those persons, and subsequent arrest information pursuant to Section 11105.2 of the Penal Code.
(3) The following shall apply to the criminal record information:
(A) If the State Department of Social Services finds that the applicant or any other person specified in subdivision (b) has been convicted of a crime, other than a minor traffic violation, the application or presence shall be denied, unless the director grants an exemption pursuant to subdivision (f).
(B) If the State Department of Social Services finds that the applicant, or any other person specified in subdivision (b), is awaiting trial for a crime other than a minor traffic violation, the State Department of Social Services may cease processing the criminal record information until the conclusion of the trial.

(C) If no criminal record information has been recorded, the Department of Justice shall provide the applicant and the State Department of Social Services with a statement of that fact.
(D) If the State Department of Social Services finds after licensure that the licensee, or any other person specified in paragraph (2) of subdivision (b), has been convicted of a crime other than a minor traffic violation, the license may be revoked, unless the director grants an exemption pursuant to subdivision (f).
(E) An applicant and any other person specified in subdivision (b) shall submit fingerprint images and related information to the Department of Justice and the Federal Bureau of Investigation, through the Department of Justice, for a state and federal level criminal offender record information search, in addition to the search required by subdivision (a). If an applicant meets all other conditions for licensure, except receipt of the Federal Bureau of Investigation's criminal history information for the applicant and persons listed in subdivision (b), the department may issue a license if the applicant and each person described by subdivision (b) has signed and submitted a statement that he or she has never been convicted of a crime in the United States, other than a traffic infraction as defined in paragraph (1) of subdivision (a) of Section 42001 of the Vehicle Code. If, after licensure, the department determines that the licensee or person specified in subdivision (b) has a criminal record, the license may be revoked pursuant to Section 1569.50. The department may also suspend the license pending an administrative hearing pursuant to Sections 1569.50 and 1569.51.
(b) In addition to the applicant, the provisions of this section shall apply to criminal record clearances and exemptions for the following persons:
(1) (A) Adults responsible for administration or direct supervision of staff.
(B) Any person, other than a client, residing in the facility. Residents of unlicensed independent senior housing facilities that are located in contiguous buildings on the same property as a residential care facility for the elderly shall be exempt from these requirements.
(C) Any person who provides client assistance in dressing, grooming, bathing, or personal hygiene. Any nurse assistant or home health aide meeting the requirements of Section 1338.5 or 1736.6, respectively, who is not employed, retained, or contracted by the licensee, and who has been certified or recertified on or after July 1, 1998, shall be deemed to meet the criminal record clearance requirements of this section. A certified nurse assistant and certified home health aide who will be providing client assistance and who falls under this exemption shall provide one copy of his or her current certification, prior to providing care, to the residential care facility for the elderly. The facility shall maintain the copy of the certification on file as long as the care is being provided by the certified nurse assistant or certified home health aide at the facility. Nothing in this paragraph restricts the right of the department to exclude a certified nurse assistant or certified home health aide from a licensed residential care facility for the elderly pursuant to Section 1569.58.
(D) Any staff person, volunteer, or employee who has contact with the clients.
(E) If the applicant is a firm, partnership, association, or corporation, the chief executive officer or other person serving in a similar capacity.
(F) Additional officers of the governing body of the applicant or other persons with a financial interest in the applicant, as determined necessary by the department by regulation. The criteria used in the development of these regulations shall be based on the person's capability to exercise substantial influence over the operation of the facility.
(2) The following persons are exempt from requirements applicable under paragraph (1):
(A) A spouse, relative, significant other, or close friend of a client shall be exempt if this person is visiting the client or provides direct care and supervision to that client only.
(B) A volunteer to whom all of the following apply:
(i) The volunteer is at the facility during normal waking hours.
(ii) The volunteer is directly supervised by the licensee or a facility employee with a criminal record clearance or exemption.
(iii) The volunteer spends no more than 16 hours per week at the facility.
(iv) The volunteer does not provide clients with assistance in dressing, grooming, bathing, or personal hygiene.
(v) The volunteer is not left alone with clients in care.
(C) A third-party contractor retained by the facility if the contractor is not left alone with clients in care.
(D) A third-party contractor or other business professional retained by a client and at the facility at the request or by permission of that client. These individuals shall not be left alone with other clients.
(E) Licensed or certified medical professionals are exempt from fingerprint and criminal background check requirements imposed by community care licensing. This exemption does not apply to a person who is a community care facility licensee or an employee of the facility.
(F) Employees of licensed home health agencies and members of licensed hospice interdisciplinary teams who have contact with a resident of a residential care facility at the request of the resident or resident's legal decisionmaker are exempt from fingerprint and criminal background check requirements imposed by community care licensing. This exemption does not apply to a person who is a community care facility licensee or an employee of the facility.
(G) Clergy and other spiritual caregivers who are performing services in common areas of the residential care facility, or who are advising an individual resident at the request of, or with permission of, the resident, are exempt from fingerprint and criminal background check requirements imposed by community care licensing. This exemption does not apply to a person who is a community care facility licensee or an employee of the facility.
(H) Any person similar to those described in this subdivision, as defined by the department in regulations.
(I) Nothing in this paragraph shall prevent a licensee from requiring a criminal record clearance of any individual exempt from the requirements of this section, provided that the individual has client contact.
(c) (1) (A) Subsequent to initial licensure, a person specified in subdivision (b) who is not exempted from fingerprinting shall obtain either a criminal record clearance or an exemption, pursuant to subdivision (f), from the State Department of Social Services prior to employment, residence, or initial presence in a facility. A person specified in subdivision (b) who is not exempt from fingerprinting shall be fingerprinted and shall sign a declaration under penalty of perjury regarding any prior criminal convictions. The licensee shall submit these fingerprint images and related information to the Department of Justice and the Federal Bureau of Investigation, through the Department of Justice, for a state and federal level criminal offender record information search, or to comply with paragraph (1) of subdivision (g) prior to the person's employment, residence, or initial presence in the residential care facility for the elderly.
(B) These fingerprint images and related information shall be electronically transmitted in a manner approved by the State Department of Social Services and the Department of Justice. A licensee's failure to submit fingerprint images and related information to the Department of Justice, or to comply with paragraph (1) of subdivision (g), as required in this section, shall result in the citation of a deficiency and an immediate assessment of civil penalties in the amount of one hundred dollars ($100) per violation per day for a maximum of five days, unless the violation is a second or subsequent violation within a 12-month period in which case the civil penalties shall be in the amount of one hundred dollars ($100) per violation for a maximum of 30 days, and shall be grounds for disciplining the licensee pursuant to Section 1569.50. The State Department of Social Services may assess civil penalties for continued violations as permitted by Section 1569.49. The licensee shall then submit these fingerprint images to the State Department of Social Services for processing. Documentation of the individual's clearance or exemption shall be maintained by the licensee and be available for inspection. The Department of Justice shall notify the department, as required by Section 1522.04, and notify the licensee by mail within 14 days of electronic transmission of the fingerprints to the Department of Justice, if the person has no criminal record. A violation of the regulations adopted pursuant to Section 1522.04 shall result in the citation of a deficiency and an immediate assessment of civil penalties in the amount of one hundred dollars ($100) per violation per day for a maximum of five days, unless the violation is a second or subsequent violation within a 12-month period in which case the civil penalties shall be in the amount of one hundred dollars ($100) per violation for a maximum of 30 days, and shall be grounds for disciplining the licensee pursuant to Section 1569.50. The department may assess civil penalties for continued violations as permitted by Section 1569.49.
(2) Within 14 calendar days of the receipt of the fingerprint images, the Department of Justice shall notify the State Department of Social Services of the criminal record information, as provided for in this subdivision. If no criminal record information has been recorded, the Department of Justice shall provide the licensee and the State Department of Social Services with a statement of that fact within 14 calendar days of receipt of the fingerprint images. If new fingerprint images are required for processing, the Department of Justice shall, within 14 calendar days from the date of receipt of the fingerprint images, notify the licensee that the fingerprint images were illegible.
(3) Except for persons specified in paragraph (2) of subdivision (b), the licensee shall endeavor to ascertain the previous employment history of persons required to be fingerprinted under this subdivision. If the State Department of Social Services determines, on the basis of the fingerprint images submitted to the Department of Justice, that the person has been convicted of a sex offense against a minor, an offense specified in Section 243.4, 273a, 273ab, 273d, 273g, or 368 of the Penal Code, or a felony, the State Department of Social Services shall notify the licensee in writing within 15 calendar days of the receipt of the notification from the Department of Justice to act immediately to terminate the person's employment, remove the person from the residential care facility for the elderly, or bar the person from entering the residential care facility for the elderly. The State Department of Social Services may subsequently grant an exemption pursuant to subdivision (f). If the conviction was for another crime, except a minor traffic violation, the licensee shall, upon notification by the State Department of Social Services, act immediately to either (1) terminate the person's employment, remove the person from the residential care facility for the elderly, or bar the person from entering the residential care facility for the elderly or (2) seek an exemption pursuant to subdivision (f). The department shall determine if the person shall be allowed to remain in the facility until a decision on the exemption is rendered by the department. A licensee's failure to comply with the department's prohibition of employment, contact with clients, or presence in the facility as required by this paragraph shall result in a citation of deficiency and an immediate assessment of civil penalties by the department against the licensee, in the amount of one hundred dollars ($100) per violation per day for a maximum of five days, unless the violation is a second or subsequent violation within a 12-month period in which case the civil penalties shall be in the amount of one hundred dollars ($100) per violation for a maximum of 30 days, and shall be grounds for disciplining the licensee pursuant to Section 1569.50.
(4) The department may issue an exemption on its own motion pursuant to subdivision (f) if the person's criminal history indicates that the person is of good character based on the age, seriousness, and frequency of the conviction or convictions. The department, in consultation with interested parties, shall develop regulations to establish the criteria to grant an exemption pursuant to this paragraph.

(5) Concurrently with notifying the licensee pursuant to paragraph (4), the department shall notify the affected individual of his or her right to seek an exemption pursuant to subdivision (f). The individual may seek an exemption only if the licensee terminates the person's employment or removes the person from the facility after receiving notice from the department pursuant to paragraph (4).

(d) (1) For purposes of this section or any other provision of this chapter, a conviction means a plea or verdict of guilty or a conviction following a plea of nolo contendere. Any action that the department is permitted to take following the establishment of a conviction may be taken when the time for appeal has elapsed, when the judgment of conviction has been affirmed on appeal or when an order granting probation is made suspending the imposition of the sentence, notwithstanding a subsequent order pursuant to the provisions of Sections 1203.4 and 1203.4a of the Penal Code permitting a person to withdraw his or her plea of guilty and to enter a plea of not guilty, or setting aside the verdict of guilty, or dismissing the accusation, information, or indictment. For purposes of this section or any other provision of this chapter, the record of a conviction, or a copy thereof certified by the clerk of the court or by a judge of the court in which the conviction occurred, shall be conclusive evidence of the conviction. For purposes of this section or any other provision of this chapter, the arrest disposition report certified by the Department of Justice or documents admissible in a criminal action pursuant to Section 969b of the Penal Code shall be prima facie evidence of the conviction, notwithstanding any other law prohibiting the admission of these documents in a civil or administrative action.

(2) For purposes of this section or any other provision of this chapter, the department shall consider criminal convictions from another state or federal court as if the criminal offense was committed in this state.

(e) (1) The State Department of Social Services shall not use a record of arrest to deny, revoke, or terminate any application, license, employment, or residence unless the department investigates the incident and secures evidence, whether or not related to the incident of arrest, that is admissible in an administrative hearing to establish conduct by the person that may pose a risk to the health and safety of any person who is or may become a client.

(2) The department shall not issue a criminal record clearance to a person who has been arrested for any crime specified in Section 290 of the Penal Code, or for violating Section 245, 273ab, or 273.5, or subdivision (b) of Section 273a of the Penal Code, or, prior to January 1, 1994, paragraph (2) of Section 273a of the Penal Code, or for any crime for which the department is prohibited from granting a record exemption pursuant to subdivision (f), prior to the department's completion of an investigation pursuant to paragraph (1).

(3) The State Department of Social Services is authorized to obtain any arrest or conviction records or reports from any law enforcement agency as necessary to the performance of its duties to inspect, license, and investigate community care facilities and individuals associated with a community care facility.

(f) (1) After review of the record, the director may grant an exemption from disqualification for a license as specified in paragraphs (1) and (4) of subdivision (a), or for employment, residence, or presence in a residential care facility for the elderly as specified in paragraphs (4), (5), and (6) of subdivision (c) if the director has substantial and convincing evidence to support a reasonable belief that the applicant and the person convicted of the crime, if other than the applicant, are of such good character as to justify issuance of the license or special permit or granting an exemption for purposes of subdivision (c). However, an exemption shall not be granted pursuant to this subdivision if the conviction was for any of the following offenses:

(A) An offense specified in Section 220, 243.4, or 264.1, subdivision (a) of Section 273a, or, prior to January 1, 1994, paragraph (1) of Section 273a, Section 273ab, 273d, 288, or 289, subdivision (c) of Section 290, or Section 368, of the Penal Code, or was a conviction of another crime against an individual specified in subdivision (c) of Section 667.5 of the Penal Code.

(B) A felony offense specified in Section 729 of the Business and Professions Code or Section 206 or 215, subdivision (a) of Section 347, subdivision (b) of Section 417, or subdivision (a) of Section 451 of the Penal Code.

(2) The director shall notify in writing to the licensee or the applicant of his or her decision within 60 days of receipt of all information from the applicant and other sources determined necessary by the director for the rendering of a decision pursuant to this subdivision.

(3) The department shall not prohibit a person from being employed or having contact with clients in a facility on the basis of a denied criminal record exemption request or arrest information unless the department complies with the requirements of Section 1569.58.

(g) (1) For purposes of compliance with this section, the department may permit an individual to transfer a current criminal record clearance, as defined in subdivision (a), from one facility to another, as long as the criminal record clearance has been processed through a state licensing district office, and is being transferred to another facility licensed by a state licensing district office. The request shall be submitted in writing to the department, and shall include a copy of the person's driver's license or valid identification card issued by the Department of Motor Vehicles, or a valid photo identification issued by another state or the United States government if the person is not a California resident. Upon request of the licensee, who shall enclose a self-addressed stamped envelope for this purpose, the department shall verify whether the individual has a clearance that can be transferred.

(2) The State Department of Social Services shall hold criminal record clearances in its active files for a minimum of two years after an employee is no longer employed at a licensed facility in order for the criminal record clearances to be transferred under this section.

(h) If a licensee or facility is required by law to deny employment or to terminate employment of any employee based on written notification from the department that the employee has a prior criminal conviction or is determined unsuitable for employment under Section 1569.58, the licensee or facility shall not incur civil liability or unemployment insurance liability as a result of that denial or termination.

(i) Notwithstanding any other law, the department may provide an individual with a copy of his or her state or federal level criminal offender record information search response as provided to that department by the Department of Justice if the department has denied a criminal background clearance based on this information and the individual makes a written request to the department for a copy specifying an address to which it is to be sent. The state or federal level criminal offender record information search response shall not be modified or altered from its form or content as provided by the Department of Justice and shall be provided to the address specified by the individual in his or her written request. The department shall retain a copy of the individual's written request and the response and date provided.

(Amended by Stats. 2014, Ch. 824, Sec. 3. (AB 2632) Effective January 1, 2015.)

1569.171.

Prior to issuance to any person of a certificate of completion of the administrator certification program pursuant to Section 1569.616, the department shall secure from an appropriate law enforcement agency a criminal record to determine if the person has been convicted of a crime other than a minor traffic violation. Based upon the criminal record information received, the department shall take appropriate action as provided for in Section 1569.17.

(Added by Stats. 1991, Ch. 848, Sec. 1.)

1569.172.

The Department of Justice may charge a fee sufficient to cover its cost in providing services in accordance with Section 1569.17 to comply with the 14-day requirement for provision to the department of the criminal record information, as contained in subdivision (c) of Section 1569.17.

(Amended by Stats. 1998, Ch. 311, Sec. 38. Effective August 19, 1998.)

1569.175.

(a) In addition to any other requirements of this chapter, any residential care facility for the elderly providing residential care for six or fewer persons at which the owner does not reside shall provide a procedure approved by the licensing agency for immediate response to incidents and complaints. This procedure shall include a method of assuring that the owner, licensee, or person designated by the owner or licensee is notified of the incident, that the owner, licensee, or person designated by the owner or licensee has personally investigated the matter, and that the person making the complaint or reporting the incident has received a response of action taken or a reason why no action needs to be taken.

(b) In order to assure the opportunity for complaints to be made directly to the owner, licensee, or person designated by the owner or licensee, and to provide the opportunity for the owner, licensee, or person designated by the owner or licensee to meet residents and learn of problems in the neighborhood, any facility with a nonresident owner shall establish a fixed time on a weekly basis when the owner, licensee, or person designated by the owner or licensee will be present.

(c) Facilities with nonresident owners shall establish procedures to comply with the requirements of this section on or before July 1, 1987.

(Added by Stats. 1986, Ch. 822, Sec. 2.)

1569.185.

(a) (1) An application fee adjusted by facility and capacity shall be charged by the department for the issuance of a license to operate a residential care facility for the elderly. After initial licensure, a fee shall be charged by the department annually on each anniversary of the effective date of the license.

The fees are for the purpose of financing activities specified in this chapter. Fees shall be assessed as follows, subject to paragraph (2):

Fee Schedule		
Capacity	Initial Application	Annual
1–3	$495.60	$495.60
4–6	$990.00	$495.60
7–15	$1,486.80	$742.80
16–30	$1,980.00	$990.00

31–49	$2,476.80	$1,238.40
50–74	$2,972.40	$1,448.00
75–100	$3,469.20	$1,734.00
101–150	$3,964.80	$1,982.40
151–200	$4,622.40	$2,311.20
201–250	$5,280.00	$2,640.00
251–300	$5,940.00	$2,970.00
301–350	$6,600.00	$3,300.00
351–400	$7,260.00	$3,630.00
401–500	$8,580.00	$4,290.00
501–600	$9,900.00	$4,950.00
601–700	$11,220.00	$5,610.00
701+	$13,200.00	$6,600.00

(2) (A) The Legislature finds that all revenues generated by fees for licenses computed under this section and used for the purposes for which they were imposed are not subject to Article XIII B of the California Constitution.

(B) The department, at least every five years, shall analyze initial application fees and annual fees issued by it to ensure the appropriate fee amounts are charged. The department shall recommend to the Legislature that fees established by the Legislature be adjusted as necessary to ensure that the amounts are appropriate.

(b) (1) In addition to fees set forth in subdivision (a), the department shall charge all of the following fees:

(A) A fee that represents 50 percent of an established application fee when an existing licensee moves the facility to a new physical address.

(B) A fee that represents 50 percent of the established application fee when a corporate licensee changes who has the authority to select a majority of the board of directors.

(C) A fee of twenty-five dollars ($25) when an existing licensee seeks to either increase or decrease the licensed capacity of the facility.

(D) An orientation fee of fifty dollars ($50) for attendance by an individual at a department-sponsored orientation session.

(E) A probation monitoring fee equal to the current annual fee, in addition to the current annual fee for that category and capacity for each year a license has been placed on probation as a result of a stipulation or decision and order pursuant to the administrative adjudication procedures of the Administrative Procedure Act (Chapter 4.5 (commencing with Section 11400) and Chapter 5 (commencing with Section 11500) of Part 1 of Division 3 of Title 2 of the Government Code).

(F) A late fee that represents an additional 50 percent of the established current annual fee when a licensee fails to pay the current annual licensing fee on or before the due date as indicated by postmark on the payment.

(G) A fee to cover any costs incurred by the department for processing payments including, but not limited to, bounced check charges, charges for credit and debit transactions, and postage due charges.

(H) A plan of correction fee of two hundred dollars ($200) when a licensee does not implement a plan of correction on or prior to the date specified in the plan.

(2) A local jurisdiction shall not impose a business license, fee, or tax for the privilege of operating a facility licensed under this chapter that serves six or fewer persons.

(c) (1) The revenues collected from licensing fees pursuant to this section shall be utilized by the department for the purpose of ensuring the health and safety of all individuals provided care or supervision by licensees and to support the activities of the licensing programs, including, but not limited to, monitoring facilities for compliance with licensing laws and regulations pursuant to this chapter, and other administrative activities in support of the licensing program, when appropriated for these purposes. The revenues collected shall be used in addition to any other funds appropriated in the annual Budget Act in support of the licensing program. The department shall adjust the fees collected pursuant to this section to ensure that they do not exceed the costs described in this paragraph.

(2) The department shall not utilize any portion of these revenues sooner than 30 days after notification in writing of the purpose and use, as approved by the Department of Finance, to the Chairperson of the Joint Legislative Budget Committee, and the chairpersons of the committee in each house that considers appropriations for each fiscal year. The department shall submit a budget change proposal to justify any positions or any other related support costs on an ongoing basis.

(d) A residential care facility for the elderly may use a bona fide business check to pay the license fee required under this section.

(e) The failure of an applicant for licensure or a licensee to pay all applicable and accrued fees and civil penalties shall constitute grounds for denial or forfeiture of a license.
(Amended by Stats. 2014, Ch. 707, Sec. 2. (SB 1382) Effective January 1, 2015.)
1569.19.
A license shall be forfeited by operation of law prior to its expiration date when one of the following occurs:

(a) The licensee sells or otherwise transfers the facility or facility property, except when change of ownership applies to transferring of stock when the facility is owned by a corporation and when the transfer of stock does not constitute a majority change in ownership. The sale of a facility shall be subject to the requirements of this chapter.

(b) The licensee surrenders the license to the department.

(c) The licensee moves a facility from one location to another. The department shall develop regulations to ensure that the facilities are not charged a full licensing fee and do not have to complete the entire application process when applying for a license for the new location.

(d) The licensee is convicted of an offense specified in Section 220, 243.4, or 264.1, or paragraph (1) of Section 273a, Section 273d, 288, or 289 of the Penal Code, or is convicted of another crime specified in subdivision (c) of Section 667.5 of the Penal Code.

(e) The licensee dies. When a licensee dies, the continued operation shall be subject to the requirements of Section 1569.193.

(f) The licensee abandons the facility. A licensee who abandons the facility and the residents in care resulting in an immediate and substantial threat to the health and safety of the abandoned residents, in addition to forfeiture of the license pursuant to this section, shall be excluded from licensure in facilities licensed by the department without the right to petition for reinstatement.
(Amended by Stats. 2014, Ch. 700, Sec. 1. (AB 1899) Effective January 1, 2015.)
1569.191.

(a) Notwithstanding Section 1569.19, in the event of a sale of a licensed facility where the sale will result in a new license being issued, the sale and transfer of property and business shall be subject to both of the following:

(1) The licensee shall provide written notice to the department and to each resident or his or her legal representative of the licensee's intent to sell the facility at least 30 days prior to the transfer of the property or business, or at the time that a bona fide offer is made, whichever period is longer.

(2) The licensee shall, prior to entering into an admission agreement, inform all residents, or their legal representatives, admitted to the facility after notification to the department, of the licensee's intent to sell the property or business.

(b) Except as provided in subdivision (e), the property and business shall not be transferred until the buyer qualifies for a license or provisional license within the appropriate provisions of this chapter.

(1) The seller shall notify, in writing, a prospective buyer of the necessity to obtain a license, as required by this chapter, if the buyer's intent is to continue operating the facility as a residential care facility for the elderly. The seller shall send a copy of this written notice to the licensing agency.

(2) The prospective buyer shall submit an application for a license, as specified in Section 1569.15, within five days of the acceptance of the offer by the seller.

(c) No sale of the facility shall be permitted until 30 days have elapsed from the date upon which notice has been provided pursuant to paragraphs (1) and (2) of subdivision (a).

(d) The department shall give priority to applications for licensure that are submitted pursuant to this section in order to ensure timely transfer of the property and business. The department shall make a decision within 60 days after a complete application is submitted on whether to issue a license pursuant to Section 1569.15.

(e) If the parties involved in the transfer of the property and business fully comply with this section, then the transfer may be completed and the buyer shall not be considered to be operating an unlicensed facility while the department makes a final determination on the application for licensure.

(f) Facilities that are subject to Chapter 10 (commencing with Section 1770) of Division 2, including Section 1789.4, shall not be subject to paragraph (1) of subdivision (a), and subdivisions (c) and (d).

(Amended by Stats. 1993, Ch. 526, Sec. 2. Effective January 1, 1994.)

1569.193.

(a) When a licensee dies, an adult relative, or other nonrelated adult, who has control of the property may be designated as the responsible party to continue operation of the facility if the following conditions are met:

(1) The licensee has filed a notarized written statement with the department designating the responsible party in the event of death, and the licensee has submitted the following information to the department:

(A) A notarized statement, signed by the designee acknowledging acceptance of designation as responsible party.

(B) A declaration signed by the designee under penalty of perjury regarding any prior criminal convictions.

(2) The designee files an application for licensure pursuant to Section 1569.15 within 20 working days of the date of death, shows evidence satisfactory to the department that he or she has the ability to operate the facility, and provides evidence of the licensee's death.

(b) A designee under this section shall notify the department of the licensee's death by the close of business on the department's next business day following the licensee's death.

(c) (1) If the designee decides not to apply for licensure, he or she shall notify the department of that decision within five working days of the licensee's death. If the designee decides not to apply, the department shall assist the designee in the development and implementation of a relocation plan.

(2) If the designee decides to apply for licensure, the department shall decide within 60 days after the application is submitted whether to issue a provisional license pursuant to Section 1569.21. A provisional license shall be granted only if the department is satisfied that the conditions specified in subdivision (a) have been met and that the health and safety of the residents of the facility will not be jeopardized.

(d) If the designee complies with this section, he or she shall not be considered to be operating an unlicensed facility while the department decides whether to grant the provisional license.

(Amended by Stats. 1998, Ch. 179, Sec. 1. Effective January 1, 1999.)

1569.194.

(a) Every residential care facility for the elderly that is licensed or has a valid special permit therefor pursuant to Section 1569.10 shall provide a copy of the disaster and mass casualty plan required pursuant to Section 87223 of Title 22 of the California Code of Regulations to any fire department, law enforcement agency, or civil defense or other disaster authority in the area or community in which the facility is located, upon request by the fire department, law enforcement agency, or civil defense or other disaster authority. Section 1569.40 shall not apply to this section.

(b) The department is not required to monitor compliance with this section as part of its regulatory monitoring functions.

(Added by Stats. 2007, Ch. 18, Sec. 2. Effective January 1, 2008.)

1569.20.

Upon the filing of the application for issuance of an initial license, the department shall, within five working days of the filing, make a determination regarding the completeness of the application. If the application is complete, the department shall immediately request a fire clearance and notify the applicant to arrange a time for the department to conduct a prelicensure inspection. If the department determines that an application is for licensure of a currently licensed facility for which there is no material change to the management or operations of the facility, the prelicensure inspection is optional at the discretion of the department. If the application is incomplete, the department shall notify the applicant and request the necessary information. Within 60 days of making a determination that the file is complete, the department shall make a determination whether the application is in compliance with this chapter and the rules and regulations of the department and shall either immediately issue the license or notify the applicant of the deficiencies. The notice shall specify whether the deficiencies constitute denial of the application or whether further corrections for compliance will likely result in approval of the application.

(Amended by Stats. 2014, Ch. 29, Sec. 22. (SB 855) Effective June 20, 2014.)

1569.21.

The director may issue provisional licenses to operate residential care facilities for the elderly for the facilities which the director determines are in substantial compliance with this chapter and the rules and regulations adopted pursuant thereto; provided, that no life safety risks are involved, as determined by the director. In determining whether any life safety risks are involved, the director shall require completion of all applicable fire clearances and criminal record clearances as otherwise required by the department's rules and regulations. This provisional license shall expire six months from the date of issuance, or at such earlier time as the director may determine, and may not be renewed. However, the director may extend the term of a provisional license for an additional six months at time of application, if it is determined that more than six months will be required to achieve full compliance with licensing standards due to circumstances beyond the control of the applicant; provided, that all other requirements for a license have been met.

(Added by Stats. 1985, Ch. 1127, Sec. 3.)

1569.22.

Immediately upon the denial of any application for a license, the department shall notify the applicant in writing. Within 15 days after the department mails the notice, the applicant may present his or her written petition for a hearing to the department. Upon receipt by the department of the petition in proper form, the petition shall be set for hearing. The proceedings shall be conducted in accordance with Chapter 5 (commencing with Section 11500) of Part 1 of Division 3 of Title 2 of the Government Code, and the department has all the powers granted therein.

(Added by Stats. 1985, Ch. 1127, Sec. 3.)

1569.23.

(a) As a requirement for licensure, the applicant shall demonstrate that he or she has successfully completed a certification program approved by the department.

(b) The certification program shall consist of both of the following:

(1) Eighty hours of coursework, at least 60 hours of which shall be attended in person.

(2) A state-administered examination consisting of no less than 100 questions. The examination shall reflect the uniform core of knowledge required pursuant to subdivision (c).

(c) The certification program shall include a uniform core of knowledge which shall include all of the following:

(1) Law, including regulations, policies, and procedural standards that impact the operations of residential care facilities for the elderly.

(2) Business operations.

(3) Management and supervision of staff.

(4) Psychosocial need of the elderly residents.

(5) Physical needs for elderly residents.

(6) Community and support services.

(7) Medication management, including use, misuse, and interaction of drugs commonly used by the elderly, including antipsychotics, and the adverse effects of psychotropic drugs for use in controlling the behavior of persons with dementia.

(8) Resident admission, retention, and assessment procedures.

(9) Managing Alzheimer's disease and related dementias, including nonpharmacologic, person-centered approaches to dementia care.

(10) Managing the physical environment, including maintenance and housekeeping.

(11) Residents' rights, and the importance of initial and ongoing training for all staff to ensure residents' rights are fully respected and implemented.

(12) Cultural competency and sensitivity in issues relating to the underserved, aging, lesbian, gay, bisexual, and transgender community.

(13) Postural supports, restricted health conditions, and hospice care.

(d) Successful completion of the certification program shall be demonstrated by passing the state-administered examination and submitting a fee of one hundred dollars ($100) to the department for the issuance of a certificate of completion.

(e) (1) The department shall establish by regulation the program content, the testing instrument, process for approving certification programs, and criteria to be used for authorizing individuals or organizations to conduct certification programs. These regulations shall be developed with the participation of provider organizations.

(2) The department shall ensure that the examination consists of at least 100 questions and allows an applicant to have access to the California Residential Care Facility for the Elderly Act and related regulations during the examination. The department, no later than July 1 of every other year, shall review and revise the examination in order to ensure the rigor and quality of the examination. Each year, the department shall ensure by January 1 that the exam is not in conflict with current law. The department may convene a stakeholder group to assist in developing and reviewing test questions.

(f) This section shall apply to all applications for licensure unless the applicant provides evidence that he or she has a current license for another residential care facility for the elderly which was initially licensed prior to July 1, 1989, or has successfully completed an approved certification program within the prior five years.

(g) If the applicant is a firm, partnership, association, or corporation, the chief executive officer, or other person serving in a like capacity, or the designated administrator of the facility, shall provide evidence of successfully completing an approved certification program.

(h) This section shall become operative on January 1, 2016.

(Repealed (in Sec. 1) and added by Stats. 2014, Ch. 698, Sec. 2. (AB 1570) Effective January 1, 2015. Section operative January 1, 2016, by its own provisions.)

1569.235.

As a requirement for licensure, the applicant shall attend an orientation given by the department which outlines the applicable rules and regulations, and the scope and responsibility for operation of a residential care facility for the elderly.

(Added by Stats. 1991, Ch. 848, Sec. 3.)

1569.24.

Within 90 days after a facility accepts its first resident for placement following its initial licensure, the department shall inspect the facility to evaluate compliance with rules and regulations and to assess the facility's continuing ability to meet regulatory requirements. The licensee shall notify the department, within five business days after accepting its first resident for placement, that the facility has commenced operation.

The department may take appropriate remedial action as provided for in this chapter.

(Amended by Stats. 2006, Ch. 902, Sec. 11. Effective January 1, 2007.)

ARTICLE 2.5. Resident's Bill of Rights [1569.261 - 1569.269]
(Article 2.5 added by Stats. 2014, Ch. 702, Sec. 1.)

1569.261.

(a) It is the intent of the Legislature in enacting this article to adopt fundamental rights for all persons residing in a residential care facility for the elderly, as defined in Section 1569.2, and to ensure that facilities respect and promote these rights.

(b) In establishing this bill of rights, the Legislature intends that persons residing in residential care facilities for the elderly be treated with dignity, kindness, and respect, and that their civil liberties be fully honored.

(c) A central purpose of the bill of rights is to strengthen a resident's right to make choices about his or her care, treatment, and daily life in the facility and to ensure that the resident's choices are respected. The Legislature intends to enhance each resident's autonomy and ability to make decisions concerning his or her life.

(d) The Legislature also intends that each residential care facility for the elderly provide a safe, comfortable, and homelike environment for its residents and that it protect residents from physical or mental abuse, neglect, exploitation, or endangerment.

(Added by Stats. 2014, Ch. 702, Sec. 1. (AB 2171) Effective January 1, 2015.)

1569.265.

(a) Rights and liberties set forth in this article do not diminish a resident's constitutional rights or any other rights set forth in other state or federal laws and regulations. Persons residing in residential care facilities for the elderly shall continue to enjoy all of their civil and legal rights.

(b) The provisions of this article apply only to privately operated residential care facilities for the elderly.

(Added by Stats. 2014, Ch. 702, Sec. 1. (AB 2171) Effective January 1, 2015.)

1569.267.

(a) At admission, a facility staff person shall personally advise a resident and the resident's representative of, and give a complete written copy of, the rights in this article and the personal rights in Section 87468 of Title 22 of the California Code of Regulations. The licensee shall have each resident and the resident's representative sign and date a copy of the resident's rights, and the licensee shall include the signed and dated copy in the resident's record.

(b) Licensees shall prominently post, in areas accessible to the residents and their representatives, a copy of the residents' rights.

(c) The rights posted pursuant to subdivision (b) shall be posted both in English and in any other language in a facility in which 5 percent or more of the residents can only read that other language.

(d) The licensee shall provide initial and ongoing training for all members of its staff to ensure that residents' rights are fully respected and implemented.

(Added by Stats. 2014, Ch. 702, Sec. 1. (AB 2171) Effective January 1, 2015.)

1569.269.

(a) Residents of residential care facilities for the elderly shall have all of the following rights:

(1) To be accorded dignity in their personal relationships with staff, residents, and other persons.

(2) To be granted a reasonable level of personal privacy in accommodations, medical treatment, personal care and assistance, visits, communications, telephone conversations, use of the Internet, and meetings of resident and family groups.

(3) To confidential treatment of their records and personal information and to approve their release, except as authorized by law.

(4) To be encouraged and assisted in exercising their rights as citizens and as residents of the facility. Residents shall be free from interference, coercion, discrimination, and retaliation in exercising their rights.

(5) To be accorded safe, healthful, and comfortable accommodations, furnishings, and equipment.

(6) To care, supervision, and services that meet their individual needs and are delivered by staff that are sufficient in numbers, qualifications, and competency to meet their needs.

(7) To be served food of the quality and in the quantity necessary to meet their nutritional needs.

(8) To make choices concerning their daily life in the facility.

(9) To fully participate in planning their care, including the right to attend and participate in meetings or communications regarding the care and services to be provided in accordance with Section 1569.80, and to involve persons of their choice in the planning process. The licensee shall provide necessary information and support to ensure that residents direct the process to the maximum extent possible, and are enabled to make informed decisions and choices.

(10) To be free from neglect, financial exploitation, involuntary seclusion, punishment, humiliation, intimidation, and verbal, mental, physical, or sexual abuse.

(11) To present grievances and recommend changes in policies, procedures, and services to the staff of the facility, the facility's management and governing authority, and to any other person without restraint, coercion, discrimination, reprisal, or other retaliatory actions. The licensee shall take prompt actions to respond to residents' grievances.

(12) To contact the State Department of Social Services, the long-term care ombudsman, or both, regarding grievances against the licensee. The licensee shall post the telephone numbers and addresses for the local offices of the State Department of Social Services and ombudsman program, in accordance with Section 9718 of the Welfare and Institutions Code, conspicuously in the facility foyer, lobby, residents' activity room, or other location easily accessible to residents.

(13) To be fully informed, as evidenced by the resident's written acknowledgement, prior to or at the time of admission, of all rules governing residents' conduct and responsibilities. In accordance with Section 1569.885, all rules established by a licensee

shall be reasonable and shall not violate any rights set forth in this chapter or in other applicable laws or regulations.

(14) To receive in the admission agreement a comprehensive description of the method for evaluating residents' service needs and the fee schedule for the items and services provided, and to receive written notice of any rate increases pursuant to Sections 1569.655 and 1569.884.

(15) To be informed in writing at or before the time of admission of any resident retention limitations set by the state or licensee, including any limitations or restrictions on the licensee's ability to meet residents' needs.

(16) To reasonable accommodation of individual needs and preferences in all aspects of life in the facility, except when the health or safety of the individual or other residents would be endangered.

(17) To reasonable accommodation of resident preferences concerning room and roommate choices.

(18) To written notice of any room changes at least 30 days in advance unless the request for a change is agreed to by the resident, required to fill a vacant bed, or necessary due to an emergency.

(19) To share a room with the resident's spouse, domestic partner, or a person of resident's choice when both spouses, partners, or residents live in the same facility and consent to the arrangement.

(20) To select their own physicians, pharmacies, privately paid personal assistants, hospice agency, and health care providers, in a manner that is consistent with the resident's contract of admission or other rules of the facility, and in accordance with this act.

(21) To have prompt access to review all of their records and to purchase photocopies. Photocopied records shall be promptly provided, not to exceed two business days, at a cost not to exceed the community standard for photocopies.

(22) To be protected from involuntary transfers, discharges, and evictions in violation of state laws and regulations. Facilities shall not involuntarily transfer or evict residents for grounds other than those specifically enumerated under state law or regulations, and shall comply with enumerated eviction and relocation protections for residents. For purposes of this paragraph, "involuntary" means a transfer, discharge, or eviction that is initiated by the licensee, not by the resident.

(23) To move from a facility.

(24) To consent to have relatives and other individuals of the resident's choosing visit during reasonable hours, privately and without prior notice.

(25) To receive written information on the right to establish an advanced health care directive and, pursuant to Section 1569.156, the licensee's written policies on honoring those directives.

(26) To be encouraged to maintain and develop their fullest potential for independent living through participation in activities that are designed and implemented for this purpose, in accordance with Section 87219 of Title 22 of the California Code of Regulations.

(27) To organize and participate in a resident council that is established pursuant to Section 1569.157.

(28) To protection of their property from theft or loss in accordance with Sections 1569.152, 1569.153, and 1569.154.

(29) To manage their financial affairs. A licensee shall not require residents to deposit their personal funds with the licensee. Except as provided in approved continuing care agreements, a licensee, or a spouse, domestic partner, relative, or employee of a licensee, shall not do any of the following:

(A) Accept appointment as a guardian or conservator of the person or estate of a resident.

(B) Become or act as a representative payee for any payments made to a resident, without the written and documented consent of the resident or the resident's representative.

(C) Serve as an agent for a resident under any general or special power of attorney.

(D) Become or act as a joint tenant on any account with a resident.

(E) Enter into a loan or promissory agreement or otherwise borrow money from a resident without a notarized written agreement outlining the terms of the repayment being given to the resident.

(30) To keep, have access to, and use their own personal possessions, including toilet articles, and to keep and be allowed to spend their own money, unless limited by statute or regulation.

(b) A licensed residential care facility for the elderly shall not discriminate against a person seeking admission or a resident based on sex, race, color, religion, national origin, marital status, registered domestic partner status, ancestry, actual or perceived sexual orientation, or actual or perceived gender identity.

(c) No provision of a contract of admission, including all documents that a resident or his or her representative is required to sign as part of the contract for, or as a condition of, admission to a residential care facility for the elderly, shall require that a resident waive benefits or rights to which he or she is entitled under this chapter or provided by federal or other state law or regulation.

(d) Residents' family members, friends, and representatives have the right to organize and participate in a family council that is established pursuant to Section 1569.158.

(e) The rights specified in this section shall be in addition to any other rights provided by law.

(f) The provisions of this section are severable. If any provision of this section or its application is held invalid, that invalidity shall not affect other provisions or applications that can be given effect without the invalid provision or application.

(Added by Stats. 2014, Ch. 702, Sec. 1. (AB 2171) Effective January 1, 2015.)

(Article 3 added by Stats. 1985, Ch. 1127, Sec. 3.)

1569.30.

(a) The department shall adopt, amend, or repeal, in accordance with Chapter 3.5 (commencing with Section 11340) of Part 1 of Division 3 of Title 2 of the Government Code, reasonable rules, regulations, and standards as may be necessary or proper to carry out the purposes and intent of this chapter and to enable the department to exercise the powers and perform the duties conferred upon it by this chapter, not inconsistent with any statute of this state.

(b) The regulations governing residential facilities for the elderly under the Community Care Facilities Act (Chapter 3 (commencing with Section 1500)) shall continue to govern residential care facilities for the elderly under this act until amended or repealed.
(Amended by Stats. 2004, Ch. 183, Sec. 190. Effective January 1, 2005.)

1569.31.

The regulations for a license shall prescribe standards of safety and sanitation for the physical plant and standards for basic care and supervision, personal care, and services to be provided.

The department's regulations shall allow for the development of new and innovative community programs.

In adopting regulations which implement this chapter, the department shall provide flexibility to allow facilities conducted by and exclusively for adherents of a well-recognized church or religious denomination who rely solely on prayer or spiritual means for healing to operate a licensed residential care facility for the elderly.
(Added by Stats. 1985, Ch. 1127, Sec. 3.)

1569.311.

Every residential care facility for the elderly shall have one or more carbon monoxide detectors in the facility that meet the standards established in Chapter 8 (commencing with Section 13260) of Part 2 of Division 12. The department shall account for the presence of these detectors during inspections.
(Added by Stats. 2014, Ch. 503, Sec. 3. (AB 2386) Effective January 1, 2015.)

1569.312.

Every facility required to be licensed under this chapter shall provide at least the following basic services:

(a) Care and supervision as defined in Section 1569.2.

(b) Assistance with instrumental activities of daily living in the combinations which meet the needs of residents.

(c) Helping residents gain access to appropriate supportive services, as defined, in the community.

(d) Being aware of the resident's general whereabouts, although the resident may travel independently in the community.

(e) Monitoring the activities of the residents while they are under the supervision of the facility to ensure their general health, safety, and well-being.

(f) Encouraging the residents to maintain and develop their maximum functional ability through participation in planned activities.
(Amended by Stats. 1986, Ch. 844, Sec. 4.)

1569.313.

Each residential care facility for the elderly shall state, on its client information form or admission agreement, and on its patient's rights form, the facility's policy concerning family visits and other communication with resident clients and shall promptly post notice of its visiting policy at a location in the facility that is accessible to residents and families. The facility's policy concerning family visits and communication shall be designed to encourage regular family involvement with the resident client and shall provide ample opportunities for family participation in activities at the facility.
(Added by Stats. 1985, Ch. 954, Sec. 3.)

1569.314.

A residential care facility for the elderly shall not require residents to purchase medications, or rent or purchase medical supplies or equipment, from any particular pharmacy or other source.

This section shall not preclude a residential care facility for the elderly from requiring that residents who need assistance with the purchasing, storing, or taking of medications comply with the facility's policies and procedures regarding storage of medications and methods of assisting residents with the taking of medications, if the policies and procedures are reasonably necessary and meet the intent of state or federal regulations.
(Amended by Stats. 1991, Ch. 888, Sec. 8.)

1569.315.

Each residential care facility for the elderly required to be licensed pursuant to this chapter shall keep a current record of clients in the facility, including the client's name and ambulatory status, and the name, address, and telephone number of the client's physician and of any person or agency responsible for the care of the client. The facility shall protect the privacy and confidentiality of this information.
(Added by Stats. 1985, Ch. 869, Sec. 4. See similar Section 1569.315 added by Stats. 1985, Ch. 1096.)

1569.315.

Each facility required to be licensed shall keep a current record of all of the following:

(a) Clients in the facility, including each client's name and ambulatory status.

(b) The name and telephone number of each client's physician.

(c) The name, address, and telephone number of any person or agency responsible for the care of a client.

The facility shall respect the privacy and confidentiality of this information.

(Added by Stats. 1985, Ch. 1096, Sec. 5.)

1569.316.

(a) The referring agency or facility, or its designee, shall provide to the administrator all information in its possession concerning any history of dangerous propensity of the client prior to the placement in the residential care facility for the elderly. However, no confidential client information shall be released pursuant to this section without the consent of the client or his or her authorized representative.

(b) In determining a person's compatibility, the licensee shall consider criteria that includes, but is not limited to, both of the following:

(1) The extent to which the person's personal and health care needs can be adequately met in the residential care facility for the elderly.

(2) The existence of a past history of violence or mental illness that would create a risk for the person or other residents of that facility.
(Added by Stats. 1996, Ch. 434, Sec. 2. Effective January 1, 1997.)

1569.317.

Every residential care facility for the elderly, as defined in Section 1569.2, shall, for the purpose of addressing issues that arise when a resident is missing from the facility, develop and comply with an absentee notification plan as part of the written record of the care the resident will receive in the facility, as described in Section 1569.80. The plan shall include and be limited to the following: a requirement that an administrator of the facility, or his or her designee, inform the resident's authorized representative when that resident is missing from the facility and the circumstances in which an administrator of the facility, or his or her designee, shall notify local law enforcement when a resident is missing from the facility.
(Added by Stats. 2013, Ch. 674, Sec. 3. (AB 620) Effective January 1, 2014.)

1569.318.

Every residential care facility for the elderly shall abide by the provisions of the Lesbian, Gay, Bisexual, and Transgender Long-Term Care Facility Residents' Bill of Rights (Chapter 2.45 (commencing with Section 1439.50)).
(Added by Stats. 2017, Ch. 483, Sec. 4. (SB 219) Effective January 1, 2018.)

1569.32.

Any duly authorized officer, employee, or agent of the department may, upon presentation of proper identification, enter and inspect any place providing personal care, supervision, and services at any time, with or without advance notice, to secure compliance with, or to prevent a violation of, this chapter.
(Added by Stats. 1985, Ch. 1127, Sec. 3.)

1569.33.

(a) Every licensed residential care facility for the elderly shall be subject to unannounced inspections by the department. The department shall inspect these facilities as often as necessary to ensure the quality of care provided.

(b) The department shall conduct an annual unannounced inspection of a facility under any of the following circumstances:

(1) When a license is on probation.

(2) When the terms of agreement in a facility compliance plan require an annual inspection.

(3) When an accusation against a licensee is pending.

(4) When a facility requires an annual inspection as a condition of receiving federal financial participation.

(5) In order to verify that a person who has been ordered out of the facility for the elderly by the department is no longer at the facility.

(c) On and after January 1, 2017, and until January 1, 2018, the following shall apply:

(1) The department shall conduct annual unannounced inspections of no less than 30 percent of residential care facilities for the elderly not subject to an inspection under subdivision (b).

(2) These unannounced inspections shall be conducted based on a random sampling methodology developed by the department.

(3) The department shall inspect a residential care facility for the elderly at least once every three years.

(d) On and after January 1, 2018, and until January 1, 2019, the following shall apply:

(1) The department shall conduct annual unannounced inspections of no less than 20 percent of residential care facilities for the elderly not subject to an evaluation under subdivision (b).

(2) These unannounced inspections shall be conducted based on a random sampling methodology developed by the department.

(3) The department shall inspect a residential care facility for the elderly at least once every two years.

(e) On and after January 1, 2019, the department shall conduct annual unannounced inspections of all residential care facilities for the elderly.

(f) (1) The department shall notify the residential care facility for the elderly in writing of all deficiencies in its compliance with the provisions of this chapter and the rules and regulations adopted pursuant to this chapter.

(2) Unless otherwise specified in the plan of correction, the residential care facility for the elderly shall remedy the deficiencies within 10 days of the notification.

(g) (1) Reports on the results of each inspection, evaluation, or consultation shall be kept on file in the department, and all inspection reports, consultation reports, lists of deficiencies, and plans of correction shall be open to public inspection.

(2) (A) The department shall post on its Internet Web site information on how to obtain an inspection report.

(B) It is the intent of the Legislature that the department shall make inspection reports available on its Internet Web site by January 1, 2020.

(h) As a part of the department's evaluation process, the department shall review the plan of operation, training logs, and marketing materials of any residential care facility for the elderly that advertises or promotes special care, special programming, or a special environment for persons with dementia to monitor compliance with Sections 1569.626 and 1569.627.

(i) (1) The department shall design, or cause to be designed, a poster that contains information on the appropriate reporting agency in case of a complaint or emergency.

(2) Each residential care facility for the elderly shall post this poster in the main entryway of its facility.

(j) This section shall become operative on January 1, 2017.

(Repealed (in Sec. 6) and added by Stats. 2015, Ch. 20, Sec. 7. (SB 79) Effective June 24, 2015. Section operative January 1, 2017, by its own provisions.)

1569.331.

The Legislature hereby finds and declares that in order to protect the health and safety of elders in care at residential care facilities for the elderly, appropriate oversight and regulation of residential care facilities for the elderly requires regular, periodic inspections of these facilities in addition to investigations in response to complaints. It is the intent of the Legislature to increase the frequency of unannounced inspections pursuant to Section 1569.33. In addition to the information that the State Department of Social Services is required to report during the 2015–16 legislative budget subcommittee hearings pursuant to Section 85 of Chapter 29 of the Statutes of 2014, the department shall also at that time report the projected costs of conducting annual inspections of residential care facilities for the elderly beginning January 1, 2018.

(Added by Stats. 2014, Ch. 704, Sec. 2. (SB 895) Effective January 1, 2015.)

1569.335.

(a) The department shall provide the Office of the State Long-Term Care Ombudsman, as defined in subdivision (c) of Section 9701 of the Welfare and Institutions Code, with a precautionary notification if the department begins to prepare to issue a temporary suspension or revocation of any license, so that the office may properly prepare to provide advocacy services if and when necessary.

(b) The department shall notify affected public placement agencies and the Office of the State Long-Term Care Ombudsman whenever the department substantiates that a violation has occurred that poses a serious threat to the health and safety of any resident when the violation results in the assessment of any penalty or causes an accusation to be filed for the revocation of a license.

(c) (1) If the violation is appealed by the facility within 15 business days, the department shall only notify placement agencies of the violation when the appeal has been exhausted.

(2) If the appeal process has not been completed within 60 days, the placement agency shall be notified with a notation that indicates that the case is still under appeal.

(3) The notice to each placement agency shall be updated monthly for the following 24-month period and shall include the name and location of the facility, the amount of the fine, the nature of the violation, the corrective action taken, the status of the revocation, and the resolution of the complaint.

(Amended by Stats. 2016, Ch. 823, Sec. 6. (AB 2231) Effective January 1, 2017.)

1569.34.

The director shall have the authority to contract for personal services as required in order to perform inspections of, or consultation with, residential care facilities for the elderly. The department shall establish by December 1, 1986, within the department an interdisciplinary team of professionals to advise the department on implementation of this chapter and to be available in crisis situations to assist local licensing evaluators on the needs of elderly residents in facilities.

This team shall include at least a geriatric nurse practitioner or a public health nurse with geriatric experience and a social worker with related experience.

(Added by Stats. 1985, Ch. 1127, Sec. 3.)

1569.345.

Upon request, the department shall provide the Office of the State Long-Term Care Ombudsman and any approved organizations of the office with copies of inspection reports for residential care facilities for the elderly.

(Added by Stats. 1985, Ch. 1127, Sec. 3.)

1569.35.

(a) Any person may request an investigation of a residential care facility for the elderly in accordance with this chapter by making a complaint to the department alleging a violation of applicable requirements prescribed by statutes or regulations of this state, including, but not limited to, a denial of access of any person authorized to enter the facility pursuant to Section 9722 of the Welfare and Institutions Code. A complaint may be made either orally or in writing.

(b) The substance of the complaint shall be provided to the licensee no earlier than at the time of the inspection. Unless the complainant specifically requests otherwise, neither the substance of the complaint provided the licensee nor any copy of the complaint or any record published, released, or otherwise made available to the licensee shall disclose the name of any person mentioned in the complaint except the name of any duly authorized officer, employee, or agent of the department conducting the investigation or inspection pursuant to this chapter.

(c) (1) Upon receipt of a complaint, other than a complaint alleging denial of a statutory right of access to a residential care facility for the elderly, the department shall make a preliminary review and, unless the department determines that the complaint is willfully intended to harass a licensee or is without any reasonable basis, it shall make an onsite inspection within 10 days after receiving the complaint except where the visit would adversely affect the licensing investigation or the investigation of other agencies,

including, but not limited to, law enforcement agencies. In either event, the complainant shall be promptly informed of the department's proposed course of action.

(2) If a local long-term care ombudsman or the State Long-Term Care Ombudsman files a complaint alleging denial of a statutory right of access to a residential care facility for the elderly under Section 9722 of the Welfare and Institutions Code, the department shall give priority to the complaint pursuant to Section 9721 of the Welfare and Institutions Code and notify the Office of the State Long-Term Care Ombudsman that an investigation has been initiated pursuant to this section.

(3) Prior to conducting an onsite investigation pursuant to this section, the department shall make a good faith effort, documented in writing, to contact and interview the complainant and inform the complainant of the department's proposed course of action and the relevant deadline for the department to complete its investigation. To the extent practicable, the officer, employee, or agent of the department who will conduct the investigation shall be the representative who interviews and makes contact with the complainant.

(d) Within 10 business days of completing the investigation of a complaint under this section, the department shall notify the complainant in writing of the department's determination as a result of the investigation.

(Amended by Stats. 2015, Ch. 486, Sec. 4. (AB 1387) Effective January 1, 2016.)

1569.351.

(a) The department shall ensure that the licensee's plan of correction is verifiable and measurable. The plan of correction shall specify what evidence is acceptable to establish that a deficiency has been corrected. This evidence shall be included in the department's facility file.

(b) The department shall specify in its licensing report all violations that, if not corrected, will have a direct and immediate risk to the health, safety, or personal rights of residents in care.

(c) The department shall complete all complaint investigations and place a note of final conclusion in the department's facility file, regardless of whether the licensee voluntarily surrendered the license.

(Added by Stats. 2008, Ch. 291, Sec. 14. Effective September 25, 2008.)

1569.355.

The director shall establish an automated license information system on licensees and former licensees of licensed residential care facilities for the elderly. The system shall maintain a record of any information that may be pertinent, as determined by the director, for licensure under this chapter. This information may include, but is not limited to, the licensees' addresses, telephone numbers, violations of any laws related to the care of clients in a residential care facility for the elderly, licenses, revocation of any licenses and, to the extent permitted by federal law, social security numbers.

(Added by Stats. 1985, Ch. 1127, Sec. 3.)

1569.356.

To the extent that the department's computer system can electronically accommodate additional residential care facility for the elderly profile information, the department shall post on its Internet Web site the current name, business address, and telephone number of the licensee, the name of the owner of the residential care facility for the elderly, if not the same as the licensee, the name of any parent organization, the licensed capacity of the facility, including the capacity for nonambulatory residents, whether the facility is permitted to accept and retain residents receiving hospice care services, whether the facility has a special care unit or program for people with Alzheimer's disease and other dementias and has a delayed egress or secured perimeter system in place, or both, and information required pursuant to subparagraph (B) of paragraph (3) of subdivision (a) of Section 1569.15.

(Added by Stats. 2015, Ch. 628, Sec. 4. (AB 601) Effective January 1, 2016.)

1569.36.

(a) Not less than 30 days prior to the expiration date of any residential care facility for the elderly license, the department shall transmit a copy to the state ombudsman in the Department of Aging as well as the local ombudsman, if one exists, of all notices sent to the facility by the department during the term of the current license as a result of a substantiated complaint regarding a violation of any of the provisions of this chapter relating to resident abuse and neglect, food, sanitation, incidental medical care, and residential supervision. During that one-year period the copy of the notices transmitted and the proof of the transmittal shall be open for public inspection.

(b) The department shall provide the names and addresses of the state ombudsman in the Department of Aging and, where applicable, the local ombudsman, to each residential care facility for the elderly.

(Amended by Stats. 1989, Ch. 1115, Sec. 13.)

1569.37.

No licensee, or officer or employee of the licensee, shall discriminate or retaliate in any manner, including, but not limited to, eviction or threat of eviction, against any person receiving the services of the licensee's residential care facility for the elderly, or against any employee of the licensee's facility, on the basis, or for the reason that, the person or employee or any other person has initiated or participated in the filing of a complaint, grievance, or a request for inspection with the department pursuant to this chapter, or has initiated or participated in the filing of a complaint, grievance, or request for investigation with the appropriate local ombudsman, or with the state ombudsman recognized pursuant to Chapter 11 (commencing with Section 9700) of Division 8.5 of the Welfare and Institutions Code.

(Amended by Stats. 2013, Ch. 295, Sec. 3. (AB 581) Effective January 1, 2014.)

1569.371.

(a) No licensee, or officer or employee of the licensee, shall discriminate or retaliate in any manner against any person receiving the services of the licensee's residential care facility for the elderly, or against any employee of the licensee's facility, on the basis, or for the reason that, the person, employee, or any other person dialed or called 911.

(b) A violation of this section is subject to civil penalty pursuant to Section 1569.49.

(c) This section shall become operative on January 1, 2016.

(Added by Stats. 2014, Ch. 705, Sec. 1. (SB 911) Effective January 1, 2015.)

1569.38.

(a) Each residential care facility for the elderly shall place in a conspicuous place copies of all licensing reports issued by the department within the preceding 12 months, and all licensing reports issued by the department resulting from the most recent annual visit of the department to the facility. This subdivision shall not apply to any portion of a licensing report referring to a complaint that was found by the department to be unfounded or unsubstantiated. The facility, during the admission process, shall inform the resident and the resident's responsible person in writing that licensing reports are available for review at the facility, and that copies of licensing reports and other documents pertaining to the facility are available from the appropriate district office of the department. The facility shall provide the telephone number and address of the appropriate district office.

(b) A licensed residential care facility for the elderly shall provide written notice to a resident, the resident's responsible party, if any, and the local long-term care ombudsman, within 10 days from the occurrence of either of the following events:

(1) The department commences proceedings to suspend or revoke the license of the facility pursuant to Section 1569.50.

(2) A criminal action that relates to the health or safety of the residents is brought against the licensed residential care facility.

(c) The notice provided to a resident and the resident's responsible party, if any, shall include the name and contact information for the local long-term care ombudsman and for the Community Care Licensing Division of the department with a statement that directs the resident or the resident's responsible party to contact the division for information on the license status of the facility.

(d) The notice, described in subdivision (b), provided to a resident and the resident's responsible party, if any, shall include the reason given for the commencement of proceedings to suspend or revoke the license of the facility, or the reason given for criminal action brought against the licensed residential care facility.

(e) Upon providing the notice described in subdivision (b), the licensed residential care facility shall also post a written notice, in at least 14-point type, in a conspicuous location in the facility, that may include where the mail boxes are located, where the facility license is posted, or any other easily accessible location in the facility. The posting shall include all of the following information:

(1) The date of the notice.

(2) The name of the residential care facility for the elderly.

(3) A statement that a copy of the most recent licensing report prepared by the department, and any additional reports of facility evaluation visits, within the preceding 12 months, may be obtained at the facility.

(4) The name and telephone number of the contact person designated by the Community Care Licensing Division of the department to provide information on the license status of the facility.

(f) The notice required to be posted pursuant to subdivision (e) shall remain posted until the deficiencies that gave rise to the notice are resolved.

(g) A licensee who fails to comply with the requirements of subdivision (b) or (c) shall be liable for civil penalties in the amount of one hundred dollars ($100) for each day of the failure to provide notification as required in this section. The total civil penalty for each day shall not exceed one hundred dollars ($100) regardless of the number of notices that the licensee fails to send that day. The total civil penalty for a continuous violation of subdivision (b) or (c) shall not exceed five thousand dollars ($5,000).

(h) For purposes of this section, "responsible party" means an individual, including the patient's relative, health care surrogate decisionmaker, or a placement agency, who assists the resident in placement or assumes varying degrees of responsibility for the well-being of the resident, as designated by the resident in writing.

(Amended by Stats. 2011, Ch. 365, Sec. 1. (AB 313) Effective January 1, 2012.)

1569.39.

(a) A residential care facility for the elderly that accepts or retains residents with prohibited health conditions, as defined by the department, in Section 87615 of Title 22 of the California Code of Regulations, shall assist residents with accessing home health or hospice services, as indicated in the resident's current appraisal, to ensure that residents receive medical care as prescribed by the resident's physician and contained in the resident's service plan.

(b) A residential care facility for the elderly that accepts or retains residents with restricted health conditions, as defined by the department, shall ensure that residents receive medical care as prescribed by the resident's physician and contained in the resident's service plan by appropriately skilled professionals acting within their scope of practice. An appropriately skilled professional may not be required when the resident is providing self-care, as defined by the department, and there is documentation in the resident's service plan that the resident is capable of providing self-care.

(c) An "appropriately skilled professional" means, for purposes of this section, an individual who has training and is licensed to perform the necessary medical procedures prescribed by a physician. This includes, but is not limited to, a registered nurse, licensed vocational nurse, physical therapist, occupational therapist, or respiratory therapist. These professionals may include, but are not limited to, those persons employed by a

home health agency, the resident, or a facility, and who are currently licensed in this state.

(d) Failure to meet or arrange to meet the needs of those residents who require health-related services as specified in the resident's written record of care, defined pursuant to Section 1569.80, or failure to notify the physician of a resident's illness or injury that poses a danger of death or serious bodily harm is a licensing violation and subject to civil penalty pursuant to Section 1569.49.

(e) This section shall become operative on January 1, 2016.

(Added by Stats. 2014, Ch. 705, Sec. 2. (SB 911) Effective January 1, 2015.)

ARTICLE 4. Offenses [1569.40 - 1569.495]

(Article 4 added by Stats. 1985, Ch. 1127, Sec. 3.)

1569.40.

(a) Any person who violates this chapter, or who willfully or repeatedly violates any rule or regulation adopted under this chapter, is guilty of a misdemeanor and upon conviction thereof shall be punished by a fine not to exceed one thousand dollars ($1,000), by imprisonment in the county jail for a period not to exceed one year, or by both the fine and imprisonment.

(b) Operation of a residential care facility for the elderly without a license shall be subject to a summons to appear in court. Unlicensed operation, establishment, management, conducting, or maintaining of a facility as prohibited by Section 1569.10 is a separate and distinct offense of this section and is punishable as a misdemeanor.

(c) A misdemeanor may be prosecuted regardless of any concurrent enforcement of civil penalties or administrative remedies available to the department.

(d) Notwithstanding any other provision of this chapter, any person, firm, partnership, association, or corporation who owns, operates, establishes, manages, conducts, or maintains a residential care facility for the elderly, as defined in subdivisions (k) and (l) of Section 1569.2 which is an unlicensed residential care facility for the elderly as defined in subdivision (a) of Section 1569.44 is guilty of a misdemeanor and upon conviction thereof shall be punished by a fine not exceeding two thousand five hundred dollars ($2,500), by imprisonment in the county jail for a period not to exceed one year, or by both the fine and imprisonment.

(Amended by Stats. 1989, Ch. 1115, Sec. 14.)

1569.405.

Upon a finding by the licensing authority that a facility is in operation without a license, a peace officer, as defined in Chapter 4.5 (commencing with Section 830) of Title 3 of Part 2 of the Penal Code, may enforce Section 1569.10 by utilizing the procedures set forth in Chapter 5 (commencing with Section 853.5) of Title 3 of Part 2 of the Penal Code. A facility violating Section 1569.10 is guilty of an infraction punishable by a fine of two hundred dollars ($200) for each day of violation. Upon a determination that a residential care facility for the elderly is in violation of Section 1569.10, and after a citation has been issued, the peace officer shall immediately notify the licensing authority in the department.

(Added by Stats. 1987, Ch. 856, Sec. 2.)

1569.406.

Any person who, without lawful authorization from a duly authorized officer, employee, or agent of the department, informs an owner, operator, employee, agent, or resident of a residential care facility for the elderly of an impending and unannounced site visit to that facility by personnel of the department, except for a site visit prior to licensing the facility, is guilty of a misdemeanor and upon conviction thereof shall be punished by a fine not to exceed one thousand dollars ($1,000), by imprisonment in the county jail for a period not to exceed 180 days, or by both a fine and imprisonment.

(Amended by Stats. 1991, Ch. 888, Sec. 9.)

1569.41.

The director may bring an action to enjoin the violation or threatened violation of Section 1569.10 or 1569.44, or both, in the superior court in and for the county in which the violation occurred or is about to occur. Any proceeding under this section shall conform to the requirements of Chapter 3 (commencing with Section 525) of Title 7 of Part 2 of the Code of Civil Procedure, except that the director shall not be required to allege facts necessary to show or tending to show lack of adequate remedy at law or irreparable damage or loss. Upon a finding by the director that the violations threaten the health or safety of persons in, or served by, a residential care facility for the elderly, the agency contracted with pursuant to Section 1569.13 may bring an action to enjoin the violation, threatened violation, or continued violation by any residential care facility for the elderly which is located in an area for which it is responsible pursuant to the terms of the contract.

With respect to any and all actions brought pursuant to this section alleging actual violation of Section 1569.10 or 1569.44, or both, the court shall, if it finds the allegations to be true, issue its order enjoining the residential care facility for the elderly from continuance of the violation.

(Added by Stats. 1985, Ch. 1127, Sec. 3.)

1569.42.

Any action brought by the director against a residential care facility for the elderly shall not abate by reason of a sale or other transfer of ownership of the residential care facility for the elderly which is a party to the action except with express written consent of the director.

(Added by Stats. 1985, Ch. 1127, Sec. 3.)

1569.43.

Notwithstanding any other provisions of this chapter, the district attorney of every county, and city attorneys in those cities which have city attorneys which prosecute misdemeanors pursuant to Section 72193 of the Government Code, shall, upon their own initiative or upon application by the state department or its authorized representative, institute and conduct the prosecution of any action for violation of this chapter within his or her jurisdiction.

(Amended by Stats. 2002, Ch. 784, Sec. 515. Effective January 1, 2003.)

1569.44.

(a) A facility shall be deemed to be an "unlicensed residential care facility for the elderly" and "maintained and operated to provide residential care" if it is unlicensed and not exempt from licensure, and any one of the following conditions is satisfied:

(1) The facility is providing care and supervision, as defined by this chapter or the rules and regulations adopted pursuant to this chapter.

(2) The facility is held out as, or represented as, providing care and supervision, as defined by this chapter or the rules and regulations adopted pursuant to this chapter.

(3) The facility accepts or retains residents who demonstrate the need for care and supervision, as defined by this chapter or the rules and regulations adopted pursuant to this chapter.

(4) The facility represents itself as a licensed residential facility for the elderly.

(b) No unlicensed residential facility for the elderly, as defined in subdivision (a), shall operate in this state.

(c) Upon discovery of an unlicensed residential care facility for the elderly, the department shall refer residents to the appropriate placement or adult protective services agency or the appropriate local or state long-term care ombudsman, if either of the following conditions exist:

(1) There is an immediate threat to the clients' health and safety.

(2) The facility will not cooperate with the licensing agency to apply for a license, meet licensing standards, and obtain a valid license.

(Amended by Stats. 1989, Ch. 1115, Sec. 16.)

1569.45.

A facility shall be licensed as a residential care facility for the elderly if it offers care and supervision, as defined, to its residents. Every residential care facility for the elderly in this state shall be licensed under this chapter.

(Added by Stats. 1985, Ch. 1127, Sec. 3.)

1569.46.

Operation of an unlicensed facility shall be an act of unfair competition and an unfair business practice within the meaning of Chapter 5 (commencing with Section 17200) of the Business and Professions Code.

(Added by Stats. 1989, Ch. 1115, Sec. 17.)

1569.47.

(a) "Placement agency" means any county welfare department, county social service department, county mental health department, county public guardian, general acute care hospital discharge planner or coordinator, state-funded program or private agency providing placement or referral services, conservator pursuant to Part 3 (commencing with Section 1800) of Division 4 of the Probate Code, conservator pursuant to Chapter 3 (commencing with Section 5350) of Part 1 of Division 5 of the Welfare and Institutions Code, and regional center for persons with developmental disabilities which is engaged in finding homes or other places for the placement of elderly persons for temporary or permanent care.

(b) A placement agency shall not place individuals in licensed residential care facilities for the elderly when the individual, because of his or her health condition, cannot be cared for within the limits of the license or requires inpatient care in a health facility. Violation of this subdivision is a misdemeanor.

(c) A placement agency or employee of a placement agency shall not place, refer, or recommend placement of a person in a facility providing care and supervision, or protective supervision, unless the facility is licensed as a residential care facility for the elderly or is exempt from licensing under Section 1569.145. Violation of this subdivision is a misdemeanor.

(d) Any employee of a placement agency who knows, or reasonably suspects, that a facility which is not exempt from licensing is operating without a license shall report the name and address of the facility to the department. Failure to report as required by this subdivision is a misdemeanor.

(e) The department shall investigate any report filed under subdivision (d). If the department has probable cause to believe that the facility which is the subject of the report is operating without a license, the department shall investigate the facility within 10 days after receipt of the report.

(f) A placement agency shall notify the appropriate licensing agency of any known or suspected incidents which would jeopardize the health or safety of residents in a residential care facility for the elderly. Reportable incidents include, but are not limited to, all of the following:

(1) Incidents of physical abuse.

(2) Any violation of personal rights.

(3) Any situation in which a facility is unclean, unsafe, unsanitary, or in poor condition.

(4) Any situation in which a facility has insufficient personnel or incompetent personnel on duty.

(5) Any situation in which residents experience mental or verbal abuse.

(Amended by Stats. 1991, Ch. 888, Sec. 10.)

1569.48.

An emergency resident contingency account may be established within the Technical Assistance Fund established under Section 1523.2 to which not more than 50 percent of each penalty assessed pursuant to Section 1569.49 is deposited for use by the Community Care Licensing Division of the department, at the discretion of the director, for the relocation and care of residents when a facility's license is revoked or temporarily

suspended. The money in the account shall cover costs, including, but not limited to, transportation expenses, expenses incurred in notifying family members, and any other costs directly associated with providing continuous care and supervision to the residents. The department shall seek the input of stakeholders and local agencies in developing policies for emergency resident care and supervision.

(Amended by Stats. 2014, Ch. 29, Sec. 23. (SB 855) Effective June 20, 2014.)

1569.481.

(a) (1) It is the intent of the Legislature in enacting this section to authorize the department to take quick, effective action to protect the health and safety of residents of residential care facilities for the elderly and to minimize the effects of transfer trauma that accompany the abrupt transfer of residents by appointing a temporary manager to assume the operation of a facility that is found to be in a condition in which continued operation by the licensee or his or her representative presents a substantial probability of imminent danger of serious physical harm or death to the residents.

(2) A temporary manager appointed pursuant to this section shall assume the operation of the facility in order to bring it into compliance with the law, facilitate a transfer of ownership to a new licensee, or ensure the orderly transfer of residents should the facility be required to close. Upon a final decision and order of revocation of the license, issuance of a temporary suspension, or a forfeiture by operation of law, the department shall immediately issue a provisional license to the appointed temporary manager. Notwithstanding the applicable sections of this code governing the revocation of a provisional license, the provisional license issued to a temporary manager shall automatically expire upon the termination of the temporary manager. The temporary manager shall possess the provisional license solely for purposes of carrying out the responsibilities authorized by this section and the duties set forth in the written agreement between the department and the temporary manager. The temporary manager does not have the right to appeal the expiration of the provisional license.

(b) For purposes of this section, "temporary manager" means the person, corporation, or other entity appointed temporarily by the department as a substitute facility licensee or administrator with authority to hire, terminate, reassign staff, obligate facility funds, alter facility procedures, and manage the facility to correct deficiencies identified in the facility's operation. The temporary manager has the final authority to direct the care and supervision activities of any person associated with the facility, including superseding the authority of the licensee and the administrator.

(c) The director, in order to protect the residents of the facility from physical or mental abuse, abandonment, or any other substantial threat to health or safety, may appoint a temporary manager when any of the following circumstances exist:

(1) The director determines that it is necessary to temporarily suspend the license of a residential care facility for the elderly pursuant to Section 1569.50 and the immediate relocation of the residents is not feasible based on transfer trauma, lack of available alternative placements, or other emergency considerations for the health and safety of the residents.

(2) The licensee is unwilling or unable to comply with the requirements of Section 1569.525 or the requirements of Section 1569.682 regarding the safe and orderly relocation of residents when ordered to do so by the department or when otherwise required by law.

(3) The licensee has opted to secure a temporary manager pursuant to Section 1569.525.

(d) (1) Upon appointment, the temporary manager shall complete its application for a license to operate a residential care facility for the elderly and take all necessary steps and make best efforts to eliminate any substantial threat to the health and safety to residents or complete the transfer of residents to alternative placements pursuant to Section 1569.525 or 1569.682. For purposes of a provisional license issued to a temporary manager, the licensee's existing fire safety clearance shall serve as the fire safety clearance for the temporary manager's provisional license.

(2) A person shall not impede the operation of a temporary manager. The temporary manager's access to, or possession of, the property shall not be interfered with during the term of the temporary manager's appointment. There shall be an automatic stay for a 60-day period subsequent to the appointment of a temporary manager of any action that would interfere with the functioning of the facility, including, but not limited to, termination of utility services, attachments, or setoffs of resident trust funds, and repossession of equipment in the facility.

(e) (1) The appointment of a temporary manager shall be immediately effective and shall continue for a period not to exceed 60 days unless otherwise extended in accordance with paragraph (2) of subdivision (h) at the discretion of the department or as permitted by paragraph (2) of subdivision (d) of Section 1569.525, or unless otherwise terminated earlier by any of the following events:

(A) The temporary manager notifies the department, and the department verifies, that the facility meets state and, if applicable, federal standards for operation, and will be able to continue to maintain compliance with those standards after the termination of the appointment of the temporary manager.

(B) The department approves a new temporary manager.

(C) A new operator is licensed.

(D) The department closes the facility.

(E) A hearing or court order ends the temporary manager appointment, including the appointment of a receiver under Section 1569.482.

(F) The appointment is terminated by the department or the temporary manager.

(2) The appointment of a temporary manager shall authorize the temporary manager to act pursuant to this section. The appointment shall be made pursuant to a written agreement between the temporary manager and the department that outlines the

circumstances under which the temporary manager may expend funds. The department shall provide the licensee and administrator with a copy of the accusation to appoint a temporary manager at the time of appointment. The accusation shall notify the licensee of the licensee's right to petition the Office of Administrative Hearings for a hearing to contest the appointment of the temporary manager as described in subdivision (f) and shall provide the licensee with a form and appropriate information for the licensee's use in requesting a hearing.

(3) The director may rescind the appointment of a temporary manager and appoint a new temporary manager at any time that the director determines the temporary manager is not adhering to the conditions of the appointment.

(f) (1) The licensee of a residential care facility for the elderly may contest the appointment of the temporary manager by filing a petition for an order to terminate the appointment of the temporary manager with the Office of Administrative Hearings within 15 days from the date of mailing of the accusation to appoint a temporary manager under subdivision (e). On the same day the petition is filed with the Office of Administrative Hearings, the licensee shall serve a copy of the petition to the office of the director.

(2) Upon receipt of a petition under paragraph (1), the Office of Administrative Hearings shall set a hearing date and time within 10 business days of the receipt of the petition. The office shall promptly notify the licensee and the department of the date, time, and place of the hearing. The office shall assign the case to an administrative law judge. At the hearing, relevant evidence may be presented pursuant to Section 11513 of the Government Code. The administrative law judge shall issue a written decision on the petition within 10 business days of the conclusion of the hearing. The 10-day time period for holding the hearing and for rendering a decision may be extended by the written agreement of the parties.

(3) The administrative law judge shall uphold the appointment of the temporary manager if the department proves, by a preponderance of the evidence, that the circumstances specified in subdivision (c) applied to the facility at the time of the appointment. The administrative law judge shall order the termination of the temporary manager if the burden of proof is not satisfied.

(4) The decision of the administrative law judge is subject to judicial review as provided in Section 1094.5 of the Code of Civil Procedure by the superior court of the county where the facility is located. This review may be requested by the licensee of the facility or the department by filing a petition seeking relief from the order. The petition may also request the issuance of temporary injunctive relief pending the decision on the petition. The superior court shall hold a hearing within 10 business days of the filing of the petition and shall issue a decision on the petition within 10 days of the hearing. The department may be represented by legal counsel within the department for purposes of court proceedings authorized under this section.

(g) If the licensee does not protest the appointment or does not prevail at either the administrative hearing under paragraph (2) of subdivision (f) or the superior court hearing under paragraph (4) of subdivision (f), the temporary manager shall continue in accordance with subdivision (e).

(h) (1) If the licensee petitions the Office of Administrative Hearings pursuant to subdivision (f), the appointment of the temporary manager by the director pursuant to this section shall continue until it is terminated by the administrative law judge or by the superior court, or it shall continue until the conditions of subdivision (e) are satisfied, whichever is earlier.

(2) At any time during the appointment of the temporary manager, the director may request an extension of the appointment by filing a petition for hearing with the Office of Administrative Hearings and serving a copy of the petition on the licensee. The office shall proceed as specified in paragraph (2) of subdivision (f). The administrative law judge may extend the appointment of the temporary manager an additional 60 days upon a showing by the department that the conditions specified in subdivision (c) continue to exist.

(3) The licensee or the department may request review of the administrative law judge's decision on the extension as provided in paragraph (4) of subdivision (f).

(i) The temporary manager appointed pursuant to this section shall meet the following qualifications:

(1) Be qualified to oversee correction of deficiencies in a residential care facility for the elderly on the basis of experience and education.

(2) Not be the subject of any pending actions by the department or any other state agency nor have ever been excluded from a department-licensed facility or had a license or certification suspended or revoked by an administrative action by the department or any other state agency.

(3) Not have a financial ownership interest in the facility and not have a member of his or her immediate family who has a financial ownership interest in the facility.

(4) Not currently serve, or within the past two years have served, as a member of the staff of the facility.

(j) Payment of the costs of the temporary manager shall comply with the following requirements:

(1) Upon agreement with the licensee, the costs of the temporary manager and any other expenses in connection with the temporary management shall be paid directly by the facility while the temporary manager is assigned to that facility. Failure of the licensee to agree to the payment of those costs may result in the payment of the costs by the department and subsequent required reimbursement of the department by the licensee pursuant to this section.

(2) Direct costs of the temporary manager shall be equivalent to the sum of the following:

(A) The prevailing fee paid by licensees for positions of the same type in the facility's geographic area.

(B) Additional costs that reasonably would have been incurred by the licensee if the licensee and the temporary manager had been in an employment relationship.

(C) Other reasonable costs incurred by the temporary manager in furnishing services pursuant to this section.

(3) Direct costs may exceed the amount specified in paragraph (2) if the department is otherwise unable to find a qualified temporary manager.

(k) (1) The responsibilities of the temporary manager may include, but are not limited to, the following:

(A) Paying wages to staff. The temporary manager shall have the full power to hire, direct, manage, and discharge employees of the facility, subject to any contractual rights they may have. The temporary manager shall pay employees at the same rate of compensation, including benefits, that the employees would have received from the licensee or wages necessary to provide adequate staff for the protection of clients and compliance with the law.

(B) Preserving resident funds. The temporary manager shall be entitled to, and shall take possession of, all property or assets of residents that are in the possession of the licensee or administrator of the facility. The temporary manager shall preserve all property, assets, and records of residents of which the temporary manager takes possession.

(C) Contracting for outside services as may be needed for the operation of the facility. A contract for outside services in excess of five thousand dollars ($5,000) shall be approved by the director.

(D) Paying commercial creditors of the facility to the extent required to operate the facility. The temporary manager shall honor all leases, mortgages, and secured transactions affecting the building in which the facility is located and all goods and fixtures in the building, but only to the extent of payments that, in the case of a rental agreement, are for the use of the property during the period of the temporary management, or that, in the case of a purchase agreement, come due during the period of the temporary management.

(E) Performing all acts that are necessary and proper to maintain and operate the facility in accordance with sound fiscal policies. The temporary manager shall take action as is reasonably necessary to protect or conserve the assets or property of which the temporary manager takes possession and may use those assets or property only in the performance of the powers and duties set forth in this section.

(2) Expenditures by the temporary manager in excess of five thousand dollars ($5,000) shall be approved by the director. Total encumbrances and expenditures by the temporary manager for the duration of the temporary management shall not exceed the sum of forty-nine thousand nine hundred ninety-nine dollars ($49,999) unless approved by the director in writing.

(3) The temporary manager shall not make capital improvements to the facility in excess of five thousand dollars ($5,000) without the approval of the director.

(l) (1) To the extent department funds are advanced for the costs of the temporary manager or for other expenses in connection with the temporary management, the department shall be reimbursed from the revenues accruing to the facility or to the licensee or an entity related to the licensee. Any reimbursement received by the department shall be redeposited in the account from which the department funds were advanced. If the revenues are insufficient to reimburse the department, the unreimbursed amount shall constitute grounds for a monetary judgment in civil court and a subsequent lien upon the assets of the facility or the proceeds from the sale thereof. Pursuant to Chapter 2 (commencing with Section 697.010) of Division 2 of Title 9 of Part 2 of the Code of Civil Procedure, a lien against the personal assets of the facility or an entity related to the licensee based on the monetary judgment obtained shall be filed with the Secretary of State on the forms required for a notice of judgment lien. A lien against the real property of the facility or an entity related to the licensee based on the monetary judgment obtained shall be recorded with the county recorder of the county where the facility of the licensee is located or where the real property of the entity related to the licensee is located. The lien shall not attach to the interests of a lessor, unless the lessor is operating the facility. The authority to place a lien against the personal and real property of the licensee for the reimbursement of any state funds expended pursuant to this section shall be given judgment creditor priority.

(2) For purposes of this section, "entity related to the licensee" means an entity, other than a natural person, of which the licensee is a subsidiary or an entity in which a person who was obligated to disclose information under Section 1569.15 possesses an interest that would also require disclosure pursuant to Section 1569.15.

(m) Appointment of a temporary manager under this section does not relieve the licensee of any responsibility for the care and supervision of residents under this chapter. The licensee, even if the license is deemed surrendered or the facility abandoned, shall be required to reimburse the department for all costs associated with operation of the facility during the period the temporary manager is in place that are not accounted for by using facility revenues or for the relocation of residents handled by the department if the licensee fails to comply with the relocation requirements of Section 1569.525 or 1569.682 when required by the department to do so. If the licensee fails to reimburse the department under this section, then the department, along with using its own remedies available under this chapter, may request that the Attorney General's office, the city attorney's office, or the local district attorney's office seek any available criminal, civil, or administrative remedy, including, but not limited to, injunctive relief, restitution, and damages in the same manner as provided for in Chapter 5 (commencing with Section 17200) of Part 2 of Division 7 of the Business and Professions Code.

(n) The department may use funds from the emergency resident contingency account pursuant to Section 1569.48 when needed to supplement the operation of the facility or the transfer of residents under the control of the temporary manager appointed under this section if facility revenues are unavailable or exhausted when needed. Pursuant to subdivision (l), the licensee shall be required to reimburse the department for any funds used from the emergency resident contingency account during the period of control of the temporary manager and any incurred costs of collection.

(o) This section does not apply to a residential care facility for the elderly that serves six or fewer persons and is also the principal residence of the licensee.

(p) Notwithstanding any other provision of law, the temporary manager shall be liable only for damages resulting from gross negligence in the operation of the facility or intentional tortious acts.

(q) All governmental immunities otherwise applicable to the state shall also apply to the state in the use of a temporary manager in the operation of a facility pursuant to this section.

(r) A licensee is not liable for any occurrences during the temporary management under this section except to the extent that the occurrences are the result of the licensee's conduct.

(s) The department may adopt regulations for the administration of this section. (Amended by Stats. 2015, Ch. 303, Sec. 281. (AB 731) Effective January 1, 2016.) 1569.482.

(a) It is the intent of the Legislature in enacting this section to authorize the department to take quick, effective action to protect the health and safety of residents of residential care facilities for the elderly and to minimize the effects of transfer trauma that accompany the abrupt transfer of residents through a system whereby the department may apply for a court order appointing a receiver to temporarily operate a residential care facility for the elderly. The receivership is not intended to punish a licensee or to replace attempts to secure cooperative action to protect the residents' health and safety. The receivership is intended to protect the residents in the absence of other reasonably available alternatives. The receiver shall assume the operation of the facility in order to bring it into compliance with law, facilitate a transfer of ownership to a new licensee, or ensure the orderly transfer of residents should the facility be required to close.

(b) (1) Whenever circumstances exist indicating that continued management of a residential care facility by the current licensee would present a substantial probability or imminent danger of serious physical harm or death to the residents, or the facility is closing or intends to terminate operation as a residential care facility for the elderly and adequate arrangements for the relocation of residents have not been made at least 30 days prior to the closing or termination, the director may petition the superior court for the county in which the facility is located for an order appointing a receiver to temporarily operate the facility in accordance with this section.

(2) The petition shall allege the facts upon which the action is based and shall be supported by an affidavit of the director. A copy of the petition and affidavit together with an order to appear and show cause why temporary authority to operate the residential care facility for the elderly should not be vested in a receiver pursuant to this section, shall be delivered to the licensee, administrator, or a responsible person at the facility to the attention of the licensee and administrator. The order shall specify a hearing date, which shall be not less than 10, nor more than 15, days following delivery of the petition and order upon the licensee, except that the court may shorten or lengthen the time upon a showing of just cause.

(c) (1) If the director files a petition pursuant to subdivision (b) for appointment of a receiver to operate a residential care facility for the elderly, in accordance with Section 564 of the Code of Civil Procedure, the director may also petition the court, in accordance with Section 527 of the Code of Civil Procedure, for an order appointing a temporary receiver. A temporary receiver appointed by the court pursuant to this subdivision shall serve until the court has made a final determination on the petition for appointment of a receiver filed pursuant to subdivision (b). A receiver appointed pursuant to this subdivision shall have the same powers and duties as a receiver would have if appointed pursuant to subdivision (b). Upon the director filing a petition for a receiver, the receiver shall complete its application for a provisional license to operate a residential care facility for the elderly. For purposes of a provisional license issued to a receiver, the licensee's existing fire safety clearance shall serve as the fire safety clearance for the receiver's provisional license.

(2) At the time of the hearing, the department shall advise the licensee of the name of the proposed receiver. The receiver shall be a certified residential care facility for the elderly administrator or other responsible person or entity, as determined by the court, from a list of qualified receivers established by the department, and, if need be, with input from providers of residential care and consumer representatives. Persons appearing on the list shall have experience in the delivery of care services to clients of community care facilities, and, if feasible, shall have experience with the operation of a residential care facility for the elderly, shall not be the subject of any pending actions by the department or any other state agency, and shall not have ever been excluded from a department licensed facility nor have had a license or certification suspended or revoked by an administrative action by the department or any other state agency. The receivers shall have sufficient background and experience in management and finances to ensure compliance with orders issued by the court. The owner, licensee, or administrator shall not be appointed as the receiver unless authorized by the court.

(3) If at the conclusion of the hearing, which may include oral testimony and cross-examination at the option of any party, the court determines that adequate grounds exist for the appointment of a receiver and that there is no other reasonably available remedy to protect the residents, the court may issue an order appointing a receiver to temporarily operate the residential care facility for the elderly and enjoining the licensee from interfering with the receiver in the conduct of his or her duties. In these proceedings,

the court shall make written findings of fact and conclusions of law and shall require an appropriate bond to be filed by the receiver and paid for by the licensee. The bond shall be in an amount necessary to protect the licensee in the event of any failure on the part of the receiver to act in a reasonable manner. The bond requirement may be waived by the licensee.

(4) The court may permit the licensee to participate in the continued operation of the facility during the pendency of any receivership ordered pursuant to this section and shall issue an order detailing the nature and scope of participation.

(5) Failure of the licensee to appear at the hearing on the petition shall constitute an admission of all factual allegations contained in the petition for purposes of these proceedings only.

(6) The licensee shall receive notice and a copy of the application each time the receiver applies to the court or the department for instructions regarding his or her duties under this section, when an accounting pursuant to subdivision (i) is submitted, and when any other report otherwise required under this section is submitted. The licensee shall have an opportunity to present objections or otherwise participate in those proceedings.

(d) A person shall not impede the operation of a receivership created under this section. The receiver's access to, or possession of, the property shall not be interfered with during the term of the receivership. There shall be an automatic stay for a 60-day period subsequent to the appointment of a receiver of any action that would interfere with the functioning of the facility, including, but not limited to, cancellation of insurance policies executed by the licensees, termination of utility services, attachments, or setoffs of resident trust funds and working capital accounts and repossession of equipment in the facility.

(e) When a receiver is appointed, the licensee may, at the discretion of the court, be divested of possession and control of the facility in favor of the receiver. If the court divests the licensee of possession and control of the facility in favor of the receiver, the department shall immediately issue a provisional license to the receiver. Notwithstanding the applicable sections of this code governing the revocation of a provisional license, the provisional license issued to a receiver shall automatically expire upon the termination of the receivership. The receiver shall possess the provisional license solely for purposes of carrying out the responsibilities authorized by this section and the duties ordered by the court. The receiver shall have no right to appeal the expiration of the provisional license.

(f) A receiver appointed pursuant to this section:

(1) May exercise those powers and shall perform those duties ordered by the court, in addition to other duties provided by statute.

(2) Shall operate the facility in a manner that ensures the safety and adequate care for the residents.

(3) Shall have the same rights to possession of the building in which the facility is located, and of all goods and fixtures in the building at the time the petition for receivership is filed, as the licensee and administrator would have had if the receiver had not been appointed.

(4) May use the funds, building, fixtures, furnishings, and any accompanying consumable goods in the provision of care and services to residents and to any other persons receiving services from the facility at the time the petition for receivership was filed.

(5) Shall take title to all revenue coming to the facility in the name of the receiver who shall use it for the following purposes in descending order of priority:

(A) To pay wages to staff. The receiver shall have full power to hire, direct, manage, and discharge employees of the facility, subject to any contractual rights they may have. The receiver shall pay employees at the same rate of compensation, including benefits, that the employees would have received from the licensee or wages necessary to provide adequate staff for the protection of the clients and compliance with the law.

(B) To preserve resident funds. The receiver shall be entitled to, and shall take, possession of all property or assets of residents that are in the possession of the licensee or operator of the facility. The receiver shall preserve all property, assets, and records of residents of which the receiver takes possession.

(C) To contract for outside services as may be needed for the operation of the residential care facility for the elderly. A contract for outside services in excess of five thousand dollars ($5,000) shall be approved by the court.

(D) To pay commercial creditors of the facility to the extent required to operate the facility. Except as provided in subdivision (h), the receiver shall honor all leases, mortgages, and secured transactions affecting the building in which the facility is located and all goods and fixtures in the building of which the receiver has taken possession, but only to the extent of payments which, in the case of a rental agreement, are for the use of the property during the period of receivership, or which, in the case of a purchase agreement, come due during the period of receivership.

(E) To receive a salary, as approved by the court.

(F) To do all things necessary and proper to maintain and operate the facility in accordance with sound fiscal policies. The receiver shall take action as is reasonably necessary to protect or conserve the assets or property of which the receiver takes possession and may use those assets or property only in the performance of the powers and duties set out in this section and by order of the court.

(G) To ask the court for direction in the treatment of debts incurred prior to the appointment, if the licensee's debts appear extraordinary, of questionable validity, or unrelated to the normal and expected maintenance and operation of the facility, or if payment of the debts will interfere with the purposes of receivership.

(g) (1) A person who is served with notice of an order of the court appointing a receiver and of the receiver's name and address shall be liable to pay the receiver, rather than the licensee, for any goods or services provided by the residential care facility for the elderly after the date of the order. The receiver shall give a receipt for each payment and shall keep a copy of each receipt on file. The receiver shall deposit amounts received in a special account and shall use this account for all disbursements. Payment to the receiver pursuant to this subdivision shall discharge the obligation to the extent of the payment and shall not thereafter be the basis of a claim by the licensee or any other person. A resident shall not be evicted nor may any contract or rights be forfeited or impaired, nor may any forfeiture be effected or liability increased, by reason of an omission to pay the licensee, operator, or other person a sum paid to the receiver pursuant to this subdivision.

(2) This section shall not be construed to suspend, during the temporary management by the receiver, any obligation of the licensee for payment of local, state, or federal taxes. A licensee shall not be held liable for acts or omissions of the receiver during the term of the temporary management.

(3) Upon petition of the receiver, the court may order immediate payment to the receiver for past services that have been rendered and billed, and the court may also order a sum not to exceed one month's advance payment to the receiver of any sums that may become payable under the Medi-Cal program.

(h) (1) A receiver shall not be required to honor a lease, mortgage, or secured transaction entered into by the licensee of the facility and another party if the court finds that the agreement between the parties was entered into for a collusive, fraudulent purpose or that the agreement is unrelated to the operation of the facility.

(2) A lease, mortgage, or secured transaction or an agreement unrelated to the operation of the facility that the receiver is permitted to dishonor pursuant to this subdivision shall only be subject to nonpayment by the receiver for the duration of the receivership, and the dishonoring of the lease, mortgage, security interest, or other agreement, to this extent, by the receiver shall not relieve the owner or operator of the facility from any liability for the full amount due under the lease, mortgage, security interest, or other agreement.

(3) If the receiver is in possession of real estate or goods subject to a lease, mortgage, or security interest that the receiver is permitted to dishonor pursuant to paragraph (1), and if the real estate or goods are necessary for the continued operation of the facility, the receiver may apply to the court to set a reasonable rent, price, or rate of interest to be paid by the receiver during the duration of the receivership. The court shall hold a hearing on this application within 15 days. The receiver shall send notice of the application to any known owner of the property involved at least 10 days prior to the hearing.

(4) Payment by the receiver of the amount determined by the court to be reasonable is a defense to any action against the receiver for payment or possession of the goods or real estate, subject to the lease or mortgage, which is brought by any person who received the notice required by this subdivision. However, payment by the receiver of the amount determined by the court to be reasonable does not relieve the owner or operator of the facility from any liability for the difference between the amount paid by the receiver and the amount due under the original lease, mortgage, or security interest.

(i) A monthly accounting shall be made by the receiver to the department of all moneys received and expended by the receiver on or before the 15th day of the following month or as ordered by the court, and the remainder of income over expenses for that month shall be returned to the licensee. A copy of the accounting shall be provided to the licensee. The licensee or owner of the residential care facility for the elderly may petition the court for a determination as to the reasonableness of any expenditure made pursuant to paragraph (5) of subdivision (f).

(j) (1) The receiver shall be appointed for an initial period of not more than three months. The initial three-month period may be extended for additional periods not exceeding three months, as determined by the court pursuant to this section. At the end of one month, the receiver shall report to the court on its assessment of the probability that the residential care facility for the elderly will meet state standards for operation by the end of the initial three-month period and will continue to maintain compliance with those standards after termination of the receiver's management. If it appears that the facility cannot be brought into compliance with state standards within the initial three-month period, the court shall take appropriate action as follows:

(A) Extend the receiver's management for an additional three months if there is a substantial likelihood that the facility will meet state standards within that period and will maintain compliance with the standards after termination of the receiver's management. The receiver shall report to the court in writing upon the facility's progress at the end of six weeks of any extension ordered pursuant to this paragraph.

(B) Order the director to revoke or temporarily suspend, or both, the license pursuant to Section 1569.50 and extend the receiver's management for the period necessary to transfer clients in accordance with the transfer plan, but for not more than three months from the date of initial appointment of a receiver, or 14 days, whichever is greater. An extension of an additional three months may be granted if deemed necessary by the court.

(2) If it appears at the end of six weeks of an extension ordered pursuant to subparagraph (A) of paragraph (1) that the facility cannot be brought into compliance with state standards for operation or that it will not maintain compliance with those standards after the receiver's management is terminated, the court shall take appropriate action as specified in subparagraph (B) of paragraph (1).

(3) In evaluating the probability that a residential care facility for the elderly will maintain compliance with state standards of operation after the termination of receiver management ordered by the court, the court shall consider at least the following factors:

(A) The duration, frequency, and severity of past violations in the facility.

(B) History of compliance in other care facilities operated by the proposed licensee.

(C) Efforts by the licensee to prevent and correct past violations.

(D) The financial ability of the licensee to operate in compliance with state standards.

(E) The recommendations and reports of the receiver.

(4) Management of a residential care facility for the elderly operated by a receiver pursuant to this section shall not be returned to the licensee, to any person related to the licensee, or to any person who served as a member of the facility's staff or who was employed by the licensee prior to the appointment of the receiver unless both of the following conditions are met:

(A) The department believes that it would be in the best interests of the residents of the facility, requests that the court return the operation of the facility to the former licensee, and provides clear and convincing evidence to the court that it is in the best interests of the facility's residents to take that action.

(B) The court finds that the licensee has fully cooperated with the department in the appointment and ongoing activities of a receiver appointed pursuant to this section, and, if applicable, any temporary manager appointed pursuant to Section 1569.481.

(5) The owner of the facility may at any time sell, lease, or close the facility, subject to the following provisions:

(A) If the owner closes the facility, or the sale or lease results in the closure of the facility, the court shall determine if a transfer plan is necessary. If the court so determines, the court shall adopt and implement a transfer plan consistent with the provisions of Section 1569.682.

(B) If the licensee proposes to sell or lease the facility and the facility will continue to operate as a residential care facility for the elderly, the court and the department shall reevaluate any proposed transfer plan. If the court and the department determine that the sale or lease of the facility will result in compliance with licensing standards, the transfer plan and the receivership shall, subject to those conditions that the court may impose and enforce, be terminated upon the effective date of the sale or lease.

(k) (1) The salary of the receiver shall be set by the court commensurate with community care facility industry standards, giving due consideration to the difficulty of the duties undertaken, and shall be paid from the revenue coming to the facility. If the revenue is insufficient to pay the salary in addition to other expenses of operating the facility, the receiver's salary shall be paid from the emergency resident contingency account as provided in Section 1569.48. State advances of funds in excess of five thousand dollars ($5,000) shall be approved by the director. Total advances for encumbrances and expenditures shall not exceed the sum of forty-nine thousand nine hundred ninety-nine dollars ($49,999) unless approved by the director in writing.

(2) To the extent state funds are advanced for the salary of the receiver or for other expenses in connection with the receivership, as limited by subdivision (g), the state shall be reimbursed from the revenues accruing to the facility or to the licensee or an entity related to the licensee. Reimbursement received by the state shall be redeposited in the account from which the state funds were advanced. If the revenues are insufficient to reimburse the state, the unreimbursed amount shall constitute grounds for a monetary judgment in civil court and a subsequent lien upon the assets of the facility or the proceeds from the sale thereof. Pursuant to Chapter 2 (commencing with Section 697.010) of Division 2 of Title 9 of Part 2 of the Code of Civil Procedure, a lien against the personal assets of the facility or an entity related to the licensee based on the monetary judgment obtained shall be filed with the Secretary of State on the forms required for a notice of judgment lien. A lien against the real property of the facility or an entity related to the licensee based on the monetary judgment obtained shall be recorded with the county recorder of the county where the facility of the licensee is located or where the real property of the entity related to the licensee is located. The lien shall not attach to the interests of a lessor, unless the lessor is operating the facility. The authority to place a lien against the personal and real property of the licensee for the reimbursement of any state funds expended pursuant to this section shall be given judgment creditor priority.

(3) For purposes of this subdivision, "entity related to the licensee" means an entity, other than a natural person, of which the licensee is a subsidiary or an entity in which any person who was obligated to disclose information under Section 1569.15 possesses an interest that would also require disclosure pursuant to Section 1569.15.

(l) (1) This section does not impair the right of the owner of a residential care facility for the elderly to dispose of his or her property interests in the facility, but any facility operated by a receiver pursuant to this section shall remain subject to that administration until terminated by the court. The termination shall be promptly effectuated, provided that the interests of the residents have been safeguarded as determined by the court.

(2) This section does not limit the power of the court to appoint a receiver under any other applicable provision of law or to order any other remedy available under law.

(m) (1) Notwithstanding any other provision of law, the receiver shall be liable only for damages resulting from gross negligence in the operation of the facility or intentional tortious acts.

(2) All governmental immunities otherwise applicable to the State of California shall also apply in the use of a receiver in the operation of a facility pursuant to this section.

(3) The licensee is not liable for any occurrences during the receivership except to the extent that the occurrences are the result of the licensee's conduct.

(n) The department may adopt regulations for the administration of this section. This section does not impair the authority of the department to temporarily suspend licenses under Section 1569.50 or to reach a voluntary agreement with the licensee for alternate management of a community care facility including the use of a temporary manager under Section 1569.481. This section does not authorize the department to interfere in a labor dispute.

(o) This section does not apply to a residential care facility for the elderly that serves six or fewer persons and is also the principal residence of the licensee.

(p) This section does not apply to a licensee that has obtained a certificate of authority to offer continuing care contracts, as defined in paragraph (8) of subdivision (c) of Section 1771.

(Amended by Stats. 2015, Ch. 303, Sec. 282. (AB 731) Effective January 1, 2016.)

1569.485.

(a) Notwithstanding any other provision of this chapter, any person who violates Section 1569.10 or 1569.44, or both, shall be assessed by the department an immediate civil penalty in the amount of one hundred dollars ($100) per resident for each day of the violation, unless other remedies available to the department, including criminal prosecution, are deemed more effective by the department.

(b) The civil penalty authorized in subdivision (a) shall be doubled if an unlicensed facility is operated and the operator refuses to seek licensure or the operator seeks licensure and the licensure application is denied and the operator continues to operate the unlicensed facility, unless other remedies available to the department, including criminal prosecution, are deemed more effective by the department.

(c) An operator may appeal the assessment to the director. The department shall adopt regulations setting forth the appeal procedure.

(Amended by Stats. 1990, Ch. 1488, Sec. 2.)

1569.49.

(a) In addition to the suspension, temporary suspension, or revocation of a license issued under this chapter, the department shall levy civil penalties as follows:

(b) (1) The amount of the civil penalty shall be one hundred dollars ($100) per day for each violation of this chapter if the facility fails to correct a deficiency after being provided a specified length of time to correct that deficiency.

(A) If a licensee or a licensee's representative submits evidence to the department that the licensee has corrected a deficiency, and the department, after reviewing that evidence, has determined that the deficiency has been corrected, the civil penalty shall cease as of the day the department received that evidence.

(B) If the department deems it necessary, the department shall inspect the facility within five working days after the department receives evidence pursuant to subparagraph (A) to confirm that the deficiency has been corrected.

(C) If the department determines that the deficiency has not been corrected, the civil penalty shall continue to accrue from the date of the original citation.

(D) If the department is able to verify that the deficiency was corrected prior to the date on which the department received the evidence pursuant to subparagraph (A), the civil penalty shall cease as of that earlier date.

(2) (A) If the department issues a notification of deficiency to a facility for a repeat violation of a violation specified in paragraph (1), the department shall assess an immediate civil penalty of two hundred fifty dollars ($250) per repeat violation and one hundred dollars ($100) for each day the repeat violation continues after citation. The notification of deficiency shall state the manner in which the deficiency constitutes a repeat violation and shall be submitted to a supervisor for review and approval.

(B) For purposes of this section, "repeat violation" means a violation within 12 months of a prior violation of a statutory or regulatory provision designated by the same combination of letters or numerals, or both letters and numerals.

(C) Notwithstanding subparagraphs (A) and (B), the department, in its sole discretion, may reduce the civil penalty for the cited repeat violation to the level of the underlying violation, as applicable, if it determines that the cited repeat violation is not substantially similar to the original violation.

(3) If the nature or seriousness of the violation or the frequency of the violation warrants a higher penalty or an immediate civil penalty assessment, or both, as provided in this chapter, a correction of the deficiency shall not impact the imposition of a civil penalty.

(c) The department shall assess an immediate civil penalty of five hundred dollars ($500) per violation and one hundred dollars ($100) for each day the violation continues after citation for any of the following serious violations:

(1) Any violation that the department determines resulted in the injury or illness of a resident.

(2) (A) Fire clearance violations, including, but not limited to, overcapacity, ambulatory status, inoperable smoke alarms, and inoperable fire alarm systems. The civil penalty shall not be assessed if the licensee has done either of the following:

(i) Requested the appropriate fire clearance based on ambulatory, nonambulatory, or bedridden status, and the decision is pending.

(ii) Initiated eviction proceedings.

(B) A licensee denied a clearance for bedridden residents may appeal to the fire authority, and, if that appeal is denied, may subsequently appeal to the Office of the State Fire Marshal, and shall not be assessed an immediate civil penalty until the final appeal is decided, or after 60 days has passed from the date of the citation, whichever is earlier.

(3) Absence of supervision as required by statute or regulation.

(4) Accessible bodies of water, when prohibited in this chapter or regulations adopted pursuant to this chapter.

(5) Accessible firearms, ammunition, or both.

(6) Refused entry to a facility or any part of a facility in violation of Section 1569.32, 1569.33, or 1569.35.

(7) The presence of a person subject to a department Order of Exclusion on the premises.

(d) If the department issues a notification of deficiency to a facility for a repeat violation of a violation specified in subdivision (c), the department shall assess an immediate civil penalty of one thousand dollars ($1,000) per repeat violation and one hundred dollars ($100) for each day the repeat violation continues after citation. The notification of deficiency shall state the manner in which the deficiency constitutes a repeat violation and shall be submitted to a supervisor for review and approval.

(e) For a violation that the department determines resulted in the death of a resident, the civil penalty shall be fifteen thousand dollars ($15,000).

(f) For a violation that the department determines constitutes physical abuse, as defined in Section 15610.63 of the Welfare and Institutions Code, or resulted in serious bodily injury, as defined in Section 15610.67 of the Welfare and Institutions Code, to a resident, the civil penalty shall be ten thousand dollars ($10,000).

(g) (1) Before the assessment of a civil penalty pursuant to subdivision (e) or (f), the decision shall be approved by the program administrator of the Community Care Licensing Division.

(2) (A) The department shall reduce the amount of a civil penalty due pursuant to subdivision (e) or (f) by the amount of the civil penalty already assessed for the underlying violation.

(B) If the amount of the civil penalty that the department has already assessed for the underlying violation exceeds the amount of the penalty pursuant to subdivision (e) or (f), the larger amount shall prevail and be due and payable as already assessed by the department.

(h) (1) A notification of a deficiency written by a representative of the department shall include a factual description of the nature of the deficiency fully stating the manner in which the licensee failed to comply with the specified statute or regulation, and, if applicable, the particular place or area of the facility in which the deficiency occurred. The department shall make a good faith effort to work with the licensee to determine the cause of the deficiency and ways to prevent any repeat violations.

(2) The department shall adopt regulations setting forth the appeal procedures for deficiencies.

(i) (1) A licensee shall have the right to submit to the department a written request for a formal review of a civil penalty assessed pursuant to subdivisions (e) and (f) within 15 business days of receipt of the notice of a civil penalty assessment and shall provide all available supporting documentation at that time. The review shall be conducted by the deputy director of the Community Care Licensing Division. The licensee may submit additional supporting documentation that was unavailable at the time of submitting the request for review within the first 30 business days after submitting the request for review. If the department requires additional information from the licensee, that information shall be requested within the first 30 business days after receiving the request for review. The licensee shall provide this additional information within 30 business days of receiving the request from the department. If the deputy director determines that the civil penalty was not assessed, or the finding of the deficiency that resulted in the assessment of the civil penalty was not made, in accordance with applicable statutes or regulations of the department, he or she may amend or dismiss the civil penalty or finding of deficiency. The licensee shall be notified in writing of the deputy director's decision within 60 business days of the date when all necessary information has been provided to the department by the licensee.

(2) Upon exhausting the review described in paragraph (1), a licensee may further appeal that decision to an administrative law judge. Proceedings shall be conducted in accordance with Chapter 5 (commencing with Section 11500) of Part 1 of Division 3 of Title 2 of the Government Code, and the department shall have all the powers granted by those provisions. In all proceedings conducted in accordance with this section, the standard of proof shall be by a preponderance of the evidence.

(3) If, in addition to an assessment of civil penalties, the department elects to file an administrative action to suspend or revoke the facility license that includes violations relating to the assessment of the civil penalties, the department review of the pending appeal shall cease and the assessment of the civil penalties shall be heard as part of the administrative action process.

(4) Civil penalties shall be due and payable when administrative appeals have been exhausted. Unless payment arrangements have been made that are acceptable to the department, a civil penalty not paid within 30 days shall be subject to late fees, as specified by the department in regulation.

(j) (1) A licensee shall have the right to submit to the department a written request for a formal review of any other civil penalty or deficiency not described in subdivision (i) within 15 business days of receipt of the notice of a civil penalty assessment or a finding of a deficiency, and shall provide all available supporting documentation at that time. The review shall be conducted by a regional manager of the Community Care Licensing Division. The licensee may submit additional supporting documentation that was unavailable at the time of submitting the request for review within the first 30 business days after submitting the request for review. If the department requires additional information from the licensee, that information shall be requested within the first 30 business days after receiving the request for review. The licensee shall provide this additional information within 30 business days of receiving the request from the department. If the regional manager determines that the civil penalty was not assessed, or the finding of the deficiency was not made, in accordance with applicable statutes or regulations of the department, he or she may amend or dismiss the civil penalty or finding of deficiency. The licensee shall be notified in writing of the regional manager's decision within 60 business days of the date when all necessary information has been provided to the department by the licensee.

(2) Upon exhausting the review described in paragraph (1), the licensee may further appeal that decision to the program administrator of the Community Care Licensing Division within 15 business days of receipt of notice of the regional manager's decision. The licensee may submit additional supporting documentation that was unavailable at the time of appeal to the program administrator within the first 30 business days after

requesting that appeal. If the department requires additional information from the licensee, that information shall be requested within the first 30 business days after receiving the request for the appeal. The licensee shall provide this additional information within 30 business days of receiving the request from the department. If the program administrator determines that the civil penalty was not assessed, or the finding of the deficiency was not made, in accordance with applicable statutes or regulations of the department, he or she may amend or dismiss the civil penalty or finding of deficiency. The licensee shall be notified in writing of the program administrator's decision within 60 business days of the date when all necessary information has been provided to the department by the licensee. The program administrator's decision is considered final and concludes the licensee's administrative appeal rights regarding the appeal conducted pursuant to this paragraph.

(3) Civil penalties shall be due and payable when administrative appeals have been exhausted. Unless payment arrangements have been made that are acceptable to the department, a civil penalty not paid within 30 days shall be subject to late fees, as specified by the department in regulation.

(k) The department shall adopt regulations implementing this section.

(l) The department shall, by January 1, 2016, amend its regulations to reflect the changes to this section made by Section 6 of Chapter 813 of the Statutes of 2014.

(m) Notwithstanding the Administrative Procedure Act (Chapter 3.5 (commencing with Section 11340) of Part 1 of Division 3 of Title 2 of the Government Code), the department may implement and administer the changes made by the act that added this subdivision through all-county letters or similar written instructions until regulations are adopted pursuant to the Administrative Procedure Act.

(n) This section shall become operative on July 1, 2017.

(Repealed (in Sec. 7) and added by Stats. 2016, Ch. 823, Sec. 8. (AB 2231) Effective January 1, 2017. Section operative July 1, 2017, by its own provisions.)
1569.495.

The civil, criminal, and administrative remedies available to the department pursuant to this article are not exclusive, and may be sought and employed in any combination deemed advisable by the state department to enforce this chapter.

(Added by Stats. 1985, Ch. 1127, Sec. 3.)

ARTICLE 5. Suspension and Revocation [1569.50 - 1569.545]

(Article 5 added by Stats. 1985, Ch. 1127, Sec. 3.)

1569.50.

(a) The department may deny an application for a license or may suspend or revoke a license issued under this chapter upon any of the following grounds and in the manner provided in this chapter:

(1) Violation by the licensee of this chapter or of the rules and regulations adopted under this chapter.

(2) Aiding, abetting, or permitting the violation of this chapter or of the rules and regulations adopted under this chapter.

(3) Conduct that is inimical to the health, morals, welfare, or safety of either an individual in or receiving services from the facility or the people of the State of California.

(4) The conviction of a licensee, or other person mentioned in Section 1569.17 at any time before or during licensure, of a crime as defined in Section 1569.17.

(5) Engaging in acts of financial malfeasance concerning the operation of a facility, including, but not limited to, improper use or embezzlement of client moneys and property or fraudulent appropriation for personal gain of facility moneys and property, or willful or negligent failure to provide services for the care of clients.

(b) The remedies provided in this section may be applied if the department finds that any employee, administrator, partner, officer, director, member, or manager of the applicant or licensee, any person who controls, as defined in Section 1569.2, the licensee, or any person who holds a beneficial ownership interest of 10 percent or more in the applicant or licensee has engaged in the conduct described in subdivision (a) related to any facility licensed pursuant to Chapter 1 (commencing with Section 1200), Chapter 2 (commencing with Section 1250), or Chapter 3 (commencing with Section 1500), or a similarly licensed facility in California or any other state.

(c) The director may temporarily suspend a license, prior to a hearing when, in the opinion of the director, the action is necessary to protect residents or clients of the facility from physical or mental abuse, abandonment, or any other substantial threat to health or safety. The director shall notify the licensee of the temporary suspension and the effective date of the temporary suspension and at the same time shall serve the provider with an accusation. Upon receipt of a notice of defense to the accusation by the licensee, the director shall, within 15 days, set the matter for hearing, and the hearing shall be held as soon as possible but not later than 30 days after receipt of the notice. The temporary suspension shall remain in effect until the time the hearing is completed and the director has made a final determination on the merits. However, the temporary suspension shall be deemed vacated if the director fails to make a final determination on the merits within 30 days after the original hearing has been completed.

(d) A licensee who abandons the facility and the residents in care resulting in an immediate and substantial threat to the health and safety of the abandoned residents, in addition to revocation of the license pursuant to this section, shall be excluded from licensure in facilities licensed by the department without the right to petition for reinstatement.

(Amended by Stats. 2015, Ch. 628, Sec. 5. (AB 601) Effective January 1, 2016.)
1569.51.

(a) Proceedings for the suspension, revocation, or denial of a license under this chapter shall be conducted in accordance with the provisions of Chapter 5 (commencing with Section 11500) of Part 1 of Division 3 of Title 2 of the Government Code, and the state department shall have all the powers granted by these provisions. In the event of conflict between this chapter and those provisions of the Government Code, the provisions of the Government Code shall prevail.

(b) In all proceedings conducted in accordance with this section, the standard of proof to be applied shall be by the preponderance of the evidence.

(c) If the license is not temporarily suspended pursuant to Section 1569.50, the hearing shall be held within 90 days after receipt of the notice of defense, unless a continuance of the hearing is granted by the department or the administrative law judge. When the matter has been set for hearing only the administrative law judge may grant a continuance of the hearing. The administrative law judge may, but need not, grant a continuance of the hearing, only upon finding the existence of one or more of the following:

(1) The death or incapacitating illness of a party, a representative or attorney of a party, a witness to an essential fact, or of the parent, child, or member of the household of such person, when it is not feasible to substitute another representative, attorney, or witness because of the proximity of the hearing date.

(2) Lack of notice of hearing as provided in Section 11509 of the Government Code.

(3) A material change in the status of the case where a change in the parties or pleadings requires postponement, or an executed settlement or stipulated findings of fact obviate the need for hearing. A partial amendment of the pleadings shall not be good cause for continuance to the extent that the unamended portion of the pleadings is ready to be heard.

(4) A stipulation for continuance signed by all parties or their authorized representatives, including, but not limited to, a representative, which is communicated with the request for continuance to the administrative law judge no later than 25 business days before the hearing.

(5) The substitution of the representative or attorney of a party upon showing that the substitution is required.

(6) The unavailability of a party, representative, or attorney of a party, or witness to an essential fact due to a conflicting and required appearance in a judicial matter if when the hearing date was set, the person did not know and could neither anticipate nor at any time avoid the conflict, and the conflict with request for continuance is immediately communicated to the administrative law judge.

(7) The unavailability of a party, a representative or attorney of a party, or a material witness due to an unavoidable emergency.

(8) Failure by a party to comply with a timely discovery request if the continuance request is made by the party who requested the discovery.

(Amended by Stats. 1992, Ch. 1315, Sec. 22. Effective January 1, 1993.)
1569.510.

(a) The department shall conduct an unannounced visit to a facility within 30 days after the effective date of a temporary suspension of a license in order to ensure that the facility is nonoperational, unless the department previously has verified that the facility is nonoperational.

(b) The department shall conduct an unannounced visit to a facility within 30 days after the effective date of a revocation of a license in order to ensure that the facility is nonoperational, unless the department previously has verified that the facility is nonoperational.

(Added by Stats. 2008, Ch. 291, Sec. 17. Effective September 25, 2008.)
1569.511.

(a) The administrative law judge conducting a hearing under this article may permit the testimony of a child witness, or a similarly vulnerable witness, including a witness who is developmentally disabled, to be taken outside the presence of the respondent or respondents if all of the following conditions exist:

(1) The administrative law judge determines that taking the witness's testimony outside the presence of the respondent or respondents is necessary to ensure truthful testimony.

(2) The witness is likely to be intimidated by the presence of the respondent or respondents.

(3) The witness is afraid to testify in front of the respondent or respondents.

(b) If the testimony of the witness is taken outside of the presence of the respondent or respondents, the department shall provide for the use of one-way closed-circuit television so the respondent or respondents can observe the testimony of the witness. Nothing in this section shall limit a respondent's right of cross-examination.

(c) The administrative law judge conducting a hearing under this section may clear the hearing room of any persons who are not a party to the action in order to protect any witness from intimidation or other harm, taking into account the rights of all persons.

(Added by Stats. 1994, Ch. 1267, Sec. 7. Effective January 1, 1995.)
1569.512.

(a) (1) An out-of-court statement made by a minor under 12 years of age who is the subject or victim of an allegation at issue is admissible evidence at an administrative hearing conducted pursuant to this article. The out-of-court statement may be used to support a finding of fact unless an objection is timely made and the objecting party establishes that the statement is unreliable because it was the product of fraud, deceit, or undue influence. However, the out-of-court statement may not be the sole basis for the finding of fact, unless the adjudicator finds that the time, content, and circumstances of the statement provide sufficient indicia of reliability.

(2) The proponent of the statement shall give reasonable notice to all parties of the intended introduction of the statement at the hearing.

(3) For purposes of this subdivision, an objection is timely if it identifies with reasonable specificity the disputed out-of-court statement and it gives the proponent of the evidence a reasonable period of time to prepare a response to the objection prior to the hearing.

(b) This section shall not be construed to limit the right of any party to the administrative hearing to subpoena a witness whose statement is admitted as evidence or to introduce admissible evidence relevant to the weight of the hearsay evidence or the credibility of the hearsay declarant.

(Added by Stats. 2002, Ch. 707, Sec. 3. Effective January 1, 2003.)

1569.515.

In addition to the witness fees and mileage provided by Section 11450.40 of the Government Code, the department may pay actual, necessary, and reasonable expenses in an amount not to exceed the per diem allowance payable to a nonrepresented state employee on travel status. The department may pay witness expenses pursuant to this section in advance of the hearing.

(Amended by Stats. 1995, Ch. 938, Sec. 62. Effective January 1, 1996. Operative July 1, 1997, by Sec. 98 of Ch. 938.)

1569.52.

The withdrawal of an application for a license after it has been filed with the department shall not, unless the department consents in writing to such withdrawal, deprive the department of its authority to institute or continue a proceeding against the applicant for the denial of the license upon any ground provided by law or to enter an order denying the license upon any such ground.

The suspension, expiration, or forfeiture by operation of law of a license issued by the department, or its suspension, forfeiture, or cancellation by order of the department or by order of a court of law, or its surrender without the written consent of the department, shall not deprive the department of its authority to institute or continue a disciplinary proceeding against the licensee upon any ground provided by law or to enter an order suspending or revoking the license or otherwise taking disciplinary action against the licensee on any such ground.

(Added by Stats. 1985, Ch. 1127, Sec. 3.)

1569.525.

(a) If the director determines that it is necessary to temporarily suspend or to revoke any license of a residential care facility for the elderly in order to protect the residents or clients of the facility from physical or mental abuse, abandonment, or any other substantial threat to health or safety pursuant to Section 1569.50, the department shall make every effort to minimize trauma for the residents.

(b) (1) (A) After a decision is made to temporarily suspend or, upon an order, to revoke the license of a residential care facility for the elderly which is likely to result in closure of the facility, the department shall contact both of the following:

(i) The Office of the State Long-Term Care Ombudsman.

(ii) Any local agency that may have placement or advocacy responsibility for the residents of a residential care facility for the elderly.

(B) The department shall work with these agencies, and the licensee if the director determines it to be appropriate, to locate alternative placement sites and to contact relatives or other persons responsible for the care of these residents, and to assist in the transfer of residents.

(2) The department shall use appropriately skilled professionals deemed appropriate by the department to provide onsite evaluation of the residents and assist in any transfers.

(3) The department shall require the licensee to prepare and submit to the licensing agency a written plan for relocation and compliance with the terms and conditions of the approved plans, and to provide other information as necessary for the enforcement of this section.

(c) Upon receipt of an order to temporarily suspend or revoke a license, the licensee shall be prohibited from accepting new residents or entering into admission agreements for new residents.

(d) Upon an order to temporarily suspend a license, the following shall apply:

(1) The licensee shall immediately provide written notice of the temporary suspension to the resident and initiate contact with the resident's responsible person, if applicable.

(2) The department may secure, or permit the licensee to secure, the services of a temporary manager who is not an immediate family member of the licensee or an entity that is not owned by the licensee to manage the day-to-day operations of the facility. The temporary manager shall be appointed and assume operation of the facility in accordance with Section 1569.481.

(e) Upon an order to revoke a license following the temporary suspension of a license pursuant to Section 1569.50 that led to the transfer of all residents, the following applies:

(1) The licensee shall provide a 60-day written notice of license revocation that may lead to closure to the resident and the resident's responsible person within 24 hours of receipt of the department's order of revocation.

(2) The department shall permit the licensee to secure the services of a temporary manager who is not an immediate family member of the licensee or an entity that is not owned by the licensee to manage the day-to-day operations of the residential care facility for the elderly for a period of at least 60 days, provided that all of the following conditions are met:

(A) A proposal is submitted to the department within 72 hours of the licensee's receipt of the department's order of revocation that includes both of the following:

(i) A completed "Application for a Community Care Facility or Residential Care Facility for the Elderly License" form (LIC 200), or similar form as determined by the department, signed and dated by both the licensee and the person or entity described in paragraph (2).

(ii) A copy of the executed agreement between the licensee and the person or entity described in paragraph (2) that delineates the roles and responsibilities of each party and specifies that the person or entity described in paragraph (2) shall have the full

authority necessary to operate the facility, in compliance with all applicable laws and regulations, and without interference from the licensee.

(B) The person or entity described in paragraph (2) shall be currently licensed and in substantial compliance to operate a residential care facility for the elderly that is of comparable size or greater and has comparable programming to the facility. For purposes of this subparagraph, the following definitions apply:

(i) "Comparable programming" includes, but is not limited to, dementia care, hospice care, and care for residents with exempted prohibited health care conditions.

(ii) "Comparable size" means a facility capacity of 1 to 15 residents, 16 to 49 residents, or 50 or more residents.

(C) The person or entity described in paragraph (2) is not subject to the application fee specified in Section 1569.185.

(D) If the department denies a proposal to secure the services of a person or entity pursuant to paragraph (2), this denial shall not be deemed a denial of a license application subject to the right to a hearing under Section 1569.22 and other procedural rights under Section 1569.51.

(f) (1) Notwithstanding Section 1569.651 or any other law, for paid preadmission fees, a resident who transfers from the facility due to the notice of temporary suspension or revocation of a license pursuant to this section is entitled to a refund in accordance with all of the following:

(A) A 100-percent refund if preadmission fees were paid within six months of either notice of closure required by this section.

(B) A 75-percent refund if preadmission fees were paid more than six months, but not more than 12 months, before either notice required by this section.

(C) A 50-percent refund if preadmission fees were paid more than 12 months, but not more than 18 months, before either notice required by this section.

(D) A 25-percent refund if preadmission fees were paid more than 18 months, but not more than 25 months, before either notice required by this section.

(2) A preadmission fee refund is not required if preadmission fees were paid 25 months or more before either notice required by this section.

(3) The preadmission fee refund required by this paragraph shall be paid within 15 days of issuing either notice required by this section. In lieu of the refund, the resident may request that the licensee provide a credit toward the resident's monthly fee obligation in an amount equal to the preadmission fee refund due.

(4) If a resident transfers from the facility due to the revocation of a license, and the resident gives notice at least five days before leaving the facility, or if the transfer is due to a temporary suspension of the license order, the licensee shall refund to the resident or his or her legal representative a proportional per diem amount of any prepaid monthly fees at the time the resident leaves the facility and the unit is vacated. Otherwise the licensee shall pay the refund within seven days from the date that the resident leaves the facility and the unit is vacated.

(g) Within 24 hours after each resident who is transferring pursuant to these provisions has left the facility, the licensee that had his or her license temporarily suspended or revoked shall, based on information provided by the resident or the resident's responsible person, submit a final list of names and new locations of all residents to the department and the local ombudsman program.

(h) If at any point during or following a temporary suspension or revocation order of a license the director determines that there is a risk to the residents of a facility of physical or mental abuse, abandonment, or any other substantial threat to health or safety, the department shall take any necessary action to minimize trauma for the residents, including, but not limited to, all of the following:

(1) Contact any local agency that may have placement or advocacy responsibility for the residents and work with those agencies to locate alternative placement sites.

(2) Contact the residents' relatives, legal representatives, authorized agents in a health care directive, or responsible parties.

(3) Assist in the transfer of residents, and, if necessary, arrange or coordinate transportation.

(4) Provide onsite evaluation of the residents and use any medical personnel deemed appropriate by the department to provide onsite evaluation of the residents and assist in any transfers.

(5) Arrange for or coordinate care and supervision.

(6) Arrange for the distribution of medications.

(7) Arrange for the preparation and service of meals and snacks.

(8) Arrange for the preparation of the residents' records and medications for transfer of each resident.

(9) Assist in any way necessary to facilitate a safe transfer of all residents.

(10) Check on the status of each transferred resident within 24 hours of transfer.

(i) The participation of the department and local agencies in the relocation of residents from a residential care facility for the elderly shall not relieve the licensee of any responsibility under this section. A licensee that fails to comply with the requirements of this section shall be required to reimburse the department and local agencies for the cost of providing those services. If the licensee fails to provide the services required in this section, the department shall request that the Attorney General's office, the city attorney's office, or the local district attorney's office seek injunctive relief and damages.

(j) Notwithstanding Section 1569.49, a licensee who fails to comply with the requirements of this section shall be liable for civil penalties in the amount of five hundred dollars ($500) per violation per day for each day that the licensee is in violation of this section, until the violation has been corrected. The civil penalties shall be issued immediately following the written notice of violation.

(k) This section does not preclude the department from amending the effective date in the order of suspension or revocation of a license and closing the facility, or from pursuing any other available remedies if necessary to protect the health and safety of the residents in care.

(Amended by Stats. 2015, Ch. 303, Sec. 283. (AB 731) Effective January 1, 2016.)

1569.53.

Any license suspended or revoked pursuant to this chapter may be reinstated pursuant to Section 11522 of the Government Code.

Whenever a license issued under this chapter for a residential care facility for the elderly is suspended, revoked, temporarily suspended, forfeited, canceled, or expires, the department shall provide written notice of the occurrence within 10 days to the local director of social services in the county in which the facility is located.

(Added by Stats. 1985, Ch. 1127, Sec. 3.)

1569.54.

(a) (1) When the department does not suspend the license of a residential care facility for the elderly pursuant to this article, the department may still order the licensee to remove a resident who has a health condition which cannot be cared for within the limits of the license or requires inpatient care in a health facility as determined by the department.

(2) Where the department determines that the resident's mental or physical condition requires immediate transfer from the facility in order to protect the health and safety of the resident, the department may order the licensee to remove the resident after the department consults with a physician or other medical professional about the transfer and ways in which transfer trauma can be minimized.

(b) (1) Where the department alleges that a resident has a health condition which cannot be cared for within the limits of the license or requires inpatient care in a health facility, the department shall give notice to the resident, his or her legal representative when appropriate, and the licensee. The notice shall specify a deadline for submitting a written plan for relocation and inform the resident of his or her right for a review and determination by an interdisciplinary team as provided for in Section 1569.34. The resident, or his or her legal representative, shall have three working days to inform the licensee of the request for review. Upon receiving a request from a resident, or his or her legal representative, for a review and determination, the licensee shall forward the request to the department within two working days of receipt. Failure or refusal by the licensee to submit the request for review and determination to the department may be subject to the civil penalties specified in Section 1569.49.

(2) The review and determination shall be completed within 30 days from the date that the resident was initially informed of the need to relocate. If the determination is made that the resident must relocate, the notice shall include a plan for transfer, including attempts to minimize transfer trauma for the resident.

The department may require the licensee to prepare and submit to the licensing agency a written plan for relocation, to comply with the terms and conditions of the approved plans and to provide other information as necessary for the enforcement of this section.

(c) The provisions allowing for a resident's right to a review prior to transfer as provided for in subdivision (b) neither negates the department's authority and responsibility to require an immediate transfer according to paragraph (2) of subdivision (a) when the department finds and provides evidence that the resident must be relocated in order to protect the health and safety of the resident, nor implies any right to a fair hearing pursuant to Chapter 7 (commencing with Section 10950) of Part 2 of Division 9 of the Welfare and Institutions Code.

The department shall specify in regulations the process provided for pursuant to this section for making relocation decisions and for appealing and reviewing these decisions. (Repealed and added by Stats. 1989, Ch. 1115, Sec. 24.)

1569.545.

(a) For purposes of this section, "suspension of new admissions" means a prohibition on admitting new residents to receive care or services in the facility.

(b) The department may order a suspension of new admissions for a facility in either of the following circumstances:

(1) The department finds that the facility has violated this chapter or any applicable regulations, the violation presents a direct and immediate risk to the health, safety, or personal rights of a resident or residents of the facility, and the violation is not corrected immediately.

(2) The facility has failed to pay a fine assessed by the department after the facility's appeal rights have been exhausted.

(c) A suspension of new admissions for a failure to pay a fine, as described in paragraph (2) of subdivision (b), shall remain in effect until the facility pays the fine assessed by the department.

(d) A suspension of new admissions under paragraph (1) of subdivision (b) shall remain in effect until the department determines that the facility has corrected the violation. The department shall conduct a followup visit to determine compliance within 10 working days following the latest date of correction specified in the notice of deficiency, unless the licensee has demonstrated that the deficiency was corrected as required in the notice. The department may make unannounced visits after the suspension of new admissions is lifted to ensure that the facility continues to maintain correction of the violation. The department may order another suspension of new admissions or take other appropriate enforcement action if the facility does not maintain correction of the violation.

(e) A licensee may appeal a suspension of new admissions ordered under this section to the director. The department shall adopt regulations that specify the appeal procedure.

(f) A suspension of new admissions ordered under this section shall not be stayed pending the facility's appeal or request for review.

(Added by Stats. 2014, Ch. 706, Sec. 1. (SB 1153) Effective January 1, 2015.)

ARTICLE 5.5. Employee Actions [1569.58 - 1569.595]

(Article 5.5 added by Stats. 1989, Ch. 825, Sec. 2.)

1569.58.

(a) The department may prohibit any person from being a licensee, owning a beneficial ownership interest of 10 percent or more in a licensed facility, or being an administrator, officer, director, member, or manager of a licensee or entity controlling a licensee, and may further prohibit any licensee from employing, or continuing the employment of, or allowing in a licensed facility, or allowing contact with clients of a licensed facility by, any employee, prospective employee, or person who is not a client and who has done any of the following:

(1) Violated, or aided or permitted the violation by any other person of, any provisions of this chapter or of any rules or regulations promulgated under this chapter.

(2) Engaged in conduct that is inimical to the health, morals, welfare, or safety of either an individual in or receiving services from the facility, or the people of the State of California.

(3) Been denied an exemption to work or to be present in a facility, when that person has been convicted of a crime as defined in Section 1569.17.

(4) Engaged in any other conduct that would constitute a basis for disciplining a licensee.

(5) Engaged in acts of financial malfeasance concerning the operation of a facility, including, but not limited to, improper use or embezzlement of client moneys and property or fraudulent appropriation for personal gain of facility moneys and property, or willful or negligent failure to provide services for the care of clients.

(b) The excluded person, the facility, and the licensee shall be given written notice of the basis of the department's action and of the excluded person's right to an appeal. The notice shall be served either by personal service or by registered mail. Within 15 days after the department serves the notice, the excluded person may file with the department a written appeal of the exclusion order. If the excluded person fails to file a written appeal within the prescribed time, the department's action shall be final.

(c) (1) The department may require the immediate removal of a member of the board of directors, an executive director, or an officer of a licensee or exclusion of an employee, prospective employee, or person who is not a client from a facility pending a final decision of the matter, when, in the opinion of the department, the action is necessary to protect residents or clients from physical or mental abuse, abandonment, or any other substantial threat to their health or safety.

(2) If the department requires the immediate removal of a member of the board of directors, an executive director, or an officer of a licensee or exclusion of an employee, prospective employee, or person who is not a client from a facility the department shall serve an order of immediate exclusion upon the excluded person that shall notify the excluded person of the basis of the department's action and of the excluded person's right to a hearing.

(3) Within 15 days after the department serves an order of immediate exclusion, the excluded person may file a written appeal of the exclusion with the department. The department's action shall be final if the excluded person does not appeal the exclusion within the prescribed time. The department shall do the following upon receipt of a written appeal:

(A) Within 30 days of receipt of the appeal, serve an accusation upon the excluded person.

(B) Within 60 days of receipt of a notice of defense by the excluded person pursuant to Section 11506 of the Government Code, conduct a hearing on the accusation.

(4) An order of immediate exclusion of the excluded person from the facility shall remain in effect until the hearing is completed and the department has made a final determination on the merits. However, the order of immediate exclusion shall be deemed vacated if the department fails to make a final determination on the merits within 60 days after the original hearing has been completed.

(d) An excluded person who files a written appeal of the exclusion order with the department pursuant to this section shall, as part of the written request, provide his or her current mailing address. The excluded person shall subsequently notify the department in writing of any change in mailing address, until the hearing process has been completed or terminated.

(e) Hearings held pursuant to this section shall be conducted in accordance with Chapter 5 (commencing with Section 11500) of Division 3 of Title 2 of the Government Code. The standard of proof shall be the preponderance of the evidence and the burden of proof shall be on the department.

(f) The department may institute or continue a disciplinary proceeding against a member of the board of directors, an executive director, or an officer of a licensee or an employee, prospective employee, or person who is not a client upon any ground provided by this section. The department may enter an order prohibiting any person from being a member of the board of directors, an executive director, or an officer of a licensee, or prohibiting the excluded person's employment or presence in the facility, or otherwise take disciplinary action against the excluded person, notwithstanding any resignation, withdrawal of employment application, or change of duties by the excluded person, or any discharge, failure to hire, or reassignment of the excluded person by the licensee or that the excluded person no longer has contact with clients at the facility.

(g) A licensee's failure to comply with the department's exclusion order after being notified of the order shall be grounds for disciplining the licensee pursuant to Section 1569.50.

(h) (1) (A) In cases in which the excluded person appealed the exclusion order and there is a decision and order of the department upholding the exclusion order, the person shall be prohibited from working in any facility or being licensed to operate any facility licensed by the department or from being a certified foster parent or resource family for the remainder of the excluded person's life, unless otherwise ordered by the department.

(B) The excluded individual may petition for reinstatement one year after the effective date of the decision and order of the department upholding the exclusion order pursuant to Section 11522 of the Government Code. The department shall provide the excluded person with a copy of Section 11522 of the Government Code with the decision and order.

(2) (A) In cases in which the department informed the excluded person of his or her right to appeal the exclusion order and the excluded person did not appeal the exclusion order, the person shall be prohibited from working in any facility or being licensed to operate any facility licensed by the department or a certified foster parent or resource family for the remainder of the excluded person's life, unless otherwise ordered by the department.

(B) The excluded individual may petition for reinstatement after one year has elapsed from the date of the notification of the exclusion order pursuant to Section 11522 of the Government Code. The department shall provide the excluded person with a copy of Section 11522 of the Government Code with the exclusion order.
(Amended by Stats. 2017, Ch. 732, Sec. 35. (AB 404) Effective January 1, 2018.)

1569.59.
(a) (1) If the department determines that a person was issued a license under this chapter or under Chapter 1 (commencing with Section 1200), Chapter 2 (commencing with Section 1250), Chapter 3.01 (commencing with Section 1568.01), Chapter 3.2 (commencing with Section 1569), Chapter 3.4 (commencing with Section 1596.70), Chapter 3.5 (commencing with Section 1596.90), or Chapter 3.6 (commencing with Section 1597.30) and the prior license was revoked within the preceding two years, the department shall exclude the person from, and remove him or her from the position of, a member of the board of directors, an executive director, or an officer of a licensee of, any facility licensed by the department pursuant to the chapter.

(2) If the department determines that a person previously was issued a certificate of approval by a foster family agency which was revoked by the department pursuant to subdivision (b) of Section 1534 within the preceding two years, the department shall exclude the person from, and remove him or her from the position of, a member of the board of directors, an executive director, or an officer of a licensee of, any facility licensed by the department pursuant to this chapter.

(b) If the department determines that the person had previously applied for a license under any of the chapters listed in paragraph (1) of subdivision (a) and the application was denied within the last year, the department shall exclude the person from, and remove him or her from the position of, a member of the board of directors, an executive director, or an officer of a licensee of, any facility licensed by the department pursuant to this chapter and as follows:

(1) In cases where the applicant petitioned for a hearing, the department shall exclude the person from, and remove him or her from the position of, a member of the board of directors, an executive director, or an officer of a licensee of, any facility licensed by the department pursuant to this chapter until one year has elapsed from the effective date of the decision and order of the department upholding a denial.

(2) In cases where the department informed the applicant of his or her right to petition for a hearing and the applicant did not petition for a hearing, the department shall exclude the person from, and remove him or her from the position of, a member of the board of directors, an executive director, or an officer of a licensee of, any facility licensed by the department pursuant to this chapter until one year has elapsed from the date of the notification of the denial and the right to petition for a hearing.

(c) If the department determines that the person had previously applied for a certificate of approval with a foster family agency and the department ordered the foster family agency to deny the application pursuant to subdivision (b) of Section 1534, the department shall exclude the person from, and remove him or her from the position of, a member of the board of directors, an executive director, or an officer of a licensee of, any facility licensed by the department pursuant to this chapter and as follows:

(1) In cases where the applicant petitioned for a hearing, the department shall exclude the person from, and remove him or her from the position of, a member of the board of directors, an executive director, or an officer of a licensee of, any facility licensed by the department pursuant to this chapter until one year has elapsed from the effective date of the decision and order of the department upholding a denial.

(2) In cases where the department informed the applicant of his or her right to petition for a hearing and the applicant did not petition for a hearing, the department shall exclude the person from, and remove him or her from the position of, a member of the board of directors, an executive director, or an officer of a licensee of, any facility licensed by the department pursuant to this chapter until one year has elapsed from the date of the notification of the denial and the right to petition for a hearing.

(d) Exclusion or removal of an individual pursuant to this section shall not be considered an order of exclusion for purposes of Section 1569.58 or any other law.

(e) The department may determine not to exclude a person from, and remove him or her from the position of, a member of the board of directors, an executive director, or an officer of a licensee of, any facility licensed by the department pursuant to this chapter if it has been determined that the reasons for the denial of the application or revocation of the facility license or certificate of approval were due to circumstances or conditions that either have been corrected or are no longer in existence.
(Amended by Stats. 1998, Ch. 311, Sec. 41. Effective August 19, 1998.)

1569.595.
The department shall conduct an unannounced visit to a facility within 30 days after the department serves an order of immediate exclusion from the facility upon the licensee or a person subject to immediate removal or exclusion from the facility pursuant to paragraph (3) of subdivision (c) of Section 1569.17 and subdivision (c) of Section 1569.58 in order to ensure that the excluded person is not within the facility, unless the department previously has verified that the excluded person is not within the facility.
(Added by Stats. 2008, Ch. 291, Sec. 18. Effective September 25, 2008.)

ARTICLE 6. Other Provisions [1569.60 - 1569.696]
(Article 6 added by Stats. 1985, Ch. 1127, Sec. 3.)

1569.60.
(a) The director shall require as a condition precedent to the issuance of any license for a residential care facility for the elderly, if the licensee handles or will handle any money of a person within the facility, that the applicant for the license file or have on file with the department a bond issued by a surety company admitted to do business in this state in a sum to be fixed by the department based upon the magnitude of the operations of the applicant, but which sum shall not be less than one thousand dollars ($1,000), running to the State of California and conditioned upon his or her faithful and honest handling of the money of persons within the facility.

(b) The failure of any licensee under this chapter to maintain on file with the state department a bond in the amount prescribed by the director or who embezzles the trust funds of a person in the facility shall constitute cause for the revocation of the license.

(c) The provisions of this section shall not apply if the licensee handles moneys of persons within the residential care facility for the elderly in amounts less than fifty dollars ($50) per person and less than five hundred dollars ($500) for all persons in any month.
(Amended by Stats. 1992, Ch. 1315, Sec. 24. Effective January 1, 1993.)

1569.601.
The director may grant a partial or total variance from the bonding requirements of Section 1569.60 for any residential care facility for the elderly if he or she finds that compliance with them is so onerous that a residential care facility for the elderly will cease to operate, and if he or she also finds that money of the persons received or cared for in the facility has been, or will be, deposited in a bank in this state, in a trust company authorized to transact a trust business in this state, or in a savings and loan association in this state, upon condition that the money may not be withdrawn except on authorization of the guardian or conservator of the person.
(Added by renumbering Section 1569.61 by Stats. 1989, Ch. 1115, Sec. 25.)

1569.605.
On and after July 1, 2015, all residential care facilities for the elderly, except those facilities that are an integral part of a continuing care retirement community, shall maintain liability insurance covering injury to residents and guests in the amount of at least one million dollars ($1,000,000) per occurrence and three million dollars ($3,000,000) in the total annual aggregate, caused by the negligent acts or omissions to act of, or neglect by, the licensee or its employees.
(Added by Stats. 2014, Ch. 205, Sec. 1. (AB 1523) Effective January 1, 2015.)

1569.61.
The department shall develop and maintain at each district office a file for each facility in that district, containing all documents regarding the facility that were received or created by the department on or after January 1, 1999, and that are not confidential under other provisions of law. This file shall be available immediately upon the request of any consumer who shall have the right to obtain copies of documents from the file upon the payment of a reasonable charge for the copies.
(Added by Stats. 1998, Ch. 306, Sec. 3. Effective January 1, 1999.)

1569.613.
Any person who becomes an administrator of a residential care facility for the elderly on or after January 1, 1992, shall, at a minimum, comply with all of the following:
(a) Be at least 21 years of age.
(b) Have a valid certificate as an administrator of a residential care facility for the elderly as required by Section 1569.616, or have submitted the documentation required to obtain a certificate pursuant to subdivision (d) of Section 1569.616.
(c) Have a high school diploma or pass a general educational development test as described in Article 3 (commencing with Section 51420) of Chapter 3 of Part 28 of the Education Code.
(d) Obtain criminal record clearance as provided for in Sections 1569.17 and 1569.171.
(Amended by Stats. 1995, Ch. 224, Sec. 1. Effective January 1, 1996.)

1569.616.
(a) (1) An administrator of a residential care facility for the elderly shall be required to successfully complete a department-approved certification program prior to employment.
(2) In those cases where the individual is both the licensee and the administrator of a facility, or a licensed nursing home administrator, the individual shall comply with the requirements of this section unless he or she qualifies for one of the exemptions provided for in subdivision (b).
(3) Failure to comply with this section shall constitute cause for revocation of the license of the facility where an individual is functioning as the administrator.
(4) The licensee shall notify the department within 30 days of any change in administrators.
(b) Individuals seeking exemptions under paragraph (2) of subdivision (a) shall meet the following criteria and fulfill the required portions of the certification program, as the case may be:
(1) An individual designated as the administrator of a residential care facility for the elderly who holds a valid license as a nursing home administrator issued in accordance with Chapter 2.35 (commencing with Section 1416) of Division 2 shall be required to complete the areas in the uniform core of knowledge required by this section that pertain to the law, regulations, policies, and procedural standards that impact the operations of

residential care facilities for the elderly, the use, misuse, and interaction of medication commonly used by the elderly in a residential setting, and resident admission, retention, and assessment procedures, equal to 12 hours of classroom instruction. An individual meeting the requirements of this paragraph shall not be required to take a written test.

(2) In those cases where the individual was both the licensee and administrator on or before July 1, 1991, the individual shall be required to complete all the areas specified for the certification program, but shall not be required to take the written test required by this section. Those individuals exempted from the written test shall be issued a conditional certification that is valid only for the administrator of the facility for which the exemption was granted.

(A) As a condition to becoming an administrator of another facility, the individual shall be required to pass the written test provided for in this section.

(B) As a condition to applying for a new facility license, the individual shall be required to pass the written test provided for in Section 1569.23.

(c) (1) The administrator certification program shall require a minimum of 80 hours of coursework, which shall include at least 60 hours of in-person instruction that provides training on a uniform core of knowledge in each of the following areas:

(A) Laws, regulations, and policies and procedural standards that impact the operations of residential care facilities for the elderly.

(B) Business operations.

(C) Management and supervision of staff.

(D) Psychosocial needs of the elderly.

(E) Community and support services.

(F) Physical needs for elderly persons.

(G) Medication management, including the use, misuse, and interaction of medication commonly used by the elderly, including antipsychotics and the adverse effects of psychotropic drugs for use in controlling the behavior of persons with dementia.

(H) Resident admission, retention, and assessment procedures.

(I) Managing Alzheimer's disease and related dementias, including nonpharmacologic, person-centered approaches to dementia care.

(J) Cultural competency and sensitivity in issues relating to the underserved aging lesbian, gay, bisexual, and transgender community.

(K) Residents' rights and the importance of initial and ongoing training for all staff to ensure that residents' rights are fully respected and implemented.

(L) Managing the physical environment, including, but not limited to, maintenance and housekeeping.

(M) Postural supports, restricted health conditions, and hospice care.

(2) Individuals applying for certification under this section shall successfully complete an approved certification program, pass a written test administered by the department within 60 days of completing the program, and submit the documentation required by subdivision (d) to the department within 30 days of being notified of having passed the test. The department may extend these time deadlines for good cause. The department shall notify the applicant of his or her test results within 30 days of administering the test.

(3) The department shall ensure the test consists of at least 100 questions and allows an applicant to have access to the California Residential Care Facilities for the Elderly Act and related regulations during the test. The department, no later than July 1 of every other year, shall review and revise the test in order to ensure the rigor and quality of the test. Each year, the department shall ensure, by January 1, that the test is not in conflict with prevailing law. The department may convene a stakeholder group to assist in developing and reviewing test questions.

(d) The department shall not begin the process of issuing a certificate until receipt of all of the following:

(1) A certificate of completion of the administrator training required pursuant to this chapter.

(2) The fee required for issuance of the certificate. A fee of one hundred dollars ($100) shall be charged by the department to cover the costs of processing the application for certification.

(3) Documentation of passing the written test or of qualifying for an exemption pursuant to subdivision (b).

(4) Submission of fingerprints. The department and the Department of Justice shall expedite the criminal record clearance for holders of certificates of completion. The department may waive the submission for those persons who have a current criminal record clearance on file.

(e) It shall be unlawful for a person not certified under this section to hold himself or herself out as a certified administrator of a residential care facility for the elderly. Any person willfully making a false representation as being a certified administrator is guilty of a misdemeanor.

(f) (1) Certificates issued under this section shall be renewed every two years and renewal shall be conditional upon the certificate holder submitting documentation of completion of 40 hours of continuing education related to the uniform core of knowledge specified in paragraph (1) of subdivision (c). No more than one-half of the required 40 hours of continuing education necessary to renew the certificate may be satisfied through online courses. All other continuing education hours shall be completed in a classroom setting. For purposes of this section, individuals who hold a valid license as a nursing home administrator issued in accordance with Chapter 2.35 (commencing with Section 1416) of Division 2 and meet the requirements of paragraph (1) of subdivision (b) shall only be required to complete 20 hours of continuing education.

(2) Every certified administrator of a residential care facility for the elderly is required to renew his or her certificate and shall complete the continuing education requirements of this subdivision whether he or she is certified according to subdivision (a) or (b). At least

eight hours of the 40-hour continuing education requirement for a certified administrator of a residential care facility for the elderly shall include instruction on serving clients with dementia, including, but not limited to, instruction related to direct care, physical environment, and admissions procedures and assessment.

(3) Certificates issued under this section shall expire every two years, on the anniversary date of the initial issuance of the certificate, except that any administrator receiving his or her initial certification on or after January 1, 1999, shall make an irrevocable election to have his or her recertification date for any subsequent recertification either on the date two years from the date of issuance of the certificate or on the individual's birthday during the second calendar year following certification. The department shall send a renewal notice to the certificate holder 90 days prior to the expiration date of the certificate. If the certificate is not renewed prior to its expiration date, reinstatement shall only be permitted after the certificate holder has paid a delinquency fee equal to three times the renewal fee and has provided evidence of completion of the continuing education required.

(4) To renew a certificate, the certificate holder shall, on or before the certificate expiration date, request renewal by submitting to the department documentation of completion of the required continuing education courses and pay the renewal fee of one hundred dollars ($100), irrespective of receipt of the department's notification of the renewal. A renewal request postmarked on or before the expiration of the certificate is proof of compliance with this paragraph.

(5) A suspended or revoked certificate is subject to expiration as provided for in this section. If reinstatement of the certificate is approved by the department, the certificate holder, as a condition precedent to reinstatement, shall pay a fee in an amount equal to the renewal fee, plus the delinquency fee, if any, accrued at the time of its revocation or suspension.

(6) A certificate that is not renewed within four years after its expiration shall not be renewed, restored, reissued, or reinstated except upon completion of a certification program, passing any test that may be required of an applicant for a new certificate at that time, and paying the appropriate fees provided for in this section.

(7) A fee of twenty-five dollars ($25) shall be charged for the reissuance of a lost certificate.

(8) A certificate holder shall inform the department of his or her employment status within 30 days of any change.

(g) The department may revoke a certificate issued under this section for any of the following:

(1) Procuring a certificate by fraud or misrepresentation.

(2) Knowingly making or giving any false statement or information in conjunction with the application for issuance of a certificate.

(3) Criminal conviction, unless an exemption is granted pursuant to Section 1569.17.

(h) The certificate shall be considered forfeited under either of the following conditions:

(1) The administrator has had a license revoked, suspended, or denied as authorized under Section 1569.50.

(2) The administrator has been denied employment, residence, or presence in a facility based on action resulting from an administrative hearing pursuant to Section 1569.58.

(i) (1) The department shall establish, by regulation, the program content, the testing instrument, the process for approving certification programs, and criteria to be used in authorizing individuals, organizations, or educational institutions to conduct certification programs and continuing education courses. These regulations shall be developed in consultation with provider and consumer organizations, and shall be made available at least six months prior to the deadline required for certification. The department may deny vendor approval to any agency or person that has not provided satisfactory evidence of their ability to meet the requirements of vendorization set out in the regulations adopted pursuant to subdivision (j).

(2) (A) A vendor of online programs for continuing education shall ensure that each online course contains all of the following:

(i) An interactive portion where the participant receives feedback, through online communication, based on input from the participant.

(ii) Required use of a personal identification number or personal identification information to confirm the identity of the participant.

(iii) A final screen displaying a printable statement, to be signed by the participant, certifying that the identified participant completed the course. The vendor shall obtain a copy of the final screen statement with the original signature of the participant prior to the issuance of a certificate of completion. The signed statement of completion shall be maintained by the vendor for a period of three years and be available to the department upon demand. Any person who certifies as true any material matter pursuant to this section that he or she knows to be false is guilty of a misdemeanor.

(B) Nothing in this subdivision shall prohibit the department from approving online programs for continuing education that do not meet the requirements of subparagraph (A) if the vendor demonstrates to the department's satisfaction that, through advanced technology, the course and the course delivery meet the requirements of this section.

(3) The department may authorize vendors to conduct the administrator certification training program pursuant to provisions set forth in this section. The department shall conduct the written test pursuant to regulations adopted by the department.

(4) The department shall prepare and maintain an updated list of approved training vendors.

(5) The department may inspect training programs, continuing education courses, and online courses, at no charge to the department, in order to determine if content and teaching methods comply with paragraphs (1) and (2), if applicable, and with regulations. If the department determines that a vendor is not complying with the intent of this

section, the department shall take appropriate action to bring the program into compliance, which may include removing the vendor from the approved list.

(6) The department shall establish reasonable procedures and timeframes, not to exceed 30 days, for the approval of vendor training programs.

(7) The department may charge a reasonable fee, not to exceed one hundred fifty dollars ($150) every two years, to certification program vendors for review and approval of the initial 80-hour training program pursuant to subdivision (c). The department may also charge the vendor a fee, not to exceed one hundred dollars ($100) every two years, for the review and approval of the continuing education courses needed for recertification pursuant to this subdivision.

(j) This section shall be operative upon regulations being adopted by the department to implement the administrator certification program as provided for in this section.

(k) The department shall establish a registry for holders of certificates that shall include, at a minimum, information on employment status and criminal record clearance.

(l) Notwithstanding any law to the contrary, vendors approved by the department who exclusively provide either initial or continuing education courses for certification of administrators of a residential care facility for the elderly, as defined in subdivision (k) of Section 1569.2, a group home facility, as defined by regulations of the department, or an adult residential care facility, as defined by regulations of the department, shall be regulated solely by the department pursuant to this chapter. No other state or local governmental entity shall be responsible for regulating the activity of those vendors.

(m) This section shall become operative on January 1, 2016.

(Repealed (in Sec. 3) and added by Stats. 2014, Ch. 705, Sec. 4. (SB 911) Effective January 1, 2015. Section operative January 1, 2016, by its own provisions.)

1569.617.

(a) (1) There is hereby created in the State Treasury, the Certification Fund from which moneys, upon appropriation of the Legislature, shall be expended by the department for the purpose of administering the residential care facilities for the elderly certification program provided under Sections 1569.23, 1569.615, and 1569.616, the adult residential facilities certification program pursuant to Section 1562.3, and the group home facilities and short-term residential therapeutic program facilities certification program pursuant to Section 1522.41.

(2) All money contained in the Residential Care Facility for the Elderly Fund on the operative date of this paragraph shall be retained in the Certification Fund for appropriation for the purposes specified in paragraph (1).

(b) The fund shall consist of specific appropriations that the Legislature sets aside for use by the fund and all fees, penalties, and fines collected pursuant to Sections 1522.41, 1562.3, 1562.23, 1569.615, and 1569.616.

(Amended by Stats. 2017, Ch. 732, Sec. 36. (AB 404) Effective January 1, 2018.)

1569.618.

(a) The administrator designated by the licensee pursuant to paragraph (11) of subdivision (a) of Section 1569.15 shall be present at the facility during normal working hours. A facility manager designated by the licensee with notice to the department, shall be responsible for the operation of the facility when the administrator is temporarily absent from the facility.

(b) At least one administrator, facility manager, or designated substitute who is at least 21 years of age and has qualifications adequate to be responsible and accountable for the management and administration of the facility pursuant to Title 22 of the California Code of Regulations shall be on the premises 24 hours per day. The designated substitute may be a direct care staff member who shall not be required to meet the educational, certification, or training requirements of an administrator. The designated substitute shall meet qualifications that include, but are not limited to, all of the following:

(1) Knowledge of the requirements for providing care and supervision appropriate to each resident of the facility.

(2) Familiarity with the facility's planned emergency procedures.

(3) Training to effectively interact with emergency personnel in the event of an emergency call, including an ability to provide a resident's medical records to emergency responders.

(c) The facility shall employ, and the administrator shall schedule, a sufficient number of staff members to do all of the following:

(1) Provide the care required in each resident's written record of care as described in Section 1569.80.

(2) Ensure the health, safety, comfort, and supervision of the residents.

(3) Ensure that at least one staff member who has cardiopulmonary resuscitation (CPR) training and first aid training is on duty and on the premises at all times. This paragraph shall not be construed to require staff to provide CPR.

(4) Ensure that the facility is clean, safe, sanitary, and in good repair at all times.

(d) "Facility manager" means a person on the premises with the authority and responsibility necessary to manage and control the day-to-day operation of a residential care facility for the elderly and supervise the clients. The facility manager, licensee, and administrator, or any combination thereof, may be the same person provided he or she meets all applicable requirements. If the administrator is also the facility manager for the same facility, he or she shall be limited to the administration and management of only one facility.

(Amended by Stats. 2015, Ch. 628, Sec. 7. (AB 601) Effective January 1, 2016.)

1569.62.

(a) The director shall ensure that licensees, administrators, and staff of residential care facilities for the elderly have appropriate training to provide the care and services for which a license or certificate is issued.

(b) The department shall develop jointly with the California Department of Aging requirements for a uniform core of knowledge for the required initial certification and continuing education for administrators, and their designated substitutes, and for recertification of administrators of residential care facilities for the elderly. This knowledge base shall include, as a minimum, basic understanding of the psychosocial and physical care needs of elderly persons, applicable laws and regulations, residents' rights, and administration. This training shall be developed in consultation with individuals or organizations with specific expertise in residential care facilities for the elderly or assisted living services, or by an outside source with expertise in residential care facilities for the elderly or assisted living services.

(1) The initial certification training for administrators shall consist of at least 80 hours.

(2) The continuing education requirement for administrators is at least 40 hours of training during each two-year certification period, as specified in paragraph (1) of subdivision (f) of Section 1569.616.

(c) (1) The department shall develop a uniform resident assessment tool to be used by all residential care facilities for the elderly. The assessment tool shall, in lay terms, help to identify resident needs for service and assistance with activities of daily living.

(2) The departments shall develop a mandatory training program on the utilization of the assessment tool to be given to administrators and their designated substitutes.

(d) This section shall become operative on January 1, 2016.

(Repealed (in Sec. 5) and added by Stats. 2014, Ch. 705, Sec. 6. (SB 911) Effective January 1, 2015. Section operative January 1, 2016, by its own provisions.)

1569.625.

(a) The Legislature finds that the quality of services provided to residents of residential care facilities for the elderly is dependent upon the training and skills of staff. It is the intent of the Legislature in enacting this section to ensure that direct-care staff have the knowledge and proficiency to carry out the tasks of their jobs.

(b) (1) The department shall adopt regulations to require staff members of residential care facilities for the elderly who assist residents with personal activities of daily living to receive appropriate training. This training shall consist of 40 hours of training. A staff member shall complete 20 hours, including six hours specific to dementia care, as required by subdivision (a) of Section 1569.626 and four hours specific to postural supports, restricted health conditions, and hospice care, as required by subdivision (a) of Section 1569.696, before working independently with residents. The remaining 20 hours shall include six hours specific to dementia care and shall be completed within the first four weeks of employment. The training coursework may utilize various methods of instruction, including, but not limited to, lectures, instructional videos, and interactive online courses. The additional 16 hours shall be hands-on training.

(2) In addition to paragraph (1), training requirements shall also include an additional 20 hours annually, eight hours of which shall be dementia care training, as required by subdivision (a) of Section 1569.626, and four hours of which shall be specific to postural supports, restricted health conditions, and hospice care, as required by subdivision (a) of Section 1569.696. This training shall be administered on the job, or in a classroom setting, or both, and may include online training.

(3) The department shall establish, in consultation with provider organizations, the subject matter required for the training required by this section.

(c) The training shall include, but not be limited to, all of the following:

(1) Physical limitations and needs of the elderly.

(2) Importance and techniques for personal care services.

(3) Residents' rights.

(4) Policies and procedures regarding medications.

(5) Psychosocial needs of the elderly.

(6) Building and fire safety and the appropriate response to emergencies.

(7) Dementia care, including the use and misuse of antipsychotics, the interaction of drugs commonly used by the elderly, and the adverse effects of psychotropic drugs for use in controlling the behavior of persons with dementia.

(8) The special needs of persons with Alzheimer's disease and dementia, including nonpharmacologic, person-centered approaches to dementia care.

(9) Cultural competency and sensitivity in issues relating to the underserved, aging, lesbian, gay, bisexual, and transgender community.

(d) This section shall not apply to certified nurse assistants, certified pursuant to Article 9 (commencing with Section 1337) of Chapter 2, licensed vocational nurses, licensed pursuant to Chapter 6.5 (commencing with Section 2840) of Division 2 of the Business and Professions Code, and registered nurses, licensed pursuant to Chapter 6 (commencing with Section 2700) of Division 2 of the Business and Professions Code, except both of the following shall apply:

(1) A licensed or certified health professional with valid certification shall receive eight hours of training on resident characteristics, resident records, and facility practices and procedures prior to providing direct care to residents.

(2) In addition to paragraph (1), a certified nurse assistant shall also receive the 12 hours of dementia care training specified in Section 1569.626 and the annual training specified in paragraph (2) of subdivision (b).

(e) This section shall become operative on January 1, 2016.

(Repealed (in Sec. 2.5) and added by Stats. 2014, Ch. 701, Sec. 2.7. (AB 2044) Effective January 1, 2015. Section operative January 1, 2016, by its own provisions.)

1569.626.

(a) All residential care facilities for the elderly shall meet the following training requirements, as described in Section 1569.625, for all direct care staff:

(1) Twelve hours of dementia care training, six of which shall be completed before a staff member begins working independently with residents, and the remaining six hours of which shall be completed within the first four weeks of employment. All 12 hours shall be devoted to the care of persons with dementia. The facility may utilize various methods of

instruction, including, but not limited to, preceptorship, mentoring, and other forms of observation and demonstration. The orientation time shall be exclusive of any administrative instruction.

(2) Eight hours of in-service training per year on the subject of serving residents with dementia. This training shall be developed in consultation with individuals or organizations with specific expertise in dementia care or by an outside source with expertise in dementia care. In formulating and providing this training, reference may be made to written materials and literature on dementia and the care and treatment of persons with dementia. This training requirement may be satisfied in one day or over a period of time. This training requirement may be provided at the facility or offsite and may include a combination of observation and practical application.

(b) This section shall become operative on January 1, 2016.

(Repealed (in Sec. 5) and added by Stats. 2014, Ch. 698, Sec. 6. (AB 1570) Effective January 1, 2015. Section operative January 1, 2016, by its own provisions.)
1569.627.

Any residential care facility for the elderly that advertises or promotes special care, special programming, or a special environment for persons with dementia shall disclose to the department the special features of the facility in its plan of operation. This information shall be provided to the public by the facility upon request. The information shall include a brief narrative description of all of the following facility features:

(a) Philosophy, including, but not limited to, program goals.
(b) Preadmission assessment.
(c) Admission.
(d) Assessment.
(e) Program.
(f) Staff.
(g) Staff training.
(h) Physical environment.
(i) Changes in condition, including, but not limited to, when and under what circumstances are changes made to a participant's care plan.
(j) Success indicators.

(Added by Stats. 2000, Ch. 434, Sec. 6. Effective January 1, 2001.)
1569.628.

A licensee of a residential care facility for the elderly that advertises or promotes special care, programming, or environments for persons with a health related condition, except as specified in Section 1569.72, shall provide to each prospective resident an accurate narrative description of these programs and services. The description shall be provided in writing prior to admission. All reasonable efforts shall be made to communicate the information in the narrative description to a person who is unable to read it himself or herself, including, but not limited to, reading the description out loud.

(Added by Stats. 2003, Ch. 322, Sec. 1. Effective January 1, 2004.)

1569.63.

The director shall insure that licensing personnel at the department have appropriate training to properly carry out this chapter.

(Added by Stats. 1985, Ch. 1127, Sec. 3.)

1569.64.

The department shall institute a staff development and training program within the organization structure to develop among staff the knowledge and understanding necessary to successfully carry out this chapter. Specifically, the department shall do all of the following:

(a) Provide staff with 36 hours of training per year that reflect the unique needs of the elderly.

(b) Give priority to applications from individuals with experience as care providers to the elderly.

(c) Provide new staff with comprehensive training within the first six months of employment. This training shall, at a minimum, include the following core areas: administrative action process, client populations, conducting facility visits, cultural awareness, documentation skills, facility operations, human relation skills, interviewing techniques, investigation processes, and regulation administration.

This training shall also provide new staff who have earned fewer than 16 semester units in gerontology or geriatric education from an accredited college at least 40 hours of preservice training in the aging process and the psycho-social and health care needs of elderly persons.

(Amended by Stats. 1992, Ch. 1319, Sec. 2. Effective January 1, 1993.)

1569.65.

(a) On or before January 1, 1987, the department shall publish a comprehensive consumer guideline brochure to assist persons in the evaluation and selection of a licensed residential care facility for the elderly. The department shall develop the brochure for publication with the advice and assistance of the Advisory Committee on Community Care Facilities and the State Department of Aging.

(b) The consumer guideline brochure shall include, but not be limited to, guidelines highlighting resident health and safety issues to be considered in the selection of a residential care facility for the elderly, locations of the licensing offices of the State Department of Social Services where facility records may be reviewed, types of local organizations which may have additional information on specific facilities, and a list of recommended inquiries to be made in the selection of a residential care facility for the elderly.

(c) Upon publication, the consumer guideline brochures shall be distributed to statewide resident advocacy groups, statewide consumer advocacy groups, state and local

ombudsmen, and all licensed residential care facilities for the elderly. The brochure shall be made available on request to all other interested persons.

(Added by Stats. 1985, Ch. 1127, Sec. 3.)
1569.651.

(a) A licensee of a residential care facility for the elderly shall not require any form of preadmission fee or deposit from a recipient under the State Supplementary Program for the Aged, Blind and Disabled (Article 5 (commencing with Section 12200) of Chapter 3 of Part 3 of Division 9 of the Welfare and Institutions Code) who applies for admission to the facility.

(b) If a licensee charges a preadmission fee, the licensee shall provide the applicant or his or her representative with a written general statement describing all costs associated with the preadmission fee charges and stating that the preadmission fee is refundable. The statement shall describe the conditions for the refund as specified in subdivision (g). A licensee shall only charge a single preadmission fee as defined in subdivision (e) per resident admission.

(c) A licensee of a residential care facility for the elderly shall not require, request, or accept any funds from a resident or a resident's representative that constitutes a deposit against any possible damages by the resident.

(d) Any fee charged by a licensee of a residential care facility for the elderly, whether prior to or after admission, shall be clearly specified in the admission agreement.

(e) For the purposes of this section, "preadmission fee" means an application fee, processing fee, admission fee, entrance fee, community fee, or other fee, however designated, that is requested or accepted by a licensee of a residential care facility for the elderly prior to admission.

(f) This section shall not apply to licensees of residential care facilities for the elderly that have obtained a certificate of authority to offer continuing care contracts, as defined in paragraph (8) of subdivision (c) of Section 1771.

(g) If the applicant decides not to enter the facility prior to the facility's completion of a preadmission appraisal or if the facility fails to provide full written disclosure of the preadmission fee charges and refund conditions, the applicant or the applicant's representative shall be entitled to a refund of 100 percent of the preadmission fee.

(h) Unless subdivision (g) applies, preadmission fees in excess of five hundred dollars ($500) shall be refunded according to the following:

(1) If the applicant does not enter the facility after a preadmission appraisal is conducted, the applicant or the applicant's representative shall be entitled to a refund of at least 80 percent of the preadmission fee amount in excess of five hundred dollars ($500).

(2) If the resident leaves the facility for any reason during the first month of residency, the resident shall be entitled to a refund of at least 80 percent of the preadmission fee amount in excess of five hundred dollars ($500).

(3) If the resident leaves the facility for any reason during the second month of residency, the resident shall be entitled to a refund of at least 60 percent of the preadmission fee amount in excess of five hundred dollars ($500).

(4) If the resident leaves the facility for any reason during the third month of residency, the resident shall be entitled to a refund of at least 40 percent of the preadmission fee amount in excess of five hundred dollars ($500).

(5) The facility may, but is not required to, make a refund of the preadmission fee for residents living in the facility for four or more months.

(i) (1) Notwithstanding subdivision (g), if a resident is evicted by a facility pursuant to subdivision (a) of Section 1569.682, the resident or the resident's legal representative shall be entitled to a refund of preadmission fees in excess of five hundred dollars ($500) in accordance with all of the following:

(A) A 100-percent refund if preadmission fees were paid within six months of notice of eviction.

(B) A 75-percent refund if preadmission fees were paid more than six months but not more than 12 months before notice of eviction.

(C) A 50-percent refund if preadmission fees were paid more than 12 months but not more than 18 months before notice of eviction.

(D) A 25-percent refund if preadmission fees were paid more than 18 months but less than 25 months before notice of eviction.

(2) No preadmission refund is required if preadmission fees were paid 25 months or more before the notice of eviction.

(3) The preadmission refund required by this subdivision shall be paid within 15 days of issuing the eviction notice.

(Amended by Stats. 2007, Ch. 686, Sec. 1. Effective January 1, 2008.)
1569.652.

(a) A residential care facility for the elderly shall not require advance notice for terminating an admission agreement upon the death of a resident. No fees shall accrue once all personal property belonging to the deceased resident is removed from the living unit.

(b) Upon the death of a resident, a licensee shall not impede the removal of the resident's personal property from the facility during reasonable hours by an individual or individuals authorized by the resident or the resident's responsible person, as identified in the admission agreement or attachment, or by a court-appointed executor or administrator of the decedent's estate, if applicable.

(c) A refund of any fees paid in advance covering the time after the resident's personal property has been removed from the facility shall be issued to the individual, individuals, or entity contractually responsible for the fees or, if the deceased resident paid the fees, to the resident's estate, within 15 days after the personal property is removed.

(d) If fees are assessed while a resident's personal property remains in a unit after the resident is deceased, a licensee shall, within three days of becoming aware of the resident's death, provide to the resident's responsible person, or other individual or individuals as identified in the admission agreement or attachment, written notice of the facility's policies regarding contract termination upon death and refunds.

(e) This section shall not apply to fees charged by a continuing care equity project as defined in paragraph (6) of subdivision (e) of Section 1771 or amounts deducted from entrance fee refunds or repayments described in paragraph (2) of subdivision (r) of Section 1771.

(Added by Stats. 2013, Ch. 290, Sec. 1. (AB 261) Effective January 1, 2014.)

1569.655.

(a) If a licensee of a residential care facility for the elderly increases the rates of fees for residents or makes increases in any of its rate structures for services, the licensee shall provide no less than 60 days' prior written notice to the residents or the residents' representatives setting forth the amount of the increase, the reason for the increase, and a general description of the additional costs, except for an increase in the rate due to a change in the level of care of the resident. This subdivision shall not apply to optional services that are provided by individuals, professionals, or organizations under a separate fee-for-service arrangement with residents.

(b) No licensee shall charge nonrecurring lump-sum assessments. The notification requirements contained in subdivision (a) shall apply to increases specified in this subdivision. For purposes of this subdivision, "nonrecurring lump-sum assessments" mean rate increases due to unavoidable and unexpected costs that financially obligate the licensee. In lieu of the lump-sum payment, all increases in rates shall be to the monthly rate amortized over a 12-month period. The prohibition against a lump-sum assessment shall not apply to charges for specific goods or services provided to an individual resident.

(c) If a licensee increases rates for a recipient under the State Supplementary Program for the Aged, Blind and Disabled, described in Article 5 (Commencing with Section 12200) of Chapter 3 of Part 3 of Division 9 of the Welfare and Institutions Code, the licensee shall meet the requirements for SSI/SSP rate increases, as prescribed by law.

(d) This section shall not apply to licensees of residential care facilities for the elderly that have obtained a certificate of authority to offer continuing care contracts, as defined in paragraph (5) of subdivision (c) of Section 1771.

(Added by Stats. 2002, Ch. 557, Sec. 2. Effective January 1, 2003.)

1569.657.

(a) For any rate increase due to a change in the level of care of the resident, the licensee shall provide the resident and the resident's representative, if any, written notice of the rate increase within two business days after initially providing services at the new level of care. The notice shall include a detailed explanation of the additional services to be provided at the new level of care and an accompanying itemization of the charges.

(b) This section shall not apply to any resident of the facility who is a recipient of benefits pursuant to Article 5 (commencing with Section 12200) of Chapter 3 of Part 3 of Division 9 of the Welfare and Institutions Code under the State Supplementary Program for Aged, Blind and Disabled.

(c) This section shall not apply to a provider who has entered into one or more continuing care contracts at a licensed residential care facility for the elderly pursuant to a certificate of authority, as defined in paragraph (5) of subdivision (c) of Section 1771.

(Added by Stats. 2004, Ch. 401, Sec. 1. Effective January 1, 2005.)

1569.658.

(a) On or before January 31 of each year, the licensee of a licensed residential care facility for the elderly shall prepare a document disclosing its average monthly rate increases, inclusive of rates for living units and service fees, for each of the previous 3 years. For purposes of this section, "service fees" do not include fees for optional services or services provided by a third party. The licensee shall disclose the average amount of the increase, as well as the average percentage of increase. Newly licensed facilities without three years of resident rate increase history shall disclose the average increase for the years during which the facility has been serving residents. This section does not apply to newly licensed facilities with no current residents.

(b) The licensee shall provide a written copy of the disclosure required by this section to every resident or resident's representative, upon signing an admission agreement to receive residential or other services from the facility. The resident or resident's representative shall sign a confirmation of receipt of the disclosure, which shall be maintained by the facility in the resident's file.

(c) The licensee shall provide a copy of the most recent disclosure required by this section to any prospective resident, or his or her representative.

(d) This section shall not apply to a licensee of a residential care facility for the elderly that has obtained a certificate of authority to offer a continuing care contract, as defined in paragraph (5) of subdivision (c) of Section 1771.

(Added by Stats. 2008, Ch. 478, Sec. 1. Effective January 1, 2009.)

1569.66.

At least annually, the director shall publish and make available to interested persons a list or lists covering all licensed residential care facilities for the elderly and the services for which each facility has been licensed. A list or lists containing changes shall be published and made available periodically, as determined by the director.

(Amended by Stats. 1986, Ch. 844, Sec. 8.)

1569.67.

(a) The department shall develop a written notice for the purpose of informing any individual who requests information regarding admission to a residential care facility for the elderly that the department's licensing analysts' inspection reports on all residential care facilities for the elderly are on file and are available for public review in the department's community care licensing district office nearest to each residential care facility for the elderly.

(b) The department shall adopt regulations requiring that each residential care facility provide this notice, as well as the address of the nearest departmental community care licensing district office, to any individual who requests information regarding admission to a residential care facility for the elderly and to any resident of the facility.

(Added by Stats. 1989, Ch. 911, Sec. 1.)

1569.68.

All residential care facilities shall be required to include their current license number in any public advertisement or correspondence.

(Added by Stats. 1989, Ch. 465, Sec. 1.)

1569.681.

(a) Each residential care facility for the elderly licensed under this chapter shall reveal its license number in all advertisements, publications, or announcements made with the intent to attract clients or residents.

(b) Advertisements, publications, or announcements subject to the requirements of subdivision (a) referred to herein include, but are not limited to, those contained in the following:

(1) Newspaper or magazine.

(2) Consumer report.

(3) Announcement of intent to commence business.

(4) Telephone directory yellow pages.

(5) Professional or service directory.

(6) Radio or television commercial.

(Added by renumbering Section 1569.314 (as added by Stats. 1989, Ch. 458) by Stats. 1990, Ch. 1137, Sec. 1.)

1569.682.

(a) A licensee of a licensed residential care facility for the elderly shall, prior to transferring a resident of the facility to another facility or to an independent living arrangement as a result of the forfeiture of a license, as described in subdivision (a), (b), or (f) of Section 1569.19, or a change of use of the facility pursuant to the department's regulations, take all reasonable steps to transfer affected residents safely and to minimize possible transfer trauma, and shall, at a minimum, do all of the following:

(1) Prepare, for each resident, a relocation evaluation of the needs of that resident, which shall include both of the following:

(A) Recommendations on the type of facility that would meet the needs of the resident based on the current service plan.

(B) A list of facilities, within a 60-mile radius of the resident's current facility, that meet the resident's present needs.

(2) Provide each resident or the resident's responsible person with a written notice no later than 60 days before the intended eviction. The notice shall include all of the following:

(A) The reason for the eviction, with specific facts to permit a determination of the date, place, witnesses, and circumstances concerning the reasons.

(B) A copy of the resident's current service plan.

(C) The relocation evaluation.

(D) A list of referral agencies.

(E) The right of the resident or resident's legal representative to contact the department to investigate the reasons given for the eviction pursuant to Section 1569.35.

(F) The contact information for the local long-term care ombudsman, including address and telephone number.

(3) Discuss the relocation evaluation with the resident and his or her legal representative within 30 days of issuing the notice of eviction.

(4) Submit a written report of any eviction to the licensing agency within five days.

(5) Upon issuing the written notice of eviction, a licensee shall not accept new residents or enter into new admission agreements.

(6) (A) For paid preadmission fees in excess of five hundred dollars ($500), the resident is entitled to a refund in accordance with all of the following:

(i) A 100-percent refund if preadmission fees were paid within six months of notice of eviction.

(ii) A 75-percent refund if preadmission fees were paid more than six months but not more than 12 months before notice of eviction.

(iii) A 50-percent refund if preadmission fees were paid more than 12 months but not more than 18 months before notice of eviction.

(iv) A 25-percent refund if preadmission fees were paid more than 18 months but less than 25 months before notice of eviction.

(B) No preadmission refund is required if preadmission fees were paid 25 months or more before the notice of eviction.

(C) The preadmission refund required by this paragraph shall be paid within 15 days of issuing the eviction notice. In lieu of the refund, the resident may request that the licensee provide a credit toward the resident's monthly fee obligation in an amount equal to the preadmission fee refund due.

(7) If the resident gives notice five days before leaving the facility, the licensee shall refund to the resident or his or her legal representative a proportional per diem amount of any prepaid monthly fees at the time the resident leaves the facility and the unit is vacated. Otherwise the licensee shall pay the refund within seven days from the date that the resident leaves the facility and the unit is vacated.

(8) Within 10 days of all residents having left the facility, the licensee, based on information provided by the resident or resident's legal representative, shall submit a final

list of names and new locations of all residents to the department and the local ombudsman program.

(b) If seven or more residents of a residential care facility for the elderly will be transferred as a result of the forfeiture of a license or change in the use of the facility pursuant to subdivision (a), the licensee shall submit a proposed closure plan to the department for approval. The department shall approve or disapprove the closure plan, and monitor its implementation, in accordance with the following requirements:

(1) Upon submission of the closure plan, the licensee shall be prohibited from accepting new residents and entering into new admission agreements for new residents.

(2) The closure plan shall meet the requirements described in subdivision (a), and describe the staff available to assist in the transfers. The department's review shall include a determination as to whether the licensee's closure plan contains a relocation evaluation for each resident.

(3) Within 15 working days of receipt, the department shall approve or disapprove the closure plan prepared pursuant to this subdivision, and, if the department approves the plan, it shall become effective upon the date the department grants its written approval of the plan.

(4) If the department disapproves a closure plan, the licensee may resubmit an amended plan, which the department shall promptly either approve or disapprove, within 10 working days of receipt by the department of the amended plan. If the department fails to approve a closure plan, it shall inform the licensee, in writing, of the reasons for the disapproval of the plan.

(5) If the department fails to take action within 20 working days of receipt of either the original or the amended closure plan, the plan, or amended plan, as the case may be, shall be deemed approved.

(6) Until the department has approved a licensee's closure plan, the facility shall not issue a notice of transfer or require any resident to transfer.

(7) Upon approval by the department, the licensee shall send a copy of the closure plan to the local ombudsman program.

(c) (1) If a licensee fails to comply with the requirements of this section, or if the director determines that it is necessary to protect the residents of a facility from physical or mental abuse, abandonment, or any other substantial threat to health or safety, the department shall take any necessary action to minimize trauma for the residents, including caring for the residents through the use of a temporary manager or receiver as provided for in Sections 1569.481 and 1569.482 when the director determines the immediate relocation of the residents is not feasible based on transfer trauma or other considerations such as the unavailability of alternative placements. The department shall contact any local agency that may have assessment, placement, protective, or advocacy responsibility for the residents, and shall work together with those agencies to locate alternative placement sites, contact relatives or other persons responsible for the care of these residents, provide onsite evaluation of the residents, and assist in the transfer of residents.

(2) The participation of the department and local agencies in the relocation of residents from a residential care facility for the elderly does not relieve the licensee of any responsibility under this section. A licensee that fails to comply with the requirements of this section shall be required to reimburse the department and local agencies for the cost of providing the relocation services or the costs incurred in caring for the residents through the use of a temporary manager or receiver as provided for in Sections 1569.481 and 1569.482. If the licensee fails to provide the relocation services required in this section, then the department may request that the Attorney General's office, the city attorney's office, or the local district attorney's office seek injunctive relief and damages in the same manner as provided for in Chapter 5 (commencing with Section 17200) of Part 2 of Division 7 of the Business and Professions Code, including restitution to the department of any costs incurred in caring for the residents through the use of a temporary manager or receiver as provided for in Sections 1569.481 and 1569.482.

(d) A licensee who fails to comply with requirements of this section shall be liable for the imposition of civil penalties in the amount of one hundred dollars ($100) per violation per day for each day that the licensee is in violation of this section, until such time that the violation has been corrected. The civil penalties shall be issued immediately following the written notice of violation. However, if the violation does not present an immediate or substantial threat to the health or safety of residents and the licensee corrects the violation within three days after receiving the notice of violation, the licensee shall not be liable for payment of any civil penalties pursuant to this subdivision related to the corrected violation.

(e) A licensee, on and after January 1, 2015, who fails to comply with this section and abandons the facility and the residents in care resulting in an immediate and substantial threat to the health and safety of the abandoned residents, in addition to forfeiture of the license pursuant to Section 1569.19, shall be excluded from licensure in facilities licensed by the department without the right to petition for reinstatement.

(f) A resident of a residential care facility for the elderly covered under this section may bring a civil action against any person, firm, partnership, or corporation who owns, operates, establishes, manages, conducts, or maintains a residential care facility for the elderly who violates the rights of a resident, as set forth in this section. Any person, firm, partnership, or corporation who owns, operates, establishes, manages, conducts, or maintains a residential care facility for the elderly who violates this section shall be responsible for the acts of the facility's employees and shall be liable for costs and attorney's fees. Any such residential care facility for the elderly may also be enjoined from permitting the violation to continue. The remedies specified in this section are in addition to any other remedy provided by law.

(g) This section does not apply to a licensee that has obtained a certificate of authority to offer continuing care contracts, as defined in paragraph (8) of subdivision (c) of Section 1771.

(Amended by Stats. 2015, Ch. 303, Sec. 284. (AB 731) Effective January 1, 2016.)
1569.683.

(a) In addition to complying with other applicable regulations, a licensee of a residential care facility for the elderly who sends a notice of eviction to a resident shall set forth in the notice to quit the reasons relied upon for the eviction, with specific facts to permit determination of the date, place, witnesses, and circumstances concerning those reasons. In addition, the notice to quit shall include all of the following:

(1) The effective date of the eviction.

(2) Resources available to assist in identifying alternative housing and care options, including public and private referral services and case management organizations.

(3) Information about the resident's right to file a complaint with the department regarding the eviction, with the name, address, and telephone number of the nearest office of community care licensing and the State Ombudsman.

(4) The following statement: "In order to evict a resident who remains in the facility after the effective date of the eviction, the residential care facility for the elderly must file an unlawful detainer action in superior court and receive a written judgment signed by a judge. If the facility pursues the unlawful detainer action, you must be served with a summons and complaint. You have the right to contest the eviction in writing and through a hearing."

(b) The licensee, in addition to either serving a 30-day notice, or seeking approval from the department and serving three days notice, on the resident, shall notify, or mail a copy of the notice to quit to, the resident's responsible person.

(Added by Stats. 2009, Ch. 617, Sec. 2. (SB 781) Effective January 1, 2010.)
1569.686.

(a) A licensee shall notify the department, the State Long-Term Care Ombudsman, all residents, and, if applicable, their legal representatives, in writing, within two business days, and shall notify all applicants for potential residence, and, if applicable, their legal representatives, prior to admission, of any of the following events, or knowledge of the event:

(1) A notice of default, notice of trustee's sale, or any other indication of foreclosure is issued on the property.

(2) An unlawful detainer action is initiated against the licensee.

(3) The licensee files for bankruptcy.

(4) The licensee receives a written notice of default of payment of rent described in Section 1161 of the Code of Civil Procedure.

(5) A utility company has sent a notice of intent to terminate electricity, gas, or water service on the property within not more than 15 days of the notice.

(b) Upon receipt of the notice required pursuant to subdivision (a), the department shall initiate a compliance plan, noncompliance conference, or other appropriate action.

(c) A licensee who fails to comply with this section may be liable for civil penalties in an amount not to exceed one hundred dollars ($100) for each day of the failure to provide notification required in this section. The total civil penalty shall not exceed two thousand dollars ($2,000). If a resident is relocated without the notification required by this section, and suffers transfer trauma or other harm to his or her health or safety, the department may also suspend or revoke the licensee's license and issue a permanent revocation of the licensee's ability to operate or act as an administrator of a facility anywhere in the state. Suspension or revocation proceedings pursuant to this subdivision shall be conducted in compliance with Section 1569.51.

(d) For purposes of this section, "property" means the land or building in which a residential care facility for the elderly is located.

(e) This section shall not apply to licensees of residential care facilities for the elderly that have obtained a certificate of authority, as defined in paragraph (5) of subdivision (c) of Section 1771, to offer continuing care contracts, as defined in paragraph (8) of subdivision (c) of Section 1771.

(Added by Stats. 2011, Ch. 376, Sec. 3. (SB 897) Effective January 1, 2012.)
1569.69.

(a) Each residential care facility for the elderly licensed under this chapter shall ensure that each employee of the facility who assists residents with the self-administration of medications meets all of the following training requirements:

(1) In facilities licensed to provide care for 16 or more persons, the employee shall complete 24 hours of initial training. This training shall consist of 16 hours of hands-on shadowing training, which shall be completed prior to assisting with the self-administration of medications, and 8 hours of other training or instruction, as described in subdivision (f), which shall be completed within the first four weeks of employment.

(2) In facilities licensed to provide care for 15 or fewer persons, the employee shall complete 10 hours of initial training. This training shall consist of 6 hours of hands-on shadowing training, which shall be completed prior to assisting with the self-administration of medications, and 4 hours of other training or instruction, as described in subdivision (f), which shall be completed within the first two weeks of employment.

(3) An employee shall be required to complete the training requirements for hands-on shadowing training described in this subdivision prior to assisting any resident in the self-administration of medications. The training and instruction described in this subdivision shall be completed, in their entirety, within the first two weeks of employment.

(4) The training shall cover all of the following areas:

(A) The role, responsibilities, and limitations of staff who assist residents with the self-administration of medication, including tasks limited to licensed medical professionals.

(B) An explanation of the terminology specific to medication assistance.

(C) An explanation of the different types of medication orders: prescription, over-the-counter, controlled, and other medications.

(D) An explanation of the basic rules and precautions of medication assistance.

(E) Information on medication forms and routes for medication taken by residents.

(F) A description of procedures for providing assistance with the self-administration of medications in and out of the facility, and information on the medication documentation system used in the facility.

(G) An explanation of guidelines for the proper storage, security, and documentation of centrally stored medications.

(H) A description of the processes used for medication ordering, refills, and the receipt of medications from the pharmacy.

(I) An explanation of medication side effects, adverse reactions, errors, the adverse effects of psychotropic drugs for use in controlling the behavior of persons with dementia, and the increased risk of death when elderly residents with dementia are given antipsychotic medications.

(5) To complete the training requirements set forth in this subdivision, each employee shall pass an examination that tests the employee's comprehension of, and competency in, the subjects listed in paragraph (4).

(6) Residential care facilities for the elderly shall encourage pharmacists and licensed medical professionals to use plain English when preparing labels on medications supplied to residents. As used in this section, "plain English" means that no abbreviations, symbols, or Latin medical terms shall be used in the instructions for the self-administration of medication.

(7) The training requirements of this section are not intended to replace or supplant those required of all staff members who assist residents with personal activities of daily living as set forth in Sections 1569.625 and 1569.696.

(8) The training requirements of this section shall be repeated if either of the following occur:

(A) An employee returns to work for the same licensee after a break of service of more than 180 consecutive calendar days.

(B) An employee goes to work for another licensee in a facility in which he or she assists residents with the self-administration of medication.

(b) Each employee who received training and passed the examination required in paragraph (5) of subdivision (a), and who continues to assist with the self-administration of medicines, shall also complete eight hours of in-service training on medication-related issues in each succeeding 12-month period.

(c) The requirements set forth in subdivisions (a) and (b) do not apply to persons who are licensed medical professionals.

(d) Each residential care facility for the elderly that provides employee training under this section shall use the training material and the accompanying examination that are developed by, or in consultation with, a licensed nurse, pharmacist, or physician. The licensed residential care facility for the elderly shall maintain the following documentation for each medical consultant used to develop the training:

(1) The name, address, and telephone number of the consultant.

(2) The date when consultation was provided.

(3) The consultant's organization affiliation, if any, and any educational and professional qualifications specific to medication management.

(4) The training topics for which consultation was provided.

(e) Each person who provides employee training under this section shall meet the following education and experience requirements:

(1) A minimum of five hours of initial, or certified continuing, education or three semester units, or the equivalent, from an accredited educational institution, on topics relevant to medication management.

(2) The person shall meet any of the following practical experience or licensure requirements:

(A) Two years of full-time experience, within the last four years, as a consultant with expertise in medication management in areas covered by the training described in subdivision (a).

(B) Two years of full-time experience, or the equivalent, within the last four years, as an administrator for a residential care facility for the elderly, during which time the individual has acted in substantial compliance with applicable regulations.

(C) Two years of full-time experience, or the equivalent, within the last four years, as a direct care provider assisting with the self-administration of medications for a residential care facility for the elderly, during which time the individual has acted in substantial compliance with applicable regulations.

(D) Possession of a license as a medical professional.

(3) The licensed residential care facility for the elderly shall maintain the following documentation on each person who provides employee training under this section:

(A) The person's name, address, and telephone number.

(B) Information on the topics or subject matter covered in the training.

(C) The times, dates, and hours of training provided.

(f) Other training or instruction, as required in paragraphs (1) and (2) of subdivision (a), may be provided offsite, and may use various methods of instruction, including, but not limited to, all of the following:

(1) Lectures by presenters who are knowledgeable about medication management.

(2) Video recorded instruction, interactive material, online training, and books.

(3) Other written or visual materials approved by organizations or individuals with expertise in medication management.

(g) Residential care facilities for the elderly licensed to provide care for 16 or more persons shall maintain documentation that demonstrates that a consultant pharmacist or nurse has reviewed the facility's medication management program and procedures at least twice a year.

(h) Nothing in this section authorizes unlicensed personnel to directly administer medications.

(i) This section shall become operative on January 1, 2016.

(Repealed (in Sec. 7) and added by Stats. 2014, Ch. 705, Sec. 8. (SB 911) Effective January 1, 2015. Section operative January 1, 2016, by its own provisions.)

1569.695.

(a) In addition to any other requirement of this chapter, a residential care facility for the elderly shall have an emergency and disaster plan that shall include, but not be limited to, all of the following:

(1) Evacuation procedures, including identification of an assembly point or points that shall be included in the facility sketch.

(2) Plans for the facility to be self-reliant for a period of not less than 72 hours immediately following any emergency or disaster, including, but not limited to, a short-term or long-term power failure. If the facility plans to shelter in place and one or more utilities, including water, sewer, gas, or electricity, is not available, the facility shall have a plan and supplies available to provide alternative resources during an outage.

(3) Transportation needs and evacuation procedures to ensure that the facility can communicate with emergency response personnel or can access the information necessary in order to check the emergency routes to be used at the time of an evacuation and relocation necessitated by a disaster. If the transportation plan includes the use of a vehicle owned or operated by the facility, the keys to the vehicle shall be available to staff on all shifts.

(4) A contact information list of all of the following:

(A) Emergency response personnel.

(B) The Community Care Licensing Division within the State Department of Social Services.

(C) The local long-term care ombudsman.

(D) Transportation providers.

(5) At least two appropriate shelter locations that can house facility residents during an evacuation. One of the locations shall be outside of the immediate area.

(6) The location of utility shut-off valves and instructions for use.

(7) Procedures that address, but are not limited to, all of the following:

(A) Provision of emergency power that could include identification of suppliers of backup generators. If a permanently installed generator is used, the plan shall include its location and a description of how it will be used. If a portable generator is used, the manufacturer's operating instructions shall be followed.

(B) Responding to an individual resident's needs if the emergency call buttons are inoperable.

(C) Process for communicating with residents, families, hospice providers, and others, as appropriate, that might include landline telephones, cellular telephones, or walkie-talkies. A backup process shall also be established. Residents and their responsible parties shall be informed of the process for communicating during an emergency.

(D) Assistance with, and administration of, medications.

(E) Storage and preservation of medications, including the storage of medications that require refrigeration.

(F) The operation of assistive medical devices that need electric power for their operation, including, but not limited to, oxygen equipment and wheelchairs.

(G) A process for identifying residents with special needs, such as hospice, and a plan for meeting those needs.

(H) Procedures for confirming the location of each resident during an emergency response.

(b) A facility shall provide training on the plan to each staff member upon hire and annually thereafter. The training shall include staff responsibilities during an emergency or disaster.

(c) A facility shall conduct a drill at least quarterly for each shift. The type of emergency covered in a drill shall vary from quarter to quarter, taking into account different emergency scenarios. An actual evacuation of residents is not required during a drill. While a facility may provide an opportunity for residents to participate in a drill, it shall not require any resident participation. Documentation of the drills shall include the date, the type of emergency covered by the drill, and the names of staff participating in the drill.

(d) A facility shall review the plan annually and make updates as necessary, including changes in floor plans and the population served. The licensee or administrator shall sign and date documentation to indicate that the plan has been reviewed and updated as necessary.

(e) A facility shall have all of the following information readily available to facility staff during an emergency:

(1) A resident roster with the date of birth for each resident.

(2) An appraisal of resident needs and services plan for each resident.

(3) A resident medication list for residents with centrally stored medications.

(4) Contact information for the responsible party and physician for each resident.

(f) A facility shall have both of the following in place:

(1) An evacuation chair at each stairwell, on or before July 1, 2019.

(2) A set of keys available to facility staff on each shift for use during an evacuation that provides access to all of the following:

(A) All occupied resident units.

(B) All facility vehicles.

(C) All facility exit doors.

(D) All facility cabinets and cupboards or files that contain elements of the emergency and disaster plan, including, but not limited to, food supplies and protective shelter supplies.

(g) A facility shall make the plan available upon request to residents onsite, any responsible party for a resident, the local long-term care ombudsman, and local emergency responders. Resident and employee information shall be kept confidential.

(h) An applicant seeking a license for a new facility shall submit the emergency and disaster plan with the initial license application required under Section 1569.15.

(i) The department's Community Care Licensing Division shall confirm, during annual licensing visits, that the emergency and disaster plan is on file at the facility and includes required content.

(j) A facility is encouraged to have the emergency and disaster plan reviewed by local emergency authorities.

(k) Nothing in this section shall create a new or additional requirement for the department to evaluate the emergency and disaster plan.

(Amended by Stats. 2018, Ch. 348, Sec. 1. (AB 3098) Effective January 1, 2019.)

1569.696.

(a) All residential care facilities for the elderly shall provide training to direct care staff on postural supports, restricted conditions or health services, and hospice care as a component of the training requirements specified in Section 1569.625. The training shall include all of the following:

(1) Four hours of training on the care, supervision, and special needs of those residents, prior to providing direct care to residents. The facility may utilize various methods of instruction, including, but not limited to, preceptorship, mentoring, and other forms of observation and demonstration. The orientation time shall be exclusive of any administrative instruction.

(2) Four hours of training thereafter of in-service training per year on the subject of serving those residents.

(b) This training shall be developed in consultation with individuals or organizations with specific expertise in the care of those residents described in subdivision (a). In formulating and providing this training, reference may be made to written materials and literature. This training requirement may be provided at the facility or offsite and may include a combination of observation and practical application.

(c) This section shall become operative on January 1, 2016.

(Added by Stats. 2014, Ch. 705, Sec. 9. (SB 911) Effective January 1, 2015. Section operative January 1, 2016, by its own provisions.)

ARTICLE 6.6. Secured Perimeters [1569.698 - 1569.7]

(Article 6.6 added by Stats. 1995, Ch. 550, Sec. 2.)

1569.698.

(a) The State Fire Marshal has proposed that the California Building Standards Commission adopt building standards to provide for locked and secured perimeters in residential care facilities for the elderly that care for persons with major neurocognitive disorder:

(1) It is acknowledged that these building standards will not become effective until October 1, 1996.

(2) It is the policy of the California Building Standards Commission that building standards be adopted exclusively into the California Building Standards Code and not into state statute.

(3) However, in recognition of the immediate need of residential care facilities for the elderly caring for persons with major neurocognitive disorder to provide a secured environment, it is the intent of the Legislature that the building standards for locked and secured perimeters proposed by the State Fire Marshal for adoption in the 1994 California Building Standards Code, as set forth in Section 1569.699, be effective October 4, 1995.

(b) (1) Upon the filing of emergency regulations with the Secretary of State pursuant to subdivision (c), a residential care facility for the elderly that cares for people with major neurocognitive disorder may utilize secured perimeter fences or locked exit doors if it meets the requirements for additional safeguards required by those regulations.

(2) For the purposes of this article, major neurocognitive disorder includes Alzheimer's disease and related disorders, diagnosed by a physician, that increase the tendency to wander and that decrease hazard awareness and the ability to communicate.

(3) It is the intent of the Legislature in enacting this article that residential care facilities for the elderly have options for the security of persons with major neurocognitive disorder who are residents of those facilities that are in addition to existing security exceptions made for individual residents. It is the further intent of the Legislature that these additional options shall include the use of waivers of certain building standards relating to fire safety, to be issued by the state department with the approval of the State Fire Marshal, to permit the care of a target group of persons with major neurocognitive disorder by means of secured perimeter fences, or the use of locked exterior doors. Each waiver request shall include a facility plan of operation that addresses elements of care to be identified by the department in regulations and demonstrates the facility's ability to meet the safety needs of persons with major neurocognitive disorder.

(4) The department shall adopt regulations that ensure that staff for secured perimeter facilities receive appropriate and adequate training in the care of residents with major neurocognitive disorder.

(5) Nothing in this section is intended to prohibit residential care facilities for the elderly from accepting or retaining persons with major neurocognitive disorder whose needs can be fully met using care options permitted by existing law and regulations.

(6) It is not the intent of the Legislature to authorize an increase in the level of care provided in a residential care facility for the elderly or to establish a supplemental rate structure based on the services provided in the facility.

(7) All admissions to residential care facilities for the elderly shall continue to be voluntary on the part of the resident or with the lawful consent of the resident's legal conservator.

(c) The department shall adopt regulations to implement subdivision (b) in accordance with those provisions of the Administrative Procedure Act contained in Chapter 3.5 (commencing with Section 11340) of Part 1 of Division 3 of Title 2 of the Government Code. The initial adoption of any emergency regulations following October 4, 1995, shall be deemed to be an emergency and necessary for the immediate preservation of the public peace, health and safety, or general welfare. Emergency regulations adopted pursuant to this subdivision shall remain in effect for no more than 180 days.

(d) In addition to the security options authorized by subdivision (b), residential care facilities for the elderly that accept or retain as residents persons with major neurocognitive disorder, and that choose to utilize the security options of egress-control devices of the time-delay type in addition to secured perimeter fences or locked exit doors, shall comply with Section 1569.699, or regulations adopted by the California Building Standards Commission, whichever is operative.

(e) A residential care facility for the elderly shall not utilize special egress-control devices of the time-delay type, secured perimeter fences, or locked exit doors unless the facility meets the requirements of Section 1569.699 or the California Building Standards Commission adopts building standards to implement this section.

(f) Any person who is not a conservatee and is entering a locked or secured perimeter facility pursuant to this section shall sign a statement of voluntary entry. The facility shall retain the original statement and shall send a copy of the statement to the department.

(Amended by Stats. 2017, Ch. 122, Sec. 1. (SB 413) Effective January 1, 2018.)

1569.699.

(a) When approved by the person responsible for enforcement, as described in Section 13146, exit doors in facilities classified as Group R, Division 2 facilities under the California Building Standards Code, licensed as residential care facilities for the elderly, and housing clients with Alzheimer's disease or major neurocognitive disorder, may be equipped with approved listed special egress-control devices of the time-delay type, provided the building is protected throughout by an approved automatic sprinkler system and an approved automatic smoke-detection system. The devices shall conform to all of the following requirements:

(1) Automatic deactivation of the egress-control device upon activation of either the sprinkler system or the detection system.

(2) Automatic deactivation of the egress-control device upon loss of electrical power to any of the following:

(A) The egress-control device.

(B) The smoke-detection system.

(C) Exit illumination as required by Section 1013 of the California Building Standards Code.

(3) Be capable of being deactivated by a signal from a switch located in an approved location.

(4) Initiate an irreversible process that will deactivate the egress-control device whenever a manual force of not more than 15 pounds (66.72 N) is applied for two seconds to the panic bar or other door-latching hardware. The egress-control device shall deactivate within an approved time period not to exceed a total of 15 seconds, except that the person responsible for enforcement, as described in Section 13146, may approve a delay not to exceed 30 seconds in residential care facilities for the elderly serving patients with Alzheimer's disease. The time delay established for each egress-control device shall not be field adjustable.

(5) Actuation of the panic bar or other door-latching hardware shall activate an audible signal at the door.

(6) The unlatching shall not require more than one operation.

(7) (A) A sign shall be provided on the door located above and within 12 inches (305mm) of the panic bar or other door-latching hardware reading:

KEEP PUSHING. THIS DOOR WILL OPEN IN ___ SECONDS. ALARM WILL SOUND.

(B) Sign letter shall be at least one inch (25mm) in height and shall have a stroke of not less than one-eighth inch (3.3mm).

(8) Regardless of the means of deactivation, relocking of the egress-control device shall be by manual means only at the door.

(b) Grounds of residential care facilities for the elderly serving persons with Alzheimer's disease or major neurocognitive disorder may be fenced, and gates therein equipped with locks, provided safe dispersal areas are located not less than 50 feet (15240mm) from the buildings. Dispersal areas shall be sized to provide an area of not less than three square feet (0.28 2) per occupant. Gates shall not be installed across corridors or passageways leading to the dispersal areas unless they comply with the exit requirements of Section 1022 of the California Building Standards Code.

(c) Exit doors may be locked in residential care facilities for the elderly that meet the requirements for Group I, Division 3 occupancies under the California Building Standards Code and that care for people with major neurocognitive disorder.

(d) This section shall become inoperative on the date the California Building Standards Commission adopts regulations regarding secured perimeters in residential care facilities for the elderly, and, as of the January 1 next following that date, is repealed, unless a later enacted statute, that becomes operative on or before that January 1, deletes or extends the dates on which it becomes inoperative and is repealed.

(Amended by Stats. 2018, Ch. 92, Sec. 134. (SB 1289) Effective January 1, 2019. Inoperative on date prescribed by its own provisions. Repealed on January 1 after inoperative date, by its own provisions.)

1569.6991.

On and after January 1, 1999, no security window bars may be installed or maintained on any residential care facility for the elderly unless the security window bars meet current state and local requirements, as applicable, for security window bars and safety release devices.
(Added by Stats. 1998, Ch. 343, Sec. 3. Effective January 1, 1999.)
1569.7.
Residential care facilities for the elderly that serve residents with Alzheimer's disease and other forms of major neurocognitive disorder should include information on sundowning as part of the training for direct care staff, and should include in the plan of operation a brief narrative description explaining activities available for residents to decrease the effects of sundowning, including, but not limited to, increasing outdoor activities in appropriate weather conditions.
(Amended by Stats. 2017, Ch. 122, Sec. 3. (SB 413) Effective January 1, 2018.)

ARTICLE 7. Levels of Care [1569.70 - 1569.74]
(Article 7 added by Stats. 1985, Ch. 1127, Sec. 3.)
1569.70.
It is the intent of the Legislature to develop and implement a plan to establish three levels of care under the residential care facility for the elderly license, subject to future Budget Act appropriations and statutory authorization to implement levels of care.
(a) The guidelines for the development of these levels of care are:
(1) Level I—Base care and supervision. Residents at this level are able to maintain a higher degree of independence and need only minimum care and supervision, as defined, and minimal personal care assistance.
(2) Level II—Nonmedical personal care. Residents at this level have functional limitations and psychosocial needs requiring not only care and supervision but frequent assistance with personal activities of daily living and active intervention to help them maintain their potential for independent living.
(3) Level III—Health related assistance. Residents at this level require the services of lower levels and rely on the facility for extensive assistance with personal activities of daily living. This level may include residents who also require the occasional services of an appropriate skilled professional due to chronic health problems and returning residents recovering from illness, injury, or treatment that required placement in facilities providing higher levels of care.
These levels are to be based on the services required by residents at each level due to their functional limitations.
(b) The levels of care plan shall include:
(1) Guidelines for meeting requirements at each level of care by utilizing appropriate community and professional services. Options shall be provided to allow facilities to meet resident needs by accessing community services or hiring appropriate staff.
(2) Assessment procedures for facility evaluation of residents' level of care needs.
(3) Process for ensuring the individual facility's ability to serve clients at each level of care they intend to provide.
(4) Recommendations for a supplemental rate structure based on the services required at Levels II and III to be provided for residents who need those levels of care and are recipients of SSI/SSP. These rates shall be in addition to the basic SSI/SSP rate for providing care supervision and shall reflect actual costs of operation for residential care facilities for the elderly.
(5) Procedures for assessment and certification of SSI/SSP recipients, by county social services departments to allow for administration of the supplemental rate structure.
(6) Procedures for evaluating and monitoring the appropriateness of the levels of care determined for SSI/SSP recipients.
(c) Implementation of the levels of care system shall consider the applicability of the 1985 level of care report developed by the California Health and Human Services Agency, so as to ensure continuity in the residential care facility for the elderly program as outlined under this chapter.
(Amended by Stats. 2004, Ch. 183, Sec. 191. Effective January 1, 2005.)
1569.71.
In consultation with the State Fire Marshal the department shall develop and expedite implementation of regulations related to nonambulatory persons that ensure resident safety but also provide flexibility to allow residents to remain in the least restrictive environment.
Following the implementation of levels of care, regulations related to nonambulatory persons shall also provide the flexibility necessary for those levels in residential care facilities for the elderly.
(Added by Stats. 1985, Ch. 1127, Sec. 3.)
1569.72.
(a) Except as otherwise provided in subdivision (d), no resident shall be admitted or retained in a residential care facility for the elderly if any of the following apply:
(1) The resident requires 24-hour, skilled nursing or intermediate care.
(2) The resident is bedridden, other than for a temporary illness or for recovery from surgery.
(b) (1) For the purposes of this section, "bedridden" means requiring assistance in turning and repositioning in bed or being unable to independently transfer to and from bed, except in a facility with appropriate and sufficient care staff, mechanical devices, if necessary, and safety precautions, as determined by the director in regulations.
(2) The determination of the bedridden status of persons with developmental disabilities shall be made by the Director of Social Services or his or her designated representative, in consultation with the Director of Developmental Services or his or her designated representative, after consulting the resident's individual safety plan. The determination of the bedridden status of all other persons with disabilities who are not developmentally

disabled shall be made by the Director of Social Services, or his or her designated representative.
(c) Notwithstanding paragraph (2) of subdivision (a), bedridden persons may be admitted to, and remain in, residential care facilities for the elderly that secure and maintain an appropriate fire clearance. A fire clearance shall be issued to a facility in which one or more bedridden persons reside if either of the following conditions are met:
(1) The fire safety requirements are met. Residents who are unable to independently transfer to and from bed, but who do not need assistance to turn or reposition in bed, shall be considered nonambulatory for purposes of this paragraph.
(2) Alternative methods of protection are approved.
(d) (1) For purposes of this section, "temporary illness" means any illness which persists for 14 days or less.
(e) A bedridden resident may be retained in a residential care facility for the elderly in excess of 14 days if all of the following requirements are satisfied:
(1) The facility notifies the department in writing regarding the temporary illness or recovery from surgery.
(2) The facility submits to the department, with the notification, a physician and surgeon's written statement to the effect that the resident's illness or recovery is of a temporary nature. The statement shall contain an estimated date upon which the illness or recovery will end or upon which the resident will no longer be confined to a bed.
(3) The department determines that the health and safety of the resident is adequately protected in that facility and that transfer to a higher level of care is not necessary.
(4) This section does not expand the scope of care and supervision of a residential care facility for the elderly.
(f) Notwithstanding the length of stay of a bedridden resident, every facility admitting or retaining a bedridden resident, as defined in this section, shall, within 48 hours of the resident's admission or retention in the facility, notify the local fire authority with jurisdiction in the bedridden resident's location of the estimated length of time the resident will retain his or her bedridden status in the facility.
(g) Nothing in this section shall be used for purposes of Section 1569.70 to determine the appropriateness of residents being admitted or retained in a residential care facility for the elderly on the basis of health-related conditions and the need for these services until the three levels of care set forth in Section 1569.70 are fully implemented. This section shall not prohibit the Community Care Licensing Division of the State Department of Social Services from continuing to implement the regulations of Article 8 (commencing with Section 87700) of Chapter 8 of Division 6 of Title 22 of the California Code of Regulations, as promulgated and approved on February 13, 1990.
(h) (1) The department and the Office of the State Fire Marshal, in consultation with the State Department of Developmental Services, shall each promulgate regulations that meet all of the following conditions:
(A) Are consistent with subdivisions (a) to (f), inclusive.
(B) Are applicable to facilities regulated under this chapter, consistent with the regulatory requirements of the California Building Standards Code for fire and life safety for the respective occupancy classifications into which the State Department of Social Services' community care licensing classifications fall.
(C) Permit residents to remain in home-like settings.
(2) At a minimum, these regulations shall do both of the following with regard to a residential care facility that provides care for six or fewer residents, at least one of whom is bedridden:
(A) Clarify the fire and life safety requirements for a fire clearance for the facility.
(B) (i) Identify procedures for requesting the approval of alternative means of providing equivalent levels of fire and life safety protection.
(ii) Either the facility, the resident or resident's representative, or local fire official may request from the Office of the State Fire Marshal a written opinion concerning the interpretation of the regulations promulgated by the State Fire Marshal pursuant to this section for a particular factual dispute. The State Fire Marshal shall issue the written opinion within 45 days following the request.
(i) For facilities that care for six or fewer clients, a local fire official may not impose fire safety requirements stricter than the fire safety regulations promulgated for the particular type of facility by the Office of the State Fire Marshal or the local fire safety requirements imposed on any other single family dwelling, whichever is more strict.
(j) This section and any regulations promulgated thereunder shall be interpreted in a manner that provides flexibility to allow bedridden persons to avoid institutionalization and be admitted to, and safely remain in, community-based residential care facilities.
(Amended by Stats. 2009, Ch. 471, Sec. 3. (AB 762) Effective January 1, 2010.)
1569.725.
(a) A residential care facility for the elderly may permit incidental medical services to be provided through a home health agency, licensed pursuant to Chapter 8 (commencing with Section 1725), when all of the following conditions are met:
(1) The facility, in the judgment of the department, has the ability to provide the supporting care and supervision appropriate to meet the needs of the resident receiving care from a home health agency.
(2) The home health agency has been advised of the regulations pertaining to residential care facilities for the elderly and the requirements related to incidental medical services being provided in the facility.
(3) There is evidence of an agreed-upon protocol between the home health agency and the residential care facility for the elderly. The protocol shall address areas of responsibility of the home health agency and the facility and the need for communication and the sharing of resident information related to the home health care plan. Resident information may be shared between the home health agency and the residential care

facility for the elderly relative to the resident's medical condition and the care and treatment provided to the resident by the home health agency including, but not limited to, medical information, as defined by the Confidentiality of Medical Information Act, Part 2.6 (commencing with Section 56) of Division 1 of the Civil Code.

(4) There is ongoing communication between the home health agency and the residential care facility for the elderly about the services provided to the resident by the home health agency and the frequency and duration of care to be provided.

(b) Nothing in this section is intended to expand the scope of care and supervision for a residential care facility for the elderly, as prescribed by this chapter.

(c) Nothing in this section shall require any care or supervision to be provided by the residential care facility for the elderly beyond that which is permitted in this chapter.

(d) The department shall not be responsible for the evaluation of medical services provided to the resident of the residential care facility for the elderly by the home health agency.

(e) Any regulations, policies, or procedures related to sharing resident information and development of protocols, established by the department pursuant to this section, shall be developed in consultation with the State Department of Health Services and persons representing home health agencies and residential care facilities for the elderly.

(Amended by Stats. 1998, Ch. 831, Sec. 6. Effective January 1, 1999.)

1569.73.

(a) Notwithstanding Section 1569.72 or any other provision of law, a residential care facility for the elderly may obtain a waiver from the department for the purpose of allowing a resident who has been diagnosed as terminally ill by his or her physician and surgeon to remain in the facility, or allowing a person who has been diagnosed as terminally ill by his or her physician and surgeon to become a resident of the facility if that person is already receiving hospice services and would continue to receive hospice services without disruption if he or she became a resident, when all the following conditions are met:

(1) The facility agrees to retain the terminally ill resident, or accept as a resident the terminally ill person, and to seek a waiver on behalf of the individual, provided the individual has requested the waiver and is capable of deciding to obtain hospice services.

(2) The terminally ill resident, or the terminally ill person to be accepted as a resident, has obtained the services of a hospice certified in accordance with federal medicare conditions of participation and licensed pursuant to Chapter 8 (commencing with Section 1725) or Chapter 8.5 (commencing with Section 1745).

(3) The facility, in the judgment of the department, has the ability to provide care and supervision appropriate to meet the needs of the terminally ill resident or the terminally ill person to be accepted as a resident, and is in substantial compliance with regulations governing the operation of residential care facilities for the elderly.

(4) The hospice has agreed to design and provide for care, services, and necessary medical intervention related to the terminal illness as necessary to supplement the care and supervision provided by the facility.

(5) An agreement has been executed between the facility and the hospice regarding the care plan for the terminally ill resident or terminally ill person to be accepted as a resident. The care plan shall designate the primary caregiver, identify other caregivers, and outline the tasks the facility is responsible for performing and the approximate frequency with which they shall be performed. The care plan shall specifically limit the facility's role for care and supervision to those tasks allowed under this chapter.

(6) The facility has obtained the agreement of those residents who share the same room with the terminally ill resident, or any resident who will share a room with the terminally ill person to be accepted as a resident, to allow the hospice caregivers into their residence.

(b) At any time that the licensed hospice, the facility, or the terminally ill resident determines that the resident's condition has changed so that continued residence in the facility will pose a threat to the health and safety to the terminally ill resident or any other resident, the facility may initiate procedures for a transfer.

(c) A facility that has obtained a hospice waiver from the department pursuant to this section need not call emergency response services at the time of a life-threatening emergency if the hospice agency is notified instead and all of the following conditions are met:

(1) The resident is receiving hospice services from a licensed hospice agency.

(2) The resident has completed an advance directive, as defined in Section 4605 of the Probate Code, requesting to forego resuscitative measures.

(3) The facility has documented that facility staff have received training from the hospice agency on the expected course of the resident's illness and the symptoms of impending death.

(d) Nothing in this section is intended to expand the scope of care and supervision for a residential care facility for the elderly as defined in this act, nor shall a facility be required to alter or extend its license in order to retain a terminally ill resident or allow a terminally ill person to become a resident of the facility as authorized by this section.

(e) Nothing in this section shall require any care or supervision to be provided by the residential care facility for the elderly beyond that which is permitted in this chapter.

(f) Nothing in this section is intended to expand the scope of life care contracts or the contractual obligation of continuing care retirement communities as defined in Section 1771.

(g) The department shall not be responsible for the evaluation of medical services provided to the resident by the hospice and shall have no liability for the independent acts of the hospice.

(h) Nothing in this section shall be construed to relieve a licensed residential care facility for the elderly of its responsibility to notify the appropriate fire authority of the presence of a bedridden resident in the facility as required under subdivision (f) of Section

1569.72, and to obtain and maintain a fire clearance as required under Section 1569.149.

(Amended by Stats. 2003, Ch. 312, Sec. 2. Effective January 1, 2004.)

1569.74.

(a) Licensed residential care facilities for the elderly that employ health care providers may establish policies to honor a request to forego resuscitative measures as defined in Section 4780 of the Probate Code.

(b) Any policy established pursuant to subdivision (a) shall meet all of the following conditions:

(1) The policy shall be in writing and specify procedures to be followed in implementing the policy.

(2) The policy and procedures shall, at all times, be available in the facility for review by the department.

(3) The licensee shall ensure that all staff are aware of the policy as well as the procedures to be followed in implementing the policy.

(4) A copy of the policy shall be given to each resident who makes a request to forego resuscitative measures and to the resident's primary physician.

(5) A copy of the resident's request to forego resuscitative measures shall be maintained in the facility and shall be immediately available for review by facility staff, the licensed health care provider, and the department.

(6) Facility staff are prohibited, on behalf of any resident, from signing any directive document as a witness or from being the legally recognized surrogate decisionmaker.

(7) The facility shall provide the resident's physician with a copy of the resident's request to forego resuscitative measures form.

(c) Any action by a facility that has established policies pursuant to subdivision (a), to honor a resident's request to forego resuscitative measures as provided for in subdivision (a) may only be taken in either of the following ways:

(1) By a licensed health care provider who is employed by the facility and on the premises at the time of the life threatening emergency.

(2) By notifying, under those conditions specified in subdivision (c) of Section 1569.73, the hospice agency that is caring for a resident receiving hospice services.

(d) Licensed residential care facilities for the elderly that have not established policies pursuant to subdivision (a), may keep an executed request to forego resuscitative measures form in the resident's file and present it to an emergency medical technician or paramedic when authorized to do so in writing by the resident or his or her legally recognized surrogate decisionmaker. The request may be honored by an emergency medical technician or by any health care provider as defined in Section 4621 of the Probate Code, who, in the course of professional or volunteer duties, responds to emergencies.

(Amended by Stats. 2003, Ch. 312, Sec. 3. Effective January 1, 2004.)

ARTICLE 7.5. Resident Participation in Decisionmaking [1569.80- 1569.80.]
(Article 7.5 added by Stats. 1998, Ch. 660, Sec. 2.)

1569.80.

(a) A resident of a residential care facility for the elderly, or the resident's representative, or both, shall have the right to participate in decisionmaking regarding the care and services to be provided to the resident. Accordingly, prior to, or within two weeks after, the resident's admission, the facility shall coordinate a meeting with the resident and the resident's representative, if any, an appropriate member or members of the facility's staff, if the resident is receiving home health services in the facility, a representative of the home health agency involved, and any other appropriate parties. The facility shall ensure that participants in the meeting prepare a written record of the care the resident will receive in the facility, and the resident's preferences regarding the services provided at the facility.

(b) Once prepared, the written record described in subdivision (a) shall be used by the facility, and, if applicable pursuant to Section 1569.725, the home health agency, to determine the care and services provided to the resident. If the resident has a regular physician, the written record shall be sent by the facility to that physician.

(c) The written record described in subdivision (a) shall be reviewed, and, if necessary, revised, at least once every 12 months, or upon a significant change in the resident's condition, as defined by regulations, whichever occurs first. The review shall take place at a meeting coordinated by the facility, and attended by the resident, the resident's representative, if any, an appropriate member or members of the facility's staff, and, if the resident is receiving home health services in the facility, a representative from the home health agency involved.

(d) This section shall not preclude a residential care facility for the elderly or home health agency from satisfying other state or federal obligations at a meeting required by subdivision (a) or (c).

(e) If the residential care facility for the elderly is a continuing care retirement community, as defined in paragraph (10) of subdivision (c) of Section 1771, this section shall apply only to residents who require care and supervision, as defined in subdivision (b) of Section 1569.2.

(Added by Stats. 1998, Ch. 660, Sec. 2. Effective January 1, 1999.)

ARTICLE 8. Local Regulation [1569.82 - 1569.87]
(Article 8 added by Stats. 1986, Ch. 844, Sec. 11.)

1569.82.

The Legislature hereby declares that it is the policy of this state that each county and city shall permit and encourage the development of sufficient numbers of residential care facilities for the elderly as are commensurate with local need.

This article shall apply equally to any chartered city, general law city, county, city and county, district, and any other local public entity.

For the purposes of this article, "six or fewer persons" does not include the licensee or members of the licensee's family or persons employed as facility staff.

(Added by Stats. 1986, Ch. 844, Sec. 11.)

1569.83.

Any person licensed under this chapter who operates, or proposes to operate a residential care facility for the elderly, the department or other public agency authorized to license the facility, or any public or private agency which uses or may use the services of the facility to place its clients, may invoke this article.

This section shall not be construed to prohibit any interested party from bringing suit to invoke this article.

(Added by Stats. 1986, Ch. 844, Sec. 11.)

1569.84.

A residential care facility for the elderly, which serves six or fewer persons shall not be subject to any business taxes, local registration fees, use permit fees, or other fees to which other family dwellings of the same type in the same zone are not likewise subject. Nothing in this section shall be construed to forbid the imposition of local property taxes, fees for water service and garbage collection, fees for inspections not prohibited by Section 1569.85, local bond assessments, and other fees, charges, and assessments to which other family dwellings of the same type in the same zone are likewise subject. Neither the State Fire Marshal nor any local public entity shall charge any fee for enforcing fire inspection regulations pursuant to state law or regulation or local ordinance, with respect to residential care facilities for the elderly which service six or fewer persons.

For the purposes of this section, "family dwelling," includes, but is not limited to, single-family dwellings, units in multifamily dwellings, including units in duplexes and units in apartment dwellings, mobilehomes, including mobilehomes located in mobilehome parks, units in cooperatives, units in condominiums, units in townhouses, and units in planned unit developments.

(Amended by Stats. 1987, Ch. 1092, Sec. 4. Effective September 24, 1987.)

1569.85.

(a) Whether or not unrelated persons are living together, a residential care facility for the elderly that serves six or fewer persons shall be considered a residential use of property for the purposes of this article. In addition, the residents and operators of the facility shall be considered a family for the purposes of any law or zoning ordinance that relates to the residential use of property pursuant to this article.

(b) For the purpose of all local ordinances, a residential care facility for the elderly that serves six or fewer persons shall not be included within the definition of a boarding house, rooming house, institution or home for the care of the aged, guest home, rest home, community residence, or other similar term that implies that the residential care facility for the elderly is a business run for profit or differs in any other way from a family dwelling.

(c) This section shall not be construed to forbid a city, county, or other local public entity from placing restrictions on building heights, setback, lot dimensions, or placement of signs of a residential care facility for the elderly that serves six or fewer persons as long as the restrictions are identical to those applied to other family dwellings of the same type in the same zone.

(d) This section shall not be construed to forbid the application to a residential care facility for the elderly of any local ordinance that deals with health and safety, building standards, environmental impact standards, or any other matter within the jurisdiction of a local public entity if the ordinance does not distinguish residential care facilities for the elderly that serve six or fewer persons from other family dwellings of the same type in the same zone and if the ordinance does not distinguish residents of the residential care facilities for the elderly from persons who reside in other family dwellings of the same type in the same zone.

(e) No conditional use permit, zoning variance, or other zoning clearance shall be required of a residential care facility for the elderly that serves six or fewer persons that is not required of a family dwelling of the same type in the same zone.

(f) Use of a family dwelling for purposes of a residential care facility for the elderly serving six or fewer persons shall not constitute a change of occupancy for purposes of Part 1.5 (commencing with Section 17910) of Division 13 or local building codes. However, nothing in this section is intended to supersede Section 13143 or 13143.6, to the extent these sections are applicable to residential care facilities for the elderly providing care for six or fewer residents.

(g) For the purposes of this section, "family dwelling," includes, but is not limited to, single-family dwellings, units in multifamily dwellings, including units in duplexes and units in apartment dwellings, mobilehomes, including mobilehomes located in mobilehome parks, units in cooperatives, units in condominiums, units in townhouses, and units in planned unit developments.

(Amended by Stats. 2014, Ch. 144, Sec. 35. (AB 1847) Effective January 1, 2015.)

1569.86.

No fire inspection clearance or other permit, license, clearance, or similar authorization shall be denied to a residential care facility for the elderly because of a failure to comply with local ordinances from which the facilities are exempt under Section 1569.85, provided that the applicant otherwise qualifies for the fire clearance, license, permit, or similar authorization.

(Added by Stats. 1986, Ch. 844, Sec. 11.)

1569.87.

For the purposes of any contract, deed, or covenant for the transfer of real property executed on or after January 1, 1979, a residential facility for the elderly which serves six or fewer persons shall be considered a residential use of property and a use of property by a single family, notwithstanding any disclaimers to the contrary.

(Added by Stats. 1986, Ch. 844, Sec. 11.)

ARTICLE 9. Admission Agreements [1569.880 - 1569.889]

(Article 9 added by Stats. 2003, Ch. 409, Sec. 2.)

1569.880.

(a) For purposes of this section, an "admission agreement" includes all documents that a resident or his or her representative must sign at the time of, or as a condition of, admission to a residential care facility for the elderly licensed under this chapter.

(b) The admission agreement shall not include any written attachment containing any provision that is prohibited from being included in the admission agreement.

(Added by Stats. 2003, Ch. 409, Sec. 2. Effective January 1, 2004.)

1569.881.

(a) Every residential care facility for the elderly shall make blank complete copies of its admission agreement available to the public immediately, subject to time required for copying or mailing, at cost, upon request.

(b) Every residential care facility for the elderly shall conspicuously post in a location accessible to the public view within the facility either a complete copy of the admission agreement, or a notice of its availability from the facility.

(Added by Stats. 2003, Ch. 409, Sec. 2. Effective January 1, 2004.)

1569.882.

(a) The admission agreement shall be printed in black type of not less than 12-point type size, on plain white paper. The print shall appear on one side of the paper only.

(b) The admission agreement shall be written in clear, coherent, and unambiguous language, using words with common and everyday meanings. It shall be appropriately divided, and each section shall be appropriately captioned.

(Added by Stats. 2003, Ch. 409, Sec. 2. Effective January 1, 2004.)

1569.883.

(a) The admission agreement shall not include unlawful waivers of facility liability for the health and safety or personal property of residents.

(b) The admission agreement shall not include any provision that the facility knows or should know is deceptive, or unlawful under state or federal law.

(Added by Stats. 2003, Ch. 409, Sec. 2. Effective January 1, 2004.)

1569.884.

The admission agreement shall include all of the following:

(a) A comprehensive description of any items and services provided under a single fee, such as a monthly fee for room, board, and other items and services.

(b) A comprehensive description of, and the fee schedule for, all items and services not included in a single fee. In addition, the agreement shall indicate that the resident shall receive a monthly statement itemizing all separate charges incurred by the resident.

(c) A facility may assess a separate charge for an item or service only if that separate charge is authorized by the admission agreement. If additional services are available through the facility to be purchased by the resident that were not available at the time the admission agreement was signed, a list of these services and charges shall be provided to the resident or the resident's representative. A statement acknowledging the acceptance or refusal to purchase the additional services shall be signed and dated by the resident or the resident's representative and attached to the admission agreement.

(d) An explanation of the use of third-party services within the facility that are related to the resident's service plan, including, but not limited to, ancillary, health, and medical services, how they may be arranged, accessed, and monitored, any restrictions on third-party services, and who is financially responsible for the third-party services.

(e) A comprehensive description of billing and payment policies and procedures.

(f) The conditions under which rates may be increased pursuant to Section 1569.655.

(g) The facility's policy concerning family visits and other communication with residents, pursuant to Section 1569.313.

(h) The facility's policy concerning refunds, including the conditions under which a refund for advanced monthly fees will be returned in the event of a resident's death, pursuant to Section 1569.652.

(i) Conditions under which the agreement may be terminated.

(j) An explanation of the facility's responsibility to prepare a relocation evaluation, for each resident and a closure plan and to provide notice in the case of an eviction pursuant to Section 1569.682.

(Amended by Stats. 2013, Ch. 290, Sec. 2. (AB 261) Effective January 1, 2014.)

1569.885.

(a) When referring to a resident's obligation to observe facility rules, the admission agreement shall indicate that the rules must be reasonable, and that there is a facility procedure for suggesting changes in the rules. A facility rule shall not violate any right set forth in this article or in other applicable laws and regulations.

(b) The admission agreement shall specify that a copy of the facility grievance procedure for resolution of resident complaints about facility practices shall be made available to the resident or his or her representative.

(c) The admission agreement shall inform a resident of the right to contact the State Department of Social Services, the long-term care ombudsman, or both, regarding grievances against the facility.

(d) A copy of any applicable resident's rights specified by law or regulation shall be an attachment to all admission agreements.

(e) The statement of resident's rights attached to admissions agreements by a residential care facility for the elderly shall include information on the reporting of suspected or known elder and dependent adult abuse, as set forth in Section 1569.889.
(Amended by Stats. 2005, Ch. 456, Sec. 1. Effective January 1, 2006.)
1569.886.
(a) The admission agreement shall not include any ground for involuntary transfer or eviction of the resident unless those grounds are specifically enumerated under state law or regulation.
(b) The admission agreement shall list the justifications for eviction permissible under state law or regulation, exactly as they are worded in the applicable law or regulation.
(c) The admission agreement shall include an explanation of the resident's right to notice prior to an involuntary transfer, discharge, or eviction, the process by which the resident may appeal the decision and a description of the relocation assistance offered by the facility.
(d) The admission agreement shall state the responsibilities of the licensee and the rights of the resident when a facility evicts residents pursuant to Section 1569.682.
(Amended by Stats. 2007, Ch. 686, Sec. 4. Effective January 1, 2008.)
1569.887.
(a) The admission agreement shall be signed and dated, acknowledging the contents of the document, by the resident or the resident's representative.
(b) The licensee shall retain in the resident's file the original signed and dated initial agreement and all subsequent modifications.
(c) The licensee shall provide a copy of the signed and dated admission agreement to the resident or the resident's representative, if any.
(d) The admission agreement shall be reviewed at the time of the compliance visit and in response to a complaint involving the admission agreement.
(Added by Stats. 2003, Ch. 409, Sec. 2. Effective January 1, 2004.)
1569.888.
(a) The requirements of this article relating to admission agreements for residential care facilities for the elderly are intended to be in addition to, and not exclusive of, any other requirements established by state law or regulation.
(b) This article shall not apply to licensees of residential care facilities for the elderly that have obtained a certificate of authority to offer continuing care contracts, as defined in paragraph (5) of subdivision (c) of Section 1771.
(Added by Stats. 2003, Ch. 409, Sec. 2. Effective January 1, 2004.)
1569.889.
(a) The personal rights form made available by the department's Community Care Licensing Division to residential care facilities for the elderly shall include a statement regarding procedures for reporting known or suspected elder and dependent adult abuse, including the toll-free telephone number of the State Long-Term Care Ombudsman's CRISISline and a blank space for the telephone number of the nearest approved organization for long-term care ombudsperson activities. A residential care facility for the elderly shall insert in the form's blank space the telephone number of the nearest approved organization for long-term care ombudsperson activities.
(b) The department's Community Care Licensing Division shall adopt or amend any regulation and revise any document or policy as necessary to implement this section.
(Added by Stats. 2005, Ch. 456, Sec. 2. Effective January 1, 2006.)

CHAPTER 3.3. California Adult Day Health Care Act [1570 - 1596.5]

(Heading of Chapter 3.3 renumbered from Chapter 3.2 by Stats. 1988, Ch. 160, Sec. 92.)

ARTICLE 1. General Provisions [1570 - 1571]
(Article 1 added by Stats. 1977, Ch. 1066.)
1570.
This chapter shall be known and may be cited as the California Adult Day Health Care Act.
(Added by Stats. 1977, Ch. 1066.)
1570.2.
The Legislature hereby finds and declares that there exists a pattern of overutilization of long-term institutional care for elderly persons or adults with disabilities, and that there is an urgent need to establish and to continue a community-based system of quality adult day health care which will enable elderly persons or adults with disabilities to maintain maximum independence. While recognizing that there continues to be a substantial need for facilities providing custodial care, overreliance on this type of care has proven to be a costly panacea in both financial and human terms, often traumatic, and destructive of continuing family relationships and the capacity for independent living.
It is, therefore, the intent of the Legislature in enacting this chapter and related provisions to provide for the development of policies and programs that will accomplish the following:
(a) Ensure that elderly persons and adults with disabilities are not institutionalized inappropriately or prematurely.
(b) Provide a viable alternative to institutionalization for those elderly persons and adults with disabilities who are capable of living at home with the aid of appropriate health care or rehabilitative and social services.
(c) Establish adult day health centers in the community for this purpose, that will be easily accessible to all participants, including economically disadvantaged elderly persons and adults with disabilities, and that will provide outpatient health, rehabilitative, and social services necessary to permit the participants to maintain personal independence and lead meaningful lives.

(d) Include the services of adult day health centers as a benefit under the Medi-Cal Act, that shall be an initial and integral part in the development of an overall plan for a coordinated, comprehensive continuum of optional long-term care services based upon appropriate need.
(e) Establish a rural alternative adult day health care program designed to meet the special needs and requirements of rural areas to enable the implementation of subdivisions (a) through (d), inclusive, for all Californians in need of those services.
(f) Ensure that all laws, regulations, and procedures governing adult day health care be enforced equitably regardless of organizational sponsorship and that all program flexibility provisions be administered equitably.
(Amended by Stats. 2008, Ch. 648, Sec. 1. Effective January 1, 2009.)
1570.7.
As used in this chapter and in any regulations promulgated thereunder:
(a) "Adult day health care" means an organized day program of therapeutic, social, and skilled nursing health activities and services provided pursuant to this chapter to elderly persons or adults with disabilities with functional impairments, either physical or mental, for the purpose of restoring or maintaining optimal capacity for self-care. Provided on a short-term basis, adult day health care serves as a transition from a health facility or home health program to personal independence. Provided on a long-term basis, it serves as an alternative to institutionalization in a long-term health care facility when 24-hour skilled nursing care is not medically necessary or viewed as desirable by the recipient or his or her family.
(b) "Adult day health center" or "adult day health care center" means a licensed facility that provides adult day health care.
(c) "Core staff" includes the positions of program director, registered nurse, social worker, activity director, and program aide.
(d) "Department" or "state department" means the State Department of Public Health.
(e) "Director" means the State Public Health Officer.
(f) "Elderly" or "older person" means a person 55 years of age or older, but also includes other adults who are chronically ill or impaired and who would benefit from adult day health care.
(g) "Extended hours" means those hours of operation prior to or following the adult day health care program hours of service, as designated by the adult day health care center in its plan of operation, during which the adult day health care center may operate an adult day program, or an Alzheimer's day care resource center, or both.
(h) "Hours of service" means the program hours defined and posted by the adult day health care center for the provision of adult day health care services, pursuant to Section 14550 of the Welfare and Institutions Code, which shall be no less than four hours, excluding transportation.
(i) "Individual plan of care" means a plan designed to provide recipients of adult day health care with appropriate treatment in accordance with the assessed needs of each individual.
(j) "License" means a basic permit to operate an adult day health care center. With respect to a health facility licensed pursuant to Chapter 2 (commencing with Section 1250), "license" means a special permit, as defined by Section 1251.5, empowering the health facility to provide adult day health care services.
(k) "Long-term absence" or "long-term vacancy" means an absence or vacancy lasting, or likely to last, more than one month. An adult day health care center's policies and procedures shall be specific regarding coverage in the situation for long-term absences or vacancies.
(l) "Maintenance program" means procedures and exercises that are provided to a participant, pursuant to Section 1580, in order to generally maintain existing function. These procedures and exercises are planned by a licensed or certified therapist and are provided by a person who has been trained by a licensed or certified therapist and who is directly supervised by a nurse or by a licensed or certified therapist.
(m) "Program director" shall be a person with both of the following:
(1) One of the following backgrounds:
(A) A person with a bachelor's degree and a minimum of two years of experience in a management, supervisory, or administrative position.
(B) A person with a master's degree and a minimum of one year of experience in a management, supervisory, or administrative position.
(C) A registered nurse with a minimum of two years experience in a management, supervisory, or administrative position.
(2) Appropriate skills, knowledge, and abilities related to the health, and mental, cognitive, and social needs of the participant group being served by the adult day health center.
(n) "Restorative therapy" means physical, occupational, and speech therapy, and psychiatric and psychological services that are planned and provided by a licensed or certified therapist. The therapy and services may also be provided by an assistant or aide under the appropriate supervision of a licensed therapist, as determined by the licensed therapist. The therapy and services are provided to restore function, when there is an expectation that the condition will improve significantly in a reasonable period of time, as determined by the multidisciplinary assessment team.
(o) "Short-term absence" or "short-term vacancy" means an absence or vacancy lasting one month or less, and includes sick leave and vacations. An adult day health care center shall ensure that appropriate staff is designated to serve in these positions during the short-term absence or vacancy and that the center's policies and procedures are specific regarding coverage of short-term absences or vacancies.
(p) "Social worker" shall be a person who meets one of the following:

(1) The person holds a master's degree in social work from an accredited school of social work.

(2) The person holds a master's degree in psychology, gerontology, or counseling from an accredited school and has one year of experience providing social services in one or more of the fields of aging, health, or long-term care services.

(3) The person is licensed by the California Board of Behavioral Sciences.

(4) The person holds a bachelor's degree in social work from an accredited school with two years of experience providing social services in one or more of the fields of aging, health, or long-term care services.

(Amended by Stats. 2011, Ch. 119, Sec. 1. (SB 91) Effective July 25, 2011.)

1570.9.

In the event of conflict between the provisions of this chapter and the provisions of Chapter 1 (commencing with Section 1200), Chapter 2 (commencing with Section 1250), or Chapter 3 (commencing with Section 1500) of this division, this chapter shall be deemed controlling. Except as provided in Section 1507, no facility which provides a specialized program of both medical and nonmedical care for the elderly or adults with disabilities on an outpatient basis shall be licensed as a health facility, clinic, or community care facility under this division, but shall be subject to licensure exclusively in accordance with the provisions of this chapter.

Review of the need and desirability of proposals for adult day health centers shall be governed by the provisions of this chapter and shall not be subject to review under Part 1.5 (commencing with Section 437) of Division 1.

(Amended by Stats. 2008, Ch. 648, Sec. 3. Effective January 1, 2009.)

1571.

Nothing in this chapter shall require any county to include adult day health care as a part of the services offered by the county hospital or to otherwise establish an adult day health center.

(Added by Stats. 1977, Ch. 1066.)

ARTICLE 2. Administration [1572 - 1574.7]

(Article 2 added by Stats. 1977, Ch. 1066.)

1572.

(a) The functions and duties of the State Department of Public Health provided for under this chapter shall be performed by the California Department of Aging commencing on the date those functions are transferred from the State Department of Public Health to the California Department of Aging. The authority, functions, and responsibility for the administration of the adult day health care program by the California Department of Aging and the State Department of Public Health shall be defined in an interagency agreement between the two departments and the State Department of Health Care Services that specifies how the departments will work together.

(b) The interagency agreement shall specify that the California Department of Aging is designated by the department as the agency responsible for community long-term care programs. At a minimum, the interagency agreement shall clarify each department's responsibilities on issues involving licensure and certification of adult day health care providers, payment of adult day health care claims, prior authorization of services, promulgation of regulations, and development of adult day health care Medi-Cal rates. This agreement shall also include provisions whereby the department and the California Department of Aging shall collaborate in the development and implementation of health programs and services for older persons and functionally impaired adults.

(c) The Director of the California Department of Aging shall make recommendations regarding licensure to the Licensing and Certification Division in the State Department of Public Health. The recommendation shall be based on all of the following criteria:

(1) An evaluation of the ability of the applicant to provide adult day health care in accordance with the requirements of this chapter and regulations adopted hereunder.

(2) Other criteria that the director deems necessary to protect public health and safety.

(Amended by Stats. 2008, Ch. 648, Sec. 4. Effective January 1, 2009.)

1574.

The state department may delegate to local health departments the authority to verify compliance with the licensing and approval provisions of this chapter, and regulations adopted pursuant to this chapter to provide consultation, and to recommend disciplinary action by the department against those licensed or approved under the provisions of this chapter. In exercising the authority so delegated, the local health department shall conform to the requirements of this chapter and to the rules and regulations of the state department. Payment to the local health departments for services performed pursuant to this section shall be in accordance with a budget submitted by the local health department and approved by the state department. Such expenditures shall not exceed amounts appropriated by the Legislature for the purpose of such inspection and enforcement.

(Added by Stats. 1980, Ch. 268.)

1574.5.

(a) All adult day health care centers shall maintain compliance with licensing requirements. These requirements shall not prohibit program flexibility for the use of alternate concepts, methods, procedures, techniques, equipment, number and qualifications of personnel, or the conducting of pilot projects, if these alternatives or pilot projects are carried out with provisions for safe and adequate care and with the prior written approval of the state department. This approval shall provide for the terms and conditions under which permission to use an alternative or pilot program is granted. Particular attention shall be given to encourage the development of models appropriate to rural areas. The department may allow the substitution of work experience for academic requirements for the position of program director, administrator, or activity coordinator.

(b) The applicant or licensee may submit a written request to the department for program flexibility, and shall submit with the request substantiating evidence supporting the request.

(c) Any approval by the department granted under this section, or a true copy thereof, shall be posted immediately adjacent to the center's license.

(Amended by Stats. 2011, Ch. 119, Sec. 2. (SB 91) Effective July 25, 2011.)

1574.7.

(a) The department and the licensing agencies with which it contracts for licensing shall review and make a final determination within 60 days of an applicant's submission of a complete application on all applications for a license to operate an adult day health center if the applicant possesses a current valid license to operate an adult day health center at another site. Applicants shall note on the application, or in a cover letter to the application, that they possess a current valid license at another site, and the number of that license.

(b) The department shall request a fire safety clearance from the appropriate fire marshal within five days of receipt of an application described in subdivision (a). The applicant shall be responsible for requesting and obtaining the required criminal record clearances.

(c) If the department for any reason is unable to comply with subdivision (a), it shall, within 60 days of receipt of the application described in subdivision (a), grant a provisional license to the applicant to operate for a period not to exceed six months, except as provided in subdivision (d). While the provisional license is in effect, the department shall continue its investigation and make a final determination on the application before the provisional license expires. The provisional license shall be granted, provided the department knows of no life safety risks, the criminal records clearances, if applicable, are complete, and the fire safety clearance is complete. The director may extend the term of a provisional license for an additional six months at the time of the application, if the director determines that more than six months will be required to achieve full compliance with licensing standards due to circumstances beyond the control of the applicant, and if all other requirements for a license have been met.

(d) If the department does not issue a provisional license pursuant to subdivision (c), the department shall issue a notice to the applicant identifying whether the provisional license has not been issued due to the existence of a life safety risk, lack of a fire safety clearance, lack of a criminal records clearance, failure to complete the application, or any combination of these reasons. If a life safety risk is identified, the risk preventing the issuance of the provisional license shall be clearly explained. If a lack of the fire safety clearance is identified, the notice shall include the dates on which the department requested the clearance and the current status of that request, and the fire marshal's name and telephone number to whom a fire safety clearance request was sent. The department shall identify the names of individuals for whom criminal records clearances are lacking. If failure to complete the application is identified, the notice shall list all of the forms or attachments that are missing or incorrect. This notice shall be sent to the applicant no later than 60 days after the applicant filed the application. If the reasons identified in the notice are corrected, the department shall issue the provisional license within five days after the corrections are made.

(e) The department shall, immediately after January 1, 1993, develop expedited procedures necessary to implement subdivisions (a), (b), (c), and (d).

(f) The department shall, immediately after January 1, 1993, develop an appeal procedure for applicants under this section for both denial of licenses and delay in processing applications.

(Added by Stats. 1992, Ch. 570, Sec. 3. Effective January 1, 1993.)

ARTICLE 3. Licensure [1575 - 1579]

(Article 3 added by Stats. 1977, Ch. 1066.)

1575.

No person or public agency within this state shall provide adult day health care in this state, without first obtaining a license therefor as provided in this chapter.

(Added by Stats. 1977, Ch. 1066.)

1575.1.

(a) (1) Each applicant for a license to operate an adult day health care center shall disclose to the department the name and business address of each general partner if the applicant is a partnership, or each director and officer if the applicant is a corporation, and each person having a beneficial ownership or control interest of 5 percent or more in the applicant corporation, company, or partnership.

(2) If any person described in paragraph (1) has served or currently serves as an administrator, general partner, trustee or trust applicant, sole proprietor of any applicant or licensee who is a sole proprietor, executor, or corporate officer or director of, or has held a beneficial ownership or control interest of 5 percent or more in, any health facility as defined in Section 1250, adult day health care center, residential care facility for the elderly, home health agency, clinic, or community care facility licensed pursuant to Chapter 3 (commencing with Section 1500), the applicant shall disclose the relationship to the department, including the name and current or last address of the health facility, adult day health care center, residential care facility for the elderly, home health agency, clinic, or community care facility and the date the relationship commenced and, if applicable, the date it was terminated.

(3) (A) If the center is operated by, or proposed to be operated in whole or in part under, a management contract, the names and addresses of any person or organization, or both, having an ownership or control interest of 5 percent or more in the management company shall be disclosed to the department.

(B) This paragraph shall not apply if the management company has submitted an application for licensure with the department and has complied with paragraph (1).

(4) If the applicant or licensee is a subsidiary of another organization, the information shall include the names and addresses of the parent organization of the subsidiary and the names and addresses of any officer or director of the parent organization.

(b) The information required by subdivision (a) shall be provided to the department upon initial application for licensure, and upon payment of the annual renewal licensure fee.

(c) Failure to comply with subdivision (a) or (b) may result in action to revoke or deny a license. The information required by subdivisions (a) and (b) shall be made available to the public upon request, and shall be included in the public file of the center.

(d) On or after January 1, 2002, no person may acquire a beneficial or control interest of 5 percent or more in any corporation, company, or partnership licensed to operate an adult day health care center or in any management company under contract with a licensee of an adult day health care center, nor may any person become an officer or director of, or a general partner in, a corporation, partnership, or management company of this type without the prior written approval of the department. Each application for departmental approval pursuant to this subdivision shall include the information specified in subdivision (a) with regard to the person for whom the application is made.

(e) The department may deny approval of a license application or of an application for approval under subdivision (d) or revoke a license if a person named in the application, as required by this section, was suspended as a Medi-Cal provider or excluded as a medicaid or Medicare provider, was an officer, director, general partner, or owner of a 5 percent or greater beneficial or control interest in a licensee of, or in a management company under contract with a licensee of, a health facility, community care facility, residential care facility for the elderly, home health agency, clinic, or adult day health care center at a time when one or more violations of law were committed therein that resulted in suspension or revocation of its license, or at a time when a court-ordered receiver was appointed pursuant to Section 1327, or at a time when a final medicaid decertification action was taken under federal law. However, the prior suspension, revocation, or court-ordered receivership of a license shall not be grounds for denial of the application if the applicant shows to the satisfaction of the department that both of the following conditions exist:

(1) The person in question took every reasonably available action to prevent the violation or violations that resulted in the disciplinary action.

(2) The person in question took every reasonably available action to correct the violation or violations once he or she knew, or with the exercise of reasonable diligence should have known, of the violation or violations.

(f) No application shall be denied pursuant to this section until the department provides the applicant with notice in writing of grounds for the proposed denial of application and affords the applicant an opportunity to submit additional documentary evidence in opposition to the proposed denial.

(g) This section shall not apply to a bank, trust company, financial institution, title insurer, controlled escrow company, or underwritten title company to which a license is issued in a fiduciary capacity.

(Added by Stats. 2001, Ch. 681, Sec. 5. Effective January 1, 2002.)

1575.2.

An applicant for initial licensure as an adult day health care center shall file with the department, pursuant to its regulations, an application on forms furnished by the department, that shall include, but not be limited to, the following:

(a) Evidence satisfactory to the department that the applicant, its directors, officers, and the person designated to manage the day-to-day affairs of the proposed adult day health care center are of reputable and responsible character.

(b) Evidence satisfactory to the department of the ability of the applicant to comply with the provisions of this chapter and of rules and regulations adopted pursuant thereto by the department.

(c) Evidence satisfactory to the department that the applicant for a license to operate an adult day health care center possesses financial resources sufficient to operate each licensed center for a period of not less than 30 calendar days and that these resources are identified for adult day health care center operations. The financial reserve requirements may be met, in whole or in part, by a line of credit or a loan.

(d) Any other information as may be required by the department for the proper administration and enforcement of this chapter.

(Amended by Stats. 2001, Ch. 681, Sec. 6. Effective January 1, 2002.)

1575.3.

(a) If an adult day health care center or an applicant for a license has not been previously licensed, the department may only issue a provisional license to the center as provided in this section.

(b) A provisional license to operate an adult day health care center shall expire one year from the date of issuance, or at an earlier time as determined by the department at the time of issuance.

(c) Within 30 days prior to the expiration of a provisional license, the department shall give the adult day health care center a full and complete inspection, and, if the adult day health care center meets all applicable requirements for licensure, a regular license shall be issued. If the adult day health care center does not meet the requirements for licensure but has made substantial progress towards meeting the requirements, as determined by the department, the initial provisional license shall be renewed for six months.

(d) If the department determines that there has not been substantial progress towards meeting licensure requirements at the time of the first full inspection provided by this section, or, if the department determines upon its inspection made within 30 days prior to

the termination of a renewed provisional license that there is lack of full compliance with the requirements, no further license shall be issued.

(e) If an applicant for a provisional license to operate an adult day health care center has been denied a license, the applicant may contest the denial by requesting an adjudicative hearing. The proceedings to review the denial shall be conducted pursuant to Section 100171.

(f) The department shall not apply less stringent criteria when issuing a provisional license pursuant to this section than it applies when issuing a regular license.

(Amended by Stats. 2000, Ch. 869, Sec. 2. Effective January 1, 2001.)

1575.4.

(a) The department may issue a provisional license to an adult day health care center if all of the following conditions are met:

(1) The adult day health care center and the applicant for licensure substantially meet the standards specified by this chapter and regulations adopted pursuant to this chapter.

(2) No violation of this chapter or regulations adopted under this chapter exists in the adult day health care center that jeopardizes the health or safety of patients.

(3) The applicant has adopted a plan for correction of any existing violations that is satisfactory to the department.

(b) A provisional license issued under this section shall expire not later than one year after the date of issuance, or at an earlier time as determined by the department at the time of issuance, and may not be renewed.

(c) At the expiration of the provisional license period, the department shall assess the adult day health care center's full compliance with licensure requirements. If the adult day health care center meets all applicable requirements for licensure, the department shall issue a regular license.

(d) The department shall not apply less stringent criteria when issuing a provisional license pursuant to this section than it applies when issuing a regular license.

(Amended by Stats. 2000, Ch. 869, Sec. 3. Effective January 1, 2001.)

1575.45.

(a) If the department determines that the adult day health care center operating under a provisional license has serious deficiencies that pose a risk to the health and safety of the participants, the department may immediately take any of the following actions, including, but not limited to:

(1) Require a plan of correction.

(2) Limit participant enrollment.

(3) Prohibit new participant enrollment.

(b) When appropriate, the California Department of Aging and the department shall coordinate an action or actions to ensure consistency and uniformity.

(c) The licensee shall have the right to dispute an action or actions taken pursuant to paragraphs (2) and (3) of subdivision (a). The department shall accept, consider, and resolve disputes filed pursuant to this subdivision by a licensee in a timely manner.

(d) The director shall ensure that public records accurately reflect the current status of any action or actions taken pursuant to this section, including any resolution of disputes.

(Added by Stats. 2000, Ch. 869, Sec. 4. Effective January 1, 2001.)

1575.6.

(a) As a prudent business practice, a licensee shall maintain sufficient financial resources for adult day health care operations to enable each licensed facility to operate for 30 calendar days.

(b) The financial resource requirement contained in subdivision (a) may be met, in whole or in part, by a line of credit, grant, or loan.

(c) Whenever a licensee fails to meet the financial resource requirement contained in subdivision (a) for a period of 10 working days, the licensee shall notify the department of that fact within 48 hours.

(Added by Stats. 2001, Ch. 681, Sec. 6.5. Effective January 1, 2002.)

1575.7.

(a) (1) The State Department of Public Health, prior to issuing a new license, shall obtain a criminal record clearance for the administrator, program director, and fiscal officer of the proposed adult day health care center. The department shall obtain the criminal record clearances each time these positions are to be filled. When the conditions set forth in paragraph (3) of subdivision (a) of Section 1265.5, subparagraph (A) of paragraph (1) of subdivision (a) of Section 1338.5, and paragraph (1) of subdivision (a) of Section 1736.6 are met, the licensing and certification program shall issue an All Facilities Letter (AFL) informing facility licensees. After the AFL is issued, facilities shall not allow newly hired administrators, program directors, and fiscal officers to have direct contact with clients or residents of the facility prior to completion of the criminal record clearance. A criminal record clearance shall be complete when the department has obtained the person's criminal offender record information search response from the Department of Justice and has determined that the person is not disqualified from engaging in the activity for which clearance is required.

(2) The criminal record clearance shall require the administrator, program director, and fiscal officer to submit electronic fingerprint images to the Department of Justice.

(3) An applicant and any other person specified in this subdivision, as part of the background clearance process, shall provide information as to whether or not the person has any prior criminal convictions, has had any arrests within the past 12-month period, or has any active arrests, and shall certify that, to the best of his or her knowledge, the information provided is true. This requirement is not intended to duplicate existing requirements for individuals who are required to submit fingerprint images as part of a criminal background clearance process. Every applicant shall provide information on any prior administrative action taken against him or her by any federal, state, or local government agency and shall certify that, to the best of his or her knowledge, the

information provided is true. An applicant or other person required to provide information pursuant to this section that knowingly or willfully makes false statements, representations, or omissions may be subject to administrative action, including, but not limited to, denial of his or her application or exemption or revocation of any exemption previously granted.

(b) A past conviction of any crime, especially any crime involving misuse of funds or involving physical abuse shall, in the discretion of the department, be grounds for denial of the license, and shall be grounds to prohibit the person from providing services in an adult day health care center.

(c) Suspension of the applicant from the Medi-Cal program or prior violations of statutory provisions or regulations relating to licensure of a health facility, community care facility, or clinic shall also be grounds for a denial of licensure, where determined by the state department to indicate a substantial probability that the applicant will not comply with this chapter and regulations adopted hereunder.

(d) No applicant which is licensed as a health facility, community care facility, or clinic may be issued a license for an adult day health care center while there exists a subsisting, uncorrected violation of the statutes or regulations relating to such licensure.

(e) The department shall develop procedures to ensure that any licensee, direct care staff, or certificate holder for whom a criminal record has been obtained pursuant to this section or Section 1265.5 or 1736 shall not be required to obtain multiple criminal record clearances.

(f) Notwithstanding any other provision of law, the department may provide an individual with a copy of his or her state or federal level criminal offender record information search response as provided to that department by the Department of Justice if the department has denied a criminal background clearance based on this information and the individual makes a written request to the department for a copy specifying an address to which it is to be sent. The state or federal level criminal offender record information search response shall not be modified or altered from its form or content as provided by the Department of Justice and shall be provided to the address specified by the individual in his or her written request. The department shall retain a copy of the individual's written request and the response and date provided.

(Amended by Stats. 2007, Ch. 483, Sec. 17. Effective January 1, 2008.)
1575.9.

Each application for a new license or renewal submitted to the state department shall be accompanied by an annual Licensing and Certification Program fee set in accordance with Section 1266.

(Amended by Stats. 2006, Ch. 74, Sec. 17. Effective July 12, 2006.)

1576.

The director shall approve an application for a new license if no substantial basis for denial of the license exists under Section 1575.7, and the applicant has met all the requirements for licensure set forth in this chapter and regulations adopted hereunder. Otherwise the director shall deny issuance of the license.

(Amended by Stats. 2003, 1st Ex. Sess., Ch. 7, Sec. 10. Effective May 5, 2003.)
1576.2.

Each license issued or renewed pursuant to this chapter shall not be transferable and the initial license shall expire 12 months from the date of its issuance. The director shall be given the discretion to approve applications for relicensure for a period of up to 24 months. Application for annual renewal of a license, accompanied by the required fee, shall be filed with the department not less than 30 days prior to the expiration date. Failure to submit a renewal application prior to that date shall result in expiration of license.

(Amended by Stats. 2011, Ch. 119, Sec. 4. (SB 91) Effective July 25, 2011.)
1576.5.

Immediately upon the denial of any application for issuance or renewal of a license, the state department shall notify the applicant in writing. Not later than 10 days after the state department mails the notice, the applicant may submit a written petition for a hearing to the state department. Upon receipt by the state department of the petition in proper form, such petition shall be set for hearing. The hearing shall be held within 60 calendar days of receipt of the petition. The proceedings shall be conducted in accordance with Chapter 5 (commencing with Section 11500) of Part 1 of Division 3 of Title 2 of the Government Code, and the state department has all the powers granted therein.

(Added by Stats. 1977, Ch. 1066.)

1578.

A provider may share space with another licensed health facility, community care facility, senior center, or other appropriate structure, upon the approval of the department, based upon a determination of all of the following:

(a) The use of the shared space does not jeopardize the welfare of the participant or other clients.

(b) The shared use does not exceed occupancy capacity established for fire safety.

(c) The space used by the adult day health care center is not essential to meet the other program's licensing requirements.

(d) Each entity schedules services and activities at separate times. This subdivision shall not apply to space used for meals or for space used by another licensed adult day services program.

For purposes of this section, "shared space" means the mutual use of exits and entrances, offices, hallways, bathrooms, treatment rooms, and dining rooms by an adult day health care center and another program.

(Added by Stats. 2001, Ch. 681, Sec. 8. Effective January 1, 2002.)
1578.1.

(a) Notwithstanding subdivisions (b) and (c) of Section 1570.7 or any other provision of law, if an adult day health care center licensee also provides adult day program services, the adult day health care license shall be the only license required to provide these additional services. Costs shall be allocated among the programs in accordance with generally accepted accounting practices.

(b) A provider choosing to add an adult day program within the adult day health care facility shall submit a notice to the department on such forms as may be required.

(c) Review and approval of the application to provide a dual program shall not require an on-site inspection.

(d) The maximum licensed capacity shall be determined by the local fire authority and shall include limits for ambulatory and nonambulatory participants.

(Amended by Stats. 2011, Ch. 119, Sec. 5. (SB 91) Effective July 25, 2011.)
1579.

(a) A rural alternative adult day health care center shall operate its programs a minimum of three days weekly, unless the program can justify, to the satisfaction of the department, fewer days of operation due to space, staff, financial, or participant reasons.

(b) Any program desiring to become a parent center and develop a satellite program may be located in an area that does not meet the population requirements of the rural service areas and need not be in the same county as a satellite. The satellite shall be located in an area that meets the population requirements of a rural service area, and shall be located within a reasonable distance of the parent center to allow sharing of administration, services, and supervision. Parent and satellite centers shall be located in the same licensing district office.

(c) Notwithstanding any other provision of law, the administrator or program director of a parent center may, with the approval of the department, serve as the administrator or program director for up to three additional satellite sites.

(d) For the purposes of this section, the following definitions apply:

(1) "Parent" means a licensed and certified adult day health care center that establishes one or more satellites. A satellite may be in the county of the parent or a rural service area. The parent center shall provide administration, supervision, and, with the approval of the department, may share services and staff with one or more satellite centers. The parent center's license and certification shall cover adult day health care services at one or more satellites.

(2) "Rural alternative adult day health care center" means an adult day health care center located in a rural service area.

(3) "Rural service area" means an identified service area within one hour driving time from the center and with two or more of the following characteristics:

(A) Is more than one-half hour direct driving time from an urban area of 50,000 population or more.

(B) Has no other adult day health care center within one-half hour direct driving time.

(C) Has geographic or climatic barriers, including, but not limited to, snow, fog, ice, mountains, inadequate highways, or weather, that make transportation to another adult day health care center impractical.

(D) Is located in a county with an overall population density of less than 100 persons per square mile.

(E) Can demonstrate in the application for licensure that a shortage of qualified professionals exists in the county or identified service area.

(4) "Satellite" means an adult day health care center established in a rural service area by an existing licensed and certified adult day health care center for the purposes of extending rural adult day health care services to another location. A satellite shall be located close enough to the adult day health center so that administration, supervision, and services may be shared in a manner that does not compromise care and makes it unnecessary for the satellite to be separately licensed. Each satellite shall meet fire and life safety regulations and laws. Prior approval from the department is required before operating or opening a satellite.

(Amended by Stats. 2004, Ch. 632, Sec. 3. Effective January 1, 2005.)

ARTICLE 4. Standards and Inspection [1580 - 1584.5]
(Article 4 added by Stats. 1977, Ch. 1066.)

1580.

The state department shall adopt and may from time to time amend or repeal, in accordance with Chapter 3.5 (commencing with Section 11340) of Part 1 of Division 3 of Title 2 of the Government Code, the reasonable rules and regulations as may be necessary or proper to carry out the purposes and intent of this chapter and to enable the state department to exercise the powers and perform the duties conferred upon it by this chapter, not inconsistent with any statute of this state. The regulations shall prescribe standards of safety and sanitation for the physical plant of adult day health centers and standards for the quality of adult day health care services, including, but not limited to, staffing with duly qualified personnel and average daily staffing requirements. For the purposes of computing average daily attendance staffing requirements, maintenance programs for elderly persons shall, as of January 1, 1992, be included in the calculation for monthly total hours of services provided. In adopting the regulations, the state department shall take into account the physical and mental capabilities and needs of the persons to be served, and consideration shall be given to flexible application of safety and sanitation standards, if necessary, to be consistent with the legislative intent of establishing adult day health care programs in locations easily accessible to economically disadvantaged older persons. Program standards contained in regulations adopted pursuant to this section shall be those specified in Chapter 8.7 (commencing with Section 14520) of Part 3 of Division 9 of the Welfare and Institutions Code.

(Amended by Stats. 1991, Ch. 985, Sec. 3.)
1580.1.

The State Department of Health Care Services, and as applicable, the State Department of Public Health and the California Department of Aging, may grant to entities contracting with the State Department of Health Care Services under the PACE program, as defined in Chapter 8.75 (commencing with Section 14591) of Part 3 of Division 9 of the Welfare and Institutions Code, exemptions from the provisions contained in this chapter in accordance with the requirements of Section 100315.

(Amended by Stats. 2011, Ch. 367, Sec. 4. (AB 574) Effective January 1, 2012.)

1580.2.

On or before December 1, 1978, the director shall by regulation adopt an equitable and uniform method of evaluating the quality of care and services provided by adult day health centers based upon the following:

(a) Compliance with regulations adopted pursuant to this chapter.

(b) Continued demonstrated community need.

(c) Conformity of the program to individual participants' assessed and reassessed needs and interests with particular attention to visual, auditory, and equipment needs.

(d) Suitability of program changes to the community and participants served.

(e) Compliance with requirements of law pertaining to fire and life and safety.

The evaluation method adopted by the state department shall be published and distributed to all licensed adult day health centers and all other interested persons.

(Added by Stats. 1977, Ch. 1066.)

1580.5.

(a) Every adult day health care center shall be periodically inspected and evaluated for quality of care by a representative or representatives designated by the director. Inspections shall be conducted prior to the expiration of certification or at least every two years and as often as necessary to ensure the quality of care being provided, whether initiated by the state department or pursuant to Section 1580.9. As resources permit, an inspection may be conducted prior to, as well as within the first 90 days of, adult day health care center operation.

(b) After each inspection, the state department shall notify the adult day health care center in writing of any deficiencies in its compliance with this chapter and the rules and regulations adopted pursuant to this chapter, and shall set a reasonable length of time for compliance by the facility. Upon a finding of noncompliance, the state department may also assess a civil penalty not to exceed fifty dollars ($50) per day for each violation continuing beyond the date fixed in the notice for correction. If the violation is not corrected within that time, the civil penalty shall accrue from the date of receipt of the notice by the licensee. If the violation continues beyond the date fixed for correction, the state department may also initiate action against the licensee in accordance with Article 7 (commencing with Section 1595).

(c) When a civil penalty is to be assessed pursuant to this section, the notice shall specify the amount thereof and shall be served upon the licensee in a manner prescribed by subdivision (c) of Section 11505 of the Government Code. Any judicial action required to collect a civil penalty assessed pursuant to this section shall be brought by the Attorney General acting on behalf of the state department in the superior court of the county in which the adult day health care center is located.

(Amended by Stats. 2000, Ch. 869, Sec. 6. Effective January 1, 2001.)

1580.9.

Any person may request an inspection of any adult day health center in accordance with the provisions of this article by transmitting to the state department notice of an alleged violation of applicable requirements prescribed by statute or regulation. Any such notice shall be in writing, specifying to a reasonable extent the details of the alleged violation, and shall be signed by the complainant. The substance of the complaint shall be provided to the licensee no earlier than at the time of the inspection.

Unless the complainant specifically requests otherwise, neither the substance of the complaint provided the licensee nor any copy of the complaint or any record published, released, or otherwise made available to the licensee or the public shall disclose the name of any person mentioned in the complaint, unless the complainant is a duly authorized officer, employee, or agent of the state department conducting the investigation or inspection pursuant to this article.

(Added by Stats. 1977, Ch. 1066.)

1581.

Upon receipt of a complaint pursuant to Section 1580.9, the state department shall make a preliminary review. Unless the state department determines that the complaint is willfully intended to harass a licensee or is without any reasonable basis, it shall make an onsite inspection within 10 days after receiving the complaint. In either event, the complainant shall be promptly informed of the state department's proposed course of action.

No licensee shall discriminate or retaliate in any manner against any person receiving the services of such licensee's adult day health center, or against any employee of such licensee's facility, on the basis or for the reason that such person or employee or any other person has initiated or participated in an inspection pursuant to Section 1580.9 or 1581.

(Added by Stats. 1977, Ch. 1066.)

1581.5.

Any duly authorized officer, employee, or agent of the department or the California Department of Aging may, upon presentation of proper identification, enter and inspect any place providing adult day health care at any time, with or without advance notice, to secure compliance with, or to prevent a violation of, any provision of this chapter or any regulation adopted hereunder.

(Amended by Stats. 2001, Ch. 681, Sec. 11. Effective January 1, 2002.)

1582.

The state department may provide consulting services upon request to any adult day health center to assist in the identification or correction of deficiencies and in the upgrading of the quality of care provided by such adult day health center.

(Added by Stats. 1977, Ch. 1066.)

1582.5.

Reports on the results of each inspection, evaluation, or consultation performed pursuant to this article shall be kept on file in the state department, and all inspection reports, consultation reports, lists of deficiencies, and plans of correction shall be open to public inspection.

(Added by Stats. 1977, Ch. 1066.)

1583.

The director shall publish and make available to interested persons a list of all licensed adult day health centers, the services which each such facility provides, and the relative evaluation rating of each adult day health center as determined pursuant to Section 1580.2.

(Added by Stats. 1977, Ch. 1066.)

1584.

(a) An adult day health care center that provides care for adults with Alzheimer's disease and other dementias may install for the safety and security of those persons secured perimeter fences or egress control devices of the time-delay type on exit doors.

(b) As used in this section, "egress control device" means a device that precludes the use of exits for a predetermined period of time. These devices shall not delay any participant's departure from the center for longer than 30 seconds. Center staff may attempt to redirect a participant who attempts to leave the center.

(c) Adult day health care centers installing security devices pursuant to this section shall meet all of the following requirements:

(1) The center shall be subject to all fire and building codes, regulations, and standards applicable to adult day health care centers using egress control devices or secured perimeter fences and shall receive a fire clearance from the fire authority having jurisdiction for the egress control devices or secured perimeter fences.

(2) The center shall maintain documentation of diagnosis by a physician of a participant's Alzheimer's disease or other dementia.

(3) The center shall provide staff training regarding the use and operation of the egress control devices utilized by the center, the protection of participants' personal rights, wandering behavior and acceptable methods of redirection, and emergency evacuation procedures for persons with dementia.

(4) All admissions to the center shall continue to be voluntary on the part of the participant or with consent of the participant's conservator, an agent of the participant under a power of attorney for health care, or other person who has the authority to act on behalf of the participant. Persons who have the authority to act on behalf of the participant include the participant's spouse or closest available relative.

(5) The center shall inform all participants, conservators, agents, and persons who have the authority to act on behalf of participants of the use of security devices. The center shall maintain a signed participation agreement indicating the use of the devices and the consent of the participant, conservator, agent, or person who has the authority to act on behalf of the participant. The center shall retain the original statement in the participant's files at the center.

(6) The use of egress control devices or secured perimeter fences shall not substitute for adequate staff. Staffing ratios shall at all times meet the requirements of applicable regulations.

(7) Emergency fire and earthquake drills shall be conducted at least once every three months, or more frequently as required by a county or city fire department or local fire prevention district. The drills shall include all center staff and volunteers providing participant care and supervision. This requirement does not preclude drills with participants as required by regulations.

(8) The center shall develop a plan of operation approved by the department that includes a description of how the center is to be equipped with egress control devices or secured perimeter fences that are consistent with regulations adopted by the State Fire Marshal pursuant to Section 13143. The plan shall include, but not be limited to, the following:

(A) A description of how the center will provide training for staff regarding the use and operation of the egress control device utilized by the center.

(B) A description of how the center will ensure the protection of the participant's personal rights consistent with applicable regulations.

(C) A description of the center's emergency evacuation procedures for persons with Alzheimer's disease and other dementias.

(d) This section does not require an adult day health care center to use security devices in providing care for persons with Alzheimer's disease and other dementias.

(Amended by Stats. 1999, Ch. 658, Sec. 3. Effective January 1, 2000. Operative July 1, 2000, by Sec. 43 of Ch. 658.)

1584.5.

Every adult day health care center shall, for the purpose of addressing issues that arise when an adult day health care participant is missing from the facility, develop and comply with an absentee notification plan, as part of the individual plan of care, as defined in Section 1570.7. The plan shall include and be limited to the following: a requirement that an administrator of the facility, or his or her designee, inform the participant's authorized representative when that participant is missing from the facility and the circumstances in which an administrator of the facility, or his or her designee, shall notify local law enforcement when a participant is missing from the facility.

(Added by Stats. 2013, Ch. 674, Sec. 4. (AB 620) Effective January 1, 2014.)

(Article 5 added by Stats. 1977, Ch. 1066.)

1585.

No member of the governing board of an adult day health center, nor any member of the immediate family of that board member, may have any direct or indirect interest in any contract for supplying services to the adult day health center.

(Amended by Stats. 2003, 1st Ex. Sess., Ch. 7, Sec. 11. Effective May 5, 2003.)

1585.2.

(a) Any operator of a health facility licensed to provide adult day health care under this chapter shall provide that adult day health care as a separate program as determined by the State Department of Health Services.

(b) Any operator of a clinic or community care facility licensed to provide adult day health care under this chapter shall provide that adult day health care as an independent program that is located in a separate, freestanding facility or in a distinct part of the clinic or community care facility.

(Amended by Stats. 1998, Ch. 728, Sec. 3. Effective January 1, 1999.)

1585.5.

Adult day health care centers shall provide services to each participant pursuant to an individual plan of care designed to maintain or restore each participant's optimal capacity for self-care.

(Amended by Stats. 1998, Ch. 151, Sec. 6. Effective January 1, 1999.)

1586.

No adult day health center shall refuse to provide adult day care health services to any person on the basis that service to such person will be reimbursed under the Medi-Cal Act (Chapter 7 (commencing with Section 14000) of Part 3 of Division 9 of the Welfare and Institutions Code).

(Added by Stats. 1977, Ch. 1066.)

1586.6.

Adult day health care centers may not require family members to attend the center or assist the participant with activities of daily living while at the center.

(Added by Stats. 2003, Ch. 105, Sec. 1. Effective January 1, 2004.)

1586.7.

(a) Adult day health care centers may not discriminate because of race, color, creed, national origin, sex, sexual orientation, or physical or mental disabilities. Centers shall accommodate individuals with physical disabilities by ensuring that they have access to bathrooms, hallways, and door entrances, and by providing safe and adequate parking and passenger loading areas. All staff at centers shall be trained and able to interact with participants with physical disabilities.

(b) Notwithstanding subdivision (a), the program may not admit any participants to the program that, in the clinical judgment of those administering the program, cannot be appropriately cared for by the program.

(Added by Stats. 2003, Ch. 105, Sec. 2. Effective January 1, 2004.)

(Article 5.5 added by Stats. 1983, Ch. 1208, Sec. 2.)

1588.

(a) The state department shall, subject to the availability of funds appropriated therefor, conduct a grants-in-aid program for the following purposes:

(1) To assist in the establishment of new adult day health care centers.

(2) To assist in stabilizing or expanding the health care operations of adult day health care centers which have been licensed for a period of two years or less.

(3) To assist in expanding the health care operations of adult day health care centers which have been licensed for a period of two years or more when identified expansion meets criteria outlined in the specific guidelines established for the grant-supported activities. Expansion under this paragraph shall be based on documented unmet need.

(b) The grants authorized pursuant to this article shall be limited in purpose to defraying operating expenses of the center, including staffing costs, required renovation costs, and facility rental costs.

(Amended by Stats. 2000, Ch. 108, Sec. 6. Effective July 10, 2000.)

1588.2.

Eligibility for grants pursuant to this article shall be limited to any public or private nonprofit agency. As a condition of making a grant, the director shall require the applicant to match not less than 20 percent of the amount granted. The required match may be cash or in-kind contributions, or a combination of both. In-kind contributions may include, but shall not be limited to, staff and volunteer services.

(Amended by Stats. 1998, Ch. 151, Sec. 7. Effective January 1, 1999.)

1588.3.

The grant amount available from funds appropriated through the Budget Act for the Adult Day Health Care Program shall not exceed one hundred twenty-five thousand dollars ($125,000) for a single project.

(Amended by Stats. 2000, Ch. 108, Sec. 7. Effective July 10, 2000.)

1588.5.

In developing policies and priorities pertaining to the allocation of grant funds, the department shall give primary consideration to the following factors:

(a) The applicant's immediate need for funds.

(b) The demonstrated community support for the project.

(c) The applicant's long-term prospects for financial stability.

(d) The applicant's demonstrated marketing strategies.

(e) The applicant's ability to provide innovative services and to coordinate with other services in the continuum of care.

(f) Special consideration shall be given to an applicant who is in one or more of the following categories:

(1) Applicants in rural areas.

(2) Applicants in counties where there are no other centers or in areas where there are no other centers within one hour driving time from the proposed site.

(3) Applicants who will deliver services in an area with a high elderly ethnic minority population when compared to the total elderly population of the area.

(4) Applicants who will deliver services in an area with a high percentage of elderly Medi-Cal beneficiaries when compared to the total elderly population of the area.

(Amended by Stats. 2004, Ch. 632, Sec. 4. Effective January 1, 2005.)

1588.7.

(a) The department, unless otherwise specified in the interagency agreement entered into pursuant to Section 1572 or pursuant to annual Budget Act requirements, shall adopt specific guidelines for the establishment of grant-supported activities, including criteria for evaluation of each activity and monitoring to assure compliance with grant conditions and applicable regulations of the department. Funds shall be awarded only after the applicant's proposal is approved by the department or the California Department of Aging pursuant to the guidelines established for these grants.

(b) The department, unless otherwise specified by annual Budget Act requirements, shall develop a contract with each selected project.

(Amended by Stats. 2004, Ch. 632, Sec. 5. Effective January 1, 2005.)

1589.

Subject to the appropriation of funds pursuant to the annual Budget Act, the department may establish planning and development grants for public or private nonprofit applicants that request assistance in conducting feasibility and needs analysis for new adult day health care centers.

(Amended by Stats. 2004, Ch. 632, Sec. 6. Effective January 1, 2005.)

1589.5.

State administrative costs on grants issued pursuant to this article shall not exceed 10 percent of the amount of the grants.

(Added by renumbering Section 1589 by Stats. 2000, Ch. 108, Sec. 10. Effective July 10, 2000.)

(Article 6 added by Stats. 1977, Ch. 1066.)

1590.

The state department may suspend or revoke any license issued under the provisions of this chapter upon any of the following grounds and in the manner provided in this article:

(a) Violation by the licensee of any of the provisions of this chapter or of the rules and regulations adopted pursuant to this chapter.

(b) Aiding, abetting, or permitting the violation of any provision of this chapter or of the rules and regulations adopted pursuant to this chapter.

(c) Conduct in the operation or maintenance, or both the operation and maintenance, of an adult day health facility which is inimical to the health, morals, welfare, or safety of either an individual receiving services from the facility or the people of the State of California.

(Added by Stats. 1977, Ch. 1066.)

1590.5.

Proceedings for the suspension, revocation, or denial of a license under this article shall be conducted in accordance with Section 100171. Except as provided in Section 1591, Section 100171 shall prevail in the event of a conflict between this chapter and Section 100171. The director shall ensure that public records accurately reflect the current status of any potential adverse action or actions, including the resolution of disputes.

(Amended by Stats. 2000, Ch. 869, Sec. 8. Effective January 1, 2001.)

1591.

(a) When the director intends to seek the suspension or revocation of a license, the director shall notify the licensee of the proposed suspension or revocation and, at the same time, shall serve the person with an accusation. Upon receipt of a notice of defense from the licensee, the director shall set the matter for hearing within five days. The director shall make a final determination as to whether to suspend or revoke the license within 30 days after the original hearing has been completed.

(b) The director may temporarily suspend a license prior to a hearing when he or she determines that the suspension is necessary to protect the health and safety of the participants. In the event of a prehearing suspension, the director shall notify the licensee of the suspension and its effective date and, at the same time, shall serve the licensee with an accusation. Within 15 days of receiving a notice of defense from the licensee, the director shall set the matter for a hearing that shall be held as soon as possible, but not later than 30 days after receipt of the notice. The temporary suspension shall remain in effect until the hearing is completed and the director has made a final determination on the merits, which shall be made within 30 days after the hearing has been completed.

(Amended by Stats. 2004, Ch. 632, Sec. 7. Effective January 1, 2005.)

1591.5.

The withdrawal of an application for a license after it has been filed with the state department shall not, unless the state department consents in writing to such withdrawal, deprive the state department of its authority to institute or continue a proceeding against the applicant for the denial of the license upon any ground provided by law or to enter an order denying the license upon any such ground.

The suspension, expiration, or forfeiture by operation of law of a license issued by the state department, or its suspension, forfeiture, or cancellation by order of the state department or by order of a court of law, or its surrender without the written consent of the state department, shall not deprive the state department of its authority to institute or

continue a disciplinary proceeding against the licensee upon any ground provided by law or to enter an order suspending or revoking the license or otherwise taking disciplinary action against the licensee on any such ground.
(Added by Stats. 1977, Ch. 1066.)

ARTICLE 7. Offenses [1595 - 1596.5]
(Article 7 added by Stats. 1977, Ch. 1066.)

1595.

Any license revoked pursuant to this article may be reinstated pursuant to the provisions of Section 11522 of the Government Code.
(Added by Stats. 1977, Ch. 1066.)

1595.2.

Any person who negligently, repeatedly, or willfully violates any of the provisions of this chapter, or regulations adopted pursuant to this chapter, is guilty of a misdemeanor and upon conviction thereof shall be punished by a fine not to exceed one thousand dollars ($1,000) or by imprisonment in the county jail for a period not to exceed six months, or by both such fine and imprisonment.
(Amended by Stats. 1983, Ch. 1092, Sec. 147. Effective September 27, 1983. Operative January 1, 1984, by Sec. 427 of Ch. 1092.)

1595.5.

The director may bring an action to enjoin the violation or threatened violation of Section 1575 in the superior court in and for the county in which the violation occurred or is about to occur. Any proceeding under the provisions of this section shall conform to the requirements of Chapter 3 (commencing with Section 525) of Title 7, of Part 2 of the Code of Civil Procedure, except that the director shall not be required to allege facts necessary to show or tending to show lack of adequate remedy at law or irreparable damage or loss.
(Added by Stats. 1977, Ch. 1066.)

1596.

Any action brought by the director against an adult day health center shall not abate by reason of a sale or other transfer of ownership of the adult day health center which is a party to the action.
(Added by Stats. 1977, Ch. 1066.)

1596.5.

The district attorney of every county shall, upon application by the state department or its authorized representative institute and conduct the prosecution of any action for violation within his county of any provisions of this chapter or of regulations adopted pursuant to this chapter.
(Added by Stats. 1977, Ch. 1066.)

CHAPTER 3.35. Child Care Provider Registration [1596.60 - 1596.68]

(Chapter 3.35 added by Stats. 1997, Ch. 843, Sec. 4.)

1596.60.

(a) For the purposes of this chapter, the following definitions shall apply:
(1) "Department" means the State Department of Social Services.
(2) "Director" means the Director of Social Services.
(3) "Trustline provider," "license exempt child care provider," or "provider" means a person 18 years of age or older who provides child care, supervision, or any person providing in-home educational or counseling services to a minor, and who is not required to be licensed pursuant to Section 1596.792. "Provider" also means a person who provides care or childcare supervision in an ancillary day care center other than the parent or guardian of the child receiving the care.
(4) "Ancillary day care center" means a day care center, as defined in Section 1596.76, that is associated with an athletic club, grocery store, or other business or group of businesses that is not required to be licensed pursuant to subdivision (k) of Section 1596.792 that provides a day care center that is ancillary to its principal business activity and that provides day care services, with or without a fee, for the children of the clients or customers of that business or group of businesses while the clients or customers are engaged in shopping for, or purchasing, goods or services from that business or group of businesses.
(b) This section shall become operative on January 1, 2011.
(Repealed (in Sec. 1) and added by Stats. 2009, Ch. 199, Sec. 2. (SB 702) Effective January 1, 2010. Section operative January 1, 2011, by its own provisions.)

1596.601.

Any child care provider who possesses any one of the following identification cards may initiate a background examination to be a trustline provider:
(a) A valid California driver's license.
(b) A valid identification card issued by the Department of Motor Vehicles.
(c) A valid Alien Registration Card.
(d) In the case of a person living in a state other than California, a valid numbered photo identification card issued by an agency of the state other than California.
(Added by Stats. 1997, Ch. 843, Sec. 4. Effective January 1, 1998. Section operative July 1, 1998, pursuant to Section 1596.68.)

1596.603.

(a) Each person initiating a background examination to be a trustline provider shall either obtain two sets of fingerprints from a law enforcement agency or other local agency on a fingerprint card authorized by the Department of Justice and shall submit the fingerprints, or send his or her fingerprints to the Department of Justice by electronic transmission in a manner approved by the department, unless exempted in subdivision

(e), and a completed trustline application to the department, or the local child care resource and referral agency which will immediately forward the application package to the department. The agency taking the fingerprints shall inscribe the serial number from the identification card described in Section 1596.601 on the fingerprint cards.
(b) A law enforcement agency or other local agency authorized to take fingerprints may charge a reasonable fee to offset the costs of fingerprinting for the purposes of this chapter.
(c) Upon receipt, the department shall transmit the fingerprint card and a copy of the application to the Department of Justice. The Department of Justice shall use the fingerprints and the application to search the state and Federal Bureau of Investigation criminal history information pursuant to Section 1596.871 and the automated child abuse system pursuant to subdivision (b) of Section 1596.877.
(d) A person who is a current licensee or employee in a facility licensed by the department need not submit fingerprints to the department and may transfer their criminal record clearance pursuant to subdivision (h) of Section 1596.871. The person shall instead submit to the department, along with the person's application, a copy of the person's identification card described in Section 1596.601 and sign a declaration verifying the person's identity. A willful false declaration is a violation of this subdivision punishable in the same manner as provided under Section 1596.890.
(Amended by Stats. 1998, Ch. 311, Sec. 43. Effective August 19, 1998.)

1596.605.

(a) (1) The department shall establish a trustline registry pursuant to this chapter and shall continuously update the registry information. Upon submission of the trustline application and fingerprints or other identification documents pursuant to either subdivision (a) or (e) of Section 1596.603, the department shall enter into the trustline registry the provider's name, identification card number, and an indicator that the provider has submitted an application and fingerprints or identification documentation. This provider shall be known as a "trustline applicant."
(2) A person shall not be entitled to apply to be a trustline provider and shall have his or her application returned without the right to appeal if the provider would not be eligible to obtain a child care license pursuant to Section 1596.851.
(b) (1) Before approving the person's application, the department shall check the individual criminal history pursuant to Section 1596.871 and against the child abuse index pursuant to subdivision (b) of Section 1596.877. Upon completion of the searches of the state summary criminal history information and the child abuse index, and, if applicable, the records of the Federal Bureau of Investigation, the department shall grant the trustline application if grounds do not exist for denial pursuant to Section 1596.607 and the department shall enter that finding in the provider's record in the trustline registry and shall notify the provider of the action. This provider shall be known as a "registered trustline child care provider."
(2) The department may transfer the criminal record clearance granted to a registered trustline child care provider and hold the registered trustline child care provider's criminal record clearance in its active files pursuant to subdivision (h) of Section 1596.871.
(Added by Stats. 1997, Ch. 843, Sec. 4. Effective January 1, 1998. Section operative July 1, 1998, pursuant to Section 1596.68.)

1596.607.

(a) (1) If the department finds that the trustline applicant has been convicted of a crime, other than a minor traffic violation, the department shall deny the application, unless the department grants an exemption pursuant to subdivision (f) of Section 1596.871.
(2) If the department finds that the trustline applicant has an arrest as described in subdivision (a) of Section 1596.871, the department may deny the application if the trustline applicant may pose a risk to the health and safety of any person who is or may become a client and the department complies with subdivision (e) of Section 1596.871.
(3) The department shall comply with the requirements of Section 1596.877 and may deny the application of a trustline applicant for substantiated child abuse that may pose a threat to the health and safety of any person who is or may become a client.
(4) The department may deny the application for registration of the trustline applicant if it discovers that the department or a county had previously revoked or rescinded a license or certificate to be a certified family home or resource family held by the trustline applicant or excluded the trustline applicant from a licensed facility, certified family home, or resource family home.
(5) The department may deny the application for registration of the trustline applicant if it discovers that the department or a county had previously denied the trustline applicant's application for a license from the department or certificate to be a certified family home or resource family.
(b) (1) If, the department denies registration pursuant to subdivision (a), it shall advise the provider of the right to appeal. The provider shall have 15 days to appeal the denial.
(2) Upon receipt by the department of the appeal, the appeal shall be set for hearing. The hearing shall be conducted in accordance with Section 1596.887.
(Amended by Stats. 2017, Ch. 732, Sec. 37. (AB 404) Effective January 1, 2018.)

1596.608.

(a) (1) The department may revoke a provider's trustline registration for any of the following:
(A) Procuring trustline registration by fraud or misrepresentation.
(B) Knowingly making or giving any false statement or information in conjunction with the application for issuance of trustline registration.
(C) Criminal conviction unless an exemption is granted pursuant to Section 1596.871.
(D) Incident of child abuse or neglect or other conduct that poses a threat to the health and safety of any person who is or may become a client.

(2) The hearing to revoke the trustline registration shall be conducted in accordance with Section 1596.887.

(b) The trustline provider's registration shall be considered forfeited under the following conditions:

(1) The trustline provider has had a license or certificate of approval revoked, suspended, or denied as authorized under Section 1534, 1550, 1568.082, 1569.50, or 1596.885.

(2) The trustline provider has been denied employment, residence, or presence in a facility based on action resulting from an administrative hearing pursuant to Section 1558, 1568.092, 1569.58, or 1596.8897.

(3) The trustline provider fails to maintain a current mailing address with the department.
(Added by Stats. 1997, Ch. 843, Sec. 4. Effective January 1, 1998. Section operative July 1, 1998, pursuant to Section 1596.68.)

1596.61.

(a) The department may charge a fee to a trustline applicant. The department may enter into an interagency agreement for the purpose of transferring funds to offset the costs incurred by the California Child Care Resource and Referral Network to implement the trustline program pursuant to this chapter.

(b) The maximum fee shall not exceed the total actual costs of all of the following:

(1) The searches of the state summary criminal history information and the child abuse index performed by the Department of Justice. The cost to check the criminal history information shall not subsidize the cost to check the criminal history of other persons by the State Department of Social Services who are not charged a fee by the Department of Justice.

(2) The cost incurred by the Department of Justice for the searches of the records of the Federal Bureau of Investigation.

(3) The information and technical assistance provided by the California Child Care Resource and Referral Network to parents, providers, and employment agencies.

(4) The implementation by the local child care resource and referral programs of the trustline program.

(5) The cost to the department to process the applications and maintain the trustline registry.
(Added by Stats. 1997, Ch. 843, Sec. 4. Effective January 1, 1998. Section operative July 1, 1998, pursuant to Section 1596.68.)

1596.615.

All moneys collected by the department to implement this chapter shall, notwithstanding Section 13340 of the Government Code, be continuously appropriated to the department without regard to fiscal year for expenditure pursuant to this chapter.
(Added by Stats. 1997, Ch. 843, Sec. 4. Effective January 1, 1998. Section operative July 1, 1998, pursuant to Section 1596.68.)

1596.616.

Notwithstanding Section 1596.61, the department shall charge a fee to each trustline applicant who provides care in an ancillary day care center, that is equal to and does not exceed the total amount required by the department to process applications and maintain the trustline registry for these providers.
(Amended by Stats. 2010, Ch. 431, Sec. 1. (AB 222) Effective September 29, 2010.)

1596.62.

(a) (1) The Department of Justice shall maintain and continually update an index of reports of child abuse by, and pertinent criminal convictions of, providers and shall inform the department of subsequent reports received from the child abuse index pursuant to Section 11170 of the Penal Code and the criminal history. The department shall continually update the trustline registry pursuant to the actions required in Section 1596.607.

(2) The trustline applicant and registered trustline provider shall inform the department of any new mailing address in writing within 10 days of the change in address.

(b) The department shall provide the California Child Care Resource and Referral Network with a continually updated record of the trustline applicants, trustline applicants that the department denied, the registered trustline child care providers, and providers whose registration that the department revoked.

(c) Notwithstanding any other law, including Part 3 (commencing with Section 900) of Division 3.6 of Title 1 of the Government Code, state officers or employees shall not be liable for any damages caused by their conduct pursuant to this chapter except for intentional acts or gross negligence.

(d) On July 1, 1998, the Department of Justice shall transfer all trustline application and registration material to the department. The department shall be responsible for all pending applications and hearings and shall transfer all trustline application and registration information.
(Added by Stats. 1997, Ch. 843, Sec. 4. Effective January 1, 1998. Section operative July 1, 1998, pursuant to Section 1596.68.)

1596.63.

It is a misdemeanor for a person to falsely represent or present himself or herself as a trustline applicant or a registered trustline child care provider.
(Added by Stats. 1997, Ch. 843, Sec. 4. Effective January 1, 1998. Section operative July 1, 1998, pursuant to Section 1596.68.)

1596.64.

(a) Both the department and the State Department of Education shall enter into a contract with the California Child Care Resource and Referral Network to administer the trustline duties as described in this chapter.

(b) The California Child Care Resources and Referral Network may subcontract with local resource and referral programs for the implementation of the trustline program at the local level.

(c) Notwithstanding any other law:

(1) Contracts or grants awarded pursuant to this chapter shall be exempt from the personal services contracting requirements of Article 4 (commencing with Section 19130) of Chapter 5 of Part 2 of Division 5 of Title 2 of the Government Code.

(2) Contracts or grants awarded pursuant to this chapter shall be exempt from the Public Contract Code and the State Contracting Manual, and shall not be subject to the approval of the Department of General Services.
(Amended by Stats. 2017, Ch. 15, Sec. 68. (AB 99) Effective June 27, 2017.)

1596.643.

(a) The California Child Care Resource and Referral Network shall have the following responsibilities:

(1) Establish and maintain a toll-free line to allow parents, employment agencies, child care referral groups and registries, alternative payment programs, and others to determine if a provider is a trustline applicant or a registered trustline child care provider.

(2) Develop a statewide promotion plan, publicize statewide existence, benefits, and methods of accessing the trustline for both parents and providers, and distribute trustline applications statewide.

(3) Monitor and provide assistance to the child care resource and referral agencies in carrying out their trustline responsibilities.

(4) Seek private financial support for the trustline.

(5) Ensure that the trustline is accessible to all persons in the state, regardless of their ability to speak English.

(b) Officers or employees of the California Child Care Resource and Referral Network shall not be liable for any injury caused by their conduct pursuant to paragraph (1) of subdivision (a), except for intentional conduct or gross negligence.
(Added by Stats. 1997, Ch. 843, Sec. 4. Effective January 1, 1998. Section operative July 1, 1998, pursuant to Section 1596.68.)

1596.645.

The California Child Care Resource and Referral Network, in consultation with representatives of private industry, parents, child care resource and referral agencies, the department, the State Department of Education, trustline providers, employment agencies, and the pediatric health sector, shall review and make recommendations concerning the operation of the trustline. This review shall include a consideration of strategies for reducing the processing time for trustline application denials, and to the extent possible, an evaluation of, or proposed methodology for measuring, whether those child care providers for whom trustline applications are denied are still providing care when denial letters are sent to them.
(Added by Stats. 1997, Ch. 843, Sec. 4. Effective January 1, 1998. Section operative July 1, 1998, pursuant to Section 1596.68.)

1596.65.

(a) An employment agency, as defined in Section 1812.501 of the Civil Code, that refers a child care provider to parents or guardians who are not required to be a licensed child day care facility shall not make a placement of a child care provider who is not a trustline applicant or a registered child care provider.

(b) Any violation of this section is a misdemeanor and shall be punishable by a fine of one hundred dollars ($100).
(Amended by Stats. 1998, Ch. 287, Sec. 2. Effective January 1, 1999.)

1596.653.

(a) It is the intent of the Legislature to protect the well-being of California children by regulating private individuals and companies that transport or accompany minors to out-of-state residential facilities or institutions.

(b) As used in this section:

(1) "Transport escort service" means any person, partnership, association, or corporation that accepts financial compensation or other consideration to accompany or transport minors who are residents of California to any residential facility or institution located outside the state.

(2) "Minor" means any person under the age of 18 years.

(3) "Department" means the State Department of Social Services.

(c) Every transport escort service that accompanies or transports a minor who is a resident of California to any residential facility or institution located outside the state, shall first provide the minor's parents, custodial parent, or legal guardian with all of the following:

(1) A description of the child care provider trustline registry established pursuant to this chapter that provides criminal history checks on child care providers.

(2) An explanation of how a parent may obtain more information about the child care provider trustline registry.

(3) A statement that a transport escort service is prohibited by law from transporting or accompanying a minor unless the person or persons transporting the minor are trustline registered child care providers.

(4) An explanation of how the parent may verify the trustline registration of the transport escort service.

(5) An explanation of the minor's right to make a complaint to a child protective agency concerning abusive treatment by the transport escort service.

(d) A transport escort service shall not transport or accompany a minor without obtaining the written permission of the minor's parents, custodial parent, or legal guardian.

(e) The transport escort service shall verify in writing that the minor's parents, custodial parent, or legal guardian has received the information required under subdivision (c).

(f) A transport escort service shall not accompany or transport a minor to any residential facility or institution located outside the state, unless the person or persons transporting or accompanying the minor are trustline registered child care providers.

(g) A minor, parent, or legal guardian claiming to be aggrieved by a violation of this section by a transport escort service may bring a civil action for injunctive relief or damages, or both.

(h) In addition to the remedy provided in subdivision (g), a violation of this section may be prosecuted as a misdemeanor punishable by a fine of not less than five hundred dollars ($500) or more than five thousand dollars ($5,000) as to each person with respect to whom a violation occurs, or imprisonment in a county jail for not more than six months.

(i) This section does not apply to the following:

(1) The transport of minors by any governmental agency or employee.

(2) The transport of minors under the jurisdiction of the juvenile court.

(3) The transport of minors by family members or relatives.

(j) Nothing in this section shall limit any claim for damages or the issuance of any injunction that a parent or child may assert against a transport escort service pursuant to any other state or federal law or regulation.

(Added by Stats. 1999, Ch. 772, Sec. 1. Effective January 1, 2000.)
1596.655.

A child care resource and referral agency established pursuant to Article 2 (commencing with Section 8210) of Chapter 2 of Part 6 of the Education Code shall have the following responsibilities in the administration of the trustline within its local geographic area of service:

(a) Implement the local elements of the promotion plan designed by the California Child Care Resource and Referral Network pursuant to Section 1596.643 and publicize the availability, purpose, and benefits of the trustline to parents, child care providers, prospective child care providers, and institutions and agencies that have frequent contact with parents and providers.

(b) Cooperate with the California Child Care Resource and Referral Network in promotional and data collection efforts.

(c) Report annually to the California Child Care Resource and Referral Network on local promotional efforts, problems encountered, and recommendations for program improvement.

(d) Ensure that the trustline is accessible to all persons in the state, regardless of their ability to speak English.

(e) Provide information and technical assistance on the trustline process to parents, child care providers, and other interested parties.

(Added by Stats. 1997, Ch. 843, Sec. 4. Effective January 1, 1998. Section operative July 1, 1998, pursuant to Section 1596.68.)
1596.656.

(a) A person 18 years of age or older, who provides child care or child care supervision in an ancillary day care center, as defined in Section 1596.60, shall be registered pursuant to Sections 1596.603 and 1596.605. Nothing in this chapter shall be construed to prevent a person under 18 years of age from being employed in an ancillary day care center.

(b) Notwithstanding any provision of law to the contrary, if a person 18 years of age or older is denied trustline registration by the department pursuant to Section 1596.605 or 1596.607, or if the department revokes a person's trustline registration pursuant to Section 1596.608, that person shall be ineligible for employment in a position providing child care or child care supervision in an ancillary day care center.

(c) If an existing employee providing child care or child care supervision in an ancillary day care center, or a prospective employee seeking employment in a position that provides child care or child care supervision in an ancillary day care center, submits an application to the department to become a registered trustline child care provider, that existing or prospective employee shall be deemed to be in compliance with the requirements of this section and permitted to work in a position providing child care or child care supervision pending the department's review of his or her trustline application. The existing or prospective employee shall become ineligible for employment providing child care or child care supervision in an ancillary day care center if the department denies his or her trustline application and any right to appeal the department's denial has been exhausted or has expired.

(d) This section shall become operative on January 1, 2011.

(Amended by Stats. 2010, Ch. 431, Sec. 2. (AB 222) Effective September 29, 2010. Section initially operative January 1, 2011, by its own provisions.)
1596.66.

(a) Each license-exempt childcare provider, as defined pursuant to Section 1596.60, who is compensated, in whole or in part, with funds provided pursuant to the Alternative Payment Program, Article 3 (commencing with Section 8220) of Chapter 2 of Part 6 of the Education Code or pursuant to the federal Child Care and Development Block Grant Program, except a provider who is, by marriage, blood, or court decree, the grandparent, aunt, or uncle of the child in care, shall be registered pursuant to Sections 1596.603 and 1596.605 in order to be eligible to receive this compensation. Registration under this chapter shall be required for providers who receive funds under Section 9858 and following of Title 42 of the United States Code only to the extent permitted by that law and the regulations adopted pursuant thereto. Registration under this chapter shall be required for providers who receive funds under the federal Child Care and Development

Block Grant Program only to the extent permitted by that program and the regulations adopted pursuant thereto.

(b) For the purposes of registration of the providers identified in subdivision (a), the following procedures shall apply:

(1) Notwithstanding subdivision (a) of Section 1596.603, the provider shall submit the fingerprints and Trustline application to the local childcare resource and referral agency established pursuant to Article 2 (commencing with Section 8210) of Chapter 2 of Part 6 of the Education Code. The local childcare resource and referral agency shall transmit the fingerprints and completed Trustline applications to the department and address any local problems that occur in the registration system. If a fee is charged by the local childcare resource and referral agency that takes a provider's fingerprints, the provider shall be reimbursed for this charge by the State Department of Education, through the local childcare resource and referral agency, from federal Child Care and Development Block Grant funds to the extent that those funds are available.

(2) The department shall adhere to the requirements of Sections 1596.603, 1596.605, 1596.606, and 1596.607 and shall notify the California Child Care Resource and Referral Network of any action it takes pursuant to Sections 1596.605, 1596.606, and 1596.607.

(3) The California Child Care Resource and Referral Network shall notify the applicable local childcare resource and referral agencies, alternative payment programs, and county welfare departments of the status of the Trustline applicants and registered Trustline childcare providers. The network shall maintain a toll-free telephone line to provide information to the local resource and referral agencies, the alternative payment programs, and the childcare recipients of the status of providers.

(c) This section shall become operative only if funds appropriated for the purposes of this article from Item 6110-196-890 of Section 2 of the Budget Act of 1991 are incorporated into and approved as part of the state plan that is required pursuant to Section 658(E)(a) of the federal Child Care Block Grant Act of 1990 (Sec. 5082, P.L. 101-508).

(Amended by Stats. 2019, Ch. 27, Sec. 9. (SB 80) Effective June 27, 2019. Section conditionally operative by its own provisions.)
1596.67.

(a) To the extent permitted by federal law, each childcare provider, as defined by Section 1596.60, who receives compensation, in whole or in part, under Stage 1 of the CalWORKs Child Care Program pursuant to Article 15.5 (commencing with Section 8350) of Chapter 2 of Part 6 of the Education Code, for providing childcare for a recipient or former recipient, except a provider who is, by marriage, blood, or court decree, the grandparent, aunt, or uncle of the child in care, shall be registered pursuant to Sections 1596.603 and 1596.605 in order to be eligible to receive this compensation. Active Trustline registration is required for providers who receive compensation under Stage 1 of the CalWORKs Child Care Program pursuant to Article 15.5 (commencing with Section 8350) of Chapter 2 of Part 6 of the Education Code, for providing childcare for a recipient or former recipient only to the extent permitted by that law and the regulations adopted pursuant thereto. This section applies only to a license-exempt childcare provider, as defined by Section 1596.60, who registers for payment under Stage 1 of the CalWORKs Child Care Program pursuant to Article 15.5 (commencing with Section 8350) of Chapter 2 of Part 6 of the Education Code, for providing childcare for a recipient or former recipient after the implementation of the Trustline registration system in those programs. A provider, as defined by Section 1596.60, who was exempted from Trustline registration because the provider was not compensated, in whole or in part, with funds provided under Stage 1 of the CalWORKs Child Care Program pursuant to Article 15.5 (commencing with Section 8350) of Chapter 2 of Part 6 of the Education Code, for providing childcare for a recipient or former recipient shall be registered, at no cost to the provider, pursuant to Sections 1596.603 and 1596.605 when either of the following occur:

(1) The provider begins to provide childcare to an eligible family for which the provider has not provided care.

(2) The provider begins to provide childcare to an eligible family subsequent to a lapse in providing care that is compensated under Stage 1 of the CalWORKs Child Care Program pursuant to Article 15.5 (commencing with Section 8350) of Chapter 2 of Part 6 of the Education Code, for providing childcare for a recipient or former recipient.

(b) Payment provided pursuant to subdivision (a) shall cease if the provider has a criminal conviction for which the department has not granted a criminal record exemption pursuant to subdivision (f) of Section 1596.871.

(c) Subdivision (a) shall not be implemented unless funding for Trustline registration is appropriated to the department for this purpose in the annual Budget Act or in other legislation. The department shall enter into a contract with the California Child Care Resource and Referral Network to administer the Trustline as it relates to providers who are compensated under Stage 1 of the CalWORKs Child Care Program pursuant to Article 15.5 (commencing with Section 8350) of Chapter 2 of Part 6 of the Education Code, for providing childcare for a recipient or former recipient.

(Amended by Stats. 2019, Ch. 27, Sec. 10. (SB 80) Effective June 27, 2019.)
1596.671.

(a) To the extent required by federal law, each license-exempt childcare provider, as defined in Section 1596.60, who receives compensation, in whole or in part, under the Emergency Child Care Bridge Program for Foster Children established pursuant to Section 11461.6 of the Welfare and Institutions Code, shall be registered pursuant to Sections 1596.603 and 1596.605. Registration shall be at no cost to the provider, and payment of the cost shall be consistent with county policies and procedures for payment of the cost for childcare providers who receive compensation under Stage 1 of the CalWORKs Child Care Program and who register with Trustline pursuant to Section 1596.67.

(b) Payment provided to a license-exempt childcare provider pursuant to Section 11461.6 of the Welfare and Institutions Code shall cease if the provider has a criminal conviction for which the department has not granted a criminal record exemption pursuant to subdivision (f) of Section 1596.871.

(c) Subdivision (a) shall not be implemented unless funding for Trustline registration is appropriated to the department for this purpose in the annual Budget Act or in other legislation.

(Added by Stats. 2019, Ch. 27, Sec. 11. (SB 80) Effective June 27, 2019.)

1596.68.

(a) This chapter shall be operative on July 1, 1998.

(b) (1) Before, on, or after July 1, 1998, the department may adopt regulations to implement this chapter.

(2) The initial adoption of any emergency regulations for purposes of this chapter following January 1, 1998, shall be deemed to be an emergency and necessary for the immediate preservation of the public peace, health, and safety, or general welfare. Emergency regulations adopted pursuant to this subdivision shall remain in effect for no more than 180 days.

(Added by Stats. 1997, Ch. 843, Sec. 4. Effective January 1, 1998. Note: This section prescribes a delayed operative date (July 1, 1998) for Chapter 3.35, commencing with Section 1596.60.)

CHAPTER 3.4. California Child Day Care Act [1596.70 - 1596.895]

(Chapter 3.4 added by Stats. 1984, Ch. 1615, Sec. 9.)

ARTICLE 1. General Provisions and Definitions [1596.70 - 1596.7996]
(Article 1 added by Stats. 1984, Ch. 1615, Sec. 9.)

1596.70.

This chapter and Chapters 3.5 (commencing with Section 1596.90) and 3.6 (commencing with Section 1597.30) may be cited as the California Child Day Care Facilities Act.

(Amended by Stats. 1985, Ch. 1064, Sec. 4.)

1596.71.

This chapter applies to Chapters 3.5 (commencing with Section 1596.90) and 3.6 (commencing with Section 1597.30). This chapter also applies to Chapter 3.65 (commencing with Section 1597.70).

(Amended by Stats. 1994, Ch. 690, Sec. 1. Effective January 1, 1995.)

1596.72.

The Legislature finds all of the following:

(a) That child day care facilities can contribute positively to a child's emotional, cognitive, and educational development.

(b) That it is the intent of this state to provide a comprehensive, quality system for licensing child day care facilities to ensure a quality day care environment.

(c) That this system of licensure requires a special understanding of the unique characteristics and needs of the children served by child day care facilities.

(d) That it is the intent of the Legislature to establish within the State Department of Social Services an organizational structure to separate licensing of child day care facilities from those facility types administered under Chapter 3 (commencing with Section 1500).

(e) That good quality child day care services are an essential service for working parents.

(Amended by Stats. 1985, Ch. 1064, Sec. 5.)

1596.73.

The purposes of this act are to:

(a) Streamline the administration of child care licensing and thereby increase the efficiency and effectiveness of this system.

(b) Encourage the development of licensing staff with knowledge and understanding of children and child care needs.

(c) Provide providers of child care with technical assistance about licensing requirements.

(d) Enhance consumer awareness of licensing requirements and the benefits of licensed child care.

(e) Recognize that affordable, quality licensed child care is critical to the well-being of parents and children in this state.

(Amended by Stats. 1985, Ch. 1064, Sec. 6.)

1596.74.

Unless the context otherwise requires, the definitions contained in this chapter govern the construction of this chapter and Chapters 3.5 (commencing with Section 1596.90) and 3.6 (commencing with Section 1597.30).

(Added by Stats. 1984, Ch. 1615, Sec. 9.)

1596.75.

"Child" means a person who is under 18 years of age who is being provided care and supervision in a child day care facility, except where otherwise specified in this act.

(Added by Stats. 1984, Ch. 1615, Sec. 9.)

1596.750.

"Child day care facility" means a facility that provides nonmedical care to children under 18 years of age in need of personal services, supervision, or assistance essential for sustaining the activities of daily living or for the protection of the individual on less than a 24-hour basis. Child day care facility includes day care centers, employer-sponsored child care centers, and family day care homes.

(Amended by Stats. 1994, Ch. 690, Sec. 2. Effective January 1, 1995.)

1596.76.

"Day care center" means a child day care facility other than a family day care home, and includes infant centers, preschools, extended day care facilities, and schoolage child care centers, and includes child care centers licensed pursuant to Section 1596.951.

(Amended by Stats. 2018, Ch. 574, Sec. 1. (AB 605) Effective January 1, 2019.)

1596.77.

"Department" means the State Department of Social Services.

(Added by Stats. 1984, Ch. 1615, Sec. 9.)

1596.770.

"Director" means the Director of Social Services.

(Added by Stats. 1984, Ch. 1615, Sec. 9.)

1596.771.

"Employer-sponsored child care center" means any child day care facility at the employer's site of business operated directly or through a provider contract by any person or entity having one or more employees, and available exclusively for the care of children of that employer, and of the officers, managers, and employees of that employer.

(Added by Stats. 1994, Ch. 690, Sec. 3. Effective January 1, 1995.)

1596.773.

(a) "Probation" means the period of time that a licensed child day care facility is required to comply with specific terms and conditions set forth by the department in order to stay or postpone the revocation of the facility's license.

(b) "Revocation" means an administrative action taken by the department to void or rescind the license of a child day care facility because of serious or chronic violations of licensing laws or regulations by the facility.

(Added by Stats. 2004, Ch. 358, Sec. 3. Effective January 1, 2005.)

1596.775.

The Legislature finds and declares all of the following:

(a) There is a severe shortage of child care for schoolage children throughout California, with many schoolage children going home to an empty, unsupervised setting after school.

(b) For nearly five years several counties have participated in a pilot program that allows for a family day care home to care for two additional children above the current number allowed pursuant to licensing regulations.

(c) As part of the pilot program, a study was conducted by the Assembly Office of Research. The results of the study demonstrated that the pilot program achieved all of the following results:

(1) Increased access to care for schoolage children.

(2) Participating providers encountered few problems and strongly support expansion of the program.

(3) Parents of children in the pilot program family day care homes strongly support the program.

(4) Participating providers with additional children were no more likely to receive substantiated complaints from licensing officials than nonparticipants.

(5) Local governments and planning officials saw little or no impact on their licensing policies and procedures.

(6) Overall quality of care was not adversely affected.

(Added by Stats. 1996, Ch. 18, Sec. 1. Effective January 1, 1997.)

1596.78.

(a) "Family day care home" means a home that regularly provides care, protection, and supervision for 14 or fewer children, in the provider's own home, for periods of less than 24 hours per day, while the parents or guardians are away, and is either a large family day care home or a small family day care home.

(b) "Large family day care home" means a home that provides family day care for 7 to 14 children, inclusive, including children under the age of 10 years who reside at the home, as set forth in Section 1597.465 and as defined in regulations.

(c) "Small family day care home" means a home that provides family day care for eight or fewer children, including children under the age of 10 years who reside at the home, as set forth in Section 1597.44 and as defined in regulations.

(Amended by Stats. 1996, Ch. 18, Sec. 2. Effective January 1, 1997.)

1596.785.

"Nonminor student" means a person 18 years of age or older who qualifies as an individual with exceptional needs, as defined in Section 56026 of the Education Code, and who qualifies for services from a regional center for persons with developmental disabilities, as a person with a developmental disability as defined in subdivision (a) of Section 4512 of the Welfare and Institutions Code. The terms "child," "children," or "minor," as used in this chapter or Chapter 3.5 (commencing with Section 1596.90), may also include a nonminor student enrolled or retained at a schoolage child care center.

(Added by Stats. 2011, Ch. 471, Sec. 1. (SB 309) Effective January 1, 2012.)

1596.79.

"Person" means an individual, partnership, association, corporation, limited liability company, or governmental entity, such as the state, a county, city, special district, school district, community college district, chartered city, or chartered city and county.

(Amended by Stats. 1994, Ch. 1010, Sec. 155. Effective January 1, 1995.)

1596.790.

"Planning agency" means the agency designated pursuant to Section 65100 of the Government Code.

(Added by Stats. 1984, Ch. 1615, Sec. 9.)

1596.791.

"Provider" means a person who operates a child day care facility and is licensed pursuant to Chapter 3.5 (commencing with Section 1596.90) or 3.6 (commencing with Section 1597.30).

(Added by Stats. 1984, Ch. 1615, Sec. 9.)

1596.7915.

"Schoolage child care center" means a day care center or part of a day care center that provides nonmedical care and supervision, personal services, or assistance essential for sustaining the activities of daily living or for the protection of schoolage children or nonminor students, or both, in a group setting for less than 24 hours per day.
(Added by Stats. 2011, Ch. 471, Sec. 2. (SB 309) Effective January 1, 2012.)
1596.792.

This chapter, Chapter 3.5 (commencing with Section 1596.90), and Chapter 3.6 (commencing with Section 1597.30) do not apply to any of the following:
(a) Any health facility, as defined by Section 1250.
(b) Any clinic, as defined by Section 1202.
(c) Any community care facility, as defined by Section 1502.
(d) Any family day care home providing care for the children of only one family in addition to the operator's own children.
(e) Any cooperative arrangement between parents for the care of their children when no payment is involved and the arrangement meets all of the following conditions:
(1) In a cooperative arrangement, parents shall combine their efforts so that each parent, or set of parents, rotates as the responsible caregiver with respect to all the children in the cooperative.
(2) Any person caring for children shall be a parent, legal guardian, stepparent, grandparent, aunt, uncle, or adult sibling of at least one of the children in the cooperative.
(3) There can be no payment of money or receipt of in-kind income in exchange for the provision of care. This does not prohibit in-kind contributions of snacks, games, toys, blankets for napping, pillows, and other materials parents deem appropriate for their children. It is not the intent of this paragraph to prohibit payment for outside activities, the amount of which may not exceed the actual cost of the activity.
(4) No more than 12 children are receiving care in the same place at the same time.
(f) Any arrangement for the receiving and care of children by a relative.
(g) Any public recreation program. "Public recreation program" means a program operated by the state, city, county, special district, school district, community college district, chartered city, or chartered city and county that meets either of the following criteria:
(1) The program is operated only during hours other than normal school hours for kindergarten and grades 1 to 12, inclusive, in the public school district where the program is located, or operated only during periods when students in kindergarten and grades 1 to 12, inclusive, are normally not in session in the public school district where the program is located, for either of the following periods:
(A) For under 20 hours per week.
(B) For a total of 14 weeks or less during a 12-month period. This total applies to any 14 weeks within any 12-month period, without regard to whether the weeks are consecutive. In determining "normal school hours" or periods when students are "normally not in session," the State Department of Social Services shall, when appropriate, consider the normal school hours or periods when students are normally not in session for students attending a year-round school.
(2) The program is provided to children who are over the age of four years and nine months and not yet enrolled in school and the program is operated during either of the following periods:
(A) For under 16 hours per week.
(B) For a total of 12 weeks or less during a 12-month period. This total applies to any 12 weeks within any 12-month period, without regard to whether the weeks are consecutive.
(3) The program is provided to children under the age of four years and nine months with sessions that run 12 hours per week or less and are 12 weeks or less in duration. A program subject to this paragraph may permit children to be enrolled in consecutive sessions throughout the year. However, the program shall not permit children to be enrolled in a combination of sessions that total more than 12 hours per week for each child.
(h) Extended day care programs operated by public or private schools.
(i) Any school parenting program or adult education child care program that satisfies both of the following:
(1) Is operated by a public school district or operated by an individual or organization pursuant to a contract with a public school district.
(2) Is not operated by an organization specified in Section 1596.793.
(j) Any child day care program that operates only one day per week for no more than four hours on that one day.
(k) Any child day care program that offers temporary child care services to parents and that satisfies both of the following:
(1) The services are only provided to parents and guardians who are on the same premises as the site of the child day care program.
(2) The child day care program is not operated on the site of a ski facility, shopping mall, department store, or any other similar site identified by the department by regulation.
(l) Any program that provides activities for children of an instructional nature in a classroom-like setting and satisfies both of the following:
(1) Is operated only during periods of the year when students in kindergarten and grades 1 to 12, inclusive, are normally not in session in the public school district where the program is located due to regularly scheduled vacations.
(2) Offers any number of sessions during the period specified in paragraph (1) that when added together do not exceed a total of 30 days when only schoolage children are enrolled in the program or 15 days when children younger than schoolage are enrolled in the program.

(m) A program facility administered by the Department of Corrections and Rehabilitation that (1) houses both women and their children, and (2) is specifically designated for the purpose of providing substance abuse treatment and maintaining and strengthening the family unit pursuant to Chapter 4 (commencing with Section 3410) of Title 2 of Part 3 of the Penal Code, or Chapter 4.8 (commencing with Section 1174) of Title 7 of Part 2 of that code.
(n) Any crisis nursery, as defined in paragraph (17) of subdivision (a) of Section 1502.
(o) (1) Commencing with the adoption of emergency regulations pursuant to paragraph (3), or no later than July 1, 2019, whichever comes first, a California state preschool program operated by a local educational agency under contract with the State Department of Education and that operates in a school building, as defined by Section 17283 of the Education Code, that meets all of the following conditions:
(A) The program is operated in a local educational agency facility that meets the requirements of the Field Act, as specified in Article 3 (commencing with Section 17280) and Article 6 (commencing with Section 17365) of Chapter 3 of Part 10.5 of Division 1 of Title 1 of, and Article 7 (commencing with Section 81130) of Chapter 1 of Part 49 of Division 7 of Title 3 of, the Education Code.
(B) The local educational agency facility is constructed consistent with California Building Standards Code pursuant to Title 24 of the California Code of Regulations.
(C) The local educational agency facility meets the requirements for kindergarten classrooms in accordance with Chapter 13 (commencing with Section 14000) of Division 1 of Title 5 of the California Code of Regulations.
(D) The program meets all other requirements of California state preschool programs pursuant to Chapter 19 (commencing with Section 17906) of Division 1 of Title 5 of the California Code of Regulations.
(2) A California state preschool program exempt under this subdivision shall be considered licensed under Division 12 (commencing with Section 101151) of Title 22 of the California Code of Regulations for purposes of establishing a rating on an early learning quality rating and improvement system matrix pursuant to Section 8203.1 of the Education Code.
(3) (A) No later than October 1, 2017, the Legislative Analyst shall convene a stakeholder process for the purpose of ensuring state preschools operated by local educational agencies are maintaining all existing necessary health and safety requirements.
(B) The stakeholder process shall identify and make recommendations on any health and safety requirements currently required under Title 22 of the California Code of Regulations, but not included in Title 5 of the California Code of Regulations, the Field Act, Title 24 of the California Code of Regulations, the California Plumbing Code, the Education Code, or this code, including, but not limited to, all of the following:
(i) Adequate outdoor shade structures.
(ii) Access to age and developmentally appropriate bathroom and drinking water facilities.
(iii) Appropriate processes for parent notification and resolution of code and regulation violations.
(C) The stakeholder process participants shall include experts on early childhood education health and safety issues from local educational agency and nonlocal educational agency state preschool program providers, and representatives from the State Department of Education, State Department of Social Services, Department of Finance, and legislative staff.
(D) No later than March 15, 2018, the Legislative Analyst shall report to the appropriate fiscal and policy committees of the Legislature, the Department of Finance, and the State Department of Education on recommendations or observations as a result of the stakeholder process. These recommendations or observations shall consider the fiscal impact on the state. No sooner than 30 days after the report is provided, the State Department of Education shall commence a process to adopt emergency regulations pursuant to Section 11346.1 of the Government Code to satisfy the requirements of this paragraph. The adoption of emergency regulations shall be deemed an emergency and necessary for the immediate preservation of the public peace, health, safety, or general welfare.
(4) For purposes of this subdivision, the following terms have the following meanings:
(A) "California state preschool program" means any classroom that is funded, in whole or in part, by funds received pursuant to Section 8235 of the Education Code.
(B) "Local educational agency" means a school district, county office of education, or charter school.
(Amended by Stats. 2018, Ch. 32, Sec. 125. (AB 1808) Effective June 27, 2018.)
1596.7925.

(a) On or before July 1, 2019, the State Department of Education shall adopt new health and safety regulations under Title 5 of the California Code of Regulations that apply to California state preschool programs that meet the conditions specified in subdivision (o) of Section 1596.792. The regulations shall require those programs to have all of the following:
(1) Outdoor shade that is safe and in good repair.
(2) Drinking water that is accessible and readily available throughout the day.
(3) Safe and sanitary restroom facilities with one toilet and handwashing fixture for every 15 children.
(4) Restroom facilities that are only available for preschoolers and kindergartners.
(5) Visual supervision of children at all times.
(6) Indoor and outdoor space that is properly contained or fenced and provides sufficient space for the number of children using the space at any given time. Playground equipment must be safe, in good repair, and age appropriate.

(b) The State Department of Education may adopt emergency regulations pursuant to Section 11346.1 of the Government Code to satisfy the requirements of this section. The adoption of emergency regulations shall be deemed an emergency and necessary for the immediate preservation of the public peace, health, safety, or general welfare.

(c) A violation of regulations adopted pursuant to subdivision (a) or (b) shall not be subject to Section 1596.890.

(Added by Stats. 2018, Ch. 32, Sec. 126. (AB 1808) Effective June 27, 2018.)

1596.793.

This chapter and Chapters 3.5 (commencing with Section 1596.90) and 3.6 (commencing with Section 1597.30) do not apply to recreation programs conducted for children by the YMCA, Girl Scouts of the USA, Boy Scouts of America, Boys and Girls Clubs, Camp Fire USA, organized camps, or similar organizations. However, child day care programs conducted by these organizations and the fees charged for those purposes shall be subject to the requirements of this chapter, Chapter 3.5 (commencing with Section 1596.90) and Chapter 3.6 (commencing with Section 1597.30).

(Amended by Stats. 2012, Ch. 652, Sec. 2. (SB 1087) Effective January 1, 2013.)

1596.794.

The department shall serve as the liaison to child day care facilities for the purposes of Sections 17608 to 17613, inclusive, of the Education Code.

(Added by Stats. 2006, Ch. 865, Sec. 7. Effective January 1, 2007.)

1596.795.

(a) The smoking of a tobacco product in a private residence that is licensed as a family day care home shall be prohibited in the home and in those areas of the family day care home where children are present. Nothing in this section shall prohibit a city or county from enacting or enforcing an ordinance relating to smoking in a family day care home if the ordinance is more stringent than this section.

(b) The smoking of a tobacco product on the premises of a licensed day care center shall be prohibited.

(c) For purposes of this section, "smoking" has the same meaning as in subdivision (c) of Section 22950.5 of the Business and Professions Code.

(d) For purposes of this section, "tobacco product" means a product or device as defined in subdivision (d) of Section 22950.5 of the Business and Professions Code.

(Amended by Stats. 2016, 2nd Ex. Sess., Ch. 7, Sec. 14. (SB 5 2x) Effective June 9, 2016.)

1596.796.

Notwithstanding any other provision of law, payments are not required to be made to any person who provides child care services and is exempt from the licensing requirements of this chapter, Chapter 3.5 (commencing with Section 1596.90), or Chapter 3.6 (commencing with Section 1597.30) if that person either is known to have tuberculosis, or to have been convicted of any crime involving violence against, or abuse or neglect of, children.

This section shall not be construed to create an affirmative duty on any individual, government body, or other entity paying for child care to investigate the person to whom payments are being made nor shall it be construed to create any liability for failure to investigate that person.

To the extent that this section is inconsistent with federal law, it shall be inoperative.

(Added by Stats. 1991, Ch. 1190, Sec. 13. Effective October 14, 1991. Provisions inoperative to extent inconsistent with federal law.)

1596.797.

(a) Blood glucose testing for the purposes of monitoring a minor child diagnosed with diabetes may be performed in a child day care facility in accordance with paragraph (6) of subdivision (b) of Section 1241 of the Business and Professions Code.

(b) Nothing in this section, or in any other provision of law, including, but not limited to, Section 1241 or 2058 of the Business and Professions Code, shall require an insulin injection to be administered to any child in a child day care facility.

(Added by Stats. 1997, Ch. 550, Sec. 3. Effective January 1, 1998.)

1596.798.

(a) Notwithstanding any other provision of law, licensees and staff of a child day care facility may administer inhaled medication to a child if all of the following requirements are met:

(1) The licensee or staff person has been provided with written authorization from the minor's parent or legal guardian to administer inhaled medication and authorization to contact the child's health care provider. The authorization shall include the telephone number and address of the minor's parent or legal guardian.

(2) The licensee or staff person complies with specific written instructions from the child's physician to which all of the following shall apply:

(A) The instructions shall contain all of the following information:

(i) Specific indications for administering the medication pursuant to the physician's prescription.

(ii) Potential side effects and expected response.

(iii) Dose-form and amount to be administered pursuant to the physician's prescription.

(iv) Actions to be taken in the event of side effects or incomplete treatment response pursuant to the physician's prescription.

(v) Instructions for proper storage of the medication.

(vi) The telephone number and address of the child's physician.

(B) The instructions shall be updated annually.

(3) The licensee or staff person that administers the inhaled medication to the child shall record each instance and provide a record to the minor's parent or legal guardian on a daily basis.

(4) Beginning January 1, 2000, a licensee or staff person who obtains or renews a pediatric first aid certificate pursuant to Section 1596.866 shall complete formal training designed to provide instruction in administering inhaled medication to children with respiratory needs. This training shall include, but not be limited to, training in the general use of nebulizer equipment and inhalers, how to clean the equipment, proper storage of inhaled medication, how a child should respond to inhaled medication, what to do in cases of emergency, how to identify side effects of the medication, and when to notify a parent or legal guardian or physician. This training shall be a component in the pediatric first aid certificate requirement as provided in Section 1596.8661.

(5) For a specified child, the licensee or staff person who administers inhaled medication has been instructed to administer inhaled medication by the child's parent or guardian.

(6) Beginning January 1, 2000, any training materials pertaining to nebulizer care that licensees or staff receive in the process of obtaining or renewing a pediatric first aid certificate pursuant to paragraph (4) shall be kept on file at the child care facility. The materials shall be made available to a licensee or staff person who administers inhaled medication. This requirement shall only apply to the extent that training materials are made available to licensees or staff who obtain or renew a pediatric first aid certificate pursuant to paragraph (4).

(b) For purposes of this section, inhaled medication shall refer to medication prescribed for the child to control lung-related illness, including, but not limited to, local held nebulizers.

(c) Nothing in this section shall be interpreted to require a certificated teacher who provides day care pursuant to Chapter 2 (commencing with Section 8200) of Part 6 of the Education Code in a public school setting to administer inhaled medication.

(Added by Stats. 1998, Ch. 625, Sec. 2. Effective September 21, 1998.)

1596.799.

(a) Notwithstanding Section 1597.05 or any other provision of law, any day care center that exclusively offers a program of services for which there is no contract or agreement between any parent and the center for the regular care of any child, and for which there is no prearranged schedule of care for any child, shall not be required to do either of the following:

(1) Verify children's immunizations or tuberculosis testing.

(2) Maintain files regarding children's immunizations or tuberculosis testing.

(b) Upon admission of a child, the parent shall sign an acknowledgment that he or she understands that verification of immunizations and tuberculosis testing is not required for any child accepted in this type of program.

(c) This section shall not be construed to exempt a day care center from any other licensing requirement.

(Added by Stats. 2002, Ch. 536, Sec. 1. Effective January 1, 2003.)

1596.7995.

(a) (1) Commencing September 1, 2016, a person shall not be employed or volunteer at a day care center if he or she has not been immunized against influenza, pertussis, and measles. Each employee and volunteer shall receive an influenza vaccination between August 1 and December 1 of each year.

(2) If a person meets all other requirements for employment or volunteering, as applicable, but needs additional time to obtain and provide his or her immunization records, the person may be employed or volunteer conditionally for a maximum of 30 days upon signing and submitting a written statement attesting that he or she has been immunized as required.

(b) A person is exempt from the requirements of this section only under any of the following circumstances:

(1) The person submits a written statement from a licensed physician declaring that because of the person's physical condition or medical circumstances, immunization is not safe.

(2) The person submits a written statement from a licensed physician providing that the person has evidence of current immunity to the diseases described in subdivision (a).

(3) The person submits a written declaration that he or she has declined the influenza vaccination. This exemption applies only to the influenza vaccine.

(4) The person was hired after December 1 of the previous year and before August 1 of the current year. This exemption applies only to the influenza vaccine during the first year of employment or volunteering.

(c) The day care center shall maintain documentation of the required immunizations or exemptions from immunization, as set forth in this section, in the person's personnel record that is maintained by the day care center.

(d) Section 1596.890 does not apply to a violation of this section.

(e) For purposes of this section, "volunteer" means any nonemployee who provides care and supervision to children in care.

(Added by Stats. 2015, Ch. 807, Sec. 1. (SB 792) Effective January 1, 2016.)

1596.7996.

(a) A licensed child day care facility, upon enrolling or reenrolling any child, shall provide the parent or guardian with written information, to be developed by the department, in consultation with the State Department of Public Health, on all of the following:

(1) Risks and effects of lead exposure.

(2) Blood lead testing recommendations and requirements.

(3) Options for obtaining blood lead testing, including any state or federally funded programs that offer free or discounted tests.

(b) For purposes of this section, "child day care facility" has the same meaning as in Section 1596.750.

(Added by Stats. 2018, Ch. 676, Sec. 1. (AB 2370) Effective January 1, 2019.)

(Article 2 added by Stats. 1984, Ch. 1615, Sec. 9.)

1596.80.

No person, firm, partnership, association, or corporation shall operate, establish, manage, conduct, or maintain a child day care facility in this state without a current valid license therefor as provided in this act.

(Amended by Stats. 1986, Ch. 1016, Sec. 7.)

1596.803.

(a) (1) An application fee adjusted by facility and capacity shall be charged by the department for the issuance of a license to operate a child day care facility. After initial licensure, a fee shall be charged by the department annually, on each anniversary of the effective date of the license. The fees are for the purpose of financing activities specified in this chapter. Fees shall be assessed as follows, subject to paragraph (2):

Fee Schedule			
Facility Type	Capacity	Original Application	Annual Fee
Family Day Care	1–8	$73	$73
	9–14	$140	$140
Day Care Centers	1–30	$484	$242
	31–60	$968	$484
	61–75	$1,210	$605
	76–90	$1,452	$726
	91–120	$1,936	$968
	121+	$2,420	$1,210

(2) (A) The Legislature finds that all revenues generated by fees for licenses computed under this section and used for the purposes for which they were imposed are not subject to Article XIII B of the California Constitution.

(B) The department, at least every five years, shall analyze initial application fees and annual fees issued by it to ensure the appropriate fee amounts are charged. The department shall recommend to the Legislature that fees established by the Legislature be adjusted as necessary to ensure that the amounts are appropriate.

(b) (1) In addition to fees set forth in subdivision (a), the department shall charge the following fees:

(A) A fee that represents 50 percent of an established application fee when an existing licensee moves the facility to a new physical address.

(B) A fee that represents 50 percent of the established application fee when a corporate licensee changes who has the authority to select a majority of the board of directors.

(C) A fee of twenty-five dollars ($25) when an existing licensee seeks to either increase or decrease the licensed capacity of the facility.

(D) An orientation fee of twenty-five dollars ($25) for attendance by any individual at a department-sponsored family child day care home orientation session, and a fifty dollar ($50) orientation fee for attendance by any individual at a department-sponsored child day care center orientation session.

(E) A probation monitoring fee equal to the current annual fee, in addition to the current annual fee for that category and capacity for each year a license has been placed on probation as a result of a stipulation or decision and order pursuant to the administrative adjudication procedures of the Administrative Procedure Act (Chapter 4.5 (commencing with Section 11400) and Chapter 5 (commencing with Section 11500) of Part 1 of Division 3 of Title 2 of the Government Code).

(F) A late fee that represents an additional 50 percent of the established current annual fee when any licensee fails to pay the current annual licensing fee on or before the due date as indicated by postmark on the payment.

(G) A fee to cover any costs incurred by the department for processing payments including, but not limited to, bounced check charges, charges for credit and debit transactions, and postage due charges.

(H) A plan of correction fee of two hundred dollars ($200) when any licensee does not implement a plan of correction on or prior to the date specified in the plan.

(2) No local jurisdiction shall impose any business license, fee, or tax for the privilege of operating a small family day care home licensed under this act.

(c) (1) The revenues collected from licensing fees pursuant to this section shall be utilized by the department for the purpose of ensuring the health and safety of all individuals provided care and supervision by licensees, and to support the activities of the licensing program, including, but not limited to, monitoring facilities for compliance with licensing laws and regulations pursuant to this act, and other administrative activities in support of the licensing program, when appropriated for these purposes. The revenues collected shall be used in addition to any other funds appropriated in the annual Budget Act in support of the licensing program. The department shall adjust the fees collected pursuant to this section as necessary to ensure they do not exceed the costs described in this paragraph.

(2) The department shall not utilize any portion of these revenues sooner than 30 days after notification in writing of the purpose and use, as approved by the Department of Finance, to the Chairperson of the Joint Legislative Budget Committee, and the chairpersons of the committee in each house that considers appropriations for each fiscal year. The department shall submit a budget change proposal to justify any positions or any other related support costs on an ongoing basis.

(d) A child day care facility may use a bona fide business or personal check to pay the license fee required under this section.

(e) The failure of an applicant for licensure or a licensee to pay all applicable and accrued fees and civil penalties shall constitute grounds for denial or forfeiture of a license.

(Amended by Stats. 2014, Ch. 29, Sec. 28. (SB 855) Effective June 20, 2014.)

1596.805.

No person, firm, partnership, association, or corporation shall provide specialized services within a child day care facility in this state without first obtaining a special permit as provided in this act.

(Added by Stats. 1984, Ch. 1615, Sec. 9.)

1596.806.

(a) A room used as a classroom by a schoolage child care program shall not be required to meet the square footage or toilet requirements for child day care centers if the program is operated on either of the following:

(1) A functioning schoolsite in the same facilities that have housed school children during the day, before or after school hours, or before and after school hours.

(2) A functioning schoolsite in facilities certified as usable as a classroom for instruction. A building owned by a school district, the state, or the schoolage child care program may meet the certification requirement if either of the following is provided to the department:

(A) Evidence that the building was approved as a classroom by the office of the State Architect.

(B) A certification statement signed by the superintendent of the schools, or his or her designee, in the district where the schoolage child care program is located, that the classroom building is of sufficient size to accommodate public instruction. The school district may make this certification regardless of the ownership of the classroom.

(b) School grounds, other than rooms used as classrooms, used by a schoolage child care program operated on a functioning schoolsite pursuant to either paragraph (1) or (2) of subdivision (a) shall be exempt from all of the following requirements imposed by the department on child day care facilities:

(1) Fencing, outdoor activity space, toilet, and isolation space requirements.

(2) Requirements to have exclusive use of the outdoor activity space or exclusive use of children's rest rooms also used by students located on school grounds.

(c) The exemptions pursuant to subdivisions (a) and (b) shall continue during school vacation and intersession periods.

(d) For purposes of this section, "schoolage child care program" means a program for children who are four years and nine months or older and are currently enrolled in a school or are dependent children living within the same household as a child attending a school, operated by an entity that contracts with the school to provide staff and program. "Schoolage child care program" includes, but is not limited to, a program pursuant to Article 22 (commencing with Section 8460) or Article 23 (commencing with Section 8485) of Chapter 2 of Part 6 of the Education Code.

(Amended by Stats. 1991, Ch. 867, Sec. 1.)

1596.807.

The State Department of Social Services, shall allow an extended day care program, whether or not exempt from licensure pursuant to subdivision (h) of Section 1596.792, to serve additional children at that school site, so long as they are four years and nine months of age or older and the number of additional children, including dependent children living within the same household as a child attending that school, does not exceed 15 percent of the total enrollment in the extended day care program. In no case shall the enrollment of the extended day care program exceed the enrollment during the regular schoolday.

(Amended by Stats. 1987, Ch. 1487, Sec. 2.)

1596.808.

(a) Commencing January 1, 2012, except as provided in subdivisions (b) and (c), a licensed child day care facility shall comply with all of the following requirements for beverages served by the day care provider to children in the provider's care:

(1) Whenever milk is served, serve only lowfat (1 percent) milk or nonfat milk to children two years of age or older.

(2) Limit juice to not more than one serving per day of 100-percent juice.

(3) Serve no beverages with added sweeteners, either natural or artificial. "Beverages with added sweeteners" does not include infant formula or complete balanced nutritional products designed for children.

(4) Make clean and safe drinking water readily available and accessible for consumption throughout the day.

(b) If a child has a medical necessity documented by a physician that includes the need for "medical food" as defined by Section 109971 of the Health and Safety Code, a licensed child day care facility shall be exempt from complying with the requirements of subdivision (a), to the extent necessary to meet the medical needs of that child.

(c) This section shall not apply to beverages at a licensed child day care facility that are provided by a parent or legal guardian for his or her child.

(d) As the Dietary Guidelines for Americans, published jointly by the federal Department of Health and Human Services and the federal Department of Agriculture, are updated every five years, the department may adapt the provisions of this section by bulletin, as necessary, so that the standards continue to reflect the most recent relevant nutrition science and continue to improve the health of children in child care.

(e) The department shall only determine compliance with this section during a regularly scheduled, authorized inspection, and shall not be required to conduct separate and independent visits.

(Added by Stats. 2010, Ch. 593, Sec. 2. (AB 2084) Effective January 1, 2011.)

1596.809.

A prospective applicant for licensure shall be notified at the time of the initial request for information regarding application for licensure that, prior to obtaining licensure, the facility shall secure and maintain a fire clearance approval from the local fire enforcing agency, as defined in Section 13244, or the State Fire Marshal, whichever has primary fire protection jurisdiction. The prospective applicant shall be notified of the provisions of Section 13235, relating to the fire safety clearance application. The prospective applicant for licensure shall be notified that the fire clearance shall be in accordance with state and local fire safety regulations.

(Added by Stats. 1989, Ch. 993, Sec. 4.)

1596.81.

(a) The department shall adopt, amend, or repeal in accordance with Chapter 3.5 (commencing with Section 11340) of Part 1 of Division 3 of Title 2 of the Government Code any rules and regulations which may be necessary to carry out this act.

(b) Licensing requirements adopted pursuant to Section 1530 shall only continue to be applicable to day care centers, and requirements adopted pursuant to Section 1597.51 shall continue to be applicable to family day care homes, until the department adopts regulations pursuant to this chapter.

(Amended by Stats. 1985, Ch. 1064, Sec. 9.)

1596.813.

The department shall adopt regulations regarding immunization requirements for children enrolled in family day care homes in accordance with Chapter 1 (commencing with Section 120325) of Part 2 of Division 105.

(Amended by Stats. 1996, Ch. 1023, Sec. 166. Effective September 29, 1996.)

1596.815.

The department shall, on or before December 31, 1991, review all child care regulations of the department with respect to clarifying or eliminating vagueness and shall issue revised regulations if necessary to correct those defects.

(Added by Stats. 1989, Ch. 301, Sec. 2.)

1596.816.

(a) The Community Care Licensing Division of the department shall regulate child care licensees through an organizational unit that is separate from that used to regulate all other licensing programs. The chief of the child care licensing branch shall report directly to the Deputy Director of the Community Care Licensing Division.

(b) All child care regulatory functions of the licensing division, including the adoption and interpretation of regulations, staff training, monitoring and enforcement functions, administrative support functions, and child care advocacy responsibilities shall be carried out by the child care licensing branch to the extent that separation of these activities can be accomplished without new costs to the department.

(c) Those persons conducting inspections of day care facilities shall meet qualifications approved by the State Personnel Board.

(d) The department shall notify the appropriate legislative committees whenever actual staffing levels of licensing program analysts within the child care licensing branch drops more than 10 percent below authorized positions.

(e) The budget for the child care licensing branch shall be included as a separate entry within the budget of the department.

(Amended by Stats. 2006, Ch. 538, Sec. 362. Effective January 1, 2007.)

1596.817.

(a) When the department conducts a site visit of a licensed child day care facility, the department shall post on, or immediately adjacent to, the interior side of the main door into the facility and adjacent to the postings required pursuant to Section 1596.8595, a notice, written in at least 14-point type, that includes all of the following:

(1) The date of the site visit.

(2) Whether the facility was cited for violating any state standards or regulations as a result of the site visit and which of the following categories was cited:

(A) A violation that, if not corrected, will have a direct and immediate risk to the health, safety, or personal rights of children in care.

(B) A violation that, if not corrected, could become a risk to the health, safety, or personal rights of children, a recordkeeping violation that would impact the care of children, or a violation that would impact those services required to meet children's needs.

(3) Whether the facility is required to post the site visit report for 30 consecutive days pursuant to Section 1596.8595.

(4) A statement explaining that copies of the site visit report, including, but not limited to, violations noted in subparagraph (B) of paragraph (2), may be obtained by contacting the department and the telephone number to call in order to obtain a copy of the site visit report.

(5) The name and telephone number of a person in the department who may be contacted for further information about the site visit report.

(b) (1) The notice posted pursuant to subdivision (a) shall remain posted for 30 consecutive days, except that a family day care home shall comply with the posting requirements contained in this subdivision only during the hours when clients are present.

(2) Failure by a licensed child day care facility or a family day care home to comply with paragraph (1) shall result in an immediate civil penalty of one hundred dollars ($100).

(Added by Stats. 2003, Ch. 403, Sec. 1. Effective January 1, 2004.)

1596.818.

(a) The department shall specify in its licensing report all violations that, if not corrected, will have a direct and immediate risk to the health, safety, or personal rights of children in care.

(b) The department shall complete all complaint investigations and place a note of final conclusion in the department's facility file, consistent with the confidentiality requirements of Section 1596.853, regardless of whether the licensee voluntarily surrendered his or her license.

(Added by Stats. 2008, Ch. 291, Sec. 19. Effective September 25, 2008.)

1596.819.

(a) Except as otherwise prohibited by law, the department shall post licensing information on its Internet Web site as follows:

(1) For each child day care facility as defined in Section 1596.750, except family day care homes, the information shall include, but is not limited to, the name and address of the facility, the licensed capacity of the facility, the status of the license, and the number of site inspections, including the number of citations, substantiated and unsubstantiated complaint inspections, and noncomplaint inspections during the preceding five-year period.

(2) For each family day care home, the information shall include, but is not limited to, the name of the home, the status of the license, and the number of site inspections, including the number of citations, substantiated and unsubstantiated complaint inspections, and noncomplaint inspections during the preceding five-year period.

(b) The department shall update the information posted under subdivision (a) on at least a monthly basis.

(Amended by Stats. 2016, Ch. 823, Sec. 9. (AB 2231) Effective January 1, 2017.)

1596.82.

The department may contract for state, county, or other public agencies to assume specified licensing, approval, or consultation responsibilities. If an agency also provides licensing, approval, or consultation responsibilities for the purpose of administering Chapter 3 (commencing with Section 1500), the agency shall maintain licensing staff positions distinct from those positions responsible for administering Chapter 3 (commencing with Section 1500). The department shall reimburse agencies for services performed pursuant to this section which shall not exceed actual cost.

(Added by Stats. 1984, Ch. 1615, Sec. 9.)

1596.83.

An applicant or licensee shall file his or her mailing address, in writing, with the department and, shall notify the department, in writing, of any change within 10 calendar days.

(Added by Stats. 1987, Ch. 1069, Sec. 8.)

1596.84.

The department may issue provisional licenses to operate day care facilities which the director determines are in substantial compliance with the provisions of the licensure requirements and the rules and regulations adopted pursuant thereto, provided, that no life safety risks are involved, as determined by the director. In determining whether any life safety risks are involved, the director shall require completion of all applicable fire clearances and criminal record clearances as otherwise required by the department's rules and regulations. The provisional license shall expire six months from the date of issuance, or at such earlier time as the director may determine. However, the director may extend the term of a provisional license for an additional six months time, if it is determined that more than six months will be required to achieve full compliance with licensing standards due to circumstances beyond the control of the applicant. provided all other requirements for a license have been met. In no case shall a provisional license be issued for more than 12 months.

(Amended by Stats. 1985, Ch. 1064, Sec. 11.)

1596.841.

Each child day care facility shall maintain a current roster of children who are provided care in the facility. The roster shall include the name, address, and daytime telephone number of the child's parent or guardian, and the name and telephone number of the child's physician. This roster shall be available to the licensing agency upon request.

(Added by Stats. 1985, Ch. 1312, Sec. 1.)

1596.842.

Following approval by the department of a list of provider rights, the Community Care Licensing Division shall print and distribute in person, to individuals or to groups, and by other appropriate methods of distribution, a list of provider rights which shall include, but not be limited to, the following:

(a) Site visit rights:

(1) The right to require licensing field staff to identify themselves.

(2) The right to be advised of the type of the visit, whether complaint, plan of correction, prelicensing, or some other type. When a site visit is made to investigate a complaint, the site visit rights described in paragraphs (4) and (9) shall be applicable at the completion of the investigation.

(3) The right to be treated as a professional and with dignity and respect.

(4) The right to receive an accurate report of the evaluator's findings listing each observed deficiency. Each deficiency shall be separately numbered, so as to clearly

indicate the number of deficiencies, shall be accompanied by a number that corresponds to a section of law or licensing regulation, and shall include a description of the evaluator's observation that led to the finding of a deficiency. The description of the evaluator's observation shall include a clear explanation of why the existing condition constitutes a deficiency, unless the description of the observation provides the explanation.

(5) The right to review licensing laws, regulations, and policy.

(6) The right to an impartial investigation of all complaints.

(7) The right, at the time of the visit, to determine and develop a plan of correction for deficiencies cited.

(8) The right to use the licensing report (LIC 809) as a means to agree or disagree with cited deficiencies.

(9) The right to an exit interview upon completion of the visit and to receive a signed copy of the LIC 809.

(10) The right to be informed on the LIC 809 of the evaluator's supervisor and his or her telephone number.

(11) The right of access to the public file on any facility and the right to purchase a copy at a reasonable cost.

(b) Initial appeal rights:

(1) The right, without prejudice, to appeal any decision, any failure to act according to law or regulation, or any failure to act within any specified timeline, through the licensing agency as specified in Sections 1596.99 and 1597.58.

(2) The right to request a meeting with district office administrators to discuss any licensing issue and with notice to bring any person to the meeting.

(3) The right to due process and the option of bringing a representative to any administrative action.

(c) The right to file a formal complaint, and receive a written response to that complaint within 30 days, for any licensing issue not covered by subdivision (b), including, but not limited to, inappropriate behavior of department employees.

(d) The department shall, by June 30, 1992, mail to all licensees a copy of this section and a full and complete copy of the appeals procedure developed to implement subdivision (b).

(e) The department shall, on all forms it requires or recommends that providers use, all notices of regulations or departmental policy, and all notices to implement this section, clearly label the department as the source of the material, including the name of the department, the name of the division responsible for implementing this chapter, and the address of that division.

(Amended by Stats. 2015, Ch. 486, Sec. 6. (AB 1387) Effective January 1, 2016.)

1596.843.

(a) Whenever a facility visit and a complaint investigation are conducted at the same time by the department, a separate licensing report shall be used to document the complaint investigation.

(b) The department shall review a random sample of licensing reports to evaluate the consistency of the application of regulations by different licensing program analysts.

(Added by Stats. 1989, Ch. 301, Sec. 4.)

1596.844.

The department shall acknowledge in writing within 10 days of receipt, the request of a licensee to review notices of deficiency or penalty, or both.

(Added by Stats. 1989, Ch. 301, Sec. 5.)

1596.845.

Prior to the issuance of a new license or special permit pursuant to this chapter, Chapter 3.5 (commencing with Section 1596.90), or Chapter 3.6 (commencing with Section 1597.30) the applicant shall attend an orientation given by the department. The orientation given by the department shall outline all of the following:

(a) The rules and regulations of the department applicable to child day care facilities.

(b) The scope of operation of a child day care facility.

(c) The responsibility entailed in operating a child day care facility.

(d) Information about the Healthy Schools Act of 2000 and integrated pest management practices.

(Amended by Stats. 2006, Ch. 865, Sec. 8. Effective January 1, 2007.)

1596.846.

(a) The Legislature finds and declares all of the following:

(1) The American Academy of Pediatrics, after reviewing the data from all the studies, concluded that baby walkers are dangerous and should be banned from all manufacturing, sale, and distribution in the United States.

(2) A jury in San Mateo County, California has determined that baby walkers are inherently unsafe and are not capable of design changes in order to prevent accidents.

(3) Citing numerous ways in which babies can be injured, Consumer Reports found that, "With a capacity to move as fast as five feet per second, a baby walker can propel your baby faster than you can rescue him."

(4) During the past 15 years, one particular product, a baby walker, has been shown to be associated with increasing numbers of injuries to infants, with the most recent reporting year, 1991, indicating that 27,800 children under the age of two years had to be admitted to an emergency room in the United States for injuries associated with a baby walker.

(b) A baby walker shall not be kept or used on the premises of a child day care facility.

(c) A "baby walker" means any article described in paragraph (4) of subdivision (a) of Section 1500.86 of Part 1500 of Title 16 of the Code of Federal Regulations.

(d) Section 1596.890 shall not apply to this section.

(Added by Stats. 1993, Ch. 336, Sec. 1. Effective January 1, 1994.)

1596.847.

(a) A child day care facility shall not use or have on the premises, on or after July 1, 1998, a full-size or non-full-size crib that is unsafe for any infant using the crib, as described in Article 1 (commencing with Section 24500) of Chapter 4.7 of Division 20. This subdivision shall not apply to any antique or collectible crib if it is not used by, or accessible to, any child in the child day care facility.

(b) The State Department of Social Services shall provide information and instructional materials regarding sudden infant death syndrome, explaining the medical effects upon infants and young children and emphasizing measures that may reduce the risk, free of charge to any child care facility licensed to provide care to children under the age of two years. This shall occur upon licensure and, on a one-time basis only, at the time of a regularly scheduled site visit.

(c) To the maximum extent practicable, the materials provided to child care facilities shall substantially reflect the information contained in materials approved by the State Department of Health Services for public circulation. The State Department of Health Services shall make available, to child care facilities, free of charge, information in camera-ready typesetting format. Nothing in this section prohibits the State Department of Social Services from obtaining free and suitable information from any other public or private agency. The information and instructional materials provided pursuant to this section shall focus upon the serious nature of the risk to infants and young children presented by sudden infant death syndrome.

(d) The requirement that informational and instructional materials be provided pursuant to this section applies only when those materials have been supplied to those persons or entities that are required to provide the materials. The persons or entities required to provide these materials shall not be subject to any legal cause of action whatsoever based on the requirements of this section.

(e) For persons or agencies providing these materials pursuant to this section, this section does not require the provision of duplicative or redundant informational and instructional materials.

(Amended by Stats. 2006, Ch. 538, Sec. 363. Effective January 1, 2007.)

1596.85.

No license or special permit issued pursuant to Chapters 3.5 (commencing with Section 15967.90) and 3.6 (commencing with Section 1597.30) shall have any property value for sale or exchange purposes and no person, including any owner, agent, or broker, shall sell or exchange the license or special permit for any commercial purpose.

(Added by Stats. 1984, Ch. 1615, Sec. 9.)

1596.851.

(a) (1) If an application for a license or special permit indicates, or the department determines during the application review process, that the applicant previously was issued a license under this act or under Chapter 1 (commencing with Section 1200), Chapter 2 (commencing with Section 1250), Chapter 3 (commencing with Section 1500), Chapter 3.01 (commencing with Section 1568.01), or Chapter 3.3 (commencing with Section 1569) and that the prior license was revoked within the preceding two years, the department shall cease any further review of the application until two years shall have elapsed from the date of the revocation.

(2) If an application for a license or special permit indicates, or the department determines during the application review process, that the applicant previously was issued a certificate of approval by a foster family agency that was revoked by the department pursuant to subdivision (b) of Section 1534 within the preceding two years, the department shall cease any further review of the application until two years have elapsed from the date of the revocation.

(3) If an application for a license or special permit indicates, or the department determines during the application review process, that the applicant was excluded from a facility licensed by the department pursuant to Section 1558, 1568.092, 1569.58, or 1596.8897, the department shall cease any further review of the application unless the excluded individual has been reinstated pursuant to Section 11522 of the Government Code by the department.

(b) If an application for a license or special permit indicates, or the department determines during the application review process, that the applicant had previously applied for a license under any of the chapters listed in paragraph (1) of subdivision (a) and the application was denied within the last year, the department shall cease further review of the application as follows:

(1) In cases where the applicant petitioned for a hearing, the department shall cease further review of the application until one year has elapsed from the effective date of the decision and order of the department upholding a denial.

(2) In cases where the department informed the applicant of his or her right to petition for a hearing as specified in Section 1596.879 and the applicant did not petition for a hearing, the department shall cease further review of the application until one year has elapsed from the date of the notification of the denial and the right to petition for a hearing.

(3) The department may continue to review the application if it has determined that the reasons for the denial of the application were due to circumstances and conditions which have been corrected or are no longer in existence. The cessation of review shall not constitute a denial of the application.

(c) If an application for a license or special permit indicates, or the department determines during the application review process, that the applicant had previously applied for a certificate of approval with a foster family agency and the department ordered the foster family agency to deny the application pursuant to subdivision (b) of Section 1534, the department shall cease further review of the application as follows:

(1) In cases where the applicant petitioned for a hearing, the department shall cease further review of the application until one year has elapsed from the effective date of the decision and order of the department upholding a denial.

(2) In cases where the department informed the applicant of his or her right to petition for a hearing and the applicant did not petition for a hearing, the department shall cease further review of the application until one year has elapsed from the date of the notification of the denial and the right to petition for a hearing.

(3) The department may continue to review the application if it has determined that the reasons for the denial of the application were due to circumstances and conditions that either have been corrected or are no longer in existence.

(d) The cessation of review shall not constitute a denial of the application for purposes of Section 1526 or any other law.

(Amended by Stats. 1997, Ch. 617, Sec. 16. Effective January 1, 1998.)

1596.852.

Any duly authorized officer, employee, or agent of the department may, upon presentation of proper identification, enter and inspect any place providing personal care, supervision, and services at any time, with or without advance notice, to secure compliance with, or to prevent a violation of, this act or the regulations adopted by the department pursuant to the act.

(Amended by Stats. 1985, Ch. 1064, Sec. 13.)

1596.853.

(a) Any person may request an inspection of any child day care facility in accordance with the California Child Day Care Facilities Act by transmitting to the department notice of an alleged violation of applicable requirements prescribed by the statutes or regulations of this state. A complaint may be made either orally or in writing.

(b) The substance of the complaint shall be provided to the licensee no earlier than at the time of the inspection. Unless the complainant specifically requests otherwise, neither the substance of the complaint provided the licensee nor any copy of the complaint or any record published, released, or otherwise made available to the licensee shall disclose the name of any person mentioned in the complaint, except the name of any duly authorized officer, employee, or agent of the department conducting the investigation or inspection pursuant to this chapter.

(c) Upon receipt of a complaint, the department shall make a preliminary review and, unless the department determines that the complaint is willfully intended to harass a licensee or is without any reasonable basis, the department shall make an onsite inspection within 10 days after receiving the complaint, except where the visit would adversely affect the licensing investigation or the investigation of other agencies, including, but not limited to, law enforcement agencies. In either event, the complainant shall be promptly informed of the department's proposed course of action.

If the department determines that the complaint is without a reasonable basis, then the complaint shall be marked confidential and shall not be disclosed to the public. The child-care provider shall be notified in writing within 30 days of the dismissal that the complaint has been dismissed.

(d) (1) The department shall notify a resource and referral program funded under Section 8210 of the Education Code, as follows:

(A) Upon the issuance or denial of a license for a child day care facility within the resource and referral program's jurisdiction.

(B) Within one business day of a finding that physical or sexual abuse has occurred at a child day care facility within the resource and referral program's jurisdiction.

(C) Within two business days of the issuance of a temporary suspension order, or the revocation or placement on probation of a license for a child day care facility within the resource and referral program's jurisdiction.

(D) The department shall also notify the resource and referral program of the final resolution of any action specified in this paragraph.

(2) With the exception of parents seeking local day care service, any other entity specified in subdivision (b) of Section 1596.86 may request that the department provide the notification described in paragraph (1).

(e) When the department substantiates an allegation that it deems to be serious in a facility funded by the Child Development Division of the State Department of Education pursuant to Chapter 2 (commencing with Section 8200) of Part 6 of the Education Code it shall notify the Child Development Division.

(Amended by Stats. 2004, Ch. 358, Sec. 4. Effective January 1, 2005.)

1596.8535.

(a) Notwithstanding any other provision of law, the department shall conduct any authorized inspection, announced site visit, or unannounced site visit of any child daycare facility only during the period beginning one hour before and ending one hour after the facility's normal business hours or at any time childcare services are being provided. This subdivision shall not apply to the investigation of any complaint received by the department if the department determines that an inspection or site visit outside the time period beginning one hour before, and ending one hour after, the facility's normal operating hours is necessary to protect the health or safety of any child in the facility.

(b) If a facility is closed for an extended period of time, the department may not perform any inspection, announced site visit, or unannounced site visit until the facility has reopened, subject to subdivision (a).

(c) The department shall develop regulations establishing a procedure by which a licensee of any childcare facility may notify the licensing agency of a planned period of inactivity in the operation of the facility. The department shall also develop regulations establishing a procedure by which the department shall determine if it will grant inactive status to a licensee after receiving this notice from the licensee.

(d) If the department grants inactive status to a licensee pursuant to subdivision (c), the license shall not be valid during the period of inactivity in the operation of the facility, the licensee shall be responsible for the payment of annual licensing fees and for maintaining licensing standards upon reactivation of operation of the facility, and the department's timeframe for required site visits shall be adjusted accordingly. However, if the department believes the licensee is operating during a period in which the department has granted inactive status to the licensee, the department may enter the facility for any inspection permitted by law.

(e) This section shall be operative July 1, 2003.

(Added by Stats. 2002, Ch. 122, Sec. 1. Effective January 1, 2003. Section operative July 1, 2003, by its own provisions.)

1596.854.

The withdrawal of an application for a license or a special permit after it has been filed with the department shall not, unless the department consents in writing to the withdrawal, deprive the department of its authority to institute or continue a proceeding against the applicant for the denial of the license or a special permit upon any ground provided by law or to enter an order denying the license or special permit upon any such ground.

The suspension, expiration, or forfeiture by operation of law of a license or a special permit issued by the department, or its suspension, forfeiture, or cancellation by order of the department or by order of a court of law, or its surrender without the written consent of the department, shall not deprive the department of its authority to institute or continue a disciplinary proceeding against the licensee or holder of a special permit upon any ground provided by law or to enter an order suspending or revoking the license or special permit or otherwise taking disciplinary action against the licensee or holder of a special permit on any such ground.

(Added by Stats. 1984, Ch. 1615, Sec. 9.)

1596.855.

(a) Upon attendance at an orientation meeting, as described in Section 1596.845, an applicant shall be provided, without charge, a printed copy of all applicable regulations by the department, a copy of Section 1596.842, and a copy of the appeals procedure specified in subdivision (b) of Section 1596.842. The department shall inform applicants of the availability of a Spanish language version of these materials and shall provide it to the applicant upon request by the applicant.

(b) The department shall mail, without charge, printed copies of all revisions of regulations to all resource and referral programs funded under Section 8210 of the Education Code, and to any association of child care agencies which requests to receive revisions of regulations. Upon request, the department shall mail, without charge, a version of these regulations in Spanish, and may mail, without charge, a version of these regulations in other languages, as available.

(c) The versions in Spanish and in other languages shall be provided as a convenience to the reader. In the event of a discrepancy between these versions and the English version, the English version shall prevail.

(Amended by Stats. 1992, Ch. 1319, Sec. 3. Effective January 1, 1993.)

1596.8555.

A licensed child day care facility shall post its license in a prominent, publicly accessible location in the facility. A family day care home shall comply with this posting requirement during the hours when clients are present.

(Added by Stats. 2004, Ch. 358, Sec. 5. Effective January 1, 2005.)

1596.856.

If the department finds that the applicant is not in compliance with this act or the regulations promulgated under this act, the department shall deny the applicant a license.

(Amended by Stats. 1992, Ch. 1315, Sec. 26. Effective January 1, 1993.)

1596.857.

(a) Upon presentation of identification, the responsible parent or guardian of a child receiving services in a child day care facility has the right to enter and inspect the facility without advance notice during the normal operating hours of the facility or at any time that the child is receiving services in the facility. Parents or guardians when inspecting shall be respectful of the children's routines and programmed activities. The facility shall inform parents and guardians of children receiving services in the facility of the right of the parents and guardians to inspect the facility pursuant to this section.

(b) No child day care facility shall discriminate or retaliate against any child or parent or guardian on the basis or for the reason that the parent or guardian has exercised his or her right under this section to inspect the facility or has lodged a complaint with the department against a facility.

(c) If any child day care facility denies a parent or legal guardian the right to enter and inspect a facility or retaliates, the department shall issue the facility a warning citation. For any subsequent violation of this right, the department may impose a civil penalty upon the facility of fifty dollars ($50) per violation. The department may take any appropriate action, including license revocation.

(d) Each child day care facility shall permanently post in a facility location accessible to parents and guardians a written notice, available from the department, of the right to make an inspection pursuant to this section and the prohibition against retaliation and the right to file a complaint. In addition, this notice shall include information stating that the specified registered sex offender database is available to the public via an Internet Web site maintained by the Department of Justice as www.meganslaw.ca.gov. The department shall make this written notice available to child day care facility licensees, and shall include on this notice a statement of the right of the parents and guardians to review licensing reports of facility visits and substantiated complaints against the facility on the site of the facility, pursuant to Section 1596.859.

(e) At the time of acceptance of each child into a child day care facility after January 1, 2007, the licensee shall provide the child's parent or guardian with a copy of the Family Child Care Home Notification of Parents' Rights provided by the State Department of Social Services, which shall include information stating that the specified registered sex offender database is available to the public via an Internet Web site maintained by the Department of Justice as www.meganslaw.ca.gov.
(f) Upon delivery of the Family Child Care Home Notification of Parents' Rights required pursuant to subdivision (e) to a parent or guardian, a provider is not required to provide any additional information regarding the location and proximity of registered sex offenders who reside in the community where the child care facility or family day care home is located. The provision of the information required by this section to parents and guardians of a child in their care shall not subject the provider to any liability or cause of action against the provider by a registered sex offender identified in the database.
(g) Notwithstanding any other provision of this section, the person present who is in charge of a child day care facility may deny access to an adult whose behavior presents a risk to children present in the facility and may deny access to noncustodial parents or guardians if so requested by the responsible parent or legal guardian.
(Amended by Stats. 2006, Ch. 208, Sec. 1. Effective January 1, 2007.)
1596.858.
A license shall be forfeited by operation of law prior to its expiration date when any one of the following occurs:
(a) The licensee sells or otherwise transfers the facility or facility property, except when change of ownership applies to transferring of stock when the facility is owned by a corporation, and when the transfer of stock does not constitute a majority change in ownership.
(b) The licensee surrenders the license to the department.
(c) The licensee moves the facility from one location to another. The department shall develop regulations to ensure that the facilities are not charged a full licensing fee and do not have to complete the entire application process when applying for license for the new location.
(d) The licensee is convicted of an offense specified in Section 220, 243.4, or 264.1, or paragraph (1) of Section 273a, Section 273d, 288, or 289 of the Penal Code, or is convicted of another crime specified in subdivision (c) of Section 667.5 of the Penal Code.
(e) The licensee dies. If an adult relative notifies the department of his or her desire to continue operation of the facility and submits an application, the department shall expedite the application. The department shall promulgate regulations for expediting applications submitted pursuant to this subdivision.
(f) The licensee abandons the facility.
(Amended by Stats. 1989, Ch. 606, Sec. 9.)
1596.859.
(a) (1) Each licensed child day care facility shall make accessible to the public a copy of any licensing report or other public licensing document pertaining to the facility that documents a facility inspection, a substantiated complaint investigation, a conference with a local licensing agency management representative and the licensee in which issues of noncompliance are discussed, or a copy of an accusation indicating the department's intent to revoke the facility's license. An individual licensing report and other licensing documents shall not be required to be maintained beyond three years from the date of issuance, and shall not include any information that would not have been accessible to the public through the State Department of Social Services Community Care Licensing Division.
(2) (A) Every child care resource and referral program established pursuant to Article 2 (commencing with Section 8210) of Chapter 2 of Part 6 of the Education Code, and every alternative payment program established pursuant to Article 3 (commencing with Section 8220) of Chapter 2 of Part 6 of the Education Code shall advise every person who requests a child care referral of his or her right to the licensing information of a licensed child day care facility required to be maintained at the facility pursuant to this section and to access any public files pertaining to the facility that are maintained by the State Department of Social Services Community Care Licensing Division.
(B) A written or oral advisement in substantially the following form, with the telephone number of the local licensing office included, will comply with the requirements of subparagraph (A):
"As a parent, you have the right to get information about any substantiated or unsubstantiated complaints about a child care provider that you select for your child. That information is public and you can get it by calling the local licensing office. This telephone number is ____."
(b) Within 30 days after the date specified by the department for a licensee to correct a deficiency, the department shall provide the licensee with a licensing report or other appropriate document verifying compliance or noncompliance. Notwithstanding any other provision of law, and with good cause, the department may provide the licensee with an alternate timeframe for providing the licensing report or other appropriate document verifying compliance or noncompliance. If the department provides the licensee with an alternate timeframe, it shall also provide the reasons for the alternate timeframe, in writing. The licensee shall make this documentation available to the public.
(Amended by Stats. 2016, Ch. 823, Sec. 10. (AB 2231) Effective January 1, 2017.)
1596.8595.
(a) (1) Each licensed child day care facility shall post a copy of any licensing report pertaining to the facility that documents either a facility inspection or a complaint investigation that results in a citation for a violation that, if not corrected, will create a direct and immediate risk to the health, safety, or personal rights of the children in care. The licensing report provided by the department shall be posted immediately upon receipt, adjacent to the postings required pursuant to Section 1596.817 and on, or immediately adjacent to, the interior side of the main door to the facility and shall remain posted for 30 consecutive days.
(2) A family day care home shall comply with the posting requirements contained in paragraph (1) during the hours when clients are present.
(3) Failure to comply with paragraph (1) shall result in an immediate civil penalty of one hundred dollars ($100).
(b) (1) Notwithstanding subdivision (b) of Section 1596.859, the licensee shall post a licensing report or other appropriate document verifying the licensee's compliance or noncompliance with the department's order to correct a deficiency that is subject to posting pursuant to paragraph (1) of subdivision (a). The licensing report or other document shall be posted immediately upon receipt, adjacent to the postings required pursuant to Section 1596.817, on, or immediately adjacent to, the interior side of the main door into the facility and shall be posted for a period of 30 consecutive days.
(2) A family day care home shall comply with the posting requirements contained in paragraph (1) during the hours when clients are present.
(3) Failure to comply with paragraph (1) shall result in an immediate civil penalty of one hundred dollars ($100).
(c) (1) A licensed child day care facility shall provide to the parents or guardians of each child receiving services in the facility copies of any licensing report that documents a citation issued pursuant to subdivision (e) or (f) of Section 1596.99 or subdivision (e) or (f) of Section 1597.58 or that represents an immediate risk to the health, safety, or personal rights of children in care as set forth in paragraph (1) of subdivision (a) of Section 1596.893b.
(2) Upon enrollment of a new child in a facility, the licensee shall provide to the parents or legal guardians of the newly enrolling child copies of any licensing report that the licensee has received during the prior 12-month period that documents a citation issued pursuant to subdivision (e) or (f) of Section 1596.99 or subdivision (e) or (f) of Section 1597.58 or that represents an immediate risk to the health, safety, or personal rights of children in care as set forth in paragraph (1) of subdivision (a) of Section 1596.893b.
(3) The licensee shall require each recipient of the licensing report described in paragraph (1) pertaining to a complaint investigation to sign a statement indicating that he or she has received the document and the date it was received.
(4) The licensee shall keep verification of receipt in each child's file.
(d) (1) A licensed child day care facility shall provide to the parents or legal guardians of each child receiving services in the facility copies of any licensing document pertaining to a conference conducted by a local licensing agency management representative with the licensee in which issues of noncompliance are discussed.
(2) Upon enrollment of a new child in a facility, the licensee shall provide to the parents or legal guardians of the newly enrolling child copies of any licensing document that the licensee has received during the prior 12-month period that pertains to a conference conducted by a local licensing agency management representative with the licensee in which issues of noncompliance are discussed.
(3) The licensee shall require each recipient of the licensing document pertaining to a conference to sign a statement indicating that he or she has received the document and the date it was received.
(4) The licensee shall keep verification of receipt in each child's file.
(e) This section shall become operative on July 1, 2017.
(Repealed (in Sec. 11) and added by Stats. 2016, Ch. 823, Sec. 12. (AB 2231) Effective January 1, 2017. Section operative July 1, 2017, by its own provisions.)
1596.86.
(a) The director shall annually publish and make available to interested persons a list or lists covering all licensed child day care facilities, other than small family day care homes, and the services for which each facility has been licensed or issued a special permit. The lists shall also specify the licensed capacity of the facility and whether it is licensed by the department or by another public agency.
(b) To encourage the recruitment of small family day care homes and protect their personal privacy, the department shall prevent the use of lists containing names, addresses and other identifying information of facilities identified as small family day care homes, except as necessary for administering the licensing program, facilitating the placement of children in these facilities, and providing the names and addresses to resource and referral agencies funded by the State Department of Education, food and nutrition programs funded by the State Department of Education, alternative payment programs funded by the State Department of Education, county programs under the Greater Avenues for Independence Act of 1985 (Article 3.2 (commencing with Section 11320) of Chapter 2 of Part 3 of Division 9 of the Welfare and Institutions Code), family day care organizations, provider organizations that have been determined to be provider organizations pursuant to subdivision (a) of Section 8432 of the Education Code, or specialized health care service plans licensed under the Knox-Keene Health Care Service Plan Act of 1975, as contained in Chapter 2.2 (commencing with Section 1340), which provide employee assistance program services that include childcare referral services. Upon request, parents seeking local day care services may receive the names and telephone numbers of local small family day care providers.
(c) The department, in consultation with the Child Development Division of the State Department of Education, shall adopt regulations relating to the confidentiality of information provided pursuant to subdivision (b) on small family day care homes. These regulations shall include procedures for updating lists or other information on small family day care providers to ensure referral only to licensed homes in good standing with the department. Any person or entity violating the regulations under this subdivision may be

denied access by the department to information on small family day care homes and shall be reported by the department to the appropriate funding or licensing department.
(Amended by Stats. 2019, Ch. 51, Sec. 66. (SB 75) Effective July 1, 2019.)
1596.861.
(a) Each child day care facility licensed under this chapter, Chapter 3.5 (commencing with Section 1596.90), or Chapter 3.6 (commencing with Section 1597.30) shall reveal its license number in all advertisements, publications, or announcements made with the intent to attract clients.
(b) Advertisements, publications, or announcements subject to the requirements of subdivision (a) include, but are not limited to, those contained in the following:
(1) Newspaper or magazine.
(2) Consumer report.
(3) Announcement of intent to commence business.
(4) Telephone directory yellow pages.
(5) Professional or service directory.
(6) Radio or television commercial.
(Amended by Stats. 1990, Ch. 216, Sec. 56.)
1596.862.
(a) The department may approve or deny a written request for enrollment or retention of a nonminor student at a schoolage child care center. The department may approve a request for enrollment or retention of a nonminor student if the department determines the schoolage child care center can meet the needs of the nonminor student and enrollment or retention of the nonminor student is not detrimental to the health and safety of the nonminor student.
(b) (1) For the purposes of retention, if a request, as described in subdivision (c), is submitted to the department at least 30 days prior to the child's 18th birthday, the nonminor student shall be retained at a schoolage child care center, unless the request is denied in writing by the department.
(2) For the purposes of enrollment, a nonminor student shall not be enrolled at a schoolage child care center until the request, as described in subdivision (c), is approved in writing by the department.
(c) A written request from a schoolage child care center for enrollment or retention of a nonminor student shall include all of the following:
(1) Confirmation that the licensee conducted a personal interview of the nonminor student or the nonminor student's authorized representative, if applicable, and a written statement from the licensee that assesses both of the following:
(A) Whether the enrollment or retention of the nonminor student would present a threat to the physical health, mental health, or safety of the nonminor student and others at the schoolage child care center.
(B) Whether the needs of the nonminor student can be met by the schoolage child care center.
(2) A copy of the nonminor student's current individualized education program and any other information requested by the department.
(d) A nonminor student enrolled or retained pursuant to this section shall be exempt from the fingerprinting and criminal record clearance requirements in Section 1596.871 and otherwise applicable regulations.
(e) An approved request may be terminated by the department and a citation of deficiency, an assessment of civil penalties, or discipline of the licensee pursuant to Section 1596.885 or Section 1596.886, or any combination thereof, may result if the licensee fails to comply with applicable laws.
(f) The department may adopt regulations necessary to implement this section.
(Added by Stats. 2011, Ch. 471, Sec. 3. (SB 309) Effective January 1, 2012.)
1596.865.
It is the intent of the Legislature to encourage any person who provides child care in a child day care facility licensed pursuant to this chapter, Chapter 3.5 (commencing with Section 1596.90), or Chapter 3.6 (commencing with Section 1597.30) to have the following elementary health care training:
(a) Cardiopulmonary resuscitation.
(b) Pediatric first aid.
(c) Preventive health practices, including food preparation, childhood nutrition, and sanitation practices that support overall health and reduce the spread of infectious diseases.
(Amended by Stats. 2013, Ch. 734, Sec. 2. (AB 290) Effective January 1, 2014.)
1596.866.
(a) (1) In addition to other required training, at least one director or teacher at each day care center, and each family day care home licensee who provides care, shall have at least 15 hours of health and safety training, and if applicable, at least one additional hour of training pursuant to clause (ii) of subparagraph (C) of paragraph (2).
(2) The training shall include the following components:
(A) Pediatric first aid.
(B) Pediatric cardiopulmonary resuscitation (CPR).
(C) (i) A preventive health practices course or courses that include instruction in the recognition, management, and prevention of infectious diseases, including immunizations, prevention of childhood injuries, and, for licenses issued on and after July 1, 2020, instruction in the prevention of lead exposure that is consistent with the most recent State Department of Public Health's training curriculum on childcare lead poisoning prevention.
(ii) For licenses issued on or after January 1, 2016, at least one director or teacher at each day care center, and each family day care home licensee who provides care, shall have at least one hour of childhood nutrition training as part of the preventive health practices course or courses.

(3) The training may include instruction in sanitary food handling, emergency preparedness and evacuation, and caring for children with special needs.
(b) Day care center directors and licensees of family day care homes shall ensure that at least one staff member who has a current course completion card in pediatric first aid and pediatric CPR issued by the American Red Cross, the American Heart Association, or by a training program that has been approved by the Emergency Medical Services Authority pursuant to this section and Section 1797.191 shall be onsite at all times when children are present at the facility, and shall be present with the children when children are offsite from the facility for facility activities. Nothing in this subdivision shall be construed to require, in the event of an emergency, additional staff members, who are onsite when children are present at the facility, to have a current course completion card in pediatric first aid and pediatric CPR.
(c) (1) The completion of health and safety training by all personnel and licensees described in subdivision (a) shall be a condition of licensure.
(2) Training in pediatric first aid and pediatric CPR by persons described in subdivisions (a) and (b) shall be current at all times. Training in preventive health practices, as described in subparagraph (C) of paragraph (2) of subdivision (a), is a one-time only requirement for persons described in subdivision (a).
(3) The department shall issue a provisional license for otherwise qualified applicants who are not in compliance with this section. This provisional license shall expire 90 days after the date of issuance and shall not be extended.
(4) A notice of deficiency shall be issued by the department at the time of a site visit to a licensee who is not in compliance with this section. The licensee shall, at the time the notice is issued, develop a plan of correction to correct the deficiency within 90 days of receiving the notice. The facility's license may be revoked if it fails to correct the deficiency within the 90-day period. Section 1596.890 shall not apply to this paragraph.
(d) Completion of the training required pursuant to subdivisions (a) and (b) shall be demonstrated, upon request of the licensing agency, by the following:
(1) Current pediatric first aid and pediatric CPR course completion cards issued by the American Red Cross, the American Heart Association, or by a training program approved by the Emergency Medical Services Authority pursuant to Section 1797.191.
(2) (A) A course completion card for a preventive health practices course or courses, as described in subparagraph (C) of paragraph (2) of subdivision (a), issued by a training program approved by the Emergency Medical Services Authority pursuant to Section 1797.191.
(B) Persons who, before September 21, 1998, have completed a course or courses in preventive health practices, as described in clause (i) of subparagraph (C) of paragraph (2) of subdivision (a), and have a certificate of completion of a course or courses in preventive health practices, or certified copies of transcripts that identify the number of hours and the specific course or courses taken for training in preventive health practices, shall be deemed to have met the training in preventive health practices.
(3) In addition to training programs specified in paragraphs (1) and (2), training programs or courses in pediatric first aid, pediatric CPR, and preventive health practices offered or approved by an accredited college or university are considered to be approved sources of training that may be used to satisfy the training requirements of paragraph (2) of subdivision (a). Completion of this training shall be demonstrated to the licensing agency by a certificate of course completion, course completion cards, or certified copies of transcripts that identify the number of hours and the specified course or courses taken for the training, as defined in paragraph (2) of subdivision (a).
(e) The training required under subdivision (a) shall not be provided by a home study course. This training may be provided through in-service training, workshops, or classes.
(f) All personnel and licensees described in subdivisions (a) and (b) shall maintain current course completion cards for pediatric first aid and pediatric CPR issued by the American Red Cross, the American Heart Association, or by a training program approved by the Emergency Medical Services Authority pursuant to Section 1797.191, or shall have current certification in pediatric first aid and pediatric CPR from an accredited college or university in accordance with paragraph (3) of subdivision (d).
(g) The department shall have the authority to grant exceptions to the requirements imposed by this section in order to meet the requirements of the federal Americans with Disabilities Act of 1990 (42 U.S.C. Sec. 12101 et seq.).
(h) The department shall adopt regulations to implement this section.
(Amended by Stats. 2018, Ch. 676, Sec. 2. (AB 2370) Effective January 1, 2019.)
1596.8661.
(a) For purposes of the training required pursuant to paragraph (4) of subdivision (a) of Section 1596.798, pediatric first aid training pursuant to Section 1596.866 shall include a component of training in the administration of inhaled medication described in paragraph (4) of subdivision (a) of Section 1596.798.
(b) The Emergency Medical Services Authority shall establish, consistent with Section 1797.191, minimum standards for a component of pediatric first aid training that satisfies the requirements of paragraph (4) of subdivision (a) of Section 1596.798. For purposes of this subdivision, the Emergency Medical Services Authority is encouraged to consult with organizations and providers with expertise in administering inhaled medication and nebulizer care, including, but not limited to, the American Lung Association, respiratory therapists, and others.
(c) For purposes of the training required pursuant to clause (ii) of subparagraph (C) of paragraph (2) of subdivision (a) of Section 1596.866, instruction in childhood nutrition shall be at least one hour in length and shall include content on age-appropriate meal patterns based on the most current Dietary Guidelines for Americans. In order to increase child care providers' capacity to serve healthy foods at a lower cost, the training shall contain information about reimbursement rates for the United States Department of

Agriculture's Child and Adult Care Food Program (CACFP) (7 C.F.R. 226.20), and shall direct child care providers to the CACFP Unit of the Nutrition Services Division of the State Department of Education for detailed information on CACFP eligibility and enrollment.

(d) Notwithstanding the rulemaking provisions of the Administrative Procedure Act (Chapter 3.5 (commencing with Section 11340) of Part 1 of Division 3 of Title 2 of the Government Code), the Emergency Medical Services Authority may, through bulletin or similar instructions from the director until regulations are adopted, establish standards for the training in childhood nutrition required pursuant to clause (ii) of subparagraph (C) of paragraph (2) of subdivision (a) of Section 1596.866 and for the training in lead poisoning required pursuant to clause (i) of subparagraph (C) of paragraph (2) of subdivision (a) of Section 1596.866.

(Amended by Stats. 2018, Ch. 676, Sec. 3. (AB 2370) Effective January 1, 2019.)
1596.8662.

(a) The department shall do all of the following:

(1) Make information available to all licensed child day care providers, administrators, and employees of licensed child day care facilities regarding detecting and reporting child abuse and neglect.

(2) Provide training including statewide guidance on the responsibilities of a mandated reporter who is a licensed day care provider or an applicant for that license, administrator, or employee of a licensed child day care facility in accordance with the Child Abuse and Neglect Reporting Act (Article 2.5 (commencing with Section 11164) of Chapter 2 of Title 1 of Part 4 of the Penal Code). The department shall provide the guidance using its free module or modules provided on the State Department of Social Services Internet Web site or as otherwise specified by the department. This guidance content shall include, but is not necessarily limited to, all of the following:

(A) Information on the identification of child abuse and neglect, including behavioral signs of abuse and neglect.

(B) Reporting requirements for child abuse and neglect, including guidelines on how to make a suspected child abuse report when suspected abuse or neglect takes place outside a child day care facility, or within a child day care facility, and to which enforcement agency or agencies a report is required to be made.

(C) Information that failure to report an incident of known or reasonably suspected child abuse or neglect, as required by Section 11166 of the Penal Code, is a misdemeanor punishable by up to six months confinement in a county jail, or by a fine of one thousand dollars ($1,000), or by both that imprisonment and fine.

(D) Information that mandated reporting duties are individual and no supervisor or administrator may impede or inhibit reporting duties, and no person making a report shall be subject to any sanction for making the report, pursuant to paragraph (1) of subdivision (i) of Section 11166 of the Penal Code. A supervisor or administrator who impedes or inhibits the duties of a mandated reporter shall be subject to punishment pursuant to Section 11166.01 of the Penal Code.

(E) Information on childhood stages of development in order to help distinguish whether a child's behavior or physical symptoms are within range for his or her age and ability, or are signs of abuse or neglect.

(3) The department shall provide training, including information about child safety and maltreatment prevention using its free training module or modules specified in paragraph (2), or as otherwise specified by the department. This information shall include, but is not necessarily limited to, all of the following:

(A) Information on protective factors that may help prevent abuse, including dangers of shaking a child, safe sleep practices, psychological effects of repeated exposure to domestic violence, safe and age-appropriate forms of discipline, how to promote a child's social and emotional health, and how to support positive parent-child relationships.

(B) Information on recognizing risk factors that may lead to abuse, such as stress and social isolation, and available resources to which a family may be referred to help prevent child abuse and neglect.

(C) When to call for emergency medical attention to prevent further injury or death.

(D) Information on how a licensed child day care provider, administrator, or employee of a licensed child day care facility might communicate with a family before and after making a suspected child abuse report.

(4) The department shall comply with the Dymally-Alatorre Bilingual Services Act of 1973 (Chapter 17.5 (commencing with Section 7290) of the Government Code), which includes, among alternative communication options, providing the same type of training materials in any non-English language spoken by a substantial number of members of the public whom the department serves.

(b) (1) On or before March 30, 2018, a person who, on January 1, 2018, is a licensed child day care provider, administrator, or employee of a licensed child day care facility shall complete the mandated reporter training provided pursuant to paragraphs (2) and (3) of subdivision (a), and shall complete renewal mandated reporter training every two years following the date on which he or she completed the initial mandated reporter training.

(2) On and after January 1, 2018, a person who applies for a license to be a provider of a child day care facility shall complete the mandated reporter training provided pursuant to paragraphs (2) and (3) of subdivision (a) as a precondition to licensure and shall complete renewal mandated reporter training every two years following the date on which he or she completed the initial mandated reporter training.

(3) On and after January 1, 2018, a person who becomes an administrator or employee of a licensed child day care facility shall complete the mandated reporter training provided pursuant to paragraphs (2) and (3) of subdivision (a) within the first 90 days that he or she is employed at the facility and shall complete renewal mandated reporter

training every two years following the date on which he or she completed the initial mandated reporter training.

(4) The licensee of a licensed child day care facility shall obtain proof from an administrator or employee of the facility that the person has completed mandated reporter training in compliance with this subdivision.

(5) A licensed child day care provider, administrator, or employee of a licensed child day care facility who does not use the online training module provided by the department shall report to, and obtain approval from, the department regarding the training that person shall use in lieu of the online training module.

(c) Current proof of completion for each licensed child day care provider or applicant for that license, administrator, and employee of a licensed child day care facility shall be submitted to the department upon inspection of the child day care or upon request by the department.

(d) (1) The department shall issue a notice of deficiency at the time of a site visit to the licensee of a licensed child day care facility who is not in compliance with this section. The licensee shall, at the time the department issues the notice of deficiency, develop a plan to correct the deficiency within 45 days.

(2) A deficiency under this subdivision is not subject to Section 1596.890.

(e) A licensed child day care provider or applicant for that license, an administrator, or employee of a licensed child care facility is exempt from the detecting and reporting child abuse training if he or she has limited English proficiency and training is not made available in his or her primary language.

(f) This section shall become operative on January 1, 2018.

(Amended by Stats. 2016, Ch. 86, Sec. 180. (SB 1171) Effective January 1, 2017.)
1596.867.

(a) All child day care facilities, as defined in Section 1596.750, shall include an Earthquake Preparedness Checklist as an attachment to the disaster plan prescribed by Section 1596.95 or 1597.54. However, the Earthquake Preparedness Checklist shall not be considered a requirement for obtaining or maintaining a license for a child day care center or family day care home. The Earthquake Preparedness Checklist shall be made accessible to the public at the child day care center, or family day care home. The licensing agency shall not monitor or be responsible for enforcing any provision contained in the Earthquake Preparedness Checklist or ensuring that the checklist is made accessible to the public.

(b) The Earthquake Preparedness Checklist shall not exceed two typewritten pages and the department may add to or delete from the list, as it deems appropriate. The checklist may include, but not be limited to, all of the procedures that are listed in the following proposed Earthquake Preparedness Checklist. A licensee of a child day care center or family day care home shall have the option of selecting from the checklist the procedures, if any, the licensee chooses to use in the child day care center or family day care home.

Earthquake Preparedness Checklist (EPC)*	
Eliminate potential hazards in classrooms and throughout the site:	
	Bolt bookcases in high traffic areas securely to wall studs
	Move heavy books and items from high to low shelves
	Secure and latch filing cabinets
	Secure cabinets in high traffic areas with child safety latches
	Secure aquariums, computers, typewriters, TV-VCR equipment to surfaces, such as by using Velcro tabs
	Make provisions for securing rolling portable items such as TV-VCRs, pianos, refrigerators
	Move children's activities and play areas away from windows, or protect windows with blinds or adhesive plastic sheeting
	Secure water heater to wall using plumber's tape
	Assess and determine possible escape routes
Establish a coordinated response plan involving all of the following:	

Involving children:

Teach children about earthquakes and what to do (see resource list below)

Practice "duck, cover, and hold" earthquake drills under tables or desks no less than 4 times a year

Involving parents:

Post, or make available to parents, copies of the school earthquake safety plan (including procedures for reuniting parents or alternate guardians with children, location of planned evacuation site, method for leaving messages and communicating)

Enlist parent and community resource assistance in securing emergency supplies or safeguarding the child day care site:

store a 3-day supply of nonperishable food (including juice, canned food items, snacks, and infant formula)

store a 3-day supply of water and juice

store food and water in an accessible location, such as portable plastic storage containers

store other emergency supplies such as flashlights, a radio with extra batteries, heavy gloves, trash bags, and tools

maintain a complete, up-to-date listing of children, emergency numbers, and contact people for each classroom stored with emergency supplies

Involving child day care personnel and local emergency agencies:

Identify and assign individual responsibilities for staff following an earthquake (including accounting for and evacuating children, injury control, damage assessment)

Involve and train all staff members about the earthquake safety plan, including location and procedure for turning off utilities and gas

Contact nearby agencies (including police, fire, Red Cross, and local government) for information and materials in developing the child day care center earthquake safety plan

*For more free resources contact:

(1) Federal Emergency Management Agency (FEMA)
(2) Office of Emergency Services
(3) Red Cross

(c) Nothing in this section shall be construed to prevent the adoption or enforcement of earthquake safety standards for child day care facilities by local ordinance.
(d) Nothing in this section shall be construed to prevent the department from adopting or enforcing regulations on earthquake safety or making earthquake safety drills mandatory.
(Amended by Stats. 2013, Ch. 352, Sec. 331. (AB 1317) Effective September 26, 2013. Operative July 1, 2013, by Sec. 543 of Ch. 352.)
1596.869.
Directors of combination child day care facilities shall be included in the teacher-child ratio during periods when they are actively supervising children and on the same basis that any other director of a day care center may be included in the teacher-child ratio.
(Repealed and added by Stats. 1991, Ch. 867, Sec. 5.)

1596.87.
The department shall institute a staff development and training program within the organizational structure to develop among staff the knowledge, understanding of children and child care, and regulatory administration necessary to successfully carry out this act. Specifically, the department shall do all of the following:
(a) Provide staff with 36 hours of training per year that reflect the unique needs of children. The training shall include training relating to regulation administration, including communication skills, writing skills, and human relations skills.
(b) Find ways to encourage applications from individuals with child care provider experience or educational backgrounds applicable to the provision of child care.
(c) Provide new staff with comprehensive training within the first six months of employment. This training shall, at a minimum, include the following core areas: administrative action process, client populations, conducting facility visits, cultural awareness, documentation skills, facility operations, human relation skills, interviewing techniques, investigation processes, and regulation administration.
This program shall also provide new staff who have earned fewer than 16 semester units in child development or early childhood education from an accredited college at least 40 hours of preservice training in child development or early childhood education.
(d) Submit for approval to the advisory committee established in Section 8286 of the Education Code a plan for meeting the provisions of subdivisions (a) and (c).
(Amended by Stats. 1992, Ch. 1319, Sec. 4. Effective January 1, 1993.)
1596.871.
The Legislature recognizes the need to generate timely and accurate positive fingerprint identification of applicants as a condition of issuing licenses, permits, or certificates of approval for persons to operate or provide direct care services in a childcare center or family childcare home. It is the intent of the Legislature in enacting this section to require the fingerprints of those individuals whose contact with child day care facility clients may pose a risk to the children's health and safety. An individual shall be required to obtain either a criminal record clearance or a criminal record exemption from the State Department of Social Services before the individual's initial presence in a child day care facility.
(a) (1) Before and, as applicable, subsequent to issuing a license or special permit to any person to operate or manage a day care facility, the department shall secure from an appropriate law enforcement agency a criminal record to determine whether the applicant or any other person specified in subdivision (b) has ever been convicted of a crime other than a minor traffic violation or arrested for any crime specified in subdivision (c) of Section 290 of the Penal Code, or for violating Section 245, 273ab, or 273.5, subdivision (b) of Section 273a or, prior to January 1, 1994, paragraph (2) of Section 273a, of the Penal Code, or for any crime for which the department is prohibited from granting a criminal record exemption pursuant to subdivision (f).
(2) The criminal history information shall include the full criminal record, if any, of those persons, and subsequent arrest information pursuant to Section 11105.2 of the Penal Code.
(3) The following shall apply to the criminal record information:
(A) If the State Department of Social Services finds that the applicant or any other person specified in subdivision (b) has been convicted of a crime, other than a minor traffic violation, the application shall be denied, unless the director grants an exemption pursuant to subdivision (f).
(B) If the State Department of Social Services finds that the applicant, or any other person specified in subdivision (b), is awaiting trial for a crime other than a minor traffic violation, the State Department of Social Services may cease processing the criminal record information until the conclusion of the trial.
(C) If no criminal record information has been recorded, the Department of Justice shall provide the applicant and the State Department of Social Services with a statement of that fact.
(D) If the State Department of Social Services finds after licensure that the licensee, or any other person specified in paragraph (2) of subdivision (b), has been convicted of a crime other than a minor traffic violation, the license may be revoked, unless the director grants an exemption pursuant to subdivision (f).
(E) An applicant and any other person specified in subdivision (b) shall submit fingerprint images and related information to the Department of Justice and the Federal Bureau of Investigation, through the Department of Justice, for a state and federal level criminal offender record information search, in addition to the search required by subdivision (a). If an applicant meets all other conditions for licensure, except receipt of the Federal Bureau of Investigation's criminal history information for the applicant and persons listed in subdivision (b), the department may issue a license if the applicant and each person described by subdivision (b) has signed and submitted a statement that the person has never been convicted of a crime in the United States, other than a traffic infraction as defined in paragraph (1) of subdivision (a) of Section 42001 of the Vehicle Code. If, after licensure, the department determines that the licensee or person specified in subdivision (b) has a criminal record, the license may be revoked pursuant to Section 1596.885. The department may also suspend the license pending an administrative hearing pursuant to Section 1596.886.
(b) (1) In addition to the applicant, this section shall be applicable to criminal record clearances and exemptions for the following persons:
(A) Adults responsible for administration or direct supervision of staff.
(B) Any person, other than a child, residing in the facility.
(C) Any person who provides care and supervision to the children.
(D) Any staff person, volunteer, or employee who has contact with the children.

(i) A volunteer providing time-limited specialized services shall be exempt from the requirements of this subdivision if this person is directly supervised by the licensee or a facility employee with a criminal record clearance or exemption, the volunteer spends no more than 16 hours per week at the facility, and the volunteer is not left alone with children in care.

(ii) A student enrolled or participating at an accredited educational institution shall be exempt from the requirements of this subdivision if the student is directly supervised by the licensee or a facility employee with a criminal record clearance or exemption, the facility has an agreement with the educational institution concerning the placement of the student, the student spends no more than 16 hours per week at the facility, and the student is not left alone with children in care.

(iii) A volunteer who is a relative, legal guardian, or foster parent of a client in the facility shall be exempt from the requirements of this subdivision.

(iv) A contracted repair person retained by the facility, if not left alone with children in care, shall be exempt from the requirements of this subdivision.

(v) Any person similar to those described in this subdivision, as defined by the department in regulations.

(E) If the applicant is a firm, partnership, association, or corporation, the chief executive officer, other person serving in like capacity, or a person designated by the chief executive officer as responsible for the operation of the facility, as designated by the applicant agency.

(F) If the applicant is a local educational agency, the president of the governing board, the school district superintendent, or a person designated to administer the operation of the facility, as designated by the local educational agency.

(G) Additional officers of the governing body of the applicant, or other persons with a financial interest in the applicant, as determined necessary by the department by regulation. The criteria used in the development of these regulations shall be based on the person's capability to exercise substantial influence over the operation of the facility.

(H) This section does not apply to employees of childcare and development programs under contract with the State Department of Education who have completed a criminal record clearance as part of an application to the Commission on Teacher Credentialing, and who possess a current credential or permit issued by the commission, including employees of childcare and development programs that serve both children subsidized under, and children not subsidized under, a State Department of Education contract. The Commission on Teacher Credentialing shall notify the department upon revocation of a current credential or permit issued to an employee of a childcare and development program under contract with the State Department of Education.

(I) This section does not apply to employees of a childcare and development program operated by a school district, county office of education, or community college district under contract with the State Department of Education who have completed a criminal record clearance as a condition of employment. The school district, county office of education, or community college district upon receiving information that the status of an employee's criminal record clearance has changed shall submit that information to the department.

(2) Nothing in this subdivision shall prevent a licensee from requiring a criminal record clearance of any individuals exempt from the requirements under this subdivision.

(c) (1) (A) Subsequent to initial licensure, a person specified in subdivision (b) who is not exempt from fingerprinting shall obtain either a criminal record clearance or an exemption from disqualification, pursuant to subdivision (f), from the State Department of Social Services prior to employment, residence, or initial presence in the facility. A person specified in subdivision (b) who is not exempt from fingerprinting shall be fingerprinted and shall sign a declaration under penalty of perjury regarding any prior criminal convictions. The licensee shall submit fingerprint images and related information to the Department of Justice and the Federal Bureau of Investigation, through the Department of Justice, or comply with paragraph (1) of subdivision (h), prior to the person's employment, residence, or initial presence in the child day care facility.

(B) These fingerprint images and related information shall be electronically submitted to the Department of Justice in a manner approved by the State Department of Social Services and the Department of Justice for the purpose of obtaining a permanent set of fingerprints. A licensee's failure to submit fingerprint images and related information to the Department of Justice or to comply with paragraph (1) of subdivision (h), as required in this section, shall result in the citation of a deficiency, and an immediate assessment of civil penalties in the amount of one hundred dollars ($100) per violation per day for a maximum of five days, unless the violation is a second or subsequent violation within a 12-month period in which case the civil penalties shall be in the amount of one hundred dollars ($100) per violation for a maximum of 30 days, and shall be grounds for disciplining the licensee pursuant to Section 1596.885 or 1596.886. The State Department of Social Services may assess civil penalties for repeated or continued violations permitted by Sections 1596.99 and 1597.58. The fingerprint images and related information shall then be submitted to the department for processing. Within 14 calendar days of the receipt of the fingerprint images, the Department of Justice shall notify the State Department of Social Services of the criminal record information, as provided in this subdivision. If no criminal record information has been recorded, the Department of Justice shall provide the licensee and the State Department of Social Services with a statement of that fact within 14 calendar days of receipt of the fingerprint images. If new fingerprint images are required for processing, the Department of Justice shall, within 14 calendar days from the date of receipt of the fingerprint images, notify the licensee that the fingerprints were illegible.

(C) Documentation of the individual's clearance or exemption shall be maintained by the licensee, and shall be available for inspection. When live-scan technology is operational,

as defined in Section 1522.04, the Department of Justice shall notify the department, as required by that section, and notify the licensee by mail within 14 days of electronic transmission of the fingerprints to the Department of Justice, if the person has no criminal record. Any violation of the regulations adopted pursuant to Section 1522.04 shall result in the citation of a deficiency and an immediate assessment of civil penalties in the amount of one hundred dollars ($100) per violation per day for a maximum of five days, unless the violation is a second or subsequent violation within a 12-month period in which case the civil penalties shall be in the amount of one hundred dollars ($100) per violation for a maximum of 30 days, and shall be grounds for disciplining the licensee pursuant to Section 1596.885 or 1596.886. The department may assess civil penalties for repeated or continued violations, as permitted by Sections 1596.99 and 1597.58.

(2) Except for persons specified in paragraph (2) of subdivision (b), the licensee shall endeavor to ascertain the previous employment history of persons required to be fingerprinted under this subdivision. If it is determined by the department, on the basis of fingerprints submitted to the Department of Justice, that the person has been convicted of a sex offense against a minor, an offense specified in Section 243.4, 273a, 273ab, 273d, 273g, or 368 of the Penal Code, or a felony, the State Department of Social Services shall notify the licensee to act immediately to terminate the person's employment, remove the person from the child day care facility, or bar the person from entering the child day care facility. The department may subsequently grant an exemption pursuant to subdivision (f). If the conviction was for another crime except a minor traffic violation, the licensee shall, upon notification by the State Department of Social Services, act immediately to either (1) terminate the person's employment, remove the person from the child day care facility, or bar the person from entering the child day care facility; or (2) seek an exemption pursuant to subdivision (f). The department shall determine if the person shall be allowed to remain in the facility until a decision on the exemption is rendered. A licensee's failure to comply with the department's prohibition of employment, contact with clients, or presence in the facility as required by this paragraph shall result in a citation of deficiency and an immediate assessment of civil penalties by the department against the licensee, in the amount of one hundred dollars ($100) per violation per day for a maximum of five days, unless the violation is a second or subsequent violation within a 12-month period in which case the civil penalties shall be in the amount of one hundred dollars ($100) per violation for a maximum of 30 days, and shall be grounds for disciplining the licensee pursuant to Section 1596.885 or 1596.886.

(3) The department may issue an exemption on its own motion pursuant to subdivision (f) if the person's criminal history indicates that the person is of good character based on the age, seriousness, and frequency of the conviction or convictions. The department, in consultation with interested parties, shall develop regulations to establish the criteria to grant an exemption pursuant to this paragraph.

(4) Concurrently with notifying the licensee pursuant to paragraph (3), the department shall notify the affected individual of the right to seek an exemption pursuant to subdivision (f). The individual may seek an exemption only if the licensee terminates the person's employment or removes the person from the facility after receiving notice from the department pursuant to paragraph (3).

(d) (1) For purposes of this section or any other provision of this chapter, a conviction means a plea or verdict of guilty or a conviction following a plea of nolo contendere. Any action that the department is permitted to take following the establishment of a conviction may be taken when the time for appeal has elapsed, when the judgment of conviction has been affirmed on appeal, or when an order granting probation is made suspending the imposition of sentence, notwithstanding a subsequent order pursuant to Sections 1203.4 and 1203.4a of the Penal Code permitting the person to withdraw a plea of guilty and to enter a plea of not guilty, or setting aside the verdict of guilty, or dismissing the accusation, information, or indictment. For purposes of this section or any other provision of this chapter, the record of a conviction, or a copy thereof certified by the clerk of the court or by a judge of the court in which the conviction occurred, shall be conclusive evidence of the conviction. For purposes of this section or any other provision of this chapter, the arrest disposition report certified by the Department of Justice, or documents admissible in a criminal action pursuant to Section 969b of the Penal Code, shall be prima facie evidence of conviction, notwithstanding any other law prohibiting the admission of these documents in a civil or administrative action.

(2) For purposes of this section or any other provision of this chapter, the department shall consider criminal convictions from another state or federal court as if the criminal offense was committed in this state.

(e) (1) The State Department of Social Services shall not use a record of arrest to deny, revoke, or terminate any application, license, employment, or residence unless the department investigates the incident and secures evidence, whether or not related to the incident of arrest, that is admissible in an administrative hearing to establish conduct by the person that may pose a risk to the health and safety of any person who is or may become a client.

(2) The department shall not issue a criminal record clearance to a person who has been arrested for any crime specified in Section 290 of the Penal Code, or for violating Section 245, 273ab, or 273.5, or subdivision (b) of Section 273a of the Penal Code, or, prior to January 1, 1994, paragraph (2) of Section 273a of the Penal Code, or for any crime for which the department is prohibited from granting a criminal record exemption pursuant to subdivision (f), prior to the department's completion of an investigation pursuant to paragraph (1).

(3) The State Department of Social Services is authorized to obtain any arrest or conviction records or reports from any law enforcement agency as necessary to the performance of its duties to inspect, license, and investigate community care facilities and individuals associated with a community care facility.

(f) (1) After review of the record, the director may grant an exemption from disqualification for a license or special permit as specified in paragraphs (1) and (4) of subdivision (a), or for employment, residence, or presence in a child day care facility as specified in paragraphs (3), (4), and (5) of subdivision (c) if the director has substantial and convincing evidence to support a reasonable belief that the applicant and the person convicted of the crime, if other than the applicant, are of good character so as to justify issuance of the license or special permit or granting an exemption for purposes of subdivision (c). However, an exemption shall not be granted pursuant to this subdivision if the conviction was for any of the following offenses:

(A) An offense specified in Section 220, 243.4, or 264.1, subdivision (a) of Section 273a, or, prior to January 1, 1994, paragraph (1) of Section 273a, Section 273ab, 273d, 288, or 289, subdivision (c) of Section 290, or Section 368, of the Penal Code, or was a conviction of another crime against an individual specified in subdivision (c) of Section 667.5 of the Penal Code.

(B) A felony offense specified in Section 729 of the Business and Professions Code or Section 206 or 215, subdivision (a) of Section 347, subdivision (b) of Section 417, or subdivision (a) or (b) of Section 451 of the Penal Code.

(2) The department shall not prohibit a person from being employed or having contact with clients in a facility on the basis of a denied criminal record exemption request or arrest information unless the department complies with the requirements of Section 1596.8897.

(g) Upon request of the licensee, who shall enclose a self-addressed stamped postcard for this purpose, the Department of Justice shall verify receipt of the fingerprint images.

(h) (1) For the purposes of compliance with this section, the department may permit an individual to transfer a current criminal record clearance, as defined in subdivision (a), from one facility to another, as long as the criminal record clearance has been processed through a state licensing district office, and is being transferred to another facility licensed by a state licensing district office. The request shall be in writing to the department, and shall include a copy of the person's driver's license or valid identification card issued by the Department of Motor Vehicles, or a valid photo identification issued by another state or the United States government if the person is not a California resident. Upon request of the licensee, who shall enclose a self-addressed stamped envelope for this purpose, the department shall verify whether the individual has a clearance that can be transferred.

(2) The State Department of Social Services shall hold criminal record clearances in its active files for a minimum of two years after an employee is no longer employed at a licensed facility in order for the criminal record clearances to be transferred.

(3) The following shall apply to a criminal record clearance or exemption from the department or a county office with department-delegated licensing authority:

(A) A county office with department-delegated licensing authority may accept a clearance or exemption from the department.

(B) The department may accept a clearance or exemption from any county office with department-delegated licensing authority.

(C) A county office with department-delegated licensing authority may accept a clearance or exemption from any other county office with department-delegated licensing authority.

(4) With respect to notifications issued by the Department of Justice pursuant to Section 11105.2 of the Penal Code concerning an individual whose criminal record clearance was originally processed by the department or a county office with department-delegated licensing authority, all of the following shall apply:

(A) The Department of Justice shall process a request from the department or a county office with department-delegated licensing authority to receive the notice, only if all of the following conditions are met:

(i) The request shall be submitted to the Department of Justice by the agency to be substituted to receive the notification.

(ii) The request shall be for the same applicant type as the type for which the original clearance was obtained.

(iii) The request shall contain all prescribed data elements and format protocols pursuant to a written agreement between the department and the Department of Justice.

(B) (i) On or before January 7, 2005, the department shall notify the Department of Justice of all county offices that have department-delegated licensing authority.

(ii) The department shall notify the Department of Justice within 15 calendar days of the date on which a new county office receives department-delegated licensing authority or a county's delegated licensing authority is rescinded.

(C) The Department of Justice shall charge the department or a county office with department-delegated licensing authority a fee for each time a request to substitute the recipient agency is received for purposes of this paragraph. This fee shall not exceed the cost of providing the service.

(i) Notwithstanding any other law, the department may provide an individual with a copy of the individual's state or federal level criminal offender record information search response as provided to that department by the Department of Justice if the department has denied a criminal background clearance based on this information and the individual makes a written request to the department for a copy specifying an address to which it is to be sent. The state or federal level criminal offender record information search response shall not be modified or altered from its form or content as provided by the Department of Justice and shall be provided to the address specified by the individual in the individual's written request. The department shall retain a copy of the individual's written request and the response and date provided.

(j) The State Department of Social Services may charge a reasonable fee for the costs of processing electronic fingerprint images and related information.
(Amended by Stats. 2019, Ch. 27, Sec. 12. (SB 80) Effective June 27, 2019.)

1596.8712.

(a) (1) Whenever an individual is excluded by the department from a licensed family day care home, the department shall prepare and provide to the licensed family day care home from which the individual was excluded, within 45 days, an addendum to the notification of parents' rights form required by Section 102419 of Title 22 of the California Code of Regulations, clearly identifying the name or names of any individual or individuals who have been excluded from the licensed family day care home. The addendum shall also identify the existence and location of a public file maintained by the department explaining the reason for the exclusion.

(2) The department shall revise the addendum if the excluded individual is reinstated by the department pursuant to Section 11522 of the Government Code.

(b) (1) Immediately upon receipt of an addendum from the department, the licensee shall provide the parent or guardian of each child under the licensee's care or supervision with a copy of the addendum identifying the excluded individual or individuals. The licensee shall also obtain the signature of the parent or guardian indicating that the parent or guardian has received a copy of the addendum. A signed copy of the addendum shall be provided to the parent or guardian, and the original signed addendum shall be retained by the licensed day care home provider, and provided to the department during the regular inspection of the home, or at any time upon the request of the department.

(2) This section shall apply to all children currently under the licensee's care or supervision, and to all children who come under the licensee's care or supervision after the implementation of this section.

(c) During its regular inspection of all licensed family day care homes where an individual or individuals have been excluded, the department shall verify that the licensee has obtained a signature from the parent or guardian of each child under the licensee's care or supervision indicating that the parent or guardian has been provided with the addendum identifying the excluded individual or individuals. The department may also request the signed addenda from the licensee at any time.

(d) A licensee shall be assessed an immediate civil penalty of one hundred dollars ($100) per violation, for failure to do any of the following:

(1) Provide a copy of the addendum to a parent or guardian of any child under the provider's care or supervision.

(2) Obtain a parent or guardian's signature indicating he or she has been provided with the addendum.

(3) Provide signed addenda to the department, when requested for all children under the provider's care.

(e) Failure to comply with this section shall constitute grounds for disciplining the licensee pursuant to Section 1596.885 or Section 1596.886.

(f) This section shall apply to any family day care home from which an individual is excluded after January 1, 2001.

(g) The department shall promulgate regulations and policies, as necessary, to implement the provisions of this section by January 1, 2002.
(Added by Stats. 2000, Ch. 549, Sec. 2. Effective January 1, 2001.)

1596.8713.

(a) The Department of Justice may charge a fee sufficient to cover its costs in providing services in accordance with Section 1596.871 to comply with the 14-day requirement for provision to the department of the criminal record information, as contained in subdivision (c) of Section 1596.871.

(b) (1) Between July 1, 2000, and July 1, 2001, no fee shall be charged by the Department of Justice or the State Department of Social Services for any costs associated with obtaining a California or Federal Bureau of Investigation criminal record or for conducting a child abuse index check, of a volunteer at a child care facility who is required to be fingerprinted pursuant to subdivision (b) of Section 1596.871, provided that the exemption does not cause an increase in fees for other providers.

(2) On or after July 1, 2001, no fee shall be charged for the purposes specified in paragraph (1) if funds for those purposes are appropriated in the annual Budget Act and the exemption does not cause an increase in fees for other providers.

(3) For purposes of this subdivision, "volunteer" means a person who provides services at a child care facility and does not receive any payment of a salary or hourly wage in exchange for these services.
(Amended by Stats. 2000, Ch. 108, Sec. 12. Effective July 10, 2000.)

1596.8714.

On or before March 1, 2000, the State Department of Social Services shall convene a workgroup to review current criminal background check requirements and processes for screening care providers. The workgroup shall study and make recommendations concerning improving the coordination of the different populations who are required to undergo multiple criminal background checks, methods to reduce the costs, and expedite the process of conducting criminal background checks. The workgroup shall include representatives from the various departments within the California Health and Human Services Agency, the Department of Justice, the Child Care Resource and Referral Network, and care provider organizations.
(Added by Stats. 1999, Ch. 934, Sec. 2. Effective January 1, 2000.)

1596.8715.

If a licensee or facility is required by law to deny employment or to terminate employment of any employee based on written notification from the state department that the employee has a prior criminal conviction or is determined unsuitable for employment under Section 1596.8897, the licensee or facility shall not incur civil liability or unemployment insurance liability as a result of that denial or termination.
(Added by Stats. 1991, Ch. 888, Sec. 12.)

1596.8716.

(a) For licensing purposes, employees of a child care and development program operated by a school district, county office of education, or community college under contract with the State Department of Education pursuant to Chapter 2 (commencing with Section 8200) of Part 6 of the Education Code who have received a physical examination as a condition of employment with the district or office are not required to have a health screening as required by Section 101216 of Title 22 of the California Code of Regulations.

(b) For licensing purposes, a school principal of a public school that operates a child care and development program under contract with the State Department of Education pursuant to Article 7 (commencing with Section 8235) of Chapter 2 of Part 6 of the Education Code shall be deemed qualified to be a day care center director pursuant to Section 101315 of Title 22 of the California Code of Regulations only when the program is located on the campus of an operating public school, with staff who are employees of the public school.

(Amended by Stats. 1994, Ch. 252, Sec. 1. Effective January 1, 1995.)

1596.872a.

(a) The department may establish a child care advocate program. Each regional office, as well as the central office of the department, may have an advocate who has knowledge of state child care laws, regulations, and programs. The advocate's duties shall include, but not be limited to, all of the following:

(1) Providing information to the general public and parents on child care licensing standards and regulations.

(2) Serving as a liaison to local business, community, law enforcement, labor, and education groups, as well as child care providers and consumers, for the purpose of providing information about licensing standards and regulations.

(3) Disseminating information on the state's licensing role and activities, child care resource and referral agencies, and other child care programs.

(4) Acting as a liaison to child care resource and referral agencies to provide current information on licensing regulations, procedures, violations, revocations, and activities.

(5) Investigating and seeking to resolve complaints and concerns communicated on behalf of children served by a child day care facility. Complaints shall be handled in an objective manner to ascertain the pertinent facts. The ombudsman may refer any complaint to the appropriate state or local government agency.

(b) The advocate shall have access to child day care facilities and shall have the authority to speak with children and staff.

(c) The department shall report to the Legislature and the Governor, on December 31, 1985, and annually thereafter, the number of complaints resolved and referred and any related followup activities, and the number of facilities visited pursuant to subdivision (a).

(d) The department shall implement this section during periods that Section 1596.872b is not being implemented in accordance with Section 18285.5 of the Welfare and Institutions Code.

(Amended by Stats. 2004, Ch. 229, Sec. 10. Effective August 16, 2004.)

1596.872b.

(a) The department may establish a child care advocate program. This program may have one child care advocate for each licensing district regional office providing child care licensing services. A chief child care advocate shall be responsible for operations of the program and shall report to the chief of the child care licensing branch.

Each child care advocate shall have knowledge of state child care laws, regulations, and programs. The child care advocate's duties shall include, but not be limited to, all of the following:

(1) Providing information to the general public and parents on child care licensing standards and regulations.

(2) Serving as a liaison to local business, community, law enforcement, labor, and education groups, as well as child care providers and consumers, for the purpose of providing information about licensing standards and regulations.

(3) Disseminating information on the state's licensing role and activities, child care resource and referral agencies, and other child care programs.

(4) Acting as a liaison to child care resource and referral agencies to provide current information on licensing regulations, procedures, violations, revocations, and activities.

(5) Evaluating and seeking to resolve complaints and concerns communicated on behalf of children served by a child day care facility. Complaints shall be handled in an objective manner to ascertain the pertinent facts. The child care advocate may refer any complaint to the appropriate state or local government agency.

(6) Seeking to mediate disputes between the department and child care licensees, where licensees allege misapplication of licensing regulations and have exercised any initial appeal rights as specified in Section 1596.842.

(b) The child care advocate shall have access to child day care facilities and shall have the authority to speak with children and staff.

(c) The department may implement this section only to the extent funds are available in accordance with Section 18285.5 of the Welfare and Institutions Code.

(Amended by Stats. 2004, Ch. 229, Sec. 11. Effective August 16, 2004.)

1596.873.

The advisory committee established pursuant to Section 8286 of the Education Code shall perform all of the following functions with regard to this act:

(a) Assist the department in developing and reviewing guidelines for the administration of this act.

(b) Review the implementation of this act.

(c) Make written recommendations to the Legislature, the Governor, and the department by December 31, 1985, with regard to possible improvements to facilitate the implementation of this act.

(d) Advise the director regarding regulations, policy, and administrative practices pertaining to the licensing of child day care facilities.

(Amended by Stats. 1985, Ch. 1064, Sec. 19.)

1596.874.

(a) The State Department of Social Services shall furnish each licensed child day care facility with a notice that shall be posted at the facility where it can be easily seen by employees and consumers. The required notice shall contain information which does all of the following:

(1) Identifies the licensing agency and how licensing regulations may be obtained.

(2) Gives local telephone numbers where complaints may be made.

(3) Contains the nonretaliation provision in Section 1596.881.

(b) The licensee of the child day care facility shall make his or her copy of current licensing regulations available to employees and consumers.

(Amended by Stats. 1985, Ch. 1064, Sec. 20.)

1596.875.

To assure compliance with this act, the department shall:

(a) Conduct ongoing in-service programs for licensing staff in cooperation with other public entities and local associations.

(b) Conduct an annual seminar for representatives of enforcement agencies, including, but not limited to, police officers, district attorneys, and judges.

(c) Work with the Department of Justice to assure that license revocations appear on criminal records.

(Added by renumbering Section 1597.64 by Stats. 1984, Ch. 1615, Sec. 23.)

1596.876.

In any case in which a child day care facility releases a minor to a peace officer pursuant to Section 305 of the Welfare and Institutions Code, the official in charge of that facility shall provide the peace officer with the address and telephone number of the minor's parent or guardian in order to enable the peace officer to make the notification required by Section 308 of the Welfare and Institutions Code.

(Added by Stats. 1985, Ch. 811, Sec. 1.)

1596.877.

(a) Prior to granting a license to, or otherwise approving, any family day care home, the department shall check the child abuse and neglect complaint records of the child protective services agency of the county in which the applicant has resided for the two years preceding the application.

(b) Prior to granting a license to or otherwise approving any individual to care for children in either a family day care home or a day care center, the department shall check the Child Abuse Registry pursuant to paragraph (3) of subdivision (b) of Section 11170 of the Penal Code. The Department of Justice shall maintain and continually update an index of reports of child abuse by providers and shall inform the department of subsequent reports received from the child abuse index pursuant to Section 11170 of the Penal Code and the criminal history.

(c) The department shall investigate any reports received from the Child Abuse Registry and investigate any information received from the county child protective services agency. However, child protective services agency information arising from a report designated as "unfounded," as defined pursuant to subdivision (a) of Section 11165.12 of the Penal Code, shall not be included in the investigation. The investigation shall include, but not be limited to, the review of the investigation report and file prepared by the child protective services agency that investigated the child abuse report. The department shall not deny a license based upon a report from the Child Abuse Registry or based on child abuse and neglect complaint records of the county child protective services agency unless child abuse is substantiated.

(d) On and after January 1, 1993, the department shall implement this section for records maintained by counties that have automated their child abuse and neglect complaint records on or before January 1, 1993. On and after July 1, 1993, the department shall implement this section for records maintained by all counties.

(Amended by Stats. 1998, Ch. 311, Sec. 46. Effective August 19, 1998.)

1596.878.

The department shall establish, administer, and monitor programs which license child day care facilities consistent with the provisions of this act.

(Added by renumbering Section 1596.871 (as added by Stats. 1984, Ch. 1615, Sec. 12) by Stats. 1985, Ch. 1064, Sec. 17.)

1596.879.

Immediately upon the denial of any application for a license or for a special permit, the department shall notify the applicant in writing. Within 15 days after the department mails the notice, the applicant may present his or her written petition for a hearing to the department. Upon receipt by the department of the petition, the petition shall be set for hearing. The hearing shall be conducted in accordance with Chapter 5 (commencing with Section 11500) of Part 1 of Division 3 of Title 2 of the Government Code, and the department has all the powers granted in that chapter.

(Added by Stats. 1985, Ch. 1064, Sec. 20.5.)

ARTICLE 3. Remedies for Employer Discrimination [1596.880 - 1596.883]

(Article 3 added by Stats. 1984, Ch. 1615, Sec. 9.)

1596.880.

For the purposes of this article:

(a) "Employee" means employee of a licensee or employee of the agent of a licensee subject to this act.

(b) "Employer" means a licensee or agent of a licensee subject to this act.

(Amended by Stats. 1985, Ch. 1064, Sec. 21.)

1596.881.

No employer shall discharge, demote, or suspend, or threaten to discharge, demote, or suspend, or in any manner discriminate against any employee who takes any of the following actions:

(a) Makes any good faith oral or written complaint of the violation of any licensing or other laws by the employer to the State Department of Social Services or other agency having statutory responsibility for enforcement of the law or to the employer or representative of the employer.

(b) Institutes, or causes to be instituted, any proceeding against the employer in relation to the violation of any licensing or other laws.

(c) Is, or will be, a witness or testify in a proceeding in relation to the violation of any licensing or other laws.

(d) Refuses to perform work in violation of a licensing law or regulation after notifying the employer of the violation.

Employees shall be notified in writing at the time of employment of their rights under this chapter, as evidenced by their signature on a notification form outlining actions protected by this section. Forms to be utilized for this purpose shall be kept on file at the facility. The department shall provide each facility with the notification forms, which shall include information regarding enforcement pursuant to relevant Labor Code sections.

"Other laws" for the purposes of this section, includes, but is not limited to, laws relating to staff-child ratios, transportation of children, or child abuse.

(Amended by Stats. 1987, Ch. 489, Sec. 1.)
1596.882.

(a) A claim by the employee alleging the violation by the employer of Section 1596.881 shall be presented to the employer within 45 days after the action as to which complaint is made and presented to the Division of Labor Standards Enforcement not later than 90 days after the action as to which complaint is made.

(b) Upon receipt of the complaint, the Division of Labor Standards Enforcement shall cause whatever investigation to be made as it deems appropriate.

(c) If upon investigation the Division of Labor Standards Enforcement determines that the employer has violated Section 1596.881, it shall bring an action in any appropriate court against the employer.

(d) In any such action, the court shall have jurisdiction, for cause shown, to issue restraining orders and order all appropriate relief, including rehiring and reinstatement of the employee of his or her former position with backpay and benefits.

(e) Within 30 days of the receipt of a complaint pursuant to this section, the Division of Labor Standards Enforcement shall review the facts of the employee's complaint and either set a hearing date or notify the employee and the employer of its decision. Where necessary, the Division of Labor Standards Enforcement shall begin the appropriate court action to enforce the decision.

(f) Except for any grievance procedure or arbitration or hearing that is available to the employee pursuant to a collective bargaining agreement, this section is the exclusive means for presenting claims under this article.

(Amended by Stats. 1987, Ch. 489, Sec. 2.)
1596.883.

Any employer who willfully refuses to rehire, promote, or otherwise restore an employee or former employee who has been determined to be eligible for the rehiring or promotion by a grievance procedure, arbitration, or hearing authorized by law, is guilty of a misdemeanor.

(Added by Stats. 1984, Ch. 1615, Sec. 9.)

ARTICLE 4. Suspension and Revocation [1596.885 - 1596.8895]
(Article 4 added by Stats. 1984, Ch. 1615, Sec. 9.)
1596.885.

The department may deny an application for or suspend or revoke any license, registration, or special permit issued under this act upon any of the following grounds and in the manner provided in this act:

(a) Violation by the licensee, registrant, or holder of a special permit of this act or of the rules and regulations promulgated under this act.

(b) Aiding, abetting, or permitting the violating of this act or of the rules and regulations promulgated under this act.

(c) Conduct which is inimical to the health, morals, welfare, or safety of either an individual in or receiving services from the facility or the people of this state.

(d) The conviction of a licensee, or other person specified in Section 1596.871, at any time before or during licensure, of a crime as defined in Section 1596.871.

(e) Engaging in acts of financial malfeasance concerning the operation of a facility, including, but not limited to, improper use or embezzlement of client moneys and property or fraudulent appropriation for personal gain of facility moneys and property, or willful or negligent failure to provide services for the care of clients.

(Amended by Stats. 1998, Ch. 311, Sec. 47. Effective August 19, 1998.)
1596.886.

The director may temporarily suspend any license, registration, or special permit prior to any hearing when, in the opinion of the director, the action is necessary to protect any child of a child day care facility from physical or mental abuse, abandonment, or any other substantial threat to health or safety. The director shall notify the licensee, registrant, or holder of the special permit of the temporary suspension and the effective date thereof and at the same time shall serve the provider with an accusation. Upon receipt of a notice of defense to the accusation by the licensee, registrant, or holder of the special permit, the director shall, within 15 days, set the matter for hearing, and the hearing shall be held as soon as possible but not later than 30 days after receipt of the notice. The temporary suspension shall remain in effect until such time as the hearing is completed and the director has made a final determination on the merits. However, the temporary

suspension shall be deemed vacated if the director fails to make a final determination on the merits within 30 days after the original hearing has been completed.

(Amended by Stats. 1985, Ch. 1, Sec. 1. Effective December 10, 1984.)
1596.8865.

(a) When a local child protective agency, as defined in Section 11165 of the Penal Code, has a reasonable suspicion, as defined in subdivision (a) of Section 11166 of the Penal Code, that the death or serious injury of a child occurred at a child day care facility because of abuse or willful neglect by the personnel of the child day care facility, the agency shall immediately notify the director.

(b) Within two working days of receipt of the evidence that the death or serious injury occurred at a child day care facility because of abuse or willful neglect by the personnel of the child day care facility, the department shall temporarily suspend the license, registration, or special permit of the facility, and shall immediately notify the licensee, registrant, or holder of the special permit of the temporary suspension and the effective date thereof and at the same time serve the provider with an accusation. The hearing shall be set and conducted in the manner provided in Section 1596.886, and the temporary suspension shall have the same effect and duration as provided in Section 1596.886.

(c) The director shall request that the city police, county sheriff, or other law enforcement agencies, and any other county agencies, investigating the death or serious injury of the child shall expedite and coordinate evidence gathering in the case, and, to the extent that providing the evidence will not adversely affect any criminal prosecution, make that evidence available as soon as possible for the purposes of the hearing on the temporary suspension.

(d) As used in this section, "serious injury" means a serious impairment of physical condition, including, but not limited to, the following: loss of consciousness; concussion; bone fracture; protracted loss or impairment of function of any bodily member or organ; a wound requiring extensive suturing; and serious disfigurement.

(Amended by Stats. 2006, Ch. 538, Sec. 364. Effective January 1, 2007.)
1596.8866.

The State Department of Social Services shall reopen an investigation into a licensed child day care facility when any person provides the department with a certified copy of a court record in which a judicial officer has determined that an injury to a child may have been inflicted while in the care and custody of a day care provider.

(Amended by Stats. 2002, Ch. 353, Sec. 1. Effective January 1, 2003.)
1596.8867.

(a) The department shall conduct an unannounced visit to a facility within 30 days after the effective date of a temporary suspension of a license, in order to ensure that the facility is nonoperational, unless the department has previously verified that the facility is nonoperational.

(b) The department shall conduct an unannounced visit to a facility within 30 days after the effective date of a revocation of a license in order to ensure that the facility is nonoperational, unless the department has previously verified that the facility is nonoperational.

(Added by Stats. 2008, Ch. 291, Sec. 20. Effective September 25, 2008.)
1596.887.

(a) Proceedings for the suspension, revocation, or denial of a license, registration, or special permit under this chapter shall be conducted in accordance with Chapter 5 (commencing with Section 11500) of Part 1 of Division 3 of Title 2 of the Government Code, and the department shall have all the powers granted by that chapter. In the event of conflict between the provisions of this chapter and those provisions of the Government Code, the provisions of the Government Code shall prevail.

(b) In all proceedings conducted in accordance with this section, the standard of proof to be applied shall be by the preponderance of the evidence.

(c) If the license is not temporarily suspended pursuant to Section 1596.8865, the hearing shall be held within 90 days after receipt of the notice of defense, unless a continuance of the hearing is granted by the department or the administrative law judge. When the matter has been set for hearing, only the administrative law judge may grant a continuance of the hearing. The administrative law judge may, but need not, grant a continuance of the hearing, only upon finding the existence of one or more of the following:

(1) The death or incapacitating illness of a party, a representative or attorney of a party, a witness to an essential fact, or of the parent, child, or member of the household of such person, when it is not feasible to substitute another representative, attorney, or witness because of the proximity of the hearing date.

(2) Lack of notice of hearing as provided in Section 11509 of the Government Code.

(3) A material change in the status of the case where a change in the parties or pleadings requires postponement, or an executed settlement or stipulated findings of fact obviate the need for hearing. A partial amendment of the pleadings shall not be good cause for continuance to the extent that the unamended portion of the pleadings is ready to be heard.

(4) A stipulation for continuance signed by all parties or their authorized representatives, including, but not limited to, a representative, which is communicated with the request for continuance to the administrative law judge no later than 25 business days before the hearing.

(5) The substitution of the representative or attorney of a party upon showing that the substitution is required.

(6) The unavailability of a party, representative, or attorney of a party, or witness to an essential fact due to a conflicting and required appearance in a judicial matter if when the hearing date was set, the person did not know and could neither anticipate nor at any

time avoid the conflict, and the conflict with request for continuance is immediately communicated to the administrative law judge.

(7) The unavailability of a party, a representative or attorney of a party, or a material witness due to an unavoidable emergency.

(8) Failure by a party to comply with a timely discovery request if the continuance request is made by the party who requested the discovery.

(Amended by Stats. 1992, Ch. 1315, Sec. 27. Effective January 1, 1993.)
1596.8871.

(a) The administrative law judge conducting a hearing under this article may permit the testimony of a child witness, or a similarly vulnerable witness, including a witness who is developmentally disabled, to be taken outside the presence of the respondent or respondents if all of the following conditions exist:

(1) The administrative law judge determines that taking the witness's testimony outside the presence of the respondent or respondents is necessary to ensure truthful testimony.

(2) The witness is likely to be intimidated by the presence of the respondent or respondents.

(3) The witness is afraid to testify in front of the respondent or respondents.

(b) If the testimony of the witness is taken outside of the presence of the respondent or respondents, the department shall provide for the use of one-way closed-circuit television so the respondent or respondents can observe the testimony of the witness. Nothing in this section shall limit a respondent's right of cross-examination.

(c) The administrative law judge conducting a hearing under this section may clear the hearing room of any persons who are not a party to the action in order to protect any witness from intimidation or other harm, taking into account the rights of all persons.

(Added by Stats. 1994, Ch. 1267, Sec. 10. Effective January 1, 1995.)
1596.8872.

(a) (1) An out-of-court statement made by a minor under 12 years of age who is the subject or victim of an allegation at issue is admissible evidence at an administrative hearing conducted pursuant to this article. The out-of-court statement may be used to support a finding of fact unless an objection is timely made and the objecting party establishes that the statement is unreliable because it was the product of fraud, deceit, or undue influence. However, the out-of-court statement may not be the sole basis for the finding of fact, unless the adjudicator finds that the time, content, and circumstances of the statement provide sufficient indicia of reliability.

(2) The proponent of the statement shall give reasonable notice to all parties of the intended introduction of the statement at the hearing.

(3) For purposes of this subdivision, an objection is timely if it identifies with reasonable specificity the disputed out-of-court statement and it gives the proponent of the evidence a reasonable period of time to prepare a response to the objection prior to the hearing.

(b) This section shall not be construed to limit the right of any party to the administrative hearing to subpoena a witness whose statement is admitted as evidence or to introduce admissible evidence relevant to the weight of the hearsay evidence or the credibility of the hearsay declarant.

(Added by Stats. 2002, Ch. 707, Sec. 4. Effective January 1, 2003.)
1596.8875.

In addition to the witness fees and mileage provided by Section 11450.40 of the Government Code, the department may pay actual, necessary, and reasonable expenses in an amount not to exceed the per diem allowance payable to a nonrepresented state employee on travel status. The department may pay witness expenses pursuant to this section in advance of the hearing.

(Amended by Stats. 1995, Ch. 938, Sec. 63. Effective January 1, 1996. Operative July 1, 1997, by Sec. 98 of Ch. 938.)
1596.888.

Any license, registration, or special permit suspended pursuant to this chapter, and any special permit revoked pursuant to this chapter, may be reinstated pursuant to Section 11522 of the Government Code.

(Added by Stats. 1984, Ch. 1615, Sec. 9.)
1596.889.

In all proceedings conducted in accordance with Section 1596.887, the preponderance of the evidence standard shall apply.

(Added by Stats. 1985, Ch. 1528, Sec. 1.)
1596.8895.

(a) Whenever the director temporarily suspends the license, registration, or special permit of a child day care facility pursuant to Section 1596.886, the director or the local licensing agency shall send written notification to the parent or legal guardian of each child receiving services in the facility. The department or the local licensing agency, if there is one, shall also post a written notice of the temporary suspension at the facility in a place readily visible and accessible to the parents or guardians of children receiving services at the facility. Removal of the posted notice while the temporary suspension is in effect is a violation of this chapter punishable by a fine of five hundred dollars ($500).

(b) If a temporary suspension order is not effected within 30 days of the filing of an accusation, the director or the local licensing agency shall send written notification that the accusation has been filed to the parent or legal guardian of each child receiving services in the facility.

(c) (1) Upon receipt of an accusation indicating the department's intent to revoke a facility's license, the licensee shall provide copies of a summary of the accusation to the parent or legal guardian of each child receiving services in the facility until that accusation is either dismissed or resolved through the administrative hearing process or stipulated agreement.

(2) Upon enrollment of a new child in a facility, the licensee shall provide to the parents or legal guardians of the newly enrolling child copies of a summary of any accusation that the licensee has received during the prior 12-month period that indicates the department's intent to revoke the facility's license.

(3) The licensee shall require each recipient of the summary of the accusation to sign a statement indicating that he or she has received the document and the date it was received.

(4) The licensee shall keep verification of receipt in each child's file.

(5) The department shall prepare and provide to the licensee the summary of the accusation.

(Amended by Stats. 2006, Ch. 545, Sec. 4. Effective January 1, 2007.)

ARTICLE 4.5. Employee Actions [1596.8897 - 1596.8899]

(Article 4.5 added by Stats. 1989, Ch. 825, Sec. 3.)
1596.8897.

(a) The department may prohibit any person from being a member of the board of directors, an executive director, or an officer of a licensee or a licensee from employing, or continuing the employment of, or allowing in a licensed facility, or allowing contact with clients of a licensed facility by, any employee, prospective employee, or person who is not a client who has:

(1) Violated, or aided or permitted the violation by any other person of, any provisions of this chapter or of any rules or regulations promulgated under this chapter.

(2) Engaged in conduct that is inimical to the health, morals, welfare, or safety of either an individual in or receiving services from the facility, or the people of the State of California.

(3) Been denied an exemption to work or to be present in a facility, when that person has been convicted of a crime as defined in Section 1596.871.

(4) Engaged in any other conduct that would constitute a basis for disciplining a licensee.

(5) Engaged in acts of financial malfeasance concerning the operation of a facility, including, but not limited to, improper use or embezzlement of client moneys and property or fraudulent appropriation for personal gain of facility moneys and property, or willful or negligent failure to provide services for the care of clients.

(b) The excluded person, the facility, and the licensee shall be given written notice of the basis of the department's action and of the excluded person's right to an appeal. The notice shall be served either by personal service or by registered mail. Within 15 days after the department serves the notice, the excluded person may file with the department a written appeal of the exclusion order. If the excluded person fails to file a written appeal within the prescribed time, the department's action shall be final.

(c) (1) The department may require the immediate removal of a member of the board of directors, an executive director, or an officer of a licensee or exclusion of an employee, prospective employee, or person who is not a client from a facility pending a final decision of the matter, when, in the opinion of the department, the action is necessary to protect residents or clients from physical or mental abuse, abandonment, or any other substantial threat to their health or safety.

(2) If the department requires the immediate removal of a member of the board of directors, an executive director, or an officer of a licensee or exclusion of an employee, prospective employee, or person who is not a client from a facility, the department shall serve an order of immediate exclusion upon the excluded person that shall notify the excluded person of the basis of the department's action and of the excluded person's right to a hearing.

(3) Within 15 days after the department serves an order of immediate exclusion, the excluded person may file a written appeal of the exclusion with the department. The department's action shall be final if the excluded person does not appeal the exclusion within the prescribed time. The department shall do the following upon receipt of a written appeal:

(A) Within 30 days of receipt of the appeal, serve an accusation upon the excluded person.

(B) Within 60 days of receipt of a notice of defense by the employee or prospective employee pursuant to Section 11506 of the Government Code, conduct a hearing on the accusation.

(4) An order of immediate exclusion of the excluded person from the facility shall remain in effect until the hearing is completed and the department has made a final determination on the merits. However, the order of immediate exclusion shall be deemed vacated if the department fails to make a final determination on the merits within 60 days after the original hearing has been completed.

(d) An excluded person who files a written appeal of the exclusion order with the department pursuant to this section shall, as part of the written request, provide his or her current mailing address. The excluded person shall subsequently notify the department in writing of any change in mailing address, until the hearing process has been completed or terminated.

(e) Hearings held pursuant to this section shall be conducted in accordance with Chapter 5 (commencing with Section 11500) of Division 3 of Title 2 of the Government Code. The standard of proof shall be the preponderance of the evidence and the burden of proof shall be on the department.

(f) The department may institute or continue a disciplinary proceeding against a member of the board of directors, an executive director, or an officer of a licensee or an employee, prospective employee, or person who is not a client upon any ground provided by this section. The department may enter an order prohibiting any person from being a member of the board of directors, the executive director, or an officer of a licensee prohibiting the excluded person's employment or presence in the facility, or otherwise take disciplinary action against the excluded person, notwithstanding any resignation, withdrawal of employment application, or change of duties by the excluded person, or any discharge, failure to hire, or reassignment of the excluded person by the licensee or that the excluded person no longer has contact with clients at the facility.

(g) A licensee's failure to comply with the department's exclusion order after being notified of the order shall be grounds for disciplining the licensee pursuant to Section 1596.885 or 1596.886.

(h) (1) (A) In cases in which the excluded person appealed the exclusion order and there is a decision and order upholding the exclusion order, the person shall be prohibited from working in any facility or being licensed to operate any facility licensed by the department or from being a certified foster parent or resource family for the remainder of the excluded person's life, unless otherwise ordered by the department.

(B) The excluded individual may petition for reinstatement one year after the effective date of the decision and order of the department upholding the exclusion order pursuant to Section 11522 of the Government Code. The department shall provide the excluded person with a copy of Section 11522 of the Government Code with the decision and order.

(2) (A) In cases in which the department informed the excluded person of his or her right to appeal the exclusion order and the excluded person did not appeal the exclusion order, the person shall be prohibited from working in any facility or being licensed to operate any facility licensed by the department or a certified foster parent or resource family for the remainder of the excluded person's life, unless otherwise ordered by the department.

(B) The excluded individual may petition for reinstatement after one year has elapsed from the date of the notification of the exclusion order pursuant to Section 11522 of the Government Code. The department shall provide the excluded person with a copy of Section 11522 of the Government Code with the exclusion order.

(Amended by Stats. 2017, Ch. 732, Sec. 38. (AB 404) Effective January 1, 2018.)
1596.8898.

(a) (1) If the department determines that a person was issued a license under this chapter or under Chapter 1 (commencing with Section 1200), Chapter 2 (commencing with Section 1250), Chapter 3.01 (commencing with Section 1568.01), Chapter 3.2 (commencing with Section 1569), Chapter 3.4 (commencing with Section 1596.70), Chapter 3.5 (commencing with Section 1596.90), or Chapter 3.6 (commencing with Section 1597.30) and the prior license was revoked within the preceding two years, the department shall exclude the person from, and remove the person from the position of a member of the board of directors, the executive director, or an officer of a licensee of, any facility licensed by the department pursuant to the chapter.

(2) If the department determines that a person previously was issued a certificate of approval by a foster family agency which was revoked by the department pursuant to subdivision (b) of Section 1534 within the preceding two years, the department shall exclude the person from, and remove the person from the position of a member of the board of directors, the executive director, or an officer of a licensee of, any facility licensed by the department pursuant to this chapter.

(b) If the department determines that the person had previously applied for a license under any of the chapters listed in paragraph (1) of subdivision (a) and the application was denied within the last year, the department shall exclude the person from, and remove the person from the position of a member of the board of directors, the executive director, or an officer of a licensee of, any facility licensed by the department pursuant to this chapter and as follows:

(1) In cases where the applicant petitioned for a hearing, the department shall exclude the person from, and remove the person from the position of a member of the board of directors, the executive director, or an officer of a licensee of, any facility licensed by the department pursuant to this chapter until one year has elapsed from the effective date of the decision and order of the department upholding a denial.

(2) In cases where the department informed the applicant of his or her right to petition for a hearing and the applicant did not petition for a hearing, the department shall exclude the person from, and remove the person from the position of a member of the board of directors, the executive director, or an officer of a licensee of, any facility licensed by the department pursuant to this chapter until one year has elapsed from the date of the notification of the denial and the right to petition for a hearing.

(c) If the department determines that the person had previously applied for a certificate of approval with a foster family agency and the department ordered the foster family agency to deny the application pursuant to subdivision (b) of Section 1534, the department shall exclude the person from, and remove the person from the position of a member of the board of directors, the executive director, or an officer of a licensee of, any facility licensed by the department pursuant to this chapter and as follows:

(1) In cases where the applicant petitioned for a hearing, the department shall exclude the person from, and remove the person from the position of a member of the board of directors, the executive director, or an officer of a licensee of, any facility licensed by the department pursuant to this chapter until one year has elapsed from the effective date of the decision and order of the department upholding a denial.

(2) In cases where the department informed the applicant of his or her right to petition for a hearing and the applicant did not petition for a hearing, the department shall exclude the person from, and remove the person from the position of a member of the board of directors, the executive director, or an officer of a licensee of, any facility licensed by the department pursuant to this chapter until one year has elapsed from the date of the notification of the denial and the right to petition for a hearing.

(d) Exclusion or removal of an individual pursuant to this section shall not be considered an order of exclusion for purposes of Section 1598.8897 or any other law.

(e) The department may determine not to exclude a person from, or remove him or her from the position of, a member of the board of directors, the executive director, or an officer of a licensee of, any facility licensed by the department pursuant to this chapter if it has been determined that the reasons for the denial of the application or revocation of the facility license or certificate of approval were due to circumstances or conditions that either have been corrected or are no longer in existence.

(Amended by Stats. 1998, Ch. 311, Sec. 49. Effective August 19, 1998.)
1596.8899.

The department shall conduct an unannounced visit to a facility within 30 days after the department serves an order of immediate exclusion from the facility upon the licensee or a person subject to immediate removal or exclusion from the facility pursuant to paragraph (2) of subdivision (c) of Section 1596.871 or subdivision (c) of Section 1596.8897 in order to ensure that the excluded person is not within the facility, unless the department previously has verified that the excluded person is not within the facility.

(Added by Stats. 2008, Ch. 291, Sec. 21. Effective September 25, 2008.)

ARTICLE 5. Offenses [1596.89 - 1596.895]
(Article 5 added by Stats. 1984, Ch. 1615, Sec. 9.)
1596.89.

The director may bring an action to enjoin the violation or threatened violation of Section 1596.80 or 1596.805 in the superior court in and for the county in which the violation occurred or is about to occur. Any proceeding under this section shall conform to the requirements of Chapter 3 (commencing with Section 525) of Title 7 of Part 2 of the Code of Civil Procedure, except that the director shall not be required to allege facts necessary to show or tending to show lack of adequate remedy at law or irreparable damage or loss. Upon a finding by the director that the violation threatens the health or safety of any child in, or served by, a child day care facility, the department or agency contracted with may bring an action to enjoin the violation, threatened violation, or continued violation by any child day care facility which is located in an area for which it is responsible pursuant to the terms of the contract.

With respect to any and all actions brought pursuant to this section alleging actual violation of Section 1596.80 or 1596.805, the court shall, if it finds such allegations to be true, issue its order enjoining the child day care facility from continuance of the violation. This section applies to family day care homes when the provider has failed to comply with Section 1596.80 or 1596.805 within 30 days of notice by the director of noncompliance, or at any time when a threat to the health and safety of children exists.

(Amended by Stats. 1985, Ch. 1064, Sec. 22.)
1596.890.

(a) Any person who willfully or repeatedly violates any provision of this chapter, or any rule or regulation promulgated under this chapter is guilty of a misdemeanor. Upon conviction thereof, such a person shall be punished by a fine not to exceed one thousand dollars ($1,000) or by imprisonment in the county jail for a period not to exceed 180 days, or by both the fine and imprisonment. The operation of a child day care facility without a license issued pursuant to this chapter shall make the owner or operator, or both, subject to a summons to appear in court.

(b) Notwithstanding subdivision (a) or any other provision of law, the sole sanction for failure of a resources and referral agency or an alternative payment program to comply with paragraph (2) of subdivision (a) of Section 1596.859 shall be set forth in the "Funding Terms and Conditions" agreement between the affected agency or program and the State Department of Education.

(Amended by Stats. 1999, Ch. 823, Sec. 8. Effective January 1, 2000.)
1596.891.

(a) A person who violates Section 1596.80 may be liable for an immediate assessment of civil penalties in the amount of two hundred dollars ($200) per day.

(b) The penalty specified in subdivision (a) shall be imposed if the operator of an unlicensed facility refuses to seek licensure or the operator seeks licensure and is denied but continues to operate, unless other remedies available to the department, including criminal prosecution, are deemed more effective by the department.

(c) The operator may appeal the assessment to the director. The department shall adopt regulations setting forth the appeals procedure.

(d) The operator shall be exempt from the civil penalty specified in subdivision (a) if a lack of liability insurance is the sole reason for nonlicensure and the reason for operating without liability insurance is not due to any fault on the part of the operator.

(Amended by Stats. 1990, Ch. 1488, Sec. 4.)
1596.8915.

Any person who, without lawful authorization from a duly authorized officer, employee, or agent of the department, informs an owner, operator, employee, or agent of a child day care facility of an impending and unannounced site visit to that facility by personnel of the department, is guilty of a misdemeanor and upon conviction thereof shall be punished by a fine not to exceed one thousand dollars ($1,000), by imprisonment in the county jail for a period not to exceed 180 days, or by both a fine and imprisonment.

(Amended by Stats. 1991, Ch. 888, Sec. 13.)
1596.892.

The civil, criminal, and administrative remedies available to the department pursuant to this article are not exclusive, and may be sought and employed in any combination deemed advisable by the department to enforce the provisions of this chapter.

(Added by Stats. 1985, Ch. 1110, Sec. 3.)
1596.893a.

(a) When the licensing agency has reason to believe that an unlicensed day care facility is operating or that a day care facility is in violation of the California Child Day Care Facilities Act or of the rules and regulations promulgated under the California Child Day

Care Facilities Act, the agency may issue a citation to the facility. Each citation shall be in writing and shall describe with particularity the nature of the violation and the action proposed by the licensing agency. If the citation has been developed pursuant to an evaluator visit, the citation shall include the plan developed by the operator and evaluator to correct each deficiency. The citation shall be served upon the facility operator personally or through registered mail.

(b) The licensing agency shall give due consideration to the appropriateness of the penalty to the alleged violation, considering each of the following factors:

(1) The gravity of the violation.

(2) The history of previous violations.

(3) The possibility of a threat to the health or safety of any child in the facility.

(4) The number of children affected by the violation.

(5) The availability of equipment or personnel necessary to correct the violation, if appropriate.

(c) If the facility desires to contest a citation or the proposed assessment of a civil penalty, the facility shall, within 10 business days after service of the citation, notify the licensing agency in writing of a request for an informal conference. The licensing agency shall hold, within 30 days from the receipt of the request, an informal conference. At the conclusion of the conference, the licensing agency may affirm, modify, or dismiss the citation or proposed penalty. The agency shall state in writing the reasons for any action taken in the informal conference.

(d) If the penalty contained in the citation is affirmed in the informal conference, the licensing agency shall pursue enforcement of the penalty, and the facility may pursue any appeal mechanisms otherwise contained in law.

(e) The department shall implement this section during periods that Section 1596.893b is not being implemented in accordance with Section 18285.5 of the Welfare and Institutions Code.

(Added by Stats. 1993, Ch. 726, Sec. 4. Effective October 4, 1993.)

1596.893b.

(a) When the licensing agency has reason to believe that an unlicensed day care facility is operating or that a day care facility is in violation of the California Child Day Care Facilities Act or of the rules and regulations promulgated under the California Child Day Care Facilities Act, the agency may issue a citation to, or impose penalties on, the facility. Each citation shall be in writing and shall describe with particularity the nature of the violation and the action proposed by the licensing agency. If the citation has been developed pursuant to an evaluator visit, the citation shall include the plan developed by the operator and evaluator to correct each deficiency. The citation shall be served upon the facility operator personally or through registered mail. Citations and penalties of licensed child care facilities shall be applied for the sole purpose of ensuring compliance with established statutes or regulations. The department shall distinguish between all of the following:

(1) Violations that present an immediate risk to the health, safety, or personal rights of the children in care.

(2) Violations that have the potential of becoming an immediate risk to the health, safety, or personal rights of the children in care.

(3) Violations that do not present an immediate or potential risk to the health, safety, or personal rights of the children in care.

(b) Civil penalties shall be imposed in accordance with Sections 1596.99 and 1597.62 only after the day care licensee fails to correct the violation in the time period specified in the plan developed pursuant to Section 1596.98 or 1597.56 and the evaluator makes a finding that the violation presents risks identified in paragraph (1) or (2) of subdivision (a). Civil penalties shall begin to accrue on the day the evaluator revisits the site and verifies that the violation was not corrected, even if the evaluator's visit is after the time period specified in the plan.

(c) The department shall adopt regulations establishing procedures for the imposition of citations or civil penalties under this section.

(d) The department shall implement this section only to the extent funds are available in accordance with Section 18285.5 of the Welfare and Institutions Code.

(Added by renumbering Section 1596.893 (as amended by Stats. 1992, Ch. 1316) by Stats. 1993, Ch. 726, Sec. 5. Effective October 4, 1993.)

1596.893c.

(a) The department shall consider, in determining whether to issue a citation or impose a civil penalty under any provision of this chapter to a child day care facility that contracts with the State Department of Education, whether the child day care facility is in the process of complying with Section 8239.1 of the Education Code.

(b) This section shall apply only to a California state preschool program described in Article 7 (commencing with Section 8235) of Chapter 2 of Part 6 of Division 1 of Title 1 of the Education Code.

(Added by Stats. 2017, Ch. 708, Sec. 3. (AB 752) Effective January 1, 2018.)

1596.894.

Any action brought by the department against an unlicensed child day care facility shall not abate by reason of sale or other transfer of ownership of the child day care facility which is a party to the action except with the written consent of the licensing agency.

(Added by renumbering Section 1596.891 (as added by Stats. 1985, Ch. 1064) by Stats. 1988, Ch. 160, Sec. 96.)

1596.895.

(a) The department shall notify resource and referral agencies funded pursuant to Section 8210 of the Education Code of any priority one violation or any allegation of a priority one violation affecting the health and safety of children that is within the geographic area served by the agency. Resource and referral agencies shall use this

information when deciding whether to make a referral to the licensee and shall maintain the confidentiality of information provided to them pursuant to this section.

(b) The Child Care Regulation Section shall notify these resource and referral agencies of the department's actions regarding these allegations of priority one violations within 30 days. The Child Care Regulation Section shall notify these resource and referral agencies of the department's actions regarding these allegations of priority one violations within 10 days after the allegations have been substantiated by the department.

(c) "Priority one violation" is defined to include sexual assault, physical abuse, ritualistic abuse, or suspicious deaths, if any of the following apply:

(1) The victim is a child in care and the suspect is the facility operator, the licensee, an employee of the facility, or is yet to be identified as any of the individuals specified in this paragraph.

(2) The facility is operating and the suspect has access to the victim or potential victim.

(3) The complaint is against an unlicensed facility and either a temporary suspension order is in effect or the license has been revoked.

(d) "Allegation of a priority one violation" is defined to include any complaints of priority one violations pursuant to subdivision (c).

(e) The department shall implement this section only to the extent funds are available in accordance with Section 18285.5 of the Welfare and Institutions Code.

(Amended by Stats. 1993, Ch. 726, Sec. 6. Effective October 4, 1993.)

CHAPTER 3.5. Day Care Centers [1596.90 - 1597.21]

(Chapter 3.5 added by Stats. 1984, Ch. 1615, Sec. 10.)

ARTICLE 1. General Provisions [1596.90- 1596.90.]

(Article 1 added by Stats. 1984, Ch. 1615, Sec. 10.)

1596.90.

No day care center for children shall be licensed under Chapter 3 (commencing with Section 1500), but shall be subject to licensure exclusively in accordance with this chapter and Chapter 3.4 (commencing with Section 1596.70).

(Added by Stats. 1984, Ch. 1615, Sec. 10.)

ARTICLE 2. Licensure Requirements [1596.95 - 1596.99]

(Article 2 added by Stats. 1984, Ch. 1615, Sec. 10.)

1596.95.

Any person desiring issuance of a license for a day care center or a special permit for specialized services in a day care center under this chapter shall file with the department pursuant to regulations, an application on forms furnished by the department, which shall include, but not be limited to, all of the following:

(a) Evidence satisfactory to the department of the ability of the applicant to comply with this act and rules and regulations adopted pursuant to this act by the department.

(b) Evidence satisfactory to the department that the applicant is a reputable and responsible character. This evidence shall include, but not be limited to, a criminal record clearance pursuant to Section 1596.871, employment history, and character references. If the applicant is a firm, association, organization, partnership, business trust, corporation, or company, evidence of reputable and responsible character shall be submitted as to the members or shareholders thereof, and the person in charge of the day care center for which application for issuance of license or special permit is made.

(c) Evidence satisfactory to the department that the applicant has sufficient financial resources to maintain the standards of service required by regulations adopted pursuant to this act. The information shall be required only upon initial application for licensure, and when requested by the department, in writing, explaining the need for the evidence as part of the department's investigative function.

(d) Disclosure of the applicant's prior or present service as an administrator, general partner, corporate officer, or director of, or as a person who has held or holds a beneficial ownership of 10 percent or more in any child day care facility or in any facility licensed pursuant to Chapter 1 (commencing with Section 1200), 2 (commencing with Section 1250), or 3 (commencing with Section 1500).

(e) Disclosure of any revocation or other disciplinary action taken, or in the process of being taken, against a license held or previously held by the entities specified in subdivision (d).

(f) Evidence satisfactory to the department that there is a fire escape and disaster plan for the facility and that fire drills and disaster drills will be conducted at least once every six months. The documentation of these drills shall be maintained at the facility on a form prepared by the department and shall include the date and time of the drills.

(g) Evidence satisfactory to the department that the applicant has posted signs at the point of entry to the facility that provide the telephone number of the local health department and state all of the following:

(1) Protect your child—it is the law.

(2) All the information specified in Sections 27360 and 27360.5 of the Vehicle Code regarding child passenger restraint systems.

(3) Call your local health department for more information.

(h) Any other information as may be required by the department for the proper administration and enforcement of this act.

(i) Failure of the applicant to cooperate with the licensing agency in the completion of the application shall result in the denial of the application. Failure to cooperate means that the information described in this section and in regulations of the department has not been provided, or not provided in the form requested by the licensing agency, or both.

(Amended by Stats. 2002, Ch. 350, Sec. 1. Effective January 1, 2003.)

1596.951.

(a) It is the intent of the Legislature to create a child care license that has individual program components that serve infant, toddler, preschool, and schoolage children. It is the intent of the Legislature that the department consider flexibility for child care providers, maximizing administrative efficiency, while supporting a continuum of services in a manner consistent with all respective health and safety requirements.

(b) The department, in consultation with stakeholders, shall adopt regulations on or before January 1, 2021, to create a child care center license to serve infant, toddler, preschool, and schoolage children with all respective health and safety requirements. Before January 1, 2024, all day care centers shall be licensed as child care centers pursuant to this section.

(c) The regulations adopted pursuant to this section shall include, but are not limited to, all of the following:

(1) Components for serving infant, toddler, preschool, and schoolage children.

(2) Health and safety standards for children in care.

(3) Enhanced ability to transition children from one age group to the next.

(d) During the development and adoption of the regulations required by subdivision (b), the department shall consider best practices for continuity of care of the children and parents being served.

(e) The department may charge an applicant for a child care center license a fee commensurate with license fee schedules established for day care centers in Section 1596.803.

(f) The department may adopt emergency regulations in accordance with Chapter 3.5 (commencing with Section 11340) of Part 1 of Division 3 of Title 2 of the Government Code, to implement this section.

(Added by Stats. 2018, Ch. 574, Sec. 2. (AB 605) Effective January 1, 2019.)

1596.952.

(a) A corporation that applies for licensure with the department shall list the facilities that any member of the board of directors, the executive director, or an officer that has been licensed to operate, been employed in or served as a member of the board of directors, the executive director, or an officer.

(b) The department shall not issue a provisional license or license to any corporate applicant that has a member of the board of directors, the executive director, or an officer who is not eligible for licensure pursuant to Sections 1596.851 and 1596.8898.

(c) The department may revoke the license of any corporate licensee that has a member of the board of directors, the executive director, or an officer who is not eligible for licensure pursuant to Sections 1596.851 and 1596.8898.

(d) Prior to instituting an administrative action pursuant to subdivision (b) or (c), the department shall notify the applicant or licensee of the person's ineligibility to be a member of the board of directors, an executive director, or an officer of the applicant or licensee. The licensee has 15 days to remove the person from that position if the person does not have client contact, or immediately upon notification if the person has client contact.

(Added by Stats. 1998, Ch. 311, Sec. 50. Effective August 19, 1998.)

1596.954.

Every licensed child day care center shall have one or more carbon monoxide detectors in the facility that meet the standards established in Chapter 8 (commencing with Section 13260) of Part 2 of Division 12. The department shall account for the presence of these detectors during inspections.

(Added by Stats. 2014, Ch. 503, Sec. 4. (AB 2386) Effective January 1, 2015.)

1596.955.

(a) The department shall develop guidelines and procedures to permit licensed child day care centers serving preschool age children to create a special program component for children between 18 months to three years of age. This optional toddler program shall be subject to the following basic conditions:

(1) An amended application is submitted to and approved by the department.

(2) Parents give permission for the placement of their children in the toddler program.

(3) A ratio of six children to each teacher is maintained for all children in attendance at the toddler program. An aide who is participating in on-the-job training may be substituted for a teacher when directly supervised by a fully qualified teacher.

(4) The maximum group size, with two teachers, or one fully qualified teacher and one aide, does not exceed 12 toddlers.

(5) The toddler program is conducted in areas separate from those used by older or younger children. Plans to alternate use of outdoor play space may be approved to achieve separation.

(6) All other regulations pertaining to preschool age children are complied with.

(b) The toddler program shall be considered an extension of the center license, without the need for a separate license.

(c) The department may extend the period for participation in the toddler program for a maximum of three months for a child in extenuating circumstances, on the request of a day care center, if the center can establish that it is unable to find an alternative placement.

(Amended by Stats. 2018, Ch. 574, Sec. 3. (AB 605) Effective January 1, 2019.)

1596.956.

(a) The department shall develop guidelines and procedures to authorize licensed child day care centers serving infants to create a special program component for children between 18 months to three years of age. The optional toddler program shall be subject to the following basic conditions:

(1) An amended application shall be submitted to and approved by the department.

(2) A child younger than 18 months of age shall not be moved into the toddler program. A child who is older than 18 months of age shall not be required to be in the toddler program.

(3) Parents shall give permission for the placement of their children in the toddler program.

(4) A ratio of six children to each teacher shall be maintained for all children in attendance at the toddler program. An aide who is participating in on-the-job training may be substituted for a teacher when directly supervised by a fully qualified teacher.

(5) The maximum group size, with two teachers, or one fully qualified teacher and one aide, shall not exceed 12 toddlers.

(6) The toddler program shall be conducted in areas separate from those used by older or younger children. Plans to alternate use of outdoor play space may be approved to achieve separation.

(7) All other regulations pertaining to infants shall be complied with.

(b) The toddler program shall be considered an extension of the infant center license, without the need for a separate license.

(c) The department may extend the period for participation in the toddler program for a maximum of three months for a child in extenuating circumstances, on the request of the day care center, if the center can established that it is unable to find an alternative placement.

(Amended by Stats. 2018, Ch. 574, Sec. 4. (AB 605) Effective January 1, 2019.)

1596.96.

(a) The department and the licensing agencies with which it contracts for licensing shall review and make a final determination within 60 days of an applicant's submission of a complete application on all applications for a license to operate a day care facility for children by an organization which possesses a current valid license to operate a day care facility for children at another site. Applicants shall note on the application, or in a cover letter to the application, that they possess a current valid license at another site, and the number of that license.

(b) The department shall request a fire safety clearance from the appropriate fire marshal within five days of receipt of an application described in subdivision (a). The department shall request criminal records clearance within five days of receipt of an application described in subdivision (a), unless the clearance requirement has been otherwise satisfied by transfer of clearance under subdivision (g) of Section 1596.871.

(c) If the department for any reason is unable to comply with subdivision (a), it shall, within 60 days of receipt of the application described in subdivision (a), grant a provisional license to the applicant to operate for a period not to exceed six months. While the provisional license is in effect, the department shall continue its investigation and make a final determination on the application before the provisional license expires. The provisional license shall be granted, provided the department knows of no life safety risks, the criminal records clearances, if applicable, are complete, and the fire safety clearance is complete. The director may extend the term of a provisional license for an additional six months at the time of the application, if the director determines that more than six months will be required to achieve full compliance with licensing standards due to circumstances beyond the control of the applicant, and if all other requirements for a license have been met.

(d) If the department does not issue a provisional license pursuant to subdivision (c), the department shall issue a notice to the applicant identifying whether the provisional license has not been issued due to the existence of a life safety risk, lack of a fire safety clearance, lack of a criminal records clearance, failure to complete the application, or any combination of these reasons. If a life safety risk is identified, the risk preventing the issuance of a provisional license shall be clearly explained. If a lack of the fire safety clearance or lack of criminal records clearance is identified, the notice shall include the dates on which the department requested the clearance and the current status of those requests, the fire marshal's name and telephone number to whom a fire safety clearance request was sent, and the names of individuals for whom criminal records clearances are lacking. If failure to complete the application is identified, the notice shall list all of the forms or attachments which are missing or incorrect. This notice shall be sent to the applicant no later than 60 days after the applicant filed the application. If the reasons identified in the notice are corrected, the department shall issue the provisional license within five days after the corrections are made.

(e) The department shall, immediately after January 1, 1992, develop expedited procedures necessary to implement subdivisions (a), (b), (c), and (d).

(f) The department shall, immediately after January 1, 1992, develop an appeal procedure for applicants under this section for both denial of licenses and delay in processing applications.

(Amended by Stats. 1991, Ch. 867, Sec. 7.)

1596.97.

A license or special permit for a day care center for children may be issued providing the licensee has been found not to be in violation of any statutory requirements or rules or regulations pursuant to this chapter and Chapter 3.4 (commencing with Section 1596.70).

(Amended by Stats. 1992, Ch. 1315, Sec. 30. Effective January 1, 1993.)

1596.98.

(a) The department shall notify the day care center in writing of all deficiencies in its compliance with this chapter and the rules and regulations adopted pursuant to this chapter, and shall set a reasonable length of time for compliance by the center. Upon a finding of noncompliance, the department may levy a civil penalty which shall be paid to the department each day until the department finds the center in compliance.

(b) In developing a plan of correction both the licensee and the department shall give due consideration to the following factors:

(1) The gravity of the violation.

(2) The history of previous violations.

(3) The possibility of a threat to the health or safety of any child in the facility.

(4) The number of children affected by the violation.

(5) The availability of equipment or personnel necessary to correct the violation, if appropriate.

(c) The department shall ensure that the licensee's plan of correction is verifiable and measurable. The plan of correction shall specify what evidence is acceptable to establish that a deficiency has been corrected. This evidence shall be included in the department's facility file.

(d) The department shall adopt regulations establishing procedures for the imposition of civil penalties under this section.

(Amended by Stats. 2008, Ch. 291, Sec. 22. Effective September 25, 2008.)

1596.99.

(a) In addition to the suspension, temporary suspension, or revocation of a license issued under this chapter or Chapter 3.4 (commencing with Section 1596.70), the department shall levy civil penalties as follows:

(b) (1) The amount of the civil penalty shall be one hundred dollars ($100) per day for each violation of this chapter if a facility fails to correct a deficiency after being provided a specified length of time to correct the deficiency.

(A) If a licensee or a licensee's representative submits evidence to the department that the licensee has corrected a deficiency, and the department, after reviewing that evidence, has determined that the deficiency has been corrected, the civil penalty shall cease as of the day the department received that evidence.

(B) If the department deems it necessary, the department shall inspect the facility within five working days after the department receives evidence pursuant to subparagraph (A) to confirm that the deficiency has been corrected.

(C) If the department determines that the deficiency has not been corrected, the civil penalty shall continue to accrue from the date of the original citation.

(D) If the department is able to verify that the deficiency was corrected prior to the date on which the department received the evidence pursuant to subparagraph (A), the civil penalty shall cease as of that earlier date.

(2) (A) If the department issues a notification of deficiency to a facility for a repeat violation of a violation specified in paragraph (1), the department shall assess an immediate civil penalty of two hundred fifty dollars ($250) per repeat violation and one hundred dollars ($100) for each day the repeat violation continues after citation. The notification of deficiency shall state the manner in which the deficiency constitutes a repeat violation and shall be submitted to a supervisor for review and approval.

(B) For purposes of this section, "repeat violation" means a violation within 12 months of a prior violation of a statutory or regulatory provision designated by the same combination of letters or numerals, or both letters and numerals.

(C) Notwithstanding subparagraphs (A) and (B), the department, in its sole discretion, may reduce the civil penalty for the cited repeat violation to the level of the underlying violation, as applicable, if it determines that the cited repeat violation is not substantially similar to the original violation.

(3) If the nature or seriousness of the violation or the frequency of the violation warrants a higher penalty or an immediate civil penalty assessment, or both, as provided in this chapter, a correction of a deficiency shall not impact the imposition of a civil penalty.

(c) The department shall assess an immediate civil penalty of five hundred dollars ($500) per violation and one hundred dollars ($100) for each day the violation continues after citation, for any of the following serious violations:

(1) Any violation that the department determines resulted in the injury or illness of a child.

(2) Fire clearance violations, including, but not limited to, overcapacity, inoperable smoke alarms, and inoperable fire alarm systems.

(3) Absence of supervision, including, but not limited to, a child left unattended, and supervision of a child by a person under 18 years of age.

(4) Accessible bodies of water, when prohibited by this chapter or regulations adopted pursuant to this chapter.

(5) Accessible firearms, ammunition, or both.

(6) Refused entry to a facility or any part of a facility in violation of Section 1596.852, 1596.853, or 1597.09.

(7) The presence of a person subject to a department Order of Exclusion on the premises.

(d) If the department issues a notification of deficiency to a facility for a repeat violation of a violation specified in subdivision (c), the department shall assess an immediate civil penalty of one thousand dollars ($1,000) per repeat violation and one hundred dollars ($100) for each day the repeat violation continues after citation. The notification of deficiency shall state the manner in which the deficiency constitutes a repeat violation and shall be submitted to a supervisor for review and approval.

(e) For a violation that the department determines resulted in the death of a child, the civil penalty shall be assessed as follows:

(1) Seven thousand five hundred dollars ($7,500) for a facility licensed to care for 30 or fewer children.

(2) Ten thousand dollars ($10,000) for a facility licensed to care for 31 to 100, inclusive, children.

(3) Fifteen thousand dollars ($15,000) for a facility licensed to care for more than 100 children.

(f) (1) For a violation that the department determines constitutes physical abuse or resulted in serious injury, as defined in Section 1596.8865, to a child, the civil penalty shall be assessed as follows:

(A) Two thousand five hundred dollars ($2,500) for a facility licensed to care for 30 or fewer children.

(B) Five thousand dollars ($5,000) for a facility licensed to care for 31 to 100, inclusive, children.

(C) Ten thousand dollars ($10,000) for a facility licensed to care for more than 100 children.

(2) For purposes of this subdivision, "physical abuse" includes physical injury inflicted upon a child by another person by other than accidental means, sexual abuse as defined in Section 11165.1 of the Penal Code, neglect as defined in Section 11165.2 of the Penal Code, or unlawful corporal punishment or injury as defined in Section 11165.4 of the Penal Code when the person responsible for the child's welfare is a licensee, administrator, or employee of any facility licensed to care for children, or an administrator or employee of a public or private school or other institution or agency.

(g) (1) Before the assessment of a civil penalty pursuant to subdivision (e) or (f), the decision shall be approved by the program administrator of the Community Care Licensing Division.

(2) (A) The department shall reduce the amount of a civil penalty due pursuant to subdivision (e) or (f) by the amount of the civil penalty already assessed for the underlying violation.

(B) If the amount of the civil penalty that the department has already assessed for the underlying violation exceeds the amount of the penalty pursuant to subdivision (e) or (f), the larger amount shall prevail and be due and payable as already assessed by the department.

(h) Notwithstanding any other law, revenues received by the state from the payment of civil penalties imposed on licensed child care centers pursuant to this chapter or Chapter 3.4 (commencing with Section 1596.70), shall be deposited in the Child Health and Safety Fund, created pursuant to Chapter 4.6 (commencing with Section 18285) of Part 6 of Division 9 of the Welfare and Institutions Code, and shall be expended, upon appropriation by the Legislature, pursuant to subdivision (f) of Section 18285 of the Welfare and Institutions Code exclusively for the technical assistance, orientation, training, and education of licensed day care center providers.

(i) (1) A notification of a deficiency written by a representative of the department shall include a factual description of the nature of the deficiency fully stating the manner in which the licensee failed to comply with the specified statute or regulation, and, if applicable, the particular place or area in which the deficiency occurred. The department shall make a good faith effort to work with the licensee to determine the cause of the deficiency and ways to prevent any repeat violations.

(2) The department shall adopt regulations setting forth the appeal procedures for deficiencies.

(j) (1) A licensee shall have the right to submit to the department a written request for a formal review of a civil penalty assessed pursuant to subdivisions (d) and (e) within 15 business days of receipt of the notice of a civil penalty assessment and shall provide all available supporting documentation at that time. The review shall be conducted by the deputy director of the Community Care Licensing Division. The licensee may submit additional supporting documentation that was unavailable at the time of submitting the request for review within the first 30 business days after submitting the request for review. If the department requires additional information from the licensee, that information shall be requested within the first 30 business days after receiving the request for review. The licensee shall provide this additional information within 30 business days of receiving the request from the department. If the deputy director determines that the civil penalty was not assessed, or the finding of the deficiency that resulted in the assessment of the civil penalty was not made, in accordance with applicable statutes or regulations of the department, he or she may amend or dismiss the civil penalty or finding of deficiency. The licensee shall be notified in writing of the deputy director's decision within 60 business days of the date when all necessary information has been provided to the department by the licensee.

(2) Upon exhausting the review described in paragraph (1), a licensee may further appeal that decision to an administrative law judge. Proceedings shall be conducted in accordance with Chapter 5 (commencing with Section 11500) of Part 1 of Division 3 of Title 2 of the Government Code, and the department shall have all the powers granted by those provisions. In all proceedings conducted in accordance with this section, the standard of proof shall be by a preponderance of the evidence.

(3) If, in addition to an assessment of civil penalties, the department elects to file an administrative action to suspend or revoke the facility license that includes violations relating to the assessment of the civil penalties, the department review of the pending appeal shall cease and the assessment of the civil penalties shall be heard as part of the administrative action process.

(4) Civil penalties shall be due and payable when administrative appeals have been exhausted. Unless payment arrangements have been made that are acceptable to the department, a civil penalty not paid within 30 days shall be subject to late fees, as specified by the department in regulation.

(k) (1) A licensee shall have the right to submit to the department a written request for a formal review of any other civil penalty or deficiency not described in subdivision (j) within 15 business days of receipt of the notice of a civil penalty assessment or a finding of a deficiency, and shall provide all available supporting documentation at that time. The review shall be conducted by a regional manager of the Community Care Licensing Division. The licensee may submit additional supporting documentation that was unavailable at the time of submitting the request for review within the first 30 business days after submitting the request for review. If the department requires additional information from the licensee, that information shall be requested within the first 30 business days after receiving the request for review. The licensee shall provide this additional information within 30 business days of receiving the request from the department. If the regional manager determines that the civil penalty was not assessed, or the finding of the deficiency was not made, in accordance with applicable statutes or regulations of the department, he or she may amend or dismiss the civil penalty or finding of deficiency. The licensee shall be notified in writing of the regional manager's decision within 60 business days of the date when all necessary information has been provided to the department by the licensee.

(2) Upon exhausting the review described in paragraph (1), the licensee may further appeal that decision to the program administrator of the Community Care Licensing Division within 15 business days of receipt of notice of the regional manager's decision. The licensee may submit additional supporting documentation that was unavailable at the time of appeal to the program administrator within the first 30 business days after requesting that appeal. If the department requires additional information from the licensee, that information shall be requested within the first 30 business days after receiving the request for the appeal. The licensee shall provide this additional information within 30 business days of receiving the request from the department. If the program administrator determines that the civil penalty was not assessed, or the finding of the deficiency was not made, in accordance with applicable statutes or regulations of the department, he or she may amend or dismiss the civil penalty or finding of deficiency. The licensee shall be notified in writing of the program administrator's decision within 60 business days of the date when all necessary information has been provided to the department by the licensee. The program administrator's decision is considered final and concludes the licensee's administrative appeal rights regarding the appeal conducted pursuant to this paragraph.

(3) Civil penalties shall be due and payable when administrative appeals have been exhausted. Unless payment arrangements have been made that are acceptable to the department, a civil penalty not paid within 30 days shall be subject to late fees, as specified by the department in regulation.

(l) The department shall, by January 1, 2016, amend its regulations to reflect the changes to this section made by Section 8 of Chapter 813 of the Statutes of 2014.

(m) Notwithstanding the Administrative Procedure Act (Chapter 3.5 (commencing with Section 11340) of Part 1 of Division 3 of Title 2 of the Government Code), the department may implement and administer the changes made by the act that added this subdivision through all-county letters or similar written instructions until regulations are adopted pursuant to the Administrative Procedure Act.

(n) This section shall become operative on July 1, 2017.

(Repealed (in Sec. 13) and added by Stats. 2016, Ch. 823, Sec. 14. (AB 2231) Effective January 1, 2017. Section operative July 1, 2017, by its own provisions.)

ARTICLE 3. Administration [1597.05 - 1597.21]

(Article 3 added by Stats. 1984, Ch. 1615, Sec. 10.)

1597.05.

(a) Licensing reviews of a child day care center shall be limited to health and safety considerations and shall not include any reviews of the content of any educational or training program of the facility.

(b) A licensee shall have 30 days after the employment of a staff person or enrollment of a child to secure records requiring information from sources not in the control of the licensee, staff person, or child. An extension can be granted where the licensee can demonstrate that further delays are beyond the control of the licensee. No additional onsite inspections for the purpose of checking completion of the designated records shall be made during the 30-day period.

"Records," for the purposes of this subdivision, mean those types of records requiring information from sources not in the control of the facilities, and include, but are not limited to, all of the following:

(1) Physical examination reports by physicians and surgeons.

(2) Confirmation of required immunizations.

(3) Submission of official data describing the educational qualifications of the facility staff.

(c) Within 90 days of employing a facility director, a licensee shall secure verification that the facility director has completed an orientation given by the department and shall maintain a copy of that verification.

(Amended by Stats. 2006, Ch. 545, Sec. 5. Effective January 1, 2007.)

1597.055.

(a) Notwithstanding any other educational requirements, a person may be hired as a teacher in a day care center if he or she satisfies all of the following conditions:

(1) Is 18 years of age or older.

(2) Possesses a regional occupation program certificate of training in child care occupations issued by a regional occupational program which is accredited by the Western Association of Schools and Colleges.

(3) Has completed at least 95 hours of classroom instruction in child care and development and child care occupations and at least 150 hours in supervised field experience in a licensed day care center or comparable group child care program.

(4) Commencing September 1, 2016, has provided evidence of current immunity or exemption from immunity, as described in Section 1596.7995.

(5) Has provided evidence of a current tuberculosis clearance, as described in subdivision (g) of Section 101216 of Title 22 of the California Code of Regulations. This requirement may be satisfied by a current certificate, as defined in subdivision (f) of

Section 121525, that indicates freedom from infectious tuberculosis as set forth in Section 121525.

(b) Subsequent to being hired pursuant to subdivision (a), a teacher shall make satisfactory progress towards meeting the educational requirement for a fully qualified teacher, as specified in departmental regulations. For purposes of this section, "satisfactory progress" shall mean completion, with passing grades, of a minimum of two units each semester or the equivalent number of units each quarter until the educational requirement is satisfied. Six of the required semester or equivalent number of quarter units of early childhood education from an accredited university or college shall be completed during the next two consecutive regular semesters or equivalent quarters.

(c) A teacher hired pursuant to this section shall not be exempt from satisfying any other noneducation requirements imposed by law on teachers in day care centers and shall have onsite supervision by a fully qualified teacher until six of the units specified in subdivision (b) are completed.

(Amended by Stats. 2015, Ch. 807, Sec. 2. (SB 792) Effective January 1, 2016.)

1597.056.

Notwithstanding any other educational requirements, a person may be hired to provide extended day care for children of a given grade level in a day care center if the person is otherwise qualified to be hired by a school district to teach children of that grade level.

(Added by Stats. 1987, Ch. 626, Sec. 1.)

1597.057.

Any requirement established by the department, pursuant to Article 1 (commencing with Section 1596.70) of Chapter 3.4, that coursework in early childhood education or child development, or both, be completed in order to fully qualify as a day care center teacher, may be satisfied with a valid child development associate credential issued by the Child Development Associate National Credentialing Program for a center-based setting with a preschool age level or infant/toddler age level endorsement. The preschool age level endorsement shall qualify the holder of the credential as a day care center teacher for ages three to five, inclusive, and the infant/toddler age level endorsement shall qualify the holder of the credential as a day care center teacher for up to, and including, age two. The child development associate credential used to qualify individuals as day care center teachers shall involve standards that are no less stringent than those in effect on January 1, 1988.

(Added by Stats. 1988, Ch. 1326, Sec. 5. Effective September 26, 1988.)

1597.059.

(a) The State Department of Social Services shall adopt guidelines and procedures to permit an aide to assist a fully qualified child care teacher in the supervision of up to 18 preschool age children, with the requirement that the aide shall complete at least two accredited postsecondary semester units or equivalent quarter units of early childhood education or child development per semester or quarter, commencing with the first semester or quarter following initial employment and continuing until six units have been completed.

(b) For purposes of this section, "preschool age children" means children who are enrolled in a child day care center licensed by the department and who are not enrolled in either an infant care center or a schoolage child day care center, as these terms are defined in Title 22 of the California Code of Regulations.

(c) This section shall not become operative prior to June 30, 1993.

(Added by Stats. 1993, Ch. 246, Sec. 3. Effective (and operative) August 2, 1993.)

1597.07.

The department shall require of every licensee a written policy statement which shall include names and qualifications of all current employees, admission policies, program philosophy, the location and telephone number of the nearest local office responsible for child day care licensing, disciplinary practices, and the licensee's policy and practice regarding preventive health and care of children with non-life-endangering illnesses. The facility shall retain an affidavit signed by the parent or guardian of every child in the facility indicating he or she has read this statement. The licensee shall also provide to all parents, at the consent of the parents involved, a list of parents of children served by the facility.

(Added by Stats. 1984, Ch. 1615, Sec. 10.)

1597.08.

All site visits shall be unannounced.

(Added by Stats. 1984, Ch. 1615, Sec. 10.)

1597.09.

(a) Each licensed child day care center shall be subject to unannounced inspections by the department. The department shall inspect these facilities as often as necessary to ensure the quality of care provided.

(b) The department shall conduct an annual unannounced inspection of a licensed child day care center under any of the following circumstances:

(1) When a license is on probation.

(2) When the terms of agreement in a facility compliance plan require an annual inspection.

(3) When an accusation against a licensee is pending.

(4) In order to verify that a person who has been ordered out of a child day care center by the department is no longer at the facility.

(c) (1) The department shall conduct an annual unannounced inspection of no less than 30 percent of facilities not subject to an evaluation under subdivision (b).

(2) These unannounced inspections shall be conducted based on a random sampling methodology developed by the department.

(d) The department shall inspect a licensed child day care center at least once every three years.

(e) It is the intent of the Legislature to achieve annual inspections for licensed child day care centers governed by this section on or before July 1, 2021.

(Amended by Stats. 2019, Ch. 27, Sec. 13. (SB 80) Effective June 27, 2019.)

1597.091.

(a) In addition to the visits required by Section 1597.09, the department shall annually make unannounced spot visits to 20 percent of all child day care centers licensed under this chapter, except schoolage child day care centers. The unannounced visits may be made at any time during the facility's business hours. At no time shall other site visit requirements described by this section prevent a timely site visit response to a complaint as required by Section 1596.853.

(b) The department shall implement this section only to the extent funds are available in accordance with Section 18285.5 of the Welfare and Institutions Code.

(Amended by Stats. 2002, Ch. 1022, Sec. 5. Effective September 28, 2002.)

1597.11.

The department shall notify the State Department of Education when a child care or development facility licensed pursuant to this chapter is found to have licensing violations which the department has determined, by regulation, to endanger the health and safety of the children receiving care. This notification shall be made no later than 15 days after the finding of the violation or violations.

(Added by Stats. 1985, Ch. 1064, Sec. 29.)

1597.13.

The department and any local agency with which it contracts for the licensing of day care centers shall grant or deny an application for license within 30 days after receipt of all appropriate licensing application materials, as determined by the department, after a site visit has been completed and the facility has been found to be in compliance with licensing standards. The department shall conduct an initial site visit within 30 days after the receipt of all appropriate licensing application materials.

(Added by renumbering Section 1597.11 (as added by Stats. 1985, Ch. 1064, Sec. 10) by Stats. 1988, Ch. 160, Sec. 97.)

1597.14.

(a) Notwithstanding Section 1596.858, in the event of a sale of a licensed child day care center where the sale will result in a new license being issued, the sale and transfer of property and business shall be subject to both of the following:

(1) The licensee shall provide written notice to the department and to the child's parent or his or her legal guardian of the licensee's intent to sell the child day care center at least 30 days prior to the transfer of the property or business, or at the time that a bona fide offer is made, whichever period is longer.

(2) The licensee shall, prior to entering into an admission agreement, inform the child's parent or his or her legal guardian, admitted to the facility after notification to the department, of the licensee's intent to sell the property or business.

(b) Except as provided in subdivision (e), the property and business shall not be transferred until the buyer qualifies for a license or provisional license pursuant to this chapter.

(1) The seller shall notify, in writing, a prospective buyer of the necessity to obtain a license, as required by this chapter, if the buyer's intent is to continue operating the facility as a child day care center. The seller shall send a copy of this written notice to the licensing agency.

(2) The prospective buyer shall submit an application for a license, as specified in Section 1596.95, within five days of the acceptance of the offer by the seller.

(c) No transfer of the facility shall be permitted until 30 days have elapsed from the date when notice has been provided to the department pursuant to paragraph (1) of subdivision (a).

(d) The department shall give priority to applications for licensure that are submitted pursuant to this section in order to ensure timely transfer of the property and business. The department shall make a decision within 60 days after a complete application is submitted on whether to issue a license pursuant to Section 1596.95.

(e) If the parties involved in the transfer of the property and business fully comply with this section, then the transfer may be completed and the buyer shall not be considered to be operating an unlicensed facility while the department makes a final determination on the application for licensure.

(Amended by Stats. 1994, Ch. 236, Sec. 1. Effective January 1, 1995.)

1597.15.

(a) The director shall authorize the University of California to conduct a pilot project pursuant to this section for a period not to extend 24 months beyond the date that funding is available for expenditure for the pilot project. The purpose of the pilot project is to test the feasibility of permitting family day care home providers and child day care center staff to undertake gastric tube feeding or the administration of medication through nebulizers under the conditions and with the precautions specified in subdivision (c).

(b) Notwithstanding any other provision of law, upon authorization from the director pursuant to subdivision (a), child day care center and family day care home licensees and staff selected by the principal investigator of the pilot project, to be known as the Access Project, or his or her staff shall be authorized to undertake gastrostomy tube feeding or the administration of medication through nebulizers on children enrolled in their facilities.

(c) For the purposes of the pilot project, the following precautions shall be taken:

(1) The principal investigator selected by the University of California shall be a person who is licensed to practice medicine in the state and is experienced in supervising programs in which nonmedical personnel perform minor health procedures.

(2) The availability of, and interaction with, experienced nurses with appropriate experience, as determined by the principal investigator, shall be part of the study design.

(3) Only children with explicit and signed permission from their personal physicians shall be included in the pilot project.

(d) The University of California shall notify the department of any family day care provider or child day care center staff selected to participate in the training and procedures described in subdivision (b) prior to undertaking these procedures.

(e) Eighteen months after the date funding for the proposed pilot became available for expenditure, the principal investigator of the Access Project shall submit an evaluation of the project to the Assembly Human Services Committee and the Senate Health and Human Services Committee of the Legislature. In preparing the evaluation, the Access Project shall consult with representatives from the State Department of Health Services, the department, family day care associations, family resource centers and networks, the child care center provider community, and child care resource and referral agencies. The principal investigator of the Access Project shall consult with the department to determine the additional data necessary for the department to make use of the evaluation. The evaluation shall include, but not be limited to, all of the following:

(1) The number of family day care home providers who participated in the project, with information identifying the procedure the provider was trained in and his or her licensed capacity and actual enrollment.

(2) The number of child day care center staff who participated in the project, with information identifying the procedure the staff was trained in, the licensed capacity and actual enrollment of the program, and the number of staff overall.

(3) The number of children who were able to be served in licensed child care programs with trained family day care home providers or child day care center staff.

(4) Overall impressions, problems encountered, and satisfaction with the pilot project by providers and staff.

(5) Overall impressions, problems encountered, and satisfaction with the pilot project by parents and children.

(6) Overall impressions, problems encountered, and satisfaction with the pilot project by licensing staff.

(7) Overall impressions, problems encountered, and satisfaction with the pilot project by those providing the training, backup, and monitoring, of a nonlicensing nature.

(8) Input from providers, staff, trainers, parents, and children as appropriate about the effectiveness of the pilot project.

(9) An assessment of the adequacy of the training, including curriculum and core competencies for the health care procedures taught; teaching methods used in the project; and the quality of health care procedures provided, including errors and incidents.

(10) The impact on health and safety from engaging in these procedures on the child needing the procedure and the other children and staff in the program, where measurable.

(11) The impact of the pilot project on increasing the ability of child care programs to serve children with special health needs.

(12) The number of nurse visits required for initial placement in the child care setting.

(13) The need for a nurse with appropriate experience, as determined by the principal investigator, after placement is arranged and initiated as an adjunct to support each child's own physician or physicians.

(14) The cost of providing the training and services.

(15) Recommendations as to whether the pilot project should be expanded to enable family day care home providers and child day care center staff throughout the state to undertake these procedures and under what specific conditions, with accompanying rationales.

(16) Recommendations for other possible procedures to be authorized in a pilot project with the reasons for those recommendations.

(17) The cost of the care provided in the project, the likely cost of the care if performed by the child day care licensees or staff pursuant to the project, and the cost for provision of that care by the child's current care providers, specifically including the cost of nursing services.

(18) The number of Medi-Cal recipients participating in the project.

(f) No provision of this section applies to the Regents of the University of California unless the Regents, by appropriate resolution, make it applicable. It is the intent of the Legislature that the project be funded from non-General Fund resources.

(g) This section shall remain in effect only until two years from the date funding is available for expenditure for the pilot project established pursuant to this section and as of that date shall be repealed, unless a later enacted statute, which is chaptered before that date, deletes or extends that date. The director shall notify the Chief Clerk of the Assembly in writing of the date this section is repealed and the Chief Clerk shall publish the notification in the Assembly Journal.

(Amended by Stats. 1996, Ch. 124, Sec. 51. Effective January 1, 1997. Repealed on date prescribed by its own provisions.)

1597.16.

(a) (1) A licensed child day care center, as defined in Section 1596.76, that is located in a building that was constructed before January 1, 2010, shall have its drinking water tested for lead contamination levels on or after January 1, 2020, but no later than January 1, 2023, and every five years after the date of the initial test.

(2) (A) A licensed child day care center subject to paragraph (1) shall collect and submit drinking water samples to a laboratory accredited pursuant to Article 3 (commencing with Section 100825) of Chapter 4 of Part 1 of Division 101. A laboratory receiving a drinking water sample pursuant to this paragraph shall, in a timely manner, electronically submit its test results to the State Water Resources Control Board using lead data submission methods that are acceptable to the State Water Resources Control Board. If the test

results show elevated lead levels, the State Water Resources Control Board shall, in a timely manner, report the results for the affected licensed child day care center to the department.

(B) The State Water Resources Control Board shall do both of the following:

(i) Notify the department if there is a change to the recommended action level for lead in water.

(ii) Post all test results received pursuant to subparagraph (A) on its Internet Web site in a timely manner. The posted test results shall be readily accessible to the public.

(3) Upon notification of elevated lead levels, an affected licensed child day care center shall immediately make inoperable and cease using the fountains and faucets where elevated lead levels may exist and shall obtain a potable source of water for children and staff at that location. Any licensed child day care center that fails to take that action is subject to the temporary suspension of their license pursuant to Section 1596.886.

(4) A licensed day care center shall notify the parents or legal guardians of children enrolled in the day care center of the requirement to test a facility's drinking water and of the test results.

(b) (1) The department shall, in consultation with the State Water Resources Control Board, adopt regulations for the implementation of the requirements of this section no later than January 1, 2021. The regulations shall include requirements to ensure the collection and submission of valid water samples.

(2) In adopting regulations under this section, the department shall include a public stakeholder process.

(3) Notwithstanding the Administrative Procedure Act (Chapter 3.5 (commencing with Section 11340) of Part 1 of Division 3 of Title 2 of the Government Code), the department may implement and administer the changes made by this section through all-county letters or similar written instructions until regulations are adopted.

(Added by Stats. 2018, Ch. 676, Sec. 4. (AB 2370) Effective January 1, 2019.)

1597.20.

The Legislature finds and declares all of the following:

(a) There is a critical need to increase opportunities for children to engage in positive activities during after school hours.

(b) There is a need for staff with the capacity to make after school programs interesting and relevant for schoolage children.

(c) California's juvenile incarceration rate is twice the national average and has increased 65 percent since 1975.

(d) Twice as many California young people were victims of homicide in 1990 than in 1974.

(e) Compared to 1960, American children spend an average of 10 to 12 fewer hours per week with their parents.

(Added by Stats. 1994, Ch. 848, Sec. 1. Effective January 1, 1995.)

1597.21.

The following requirements shall apply to schoolage day care centers:

(a) The State Department of Social Services shall permit the substitution of 20 training hours for each required unit of education.

(b) In addition to an administration course consisting of three units or 60 training hours and three units or 60 training hours in early childhood education, child development, or schoolage child courses, the site director may, as an alternative to existing regulations, complete nine core units or 180 training hours from the following:

(1) Recreation, which includes, but is not limited to, art, music, and dance.

(2) Physical education, which includes, but is not limited to, indoor and outdoor sports activities.

(3) Human services and social welfare, which includes, but is not limited to, nursing, psychology, sociology, or home economics.

(4) Units earned toward an elementary or middle school teaching credential.

(5) Early childhood education, child development, or schoolage child units.

A director is required to complete 12 units or 240 training hours prior to employment. The remaining three units must be completed within one year of employment.

(c) The State Department of Social Services shall expand the list of college degrees that satisfy current site director educational requirements to include degrees in recreation, physical education, human services, and social welfare, as described in paragraph (3) of subdivision (b), and education, as described in paragraphs (2) and (4) of subdivision (b).

(d) As an alternative to satisfying the educational requirements of teachers contained in the regulations, a teacher may substitute 12 units or 240 training hours in any combination of the following:

(1) Recreation, which includes, but is not limited to, art, music, and dance.

(2) Physical education, which includes, but is not limited to, indoor and outdoor sports activities.

(3) Human services and social welfare, which includes, but is not limited to, nursing, psychology, sociology, or home economics.

(4) Units earned toward an elementary or middle school teaching credential.

(5) Early childhood education, child development, or schoolage child units.

A teacher is required to complete six units or 120 training hours prior to employment.

(e) The department shall accept the following alternative types of experience for site directors and teachers, if the experience was obtained working directly with children: classroom teaching or teacher assisting experience in elementary or middle school education; paid or volunteer work experience in physical education or recreation programs; college work-study or internship in recreation or youth development; paid or volunteer work experience in human services as described in paragraph (3) of

subdivision (b); or paid or volunteer work experience in school guidance or in other counseling programs.

(f) In addition to existing approved sources of education, the following are approved sources of education that may be used to satisfy the education required of staff at a schoolage child care center:

(1) Vocational school training in recreation, physical education, human services, social welfare, and education as described in subdivisions (b) and (d).

(2) Professional training that qualifies as continuing education credits in the child care or elementary education area.

(3) Standard training programs that are provided by statewide or nationally recognized or community-based youth service organizations and offered or approved by an accredited educational institution or the Commission on Teacher Credentialing.

(g) Upon the receipt of a completed application for a license to operate a schoolage day care program at a functioning schoolsite from an organization that is currently licensed to operate a schoolage day care program at another site, the department shall have 30 days to make a final determination on whether to issue a license to operate the program. A functioning schoolsite shall meet the requirements of paragraphs (1) and (2) of subdivision (a) of Section 1596.806.

(h) (1) If the department, for any reason, is unable to comply with subdivision (g), it shall, within 30 days of the receipt of the application described in subdivision (g), grant a provisional license to the applicant to operate for a period not to exceed six months. The provisional license shall be granted provided the department has conducted a site visit and has not found any life safety risks, the criminal records clearances are complete, and the school fire inspection has been verified. The requirement for criminal records clearances may be satisfied by transfer of current criminal records clearances, pursuant to subdivision (g) of Section 1596.871. For purposes of a schoolage day care program operating on a functioning schoolsite, the school fire inspection shall be accepted as sufficient fire clearance.

(2) While a provisional license is in effect, the department shall continue its investigation and shall make a final determination on the application prior to the expiration of the provisional license. If the department does not issue a provisional license pursuant to paragraph (1), the department shall follow the procedures for notifying applicants as set forth in subdivision (d) of Section 1596.96.

(Added by Stats. 1994, Ch. 848, Sec. 2. Effective January 1, 1995.)

CHAPTER 3.6. Family Day Care Homes [1597.30 - 1597.622]

(Heading of Chapter 3.6 amended by Stats. 1984, Ch. 1615, Sec. 10.5.)

1597.30.

The Legislature finds and declares:

(a) It has a responsibility to ensure the health and safety of children in family homes that provide day care.

(b) That there are insufficient numbers of regulated family day care homes in California.

(c) There will be a growing need for child day care facilities due to the increase in working parents.

(d) Many parents prefer child day care located in their neighborhoods in family homes.

(e) There should be a variety of child care settings, including regulated family day care homes, as suitable alternatives for parents.

(f) That the program to be operated by the state should be cost effective, streamlined, and simple to administer in order to ensure adequate care for children placed in family day care homes, while not placing undue burdens on the providers.

(g) That the state should maintain an efficient program of regulating family day care homes that ensures the provision of adequate protection, supervision, and guidance to children in their homes.

(Added by renumbering Section 1597.50 by Stats. 1983, Ch. 1233, Sec. 1.)

1597.36.

The department shall provide written documentation to providers of the need for repairs, renovations, or additions when requested for an application for a loan guarantee pursuant to subdivision (d) of Section 8277.6 of the Education Code whenever the repairs, renovations, or additions are required by the department in order for the licensee to maintain or obtain a license for more than six children.

(Added by Stats. 1997, Ch. 270, Sec. 20. Effective August 11, 1997. Operative January 1, 1998, by Sec. 183 of Ch. 270.)

1597.40.

(a) It is the intent of the Legislature that family day care homes for children should be situated in normal residential surroundings so as to give children the home environment which is conducive to healthy and safe development. It is the public policy of this state to provide children in a family day care home the same home environment as provided in a traditional home setting.

The Legislature declares this policy to be of statewide concern with the purpose of occupying the field to the exclusion of municipal zoning, building and fire codes and regulations governing the use or occupancy of family day care homes for children, except as specifically provided for in this chapter, and to prohibit any restrictions relating to the use of single-family residences for family day care homes for children except as provided by this chapter.

(b) Every provision in a written instrument entered into relating to real property which purports to forbid or restrict the conveyance, encumbrance, leasing, or mortgaging of the real property for use or occupancy as a family day care home for children, is void and every restriction or prohibition in any such written instrument as to the use or occupancy of the property as a family day care home for children is void.

(c) Except as provided in subdivision (d), every restriction or prohibition entered into, whether by way of covenant, condition upon use or occupancy, or upon transfer of title to real property, which restricts or prohibits directly, or indirectly limits, the acquisition, use, or occupancy of such property for a family day care home for children is void.

(d) (1) A prospective family day care home provider, who resides in a rental property, shall provide 30 days' written notice to the landlord or owner of the rental property prior to the commencement of operation of the family day care home.

(2) For family day care home providers who have relocated an existing licensed family day care home program to a rental property on or after January 1, 1997, less than 30 days' written notice may be provided in cases where the department approves the operation of the new location of the family day care home in less than 30 days, or the home is licensed in less than 30 days, in order that service to the children served in the former location not be interrupted.

(3) A family day care home provider in operation on rental or leased property as of January 1, 1997, shall notify the landlord or property owner in writing at the time of the annual license fee renewal, or by March 31, 1997, whichever occurs later.

(4) Notwithstanding any other provision of law, upon commencement of, or knowledge of, the operation of a family day care home on his or her property, the landlord or property owner may require the family day care home provider to pay an increased security deposit for operation of the family day care home. The increase in deposit may be required notwithstanding that a lesser amount is required of tenants who do not operate family day care homes. In no event, however, shall the total security deposit charged exceed the maximum allowable under existing law.

(5) Section 1596.890 shall not apply to this subdivision.

(Amended by Stats. 1996, Ch. 449, Sec. 2. Effective January 1, 1997.)

1597.43.

The Legislature finds and declares all of the following:

(a) Family day care homes operated under the standards of state law constitute accessory uses of residentially zoned and occupied properties and do not fundamentally alter the nature of the underlying residential uses. Family day care homes draw clients and vehicles to their sites during a limited time of day and do not require the attendance of a large number of employees and equipment.

(b) The uses of congregate care facilities are distinguishable from the uses of family day care homes operated under the standards of state law. For purposes of this section, a "congregate care facility" means a "residential facility," as defined in paragraph (1) of subdivision (a) of Section 1502. Congregate care facilities are used throughout the day and night, and the institutional uses of these facilities are primary uses of the facilities, not accessory uses, and draw a large number of employees, vehicles, and equipment compared to that drawn to family day care homes.

(c) The expansion permitted for family day care homes by Sections 1597.44 and 1597.465 is not appropriate with respect to congregate care facilities, or any other facilities with quasi-institutional uses. Therefore, with these provisions, the Legislature does not intend to alter the legal standards governing congregate care facilities and these provisions are not intended to encourage, or be a precedent for, changes in statutory and case law governing congregate care facilities.

(Added by Stats. 1996, Ch. 18, Sec. 3.5. Effective January 1, 1997.)

1597.44.

A small family day care home may provide care for more than six and up to eight children, without an additional adult attendant, if all of the following conditions are met:

(a) At least one child is enrolled in and attending kindergarten or elementary school and a second child is at least six years of age.

(b) No more than two infants are cared for during any time when more than six children are cared for.

(c) The licensee notifies each parent that the facility is caring for two additional schoolage children and that there may be up to seven or eight children in the home at one time.

(d) The licensee obtains the written consent of the property owner when the family day care home is operated on property that is leased or rented.

(Amended by Stats. 2003, Ch. 744, Sec. 1. Effective January 1, 2004.)

1597.45.

All of the following shall apply to small family day care homes:

(a) The use of a single-family residence as a small family day care home shall be considered a residential use of property for the purposes of all local ordinances.

(b) No local jurisdiction shall impose a business license, fee, or tax for the privilege of operating a small family day care home.

(c) Use of a single-family dwelling for purposes of a small family day care home shall not constitute a change of occupancy for purposes of Part 1.5 (commencing with Section 17910) of Division 13 (State Housing Law) or for purposes of local building codes.

(d) A small family day care home shall not be subject to Article 1 (commencing with Section 13100) or Article 2 (commencing with Section 13140) of Chapter 1 of Part 2 of Division 12, except that a small family day care home shall contain a fire extinguisher and smoke detector device that meet standards established by the State Fire Marshal and one or more functioning carbon monoxide detectors that meet the requirements of Chapter 8 (commencing with Section 13260) of Part 2 of Division 12. The department shall account for the presence of the carbon monoxide detectors during inspections.

(Amended by Stats. 2014, Ch. 503, Sec. 5. (AB 2386) Effective January 1, 2015.)

1597.46.

All of the following shall apply to large family day care homes:

(a) A city, county, or city and county shall not prohibit large family day care homes on lots zoned for single-family dwellings, but shall do one of the following:

(1) Classify these homes as a permitted use of residential property for zoning purposes.

(2) Grant a nondiscretionary permit to use a lot zoned for a single-family dwelling to a large family day care home that complies with local ordinances prescribing reasonable standards, restrictions, and requirements concerning spacing and concentration, traffic control, parking, and noise control relating to those homes, and complies with subdivision (e) and regulations adopted by the State Fire Marshal pursuant to that subdivision. Noise standards shall be consistent with local noise ordinances implementing the noise element of the general plan and shall take into consideration the noise level generated by children. The permit issued pursuant to this paragraph shall be granted by the zoning administrator or, if there is no zoning administrator, by the person or persons designated by the planning agency to grant these permits, upon the certification without a hearing.

(3) Require a large family day care home to apply for a permit to use a lot zoned for single-family dwellings. The zoning administrator or, if there is no zoning administrator, the person or persons designated by the planning agency to handle the use permits, shall review and decide the applications. The use permit shall be granted if the large family day care home complies with local ordinances, if any, prescribing reasonable standards, restrictions, and requirements concerning the following factors: spacing and concentration, traffic control, parking, and noise control relating to those homes, and complies with subdivision (e) and regulations adopted by the State Fire Marshal pursuant to that subdivision. Noise standards shall be consistent with local noise ordinances implementing the noise element of the general plan and shall take into consideration the noise levels generated by children. The local government shall process a required permit as economically as possible.

Fees charged for review shall not exceed the costs of the review and permit process. An applicant may request a verification of fees, and the city, county, or city and county shall provide the applicant with a written breakdown within 45 days of the request. Beginning July 1, 2007, the application form for large family day care home permits shall include a statement of the applicant's right to request the written fee verification.

Not less than 10 days prior to the date on which the decision will be made on the application, the zoning administrator or person designated to handle the use permits shall give notice of the proposed use by mail or delivery to all owners shown on the last equalized assessment roll as owning real property within a 100-foot radius of the exterior boundaries of the proposed large family day care home. A hearing on the application for a permit issued pursuant to this paragraph shall not be held before a decision is made unless a hearing is requested by the applicant or other affected person. The applicant or other affected person may appeal the decision. The appellant shall pay the cost, if any, of the appeal.

(b) In connection with an action taken pursuant to paragraph (2) or (3) of subdivision (a), a city, county, or city and county shall do all of the following:

(1) Upon the request of an applicant, provide a list of the permits and fees that are required by the city, county, or city and county, including information about other permits that may be required by other departments in the city, county, or city and county, or by other public agencies. The city, county, or city and county shall, upon request of an applicant, also provide information about the anticipated length of time for reviewing and processing the permit application.

(2) Upon the request of an applicant, provide information on the breakdown of any individual fees charged in connection with the issuance of the permit.

(3) If a deposit is required to cover the cost of the permit, provide information to the applicant about the estimated final cost to the applicant of the permit, and procedures for receiving a refund from the portion of the deposit not used.

(c) A large family day care home shall not be subject to the provisions of Division 13 (commencing with Section 21000) of the Public Resources Code.

(d) Use of a single-family dwelling for the purposes of a large family day care home shall not constitute a change of occupancy for purposes of Part 1.5 (commencing with Section 17910) of Division 13 (State Housing Law), or for purposes of local building and fire codes.

(e) A large family day care home shall have one or more functioning carbon monoxide detectors that meet the requirements of Chapter 8 (commencing with Section 13260) of Part 2 of Division 12. The department shall account for the presence of the carbon monoxide detectors during inspections.

(f) Large family day care homes shall be considered as single-family residences for the purposes of the State Uniform Building Standards Code and local building and fire codes, except with respect to any additional standards specifically designed to promote the fire and life safety of the children in these homes adopted by the State Fire Marshal pursuant to this subdivision. The State Fire Marshal shall adopt separate building standards specifically relating to the subject of fire and life safety in large family day care homes, which shall be published in Title 24 of the California Code of Regulations. These standards shall apply uniformly throughout the state and shall include, but not be limited to: (1) the requirement that a large family day care home contain a fire extinguisher or smoke detector device, or both, that meets standards established by the State Fire Marshal; (2) specification as to the number of required exits from the home; and (3) specification as to the floor or floors on which day care may be provided. Enforcement of these provisions shall be in accordance with Sections 13145 and 13146. No city, county, city and county, or district shall adopt or enforce a building ordinance or local rule or regulation relating to the subject of fire and life safety in large family day care homes that is inconsistent with those standards adopted by the State Fire Marshal, except to the extent the building ordinance or local rule or regulation applies to single-family residences in which day care is not provided.

(g) The State Fire Marshal shall adopt the building standards required in subdivision (d) and any other regulations necessary to implement this section.
(Amended by Stats. 2014, Ch. 503, Sec. 6. (AB 2386) Effective January 1, 2015.)
1597.465.
A large family day care home may provide care for more than 12 children and up to and including 14 children, if all of the following conditions are met:
(a) At least one child is enrolled in and attending kindergarten or elementary school and a second child is at least six years of age.
(b) No more than three infants are cared for during any time when more than 12 children are being cared for.
(c) The licensee notifies a parent that the facility is caring for two additional schoolage children and that there may be up to 13 or 14 children in the home at one time.
(d) The licensee obtains the written consent of the property owner when the family day care home is operated on property that is leased or rented.
(Amended by Stats. 2003, Ch. 744, Sec. 2. Effective January 1, 2004.)
1597.467.
(a) Whenever any licensee under this chapter has reasonable cause to believe that a child in his or her care has suffered any injury or has been subjected to any act of violence while under the licensee's care, the licensee shall, as soon as possible, report that injury or act of violence to the parent, parents, or guardian of that child.
(b) (1) A report shall be made to the department by telephone or fax during the department's normal business hours before the close of the next working day following the occurrence during the operation of a family day care home of any of the following events:
(A) Death of any child from any cause.
(B) Any injury to any child that requires medical treatment.
(C) Any unusual incident or child absence that threatens the physical or emotional health or safety of any child.
(2) In addition to the report required pursuant to paragraph (1), a written report shall be submitted to the department within seven days following the occurrence of any events specified in paragraph (1). The report shall contain all of the following information:
(A) Child's name, age, sex, and date of admission.
(B) Date and nature of the event.
(C) Attending physician's name and findings and treatment, if any.
(D) Disposition of the case.
(c) The department may develop the report form to be used for reporting purposes pursuant to this section, and shall maintain all reports filed under this section in a manner that allows the department to report the data to the Legislature.
(d) The failure of a licensee to report, as prescribed by this section, any injury of, or act of violence to, a child under the licensee's care may be grounds for the suspension of his or her license pursuant to this chapter, but shall not constitute a misdemeanor.
(e) Nothing in this section shall relieve any licensee of any obligation imposed by other law including, but not limited to, laws relating to seeking medical attention for a child or reporting suspected child abuse.
(Added by Stats. 2001, Ch. 679, Sec. 1. Effective January 1, 2002.)
1597.47.
The provisions of this chapter shall not be construed to preclude any city, county, or other local public entity from placing restrictions on building heights, setback, or lot dimensions of a family day care facility as long as such restrictions are identical to those applied to other single-family residences. The provisions of this chapter shall not be construed to preclude the application to a family day care facility for children of any local ordinance which deals with health and safety, building standards, environmental impact standards, or any other matter within the jurisdiction of a local public entity. The provisions of this chapter also shall not be construed to prohibit or restrict the abatement of nuisances by a city, county, or city and county. However, such ordinance or nuisance abatement shall not distinguish family day care facilities from other single-family dwellings, except as otherwise provided in this chapter.
(Added by Stats. 1983, Ch. 1233, Sec. 6.)
1597.52.
(a) Licensing reviews of a family day care home for children shall be limited to health and safety considerations and shall not include any reviews of the content of any educational or training programs of the facility.
(b) No home shall be licensed or registered as a large family day care home after January 1, 1984, unless the provider has at least one year's experience as a regulated small family day care home operator or as an administrator of a licensed day care center. The director may waive this requirement upon a finding that the applicant has sufficient qualifying experience.
(Amended by Stats. 1985, Ch. 1064, Sec. 30.)
1597.53.
No family day care home for children shall be licensed under Chapter 3 (commencing with Section 1500), but shall be subject to licensure exclusively in accordance with this chapter and Chapter 3.4 (commencing with Section 1596.70) which shall apply to family day care homes.
(Amended by Stats. 1984, Ch. 1615, Sec. 14.)
1597.531.
(a) All family day care homes for children shall maintain in force either liability insurance covering injury to clients and guests in the amount of at least one hundred thousand dollars ($100,000) per occurrence and three hundred thousand dollars ($300,000) in the total annual aggregate, sustained on account of the negligence of the licensee or its employees, or a bond in the aggregate amount of three hundred thousand dollars

($300,000). In lieu of the liability insurance or the bond, the family day care home may maintain a file of affidavits signed by each parent with a child enrolled in the home which meets the requirements of this subdivision. The affidavit shall state that the parent has been informed that the family day care home does not carry liability insurance or a bond according to standards established by the state. If the provider does not own the premises used as the family day care home, the affidavit shall also state that the parent has been informed that the liability insurance, if any, of the owner of the property or the homeowners' association, as appropriate, may not provide coverage for losses arising out of, or in connection with, the operation of the family day care home, except to the extent that the losses are caused by, or result from, an action or omission by the owner of the property or the homeowners' association, for which the owner of the property or the homeowners' association would otherwise be liable under the law. These affidavits shall be on a form provided by the department and shall be reviewed at each licensing inspection.
(b) A family day care home that maintains liability insurance or a bond pursuant to this section, and that provides care in premises that are rented or leased or uses premises which share common space governed by a homeowners' association, shall name the owner of the property or the homeowners' association, as appropriate, as an additional insured party on the liability insurance policy or bond if all of the following conditions are met:
(1) The owner of the property or governing body of the homeowners' association makes a written request to be added as an additional insured party.
(2) The addition of the owner of the property or the homeowners' association does not result in cancellation or nonrenewal of the insurance policy or bond carried by the family day care home.
(3) Any additional premium assessed for this coverage is paid by the owner of the property or the homeowners' association.
(c) As used in this section, "homeowners' association" means an association of a common interest development, as defined in Sections 4080 and 4100 of the Civil Code.
(Amended by Stats. 2012, Ch. 181, Sec. 62. (AB 806) Effective January 1, 2013. Operative January 1, 2014, by Sec. 86 of Ch. 181.)
1597.54.
All family day care homes for children, shall apply for a license under this chapter, except that any home which on June 28, 1981, had a valid and unexpired license to operate as a family day care home for children under other provisions of law shall be deemed to have a license under this chapter for the unexpired term of the license at which time a new license may be issued upon fulfilling the requirements of this chapter.
An applicant for licensure as a family day care home for children shall file with the department, pursuant to its regulations, an application on forms furnished by the department, which shall include, but not be limited to, all of the following:
(a) A brief statement confirming that the applicant is financially secure to operate a family day care home for children. The department shall not require any other specific or detailed financial disclosure.
(b) (1) Evidence that the small family day care home contains a fire extinguisher or smoke detector device, or both, which meets standards established by the State Fire Marshal under subdivision (d) of Section 1597.45, or evidence that the large family day care home meets the standards established by the State Fire Marshal under subdivision (d) of Section 1597.46.
(2) Evidence satisfactory to the department that there is a fire escape and disaster plan for the facility and that fire drills and disaster drills will be conducted at least once every six months. The documentation of these drills shall be maintained at the facility on a form prepared by the department and shall include the date and time of the drills.
(c) The fingerprints of any applicant of a family day care home license, and any other adult, as required under subdivision (b) of Section 1596.871.
(d) Evidence of a current tuberculosis clearance, as defined in regulations that the department shall adopt, for any adult in the home during the time that children are under care. This requirement may be satisfied by a current certificate, as defined in subdivision (f) of Section 121525, that indicates freedom from infectious tuberculosis as set forth in Section 121525.
(e) Commencing September 1, 2016, evidence of current immunity or exemption from immunity, as described in Section 1597.622, for the applicant and any other person who provides care and supervision to the children.
(f) Evidence satisfactory to the department of the ability of the applicant to comply with this chapter and Chapter 3.4 (commencing with Section 1596.70) and the regulations adopted pursuant to those chapters.
(g) Evidence satisfactory to the department that the applicant and all other persons residing in the home are of reputable and responsible character. The evidence shall include, but not be limited to, a criminal record clearance pursuant to Section 1596.871, employment history, and character references.
(h) Failure of the applicant to cooperate with the licensing agency in the completion of the application shall result in the denial of the application. Failure to cooperate means that the information described in this section and in regulations of the department has not been provided, or not provided in the form requested by the licensing agency, or both.
(i) Other information as may be required by the department for the proper administration and enforcement of the act.
(Amended by Stats. 2015, Ch. 807, Sec. 3. (SB 792) Effective January 1, 2016.)
1597.541.
(a) The department shall adopt regulations regarding age-appropriate immunization requirements for enrolled children for family day care homes.

(b) All family day care homes for children shall maintain evidence that enrolled children have met the age-appropriate immunization requirements adopted pursuant to this section.
(Added by Stats. 1992, Ch. 1316, Sec. 9. Effective January 1, 1993.)
1597.542.
(a) The Division of Child Care Licensing in the department shall clearly differentiate degrees of violations of the regulations adopted for purposes of this chapter by the impact upon children in care.
(b) The department shall implement this section only to the extent funds are available in accordance with Section 18285.5 of the Welfare and Institutions Code.
(Amended by Stats. 1993, Ch. 726, Sec. 9. Effective October 4, 1993.)
1597.543.
Every family day care home for children shall have one or more carbon monoxide detectors in the facility that meet the standards established in Chapter 8 (commencing with Section 13260) of Part 2 of Division 12. The department shall account for the presence of these detectors during inspections.
(Added by Stats. 2014, Ch. 503, Sec. 7. (AB 2386) Effective January 1, 2015.)
1597.55a.
(a) Every family day care home shall be subject to unannounced inspections by the department, as provided in this section. The department shall inspect these facilities as often as necessary to ensure the quality of care provided.
(b) The department shall conduct an announced site inspection prior to the initial licensing of the applicant.
(c) The department shall conduct an annual unannounced inspection of a facility under any of the following circumstances:
(1) When a license is on probation.
(2) When the terms of agreement in a facility compliance plan require an annual inspection.
(3) When an accusation against a licensee is pending.
(4) In order to verify that a person who has been ordered out of a family day care home by the department is no longer at the facility.
(d) (1) The department shall conduct annual unannounced inspections of no less than 30 percent of facilities not subject to an inspection under subdivision (c).
(2) These unannounced inspections shall be conducted based on a random sampling methodology developed by the department.
(e) The department shall inspect a licensed family day care home at least once every three years.
(f) A public agency under contract with the department may make spot checks if it does not result in any cost to the state. However, spot checks shall not be required by the department.
(g) The department or licensing agency shall make an unannounced site inspection on the basis of a complaint and a followup inspection, as provided in Section 1596.853.
(h) An unannounced site inspection shall adhere to both of the following conditions:
(1) The inspection shall take place only during the facility's normal business hours or at any time family day care services are being provided.
(2) The inspection of the facility shall be limited to those parts of the facility in which family day care services are provided or to which the children have access.
(i) The department shall implement this section during periods that Section 1597.55b is not being implemented in accordance with Section 18285.5 of the Welfare and Institutions Code.
(j) It is the intent of the Legislature to achieve annual inspections for licensed family day care homes and facilities governed by this section on or before July 1, 2021.
(Amended by Stats. 2019, Ch. 27, Sec. 14. (SB 80) Effective June 27, 2019.)
1597.55b.
No site visits, unannounced visits, or spot checks, shall be made under this chapter except as provided in this section.
(a) An announced site visit shall be required prior to the licensing of the applicant.
(b) A public agency under contract with the department may make spot checks if they do not result in any cost to the state. However, spot checks shall not be required by the department.
(c) An unannounced site visit to all licensed family day care homes shall be made annually and as often as necessary to ensure compliance.
(d) The department or licensing agency shall make an unannounced site visit on the basis of a complaint and a followup visit as provided in Section 1596.853. At no time shall other site visit requirements described by this section prevent a timely site visit response to a complaint.
(e) The department shall annually make unannounced spot visits on 20 percent of all family day care homes for children licensed under this chapter. The unannounced visits may be made at any time, and shall be in addition to the visits required by subdivisions (b) and (c).
(f) An unannounced site visit shall comply with both of the following conditions:
(1) The visit shall take place only during the facility's normal business hours or at any time family day care services are being provided.
(2) The inspection of the facility shall be limited to those parts of the facility in which family day care services are provided or to which the children have access.
(g) The department shall implement this section only to the extent funds are available in accordance with Section 18285.5 of the Welfare and Institutions Code.
(Amended by Stats. 2003, Ch. 225, Sec. 18. Effective August 11, 2003.)
1597.56.

(a) The department shall notify a family day care home in writing of all deficiencies in its compliance with this act and the rules and regulations adopted pursuant to this act, and shall set a reasonable length of time for compliance by the family day care home. Upon a finding of noncompliance with a plan of correction, the department may levy a civil penalty that shall be paid to the department each day until the department finds the family day care home in compliance.
(b) In developing a plan of correction, both the licensee and the department shall give due consideration to the following factors:
(1) The gravity of the violation.
(2) The history of previous violations.
(3) The possibility of a threat to the health or safety of any child in the facility.
(4) The number of children affected by the violation.
(5) The availability of equipment or personnel necessary to correct the violation, if appropriate.
(c) The department shall ensure that the licensee's plan of correction is verifiable and measurable. The plan of correction shall specify what evidence is acceptable to establish that a deficiency has been corrected. This evidence shall be included in the department's facility file.
(d) The department shall adopt regulations establishing procedures for the imposition of civil penalties under this section.
(Amended by Stats. 2008, Ch. 291, Sec. 24. Effective September 25, 2008.)
1597.57.
The department shall do all of the following:
(a) Develop and utilize one application form for all family day care homes for children requesting a new license.
(b) Establish for parents a consumer education program annually on the law and regulations governing family day care homes for children under this chapter and the role of the state and other public entities and local associations in relation to family day care homes for children. In planning this program, the department shall seek the assistance of other public entities and local associations.
(c) Administer an orientation program for new operators of family day care homes for children that may be conducted directly by the department or by contract with local governments or family day care home associations.
(Amended by Stats. 1992, Ch. 1315, Sec. 34. Effective January 1, 1993.)
1597.58.
(a) In addition to the suspension, temporary suspension, or revocation of a license issued under this chapter, the department shall levy a civil penalty.
(b) (1) The amount of the civil penalty shall be one hundred dollars ($100) per day for each violation of this chapter if a facility fails to correct a deficiency after being provided a specified length of time to correct that deficiency.
(A) If a licensee or a licensee's representative submits evidence to the department that the licensee has corrected a deficiency, and the department, after reviewing that evidence, has determined that the deficiency has been corrected, the civil penalty shall cease as of the day the department received that evidence.
(B) If the department deems it necessary, the department shall inspect the facility within five working days after the department receives evidence pursuant to subparagraph (A) to confirm that the deficiency has been corrected.
(C) If the department determines that the deficiency has not been corrected, the civil penalty shall continue to accrue from the date of the original citation.
(D) If the department is able to verify that the deficiency was corrected prior to the date on which the department received the evidence pursuant to subparagraph (A), the civil penalty shall cease as of that earlier date.
(2) (A) If the department issues a notification of deficiency to a facility for a repeat violation of a violation specified in paragraph (1), the department shall assess an immediate civil penalty of two hundred fifty dollars ($250) per repeat violation and one hundred dollars ($100) for each day the repeat violation continues after citation. The notification of deficiency shall state the manner in which the deficiency constitutes a repeat violation and shall be submitted to a supervisor for review and approval.
(B) For purposes of this section, "repeat violation" means a violation within 12 months of a prior violation of a statutory or regulatory provision designated by the same combination of letters or numerals, or both letters and numerals.
(C) Notwithstanding subparagraphs (A) and (B), the department, in its sole discretion, may reduce the civil penalty for the cited repeat violation to the level of the underlying violation, as applicable, if it determines that the cited repeat violation is not substantially similar to the original violation.
(3) If the nature or seriousness of the violation or the frequency of the violation warrants a higher penalty or an immediate civil penalty assessment, or both, as provided in this chapter, a correction of the deficiency shall not impact the imposition of a civil penalty.
(c) The department shall assess an immediate civil penalty of five hundred dollars ($500) per violation and one hundred dollars ($100) for each day the violation continues after citation, for any of the following serious violations:
(1) Any violation that the department determines resulted in the injury or illness of a child.
(2) Absence of supervision, including, but not limited to, a child left unattended and a child left alone with a person under 18 years of age.
(3) Accessible bodies of water, when prohibited by this chapter or regulations adopted pursuant to this chapter.
(4) Accessible firearms, ammunition, or both.
(5) Refused entry to a facility or any part of a facility in violation of Sections 1596.852, 1596.853, 1597.55a, and 1597.55b.

(6) The presence of a person subject to a department Order of Exclusion on the premises.

(d) If the department issues a notification of deficiency to a facility for a repeat violation of a violation specified in subdivision (c), the department shall assess an immediate civil penalty of one thousand dollars ($1,000) per repeat violation and one hundred dollars ($100) for each day the repeat violation continues after citation. The notification of deficiency shall state the manner in which the deficiency constitutes a repeat violation and shall be submitted to a supervisor for review and approval.

(e) For a violation that the department determines resulted in the death of a child, the civil penalty shall be assessed as follows:

(1) Five thousand dollars ($5,000) for a small family day care home, as described in Section 1597.44.

(2) Seven thousand five hundred dollars ($7,500) for a large family day care home, as described in Section 1597.465.

(f) (1) For a violation that the department determines constitutes physical abuse or resulted in serious injury, as defined in Section 1596.8865, to a child, the civil penalty shall be assessed as follows:

(A) One thousand dollars ($1,000) for a small family day care home, as described in Section 1597.44.

(B) Two thousand dollars ($2,000) for a large family day care home, as described in Section 1597.465.

(2) For purposes of this subdivision, "physical abuse" includes physical injury inflicted upon a child by another person by other than accidental means, sexual abuse as defined in Section 11165.1 of the Penal Code, neglect as defined in Section 11165.2 of the Penal Code, or unlawful corporal punishment or injury as defined in Section 11165.4 of the Penal Code when the person responsible for the child's welfare is a licensee, administrator, or employee of any facility licensed to care for children, or an administrator or employee of a public or private school or other institution or agency.

(g) (1) Before the assessment of a civil penalty pursuant to subdivision (e) or (f), the decision shall be approved by the program administrator of the Community Care Licensing Division.

(2) (A) The department shall reduce the amount of a civil penalty due pursuant to subdivision (e) or (f) by the amount of the civil penalty already assessed for the underlying violation.

(B) If the amount of the civil penalty that the department has already assessed for the underlying violation exceeds the amount of the penalty pursuant to subdivision (e) or (f), the larger amount shall prevail and be due and payable as already assessed by the department.

(h) Notwithstanding any other law, revenues received by the state from the payment of civil penalties imposed on licensed family day care homes pursuant to this chapter or Chapter 3.4 (commencing with Section 1596.70), shall be deposited in the Child Health and Safety Fund, created pursuant to Chapter 4.6 (commencing with Section 18285) of Part 6 of Division 9 of the Welfare and Institutions Code, and shall be expended, upon appropriation by the Legislature, pursuant to subdivision (f) of Section 18285 of the Welfare and Institutions Code exclusively for the technical assistance, orientation, training, and education of licensed family day care home providers.

(i) (1) A notification of a deficiency written by a representative of the department shall include a factual description of the nature of the deficiency fully stating the manner in which the licensee failed to comply with the specified statute or regulation, and, if applicable, the particular place or area in which the deficiency occurred. The department shall make a good faith effort to work with the licensee to determine the cause of the deficiency and ways to prevent any repeat violations.

(2) The department shall adopt regulations setting forth appeal procedures for deficiencies.

(j) (1) A licensee shall have the right to submit to the department a written request for a formal review of a civil penalty assessed pursuant to subdivisions (d) and (e) within 15 business days of receipt of the notice of a civil penalty assessment and shall provide all available supporting documentation at that time. The review shall be conducted by the deputy director of the Community Care Licensing Division. The licensee may submit additional supporting documentation that was unavailable at the time of submitting the request for review within the first 30 business days after submitting the request for review. If the department requires additional information from the licensee, that information shall be requested within the first 30 business days after receiving the request for review. The licensee shall provide this additional information within 30 business days of receiving the request from the department. If the deputy director determines that the civil penalty was not assessed, or the finding of the deficiency that resulted in the assessment of the civil penalty was not made, in accordance with applicable statutes or regulations of the department, he or she may amend or dismiss the civil penalty or finding of deficiency. The licensee shall be notified in writing of the deputy director's decision within 60 business days of the date when all necessary information has been provided to the department by the licensee.

(2) Upon exhausting the review described in paragraph (1), a licensee may further appeal that decision to an administrative law judge. Proceedings shall be conducted in accordance with Chapter 5 (commencing with Section 11500) of Part 1 of Division 3 of Title 2 of the Government Code, and the department shall have all the powers granted by those provisions. In all proceedings conducted in accordance with this section, the standard of proof shall be by a preponderance of the evidence.

(3) If, in addition to an assessment of civil penalties, the department elects to file an administrative action to suspend or revoke the facility license that includes violations relating to the assessment of the civil penalties, the department review of the pending appeal shall cease and the assessment of the civil penalties shall be heard as part of the administrative action process.

(4) Civil penalties shall be due and payable when administrative appeals have been exhausted. Unless payment arrangements have been made that are acceptable to the department, a civil penalty not paid within 30 days shall be subject to late fees, as specified by the department in regulation.

(k) (1) A licensee shall have the right to submit to the department a written request for a formal review of any other civil penalty or deficiency not described in subdivision (j) within 15 business days of receipt of the notice of a civil penalty assessment or a finding of a deficiency, and shall provide all available supporting documentation at that time. The review shall be conducted by a regional manager of the Community Care Licensing Division. The licensee may submit additional supporting documentation that was unavailable at the time of submitting the request for review within the first 30 business days after submitting the request for review. If the department requires additional information from the licensee, that information shall be requested within the first 30 business days after receiving the request for review. The licensee shall provide this additional information within 30 business days of receiving the request from the department. If the regional manager determines that the civil penalty was not assessed, or the finding of the deficiency was not made, in accordance with applicable statutes or regulations of the department, he or she may amend or dismiss the civil penalty or finding of deficiency. The licensee shall be notified in writing of the regional manager's decision within 60 business days of the date when all necessary information has been provided to the department by the licensee.

(2) Upon exhausting the review described in paragraph (1), the licensee may further appeal that decision to the program administrator of the Community Care Licensing Division within 15 business days of receipt of notice of the regional manager's decision. The licensee may submit additional supporting documentation that was unavailable at the time of appeal to the program administrator within the first 30 business days after requesting that appeal. If the department requires additional information from the licensee, that information shall be requested within the first 30 business days after receiving the request for the appeal. The licensee shall provide this additional information within 30 business days of receiving the request from the department. If the program administrator determines that the civil penalty was not assessed, or the finding of the deficiency was not made, in accordance with applicable statutes or regulations of the department, he or she may amend or dismiss the civil penalty or finding of deficiency. The licensee shall be notified in writing of the program administrator's decision within 60 business days of the date when all necessary information has been provided to the department by the licensee. The program administrator's decision is considered final and concludes the licensee's administrative appeal rights regarding the appeal conducted pursuant to this paragraph.

(3) Civil penalties shall be due and payable when administrative appeals have been exhausted. Unless payment arrangements have been made that are acceptable to the department, a civil penalty not paid within 30 days shall be subject to late fees, as specified by the department in regulation.

(l) Notwithstanding the Administrative Procedure Act (Chapter 3.5 (commencing with Section 11340) of Part 1 of Division 3 of Title 2 of the Government Code), the department may implement and administer the changes made by the act that added this subdivision through all-county letters or similar written instructions until regulations are adopted pursuant to the Administrative Procedure Act.

(m) This section shall become operative on July 1, 2017.

(Repealed (in Sec. 15) and added by Stats. 2016, Ch. 823, Sec. 16. (AB 2231) Effective January 1, 2017. Section operative July 1, 2017, by its own provisions.)

1597.59.

The department and the local agencies with which it contracts for the licensing of family day care homes for children shall grant or deny a license to a family day care home for children within 30 days after receipt of all appropriate licensing application materials as determined by the department, provided both of the following conditions are met:

(a) A site visit has been completed and the family day care home has been found to be in compliance with licensing standards.

(b) The applicant and each person described by subdivision (b) of Section 1596.871 has obtained a criminal record clearance, or been granted a criminal record exemption by the department or the local contracting agency.

The department shall conduct an initial site visit within 30 days after the receipt of all appropriate licensing application materials.

(Amended by Stats. 1997, Ch. 606, Sec. 11. Effective October 3, 1997.)

1597.61.

(a) When the department determines that a family day care home for children is operating without a license and notifies the unlicensed provider of the requirement for the license, the licensing agency may issue a cease and desist order only if it finds and documents that continued operation of the facility will be dangerous to the health and safety of the children or if a license held by the facility has been revoked by the department within two years preceding the determination of unlicensed operation. In all other cases where the licensing agency determines such a facility is operating without a license and notifies the unlicensed provider of the requirements for the license, the licensing agency may issue a cease and desist order only if the unlicensed provider does not apply for a license within a reasonable time after the notice.

(b) If an unlicensed family day care home fails to respond to a cease and desist order issued pursuant to subdivision (a), or if the department determines it necessary to protect the immediate health and safety of the children, the licensing agency may bring an action to enjoin such a home from continuing to operate pursuant to Section 1596.89.

(c) The district attorney of a county shall, upon application by the department, institute and conduct the prosecution of any action brought by the licensing agency against an unlicensed family day care home located in that county.

(Amended by Stats. 1988, Ch. 1098, Sec. 4.)

1597.62.

(a) The department may impose civil penalties of not less than twenty-five dollars ($25) and not more than fifty dollars ($50) per day per violation for uncorrected violations that present an immediate or potential risk to the health and safety of children in care. The penalties shall be imposed in accordance with Sections 1596.893b and 1597.56.

(b) The department shall implement this section only to the extent funds are available in accordance with Section 18285.5 of the Welfare and Institutions Code.

(Amended by Stats. 2008, Ch. 291, Sec. 25.2. Effective September 25, 2008.)

1597.621.

Family day care homes that, on December 31, 1983, have a valid unexpired registration to operate as a family day care home for children pursuant to Section 1597.62 in one of the pilot counties shall be deemed to be issued a family day care license effective January 1, 1984. Licensure pursuant to this section shall not require a visit pursuant to the requirement set forth in subdivision (a) of Section 1597.55. However, all other requirements of licensing shall continue to be met. Complaint and revocation procedures may be enforced.

(Amended by Stats. 1992, Ch. 1315, Sec. 37. Effective January 1, 1993.)

1597.622.

(a) (1) Commencing September 1, 2016, a person shall not be employed or volunteer at a family day care home if he or she has not been immunized against influenza, pertussis, and measles. Each employee and volunteer shall receive an influenza vaccination between August 1 and December 1 of each year.

(2) If a person meets all other requirements for employment or volunteering, as applicable, but needs additional time to obtain and provide his or her immunization records, the person may be employed or volunteer conditionally for a maximum of 30 days upon signing and submitting a written statement attesting that he or she has been immunized as required.

(b) A person is exempt from the requirements of this section only under any of the following circumstances:

(1) The person submits a written statement from a licensed physician declaring that because of the person's physical condition or medical circumstances, immunization is not safe.

(2) The person submits a written statement by a licensed physician providing that the person has evidence of current immunity to the diseases described in subdivision (a).

(3) The person submits a written declaration that he or she has declined the influenza vaccination. This exemption applies only to the influenza vaccine.

(4) The person was hired after December 1 of the previous year and before August 1 of the current year. This exemption applies only to the influenza vaccine during the first year of employment or volunteering.

(c) The family day care home shall maintain documentation of the required immunizations or exemptions from immunization, as set forth in this section, in the person's personnel record that is maintained by the family day care home.

(d) For purposes of this section, "volunteer" means any nonemployee who provides care and supervision to children in care.

(Added by Stats. 2015, Ch. 807, Sec. 4. (SB 792) Effective January 1, 2016.)

CHAPTER 3.65. Employer-Sponsored Child Care Centers [1597.70 - 1597.71]

(Chapter 3.65 added by Stats. 1994, Ch. 690, Sec. 4.)

ARTICLE 1. General Provisions [1597.70- 1597.70.]

(Article 1 added by Stats. 1994, Ch. 690, Sec. 4.)

1597.70.

The Legislature finds and declares the following:

(a) It is significant that the Santa Clara County Intergovernmental Council has found that due to changes in the labor force and an increase in the child population, 25 percent of the nation's workers must make child care arrangements.

(b) Californians will benefit from investment in child care. According to the House Select Committee on Children, Youth, and Families, one dollar invested in preschool education results in a savings of four dollars and seventy-five cents ($4.75) in social costs.

(c) Allowing and encouraging businesses to open onsite or nearsite employer-sponsored child care centers has had a number of positive effects for Californians, including reduced job absenteeism, closer parent-child relationships, and increased worker productivity.

(d) In a 1990 study, the Department of General Services found that working parents add five to six miles to their daily commute for transporting their children to child care and school, and that the effect of this commute is 1,352 extra miles driven each year and an additional 56 pounds of auto emissions per person per year.

(Added by Stats. 1994, Ch. 690, Sec. 4. Effective January 1, 1995.)

ARTICLE 2. Licensing Waivers for Small Businesses [1597.71- 1597.71.]

(Article 2 added by Stats. 1994, Ch. 690, Sec. 4.)

1597.71.

To encourage and facilitate the establishment of employer-sponsored child day care centers, the department shall allow for reasonable waivers of those regulations presenting difficulties to small businesses for licensure, provided that the health and

safety of all children is maintained and that the applicant has agreed to alternative methods of meeting the purpose and intent of any regulation waived.

(Added by renumbering Section 1571.71 by Stats. 2009, Ch. 140, Sec. 104. (AB 1164) Effective January 1, 2010.)

CHAPTER 3.7. Local Rape Victim Counseling Centers [1598 - 1598.5]

(Chapter 3.7 added by Stats. 1978, Ch. 1312.)

1598.

It is the intent of the Legislature in the enactment of this chapter to establish a grant program administered by the State Department of Social Services to provide support to existing local rape victim counseling centers and to encourage the establishment of such local centers.

(Added by Stats. 1978, Ch. 1312.)

1598.1.

The State Department of Social Services shall provide grants to proposed and existing local rape victim counseling centers. Such centers shall maintain a 24-hour telephone counseling service for rape victims, appropriate in-person counseling and referred service during normal business hours, and maintain other standards or services which shall be determined to be appropriate by the advisory committee established pursuant to Section 13836 of the Penal Code as grant conditions. The advisory committee shall identify the criteria to be utilized in awarding the grants provided by this chapter before any funds are allocated.

In order to be eligible for funding pursuant to this chapter, the centers shall demonstrate an ability to receive and make use of any funds available from governmental, voluntary, philanthropic, or other sources which may be used to augment any state funds appropriated for purposes of this chapter. Each center receiving funds pursuant to this chapter shall make every attempt to qualify for any available federal funding.

State funds provided to establish centers shall be utilized when possible, as determined by the advisory committee, to expand the program and shall not be expended to reduce fiscal support from other public or private sources. The centers shall maintain quarterly and final fiscal reports in a form to be prescribed by the advisory committee. In granting funds, the advisory committee shall give priority to centers which are operated in close proximity to medical treatment facilities.

(Amended by Stats. 1980, Ch. 917.)

1598.5.

The sum of one hundred thousand dollars ($100,000) is hereby appropriated from the General Fund to the State Department of Social Services for expenditure during the 1978–79 fiscal year. Only 5 percent of such funds shall be used for the state administration of the grant program. After the 1978–79 fiscal year, the grant program provided pursuant to Section 1598.1 shall be funded through the regular budgetary process. The funds shall be administered through the Violent Crime Victim Assistance Commission, if created.

(Added by Stats. 1978, Ch. 1312.)

CHAPTER 3.9. Skilled Nursing and Intermediate Care Facility Patient's Bill of Rights [1599 - 1599.4]

(Chapter 3.9 added by Stats. 1979, Ch. 893.)

1599.

It is the intent of the Legislature in enacting this chapter to expressly set forth fundamental human rights which all patients shall be entitled to in a skilled nursing, intermediate care facility, or hospice facility, as defined in Section 1250, and to ensure that patients in such facilities are advised of their fundamental rights and the obligations of the facility.

(Amended by Stats. 2012, Ch. 673, Sec. 6. (SB 135) Effective January 1, 2013.)

1599.1.

Written policies regarding the rights of patients shall be established and shall be made available to the patient, to any guardian, next of kin, sponsoring agency or representative payee, and to the public. Those policies and procedures shall ensure that each patient admitted to the facility has the following rights and is notified of the following facility obligations, in addition to those specified by regulation:

(a) The facility shall employ an adequate number of qualified personnel to carry out all of the functions of the facility.

(b) Each patient shall show evidence of good personal hygiene and be given care to prevent bedsores, and measures shall be used to prevent and reduce incontinence for each patient.

(c) The facility shall provide food of the quality and quantity to meet the patients' needs in accordance with physicians' orders.

(d) The facility shall provide an activity program staffed and equipped to meet the needs and interests of each patient and to encourage self-care and resumption of normal activities. Patients shall be encouraged to participate in activities suited to their individual needs.

(e) The facility shall be clean, sanitary, and in good repair at all times.

(f) A nurses' call system shall be maintained in operating order in all nursing units and provide visible and audible signal communication between nursing personnel and patients. Extension cords to each patient's bed shall be readily accessible to patients at all times.

(g) (1) If a facility has a significant beneficial interest in an ancillary health service provider or if a facility knows that an ancillary health service provider has a significant beneficial interest in the facility, as provided by subdivision (a) of Section 1323, or if the facility has a significant beneficial interest in another facility, as provided by subdivision (c) of Section 1323, the facility shall disclose that interest in writing to the patient, or his or her representative, and advise the patient, or his or her representative, that the patient may choose to have another ancillary health service provider, or facility, as the case may be, provide any supplies or services ordered by a member of the medical staff of the facility.

(2) A facility is not required to make any disclosures required by this subdivision to any patient, or his or her representative, if the patient is enrolled in an organization or entity that provides or arranges for the provision of health care services in exchange for a prepaid capitation payment or premium.

(h) (1) If a resident of a long-term health care facility has been hospitalized in an acute care hospital and asserts his or her rights to readmission pursuant to bed hold provisions, or readmission rights of either state or federal law, and the facility refuses to readmit him or her, the resident may appeal the facility's refusal.

(2) The refusal of the facility as described in this subdivision shall be treated as if it were an involuntary transfer under federal law, and the rights and procedures that apply to appeals of transfers and discharges of nursing facility residents shall apply to the resident's appeal under this subdivision.

(3) If the resident appeals pursuant to this subdivision, and the resident is eligible under the Medi-Cal program, the resident shall remain in the hospital and the hospital may be reimbursed at the administrative day rate, pending the final determination of the hearing officer, unless the resident agrees to placement in another facility.

(4) If the resident appeals pursuant to this subdivision, and the resident is not eligible under the Medi-Cal program, the resident shall remain in the hospital if other payment is available, pending the final determination of the hearing officer, unless the resident agrees to placement in another facility.

(5) If the resident is not eligible for participation in the Medi-Cal program and has no other source of payment, the hearing and final determination shall be made within 48 hours.

(i) (1) Effective July 1, 2007, Sections 483.10, 483.12, 483.13, and 483.15 of Title 42 of the Code of Federal Regulations in effect on July 1, 2006, shall apply to each skilled nursing facility and intermediate care facility, regardless of a resident's payment source or the Medi-Cal or Medicare certification status of the skilled nursing facility or intermediate care facility in which the resident resides, except that a noncertified facility is not obligated to provide notice of Medicaid or Medicare benefits, covered services, or eligibility procedures.

(2) Effective January 1, 2013, Sections 483.10, 483.12, 483.13, and 483.15 of Title 42 of the Code of Federal Regulations in effect on July 1, 2006, shall apply to each hospice facility, regardless of a resident's payment source or the Medi-Cal or Medicare certification status of the hospice facility in which the resident resides, except that a noncertified facility is not obligated to provide notice of Medicaid or Medicare benefits, covered services, or eligibility procedures and a hospice facility is not obligated to comply with the provisions of subdivision (f) of Section 483.15 of Title 42 of the Code of Federal Regulations.

(Amended by Stats. 2012, Ch. 673, Sec. 7. (SB 135) Effective January 1, 2013.)
1599.2.

Written information informing patients of their rights shall include a preamble or preliminary statement in substantial form as follows:

(a) Further facility requirements are set forth in the Health and Safety Code, and in Title 22 of the California Administrative Code.

(b) Willful or repeated violations of either code may subject a facility and its personnel to civil or criminal proceedings.

(c) Patients have the right to voice grievances to facility personnel free from reprisal and can submit complaints to the State Department of Health Services or its representative.
(Added by Stats. 1979, Ch. 893.)
1599.3.

Any rights under this chapter of a patient judicially determined to be incompetent, or who is found by his physician to be medically incapable of understanding such information, or who exhibits a communication barrier, shall devolve to such patient's guardian, conservator, next of kin, sponsoring agency, or representative payer, except when the facility itself is the representative payer.
(Added by Stats. 1979, Ch. 893.)
1599.4.

In no event shall this chapter be construed or applied in a manner which imposes new or additional obligations or standards on skilled nursing, intermediate care facilities, or hospice facilities or their personnel, other than in regard to the notification and explanation of patient's rights or unreasonable costs.
(Amended by Stats. 2012, Ch. 673, Sec. 8. (SB 135) Effective January 1, 2013.)

CHAPTER 3.93. Admission Contracts for Long-Term Health Care Facilities [1599.60 - 1599.84]

(Heading of Chapter 3.93 renumbered from Chapter 3.95 (as added by Stats. 1987, Ch. 625) by Stats. 1990, Ch. 216, Sec. 57.)
1599.60.
As used in this chapter:

(a) "Abbreviated contract of admission" means a contract which meets the provisions of this chapter, except as otherwise provided, for a resident who is receiving respite care services, as defined in Section 1418.1. The following provisions of this chapter shall not apply to an abbreviated contract of admission: subdivision (b) of Section 1599.65, subdivision (b) of Section 1599.67, Section 1599.69, subdivision (b) of Section 1599.76, and Section 1599.79.

(b) "Contract of admission" includes all documents which a resident or his or her representative must sign at the time of, or as a condition of, admission to a long-term health care facility, as defined in Section 1326.

(c) "Department" means the State Department of Health Services or its designee.
(Amended by Stats. 1990, Ch. 1329, Sec. 4.5. Effective September 26, 1990.)
1599.61.

(a) By January 1, 2000, all skilled nursing facilities, as defined in subdivision (c) of Section 1250, intermediate care facilities, as defined in subdivision (d) of Section 1250, and nursing facilities, as defined in subdivision (k) of Section 1250, shall use a standard admission agreement developed and adopted by the department. This standard agreement shall comply with all applicable state and federal laws.

(b) (1) No facility shall alter the standard agreement unless so directed by the department.

(2) The department may develop an abbreviated admission agreement for patients whose length of stay is anticipated to be 14 days or less. This abbreviated agreement may be developed to coordinate with the standard admission agreement. If the patient's stay exceeds 14 days, the nursing facility shall obtain agreement to the remainder of the standard admission agreement.

(3) Nothing in this section shall prevent a skilled nursing facility, an intermediate care facility, or a nursing facility from distributing written explanations of facility-specific rules and procedures, provided that the written explanations are not included or incorporated in, or attached to the standard admission agreement, nor signed by the resident or his or her representative.

(c) Subdivisions (a) and (b) shall apply to all new admissions to skilled nursing facilities, intermediate care facilities, and nursing facilities that occur after December 31, 1999.

(d) By January 1, 2000, the department shall consolidate and develop one comprehensive Patients' Bill of Rights that includes the provisions contained in Chapter 3.9 (commencing with Section 1599), the regulatory resident rights for skilled nursing facilities under Section 72527 of Title 22 of the California Code of Regulations, the regulatory resident rights for intermediate care facilities under Section 73523 of Title 22 of the California Code of Regulations, and the rights afforded residents under Section 483.10 et seq. of Title 42 of the Code of Federal Regulations.

This comprehensive Patients' Bill of Rights shall be a mandatory attachment to all skilled nursing facility, intermediate care facility, and nursing facility contracts as specified in Section 1599.74 of this chapter.

(e) By January 1, 2000, the department shall ensure the translation of the Patients' Bill of Rights described in subdivision (d) into Spanish, Chinese, and other languages as needed to provide copies of the Patients' Bill of Rights to members of any ethnic group that represents at least 1 percent of the state's skilled nursing facility, intermediate care facility, and nursing facility population.

(f) Translated copies of the Patients' Bill of Rights shall be made available to all long-term health care facilities in the state, including skilled nursing facilities, intermediate care facilities, and nursing facilities. It shall be the responsibility of the long-term health care facilities to duplicate and distribute the translated versions of the Patients' Bill of Rights with admissions agreements, when appropriate.

(g) Nothing in this section is intended to change existing statutory or regulatory requirements governing the care provided to nursing facility residents. Similarly, nothing in this section is intended to create a new cause of action against a skilled nursing facility, an intermediate care facility, or a nursing facility as defined in Section 1250, related to its compliance with those existing statutory or regulatory requirements governing the care provided to nursing facility residents.
(Repealed and added by Stats. 1997, Ch. 631, Sec. 3. Effective January 1, 1998.)
1599.62.

(a) Contracts of admission shall not include unlawful waivers of facility liability for the health and safety or personal property of residents. No contract of admission shall include any provision which the facility knows or should know to be deceptive or unlawful under state or federal law.

(b) Violation of this chapter shall result in a Class B citation or a deficiency from the department. For purposes of this section, the admission agreement shall be viewed as a whole and shall result in only one citation.

(c) Unless otherwise expressly provided, the remedies or penalties provided by this chapter do not preclude a resident from seeking any other remedy and penalties available under all other laws of this state.
(Added by Stats. 1987, Ch. 625, Sec. 1.)
1599.63.

(a) Every long-term health care facility shall make complete blank copies of its admission contract immediately available to the public at cost, upon request.

(b) Every long-term health care facility shall post conspicuously in a location accessible to public view within the facility either a complete copy of its admission contract or notice of the availability of it from the facility.

(Added by Stats. 1987, Ch. 625, Sec. 1.)

1599.64.

(a) All abbreviated contracts of admission and contracts of admission shall be printed in black type of not less than 10-point type size, on plain white paper. The print shall appear on one side of the paper only.

(b) The contract shall be written in clear, coherent, and unambiguous language, using words with common and everyday meanings. It shall be appropriately divided, and each section captioned.

(c) The contract for a skilled nursing facility shall have an attachment that is placed before any other attachment and that shall disclose the name of the owner and licensee of the skilled nursing facility and the name and contact information of a single entity that is responsible for all aspects of patient care and the operation of the facility.

(d) An abbreviated contract of admission shall include a statement indicating that respite care services, as defined in Section 1418.1, provided by the skilled nursing facility or intermediate care facility is not a Medi-Cal covered service and can only be provided by the facility on a private-pay or third-party payor basis, unless the person is participating in a Medicaid waiver program pursuant to Section 1396n of Title 42 of the United States Code, or other respite care service already covered by the Medi-Cal program.

(e) An abbreviated contract of admission shall specify the discharge date agreed to upon admission by the skilled nursing facility or intermediate care facility and the person being admitted or his or her representative. This discharge date shall be binding as a ground for discharge in addition to any other ground for discharge pursuant to federal or state law and regulations.

(f) An abbreviated contract of admission shall include a statement informing the person being admitted for respite care services that the contract is designed specifically for the provision of respite care services and cannot be used for any other type of admission to the facility.

(Amended by Stats. 2009, Ch. 532, Sec. 1. (AB 1457) Effective January 1, 2010.)

1599.645.

(a) Within 30 days of approval of a change of ownership by the State Department of Public Health, the skilled nursing facility shall send written notification to all current residents and patients and to the primary contacts listed in the admission agreement of each resident and patient. The notice shall disclose the name of the owner and licensee of the skilled nursing facility and the name and contact information of a single entity that is responsible for all aspects of patient care and the operation of the facility.

(b) The department shall accept a copy of the written notice and a copy of the list of individuals and mailing addresses to whom the facility sent the notification as satisfactory evidence that the facility provided the required written notification.

(Amended by Stats. 2010, Ch. 328, Sec. 125. (SB 1330) Effective January 1, 2011.)

1599.65.

(a) Prior to or at the time of admission, the facility shall make reasonable efforts to communicate the content of the contract to, and obtain on the contract the signature of, the person who is to be admitted to the facility. Unless the prospective resident has been declared legally incompetent or is unable to understand and sign the contract because of his or her medical condition, he or she shall sign or cosign the admission agreement. In the event the patient is unable to sign the contract, the reason shall be documented in the resident's medical record by the admitting physician. This provision does not preclude the facility from obtaining the signature of an agent, responsible party, or a legal representative, if applicable.

(b) The contract of admission for facilities certified to be reimbursed by Medi-Cal shall set forth, in bold capital letters of not less than 10-point type, the prohibition in Section 14110.8 of the Welfare and Institutions Code that no facility may require or solicit as a condition of admission that a Medi-Cal beneficiary have a responsible party sign or cosign the contract of admission. If the Medi-Cal beneficiary has an agent, then the signature of the agent may be required on the contract of admission.

(Added by Stats. 1987, Ch. 625, Sec. 1.)

1599.651.

A person who seeks to be admitted to the same long-term health care facility for which there exists a prior executed contract of admission which was signed by that person, or his or her legal representative, responsible party, or agent, in accordance with this chapter shall not be required to execute a new contract of admission if the person, or his or her legal representative, responsible party, or agent, either prior to or upon readmission, signs a written statement prepared by the facility which lists the modifications to the contract of admission.

The written statement shall indicate the date upon which the person's signature was obtained. The written statement shall be kept on file by the facility with the person's previously signed contract of admission.

This section shall not apply to any person who has been declared legally incompetent subsequent to the time he or she signed the contract of admission. This section shall not apply to any person when the physician and surgeon of that person has determined that the person is unable to understand and sign the written statement because of his or her medical condition.

No written statement shall contain any provision that is prohibited from being included in a contract of admission.

A new contract of admission or a written statement which lists the modifications need not be signed by the person, or his or her legal representative, responsible party, or agent, in the case of a transfer during a bedhold period.

(Added by Stats. 1990, Ch. 353, Sec. 1.)

1599.652.

A person who seeks to be admitted to the same skilled nursing facility or intermediate care facility to receive respite care services for which there already exists a prior executed abbreviated contract of admission which was signed by that person, or his or her legal representative or responsible party, in accordance with this chapter shall not be required to execute a new abbreviated contract of admission if the person, or his or her legal representative or responsible party, either prior to or upon admission, signs a written statement prepared by the facility which lists the modifications to the abbreviated contract of admission.

The written statement shall indicate the date upon which the person's signature was obtained. The written statement shall be kept on file by the facility with the person's previously signed abbreviated contract of admission.

This section shall not apply to any person who has been declared legally incompetent subsequent to the time he or she signed the abbreviated contract of admission. This section shall not apply to any person when the physician and surgeon of that person has determined that the person is unable to understand and sign the written statement because of his or her medical condition.

(Added by Stats. 1990, Ch. 1329, Sec. 6. Effective September 26, 1990.)

1599.66.

Every contract of admission shall clearly and explicitly state whether the facility participates in the Medi-Cal program.

(Added by Stats. 1987, Ch. 625, Sec. 1.)

1599.67.

(a) Every contract of admission shall state clearly what services and supplies are covered by the facility's basic daily rate. In addition, the agreement shall specify in detail which services are optional, and the charges for these services, and indicate that residents will receive monthly statements itemizing all charges incurred by them.

(b) The contract of a facility that is a provider pursuant to Medicare, or Medi-Cal, or both, shall state that optional and covered services may be different for residents in those programs than for private pay residents. When a resident converts from Medicare or private pay to Medi-Cal, the facility shall give the resident a form listing Medi-Cal optional and covered services.

(c) Every contract of admission shall clearly state that the facility is required by law to provide no less than 30 days written notice to the residents of any increase for optional services or in the daily room rate charged by the facility, except as provided in subdivision (b) of Section 1288.

(Added by Stats. 1987, Ch. 625, Sec. 1.)

1599.68.

Any long-term health care facility that imposes interest charges on delinquent accounts shall clearly state in the contract of admission the rate of interest so charged and the method of computation.

(Added by Stats. 1987, Ch. 625, Sec. 1.)

1599.69.

(a) The contract of admission for any long-term health care facility that is a Medi-Cal certified facility shall state in bold capital letters of not less than 10-point type that neither the prospective resident, nor his or her representative, may be required to pay privately for any period during which the resident has been approved for payment by Medi-Cal, and that as provided by Section 14019.3 of the Welfare and Institutions Code, upon presentation of the Medi-Cal card or other proof of eligibility, the facility shall submit a Medi-Cal claim for reimbursement, subject to the rules and regulations of the Medi-Cal program, and the facility shall return any and all payments made by the beneficiary, or any person on behalf of the beneficiary, for Medi-Cal program covered services upon receipt of Medi-Cal payment. The contract shall state in bold capital letters of not less than 10-point type that no certified facility may require as a condition of admission, either in its contract of admission or by oral promise prior to signing the contract, that residents remain in private pay status for a specified period of time.

(b) No contract of admission may require notice of a resident's intent to convert to Medi-Cal status prior to the date of the resident's application for Medi-Cal status. This subdivision does not preclude the facility from requesting notice from a resident who has been admitted.

(Added by Stats. 1987, Ch. 625, Sec. 1.)

1599.70.

(a) No contract of admission may require a security deposit from a Medi-Cal beneficiary who applies for admission to the facility as a Medi-Cal patient.

(b) Any security deposit from a person paying privately upon admission shall be returned within 14 days of the private account being closed, or first Medi-Cal payment, whichever is later, and with no deduction for administration or handling charges.

(Added by Stats. 1987, Ch. 625, Sec. 1.)

1599.71.

(a) No contract of admission shall require the resident to pay for days beyond the date of his or her death or involuntary discharge from the facility, except that a facility may charge the resident for a maximum of three days at the basic daily rate in the event that the resident is voluntarily discharged from the facility less than three days following his or her admission. This section does not affect the provision for a maximum of seven days' payment under the bedhold regulation as specified in Section 72520 of Title 22 of the California Administrative Code.

(b) No contract of admission shall require advance notice of voluntary discharge from a facility.
(Added by Stats. 1987, Ch. 625, Sec. 1.)
1599.72.
No contract of admission shall include a clause requiring residents to sign a consent to all treatment ordered by any physician. Contracts of admission may require consent only for routine nursing care or emergency care. The admission contract shall contain a clause which informs the patient of the right to refuse treatments as set forth in paragraph (4) of subdivision (a) of Section 72527 of Title 22 of the California Administrative Code.
(Added by Stats. 1987, Ch. 625, Sec. 1.)
1599.73.
(a) Every contract of admission shall state that residents have a right to confidential treatment of medical information.
(b) The contract shall provide a means by which the resident may authorize the disclosure of information to specific persons, by attachment of a separate sheet that conforms to the specifications of Section 56 of the Civil Code. After admission, the facility shall encourage residents having capacity to make health care decisions to execute an advance health care directive in the event that he or she becomes unable to give consent for disclosure. The facility shall make available upon request to the long-term care ombudsman a list of newly admitted patients.
(Amended by Stats. 1999, Ch. 658, Sec. 4. Effective January 1, 2000. Operative July 1, 2000, by Sec. 43 of Ch. 658.)
1599.74.
(a) The department shall translate both the statutory Patients' Bill of Rights, as provided in Chapter 3.9 (commencing with Section 1599), the regulatory Patients' Bill of Rights for Skilled Nursing Facilities (commencing with Section 72527 of Title 22 of the California Administrative Code), and, if appropriate, the regulatory Patients' Bill of Rights for Intermediate Care Facilities (commencing with Section 73523 of Title 22 of the California Administrative Code), into Spanish and Chinese, and into other languages as needed for ethnic groups representing 1 percent or more of the nursing home population in the state. The department shall also translate the Patients' Bill of Rights into Braille or have it recorded for the use of blind patients, or both. These translations shall be sent to all long-term health care facilities in the state.
(b) Every contract of admission shall contain a complete copy of both the statutory and regulatory Patients' Bill of Rights. Notwithstanding any other provision of law, the text of the Patients' Bill of Rights shall be in legible print of no less than 12-point type. If a translation has been provided by the department, the text given to non-English-speaking residents shall be in their language.
(c) The contract shall also contain a separate written acknowledgement that the resident has been informed of the Patients' Bill of Rights.
Written acknowledgement by the resident or the resident's representative must be made either on a separate document or in the agreement itself next to the clause informing the resident of these regulatory rights. Written acknowledgement by use of the signature on the agreement as a whole does not meet this requirement.
(Amended by Stats. 2002, Ch. 550, Sec. 1. Effective January 1, 2003.)
1599.75.
(a) When referring to a resident's obligation to observe facility rules, the contract of admission shall indicate that the rules must be reasonable, and that there is a facility procedure for suggesting changes in the rules.
(b) The contract of admission shall specify that a copy of the facility grievance procedure, for resolution of resident complaints about facility practices, is available.
(c) The agreement shall also inform residents of their right to contact the State Department of Health Services or the long-term care ombudsman, or both, regarding grievances against the facility.
(Added by Stats. 1987, Ch. 625, Sec. 1.)
1599.76.
(a) No contract of admission shall list any ground for involuntary transfer or discharge of the resident except those grounds which are specifically enumerated in either federal or state law.
(b) Every contract of admission to a long-term health care facility that participates in the Medi-Cal program shall state that the facility may not transfer or seek to evict any resident solely as a result of the resident changing his or her manner of purchasing the services from private payment or Medicare to Medi-Cal.
(Added by Stats. 1987, Ch. 625, Sec. 1.)
1599.77.
With respect to transfer or eviction of a resident pursuant to Section 1439.7:
(a) Contracts of admission shall speak only of "material" or "fraudulent" misrepresentation of finances as possible grounds for discharge under that section.
(b) All contracts of admission shall state that the resident may file a complaint with the Office of the State Long-Term Care Ombudsman, or the department, or both, regarding any notice of discharge for material or fraudulent misrepresentation.
(Added by Stats. 1987, Ch. 625, Sec. 1.)
1599.78.
All contracts of admission shall state that except in an emergency, no resident may be involuntarily transferred within or discharged from a long-term health care facility unless he or she is given reasonable notice in writing and transfer or discharge planning as required by law. The written notice shall state the reason for the transfer or discharge. The facility shall immediately notify the Office of the State Long-Term Care Ombudsman in every case of involuntary discharge as specified in Section 1439.7.
(Amended by Stats. 1989, Ch. 1360, Sec. 86.)

1599.79.
Every contract of admission shall meet the requirements of Section 72520 of Title 22 of the California Administrative Code, which requires that the facility offer to hold a bed for the resident in the event the resident must be transferred to an acute care hospital for seven days or less. The facility shall also give the resident, or a representative for the resident, notice of the rights to a bedhold at the time of transfer. The resident or representative for the resident has 24 hours from receipt of notice to request the bedhold. The contract of admission shall state that the facility shall offer the next available appropriate bed to the resident in the event the facility fails to follow this required procedure. The facility shall inform the resident that Medi-Cal will pay for up to seven bedhold days.
(Added by Stats. 1987, Ch. 625, Sec. 1.)
1599.80.
Facilities that wish to photograph a resident for other than staff identification or health care purposes shall obtain permission from the resident whether for one photograph or for multiple photographs for one particular purpose on a document separate from the admission contract as a whole. This document shall describe the specific use to be made of the photograph and indicate that the photograph will be used only for that purpose.
(Added by Stats. 1987, Ch. 625, Sec. 1.)
1599.81.
(a) All contracts of admission that contain an arbitration clause shall clearly indicate that agreement to arbitration is not a precondition for medical treatment or for admission to the facility.
(b) All arbitration clauses shall be included on a form separate from the rest of the admission contract. This attachment shall contain space for the signature of any applicant who agrees to arbitration of disputes.
(c) On the attachments, clauses referring to arbitration of medical malpractice claims, as provided for under Section 1295 of the Code of Civil Procedure, shall be clearly separated from other arbitration clauses, and separate signatures shall be required for each clause.
(d) In the event the contract contains an arbitration clause, the contract attachment pertaining to arbitration shall contain notice that under Section 1430, the patient may not waive his or her ability to sue for violation of the Patient's Bill of Rights.
(Added by Stats. 1987, Ch. 625, Sec. 1.)
1599.82.
No contract of admission shall include a clause that purports to alter the statutory period for filing an action against a facility.
(Added by Stats. 1987, Ch. 625, Sec. 1.)
1599.83.
If a provision for the payment of attorney's fees is included in the admission contract, it shall state that in disputes arising from the admission contract, the prevailing party shall be entitled to attorney's fees.
(Added by Stats. 1987, Ch. 625, Sec. 1.)
1599.84.
This chapter applies to new admissions to skilled nursing and intermediate care facilities on and after January 1, 1988. This chapter shall not be construed to require the execution of new admission agreements for patients who were residing in those facilities prior to the enactment of this chapter. However, those patients shall be given notice of changes in admission contracts pursuant to this chapter.
(Amended by Stats. 1988, Ch. 160, Sec. 98.)

CHAPTER 3.95. Seniors Nursing Home Disclosure [1599.85 - 1599.89]

(Chapter 3.95 added November 8, 1988, by initiative Proposition 105, Sec. 4.)
1599.85.
Long-term health care facilities must prominently and clearly display the following notice on all contracts of admission, and all advertisements used to solicit consumers to enter into contracts of admission: "For more information about our facility, you may call the State Ombudsman's Office at (insert toll-free number)."
(Added November 8, 1988, by initiative Proposition 105. Operative January 1, 1990. Invalidated in 1991 by court decision.)
1599.86.
"Contract of admission," as used in this chapter, includes all documents which a resident or his or her representative must sign at the time of, or as a condition of, admission to a long-term care health facility as defined in Health and Safety Code Section 1326.
(Added November 8, 1988, by initiative Proposition 105. Operative January 1, 1990. Invalidated in 1991 by court decision.)
1599.87.
The Department of Health Services (the Department) shall compile a list of approximately twenty five % (25%) of the long-term health care facilities with the most serious records of violations of laws or regulations by virtue of proven or admitted Class AA and Class A citations. Those facilities on this list shall include this statement on all contracts of admission, and all advertisements used to solicit consumers to enter into contracts of admission: "This facility's record of citations is posted at the facility, and a copy may be obtained from the Department of Health Services."
(Added November 8, 1988, by initiative Proposition 105. Operative January 1, 1990. Invalidated in 1991 by court decision.)
1599.88.

The Department shall issue regulations to implement this Chapter, including permitting one disclosure to satisfy the requirements of Section 1599.85 for all advertisements on the same page.
(Added November 8, 1988, by initiative Proposition 105. Operative January 1, 1990. Invalidated in 1991 by court decision.)

1599.89.
The remedies for violations of this Chapter are as provided in Government Code Section 12269.
(Added November 8, 1988, by initiative Proposition 105. Operative January 1, 1990. Invalidated in 1991 by court decision.)

CHAPTER 4. Human Whole Blood, Human Whole Blood Derivatives, and Other Biologics [1600 - 1630]

(Chapter 4 repealed and added by Stats. 1963, Ch. 1055.)

ARTICLE 1. Definitions [1600 - 1600.9]
(Article 1 added by Stats. 1963, Ch. 1055.)

1600.
Unless the context otherwise requires, the definitions in this article govern the construction of this chapter.
(Repealed and added by Stats. 1963, Ch. 1055.)

1600.1.
"Biologics" includes the following products which are offered for sale or distribution for the prevention or treatment of disease, except biologics which are registered pursuant to Chapter 1.5 (commencing with Section 9201), Part 1, Division 5 of the Food and Agricultural Code:
(a) Human whole blood.
(b) Human whole blood derivatives specified by regulations.
(c) Serum, vaccine, live vaccine, killed vaccine, tissue vaccine, autogenous vaccine, live virus, killed virus, live bacterial culture, killed bacterial culture, bacterin, hormone, tissue extract, gland extract, gland preparation, insulin, and similar products made from human or animal tissues or micro-organisms.
The amendments to this section enacted at the 1973–74 Regular Session of the Legislature shall become operative on July 1, 1975.
(Amended by Stats. 1974, Ch. 776.)

1600.2.
"Blood bank" means any place where human whole blood, and human whole blood derivatives specified by regulation, are collected, prepared, tested, processed, or stored, or from which human whole blood or human whole blood derivatives specified by regulation are distributed.
(Added by Stats. 1963, Ch. 1055.)

1600.21.
"Blood collection center" means a stationary auxiliary to a blood bank which is designed, equipped, and staffed to procure human whole blood or blood components which are to be transported to the blood bank for processing, storing, and distribution.
(Added by Stats. 1991, Ch. 800, Sec. 2.)

1600.22.
"Stationary" means a nonmobile room or building maintained at a fixed address.
(Added by Stats. 1991, Ch. 800, Sec. 3.)

1600.25.
"Mobile unit" means a transportable auxiliary to a blood bank designed, equipped, and staffed to procure human whole blood and to transport this blood to the bank for processing, storing, and distribution.
(Added by Stats. 1991, Ch. 800, Sec. 4.)

1600.3.
"Blood bank depository" means any place other than a blood bank where human whole blood and human whole blood derivatives specified by regulation are stored and held for transfusion. Such blood bank depositories shall be clinical laboratories, licensed in accordance with the provisions of Chapter 3 (commencing with Section 1200), Division 2 of the Business and Professions Code, or such other places where services essentially equivalent are maintained, as determined by the department.
(Added by Stats. 1963, Ch. 1055.)

1600.35.
"Blood component" or "blood derivative" means any product produced from whole blood.
(Added by Stats. 1991, Ch. 800, Sec. 5.)

1600.4.
"Distribution" includes sale and exchange.
(Added by Stats. 1963, Ch. 1055.)

1600.5.
"Production" includes collection, preparation, testing, processing, storage, and distribution of biologics under a license issued by the department.
(Added by Stats. 1963, Ch. 1055.)

1600.6.
"Department" means the State Department of Health Services.
(Amended by Stats. 1977, Ch. 1252.)

1600.7.
"Carrier donor" means any donor of human whole blood whose blood donation has been found, either by laboratory tests or by the tracing of a transfusion-associated hepatitis

case where there was a single donor, to contain viral hepatitis, or any donor of human whole blood who has twice been determined by the department to be a possible carrier donor.
(Added by Stats. 1974, Ch. 985.)

1600.8.
"Possible carrier donor" means any donor of human whole blood whose blood donation was administered where multiple transfusions from multiple donors were administered to a recipient and such transfusions result in a case diagnosed by a physician as transfusion-associated hepatitis.
(Added by Stats. 1974, Ch. 985.)

1600.9.
"Carrier of viral hepatitis" means a person under treatment by a physician who has contracted viral hepatitis which has been confirmed by voluntary laboratory tests or who exhibits symptoms which lead a physician to render a diagnostic opinion that the person has contracted viral hepatitis.
(Added by Stats. 1974, Ch. 985.)

ARTICLE 2. Human Whole Blood and Human Whole Blood Derivatives [1602.5 - 1608]
(Article 2 added by Stats. 1963, Ch. 1055.)

1602.5.
(a) No person shall engage in the production of human whole blood or human whole blood derivatives unless the person is licensed under this chapter and the human whole blood or human whole blood derivative is collected, prepared, labeled, and stored in accordance with both of the following:
(1) The standards set forth in the 13th Edition of "Standards for Blood Banks and Transfusion Services," as published by the American Association of Blood Banks and in effect on November 15, 1989, or any amendments thereto or later published editions or amendments thereto. These shall be the standards for all licensed blood banks and blood transfusion services in the state.
(2) Those provisions of Title 17 of the California Code of Regulations that are continued in effect by subdivision (c) or that are adopted pursuant to subdivision (b).
(b) The department may, by the adoption of regulations, establish and require compliance with requirements in addition to, or in lieu of, those in subdivision (a) as the department deems appropriate to reflect changing technology or to improve the safety of human whole blood or human whole blood derivatives. Any standards adopted pursuant to this subdivision shall be adopted after consultation with representatives of the American Association of Blood Banks.
(c) Until the time superseded by any regulation adopted pursuant to this section, all of the provisions of Group 1 (commencing with Section 950) of Subchapter 1 of Chapter 2 of Part 1 of Title 17 of the California Code of Regulations shall remain in effect with the exception of the following:
(1) Subdivisions (i) to (k), inclusive, of Section 997.
(2) Sections 999 and 1001.
(3) Subdivisions (a) to (c), inclusive, of Section 1002.
(4) Paragraphs (2) and (3) of subdivision (e) of Section 1002.
(5) Subdivisions (f) and (g) of Section 1002.
(6) Paragraphs (2) to (6), inclusive, of subdivision (h) of Section 1002.
(7) Subdivisions (i), (k), and (l) of Section 1002.
(8) Subdivisions (a) to (c), inclusive, of Section 1004.
(9) Sections 1010, 1012, 1013, 1014, 1024, and 1024.1.
(10) Subdivisions (a), (b), and (e) of Section 1025.
(11) Paragraphs (1) to (3), inclusive, of subdivision (c) of Section 1025.
(d) (1) Any amendment to the 13th Edition of "Standards for Blood Banks and Transfusion Services," any later editions, or any amendments thereto, published by the American Association of Blood Banks shall become effective in California 90 days after the effective date of this section, or 90 days after publication by the association, unless the department sends written notice, within such a 90-day period, to all persons licensed under this chapter to engage in the production of human whole blood or human whole blood derivatives, indicating which portions shall not become effective.
(2) The department may determine that no portion of any amendments or later editions shall become effective. The department shall determine that no portion of an amendment or later edition shall become effective pursuant to this section whenever the department has not received a copy of the amendment or later edition by the date it is published by the American Association of Blood Banks.
(Amended by Stats. 1998, Ch. 416, Sec. 2. Effective January 1, 1999.)

1602.6.
(a) No person shall import any human whole blood or human whole blood derivative produced outside the state unless that blood or blood product meets the standards set forth in the latest edition of the "Standards for Blood Banks and Transfusion Services," as published by the American Association of Blood Banks, or any later published editions or amendments thereto.
(b) Any later editions of the "Standards for Blood Banks and Transfusion Services," or amendments thereto, published by the American Association of Blood Banks, shall become effective for purposes at this section 90 days after the effective date of this section, or 90 days after publication by the association, whichever is later, unless the department sends written notice, within the 90-day period, to all persons who import human whole blood or human whole blood derivatives produced outside the state that have requested this notice, stating the portions of those later editions or amendments that shall not become effective.

(c) The department may determine that no portion of any later editions or amendments shall become effective for purposes of this section. The department shall determine that no portion of a later edition or amendment shall become effective for purposes of this section whenever the department has not received a copy of the later edition or amendment by the date it is published by the American Association of Blood Banks.

(d) The department shall administer and enforce this section in accordance with this chapter and in a manner that assures, to the greatest degree, consistency with Section 1602.5.

(Added by Stats. 1992, Ch. 760, Sec. 1. Effective January 1, 1993.)

1603.1.

(a) Except as provided in this subdivision, no blood or blood components shall be used in vivo for humans in this state, unless the blood or blood components have been tested and found nonreactive for HIV or the blood or blood components are used for research or vaccination programs pursuant to an informed consent.

Additional exceptions to the requirement of this subdivision are as follows:

(1) Blood or blood components released for transfusion in emergency circumstances, as determined by the department.

(2) Blood or blood components used for autologous purposes.

(b) Blood banks and plasma centers shall make laboratory tests of all human whole blood and blood components received to detect the presence of viral hepatitis and HIV in the manner specified in Section 1603.3. If the blood bank or plasma center finds the presence of viral hepatitis, or an antigen thereof, in the blood or blood components tested, it shall report that finding, the date of the human whole blood or blood components donation, the name, address, and social security number of the person who donated the blood or blood components, and the name and address of the blood bank or plasma center that received the human whole blood or blood components from the person and any additional information required by the department, to the local health officer within 72 hours of the confirmation of the presence of viral hepatitis, or an antigen thereof, in the blood or blood components tested.

(c) A physician, hospital, or other health care provider shall report all AIDS cases, HIV infections, and viral hepatitis infections. including transfusion-associated cases or infections, to the local health officer with the information required, and within the timeframes established by the department, pursuant to Title 17 of the California Code of Regulations.

(d) Upon receipt of a report concerning any transfusion-associated hepatitis or transfusion-associated HIV or AIDS cases, the local health officer shall identify which blood bank or plasma center is the source of the infectious blood or blood components and shall report this fact to the blood bank or plasma center that issued the blood or blood components. The blood bank or plasma center shall undertake an investigation to determine the donor source of the infectious blood or blood components.

(e) Local health officials shall contact all persons who have confirmed cases of AIDS, as determined by a person responsible for the care and treatment of the person with AIDS, to suggest appropriate treatment alternatives and for the purposes of epidemiological studies and followup.

(f) The department may adopt regulations governing the procedures in this section as it deems necessary to protect the public health and safety.

(g) "Plasma center," as used in this chapter, means any place where the process of plasmapheresis is conducted, as defined in Section 1025 of Title 17 of the California Code of Regulations and includes a place where leukopheresis or platelet pheresis, or both, is conducted.

(h) "AIDS," as used in this chapter, means acquired immune deficiency syndrome.

(i) "HIV," as used in this chapter, means human immunodeficiency virus.

(j) "Blood components," as used in this chapter, means preparations separated from single units of whole blood or prepared for hemapheresis and intended for use as final products for transfusions.

(k) A local health officer may disclose to a blood bank or plasma center, on a confidential basis, whether blood or blood components previously transfused may have been donated by a person infected with HIV, in order to implement the blood bank's or plasma center's program to notify a recipient of blood or blood components that might have transmitted HIV. The blood bank or plasma center may not disclose information that would identify a donor to which this subdivision applies and shall destroy information communicated to it as authorized by this subdivision immediately after reviewing its records as necessary to implement this program.

(Amended by Stats. 2003, Ch. 419, Sec. 1. Effective January 1, 2004.)

1603.2.

(a) Each blood bank or plasma center shall require as identification either a photographic driver's license or other photographic identification that is issued by the Department of Motor Vehicles, pursuant to Division 6 (commencing with Section 12500) of the Vehicle Code, from all donors of human whole blood or blood components who receive payment in return for the donation of that blood or blood components.

(b) For the purposes of this section, "payment" means the transfer by a blood bank or plasma center to any person of money or any other valuable consideration that can be converted to money by the recipient, except that payment shall not include any of the following:

(1) Cancellation or refund of the nonreplacement fees or related blood or blood components transfusion charges.

(2) Blood assurance benefits to a person as a result of a blood or blood components donation to a donor club or blood assurance program.

(3) Time away from employment granted by an employer to an employee in order to donate blood or blood components.

(Amended by Stats. 2003, Ch. 419, Sec. 2. Effective January 1, 2004.)

1603.3.

(a) Before donation of blood or blood components, a donor shall be notified in writing of, and shall have signed a written statement confirming the notification of, all of the following:

(1) That the blood or blood components shall be tested for evidence of antibodies to HIV.

(2) That the donor shall be notified of the test results in accordance with the requirements described in subdivision (c).

(3) That the donor blood or blood component that is found to have the antibodies shall not be used for transfusion.

(4) That blood or blood components shall not be donated for transfusion purposes by a person if the person may have reason to believe that he or she has been exposed to HIV or AIDS.

(5) That the donor is required to complete a health screening questionnaire to assist in the determination as to whether he or she may have been exposed to HIV or AIDS.

(b) A blood bank or plasma center shall incorporate voluntary means of self-deferral for donors. The means of self-deferral may include, but are not limited to, a form with checkoff boxes specifying that the blood or blood components are for research or test purposes only and a telephone callback system for donors to use in order to inform the blood bank or plasma center that blood or blood components donated should not be used for transfusion. The blood bank or plasma center shall inform the donor, in a manner that is understandable to the donor, that the self-deferral process is available and should be used if the donor has reason to believe that he or she is infected with HIV.

(c) Blood or blood components from any donor initially found to have serologic evidence of antibodies to HIV shall be retested for confirmation. Only if a further test confirms the conclusion of the earlier test shall the donor be notified of a reactive result by the blood bank or plasma center.

The department shall develop permissive guidelines for blood banks and plasma centers on the method to be used to notify a donor of a test result.

(d) Each blood bank or plasma center operating in California shall prominently display at each of its collection sites a notice that provides the addresses and telephone numbers of sites, within the proximate area of the blood bank or plasma center, where anonymous HIV antibody testing provided pursuant to Chapter 3 (commencing with Section 120885) of Part 4 of Division 105 may be administered without charge.

(e) The department may promulgate any additional regulations it deems necessary to enhance the safety of donated blood and blood components. The department may also promulgate regulations it deems necessary to safeguard the consistency and accuracy of HIV test results by requiring any confirmatory testing the department deems appropriate for the particular types of HIV tests that have yielded "reactive," "positive," "indeterminate," or other similarly labeled results.

(f) Notwithstanding any other provision of law, civil liability or criminal sanction shall not be imposed for disclosure of test results to a local health officer if the disclosure is necessary to locate and notify a blood or blood components donor of a reactive result if reasonable efforts by the blood bank or plasma center to locate the donor have failed. Upon completion of the local health officer's efforts to locate and notify a blood or blood components donor of a reactive result, all records obtained from the blood bank or plasma center pursuant to this subdivision, or maintained pursuant to this subdivision, including, but not limited to, any individual identifying information or test results, shall be expunged by the local health officer.

(Amended by Stats. 2017, Ch. 537, Sec. 1. (SB 239) Effective January 1, 2018.)

1603.4.

(a) Notwithstanding Chapter 7 (commencing with Section 120975) of Part 4 of Division 105, or any other provision of law, no public entity or any private blood bank or plasma center shall be liable for an inadvertent, accidental, or otherwise unintentional disclosure of the results of an HIV test.

As used in this section, "public entity" includes, but is not limited to, any publicly owned or operated blood bank or plasma center, local health officer, and the department.

(b) Neither the department nor any blood bank or plasma center, including a blood bank or plasma center owned or operated by a public entity, or local health officer shall be held liable for any damage resulting from the notification of test results, as set forth in paragraph (2) of subdivision (a) of, or in subdivision (c) of, Section 1603.3.

(Amended by Stats. 2003, Ch. 419, Sec. 4. Effective January 1, 2004.)

1603.5.

(a) Notwithstanding any other provision of law, every person engaged in the production of blood shall, if the product is intended for transfusion, label each container of blood which the person produces with a label, upon which the following designations shall be printed in letters the size of which shall be no less prominent than the proper name of the product.

(1) If the person giving the blood received no payment for the blood, the designation shall be "volunteer donor."

(2) If the person giving the blood received payment for the blood, the designation shall be "paid donor."

(b) As used in this section:

(1) "Blood" means human whole blood or components of human blood, including plasma, which are prepared from human whole blood by physical, rather than chemical processes, but does not include blood derivatives manufactured or processed by industrial use.

(2) "Industrial use" means a use of blood in which the blood is modified by physical or chemical means to produce derivatives for therapeutic or pharmaceutic biologics, laboratory reagents, or in vitro diagnostics.

(3) "Payment" means the transfer by a blood bank, or any other party, to any person of money or any other valuable consideration which can be converted to money by the recipient, except that "payment" shall not include any of the following:

(i) Cancellation or refund of the nonreplacement fees or related blood transfusion charges.

(ii) Blood assurance benefits to a person as a result of a blood donation to a donor club or blood assurance program.

(iii) Time away from employment granted by an employer to an employee in order to donate blood.

(c) Any blood bank receiving blood from a blood bank outside of California shall comply with the labeling requirements of this chapter. Any blood bank receiving this blood may label the blood as "volunteer donor" blood only if the blood bank receives with the blood a certificate from the out-of-state blood bank which states either that the particular shipment of blood was acquired from volunteer donors not receiving payment or that all blood processed by the out-of-state blood bank is acquired from volunteer donors not receiving payment. If the blood bank receiving such blood receives no such certificate with the blood, the blood shall be labeled as "paid donor" blood.

(d) No warranty shall be implied from the fact that any blood is labeled in accordance with the requirements of this section.

(Amended by Stats. 1989, Ch. 513, Sec. 1.)

1604.

The distribution or release for distribution by blood banks of human whole blood, or those human whole blood derivatives specified by regulation, shall be made only to blood bank depositories or to other licensed blood banks.

(Repealed and added by Stats. 1963, Ch. 1055.)

1604.6.

(a) Notwithstanding any other provision of law, in order to provide umbilical cord blood banking storage services, a blood bank shall be licensed pursuant to this chapter. Any additional standards for blood banks to store umbilical cord blood may be implemented by the department through the adoption of regulations.

(b) (1) The department may adopt emergency regulations to implement and make specific subdivision (a) in accordance with Chapter 3.5 (commencing with Section 11340) of Part 1 of Division 3 of Title 2 of the Government Code. For purposes of the Administrative Procedure Act, the adoption of regulations shall be deemed an emergency and necessary for the immediate preservation of the public peace, health and safety, or general welfare.

(2) (A) Notwithstanding Chapter 3.5 (commencing with Section 11340) of Part 1 of Division 3 of Title 2 of the Government Code, these emergency regulations shall not be subject to the review and approval of the Office of Administrative Law. Notwithstanding Sections 11346.1 and 11349.6 of the Government Code, the department shall submit these regulations directly to the Secretary of State for filing.

(B) Emergency regulations adopted pursuant to this section shall become effective immediately upon filing by the Secretary of State, shall be subject to public hearing within 120 days of filing with the Secretary of State, and shall comply with Sections 11346.8 and 11346.9 of the Government Code, or shall be repealed by the department.

(3) The Office of Administrative Law shall provide for the printing and publication of emergency regulations adopted pursuant to this section in the California Code of Regulations.

(4) Notwithstanding Chapter 3.5 (commencing with Section 11340) of Part 1 of Division 3 of Title 2 of the Government Code, and subject to subparagraph (B) of paragraph (2), the emergency regulations adopted pursuant to this subdivision shall not be repealed by the Office of Administrative Law and shall remain in effect until revised or repealed by the department.

(Amended by Stats. 2007, Ch. 130, Sec. 160. Effective January 1, 2008.)

1605.

Establishments which receive human whole blood and human whole blood derivatives specified by regulation and are not subject to license in accordance with this chapter shall be considered as blood bank depositories. Laboratory tests and other procedures with respect to the preparation of blood for transfusion shall be the sole responsibility of the blood bank depository.

(Repealed and added by Stats. 1963, Ch. 1055.)

1606.

The procurement, processing, distribution, or use of whole blood, plasma, blood products, and blood derivatives for the purpose of injecting or transfusing the same, or any of them, into the human body shall be construed to be, and is declared to be, for all purposes whatsoever, the rendition of a service by each and every person, firm, or corporation participating therein, and shall not be construed to be, and is declared not to be, a sale of such whole blood, plasma, blood products, or blood derivatives, for any purpose or purposes whatsoever.

(Repealed and added by Stats. 1963, Ch. 1055.)

1607.

(a) Notwithstanding any other provision of law, licensed clinical laboratory bioanalysts, licensed clinical laboratory technologists, registered clinical laboratory technologist trainees, licensed vocational nurses, registered nurses, and blood donor phlebotomists, as defined by the American Association of Blood Banks, may perform skin puncture and venipuncture for the purposes of collecting human blood if both of the following are satisfied:

(1) The acts are performed in a blood bank licensed pursuant to this chapter and personnel training and standards meet accreditation requirements of the American Association of Blood Banks.

(2) The acts are performed under the direct and responsible supervision of a licensed physician and surgeon. The licensing and registration referred to in this section shall be licensing and registration pursuant to the Business and Professions Code.

(b) In accordance with the American Association of Blood Banks standards, the medical director of the blood bank shall be responsible for all medical and technical policies and procedures that relate to the safety of staff members, donors, and patients, including, but not limited to, ensuring that the blood bank has a qualified and competent staff to perform all tasks involved in the collection, storage, processing, and distribution of blood and blood components. The employer blood bank shall be responsible for determining the appropriate mix of qualified, competent employees that meets the accreditation requirements of the American Association of Blood Banks and is consistent with the services rendered.

(c) Personnel who are explicitly authorized by the blood bank and who meet the education, training, and competency standards of the blood bank, may obtain a predonation medical history and perform predonation screening. When unlicensed personnel perform these duties, the review of work required by federal regulations relating to good manufacturing practices, as set forth in Part 211 and Part 606 of Title 21 of the Code of Federal Regulations, shall be performed by those staff members who are licensed health care personnel.

(d) The collection of blood from autologous patients and other individuals who do not meet the American Association of Blood Banks criteria for regular volunteer donation shall be conducted by licensed health care personnel.

(e) Nothing in this chapter shall prohibit the collection of blood at a state institution, a blood bank licensed pursuant to this chapter, or other establishment, under conditions established and acceptable to the department, by the personnel of the collecting entity.

(f) A staff position for a blood donor phlebotomist created as a consequence of this section shall not be the only cause for the displacement of any licensed personnel employed in a licensed blood bank as of the effective date of the statute amending this section during the 1995-96 Regular Legislative Session. As used in this section, the term "displacement" shall mean a reduction in hours of nonovertime work, the loss of wages, or the loss of employment.

(g) Nothing in this section shall be construed to limit the rights of employees or employee organizations to bargain in good faith on matters of wages, hours, or other terms and conditions of employment, including the negotiation of workplace standards within the scope of collective bargaining as authorized by state and federal law.

(Amended by Stats. 1995, Ch. 703, Sec. 1. Effective January 1, 1996.)

1607.5.

(a) Notwithstanding any other provision of law, a person who has attained the age of 17 may consent to the donation of his or her blood and to the penetration of tissue which is necessary to accomplish such donation, and a blood bank may accept such donation.

(b) Notwithstanding any other provision of law, a person who has attained the age of 15 may consent to the donation of his or her blood and to the penetration of tissue which is necessary to accomplish such donation, and a blood bank may accept such donation, if he or she has the written consent of his or her parents or a guardian, and the written authorization of a physician and surgeon.

(c) As used in this section "donation of blood" means a giving of blood in which the donor of the blood receives no payment therefor.

(Amended by Stats. 1981, Ch. 23.)

1608.

This chapter does not repeal or in any manner affect any provision of the Business and Professions Code relating to the practice of medicine.

(Repealed and added by Stats. 1963, Ch. 1055.)

ARTICLE 3. Biologics Other Than Human Whole Blood and Human Whole Blood Derivatives [1609 - 1611]

(Article 3 added by Stats. 1963, Ch. 1055.)

1609.

No person shall engage in the production of biologics other than human whole blood and human whole blood derivatives unless:

(a) In a laboratory licensed by the Public Health Service, United States Department of Health, Education and Welfare.

(b) In a laboratory licensed by the Animal Inspection and Quarantine Branch, Agricultural Research Service, United States Department of Agriculture.

(c) Under the provisions of this chapter.

(Repealed and added by Stats. 1963, Ch. 1055.)

1610.

The department shall make rules and regulations governing the production of all biologics produced in establishments under subdivision (c) of Section 1609.

(Repealed and added by Stats. 1963, Ch. 1055.)

1611.

The department may make rules and regulations governing the transportation or distribution of cultures of micro-organisms which may produce disease in man or animals.

(Repealed and added by Stats. 1963, Ch. 1055.)

ARTICLE 4. Licenses [1613 - 1615]

(Article 4 added by Stats. 1963, Ch. 1055.)

1613.

Applications for licenses issued under this chapter shall be made upon forms issued by the department. The applications shall contain at least the following:

(a) The name and address of the person owning the place, establishment, or institution in which biologics production is planned.

(b) The name and address of the person to be in charge of biologics production.

(c) The types of biologics to be produced.

(d) A full description of the building, its location, facilities, equipment, and apparatus to be used in biologics production.

(e) The name and address of each blood collection center operated by the applicant and whether the applicant operates any mobile units.

(f) Any additional information as the department may require.

(Amended by Stats. 1991, Ch. 800, Sec. 12.)

1614.

If the department does not within 60 days after the filing of the application issue a license, it shall state the grounds and reasons for its refusal in writing, serving a copy upon the applicant.

The notice may be served by registered mail addressed to the applicant at his last known address.

(Amended by Stats. 1991, Ch. 800, Sec. 13.)

1615.

(a) A license shall be automatically revoked when there is a change of address, ownership, or person in charge of biologics production. However, a new license may be secured for the new location, owner, or person in charge prior to the actual change if the contemplated change is in compliance with all the provisions of this chapter and regulations pertaining thereto.

(b) Proceedings for denial of license shall be conducted in accordance with Section 100171.

(Amended by Stats. 1997, Ch. 220, Sec. 18. Effective August 4, 1997.)

ARTICLE 5. Revenue [1616 - 1616.5]

(Article 5 added by Stats. 1963, Ch. 1055.)

1616.

(a) Each application for a license or license renewal under this chapter shall be accompanied by a fee determined by the director by regulations and in an amount sufficient to cover the cost of administering this chapter but not to exceed those costs, as specified pursuant to Section 1616.5.

(b) The state department shall receive and account for all moneys received pursuant to this chapter and shall deposit them with the Treasurer for deposit in the Clinical Laboratory Improvement Fund established pursuant to Section 1302 of the Business and Professions Code. All funds received pursuant to this chapter shall, upon appropriation, be expended to administer this chapter.

(c) Each license issued under this chapter shall expire 12 months from the date of its issuance. Application for renewal of license accompanied by the fee shall be filed with the department not less than 10 days prior to the expiration each year. Failure to make a timely renewal shall result in expiration of the license.

(Amended by Stats. 1994, Ch. 492, Sec. 5. Effective January 1, 1995.)

1616.5.

(a) The fee required pursuant to Section 1616 for the calendar year commencing January 1, 1992, and for each fiscal year thereafter unless adjusted pursuant to subdivision (b), shall not exceed the following:

One thousand five hundred dollars ($1,500) for a blood bank and no more than one blood collection center operated at the same location as the blood bank. In addition and irrespective of the location of the blood collection center, a fee of five hundred dollars ($500) for each additional blood collection center operated by the blood bank up to a maximum of one thousand five hundred dollars ($1,500) for three or more blood collection centers.

(b) The maximum application and renewal fees for blood bank licenses pursuant to subdivision (a) shall be adjusted annually in the manner specified in Section 100450. The adjustments shall be rounded off to the nearest whole dollar.

(c) This chapter shall not be interpreted to exempt the state, a district, city, county, or city and county, from payment of fees or from meeting the requirements established pursuant to this chapter or regulations adopted thereunder.

(Amended by Stats. 1996, Ch. 1023, Sec. 169. Effective September 29, 1996.)

ARTICLE 6. Enforcement [1617 - 1620]

(Article 6 added by Stats. 1963, Ch. 1055.)

1617.

(a) The department shall administer this chapter.

(b) In order to carry out this chapter, any duly authorized representative of the department may do any of the following:

(1) Enter or inspect on an announced or unannounced basis any building, premise, equipment, materials, records, or information at any reasonable time to secure compliance with, or prevent a violation of, this chapter or the regulations adopted pursuant thereto.

(2) Inspect, photograph, or copy any records, reports, test results, test specimens, or other information related to the requirements of this chapter or the regulations adopted pursuant thereto.

(3) Secure any sample, photograph, or other evidence from any building or premise for the purpose of enforcing this chapter or the regulations adopted pursuant thereto.

(Amended by Stats. 1991, Ch. 800, Sec. 16.)

1618.

(a) Licenses shall be suspended or revoked by the department for the violation of any provision of this chapter, or of any rule or regulation made by the department under authority conferred by this chapter. The proceedings shall be conducted in accordance with Section 100171.

(b) Licenses may be denied for any reason applicable to revocation and suspension of licenses.

(c) District and city attorneys shall prosecute violations of this chapter upon evidence of violations within their respective jurisdictions submitted by the department.

(Amended by Stats. 1997, Ch. 220, Sec. 19. Effective August 4, 1997.)

1619.

Nothing in this chapter shall be considered to be in conflict with Part 5 (commencing with Section 109875) of Division 104 of this code and all provisions of that division shall apply to biologics within the meaning of this chapter, except that this chapter shall not apply to products of:

(a) A laboratory licensed by the Public Health Service, United States Department of Health, Education and Welfare.

(b) A laboratory licensed by the Animal Inspection and Quarantine Branch, Agricultural Research Service, United States Department of Agriculture.

(Amended by Stats. 1996, Ch. 1023, Sec. 170. Effective September 29, 1996.)

1620.

The violation of any provision of this chapter is a misdemeanor punishable by a fine of not less than one hundred dollars ($100) nor more than one thousand dollars ($1,000), or by imprisonment for not more than 30 days, or by both.

(Amended by Stats. 1983, Ch. 1092, Sec. 148. Effective September 27, 1983. Operative January 1, 1984, by Sec. 427 of Ch. 1092.)

ARTICLE 7. Blood Donations [1625 - 1626]

(Article 7 added by Stats. 1976, Ch. 917.)

1625.

As used in this article:

(a) "Blood" means human whole blood or components of human blood, including plasma, which are prepared from human whole blood by physical, rather than chemical processes, but does not include blood derivatives manufactured or processed for industrial use.

(b) "Cytapheresis" means the separation and collection of blood cells by hemapheresis.

(c) "Hemapheresis" means the removal of whole blood from a donor, separation of the blood into components, retention of the desired components, and return of the recombined remaining elements to the donor.

(d) "Industrial use" means a use of blood in which the blood is modified by physical or chemical means to produce derivatives for therapeutic or pharmaceutic biologics, laboratory reagents, or in vitro diagnostics.

(e) "Paid donor" means a person who donates blood and who receives payment in return for the donation of such blood.

(f) "Payment" means the transfer by a blood bank to any person of money or any other valuable consideration which can be converted to money by the recipient, except that payment shall not include any of the following:

(1) Cancellation or refund of the nonreplacement fees or related blood transfusion charges.

(2) Blood assurance benefits to a person as a result of a blood donation to a donor club or blood assurance program.

(3) Time away from employment, with or without pay, granted by an employer to an employee in order to donate blood.

(g) "Person" means any individual, blood bank, hospital, firm, corporation, or any other entity.

(h) "Transfusion" means a use of blood in which the blood is administered to a human being for treatment of sickness or injury.

(Amended by Stats. 1986, Ch. 1007, Sec. 2.)

1625.1.

In addition to the requirements of Section 1602.1, subdivisions (a) to (c), inclusive, of Section 1002 of Title 17 of the California Administrative Code, and any other requirements identified by the State Department of Health Services, hemapheresis donors shall provide a medical history questionnaire completed by a trained interviewer who questions and verifies the accuracy of responses before every donation.

The department may require testing or examinations to reflect changing technology and to increase the safety of blood products.

(Added by Stats. 1986, Ch. 1007, Sec. 3.)

1626.

(a) Except as provided in subdivisions (b) and (c), it shall be unlawful, in any transfusion of blood, to use any blood that was obtained from a paid donor.

(b) Subdivision (a) shall not be applicable to any transfusion of blood that was obtained from a paid donor if the physician and surgeon performing the transfusion has determined, taking into consideration the condition of the patient who is the recipient of the transfusion, that other blood of a type compatible with the blood type of the patient cannot reasonably be obtained for the transfusion.

(c) Subdivision (a) shall not apply to blood platelets secured from paid donors through the hemapheresis process if all of the following requirements are satisfied:

(1) The blood platelets are ordered by a doctor holding a valid California physician's and surgeon's certificate.

(2) The blood platelets are secured from a single donor and are sufficient to constitute a complete platelet transfusion.

(3) The donor's identification number is recorded on the platelet label and is kept in the records of the entity providing the blood platelets for a minimum of five years.

(4) The donor has been examined by a doctor holding a valid California physician's and surgeon's certificate, and a repeat donor is reexamined at least annually.

(5) The transfusion is performed in a general acute care hospital.

(6) The blood platelets are processed according to standards issued by the American Association of Blood Banks, pursuant to Section 1602.1.

(7) The donor and blood are tested in accordance with regulations issued by the State Department of Health Services.

(8) The entity providing the blood platelets is licensed by the State Department of Health Services.

(9) The information that the donor of the blood platelets was compensated is printed on the label in accordance with Section 1603.5.

(10) In all instances, a potential donor shall provide a blood sample, which shall be tested with the standard panel of blood tests required by the State Department of Health Services for all blood donations. The results of the testing shall be obtained, evaluated, and determined to be acceptable prior to allowing the potential donor to provide his or her first donation of platelets. In addition, all donors shall be required to schedule an appointment for platelet donation.

(11) Any entity that is not collecting blood platelets from paid donors on August 1, 2000, shall obtain written permission from the director prior to compensating any donor for blood platelets.

(d) Subdivision (c) shall become inoperative on January 1, 2003.

(Amended by Stats. 2012, Ch. 728, Sec. 83. (SB 71) Effective January 1, 2013.)

ARTICLE 8. Umbilical Cord Blood Program [1627 - 1630]

(Article 8 added by Stats. 2007, Ch. 516, Sec. 2.)

1627.

(a) (1) On or before July 1, 2011, the University of California is requested to develop a plan to establish and administer the Umbilical Cord Blood Collection Program for the purpose of collecting units of umbilical cord blood for public use in transplantation and providing nonclinical units for research pertaining to biology and new clinical utilization of stem cells derived from the blood and tissue of the placenta and umbilical cord. The program shall conclude no later than January 1, 2023.

(2) For purposes of this article, "public use" means both of the following:

(A) The collection of umbilical cord blood units from genetically diverse donors that will be owned by the University of California. This inventory shall be accessible by the National Registry and by qualified California-based and other United States and international registries and transplant centers to increase the likelihood of providing suitably matched donor cord blood units to patients or research participants who are in need of a transplant.

(B) Cord blood units with a lower number of cells than deemed necessary for clinical transplantation and units that meet clinical requirements, but for other reasons are unsuitable, unlikely to be transplanted, or otherwise unnecessary for clinical use, may be made available for research.

(b) (1) In order to implement the collection goals of this program, the University of California may, commensurate with available funds appropriated to the University of California for this program, contract with one or more selected applicant entities that have demonstrated the competence to collect and ship cord blood units in compliance with federal guidelines and regulations.

(2) It is the intent of the Legislature that, if the University of California contracts with another entity pursuant to this subdivision, the following shall apply:

(A) The University of California may use a competitive process to identify the best proposals submitted by applicant entities to administer the collection and research objectives of the program, to the extent that the University of California chooses not to undertake these activities itself.

(B) In order to qualify for selection under this section to receive, process, cryopreserve, or bank cord blood units, the entity shall, at a minimum, have obtained an investigational new drug (IND) exemption from the FDA or a biologic license from the FDA, as appropriate, to manufacture clinical grade cord blood stem cell units for clinical indications.

(C) In order to qualify to receive appropriate cord blood units and placental tissue to advance the research goals of this program, an entity shall, at a minimum, be a laboratory recognized as having performed peer-reviewed research on stem and progenitor cells, including those derived from placental or umbilical cord blood and postnatal tissue.

(3) A medical provider or research facility shall comply with, and shall be subject to, existing penalties for violations of all applicable state and federal laws with respect to the protection of any medical information, as defined in Section 56.05 of the Civil Code, and any personally identifiable information contained in the umbilical cord blood inventory.

(c) The University of California is encouraged to make every effort to avoid duplication or conflicts with existing and ongoing programs and to leverage existing resources.

(d) (1) All information collected pursuant to the program shall be confidential, and shall be used solely for the purposes of the program, including research. Access to confidential information shall be limited to authorized persons who are bound by appropriate institutional policies or who otherwise agree, in writing, to maintain the confidentiality of that information.

(2) Any person who, in violation of applicable institutional policies or a written agreement to maintain confidentiality, discloses any information provided pursuant to this section, or who uses information provided pursuant to this section in a manner other than as approved pursuant to this section, may be denied further access to any confidential information maintained by the University of California, and shall be subject to a civil penalty not exceeding one thousand dollars ($1,000). The penalty provided for in this section shall not be construed to limit or otherwise restrict any remedy, provisional or otherwise, provided by law for the benefit of the University of California or any other person covered by this section.

(3) Notwithstanding the restrictions of this section, an individual to whom the confidential information pertains shall have access to his or her own personal information.

(e) It is the intent of the Legislature that the plan and implementation of the program provide for both of the following:

(1) Limit fees for access to cord blood units to the reasonable and actual costs of storage, handling, and providing units, as well as for related services such as donor matching and testing of cord blood and other programs and services typically provided by cord blood banks and public use programs.

(2) The submittal of the plan developed pursuant to subdivision (a) to the health and fiscal committees of the Legislature.

(f) It is additionally the intent of the Legislature that the plan and implementation of the program attempt to provide for all of the following:

(1) Development of a strategy to increase voluntary participation by hospitals in the collection and storage of umbilical cord blood and identify funding sources to offset the financial impact on hospitals.

(2) Consideration of a medical contingency response program to prepare for and respond effectively to biological, chemical, or radiological attacks, accidents, and other public health emergencies where victims potentially benefit from treatment.

(3) Exploration of the feasibility of operating the program as a self-funding program, including the potential for charging users a reimbursement fee.

(Amended by Stats. 2017, Ch. 38, Sec. 1. (AB 114) Effective July 10, 2017. Repealed as of January 1, 2023, pursuant to Section 1630.)

1628.

(a) The University of California may accept public and private funds for the purpose of implementing this article.

(b) The Umbilical Cord Blood Collection Program Fund is hereby created in the State Treasury. Any fees collected pursuant to Section 103625 shall be deposited into the fund. Moneys in the fund shall be available, upon appropriation by the Legislature, for purposes of this article.

(c) The fund may include additional federal, state, and private funds made available for purposes of the program, including, but not limited to, the fees collected for the fund pursuant to Section 103625, and, notwithstanding Section 16305.7 of the Government Code, any interest earned on moneys in the fund.

(d) (1) Funds shall be appropriated for the purposes of this article to the extent the plan the University of California is requested to develop pursuant to subdivision (a) of Section 1627 and the implementation of the plan are consistent with the goals and intent of this article.

(2) In the event that funds are not appropriated for the program as described in this article, it is the intent of the Legislature that the University of California shall not implement the program.

(Amended by Stats. 2010, Ch. 529, Sec. 3. (AB 52) Effective September 29, 2010. Repealed as of January 1, 2023, pursuant to Section 1630.)

1629.

In implementing the program, the department shall make every effort to avoid duplication or conflicts with existing and ongoing programs and to leverage existing resources.

(Added by Stats. 2007, Ch. 516, Sec. 2. Effective January 1, 2008. Repealed as of January 1, 2023, pursuant to Section 1630.)

1629.5.

(a) On or before January 1, 2022, if it elects to administer the Umbilical Cord Blood Collection Program, the University of California shall provide a report to the Assembly and Senate Committees on Health that addresses, at a minimum, all of the following:

(1) The number of cord blood units collected and registered under the program, disaggregated by race and ethnicity.

(2) The number of registered units transplanted as a result of the program, disaggregated by race and ethnicity.

(3) The number of California residents receiving a transplant as a result of the program.

(4) The number of units made available for research and a summary of key research findings as a result of the program.

(5) Annual budget information on the program, including revenues, spending, and beginning- and end-of-year balances.

(6) Budget information for each participating cord blood bank, including collection and storage costs and available revenues to cover those costs.

(7) Fees charged by participating cord blood banks for collecting, storing, handling, and providing units, and a summary of how these fees were determined.

(8) Nationwide data on cord blood units collected, registered, and transplanted, disaggregated by race and ethnicity.

(9) A summary of available cell sources for a hematopoietic stem cell transplant and research on the ability of underrepresented groups to find a suitable match for a transplant.

(10) Any other outcomes or data regarding the impact of the program.

(b) The requirement for submitting a report imposed under subdivision (a) is inoperative on December 31, 2022, pursuant to Section 10231.5 of the Government Code.

(Added by Stats. 2017, Ch. 38, Sec. 2. (AB 114) Effective July 10, 2017. Repealed as of January 1, 2023, pursuant to Section 1630.)

1630.

This article shall remain in effect only until January 1, 2023, and as of that date is repealed, unless a later enacted statute, that is enacted before January 1, 2023, deletes or extends that date.

(Amended by Stats. 2017, Ch. 38, Sec. 3. (AB 114) Effective July 10, 2017. Repealed as of January 1, 2023, by its own provisions. Note: Repeal affects Article 8, commencing with Section 1627.)

CHAPTER 4.1. Tissue Banks [1635 - 1643.2]

(Chapter 4.1 added by Stats. 1991, Ch. 801, Sec. 2.)

ARTICLE 1. Definitions, Licensure, and Exceptions [1635 - 1635.2]
(Article 1 added by Stats. 1991, Ch. 801, Sec. 2.)

1635.
(a) "Department" means the State Department of Public Health.
(b) "Donor" means an individual, living or deceased, from whom tissue is removed.
(c) "Gamete bank" means a tissue bank that collects, processes, stores, or distributes gametes, including a facility that provides professional reproductive services, other than those facilities exempt from tissue bank licensure.
(d) "Person" means an individual, corporation, business trust, estate trust, partnership, association, state or local government, or subdivision or agency thereof, or any other legal entity.
(e) (1) "Tissue" means a human cell, group of cells, including the cornea, sclera, or vitreous humor and other segments of, or the whole eye, bones, skin, arteries, sperm, blood, other fluids, and any other portion of a human body, but shall not include an organ when recovered for transplantation or research purposes.
(2) For purposes of paragraph (1), "organ" means a human kidney, liver, heart, lung, pancreas, intestine (including the esophagus, stomach, small or large intestine, or any portion of the gastrointestinal tract), or vascularized composite allograft, and associated blood vessels recovered from an organ donor during the recovery of the organ.
(f) "Tissue bank" means a place, establishment, or institution that collects, processes, stores, or distributes tissue for transplantation into human beings.
(g) "Transplantation" means the act or process of transferring tissue, including by ingestion, from a donor to the body of the donor or another human being.
(Amended by Stats. 2018, Ch. 876, Sec. 66. (AB 2684) Effective January 1, 2019.)
1635.1.
(a) Except as provided in subdivision (b), every tissue bank operating in California on or after July 1, 1992, shall have a current and valid tissue bank license issued or renewed by the department pursuant to Section 1639.2 or 1639.3.
(b) This chapter does not apply to any of the following:
(1) The collection, processing, storage, or distribution of human whole blood or its derivatives by blood banks licensed pursuant to Chapter 4 (commencing with Section 1600) or any person exempt from licensure under that chapter.
(2) The collection, processing, storage, or distribution of tissue for autopsy, biopsy, training, education, or for other medical or scientific research or investigation, when transplantation of the tissue is not intended or reasonably foreseeable.
(3) The collection of tissue by an individual physician and surgeon from his or her patient or the implantation of tissue by an individual physician and surgeon into his or her patient. This exemption shall not be interpreted to apply to any processing or storage of the tissue, except for the processing and storage of semen by an individual physician and surgeon when the semen was collected by that physician and surgeon from a semen donor or obtained by that physician and surgeon from a tissue bank licensed under this chapter.
(4) The collection, processing, storage, or distribution of fetal tissue or tissue derived from a human embryo or fetus.
(5) The collection, processing, storage, or distribution by an organ procurement organization (OPO), as defined in Section 486.302 of Title 42 of the Code of Federal Regulations, if the OPO, at the time of collection, processing, storage, and distribution of the tissue, has been designated by the Secretary of Health and Human Services as an OPO and meets the requirements of Sections 486.304 and 486.306 of Title 42 of the Code of Federal Regulations, as applicable.
(6) The storage of prepackaged, freeze-dried bone by a general acute care hospital.
(7) The storage of freeze-dried bone and dermis by any licensed dentist practicing in a lawful practice setting, if the freeze-dried bone and dermis have been obtained from a licensed tissue bank, are stored in strict accordance with a kit's package insert and any other manufacturer instructions and guidelines, and are used for the express purpose of implantation into a patient.
(8) The storage of a human cell, tissue, or cellular- or tissue-based product (HCT/P), as defined by the federal Food and Drug Administration (FDA), that is either a medical device approved pursuant to Section 510 or 515 of the Federal Food, Drug, and Cosmetic Act (21 U.S.C. Sec. 360 et seq.) or that is a biologic product approved under Section 351 of the federal Public Health Service Act (42 U.S.C. Sec. 262) by a licensed physician or podiatrist acting within the scope and authority of his or her license and practicing in a lawful practice setting. The medical device or biologic product must have been obtained from a California-licensed tissue bank, been stored in strict accordance with the device's or product's package insert and any other manufacturer instructions, and used solely for the express purpose of direct implantation into or application on the practitioner's own patient. In order to be eligible for the exemption in this paragraph, the entity or organization where the physician or podiatrist who is eligible for the exemption is practicing shall notify the department, in writing, that the practitioner is licensed and meets the requirements of this paragraph. The notification shall include all of the following:
(A) A list of all practitioners to whom the notice applies.

(B) Acknowledgment that each listed practitioner uses the medical device or biologic product in the scope and authority of his or her license and practice for the purposes of direct patient care as described in this paragraph.
(C) A statement that each listed practitioner agrees to strictly abide by the directions for storage in the device's or product's package insert and any other manufacturer instructions and guidelines.
(D) Acknowledgment by each practitioner that the medical device or biologic product shall not be resold or distributed.
(9) The collection, processing, storage, or distribution of any organ, as defined in paragraph (2) of subdivision (c) of Section 1635, within a single general acute care hospital, as defined in subdivision (a) of Section 1250, operating a Medicare-approved transplant program.
(10) The storage of allograft tissue by a person if all of the following apply:
(A) The person, as defined in Section 1635, is a hospital, or an outpatient setting regulated by the Medical Board of California pursuant to Chapter 1.3 (commencing with Section 1248), including an ambulatory surgical center.
(B) The person maintains a log that includes the date on which the allograft tissue was received, the expiration date of the allograft tissue, the date on which each allograft tissue is used for clinical purposes, and the disposition of any allograft tissue samples that remain unused at the time the allograft tissue expires.
(C) The allograft tissue meets all of the following:
(i) The allograft tissue was obtained from a tissue bank licensed by the state.
(ii) Each allograft tissue is individually boxed and labeled with a unique identification number and expiration date so that opening the shipping container will not disturb or otherwise alter any of the allograft tissue that is not being utilized.
(iii) The allograft tissue is intended for the express purpose of implantation into or application on a patient.
(iv) The allograft tissue is not intended for further distribution.
(v) The allograft tissue is registered with the FDA and designated to be maintained at ambient room temperature requiring no refrigeration.
(Amended by Stats. 2016, Ch. 273, Sec. 1. (AB 2750) Effective January 1, 2017.)
1635.2.
The Legislature hereby declares its intent that the collection, processing, storage, or distribution of tissue for the purpose of transplantation, as regulated by this chapter, shall be deemed a service by these persons engaged in these activities. Therefore, the collection, processing, storage, or distribution of tissue for the purpose of transplantation, as regulated by this chapter, shall not be subject to the requirements of Division 2 (commencing with Section 2101) of the Commercial Code.
(Added by Stats. 1991, Ch. 801, Sec. 2.)

ARTICLE 2. Regulation of Tissue Banks [1639 - 1641.1]
(Article 2 added by Stats. 1991, Ch. 801, Sec. 2.)

1639.
(a) The department may adopt rules and regulations governing the administration and enforcement of this chapter.
(b) Regulations adopted by the department may include minimum standards for the following:
(1) Safe preservation, transportation, storage, and handling of tissue acquired or used for transplantation.
(2) Testing of donors to determine compatibility when appropriate.
(3) Testing or assessment of donors to prevent the spread of disease through transplantation.
(4) Equipment.
(5) Methods.
(6) Personnel qualifications.
(7) Any other area concerning the operation or maintenance of a tissue bank, not inconsistent with this chapter, as may be necessary to carry out this chapter.
(c) The department shall report to the Legislature by January 1, 2004, on the status of the regulations developed pursuant to this section.
(Amended by Stats. 2003, Ch. 464, Sec. 1. Effective January 1, 2004.)
1639.01.
(a) Notwithstanding Section 1639, the state department shall adopt, on or before July 1, 2004, rules and regulations governing licensed tissue banks engaged in the collection of human musculoskeletal tissue, skin, and veins for transplantation in humans. The regulations shall be substantially based upon the criteria used by tissue bank trade associations in their respective accreditation processes including, but not limited to, those of the Eye Bank Association of America and the American Association of Tissue Banks, and the scientific and technical data submitted by individual tissue banks.
(b) Regulations adopted by the state department, pursuant to subdivision (a), shall include minimum standards for all of the following:
(1) Safe preservation, transportation, storage, and handling of tissue acquired or used for transplantation.
(2) Testing of donors to determine compatibility when appropriate.
(3) Testing or assessment of donors to prevent the spread of disease through transplantation.
(4) Equipment.
(5) Methods.
(6) Personnel qualifications.
(7) Any other area concerning the operation or maintenance of a tissue bank, not inconsistent with this chapter, as may be necessary to carry out this chapter.

(c) On or before July 1, 2003, the department shall report to the appropriate policy and fiscal committees of the Legislature regarding the status of the proposed regulations.
(Added by Stats. 2002, Ch. 929, Sec. 1. Effective January 1, 2003.)
1639.1.
Any person desiring a license issued pursuant to Section 1639.3 shall file with the state department a verified application on forms prescribed by the state department containing all of the following:
(a) The name of the applicant for licensure.
(b) The street address of the tissue bank. If more than one street address is occupied by the tissue bank, all occupied street addresses shall be listed.
(c) Whether the applicant is an individual, partnership, unincorporated association, or corporation.
(d) Whether the applicant does business under a fictitious name, and, if so, the fictitious name and the name of the locality wherein any fictitious name permit is filed.
(e) If the applicant is a partnership, the names of all the members of the partnership, or unincorporated association, whether general or limited.
(f) If the applicant is a corporation, the name of the officers, directors, shareholders holding a 5 percent or more interest in the corporation, and any person, partnership, or corporation who or which has the responsibility to manage or conduct the day-to-day operation of the tissue bank.
(g) The type of tissue collected, processed, stored, or distributed by the tissue bank.
(h) The names, titles, and qualifications of the persons responsible for the collection, processing, storage, or distribution of tissue by the tissue bank.
(i) Any process utilized by the tissue bank to ensure safe preservation, transportation, storage, and handling, of tissue acquired or used by the tissue bank.
(j) Any process utilized by the tissue bank to determine if, when appropriate, donors have been tested to determine compatibility.
(k) Any process utilized by the tissue bank to determine if donors have been tested or assessed for the transmission of disease through transplantation.
(Added by Stats. 1991, Ch. 801, Sec. 2.)
1639.2.
(a) Each license issued pursuant to subdivision (a) of Section 1639.3 before July 1, 1992, shall expire July 1, 1993. Every other license issued pursuant to subdivision (a) of Section 1639.3 shall expire 12 months from the date of issuance.
(b) An application for renewal of a license issued pursuant to subdivision (a) of Section 1639.3 shall be filed with the state department not less than 30 days prior to its expiration date and shall be accompanied by the annual renewal fee required in Section 1639.5. Failure to make timely application or payment for renewal shall result by operation of law in expiration of the license on its expiration date.
(c) Upon application and payment of the required fee, a renewal license issued under subdivision (a) of Section 1639.3 shall be renewed for one- or two-year periods, at the option of the licensee, as long as the licensee has been found to be in substantial compliance with this chapter and the rules and regulations adopted under this chapter during the preceding license period.
(d) Any license issued pursuant to this chapter shall be forfeited by operation of law prior to its expiration date when one of the following occurs:
(1) The tissue bank is sold or otherwise transferred.
(2) The license is surrendered to the state department.
(Added by Stats. 1991, Ch. 801, Sec. 2.)
1639.3.
(a) Upon the filing of the verified application for licensure required by Section 1639.1, payment of the application fee in the amount required in Section 1639.5, and full compliance with this chapter and the rules and regulations adopted by the state department, the state department shall issue a license to operate a tissue bank to the applicant.
(b) If the state department finds that the applicant is not in compliance with this chapter or the rules or regulations adopted under this chapter, or if it finds that the applicant has acted in a manner which would justify the revocation or suspension of a tissue bank license as described in Section 1643, the license shall be denied.
(c) The state department may, prior to a determination under subdivision (a) that the applicant is in full compliance, but after the filing of a complete and verified application and payment of the application fee, issue a provisional license to operate a tissue bank to the applicant. The provisional license shall remain in effect until a license is either granted under subdivision (a) or denied under subdivision (b).
If this period is longer than a year from the date of filing the application for licensure, the applicant shall pay an additional annual fee of nine hundred fifty dollars ($950) in order for the provisional license to remain in effect for an additional one-year period. Failure to pay the additional annual fee shall result, by operation of law, in automatic expiration of the provisional license one year from the date of its original issuance. If the provisional license does so expire, the applicant may not continue to operate a tissue bank pending the department's determination of whether a license shall be granted or denied.
(Added by Stats. 1991, Ch. 801, Sec. 2.)
1639.35.
Any person, when submitting an application for a license, including the renewal thereof, pursuant to this chapter, shall also submit, with the application, a copy of the applicant's standard informed consent form required pursuant to Section 7158.3.
(Added by Stats. 2003, Ch. 464, Sec. 2. Effective January 1, 2004.)
1639.4.
Immediately upon the denial of any application for a license, the state department shall notify the applicant in writing. Within 20 days after the state department mails the notice,

the applicant may present a written petition for a hearing to the state department. Upon receipt by the state department of the petition in proper form, the petition shall be set for hearing. The proceedings shall be conducted in accordance with Section 100171.
(Amended by Stats. 1997, Ch. 220, Sec. 20. Effective August 4, 1997.)
1639.5.
(a) The application and annual renewal fee for a tissue bank license shall be nine hundred fifty dollars ($950). Upon application for renewal of a license issued pursuant to subdivision (a) of Section 1639.3, the amount of the annual renewal fee required shall be determined by the period of time for which renewal is sought, which shall be either a one- or two-year period. The amount due shall be the amount prorated to the length of time the renewal is sought, based on the annual nine hundred fifty dollar ($950) fee.
(b) Notwithstanding subdivision (a), no license fee shall be required for any tissue bank operated by the state or any state agency, or by a district, city, county, or city and county, or any subdivision or agency thereof, or by a "mothers' milk bank," as defined in subdivision (b) of Section 14132.34 of the Welfare and Institutions Code, that has applied for tissue bank licensure prior to January 1, 1995.
(Amended by Stats. 1994, Ch. 639, Sec. 1. Effective January 1, 1995.)
1639.55.
(a) There is hereby established in the State Treasury the Tissue Bank License Fund. Notwithstanding any other provision of law, if, at the end of any fiscal year, the unencumbered balance in any account in the Tissue Bank License Fund exceeds 110 percent of the amount appropriated from the account for the following fiscal year, the state department shall reduce the application and annual renewal fees which are deposited into the account. The amount of the reduction shall be sufficient to reduce the unencumbered balance in the account at the end of the following fiscal year to less than 110 percent of the amount appropriated in that fiscal year. The adjustment of fees pursuant to this section shall not be subject to the requirements of Chapter 3.5 (commencing with Section 11340) of Part 1 of Division 3 of Title 2 of the Government Code.
(b) The state department shall receive and account for all money received pursuant to this chapter and shall deposit it with the Treasurer who shall keep the money in the Tissue Bank License Fund.
(c) Moneys deposited to the credit of the Tissue Bank License Fund which are appropriated in the Budget Act or any other appropriation act for support of or expenditure by the state department shall be used by the state department to administer this chapter.
(d) Upon the request of the State Director of Health Services, the Director of Finance may make a loan to the Tissue Bank License Fund from funds appropriated from the General Fund for that purpose. The amount of any such loan shall be approved by the Director of Finance and be repaid under those terms and conditions as prescribed by the Director of Finance, but shall, in any event, be repaid not later than June 30, 1995.
(Added by Stats. 1991, Ch. 801, Sec. 2.)
1639.56.
The department shall submit a report to the Legislature no later than January 1, 2003, including, but not limited to, examining and evaluating all of the following:
(a) Administrative expenditures of tissue banks.
(b) Current use of informed consent by tissue banks in tissue donation and recovery, including recommendations for improving and expanding informed consent policy.
(c) Full disclosure requirements by tissue banks to the donor or the person authorized to make a donation on behalf of a decedent of all potential uses of donated and recovered tissues.
(d) A system in which individuals with medically necessary conditions for which donated tissues are part of the prescribed treatment are given priority in receiving donated tissues, and the feasibility of state subsidies to implement the system.
(e) The current process for tissue recovery and distribution, including recommendations for improvement, where necessary.
(Added by Stats. 2000, Ch. 829, Sec. 1. Effective January 1, 2001.)
1639.6.
(a) In order to carry out the purpose of this chapter, any duly authorized representative of the department may do any of the following:
(1) Enter or inspect on an announced or unannounced basis any building, premise, equipment, materials, records, or information at any reasonable time to secure compliance with, or prevent a violation of, this chapter or the rules or regulations adopted by the state department.
(2) Inspect, photograph, or copy any records, reports, test results, test specimens, or other information related to the requirements of this chapter or the rules or regulations adopted by the state department.
(3) Secure any sample, photograph, or other evidence from any building or premise for the purpose of enforcing this chapter or the rules or regulations adopted by the state department.
(b) The state department may require licensed tissue banks to demonstrate satisfactory performance in a proficiency testing program approved by the state department in laboratory procedures which the tissue bank performs.
(Added by Stats. 1991, Ch. 801, Sec. 2.)
1641.
Any person who violates this chapter or who willfully and repeatedly violates any rule or regulation adopted under this chapter, is guilty of a misdemeanor and upon conviction thereof shall be punished by a fine not to exceed one thousand dollars ($1,000) or by imprisonment in a county jail for a period not to exceed 180 days, or by both fine and imprisonment.

(Added by Stats. 1991, Ch. 801, Sec. 2.)
1641.1.
The state department may bring an action to enjoin the violation or threatened violation of Section 1635.1 in the superior court in and for the county in which the violation occurred or is about to occur. Any proceeding under this section shall conform to the requirements of Chapter 3 (commencing with Section 525) of Title 7 of Part 2 of the Code of Civil Procedure, except that the state department shall not be required to allege facts necessary to show or tending to show lack of adequate remedy at law or irreparable damage or loss. With respect to any action brought pursuant to this section alleging actual violation of Section 1635.1, the court shall, if it finds the allegations to be true, issue its order enjoining the continuance of the violation.
(Added by Stats. 1991, Ch. 801, Sec. 2.)

ARTICLE 3. Suspension or Revocation of License [1643 - 1643.2]
(Article 3 added by Stats. 1991, Ch. 801, Sec. 2.)
1643.
The state department may suspend or revoke any license issued under this chapter for any of the following reasons:
(a) Violation by the licensee of this chapter or any rule or regulation adopted under this chapter.
(b) Aiding, abetting, or permitting the violation of any provision of this chapter, the rules or regulations adopted under this chapter or the Medical Practice Act (Chapter 5 (commencing with Section 2000) of Division 2 of the Business and Professions Code).
(c) Proof that the licensee has made false statements in any material regard on the application for a tissue bank license.
(d) Conduct inimical to the public health, morals, welfare, or safety of the people of the State of California in the maintenance or operation of the premises or services for which a license is issued.
(e) Conduct prohibited under Section 367f of the Penal Code and under Section 274e of Title 42 of the United States Code.
(f) The conviction of a licensee or the person in charge of the tissue bank of any crime which is substantially related to the qualifications or duties of the licensee or the person in charge of the tissue bank or which is substantially related to the functions of the tissue bank. For purposes of this section, a conviction means a plea or verdict of guilty or a conviction following a plea of nolo contendere. An action to revoke or suspend the license may be taken when the time for appeal has elapsed or the judgment of conviction has been affirmed on appeal or when an order granting probation is made suspending the imposition of sentence, notwithstanding a subsequent order pursuant to Section 1203.4 of the Penal Code permitting withdrawal of a plea of guilty and entry of a plea of not guilty, or setting aside the verdict of guilty, or dismissing the accusation, information or indictment. The director shall take into account all competent evidence of rehabilitation furnished by the licensee or person in charge of the tissue bank.
(Added by Stats. 1991, Ch. 801, Sec. 2.)
1643.1.
Proceedings for the suspension or revocation of licenses under this chapter shall be conducted in accordance with Section 100171.
(Amended by Stats. 1997, Ch. 220, Sec. 21. Effective August 4, 1997.)
1643.2.
The state department may temporarily suspend any license issued under this chapter prior to any hearing, when it has determined that the action is necessary to protect the public welfare. The state department shall notify the licensee of the temporary suspension and the effective date thereof and at the same time shall serve the licensee with an accusation. Upon receipt of a notice of defense by the licensee, the matter shall, within 15 days, be set for hearing. The hearing shall be held as soon as possible but not later than 30 days after receipt of such notice. The temporary suspension shall remain in effect until such time as the hearing is completed and the state department has made a final determination on the merits. However, the temporary suspension shall be deemed vacated if the state department fails to make a final determination on the merits within 60 days after the original hearing has been completed.
(Added by Stats. 1991, Ch. 801, Sec. 2.)

CHAPTER 4.2. Donations of Organs, Tissues, or Body Fluids [1644 - 1644.6]

(Heading of Chapter 4.2 renumbered from Chapter 4.1 by Stats. 1991, Ch. 801, Sec. 3.)
1644.
(a) For purposes of this chapter, "donor," "person," "tissue," "transplantation," and "department" shall have the meaning as defined for those terms in Section 1635.
(b) For purposes of this chapter, "HIV" shall mean human immunodeficiency virus.
(c) "Identifying information" means the full name of the donor, the donor's date of birth, and the permanent and, if different, current address of the donor at the time of donation.
(d) "Medical information" means information regarding a present illness of the donor, past illness of the donor, and social, genetic, and family history of the donor.
(Amended by Stats. 2018, Ch. 876, Sec. 67. (AB 2684) Effective January 1, 2019.)
1644.1.
(a) (1) Except as provided in paragraph (2), a gamete bank licensed in this state shall collect and retain from a gamete donor the donor's identifying information and medical information at the time of the donation. If the gamete bank sends the gametes of a donor to another gamete bank, the sending gamete bank shall forward any identifying information and medical information, including the donor's signed declaration under

Section 1644.2 regarding identity disclosure, to the receiving gamete bank and shall no longer be required to retain the information. A receiving gamete bank licensed in this state shall collect and retain the information about the donor and each sending gamete bank.
(2) A gamete bank obtaining gametes for the purpose of clinical utilization within one month from receipt shall not be considered a receiving gamete bank responsible for long-term retention of any identifying information or medical information other than what is typically documented in the medical record, and shall not be responsible for responding to any request under Section 1644.3 other than to identify the sending gamete bank.
(b) This section shall apply only to gametes collected on or after January 1, 2020.
(Added by Stats. 2018, Ch. 876, Sec. 68. (AB 2684) Effective January 1, 2019.)
1644.2.
(a) A gamete bank licensed in this state that collects gametes from a donor shall do both of the following:
(1) Provide the donor with information in a record about the donor's choice regarding identity disclosure.
(2) Obtain a declaration from the donor regarding identity disclosure.
(b) A gamete bank licensed in this state shall give a donor the choice to sign a declaration, attested by a notary or witnessed, that does either of the following:
(1) States that the donor agrees to disclose his or her identity to a child conceived by assisted reproduction with the donor's gametes, on request, once the child attains 18 years of age.
(2) States that the donor does not agree presently to disclose the donor's identity to the child.
(c) A gamete bank licensed in this state shall permit a donor who has signed a declaration under paragraph (2) of subdivision (b) to withdraw the declaration at any time by signing a declaration under paragraph (1) of subdivision (b).
(d) This section shall apply only to gametes collected on or after January 1, 2020.
(Added by Stats. 2018, Ch. 876, Sec. 69. (AB 2684) Effective January 1, 2019.)
1644.3.
(a) On request of a child conceived by assisted reproduction who attains 18 years of age, a gamete bank licensed in this state that collected, stored, or released for use the gametes used in the assisted reproduction shall provide the child with identifying information of the donor who provided the gamete, unless the donor signed and did not withdraw a declaration under paragraph (2) of subdivision (b) of Section 1644.2. If the donor signed and did not withdraw the declaration, the gamete bank shall make a good faith effort to notify the donor, who may elect under subdivision (c) of Section 1644.2 to withdraw the declaration.
(b) Regardless whether a donor signed a declaration under paragraph (2) of subdivision (b) of Section 1644.2, on request from a child conceived by assisted reproduction who attains 18 years of age, or, if the child is a minor, by a parent or guardian of the child, a gamete bank licensed in this state shall provide the child or, if the child is a minor, the parent or guardian of the child, access to nonidentifying medical information provided by the donor.
(c) This section shall apply only to gametes collected on or after January 1, 2020.
(Added by Stats. 2018, Ch. 876, Sec. 70. (AB 2684) Effective January 1, 2019.)
1644.5.
(a) Except as provided in subdivision (c) or (d), tissues shall not be transferred into the body of another person by means of transplantation, unless the donor of the tissues has been screened and found nonreactive by laboratory tests for evidence of infection with human immunodeficiency virus (HIV), agents of viral hepatitis (HBV and HCV), and syphilis. For tissues that are rich in viable leukocytes, the tissue shall be tested for evidence of infection with human T-lymphotropic virus (HTLV) and found nonreactive. The department may adopt regulations requiring additional screening tests of donors of tissues when, in the opinion of the department, the action is necessary for the protection of the public, donors, or recipients.
(b) Notwithstanding subdivision (a), infectious disease screening of blood and blood products shall be carried out solely in accordance with Article 2 (commencing with Section 1602.5) of Chapter 4.
(c) All donors of sperm shall be screened and found nonreactive as required under subdivision (a), except in the following instances:
(1) A recipient of sperm, from a sperm donor known to the recipient, may waive a second or other repeat testing of that donor if the recipient is informed of the requirements for testing donors under this section and signs a written waiver.
(2) A recipient of sperm may consent to therapeutic insemination of sperm or use of sperm in other assisted reproductive technologies even if the sperm donor is found reactive for hepatitis B, hepatitis C, syphilis, HIV, or HTLV if the sperm donor is the spouse of, partner of, or designated donor for that recipient. The physician providing insemination or assisted reproductive technology services shall advise the donor and recipient of the potential medical risks associated with receiving sperm from a reactive donor. The donor and the recipient shall sign a document affirming that each person comprehends the potential medical risks of using sperm from a reactive donor for the proposed procedure and that each consents to it. Copies of the document shall be placed in the medical records of the donor and the recipient.
(3) (A) Sperm whose donor has tested reactive for syphilis may be used for the purposes of insemination or assisted reproductive technology only after the donor has been treated for syphilis. Sperm whose donor has tested reactive for hepatitis B may be used for the purposes of insemination or assisted reproductive technology only after the recipient has been vaccinated against hepatitis B.

(B) (i) Sperm whose donor has tested reactive for HIV or HTLV may be used for the purposes of insemination or assisted reproductive technology for a recipient testing negative for HIV or HTLV only after the donor's sperm has been effectively processed to minimize the likelihood of transmission through the sperm for that specific donation and if informed and mutual consent has occurred.

(ii) The department shall adopt regulations regulating facilities that perform sperm processing, pursuant to this subparagraph, that prescribe standards for the handling and storage of sperm samples of carriers of HIV, HTLV, or any other virus as deemed appropriate by the department. The department may propose to adopt, as initial regulations, the most relevant and up-to-date recommendations published by the American Society for Reproductive Medicine. Notice of the department's proposed adoption of the regulations shall be posted on the department's Internet Web site for at least 45 days. Public comment shall be accepted by the department for at least 30 days after the conclusion of the 45-day posting period. If a member of the public requests a public hearing during the 30-day comment period, the hearing shall be held prior to the adoption of the regulations. If no member of the public requests a public hearing, the regulations shall be deemed adopted at the conclusion of the 30-day comment period. Comments received shall be considered prior to the adoption of the final initial regulations. The department may modify any recommendations published by the American Society for Reproductive Medicine. Adoption of initial regulations by the department pursuant to this subdivision shall not be subject to the rulemaking requirements of Chapter 3.5 (commencing with Section 11340) of Part 1 of Division 3 of Title 2 of the Government Code and written responses to public comments shall not be required. Updates to the regulations shall be adopted pursuant to the same process. Until the department adopts these regulations, facilities that perform sperm processing pursuant to this section shall follow facility and sperm processing recommendations for the reduction of viral transmission developed by the American Society for Reproductive Medicine. This section does not prevent the department from monitoring and inspecting facilities that process sperm to ensure adherence to the regulations, or, until regulations are adopted, to the recommendations set forth by the American Society for Reproductive Medicine.

(iii) Before insemination or other assisted reproductive technology services are performed, the physician providing the services shall inform the recipient of sperm from a spouse, partner, or designated donor who has tested reactive for HIV or HTLV of all of the following:

(I) That sperm processing may not eliminate all of the risks of HIV or HTLV transmission.

(II) That the sperm may be tested to determine whether or not it is reactive for HIV or HTLV.

(III) That the recipient shall provide documentation to the physician providing insemination or assisted reproductive technology services prior to treatment that she has established an ongoing relationship with another physician to provide for her medical care during and after completion of fertility services.

(IV) The most relevant and up-to-date recommendations published by the American Society for Reproductive Medicine regarding followup testing for HIV and HTLV after use of sperm from an HIV or HTLV reactive donor and have the recommendations regarding followup testing be documented in the recipient's medical record.

(iv) The physician providing insemination or assisted reproductive technology services shall also verify, and document in the recipient's medical record, that the donor of sperm who tests reactive for HIV or HTLV is under the care of a physician managing the HIV or HTLV.

(v) The physician providing insemination or assisted reproductive technology services shall recommend to the physician who will be providing ongoing care to the recipient recommended followup testing for HIV and HTLV according to the most relevant and up-to-date guidelines published by the American Society for Reproductive Medicine, which shall be documented in the recipient's medical record.

(vi) If the recipient becomes HIV or HTLV positive, the physician assuming ongoing care of the recipient shall treat or provide information regarding referral to a physician who can provide ongoing treatment of the HIV or HTLV.

(4) A recipient of sperm donated by a sexually intimate partner of the recipient for reproductive use may waive a second or repeat testing of that donor if the recipient is informed of the donor testing requirements of this section and signs a written waiver. For purposes of this paragraph, "sexually intimate partner of the recipient" includes a known or designated donor to whose sperm the recipient has previously been exposed in a nonmedical setting in an attempt to conceive.

(d) Subdivision (a) does not apply to the transplantation of tissue from a donor who has not been tested or, with the exception of HTLV, has been found reactive for the infectious diseases listed in subdivision (a) or for which the department has, by regulation, required additional screening tests, if all of the following conditions are satisfied:

(1) The physician and surgeon performing the transplantation has determined any one or more of the following:

(A) Without the transplantation the intended recipient will most likely die during the period of time necessary to obtain other tissue or to conduct the required tests.

(B) The intended recipient already is diagnosed with the infectious disease for which the donor has tested positive.

(C) The symptoms from the infectious disease for which the donor has tested positive will most likely not appear during the intended recipient's likely lifespan after transplantation with the tissue or may be treated prophylactically if they do appear.

(2) The physician and surgeon performing the transplantation has ensured that an organ from an individual who has been found reactive for HIV may be transplanted only into an individual who satisfies both of the following:

(A) The individual has been found reactive for HIV before receiving the organ.

(B) The individual is either participating in clinical research approved by an institutional review board under the criteria, standards, and regulations described in subsections (a) and (b) of Section 274f-5 of Title 42 of the United States Code, or, if the United States Secretary of Health and Human Services determines under subsection (c) of Section 274f-5 of Title 42 of the United States Code that participation in this clinical research is no longer warranted as a requirement for transplants, the individual is receiving the transplant under the standards and regulations under subsection (c) of Section 274f-5 of Title 42 of the United States Code.

(3) Consent for the use of the tissue has been obtained from the recipient, if possible, or if not possible, from a member of the recipient's family, or the recipient's legal guardian. For purposes of this section, "family" means spouse, adult son or daughter, either parent, adult brother or sister, or grandparent.

(e) The penalties prescribed in Section 120290 do not apply to a sperm donor covered under subdivision (c) or an organ or tissue donor who donates an organ or tissue for transplantation or research purposes.

(f) Human breast milk from donors who test reactive for agents of viral hepatitis (HBV and HCV), HTLV, HIV, or syphilis shall not be used for deposit into a milk bank for human ingestion in California.

(Amended by Stats. 2017, Ch. 537, Sec. 3. (SB 239) Effective January 1, 2018.)

1644.6.

(a) No physician and surgeon shall be subject to liability for damages for any cause of action based solely on the use of sperm donated by a sexually intimate partner of the recipient if both of the following conditions are met:

(1) The physician and surgeon provides insemination or assisted reproductive technology services and has obtained the informed consent of the recipient, who waives second or other repeat testing of the sexually intimate partner and acknowledges and accepts the risks of using sperm from a sexually intimate partner who has not undergone repeat testing, in accordance with paragraph (1) of subdivision (c) of Section 1644.5.

(2) The physician and surgeon complies with the applicable requirements specified in Section 1644.5.

(b) No physician and surgeon shall be subject to disciplinary action against his or her professional license, or subject to peer review by a professional association peer review body, as defined in clause (iii) of subparagraph (B) of paragraph (1) of subdivision (a) of Section 805 of the Business and Professions Code, because the physician and surgeon used sperm donated by a sexually intimate partner of the recipient in providing insemination or assisted reproductive technology services if both of the following conditions are met:

(1) The physician and surgeon has obtained the informed consent of the recipient who waives second or other repeat testing of the sexually intimate partner and acknowledges and accepts the risks of using sperm from a sexually intimate partner who has not undergone repeat testing, in accordance with paragraph (1) of subdivision (c) of Section 1644.5.

(2) The physician and surgeon complies with the applicable requirements specified in Section 1644.5.

(c) A tissue bank that is owned and operated by a physician and surgeon shall not be subject to disciplinary action against its license because of the use of sperm donated by a sexually intimate partner of the recipient in providing insemination or assisted reproductive technology services if both of the following conditions are met:

(1) A physician and surgeon affiliated with the tissue bank has obtained the informed consent of the recipient, who waives second or other repeat testing of the sexually intimate partner and acknowledges and accepts the risks of using sperm from a sexually intimate partner who has not undergone repeat testing, in accordance with paragraph (1) of subdivision (c) of Section 1644.5.

(2) The physician and surgeon complies with the applicable requirements specified in Section 1644.5.

(d) Nothing in this section shall create a duty for a physician and surgeon to use sperm donated by a sexually intimate partner of the recipient in providing insemination or assisted reproductive technology services if the physician and surgeon reasonably concludes that the insemination or services do not meet the 2008 American Society for Reproductive Medicine guidelines for gamete and embryo donation.

(e) Nothing in this section shall be construed to affect any liability that may be imposed pursuant to a federal rule or regulation when a physician and surgeon, or tissue bank provides insemination or assisted reproductive technology services.

(f) For purposes of this section, "sexually intimate partner" includes a known or designated donor to whose sperm the recipient has previously been exposed in a nonmedical setting in an attempt to conceive.

(Added by Stats. 2012, Ch. 699, Sec. 3. (AB 2356) Effective January 1, 2013.)

CHAPTER 4.4. Genetic Depositories [1644.7 - 1644.9]

(Chapter 4.4 added by Stats. 2004, Ch. 775, Sec. 2.5.)

1644.7.

Any entity that receives genetic material of a human being that may be used for conception shall provide to the person depositing his or her genetic material a form for use by the depositor that, if signed by the depositor, would satisfy the conditions set forth in Section 249.5 of the Probate Code, regarding the decedent's intent for the use of that material. The use of the form is not mandatory, and the form is not the exclusive means of expressing a depositor's intent. The form shall include advisements in substantially the following form:

"The use of this form for designating whether a child conceived after your death will be your heir is not mandatory. However, if you wish to allow a child conceived after your death to be considered as your heir (or beneficiary of other benefits such as life insurance or retirement) you must specify that in writing and you must sign that written expression of intent.

This specification can be revoked or amended only in writing signed by you (and not by spoken words).

You should consider how having a child conceived after your death affects your estate planning (including your will, trust, and other beneficiary designations for retirement benefits, life insurance, financial accounts, etc.) These issues can be complex, and you should discuss them with your attorney."

(Added by Stats. 2004, Ch. 775, Sec. 2.5. Effective January 1, 2005.)

1644.8.

Any entity that receives genetic material of a human being that may be used for conception shall make available to the person depositing his or her genetic material a form that, if signed by the depositor, would revoke any previous expression of intent regarding the use of his or her genetic material necessary to satisfy the conditions set forth in Section 249.5 of the Probate Code. The use of the form is not mandatory, and the form is not the exclusive means of expressing a depositor's intent with respect to revocation or amendment of a prior expression of intent. The form shall include advisements in substantially the following form:

"The use of this form to revoke or amend a previous form for designating whether a child conceived after your death will be your heir is not mandatory. This specification can be revoked or amended only in a writing signed by you (and not by spoken words). These issues can be complex, and you should discuss them with your attorney."

(Added by Stats. 2004, Ch. 775, Sec. 2.5. Effective January 1, 2005.)

1644.9.

This chapter does not apply to the application of somatic nuclear transfer technology to the creation of a human being that shares all of its nuclear genes with the person donating the implanted nucleus, commonly known as human cloning. For purposes of this section, the phrase "somatic cell nuclear transfer" means the process in which the nucleus of a somatic cell of an organism is transferred into an enucleated oocyte.

(Added by Stats. 2004, Ch. 775, Sec. 2.5. Effective January 1, 2005.)

CHAPTER 4.5. The Paul Gann Blood Safety Act [1645- 1645.]

(Chapter 4.5 added by Stats. 1989, Ch. 1365, Sec. 2.)

1645.

(a) Whenever there is a reasonable possibility, as determined by a physician and surgeon or doctor of podiatric medicine, that a blood transfusion may be necessary as a result of a medical or surgical procedure, the physician and surgeon or doctor of podiatric medicine, by means of a standardized written summary as most recently developed or revised by the State Department of Public Health pursuant to subdivision (e), shall inform, either directly or through a nurse practitioner, certified nurse midwife, or a physician assistant, who is licensed in the state and authorized to order a blood transfusion, the patient of the positive and negative aspects of receiving autologous blood and directed and nondirected homologous blood from volunteers. For purposes of this section, the term "autologous blood" includes, but is not limited to, predonation, intraoperative autologous transfusion, plasmapheresis, and hemodilution.

(b) The person who provided the patient with the standardized written summary pursuant to subdivision (a) shall note on the patient's medical record that the standardized written summary was given to the patient.

(c) Subdivisions (a) and (b) shall not apply when medical contraindications or a life-threatening emergency exists.

(d) When there is no life-threatening emergency and there are no medical contraindications, the physician and surgeon or doctor of podiatric medicine shall allow adequate time prior to the procedure for predonation to occur. Notwithstanding this chapter, if a patient waives allowing adequate time prior to the procedure for predonation to occur, a physician and surgeon or doctor of podiatric medicine shall not incur any liability for his or her failure to allow adequate time prior to the procedure for predonation to occur.

(e) The State Department of Public Health shall develop and annually review, and if necessary revise, a standardized written summary which explains the advantages, disadvantages, risks, and descriptions of autologous blood, and directed and nondirected homologous blood from volunteer donors. These blood options shall include, but not be limited to, the blood options described in subdivision (a). The summary shall be written so as to be easily understood by a layperson.

(f) The Medical Board of California shall publish the standardized written summary prepared pursuant to subdivision (e) by the State Department of Public Health and shall distribute copies thereof, upon request, to physicians and surgeons and doctors of podiatric medicine. The Medical Board of California shall make the summary available for a fee not exceeding in the aggregate the actual costs to the State Department of Public Health and the Medical Board of California for developing, updating, publishing and distributing the summary. Physicians and surgeons and doctors of podiatric medicine shall purchase the written summary from the Medical Board of California for, or purchase or otherwise receive the written summary from the Web site of the board or any other

entity for, distribution to their patients as specified in subdivision (a). Clinics, health facilities, and blood collection centers may purchase the summary if they desire.

(g) Any entity may reproduce the written summary prepared pursuant to subdivision (e) by the State Department of Public Health and distribute the written summary to physicians and surgeons and doctors of podiatric medicine.

(Amended by Stats. 2007, Ch. 88, Sec. 1. Effective January 1, 2008.)

CHAPTER 4.75. Human Milk [1647 - 1648]

(Chapter 4.75 added by Stats. 1999, Ch. 87, Sec. 2.)

1647.

The procurement, processing, distribution, or use of human milk for the purpose of human consumption shall be construed to be, and is declared to be for all purposes, the rendition of a service by each and every nonprofit organization and its employees participating therein, and shall not be construed to be, and is declared not to be, a sale of the human milk for any purpose or purposes.

(Added by Stats. 1999, Ch. 87, Sec. 2. Effective January 1, 2000.)

1648.

(a) A hospital that collects, processes, stores, or distributes human milk collected from a mother exclusively for her own child shall comply with the most current standards established for the collection, processing, storage, or distribution of human milk by the Human Milk Banking Association of North America until or unless the department approves alternative standards.

(b) A hospital shall be exempt from the requirements of Chapter 4.1 (commencing with Section 1635) for the purpose of collecting, processing, storing, or distributing human milk collected from a mother exclusively for her own child.

(c) Notwithstanding any other provision of law, no screening tests shall be required to be performed on human milk collected from a mother exclusively for her own child.

(d) The department shall assess hospital processes for collecting, processing, storing, or distributing human milk pursuant to its current practice, as required by Chapter 2 (commencing with Section 1250).

(e) This section does not apply to any hospital that collects, processes, stores, or distributes milk from human milk banks or other outside sources.

(Added by Stats. 2006, Ch. 480, Sec. 2. Effective January 1, 2007.)

CHAPTER 5. Regulation of Use of Animals in Diagnostic Procedures and Medical Research [1650 - 1677]

(Chapter 5 added by Stats. 1951, Ch. 1750.)

ARTICLE 1. General Provisions [1650 - 1651]

(Article 1 added by Stats. 1951, Ch. 1750.)

1650.

The public health and welfare depend on the humane use of animals for scientific advancement in the diagnosis and treatment of human and animal diseases, for education, for research in the advancement of veterinary, dental, medical and biologic sciences, for research in animal and human nutrition, and improvement and standardization of laboratory procedures of biologic products, pharmaceuticals and drugs.

(Added by Stats. 1951, Ch. 1750.)

1651.

The State Department of Health Services shall administer the provisions of this chapter. Every provision of this chapter shall be liberally construed to protect the interests of all persons and animals affected.

As used in this chapter, "person" includes: laboratory, firm, association, corporation, copartnership, and educational institution.

As used in this chapter, "board" or "department" means the State Department of Health Services.

(Amended by Stats. 1977, Ch. 1252.)

ARTICLE 2. Administration and Regulation [1660 - 1662]

(Article 2 added by Stats. 1951, Ch. 1750.)

1660.

The department shall make and promulgate, and may thereafter modify, amend or rescind, reasonable rules and regulations to carry out the purposes of this chapter, including the control of the humane use of animals for the diagnosis and treatment of human and animal diseases, for research in the advancement of veterinary, dental, medical and biologic sciences, for research in animal and human nutrition, and for the testing and diagnosis, improvement and standardization of laboratory specimens, biologic products, pharmaceuticals and drugs. Such rules and regulations shall include requirements for satisfactory shelter, food, sanitation, record keeping, and for the humane treatment of animals by persons authorized by the board to raise, keep or to use animals under the provision of this chapter. The department shall not make or promulgate any rule compelling the delivery of animals for the purpose of research, demonstration, diagnosis, or experimentation.

(Added by Stats. 1951, Ch. 1750.)

1661.

The provisions of Chapter 3.5 (commencing with Section 11340) of Part 1 of Division 3 of Title 2 of the Government Code, shall be applicable to all the rules and regulations promulgated by the department under this chapter.

(Amended by Stats. 1983, Ch. 101, Sec. 105.)

1662.

The department is hereby authorized to inspect any premises or property on or in which animals are kept for experimental or diagnostic purposes, for the purpose of investigation of compliance with the rules and regulations adopted hereunder. Such inspection or other method of control shall be enforced only by employees of the department and such power and authority may not be delegated to any other persons or agency.

(Added by Stats. 1951, Ch. 1750.)

ARTICLE 3. Application of the Chapter [1666 - 1670]
(Article 3 added by Stats. 1951, Ch. 1750.)

1666.

No person shall keep or use animals for diagnostic purposes, education or research unless approved by the board.

(Added by Stats. 1951, Ch. 1750.)

1667.

The board shall prescribe the rules under which approval shall be granted including the standards regarding the care and treatment of such animals employed. Any person desiring approval to use animals for the purposes covered by this chapter shall make application to the department for such approval on forms provided by the department. The board shall grant approval on forms provided by the department to any person who has made application in accordance with the provisions of this article and who is found to be in compliance with the provisions of this chapter and the rules and regulations of the board. Any person keeping or using animals under the provisions of this chapter shall display in a prominent place the certificate of approval granted for such purpose. Such approval shall remain in effect for one fiscal year if not revoked by the board. If the board does not within ninety (90) days after the filing of this application grant approval it shall state the grounds and reasons for its refusal in writing, serving a copy upon the applicant, the notice may be served by registered mail addressed to the applicant at his last known address.

(Added by Stats. 1951, Ch. 1750.)

1668.

The board may, upon its own motion, and shall upon the verified complaint in writing of any person, investigate the actions of any person keeping or using animals for research or diagnostic purposes within this State, and it may temporarily suspend or permanently revoke a certificate of approval at any time where the holder of such a certificate, within the immediately preceding three years, while a holder of a certificate of approval, in performing or attempting to perform any of the acts within the scope of this chapter, has been guilty of the breach of any of the provisions of this chapter or of any reasonable rule or regulation adopted by the board for the purpose of carrying out the provisions of this chapter. The board may promulgate and adopt reasonable rules and regulations concerning the procedure for the drafting, filing and disposition of verified complaints of individuals. Procedure for revocation or suspension of approval shall be in accordance with the provision of the Administrative Procedure Act Government Code, Title 2, Division 3, Part 1, Chapter 5, and the department shall have all the powers granted therein.

(Added by Stats. 1951, Ch. 1750.)

1669.

This chapter does not apply to any veterinary licensed to practice veterinary medicine in this State or to any place of business operated by such veterinary, nor to animal training, animal cosmetics and routine animal husbandry practices, nor to laboratories subject to control or regulation by the National Institutes of Health or the Federal Bureau of Animal Industry.

(Added by Stats. 1951, Ch. 1750.)

1670.

Nothing contained in this chapter shall be construed to limit or restrict the right of counties, cities, cities and counties, towns or townships, to adopt or enforce ordinances or other regulations regulating the use or procurement of animals for diagnostic procedures or medical research, and any such ordinances or regulations now in effect are not affected by this chapter. It is the intent of this chapter to provide state regulation of the use of animals in diagnostic procedures and medical research concurrently with and supplementary to local regulations, but not to preclude the exercise by counties, cities, cities and counties, towns or townships, of such regulatory power as they may possess in this field under the Constitution and statutes of this State.

(Added by Stats. 1951, Ch. 1750.)

ARTICLE 4. Offenses Against the Chapter [1672 - 1673]
(Article 4 added by Stats. 1951, Ch. 1750.)

1672.

It is unlawful for any person to use animals for the purposes provided for in this chapter without the approval of the board.

(Added by Stats. 1951, Ch. 1750.)

1673.

Any person who violates this chapter is guilty of a misdemeanor.

(Added by Stats. 1951, Ch. 1750.)

ARTICLE 5. Revenue [1676 - 1677]
(Article 5 added by Stats. 1951, Ch. 1750.)

1676.

An annual fee, to be employed for the enforcement of this act, shall accompany each application for approval. The fee shall be determined by the director by regulations based on the number of animals used for the purposes of this chapter and in an amount sufficient to cover the cost of administering this chapter.

(Amended by Stats. 1972, Ch. 1148.)

1677.

Annual fees payable under this chapter shall become due and payable by each person approved by the board 12 months from the date of its issuance. Such fees shall be paid by the department into the General Fund in the State Treasury. It is the intention of the Legislature that the cost of administering this act shall be substantially covered by the revenues collected hereunder.

(Amended by Stats. 1972, Ch. 1148.)

CHAPTER 6. Audiometrists [1685 - 1686]

(Chapter 6 added by Stats. 1957, Ch. 205.)

1685.

The governing body of a city, county, city and county or school district may employ one or more school audiometrists, each of whom shall be registered with the State Department of Health Services and possess such qualifications as may at the date of registration be prescribed by the state department.

Audiometric testing as conducted by the qualified school audiometrist, pursuant to Section 13300 of the Education Code, or by other qualified certificated school personnel, as defined in Sections 11751 and 11824 of the Education Code, shall meet the standards which the State Department of Health Services determines necessary to insure the adequacy of hearing testing in the schools. Subject to Section 11822 of the Education Code, audiometric tests may be administered to school and preschool children in school buildings and other places as are or may be used by schools, health departments or other agencies that provide qualified personnel to conduct such tests.

(Amended by Stats. 1977, Ch. 1252.)

1686.

The State Department of Health Services shall, subject to the provisions of Section 1685, issue certificates of registration to school audiometrists and to qualified supervisors of health, pursuant to Sections 11751 and 11823 of the Education Code. The department shall prescribe such qualifications as may be necessary for the testing of the hearing of schoolchildren.

Candidates for registration who present evidence of having satisfactorily completed the required training in audiology and audiometry at an accredited university or college, as prescribed by the State Department of Health Services, may be issued certificates of registration without further examination.

The state department shall require a registration fee not in excess of ten dollars ($10) for each certificate issued. Such fee shall be based upon a determination by the department as to the amount that is reasonably necessary to pay for the costs of the issuance of certificates of registration.

(Amended by Stats. 1977, Ch. 1252.)

CHAPTER 6.5. Hysterectomies [1690 - 1691]

(Chapter 6.5 added by Stats. 1987, Ch. 1387, Sec. 1.)

1690.

(a) Prior to the performance of a hysterectomy, physicians and surgeons shall obtain verbal and written informed consent. The informed consent procedure shall ensure that at least all of the following information is given to the patient verbally and in writing:

(1) Advice that the individual is free to withhold or withdraw consent to the procedure at any time before the hysterectomy without affecting the right to future care or treatment and without loss or withdrawal of any state or federally funded program benefits to which the individual might be otherwise entitled.

(2) A description of the type or types of surgery and other procedures involved in the proposed hysterectomy, and a description of any known available and appropriate alternatives to the hysterectomy itself.

(3) Advice that the hysterectomy procedure is considered to be irreversible, and that infertility will result; except as provided in subdivision (b).

(4) A description of the discomforts and risks that may accompany or follow the performing of the procedure, including an explanation of the type and possible effects of any anesthetic to be used.

(5) A description of the benefits or advantages that may be expected as a result of the hysterectomy.

(6) Approximate length of hospital stay.

(7) Approximate length of time for recovery.

(8) Financial cost to the patient of the physician and surgeon's fees.

(b) A woman shall sign a written statement prior to the performance of the hysterectomy procedure, indicating she has read and understood the written information provided pursuant to subdivision (a), and that this information has been discussed with her by her physician and surgeon, or his or her designee. The statement shall indicate that the patient has been advised by her physician or designee that the hysterectomy will render her permanently sterile and incapable of having children and shall accompany the claim, unless the patient has previously been sterile or is postmenopausal.

(c) The informed consent procedure shall not pertain when the hysterectomy is performed in a life-threatening emergency situation in which the physician determines prior written informed consent is not possible. In this case, a statement, handwritten and signed by the physician, certifying the nature of the emergency, shall accompany the claim.

(d) The State Department of Health Services may develop regulations establishing verbal and written informed consent procedures that shall be obtained prior to performance of a

hysterectomy, that indicate the medically accepted justifications for performance of a hysterectomy, pursuant to this chapter.
(Added by Stats. 1987, Ch. 1387, Sec. 1.)
1691.
The failure of a physician and surgeon to inform a patient by means of written consent, in layman's language and in a language understood by the patient of alternative efficacious methods of treatment which may be medically viable, when a hysterectomy is to be performed, constitutes unprofessional conduct within the meaning of Chapter 5 (commencing with Section 2000) of Division 2 of the Business and Professions Code.
(Added by Stats. 1987, Ch. 1387, Sec. 1.)

CHAPTER 6.6. Neonatal Group B Streptococcal Infection [1695- 1695.]

(Chapter 6.6 added by Stats. 1994, Ch. 758, Sec. 1.)
1695.
To the extent that funds are available in the State Department of Health Services' budget for the 1994–95 fiscal year for this purpose, the department shall convene a consensus conference to address the issue of testing or treatment to prevent neonatal group B streptococcal disease (chemoprophylaxis). The conferees shall include, but not be limited to, representation from the California Chapter of the American Academy of Pediatrics, the American College of Obstetricians and Gynecologists District IX, the California Medical Association, the California Conference of Local Health Officers, and the Group B Strep Association. The conference shall convene at least once during the 1994–95 fiscal year. The department shall develop, based on the proceedings of the consensus conference, a standardized written summary on group B streptococcal disease and guidelines on the prevention of neonatal group B streptococcal disease, no later than July 1, 1995. If the department determines that state funds are not available, the department shall make every effort to obtain appropriate federal funds for this purpose.
(Added by Stats. 1994, Ch. 758, Sec. 1. Effective January 1, 1995.)

CHAPTER 8. Home Health Agencies [1725 - 1742]

(Chapter 8 added by Stats. 1966, 1st Ex. Sess., Ch. 79.)
1725.
(a) The purpose of this chapter is to require licensure of home health agencies in order to protect the health and safety of the people of California.
(b) All organizations that provide skilled nursing services to patients in the home shall obtain a home health agency license issued by the department.
(c) The department shall establish high standards of quality for home health agencies and ensure that unlicensed entities are not providing skilled nursing services in the home, except as set forth in Section 1726.
(d) The department shall require that the appropriate field staff be informed of the proper protocols and procedures to document, report, and investigate reported incidents of unlicensed facilities providing skilled nursing services in the home in order to protect public health and to facilitate statewide consistency in documenting and investigating those entities.
(Amended by Stats. 2005, Ch. 335, Sec. 1. Effective January 1, 2006.)
1726.
(a) No private or public organization, including, but not limited to, any partnership, corporation, political subdivision of the state, or other governmental agency within the state, shall provide, or arrange for the provision of, skilled nursing services in the home in this state without first obtaining a home health agency license.
(b) No private or public organization, including, but not limited to, any partnership, corporation, or political subdivision of the state, or other governmental agency within the state, shall do any of the following unless it is licensed under this chapter:
(1) Represent itself to be a home health agency by its name or advertisement, soliciting, or any other presentments to the public, or in the context of services within the scope of this chapter imply that it is licensed to provide those services or to make any reference to employee bonding in relation to those services.
(2) Use the words "home health agency," "home health," "home-health," "homehealth," or "in-home health," or any combination of those terms, within its name.
(3) Use the words "skilled" or "nursing," or any combination of those terms within its name, to imply that it is licensed as a home health agency to provide those services.
(c) In implementing the system of licensing for home health agencies, the department shall distinguish between the functions of a home health agency and the functions of an employment agency or a licensed nurses' registry pursuant to Title 2.91 (commencing with Section 1812.500) of Part 4 of Division 3 of the Civil Code. An employment agency or a licensed nurses' registry performing its functions as specified in Title 2.91 (commencing with Section 1812.500) of Part 4 of Division 3 of the Civil Code is not required to secure a home health agency license under subdivision (a), unless it is performing the functions of a home health agency, as defined in this chapter. However, subdivision (b) shall apply to an employment agency or a licensed nurses' registry that is not licensed under this chapter.
(d) A hospice is not required to secure a home health agency license under subdivision (a). However, subdivision (b) shall apply to a hospice that is not licensed under this chapter.
(Amended by Stats. 2005, Ch. 335, Sec. 2. Effective January 1, 2006.)
1727.

(a) "Home health agency" means a private or public organization, including, but not limited to, any partnership, corporation, political subdivision of the state, or other government agency within the state, which provides, or arranges for the provision of, skilled nursing services, to persons in their temporary or permanent place of residence.
(b) "Skilled nursing services" means services provided by a registered nurse or licensed vocational nurse.
(c) "Home Health Aide" means an aide who has successfully completed a state-approved training program, is employed by a home health agency or hospice program, and provides personal care services in the patient's home.
(d) "Home health aide services" means personal care services provided under a plan of treatment prescribed by the patient's physician and surgeon who is licensed to practice medicine in the state. Home health aide services shall be provided by a person certified by the state department as a home health aide pursuant to this chapter. Services which do not involve personal care services provided under a plan of treatment prescribed by a physician and surgeon may be provided by a person who is not a certified home health aide. Home health aide services shall not include services provided pursuant to Article 7 (commencing with Section 12300) of Chapter 3 of Part 3 of Division 9 of the Welfare and Institutions Code.
(Amended by Stats. 1994, Ch. 1246, Sec. 9. Effective January 1, 1995.)
1727.1.
A licensed home health agency may also provide, or arrange for the provision of, other therapeutic services to persons in their temporary or permanent place of residence. Therapeutic services include, but are not limited to, physical, speech, or occupational therapy, medical social services, and home health aide services.
(Added by Stats. 1989, Ch. 856, Sec. 6.)
1727.5.
Each home health agency providing home health agency services shall do all of the following:
(a) Provide for a plan of treatment for patients receiving skilled nursing services.
(b) Maintain clinical records on all patients.
(c) Provide for the supervision of licensed and unlicensed personnel by a registered nurse or physical, speech, or occupational therapist when within the therapist's scope of practice.
(d) Maintain policies regarding the delivery and supervision of patient care that are reviewed annually by a group of professional personnel including a physician and surgeon and a registered nurse and revised as needed.
(e) Meet all applicable federal, state, and local requirements.
(f) Maintain, and revise as needed, and implement policies regarding the purchase, storage, furnishing, and transportation of legend devices that are reviewed annually by a group of professional personnel, including a physician and surgeon, pharmacist, and a registered nurse. As used in this subdivision, "legend devices" means any device that bears the label "Caution: federal law restricts this device to sale by or on the order of a _____" or words of similar meaning.
(g) Meet other standards, rules, and regulations adopted by the state department in order to implement this chapter.
(Amended by Stats. 1992, Ch. 1104, Sec. 4. Effective September 29, 1992.)
1727.7.
(a) The Legislature finds and declares the following:
(1) Thousands of patients receive home health care each year, thus preventing, postponing, and limiting the need for unnecessary institutionalization.
(2) The adoption of emergency home health agency licensing regulations is necessary in order to conform existing home health agency licensing regulations to state law and the current scope and practice of home health care.
(3) The adoption of emergency home health agency regulations is necessary due to the increased provider and consumer demands for home care services and advances in health care technology.
(4) The adoption of emergency home health agency regulations is necessary due to the emerging influences of health care reform and changing expectations of managed care programs and insurance providers.
(b) The director shall adopt revised home health agency licensure regulations. These revised regulations shall be adopted on an emergency basis. Until January 1, 1996, the adoption of any emergency regulations pursuant to Chapter 3.5 (commencing with Section 11340) of Part 1 of Division 3 of Title 2 of the Government Code to implement this section shall be deemed to be an emergency by the Office of Administrative Law as necessary for the immediate preservation of the public peace, health and safety, or general welfare.
(c) It is the intent of the Legislature that the adoption of home health agency licensure regulations pursuant to this chapter shall in no way prohibit interested parties from participating in review of the revised regulations. It is also the intent of the Legislature that the adoption of the revised regulations shall in no way narrow the existing scope of practice of registered nurses or licensed vocational nurses or lessen the quality of nurse supervision or care in the home health care setting.
(Added by Stats. 1994, Ch. 551, Sec. 1. Effective September 12, 1994.)
1728.
Any person, organization, political subdivision of the state or governmental agency desiring a license under the provisions of this chapter or a hospital as defined in Section 1401 of this division which desires to establish, conduct, or maintain a home health agency shall file with the state department a verified application on a form prescribed, prepared and furnished by the state department, containing information as may be

required by the state department for the proper administration and enforcement of this chapter.

(Added by Stats. 1966, 1st Ex. Sess., Ch. 79.)

1728.1.

(a) To qualify for a home health agency license, the following requirements shall be met:

(1) Every applicant shall satisfy the following conditions:

(A) Be of good moral character. If the applicant is a firm, association, organization, partnership, business trust, corporation, or company, all principal managing members thereof, and the person in charge of the agency for which application for license is made, shall satisfy this requirement. If the applicant is a political subdivision of the state or other governmental agency, the person in charge of the agency for which application for license is made, shall satisfy this requirement.

(B) Possess and demonstrate the ability to comply with this chapter and the rules and regulations adopted under this chapter by the state department.

(C) File his or her application pursuant to and in full compliance with this chapter.

(2) (A) The following persons shall submit to the State Department of Public Health an application and shall submit electronic fingerprint images to the Department of Justice for the furnishing of the person's criminal record to the state department, at the person's expense as provided in subdivision (b), for the purpose of a criminal record review:

(i) The owner or owners of a private agency if the owners are individuals.

(ii) If the owner of a private agency is a corporation, partnership, or association, any person having a 10 percent or greater interest in that corporation, partnership, or association.

(iii) The administrator of a home health agency.

(B) When the conditions set forth in paragraph (3) of subdivision (a) of Section 1265.5, subparagraph (A) of paragraph (1) of subdivision (a) of Section 1338.5, and paragraph (1) of subdivision (a) of Section 1736.6 are met, the licensing and certification program shall issue an All Facilities Letter (AFL) informing facility licensees. After the AFL is issued, facilities must not allow newly hired administrators, program directors, and fiscal officers to have direct contact with clients or residents of the facility prior to completion of the criminal record clearance. A criminal record clearance shall be complete when the department has obtained the person's criminal offender record information search response from the Department of Justice and has determined that the person is not disqualified from engaging in the activity for which clearance is required.

(b) The persons specified in paragraph (2) of subdivision (a) shall be responsible for any costs associated with transmitting the electronic fingerprint images. The fee to cover the processing costs of the Department of Justice, not including the costs associated with capturing or transmitting the fingerprint images and related information, shall not exceed thirty-two dollars ($32) per submission.

(c) If the criminal record review conducted pursuant to paragraph (2) of subdivision (a) discloses a conviction for a felony or any crime that evidences an unfitness to provide home health services, the application for a license shall be denied or the person shall be prohibited from providing service in the home health agency applying for a license. This subdivision shall not apply to deny a license or prohibit the provision of service if the person presents evidence satisfactory to the state department that the person has been rehabilitated and presently is of such good character as to justify the issuance of the license or the provision of service in the home health agency.

(d) An applicant and any other person specified in this section, as part of the background clearance process, shall provide information as to whether or not the person has any prior criminal convictions, has had any arrests within the past 12-month period, or has any active arrests, and shall certify that, to the best of his or her knowledge, the information provided is true. This requirement is not intended to duplicate existing requirements for individuals who are required to submit fingerprint images as part of a criminal background clearance process. Every applicant shall provide information on any prior administrative action taken against him or her by any federal, state, or local government agency and shall certify that, to the best of his or her knowledge, the information provided is true. An applicant or other person required to provide information pursuant to this section that knowingly or willfully makes false statements, representations, or omissions may be subject to administrative action, including, but not limited to, denial of his or her application or exemption or revocation of any exemption previously granted.

(Amended by Stats. 2007, Ch. 483, Sec. 18. Effective January 1, 2008.)

1728.2.

(a) If a home health agency or an applicant for a license has not been previously licensed, the state department may only issue a provisional license to the agency as provided in this section.

(b) A provisional license to operate a home health agency shall terminate six months from the date of issuance.

(c) Within 30 days prior to the termination of a provisional license, the state department shall give the agency a full and complete inspection, and, if the agency meets all applicable requirements for licensure, a regular license shall be issued. If the home health agency does not meet the requirements for licensure but has made substantial progress towards meeting the requirements, as determined by the state department, the initial provisional license shall be renewed for six months.

(d) If the state department determines that there has not been substantial progress towards meeting licensure requirements at the time of the first full inspection provided by this section, or, if the state department determines upon its inspection made within 30 days of the termination of a renewed provisional license that there is lack of full compliance with the requirements, no further license shall be issued.

(e) If an applicant for a provisional license to operate a home health agency has been denied provisional licensing by the state department, the applicant may contest the denial by filing a request for a hearing pursuant to Section 100171.

(f) The department shall not apply less stringent criteria when granting a provisional license pursuant to this section than it applies when granting a permanent license.

(Amended by Stats. 1997, Ch. 220, Sec. 22. Effective August 4, 1997.)

1728.3.

Notwithstanding Sections 1728.1 and 1732, the state department may issue a provisional license to a home health agency if:

(a) The agency and the applicant for licensure substantially meet the standards specified by this chapter and regulations adopted pursuant to this chapter.

(b) No violation of this chapter or regulations adopted under this chapter exists in the agency which jeopardizes the health or safety of patients.

(c) The applicant has adopted a plan for correction of any existing violations which is satisfactory to the state department.

A provisional license issued under this section shall expire not later than six months after the date of issuance, or at an earlier time as determined by the state department at the time of issuance, and may not be renewed.

The department shall not apply less stringent criteria when granting a provisional license pursuant to this section than it applies when granting a permanent license.

(Amended by Stats. 1988, Ch. 160, Sec. 100.)

1728.7.

(a) Notwithstanding any other provision of this chapter, the department shall issue a license to a home health agency that applies to the department for a home health agency license and meets all of the following requirements:

(1) Is accredited as a home health agency by an entity approved by the federal Centers for Medicare and Medicaid Services as a national accreditation organization, and the national accreditation organization forwards to the department copies of all initial and subsequent survey and other accreditation reports or findings.

(2) Files an application with fees pursuant to this chapter.

(3) Meets any other additional licensure requirements of, or regulations adopted pursuant to, this chapter that the department identifies, after consulting with the national accreditation organizations, as more stringent than the accreditation requirements of the national accreditation organizations.

(b) The department may conduct a survey of an accredited home health agency to ensure the accreditation requirements are met. These surveys shall be conducted using a selective sample basis.

(c) The department may conduct a survey of an accredited home health agency to investigate complaints against an accredited home health agency for substantial noncompliance, as determined by the department, with these accreditation standards.

(d) Notwithstanding subdivisions (a), (b), and (c), the department shall retain its full range of authority over accredited home health agencies to ensure the licensure and accreditation requirements are met. This authority shall include the entire scope of enforcement sanctions and options available for unaccredited home health agencies.

(Amended by Stats. 2018, Ch. 424, Sec. 2. (SB 1495) Effective January 1, 2019.)

1728.8.

(a) It is the intent of the Legislature to ensure that the department licenses and certifies home health agencies in a reasonable and timely manner to ensure that Californians have access to critical home- and community-based services. Home health agencies have significant startup costs and regulatory requirements, which make home health agencies vulnerable to delays in licensing and certification surveys. Home health agencies help the state protect against the unnecessary institutionalization of individuals and are integral in ensuring the state's compliance with the United States Supreme Court decision in Olmstead v. L.C. (1999) 527 U.S. 581, which requires public agencies to provide services in the most integrated setting appropriate to the needs of qualified individuals with disabilities.

(b) No later than 90 calendar days after the department receives an initial and complete parent, branch, or change of ownership home health agency application, the department shall make every effort to complete the application paperwork and conduct a licensure survey, if necessary, to inspect the agency and evaluate the agency's compliance with state requirements. The department shall forward its recommendation, if necessary, and all other information, to the federal Centers for Medicare and Medicaid Services within the same 90 calendar days.

(c) (1) For those applicants seeking to receive reimbursement under the Medicare or Medi-Cal programs, the department shall make every effort to complete the initial application paperwork and conduct an unannounced certification survey, if necessary, no later than 90 calendar days after the department conducts the licensure survey required by subdivision (a), or no later than 90 days after the department's receipt of a letter from the home health agency notifying the department of its readiness for the certification survey from a parent or branch agency.

(2) No later than 30 calendar days after the certification survey, the department shall forward the results of its licensure and certification surveys and all other information necessary for certification to the federal Centers for Medicare and Medicaid Services.

(d) This section shall apply to all licensing and certification entities, including a county that contracts with the state to provide licensing and certification services on behalf of the state.

(e) If the department is unable to meet the 90-day timelines for licensing or certification required pursuant to this section, the department shall notify the applicant in writing of the delay and the anticipated date of the survey.

(f) This section shall become operative on July 1, 2008.

(Amended by Stats. 2008, Ch. 179, Sec. 144. Effective January 1, 2009.)

1729.

Each application for a license under this chapter, except applications by the State of California or any state department, authority, bureau, commission, or officer, shall be accompanied by a Licensing and Certification Program fee for the headquarters or main office of the agency and for each additional branch office maintained and operated by the agency in the amount set in accordance with Section 1266. The department shall work with the home health agency industry association and providers to restructure home health agency licensing and certification program fees in a budget neutral capacity for the 2008–09 fiscal year.

(Amended by Stats. 2007, Ch. 620, Sec. 2. Effective January 1, 2008.)

1730.

(a) Each license issued under this chapter shall expire 12 months from the date of its issuance. Application for renewal of license accompanied by the necessary fee shall be filed with the state department annually, not less than 30 days prior to expiration date. Failure to make a timely renewal shall result in expiration of the license.

(b) (1) At least 45 days prior to the expiration of a license issued pursuant to this chapter, the department shall mail an application for renewal to the licensee.

(2) Any application for a license renewal shall be submitted with the necessary fee in accordance with subdivision (a). A license shall be deemed renewed upon payment of the necessary fee, commencing from the license's expiration date. If the requirements of this section are met, the department shall issue a license to the agency and its branches by the expiration date of the license to ensure the provider remains in good standing. The agency's license shall be mailed within 30 calendar days after the date the department receives the renewal fee.

(Amended by Stats. 2007, Ch. 620, Sec. 3. Effective January 1, 2008.)

1731.

No person, public or private organization, political subdivision of the state, or other governmental agency within the state, shall continue to operate, conduct, or maintain an existing home health agency after September 30, 1966, without having applied for and obtained a license as provided in this chapter or in the case of a hospital as defined in Section 1401 of this division, having been approved by the state department to establish, conduct, or maintain a home health agency.

(Added by Stats. 1966, 1st Ex. Sess., Ch. 79.)

1732.

Upon filing of the application for a license provided for in, and upon full compliance with, the provisions of this chapter and the rules and regulations promulgated under this chapter by the state department, the state department shall issue to the applicant the license applied for. However, any hospital, as defined in Section 1401 which is licensed under the provisions of Chapter 2.3 (commencing with Section 1400) is not required to obtain a license. In order for a hospital to establish, conduct, or maintain a home health agency, it shall comply with all the provisions of this chapter and be approved by the state department. The approval shall be deemed to be licensure and shall not extend past midnight on the 31st day of December of each calendar year. The fee set forth in Section 1729 shall be paid before approval is granted. Approval may be denied or withdrawn by the state department on the same grounds as provided for denial, suspension, or revocation of a home health agency license. The state department may take the same action against any approved hospital home health agency as it may against any licensed home health agency under this chapter.

(Amended by Stats. 1981, Ch. 714.)

1733.

Every home health agency for which a license has been issued, except a facility that is certified to participate either in the Medicare program under Title XVIII (42 U.S.C. Sec. 1395 et seq.) of the federal Social Security Act, or the medicaid program under Title XIX (42 U.S.C. Sec. 1396 et seq.) of the federal Social Security Act, or both, shall be periodically inspected by a duly authorized representative of the state department no less than once a year. Reports of each such inspection shall be prepared by the representative conducting it upon forms prepared and furnished by the state department and filed with the state department. Such inspection shall be for the purpose of ensuring that the provisions of this chapter and the rules and regulations of the department are being followed. The state department is directed to ensure by such inspection that the home health agency is providing high quality care to its patients in accordance with the orders of the patient's physician.

(Amended by Stats. 1992, Ch. 709, Sec. 14. Effective September 15, 1992.)

1734.

(a) The state department shall adopt, and may thereafter modify, amend, or rescind, reasonable rules and regulations to carry out the purposes of this chapter, including, the prohibition of specific conduct, determined by the state department to be inimical to the public health, morals, welfare or safety of the people of the State of California in the maintenance and operation of the home health agency for which a license is issued. In adopting, modifying, amending or rescinding the rules and regulations, the state department shall consult with, and receive recommendations from among other physicians and surgeons, pharmacists, public health nurses, and persons representing hospitals, nonprofit home health agencies, proprietary home health agencies and counties whose health department or hospital has a home health agency. The state department shall also comply with Chapter 3.5 (commencing with Section 11340) of Part 1 of Division 3 of Title 2 of the Government Code.

(b) The state department shall adopt rules and regulations regarding the purchase, storage, furnishing, and transportation of legend devices for a patient of a home health agency. As used in this subdivision, "legend devices" means any device that bears the label "Caution: federal law restricts this device to sale by or on the order of a _____" or words of similar meaning.

(Amended by Stats. 1992, Ch. 1104, Sec. 5. Effective September 29, 1992.)

1734.5.

The department may grant to entities contracting with the department under the PACE program, as defined in Chapter 8.75 (commencing with Section 14591) of Part 3 of Division 9 of the Welfare and Institutions Code, exemptions from the provisions contained in this chapter in accordance with the requirements of Section 100315.

(Amended by Stats. 2011, Ch. 367, Sec. 5. (AB 574) Effective January 1, 2012.)

1735.

The state department may deny any application for, or suspend or revoke any license issued under the provisions of this chapter upon any of the following grounds and in the manner hereinafter provided:

(a) Violation by the licensee of any of the provisions of this chapter or of any other law of this state or of the rules and regulations promulgated under this chapter.

(b) Aiding, abetting or permitting the commission of any illegal act.

(c) Misrepresentation of a material fact in the application for a license.

(Added by Stats. 1966, 1st Ex. Sess., Ch. 79.)

1736.

Proceedings for the denial, suspension or revocation of licenses or denial or withdrawal of approval under this chapter shall be conducted in accordance with Section 100171. The suspension, expiration, or forfeiture by operation of law of a license issued by the state department; its suspension, forfeiture, or cancellation by order of the state department or by order of a court of law; or its surrender without the written consent of the state department, shall not deprive the state department of its authority to institute or continue a disciplinary proceeding against the licensee upon any ground provided by law or to enter an order suspending or revoking the license or otherwise taking disciplinary action against the licensee on any such ground.

(Amended by Stats. 1997, Ch. 220, Sec. 23. Effective August 4, 1997.)

1736.1.

(a) An applicant for certification as a certified home health aide shall comply with each of the following requirements:

(1) Have successfully completed a training program with a minimum of 75 hours or an equivalent competency evaluation program approved by the department pursuant to applicable federal and state regulations.

(2) Obtain a criminal record clearance pursuant to Section 1736.6.

(b) (1) No later than July 1, 2019, the department shall require the applicant to provide either the individual taxpayer identification number or social security number for purposes of applying for a certificate or the renewal of a certificate.

(2) If the department utilizes a national examination to issue a certificate, and if a reciprocity agreement or comity exists between the State of California and the state requesting release of the individual taxpayer identification number or social security number, any deputy, agent, clerk, officer, or employee of the department may release an individual's taxpayer identification number or social security number to an examination or certifying entity, only for the purpose of verification of certification or examination status.

(3) The individual taxpayer identification or the social security number shall serve to establish the identification of persons affected by state tax laws and for purposes of establishing compliance with subsection (a) of Section 666 of Title 42 of the United States Code, Section 60.15 of Title 45 of the Code of Federal Regulations, Section 17520 of the Family Code, and Section 11105 of the Penal Code, and to that end, the information furnished pursuant to this section shall be used exclusively for those purposes.

(4) The department shall not do either of the following:

(A) Require an applicant to disclose citizenship status or immigration status for purposes of the application or renewal of a certificate.

(B) Deny licensure to an otherwise qualified and eligible applicant based solely on his or her citizenship status or immigration status.

(c) Any person who violates this article is guilty of a misdemeanor and, upon a conviction thereof, shall be punished by imprisonment in the county jail for not more than 180 days, or by a fine of not less than twenty dollars ($20) nor more than one thousand dollars ($1,000), or by both that fine and imprisonment.

(Amended by Stats. 2018, Ch. 838, Sec. 9. (SB 695) Effective January 1, 2019.)

1736.2.

(a) Certificates issued for certified home health aides shall be renewed every two years and renewal shall be conditioned on the certificate holder obtaining a criminal record clearance pursuant to Section 1736.6.

(b) Certificates issued to certified home health aides shall expire on the certificate holder's birthday.

(c) To renew an unexpired certificate, the certificate holder shall, on or before the certificate expiration date, apply for renewal on a form provided by the state.

(d) The department shall give written notice to a certificate holder 90 days in advance of the renewal date and 90 days in advance of the expiration of the fourth year that an application has not been submitted, and shall give written notice informing the certificate holder in general terms of the provisions governing certificate renewal for certified home health aides. Nonreceipt of the renewal notice does not relieve the certificate holder of the obligation to make a timely renewal. Failure to make a timely renewal shall result in expiration of the certificate.

(e) Except as otherwise provided in this article, an expired certificate may be renewed at any time within four years after its expiration on the filing of an application for renewal on a form prescribed by the department.

Renewal under this article shall be effective on the date on which the application is filed. If renewed, the certificate shall continue in effect until the date provided for in this section, when it shall expire if it is not again renewed.
(f) If a certified home health aide applies for renewal more than 30 days after expiration but within four years after the expiration, and demonstrates in writing to the department's satisfaction why the renewal application was late, then the state department shall issue a renewal. A suspended certificate is subject to expiration and shall be renewed as provided in this article, but this renewal does not entitle the certificate holder, while the certificate remains suspended, and until it is reinstated, to engage in the certified activity, or in any other activity or conduct in violation of the order or judgment by which the certificate was suspended.
(g) A revoked certificate is subject to expiration as provided in this section, but it cannot be renewed.
(h) A certificate that is not renewed within four years after its expiration cannot be renewed, restored, reissued, or reinstated except upon completion of a certification training program unless deemed otherwise by the state department if both of the following conditions are met:
(1) No fact, circumstance, or condition exists that, if the certificate were issued, would justify its revocation or suspension.
(2) The person takes and passes any examination that may be required of an applicant for a new certificate at that time, that shall be given by an approved provider of a certification training program.
(i) Certificate holders shall notify the department within 60 days of any change of address. Any notice sent by the department shall be effective if mailed to the current address filed with the department.
(j) Certificate holders that have been certified as both nurse assistants pursuant to Article 9 (commencing with Section 1337) of Chapter 2 of Division 2 and home health aides pursuant to this chapter shall renew their certificates at the same time on one application.
(Amended by Stats. 2006, Ch. 74, Sec. 21. Effective July 12, 2006.)
1736.4.
(a) The state department shall investigate complaints concerning misconduct by certified home health aides and may take disciplinary action pursuant to Section 1736.5.
(b) The department shall maintain a registry that includes the certification status of all certified home health aides, including the status of any proposed or completed disciplinary actions.
(c) Home health agencies, as defined in subdivision (a) of Section 1727, and hospice providers, as defined in subdivision (b) of Section 1745, that hire certified home health aides after July 1, 1997, shall consult the state department's registry prior to hiring these individuals or placing them in direct contact with patients.
(Added by Stats. 1994, Ch. 1246, Sec. 13. Effective January 1, 1995.)
1736.5.
(a) The department shall deny a training application and deny, suspend, or revoke a certificate issued under this article if the applicant or certificate holder has been convicted of a violation or attempted violation of any of the following Penal Code provisions: Section 187, subdivision (a) of Section 192, Section 203, 205, 206, 207, 209, 210, 210.5, 211, 220, 222, 243.4, 245, 261, 262, or 264.1, Sections 265 to 267, inclusive, Section 273a, 273d, 273.5, or 285, subdivisions (c), (d), (f), and (g) of Section 286, Section 288, subdivisions (c), (d), (f), and (g) of Section 287 or former Section 288a, Section 288.5, 289, 289.5, 368, 451, 459, 470, 475, 484, or 484b, Sections 484d to 484j, inclusive, Section 487, subdivision (a) of Section 487a, or Section 488, 496, 503, 518, or 666, unless any of the following applies:
(1) The person was convicted of a felony and has obtained a certificate of rehabilitation under Chapter 3.5 (commencing with Section 4852.01) of Title 6 of Part 3 of the Penal Code and the information or accusation against him or her has been dismissed pursuant to Section 1203.4 of the Penal Code.
(2) The person was convicted of a misdemeanor and the information or accusation against him or her has been dismissed pursuant to Section 1203.4 or 1203.4a of the Penal Code.
(3) The certificate holder was convicted of a felony or a misdemeanor, but has previously disclosed the fact of each conviction to the department, and the department has made a determination in accordance with law that the conviction does not disqualify the applicant from certification.
(b) An application or certificate shall be denied, suspended, or revoked upon conviction in another state of an offense that, if committed or attempted in this state, would have been punishable as one or more of the offenses set forth in subdivision (a), unless evidence of rehabilitation comparable to the certificate of rehabilitation or dismissal of a misdemeanor set forth in paragraph (1) or (2) of subdivision (a) is provided.
(c) (1) The department may deny an application or deny, suspend, or revoke a certificate issued under this article for any of the following:
(A) Unprofessional conduct, including, but not limited to, incompetence, gross negligence, physical, mental, or verbal abuse of patients, or misappropriation of property of patients or others.
(B) Conviction of a crime substantially related to the qualifications, functions, and duties of a home health aide, irrespective of a subsequent order under Section 1203.4, 1203.4a, or 4852.13 of the Penal Code, where the department determines that the applicant or certificate holder has not adequately demonstrated that he or she has been rehabilitated and will present a threat to the health, safety, or welfare of patients.
(C) Conviction for, or use of, any controlled substance as defined in Division 10 (commencing with Section 11000) of this code, or any dangerous drug, as defined in Section 4022 of the Business and Professions Code, or alcoholic beverages, to an extent or in a manner dangerous or injurious to the home health aide, any other person, or the public, to the extent that this use would impair the ability to conduct, with safety to the public, the practice authorized by a certificate.
(D) Procuring a home health aide certificate by fraud, misrepresentation, or mistake.
(E) Making or giving any false statement or information in conjunction with the application for issuance of a home health aide certificate or training and examination application.
(F) Impersonating any applicant, or acting as proxy for an applicant, in any examination required under this article for the issuance of a certificate.
(G) Impersonating another home health aide, a licensed vocational nurse, or a registered nurse, or permitting or allowing another person to use a certificate for the purpose of providing nursing services.
(H) Violating or attempting to violate, directly or indirectly, or assisting in or abetting the violation of, or conspiring to violate any provision or term of, this article.
(2) In determining whether or not to deny an application or deny, suspend, or revoke a certificate issued under this article pursuant to this subdivision, the department shall take into consideration the following factors as evidence of good character and rehabilitation:
(A) The nature and seriousness of the offense under consideration and its relationship to the person's employment duties and responsibilities.
(B) Activities since conviction, including employment or participation in therapy or education, that would indicate changed behavior.
(C) The time that has elapsed since the commission of the conduct or offense referred to in subparagraph (A) or (B) and the number of offenses.
(D) The extent to which the person has complied with any terms of parole, probation, restitution, or any other sanction lawfully imposed against the person.
(E) Any rehabilitation evidence, including character references, submitted by the person.
(F) Employment history and current employer recommendations.
(G) Circumstances surrounding the commission of the offense that would demonstrate the unlikelihood of repetition.
(H) Granting by the Governor of a full and unconditional pardon.
(I) A certificate of rehabilitation from a superior court.
(d) When the department determines that a certificate shall be suspended, the department shall specify the period of actual suspension. The department may determine that the suspension shall be stayed, placing the certificate holder on probation with specified conditions for a period not to exceed two years. When the department determines that probation is the appropriate action, the certificate holder shall be notified that in lieu of the department proceeding with a formal action to suspend the certification and in lieu of an appeal pursuant to subdivision (g), the certificate holder may request to enter into a diversion program agreement. A diversion program agreement shall specify terms and conditions related to matters including, but not limited to, work performance, rehabilitation, training, counseling, progress reports, and treatment programs. If a certificate holder successfully completes a diversion program, no action shall be taken upon the allegations that were the basis for the diversion agreement. Upon failure of the certificate holder to comply with the terms and conditions of an agreement, the department may proceed with a formal action to suspend or revoke the certification.
(e) A plea or verdict of guilty, or a conviction following a plea of nolo contendere, shall be deemed a conviction within the meaning of this article. The department may deny an application or deny, suspend, or revoke a certification based on a conviction as provided in this article when the judgment of conviction is entered or when an order granting probation is made suspending the imposition of sentence.
(f) Upon determination to deny an application or deny, revoke, or suspend a certificate, the department shall notify the applicant or certificate holder in writing by certified mail of both of the following:
(1) The reasons for the determination.
(2) The applicant's or certificate holder's right to appeal the determination if the determination was made under subdivision (c).
(g) (1) Upon written notification that the department has determined that an application shall be denied or a certificate shall be denied, suspended, or revoked under subdivision (c), the applicant or certificate holder may request an administrative hearing by submitting a written request to the department within 20 business days of receipt of the written notification. Upon receipt of a written request, the department shall hold an administrative hearing pursuant to the procedures specified in Section 100171, except where those procedures are inconsistent with this section.
(2) A hearing under this section shall be conducted by a hearing officer or administrative law judge designated by the director at a location, other than the work facility, that is convenient to the applicant or certificate holder. The hearing shall be audio or video recorded and a written decision shall be sent by certified mail to the applicant or certificate holder within 30 calendar days of the hearing. Except as specified in subdivision (h), the effective date of an action to revoke or suspend a certificate shall be specified in the written decision, or if no administrative hearing is timely requested, the effective date shall be 21 business days from written notification of the department's determination to revoke or suspend.
(h) The department may revoke or suspend a certificate prior to any hearing when immediate action is necessary in the judgment of the director to protect the public welfare. Notice of this action, including a statement of the necessity of immediate action to protect the public welfare, shall be sent in accordance with subdivision (f). If the certificate holder requests an administrative hearing pursuant to subdivision (g), the department shall hold the administrative hearing as soon as possible but not later than 30 calendar days from receipt of the request for a hearing. A written hearing decision upholding or setting aside the action shall be sent by certified mail to the certificate holder within 30 calendar days of the hearing.

(i) Upon the expiration of the term of suspension, the certificate holder shall be reinstated by the department and shall be entitled to resume practice unless it is established to the satisfaction of the department that the person has practiced as a home health aide in California during the term of suspension. In this event, the department shall revoke the person's certificate.

(j) Upon a determination to deny an application or deny, revoke, or suspend a certificate, the department shall notify the employer of the applicant or certificate holder in writing of that determination, and whether the determination is final, or whether a hearing is pending relating to this determination. If a licensee or facility is required to deny employment or terminate employment of the employee based upon notice from the state that the employee is determined to be unsuitable for employment under this section, the licensee or facility shall not incur criminal, civil, unemployment insurance, workers' compensation, or administrative liability as a result of that denial or termination.
(Amended by Stats. 2018, Ch. 423, Sec. 34. (SB 1494) Effective January 1, 2019.)
1736.6.

(a) (1) A criminal record clearance shall be conducted by the department for all home health aides by electronically submitting fingerprint images and related information to the Department of Justice. The Licensing and Certification Program shall issue an All Facilities Letter (AFL) to facility licensees when it determines that both of the following criteria have been met for a period of 30 days:

(A) The program receives, within three business days, 95 percent of its total responses indicating no evidence of recorded criminal information from the Department of Justice.

(B) The program processes 95 percent of its total responses requiring disqualification with notices mailed to the individual in accordance with subdivision (a) of Section 1736.5, no later than 45 days after the date that the report is received from the Department of Justice.

(2) After the AFL is issued, facilities must not allow newly hired administrators, program directors, and fiscal officers to have direct contact with clients or residents of the facility prior to completion of the criminal record clearance. A criminal record clearance shall be complete when the department has obtained the person's criminal offender record information search response from the Department of Justice and has determined that the person is not disqualified from engaging in the activity for which clearance is required. Applicants shall be responsible for any costs associated with capturing or transmitting the fingerprint images and related information. The fee to cover the processing costs of the Department of Justice, not including the costs associated with capturing or transmitting the fingerprint images and related information, shall not exceed thirty-two dollars ($32) per submission.

(3) An applicant or certificate holder who may be disqualified on the basis of a criminal conviction shall provide the department with a certified copy of the judgment of each conviction. In addition, the individual may, during a period of two years after the department receives the criminal record report, provide the department with evidence of good character and rehabilitation in accordance with subdivision (a) of Section 1736.5. Upon receipt of a new application for certification of the individual, the department may receive and consider the evidence during the two-year period without requiring additional fingerprint imaging to clear the individual.

(4) The department's Licensing and Certification Program shall explore and implement methods for maximizing its efficiency in processing criminal record clearances within the requirements of law, including a streamlined clearance process for persons that have been disqualified in the basis of criminal convictions that do not require automatic denial pursuant to subdivision (a) of Section 1736.5.

(b) Upon enrollment in a training program for home health aide certification, and prior to direct contact with residents, a candidate for training shall submit a training and examination application to the department and submit electronic fingerprint images and related information to receive a criminal record review through the Department of Justice. This criminal record clearance shall be completed prior to direct contact with residents. Submission of the fingerprint images to the Federal Bureau of Investigation, through the Department of Justice, shall be at the discretion of the state department.

(c) A criminal record clearance, consistent with this section shall be implemented for home health aide applicants beginning July 1, 1998, and phased in for all certified home health aides by June 30, 2000.

(d) The department shall develop procedures to ensure that any licensee, direct care staff, or certificate holder for whom a criminal record has been obtained pursuant to this section or Section 1265.6 or 1338.5 shall not be required to obtain multiple criminal record clearances.

(e) An applicant and any other person specified in this subdivision, as part of the background clearance process, shall provide information as to whether or not the person has any prior criminal convictions, has had any arrests within the past 12-month period, or has any active arrests, and shall certify that, to the best of his or her knowledge, the information provided is true. This requirement is not intended to duplicate existing requirements for individuals who are required to submit fingerprint images as part of a criminal background clearance process. Every applicant shall provide information on any prior administrative action taken against him or her by any federal, state, or local government agency and shall certify that, to the best of his or her knowledge, the information provided is true. An applicant or other person required to provide information pursuant to this section that knowingly or willfully makes false statements, representations, or omissions may be subject to administrative action, including, but not limited to, denial of his or her application or exemption or revocation of any exemption previously granted.

(f) If, at any time, the department determines that it does not meet the standards specified in subparagraphs (A) and (B) of paragraph (1) of subdivision (a) for a period of 90 consecutive days, the requirements in subdivision (a) shall be inoperative until the department determines that that it has met those standards for a period of 90 consecutive days.

(g) During any period of time in which the requirements of subdivision (a) are inoperative, home health agencies may allow newly hired home health aides to have direct contact with patients after those persons have submitted live-scan fingerprint images to the Department of Justice, and the department shall issue an AFL advising facilities of this change in the statutory requirement.

(h) Notwithstanding any other provision of law, the department may provide an individual with a copy of his or her state or federal level criminal offender record information search response as provided to that department by the Department of Justice if the department has denied a criminal background clearance based on this information and the individual makes a written request to the department for a copy specifying an address to which it is to be sent. The state or federal level criminal offender record information search response shall not be modified or altered from its form or content as provided by the Department of Justice and shall be provided to the address specified by the individual in his or her written request. The department shall retain a copy of the individual's written request and the response and date provided.
(Amended by Stats. 2006, Ch. 902, Sec. 15. Effective January 1, 2007.)
1736.7.

(a) The state department may request and maintain employment information for home health aides.

(b) Within five working days of receipt of a criminal record or information from the Department of Justice pursuant to Section 1736.6, the state department shall notify the licensee and applicant of any criminal convictions.

(c) The state department shall conduct a feasibility study to assess the additional technology requirements necessary to include previous and current employment information on its registry and to make that information available to potential employers. The state department shall report to the Legislature by July 1, 2000, as to the results of the study.
(Added by Stats. 1998, Ch. 716, Sec. 2. Effective January 1, 1999.)
1737.

Any license revoked pursuant to this chapter may be reinstated pursuant to the provisions of Section 11522 of the Government Code.
(Added by Stats. 1966, 1st Ex. Sess., Ch. 79.)
1737.5.

Any licensee may, with the approval of the state department, surrender his license for suspension or cancellation by the state department. Any license suspended or canceled pursuant to this section may be reinstated by the state department on receipt of an application showing compliance with the requirements of Section 1728.
(Added by Stats. 1966, 1st Ex. Sess., Ch. 79.)
1738.

The provisions of this chapter do not apply to any home health agency conducted by and for the adherents of any well recognized church or religious denomination for the purpose of providing facilities for the care or treatment of the sick who depend upon prayer or spiritual means for healing in the practice of the religion of such church or denomination.
(Added by Stats. 1966, 1st Ex. Sess., Ch. 79.)
1739.

Any person who violates any of the provisions of this chapter or of the rules and regulations promulgated under this chapter is guilty of a misdemeanor and upon conviction thereof shall be punished by a fine not to exceed one thousand dollars ($1,000) or by imprisonment in the county jail for a period not to exceed 180 days or by both such fine and imprisonment.
(Amended by Stats. 1983, Ch. 1092, Sec. 149. Effective September 27, 1983. Operative January 1, 1984, by Sec. 427 of Ch. 1092.)
1740.

The director may bring an action to enjoin the violation or threatened violation of Section 1726 in the superior court in and for the county in which the violation occurred or is about to occur. Any proceeding under the provisions of this section shall conform to the requirements of Chapter 3 (commencing with Section 525) of Title 7 of Part 2 of the Code of Civil Procedure, except that the director shall not be required to allege facts necessary to show or tending to show lack of adequate remedy at law or to show or tending to show irreparable damage or loss.
(Added by Stats. 1966, 1st Ex. Sess., Ch. 79.)
1741.

Any officer, employee, or agent of the state department may enter and inspect any building, premises, record or file of a licensee at any reasonable time to secure compliance with, or to prevent a violation of, any provision of this chapter.
(Added by Stats. 1966, 1st Ex. Sess., Ch. 79.)
1742.

The district attorney of every county shall, upon application by the state department or its authorized representative, institute and conduct the prosecution of any action for violation within his county or any provisions of this chapter.
(Added by Stats. 1966, 1st Ex. Sess., Ch. 79.)

CHAPTER 8.3. Private Duty Nursing Agencies [1743 - 1743.37]

(Chapter 8.3 added by Stats. 2001, Ch. 242, Sec. 1.)
1743.

(a) The Legislature finds and declares all of the following:

(1) There is currently a crisis in accessing home health care.

(2) Approximately 300 home health agencies have closed in the past two years.

(3) The reduction in the number of home health agencies has made it difficult for many children and adults needing skilled nursing services provided on a shift basis under home- and community-based waivers to receive the services they need, and also jeopardizes the ability of people with disabilities and others from remaining in home- and community-based settings.

(4) Home health agencies have historically been designed as a model of care for elderly Medicare beneficiaries, but this model is not well-suited for the kind of care required by adults and children with disabilities.

(b) It is the intent of the Legislature in enacting this chapter to ensure adequate access to home- and community-based skilled nursing services provided on a shift basis for people who need these services, including people with disabilities.

(c) It is the intent of the Legislature, in adopting a new licensure category for private duty nursing agencies, to provide appropriate nursing care while upholding the same strong consumer protections applicable to home health agencies under Title 22 of the California Code of Regulations.

(Added by Stats. 2001, Ch. 242, Sec. 1. Effective January 1, 2002.)

1743.2.

(a) "Private duty nursing agency" means a private or public organization, including, but not limited to, any partnership, corporation, political subdivision of the state, or other government agency within the state, that provides, or arranges for the provision of, private duty nursing services, as described in Section 1743.3.

(b) "Private duty nursing services" means skilled nursing services provided on a shift basis for patients who require individual and continuous nursing care, and that meets all of the following requirements:

(1) Is provided by a registered nurse or a licensed vocational nurse, except that any person accepted for service whose care requires medical orders shall be under the care of a physician, dentist, podiatrist, or other licensed practitioner within his or her scope of practice.

(2) Is provided to the patient in his or her temporary or permanent place of residence or other community-based setting and includes, one or both of the following locations:

(A) The patient's home.

(B) Outside of the patient's home, as necessitated by normal life activities.

(Added by Stats. 2001, Ch. 242, Sec. 1. Effective January 1, 2002.)

1743.3.

Each private duty nursing agency providing services shall do all of the following:

(a) Provide for a plan of treatment for patients receiving private duty nursing services.

(b) Maintain clinical records on all patients.

(c) Maintain policies regarding the delivery and supervision of patient care that are reviewed annually by a group of professional personnel including a physician and surgeon and a registered nurse and revised as needed.

(d) Meet all applicable federal, state, and local requirements.

(e) Maintain, and revise as needed, and implement policies regarding the purchase, storage, furnishing, and transportation of legend devices that are reviewed annually by a group of professional personnel, including a physician and surgeon, pharmacist, and a registered nurse. As used in this subdivision, "legend devices" means any device that bears the label "Caution: federal law restricts this device to sale by or on the order of a _____" or words of similar meaning.

(f) Meet other standards, rules, and regulations adopted by the department in order to implement this chapter.

(Added by Stats. 2001, Ch. 242, Sec. 1. Effective January 1, 2002.)

1743.7.

Any person, organization, political subdivision of the state or governmental agency desiring a license under this chapter, or any health facility as defined in Section 1250 that desires to establish, conduct, or maintain a private duty nursing agency, shall file with the department a verified application on a form prescribed, prepared, and furnished by the department, containing information as may be required by the department for the proper administration and enforcement of this chapter.

(Added by Stats. 2001, Ch. 242, Sec. 1. Effective January 1, 2002.)

1743.9.

(a) To qualify for a private duty nursing agency license, the following requirements shall be met:

(1) Every applicant shall satisfy the following conditions:

(A) Be of good moral character. If the applicant is a firm, association, organization, partnership, business trust, corporation, or company, all principal managing members thereof, and the person in charge of the agency for which application for a license is made, shall satisfy this requirement. If the applicant is a political subdivision of the state or other governmental agency, the person in charge of the agency for which application for a license is made shall satisfy this requirement.

(B) Possess and demonstrate the ability to comply with this chapter and the rules and regulations adopted under this chapter by the department.

(C) File his or her application pursuant to and in full compliance with this chapter.

(2) (A) The following persons shall submit to the department an application, and shall submit fingerprint images and related information to the Department of Justice, for the furnishing of the person's criminal record to the department, at the person's expense as provided in subdivision (b), for the purpose of a criminal record review:

(i) The owner or owners of a private agency if the owners are individuals.

(ii) If the owner of a private agency is a corporation, partnership, or association, any person having a 10 percent or greater interest in that corporation, partnership, or association.

(iii) The administrator of a private duty nursing agency.

(3) When the conditions set forth in paragraph (3) of subdivision (a) of Section 1265.5, subparagraph (A) of paragraph (1) of subdivision (a) of Section 1338.5, and paragraph (1) of subdivision (a) of Section 1736.6 are met, the licensing and certification program shall issue an All Facilities Letter (AFL) informing facility licensees. After the AFL is issued, facilities shall not allow newly hired administrators, program directors, and fiscal officers to have direct contact with clients or residents of the facility prior to completion of the initial record clearance. A criminal record clearance shall be complete when the department has obtained the person's criminal offender record information search response from the Department of Justice and has determined that the person is not disqualified from engaging in the activity for which the clearance is required.

(b) Notwithstanding any other provision of law, the department may provide an individual with a copy of his or her state or federal level criminal offender record information search response as provided to that department by the Department of Justice if the department has denied a criminal background clearance based on this information and the individual makes a written request to the department for a copy specifying an address to which it is to be sent. The state or federal level criminal offender record information search response shall not be modified or altered from its form or content as provided by the Department of Justice and shall be provided to the address specified by the individual in his or her written request. The department shall retain a copy of the individual's written request and the response and date provided.

(4) An applicant and any other person specified in this subdivision, as part of the background clearance process, shall provide information as to whether or not the person has any prior criminal convictions, has had any arrests within the past 12-month period, or has any active arrests, and shall certify that, to the best of his or her knowledge, the information provided is true. This requirement is not intended to duplicate existing requirements for individuals who are required to submit fingerprint images as part of a criminal background clearance process. Every applicant shall provide information on any prior administrative action taken against him or her by any federal, state, or local government agency and shall certify that, to the best of his or her knowledge, the information provided is true. An applicant or other person required to provide information pursuant to this section that knowingly or willfully makes false statements, representations, or omissions may be subject to administrative action, including, but not limited to, denial of his or her application or exemption or revocation of any exemption previously granted.

(c) The persons specified in paragraph (2) of subdivision (a) shall be responsible for any costs associated with capturing or transmitting the fingerprint images and related information. The fee to cover the processing costs of the Department of Justice, not including the costs associated with capturing or transmitting the electronic fingerprint images and related information, shall not exceed thirty-two dollars ($32) per submission.

(d) If the criminal record review conducted pursuant to paragraph (2) of subdivision (a) discloses a conviction for a felony or any crime that evidences an unfitness to provide private duty nursing services, the application for a license shall be denied, or the person shall be prohibited from providing service in the private duty nursing agency applying for a license. This subdivision shall not apply to deny a license or prohibit the provision of service if the person presents evidence satisfactory to the department that the person has been rehabilitated and presently is of that good character that justifies the issuance of the license or the provision of service in the private duty nursing agency.

(Amended by Stats. 2006, Ch. 902, Sec. 16. Effective January 1, 2007.)

1743.11.

(a) If a private duty nursing agency or an applicant for a license has not been previously licensed, the department may only issue a provisional license to the agency as provided in this section.

(b) A provisional license to operate a private duty nursing agency shall terminate six months from the date of issuance.

(c) Within 30 days prior to the termination of a provisional license, the department shall give the agency a full and complete inspection, and, if the agency meets all applicable requirements for licensure, a regular license shall be issued. If the private duty nursing agency does not meet the requirements for licensure, but has made substantial progress towards meeting the requirements, as determined by the department, the initial provisional license shall be renewed for six months.

(d) If the department determines that there has not been substantial progress towards meeting licensure requirements at the time of the first full inspection provided by this section, or, if the department determines upon its inspection made within 30 days of the termination of a renewed provisional license that there is lack of full compliance with the requirements, no further license shall be issued.

(e) If an applicant for a provisional license to operate a private duty nursing agency has been denied provisional licensing by the state department, the applicant may contest the denial by filing a request for a hearing pursuant to Section 100171.

(f) The department shall not apply less stringent criteria when granting a provisional license pursuant to this section than it applies when granting a permanent license.

(Added by Stats. 2001, Ch. 242, Sec. 1. Effective January 1, 2002.)

1743.13.

(a) Notwithstanding Sections 1743.9 and 1743.15, if a private duty nursing agency or an applicant for a license has been previously licensed as a home health agency, the department may issue a provisional license to the private duty nursing agency if all of the following conditions are satisfied:

(1) The agency and the applicant for licensure substantially meet the standards specified by this chapter and regulations adopted pursuant to this chapter.

(2) No violation of this chapter or regulations adopted under this chapter exists in the agency that jeopardizes the health or safety of patients.

(3) The applicant has adopted a plan for correction of any existing violations that is satisfactory to the department.

(b) A provisional license issued under this section shall expire not later than six months after the date of issuance, or at an earlier time as determined by the department at the time of issuance, and may not be renewed.

(c) The department shall not apply less stringent criteria when granting a provisional license pursuant to this section than it applies when granting a permanent license.

(Added by Stats. 2001, Ch. 242, Sec. 1. Effective January 1, 2002.)

1743.15.

(a) Upon filing an application for a private duty nursing agency license as provided for in, and upon the full compliance with, the provisions of this chapter and the rules and regulations promulgated under this chapter by the department, the department shall issue a private duty nursing agency license to the applicant.

(b) Notwithstanding subdivision (a), any health facility, as defined in Section 1250 that is licensed under Chapter 2 (commencing with Section 1250) is not required to obtain a license. In order for a health facility to establish, conduct, or maintain a private duty nursing agency, it shall comply with all the provisions of this chapter and be approved by the department. The approval shall be deemed to be licensure and shall not extend past midnight on the 31st day of December of each calendar year. The fee set forth in Section 1743.17 shall be paid before approval is granted. Approval may be denied or withdrawn by the department on the same grounds as provided for denial, suspension, or revocation of a private duty nursing agency license. The department may take the same action against an approved health facility private duty nursing agency as it may against any licensed private duty nursing agency under this chapter.

(c) As an alternative to subdivision (a), the department may issue a license to a private duty nursing agency that meets the requirements for a home health agency as provided in subdivision (a) of Section 1728.7, including accreditation, except the application and fees shall be submitted pursuant to this chapter. If the department issues a license pursuant to this subdivision, subdivisions (b), (c), and (d) of Section 1728.7 as they apply to home health agencies shall apply to private duty nursing agencies.

(d) A currently licensed home health agency may apply for conversion of that license to a private duty nursing license by filing a written request with the department. If the home health agency holds a valid license and is in good standing, the department shall issue a private duty nursing agency license to that applicant within 30 days of receiving the application.

(Added by Stats. 2001, Ch. 242, Sec. 1. Effective January 1, 2002.)

1743.17.

Each application for a private duty nursing agency license under this chapter, except applications by this state or any state department, authority, bureau, commission, or officer, shall be accompanied by a Licensing and Certification Program fee for the headquarters or main office of the agency and for each additional branch office maintained and operated by the agency in the amount set in accordance with Section 1266.

(Amended by Stats. 2006, Ch. 74, Sec. 23. Effective July 12, 2006.)

1743.19.

Each private duty nursing agency license issued under this chapter shall expire 12 months from the date of its issuance. Application for renewal of license accompanied by the necessary fee shall be filed with the department annually, not less than 30 days prior to expiration date. Failure to make a timely renewal shall result in expiration of the license.

(Amended by Stats. 2006, Ch. 74, Sec. 24. Effective July 12, 2006.)

1743.21.

(a) Every private duty nursing agency for which a license has been issued, except a facility that is certified to participate either in the Medicare program under Title XVIII (42 U.S.C. Sec. 1395 et seq.) of the federal Social Security Act, or the medicaid program under Title XIX (42 U.S.C. Sec. 1396 et seq.) of the federal Social Security Act, or both, shall be periodically inspected by a duly authorized representative of the department. Reports of each inspection shall be prepared by the representative conducting it upon forms prepared and furnished by the department and filed with the department. These inspections shall be for the purpose of ensuring that the provisions of this chapter and the rules and regulations of the department are being followed. The department is directed to ensure by these inspections that the private duty nursing agency is providing high quality care to its patients in accordance with the orders of the patient's physician.

(b) Nothing in this chapter shall be deemed to require a private duty nursing agency to comply with federal Medicare conditions of participation, if the agency is not serving medicare beneficiaries.

(Added by Stats. 2001, Ch. 242, Sec. 1. Effective January 1, 2002.)

1743.23.

(a) The department shall apply its current regulations governing home health agencies to home health agencies and to private duty nursing agencies and may thereafter modify, amend, or rescind, reasonable rules and regulations to carry out the purposes of this chapter, including, the prohibition of specific conduct, determined by the department to be inimical to the public health, morals, welfare, or safety of the people of the State of California in the maintenance and operation of a private duty nursing services agency for which a license is issued. In adopting, modifying, amending, or rescinding the rules and regulations, the department shall consult with, and receive recommendations from,

among others, physicians and surgeons, pharmacists, public health nurses, and persons representing hospitals, nonprofit home health and private duty nursing agencies, proprietary home health and private duty nursing agencies, and counties whose health department or hospital has a home health or private duty nursing agency. The department shall also comply with Chapter 3.5 (commencing with Section 11340) of Part 1 of Division 3 of Title 2 of the Government Code.

(b) The department shall apply current rules and regulations governing home health agencies regarding the purchase, storage, furnishing, and transportation of legend devices for a patient of a private duty nursing agency. As used in this subdivision, "legend devices" means any device that bears the label "Caution: federal law restricts this device to sale by or on the order of a _____" or words of similar meaning.

(c) It is the intent of the Legislature that the department apply current regulations governing home health agencies to private duty nursing facilities that are similar to those that govern home health agencies including, but not limited to, those regulations related to services and the scope and duration of benefits, except to the extent the regulations would be inconsistent with the authority provided under, and the restrictions prescribed by, this chapter.

(Added by Stats. 2001, Ch. 242, Sec. 1. Effective January 1, 2002.)

1743.25.

(a) The department may deny any application for, or suspend or revoke, any private duty nursing license issued under this chapter upon any of the following grounds and in the manner provided in this chapter:

(1) Violation by the licensee of any of the provisions of this chapter or of any other law of this state or of the rules and regulations promulgated under this chapter.

(2) Aiding, abetting, or permitting the commission of any illegal act.

(3) Misrepresentation of a material fact in the application for a license.

(b) (1) Proceedings for the denial, suspension, or revocation of licenses or the denial or withdrawal of approval under this chapter shall be conducted in accordance with Section 100171.

(2) The suspension, expiration, or forfeiture by operation of law of a license issued by the department; its suspension, forfeiture, or cancellation by order of the department or by order of a court of law; or its surrender without the written consent of the department, shall not deprive the department of its authority to institute or continue a disciplinary proceeding against the licensee upon any ground provided by law or to enter an order suspending or revoking the license or otherwise taking disciplinary action against the licensee on any ground provided by law.

(Added by Stats. 2001, Ch. 242, Sec. 1. Effective January 1, 2002.)

1743.27.

(a) Any license revoked pursuant to this chapter may be reinstated pursuant to Section 11522 of the Government Code.

(b) Any licensee may, with the approval of the department, surrender his or her license for suspension or cancellation by the department. Any license suspended or canceled pursuant to this section may be reinstated by the department on receipt of an application showing compliance with the requirements of Section 1743.7.

(Added by Stats. 2001, Ch. 242, Sec. 1. Effective January 1, 2002.)

1743.29.

The provisions of this chapter do not apply to the adherents of any well recognized church or religious denomination that provides for the care or treatment of the sick who depend upon prayer or spiritual means for healing in the practice of the religion of the church or denomination.

(Added by Stats. 2001, Ch. 242, Sec. 1. Effective January 1, 2002.)

1743.31.

Any person who violates any of the provisions of this chapter, or of the rules and regulations promulgated under this chapter, is guilty of a misdemeanor and upon conviction thereof shall be punished by a fine not to exceed one thousand dollars ($1,000), by imprisonment in a county jail for a period not to exceed 180 days, or by both the fine and imprisonment.

(Added by Stats. 2001, Ch. 242, Sec. 1. Effective January 1, 2002.)

1743.33.

The director may bring an action to enjoin the violation or threatened violation of Section 1743 in the superior court in and for the county in which the violation occurred or is about to occur. Any proceeding under this section shall conform to the requirements of Chapter 3 (commencing with Section 525) of Title 7 of Part 2 of the Code of Civil Procedure, except that the director shall not be required to allege facts necessary to show or tending to show lack of adequate remedy at law or to show or tending to show irreparable damage or loss.

(Added by Stats. 2001, Ch. 242, Sec. 1. Effective January 1, 2002.)

1743.35.

Any officer, employee, or agent of the department may enter and inspect any building, premises, record, or file of a private duty nursing agency licensee at any reasonable time to secure compliance with, or to prevent a violation of, any provision of this chapter.

(Added by Stats. 2001, Ch. 242, Sec. 1. Effective January 1, 2002.)

1743.37.

The district attorney of every county shall, upon application by the department or its authorized representative, institute and conduct the prosecution of any action for violation within the district attorney's county or any provisions of this chapter.

(Added by Stats. 2001, Ch. 242, Sec. 1. Effective January 1, 2002.)

CHAPTER 8.5. California Hospice Licensure Act of 1990 [1745 - 1759]

(Chapter 8.5 added by Stats. 1990, Ch. 1343, Sec. 1.)

ARTICLE 1. General [1745 - 1746]

(Article 1 added by Stats. 1990, Ch. 1343, Sec. 1.)

1745.

(a) The purposes of this chapter are to provide for the licensure of hospices by the state department in order to ensure the health and safety of patients, who by definition, are experiencing the last phases of life due to the existence of a terminal disease, and to permit qualified persons, political subdivisions of the state, and governmental agencies to comply with requirements of federal law regarding the provision of hospice care.

(b) In enacting this chapter, it is the intent of the Legislature to allow all qualified persons, political subdivisions of the state, and governmental agencies to provide hospice services to the people of California. It is also the intent of the Legislature to distinguish between the functions of a volunteer hospice and a hospice requiring licensure. It is further the intent of the Legislature to require the state department to establish standards of quality care for licensed hospices.

(c) It is the intent of the Legislature that regulations adopted by the state department pursuant to this chapter not be so burdensome or costly, or both, in terms of implementation, that hospices located in rural areas are forced to stop providing care. Therefore, the state department shall exercise discretion and program flexibility in regard to licensing hospices which are located in rural areas of the state.

(Added by Stats. 1990, Ch. 1343, Sec. 1.)

1746.

For the purposes of this chapter, the following definitions apply:

(a) "Bereavement services" means those services available to the surviving family members for a period of at least one year after the death of the patient, including an assessment of the needs of the bereaved family and the development of a care plan that meets these needs, both prior to and following the death of the patient.

(b) "Home health aide" has the same meaning as that term is defined in subdivision (c) of Section 1727.

(c) "Home health aide services" means those services described in subdivision (d) of Section 1727 that provide for the personal care of the terminally ill patient and the performance of related tasks in the patient's home in accordance with the plan of care in order to increase the level of comfort and to maintain personal hygiene and a safe, healthy environment for the patient.

(d) "Hospice" means a specialized form of interdisciplinary health care that is designed to provide palliative care, alleviate the physical, emotional, social, and spiritual discomforts of an individual who is experiencing the last phases of life due to the existence of a terminal disease, and provide supportive care to the primary caregiver and the family of the hospice patient, and that meets all of the following criteria:

(1) Considers the patient and the patient's family, in addition to the patient, as the unit of care.

(2) Utilizes an interdisciplinary team to assess the physical, medical, psychological, social, and spiritual needs of the patient and the patient's family.

(3) Requires the interdisciplinary team to develop an overall plan of care and to provide coordinated care that emphasizes supportive services, including, but not limited to, home care, pain control, and limited inpatient services. Limited inpatient services are intended to ensure both continuity of care and appropriateness of services for those patients who cannot be managed at home because of acute complications or the temporary absence of a capable primary caregiver.

(4) Provides for the palliative medical treatment of pain and other symptoms associated with a terminal disease, but does not provide for efforts to cure the disease.

(5) Provides for bereavement services following death to assist the family in coping with social and emotional needs associated with the death of the patient.

(6) Actively utilizes volunteers in the delivery of hospice services.

(7) To the extent appropriate, based on the medical needs of the patient, provides services in the patient's home or primary place of residence.

(e) "Hospice facility" means a health facility as defined in subdivision (n) of Section 1250.

(f) "Inpatient care arrangements" means arranging for those short inpatient stays that may become necessary to manage acute symptoms or because of the temporary absence, or need for respite, of a capable primary caregiver. The hospice shall arrange for these stays, ensuring both continuity of care and the appropriateness of services.

(g) "An interdisciplinary team" means the hospice care team that includes, but is not limited to, the patient and patient's family, a physician and surgeon, a registered nurse, a social worker, a volunteer, and a spiritual caregiver. The team shall be coordinated by a registered nurse and shall be under medical direction. The team shall meet regularly to develop and maintain an appropriate plan of care.

(h) "Medical direction" means those services provided by a licensed physician and surgeon who is charged with the responsibility of acting as a consultant to the interdisciplinary team, a consultant to the patient's attending physician and surgeon, as requested, with regard to pain and symptom management, and a liaison with physician and surgeons in the community.

(i) "Multiple location" means a location or site from which a hospice makes available basic hospice services within the service area of the parent agency. A multiple location shares administration, supervision, policies and procedures, and services with the parent agency in a manner that renders it unnecessary for the site to independently meet the licensing requirements.

(j) "Palliative care" means patient and family-centered care that optimizes quality of life of a patient with a terminal illness by anticipating, preventing, and treating suffering. Palliative care throughout the continuum of illness involves addressing physical, intellectual, emotional, social, and spiritual needs and to facilitate patient autonomy, access to information, and choice.

(k) "Parent agency" means the part of the hospice that is licensed pursuant to this chapter and that develops and maintains administrative control of multiple locations. All services provided from each multiple location and parent agency are the responsibility of the parent agency.

(l) "Plan of care" means a written plan developed by the attending physician and surgeon, the medical director or physician and surgeon designee, and the interdisciplinary team that addresses the needs of a patient and family admitted to the hospice organization. The hospice shall retain overall responsibility for the development and maintenance of the plan of care and quality of services delivered.

(m) "Preliminary services" means those services authorized pursuant to subdivision (d) of Section 1749.

(n) "Skilled nursing services" means nursing services provided by or under the supervision of a registered nurse under a plan of care developed by the interdisciplinary team and the patient's physician and surgeon to a patient and his or her family that pertain to the palliative, supportive services required by patients with a terminal illness. Skilled nursing services include, but are not limited to, patient assessment, evaluation and case management of the medical nursing needs of the patient, the performance of prescribed medical treatment for pain and symptom control, the provision of emotional support to both the patient and his or her family, and the instruction of caregivers in providing personal care to the patient. Skilled nursing services shall provide for the continuity of services for the patient and his or her family. Skilled nursing services shall be available on a 24-hour on-call basis.

(o) "Social services/counseling services" means those counseling and spiritual care services that assist the patient and his or her family to minimize stresses and problems that arise from social, economic, psychological, or spiritual needs by utilizing appropriate community resources, and maximize positive aspects and opportunities for growth.

(p) "Terminal disease" or "terminal illness" means a medical condition resulting in a prognosis of life of one year or less, if the disease follows its natural course.

(q) "Volunteer services" means those services provided by trained hospice volunteers who have agreed to provide service under the direction of a hospice staff member who has been designated by the hospice to provide direction to hospice volunteers. Hospice volunteers may be used to provide support and companionship to the patient and his or her family during the remaining days of the patient's life and to the surviving family following the patient's death.

(Amended by Stats. 2012, Ch. 673, Sec. 9. (SB 135) Effective January 1, 2013.)

ARTICLE 2. Licensure [1747 - 1751.5]

(Article 2 added by Stats. 1990, Ch. 1343, Sec. 1.)

1747.

(a) No person, political subdivision of the state, or other governmental agency, that is not operating a hospice as of January 1, 1991, shall establish or operate a hospice without first obtaining a license under this chapter.

(b) Any person, political subdivision of the state, or other governmental agency, that is operating a hospice as of January 1, 1991, may continue to operate the hospice only under the following conditions:

(1) The person, political subdivision of the state, or other governmental agency shall apply to the state department for a license under this chapter within 60 days after forms for the application of licensure under this chapter are available from the state department.

(2) The person, political subdivision of the state, or other governmental agency shall cease calling or referring to itself as a hospice upon the final decision of the director upholding the state department's denial of an application for licensure under this chapter.

(c) Nothing in this chapter shall preclude the ongoing use of the title "volunteer hospice" by those organizations that satisfy all of the following:

(1) They do not provide skilled nursing services.

(2) They do not charge patients or families for hospice services, and they do not receive third-party insurance payments for services rendered.

(3) They satisfy the disclosure requirements specified in subdivision (c) of Section 1748.

(d) A small and rural hospice is exempt from the licensing provisions of this chapter and the disclosure requirements of subdivision (c) of Section 1748. A small and rural hospice may provide skilled nursing services and may use the title "volunteer hospice." For purposes of this chapter, a "small and rural hospice" means a hospice that provides services to less than 50 patients per year, does not charge for services, does not receive third-party payment for services rendered, and is not located in a standard metropolitan statistical area.

(Amended by Stats. 1997, Ch. 492, Sec. 2. Effective January 1, 1998.)

1747.1.

A hospice program certified in accordance with federal Medicare hospice conditions of participation shall be exempt from subdivision (a) of Section 1747, but shall be subject to Section 1726 unless it elects to apply for hospice licensure. A hospice program that elects to apply for hospice licensure shall thereafter be subject to all the hospice licensure requirements set forth in this chapter.

(Added by Stats. 1994, Ch. 985, Sec. 1.5. Effective January 1, 1995.)

1747.3.

(a) Notwithstanding any other law, beginning January 1, 2018, a licensee pursuant to this chapter may provide any interdisciplinary hospice services described in this chapter, including, but not limited to, palliative care, to a patient with a serious illness as determined by the physician and surgeon in charge of the care of the patient, including, among other kinds of patients, a patient who continues to receive curative treatment from other licensed health care professionals.

(b) A licensee that elects to provide palliative care pursuant to this section shall provide the department with the date the licensee intends to begin providing the palliative care no less than 45 days before that date and all of the following:

(1) The completed relevant portions of a form HS 200, or a successor form, as determined by the department.

(2) A complete federal form CMS 417, or a successor form, as determined by the department.

(c) (1) The department shall not require the documents submitted pursuant to subdivision (b) to be approved prior to the licensee providing palliative care pursuant to this section.

(2) The department shall not charge an application fee to provide any care or services pursuant to this section.

(d) On or before January 1, 2019, January 1, 2020, and January 1, 2021, a licensee shall provide the department with all of the following information for the period of time the licensee provided palliative care pursuant to this section on a form prescribed by the department:

(1) The number of non-hospice patients who received palliative care pursuant to this section.

(2) The number of patients enrolled in hospice.

(3) The primary diagnoses of the patients for which the licensee provided palliative care pursuant to this section.

(4) The numbers and types of providers hired during the previous 12 months.

(5) The numbers and types of providers who left employment during the previous 12 months.

(6) Complaints received by the licensee during the previous 12 months that related to all the following:

(A) Events that caused or were likely to cause serious injury, harm, impairment, or death.

(B) Events or incidents that negatively impacted a patient's mental, physical, or psychosocial status and were of such consequence to the patient's well-being that a rapid response was required.

(C) Delays in patient care for hospice and non-hospice patients who received palliative care pursuant to this section.

(D) Qualifications of staff.

(e) During the period of time a licensee provides palliative care pursuant to this section, the licensee shall simultaneously submit to the department all information the licensee provides to the Office of Statewide Health Planning and Development.

(f) Notwithstanding the rulemaking provisions of the Administrative Procedure Act (Chapter 3.5 (commencing with Section 11340) of Part 1 of Division 3 of Title 2 of the Government Code), the department may implement, interpret, or make specific the provisions of this section by means of all-facility letters, or similar instructions, without taking regulatory action.

(g) If the licensee ceases to provide palliative care services pursuant to this section on or before January 1, 2022, the licensee shall submit to the department the same documents as required in subdivision (b).

(h) The provisions of this section shall not be applicable to a hospice facility established pursuant to subdivision (n) of Section 1250, or Section 1339.30 or 1339.40.

(i) This section shall not be deemed to modify the provision of hospice care required pursuant to Section 1368.2.

(j) On or before June 1, 2021, the department shall convene a stakeholder meeting to discuss the results of the information collected pursuant to this section. The department may, at its discretion, use electronic means, such as a webinar, to convene the stakeholder meeting.

(k) For purposes of this section, "serious illness" shall mean a condition that may result in death, regardless of the estimated length of the patient's remaining period of life.

(l) This section shall remain in effect only until January 1, 2022, and as of that date is repealed.

(Added by Stats. 2017, Ch. 515, Sec. 1. (SB 294) Effective January 1, 2018. Repealed as of January 1, 2022, by its own provisions.)

1747.5.

Each hospice licensed pursuant to this chapter shall maintain, and revise as needed, and implement policies regarding the purchase, storage, furnishing, and transportation of legend devices that are reviewed annually by a group of professional personnel, including a physician and surgeon, a pharmacist, and a registered nurse, and are revised as needed. As used in this section, legend devices means any device that bears the label "Caution: federal law restricts this device to sale by or on the order of a _____," or words of similar meaning.

(Added by Stats. 1992, Ch. 1104, Sec. 6. Effective September 29, 1992.)

1748.

(a) Except as otherwise provided in subdivision (b) or (d) of Section 1747, no person, political subdivision of the state, or other governmental agency shall establish, conduct, maintain, or represent itself as a hospice unless a license has been issued under this chapter. Multiple locations need not obtain a separate license. Multiple locations shall be listed on the license of the parent agency and each shall pay a licensing fee in the amount prescribed by subdivision (a) of Section 1750.

(b) Any person, political subdivision of the state, or other governmental agency desiring a license to establish a hospice shall file with the state department a verified application on a form prescribed and furnished by the state department which contains any information as may be required by the state department for the proper administration and enforcement of this chapter.

(c) Any hospice that is not required to obtain a license under this chapter shall disclose in all advertisements and information provided to the public all of the following information:

(1) It is not required to be licensed and is not regulated by the state department.

(2) Any complaint against the hospice should be directed to the local district attorney and the state department.

(3) Any complaint against personnel licensed by a board or committee within the Department of Consumer Affairs and employed by the hospice should be directed to the respective board or committee. Any complaint against a certified home health aide or certified nurse assistant shall be directed to the state department.

The address and phone number of any state agency, board, or committee which is responsible for addressing complaints shall be provided by the hospice, upon request, to any patient of the hospice.

(Amended by Stats. 1997, Ch. 492, Sec. 3. Effective January 1, 1998.)

1749.

(a) To qualify for a license under this chapter, an applicant shall satisfy all of the following:

(1) Be of good moral character. If the applicant is a franchise, franchisee, firm, association, organization, partnership, business trust, corporation, company, political subdivision of the state, or governmental agency, the person in charge of the hospice for which the application for a license is made shall be of good moral character.

(2) Demonstrate the ability of the applicant to comply with this chapter and any rules and regulations promulgated under this chapter by the state department.

(3) File a completed application with the state department that was prescribed and furnished pursuant to Section 1748.

(b) In order for a person, political subdivision of the state, or other governmental agency to be licensed as a hospice it shall satisfy the definition of a hospice contained in Section 1746, and also provide, or make provision for, the following basic services:

(1) Skilled nursing services.

(2) Social services/counseling services.

(3) Medical direction.

(4) Bereavement services.

(5) Volunteer services.

(6) Inpatient care arrangements.

(7) Home health aide services.

(c) The services required to be provided pursuant to subdivision (b) shall be provided in compliance with the "Standards for Quality Hospice Care, 2003," as available from the California Hospice and Palliative Care Association, until the state department adopts regulations establishing alternative standards pursuant to subdivision (e).

(d) (1) Notwithstanding any provision of law to the contrary, to meet the unique needs of the community, licensed hospices may provide, in addition to hospice services authorized in this chapter, any of the following preliminary services for any person in need of those services, as determined by the physician and surgeon, if any, in charge of the care of a patient, or at the request of the patient or family:

(A) Preliminary palliative care consultations.

(B) Preliminary counseling and care planning.

(C) Preliminary grief and bereavement services.

(2) Preliminary services authorized pursuant to this subdivision may be provided concurrently with curative treatment to a person who does not have a terminal prognosis or who has not elected to receive hospice services only by licensed and certified hospices. These services shall be subject to the schedule of benefits under the Medi-Cal program, pursuant to subdivision (w) of Section 14132 of the Welfare and Institutions Code.

(e) The state department may adopt regulations establishing standards for any or all of the services required to be provided under subdivision (b). The regulations of the state department adopted pursuant to this subdivision shall supersede the standards referenced in subdivision (c) to the extent the regulations duplicate or replace those standards.

(Amended by Stats. 2004, Ch. 825, Sec. 3. Effective January 1, 2005.)

1749.5.

The Legislature recognizes that hospices can apply for certification for their hospice programs from the federal Medicare program. If the department has determined during any combined licensing and certification survey that a hospice is in substantial compliance with a requirement, the department shall not be redundant by also reviewing the similar licensing or certification requirements.

(Added by Stats. 1990, Ch. 1343, Sec. 1.)

1750.

(a) Each new and renewal application for a license under this chapter shall be accompanied by an annual Licensing and Certification Program fee set in accordance with Section 1266.

(b) All hospices shall maintain compliance with the licensing requirements. These requirements shall not, however, prohibit the use of alternate concepts, methods, procedures, techniques, space, equipment, personnel qualifications, or the conducting of pilot projects, necessary for program flexibility. Program flexibility shall be carried out with provision for safe and adequate patient care and with prior written approval of the state department. A written request for program flexibility and substantiating evidence supporting the request shall be submitted by the applicant or licensee to the state department. The state department shall approve or deny the request within 60 days of submission. Approval shall be in writing and shall provide for the terms and conditions under which program flexibility is approved. A denial shall be in writing and shall specify the basis therefor. If after investigation the state department determines that a hospice using program flexibility pursuant to this section is operating in a manner contrary to the terms or conditions of the approval for program flexibility, the director shall immediately revoke that approval.

(c) Each hospice shall, on or before March 15 of each year, file with the Office of Statewide Health Planning and Development (OSHPD), upon forms furnished by OSHPD, a verified report for the preceding calendar year upon all matters requested by OSHPD. This report may include, but not be limited to, data pertaining to age of patients, diagnostic categories of patients, and number of visits by service provided.
(Amended by Stats. 2006, Ch. 74, Sec. 25. Effective July 12, 2006.)

1751.

(a) Upon an applicant's filing an application for licensure under this chapter and compliance with this chapter and the rules and regulations adopted by the state department under this chapter, the state department shall issue to the applicant a license to operate as a hospice. Any fees required pursuant to Section 1750 shall be paid before a license is issued. Licensure also may be denied by the state department as specified in Section 1755.

(b) Each license issued under this chapter shall expire 24 months from the date of its issuance.

(c) A biennial application for the renewal of a license, accompanied by any fee required pursuant to subdivision (b) of Section 1750, shall be filed with the state department no less than 30 days prior to the expiration date of the license. The failure to file an application for renewal within the time required by this subdivision shall result in the expiration of the license.
(Added by Stats. 1990, Ch. 1343, Sec. 1.)

1751.5.

(a) Notwithstanding any other provision of this chapter, the department shall issue a license to a hospice that applies to the department for a hospice license and meets all of the following requirements:

(1) Is accredited as a hospice by an entity approved by the federal Centers for Medicare and Medicaid Services as a national accreditation organization, and the national accreditation organization forwards to the department copies of all initial and subsequent survey and other accreditation reports or findings.

(2) Files an application with fees pursuant to this chapter.

(3) Meets any other additional licensure requirements of, or regulations adopted if necessary pursuant to, this chapter that the department identifies, after consulting with the national accreditation organization, as more stringent than the accreditation requirements of the national accreditation organization.

(b) The department may conduct a survey of an accredited hospice to ensure the accreditation requirements are met. These surveys shall be conducted using a selective sample basis.

(c) The department may conduct a survey of an accredited hospice to investigate complaints against an accredited hospice for substantial noncompliance, as determined by the department, with these accreditation standards.

(d) Notwithstanding subdivisions (a), (b), and (c), the department shall retain its full range of authority over accredited hospices to ensure the licensure and accreditation requirements are met. This authority shall include the entire scope of enforcement sanctions and options available for unaccredited hospices.
(Added by Stats. 2018, Ch. 424, Sec. 3. (SB 1495) Effective January 1, 2019.)

ARTICLE 3. Enforcement [1752 - 1759]
(Article 3 added by Stats. 1990, Ch. 1343, Sec. 1.)

1752.

(a) A licensed hospice, at the state department's option, may periodically be inspected by a duly authorized representative of the state department. Reports of each inspection shall be prepared by the representative who conducted the inspection, upon forms prepared and furnished by the state department, and filed with the state department. The inspection shall be for the purpose of ensuring that this chapter and the rules and regulations adopted under this chapter are being followed.

(b) Any officer, employee, or agent of the state department, who has been assigned the responsibility of enforcing this chapter, may enter and inspect any building or premises where hospice care is being provided, as well as any form, record, or file of a licensee at any reasonable time to assure compliance with, or to prevent the violation of, any provision of this chapter.
(Added by Stats. 1990, Ch. 1343, Sec. 1.)

1753.

(a) The state department shall adopt, amend, or repeal, in accordance with Chapter 3.5 (commencing with Section 11340) of Part 1 of Division 3 of Title 2 of the Government Code, reasonable rules and regulations as may be necessary or proper to carry out the purposes and intent of this chapter and to enable the state department to exercise the powers and perform the duties conferred upon it by this chapter. The state department shall adopt any regulation needed to commence the licensing of hospices pursuant to this chapter on or before June 30, 1992. The department shall consult with licensed hospices, small and rural hospices, and volunteer hospice providers in developing regulations pursuant to this chapter.

(b) The state department shall adopt rules and regulations regarding the purchase, storage, furnishing, and transportation of legend devices for a patient of a hospice. As used in this subdivision, "legend devices" means any device that bears the label

"Caution: federal law restricts this device to sale by or on the order of a _____" or words of similar meaning.
(Amended by Stats. 1992, Ch. 1104, Sec. 7. Effective September 29, 1992.)

1754.

(a) Any licensee may, with the approval of the state department, surrender his or her license for suspension or cancellation by the state department.

(b) Any license suspended or canceled pursuant to this section may be reinstated by the state department upon receipt of an application showing compliance with this chapter.
(Added by Stats. 1990, Ch. 1343, Sec. 1.)

1755.

(a) The state department may deny any application for licensure, or suspend or revoke any license issued, under this chapter upon any of the following grounds:

(1) Violation by the applicant or licensee of this chapter or any rules and regulations promulgated by the state department under this chapter.

(2) Any felony conviction of the applicant or licensee for the violation of any law of this state.

(3) Any conviction of the applicant or licensee for aiding, abetting, or permitting the commission of any act that is a felony in this state.

(4) The applicant's or licensee's misrepresentation of a material fact in the application for a license under this chapter.

(b) Proceedings for the denial, suspension, or revocation of licenses under this chapter shall be conducted in accordance with Chapter 5 (commencing with Section 11500) of Part 1 of Division 3 of Title 2 of the Government Code. In the case of a conflict between this chapter and Chapter 5 (commencing with Section 11500) of Part 1 of Division 3 of Title 2 of the Government Code, Chapter 5 (commencing with Section 11500) shall control.
(Added by Stats. 1990, Ch. 1343, Sec. 1.)

1756.

(a) The suspension, expiration, or forfeiture by operation of law of a license issued by the state department under this chapter, the suspension or cancellation of a license by order of the state department or by order of a court of law, or the surrender of a license without the written consent of the state department shall not deprive the state department of its authority to institute or continue any disciplinary proceeding against the licensee pursuant to this chapter.

(b) Any license revoked pursuant to this chapter may be reinstated pursuant to Section 11522 of the Government Code.
(Added by Stats. 1990, Ch. 1343, Sec. 1.)

1757.

Any person who violates any provision of this chapter or any rule or regulation promulgated under this chapter is guilty of a misdemeanor, and upon conviction thereof, shall be punished by a fine not to exceed five hundred dollars ($500), by imprisonment in the county jail for a period not to exceed 180 days, or by both the fine and imprisonment.
(Added by Stats. 1990, Ch. 1343, Sec. 1.)

1758.

The director may bring an action to enjoin the violation or threatened violation of Section 1748 in the superior court in and for the county in which the violation occurred or is about to occur. Any proceeding under this section shall conform to the requirements of Chapter 3 (commencing with Section 525) of Title 7 of Part 2 of the Code of Civil Procedure, except that the director shall not be required to allege facts necessary to show or tending to show the lack of an adequate remedy at law or to allege facts necessary to show or tending to show irreparable damage or loss.
(Added by Stats. 1990, Ch. 1343, Sec. 1.)

1759.

The district attorney of every county shall, upon application by the state department or its authorized representative, institute and conduct the prosecution within his or her county of any action for violation of this chapter.
(Added by Stats. 1990, Ch. 1343, Sec. 1.)

CHAPTER 8.6. Pediatric Day Health and Respite Care Facilities [1760 - 1763.4]
(Chapter 8.6 added by Stats. 1990, Ch. 1227, Sec. 8.)

1760.

In enacting this chapter, it is the intent of the Legislature to create, within the state department, a program for licensing pediatric day health and respite care facilities to serve the needs of medically fragile and terminally ill children and their families.
(Added by Stats. 1990, Ch. 1227, Sec. 8. Effective September 24, 1990.)

1760.2.

As used in this chapter, the following definitions shall apply:

(a) (1) "Pediatric day health and respite care facility" means a facility that provides an organized program of therapeutic social and day health activities and services and limited 24-hour inpatient respite care to medically fragile children 21 years of age or younger, including terminally ill and technology-dependent patients, except as provided in paragraph (2) and Section 1763.4.

(2) An individual who is 22 years of age or older may continue to receive care in a pediatric day health and respite care facility if the facility receives approval from the state department for a Transitional Health Care Needs Optional Service Unit pursuant to Section 1763.4. A patient who previously received services from a pediatric day health and respite care facility, who is 22 years of age or older, and who satisfies the requirements of Section 1763.4, may also receive services in an optional service unit.

(b) "Medically fragile" means having an acute or chronic health problem that requires therapeutic intervention and skilled nursing care during all or part of the day. Medically fragile problems include, but are not limited to, HIV disease, severe lung disease requiring oxygen, severe lung disease requiring ventilator or tracheostomy care, complicated spina bifida, heart disease, malignancy, asthmatic exacerbations, cystic fibrosis exacerbations, neuromuscular disease, encephalopathies, and seizure disorders.

(c) "Technology-dependent patient" means a person who, from birth, has a chronic disability, requires the routine use of a specific medical device to compensate for the loss of use of a life-sustaining body function, and requires daily, ongoing care or monitoring by trained personnel.

(d) "Respite care" means day and 24-hour relief for the parent or guardian and care for the patient. 24-hour inpatient respite care includes, but is not limited to, 24-hour nursing care, meals, socialization, and developmentally appropriate activities. As used in this chapter, "24-hour inpatient respite care" is limited to no more than 30 intermittent or continuous whole calendar days per patient per calendar year.

(e) "Comprehensive case management" means locating, coordinating, and monitoring services for the eligible patient population and includes all of the following:

(1) Screening of patient referrals to identify those persons who can benefit from the available services.

(2) Comprehensive patient assessment to determine the services needed.

(3) Coordinating the development of an interdisciplinary comprehensive care plan.

(4) Determining individual case cost effectiveness and available sources of funding.

(5) Identifying and maximizing informal sources of care.

(6) Ongoing monitoring of service delivery to determine the optimum type, amount, and duration of services provided.

(f) "License" means a basic permit to operate a pediatric day health and respite care facility. With respect to a health facility licensed pursuant to Chapter 2 (commencing with Section 1250), "license" means a special permit authorizing the health facility to provide pediatric day health and respite care services as a separate program in a distinct part of the facility.

(g) "State department" means the State Department of Public Health.

(Amended by Stats. 2016, Ch. 86, Sec. 181. (SB 1171) Effective January 1, 2017.)

1760.4.

(a) The state department shall develop and adopt regulations for the licensure of, and shall license, pediatric day health and respite care facilities. The regulations shall include minimum standards for the following:

(1) Adequacy, safety, and sanitation of the physical plant and equipment.

(2) Staffing with duly qualified personnel.

(3) Training of the staff.

(4) Providing the services offered.

These regulations shall be filed with the Secretary of State no later than July 1, 1993.

(b) The state department shall establish within the state department an advisory committee of experts to assist in the development of the regulations required pursuant to this section. A representative of the state department shall act as chairperson of the committee. The members of the committee shall serve without compensation, but shall be reimbursed by the state department for all necessary expenses incurred in the actual performance of their duties. To the extent sufficient funds have been appropriated in the Budget Act, the state department may provide staff support to the committee as the state department deems is necessary for the conduct of the committee's business. The committee shall meet at the state director's pleasure until the time that the proposed regulations are presented for adoption at the public hearing.

(c) Pending adoption of the regulations pursuant to subdivision (b), an entity may be licensed as a pediatric day health and respite care facility if it meets interim regulations administered by the state department for congregate living health facilities pursuant to Section 1267.13.

(d) (1) In addition to the exceptions from regulations described in subdivision (n) of Section 1267.13, a pediatric day health and respite care facility shall not be required to conform to the following regulations contained in Chapter 3 of Division 5 of Title 22 of the California Code of Regulations: 72329.1, 72353, 72359, 72363, 72365, 72371, subdivisions (b) and (c) of Section 72375, subdivision (b) of Section 72377, 72516, 72525, and 72531.

(2) A pediatric day health and respite care facility shall not be required to meet the requirements of Section 72367 of Article 3 of Chapter 3 of Division 5 of Title 22 of the California Code of Regulations, except that medications brought by or with the patient on admission to the facility shall not be used unless, after admission by the facility, the contents of the containers have been examined and positively identified by a licensed nurse, in accordance with his or her scope of practice.

(e) A pediatric day health and respite care facility shall have a patient care committee to address quality of care provided in the facility, including, but not limited to, patient care policies, pharmacy services, and infection control.

(1) The pediatric day health and respite care facility shall maintain minutes of every committee meeting and indicate the names of members present, the date, the length of the meeting, the subject matter discussed, and any action taken.

(2) The patient care committee shall include the medical director, dietician, pharmacist, nursing staff, nurse supervisor, center administrator or director, and other staff as may be required by facility policies and procedures.

(3) The patient care committee shall meet at least twice per year or more often if a need or problem is identified by the committee.

(4) The patient care committee shall be responsible for all of the following:

(A) Reviewing and approving all policies relating to patient care. Based on reports received from the pediatric day health and respite care facility's administrator, the committee shall review the effectiveness of policy implementation and shall make recommendations to the administrator of the facility for the improvement of patient care. The committee shall review patient care policies annually and revise the policies as necessary. The committee's minutes shall list the policies the committee reviewed.

(B) Infection control in the facility, which shall include, but not be limited to, establishing, reviewing, monitoring, and approving policies and procedures for investigating, controlling, and preventing infections in the facility, and maintaining, reviewing, and reporting statistics of the number, types, sources, and locations of infections within the pediatric day health and respite care facility.

(C) Establishing, reviewing, and monitoring the storage and administration of drugs and biologicals, reviewing and taking appropriate action based on any findings from a pharmacist hired to consult with the committee and internal quality assurance reviews, and recommending improvements of services to the administrator of the facility.

(f) (1) A pediatric day health and respite care facility shall comply with licensing requirements. The state department may, upon written request of an applicant or licensee, approve the use of alternate concepts, methods, procedures, techniques, equipment, personnel qualifications, or conducting pilot projects, provided those alternatives are carried out with safe and adequate care for the patients and with the prior written approval of the state department. The state department's approval shall provide for the terms and conditions under which the alternatives are granted. An applicant's or licensee's written request shall be accompanied by substantiating evidence supporting the request pursuant to this paragraph.

(2) The state department's review of written requests submitted under this subdivision shall consider the unique nature of services provided to individuals served by the pediatric day health and respite care facility when compared to the requirements for congregate living health facilities for individuals requiring inpatient care.

(3) If the state department grants an approval under this subdivision, a pediatric day health and respite care facility shall immediately post that approval, or a true copy of that approval, adjacent to the facility's license.

(Amended by Stats. 2015, Ch. 206, Sec. 2. (AB 1147) Effective August 13, 2015.)

1760.5.

The annual Licensing and Certification Program fee for a pediatric day health and respite care facility, as defined in Section 1760.2, shall be set in accordance with Section 1266. (Added by Stats. 2006, Ch. 74, Sec. 26. Effective July 12, 2006.)

1760.6.

(a) A pediatric day health and respite care facility shall provide all of the following services:

(1) Medical.

(2) Nursing.

(3) Pharmacy.

(4) Nutrition.

(5) Socialization.

(6) Developmentally appropriate activities.

(b) Services which may be provided by a pediatric day health and respite care facility include, but are not limited to, any of the following:

(1) Physical therapy.

(2) Developmental services.

(3) Occupational and speech therapy.

(4) Educational and psychological services.

(5) Respite care.

(6) Instruction for parents or guardians.

(7) Comprehensive case management, if not otherwise available for the client.

(Added by Stats. 1990, Ch. 1227, Sec. 8. Effective September 24, 1990.)

1760.7.

A pediatric day health and respite care facility shall provide pharmacy services that satisfy all of the following:

(a) (1) Medications shall be supplied to the licensed nursing personnel of the pediatric day health and respite care facility by the patient's parent, foster parent, or legal guardian in the original dispensing container that specifies administration instructions.

(2) Medications shall be administered only upon written and signed orders of the patient's attending physician.

(3) The pediatric day health and respite care facility shall not order medications from a pharmacy or take delivery of medications from a pharmacy.

(4) The pediatric day health and respite care facility shall not accept a patient into the facility if the patient's medications have expired or are scheduled to expire during the patient's stay at the facility.

(b) (1) Physician orders shall be current and maintained in the patient's medical record at the pediatric day health and respite care facility. Verbal orders from the attending physician for services to be rendered at the facility may be received and recorded by licensed nursing personnel in the patient's medical record at the facility and shall be signed by the attending physician within 30 working days.

(2) Medications shall not be administered to a patient unless the facility first verifies that the medication was ordered by a physician. Verification may be obtained by contacting the physician's office or by being provided with a copy of the physician's order for the medication.

(c) The pediatric day health and respite care facility shall maintain records of medication administered for at least one year, unless a longer period is required by state or federal law. The records of medication administered shall be a part of the patient's plan of care.

(d) The pediatric day health and respite care facility may treat changes in the patient's condition, such as new onset pain, nausea, diarrhea, infections, or other similar changes, in accordance with the patient's plan of care if the patient has been prescribed medications to treat these anticipated symptoms, and the treatment does not present a risk to the health and safety of themselves, other patients, staff, or other individuals with whom the patient may come into contact. A patient who presents with symptoms that are not anticipated or planned for in the plan of care shall not remain in the facility.

(e) Other requirements as specified in subdivision (a) of Section 72375, and subdivision (a) of Section 72377, of Article 3 of Chapter 3 of Division 5 of Title 22 of the California Code of Regulations.

(f) Only licensed nursing personnel, acting in accordance with their scope of practice, may accept, inspect the condition of medical containers, and record the receipt and the return of all medications in a pediatric day health and respite care facility. The facility shall comply with Section 72313 of Title 22 of the California Code of Regulations with regard to the administration of medication.

(g) A pediatric day health and respite care facility shall comply with all applicable state and federal laws regarding the labeling condition of medication containers.
(Added by Stats. 2015, Ch. 206, Sec. 3. (AB 1147) Effective August 13, 2015.)
1760.8.
(a) A pediatric day health and respite care facility may establish admission criteria based upon the compatibility of the developmental needs of the persons served and the facility's ability to meet those needs. All admission criteria established by the facility shall be approved by the state department.

(b) A child accepted for care in a pediatric day health and respite care facility shall satisfy all of the following criteria:

(1) Be medically stable, as determined by the child's attending physician and surgeon.

(2) Be under the care of a physician and surgeon who approves the plan of care.

(3) Have current immunization records unless medically contraindicated as stated by the child's attending physician and surgeon at the time of admission and pose no significant risk of infection to others in the facility.

(4) Have the consent of the parent or legal guardian for the admission.
(Added by Stats. 1990, Ch. 1227, Sec. 8. Effective September 24, 1990.)
1760.9.
A pediatric day health and respite care facility may implement policies and procedures that prohibit smoking by patients, parents, staff, visitors, or consultants within the facility or on the premises, if the prohibition is clearly stated in the admission agreement, and notices are posted at the facility.
(Added by Stats. 2015, Ch. 206, Sec. 4. (AB 1147) Effective August 13, 2015.)
1761.
Pediatric day health and respite care facilities shall be separately licensed.
(Added by Stats. 1990, Ch. 1227, Sec. 8. Effective September 24, 1990.)
1761.2.
(a) Pediatric day health and respite care facilities shall meet the same fire safety standards adopted by the State Fire Marshal that apply to community care facilities, as defined in Section 1502, of similar size and with clients of similar age and ambulatory status. No other state or local requirements relating to fire safety shall apply to these facilities and the requirements in this section shall be uniformly enforced by state and local fire authorities.

(b) Pediatric day health and respite care facilities shall meet the same seismic safety standards that apply to community care facilities, as defined in Section 1502, of similar size and with clients of similar age and ambulatory status. No additional state or local requirements relating to seismic safety shall apply to these facilities.
(Added by Stats. 1990, Ch. 1227, Sec. 8. Effective September 24, 1990.)
1761.4.
A pediatric day health and respite care facility of six beds or less shall be considered a residential use of property for purposes of any zoning ordinance or law related to the residential use of property. This section does not prohibit any city, county, or other local public entity from placing restrictions on building heights, setback, lot dimensions, or placement of signs of a pediatric day health and respite care facility as long as those restrictions are identical to those applied to single-family residences.
(Added by Stats. 1990, Ch. 1227, Sec. 8. Effective September 24, 1990.)
1761.6.
A pediatric day health and respite care facility shall conspicuously post the license, or a true copy thereof, in a location accessible to public view.
(Added by Stats. 1990, Ch. 1227, Sec. 8. Effective September 24, 1990.)
1761.8.
A pediatric day health and respite care facility shall not be subject to architectural plan review or field inspection by the Office of Statewide Health Planning and Development. However, as part of the application for licensure, an applicant shall submit evidence of compliance with local building code requirements. In addition, the physical environment shall be adequate to provide the level of care and service required by the clients of the facility as determined by the state department.
(Added by Stats. 1990, Ch. 1227, Sec. 8. Effective September 24, 1990.)
1761.85.
Sections 1761.2, 1761.4, and 1761.8 do not prohibit the use of alternate space utilization, new concepts of design, treatment techniques, equipment and alternate finish materials, or other flexibility, if written approval is granted by the local building authority.
(Added by Stats. 2015, Ch. 206, Sec. 5. (AB 1147) Effective August 13, 2015.)
1762.

(a) In order to obtain a license under the provisions of this chapter to establish, conduct, or maintain a pediatric day health and respite care facility, a person, entity, political subdivision of the state, or governmental agency shall file with the state department a verified application on a form prescribed, prepared, and furnished by the state department, containing information as may be required by the state department for the proper administration and enforcement of this chapter.

(b) The state department shall initiate an initial licensing inspection of a Transitional Health Care Needs Optional Service Unit within 60 days of receipt of a completed application.
(Added by Stats. 2015, Ch. 206, Sec. 6. (AB 1147) Effective August 13, 2015.)
1762.2.
(a) If a pediatric day health and respite care facility or an applicant for a license has not been previously licensed, the state department shall issue a provisional license to the facility only as provided in this section.

(b) The state department shall not issue a provisional license unless, after an onsite survey by the state department, the state department finds that the pediatric day health and respite care facility is in substantial compliance with the requirements of this chapter.

(c) A provisional license to operate a pediatric day health and respite care facility shall terminate six months from the date of issuance, or the date that the state department is able to conduct a full and complete inspection, whichever is later.

(d) Within 30 days prior to the termination of a provisional license, the state department shall give the facility a full and complete inspection, and, if the facility meets all applicable requirements for licensure, a regular license shall be issued. If the facility does not meet the requirements for licensure but has made substantial progress towards meeting the requirements, as determined by the state department, the initial provisional license shall be renewed for six months.

(e) If the state department determines that there has not been substantial progress towards meeting licensure requirements at the time of the first full inspection provided by this section, or, if the state department determines upon its inspection made within 30 days of the termination of a renewed provisional license that there is lack of full compliance with the requirements, the state department shall not issue a further license.

(f) If an applicant for a provisional license to operate a pediatric day health and respite care facility has been denied provisional licensing by the state department, the applicant may contest the denial by filing a request for a hearing pursuant to Section 131071.

(g) The state department shall not apply less stringent criteria when granting a provisional license pursuant to this section than it applies when granting a permanent license.
(Added by Stats. 2015, Ch. 206, Sec. 7. (AB 1147) Effective August 13, 2015.)
1762.4.
(a) A license issued under this chapter shall expire 12 months from the date of its issuance. The licensee shall pay a fee, not to exceed the reasonable regulatory cost to the state department, to the state department annually, not less than 30 days prior to expiration date, subject to the state department mailing the notice of renewal in accordance with subdivision (b).

(b) (1) At least 45 days prior to the expiration of a license issued pursuant to this chapter, the state department shall mail a notice for renewal to the licensee.

(2) A license renewal shall be submitted with the necessary fee in accordance with subdivision (a). A license shall be deemed renewed upon payment of the necessary fee, commencing from the license's expiration date. If the requirements of this section are satisfied, the state department shall issue a license to the facility by the expiration date of the license to ensure the provider remains in good standing. The facility's license shall be mailed within 15 calendar days after the date the state department receives the renewal fee.
(Added by Stats. 2015, Ch. 206, Sec. 8. (AB 1147) Effective August 13, 2015.)
1762.6.
Every pediatric day health and respite care facility for which a license has been issued shall be periodically inspected by a duly authorized representative of the state department. Reports of each inspection shall be prepared by the representative upon forms prepared and furnished by the state department and filed with the state department. The inspection shall be for the purpose of ensuring that the pediatric day health and respite care facility is complying with the provisions of this chapter and the rules and regulations of the state department.
(Added by Stats. 2015, Ch. 206, Sec. 9. (AB 1147) Effective August 13, 2015.)
1762.8.
The state department may deny an application for, or suspend or revoke a license issued under the provisions of this chapter in the manner provided in Section 1763 upon, any of the following grounds:

(a) A serious violation by the licensee of any of the provisions of this chapter, of any other law, or of the rules and regulations promulgated under this chapter that jeopardizes the health and safety of patients.

(b) Aiding, abetting, or permitting the commission of any illegal act.

(c) Willful omission or falsification of a material fact in the application for a license.
(Added by Stats. 2015, Ch. 206, Sec. 10. (AB 1147) Effective August 13, 2015.)
1763.
Proceedings for the denial, suspension, or revocation of licenses, or denial or withdrawal of approval under this chapter shall be conducted in accordance with Section 131071. The suspension, expiration, or forfeiture by operation of law of a license issued by the state department, its suspension, forfeiture, or cancellation by order of the state department or by order of a court, or its surrender without the written consent of the state department, shall not deprive the state department of its authority to institute or

continue a disciplinary proceeding against the licensee upon any ground provided by law or to enter an order suspending or revoking the license or otherwise taking disciplinary action against the licensee on any of those grounds.

(Added by Stats. 2015, Ch. 206, Sec. 11. (AB 1147) Effective August 13, 2015.)

1763.2.

The state department has authority to make reasonable accommodation for exceptions to the standards in this chapter if the health, safety, and quality of patient care is not compromised. Prior written approval communicating the terms and conditions under which the exception is granted shall be required. An applicant shall request an exception in writing accompanied by detailed supporting documentation.

(Added by Stats. 2015, Ch. 206, Sec. 12. (AB 1147) Effective August 13, 2015.)

1763.4.

(a) For purposes of this chapter, the following definitions shall apply:

(1) "Distinct part" means an identifiable unit accommodating beds or patient space, including, but not limited to, contiguous beds or patient space, a wing, floor, or building approved by the state department for a specific purpose.

(2) "Older children" means patients who are 18 to 21 years of age, inclusive.

(3) "Transitional Health Care Needs Optional Service Unit" or "optional service unit" means a functional unit of a pediatric day health and respite care facility that is organized, staffed, and equipped to provide care to individuals who are 22 years of age or older.

(A) Patients receiving care in the optional service unit shall be in age-appropriate groupings as provided for in the pediatric day health and respite care facility's policies and procedures. Older children are not precluded from being cared for in the same optional service unit as the patients who are 22 years of age or older. If a pediatric day health and respite care facility proposes to provide care to older children in the optional service unit, the facility shall have policies, procedures, equipment, and supplies to meet the needs of those patients. Patients who are 15 to 17 years of age, inclusive, may also be considered for care in the optional service unit if the pediatric day health and respite care facility obtains an individual age waiver from the regional center, with the concurrence of the department. A pediatric day health and respite care facility is not required to operate an optional service unit.

(B) In order to continue receiving care in the pediatric day health and respite care facility, patients who are 22 years of age or older shall have a developmental age of 18 years of age or younger, as evidenced by the patient's Individual Education Plan (IEP), Regional Center Assessment, physician's assessment, or other assessment using a standardized assessment tool that is nationally recognized in the field. A patient who previously received services from a pediatric day health and respite care facility, who is 22 years of age or older, and who satisfies the requirements of this subparagraph may also receive services in an optional service unit.

(b) An optional service unit shall be subject to the approval of the state department. A pediatric day health and respite care facility desiring approval for an optional service unit shall file an application on forms furnished by the state department. The state department shall list on the facility license each optional service for which approval is granted.

(c) Except as provided in subparagraph (A) of paragraph (3) of subdivision (a), care for patients who are 22 years of age or older shall be provided in a distinct part of the pediatric day health and respite care facility or optional service unit, separate from the area where care is provided to patients who are 21 years of age or younger. The facility shall establish and implement policies and procedures for determining the age ranges of patients who are cared for in the optional service unit. These policies and procedures shall include, but not be limited to, consideration of the patient's chronological age, developmental age, and size, and shall reflect the needs of individual patients through a comprehensive assessment.

(d) The pediatric day health and respite care facility shall ensure that its staffing and equipment are sufficient to provide services to patients who are 22 years of age or older.

(e) A Transitional Health Care Needs Optional Service Unit shall have written policies and procedures for the management of the service. The policies and procedures shall be established and implemented by the patient care policy committee described in Section 1760.4

(f) (1) The state department may review and approve the policies and procedures for an optional service unit.

(2) The State Department of Developmental Services and the regional centers may review the policies and procedures for an optional service unit.

(Added by Stats. 2015, Ch. 206, Sec. 13. (AB 1147) Effective August 13, 2015.)

CHAPTER 9. Mobile Health Care Units [1765.101 - 1765.175]

(Chapter 9 added by Stats. 1993, Ch. 1020, Sec. 2.)

1765.101.

This chapter shall be known, and may be cited as, the Mobile Health Care Services Act.

(Added by Stats. 1993, Ch. 1020, Sec. 2. Effective January 1, 1994.)

1765.105.

As used in this chapter, the following definitions shall apply:

(a) "Parent facility" means a health facility licensed pursuant to Chapter 2 (commencing with Section 1250) of Division 2, or a clinic licensed pursuant to Chapter 1 (commencing with Section 1200) of Division 2.

(b) (1) "Mobile service unit" or "mobile unit" means a special purpose commercial coach as defined in Section 18012.5, or a commercial coach as defined in Section 18001.8, that provides services as set forth in Section 1765.110, and meets any of the following criteria:

(A) Is approved pursuant to this chapter by the state department as a service of a licensed health facility, as defined in Section 1250.

(B) Is approved by the state department pursuant to this chapter as a service of a licensed clinic, as defined in Section 1200.

(C) Is licensed pursuant to this chapter by the state department as a clinic, as defined in Section 1200.

(D) Is licensed pursuant to this chapter as an "other" type of approved mobile unit by the state department. "Other" types of approved mobile units shall be limited to mobile units performing services within new health facility or clinic licensure categories created after the effective date of this chapter. The State Department of Health Services shall not create a new health facility or clinic licensure category under this subparagraph absent a legislative mandate.

(2) "Mobile service unit" or "mobile unit" does not mean a modular, relocatable, or transportable unit that is designed to be placed on a foundation when it reaches its destination, nor does it mean any entity that is exempt from licensure pursuant to Section 1206.

(Added by Stats. 1993, Ch. 1020, Sec. 2. Effective January 1, 1994.)

1765.110.

The purpose of this chapter is to provide for the use of mobile units to provide medical, diagnostic, and treatment services, in order to help ensure the availability of quality health care services for patients who receive care in remote or underserved areas and for patients who need specialized types of medical care provided in a cost-effective way.

(Added by Stats. 1993, Ch. 1020, Sec. 2. Effective January 1, 1994.)

1765.115.

A mobile unit may operate as one of the following:

(a) As an adjunct to a licensed health facility or to a licensed clinic.

(b) As an independent-freestanding clinic pursuant to Chapter 1 (commencing with Section 1200).

(c) As an "other" type of approved mobile unit.

(Added by Stats. 1993, Ch. 1020, Sec. 2. Effective January 1, 1994.)

1765.117.

The state department shall charge applicants a licensure fee as follows:

(a) Pursuant to Chapter 1 (commencing with Section 1200), or Chapter 2 (commencing with Section 1250).

(b) Pursuant to the applicable section of the Health and Safety Code that creates a new health facility or clinic licensure category.

(c) No additional licensure fee will be imposed solely because a service is to be provided in a mobile unit.

(Added by Stats. 1993, Ch. 1020, Sec. 2. Effective January 1, 1994.)

1765.120.

Compliance with all of the following criteria shall be required prior to licensure:

(a) The mobile unit shall comply with the applicable requirements of the Vehicle Code, and shall have a vehicle identification number.

(b) The mobile unit shall bear an insignia issued by the Department of Housing and Community Development pursuant to Section 18026.

(Added by Stats. 1993, Ch. 1020, Sec. 2. Effective January 1, 1994.)

1765.125.

(a) Except as provided in subdivision (b), no person, political subdivision of the state, or governmental agency shall operate a mobile service unit without first obtaining a license or an addition to existing licensure under this chapter unless exempt from licensure under Section 1206.

(b) Any person, political subdivision of the state, or governmental agency, that was operating a mobile unit as of January 1, 1994, may continue to operate the mobile unit only under the following conditions:

(1) The person, political subdivision of the state, or governmental agency shall apply to the state department for a mobile unit license, or an addition to existing licensure, via a request for licensure under this chapter by March 1, 1994.

(2) The person, political subdivision of the state, or governmental agency shall cease operating the mobile unit upon a final decision of the state department denying the application for licensure or addition to licensure under this chapter.

(c) Notwithstanding any other provision of this chapter, after the initial licensure, or the initial approval of the addition to existing licensure of a parent facility, to operate a mobile service unit, the department shall not require that each site where the mobile unit operates be licensed or approved by the department unless the mobile unit will be operating outside of the proposed area or areas specified in the application pursuant to paragraph (4) of subdivision (b) of Section 1765.130.

(Amended by Stats. 2002, Ch. 111, Sec. 2. Effective January 1, 2003.)

1765.130.

(a) Any applicant under this chapter shall file with the state department an application. The application shall be on forms prescribed and furnished by the state department that shall contain any information as may be required by the state department for the proper administration and enforcement of this chapter.

(b) An applicant health facility or clinic pursuant to this chapter shall submit an application to the licensing and certification district office of the state department stating with specificity all of the following:

(1) The proposed service to be provided.

(2) The expected hours and days of operation.

(3) The type and the manufacturer of the mobile unit contemplated.

(4) The proposed area or areas where the mobile unit will be providing services.

(c) An applicant for licensure as an independently licensed clinic under this chapter shall submit a verified application to the state department on the appropriate forms for the type of clinic for which it wishes to obtain licensure.

(d) Prior to granting approval to an applicant parent facility for operation of a mobile unit under the parent facility's existing licensure pursuant to this chapter, or prior to granting license for an independent mobile unit, the state department shall conduct an onsite inspection, including, but not limited to, a review of policies and procedures.

(e) Supplemental services offered via mobile units shall be listed by the state department as an approved or supplemental service on the license of the parent facility.

(f) Licenses issued by the state department authorizing operation of a mobile unit as an addition to existing parent facility licensure shall be posted at the parent facility. Licenses authorizing operation of a clinic as a mobile unit shall be posted at the administrative headquarters of the licensee. A true copy of the license shall be posted within the mobile unit.

(Added by Stats. 1993, Ch. 1020, Sec. 2. Effective January 1, 1994.)
1765.135.

(a) To qualify for a license under this chapter, an applicant shall satisfy all the requirements of this chapter, the applicable requirements of Chapter 1 (commencing with Section 1200) or of Chapter 2 (commencing with Section 1250) of Division 2, and all applicable regulations.

(b) The applicant shall file a completed application with the state department.
(Added by Stats. 1993, Ch. 1020, Sec. 2. Effective January 1, 1994.)
1765.140.

(a) Mobile units that provide services as an addition to the existing license of a parent facility shall be subject to the same requirements and regulations as the parent facility, except that, instead of complying with the physical plant requirements applicable to the parent facility, they shall comply with the mobile unit requirements contained in this chapter.

(b) Clinics licensed as mobile units shall be subject to the same requirements and regulations as any other clinic, except that, instead of complying with the physical plant requirements applicable to the clinic, the mobile unit shall comply with the mobile unit requirements contained in this chapter.

(Added by Stats. 1993, Ch. 1020, Sec. 2. Effective January 1, 1994.)
1765.145.

(a) A licensee using mobile services pursuant to this chapter shall, at the department's option, be periodically inspected, in addition to any inspections required pursuant to the parent facility licensure requirements, by a duly authorized representative of the department. Reports of each inspection shall be prepared by the representative conducting it upon forms prepared and furnished by the department and filed with the department. The inspection shall be for the purpose of ensuring that this chapter and the rules and regulations of the department adopted under this chapter are being followed.

(b) Any officer, employee, or agent of the department may enter and inspect any building, premises, or vehicle and may have access to and inspect any document, file, or other record, of a mobile unit or of a parent facility operating a mobile unit, at any reasonable time to assure compliance with, or to prevent violation of, this chapter.

(c) After the initial licensure, or the initial approval of the addition to existing licensure of a parent facility, the mobile unit shall be periodically reviewed for compliance. When approved as additions to the existing licensure of a parent facility, reviews shall be conducted as a part of the parent facility's regular inspection. When the mobile unit is an independently licensed clinic, it shall be reviewed in accordance with the licensing inspection schedule for clinics.

(d) Demonstration of a mock emergency drill shall be observed by department staff in the mobile unit on a site where patient mobility is limited.
(Amended by Stats. 2006, Ch. 538, Sec. 366. Effective January 1, 2007.)
1765.150.

(a) The mobile unit shall be of sufficient size and shall be arranged in a manner that is appropriate for the provision of those health care services that it is licensed to provide.

(b) The mobile unit shall be equipped with appropriate utilities for the comfort and safety of patients. The Office of Statewide Health Planning and Development shall review and approve hospital-provided utility connections for mobile units that require utility hookups with general acute care hospitals.

(c) The mobile unit shall be maintained in good repair and in a clean and sanitary manner.

(d) All proposed modifications to previously approved services and procedures shall be reviewed and approved by the state department before they are implemented. Modifications to the mobile service unit shall be approved by the Department of Housing and Community Development pursuant to Section 18029.

(e) The licensee shall report to the department the location of the site at least 24 hours prior to the operation of a mobile unit at any site for the first time.

(f) Notification required by subdivision (e) shall be waived when the mobile unit operates at any site for the first time at the request of federal, state, or local authorities for the purposes of responding to state or locally declared emergencies as defined in subdivisions (a), (b), and (c) of Section 8558 of the Government Code, federally declared emergencies, and declared public health emergencies as defined in Section 101080 for the duration of the emergency.

(Amended by Stats. 2008, Ch. 360, Sec. 1. Effective January 1, 2009.)
1765.155.

(a) The licensed parent facility or clinic shall be responsible for obtaining approvals for the site or sites of the mobile unit as required by the local planning, zoning, and fire authorities.

(b) The mobile unit shall be situated for safe and comfortable patient access. The mobile unit shall comply with all local parking laws. Any parking restrictions developed by a parent facility or clinic for mobile units shall be strictly enforced by the parent facility or clinic.

(c) The parent facility or clinic shall ensure that there is sufficient lighting around the perimeter of the site from which the mobile unit provides any services.
(Amended by Stats. 2008, Ch. 360, Sec. 2. Effective January 1, 2009.)
1765.160.

Any licensee using mobile services pursuant to this chapter shall do all of the following:

(a) Have written policies established by the governing body of the licensee, to govern the services that the mobile unit provides. The policies shall include, but shall not be limited to, policies related to patient care, personnel training and orientation, personnel supervision, and evaluation of services provided by the mobile unit.

(b) Have written policies regarding patient selection criteria.

(c) Develop and implement the written policies and procedures for the mobile unit in consultation with other appropriate health care professionals.

(d) Ensure that the written policies and procedures are consistent with the policies and procedures of the parent facility, if any.

(e) Ensure that the policies and written procedures shall be approved by the governing body, administration, and medical staff of the licensee, where appropriate.

(f) Ensure that the written policies and procedures include, but are not limited to, all of the following:

(1) Scope of services.

(2) Procedures for the performance of the services provided.

(3) Quality assurance.

(4) Infection control.

(5) Medical record documentation of services provided, as appropriate.

(6) Transport of patients, including, but not limited to, method, special equipment, necessary personnel, and protection from inclement weather.

(7) Emergency services and evacuation plan for the mobile unit.

(A) A licensee using mobile services pursuant to this chapter shall specify in writing policies and procedures for emergencies including fire, natural disaster, and medical emergencies. In its policies and procedures, the mobile unit shall address the emergency plan required of the parent facility and state how the plans shall be coordinated.

(B) A licensee using mobile services pursuant to this chapter shall familiarize its employees and each patient with the policies and procedures adopted pursuant to subparagraph (A).

(C) A licensee using mobile services pursuant to this chapter shall maintain written transfer agreements that shall include, but shall not be limited to, provisions for communication with, and transportation to, one or more nearby hospitals and other health facilities as needed to meet medical emergencies. The mobile unit shall develop procedures that include personnel needed to assist in the transfer, as well as provisions for meeting medical needs to accommodate the emergency transfer.

(8) Location.

(9) Schedule of mobile unit services.

(g) Maintain clinical records on each patient, in accordance with regulations.

(h) Maintain a mobile unit services log that shall include, but shall not be limited to, all of the following:

(1) Patient chart or identification number.

(2) Name, age, and sex of patient.

(3) Site, date, time, and as appropriate, duration of procedure.
(Added by Stats. 1993, Ch. 1020, Sec. 2. Effective January 1, 1994.)
1765.165.

(a) For general acute care hospitals, mobile unit services shall not be utilized as a primary source for a basic hospital service, as defined in subdivision (a) of Section 1250, unless in response to a natural disaster or other emergency situation.

(b) The mobile services provided in a mobile unit operated by a parent facility shall be licensed to the parent facility, even though it may be operated pursuant to a contract. When a contract of this type exists with a licensed parent facility for the provision of mobile unit services, all of the following shall apply:

(1) Mobile units shall be treated as part of the parent facility for licensure purposes.

(2) Each parent facility shall document the designated service and staff that have administrative responsibility for the mobile unit.

(3) The parent facility shall maintain the administrative and professional responsibility for the mobile unit. All liabilities for noncompliance regarding the provisions of services in the mobile unit shall be that of the parent facility.

(4) Procedures and services to be provided in the mobile unit shall be in accordance with recognized acceptable standards of practice.

(5) Coordination with the owner of the mobile unit vehicle for availability of the vehicle at the site for required inspections shall be the responsibility of the parent facility.
(Added by Stats. 1993, Ch. 1020, Sec. 2. Effective January 1, 1994.)
1765.170.

The mobile unit shall comply with all of the following:

(a) It shall have supplies and equipment to meet the needs of the patients served.

(b) Any mobile unit X-ray equipment shall be in compliance with the requirements in the California Radiation Control Regulations, Title 17, California Code of Regulations.

(c) The mobile unit shall have fire safety equipment as specified by the fire authority having jurisdiction, including but not limited to, at least two fire extinguishers of 2A:20 BC rating.

(d) Documented evidence of preventative maintenance and calibration procedures of mobile unit equipment shall conform to the manufacturer's specifications.

(e) Use of the equipment in mobile units shall conform to the manufacturer's specifications.

(f) The mobile unit shall have a telecommunications device.

(Added by Stats. 1993, Ch. 1020, Sec. 2. Effective January 1, 1994.)

1765.175.

The state department shall adopt, amend, or repeal, in accordance with Chapter 3.5 (commencing with Section 11340) of Part 1 of Division 3 of Title 2 of the Government Code, rules and regulations as it determines may be necessary to carry out the purposes and intent of this chapter and to enable the state department to exercise the powers and perform the duties conferred upon it by this chapter. Until the state department adopts regulations relating to provision of services by a chronic hemodialysis clinic, a surgery clinic, or a rehabilitation clinic, mobile units licensed or seeking licensure, in these categories shall comply with federal certification standards for end stage renal disease clinics, ambulatory surgery clinics, or comprehensive outpatient rehabilitation facilities, as applicable.

(Added by Stats. 1993, Ch. 1020, Sec. 2. Effective January 1, 1994.)

CHAPTER 10. Continuing Care Contracts [1770 - 1793.91]

(Chapter 10 repealed and added by Stats. 1990, Ch. 875, Sec. 2.)

ARTICLE 1. General Provisions [1770 - 1778]

(Article 1 added by Stats. 1990, Ch. 875, Sec. 2.)

1770.

The Legislature finds, declares, and intends all of the following:

(a) Continuing care retirement communities are an alternative for the long-term residential, social, and health care needs of California's elderly residents and seek to provide a continuum of care, minimize transfer trauma, and allow services to be provided in an appropriately licensed setting.

(b) Because elderly residents often both expend a significant portion of their savings in order to purchase care in a continuing care retirement community and expect to receive care at their continuing care retirement community for the rest of their lives, tragic consequences can result if a continuing care provider becomes insolvent or unable to provide responsible care.

(c) There is a need for disclosure concerning the terms of agreements made between prospective residents and the continuing care provider, and concerning the operations of the continuing care retirement community.

(d) Providers of continuing care should be required to obtain a certificate of authority to enter into continuing care contracts and should be monitored and regulated by the State Department of Social Services.

(e) This chapter applies equally to for-profit and nonprofit provider entities.

(f) This chapter states the minimum requirements to be imposed upon any entity offering or providing continuing care.

(g) Because the authority to enter into continuing care contracts granted by the State Department of Social Services is neither a guarantee of performance by the providers nor an endorsement of any continuing care contract provisions, prospective residents must carefully consider the risks, benefits, and costs before signing a continuing care contract and should be encouraged to seek financial and legal advice before doing so.

(Amended by Stats. 2000, Ch. 820, Sec. 1. Effective January 1, 2001.)

1771.

Unless the context otherwise requires, the definitions in this section govern the interpretation of this chapter.

(a) (1) "Affiliate" means any person, corporation, limited liability company, business trust, trust, partnership, unincorporated association, or other legal entity that directly or indirectly controls, is controlled by, or is under common control with, a provider or applicant.

(2) "Affinity group" means a grouping of entities sharing a common interest, philosophy, or connection (e.g., military officers, religion).

(3) "Annual report" means the report each provider is required to file annually with the department, as described in Section 1790.

(4) "Applicant" means any entity, or combination of entities, that submits and has pending an application to the department for a permit to accept deposits and a certificate of authority.

(5) "Assisted living services" includes, but is not limited to, assistance with personal activities of daily living, including dressing, feeding, toileting, bathing, grooming, mobility, and associated tasks, to help provide for and maintain physical and psychosocial comfort.

(6) "Assisted living unit" means the living area or unit within a continuing care retirement community that is specifically designed to provide ongoing assisted living services.

(7) "Audited financial statement" means financial statements prepared in accordance with generally accepted accounting principles, including the opinion of an independent certified public accountant, and notes to the financial statements considered customary or necessary to provide full disclosure and complete information regarding the provider's financial statements, financial condition, and operation.

(b) (reserved)

(c) (1) "Cancel" means to destroy the force and effect of an agreement or continuing care contract.

(2) "Cancellation period" means the 90-day period, beginning when the resident physically moves into the continuing care retirement community, during which the resident may cancel the continuing care contract, as provided in Section 1788.2.

(3) "Care" means nursing, medical, or other health-related services, protection or supervision, assistance with the personal activities of daily living, or any combination of those services.

(4) "Cash equivalent" means certificates of deposit and United States treasury securities with a maturity of five years or less.

(5) "Certificate" or "certificate of authority" means the certificate issued by the department, properly executed and bearing the State Seal, authorizing a specified provider to enter into one or more continuing care contracts at a single specified continuing care retirement community.

(6) "Condition" means a restriction, specific action, or other requirement imposed by the department for the initial or continuing validity of a permit to accept deposits, a provisional certificate of authority, or a certificate of authority. A condition may limit the circumstances under which the provider may enter into any new deposit agreement or contract, or may be imposed as a condition precedent to the issuance of a permit to accept deposits, a provisional certificate of authority, or a certificate of authority.

(7) "Consideration" means some right, interest, profit, or benefit paid, transferred, promised, or provided by one party to another as an inducement to contract. Consideration includes some forbearance, detriment, loss, or responsibility, that is given, suffered, or undertaken by a party as an inducement to another party to contract.

(8) "Continuing care contract" means a contract that includes a continuing care promise made, in exchange for an entrance fee, the payment of periodic charges, or both types of payments. A continuing care contract may consist of one agreement or a series of agreements and other writings incorporated by reference.

(9) "Continuing care promise" means a promise, expressed or implied, by a provider to provide one or more elements of care to an elderly resident for the duration of his or her life or for a term in excess of one year. Any such promise or representation, whether part of a continuing care contract, other agreement, or series of agreements, or contained in any advertisement, brochure, or other material, either written or oral, is a continuing care promise.

(10) "Continuing care retirement community" means a facility located within the State of California where services promised in a continuing care contract are provided. A distinct phase of development approved by the department may be considered to be the continuing care retirement community when a project is being developed in successive distinct phases over a period of time. When the services are provided in residents' own homes, the homes into which the provider takes those services are considered part of the continuing care retirement community.

(11) "Control" means directing or causing the direction of the financial management or the policies of another entity, including an operator of a continuing care retirement community, whether by means of the controlling entity's ownership interest, contract, or any other involvement. A parent entity or sole member of an entity controls a subsidiary entity provider for a continuing care retirement community if its officers, directors, or agents directly participate in the management of the subsidiary entity or in the initiation or approval of policies that affect the continuing care retirement community's operations, including, but not limited to, approving budgets or the administrator for a continuing care retirement community.

(d) (1) "Department" means the State Department of Social Services.

(2) "Deposit" means any transfer of consideration, including a promise to transfer money or property, made by a depositor to any entity that promises or proposes to promise to provide continuing care, but is not authorized to enter into a continuing care contract with the potential depositor.

(3) "Deposit agreement" means any agreement made between any entity accepting a deposit and a depositor. Deposit agreements for deposits received by an applicant prior to the department's release of funds from the deposit escrow account shall be subject to the requirements described in Section 1780.4.

(4) "Depository" means a bank or institution that is a member of the Federal Deposit Insurance Corporation or a comparable deposit insurance program.

(5) "Depositor" means any prospective resident who pays a deposit. Where any portion of the consideration transferred to an applicant as a deposit or to a provider as consideration for a continuing care contract is transferred by a person other than the prospective resident or a resident, that third-party transferor shall have the same cancellation or refund rights as the prospective resident or resident for whose benefit the consideration was transferred.

(6) "Director" means the Director of Social Services.

(e) (1) "Elderly" means an individual who is 60 years of age or older.

(2) "Entity" means an individual, partnership, corporation, limited liability company, and any other form for doing business. Entity includes a person, sole proprietorship, estate, trust, association, and joint venture.

(3) "Entrance fee" means the sum of any initial, amortized, or deferred transfer of consideration made or promised to be made by, or on behalf of, a person entering into a continuing care contract for the purpose of ensuring care or related services pursuant to that continuing care contract or as full or partial payment for the promise to provide care for the term of the continuing care contract. Entrance fee includes the purchase price of a condominium, cooperative, or other interest sold in connection with a promise of continuing care. An initial, amortized, or deferred transfer of consideration that is greater in value than 12 times the monthly care fee shall be presumed to be an entrance fee.

(4) "Equity" means the value of real property in excess of the aggregate amount of all liabilities secured by the property.

(5) "Equity interest" means an interest held by a resident in a continuing care retirement community that consists of either an ownership interest in any part of the continuing care retirement community property or a transferable membership that entitles the holder to reside at the continuing care retirement community.

(6) "Equity project" means a continuing care retirement community where residents receive an equity interest in the continuing care retirement community property.

(7) "Equity securities" shall refer generally to large and midcapitalization corporate stocks that are publicly traded and readily liquidated for cash, and shall include shares in mutual funds that hold portfolios consisting predominantly of these stocks and other qualifying assets, as defined by Section 1792.2. Equity securities shall also include other similar securities that are specifically approved by the department.

(8) "Escrow agent" means a bank or institution, including, but not limited to, a title insurance company, approved by the department to hold and render accountings for deposits of cash or cash equivalents.

(f) "Facility" means any place or accommodation where a provider provides or will provide a resident with care or related services, whether or not the place or accommodation is constructed, owned, leased, rented, or otherwise contracted for by the provider.

(g) (reserved)

(h) (reserved)

(i) (1) "Inactive certificate of authority" means a certificate that has been terminated under Section 1793.8.

(2) "Investment securities" means any of the following:

(A) Direct obligations of the United States, including obligations issued or held in book-entry form on the books of the United States Department of the Treasury or obligations the timely payment of the principal of, and the interest on, which are fully guaranteed by the United States.

(B) Obligations, debentures, notes, or other evidences of indebtedness issued or guaranteed by any of the following:

(i) The Federal Home Loan Bank System.

(ii) The Export-Import Bank of the United States.

(iii) The Federal Financing Bank.

(iv) The Government National Mortgage Association.

(v) The Farmers Home Administration.

(vi) The Federal Home Loan Mortgage Corporation of the Federal Housing Administration.

(vii) Any agency, department, or other instrumentality of the United States if the obligations are rated in one of the two highest rating categories of each rating agency rating those obligations.

(C) Bonds of the State of California or of any county, city and county, or city in this state, if rated in one of the two highest rating categories of each rating agency rating those bonds.

(D) Commercial paper of finance companies and banking institutions rated in one of the two highest categories of each rating agency rating those instruments.

(E) Repurchase agreements fully secured by collateral security described in subparagraph (A) or (B), as evidenced by an opinion of counsel, if the collateral is held by the provider or a third party during the term of the repurchase agreement, pursuant to the terms of the agreement, subject to liens or claims of third parties, and has a market value, which is determined at least every 14 days, at least equal to the amount so invested.

(F) Long-term investment agreements, which have maturity dates in excess of one year, with financial institutions, including, but not limited to, banks and insurance companies or their affiliates, if the financial institution's paying ability for debt obligations or long-term claims or the paying ability of a related guarantor of the financial institution for these obligations or claims, is rated in one of the two highest rating categories of each rating agency rating those instruments, or if the short-term investment agreements are with the financial institution or the related guarantor of the financial institution, the long-term or short-term debt obligations, whichever is applicable, of which are rated in one of the two highest long-term or short-term rating categories, of each rating agency rating the bonds of the financial institution or the related guarantor, provided that if the rating falls below the two highest rating categories, the investment agreement shall allow the provider the option to replace the financial institution or the related guarantor of the financial institution or shall provide for the investment securities to be fully collateralized by investments described in subparagraph (A), and, provided further, if so collateralized, that the provider has a perfected first security lien on the collateral, as evidenced by an opinion of counsel and the collateral is held by the provider.

(G) Banker's acceptances or certificates of deposit of, or time deposits in, any savings and loan association that meets any of the following criteria:

(i) The debt obligations of the savings and loan association, or in the case of a principal bank, of the bank holding company, are rated in one of the two highest rating categories of each rating agency rating those instruments.

(ii) The certificates of deposit or time deposits are fully insured by the Federal Deposit Insurance Corporation.

(iii) The certificates of deposit or time deposits are secured at all times, in the manner and to the extent provided by law, by collateral security described in subparagraph (A) or (B) with a market value, valued at least quarterly, of no less than the original amount of moneys so invested.

(H) Taxable money market government portfolios restricted to obligations issued or guaranteed as to payment of principal and interest by the full faith and credit of the United States.

(I) Obligations the interest on which is excluded from gross income for federal income tax purposes and money market mutual funds whose portfolios are restricted to these obligations, if the obligations or mutual funds are rated in one of the two highest rating categories by each rating agency rating those obligations.

(J) Bonds that are not issued by the United States or any federal agency, but that are listed on a national exchange and that are rated at least "A" by Moody's Investors Service, or the equivalent rating by Standard and Poor's Corporation or Fitch Investors Service.

(K) Bonds not listed on a national exchange that are traded on an over-the-counter basis, and that are rated at least "Aa" by Moody's Investors Service or "AA" by Standard and Poor's Corporation or Fitch Investors Service.

(j) (reserved)

(k) (reserved)

(l) "Life care contract" means a continuing care contract that includes a promise, expressed or implied, by a provider to provide or pay for routine services at all levels of care, including acute care and the services of physicians and surgeons, to the extent not covered by other public or private insurance benefits, to a resident for the duration of his or her life. Care shall be provided under a life care contract in a continuing care retirement community having a comprehensive continuum of care, including a skilled nursing facility, under the ownership and supervision of the provider on or adjacent to the premises. A change shall not be made in the monthly fee based on level of care. A life care contract shall also include provisions to subsidize residents who become financially unable to pay their monthly care fees.

(m) (1) "Monthly care fee" means the fee charged to a resident in a continuing care contract on a monthly or other periodic basis for current accommodations and services, including care, board, or lodging. Periodic entrance fee payments or other prepayments shall not be monthly care fees.

(2) "Monthly fee contract" means a continuing care contract that requires residents to pay monthly care fees.

(n) "Nonambulatory person" means a person who is unable to leave a building unassisted under emergency conditions in the manner described by Section 13131.

(o) (reserved)

(p) (1) "Per capita cost" means a continuing care retirement community's operating expenses, excluding depreciation, divided by the average number of residents.

(2) "Periodic charges" means fees paid by a resident on a periodic basis.

(3) "Permanent closure" means the voluntary or involuntary termination or forfeiture, as specified in subdivisions (a), (b), (g), (h), and (i) of Section 1793.7, of a provider's certificate of authority or license, or another action that results in the permanent relocation of residents. Permanent closure does not apply in the case of a natural disaster or other event out of the provider's control.

(4) "Permit to accept deposits" means a written authorization by the department permitting an applicant to enter into deposit agreements regarding a single specified continuing care retirement community.

(5) "Prepaid contract" means a continuing care contract in which the monthly care fee, if any, may not be adjusted to cover the actual cost of care and services.

(6) "Preferred access" means that residents who have previously occupied a residential living unit have a right over other persons to any assisted living or skilled nursing beds that are available at the community.

(7) "Processing fee" means a payment to cover administrative costs of processing the application of a depositor or prospective resident.

(8) "Promise to provide one or more elements of care" means any expressed or implied representation that one or more elements of care will be provided or will be available, such as by preferred access.

(9) "Proposes" means a representation that an applicant or provider will or intends to make a future promise to provide care, including a promise that is subject to a condition, such as the construction of a continuing care retirement community or the acquisition of a certificate of authority.

(10) "Provider" means an entity that provides continuing care, makes a continuing care promise, or proposes to promise to provide continuing care. "Provider" also includes any entity that controls an entity that provides continuing care, makes a continuing care promise, or proposes to promise to provide continuing care. The department shall determine whether an entity controls another entity for purposes of this article. No homeowner's association, cooperative, or condominium association may be a provider.

(11) "Provisional certificate of authority" means the certificate issued by the department, properly executed and bearing the State Seal, under Section 1786. A provisional certificate of authority shall be limited to the specific continuing care retirement community and number of units identified in the applicant's application.

(q) (reserved)

(r) (1) "Refund reserve" means the reserve a provider is required to maintain, as provided in Section 1792.6.

(2) "Refundable contract" means a continuing care contract that includes a promise, expressed or implied, by the provider to pay an entrance fee refund or to repurchase the transferor's unit, membership, stock, or other interest in the continuing care retirement community when the promise to refund some or all of the initial entrance fee extends beyond the resident's sixth year of residency. Providers that enter into refundable contracts shall be subject to the refund reserve requirements of Section 1792.6.

(3) "Repayable contract" means a continuing care contract that includes a promise to repay all or a portion of an entrance fee that is conditioned upon reoccupancy or resale of the unit previously occupied by the resident. A repayable contract shall not be considered a refundable contract for purposes of the refund reserve requirements of

Section 1792.6, provided that this conditional promise of repayment is not referred to by the applicant or provider as a "refund." A provider may repay all or a portion of an entrance fee that is conditioned upon resale of the unit before the resale of the unit. The repayment of an entrance fee before the resale of the unit shall not cause any other entrance fee to be subject to the refund reserve requirements of Section 1792.6, provided that the provider does not promise, at the time of contracting or thereafter, to make this type of early repayment, represent that the provider intends to make this type of early repayment, or indicate that the provider has a practice of making this type of early repayment.

(4) "Resale fee" means a levy by the provider against the proceeds from the sale of a transferor's equity interest.

(5) "Reservation fee" refers to consideration collected by an entity that has made a continuing care promise or is proposing to make this promise and has complied with Section 1771.4.

(6) "Resident" means a person who enters into a continuing care contract with a provider, or who is designated in a continuing care contract to be a person being provided or to be provided services, including care, board, or lodging.

(7) "Residential care facility for the elderly" means a housing arrangement as defined by Section 1569.2.

(8) "Residential living unit" means a living unit in a continuing care retirement community that is not used exclusively for assisted living services or nursing services.

(9) "Residential temporary relocation" means the relocation of one or more residents, except in the case of a natural disaster that is out of the provider's control, from one or more residential living units, assisted living units, skilled nursing units, or a wing, floor, or entire continuing care retirement community building, due to a change of use or major repairs or renovations. A residential temporary relocation shall mean a relocation pursuant to this subdivision that lasts for a period of at least 9 months but that does not exceed 18 months without the written agreement of the resident.

(s) (reserved)

(t) (1) "Termination" means the ending of a continuing care contract as provided for in the terms of the continuing care contract.

(2) "Transfer trauma" means death, depression, or regressive behavior, that is caused by the abrupt and involuntary transfer of an elderly resident from one home to another and results from a loss of familiar physical environment, loss of well-known neighbors, attendants, nurses and medical personnel, the stress of an abrupt break in the small routines of daily life, or the loss of visits from friends and relatives who may be unable to reach the new facility.

(3) "Transferor" means a person who transfers, or promises to transfer, consideration in exchange for care and related services under a continuing care contract or proposed continuing care contract, for the benefit of another. A transferor shall have the same rights to cancel and obtain a refund as the depositor under the deposit agreement or the resident under a continuing care contract.

(Amended by Stats. 2016, Ch. 112, Sec. 1. (SB 939) Effective January 1, 2017.)

1771.2.

(a) An entity shall apply for and hold a currently valid permit to accept deposits before it may enter into a deposit agreement or accept a deposit.

(b) A provider shall hold a currently valid provisional certificate of authority or certificate of authority before it may enter into a continuing care contract.

(c) Before a provider subcontracts or assigns to another entity the responsibility to provide continuing care, that other entity shall have a current and valid certificate of authority. A provider holding a certificate of authority may contract for the provision of a particular aspect of continuing care, such as medical care, with another entity that does not possess a certificate of authority, if that other entity is appropriately licensed under laws of this state to provide that care, and the provider has not paid in advance for more than one year for that care.

(d) If an entity enters into an agreement to provide care for life or for more than one year to a person under 60 years of age in return for consideration, and the agreement includes the provision of services to that person after age 60, when the person turns 60 years of age, the promising entity shall comply with all the requirements imposed by this chapter.

(Amended by Stats. 2000, Ch. 820, Sec. 3. Effective January 1, 2001.)

1771.3.

(a) This chapter shall not apply to either of the following:

(1) An arrangement for the care of a person by a relative.

(2) An arrangement for the care of a person or persons from only one family by a friend.

(b) This chapter shall not apply to any admission or residence agreements offered by residential communities for the elderly or residential care facilities for the elderly that promise residents preferred access to assisted living services or nursing care, when each of the following conditions is satisfied:

(1) Residents pay on a fee-for-service basis for available assisted living services and nursing care.

(2) The fees paid for available assisted living services and nursing care are the same for residents who have previously occupied a residential living unit as for residents who have not previously occupied a residential living unit.

(3) No entrance fee or prepayment for future care or access, other than monthly care fees, is paid by, or charged to, any resident at the community or facility. For purposes of this paragraph, the term entrance fee shall not include initial, deferred, or amortized payments that cumulatively do not exceed seven thousand five hundred dollars ($7,500).

(4) The provider has not made a continuing care promise of preferred access, other than a promise as described in paragraph (5).

(5) The admission or residence agreement states:

(A) "This agreement does not guarantee that an assisted living or nursing bed will be available for residents, but, instead, promises preferred access to any assisted living or nursing beds that are available at the community or facility. The promise of preferred access gives residents who have previously occupied a residential living unit a right over other persons to such beds."

(B) "A continuing care contract promises that care will be provided to residents for life or for a term in excess of a year. (Name of community or facility) is not a continuing care retirement community and (name of provider) does not hold a certificate of authority to enter into continuing care contracts and is not required to have the same fiscal reserves as a continuing care provider. This agreement is not a continuing care contract and is exempted from the continuing care statutes under subdivision (b) of Section 1771.3 of the Health and Safety Code so long as the conditions set forth in that section are met."

(6) The admission or residence agreement also states the policies and procedures regarding transfers to higher levels of care within the community or facility.

(c) Any entity may apply to the department for a Letter of Exemption stating that the requesting entity satisfies the requirements for an exemption under this section.

(d) The department shall issue a Letter of Exemption to a requesting entity if the department determines either of the following:

(1) The requesting entity satisfies each of the requirements for an exemption under subdivision (b).

(2) The requesting entity satisfies each of the requirements for an exemption under subdivision (b) other than the requirements of paragraph (2) of subdivision (b), and there is no substantial difference between the following:

(A) The fees for available assisted living services and skilled nursing care paid by residents who have previously occupied a residential living unit.

(B) The fees for available assisted living services and skilled nursing care paid by residents who have not previously occupied a residential living unit.

(e) An application to the department for a Letter of Exemption shall include all of the following:

(1) A nonrefundable one thousand dollar ($1,000) application fee.

(2) The name and business address of the applicant.

(3) A description of the services and care available or provided to residents of the community or facility.

(4) Documentation establishing that the requesting entity satisfies the requirements for an exemption under this section, including all of the following:

(A) A schedule showing all fees for assisted living services and skilled nursing care charged to residents at the facility or community who have previously occupied a residential living unit.

(B) A schedule showing all fees for assisted living services and skilled nursing care charged to residents at the facility or community who have not previously occupied a residential living unit.

(C) A description of the differences between the fees for assisted living services and skilled nursing care charged to residents who have not previously occupied a residential unit and the fees for assisted living services and skilled nursing care charged to residents who have previously occupied a residential unit.

(D) A schedule showing any other fees charged to residents of the community or facility.

(E) Copies of all admission and residence agreement forms that have been entered into, or will be entered into, with residents at the community or facility.

(5) Any other information reasonably requested by the department.

(f) If at any time any of the conditions stated in this section are not satisfied, then the requirements of this chapter apply, and the department may impose appropriate remedies and penalties set forth in Article 7 (commencing with Section 1793.5).

(Added by Stats. 2000, Ch. 820, Sec. 4. Effective January 1, 2001.)

1771.4.

An entity may conduct a market test for a proposed continuing care retirement community and collect reservation fees from persons interested in residing at the proposed continuing care retirement community without violating this chapter if all of the following conditions are met:

(a) The entity has filed with the department an application for a permit to accept deposits and a certificate of authority for the project.

(b) The entity's application includes the proposed reservation agreement form and a proposed escrow agreement that provide all of the following:

(1) All fees shall be deposited in escrow.

(2) Refunds shall be made within 10 calendar days after the payer's or proposed resident's request or 10 days after denial of the application for a permit to accept deposits.

(3) All reservation fees shall be converted to deposits within 15 days after a permit to accept deposits is issued.

(c) The department has acknowledged in writing its receipt of the entity's application and its approval of the entity's proposed reservation agreement between the payer and the entity and the escrow agreement between the escrow holder and the entity.

(d) The amount of any reservation fee collected by the entity does not exceed one thousand dollars ($1,000) or 1 percent of the average entrance fee amount as determined from the entity's application, whichever is greater.

(e) The entity places all reservation fees collected by the entity into an escrow under the terms of the approved reservation agreement and escrow agreement.

(Repealed and added by Stats. 2000, Ch. 820, Sec. 6. Effective January 1, 2001.)

1771.5.

The department shall not issue a provisional certificate of authority or a certificate of authority to an applicant until the applicant has obtained licenses for the entire continuing care retirement community, including a license to operate the residential living and assisted living units, pursuant to Chapter 3.2 (commencing with Section 1569) and if a skilled nursing facility is on the premises, a license for the facility pursuant to Chapter 2 (commencing with Section 1250).

(Repealed and added by Stats. 2000, Ch. 820, Sec. 8. Effective January 1, 2001.)

1771.6.

(a) Any entity may apply to the department for a Letter of Nonapplicability for reasons other than those specified in Section 1771.3, which states that the provisions of this chapter do not apply to its community, project, or proposed project.

(b) Applications for Letters of Nonapplicability shall be made to the department in writing and include the following:

(1) A nonrefundable one thousand dollar ($1,000) application fee.

(2) A list of the reasons why the existing or proposed project may not be subject to this chapter.

(3) A copy of the existing or proposed contract between the entity and residents.

(4) Copies of all advertising material.

(5) Any other information reasonably requested by the department.

(c) The department shall do both of the following:

(1) Within seven calendar days, acknowledge receipt of the request for a Letter of Nonapplicability.

(2) Within 30 calendar days after all materials are received, either issue the Letter of Nonapplicability or notify the entity of the department's reasons for denial of the request.

(d) (1) If the department determines that the entity does not qualify for a Letter of Nonapplicability, the entity shall refrain from, or immediately cease, entering into continuing care contracts.

(2) If an entity to which this subdivision applies intends to provide continuing care, an application for a certificate of authority shall be required to be filed with the department pursuant to this chapter.

(3) If an entity to which this subdivision applies does not intend to provide continuing care, it shall alter its plan of operation so that the project is not subject to this chapter. To obtain a Letter of Nonapplicability for the revised project, the entity shall submit a new application and fee.

(Repealed and added by Stats. 2000, Ch. 820, Sec. 10. Effective January 1, 2001.)

1771.7.

(a) No resident of a continuing care retirement community shall be deprived of any civil or legal right, benefit, or privilege guaranteed by law, by the California Constitution, or by the United States Constitution, solely by reason of status as a resident of a community. In addition, because of the discretely different character of residential living unit programs that are a part of continuing care retirement communities, this section shall augment Chapter 3.9 (commencing with Section 1599), Sections 72527 and 87572 of Title 22 of the California Code of Regulations, and other applicable state and federal law and regulations.

(b) A prospective resident shall have the right to visit each of the different care levels and to inspect assisted living and skilled nursing home licensing reports including, but not limited to, the most recent inspection reports and findings of complaint investigations covering a period of no less than two years, prior to signing a continuing care contract.

(c) All residents in residential living units shall have all of the following rights:

(1) To live in an attractive, safe, and well maintained physical environment.

(2) To live in an environment that enhances personal dignity, maintains independence, and encourages self-determination.

(3) To participate in activities that meet individual physical, intellectual, social, and spiritual needs.

(4) To expect effective channels of communication between residents and staff, and between residents and the administration or provider's governing body.

(5) To receive a clear and complete written contract that establishes the mutual rights and obligations of the resident and the continuing care retirement community.

(6) To manage his or her financial affairs.

(7) To be assured that all donations, contributions, gifts, or purchases of provider-sponsored financial products shall be voluntary, and may not be a condition of acceptance or of ongoing eligibility for services.

(8) To maintain and establish ties to the local community.

(9) To organize and participate freely in the operation of independent resident organizations and associations.

(d) A continuing care retirement community shall maintain an environment that enhances the residents' self-determination and independence. The provider shall do both of the following:

(1) Encourage the formation of a resident association by interested residents who may elect a governing body. The provider shall provide space and post notices for meetings, and provide assistance in attending meetings for those residents who request it. In order to promote a free exchange of ideas, at least part of each meeting shall be conducted without the presence of any continuing care retirement community personnel. The association may, among other things, make recommendations to management regarding resident issues that impact the residents' quality of life, quality of care, exercise of rights, safety and quality of the physical environment, concerns about the contract, fiscal matters, or other issues of concern to residents. The management shall respond, in writing, to a written request or concern of the resident association within 20 working days of receiving the written request or concern. Meetings shall be open to all residents to

attend as well as to present issues. Executive sessions of the governing body shall be attended only by the governing body.

(2) Establish policies and procedures that promote the sharing of information, dialogue between residents and management, and access to the provider's governing body. The provider shall biennially conduct a resident satisfaction survey that shall be made available to the resident association or its governing body, or, if neither exists, to a committee of residents at least 14 days prior to the next semiannual meeting of residents and the governing board of the provider required by subdivision (c) of Section 1771.8. A copy of the survey shall be posted in a conspicuous location at each facility.

(e) In addition to any statutory or regulatory bill of rights required to be provided to residents of residential care facilities for the elderly or skilled nursing facilities, the provider shall provide a copy of the bill of rights prescribed by this section to each resident at the time or before the resident signs a continuing care contract, and at any time when the resident is proposed to be moved to a different level of care.

(f) Each continuing care retirement community shall prominently post in areas accessible to the residents and visitors a notice that a copy of rights applicable to residents pursuant to this section and any governing regulation issued by the Continuing Care Contracts Branch of the State Department of Social Services is available upon request from the provider. The notice shall also state that the residents have a right to file a complaint with the Continuing Care Contracts Branch for any violation of those rights and shall contain information explaining how a complaint may be filed, including the telephone number and address of the Continuing Care Contracts Branch.

(g) The resident has the right to freely exercise all rights pursuant to this section, in addition to political rights, without retaliation by the provider.

(h) The department may, upon receiving a complaint of a violation of this section, request a copy of the policies and procedures along with documentation on the conduct and findings of any self-evaluations.

(i) Failure to comply with this section shall be grounds for the imposition of conditions on, suspension of, or revocation of the provisional certificate of authority or certificate of authority pursuant to Section 1793.21.

(j) Failure to comply with this section constitutes a violation of residents' rights. Pursuant to Section 1569.49 of the Health and Safety Code, the department shall impose and collect a civil penalty of not more than one hundred fifty dollars ($150) per violation upon a continuing care retirement community that violates a right guaranteed by this section.

(Amended by Stats. 2011, Ch. 32, Sec. 5. (AB 106) Effective June 29, 2011. Operative January 1, 2012, by Sec. 73 of Stats. 2011, Ch. 32.)

1771.8.

(a) The Legislature finds and declares all of the following:

(1) The residents of continuing care retirement communities have a unique and valuable perspective on the operations of, and services provided in, the community in which they live.

(2) Resident input into decisions made by the provider is an important factor in creating an environment of cooperation, reducing conflict, and ensuring timely response and resolution to issues that may arise.

(3) Continuing care retirement communities are strengthened when residents know that their views are heard and respected.

(b) The Legislature encourages continuing care retirement communities to exceed the minimum resident participation requirements established by this section by, among other things, the following:

(1) Encouraging residents to form a resident association, and assisting the residents, the resident association, and its governing body to keep informed about the operation of the continuing care retirement community.

(2) Encouraging residents of a continuing care retirement community or their elected representatives to select residents to participate as members of the governing body of the provider.

(3) Quickly and fairly resolving any dispute, claim, or grievance arising between a resident and the continuing care retirement community.

(c) The governing body of a provider, or the designated representative of the provider, shall hold, at a minimum, semiannual meetings with the residents of the continuing care retirement community, or the resident association or its governing body, for the purpose of the free discussion of subjects including, but not limited to, income, expenditures, and financial trends and issues as they apply to the continuing care retirement community and proposed changes in policies, programs, and services. This section does not preclude a provider from taking action or making a decision at any time, without regard to the meetings required under this subdivision.

(d) At least 30 days prior to the implementation of an increase in the monthly care fee, the designated representative of the provider shall convene a meeting, to which all residents shall be invited, for the purpose of discussing the reasons for the increase, the basis for determining the amount of the increase, and the data used for calculating the increase. This meeting may coincide with the semiannual meetings required in subdivision (c). At least 14 days prior to the meeting to discuss an increase in the monthly care fee, the provider shall make available to each resident or resident household comparative data showing the budget for the upcoming year, the current year's budget, and actual and projected expenses for the current year, and a copy shall be posted in a conspicuous location at each facility.

(e) The governing body of a provider or the designated representative of the provider shall provide residents with at least 14 days' advance notice of each meeting provided for in subdivisions (c) and (d), and shall permit residents attending the meeting to present issues orally and in writing. The governing body of a provider or the designated representative of the provider shall post the notice of, and the agenda for, the meeting in

434

a conspicuous place in the continuing care retirement community at least 14 days prior to the meeting. The governing body of a provider or the designated representative of the provider shall make available to residents of the continuing care retirement community upon request the agenda and accompanying materials at least seven days prior to the meeting.
(f) A provider shall make available to the resident association or its governing body, or if neither exists, to a committee of residents, a financial statement of activities for that facility comparing actual costs to budgeted costs broken down by expense category, not less than quarterly, with a written explanation of all significant budget variances, and shall consult with the resident association or its governing body, or, if neither exists, with a committee of residents, during the annual budget planning process. The effectiveness of consultations during the annual budget planning process shall be evaluated at a minimum every two years by the continuing care retirement community administration. The evaluation, including any policies adopted relating to cooperation with residents, shall be made available to the resident association or its governing body, or, if neither exists, to a committee of residents at least 14 days prior to the next semiannual meeting of residents and the provider's governing body provided for in subdivision (c), and a copy of the evaluation shall be posted in a conspicuous location at each facility.
(g) A provider shall, within 10 days after the annual report required pursuant to Section 1790 is submitted to the department, provide, at a central and conspicuous location in the community and in a conspicuous location on the provider's Internet Web site, a copy of the annual report, including the multifacility statement of activities and a copy of the annual audited financial statement, but excluding personal confidential information.
(h) A provider shall maintain, as public information, available upon request to residents, prospective residents, and the public, minutes of the meetings held by the provider's governing body and shall retain these records for at least three years from the date the records were filed or issued.
(i) Except as provided in subdivision (s), the governing body of a provider that is not part of a multifacility organization with more than one continuing care retirement community in the state shall accept both of the following:
(1) At least one resident of the continuing care retirement community it operates to participate as a nonvoting resident representative to the provider's governing body.
(2) At least one resident, or two residents for a governing body with 21 or more members, of the continuing care retirement community it operates to participate as a voting member of the provider's governing body. A provider's governing body shall not be required to meet the requirements of this paragraph until there is a vacancy on the provider's governing body or upon the next regularly scheduled selection of the provider's governing body occurring on or after January 1, 2015. A resident member shall perform his or her duties in a manner that complies with the standards of conduct and fiduciary duties of all other members of the governing board.
(j) Except as provided in subdivision (s), in a multifacility organization having more than one continuing care retirement community in the state, the governing body of the multifacility organization shall do both of the following:
(1) Elect either to have at least one nonvoting resident representative to the provider's governing body for each California-based continuing care retirement community the provider operates or to have a resident-elected committee composed of representatives of the residents of each California-based continuing care retirement community that the provider operates select or nominate at least one nonvoting resident representative to the provider's governing body for every three California-based continuing care retirement communities, or fraction thereof, that the provider operates. If a multifacility organization elects to have one representative for every three communities that the provider operates, the provider shall provide to the president of the residents association of each of the communities that do not have a resident representative the same notice of meetings, packets, minutes, and other materials as the resident representative. At the reasonable discretion of the provider, information related to litigation, personnel, competitive advantage, or confidential information that is not appropriate to disclose, may be withheld.
(2) (A) Elect to have at least one resident, or two residents for a governing body with 21 or more members, from any of the continuing care retirement communities it operates to participate as voting members of the provider's governing body. A provider's governing body shall not be required to meet the requirements of this subparagraph until there is a vacancy on the provider's governing body or upon the next regularly scheduled selection of the provider's governing body occurring on or after January 1, 2015. A resident member shall perform his or her duties in a manner that complies with the standards of conduct and fiduciary duties of all other members of the governing board.
(B) If there are communities that do not have a resident from the community as a voting member of the provider's governing body, the provider shall provide to the president of the resident association of each of those communities the same notice of meetings, packets, minutes, and other materials as the resident voting members. At the reasonable discretion of the provider, information related to litigation, personnel, competitive advantage, or confidential information that is not appropriate to disclose may be withheld.
(k) In order to encourage innovative and alternative models of resident involvement, residents selected pursuant to paragraph (1) of subdivision (i) or paragraph (1) of subdivision (j) to participate as a resident representative to the provider's governing body may, at the option of the resident association, be selected in any one of the following ways:
(1) By a majority vote of the resident association of a provider or by a majority vote of a resident-elected committee of residents of a multifacility organization.
(2) If no resident association exists, any resident may organize a meeting of the majority of the residents of the continuing care retirement community to select or nominate residents to represent them on the governing body.
(3) Any other method designated by the resident association.
(l) A resident member of the provider's governing body selected pursuant to paragraph (2) of subdivision (i) or paragraph (2) of subdivision (j) shall be nominated to participate on the provider's governing body by the resident association or, if a resident association does not exist, a committee of residents. The resident association or committee of residents may nominate multiple nominees from which the provider's governing body may approve a resident member. If the governing body disapproves of the resident association's nominations, the resident association or the committee of residents shall nominate additional resident members for the governing body's approval or disapproval until the vacancy is filled.
(m) The resident association, organizing resident, or, in the case of a multifacility organization, the resident-elected committee of residents, shall give residents of the continuing care retirement community at least 30 days' advance notice of the meeting to select a resident representative and resident members of the governing body and shall post the notice in a conspicuous place at the continuing care retirement community.
(n) (1) Except as provided in subdivision (o), resident representatives shall receive the same notice of meetings, packets, minutes, and other materials as members of the provider's governing body and shall be permitted to attend, speak, and participate in all meetings of the governing body.
(2) Resident representatives may share information from meetings with other residents, unless the information is confidential or doing so would violate fiduciary duties to the provider. A resident representative shall be permitted to attend meetings of the governing body committee or committees that review the annual budget of the facility or facilities and recommend increases in monthly care fees. The resident representative shall receive the same notice of meetings, information, packets, minutes, and other materials as committee members, and shall be permitted to attend, speak, and participate in the committee meetings. Resident representatives shall perform their duties in good faith and with such care, including reasonable inquiry, as an ordinarily prudent person in a like position would use under similar circumstances.
(o) Notwithstanding subdivision (n), the provider's governing body may exclude resident representatives from its executive sessions and from receiving meeting materials to be discussed during executive session. However, resident representatives shall be included in executive sessions and shall receive all meeting materials to be discussed during executive sessions related to discussions of the annual budgets, increases in monthly care fees, indebtedness, and expansion of new and existing continuing care retirement communities.
(p) The provider shall pay all reasonable travel costs for resident representatives and resident members of the governing body.
(q) The provider shall disclose in writing the extent of resident involvement with the governing body to prospective residents.
(r) A provider is not prohibited from exceeding the minimum resident participation requirements of this section by, for example, having more resident meetings, more resident representatives or resident members of the governing body to the provider's governing body than required, or by having one or more residents on the provider's governing body who are selected with the active involvement of residents.
(s) (1) If a provider having at least one continuing care retirement community in the state does not have a governing body within the state, the provider shall, in lieu of appointing a voting member pursuant to subdivision (i) or (j), appoint a select committee of its governing body members to meet pursuant to paragraph (6) of subdivision (a) of Section 307 of the Corporations Code, or in a location that has been designated in the notice of the meeting, with the resident association or a resident-elected committee of residents no less frequently than a reasonable period prior to any regularly scheduled meeting of the governing body at each of its facilities in the state to address concerns of the residents and to ensure that the opinions of the residents are relayed to all governing body members of the provider.
(2) (A) For a provider that is a sole proprietorship, general partnership, limited partnership, limited liability company, or a closely held corporation, the provider may, in lieu of appointing a voting member pursuant to paragraph (2) of subdivision (i) or paragraph (2) of subdivision (j), appoint a select committee of its members to, or, if it is a sole proprietorship, the sole proprietor shall, meet in a location that has been designated in the notice of the meeting with the resident association or a resident-elected committee of residents at each of its facilities semiannually and at least 60 days prior to any financial or administrative changes, including, but not limited to, any proposed increase in monthly fees, indebtedness of the provider, expansion or contraction of the community facility, or other changes that would result in a budget variance, or any policies, programs, or services that would materially change the operation or environment of the community, to address concerns of the residents and to ensure that the opinions of the residents are relayed to all members of the provider.
(B) If any member of a limited liability company is a corporation, a nonvoting resident representative elected pursuant to paragraph (1) of subdivision (i) or paragraph (1) of subdivision (j) shall be invited to the meetings of the governing body of that corporation that address any of the proposed changes specified in subparagraph (A) and shall be permitted to address those proposed changes. The governing body of the corporation shall provide the nonvoting resident representative with at least 30 days' advance notice of the meeting. If more than one member of the limited liability company is a corporation, only the corporation with the largest interest in the limited liability company shall comply with this subparagraph.

(Amended by Stats. 2014, Ch. 699, Sec. 1. (AB 1751) Effective January 1, 2015.)
1771.10.
Each provider shall adopt a comprehensive disaster preparedness plan specifying policies for evacuation, relocation, continued services, reconstruction, organizational structure, insurance coverage, resident education, and plant replacement.
(Added by renumbering Section 1771.11 by Stats. 2000, Ch. 820, Sec. 15. Effective January 1, 2001.)
1772.
(a) No report, circular, public announcement, certificate, financial statement, or any other printed matter or advertising material, or oral representation, that states or implies that an entity sponsors, guarantees, or assures the performance of any continuing care contract, shall be published or presented to any prospective resident unless both of the following have been met:
(1) Paragraph (5) of subdivision (a) of Section 1788 applies and the requirements of that paragraph have been satisfied.
(2) The entity files with the department a duly authorized and executed written declaration that it accepts full financial responsibility for each continuing care contract. The filing entity shall be subject to the application requirements set forth in Article 2 (commencing with Section 1779), shall be a coobligor for the subject contracts, and shall be a coprovider on the applicable provisional certificate of authority and certificate of authority.
(b) Implied sponsorship includes the use of the entity's name for the purpose of implying that the entity's reputation may be relied upon to ensure the performance of the continuing care contract.
(c) Any implication that the entity may be financially responsible for these contracts may be rebutted by a conspicuous statement, in all continuing care contracts and marketing materials, that clearly discloses to prospective residents and all transferors that the entity is not financially responsible.
(d) On written appeal to the department, and for good cause shown, the department may, in its discretion, allow an affinity group exemption from this section. If an exemption is granted, every continuing care contract shall include a conspicuous statement which clearly discloses to prospective residents and all transferors that the affinity group entity is not financially responsible.
(e) If the name of an entity, including, but not limited to, a religion, is used in connection with the development, marketing, or continued operation of a continuing care retirement community, but that entity does not actually own, control, manage, or otherwise operate the continuing care retirement community, the provider shall clearly disclose the absence of that affiliation, involvement, or association with the continuing care retirement community in the continuing care contract.
(Amended by Stats. 2000, Ch. 820, Sec. 16. Effective January 1, 2001.)
1772.2.
(a) All printed advertising materials, including brochures, circulars, public announcements, and similar publications pertaining to continuing care or a continuing care retirement community shall specify the number on the provider's provisional certificate of authority or certificate of authority.
(b) If the provider has not been issued a certificate of authority, all advertising materials shall specify both of the following:
(1) Whether an application has been filed.
(2) If applicable, that a permit to accept deposits or a provisional certificate of authority has been issued.
(Added by Stats. 2000, Ch. 820, Sec. 17. Effective January 1, 2001.)
1773.
(a) A provisional certificate of authority or certificate of authority may not be sold, transferred, or exchanged in any manner. A provider may not sell or transfer ownership of the continuing care retirement community without the approval of the department. Any violation of this section shall cause the applicable provisional certificate of authority or certificate of authority to be forfeited by operation of law pursuant to subdivision (c) of Section 1793.7.
(b) A provider may not enter into a contract with a third party for overall management of the continuing care retirement community without the approval of the department. The department shall review the transaction for consistency with this chapter.
(c) Any violation of this section shall be grounds for revocation for the provider's provisional certificate of authority or certificate of authority under Section 1793.21.
(Amended by Stats. 2000, Ch. 820, Sec. 18. Effective January 1, 2001.)
1774.
No arrangement allowed by a permit to accept deposits, a provisional certificate or authority, or a certificate of authority issued by the department under this chapter may be deemed a security for any purpose.
(Amended by Stats. 2000, Ch. 820, Sec. 19. Effective January 1, 2001.)
1775.
(a) To the extent that this chapter, as interpreted by the department, conflicts with the statutes, regulations, or interpretations governing the sale or hire of real property, this chapter shall prevail.
(b) Notwithstanding any law or regulation to the contrary, a provider for a continuing care retirement community may restrict or abridge the right of any resident, whether or not the resident owns an equity interest, to sell, lease, encumber, or otherwise convey any interest in the resident's unit, and may require that the resident only sell, lease, or otherwise convey the interest to persons approved by the provider. Provider approval may be based on factors which include, but are not limited to, age, health status,

insurance risk, financial status, or burden on the provider's personnel, resources, or physical facility. The provider shall record any restrictions on a real property interest.
(c) To the extent that this chapter conflicts with Sections 51.2 and 51.3 of the Civil Code, this chapter shall have precedence. A continuing care provider, at its discretion, may limit entrance based on age.
(d) This chapter imposes minimum requirements upon any entity promising to provide, proposing to promise to provide, or providing continuing care.
(e) This chapter shall be liberally construed for the protection of persons attempting to obtain or receiving continuing care.
(f) A resident's entry into a continuing care contract described in this chapter shall be presumptive evidence of the resident's intent not to return to his or her prior residence to live for purposes of qualifying for Medi-Cal coverage under Sections 14000 et seq. of the Welfare and Institutions Code and Section 50425 of Title 22 of the California Code of Regulations.
(Amended by Stats. 2000, Ch. 820, Sec. 20. Effective January 1, 2001.)
1776.
The department shall adopt, amend, or repeal, in accordance with Chapter 3.5 (commencing with Section 11340) of Part 1 of Division 3 of Title 2 of the Government Code, reasonable regulations as may be necessary or proper to carry out the purposes and intent of this chapter and to protect the rights of the elderly.
(Repealed and added by Stats. 1990, Ch. 875, Sec. 2.)
1776.2.
The department may, by any duly authorized representative, inspect and examine any continuing care retirement community, including the books and records thereof, or the performance of any service required by the continuing care contracts.
(Amended by Stats. 1995, Ch. 920, Sec. 10. Effective January 1, 1996.)
1776.3.
(a) The Continuing Care Contracts Branch of the department shall enter and review each continuing care retirement community in the state at least once every three years to augment the branch's assessment of the provider's financial soundness.
(b) During its facility visits, the branch shall consider the condition of the facility, whether the facility is operating in compliance with applicable state law, and whether the provider is performing the services it has specified in its continuing care contracts.
(c) The branch shall issue guidelines that require each provider to adopt a comprehensive disaster preparedness plan, update that plan at least every three years, submit a copy to the department, and make copies available to residents in a prominent location in each continuing care retirement community facility.
(d) (1) The branch shall respond within 15 business days to residents' rights, service-related, and financially related complaints by residents, and shall furnish to residents upon request and within 15 business days any document or report filed with the department by a continuing care provider, except documents protected by privacy laws.
(2) The provider shall disclose any citation issued by the department pursuant to Section 1793.6 in its disclosure statement to residents as updated annually, and shall post a notice of the citation in a conspicuous location in the facility. The notice shall include a statement indicating that residents may obtain additional information regarding the citation from the provider and the department.
(Amended by Stats. 2011, Ch. 32, Sec. 7. (AB 106) Effective June 29, 2011. Operative January 1, 2012, by Sec. 73 of Stats. 2011, Ch. 32.)
1776.4.
The department may contract with any entity to provide consultation services. In providing the services, the entity shall conform to the requirements of this chapter and to the rules, regulations, and standards of the department. The department shall reimburse an entity for services performed pursuant to this section.
(Added by Stats. 1990, Ch. 875, Sec. 2.)
1776.6.
(a) Pursuant to the California Public Records Act (Chapter 3.5 (commencing with Section 6250) of Division 7 of Title 1 of the Government Code) and the Information Practices Act of 1977 (Chapter 1 (commencing with Section 1798) of Title 1.8 of Part 4 of Division 3 of the Civil Code), the following documents are public information and shall be provided by the department upon request: audited financial statements, annual reports and accompanying documents, compliance or noncompliance with reserve requirements, whether an application for a permit to accept deposits and certificate of authority has been filed, whether a permit or certificate has been granted or denied, and the type of care offered by the provider.
(b) The department shall regard resident data used in the calculation of reserves as confidential.
(Amended by Stats. 2000, Ch. 820, Sec. 21. Effective January 1, 2001.)
1778.
(a) There is hereby created in the State Treasury a fund which shall be known as the Continuing Care Provider Fee Fund. The fund shall consist of fees received by the department pursuant to this chapter. Notwithstanding Section 13340 of the Government Code, the Continuing Care Provider Fee Fund is hereby continuously appropriated to the department, without regard to fiscal years.
(b) Use of the funds appropriated pursuant to this section shall include funding of the following:
(1) Program personnel salary costs, to include but not be limited to: Continuing Care Contracts Program Manager at a level consistent with other management classifications that direct a regulatory program with statewide impact requiring skills and knowledge at the highest level with responsibility for work of the most critical or sensitive nature as it relates to the department's mission, including protecting vulnerable elderly persons,

supervising technical staff with oversight of highly complex operations and responsibility for policy and program evaluation and recommendations; full-time legal counsel with a working knowledge of all laws relating to the regulation of continuing care retirement communities and residential care facilities for the elderly; financial analyst with working knowledge of generally accepted accounting principles and auditing standards; and other appropriate analytical and technical support positions.

(2) Contracts with technically qualified persons, to include but not be limited to financial, actuarial, and marketing consultants, as necessary to provide advice regarding the feasibility or viability of continuing care retirement communities and providers.

(3) Other program costs or costs directly supporting program staff.

(4) The department shall use no more than 5 percent of the fees collected pursuant to this section for overhead costs, including facilities operation, and indirect department and division costs.

(c) If the balance in the Continuing Care Provider Fee Fund is projected to exceed five hundred thousand dollars ($500,000) for the next budget year, the department shall adjust the calculations for the application fees under Section 1779.2 and annual fees under Section 1791 to reduce the amounts collected.

(d) The intent of the Legislature is to empower the program administrator with the ability and authorization to obtain necessary resources or staffing to carry out the program objectives.

(Amended by Stats. 1995, Ch. 920, Sec. 14. Effective January 1, 1996.)

ARTICLE 2. Application [1779 - 1779.10]

(Article 2 added by Stats. 1990, Ch. 875, Sec. 2.)

1779.

(a) An entity shall file an application for a permit to accept deposits and for a certificate of authority with the department, as set forth in this chapter, before doing any of the following:

(1) Accepting any deposit, reservation fee, or any other payment that is related to a promise or proposal to promise to provide continuing care.

(2) Entering into any reservation agreement, deposit agreement, or continuing care contract.

(3) Commencing construction of a prospective continuing care retirement community. If the project is to be constructed in phases, the application shall include all planned phases.

(4) Expanding an existing continuing care retirement community whether by converting existing buildings or by new construction.

(5) Converting an existing structure to a continuing care retirement community.

(6) Recommencing marketing on a planned continuing care retirement community when the applicant has previously forfeited a permit to accept deposits pursuant to Section 1703.7.

(7) Executing new continuing care contracts after a provisional certificate of authority or certificate of authority has been inactivated, revoked, surrendered, or forfeited.

(8) Closing the sale or transfer of a continuing care retirement community or assuming responsibility for continuing care contracts.

(b) For purposes of paragraph (4) of subdivision (a), an expansion of a continuing care retirement community shall be deemed to occur when there is an increase in the capacity stated on the residential care facility for the elderly license issued to the continuing care retirement community, an increase in the number of units at the continuing care retirement community, an increase in the number of skilled nursing beds, or additions to or replacement of existing continuing care retirement community structures that may affect obligations to current residents.

(c) Any provider that alters, or proposes to alter, its organization, including by means of a change in the type of entity it is, separation from another entity, merger, affiliation, spinoff, or sale, shall file a new application and obtain a new certificate of authority before the new entity may enter into any new continuing care contracts.

(d) A new application shall not be required for an entity name change if there is no change in the entity structure or management. If the provider undergoes a name change, the provider shall notify the department in writing of the name change and shall return the previously issued certificate of authority for reissuance under the new name.

(e) Within 10 days of submitting an application for a certificate of authority pursuant to paragraph (3), (4), (7), or (8) of subdivision (a), the provider shall notify residents of the provider's existing community or communities of its application. The provider shall notify its resident associations of any filing with the department to obtain new financing, additional financing for a continuing care retirement community, the sale or transfer of a continuing care retirement community, any change in structure, and of any applications to the department for any expansion of a continuing care retirement community. A summary of the plans and application shall be posted in a prominent location in the continuing care retirement community so as to be accessible to all residents and the general public, indicating in the summary where the full plans and application may be inspected in the continuing care retirement community.

(f) When the department determines that it has sufficient information on the provider or determines that the provisions do not apply and the protections provided by this article are not compromised, the department may eliminate all or portions of the application contents required under Section 1779.4 for applications filed pursuant to paragraphs (4), (5), (6), (7), and (8) of subdivision (a) or pursuant to subdivision (c).

(Amended by Stats. 2000, Ch. 820, Sec. 25. Effective January 1, 2001.)

1779.2.

(a) Any entity filing an application for a permit to accept deposits and a certificate of authority shall pay an application fee.

(b) The applicant shall pay 80 percent of the application fee for all planned phases at the time the applicant submits its application. The 80 percent payment shall be made by check payable to the Continuing Care Provider Fee Fund. The department shall not process the application until it has received this fee.

(c) For new continuing care retirement communities or for the sale or transfer of existing continuing care retirement communities, the application fee shall be calculated as one-tenth of 1 percent of the purchase price of the continuing care retirement community, or the estimated construction cost, including the purchase price of the land or the present value of any long-term lease and all items listed in subparagraph (D) of paragraph (2) of subdivision (y) of Section 1779.4.

(d) For existing continuing care retirement communities that are proposing new phases, remodeling or an expansion, the application fee shall be calculated as one-tenth of 1 percent of the cost of the addition, annexation, or renovation, including the value of the land and improvements and all items listed in subparagraph (D) of paragraph (2) of subdivision (y) of Section 1779.4.

(e) For existing facilities converting to continuing care retirement communities, the application fee shall be calculated as one-tenth of 1 percent of the current appraised value of the facility, including the land, or present value of any long-term lease.

(f) For organizational changes, the application fee shall be determined by the department based on the time and resources it considers reasonably necessary to process the application, including any consultant fees. The minimum application fee for those applications shall be two thousand dollars ($2,000).

(g) The applicant shall pay the remainder of the application fee before the provisional certificate of authority is issued, or in the case of expansions or remodeling, before final approval of the project is granted. The applicant shall make this payment by check payable to the Continuing Care Provider Fee Fund.

(Amended by Stats. 2000, Ch. 820, Sec. 26. Effective January 1, 2001.)

1779.4.

An application shall contain all of the following:

(a) A statement signed by the applicant under penalty of perjury certifying that to the best of the applicant's knowledge and belief, the items submitted in the application are correct. If the applicant is a corporation, the chief executive officer shall sign the statement. If there are multiple applicants, these requirements shall apply to each applicant.

(b) The name and business address of the applicant.

(c) An itemization of the total fee calculation, including sources of figures used, and a check in the amount of 80 percent of the total application fee.

(d) The name, address, and a description of the real property of the continuing care retirement community.

(e) An estimate of the number of continuing care residents at the continuing care retirement community.

(f) A description of the proposed continuing care retirement community, including the services and care to be provided to residents or available for residents.

(g) A statement indicating whether the application is for a certificate of authority to enter into continuing care or life care contracts.

(h) A license to operate the proposed continuing care retirement community as a residential care facility for the elderly or documentation establishing that the applicant has received a preliminary approval for licensure from the department's Community Care Licensing Division.

(i) A license to operate the proposed skilled nursing facility or evidence that an application has been filed with the Licensing and Certification Division of the State Department of Health Services, if applicable.

(j) A statement disclosing any revocation or other disciplinary action taken, or in the process of being taken, against a license, permit, or certificate held or previously held by the applicant.

(k) A description of any matter in which any interested party involved with the proposed continuing care retirement community has been convicted of a felony or pleaded nolo contendere to a felony charge, or been held liable or enjoined in a civil action by final judgment, if the felony or civil action involved fraud, embezzlement, fraudulent conversion, or the misappropriation of property. For the purpose of this subdivision, "interested party" includes any representative of the developer of the proposed continuing care retirement community or the applicant, including all general partners, executive officers, or chief operating officers and board members of corporations; and managing members and managers of limited liability companies for each entity; who has significant decisionmaking authority with respect to the proposed continuing care retirement community.

(l) If the applicant is an entity other than an individual, the following information shall also be submitted:

(1) A statement identifying the type of legal entity and listing the interest and extent of the interest of each principal in the legal entity. For the purposes of this paragraph, "principal" means any person or entity having a financial interest in the legal entity of 10 percent or more. When the application is submitted in the name of a corporation, the parent, sole corporate shareholder, or sole corporate member who controls the operation of the continuing care retirement community shall be listed as an applicant. When multiple corporate applicants exist, they shall be listed jointly by corporate name on the application, and the certificate of authority shall be issued in the joint names of the corporations. When the application is submitted by a partnership, all general partners shall be named as coapplicants and the department shall name them as coproviders on any certificate of authority it issues.

(2) The names of the members of the provider's governing body.

(3) A statement indicating whether the applicant was or is affiliated with a religious, charitable, nonprofit or for-profit organization, and the extent of any affiliation. The statement shall also include the extent, if any, to which the affiliate organization will be responsible for the financial and contract obligations of the applicant and shall be signed by a responsible officer of the affiliate organization.

(4) A statement identifying any parent entity or other affiliate entity, the primary activities of each entity identified, the relationship of each entity to the applicant, and the interest in the applicant held by each entity.

(5) Copies of all contracts, management agreements, or other documents setting forth the relationships with each of the other entities.

(6) A statement indicating whether the applicant, a principal, a parent entity, affiliate entity, subsidiary entity, any responsible employee, manager, or board member, or anyone who profits from the continuing care retirement community has had applied against it any injunctive or restrictive order of a court of record, or any suspension or revocation of any state or federal license, permit, or certificate, arising out of or relating to business activity of health or nonmedical care, including, but not limited to, actions affecting a license to operate a health care institution, nursing home, intermediate care facility, hospital, home health agency, residential care facility for the elderly, community care facility, or child day care facility.

(m) A description of the business experience of the applicants in the operation or management of similar facilities.

(n) A copy of any advertising material regarding the proposed continuing care retirement community prepared for distribution or publication.

(o) Evidence of the bonds required by Section 1789.8.

(p) A copy of any proposed reservation agreement.

(q) A copy of the proposed deposit agreements.

(r) The name of the proposed escrow agent and depository.

(s) Any copies of reservation and deposit escrow account agreements.

(t) A copy of any proposed continuing care contracts.

(u) A statement of any monthly care fees to be paid by residents, the components and services considered in determining the fees, and the manner by which the provider may adjust these fees in the future. If the continuing care retirement community is already in operation, or if the provider operates one or more similar continuing care retirement communities within this state, the statement shall include tables showing the frequency and each percentage increase in monthly care rates at each continuing care retirement community for the previous five years, or any shorter period for which each continuing care retirement community may have been operated by the provider or his or her predecessor in interest.

(v) A statement of the actions that have been, or will be, taken by the applicant to fund reserves as required by Section 1792 or 1792.6 and to otherwise ensure that the applicant will have adequate finances to fully perform continuing care contract obligations. The statement shall describe actions such as establishing restricted accounts, sinking funds, trust accounts, or additional reserves. If the applicant is purchasing an existing continuing care retirement community from a selling provider, the applicant shall provide an actuarial report to determine the liabilities of existing continuing care contracts and demonstrate the applicant's ability to fund those obligations.

(w) A copy of audited financial statements for the three most recent fiscal years of the applicant or any shorter period of time the applicant has been in existence, prepared in accordance with generally accepted accounting principles and accompanied by an independent auditor's report from a reputable firm of certified public accountants. The audited financial statements shall be accompanied by a statement signed and dated by both the chief financial officer and chief executive officer for the applicant or, if applicable, by each general partner, or each managing member and manager, stating that the financial statements are complete, true, and correct in all material matters to the best of their knowledge.

(x) Unaudited interim financial statements shall be included if the applicant's fiscal year ended more than 90 days prior to the date of filing. The statements shall be either quarterly or monthly, and prepared on the same basis as the annual audited financial statements or any other basis acceptable to the department.

(y) A financial study and a marketing study that reasonably project the feasibility of the proposed continuing care retirement community and are prepared by a firm or firms acceptable to the department. These studies shall address and evaluate, at a minimum, all of the following items:

(1) The applicant and its prior experience, qualifications, and management, including a detailed description of the applicant's proposed continuing care retirement community, its service package, fee structure, and anticipated opening date.

(2) The construction plans, construction financing, and permanent financing for the proposed continuing care retirement community, including a description of the anticipated source, cost, terms, and use of all funds to be used in the land acquisition, construction, and operation of the continuing care retirement community. This proposal shall include, at a minimum, all of the following:

(A) A description of all debt to be incurred by the applicant for the continuing care retirement community, including the anticipated terms and costs of the financing. The applicant's outstanding indebtedness related to the continuing care retirement community may not, at any time, exceed the appraised value of the continuing care retirement community.

(B) A description of the source and amount of the equity to be contributed by the applicant.

(C) A description of the source and amount of all other funds, including entrance fees, that will be necessary to complete and operate the continuing care retirement community.

(D) A statement itemizing all estimated project costs, including the real property costs and the cost of acquiring or designing and constructing the continuing care retirement community, and all other similar costs that the provider expects to incur prior to the commencement of operation. This itemization shall identify all costs related to the continuing care retirement community or project, including financing expenses, legal expenses, occupancy development costs, marketing costs, and furniture and equipment.

(E) A description of the interest expense, insurance premiums, and property taxes that will be incurred prior to opening.

(F) An estimate of any proposed continuing care retirement community reserves required for items such as debt service, insurance premiums, and operations.

(G) An estimate of the amount of funds, if any, that will be necessary to fund startup losses, fund statutory and refundable contract reserves, and to otherwise provide additional financial resources in an amount sufficient to ensure full performance by the provider of its continuing care contract obligations.

(3) An analysis of the potential market for the applicant's continuing care retirement community, addressing such items as:

(A) A description of the service area, including its demographic, economic, and growth characteristics.

(B) A forecast of the market penetration the continuing care retirement community will achieve based on the proposed fee structure.

(C) Existing and planned competition in and about the primary service area.

(4) A detailed description of the sales and marketing plan, including all of the following:

(A) Marketing projections, anticipated sales, and cancellation rates.

(B) Month-by-month forecast of unit sales through sellout.

(C) A description of the marketing methods, staffing, and advertising media to be used by the applicant.

(D) An estimate of the total entrance fees to be received from residents prior to opening the continuing care retirement community.

(5) Projected move-in rates, deposit collections, and resident profiles, including couple mix by unit type, age distribution, care and nursing unit utilization, and unit turnover or resale rates.

(6) A description or analysis of development-period costs and revenues throughout the development of the proposed continuing care retirement community.

(z) Projected annual financial statements for the period commencing on the first day of the applicant's current fiscal year through at least the fifth year of operation.

(1) Projected annual financial statements shall be prepared on an accrual basis using the same accounting principles and procedures as the audited financial statements furnished pursuant to subdivision (x).

(2) Separate projected annual cash-flow statements shall be provided. These statements shall show projected annual cash-flows for the duration of any debt associated with the continuing care retirement community. If the continuing care retirement community property is leased, the cash-flow statement shall demonstrate the feasibility of closing the continuing care retirement community at the end of the lease period.

(A) The projected annual cash-flow statements shall be submitted using prevailing rates of interest, and assume no increase of revenues and expenses due to inflation.

(B) The projected annual cash-flow statements shall include all of the following:

(i) A detailed description and a full explanation of all assumptions used in preparing the projections, accompanied by supporting supplementary schedules and calculations, all to be consistent with the financial study and marketing study furnished pursuant to subdivision (y). The department may require such other supplementary schedules, calculations, or projections as it determines necessary for an adequate application.

(ii) Cash-flow from monthly operations showing projected revenues for monthly fees received from continuing care contracts, medical unit fees if applicable, other periodic fees, gifts and bequests used in operations, and any other projected source of revenue from operations less operating expenses.

(iii) Contractual cash-flow from activities showing projected revenues from presales, deposit receipts, entrance fees, and all other projected sources of revenue from activities, less contract acquisition, marketing, and advertising expenditures.

(iv) Cash-flows from financing activities, including, but not limited to, bond or loan proceeds less bond issue or loan costs and fees, debt service including CAL Mortgage Insurance premiums, trustee fees, principal and interest payments, leases, contracts, rental agreements, or other long-term financing.

(v) Cash-flows from investment activities, including, but not limited to, construction progress payments, architect and engineering services, furnishings, and equipment not included in the construction contract, project development, inspection and testing, marketable securities, investment earnings, and interfund transfers.

(vi) The increase or decrease in cash during the projection period.

(vii) The beginning cash balance, which means cash, marketable securities, reserves, and other funds on hand, available, and committed to the proposed continuing care retirement community.

(viii) The cash balance at the end of the period.

(ix) Details of the components of the ending cash balance shall be provided for each period presented, including, but not limited to, the ending cash balances for bond reserves, other reserve funds, deposit funds, and construction funds balance.

(3) If the cash-flow statements required by paragraph (2) indicate that the provider will have cash balances exceeding two months' projected operating expenses of the continuing care retirement community, a description of the manner in which the cash balances will be invested, and the persons who will be making the investment decisions, shall accompany the application.

(4) The department may require the applicant to furnish additional data regarding its operating budgets, projections of cash required for major repairs and improvements, or any other matter related to its projections including additional information, schedules, and calculations regarding occupancy rate projections, unit types, couple mix, sex and age estimates for resident mix, turnover rates, refund obligations, and sales.

(aa) (1) A declaration by the applicant acknowledging that it is required to execute and record a Notice of Statutory Limitation on Transfer relating to continuing care retirement community property.

(2) The notice required in this subdivision shall be acknowledged and suitable for recordation, describe the property, declare the applicant's intention to use all or part of the described property for the purposes of a continuing care retirement community pursuant to this chapter, and shall be in substantially the following form:

"NOTICE OF STATUTORY LIMITATION ON TRANSFER

Notice is hereby given that the property described below is licensed, or proposed to be licensed, for use as a continuing care retirement community and accordingly, the use and transfer of the property is subject to the conditions and limitations as to use and transfer set forth in Sections 1773 and 1789.4 of the Health and Safety Code. This notice is recorded pursuant to subdivision (aa) of Section 1779.4 of the Health and Safety Code. The real property, which is legally owned by (insert the name of the legal owner) and is the subject of the statutory limitation to which this notice refers, is more particularly described as follows: (Insert the legal description and the assessor's parcel number of the real property to which this notice applies.)"

(3) The Notice of Statutory Limitation on Transfer shall remain in effect until notice of release is given by the department. The department shall execute and record a release of the notice upon proof of complete performance of all obligations to residents.

(4) Unless a Notice of Statutory Limitation on Transfer has been recorded with respect to the land on which the applicant or provider is operating, or intends to operate a continuing care retirement community, prior to the date of execution of any trust deed, mortgage, or any other lien or encumbrance securing or evidencing the payment of money and affecting land on which the applicant or provider intends to operate a continuing care retirement community, the applicant or provider shall give the department advance written notice of the proposed encumbrance. Upon the giving of notice to the department, the applicant or provider shall execute and record the Notice of Statutory Limitation on Transfer in the office of the county recorder in each county in which any portion of the continuing care retirement community is located prior to encumbering the continuing care retirement community property with the proposed encumbrance.

(5) In the event that the applicant or provider and the owner of record are not the same entity on the date on which execution and recordation of the notice is required, the leasehold or other interest in the continuing care retirement community property held by the applicant or provider shall survive in its entirety and without change, any transfer of the continuing care retirement community property by the owner. In addition, the applicant or provider shall record a memorandum of leasehold or other interest in the continuing care retirement community property that includes a provision stating that its interest in the property survives any transfer of the property by the owner. The applicant or provider shall provide a copy of the notice and the memorandum of interest to the owner of record by certified mail and to the department.

(6) The notice shall, and, if applicable, the memorandum of interest shall be indexed by the recorder in the grantor-grantee index to the name of the owner of record and the name of the applicant or provider.

(ab) A statement that the applicant will keep the department informed of any material changes to the proposed continuing care retirement community or its application.

(ac) Any other information that may be required by the department for the proper administration and enforcement of this chapter.

(Amended by Stats. 2000, Ch. 820, Sec. 27. Effective January 1, 2001.)

1779.6.

(a) Within seven calendar days of receipt of an initial application for a permit to accept deposits and a certificate of authority, the department shall acknowledge receipt of the application in writing.

(b) Within 30 calendar days following its receipt of an application, the department shall determine if the application is complete and inform the applicant of its determination. If the department determines that the application is incomplete, its notice to the applicant shall identify the additional forms, documents, information, and other materials required to complete the application. The department shall allow the applicant adequate time to submit the requested information and materials. This review may not determine the adequacy of the materials included in the application.

(c) Within 120 calendar days after the department determines that an application is complete, the department shall review the application for adequacy. An application shall be adequate if it complies with all the requirements imposed by this chapter, and both the financial study and marketing study reasonably project the feasibility of the proposed continuing care retirement community, as well as demonstrate the financial soundness of the applicant. The department shall either approve the application as adequate under this chapter or notify the applicant that its application is inadequate. If the application is inadequate, the department shall identify the deficiencies in the application, provide the appropriate code references, and give the applicant an opportunity to respond.

(d) Within 60 calendar days after receiving any additional information or clarification required from the applicant, the department shall respond to the applicant's submission in writing and state whether each specific deficiency has been addressed sufficiently to make the application adequate. If the department determines that the application is adequate and in compliance with this chapter, the department shall issue the permit to accept deposits. If the department determines that the response is inadequate, it may request additional information or clarification from the applicant pursuant to subdivision (c) or deny the application pursuant to Section 1779.10.

(e) If the applicant does not provide the department with the additional information within 90 days after the department's notice described in subdivision (c), the application may be denied for being inadequate. Any new application shall require an application fee. (Amended by Stats. 2000, Ch. 820, Sec. 28. Effective January 1, 2001.)

1779.7.

(a) Where any portion of the consideration transferred to an applicant as a deposit or to a provider as consideration for a continuing care contract is transferred by a person other than the prospective resident or a resident, that third-party transferor shall have the same cancellation or refund rights as the prospective resident or resident for whose benefit this consideration was transferred.

(b) A transferor shall have the same rights to cancel and obtain a refund as the depositor under the deposit agreement or the resident under a continuing care contract. (Added by Stats. 2000, Ch. 820, Sec. 28.5. Effective January 1, 2001.)

1779.8.

(a) The applicant shall notify the department of material changes in the application information submitted to the department, including the applicant's financial and marketing projections.

(b) An applicant shall provide to the department at least 60 days' advance written notice of any proposal to make any changes in the applicant's corporate name, structure, organization, operation, or financing.

(c) Within 30 calendar days after receiving notice of a change affecting the applicant or the application, the department shall advise the applicant:

(1) Whether additional information is required to process the pending application.

(2) Whether an additional application fee is required.

(3) Whether a new application and application fee must be submitted. The new application fee shall be twice the actual cost of additional review time caused by the change. This additional fee is payable to the department on demand.

(d) The department shall suspend the applicant's application and, if applicable, its permit to accept deposits if the applicant fails to give written notice of changes required by this section. The suspension shall remain in effect until the department has both assessed the potential impact of the changes on the interests of depositors and taken such action as necessary under this chapter to protect these interests.

(Amended by Stats. 2000, Ch. 820, Sec. 29. Effective January 1, 2001.)

1779.10.

(a) The department shall deny an application for a permit to accept deposits and a certificate of authority if the applicant fails to do any of the following:

(1) Pay the application fee as required by Section 1779.2.

(2) Submit all information required by this chapter.

(3) Submit evidence to support a reasonable belief that any interested party of the proposed continuing care retirement community who has committed any offenses listed in subdivision (k) of Section 1779.4 is of such good character as to indicate rehabilitation.

(4) Submit evidence to support a reasonable belief that the applicant is capable of administering the continuing care retirement community in compliance with applicable laws and regulations when an action specified in subdivision (j) or (k) of Section 1779.4 has been taken against the applicant.

(5) Demonstrate the feasibility of the proposed continuing care retirement community.

(6) Comply with residential care facility for the elderly licensing requirements.

(b) If the application is denied, no portion of the paid application fee shall be refundable or refunded.

(c) Immediately upon the denial of an application, the department shall notify the applicant in writing.

(d) The Notice of Denial from the department shall contain all of the following:

(1) A statement that the application is denied.

(2) The grounds for the denial.

(3) A statement informing the applicant that it has the right to appeal.

(4) A statement that the applicant has 30 calendar days from the date that the Notice of Denial was mailed to appeal the denial, and where to send the appeal.

(e) If the applicant appeals the denial, further proceedings shall be conducted in accordance with Chapter 5 (commencing with Section 11500) of Part 1 of Division 3 of Title 2 of the Government Code.

(Amended by Stats. 2000, Ch. 820, Sec. 30. Effective January 1, 2001.)

ARTICLE 3. Deposit Subscription Period [1780 - 1785]

(Article 3 added by Stats. 1990, Ch. 875, Sec. 2.)

1780.

The department shall issue a permit to accept deposits when it has done all of the following:

(a) Determined that the application is adequate.

(b) Determined that the proposed continuing care retirement community financial and marketing studies are acceptable.

(c) Reviewed and approved the deposit agreements.

(d) Reviewed and approved the deposit escrow account agreement.

(Amended by Stats. 2000, Ch. 820, Sec. 31. Effective January 1, 2001.)

1780.2.

(a) A deposit may be paid in one or several payments, at or after the time the parties enter into the deposit agreement.

A deposit shall be paid by cash or cash equivalent, jointly payable to the applicant and the escrow agent or depository. Possession and control of any deposit agreement shall be transferred to the escrow agent at the time the deposit is paid.

(b) A processing fee may be added to the deposit.

(1) The processing fee shall not exceed 1 percent of the amount of the average entrance fee or five hundred dollars ($500), whichever is greater.

(2) A nonrefundable processing fee may be paid directly to the applicant without being placed in the deposit escrow account.

(c) Payments made by a depositor for upgrades or modifications to the living unit shall not be placed in escrow with deposits. The applicant shall provide written refund policies to the depositor before accepting any payments for modifications or upgrades.

(d) The applicant shall furnish to the department within the first 10 days of each calendar month a list of all residents who have made payments for modifications or upgrades, the amounts each resident has paid, the date of each payment, and the unit to be modified or upgraded for each resident.

(e) All payments for modifications or upgrades shall be refunded to the depositor with interest if the applicant does not receive a certificate of authority for the proposed continuing care retirement community or expansion.

(f) The department may record a lien against the continuing care retirement community property, or any portion of the continuing care retirement community property, to secure the applicant's obligations to refund the depositor's payments made for modifications or upgrades. Any lien created under this section shall be to protect depositors and shall be governed by Section 1793.15.

(Amended by Stats. 2000, Ch. 820, Sec. 32. Effective January 1, 2001.)

1780.4.

(a) All deposit agreements between the applicant and the depositor shall be in writing and shall contain all information required by this section.

(b) All deposit agreement forms shall be approved by the department prior to their use.

(c) The requirements of this chapter and Chapter 3.2 (commencing with Section 1569) shall be the bases for approval of the forms by the department.

(d) All text in deposit agreement forms shall be printed in at least 10-point typeface.

(e) The deposit agreement form shall provide all of the following:

(1) An estimated date for commencement of construction of the proposed continuing care retirement community or, if applicable, each phase not to exceed 36 months from the date the permit to accept deposits is issued.

(2) A statement to the effect that the applicant will notify depositors of any material change in the application.

(3) The identity of the specific unit reserved and the total deposit for that unit.

(4) Processing fee terms and conditions, including:

(A) The amount.

(B) A statement explaining the applicant's policy regarding refund or retention of the processing fee in the event of death of the depositor or voluntary cancellation by the depositor.

(C) Notice that the processing fee shall be refunded within 30 days if the applicant does not accept the depositor for residency, or the applicant fails to construct the continuing care retirement community before the estimated date of completion and the department determines that there is no satisfactory cause for the delay.

(5) Requirements for payment of the deposit by the depositor.

(6) A statement informing the depositor that their deposit payments will be converted to an entrance fee payment at the time the continuing care contract is executed.

(7) A statement informing the depositor that deposits shall be refunded within 30 calendar days of the depositor's nonacceptance for residency or notice to the applicant of the death of the depositor.

(8) A statement informing the depositor that all deposits shall be refunded to the depositors if the continuing care retirement community is not constructed by the estimated date of completion and the department determines that there is no satisfactory cause for the delay.

(9) A statement informing the depositor that a refund of the deposit within 10 calendar days of notice of cancellation by the depositor. The deposit agreement shall state that depositors who have deposited more than one thousand dollars ($1,000) or 5 percent of the entrance fee, whichever is greater, and who have been notified that construction of the proposed continuing care retirement community has commenced, will not be entitled to a refund of their deposit until the provisional certificate of authority is issued or after one of the following occurs:

(A) Another depositor has reserved the canceling depositor's specific residential unit and paid the necessary deposit.

(B) The depositor no longer meets financial or health requirements for admission.

(C) The applicant fails to meet the requirements of Section 1786 or 1786.2.

(10) A statement to depositors that specifies when funds may be released from escrow to the applicant and explains that thereafter the depositor's funds will not have escrow protection.

(11) A statement advising the depositor whether interest will be paid to the depositor on deposits placed in the deposit escrow account.

(f) If cash equivalents are to be accepted in lieu of cash, all of the following shall also be included in the deposit agreement:

(1) A statement that cash equivalents that may be accepted as deposits shall be either certificates of deposit or United States securities with maturities of five years or less.

(2) A statement that the instruments will be held by the escrow agent in the form in which they were delivered and assigned by the depositor until they are replaced by cash or converted to cash.

(3) A statement that the depositor will be required to assign the instruments to a neutral third-party escrow agent. If the bank or entity that issued the instruments refuses to allow this assignment, the escrow agent shall not accept the instruments. These instruments shall be reassigned to the depositor if the depositor terminates the deposit agreement before the instruments mature. If the depositor terminates the deposit agreement after the instruments mature, the depositor shall receive a cash refund of the portion of the deposit represented by the matured instruments.

(4) A statement that any amount by which the face value of the deposited instruments exceeds the required deposit shall be deemed part of the deposit and shall be applied against the depositor's obligations under the deposit agreement.

(5) A statement that the instruments shall be converted to, or replaced with, cash prior to the department's authorization for the release of deposits to the applicant. The depositor shall be advised that if the depositor does not substitute cash in the amount equal to the deposit, the applicant may do either of the following:

(A) Direct the escrow agent to sell, redeem, or otherwise convert the instruments to cash and to treat the proceeds in the same manner as it treats cash deposits under the deposit agreement. The costs of any such sale, redemption, or conversion, including, without limitation, transaction fees and any early withdrawal penalties, may be charged to the depositor and paid out of the cash or other instruments received from the depositor in escrow. If there is a shortfall, the depositor may be immediately obligated to pay the shortfall by check jointly payable to the applicant and the escrow agent.

(B) Terminate the deposit agreement. In this event, the escrow agent shall reassign the property to the depositor and refund all cash in escrow within the time periods specified in the deposit agreement.

(g) A statement that deposits will be invested in instruments guaranteed by the federal government or an agency of the federal government, or in investment funds secured by federally guaranteed instruments.

(h) A statement that no funds deposited in a deposit escrow account shall be subject to any liens, judgments, garnishments, or creditor's claims against the applicant, the proposed continuing care retirement community property, or the continuing care retirement community. The deposit agreement shall also provide that deposits may not be subject to any liens or charges by the escrow agent, except that cash equivalent deposits may be subject to transactions fees, commissions, prepayment penalties, and other fees incurred in connection with these deposits.

(i) A schedule of projected monthly care fees estimated to be charged to residents for each of the first five years of the continuing care retirement community's existence shall be attached to each deposit agreement. This schedule shall contain a conspicuous statement in at least 10-point boldface type that the projected fees are an estimate only and may be changed without notice.

(Amended by Stats. 2000, Ch. 820, Sec. 33. Effective January 1, 2001.)

1781.

(a) All deposits, excluding processing fees, shall be placed in an escrow account. All terms governing the deposit escrow account shall be approved in advance by the department.

(b) The deposit escrow account shall be established by an escrow agent and all deposits shall be deposited in a depository located in California and approved by the department. The department's approval of the depository shall be based, in part, upon its ability to ensure the safety of funds and properties entrusted to it and its qualifications to perform the obligations of the depository pursuant to the deposit escrow account agreement and this chapter. The depository may be the same entity as the escrow agent. All deposits shall be kept and maintained in a segregated account without any commingling with other funds, including any funds or accounts owned by the applicant.

(c) If the escrow agent is a title company, it shall meet the following requirements:

(1) A Standard and Poors rating of "A" or better or a comparable rating from a comparable rating service.

(2) Licensure in good standing with the Department of Insurance.

(3) Tangible net equity as required by the Department of Insurance.

(4) Reserves as required by the Department of Insurance.

(d) All deposits shall remain in escrow until the department has authorized release of the deposits, as provided in Section 1783.3.

(e) Deposits shall be invested in instruments guaranteed by the federal government or an agency of the federal government, or in investment funds secured by federally guaranteed instruments.

(f) No funds deposited in a deposit escrow account shall be subject to any liens, judgments, garnishments, or creditor's claims against the applicant or the continuing care retirement community. The deposit agreement shall also provide that deposits may not be subject to any liens or charges by the escrow agent except that cash equivalent deposits may be subject to transaction fees, commissions, prepayment penalties, and other fees incurred in connection with those deposits.

(Amended by Stats. 2000, Ch. 820, Sec. 34. Effective January 1, 2001.)

1781.2.

(a) All deposits shall be delivered to the escrow agent and deposited into the deposit escrow account within five business days after receipt by the applicant. The deposit escrow account shall be accounted for in a separate escrow account.

(b) The applicant shall provide, with all deposits delivered to the escrow holder, a copy of the executed deposit agreement, a copy of the receipt given to the depositor, a summary of all deposits made on that date, and any other materials required by the escrow holder.

(Amended by Stats. 2000, Ch. 820, Sec. 35. Effective January 1, 2001.)

1781.4.

The deposit escrow account agreement between the applicant and the escrow agent shall include all of the following:

(a) The amount of the processing fee.

(b) A provision requiring that all deposits shall be placed into the deposit escrow account upon delivery.

(c) A provision requiring that monthly progress reports be sent by the escrow agent directly to the department, beginning the month after the deposit escrow account is opened and continuing through the month funds are released from escrow. These reports shall be prepared every month that there are any funds in the account and shall show each of the following in separate columns:

(1) The name and address of each depositor or resident.

(2) The designation of the living unit being provided.

(3) Any processing fee which is deposited into escrow.

(4) The total deposit required for the unit.

(5) The total entrance fee for the unit.

(6) Twenty percent of the total entrance fee.

(7) Each deposit payment made by or on behalf of the depositor and any refunds paid to the depositor.

(8) The unpaid balance for each depositor's deposit.

(9) The unpaid balance for each depositor's entrance fee.

(10) The current balance in the deposit escrow account for each depositor and the collective balance.

(11) The dollar amount, type, and maturity date of any cash equivalent paid by each depositor.

(d) A provision for investment of escrow account funds in a manner consistent with Section 1781.

(e) A provision for refunds to depositors in the manner specified by Section 1783.2.

(f) A provision regarding the payment of interest earned on the funds held in escrow in the manner specified in the applicant's deposit agreement.

(g) Release of deposit escrow account funds in the manner specified in Section 1783.3, including to whom payment of interest earned on the funds will be made.

(h) Representations by the escrow agent that it is not, and shall not be during the term of the deposit escrow account, a lender to the applicant or for the proposed continuing care retirement community, or a fiduciary for any lender or bondholder for that continuing care retirement community, unless approved by the department.

(i) If cash equivalents may be accepted as a deposit in lieu of cash, the deposit escrow account agreement shall also include all of the following:

(1) Authorization for the escrow agent to convert instruments to cash when they mature. The escrow agent may notify all financial institutions whose securities are held by the escrow agent that all interest and other payments due upon these instruments shall be paid to the escrow agent. The escrow agent shall collect, hold, invest, and disburse these funds as provided under the escrow agreement.

(2) Authorization for the escrow agent to deliver the instruments in its possession and release funds from escrow according to written directions from the applicant, consistent with the terms provided in the applicant's deposit escrow account agreement. The escrow agent shall distribute cash and other property to an individual depositor only upon either of the following occurrences:

(A) The depositor's written request to receive monthly payments of interest accrued on his or her deposits.

(B) Receipt of notice from the applicant to pay a refund to the depositor.

(3) A provision that the escrow agent shall maintain, at all times, adequate records showing the beneficial ownership of the instruments.

(4) A provision that the escrow agent shall have no responsibility or authority to initiate any transfer of the instruments or conduct any other transaction without specific written instructions from the applicant.

(5) A provision authorizing, instructing, and directing the escrow agent to do all of the following:

(A) Redeem and roll over matured investments into money market accounts or other department approved instruments with the escrow agent or an outside financial institution.

(B) Collect and receive interest, principal, and other things of value in connection with the instruments.

(C) Sign for the depositors any declarations, affidavits, certificates, and other documents that may be required to collect or receive payments or distributions with respect to the instruments.

(Amended by Stats. 2000, Ch. 820, Sec. 36. Effective January 1, 2001.)

1781.6.

All changes to a deposit agreement or deposit escrow account agreement form shall be submitted to, and approved by, the department before use by the applicant.

(Amended by Stats. 2000, Ch. 820, Sec. 37. Effective January 1, 2001.)

1781.8.

(a) Deposits held in escrow shall be placed in an interest bearing account or invested as provided under subdivision (e) of Section 1781.

(b) Interest, income, and other gains derived from deposits held in a deposit escrow account may not be released or distributed from the deposit escrow account except upon written approval of the department.

(c) Approval by the department for the release of earnings generated from funds held in escrow shall be based upon an assessment that funds remaining in the deposit escrow account will be sufficient to pay refunds and any interest promised to all depositors, as well as administrative costs owed to the escrow agent.

(d) When released by the department, interest earned by the funds in the deposit escrow account shall be distributed in accordance with the terms of the deposit agreement.

(Amended by Stats. 2000, Ch. 820, Sec. 38. Effective January 1, 2001.)

1781.10.

No deposit or any other asset held in a deposit escrow account, shall be encumbered or used as collateral for any obligation of the applicant or any other person, unless the applicant obtains prior written approval from the department for the encumbrance or use as collateral. The department shall not approve any encumbrance or use as collateral under this section unless the encumbrance or use as collateral is expressly subordinated to the rights of depositors under this chapter to refunds of their deposits.

(Amended by Stats. 2000, Ch. 820, Sec. 39. Effective January 1, 2001.)

1782.

(a) An applicant shall not begin construction on any phase of a continuing care retirement community without first obtaining a written acknowledgment from the department that all of the following prerequisites have been met:

(1) A completed application has been submitted to the department.

(2) A permit to accept deposits has been issued to the applicant or, in the case of continuing care retirement community renovation projects, the department has issued a written approval of the applicant's application.

(3) For new continuing care retirement communities, or construction projects adding new units to an existing continuing care retirement community, deposits equal to at least 10 percent of each depositor's applicable entrance fee have been placed into escrow for each phase for at least 50 percent of the number of residential living units to be constructed.

(b) Applicants shall notify depositors in writing when construction is commenced.

(c) For purposes of this chapter only, construction shall not include site preparation, demolition, or the construction of model units.

(Amended by Stats. 2006, Ch. 529, Sec. 2. Effective January 1, 2007.)

1783.

(a) (1) An applicant proposing to convert an existing building to continuing care use shall comply with all the application requirements in Section 1779.4 identified by the department as necessary for the department to assess the feasibility of the proposed continuing care retirement community or conversion.

(2) If the proposed continuing care retirement community is already occupied and only a portion of the existing residential units will be converted into continuing care units, the department may modify the presale requirements of paragraph (3) of subdivision (a) of Section 1782 and paragraph (2) of subdivision (a) of Section 1783.3.

(b) Any applicant proposing to convert an existing building into continuing care units shall indicate the portion of the facility to be used for continuing care contract services. The continuing care allocation specified by the applicant shall be reflected in all financial and marketing studies and shall be used to determine the applicant's compliance with the percentage requirements stated in paragraph (3) of subdivision (a) of Section 1782 and paragraph (2) of subdivision (a) of Section 1783.3.

(Amended by Stats. 2000, Ch. 820, Sec. 41. Effective January 1, 2001.)

1783.2.

(a) An escrow agent shall refund to the depositor all amounts required by the depositor's deposit agreement upon receiving written notice from the applicant that a depositor has canceled the deposit agreement. Refunds required by this subdivision shall be paid to the depositor within 10 days after the depositor gives notice of cancellation to the applicant.

(b) Depositors who have deposited more than one thousand dollars ($1,000) or 5 percent of the entrance fee, whichever is greater, and who have been notified that construction of the proposed continuing care retirement community has commenced, shall not be entitled to a refund of their deposit until any of the following occurs:

(1) The continuing care retirement community is opened for operation.

(2) Another depositor has reserved the canceling depositor's specific residential unit and paid the necessary deposit.

(3) The depositor no longer meets financial or health requirements for admission.

(Amended by Stats. 2000, Ch. 820, Sec. 42. Effective January 1, 2001.)

1783.3.

(a) In order to seek a release of escrowed funds, the applicant shall petition in writing to the department and certify to each of the following:

(1) The construction of the proposed continuing care retirement community or phase is at least 50 percent completed.

(2) At least 10 percent of the total of each applicable entrance fee has been received and placed in escrow for at least 60 percent of the total number of residential living units. Any unit for which a refund is pending may not be counted toward that 60-percent requirement.

(3) Deposits made with cash equivalents have been either converted into, or substituted with, cash or held for transfer to the provider. A cash equivalent deposit may be held for transfer to the provider, if all of the following conditions exist:

(A) Conversion of the cash equivalent instrument would result in a penalty or other substantial detriment to the depositor.

(B) The provider and the depositor have a written agreement stating that the cash equivalent will be transferred to the provider, without conversion into cash, when the deposit escrow is released to the provider under this section.

(C) The depositor is credited the amount equal to the value of the cash equivalent.

(4) The applicant's average performance over any six-month period substantially equals or exceeds its financial and marketing projections approved by the department, for that period.

(5) The applicant has received a commitment for any permanent mortgage loan or other long-term financing.

(b) The department shall instruct the escrow agent to release to the applicant all deposits in the deposit escrow account when all of the following requirements have been met:

(1) The department has confirmed the information provided by the applicant pursuant to subdivision (a).

(2) The department has determined that there has been substantial compliance with projected annual financial statements that served as a basis for issuance of the permit to accept deposits.

(3) The applicant has complied with all applicable licensing requirements in a timely manner.

(4) The applicant has obtained a commitment for any permanent mortgage loan or other long-term financing that is satisfactory to the department.

(5) The applicant has complied with any additional reasonable requirements for release of funds placed in the deposit escrow accounts, established by the department under Section 1785.

(c) The escrow agent shall release the funds held in escrow to the applicant only when the department has instructed it to do so in writing.

(d) When an application describes different phases of construction that will be completed and commence operating at different times, the department may apply the 50-percent construction completion requirement to any one or group of phases requested by the applicant, provided the phase or group of phases is shown in the applicant's projections to be economically viable.

(Amended by Stats. 2011, Ch. 32, Sec. 11. (AB 106) Effective June 29, 2011. Operative January 1, 2012, by Sec. 73 of Stats. 2011, Ch. 32.)

1784.

(a) If construction of the proposed continuing care retirement community, or applicable phase, has not commenced within 36 months from the date the permit to accept deposits is issued, an applicant may request an extension of the permit to accept deposits. The request for extension shall be made to the department in writing and shall include the reasons why construction of the proposed continuing care retirement community was not commenced within the required 36-month period. The request for extension shall also state the new estimated date for commencement of construction.

(b) In response to a request for an extension, the department may do one of the following:

(1) If the department determines there is satisfactory cause for the delay in commencement of construction of the proposed continuing care retirement community or applicable phase, the department may extend the permit to accept deposits for up to one year.

(2) If the department determines that there is no satisfactory cause for the delay, the department may instruct the escrow agent to refund to depositors all deposits held in escrow, plus any interest due under the terms of the deposit subscription agreements, and require the applicant to file a new application and application fee. The applicant shall also refund all processing fees paid by the depositors.

(c) Within 10 calendar days the applicant shall notify each depositor of the department's approval or denial of the extension, of any expiration of the permit to accept deposits and of any right to a refund of their deposits.

(Amended by Stats. 2000, Ch. 820, Sec. 44. Effective January 1, 2001.)

1785.

(a) If, at any time prior to issuance of a certificate of authority, the applicant's average performance over any six-month period does not substantially equal or exceed the applicant's projections for that period, the department may take any of the following actions:

(1) Cancel the permit to accept deposits and require that all funds in escrow be returned to depositors immediately.

(2) Increase the required percentages of construction completed, units reserved, or entrance fees to be deposited as required under Sections 1782, 1783.3, 1786, and 1786.2.

(3) Increase the reserve requirements under this chapter.

(b) Prior to taking any actions specified in subdivision (a), the department shall give the applicant an opportunity to submit a feasibility study from a consultant in the area of continuing care, approved by the department, to determine whether in his or her opinion the proposed continuing care retirement community is still viable, and if so, to submit a plan of correction. The department shall determine if the plan is acceptable.

(c) In making its determination, the department shall take into consideration the overall performance of the proposed continuing care retirement community to date.

(d) If deposits have been released from escrow, the department may further require the applicant to reopen the escrow as a condition of receiving any further entrance fee payments from depositors or residents.

(e) The department may require the applicant to notify all depositors and, if applicable, all residents, of any actions required by the department under this section.

(Amended by Stats. 2011, Ch. 32, Sec. 12. (AB 106) Effective June 29, 2011. Operative January 1, 2012, by Sec. 73 of Stats. 2011, Ch. 32.)

ARTICLE 4. Certificate of Authority [1786 - 1786.2]

(Article 4 added by Stats. 1990, Ch. 875, Sec. 2.)

1786.

(a) The department shall issue a provisional certificate of authority when an applicant has done all of the following:

(1) Complied with the approved marketing plans.

(2) Met and continues to meet the requirements imposed under subdivision (a) of Section 1783.3. The issuance of the provisional certificate of authority shall not require, and shall not be dependent upon the release of escrowed funds. Release of escrowed funds shall be governed by Section 1783.3.

(3) Completed construction of the continuing care retirement community or applicable phase.

(4) Obtained the required licenses.

(5) Paid the remainder of the application fee.

(6) Executed a permanent mortgage loan or other long-term financing.

(7) Provided the department with a recorded copy of the Notice of Statutory Limitation on Transfer required by subdivision (aa) of Section 1779.4.

(8) Met all applicable provisions of this chapter.

(b) The provisional certificate of authority shall expire 12 months after issuance unless both of the following occur:

(1) No later than 60 days prior to the expiration of the provisional certificate of authority, the provider petitions the department and demonstrates good cause in writing for an extension of the provisional certificate of authority.

(2) The department determines that the provider is capable of meeting the requirements of Section 1786.2 during the extension period.

(c) The department shall exercise its discretion to determine the length of the extension period.

(d) After the provisional certificate of authority is issued providers may continue to take deposits by modifying the deposit agreement as appropriate. The new deposit agreement shall clearly state the rights of the depositor and the provider. The applicant shall submit the agreements to the department for review and approval prior to use. A provider that holds a provisional certificate of authority or certificate of authority may accept fees paid by potential residents to be placed on a waiting list without using a deposit agreement. These waiting list fees may not exceed five hundred dollars ($500), and shall be refunded to the potential resident upon written request.

(e) All holders of a provisional certificate of authority shall request in writing a certificate of authority when the requirements of Section 1786.2 have been met.

(Amended by Stats. 2000, Ch. 820, Sec. 46. Effective January 1, 2001.)

1786.2.

(a) The department shall not issue a certificate of authority to an applicant or a provider, until the department determines that each of the following has occurred:

(1) A provisional certificate of authority has been issued or all of the requirements for a provisional certificate of authority have been satisfied. In the case of an application for a new certificate of authority due to an organizational change, if the continuing care retirement community is financially sound and operating in compliance with this chapter, it shall be sufficient for the purposes of this paragraph that the department has approved the application in writing.

(2) One of the following requirements has been met:

(A) At a minimum, continuing care contracts have been executed for 80 percent of the total residential living units in the continuing care retirement community, with payment in full of the entrance fee.

(B) At a minimum, continuing care contracts have been executed for 70 percent of the total residential living units in the continuing care retirement community, with payment in full of the entrance fee, and the provider has submitted an updated financial and marketing plan, satisfactory to the department, demonstrating that the proposed continuing care retirement community will be financially viable.

(C) At a minimum, continuing care contracts have been executed for 50 percent of the total residential living units in the continuing care retirement community, with payment in full of the entrance fee, and the provider furnishes and maintains a letter of credit or other security, satisfactory to the department, sufficient to bring the total amount of payments to a level equivalent to 80 percent of the total entrance fees for the entire continuing care retirement community.

(3) A minimum five-year financial plan of operation remains satisfactory to the department.

(4) Adequate reserves exist as required by Sections 1792 and 1792.6. For a new continuing care retirement community without an operating history, the department may approve calculation of required reserves on a pro forma basis in conjunction with compliance with approved marketing plans.

(5) All applicable provisions of this chapter have been met.

(b) When issued, the certificate of authority, whether full or conditioned, shall remain in full force unless forfeited by operation of law under Section 1793.7, inactivated under Section 1793.8, or suspended or revoked by the department pursuant to Section 1793.21.

(c) The provider shall display the certificate of authority in a prominent place within the continuing care retirement community.

(Amended by Stats. 2000, Ch. 820, Sec. 47. Effective January 1, 2001.)

ARTICLE 5. Contract [1787 - 1788.4]

(Article 5 added by Stats. 1990, Ch. 875, Sec. 2.)

1787.

(a) All continuing care contracts shall be in writing and shall contain all the information required by Section 1788.

(b) All continuing care contract forms, including all addenda, exhibits, and any other related documents, incorporated therein, as well as any modification to these items, shall be approved by the department prior to their use.

(c) The department shall approve continuing care contract forms that comply with this chapter. The requirements of this chapter and Chapter 3.2 (commencing with Section 1569) shall be the bases for approval by the department. To the extent that this chapter conflicts with Chapter 3.2 (commencing with Section 1569), this chapter shall prevail.

(d) A continuing care contract approved by the department shall constitute the full and complete agreement between the parties.

(e) More than one continuing care contract form may be used by a provider if multiple program options are available.

(f) All text in continuing care contract forms shall be printed in at least 10-point typeface.

(g) A clearly legible copy of the continuing care contract, executed by each provider named on the provisional certificate of authority or the certificate of authority, the resident, and any transferor, shall be furnished with all required or included attachments to the resident at the time the continuing care contract is executed. A copy shall also be furnished within 10 calendar days to any transferor who is not a resident.

(h) The provider shall require a written acknowledgment from the resident (and any transferor who is not a resident) that the executed copy of the continuing care contract and attachments have been received.

(i) The continuing care contract shall be an admissions agreement for purposes of the residential care facility for the elderly and long-term health care facility requirements and shall state the resident's entitlement to receive these levels of care. The continuing care contract may state the entitlement for skilled nursing care in accordance with the provisions of law governing admissions to long-term health care facilities in effect at the time of admission to the skilled nursing facility. The parties may agree to the terms of nursing facility admission at the time the continuing care contract is executed, or the provider may present an exemplar of the then-current nursing facility admission agreement and require the resident to execute the form of agreement in effect at the time of admission to the nursing facility. The terms shall include the nursing fee, or the method of determining the fee, at the time of the execution of the continuing care contract, the services included in and excluded from the fee, the grounds for transfers and discharges, and any other terms required to be included under applicable law.

(j) Only the skilled nursing admission agreement sections of continuing care contracts which cover long-term health care facility services are subject to Chapter 3.95 (commencing with Section 1599.60). The provider shall use a skilled nursing admission nursing agreement that complies with the requirements of Chapter 3.95 (commencing with Section 1599.85).

(Amended by Stats. 2000, Ch. 820, Sec. 48. Effective January 1, 2001.)

1788.

(a) A continuing care contract shall contain all of the following:

(1) The legal name and address of each provider.

(2) The name and address of the continuing care retirement community.

(3) The resident's name and the identity of the unit the resident will occupy.

(4) If there is a transferor other than the resident, the transferor shall be a party to the contract and the transferor's name and address shall be specified.

(5) If the provider has used the name of any charitable or religious or nonprofit organization in its title before January 1, 1979, and continues to use that name, and that organization is not responsible for the financial and contractual obligations of the provider or the obligations specified in the continuing care contract, the provider shall include in every continuing care contract a conspicuous statement that clearly informs the resident that the organization is not financially responsible.

(6) The date the continuing care contract is signed by the resident and, where applicable, any other transferor.

(7) The duration of the continuing care contract.

(8) A list of the services that will be made available to the resident as required to provide the appropriate level of care. The list of services shall include the services required as a condition for licensure as a residential care facility for the elderly, including all of the following:

(A) Regular observation of the resident's health status to ensure that his or her dietary needs, social needs, and needs for special services are satisfied.

(B) Safe and healthful living accommodations, including housekeeping services and utilities.

(C) Maintenance of house rules for the protection of residents.

(D) A planned activities program, which includes social and recreational activities appropriate to the interests and capabilities of the resident.

(E) Three balanced, nutritious meals and snacks made available daily, including special diets prescribed by a physician as a medical necessity.

(F) Assisted living services.

(G) Assistance with taking medications.

(H) Central storing and distribution of medications.

(I) Arrangements to meet health needs, including arranging transportation.

(9) An itemization of the services that are included in the monthly fee and the services that are available at an extra charge. The provider shall attach a current fee schedule to the continuing care contract. The schedule shall state that a provider is prohibited from charging the resident or his or her estate a monthly fee once a unit has been permanently vacated by the resident, unless the fee is part of an equity interest contract.

(10) The procedures and conditions under which a resident may be voluntarily and involuntarily transferred from a designated living unit. The transfer procedures, at a minimum, shall include provisions addressing all of the following circumstances under which a transfer may be authorized:

(A) A continuing care retirement community may transfer a resident under the following conditions, taking into account the appropriateness and necessity of the transfer and the goal of promoting resident independence:

(i) The resident is nonambulatory. The definition of "nonambulatory," as provided in Section 13131, shall either be stated in full in the continuing care contract or be cited. If Section 13131 is cited, a copy of the statute shall be made available to the resident, either as an attachment to the continuing care contract or by specifying that it will be provided upon request. If a nonambulatory resident occupies a room that has a fire clearance for nonambulatory residents, transfer shall not be necessary.

(ii) The resident develops a physical or mental condition that is detrimental to or endangers the health, safety, or well-being of the resident or another person.

(iii) The resident's condition or needs require the resident's transfer to an assisted living care unit or skilled nursing facility, because the level of care required by the resident exceeds that which may be appropriately provided in the living unit.

(iv) The resident's condition or needs require the resident's transfer to a nursing facility, hospital, or other facility, and the provider has no facilities available to provide that level of care.

(B) Before the continuing care retirement community transfers a resident under any of the conditions set forth in subparagraph (A), the community shall satisfy all of the following requirements:

(i) Involve the resident and the resident's responsible person, as defined in paragraph (6) of subdivision (r) of Section 87101 of Title 22 of the California Code of Regulations, and upon the resident's or responsible person's request, family members, or the resident's physician or other appropriate health professional, in the assessment process that forms the basis for the level of care transfer decision by the provider. The provider shall offer an explanation of the assessment process, which shall include, but not be limited to, an evaluation of the physical and cognitive capacities of the resident. An assessment tool or tools, including scoring and evaluating criteria, shall be used in the determination of the appropriateness of the transfer. The provider shall make copies of the completed assessment to share with the resident or the resident's responsible person.

(ii) Prior to sending a formal notification of transfer, the provider shall conduct a care conference with the resident and the resident's responsible person, and, upon the resident's or responsible person's request, family members, and the resident's health care professionals, to explain the reasons for transfer.

(iii) Notify the resident and the resident's responsible person of the reasons for the transfer in writing.

(iv) Notwithstanding any other provision of this subparagraph, if the resident does not have impairment of cognitive abilities, the resident may request that his or her responsible person not be involved in the transfer process.

(v) The notice of transfer shall be made at least 30 days before the transfer is expected to occur, except when the health or safety of the resident or other residents is in danger, or the transfer is required by the resident's urgent medical needs. Under those circumstances, the written notice shall be made as soon as practicable before the transfer.

(vi) The written notice shall contain the reasons for the transfer, the effective date, the designated level of care or location to which the resident will be transferred, a statement of the resident's right to a review of the transfer decision at a care conference, as provided for in subparagraph (C), and for disputed transfer decisions, the right to review by the Continuing Care Contracts Branch of the State Department of Social Services, as provided for in subparagraph (D). The notice shall also contain the name, address, and telephone number of the department's Continuing Care Contracts Branch.

(vii) The continuing care retirement community shall provide sufficient preparation and orientation to the resident to ensure a safe and orderly transfer and to minimize trauma.

(viii) For disputed transfer decisions, the provider shall provide documentation of the resident's medical reports, other documents showing the resident's current mental and physical function, the prognosis, and the expected duration of relevant conditions, if applicable. The documentation shall include an explanation of how the criteria set out in subparagraph (A) are met. The provider shall make copies of the completed report to share with the resident or the resident's responsible person.

(C) The resident has the right to review and dispute the transfer decision at a subsequent care conference that shall include the resident, the resident's responsible person, and, upon the resident's or responsible person's request, family members, the resident's physician or other appropriate health care professional, and members of the provider's interdisciplinary team. The local ombudsperson may also be included in the care conference, upon the request of the resident, the resident's responsible person, or the provider.

(D) For disputed transfer decisions, the resident or the resident's responsible person has the right to a prompt and timely review of the transfer process by the Continuing Care Contracts Branch of the State Department of Social Services. The branch of the department shall provide a description of the steps a provider took and the factors a provider considered in deciding to transfer a resident, including the assessment tool or tools and the scoring and evaluating criteria used by the provider to justify the transfer.

(E) The decision of the department's Continuing Care Contracts Branch shall be in writing and shall determine whether the provider failed to comply with the transfer process pursuant to subparagraphs (A) to (C), inclusive, and whether the transfer is appropriate and necessary. Pending the decision of the Continuing Care Contracts Branch, the provider shall specify any additional care the provider believes is necessary in order for the resident to remain in his or her unit. The resident may be required to pay for the extra care, as provided in the contract.

(F) Transfer of a second resident when a shared accommodation arrangement is terminated.

(11) Provisions describing any changes in the resident's monthly fee and any changes in the entrance fee refund payable to the resident that will occur if the resident transfers from any unit, including, but not limited to, terminating his or her contract after 18 months of residential temporary relocation, as defined in paragraph (9) of subdivision (r) of Section 1771. Unless the fee is part of an equity interest contract, a provider is prohibited from charging the resident or his or her estate a monthly fee once a unit has been permanently vacated by the resident.

(12) The provider's continuing obligations, if any, in the event a resident is transferred from the continuing care retirement community to another facility.

(13) The provider's obligations, if any, to resume care upon the resident's return after a transfer from the continuing care retirement community.

(14) The provider's obligations to provide services to the resident while the resident is absent from the continuing care retirement community.

(15) The conditions under which the resident must permanently release his or her living unit.

(16) If real or personal properties are transferred in lieu of cash, a statement specifying each item's value at the time of transfer, and how the value was ascertained.

(A) An itemized receipt that includes the information described above is acceptable if incorporated as a part of the continuing care contract.

(B) When real property is or will be transferred, the continuing care contract shall include a statement that the deed or other instrument of conveyance shall specify that the real property is conveyed pursuant to a continuing care contract and may be subject to rescission by the transferor within 90 days from the date that the resident first occupies the residential unit.

(C) The failure to comply with this paragraph shall not affect the validity of title to real property transferred pursuant to this chapter.

(17) The amount of the entrance fee.

(18) In the event two parties have jointly paid the entrance fee or other payment that allows them to occupy the unit, the continuing care contract shall describe how any refund of entrance fees is allocated.

(19) The amount of any processing fee.

(20) The amount of any monthly care fee.

(21) For continuing care contracts that require a monthly care fee or other periodic payment, the continuing care contract shall include the following:

(A) A statement that the occupancy and use of the accommodations by the resident is contingent upon the regular payment of the fee.

(B) The regular rate of payment agreed upon (per day, week, or month).

(C) A provision specifying whether payment will be made in advance or after services have been provided.

(D) A provision specifying the provider will adjust monthly care fees for the resident's support, maintenance, board, or lodging, when a resident requires medical attention while away from the continuing care retirement community.

(E) A provision specifying whether a credit or allowance will be given to a resident who is absent from the continuing care retirement community or from meals. This provision shall also state, when applicable, that the credit may be permitted at the discretion or by special permission of the provider.

(F) A statement of billing practices, procedures, and timelines. A provider shall allow a minimum of 14 days between the date a bill is sent and the date payment is due. A charge for a late payment may only be assessed if the amount and any condition for the penalty is stated on the bill.

(G) A statement that the provider is prohibited from charging the resident or his or her estate a monthly fee once a unit has been permanently vacated by the resident, unless the fee is part of an equity interest contract.

(22) All continuing care contracts that include monthly care fees shall address changes in monthly care fees by including either of the following provisions:

(A) For prepaid continuing care contracts, which include monthly care fees, one of the following methods:

(i) Fees shall not be subject to change during the lifetime of the agreement.

(ii) Fees shall not be increased by more than a specified number of dollars in any one year and not more than a specified number of dollars during the lifetime of the agreement.

(iii) Fees shall not be increased in excess of a specified percentage over the preceding year and not more than a specified percentage during the lifetime of the agreement.

(B) For monthly fee continuing care contracts, except prepaid contracts, changes in monthly care fees shall be based on projected costs, prior year per capita costs, and economic indicators.

(23) A provision requiring that the provider give written notice to the resident at least 30 days in advance of any change in the resident's monthly care fees or in the price or scope of any component of care or other services.

(24) A provision indicating whether the resident's rights under the continuing care contract include any proprietary interests in the assets of the provider or in the continuing care retirement community, or both. Any statement in a contract concerning an ownership interest shall appear in a large-sized font or print.

(25) If the continuing care retirement community property is encumbered by a security interest that is senior to any claims the residents may have to enforce continuing care contracts, a provision shall advise the residents that any claims they may have under the

continuing care contract are subordinate to the rights of the secured lender. For equity projects, the continuing care contract shall specify the type and extent of the equity interest and whether any entity holds a security interest.

(26) Notice that the living units are part of a continuing care retirement community that is licensed as a residential care facility for the elderly and, as a result, any duly authorized agent of the department may, upon proper identification and upon stating the purpose of his or her visit, enter and inspect the entire premises at any time, without advance notice.

(27) A conspicuous statement, in at least 10-point boldface type in immediate proximity to the space reserved for the signatures of the resident and, if applicable, the transferor, that provides as follows: "You, the resident or transferor, may cancel the transaction without cause at any time within 90 days from the date you first occupy your living unit. See the attached notice of cancellation form for an explanation of this right."

(28) Notice that during the cancellation period, the continuing care contract may be canceled upon 30 days' written notice by the provider without cause, or that the provider waives this right.

(29) The terms and conditions under which the continuing care contract may be terminated after the cancellation period by either party, including any health or financial conditions.

(30) A statement that, after the cancellation period, a provider may unilaterally terminate the continuing care contract only if the provider has good and sufficient cause.

(A) Any continuing care contract containing a clause that provides for a continuing care contract to be terminated for "just cause," "good cause," or other similar provision, shall also include a provision that none of the following activities by the resident, or on behalf of the resident, constitutes "just cause," "good cause," or otherwise activates the termination provision:

(i) Filing or lodging a formal complaint with the department or other appropriate authority.

(ii) Participation in an organization or affiliation of residents, or other similar lawful activity.

(B) The provision required by this paragraph shall also state that the provider shall not discriminate or retaliate in any manner against any resident of a continuing care retirement community for contacting the department, or any other state, county, or city agency, or any elected or appointed government official to file a complaint or for any other reason, or for participation in a residents' organization or association.

(C) This paragraph does not diminish the provider's ability to terminate the continuing care contract for good and sufficient cause.

(31) A statement that at least 90 days' written notice to the resident is required for a unilateral termination of the continuing care contract by the provider.

(32) A statement concerning the length of notice that a resident is required to give the provider to voluntarily terminate the continuing care contract after the cancellation period.

(33) The policy or terms for refunding or repaying a lump sum of any portion of the entrance fee, in the event of cancellation, termination, or death. Every continuing care contract that provides for a refund or repaying a lump sum of all or a part of the entrance fee shall also do all of the following:

(A) Specify the amount, if any, the resident has paid or will pay for upgrades, special features, or modifications to the resident's unit.

(B) State that if the continuing care contract is canceled or terminated by the provider, the provider shall do both of the following:

(i) Amortize the specified amount at the same rate as the resident's entrance fee.

(ii) Refund the unamortized balance to the resident at the same time the provider pays the resident's entrance fee refund.

(C) State that the resident has a right to terminate his or her contract after 18 months of residential temporary relocation, as defined in paragraph (9) of subdivision (r) of Section 1771. Provisions for refunds due to cancellation pursuant to this subparagraph shall be set forth in the contract.

(D) State the provider shall make a good-faith effort to reoccupy or resell a unit for which a lump-sum payment is conditioned upon resale of the unit. No later than July 1, 2017, a provider shall provide notice to all current residents with contracts applicable to this subparagraph regarding the statement required by this subparagraph as a clarification of the resident's existing contract.

(E) For all contracts with a repayment of all or a portion of the entrance fee conditioned upon the resale of the unit, the provider shall state the average and longest amount of time that it has taken to resell a unit within the last five calendar years.

(34) The following notice at the bottom of the signatory page:

| "NOTICE" | (date) |

"This is a continuing care contract as defined by paragraph (8) of subdivision (c) or subdivision (l) of Section 1771 of the California Health and Safety Code. This continuing care contract form has been approved by the State Department of Social Services as required by subdivision (b) of Section 1787 of the California Health and Safety Code. The basis for this approval was a determination that (provider name) has submitted a contract that complies with the minimum statutory requirements applicable to continuing care contracts. The department does not approve or disapprove any of the financial or health care coverage provisions in this contract. Approval by the department is NOT a guaranty of performance or an endorsement of any continuing care contract provisions. Prospective transferors and residents are strongly encouraged to carefully consider the benefits and risks of this continuing care contract and to seek financial and legal advice before signing."

(35) The provider shall not attempt to absolve itself in the continuing care contract from liability for its negligence by any statement to that effect, and shall include the following statement in the contract: "Nothing in this continuing care contract limits either the provider's obligation to provide adequate care and supervision for the resident or any liability on the part of the provider which may result from the provider's failure to provide this care and supervision."

(36) Provisions describing how the provider will proceed in the event of a closure, including an explanation of how the provider will comply with Sections 1793.80, 1793.81, 1793.82, and 1793.83.

(b) A life care contract shall also provide that:

(1) All levels of care, including acute care and physicians' and surgeons' services, will be provided to a resident.

(2) Care will be provided for the duration of the resident's life unless the life care contract is canceled or terminated by the provider during the cancellation period or after the cancellation period for good cause.

(3) A comprehensive continuum of care will be provided to the resident, including skilled nursing, in a facility under the ownership and supervision of the provider on, or adjacent to, the continuing care retirement community premises.

(4) Monthly care fees will not be changed based on the resident's level of care or service.

(5) A resident who becomes financially unable to pay his or her monthly care fees shall be subsidized provided the resident's financial need does not arise from action by the resident to divest the resident of his or her assets.

(c) Continuing care contracts may include provisions that do any of the following:

(1) Subsidize a resident who becomes financially unable to pay for his or her monthly care fees at some future date. If a continuing care contract provides for subsidizing a resident, it may also provide for any of the following:

(A) The resident shall apply for any public assistance or other aid for which he or she is eligible and that the provider may apply for assistance on behalf of the resident.

(B) The provider's decision shall be final and conclusive regarding any adjustments to be made or any action to be taken regarding any charitable consideration extended to any of its residents.

(C) The provider is entitled to payment for the actual costs of care out of any property acquired by the resident subsequent to any adjustment extended to the resident under this paragraph, or from any other property of the resident that the resident failed to disclose.

(D) The provider may pay the monthly premium of the resident's health insurance coverage under Medicare to ensure that those payments will be made.

(E) The provider may receive an assignment from the resident of the right to apply for and to receive the benefits, for and on behalf of the resident.

(F) The provider is not responsible for the costs of furnishing the resident with any services, supplies, and medication, when reimbursement is reasonably available from any governmental agency, or any private insurance.

(G) Any refund due to the resident at the termination of the continuing care contract may be offset by any prior subsidy to the resident by the provider.

(2) Limit responsibility for costs associated with the treatment or medication of an ailment or illness existing before the date of admission. In these cases, the medical or surgical exceptions, as disclosed by the medical entrance examination, shall be listed in the continuing care contract or in a medical report attached to and made a part of the continuing care contract.

(3) Identify legal remedies that may be available to the provider if the resident makes any material misrepresentation or omission pertaining to the resident's assets or health.

(4) Restrict transfer or assignments of the resident's rights and privileges under a continuing care contract due to the personal nature of the continuing care contract.

(5) Protect the provider's ability to waive a resident's breach of the terms or provisions of the continuing care contract in specific instances without relinquishing its right to insist upon full compliance by the resident with all terms or provisions in the contract.

(6) Provide that the resident shall reimburse the provider for any uninsured loss or damage to the resident's unit, beyond normal wear and tear, resulting from the resident's carelessness or negligence.

(7) Provide that the resident agrees to observe the off-limit areas of the continuing care retirement community designated by the provider for safety reasons. The provider shall not include any provision in a continuing care contract that absolves the provider from liability for its negligence.

(8) Provide for the subrogation to the provider of the resident's rights in the case of injury to a resident caused by the acts or omissions of a third party, or for the assignment of the resident's recovery or benefits in this case to the provider, to the extent of the value of the goods and services furnished by the provider to or on behalf of the resident as a result of the injury.

(9) Provide for a lien on any judgment, settlement, or recovery for any additional expense incurred by the provider in caring for the resident as a result of injury.

(10) Require the resident's cooperation and assistance in the diligent prosecution of any claim or action against any third party.

(11) Provide for the appointment of a conservator or guardian by a court with jurisdiction in the event a resident becomes unable to handle his or her personal or financial affairs.

(12) Allow a provider, whose property is tax exempt, to charge the resident, on a pro rata basis, property taxes, or in-lieu taxes, that the provider is required to pay.

(13) Make any other provision approved by the department.

(d) A copy of the resident's rights as described in Section 1771.7 shall be attached to every continuing care contract.

(e) A copy of the current audited financial statement of the provider shall be attached to every continuing care contract. For a provider whose current audited financial statement does not accurately reflect the financial ability of the provider to fulfill the continuing care contract obligations, the financial statement attached to the continuing care contract shall include all of the following:

(1) A disclosure that the reserve requirement has not yet been determined or met, and that entrance fees will not be held in escrow.

(2) A disclosure that the ability to provide the services promised in the continuing care contract will depend on successful compliance with the approved financial plan.

(3) A copy of the approved financial plan for meeting the reserve requirements.

(4) Any other supplemental statements or attachments necessary to accurately represent the provider's financial ability to fulfill its continuing care contract obligations.

(f) A schedule of the average monthly care fees charged to residents for each type of residential living unit for each of the five years preceding execution of the continuing care contract shall be attached to every continuing care contract. The provider shall update this schedule annually at the end of each fiscal year. If the continuing care retirement community has not been in existence for five years, the information shall be provided for each of the years the continuing care retirement community has been in existence.

(g) If any continuing care contract provides for a health insurance policy for the benefit of the resident, the provider shall attach to the continuing care contract a binder complying with Sections 382 and 382.5 of the Insurance Code.

(h) The provider shall attach to every continuing care contract a completed form in duplicate, captioned "Notice of Cancellation." The notice shall be easily detachable, and shall contain, in at least 10-point boldface type, the following statement:

```
"NOTICE OF CANCELLATION"                        (date)


Your first date of occupancy under this contract _____


is: _____
```

"You may cancel this transaction, without any penalty within 90 calendar days from the above date.

If you cancel, any property transferred, any payments made by you under the contract, and any negotiable instrument executed by you will be returned within 14 calendar days after making possession of the living unit available to the provider. Any security interest arising out of the transaction will be canceled.

If you cancel, you are obligated to pay a reasonable processing fee to cover costs and to pay for the reasonable value of the services received by you from the provider up to the date you canceled or made available to the provider the possession of any living unit delivered to you under this contract, whichever is later.

If you cancel, you must return possession of any living unit delivered to you under this contract to the provider in substantially the same condition as when you took possession. Possession of the living unit must be made available to the provider within 20 calendar days of your notice of cancellation. If you fail to make the possession of any living unit available to the provider, then you remain liable for performance of all obligations under the contract.

To cancel this transaction, mail or deliver a signed and dated copy of this cancellation notice, or any other written notice, or send a telegram

```
to _____


(Name of provider)


at _____


(Address of provider's place of business)


not later than midnight of_____ (date).


I hereby cancel this
transaction


                            (Resident's or
                            Transferor's signature)"
```

(Amended by Stats. 2018, Ch. 92, Sec. 135. (SB 1289) Effective January 1, 2019.)

1788.2.

(a) A continuing care contract may be canceled without cause by written notice from either party within 90 days from the date of the resident's initial occupancy.

(b) For all continuing care contracts, death of the resident before or during the cancellation period shall constitute a cancellation of the continuing care contract under subdivision (a), unless the continuing care contract includes specific provisions otherwise.

(c) The cancellation period and the associated refund obligations shall apply as follows:

(1) To all executed continuing care contracts regarding a unit in a continuing care retirement community that is not an equity continuing care retirement community.

(2) To continuing care contracts executed in conjunction with a purchase of an equity interest from a provider but not to continuing care contracts executed in conjunction with sales of an equity interest by one resident to another.

(d) The following fees may be charged before or during the 90-day cancellation period:

(1) If possession of the living unit in a continuing care retirement community that is not an equity continuing care retirement community is returned to the provider in substantially the same condition as when received, the resident's only obligations shall be to pay a reasonable fee to cover costs and to pay the reasonable value of services rendered pursuant to the canceled continuing care contract.

(2) Equity project providers may impose a resale fee on sellers. For contracts entered into after January 1, 1996, upon the cancellation of a continuing care contract executed in conjunction with the purchase of an equity interest from the provider, the provider may charge a resale fee not to exceed the excess of the gross resale price of the equity interest over the purchase price paid by the resident or on behalf of the resident for the interest.

(e) No resale fee shall exceed the sum of 10 percent of either the original or resale price of the equity interest and 100 percent of the excess if any, of the gross resale price of the equity interest over the purchase price paid by the resident or on behalf of the resident for the interest if either of the following applies:

(1) The continuing care contract involved the purchase of an equity interest from the provider and is terminated after the cancellation period.

(2) The continuing care contract involved the purchase of an equity interest from another resident and is terminated at any time.

(f) For purposes of this section, "gross resale price" means the resale price before any deductions for resale fees, transfer taxes, real estate commissions, periodic fees, late charges, interest, escrow fees, or any other fees incidental to the sale of real property.

(g) This section may not be construed to limit the provider's ability to withhold delinquent periodic fees, late charges, accrued interest, or assessments from the sale proceeds, as provided by the continuing care contract or the real estate documents governing the equity continuing care retirement community.

(Amended by Stats. 2000, Ch. 820, Sec. 50. Effective January 1, 2001.)

1788.4.

(a) During the cancellation period, the provider shall pay all refunds owed to a resident within 14 calendar days after a resident makes possession of the living unit available to the provider.

(b) After the cancellation period, any refunds due to a resident under a continuing care contract shall be paid within 14 calendar days after a resident makes possession of the living unit available to the provider or 90 calendar days after death or receipt of notice of termination, whichever is later.

(c) In nonequity projects, if the continuing care contract is canceled by either party during the cancellation period or terminated by the provider after the cancellation period, the resident shall be refunded the difference between the total amount of entrance, monthly, and optional fees paid and the amount used for care of the resident.

(d) If a resident has paid additional amounts for upgrades, special features, or modifications to the living unit and the provider terminates the resident's continuing care contract, the provider shall amortize those additional amounts at the same rate as the entrance fee and shall refund the unamortized balance to the resident.

(e) A lump-sum payment after termination of a repayable contract, as defined in paragraph (3) of subdivision (r) of Section 1771, shall not be considered to be a refund and may not be characterized or advertised as a refund. The full lump sum owed, including any interest accrued, shall be paid to the resident or the resident's estate within 14 calendar days after resale of the unit.

(f) (1) Any balance of the lump sum owed that has not been paid to the resident or the resident's estate within 180 days after termination of a repayable contract shall accrue interest at a rate calculated pursuant to paragraph (2). Any balance of the lump sum owed that has not been paid to the resident or the resident's estate within 240 days after termination of a repayable contract shall accrue interest at a rate calculated pursuant to paragraph (3). Interest shall continue to accrue annually pursuant to paragraph (4) until the date the full lump sum owed is paid to the resident or the resident's estate. This subdivision shall apply only to repayable contracts entered into on or after January 1, 2017.

(2) Any amount owed that is not paid to the resident or the resident's estate within the 180-day period pursuant to paragraph (1) shall accrue simple interest at a rate of 4 percent of the amount owed.

(3) Any amount owed that is not paid to the resident or the resident's estate within the 240-day period pursuant to paragraph (1) shall accrue simple interest at a rate of 6 percent of the amount owed.

(4) Any amount owed that is not paid to the resident or the resident's estate within one year after the 240-day period pursuant to paragraph (3) shall accrue interest at a rate of 6 percent, compounded annually.

(5) Until January 1, 2018, this subdivision shall not apply to a project that is in development prior to January 1, 2017, including current repayable agreements, current deposit agreements that contemplate repayable entrance fees, and other projects that have received department approval to market units pursuant to Section 1771.4, or have received issuer, lender, or bond insurer approval to obtain bond financing, or other governmental approval based on a repayable entrance fee option, if the initial contract for the project is entered into on or before January 1, 2018.

(g) Except as otherwise obligated by an equity interest contract, once the unit has been vacated and made available to the provider, the provider shall not make any further charges to the resident or his or her estate or charges against the lump sum owed to the

resident or the resident's estate for purposes of continued monthly payments to the provider or for maintenance or housekeeping on the vacated unit.

(h) Nothing in this section shall be construed to limit or alter any legal remedies otherwise available to a resident or his or her estate.

(Amended by Stats. 2016, Ch. 112, Sec. 3. (SB 939) Effective January 1, 2017.)

ARTICLE 6. Reporting and Reserve Requirements [1789 - 1793]
(Article 6 added by Stats. 1990, Ch. 875, Sec. 2.)

1789.

(a) A provider shall notify the department and obtain its approval before making any changes to any of the following: its name; its business structure or form of doing business; the overall management of its continuing care retirement community; or the terms of its financing.

(b) The provider shall give written notice of proposed changes to the department at least 60 calendar days in advance of making the changes described in this section.

(c) This notice requirement does not apply to routine facility staff changes.

(d) Within 10 calendar days of submitting notification to the department of any proposed changes under subdivision (a), the provider shall notify the resident association of the proposed changes in the manner required by subdivision (e) of Section 1779.

(Amended by Stats. 2000, Ch. 820, Sec. 52. Effective January 1, 2001.)

1789.1.

(a) Before executing a deposit agreement or continuing care agreement, or receiving any payment from a depositor or prospective resident, a provider shall deliver to the other parties in the deposit or continuing care agreement a disclosure statement in the form prescribed by the department.

(b) The department shall issue a disclosure statement form that shall generally require disclosure, at a minimum, of the following information:

(1) General information regarding the provider and the continuing care retirement community, including at a minimum all of the following:

(A) The continuing care retirement community's name, address, and telephone number.

(B) The type of ownership, names of the continuing care retirement community's owner and operator, the names of any affiliated facilities, and any direct religious affiliation.

(C) Whether accredited and by what organization.

(D) The year the continuing care retirement community opened and the distance to the nearest shopping center and hospital.

(E) Whether the continuing care retirement community offers life care contracts or continuing care contracts, and whether the continuing care retirement community is single story or multistory.

(F) The number of the continuing care retirement community's studio units, one bedroom units, two bedroom units, cottages or houses, assisted living beds, and skilled nursing beds.

(G) The continuing care retirement community's percentage occupancy at the provider's most recent fiscal yearend.

(H) The form of contracts offered, the range of entrance fees, the percentages of a resident's entrance fees that may be refunded, and the health care benefits included in contract.

(I) Any age and insurance requirements for admission.

(J) A listing of common area amenities and other services included with the monthly service fee, and a listing of those amenities and services that are available for an additional charge.

(K) The number of meals each day included in the monthly service fee, the number of meals available for an extra charge, the frequency of housekeeping services, and additional cost, if any , for housekeeping services.

(2) Income from operations during the most recent five years for which audited financial statements have been completed, including all of the following:

(A) Operating income (excluding amortization of entrance fee income).

(B) Operating expense (excluding depreciation, amortization, and interest).

(C) Net income from operations.

(D) Interest expense.

(E) Unrestricted contributions.

(F) Nonoperating income or expense, excluding extraordinary items.

(G) Net income or loss before entrance fees.

(H) Net cash-flow from entrance fees, that is the total deposits less refunds.

(3) The name of the lender, outstanding balance, interest rate, date of origination, date of maturity, and amortization period for all secured debt.

(4) Financial ratios for each of the three most recent years for which audited financial statements have been prepared, including all of the following: debt-to-asset ratio, operating ratio, debt service coverage ratio, and days cash-on-hand. The formulas for each ratio shall be determined by the department after consultation with the Continuing Care Advisory Committee.

(5) The average monthly service fees charged during the most recent five years, and the percentage changes in the average from year to year, for each of the following: studio units, one bedroom units, two bedroom units, cottages and houses, assisted living units, and skilled nursing units.

(6) Comments from the provider explaining any of the information included in the disclosure form.

(c) Each provider shall update its disclosure statement at least annually when it completes its annual audited financial statements. Each provider shall file its updated version of the disclosure statement with the department not later than the final filing date for its annual report.

(d) The form prescribed by the department under this section shall be used by providers to comply with the requirements of this section.
(Added by Stats. 2000, Ch. 820, Sec. 53. Effective January 1, 2001.)
1789.2.
(a) A provider shall provide the department with written notice at least 90 calendar days prior to closing any transaction that results in an encumbrance or lien on a continuing care retirement community property or its revenues.
(b) The written notice required by this section shall include all of the following:
(1) A description of the terms and amount of the proposed transaction.
(2) An analysis of the sources of funds for repayment of principal and interest.
(3) An analysis of the impact of the proposed transaction on monthly care fees.
(4) An analysis of the impact that the proposed encumbrance would have on assets available for liquid reserves required by Section 1792, and refund reserves required by Section 1792.6.
(c) Within seven calendar days of receipt of notice of proposed changes, the department shall acknowledge receipt of the notice in writing.
(d) Within 30 calendar days following its receipt of the notice, the department shall inform the provider in writing whether additional materials are required to evaluate the transaction.
(e) Within 90 calendar days following its receipt of additional materials, the department shall inform the provider of its approval or denial of the proposed transaction.
(f) Providers shall not execute the proposed financial transaction for which notice has been given pursuant to subdivision (a) without the department's written authorization unless either the 30-day response period or the 90 calendar day period for the department's review of the provider's request has expired without any response by the department.
(g) If the department determines that the proposed financial transaction will materially increase monthly care fees or impair the provider's ability to maintain required reserves, the department may:
(1) Refuse to approve the transaction.
(2) Record a notice of lien on the provider's property pursuant to Section 1793.15 after notifying the provider and giving the provider an opportunity to withdraw the planned transaction.
(3) Take both actions and any other action that it determines is necessary to protect the best interests of the residents.
(h) Within 10 calendar days of submitting notification to the department of any proposed encumbrance to the community property, the provider shall notify the resident governing body or association of the proposed encumbrance in the manner required by subdivision (e) of Section 1779.
(Amended by Stats. 2000, Ch. 820, Sec. 54. Effective January 1, 2001.)
1789.4.
(a) A provider for a continuing care retirement community shall obtain approval from the department before consummating any sale or transfer of the continuing care retirement community or any interest in that community, other than sale of an equity interest in a unit to a resident or other transferor.
(b) The provider shall provide written notice to the department at least 120 calendar days prior to consummating the proposed transaction.
(c) The notice required by this section shall include all of the following:
(1) The identity of the purchaser.
(2) A description of the terms of the transfer or sale, including the sales price.
(3) A plan for ensuring performance of the existing continuing care contract obligations.
(d) The provider shall give written notice to all continuing care contract residents and depositors 120 calendar days prior to the sale or transfer. The notice shall do all of the following:
(1) Describe the parties.
(2) Describe the proposed sale or transfer.
(3) Describe the arrangements for fulfilling continuing care contract obligations.
(4) Describe options available to any depositor or resident who does not wish to have his or her contract assumed by a new provider.
(5) Include an acknowledgment of receipt of the notice to be signed by the resident.
(e) Unless a new provider assumes all of the continuing care obligations of the selling provider at the close of the sale or transfer, the selling provider shall set up a trust fund or secure a performance bond to ensure the fulfillment of all its continuing care contract obligations.
(f) The purchaser shall make applications for, and obtain, the appropriate licenses and a certificate of authority before executing any continuing care contracts or assuming the selling provider's continuing care contract obligations.
(Amended by Stats. 2000, Ch. 820, Sec. 55. Effective January 1, 2001.)
1789.6.
A provider shall record with the county recorder a "Notice of Statutory Limitation on Transfer" for each community as required by subdivision (aa) of Section 1779.4 and Section 1786.
(Amended by Stats. 2000, Ch. 820, Sec. 56. Effective January 1, 2001.)
1789.8.
Each provider shall obtain and maintain in effect insurance or a fidelity bond for each agent or employee, who, in the course of his or her agency or employment, has access to any substantial amount of funds. This requirement is separate from the bonding requirements of residential care facility for the elderly regulations.
(Amended by Stats. 2000, Ch. 820, Sec. 57. Effective January 1, 2001.)
1790.

(a) Each provider that has obtained a provisional or final certificate of authority and each provider that possesses an inactive certificate of authority shall submit an annual report of its financial condition. The report shall consist of audited financial statements and required reserve calculations, with accompanying certified public accountants' opinions thereon, the reserve information required by paragraph (2), Continuing Care Provider Fee and Calculation Sheet, evidence of fidelity bond as required by Section 1789.8, and certification that the continuing care contract in use for new residents has been approved by the department, all in a format provided by the department, and shall include all of the following information:
(1) A certification, if applicable, that the entity is maintaining reserves for prepaid continuing care contracts, statutory reserves, and refund reserves.
(2) Full details on the status, description, and amount of all reserves that the provider currently designates and maintains, and on per capita costs of operation for each continuing care retirement community operated.
(3) Disclosure of any amounts accumulated or expended for identified projects or purposes, including, but not limited to, projects designated to meet the needs of the continuing care retirement community as permitted by a provider's nonprofit status under Section 501(c)(3) of the Internal Revenue Code, and amounts maintained for contingencies. The disclosure of a nonprofit provider shall state how the project or purpose is consistent with the provider's tax-exempt status. The disclosure of a for-profit provider shall identify amounts accumulated for specific projects or purposes and amounts maintained for contingencies. Nothing in this subdivision shall be construed to require the accumulation of funds or funding of contingencies, nor shall it be interpreted to alter existing law regarding the reserves that are required to be maintained.
(4) Full details on any increase in monthly care fees, the basis for determining the increase, and the data used to calculate the increase.
(5) The required reserve calculation schedules shall be accompanied by the auditor's opinion as to compliance with applicable statutes.
(6) Any other information as the department may require.
(b) Each provider shall file the annual report with the department within four months after the provider's fiscal yearend. If the complete annual report is not received by the due date, a one thousand dollar ($1,000) late fee shall accompany submission of the reports. If the reports are more than 30 days past due, an additional fee of thirty-three dollars ($33) for each day over the first 30 days shall accompany submission of the report. The department may, at its discretion, waive the late fee for good cause.
(c) The annual report and any amendments thereto shall be signed and certified by the chief executive officer of the provider, stating that, to the best of his or her knowledge and belief, the items are correct.
(d) A copy of the most recent annual audited financial statement shall be transmitted by the provider to each transferor requesting the statement.
(e) A provider shall amend its annual report on file with the department at any time, without the payment of any additional fee, if an amendment is necessary to prevent the report from containing a material misstatement of fact or omitting a material fact.
(f) If a provider is no longer entering into continuing care contracts, and currently is caring for 10 or fewer continuing care residents, the provider may request permission from the department, in lieu of filing the annual report, to establish a trust fund or to secure a performance bond to ensure fulfillment of continuing care contract obligations. The request shall be made each year within 30 days after the provider's fiscal yearend. The request shall include the amount of the trust fund or performance bond determined by calculating the projected life costs, less the projected life revenue, for the remaining continuing care residents in the year the provider requests the waiver. If the department approves the request, the following shall be submitted to the department annually:
(1) Evidence of trust fund or performance bond and its amount.
(2) A list of continuing care residents. If the number of continuing care residents exceeds 10 at any time, the provider shall comply with the requirements of this section.
(3) A provider fee as required by subdivision (c) of Section 1791.
(g) If the department determines a provider's annual audited report needs further analysis and investigation, as a result of incomplete and inaccurate financial statements, significant financial deficiencies, development of work out plans to stabilize financial solvency, or for any other reason, the provider shall reimburse the department for reasonable actual costs incurred by the department or its representative. The reimbursed funds shall be deposited in the Continuing Care Contract Provider Fee Fund.
(Amended by Stats. 2009, Ch. 513, Sec. 1. (AB 1169) Effective January 1, 2010.)
1791.
(a) An annual fee shall be required of each provider which has obtained a provisional or final certificate of authority.
(b) Each annual report submitted pursuant to Section 1790 shall be accompanied by a payment to the Continuing Care Provider Fee Fund in the amount of one-tenth of 1 percent of the portion of total operating expenses, excluding debt service and depreciation from audited financial statements, which has been allocated to continuing care contract residents. The allocation shall be based on the ratio of the mean number of total residents.
(c) If a provider is granted an exemption from filing annual reports to the department pursuant to subdivision (f) of Section 1790, the minimum annual provider fee shall be two hundred fifty dollars ($250). This fee shall be submitted after the end of the provider's fiscal year with proof of trust fund or performance bond as required by subdivision (f) of Section 1790.
(Amended by Stats. 1995, Ch. 920, Sec. 45. Effective January 1, 1996.)
1792.

(a) A provider shall maintain at all times qualifying assets as a liquid reserve in an amount that equals or exceeds the sum of the following:

(1) The amount the provider is required to hold as a debt service reserve under Section 1792.3.

(2) The amount the provider must hold as an operating expense reserve under Section 1792.4.

(b) The liquid reserve requirement described in this section is satisfied when a provider holds qualifying assets in the amount required. Except as may be required under subdivision (d), a provider is not required to set aside, deposit into an escrow, or otherwise restrict the assets it holds as its liquid reserve.

(c) A provider shall not allow the amount it holds as its liquid reserve to fall below the amount required by this section. In the event the amount of a provider's liquid reserve is insufficient, the provider shall prudently eliminate the deficiency by increasing its assets qualifying under Section 1792.2.

(d) The department may increase the amount a provider is required to hold as its liquid reserve or require that a provider immediately place its liquid reserve into an escrow account meeting the requirements of Section 1781 if the department has reason to believe the provider is any of the following:

(1) Insolvent.

(2) In imminent danger of becoming insolvent.

(3) In a financially unsound or unsafe condition.

(4) In a condition such that it may otherwise be unable to fully perform its obligations pursuant to continuing care contracts.

(e) For providers that have voluntarily and permanently discontinued entering into continuing care contracts, the department may allow a reduced liquid reserve amount if the department finds that the reduction is consistent with the financial protections imposed by this article. The reduced liquid reserve amount shall be based upon the percentage of residents at the continuing care retirement community who have continuing care contracts.

(Amended by Stats. 2004, Ch. 129, Sec. 2. Effective January 1, 2005.)

1792.2.

(a) A provider shall satisfy its liquid reserve obligation with qualifying assets. Qualifying assets are:

(1) Cash.

(2) Cash equivalents as defined in paragraph (4) of subdivision (c) of Section 1771.

(3) Investment securities, as defined in paragraph (2) of subdivision (i) of Section 1771.

(4) Equity securities, including mutual funds, as defined in paragraph (7) of subdivision (e) of Section 1771.

(5) Lines of credit and letters of credit that meet the requirements of this paragraph. The line of credit or letter of credit shall be issued by a state or federally chartered financial institution approved by the department or whose long-term debt is rated in the top three long-term debt rating categories by either Moody's Investors Service, Standard and Poor's Corporation, or a recognized securities rating agency acceptable to the department. The line of credit or letter of credit shall obligate the financial institution to furnish credit to the provider.

(A) The terms of the line of credit or letter of credit shall at a minimum provide both of the following:

(i) The department's approval shall be obtained by the provider and communicated in writing to the financial institution before any modification.

(ii) The financial institution shall fund the line of credit or letter of credit and pay the proceeds to the provider no later than four business days following written instructions from the department that, in the sole judgment of the department, funding of the provider's minimum liquid reserve is required.

(B) The provider shall provide written notice to the department at least 14 days before the expiration of the line of credit or letter of credit if the term has not been extended or renewed by that time. The notice shall describe the qualifying assets the provider will use to satisfy the liquid reserve requirement when the line of credit or letter of credit expires.

(C) A provider may satisfy all or a portion of its liquid reserve requirement with the available and unused portion of a qualifying line of credit or letter of credit.

(6) For purposes of satisfying all or a portion of a provider's debt service reserve requirement described in Section 1792.3, restricted assets that are segregated or held in a separate account or escrow as a debt service reserve under the terms of the provider's long-term debt instruments are qualifying assets, subject to all of the following conditions:

(A) The assets are restricted by the debt instrument so that they may be used only to pay principal, interest, and credit enhancement premiums.

(B) The provider furnishes to the department a copy of the agreement under which the restricted assets are held and certifies that it is a correct and complete copy. The provider, escrow holder, or other entity holding the assets must agree to provide to the department any information the department may request concerning the debt service reserve it holds.

(C) The market value, or guaranteed value, if applicable, of the restricted assets, up to the amount the provider must hold as a debt reserve under Section 1792.3, will be included as part of the provider's liquid reserve.

(D) The restricted assets described in this paragraph will not reduce or count towards the amount the provider must hold in its liquid reserve for operating expenses.

(7) For purposes of satisfying all or a portion of a provider's operating expense reserve requirement described in Section 1792.4, restricted assets that are segregated or held in a separate account or escrow as a reserve for operating expenses, are qualifying assets subject to all of the following conditions:

(A) The governing instrument restricts the assets so that they may be used only to pay operating costs when operating funds are insufficient.

(B) The provider furnishes to the department a copy of the agreement under which the assets are held, certified by the provider to be a correct and complete copy. The provider, escrow holder, or other entity holding the assets shall agree to provide to the department any information the department may request concerning the account.

(C) The market value, or the guaranteed value, if applicable, of the restricted assets, up to the amount the provider is required to hold as an operating expense reserve under Section 1792.4, will be included as part of the provider's liquid reserve.

(D) The restricted assets described in this paragraph shall not reduce or count towards the amount the provider is required to hold in its liquid reserve for long-term debt.

(b) Except as otherwise provided in this subdivision, the assets held by the provider as its liquid reserve may not be subject to any liens, charges, judgments, garnishments, or creditors' claims and may not be hypothecated, pledged as collateral, or otherwise encumbered in any manner. A provider may encumber assets held in its liquid reserve as part of a general security pledge of assets or similar collateralization that is part of the provider's long-term capital debt covenants and is included in the provider's long-term debt indenture or similar instrument.

(Repealed and added by Stats. 2000, Ch. 820, Sec. 57.25. Effective January 1, 2001.)

1792.3.

(a) Each provider shall include in its liquid reserve a reserve for its long-term debt obligations in an amount equal to the sum of all of the following:

(1) All regular principal and interest payments, as well as credit enhancement premiums, paid by the provider during the immediately preceding fiscal year on account of any fully amortizing long-term debt owed by the provider. If a provider has incurred new long-term debt during the immediately preceding fiscal year, the amount required by this paragraph for that debt is 12 times the provider's most recent monthly payment on the debt.

(2) Facility rental or leasehold payments, and any related payments such as lease insurance, paid by the provider during the immediately preceding fiscal year.

(3) All payments paid by the provider during the immediately preceding fiscal year on account of any debt that provides for a balloon payment. If the balloon payment debt was incurred within the immediately preceding fiscal year, the amount required by this paragraph for that debt is 12 times the provider's most recent monthly payment on the debt made during the fiscal year.

(b) If any balloon payment debt matures within the next 24 months, the provider shall submit with its annual report a plan for refinancing the debt or repaying the debt with existing assets.

(c) When principal and interest payments on long-term debt are paid to a trust whose beneficial interests are held by the residents, the department may waive all or any portion of the debt service reserve required by this section. The department shall not waive any debt service reserve requirement unless the department finds that the waiver is consistent with the financial protections imposed by this chapter.

(Added by Stats. 2000, Ch. 820, Sec. 57.3. Effective January 1, 2001.)

1792.4.

(a) Each provider shall include in its liquid reserve a reserve for its operating expenses in an amount that equals or exceeds 75 days' net operating expenses. For purposes of this section:

(1) Seventy-five days net operating expenses shall be calculated by dividing the provider's operating expenses during the immediately preceding fiscal year by 365, and multiplying that quotient by 75.

(2) "Net operating expenses" includes all expenses except the following:

(A) The interest and credit enhancement expenses factored into the provider's calculation of its long-term debt reserve obligation described in Section 1792.3.

(B) Depreciation or amortization expenses.

(C) An amount equal to the reimbursement paid to the provider during the past 12 months for services to residents other than residents holding continuing care contracts.

(D) Extraordinary expenses that the department determines may be excluded by the provider. A provider shall apply in writing for a determination by the department and shall provide supporting documentation prepared in accordance with generally accepted accounting principles.

(b) A provider that has been in operation for less than 12 months shall calculate its net operating expenses by using its actual expenses for the months it has operated and, for the remaining months, the projected net operating expense amounts it submitted to the department as part of its application for a certificate of authority.

(Amended by Stats. 2004, Ch. 129, Sec. 4. Effective January 1, 2005.)

1792.5.

(a) The provider shall compute its liquid reserve requirement as of the end of the provider's most recent fiscal yearend based on its audited financial statements for that period and, at the time it files its annual report, shall file a form acceptable to the department certifying all of the following:

(1) The amount the provider is required to hold as a liquid reserve, including the amounts required for the debt service reserve and the operating expense reserve.

(2) The qualifying assets, and their respective values, the provider has designated for its debt service reserve and for its operating expense reserve.

(3) The amount of any deficiency or surplus for the provider's debt service reserve and the provider's operating expense reserve.

(b) For the purpose of calculating the amount held by the provider to satisfy its liquid reserve requirement, all qualifying assets used to satisfy the liquid reserve requirements shall be valued at their fair market value as of the end of the provider's most recently completed fiscal year. Restricted assets that have guaranteed values and are designated as qualifying assets under paragraph (6) or (7) of subdivision (a) of Section 1792.2 may be valued at their guaranteed values.

(Amended by Stats. 2004, Ch. 129, Sec. 5. Effective January 1, 2005.)

1792.6.

(a) Any provider offering a refundable contract, or other entity assuming responsibility for refundable contracts, shall maintain a refund reserve in trust for the residents. The amount of the refund reserve shall be revised annually by the provider and the provider shall submit its calculation of the refund reserve amount to the department in conjunction with the annual report required by Section 1790. This reserve shall accumulate interest and earnings and shall be invested in any of the following:

(1) Qualifying assets as defined in Section 1792.2.

(2) Real estate, subject to all of the following conditions:

(A) To the extent approved by the department, the trust account may invest up to 70 percent of the refund reserves in real estate that is both used to provide care and housing for the holders of the refundable continuing care contracts and is located on the same campus where these continuing care contractholders reside.

(B) Investments in real estate shall be limited to 50 percent of the providers' net equity in the real estate. The net equity shall be the book value, assessed value, or current appraised value within 12 months prior to the end of the fiscal year, less any depreciation, and encumbrances, all according to audited financial statements acceptable to the department.

(b) Each refund reserve trust shall be established at an institution qualified to be an escrow agent. The escrow agreement between the provider and the institution shall be in writing and include the terms and conditions described in this section. The escrow agreement shall be submitted to and approved by the department before it becomes effective.

(c) The amount to be held in the reserve shall be the total of the amounts calculated with respect to each individual resident holding a refundable contract as follows:

(1) Determine the age in years and the portion of the entry fee for the resident refundable for the seventh year of residency and thereafter.

(2) Determine life expectancy of that individual based on all of the following rules:

(A) The following life expectancy table shall be used in connection with all continuing care contracts:

Age	Females	Males	Age	Females	Males
55	26.323	23.635	83	7.952	6.269
56	25.526	22.863	84	7.438	5.854
57	24.740	22.101	85	6.956	5.475
58	23.964	21.350	86	6.494	5.124
59	23.199	20.609	87	6.054	4.806
60	22.446	19.880	88	5.613	4.513
61	21.703	19.163	89	5.200	4.236
62	20.972	18.457	90	4.838	3.957
63	20.253	17.764	91	4.501	3.670
64	19.545	17.083	92	4.175	3.388
65	18.849	16.414	93	3.862	3.129
66	18.165	15.759	94	3.579	2.903
67	17.493	15.116	95	3.329	2.705
68	16.832	14.486	96	3.109	2.533
69	16.182	13.869	97	2.914	2.384
70	15.553	13.268	98	2.741	2.254
71	14.965	12.676	99	2.584	2.137
72	14.367	12.073	100	2.433	2.026
73	13.761	11.445	101	2.289	1.919
74	13.189	10.830	102	2.152	1.818
75	12.607	10.243	103	2.022	1.723
76	12.011	9.673	104	1.899	1.637
77	11.394	9.139	105	1.784	1.563
78	10.779	8.641	106	1.679	1.510
79	10.184	8.159	107	1.588	1.500
80	9.620	7.672	108	1.522	1.500
81	9.060	7.188	109	1.500	1.500
82	8.501	6.719	110	1.500	1.500

(B) If there is a couple, the life expectancy for the person with the longer life expectancy shall be used.

(C) The life expectancy table set forth in this paragraph shall be used until expressly provided to the contrary through the amendment of this section.

(D) For residents over 110 years of age, 1.500 years shall be used in computing life expectancy.

(E) If a continuing care retirement community has contracted with a resident under 55 years of age, the continuing care retirement community shall provide the department with the methodology used to determine that resident's life expectancy.

(3) For that resident, use an interest rate of 6 percent or lower to determine from compound interest tables the factor that, when multiplied by one dollar ($1), represents the amount, at the time the computation is made, that will grow at the assumed compound interest rate to one dollar ($1) at the end of the period of the life expectancy of the resident.

(4) Multiply the refundable portion of the resident's entry fee amount by the factor obtained in paragraph (3) to determine the amount of reserve required to be maintained.

(5) The sum of these amounts with respect to each resident shall constitute the reserve for refundable contracts.

(6) The reserve for refundable contracts shall be revised annually as provided for in subdivision (a), using the interest rate, refund obligation amount, and individual life expectancies current at that time.

(d) Withdrawals may be made from the trust to pay refunds when due under the terms of the refundable entrance fee contracts and when the balance in the trust exceeds the required refund reserve amount determined in accordance with subdivision (c).

(e) Deposits shall be made to the trust with respect to new residents when the entrance fee is received and in the amount determined with respect to that resident in accordance with subdivision (c).

(f) Additional deposits shall be made to the trust fund within 30 days of any annual reporting date on which the trust fund balance falls below the required reserve in accordance with subdivision (c) and the deposits shall be in an amount sufficient to bring the trust balance into compliance with this section.

(g) Providers who have used a method previously allowed by statute to satisfy their refund reserve requirement may continue to use that method.

(Added by Stats. 2000, Ch. 820, Sec. 57.36. Effective January 1, 2001.)

1792.7.

(a) The Legislature finds and declares all of the following:

(1) In continuing care contracts, providers offer a wide variety of living accommodations and care programs for an indefinite or extended number of years in exchange for substantial payments by residents.

(2) The annual reporting and reserve requirements for each continuing care provider should include a report that summarizes the provider's recent and projected performance in a form useful to residents, prospective residents, and the department.

(3) Certain providers enter into "life care contracts" or similar contracts with their residents. Periodic actuarial studies that examine the actuarial financial condition of these providers will help to assure their long-term financial soundness.

(b) Each provider shall annually file with the department a report that shows certain key financial indicators for the provider's past five years, based on the provider's actual experience, and for the upcoming five years, based on the provider's projections. Providers shall file their key indicator reports in the manner required by Section 1792.9 and in a form prescribed by the department.

(c) Each provider that has entered into Type A contracts shall file with the department an actuary's opinion as to the actuarial financial condition of the provider's continuing care operations in the manner required by Section 1792.10.
(Added by Stats. 2004, Ch. 129, Sec. 6. Effective January 1, 2005.)
1792.8.
(a) For purposes of this article, "actuarial study" means an analysis that addresses the current actuarial financial condition of a provider that is performed by an actuary in accordance with accepted actuarial principles and the standards of practice adopted by the Actuarial Standards Board. An actuarial study shall include all of the following:
(1) An actuarial report.
(2) A statement of actuarial opinion.
(3) An actuarial balance sheet.
(4) A cohort pricing analysis.
(5) A cashflow projection.
(6) A description of the actuarial methodology, formulae, and assumptions.
(b) "Actuary" means a member in good standing of the American Academy of Actuaries who is qualified to sign a statement of actuarial opinion.
(c) "Type A contract" means a continuing care contract that has an up-front entrance fee and includes provision for housing, residential services, amenities, and unlimited specific health-related services with little or no substantial increases in monthly charges, except for normal operating costs and inflation adjustments.
(Added by Stats. 2004, Ch. 129, Sec. 7. Effective January 1, 2005.)
1792.9.
(a) All providers shall file annually with the department a financial report disclosing key financial ratios and other key indicators in a form determined by the department.
(b) The department shall issue a "Key Indicators Report" form to providers that shall be used to satisfy the requirements of subdivision (a). The Key Indicators Report shall require providers to disclose the following information:
(1) Operational data indicating the provider's average annual occupancy by facility.
(2) Margin ratios indicating the provider's net operating margin and net operating margin adjusted to reflect net proceeds from entrance fees.
(3) Liquidity indicators stating both the provider's total cash and investments available for operational expenses and the provider's days cash on hand.
(4) Capital structure indicators stating the provider's dollar figures for deferred revenue from entrance fees, net annual entrance fee proceeds, unrestricted net assets, and annual capital expenditure.
(5) Capital structure ratios indicating the provider's annual debt service coverage, annual debt service coverage adjusted to reflect net proceeds from entrance fees, annual debt service over revenue percentage, and unrestricted cash over long-term debt percentage.
(6) Capital structure indicators stating the provider's average age of facility calculation based on accumulated depreciation and the provider's average annual effective interest rate.
(c) The department shall determine the appropriate formula for calculating each of the key indicators included in the Key Indicator Report. The department shall base each formula on generally accepted standards and practices related to the financial analysis of continuing care providers and entities engaged in similar enterprises.
(d) Each provider shall file its annual Key Indicators Report within 30 days following the due date for the provider's annual report. If the Key Indicators Report is not received by the department by the date it is due, the provider shall pay a one thousand dollar ($1,000) late fee at the time the report is submitted. The provider shall pay an additional late fee of thirty-three dollars ($33) for each day the report is late beyond 30 days. For purposes of this section, a provider's Key Indicators Report is not submitted to the department until the provider has paid all accrued late fees.
(Added by Stats. 2004, Ch. 129, second Sec. 7 (Sec. 7.5). Effective January 1, 2005.)
1792.10.
(a) Each provider that has entered into Type A contracts shall submit to the department, at least once every five years, an actuary's opinion as to the provider's actuarial financial condition. The actuary's opinion shall be based on an actuarial study completed by the opining actuary in a manner that meets the requirements described in Section 1792.8. The actuary's opinion, and supporting actuarial study, shall examine, refer to, and opine on the provider's actuarial financial condition as of a specified date that is within four months of the date the opinion is provided to the department.
(b) Each provider required to file an actuary's opinion under subdivision (a) that held a certificate of authority on December 31, 2003, shall file its actuary's opinion before the expiration of five years following the date it last filed an actuarial study or opinion with the department. Thereafter, the provider shall file its required actuary's opinion before the expiration of five years following the date it last filed an actuary's opinion with the department.
(c) Each provider required to file an actuary's opinion under subdivision (a) that did not hold a certificate of authority on December 31, 2003, shall file its first actuary's opinion within 45 days following the due date for the provider's annual report for the fiscal year in which the provider obtained its certificate of authority. Thereafter, the provider shall file its required actuary's opinion before the expiration of five years following the date it last filed an actuary's opinion with the department.
(d) The actuary's opinion required by subdivision (a) shall comply with generally accepted actuarial principles and the standards of practice adopted by the Actuarial Standards Board. The actuary's opinion shall also include statements that the data and assumptions used in the underlying actuarial study are appropriate and that the methods employed in the actuarial study are consistent with sound actuarial principles and practices. The actuary's opinion must state whether the provider has adequate resources to meet all its actuarial liabilities and related statement items, including an appropriate surplus, and whether the provider's financial condition is actuarially sound.
(Added by Stats. 2004, Ch. 129, Sec. 8. Effective January 1, 2005.)
1793.
(a) Any provider offering a refundable contract, or other entity assuming responsibility for refundable contracts, shall maintain a refund reserve fund in trust for the residents. This trust fund shall remain intact to accumulate interest earnings resulting from investments of liquid reserves in accordance with paragraph (1) of subdivision (e) and subparagraphs (A) through (E), inclusive, of paragraph (3) of subdivision (e) of Section 1792.2. The amount of the refund reserve shall be revised annually by the provider and submitted to the department in conjunction with the annual report required by Section 1790.
(b) Any providers or other entity assuming responsibility for refundable contracts, which has not executed refundable contracts in a continuing care retirement community prior to January 1, 1996, and proposes to execute these contracts in that continuing care retirement community after that date, shall maintain a refund reserve fund in trust for the residents holding such contracts.
(1) Except as noted in paragraph (2), this trust fund shall remain intact as specified in subdivision (a).
(2) To the extent approved by the department, the trust account may invest up to 70 percent of the refund reserves in real estate that is used to provide care and housing for the holders of the refundable continuing care contracts and is located on the same campus where these continuing care contract holders reside.
These investments in real estate shall be limited to 50 percent of the providers' net equity in the real estate. The net equity shall be the book value, assessed value, or current appraised value within 12 months prior to the end of the fiscal year, less any depreciation, encumbrances, and the amount required for statutory reserves under Section 1792.2, all according to audited financial statements acceptable to the department. This paragraph shall apply to applications, and for those phases of the project that were identified as part of applications, submitted after May 31, 1995.
(3) Any provider who submitted an application on or before May 31, 1995, may provide for the refund obligation of this section with a trust account that invests up to 85 percent of the refund reserves in the continuing care retirement community's real estate and the remaining 15 percent in the form of either cash or an unconditional, irrevocable letter of credit to be phased in over a two-year period beginning with initial occupancy in the facility.
(4) Each refund reserve trust fund shall be established at an institution qualified to be an escrow agent pursuant to an agreement between the provider and the institution based on this section and approved in advance by the department.
(5) The amount to be held in the reserve fund shall be the total of the amounts calculated with respect to each individual resident as follows:
(A) Determine the age in years and the portion of the entry fee for the resident refundable for the seventh year of residency and thereafter.
(B) Determine life expectancy of that individual from the life expectancy table in paragraph (1) of subdivision (b) of Section 1792.2. If there is a couple, use the life expectancy for the individual with the longer life expectancy.
(C) For that resident, use an interest rate of 6 percent or lower to determine from compound interest tables the factor which represents the amount required today to grow at compound interest to one dollar ($1) at the end of the period of the life expectancy of the resident.
(D) Multiply the refundable portion of the resident's entry fee amount by the factor obtained in subparagraph (C) to determine the amount of reserve required to be maintained.
(E) The sum of these amounts with respect to each resident shall constitute the reserve for refundable contracts.
(F) The reserve for refundable contracts will be revised annually as provided for in subdivision (a), using the interest rate, refund obligation amount, and individual life expectancies current at that time.
(6) Withdrawals may be made from the trust fund to pay refunds when due under the terms of the refundable entry fee contracts and when the balance in the trust fund exceeds the required refund reserve amount determined in accordance with paragraph (5) of subdivision (b).
(7) Deposits shall be made to the trust fund with respect to new residents when the entry fee is received and in the amount determined with respect to that resident in accordance with paragraph (5) of subdivision (b).
(8) Additional deposits shall be made to the trust fund within 30 days of any annual reporting date on which the trust fund balance falls below the required reserve in accordance with paragraph (5) of subdivision (b) and such deposits shall be in an amount sufficient to bring the trust fund balance into compliance with this section.
(c) Any provider which has executed refundable contracts in a continuing care retirement community prior to January 1, 1996, and which has not executed refundable contracts in a continuing care retirement community prior to January 1, 1991, shall submit, for the department's approval, a method of determining a refund reserve to be held in trust for the residents. Approved methods include any of the following:
(1) The establishment, at the time continuing care contracts are signed, of a reserve fund in trust for the full amount of the refunds promised.
(2) The purchase from an insurance company, authorized to do business in the State of California, of fully paid life insurance policies for the full amount of the refunds promised.
(3) A method approved by the American Academy of Actuaries in their Actuarial Standards of Practice Relating to Continuing Care Retirement Communities, which method

provides for fully funding the refund obligations in a separate trust fund as provided in subdivision (b).

(d) Any provider offering a refundable contract, or other entity assuming responsibility for refundable contracts prior to January 1, 1991, shall maintain a refund reserve bank account in trust for the residents as described in subdivision (b) except that the amount of refund reserves shall be calculated based on the following assumptions and methods of calculation:

(1) The continuing care retirement community will no longer receive entry fee income after a period of 40 years following the commencement of operation.

(2) Approved long-term investments, such as treasury notes, will earn 3 percent more than the rate of inflation.

(3) Entrance fees will increase at the rate of inflation.

(4) Land values will increase at the rate of inflation.

(5) Investments in the refund reserve trust will increase at the rate for approved long-term investments.

(6) Calculate the number of units to be resold each year at the approved rate of turnover.

(7) Determine the mean entrance fee, as of the current date.

(8) Determine the factor for inflating the mean entrance fee at the rate of 3 percent below the interest rate on new 30-year treasury bonds, for each year from the current date to the 40th year of operation, or until all units have been turned over.

(9) Calculate the inflated mean entrance fees for the 40th year and for each preceding year, until all units have been turned over.

(10) Multiply the inflated mean entrance fee for the 40th year, and each preceding year, as specified in paragraph (9), by the annual turnover, as specified in paragraph (6), until the total of the annual turnovers used in the calculations equals the total number of units in the continuing care retirement community.

(11) The projected refund liability shall be the sum of the products obtained pursuant to paragraph (10), multiplied by the rate of refund for the seventh year of residency, specified by current continuing care contracts, multiplied by the percentage of current continuing care contracts which specify this rate of refund. The projected refund liability amount shall be calculated for each rate, if existing continuing care contracts specify several rates.

(12) The projected refund liability, or the aggregate of these liabilities, if several rates are obtained pursuant to paragraph (11), may be reduced by the value of the land used for the continuing care retirement community, inflated to the 40th year of operation, as determined pursuant to paragraph (4), if the provider agrees to a lien pursuant to Section 1793.15 to secure this commitment.

(13) Calculate the present value of the projected refund liability at the current rate of interest for new 30-year treasury bonds. The result is the required refund reserve.

(e) Any entity which holds a certificate of authority, provisional certificate of authority, or permit to sell deposit subscriptions on or before September 23, 1986, shall be exempted from the refund reserve requirement established by this section, if the entity has an equity balance of five times the amount of the refund reserves calculated pursuant to subdivision (c).

(1) The equity balance shall be verified by one or more of the following means:

(A) The "stockholders' equity," or equivalent amount, as reflected on the most recent Form 10K (which may be on a consolidated basis or on a consolidated and combined basis) filed with the Securities and Exchange Commission.

(B) The "total fund balance of net worth," or equivalent amount, as reflected on Form 990 or Form 990-PF filed with the Internal Revenue Service.

(C) The "total net worth," or equivalent amount, as reflected on the most recent Form 109 filed with the Franchise Tax Board.

(2) The amount of the requirement for the equity balance shall be revised annually pursuant to this section.

(3) Compliance shall be based on review, by the department, of financial statements prepared in accordance with generally accepted accounting principles, accompanied by an unqualified opinion by a certified public accountant.

(4) If the equity balance is determined by the department to be less than the required amount, the provider or other entity assuming responsibility shall deposit, in a form satisfactory to the department, an amount equal to the refund reserve required within 60 days.

(f) All continuing care retirement communities offering refundable entrance fees that are not secured by cash reserves, except those facilities that were issued a certificate of authority prior to May 31, 1995, shall clearly disclose this fact in all marketing materials and continuing care contracts.

(Amended by Stats. 1995, Ch. 920, Sec. 48. Effective January 1, 1996.)

ARTICLE 7. Offenses and Penalties [1793.5 - 1793.31]

(Article 7 added by Stats. 1990, Ch. 875, Sec. 2.)

1793.5.

(a) An entity that accepts deposits and proposes to promise to provide care without having a current and valid permit to accept deposits is guilty of a misdemeanor.

(b) An entity that accepts deposits and fails to place any deposit received into an escrow account as required by this chapter is guilty of a misdemeanor.

(c) An entity that executes a continuing care contract without holding a current and valid provisional certificate of authority or certificate of authority is guilty of a misdemeanor.

(d) An entity that abandons a continuing care retirement community or its obligations under a continuing care contract is guilty of a misdemeanor. An entity that violates this section shall be liable to the injured resident for treble the amount of damages assessed in any civil action brought by or on behalf of the resident in any court having proper

jurisdiction. The court may, in its discretion, award all costs and attorney fees to the injured resident, if that resident prevails in the action.

(e) Each violation of subdivision (a), (b), (c), or (d) is subject to a fine not to exceed ten thousand dollars ($10,000), or by imprisonment in the county jail for a period not to exceed one year, or by both.

(f) An entity that issues, delivers, or publishes, or as manager or officer or in any other administrative capacity, assists in the issuance, delivery, or publication of any printed matter, oral representation, or advertising material which does not comply with the requirements of this chapter is guilty of a misdemeanor.

(g) A violation of subdivision (f) by an entity will constitute cause for the suspension of all and any licenses, permits, provisional certificates of authority, and certificates of authority issued to that entity by any agency of the state.

(h) A violation under this section is an act of unfair competition as defined in Section 17200 of the Business and Professions Code.

(Amended by Stats. 2000, Ch. 820, Sec. 58. Effective January 1, 2001.)

1793.6.

(a) The department may issue citations pursuant to this section containing orders of abatement and assessing civil penalties against any entity that violates Section 1771.2 or 1793.5.

(b) If upon inspection or investigation, the department has probable cause to believe that an entity is violating Section 1771.2 or 1793.5, the department may issue a citation to that entity. Each citation shall be in writing and shall describe with particularity the basis of the citation. Each citation shall contain an order of abatement. In addition to the administrative fines imposed pursuant to Section 1793.27, an entity that violates the abatement order shall be liable for a civil penalty in the amount of two hundred dollars ($200) per day for violation of the abatement order.

(c) The civil penalty authorized in subdivision (b) shall be imposed if a continuing care retirement community is operated without a provisional certificate of authority or certificate of authority and the operator refuses to seek a certificate of authority or the operator seeks a certificate of authority and the application is denied and the operator continues to operate the continuing care retirement community without a provisional certificate of authority or certificate of authority, unless other remedies available to the department, including prosecution, are deemed more appropriate by the department.

(d) Service of a citation issued under this section may be made by certified mail at the last known business address or residence address of the entity cited.

(e) Within 15 days after service of a citation under this section, an entity may appeal in writing to the department with respect to the violations alleged, the scope of the order of abatement, or the amount of civil penalty assessed.

(f) If the entity cited fails without good cause to appeal in writing to the department within 15 business days after service of the citation, the citation shall become a final order of the department. The department may extend the 15-day period for good cause, to a maximum of 15 additional days.

(g) If the entity cited under this section makes a timely appeal of the citation, the department shall provide an opportunity for a hearing. The department shall thereafter issue a decision, based on findings of fact, affirming, modifying, or vacating the citation or directing other appropriate relief. The proceedings under this section shall be conducted in accordance with the provisions of Chapter 5 (commencing with Section 11500) of Part 1 of Division 3 of Title 2 of the Government Code, and the department shall have all the powers granted therein.

(h) After exhaustion of the review procedures specified in this section, the department may apply to the appropriate superior court for a judgment in the amount of the civil penalty and an order compelling the cited entity to comply with the order of abatement. The application, which shall include a certified copy of the final order of the department shall be served upon the cited entity who shall have five business days to file that entity's response in writing in the superior court. This period may be extended for good cause. Failure on the part of the cited entity to respond shall constitute grounds for entry of a default judgment against that entity. In the event a response is timely filed in superior court, the action shall have priority for trial over all other civil matters.

(i) Notwithstanding any other provision of law, the department may waive part or all of the civil penalty if the entity against whom the civil penalty is assessed satisfactorily completes all the requirements for, and is issued, a provisional certificate of authority or certificate of authority.

(j) Civil penalties recovered pursuant to this section shall be deposited into the Continuing Care Provider Fee Fund.

(Amended by Stats. 2000, Ch. 820, Sec. 59. Effective January 1, 2001.)

1793.7.

A permit to accept deposits, a provisional certificate of authority, or a certificate of authority shall be forfeited by operation of law when any one of the following occurs:

(a) The applicant terminates marketing for the proposed continuing care retirement community.

(b) The applicant or provider surrenders to the department its residential care facility for the elderly license, the permit to accept deposits, provisional certificate of authority, or certificate of authority for a continuing care retirement community.

(c) The applicant or provider sells or otherwise transfers all or part of the continuing care retirement community.

(d) A change occurs in the majority ownership of the continuing care retirement community or the certificate of authority holder.

(e) The applicant or provider merges with another entity.

(f) The applicant or entity makes a material change in a pending application which requires a new application pursuant to subdivision (c) of Section 1779.8.

(g) The applicant or provider moves the continuing care retirement community from one location to another without the department's prior approval.

(h) The applicant or provider abandons the continuing care retirement community or its obligations under the continuing care contracts.

(i) The applicant or provider is evicted from the continuing care retirement community premises.

(Amended by Stats. 2000, Ch. 820, Sec. 60. Effective January 1, 2001.)

1793.8.

A Certificate of Authority shall be automatically inactivated when a provider voluntarily ceases to enter into continuing care contracts with new residents. The provider shall notify the department of its intention to cease entering into continuing care contracts and shall continue to comply with all provisions of this chapter until all continuing care contract obligations have been fulfilled.

(Amended by Stats. 2000, Ch. 820, Sec. 61. Effective January 1, 2001.)

1793.9.

(a) In the event of receivership or liquidation, all claims made against a provider based on the provider's continuing care contracts shall be preferred claims against all assets owned by the provider. However, these preferred claims shall be subject to any perfected claims secured by the provider's assets.

(b) If the provider is liquidated, residents who have executed a refundable continuing care contract shall have a preferred claim to liquid assets held in the refund reserve pursuant to Section 1792.6. This preferred claim shall be superior to all other claims from residents without refundable contracts or other creditors. If this fund and any other available assets are not sufficient to fulfill the refund obligations, each resident shall be distributed a proportionate amount of the refund reserve funds determined by dividing the amount of each resident's refund due by the total refunds due and multiplying that percentage by the total funds available.

(c) For purposes of computing the reserve required pursuant to Sections 1792.2 and 1793, the liens required under Section 1793.15 are not required to be deducted from the value of real or personal property.

(Amended by Stats. 2002, Ch. 553, Sec. 5. Effective January 1, 2003.)

1793.11.

(a) Any transfer of money or property, pursuant to a continuing care contract found by the department to be executed in violation of this chapter, is voidable at the option of the resident or transferor for a period of 90 days from the execution of the transfer.

(b) Any deed or other instrument of conveyance shall contain a recital that the transaction is made pursuant to rescission by the resident or transferor within 90 days from the date of first occupancy.

(c) No action may be brought for the reasonable value of any services rendered between the date of transfer and the date the resident disaffirms the continuing care contract.

(d) With respect to real property, the right of disaffirmance or rescission is conclusively presumed to have terminated if a notice of intent to rescind is not recorded with the county recorder of the county in which the real property is located within 90 days from the date of first occupancy of the residential living unit.

(e) A transfer of money or property, real or personal, to anyone pursuant to a continuing care contract that was not approved by the department is voidable at the option of the department or transferor or his or her assigns or agents.

(f) A transaction determined by the department to be in violation of this chapter is voidable at the option of the resident or his or her assignees or agents.

(Amended by Stats. 2000, Ch. 820, Sec. 63. Effective January 1, 2001.)

1793.13.

(a) The department may require a provider to submit a financial plan, if either of the following applies:

(1) A provider fails to file a complete annual report as required by Section 1790.

(2) The department has reason to believe that the provider is insolvent, is in imminent danger of becoming insolvent, is in a financially unsound or unsafe condition, or that its condition is such that it may otherwise be unable to fully perform its obligations pursuant to continuing care contracts.

(b) A provider shall submit its financial plan to the department within 60 days following the date of the department's request. The financial plan shall explain how and when the provider will rectify the problems and deficiencies identified by the department.

(c) The department shall approve or disapprove the plan within 30 days of its receipt.

(d) If the plan is approved, the provider shall immediately implement the plan.

(e) If the plan is disapproved, or if it is determined that the plan is not being fully implemented, the department may consult with its financial consultants to develop a corrective action plan at the provider's expense, or require the provider to obtain new or additional management capability approved by the department to solve its difficulties. A reasonable period, as determined by the department, shall be allowed for the reorganized management to develop a plan which, subject to the approval of the department, will reasonably assure that the provider will meet its responsibilities under the law.

(Amended by Stats. 2011, Ch. 32, Sec. 13. (AB 106) Effective June 29, 2011. Operative January 1, 2012, by Sec. 73 of Stats. 2011, Ch. 32.)

1793.15.

(a) When necessary to secure an applicant's or a provider's performance of its obligations to depositors or residents, the department may record a notice or notices of lien on behalf of the depositors or residents. From the date of recording, the lien shall attach to all real property owned or acquired by the provider during the pendency of the lien, provided the real property is not exempt from the execution of a lien and is located within the county in which the lien is recorded. The lien shall have the force, effect, and priority of a judgment lien.

(b) The department may record a lien on any real property owned by the provider if the provider's annual report indicates the provider has an unfunded statutory or refund requirement. A lien filed pursuant to this section shall have the effect, force, and priority of a judgment lien filed against the property.

(c) The department shall file a release of the lien if the department determines that the lien is no longer necessary to secure the applicant's or provider's performance of its obligations to the depositors or residents.

(d) Within 10 days following the department's denial of a request for a release of the lien, the applicant or provider may file an appeal with the department.

(e) The department's final decision shall be subject to court review pursuant to Section 1094.5 of the Code of Civil Procedure, upon petition of the applicant or provider filed within 30 days of service of the decision.

(Amended by Stats. 2000, Ch. 820, Sec. 65. Effective January 1, 2001.)

1793.17.

(a) When necessary to secure the interests of depositors or residents, the department may require that the applicant or provider reestablish an escrow account, return previously released moneys to escrow, and escrow all future entrance fee payments.

(b) The department may release funds from escrow as it deems appropriate or terminate the escrow requirement when it determines that the escrow is no longer necessary to secure the performance of all obligations of the applicant or provider to depositors or residents.

(Amended by Stats. 2000, Ch. 820, Sec. 66. Effective January 1, 2001.)

1793.19.

The civil, criminal, and administrative remedies available to the department pursuant to this article are not exclusive and may be sought and employed by the department, in any combination to enforce this chapter.

(Amended by Stats. 2000, Ch. 820, Sec. 67. Effective January 1, 2001.)

1793.21.

The department, in its discretion, may condition, suspend, or revoke any permit to accept deposits, provisional certificate of authority, or certificate of authority issued under this chapter if it finds that the applicant or provider has done any of the following:

(a) Violated this chapter or the rules and regulations adopted under this chapter.

(b) Aided, abetted, or permitted the violation of this chapter or the rules and regulations adopted under this chapter.

(c) Had a license suspended or revoked pursuant to the licensing provisions of Chapter 2 (commencing with Section 1250) or Chapter 3.2 (commencing with Section 1569).

(d) Made a material misstatement, misrepresentation, or fraud in obtaining the permit to accept deposits, provisional certificate of authority, or certificate of authority.

(e) Demonstrated a lack of fitness or trustworthiness.

(f) Engaged in any fraudulent or dishonest practices of management in the conduct of business.

(g) Misappropriated, converted, or withheld moneys.

(h) After request by the department for an examination, access to records, or information, refused to be examined or to produce its accounts, records, and files for examination, or refused to give information with respect to its affairs, or refused to perform any other legal obligations related to an examination.

(i) Manifested an unsound financial condition.

(j) Used methods and practices in the conduct of business so as to render further transactions by the provider or applicant hazardous or injurious to the public.

(k) Failed to maintain at least the minimum statutory reserves required by Section 1792.2.

(l) Failed to maintain the reserve fund escrow account for prepaid continuing care contracts required by Section 1792.

(m) Failed to comply with the refund reserve requirements stated in Section 1793.

(n) Failed to comply with the requirements of this chapter for maintaining escrow accounts for funds.

(o) Failed to file the annual report described in Section 1790.

(p) Violated a condition on its permit to accept deposits, provisional certificate of authority, or certificate of authority.

(q) Failed to comply with its approved financial and marketing plan or to secure approval of a modified plan.

(r) Materially changed or deviated from an approved plan of operation without the prior consent of the department.

(s) Failed to fulfill his or her obligations under continuing care contracts.

(t) Made material misrepresentations to depositors, prospective residents, or residents of a continuing care retirement community.

(u) Failed to submit proposed changes to continuing care contracts prior to use, or using a continuing care contract that has not been previously approved by the department.

(v) Failed to diligently submit materials requested by the department or required by the statute.

(Amended by Stats. 2000, Ch. 820, Sec. 68. Effective January 1, 2001.)

1793.23.

(a) If the department conditions, suspends, or revokes any permit to accept deposits, provisional certificate of authority, or certificate of authority issued pursuant to this chapter, the provider shall have a right of appeal to the department. The proceedings shall be conducted in accordance with Chapter 5 (commencing with Section 11500) of Part 1 of Division 3 of Title 2 of the Government Code, and the department shall have all of the powers granted therein. A suspension, condition, or revocation shall remain in effect until completion of the proceedings in favor of the provider. In all proceedings conducted in accordance with this section, the standard of proof to be applied shall be by a preponderance of the evidence.

(b) The department may, upon finding of changed circumstances, remove a suspension or condition.

(Amended by Stats. 2011, Ch. 32, Sec. 14. (AB 106) Effective June 29, 2011. Operative January 1, 2012, by Sec. 73 of Stats. 2011, Ch. 32.)

1793.25.

(a) During the period that the revocation or suspension action is pending against the permit to accept deposits, provisional certificate of authority, or certificate of authority, the provider shall not enter into any new deposit agreements or continuing care contracts.

(b) The suspension or revocation by the department, or voluntary return of the provisional certificate of authority or certificate of authority by the provider, shall not release the provider from obligations assumed at the time the continuing care contracts were executed.

(Amended by Stats. 2000, Ch. 820, Sec. 70. Effective January 1, 2001.)

1793.27.

(a) If the department finds that any entity has violated Section 1793.5 or one or more grounds exist for conditioning, revoking, or suspending a permit to accept deposits, provisional certificate of authority, or a certificate of authority issued under this chapter, the department, in lieu of the condition, revocation, or suspension, may impose an administrative fine upon an applicant or provider in an amount not to exceed one thousand dollars ($1,000) per violation.

(b) The administrative fine shall be deposited in the Continuing Care Provider Fee Fund and shall be disbursed for the specific purposes of offsetting the costs of investigation and litigation and to compensate court-appointed administrators when continuing care retirement community assets are insufficient.

(Amended by Stats. 2000, Ch. 820, Sec. 71. Effective January 1, 2001.)

1793.29.

In the case of any violation or threatened violation of this chapter, the department may institute a proceeding or may request the Attorney General to institute a proceeding to obtain injunctive or other equitable relief in the superior court in and for the county in which the violation has occurred or will occur, or in which the principal place of business of the provider is located. The proceeding under this section shall conform with the requirements of Chapter 3 (commencing with Section 525) of Title 7 of Part 2 of the Code of Civil Procedure, except that no undertaking shall be required of the department in any action commenced under this section, nor shall the department be required to allege facts necessary to show lack of adequate remedy at law, or to show irreparable loss or damage.

(Amended by Stats. 2000, Ch. 820, Sec. 72. Effective January 1, 2001.)

1793.31.

(a) The district attorney of every county may, upon application by the department or its authorized representative, institute and conduct the prosecution of any action for violation of this chapter within his or her county.

(b) This chapter shall not limit or qualify the powers of the district attorney to institute and conduct the prosecution of any action brought for the violation within his or her county of this chapter or any other provision of law, including, but not limited to, actions for fraud or misrepresentation.

(c) The department shall provide access to any records in its control on request of a district attorney and shall cooperate in any investigation by a district attorney.

(Amended by Stats. 1995, Ch. 920, Sec. 64. Effective January 1, 1996.)

ARTICLE 8. Appointment of Administrators [1793.50 - 1793.62]
(Article 8 added by Stats. 1990, Ch. 875, Sec. 2.)

1793.50.

(a) The department may petition the superior court for an order appointing a qualified administrator to operate a continuing care retirement community, and thereby mitigate imminent crisis situations where elderly residents could lose support services or be moved without proper preparation, in any of the following circumstances:

(1) The provider is insolvent or in imminent danger of becoming insolvent.

(2) The provider is in a financially unsound or unsafe condition.

(3) The provider has failed to establish or has substantially depleted the reserves required by this chapter.

(4) The provider has failed to submit a plan, as specified in Section 1793.13, the department has not approved the plan submitted by the provider, the provider has not fully implemented the plan, or the plan has not been successful.

(5) The provider is unable to fully perform its obligations pursuant to continuing care contracts.

(6) The residents are otherwise placed in serious jeopardy.

(b) The administrator may only assume the operation of the continuing care retirement community in order to accomplish one or more of the following: rehabilitate the provider to enable it fully to perform its continuing care contract obligations; implement a plan of reorganization acceptable to the department; facilitate the transition where another provider assumes continuing care contract obligations; or facilitate an orderly liquidation of the provider.

(c) With each petition, the department shall include a request for a temporary restraining order to prevent the provider from disposing of or transferring assets pending the hearing on the petition.

(d) The provider shall be served with a copy of the petition, together with an order to appear and show cause why management and possession of the provider's continuing care retirement community or assets should not be vested in an administrator.

(e) The order to show cause shall specify a hearing date, which shall be not less than five nor more than 10 days following service of the petition and order to show cause on the provider.

(f) Petitions to appoint an administrator shall have precedence over all matters, except criminal matters, in the court.

(g) At the time of the hearing, the department shall advise the provider and the court of the name of the proposed administrator.

(h) If, at the conclusion of the hearing, including such oral evidence as the court may consider, the court finds that any of the circumstances specified in subdivision (a) exist, the court shall issue an order appointing an administrator to take possession of the property of the provider and to conduct the business thereof, enjoining the provider from interfering with the administrator in the conduct of the rehabilitation, and directing the administrator to take steps toward removal of the causes and conditions which have made rehabilitation necessary, as the court may direct.

(i) The order shall include a provision directing the issuance of a notice of the rehabilitation proceedings to the residents at the continuing care retirement community and to other interested persons as the court may direct.

(j) The court may permit the provider to participate in the continued operation of the continuing care retirement community during the pendency of any appointments ordered pursuant to this section and shall specify in the order the nature and scope of the participation.

(k) The court shall retain jurisdiction throughout the rehabilitation proceeding and may issue further orders as it deems necessary to accomplish the rehabilitation or orderly liquidation of the continuing care retirement community in order to protect the residents of the continuing care retirement community.

(Amended by Stats. 2011, Ch. 32, Sec. 15. (AB 106) Effective June 29, 2011. Operative January 1, 2012, by Sec. 73 of Stats. 2011, Ch. 32.)

1793.52.

The court-appointed administrator shall immediately notify the residents of that appointment and of the status of the continuing care retirement community management.

(Amended by Stats. 1995, Ch. 920, Sec. 66. Effective January 1, 1996.)

1793.54.

If an administrator is appointed to rehabilitate a provider, the administrator may do any of the following:

(a) Take possession of and preserve, protect and recover any assets, books, records, or property of the provider, including, but not limited to, claims or causes of action belonging to, or which may be asserted by, the provider.

(b) Deal with the property in the administrator's name in the capacity as administrator, and purchase at any sale any real estate or other asset upon which the provider may hold any lien or encumbrance or in which the provider may have an interest.

(c) File, prosecute, and defend or compromise any suit or suits which have been filed, or which may thereafter be filed, by or against the provider as necessary to protect the provider or the residents or any property affected thereby.

(d) Deposit and invest any of the provider's available funds.

(e) Pay all expenses of the rehabilitation.

(f) Perform all duties of the provider in the provision of care and services to residents in the continuing care retirement community at the time the administrator takes possession.

(g) Facilitate the orderly transfer of residents should the provider ultimately fail.

(h) Exercise any other powers and duties as may be authorized by law or provided by order of the court.

(Amended by Stats. 1995, Ch. 920, Sec. 67. Effective January 1, 1996.)

1793.56.

(a) The appointed administrator is entitled to reasonable compensation.

(b) The costs compensating the administrator may be charged against the assets of the provider. When the provider's assets and assets from the continuing care retirement community are insufficient, the department, in its discretion, may compensate the administrator from the Continuing Care Provider Fee Fund.

(c) Any individual appointed administrator, pursuant to Section 1793.50, shall be held harmless for any negligence in the performance of his or her duties and the provider shall indemnify the administrator for all costs of defending actions brought against him or her in his or her capacity as administrator.

(Amended by Stats. 2000, Ch. 820, Sec. 74. Effective January 1, 2001.)

1793.58.

(a) The department, administrator, or any interested person, upon due notice to the administrator, at any time, may apply to the court for an order terminating the rehabilitation proceedings and permitting the provider to resume possession of the provider's property and the conduct of the provider's business.

(b) The court shall not issue the order requested pursuant to subdivision (a) unless, after a full hearing, the court has determined that the purposes of the proceeding have been fully and successfully accomplished and that the continuing care retirement community can be returned to the provider's management without further jeopardy to the residents of the continuing care retirement community, creditors, owners of the continuing care retirement community, and to the public.

(c) Before issuing any order terminating the rehabilitation proceeding the court shall consider a full report and accounting by the administrator regarding the provider's affairs, including the conduct of the provider's officers, employees, and business during the rehabilitation and the provider's current financial condition.

(d) Upon issuance of an order terminating the rehabilitation, the department shall reinstate the provisional certificate of authority or certificate of authority. The department may condition, suspend, or revoke the reinstated certificate only upon a change in the conditions existing at the time of the order or upon the discovery of facts which the department determines would have resulted in a denial of the request for an order terminating the rehabilitation had the court been aware of these facts.

(Amended by Stats. 2000, Ch. 820, Sec. 75. Effective January 1, 2001.)

1793.60.

(a) If at any time the department determines that further efforts to rehabilitate the provider would not be in the best interest of the residents or prospective residents, or would not be economically feasible, the department may apply to the court for an order of liquidation and dissolution or may apply for other appropriate relief for dissolving the property and bringing to conclusion its business affairs.

(b) Upon issuance of an order directing the liquidation or dissolution of the provider, the department shall revoke the provider's provisional certificate of authority or certificate of authority.

(Amended by Stats. 2011, Ch. 32, Sec. 16. (AB 106) Effective June 29, 2011. Operative January 1, 2012, by Sec. 73 of Stats. 2011, Ch. 32.)

1793.62.

(a) The department, administrator, or any interested person, upon due notice to the parties, may petition the court for an order terminating the rehabilitation proceedings when the rehabilitation efforts have not been successful, the continuing care retirement community has been sold at foreclosure sale, the provider is the subject of an order for relief in bankruptcy, or the provider has otherwise been shown to be unable to perform its obligations under the continuing care contracts.

(b) The court shall not issue the order requested pursuant to subdivision (a) unless all of the following have occurred:

(1) There has been a full hearing and the court has determined that the provider is unable to perform its contractual obligations.

(2) The administrator has given the court a full and complete report and financial accounting signed by the administrator as being a full and complete report and accounting.

(3) The court has determined that the residents of the continuing care retirement community have been protected to the extent possible and has made such orders in this regard as the court deems proper.

(Amended by Stats. 2009, Ch. 500, Sec. 49. (AB 1059) Effective January 1, 2010.)

ARTICLE 9. Continuing Care Retirement Community Closures [1793.80 - 1793.84]

(Article 9 added by Stats. 2009, Ch. 442, Sec. 3.)

1793.80.

(a) Notwithstanding any other provisions of law, a provider regulated under this chapter shall, no less than 120 days prior to the intended date of the permanent closure of a continuing care retirement community facility, as defined in paragraph (3) of subdivision (p) of Section 1771, provide written notice to the department and to the affected residents and their designated representatives. The notice shall contain the following statement of residents' rights under this article, in no less than 12-point type:

"This facility is planned for permanent closure on or after [state date of closure] that will require you to vacate your living unit. Residents of continuing care retirement communities in California have certain rights and continuing care community providers have certain responsibilities when a continuing care community closes. Those rights include, but are not limited to, the following:

1. Prior to closing, the provider shall provide a permanent closure plan to the Continuing Care Contracts Branch of the State Department of Social Services that describes the options available to residents for relocating to another part of the facility, or another facility or the compensation to be provided to residents.

2. No action can be taken to relocate any resident or to close the facility until the permanent closure and relocation plan has been prepared and provided to the department, the affected residents of the facility and their designated representatives, and to the local long-term care ombudsman program."

(b) Upon service of the closure notice when closure is planned for all units in a facility, the provider is prohibited from accepting new residents or entering into new continuing care contracts at the facility being closed.

(Added by Stats. 2009, Ch. 442, Sec. 3. (AB 407) Effective January 1, 2010.)

1793.81.

No less than 90 days prior to the permanent closure of the continuing care retirement community facility, as defined in paragraph (3) of subdivision (p) of Section 1771, the provider shall provide to the department, the affected residents of the facility and their designated representatives, and to the local long-term care ombudsman program, a written closure and relocation plan. The plan shall contain all of the following information:

(a) The number of affected residents at each level of care in the continuing care retirement community facility.

(b) Assessment of unique service and care needs, if applicable, for all of the following:

(1) Affected residents in skilled nursing and special care.

(2) Affected residents in assisted living units.

(3) Affected residents in the residential living units who require assistance with three or more activities of daily living, and other residents upon request.

(c) An explanation on how comparable care, if applicable, and comparable replacement housing will be provided.

(d) A detailed description of the services the provider will provide to residents to assist them in relocating, including, but not limited to, reasonable costs of moving, storage, if applicable, and transportation that shall be arranged by the provider in consultation with the resident and his or her designated representative, and paid for directly by the provider.

(e) The names and addresses of other continuing care retirement communities operated by the provider and whether there are openings available to the residents.

(f) The names and addresses of other continuing care retirement communities within 30 miles of the closing continuing care retirement community facility that provide comparable replacement housing and care, if applicable, to those offered at the facility that is scheduled for closure, and whether the facilities have immediate openings available to residents of the closing facility.

(g) A description of how the facility will comply with the requirements of Section 1793.82. The plan shall describe or identify the replacement facility or facilities and the procedure by which a resident can select a replacement facility. In no case shall the plan for replacement housing require a resident to pay more than he or she is presently paying for comparable housing and care, other than normal rate increases. Any proposed monetary compensation shall be fair and reasonable and shall represent the estimated cost to the resident of securing comparable replacement housing and care under terms similar to the contract between resident and provider.

(h) A statement regarding the availability of a licensed medical or geriatric professional to advise the resident, the resident's representative, and the provider regarding the transfer of the resident. Upon request by the resident or the resident's representative, the provider shall make available the services of a licensed medical or geriatric professional to advise the resident, the resident's representative, and the provider regarding the transfer of the resident. The provider may place a reasonable limit on the cost of the services of the medical or geriatric professional.

(Added by Stats. 2009, Ch. 442, Sec. 3. (AB 407) Effective January 1, 2010.)

1793.82.

(a) In the case of a permanent closure, the provider shall offer the resident the choice of the following four options, the terms of which shall not be less than the terms of the continuing care contract entered into between the resident and the provider as if that contract had been fully performed:

(1) Relocation to another continuing care facility owned or operated by the provider, if available.

(2) Relocation to a continuing care facility that is not owned by the provider.

(3) Monetary compensation equal to the value of the remainder of the contract as if the contract had been fully performed.

(4) An alternative arrangement that is mutually agreed upon by the provider and the resident or his or her representative.

(b) Replacement housing offered pursuant to paragraph (1) or (2) of subdivision (a) shall be housing that is, overall, comparable in cost, size, services, features, and amenities to the unit being vacated. If the resident chooses either of the replacement housing options in paragraph (1) or (2) of subdivision (a), the provider shall provide the reasonable costs of moving, storage, if applicable, and transportation.

(c) Notwithstanding subdivision (a), for a resident under a life care contract, the provider shall secure replacement housing and care at a comparable facility for the resident at no additional cost to the resident. The replacement housing and care shall comply with subdivision (l) of Section 1771 and subdivision (b) of Section 1788.

(d) The provider may provide relocation pursuant to paragraph (2) of subdivision (a) on a month-to-month basis, provided that the terms are otherwise consistent with subdivision (a). After 120 days, a resident selecting a facility not owned by the provider may not seek monetary compensation pursuant to paragraph (3) of subdivision (a).

(Added by Stats. 2009, Ch. 442, Sec. 3. (AB 407) Effective January 1, 2010.)

1793.83.

(a) When there is a permanent closure, as defined in paragraph (3) of subdivision (p) of Section 1771, within 30 days of submitting the relocation plan to the department, the provider shall fund a reserve, set up a trust fund, or secure a performance bond to ensure the fulfillment of the obligations and commitments associated with the relocation plan. The amount of the reserve trust fund or performance bond shall be equal to or greater than the estimated costs of relocating residents and the costs associated with the relocation options pursuant to Section 1793.81 and subdivision (a) of Section 1793.82.

(b) The reserve, trust fund, or performance bond shall be funded with qualifying assets enumerated in paragraphs (1) to (5), inclusive, of subdivision (a) of Section 1792.2 and shall not be subject to any liens, judgments, garnishments, or creditor's claims.

(Added by Stats. 2009, Ch. 442, Sec. 3. (AB 407) Effective January 1, 2010.)

1793.84.

(a) The provider shall submit monthly progress reports to the department detailing the progress and problems associated with the permanent closure, as defined in paragraph (3) of subdivision (p) of Section 1771, until all affected residents are relocated and all required payments to, or on behalf of, affected residents are made.

(b) The department shall monitor the implementation of the permanent closure as defined in paragraph (3) of subdivision (p) of Section 1771 and relocation plan as necessary to ensure full compliance by the provider. If the department determines that a provider is closing a facility in violation of this article or is doing so in a manner that endangers the health or safety of residents, it shall exercise its powers under Article 7 (commencing with Section 1793.5).

(c) No action shall be taken by the provider to relocate any resident or to close the facility until the relocation plan required by Section 1793.81 has been prepared and provided to the department, the affected residents of the facility and their designated representatives, and to the local long-term ombudsman program.
(Added by Stats. 2009, Ch. 442, Sec. 3. (AB 407) Effective January 1, 2010.)

ARTICLE 10. Temporary Relocation of Residents [1793.90 - 1793.91]
(Article 10 added by Stats. 2010, Ch. 443, Sec. 3.)
1793.90.
(a) All providers shall include in resident contracts the procedures to be followed to ensure that residential temporary relocations provide comparable levels of care, services, and living accommodations as described in the resident's contract.
(b) The provider shall notify the resident of the impending relocation at least 60 days in advance of the relocation.
(c) The provider shall meet with the resident and, at the resident's request, family members or other individuals, at least 30 days in advance of the transfer to discuss all aspects of the transfer, including, but not limited to, the rights, requirements, and procedures set forth in this article. Notice of this meeting shall be provided in writing and at least seven days in advance of the meeting and shall include all of the following information:
(1) The date of the transfer.
(2) The available replacement unit or units and monthly fees.
(3) The time when the resident will be able to inspect the replacement unit or units.
(4) The estimated date when the resident will be able to return to his or her unit or may move to a substitute permanent unit.
(d) If accommodations are not available at a continuing care retirement community operated by the provider within a 30-mile radius, the provider shall be required to provide a unit in a facility, agreed to by the resident, that most closely provides the services, size, features, and amenities provided in the unit being vacated.
(e) The provider shall be required to arrange and pay for all moving costs to the new facility and moving costs to the reconstructed facility, if the resident returns, as well as storage costs.
(f) The resident shall only be required to pay to the provider the monthly fee required in the resident's contract, or the monthly fee in the new facility, whichever is less. The provider shall be required to make payment to the facility to which the resident is relocated.
(g) Upon request by the resident or the resident's representative, the provider shall make available the services of a licensed medical or geriatric professional to advise the resident, the resident's representative, and the provider regarding the relocation of the resident. The provider may place a reasonable limit on the cost of the services of the medical or geriatric professional.
(h) The provider shall identify unique service and care needs, if applicable, for a resident directly affected by the residential temporary relocation. The unique services and care needs identified shall be in writing and shall become a part of the resident's plan of care.
(Amended by Stats. 2011, Ch. 296, Sec. 148. (AB 1023) Effective January 1, 2012.)
1793.91.
The provider shall set forth specific procedures for the resident to follow regarding relocation to the unit originally vacated, the selection of a new unit, and timeframes for making choices. Procedures for returning the relocated resident when residential units will be ready for occupancy shall include all of the following:
(a) The provider shall provide the resident at least 60 days notice of the return to his or her unit or a substitute permanent unit. and subsequent notices 30 days and seven days prior to the return date.
(b) The resident shall have the right to return to his or her previously occupied unit or a unit comparable in services, size, features, and amenities to the unit originally vacated, without payment of any further entrance or accommodation fee. The provider is not required to guarantee a specific unit. Assignment of units shall be based upon the length of occupancy of returning residents.
(c) If the residential temporary relocation of a resident of a continuing care retirement community will exceed 18 months, the resident shall have all options allowed by Section 1793.82, unless there is a written agreement between the affected resident and the provider as described in subdivision (d).
(d) If a provider determines that the period of residential temporary relocation, as defined in paragraph (8) of subdivision (r) of Section 1771, will exceed 18 months, the provider may extend the period of residential temporary relocation for up to six months for an affected resident if that resident has agreed to the extension in writing. The written agreement shall state that by signing, the resident waives all rights to relocation options offered in Section 1793.82 for the period of the extension.
(Added by Stats. 2010, Ch. 443, Sec. 3. (AB 1433) Effective January 1, 2011.)

CHAPTER 12. Family Notification [1795-1795.]

(Chapter 12 added by Stats. 2002, Ch. 272, Sec. 1.)
1795.
(a) Notwithstanding any other provision of law, a skilled nursing facility as defined in subdivision (c) of Section 1250, any intermediate care facility, as defined in subdivision (d), (e), (g), and (h) of Section 1250, a congregate living facility, as defined in subdivision (i) of Section 1250, or a hospice facility, as defined in subdivision (n) of Section 1250, shall make reasonable efforts to contact the person named in the resident's admission agreement as the resident's contact person, or the resident's

responsible person, within 24 hours after a significant change in the resident's health or mental status.
(b) Notwithstanding any other provision of law, a residential care facility for the elderly, as defined in subdivision (k) of Section 1569.2, shall make reasonable efforts to contact the person named in the resident's admission agreement as the resident's contact person, or the resident's responsible person, within 24 hours after a significant change in the resident's health or mental status.
(Amended by Stats. 2012, Ch. 673, Sec. 10. (SB 135) Effective January 1, 2013.)

CHAPTER 13. Home Care Services [1796.10 - 1796.63]

(Chapter 13 added by Stats. 2013, Ch. 790, Sec. 1.)

ARTICLE 1. General Provisions [1796.10 - 1796.12]
(Article 1 added by Stats. 2013, Ch. 790, Sec. 1.)
1796.10.
This chapter shall be known, and may be cited, as the Home Care Services Consumer Protection Act.
(Added by Stats. 2013, Ch. 790, Sec. 1. (AB 1217) Effective January 1, 2014. Provisions implemented as of January 1, 2016, pursuant to Section 1796.61.)
1796.11.
The State Department of Social Services shall administer and enforce this chapter.
(Added by Stats. 2013, Ch. 790, Sec. 1. (AB 1217) Effective January 1, 2014. Provisions implemented as of January 1, 2016, pursuant to Section 1796.61.)
1796.12.
For purposes of this chapter, the following definitions shall apply:
(a) "Affiliated home care aide" means an individual, 18 years of age or older, who is employed by a home care organization to provide home care services to a client and is listed on the home care aide registry.
(b) "Child" or "children" means an individual or individuals under 18 years of age.
(c) "Client" means an individual who receives home care services from a registered home care aide.
(d) "Department" means the State Department of Social Services.
(e) "Director" means the Director of Social Services.
(f) "Family member" means any spouse, by marriage or otherwise, domestic partner, child or stepchild, by natural birth or by adoption, parent, brother, sister, half-brother, half-sister, parent-in-law, brother-in-law, sister-in-law, nephew, niece, aunt, uncle, first cousin, or any person denoted by the prefix "grand" or "great," or the spouse of any of these persons, even if the marriage has been terminated by death or dissolution.
(g) "Home care aide applicant" means an individual, 18 years of age or older, who is requesting to become a registered home care aide and the department has received and is processing the individual's complete home care aide application and nonrefundable application fee.
(h) "Home care aide application" means the official form, designated by the department, to request to become a registered home care aide.
(i) "Home care aide registry" means a department-established and department-maintained Internet Web site of registered home care aides and home care aide applicants, which includes all of the following: the individual's name, registration number, registration status, registration expiration date, and, if applicable, the home care organization to which the affiliated home care aide or affiliated home care aide applicant is associated.
(j) "Home care organization" means an individual, 18 years of age or older, firm, partnership, corporation, limited liability company, joint venture, association, or other entity that arranges for home care services by an affiliated home care aide to a client, and is licensed pursuant to this chapter.
(k) "Home care organization applicant" means an individual, 18 years of age or older, or a firm, partnership, corporation, limited liability company, joint venture, association, or other entity where the individual or individuals applying for the license are 18 years of age or older and are requesting to become a home care organization licensee and the department has received and is processing the complete home care organization application and nonrefundable application fee.
(l) "Home care organization application" means the official form, designated by the department, to request to become a licensed home care organization.
(m) "Home care organization licensee" means an individual, 18 years of age or older, firm, partnership, corporation, limited liability company, joint venture, association, or other entity having the authority and responsibility for the operation or management of a licensed home care organization.
(n) "Home care services" means nonmedical services and assistance provided by a registered home care aide to a client who, because of advanced age or physical or mental disability, cannot perform these services. These services enable the client to remain in his or her residence and include, but are not limited to, assistance with the following: bathing, dressing, feeding, exercising, personal hygiene and grooming, transferring, ambulating, positioning, toileting and incontinence care, assisting with medication that the client self-administers, housekeeping, meal planning and preparation, laundry, transportation, correspondence, making telephone calls, shopping for personal care items or groceries, and companionship. This subdivision shall not authorize a registered home care aide to assist with medication that the client self-administers that would otherwise require administration or oversight by a licensed health care professional.
(o) "Registered home care aide" means an affiliated home care aide or independent home care aide, 18 years of age or older, who is listed on the home care aide registry.

(p) "Independent home care aide" means an individual, 18 years of age or older, who is not employed by a home care organization, but who is listed on the home care aide registry and is providing home care services through a direct agreement with a client. (Amended by Stats. 2014, Ch. 29, Sec. 30. (SB 855) Effective June 20, 2014. Provisions implemented as of January 1, 2016, pursuant to Section 1796.61.)

ARTICLE 2. Registry and Exemptions [1796.14 - 1796.17]
(Article 2 added by Stats. 2013, Ch. 790, Sec. 1.)
1796.14.
(a) Individuals who are not employed by a home care organization but who provide home care services to a client may be listed on the home care aide registry.
(b) An affiliated home care aide shall be listed on the home care aide registry prior to providing home care services to a client.
(c) (1) Home care aides shall not include individuals who are providing home care services as part of their job duties through one of the following entities:
(A) Services authorized to be provided by a licensed home health agency under Chapter 8 (commencing with Section 1725).
(B) Services authorized to be provided by a licensed hospice pursuant to Chapter 8.5 (commencing with Section 1745).
(C) Services authorized to be provided by a licensed health facility pursuant to Chapter 2 (commencing with Section 1250).
(D) In-home supportive services provided pursuant to Article 7 (commencing with Section 12300) of Chapter 3 of Part 3 of Division 9 of, or Section 14132.95, 14132.952, or 14132.956 of, the Welfare and Institutions Code.
(E) A community care facility licensed pursuant to Chapter 3 (commencing with Section 1500), a residential care facility for persons with chronic life-threatening illness licensed pursuant to Chapter 3.01 (commencing with Section 1568.01), a residential care facility for the elderly licensed pursuant to Chapter 3.2 (commencing with Section 1569), or a facility licensed pursuant to the California Child Day Care Facilities Act, (Chapter 3.4 (commencing with Section 1596.70)), which includes day care centers, as described in Chapter 3.5 (commencing with Section 1596.90), family day care homes, as described in Chapter 3.6 (commencing with Section 1597.30), and employer-sponsored child care centers, as described in Chapter 3.65 (commencing with Section 1597.70).
(F) A clinic licensed pursuant to Section 1204 or 1204.1.
(G) A home medical device retail facility licensed pursuant to Section 111656.
(H) An organization vendored or contracted through a regional center or the State Department of Developmental Services pursuant to the Lanterman Developmental Disabilities Services Act (Chapter 1 (commencing with Section 4500) of Division 4.5 of the Welfare and Institutions Code) and the California Early Intervention Services Act (Title 14 (commencing with Section 95000) of the Government Code) to provide services and supports for persons with developmental disabilities, as defined in Section 4512 of the Welfare and Institutions Code, when funding for those services is provided through the State Department of Developmental Services and more than 50 percent of the recipients of the home care services provided by the organization are persons with developmental disabilities.
(I) An alcoholism or drug abuse recovery or treatment facility as defined in Section 11834.02.
(J) A facility in which only Indian children who are eligible under the federal Indian Child Welfare Act (25 U.S.C. Sec. 1901 et seq.) are placed and is either of the following:
(i) An extended family member of the Indian child, as defined in Section 1903 of Title 25 of the United States Code.
(ii) A foster home that is licensed, approved, or specified by the Indian child's tribe pursuant to Section 1915 of Title 25 of the United States Code.
(2) Home care aides shall not include individuals providing services authorized to be provided pursuant to Section 2731 of the Business and Professions Code.
(d) Home care aides shall not include a nonrelative extended family member, as defined in Section 362.7 of the Welfare and Institutions Code.
(e) In the event of a conflict between this chapter and a provision listed in subdivision (b), (c), or (d), the provision in subdivision (b), (c), or (d) shall control.
(Amended by Stats. 2014, Ch. 29, Sec. 31. (SB 855) Effective June 20, 2014. Provisions implemented as of January 1, 2016, pursuant to Section 1796.61.)
1796.15.
This chapter shall not prohibit an individual from employing an individual not listed on the home care aide registry to provide home care services. The department shall have responsibility only for the maintenance of the home care aide registry regarding registered home care aides.
(Added by Stats. 2013, Ch. 790, Sec. 1. (AB 1217) Effective January 1, 2014. Provisions implemented as of January 1, 2016, pursuant to Section 1796.61.)
1796.16.
 (a) A registered home care aide may provide home care services to more than one child for a family, but may not provide home care services for a child or children from more than one family at the same time. This chapter shall not preclude a registered home care aide from providing home care services for a child or children of multiple families at different times. This chapter shall not override provisions of the California Child Day Care Facilities Act (Chapter 3.4 (commencing with Section 1596.70)), which includes Chapter 3.5 (commencing with Section 1596.90), Chapter 3.6 (commencing with Section 1597.30), and Chapter 3.65 (commencing with Section 1597.70).
(b) This chapter does not override provisions of the California Community Care Facilities Act (Chapter 3 (commencing with Section 1500)), Residential Care Facilities for Persons With Chronic Life-Threatening Illness Act (Chapter 3.01 (commencing with Section

1568.01)), or the California Residential Care Facilities for the Elderly Act (Chapter 3.2 (commencing with Section 1569)).
(Amended by Stats. 2014, Ch. 29, Sec. 32. (SB 855) Effective June 20, 2014. Provisions implemented as of January 1, 2016, pursuant to Section 1796.61.)
1796.17.
(a) Each home care organization shall be separately licensed. This chapter does not prevent a licensee from obtaining more than one home care organization license or obtaining a home care organization license in addition to other licenses issued by the department, or both.
(b) A home care organization does not include the following:
(1) A home health agency licensed under Chapter 8 (commencing with Section 1725).
(2) A hospice licensed under Chapter 8.5 (commencing with Section 1745).
(3) A health facility licensed under Chapter 2 (commencing with Section 1250).
(4) A person who performs services through the In-Home Supportive Services program pursuant to Article 7 (commencing with Section 12300) of Chapter 3 of Part 3 of Division 9 of, or Section 14132.95, 14132.952, or 14132.956 of, the Welfare and Institutions Code.
(5) A home medical device retail facility licensed under Section 111656.
(6) An organization vendored or contracted through a regional center or the State Department of Developmental Services pursuant to the Lanterman Developmental Disabilities Services Act (Division 4.5 (commencing with Section 4500) of the Welfare and Institutions Code) and the California Early Intervention Services Act (Title 14 (commencing with Section 95000) of the Government Code) to provide services and supports for persons with developmental disabilities, as defined in Section 4512 of the Welfare and Institutions Code, when funding for those services is provided through the State Department of Developmental Services and more than 50 percent of the recipients of the home care services provided by the organization are persons with developmental disabilities.
(7) An employment agency, as defined in Section 1812.5095 of the Civil Code, that procures, offers, refers, provides, or attempts to provide an independent home care aide who provides home care services to clients.
(8) A community care facility licensed pursuant to Chapter 3 (commencing with Section 1500), a residential care facility for persons with chronic life-threatening illness licensed pursuant to Chapter 3.01 (commencing with Section 1568.01), a residential care facility for the elderly licensed pursuant to Chapter 3.2 (commencing with Section 1569), or a facility licensed pursuant to the California Child Day Care Facilities Act (Chapter 3.4 (commencing with Section 1596.70)), which includes day care centers, as described in Chapter 3.5 (commencing with Section 1596.90), family day care homes, as described in Chapter 3.6 (commencing with Section 1597.30), and employer-sponsored child care centers, as described in Chapter 3.65 (commencing with Section 1597.70).
(9) An alcoholism or drug abuse recovery or treatment facility as defined in Section 11834.02.
(10) A person providing services authorized pursuant to Section 2731 of the Business and Professions Code.
(11) A clinic licensed pursuant to Section 1204 or 1204.1.
(12) A nonrelative extended family member, as defined in Section 362.7 of the Welfare and Institutions Code.
(13) A facility providing home care services in which only Indian children who are eligible under the federal Indian Child Welfare Act (25 U.S.C. Sec. 1901 et seq.) are placed and which satisfies either of the following:
(A) An extended family member of the Indian child, as defined in Section 1903 of Title 25 of the United States Code.
(B) A foster home that is licensed, approved, or specified by the Indian child's tribe pursuant to Section 1915 of Title 25 of the United States Code.
(14) Any other individual or entity providing services similar to those described in this chapter, as determined by the director.
(c) In the event of a conflict between this chapter and a provision listed in subdivision (b), the provision in subdivision (b) controls.
(Amended by Stats. 2015, Ch. 303, Sec. 287. (AB 731) Effective January 1, 2016.)

ARTICLE 3. Home Care Aide Applicants [1796.19- 1796.19.]
(Article 3 added by Stats. 2013, Ch. 790, Sec. 1.)
1796.19.
(a) The department shall consider, but is not limited to, the following when determining whether to approve a registration application:
(1) Evidence satisfactory to the department of the ability of the home care aide applicant to comply with this chapter and the rules and regulations promulgated under this chapter by the department.
(2) Evidence satisfactory to the department that the home care aide applicant is of reputable and responsible character. The evidence shall include, but is not limited to, a review of the independent home care aide applicant's criminal offender record information pursuant to Section 1522.
(3) Any revocation or other disciplinary action taken, or in the process of being taken, related to the care of individuals against the home care aide applicant.
(4) Any other information that may be required by the department for the proper administration and enforcement of this chapter.
(b) Failure of the home care aide applicant to cooperate with the department in the completion of the Home Care Aide application shall result in the withdrawal of the registration application. "Failure to cooperate" means that the information described in this chapter and by any rules and regulations promulgated under this chapter has not

been provided, or has not been provided in the form requested by the department, or both.

(Amended by Stats. 2014, Ch. 29, Sec. 34. (SB 855) Effective June 20, 2014. Provisions implemented as of January 1, 2016, pursuant to Section 1796.61.)

ARTICLE 4. Registration [1796.21 - 1796.29]

(Article 4 added by Stats. 2013, Ch. 790, Sec. 1.)

1796.21.

A registered home care aide shall be 18 years of age or older.

(Added by Stats. 2013, Ch. 790, Sec. 1. (AB 1217) Effective January 1, 2014. Provisions implemented as of January 1, 2016, pursuant to Section 1796.61.)

1796.22.

Any individual who has submitted a home care aide application and who possesses any one of the following identification cards may initiate a background examination to be a registered home care aide:

(a) A valid California driver's license.

(b) A valid identification card issued by the Department of Motor Vehicles.

(c) A valid Alien Registration Card.

(d) In the case of a person living in a state other than California, a valid numbered photo identification card issued by an agency of the state other than California.

(Amended by Stats. 2014, Ch. 29, Sec. 35. (SB 855) Effective June 20, 2014. Provisions implemented as of January 1, 2016, pursuant to Section 1796.61.)

1796.23.

(a) Each person initiating a background examination to be a registered home care aide shall submit his or her fingerprints to the Department of Justice by electronic transmission in a manner approved by the department, unless exempt under subdivision (d). Each person initiating a background examination to be a registered home care aide shall also submit to the department a signed declaration under penalty of perjury regarding any prior criminal convictions pursuant to Section 1522 and a completed home care aide application.

(b) A law enforcement agency or other local agency authorized to take fingerprints may charge a reasonable fee to offset the costs of fingerprinting for the purposes of this chapter. The fee revenues shall be deposited in the Fingerprint Fees Account.

(c) The Department of Justice shall use the fingerprints to search state and Federal Bureau of Investigation criminal offender record information pursuant to Section 1522.

(d) A person who is a current licensee or employee in a facility licensed by the department, a certified foster parent, a certified administrator, or a registered TrustLine provider need not submit fingerprints to the department, and may transfer his or her current criminal record clearance or exemption pursuant to paragraph (1) of subdivision (h) of Section 1522. The person shall instead submit to the department, along with the person's registration application, a copy of the person's identification card described in Section 1796.22 and sign a declaration verifying the person's identity.

(Amended by Stats. 2015, Ch. 303, Sec. 288. (AB 731) Effective January 1, 2016.)

1796.24.

(a) (1) The department shall establish a home care aide registry pursuant to this chapter and shall continuously update the registry information. Upon submission of the home care aide application and fingerprints or other identification documents pursuant to Section 1796.22, the department shall enter into the home care aide registry the person's name, identification number, and an indicator that the person has submitted a home care aide application and fingerprints or identification documentation. This person shall be known as a "home care aide applicant."

(2) A person shall not be entitled to apply to be a registered home care aide and shall have his or her registration application returned without the right to appeal if the person would not be eligible to obtain a license pursuant to Section 1796.40 or 1796.41.

(b) (1) Before approving an individual for registration, the department shall check the individual's criminal history pursuant to Section 1522. Upon completion of the searches of the state summary criminal offender record information and the records of the Federal Bureau of Investigation, the home care aide applicant shall be issued a criminal record clearance or granted a criminal record exemption if grounds do not exist for denial pursuant to Section 1522. The department shall enter that finding in the person's record in the home care aide registry and shall notify the person of the action. This person shall be known as a "registered home care aide." If the home care aide applicant meets all of the conditions for registration, except receipt of the Federal Bureau of Investigation's criminal offender record information search response, the department may issue a clearance if the home care aide applicant has signed and submitted a statement that he or she has never been convicted of a crime in the United States, other than a minor traffic violation. If, after approval, the department determines that the registrant has a criminal record, registration may be revoked pursuant to Section 1796.26.

(2) For purposes of compliance with this section, the department may permit a home care organization applicant or a home care organization licensee to request the transfer of a home care aide's current criminal record clearance or exemption for a licensed care facility issued by the department. A signed criminal record clearance or exemption transfer request shall be submitted to the department and shall include a copy of the person's driver's license or valid identification card issued by the Department of Motor Vehicles, or a valid photo identification issued by another state or the United States government if the person is not a California resident. Upon request of the licensee or home care aide applicant, the department shall verify whether the individual has a clearance or exemption that can be transferred pursuant to the requirements of this chapter.

(3) The department shall hold criminal record clearances and exemptions in its active files for a minimum of three years after the individual is no longer on the registry in order to facilitate a transfer request.

(Amended by Stats. 2014, Ch. 29, Sec. 37. (SB 855) Effective June 20, 2014. Provisions implemented as of January 1, 2016, pursuant to Section 1796.61.)

1796.25.

(a) (1) If the department finds that the home care aide applicant or the registered home care aide has been convicted of a crime, other than a minor traffic violation, the department shall deny the home care aide application, or revoke the registered home care aide's registration unless the department grants an exemption pursuant to subdivision (g) of Section 1522.

(2) If the department finds that the home care aide applicant or registered home care aide has an arrest as described in subdivision (a) of Section 1522, the department may deny the registration application or registration renewal application, or revoke the registered home care aide's registration, if the home care aide or registered home care aide may pose a risk to the health and safety of any person who is or may become a client and the department complies with subdivision (e) of Section 1522.

(3) The department may deny the home care aide application or the renewal application of a registered home care aide, or revoke the home care aide registration, if the department discovers that the department or a county had previously revoked or rescinded a license or certificate to be a certified family home or resource family, a certified administrator, or a registered trustline provider held by the home care aide applicant or registered home care aide, or that the department had excluded the home care aide applicant or registered home care aide from a licensed facility, certified family home, or resource family home.

(4) The department may deny the home care aide application or registered home care aide registration renewal application for placement or retention upon the home care aide registry, or revoke the registered home care aide's registration, if the department discovers that the department or a county had previously denied the home care aide applicant's or registered home care aide's application for a license from the department or certificate to be a certified family home or resource family, a certified administrator, or a registered trustline provider.

(b) (1) If the department revokes or denies a home care aide application or registered home care aide's renewal application pursuant to subdivision (a), the department shall advise the home care aide applicant or registered home care aide, by written notification, of the right to appeal. The home care aide applicant or registered home care aide shall have 15 days from the date of the written notification to appeal the denial or revocation.

(2) Upon receipt by the department of the appeal, the appeal shall be set for hearing. The hearing shall be conducted in accordance with Section 1551.

(c) If the home care aide application or registered home care aide renewal application is denied, the home care aide applicant or registered home care aide shall not reapply until he or she meets the timeframe set forth in Sections 1796.40 and 1796.41.

(Amended by Stats. 2017, Ch. 732, Sec. 39. (AB 404) Effective January 1, 2018.)

1796.26.

(a) (1) The department may revoke or deny a registered home care aide's registration or request for registration renewal if any of the following apply to the registered home care aide:

(A) He or she procured or attempted to procure his or her registered home care aide registration or renewal by fraud or misrepresentation.

(B) He or she has a criminal conviction, other than a minor traffic violation, unless an exemption is granted pursuant to Section 1522.

(C) He or she engages or has engaged in conduct that is inimical to the health, morals, welfare, or safety of the people of the State of California or an individual receiving or seeking to receive home care services.

(2) An individual whose registration has been revoked shall not reapply until he or she meets the timeframe as set forth in Section 1796.40 or 1796.41.

(3) An individual whose criminal record exemption has been denied shall not reapply for two years from the date of the exemption denial.

(4) The hearing to revoke or deny the registered home care aide registration or registration renewal request shall be conducted in accordance with Section 1551.

(b) (1) The registered home care aide's registration shall be considered forfeited under the following conditions:

(A) The registered home care aide has had a license or certificate of approval revoked, suspended, or denied as authorized under Section 1534, 1550, 1568.082, 1569.50, 1596.608, or 1596.885.

(B) The registered home care aide has been denied employment, residence, or presence in a facility or client's home based on action resulting from an administrative hearing pursuant to Section 1558, 1568.092, 1569.58, or 1596.8897.

(C) The registered home care aide fails to maintain a current mailing address with the department.

(D) The registered home care aide's registration is not renewed.

(E) The registered home care aide surrenders his or her registration to the department.

(F) The registered home care aide dies.

(2) An individual whose registered home care aide registration has been forfeited shall not reapply until he or she meets the timeframe set forth by the department in Sections 1796.40 and 1796.41.

(c) A registered home care aide's registration shall not be transferred or sold to another individual or entity.

(Amended by Stats. 2015, Ch. 303, Sec. 290. (AB 731) Effective January 1, 2016.)

1796.28.

(a) The Department of Justice shall maintain and continually update pertinent criminal offender record information of registered home care aides and shall inform the department of subsequent reports received pursuant to Section 11105.2 of the Penal Code. The department shall continually update the home care aide registry pursuant to the actions required in this chapter.

(1) Registered home care aides and home care aide applicants shall maintain a current mailing address with the department.

(2) Registered home care aides and home care aide applicants shall inform the department of any new mailing address in writing within 10 days of a change in address.

(b) Notwithstanding any other law, including Part 3 (commencing with Section 900) of Division 3.6 of Title 1 of the Government Code, state officers or employees shall not be liable for any damages caused by their conduct pursuant to this chapter except for intentional acts or gross negligence.

(Added by Stats. 2013, Ch. 790, Sec. 1. (AB 1217) Effective January 1, 2014. Provisions implemented as of January 1, 2016, pursuant to Section 1796.61.)

1796.29.

The department shall do all of the following in the administration of the home care aide registry:

(a) Establish and maintain on the department's Internet Web site the registry of registered home care aides and home care aide applicants.

(1) To expedite the ability of a consumer to determine if a registered home care aide or home care aide applicant has passed a background examination, pursuant to Section 1796.23, the Internet Web site shall enable consumers to look up the registration status by providing the registered home care aide's or home care aide applicant's name and registration number. The Internet Web site shall provide the registration status, the registration expiration date, and, if applicable, the home care organization with which the affiliated home care aide is associated.

(2) The Internet Web site shall not provide any additional, individually identifiable information about a registered home care aide or home care aide applicant. The department may request and may maintain additional information for registered home care aides or home care aide applicants, as necessary for the administration of this chapter, that shall not be publicly available on the home care aide registry.

(b) Update the home care aide registry upon receiving notification from a home care organization that an affiliated home care aide is no longer employed by the home care organization.

(c) Notwithstanding any other provision of this chapter to the contrary, information regarding a registered home care aide or registered home care aide applicant is not subject to public disclosure pursuant to this chapter, except as provided in subdivision (d).

(d) (1) For any new registration or renewal of registration occurring on and after July 1, 2019, the department shall provide an electronic copy of a registered home care aide's name, telephone number, and cellular telephone number on file with the department, upon its request, to a labor organization in which a provider of in-home supportive services, as described in Article 7 (commencing with Section 12300) of Chapter 3 of Part 3 of Division 9 of the Welfare and Institutions Code, or a registered home care aide, already participates and which exists for the purpose, in whole or in part, of dealing with employers of home care aides concerning access to training, grievances, labor disputes, wages, rates of pay, hours of employment, or conditions of work. The labor organization shall not use this information for any purpose other than employee organizing, representation, and assistance activities. The labor organization shall not disclose this information to any other party.

(2) The department shall establish a simple opt-out procedure by which a registered home care aide or registered home care aide applicant may request that his or her contact information on file with the department not be disclosed in response to a request described in paragraph (1).

(e) At the time of any registration or renewal of registration occurring on and after July 1, 2019, the department shall do both of the following:

(1) Provide a written notice to the registering or registered home care aide that his or her information may be shared with a labor organization, as described in paragraph (1) of subdivision (d).

(2) Provide written instructions on how to utilize the simple opt-out procedure described in paragraph (2) of subdivision (d).

(f) This section applies solely to an individual who provides services as a home care aide under this chapter.

(Amended by Stats. 2018, Ch. 917, Sec. 2. (AB 2455) Effective January 1, 2019.)

ARTICLE 5. Renewal [1796.31- 1796.31.]

(Article 5 added by Stats. 2013, Ch. 790, Sec. 1.)

1796.31.

(a) To remain on the home care aide registry, a registered home care aide shall renew his or her registration every two years.

(1) A registered home care aide's registration shall expire every two years, on the anniversary date of the initial registration date. If the registration is not renewed on or prior to its expiration date, the registration shall be forfeited pursuant to subdivision (b) of Section 1796.26.

(2) To renew a registration, the registered home care aide shall, on or before the registration expiration date, request renewal by submitting to the department the registration renewal application form and paying the nonrefundable registration renewal application fee in the amount determined by the department.

(b) Renewal of a registered home care aide's registration is conditioned on compliance with all of the following:

(1) Submitting a complete registration renewal application form and payment of the nonrefundable renewal fee, both of which shall be postmarked on or before the expiration of the registration.

(2) Continuing to satisfy the requirements set forth in this chapter.

(3) Cooperating with the department in the completion of the renewal process. Failure of the registered home care aide to cooperate shall result in the withdrawal of the registration renewal application by the department. For purposes of this section, "failure to cooperate" means that the information described in this chapter and in any rules and regulations promulgated under this chapter has not been provided, or has not been provided in the form requested by the department, or both.

(c) (1) The department shall notify a registered home care aide in writing of his or her registration expiration date and the process of renewal.

(2) Written notification pursuant to this subdivision shall be mailed to the registered home care aide's mailing address of record at least 60 days before the registration expiration date.

(Amended by Stats. 2014, Ch. 29, Sec. 41. (SB 855) Effective June 20, 2014. Provisions implemented as of January 1, 2016, pursuant to Section 1796.61.)

ARTICLE 6. Licensure of Home Care Organizations [1796.32 - 1796.41]

(Article 6 added by Stats. 2013, Ch. 790, Sec. 1.)

1796.32.

Any individual who has submitted an application and who possesses any one of the following identification cards may initiate a background examination to be a licensed home care organization:

(a) A valid California driver's license.

(b) A valid identification card issued by the Department of Motor Vehicles.

(c) A valid Alien Registration Card.

(d) In the case of a person living in a state other than California, a valid numbered photo identification card issued by an agency of the state other than California.

(Added by renumbering Section 1796.33 by Stats. 2014, Ch. 29, Sec. 42. (SB 855) Effective June 20, 2014. Provisions implemented as of January 1, 2016, pursuant to Section 1796.61.)

1796.33.

In order to obtain a home care organization license, the following individual or individuals shall consent to the background examination described in Section 1796.23:

(a) The owner of the home care organization, if the owner is an individual.

(b) If the owner of a home care organization is a corporation, limited liability company, joint venture, association, or other entity, an individual having a 10-percent or greater ownership in that entity and the chief executive officer or other person serving in a similar capacity. The department shall not issue a provisional license or license to any corporate home care organization applicant that has a member of the board of directors, executive director, or officer who is not eligible for licensure pursuant to Sections 1796.40 and 1796.41.

(Added by renumbering Section 1796.34 by Stats. 2014, Ch. 29, Sec. 43. (SB 855) Effective June 20, 2014. Provisions implemented as of January 1, 2016, pursuant to Section 1796.61.)

1796.34.

(a) A person or a private or public organization, with the exception of any person who performs in-home supportive services through the In-Home Supportive Services program pursuant to Article 7 (commencing with Section 12300) of Chapter 3 of Part 3 of Division 9 of the Welfare and Institutions Code, or Section 14132.95, 14132.952, or 14132.956 of the Welfare and Institutions Code, and the exceptions provided for in subdivision (b), shall not do any of the following, unless he, she, or it is licensed pursuant to this chapter:

(1) Own, manage, or represent himself, herself or itself to be a home care organization by name, advertising, solicitation, or any other presentments to the public, or in the context of services within the scope of this chapter, imply that he, she, or it is licensed to provide those services or to make any reference to employee bonding in relation to those services.

(2) Use the terms "home care organization," "home care," "in-home care," or any combination of those terms, within its name.

(b) This section does not apply to either of the following:

(1) Any person who performs in-home supportive services through the In-Home Supportive Services program pursuant to Article 7 (commencing with Section 12300) of Chapter 3 of Part 3 of Division 9 of, or Section 14132.95, 14132.952, or 14132.956 of, the Welfare and Institutions Code.

(2) An employment agency, as defined in Section 1812.5095 of the Civil Code, that procures, offers, refers, provides, or attempts to provide an independent home care aide who provides home care to clients.

(Amended by Stats. 2015, Ch. 303, Sec. 292. (AB 731) Effective January 1, 2016.)

1796.35.

(a) Subject to the exceptions set forth in Section 1796.17, an individual, partnership, corporation, limited liability company, joint venture, association, or other entity shall not arrange for the provision of home care services by a registered home care aide to a client in this state before obtaining a license pursuant to this chapter. This shall be deemed "unlicensed home care services."

(b) Upon discovering an individual or entity is in violation of subdivision (a), the department shall send a written notice of noncompliance to the individual or entity and assess a civil penalty of nine hundred dollars ($900) per day for each calendar day of each violation.

(c) Upon discovering that an individual or entity is in violation of subdivision (a), the department shall send a copy of the written notice of noncompliance to the individual or entity and to the Attorney General or appropriate district attorney or city attorney.

(d) Upon receiving this notice, the Attorney General, district attorney, or city attorney may do any or all of the following:

(1) Issue a cease and desist order, which shall remain in effect until the individual or entity has obtained a license pursuant to this chapter. If the individual or entity fails to comply with the cease and desist order within 20 calendar days, the Attorney General, district attorney, or city attorney may apply for an injunction.

(2) Bring an action against the individual or entity under Chapter 5 (commencing with Section 17200) of Part 2 of Division 7 of the Business and Professions Code.

(Added by renumbering Section 1796.36 by Stats. 2014, Ch. 29, Sec. 45. (SB 855) Effective June 20, 2014. Provisions implemented as of January 1, 2016, pursuant to Section 1796.61.)

1796.36.

(a) A home care organization that has its principal place of business in another state, in addition to the other requirements of this chapter, before arranging for home care services provided by an affiliated home care aide to a client in the state, shall comply with all of the following:

(1) Have an office in California.

(2) Maintain all pertinent records of the operation in California at the California office. All records shall be available to review, copy, audit, and inspect by the department.

(b) If the home care organization is a foreign corporation, foreign limited liability company, foreign limited partnership, foreign association, or a foreign limited liability partnership, as defined in Sections 170, 171, 171.03, 171.05, and 16101 of the Corporations Code, before arranging for home care services provided by an affiliated home care aide to a client in the state, the home care organization shall have an office in California and shall comply with both of the following:

(1) Register with the Secretary of State to conduct intrastate business in California.

(2) Maintain all pertinent records of the operation in California at the California office. All records shall be available to review, copy, audit, and inspect by the department.

(Added by renumbering Section 1796.37 by Stats. 2014, Ch. 29, Sec. 46. (SB 855) Effective June 20, 2014. Provisions implemented as of January 1, 2016, pursuant to Section 1796.61.)

1796.37.

(a) The department may issue a home care organization license to a home care organization applicant that satisfies the requirements set forth in this chapter, including all of the following:

(1) Files a complete home care organization application, including the fees required pursuant to Section 1796.49.

(2) Submits proof of general and professional liability insurance in the amount of at least one million dollars ($1,000,000) per occurrence and three million dollars ($3,000,000) in the aggregate.

(3) Submits proof of a valid workers' compensation policy covering its affiliated home care aides. The proof shall consist of the policy number, the effective and expiration dates of the policy, and the name and address of the policy carrier.

(4) Submits proof of an employee dishonesty bond, including third-party coverage, with a minimum limit of ten thousand dollars ($10,000). This proof shall be submitted at each subsequent renewal.

(5) Provides the department, upon request, with a complete list of its affiliated home care aides, and proof that each satisfies the requirements of Sections 1796.43, 1796.44, and 1796.45.

(6) Passes a background examination, as required pursuant to Section 1796.33.

(7) Completes a department orientation.

(8) Does not have any outstanding fees or civil penalties due to the department.

(9) Discloses prior or present service as an administrator, general partner, corporate officer, or director of, or discloses that he or she has held or holds a beneficial ownership of 10 percent or more in, any of the following:

(A) A community care facility, as defined in Section 1502.

(B) A residential care facility, as defined in Section 1568.01.

(C) A residential care facility for the elderly, as defined in Section 1569.2.

(D) A child day care facility, as defined in Section 1596.750.

(E) A day care center, as described in Chapter 3.5 (commencing with Section 1596.90).

(F) A family day care home, as described in Chapter 3.6 (commencing with Section 1597.30).

(G) An employer-sponsored child care center, as described in Chapter 3.65 (commencing with Section 1597.70).

(H) A home care organization licensed pursuant to this chapter.

(10) Discloses any revocation or other disciplinary action taken, or in the process of being taken, against a license held or previously held by the entities specified in paragraph (9).

(11) Provides evidence that every member of the board of directors, if applicable, understands his or her legal duties and obligations as a member of the board of directors and that the home care organization's operation is governed by laws and regulations that are enforced by the department.

(12) Provides any other information as may be required by the department for the proper administration and enforcement of this chapter.

(13) Cooperates with the department in the completion of the home care organization license application process. Failure of the home care organization licensee to cooperate may result in the withdrawal of the home care organization license application. "Failure to

cooperate" means that the information described in this chapter and in any rules and regulations promulgated pursuant to this chapter has not been provided, or not provided in the form requested by the department, or both.

(b) A home care organization licensee shall renew the home care organization license every two years. The department may renew a home care organization license if the licensee satisfies the requirements set forth in this chapter, including all of the following:

(1) Files a complete home care organization license renewal application, including the nonrefundable fees required pursuant to Section 1796.49, both of which shall be postmarked on or before the expiration of the license.

(2) Submits proof of general and professional liability insurance in the amount of at least one million dollars ($1,000,000) per occurrence and three million dollars ($3,000,000) in the aggregate.

(3) Submits proof of a valid workers' compensation policy covering its affiliated home care aides. The proof shall consist of the policy number, the effective and expiration dates of the policy, and the name and address of the policy carrier.

(4) Submits proof of an employee dishonesty bond, including third-party coverage, with a minimum limit of ten thousand dollars ($10,000).

(5) Does not have any outstanding fees or civil penalties due to the department.

(6) Provides any other information as may be required by the department for the proper administration and enforcement of this chapter.

(7) Cooperates with the department in the completion of the home care organization license renewal process. Failure of the home care organization licensee to cooperate may result in the withdrawal of the home care organization license renewal application. "Failure to cooperate" means that the information described in this chapter and in any rules and regulations promulgated pursuant to this chapter has not been provided, or not provided in the form requested by the department, or both.

(c) (1) The department shall notify a licensed home care organization in writing of its registration expiration date and the process of renewal.

(2) Written notification pursuant to this subdivision shall be mailed to the registered home care organization's mailing address of record at least 60 days before the registration expiration date.

(Amended by Stats. 2015, Ch. 303, Sec. 293. (AB 731) Effective January 1, 2016.)

1796.38.

The department may deny an application for licensure or suspend or revoke any license issued pursuant to this chapter, pursuant to Sections 1550.5 and 1551 and in the manner provided in this chapter on any of the following grounds:

(a) Violation by the licensee of this chapter or of the rules and regulations promulgated under this chapter.

(b) Aiding, abetting, or permitting the violation of this chapter or of the rules and regulations promulgated under this chapter.

(c) Conduct that is inimical to the health, morals, welfare, or safety of either an individual receiving home care services or the people of the State of California.

(d) The conviction of a licensee, or other person mentioned in Section 1522, at any time before or during licensure, of a crime described in Section 1522.

(e) Engaging in acts of financial malfeasance concerning the operation of a home care organization.

(Amended by Stats. 2015, Ch. 303, Sec. 294. (AB 731) Effective January 1, 2016.)

1796.40.

(a) (1) If an application for a home care organization license indicates, or the department determines during the application review process, that the home care organization applicant was previously issued a license under this chapter or under Chapter 1 (commencing with Section 1200), Chapter 2 (commencing with Section 1250), Chapter 3 (commencing with Section 1500), Chapter 3.01 (commencing with Section 1568.01), Chapter 3.2 (commencing with Section 1569), Chapter 3.4 (commencing with Section 1596.70), Chapter 3.5 (commencing with Section 1596.90), Chapter 3.6 (commencing with Section 1597.30), or Chapter 3.65 (commencing with Section 1597.70), and the prior license was revoked within the preceding two years, the department shall cease any further review of the application until two years have elapsed from the date of the revocation. All home care organizations are exempt from the health planning requirements contained in Part 2 (commencing with Section 127125) of Division 107.

(2) If an application for a license indicates, or the department determines during the application review process, that the home care organization applicant previously was issued a certificate of approval by a foster family agency that was revoked by the department pursuant to subdivision (b) of Section 1534 within the preceding two years, the department shall cease any further review of the application until two years have elapsed from the date of the revocation.

(3) If an application for a license indicates, or the department determines during the application review process, that the home care organization applicant was excluded from a facility licensed by the department pursuant to Section 1558, 1568.092, 1569.58, or 1596.8897, the department shall cease any further review of the application unless the excluded individual has been reinstated pursuant to Section 11522 of the Government Code by the department.

(b) If an application for a license indicates, or the department determines during the application review process, that the home care organization applicant had previously applied for a license pursuant to any of the chapters listed in paragraph (1) of subdivision (a) and the application was denied within the last year, the department shall cease further review of the application until one year has elapsed from the date of the denial letter. In those circumstances in which denials are appealed and upheld at an administrative hearing, review of the application shall cease for one year from the date of the decision and order of the department.

(c) If an application for a license indicates, or the department determines during the application review process, that the home care organization applicant had previously applied for a certificate of approval with a foster family agency and the department ordered the foster family agency to deny the application pursuant to subdivision (b) of Section 1534, the department shall cease further review of the application as follows:

(1) In cases where the home care organization applicant petitioned for a hearing, the department shall cease further review of the application until one year has elapsed from the effective date of the decision and order of the department upholding the denial.

(2) In cases where the department informed the home care organization applicant of his or her right to petition for a hearing and the home care organization applicant did not petition for a hearing, the department shall cease further review of the application until one year has elapsed from the date of the notification of the denial and the right to petition for a hearing.

(3) The department may continue to review the application if it has determined that the reasons for the denial of the application were due to circumstances and conditions that either have been corrected or are no longer in existence.

(d) Cessation of review pursuant to this section does not constitute a denial of the application.

(Added by Stats. 2014, Ch. 29, Sec. 50. (SB 855) Effective June 20, 2014. Provisions implemented as of January 1, 2016, pursuant to Section 1796.61.)

1796.41.

(a) (1) If the department determines that a person was issued a license pursuant to this chapter or Chapter 1 (commencing with Section 1200), Chapter 2 (commencing with Section 1250), Chapter 3 (commencing with Section 1500), Chapter 3.01 (commencing with Section 1568.01), Chapter 3.2 (commencing with Section 1569), Chapter 3.4 (commencing with Section 1596.70), Chapter 3.5 (commencing with Section 1596.90), Chapter 3.6 (commencing with Section 1597.30), or Chapter 3.65 (commencing with Section 1597.70), and the prior license was revoked within the preceding two years, the department shall exclude the person from acting as, and require the home care organization to remove him or her from his or her position as, a member of the board of directors, an executive director, or an officer of a licensee of any home care organizations licensed by the department pursuant to this chapter.

(2) If the department determines that a person was previously issued a certificate of approval by a foster family agency that was revoked by the department pursuant to subdivision (b) of Section 1534 within the preceding two years, the department shall exclude the person from acting as, and require the home care organization to remove him or her from his or her position as, a member of the board of directors, an executive director, or an officer of a licensee of, any home care organizations licensed by the department pursuant to this chapter.

(b) If the department determines that the person had previously applied for a license under any of the chapters listed in paragraph (1) of subdivision (a) and the application was denied within the last year, the department shall exclude the person from acting as, and require the home care organization to remove him or her from his or her position as, a member of the board of directors, an executive director, or an officer of a licensee of any home care organizations licensed by the department pursuant to this chapter as follows:

(1) In cases in which the home care organization applicant petitioned for a hearing, the department shall exclude the person from acting as, and require the home care organization to remove him or her from his or her position as, a member of the board of directors, an executive director, or an officer of a licensee of, any home care organizations licensed by the department pursuant to this chapter until one year has elapsed from the effective date of the decision and order of the department upholding a denial.

(2) In cases in which the department informed the home care organization applicant of his or her right to petition for a hearing and the home care organization applicant did not petition for a hearing, the department shall exclude the person from acting as, and require the home care organization to remove him or her from his or her position as, a member of the board of directors, an executive director, or an officer of a licensee of, any home care organizations licensed by the department pursuant to this chapter until one year has elapsed from the date of the notification of the denial and the right to petition for a hearing.

(c) If the department determines that the person had previously applied for a certificate of approval with a foster family agency and the department ordered the foster family agency to deny the application pursuant to subdivision (b) of Section 1534, the department shall exclude the person from acting as, and require the home care organization to remove him or her from his or her position as, a member of the board of directors, an executive director, or an officer of a licensee of, any home care organizations licensed by the department pursuant to this chapter and as follows:

(1) In cases in which the home care organization applicant petitioned for a hearing, the department shall exclude the person from acting as, and require the home care organization to remove him or her from his or her position as, a member of the board of directors, an executive director, or an officer of a licensee of, any home care organizations licensed by the department pursuant to this chapter until one year has elapsed from the effective date of the decision and order of the department upholding a denial.

(2) In cases in which the department informed the home care organization applicant of his or her right to petition for a hearing and the home care organization applicant did not petition for a hearing, the department shall exclude the person from acting as, and require the home care organization to remove him or her from his or her position as, a member of the board of directors, an executive director, or an officer of a licensee of, any

home care organizations licensed by the department pursuant to this chapter until one year has elapsed from the date of the notification of the denial and the right to petition for a hearing.

(d) Exclusion or removal of an individual pursuant to this section shall not be considered an order of exclusion for purposes of Section 1796.25 or any other law.

(e) The department may determine not to exclude a person from acting, or require that he or she be removed from his or her position, as a member of the board of directors, an executive director, or an officer of a licensee of, any home care organizations licensed by the department pursuant to this chapter if it has been determined that the reasons for the denial of the application or revocation of the facility license or certificate of approval were due to circumstances or conditions that either have been corrected or are no longer in existence.

(Amended by Stats. 2015, Ch. 303, Sec. 295. (AB 731) Effective January 1, 2016.)

ARTICLE 7. Home Care Organization Operating Requirements [1796.42 - 1796.43]

(Article 7 added by Stats. 2013, Ch. 790, Sec. 1.)

1796.42.

A home care organization licensee shall do all of the following:

(a) Post its license, business hours, and any other information required by the department in its place of business in a conspicuous location, visible both to clients and affiliated home care aides.

(b) Maintain and abide by a valid workers' compensation policy covering its affiliated home care aides.

(c) Maintain and abide by an employee dishonesty bond, including third-party coverage, with a minimum limit of ten thousand dollars ($10,000).

(d) Maintain proof of general and professional liability insurance in the amount of at least one million dollars ($1,000,000) per occurrence and three million dollars ($3,000,000) in the aggregate.

(e) Report any suspected or known dependent adult or elder abuse as required by Section 15630 of the Welfare and Institutions Code and suspected or known child abuse as required by Sections 11164 to 11174.3, inclusive, of the Penal Code. A copy of each suspected abuse report shall be maintained and available for review by the department during normal business hours.

(Added by renumbering Section 1796.41 by Stats. 2014, Ch. 29, Sec. 51. (SB 855) Effective June 20, 2014. Provisions implemented as of January 1, 2016, pursuant to Section 1796.61.)

1796.43.

(a) Home care organizations that employ affiliated home care aides shall ensure the affiliated home care aides are cleared on the home care aide registry before placing the individual in direct contact with clients. In addition, the home care organization shall do all of the following:

(1) Ensure any staff person, volunteer, or employee of a home care organization who has contact with clients, prospective clients, or confidential client information that may pose a risk to the clients' health and safety has met the requirements of Sections 1796.23, 1796.24, 1796.25, 1796.26, and 1796.28 before there is contact with clients or prospective clients or access to confidential client information.

(2) Require home care aides to demonstrate that they are free of active tuberculosis disease, pursuant to Section 1796.45.

(3) Immediately notify the department when the home care organization no longer employs an individual as an affiliated home care aide.

(b) This section shall not prevent a licensee from requiring a criminal record clearance of any individual exempt from the requirements of this section, provided that the individual has client contact.

(Added by renumbering Section 1796.42 by Stats. 2014, Ch. 29, Sec. 53. (SB 855) Effective June 20, 2014. Provisions implemented as of January 1, 2016, pursuant to Section 1796.61.)

ARTICLE 8. Affiliated Home Care Aides [1796.44 - 1796.45]

(Article 8 added by Stats. 2013, Ch. 790, Sec. 1.)

1796.44.

(a) A licensee shall ensure that prior to providing home care services, an affiliated home care aide shall complete the training requirements specified in this section.

(b) An affiliated home care aide shall complete a minimum of five hours of entry-level training prior to presence with a client, as follows:

(1) Two hours of orientation training regarding his or her role as caregiver and the applicable terms of employment.

(2) Three hours of safety training, including basic safety precautions, emergency procedures, and infection control.

(c) In addition to the requirements in subdivision (b), an affiliated home care aide shall complete a minimum of five hours of annual training. The annual training shall relate to core competencies and be population specific, which shall include, but not be limited to, the following areas:

(1) Clients' rights and safety.

(2) How to provide for, and respond to, a client's daily living needs.

(3) How to report, prevent, and detect abuse and neglect.

(4) How to assist a client with personal hygiene and other home care services.

(5) If transportation services are provided, how to safely transport a client.

(d) The entry-level training and annual training described in subdivisions (b) and (c) may be completed through an online training program.

(Amended by Stats. 2015, Ch. 303, Sec. 296. (AB 731) Effective January 1, 2016.)

1796.45.

(a) Affiliated home care aides hired on or after January 1, 2016, shall submit to an examination 90 days prior to employment, or within seven days after employment, to determine that the individual is free of active tuberculosis disease.

(b) For purposes of this section, "examination" means a test for tuberculosis infection that is recommended by the federal Centers for Disease Control and Prevention (CDC) and licensed by the federal Food and Drug Administration (FDA) and, if that test is positive, an X-ray of the lungs. The aide shall not work as an affiliated home care aide unless the licensee obtains documentation from a licensed medical professional that there is no risk of spreading the disease.

(c) After submitting to an examination, an affiliated home care aide whose test for tuberculosis infection is negative shall be required to undergo an examination at least once every two years. Once an affiliated home care aide has a documented positive test for tuberculosis infection that has been followed by an X-ray, the examination is no longer required.

(d) After each examination, an affiliated home care aide shall submit, and the home care organization shall keep on file, a certificate from the examining practitioner showing that the affiliated home care aide was examined and found free from active tuberculosis disease.

(e) The examination is a condition of initial and continuing employment with the home care organization.

(f) An affiliated home care aide who transfers employment from one home care organization to another shall be deemed to meet the requirements of subdivision (a) or (c) if the affiliated home care aide can produce a certificate showing that he or she submitted to the examination within the past two years and was found to be free of active tuberculosis disease, or if it is verified by the home care organization previously employing him or her that it has a certificate on file that contains that showing and a copy of the certificate is provided to the new home care organization prior to the affiliated home care aide beginning employment.

(Amended by Stats. 2015, Ch. 303, Sec. 297. (AB 731) Effective January 1, 2016.)

ARTICLE 9. Revenues [1796.47 - 1796.49]

(Article 9 added by Stats. 2013, Ch. 790, Sec. 1.)

1796.47.

(a) (1) Administration of this program shall be fully supported by fees and not civil penalties. Initial costs to implement this chapter may be provided through a General Fund loan that is to be repaid in accordance with a schedule provided by the Department of Finance. The department shall assess fees for home care organization licensure, and home care aide registration related to activities authorized by this chapter. The department may adjust fees as necessary to fully support the administration of this chapter. Except for General Fund moneys that are otherwise transferred or appropriated for the initial costs of administering this chapter, or penalties collected pursuant to this chapter that are appropriated by the Legislature for the purposes of this chapter, no General Fund moneys shall be used for any purpose under this chapter.

(2) A portion of moneys collected in the administration of this chapter, as designated by the department, may be used for community outreach consistent with this chapter.

(b) The Home Care Fund is hereby created within the State Treasury for the purpose of this chapter. All licensure and registration fees authorized by this chapter shall be deposited into the Home Care Fund, except the fingerprint fees collected pursuant to Section 1796.23, which shall be deposited into the Fingerprint Fees Account. Moneys in this fund shall, upon appropriation by the Legislature, be made available to the department for purposes of administering this chapter.

(c) Any fines and penalties collected pursuant to this chapter shall be deposited into the Home Care Technical Assistance Fund, which is hereby created as a subaccount within the Home Care Fund. Moneys in the Home Care Technical Assistance Fund shall, upon appropriation by the Legislature, be available to the department for the purposes of providing technical assistance, training, and education pursuant to this chapter.

(Amended by Stats. 2014, Ch. 29, Sec. 56. (SB 855) Effective June 20, 2014. Provisions implemented as of January 1, 2016, pursuant to Section 1796.61.)

1796.48.

(a) The department may charge a nonrefundable application and nonrefundable renewal fee to become a registered home care aide and to renew a registered home care aide's registration.

(b) The maximum fee shall not exceed the total actual costs, which include, but are not limited to, of all of the following:

(1) The searches for criminal offender records performed by the Department of Justice.

(2) The cost incurred by the Department of Justice for the searches of the records of the Federal Bureau of Investigation.

(3) The cost to the department to process the applications and maintain the home care aide registry and perform the duties required by this chapter and any rules and regulations promulgated pursuant to this chapter.

(c) The fees collected shall be deposited into the Home Care Fund pursuant to subdivision (b) of Section 1796.47, except the fingerprint fees collected pursuant to Section 1796.23, which shall be deposited into the Fingerprint Fees Account.

(Amended by Stats. 2014, Ch. 29, Sec. 57. (SB 855) Effective June 20, 2014. Provisions implemented as of January 1, 2016, pursuant to Section 1796.61.)

1796.49.

(a) A licensee shall pay the following fees:

(1) A nonrefundable 24-month initial license fee, as prescribed by the department, for a licensee not currently licensed to provide home care services in the state.

(2) A two-year nonrefundable renewal fee, as determined by the department, based on the number of full-time equivalents (FTEs), including paid personnel or contractors needed to oversee the enforcement of this chapter.

(3) Other reasonable fees as prescribed by the department necessary for the administration of this chapter.

(b) The fees collected shall be deposited into the Home Care Fund pursuant to subdivision (b) of Section 1796.47, except the fingerprint fees collected pursuant to Section 1796.23, which shall be deposited into the Fingerprint Fees Account.

(Amended by Stats. 2014, Ch. 29, Sec. 58. (SB 855) Effective June 20, 2014. Provisions implemented as of January 1, 2016, pursuant to Section 1796.61.)

ARTICLE 10. Complaints, Inspections, and Investigations [1796.51 - 1796.53]

(Article 10 added by Stats. 2013, Ch. 790, Sec. 1.)

1796.51.

In order to carry out the provisions of this chapter, the department may establish procedures for the receipt, investigation, and resolution of complaints against home care organizations.

(Added by Stats. 2013, Ch. 790, Sec. 1. (AB 1217) Effective January 1, 2014. Provisions implemented as of January 1, 2016, pursuant to Section 1796.61.)

1796.52.

(a) The department may review and, if it determines necessary, investigate complaints filed against home care organizations regarding violations of this chapter or any rules or regulations promulgated pursuant to this chapter.

(b) The department shall verify through random, unannounced inspections that a home care organization meets the requirements of this chapter and the rules and regulations promulgated pursuant to this chapter.

(c) An investigation or inspection conducted by the department pursuant to this chapter may include, but is not limited to, inspection of the books, records, or premises of a home care organization. A home care organization's refusal to make records, books, or premises available shall constitute cause for the revocation of the home care organization's license.

(d) Other than maintaining the home care registry, the department shall have no oversight responsibility regarding registered home care aides.

(e) Upon receipt of a report of suspected or known abuse, as set forth in subdivision (e) of Section 1796.42, the department shall cross-report the suspected or known abuse to local law enforcement and Adult Protective Services if the alleged victim is 18 years of age or older, or local law enforcement and Child Protective Services if the alleged victim is under 18 years of age. Other than the cross-reporting required by this subdivision, the department shall not be required to investigate suspected or known abuse or have other responsibilities related to the suspected or known abuse. This subdivision shall not supersede the existing duty of home health aides and home health agencies as mandated reporters to report directly to local law enforcement or county adult protective services pursuant to Section 15630.

(Amended by Stats. 2014, Ch. 29, Sec. 59. (SB 855) Effective June 20, 2014. Provisions implemented as of January 1, 2016, pursuant to Section 1796.61.)

1796.53.

A duly authorized officer, employee, or agent of the department may, upon presentation of proper identification, enter a home care organization during posted business hours, with or without advance notice, to secure compliance with, or to prevent a violation of, any provision of this chapter or any provision promulgated under this chapter.

(Added by Stats. 2013, Ch. 790, Sec. 1. (AB 1217) Effective January 1, 2014. Provisions implemented as of January 1, 2016, pursuant to Section 1796.61.)

ARTICLE 11. Enforcement [1796.55 - 1796.59]

(Article 11 added by Stats. 2013, Ch. 790, Sec. 1.)

1796.55.

(a) A home care organization that operates in violation of any requirement or obligation imposed by this chapter or any rule or regulation promulgated pursuant to this chapter may be subject to the fines levied or licensure action taken by the department as specified in this chapter.

(b) When the department determines that a home care organization is in violation of this chapter or any rules or regulations promulgated pursuant to this chapter, a notice of violation shall be served upon the licensee. Each notice of violation shall be prepared in writing and shall specify the nature of the violation and the statutory provision, rule, or regulation alleged to have been violated. The notice shall inform the licensee of any action the department may take pursuant to this chapter, including the requirement of a plan of correction, assessment of a penalty, or action to suspend, revoke, or deny renewal of the license. The director or his or her designee shall also inform the licensee of rights to a hearing pursuant to this chapter.

(c) The department may impose a fine of up to nine hundred dollars ($900) per violation per day commencing on the date the violation was identified and ending on the date each violation is corrected.

(d) The department shall adopt regulations establishing procedures for notices, correction plans, appeals, and hearings.

(Amended by Stats. 2014, Ch. 29, Sec. 60. (SB 855) Effective June 20, 2014. Provisions implemented as of January 1, 2016, pursuant to Section 1796.61.)

1796.57.

It is a misdemeanor for a person to falsely represent or present himself or herself as a home care aide applicant or registered home care aide.

(Added by Stats. 2013, Ch. 790, Sec. 1. (AB 1217) Effective January 1, 2014. Provisions implemented as of January 1, 2016, pursuant to Section 1796.61.)

1796.58.

Any person who violates this chapter, or who willfully or repeatedly violates a rule or regulation promulgated under this chapter, is guilty of a misdemeanor and, upon conviction thereof, shall be punished by a fine not to exceed one thousand dollars ($1,000) or by imprisonment in a county jail for a period not to exceed 180 days, or by both that fine and imprisonment.

(Amended by Stats. 2014, Ch. 54, Sec. 6. (SB 1461) Effective January 1, 2015. Provisions implemented as of January 1, 2016, pursuant to Section 1796.61.)

1796.59.

(a) Notwithstanding any other provision of this chapter, the district attorney of every county, and city attorneys in cities that have city attorneys who have jurisdiction to prosecute misdemeanors pursuant to Section 72193 of the Government Code, may, upon their own initiative or upon application by the department or its authorized representative, institute and conduct the prosecution of any action for violation within their county of this chapter or a rule or regulation promulgated under this chapter.

(b) The civil, criminal, and administrative remedies available to the department pursuant to this chapter are not exclusive, and may be sought and employed in any combination as determined by the department to enforce this chapter or a rule or regulation promulgated under this chapter.

(Added by Stats. 2013, Ch. 790, Sec. 1. (AB 1217) Effective January 1, 2014. Provisions implemented as of January 1, 2016, pursuant to Section 1796.61.)

ARTICLE 12. Operation [1796.61 - 1796.63]

(Article 12 added by Stats. 2013, Ch. 790, Sec. 1.)

1796.61.

(a) This chapter shall be implemented on January 1, 2016.

(b) Home care organization applicants and home care aide applicants who submit applications prior to January 1, 2016, shall be authorized to provide home care services without meeting the requirements of Section 1796.45, provided the requirements of that section are met no later than July 1, 2016.

(c) The applicants described in subdivision (b) shall meet all the requirements of this chapter no later than July 1, 2016, in order to continue to provide home care services.

(Amended by Stats. 2014, Ch. 29, Sec. 62. (SB 855) Effective June 20, 2014. Provisions implemented as of January 1, 2016, pursuant to Section 1796.61. Note: This section prescribes a delayed implementation date (Jan. 1, 2016) for Chapter 13, commencing with Section 1796.10.)

1796.62.

This chapter and any rules and regulations promulgated pursuant to this chapter shall only be implemented to the extent that funds are made available through an appropriation in the annual Budget Act.

(Added by Stats. 2013, Ch. 790, Sec. 1. (AB 1217) Effective January 1, 2014. Provisions implemented as of January 1, 2016, pursuant to Section 1796.61.)

1796.63.

(a) The department shall adopt, amend, or repeal, in accordance with Chapter 3.5 (commencing with Section 11340) of the Government Code, any reasonable rules, regulations, and standards as may be necessary or proper to carry out the purpose and intent of this chapter and to enable the department to exercise the powers and perform the duties conferred upon it by this chapter, not inconsistent with any of the provisions of any statute of this state. Notwithstanding the rulemaking provisions of the Administrative Procedure Act (Chapter 3.5 (commencing with Section 11340) of Part 1 of Division 3 of Title 2 of the Government Code), the department may implement and administer this chapter through written directives, without taking regulatory action, subject to the limitations provided in subdivision (b).

(b) The department's authority to implement and administer this chapter through written directives shall expire no later than January 1, 2018, or upon the effective date of regulations promulgated in accordance with the Administrative Procedure Act (Chapter 3.5 (commencing with Section 11340) of Part 1 of Division 3 of Title 2 of the Government Code), whichever occurs sooner.

(c) The department may adopt emergency regulations to implement and administer the provisions of this chapter. The department may readopt any emergency regulations that are the same as, or substantially equivalent to, any emergency regulations previously adopted. The initial adoption and readoption of emergency regulations for the implementation and administration of this chapter pursuant to this subdivision shall be deemed to be an emergency and necessary for the immediate preservation of the public peace, health, safety, or general welfare. The initial and readopted emergency regulations shall be exempt from review by the Office of Administrative Law. The initial and readopted emergency regulations shall be submitted to the Office of Administrative Law for filing with the Secretary of State and each adoption or readoption shall remain in effect for no more than 180 days.

(Amended by Stats. 2014, Ch. 29, Sec. 63. (SB 855) Effective June 20, 2014. Provisions implemented as of January 1, 2016, pursuant to Section 1796.61.)

CHAPTER 14. Rehabilitation Innovation Centers [1797.8- 1797.8.]

(Chapter 14 added by Stats. 2017, Ch. 386, Sec. 3.)

1797.8.

For purposes of this chapter, "rehabilitation innovation center" means a not-for-profit or government-owned rehabilitation facility that meets all of the following:

(a) Is classified as a not-for-profit entity or as a government-owned institution under the Centers for Medicare and Medicaid Services Provider of Services file.

(b) Holds at least one federal rehabilitation research and training designation for research projects on traumatic brain injury, spinal cord injury, or stroke rehabilitation research from the Rehabilitation Research and Training Centers, the Rehabilitation Engineering Research Center, or the Model Spinal Cord Injury Systems at the National Institute on Disability, Independent Living, and Rehabilitation Research at the federal Department of Health and Human Services.

(c) Has at least 200 Medi-Cal discharges per year.

(Added by Stats. 2017, Ch. 386, Sec. 3. (AB 1411) Effective January 1, 2018. See same-numbered section in Division 2.5, Chapter 1.)

DIVISION 2.5. EMERGENCY MEDICAL SERVICES [1797 - 1799.207]

(Division 2.5 added by Stats. 1980, Ch. 1260.)

CHAPTER 1. General Provisions [1797 - 1797.10]

(Chapter 1 added by Stats. 1980, Ch. 1260.)

1797.

This division shall be known and may be cited as the Emergency Medical Services System and the Prehospital Emergency Medical Care Personnel Act.

(Amended by Stats. 1986, Ch. 248, Sec. 121.)

1797.1.

The Legislature finds and declares that it is the intent of this act to provide the state with a statewide system for emergency medical services by establishing within the Health and Welfare Agency the Emergency Medical Services Authority, which is responsible for the coordination and integration of all state activities concerning emergency medical services.

(Amended by Stats. 1983, Ch. 1246, Sec. 6.)

1797.2.

It is the intent of the Legislature to maintain and promote the development of EMT-P paramedic programs where appropriate throughout the state and to initiate EMT-II limited advanced life support programs only where geography, population density, and resources would not make the establishment of a paramedic program feasible.

(Added by Stats. 1980, Ch. 1260.)

1797.3.

The provisions of this division do not preclude the adoption of additional training standards for EMT-II and EMT-P personnel by local EMS agencies, consistent with standards adopted pursuant to Sections 1797.171, 1797.172, and 1797.214.

(Amended by Stats. 1989, Ch. 1362, Sec. 1. Effective October 2, 1989.)

1797.4.

Any reference in any provision of law to mobile intensive care paramedics subject to former Article 3 (commencing with Section 1480) of Chapter 2.5 of Division 2 shall be deemed to be a reference to persons holding valid certificates under this division as an EMT-I, EMT-II, or EMT-P. Any reference in any provision of law to mobile intensive care nurses subject to former Article 3 (commencing with Section 1480) of Chapter 2.5 of Division 2 shall be deemed to be a reference to persons holding valid authorization under this division as an MICN.

(Added by Stats. 1988, Ch. 260, Sec. 1.)

1797.5.

It is the intent of the Legislature to promote the development, accessibility, and provision of emergency medical services to the people of the State of California.

Further, it is the policy of the State of California that people shall be encouraged and trained to assist others at the scene of a medical emergency. Local governments, agencies, and other organizations shall be encouraged to offer training in cardiopulmonary resuscitation and lifesaving first aid techniques so that people may be adequately trained, prepared, and encouraged to assist others immediately.

(Added by Stats. 1983, Ch. 1246, Sec. 8.)

1797.6.

(a) It is the policy of the State of California to ensure the provision of effective and efficient emergency medical care. The Legislature finds and declares that achieving this policy has been hindered by the confusion and concern in the 58 counties resulting from the United States Supreme Court's holding in Community Communications Company, Inc. v. City of Boulder, Colorado, 455 U.S. 40, 70 L. Ed. 2d 810, 102 S. Ct. 835, regarding local governmental liability under federal antitrust laws.

(b) It is the intent of the Legislature in enacting this section and Sections 1797.85 and 1797.224 to prescribe and exercise the degree of state direction and supervision over emergency medical services as will provide for state action immunity under federal antitrust laws for activities undertaken by local governmental entities in carrying out their prescribed functions under this division.

(Added by Stats. 1984, Ch. 1349, Sec. 1.)

1797.7.

(a) The Legislature finds and declares that the ability of some prehospital emergency medical care personnel to move from the jurisdiction of one local EMS agency which issued certification and authorization to the jurisdiction of another local EMS agency which utilizes the same level of emergency medical care personnel will be unreasonably hindered if those personnel are required to be retested and recertified by each local EMS agency.

(b) It is the intent of the Legislature in enacting this section and Section 1797.185 to ensure that EMT-P personnel who have met state competency standards for their basic scope of practice, as defined in Chapter 4 (commencing with Section 100135) of Division 9 of Title 22 of the California Code of Regulations, and are currently certified are recognized statewide without having to repeat testing or certification for that same basic scope of practice.

(c) It is the intent of the Legislature that local EMS agencies may require prehospital emergency medical care personnel who were certified in another jurisdiction to be oriented to the local EMS system and receive training and demonstrate competency in any optional skills for which they have not received accreditation. It is also the intent of the Legislature that no individual who possesses a valid California EMT-P certificate shall be prevented from beginning working within the standard statewide scope of practice of an EMT-P if he or she is accompanied by a EMT-P who is currently certified in California and is accredited by the local EMS agency. It is further the intent of the Legislature that the local EMS agency provide, or arrange for the provision of, training and accreditation testing in local EMS operational policies and procedures and any optional skills utilized in the local EMS system within 30 days of application for accreditation as an EMT-P by the local EMS agency.

(d) It is the intent of the Legislature that subdivisions (a), (b), and (c) not be construed to hinder the ability of local EMS agencies to maintain medical control within their EMS system in accordance with the requirements of this division.
(Amended by Stats. 1989, Ch. 1362, Sec. 2. Effective October 2, 1989.)

1797.8.

(a) For purposes of this section, the following definitions apply:

(1) "EMT-I" means any person who has training and a valid certificate as prescribed by Section 1797.80.

(2) "EMT certifying authority" means the medical director of the local emergency medical services agency.

(b) Any county may, at the discretion of the county or regional medical director of emergency medical services, develop a program to certify an EMT-I to administer naloxone hydrochloride by means other than intravenous injection.

(c) Any county that chooses to implement a program to certify an EMT-I to administer naloxone hydrochloride, as specified in subdivision (b), shall approve and administer a training and testing program leading to certification consistent with guidelines established by the state Emergency Medical Services Authority.

(d) On or before July 1, 2003, the state Emergency Medical Services Authority shall develop guidelines relating to the county certification programs authorized pursuant to subdivision (b).

(e) An EMT-I may be authorized by the EMT certifying authority to administer naloxone hydrochloride by means other than intravenous injection only if the EMT-I has completed training and passed an examination administered or approved by the EMT certifying authority in the area.

(f) This section shall be operative only until the operative date of regulations that revise the regulations set forth in Chapter 3 (commencing with Section 100101) of Division 9 of Title 22 of the California Code of Regulations and that authorize an EMT-I to receive EMT-II training in administering naloxone hydrochloride without having to complete the entire EMT-II certification course.
(Added by Stats. 2002, Ch. 678, Sec. 2. Effective January 1, 2003. Conditionally inoperative as provided in subd. (f). See same-numbered section in Division 2, Chapter 14.)

1797.9.

(a) This division shall not be construed to regulate or authorize state or local regulation of any nonmedical aspects of the following:

(1) Public aircraft certification or configuration.

(2) Public aircraft maintenance procedures and documentation.

(3) Piloting techniques and methods of piloting public aircraft.

(4) Public aircraft crewmember qualifications.

(5) Pilot certification or qualifications for public aircraft.

(b) For purposes of this section, "public aircraft" has the same meaning as in Section 1.1 of Title 14 of the Code of Federal Regulations.
(Added by Stats. 2008, Ch. 289, Sec. 2. Effective January 1, 2009.)

1797.10.

(a) The County of San Bernardino is authorized to work with the Inland Counties Emergency Medical Agency to conduct a pilot project, commencing January 1, 2019, that would authorize emergency transportation for a police dog injured in the line of duty to a facility that is capable of providing veterinary medical services to the injured police dog if all of the following conditions apply:

(1) A request for transport is made by the injured police dog's canine handler.

(2) An ambulance is present at the scene of the injury at the time the request for transport is made.

(3) No person at the scene of the incident requires medical attention or medical transportation at the time the request for transport is made.

(4) The owner of the ambulance has a policy that permits the transport of an injured police dog.

(5) The canine handler accompanies the injured police dog and remains in full control of the dog during transport.

(6) The canine handler provides the location of the nearest facility that is capable of providing veterinary medical services to the injured police dog.

(7) The canine handler remains responsible for any first aid rendered to the injured police dog during transport.

(b) For purposes of this section, "police dog" means a dog being used by a peace officer in the discharge or attempted discharge of his or her duties and includes, but is not limited to, a search and rescue dog or a passive alert dog.

(c) (1) The Inland Counties Emergency Medical Agency shall collect data on the number of police dogs transported pursuant to this section, the location where the police dogs were transported to, and the outcome of those transports.

(2) The Inland Counties Emergency Medical Agency shall submit a report to the Legislature that includes the data described in paragraph (1) by January 1, 2022. The report shall be submitted in compliance with Section 9795 of the Government Code.

(d) This section shall remain in effect only until January 1, 2022, and as of that date is repealed.
(Added by Stats. 2018, Ch. 272, Sec. 1. (AB 1776) Effective January 1, 2019. Repealed as of January 1, 2022, by its own provisions.)

CHAPTER 2. Definitions [1797.50 - 1797.97]

(Chapter 2 added by Stats. 1980, Ch. 1260.)

1797.50.

Unless the context otherwise requires, the definitions contained in this chapter shall govern the provisions of this division.
(Amended by Stats. 1986, Ch. 248, Sec. 123.)

1797.52.

"Advanced life support" means special services designed to provide definitive prehospital emergency medical care, including, but not limited to, cardiopulmonary resuscitation, cardiac monitoring, cardiac defibrillation, advanced airway management, intravenous therapy, administration of specified drugs and other medicinal preparations, and other specified techniques and procedures administered by authorized personnel under the direct supervision of a base hospital as part of a local EMS system at the scene of an emergency, during transport to an acute care hospital, during interfacility transfer, and while in the emergency department of an acute care hospital until responsibility is assumed by the emergency or other medical staff of that hospital.
(Amended by Stats. 1984, Ch. 1391, Sec. 4.)

1797.53.

"Alternative base station" means a facility or service operated and directly supervised by, or directly supervised by, a physician and surgeon who is trained and qualified to issue advice and instructions to prehospital emergency medical care personnel, which has been approved by the medical director of the local EMS agency to provide medical direction to advanced life support or limited advanced life support personnel responding to a medical emergency as part of the local EMS system, when no qualified hospital is available to provide that medical direction.
(Added by Stats. 1988, Ch. 1390, Sec. 1.)

1797.54.

"Authority" means the Emergency Medical Services Authority established by this division.
(Amended by Stats. 1986, Ch. 248, Sec. 124.)

1797.56.

"Authorized registered nurse," "mobile intensive care nurse," or "MICN" means a registered nurse who is functioning pursuant to Section 2725 of the Business and Professions Code and who has been authorized by the medical director of the local EMS agency as qualified to provide prehospital advanced life support or to issue instructions to prehospital emergency medical care personnel within an EMS system according to standardized procedures developed by the local EMS agency consistent with statewide guidelines established by the authority. Nothing in this section shall be deemed to abridge or restrict the duties or functions of a registered nurse or mobile intensive care nurse as otherwise provided by law.
(Amended by Stats. 1984, Ch. 1391, Sec. 5.)

1797.58.

"Base hospital" means one of a limited number of hospitals which, upon designation by the local EMS agency and upon the completion of a written contractual agreement with the local EMS agency, is responsible for directing the advanced life support system or limited advanced life support system and prehospital care system assigned to it by the local EMS agency.
(Amended by Stats. 1984, Ch. 1391, Sec. 6.)

1797.59.

"Base hospital physician" or "BHP" means a physician and surgeon who is currently licensed in California, who is assigned to the emergency department of a base hospital, and who has been trained to issue advice and instructions to prehospital emergency medical care personnel consistent with statewide guidelines established by the authority. Nothing in this section shall be deemed to abridge or restrict the duties or functions of a physician and surgeon as otherwise provided by law.
(Added by Stats. 1984, Ch. 1391, Sec. 7.)

1797.60.

"Basic life support" means emergency first aid and cardiopulmonary resuscitation procedures which, as a minimum, include recognizing respiratory and cardiac arrest and starting the proper application of cardiopulmonary resuscitation to maintain life without invasive techniques until the victim may be transported or until advanced life support is available.

(Added by Stats. 1980, Ch. 1260.)

1797.61.

(a) "Certificate" or "license" means a specific document issued to an individual denoting competence in the named area of prehospital service.

(b) "Certificate status" or "license status" means the active, expired, denied, suspended, revoked, or placed on probation designation applied to a certificate or license issued pursuant to this division.

(Added by Stats. 2008, Ch. 274, Sec. 2. Effective January 1, 2009.)

1797.62.

"Certifying entity" means a public safety agency or the office of the State Fire Marshal if the agency has a training program for EMT-I personnel that is approved pursuant to the standards developed pursuant to Section 1797.109, or the medical director of a local EMS agency.

(Repealed and added by Stats. 2008, Ch. 274, Sec. 4. Effective January 1, 2009.)

1797.63.

"Certifying examination" or "examination for certification" means an examination designated by the authority for a specific level of prehospital emergency medical care personnel that must be satisfactorily passed prior to certification or recertification at the specific level and may include any examination or examinations designated by the authority, including, but not limited to, any of the following options determined appropriate by the authority:

(a) An examination developed either by the authority or under the auspices of the authority or approved by the authority and administered by the authority or any entity designated by the authority to administer the examination.

(b) An examination developed and administered by the National Registry of Emergency Medical Technicians.

(c) An examination developed administered, or approved by a certifying agency pursuant to standards adopted by the authority for the certification examination.

(Added by Stats. 1989, Ch. 1362, Sec. 3. Effective October 2, 1989.)

1797.64.

"Commission" means the Commission on Emergency Medical Services created pursuant to the provisions of Section 1799.

(Added by Stats. 1980, Ch. 1260.)

1797.66.

"Competency based curriculum" means a curriculum in which specific objectives are defined for each of the separate skills taught in training programs with integrated didactic and practical instruction and successful completion of an examination demonstrating mastery of every skill.

(Added by Stats. 1980, Ch. 1260.)

1797.67.

"Designated facility" means a hospital which has been designated by a local EMS agency to perform specified emergency medical services systems functions pursuant to guidelines established by the authority.

(Added by Stats. 1983, Ch. 1246, Sec. 12.)

1797.68.

"Director" means the Director of the Emergency Medical Services Authority.

(Amended by Stats. 1983, Ch. 1246, Sec. 13.)

1797.70.

"Emergency" means a condition or situation in which an individual has a need for immediate medical attention, or where the potential for such need is perceived by emergency medical personnel or a public safety agency.

(Added by Stats. 1980, Ch. 1260.)

1797.72.

"Emergency medical services" means the services utilized in responding to a medical emergency.

(Added by Stats. 1980, Ch. 1260.)

1797.74.

"Emergency medical services area" or "EMS area" means the geographical area within the jurisdiction of the designated local EMS agency.

(Amended by Stats. 1984, Ch. 1391, Sec. 8.)

1797.76.

"Emergency medical services plan" means a plan for the delivery of emergency medical services consistent with state guidelines addressing the components listed in Section 1797.103.

(Amended by Stats. 1983, Ch. 1246, Sec. 14.)

1797.78.

"Emergency medical services system" or "system" means a specially organized arrangement which provides for the personnel, facilities, and equipment for the effective and coordinated delivery in an EMS area of medical care services under emergency conditions.

(Added by Stats. 1980, Ch. 1260.)

1797.80.

"Emergency Medical Technician-I" or "EMT-I" means an individual trained in all facets of basic life support according to standards prescribed by this part and who has a valid certificate issued pursuant to this part. This definition shall include, but not be limited to, EMT-I (FS) and EMT-I-A.

(Added by Stats. 1980, Ch. 1260.)

1797.82.

"Emergency Medical Technician-II," "EMT-II," "Advanced Emergency Medical Technician," or "Advanced EMT" means an EMT-I with additional training in limited advanced life support according to standards prescribed by this part and who has a valid certificate issued pursuant to this part.

(Amended by Stats. 2008, Ch. 275, Sec. 2. Effective January 1, 2009.)

1797.84.

"Emergency Medical Technician-Paramedic," "EMT-P," "paramedic" or "mobile intensive care paramedic" means an individual whose scope of practice to provide advanced life support is according to standards prescribed by this division and who has a valid certificate issued pursuant to this division.

(Amended by Stats. 1986, Ch. 248, Sec. 125.)

1797.85.

"Exclusive operating area" means an EMS area or subarea defined by the emergency medical services plan for which a local EMS agency, upon the recommendation of a county, restricts operations to one or more emergency ambulance services or providers of limited advanced life support or advanced life support.

(Added by Stats. 1984, Ch. 1349, Sec. 2.)

1797.86.

"Health systems agency" means a health systems agency as defined in subsection (a) of Section 300(

l)-1 of Title 42 of the United States Code.

(Added by Stats. 1980, Ch. 1260.)

1797.88.

"Hospital" means an acute care hospital licensed under Chapter 2 (commencing with Section 1250) of Division 2, with a permit for basic emergency service or an out-of-state acute care hospital which substantially meets the requirements of Chapter 2 (commencing with Section 1250) of Division 2, as determined by the local EMS agency which is utilizing the hospital in the emergency medical services system, and is licensed in the state in which it is located.

(Amended by Stats. 1986, Ch. 1162, Sec. 1. Effective September 26, 1986.)

1797.90.

"Medical control" means the medical management of the emergency medical services system pursuant to the provisions of Chapter 5 (commencing with Section 1798).

(Added by Stats. 1980, Ch. 1260.)

1797.92.

"Limited advanced life support" means special service designed to provide prehospital emergency medical care limited to techniques and procedures that exceed basic life support but are less than advanced life support and are those procedures specified pursuant to Section 1797.171.

(Added by Stats. 1980, Ch. 1260.)

1797.94.

"Local EMS agency" means the agency, department, or office having primary responsibility for administration of emergency medical services in a county and which is designated pursuant to Chapter 4 (commencing with Section 1797.200).

(Added by Stats. 1980, Ch. 1260.)

1797.97.

"Poison control center" or "PCC" means a hospital-based facility or other facility which, as a minimum, provides information and advice regarding the management of individuals who have or may have ingested or otherwise been exposed to poisonous or possibly toxic substances, and which has been designated by the Emergency Medical Services Authority according to the standards prescribed by this division.

(Amended by Stats. 1987, Ch. 972, Sec. 1.)

CHAPTER 2.5. The Maddy Emergency Medical Services Fund [1797.98a - 1797.98g]

(Heading of Chapter 2.5 amended by Stats. 1998, Ch. 58, Sec. 2.)

1797.98a.

(a) The fund provided for in this chapter shall be known as the Maddy Emergency Medical Services (EMS) Fund.

(b) (1) Each county may establish an emergency medical services fund, upon the adoption of a resolution by the board of supervisors. The moneys in the fund shall be available for the reimbursements required by this chapter. The fund shall be administered by each county, except that a county electing to have the state administer its medically indigent services program may also elect to have its emergency medical services fund administered by the state.

(2) Costs of administering the fund shall be reimbursed by the fund in an amount that does not exceed the actual administrative costs or 10 percent of the amount of the fund, whichever amount is lower.

(3) All interest earned on moneys in the fund shall be deposited in the fund for disbursement as specified in this section.

(4) Each administering agency may maintain a reserve of up to 15 percent of the amount in the portions of the fund reimbursable to physicians and surgeons, pursuant to subparagraph (A) of, and to hospitals, pursuant to subparagraph (B) of, paragraph (5). Each administering agency may maintain a reserve of any amount in the portion of the fund that is distributed for other emergency medical services purposes as determined by each county, pursuant to subparagraph (C) of paragraph (5).

(5) The amount in the fund, reduced by the amount for administration and the reserve, shall be utilized to reimburse physicians and surgeons and hospitals for patients who do not make payment for emergency medical services and for other emergency medical services purposes as determined by each county according to the following schedule:

(A) Fifty-eight percent of the balance of the fund shall be distributed to physicians and surgeons for emergency services provided by all physicians and surgeons, except those physicians and surgeons employed by county hospitals, in general acute care hospitals that provide basic, comprehensive, or standby emergency services pursuant to paragraph (3) or (5) of subdivision (f) of Section 1797.98e up to the time the patient is stabilized.

(B) Twenty-five percent of the fund shall be distributed only to hospitals providing disproportionate trauma and emergency medical care services.

(C) Seventeen percent of the fund shall be distributed for other emergency medical services purposes as determined by each county, including, but not limited to, the funding of regional poison control centers. Funding may be used for purchasing equipment and for capital projects only to the extent that these expenditures support the provision of emergency services and are consistent with the intent of this chapter.

(c) The source of the moneys in the fund shall be the penalty assessment made for this purpose, as provided in Section 76000 of the Government Code.

(d) Any physician and surgeon may be reimbursed for up to 50 percent of the amount claimed pursuant to subdivision (a) of Section 1797.98c for the initial cycle of reimbursements made by the administering agency in a given year, pursuant to Section 1797.98e. All funds remaining at the end of the fiscal year in excess of any reserve held and rolled over to the next year pursuant to paragraph (4) of subdivision (b) shall be distributed proportionally, based on the dollar amount of claims submitted and paid to all physicians and surgeons who submitted qualifying claims during that year.

(e) Of the money deposited into the fund pursuant to Section 76000.5 of the Government Code, 15 percent shall be utilized to provide funding for all pediatric trauma centers throughout the county, both publicly and privately owned and operated. The expenditure of money shall be limited to reimbursement to physicians and surgeons, and to hospitals for patients who do not make payment for emergency care services in hospitals up to the point of stabilization, or to hospitals for expanding the services provided to pediatric trauma patients at trauma centers and other hospitals providing care to pediatric trauma patients, or at pediatric trauma centers, including the purchase of equipment. Local emergency medical services (EMS) agencies may conduct a needs assessment of pediatric trauma services in the county to allocate these expenditures. Counties that do not maintain a pediatric trauma center shall utilize the money deposited into the fund pursuant to Section 76000.5 of the Government Code to improve access to, and coordination of, pediatric trauma and emergency services in the county, with preference for funding given to hospitals that specialize in services to children, and physicians and surgeons who provide emergency care for children. Funds spent for the purposes of this section shall be known as Richie's Fund. This subdivision shall remain in effect until January 1, 2027.

(f) Costs of administering money deposited into the fund pursuant to Section 76000.5 of the Government Code shall be reimbursed from the money collected in an amount that does not exceed the actual administrative costs or 10 percent of the money collected, whichever amount is lower. This subdivision shall remain in effect until January 1, 2027.

(Amended by Stats. 2016, Ch. 147, Sec. 2. (SB 867) Effective January 1, 2017.)

1797.98b.

(a) Each county establishing a fund, on January 1, 1989, and on each April 15 thereafter, shall report to the authority on the implementation and status of the Emergency Medical Services Fund. Notwithstanding Section 10231.5 of the Government Code, the authority shall compile and forward a summary of each county's report to the appropriate policy and fiscal committees of the Legislature. Each county report, and the summary compiled by the authority, shall cover the immediately preceding fiscal year, and shall include, but not be limited to, all of the following:

(1) The total amount of fines and forfeitures collected, the total amount of penalty assessments collected, and the total amount of penalty assessments deposited into the Emergency Medical Services Fund, or, if no moneys were deposited into the fund, the reason or reasons for the lack of deposits. The total amounts of penalty assessments shall be listed on the basis of each statute that provides the authority for the penalty assessment, including Sections 76000, 76000.5, and 76104 of the Government Code, and Section 42007 of the Vehicle Code.

(2) The amount of penalty assessment funds collected under Section 76000.5 of the Government Code that are used for the purposes of subdivision (e) of Section 1797.98a.

(3) The fund balance and the amount of moneys disbursed under the program to physicians and surgeons, for hospitals, and for other emergency medical services purposes, and the amount of money disbursed for actual administrative costs. If funds were disbursed for other emergency medical services, the report shall provide a description of each of those services.

(4) The number of claims paid to physicians and surgeons, and the percentage of claims paid, based on the uniform fee schedule, as adopted by the county.

(5) The amount of moneys available to be disbursed to physicians and surgeons, descriptions of the physician and surgeon claims payment methodologies, the dollar amount of the total allowable claims submitted, and the percentage at which those claims were reimbursed.

(6) A statement of the policies, procedures, and regulatory action taken to implement and run the program under this chapter.

(7) The name of the physician and surgeon and hospital administrator organization, or names of specific physicians and surgeons and hospital administrators, contacted to review claims payment methodologies.

(8) A description of the process used to solicit input from physicians and surgeons and hospitals to review payment distribution methodology as described in subdivision (a) of Section 1797.98e.

(9) An identification of the fee schedule used by the county pursuant to subdivision (e) of Section 1797.98c.

(10) (A) A description of the methodology used to disburse moneys to hospitals pursuant to subparagraph (B) of paragraph (5) of subdivision (b) of Section 1797.98a.

(B) The amount of moneys available to be disbursed to hospitals.

(C) If moneys are disbursed to hospitals on a claims basis, the dollar amount of the total allowable claims submitted and the percentage at which those claims were reimbursed to hospitals.

(11) The name and contact information of the entity responsible for each of the following:

(A) Collection of fines, forfeitures, and penalties.

(B) Distribution of penalty assessments into the Emergency Medical Services Fund.

(C) Distribution of moneys to physicians and surgeons.

(b) (1) Each county, upon request, shall make available to any member of the public the report provided to the authority under subdivision (a).

(2) Each county, upon request, shall make available to any member of the public a listing of physicians and surgeons and hospitals that have received reimbursement from the Emergency Medical Services Fund and the amount of the reimbursement they have received. This listing shall be compiled on a semiannual basis.

(Amended by Stats. 2014, Ch. 442, Sec. 5. (SB 1465) Effective September 18, 2014.)

1797.98c.

(a) Physicians and surgeons wishing to be reimbursed shall submit their claims for emergency services provided to patients who do not make any payment for services and for whom no responsible third party makes any payment.

(b) If, after receiving payment from the fund, a physician and surgeon is reimbursed by a patient or a responsible third party, the physician and surgeon shall do one of the following:

(1) Notify the administering agency, and, after notification, the administering agency shall reduce the physician and surgeon's future payment of claims from the fund. In the event there is not a subsequent submission of a claim for reimbursement within one year, the physician and surgeon shall reimburse the fund in an amount equal to the amount collected from the patient or third-party payer, but not more than the amount of reimbursement received from the fund.

(2) Notify the administering agency of the payment and reimburse the fund in an amount equal to the amount collected from the patient or third-party payer, but not more than the amount of the reimbursement received from the fund for that patient's care.

(c) Reimbursement of claims for emergency services provided to patients by any physician and surgeon shall be limited to services provided to a patient who does not have health insurance coverage for emergency services and care, cannot afford to pay for those services, and for whom payment will not be made through any private coverage or by any program funded in whole or in part by the federal government, with the exception of claims submitted for reimbursement through Section 1011 of the federal Medicare Prescription Drug, Improvement and Modernization Act of 2003, and where all of the following conditions have been met:

(1) The physician and surgeon has inquired if there is a responsible third-party source of payment.

(2) The physician and surgeon has billed for payment of services.

(3) Either of the following:

(A) At least three months have passed from the date the physician and surgeon billed the patient or responsible third party, during which time the physician and surgeon has made two attempts to obtain reimbursement and has not received reimbursement for any portion of the amount billed.

(B) The physician and surgeon has received actual notification from the patient or responsible third party that no payment will be made for the services rendered by the physician and surgeon.

(4) The physician and surgeon has stopped any current, and waives any future, collection efforts to obtain reimbursement from the patient, upon receipt of moneys from the fund.

(d) A listing of patient names shall accompany a physician and surgeon's submission, and those names shall be given full confidentiality protections by the administering agency.

(e) Notwithstanding any other restriction on reimbursement, a county shall adopt a fee schedule and reimbursement methodology to establish a uniform reasonable level of reimbursement from the county's emergency medical services fund for reimbursable services.

(f) For the purposes of submission and reimbursement of physician and surgeon claims, the administering agency shall adopt and use the current version of the Physicians' Current Procedural Terminology, published by the American Medical Association, or a similar procedural terminology reference.

(g) Each administering agency of a fund under this chapter shall make all reasonable efforts to notify physicians and surgeons who provide, or are likely to provide, emergency services in the county as to the availability of the fund and the process by which to submit a claim against the fund. The administering agency may satisfy this requirement by sending materials that provide information about the fund and the process to submit a claim against the fund to local medical societies, hospitals, emergency rooms, or other organizations, including materials that are prepared to be posted in visible locations.

(Amended by Stats. 2005, Ch. 671, Sec. 3. Effective January 1, 2006.)

1797.98e.

(a) It is the intent of the Legislature that a simplified, cost-efficient system of administration of this chapter be developed so that the maximum amount of funds may be utilized to reimburse physicians and surgeons and for other emergency medical services purposes. The administering agency shall select an administering officer and shall establish procedures and time schedules for the submission and processing of proposed reimbursement requests submitted by physicians and surgeons. The schedule shall provide for disbursements of moneys in the Emergency Medical Services Fund on at least a quarterly basis to applicants who have submitted accurate and complete data for payment. When the administering agency determines that claims for payment for physician and surgeon services are of sufficient numbers and amounts that, if paid, the claims would exceed the total amount of funds available for payment, the administering agency shall fairly prorate, without preference, payments to each claimant at a level less than the maximum payment level. Each administering agency may encumber sufficient funds during one fiscal year to reimburse claimants for losses incurred during that fiscal year for which claims will not be received until after the fiscal year. The administering agency may, as necessary, request records and documentation to support the amounts of reimbursement requested by physicians and surgeons and the administering agency may review and audit the records for accuracy. Reimbursements requested and reimbursements made that are not supported by records may be denied to, and recouped from, physicians and surgeons. Physicians and surgeons found to submit requests for reimbursement that are inaccurate or unsupported by records may be excluded from submitting future requests for reimbursement. The administering officer shall not give preferential treatment to any facility, physician and surgeon, or category of physician and surgeon and shall not engage in practices that constitute a conflict of interest by favoring a facility or physician and surgeon with which the administering officer has an operational or financial relationship. A hospital administrator of a hospital owned or operated by a county of a population of 250,000 or more as of January 1, 1991, or a person under the direct supervision of that person, shall not be the administering officer. The board of supervisors of a county or any other county agency may serve as the administering officer. The administering officer shall solicit input from physicians and surgeons and hospitals to review payment distribution methodologies to ensure fair and timely payments. This requirement may be fulfilled through the establishment of an advisory committee with representatives comprised of local physicians and surgeons and hospital administrators. In order to reduce the county's administrative burden, the administering officer may instead request an existing board, commission, or local medical society, or physicians and surgeons and hospital administrators, representative of the local community, to provide input and make recommendations on payment distribution methodologies.

(b) Each provider of health services that receives payment under this chapter shall keep and maintain records of the services rendered, the person to whom rendered, the date, and any additional information the administering agency may, by regulation, require, for a period of three years from the date the service was provided. The administering agency shall not require any additional information from a physician and surgeon providing emergency medical services that is not available in the patient record maintained by the entity listed in subdivision (f) where the emergency medical services are provided, nor shall the administering agency require a physician and surgeon to make eligibility determinations.

(c) During normal working hours, the administering agency may make any inspection and examination of a hospital's or physician and surgeon's books and records needed to carry out this chapter. A provider who has knowingly submitted a false request for reimbursement shall be guilty of civil fraud.

(d) Nothing in this chapter shall prevent a physician and surgeon from utilizing an agent who furnishes billing and collection services to the physician and surgeon to submit claims or receive payment for claims.

(e) All payments from the fund pursuant to Section 1797.98c to physicians and surgeons shall be limited to physicians and surgeons who, in person, provide onsite services in a clinical setting, including, but not limited to, radiology and pathology settings.

(f) All payments from the fund shall be limited to claims for care rendered by physicians and surgeons to patients who are initially medically screened, evaluated, treated, or stabilized in any of the following:

(1) A basic or comprehensive emergency department of a licensed general acute care hospital.

(2) A site that was approved by a county prior to January 1, 1990, as a paramedic receiving station for the treatment of emergency patients.

(3) A standby emergency department that was in existence on January 1, 1989, in a hospital specified in Section 124840.

(4) For the 1991–92 fiscal year and each fiscal year thereafter, a facility which contracted prior to January 1, 1990, with the National Park Service to provide emergency medical services.

(5) A standby emergency room in existence on January 1, 2007, in a hospital located in Los Angeles County that meets all of the following requirements:

(A) The requirements of subdivision (m) of Section 70413 and Sections 70415 and 70417 of Title 22 of the California Code of Regulations.

(B) Reported at least 18,000 emergency department patient encounters to the Office of Statewide Health Planning and Development in 2007 and continues to report at least 18,000 emergency department patient encounters to the Office of Statewide Health Planning and Development in each year thereafter.

(C) A hospital with a standby emergency department meeting the requirements of this paragraph shall do both of the following:

(i) Annually provide the State Department of Public Health and the local emergency medical services agency with certification that it meets the requirements of subparagraph (A). The department shall confirm the hospital's compliance with subparagraph (A).

(ii) Annually provide to the State Department of Public Health and the local emergency medical services agency the emergency department patient encounters it reports to the Office of Statewide Health Planning and Development to establish that it meets the requirement of subparagraph (B).

(g) Payments shall be made only for emergency medical services provided on the calendar day on which emergency medical services are first provided and on the immediately following two calendar days.

(h) Notwithstanding subdivision (g), if it is necessary to transfer the patient to a second facility providing a higher level of care for the treatment of the emergency condition, reimbursement shall be available for services provided at the facility to which the patient was transferred on the calendar day of transfer and on the immediately following two calendar days.

(i) Payment shall be made for medical screening examinations required by law to determine whether an emergency condition exists, notwithstanding the determination after the examination that a medical emergency does not exist. Payment shall not be denied solely because a patient was not admitted to an acute care facility. Payment shall be made for services to an inpatient only when the inpatient has been admitted to a hospital from an entity specified in subdivision (f).

(j) The administering agency shall compile a quarterly and yearend summary of reimbursements paid to facilities and physicians and surgeons. The summary shall include, but shall not be limited to, the total number of claims submitted by physicians and surgeons in aggregate from each facility and the amount paid to each physician and surgeon. The administering agency shall provide copies of the summary and forms and instructions relating to making claims for reimbursement to the public, and may charge a fee not to exceed the reasonable costs of duplication.

(k) Each county shall establish an equitable and efficient mechanism for resolving disputes relating to claims for reimbursements from the fund. The mechanism shall include a requirement that disputes be submitted either to binding arbitration conducted pursuant to arbitration procedures set forth in Chapter 3 (commencing with Section 1282) and Chapter 4 (commencing with Section 1285) of Part 3 of Title 9 of the Code of Civil Procedure, or to a local medical society for resolution by neutral parties.

(l) Physicians and surgeons shall be eligible to receive payment for patient care services provided by, or in conjunction with, a properly credentialed nurse practitioner or physician's assistant for care rendered under the direct supervision of a physician and surgeon who is present in the facility where the patient is being treated and who is available for immediate consultation. Payment shall be limited to those claims that are substantiated by a medical record and that have been reviewed and countersigned by the supervising physician and surgeon in accordance with regulations established for the supervision of nurse practitioners and physician assistants in California.

(Amended by Stats. 2008, Ch. 288, Sec. 2. Effective January 1, 2009.)

1797.98f.

Notwithstanding any other provision of this chapter, an emergency physician and surgeon, or an emergency physician group, with a gross billings arrangement with a hospital shall be entitled to receive reimbursement from the Emergency Medical Services Fund for services provided in that hospital, if all of the following conditions are met:

(a) The services are provided in a basic or comprehensive general acute care hospital emergency department, or in a standby emergency department in a small and rural hospital as defined in Section 124840.

(b) The physician and surgeon is not an employee of the hospital.

(c) All provisions of Section 1797.98c are satisfied, except that payment to the emergency physician and surgeon, or an emergency physician group, by a hospital pursuant to a gross billings arrangement shall not be interpreted to mean that payment for a patient is made by a responsible third party.

(d) Reimbursement from the Emergency Medical Services Fund is sought by the hospital or the hospital's designee, as the billing and collection agent for the emergency physician and surgeon, or an emergency physician group.

For purposes of this section, a "gross billings arrangement" is an arrangement whereby a hospital serves as the billing and collection agent for the emergency physician and surgeon, or an emergency physician group, and pays the emergency physician and surgeon, or emergency physician group, a percentage of the emergency physician and surgeon's or group's gross billings for all patients.

(Amended by Stats. 1998, Ch. 1016, Sec. 3. Effective January 1, 1999.)

1797.98g.

The moneys contained in an Emergency Medical Services Fund, other than moneys contained in a Physician Services Account within the fund pursuant to Section 16952 of the Welfare and Institutions Code, shall not be subject to Article 3.5 (commencing with Section 16951) of Chapter 5 of Part 4.7 of Division 9 of the Welfare and Institutions Code.

(Added by Stats. 1991, Ch. 1169, Sec. 4.)

CHAPTER 3. State Administration [1797.100 - 1797.197a]

(Chapter 3 added by Stats. 1980, Ch. 1260.)

ARTICLE 1. The Emergency Medical Services Authority [1797.100 - 1797.120]

(Article 1 added by Stats. 1980, Ch. 1260.)

1797.100.

There is in the state government in the Health and Welfare Agency, the Emergency Medical Services Authority.

(Amended by Stats. 1983, Ch. 1246, Sec. 16.)

1797.101.

The Emergency Medical Services Authority shall be headed by the Director of the Emergency Medical Services Authority who shall be appointed by the Governor upon nomination by the Secretary of California Health and Human Services. The director shall be a physician and surgeon licensed in California pursuant to the provisions of Chapter 5 (commencing with Section 2000) of Division 2 of the Business and Professions Code, and who has substantial experience in the practice of emergency medicine.

(Amended by Stats. 2008, Ch. 274, Sec. 5. Effective January 1, 2009.)

1797.102.

The authority, utilizing regional and local information, shall assess each EMS area or the system's service area for the purpose of determining the need for additional emergency medical services, coordination of emergency medical services, and the effectiveness of emergency medical services.

(Added by Stats. 1980, Ch. 1260.)

1797.103.

The authority shall develop planning and implementation guidelines for emergency medical services systems which address the following components:

(a) Manpower and training.

(b) Communications.

(c) Transportation.

(d) Assessment of hospitals and critical care centers.

(e) System organization and management.

(f) Data collection and evaluation.

(g) Public information and education.

(h) Disaster response.

(Added by Stats. 1980, Ch. 1260.)

1797.104.

The authority shall provide technical assistance to existing agencies, counties, and cities for the purpose of developing the components of emergency medical services systems.

(Added by Stats. 1980, Ch. 1260.)

1797.105.

(a) The authority shall receive plans for the implementation of emergency medical services and trauma care systems from local EMS agencies.

(b) After the applicable guidelines or regulations are established by the authority, a local EMS agency may implement a local plan developed pursuant to Section 1797.250, 1797.254, 1797.257, or 1797.258 unless the authority determines that the plan does not effectively meet the needs of the persons served and is not consistent with coordinating activities in the geographical area served, or that the plan is not concordant and consistent with applicable guidelines or regulations, or both the guidelines and regulations, established by the authority.

(c) A local EMS agency may appeal a determination of the authority pursuant to subdivision (b) to the commission.

(d) In an appeal pursuant to subdivision (c), the commission may sustain the determination of the authority or overrule and permit local implementation of a plan, and the decision of the commission is final.

(Amended by Stats. 1984, Ch. 1735, Sec. 1. Effective September 30, 1984.)

1797.106.

(a) Regulations, standards, and guidelines adopted by the authority and by local EMS agencies pursuant to the provisions of this division shall not prohibit hospitals which contract with group practice prepayment health care service plans from providing necessary medical services for the members of those plans.

(b) Regulations, standards, and guidelines adopted by the authority and by local EMS agencies pursuant to the provisions of this division shall provide for the transport and transfer of a member of a group practice prepayment health care service plan to a hospital that contracts with the plan when the base hospital determines that the condition of the member permits the transport or when the condition of the member permits the transfer, except that when the dispatching agency determines that the transport by a transport unit would unreasonably remove the transport unit from the area, the member may be transported to the nearest hospital capable of treating the member.

(Amended by Stats. 1986, Ch. 248, Sec. 127.)

1797.107.

The authority shall adopt, amend, or repeal, after approval by the commission and in accordance with the provisions of Chapter 3.5 (commencing with Section 11340) of Part 1 of Division 3 of Title 2 of the Government Code, such rules and regulations as may be reasonable and proper to carry out the purposes and intent of this division and to enable the authority to exercise the powers and perform the duties conferred upon it by this division not inconsistent with any of the provisions of any statute of this state.

(Amended by Stats. 1986, Ch. 248, Sec. 128.)

1797.108.

Subject to the availability of funds appropriated therefor, the authority may contract with local EMS agencies to provide funding assistance to those agencies for planning, organizing, implementing, and maintaining regional emergency medical services systems. In addition, the authority may provide special funding to multicounty EMS agencies which serve rural areas with extensive tourism, as determined by the authority, to reduce the burden on the rural EMS agency of providing the increased emergency medical services required due to that tourism.

Each local or multicounty EMS agency receiving funding pursuant to this section shall make a quarterly report to the authority on the functioning of the local EMS system. The authority may continue to transfer appropriated funds to the local EMS agency upon satisfactory operation.

(Added by Stats. 1983, Ch. 191, Sec. 3. Effective July 11, 1983.)

1797.109.

(a) The director may develop, or prescribe standards for and approve, an emergency medical technician training and testing program for the Department of the California Highway Patrol, Department of Forestry and Fire Protection, California Fire Fighter Joint Apprenticeship Committee, and other public safety agency personnel, upon the request of, and as deemed appropriate by, the director for the particular agency.

(b) The director may, with the concurrence of the Department of the California Highway Patrol, designate the California Highway Patrol Academy as a site where the training and testing may be offered.

(c) The director may prescribe that each person, upon successful completion of the training course and upon passing a written and a practical examination, be certified as an emergency medical technician of an appropriate classification. A suitable identification card may be issued to each certified person to designate that person's emergency medical skill level.

(d) The director may prescribe standards for refresher training to be given to persons trained and certified under this section.

(e) The Department of the California Highway Patrol shall, subject to the availability of federal funds, provide for the initial training of its uniformed personnel in the rendering of emergency medical technician services to the public in specified areas of the state as designated by the Commissioner of the California Highway Patrol.

(Amended by Stats. 2000, Ch. 157, Sec. 1. Effective January 1, 2001.)

1797.110.

The Legislature finds that programs funded through the authority are hindered by the length of time required for the state process to execute approved contracts and payment of vendor claims. These programs include, but are not limited to, general fund assistance to rural multicounty EMS agencies and dispersal of federal grant moneys for EMS systems development to local EMS agencies. This hardship is particularly felt by new or rural community based EMS agencies with modest reserves and cash flow problems. It is the intent of the Legislature that advance payment authority be established for the authority in order to alleviate such problems for those types of contractors to the extent possible. Notwithstanding any other provision of law, the authority may, to the extent funds are available, provide for advanced payments under any financial assistance contract which the authority determines has been entered into with any small, rural, or new EMS agency with modest reserves and potential cash flow problems, as determined by the authority. Such programs include, but are not limited to, local county or multicounty EMS agencies. No advance payment or aggregate of advance payments made pursuant to this section shall exceed 25 percent of the total annual contract amount. No advance payment should be made pursuant to this section if the applicable federal law prohibits advance payment.

(Added by Stats. 1983, Ch. 191, Sec. 4. Effective July 11, 1983.)

1797.111.

With the approval of the Department of Finance, and for use in the furtherance of the work of the authority, the director may accept all of the following:

(a) Grants of interest in real property.

(b) Gifts of money from public agencies or from organizations or associations organized for scientific, educational, or charitable purpose.

(Added by Stats. 1983, Ch. 1246, Sec. 18.)

1797.112.

(a) The Emergency Medical Services Personnel Fund is hereby created in the State Treasury, the funds in which are to be held in trust for the benefit of the authority's testing and personnel licensure program and for the purpose of making reimbursements to entities for the performance of functions for which fees are collected pursuant to Section 1797.172, for expenditure upon appropriation by the Legislature.

(b) The authority may transfer unused portions of the Emergency Medical Services Personnel Fund to the Surplus Money Investment Fund. Funds transferred to the Surplus Money Investment Fund shall be placed in a separate trust account, and shall be available for transfer to the Emergency Medical Services Personnel Fund, together with interest earned, when requested by the authority.

(c) The authority shall maintain a reserve balance in the Emergency Medical Services Personnel Fund of five percent. Any increase in the fees deposited in the Emergency Medical Services Personnel Fund shall be effective upon a determination by the authority that additional moneys are required to fund expenditures of the personnel licensure program, including, but not limited to, reimbursements to entities set forth in subdivision (a).

(Amended by Stats. 2000, Ch. 93, Sec. 14. Effective July 7, 2000.)

1797.113.

The Emergency Medical Services Training Program Approval Fund is hereby established in the State Treasury and, notwithstanding Section 13340 of the Government Code, is continuously appropriated to the authority for the authority's training program review and approval activities. The fees charged by the authority under Section 1797.191 shall be deposited in this fund. The authority may transfer unexpended and unencumbered moneys contained in the Emergency Medical Services Training Program Approval Fund to the Surplus Money Investment Fund for investment pursuant to Article 4 (commencing with Section 16470) of Chapter 3 of Part 2 of Division 4 of Title 2 of the Government Code. All interest, dividends, and pecuniary gains from these investments or deposits shall accrue to the Emergency Medical Services Training Program Approval Fund.

(Amended by Stats. 1998, Ch. 666, Sec. 2. Effective September 21, 1998.)

1797.114.

The rules and regulations of the authority established pursuant to Section 1797.107 shall include a requirement that a local EMS agency local plan developed pursuant to this division shall require that in providing emergency medical transportation services to any patient, the patient shall be transported to the closest appropriate medical facility, if the emergency health care needs of the patient dictate this course of action. Emergency health care need shall be determined by the prehospital emergency medical care personnel under the direction of a base hospital physician and surgeon or in conformance with the regulations of the authority adopted pursuant to Section 1797.107. (Added by Stats. 1998, Ch. 979, Sec. 4. Effective January 1, 1999.)

1797.115.

(a) To the extent permitted by federal law and upon appropriation in the annual Budget Act or another statute, the Director of Finance may transfer any moneys in the Federal Trust Fund established pursuant to Section 16360 of the Government Code to the Emergency Medical Services Authority if the money is made available by the United States for expenditure by the state for purposes consistent with the implementation of this section.

(b) Moneys appropriated pursuant to subdivision (a) shall be allocated by the authority to the California Fire Fighter Joint Apprenticeship Program to do all of the following:

(1) Offset the cost of paramedic training course development.

(2) Enter into reimbursement contracts with eligible state and local agencies that in turn may contract with educational institutions for the delivery of paramedic training conducted in compliance with the requirements of subdivision (a) of Section 1797.172.

(3) Allocate funds, in the form of grants, to eligible state and local agencies to defray the cost of providing paramedic training for fire services personnel, including, but not limited to, instructional supplies and trainee compensation expenses.

(c) To the extent permitted by federal law, the authority shall recover its costs for administration of this section from the funds transferred pursuant to subdivision (a).

(d) In order to be eligible for a grant under paragraph (3) of subdivision (b), a state or local agency shall demonstrate a need for additional paramedics.

(e) For purposes of this section, the following definitions apply:

(1) "Fire service personnel" includes, but is not limited to, a firefighter or prehospital emergency medical worker employed by a state or local agency.

(2) "Local agency" means any city, county, city and county, fire district, special district, joint powers agency, or any other political subdivision of the state that provides fire protection services.

(3) "State agency" means any state agency that provides residential or institutional fire protection, including, but not limited to, the Department of Forestry and Fire Protection. (Amended by Stats. 2003, Ch. 62, Sec. 180. Effective January 1, 2004.)

1797.116.

(a) The authority shall establish additional training standards that include the criteria for the curriculum content recommended by the Curriculum Development Advisory Committee established pursuant to Section 8588.10 of the Government Code, involving the responsibilities of first responders to terrorism incidents and to address the training needs of those identified as first responders. Training standards shall include, but not be limited to, criteria for coordinating between different responding entities.

(b) Every EMT I, EMT II, and EMT-P, as defined in Sections 1797.80, 1797.82, and 1797.84, may receive the appropriate training described in this section. Pertinent training previously completed by any jurisdiction's EMT I, EMT II, or EMT-P personnel and meeting the training requirements of this section may be submitted to the training program approving authority to assess its content and determine whether it meets the training standards prescribed by the authority. (Amended by Stats. 2014, Ch. 668, Sec. 3. (AB 1598) Effective January 1, 2015.)

1797.117.

(a) The authority shall establish and maintain a centralized registry system for the monitoring and tracking of each EMT-I and EMT-II certificate status and each EMT-P license status. This centralized registry system shall be used by the certifying entities as part of the certification process for an EMT-I and EMT-II and by the authority as part of the licensure process for an EMT-P license. The authority shall, by regulation, specify the data elements to be included in the centralized registry system, the requirements for certifying entities to report the data elements for inclusion in the registry, including reporting deadlines, the penalties for failure of a certifying entity to report certification status changes within these deadlines, and requirements for submission to the Department of Justice fingerprint images and related information required by the Department of Justice of, except as otherwise provided in this division, EMT-I and EMT-II certificate candidates or holders and EMT-P license candidates or holders for the purposes described in subdivision (c). The data elements to be included in the centralized registry system shall include, but are not limited to, data elements that are to be made publicly available pursuant to subdivision (b).

(b) The information made available to the public through the centralized registry system shall include all of the following data elements: the full name of every individual who has been issued an EMT-I or EMT-II certificate or EMT-P license, the name of the entity that issued the certificate or license, the certificate or license number, the date of issuance of the license or certificate, and the license or certificate status.

(c) (1) As part of the centralized registry system, the authority shall electronically submit to the Department of Justice fingerprint images and related information required by the Department of Justice of all EMT-I and EMT-II certificate candidates or holders, and of all EMT-P license applicants, for the purposes of obtaining information as to the existence and content of a record of state or federal convictions and state or federal arrests and also information as to the existence and content of a record of state or federal arrests for which the Department of Justice establishes that the person is free on bail or on his or her recognizance pending trial or appeal.

(2) When received, the Department of Justice shall forward to the Federal Bureau of Investigation requests for federal summary criminal history information received pursuant to this subdivision. The Department of Justice shall review the information returned from the Federal Bureau of Investigation and compile and electronically disseminate a primary response to the authority and electronically disseminate a dual response to one government agency certifying entity.

(3) The Department of Justice shall electronically provide the primary response to the authority and also electronically, the dual response to one certifying entity that is a government agency, pursuant to paragraph (1) of subdivision (p) of Section 11105 of the Penal Code.

(d) The authority shall request the Department of Justice to provide subsequent arrest notification service, as provided pursuant to Section 11105.2 of the Penal Code, for persons described in subdivision (c). All subsequent arrest notifications provided to the authority for persons described in subdivision (c) shall be electronically submitted to one government agency certifying entity, as a dual response by the Department of Justice.

(e) The Department of Justice shall charge a fee sufficient to cover the cost of processing the request described in this section. (Added by Stats. 2008, Ch. 274, Sec. 6. Effective January 1, 2009.)

1797.118.

(a) On and after July 1, 2010, and except as provided in subdivision (b), every EMT-I and EMT-II certificate candidate or holder shall have their fingerprint images and related information submitted to the authority for submission to the Department of Justice pursuant to the regulations adopted pursuant to Section 1797.117 for a state and federal level criminal offender record information search, including subsequent arrest information.

(b) If a state level criminal offender record information search, including subsequent arrest information, has been conducted on a currently certified EMT-I or EMT-II, who was certified prior to July 1, 2010, for the purposes of employment or EMT-I or EMT-II certification, then the certifying entity or employer as identified in paragraph (2) of subdivision (a) of Section 1798.200 shall verify in writing to the authority pursuant to regulations adopted pursuant to Section 1797.117 that a state level criminal offender record information search, including subsequent arrest information, has been conducted and that nothing in the criminal offender record information search precluded the individual from obtaining EMT-I or EMT-II certification. (Added by Stats. 2008, Ch. 274, Sec. 7. Effective January 1, 2009.)

1797.120.

(a) The authority shall develop, using input from stakeholders, including, but not limited to, hospitals, local EMS agencies, and public and private EMS providers, and, after approval by the commission pursuant to Section 1799.50, adopt a statewide standard methodology for the calculation and reporting by a local EMS agency of ambulance patient offload time.

(b) For the purposes of this section, "ambulance patient offload time" is defined as the interval between the arrival of an ambulance patient at an emergency department and the time that the patient is transferred to an emergency department gurney, bed, chair, or other acceptable location and the emergency department assumes responsibility for care of the patient. (Added by Stats. 2015, Ch. 379, Sec. 1. (AB 1223) Effective January 1, 2016.)

ARTICLE 2. Reports [1797.121 - 1797.123]

(Heading of Article 2 amended by Stats. 1987, Ch. 1058, Sec. 1.)

1797.121.

The authority shall report to the Legislature on the effectiveness of the systems provided for in this division on or before January 1, 1984, and annually thereafter, including within this report, systems impact evaluations on death and disability. (Added by Stats. 1980, Ch. 1260.)

1797.122.

(a) Notwithstanding any other law, a health facility as defined in subdivision (a) or (b) of Section 1250 may release patient-identifiable medical information under the following circumstances:

(1) To an EMS provider, information regarding a patient who was treated, or transported to the hospital by, that EMS provider, to the extent that specific data elements are requested for quality assessment and improvement purposes.

(2) To the authority or the local EMS agency, to the extent that specific data elements are requested for quality assessment and improvement purposes.

(b) An EMS provider, local EMS agency, and the authority shall request only those data elements that are minimally necessary in compliance with Section 164.502 (b) and Section 164.514 (d) of Title 45 of the Code of Federal Regulations.

(c) The authority may develop minimum standards for the implementation of data collection for system operation, patient outcome, and performance quality improvement.

(d) For purposes of this section, "EMS provider" means an organization employing an Emergency Medical Technician-I, Advanced Emergency Medical Technician, Emergency Medical Technician-Paramedic, registered nurse, or physician for the delivery of emergency medical care to the sick and injured at the scene of an emergency, during transport, or during an interfacility transfer. (Added by Stats. 2015, Ch. 362, Sec. 2. (AB 503) Effective January 1, 2016.)

1797.123.

(a) Upon receipt of data reported by a local EMS agency to the authority pursuant to Section 1797.228, the authority shall calculate ambulance patient offload time by local EMS agency jurisdiction and by each facility in a local EMS agency jurisdiction.

(b) The authority shall report twice per year to the Commission on Emergency Medical Services the ambulance patient offload time by local EMS agency jurisdiction and by each facility in a local EMS agency jurisdiction.

(c) On or before December 1, 2020, the authority, in collaboration with local EMS agencies, shall submit a report to the Legislature on ambulance patient offload time and recommendations to reduce or eliminate ambulance patient offload time. The report shall be submitted in compliance with Section 9795 of the Government Code.

(Added by Stats. 2018, Ch. 656, Sec. 2. (AB 2961) Effective January 1, 2019.)

ARTICLE 3. Coordination With Other State Agencies [1797.130 - 1797.134]

(Article 3 added by Stats. 1980, Ch. 1260.)

1797.130.

The director shall chair an Interdepartmental Committee on Emergency Medical Services established pursuant to Section 1797.132.

(Added by Stats. 1980, Ch. 1260.)

1797.132.

An Interdepartmental Committee on Emergency Medical Services is hereby established. This committee shall advise the authority on the coordination and integration of all state activities concerning emergency medical services. The committee shall include a representative from each of the following state agencies and departments: the Office of Emergency Services, the Department of the California Highway Patrol, the Department of Motor Vehicles, a representative of the administrator of the California Traffic Safety Program as provided by Chapter 5 (commencing with Section 2900) of Division 2 of the Vehicle Code, the Medical Board of California, the State Department of Public Health, the Board of Registered Nursing, the State Department of Education, the National Guard, the Office of Statewide Health Planning and Development, the State Fire Marshal, the California Conference of Local Health Officers, the Department of Forestry and Fire Protection, the Chancellor's Office of the California Community Colleges, and the Department of General Services.

(Amended by Stats. 2013, Ch. 352, Sec. 332. (AB 1317) Effective September 26, 2013. Operative July 1, 2013, by Sec. 543 of Ch. 352.)

1797.133.

The director may appoint select resource committees of experts and may contract with special medical consultants for assistance in the implementation of this division.

(Amended by Stats. 1986, Ch. 248, Sec. 129.)

1797.134.

The Interdepartmental Committee on Emergency Medical Services or another committee designated by the director shall consult with the Commission on Peace Officer Standards and Training regarding emergency medical services integration and coordination with peace officer training.

(Added by Stats. 2014, Ch. 668, Sec. 4. (AB 1598) Effective January 1, 2015.)

ARTICLE 4. Medical Disasters [1797.150 - 1797.153]

(Article 4 added by Stats. 1980, Ch. 1260.)

1797.150.

In cooperation with the Office of Emergency Services, the authority shall respond to any medical disaster by mobilizing and coordinating emergency medical services mutual aid resources to mitigate health problems.

(Amended by Stats. 2013, Ch. 352, Sec. 333. (AB 1317) Effective September 26, 2013. Operative July 1, 2013, by Sec. 543 of Ch. 352.)

1797.151.

The authority shall coordinate, through local EMS agencies, medical and hospital disaster preparedness with other local, state, and federal agencies and departments having a responsibility relating to disaster response, and shall assist the Office of Emergency Services in the preparation of the emergency medical services component of the State Emergency Plan as defined in Section 8560 of the Government Code.

(Amended by Stats. 2013, Ch. 352, Sec. 334. (AB 1317) Effective September 26, 2013. Operative July 1, 2013, by Sec. 543 of Ch. 352.)

1797.152.

(a) The director and the State Public Health Officer may jointly appoint a regional disaster medical and health coordinator for each mutual aid region of the state. A regional disaster medical and health coordinator shall be either a county health officer, a county coordinator of emergency services, an administrator of a local EMS agency, or a medical director of a local EMS agency. Appointees shall be chosen from among persons nominated by a majority vote of the local health officers in a mutual aid region.

(b) In the event of a major disaster which results in a proclamation of emergency by the Governor, and in the need to deliver medical or public and environmental health mutual aid to the area affected by the disaster, at the request of the authority, the State Department of Public Health, or the Office of Emergency Services, a regional disaster medical and health coordinator in a region unaffected by the disaster may coordinate the acquisition of requested mutual aid resources from the jurisdictions in the region.

(c) A regional disaster medical and health coordinator may develop plans for the provision of medical or public health mutual aid among the counties in the region.

(d) No person may be required to serve as a regional disaster medical and health coordinator. No state compensation shall be paid for a regional disaster medical and health coordinator position, except as determined appropriate by the state, if funds become available.

(Amended by Stats. 2013, Ch. 352, Sec. 335. (AB 1317) Effective September 26, 2013. Operative July 1, 2013, by Sec. 543 of Ch. 352.)

1797.153.

(a) In each operational area the county health officer and the local EMS agency administrator may act jointly as the medical health operational area coordinator (MHOAC). If the county health officer and the local EMS agency administrator are unable to fulfill the duties of the MHOAC they may jointly appoint another individual to fulfill these responsibilities. If an operational area has a MHOAC, the MHOAC in cooperation with the county office of emergency services, local public health department, the local office of environmental health, the local department of mental health, the local EMS agency, the local fire department, the regional disaster and medical health coordinator (RDMHC), and the regional office of the Office of Emergency Services, shall be responsible for ensuring the development of a medical and health disaster plan for the operational area. The medical and disaster plans shall follow the Standard Emergency Management System and National Incident Management System. The MHOAC shall recommend to the operational area coordinator of the Office of Emergency Services a medical and health disaster plan for the provision of medical and health mutual aid within the operational area.

(b) For purposes of this section, "operational area" has the same meaning as that term is defined in subdivision (b) of Section 8559 of the Government Code.

(c) The medical and health disaster plan shall include preparedness, response, recovery, and mitigation functions consistent with the State Emergency Plan, as established under Sections 8559 and 8560 of the Government Code, and, at a minimum, the medical and health disaster plan, policy, and procedures shall include all of the following:

(1) Assessment of immediate medical needs.

(2) Coordination of disaster medical and health resources.

(3) Coordination of patient distribution and medical evaluations.

(4) Coordination with inpatient and emergency care providers.

(5) Coordination of out-of-hospital medical care providers.

(6) Coordination and integration with fire agencies personnel, resources, and emergency fire prehospital medical services.

(7) Coordination of providers of nonfire based prehospital emergency medical services.

(8) Coordination of the establishment of temporary field treatment sites.

(9) Health surveillance and epidemiological analyses of community health status.

(10) Assurance of food safety.

(11) Management of exposure to hazardous agents.

(12) Provision or coordination of mental health services.

(13) Provision of medical and health public information protective action recommendations.

(14) Provision or coordination of vector control services.

(15) Assurance of drinking water safety.

(16) Assurance of the safe management of liquid, solid, and hazardous wastes.

(17) Investigation and control of communicable disease.

(d) In the event of a local, state, or federal declaration of emergency, the MHOAC shall assist the agency operational area coordinator in the coordination of medical and health disaster resources within the operational area, and be the point of contact in that operational area, for coordination with the RDMHC, the agency, the regional office of the agency, the State Department of Public Health, and the authority.

(e) Nothing in this section shall be construed to revoke or alter the current authority for disaster management provided under either of the following:

(1) The State Emergency Plan established pursuant to Section 8560 of the Government Code.

(2) The California standardized emergency management system established pursuant to Section 8607 of the Government Code.

(Amended by Stats. 2013, Ch. 352, Sec. 336. (AB 1317) Effective September 26, 2013. Operative July 1, 2013, by Sec. 543 of Ch. 352.)

ARTICLE 5. Personnel [1797.160 - 1797.197a]

(Article 5 added by Stats. 1980, Ch. 1260.)

1797.160.

No owner of a publicly or privately owned ambulance shall permit the operation of the ambulance in emergency service unless the attendant on duty therein, or, if there is no attendant on duty therein, the operator, possesses evidence of that specialized training as is reasonably necessary to ensure that the attendant or operator is competent to care for sick or injured persons who may be transported by the ambulance, as set forth in the emergency medical training and educational standards for ambulance personnel established by the authority pursuant to this article. This section shall not be applicable in any state of emergency declared pursuant to the California Emergencies Services Act (Chapter 7 (commencing with Section 8550) of Division 1 of Title 2 of the Government Code), when it is necessary to fully utilize all available ambulances in an area and it is not possible to have the ambulance operated or attended by persons with the qualifications required by this section.

(Added by Stats. 1983, Ch. 1246, Sec. 20.)

1797.165.

(a) (1) Notwithstanding any other law, the Department of Forestry and Fire Protection, also known as CAL-FIRE pursuant to Section 701.6 of the Public Resources Code, may certify an individual as an Emergency Medical Responder (EMR) if he or she meets both of the following conditions:

(A) The individual is a graduate of the CAL-FIRE training program at a conservation camp under the Department of Corrections and Rehabilitation and received a letter of recommendation from the Director of CAL-FIRE.

(B) While participating in the training program described in subparagraph (A), the individual was working toward a high school diploma or its equivalent, unless he or she already earned one.

(2) Except as provided in subdivision (b), an individual certified as an EMR pursuant to this section shall meet the training requirements developed by the authority pursuant to this division, including, but not limited to, the requirements of Chapter 1.5 of Title 22 of Division 9 of the California Code of Regulations.

(b) (1) Any individual certified pursuant to paragraph (1) of subdivision (a) is not disqualified from certification as an EMR for having committed any of the actions described in subdivision (c) of Section 1798.200. This subdivision does not apply to an individual who committed any of those actions after he or she received certification pursuant to this section.

(2) The certification of an individual as an EMR pursuant to this section shall be recognized statewide as a valid EMR certification without an individual having to repeat testing or certification.

(c) The authority, in consultation with CAL-FIRE, shall, after approval by the commission pursuant to Section 1799.50, promulgate emergency regulations for the process of establishing the certification process pursuant to this section. The emergency regulations promulgated pursuant to this section shall be adopted in accordance with Chapter 3.5 (commencing with Section 11340) of Part 1 of Division 3 of Title 2 of the Government Code, and, for purposes of that chapter, including Section 11349.6 of the Government Code, the adoption of the regulations is an emergency and shall be considered by the Office of Administrative Law as necessary for the immediate preservation of the public peace, health and safety, and general welfare.
(Amended by Stats. 2018, Ch. 457, Sec. 3. (SB 879) Effective September 17, 2018.)
1797.170.

(a) The authority shall develop and, after approval by the commission pursuant to Section 1799.50, adopt regulations for the training and scope of practice for EMT-I certification.

(b) (1) No later than July 1, 2019, the authority, local EMS agency, and certifying entity shall require an applicant to provide either the individual taxpayer identification number or social security number for purposes of applying for a certificate or the renewal of a certificate.

(2) If the authority, local EMS agency, or certifying entity utilizes a national examination to issue a certificate, and if a reciprocity agreement or comity exists between the State of California and the state requesting release of the individual taxpayer identification number or social security number, any deputy, agent, clerk, officer, or employee of the authority or agency may release an individual's taxpayer identification number or social security number to an examination or certifying entity, only for the purpose of verification of certification or examination status.

(3) The individual taxpayer identification or the social security number shall serve to establish the identification of persons affected by state tax laws and for purposes of establishing compliance with subsection (a) of Section 666 of Title 42 of the United States Code, Section 60.15 of Title 45 of the Code of Federal Regulations, Section 17520 of the Family Code, and Section 11105 of the Penal Code, and to that end, the information furnished pursuant to this section shall be used exclusively for those purposes.

(4) The authority, local EMS agency, and certifying entity shall not do either of the following:

(A) Require an applicant to disclose citizenship status or immigration status for purposes of the application or renewal of a certificate.

(B) Deny certification to an otherwise qualified and eligible applicant based solely on his or her citizenship status or immigration status.

(c) Any individual certified as an EMT-I pursuant to this division shall be recognized as an EMT-I on a statewide basis, and recertification shall be based on statewide standards.

(d) Effective July 1, 1990, any individual certified as an EMT-I pursuant to this act shall complete a course of training on the nature of sudden infant death syndrome which is developed by the California SIDS program in the State Department of Public Health in consultation with experts in the field of sudden infant death syndrome.

(e) On or before July 1, 2016, the authority shall develop and, after approval by the commission pursuant to Section 1799.50, adopt regulations to include the administration of naloxone hydrochloride in the training and scope of practice of EMT-I certification. These regulations shall be substantially similar to existing regulations set forth in Chapter 3 (commencing with Section 100101) of Division 9 of Title 22 of the California Code of Regulations that authorize an EMT-I to receive EMT-II training in the administration of naloxone hydrochloride without having to complete the entire EMT-II certification course. This subdivision shall be implemented in accordance with Chapter 5 (commencing with Section 1798).
(Amended by Stats. 2018, Ch. 838, Sec. 10. (SB 695) Effective January 1, 2019.)
1797.171.

(a) The authority shall develop, and after approval of the commission pursuant to Section 1799.50, shall adopt, minimum standards for the training and scope of practice for EMT-II.

(b) (1) No later than July 1, 2019, the authority, local EMS agency, and certifying entity shall require an applicant to provide either the individual taxpayer identification number or social security number for purposes of applying for a certificate or the renewal of a certificate.

(2) If the authority, local EMS agency, or certifying entity utilizes a national examination to issue a certificate, and if a reciprocity agreement or comity exists between the State of California and the state requesting release of the individual taxpayer identification number or social security number, any deputy, agent, clerk, officer, or employee of the authority or agency may release an individual's taxpayer identification number or social security number to an examination or certifying entity, only for the purpose of verification of certification or examination status.

(3) The individual taxpayer identification or the social security number shall serve to establish the identification of persons affected by state tax laws and for purposes of establishing compliance with subsection (a) of Section 666 of Title 42 of the United States Code, Section 60.15 of Title 45 of the Code of Federal Regulations, Section 17520 of the Family Code, and Section 11105 of the Penal Code, and to that end, the information furnished pursuant to this section shall be used exclusively for those purposes.

(4) The authority, local EMS agency, and certifying entity shall not do either of the following:

(A) Require an applicant to disclose citizenship status or immigration status for purposes of the application or renewal of a certificate.

(B) Deny certification to an otherwise qualified and eligible applicant based solely on his or her citizenship status or immigration status.

(c) An EMT-II shall complete a course of training on the nature of sudden infant death syndrome in accordance with subdivision (b) of Section 1797.170.

(d) In rural or remote areas of the state where patient transport times are particularly long and where local resources are inadequate to support an EMT-P program for EMS responses, the director may approve additions to the scope of practice of EMT-IIs serving the local system, if requested by the medical director of the local EMS agency, and if the EMT-II has received training equivalent to that of an EMT-P. The approval of the director, in consultation with a committee of local EMS medical directors named by the Emergency Medical Directors Association of California, is required prior to implementation of any addition to a local optional scope of practice for EMT-IIs proposed by the medical director of a local EMS agency. No drug or procedure that is not part of the basic EMT-P scope of practice, including, but not limited to, any approved local options, shall be added to any EMT-II scope of practice pursuant to this subdivision.
Approval of additions to the scope of practices pursuant to this subdivision may be given only for EMT-II programs in effect on January 1, 1994.
(Amended by Stats. 2018, Ch. 838, Sec. 11. (SB 695) Effective January 1, 2019.)
1797.172.

(a) The authority shall develop and, after approval by the commission pursuant to Section 1799.50, adopt minimum standards for the training and scope of practice for EMT-P.

(b) The approval of the director, in consultation with a committee of local EMS medical directors named by the EMS Medical Directors Association of California, is required prior to implementation of any addition to a local optional scope of practice for EMT-Ps proposed by the medical director of a local EMS agency.

(c) (1) Notwithstanding any other provision of law, the authority shall be the agency solely responsible for licensure and licensure renewal of EMT-Ps who meet the standards and are not precluded from licensure because of any of the reasons listed in subdivision (c) of Section 1798.200. No later than July 1, 2019, the authority shall require an applicant to provide an individual taxpayer identification number or the social security number in order to establish the identity of the applicant. The information obtained as a result of a state and federal level criminal offender record information search shall be used in accordance with Section 11105 of the Penal Code, and to determine whether the applicant is subject to denial of licensure or licensure renewal pursuant to this division. Submission of fingerprint images to the Department of Justice may not be required for licensure renewal upon determination by the authority that fingerprint images have previously been submitted to the Department of Justice during initial licensure, or a previous licensure renewal, provided that the license has not lapsed and the applicant has resided continuously in the state since the initial licensure.

(2) The individual taxpayer identification or the social security number shall serve to establish the identification of persons affected by state tax laws and for purposes of establishing compliance with subsection (a) of Section 666 of Title 42 of the United States Code, Section 60.15 of Title 45 of the Code of Federal Regulations, Section 17520 of the Family Code, and Section 11105 of the Penal Code, and to that end, the information furnished pursuant to this section shall be used exclusively for those purposes.

(3) If the authority utilizes a national examination to issue a certificate, and if a reciprocity agreement or comity exists between the State of California and the state requesting release of the individual taxpayer identification number or social security number, any deputy, agent, clerk, officer, or employee of the authority may release an individual's taxpayer identification number or social security number to an examination or certifying entity, only for the purpose of verification of certification or examination status.

(4) The authority shall not do either of the following:

(A) Require an applicant to disclose citizenship status or immigration status for purposes of the application or renewal of a certificate.

(B) Deny certification to an applicant based solely on his or her citizenship status or immigration status.

(d) The authority shall charge fees for the licensure and licensure renewal of EMT-Ps in an amount sufficient to support the authority's licensure program at a level that ensures the qualifications of the individuals licensed to provide quality care. The basic fee for licensure or licensure renewal of an EMT-P shall not exceed one hundred twenty-five dollars ($125) until the adoption of regulations that specify a different amount that does not exceed the authority's EMT-P licensure, license renewal, and enforcement programs. The authority shall annually evaluate fees to determine if the fee is sufficient to fund the actual costs of the authority's licensure, licensure renewal, and enforcement programs. If the evaluation shows that the fees are excessive or are insufficient to fund the actual costs of the authority's EMT-P licensure, licensure renewal, and enforcement programs, then the fees shall be adjusted accordingly through the rulemaking process described in the Administrative Procedure Act (Chapter 3.5 (commencing with Section 11340) of Part

1 of Division 3 of Title 2 of the Government Code). Separate additional fees may be charged, at the option of the authority, for services that are not shared by all applicants for licensure and licensure renewal, including, but not limited to, any of the following services:

(1) Initial application for licensure as an EMT-P.

(2) Competency testing, the fee for which shall not exceed thirty dollars ($30), except that an additional fee may be charged for the cost of any services that provide enhanced availability of the exam for the convenience of the EMT-P, such as on-demand electronic testing.

(3) Fingerprint and criminal record check. The applicant shall, if applicable according to subdivision (c), submit fingerprint images and related information for criminal offender record information searches with the Department of Justice and the Federal Bureau of Investigation.

(4) Out-of-state training equivalency determination.

(5) Verification of continuing education for a lapse in licensure.

(6) Replacement of a lost licensure card. The fees charged for individual services shall be set so that the total fees charged to EMT-Ps shall not exceed the authority's actual total cost for the EMT-P licensure program.

(e) The authority may provide nonconfidential, nonpersonal information relating to EMS programs to interested persons upon request, and may establish and assess fees for the provision of this information. These fees shall not exceed the costs of providing the information.

(f) At the option of the authority, fees may be collected for the authority by an entity that contracts with the authority to provide any of the services associated with the EMT-P program. All fees collected for the authority in a calendar month by any entity designated by the authority pursuant to this section to collect fees for the authority shall be transmitted to the authority for deposit into the Emergency Medical Services Personnel Fund within 30 calendar days following the last day of the calendar month in which the fees were received by the designated entity, unless the contract between the entity and the authority specifies a different timeframe.

(Amended by Stats. 2018, Ch. 838, Sec. 12. (SB 695) Effective January 1, 2019.)

1797.173.

The authority shall assure that all training programs for EMT-I, EMT-II, and EMT-P are located in an approved licensed hospital or an educational institution operated with written agreements with an acute care hospital, including a public safety agency that has been approved by the local emergency medical services agency to provide training. The authority shall also assure that each training program has a competency-based curriculum. EMT-I training and testing for fire service personnel may be offered at sites approved by the State Board of Fire Services and training for officers of the California Highway Patrol may be provided at the California Highway Patrol Academy.

(Amended by Stats. 1983, Ch. 1246, Sec. 22.)

1797.174.

In consultation with the commission, the Emergency Medical Directors Association of California, and other affected constituencies, the authority shall develop statewide guidelines for continuing education courses and approval of continuing education courses for EMT-Ps and for quality improvement systems which monitor and promote improvement in the quality of care provided by EMT-Ps throughout the state.

(Added by Stats. 1993, Ch. 997, Sec. 5. Effective January 1, 1994.)

1797.175.

The authority shall establish the standards for continuing education and shall designate the examinations for certification and recertification of all prehospital personnel.

The authority shall consider including training regarding the characteristics and method of assessment and treatment of acquired immune deficiency syndrome (AIDS).

(Amended by Stats. 1989, Ch. 1362, Sec. 6. Effective October 2, 1989.)

1797.176.

The authority shall establish the minimum standards for the policies and procedures necessary for medical control of the EMS system.

(Amended by Stats. 1988, Ch. 1390, Sec. 3.)

1797.177.

No individual shall hold himself or herself out to be an EMT-I, EMT-II, EMT-P, or paramedic unless that individual is currently certified as such by the local EMS agency or other certifying authority.

(Added by Stats. 1980, Ch. 1260.)

1797.178.

No person or organization shall provide advanced life support or limited advanced life support unless that person or organization is an authorized part of the emergency medical services system of the local EMS agency or of a pilot program operated pursuant to the Wedworth-Townsend Paramedic Act, Article 3 (commencing with Section 1480) of Chapter 2.5 of Division 2.

(Added by Stats. 1980, Ch. 1260.)

1797.179.

Notwithstanding any other provision of law, and to the extent federal financial participation is available, any city, county or special district providing paramedic services as set forth in Section 1797.172, shall reimburse the Health Care Deposit Fund for the state costs of paying such medical claims. Funds allocated to the county from the County Health Services Fund pursuant to Part 4.5 (commencing with Section 16700) of Division 9 of the Welfare and Institutions Code may be utilized by the county or city to make such reimbursement.

(Added by Stats. 1980, Ch. 1322.)

1797.180.

No agency, public or private, shall advertise or disseminate information to the public that the agency provides EMT-II or EMT-P rescue or ambulance services unless that agency does in fact provide this service on a continuous 24 hours-per-day basis. If advertising or information regarding that agency's EMT-II or EMT-P rescue or ambulance service appears on any vehicle it may only appear on those vehicles utilized solely to provide that service on a continuous 24 hours-per-day basis.

(Added by Stats. 1983, Ch. 1246, Sec. 23.)

1797.181.

The authority may, by regulation, prescribe standardized insignias or emblems for patches which may be affixed to the clothing of an EMT-I, EMT-II, or EMT-P.

(Added by Stats. 1983, Ch. 1246, Sec. 24.)

1797.182.

All ocean, public beach, and public swimming pool lifeguards and all firefighters in this state, except those whose duties are primarily clerical or administrative, shall be trained to administer first aid and cardiopulmonary resuscitation. The training shall meet standards prescribed by the authority, and shall be satisfactorily completed by such persons as soon as practical, but in no event more than one year after the date of employment. Satisfactory completion of a refresher course which meets the standards prescribed by the authority in cardiopulmonary resuscitation and other first aid shall be required at least every three years.

The authority may designate a public agency or private nonprofit agency to provide for each county the training required by this section. The training shall be provided at no cost to the trainee.

As used in this section, "lifeguard" means any regularly employed and paid officer, employee, or member of a public aquatic safety department or marine safety agency of the State of California, a city, county, city and county, district, or other public or municipal corporation or political subdivision of this state.

As used in this section, "firefighter" means any regularly employed and paid officer, employee, or member of a fire department or fire protection or firefighting agency of the State of California, a city, county, city and county, district, or other public or municipal corporation or political subdivision of this state or member of an emergency reserve unit of a volunteer fire department or fire protection district.

(Added by Stats. 1983, Ch. 1246, Sec. 25.)

1797.183.

All peace officers described in Section 13518 of the Penal Code, except those whose duties are primarily clerical or administrative, shall be trained to administer first aid and cardiopulmonary resuscitation (CPR). The training shall meet standards prescribed by the authority, in consultation with the Commission on Peace Officers Standards and Training, and shall be satisfactorily completed by those officers as soon as practical, but in no event more than one year after the date of employment. Satisfactory completion of either refresher training or appropriate testing, which meets the standards of the authority, in cardiopulmonary resuscitation and other first aid, shall be required at periodic intervals as determined by the authority.

(Added by Stats. 1983, Ch. 1246, Sec. 26.)

1797.184.

The authority shall develop and, after approval by the commission pursuant to Section 1799.50, adopt all of the following:

(a) Guidelines for disciplinary orders, temporary suspensions, and conditions of probation for EMT-I and EMT-II certificate holders that protects the public health and safety.

(b) Regulations for the issuance of EMT-I and EMT-II certificates by a certifying entity that protects the public health and safety.

(c) Regulations for the recertification of EMT-I and EMT-II certificate holders that protect the public health and safety.

(d) Regulations for disciplinary processes for EMT-I and EMT-II applicants and certificate holders that protect the public health and safety. These disciplinary processes shall be in accordance with Chapter 5 (commencing with Section 11500) of Part 1 of Division 3 of Title 2 of the Government Code.

(Added by Stats. 2008, Ch. 274, Sec. 10. Effective January 1, 2009.)

1797.185.

(a) The authority shall establish criteria for the statewide recognition of the certification of EMT-P personnel in the basic scope of practice of those personnel. The criteria shall include, but need not be limited to, the following:

(1) Standards for training, testing, certification, and revocation of certification, as required for statewide recognition of certification. The standards may include designation by the authority of the specific examinations required for certification, including, at the option of the authority, an examination provided by the authority. At the option of the authority, the standards may include a requirement for registration of prehospital emergency care personnel with the authority or other entity designated by the authority.

(2) Conditions for local accreditation of certified EMT-P personnel which are reasonable in order to maintain medical control and the integrity of the local EMS system, as determined by the authority and approved by the commission.

(3) Provisions for local accreditation in approved optional scope of practice, if any, as allowed by applicable state regulations and statutes.

(4) Provisions for the establishment and collection of fees by the appropriate agency, which may be the authority or an entity designated by the authority to collect fees for the authority, for testing, certification, accreditation, and registration with the appropriate state or local agency in the appropriate scope of practice. All fees collected for the authority in a calendar month by any entity designated by the authority pursuant to this section to collect fees for the authority shall be transmitted to the authority for deposit into the Emergency Medical Services Personnel Fund within 30 calendar days following

the last day of the calendar month in which the fees were received by the designated entity.

(b) After January 1, 1991, all regulations for EMT-P personnel adopted by the authority shall, where relevant, include provisions for statewide recognition of certification or authorization for the scope of practice of those personnel.

(c) On or before July 1, 1991, the authority shall amend all relevant regulations for EMT-P personnel to include criteria developed pursuant to subdivision (c) of Section 1797.7 and subdivision (b) of Section 1797.172 to insure statewide recognition of certification for the scope of practice of those personnel.

(d) All future regulations for EMT-P personnel adopted by the authority shall, where relevant, include provisions for statewide recognition of certification or authorization for the scope of practice of those personnel.
(Amended by Stats. 1989, Ch. 1362, Sec. 7. Effective October 2, 1989.)
1797.186.

All persons described in Sections 1797.170, 1797.171, 1797.172, 1797.182, and 1797.183, whether volunteers, partly paid, or fully paid, shall be entitled to prophylactic medical treatment to prevent the onset of disease, provided that the person demonstrates that he or she was exposed, while in the service of the department or unit, to a contagious disease, as listed in Section 2500 of Title 17 of the California Administrative Code, while performing first aid or cardiopulmonary resuscitation services to any person.

Medical treatment under this section shall not affect the provisions of Division 4 (commencing with Section 3200) or Division 5 (commencing with Section 6300) of the Labor Code or the person's right to make a claim for work-related injuries, at the time the contagious disease manifests itself.
(Added by Stats. 1985, Ch. 1543, Sec. 1.)
1797.187.

A peace officer as described in Section 830.1, subdivision (a) of Section 830.2, or subdivision (g) of Section 830.3 of the Penal Code, while in the service of the agency or local agency which employs him or her, shall be notified by the agency or local agency if the peace officer is exposed to a known carcinogen, as defined by the International Agency for Research on Cancer, or as defined by its director, during the investigation of any place where any controlled substance, as defined in Section 11007 is suspected of being manufactured, stored, transferred, or sold, or any toxic waste spills, accidents, leaks, explosions, or fires.

The Commission on Peace Officers Standards and Training basic training course, and other training courses as the commission determines appropriate, shall include, on or before January 1, 1990, instruction on, but not limited to, the identification and handling of possible carcinogenic materials and the potential health hazards associated with these materials, protective equipment, and clothing available to minimize contamination, handling, and disposing of materials and measures and procedures that can be adopted to minimize exposure to possible hazardous materials.
(Amended by Stats. 1998, Ch. 606, Sec. 4. Effective January 1, 1999.)
1797.188.

(a) As used in this section:

(1) "Prehospital emergency medical care person or personnel" means any of the following: an authorized registered nurse or mobile intensive care nurse, emergency medical technician-I, emergency medical technician-II, emergency medical technician-paramedic, lifeguard, firefighter, or peace officer, as defined or described by Sections 1797.56, 1797.80, 1797.82, 1797.84, 1797.182, and 1797.183, respectively, or a physician and surgeon who provides prehospital emergency medical care or rescue services.

(2) "Reportable communicable disease or condition" or "a communicable disease or condition listed as reportable" means those diseases prescribed by Subchapter 1 (commencing with Section 2500) of Chapter 4 of Title 17 of the California Code of Regulations, as may be amended from time to time.

(3) "Exposed" means at risk for contracting the disease, as defined by regulations of the state department.

(4) "Health facility" means a health facility, as defined in Section 1250, including a publicly operated facility.

(5) "Health facility infection control officer" means the official or officer who has been designated by the health facility to communicate with a designated officer, or his or her designee.

(6) "Designated officer" means the official or officer of an employer of a prehospital emergency medical care person or personnel who has been designated by the state's public health officer or the employer.

(7) "Urgency reporting requirement" means a disease required to be reported immediately by telephone or reported by telephone within one working day pursuant to subdivisions (h) and (i) of Section 2500 of Title 17 of the California Code of Regulations.

(b) In addition to the communicable disease testing and notification procedures applicable under Chapter 3.5 (commencing with Section 120260) of Part 1 of Division 105, all prehospital emergency medical care personnel, whether volunteers, partly paid, or fully paid, who have provided emergency medical or rescue services and have been exposed to a person afflicted with a communicable disease or condition listed as reportable, which can, as determined by the county health officer, be transmitted through physical or oral contact or secretions of the body, including blood, shall be notified that they have been exposed to the disease or condition in accordance with the following:

(1) If the prehospital emergency medical care person, who has rendered emergency medical or rescue services and believes that he or she may have been exposed to a person afflicted with a reportable communicable disease or condition in a manner that could result in transmission of a reportable communicable disease or condition, and provides the health facility infection control officer with his or her name and telephone number at the time the patient is transferred from that prehospital emergency medical care person to the admitting health facility; or the party transporting the person afflicted with the reportable communicable disease or condition provides that health facility with the name and telephone number of the prehospital emergency medical care person who provided the emergency medical or rescue services and believes he or she may have been exposed to a person afflicted with a reportable communicable disease or condition in a manner that could result in transmission of a communicable disease or condition, the health facility infection control officer, upon determining that the person to whom the prehospital emergency medical care person provided the emergency medical or rescue services is diagnosed as being afflicted with a reportable communicable disease or condition, and that the reportable communicable disease or condition may have been transmitted during the provision of emergency medical or rescue services, shall immediately notify the designated officer of the prehospital emergency medical care person if the reportable communicable disease or condition has an urgency reporting requirement on the list of reportable diseases or conditions, or if the conditions of the exposure may have included direct contact between the unprotected skin, eyes, or mucous membranes of the prehospital emergency medical care person and the blood of the person afflicted with the reportable communicable disease or condition. Otherwise, the health facility infection control officer shall notify the designated officer consistent with Section 2500 of Title 17 of the California Code of Regulations. The health facility infection control officer shall also report the name and telephone number of the prehospital emergency medical care person to the county health officer. The designated officer shall immediately notify the prehospital emergency medical care person if the reportable communicable disease or condition has an urgency reporting requirement on the list of reportable diseases or conditions, or if the conditions of the exposure may have included direct contact between the unprotected skin, eyes, or mucous membranes of the prehospital emergency medical care person and the blood of the person afflicted with the reportable communicable disease or condition. Otherwise, the designated officer shall notify the prehospital emergency medical care person consistent with Section 2500 of Title 17 of the California Code of Regulations.

(2) If the prehospital emergency medical care person who has rendered emergency medical or rescue services and has been exposed to a person afflicted with a reportable communicable disease or condition, but has not provided the health facility infection control officer with his or her name and telephone number pursuant to paragraph (1), the health facility infection control officer, upon determining that the person to whom the prehospital emergency medical care person provided the emergency medical or rescue services is diagnosed as being afflicted with a reportable communicable disease or condition that may have been transmitted during provision of emergency medical or rescue services, shall immediately notify the designated officer of the employer of the prehospital emergency medical care person and the county health officer if the reportable communicable disease or condition has an urgency reporting requirement on the list of reportable diseases or conditions, or if the conditions of the exposure may have included direct contact between the unprotected skin, eyes, or mucous membranes of the prehospital emergency medical care person and the blood of the person afflicted with the reportable communicable disease or condition. Otherwise, the health facility infection control officer shall notify the designated officer consistent with Section 2500 of Title 17 of the California Code of Regulations. The designated officer shall immediately notify the prehospital emergency medical care person if the reportable communicable disease or condition has an urgency reporting requirement on the list of reportable diseases or conditions, or if the conditions of the exposure may have included direct contact between the unprotected skin, eyes, or mucous membranes of the prehospital emergency medical care person and the blood of the person afflicted with the reportable communicable disease or condition. Otherwise, the designated officer shall notify the prehospital emergency medical care person consistent with Section 2500 of Title 17 of the California Code of Regulations.

(c) The county health officer shall immediately notify the prehospital emergency medical care person who has provided emergency medical or rescue services and has been exposed to a person afflicted with a communicable disease or condition listed as reportable, which can, as determined by the county health officer, be transmitted through oral contact or secretions of the body, including blood, if the reportable communicable disease or condition has an urgency reporting requirement on the list of reportable diseases or conditions, or if the conditions of the exposure may have included direct contact between the unprotected skin, eyes, or mucous membranes of the prehospital emergency medical care person and the blood of the person afflicted with the reportable communicable disease or condition, upon receiving the report from a health facility pursuant to paragraph (1) of subdivision (b). Otherwise, the county health officer shall notify the prehospital emergency medical care person consistent with Section 2500 of Title 17 of the California Code of Regulations. The county health officer shall not disclose the name of the patient or other identifying characteristics to the prehospital emergency medical care person.

(d) An employer of a prehospital emergency medical care person or personnel that maintains an Internet Web site shall post the title and telephone number of the designated officer in a conspicuous location on its Internet Web site accessible from the home page. A health facility that maintains an Internet Web site shall post the title and telephone number of the health facility infection control officer in a conspicuous location on its Internet Web site accessible from the home page.

(e) (1) The health facility infection control officer, or his or her designee, shall be available either onsite or on call 24 hours per day.

(2) The designated officer, or his or her designee, shall be available either onsite or on call 24 hours per day.

(f) An employer of a health facility infection control officer and an employer of a prehospital emergency medical care person or personnel shall inform those employees of this law as part of the Cal-OSHA Injury and Illness Prevention Program training required by paragraph (7) of subdivision (a) of Section 3203 of Title 8 of the California Code of Regulations.

(g) Nothing in this section shall be construed to authorize the further disclosure of confidential medical information by the health facility, the designated officer, or any prehospital emergency medical care personnel described in this section except as otherwise authorized by law.

(h) In the event of the demise of the person afflicted with the reportable communicable disease or condition, the health facility or county health officer shall notify the funeral director, charged with removing the decedent from the health facility, of the reportable communicable disease or condition prior to the release of the decedent from the health facility to the funeral director.

(i) Notwithstanding Section 1798.206, a violation of this section is not a misdemeanor. (Amended by Stats. 2018, Ch. 424, Sec. 4. (SB 1495) Effective January 1, 2019.)
1797.189.

(a) As used in this section:

(1) "Chief medical examiner-coroner" means the chief medical examiner or the coroner as referred to in subdivision (m) of Section 24000, Section 24010, subdivisions (k), (m), and (n) of Section 24300, subdivisions (k), (m), and (n) of Section 24304, and Sections 27460 to 27530, inclusive, of the Government Code, and Section 102850.

(2) "Prehospital emergency medical care person or personnel" means any of the following: authorized registered nurse or mobile intensive care nurse, emergency medical technician-I, emergency medical technician-II, emergency medical technician-paramedic, lifeguard, firefighter, or peace officer, as defined or described by Sections 1797.56, 1797.80, 1797.82, 1797.84, 1797.182, and 1797.183, respectively, or a physician and surgeon who provides prehospital emergency medical care or rescue services.

(3) "Reportable disease or condition" or "a disease or condition listed as reportable" means those diseases specified in Subchapter 1 (commencing with Section 2500) of Chapter 4 of Title 17 of the California Administrative Code, as may be amended from time to time.

(4) "Exposed" means at risk for contracting a disease, as defined by regulations of the state department.

(5) "Health facility" means a health facility, as defined in Section 1250, including a publicly operated facility.

(b) Any prehospital emergency medical care personnel, whether volunteers, partly paid, or fully paid who have provided emergency medical or rescue services and have been exposed to a person afflicted with a disease or condition listed as reportable, that can, as determined by the county health officer, be transmitted through oral contact or secretions of the body, including blood, shall be notified that they have been exposed to the disease and should contact the county health officer if all of the following conditions are met:

(1) The prehospital emergency medical care person, who has rendered emergency medical or rescue services and has been exposed to a person afflicted with a reportable disease or condition, provides the chief medical examiner-coroner with his or her name and telephone number at the time the patient is transferred from that prehospital medical care person to the chief medical examiner-coroner; or the party transporting the person afflicted with the reportable disease or condition provides that chief medical examiner-coroner with the name and telephone number of the prehospital emergency medical care person who provided the emergency medical or rescue services.

(2) The chief medical examiner-coroner reports the name and telephone number of the prehospital emergency medical care person to the county health officer upon determining that the person to whom the prehospital emergency medical care person provided the emergency medical or rescue services is diagnosed as being afflicted with a reportable disease or condition.

(c) The county health officer shall immediately notify the prehospital emergency medical care person who has provided emergency medical or rescue services and has been exposed to a person afflicted with a disease or condition listed as reportable, that can, as determined by the county health officer, be transmitted through oral contact or secretions of the body, including blood, upon receiving the report from a health facility pursuant to paragraph (1) of subdivision (b). The county health officer shall not disclose the name of the patient or other identifying characteristics to the prehospital emergency medical care person.

Nothing in this section shall be construed to authorize the further disclosure of confidential medical information by the chief medical examiner-coroner or any of the prehospital emergency medical care personnel described in this section except as otherwise authorized by law.

The chief medical examiner-coroner, or the county health officer shall notify the funeral director, charged with removing or receiving the decedent afflicted with a reportable disease or condition from the chief medical examiner-coroner, of the reportable disease prior to the release of the decedent from the chief medical examiner-coroner to the funeral director.

Notwithstanding Section 1798.206, violation of this section is not a misdemeanor. (Amended by Stats. 1996, Ch. 1023, Sec. 173. Effective September 29, 1996.)
1797.190.

The authority may establish minimum standards for the training and use of automatic external defibrillators.

(Amended by Stats. 2002, Ch. 718, Sec. 2. Effective January 1, 2003.)

1797.191.

(a) The authority shall establish minimum standards for the training in pediatric first aid, pediatric cardiopulmonary resuscitation (CPR), and preventive health practices required by Section 1596.866.

(b) (1) The authority shall establish a process for the ongoing review and approval of training programs in pediatric first aid, pediatric CPR, and preventive health practices as specified in paragraph (2) of subdivision (a) of Section 1596.866 to ensure that those programs meet the minimum standards established pursuant to subdivision (a). The authority shall charge fees equal to its costs incurred for the pediatric first aid and pediatric CPR training standards program and for the ongoing review and approval of these programs.

(2) The authority shall establish, in consultation with experts in pediatric first aid, pediatric CPR, and preventive health practices, a process to ensure the quality of the training programs, including, but not limited to, a method for assessing the appropriateness of the courses and the qualifications of the instructors.

(c) (1) The authority may charge a fee equal to its costs incurred for the preventive health practices program and for the initial review and approval and renewal of approval of the program.

(2) If the authority chooses to establish a fee process based on the use of course completion cards for the preventive health practices program, the cost shall not exceed seven dollars ($7) per card for each training participant until January 1, 2001, at which time the authority may evaluate its administrative costs. After evaluation of the costs, the authority may establish a new fee scale for the cards so that revenue does not exceed the costs of the ongoing review and approval of the preventive health practices training.

(d) For the purposes of this section, "training programs" means programs that apply for approval by the authority to provide the training in pediatric first aid, pediatric CPR, or preventive health practices as specified in paragraph (2) of subdivision (a) of Section 1596.866. Training programs include all affiliated programs that also provide any of the authority-approved training required by this division. "Affiliated programs" means programs that are overseen by persons or organizations that have an authority-approved training program in pediatric first aid, pediatric CPR, or preventive health practices. Affiliated programs also include programs that have purchased an authority-approved training program in pediatric first aid, pediatric CPR, or preventive health practices. Training programs and their affiliated programs shall comply with this division and with the regulations adopted by the authority pertaining to training programs in pediatric first aid, pediatric CPR, or preventive health practices.

(e) The director of the authority may, in accordance with regulations adopted by the authority, deny, suspend, or revoke any approval issued under this division or may place any approved program on probation, upon the finding by the director of the authority of an imminent threat to the public health and safety as evidenced by the occurrence of any of the actions listed in subdivision (f).

(f) Any of the following actions shall be considered evidence of a threat to the public health and safety, and may result in the denial, suspension, probation, or revocation of a program's approval or application for approval pursuant to this division.

(1) Fraud.

(2) Incompetence.

(3) The commission of any fraudulent, dishonest, or corrupt act that is substantially related to the qualifications, functions, and duties of training program directors and instructors.

(4) Conviction of any crime that is substantially related to the qualifications, functions, and duties of training program directors and instructors. The record of conviction or a certified copy of the record shall be conclusive evidence of the conviction.

(5) Violating or attempting to violate, directly or indirectly, or assisting in or abetting the violation of, or conspiring to violate, this division or the regulations promulgated by the authority pertaining to the review and approval of training programs in pediatric first aid, pediatric CPR, and preventive health practices as specified in paragraph (2) of subdivision (a) of Section 1596.866.

(g) In order to ensure that adequate qualified training programs are available to provide training in the preventive health practices course to all persons who are required to have that training, the authority may, after approval of the Commission on Emergency Medical Services pursuant to Section 1799.50, establish temporary standards for training programs for use until permanent standards are adopted pursuant to Chapter 3.5 (commencing with Section 11340) of Part 1 of Division 3 of Title 2 of the Government Code.

(h) Persons who, prior to the date on which the amendments to this section enacted in 1998 become operative, have completed a course or courses in preventive health practices as specified in subparagraph (C) of paragraph (2) of subdivision (a) of Section 1596.866, and have a certificate of completion card for a course or courses in preventive health practices, or certified copies of transcripts that identify the number of hours and the specific course or courses taken for training in preventive health practices shall be deemed to have met the requirement for training in preventive health practices.

(Amended by Stats. 1999, Ch. 83, Sec. 106. Effective January 1, 2000.)
1797.192.

On or before July 1, 1991, the authority shall adopt standards for a standard statewide scope of practice which shall be utilized for the training and certification testing of EMT-P personnel for certification as EMT-P's. Local EMS systems shall not be required to utilize the entire standard scope of practice. Testing of EMT-P personnel for local accreditation to practice shall only include local operational policies and procedures, and drug, device, or treatment procedures being utilized within that local EMS system pursuant to Sections 1797.172 and 1797.221.

(Added by Stats. 1989, Ch. 1362, Sec. 8. Effective October 2, 1989.)
1797.193.

(a) By July 1, 1992, existing firefighters in this state shall complete a course on the nature of sudden infant death syndrome taught by experts in the field of sudden infant death syndrome. All persons who become firefighters after January 1, 1990, shall complete a course on this topic as part of their basic training as firefighters. The course shall include information on the community resources available to assist families who have lost children to sudden infant death syndrome.

(b) For purposes of this section, the term "firefighter" has the same meaning as that specified in Section 1797.182.

(c) When the instruction and training are provided by a local agency, a fee shall be charged sufficient to defray the entire cost of the instruction and training.
(Added by renumbering Section 1797.192 (as added by Stats. 1989, Ch. 1111) by Stats. 1990, Ch. 216, Sec. 61.)
1797.194.

The purpose of this section is to provide for the state licensure of EMT-P personnel. Notwithstanding any provision of law, including, but not limited to, Sections 1797.208 and 1797.214, all of the following applies to EMT-P personnel:

(a) Any reference to EMT-P certification pursuant to this division shall be equivalent to EMT-P licensure pursuant to this division, including, but not limited to, any provision in this division relating to the assessment of fees.

(b) The statewide examination designated by the authority for licensure of EMT-P personnel and the licensure issued by the authority shall be the single sufficient examination and licensure required for practice as an EMT-P.

(c) EMT-P licenses shall be renewed every two years upon submission to the authority of proof of satisfactory completion of continuing education or other educational requirements established by regulations of the authority, upon approval by the commission. If the evaluation and recommendations of the authority required pursuant to Section 8 of Chapter 997 of the Statutes of 1993, so concludes, the renewal of EMT-P licenses shall, in addition to continuing education requirements, be contingent upon reexamination at 10-year intervals to ensure competency.

(d) Every EMT-P licensee may be disciplined by the authority for violations of this division. The proceedings under this subdivision shall be conducted in accordance with Chapter 5 (commencing with Section 11500) of Part 1 of Division 3 of Title 2 of the Government Code, and the authority shall have all the powers granted therein for this purpose.

(e) Nothing in this section shall be construed to extend the scope of practice of an EMT-P beyond prehospital settings, as defined by regulations of the authority.

(f) Nothing in this section shall be construed to alter or interfere with the local EMS agency's ability to locally accredit licensed EMT-Ps.

(g) Nothing in this section shall be construed to hinder the ability of the medical director of the local EMS agency to maintain medical control within the local EMS system in accordance with this division, including, but not limited to, Chapter 5 (commencing with Section 1798).
(Added by Stats. 1994, Ch. 709, Sec. 4. Effective January 1, 1995.)
1797.195.

(a) Notwithstanding any other provision of law to the contrary, an EMT-I, EMT-II, or EMT-P may provide emergency medical care pursuant to this section in the emergency department of a hospital that meets the definition of small and rural hospital pursuant to Section 1188.855, except that in the case of a hospital meeting the definition contained in Section 1188.855 the population of the incorporated place or census designated place where the hospital is located shall not have increased to more than 20,000 since 1980, and all of the following conditions are met:

(1) The EMT-I, EMT-II, or EMT-P is on duty as a prehospital emergency medical care provider.

(2) The EMT-I, EMT-II, or EMT-P shall function under direct supervision as defined in hospital protocols that have been issued pursuant to paragraph (3), and only where the physician and surgeon or the registered nurse determines that the emergency department is faced with a patient crisis, and that the services of the EMT-I, EMT-II, or EMT-P are necessary to temporarily meet the health care needs of the patients in the emergency department.

(3) The utilization of an EMT-I, EMT-II, or EMT-P in the emergency department is done pursuant to hospital protocols that have been developed by the hospital's nursing staff, the physician and surgeon medical director of the emergency department, and the administration of the hospital, with the approval of the medical staff, and that shall include at least all of the following:

(A) A requirement that the EMT-I, EMT-II, or EMT-P successfully complete a hospital training program on the protocols and procedures of the hospital emergency department. The program shall include, but not be limited to, features of the protocols for which the EMT-I, EMT-II, or EMT-P has not previously received training and a postprogram evaluation.

(B) A requirement that the EMT-I, EMT-II, or EMT-P annually demonstrates and documents to the hospital competency in the emergency department procedures.

(C) The emergency medical care to be provided in the emergency department by the EMT-I, EMT-II, or EMT-P shall be set forth or referenced in the protocols and shall be limited to that which is otherwise authorized by their certification or licensure as defined in statute or regulation. The protocols shall not include patient assessment in this setting, except when the assessment is directly related to the specific task the EMT-I, EMT-II, and EMT-P is performing.

(D) A process for continuity of patient care when the EMT-I, EMT-II, or EMT-P is called to an off-site emergency situation.

(E) Procedures for the supervision of the EMT-I, EMT-II, or EMT-P.

(4) The protocols for utilization of an EMT-I, EMT-II, or EMT-P in the emergency department are developed in consultation with the medical director of the local EMS agency and the emergency medical care committee, if a committee has been formed.

(5) A written contract shall be in effect relative to the services provided pursuant to this section, between the ambulance company and the hospital, where the EMT-I, EMT-II, or EMT-P is employed by an ambulance company that is not owned by the hospital.

(b) When services of emergency personnel are called upon pursuant to this section, responsibility for the medical direction of the EMT-I, EMT-II, or EMT-P rests with the hospital, pursuant to the hospital protocols as set forth in paragraph (3) of subdivision (a).

(c) Although this section authorizes the provision of services in an emergency department of certain small and rural hospitals, nothing in this section is intended to expand or restrict the types of services or care to be provided by EMT-I, EMT-II, or EMT-P pursuant to this article.
(Added by Stats. 1995, Ch. 239, Sec. 2. Effective January 1, 1996.)
1797.196.

(a) For purposes of this section, "AED" or "defibrillator" means an automated external defibrillator.

(b) (1) In order to ensure public safety, a person or entity that acquires an AED shall do all of the following:

(A) Comply with all regulations governing the placement of an AED.

(B) Notify an agent of the local EMS agency of the existence, location, and type of AED acquired.

(C) Ensure that the AED is maintained and tested according to the operation and maintenance guidelines set forth by the manufacturer.

(D) Ensure that the AED is tested at least biannually and after each use.

(E) Ensure that an inspection is made of all AEDs on the premises at least every 90 days for potential issues related to operability of the device, including a blinking light or other obvious defect that may suggest tampering or that another problem has arisen with the functionality of the AED.

(F) Ensure that records of the maintenance and testing required pursuant to this paragraph are maintained.

(2) When an AED is placed in a building, the building owner shall do all of the following:

(A) At least once a year, notify the tenants as to the location of the AED units and provide information to tenants about who they can contact if they want to voluntarily take AED or CPR training.

(B) At least once a year, offer a demonstration to at least one person associated with the building so that the person can be walked through how to use an AED properly in an emergency. The building owner may arrange for the demonstration or partner with a nonprofit organization to do so.

(C) Next to the AED, post instructions, in no less than 14-point type, on how to use the AED.

(3) A medical director or other physician and surgeon is not required to be involved in the acquisition or placement of an AED.

(c) (1) When an AED is placed in a public or private K–12 school, the principal shall ensure that the school administrators and staff annually receive information that describes sudden cardiac arrest, the school's emergency response plan, and the proper use of an AED. The principal shall also ensure that instructions, in no less than 14-point type, on how to use the AED are posted next to every AED. The principal shall, at least annually, notify school employees as to the location of all AED units on the campus.

(2) This section does not prohibit a school employee or other person from rendering aid with an AED.

(d) A manufacturer or retailer supplying an AED shall provide to the acquirer of the AED all information governing the use, installation, operation, training, and maintenance of the AED.

(e) A violation of this section is not subject to penalties pursuant to Section 1798.206.

(f) Nothing in this section or Section 1714.21 of the Civil Code may be construed to require a building owner or a building manager to acquire and have installed an AED in any building.

(g) For purposes of this section, "local EMS agency" means an agency established pursuant to Section 1797.200.

(h) This section does not apply to facilities licensed pursuant to subdivision (a), (b), (c), or (f) of Section 1250.
(Amended by Stats. 2015, Ch. 264, Sec. 2. (SB 658) Effective January 1, 2016.)
1797.197.

(a) The authority shall establish training and standards for all prehospital emergency medical care personnel, as defined in paragraph (2) of subdivision (a) of Section 1797.189, regarding the characteristics and method of assessment and treatment of anaphylactic reactions and the use of epinephrine. The authority shall promulgate regulations regarding these matters for use by all prehospital emergency medical care personnel.

(b) (1) The authority shall develop and, after approval by the commission pursuant to Section 1799.50, adopt training and standards for all prehospital emergency medical care personnel, as defined in paragraph (2) of subdivision (a) of Section 1797.189, regarding the use and administration of naloxone hydrochloride and other opioid antagonists. The authority shall promulgate regulations regarding these matters for use by all prehospital emergency medical care personnel. The authority may adopt existing training and standards for prehospital emergency medical care personnel regarding the statewide use and administration of naloxone hydrochloride or another opioid antagonist to satisfy the requirements of this section.

(2) The medical director of a local EMS agency may, pursuant to Section 1797.221, approve or conduct a trial study of the use and administration of naloxone hydrochloride or other opioid antagonists by any level of prehospital emergency medical care personnel. Training received by prehospital emergency medical care personnel specific to the use and administration of naloxone hydrochloride or another opioid antagonist during this trial study may be used towards satisfying the training requirements established pursuant to paragraph (1) regarding the use and administration of naloxone hydrochloride and other opioid antagonists by prehospital emergency medical care personnel.

(3) The training described in paragraphs (1) and (2) shall satisfy the requirements of paragraph (1) of subdivision (d) of Section 1714.22 of the Civil Code.
(Amended by Stats. 2014, Ch. 491, Sec. 2. (SB 1438) Effective January 1, 2015.)
1797.197a.

(a) For purposes of this section, the following definitions shall apply:

(1) "Anaphylaxis" means a potentially life-threatening hypersensitivity or allergic reaction to a substance.

(A) Symptoms of anaphylaxis may include shortness of breath, wheezing, difficulty breathing, difficulty talking or swallowing, hives, itching, swelling, shock, or asthma.

(B) Causes of anaphylaxis may include, but are not limited to, insect stings or bites, foods, drugs, and other allergens, as well as idiopathic or exercise-induced anaphylaxis.

(2) "Authorized entity" means any for-profit, nonprofit, or government entity or organization that employs at least one person or utilizes at least one volunteer or agent that has voluntarily completed a training course as described in subdivision (c).

(3) "Epinephrine auto-injector" means a disposable delivery device designed for the automatic injection of a premeasured dose of epinephrine into the human body to prevent or treat a life-threatening allergic reaction.

(4) "Lay rescuer" means any person who has met the training standards and other requirements of this section but who is not otherwise licensed or certified to use an epinephrine auto-injector on another person.

(5) "Prehospital emergency medical care person" has the same meaning as defined in paragraph (2) of subdivision (a) of Section 1797.189.

(b) A prehospital emergency medical care person or lay rescuer may use an epinephrine auto-injector to render emergency care to another person if all of the following requirements are met:

(1) The epinephrine auto-injector is legally obtained by prescription from an authorized health care provider or from an authorized entity that acquired the epinephrine auto-injector pursuant to subdivision (e).

(2) The epinephrine auto-injector is used on another, with the expressed or implied consent of that person, to treat anaphylaxis.

(3) The epinephrine auto-injector is stored and maintained as directed by the manufacturer's instructions for that product.

(4) The person using the epinephrine auto-injector has successfully completed a course of training with an authorized training provider, as described in subdivision (c), and has current certification of training issued by the provider.

(5) The epinephrine auto-injectors obtained by prehospital emergency medical care personnel pursuant to Section 4119.3 of the Business and Professions Code shall be used only when functioning outside the course of the person's occupational duties, or as a volunteer, pursuant to this section.

(6) The Emergency Medical Services System is activated as soon as practicable when an epinephrine auto-injector is used.

(c) (1) The authorized training providers shall be approved, and the minimum standards for training and the use and administration of epinephrine auto-injectors pursuant to this section shall be established and approved, by the authority. The authority may designate existing training standards for the use and administration of epinephrine auto-injectors by prehospital emergency medical care personnel to satisfy the requirements of this section.

(2) The minimum training and requirements shall include all of the following components:

(A) Techniques for recognizing circumstances, signs, and symptoms of anaphylaxis.

(B) Standards and procedures for proper storage and emergency use of epinephrine auto-injectors.

(C) Emergency followup procedures, including activation of the Emergency Medical Services System, by calling the emergency 911 telephone number or otherwise alerting and summoning more advanced medical personnel and services.

(D) Compliance with all regulations governing the training, indications, use, and precautions concerning epinephrine auto-injectors.

(E) Written material covering the information required under this provision, including the manufacturer product information sheets on commonly available models of epinephrine auto-injectors.

(F) Completion of a training course in cardiopulmonary resuscitation and the use of an automatic external defibrillator (AED) for infants, children, and adults that complies with regulations adopted by the authority and the standards of the American Heart Association or the American Red Cross, and a current certification for that training.

(3) Training certification shall be valid for no more than two years, after which recertification with an authorized training provider is required.

(4) The director may, in accordance with regulations adopted by the authority, deny, suspend, or revoke any approval issued under this subdivision or may place any approved training provider on probation upon a finding by the director of an imminent threat to public health and safety, as evidenced by any of the following:

(A) Fraud.

(B) Incompetence.

(C) The commission of any fraudulent, dishonest, or corrupt act that is substantially related to the qualifications, functions, or duties of training program directors or instructors.

(D) Conviction of any crime that is substantially related to the qualifications, functions, or duties of training program directors or instructors. The record of conviction or a certified copy of the record shall be conclusive evidence of the conviction.

(E) Violating or attempting to violate, directly or indirectly, or assisting in or abetting the violation of, or conspiring to violate, any provision of this section or the regulations promulgated by the authority pertaining to the review and approval of training programs in anaphylaxis and the use and administration of epinephrine auto-injectors, as described in this subdivision.

(d) (1) The authority shall assess a fee pursuant to regulation sufficient to cover the reasonable costs incurred by the authority for the ongoing review and approval of training and certification under subdivision (c).

(2) The fees shall be deposited in the Specialized First Aid Training Program Approval Fund, which is hereby created in the State Treasury. All moneys deposited in the fund shall be made available, upon appropriation, to the authority for purposes described in paragraph (1).

(3) The authority may transfer unused portions of the Specialized First Aid Training Program Approval Fund to the Surplus Money Investment Fund. Funds transferred to the Surplus Money Investment Fund shall be placed in a separate trust account, and shall be available for transfer to the Specialized First Aid Training Program Approval Fund, together with the interest earned, when requested by the authority.

(4) The authority shall maintain a reserve balance in the Specialized First Aid Training Program Approval Fund of 5 percent of annual revenues. Any increase in the fees deposited in the Specialized First Aid Training Program Approval Fund shall be effective upon determination by the authority that additional moneys are required to fund expenditures pursuant to subdivision (c).

(e) (1) An authorized health care provider may issue a prescription for an epinephrine auto-injector to a prehospital emergency medical care person or a lay rescuer for the purpose of rendering emergency care to another person upon presentation of a current epinephrine auto-injector certification card issued by the authority demonstrating that the person is trained and qualified to administer an epinephrine auto-injector pursuant to this section or any other law.

(2) An authorized health care provider may issue a prescription for an epinephrine auto-injector to an authorized entity if the authorized entity submits evidence it employs at least one person, or utilizes at least one volunteer or agent, who is trained and has a current epinephrine auto-injector certification card issued by the authority demonstrating that the person is qualified to administer an epinephrine auto-injector pursuant to this section.

(f) An authorized entity that possesses and makes available epinephrine auto-injectors shall do both of the following:

(1) Create and maintain on its premises an operations plan that includes all of the following:

(A) The name and contact number for the authorized health care provider who prescribed the epinephrine auto-injector.

(B) Where and how the epinephrine auto-injector will be stored.

(C) The names of the designated employees or agents who have completed the training program required by this section and who are authorized to administer the epinephrine auto-injector.

(D) How and when the epinephrine auto-injector will be inspected for an expiration date.

(E) The process to replace the expired epinephrine auto-injector, including the proper disposal of the expired epinephrine auto-injector or used epinephrine auto-injector in a sharps container.

(2) Submit to the authority, in a manner identified by the authority, a report of each incident that involves the use of an epinephrine auto-injector, not more than 30 days after each use. The authority shall annually publish a report that summarizes all reports submitted to it under this subdivision.

(g) This section does not apply to a school district or county office of education, or its personnel, that provides and utilizes epinephrine auto-injectors to provide emergency medical aid pursuant to Section 49414 of the Education Code.

(h) This section shall not be construed to limit or restrict the ability of prehospital emergency medical care personnel, under any other statute or regulation, to administer epinephrine, including the use of epinephrine auto-injectors, or to require additional training or certification beyond what is already required under the other statute or regulation.
(Amended by Stats. 2017, Ch. 561, Sec. 109. (AB 1516) Effective January 1, 2018.)

CHAPTER 3.75. Trauma Care Fund
[1797.198 - 1797.199]

(Chapter 3.75 added by Stats. 2001, Ch. 171, Sec. 2.5.)
1797.198.
The Legislature finds and declares all of the following:

(a) Trauma care is an essential public service. It is as vital to the safety of the public as the services provided by law enforcement and fire departments. In communities with access to trauma centers, mortality and morbidity rates from traumatic injuries are significantly reduced. For the same reasons that each community in California needs timely access to the services of skilled police, paramedics, and fire personnel, each community needs access to the services provided by certified trauma centers.

(b) Trauma centers save lives by providing immediate coordination of highly specialized care for the most life-threatening injuries.

(c) Trauma centers save lives, and also save money, because access to trauma care can mean the difference between full recovery from a traumatic injury, and serious disability necessitating expensive long-term care.

(d) Trauma centers do their job most effectively as part of a system that includes a local plan with a means of immediately identifying trauma cases and transporting those patients to the nearest trauma center.

(e) It is essential for persons in need of trauma care to receive that care within the 60-minute period immediately following injury. It is during this period, referred to as the "golden hour," when the potential for survival is greatest, and the need for treatment for shock or injury is most critical.

(f) It is the intent of the Legislature in enacting this act to promote access to trauma care by ensuring the availability of services through EMS agency-designated trauma centers. (Amended by Stats. 2005, Ch. 80, Sec. 1.1. Effective July 19, 2005.)

1797.199.

(a) There is hereby created in the State Treasury, the Trauma Care Fund, which, notwithstanding Section 13340 of the Government Code, is hereby continuously appropriated without regard to fiscal years to the authority for the purposes specified in subdivision (c).

(b) The fund shall contain any moneys deposited in the fund pursuant to appropriation by the Legislature or from any other source, as well as, notwithstanding Section 16305.7 of the Government Code, any interest and dividends earned on moneys in the fund.

(c) Moneys in the fund shall be expended by the authority to provide for allocations to local EMS agencies, for distribution to local EMS agency-designated trauma centers provided for by this chapter.

(d) Within 30 days of the effective date of the enactment of an appropriation for purposes of implementing this chapter, the authority shall request all local EMS agencies with an approved trauma plan, that includes at least one designated trauma center, to submit within 45 days of the request the total number of trauma patients and the number of trauma patients at each facility that were reported to the local trauma registry for the most recent fiscal year for which data are available, pursuant to Section 100257 of Title 22 of the California Code of Regulations. However, the local EMS agency's report shall not include any registry entry that is in reference to a patient who is discharged from the trauma center's emergency department without being admitted to the hospital unless the nonadmission is due to the patient's death or transfer to another facility. Any local EMS agency that fails to provide these data shall not receive funding pursuant to this section.

(e) Except as provided in subdivision (m), the authority shall distribute all funds to local EMS agencies with an approved trauma plan that includes at least one designated trauma center in the local EMS agency's jurisdiction as of July 1 of the fiscal year in which funds are to be distributed.

(1) The amount provided to each local EMS agency shall be in the same proportion as the total number of trauma patients reported to the local trauma registry for each local EMS agency's area of jurisdiction compared to the total number of all trauma patients statewide as reported under subdivision (d).

(2) The authority shall send a contract to each local EMS agency that is to receive funds within 30 days of receiving the required data and shall distribute the funds to a local EMS agency within 30 days of receiving a signed contract and invoice from the agency.

(f) Local EMS agencies that receive funding under this chapter shall distribute all those funds to eligible trauma centers, except that an agency may expend 1 percent for administration. It is the intent of the Legislature that the funds distributed to eligible trauma centers be spent on trauma services. The funds shall not be used to supplant existing funds designated for trauma services or for training ordinarily provided by the trauma hospital. The local EMS agency shall utilize a competitive grant-based system. All grant proposals shall demonstrate that funding is needed because the trauma center cares for a high percentage of uninsured patients. Local EMS agencies shall determine distribution of funds based on whether the grant proposal satisfies one or more of the following criteria:

(1) The preservation or restoration of specialty physician and surgeon oncall coverage that is demonstrated to be essential for trauma services within a specified hospital.

(2) The acquisition of equipment that is demonstrated to be essential for trauma services within a specified hospital.

(3) The creation of overflow or surge capacity to allow a trauma hospital to respond to mass casualties resulting from an act of terrorism or natural disaster.

(4) The coordination or payment of emergency, nonemergency, and critical care ambulance transportation that would allow for the time-urgent movement or transfer of critically injured patients to trauma centers outside of the originating region so that specialty services or a higher level of care may be provided as necessary without undue delay.

(g) A trauma center shall be eligible for funding under this section if it is designated as a trauma center by a local EMS agency pursuant to Section 1798.165 and complies with the requirements of this section. Both public and private hospitals designated as trauma centers shall be eligible for funding.

(h) A trauma center that receives funding under this section shall agree to remain a trauma center through June 30 of the fiscal year in which it receives funding. If the trauma center ceases functioning as a trauma center, it shall pay back to the local EMS agency a pro rata portion of the funding that has been received. If there are one or more trauma centers remaining in the local EMS agency's service area, the local EMS agency shall

distribute the funds among the other trauma centers. If there is no other trauma center within the local EMS agency's service area, the local EMS agency shall return the moneys to the authority.

(i) In order to receive funds pursuant to this section, an eligible trauma center shall submit, pursuant to a contract between the trauma center and the local EMS agency, relevant and pertinent data requested by the local EMS agency. A trauma center shall demonstrate that it is appropriately submitting data to the local EMS agency's trauma registry and a local EMS agency shall audit the data annually within two years of a distribution from the local EMS agency to a trauma center. Any trauma center receiving funding pursuant to this section shall report to the local EMS agency how the funds were used to support trauma services.

(j) It is the intent of the Legislature that all moneys appropriated to the fund be distributed to local EMS agencies during the same year the moneys are appropriated. To the extent that any moneys are not distributed by the authority during the fiscal year in which the moneys are appropriated, the moneys shall remain in the fund and be eligible for distribution pursuant to this section during subsequent fiscal years.

(k) By October 31, 2002, the authority shall develop criteria for the standardized reporting of trauma patients to local trauma registries. The authority shall seek input from local EMS agencies to develop the criteria. All local EMS agencies shall utilize the trauma patient criteria for reporting trauma patients to local trauma registries by July 1, 2003.

(l) By December 31 of the fiscal year following any fiscal year in which funds are distributed pursuant to this section, a local EMS agency that has received funds from the authority pursuant to this chapter shall provide a report to the authority that details the amount of funds distributed to each trauma center, the amount of any balance remaining, and the amount of any claims pending, if any, and describes how the respective centers used the funds to support trauma services. The report shall also describe the local EMS agency's mechanism for distributing the funds to trauma centers, a description of their audit process and criteria, and a summary of the most recent audit results.

(m) The authority may retain from any appropriation to the fund an amount sufficient to implement this section, up to two hundred eighty thousand dollars ($280,000). This amount may be adjusted to reflect any increases provided for wages or operating expenses as part of the authority's budget process.

(Amended by Stats. 2005, Ch. 80, Sec. 1.2. Effective July 19, 2005.)

CHAPTER 4. Local Administration [1797.200 - 1797.276]

(Chapter 4 added by Stats. 1980, Ch. 1260.)

ARTICLE 1. Local EMS Agency [1797.200 - 1797.229]

(Article 1 added by Stats. 1980, Ch. 1260.)

1797.200.

Each county may develop an emergency medical services program. Each county developing such a program shall designate a local EMS agency which shall be the county health department, an agency established and operated by the county, an entity with which the county contracts for the purposes of local emergency medical services administration, or a joint powers agency created for the administration of emergency medical services by agreement between counties or cities and counties pursuant to the provisions of Chapter 5 (commencing with Section 6500) of Division 7 of Title 1 of the Government Code.

(Added by Stats. 1980, Ch. 1260.)

1797.201.

Upon the request of a city or fire district that contracted for or provided, as of June 1, 1980, prehospital emergency medical services, a county shall enter into a written agreement with the city or fire district regarding the provision of prehospital emergency medical services for that city or fire district. Until such time that an agreement is reached, prehospital emergency medical services shall be continued at not less than the existing level, and the administration of prehospital EMS by cities and fire districts presently providing such services shall be retained by those cities and fire districts, except the level of prehospital EMS may be reduced where the city council, or the governing body of a fire district, pursuant to a public hearing, determines that the reduction is necessary. Notwithstanding any provision of this section the provisions of Chapter 5 (commencing with Section 1798) shall apply.

(Added by Stats. 1980, Ch. 1260.)

1797.202.

(a) Every local EMS agency shall have a full- or part-time licensed physician and surgeon as medical director, who has substantial experience in the practice of emergency medicine, as designated by the county or by the joint powers agreement, to provide medical control and to assure medical accountability throughout the planning, implementation and evaluation of the EMS system. The authority director may waive the requirement that the medical director have substantial experience in the practice of emergency medicine if the requirement places an undue hardship on the county or counties.

(b) The medical director of the local EMS agency may appoint one or more physicians and surgeons as assistant medical directors to assist the medical director with the discharge of the duties of medical director or to assume those duties during any time that the medical director is unable to carry out those duties as the medical director deems necessary.

(c) The medical director may assign to administrative staff of the local EMS agency for completion under the supervision of the medical director, any administrative functions of

his or her duties which do not require his or her professional judgment as medical director.
(Amended by Stats. 1989, Ch. 1362, Sec. 9. Effective October 2, 1989.)
1797.204.
The local EMS agency shall plan, implement, and evaluate an emergency medical services system, in accordance with the provisions of this part, consisting of an organized pattern of readiness and response services based on public and private agreements and operational procedures.
(Added by Stats. 1980, Ch. 1260.)
1797.206.
The local EMS agency shall be responsible for implementation of advanced life support systems and limited advanced life support systems and for the monitoring of training programs.
(Amended by Stats. 1983, Ch. 1246, Sec. 27.)
1797.208.
The local EMS agency shall be responsible for determining that the operation of training programs at the EMT-I, EMT-II, and EMT-P levels are in compliance with this division, and shall approve the training programs if they are found to be in compliance with this division. The training program at the California Highway Patrol Academy shall be exempt from the provisions of this section.
(Amended by Stats. 1986, Ch. 248, Sec. 131.)
1797.210.
(a) The medical director of the local EMS agency shall issue a certificate, except an EMT-P certificate, to an individual upon proof of satisfactory completion of an approved training program, passage of the certifying examination designated by the authority, completion of any other requirements for certification established by the authority, and a determination that the individual is not precluded from certification for any of the reasons listed in Section 1798.200. The certificate shall be proof of the individual's initial competence to perform at the designated level.
(b) The medical director of the local EMS agency shall, at the interval specified by the authority, recertify an EMT-I or EMT-II upon proof of the individual's satisfactory passage of the examination for recertification designated by the authority, completion of any continuing education or other requirements for recertification established by the authority, and a determination that the individual is not precluded from recertification because of any of the reasons listed in Section 1798.200.
(Amended by Stats. 1993, Ch. 64, Sec. 5. Effective June 30, 1993.)
1797.211.
Each local EMS agency shall submit certificate status updates to the authority within three working days after a final determination is made regarding a certification disciplinary action taken by the medical director that results in a change to an EMT-I or EMT-II certificate status.
(Added by Stats. 2008, Ch. 274, Sec. 11. Effective January 1, 2009.)
1797.212.
The local EMS agency may establish a schedule of fees for certification in an amount sufficient to cover the reasonable cost of administering the certification provisions of this division. However, a local EMS agency shall not collect fees for the certification or recertification of an EMT-P.
(Amended by Stats. 1993, Ch. 64, Sec. 6. Effective June 30, 1993.)
1797.213.
(a) Any local EMS agency conducting a program pursuant to this article may provide courses of instruction and training leading to certification as an EMT-I, EMT-II, EMT-P, or authorized registered nurse. When such instruction and training are provided, a fee may be charged sufficient to defray the cost of such instruction and training.
(b) Effective July 1, 1990, any courses of instruction and training leading to certification as an EMT-I, EMT-II, EMT-P, or authorized registered nurse shall include a course of training on the nature of sudden infant death syndrome which is developed by the California SIDS program in the State Department of Health Services in consultation with experts in the field of sudden infant death syndrome, and effective January 1, 1990, any individual certified as an EMT-I, EMT-II, EMT-P, or authorized registered nurse shall complete that course of training. The course shall include information on the community resources available to assist families who have lost a child to sudden infant death syndrome. An individual who was certified as an EMT-I, EMT-II, EMT-P, or authorized registered nurse prior to January 1, 1990, shall complete supplementary training on this topic on or before January 1, 1992.
(Amended by Stats. 1989, Ch. 1111, Sec. 6.)
1797.214.
A local EMS agency may require additional training or qualifications, for the use of drugs, devices, or skills in either the standard scope of practice or a local EMS agency optional scope of practice, which are greater than those provided in this chapter as a condition precedent for practice within such EMS area in an advanced life support or limited advanced life support prehospital care system consistent with standards adopted pursuant to this division.
(Amended by Stats. 1989, Ch. 1362, Sec. 11. Effective October 2, 1989.)
1797.215.
Notwithstanding any other provision of law, EMT-I's, EMT-II's, and EMT-P's shall be required to renew their cardiopulmonary resuscitation certificate no more than once every two years.
(Added by Stats. 1983, Ch. 774, Sec. 1.)
1797.216.

Public safety agencies that are certifying entities may certify and recertify public safety personnel as EMT-I. The state fire marshal, subject to policy guidance and advice from the State Board of Fire Services, may certify and recertify fire safety personnel as EMT-I. All persons certified shall have completed a program of training approved by the local EMS agency or the authority and have passed a competency-based examination.
(Amended by Stats. 2008, Ch. 274, Sec. 12. Effective January 1, 2009.)
1797.217.
(a) Every certifying entity shall submit to the authority certification data required by Section 1797.117.
(b) The authority shall collect fees from each certifying entity for the certification and certification renewal of each EMT-I and EMT-II in an amount sufficient to support the authority's central registry program and the local EMS agency administrative law judge reimbursement program. Separate additional fees may be charged, at the option of the authority, for services that are not shared by all applicants.
(c) The authority's fees shall be established in regulations, and fees charged for individual services shall be set so that the total fees charged shall not exceed the authority's actual total cost for the authority's central registry program, state and federal criminal offender record information search response program, and the local EMS agency administrative law judge reimbursement program.
(d) In addition to any fees collected by EMT-I or EMT-II certifying entities to support their certification, recertification, or enforcement programs, EMT-I or EMT-II certifying entities shall collect fees to support the authority's central registry program, and the local EMS agency administrative law judge reimbursement program. In lieu of collecting fees from an individual, pursuant to an employer choice, a collective bargaining agreement, or other employment contract, the certifying entity shall provide the appropriate fees to the authority pursuant to this subdivision.
(e) All fees collected for or provided to the authority in a calendar month by an EMT-I or EMT-II certifying entity pursuant to this section shall be transmitted to the authority for deposit into the Emergency Medical Technician Certification Fund within 30 calendar days following the last day of the calendar month in which the fees were received by the certifying entity, unless a contract between the certifying entity and the authority specifies a different timeframe.
(f) At the option of the authority, fees may be collected for the authority by an entity that contracts with the authority to provide any of the services associated with the registry program, or the state and federal criminal offender record information search response program, or the local EMS agency administrative law judge reimbursement program. All fees collected for the authority in a calendar month by any entity designated by the authority pursuant to this section to collect fees for the authority shall be transmitted to the authority for deposit into the Emergency Medical Technician Certification Fund within 30 calendar days following the last day of the calendar month in which the fees were received by the designated entity, unless the contract between the entity and the authority specifies a different timeframe.
(g) The authority shall annually evaluate fees to determine if the fee is sufficient to fund the actual costs of the authority's central registry program, state and federal criminal offender record information search response program, and local EMS agency administrative law judge reimbursement program. If the evaluation shows that the fees are excessive or are insufficient to fund the actual costs of these programs, then the fees will be adjusted accordingly through the rulemaking process as outlined in the Administrative Procedure Act (Chapter 3.5 (commencing with Section 11340) of Part 1 of Division 3 of Title 2 of the Government Code).
(h) The Emergency Medical Technician Certification Fund is hereby created in the State Treasury. All moneys deposited in the fund shall be made available, upon appropriation, to the authority for purposes of the central registry program, state and federal criminal offender record information search response program, and the local EMS agency administrative law judge reimbursement program. The local EMS agency administrative law judge reimbursement program is solely for the purpose of making reimbursements to local emergency medical service agencies for actual administrative law judge costs regarding EMT-I or EMT-II disciplinary action appeals. Reimbursement to the local emergency medical service agencies shall only be made if adequate funds are available from fees collected for the authority's local EMS agency administrative law judge reimbursement program.
(i) The authority may transfer unused portions of the Emergency Medical Technician Certification Fund to the Surplus Money Investment Fund. Funds transferred to the Surplus Money Investment Fund shall be placed in a separate trust account, and shall be available for transfer to the Emergency Medical Technician Certification Fund, together with interest earned, when requested by the authority.
(j) The authority shall maintain a reserve balance in the Emergency Medical Technician Certification Fund of 5 percent of annual revenues. Any increase in the fees deposited in the Emergency Medical Technician Certification Fund shall be effective upon a determination by the authority that additional moneys are required to fund expenditures of this section.
(Amended by Stats. 2011, Ch. 296, Sec. 150. (AB 1023) Effective January 1, 2012.)
1797.218.
Any local EMS agency may authorize an advanced life support or limited advanced life support program which provides services utilizing EMT-II or EMT-P, or both, for the delivery of emergency medical care to the sick and injured at the scene of an emergency, during transport to a general acute care hospital, during interfacility transfer, while in the emergency department of a general acute care hospital until care responsibility is assumed by the regular staff of that hospital, and during training within the facilities of a participating general acute care hospital.

(Amended by Stats. 1983, Ch. 1246, Sec. 34.)
1797.219.

All investigatory and disciplinary processes for EMT-I and EMT-II certificate holders shall be, subject to Chapter 9.6 (commencing with Section 3250) of Division 4 of Title 1 of the Government Code, with respect to certificate holders who are firefighters otherwise subject to these provisions, and Chapter 9.7 (commencing with Section 3300) of Division 4 of Title 1 of the Government Code, with respect to certificate holders who are peace officers otherwise subject to these provisions.
(Added by Stats. 2008, Ch. 274, Sec. 14. Effective January 1, 2009.)
1797.220.

The local EMS agency, using state minimum standards, shall establish policies and procedures approved by the medical director of the local EMS agency to assure medical control of the EMS system. The policies and procedures approved by the medical director may require basic life support emergency medical transportation services to meet any medical control requirements including dispatch, patient destination policies, patient care guidelines, and quality assurance requirements.
(Amended by Stats. 1988, Ch. 1390, Sec. 5.)
1797.221.

The medical director of the local EMS agency may approve or conduct any scientific or trial study of the efficacy of the prehospital emergency use of any drug, device, or treatment procedure within the local EMS system, utilizing any level of prehospital emergency medical care personnel. The study shall be consistent with any requirements established by the authority for scientific or trial studies conducted within the prehospital emergency medical care system, and, where applicable, with Article 5 (commencing with Section 111550) of Chapter 6 of Part 5 of Division 104. No drug, device, or treatment procedure which has been specifically excluded by the authority from usage in the EMS system shall be included in such a study.
(Amended by Stats. 1996, Ch. 1023, Sec. 174. Effective September 29, 1996.)
1797.222.

A county, upon the recommendation of its local EMS agency, may adopt ordinances governing the transport of a patient who is receiving care in the field from prehospital emergency medical personnel, when the patient meets specific criteria for trauma, burn, or pediatric centers adopted by the local EMS agency.

The ordinances shall, to the extent possible, ensure that individual patients receive appropriate medical care while protecting the interests of the community at large by making maximum use of available emergency medical care resources. These ordinances shall be consistent with Sections 1797.106, 1798.100, and 1798.102, and shall not conflict with any state regulations or any guidelines adopted by the Emergency Medical Service Authority.

This section shall not be construed as prohibiting the helicopter program of the Department of the California Highway Patrol from a role in providing emergency medical services when the best medically qualified person at the scene of an accident determines it is in the best interests of any injured party.
(Added by Stats. 1983, Ch. 1237, Sec. 2.)
1797.224.

A local EMS agency may create one or more exclusive operating areas in the development of a local plan, if a competitive process is utilized to select the provider or providers of the services pursuant to the plan. No competitive process is required if the local EMS agency develops or implements a local plan that continues the use of existing providers operating within a local EMS area in the manner and scope in which the services have been provided without interruption since January 1, 1981. A local EMS agency which elects to create one or more exclusive operating areas in the development of a local plan shall develop and submit for approval to the authority, as part of the local EMS plan, its competitive process for selecting providers and determining the scope of their operations. This plan shall include provisions for a competitive process held at periodic intervals. Nothing in this section supersedes Section 1797.201.
(Added by Stats. 1984, Ch. 1349, Sec. 3.)
1797.225.

(a) A local EMS agency may adopt policies and procedures for calculating and reporting ambulance patient offload time, as defined in subdivision (b) of Section 1797.120.
(b) A local EMS agency that adopts policies and procedures for calculating and reporting ambulance patient offload time pursuant to subdivision (a) shall do all of the following:
(1) Use the statewide standard methodology for calculating and reporting ambulance patient offload time developed by the authority pursuant to Section 1797.120.
(2) Establish criteria for the reporting of, and quality assurance followup for, a nonstandard patient offload time, as defined in subdivision (c).
(c) (1) For the purposes of this section, a "nonstandard patient offload time" means that the ambulance patient offload time for a patient exceeds a period of time designated in the criteria established by the local EMS agency pursuant to paragraph (2) of subdivision (b).
(2) "Nonstandard patient offload time" does not include instances in which the ambulance patient offload time exceeds the period set by the local EMS agency due to acts of God, natural disasters, or manmade disasters.
(Added by Stats. 2015, Ch. 379, Sec. 2. (AB 1223) Effective January 1, 2016.)
1797.226.

Without altering or otherwise affecting the meaning of any portion of this division as to any other county, as to San Bernardino County only, it shall be competent for any local EMS agency which establishes exclusive operating areas pursuant to Section 1797.224 to determine the following:

(a) That a minor alteration in the level of life support personnel or equipment, which does not significantly reduce the level of care available, shall not constitute a change in the manner and scope of providing services.
(b) That a successor to a previously existing emergency services provider shall qualify as an existing provider if the successor has continued uninterrupted the emergency transportation previously supplied by the prior provider.
(Added by Stats. 1986, Ch. 965, Sec. 1.)
1797.227.

(a) An emergency medical care provider shall do both of the following when collecting and submitting data to a local EMS agency:
(1) Use an electronic health record system that exports data in a format that is compliant with the current versions of the California Emergency Medical Services Information System (CEMSIS) and the National Emergency Medical Services Information System (NEMSIS) standards and includes those data elements that are required by the local EMS agency.
(2) Ensure that the electronic health record system can be integrated with the local EMS agency's data system, so that the local EMS agency may collect data from the provider.
(b) A local EMS agency shall not mandate that a provider use a specific electronic health record system to collect and share data with the local EMS agency.
(c) This section does not modify or affect a written contract or agreement executed before January 1, 2016, between a local EMS agency and an emergency medical care provider.
(Added by Stats. 2015, Ch. 377, Sec. 1. (AB 1129) Effective January 1, 2016.)
1797.228.

(a) (1) On or before July 1, 2019, a local EMS agency shall transmit ambulance patient offload time data quarterly to the authority, consistent with the policies and procedures developed pursuant to Section 1797.225.
(2) The data must be sufficient for the authority to calculate ambulance patient offload time, as defined in subdivision (b) of Section 1797.120, by local EMS agency jurisdiction and by each facility in a local EMS agency jurisdiction.
(b) Notwithstanding Section 1797.122, the local EMS agency shall ensure that personally identifying patient data is not included in the submission of data to calculate patient offload time.
(Added by Stats. 2018, Ch. 656, Sec. 3. (AB 2961) Effective January 1, 2019.)
1797.229.

(a) Each local EMS agency and other certifying entities shall annually submit to the authority, by July 1 of each year, data on the approval or denial of EMT-I or EMT-II applicants. The data submitted to the authority shall include, at a minimum, all of the following information with respect to the preceding calendar year:
(1) The total number of applicants who applied for initial certification.
(2) The total number of applicants with a prior criminal conviction who applied for initial certification.
(3) The number of applicants who were denied, the number of applicants who were approved, and the number of applicants who were approved with restrictions.
(4) The number of applicants with a prior criminal conviction who were denied, the number of applicants with a prior criminal conviction who were approved, and the number of applicants with a prior criminal conviction who were approved with restrictions.
(5) The reason or reasons stated for denying an applicant with a prior criminal conviction, or the reason or reasons stated for approving with restrictions an applicant with a prior criminal conviction.
(6) The restrictions imposed on approved applicants with a prior criminal conviction, and the duration of those imposed restrictions.
(7) Race, ethnicity, gender, and age demographic data for all applicants who were denied, approved, or approved with restrictions.
(b) The authority shall annually report to the commission on the extent to which prior criminal history may be an obstacle to certification as an EMT-I or EMT-II. The authority shall annually submit the same report to the Legislature, in compliance with Section 9795 of the Government Code, and shall make the report easily accessible on the authority's Internet Web site.
(c) Data submitted to the authority pursuant to subdivision (a) and the reports described in subdivision (b) shall not contain any personal identifying information of the EMT-I or EMT-II applicants.
(d) This section shall become inoperative on July 1, 2024, and, as of January 1, 2025, is repealed.
(Added by Stats. 2018, Ch. 342, Sec. 1. (AB 2293) Effective January 1, 2019. Section inoperative July 1, 2024. Repealed as of January 1, 2025, by its own provisions.)

ARTICLE 2. Local Emergency Medical Services Planning [1797.250 - 1797.258]

(Article 2 added by Stats. 1980, Ch. 1260.)
1797.250.

In each designated EMS area, the local EMS agency may develop and submit a plan to the authority for an emergency medical services system according to the guidelines prescribed pursuant to Section 1797.103.
(Added by Stats. 1980, Ch. 1260.)
1797.252.

The local EMS agency shall, consistent with such plan, coordinate and otherwise facilitate arrangements necessary to develop the emergency medical services system.
(Added by Stats. 1980, Ch. 1260.)
1797.254.

Local EMS agencies shall annually submit an emergency medical services plan for the EMS area to the authority, according to EMS Systems, Standards, and Guidelines established by the authority.
(Amended by Stats. 1996, Ch. 197, Sec. 2. Effective July 22, 1996.)
1797.256.
A local EMS agency may review applications for grants and contracts for federal, state, or private funds concerning emergency medical services or related activities in its EMS area.
(Added by Stats. 1980, Ch. 1260.)
1797.257.
A local EMS agency which elects to implement a trauma care system on or after the effective date of the regulations adopted pursuant to Section 1798.161 shall develop and submit a plan for that trauma care system to the authority according to the requirements of the regulations prior to the implementation of that system.
(Added by Stats. 1984, Ch. 1735, Sec. 3. Effective September 30, 1984.)
1797.258.
After the submission of an initial trauma care system plan, a local EMS agency which has implemented a trauma care system shall annually submit to the authority an updated plan which identifies all changes, if any, to be made in the trauma care system.
(Added by Stats. 1984, Ch. 1735, Sec. 4. Effective September 30, 1984.)

ARTICLE 3. Emergency Medical Care Committee [1797.270 - 1797.276]
(Article 3 added by Stats. 1983, Ch. 1246, Sec. 35.)
1797.270.
An emergency medical care committee may be established in each county in this state. Nothing in this division should be construed to prevent two or more adjacent counties from establishing a single committee for review of emergency medical care in these counties.
(Amended by Stats. 1993, Ch. 64, Sec. 7. Effective June 30, 1993.)
1797.272.
The county board of supervisors shall prescribe the membership, and appoint the members, of the emergency medical care committee. If two or more adjacent counties establish a single committee, the county boards of supervisors shall jointly prescribe the membership, and appoint the members of the committee.
(Added by Stats. 1983, Ch. 1246, Sec. 35.)
1797.274.
The emergency medical care committee shall, at least annually, review the operations of each of the following:
(a) Ambulance services operating within the county.
(b) Emergency medical care offered within the county, including programs for training large numbers of people in cardiopulmonary resuscitation and lifesaving first aid techniques.
(c) First aid practices in the county.
(Added by Stats. 1983, Ch. 1246, Sec. 35.)
1797.276.
Every emergency medical care committee shall, at least annually, report to the authority, and the local EMS agency its observations and recommendations relative to its review of the ambulance services, emergency medical care, and first aid practices, and programs for training people in cardiopulmonary resuscitation and lifesaving first aid techniques, and public participation in such programs in that county. The emergency medical care committee shall submit its observations and recommendations to the county board or boards of supervisors which it serves and shall act in an advisory capacity to the county board or boards of supervisors which it serves, and to the local EMS agency, on all matters relating to emergency medical services as directed by the board or boards of supervisors.
(Amended by Stats. 1988, Ch. 260, Sec. 5.)

CHAPTER 5. Medical Control [1798 - 1798.6]

(Chapter 5 added by Stats. 1980, Ch. 1260.)
1798.
(a) The medical direction and management of an emergency medical services system shall be under the medical control of the medical director of the local EMS agency. This medical control shall be maintained in accordance with standards for medical control established by the authority.
(b) Medical control shall be within an EMS system which complies with the minimum standards adopted by the authority, and which is established and implemented by the local EMS agency.
(c) In the event a medical director of a base station questions the medical effect of a policy of a local EMS agency, the medical director of the base station shall submit a written statement to the medical director of the local EMS agency requesting a review by a panel of medical directors of other base stations. Upon receipt of the request, the medical director of a local EMS agency shall promptly convene a panel of medical directors of base stations to evaluate the written statement. The panel shall be composed of all the medical directors of the base stations in the region, except that the local EMS medical director may limit the panel to five members.
This subdivision shall remain in effect only until the authority adopts more comprehensive regulations that supersede this subdivision.
(Amended by Stats. 1988, Ch. 1390, Sec. 6.)
1798.2.

The base hospital shall implement the policies and procedures established by the local EMS agency and approved by the medical director of the local EMS agency for medical direction of prehospital emergency medical care personnel.
(Amended by Stats. 1988, Ch. 1390, Sec. 7.)
1798.3.
Advanced life support and limited advanced life support personnel may receive medical direction from an alternative base station in lieu of a base hospital when the following conditions are met:
(a) The alternative base station has been designated by the local EMS agency and approved by the medical director of the local EMS agency, pursuant to Section 1798.105, to provide medical direction to prehospital personnel because no base hospital is available to provide medical direction for the geographical area assigned.
(b) The medical direction is provided by either of the following:
(1) A physician and surgeon who is trained and qualified to issue advice and instructions to prehospital emergency medical care personnel.
(2) A mobile intensive care nurse who has been authorized by the medical director of the local EMS agency, pursuant to Section 1797.56, as qualified to issue instructions to prehospital emergency medical care personnel.
(Added by Stats. 1988, Ch. 1390, Sec. 8.)
1798.6.
(a) Authority for patient health care management in an emergency shall be vested in that licensed or certified health care professional, which may include any paramedic or other prehospital emergency personnel, at the scene of the emergency who is most medically qualified specific to the provision of rendering emergency medical care. If no licensed or certified health care professional is available, the authority shall be vested in the most appropriate medically qualified representative of public safety agencies who may have responded to the scene of the emergency.
(b) If any county desires to establish a unified command structure for patient management at the scene of an emergency within that county, a committee may be established in that county comprised of representatives of the agency responsible for county emergency medical services, the county sheriff's department, the California Highway Patrol, public prehospital-care provider agencies serving the county, and public fire, police, and other affected emergency service agencies within the county. The membership and duties of the committee shall be established by an agreement for the joint exercise of powers under Chapter 5 (commencing with Section 6500) of Division 7 of Title 1 of the Government Code.
(c) Notwithstanding subdivision (a), authority for the management of the scene of an emergency shall be vested in the appropriate public safety agency having primary investigative authority. The scene of an emergency shall be managed in a manner designed to minimize the risk of death or health impairment to the patient and to other persons who may be exposed to the risks as a result of the emergency condition, and priority shall be placed upon the interests of those persons exposed to the more serious and immediate risks to life and health. Public safety officials shall consult emergency medical services personnel or other authoritative health care professionals at the scene in the determination of relevant risks.
(Added by Stats. 1983, Ch. 206, Sec. 2.)

CHAPTER 6. Facilities [1798.100 - 1798.183]

(Chapter 6 added by Stats. 1980, Ch. 1260.)

ARTICLE 1. Base Hospitals [1798.100 - 1798.105]
(Heading of Article 1 amended by Stats. 1984, Ch. 1391, Sec. 5.)
1798.100.
In administering the EMS system, the local EMS agency, with the approval of its medical director, may designate and contract with hospitals or other entities approved by the medical director of the local EMS agency pursuant to Section 1798.105 to provide medical direction of prehospital emergency medical care personnel, within its area of jurisdiction, as either base hospitals or alternative base stations, respectively. Hospitals or other entities so designated and contracted with as base hospitals or alternative base stations shall provide medical direction of prehospital emergency medical care provided for the area defined by the local EMS agency in accordance with policies and procedures established by the local EMS agency and approved by the medical director of the local EMS agency pursuant to Sections 1797.220 and 1798.
(Amended by Stats. 1988, Ch. 1390, Sec. 10.)
1798.101.
(a) In rural areas, as determined by the authority, where the use of a base hospital having a basic emergency medical service special permit pursuant to subdivision (c) of Section 1277 is precluded because of geographic or other extenuating circumstances, a local EMS agency, in order to assure medical direction to prehospital emergency medical care personnel, may utilize other hospitals which do not have a basic emergency medical service permit but which have been approved by the medical director of the local EMS agency for utilization as a base hospital, if both of the following apply:
(1) Medical control is maintained in accordance with policies and procedures established by the local EMS agency, with the approval of the medical director of the local EMS agency.
(2) Approval is secured from the authority.
(b) (1) In rural areas, as determined by the authority, when the use of a hospital having a basic emergency medical service special permit is precluded because of geographic or other extenuating circumstances, as determined by the authority, the medical director of the local EMS agency may authorize another facility which does not have this special permit to receive patients requiring emergency medical services if the facility has

adequate staff and equipment to provide these services, as determined by the medical director of the local EMS agency.

(2) A local EMS agency which utilizes in its EMS system any facility which does not have a special permit to receive patients requiring emergency medical care pursuant to paragraph (1) shall submit to the authority, as part of the plan required by Section 1797.254, protocols approved by the medical director of the local EMS agency to ensure that the use of that facility is in the best interests of patient care. The protocols addressing patient safety and the use of the nonpermit facility shall take into account, but not be limited to, the following:

(A) The medical staff, and the availability of the staff at various times to care for patients requiring emergency medical services.

(B) The ability of staff to care for the degree and severity of patient injuries.

(C) The equipment and services available at the facility necessary to care for patients requiring emergency medical services and the severity of their injuries.

(D) The availability of more comprehensive emergency medical services and the distance and travel time necessary to make the alternative emergency medical services available.

(E) The time of day and any limitations which may apply for a nonpermit facility to treat patients requiring emergency medical services.

(3) Any change in the status of a nonpermit facility, authorized pursuant to this subdivision to care for patients requiring emergency medical services, with respect to protocols and the facility's ability to care for the patients shall be reported by the facility to the local EMS agency.

(Amended by Stats. 1988, Ch. 1390, Sec. 11.)

1798.102.

The base hospital shall supervise prehospital treatment, triage, and transport, advanced life support or limited advanced life support, and monitor personnel program compliance by direct medical supervision.

(Amended by Stats. 1984, Ch. 1391, Sec. 17.)

1798.104.

The base hospital shall provide, or cause to be provided, EMS prehospital personnel training and continuing education in accordance with local EMS policies and procedures.

(Amended by Stats. 1984, Ch. 1391, Sec. 18.)

1798.105.

The medical director of the local EMS agency may approve an alternative base station, as defined in Section 1798.53, to provide medical direction to advanced life support or limited advanced life support personnel for an area of the local EMS system for which no qualified base hospital is available, to provide that medical direction, providing that both the following conditions are met:

(a) Medical control is maintained in accordance with policies and procedures established by the local EMS agency, with the approval of the medical director of the local EMS agency.

(b) Any responsibilities of a base station hospital, including review of run reports or provision of continuing education, which are not assigned to the alternative base station, are assigned to either the local EMS agency, a base hospital for another area of the local EMS system, or a receiving hospital which has been approved by the medical director to, and has agreed to, assume the responsibilities.

(Added by Stats. 1988, Ch. 1390, Sec. 12.)

ARTICLE 2. Critical Care [1798.150- 1798.150.]

(Article 2 added by Stats. 1980, Ch. 1260.)

1798.150.

The authority may establish, in cooperation with affected medical organizations, guidelines for hospital facilities according to critical care capabilities.

(Added by Stats. 1980, Ch. 1260.)

ARTICLE 2.5. Regional Trauma Systems [1798.160 - 1798.169]

(Article 2.5 added by Stats. 1983, Ch. 1067, Sec. 2.)

1798.160.

Except where the context otherwise requires, the following definitions govern the construction of this article:

(a) "Trauma case" means any injured person who has been evaluated by prehospital personnel according to policies and procedures established by the local EMS agency pursuant to Section 1798.163 and who has been found to require transportation to a trauma facility.

(b) "Trauma facility" means a health facility, as defined by regulation, which is capable of treating one or more types of potentially seriously injured persons and which has been designated as part of the regional trauma care system by the local EMS agency. A facility may be a trauma facility for one or more services, as designated by the local EMS agency.

(c) "Trauma care system" means an arrangement under which trauma cases are transported to, and treated by, the appropriate trauma facility.

(Amended by Stats. 1984, Ch. 1735, Sec. 5. Effective September 30, 1984.)

1798.161.

(a) The authority shall submit draft regulations specifying minimum standards for the implementation of trauma care systems to the commission on or before July 1, 1984, and shall adopt the regulations on or before July 1, 1985. These regulations shall provide specific requirements for the care of trauma cases and shall ensure that the trauma care system is fully coordinated with all elements of the existing emergency medical services system. The regulations shall be adopted as provided in Section 1799.50, and shall include, but not be limited to, all of the following:

(1) Prehospital care management guidelines for triage and transportation of trauma cases.

(2) Flow patterns of trauma cases and geographic boundaries regarding trauma and nontrauma cases.

(3) The number and type of trauma cases necessary to assure that trauma facilities will provide quality care to trauma cases referred to them.

(4) The resources and equipment needed by trauma facilities to treat trauma cases.

(5) The availability and qualifications of the health care personnel, including physicians and surgeons, treating trauma cases within a trauma facility.

(6) Data collection regarding system operation and patient outcome.

(7) Periodic performance evaluation of the trauma system and its components.

(b) The authority may grant an exception to a portion of the regulations adopted pursuant to subdivision (a) upon substantiation of need by a local EMS agency that, as defined in the regulations, compliance with that requirement would not be in the best interests of the persons served within the affected local EMS area.

(Amended by Stats. 1984, Ch. 1735, Sec. 6. Effective September 30, 1984.)

1798.162.

(a) A local emergency medical services agency may implement a trauma care system only if the system meets the minimum standards set forth in the regulations for implementation established by the authority and the plan required by Section 1797.257 has been submitted to, and approved by, the authority. Prior to submitting the plan for the trauma care system to the authority, a local emergency medical services agency shall hold a public hearing and shall give adequate notice of the public hearing to all hospitals and other interested parties in the area proposed to be included in the system. This subdivision does not preclude a local EMS agency from adopting trauma care system standards which are more stringent than those established by the regulations.

(b) Notwithstanding subdivision (a) or any other provision of this article, the Santa Clara County Emergency Medical Services Agency may implement a trauma care system prior to the adoption of regulations by the authority pursuant to Section 1798.161. If the Santa Clara County Emergency Medical Services Agency implements a trauma care system pursuant to this subdivision prior to the adoption of those regulations by the authority, the agency shall prepare and submit to the authority a trauma care system plan which conforms to any regulations subsequently adopted by the authority.

(Amended by Stats. 1984, Ch. 1735, Sec. 7. Effective September 30, 1984.)

1798.163.

A local emergency medical services agency implementing a trauma care system shall establish policies and procedures which are concordant and consistent with the minimum standards set forth in the regulations adopted by the authority. This section does not preclude a local EMS agency from adopting trauma care system standards which are more stringent than those established by the regulations.

(Amended by Stats. 1984, Ch. 1735, Sec. 8. Effective September 30, 1984.)

1798.164.

(a) A local emergency medical services agency may charge a fee to an applicant seeking initial or continuing designation as a trauma facility in an amount sufficient to cover the costs directly related to the designation of trauma facilities pursuant to Section 1798.165 and to the development of the plans prepared pursuant to Sections 1797.257 and 1797.258, and subdivision (b) of Section 1798.162.

(b) Each local emergency medical services agency charging fees pursuant to subdivision (a) shall annually provide a report to the authority and to each trauma facility having paid a fee to the agency. The report shall contain sufficient detail to apprise facilities of the specific application of fees collected and to assure the authority that fees collected were expended in compliance with subdivision (a).

(c) The authority may establish a prescribed format for the report required in subdivision (b).

(Amended by Stats. 1988, Ch. 768, Sec. 1.)

1798.165.

(a) Local emergency medical services agencies may designate trauma facilities as part of their trauma care system pursuant to the regulations promulgated by the authority.

(b) The health facility shall only be designated to provide the level of trauma care and service for which it is qualified and which is included within the system implemented by the agency.

(c) No health care provider shall use the terms "trauma facility," "trauma hospital," "trauma center," "trauma care provider," "trauma vehicle," or similar terminology in its signs or advertisements, or in printed materials and information it furnishes to the general public, unless the use is authorized by the local EMS agency.

(Amended by Stats. 1985, Ch. 570, Sec. 1.)

1798.166.

A local emergency medical services agency which elects to implement a trauma care system on or after January 1, 1984, shall develop and submit a plan to the authority according to the regulations established prior to the implementation.

(Added by Stats. 1983, Ch. 1067, Sec. 2.)

1798.167.

Nothing in this article shall be construed to restrict the authority of a health care facility to provide a service for which it has received a license pursuant to Chapter 2 (commencing with Section 1250) of Division 2.

(Added by Stats. 1983, Ch. 1067, Sec. 2.)

1798.168.

Nothing in this article shall be construed as changing the boundaries of any local emergency medical services agency in existence on January 1, 1984.

(Added by Stats. 1983, Ch. 1067, Sec. 2.)

1798.169.

Nothing in this article shall be construed as restricting the use of a helicopter of the Department of the California Highway Patrol from performing missions which the department determines are in the best interests of the people of the State of California. (Added by Stats. 1983, Ch. 1067, Sec. 2.)

ARTICLE 3. Transfer Agreements [1798.170 - 1798.172]

(Article 3 added by Stats. 1980, Ch. 1260.)
1798.170.
A local EMS agency may develop triage and transfer protocols to facilitate prompt delivery of patients to appropriate designated facilities within and without its area of jurisdiction. Considerations in designating a facility shall include, but shall not be limited to, the following:
(a) A general acute care hospital's consistent ability to provide on-call physicians and services for all emergency patients regardless of ability to pay.
(b) The sufficiency of hospital procedures to ensure that all patients who come to the emergency department are examined and evaluated to determine whether or not an emergency condition exists.
(c) The hospital's compliance with local EMS protocols, guidelines, and transfer agreement requirements.
(Amended by Stats. 1987, Ch. 1240, Sec. 16.)
1798.172.
(a) The local EMS agency shall establish guidelines and standards for completion and operation of formal transfer agreements between hospitals with varying levels of care in the area of jurisdiction of the local EMS agency consistent with Sections 1317 to 1317.9a, inclusive, and Chapter 5 (commencing with Section 1798). Each local EMS agency shall solicit and consider public comment in drafting guidelines and standards. These guidelines shall include provision for suggested written agreements for the type of patient, initial patient care treatments, requirements of interhospital care, and associated logistics for transfer, evaluation, and monitoring of the patient.
(b) Notwithstanding subdivision (a), and in addition to Section 1317, a general acute care hospital licensed under Chapter 2 (commencing with Section 1250) of Division 2 shall not transfer a person for nonmedical reasons to another health facility unless that other facility receiving the person agrees in advance of the transfer to accept the transfer. (Amended by Stats. 1988, Ch. 888, Sec. 6. Effective September 14, 1988.)

ARTICLE 3.5. Use of "Emergency" [1798.175- 1798.175.]

(Article 3.5 added by Stats. 1986, Ch. 1377, Sec. 1.)
1798.175.
(a) No person or public agency shall advertise itself as, or hold itself out as, providing emergency medical services, by using in its name or advertising the word "emergency," or any derivation thereof, or any words which suggest that it is staffed and equipped to provide emergency medical services, unless the person or public agency satisfies one of the following requirements:
(1) Is a general acute care hospital providing approved standby, basic, or comprehensive emergency medical services regulated by this chapter.
(2) Meets all of the following minimum standards:
(A) Emergency services are available in the facility seven days a week, 24 hours a day.
(B) Has equipment, medication, and personnel experienced in the provision of services needed to treat life-, limb-, or function-threatening conditions.
(C) Diagnostic radiology and clinical laboratory services are provided by persons on duty or on call and available when needed.
(D) At least one physician who is trained and experienced in the provision of emergency medical care who is on duty or on call so as to be immediately available to the facility.
(E) Medical records document the name of each patient who seeks care, as well as the disposition of each patient upon discharge.
(F) A roster of speciality physicians who are available for referral, consultation, and speciality services is maintained and available.
(G) Policies and procedures define the scope and conduct of treatment provided, including procedures for the management of specific types of emergencies.
(H) The quality and appropriateness of emergency services are evaluated at least annually as part of a quality assurance program.
(I) Provides information to the public that describes the capabilities of the facility, including the scope of services provided, the manner in which the facility complies with the requirements of this section pertaining to the availability and qualifications of personnel or services, and the manner in which the facility cooperates with the patient's primary care physician in followup care.
(J) Clearly identifies the responsible professional or professionals and the legal owner or owners of the facility in its promotion, advertising, and solicitations.
(K) Transfer agreements are in effect at all times with one or more general acute care hospitals which provide basic or comprehensive emergency medical services wherein patients requiring more definitive care will be expeditiously transferred and receive prompt hospital care. Reasonable care shall be exercised to determine whether an emergency requiring more definitive care exists and the person seeking emergency care shall be assisted in obtaining these services, including transportation services, in every way reasonable under the circumstances.
(b) Nothing in this article shall be construed to require the licensing or certification of any person or public agency meeting the minimum standards of paragraph (2) of subdivision (a), nor to exempt from licensure those health facilities covered by paragraph (1) of subdivision (a).
(c) Nothing in this article shall be construed to:

(1) Prohibit a physician in private practice, an outpatient department of a general acute care hospital whether located on or off the premises of the hospital, or other entity authorized to offer medical services from advertising itself as, or otherwise holding itself out as, providing urgent, immediate, or prompt medical services, or from using in its name or advertising the words "urgent," "prompt," "immediate," any derivative thereof, or other words which suggest that it is staffed and equipped to provide urgent, prompt, or immediate medical services.
(2) Prohibit prehospital emergency medical care personnel certified pursuant to, or any state or local agencies established pursuant to, this division, or any emergency vehicle operating within the emergency medical services system from using the word "emergency" in the title, classification, or designation of the personnel, agency, or vehicle.
(d) Any person or public agency using the word "emergency" or any derivation thereof in its name or advertising on January 1, 1987, but which would be prohibited from using the word or derivation thereof by this article, shall have until January 1, 1988, to comply with this article.
(Added by Stats. 1986, Ch. 1377, Sec. 1.)

ARTICLE 4. Poison Control Centers [1798.180 - 1798.183]

(Article 4 added by Stats. 1984, Ch. 1391, Sec. 19. }
1798.180.
(a) The authority shall establish minimum standards for the operation of poison control centers.
(b) The authority shall establish geographical service areas and criteria for designation of regional poison control centers. The authority may designate poison control centers which have met the standards established pursuant to subdivision (a), in accordance with the criteria adopted pursuant to this subdivision.
(c) No person or persons, business, agency, organization, or other entity, whether public or private, shall hold itself out as providing a poison advice service or use the term poison control center, poison advice center, or any other term which implies that it is qualified to provide advice on the treatment or handling of poisons in its advertising, name, or in printed materials and information it furnishes to the general public unless that entity meets one of the following conditions:
(1) Has been designated as a poison control center by the authority.
(2) Is a company or organization which provides a poison information service for products or chemicals which it manufactures or distributes.
(d) Nothing in this section shall prohibit a qualified health care professional, within his or her level of professional expertise, from providing advice regarding poisoning or poisons to his or her patient or patients upon request or whenever he or she deems it warranted in the exercise of his or her professional judgment, as otherwise permitted by law. (Amended by Stats. 1987, Ch. 972, Sec. 2.)
1798.181.
The authority shall consolidate the number of poison control centers if it is determined by the authority that the consolidation will result in cost savings.
(Added by Stats. 1992, Ch. 1366, Sec. 1. Effective October 27, 1992.)
1798.182.
The authority may authorize a poison control center, instead of providing poison control services directly, to contract with an entity in another state to provide poison control services during any part of the 24-hour period for which the center is required to provide poison control services, if both of the following conditions are met:
(a) The center is unable to provide poison control services 24 hours a day.
(b) The entity in the other state provides substantially the same poison control services as required under Section 1798.180, and regulations adopted pursuant thereto. An entity in another state shall not be deemed not to provide substantially the same poison control services solely because the staff of the entity is licensed in the other state, and not licensed in the State of California.
(Added by Stats. 1993, Ch. 236, Sec. 1. Effective January 1, 1994.)
1798.183.
The authority may authorize a poison control center to provide poison control services for fewer than 24 hours a day, as the authority deems necessary.
(Added by Stats. 1993, Ch. 236, Sec. 2. Effective January 1, 1994.)

CHAPTER 7. Penalties [1798.200 - 1798.211]

(Chapter 7 added by Stats. 1980, Ch. 1260.)
1798.200.
(a) (1) (A) Except as provided in paragraph (2), an employer of an EMT-I or EMT-II may conduct investigations, as necessary, and take disciplinary action against an EMT-I or EMT-II who is employed by that employer for conduct in violation of subdivision (c). The employer shall notify the medical director of the local EMS agency that has jurisdiction in the county in which the alleged violation occurred within three days when an allegation has been validated as a potential violation of subdivision (c).
(B) Each employer of an EMT-I or EMT-II employee shall notify the medical director of the local EMS agency that has jurisdiction in the county in which a violation related to subdivision (c) occurred within three days after the EMT-I or EMT-II is terminated or suspended for a disciplinary cause, the EMT-I or EMT-II resigns following notification of an impending investigation based upon evidence that would indicate the existence of a disciplinary cause, or the EMT-I or EMT-II is removed from EMT-related duties for a disciplinary cause after the completion of the employer's investigation.

(C) At the conclusion of an investigation, the employer of an EMT-I or EMT-II may develop and implement, in accordance with the guidelines for disciplinary orders, temporary suspensions, and conditions of probation adopted pursuant to Section 1797.184, a disciplinary plan for the EMT-I or EMT-II. Upon adoption of the disciplinary plan, the employer shall submit that plan to the local EMS agency within three working days. The employer's disciplinary plan may include a recommendation that the medical director of the local EMS agency consider taking action against the holder's certificate pursuant to paragraph (3).

(2) If an EMT-I or EMT-II is not employed by an ambulance service licensed by the Department of the California Highway Patrol or a public safety agency or if that ambulance service or public safety agency chooses not to conduct an investigation pursuant to paragraph (1) for conduct in violation of subdivision (c), the medical director of a local EMS agency shall conduct the investigations, and, upon a determination of disciplinary cause, take disciplinary action as necessary against the EMT-I or EMT-II. At the conclusion of these investigations, the medical director shall develop and implement, in accordance with the recommended guidelines for disciplinary orders, temporary orders, and conditions of probation adopted pursuant to Section 1797.184, a disciplinary plan for the EMT-I or EMT-II. The medical director's disciplinary plan may include action against the holder's certificate pursuant to paragraph (3).

(3) The medical director of the local EMS agency may, upon a determination of disciplinary cause and in accordance with regulations for disciplinary processes adopted pursuant to Section 1797.184, deny, suspend, or revoke any EMT-I or EMT-II certificate issued under this division, or may place any EMT-I or EMT-II certificate holder on probation, upon the finding by that medical director of the occurrence of any of the actions listed in subdivision (c) and the occurrence of one of the following:

(A) The EMT-I or EMT-II employer, after conducting an investigation, failed to impose discipline for the conduct under investigation, or the medical director makes a determination that the discipline imposed was not according to the guidelines for disciplinary orders and conditions of probation and the conduct of the EMT-I or EMT-II certificate holder constitutes grounds for disciplinary action against the certificate.

(B) Either the employer of an EMT-I or EMT-II further determines, after an investigation conducted under paragraph (1), or the medical director determines after an investigation conducted under paragraph (2), that the conduct requires disciplinary action against the certificate.

(4) The medical director of the local EMS agency, after consultation with the employer of an EMT-I or EMT-II, may temporarily suspend, prior to a hearing, any EMT-I or EMT-II certificate or both EMT-I and EMT-II certificates upon a determination that both of the following conditions have been met:

(A) The certificate holder has engaged in acts or omissions that constitute grounds for revocation of the EMT-I or EMT-II certificate.

(B) Permitting the certificate holder to continue to engage in the certified activity without restriction would pose an imminent threat to the public health or safety.

(5) If the medical director of the local EMS agency temporarily suspends a certificate, the local EMS agency shall notify the certificate holder that his or her EMT-I or EMT-II certificate is suspended and shall identify the reasons therefor. Within three working days of the initiation of the suspension by the local EMS agency, the agency and employer shall jointly investigate the allegation in order for the agency to make a determination of the continuation of the temporary suspension. All investigatory information not otherwise protected by law held by the agency and employer shall be shared between the parties via facsimile transmission or overnight mail relative to the decision to temporarily suspend. The local EMS agency shall decide, within 15 calendar days, whether to serve the certificate holder with an accusation pursuant to Chapter 5 (commencing with Section 11500) of Part 1 of Division 3 of Title 2 of the Government Code. If the certificate holder files a notice of defense, the hearing shall be held within 30 days of the local EMS agency's receipt of the notice of defense. The temporary suspension order shall be deemed vacated if the local EMS agency fails to make a final determination on the merits within 15 days after the administrative law judge renders the proposed decision.

(6) The medical director of the local EMS agency shall refer, for investigation and discipline, any complaint received on an EMT-I or EMT-II to the relevant employer within three days of receipt of the complaint, pursuant to subparagraph (A) of paragraph (1) of subdivision (a).

(b) The authority may deny, suspend, or revoke any EMT-P license issued under this division, or may place any EMT-P license issued under this division, or may place any EMT-P licenseholder on probation upon the finding by the director of the occurrence of any of the actions listed in subdivision (c). Proceedings against any EMT-P license or licenseholder shall be held in accordance with Chapter 5 (commencing with Section 11500) of Part 1 of Division 3 of Title 2 of the Government Code.

(c) Any of the following actions shall be considered evidence of a threat to the public health and safety and may result in the denial, suspension, or revocation of a certificate or license issued under this division, or in the placement on probation of a certificate holder or licenseholder under this division:

(1) Fraud in the procurement of any certificate or license under this division.

(2) Gross negligence.

(3) Repeated negligent acts.

(4) Incompetence.

(5) The commission of any fraudulent, dishonest, or corrupt act that is substantially related to the qualifications, functions, and duties of prehospital personnel.

(6) Conviction of any crime which is substantially related to the qualifications, functions, and duties of prehospital personnel. The record of conviction or a certified copy of the record shall be conclusive evidence of the conviction.

(7) Violating or attempting to violate directly or indirectly, or assisting in or abetting the violation of, or conspiring to violate, any provision of this division or the regulations adopted by the authority pertaining to prehospital personnel.

(8) Violating or attempting to violate any federal or state statute or regulation that regulates narcotics, dangerous drugs, or controlled substances.

(9) Addiction to, the excessive use of, or the misuse of, alcoholic beverages, narcotics, dangerous drugs, or controlled substances.

(10) Functioning outside the supervision of medical control in the field care system operating at the local level, except as authorized by any other license or certification.

(11) Demonstration of irrational behavior or occurrence of a physical disability to the extent that a reasonable and prudent person would have reasonable cause to believe that the ability to perform the duties normally expected may be impaired.

(12) Unprofessional conduct exhibited by any of the following:

(A) The mistreatment or physical abuse of any patient resulting from force in excess of what a reasonable and prudent person trained and acting in a similar capacity while engaged in the performance of his or her duties would use if confronted with a similar circumstance. Nothing in this section shall be deemed to prohibit an EMT-I, EMT-II, or EMT-P from assisting a peace officer, or a peace officer who is acting in the dual capacity of peace officer and EMT-I, EMT-II, or EMT-P, from using that force that is reasonably necessary to effect a lawful arrest or detention.

(B) The failure to maintain confidentiality of patient medical information, except as disclosure is otherwise permitted or required by law in Part 2.6 (commencing with Section 56) of Division 1 of the Civil Code.

(C) The commission of any sexually related offense specified under Section 290 of the Penal Code.

(d) The information shared among EMT-I, EMT-II, and EMT-P employers, medical directors of local EMS agencies, the authority, and EMT-I and EMT-II certifying entities shall be deemed to be an investigative communication that is exempt from public disclosure as a public record pursuant to subdivision (f) of Section 6254 of the Government Code. A formal disciplinary action against an EMT-I, EMT-II, or EMT-P shall be considered a public record available to the public, unless otherwise protected from disclosure pursuant to state or federal law.

(e) For purposes of this section, "disciplinary cause" means an act that is substantially related to the qualifications, functions, and duties of an EMT-I, EMT-II, or EMT-P and is evidence of a threat to the public health and safety described in subdivision (c). (Amended by Stats. 2010, Ch. 328, Sec. 127. (SB 1330) Effective January 1, 2011.)

1798.201.

(a) When information comes to the attention of the medical director of the local EMS agency that an EMT-P licenseholder has committed any act or omission that appears to constitute grounds for disciplinary action under this division, the medical director of the local EMS agency may evaluate the information to determine if there is reason to believe that disciplinary action may be necessary.

(b) If the medical director sends a recommendation to the authority for further investigation or discipline of the licenseholder, the recommendation shall include all documentary evidence collected by the medical director in evaluating whether or not to make that recommendation. The recommendation and accompanying evidence shall be deemed in the nature of an investigative communication and be protected by Section 6254 of the Government Code. In deciding what level of disciplinary action is appropriate in the case, the authority shall consult with the medical director of the local EMS agency. (Added by Stats. 1994, Ch. 709, Sec. 6. Effective January 1, 1995.)

1798.202.

(a) The director of the authority or the medical director of the local EMS agency, after consultation with the relevant employer, may temporarily suspend, prior to hearing, any EMT-P license upon a determination that: (1) the licensee has engaged in acts or omissions that constitute grounds for revocation of the EMT-P license; and (2) permitting the licensee to continue to engage in the licensed activity, or permitting the licensee to continue in the licensed activity without restriction, would present an imminent threat to the public health or safety. When the suspension is initiated by the local EMS agency, subdivision (b) shall apply. When the suspension is initiated by the director of the authority, subdivision (c) shall apply.

(b) The local EMS agency shall notify the licensee that his or her EMT-P license is suspended and shall identify the reasons therefor. Within three working days of the initiation of the suspension by the local EMS agency, the agency shall transmit to the authority, via facsimile transmission or overnight mail, all documentary evidence collected by the local EMS agency relative to the decision to temporarily suspend. Within two working days of receipt of the local EMS agency's documentary evidence, the director of the authority shall determine the need for the licensure action. Part of that determination shall include an evaluation of the need for continuance of the suspension during the licensure action review process. If the director of the authority determines that the temporary suspension order should not continue, the authority shall immediately notify the licensee that the temporary suspension is lifted. If the director of the authority determines that the temporary suspension order should continue, the authority shall immediately notify the licensee of the decision to continue the temporary suspension and shall, within 15 calendar days of receipt of the EMS agency's documentary evidence, serve the licensee with a temporary suspension order and accusation pursuant to Chapter 5 (commencing with Section 11500) of Part 1 of Division 3 of Title 2 of the Government Code.

(c) The director of the authority shall initiate a temporary suspension with the filing of a temporary suspension order and accusation pursuant to Chapter 5 (commencing with

Section 11500) of Part 1 of Division 3 of Title 2 of the Government Code and shall notify the director of the local EMS agency, and the relevant employer.

(d) If the licensee files a notice of defense, the hearing shall be held within 30 days of the authority's receipt of the notice of defense. The temporary suspension order shall be deemed vacated if the authority fails to make a final determination on the merits within 15 days after the administrative law judge renders the proposed decision.

(Repealed and added by Stats. 1994, Ch. 709, Sec. 8. Effective January 1, 1995.)
1798.204.

Proceedings for probation, suspension, revocation, or denial of a certificate, or a denial of a renewal of a certificate, under this division shall be conducted in accordance with guidelines established by the Emergency Medical Services Authority.

(Amended by Stats. 1986, Ch. 248, Sec. 135.)
1798.205.

Any alleged violations of local EMS agency transfer protocols, guidelines, or agreements shall be evaluated by the local EMS agency. If the local EMS agency has concluded that a violation has occurred, it shall take whatever corrective action it deems appropriate within its jurisdiction, including referrals to the district attorney under Sections 1798.206 and 1798.208 and shall notify the State Department of Health Services if it concludes that any violation of Sections 1317 to 1317.9a, inclusive, has occurred.

(Added by Stats. 1987, Ch. 1240, Sec. 18.)
1798.206.

Any person who violates this part, the rules and regulations adopted pursuant thereto, or county ordinances adopted pursuant to this part governing patient transfers, is guilty of a misdemeanor. The Attorney General or the district attorney may prosecute any of these misdemeanors which falls within his or her jurisdiction.

(Amended by Stats. 1987, Ch. 1225, Sec. 17.)
1798.207.

(a) It is a misdemeanor for any person to knowingly and willfully engage in conduct that subverts or attempts to subvert any licensing or certification examination, or the administration of any licensing or certification examination, conducted pursuant to this division, including, but not limited to, any of the following:

(1) Conduct that violates the security of the examination material.

(2) Removing from the examination room any examination materials without authorization.

(3) The unauthorized reproduction by any means of any portion of the actual licensing or certification examination.

(4) Aiding by any means the unauthorized reproduction of any portion of the actual licensing or certification examination.

(5) Paying or using professional or paid examination-takers, for the purpose of reconstructing any portion of the licensing or certification examination.

(6) Obtaining or attempting to obtain examination questions or other examination material from examinees or by any other method, except by specific authorization either before, during, or after an examination.

(7) Using or purporting to use any examination questions or materials that were improperly removed or taken from any examination for the purpose of instructing or preparing any applicant for examination.

(8) Selling, distributing, buying, receiving, or having unauthorized possession of any portion of a future, current, or previously administered licensing or certification examination.

(9) Communicating with any other examinee during the administration of a licensing or certification examination.

(10) Copying answers from another examinee or permitting one's answers to be copied by another examinee.

(11) Having in one's possession during the administration of the licensing or certification examination any books, equipment, notes written or printed materials, or data of any kind, other than the examination materials distributed, or otherwise authorized to be in one's possession during the examination.

(12) Impersonating any examinee or having an impersonator take the licensing or certification examination on one's behalf.

(b) The penalties provided in this section are not exclusive remedies and shall not preclude remedies provided pursuant to any other provision of law.

(c) In addition to any other penalties, a person found guilty of violating this section shall be liable for the actual damages sustained by the agency administering the examination not to exceed ten thousand dollars ($10,000) and the costs of litigation.

(Added by Stats. 1992, Ch. 215, Sec. 1. Effective January 1, 1993.)
1798.208.

Whenever any person who has engaged, or is about to engage, in any act or practice which constitutes, or will constitute, a violation of any provision of this division, the rules and regulations promulgated pursuant thereto, or local EMS agency mandated protocols, guidelines, or transfer agreements, the superior court in and for the county wherein the acts or practices take place or are about to take place may issue an injunction or other appropriate order restraining the conduct on application of the authority, the Attorney General, or the district attorney of the county. The proceedings under this section shall be governed by Chapter 3 (commencing with Section 525) of Title 7 of Part 2 of the Code of Civil Procedure, except that no undertaking shall be required.

(Amended by Stats. 1987, Ch. 1240, Sec. 19.)
1798.209.

The local EMS agency may place on probation, suspend, or revoke the approval under this division of any training program for failure to comply with this division or any rules or regulations adopted pursuant thereto.

(Added by Stats. 1994, Ch. 709, Sec. 9. Effective January 1, 1995.)
1798.210.

(a) The authority may impose an administrative fine of up to two thousand five hundred dollars ($2,500) per violation on any licensed paramedic found to have committed any of the actions described by subdivision (c) of Section 1798.200 that did not result in actual harm to a patient. Fines may not be imposed if a paramedic has previously been disciplined by the authority for any other act committed within the immediately preceding five-year period.

(b) The authority shall adopt regulations establishing an administrative fine structure, taking into account the nature and gravity of the violation. The administrative fine shall not be imposed in conjunction with a suspension for the same violation, but may be imposed in conjunction with probation for the same violation except when the conditions of the probation require a paramedic's personal time or expense for training, clinical observation, or related corrective instruction.

(c) In assessing the fine, the authority shall give due consideration to the appropriateness of the amount of the fine with respect to factors that include the gravity of the violation, the good faith of the paramedic, the history of previous violations, any discipline imposed by the paramedic's employer for the same occurrence of that conduct, as reported pursuant to Section 1799.112, and the totality of the discipline to be imposed. The imposition of the fine shall be subject to the administrative adjudication provisions set forth in Chapter 5 (commencing with Section 11500) of Part 1 of Division 3 of Title 2 of the Government Code.

(d) If a paramedic does not pay the administrative fine imposed by the authority and chooses not to renew his or her license, the authority may enforce the order for repayment in any appropriate court. This right of enforcement shall be in addition to any other rights the authority may have to require a paramedic to pay costs.

(e) In any action for collection of an administrative fine, proof of the authority's decision shall be conclusive proof of the validity of the order of payment and the terms for payment.

(f) (1) Except as provided in paragraph (2), the authority shall not license or renew the license of any paramedic who has failed to pay an administrative fine ordered under this section.

(2) The authority may, in its discretion, conditionally license or renew for a maximum of one year the license of any paramedic who demonstrates financial hardship and who enters into a formal agreement with the authority to reimburse the authority within that one-year period for the unpaid fine.

(g) All funds recovered under this section shall be deposited into the state General Fund.

(h) Nothing in this section shall preclude the authority from imposing an administrative fine in any stipulated settlement.

(i) For purposes of this section, "licensed paramedic" includes a paramedic whose license has lapsed or has been surrendered.

(Added by Stats. 2004, Ch. 513, Sec. 1. Effective January 1, 2005.)
1798.211.

When making a decision regarding a disciplinary action pursuant to Section 1798.200 or Section 1798.210, the authority, and when applicable the administrative law judge, shall give credit for discipline imposed by the employer and for any immediate suspension imposed by the local EMS agency for the same conduct.

(Added by Stats. 2004, Ch. 513, Sec. 2. Effective January 1, 2005.)

CHAPTER 8. The Commission on Emergency Medical Services [1799 - 1799.56]

(Chapter 8 added by Stats. 1980, Ch. 1260.)

ARTICLE 1. The Commission [1799 - 1799.8]

(Article 1 added by Stats. 1980, Ch. 1260.)

1799.

The Commission on Emergency Medical Services is hereby created in the California Health and Human Services Agency.

(Amended by Stats. 2008, Ch. 275, Sec. 3. Effective January 1, 2009.)
1799.2.

The commission shall consist of 18 members appointed as follows:

(a) One full-time physician and surgeon, whose primary practice is emergency medicine, appointed by the Senate Committee on Rules from a list of three names submitted by the California Chapter of the American College of Emergency Physicians.

(b) One physician and surgeon, who is a trauma surgeon, appointed by the Speaker of the Assembly from a list of three names submitted by the California Chapter of the American College of Surgeons.

(c) One physician and surgeon appointed by the Senate Committee on Rules from a list of three names submitted by the California Medical Association.

(d) One county health officer appointed by the Governor from a list of three names submitted by the California Conference of Local Health Officers.

(e) One registered nurse, who is currently, or has been previously, authorized as a mobile intensive care nurse and who is knowledgeable in state emergency medical services programs and issues, appointed by the Governor from a list of three names submitted by the Emergency Nurses Association.

(f) One full-time paramedic or EMT-II, who is not employed as a full-time peace officer, appointed by the Senate Committee on Rules from a list of three names submitted by the California Rescue and Paramedic Association.

(g) One prehospital emergency medical service provider from the private sector, appointed by the Speaker of the Assembly from a list of three names submitted by the California Ambulance Association.

(h) One management member of an entity providing fire protection and prevention services appointed by the Governor from a list of three names submitted by the California Fire Chiefs Association.

(i) One physician and surgeon who is board prepared or board certified in the specialty of emergency medicine by the American Board of Emergency Medicine and who is knowledgeable in state emergency medical services programs and issues appointed by the Speaker of the Assembly.

(j) One hospital administrator of a base hospital who is appointed by the Governor from a list of three names submitted by the California Association of Hospitals and Health Systems.

(k) One full-time peace officer, who is either an EMT-II or a paramedic, who is appointed by the Governor from a list of three names submitted by the California Peace Officers Association.

(l) Two public members who have experience in local EMS policy issues, at least one of whom resides in a rural area as defined by the authority, and who are appointed by the Governor.

(m) One administrator from a local EMS agency appointed by the Governor from a list of four names submitted by the Emergency Medical Services Administrator's Association of California.

(n) One medical director of a local EMS agency who is an active member of the Emergency Medical Directors Association of California and who is appointed by the Governor.

(o) One person appointed by the Governor, who is an active member of the California State Firemen's Association.

(p) One person who is employed by the Department of Forestry and Fire Protection (CAL-FIRE) appointed by the Governor from a list of three names submitted by the California Professional Firefighters.

(q) One person who is employed by a city, county, or special district that provides fire protection appointed by the Governor from a list of three names submitted by the California Professional Firefighters.

(Amended by Stats. 2008, Ch. 275, Sec. 4. Effective January 1, 2009.)

1799.3.

At the discretion of the appointing power or body, a member of the commission may be reappointed or may continue to serve if he or she no longer continues to function in the capacity which originally qualified him or her for appointment. However, where Section 1799.2 requires that an appropriate organization submit names to the appointing power or body, a person shall not be reappointed pursuant to this section unless his or her name is submitted by that appropriate organization.

(Added by Stats. 1985, Ch. 42, Sec. 2. Effective May 15, 1985.)

1799.4.

(a) Except as otherwise provided in this section, the terms of the members of the commission shall be three calendar years, commencing January 1 of the year of appointment. No member shall serve more than two consecutive full terms; provided, however, that a term or part of a term served pursuant to paragraph (1) or (2) of subdivision (b) shall not be included in this limitation.

(b) (1) The first members appointed on or after January 1, 1985, pursuant to subdivisions (a), (b), (c), and (d) of Section 1799.2 shall serve from the date of appointment to the end of that calendar year, plus one additional year.

(2) The first members appointed on or after January 1, 1985, pursuant to subdivisions (e), (f), (g), (h), and (i) of Section 1799.2 shall serve from the date of appointment to the end of that calendar year, plus two additional years.

(3) The first members appointed on or after January 1, 1985, pursuant to subdivisions (j), (k), and (m) of Section 1799.2 shall be from the date of appointment to the end of that calendar year, plus three additional years.

(4) The first member appointed on or after January 1, 1985, pursuant to subdivision (l) of Section 1799.2 shall serve from the date of appointment to the end of that calendar year, plus one additional year, and the second member shall serve from the date of appointment to the end of that calendar year, plus two additional years.

(5) The first member appointed pursuant to subdivision (n) of Section 1799.2 shall serve from the date of appointment to the end of the 1991 calendar year.

(6) It is the purpose of this subdivision to provide for staggered terms for the members of the commission.

(Amended by Stats. 1987, Ch. 1102, Sec. 3.)

1799.6.

The members of the commission shall receive no compensation for their services, but shall be reimbursed for their actual, necessary, traveling and other expenses incurred in the discharge of their duties.

(Added by Stats. 1980, Ch. 1260.)

1799.8.

The commission shall select a chairperson from its members and shall meet at least quarterly on the call of the director, the chairperson, or three members of the commission.

(Added by Stats. 1980, Ch. 1260.)

ARTICLE 2. Duties of the Commission [1799.50 - 1799.56]

(Article 2 added by Stats. 1980, Ch. 1260.)

1799.50.

The commission shall review and approve regulations, standards, and guidelines to be developed by the authority for implementation of this division.

(Amended by Stats. 1986, Ch. 248, Sec. 138.)

1799.51.

The commission shall advise the authority on the development of an emergency medical data collection system.

(Added by Stats. 1980, Ch. 1260.)

1799.52.

The commission shall advise the director concerning the assessment of emergency facilities and services.

(Added by Stats. 1980, Ch. 1260.)

1799.53.

The commission shall advise the director with regard to communications, medical equipment, training personnel, facilities, and other components of an emergency medical services system.

(Added by Stats. 1980, Ch. 1260.)

1799.54.

The commission shall review and comment upon the emergency medical services portion of the State Health Facilities and Service Plan developed pursuant to Section 127155.

(Amended by Stats. 1996, Ch. 1023, Sec. 175. Effective September 29, 1996.)

1799.55.

Based upon evaluations of the EMS systems in the state and their coordination, the commission shall make recommendations for further development and future directions of the emergency medical services in the state.

(Added by Stats. 1980, Ch. 1260.)

1799.56.

The commission may utilize technical advisory panels established pursuant to the provisions of Section 1797.133 as are needed to assist in developing standards for emergency medical services.

(Added by Stats. 1980, Ch. 1260.)

CHAPTER 9. Liability Limitation [1799.100 - 1799.112]

(Chapter 9 added by Stats. 1980, Ch. 1260.)

1799.100.

In order to encourage local agencies and other organizations to train people in emergency medical services, no local agency, entity of state or local government, private business or nonprofit organization included on the statewide registry that voluntarily and without expectation and receipt of compensation donates services, goods, labor, equipment, resources, or dispensaries or other facilities, in compliance with Section 8588.2 of the Government Code, or other public or private organization which sponsors, authorizes, supports, finances, or supervises the training of people, or certifies those people, excluding physicians and surgeons, registered nurses, and licensed vocational nurses, as defined, in emergency medical services, shall be liable for any civil damages alleged to result from those training programs.

(Amended by Stats. 2008, Ch. 363, Sec. 3. Effective January 1, 2009.)

1799.102.

(a) No person who in good faith, and not for compensation, renders emergency medical or nonmedical care at the scene of an emergency shall be liable for any civil damages resulting from any act or omission. The scene of an emergency shall not include emergency departments and other places where medical care is usually offered. This subdivision applies only to the medical, law enforcement, and emergency personnel specified in this chapter.

(b) (1) It is the intent of the Legislature to encourage other individuals to volunteer, without compensation, to assist others in need during an emergency, while ensuring that those volunteers who provide care or assistance act responsibly.

(2) Except for those persons specified in subdivision (a), no person who in good faith, and not for compensation, renders emergency medical or nonmedical care or assistance at the scene of an emergency shall be liable for civil damages resulting from any act or omission other than an act or omission constituting gross negligence or willful or wanton misconduct. The scene of an emergency shall not include emergency departments and other places where medical care is usually offered. This subdivision shall not be construed to alter existing protections from liability for licensed medical or other personnel specified in subdivision (a) or any other law.

(c) Nothing in this section shall be construed to change any existing legal duties or obligations, nor does anything in this section in any way affect the provisions in Section 1714.5 of the Civil Code, as proposed to be amended by Senate Bill 39 of the 2009–10 Regular Session of the Legislature.

(d) The amendments to this section made by the act adding subdivisions (b) and (c) shall apply exclusively to any legal action filed on or after the effective date of that act.

(Amended by Stats. 2009, Ch. 77, Sec. 1. Effective August 6, 2009. Note: As referenced in subd. (d), subds. (b) and (c) were added in the amendment by Stats. 2009, Ch. 77.)

1799.103.

(a) An employer shall not adopt or enforce a policy prohibiting an employee from voluntarily providing emergency medical services, including, but not limited to, cardiopulmonary resuscitation, in response to a medical emergency, except as provided in subdivisions (b) and (c).

(b) Notwithstanding subdivision (a), an employer may adopt and enforce a policy authorizing employees trained in emergency services to provide those services. However, in the event of an emergency, any available employee may voluntarily provide emergency medical services if a trained and authorized employee is not immediately available or is otherwise unable or unwilling to provide emergency medical services.

(c) Notwithstanding subdivision (a), an employer may adopt and enforce a policy prohibiting an employee from performing emergency medical services, including, but not limited to, cardiopulmonary resuscitation, on a person who has expressed the desire to forgo resuscitation or other medical interventions through any legally recognized means, including, but not limited to, a do-not-resuscitate order, a Physician Orders for Life Sustaining Treatment form, an advance health care directive, or a legally recognized health care decisionmaker.

(d) This section does not impose any express or implied duty on an employer to train its employees regarding emergency medical services or cardiopulmonary resuscitation.
(Added by Stats. 2013, Ch. 591, Sec. 1. (AB 633) Effective January 1, 2014.)
1799.104.

(a) No physician or nurse, who in good faith gives emergency instructions to an EMT-II or mobile intensive care paramedic at the scene of an emergency, shall be liable for any civil damages as a result of issuing the instructions.

(b) No EMT-II or mobile intensive care paramedic rendering care within the scope of his duties who, in good faith and in a nonnegligent manner, follows the instructions of a physician or nurse shall be liable for any civil damages as a result of following such instructions.
(Added by Stats. 1980, Ch. 1260.)
1799.105.

(a) A poison control center which (1) meets the minimum standards for designation and operation established by the authority pursuant to Section 1798.180, (2) has been designated a regional poison control center by the authority, and (3) provides information and advice for no charge on the management of exposures to poisonous or toxic substances, shall be immune from liability in civil damages with respect to the emergency provision of that information or advice, for acts or omissions by its medical director, poison information specialist, or poison information provider as provided in subdivisions (b) and (c).

(b) Any poison information specialist or poison information provider who provides emergency information and advice on the management of exposures to poisonous or toxic substances, through, and in accordance with, protocols approved by the medical director of a poison control center specified in subdivision (a), shall only be liable in civil damages, with respect to the emergency provision of that information or advice, for acts or omissions performed in a grossly negligent manner or acts or omissions not performed in good faith. This subdivision shall not be construed to immunize the negligent adoption of a protocol.

(c) The medical director of a poison control center specified in subdivision (a) who provides emergency information and advice on the management of exposures to poisonous or toxic substances, where the exposure is not covered by an approved protocol, shall be liable only in civil damages, with respect to the emergency provision of that information or advice, for acts or omissions performed in a grossly negligent manner or acts or omissions not performed in good faith. This subdivision shall neither be construed to immunize the negligent failure to adopt adequate approved protocols nor to confer liability upon the medical director for failing to develop or approve a protocol when the development of a protocol for a specific situation is not practical or the situation could not have been reasonably foreseen.
(Added by Stats. 1988, Ch. 1192, Sec. 1.)
1799.106.

(a) In addition to the provisions of Section 1799.104 of this code, Section 2727.5 of the Business and Professions Code, and Section 1714.2 of the Civil Code, and in order to encourage the provision of emergency medical services by firefighters, police officers or other law enforcement officers, EMT-I, EMT-II, EMT-P, or registered nurses, a firefighter, police officer or other law enforcement officer, EMT-I, EMT-II, EMT-P, or registered nurse who renders emergency medical services at the scene of an emergency or during an emergency air or ground ambulance transport shall only be liable in civil damages for acts or omissions performed in a grossly negligent manner or acts or omissions not performed in good faith. A public agency employing such a firefighter, police officer or other law enforcement officer, EMT-I, EMT-II, EMT-P, or registered nurse shall not be liable for civil damages if the firefighter, police officer or other law enforcement officer, EMT-I, EMT-II, EMT-P, or registered nurse is not liable.

(b) For purposes of this section, "registered nurse" means a registered nurse trained in emergency medical services and licensed pursuant to Chapter 6 (commencing with Section 2700) of Division 2 of the Business and Professions Code.
(Amended by Stats. 2012, Ch. 69, Sec. 2. (SB 1365) Effective January 1, 2013.)
1799.107.

(a) The Legislature finds and declares that a threat to the public health and safety exists whenever there is a need for emergency services and that public entities and emergency rescue personnel should be encouraged to provide emergency services. To that end, a qualified immunity from liability shall be provided for public entities and emergency rescue personnel providing emergency services.

(b) Except as provided in Article 1 (commencing with Section 17000) of Chapter 1 of Division 9 of the Vehicle Code, neither a public entity nor emergency rescue personnel shall be liable for any injury caused by an action taken by the emergency rescue personnel acting within the scope of their employment to provide emergency services, unless the action taken was performed in bad faith or in a grossly negligent manner.

(c) For purposes of this section, it shall be presumed that the action taken when providing emergency services was performed in good faith and without gross negligence. This presumption shall be one affecting the burden of proof.

(d) For purposes of this section, "emergency rescue personnel" means any person who is an officer, employee, or member of a fire department or fire protection or firefighting agency of the federal government, the State of California, a city, county, city and county, district, or other public or municipal corporation or political subdivision of this state, or of a private fire department, whether that person is a volunteer or partly paid or fully paid, while he or she is actually engaged in providing emergency services as defined by subdivision (e).

(e) For purposes of this section, "emergency services" includes, but is not limited to, first aid and medical services, rescue procedures and transportation, or other related activities necessary to insure the health or safety of a person in imminent peril.
(Amended by Stats. 1998, Ch. 617, Sec. 1. Effective January 1, 1999.)
1799.108.

Any person who has a certificate issued pursuant to this division from a certifying agency to provide prehospital emergency field care treatment at the scene of an emergency, as defined in Section 1799.102, shall be liable for civil damages only for acts or omissions performed in a grossly negligent manner or acts or omissions not performed in good faith.
(Amended by Stats. 1986, Ch. 248, Sec. 139.)
1799.109.

(a) The Legislature finds and declares all of the following:

(1) California residents receive comfort and unconditional love on a daily basis from their household pets, particularly dogs and cats.

(2) California residents benefit from the special support, comfort, guidance, companionship, and therapy provided by dogs and cats.

(3) Pets provide critical support to many California residents with disabilities.

(4) Pets provide assistance and aid in the official duties of military personnel, peace officers, law enforcement agencies, fire departments, and search-and-rescue agencies.

(5) Personnel of some fire districts and other first responder agencies currently provide stabilizing, life-saving emergency care to dogs and cats, which violates the Veterinary Medicine Practice Act.

(6) In enacting this section, it is the intent of the Legislature to authorize emergency responders to provide, on a voluntary basis, basic first aid to dogs and cats without exposure to criminal prosecution or professional discipline for the unlawful practice of veterinary medicine.

(b) Notwithstanding the Veterinary Medicine Practice Act, as set forth in Chapter 11 (commencing with Section 4800) of Division 2 of the Business and Professions Code, an emergency responder may provide basic first aid to dogs and cats to the extent that the provision of that care is not prohibited by the responder's employer, and the responder shall not be subject to criminal prosecution for a violation of Section 4831 of the Business and Professions Code.

(c) Civil liability for a person who provides care to a pet or other domesticated animal during an emergency is governed by the following:

(1) Section 4826.1 of the Business and Professions Code governs care provided by a veterinarian.

(2) Subdivision (a) of Section 1799.102 governs care provided by an emergency responder, or law enforcement and emergency personnel specified in this chapter.

(3) Subdivision (b) of Section 1799.102 governs care provided by any person other than an individual described in paragraph (1) or (2).

(d) Notwithstanding any other law, this section does not impose a duty or obligation upon an emergency responder or any other person to transport or provide care to an injured pet or other domesticated animal during an emergency.

(e) For purposes of this section, the following definitions apply:

(1) "Cat" means a small domesticated feline animal that is kept as a pet. "Cat" does not include nondomesticated wild animals.

(2) "Dog" means a domesticated canine animal owned for companionship, service, therapeutic, or assistance purposes.

(3) "Emergency responder" means a person who is certified or licensed to provide emergency medical services.

(4) "Employer" means an entity or organization that employs or enlists the services of an emergency responder.

(5) "Basic first aid to dogs and cats" means providing immediate medical care to a dog or cat by an emergency responder, in an emergency situation to which the emergency responder is responding, that is intended to stabilize the dog or cat so that the dog or cat can be transported by the owner as soon as practical to a veterinarian for treatment and which is provided through the following means:

(A) Administering oxygen.

(B) Managing ventilation by mask.

(C) Manually clearing the upper airway, not including tracheal intubation or surgical procedures.

(D) Controlling hemorrhage with direct pressure.

(E) Bandaging for the purpose of stopping bleeding.

(f) This section does not require or authorize the provision of emergency services to dogs or cats in response to a telephone call to the 911 emergency system and is not a basis for liability for the failure to provide emergency services to dogs or cats in response to a telephone call to the 911 emergency system.
(Added by Stats. 2018, Ch. 900, Sec. 1. (SB 1305) Effective January 1, 2019.)
1799.110.

(a) In any action for damages involving a claim of negligence against a physician and surgeon arising out of emergency medical services provided in a general acute care hospital emergency department, the trier of fact shall consider, together with all other relevant matters, the circumstances constituting the emergency, as defined herein, and the degree of care and skill ordinarily exercised by reputable members of the physician and surgeon's profession in the same or similar locality, in like cases, and under similar emergency circumstances.

(b) For the purposes of this section, "emergency medical services" and "emergency medical care" means those medical services required for the immediate diagnosis and treatment of medical conditions which, if not immediately diagnosed and treated, could lead to serious physical or mental disability or death.

(c) In any action for damages involving a claim of negligence against a physician and surgeon providing emergency medical coverage for a general acute care hospital emergency department, the court shall admit expert medical testimony only from physicians and surgeons who have had substantial professional experience within the last five years while assigned to provide emergency medical coverage in a general acute care hospital emergency department. For purposes of this section, "substantial professional experience" shall be determined by the custom and practice of the manner in which emergency medical coverage is provided in general acute care hospital emergency departments in the same or similar localities where the alleged negligence occured.
(Added by Stats. 1983, Ch. 1246, Sec. 41.)

1799.111.

(a) Subject to subdivision (b), a licensed general acute care hospital, as defined in subdivision (a) of Section 1250, that is not a county-designated facility pursuant to Section 5150 of the Welfare and Institutions Code, a licensed acute psychiatric hospital, as defined in subdivision (b) of Section 1250, that is not a county-designated facility pursuant to Section 5150 of the Welfare and Institutions Code, licensed professional staff of those hospitals, or any physician and surgeon, providing emergency medical services in any department of those hospitals to a person at the hospital shall not be civilly or criminally liable for detaining a person if all of the following conditions exist during the detention:

(1) The person cannot be safely released from the hospital because, in the opinion of the treating physician and surgeon, or a clinical psychologist with the medical staff privileges, clinical privileges, or professional responsibilities provided in Section 1316.5, the person, as a result of a mental disorder, presents a danger to himself or herself, or others, or is gravely disabled. For purposes of this paragraph, "gravely disabled" means an inability to provide for his or her basic personal needs for food, clothing, or shelter.

(2) The hospital staff, treating physician and surgeon, or appropriate licensed mental health professional, have made, and documented, repeated unsuccessful efforts to find appropriate mental health treatment for the person.

(A) Telephone calls or other contacts required pursuant to this paragraph shall commence at the earliest possible time when the treating physician and surgeon has determined the time at which the person will be medically stable for transfer.

(B) In no case shall the contacts required pursuant to this paragraph begin after the time when the person becomes medically stable for transfer.

(3) The person is not detained beyond 24 hours.

(4) There is probable cause for the detention.

(b) If the person is detained pursuant to subdivision (a) beyond eight hours, but less than 24 hours, both of the following additional conditions shall be met:

(1) A discharge or transfer for appropriate evaluation or treatment for the person has been delayed because of the need for continuous and ongoing care, observation, or treatment that the hospital is providing.

(2) In the opinion of the treating physician and surgeon, or a clinical psychologist with the medical staff privileges or professional responsibilities provided for in Section 1316.5, the person, as a result of a mental disorder, is still a danger to himself or herself, or others, or is gravely disabled, as defined in paragraph (1) of subdivision (a).

(c) In addition to the immunities set forth in subdivision (a), a licensed general acute care hospital, as defined in subdivision (a) of Section 1250 that is not a county-designated facility pursuant to Section 5150 of the Welfare and Institutions Code, a licensed acute psychiatric hospital as defined by subdivision (b) of Section 1250 that is not a county-designated facility pursuant to Section 5150 of the Welfare and Institutions Code, licensed professional staff of those hospitals, or any physician and surgeon, providing emergency medical services in any department of those hospitals to a person at the hospital shall not be civilly or criminally liable for the actions of a person detained up to 24 hours in those hospitals who is subject to detention pursuant to subdivision (a) after that person's release from the detention at the hospital, if all of the following conditions exist during the detention:

(1) The person has not been admitted to a licensed general acute care hospital or a licensed acute psychiatric hospital for evaluation and treatment pursuant to Section 5150 of the Welfare and Institutions Code.

(2) The release from the licensed general acute care hospital or the licensed acute psychiatric hospital is authorized by a physician and surgeon or a clinical psychologist with the medical staff privileges or professional responsibilities provided for in Section 1316.5, who determines, based on a face-to-face examination of the person detained, that the person does not present a danger to himself or herself or others and is not gravely disabled, as defined in paragraph (1) of subdivision (a). In order for this paragraph to apply to a clinical psychologist, the clinical psychologist shall have a collaborative treatment relationship with the physician and surgeon. The clinical psychologist may authorize the release of the person from the detention, but only after he or she has consulted with the physician and surgeon. In the event of a clinical or

professional disagreement regarding the release of a person subject to the detention, the detention shall be maintained unless the hospital's medical director overrules the decision of the physician and surgeon opposing the release. Both the physician and surgeon and the clinical psychologist shall enter their findings, concerns, or objections in the person's medical record.

(d) Nothing in this section shall affect the responsibility of a general acute care hospital or an acute psychiatric hospital to comply with all state laws and regulations pertaining to the use of seclusion and restraint and psychiatric medications for psychiatric patients. Persons detained under this section shall retain their legal rights regarding consent for medical treatment.

(e) A person detained under this section shall be credited for the time detained, up to 24 hours, in the event he or she is placed on a subsequent 72-hour hold pursuant to Section 5150 of the Welfare and Institutions Code.

(f) The amendments to this section made by the act adding this subdivision shall not be construed to limit any existing duties for psychotherapists contained in Section 43.92 of the Civil Code.

(g) Nothing in this section is intended to expand the scope of licensure of clinical psychologists.
(Amended by Stats. 2009, Ch. 612, Sec. 1. (SB 743) Effective January 1, 2010.)

1799.112.

(a) EMT-P employers shall report in writing to the local EMS agency medical director and the authority and provide all supporting documentation within 30 days of whenever any of the following actions are taken:

(1) An EMT-P is terminated or suspended for disciplinary cause or reason.

(2) An EMT-P resigns following notice of an impending investigation based upon evidence indicating disciplinary cause or reason.

(3) An EMT-P is removed from paramedic duties for disciplinary cause or reason following the completion of an internal investigation.

(b) The reporting requirements of subdivision (a) do not require or authorize the release of information or records of an EMT-P who is also a peace officer protected by Section 832.7 of the Penal Code.

(c) For purposes of this section, "disciplinary cause or reason" means only an action that is substantially related to the qualifications, functions, and duties of a paramedic and is considered evidence of a threat to the public health and safety as identified in subdivision (c) of Section 1798.200.

(d) Pursuant to subdivision (i) of Section 1798.24 of the Civil Code, upon notification to the paramedic, the authority may share the results of its investigation into a paramedic's misconduct with the paramedic's employer, prospective employer when requested in writing as part of a preemployment background check, and the local EMS agency.

(e) The information reported or disclosed in this section shall be deemed in the nature of an investigative communication and is exempt from disclosure as a public record by subdivision (f) of Section 6254 of the Government Code.

(f) A paramedic applicant or licensee to whom the information pertains may view the contents, as set forth in subdivision (a) of Section 1798.24 of the Civil Code, of a closed investigation file upon request during the regular business hours of the authority.
(Added by Stats. 2004, Ch. 513, Sec. 3. Effective January 1, 2005.)

CHAPTER 11. Emergency and Critical Care Services for Children [1799.200 - 1799.201]

(Chapter 11 added by Stats. 1989, Ch. 1206, Sec. 2.)

1799.200.

(a) The State Department of Health Services shall contract with an organization with expertise in program evaluation, pediatric emergency medical services, and critical care, for the purposes specified in subdivision (b).

(b) The contractor, in consultation with a professional pediatric association, a professional emergency physicians association, a professional emergency medical services medical directors association, the Emergency Medical Services Authority, and the State Department of Health Services, shall perform a study that will identify the outcome criteria which can be used to evaluate pediatric critical care systems. This study shall include, but not be limited to, all of the following:

(1) Development of criteria to identify how changes in pediatric critical care systems affect the treatment of critically ill and injured children.

(2) Development of criteria to compare the systems in place in various areas of the state.

(3) Determination of whether the necessary data is currently available.

(4) Estimate of the cost to providers, such as emergency medical service agencies and hospitals, of collecting this data.

(5) Recommendations concerning the most reliable and cost-effective monitoring plan for use by agencies and facilities at the state, regional, and local levels.
(Added by renumbering Section 1199.200 by Stats. 1991, Ch. 1091, Sec. 68.)

1799.201.

The contractor shall submit the results of the study to the Legislature and the Governor not later than January 1, 1991.
(Added by renumbering Section 1199.201 by Stats. 1991, Ch. 1091, Sec. 69.)

CHAPTER 12. Emergency Medical Services System for Children [1799.202 - 1799.207]

(Chapter 12 added by Stats. 1996, Ch. 197, Sec. 3.)

1799.202.

This chapter shall be known and may be cited as the California Emergency Medical Services for Children Act of 1996.

(Added by Stats. 1996, Ch. 197, Sec. 3. Effective July 22, 1996.)

1799.204.

(a) For purposes of this chapter, the following definitions apply:

(1) "EMSC Program" means the Emergency Medical Services For Children Program administered by the authority.

(2) "Technical advisory committee" means a multidisciplinary committee with pediatric emergency medical services, pediatric critical care, or other related expertise.

(3) "EMSC component" means the part of the local agency's EMS plan that outlines the training, transportation, basic and advanced life support care requirements, and emergency department and hospital pediatric capabilities within a local jurisdiction.

(b) Contingent upon available funding, an Emergency Medical Services For Children Program is hereby established within the authority.

(c) The authority shall do the following to implement the EMSC Program:

(1) Employ or contract with professional, technical, research, and clerical staff as necessary to implement this chapter.

(2) Provide advice and technical assistance to local EMS agencies on the integration of an EMSC Program into their EMS system.

(3) Oversee implementation of the EMSC Program by local EMS agencies.

(4) Establish an EMSC technical advisory committee.

(5) Facilitate cooperative interstate relationships to provide appropriate care for pediatric patients who must cross state borders to receive emergency and critical care services.

(6) Work cooperatively and in a coordinated manner with the State Department of Health Services and other public and private agencies in the development of standards and policies for the delivery of emergency and critical care services to children.

(7) On or before March 1, 2000, produce a report for the Legislature describing any progress on implementation of this chapter. The report shall contain, but not be limited to, a description of the status of emergency medical services for children at both the state and local levels, the recommendation for training, protocols, and special medical equipment for emergency services for children, an estimate of the costs and benefits of the services and programs authorized by this chapter, and a calculation of the number of children served by the EMSC system.

(Amended by Stats. 2001, Ch. 171, Sec. 3. Effective August 10, 2001.)

1799.205.

A local EMS agency may develop an EMSC Program in its jurisdiction, contingent upon available funding. If a local EMS agency develops an EMSC Program in its jurisdiction, the local EMS agency shall develop and incorporate in its EMS plan an EMSC component that complies with EMS plan requirements. The EMSC component shall include, but need not be limited to, the following:

(a) EMSC system planning, implementation, and management.

(b) Injury and illness prevention planning, that includes, among other things, coordination, education, and data collection.

(c) Care rendered to patients outside the hospital.

(d) Emergency department care.

(e) Interfacility consultation, transfer, and transport.

(f) Pediatric critical care and pediatric trauma services.

(g) General trauma centers with pediatric considerations.

(h) Pediatric rehabilitation plans that include, among other things, data collection and evaluation, education on early detection of need for referral, and proper referral of pediatric patients.

(i) Children with special EMS needs outside the hospital.

(j) Information management and system evaluation.

(Added by Stats. 1996, Ch. 197, Sec. 3. Effective July 22, 1996.)

1799.207.

The authority may solicit and accept grant funding from public and private sources to supplement state funds.

(Added by Stats. 1996, Ch. 197, Sec. 3. Effective July 22, 1996.)

DIVISION 3. PEST ABATEMENT [2000 - 2910]

(Heading of Division 3 amended by Stats. 1957, Ch. 205.)

CHAPTER 1. Mosquito Abatement and Vector Control Districts [2000 - 2093]

(Chapter 1 added by Stats. 2002, Ch. 395, Sec. 6.)

ARTICLE 1. General Provisions [2000 - 2007]

(Article 1 added by Stats. 2002, Ch. 395, Sec. 6.)

2000.

This chapter shall be known and may be cited as the Mosquito Abatement and Vector Control District Law.

(Added by Stats. 2002, Ch. 395, Sec. 6. Effective January 1, 2003.)

2001.

(a) The Legislature finds and declares all of the following:

(1) California's climate and topography support a wide diversity of biological organisms.

(2) Most of these organisms are beneficial, but some are vectors of human disease pathogens or directly cause other human diseases such as hypersensitivity, envenomization, and secondary infections.

(3) Some of these diseases, such as mosquitoborne viral encephalitis, can be fatal, especially in children and older individuals.

(4) California's connections to the wider national and international economies increase the transport of vectors and pathogens.

(5) Invasions of the United States by vectors such as the Asian tiger mosquito and by pathogens such as the West Nile virus underscore the vulnerability of humans to uncontrolled vectors and pathogens.

(b) The Legislature further finds and declares:

(1) Individual protection against the vectorborne diseases is only partially effective.

(2) Adequate protection of human health against vectorborne diseases is best achieved by organized public programs.

(3) The protection of Californians and their communities against the discomforts and economic effects of vectorborne diseases is an essential public service that is vital to public health, safety, and welfare.

(4) Since 1915, mosquito abatement and vector control districts have protected Californians and their communities against the threats of vectorborne diseases.

(c) In enacting this chapter, it is the intent of the Legislature to create and continue a broad statutory authority for a class of special districts with the power to conduct effective programs for the surveillance, prevention, abatement, and control of mosquitoes and other vectors.

(d) It is also the intent of the Legislature that mosquito abatement and vector control districts cooperate with other public agencies to protect the public health, safety, and welfare. Further, the Legislature encourages local communities and local officials to adapt the powers and procedures provided by this chapter to meet the diversity of their own local circumstances and responsibilities.

(Added by Stats. 2002, Ch. 395, Sec. 6. Effective January 1, 2003.)

2002.

As used in this chapter:

(a) "Abate" means to put an end to a public nuisance, or to reduce the degree or the intensity of a public nuisance.

(b) "Board of trustees" means the legislative body of a district.

(c) "City" means any city, whether general law or chartered, including a city and county, and including any city the name of which includes the word "town."

(d) "Control" means to prevent or reduce vectors.

(e) "Department" means the State Department of Health Services.

(f) "District" means any mosquito abatement and vector control district created pursuant to this chapter or any of its statutory predecessors.

(g) "Principal county" means the county having all or the greater portion of the entire assessed value, as shown on the last equalized assessment roll of the county or counties, of all taxable property within a district at the time of formation.

(h) "Property" means land and improvements, and includes water.

(i) "Public agency" means any state agency, board, or commission, including the California State University and the University of California, any county, city and county, city, regional agency, school district, special district, redevelopment agency, or other political subdivision.

(j) "Public nuisance" means any of the following:

(1) Any property, excluding water, that has been artificially altered from its natural condition so that it now supports the development, attraction, or harborage of vectors. The presence of vectors in their developmental stages on a property is prima facie evidence that the property is a public nuisance.

(2) Any water that is a breeding place for vectors. The presence of vectors in their developmental stages in the water is prima facie evidence that the water is a public nuisance.

(3) Any activity that supports the development, attraction, or harborage of vectors, or that facilitates the introduction or spread of vectors.

(k) "Vector" means any animal capable of transmitting the causative agent of human disease or capable of producing human discomfort or injury, including, but not limited to, mosquitoes, flies, mites, ticks, other arthropods, and rodents and other vertebrates.

(l) "Voter" means a voter as defined by Section 359 of the Elections Code.

(Added by Stats. 2002, Ch. 395, Sec. 6. Effective January 1, 2003.)

2003.

(a) This chapter provides the authority for the organization and powers of mosquito abatement and vector control districts. This chapter succeeds the former Chapter 5 (commencing with Section 2200) as added by Chapter 60 of the Statutes of 1939, as subsequently amended, and any of its statutory predecessors.

(b) Any mosquito abatement and vector control district formed pursuant to the former Chapter 5 (commencing with Section 2200) or any of its statutory predecessors that was in existence on January 1, 2003, shall remain in existence as if it had been organized pursuant to this chapter. Any zone of a mosquito abatement and vector control district formed pursuant to former Section 2291 to former Section 2291.4, inclusive, and any of their statutory predecessors that was in existence on January 1, 2003, shall remain in existence as if it had been formed pursuant to this chapter.

(c) Any indebtedness, special tax, benefit assessment, fee, election, ordinance, resolution, regulation, rule, or any other action of a district taken pursuant to the former Chapter 5 (commencing with Section 2200) or any of its statutory predecessors that was

taken before January 1, 2003, shall not be voided solely because of any error, omission, informality, misnomer, or failure to comply strictly with this chapter.
(Added by Stats. 2002, Ch. 395, Sec. 6. Effective January 1, 2003.)

2004.

This chapter is necessary to protect the public health, safety, and welfare, and shall be liberally construed to effectuate its purposes.
(Added by Stats. 2002, Ch. 395, Sec. 6. Effective January 1, 2003.)

2005.

If any provision of this chapter or the application of any provision of this chapter in any circumstance or to any person, city, county, special district, school district, the state, or any agency or subdivision of the state, including the California State University and the University of California, is held invalid, that invalidity shall not affect other provisions or applications of this chapter that can be given effect without the invalid provision or application of the invalid provision, and to this end the provisions of this chapter are severable.
(Added by Stats. 2002, Ch. 395, Sec. 6. Effective January 1, 2003.)

2006.

(a) Any action to determine the validity of either the organization, or any action, of a district shall be brought pursuant to Chapter 9 (commencing with Section 860) of Title 10 of Part 2 of the Code of Civil Procedure.
(b) Any judicial review of an action taken pursuant to this chapter shall be conducted pursuant to Chapter 2 (commencing with Section 1084) of Title 1 of Part 3 of the Code of Civil Procedure.
(Added by Stats. 2002, Ch. 395, Sec. 6. Effective January 1, 2003.)

2007.

(a) Except as provided in this section, territory, whether incorporated or unincorporated, whether contiguous or noncontiguous, may be included in a district. Territory that is already within a mosquito abatement and vector control district formed pursuant to this chapter may not be included within another mosquito abatement and vector control district.
(b) Except as otherwise provided in this chapter, the Cortese-Knox-Hertzberg Local Government Reorganization Act of 2000, Division 3 (commencing with Section 56000) of Title 5 of the Government Code, shall govern any change of organization or reorganization of a district. In the case of any conflict between that division and this chapter, the provisions of this chapter shall prevail.
(c) A district shall be deemed an "independent special district," as defined by Section 56044 of the Government Code.
(Added by Stats. 2002, Ch. 395, Sec. 6. Effective January 1, 2003.)

ARTICLE 2. Formation [2010 - 2014]

(Article 2 added by Stats. 2002, Ch. 395, Sec. 6.)

2010.

A new district may be formed pursuant to this article.
(Added by Stats. 2002, Ch. 395, Sec. 6. Effective January 1, 2003.)

2011.

(a) A proposal to form a new district may be made by petition. The petition shall do all of the things required by Section 56700 of the Government Code. In addition, the petition shall:
(1) Set forth the methods by which the district will be financed, including, but not limited to, special taxes, special benefit assessments, and fees.
(2) Propose a name for the district.
(3) Specify the size of the initial board of trustees and the method of their appointment.
(b) The petitions, the proponents, and the procedures for certifying the sufficiency of the petitions shall comply with Chapter 2 (commencing with Section 56700) of Part 3 of Division 3 of Title 5 of the Government Code. In the case of any conflict between Chapter 2 (commencing with Section 56700) of Part 3 of Division 3 of Title 5 of the Government Code and this article, the provisions of this article shall prevail.
(c) The petition shall be signed by not less than 25 percent of the registered voters residing in the area to be included in the district, as determined by the local agency formation commission.
(Added by Stats. 2002, Ch. 395, Sec. 6. Effective January 1, 2003.)

2012.

(a) Before circulating any petition, the proponents shall publish a notice of intention that includes a written statement not to exceed 500 words in length, setting forth the reasons for forming the district and the methods by which the district will be financed. The notice shall be published pursuant to Section 6061 of the Government Code in one or more newspapers of general circulation within the territory proposed to be included in the district. If the territory proposed to be included in the district is located in more than one county, publication of the notice shall be made in at least one newspaper of general circulation in each of the counties.
(b) The following shall be signed by a representative of the proponent, and shall be in substantially the following form:
"Notice of Intent to Circulate Petition
"Notice is hereby given of the intention to circulate a petition proposing to form the _____ (name of the district). The reasons for forming the proposed district are: _____. The method(s) by which the proposed district will be financed are: _____."
(c) Within five days after the date of publication, the proponents shall file with the executive officer of the local agency formation commission of the principal county a copy of the notice together with an affidavit made by a representative of the newspaper in which the notice was published certifying to the fact of the publication.

(d) After the filing required pursuant to subdivision (c), the petition may be circulated for signatures.
(Added by Stats. 2002, Ch. 395, Sec. 6. Effective January 1, 2003.)

2013.

(a) A proposal to form a new district may also be made by the adoption of a resolution of application by the legislative body of any county or city that contains the territory proposed to be included in the district. Except for the provisions regarding the signers, signatures, and the proponents, a resolution of application shall contain all of the matters required for inclusion in a petition in Section 2011.
(b) Before adopting a resolution of application, the legislative body shall hold a public hearing on the resolution. Notice of the hearing shall be published pursuant to Section 6061 of the Government Code in one or more newspapers of general circulation within the county or city. At least 20 days before the hearing, the legislative body shall give mailed notice of its hearing to the executive officer of the local agency formation commission of the principal county. The notice shall generally describe the proposed formation of the district and the territory proposed to be included in the district.
(c) At the hearing required by subdivision (b), the legislative body shall give any person an opportunity to present his or her views on the resolution.
(d) The clerk of the legislative body shall file a certified copy of the resolution of application with the executive officer of the local agency formation commission of the principal county.
(Added by Stats. 2002, Ch. 395, Sec. 6. Effective January 1, 2003.)

2014.

(a) Once the proponents have filed a sufficient petition or a legislative body has filed a resolution of application, the local agency formation commission shall proceed pursuant to Part 3 (commencing with Section 56650) of Division 3 of Title 5 of the Government Code.
(b) If the local agency formation commission approves the proposal for the formation of a district, then, notwithstanding Section 57007 of the Government Code, the commission shall proceed pursuant to Part 4 (commencing with Section 57000) of Division 3 of Title 5 of the Government Code.
(c) Notwithstanding Section 57075 of the Government Code, the local agency formation commission shall take one of the following actions:
(1) If a majority protest exists in accordance with Section 57078 of the Government Code, the commission shall terminate proceedings.
(2) If no majority protest exists, the commission shall either:
(A) Order the formation without an election.
(B) Order the formation subject to the approval by the voters of a special tax or the approval by the property owners of a special benefit assessment.
(d) If the local agency formation commission orders the formation of a district pursuant to subparagraph (B) of paragraph (2) of subdivision (c), the commission shall direct the board of supervisors to direct county officials to conduct the necessary elections on behalf of the proposed district.
(Added by Stats. 2002, Ch. 395, Sec. 6. Effective January 1, 2003.)

ARTICLE 3. Boards of Trustees and Officers [2020 - 2030]

(Article 3 added by Stats. 2002, Ch. 395, Sec. 6.)

2020.

A legislative body of at least five members known as the board of trustees shall govern every district. The board of trustees shall establish policies for the operation of the district. The board of trustees shall provide for the faithful implementation of those policies which is the responsibility of the employees of the district.
(Added by Stats. 2002, Ch. 395, Sec. 6. Effective January 1, 2003.)

2021.

Within 30 days after the effective date of the formation of a district, a board of trustees shall be appointed as follows:
(a) In the case of a district that contains only unincorporated territory in a single county, the board of supervisors shall appoint five persons to the board of trustees.
(b) In the case of a district that is located entirely within a single county and contains both incorporated territory and unincorporated territory, the board of supervisors may appoint one person to the board of trustees, and the city council of each city that is located in whole or in part within the district may appoint one person to the board of trustees. If those appointments result in a board of trustees with less than five trustees, the board of supervisors shall appoint enough additional persons to make a board of trustees of five members.
(c) In the case of a district that contains only unincorporated territory in more than one county, the board of supervisors of each county may appoint one person to the board of trustees. If those appointments result in a board of trustees with less than five persons, the board of supervisors of the principal county shall appoint enough additional persons to make a board of trustees of five members.
(d) In the case of a district that is located in two or more counties and contains both incorporated territory and unincorporated territory, the board of supervisors of each county may appoint one person to the board of trustees, and the city council of each city that is located in whole or part within the district may appoint one person to the board of trustees. If those appointments result in less than five persons, the board of supervisors of the principal county shall appoint enough additional persons to make a board of trustees of five members.
(Added by Stats. 2002, Ch. 395, Sec. 6. Effective January 1, 2003.)

2021.5.

(a) Notwithstanding Section 2021, the Board of Trustees of the San Mateo County Mosquito and Vector Control District may be appointed as follows:

(1) The San Mateo County Board of Supervisors shall appoint two trustees.

(2) The city selection committee in the County of San Mateo, established pursuant to Article 11 (commencing with Section 50270) of Chapter 1 of Part 1 of Division 1 of Title 5 of the Government Code, shall appoint one trustee from each county supervisorial district; however, the committee shall not appoint a trustee to serve on the board at the same time as another trustee if both trustees would represent the same city as a result of that appointment.

(b) This section shall apply only if a majority of the legislative bodies that include the city councils in, and the Board of Supervisors of, the County of San Mateo adopt resolutions approving the change in board composition.

(c) Upon adoption of a resolution pursuant to subdivision (b), the city council or board of supervisors shall forward a copy of the resolution to the local agency formation commission. If a majority of the legislative bodies that include the city councils in, and the Board of Supervisors of, the County of San Mateo adopt a resolution, the local agency formation commission shall adopt procedures for the reorganization of the board of trustees and notify the San Mateo County Mosquito and Vector Control District and the city selection committee in the County of San Mateo.

(Added by Stats. 2016, Ch. 288, Sec. 1. (AB 1362) Effective January 1, 2017.)

2022.

(a) Each person appointed by a board of supervisors to be a member of a board of trustees shall be a voter in that county and a resident of that portion of the county that is within the district.

(b) Each person appointed by a city council to be a member of a board of trustees shall be a voter in that city and a resident of that portion of the city that is within the district.

(c) Notwithstanding any other provision of law including the common law doctrine that precludes the simultaneous holding of incompatible offices, a member of a city council may be appointed and may serve as a member of a board of trustees if that person also meets the other applicable qualifications of this chapter.

(d) It is the intent of the Legislature that persons appointed to boards of trustees have experience, training, and education in fields that will assist in the governance of the districts.

(e) All trustees shall exercise their independent judgment on behalf of the interests of the residents, property owners, and the public as a whole in furthering the purposes and intent of this chapter. The trustees shall represent the interests of the public as a whole and not solely the interests of the board of supervisors or the city council that appointed them.

(Added by Stats. 2002, Ch. 395, Sec. 6. Effective January 1, 2003.)

2023.

(a) The initial board of trustees of a district formed on or after January 1, 2003, shall be determined pursuant to this section.

(b) The persons appointed to the initial board of trustees shall meet on the first Monday after 45 days after the effective date of the formation of the district.

(c) At the first meeting of the initial board of trustees, the trustees shall classify themselves by lot into two classes, as nearly equal as possible. The term of office of the class having the greater number shall expire at noon on the first Monday in January that is closest to the second year from the appointments made pursuant to Section 2021. The term of office of the class having the lesser number shall expire at noon on the first Monday in January that is closest to the first year from the appointments made pursuant to Section 2021.

(Added by Stats. 2002, Ch. 395, Sec. 6. Effective January 1, 2003.)

2024.

(a) Except as provided in Section 2023, the term of office for a member of the board of trustees shall be for a term of two or four years, at the discretion of the appointing authority. Terms of office commence at noon on the first Monday in January.

(b) Any vacancy in the office of a member appointed to a board of trustees shall be filled pursuant to Section 1779 of the Government Code. Any person appointed to fill a vacant office shall fill the balance of the unexpired term.

(Added by Stats. 2002, Ch. 395, Sec. 6. Effective January 1, 2003.)

2025.

(a) Under no circumstances shall a board of trustees consist of less than five members. Except as provided in Section 2026, the number of members who represent the unincorporated territory of a county may not exceed five members.

(b) A board of trustees may adopt a resolution requesting the board of supervisors of any county that contains territory within the district to increase or decrease the number of members of the board of trustees who represent the unincorporated territory of that county within the district. The resolution shall specify the number of members and the areas of the unincorporated territory for which the board of trustees requests the increase or decrease.

(c) Within 60 days of receiving a resolution adopted pursuant to subdivision (b), the board of supervisors shall order the increase or decrease in the number of members of the board of trustees, consistent with the board of trustees' resolution.

(d) If the board of supervisors orders an increase in the number of members of the board of trustees, the board of supervisors shall appoint a person or persons to the board of trustees and specify their term of office, consistent with the requirements of this chapter. If the board of supervisors orders a decrease in the number of members of the board of trustees, the board of supervisors shall designate the trustee or trustees whose office shall be eliminated at the termination of the trustee's current term of office. Any trustee whose office is designated to be eliminated shall continue to serve until his or her term of office expires.

(Added by Stats. 2002, Ch. 395, Sec. 6. Effective January 1, 2003.)

2026.

(a) A local agency formation commission, in approving either a consolidation of districts or the reorganization of two more districts into a single district, may, pursuant to subdivisions (k) and (n) of Section 56886 of the Government Code, change the number of members on the board of trustees of the consolidated or reorganized district, provided that the resulting number of trustees shall be an odd number but not less than five.

(b) Upon the expiration of the terms of the members of the board of trustees of the consolidated or reorganized district whose terms first expire following the effective date of the consolidation or reorganization, the total number of members on the board of trustees shall be reduced until the number equals the number of members determined by the local agency formation commission.

(c) Notwithstanding subdivision (b) of Section 2024, in the event of a vacancy on the board of trustees of the consolidated or reorganized district at a time when the number of members of the board of trustees is greater than the number determined by the local agency formation commission, the vacancy shall not be filled and the membership of the board of trustees shall be reduced by one member.

(Added by Stats. 2002, Ch. 395, Sec. 6. Effective January 1, 2003.)

2027.

(a) At the first meeting of the initial board of trustees of a newly formed district, and in the case of an existing district at the first meeting in January every year or every other year, the board of trustees shall elect its officers.

(b) The officers of a board of trustees are a president and a secretary. The president shall be a trustee. The secretary may be either a trustee or a district employee. A board of trustees may create additional officers and elect members to those positions. No trustee shall hold more than one office.

(c) Except as provided in Section 2077, the county treasurer of the principal county shall act as the district treasurer. The county treasurer shall receive no compensation for the receipt and disbursement of money of the district.

(Added by Stats. 2002, Ch. 395, Sec. 6. Effective January 1, 2003.)

2028.

A board of trustees shall meet at least once every three months. Meetings of the board of trustees are subject to the provisions of the Ralph M. Brown Act, Chapter 9 (commencing with Section 54950) of Part 1 of Division 2 of Title 5 of the Government Code.

(Added by Stats. 2002, Ch. 395, Sec. 6. Effective January 1, 2003.)

2029.

(a) A majority of the board of trustees shall constitute a quorum for the transaction of business.

(b) Except as otherwise specifically provided to the contrary in this chapter, a recorded vote of a majority of those trustees present and voting is required on each action.

(c) The board of trustees shall act only by ordinance, resolution, or motion.

(d) The board of trustees shall keep a record of all of its acts, including financial transactions.

(e) The board of trustees shall adopt rules for its proceedings.

(Added by Stats. 2002, Ch. 395, Sec. 6. Effective January 1, 2003.)

2030.

(a) The members of the board of trustees shall serve without compensation.

(b) The members of the board of trustees may receive their actual and necessary traveling and incidental expenses incurred while on official business. In lieu of paying for actual expenses, the board of trustees may by resolution provide for the allowance and payment to each trustee a sum not to exceed one hundred dollars ($100) per month for expenses incurred while on official business. A trustee may waive the payments permitted by this subdivision.

(c) Notwithstanding subdivision (a), the secretary of the board of trustees may receive compensation in an amount determined by the board of trustees.

(d) Reimbursement for these expenses is subject to Sections 53232.2 and 53232.3 of the Government Code.

(Amended by Stats. 2005, Ch. 700, Sec. 8. Effective January 1, 2006.)

ARTICLE 4. Powers [2040 - 2055]

(Article 4 added by Stats. 2002, Ch. 395, Sec. 6.)

2040.

Within the district's boundaries or in territory that is located outside the district from which vectors and vectorborne diseases may enter the district, a district may do all of the following:

(a) Conduct surveillance programs and other appropriate studies of vectors and vectorborne diseases.

(b) Take any and all necessary or proper actions to prevent the occurrence of vectors and vectorborne diseases.

(c) Take any and all necessary or proper actions to abate or control vectors and vectorborne diseases.

(d) Take any and all actions necessary for or incidental to the powers granted by this chapter.

(Added by Stats. 2002, Ch. 395, Sec. 6. Effective January 1, 2003.)

2041.

A district shall have and may exercise all rights and powers, expressed or implied, necessary to carry out the purposes and intent of this chapter, including, but not limited to, all of the following powers:

(a) To sue and be sued.

(b) To acquire by purchase, eminent domain, or other lawful means, any real property within the district or any personal property that may be necessary or proper to carry out the purposes and intent of this chapter.

(c) To sell, lease, or otherwise dispose of any real or personal property. Every sale of property shall be to the highest bidder. The board shall publish notice of the sale pursuant to Section 6066 of the Government Code. A board of trustees may exchange equivalent properties if the board determines that the exchange is in the best interests of the district.

(d) To donate any surplus real or personal property to any public agency or nonprofit organization.

(e) To purchase the supplies and materials, employ the personnel, and contract for the services that may be necessary or proper to carry out the purposes and intent of this chapter.

(f) To build, repair, and maintain on any land the dikes, levees, cuts, canals, or ditches that may be necessary or proper to carry out the purposes and intent of this chapter.

(g) To contract to indemnify or compensate any property owner for any injury or damage necessarily caused by the use or taking of real or personal property for dikes, levees, cuts, canals, or ditches.

(h) To engage necessary personnel, to define their qualifications and duties, and to provide a schedule of compensation for the performance of their duties.

(i) To engage counsel and other professional services.

(j) To adopt a seal and alter it at pleasure.

(k) To provide insurance pursuant to Part 6 (commencing with Section 989) of Division 3.6 of Title 1 of the Government Code.

(l) To participate in, review, comment, and make recommendations regarding local, state, or federal land use planning and environmental quality processes, documents, permits, licenses, and entitlements for projects and their potential effects on the purposes and intent of this chapter.

(m) To take any and all actions necessary for, or incidental to, the powers expressed or implied by this chapter.

(Added by Stats. 2002, Ch. 395, Sec. 6. Effective January 1, 2003.)

2042.

When acquiring, improving, or using any real property, a district shall comply with Article 5 (commencing with Section 53090) of Chapter 1 of Part 1 of Division 2 of Title 5, and Article 7 (commencing with Section 65400) of Chapter 1 of Division 1 of Title 7 of the Government Code.

(Added by Stats. 2002, Ch. 395, Sec. 6. Effective January 1, 2003.)

2043.

(a) A district shall have perpetual succession.

(b) A board of trustees may, by a two-thirds vote of its total membership, adopt a resolution to change the name of the district. The name shall contain the words "mosquito abatement district," "vector control district," "mosquito and vector control district," "mosquito control district," or "vector management district." The resolution shall comply with the requirements of Chapter 23 (commencing with Section 7530) of Division 7 of Title 1 of the Government Code. Within 10 days of its adoption, the board of trustees shall file a copy of its resolution with the Secretary of State, the county clerk, the board of supervisors, and the local agency formation commission of each county in which the district is located.

(c) A district may destroy a record pursuant to Chapter 7 (commencing with Section 60200) of Division 1 of Title 6 of the Government Code.

(Amended by Stats. 2005, Ch. 158, Sec. 18. Effective January 1, 2006.)

2044.

(a) A district may cooperate with any public agency or federal agency to carry out the purposes and intent of this chapter. To that end, a district may enter into agreements with those other public agencies or federal agencies to take any and all actions necessary or convenient for carrying out the purposes and intent of this chapter.

(b) A district may jointly acquire, construct, improve, maintain, and operate any facilities, projects, or programs with any other public agency or federal agency to carry out the purposes and intent of this chapter. Nothing in this chapter shall be construed to prohibit any joint or cooperative action with other public agencies or federal agencies.

(c) A district may enter into joint powers agreements pursuant to the Joint Exercise of Powers Act, Chapter 5 (commencing with Section 6500) of Division 7 of Title 1 of the Government Code.

(Added by Stats. 2002, Ch. 395, Sec. 6. Effective January 1, 2003.)

2045.

A district may contract with other public agencies and federal agencies to provide any service, project, or program authorized by this chapter within the district's boundaries. A district may contract with other public agencies and federal agencies to provide any service, project, or program authorized by this chapter within the boundaries of the other public agencies and federal agencies.

(Added by Stats. 2002, Ch. 395, Sec. 6. Effective January 1, 2003.)

2046.

(a) Each district shall adopt policies and procedures, including bidding regulations, governing the purchase of supplies and equipment. Each district shall adopt these policies and procedures by rule or regulation pursuant to Article 7 (commencing with Section 54201) of Chapter 5 of Division 2 of the Government Code.

(b) A district may request the State Department of General Services to make purchases of materials, equipment, or supplies on its behalf pursuant to Section 10298 of the Public Contract Code.

(c) A district may request the purchasing agent of the principal county to make purchases on materials, equipment, or supplies on its behalf pursuant to Article 7 (commencing with Section 25500) of Chapter 5 of Division 2 of Title 3 of the Government Code.

(d) A district may request the purchasing agent of the principal county to contract with persons to provide services, projects, and programs authorized by this chapter pursuant to Article 7 (commencing with Section 25500) of Chapter 5 of Division 2 of Title 3 of the Government Code.

(Added by Stats. 2002, Ch. 395, Sec. 6. Effective January 1, 2003.)

2047.

Any person who restrains, hinders, obstructs, or threatens any officer or employee of a district in the performance of that person's duties, or any person who interferes with any work done by, or under the direction of, the district is guilty of a misdemeanor.

(Added by Stats. 2002, Ch. 395, Sec. 6. Effective January 1, 2003.)

2048.

(a) The Meyers-Milias-Brown Act, Chapter 10 (commencing with Section 3500) of Division 4 of Title 1 of the Government Code applies to all districts.

(b) A board of trustees may adopt an ordinance establishing an employee relations system that may include, but is not limited to, a civil service system or a merit system.

(Added by Stats. 2002, Ch. 395, Sec. 6. Effective January 1, 2003.)

2049.

A board of trustees may require any employee or officer to be bonded. The district shall pay the cost of the bonds.

(Added by Stats. 2002, Ch. 395, Sec. 6. Effective January 1, 2003.)

2050.

A board of trustees may provide for any programs for the benefit of its employees and members of the board of trustees pursuant to Chapter 2 (commencing with Section 53200) of Part 1 of Division 2 of Title 5 of the Government Code.

(Added by Stats. 2002, Ch. 395, Sec. 6. Effective January 1, 2003.)

2051.

A district may authorize the members of its board of trustees and its employees to attend professional, educational, or vocational meetings, and pay their actual and necessary traveling and incidental expenses while on official business. The payment of expenses pursuant to this section may be in addition to the payments made pursuant to Section 2030. Reimbursement for these expenses is subject to Sections 53232.2 and 53232.3 of the Government Code.

(Amended by Stats. 2006, Ch. 643, Sec. 23. Effective January 1, 2007.)

2052.

(a) Pursuant to Article 4 (commencing with Section 106925) of Chapter 4 of Part 1 of Division 104, every district employee who handles, applies, or supervises the use of any pesticide for public health purposes shall be certified by the department as a vector control technician in at least one of the following categories commensurate with the assigned duties:

(1) Mosquito control.

(2) Terrestrial invertebrate vector control.

(3) Vertebrate vector control.

(b) The department may establish, by regulation, exemptions from the requirements of this section that the department deems reasonably necessary to further the purposes of this section.

(Added by Stats. 2002, Ch. 395, Sec. 6. Effective January 1, 2003.)

2053.

(a) A district may request an inspection and abatement warrant pursuant to Title 13 (commencing with Section 1822.50) of Part 3 of the Code of Civil Procedure. A warrant issued pursuant to this section shall apply only to the exterior of places, dwellings, structures, and premises. The warrant shall state the geographic area which it covers and shall state its purposes. A warrant may authorize district employees to enter property only to do the following:

(1) Inspect to determine the presence of vectors or public nuisances.

(2) Abate public nuisances, either directly or by giving notice to the property owner to abate the public nuisance.

(3) Determine if a notice to abate a public nuisance has been complied with.

(4) Control vectors and treat property with appropriate physical, chemical, or biological control measures.

(b) Subject to the limitations of the United States Constitution and the California Constitution, employees of a district may enter any property, either within the district or property that is located outside the district from which vectors may enter the district, without hindrance or notice for any of the following purposes:

(1) Inspect the property to determine the presence of vectors or public nuisances.

(2) Abate public nuisances pursuant to this chapter, either directly or by giving notice to the property owner to abate the public nuisance.

(3) Determine if a notice to abate a public nuisance has been complied with.

(4) Control vectors and treat property with appropriate physical, chemical, or biological control measures.

(Added by Stats. 2002, Ch. 395, Sec. 6. Effective January 1, 2003.)

2054.

Whenever the boundaries of a district or a zone change, the district shall comply with Chapter 8 (commencing with Section 54900) of Part 1 of Division 2 of Title 5 of the Government Code.

(Amended by Stats. 2005, Ch. 158, Sec. 19. Effective January 1, 2006.)

2055.

(a) In any dispute between a district and another public agency over the need to prevent, abate, or control, or the methods and materials used to prevent, abate, or control vectors or vectorborne diseases, the district or the other public agency may appeal the decision to the director of the department within 10 days of the decision.

(b) Within 30 days of receiving an appeal pursuant to subdivision (a), the director of the department shall consult with the affected agencies, take written and oral testimony, decide the appeal, and convey the decision to the affected agencies. The director's decision shall be consistent with the purposes of this chapter. The decision of the director of the department shall be final and conclusive.
(Added by Stats. 2002, Ch. 395, Sec. 6. Effective January 1, 2003.)

(Article 5 added by Stats. 2002, Ch. 395, Sec. 6.)
2060.
(a) A district may abate a public nuisance pursuant to this article.
(b) The person or agency claiming ownership, title, or right to property or who controls the diversion, delivery, conveyance, or flow of water shall be responsible for the abatement of a public nuisance that is caused by, or as a result of, that property or the diversion, delivery, conveyance, or control of that water.
(Added by Stats. 2002, Ch. 395, Sec. 6. Effective January 1, 2003.)
2061.
(a) Whenever a public nuisance exists on any property within a district or on any property that is located outside the district from which vectors may enter the district, the board of trustees may notify the owner of the property of the existence of the public nuisance.
(b) The notice required by subdivision (a) shall do all of the following:
(1) State that a public nuisance exists on the property, describe the public nuisance, and describe the location of the public nuisance on the property.
(2) Direct the owner of the property to abate the nuisance within a specified time.
(3) Direct the owner of the property to take any necessary action within a specified time to prevent the recurrence of the public nuisance.
(4) Inform the owner of the property that the failure to comply with the requirements of the notice within the specified times may result in the district taking the necessary actions, and that the owner shall be liable for paying the costs of the district's actions.
(5) Inform the owner of the property that the failure to comply with the requirements of the notice within the specified times may result in the imposition of civil penalties of up to one thousand dollars ($1,000) per day for each day that the public nuisance continues after the specified times.
(6) Inform the owner of the property that before complying with the requirements of the notice, the owner may appear at a hearing of the board of trustees at a time and place stated in the notice.
(c) The board of trustees shall cause the notice required by subdivision (a) to be served on the owner of the property in the same manner as a summons in a civil action. If, after a diligent search, the notice cannot be served on the owner of the property, the board of trustees shall cause the notice to be posted in a conspicuous place on the property for not less than 10 days before the hearing. Not less than 10 days before the hearing, the board of trustees shall also cause a copy of the notice to be mailed by certified mail to the owner of the property at the address shown on the most recent assessment roll of the county in which the property is located.
(d) At the hearing before the board of trustees at the time and place stated in the notice, the board of trustees shall accept written and oral testimony from the property owner and other persons. At the close of the hearing, the board of trustees shall find, based on substantial evidence in the record, whether a public nuisance exists on the property. If the board of trustees finds that a public nuisance exists, the board of trustees shall order the owner of the property to abate the public nuisance and to take other necessary actions to prevent the recurrence of the public nuisance. The board of trustees shall specify a reasonable time by which the owner of the property shall comply with these requirements.
(e) If the owner of the property does not abate the public nuisance and take the necessary actions to prevent the recurrence of the public nuisance within the time specified by the board of trustees, the district may abate the public nuisance and take the necessary actions to prevent the recurrence of the public nuisance. In addition, the board of trustees may impose civil penalties pursuant to Section 2063.
(Added by Stats. 2002, Ch. 395, Sec. 6. Effective January 1, 2003.)
2062.
(a) A board of trustees shall not declare an agricultural operation to be a public nuisance because of the presence of immature flies if the board determines that the agricultural operation is designed and managed consistent with the accepted standards and practices for controlling fly development on similar agricultural operations.
(b) As used in this section, "accepted standards and practices" means those standards and practices determined by the University of California Cooperative Extension, the department, or local public health agencies. These standards and practices include, but are not limited to, all of the following:
(1) Property design and layout of the agricultural operation to minimize the opportunity for fly development.
(2) A comprehensive system for manure management to include storage, removal, and disposal.
(3) A comprehensive system for green waste management to include storage, removal, and disposal.
(4) An integrated pest management program to control the development and harborage of flies, including the components of surveillance, management, containment, and control.
(Added by Stats. 2002, Ch. 395, Sec. 6. Effective January 1, 2003.)
2063.
In addition to abating the public nuisance and taking any necessary actions to prevent the recurrence of the public nuisance, a board of trustees may impose a civil penalty on the owner of the property for failure to comply with the requirements of Section 2061. The

civil penalty may not exceed one thousand dollars ($1,000) per day for each day that the owner of the property fails to comply with the district's requirements.
(Added by Stats. 2002, Ch. 395, Sec. 6. Effective January 1, 2003.)
2064.
A board of trustees may consider any recurrence of a public nuisance abated pursuant to Section 2061 to be a continuation of the original public nuisance.
(Added by Stats. 2002, Ch. 395, Sec. 6. Effective January 1, 2003.)
2065.
(a) The owner of the property abated pursuant to Section 2061 shall pay the district for the cost of abating the public nuisance and the cost of any necessary actions to prevent the recurrence of the public nuisance. The owner shall also pay any civil penalty imposed pursuant to Section 2063.
(b) If the owner of the property fails to pay the district's costs within 60 days, the board of trustees may order the costs and any civil penalties charged and collected against the property. The charge shall be collected at the same time and in the same manner as ordinary county taxes are collected, and shall be subject to the same penalties and the same procedure and sale in case of delinquency as are provided for ordinary county taxes. All laws applicable to the levy, collection, and enforcement of county taxes are applicable to the costs and civil penalties charged and collected against the property.
(c) If the board of trustees charges the costs and any civil penalties against the parcel, the board of trustees may also cause the notice of abatement lien to be recorded. The notice shall, at a minimum, identify the record owner of the property, set forth the last known address of the record owner, set forth the date upon which the abatement of the public nuisance was ordered by the board of trustees, set forth the date upon which the abatement and any necessary actions to prevent the recurrence of the public nuisance was complete, and include a description of the real property subject to the lien and the amount of the cost and any civil penalties.
(d) However, if the board of trustees does not cause the recordation of a notice of abatement lien pursuant to subdivision (c), and any real property to which the costs and any civil penalties relate has been transferred or conveyed to a bona fide purchaser for value, or a lien on a bona fide encumbrancer for value has been created and attaches to that property, prior to the date on which the first installment of county taxes would become delinquent, then the cost and any civil penalties may not result in a lien against that real property but shall be transferred to the unsecured roll for collection.
(e) Recordation of a notice of abatement lien pursuant to subdivision (c) shall have the same effect as recordation of an abstract of a money judgment recorded pursuant to Article 2 (commencing with Section 697.310) of Chapter 2 of Division 2 of Title 9 of Part 2 of the Code of Civil Procedure. The lien created shall have the same priority as a judgment lien on real property and shall continue in effect until released. Upon order of the board of trustees, an abatement lien created under this section may be released or subordinated in the same manner as a judgment lien on real property may be released or subordinated.
(Added by Stats. 2002, Ch. 395, Sec. 6. Effective January 1, 2003.)
2066.
The lien provisions of this article shall not apply to property owned by a public agency. Notwithstanding Section 6103 of the Government Code or any other provision of law, a public agency shall pay the district for the cost of abating the public nuisance, the cost of any necessary actions to prevent the recurrence of the public nuisance, and any civil penalties.
(Added by Stats. 2002, Ch. 395, Sec. 6. Effective January 1, 2003.)
2067.
Any money collected by a county from a lien authorized pursuant to this article, other than the amounts authorized pursuant to Section 29304 of the Government Code, shall be paid to the district.
(Added by Stats. 2002, Ch. 395, Sec. 6. Effective January 1, 2003.)

(Article 6 added by Stats. 2002, Ch. 395, Sec. 6.)
2070.
(a) On or before August 1 of each year, the board of trustees shall adopt a final budget, which shall conform to the accounting and budgeting procedures for special districts contained in Subchapter 3 (commencing with Section 1031.1) of, and Article 1 (commencing with Section 1121) of Subchapter 4 of Division 2 of Title 2 of the California Code of Regulations. The board of trustees may divide the annual budget into categories, including, but not limited to:
(1) Maintenance and operation.
(2) Employee compensation.
(3) Capital outlay.
(4) Interest and redemption for indebtedness.
(5) Restricted reserve for public health emergencies.
(6) Restricted reserve for capital and asset preservation.
(7) Restricted reserve for contingencies.
(8) Unallocated general reserve.
(b) The board of trustees shall forward a copy of the final budget to the auditor of each county in which the district is located.
(Added by Stats. 2002, Ch. 395, Sec. 6. Effective January 1, 2003.)
2071.
(a) In its annual budget, the board of trustees may establish one or more restricted reserves. When the board of trustees establishes a restricted reserve, it shall declare the exclusive purposes for which the funds in the reserve may be spent. The funds in the restricted reserve shall be spent only for the exclusive purposes for which the board of

trustees established the restricted reserve. The reserves shall be maintained according to generally accepted accounting principles.

(b) Any time after the establishment of a restricted reserve, the board of trustees may transfer any funds to that restricted reserve.

(c) Notwithstanding any other provision of this section, in a public health emergency, a board of trustees may, by majority vote of the total membership of the board of trustees, temporarily transfer funds from other restricted reserves to the restricted reserve for public health emergencies.

(d) If the board of trustees finds that the funds in a restricted reserve are no longer required for the purpose for which the restricted reserve was established, the board of trustees may, by a four-fifths vote of the total membership of the board of trustees, discontinue the restricted reserve or transfer the funds that are no longer required from the restricted reserve to the district's general fund.

(Added by Stats. 2002, Ch. 395, Sec. 6. Effective January 1, 2003.)

2072.

(a) On or before July 1 of each year, the board of trustees shall adopt a resolution establishing its appropriations limit and make other necessary determinations for the following fiscal year pursuant to Article XIII B of the California Constitution and Division 9 (commencing with Section 7900) of the Government Code.

(b) Pursuant to subdivision (c) of Section 9 of Article XIII B of the California Constitution, this section shall not apply to a district which existed on January 1, 1978, and that did not as of the 1977–78 fiscal year levy an ad valorem tax on property in excess of twelve and one-half cents ($0.125) per one hundred dollars ($100) of assessed value.

(Added by Stats. 2002, Ch. 395, Sec. 6. Effective January 1, 2003.)

2073.

The auditor of each county in which a district is located shall allocate to the district its share of property tax revenue pursuant to Chapter 6 (commencing with Section 95) of Part 0.5 of Division 1 of the Revenue and Taxation Code.

(Added by Stats. 2002, Ch. 395, Sec. 6. Effective January 1, 2003.)

2074.

(a) A district may accept any revenue, money, grants, goods, or services from any federal, state, regional, or local agency or from any person for any lawful purpose of the district.

(b) In addition to any other existing authority, a district may borrow money and incur indebtedness pursuant to Article 7 (commencing with Section 53820), Article 7.4 (commencing with Section 53835), Article 7.5 (commencing with Section 53840), Article 7.6 (commencing with Section 53850), and Article 7.7 (commencing with Section 53859) of Chapter 4 of Part 1 of Division 2 of Title 5 of the Government Code.

(Amended by Stats. 2010, Ch. 699, Sec. 25.1. (SB 894) Effective January 1, 2011.)

2075.

All claims for money or damages against a district are governed by Part 3 (commencing with Section 900) and Part 4 (commencing with Section 940) of Division 3.6 of Title 1 of the Government Code.

(Added by Stats. 2002, Ch. 395, Sec. 6. Effective January 1, 2003.)

2076.

(a) All claims against a district shall be audited, allowed, and paid by the board of trustees by warrants drawn on the county treasurer.

(b) As an alternative to subdivision (a), the board of trustees may instruct the county treasurer to audit, allow, and draw his or her warrant on the county treasury for all legal claims presented to him or her and authorized by the board of trustees.

(c) The county treasurer shall pay the warrants in the order in which they are presented.

(d) If a warrant is presented for payment and the county treasurer cannot pay it for want of funds in the account on which it is drawn, the treasurer shall endorse the warrant, "NOT PAID BECAUSE OF INSUFFICIENT FUNDS" and sign his or her name and the date and time the warrant was presented. From that time until it is paid, the warrant bears interest at the maximum rate permitted pursuant to Article 7 (commencing with Section 53530) of Chapter 3 of Part 1 of Division 2 of Title 5 of the Government Code.

(Added by Stats. 2002, Ch. 395, Sec. 6. Effective January 1, 2003.)

2077.

(a) Notwithstanding Section 2076, a district that has total annual revenues greater than two hundred fifty thousand dollars ($250,000) may withdraw its funds from the control of the county treasurer pursuant to this section.

(b) The board of trustees shall adopt a resolution that does each of the following:

(1) States its intent to withdraw its funds from the county treasury.

(2) Adopt a procedure for the appointment of a district treasurer. The board of trustees may appoint the district treasurer, or the board of trustees may delegate the appointment of the district treasurer to the district's general manager. The district treasurer may be a member of the board of trustees, the secretary of the board of trustees, the general manager, or a district employee.

(3) Fix the amount of the bond for the district treasurer and other district employees who will be responsible for handling the district's finances.

(4) Adopt a system of accounting and auditing that shall completely and at all times show the district's financial condition. The system of accounting and auditing shall adhere to generally accepted accounting principles.

(5) Adopt a procedure for drawing and signing warrants, provided that the procedure adheres to generally accepted accounting principles. The procedure shall provide that bond principal and salaries shall be paid when due. The procedure may provide that warrants to pay claims and demands need not be approved by the board of trustees before payment if the district treasurer determines that the claims and demands conform to the district's approved budget.

(6) Designate a bank or a savings and loan association as the depositary of the district's funds. A bank or savings and loan association may act as a depositary, paying agent, or fiscal agency for the holding or handling of the district's funds, notwithstanding the fact that a member of the board of trustees whose funds are on deposit in that bank or savings and loan association is an officer, employee, or stockholder of that bank or savings and loan association, or of a holding company that owns any of the stock of that bank or savings and loan association.

(c) The board of trustees and the board of supervisors of the principal county shall determine a mutually acceptable date for the withdrawal of the district's funds from the county treasury, not to exceed 15 months from the date on which the board of trustees adopts its resolution.

(d) In implementing this section, the district shall comply with Article 1 (commencing with Section 53600) and Article 2 (commencing with Section 53630) of Chapter 4 of Part 1 of Division 2 of Title 5 of the Government Code. Nothing in this section shall preclude the district treasurer from depositing the district's funds in the county treasury of the principal county or the State Treasury pursuant to Article 11 (commencing with Section 16429.1) of Chapter 2 of Part 2 of Division 4 of Title 2 of the Government Code.

(e) The district treasurer shall make annual or more frequent written reports to the board of trustees, as the board of trustees shall determine, regarding the receipts and disbursements and balances in the accounts controlled by the district treasurer. The district treasurer shall sign the reports and file them with the secretary.

(Added by Stats. 2002, Ch. 395, Sec. 6. Effective January 1, 2003.)

2078.

The board of trustees may establish a revolving fund pursuant to Article 15 (commencing with Section 53950) of Chapter 4 of Part 1 of Division 2 of Title 5 of the Government Code to make change and pay small bills directly.

(Added by Stats. 2002, Ch. 395, Sec. 6. Effective January 1, 2003.)

2079.

(a) The board of trustees shall provide for regular audits of the district's accounts and records pursuant to Section 26909 of the Government Code.

(b) The board of trustees shall provide for the annual financial reports to the Controller pursuant to Article 9 (commencing with Section 53890) of Chapter 4 of Part 1 of Division 2 of Title 5 of the Government Code.

(Added by Stats. 2002, Ch. 395, Sec. 6. Effective January 1, 2003.)

ARTICLE 7. Alternative Revenues [2080 - 2085]

(Article 7 added by Stats. 2002, Ch. 395, Sec. 6.)

2080.

Whenever a board of trustees determines that the amount of revenues available to the district or any of its zones is inadequate to meet the costs of providing facilities, programs, projects, and services, the board of trustees may raise revenues pursuant to this article or any other provision of law.

(Added by Stats. 2002, Ch. 395, Sec. 6. Effective January 1, 2003.)

2081.

A district may levy special taxes pursuant to:

(a) Article 3.5 (commencing with Section 50075) of Chapter 1 of Part 1 of Division 1 of Title 5 of the Government Code.

(b) The Mello-Roos Community Facilities Act of 1982, Chapter 2.5 (commencing with Section 53311) of Part 1 of Division 2 of Title 5 of the Government Code.

(Added by Stats. 2002, Ch. 395, Sec. 6. Effective January 1, 2003.)

2082.

(a) A district may levy special benefit assessments consistent with the requirements of Article XIII D of the California Constitution to finance vector control projects and programs.

(b) Before beginning a vector control project or program proposed to be financed pursuant to this section, the board of trustees shall adopt a resolution that does all of the following:

(1) Specifies its intent to undertake the project or program.

(2) Generally describes the project or program.

(3) Estimates the cost of the project or program.

(4) Estimates the duration of the proposed special benefit assessment.

(c) After adopting its resolution pursuant to subdivision (b), the board of trustees shall proceed pursuant to Section 53753 of the Government Code.

(d) The special benefit assessments levied pursuant to this section shall be collected at the same time and in the same manner as county taxes. The county may deduct an amount not to exceed its actual costs incurred for collecting the special benefit assessments before remitting the balance to the district. The special benefit assessments shall be a lien on all the property benefited. Liens for the assessments shall be of the same force and effect as liens for property taxes, and their collection may be enforced by the same means as provided for the enforcement of liens for county taxes.

(Added by Stats. 2002, Ch. 395, Sec. 6. Effective January 1, 2003.)

2083.

A district may levy special benefit assessments consistent with the requirements of Article XIII D of the California Constitution to finance capital improvements, including, but not limited to, special benefit assessments levied pursuant to:

(a) The Improvement Act of 1911, Division 7 (commencing with Section 5000) of the Streets and Highways Code.

(b) The Improvement Bond Act of 1915, Division 10 (commencing with Section 8500) of the Streets and Highways Code.

(c) The Municipal Improvement Act of 1913, Division 12 (commencing with Section 10000) of the Streets and Highways Code.

(d) Any other statutory authorization enacted in the future.
(Added by Stats. 2002, Ch. 395, Sec. 6. Effective January 1, 2003.)
2084.
Pursuant to Section 5 of Article XIII D of the California Constitution and Section 53753.5 of the Government Code, any assessment existing on November 6, 1996, that was imposed exclusively to finance the capital costs or maintenance and operation expenses for vector control shall be exempt from the procedures and approval process set forth in Section 4 of Article XIII D of the California Constitution and Section 2082. Subsequent increases in those assessments shall be subject to the procedures and approval process set forth in Section 4 of Article XIII D of the California Constitution and Section 2082.
(Added by Stats. 2002, Ch. 395, Sec. 6. Effective January 1, 2003.)
2085.
(a) A board of trustees may charge a fee to cover the cost of any service that the district provides or the cost of enforcing any regulation for which the fee is charged. No fee shall exceed the costs reasonably borne by the district in providing the service or enforcing the regulation for which the fee is charged.
(b) Before imposing or increasing any fee for property-related services, a board of trustees shall follow the procedures in Section 6 of Article XIII D of the California Constitution.
(c) Notwithstanding Section 6103 of the Government Code, a board of trustees may charge a fee authorized by this section to other public agencies.
(d) A board of trustees may charge residents or taxpayers of the district a fee authorized by this section which is less than the fee that it charges to nonresidents or nontaxpayers of the district.
(e) A board of trustees may authorize district employees to waive the payment, in whole or in part, of a fee authorized by this section when the board of trustees determines that the payment would not be in the public interest. Before authorizing any waiver, a board of trustees shall adopt a resolution that specifies the policies and procedures governing waivers.
(Added by Stats. 2002, Ch. 395, Sec. 6. Effective January 1, 2003.)

ARTICLE 8. Zones [2090 - 2093]

(Article 8 added by Stats. 2002, Ch. 395, Sec. 6.)
2090.
(a) Whenever a board of trustees determines that it is in the public interest to provide different services, to provide different levels of service, or to raise additional revenue within specific areas of the district, it may form one or more zones pursuant to this article.
(b) The board of trustees shall initiate proceedings for the formation of a new zone by adopting a resolution that does all of the following:
(1) States that the proposal is made pursuant to this article.
(2) Sets forth a description of the boundaries of the territory to be included in the zone.
(3) States the different services, the different levels of service, or additional revenues which the zone will provide.
(4) Sets forth the methods by which those services or levels of service will be financed.
(5) States the reasons for forming the zone.
(6) Proposes a name or number for the zone.
(c) A proposal to form a new zone may also be initiated by a petition signed by not less than 10 percent of the registered voters residing within the proposed zone. The petition shall contain all of the matters required by subdivision (b).
(d) Upon the adoption of a resolution or the receipt of a valid petition, the board of trustees shall fix the date, time, and place for the public hearing on the formation of the zone. The board of trustees shall publish notice of the hearing, including the information required by subdivision (b), pursuant to Section 6061 of the Government Code in one or more newspapers of general circulation in the district. The board of trustees shall mail the notice at least 45 days before the date of the hearing to all owners of property within the proposed zone. The board of trustees shall post the notice in at least three public places within the territory of the proposed zone.
(Added by Stats. 2002, Ch. 395, Sec. 6. Effective January 1, 2003.)
2091.
(a) At the hearing, the board of trustees shall hear and consider any protests to the formation of a zone pursuant to this article. The board of trustees shall terminate the proceedings, if, at the conclusion of the hearing, it determines either of the following:
(1) More than 50 percent of the total number of voters residing within the proposed zone have filed written objections to the formation.
(2) Property owners who own more than 50 percent of the assessed value of all taxable property within the proposed zone have filed written objections to the formation. If the board of trustees determines that the written objections have been filed by 50 percent or less of those voters or property owners, then the board of trustees may proceed to form the zone.
(b) If the resolution or petition for formation of a zone proposes that the zone use special taxes, special benefit assessments, or fees for property-related services to finance its purposes, the board of trustees shall proceed according to law. If the voters or property owners do not approve those funding methods, the zone shall not be formed.
(Added by Stats. 2002, Ch. 395, Sec. 6. Effective January 1, 2003.)
2092.
(a) A board of trustees may change the boundaries of a zone or dissolve a zone by following the procedures in Sections 2090 and 2091.
(b) Except as provided in Section 56886 of the Government Code, a local agency formation commission shall have no power or duty to review and approve or disapprove a proposal to form a zone, a proposal to change the boundaries of a zone, or a proposal to dissolve a zone.
(Added by Stats. 2002, Ch. 395, Sec. 6. Effective January 1, 2003.)
2093.
(a) As determined by the board of trustees, a zone may provide any service at any level or levels within its boundaries that the district may provide.
(b) As determined by the board of trustees and pursuant to the requirements of this chapter, a zone may exercise any fiscal powers within its boundaries that the district may exercise.
(c) Any special taxes, special benefit assessments, or fees which are intended solely for the support of services within a zone shall be levied, assessed, and charged within the boundaries of the zone.
(Added by Stats. 2002, Ch. 395, Sec. 6. Effective January 1, 2003.)

CHAPTER 8. Pest Abatement Districts [2800 - 2910]

(Chapter 8 enacted by Stats. 1939, Ch. 60.)

ARTICLE 1. Definitions and General Provisions [2800 - 2805]
(Article 1 enacted by Stats. 1939, Ch. 60.)
2800.
"Pest," as used in this chapter, includes any plant, animal, insect, fish, or other matter or material, not under human control, which is offensive to the senses or interferes with the comfortable enjoyment of life, or which is detrimental to the agricultural industry of the State, and is not protected under any other provision of law.
(Amended by Stats. 1945, Ch. 957.)
2800.5.
As used in this chapter, "public nuisance" includes, but is not limited to, both of the following:
(a) Any breeding place or place of growth of a pest for which a district may be initiated under Section 2822, which exists by reason of any use made of the land on which it is found, or which exists by reason of any artificial change in the natural condition of the land on which it is found. The presence of any immature stages of any pest, or the rooted stages of any plant pest, shall constitute prima facie evidence the place is a breeding place for the pest.
(b) Water which is a breeding place for any pest for which a district may be initiated under Section 2822.
(Repealed and added by Stats. 1984, Ch. 911, Sec. 43. Effective September 7, 1984.)
2801.
This chapter is supplemental to any other provision of law relating to the abatement of pests or nuisances.
(Enacted by Stats. 1939, Ch. 60.)
2802.
"District," as used in this chapter, means any pest abatement district formed pursuant to this chapter or pursuant to any law which it supersedes.
(Enacted by Stats. 1939, Ch. 60.)
2803.
Any person who restrains, hinders, obstructs, or threatens any officer or employee of a district in the performance of that person's duties as an officer or employee, or any person who interferes with any work done by, or under the direction of, the district, is guilty of a misdemeanor.
(Amended by Stats. 1984, Ch. 911, Sec. 44. Effective September 7, 1984.)
2804.
In case of a dispute between governmental agencies on the need, or the methods and materials to be used, to abate or prevent a public nuisance under this chapter, the matter shall be subject to appeal to the State Director of Health Services within 10 days from the date the dispute arises. The director shall take testimony on the issue, shall decide the matter on appeal, and shall convey his decision to the parties within 30 days of the receipt of the appeal. The decision of the director shall be final and conclusive.
(Added by Stats. 1984, Ch. 911, Sec. 45. Effective September 7, 1984.)
2805.
(a) Except as otherwise provided in subdivision (b), every pest abatement district employee who handles, applies, or supervises the use of any pesticide for public health purposes, shall be certified by the state department as a vector control technician in at least one of the following categories commensurate with assigned duties:
(1) Mosquito control.
(2) Terrestrial invertebrate vector control.
(3) Vertebrate vector control.
(b) The state department may establish by regulation exemptions from the requirements of this section that are deemed reasonably necessary to further the purposes of this section.
(c) The state department shall establish by regulation minimum standards for continuing education for any government agency employee certified under Section 116110 and regulations adopted pursuant thereto, who handles, applies, or supervises the use of any pesticide for public health purposes.
(d) An official record of the completed continuing education units shall be maintained by the state department. If a certified technician fails to meet the requirements set forth under subdivision (c), the state department shall suspend the technician's certificate or certificates and immediately notify the technician and the employing district. The state

department shall establish by regulation procedures for reinstating a suspended certificate.

(e) The state department shall charge and collect a nonreturnable renewal fee of one hundred twenty dollars ($120) to be paid by each continuing education certificant on or before the first day of July, or on any other date that is determined by the state department. Each person employed on September 29, 1996, in a position that requires certification shall first pay the annual fee the first day of the first July following that date. All new certificants shall first pay the annual fee the first day of the first July following their certification.

(f) The state department shall collect and account for all money received pursuant to this section and shall deposit it in the Vectorborne Disease Account provided for in Section 116112. Notwithstanding Section 116112, fees deposited in the Vectorborne Disease Account pursuant to this section shall be available for expenditure, upon appropriation by the Legislature, to implement this section.

(g) Fees collected pursuant to this section shall be subject to the annual fee increase provisions of Section 100425.
(Amended by Stats. 2008, Ch. 758, Sec. 8. Effective September 30, 2008.)

ARTICLE 2. Formation [2822 - 2835]
 (Article 2 enacted by Stats. 1939, Ch. 60.)
2822.
The organization of a pest abatement district may be initiated by a petition, describing the exterior boundaries of the proposed district, and the nature of the pest or pests to be controlled or abated.
(Enacted by Stats. 1939, Ch. 60.)
2822.5.
The petition shall state the basis on which the property in the district shall be taxed for district purposes. The petition may include a plan for zones of benefit or other proposal which would provide equity in financing the district's purposes.
(Amended by Stats. 1984, Ch. 911, Sec. 46. Effective September 7, 1984.)
2823.
The petition may fix the maximum rate of assessments that may be levied by the district.
(Enacted by Stats. 1939, Ch. 60.)
2824.
The petition shall be signed by registered voters residing in the proposed district equal in number to ten per cent of the votes cast in the proposed district for Governor at the last preceding gubernatorial election. The petition may consist of any number of separate instruments, which shall be duplicates, except for the signatures and addresses of the signers. Each person who signs the petition shall also state his address.
(Enacted by Stats. 1939, Ch. 60.)
2825.
The petition shall be presented to the clerk of the county in which the land in the proposed district is situated. The clerk shall compare the signatures on the petition with the signatures of the registered voters on his records for the purpose of ascertaining whether the petition meets the signature requirements of this article.
(Enacted by Stats. 1939, Ch. 60.)
2826.
If the petition lacks sufficient signatures the county clerk shall certify that fact, and at any time within sixty days thereafter additional signatures may be presented to supplement the signatures on the original petition. The additional signatures shall be compared by the clerk in the same manner as the original signatures. If sufficient additional signatures are not presented, proceedings under the petition shall be terminated, without prejudice to the right to file a new petition.
(Enacted by Stats. 1939, Ch. 60.)
2827.
If the petition contains the requisite number of signatures the clerk shall make a certificate to that effect, and shall present the petition and his certificate to the board of supervisors.
(Enacted by Stats. 1939, Ch. 60.)
2828.
If the board of supervisors finds that the petition has been properly presented, the board shall, by resolution, fix a time for hearing the petition, which shall be not less than two nor more than five weeks from the time of its presentation. It shall also publish a notice of the time and place of the hearing in a newspaper of general circulation, printed and published in the county, for not less than two weeks prior to the time of the hearing.
(Enacted by Stats. 1939, Ch. 60.)
2829.
At the time of the hearing, or at any time to which it may be adjourned, the board of supervisors shall hear and consider all competent and relevant testimony or evidence offered in support of, or in opposition to, the formation of the district, and the proposed method of financing.
(Amended by Stats. 1984, Ch. 911, Sec. 47. Effective September 7, 1984.)
2830.
The board of supervisors may make such changes in the proposed boundaries of the district as it may consider advisable. It may exclude any land in the proposed district upon the application of the owner, or it may include any land outside and contiguous to the proposed district upon the application of the owner, if it determines that the exclusion or inclusion is proper.
(Enacted by Stats. 1939, Ch. 60.)
2831.

If, upon the hearing, the board of supervisors determines that the public interest or welfare of the proposed territory and its inhabitants requires the formation of the district, it shall, by resolution, declare its findings and order that the territory within the boundaries determined by it is a district, under an appropriate name to be selected by it.
(Enacted by Stats. 1939, Ch. 60.)
2832.
The clerk of the board of supervisors shall immediately record a certified copy of the order in the office of the county recorder in which the district is situated and also file a certified copy with the Secretary of State. The district is then formed as a pest abatement district, with all of the rights, privileges, and powers set forth in this chapter, and those necessarily incident thereto.
(Amended by Stats. 1959, Ch. 504.)
2833.
If at any time after the board of supervisors has entered its order for organization good cause appears therefor, the district board may, by a two-thirds vote of its members, adopt a resolution reciting the facts, declaring the advisability for a change of the district's name, and setting forth therein a new name for the district. A certified copy of such resolution shall be transmitted to the board of supervisors of the county in which the district is situated.
(Added by Stats. 1971, Ch. 276.)
2834.
Upon receipt of the certified copy of the resolution the board of supervisors shall:
(a) Enter an order changing the district's name to the name set forth in the resolution.
(b) Record a certified copy of the order in the office of the county recorder of the county in which the district is situated.
(c) File a certified copy of the order in the office of the Secretary of State.
(d) File a certified copy of the order in the office of the State Board of Equalization.
From and after the date of the filing of the certified copy with the Secretary of State the new name shall be the official name of the district.
(Added by Stats. 1971, Ch. 276.)
2835.
Upon a petition adopted by a four-fifths vote of the district board, or upon its own motion following the notice the board of supervisors deems sufficient and a public hearing, the board of supervisors, may, with the concurrence of the district board, add to, or delete from, the list of pests which the district may control. The board of supervisors at the hearing may also consider, and make changes in, the method of district taxation, as authorized by Section 2822.5, as though a new district were being formed.
(Added by Stats. 1984, Ch. 911, Sec. 48. Effective September 7, 1984.)

ARTICLE 3. Administration [2850 - 2853]
 (Article 3 enacted by Stats. 1939, Ch. 60.)
2850.
Within 30 days after incorporation the board of supervisors shall appoint a board of trustees, consisting of not less than five nor more than nine members to act as the governing body of the district. At any time after the appointment of the initial board of trustees the board of supervisors may, at the request of the existing board of trustees of the district, increase or decrease the number of members of the board of trustees, but such board shall under no circumstances consist of less than five nor more than nine members.
(Amended by Stats. 1947, Ch. 890.)
2851.
The members of the district board shall hold office at the pleasure of the board of supervisors. They shall serve without compensation, but shall be allowed their necessary traveling and other expenses incurred in performance of their official duties. In lieu of expenses, the district board may, by resolution, provide for the allowance and payment to each member of the board of a sum not exceeding one hundred dollars ($100) as expenses incurred in attending each business meeting of the board. Reimbursement for these expenses is subject to Sections 53232.2 and 53232.3 of the Government Code.
(Amended by Stats. 2005, Ch. 700, Sec. 9. Effective January 1, 2006.)
2852.
The district board may take all necessary or proper steps for the extermination of the pest or pests mentioned in the petition for the organization of the district, subject to the control of city or other public authorities having jurisdiction in the matter.
(Enacted by Stats. 1939, Ch. 60.)
2853.
A district may destroy a record pursuant to Chapter 7 (commencing with Section 60200) of Division 1 of Title 6 of the Government Code.
(Added by Stats. 2005, Ch. 158, Sec. 20. Effective January 1, 2006.)

ARTICLE 3.5. District Powers [2855 - 2868]
 (Article 3.5 added by Stats. 1974, Ch. 465.)
2855.
The district board may do all of the following:
(a) Purchase supplies and other personal property.
(b) Employ necessary labor.
(c) Acquire by purchase, condemnation, or otherwise, in the name of the district, any lands, rights-of-way, easements, or other real property necessary for the district.
(d) Sell or lease any lands, rights-of-way, easements, material, or other property, real or personal, acquired by the district.

(e) Make contracts to indemnify or compensate any owner of land or other property for any injury or damage caused by the exercise of the powers conferred by this chapter or of powers incident to those powers.

(f) Sue and be sued.

(g) Enter upon, without hindrance or notice, any property, either within the district or so reasonably adjacent that pests may disperse into the district, for any of the following purposes:

(1) To inspect to ascertain the presence of pests or their breeding places.

(2) To abate public nuisances in accordance with this article through direct control or through notice to the property owner to abate the public nuisance.

(3) To ascertain if a notice to abate a public nuisance has been complied with.

(4) To treat the property with any physical, chemical, or biological control measures deemed appropriate by the district board.

(h) Assess civil penalties, as determined in the discretion of the district board, but not to exceed five hundred dollars ($500) per day for each day that a notice or hearing order to abate a nuisance has not been complied with.

(i) Exercise the powers authorized by Section 2270 if the pests the district is empowered to control fall within the meaning of "vector," as defined in subdivision (f) of Section 2200.

(j) Do everything necessary to carry out the powers conferred by this chapter and carry out the objects of the formation of the district.

(Amended by Stats. 1984, Ch. 911, Sec. 50. Effective September 7, 1984.)

2855.3.

Every sale of real property made pursuant to subdivision (d) of Section 2855 shall be made at such place within the district as the district board shall specify, and such real property shall be sold to the highest bidder at public auction, after notice of sale is published once a week for two successive weeks in a newspaper of general circulation published in the district or county. If a newspaper of general circulation is not printed and published within such district or county, public notice of the sale shall be given for at least two weeks by notices posted in three public places in the district.

(Added by Stats. 1974, Ch. 465.)

2855.7.

The district board may borrow money in any fiscal year, which shall not exceed the anticipated revenue of that fiscal year and which shall be repaid in the same fiscal year. Such money shall be borrowed upon such other terms as the board shall fix; provided, that interest shall not exceed 6 percent, computed annually or semiannually.

The district board may also issue warrants payable upon a future date in the same fiscal year as issued, which shall be evidentiary of the obligation to repay the money so borrowed and interest thereon, and for that purpose such warrant may bear such interest as is fixed by the terms of the agreement to repay.

(Added by Stats. 1974, Ch. 465.)

2856.

Any nuisance may be abated in any action or proceeding by any remedy provided by this article or any other law.

(Added by Stats. 1974, Ch. 465.)

2857.

Whenever a nuisance exists upon any property, either in the district or in territory not in the district but so situated with respect to the district that pests from the territory migrate into, or otherwise encroach upon, the district, the district board may notify in writing the owner or party in possession, or the agent of either, of the existence of the nuisance. The contents of the written notice shall conform to the requirements of Section 2858.

(Amended by Stats. 1984, Ch. 911, Sec. 51. Effective September 7, 1984.)

2858.

The notice required by Section 2857 shall include all of the following:

(a) State the finding of the district that a public nuisance exists on the property and the location of the nuisance on the property.

(b) Direct the owner or party in possession to abate the nuisance within a specified time by destroying the pests which are present.

(c) Direct the owner or party in possession to perform, within a specified time, any work necessary to prevent the recurrence of the pests in the places specified in the notice.

(d) Inform the owner or party in possession that failure to comply with the requirements of subdivision (b) shall subject the owner or party in possession to civil penalties of not more than five hundred dollars ($500) per day for each day the nuisance continues after the time specified for the abatement of the nuisance in the notice.

(e) Inform the owner or party in possession that before complying with the requirements of the notice, the owner or party in possession may appear at a hearing before the district board at a time and place stated in the notice.

The notice shall be served upon the owner of record and the person having charge or possession, if other than the owner of record, of the property upon which the nuisance exists, and may be served by any person authorized by the district board in the same manner as a summons in a civil action.

(Amended by Stats. 1984, Ch. 911, Sec. 52. Effective September 7, 1984.)

2860.

If the property is owned by a person who is not a resident of the district, and is not in charge or possession of any person, and there is no tenant or agent of the owner upon whom service can be made, who can after diligent search be found; or if the owner of record of the property cannot after diligent search be found, the notice may be served by posting a copy in a conspicuous place upon the property for a period of 10 days, and by mailing a copy to the owner of record addressed to his address as given on the last completed assessment roll of the county in which the property is situated, or, in the absence of an address on the roll, to his last known address.

(Added by Stats. 1974, Ch. 465.)

2861.

Before complying with the requirements of the notice, the owner or party in possession may appear at a hearing before the board at a time and place fixed by the board and stated in the notice. At the hearing the district board shall determine whether the initial finding as set forth in the notice is correct and shall permit the owner or party in possession to present testimony in his behalf. If, after hearing all the facts, the board makes a determination that a nuisance exists on the property, the board shall order compliance with the requirements of the notice or with alternate instructions issued by the board.

Any failure to comply with any such order of the board issued pursuant to this section shall subject the owner or party in possession, if other than the owner of record, to civil penalties of not to exceed five hundred dollars ($500) per day for each day such order is not complied with.

(Added by Stats. 1974, Ch. 465.)

2861.5.

Any judicial review of administrative procedure provided for in this chapter shall be pursuant to Section 1094.5 of the Code of Civil Procedure.

(Added by Stats. 1974, Ch. 465.)

2861.7.

Any recurrence of the nuisance may be deemed to be a continuation of the original nuisance.

(Amended by Stats. 1984, Ch. 911, Sec. 53. Effective September 7, 1984.)

2862.

If the nuisance is not abated within the time specified in the notice or an order following the hearing, the district board may abate the nuisance.

(Amended by Stats. 1984, Ch. 911, Sec. 54. Effective September 7, 1984.)

2862.5.

The cost of abating a nuisance shall be repaid to the district by the owner of the property. However, the owner shall not be required to pay for the costs unless, either prior to or subsequent to the abatement by the district, a hearing is held by the district board, at which the property owner is afforded an opportunity to be heard, and the district board determines that a nuisance actually exists or that a nuisance existed prior to the abatement by the district.

(Added by Stats. 1984, Ch. 911, Sec. 55. Effective September 7, 1984.)

2863.

When any nuisance is found to exist on any property subject to the control of any state or local agency, the district shall notify the state or local agency of the existence of the nuisance. Sections 2858, 2860, 2861, 2861.5, and 2862 shall govern the contents of the notice and the manner of serving it, the right of the state or local agency to a hearing before the board, the hearing before the board, and the power of the district to abate the nuisance if it is not abated by the state or local agency. If the state or local agency determines that the order to prevent recurrence of the breeding specified in the notice to abate the nuisance is excessive or inappropriate for the intended use of the land, or if the state or local agency determines that a nuisance, as specified in Section 2800.5, does not exist, the agency may appeal the decision of the board to the State Director of Health Services within 10 days subsequent to the hearing. The director shall decide the matters on appeal and convey his or her decision to the agency and district within 30 days of the receipt of the appeal. The decision of the director shall be final and conclusive. If the control of the nuisance is performed by the district, the cost for that control is a charge against, and shall be paid from, the maintenance fund or from other funds for the support of the state or local agency.

Any state or local agency and a district may enter into contractual agreements to provide control of nuisances. The authority which is granted by this paragraph is in addition to any other authority which a state or local agency and a district may have to enter into contractual agreements for the control of public nuisances, as defined in Section 2800.5. As used in this section, "state agency" means an agency defined in Section 11000 of the Government Code, and "local agency" means a city, county, city and county, district, or other public corporation.

(Amended by Stats. 1984, Ch. 911, Sec. 56. Effective September 7, 1984.)

2864.

Upon the failure of the property owner or the person in possession of the property to pay the district for all sums expended by the district in abating a nuisance or preventing its recurrence, or upon the failure to pay all civil penalties, the costs or penalties, or both, shall become a lien upon the property on which the nuisance was abated or its recurrence prevented when notice of the lien is filed and recorded. However, if the property has been conveyed prior to the recordation of the lien, the lien shall not attach to the real property, but shall remain the debt of the person who owned the land at the time the costs were incurred, and the debt may be recovered by the district board against the debtor, as provided in Section 2866.

(Repealed and added by Stats. 1984, Ch. 911, Sec. 58. Effective September 7, 1984.)

2864.7.

A copy of the filed and recorded lien may be given to the county assessor and tax collector, who, upon receipt of the lien, shall add the amount of the lien to the next regular tax bill levied against the parcel for district purposes.

(Amended by Stats. 1984, Ch. 911, Sec. 59. Effective September 7, 1984.)

2865.

If the county assessor and the tax collector assess property and collect taxes for the district, a certified copy of the lien shall be filed with the county auditor on or before August 10th. The descriptions of the parcels reported shall be those used for the same parcels on the county assessor's map books for the current year.
(Amended by Stats. 1984, Ch. 911, Sec. 60. Effective September 7, 1984.)
2865.5.

The county auditor shall enter each lien on the county tax roll opposite the parcel of land.
(Amended by Stats. 1984, Ch. 911, Sec. 61. Effective September 7, 1984.)
2866.

The amount of the lien shall be collected at the same time and in the same manner as ordinary county taxes are collected, and shall be subject to the same penalties and the same procedure and sale in case of delinquency, as provided for ordinary county taxes. All laws applicable to the levy, collection, and enforcement of county taxes shall be applicable to the lien, except that if any real property to which the cost of abatement relates has been transferred or conveyed to a bona fide purchaser for value, or if a lien of a bona fide encumbrancer for value has been created and attaches thereon, prior to the date on which the first installment of taxes would become delinquent, then the cost of abatement shall not result in a lien against the real property, but instead shall be transferred to the unsecured roll for collection.
(Amended by Stats. 1985, Ch. 48, Sec. 4. Effective May 20, 1985.)
2867.

The lien provisions of this article do not apply to the property of any county, city, district, or other public corporation. However, the governing body of the county, city, district, or other public corporation shall repay to a district the amount expended by the district upon any of its property under this article upon presentation by the district board of a verified claim or bill.
(Added by Stats. 1974, Ch. 465.)
2868.

Any amounts collected by a county on account of a lien authorized by this article, other than the amounts requested to be paid into the county general fund pursuant to Section 29304 of the Government Code, shall be paid to the district.
(Amended by Stats. 1984, Ch. 911, Sec. 63. Effective September 7, 1984.)

ARTICLE 4. Taxation [2870 - 2876]
(Article 4 enacted by Stats. 1939, Ch. 60.)
2870.

The district board shall annually before July 10 prepare a written estimate of the amount of money necessary for the purposes of the district during the ensuing fiscal year.
(Amended by Stats. 1984, Ch. 911, Sec. 64. Effective September 7, 1984.)
2871.

The county auditor shall allocate to a district its share of property tax revenue pursuant to Chapter 6 (commencing with Section 95) of Part 0.5 of Division 1 of the Revenue and Taxation Code.
(Repealed and added by Stats. 1984, Ch. 911, Sec. 66. Effective September 7, 1984.)
2871.5.

(a) If the petition for formation of the district states that the property shall be taxed on the basis of area, the rate shall be based on area of land, regardless of assessed valuation.
(b) If the petition for formation of the district states that property shall be taxed on the basis of a combination of area and some other basis, the district board shall, after a public hearing, determine the proportion of each source of revenue, and may consider zones of benefit or other equitable methods of establishing the rate to be charged based on area.
(c) The county assessor of each county shall prepare an assessment roll showing the names and addresses and the acreage owned by each person owning land within a district, which roll shall be the basis for the tax provided for in this section.
(Amended by Stats. 1984, Ch. 911, Sec. 67. Effective September 7, 1984.)
2871.7.

After a public hearing, the district board shall determine the rate of the tax.
(Repealed and added by Stats. 1984, Ch. 911, Sec. 69. Effective September 7, 1984.}
2871.8.

(a) Whenever it appears to the district board that the amount of funds required during an ensuing fiscal year will exceed the amount available, the district board may call an election to submit to the electors of the district the question of whether a special tax shall be voted for raising the additional funds, pursuant to Article 3.5 (commencing with Section 50075) of Chapter 1 of Part 1 of Division 1 of Title 5 of the Government Code.
(b) Notice of the election shall be published for at least four weeks prior to the election.
(c) No particular form of ballot shall be required, nor shall any informalities in conducting the election invalidate it if it is otherwise fairly conducted.
(d) At the election the ballots shall contain the words "Shall the district vote a tax to raise the additional sum of _____ ?" or words equivalent thereto.
(e) The district board shall canvass the votes cast at the election, and, if two-thirds of the votes cast are in favor of the imposition of the tax, shall report the result to the board of supervisors of the county in which the district is situated, stating the additional amount of money required to be raised. If the district is in more than one county, the additional amount shall be prorated for each county by the district board in the same way that the district's original total estimate of funds is prorated. The district board shall furnish the board of supervisors and auditor of each county a written statement of the apportionment for each county.
(Added by Stats. 1984, Ch. 911, Sec. 70. Effective September 7, 1984.)
2871.9.

Any district formed prior to January 1, 1985, may petition the board of supervisors for a change in the method of financing the district's operations, as provided in this chapter. The board of supervisors shall accept the petition, in lieu of the petition required by Section 2822.5, and shall proceed to consider changes in the method of district financing consistent with Article 2 (commencing with Section 2210) of Chapter 5.
(Added by Stats. 1984, Ch. 911, Sec. 71. Effective September 7, 1984.)
2872.

All taxes and assessments levied under this chapter shall be assessed and collected at the same time and in the same manner as other taxes are collected for county purposes, and shall be paid into the county treasury to the credit of the district.
(Amended by Stats. 1984, Ch. 911, Sec. 72. Effective September 7, 1984.)
2873.

The funds of the district shall be withdrawn from the treasury upon the warrant of the district board.
(Enacted by Stats. 1939, Ch. 60.)
2874.

The board of supervisors, from time to time, may order a temporary transfer of money from other available funds in the county treasury to the credit of the district fund. The transfer shall be made only upon resolution adopted by the board of supervisors directing the treasurer to make the transfer. It shall not exceed eighty-five per cent of the taxes accruing to the district, and shall not be made prior to the first day of the fiscal year nor after the last Monday in April of the current fiscal year. Any funds transferred shall be replaced from the taxes accruing to the district before any other obligation of the district is met from those taxes.
(Enacted by Stats. 1939, Ch. 60.)
2876.

Notwithstanding the basis upon which property in the district is taxed, if a district is organized in any year too late for the levy of a tax in that year or in the next ensuing year, the board of supervisors is authorized to transfer funds of the county not immediately needed for county purposes to the district fund to be used for the payment of the expenses of the district until the district's special assessment tax receipts are available to it. The board of supervisors shall include, in the levy of taxes for the district for the first fiscal year in which a tax may be levied, a sum sufficient to repay to the county the amounts transferred to the district for the portion or portions of the preceding fiscal year or years for which no levy of taxes was made for that purpose. The amounts transferred shall be retransferred to the county treasury from the district fund out of the first available receipts from the tax levy.
(Amended by Stats. 1984, Ch. 911, Sec. 74. Effective September 7, 1984.)

ARTICLE 4.1. Standby Charges for Public Health Emergencies [2877 - 2878]
(Article 4.1 added by Stats. 1983, Ch. 1055, Sec. 5.)
2877.

The Legislature finds that unabated outbreaks of mosquitoes pose a serious threat to the public health and safety. The Legislature further finds that public agencies, including pest abatement districts, must be prepared to abate extraordinary outbreaks of mosquitoes. The Legislature further finds and declares that to protect the public health and safety from unabated outbreaks of mosquitoes, it is necessary to enact this article to provide pest abatement districts with the ability to abate mosquitoes.
(Added by Stats. 1983, Ch. 1055, Sec. 5.)
2878.

A pest abatement district may adopt an ordinance to fix an emergency mosquito abatement standby charge pursuant to the provisions of Article 5.1 (commencing with Section 2315) of Chapter 5, except to the extent that the provisions of that article conflict with the provisions of this chapter, in which case the provisions of this chapter shall be in addition to the provisions of that article.
(Added by Stats. 1983, Ch. 1055, Sec. 5.)

ARTICLE 4.5. Claims [2880- 2880.]
(Article 4.5 added by Stats. 1959, Ch. 1727.)
2880.

All claims for money or damages against the district are governed by Part 3 (commencing with Section 900) and Part 4 (commencing with Section 940) of Division 3.6 of Title 1 of the Government Code except as provided therein, or by other statutes or regulations expressly applicable thereto.
(Amended by Stats. 1963, Ch. 1715.)

ARTICLE 5. Annexation [2900 - 2901]
(Article 5 enacted by Stats. 1939, Ch. 60.)
2900.

At any time after the incorporation of a district, land contiguous to it may be annexed, if the board of trustees finds that the annexation will benefit both the land to be annexed and the district.
(Amended by Stats. 1965, Ch. 2043.)
2901.

Annexations may proceed under Article 2 (commencing with Section 2822), as though territory to be annexed were a new district, except that the pest or pests to be controlled shall be the same as those which the annexing district is authorized to control.
(Added by Stats. 1984, Ch. 911, Sec. 75. Effective September 7, 1984.)

ARTICLE 5a. Consolidation [2910- 2910.]
(Article 5a added by Stats. 1947, Ch. 1458.)
2910.

Two or more contiguous pest abatement districts may be consolidated.

(Amended by Stats. 1965, Ch. 2043.)

DIVISION 5. SANITATION [4600 - 6127]

(Division 5 enacted by Stats. 1939, Ch. 60.)

PART 3. COMMUNITY FACILITIES [4600 - 6127]

(Heading of Part 3 amended by Stats. 1970, Ch. 420.)

CHAPTER 1. Community Facilities Law of 1911 [4600 - 4650]

(Heading of Chapter 1 amended by Stats. 1970, Ch. 420.)

ARTICLE 1. Definitions and General Provisions [4600 - 4603]

(Article 1 enacted by Stats. 1939, Ch. 60.)

4600.

This chapter shall be known as the Community Facilities Law of 1911.

(Amended by Stats. 1970, Ch. 420.)

4601.

Unless the context otherwise requires, the definitions in this article govern the construction of this chapter.

(Added by Stats. 1963, Ch. 756.)

4602.

"City" means the city in which the district is located. If a district is not entirely within the boundaries of a single city, "city" means the initiating city.

(Added by Stats. 1963, Ch. 756.)

4602.1.

"District" means any district which is formed pursuant to this chapter or pursuant to any law which it supersedes.

(Added by renumbering Section 4600 by Stats. 1963, Ch. 756.)

4602.2.

"Governing body" means the city council or other legislative body of the city.

(Added by Stats. 1963, Ch. 756.)

4602.3.

"Initiating city" means the city whose governing body initiated the proceeding for the formation of a district which is not entirely within the boundaries of a single city.

(Added by Stats. 1963, Ch. 756.)

4602.4.

Improvement means any or all of the following:

(a) The acquisition or construction of sanitary sewers of all types, including, but not limited to, outfall, trunk, intercepting, connecting, lateral, and house connection sewers.

(b) The acquisition or construction of sewage treatment plants, works, or systems.

(c) The acquisition or construction of other improvements, works, or system for the collection, transmission, treatment, or disposal of sewage or industrial waste.

(d) The acquisition or construction of sewers, drains, pipelines, conduits, culverts, or ditches for the collection, transmission, or disposal of surface or storm water.

(e) The acquisition or construction of other improvements, works, or system for the purpose of surface or storm water drainage or for the purpose of flood control.

(f) The acquisition, construction, or extension of waterworks, water systems or water distribution systems.

(g) The acquisition or construction of works or improvements appurtenant or related to any of the works, improvements, or systems described in subdivisions (a) to (f), inclusive.

(h) Additions to, or the reconstruction or improvement of, any of the works, improvements, or systems described in subdivisions (a) to (g), inclusive.

(i) The acquisition of any land, rights-of-way, capacity rights, rights of use, or other property needed for any of the works, improvements, or systems described in subdivisions (a) to (h), inclusive.

(Added by Stats. 1986, Ch. 195, Sec. 34.)

4602.5.

In cities within a county of the 20th class, as defined in Section 28041 of the Government Code, improvement shall also mean the acquisition, construction, maintenance, and operation of any public buildings which would serve as a community center facility, including, but not limited to, an exhibition building, an auditorium, a stadium, and a sports arena; and the acquisition and improvement of any land, rights-of-way, rights of use, or other property needed for any of the improvements described in this section, or for offstreet parking facilities therefor.

For the purposes of this section, at the hearing held pursuant to Section 4611, the governing body may exclude from the proposed district any territory the inhabitants of which would not be benefited by the proposed improvements as finally determined.

(Added by Stats. 1986, Ch. 195, Sec. 35.)

4603.

This chapter does not affect any other law under which improvements may be made within or by any city but it provides an alternate system of proceedings for sewer work or improvement. Improvements may be made either pursuant to this chapter, or pursuant to any other law. If, however, any proceedings are commenced pursuant to this chapter, its provisions apply to any improvement made under those proceedings until such improvement is completed.

If, after an improvement has been made pursuant to this chapter, the governing body of any city determines that it is necessary or convenient to make any additional improvement, the governing body may proceed to do so either pursuant to this chapter or under any other appropriate law. If the additional improvement is made pursuant to this chapter for the same district, the procedure shall be the same as that which is provided under this chapter for the making of the initial improvement. It is not necessary to reform the district if the governing body finds, following the hearing which is provided for by Section 4611 that the additional improvement is of benefit to the entire district which was previously formed under this chapter as such district is then constituted. As an alternative method, the governing body may make such additional improvement by forming a new district pursuant to this chapter which may include, in whole or in part, territory which is included in any district previously formed pursuant to this chapter.

(Amended by Stats. 1965, Ch. 828.)

ARTICLE 2. Formation [4605 - 4613]

(Article 2 enacted by Stats. 1939, Ch. 60.)

4605.

The governing body of any city may create an improvement district within the city pursuant to this chapter whenever in its judgment the district is necessary or convenient for any improvement authorized by this chapter.

(Amended by Stats. 1970, Ch. 420.)

4606.

A district may be formed to make any improvement and to provide for the incurring of indebtedness to pay for the costs and expenses of such improvement.

(Amended by Stats. 1965, Ch. 828.)

4607.

Whenever the governing body of a city determines that the public interest or convenience requires the making of any improvement in any part of the territory of the city, it may pass a resolution to that effect. The resolution shall be passed by a vote of at least two-thirds of the members of the governing body. It shall describe the improvement in general terms. For the purpose of such description, reference may be made to maps, plats, plans, or other documents on file in the office of the clerk of the city. Any improvements may be combined into a single project, the indebtedness for which is to be submitted to the electors as a single proposition.

The resolution shall also contain the total dollar amount of a general estimate of the costs and expenses of the proposed improvement. In arriving at such estimate, the governing body may include the estimated amounts of any or all of the items which are set forth in Section 4625. The resolution need not, however, itemize or separately state any of the items included in the costs and expenses.

(Amended by Stats. 1965, Ch. 828.)

4609.

The resolution shall do all of the following:

(a) Describe the boundaries of the proposed district. The district may consist of two or more noncontiguous parcels.

(b) Designate the district by a distinctive name and number.

(c) Declare the district to be the district benefited by the proposed improvement.

(d) Name a time and place for the hearing of objections by any person interested in the formation of the district, in the inclusion within the district of any land within the boundaries described in the resolution or in the making of the proposed improvement.

(Amended by Stats. 1965, Ch. 828.)

4610.

The resolution, together with the names of the members of the governing body voting for and against it shall be published once a week for at least two successive weeks in a newspaper of general circulation printed and published in the city. The first publication shall not be more than 60 nor less than 30 days prior to the date fixed for the hearing. If there is no newspaper of general circulation printed and published in the city, the resolution shall be so published in a newspaper of general circulation printed and published in the county in which the city is located.

(Amended by Stats. 1963, Ch. 756.)

4610.5.

Copies of the resolution shall also be posted in three public places within the proposed district not earlier than the 60th day or later than the 30th day prior to the hearing. Not earlier than 60 nor later than 30 days prior to the hearing, a copy of the resolution shall also be mailed, postage prepaid, to each person to whom land in the proposed district is assessed as such owner is shown on the last equalized county assessment roll, at his address as shown upon the roll, and to each person who has any interest in any land within the proposed district whose name and address and a designation of the land in which he is interested is on file in the office of the city clerk. Any error, omission, or mistake in such mailing, or any failure of any person to receive such copy shall not invalidate the proceedings pursuant to this chapter.

(Added by Stats. 1963, Ch. 756.)

4611.

On the day fixed for the hearing, or any day to which the hearing is continued, the governing body shall hear and consider all written and oral objections presented to the formation of the district, the inclusion of any lands in the district, or the making of the improvement which is proposed.

At the hearing, the governing body may make changes in the improvement but the estimated costs and expenses of the improvement as changed, as determined by the governing body at the time of the change, shall not exceed by more than 10 percent the amount determined under Section 4607.

At the hearing, the governing body may exclude from the district any territory that in its opinion would not be benefited by the improvement as finally determined. The governing body shall not, however, modify the boundaries of the proposed district so as to exclude from it any land which would in the judgment of the governing body be benefited by the improvement as finally determined nor shall the governing body include in the proposed district any lands which will not in its judgment be so benefited.
(Amended by Stats. 1965, Ch. 828.)

4611.5.

At the hearing, the governing body may add territory to the district if the owners of all of the land in the territory which is proposed to be added to the district have requested such addition in writing, or the governing body has first adopted a resolution of intention to do so. The resolution shall describe the boundaries of the territory which is proposed to be added to the district and shall state the time and place to which the hearing will be continued for the purpose of hearing objections to the proposed addition. Not later than 20 days before the time of such continued hearing, a copy of such resolution shall be mailed, postage prepaid, to each person to whom land in the territory which is proposed to be added to the district is assessed, as such owner is shown on the last equalized county assessment roll, at his address as shown upon the roll. A copy of such resolution shall also be mailed to each person who has any interest in any land within such territory whose name and address and a designation of the land in which he is interested as on file in the office of the city clerk. Any error, omission, or mistake in such mailing, or any failure of any person to receive such copy shall not invalidate the proceedings pursuant to this chapter.

At the continued hearing, the governing body shall hear all objections to the proposed addition and may then take action adding to the district all or part of the territory which is described in the resolution of intention.
(Added by Stats. 1963, Ch. 756.)

4612.

After making all necessary and proper changes in the boundaries, or in the improvement, the governing body may, by a resolution which is passed by a vote of two-thirds of all of its members, establish the district, fix and determine its boundaries, and generally describe the improvement as finally determined. This resolution, together with the names of the members of the governing body voting for and against it shall be spread upon the minutes of the governing body.
(Amended by Stats. 1965, Ch. 828.)

4613.

A certified copy of the resolution which establishes the district shall be recorded in the office of the county recorder. Certified copies of such resolution, together with a map or plat which shows such boundaries, shall also be filed with the county assessor, the county clerk, and the State Board of Equalization. Upon such recordation in the office of the county recorder, the district is organized. No action or proceeding which contests the validity of the district or its organization shall be had or taken in any court, state or federal, unless it is commenced within 60 days from the date of the recordation of the resolution establishing the district in the office of the county recorder.
(Added by Stats. 1963, Ch. 756.)

ARTICLE 2a. Formation of Districts in Two or More Municipal Corporations and Also in Unincorporated Territory [4614.1 - 4614.15]

(Article 2a added by Stats. 1956, 1st Ex. Sess., Ch. 8.)

4614.1.

Districts may be formed pursuant to this article for the purpose of making any improvement which will be of benefit to territory partially within the initiating city and partially within any other city or within unincorporated area of the same county, or both.
(Amended by Stats. 1965, Ch. 828.)

4614.2.

Any city may initiate proceedings for the formation of a district and the making of improvements pursuant to this article whenever the governing body of such city determines that it is desirable that a district be organized pursuant to this article. Except as otherwise provided in this article, the procedure for the formation of a district pursuant to this article shall be the same as the procedure which is provided in this chapter where the district is within a single city.
(Amended by Stats. 1965, Ch. 828.)

4614.3.

If the proposed district includes any part of any other incorporated city, the governing body of the initiating city shall file with the governing body of each such other city a certified copy of its resolution adopted pursuant to Section 4607, which resolution shall contain a request that the governing body of each such other city consent to the formation of such district. The governing body of the initiating city shall not form the district unless prior to the conclusion of the hearing which is provided for by Section 4611 the governing body of each city, any part of which is proposed to be included in the district, by resolution, consents to the formation of the district.
(Amended by Stats. 1963, Ch. 756.)

4614.4.

If any part of the district includes any unincorporated territory of the county, the governing body of the initiating city shall file with the board of supervisors of the county in which such unincorporated territory is situated a certified copy of its resolution adopted pursuant to Section 4607, which resolution shall contain a request that the board of supervisors consent to the formation of such district. The governing body of the initiating city shall not form the district unless prior to the conclusion of the hearing which is

provided for by Section 4611 the board of supervisors of the county in which such unincorporated territory is located, by resolution, consents to the formation of the district which will include such unincorporated territory within its boundaries.
(Amended by Stats. 1963, Ch. 756.)

4614.5.

Whenever the governing body of each city which is included in whole or in part within the district which is to be organized, and the board of supervisors if the district includes any unincorporated territory, has consented to the formation of the district by filing a resolution of concurrence with the governing body of the initiating city, the governing body of the initiating city has full jurisdiction to proceed with the formation of the proposed district. Upon the filing with the governing body of the initiating city of all necessary concurring resolutions of the governing body of any city or of the board of supervisors of the county, as the case may be, the governing body of the initiating city has the sole and exclusive jurisdiction to proceed with the formation of the district, to conduct all hearings on the formation of the district, to make all necessary changes in the boundaries of the proposed district or improvement, to conduct all proceedings on the formation of the district and to take any other action permitted by this chapter with like force and effect as though such district were wholly within the boundaries of the initiating city. The governing body of the initiating city shall not, however, add to the district at the hearing which is provided for by Section 4611 any territory within another city or within unincorporated territory unless it first obtains a consent to such addition which is expressed by a resolution adopted by the governing body of such other city or by the board of supervisors, as the case may be.
(Amended by Stats. 1965, Ch. 828.)

4614.11.

Upon the formation of any district pursuant to this article, the district shall be governed by and under the jurisdiction of the governing body of the initiating city. The governing body of the initiating city may conduct all of the affairs of the district, call and hold bond elections in the district, construct all improvements in the district, cause taxes to be levied and collected upon all taxable property in the district, and pass such necessary legislation as may be required for such improvements, with the same force and effect as though all of the area in the district were included within the boundaries of the initiating city.
(Amended by Stats. 1970, Ch. 420.)

4614.13.

If bonds are authorized and are issued or are expected to be issued on behalf of any district which is organized pursuant to this article, the governing body of the initiating city shall, on or before the 15th day of July of each year, certify to the board of supervisors of the county in which the district is located, the amount to be raised for the payment of the principal of and interest on the bonds in accordance with Section 4638 and, if applicable, Section 4639.5. The county auditor shall determine the rate of taxation which shall be clearly sufficient to raise such amount. The county auditor shall compute and enter in a separate column in the county assessment roll the respective sums to be paid as the district tax on the taxable property in the district. The board of supervisors of the county in which the district is located shall, at the time of fixing the general county tax levy and in the manner which is provided for such tax levy, levy and collect each year upon all of the taxable property in the district a tax in accordance with Section 4638 and, if applicable, Section 4639.5. The taxes so levied shall be in addition to all other taxes levied for county or city purposes and in addition to taxes levied pursuant to Section 4614.14 and shall be collected at the same time and in the same manner as county taxes are collected. When such taxes are collected they shall be paid to the county treasurer who shall forthwith remit them to the city treasurer of the initiating city. The taxes are a lien on all taxable property in the district and shall be of the same force and effect as the lien for county taxes. Their collection shall be enforced by the same means as provided for the enforcement of the lien of county taxes. The city treasurer of the initiating city shall hold such taxes in trust, separate and apart from all other city funds and use and apply them solely to the payment of bond principal and interest.
(Amended by Stats. 1963, Ch. 756.)

4614.15.

This chapter does not prevent two or more cities or the board of supervisors of any county from entering into co-operation agreements for the joint acquisition, construction, or use of joint sanitary sewage facilities, flood control works, and storm water drainage systems.
(Amended by Stats. 1963, Ch. 756.)

ARTICLE 3. Issuance of Bonds [4615 - 4625]

(Article 3 enacted by Stats. 1939, Ch. 60.)

4615.

At any meeting after the passage and recording of the resolution establishing the district, the governing body may, by a resolution passed by a vote of two-thirds of all its members, call an election to be held in the district for the purpose of voting on the question of incurring indebtedness for the purpose of making the improvement as finally determined.
(Amended by Stats. 1965, Ch. 828.)

4616.

The resolution calling the special election shall do all of the following:
(a) Describe the boundaries of the district as finally determined and refer to the district by its name and number.
(b) Describe in general terms the improvement as finally determined and state the dollar amount of the estimated cost and expenses of the proposed improvement, which amount shall not exceed by more than 10 percent the amount determined under Section 4607.

(c) State the amount of the principal of the indebtedness to be incurred for the purpose of paying the costs and expenses, which amount shall not exceed the estimate under subdivision (b) of this section.

(d) State the rate of interest or a maximum rate of interest to be paid on the indebtedness, which rate shall not be more than the rate specified in this chapter.

(e) Fix the date on which the special election shall be held.

(f) Determine the manner of holding the election, and the manner of voting for or against the incurring of the indebtedness.

(Amended by Stats. 1965, Ch. 828.)

4617.

In all particulars not recited in this chapter or in the resolution, the election shall be held as is provided by law for holding general elections in the city. At the election, the measure of incurrring indebtedness for the purposes set forth in the resolution shall be submitted to the voters of the district.

(Amended by Stats. 1963, Ch. 756.)

4618.

The maximum rate of interest to be paid on the bonded indebtedness shall be 8 percent per annum, and shall be payable semiannually. The first interest payable on the bonds or any series of the bonds may, however, be for any period not exceeding one year, as determined by the governing body.

(Amended by Stats. 1975, Ch. 130.)

4619.

The resolution calling the election shall be published once a week for two successive weeks prior to the date set for the election in a newspaper of general circulation, which is printed and published in the city. The first publication shall be not less than 30 days prior to the date of the election.

In any city where no newspaper is printed and published, the resolution shall be posted in three public places in the district not later than 30 days prior to the date set for the election. No other notice of the election need be given.

(Amended by Stats. 1963, Ch. 756.)

4620.

If two-thirds of the votes cast upon the measure are in favor of the issuance of the bonds, the bonds may be issued and the indebtedness incurred.

If less than two-thirds of the votes cast are in favor of the issuance of the bonds, the governing body of the city shall not within six months after the election pass any resolution which calls another election for incurring any indebtedness for sewer work or improvement within that district or in any district which has within its boundaries any of the territory of that district.

(Amended by Stats. 1963, Ch. 756.)

4621.

All bonds issued under this chapter shall be issued in the name of the city in which the district has been formed, or in the name of the initiating city, as the case may be, shall be in such form as the governing body may determine, and shall be payable at the time and in the manner determined by the governing body, at a place within the United States, to be fixed by the governing body and designated in the bonds. The maturity date of a bond need not be an anniversary of its date. The governing body may divide the principal amount of any issue of bonds into two or more series and fix different dates for the bonds of each series. The bonds of one series may be made payable at different times from those of any other series. The final maturity date of any issue of bonds, or of any series, shall not exceed 40 years from the date of such bonds, or the date of such series of the bonds. Bonds issued pursuant to this chapter shall not constitute indebtedness within the meaning of Section 29909 or Section 43605 of the Government Code.

The governing body may provide for the call and redemption of any bond prior to maturity at such time or times and at such price or prices and upon such other terms as it may specify, but no bond shall be subject to call or redemption prior to maturity unless a statement to that effect is printed on the bond.

(Amended by Stats. 1963, Ch. 756.)

4622.

The bonds shall be issued in any denominations which the governing body may determine.

The bonds shall be signed by the mayor, or by such other officer of the city as shall be designated for that purpose by the governing body by resolution, and shall also be signed by the city treasurer and countersigned by the city clerk or a deputy clerk.

The coupons of the bonds shall be numbered consecutively and signed by the treasurer. All signatures and countersignatures on the bonds and coupons, except that of the clerk or his deputy, may be printed, lithographed, or engraved.

If any officer whose signature or countersignature appears on the bonds or coupons ceases to be an officer before the delivery of the bonds to the purchaser, his signature or countersignature is as valid and sufficient for all purposes, as if he had remained in office.

(Amended by Stats. 1963, Ch. 756.)

4623.

The governing body may issue and sell the bonds at not less than their par value. The proceeds of the sale shall be placed in the city treasury to the credit of the proper improvement district fund and shall be applied exclusively to the purposes and objects specified in the resolution calling the election.

(Amended by Stats. 1965, Ch. 828.)

4623.1.

(a) When the purposes and objects specified in any measure incurring bonded indebtedness submitted at any special election called for that purpose have been accomplished and any proceeds of sale of bonds authorized at the special election

remain unexpended, or any bonds authorized at the special election remain unissued and unsold (the unexpended proceeds and the proceeds of sale of the then unissued bonds being hereinafter in this section together referred to as "unexpended bond proceeds"), the unexpended bond proceeds may be applied to payment of the costs (including any or all of the items specified in Section 4625) of any improvements, additions, betterments or extensions (hereinafter in this section collectively referred to as "improvements") to the sewer work or improvement described in the resolution or ordinance calling the special election if the governing body shall first find and determine that:

(1) The improvements are reasonably related to the purposes and objects included within the terms of the bond measure approved at the special election or are necessary to carry out the purposes and objects.

(2) The improvements will be acquired or constructed entirely within the area of and will benefit the district as it existed on the date on which the special election was called to authorize the bonds sold, or to be sold, to provide the unexpended bond proceeds.

(3) The resolution providing for the issuance of the bonds authorized at the special election and already outstanding does not prohibit, or can be and is amended to permit, the application of the unexpended bond proceeds to payment of the costs of the improvements; and if a hearing is duly called, noticed and held and resolutions are adopted by the governing body as provided in paragraph (b) of this section.

(b) Before so applying the unexpended bond proceeds the governing body shall adopt a resolution stating the following:

(1) The name and number of the district and a reference by date of adoption to the resolution or resolutions in which the boundaries of the district are set forth.

(2) The date of the special election at which the bonds (which provided, or which when sold will provide, the unexpended bond proceeds) were authorized, the aggregate principal amount of bonds outstanding, the amount (if any) of unexpended bond proceeds provided by bonds theretofore sold and the principal amount of authorized, but unissued bonds (if any), proposed to be sold to provide unexpended bond proceeds.

(3) A general description of the improvements proposed to be acquired or constructed, the estimated costs thereof and the amount of unexpended bond proceeds to be applied to payment of the costs.

(4) A time and place for the hearing of objections to the proposed improvements or to the proposed expenditure of the unexpended bond proceeds by any person who is on the date of the hearing an owner of land or a registered voter within the boundaries of the district as it existed on the date of the special election at which the bonds were authorized.

The resolution shall be published, posted and mailed as provided in Sections 4610 and 4610.5 for a resolution relating to formation of a district. On the day fixed for the hearing, or on any date to which the hearing is continued, the governing body shall hear and consider all written and oral objections presented to the proposed improvements or to the proposed expenditure of the unexpended bond proceeds. At the hearing, the governing body may make any changes in the proposed improvements or proposed expenditures as appear necessary in the public interest; and the governing body may not exclude any land from the district and shall abandon the proceedings if it finds that any land within the boundaries of the district as it existed on the date the special election was called will not be benefited by the proposed improvements.

At the conclusion of the hearing, if the proceedings are not abandoned and if the governing body overrules all protests and objections and finds that the provisions of this section are complied with, the governing body may by a resolution which is passed by a vote of two-thirds of all its members approve the proposed improvements and proposed expenditure of the unexpended bond proceeds and, if bonds are to be issued and sold, may also, by the resolution provide for the issue and sale of the bonds.

(Added by Stats. 1965, Ch. 5.)

4623.5.

Before selling the bonds, or any part of the bonds, the governing body shall give notice inviting sealed bids in such manner and for such time as the governing body may prescribe. If satisfactory bids are received, the bonds offered for sale shall be awarded to the highest responsible bidder. If no bids are received, or if the governing body determines that the bids received are not satisfactory as to price or responsibility of the bidders, the governing body may reject all bids received, if any, and either readvertise or sell the bonds at private sale.

(Added by Stats. 1963, Ch. 756.)

4624.

An action to determine the validity of bonds issued pursuant to this chapter may be brought pursuant to Chapter 9 (commencing with Section 860), Title 10, Part 2 of the Code of Civil Procedure.

(Amended by Stats. 1963, Ch. 756.)

4625.

In determining the amount of bonds to be issued, the legislative body may include all of the following:

(a) All costs and expenses and estimated costs and expenses incidental to or connected with the acquisition, construction, improving, or financing of the improvement.

(b) All engineering, inspection, legal, and fiscal agent's fees, expenses in connection with the formation of the district, costs of the bond election and of the issuance of the bonds, bond reserve funds and working capital, and bond interest estimated to accrue during the construction period and for a period of not to exceed 12 months after completion of construction.

(Amended by Stats. 1965, Ch. 828.)

ARTICLE 3.5. Performance of Work [4636- 4636.]
(Heading of Article 3.5 added by Stats. 1988, Ch. 160, Sec. 102.)

4636.

The governing body of each city in which an improvement is being made or acquired pursuant to this chapter may make all necessary rules and regulations for carrying out and maintaining the improvement, and may appoint all agents, superintendents, and engineers necessary to look after the construction and operation of the improvement. However, in any city operating under a charter framed pursuant to Sections 3 and 5 of Article XI of the California Constitution which has a board or department of public works, the powers and duties of the governing body which are stated in this section may be exercised and performed by the city board or department of public works.

(Added by Stats. 1986, Ch. 195, Sec. 36.)

ARTICLE 4. Taxation and Finances [4638 - 4640.6]

(Heading of Article 4 renumbered from Article 5 by Stats. 1986, Ch. 248, Sec. 141.)

4638.

Until the bonds are paid, or until there is a sum in the city treasury set aside for the purpose, sufficient to meet all sums coming due for the principal and interest on the bonds, the city governing body shall, at the time of fixing, and in the manner provided for the general city tax levy, levy and collect each year upon the taxable property situated in the district, and upon that property only, a tax sufficient to pay the interest on the bonds as it falls due, and also such part of the principal as will become due before the proceeds of a tax levied at the next general tax levy will be available. However, if the maturity of the indebtedness created by the issuance of the bonds, or any series of the bonds, is made to begin more than two years after date of the bonds or such series, the tax shall be levied and collected annually, sufficient to pay the interest on the indebtedness as it falls due, and also to constitute a sinking fund for the payment of the principal on or before maturity.

(Amended by Stats. 1963, Ch. 756.)

4639.

The taxes required to be levied and collected by Section 4638 shall be in addition to all other taxes levied for city purposes and in addition to the taxes levied pursuant to Section 4640. The proceeds of such taxes shall be used for no purpose other than the payment of the principal and interest due on the bonds or series of the bonds.

(Amended by Stats. 1963, Ch. 756.)

4639.5.

Chapter 5 (commencing with Section 5400), Division 6, Title 1 of the Government Code shall apply to bonds issued pursuant to this chapter, except that the proceeds referred to in Section 5404 of the Government Code shall be used only for some purpose which is of special benefit to the district including, but not limited to, the payment of or reimbursement for such of the cost and expenses listed in Section 4625 as have already been paid or incurred for the benefit of the district and which could have been included in determining the amount of bonds to be issued, or the payment of principal of or interest on bonded indebtedness previously incurred on behalf of the district.

(Added by Stats. 1963, Ch. 756.)

4640.6.

The governing body of a city may, by a two-thirds vote, require the owners of property within a district to pay a reasonable fee for connecting to any sanitary sewer improvement acquired or constructed pursuant to this chapter.

(Added by Stats. 1967, Ch. 1100.)

ARTICLE 5. Annexation [4641 - 4648]

(Heading of Article 5 renumbered from Article 6 by Stats. 1986, Ch. 248, Sec. 143.)

4641.

Territory which is either within or without the boundaries of the city and which is not within the boundaries of any other improvement district formed pursuant to this chapter may be annexed to any existing improvement district by the governing body of the city.

(Amended by Stats. 1965, Ch. 828.)

4641.5.

Territory which is outside the boundaries of the city, or the initiating city, as the case may be, shall not be annexed unless the governing body of the city within which such outside territory is situated, or, in the case of unincorporated territory, the board of supervisors of the county in which such territory is situated, consents to such annexation by resolution adopted at any time prior to the conclusion of the hearing which is provided for by Section 4646 on the annexation. Any district which as a result of any annexation includes territory not solely within the boundaries of a single city shall thereafter be deemed to be a district formed pursuant to Article 2a (commencing with Section 4614.1) of this chapter even though it was not originally formed pursuant to that article.

(Added by Stats. 1963, Ch. 756.)

4642.

Whenever the governing body of the city determines and finds that additional territory will be benefited by annexation to the district, it may pass a resolution to that effect.

(Amended by Stats. 1963, Ch. 756.)

4643.

The resolution shall be passed by a vote of two-thirds of all the members of the governing body of the city.

(Amended by Stats. 1963, Ch. 756.)

4644.

The resolution shall do all of the following:

(a) Describe the boundaries of the territory proposed to be annexed.

(b) Designate the proposed annexation by an appropriate number.

(c) Declare that the area to be annexed to the district will be benefited by such annexation.

(d) Name the time and place for the hearing of objections by any person interested in the proposed annexation, to the inclusion in the district of any land described in the resolution.

(Amended by Stats. 1963, Ch. 756.)

4645.

The resolution, together with the names of the members of the governing body voting for and against it, shall be published, posted, and mailed as provided in Sections 4610 and 4610.5, except that in applying such sections the word "district" shall mean the territory proposed to be annexed.

(Amended by Stats. 1963, Ch. 756.)

4646.

On the day fixed for the hearing, or any day to which the hearing is continued, the governing body shall hear and consider any objections presented to the annexation of the territory to the district or to the inclusion of any territory proposed to be annexed. At the hearing the governing body shall exclude from the proposed annexation any territory which in its opinion will not be benefited by such annexation.

(Amended by Stats. 1963, Ch. 756.)

4647.

After making all necessary and proper changes in the boundaries, the governing body may, by a resolution passed by a two-thirds vote of all its members order the annexation to the district of all or such part of the territory originally proposed to be annexed as the governing body determines will be benefited by such annexation and shall describe the boundaries of the territory annexed. This resolution, together with the names of the members of the governing body voting for and against the resolution, shall be spread upon the minutes of the governing body. Certified copies of the resolution shall be recorded and filed in the manner and with the same force and effect as provided in Section 4613.

(Amended by Stats. 1963, Ch. 756.)

4648.

Upon the recordation of such resolution the territory annexed is a part of the district and is subject to all the liabilities and entitled to all the benefits of the district.

(Amended by Stats. 1963, Ch. 756.)

ARTICLE 6. Withdrawal [4650- 4650.]

(Heading of Article 6 renumbered from Article 7 by Stats. 1986, Ch. 248, Sec. 143.)

4650.

Territory within the Atherton Channel Drainage District may be withdrawn from such district pursuant to Division 1 (commencing with Section 56000) of Title 6 of the Government Code.

(Added by Stats. 1969, Ch. 1301.)

CHAPTER 3. County Sanitation Districts [4700 - 4859]

(Chapter 3 enacted by Stats. 1939, Ch. 60.)

ARTICLE 1. General Provisions [4700 - 4703]

(Article 1 enacted by Stats. 1939, Ch. 60.)

4700.

This chapter shall be known and cited as the "county sanitation district act."

(Enacted by Stats. 1939, Ch. 60.)

4701.

"District," as used in this chapter, means any county sanitation district formed pursuant to this chapter or pursuant to any law which it supersedes.

(Enacted by Stats. 1939, Ch. 60.)

4702.

"District board," as used in this chapter, means the board of directors of a district.

(Enacted by Stats. 1939, Ch. 60.)

4703.

Districts may be formed, maintained, and governed in any county as provided in this chapter.

(Enacted by Stats. 1939, Ch. 60.)

ARTICLE 2. Formation [4710 - 4718]

(Article 2 enacted by Stats. 1939, Ch. 60.)

4710.

A board of supervisors desiring to form a county sanitation district shall adopt a resolution of its intention to do so. The resolution shall contain all of the following:

(a) A statement of the intention to form a district.

(b) The boundaries of the proposed district or some other designation of its territorial extent.

(c) The name of the proposed district.

(d) The time and place where objections to the formation of the district or to its extent will be heard.

(e) Instructions to the clerk of the board to publish the resolution and notices of hearing.

(f) When the proposed district includes parcels of noncontiguous territory, a statement that the proposed district will be in accordance with the master plan of county sanitation service as adopted by the board of supervisors or if the county has not adopted such a master plan then a statement that the proposed district is within the same watershed. Watershed as used in this section means to include only that area drained by gravity to the trunk sewer or sewers.

(Amended by Stats. 1961, Ch. 2130.)

4711.

The district as formed may include unincorporated or incorporated territory, or both. The incorporated territory included in the district may include the whole or part of one or more cities. However, less than the whole of a city shall not be included in the district except by the vote of a majority of the governing body of the city.

The district shall not include the whole or any part of another sanitation district or any other district formed for similar purposes unless the governing body of such other district shall consent thereto and the board of supervisors, after a hearing, shall find and determine by resolution duly adopted that the proposed inclusion of the whole or part of such other district within the district is in the public interest and the territory affected will benefit thereby.

Notice of such hearing shall be given by publication in at least two successive issues, not more than 30 nor less than 10 days prior to the hearing, in a newspaper of general circulation published within the county.

(Amended by Stats. 1965, Ch. 1848.)

4711.5.

The land proposed to be formed into a district need not consist of contiguous parcels.

(Added by Stats. 1961, Ch. 2130.)

4712.

The time to be fixed for the hearing of objections shall be not less than thirty days after the adoption of the resolution. The hearing shall be held at the regular meeting place of the board of supervisors or else at some place in the proposed district.

(Amended by Stats. 1939, Ch. 596.)

4713.

Prior to the time of hearing, the resolution shall be published at length twice in at least one newspaper of general circulation in the proposed district and brief notices of the passage of the resolution and the time and place of the hearing may be published in one or more daily or weekly newspapers published and circulated in the proposed district.

(Amended by Stats. 1939, Ch. 596.)

4714.

At the time provided in the resolution of intention or at any time to which the hearing is continued, the board of supervisors shall hear any objections to the formation of the district or to its extent. At the hearing the board of supervisors may exclude any territory that in its opinion will not be benefited by being in the district.

(Enacted by Stats. 1939, Ch. 60.)

4714.5.

If the board of supervisors finds that protests have been made, prior to its final determination for formation of the district, by the owners of real property within the proposed district the assessed value of which, as shown by the last equalized assessment roll, constitutes more than one-half of the total assessed value of the real property within the proposed district, the proceeding shall terminate. The board of supervisors shall order the proceeding terminated when such protests are received.

(Added by Stats. 1959, Ch. 152.)

4715.

If written objection to the formation of the district, signed by 5 percent of the voters registered in the district if the district contains less than 2001 registered voters, or by 2 percent of the registered voters, but not less than 100 registered voters, if the district contains 2001, or more, registered voters, is filed with the board, it shall, and in any event it may, either adopt an order abandoning the formation of the proposed district or order the matter of the formation of the district with the boundary lines determined at the close of the hearing submitted to the voters of the proposed district at an election.

(Amended by Stats. 1959, Ch. 566.)

4716.

At the election only voters registered in the proposed district may vote. Election precincts shall be established by the board of supervisors, and precinct boards, composed of one inspector, one judge, and one clerk, shall be appointed. At least one week prior to the election, notice of the election shall be given by publication in a newspaper of general circulation in the proposed district. In other particulars the election shall be conducted in the manner ordered by the board of supervisors.

(Enacted by Stats. 1939, Ch. 60.)

4716.1.

Within five days after the district formation election has been called, the legislative body which has called the election shall transmit, by registered mail, a written notification of the election call to the executive officer of the local agency formation commission of the county or principal county in which the territory or major portion of the territory of the proposed district is located. Such written notice shall include the name and a description of the proposed district, and may be in the form of a certified copy of the resolution adopted by the legislative body calling the district formation election.

The executive officer, within five days after being notified that a district formation election has been called, shall submit to the commission, for its approval or modification, an impartial analysis of the proposed district formation.

The impartial analysis shall not exceed 500 words in length and shall include a specific description of the boundaries of the district proposed to be formed.

The local agency formation commission, within five days after the receipt of the executive officer's analysis, shall approve or modify the analysis and submit it to the officials in charge of conducting the district formation election.

(Added by Stats. 1970, Ch. 736.)

4716.2.

The board of supervisors or any member or members of the board authorized by the board, or any individual voter or bona fide association of citizens entitled to vote on the district formation proposition, or any combination of such voters and associations of citizens, may file a written argument for or a written argument against the proposed district formation.

Arguments shall not exceed 300 words in length and shall be filed with the officials in charge of conducting the election not less than 54 days prior to the date of the district formation election.

(Added by Stats. 1970, Ch. 736.)

4716.3.

If more than one argument for or more than one argument against the proposed district formation is filed with the election officials within the time prescribed, such election officials shall select one of the arguments for printing and distribution to the voters.

In selecting the arguments, the election officials shall give preference and priority in the order named to the arguments of the following:

(a) The board of supervisors or any member or members of the board authorized by the board.

(b) Individual voters or bona fide associations of citizens or a combination of such voters and associations.

(Added by Stats. 1970, Ch. 736.)

4716.4.

The elections officials in charge of conducting the election shall cause a ballot pamphlet concerning the district formation proposition to be voted on to be printed and mailed to each voter entitled to vote on the district formation question.

The ballot pamphlet shall contain the following, in the order prescribed:

(a) The complete text of the proposition.

(b) The impartial analysis of the proposition, prepared by the local agency formation commission.

(c) The argument for the proposed district formation.

(d) The argument against the proposed district formation.

The elections officials shall mail a ballot pamphlet to each voter entitled to vote in the district formation election at least 10 days prior to the date of the election. The ballot pamphlet is "official matter" within the meaning of Section 13303 of the Elections Code.

(Amended by Stats. 1994, Ch. 923, Sec. 119. Effective January 1, 1995.)

4717.

At the conclusion of the hearing, or if an election is held and the canvass of the election returns shows that a majority of all the votes cast in the entire proposed district and that a majority of the votes cast on the question in each city or part thereof in the proposed district were in favor of the formation of the district, the board of supervisors may, if it deems best, make an order forming the district.

(Amended by Stats. 1939, Ch. 596.)

4718.

The order of formation shall contain the name of the district, and a description of the boundaries or otherwise indicate its territory. The order is conclusive evidence of the regularity of all prior proceedings, except the adoption and publication in full of the resolution of intention and of the fact of the hearing.

(Enacted by Stats. 1939, Ch. 60.)

ARTICLE 3. Officers [4730 - 4735]

(Article 3 enacted by Stats. 1939, Ch. 60.)

4730.

The governing body of a sanitation district is a board of directors of not less than three members. The presiding officer of the governing body of each city, the whole or part of which is included in the sanitation district, is a member of the board. A member of the governing body of each sanitary district, the whole or part of which is included in the sanitation district, is a member of the board.

If the sanitation district includes territory which is unincorporated and not included in a sanitary district, then the presiding officer of the county board of supervisors is a member of the board.

The governing body of each city with a population of under 2,500,000, as found by the latest census, and the board of supervisors shall each select one of its members, other than its presiding officer, as an alternate director to act as a member of the district board in place of the presiding officer, or in place of the other member of the governing body of the city or county where there are two members from the city or county on the board of directors of the district, during such person's absence, inability, or refusal to act.

The presiding officer of the governing body of a city with a population of 2,500,000 or over shall select one of the other members of the governing body as an alternate director to act as a member of the district board in place of the presiding officer, or in place of the other member of the governing body of the city where there are two members from the city on the board of directors of the district, during such person's absence, inability, or refusal to act. The governing body of each sanitary district represented on the board of directors of a sanitation district shall select one of its members as an alternate director to act as a member of the district board in place of its regular director, or in place of the other member of the governing body of the sanitary district where there are two members from the sanitary district on the board of directors of the district, during such person's absence, inability, or refusal to act.

If the sanitation district includes unincorporated territory and all or part of one city and no sanitary district, or unincorporated territory and one sanitary district and no city, then the presiding officer and one other member of the board of supervisors are members of the board, unless the population included in the city or sanitary district is more than half of the population of the whole sanitation district, in which case the presiding officer of the board of supervisors and the presiding officer and one other member of the governing body of the city or two members of the governing body of the sanitary district, as the case may be, constitute the board of directors.

If the total number of cities and sanitary districts included in the sanitation district in whole or in part is two and if the sanitation district does not include any territory not in cities or sanitary districts, then the district board includes the presiding officer and one other member of the governing body of the city or two members of the governing body of the sanitary district having the greatest population and the presiding officer of the governing body of the city or one member of the governing body of the sanitary district having the least population.

If the total number of cities and of sanitary districts wholly or in part within the sanitation district is two or more, and if, in addition, the district contains unincorporated territory, then the district board includes the presiding officer of the board of supervisors, the presiding officer of the governing board of each city, and a member of the governing board of each sanitary district.

If the district includes no territory which is in cities or sanitary districts, then the county board of supervisors is the board of directors of the district.

If the territory of the district lies wholly within a city, the legislative body of said city is the board of directors of the district.

A city within a sanitation district, the sewered portion of which city lies entirely within a sanitary district, shall have no representation on the board.

Notwithstanding the foregoing provisions of this section, whenever a sanitation district includes unincorporated territory and all or part of one city and no sanitary district, the governing body of such city may designate the board of supervisors of the county as the district board of directors, unless the population of the incorporated portion of the sanitation district is more than half of the population of the whole district. If the population of the incorporated portion of the sanitation district is more than half of the population of the whole district, the board of supervisors of the county may designate the governing body of the city as the district board of directors.

The term "sanitary district" as used in this section shall mean a sanitary district formed prior to the formation of the sanitation district in which it is included in whole or in part. The term "sanitary district" as used in this section shall also include a county water district which on or before July 1, 1977, assumed the responsibilities, rights, duties, assets, liabilities, and obligations of a sanitary district which at the time of such assumption had representation on the board of directors of the sanitation district by the provisions of this section.

(Amended by Stats. 1979, Ch. 35.)

4730.1.

(a) Notwithstanding the provisions of Section 4730, the resolution of intention to form the district and the order of formation of the district may provide that the governing body of the sanitation district shall be constituted in accordance with this subdivision or subdivision (b) or (c).

(1) If the district includes no territory which is within a city, other sanitation district, or public agency, the county board of supervisors is the board of directors.

(2) If the district includes territory which is within a city, other sanitation district, or public agency, the board of directors shall be composed of the presiding officer of the governing body of each city, other sanitation district, and public agency and the chairman of the county board of supervisors. If the chairman of the county board of supervisors and the presiding officer of the governing body of each city, sanitation district, and public agency constitute an even number, a member of the county board of supervisors appointed by the board of supervisors or, in the alternate as determined by the board of directors, a resident of the district elected by the registered voters of the district for a four-year term, shall be a member of the board of directors of the district.

(3) The governing body of each county, city, sanitation district, and public agency having a representative on the board of directors may designate one of its members to act in the place of its regular member in his or her absence or his or her inability or refusal to act.

(4) The governing body of any city, sanitation district, or other public agency may designate a member of the county board of supervisors to serve as its representative member on the board of directors of the district in the place of the presiding officer of its governing body; in that case, the supervisor shall have one vote for each city, sanitation district, and public agency represented by him or her.

(b) (1) The board of directors may be composed of directors who are residents of the district elected by the registered voters of the district for four-year terms.

(2) The number of directors on an elected board shall be determined, subject to the requirements of Section 4730 and subdivision (c), by the board of directors of the district, if any, in existence prior to the election.

(c) (1) In the Arvin Sanitation District in Kern County only, if no board of directors is in existence prior to the election, the county board of supervisors shall determine, subject to the requirements of Section 4730 and subdivision (d), the number of directors on an elected board.

(2) The district shall reimburse the county for any reasonable costs incurred by it for the conduct of elections required by this subdivision.

(d) The governing body of a sanitation district is a board of directors composed of an odd number of not less than three members.

(e) "Public agency" as used in this section means any sanitary district, public utility district, resort district, county water district, municipal water district, sewer maintenance district, or county maintenance district, engaged in the collection, transportation, treatment, or disposal of sewage or any other public agency empowered to, and engaged in, the collection, transportation, treatment, or disposal of sewage.

(Amended by Stats. 1986, Ch. 982, Sec. 23.)

4730.2.

A sanitation district heretofore or hereafter established may elect to be governed by a board of directors constituted as set forth in Section 4730.1 by complying with the provisions of this section.

The board of directors of the district may adopt a resolution of intention to establish a governing body in accordance with Section 4730.1. The resolution shall contain:

1. A statement of intention to establish a board of directors composed of representatives as set forth in Section 4730.1 of the Health and Safety Code.

2. The time and place where objections to the proposal will be heard.

The time fixed for hearing said objections shall be not less than 30 days after the adoption of the resolution. The resolution of intention shall be published at length twice in at least one newspaper of general circulation in the district. At the time provided in the resolution of intention for the hearing, or at any time to which the hearing is continued, the district board shall hear any objections to the proposal. At the conclusion of the hearing, the board of directors may order that the governing body of the district be constituted as set forth in Section 4730.1. A copy of said order shall be furnished to the board of supervisors and to the governing body of each city, sanitation district and public district to be represented on the new board of directors.

(Added by Stats. 1961, Ch. 1745.)

4730.4.

(a) Notwithstanding Sections 4730, 4730.1 and 4730.2, the local agency formation commission, in approving either a consolidation of districts or the reorganization of two or more districts into a single county sanitation district may, pursuant to subdivisions (k) and (n) of Section 56886 of the Government Code, increase the number of directors to serve on the board of directors of the consolidated or reorganized district to 7, 9, or 11, who shall be members of the board of directors of the districts to be consolidated or reorganized as of the effective date of the consolidation or reorganization.

(b) Upon the expiration of the terms of the members of the board of directors of the consolidated district, or a district reorganized as described in subdivision (a), whose terms first expire following the effective date of the consolidation or reorganization, the total number of members on the board of directors shall be reduced until the number equals the number of members permitted by the principal act of the consolidated or reorganized district, or any larger number as may be specified by the local agency formation commission in approving the consolidation or reorganization.

(c) In addition to the powers granted under Section 1780 of the Government Code, in the event of a vacancy on the board of directors of the consolidated district or a district reorganized as described in subdivision (a) at which time the total number of directors is greater than five, the board of directors may, by majority vote of the remaining members of the board, choose not to fill the vacancy. In that event, the total membership of the board of directors shall be reduced by one board member. Upon making the determination not to fill a vacancy, the board of directors shall notify the board of supervisors of its decision.

(d) For the purposes of this section: "consolidation" means consolidation, as defined in Section 56030 of the Government Code; "district" or "special district" means district or special district, as defined in Section 56036 of the Government Code; and "reorganization" means reorganization, as defined in Section 56073 of the Government Code.

(Amended by Stats. 2006, Ch. 172, Sec. 10. Effective January 1, 2007.)

4730.5.

(a) Notwithstanding the provisions of Sections 4730, 4730.1, and 4730.2, or any other provision of law, the governing body of the Monterey Regional County Sanitation District shall be constituted in accordance with this section.

The governing body of the Monterey Regional County Sanitation District shall be a board of directors composed of not less than three members. The district board shall be appointed as follows:

When territory of the district is within a city or other sanitation district or public agency, as defined in Section 4730.1, the governing body of each such city, other sanitation district, and public agency shall appoint one member to represent such city, other sanitation district, or public agency. When territory of the district is within unincorporated territory which is not also included in such other sanitation district or public agency, the county board of supervisors shall appoint one member to represent such unincorporated territory. In the event that the selection of members pursuant to this subdivision results in the governing body having less than three members, the county board of supervisors shall appoint additional members for purposes of increasing the number of board members to three.

The governing body of the county and each city, sanitation district, and public agency having a representative on the district board of directors may designate one alternate representative to act in the place of such body's regular member in such person's absence, inability to act, or refusal to act.

The regular member and alternate member on the district board shall be either an elected official, officer, or employee of the county, city, other sanitation district, or public agency, and shall serve solely at the pleasure of the appointing county, city, other sanitation district, or public agency.

All vacancies shall be filled in the same manner as the original appointment.

(b) Notwithstanding any other provision of law, each member of the Board of Directors of the Monterey Regional County Sanitation District shall have one vote; provided, however, that upon the call and request of any board member, present and able to vote, a weighted voting formula shall apply for any vote to be taken by the district board, with each member having one or more votes based upon the population of the city, other sanitation district, public agency, or unincorporated territory such member represents, as follows:

Population	No. of Votes
0 to 9,999	1
10,000 to 24,999	2
25,000 to 49,999	3
50,000 to 74,999	4
75,000 to 99,999	5
100,000 and above	6

For the purpose of determining the population of a city, other sanitation district, public agency, or unincorporated territory, the district board shall consider the last official United States census or the California Finance Department population estimate, whichever is more recent for a particular area.

In determining such population basis, those portions of the population of a city, other sanitation district, public agency, or unincorporated territory which are attributable to and located on the U.S. Army Military Reservation at Fort Ord, California, shall not be included within the population computation of such city, other sanitation district, public agency, or unincorporated territory.

No vote may be taken at any meeting of the Monterey Regional County Sanitation District unless a quorum of the members of such district board is in attendance. A quorum for purposes of this subdivision is a majority of all district board members.

(c) The governing board of the Monterey Regional County Sanitation District may designate any depository or depositories for the custody of any or all revenue collected or received for operation and maintenance purposes pursuant to Article 2 (commencing with Section 53630) of Chapter 4 of Part 1 of Division 2 of Title 5 of the Government Code. All other district revenue, including any moneys collected or received for the payment of principal and interest upon district bonds or any moneys designated for capital outlay expenditure, shall be paid into the treasury of the county to the credit of the district. A depository shall give security sufficient to secure the district against possible loss and shall pay the warrants drawn by the district for demands against the district under such rules as the governing board may prescribe.
(Added by Stats. 1979, Ch. 35.)

4730.6.
(a) Notwithstanding Sections 4730, 4730.1, and 4730.2 or any other provision of law, the governing board of the Ventura Regional Sanitation District shall be a board of directors appointed in accordance with this section. Unless the context otherwise indicates, as used in this section, "district" means the Ventura Regional Sanitation District.
(b) The legislative body of each city located wholly or partially within the district's boundaries shall designate one of its members to be a member of the district's board of directors. Each legislative body may designate one of its members as an alternate to act in the place of its regular member in the case of the absence or disqualification of the regular member. An alternate member shall have the full voting rights of the regular member.
(c) The special district committee, which shall consist of the presiding officers of all special districts that have a governing board separately elected, in whole or in part, from any board of supervisors or city council, and would be entitled to representation on the Ventura Regional Sanitation District Board of Directors under Section 4730.1, if that section were applicable to the Ventura Regional Sanitation District, shall designate one separately elected member of a board of directors of a special district represented on the committee to be a member of the district's board of directors. The special district committee may designate one separately elected member as an alternate to act in the place of the regular member in the case of the absence or disqualification of the regular member. An alternate member shall have the full voting rights of the regular member.
(d) Each member of the district's board of directors shall have one vote.
(e) No action shall be taken at any meeting of the district's board of directors unless a majority of all authorized members of the board of directors is in attendance.
(f) A majority of the members of the board of directors present shall be required to approve or otherwise act on any matter except as otherwise required by law.
(Amended by Stats. 1999, Ch. 550, Sec. 26. Effective September 28, 1999. Operative January 1, 2000, by Sec. 33 of Ch. 550.)

4730.65.
(a) Notwithstanding Sections 4730, 4730.1, and 4730.2, or any other law, the governing body of the Orange County Sanitation District shall be a board of directors composed of all of the following:
(1) One member of the city council of each city located wholly or partially within the district's boundaries, except the City of Yorba Linda, provided, however, a city within the Orange County Sanitation District, the sewered portion of which city lies entirely within another sanitary district, shall have no representation on the board.
(2) One member of the county board of supervisors.

(3) One member of the governing body of each sanitary district, the whole or part of which is included in the Orange County Sanitation District.
(4) One member of the governing body of a public agency empowered to and engaged in the collection, transportation, treatment, or disposal of sewage and that was a member agency of a sanitation district consolidated into the Orange County Sanitation District.
(5) One member of the governing body of the Yorba Linda Water District.
(b) The governing body of the county and each city, sanitary district, and public agency that is a member agency having a representative on the board of directors of the Orange County Sanitation District, may designate one of its members to act in the place of its regular member in his or her absence or his or her inability to act.
(c) An action shall not be taken at any meeting of the Orange County Sanitation District's board of directors unless a majority of all authorized members of the board of directors is in attendance.
(d) A majority of the members of the board of directors present is required to approve or otherwise act on any matter except as otherwise required by law.
(Amended by Stats. 2015, Ch. 303, Sec. 298. (AB 731) Effective January 1, 2016.)
4730.66.
(a) This section applies only to the consolidated sanitation district in Orange County described in Section 4730.65. The powers granted in this section supplement the existing powers of the district.
(b) The district may acquire, construct, operate, maintain, and furnish facilities for all or any of the following purposes:
(1) The diversion of urban runoff from drainage courses within the district.
(2) The treatment of the urban runoff.
(3) The return of the water to the drainage courses.
(4) The beneficial use of the water.
(c) In order to carry out the powers and purposes granted under this section, the district may exercise any of the powers otherwise granted to a district by this chapter to the extent those powers may be made applicable.
(d) Nothing in this section affects any obligation of the district to obtain a permit that may be required by law for the activities undertaken pursuant to this section.
(Added by Stats. 2002, Ch. 79, Sec. 1. Effective June 30, 2002.)
4730.68.
(a) This section applies only to county sanitation district numbers 1, 2, 3, 4, 5, 8, 9, 14, 15, 16, 17, 18, 19, 20, 21, 22, 23, 27, 28, 29, and 34 of Los Angeles County, Newhall Ranch Sanitation District of Los Angeles County, South Bay Cities Sanitation District of Los Angeles County, and Santa Clarita Valley Sanitation District of Los Angeles County. The powers granted in this section supplement the existing powers of each district.
(b) A district may acquire, construct, operate, maintain, and furnish facilities for any of the following purposes:
(1) The diversion of stormwater and dry weather runoff from the stormwater drainage system within the district.
(2) The management and treatment of the stormwater and dry weather runoff.
(3) The discharge of the water to the stormwater drainage system or receiving waters.
(4) The beneficial use of the water.
(c) In order to carry out the powers and purposes granted under this section, the district may exercise any of the powers otherwise granted to a district by this chapter to the extent those powers may be made applicable.
(d) (1) Prior to initiating a stormwater or dry weather runoff program or project within the boundaries of an adjudicated groundwater basin, a district shall consult with the relevant watermaster for a preliminary determination as to whether the project is inconsistent with the adjudication. If the watermaster deems the project to be inconsistent with the adjudication, the watermaster shall recommend, in writing, the measures that are necessary in order to conform the project to the adjudication.
(2) Prior to initiating a stormwater or dry weather runoff project within the service area of a water replenishment district, a district shall consult with the water replenishment district for the purpose of avoiding potential conflicts with water replenishment activities.
(3) Prior to initiating a stormwater or dry weather runoff project, a district shall consult with the Los Angeles County Flood Control District for the purpose of avoiding potential conflicts with flood protection and water conservation activities.
(e) This section does not affect any obligation of a district to obtain a permit that may be required by law for the activities undertaken pursuant to this section.
(f) For purposes of this section, "stormwater" and "dry weather runoff" have the same meaning as in Section 10561.5 of the Water Code.
(g) Nothing in this section shall be construed to require any local agency to participate, financially or otherwise, in a project pursued under the authority granted by this section.
(h) Nothing in this section shall be construed to alter or interfere with any of the following:
(1) Existing water rights to water from any source, including any adjudicated rights allocated by a court judgment or order, including any physical solution, rights issued by the state or a state agency, and rights acquired pursuant to any federal or state statute.
(2) Existing water rights law.
(3) Any rights, remedies, or obligations that may exist pursuant to Article 1 (commencing with Section 1200) or Article 1.5 (commencing with Section 1210) of Chapter 1 of Part 2 of Division 2 of the Water Code, Chapter 10 (commencing with Section 1700) of Part 2 of Division 2 of the Water Code, or Chapter 8.5 (commencing with Section 1501) of Part 1 of Division 1 of the Public Utilities Code.
(Added by Stats. 2015, Ch. 678, Sec. 2. (SB 485) Effective January 1, 2016.)
4730.7.

The governing board of the Delta Diablo Sanitation District may designate any depository or depositories pursuant to Article 2 (commencing with Section 53630) of Chapter 4 of Part 1 of Division 2 of Title 5 of the Government Code for the custody of any or all revenue collected or received for operation and maintenance purposes. All moneys deposited with a designated depository or depositories shall be invested in checking accounts, savings accounts, certificates of deposit, or other insured accounts. All other district revenue, including any moneys collected or received for the payment of principal and interest on district bonds, other indebtedness, or certificates of participation, and any moneys designated for capital outlay expenditure shall be paid into the county treasury to the credit of the district. Every designated depository shall give security sufficient to secure the district against possible loss and shall pay the warrants or checks drawn by the district for demands against the district under any rules as the governing board may prescribe.

(Added by Stats. 1989, Ch. 789, Sec. 17.)

4730.8.

(a) Notwithstanding Sections 4730, 4730.1, and 4730.2, or any other provision of law, the governing board of a sanitation district in the County of Riverside that includes no territory within a city shall be the county board of supervisors.

(b) The sanitation district may include all or a part of the territory of one or more previously existing sanitary districts that lie within the unincorporated territory of the county.

(c) If the sanitation district includes any part of a sanitary district, the sanitation district shall not perform any of the functions of the sanitary district within the boundaries of the sanitary district if the sanitary district has performed that function within the 10 years immediately preceding January 1, 1994.

(d) The sanitation district may handle, treat, and manage solid waste, as defined pursuant to the California Integrated Waste Management Act of 1989 (Division 30 (commencing with Section 40000) of the Public Resources Code), in the same manner as the County of Riverside is authorized pursuant to that act.

(Amended by Stats. 2006, Ch. 538, Sec. 367. Effective January 1, 2007.)

4730.9.

The governing board of the Napa Sanitation District shall be a board of directors constituted in accordance with this article, except that the board shall additionally include both of the following:

(a) One public member appointed by the Napa City Council.

(b) One public member appointed by the Napa County Board of Supervisors.

(Added by Stats. 1995, Ch. 430, Sec. 1. Effective January 1, 1996.)

4730.10.

(a) Notwithstanding Sections 4730, 4730.1, and 4730.2, or any other law, beginning on January 1, 1996, the governing body of the South San Luis Obispo County Sanitation District shall be constituted as set forth in this article, except that a member of the San Luis Obispo County Board of Supervisors may not serve as a member of the governing body unless, in the absence of that supervisor, there would otherwise be an even number of members of the governing body.

(b) This section applies only to members appointed to the South San Luis Obispo County Sanitation District on or after January 1, 1996.

(Amended by Stats. 1996, Ch. 308, Sec. 1. Effective July 29, 1996.)

4730.11.

(a) Notwithstanding any other provision of this article, the governing body of the Sacramento Area Sewer District, formerly known as the Sacramento County Sanitation District No. 1, shall be a board of directors composed of not less than five members.

(b) If the district includes no territory that is within a city, the Sacramento County Board of Supervisors shall be the board of directors of the district. If the district includes territory that is within a city, the board of directors shall be composed of the Sacramento County Board of Supervisors and a member of the governing body of each included city, appointed by that city's governing body.

(c) The governing body of each city located within the district may appoint one of its members to serve as an alternate to act in the absence, inability, or refusal to act, of its appointed member.

(d) (1) Each member or alternate member of the board of directors shall have one vote.

(2) Notwithstanding paragraph (1), if the members of the board of directors constitute an even number and if the vote is tied, the chairperson of the board of directors shall have an additional vote.

(Amended by Stats. 2008, Ch. 709, Sec. 14. Effective January 1, 2009.)

4730.12.

(a) Notwithstanding any other provision of this article, the governing body of the Sacramento Regional County Sanitation District shall be a board of directors composed of all of the following:

(1) The Sacramento County Board of Supervisors.

(2) A member or members of the governing body of each city included in the district, appointed by the governing body of each of those cities.

(3) That member of the Yolo County Board of Supervisors whose supervisorial district includes all, or the greater portion, of the population of the City of West Sacramento.

(b) The governing body of each city located within the district shall appoint a member or members to the board of directors based on that city's population, as follows:

City Population	Number of Board Members

0 to 150,000	1
150,001 to 250,000	2
250,001 to 350,000	3
350,001 to 450,000	4
450,001 to 550,000	5
550,001 to 650,000	6
650,001 to 750,000	7
750,001 and above	8

(c) For the purpose of determining the population of a city, the governing body of each city shall rely on the most recent decennial United States Census or the latest population estimate by the Department of Finance, whichever is more recent.

(d) The governing body of each city located within the district may appoint one of its members to serve as an alternate to act in the absence, inability, or refusal to act, of each appointed member. The Yolo County Board of Supervisors may appoint one of its members to serve as an alternate to act in the absence, inability, or refusal to act, of its member.

(e) (1) Each member or alternate member of the board of directors shall have one vote.

(2) Notwithstanding paragraph (1), if the members of the board of directors constitute an even number and if the vote is tied, the chairperson of the board of directors shall have an additional vote.

(Added by Stats. 2004, Ch. 199, Sec. 2. Effective January 1, 2005.)

4731.

If additional territory is annexed to the district as well as whenever any change takes place in the character of the territory, by the incorporation of a city or otherwise, resulting in a condition which makes it necessary for a change to be made in the membership of the district board, the change in the membership of the district board takes place and becomes effective immediately.

(Enacted by Stats. 1939, Ch. 60.)

4732.

The county auditor of the county in which the district is formed is ex officio the auditor of the district.

(Enacted by Stats. 1939, Ch. 60.)

4733.

(a) The district board may fix the amount of compensation per meeting to be paid each member of the board for services for each meeting attended by the member. Subject to subdivision (b), the compensation shall not exceed one hundred dollars ($100) for each meeting of the district board attended by the member or for each day's service rendered as a member by request of the board, not exceeding a total of six days in any calendar month, together with any expenses incident thereto.

(b) The district board, by ordinance adopted pursuant to Chapter 2 (commencing with Section 20200) of Division 10 of the Water Code, may increase the compensation received by the district board members above the amount of one hundred dollars ($100) per day.

(c) For purposes of this section, the determination of whether a director's activities on any specific day are compensable shall be made pursuant to Article 2.3 (commencing with Section 53232) of Chapter 2 of Part 1 of Division 2 of Title 5 of the Government Code.

(d) Reimbursement for these expenses is subject to Sections 53232.2 and 53232.3 of the Government Code.

(Amended by Stats. 2005, Ch. 700, Sec. 10. Effective January 1, 2006.)

4733.5.

Where two or more county sanitation districts have joined in the purchase, ownership, use, construction, maintenance, or operation of a sewerage system, or sewage disposal or treatment plant, or refuse transfer or disposal system, or both, either within or without the districts, or have so joined for any combination of these purposes, as provided in Section 4742, and the districts hold their meetings jointly, and one or more of the directors serve as a director on more than one of these districts meeting jointly, the districts may, by joint resolution approved by each district, limit the compensation of a director to compensation equal to not more than fifty dollars ($50) for each jointly held meeting attended by him or her, not to exceed one hundred dollars ($100) in any one month for attendance at jointly held meetings. For purposes of this section, the determination of whether a director's activities on any specific day are compensable shall be made pursuant to Article 2.3 (commencing with Section 53232) of Chapter 2 of Part 1 of Division 2 of Title 5 of the Government Code.

(Amended by Stats. 2005, Ch. 700, Sec. 11. Effective January 1, 2006.)

4734.

Where two or more county sanitation districts have joined in the purchase, ownership, use, construction, maintenance, or operation of a sewerage system or sewage disposal or treatment plant or a refuse transfer or disposal system, or both, either within or without the districts, or have so joined for any combination of these purposes, as provided in Section 4742, and the districts hold their meetings jointly and such meetings are presided over by a director of one of the districts acting as joint chairman for and on behalf of the joint organization, each district so participating may pay the joint chairman the same compensation as a director of such district is paid.

(Added by Stats. 1963, Ch. 405.)

4735.

If the withdrawal of the city results in less than three members remaining on the district board, the vacancy shall be filled in accordance with the provisions of this chapter for changes in the membership of the district board.

(Added by renumbering Section 4845.11 by Stats. 1965, Ch. 2043.)

ARTICLE 4. District Powers [4738 - 4767.5]

(Article 4 enacted by Stats. 1939, Ch. 60.)

4738.

A county sanitation district may sue and be sued by its own name.

(Added by Stats. 1951, Ch. 1000.)

4739.

A county sanitation district may employ such sanitation experts, surveyors, counsel, and other persons as are needed to carry into effect any powers of the district.

(Enacted by Stats. 1939, Ch. 60.)

4739.5.

By resolution, the board may change the name of the district. The change of name shall be effective upon recording a certified copy in the office of the county recorder of the county or counties in which the district is situated.

(Amended by Stats. 1998, Ch. 829, Sec. 37. Effective January 1, 1999.)

4740.

The district may acquire by gift, purchase, condemnation, or otherwise, in the name of the district, and own, control, manage, and dispose of any interest in real or personal property necessary or convenient for the construction, maintenance, and operation of a sewerage system and sewage disposal or treatment plant, or a refuse transfer or disposal system, or both. As used in this article "refuse" shall include all of the following: (a) animal, fruit and vegetable refuse; (b) offal; (c) leaves and cuttings, trimmings from trees, shrubs and grass; (d) inorganic refuse and rubbish; (e) garbage; (f) anything thrown away as worthless.

(Amended by Stats. 1957, Ch. 168.)

4741.

A district may acquire, construct, and complete within or without the district, sewage collection, treatment and disposal works, including sewage treatment plants, outfalls, intercepting, collecting and lateral sewers, pipes, pumps, machinery, easements, rights-of-way, and other works, property or structures necessary or convenient for sewage collection, treatment, and disposal. No sewerage system shall be constructed, maintained, or operated in any city not in the district except by consent granted by an affirmative vote by a majority of the full membership of the governing body of the city; provided, however, that the district may construct, operate, and maintain intercepting, trunk and outfall sewerlines, other than ocean outfall lines and other terminal outfall lines, together with pumps and like machinery necessary for sewage transportation, in a city pursuant to Section 4759.1. For the purposes of this section, the term "terminal outfall lines" means any outfall sewerlines that discharge within the city any effluent from a sewer treatment plant or any sewage.

It may also acquire lands and acquire and construct refuse transfer or disposal facilities, or both, within or without the district, and it may maintain and operate within the district boundaries a system for transfer or disposal of refuse, or both; provided, however, that the system shall not include "refuse collection" which is defined as the house-to-house pickup of refuse or any part thereof.

A district shall not acquire land for, or establish and operate, a refuse transfer or disposal facility within either a city or the unincorporated area of a county until the city council, if the facility is proposed to be located in the city, or the board of supervisors of the county, if it is proposed to be located in the unincorporated area of the county, has by resolution, consented to the use of the proposed site for that purpose.

If 90 percent or more of the total area of the district is unincorporated territory and the land proposed to be acquired for a refuse transfer or disposal facility is located in the unincorporated territory of the county, the board of supervisors, before adopting any resolution consenting to the use of land for that purpose, shall hold a public hearing upon the question of the adoption of the resolution. Notice of the hearing shall be given by publication in the area pursuant to Section 6066 of the Government Code, not more than 30 nor less than 10 days prior to the hearing. If at any time before the hearing, there is filed with the board of supervisors a written objection to the use of the proposed site for a refuse transfer or disposal facility, signed by 2 percent or more of the registered voters of the district, the board shall submit the matter of the proposed use to the voters of the district at an election. The proposition shall be submitted to the voters in the manner and under the procedure prescribed in Article 5 (commencing with Section 4780) of Chapter 3 of this part for submission of the proposition of incurring a bonded indebtedness. If a majority of the votes cast in an election are in favor of the proposed use, the board shall adopt the resolution consenting thereto, but if a majority of the votes cast are against the proposed use, the board shall dismiss the proceedings, and no resolution consenting to the use of any of such land shall be adopted by the board for at least one year from the date of the election.

(Added by Stats. 1986, Ch. 195, Sec. 37.)

4741.1.

A district board desiring to construct, maintain and operate a refuse transfer or disposal system, or both, within or without the district in addition to its sewage collection, treatment and disposal system shall adopt a resolution of its intention to do so. The resolution shall contain the following:

(a) A statement of the intention to construct, maintain and operate a refuse transfer or disposal system, or both;

(b) A statement that in the absence of any exclusion as provided in Section 4741.2, the boundaries of the proposed refuse transfer or disposal system, or both, shall coincide with the existing district boundaries;

(c) The name of the county sanitation district proposing to construct, maintain and operate said system;

(d) Instructions to the secretary of the district board to deliver within 10 days after the passage of said resolution of intention a certified copy thereof to the governing body of each political subdivision having representation on said district board;

(e) A statement that any political subdivision having representation on the district board may be excluded from said system and relieved of all liability in connection therewith upon complying with the provisions of Section 4741.2.

(Repealed and added by Stats. 1957, Ch. 168.)

4741.2.

That portion of a political subdivision lying within a district and having representation on the district board of directors, shall be excluded from the proposed refuse transfer or disposal system, or both, and shall not be liable for any cost incurred by said district in acquiring, constructing, operating and maintaining such system; provided, that the governing body of said political subdivision within 90 days after passage of the resolution of intention by the district to form such system, delivers to said district a certified copy of its resolution requesting exclusion from the proposed refuse transfer or disposal system, or both.

(Repealed and added by Stats. 1957, Ch. 168.)

4741.3.

At the expiration of not less than 90 days after adoption of the resolution of intention to construct, maintain and operate a refuse transfer or disposal system, or both, the district board may, in its discretion, adopt a resolution declaring the system formed or may rescind its resolution of intention to form said system and declare all prior proceedings in connection therewith void.

Any existing refuse collection and disposal system of a district shall be dissolved without further action by the board upon the adoption by the same district board of a resolution declaring a refuse transfer or disposal system, or both, formed.

(Repealed and added by Stats. 1957, Ch. 168.)

4741.4.

The board of directors of a county sanitation district shall be the same for all district purposes, activities, and objectives, whether for collection, treatment and disposal of sewage or the acquisition and operation of a refuse transfer or disposal system, or both, and no director shall be excluded from the board of directors because the political subdivision which he represents on the board has excluded itself from the said refuse transfer or disposal system, or both.

(Repealed and added by Stats. 1957, Ch. 168.)

4741.5.

When a refuse transfer or disposal system, or both, is established by a district pursuant to the provisions of this article, the district shall comply with the provisions of Sections 54900 to 54903, inclusive, of the Government Code, by furnishing a statement and map or plat to each assessor whose roll is used for the levy as provided in Section 4815 of this code and to the State Board of Equalization, showing the boundaries of said refuse transfer or disposal system or both.

(Repealed and added by Stats. 1957, Ch. 168.)

4741.6.

The provisions of Sections 4741.1 through 4741.5 shall not apply to any district whose resolution of intention pursuant to Section 4710 discloses that the district was formed for the purposes of constructing, maintaining and operating both sewage collection and disposal systems and refuse collection and disposal systems. Also nothing contained in this chapter shall be construed to preclude any district from using its sewerage system to dispose of ground garbage or other acceptable material which is ground into the form of slurry.

(Added by Stats. 1953, Ch. 1495.)

4741.7.

Notwithstanding any of the provisions of this chapter, or of Article 4 (commencing with Section 5470) to the contrary, a district may fix and collect a fee or charge in connection with its refuse transfer or disposal system only pursuant to the provisions of Section 5471, and for these purposes "sanitation or sewerage system" includes a refuse transfer or disposal system. Any entity which collects such a fee or charge for a district pursuant to the provisions of Section 5471 may deduct the administrative costs of these collections from the revenue produced from such fee or charge. The revenues of these charges shall not be used for acquisition, construction, maintenance, or operation of any refuse transfer or disposal system, whether by the district, jointly, by contract, or otherwise, unless the system is either a facility for the conversion of solid waste into energy, synthetic fuels, or reusable materials or is open for use by all persons in the district. For the purposes of this section, "person" includes an individual, company, public or private corporation, or public entity.

(Amended by Stats. 1982, Ch. 1158, Sec. 7.)

4742.

It may join with any other district, city or other governmental agency in the purchase, ownership, use, construction, maintenance, or operation of a sewerage system or sewage disposal or treatment plant, or a refuse transfer or disposal system, or both, either within or without the district, or so join for any combination of these purposes, but no sewage disposal or treatment plan shall be constructed or maintained in any city not in the district, except by consent granted by the unanimous vote of the governing body of the city.

(Amended by Stats. 1957, Ch. 168.)

4742.1.

It may contract with any district, city, governmental agency, or person, for the handling, treatment or disposal by the district of refuse, sewage, or industrial wastes originating within the district or county or within areas outside of the district or county when, in the judgment of the district board, it is for the best interest of the district to do so, upon such terms and conditions as may be agreed upon; provided, that the contract shall be for such term as agreed upon, but in no event for a term in excess of 50 years, or for such time as in the judgment of the district board the district shall have the capacity for handling, treatment or disposal of such refuse, sewage, or industrial wastes.

(Amended by Stats. 1959, Ch. 1303.)

4742.3.

Whenever a person installs sewers or other facilities for sewers and the district board determines that it is necessary that such sewers or other facilities be constructed so that they can be or will be used for the benefit of property other than that of the person making the installation and such sewers or other facilities are dedicated to the public or become the property of the district, the district board may by contract agree to reimburse such person for such sewers or other facilities. Such contract may provide that the district may collect from any person using such sewer or other facility for the benefit of property not owned by the person making the installation a reasonable fee or charge.

(Added by Stats. 1961, Ch. 1380.)

4742.4.

Any county sanitation district and any county may enter into a contract agreeing to pay and apportion between them the costs of locating, removing, repairing, or relocating any facilities owned or to be owned by either party on the roads or other property of the other in such proportion and upon such terms as the governing boards of the parties shall determine to be equitable.

(Added by Stats. 1967, Ch. 164.)

4742.5.

It may make provision for street-cleaning and streetsweeping services upon the roads and streets within the boundaries of the district. It may contract with any district, city, governmental agency or person for the operation of a street-cleaning and streetsweeping service upon the roads and streets within the boundaries of the district, when, in the judgment of the district board, it is for the best interest of the district to do so, upon such terms and conditions as may be agreed upon.

(Added by Stats. 1967, Ch. 780.)

4743.

It may sell, lease, or otherwise dispose of any property of the district or any interest therein whenever it is no longer required for the purposes of the district, or when its use may be permitted without interfering with its use by the district.

(Enacted by Stats. 1939, Ch. 60.)

4744.

It may sell, or otherwise dispose of, any water, sewage effluent, fertilizer, or other by-product resulting from the operation of a sewerage system, sewage disposal plant, refuse disposal plant or process, or treatment plant, and construct, maintain, and operate such pipe lines and other works as may be necessary for that purpose.

(Amended by Stats. 1949, Ch. 721.)

4745.

It may construct, maintain, and operate such pipe lines or other works as may be necessary to conserve and put to beneficial use any water or sewage effluent recovered from the operation of the sewerage system, plant, or works, by sale or disposition for agricultural or industrial purposes, or by discharging or spreading the water or sewage effluent in such a manner as to percolate into the underground gravels and replenish the natural water resources.

(Enacted by Stats. 1939, Ch. 60.)

4746.

It may issue bonds.

(Enacted by Stats. 1939, Ch. 60.)

4746.1.

If funds are needed to meet current expenses of maintenance and operation, a district may incur indebtedness by the issuance of negotiable promissory notes pursuant to this section, without an election. The notes shall be general obligations of the district payable in the same manner as bonds of the district, shall mature not later than two years from the date thereof, and shall bear interest at a rate not to exceed 7 percent per annum, payable as provided therein. The aggregate amount of the notes outstanding at any one time shall not exceed an amount equal to seven cents ($0.07) on each one hundred dollars ($100) of the assessed valuation of the taxable real property within the district as shown on the last equalized assessment roll of the county. If such assessed valuation is not obtainable, the county auditor's estimate of the assessed valuation of the taxable real property within the district for the fiscal year in which the indebtedness is to be incurred shall be used.

All such notes shall be issued after the adoption of a resolution by a four-fifths vote of the district board setting forth the following:

(a) The necessity for such borrowing.

(b) The assessed valuation of the taxable real property within the district, or the auditor's estimate thereof.

(c) The amount of funds to be borrowed.

(d) The date, maturity, denomination, and form of such notes.

The notes shall be signed by the chairman of the district board and countersigned by the county treasurer and the seal of the district board shall be affixed.

The district board shall cause the board of supervisors to levy and collect taxes to pay the interest on and the principal of the notes as the same comes due and, if the maturity of the notes begins more than one year after the date thereof, to constitute a sinking fund for the payment of the principal thereof at maturity.

Before selling such notes, the district board shall give notice inviting sealed bids in such manner as the board may prescribe. If satisfactory bids are received, the notes offered for sale shall be awarded to the highest responsible bidder. If no bids are received, or if the district board determines that the bids received are not satisfactory as to price or responsibility of the bidders, the district board may reject all bids received, if any, and either readvertise or sell the notes at private sale.

(Amended by Stats. 1972, Ch. 1384.)

4746.2.

(a) If the district board determines by resolution that funds are needed to meet current expenses of maintenance and repair of damage caused by disaster, a district may borrow and repay county funds not to exceed 85 percent of the district's anticipated revenue for the fiscal year in which they are borrowed or for the next ensuing fiscal year. In levying taxes as authorized by this article the district may raise sufficient revenues to repay such loans.

(b) The district may also borrow funds from another sanitation district and may lend available district funds to another sanitation district, subject to the same terms and conditions as apply to loans of county funds.

(c) At no time shall a district borrow funds pursuant to this section in an amount exceeding 85 percent of the district's anticipated revenue for the fiscal year in which the funds are borrowed or for the next ensuing fiscal year.

(d) As used in this section, "disaster" includes any fire, earthquake, landslide, mudslide, flood, or tidal wave.

(Added by Stats. 1969, Ch. 419.)

4746.3.

Notwithstanding any other provisions of law, the funds, when borrowed by a sanitation district pursuant to Section 4746.2, shall forthwith increase the appropriations of the district for which they are needed. The board of supervisors may specify the date and manner in which the funds shall be repaid. In no case shall repayment of the loan be deferred longer than 10 calendar years.

(Added by Stats. 1969, Ch. 419.)

4746.4.

The district shall pay interest to the county on all funds borrowed pursuant to Section 4746.2 at the same rate that the county applies to funds of the district on deposit with the county.

(Added by Stats. 1969, Ch. 419.)

4747.

It may cause to be levied and collected taxes upon all the taxable real property in the district sufficient to meet the obligations evidenced by its bonds, to maintain the works of the district, and to defray all other expenses incidental to the exercise of the district powers.

(Enacted by Stats. 1939, Ch. 60.)

4748.

The district board shall, by resolution, employ one or more sanitation engineers to make a survey of the problems of the district concerning sanitation especially with reference to the matters of sewage collection, treatment, and disposal, and refuse transfer or disposal, or both, the resolution shall direct the engineer or engineers to prepare and file with the district board of the district a report setting forth:

(a) A general description of existing facilities for sewage collection, treatment, and disposal, or a general description of existing facilities for refuse transfer or disposal, or both.

(b) A general description of the work proposed to be done to carry out the objects of the district.

(c) A general plan and general specifications of the work.

(d) A general description of the property proposed to be acquired or damaged in carrying out the work.

(e) A map showing the boundaries of the district and in general the location of the work proposed to be done, property taken or damaged, and any other information useful to an understanding of the proposed work.

(f) An estimate of the cost of the proposed work.

(Amended by Stats. 1957, Ch. 168.)

4749.

The engineer or engineers may, subject to the direction of the district board, employ such surveyors and others as may be necessary to prepare the report. The district board at any time may remove any or all engineers or other persons employed, and may fill all vacancies.

(Enacted by Stats. 1939, Ch. 60.)

4750.

When the engineers' report is filed the district board shall examine it and may thereupon (a) reject it and direct that a new report be prepared; (b) direct that changes be made in it; or (c) if it complies with the provisions of this chapter and is satisfactory to the board it shall fix a time and place for hearing objections to the report and to doing all or any part of the work referred to in the report.
(Enacted by Stats. 1939, Ch. 60.)

4751.

Notice of the hearing shall be given by the district board by publishing the notice for at least five times in a daily, or twice in a weekly, newspaper circulated in the district, as the district board may direct. At the time and place so fixed, or at the time and place to which the hearing may be from time to time continued, the board shall hear all objections.
(Enacted by Stats. 1939, Ch. 60.)

4752.

At the conclusion of the hearing the district board shall either order the report changed to conform to some or all the objections made or shall approve and adopt the report as made. If changes in the report are ordered a further hearing shall be had upon it as amended and further hearings shall be had until the district board approves and adopts the report.
(Enacted by Stats. 1939, Ch. 60.)

4753.

The district board may, thereafter, have such portions of the report as are adapted to publication, or a resume, published for free public distribution.
(Enacted by Stats. 1939, Ch. 60.)

4754.

The engineers employed by the district board to make the report required by this chapter, or other engineers, shall be directed by the district board to superintend the doing of the work recommended to be done in the report as approved and adopted.
(Enacted by Stats. 1939, Ch. 60.)

4758.

Any work recommended to be done in the report approved and adopted by the district board shall be done in conformity with the general plans and specifications contained in the report unless the district board, by a four-fifths vote, adopts a resolution declaring that the public interest requires a modification of or departure from the plans and specifications, which resolution shall contain a statement of the manner in which the modification is required or departure is to be made.
(Enacted by Stats. 1939, Ch. 60.)

4759.

A right of way in or across any public highway, street, or property in the district is hereby granted to the district wherever the right of way is found by the district board to be necessary or convenient for doing any of the work.
(Enacted by Stats. 1939, Ch. 60.)

4759.1.

(a) There is granted to every district the right to construct, operate and maintain outfall, intercepting and trunk sewerlines, other than ocean outfall lines and other terminal outfall lines, together with pumps and like machinery necessary for sewage transportation, across, along, in, under, over or upon any road, street, alley, avenue or highway within any city, in such a manner as to afford security for life and property. For the purposes of this section the term "terminal outfall lines" means any outfall sewerlines that discharge within the city any effluent from a sewage treatment plant or any sewage. Any use, under this section, of a public highway now or hereafter constituted a state highway shall be subject to the provisions of Chapter 3 (commencing with Section 660) of Division 1 of the Streets and Highways Code.
(b) A district exercising its rights under this section shall restore the road, street, alley, avenue or highway so used to its former state of usefulness as nearly as may be, and shall locate such sewerlines and machinery so as to interfere as little as possible with other existing uses of such road, street, alley, avenue or highway.
(c) Before any district uses any street, alley, avenue or highway within any city, it shall request the city in which the street, alley, avenue or highway is situated to agree with it upon the location of such sewerlines and machinery and the terms and conditions to which the construction, operation and maintenance of such sewerlines shall be subject.
(d) If the district and the city are unable to agree on the terms and conditions and location of such sewerlines and machinery within three months after a proposal to do so, the district may bring an action in the superior court of the county in which the street, alley, avenue or highway is situated against the city to have the terms and conditions and location determined. The superior court may determine and adjudicate the terms and conditions to which the use of the street, alley, avenue or highway shall be subject, and the location thereof, and upon the making of the final judgment the district may enter and use the street, alley, avenue or highway upon the terms and conditions and at the location specified in the judgment.
(Added by Stats. 1963, Ch. 530.)

4760.

The district board may, by agreement with any city or other public agency, take possession of, or acquire by condemnation or in any other manner any sewerage system, or any sewage or refuse disposal or treatment plant, or any combination of the foregoing necessary or convenient to carry out any of the objects of the district, or may acquire by agreement or in any manner the right to use them, and any city or other public agency may enter into such an agreement with a county sanitation district.

A compliance with this chapter is sufficient to authorize such an agreement by either a county sanitation district, city, or other public agency entering into such a contract with a county sanitation district.

Whenever any sewerage or refuse disposal system, or sewage or refuse disposal or treatment plant so taken possession of or otherwise acquired was built from the proceeds of a bond issue, the district may assume and pay out of its funds the outstanding bonds of the city or public agency according to their terms, and in that case the principal sum remaining unpaid shall be credited to it and deducted from any sum to be paid by it to the city or public agency.

Funds may be obtained by the county sanitation districts to pay the principal and interest on the assumed bonds in the manner as is provided for paying the principal and interest on its own bonds.
(Amended by Stats. 1957, Ch. 125.)

4761.

Any city or public agency in the district may enter into an agreement with the district for the use, or entire possession and operation, by the county sanitation district of any sewerage or refuse disposal system, or sewage or refuse disposal or treatment plant owned or operated by the city or public agency.
(Amended by Stats. 1949, Ch. 721.)

4762.

Whenever any area in the district is provided with a sewerage system the governing body of the city in which the area lies may declare the further maintenance or use of cesspools or other local means of sewage disposal to be a public nuisance, and may require all buildings inhabited or used by human beings to be connected with the sewerage system. The board of supervisors may prohibit the use of cesspools or other local means of sewage disposal and declare the same to be a public nuisance in any area in the district which is outside of any incorporated city, and may require all buildings inhabited or used by human beings to be connected with the sewerage system.
(Amended by Stats. 1963, Ch. 1097.)

4762.1.

All connections of lateral or other sewerlines to the sewerage system of the district, whether within or without any city, shall be made at points and in the manner to be directed by the engineers of the district under instructions from the district board, subject to such terms and conditions as the district board may prescribe. The district board may prescribe standards for installation and maintenance of laterals or sewerlines connecting to the sewerage system of the district, including, but not limited to, installation and maintenance by property owners of cleanouts and backflow protective devices.
(Added by Stats. 1963, Ch. 1097.)

4763.

All powers of the district shall be exercised by the district board unless otherwise specified.
(Added by Stats. 1939, Ch. 596.)

4764.

It may borrow money and incur indebtedness and guarantee the performance of its legal or contractual obligations whether heretofore or hereafter incurred; and also refund or retire any public indebtedness or lien that may exist against the district or any property therein which shall have arisen out of the transaction of the affairs of the district. It shall not, however, incur any bonded indebtedness unless it submits the proposition for incurring the bonded indebtedness to the voters of the district, or if the bonded indebtedness is for an improvement district, to the voters of the improvement district, at a regular election or a special election called for that purpose and at least two-thirds of the votes cast at the election are in favor of incurring the bonded indebtedness as proposed.
(Amended by Stats. 1957, Ch. 2123.)

4765.

Any district, directly or through a representative, may attend the Legislature and any committees thereof and present information to aid the passage of legislation which the district deems beneficial to the district or to prevent the passage of legislation which the governing board of the district deems detrimental to the district. The cost and expense incident thereto are proper charges against the district. Such districts may enter into and provide for participation in the business of associations and through a representative of the associations attend the Legislature, and any committees thereof, and present information to aid the passage of legislation which the association deems beneficial to the districts in the association, or to prevent the passage of legislation which the association deems detrimental to the districts in the association. The cost and expense incident thereto are proper charges against the districts comprising the association.

Each member of the district board engaging in such activities on behalf of the district shall be allowed eleven cents ($0.11) per mile, without any constructive mileage, for his expenses of traveling necessarily done by automobile, and his actual traveling expenses when he travels by public conveyance.
(Amended by Stats. 1968, Ch. 1095.)

4766.

The district board may adopt ordinances to carry out the provisions of Sections 5473 to 5473.11, inclusive, of the Health and Safety Code and this chapter; the procedure for the adoption of said ordinances shall be the same as is provided for in Article 7 (commencing with Section 25120), Chapter 1, Part 2, Division 2, Title 3 of the Government Code for counties. In the absence of county or city regulation, the district board may also adopt ordinances for the purpose of exercise and effect of any of it powers, or for the purposes for which it was formed. Any ordinance adopted by the district board shall impose restrictions equal to or greater than those imposed by the State Housing Law, Part 1.5 (commencing with Section 17910), Division 13 of this code, and the rules and regulations promulgated pursuant thereto by the Commission of Housing and Community Development. A violation of a regulation or ordinance of a district is a misdemeanor,

punishable by a fine not to exceed one thousand dollars ($1,000), imprisonment not to exceed 30 days, or both.
(Amended by Stats. 1976, Ch. 898.)

4766.1.

The board of supervisors of any county may adopt a model county sanitation district ordinance. The procedure for the adoption of said ordinance shall be the same as is provided for in Article 7 (commencing with Section 25120) of Chapter 1, Part 2, Division 2, Title 3 of the Government Code for the adoption of county ordinances. The ordinance may be amended by the same procedure used for the adoption of the ordinance. The ordinance and amendments thereto shall be effective only as to districts which have adopted it by reference as hereinafter provided.
(Added by Stats. 1975, Ch. 489.)

4766.2.

The district board is hereby authorized to enact an ordinance which adopts by reference all or any part of a model county sanitation district ordinance. The adopting ordinance may also enact provisions to add to or amend the model sanitation district ordinance as it is applied to that district.
(Added by Stats. 1975, Ch. 489.)

4766.3.

Prior to adoption of any ordinance which adopts by reference all or any part of a model county sanitation district ordinance, the district board shall give notice that copies of the model ordinance being considered for adoption are on file with the clerk of the district and are open to public inspection. Such notice shall be published pursuant to Section 6066 of the Government Code in a newspaper of general circulation in the district. If there is no newspaper of general circulation in the district, the notice shall be posted in the manner as provided for the posting of any proposed ordinance.
(Added by Stats. 1975, Ch. 489.)

4766.4.

Nothing contained in this article shall be deemed to relieve any district from the requirement of publishing in full the ordinance which adopts by reference the model sanitation district ordinance; and all provisions applicable to such publication shall be fully carried out. Such publication shall contain notice that copies of the model county sanitation district ordinance are on file with the clerk of the district and are open to public inspection.
(Added by Stats. 1975, Ch. 489.)

4766.5.

If at any time the model sanitation district ordinance is amended by the county board of supervisors, then the district board may adopt such amendment or amended model sanitation district ordinance by reference as provided in this article; or an ordinance may be enacted in the regular manner, setting forth the entire text of such amendment.
(Added by Stats. 1975, Ch. 489.)

4766.6.

If the board of directors of the district is the board of supervisors, the district may adopt the model county sanitation district ordinance and any amendments thereto by reference without following the procedures contained in Section 4766.3.
(Added by Stats. 1983, Ch. 117, Sec. 1.)

4766.7.

A district may destroy a record pursuant to Chapter 7 (commencing with Section 60200) of Division 1 of Title 6 of the Government Code.
(Added by renumbering Section 4766.5 (as added by Stats. 2005, Ch. 158, Sec. 21) by Stats. 2015, Ch. 303, Sec. 299. (AB 731) Effective January 1, 2016.)

4767.

Any county sanitation district may, in addition to its other powers, acquire, construct, control, operate, and maintain waterworks, conduits, reservoirs, storage sites, and other works and facilities for the production, treatment, storage and distribution of a water supply for domestic and other uses. The district may also purchase water from any other utility district, public agency, person, or private company, and distribute it.
The district may only distribute and sell to retail customers domestic water supplies outside the district by means of facilities designed primarily to serve inside the district. Before a district may so distribute and sell to retail customers domestic water supplies within the boundaries of another district or municipality which has the same or similar powers with respect to domestic water supplies, it shall secure the consent of the governing body of such other district or municipality to do so.
(Amended by Stats. 1968, Ch. 1096.)

4767.5.

A district may contract with any state agency to finance any district improvement authorized by Section 4767. The terms of the contract shall be consistent with this chapter. Notwithstanding any other provision in this chapter, the term of the contract may extend up to 30 years.
(Added by Stats. 2001, Ch. 606, Sec. 3. Effective October 9, 2001.)

ARTICLE 4.1. District Employees [4768- 4768.]
(Article 4.1 added by Stats. 1957, ch. 2123.)

4768.

Section 19990 of the Government Code shall apply to employees of the district.
(Amended by Stats. 2011, Ch. 382, Sec. 8.5. (SB 194) Effective January 1, 2012.)

ARTICLE 4.5. Application of Other Statutes [4770 - 4774]
(Article 4.5 added by Stats. 1939, Ch. 1124.)

4770.

Except as to State highways where the State Highway Engineer refuses to issue a permit, with the consent of the legislative body having jurisdiction of the territory within which it is proposed so to do, expressed by resolution of such governing body, the board of any district organized subsequent to the effective date of this amendment may order the construction of sewers and appurtenances in the whole or any portion of any of the streets, highways, or public places of the district, or in property or in rights of way owned by the district, and acquire or construct trunk and collection lines and laterals, sewage disposal and treatment plants, and acquire rights of way, and easements therefor, and may provide that the cost shall be assessed upon the fronting lots and lands or upon a special district.
(Added by Stats. 1939, Ch. 1124.)

4771.

The Improvement Act of 1911, the Municipal Improvement Act of 1913 and the Improvement Bond Act of 1915 are applicable to districts.
(Amended by Stats. 1974, Ch. 426.)

4772.

In the application of those acts to proceedings under this article the terms used in those acts shall have the following meanings:
(a) "City council," and "council," mean board.
(b) "City," and "municipality," mean district.
(c) "Clerk," and "city clerk," mean secretary.
(d) "Superintendent of streets," "street superintendent," and "city engineer" mean the engineer of the district, or any other person appointed to perform such duties.
(e) "Tax collector," means county tax collector.
(f) "Treasurer," and "city treasurer," mean any person or official who has charge of and makes payment of the funds of the district.
(g) "Right of way," means any parcel of land through which a right of way has been granted to the district for the purpose of constructing and maintaining a sewer.
(Added by Stats. 1939, Ch. 1124.)

4773.

The powers and duties conferred by those acts and supplementary acts upon boards, officers, and agents of cities shall be exercised by the respective boards, officers, and agents of the district.
(Added by Stats. 1939, Ch. 1124.)

4774.

The improvements authorized to be constructed or acquired under this article are restricted to those permitted to be constructed or acquired by such districts under Article 4 of this chapter.
(Added by Stats. 1941, Ch. 1072.)

ARTICLE 5. Bonds [4780 - 4803]
(Article 5 enacted by Stats. 1939, Ch. 60.)

4780.

After the approval and adoption of an engineers' report the district board shall submit to the voters of the district the proposition of incurring a bonded indebtedness to obtain funds with which to acquire the property and do the work set forth in the report. For that purpose a special election shall be called by resolution.
(Enacted by Stats. 1939, Ch. 60.)

4781.

The resolution shall state all of the following:
(a) The general objects and purposes for which it is proposed to incur an indebtedness.
(b) A reference to the report filed with the district board for particulars.
(c) The amount of the bonds proposed to be issued.
(d) The number of years not to exceed which the whole of the bonds are to run.
(e) The rate of interest or a maximum rate of interest to be paid, which rate shall not be more than the rate specified in this chapter, payable at the time specified in this chapter.
(f) The date of the election.
(g) The election precincts, polling places, and election officers.
(Amended by Stats. 1949, Ch. 168.)

4782.

For the purposes of the bond election the district board may consolidate into one precinct several precincts established for general election purposes and describe the precinct by reference to the general election precincts.
(Enacted by Stats. 1939, Ch. 60.)

4783.

An election board consisting of one inspector, one judge, and one clerk shall be appointed by the district board for each precinct.
(Enacted by Stats. 1939, Ch. 60.)

4784.

Only voters registered in the district are eligible to vote at the bond election.
(Enacted by Stats. 1939, Ch. 60.)

4785.

The resolution calling the election shall be published once a week for three successive weeks in a newspaper having a general circulation in the district and designated by the district board. No other notice of the election need be given.
(Enacted by Stats. 1939, Ch. 60.)

4786.

If two-thirds of the votes cast are in favor of incurring the bonded indebtedness as proposed, bonds of the district for the amount stated in the resolution calling the election shall be issued and sold.
(Enacted by Stats. 1939, Ch. 60.)

4787.

The validity of the bonds after their issuance shall not be questioned in any court except upon the ground that the provisions of this chapter authorizing their issuance are unconstitutional, or that the required hearing regarding the formation of the district was not legally held or proper notice of it was not given.

(Amended by Stats. 1939, Ch. 596.)

4788.

The district board shall prescribe by resolution the form of the bonds, and interest coupons. The bonds shall be payable at such times and at a place to be fixed by the board, and designated in the bonds, together with interest on all sums unpaid on that date until the whole of the indebtedness has been paid. The term of bonds issued shall not exceed forty years.

(Amended by Stats. 1949, Ch. 168.)

4789.

The bonds shall be issued in such denomination or denominations as the district board may determine. They shall be payable on the day and at the place fixed in the bonds, and with interest at the rate specified in the bonds, which rate shall not be in excess of 8 percent per annum, and shall, after the first year, be payable semiannually.

(Amended by Stats. 1975, Ch. 130.)

4790.

The bonds shall be signed by the chairman of the district board, and countersigned by the county treasurer, and the seal of the district board shall be affixed. The interest coupons of the bonds shall be numbered consecutively and signed by the county treasurer. All such signatures and countersignatures may be printed, lithographed, engraved, or otherwise mechanically reproduced except that one of said signatures or countersignatures to said bonds shall be manually affixed. Any such signature may be affixed in accordance with the provisions of the Uniform Facsimile Signatures of Public Officials Act, Chapter 6 (commencing with Section 5500) of Title 1 of the Government Code.

(Amended by Stats. 1972, Ch. 1384.)

4791.

If any officer whose signature or countersignature appears on the bonds ceases to be an officer before the delivery of the bonds to the purchaser, his signature or countersignature shall be as valid as if he had remained in office until the delivery of the bonds.

(Amended by Stats. 1939, Ch. 596.)

4792.

The board may issue and sell the bonds of the district at not less than par value, and the proceeds shall be placed in the treasury of the county.

All premiums and accrued interest received shall be paid into the fund to be used for the payment of principal and interest on the bonds and the remainder of the proceeds of the sale shall be paid into the construction fund of the district, and proper records of the transactions shall be placed upon the books of the treasurer.

(Enacted by Stats. 1939, Ch. 60.)

4792.1.

When the board of supervisors is the district board of a district and such board deems it in the best interests of the district, it may authorize the county treasurer, upon such terms and conditions as may be fixed by such board, to issue notes, on a competitive-bid basis, maturing within a period not to exceed one year, in anticipation of the sale of district bonds duly authorized at the time such notes are issued. The proceeds from the sale of such notes shall be used only for the purposes for which may be used the proceeds of the sale of bonds in anticipation whereof the notes were issued.

All notes issued and any renewal thereof shall be payable at a fixed time, solely from the proceeds of the sale of the bonds and not otherwise, except that in the event that the sale of the bonds shall not have occurred prior to the maturity of the notes issued in anticipation of the sale, the county treasurer shall, in order to meet the notes then maturing, issue renewal notes for such purpose. No renewal of a note shall be issued after the sale of bonds in anticipation of which the original note was issued. There shall be only one renewal of such note or notes.

Every note and any renewal thereof shall be payable from the proceeds of the sale of bonds and not otherwise. The total amount of such notes or renewals thereof issued and outstanding shall at no time exceed the total amount of the unsold bonds.

Interest on the notes shall be payable from proceeds of the sale of bonds.

(Added by Stats. 1973, Ch. 317.)

4793.

The construction fund shall be applied exclusively to the purposes and objects mentioned in the resolution calling the bond election.

Payments from the construction fund shall be made upon demands allowed by the district board, and prepared, presented, and audited in the same manner as demands upon the funds of the county.

(Enacted by Stats. 1939, Ch. 60.)

4793.1.

When the purposes and objects mentioned in the resolution calling the bond election have been accomplished, any moneys remaining in the construction fund may be transferred to the fund to be used for the payment of principal and interest on the bonds. The district board by a vote of two-thirds of the members thereof may use said remaining moneys for some other county sanitation district purpose which will benefit the property in the district or improvement district, as the case may be; provided, however, that with respect to improvement districts such general objectives and purposes shall not include the acquisition or construction of new local street sewers or laterals as distinguished from main trunks, interceptors, and outfall sewers. Said moneys may not be used for said other county sanitation district purposes until two-thirds of the qualified electors of said district or improvement district thereof, as the case may be, have consented thereto at a special election called in said district or improvement district by the district board. Notice of said election shall be given and said election shall be held and conducted in the manner provided for bond elections in said county sanitation district or improvement district, as the case may be.

(Amended by Stats. 1955, Ch. 1535.)

4794.

If the proposition of issuing bonds submitted at a bond election fails to receive the requisite number of votes, the district board may, at the expiration of six months after that election, call or order another bond election, either for the same objects and purposes, or for any other object or purpose of the district.

(Enacted by Stats. 1939, Ch. 60.)

4795.

If the district board by resolution passed by a vote of a majority of all its members determines that the public interest or necessity of the district demands the issuance of additional bonds for carrying out any of the objects of the district, the district board may again have a report made, and submit to the voters the question of issuing additional bonds in the same manner as for a first issue. All the provisions of this chapter for the issuance and sale of bonds, and for the expenditure of the proceeds apply to the issuance of additional bonds.

(Amended by Stats. 1963, Ch. 1097.)

4796.

Bonds and the interest thereon shall be paid by revenue derived from an annual tax upon the real property in the district, and all the real property in the district shall be and remain liable to be taxed for such payments. Said bonds and the interest thereon shall not be taxable in this State.

(Amended by Stats. 1939, Ch. 596.)

4797.

In determining the amount of bonds to be issued, the legislative body may include:

(a) All costs and estimated costs incidental to or connected with the acquisition, construction, improving or financing of the project.

(b) All engineering, inspection, legal and fiscal agent's fees, costs of the bond election and of the issuance of said bonds, bond reserve funds and working capital and bond interest estimated to accrue during the construction period and for a period of not to exceed 12 months after completion of construction.

(Added by Stats. 1957, Ch. 1378.)

4799.

Nothing in this chapter shall affect the validity of, or the right to issue and sell, bonds voted prior to the date when this code goes into effect.

(Added by Stats. 1939, Ch. 596.)

4801.

(1) An issue of bonds is hereby defined to be the aggregate principal amount of all of the bonds authorized to be issued in accordance with a proposal submitted to and approved by the electors of the district, but no indebtedness will be deemed to have been contracted until bonds shall have been sold and delivered and then only to the extent of the principal amount of bonds so sold and delivered.

(2) The board of directors of any district issuing any bonds heretofore or hereafter authorized may, in its discretion, divide the aggregate principal amount of such issue into two or more divisions or series and fix different dates for the bonds of each separate division or series. In the event any authorized issue is divided into two or more divisions or series, the bonds of each division or series may be made payable at such time or times as may be fixed by the legislative body of the district separate and distinct from the time or times the payment of bonds of any other division or series of the same issue.

(Added by Stats. 1949, Ch. 168.)

4802.

Bonds may be made payable on a date subsequent to the time fixed for the collection of the second installment of general district taxes with which the first levy of taxes for the payment of the principal and interest of said bonds is to be collected. In such event, the first interest coupons shall be for interest from the date of said bonds of such issue or series or division to the maturity date of said coupons.

(Added by Stats. 1951, Ch. 1648.)

4803.

An action to determine the validity of bonds may be brought pursuant to Chapter 9 (commencing with Section 860) of Title 10 of Part 2 of the Code of Civil Procedure.

(Amended by Stats. 1961, Ch. 1556.)

ARTICLE 5.5. Revenue Bonds [4805- 4805.]

(Article 5.5 added by Stats. 1953, Ch. 95.)

4805.

The provisions of the Revenue Bond Law of 1941 as amended shall be applicable to county sanitation districts, and the term "local agency" as used in Chapter 6 of Part 1, Division 2, Title 5 of the Government Code shall be deemed to include a county sanitation district.

Notwithstanding any provision of the Revenue Bond Law of 1941, including, but not limited to, Section 54382 of the Government Code, any county sanitation district may issue bonds, pursuant to such law which have an interest rate which is not in excess of 7 percent per annum.

(Amended by Stats. 1968, Ch. 671.)

ARTICLE 5.6. Bonds for Improvement of a Portion of a District [4806 - 4809.3]

(Article 5.6 added by Stats. 1955, Ch. 707.)

4806.

As an alternative method of issuing bonds the district board may, after the approval and adoption of an engineer's report for a portion of the district, if it deems it necessary to incur a bonded indebtedness to obtain funds with which to acquire the property and do the work set forth in the report, by resolution so declare and state: (a) the general objects and purposes for which the proposed debt is to be incurred; provided, however, that such general objectives and purposes shall not include the acquisition or construction of new local street sewers or laterals as distinguished from main trunk, interceptor and outfall sewers; (b) the amount of debt to be incurred; (c) that the district board intends to form an improvement district of that portion of the district which in the opinion of said board will be benefited, the exterior boundaries of which portion are set forth on a map on file with said board, which map shall govern for all details as to the extent of the proposed improvement district, and to call an election in such improvement district on a date to be fixed, for the purpose of submitting to the qualified voters thereof the proposition of incurring indebtedness by the issuance of bonds of the district for said improvement district; (d) that taxes for the payment of said bonds and the interest thereon shall be derived exclusively from an annual tax upon the real property in the improvement district; (e) that the engineer's report, together with a map showing the exterior boundaries of said proposed improvement district with relation to the territory immediately contiguous thereto and to the proposed improvement, are on file with the district board and are available for inspection by any person interested; (f) the time and place for a hearing by the board on the questions of the formation of said proposed improvement district, the extent thereof, the proposed improvement and the amount of debt to be incurred; and (g) that at the time and place specified in the resolution any person interested, including any persons owning property in the district or in the proposed improvement district, will be heard.

(Added by Stats. 1955, Ch. 707.)

4806.5.

As an alternative method of issuing bonds the district board may, after the approval and adoption of an engineer's report for a portion of the district, if it deems it necessary to incur a bonded indebtedness to obtain funds with which to acquire the property and do the work set forth in the report, by resolution so declare and state: (a) the general objects and purposes for which the proposed debt is to be incurred, including, but not limited to, the acquisition or construction or reconstruction of new local street sewers or laterals as distinguished from main trunk, interceptor and outfall sewers; (b) the amount of debt to be incurred; (c) that the district board intends to form an improvement district of that portion of the district which in the opinion of the board will be benefited, the exterior boundaries of which portion are set forth on a map on file with the board, which map shall govern for all details as to the extent of the proposed improvement district, and to call an election in such improvement district on a date to be fixed, for the purpose of submitting to the qualified voters thereof the proposition of incurring indebtedness by the issuance of bonds of the district for said improvement district; (d) that taxes for the payment of such bonds and the interest thereon shall be derived exclusively from an annual tax upon the real property in the improvement district; (e) that special rates or charges to finance the construction, reconstruction, maintenance, or operation of the improvement may be collected within the improvement district where, in the judgment of the board, the improvement will not be of districtwide benefit; (f) that the engineer's report, together with a map showing the exterior boundaries of such proposed improvement district with relation to the territory immediately contiguous thereto and to the proposed improvement, are on file with the district board and are available for inspection by any person interested; (g) the time and place for a hearing by the board on the questions of the formation of such proposed improvement district, the extent thereof, the proposed improvement and the amount of debt to be incurred; and (h) that at the time and place specified in the resolution any person interested, including all persons owning property in the district or in the proposed improvement district, will be heard.

This section shall only be applicable to a district within a county of the 13th class as defined in Section 28036 of the Government Code and Section 4806 shall not be applicable to a district within a county of the 13th class.

(Amended by Stats. 1974, Ch. 545.)

4807.

Notice of the hearing shall be given by publishing a copy of the resolution pursuant to Section 6066 of the Government Code prior to the time fixed for the hearing in a newspaper having general circulation in the county sanitation district. Such notice shall also be given by posting a copy of the resolution in three public places within the proposed improvement district at least two weeks before the time fixed for the hearing.

(Amended by Stats. 1957, Ch. 357.)

4808.

At the time and place so fixed, or at any time and place to which the hearing is adjourned, the district board shall proceed with the hearing. At the hearing any person interested, including any person owning property within the district or within the proposed improvement district, may appear and protest the inclusion of his property within the proposed improvement district and/or present any other matters material to the questions set forth in the resolution declaring the necessity for incurring the bonded indebtedness.

The district board shall have power to change the purpose for which the proposed debt is to be incurred, or the amount of bonded debt to be incurred, or the boundaries of said proposed improvement district, or one or all of said matters; provided, however, that said board shall not change such boundaries so as to include any territory which will not, in its judgment, be benefited by said improvement; and provided further, that said board shall exclude from the proposed improvement district any territory which it finds will not be benefited by inclusion therein. If the district board proposes to change the purposes for which the proposed debt is to be incurred, it shall cause appropriate changes to be made in the report before giving notice of such change. The purpose, amount of bonded debt and boundaries shall not be changed by said board except after notice of its intention to do so, given pursuant to Section 6061 of the Government Code in a newspaper having general circulation in said county sanitation district, and by posting in three public places within said proposed improvement district. Said notice shall state the changed purpose and debt proposed and that the engineer's report as changed by said board, together with a map showing exterior boundaries as proposed to be changed, are on file with the district board and are available for inspection by any person interested, and specify the time and place for hearing on such change, which time shall be at least 10 days after publication or posting of said notice. At the time and place so fixed, or at any time and place to which the hearing is adjourned, said board shall continue with the hearing. At the hearing any person interested, including any person owning property within the district or the proposed improvement district, may appear and present any matters material to the changes stated in the notice.

At the conclusion of the hearing the board shall by resolution determine whether it is deemed necessary to incur the bonded indebtedness, and, if so, the resolution shall also state the purpose for which said proposed debt is to be incurred (which purpose shall not include the acquisition or construction of new local street sewers or laterals as distinguished from main trunk, interceptor and outfall sewers) the amount of the proposed debt, that the exterior boundaries of the portion of the district which will be benefited are set forth on a map on file with the district board, which map shall govern for all details as to the extent of the improvement district, and that said portion of the district set forth on said map shall thereupon constitute and be known as "Improvement District No. __ of _____ (name of county sanitation district)," and the determination made in said resolution shall be final and conclusive. After the formation of such improvement district within a county sanitation district, all proceedings for the purpose of a bond election shall be limited and shall apply only to the improvement district, and taxes for the payment of said bonds and the interest thereon shall be derived exclusively from an annual tax upon the real property in the improvement district.

(Amended by Stats. 1957, Ch. 357.)

4808.5.

At the time and place so fixed, or at any time and place to which the hearing is adjourned, the district board shall proceed with the hearing. At the hearing any person interested, including any person owning property within the district or within the proposed improvement district, may appear and protest the inclusion of his property within the proposed improvement district or present any other matters material to the questions set forth in the resolution declaring the necessity for incurring the bonded indebtedness, or do both.

The district board shall have power to change the purpose for which the proposed debt is to be incurred, or the amount of bonded debt to be incurred, or the boundaries of the proposed improvement district, or one or all of such matters; provided, however, that the board shall not change such boundaries so as to include any territory which will not, in its judgment, be benefited by such improvement; and provided further, that the board shall exclude from the proposed improvement district any territory which it finds will not be benefited by inclusion therein. If the district board proposes to change the purposes for which the proposed debt is to be incurred, it shall cause appropriate changes to be made in the report before giving notice of such change. The purpose, amount of bonded debt and boundaries shall not be changed by the board except after notice of its intention to do so, given pursuant to Section 6061 of the Government Code in a newspaper having general circulation in such county sanitation district, and by posting in three public places within such proposed improvement district. Such notice shall state the changed purpose and debt proposed and that the engineer's report as changed by the board, together with a map showing exterior boundaries as proposed to be changed, are on file with the district board and are available for inspection by any person interested, and specify the time and place for hearing on such change, which time shall be at least 10 days after publication or posting of such notice. At the time and place so fixed, or at any time and place to which the hearing is adjourned, the board shall continue with the hearing. At the hearing any person interested, including any person owning property within the district or the proposed improvement district, may appear and present any matters material to the changes stated in the notice.

At the conclusion of the hearing, the board shall by resolution determine whether it is deemed necessary to incur the bonded indebtedness, and, if so, the resolution shall also state the purpose for which such proposed debt is to be incurred, the amount of the proposed debt, that the exterior boundaries of the portion of the district which will be benefited are set forth on a map on file with the district board, which map shall govern for all details as to the extent of the improvement district, and that such portion of the district set forth on such map shall thereupon constitute and be known as "Improvement District No. __ of _____ (name of county sanitation district)," and the determination made in such resolution shall be final and conclusive. After the formation of such improvement district within a county sanitation district, all proceedings for the purpose of a bond election shall be limited and shall apply only to the improvement district, and taxes for the payment of such bonds and the interest thereon shall be derived exclusively from an annual tax upon the real property in the improvement district.

This section shall only be applicable to a district within a county of the 15th class as defined in Section 28036 of the Government Code and Section 4808 shall not be applicable to a district within a county of the 15th class.
(Added by Stats. 1969, Ch. 881.)

4809.

When the board has made its determinations as provided in Section 4808 and if the board deems it necessary to incur the bonded indebtedness, the board shall by resolution call a special election in said improvement district for the purpose of submitting to the qualified voters thereof the proposition of incurring indebtedness by the issuance of bonds of the district for said improvement district. Said resolution shall state: (a) that the board deems it necessary to incur the bonded indebtedness; (b) the purpose for which the bonded indebtedness will be incurred; (c) the amount of debt to be incurred; (d) the name of the improvement district to be benefited by said indebtedness, as set forth in the resolution making determinations, and that a map showing the exterior boundaries of said improvement district is on file with the district board, which map shall govern for all details as to the extent of the improvement district; (e) that taxes for the payment of such bonds and the interest thereon shall be derived exclusively from an annual tax upon the real property in said improvement district; (f) the maximum term the bonds proposed to be issued shall run before maturity, which shall not exceed 40 years; (g) the maximum rate of interest to be paid, which shall not be more than the rate specified in this chapter for bonds of the district, payable at the time specified in this chapter for bonds of the district; (h) the measure to be submitted to the voters; (i) the date of the election; and (j) the election precincts, polling places and election officers.
(Added by Stats. 1955, Ch. 707.)

4809.1.

Except as otherwise provided in this article, notice of the election shall be given and the election shall be held and conducted in the same manner as elections for the authorization of bonds of the entire county sanitation district, and if two-thirds of the votes cast are in favor of incurring the bonded indebtedness as proposed, bonds of the district, issued in the name of the district and designated "Bonds of _____ (naming the county sanitation district) for Improvement District No. __" shall be issued and sold for the amount stated in the resolution calling the election in the same form and manner as bonds of the entire county sanitation district. Each bond of the district for an improvement district and all interest coupons thereof shall state that taxes for the payment thereof shall be derived exclusively from an annual tax upon the real property in the improvement district.
(Added by Stats. 1955, Ch. 707.)

4809.2.

No irregularities or informalities in conducting such election shall invalidate the same, if the election shall have otherwise been fairly conducted. Any action or proceedings, wherein the validity of the formation of the improvement district or of any bonds issued for it or of the proceedings in relation thereto is contested, questioned or denied, shall be commenced within three months from the date of such election; otherwise, said bonds and all proceedings in relation thereto, including the formation of the improvement district, shall be held to be valid and in every respect legal and incontestable.
(Added by Stats. 1955, Ch. 707.)

4809.3.

Bonds issued as bonds of the district for an improvement district therein and the interest thereon shall be paid by revenue derived exclusively from an annual tax upon the real property in the improvement district of such county sanitation district, and all the real property within the improvement district of such county sanitation district shall be and remain liable to be taxed for such payments. The board of supervisors of the county shall annually, at the time and in the manner of levying other county taxes, levy and cause to be collected a tax upon the taxable real property in the improvement district, based upon the last equalized assessment roll of the county sufficient to pay the interest on the bonds for that year and such portion of the principal as is to become due before the time for making the next general tax levy. Said bonds and the interest thereon shall not be taxable in this State.
(Added by Stats. 1955, Ch. 707.)

ARTICLE 6. Finance and Taxation [4810 - 4820]
(Article 6 enacted by Stats. 1939, Ch. 60.)

4810.

Annually, on or before the first day of August the district board shall furnish to the board of supervisors and the county auditor a written statement of the amount necessary to pay the interest on bonds for that year, and the portion of the principal that is to become due before the time for making the next general tax levy.
(Amended by Stats. 1974, Ch. 208.)

4811.

The board of supervisors of the county shall annually, at the time and in the manner of levying other county taxes, levy and cause to be collected a tax upon the taxable real property in the district, based upon the last equalized assessment roll of the county sufficient to pay the interest on the bonds for that year and such portion of the principal as is to become due before the time for making the next general tax levy.
(Enacted by Stats. 1939, Ch. 60.)

4812.

If the district board fails to furnish to the board of supervisors the written statement of the amount necessary, the board of supervisors of the county shall ascertain the amount necessary to pay the interest on the bonds for that year and the portion of the principal that is to become due before the time for making the next general tax levy, and shall levy and cause to be collected the necessary amount.

(Enacted by Stats. 1939, Ch. 60.)

4813.

The tax shall be collected at the same time and in the same manner as the general tax levy for county purposes, and when collected shall be paid into the treasury of the county to the credit of the district, and shall be used for the payment of the principal and interest upon the bonds, and for no other purpose.
(Enacted by Stats. 1939, Ch. 60.)

4814.

The principal and interest on the bonds shall be paid by the treasurer of the county in the manner now or hereafter provided by law for the payment of principal and interest on the bonds of the county.
(Enacted by Stats. 1939, Ch. 60.)

4815.

In any year, at least 15 days before the first day of the month in which the board of supervisors of the county in which the district is located, is required by law to levy the amount of taxes required by law for county purposes, the district board shall furnish to the board of supervisors a written statement of the amount necessary; (a) to maintain, operate, extend, or repair any work or improvements of the district, for the collection, treatment and disposal of sewage and to defray all other expenses incidental to the exercise of any of the district's powers, except the amounts necessary to acquire, construct, maintain and operate a refuse transfer or disposal system, or both, and any other expenses incidental to the operation of said system and (b) to acquire, construct, operate and maintain any work or improvement of the district for a refuse transfer or disposal system, or both. The board of supervisors of the county shall, at the time and in the manner of levying other county taxes, levy separately and cause to be collected a tax upon the taxable real property in the district, based upon the last equalized assessment roll of the county sufficient to pay: (1) the cost of maintaining, operating, extending, or repairing any work or improvements of the district for the collection, treatment and disposal sewage and of defraying all other expenses incidental to the exercise of any of the district's powers except those relating to the acquisition, construction, operation and maintenance of a refuse transfer or disposal system, or both, and (2) the cost of acquiring, constructing, operating and maintaining, extending or repairing a refuse transfer or disposal system, or both; provided, the latter levy shall be made only on the real property located in said refuse transfer or disposal system, or both.
(Amended by Stats. 1957, Ch. 168.)

4816.

The tax shall be levied and collected at the same time and in the same manner as the general tax levy for county purposes, and the revenue derived from the tax shall be paid into the county treasury to the credit of the operating fund of the district, unless the board has designated a depository or depositories pursuant to Section 4730.5 or Section 4730.7 in which case the revenue shall be paid into the depository or depositories, as directed by the board, and the district board shall control and order its expenditure.
(Amended by Stats. 1989, Ch. 789, Sec. 18.)

4817.

Claims for money or damages against the district are governed by Part 3 (commencing with Section 900) and Part 4 (commencing with Section 940) of Division 3.6 of Title 1 of the Government Code, except as provided therein. Claims not governed thereby or by other statutes or by ordinances or regulations authorized by law and expressly applicable to such claims shall be prepared and presented to the governing body, and all claims shall be audited and paid, in the same manner and with the same effect as are similar claims against the county.
(Amended by Stats. 1963, Ch. 1715.)

4818.

The cost of preparing the engineer's report, including the compensation paid engineers and other employees of the district, is a charge against the district and shall be paid from the first available funds of the district.
(Enacted by Stats. 1939, Ch. 60.)

4819.

The cost of the engineer's report, employees' salaries, costs of engineering surveys, bond counsel fees, and other initial costs and expenses, not to exceed five thousand dollars ($5,000), incurred after formation of a district and prior to receipt of its first available funds, may be advanced by another county sanitation district or districts situated within the same county, upon such terms and conditions as may be agreed upon; said funds must be repaid by the borrowing district from its first available funds.
(Added by Stats. 1957, Ch. 146.)

4820.

The board of directors of a county sanitation district engaging in refuse disposal operations may, by resolution, establish a cash difference fund in an amount not to exceed one hundred dollars ($100), in the same manner and by the same procedures as prescribed by Sections 29370 to 29379, inclusive, of the Government Code.
(Added by Stats. 1959, Ch. 1334.)

ARTICLE 7. Annexation [4830 - 4839]
(Article 7 enacted by Stats. 1939, Ch. 60.)

4830.

Territory, whether situated within the same or another county and whether incorporated or unincorporated, which is not included in any other county sanitation district or other district formed for similar purposes, may be annexed to a county sanitation district if the directors find and determine that the additional territory will be benefited by annexation. Notwithstanding the provisions of the preceding sentence, territory, whether situated within the same or another county and whether incorporated or unincorporated, which is

included in any district, which district is not, at the time of the proposed annexation, performing similar services in the area proposed to be annexed, may be annexed to a county sanitation district if the board of directors finds and determines that the additional territory will be benefited by the annexation. The land proposed to be annexed need not consist of contiguous parcels nor be contiguous with the county sanitation district when such land is within the same county. When land proposed to be annexed is not within the same county such land shall be contiguous to the district.
(Amended by Stats. 1967, Ch. 929.)

4831.
If a refuse transfer or disposal system of the district, or both, is in existence, any territory proposed to be annexed to the district shall be and become a part of said system unless an express finding is made by the district board that said territory proposed to be annexed will not be benefited by its inclusion in said system.
(Amended by Stats. 1965, Ch. 2043.)

4831.5.
Property contiguous to a sanitation district but which is situated in a county other than the county in which the sanitation district has been organized may be annexed to said sanitation district and to any improvement district therein.
(Amended by Stats. 1965, Ch. 2043.)

4832.5.
Whenever any territory in another county is annexed to a district it thereupon becomes a part of the district. The board of supervisors of the county in which is situated the annexing territory shall appoint one of its members to sit as a member of the board of directors of said district. All ordinances theretofore and thereafter adopted by the board of directors shall have full force and effect in all portions of the district regardless in which county the property is situated.
(Amended by Stats. 1965, Ch. 2043.)

4832.6.
Notwithstanding the provisions of Section 4832.5, whenever territory of less than 50 acres in another county is annexed to the Selma-Kingsburg-Fowler County Sanitation District, and if the board of supervisors of the county in which the territory to be annexed is situated consents, no member of the board of supervisors of the county in which the territory to be annexed is situated shall become a member of the board of directors of the district.
(Added by Stats. 1980, Ch. 339.)

4833.
Taxes for a district which is situated in more than one county as provided in this article shall be levied in accordance with the following procedure:
(a) The board of directors shall annually, before the time of fixing the general tax levy for county purposes, estimate the amount of money necessary to be raised by taxation to meet the requirements for operation, maintenance, and payment of principal and interest on outstanding bonds which will become payable before the proceeds of another tax levy made at the time of the next general tax levy for county purposes can be made available for payment of such operation, maintenance, principal and interest.
(b) The total estimate shall be divided by the board of directors in proportion to the value of the real property of the district and any improvement district in each county. The value shall be determined from the equalized values of the last assessment rolls of the counties. When the division of the estimate has been made, the board of directors shall promptly certify to the boards of supervisors of the counties in which the district is situated the respective parts of the estimate apportioned to each county.
(c) The board of supervisors of each county in which is situated any part of a district shall annually, at the time of levying county taxes, levy a tax upon all the property within the district or any improvement district situated in the county sufficient to raise the amount so certified to the board of supervisors by the board of directors.
(d) The tax shall be collected by the same officers and in the same manner as other county taxes, and the money so collected shall be deposited in the county treasury of the county in which the original district was created and credited to the account of said district.
(e) The treasurer of the county in which is situated the annexing territory shall at any time, but not oftener than twice a year, upon order of the board of directors, settle with the board of directors and pay over to the county treasurer, who is the repository of the funds of said district, all money in his possession belonging to said district.
(Amended by Stats. 1961, Ch. 1975.)

4834.
Territory already a part of a county sanitation district may be annexed to an improvement district of that county sanitation district under the procedure set forth in Sections 4835 to 4839, inclusive. Whenever territory is so annexed to an improvement district of a county sanitation district, the annexed territory shall be subject to all the liabilities and entitled to all the benefits of the improvement district.
(Added by Stats. 1968, Ch. 39.)

4835.
The district board shall adopt a resolution initiating proceedings for annexation pursuant to Section 4834, which resolution shall contain all the following:
(a) Set forth the exterior boundaries of the territory proposed for annexation.
(b) State that the territory will be benefitted by annexation to the improvement district.
(c) Fix a time, date, and place of hearing on the proposed annexation, which shall be not less than 15 days nor more than 60 days after the date of adoption of the resolution initiating proceedings.
(d) State that any interested person desiring to make written protest against such annexation shall do so by written communication, containing the signature and street

address of the protestant, filed with the clerk of the district not later than the hour set for hearing.
(Added by Stats. 1968, Ch. 39.)

4836.
The clerk of the district shall give notice of the hearing by mailing a copy of such notice to all landowners owning land within the territory proposed to be annexed, and by publishing notice thereof in at least two successive issues, not more than 30 nor less than 10 days prior to the hearing, in a newspaper of general circulation published in the county.
(Added by Stats. 1968, Ch. 39.)

4837.
A majority protest shall be deemed to exist, and the proposed annexation shall be abandoned, if the district board shall find that written protests filed and not withdrawn prior to the conclusion of the hearing represent more than 50 percent of the assessed value of the land therein.
(Added by Stats. 1968, Ch. 39.)

4838.
At the hearing, all interested persons shall be given the opportunity to present evidence and testimony for or against the proposed annexation. Any person who shall have filed a written protest may withdraw the written protest at any time prior to the conclusion of the hearing.
If a majority protest shall not have been filed, the district board, not later than 30 days after the conclusion of the hearing, shall adopt a resolution making one of the following determinations:
(a) Disapproving the proposed annexation.
(b) Approving the proposed annexation.
(c) Approving the annexation, but excluding any lands which the board finds will not be benefitted by becoming a part of such improvement district.
(Added by Stats. 1968, Ch. 39.)

4839.
If the district board approves the proposed annexation, or approves the annexation but excludes any lands, a certified copy of the resolution of the district board, together with a map or plat of the new boundaries of the improvement district, shall be filed with the agencies designated in and as required by Sections 54900, 54901, and 54902 of the Government Code. Upon such filing, the annexation of the territory to the improvement district shall be effective.
(Added by Stats. 1968, Ch. 39.)

ARTICLE 8. Joint Operation [4840 - 4843]
(Article 8 enacted by Stats. 1939, Ch. 60.)
4840.
Whenever two or more sanitation districts find and declare by resolution adopted by their respective district boards that it is for the interest or advantage of the districts to do so, the districts by their respective district boards may enter into an agreement for the maintenance of a centralized and joint administrative organization to care for the general administration of the affairs of each of the districts, and the construction, supervision, operation, and maintenance of the work of each of the districts, and for that purpose the districts may agree to employ the same engineers, surveyors, counsel, and other persons needed to carry out the purposes of the districts.
Such agreement may also provide for participation by said sanitation districts in the State Employees' Retirement System of the State of California and for the payment of apportionments of costs and the collection, receipt and distribution of pension payments by one district designated for the purpose and acting on behalf of all districts participating in the agreement in the same manner as provided by Sections 4841 and 4842 of this code. When the agreement so provides, the designated district shall have all the powers and perform all the duties of a public agency for the purposes of the State Employees' Retirement Law, both in respect to the joint officers and employees of the participating districts and in respect to the officers and employees separately employed by the participating districts.
(Amended by Stats. 1945, Ch. 490.)

4841.
The agreement shall specify the proportionate amount to be paid by each district toward the costs and expenses of the organization and the salaries, wages, or other compensation of all persons employed jointly by the districts.
(Enacted by Stats. 1939, Ch. 60.)

4842.
For the purpose of facilitating the payment of the joint costs, expenses, salaries, wages, or other compensation, the agreement may also provide for the payment by each district of its proportionate share of the costs, expenses, salaries, wages, or other compensation, into the funds of any one of the districts which may be designated for the purpose, and the designated district shall thereafter pay all the costs, expenses, salaries, wages, or other compensation incurred by, or to be paid in connection with the maintenance of the joint organization.
(Enacted by Stats. 1939, Ch. 60.)

4843.
The district may contract with the Federal Government of the United States or any branch thereof, or with any county, city and county, municipal corporation, district or other public corporation or with any person, firm or corporation, for the joint acquisition or construction or use of any sewer or sewers or other works or facilities for the handling, treatment or disposal of sewage or industrial waste from the district and such other area as may be designated in said contract, when in the judgment of the legislative body of said district it is for the best interests of the district so to do. Any such contract may

provide for the construction and maintenance of such sewer or sewers, or such other works or facilities, and for the payment by or for the parties thereto of such proportionate part of the cost of the acquisition, construction or maintenance of such sewer or sewers or other works or facilities as may be stated in said contract, the payments to be made at such times and in such amounts as may be provided by said contract. Any such contract may provide for the joint use of any sewer or sewers, works or facilities for the handling, treatment or disposal of sewage or industrial waste upon such terms and conditions as may be agreed upon by the parties thereto, and for the flowage, treatment or disposal of sewage or industrial waste from such area for each of the parties thereto as may be described in the contract.

Any district which has acquired or constructed or which proposes to acquire or construct, any sewer or sewers, or works or other facilities for the handling, treatment or disposal of sewage or industrial waste, may contract with the Federal Government of the United States or any branch thereof, or with any county, city and county, municipal corporation, district or other public corporation or with any person, firm or corporation for the use of any such sewer or sewers, works or facilities by any such county, city and county, municipal corporation, district or other public corporation, or for the flowage, treatment or disposal of sewage or industrial waste from any area designated by such person, firm or corporation so contracting, upon such terms and conditions as may be provided in said contract.
(Added by Stats. 1949, Ch. 843.)

ARTICLE 9. Special Zones [4850 - 4858]
(Article 9 added by Stats. 1968, Ch. 794.)
4850.
The district board may, by resolution, establish zones within the district, or amend the boundaries of an existing zone by annexing property to or by withdrawing property from such zone.
(Added by Stats. 1968, Ch. 794.)
4851.
The resolution declaring the intention to form a special zone shall describe the boundaries of the proposed zone, declare that the district board finds that the area within the proposed zone will be benefited by the maintenance and operation of facilities within the zone and that the public interest and necessity demands its creation, and state the reasons therefor and the name of the proposed zone, and set the time and place for a public hearing on the question of the creation of the zone.
(Added by Stats. 1968, Ch. 794.)
4852.
The resolution declaring the intention to annex territory to an existing zone shall describe the boundaries of the proposed annexation, declare that the district board finds that the additional territory will be benefited by the maintenance and operation of facilities in the zone, and set the time and place for a public hearing on the question of the annexation.
(Added by Stats. 1968, Ch. 794.)
4853.
Notice of a hearing shall be given by publication at least once a week for two successive weeks, not more than 30 nor less than 10 days prior to the hearing in a newspaper of general circulation published within the county.
(Added by Stats. 1968, Ch. 794.)
4854.
Any interested person, at or before the hearing, may file with the district board a written objection to the creation of the zone or to the inclusion of his property in it. At the hearing the district board shall hear and pass upon all protests and objections. At the conclusion of the hearing, the district board may order that the zone shall be formed or the boundaries of an existing zone be amended, as described in the original resolution, or that any or all properties within such boundaries will not be benefited and shall be excluded.
(Added by Stats. 1968, Ch. 794.)
4855.
A copy of the resolution ordering the formation of the zone, or amending the boundaries of an existing zone, shall be filed in the office of the county assessor, and the county assessor shall thereafter, in making the assessment roll, segregate the property included within such zone on the assessment roll under the designation contained in the resolution.
(Added by Stats. 1968, Ch. 794.)
4856.
The district board shall thereafter in each year, prior to the time of fixing the county tax rate, furnish to the board of supervisors a written statement of the amount of tax revenue necessary to maintain and operate any work or improvements within the zone.
(Added by Stats. 1968, Ch. 794.)
4857.
The board of supervisors shall fix a special tax rate and levy a special assessment tax each year upon the real property in such zone, based upon the last equalized assessment roll of the county, sufficient to pay such expenses or the portion thereof which must be paid by the zone.
(Added by Stats. 1968, Ch. 794.)
4858.
Any special zone may be abolished or territory withdrawn therefrom by resolution of the district board, after hearing held in the manner provided for in this article for the original creation of the zone or annexations thereto, whenever the district board finds that the area proposed for abolition or withdrawal is no longer benefited by the maintenance and operation of facilities within the zone.

(Added by Stats. 1968, Ch. 794.)

ARTICLE 10. Santa Clarita Valley Sanitation District [4859- 4859.]
(Article 10 added by Stats. 2015, Ch. 342, Sec. 1.)
4859.
(a) Paragraph (4) of subdivision (b) of Section 54954 of the Government Code does not apply to the regular and special meetings of the Santa Clarita Valley Sanitation District where decisions are being made upon policy items relating to a total maximum daily load (TMDL) of any pollutant.
(b) For purposes of this section, "meetings" has the same definition as that term is defined in Section 54952.2 of the Government Code.
(Added by Stats. 2015, Ch. 342, Sec. 1. (AB 951) Effective January 1, 2016.)

CHAPTER 4. Sewer Maintenance Districts [4860 - 4927]
(Chapter 4 enacted by Stats. 1939, Ch. 60.)

ARTICLE 1. General Provisions and Definitions [4860 - 4866]
(Article 1 enacted by Stats. 1939, Ch. 60.)
4860.
This chapter shall be known and may be cited as the sewer maintenance district act.
(Enacted by Stats. 1939, Ch. 60.)
4861.
"District," as used in this chapter, means a sewer maintenance district formed pursuant to this chapter or pursuant to any law which it supersedes.
(Enacted by Stats. 1939, Ch. 60.)
4862.
"Board," as used in this chapter, means the board of supervisors of the county in which a district is formed, or in which it is proposed to form a district.
(Enacted by Stats. 1939, Ch. 60.)
4863.
"Clerk," as used in this chapter, means the clerk of the board of supervisors.
(Enacted by Stats. 1939, Ch. 60.)
4864.
This chapter does not repeal any law providing for the organization of sanitary districts or county sanitation districts nor authorize the governing body of a sewer maintenance district to manage, control, or otherwise interfere with the maintenance or repair of any sewers under the control of a sanitary district or county sanitation district.
(Enacted by Stats. 1939, Ch. 60.)
4866.
"Sewers" as used in this chapter includes lateral and collecting sewers, septic tanks and all other means of handling, gathering and disposing of sewage in the district.
(Added by Stats. 1943, Ch. 765.)

ARTICLE 2. Formation [4870 - 4878]
(Article 2 enacted by Stats. 1939, Ch. 60.)
4870.
Any portion of the territory of a county, whether incorporated or unincorporated, in which lateral or collecting sanitary sewers have been installed, for the maintenance and repair of which provision is not otherwise made, may be formed into a district, except that no portion of any city shall be included within such a district unless consent of the governing body of the city is first obtained.
(Amended by Stats. 1955, Ch. 167.)
4871.
The board of supervisors of any county may determine by resolution that any portion of the unincorporated area of the county not already included in a district is in need of sewer maintenance and should be formed into a district.
(Enacted by Stats. 1939, Ch. 60.)
4872.
The board shall fix a time and place to hear the proposal to form a district.
(Enacted by Stats. 1939, Ch. 60.)
4873.
The board shall direct the clerk to give notice of the hearing. The notice shall have the heading "Notice of the proposed formation of _____ sewer maintenance district", stating the name of the proposed district. It shall:
(a) State the time and place for the hearing.
(b) Set forth the exterior boundaries of the territory proposed to be organized into a district.
(Enacted by Stats. 1939, Ch. 60.)
4874.
The board shall direct the clerk to publish the notice once a week for two successive weeks in the newspaper of general circulation circulated in the territory which it is proposed to organize into a district that the board deems most likely to give notice to the inhabitants of the proposed district.
(Enacted by Stats. 1939, Ch. 60.)
4875.
The board shall also direct the clerk to post the notice in three public places in the proposed district at least 10 days prior to the date set for the hearing. The heading of each posted notice shall be in letters of not less than one inch in height.
(Enacted by Stats. 1939, Ch. 60.)
4876.

At any time prior to the time fixed for the hearing any interested person may file with the clerk written objections to the formation of the proposed district.

(Enacted by Stats. 1939, Ch. 60.)

4877.

At the time and place fixed for the hearing or at any time to which the hearing is continued, the board shall consider and pass on all written objections filed.

(Enacted by Stats. 1939, Ch. 60.)

4878.

If the board overrules the objections to the formation it shall hear any person objecting to the inclusion in the proposed district of any particular territory and may, upon the hearing, exclude any territory that would not be benefited by inclusion. At the conclusion of the hearing the board may by resolution abandon the proposed formation of the district, or it may form the district and fix its boundaries either as set forth in the notice or as modified upon the hearing. The boundaries shall not be changed to include any territory outside the boundaries described in the notice.

(Enacted by Stats. 1939, Ch. 60.)

ARTICLE 2.3. Inclusion in County Sanitation District [4879 - 4880]
  (Article 2.3 added by Stats. 1947, Ch. 1367.)

4879.

Any district organized under the provisions of this act may become a part of a county sanitation district after the board of supervisors of the county within which the district is located, has, after a hearing, pursuant to the County Sanitation District Act, found and determined by resolution duly adopted that such inclusion is for the best interest of the district and the governing body of the district consents thereto by resolution adopted by the affirmative vote of four-fifths of its members.

(Added by Stats. 1947, Ch. 1367.)

4880.

A district which becomes a part of the county sanitation district as hereinabove provided for is not thereby dissolved, but may continue to function, except as otherwise provided in Part 1 of Division 6 of this code, in the same manner as heretofore.

(Added by Stats. 1947, Ch. 1367.)

ARTICLE 3. Officers and Powers [4885 - 4889]
  (Article 3 enacted by Stats. 1939, Ch. 60.)

4885.

The board is the governing body of the district and may make and enforce all rules and regulations necessary for the administration and government of the district and for the cleaning, repair, reconstruction, renewal, replacement, operation, and maintenance of lateral and collecting sewers in it.

(Added by Stats. 1986, Ch. 195, Sec. 38.)

4886.

The board may acquire by gift, condemnation, purchase, or otherwise in the name of the county, and own, control, manage, and dispose of, real and personal property necessary or convenient for the purposes of this chapter, and may perform all of the acts necessary or proper to accomplish such purposes.

(Amended by Stats. 1959, Ch. 1439.)

4887.

The board may appoint the county surveyor to supervise the work of cleaning, repairing, reconstructing, renewing, replacing, operating, and maintaining the sewers and their appurtenances and may enter into contracts for the purchase of water to be used in flushing the sewers and for the disposal of sewage collected in the district.

(Enacted by Stats. 1939, Ch. 60.)

4887.5.

The board may by resolution change the name of any district to conform with a change in the street name or other designation which the district bears. The clerk shall file in the office of the county assessor and with the State Board of Equalization a certified copy of every such resolution, and upon such filing the name of the district shall be changed for all purposes.

(Added by Stats. 1953, Ch. 694.)

4889.

If a district has a boundary which is contiguous to a boundary of a city and the district has a contract with that city under which the city is responsible for the operation and maintenance of all facilities of the district, the governing board of the district may, by a resolution adopted by a ⁴/₅ vote of the board, declare the board dissolved and thereafter the governing body of the city shall be ex officio the governing board of the district.

(Added by Stats. 1965, Ch. 588.)

ARTICLE 4. Finances and Taxation [4890 - 4894.1]
  (Article 4 enacted by Stats. 1939, Ch. 60.)

4890.

The clerk shall file in the office of the county assessor a certified copy of each resolution of the board that affects a district in any of the following ways:

(a) Establishes it.

(b) Annexes territory to it.

(c) Withdraws territory from it.

(d) Dissolves it.

The county assessor shall thereafter in making up the assessment roll segregate on it the property included in the district.

(Amended by Stats. 1949, Ch. 699.)

4891.

The board may levy a tax each year upon the real property in the district sufficient to defray the cost of maintaining, operating, and repairing the sewers in the district, of maintaining the district, and of meeting such other expenditures as are authorized by this chapter. The amount of taxes to be collected from the levy made upon property located within the incorporated area of a city may be paid in whole by the city, if the city elects to make such payment as provided in Section 4892.1.

If a district is divided into zones, the board of supervisors may determine what portion of the amount of money to be secured from the levy of taxes shall be secured from each zone within the district.

(Amended by Stats. 1969, Ch. 782.)

4891.1.

The annual tax levy may include a reserve for contingencies not to exceed 10 percent of the total levy. The contingency reserve shall be available for expenditure during the fiscal year for which the levy was made for necessary expenses of the district for which no specific appropriation has been made. The board may provide for the cancellation of the contingency reserve at the end of each fiscal year and for the establishment of such reserve as a specific appropriation or reserve or both or may carry it forward as encumbered surplus and add to it.

(Added by Stats. 1961, Ch. 158.)

4892.

The tax shall be levied and collected at the same time and in the same manner as general county taxes levied for county purposes and when collected shall be paid into the county treasury to the credit of the maintenance fund of the district and shall be used only in furtherance of the purposes of this chapter.

(Enacted by Stats. 1939, Ch. 60.)

4892.1.

On or before the first day of July the governing body of any city, the area of which, in whole or in part, is included within one or more sewer maintenance districts, may elect to pay out of municipal funds, in lieu of providing sewer maintenance service to such territory, the whole of the amount of taxes which will be levied for district purposes for the fiscal year commencing upon said first day of July upon property located within such city. The election shall be made by the adoption of an order reciting that the city, pursuant to this section, elects to pay the whole of the amount of taxes which will be levied by said district or districts upon property located within the incorporated limits of the city and stating the time and manner in which payment shall be made.

Upon the adoption of the order a certified copy of the same shall be presented to the governing body of the district or districts for approval. If the governing body of the district or districts is satisfied that the financial condition of the city reasonably will assure such payment and if the time and manner of payment is acceptable, the governing body of the district or districts shall by order approve the city's election to pay taxes. Immediately upon the adoption of the order approving the city's election to pay the taxes, certified copies of each order shall be filed with the county auditor, county assessor and county tax collector.

Thereafter, if the whole of the taxes which are levied on property within the city is to be paid by the city, the county auditor shall not extend the district tax on such property.

If the payment made by any city shall exceed the amount of district taxes which have been levied against property within the city, the amount of such excess without interest shall be refunded to the city prior to the close of the fiscal year for which the payment was made. Any election to pay taxes pursuant to this section shall be effective only for the fiscal year for which made.

(Added by Stats. 1961, Ch. 158.)

4893.

If a district is organized in any year too late for the levy of a tax in that year or in the next ensuing year, the board is hereby authorized to transfer funds of the county not immediately needed for county purposes to the maintenance fund of the district to be used for the payment of the expenses of such district until such time as special assessment tax receipts are available therefor. The board shall include in the levy of taxes for the district for the first fiscal year in which a tax may be levied, a sum sufficient to repay to the county the amounts so transferred to the district for the portion or portions of the preceding fiscal year or years for which no levy of taxes was made for that purpose and the amounts so transferred shall be retransferred from the maintenance fund of the district out of the first available receipts from the tax levy.

(Added by Stats. 1947, Ch. 599.)

4894.

Pursuant to a resolution adopted by its board of supervisors, a county may lend any of its available funds to a county sewer maintenance district located wholly within the county for use by the district in emergency situations for the construction, reconstruction, and repair of sewer systems, for replacement of obsolete equipment, or to defray unusual maintenance costs within the district. Any such loan may be restricted for use in a temporary zone formed under the provisions of Section 4894.1 in a district. The loan shall not exceed 100 percent of the total revenues of the district or zone for the year in which the loan is made.

The board of supervisors in the resolution shall specify the date and manner in which the funds shall be repaid. The resolution may provide for the payment of interest on the loan and the loan shall be repaid at the times and in the manner specified in the resolution which time shall not in any event exceed 10 years.

Funds so loaned shall be deemed to have been appropriated by the district or temporary zone in a district for the purposes for which the loan was made. Any area of a district, or of a temporary zone in a district, which is included in a city by annexation or incorporation after a loan has been made shall continue to be taxed for the repayment of its proportionate part of the unpaid balance of the loan.

If a zone is formed to be responsible for the loan, the board of supervisors shall, in the first fiscal year in which a special tax may be levied in said zone, and in each succeeding year of the duration of the zone, levy a special tax upon the taxable property in the zone for the purpose of repaying the amount lent to the district by the county. When the loan has been repaid, the zone shall terminate.

The board may also borrow funds from another sewer maintenance district, and the board may lend available district funds to another sewer maintenance district, subject to the same terms and conditions as apply to loans of county funds.

(Amended by Stats. 1982, Ch. 361, Sec. 1.)

4894.1.

When the board of supervisors has so declared in its resolution of intention to order the formation of a sewer maintenance district or any annexation thereto, the board of supervisors may, in its resolution ordering the formation of a sewer maintenance district or any annexation thereto, order the district divided into tax assessment zones. Tax assessment zones may be formed at a time other than at the formation of the district or any annexation thereto if pursuant to the same procedure of resolution, notice, and hearing as are applicable under this chapter to the annexation of territory.

No district shall be divided into zones unless the board of supervisors finds that a tax assessment zone requires special services or special facilities in addition to those provided generally by the sewer maintenance district or the replacement of obsolete facilities or equipment, and that the tax levy is commensurate with the special benefits to be provided in the zone. The boundaries of tax assessment zones may be changed or a zone may be dissolved in the same manner that a zone may be formed in an existing district.

(Added by Stats. 1969, Ch. 782.)

ARTICLE 5. Annexation [4895 - 4903]

(Article 5 enacted by Stats. 1939, Ch. 60.)

4895.

Outlying territory, whether incorporated or unincorporated, and whether contiguous or not, may be annexed to a district as provided in this article, except that no portion of any city shall be annexed unless consent of the governing body of the city is first obtained.

(Amended by Stats. 1955, Ch. 167.)

4896.

The board may by resolution fix a time and place for a hearing upon the question of the annexation of territory to a district. The resolution shall describe the boundaries of the territory proposed to be annexed.

(Enacted by Stats. 1939, Ch. 60.)

4897.

The date set for the hearing on the proposed annexation shall be at least three weeks after the date of the adoption of the resolution setting the hearing.

(Enacted by Stats. 1939, Ch. 60.)

4898.

The board shall cause notices of the hearing to be posted in at least three conspicuous places in the territory proposed to be annexed and in at least three conspicuous places in the district. However, if the territory proposed to be annexed is in more than one existing district the notices shall be posted in at least three conspicuous places in each district in which is situated any of the territory proposed to be annexed.

(Enacted by Stats. 1939, Ch. 60.)

4899.

The notices shall be headed "notice of hearing" in letters not less than one inch in height and shall contain a description of the territory proposed to be annexed and a statement of the time and place of the hearing. In lieu of the description the boundaries of territory proposed to be annexed may be shown by means of a diagram printed upon the notice. The notices shall be posted not less than ten days prior to the date set for the hearing. In addition to the notices the board shall direct its clerk to publish a notice once a week for two successive weeks in the newspaper of general circulation circulated in the district and another in the territory proposed to be annexed that the board deems most likely to give notice of the hearing to the inhabitants of each.

(Enacted by Stats. 1939, Ch. 60.)

4900.

At the time fixed for the hearing or at any time to which it is continued the board shall hear and pass upon the proposal and any objections that may be filed to the inclusion of any property in the proposed annexation.

The board may, by order entered upon its minutes, determine that the territory proposed to be annexed or any part will be benefited by annexation and may order that the boundaries of the district be altered to include that territory.

(Enacted by Stats. 1939, Ch. 60.)

4901.

If the territory annexed to the district comprises a portion of another district formed under the provisions of this chapter, or under the provisions of Chapter 26 (commencing at Section 5820), Part 3, Division 7 of the Streets and Highways Code, upon the annexation becoming complete the territory shall thereupon be withdrawn from the district of which it theretofore formed a part.

(Amended by Stats. 1957, Ch. 772.)

4902.

If the territory annexed to the district comprises all of another district, formed under the provisions of this chapter, or under the provisions of Chapter 26 (commencing at Section 5820), Part 3, Division 7 of the Streets and Highways Code, the theretofore existing

district is thereupon dissolved. The funds of the dissolved district shall be transferred to the district to which all its territory has been annexed and all contracts or obligations of the dissolved district become the obligations of the district to which the territory has been annexed.

(Amended by Stats. 1959, Ch. 151.)

4903.

The exclusion of territory from one district and its annexation to another district shall not be effective until all outstanding contracts of the district from which it is excluded have expired or the contracts, with the consent of the parties, have been modified or canceled so as to relieve the district of further obligation to pay for future maintenance in the territory excluded, and until the funds remaining on hand upon the completion of the exclusion and annexation have been apportioned between the district to which the territory was annexed and the district from which it was excluded.

The division of the funds shall be prorated in the proportion that the assessed value of the real property of the territory so excluded bore to the total assessed value of the real property in the district immediately prior to the exclusion.

(Enacted by Stats. 1939, Ch. 60.)

ARTICLE 6. Exclusion [4905 - 4911]

(Article 6 enacted by Stats. 1939, Ch. 60.)

4905.

Any portion of a district that will not be benefited by remaining in the district may be excluded as provided in this article.

(Enacted by Stats. 1939, Ch. 60.)

4906.

A petition to exclude territory shall be signed by 50 or more freeholders in the portion proposed to be excluded from the district, or by a majority of the freeholders, if there are less than one hundred freeholders in the portion proposed to be excluded. The petition shall request the exclusion of that territory from the district on the ground that it will not be benefited by remaining in the district.

(Enacted by Stats. 1939, Ch. 60.)

4906.1.

As an alternative to the procedure outlined in Section 4906, the board may by resolution entered in its minutes fix a time for a hearing on the question of the exclusion of any portion of a district which will not be benefited by remaining in the district. The time fixed for the hearing shall not be less than 15 or more than 30 days from and after passage of the resolution.

(Added by Stats. 1955, Ch. 167.)

4907.

Upon receiving a petition to exclude territory the board shall fix a time for hearing it and for hearing protests to the continuance of the remaining territory as a district. The time of hearing shall not be less than fifteen nor more than thirty days after the receipt of the petition.

(Enacted by Stats. 1939, Ch. 60.)

4908.

At least ten days prior to the time fixed, the board shall publish a notice of the hearing by one insertion in the newspaper circulated in the district that the board deems most likely to give notice to the district's inhabitants of the proposed exclusion.

(Enacted by Stats. 1939, Ch. 60.)

4909.

Any person interested may appear at the hearing and object to the exclusion of the territory from the district, or may object to the continuance of the remaining territory as a district, and the board shall consider all objections and shall pass upon them.

(Enacted by Stats. 1939, Ch. 60.)

4910.

If the board finds that the territory proposed to be excluded will not be benefited by remaining in the district, and that the territory not proposed to be excluded will be benefited by continuing as a district, it shall by resolution declare the district re-established excluding therefrom the territory found not benefited by remaining in the district.

(Amended by Stats. 1955, Ch. 167.)

4911.

Upon the exclusion of any territory from the district all property acquired for the district shall remain vested in the county and be used for the purposes of the district.

(Enacted by Stats. 1939, Ch. 60.)

ARTICLE 7. Dissolution [4915 - 4927]

(Article 7 enacted by Stats. 1939, Ch. 60.)

4915.

A district may be dissolved by the board as provided in this chapter.

(Enacted by Stats. 1939, Ch. 60.)

4916.

A petition for dissolution, signed by 50 or more freeholders and residents of the district, or by a majority of the freeholders and residents if there are less than 100 freeholders and residents in the district, may be filed with the board to initiate dissolution proceedings, or the board may by resolution initiate dissolution proceedings.

(Amended by Stats. 1961, Ch. 827.)

4917.

Upon receiving a petition for dissolution, or adopting a resolution to initiate dissolution proceedings, the board shall fix a time for a hearing of the petition or resolution, which shall not be less than 15 nor more than 30 days after its receipt or adoption.

(Amended by Stats. 1961, Ch. 827.)

4918.

At least ten days prior to the time fixed, the board shall publish a notice of the hearing by one insertion in a newspaper circulated in the district.

(Enacted by Stats. 1939, Ch. 60.)

4919.

At the time appointed for the hearing or at any time to which it is continued, the board shall hear and pass upon the petition or resolution and may grant or deny the proposed dissolution, and its decision is final.

(Amended by Stats. 1961, Ch. 827.)

4920.

If the proposed dissolution is granted, the board shall by resolution order the dissolution of the district and the district is thereupon dissolved. The property of the district remains the property of the county in which the district is located.

If at the time of the dissolution there is any indebtedness of the district outstanding, the district shall be dissolved for all purposes except the levy and collection of taxes for the payment of such outstanding indebtedness. From the time the district is thus dissolved until the indebtedness is fully paid, the board of supervisors of the county wherein the district is located shall be the ex officio governing body of the district. That body shall levy such taxes and perform such other acts as may be necessary to pay the outstanding indebtedness of the district.

(Amended by Stats. 1961, Ch. 827.)

4921.

Upon the inclusion of all the territory of a district in one or more cities, either by reason of annexation or by reason of the incorporation of one or more cities, all funds paid into the county treasury to the credit of the district shall be paid over by the board as provided in this article.

(Enacted by Stats. 1939, Ch. 60.)

4922.

If all of the district is included in one city, the fund shall be paid to the treasurer of the city and administered by the governing body of the city.

(Enacted by Stats. 1939, Ch. 60.)

4923.

If a part only of the district is so included in one city and the remaining part of the district is included in one or more other cities then such proportionate part of the funds shall be paid to the treasurer of each city as the assessed valuation of the real property of the portion of the district included in each city bore, before being so included, to the total assessed valuation of the real property of the district.

(Enacted by Stats. 1939, Ch. 60.)

4924.

The funds paid over by the district to a city shall be administered by its governing body for the benefit of such portions of the district as are included in the city, and for the purpose of operating and maintaining the sewers in it formerly maintained by the district.

(Enacted by Stats. 1939, Ch. 60.)

4925.

When all territory in a district has been included in a city the district is thereupon, by reason of the inclusion, dissolved.

(Enacted by Stats. 1939, Ch. 60.)

4926.

If less than the whole of a district is included in a city either by reason of annexation or by reason of incorporation proceedings, the territory so included within the city shall continue to remain a part of the district for all purposes until a copy of a resolution adopted by the city requesting exclusion of such territory from the district is received by the board. Upon receipt of such a resolution requesting exclusion of the territory contained within the city, such territory shall be excluded from the district and the remaining territory shall continue as a district. But the exclusion of such territory from the district shall not be effective until all outstanding contracts of the districts have expired or the contracts, with the consent of the parties, have been modified or canceled so as to relieve the district of further obligation to pay for future maintenance in the affected territory.

(Amended by Stats. 1955, Ch. 167.)

4927.

If all of the district is included within a sanitary district, the district is dissolved upon the filing with the Secretary of State of a resolution adopted by the district board of the sanitary district and approved by the board of supervisors which states that the sanitary district is able to provide the same service as is being provided by the sewer maintenance district and declares that the sewer maintenance district is dissolved. A copy of the resolution shall be filed with the board of supervisors.

Upon the dissolution of the sewer maintenance district, the property and funds which are held by the county for the sewer maintenance district vest in the sanitary district and the county shall convey such property and pay over such funds, to the sanitary district. The sanitary district shall also succeed to any liability or outstanding obligation of the sewer maintenance district at the time of its dissolution.

(Added by Stats. 1961, Ch. 938.)

CHAPTER 5. Sewer Revenue Bonds [4950 - 5072]

(Chapter 5 enacted by Stats. 1939, Ch. 60.)

ARTICLE 1. General Provisions and Definitions [4950 - 4961]

(Article 1 enacted by Stats. 1939, Ch. 60.)

4950.

"Works," as used in this chapter, includes any or all of the following facilities, including, but not limited to, necessary lands, rights-of-way, or other property:

(a) Sewage treatment plants.

(b) Intercepting and collecting sewers.

(c) Outfall sewers.

(d) Force mains.

(e) Pumping stations.

(f) Ejector stations.

(g) All other appurtenances necessary, useful, or convenient, for the collection, treatment, purification, or disposal of sewage.

(h) Facilities for the recycling of water, including, but not limited to, all of the following:

(1) Treatment facilities.

(2) Pumping facilities.

(3) Storage facilities.

(4) Distribution and dispersal facilities of all types including, but not limited to, related distribution mains, laterals, and appurtenances.

(Amended by Stats. 1996, Ch. 75, Sec. 1. Effective January 1, 1997.)

4951.

"District," as used in this chapter, includes city, county, city and county, or any municipal or public corporation or district which is authorized to acquire, construct, own, or operate a sewer system.

(Amended by Stats. 1951, Ch. 500.)

4952.

"Governing body," as used in this chapter, means the governing body of the district.

(Enacted by Stats. 1939, Ch. 60.)

4953.

"Clerk," as used in this chapter, means the clerk or secretary of the governing body or of the district.

(Enacted by Stats. 1939, Ch. 60.)

4954.

"Area," as used in this chapter, means the area served, or proposed to be served, by the works, or proposed works.

(Enacted by Stats. 1939, Ch. 60.)

4955.

"Rates," as used in this chapter, includes rates and charges.

(Enacted by Stats. 1939, Ch. 60.)

4956.

"Bonds," as used in this chapter, means revenue bonds authorized by this chapter.

(Enacted by Stats. 1939, Ch. 60.)

4957.

"Treasurer," as used in this chapter, means the treasurer of the district.

(Enacted by Stats. 1939, Ch. 60.)

4958.

"Owners of improved real property," as used in this chapter, means persons who are recorded on the books of the assessor and tax collector as the owners of lots or parcels of land in the area that are improved by buildings that would be subject to service of works under the provisions of this chapter, on completion of the project.

(Enacted by Stats. 1939, Ch. 60.)

4959.

The provisions of this chapter regarding a referendum shall be liberally construed to effect the objects of this chapter, and no irregularity or informality shall invalidate the election when it appears that the provisions of law have been substantially complied with.

(Enacted by Stats. 1939, Ch. 60.)

4960.

This chapter is an additional and alternative method to those already provided for the acquisition, construction, extension, and operation of the works referred to in this chapter.

(Enacted by Stats. 1939, Ch. 60.)

4961.

If any section, subsection, sentence, clause, or phrase of this chapter, or the application thereof to any person or circumstance, is for any reason held invalid, the validity of the remainder of the chapter, or the application of such provision to other persons or circumstances, shall not be affected thereby. The Legislature hereby declares that it would have passed this chapter, and each section, subsection, sentence, clause, and phrase thereof, irrespective of the fact that one or more sections, subsections, sentences, clauses or phrases, or the application thereof to any person or circumstance, be held invalid.

(Added by Stats. 1973, Ch. 910.)

ARTICLE 2. Resolution [4965 - 4967]

(Article 2 enacted by Stats. 1939, Ch. 60.)

4965.

Before a district acquires or constructs any works under this chapter, its governing body shall adopt a resolution declaring its intention to do so.

(Enacted by Stats. 1939, Ch. 60.)

4966.

The resolution of intention shall contain all of the following:

(a) A brief and general description of the works. If they are to be constructed, a reference to the plans and specifications that have been prepared and filed by the engineer chosen by the governing body.

(b) The estimated cost of the works to be acquired or constructed, and the amount of bonds to be issued and sold.

(c) A general description of the area to be served by the proposed works, referring to a plat of the area, which shall govern for all details.

(d) An estimate of the number and character of the places and properties to be served by the works, including those ready for immediate service and those in expectancy.

(e) An estimate of the immediate revenue that would be received from the operation of the works, and of future revenues in expectancy.

(f) A statement that revenue bonds of the district will be issued to cover the cost of the works.

(g) A notice of the time and place when persons interested may appear before the governing body and be heard as to any protests or objections they may have against the acquisition or construction of the proposed works and the issuance and sale of bonds.
(Amended by Stats. 1939, Ch. 1124.)

4967.

The owner of property that may be benefited by the acquisition, construction, extension, or operation of the works referred to in this chapter may file with the district a request that a particular work be undertaken. The request may, but need not, include the descriptions and estimates referred to in Section 4966 and shall not be denied without a public hearing.
(Added by Stats. 1975, Ch. 1240.)

ARTICLE 3. Notice, Hearing, and Election [4970 - 4979]
(Article 3 enacted by Stats. 1939, Ch. 60.)

4970.

The time set for the hearing shall be not less than twenty nor more than forty days after the adoption of the resolution.
(Enacted by Stats. 1939, Ch. 60.)

4971.

The governing body shall cause the resolution to be published twice in one or more newspapers published and circulated in the district. If no newspaper is published in the district, then the publication shall be made in a newspaper published in the county in which the district is located.
(Enacted by Stats. 1939, Ch. 60.)

4972.

A copy of the resolution headed "Notice of Sewer Work," in letters not less than one inch in height, shall be posted in the district along the entire length of that street in the district which, in the opinion of the governing body, is traversed by the largest number of people. The notices shall be posted not less than 300 feet in distance apart, and not less than three notices shall be posted in any case.
(Enacted by Stats. 1939, Ch. 60.)

4973.

Both the posting and the publication shall be completed at least ten days before the time set for the hearing. Affidavits of publication and of posting shall be filed with the clerk.
(Enacted by Stats. 1939, Ch. 60.)

4974.

At the time set for the hearing, the governing body shall hear all persons or their representatives having any objections to the acquisition or construction of the works as proposed, also any suggestions that may be offered in the way of an amendment or modification of the proposition. The governing body may continue the hearing from time to time, and modify the boundaries of the area by eliminating territory, but no new territory shall be added.
(Enacted by Stats. 1939, Ch. 60.)

4975.

If, before the conclusion of the hearing, a petition signed by not less than 15 percent of the owners or by not less than 15 percent of the registered voters in the specified area is filed with the governing body requesting that body to submit the proposition of acquiring or constructing the proposed works to an election of the registered voters in the area, the governing body shall forthwith call an election in the area for that purpose.
(Amended by Stats. 1973, Ch. 910.)

4976.

If called, the election shall be held and conducted, the votes received and canvassed, and the returns made, determined, and declared, so far as practicable, in accordance with the laws governing the enactment or rejection of city ordinances by means of the initiative or referendum.
(Amended by Stats. 1970, Ch. 406.)

4979.

If the proposal is not rejected at a referendum election, the governing body acquires jurisdiction to proceed.
(Amended by Stats. 1973, Ch. 910.)

ARTICLE 4. Bonds [4985 - 4997]
(Article 4 enacted by Stats. 1939, Ch. 60.)

4985.

The cost of the acquisition or construction of the works for which bonds may be issued includes all of the following:

(a) The cost of all property, rights, easements, and franchises deemed necessary or convenient therefor.

(b) Engineering, clerical, legal, financial, paying and fiscal agent's fees and expenses, cost of bond proceedings, bond reserve funds and working capital and bond interest estimated to accrue during the construction period and for a period of not to exceed twelve (12) months after completion of construction.

(c) All other expenses connected with or incident to the works in the operation and performance of the acts required by this chapter to be done.
(Amended by Stats. 1957, Ch. 8.)

4986.

Bonds issued and sold under this chapter shall be revenue bonds of the character and form known as "serials." Each bond shall be entitled "sewer revenue bond," and shall be paid and discharged within forty years from its date.
(Amended by Stats. 1939, Ch. 1124.)

4987.

Each bond, except those of the last installment, or one of each annual installment, shall be in multiples of one hundred dollars, in such amount as the governing body determines, but no bond shall be of greater denomination than one thousand dollars.
(Enacted by Stats. 1939, Ch. 60.)

4988.

The bonds shall bear interest, as the governing body shall determine, at a rate not to exceed 8 percent per annum, and shall, after the first principal maturity, be payable semiannually by coupon.
(Amended by Stats. 1975, Ch. 130.)

4989.

The governing body shall prescribe the form of the bonds, and provide that of the indebtedness represented thereby a part shall be payable each year after their date, at a time and place to be designated in the bonds, together with interest, until the whole of the indebtedness has been paid.

The maturity date of the first bond or series of bonds may be deferred for a period not exceeding five years from the date of the bonds.
(Enacted by Stats. 1939, Ch. 60.)

4990.

The number of bonds to be paid each year need not be the same, and the governing body may fix maturities so that the number of bonds retired each year will, in the discretion of the governing body, be most equitable and just; however, all bonds shall be completely paid within forty years from date of issue.
(Enacted by Stats. 1939, Ch. 60.)

4991.

If the district is a city, the bonds shall be signed by the mayor if there is one; otherwise by the president or chairman of the governing body, and countersigned by the clerk. The seal of the district shall be affixed to the bond. The coupons shall be signed by the treasurer by his engraved or lithographed signature.

If any officer whose signature or countersignature appears on the bonds or coupons ceases to be such officer before the delivery of the bonds to the purchaser, his signature or countersignature is nevertheless as valid and sufficient for all purposes as if he had remained in office.
(Enacted by Stats. 1939, Ch. 60.)

4992.

In the ordinance authorizing the issuance of the bonds, provision may be made, but are not limited to provisions:

(a) That all or part of the bonds are callable, the manner of the call and the premiums to be paid thereon;

(b) That all or part of the bonds are payable at the office of a paying or fiscal agent, within or without the State, and for the payment of fees therefor;

(c) For the pledge of revenues, its nature, and its parity with other sewer revenue bonds issued or to be issued;

(d) For the percentage that annual net revenues shall bear to bond and interest payments;

(e) For reserve, surplus and other funds usual in the issuance of revenue bonds;

(f) For the duties and obligations of the district;

(g) For the remedies of bondholders, which may be in addition to those provided herein;

(h) For the manner of amending or abrogating the bond ordinance or refunding any or all bonds thereunder;

(i) For occurrences in the event of default and the rights and remedies arising therefrom; and

(j) For usual and customary covenants for the security and protection of the payment of the bonds.
(Added by Stats. 1957, Ch. 8.)

4993.

If the proceeds of the bonds for any reason are less than the cost of the works, additional bonds may in like manner be issued and sold to provide for the amount of the deficit, but not to exceed the amount necessary to complete the works according to the original plans and specifications. Such deficiency bonds shall be deemed to be the same in all respects as the original issue, and shall be entitled to payment, without preference or priority over the bonds first issued, and shall be disposed of in like manner.
(Enacted by Stats. 1939, Ch. 60.)

4994.

No error, defect, irregularity, informality, and no neglect or omission of any officer of any district in any proceedings under this chapter, that does not affect the jurisdiction of the governing body to order the doing of the acts proposed to be done, avoids or invalidates

the proceedings or any bond. The exclusive remedy of any person affected or aggrieved thereby shall be to the governing body as provided in this chapter.
(Enacted by Stats. 1939, Ch. 60.)

4995.

Bonds may be made payable on a date subsequent to the time fixed for the collection of the second installment of general district taxes with which the first levy of taxes for the payment of the principal and interest of said bonds is to be collected. In such event, the first interest coupons shall be for interest from the date of said bonds of such issue or series or division to the maturity date of said coupons.
(Added by Stats. 1951, Ch. 1648.)

4996.

An action to determine the validity of bonds may be brought pursuant to Chapter 9 (commencing with Section 860) of Title 10 of Part 2 of the Code of Civil Procedure.
(Amended by Stats. 1961, Ch. 1517.)

4997.

In determining the amount of bonds to be issued, the legislative body may include:

(a) All costs and estimated costs incidental to or connected with the acquisition, construction, improving or financing of the project.

(b) All engineering, inspection, legal and fiscal agent's fees, costs of the bond election and of the issuance of said bonds, bond reserve funds and working capital and bond interest estimated to accrue during the construction period and for a period of not to exceed 12 months after completion of construction.
(Added by Stats. 1957, Ch. 1378.)

ARTICLE 5. Powers [5000 - 5022]

(Article 5 enacted by Stats. 1939, Ch. 60.)

5000.

Any district may acquire, construct, and operate works within or without its limits.
(Enacted by Stats. 1939, Ch. 60.)

5001.

It may acquire by gift, purchase, condemnation, or otherwise, all lands, rights of way, or other property necessary therefor.
(Enacted by Stats. 1939, Ch. 60.)

5002.

It may issue and sell bonds for the acquisition and construction of works.
(Amended by Stats. 1939, Ch. 1124.)

5003.

The governing body shall have supervision and control over the construction, acquisition, and operation of the works, and the collection of rates for their use.
(Enacted by Stats. 1939, Ch. 60.)

5004.

The governing body may take all steps and proceedings and make and enter into all contracts or agreements necessary, convenient, or incidental to the performance of its duties or the execution of its powers under this chapter.
(Enacted by Stats. 1939, Ch. 60.)

5005.

It may employ engineers, architects, inspectors, superintendents, a manager, collectors, attorneys, and such other employees as in its judgment are necessary or convenient in the execution of its powers and duties, and may fix their compensation.
(Enacted by Stats. 1939, Ch. 60.)

5006.

The governing body shall establish rules and regulations for the use of the works, including all sewers and works connected therewith, as may be necessary or expedient to insure the successful operation of the works.
(Enacted by Stats. 1939, Ch. 60.)

5007.

The governing body shall provide that all public ways or public works damaged or destroyed in carrying out the provisions of this chapter shall be restored or repaired, and placed in their original condition, as nearly as practicable, out of funds provided under this chapter.
(Enacted by Stats. 1939, Ch. 60.)

5008.

In the operation of the works, the district may do any or all of the following:

(a) Sell, or otherwise dispose of any water, sewage effluent, fertilizer, or other by-products resulting from the operation of a sewerage system or sewage treatment or disposal plant, and construct, maintain, and operate such pipe lines and other works as may be necessary for those purposes.

(b) Construct, maintain, and operate pipe lines or such other works as may be necessary to conserve and put to beneficial use any water or sewage effluent recovered from the operation of the sewerage system, plant, or works by sale or disposition for agricultural or industrial purposes, including irrigation, or by discharging or spreading the water or sewage effluent in such manner as to percolate into the underground gravels and replenish natural water resources.

(c) Exercise the power of eminent domain under the Constitution and laws of the State in so far as it may be necessary to carry out the provisions of this chapter.

(d) Make such contracts with the Reconstruction Finance Corporation or other fiscal agency of the United States as are necessary to meet the requirements of the Emergency Relief and Construction Act of 1932.
(Enacted by Stats. 1939, Ch. 60.)

5009.

Whenever any community in the district is provided with a sewerage system under this chapter the governing body having jurisdiction over that community shall declare the further maintenance or use of cesspools or other local means of sewage disposal to be a public nuisance and shall require all buildings inhabited or used by human beings to be connected with the sewerage system, within ninety days from completion, if the buildings to be served thereby are within one hundred feet of the system.
(Enacted by Stats. 1939, Ch. 60.)

5010.

All works acquired or constructed under this chapter where the expense involved exceeds five hundred dollars, shall be done by contract which shall be awarded to the lowest responsible bidder as provided in this chapter. If the bonds are purchased by the Reconstruction Finance Corporation or other fiscal agency of the United States on condition or request that the governing body have the work performed by day labor instead of by contract, the governing body may comply with the condition or request and the work need not be done by contract.
(Enacted by Stats. 1939, Ch. 60.)

5011.

The governing body shall comply with all the conditions and requirements of the Emergency Relief and Construction Act of 1932, respecting the employment of labor, and other matters in connection therewith unless they are in conflict with the Constitution and laws of this State.
(Enacted by Stats. 1939, Ch. 60.)

5012.

Before awarding any contract for construction of works the governing body shall cause to be published a notice inviting sealed bids for doing it.

The notice shall refer to the plans and specifications on file. It shall be published twice in a daily, semi-weekly, or weekly newspaper, published and circulated in the district, and designated by the governing body. If there is no newspaper published in the district, and the district is less than a county, the notice shall be published in a newspaper in the county in which the district is located.

The time fixed for receiving bids shall be not less than ten days from the first publication of the notice.
(Enacted by Stats. 1939, Ch. 60.)

5013.

All bids shall be accompanied by a certified check payable to the district for an amount that is not less than ten per cent of the aggregate of the bid. No bid shall be considered unless accompanied by the check.
(Enacted by Stats. 1939, Ch. 60.)

5014.

The bids shall be delivered to the clerk. The governing body shall, in open session, publicly open, examine, and declare them.
(Enacted by Stats. 1939, Ch. 60.)

5015.

The governing body may reject all bids if it deems this for the public good, and shall reject all bids other than the lowest regular responsible bidder, and may award the contract to him at the price named in his bid.
(Enacted by Stats. 1939, Ch. 60.)

5016.

If the bids are rejected or if no bids are received, the governing body may readvertise for bids as in the first instance without further proceedings.
(Enacted by Stats. 1939, Ch. 60.)

5017.

If the successful bidder fails, neglects, or refuses for twenty days after written notice of the award has been mailed him to enter into the contract to perform the work, the check accompanying his bid, and the amount therein named, shall be declared forfeited to the district, and shall be collected by it and paid into its general fund.
(Enacted by Stats. 1939, Ch. 60.)

5018.

Each contractor shall, at the time of entering into the contract, execute a surety bond to the satisfaction and approval of the governing body in a sum not less than twenty-five per cent of the amount of the contract, conditioned upon its faithful performance.
(Enacted by Stats. 1939, Ch. 60.)

5019.

The contract shall provide that the work shall be commenced within twenty days after the contractor has received written notice from the clerk that there is sufficient money or revenue bonds in the special fund provided to pay the contract price.
(Enacted by Stats. 1939, Ch. 60.)

5020.

At the time of entering into the contract the contractor shall execute, deliver, and file with the governing body a good and sufficient surety bond, in a sum not less than one-half the total amount payable by the terms of the contract, conditioned upon the payment by the contractor or his subcontractors, for any and all materials, provisions, provender, other supplies, or teams, or the use of implements or machinery used in, upon, or about the performance of the work.
(Enacted by Stats. 1939, Ch. 60.)

5021.

All provisions of the codes and general laws relating to notice and the foreclosure of such liens are applicable, but suit may only be brought on the bond within six months after the expiration of the period for the filing of verified claims.
(Enacted by Stats. 1939, Ch. 60.)

5022.

In all respects not otherwise provided for in this chapter the bond shall be in conformity with the requirements of the general law of the State regarding contractor's bonds for the benefit of laborers and materialmen, who shall have a first lien against any moneys or bonds due or about to become due the contractor.

(Enacted by Stats. 1939, Ch. 60.)

ARTICLE 6. Finances [5025 - 5034]

(Article 6 enacted by Stats. 1939, Ch. 60.)

5025.

All necessary preliminary expenses incurred by the governing body in carrying out this chapter, including the making of surveys, plans, and estimates of costs and revenues, compensation of employees, the giving of notices, taking of options, and all other expenses of whatsoever nature, necessary to be paid prior to the issue and sale of the bonds, may be advanced out of the general fund of the district. The general fund shall be fully reimbursed out of the first money received from the sale of the bonds, and before any other disbursements are made therefrom.

(Enacted by Stats. 1939, Ch. 60.)

5026.

All compensation of employees, and all other expenses, incurred in carrying out the provisions of this chapter shall be paid solely from funds provided under the authority of this chapter.

(Enacted by Stats. 1939, Ch. 60.)

5027.

After reimbursement and repayment to the district of all amounts advanced for preliminary expenses, all money, other than premiums and accrued interest, received from the sale of bonds shall be applied solely to the cost of the works.

(Enacted by Stats. 1939, Ch. 60.)

5028.

The money received from the collection of the rates, together with any other revenue derived from the operation of the works, shall be deposited in a bank by the treasurer in the same manner that public money is deposited by cities. The money so deposited shall be kept in a fund or funds and shall be applied as provided in this chapter.

(Amended by Stats. 1963, Ch. 1659.)

5029.

In the ordinance for the issuance of bonds the governing body shall provide that the revenues derived from the operation of the works shall be used only for:

(a) The payment or providing for payment, including payments into any reserve or sinking funds, as the same falls due, of the principal of and the interest on the bonds;

(b) The management, maintenance, operation and repair costs of the works.

After provision has been made for the payment of the foregoing, any surplus remaining may be used as follows: (a) for the purchase in the open market of the outstanding unmatured bonds of the district; (b) for extensions, or for the enlargement, replacement or betterment of the works; (c) for any lawful purpose of the district.

(Amended by Stats. 1963, Ch. 1659.)

5030.

In its discretion the governing body may provide in the ordinance providing for the issuance of bonds that the management, maintenance, operation and repair costs of the works shall be paid from the revenue derived from the operation of the works prior to paying the principal, interest and sums for other security funds.

(Amended by Stats. 1963, Ch. 1659.)

5031.

All money received for premium and accrued interest shall be paid into a fund for the payment of interest on the bonds and used for the purposes for which it was created.

(Amended by Stats. 1963, Ch. 1659.)

5032.

A district issuing bonds shall install and maintain a proper system of accounts, showing the amount of revenue received and its application. The district shall at least once a year cause the accounts to be properly audited by a competent auditor. The report of the audit shall be open for inspection at all times by any taxpayer, user of the works, holder of bonds, or any representative of such person.

(Enacted by Stats. 1939, Ch. 60.)

5033.

The treasurer is custodian of the funds derived from income received from the works constructed or acquired under the provisions of this chapter.

(Enacted by Stats. 1939, Ch. 60.)

5034.

The treasurer shall give a proper surety bond for the faithful discharge of his duties as custodian, which bond shall be fixed and approved by the governing body. The premium on the surety bond shall be paid by the district.

(Enacted by Stats. 1939, Ch. 60.)

ARTICLE 7. Rates and Collection [5040 - 5056]

(Article 7 enacted by Stats. 1939, Ch. 60.)

5040.

The governing body shall establish just and equitable rates for the use and maintenance of the works, to be paid by the person leasing or occupying the building or premises served thereby or that in any way uses or is served by the works, and may change and readjust the rates from time to time. The rates shall be sufficient in each year for the payment of the proper and reasonable expenses of operation, repair, replacement, and

maintenance of the works, and for payment of the principal of and the interest on the bonds.

(Amended by Stats. 1963, Ch. 1659.)

5041.

The governing body shall establish rates that, beyond all reasonable doubt, will bring in sufficient money to meet the interest and principal on all outstanding bonds as they fall due, in addition to the expense of operation.

(Enacted by Stats. 1939, Ch. 60.)

5042.

Whenever it appears that the rates are insufficient to provide enough money to pay the principal and interest, in addition to the operating expenses, and the governing body neglects or refuses to fix adequate rates therefor, any bondholder may petition the superior court for a writ of mandate to compel the governing body to increase the rates to such an extent as will make them sufficient to provide enough money for those purposes.

(Enacted by Stats. 1939, Ch. 60.)

5043.

The governing body may establish variable rates for different classes of users, or for different parts of the area, where all or any portion of the sewage works have been previously installed and financed under other laws or methods, so that the variable rates may be most equitable and just to all concerned.

(Enacted by Stats. 1939, Ch. 60.)

5044.

However, the rates may only be imposed and collected from the users of all or any portion of such works as are constructed with money derived from the sale of the bonds.

(Enacted by Stats. 1939, Ch. 60.)

5045.

If the users of all or any portion of any works previously acquired and financed by other methods receive any additional benefits from the construction or operation of all or any portion of the works subsequently constructed or acquired from the proceeds of the bonds, the governing body may impose reasonable rates on the works previously acquired, but only sufficient to cover the value of the additional benefits.

(Enacted by Stats. 1939, Ch. 60.)

5046.

No rates shall be established until after a public hearing, at which all the users of the works and owners of property served or proposed to be served thereby and others interested have opportunity to be heard concerning the proposed rates.

(Enacted by Stats. 1939, Ch. 60.)

5047.

After introduction of the ordinance, resolution, or order fixing the rate, and before it is finally enacted, notice of the hearing, setting forth the proposed schedule of rates shall be given by one publication in a newspaper published in the district, if there is such a newspaper, but otherwise in a newspaper having general circulation in the district. The notice shall be published at least ten days before the date fixed in the notice for the hearing. The hearing may be adjourned from time to time.

(Enacted by Stats. 1939, Ch. 60.)

5048.

After the hearing the ordinance, resolution, or order establishing rates, either as originally introduced or as modified and amended, shall be passed and put into effect.

(Enacted by Stats. 1939, Ch. 60.)

5049.

A copy of the schedule of the rates shall be kept on file in the office of the clerk, and shall be open to inspection by any interested person.

(Enacted by Stats. 1939, Ch. 60.)

5050.

The rates for any class of users or property served may be extended to cover any additional premises thereafter served which fall within the same class, without the necessity of hearing or notice.

(Enacted by Stats. 1939, Ch. 60.)

5051.

Any change or readjustment of the rates shall be made in the same manner as the rates were originally established.

(Enacted by Stats. 1939, Ch. 60.)

5052.

If the rate is not paid when due, on the first day of each calendar month thereafter a penalty of ten per cent of the amount of the delinquent rate shall be added.

(Enacted by Stats. 1939, Ch. 60.)

5053.

The rates and penalties may be collected in the following manner:

(a) An action may be brought in the name of the district against the person who occupied the property when the service was rendered for the collection of the amount of the delinquent rate and all penalties. A reasonable attorney's fee shall be awarded the plaintiff.

(b) The governing body may provide that the rates shall be collected with the rates for any other utility service rendered by the district and all the rates shall be itemized, billed upon the same bill, and collected as one item, together with and not separate from such other utility service charge.

(c) Such rates may be collected with the rates for any other utility service furnished by a department or agency of such district over which the legislative body thereof does not exercise control, or with a publicly or privately owned public utility, with the written consent and agreement of said department or agency or public utility owner, which agreement shall establish the terms and conditions upon which such collections shall be made. Such agreement, in the discretion of such department or agency or public utility owner making the collections, also may provide that said rates shall be itemized, billed upon the same bill, and collected as one item, together with and not separately from such other utility service charge.

(Amended by Stats. 1949, Ch. 1507.)

5054.

The remedies specified for collecting and enforcing rates are cumulative and may be pursued alternatively or may be used consecutively when the governing body so determines.

If any remedy is invalid, all valid remedies shall remain effectual.

(Enacted by Stats. 1939, Ch. 60.)

5055.

Until the principal and interest of the bonds are fully paid any holder of any bond outstanding at any time may compel the use of any or all of the remedies provided in this chapter.

(Enacted by Stats. 1939, Ch. 60.)

5056.

After rates are fixed pursuant to this article, any person may pay such rates under protest and bring an action against the governing body in the superior court to recover any money which the governing body refuses to refund. Payments made and actions brought under this section, shall be made and brought in the manner provided for the payment of taxes under protest and actions for refund thereof in Article 2, Chapter 5, Part 9, Division 1 of the Revenue and Taxation Code, insofar as those provisions are applicable.

(Added by Stats. 1949, Ch. 865.)

ARTICLE 8. Leases [5060 - 5063]
(Article 8 enacted by Stats. 1939, Ch. 60.)

5060.

Any district owning or operating works may contract with one or more other cities, counties, sanitation districts, or sanitary districts for the use of the works, but only to the extent of their capacity and without impairing their usefulness, upon such terms and conditions as may be fixed and approved by ordinances of the respective contracting entities. Contracts shall not be made for a period of more than fifteen years nor in violation of the provisions of the ordinance authorizing the bonds.

(Enacted by Stats. 1939, Ch. 60.)

5061.

The governing body of the district may by ordinance establish, change, and adjust rates for the service rendered in the lessee-district by the works, against the owners of the premises served, in the manner provided for establishing, changing, and adjusting rates for the service rendered in the district where the works are owned and operated, and the rates constitute a lien on the property served, and shall be collected as provided for rates made by the owner-district.

(Enacted by Stats. 1939, Ch. 60.)

5062.

The necessary intercepting sewers and appurtenant works for connecting the works of the owner-district with the sewerage system of the lessee-district shall be constructed by the owner-district or the lessee-district, or both, upon such terms and conditions as are set forth in the contract, and the cost or that part of the cost which is to be borne by the owner-district may be paid as part of the cost of the works from the proceeds of the bonds unless otherwise provided by the ordinance.

(Enacted by Stats. 1939, Ch. 60.)

5063.

The income received by the owner-district under the contract shall, if so provided in the ordinance, be deemed to be a part of the revenue of the works. The owner-district shall deduct from the whole cost and expenses such part as shall be paid by the lessee-district pursuant to the provision of the contract; but no rates shall be imposed or collected from the users of the works or portions thereof except in cases where the works or portions thereof have been acquired by means of the bonds, and unless additional benefits will be derived by the users as a result of the contract. In that case the rates shall be only sufficient to cover the value of the additional benefits.

(Enacted by Stats. 1939, Ch. 60.)

ARTICLE 9. Annexation and Exclusion [5070 - 5072]
(Article 9 added by Stats. 1951, Ch. 629.)

5070.

Territory which has become annexed to a district which has authorized the issuance of bonds pursuant to this chapter, and which territory shall use the works, shall become subject to the rates and charges imposed by the district for the use and maintenance of the works.

(Added by Stats. 1951, Ch. 629.)

5071.

Territory which has been withdrawn from a district which has authorized the issuance of bonds pursuant to this chapter, and which territory continues to use the works, shall remain liable for the payment of its pro rata share of the rates and charges imposed by the district for the use and maintenance of the works.

(Added by Stats. 1951, Ch. 629.)

5072.

A city to which any territory has been annexed, whether or not said territory has been withdrawn from a district which has authorized the issuance of bonds pursuant to this chapter, and which territory continues to use the works, may contract with the district to pay the district annually or at lesser intervals a sum or sums in lieu of the payment by the owners or residents within said territory of the rates and charges imposed by the district for the use and maintenance of the works.

(Added by Stats. 1951, Ch. 629.)

CHAPTER 6. General Provisions with Respect to Sewers [5400 - 5474.10]
(Chapter 6 enacted by Stats. 1939, Ch. 60.)

ARTICLE 1. Rights of Way for Sewers and Drainage [5400- 5400.]
(Article 1 enacted by Stats. 1939, Ch. 60.)

5400.

The board of supervisors of a county may vacate or abandon easements for sewage or drainage purposes whenever it determines that they are no longer required for public use.

(Enacted by Stats. 1939, Ch. 60.)

ARTICLE 2. Sewage and Other Waste [5410 - 5416]
(Heading of Article 2 amended by Stats. 1967, Ch. 1447.)

5410.

As used in this chapter:

(a) "Waste" includes sewage and any and all other waste substances, liquid, solid, gaseous, or radioactive, associated with human habitation, or of human or animal origin, or from any producing, manufacturing, or processing operation of whatever nature.

(b) "Person" as used in this article also includes any city, county, district, the state or any department or agency thereof.

(c) "Waters of the state" means any water, surface or underground, including saline waters, within the boundaries of the state.

(d) "Contamination" means an impairment of the quality of the waters of the state by waste to a degree which creates a hazard to the public health through poisoning or through the spread of disease. "Contamination" shall include any equivalent effect resulting from the disposal of waste, whether or not waters of the state are affected.

(e) "Pollution" means an alteration of the quality of the waters of the state by waste to a degree which unreasonably affects: (1) such waters for beneficial uses, or (2) facilities which serve such beneficial uses. "Pollution" may include "contamination."

(f) "Nuisance" means anything which: (1) is injurious to health, or is indecent or offensive to the senses, or an obstruction to the free use of property, so as to interfere with the comfortable enjoyment of life or property, and (2) affects at the same time an entire community or neighborhood, or any considerable number of persons, although the extent of the annoyance or damage inflicted upon individuals may be unequal, and (3) occurs during, or as a result of, the treatment or disposal of wastes.

(g) "Regional board" means any California regional water quality control board created pursuant to Section 13201 of the Water Code.

(Amended by Stats. 1969, Ch. 482.)

5411.

No person shall discharge sewage or other waste, or the effluent of treated sewage or other waste, in any manner which will result in contamination, pollution or a nuisance.

(Amended by Stats. 1967, Ch. 1447.)

5411.5.

(a) Any person who, without regard to intent or negligence, causes or permits any sewage or other waste, or the effluent of treated sewage or other waste, to be discharged in or on any waters of the state, or discharged in or deposited where it is, or probably will be, discharged in or on any waters of the state, shall, as soon as that person has knowledge of the discharge, immediately notify the local health officer or the director of environmental health of the discharge.

(b) A person who fails to provide the notice required by this section is guilty of a misdemeanor and shall be punished by a fine of not less than five hundred dollars ($500) nor more than one thousand dollars ($1,000), or imprisonment for less than one year, or both the fine and imprisonment.

(c) The notification required by this section shall not apply to a discharge authorized by law and in compliance with waste discharge requirements or other requirements established by the appropriate regional water quality control board or the State Water Resources Control Board.

(d) The notification required by this section shall not apply to an unauthorized discharge of effluent of treated sewage defined as recycled water pursuant to Section 13050 or 13529.2 of the Water Code.

(Amended by Stats. 2013, Ch. 635, Sec. 2. (AB 803) Effective January 1, 2014.)

5412.

Whenever the state department or any local health officer finds that a contamination exists, the state department or officer shall order the contamination abated, as provided in this chapter, and, commencing July 1 of a year in which the Legislature has appropriated sufficient funds for this purpose, shall submit any report required pursuant to subdivision (d) of Section 13193 of the Water Code.

(Amended by Stats. 2001, Ch. 498, Sec. 2. Effective January 1, 2002.)

5412.5.

(a) Any person who, without regard to intent or negligence, causes or permits any sewage or other waste, or the effluent of treated sewage or other waste to be discharged in or on any waters of the state, or discharged in or deposited where it is, or probably will be, discharged in or on any waters of the state that may cause contamination of waters used for a water-contact sport, as defined in Section 24155, shall reimburse the local health officer or the director of environmental health for the necessary and actual costs incurred to mitigate the threat of contamination and to protect the health and safety of the public.

(b) The governing body of the county shall establish the amount of payment at a level sufficient to pay the necessary and reasonable costs incurred by the local health officer or environmental health director administering this section and Section 5411.5.

(c) For the purposes of this section "mitigate" includes, but is not limited to, actions taken by the local health officer or the director of environmental health in the affected tributaries and waters used for a water-contact sport to investigate the waste discharge, to collect and analyze water samples to determine the areas of contamination, to close or restrict use, to post closure signs, and to notify the public of closures or restrictions.

(d) This section shall not apply to discharge authorized by law and in compliance with waste discharge requirements or other requirements established by the appropriate regional water quality control board or the State Water Resources Control Board.

(Added by Stats. 1992, Ch. 410, Sec. 2. Effective January 1, 1993.)

5413.

Whenever the state department finds that a pollution or nuisance does, in fact, exist, that condition shall be immediately referred by the state department to the proper regional board for action, together with any recommendations for correction, and, commencing July 1 of a year in which the Legislature has appropriated sufficient funds for this purpose, the state department shall submit any report required pursuant to subdivision (d) of Section 13193 of the Water Code. Upon request of a regional board, the state department shall inspect and report to the board on any technical factors involved in any condition of pollution or nuisance.

(Amended by Stats. 2001, Ch. 498, Sec. 3. Effective January 1, 2002.)

5414.

With respect to any condition of contamination, the state department may accept the action of any state, county, or municipal officer or agency having jurisdiction over the matter as sufficient.

(Repealed and added by Stats. 1949, Ch. 1550.)

5415.

No provision in this chapter is a limitation on any of the following:

(a) The authority of a city or county to adopt and enforce additional regulations not in conflict with this chapter imposing additional conditions, restrictions, or limitations relating to the disposal of sewage or other waste.

(b) The authority of any city or county to declare, prohibit, and abate nuisances.

(c) The authority of a state agency in the enforcement or administration of any provision of law which it is specifically permitted or required to enforce or administer.

(d) The right of any person to maintain at any time any appropriate action for relief against any private nuisance as defined in the Civil Code or for relief against any contamination or pollution.

(e) The authority of a city or county to adopt and enforce regulations relating to the use of recycled water in accordance with Chapter 7 (commencing with Section 13500) of Division 7 of the Water Code.

(Amended by Stats. 1995, Ch. 28, Sec. 5. Effective January 1, 1996.)

5416.

(a) There shall be not less than one water closet for each 20 employees or fractional part thereof working at a construction job site.

(b) The water closet shall consist of a patented chemical type privy, or a pit privy; provided, however, that a pit privy shall consist of a pit at least four feet deep with a well-constructed shelter, the openings of which shall be flyproofed, and with respect to which adequate sanitary and safe flooring shall be provided. With the approval of the local health officer other types of toilet facilities or modifications of those specified may be allowed.

(c) For the purpose of this section the term construction site shall mean the location on which actual construction of a building is in progress.

(d) A violation of this section shall constitute a misdemeanor.

(Amended by Stats. 1953, Ch. 433.)

ARTICLE 3. Procedure for Abatement [5460 - 5465]

(Article 3 repealed and added by Stats. 1949, Ch. 1550.)

5460.

The state department or local health officer may issue a peremptory order requiring the abatement of a contamination, and shall immediately furnish to the proper regional board a report of information and data relating thereto.

Coincident with issuing such order, or if any order or regulation is not complied with, the director or local health officer may bring and prosecute an action for an injunction in the superior court of the county in which the contamination occurs.

The state department or local health officer shall render to persons subject to such order all possible assistance in complying with the order, including all possible assistance in securing any necessary funds for such purpose.

(Amended by Stats. 1970, Ch. 1464.)

5461.

Any person who discharges sewage or other waste in any manner which results in contamination is guilty of a misdemeanor.

(Amended by Stats. 1967, Ch. 1447.)

5462.

Any action taken pursuant to this article with respect to the abatement of contamination created by the disposal of sewage or other waste from a community or cooperative sewerage system, shall be taken only against the agent or the agency operating such system and the contributor or contributors to the system whose waste in and of itself creates a contamination.

(Amended by Stats. 1967, Ch. 1447.)

5463.

Any health officer or governing board of any city, county, sanitary district, or other district having the power to operate and maintain a sewerage system, having served written notice upon the owner or reputed owner of land upon which there is a dwelling house, and the owner or reputed owner, after 30 days, having refused, neglected, or failed to connect the dwelling house, together with all toilets, sinks, and other plumbing therein, properly vented, and in a sanitary manner, with the adjoining street sewer, may construct the same at a reasonable cost, and the person doing that work at the request of the health officer or governing board has a lien upon that real estate for his or her work done and materials furnished, and the work done and materials furnished shall be held to have been done and furnished at the instance of the owner or reputed owner, or person claiming or having any interest therein. The governing board may pay all or any part of the cost or price of such connection to the person or persons who furnished labor, materials, or equipment for the same, and, to the extent the governing board pays the cost or price of the connection, it shall succeed to and have all the rights, including the lien provided for above, of the person or persons against the real estate and against the owner or reputed owner thereof.

As an alternative power to the enforcement of the lien provided for in this section, the governing body of the public agency performing the work of connection to the public sewer may, by order entered upon its minutes, declare that the amount of the costs of the work and the administrative expenses incurred by the governing body incident to the proceedings, together with other charges uniformly applicable within the jurisdiction of the governing body for the connection of the premises to the public sewer, shall be transmitted to the assessor and tax collector of the public agency, whereupon it shall be the duty of those officers to add the amount of the assessment to the next regular bill for taxes levied against the lot or parcel of land.

The liens provided for by this section shall be enforced in the same manner as those provided for by Part 6 (commencing with Section 8000) of Division 4, of the Civil Code. The governing board may also use the procedures in Section 5474 for levying the costs incurred for the construction of the improvements for the connection of the premises to the public sewer.

(Amended by Stats. 2010, Ch. 697, Sec. 37. (SB 189) Effective January 1, 2011. Operative July 1, 2012, by Sec. 105 of Ch. 697.)

5464.

An owner or reputed owner, who has his or her property included within an assessment district for the construction of a main trunkline or collector sewer lines, may request the governing board to construct all necessary plumbing to connect his or her property to the adjoining street public sewer system. The person employed by the governing board to do the work shall have a lien upon the property, for work done and materials furnished, and the work done and materials furnished shall be deemed to have been done and furnished at the request of the owner, reputed owner, or person claiming or having an interest in the property. The governing board may pay all, or any part, of the cost or price of the connection to the person or persons who furnished labor, materials, or equipment and, to the extent that the governing board pays the cost or price of the connection, it shall succeed to and have all the rights, including the lien, of the person or persons against the property and the owner or reputed owner of the property.

As an alternative power to the enforcement of the lien provided for in this section, the governing body of the public agency performing the work of connection to the public sewer may, by the power of ordinance approved by two-thirds vote of the members of the legislative body, fix the cost of improvement for connection to the sanitation or sewerage facilities, fix the times at which such costs shall become due, provide for the payment of the costs prior to the construction and connection or in installments over a period, not to exceed 30 years, provide a rate of interest, not to exceed 12 percent per annum, to be charged on the unpaid balance of the costs, and provide that the amount of the costs and the interest shall constitute a lien against the respective lots or parcels upon which the facilities are constructed.

The governing body may use the procedures specified in Section 5474 to implement the levying of the costs for the construction and connection of the premises to the public sewer.

(Amended by Stats. 2011, Ch. 106, Sec. 1. (AB 741) Effective January 1, 2012.)

5465.

(a) The procedures specified in this section may be used by a public agency that is an entity, as defined in Section 5470.

(b) An entity may use the procedures specified in Section 5464 for either of the following purposes, whether or not an order or other action has been issued or taken for an abatement of contamination created by sewage disposal:

(1) Converting properties from onsite septic systems and connecting them to a sewer system. The conversion improvements and costs may include, but are not limited to, pipes, pumps, and other equipment, septic system abandonment, and associated sewage treatment capacity.

(2) Replacing or repairing existing sewer laterals connecting pipes to a sewer system. The cost of the lateral replacement or repair shall constitute the cost of an improvement for connection to a sewer system.

(c) For purposes of this section, and in addition to any other power, an entity may exercise the powers specified in Article 4 (commencing with Section 5470).

(d) The authority granted by this section shall be in addition to, shall not be in derogation of, and shall not affect, any authority granted by other law relating to recovering the cost incurred by an entity for connecting properties to the public sewer system, or the entity's exercise of powers pursuant to any other law. This section shall be deemed to provide a complete and supplemental method for exercising the powers authorized by this section, and shall be deemed supplemental to the powers conferred by other applicable laws.

(e) For purposes of this section, the following definitions shall apply:

(1) "Assessment district" as used in statutes referenced in this section also means an improvement district or any other area served by the entity's sewer collection system.

(2) "Governing board" and "governing body" mean the governing body of the entity.

(3) "Ordinance" as used in statutes referenced in this section also means a resolution.

(Added by Stats. 2011, Ch. 106, Sec. 2. (AB 741) Effective January 1, 2012.)

ARTICLE 4. Sanitation and Sewerage Systems [5470 - 5474.10]

(Article 4 added by Stats. 1945, Ch. 979.)

5470.

The following words wherever used in this article shall be construed as defined in this section, unless from the context a different meaning is intended, or unless a different meaning is specifically defined and more particularly directed to the use of such words:

(a) Assessment Roll. "Assessment roll" refers to the assessment roll upon which general taxes of the entity are collected.

(b) Auditor. "Auditor" means the financial officer of the entity.

(c) Clerk. "Clerk" means the clerk of the legislative body or secretary of the entity.

(d) Chambers. "Chambers" refers to the place where the regular meetings of the legislative body of the entity are held.

(e) Entity. "Entity" means and includes counties, cities and counties, cities, sanitary districts, county sanitation districts, county service areas, sewer maintenance districts, and other public corporations and districts authorized to acquire, construct, maintain and operate sanitary sewers and sewerage systems.

(f) Rates or Charges. "Rates or charges" shall mean fees, tolls, rates, rentals, or other charges for services and facilities furnished by an entity in connection with its sanitation or sewerage systems, including garbage and refuse collection.

(g) Real Estate. "Real estate" includes:

(1) The possession of, claim to, ownership of, or right to possession of land; and

(2) Improvements on land.

(h) Tax Collector. "Tax collector" means the officer who collects general taxes for the entity.

The amendment of this section made by the 1972 Regular Session of the Legislature does not constitute a change in, but is declaratory of, the preexisting law.

(Amended by Stats. 2015, Ch. 269, Sec. 18. (SB 184) Effective January 1, 2016.)

5471.

(a) In addition to the powers granted in the principal act, any entity shall have power, by an ordinance or resolution approved by a two-thirds vote of the members of the legislative body thereof, to prescribe, revise and collect, fees, tolls, rates, rentals, or other charges for services and facilities furnished by it, either within or without its territorial limits, in connection with its water, sanitation, storm drainage, or sewerage system.

(b) In addition to the powers granted in the principal act, any entity shall have power, pursuant to the notice, protest, and hearing procedures in Section 53753 of the Government Code, to prescribe, revise, and collect water, sewer, or water and sewer standby or immediate availability charges for services and facilities furnished by it, either within or without its territorial limits, in connection with its water, sanitation, storm drainage, or sewerage system.

(c) The entity may provide that the charge for the service shall be collected with the rates, tolls, and charges for any other utility, and that any or all of these charges may be billed upon the same bill. Where the charge is to be collected with the charges for any other utility service furnished by a department or agency of the entity and over which its legislative body does not exercise control, the consent of the department or agency shall be obtained prior to collecting water, sanitation, storm drainage, or sewerage charges with the charges for any other utility. Revenues derived under the provisions in this section, shall be used only for the acquisition, construction, reconstruction, maintenance, and operation of water systems and sanitation, storm drainage, or sewerage facilities, to repay principal and interest on bonds issued for the construction or reconstruction of these water systems and sanitary, storm drainage, or sewerage facilities and to repay federal or state loans or advances made to the entity for the construction or reconstruction of water systems and sanitary, storm drainage, or sewerage facilities. However, the revenue shall not be used for the acquisition or construction of new local street sewers or laterals as distinguished from main trunk, interceptor, and outfall sewers.

(d) If the procedures set forth in this section as it read at the time a standby charge was established were followed, the entity may, by ordinance or resolution adopted by a two-thirds vote of the members of the legislative body thereof, continue the charge pursuant to this section in successive years at the same rate. If new, increased, or extended assessments are proposed, the entity shall comply with the notice, protest, and hearing procedures in Section 53753 of the Government Code.

(Amended by Stats. 2016, Ch. 366, Sec. 16. (SB 974) Effective January 1, 2017.)

5472.

After fees, rates, tolls, rentals or other charges are fixed pursuant to this article, any person may pay such fees, rates, tolls, rentals or other charges under protest and bring an action against the city or city and county in the superior court to recover any money which the legislative body refuses to refund. Payments made and actions brought under this section, shall be made and brought in the manner provided for payment of taxes under protest and actions for refund thereof in Article 2, Chapter 5, Part 9, of Division 1 of the Revenue and Taxation Code, insofar as those provisions are applicable.

(Added by Stats. 1949, Ch. 865.)

5472.5.

The rates may be collected with the rates for any other utility service furnished by a department or agency of that entity over which the legislative body thereof does not exercise control, or with a publicly or privately owned public utility, with the written consent and agreement of that department or agency or public utility owner, which agreement shall establish the terms and conditions upon which the collections shall be made. The agreement, in the discretion of the department or agency or public utility owner making the collections, also may provide that those rates shall be itemized, billed upon the same bill, and collected as one item, together with, and not separately from, the other utility service charge.

(Added by renumbering Section 5472 (as amended by Stats. 1953, Ch. 862) by Stats. 1981, Ch. 714.)

5473.

Any entity which has adopted an ordinance or resolution pursuant to this article or an order pursuant to Section 6520.5 may, by such ordinance or resolution or by separate ordinances or resolutions approved by a two-thirds vote of the members of the legislative body thereof, elect to have such charges collected on the tax roll in the same manner, by the same persons, and at the same time as, together with and not separately from, its general taxes. In such event, it shall cause a written report to be prepared each year and filed with the clerk, which shall contain a description of each parcel of real property receiving such services and facilities and the amount of the charge for each parcel for the year, computed in conformity with the charges prescribed by the ordinance or resolution. Any ordinance or resolution adopted pursuant to this section authorizing the collection of charges on the tax roll shall remain in effect for the time specified in the ordinance or resolution or, if no time is specified in the ordinance or resolution, until repealed or until a change is made in the rates charged by the entity.

The powers authorized by this section shall be alternative to all other powers of any entity, and alternative to other procedures adopted by the legislative body thereof for the collection of such charges.

The real property may be described by reference to maps prepared in accordance with Section 327 of the Revenue and Taxation Code, and on file in the office of the county assessor or by reference to plats or maps on file in the office of the clerk.

(Amended by Stats. 2016, Ch. 366, Sec. 17. (SB 974) Effective January 1, 2017.)

5473a.

Any entity may make the election specified in Section 5473 with respect only to delinquent charges and may do so by preparing and filing the written report, giving notice and holding the hearing therein required only as to such delinquencies.

(Added by Stats. 1953, Ch. 1259.)

5473.1.

The clerk shall cause notice of the filing of said report and of a time and place of hearing thereon to be published pursuant to Section 6066 of the Government Code prior to the date set for hearing, in a newspaper of general circulation printed and published within the entity if there is one and if not then in such paper printed and published in the county within which the greater part of such district is located.

Before any entity may have such charges collected on the tax roll for the first time following the effective date of this section, the clerk shall cause a notice in writing of the filing of said report proposing to have such charges for the forthcoming fiscal year collected on the tax roll and of the time and place of hearing thereon, to be mailed to each person to whom any parcel or parcels of real property described in said report is assessed in the last equalized assessment roll available on the date said report is prepared, at the address shown on said assessment roll or as known to said clerk. If the legislative body adopts the report, then the requirements for notice in writing to the persons to whom parcels of real property are assessed shall not apply to hearings on reports prepared in subsequent fiscal years but notice by publication as herein provided shall be adequate.

(Amended by Stats. 1957, Ch. 357.)

5473.2.

At the time stated in the notice, the legislative body shall hear and consider all objections or protests, if any, to said report referred to in said notice and may continue the hearing from time to time. If the legislative body finds that protest is made by the owners of a majority of separate parcels of property described in the report, then the report shall not be adopted and the charges shall be collected separately from the tax roll and shall not constitute a lien against any parcel or parcels of land.

(Amended by Stats. 1953, Ch. 862.)

5473.3.

Upon the conclusion of the hearing, the legislative body may adopt, revise, change, reduce or modify any charge or overrule any or all objections and shall make its determination upon each charge as described in said report which determination shall be final.

(Amended by Stats. 1953, Ch. 862.)

5473.4.

On or before August 10 of each year following the final determination upon each charge, the clerk shall file with the county auditor a copy of the report prepared pursuant to Section 5473 with a statement endorsed on the report over his or her signature that the report has been finally adopted by the legislative body of the entity and the county auditor shall enter the amounts of the charges against the respective lots or parcels of land as they appear on the current assessment roll. Where any of the parcels are outside the boundaries of the entity they shall be added to the assessment roll of the entity for the purpose of collecting the charges. If the property is not described on the roll, the county auditor may enter the description on the roll together with the amounts of the charges, as shown in the report.

(Amended by Stats. 2015, Ch. 269, Sec. 19. (SB 184) Effective January 1, 2016.)

5473.5.

Except as provided in Section 5473.8, the amount of the charges shall constitute a lien against the lot or parcel of land against which the charge has been imposed as of noon on the first Monday in March immediately preceding the date of levy.

(Amended by Stats. 1973, Ch. 861.)

5473.6.

The tax collector shall include the amount of the charges on bills for taxes levied against the respective lots and parcels of land.

(Added by renumbering Section 5473.5 by Stats. 1953, Ch. 862.)

5473.7.

Thereafter the amount of the charges shall be collected at the same time and in the same manner and by the same persons as, together with and not separately from, the general taxes for the entity, and shall be delinquent at the same time and thereafter be subject to the same delinquency penalties.

(Added by renumbering Section 5473.6 by Stats. 1953, Ch. 862.)

5473.8.

All laws applicable to the levy, collection, and enforcement of general taxes of the entity, including, but not limited to, those pertaining to the matters of delinquency, correction, cancellation, refund, and redemption, are applicable to the charges authorized pursuant to this article, except that if any real property to which these charges relate has been transferred or conveyed to a bona fide purchaser for value or a lien of a bona fide encumbrancer for value has been created and attaches thereon during the year prior to the date on which the first installment of the general taxes that include the charges appears on the assessment roll, then the lien which would otherwise be imposed by Section 5473.5 shall not attach to the real property and the charges relating to that property shall be transferred to the unsecured roll of collection.

(Amended by Stats. 2012, Ch. 330, Sec. 17. (SB 1090) Effective January 1, 2013.)

5473.9.

The tax collector may, in his discretion, issue separate bills for such charges and separate receipts for collection on account of such charges. The county shall be compensated for services rendered in connection with the levy, collection and enforcement of such charges for an entity other than the county in an amount to be fixed by agreement between the board of supervisors and the legislative body of the entity. The compensation shall not exceed five dollars ($5) for each account handled, or 1 percent of all money collected, whichever is greater. The compensation shall be paid into the county salary fund.

(Amended by Stats. 1969, Ch. 318.)

5473.10.

The entity may provide for a basic penalty of not more than 10 percent for nonpayment of the charges within the time and in the manner prescribed by it, and in addition may provide for a penalty of not exceeding 1 and one-half percent per month for nonpayment of the charges and basic penalty. It may provide for collection of the penalties herein provided for.

(Amended by Stats. 1985, Ch. 341, Sec. 1.)

5473.11.

(a) An entity shall notify the assessee shown on the latest equalized assessment roll whenever delinquent and unpaid charges for services which would become a lien on the property pursuant to subdivision (b) remain delinquent and unpaid for 60 days.

(b) The amount of the unpaid charges may, in the discretion of the entity, be secured at any time by filing for record in the office of the county recorder of any county, a certificate specifying the amount of the unpaid charges and the name and address of the person liable for those unpaid charges. From the time of recordation of the certificate, the amount required to be paid together with interest and penalty constitutes a lien upon all real property in the county owned by the person or afterwards, and before the lien expires, acquired by him or her. The lien shall have the force, priority, and effect of a judgment lien and shall continue for 10 years from the date of the filing of the certificate unless sooner released or otherwise discharged. The lien may, within 10 years from the filing of the certificate or within 10 years from the date of the last extension of the lien in the manner herein provided, be extended by filing for record a new certificate in the office of the county recorder of any county and from the time of this filing the lien shall be extended to the real property in this county for 10 years unless sooner released or otherwise discharged.

(Amended by Stats. 2012, Ch. 330, Sec. 18. (SB 1090) Effective January 1, 2013.)

5474.

An entity shall have the power by ordinance or resolution approved by two-thirds vote of the members of the legislative body thereof to fix fees or charges for the privilege of connecting to its sanitation or sewerage facilities and improvements constructed by the entity pursuant to Sections 5463 and 5464, to fix the time or times at which the fees or charges shall become due, to provide for the payment of the fees or charges prior to connection or in installments over a period of not to exceed 30 years, to provide the rate of interest, not to exceed 12 percent per annum, to be charged on the unpaid balance of the fees or charges, and to provide that the amount of the fees or charges and the interest thereon shall constitute a lien against the respective lots or parcels of land to which the facilities are connected at the time and in the manner specified in Sections 5473.5 and 5473.8. Prior to making the fees or charges a lien against the land, the legislative body shall give notice to the owners of the lots or parcels of land affected, and the notice shall set forth all of the following:

(a) The schedule of fees or charges to be imposed by the entity.

(b) A description of the property subject to the fees or charges, which description may be by reference to a plat or diagram on file in the office of the clerk of the legislative body, or to maps prepared in accordance with Section 327 of the Revenue and Taxation Code, and on file in the office of the county assessor.

(c) The time or times at which the fees or charges shall become due.

(d) The number of installments in which the fees or charges shall be payable.

(e) The rate of interest, not to exceed 12 percent per annum, to be charged on the unpaid balance of the fees or charges.

(f) That it is proposed that the fees or charges and interest thereon shall constitute a lien against the lots or parcels of land to which the facilities are furnished.

(g) The time and place at which the legislative body will hold a hearing at which persons may appear and present any and all objections they may have to the imposition of the fees or charges as a lien against the land.

(Amended by Stats. 2016, Ch. 366, Sec. 18. (SB 974) Effective January 1, 2017.)

5474.1.

The notice shall be published pursuant to Section 6063 of the Government Code prior to the date set for hearing. At least 10 days prior to the date of hearing written notice thereof shall be mailed to all persons owning land subject to such fees or charges, whose names and addresses appear on the last equalized assessment roll.

(Amended by Stats. 1961, Ch. 754.)

5474.2.

At the time stated in the notice the legislative body shall hear and consider all objections or protests, if any, to the imposition of the fees or charges as set forth in said notice and may continue the hearing from time to time.

(Added by Stats. 1953, Ch. 578.)

5474.3.

Upon the conclusion of the hearing, the legislative body may adopt, revise, change, reduce or modify the fees or charges or may overrule any or all objections and make its determination, which determination shall be final.

(Added by Stats. 1953, Ch. 578.)

5474.4.

On or before August 10 of each year following the final determination, the legislative body shall certify to the county auditor a list of the lots or parcels of land, as they appear on the current assessment roll, subject to any fees or charges and the amounts of the installments of those fees or charges and interest to be entered against the lots or parcels on the assessment roll. In the event a lot or parcel connected to the facilities is subsequently divided into two or more lots or parcels as shown on the current assessment roll, the legislative body shall designate the lot or parcel that remains connected to the facilities and against which the installments of the fees or charges and interest are to be entered.

(Amended by Stats. 2015, Ch. 269, Sec. 20. (SB 184) Effective January 1, 2016.)

5474.5.

The county auditor shall enter on the current assessment roll the amounts of the installments of any fees or charges and interest and, except as provided in Section 5474.6, the amounts thereof shall constitute a lien against the lot or parcel of land against which levied as of noon on the first Monday in March immediately preceding the date of entry.

(Amended by Stats. 2015, Ch. 269, Sec. 21. (SB 184) Effective January 1, 2016.)

5474.6.

(a) The tax collector shall include the amounts of the installments of fees or charges and the interest on bills for taxes levied against the respective lots and parcels of land. Thereafter, all laws applicable to the levy, collection and enforcement of taxes of the entity, including penalties and interest thereon and cancellation or refund thereof, shall be applicable to those installments of fees or charges and interest, except that, if any real property to which the fees or charges relate has been transferred or conveyed to a bona fide purchaser for value or a lien of a bona fide encumbrancer for value has been created and attaches thereon during the year prior to the date on which the first installment of the general taxes that include the fees or charges appears on the assessment roll, then the lien which would otherwise be imposed by Section 5474.5 shall not attach to the real property and the fees or charges and interest shall be transferred to the unsecured roll for collection.

(b) The amount of the unpaid installments of fees or charges and interest may, in the discretion of the entity, be secured at any time by filing for record in the office of the county recorder of any county, a certificate specifying the amount of the fees or charges and interest and the name and address of the person liable therefor. From the time of recordation of the certificate, the amount required to be paid together with interest and penalty constitutes a lien upon all real property in the county owned by the person or afterwards, and before the lien expires, acquired by him or her. The lien shall have the force, priority, and effect of a judgment lien and shall continue for 10 years from the date of the filing of the certificate unless sooner released or otherwise discharged. The lien may, within 10 years from the filing of the certificate or within 10 years from the date of the last extension of the lien in the manner herein provided, be extended by filing for record a new certificate in the office of the county recorder of any county and from the time of this filing the lien shall be extended to the real property in this county for 10 years unless sooner released or otherwise discharged.

(Amended by Stats. 2012, Ch. 330, Sec. 19. (SB 1090) Effective January 1, 2013.)

5474.7.

The tax collector may, in his discretion, issue separate bills for such installments of fees or charges and interest. The county shall be compensated for services, if any, rendered in connection with the levy, collection and enforcement of such installments of fees or charges and interest in an amount to be fixed by agreement between the board of supervisors and the legislative body of the entity. The compensation shall not exceed 1 percent of all money collected for the entity.

(Amended by Stats. 1961, Ch. 754.)

5474.8.

Fees or charges imposed by an entity by ordinance or resolution adopted pursuant to Section 5474 may differ in amount or method of computation from fees or charges imposed by any other ordinance or resolution of such entity adopted pursuant to Section 5474.

(Amended by Stats. 2016, Ch. 366, Sec. 19. (SB 974) Effective January 1, 2017.)

5474.9.

Revenues derived from fees or charges imposed pursuant to Section 5474 shall be used only for the acquisition, construction, reconstruction, maintenance and operation of sanitation or sewerage facilities, to pay municipalities for sewer service collection charges, to repay principal and interest on bonds issued for construction or reconstruction of such sanitation or sewerage facilities and to repay federal or state loans or advances made to entities for the construction or reconstruction of sanitation or sewerage facilities; provided, however, that such revenue shall not be used for the acquisition or construction of new local street sewers or laterals as distinguished from main trunk, interceptor and outfall sewers.

(Amended by Stats. 1961, Ch. 754.)

5474.10.

The authority for the imposition of fees or charges by entities pursuant to Section 5474 shall be in addition to the authority granted to such entities by any other law authorizing such entities to establish fees, tolls, rates, rentals or other charges.

(Amended by Stats. 1961, Ch. 754.)

CHAPTER 7. Effect on Previous Laws [5475- 5475.]

(Chapter 7 enacted by Stats. 1939, Ch. 60.)

5475.

No right or obligation accrued by the formation or operation of a municipal sewer district pursuant to the provisions of Chapter 673, Statutes of 1909, is affected by the repeal of that act, and any district organized may continue in existence and subject to that act.

(Enacted by Stats. 1939, Ch. 60.)

CHAPTER 9. Joint Municipal Sewage Disposal District Act [5745- 5745.]

(Chapter 9 (Sections 5700 to 5830.08) added by Stats. 1951, Ch. 439.)

ARTICLE 5.5. Claims [5745- 5745.]

(Article 5.5 added by Stats. 1959, Ch. 1727.)

5745.

All claims for money or damages against the district are governed by Part 3 (commencing with Section 900) and Part 4 (commencing with Section 940) of Division 3.6 of Title 1 of the Government Code except as provided therein, or by other statutes or regulations expressly applicable thereto.

(Amended (as added by Stats. 1959, Ch. 1727) by Stats. 1963, Ch. 1715. Note: This article was added to Chapter 9 (formerly comm. with Section 5700), which was repealed by Stats. 1959, Ch. 1309.)

CHAPTER 10. Regional Sewage Disposal Districts [6096- 6096.]

(Chapter 10 (Sections 5900 to 6110) added by Stats. 1955, Ch. 1922.)

6096.

Claims for money or damages against the district are governed by Part 3 (commencing with Section 900) and Part 4 (commencing with Section 940) of Division 3.6 of Title 1 of the Government Code, except as provided therein. Claims not governed thereby or by other statutes or by ordinances or regulations authorized by law and expressly applicable to such claims shall be prepared and presented to the governing body, and all claims shall be audited and paid, in the same manner and with the same effect as are similar claims against the county.

(Amended (as added by Stats. 1959, Ch. 1727) by Stats. 1963, Ch. 1715. Note: This section was added by Stats. 1959, Ch. 1727, to Chapter 10 (formerly comm. with Section 5900), which was repealed by Stats. 1959, Ch. 1309.)

CHAPTER 11. Assistance to Small Rural Communities [6120 - 6127]

(Chapter 11 added by Stats. 1983, Ch. 1152, Sec. 1.)

6120.

Unless the context otherwise requires, the definitions in this section govern the construction of this chapter.

(a) "Community facility" means a public or mutual water system, or publicly operated waste water system.

(b) "Department" means the Department of Housing and Community Development.

(c) "Eligible grantee" means a local governmental entity or a private nonprofit organization which has demonstrated capacity to provide technical assistance on all subjects specified in subdivision (g).

(d) "Low-income community" means a community in which the median income of the persons in the community, area, or city is less than 70 percent of the median income in the state.

(e) "Rural community" means any community, area, or city with less than 5,000 population.

(f) "Seed money" means funds granted by the department pursuant to the provisions of this chapter for project organization and development, test wells, preliminary engineering, professional fees, and other costs which are necessary to get a project approved for financing from local, state, or federal sources.

(g) "Technical assistance" means assistance and advice on all of the following subjects:

(1) Organization, including formation, financing, and operation, of public and private nonprofit service entities.

(2) Community responsibilities, including the conduct of meetings, maintenance of minutes of meetings, preparation and analysis of budgets, keeping of fiscal records, and supervision of staff.

(3) Operation and maintenance, including schedules and techniques pertaining to all parts of a facility, and maintenance control systems and maintenance recordkeeping to assure adequate maintenance, including schedules and techniques pertaining to all parts of a facility, and maintenance control systems and maintenance recordkeeping to assure adequate maintenance is performed on a facility.

(4) Project development, including, but not limited to:

(A) The preparation of plans for needed expansion, creation of services, and schedules for expected major repairs or replacement needs.

(B) Negotiation of contracts for professional services.

(C) An examination of various funding alternatives, and packaging applications for assistance.

(D) Review of engineering plans and specifications for development projects.

(E) Compliance with appropriate regulations relative to funding agencies.

(5) Financial assistance available from the department in seed money grants pursuant to this chapter.

(Amended by Stats. 1984, Ch. 744, Sec. 1.)

6121.

The Legislature finds and declares that small rural communities are unable to take advantage of various local, state, and federal facility development programs due to their lack of technical expertise, staff, and seed money. The Legislature finds and declares that changing state and federal regulations relative to the provision of domestic water and waste water disposal are creating an extra hardship upon rural areas. The Legislature further finds and declares that the provisions of this chapter are necessary in order to provide assistance to rural areas so that they may take advantage of existing programs and develop self-help expertise enabling them to assist themselves in the future.

(Added by Stats. 1983, Ch. 1152, Sec. 1.)

6122.

The department shall establish a Rural Community Facilities Technical Assistance Program, under which, subject to the availability of funds therefor, contracts shall be made by the department with public entities and nonprofit corporations for the provision of technical assistance to rural and low-income communities in the operation, maintenance, and development of community facilities.

(Added by Stats. 1983, Ch. 1152, Sec. 1.)

6123.

The program shall be administered by the Director of Housing and Community Development.

(Added by Stats. 1983, Ch. 1152, Sec. 1.)

6124.

The program shall be for the purpose of helping rural and low-income communities to take advantage of various local, state, and federal financing programs to develop community facilities, ensuring that these facilities are developed and operated in such a manner that the facilities or services last for a normal period of time, as determined by the department, and ensuring that, wherever possible, reasonable user rates are charged for use of the facilities. The department shall provide in the administration of the program that funds pursuant to this program shall, to the greatest extent practicable, be used with the greatest amount of matching nonprogram funds.

(Added by Stats. 1983, Ch. 1152, Sec. 1.)

6125.

The Rural Community Facility Grant Fund is hereby created in the State Treasury. The fund is continuously appropriated, without regard to fiscal years, notwithstanding Section 13340 of the Government Code, to the department for expenditure for the purpose of making grants pursuant to the provisions of this chapter and to pay the costs incurred by the department in administering the grant program.

(Added by Stats. 1983, Ch. 1152, Sec. 1.)

6126.

The department shall grant funds by contract with eligible grantees under the following conditions:

(a) That grantees shall have the ability to provide all aspects of technical assistance on at least a countywide basis.

(b) That grantees shall use no more than 80 percent of those funds for staff and administrative costs connected with the provision of that technical assistance.

(c) That each community designated by a grantee to receive seed money shall be reviewed and certified by the department as eligible for those funds.

(d) That any community designated to receive seed money shall also receive technical assistance.

(e) That no community shall receive seed money which is greater than the sum of seven thousand five hundred dollars ($7,500) or two hundred dollars ($200) per family in such community, whichever is less.

(f) The department and the grantee shall place seed money funds in a joint savings account which requires both the department and grantee to give authorization prior to the withdrawal of those funds.

(Amended by Stats. 1984, Ch. 744, Sec. 2.)

6127.

The department shall develop and adopt rules and regulations to implement the provisions of this chapter.

(Added by Stats. 1983, Ch. 1152, Sec. 1.)

DIVISION 6. SANITARY DISTRICTS [6400 - 6982]

(Division 6 enacted by Stats. 1939, Ch. 60.)

PART 1. SANITARY DISTRICT ACT OF 1923 [6400 - 6830]

(Heading of Part 1 amended by Stats. 1939, Ch. 1124.)

CHAPTER 1. General Provisions and Definitions [6400 - 6408]

(Chapter 1 enacted by Stats. 1939, Ch. 60.)

6400.

"District," as used in this part, means a district formed pursuant to this part or pursuant to any law which it supersedes.

(Enacted by Stats. 1939, Ch. 60.)

6401.

"Board" or "district board," as used in this part, means the governing board of a district.

(Enacted by Stats. 1939, Ch. 60.)

6402.

"Secretary," as used in this part, means the secretary of a district.

(Enacted by Stats. 1939, Ch. 60.)

6403.

"Assessor," as used in this part, means the assessor of a district.

(Enacted by Stats. 1939, Ch. 60.)

6404.

"Tax collector," as used in this part, means the tax collector of the county or counties in which a district is located.

(Amended by Stats. 1961, Ch. 1629.)

6405.

"Treasurer," as used in this part, means the treasurer of the county or counties in which a district is located.

(Amended by Stats. 1961, Ch. 1629.)

6406.

"Garbage," as used in this part, shall include all of the following: (a) animal, fruit and vegetable refuse; (b) offal; (c) leaves and cuttings, trimmings from trees, shrubs and grass; (d) inorganic refuse and rubbish; (e) anything thrown away as worthless.

(Added by Stats. 1939, Ch. 304.)

6408.

"Board of supervisors," as used in this part, means the board of supervisors of the county in which the greatest portion of the area of the district, is situated at the time of the filing of the petition for formation, unless another meaning is specified.

(Added by Stats. 1961, Ch. 1629.)

CHAPTER 2. Formation [6420 - 6466]

(Chapter 2 enacted by Stats. 1939, Ch. 60.)

ARTICLE 1. Petition [6420 - 6425]

(Article 1 enacted by Stats. 1939, Ch. 60.)

6420.

Whenever 25 persons in any county, or in two or more counties within the same natural watershed area, desire the formation of a sanitary district within the area, they may sign and present a petition to the board of supervisors of the county in which the greatest portion of the area of the proposed district is situated at the time of the filing of the petition. If the district is to be located in more than one county, the petition shall be signed by no fewer than 15 persons in the county in which the greatest portion of the district is located and by no fewer than 10 persons in each other county in which the district is located.

(Amended by Stats. 1961, Ch. 1629.)

6421.

The petition shall contain:

(a) The name of the proposed district.

(b) The boundaries of the proposed district.

(c) A request that the territory within the boundaries be formed into a district as provided by this part.

(Enacted by Stats. 1939, Ch. 60.)

6422.

Each petitioner shall be a resident and freeholder in the proposed district.

(Enacted by Stats. 1939, Ch. 60.)

6423.

The petition shall be verified by the affidavit of one of the petitioners.

(Enacted by Stats. 1939, Ch. 60.)

6424.

The petition shall be published for at least two weeks preceding the hearing in a newspaper of general circulation published in each county in which the district is located.

(Amended by Stats. 1961, Ch. 1629.)

6425.

With the petition there shall be published a notice stating the time when the petition will be presented to the board of supervisors, and that all persons interested may appear and be heard.

(Enacted by Stats. 1939, Ch. 60.)

ARTICLE 2. Hearing [6440 - 6448]

(Article 2 enacted by Stats. 1939, Ch. 60.)

6440.

At the time designated the board of supervisors shall hear the petition, and may adjourn the hearing from time to time.

(Enacted by Stats. 1939, Ch. 60.)

6441.

The board of supervisors shall not modify the boundaries of the proposed district as set forth in the petition so as to exclude from the proposed district any land which would be benefited by the formation of the district, nor shall there be included in the proposed district any lands which will not in the judgment of the board be benefited.

(Enacted by Stats. 1939, Ch. 60.)

6442.

If the board of supervisors concludes that any land has been improperly omitted from the proposed district and the owner has not appeared at the hearing, it shall continue the further hearing of the petition, and shall order notice given to the nonappearing owner, requiring him to appear before it and show cause, if any he has, why his land should not be included in the proposed district.

(Enacted by Stats. 1939, Ch. 60.)

6443.

The notice shall be given either by publication in the same manner as the original petition and for the same period, or by personal service on each nonappearing owner.

(Enacted by Stats. 1939, Ch. 60.)

6444.

If the notice is given by personal service, it shall be given at least three days prior to the date fixed for the further hearing.

(Enacted by Stats. 1939, Ch. 60.)

6445.

The board of supervisors may grant further continuances, by order entered in its minutes, to the end that a full hearing may be had.

(Enacted by Stats. 1939, Ch. 60.)

6446.

Upon the final hearing of the petition, the board of supervisors, if it approves the petition as originally presented or in a modified form, shall make an order containing:

(a) A description of the exterior boundaries of the proposed district, as determined by the board of supervisors.

(b) The date on which an election will be held in the proposed district.

(Enacted by Stats. 1939, Ch. 60.)

6447.

The order shall:

(a) Fix the day of the election, which shall be held on the next established election date not less than 74 days from the date of the order.

(b) State that at the election there shall be elected a district assessor, and five members of the board.

(Amended by Stats. 1973, Ch. 1146.)

6448.

The order shall be entered in the minutes of the board of supervisors, and is conclusive evidence of the due presentation of a proper petition, and of the fact that each of the petitioners was, at the time of the signature and presentation of the petition, a resident and freeholder in the proposed district.

(Enacted by Stats. 1939, Ch. 60.)

ARTICLE 3. Election on Formation and for Officers [6460 - 6466]

(Article 3 enacted by Stats. 1939, Ch. 60.)

6460.

Except as otherwise specifically provided in this article, the provisions of the chapter of this part on elections govern the election on the question of organizing a district and the election of the first district officers, and the board of supervisors of the county and the county clerk shall perform the duties conferred by that chapter on the district board and its secretary, respectively.

(Enacted by Stats. 1939, Ch. 60.)

6461.

A copy of the order shall be posted for four successive weeks prior to the election in three public places in the proposed district at least one of which shall be in each county in which the district is located, and shall be published once a week for four successive weeks prior to the election in a newspaper of general circulation published in each county in which the district is located.

(Amended by Stats. 1961, Ch. 1629.)

6461.1.

Within five days after the district formation election has been called, the legislative body which has called the election shall transmit, by registered mail, a written notification of the election call to the executive officer of the local agency formation commission of the county or principal county in which the territory or major portion of the territory of the proposed district is located. Such written notice shall include the name and a description of the proposed district, and may be in the form of a certified copy of the resolution adopted by the legislative body calling the district formation election.

The executive officer, within five days after being notified that a district formation election has been called, shall submit to the commission, for its approval or modification, an impartial analysis of the proposed district formation.

The impartial analysis shall not exceed 500 words in length and shall include a specific description of the boundaries of the district proposed to be formed.

The local agency formation commission, within five days after the receipt of the executive officer's analysis, shall approve or modify the analysis and submit it to the officials in charge of conducting the district formation election.

(Added by Stats. 1970, Ch. 736.)

6461.2.

The board of supervisors or any member or members of the board authorized by the board, or any individual voter or bona fide association of citizens entitled to vote on the district formation proposition, or any combination of such voters and associations of citizens, may file a written argument for or a written argument against the proposed district formation.

Arguments shall not exceed 300 words in length and shall be filed with the officials in charge of conducting the election not less than 54 days prior to the date of the district formation election.

(Added by Stats. 1970, Ch. 736.)

6461.3.

If more than one argument for or more than one argument against the proposed district formation is filed with the election officials within the time prescribed, such election officials shall select one of the arguments for printing and distribution to the voters.

In selecting the arguments, the election officials shall give preference and priority in the order named to the arguments of the following:

(a) The board of supervisors or any member or members of the board authorized by the board.

(b) Individual voters or bona fide associations of citizens or a combination of such voters and associations.

(Added by Stats. 1970, Ch. 736.)

6461.4.

The elections officials in charge of conducting the election shall cause a ballot pamphlet concerning the district formation proposition to be voted on to be printed and mailed to each voter entitled to vote on the district formation question.

The ballot pamphlet shall contain the following, in the order prescribed:

(a) The complete text of the proposition.

(b) The impartial analysis of the proposition, prepared by the local agency formation commission.

(c) The argument for the proposed district formation.

(d) The argument against the proposed district formation.

The elections officials shall mail a ballot pamphlet to each voter entitled to vote in the district formation election at least 10 days prior to the date of the election. The ballot pamphlet is "official matter" within the meaning of Section 13303 of the Elections Code.

(Amended by Stats. 1994, Ch. 923, Sec. 120. Effective January 1, 1995.)

6462.

At least 15 days prior to the election, the board of supervisors shall select one, and may select two or more, polling places in the proposed district, and shall make suitable arrangements for the election.

(Amended by Stats. 1945, Ch. 1337.)

6463.

The ballots shall contain the words, "sanitary district: yes," and "sanitary district: no," or equivalent words, and the names of the persons to be voted for at the election.

(Enacted by Stats. 1939, Ch. 60.)

6464.

At the election there shall be elected an assessor and the members of the board who shall be resident electors of the district.

(Amended by Stats. 1959, Ch. 155.)

6465.

If a majority of the votes cast in each county are in favor of formation of the district, the board of supervisors shall make and cause to be entered in its minutes an order that a district of the name and with the boundaries stated in the order calling the election, setting forth the boundaries, has been established.

The board shall immediately file for record in the office of the county recorder of each county within which the district is located a certified copy of the order declaring the district established.

The order is conclusive evidence of the fact and regularity of all prior proceedings required by this part or by law, and of the existence and validity of the district.

(Amended by Stats. 1961, Ch. 1629.)

6466.

If a majority of the votes cast are against formation of the district, the board of supervisors shall by order entered in its minutes so declare, and no other proceeding shall be taken in relation thereto until the expiration of one year from the date of the presentation of the petition to the board of supervisors.

(Enacted by Stats. 1939, Ch. 60.)

CHAPTER 3. Officers [6480 - 6501]

(Chapter 3 enacted by Stats. 1939, Ch. 60.)

6480.

(a) The officers of the district are an assessor and five members of the board.

(b) Any member of the legislative body of a city whose territory is encompassed, in whole or in part, by the boundaries of the district is not disqualified from holding office as a member of the board solely because of his membership on such legislative body.

(Amended by Stats. 1970, Ch. 22.)

6480.1.

(a) Notwithstanding Section 6480, the local agency formation commission, in approving either a consolidation of districts or the reorganization of two or more districts into a single sanitary district may, pursuant to subdivisions (k) and (n) of Section 56886 of the Government Code, increase the number of directors to serve on the board of directors of the consolidated or reorganized district to 7, 9, or 11, who shall be members of the board of directors of the districts to be consolidated or reorganized as of the effective date of the consolidation or reorganization.

(b) Upon the expiration of the terms of the members of the board of directors of the consolidated district, or a district reorganized as described in subdivision (a), whose terms first expire following the effective date of the consolidation or reorganization, the total number of members on the board of directors shall be reduced until the number equals the number of members permitted by the principal act of the consolidated or reorganized district, or any larger number as may be specified by the local agency formation commission in approving the consolidation or reorganization.

(c) In addition to the powers granted under Section 1780 of the Government Code, in the event of a vacancy on the board of directors of the consolidated district or a district reorganized as described in subdivision (a) at which time the total number of directors is greater than five, the board of directors may, by majority vote of the remaining members of the board, choose not to fill the vacancy. In that event, the total membership of the board of directors shall be reduced by one board member. Upon making the determination not to fill a vacancy, the board of directors shall notify the board of supervisors of its decision.

(d) For the purposes of this section: "consolidation" means consolidation, as defined in Section 56030 of the Government Code; "district" or "special district" means district or special district, as defined in Section 56036 of the Government Code; and "reorganization" means reorganization, as defined in Section 56073 of the Government Code.

(Amended by Stats. 2006, Ch. 172, Sec. 11. Effective January 1, 2007.)

6480.5.

At any time within two years after a sanitary district consolidates with or annexes the territory of a district having powers and functions substantially identical to those of a sanitary district formed pursuant to this part, the board of directors of the sanitary district may, by resolution, increase the number of members of the board from five to seven, and may designate the first two additional members to serve on the enlarged board. If the board is enlarged subsequent to the consolidation with, or the annexation of the territory of, another district, the first two additional directors so designated shall be resident voters of such consolidated or annexed territory. The board shall determine the term of office of each of the new directors so appointed, but in no event shall such term designated by the board be for more than four years. The terms of office thus created shall be determined in such a manner as to keep as nearly equal as practicable the number of directors to be elected at each subsequent general district election. Upon the expiration of such term so designated by the board, the membership shall be filled at the next general district election and general district elections held thereafter for the election of officers of the district.

Any references to five members of the board in this part mean seven members as applied to a board increased in size pursuant to this section. In the same manner, references to three members mean four members and to two members mean three members, and references to a four-fifths vote mean a five-sevenths vote, as applied to an enlarged board.

(Added by Stats. 1971, Ch. 385.)

6480.7.

If a consolidation involving the Capistrano Beach Sanitary District and the Dana Point Sanitary District is approved, the board of directors of the consolidated district shall initially consist of 10 members who shall be the members of the boards of directors of the two districts as of the effective date of the consolidation. Notwithstanding Section 56844 of the Government Code, those board members shall determine within 60 days from the effective date of the consolidation whether the board of directors shall consist of 5, 7, 9, or 11 members, and they shall further determine within that time the persons who shall thereafter be members of the board of directors. If those board members determine that the board of directors shall consist of 11 members, they shall appoint the eleventh member whose term shall be the same as the terms of the members of the board of directors whose terms will first expire. Upon making those determinations, the members so selected shall notify by resolution the Board of Supervisors and the Registrar of Voters of the County of Orange of the number of members and the names of the persons who have been selected or appointed as members of the board of directors, and of the expiration dates of their terms of office. If that selection and appointment process is not completed within 60 days of the effective date of the consolidation, the Board of Supervisors of the County of Orange shall determine the number of members of the board of directors and shall select the members of the board of directors from among those 10 persons, or call a special election for the election of the directors of the consolidated district on the next available election date. In that event, those 10 persons shall serve as the board of directors until the results of the special election are declared by the board of supervisors.

(Added by Stats. 1993, Ch. 1195, Sec. 19. Effective January 1, 1994.)

6481.

The board is the governing power of the district, and exercises all district powers, except the making of an assessment roll in the first instance.

(Enacted by Stats. 1939, Ch. 60.)

6482.

Except as to those members of the board who are elected at the election on formation, the term of office of each member of the board is four years and each holds office until the election and qualification of his successors or his resignation or termination of residence within the district.

(Amended by Stats. 1959, Ch. 156.)

6483.

Vacancies in the membership of the board shall be filled pursuant to Section 1780 of the Government Code.

(Amended by Stats. 1975, Ch. 1059.)

6484.

The members of the board elected at the election as a result of which the district was organized or, if the district is reorganized under this part, then the five members in office at the time of the reorganization shall, at their first meeting, or as soon thereafter as may be practicable, so classify themselves, by lot, that they shall go out of office as follows:

(a) Two shall serve until the election held in the first even-numbered year after the year in which the district is formed or reorganized, and until the election and qualification of their successors.

(b) Three shall serve until the second even-numbered year after the district is formed or reorganized, and until the election and qualification of their successors.

Notwithstanding any other provision of this part, except in districts that consolidate the election of directors with the direct primary election, the terms of office of members of the board in all districts existing on January 1, 1967, shall be determined as provided in Section 10507 of the Elections Code, and the terms of office of members of the board in all new districts shall be determined as provided in Section 10505 of the Elections Code.

(Amended by Stats. 1994, Ch. 923, Sec. 121. Effective January 1, 1995.)

6486.

At its first meeting, or as soon thereafter as may be practicable, the board shall choose one of its members as president, and shall appoint a secretary who may be a member of the board.

(Amended by Stats. 1945, Ch. 1337.)

6487.

All contracts, deeds, warrants, releases, receipts, and documents shall be signed in the name of the district by its president, and countersigned by its secretary, except that the board may, by resolution, authorize the district manager or other district employees specified by the board to sign contracts, warrants, releases, receipts, and similar documents in the name of the district.

(Amended by Stats. 1993, Ch. 1195, Sec. 20. Effective January 1, 1994.)

6488.

The board shall hold such meetings, either in the day or in the evening, as may be convenient.

In case of the absence or inability of the president or secretary to act, the board shall choose a president pro tem., or secretary pro tem., or both as the case may be.

(Enacted by Stats. 1939, Ch. 60.)

6489.

(a) Subject to subdivision (b), each of the members of the board shall receive compensation in an amount not to exceed one hundred dollars ($100) per day for each day's attendance at meetings of the board or for each day's service rendered as a director by request of the board, not exceeding a total of six days in any calendar month, together with any expenses incident thereto.

(b) The district board, by ordinance adopted pursuant to Chapter 2 (commencing with Section 20200) of Division 10 of the Water Code, may increase the compensation received by board members above the amount of one hundred dollars ($100) per day.

(c) The secretary of the sanitary board shall receive compensation to be set by the sanitary district board, which compensation shall be in lieu of any other compensation to which he or she may be entitled by reason of attendance at the meeting or meetings of the sanitary board.

(d) For purposes of this section, the determination of whether a director's activities on any specific day are compensable shall be made pursuant to Article 2.3 (commencing

with Section 53232) of Chapter 2 of Part 1 of Division 2 of Title 5 of the Government Code.

(e) Reimbursement for these expenses is subject to Sections 53232.2 and 53232.3 of the Government Code.

(Amended by Stats. 2005, Ch. 700, Sec. 12. Effective January 1, 2006.)

6490.

(a) A general regulation of the board shall be entered in its minutes, and shall be published once in a newspaper published in the district, if there is one, and if not, then it shall be posted for one week in three public places in the district.

(b) The publication or posting of general regulations, as required by subdivision (a), may be satisfied by either of the following actions:

(1) The board of directors may publish a summary of a proposed regulation or ordinance or proposed amendment to an existing regulation or ordinance. This summary shall be prepared by an official designated by the board. A summary shall be published along with the names of those board members voting for and against the regulation or ordinance or amendment, and a certified copy of the full text of the proposed regulation or ordinance or proposed amendment to same shall be posted in the office of the clerk of the board, along with the names of those board members voting for and against the regulation, ordinance, or amendment.

(2) If the official designated by the board determines that it is not feasible to prepare a fair and adequate summary of the regulation or ordinance or amendment to same, and if the board so orders, a display advertisement of at least one-quarter of a page in a newspaper published in the district shall be published. The advertisement shall indicate the general nature of, and provide information about, the regulation, ordinance, or amendment, including information sufficient to enable the public to obtain copies of the complete text of the regulation or ordinance or amendment to same, and the names of those board members voting for and against the regulation, ordinance, or amendment.

(c) A subsequent order of the board that publication or posting has been made is conclusive evidence that the publication or posting has been properly made.

(d) A general regulation takes effect upon expiration of the week of publication or posting.

(Amended by Stats. 1987, Ch. 1184, Sec. 9.)

6491.

Unless otherwise provided by this part, orders not establishing a general regulation need not be published or posted, but shall be entered in the minutes and shall take effect upon adoption.

(Amended by Stats. 1953, Ch. 765.)

6491.1.

The district board may, by general regulation, adopt codes or specifications controlling the manner of construction, repair, maintenance and operation of facilities referred to in Sections 6512 and 6522. Such codes or specifications need not be set out in full in such general regulation but may be incorporated therein by reference. Copies of such codes or specifications shall be available for examination in the office of the secretary at all times.

(Added by Stats. 1957, Ch. 1491.)

6491.2.

The district board may, by general regulation, adopt a code by reference in the same manner as legislative bodies of local agencies are authorized to adopt primary and secondary codes by reference pursuant to Section 50022.1 to 50022.8, inclusive, of the Government Code, and for the purposes of such sections of the Government Code the district board shall be deemed a legislative body and the district shall be deemed a local agency.

Any code adopted by the district board, by reference, shall impose restrictions equal to or greater than those imposed by the State Housing Law, Part 1.5 (commencing with Section 17910), Division 13 of this code, and the rules and regulations promulgated pursuant thereto by the Commission of Housing and Community Development.

No penalty clauses or sanctions contained in any code adopted by reference pursuant to this section shall be effective.

Every person who violates any provision of a general regulation adopted pursuant to this section or of a code adopted by reference in such general regulation is guilty of a misdemeanor.

(Amended by Stats. 1969, Ch. 39.)

6491.3.

Ordinances of the district may be enacted in the same manner as general regulations of the board and shall have the same force and effect as such general regulations.

(Added by Stats. 1971, Ch. 406.)

6491.5.

A district may destroy a record pursuant to Chapter 7 (commencing with Section 60200) of Division 1 of Title 6 of the Government Code.

(Added by Stats. 2005, Ch. 158, Sec. 22. Effective January 1, 2006.)

6492.

The board may instruct the district attorney of the county to commence and prosecute any or all actions and proceedings necessary or proper to enforce any of its regulations or orders, and may call upon him for advice as to any sanitary subject; and the district attorney shall obey the instructions and give advice when requested by the board.

(Enacted by Stats. 1939, Ch. 60.)

6492.5.

The board may provide, by resolution, that the health officer of the county in which the district is situated shall be the health officer of the district. Upon the adoption of such resolution, it shall be presented to the board of supervisors and, if it is approved by the board of supervisors, such county health officer shall become the ex officio health officer

of the district and it shall be his duty to give advice when requested by the board and to aid the district in doing any act necessary or proper to the complete exercise and effect of any of its powers, or for the purposes for which it is formed.
(Added by Stats. 1972, Ch. 158.)

6493.

The board may at any time employ special counsel for any purpose.
(Enacted by Stats. 1939, Ch. 60.)

6494.

There shall be an election for assessor in each even-numbered year in which members of the board are elected, and at the same time, place, and manner; provided, however, that if a district board has elected to avail itself of the county assessment roll for district taxation pursuant to Article 6 of Chapter 7 of this part, no assessor shall thereafter be elected until it shall again elect the use of its own tax roll.

The assessor holds office for two years, and until the election and qualification of his successor except that the first assessor elected holds office until the election and qualification of his successor.

If a vacancy occurs in the office of assessor, the board shall appoint a suitable person to fill the vacancy until the next election at which an assessor may be elected under this part.
(Amended by Stats. 1951, Ch. 584.)

6495.

The assessor's duties are fixed by this part and he shall perform such other duties as are ordered or required by the board.
(Enacted by Stats. 1939, Ch. 60.)

6496.

The assessor shall receive such compensation as shall be fixed by the board.
(Enacted by Stats. 1939, Ch. 60.)

6497.

(1) The sanitary board of sanitary districts may classify all the places of employment in or under the district, and in or under all the offices and departments of the district, with reference to the examinations hereinafter provided for. The places so classified by the sanitary board may constitute the classified civil service of the district, and no appointment to any such place shall be made except according to the rules hereinafter mentioned.

(2) The sanitary board may make rules to carry out the purposes of this section, and for examinations, appointments, promotions, and removals, and may from time to time make changes in existing rules. All rules and all changes therein shall be forthwith printed for distribution by the sanitary board.

(3) The examinations shall be practical in their character, and shall relate to those matters only which will fairly test the relative capacity of the persons examined to discharge the duties of the positions to which they seek to be appointed, and shall include, when appropriate, tests of manual or professional skill. The selection of laborers shall be governed by priority of application as far as may be practicable. No questions in any examination shall relate to political or religious opinions or affiliations. The sanitary board shall control all examinations.
(Amended by Stats. 1957, Ch. 1491.)

6499.

Any county officer required to act as an officer of the district and perform services for the district by virtue of his office, or any county health officer who becomes the ex officio health officer of the district pursuant to Section 6492.5, shall be entitled to reimbursement from the district for the reasonable and actual expenses incurred by him while acting on behalf of the district, to be paid into the county treasury. The amount of such reimbursement shall not exceed the actual expense which he incurred.
(Amended by Stats. 1972, Ch. 158.)

6500.

If a district has a boundary which is contiguous to the boundary of a city and the district has a contract with that city under which the city is responsible for the operation and maintenance of all facilities of the district, the governing board of the district may, by a resolution adopted by a $^4/_5$ vote of the board, declare the board dissolved and thereafter the governing body of the city shall be ex officio the governing board of the district.
(Added by Stats. 1965, Ch. 588.)

6501.

By resolution, the board may change the name of the district. Any name resulting from a change shall include the words "Sanitary District" or shall be a name that is descriptive of the functions of the district. The change of name shall be effective upon recording a certified copy in the office of the county recorder of the county or counties in which the district is situated.
(Amended by Stats. 1998, Ch. 829, Sec. 38. Effective January 1, 1999.)

CHAPTER 4. District Powers [6510 - 6550.26]

(Chapter 4 enacted by Stats. 1939, Ch. 60.)

ARTICLE 1. Generally [6510 - 6523.3]

(Article 1 enacted by Stats. 1939, Ch. 60.)

6510.

A district may use a seal, alterable at the pleasure of the board.
(Enacted by Stats. 1939, Ch. 60.)

6511.

It may sue and be sued by its name.

(Enacted by Stats. 1939, Ch. 60.)

6512.

(a) A district may acquire, plan, construct, reconstruct, alter, enlarge, lay, renew, replace, maintain, and operate garbage dumpsites and garbage collection and disposal systems, sewers, drains, septic tanks, and sewerage collection, outfall, treatment works and other sanitary disposal systems, and storm water drains and storm water collection, outfall and disposal systems, and water recycling and distribution systems, as the board deems necessary and proper, and in the performance of these functions, either in or out of the district, it may join through joint powers agreements pursuant to the provisions of Chapter 5 (commencing with Section 6500) of Division 7 of Title 1 of the Government Code, or through other means with any county or municipality or any other district or governmental agency.

(b) Before any garbage dump is established, the location shall first be approved by the county health officer, and, in addition, if the location is within two miles of any city, the consent of the governing body of the city shall first be secured.

(c) (1) If the district includes any part of a city, water district, or other local agency that provides water service to any territory in the district, the district shall not supply water service to the territory unless the district first obtains the consent of the city, water district, or other local agency. The consent shall not be revoked, if the revocation will result in a decrease of the revenues available to pay the outstanding bonds of the district.

(2) Paragraph (1) does not apply to the provision of recycled water by a district.

(3) (A) Subject to subparagraph (B), a district may not supply water service using recycled water to the territory of any part of a city, water district, or other local public entity providing water service, or commence construction of facilities for that service, prior to offering to consult with that city, water district, or other local public entity, and providing notification of availability for consultation. The obligation to consult terminates if that local public entity providing water service fails to make itself available for consultation within 60 days of written notification to that local public entity.

(B) The consultation and notification requirements described in subparagraph (A) do not apply to a district if the district, prior to supplying water or commencing construction as described in subparagraph (A), provides notification to the local public entity pursuant to Section 65604 of the Government Code or submits a written request to the local public entity pursuant to subdivision (b) of Section 13580 of the Water Code.

(d) The Department of Water Resources may assist sanitary districts in applying for, and in obtaining approval of, federal and state funding and permits for cost-effective water recycling projects and shall confer and cooperate with the legislative body of the district during the application and approval process.
(Amended by Stats. 2002, Ch. 261, Sec. 2. Effective January 1, 2003.)

6512.5.

Notwithstanding any other provision of law, for the purpose of furnishing water in the district for any present or future beneficial use, the Winton Sanitary District may exercise any of the powers of a county water district, including the power to acquire, operate, finance, and control water rights, works, property, rights, and privileges useful or necessary to convey, supply, store, or make use of water for any useful purpose, all in the same manner as county water districts formed under the County Water District Law (Division 12 (commencing with Section 30000) of the Water Code). However, the Winton Sanitary District shall otherwise continue to be governed in all respects as a sanitary district under the provisions of this part, and the provisions of this section are intended only to vest additional powers in the district which the district may elect to exercise.
(Added by Stats. 1982, Ch. 1360, Sec. 1.)

6512.6.

Notwithstanding any other provision of law, for the purpose of furnishing water in the district for any present or future beneficial use, the Lost Hills Sanitary District may exercise any of the powers of a county water district, including the power to acquire, operate, finance, and control water rights, works, property, rights, and privileges useful or necessary to convey, supply, store, or make use of water for any useful purpose, all in the same manner as county water districts formed under the County Water District Law (Division 12 (commencing with Section 30000) of the Water Code). However, the Lost Hills Sanitary District shall otherwise continue to be governed in all respects as a sanitary district under the provisions of this part, and the provisions of this section are intended only to vest additional powers in the district which the district may elect to exercise.
(Added by Stats. 1986, Ch. 106, Sec. 1. Effective May 27, 1986.)

6512.7.

(a) Notwithstanding Section 6512 and the Cortese-Knox-Hertzberg Local Government Reorganization Act of 2000 (Division 3 (commencing with Section 56000) of Title 5 of the Government Code), for the purpose of furnishing water in the district for any present or future beneficial use, the Montara Sanitary District may, pursuant to subdivision (b), exercise any of the powers of a county water district, including the power to acquire, operate, finance, and control water rights, works, property, rights and privileges useful or necessary to convey, supply, store or make use of water for any useful purpose, all in the same manner as county water districts formed under the County Water District Law (Division 12 (commencing with Section 30000) of the Water Code). The Montara Sanitary District shall otherwise continue to be governed in all respects as a sanitary district under this part, and the provisions of this section are intended only to vest additional powers in the district which the district may elect to exercise.

(b) If the governing body of the Montara Sanitary District determines, by resolution, entered in the minutes, that it is feasible, economically sound, and in the public interest for the district to exercise the powers specified in subdivision (a), the governing body shall submit to the electors of the district the question of whether the district should adopt those additional powers. The question submitted to the electors shall be in substantially the following form: "Shall the Montara Sanitary District exercise the powers of a county water district for the purpose of furnishing water in the district?" The district may exercise those powers only if a majority of the voters voting on the proposition vote in favor of the question. The costs of that election, including any additional costs incurred by the County of San Mateo for purposes of meeting legal requirements directly associated with the conduct of the election, shall be borne by the district.

(c) If the electors of the district authorize the district to exercise the powers specified in subdivision (a), the district shall include in any revenue plan developed as part of its exercise of those powers an item to reimburse the County of San Mateo the sum of one hundred eighteen thousand dollars ($118,000) for costs incurred with respect to its effort to acquire the existing water system serving the Montara Sanitary District service area. Reimbursement to the county shall occur within 180 days after the district receives any revenues from the sale of bonds, the levy of assessments, or the receipt of any other revenues to be used by the district in the exercise of its powers pursuant to this section.

(d) If the Montara Sanitary District assumes authority to exercise the powers of a county water district pursuant to this section, thereafter the district shall be subject to the Cortese-Knox-Hertzberg Local Government Reorganization Act of 2000 (Division 3 (commencing with Section 56000) of Title 5 of the Government Code).

(e) In enacting this section it is the intent of the Legislature that any service by the Montara Sanitary District not affect the approval or development of a project that includes units for lower income persons, as defined in Section 50079.5, and persons and families of moderate income, as defined in Section 50093.

(f) Upon request of the governing body of the Montara Sanitary District, the County of San Mateo shall provide the district with all books, papers, records, documents and other information, including all writings as defined in Section 250 of the Evidence Code, resulting from, or produced by, the expenditure of funds by the county to determine if the acquisition of the existing water system serving the Montara Sanitary District service area is feasible.

(Amended by Stats. 2003, Ch. 296, Sec. 22. Effective January 1, 2004.)

6513.
It may permit the use of any property of the district by any county or municipality, or any other district or governmental agency.
(Amended by Stats. 1944, 4th Ex. Sess., Ch. 53.)

6514.
It may, for the purposes specified in this part, acquire by purchase, gift, devise, condemnation proceedings, or otherwise, such real and personal property and rights of way, either within or without the limits of the district, as in the judgment of the board are necessary or proper to the exercise of its powers, and particularly for the purpose of permitting ingress to and egress from such real or personal property, and pay for and hold them, and it may dispose of such of its property as the board finds to be no longer required for the purposes of the district.

The district shall not condemn property outside of the county or counties in which it is located unless the board of supervisors of each county in which such property is located has consented to such acquisition by resolution.
(Amended by Stats. 1961, Ch. 1629.)

6514.1.
(a) A district may lease, for a term not exceeding 99 years, subject to periodic review, district property that will not be needed for district purposes during the term of the lease, as a means of providing revenues to the district for the operation and maintenance of sanitary sewer system and waste water treatment and disposal facilities of the district, and to finance the acquisition, construction, and improvement of these facilities.

(b) Prior to entering into a lease, the board shall, except as otherwise provided in subdivision (e), publish notice pursuant to Section 6066 of the Government Code of the time and place of the meeting of the board at which the proposed lease will be considered, and at that time and place shall afford all persons present an opportunity to be heard with respect to the proposed lease.

(c) If the board finds that the subject property will not be needed by the district and that it is in the best interests of the district and the users of its sanitary sewer system that the lease be entered into, it may, by ordinance setting forth the findings, authorize the lease. The ordinance shall be subject to Article 2 (commencing with Section 9340) of Chapter 4 of Division 9 of the Elections Code.

(d) Every lease shall be awarded to the bidder which, in the determination of the legislative body, offers the greatest economic return to the district after competitive bidding conducted in the manner determined by the legislative body. Notice inviting bids may be published pursuant to Section 6066 in one or more newspapers of general circulation within the district.

(e) If the board makes a finding at a noticed public hearing that the subject property will be used for compatible uses, that it will be of public benefit, and that the term of the lease will not exceed 10 years, subdivisions (c) and (d) shall be optional.
(Amended by Stats. 1994, Ch. 923, Sec. 122. Effective January 1, 1995.)

6515.
It may make and accept contracts, deeds, releases, and documents that, in the judgment of the board, are necessary or proper in the exercise of any of the powers of the district.
(Enacted by Stats. 1939, Ch. 60.)

6516.
It may pay lawful claims and demands against it.
(Enacted by Stats. 1939, Ch. 60.)

6517.
It may employ and pay necessary agents and assistants.
(Enacted by Stats. 1939, Ch. 60.)

6518.
It may lay its sewers and drains in any public street or road in the county, and for this purpose enter upon it and make all necessary and proper excavations, restoring it to proper condition. The work of restoring and repairing any such public street or road in the county shall be done under the supervision and control of the county engineer or road commissioner at the cost of the district, and in accordance with the standards established by ordinance of the board of supervisors for restoring and repairing county roads. If the street or road is in a city the consent of the proper city authorities shall first be obtained. If the street or road is in the unincorporated area of the county, the consent of the proper county authorities shall first be obtained.
(Amended by Stats. 1953, Ch. 1568.)

6518.5.
It may collect waste and garbage.
(Added by Stats. 1939, Ch. 303.)

6519.
It may call and conduct all necessary or proper elections.
(Enacted by Stats. 1939, Ch. 60.)

6520.
It may compel all residents and property owners in the district to connect their houses and habitations and structures requiring sewerage or drainage disposal service with the sewers and storm drains in streets and to use the garbage collection and disposal system.
(Amended by Stats. 1944, 4th Ex. Sess., Ch. 53.)

6520.1.
It may prohibit any resident or property owner in the district from connecting any house, habitation, or structure requiring sewerage or drainage disposal service to any privately owned sewer or storm drain in the district.
(Added by Stats. 1961, Ch. 1090.)

6520.2.
It may require any resident or property owner in the district who desires to have any house, habitation, or structure connected to a sewer or drainage disposal line owned by the district to pay his proportionate share of the cost of the line, either by an increased installation charge or by other arrangement with the district, if he did not contribute to the cost of the acquisition, construction, or installation of the line by the district.
(Added by Stats. 1961, Ch. 1090.)

6520.3.
Any sanitary district and any county may enter into a contract agreeing to pay and apportion between them the costs of locating, removing, repairing, or relocating any facilities owned or to be owned by either party on the roads or other property of the other in such proportion and upon such terms as the governing boards of the parties shall determine to be equitable.
(Added by Stats. 1967, Ch. 164.)

6520.5.
It may, by an order approved by a two-thirds vote of the members of the board, prescribe, revise and collect, fees, tolls, rates, rentals, or other charges for services and facilities furnished by it in connection with its sanitation or sewerage systems. Revenues derived by the district under the provisions of this section may be used for any purpose except the acquisition or construction of additional local street sewers or laterals which are an augmentation to an existing sewer system.
(Amended by Stats. 1965, Ch. 850.)

6520.6.
The district board may, by resolution, abandon action for the collection of any district tax assessment, connection charge, service charge, penalty, cost, fee, assessment, fine, or other money owed the district under this part or pursuant to any other provision of law which the district board determines is in an amount too small to justify the cost of collection. Such a resolution shall discharge all district officers and employees, and any other public officer or employee charged with the collection thereof, from further accountability with respect to collection of the amount owed. However, the resolution shall not extinguish the claim nor constitute a release of any person from liability for the payment of any amounts which are due and owing.

The addition of this section does not constitute a change in, but is declaratory of, the preexisting law.
(Added by Stats. 1976, Ch. 221.)

6520.7.
It may sell, or otherwise dispose of, any water, sewage effluent, fertilizer, or other byproduct resulting from the operation of a sewerage system, sewage disposal plant, refuse disposal plant or process, or treatment plant, and construct, maintain, and operate such pipelines and other works as may be necessary for that purpose.

The addition of this section made at the 1972 Regular Session of the Legislature does not constitute a change in, but is declaratory of, the existing law.
(Added by Stats. 1972, Ch. 352.)

6520.9.
It may construct, maintain, and operate such pipelines or other works as may be necessary to conserve and put to beneficial use any water or recycled effluent recovered from the operation of the wastewater system, plant, or works, by sale or disposition for agricultural or industrial purposes, or by discharging or spreading the water or recycled effluent in such a manner as to percolate into the underground gravels and replenish the natural water resources.

The addition of this section made at the 1972 Regular Session of the Legislature does not constitute a change in, but is declaratory of, the existing law.

(Amended by Stats. 1995, Ch. 28, Sec. 7. Effective January 1, 1996.)

6520.10.

On or before August 10, the board may certify to the board of supervisors and county auditor a statement of any delinquent and unpaid charges for sewer and other services, or either, requested in writing by the owner of the property that remain delinquent and unpaid for a period of 60 days or more on July 1.

The amount of any charges for sewer and other services, or either, included in the statement of delinquent and unpaid charges shall be added to and become a part of the annual taxes next levied upon the property for which the sewer service was provided and upon the property subject to the charges for any other district services and shall constitute a lien on that property as of the same time and in the same manner as does the tax lien securing the annual taxes. All laws applicable to the levy, collection, and enforcement of ad valorem taxes shall be applicable to the charges, except that if any real property to which the lien would attach has been transferred or conveyed to a bona fide purchaser for value, or if a lien of a bona fide encumbrancer for value has been created and attaches thereon prior to the date on which the first installment of the taxes would become delinquent, then the lien which would otherwise be imposed by this section shall not attach to the real property and the charges relating to the property shall be transferred to the unsecured roll for collection. The county shall deduct from the charges collected an amount sufficient to compensate the county for costs incurred in collecting the delinquent and unpaid charges. The amount of the compensation shall be fixed by agreement between the board of supervisors and the district's board of directors.

(Added by Stats. 1991, Ch. 248, Sec. 4.)

6520.11.

A district shall notify the assessee shown on the latest equalized assessment roll whenever delinquent and unpaid charges for sewer and other services, or either, which could become a lien on the property pursuant to Section 6520.10 remain delinquent and unpaid for 60 days.

(Added by Stats. 1991, Ch. 248, Sec. 5.)

6520.12.

In the event any charges for sewer and other services, or either, remain unpaid the amount of the unpaid charges may in the discretion of the district be secured at any time by recording in the office of the county recorder of any county, a certificate specifying the amount of the charges and the name and address of the person liable therefor.

From the time of recordation of the certificate, the amount required to be paid together with interest and penalty constitutes a lien upon all real property in the county owned by the person or afterwards, and before the lien expires, acquired by him or her. The lien has the force, priority, and effect of a judgment lien and shall continue for 10 years from the date of the recording of the certificate unless sooner released or otherwise discharged. The lien may, within 10 years from the recording of the certificate or within 10 years from the date of the last extension of the lien in the manner herein provided, be extended by recording a new certificate in the office of the county recorder of any county and from the time of the recording the lien shall be extended to the real property in the county for 10 years unless sooner released or otherwise discharged.

(Added by Stats. 1991, Ch. 248, Sec. 6.)

6521.

It may make and enforce all necessary and proper regulations for:

(a) The removal of garbage.

(b) The cleanliness of the roads and streets of the district.

(c) All other sanitary purposes not in conflict with the laws of this State.

(Enacted by Stats. 1939, Ch. 60.)

6521.5.

Any district may exercise the power granted to sanitation districts by Section 4765 of this code.

(Added by Stats. 1949, Ch. 1018.)

6522.

It may do any act necessary or proper to the complete exercise and effect of any of its powers, or for the purposes for which it is formed.

(Enacted by Stats. 1939, Ch. 60.)

6522.1.

No regulation or ordinance of a district which regulates or prescribes standards for the installation of plumbing inside of buildings and structures, shall be effective within any county, city and county, or city which has adopted an ordinance, regulation, or code incorporated in an ordinance governing such installations.

(Added by Stats. 1953, Ch. 1155.)

6523.

A violation of a regulation or ordinance of a district is a misdemeanor punishable by imprisonment in the county jail not to exceed 30 days, or by a fine not to exceed one thousand dollars ($1,000), or by both.

(Amended by Stats. 1976, Ch. 651.)

6523.1.

It may borrow money and incur indebtedness and guarantee the performance of its legal or contractual obligations whether heretofore or hereafter incurred; and also refund or retire any public indebtedness or lien that may exist or be created against the district or any property therein which shall have arisen out of the transaction of the affairs of the district.

(Added by Stats. 1947, Ch. 1375.)

6523.2.

In order to effect its powers, it may enter upon private property for the purpose of inspection and maintenance of sanitary and waste disposal facilities and may terminate service to property in which a violation of any rule or regulation is found to exist.

Prior to termination of service, however, the district board shall notify, in writing, the owner and tenant, if any, of such property that service is intended to be so terminated and conduct a hearing thereon as herein provided. Such notice shall be mailed to the owner at the address shown on the records of the assessor of the county or as known to the clerk, and a copy shall be delivered to the tenant or posted conspicuously on the property. The notice shall state the date of proposed termination of service and the reasons therefor and the date the district board shall hold a hearing upon such intended termination. Such hearing shall not be held less than 10 days subsequent to the giving of notice as herein required.

(Added by Stats. 1959, Ch. 1068.)

6523.3.

In order to enforce the provisions of any ordinance of the district, the district may correct any violation of an ordinance of the district. The cost of such correction may be added to any sewer service charge payable by the person violating the ordinance or the owner or tenant of the property upon which the violation occurred, and the district shall have such remedies for the collection of such costs as it has for the collection of sewer service charges. The district may also petition the superior court for the issuance of a preliminary or permanent injunction, or both, as may be appropriate, restraining any person from the continued violation of any ordinance of the district.

(Added by Stats. 1971, Ch. 406.)

ARTICLE 1.5. Inclusion in County Sanitation District [6524 - 6529]

(Article 1.5 added by Stats. 1947, Ch. 1375.)

6524.

Any district organized under the provisions of this act may become a part of a county sanitation district after the board of supervisors of the county within which the district is located, has, after a hearing, pursuant to the County Sanitation District Act, found and determined by resolution duly adopted that such inclusion is for the best interest of the district and the governing body of the district consents thereto by resolution adopted by the affirmative vote of four-fifths of its members.

(Added by Stats. 1947, Ch. 1375.)

6525.

A sanitary district which becomes a part of a county sanitation district as hereinabove provided for is not thereby dissolved, but may continue to function, except as herein otherwise provided, in the same manner as heretofore.

(Added by Stats. 1947, Ch. 1375.)

6526.

When a sanitary district is not included in a county sanitation district at the time of formation of the latter, it may subsequently become included within such county sanitation district, upon its sanitary board adopting a resolution, by the affirmative vote of four-fifths of its members, declaring its intention so to do.

(Added by Stats. 1947, Ch. 1375.)

6527.

Following the formation of such county sanitation district it shall have no jurisdiction within such sanitary district until the legislative body of such sanitary district shall, by resolution adopted by the affirmative vote of no less than four-fifths of its members, determine what facilities and functions of constructing, maintaining and operating sanitary sewerage facilities of such sanitary district shall be transferred to such county sanitation district.

(Added by Stats. 1947, Ch. 1375.)

6528.

Copies of the resolutions herein mentioned, duly certified by the clerk or secretary of the respective legislative bodies, shall be filed with the county clerk, in the respective files of such sanitary district and county sanitation district, and with the county assessor, and such resolutions shall not be effective until said copies are so filed.

(Added by Stats. 1947, Ch. 1375.)

6529.

Nothing herein shall prevent any territory within a county sanitation district from being formed into or annexed to any sanitary district, and such territory shall thereafter become subject to this article.

(Added by Stats. 1947, Ch. 1375.)

ARTICLE 2. Sewer Maintenance in Cities [6530 - 6531]

(Article 2 enacted by Stats. 1939, Ch. 60.)

6530.

At any time after the sewer or other sanitary system is constructed the governing body of any city lying within the limits of the district may elect to keep and maintain the lateral sewer lying within the city in order to keep and repair and may enter into an agreement with the board to do so.

From the date of the agreement the governing body shall keep the lateral in repair and the board is not required to keep it in order or repair.

After a city elects to keep the lateral sewers within its corporate limits in order and repair the property within the corporate limits of the city shall not be taxed for running expenses necessary to keep and maintain the lateral sewer lying within the city in order and repair but shall be taxed for the inspection and repairs of the main sewers lying within the city together with the expense of those functions other than sewerage collection within the city performed by the district pursuant to Section 6512 hereof.

(Amended by Stats. 1949, Ch. 1201.)

6530.1.

Whenever any portion of a district has been included within a city by annexation, incorporation, or otherwise, the governing body of such city may elect, upon agreement by the district, to construct new storm water drains and storm water collection, outfall and disposal facilities within the city limits, and acquire title to and reconstruct, alter, enlarge, renew, replace, maintain and operate existing storm water drains and storm water collection, outfall and disposal facilities, lying within the city and may enter into an agreement with the board to do so.

From the date fixed in the agreement the city shall have exclusive jurisdiction to perform the functions described in the first paragraph of this section and in the agreement in that portion of the district lying within the city, and the board is not required to exercise any functions pertaining to such storm water drains and storm water collection, outfall and disposal facilities, and is relieved of all liability in connection therewith.

If the city elects to perform such functions within the city, the property within the corporate limits of the city shall not be taxed by the district for any costs necessary to construct, maintain, and keep in repair such storm drains and storm water collection, outfall and disposal facilities lying within the city which are taxed by the city for those functions, other than storm drains and storm water collection, outfall and disposal facilities within the city which continue to be owned, maintained and operated by the district pursuant to Section 6512 of this code.

(Added by Stats. 1961, Ch. 419.)

6531.

Where an entire district shall have heretofore become located within the boundaries of a city by reason of the incorporation thereof, and said district shall have continued thereafter to function as a sanitary district, and no court having jurisdiction of the subject matter shall have adjudicated that said district has merged with said city, and a portion of the boundary of said district shall thereafter have become extended beyond the territorial limits of said city by reason of annexation thereto, said district shall during all said times be and constitute a legally existing sanitary district and shall not thereafter be deemed or adjudged to have merged with said city by reason of said original inclusion therein.

(Added by Stats. 1949, Ch. 977.)

ARTICLE 3. Application of Other Statutes [6540 - 6544]
(Article 3 enacted by Stats. 1939, Ch. 60.)

6540.

The governing board may order the construction of sewers, drains, septic tanks, and sewerage collection, outfall, treatment works and other sanitary disposal systems, and storm water drains and storm water collection, outfall and disposal systems, and appurtenances and appurtenant work in the whole or any portion of any of the streets, highways, or public places either in or out of the district, or in property or in rights of way owned by the district, and acquire property, rights of way, and easements therefor, and may provide that the cost shall be assessed upon the fronting lots and lands or on a special assessment district; provided, that said district shall first obtain the consent to said work and the assumption of jurisdiction thereover from the legislative body having jurisdiction of the territory within which any of the proposed work is to be done; and provided further, that if any of the territory proposed to be assessed shall be outside the boundaries of the district, the consent of the legislative body having jurisdiction over such territory shall be obtained to the formation of the special assessment district.

(Amended by Stats. 1953, Ch. 765.)

6541.

The Improvement Act of 1911, the Improvement Bond Act of 1915, and the Municipal Improvement Act of 1913 are applicable to districts.

(Amended by Stats. 1974, Ch. 426.)

6542.

In the application of those acts to proceedings under this article the terms used in those acts shall have the following meanings:

(a) "City council" and "council" mean board.

(b) "City" and "municipality" mean district.

(c) "Clerk" and "city clerk" mean secretary.

(d) "Superintendent of streets," "street superintendent," and "city engineer" mean the engineer of the district, or any other person appointed to perform the duties.

(e) "Tax collector" means county tax collector.

(f) "Treasurer" and "city treasurer" mean any person or official who has charge of and makes payment of the funds of the district.

(g) "Right-of-way" means any parcel of land in, on, under or through which a right-of-way or easement has been granted to the district for the purpose of constructing and maintaining any of the works or improvements mentioned in Section 6540.

(h) "Health officer" means the health officer appointed by the legislative body having jurisdiction over all or any portion of the territory to be served by any of the works mentioned in Section 6540, except that as to cities that have consented to or contracted for health administration by the county health officer pursuant to Article 2 (commencing with Section 101375) of, or Article 3 (commencing with Section 101400) of, Chapter 4 of Part 3 of Division 101, it shall mean the county health officer.

(Amended by Stats. 1996, Ch. 1023, Sec. 189. Effective September 29, 1996.)

6543.

The powers and duties conferred by those acts and supplementary acts upon boards, officers, and agents of cities shall be exercised by the respective boards, officers, and agents of the district.

(Enacted by Stats. 1939, Ch. 60.)

6544.

The improvements authorized to be constructed or acquired by this article are restricted to those permitted to be constructed or acquired by such districts under Article 1 of this chapter.

(Added by Stats. 1941, Ch. 1072.)

ARTICLE 4. Improvement Districts [6550.1 - 6550.26]
(Article 4 added by Stats. 1968, Ch. 1055.)

6550.1.

An improvement district may be formed to undertake any project for any one or more of the purposes stated in Section 6512 that is of special benefit to the area of such improvement district, including in any such project, any required investigation, study, analysis, appraisal or financing plan.

(Added by Stats. 1968, Ch. 1055.)

6550.2.

The formation of an improvement district shall be initiated by a resolution of the district board which shall contain all of the following:

(a) A description of the proposed boundaries of the improvement district proposed to be formed.

(b) A brief general description of the project proposed to be undertaken within such improvement district.

(c) A statement that the proposed project will be a special benefit to such improvement district.

(d) A statement of the district board's intention to undertake the project.

(e) An estimate of the cost of the proposed project.

(f) The method by which the proposed project is proposed to be financed, including the amount of bonded debt, if any, to be incurred; and, to the extent that the project is to be financed by taxes levied in such improvement district for purposes other than the payment of the principal of, and interest on, bonds, the proposed maximum amount of such tax which may be levied in any year, which maximum shall not exceed one dollar ($1) per one hundred dollars ($100) of the assessed value of the taxable property in such improvement district.

(g) The time, place, and date for a hearing by the district board on the matters stated in such resolution, which shall be not less than 15 nor more than 60 days after the date of adoption of the resolution initiating formation proceedings.

(Added by Stats. 1968, Ch. 1055.)

6550.3.

The secretary shall give notice of the time and place of the hearing by causing a copy of the resolution adopted pursuant to Section 6550.2 to be published for the time provided by Section 6066 of the Government Code in a newspaper of general circulation, circulated in the proposed improvement district, but if there is no such newspaper, then in one circulated in the county in which the proposed improvement district is situated. The secretary shall also mail copies of the resolution to all landowners owning land within the proposed improvement district.

(Added by Stats. 1968, Ch. 1055.)

6550.4.

The hearing on the proposed improvement district shall be held by the board of directors upon the date and at the time specified in the resolution initiating proceedings. At the hearing the board of directors shall hear and receive any oral or written protests, objections, or evidence which shall be made, presented, or filed. Any person who shall have filed a written protest may withdraw the same at any time prior to the conclusion of the hearing.

(Added by Stats. 1968, Ch. 1055.)

6550.5.

The district board shall have power to change the boundaries of the proposed improvement district, the project to be undertaken, the estimate of the cost of the project, the method by which the project is to be financed, or any two or more of such matters; provided, however, that the board shall not change such boundaries so as to include any territory which will not, in its judgment, be benefited by such improvement and shall exclude from the proposed improvement district any territory which it finds will not be benefited by inclusion therein.

(Added by Stats. 1968, Ch. 1055.)

6550.6.

If the district board proposes to change the boundaries of the proposed improvement district by adding territory thereto, the project, the estimate of cost, or the method by which the project is to be financed or to increase the proposed maximum amount of the tax, it shall state the proposed change and the time and place for a hearing thereon in a resolution and give notice of such hearing in the manner required by Section 6550.3. At the time and place fixed for the hearing, or at any time and place to which the hearing is adjourned, the district board shall continue with the hearing. At the hearing any person interested, including any person owning property within the district or within the proposed improvement district, may appear and present any matters material to the changes stated in the notice.

(Added by Stats. 1968, Ch. 1055.)

6550.7.

If prior to the conclusion of the hearing written protests against the formation of the proposed improvement district or the proposed project signed by the current holders of title to taxable property within the proposed improvement district which, as shown by the last equalized assessment roll, constitutes more than one-half of the total assessed value of taxable property within the proposed improvement district, are filed with the district board, further proceedings relating to the proposed improvement district and the proposed project shall be terminated and no proceedings for the formation of any improvement district to undertake the proposed project shall be instituted for a period of six months following the date of the conclusion of the hearing.

Where taxable property is owned in joint tenancy, tenancy in common, or any other multiple ownership, the first one of such owners who signs the written protest shall commit all such property to the protest.
(Added by Stats. 1968, Ch. 1055.)

6550.8.

At the conclusion of the hearing, if the proceedings are not terminated pursuant to Section 6550.7, the district board shall by resolution determine whether it is deemed necessary to form the improvement district and to undertake the project and, if so, the amount of any proposed debt to be incurred to finance the project, that the exterior boundaries of the portion of the district which will be benefited are set forth on a map on file with the district board (which map shall govern for all details as to the extent of the improvement district), and that such portion of the district set forth on such map shall thereupon constitute and be known as "Improvement District No. ___ of _____ (name of sanitary district)," and the determination made in said resolution shall be final and conclusive. After the formation of such improvement district within a sanitary district, all proceedings for the purpose of any bond election for the project for which the improvement district was formed shall be limited and shall apply only to such improvement district, and taxes for the payment of such bonds and the interest thereon, shall be derived exclusively from an annual tax upon the taxable property in such improvement district.
(Added by Stats. 1968, Ch. 1055.)

6550.9.

When the district board has made its determinations as provided in Section 6550.8, and if the board deems it necessary to incur a bonded indebtedness to finance the project for which the improvement district was formed, the board shall by resolution call a special election in such improvement district for the purpose of submitting to the qualified voters thereof, the proposition of incurring such indebtedness by the issuance of bonds of the district for such improvement district. Such resolution shall state:
(a) That the board deems it necessary to incur the bonded indebtedness.
(b) The purpose for which the bonded indebtedness will be incurred.
(c) The amount of debt to be incurred.
(d) The name of the improvement district to be benefited by such indebtedness, and that a map showing the exterior boundaries of such improvement district is on file with the district board, which map shall govern for all details as to the extent of the improvement district.
(e) That taxes for the payment of such bonds and the interest thereon shall be derived exclusively from an annual tax upon the taxable property in such improvement district.
(f) The maximum term the bonds proposed to be issued shall run before maturity, which shall not exceed 40 years.
(g) The maximum rate of interest to be paid, which shall not be more than the rate specified in this part for bonds of the district, payable at the times specified in this chapter for bonds of the district.
(h) The measure to be submitted to the voters.
(i) The date of the election.
(j) The election precincts, polling places and election officers.
(Added by Stats. 1968, Ch. 1055.)

6550.10.

Except as otherwise provided in this article, notice of the election shall be given and the election shall be held and conducted in the same manner as elections for the authorization of bonds of the entire sanitary district, and if two-thirds of the votes cast are in favor of incurring the bonded indebtedness, as proposed, bonds of the district, issued in the name of the district and designated "Bonds of _____ (naming the sanitary district) for Improvement District No. ___", shall be issued and sold for the amount stated in the resolution calling the election in the same form and manner as bonds of the entire sanitary district. Each bond of the district for an improvement district and all interest coupons thereof, shall state that taxes for the payment thereof shall be derived exclusively from an annual tax upon the taxable property in the improvement district.
(Added by Stats. 1968, Ch. 1055.)

6550.11.

No irregularities or informalities in conducting such election shall invalidate the same, if the election shall have otherwise been fairly conducted. Any action or proceedings, wherein the validity of the formation of the improvement district or of any bonds issued for it or of the proceedings in relation thereto is contested, questioned or denied, shall be commenced within three months from the date of such election; otherwise, such bonds and all proceedings in relation thereto, including the formation of the improvement district, shall be held to be valid and in every respect legal and incontestable.
(Added by Stats. 1968, Ch. 1055.)

6550.12.

Any moneys required to be raised from taxes for the purpose of paying the principal of and interest on bonds of the district for an improvement district shall be derived exclusively from an annual tax upon the taxable property in the improvement district of such sanitary district, and all the taxable property within the improvement district of such sanitary district shall be and remain liable to be taxed for such payments. The district board shall annually, at the time and in the manner of levying other district taxes, levy and cause to be collected a tax upon the taxable property in the improvement district, based upon the last equalized assessment roll of the district, sufficient to pay the interest on the bonds for that year and such portion of the principal as is to become due before

the time for making the next general tax levy. Such bonds and the interest thereon shall not be taxable in this state.
(Added by Stats. 1968, Ch. 1055.)

6550.13.

Subject to such limitations as may be contained in the resolution declaring the improvement district to be formed, the district board shall have the power in any year to cause taxes to be levied and collected in any improvement district to finance any project of such improvement district and to pay the costs of administration, maintenance, and operation of any works or facilities of, or for, such improvement district.
(Added by Stats. 1968, Ch. 1055.)

6550.14.

The procedure for levying and collecting taxes in any improvement district shall be the same as is provided in Chapter 7 (commencing at Section 6695) of this part for taxes on property in districts.
(Added by Stats. 1968, Ch. 1055.)

6550.15.

All taxes collected pursuant to this article shall be expended only for the payment of bond principal and interest, or only for the improvement district project for which levied, except that any surplus tax proceeds levied otherwise than for payment of bond principal and interest which remain after the completion of any improvement district project for which levied shall be transferred to the bond interest and redemption fund of such improvement district, if any, otherwise to the district's general fund.
(Added by Stats. 1968, Ch. 1055.)

6550.16.

For the purpose of any tax levied under this article, the properties within any improvement district shall be deemed to be equally benefited.
(Added by Stats. 1968, Ch. 1055.)

6550.17.

Territory within a district, but not a part of an improvement district created pursuant to this article, may be annexed to such improvement district whether or not contiguous thereto.
(Added by Stats. 1968, Ch. 1055.)

6550.18.

Annexation of territory to an improvement district shall be initiated by a resolution of the district board which shall contain at least all of the following:
(a) A description of the territory proposed to be annexed.
(b) A statement that the area to be annexed to the improvement district will be benefited by such annexation.
(c) The time, place, and date for a hearing by the district board on the proposed annexation, which shall not be less than 15 nor more than 60 days after the date of adoption of the resolution initiating annexation proceedings.
(d) Any additional matters which the district board may determine are necessary or convenient to the annexation proceedings.
(Added by Stats. 1968, Ch. 1055.)

6550.19.

The resolution shall be published and notice of the hearing on the proposed annexation shall be given, in the manner required by Section 6550.3, except that in applying such section the words "improvement district" shall mean the territory proposed to be annexed.
(Added by Stats. 1968, Ch. 1055.)

6550.20.

The hearing on the proposed annexation shall be held in the manner required by Section 6550.4, except that in applying such section the words, "improvement district" shall mean the territory proposed to be annexed.
(Added by Stats. 1968, Ch. 1055.)

6550.21.

The district board shall have the power to change the boundaries of territory proposed to be annexed to an improvement district, but shall not include any territory which, in its judgment, will not be benefited by inclusion within the improvement district, nor shall it exclude any territory which it finds would be benefited by inclusion within the improvement district.
(Added by Stats. 1968, Ch. 1055.)

6550.22.

If the district board proposes to change the boundaries of the territory proposed to be annexed by adding territory thereto, it shall give notice thereof in the manner provided in Section 6550.19. Owners of land within the affected territory shall be given an opportunity to appear before the district board pursuant to Section 6550.20 and to register any protests.
(Added by Stats. 1968, Ch. 1055.)

6550.23.

At the conclusion of the hearing, the district board may, by resolution, order the annexation to the improvement district of such territory as it determines will be benefited by inclusion therein.
(Added by Stats. 1968, Ch. 1055.)

6550.24.

If all the owners of land within the territory proposed to be annexed have given their written assent to such annexation, the board may, by resolution, order such an annexation without notice and hearing by the board.
(Added by Stats. 1968, Ch. 1055.)

6550.25.

After the adoption of a resolution ordering such annexation, or a resolution confirming an order of annexation following an election thereon, the secretary shall file a certified copy thereof with a map of the territory thus annexed with the county assessor and the county tax collector of each county in which such annexed territory is situated and with the State Board of Equalization.

(Added by Stats. 1968, Ch. 1055.)

6550.26.

Territory annexed to an improvement district shall be subject to existing bond issues and indebtedness of the improvement district from and after the filing with the county assessor specified in Section 6550.25.

(Added by Stats. 1968, Ch. 1055.)

CHAPTER 5. Elections [6560 - 6613]

(Chapter 5 enacted by Stats. 1939, Ch. 60.)

ARTICLE 1. Generally [6560 - 6563]

(Article 1 enacted by Stats. 1939, Ch. 60.)

6560.

The election on the question of formation of a district shall be conducted as nearly as practicable in accordance with the Uniform District Election Law.

Except as otherwise provided in this part, general district elections shall be conducted pursuant to the Uniform District Election Law.

(Amended by Stats. 1966, 1st Ex. Sess., Ch. 15.)

6561.

Every voter resident within the district or a proposed district for the period requisite to enable him to vote at a general election, is entitled to vote at district elections.

(Enacted by Stats. 1939, Ch. 60.)

6562.

At an annexation election every qualified voter resident in the territory proposed to be annexed for the length of time necessary to enable him to vote at a general election may vote.

(Amended by Stats. 1949, Ch. 977.)

6563.

At district elections the last great register of the county shall be used, and any person otherwise entitled to vote whose name is not upon the register is entitled to vote upon producing and filing with the election board a certificate, under the hand and seal of the county clerk, showing that his name is registered and uncanceled upon the great register of the county.

(Enacted by Stats. 1939, Ch. 60.)

ARTICLE 2. Election of Officers [6580 - 6585]

(Article 2 enacted by Stats. 1939, Ch. 60.)

6580.

Except as provided in Sections 6580.1 and 6580.2, all elections of officers after the formation of the district, which elections shall be known as "general district elections," shall be held on the first Tuesday after the first Monday in November in each odd-numbered year.

(Amended by Stats. 1966, 1st Ex. Sess., Ch. 15.)

6580.1.

The election of officers may be consolidated with the direct primary election if the board of directors passes a resolution to that effect on or before the first day of August of the preceding odd-numbered year, and states in the resolution those offices of director to be filled at the first consolidated election. The offices that may be filled at the first consolidated election in those districts whose general district elections are held pursuant to the Uniform District Election Law are those offices that would have expired on the last Friday of December of the year preceding the direct primary election and in all other districts are those offices that would have expired in the year of the consolidated election or in the year next following. Upon a determination to consolidate pursuant to this section, the affected officers shall hold office until the first meeting of the board following the entry of the statement of the result of the consolidated election on the records of the board of supervisors or until the end of the terms for which they were elected, whichever is shorter. In the event this consolidation procedure is used, all other elective offices shall expire and be filled in the same manner at the next succeeding consolidated election. Any vacant office resulting from the operation of this section shall be filled by appointment by the board.

If the election of directors is consolidated, and if there is to be but one person to be elected to the office, the candidate receiving the highest number of votes cast for the candidates for that office shall be declared elected. If there are two or more persons to be elected to the office, those candidates equal in number to the number to be elected who receive the highest number of votes for the office shall be declared elected. If a tie vote makes it impossible to determine which of two or more candidates has been elected, the governing board shall forthwith notify the candidates who have received the tie votes to appear before it either personally or by representative, at a time and place designated by the governing body. The governing body shall then determine the tie by lot and the results thereof shall be declared by the governing body. The candidate so chosen shall qualify, take office and serve as though elected at the preceding general district election. For consolidated elections, candidates shall declare their candidacy and shall be nominated, election returns shall be canvassed, the election shall be held and conducted, the results shall be declared, and the certificates of election shall be issued, in the same manner as the declaration of candidacy, nomination, election, canvassing of returns, declaration of results, and issuance of certificates of election for county officers are made,

declared, held, and conducted, and issued, so far as consistent with the provisions of this section. Directors elected under this section, except the first board of directors, shall take office at the first meeting of the board following the entry of the statement of the result of the consolidated election on the records of the board of supervisors. Elections held under this section at the time of the direct primary election and consolidated therewith shall be known as the general district election, and each other election in a district holding elections under this section which may be held by authority of this law, the Elections Code, or other law applicable thereto, shall be known as a special district election. Part 3 (commencing with Section 10400) of Division 10 of, and Section 10515 of the Elections Code shall apply to every consolidation under this section.

(Amended by Stats. 1994, Ch. 923, Sec. 123. Effective January 1, 1995.)

6580.2.

An officer elected or appointed pursuant to Section 6580.1 shall hold office until the election or appointment and qualification of his or her successor.

A district that has determined to consolidate its general district elections with the direct primary election may thereafter determine to conduct its general district elections pursuant to the Uniform District Election Law. In such event, the district board shall, at any time on or before July 15 of any odd-numbered year, adopt a resolution to that effect. A certified copy of the resolution shall be filed with the county elections official no later than July 20 of that year. Thereafter, the terms of each elective officer shall be determined pursuant to Section 10507 of the Elections Code, and, commencing with the first Tuesday after the first Monday in November of said year, all subsequent general district elections shall be held in the time and manner set forth in the Uniform District Election Law.

(Amended by Stats. 1994, Ch. 923, Sec. 124. Effective January 1, 1995.)

6585.

The nominating petition may be upon one or more sheets of paper.

Each petition shall contain the name of only one candidate who shall be a resident elector of the district.

(Amended by Stats. 1959, Ch. 154.)

ARTICLE 2.5. Central Contra Costa Sanitary District [6590 - 6595]

(Article 2.5 added by Stats. 1999, Ch. 696, Sec. 1.)

6590.

Notwithstanding any other provision of law, this article shall apply only to the Central Contra Costa Sanitary District.

(Added by Stats. 1999, Ch. 696, Sec. 1. Effective January 1, 2000.)

6591.

(a) In the case of an elected district board, the directors may be elected by divisions if a majority of the voters voting upon the question are in favor of the question at a general district or special election. Conversely, in the case of a district that has an elected district board which is elected by election division, the directors may be elected at large if a majority of the voters voting upon the question are in favor of the question at a general district or special election.

(b) As used in this section, "election by division" means the election of each member of the district board by voters of only the respective election division.

(c) The district board may adopt a resolution placing the question on the ballot. Alternatively, upon receipt of a petition signed by at least 5 percent of the registered voters of the district, the district board shall adopt a resolution placing the question on the ballot.

(d) If the question is submitted to the voters at a general district election, the notice required by Section 12112 of the Elections Code shall contain a statement of the question to appear on the ballot. If the question is submitted to the voters at a special election, the notice of election and ballot shall contain a statement of the question.

(e) If the majority of voters voting upon the question approves the election of directors by divisions, the district board shall promptly adopt a resolution dividing the district into as many divisions as there are directors. The resolution shall assign a number to each division. Using the last decennial census as a basis, the divisions shall be as nearly equal in population as possible. In establishing the boundaries of the divisions the district board may give consideration to the following factors: (1) topography, (2) geography, (3) cohesiveness, contiguity, integrity, and compactness of territory, and (4) community of interests of the divisions.

(f) If the majority of voters voting upon the question approves the election of directors by division, the board members shall be elected by election divisions and each member elected shall be a resident of the election division from which he or she is elected. At the district general election following the approval by the voters of the election of directors by divisions, the district board shall assign vacancies on the board created by the expiration of terms to the respective election divisions and the vacancies shall be filled from those election divisions.

(g) If the majority of voters voting upon the question approves the election of directors at large, the district board shall promptly adopt a resolution dissolving the election divisions which had existed.

(Added by Stats. 1999, Ch. 696, Sec. 1. Effective January 1, 2000.)

6592.

In the case of a district board elected by election divisions, the district board shall adjust the boundaries of the election divisions before November 1 of the year following the year in which each decennial federal census is taken. If at any time between each decennial federal census a change of organization alters the population of the district or the district increases or decreases the number of members of the district board, the district board shall reexamine the boundaries of its election divisions. If the district board finds that the population of any election division has varied so that the divisions no longer meet the criteria specified in subdivision (c) of Section 6591, the district board shall adjust the boundaries of the election divisions so that the divisions shall be as nearly equal in population as possible. The district board shall make this change within 60 days of the effective date of the change of organization or an increase or decrease in the number of members of the district board.

(Added by Stats. 1999, Ch. 696, Sec. 1. Effective January 1, 2000.)

6593.

(a) Before circulating any petition pursuant to Section 6591, the chief petitioners shall publish a notice of intention which shall include a written statement not to exceed 500 words in length, setting forth the reasons for the proposal. The notice shall be published pursuant to Section 6061 of the Government Code in one or more newspapers of general circulation within the district. If the district is located in more than one county, publication of the notice shall be made in at least one newspaper of general circulation in each of the counties.

(b) The notice shall be signed by at least one, but not more than three, chief petitioners and shall be in substantially the following form:

"Notice of Intent to Circulate Petition

Notice is hereby given of the intention to circulate a petition affecting the Board of Directors of the _____ (name of the district). The petition proposes that _____ (description of the proposal)."

(c) Within five days after the date of publication, the chief petitioners shall file with the secretary of the district board a copy of the notice together with an affidavit made by a representative of the newspaper in which the notice was published certifying to the fact of publication.

(d) After the filing required pursuant to subdivision (c), the petition may be circulated for signatures.

(Added by Stats. 1999, Ch. 696, Sec. 1. Effective January 1, 2000.)

6594.

(a) Sections 100 and 104 of the Elections Code shall govern the signing of the petition and the format of the petition.

(b) A petition may consist of a single instrument or separate counterparts. The chief petitioner or petitioners shall file the petition, together with all counterparts, with the secretary of the district board. The secretary shall not accept a petition for filing unless the signatures have been secured within six months of the date on which the first signature was obtained and the chief petitioner or petitioners submitted the petition to the secretary for filing within 60 days after the last signature was obtained.

(Added by Stats. 1999, Ch. 696, Sec. 1. Effective January 1, 2000.)

6595.

(a) Within 30 days after the date of filing a petition, the secretary of the district board shall cause the petition to be examined and shall prepare a certificate of sufficiency indicating whether the petition is signed by the requisite number of signers.

(b) The secretary shall cause the names of the signers on the petition to be compared with the voters' register in the office of the county clerk or registrar of voters and ascertain (1) the number of registered voters in the district, and (2) the number of qualified signers appearing upon the petition.

(c) If the certificate of the secretary shows the petition to be insufficient, the secretary shall immediately give notice by certified mail of the insufficiency to the chief petitioners. That mailed notice shall state in what amount the petition is insufficient. Within 15 days after the date of the notice of insufficiency, the chief petitioners may file with the secretary a supplemental petition bearing additional signatures.

(d) Within 10 days after the date of filing a supplemental petition, the secretary shall examine the supplemental petition and certify in writing the results of his or her examination.

(e) The secretary shall sign and date a certificate of sufficiency. That certificate shall also state the minimum signature requirements for a sufficient petition and show the results of the secretary's examination. The secretary shall mail a copy of the certificate of sufficiency to the chief petitioners.

(f) Once the chief petitioners have filed a sufficient petition, the district board shall take the actions required pursuant to Section 6591.

(Added by Stats. 1999, Ch. 696, Sec. 1. Effective January 1, 2000.)

ARTICLE 3. Bond Elections [6610 - 6613]
(Article 3 enacted by Stats. 1939, Ch. 60.)

6610.

Notice of bond elections shall be given by posting notices, signed by not less than a majority of the board, in three public places in the district, at least one of which shall be in each county in which the district is located, not less than 20 days before the election, and by publishing the notice not less than once a week for three successive weeks before the election in a newspaper published in the district, if there is one, and if not, in a newspaper published in each county in which the district is located.

(Amended by Stats. 1961, Ch. 1629.)

6611.

The notice shall contain:

(a) Time and place of holding the election.

(b) The names of the officers of election appointed to conduct it.

(c) The hours during the day in which the polls will be open.

(d) A statement of the purpose for which the election is held.

(e) The amount of the proposed bonds, the rate of interest or maximum rate of interest to be paid and the number of years not to exceed which the whole of the bonds are to run.

(Amended by Stats. 1949, Ch. 977.)

6612.

The vote shall be by ballot, without reference to the general law in regard to form of ballot.

The ballot shall contain the words "Bonds—Yes" and "Bonds—No," and the person voting at the election shall put a cross (+) upon his ballot after the "Yes" or "No" to indicate whether he has voted for or against the bonds.

(Enacted by Stats. 1939, Ch. 60.)

6613.

After the votes have been announced the ballots shall be sealed and delivered to the secretary or president of the board, which board shall on the seventh day after the election meet and canvass the returns and enter the results in its minutes.

The entry is conclusive evidence of the fact and regularity of all prior proceedings and of the facts stated in the entry.

(Amended by Stats. 1953, Ch. 765.)

CHAPTER 6. Bonds [6640 - 6694.3]

(Chapter 6 enacted by Stats. 1939, Ch. 60.)

ARTICLE 1. Generally [6640 - 6655]
(Article 1 enacted by Stats. 1939, Ch. 60.)

6640.

A district may issue bonds as provided in this part.

(Enacted by Stats. 1939, Ch. 60.)

6641.

A district may issue bonds to raise money for any of the purposes stated in Section 6512 hereof.

(Amended by Stats. 1944, 4th Ex. Sess., Ch. 53.)

6642.

By order entered in its minutes, when in its judgment it is advisable, the board may and shall, upon a petition of a majority of the qualified electors residing in the district, call an election and submit to the electors of the district the question whether bonds shall be issued.

(Enacted by Stats. 1939, Ch. 60.)

6643.

The order calling the election may submit as one proposal the question of issuing bonds to make all of the outlays, or so many of them as may be selected, or the order may submit at the election as separate questions the issuance of bonds for any of the outlays singly or in combination.

(Amended by Stats. 1953, Ch. 765.)

6644.

If, at the election, two-thirds of the votes cast are in favor of the issuance of bonds, the board may issue and dispose of the bonds as proposed in the order calling the election.

(Amended by Stats. 1955, Ch. 1874.)

6645.

Bonds issued by the district under the provisions of this part shall be of such denomination or denominations as the board determines.

(Amended by Stats. 1963, Ch. 736.)

6646.

The bonds shall be payable in lawful money of the United States at the office of the treasurer and bear interest at a rate not exceeding 8 percent per annum, payable semiannually in like lawful money. The interest for the first year may be payable in one installment at the end of such year, or the interest for the period from the date of the bonds to a date not later than 30 days after the date the second installment of the first district taxes levied after the date of said bonds will become delinquent may be payable in one installment at the end of such period.

(Amended by Stats. 1975, Ch. 130.)

6647.

No bonds shall be payable in installments, but each shall be payable in full on the date specified therein by the board, which need not be an anniversary of the date of the bond. The board may provide that any bond issued by the district may be subject to call and retirement prior to maturity at such times and prices and upon such other terms as the board may specify. If a bond is subject to call and retirement prior to maturity that fact shall be stated in the bond.

(Amended by Stats. 1953, Ch. 765.)

6648.

Each bond shall be signed by the president and countersigned by the secretary.

The bonds shall be numbered consecutively, beginning with number one, and shall have coupons attached referring to the number of the bond.

(Enacted by Stats. 1939, Ch. 60.)

6649.

The bonds shall be sold by the board in such manner and in such quantities as may be determined by it in its discretion but not less than 95 percent of the par value thereof. Before selling the bonds, or any part thereof, the board shall give notice inviting sealed bids in such manner as the board may prescribe. If satisfactory bids are received, the bonds offered for sale shall be awarded to the highest responsible bidder. If no bids are received, or if the board determines that the bids received are not satisfactory as to price or responsibility of the bidders, the board may reject all bids received, if any, and either again give notice inviting bids or sell the bonds at private sale.

(Amended by Stats. 1969, Ch. 194.)

6650.

The term of bonds issued shall not exceed forty years.

(Enacted by Stats. 1939, Ch. 60.)

6651.

The outstanding bonds of the district shall not at any one time exceed 15 percent of the assessed value of the real and personal property of the district, except where the board elects to use the county assessor's tax roll pursuant to Article 6 (commencing with Section 6780) of Chapter 7 of this part, in which case the outstanding bonds of the district may equal an amount not to exceed 20 percent of the assessed value of the real and personal property of the district.

Within the meaning of this section the term "bonds" means only bonds payable from the proceeds of taxes levied upon taxable property in the district.

(Amended by Stats. 1965, Ch. 1881.)

6653.

An action to determine the validity of bonds may be brought pursuant to Chapter 9 (commencing with Section 860) of Title 10 of Part 2 of the Code of Civil Procedure.

(Amended by Stats. 1961, Ch. 1558.)

6654.

(1) An issue of bonds is hereby defined to be the aggregate principal amount of all of the bonds authorized to be issued in accordance with a proposal submitted to and approved by the electors of the district, but no indebtedness will be deemed to have been contracted until bonds shall have been sold and delivered and then only to the extent of the principal amount of bonds so sold and delivered.

(2) The sanitary board of any district issuing any bonds heretofore or hereafter authorized may, in its discretion, divide the aggregate principal amount of such issue into two or more divisions or series and fix different dates for the bonds of each separate division or series. In the event any authorized issue is divided into two or more divisions or series, the bonds of each division or series may be made payable at such time or times as may be fixed by the legislative body of the district separate and distinct from the time or times of payment of bonds of any other division or series of the same issue.

(3) The provisions of this section shall also apply to bonds issued in an annexed territory and to reconstruction bonds and refunding bonds.

(Added by Stats. 1949, Ch. 977.)

6655.

In determining the amount of bonds to be issued, the legislative body may include:

(a) All costs and estimated costs incidental to or connected with the acquisition, construction, improving or financing of the project.

(b) All engineering, inspection, legal and fiscal agent's fees, costs of the bond election and of the issuance of said bonds, bond reserve funds and working capital and bond interest estimated to accrue during the construction period and for a period of not to exceed 12 months after completion of construction.

(Added by Stats. 1957, Ch. 1378.)

ARTICLE 2. Bonds of Annexed Territory [6660 - 6661]

(Article 2 added by Stats. 1967, Ch. 920.)

6660.

At any time after the annexation of territory, the board may issue bonds to raise money for any of the purposes stated in Section 6512 hereof in or for the benefit of said annexed area in the same manner as in any other part of the district, except, only qualified electors resident within the annexed territory are entitled to petition or vote in the proceedings. In the event any such bonds are issued in such annexed territory, or in lieu thereof proceedings are had under Article 3 of Chapter 4 of this part, said territory shall not be subject to taxation for any bonds of the district or of any area previously annexed thereto theretofore authorized to be issued for one or more of the same purposes under Article 1 of Chapter 6 of this part. When no such bond proceedings are intended to be taken in such territory, then in the order of the sanitary board fixing the boundaries thereof, or by resolution adopted subsequently thereto when it is found by said sanitary board to be necessary in order to provide equality of taxation in said annexed area, said sanitary board may determine that said annexed area shall not be subject to taxation for any prior indebtedness of said district or of any other part thereof. Certified copies of said resolution shall be filed with the county clerk and also with the county assessor and with the State Board of Equalization in Sacramento and thereafter said annexed area shall not be subject to taxation for any such prior indebtedness.

(Added by Stats. 1967, Ch. 920.)

6661.

The provisions of this part with reference to bonds in annexed territory do not limit the powers or alter the procedure provided for the issuance of bonds by an entire district and payable out of taxes levied upon all taxable property whether the boundaries of the district remain as originally established or have been altered by annexation.

(Added by Stats. 1967, Ch. 920.)

ARTICLE 3. Reconstruction Bonds [6670.1- 6670.1.]

(Article 3 enacted by Stats. 1939, Ch. 60.)

6670.1.

Bonds of the district for the purpose of providing funds for the construction of a larger main sewer or a different system shall be authorized and issued in the same manner as that provided in this part for other bonds of the district.

(Added by Stats. 1953, Ch. 765.)

ARTICLE 4. Exchange of Bonds [6680 - 6683]

(Article 4 enacted by Stats. 1939, Ch. 60.)

6680.

After a district organized under the Sanitary District Act of 1891, or Chapter 161, Statutes of 1891, has been reorganized under this part the entire amount of bonds issued by it

under either act may be presented by the holder to the board, and there shall be issued in exchange to the holder, by the board, bonds issued in accordance with this part for the various amounts of the bonds surrendered.

(Enacted by Stats. 1939, Ch. 60.)

6681.

The new bonds shall be payable as nearly as practicable at the same time as the installments on the old bonds and in equal amounts.

Interest on the new bonds shall be paid at the same time and rate as on the old bonds. The amount of the new bonds payable in any one year shall equal the amount of the installments on the old bonds payable in that year.

(Enacted by Stats. 1939, Ch. 60.)

6682.

The expenses of the exchange shall be borne by the holder of the bonds presented for exchange.

(Enacted by Stats. 1939, Ch. 60.)

6683.

After the exchange the old bonds shall be canceled by punching holes in the signatures, and shall be retained by the county treasurer.

(Enacted by Stats. 1939, Ch. 60.)

ARTICLE 5. Refunding Bonds [6690 - 6694.3]

(Article 5 added by Stats. 1939, Ch. 304.)

6690.

The board may cause refunding bonds to be issued for the purpose of refunding any or all outstanding bonds of the district.

(Added by Stats. 1939, Ch. 304.)

6691.

Refunding bonds shall be issued and delivered only when the bonds to be refunded have matured or are about to mature or are subject to retirement before maturity, or, if the outstanding bonds are not subject to retirement the retirement thereof shall have been assured or obtained by consent of the holders thereof.

(Added by Stats. 1939, Ch. 304.)

6692.

Except as otherwise provided in this article, refunding bonds shall be issued in substantially the manner and form prescribed for the issuance of other bonds under this part and the provisions of this part concerning the authorization, certification, issuance, and sale of bonds shall be applicable to bonds issued under this article.

(Added by Stats. 1939, Ch. 304.)

6693.

The board desiring to refund any of its bonds may formulate a proposed plan for that purpose and shall call an election for the purpose of authorizing the issuance of such refunding bonds.

The election shall be called and held and the result thereof determined and declared substantially in the same manner as provided by this part for the issuance of other bonds of the district.

(Added by Stats. 1939, Ch. 304.)

6694.

Only a majority vote shall be required to authorize the issuance of refunding bonds.

(Added by Stats. 1939, Ch. 304.)

6694.1.

The maturity date of refunding bonds shall be fixed by the board but in no case shall the maturity of any such bonds be more than forty years from the date thereof.

(Added by Stats. 1939, Ch. 304.)

6694.2.

The rate of interest on refunding bonds shall not exceed 8 percent per annum payable semiannually.

(Amended by Stats. 1975, Ch. 130.)

6694.3.

Refunding bonds may be issued in a principal amount sufficient to provide funds for the payment of the bonds to be refunded thereby and in addition all expenses incidental to the calling, retiring or payment of such outstanding bonds and the issuance of such refunding bonds.

(Added by Stats. 1939, Ch. 304.)

CHAPTER 7. Finances and Taxation [6695 - 6805]

(Chapter 7 enacted by Stats. 1939, Ch. 60.)

ARTICLE 1. Generally [6695 - 6701]

(Article 1 enacted by Stats. 1939, Ch. 60.)

6695.

(a) Except as otherwise provided in this part, no more than sixty cents ($0.60) on each one hundred dollars ($100) assessed valuation shall be levied for all the district purposes in any one year, besides what is required for the payment of the bond principal and interest for that year.

(b) Except as otherwise provided in this part, if the board elects to use the county assessor's tax roll pursuant to Article 6 (commencing with Section 6780) of this chapter, no more than one dollar ($1) on each one hundred dollars ($100) assessed valuation shall be levied for all the district purposes in any one year, besides what is required for the payment of the bond principal and interest for that year.

(Amended by Stats. 1961, Ch. 990.)

6696.

The board may prescribe the time and manner of assessing, levying, and collecting taxes for district purposes, except as otherwise provided in this part.

(Enacted by Stats. 1939, Ch. 60.)

6697.

District taxes may be assessed, levied, and collected for any or all of the following purposes:

(a) To pay the principal and interest of the bonds issued by the district.

(b) To raise money for any of the purposes stated in Sections 6512 and 6660 hereof.

(c) To pay any lawful claims against the district.

(d) To pay the running expenses of the district.

(Amended by Stats. 1944, 4th Ex. Sess., Ch. 53.)

6698.

The board shall annually levy a tax upon the taxable property in the district sufficient to pay the interest on bonds for the year, and such portion of the principal as is due or is to become due during the year, so that the entire amount of principal and interest of the bonds shall be paid at or before maturity, and in any event within forty years of the date of issuance of the bonds.

(Enacted by Stats. 1939, Ch. 60.)

6699.

If any portion of the interest or principal due for any year remains unpaid, it shall be added to the levy for the next year, and shall be collected and paid accordingly.

(Enacted by Stats. 1939, Ch. 60.)

6700.

The payment of the principal and interest of all bonds, within forty years from their issuance, is the obligation of the district; and, if necessary to accomplish that purpose, a special tax shall be levied.

(Enacted by Stats. 1939, Ch. 60.)

6701.

Taxes for the payment of the principal and interest of bonds of annexed territory shall be limited to the taxable property in the annexed territory.

(Amended by Stats. 1944, 4th Ex. Sess., Ch. 53.)

ARTICLE 2. Assessment by District Assessor [6715 - 6718]

(Article 2 enacted by Stats. 1939, Ch. 60.)

6715.

Between the first Mondays in March and July annually the assessor shall assess all taxable property in the district to the persons by whom it was owned or claimed, or in whose possession or control it was at twelve o'clock noon of the first Monday in March next preceding.

(Enacted by Stats. 1939, Ch. 60.)

6716.

No mistake in the name of the owner of any property, or any informality in the description or in other parts of the assessment, shall invalidate the assessment.

(Enacted by Stats. 1939, Ch. 60.)

6717.

The assessor shall verify his assessment roll, and shall deposit it with the board on the first Monday in July in each year, or as soon thereafter as is practicable.

(Enacted by Stats. 1939, Ch. 60.)

6718.

All the provisions of law relating to assessment of property by county assessor shall, so far as applicable, apply to and govern the acts of the assessor in the assessment of taxable property in the district.

(Enacted by Stats. 1939, Ch. 60.)

ARTICLE 3. Equalization of Assessments by District Assessor [6730 - 6734]

(Article 3 enacted by Stats. 1939, Ch. 60.)

6730.

Annually, on the first Monday of July at seven thirty p.m. the board shall meet as a board of equalization.

(Enacted by Stats. 1939, Ch. 60.)

6731.

If the district assessor has returned the assessment roll for the year the board shall proceed to equalize the assessments.

(Enacted by Stats. 1939, Ch. 60.)

6732.

If the assessment roll has not been returned by the district assessor the board shall adjourn from time to time until the roll has been returned, and for the purpose of adjournment one or more of the members of the board present may make and announce the adjournment.

(Amended by Stats. 1959, Ch. 161.)

6733.

When the assessment roll is returned by the district assessor, the board shall equalize the assessments, and the board shall continue in session as a board of equalization with reasonable intermissions until the roll has been examined, rectified, and equalized.

(Enacted by Stats. 1939, Ch. 60.)

6734.

The board may hear complaints as to the proceedings of the district assessor and adjudicate and determine the controversy. It may of its own motion raise an assessment,

after such reasonable notice to the party whose assessment is to be raised, as may be ordered by the board.

(Enacted by Stats. 1939, Ch. 60.)

ARTICLE 4. Levy of Tax [6745 - 6747]

(Article 4 enacted by Stats. 1939, Ch. 60.)

6745.

After the equalization of the assessments has been completed, the board shall, by resolution, fix the rate of taxation for district purposes, designating the number of cents on each one hundred dollars to be levied for each fund and shall designate the fund into which the proceeds shall be paid.

(Enacted by Stats. 1939, Ch. 60.)

6746.

After the entry in the minutes of the resolution fixing the rate of the tax the board shall cause the district assessor to compute the amount of the tax upon each item of real and personal property, and enter the amount on the assessment roll.

(Enacted by Stats. 1939, Ch. 60.)

6747.

When completed, the roll shall be verified by the district assessor and signed by the president and secretary.

The amount of the tax then is a lien on the property against which it is assessed, and has the effect of a judgment against the owner.

The lien has the force and effect of an execution duly levied against all the property of the delinquent, and is not satisfied and the lien is not extinguished until the taxes are paid or the property sold to satisfy them. The statute of limitations shall not apply.

(Enacted by Stats. 1939, Ch. 60.)

ARTICLE 5. Collection [6760 - 6767]

(Article 5 enacted by Stats. 1939, Ch. 60.)

6760.

As soon as practicable, but not later than the third Monday in August, after the taxes have been computed and extended on the assessment roll, verified by the district assessor and signed by the president and secretary of the board, the board shall transmit, or cause the district assessor to transmit, the roll or a duplicate to the tax collector of the county.

(Enacted by Stats. 1939, Ch. 60.)

6761.

The tax collector shall collect the taxes shown to be due, in the same manner as he collects the county taxes.

(Enacted by Stats. 1939, Ch. 60.)

6762.

All the provisions of the laws of the state as to the collection of taxes and delinquent taxes, and the enforcement of their payment, so far as applicable, apply to the collection of district taxes.

(Enacted by Stats. 1939, Ch. 60.)

6763.

The board may direct the district attorney of the county to commence and prosecute suits for the collection of the whole or any portion of the delinquent taxes.

The district attorney shall carry out such directions of the board.

The district attorney and the sureties on his official bond are responsible for the due performance of the duty imposed upon him by this part.

(Enacted by Stats. 1939, Ch. 60.)

6764.

All money collected for district purposes by the district attorney under this part shall be at once paid to the treasurer.

(Enacted by Stats. 1939, Ch. 60.)

6765.

The board may at any time, by order entered in its minutes, provide a system for the collection of delinquent taxes, or make any change in the manner of their collection.

(Enacted by Stats. 1939, Ch. 60.)

6766.

The tax collector shall immediately pay to the treasurer all money collected by him for district purposes and the treasurer shall keep it in the county treasury as provided in this part.

(Enacted by Stats. 1939, Ch. 60.)

6767.

The tax collector and the sureties on his official bond are responsible for the due performance of the duties imposed upon him by this part.

(Enacted by Stats. 1939, Ch. 60.)

ARTICLE 6. Use of County Assessor's Roll [6780 - 6787]

(Article 6 enacted by Stats. 1939, Ch. 60.)

6780.

The board may elect to avail itself of the assessment made by the assessor of the county in which the district is situated, and may take that assessment as the basis for district taxation.

(Enacted by Stats. 1939, Ch. 60.)

6781.

The board shall declare its election by resolution and shall file a certified copy with the auditor and the assessor of the county on or before the first Monday in February of the year in which the district proposes to use the county assessment roll.

Until the board by resolution elects otherwise all taxes shall be levied by the board of supervisors of the county in which the district is situated and collected by the county assessor and tax collector of the county.
(Amended by Stats. 1939, Ch. 1059.)

6782.

Following the board's election, the county auditor shall on or about the third Monday of August of each year transmit to the board a written statement showing the total value of all property in the district, which value shall be ascertained from the assessment roll used by the county for that year.
(Amended by Stats. 1963, Ch. 426.)

6783.

The board shall, then, before September 1st, estimate the amount of money needed and fix the rate of taxation for district purposes and for the payment of the principal and interest of that year upon outstanding bonds and the payment of the principal and interest that the board believes will become due during the year on bonds authorized but not sold.
(Amended by Stats. 1963, Ch. 426.)

6784.

The board shall designate the number of cents on each one hundred dollars ($100) to be levied for each fund and the fund into which the proceeds shall be paid, using as a basis the value of property as assessed on the county roll. These acts by the board are a valid assessment of the property and a valid levy of the taxes so fixed.
(Amended by Stats. 1970, Ch. 17.)

6785.

The board shall by September 1st of each year certify to the county auditor of the county in which the district is situated the rate of taxation fixed.
(Amended by Stats. 1984, Ch. 884, Sec. 11.)

6786.

The county auditor shall compute and enter in the county assessment roll the respective sums to be paid as a district tax on the property in the district, using the rate of levy as fixed by the board and the assessed value as found on the assessment roll.
The taxes shall be collected at the same time and in the same manner as county taxes are collected, and when collected shall be at once paid to the treasurer.
(Amended by Stats. 1963, Ch. 426.)

6787.

The taxes are a lien on all the property in the district, and the taxes, whether for the payment of a bonded indebtedness, or for other purposes, shall be of the same force and effect as other liens for taxes, and their collection shall be enforced by the same means as provided for the enforcement of liens for county taxes.
(Enacted by Stats. 1939, Ch. 60.)

ARTICLE 6.5. Districts in More Than One County [6789- 6789.]
(Article 6.5 added by Stats. 1961, Ch. 1629.)

6789.

Taxes for a district which is situated in more than one county and which has availed itself of the county assessor's roll pursuant to Sections 6780 and 6781 shall be levied in accordance with the following procedure:
(a) The district board shall annually, before the time of fixing the general tax levy for county purposes, estimate the amount of money necessary to be raised by taxation to meet the requirements for district purposes, including, but not limited to, operation, maintenance, and payment of principal and interest on outstanding bonds which will become payable before the proceeds of another tax levy made at the time of the next general tax levy for county purposes can be made available for payment of such operation, maintenance, principal and interest.
(b) The total estimate shall be divided by the district board in proportion to the value of the real property of the district in each county. The value shall be determined from the equalized values of the last assessment rolls of the counties. When the division of the estimate has been made, the district board shall promptly certify to the boards of supervisors of the counties in which the district is situated the respective parts of the estimate apportioned to each county.
(c) The board of supervisors of each county in which is situated any part of a district shall annually, at the time of levying county taxes, levy a tax upon all the property within the district situated in the county sufficient to raise the amount so certified to the board of supervisors by the district board.
(d) The tax shall be collected by the same officers and in the same manner as other county taxes, and the money so collected shall be transmitted to the district treasurer.
(Added by Stats. 1961, Ch. 1629.)

ARTICLE 7. Funds [6790 - 6801]
(Article 7 enacted by Stats. 1939, Ch. 60.)

6790.

In a fund called the "bond fund of sanitary district" (naming it) the treasurer shall keep the money levied by the board for that fund.
(Enacted by Stats. 1939, Ch. 60.)

6791.

No part of the money in the bond fund may be transferred to any other fund or be used for any purpose other than the payment of the principal and interest of the bonds of the district, and for the retirement of bonds that have been issued by a district that formerly formed a part of the district while any bonds are unpaid.
(Enacted by Stats. 1939, Ch. 60.)

6792.

In a fund called the "running expense fund of ____ Sanitary District" (naming it) the treasurer shall place and keep the money levied by the board for that fund.
(Enacted by Stats. 1939, Ch. 60.)

6793.

The whole or any part of the money in the running expense fund shall be transferred to the bond fund, or to any other fund provided for in this part, on the order of the board.
(Enacted by Stats. 1939, Ch. 60.)

6794.

The treasurer shall pay out money of the district only upon the written order of the board, signed by the president and countersigned by the secretary.
The order shall specify the name of the person to whom the money is to be paid, the fund from which it is to be paid, and shall state generally the purpose for which the payment is to be made.
The order shall be entered in the minutes of the board.
(Enacted by Stats. 1939, Ch. 60.)

6795.

The treasurer shall keep the order as his voucher, and shall keep a specific account of receipts and disbursements for the district.
(Enacted by Stats. 1939, Ch. 60.)

6796.

The proceeds of the sale of bonds shall be deposited with the treasurer and shall be by him placed in the fund to be called the "sewer construction fund of ____ sanitary district" (naming it).
(Enacted by Stats. 1939, Ch. 60.)

6797.

The money in the sewer construction fund shall be used for the purpose indicated in the order calling the election upon the question of the issuance of the bonds, and for no other purpose, but, if after those purposes are entirely fulfilled any balance remains in the fund, the balance may, upon the order of the board, be transferred to either of the other funds provided by this part.
(Enacted by Stats. 1939, Ch. 60.)

6798.

All fines for the violation of any regulation or order of the board shall, after the expenses of the prosecution are deducted, be paid to the secretary, who shall forthwith deposit them with the treasurer, who shall place them in the running expense fund of the district.
(Enacted by Stats. 1939, Ch. 60.)

6799.

The county treasurer and sureties upon his official bond are liable for the due performance of the duties imposed upon him by this part.
(Enacted by Stats. 1939, Ch. 60.)

6800.

Notwithstanding the provisions of any other section of this article, the board may, out of any surplus funds remaining in the bond fund, the running expense fund or the sewer construction fund, purchase in the open market its outstanding unmatured bonds.
No bonds shall be purchased at a price above par and accrued interest plus an allowance of six months interest from the date of purchase. All bonds so purchased shall be canceled.
(Added by Stats. 1939, Ch. 304.)

6801.

As an alternative to the functions of the treasurer, the district board may elect to disburse funds of the district. Such election shall be made by resolution of the board and the filing of a certified copy thereof with the treasurer. The treasurer shall thereupon and thereafter deliver to the district all funds of the district. Such funds shall be deposited by the board in a bank or banks, or savings and loan association or savings and loan associations, approved for deposit of public funds and shall be withdrawn only by written order of the district board, signed by the president and secretary. The order shall specify the name of the payee, the fund from which it is to be paid and state generally the purpose for which payment is to be made. Such order shall be entered in the minutes of the board. The district board shall appoint a treasurer who shall be responsible for the deposit and withdrawal of funds of the district. The treasurer shall deposit with the district, prior to October 1st of each year, a surety bond in the annual amount fixed by the district board. The deposit and withdrawal of funds of the district shall thereafter be subject to the provisions of Article 2 (commencing at Section 53630), Chapter 4, Part 1, Division 2, Title 5, of the Government Code.
(Amended by Stats. 1976, Ch. 349.)

ARTICLE 8. Claims [6805- 6805.]
(Article 8 added by Stats. 1959, Ch. 1727.)

6805.

All claims for money or damages against the district are governed by Part 3 (commencing with Section 900) and Part 4 (commencing with Section 940) of Division 3.6 of Title 1 of the Government Code except as provided therein, or by other statutes or regulations expressly applicable thereto.
(Amended by Stats. 1963, Ch. 1715.)

CHAPTER 8. Reorganization [6810 - 6823]

(Chapter 8 enacted by Stats. 1939, Ch. 60.)

6810.

A district organized under Chapter 161, Statutes of 1891, or under the Sanitary District Act of 1919 may be reorganized as a district under this part.
(Enacted by Stats. 1939, Ch. 60.)

6811.

To effect the reorganization a petition, signed by not less than twenty-five residents and freeholders within the district, and also by a majority of the members of the district board, shall be presented to the board of supervisors.

(Enacted by Stats. 1939, Ch. 60.)

6812.

The petition shall be verified by at least one of the petitioners in the manner prescribed by law for the verification of pleadings, and shall set forth the boundaries and name of the district and pray that it be reorganized under this part.

(Enacted by Stats. 1939, Ch. 60.)

6813.

The petition shall be published for at least two weeks preceding the hearing in a newspaper of general circulation published in the county, together with a notice stating the time when the petition will be presented to the board of supervisors, and that all persons interested may appear and be heard.

(Enacted by Stats. 1939, Ch. 60.)

6814.

At that time the board of supervisors shall hear the petition.

The board of supervisors shall not modify the boundaries of the district as set forth in the petition so as to exclude from the district any land which would be benefited by the reorganization of the district under this part, nor shall any lands which will not in the judgment of the board of supervisors be benefited by the reorganized district be included within the district.

(Enacted by Stats. 1939, Ch. 60.)

6815.

If the board of supervisors finds, upon the final hearing of the petition, that the statements therein are correct the board shall make an order approving the petition, describing the boundaries of the territory included within the district, and declaring that the territory is organized as a district under this part.

(Enacted by Stats. 1939, Ch. 60.)

6816.

From and after the making of the order of reorganization by the board of supervisors, the district is organized under this part with all the powers conferred by this part.

The persons in office at the time of the reorganization are entitled immediately to enter upon the duties of the like offices of the reorganized district and shall continue to serve until the election and qualification of their respective successors in accordance with this part.

(Enacted by Stats. 1939, Ch. 60.)

6817.

A district reorganized under this part is for all purposes the district previously existing.

(Enacted by Stats. 1939, Ch. 60.)

6818.

Reorganization shall not affect or impair the title to any property owned or held by or in trust for the district, or any debt, demand, liability, or obligation existing in favor of or against the district, or any proceeding then pending.

(Enacted by Stats. 1939, Ch. 60.)

6819.

Reorganization shall not operate to repeal or affect in any manner any ordinance previously passed or adopted and remaining unrepealed, or to discharge any person from any liability then existing for any violation of the ordinance. Proceedings commenced before reorganization shall, after reorganization, be conducted in accordance with this part.

(Enacted by Stats. 1939, Ch. 60.)

6823.

The district may contract with the Federal Government of the United States or any branch thereof, or with any county, city and county, municipal corporation, district or other public corporation or with any person, firm or corporation, for the joint acquisition or construction or use of any sewer or sewers or other works or facilities for the handling, treatment or disposal of sewage or industrial waste from the district and such other area as may be designated in said contract, when in the judgment of the legislative body of said district it is for the best interests of the district so to do. Any such contract may provide for the construction and maintenance of such sewer or sewers, or such other works or facilities, and for the payment by or for the parties thereto of such proportionate part of the cost of the acquisition, construction or maintenance of such sewer or sewers or other works or facilities as may be stated in said contract, the payments to be made at such times and in such amounts as may be provided by said contract. Any such contract may provide for the joint use of any sewer or sewers, works or facilities for the handling, treatment or disposal of sewage or industrial waste upon such terms and conditions as may be agreed upon by the parties thereto, and for the flowage, treatment or disposal of sewage or industrial waste from such area for each of the parties thereto as may be described in the contract.

Any district which has acquired or constructed or which proposes to acquire or construct, any sewer or sewers, or works or other facilities for the handling, treatment or disposal of sewage or industrial waste, may contract with the Federal Government of the United States or any branch thereof, or with any county, city and county, municipal corporation, district or other public corporation or with any person, firm or corporation for the use of any such sewer or sewers, works or facilities by any such county, city and county, municipal corporation, district or other public corporation, or for the flowage, treatment or disposal of sewage or industrial waste from any area designated by such person, firm or

corporation so contracting, upon such terms and conditions as may be provided in said contract.

(Added by Stats. 1949, Ch. 843.)

CHAPTER 8.5. District Reorganized From County Sanitation District [6825- 6825.]

(Chapter 8.5 added by Stats. 1955, Ch. 1636.)

6825.

Any duty imposed by this part on any county officer shall be deemed imposed on the county officers of the respective counties in which is situated a sanitary district reorganized under Section 4857 of this code from a county sanitation district encompassing territory in more than one county; provided, that where appropriate, the board may select the officers of one county to perform such duties for the entire district.

(Added by Stats. 1955, Ch. 1636.)

CHAPTER 9. Annexation [6830- 6830.]

(Chapter 9 enacted by Stats. 1939, Ch. 60.)

ARTICLE 1. Generally [6830- 6830.]

(Article 1 enacted by Stats. 1939, Ch. 60.)

6830.

There may be annexed to a district any of the following territory which is in the same county as the district or which is within another county but in the natural watershed area of the district:

(a) Any territory contiguous to the district.

(b) Any territory any point of which touches any point of the district.

(c) Any territory separated from the district by a "separating barrier," which term includes a street, road, highway, railway line, railway crossing, railway right-of-way, watercourse, lagoon, or other natural barrier.

(d) Any territory not contiguous to the district that will, in the opinion of the district board, be benefited by inclusion in the district.

Any territory specified in this section may consist of one or more separate parcels of land, but it is not necessary that all parcels shall constitute in the aggregate one tract of land.

(Amended by Stats. 1965, Ch. 2043.)

PART 2. OTHER SANITARY DISTRICT ACTS [6935 - 6982]

(Part 2 added by Stats. 1941, Ch. 990.)

CHAPTER 1. General [6935 - 6936]

(Chapter 1 added by Stats. 1941, Ch. 990.)

6935.

No right or obligation accrued by the formation, organization, reorganization or operation of a sanitary district pursuant to the provisions of Chapter 161 of the Statutes of 1891 or the provisions of the Sanitary District Act of 1919 is affected by the repeal of those acts and any district so organized or reorganized may continue in existence and subject to the act under which it was organized or reorganized or may reorganize pursuant to this part.

(Added by Stats. 1941, Ch. 990.)

6936.

Pursuant to Section 1002 of the Elections Code, any election held under Chapter 161 of the Statutes of 1891 or the Sanitary District Act of 1919 shall be held on the second Tuesday in March rather than the first Tuesday after the first Monday in March.

(Amended by Stats. 1994, Ch. 923, Sec. 125. Effective January 1, 1995.)

CHAPTER 2. Use of County Assessor's Roll [6940 - 6941.9]

(Chapter 2 added by Stats. 1941, Ch. 990.)

6940.

Notwithstanding the provisions of Chapter 161 of the Statutes of 1891, or the provisions of the Sanitary District Act of 1919, as the provisions of these acts existed at the time of their repeal, the board of any sanitary district organized or reorganized under and continuing in existence and subject to these acts may elect to avail itself of the assessment roll of the properties within the district, used by the county in which the district is situated, and may take that assessment as the basis for district taxation.

(Added by Stats. 1941, Ch. 990.)

6940.3.

The board shall declare its election by resolution and shall file a certified copy with the auditor and the assessor of the county on or before the first Monday in February of the year in which the district proposes to use the county assessment roll.

Thereafter, until the board by resolution elects otherwise all taxes shall be collected by the county assessor and tax collector of the county.

(Added by Stats. 1941, Ch. 990.)

6940.6.

Following the board's election, the county auditor shall on or about the third Monday in August of each year transmit to the board a written statement showing the total value of all property in the district, which value shall be ascertained from the assessment roll used by the county for that year.

(Amended by Stats. 1963, Ch. 426.)

6940.9.

Before the first day of September the district board shall fix the rate of taxation for district purposes and for the payment of the principal and interest of that year upon outstanding bonds and the payment of the principal and interest that the board believes will become due during the year on bonds authorized but not sold.

(Amended by Stats. 1963, Ch. 426.)

6941.3.

The board shall designate the number of cents on each one hundred dollars ($100) to be levied for each fund and the fund into which the proceeds shall be paid, using as a basis the value of property as assessed on the county roll.

The district board shall immediately transmit to the auditor of the county in which the district is situated a statement of the tax rate fixed.

(Added by Stats. 1941, Ch. 990.)

6941.6.

The county auditor shall compute and enter in the county assessment roll the respective sums to be paid as a district tax on the property in the district, using the rate of levy as fixed by the board and the assessed value as found on the assessment roll.

The taxes so levied shall be collected at the same time and in the same manner as county taxes are collected, and when collected shall be at once paid to the treasurer.

(Amended by Stats. 1963, Ch. 426.)

6941.9.

The taxes are a lien on all the property in the district, and the taxes, whether for the payment of a bonded indebtedness, or for other purposes, shall be of the same force and effect as other liens for taxes, and their collection shall be enforced by the same means as provided for the enforcement of liens for county taxes.

(Added by Stats. 1941, Ch. 990.)

CHAPTER 3. On-Site Wastewater Disposal Zones [6950 - 6982]

(Chapter 3 added by Stats. 1977, Ch. 1125.)

ARTICLE 1. Definitions [6950 - 6954]

(Article 1 added by Stats. 1977, Ch. 1125.)

6950.

"Board" or "board of directors" means the governing authority of a public agency.

(Added by Stats. 1977, Ch. 1125.)

6951.

"Public agency" means a city, a county, a special district, or any other political subdivision of the state which is otherwise authorized to acquire, construct, maintain, or operate sanitary sewers or sewage systems.

"Public agency" does not mean an improvement district organized pursuant to the Improvement Act of 1911 (Division 7 (commencing with Section 5000), Streets and Highways Code), or the Municipal Improvement Act of 1913 (Division 12 (commencing with Section 10000), Streets and Highways Code) or the Improvement Bond Act of 1915 (Division 10 (commencing with Section 8500), Streets and Highways Code), or a county maintenance district.

(Amended by Stats. 1978, Ch. 445.)

6952.

"On-site wastewater disposal system" means any of several works, facilities, devices, or other mechanisms used to collect, treat, recycle, or dispose of wastewater without the use of communitywide sanitary sewers or sewage systems.

(Amended by Stats. 1995, Ch. 28, Sec. 8. Effective January 1, 1996.)

6952.5.

"Owner of real property" means any public agency owning land and any person shown as the owner of land on the last equalized assessment roll; provided that where such person is no longer the owner, the term means any person entitled to be shown as owner on the next assessment roll and where land is subject to a recorded written agreement of sale, the term means any person shown therein as purchaser.

(Added by Stats. 1978, Ch. 445.)

6953.

"Zone" means an on-site wastewater disposal zone formed pursuant to this chapter.

(Added by Stats. 1977, Ch. 1125.)

6954.

"Real property" means both land and improvements to land which benefit, directly or indirectly from, or on behalf of, the activities of the zone.

(Added by Stats. 1977, Ch. 1125.)

ARTICLE 2. Formation [6955 - 6974.5]

(Article 2 added by Stats. 1977, Ch. 1125.)

6955.

Whenever the board of directors of a public agency deems it necessary to form an on-site wastewater disposal zone in all or a portion of the public agency's jurisdiction, the board shall by resolution declare that it intends to form such a zone.

(Added by Stats. 1977, Ch. 1125.)

6955.1.

A proposed zone shall contain at least 12 voters, as defined in Section 359 of the Elections Code. However, where there are fewer than 12 registered voters within a proposed zone, the public agency may form a zone if the county health officer determines that an existing or potential public health hazard exists. The board of supervisors shall receive a notice of this determination.

(Amended by Stats. 1994, Ch. 923, Sec. 126. Effective January 1, 1995.)

6956.

The resolution of intention shall also state:

(a) A description of the boundaries of the territory proposed to be included within the zone. The description may be accompanied by a map showing such boundaries.

(b) The public benefit to be derived from the establishment of such a zone.

(c) A description of the proposed types of on-site wastewater disposal systems and a proposed plan for wastewater disposal.

(d) The number of residential units and commercial users in the proposed zone which the public agency proposes to serve.

(e) The proposed means of financing the operations of the zone.

(f) The time and place for a hearing by the board on the question of the formation and extent of the proposed zone, and the question of the number and type of the residential units and commercial units that the public agency proposes to serve in the proposed zone.

(g) That at such time and place any interested persons will be heard.

(Added by Stats. 1977, Ch. 1125.)

6956.5.

The resolution of intention shall be filed for record in the office of the county recorder of the county in which all or the greater portion of the land in the proposed zone is situated.

(Added by Stats. 1977, Ch. 1125.)

6957.

(a) A proposal to form a zone within a public agency may also be initiated by filing a petition with the board. Such a petition shall contain all the matters specified in subdivisions (a), (b), (c), and (d) of Section 6956. Such a petition shall be signed as provided in either of the following:

(1) By not less than 10 percent of the voters who reside within the territory proposed to be included within the zone.

(2) By not less than 10 percent of the number of owners of real property, including both land and improvements to land, within the territory proposed to be included within the zone who also own not less than 10 percent of the assessed value of the real property within such territory.

(b) Each signer of a petition shall add to his or her signature, the date of signing. If the signer is signing the petition as a voter, he or she shall add to his or her signature his or her place of residence, giving street and number, or a designation sufficient to enable the place of residence to be readily ascertained. If the signer is signing the petition as an owner of real property, he or she shall add to his or her signature a description of the real property owned by him or her sufficient to identify the real property.

(c) Following certification of the petition, the board shall set the time and place of the hearing on the question of the formation of the proposed zone.

(Added by Stats. 1977, Ch. 1125.)

6958.

(a) Notice of the hearing shall be given by publishing a copy of the resolution of intention or the petition, pursuant to Section 6066 of the Government Code, prior to the time fixed for the hearing in a newspaper circulated in the public agency.

(b) Notice of the hearing shall also be given to the local health officer, the board of supervisors, the governing body of any other public agency within the boundaries of the proposed zone, the governing body of any public agency whose sphere of influence, as determined pursuant to the provisions of Section 54774 of the Government Code, includes the proposed zone, the affected local agency formation commission, and the regional water quality control board in whose jurisdiction the proposed zone lies.

(Added by Stats. 1977, Ch. 1125.)

6959.

The hearing by the board on the question of the formation of the proposed zone shall be commenced no less than 45 days nor more than 60 days from adoption of a resolution of intention or the receipt of a petition containing a sufficient number of signatures and shall be completed no more than 90 days after the first day of the hearing.

(Amended by Stats. 1978, Ch. 445.)

6960.

After receiving notice pursuant to subdivision (b) of Section 6958, a local health officer shall review the proposed formation and report his or her findings in writing to the board of directors of the public agency. The report shall specify the maximum number, type, volume, and location of on-site wastewater disposal systems which could be operated within the proposed zone without individually or collectively, directly or indirectly, resulting in a nuisance or hazard to public health. The local health officer may require from the public agency such information as may be reasonably necessary to make the findings required in this section.

(Added by Stats. 1977, Ch. 1125.)

6960.1.

After receiving notice pursuant to subdivision (b) of Section 6958, the affected regional water quality control board shall review the proposed formation and report its findings in writing to the board of directors of the public agency. The report shall specify the maximum number, type, volume, and location of on-site wastewater disposal systems which could be operated within the proposed zone without individually or collectively, directly or indirectly, resulting in a pollution or nuisance, or adversely affecting water quality. The regional water quality control board may require from the public agency such information as may be reasonably necessary to make the findings required in this section.

(Added by Stats. 1977, Ch. 1125.)

6960.2.

The number, type, volume, and location of on-site wastewater disposal systems to be operated within the zone shall not exceed the number specified pursuant to either Section 6960 or Section 6960.1.
(Added by Stats. 1977, Ch. 1125.)
6960.3.
The formation of an on-site wastewater disposal zone shall be subject to review and approval by a local agency formation commission which has adopted rules and regulations affecting the functions and services of special districts pursuant to Chapter 5 (commencing with Section 56450) of Part 2 of Division 3 of Title 5 of the Government Code.
(Amended by Stats. 1989, Ch. 323, Sec. 8.)
6960.4.
Prior to any decision on the question of the formation of the proposed zone, the board shall obtain approval for the proposed plan for wastewater disposal from the affected regional water quality control board if such plan involves the disposal of wastewater to a wastewater treatment facility. For any other method of wastewater disposal, and prior to any decision, the board shall obtain approval for the proposed plan from the local health officer and the affected regional water quality control board. The affected regional water quality control board or the local health officer shall not approve any plan which does not comply with applicable requirements of federal, state, regional, or local law, order, regulation, or rule relating to water pollution, the disposal of waste, or public health.
(Added by Stats. 1977, Ch. 1125.)
6961.
At the time and place fixed in the resolution of intention or the petition, or at any time or place to which the hearing is adjourned, any interested person may appear and present any matters material to the questions set forth in the resolution of intention or the petition. At the hearing the board shall also hear the reports of any local health officer, and any public agency with statutory responsibilities for setting water quality standards, regarding any matters material to the questions set forth in the resolution of intention or the petition.
(Added by Stats. 1977, Ch. 1125.)
6962.
At the hearing the board shall also hear and receive any oral or written protests, objections, or evidence which shall be made, presented, or filed. Any person who shall have filed a written protest may withdraw the same at any time prior to the conclusion of the hearing. The board shall have the following powers and duties:
(a) To exclude any territory proposed to be included in a zone when the board finds that such territory will not be benefited by becoming a part of such zone.
(b) To include any additional territory in a proposed zone when the board finds that such territory will be benefited by becoming a part of such zone.
(Added by Stats. 1977, Ch. 1125.)
6963.
At the close of the hearing the board shall find and declare by resolution that written protests, filed and not withdrawn prior to the conclusion of the hearing, represent one of the following:
(a) Less than 35 percent of either of the following:
(1) The number of voters who reside in the proposed zone.
(2) The number of owners of real property in the proposed zone who also own not less than 35 percent of the assessed value of the real property within the proposed zone.
(b) Not less than 35 percent but less than 50 percent of either of the following:
(1) The number of voters who reside in the proposed zone.
(2) The number of owners of real property in the proposed zone who also own not less than 35 percent but less than 50 percent of the assessed value of the real property within the proposed zone.
(c) Not less than 50 percent of either of the following:
(1) The number of voters who reside in the proposed zone.
(2) The number of owners of real property in the proposed zone who also own not less than 50 percent of the assessed value of the real property within the proposed zone.
(Added by Stats. 1977, Ch. 1125.)
6964.
If the number of written protests filed and not withdrawn is the number described in subdivision (c) of Section 6963, the board shall abandon any further proceedings on the question of forming a proposed zone.
(Added by Stats. 1977, Ch. 1125.)
6965.
If the number of written protests filed and not withdrawn is the number described in subdivision (a) of Section 6963, the board shall find and declare by resolution all of the following:
(a) A description of the exterior boundaries of the zone as proposed or modified.
(b) The number of on-site wastewater disposal systems which the public agency proposes to acquire, operate, maintain, or monitor.
(c) That the operation of the proposed zone will not result in land uses that are not consistent with applicable general plans, zoning ordinances, or other land use regulations.
(d) The method of financing the operations of the zone.
(Amended by Stats. 1978, Ch. 445.)
6966.
The board may order the formation of the zone either without election or subject to confirmation by the voters within the zone upon the question of such formation. However, the board shall not order any such formation without an election if the number of written

protests filed and not withdrawn is a number described in subdivision (b) of Section 6963.
(Amended by Stats. 1978, Ch. 445.)
6967.
If the board does not order the formation of the proposed zone, an election on the question shall be conducted if, within 30 days of the date upon which the board did not order the formation, the board receives a petition requesting such an election signed by either of the following:
(a) Not less than 35 percent of the voters who reside within the territory proposed to be included within the zone.
(b) Not less than 35 percent of the number of owners of real property within the territory proposed to be included within the zone who also own not less than 35 percent of the assessed value of the real property within such territory.
(Added by Stats. 1977, Ch. 1125.)
6968.
Any election conducted pursuant to the provisions of this chapter shall be conducted pursuant to the provisions of law pertaining to regular or special elections held in the public agency.
(Amended by Stats. 1978, Ch. 445.)
6969.
After the canvass of returns of any election on the question of forming a proposed zone, the board shall adopt a resolution ordering the formation of the zone if a majority of votes cast at such election are in favor of such formation.
(Added by Stats. 1977, Ch. 1125.)
6970.
No public agency shall form a zone which includes any territory already included within another zone.
(Added by Stats. 1977, Ch. 1125.)
6971.
No public agency shall form a zone if such formation will permit other land uses which are not consistent with the general plans, zoning ordinances, or other land use regulations of any county or city within which the proposed zone is located.
(Added by Stats. 1977, Ch. 1125.)
6972.
After the formation of the zone pursuant to this article, all taxes levied to carry out the purposes of the zone shall be levied exclusively upon the property taxable in the zone by the public agency.
(Added by Stats. 1977, Ch. 1125.)
6973.
If the board does not form a zone after the close of a hearing in accordance with Section 6967 and no petition is filed pursuant to Section 6967, or if the board abandons proceedings on the proposal to form a zone, or if the formation of a zone is not confirmed by the voters, no further proceeding shall be taken thereon. No application for a subsequent proposal involving substantially the same territory and undertaken pursuant to the provisions of this chapter shall be considered or acted upon by the public agency for at least one year after the date of disapproval of, abandonment of, or election on the proceedings.
(Amended by Stats. 1978, Ch. 445.)
6974.
Territory within the public agency may be annexed to a zone, provided that such territory is not part of another zone. The requirements and proceedings for the annexation of territory shall be the same as the requirements and proceedings for formation of a zone.
(Added by Stats. 1978, Ch. 445.)
6974.5.
Land already a part of a zone may be detached if the board finds and determines, following notice and hearing in the same manner provided for formation of the zone, that the land will not be benefitted by its continued inclusion in the zone.
(Added by Stats. 1978, Ch. 445.)

ARTICLE 3. Powers [6975 - 6982]
(Article 3 added by Stats. 1977, Ch. 1125.)
6975.
An on-site wastewater disposal zone may be formed to achieve water quality objectives set by regional water quality control boards, to protect existing and future beneficial water uses, protect public health, and to prevent and abate nuisances. Whenever an on-site wastewater disposal zone has been formed pursuant to this chapter, the public agency shall have the powers set forth in this article, which powers shall be in addition to any other powers provided by law. A public agency shall exercise its powers on behalf of a zone.
(Added by Stats. 1977, Ch. 1125.)
6976.
An on-site waste water disposal zone shall have the following powers:
(a) To collect, treat, reclaim, or dispose of waste water without the use of communitywide sanitary sewers or sewage systems and without degrading water quality within or outside the zone.
(b) To acquire, design, own, construct, install, operate, monitor, inspect, and maintain on-site wastewater disposal systems, not to exceed the number of systems specified pursuant to either Section 6960 or Section 6960.1, within the zone in a manner which will promote water quality, prevent the pollution, waste, and contamination of water, and abate nuisances.

(c) To conduct investigations, make analyses, and monitor conditions with regard to water quality within the zone.

(d) To adopt and enforce reasonable rules and regulations necessary to implement the purposes of the zone. Such rules and regulations may be adopted only after the board conducts a public hearing after giving public notice pursuant to Section 6066 of the Government Code.

(Amended by Stats. 1978, Ch. 445.)

6977.

The public agency shall do all such acts as are reasonably necessary to secure compliance with any federal, state, regional, or local law, order, regulation, or rule relating to water pollution or the discharge of pollutants, waste, or any other material within the zone. For such purpose, any authorized representative of the public agency, upon presentation of his credentials, or, if necessary under the circumstances, after obtaining an inspection warrant pursuant to Title 13 (commencing with Section 1822.50) of Part 3 of the Code of Civil Procedure, shall have the right of entry to any premises on which a water pollution, waste, or contamination source, including, but not limited to, septic tanks, is located for the purpose of inspecting such source, including securing samples of discharges therefrom, or any records required to be maintained in connection therewith by federal, state, or local law, order, regulation, or rule.

(Amended by Stats. 1978, Ch. 445.)

6978.

(a) Violation of any of the provisions of a rule or regulation adopted pursuant to subdivision (d) of Section 6976 may be abated as a public nuisance by the board. The board may by regulation establish a procedure for the abatement of such a nuisance and to assess the cost of such abatement to the violator. If the violator maintains the nuisance upon real property in which he has a fee title interest, the assessment shall constitute a lien upon such real property in the manner provided in subdivision (b).

(b) The amount of any costs, which are incurred by the zone in abating such a nuisance upon real property, shall be assessed to such real property and shall be added to, and become part of, the annual taxes next levied upon the real property subject to abatement and shall constitute a lien upon that real property as of the same time and in the same manner as does the tax lien securing such annual taxes. All laws applicable to the collection and enforcement of county ad valorem taxes shall be applicable to such assessment, except that if any real property to which such lien would attach has been transferred or conveyed to a bona fide purchaser for value, or if a lien of a bona fide encumbrancer for value has been created and attached thereon, prior to the date on which such delinquent charges appear on the assessment roll, then a lien which would otherwise be imposed by this section shall not attach to such real property and the delinquent and unpaid charges relating to such property shall be transferred to the unsecured roll for collection. Any amounts of such assessments collected are to be credited to the funds of the zone from which the costs of abatement were expended.

(Added by Stats. 1977, Ch. 1125.)

6979.

(a) The owner of any real property upon which is located an on-site wastewater disposal system, which system is subject to abatement as a public nuisance by the public agency, may request the public agency to replace or repair, as necessary, such system. If replacement or repair is feasible, the board may provide for the necessary replacement or repair work.

(b) The person or persons employed by the board to do the work shall have a lien, subject to the provisions of subdivision (b) of Section 6978, for work done and materials furnished, and the work done and materials furnished shall be deemed to have been done and furnished at the request of the owner. The zone, in the discretion of the board, may pay all, or any part, of the cost or price of the work done and materials furnished; and, to the extent that the zone pays the cost or price of the work done and materials furnished, the zone shall succeed to and have all the rights, including, but not limited to, the lien, of such person or persons employed to do the work against the real property and the owner.

(Amended by Stats. 1978, Ch. 445.)

6980.

A board may exercise all of the public agency's existing financial powers on behalf of a zone, excepting that any assessment or tax levied upon the real property of a zone shall be subject to the provisions of Sections 6978 and 6981.

(Added by Stats. 1977, Ch. 1125.)

6981.

Notwithstanding any other provision of law, a public agency may levy an assessment reasonably proportional to the benefits derived from the zone, as determined by the board, and subject to the approval of the voters pursuant to the provisions of Article 6 (commencing with Section 2285) of Chapter 3 of Part 4 of Division 1 of the Revenue and Taxation Code. Such benefit assessment shall be in addition to any other charges, assessments, or taxes otherwise levied by the public agency upon the property in the zone.

(Amended by Stats. 1978, Ch. 445.)

6982.

(a) Notwithstanding Section 6952, the West Bay Sanitary District may use the procedures in this chapter to provide alternative or innovative wastewater technologies in the district's jurisdiction.

(b) The determination of a public health officer pursuant to Section 6955.1 shall include written findings, adopted by the district board of directors, regarding the existing or potential public health hazard.

(c) "Alternative or innovative wastewater technologies" means either (1) an onsite wastewater disposal system, as defined in Section 6952, or (2) such a system in conjunction with communitywide sewer or sewage systems, if one or more of the components of the system is located on or in close proximity to the real property and employs innovative or alternative wastewater technologies, including, but not limited to, grinder pump pressure sewer systems, septic tank effluent pump pressure sewer systems, vacuum sewer systems, or small-diameter gravity septic tank systems.

(Amended by Stats. 2004, Ch. 193, Sec. 78. Effective January 1, 2005.)

DIVISION 7. DEAD BODIES [7000 - 8030]

(Division 7 enacted by Stats. 1939, Ch. 60.)

PART 1. GENERAL PROVISIONS [7000 - 7355]

(Part 1 enacted by Stats. 1939, Ch. 60.)

CHAPTER 1. Definitions [7000 - 7025]

(Chapter 1 enacted by Stats. 1939, Ch. 60.)

7000.

The definitions in this chapter apply to this division, Division 8 (commencing with Section 8100) and Division 102 (commencing with Section 102100) of this code and Chapter 12 (commencing with Section 7600) of Division 3 of the Business and Professions Code.

(Amended by Stats. 2018, Ch. 571, Sec. 31. (SB 1480) Effective January 1, 2019.)

7001.

"Human remains" or "remains" means the body of a deceased person, regardless of its stage of decomposition, and cremated remains.

(Amended by Stats. 2001, Ch. 436, Sec. 2. Effective January 1, 2002.)

7002.

"Cremated remains" means the ashes and bone fragments of a human body that are left after cremation in a crematory, and includes ashes from the cremation container. "Cremation remains" does not include foreign materials, pacemakers, or prostheses.

(Amended by Stats. 2001, Ch. 436, Sec. 3. Effective January 1, 2002.)

7002.5.

(a) "Hydrolyzed human remains" means bone fragments of a human body that are left after hydrolysis in a hydrolysis facility. "Hydrolyzed human remains" does not include foreign materials, pacemakers, or prostheses.

(b) This section shall become operative on July 1, 2020.

(Added by Stats. 2017, Ch. 846, Sec. 27. (AB 967) Effective January 1, 2018. Section operative July 1, 2020, by its own provisions.)

7003.

(a) "Cemetery" means either of the following:

(1) Any of the following that is used or intended to be used and dedicated for cemetery purposes:

(A) A burial park, for earth interments.

(B) A mausoleum, for crypt or vault interments.

(C) A crematory and columbarium, for cinerary interments.

(2) A place where six or more human bodies are buried.

(b) This section shall remain in effect only until July 1, 2020, and as of that date is repealed.

(Amended by Stats. 2017, Ch. 846, Sec. 28. (AB 967) Effective January 1, 2018. Repealed as of July 1, 2020, by its own provisions. See later operative version added by Sec. 29 of Stats. 2017, Ch. 846.)

7003.

(a) "Cemetery" means either of the following:

(1) Any of the following that is used or intended to be used and dedicated for cemetery purposes:

(A) A burial park, for earth interments.

(B) A mausoleum, for crypt or vault interments.

(C) A crematory and columbarium, for interment of cremated remains or hydrolyzed human remains.

(2) A place where six or more human bodies are buried.

(b) This section shall become operative on July 1, 2020.

(Repealed (in Sec. 28) and added by Stats. 2017, Ch. 846, Sec. 29. (AB 967) Effective January 1, 2018. Section operative July 1, 2020, by its own provisions.)

7004.

"Burial park" means a tract of land for the burial of human remains in the ground, used or intended to be used, and dedicated, for cemetery purposes.

(Enacted by Stats. 1939, Ch. 60.)

7005.

Except in Part 5 (commencing with Section 9501) of Division 8, "mausoleum" means a structure or building for the entombment of human remains in crypts or vaults in a place used, or intended to be used, and dedicated, for cemetery purposes.

(Amended by Stats. 2001, Ch. 436, Sec. 5. Effective January 1, 2002.)

7006.

"Crematory" means a building or structure containing one or more furnaces for the reduction of bodies of deceased persons to cremated remains.

(Enacted by Stats. 1939, Ch. 60.)

7006.1.

(a) "Hydrolysis facility" means a building or structure containing one or more chambers for the reduction of bodies of deceased persons by alkaline hydrolysis.

(b) This section shall become operative on July 1, 2020.

(Added by Stats. 2017, Ch. 846, Sec. 30. (AB 967) Effective January 1, 2018. Section operative July 1, 2020, by its own provisions.)

7006.3.

"Cremation chamber" means the enclosed space within which the cremation of human remains is performed.

(Added by Stats. 1993, Ch. 1232, Sec. 6. Effective January 1, 1994.)

7006.4.

(a) "Hydrolysis chamber" means the enclosed space within which the hydrolysis of human remains is performed and any other attached, nonenclosed, mechanical components that are necessary for the safe and proper functioning of the equipment. Allowable hydrolysis chambers for the disposition of human remains shall meet or exceed State Department of Public Health and federal Centers for Disease Control and Prevention requirements applicable for destruction of human pathogens, specified in the hydrolysis chamber approval issued pursuant to Section 7639.08 of the Business and Professions Code.

(b) This section shall become operative on July 1, 2020.

(Added by Stats. 2017, Ch. 846, Sec. 31. (AB 967) Effective January 1, 2018. Section operative July 1, 2020, by its own provisions.)

7006.5.

"Cremation container" means a combustible, closed container resistant to leakage of bodily fluids into which the body of a deceased person is placed prior to insertion in a cremation chamber for cremation.

(Added by Stats. 1993, Ch. 1232, Sec. 7. Effective January 1, 1994.)

7006.6.

(a) "Hydrolysis container" means a hydrolyzable body wrapping into which the body of a deceased person is placed prior to insertion into a hydrolysis chamber. The wrapping must consist of 100-percent protein-based material, such as silk, suede, leather, feather, fur, or wool.

(b) This section shall become operative on July 1, 2020.

(Added by Stats. 2017, Ch. 846, Sec. 32. (AB 967) Effective January 1, 2018. Section operative July 1, 2020, by its own provisions.)

7006.7.

"Cremated remains container" means a receptacle in which cremated remains are placed after cremation.

(Added by Stats. 1993, Ch. 1232, Sec. 8. Effective January 1, 1994.)

7006.8.

(a) "Hydrolyzed human remains container" means a receptacle in which hydrolyzed human remains are placed after hydrolysis.

(b) This section shall become operative on July 1, 2020.

(Added by Stats. 2017, Ch. 846, Sec. 33. (AB 967) Effective January 1, 2018. Section operative July 1, 2020, by its own provisions.)

7007.

Except in Part 5 (commencing with Section 9501) of Division 8, "columbarium" means a structure, room, or other space in a building or structure containing niches for inurnment of cremated human remains in a place used, or intended to be used, and dedicated, for cemetery purposes.

(Amended by Stats. 2001, Ch. 436, Sec. 6. Effective January 1, 2002.)

7008.

"Crematory and columbarium" means a building or structure containing both a crematory and columbarium.

(Enacted by Stats. 1939, Ch. 60.)

7009.

"Interment" means the disposition of human remains by entombment or burial in a cemetery or, in the case of cremated remains, by inurnment, placement or burial in a cemetery, or burial at sea as provided in Section 7117.

(Amended by Stats. 1993, Ch. 1232, Sec. 9. Effective January 1, 1994.)

7010.

"Cremation" means the process by which the following three steps are taken:

(a) The reduction of the body of a deceased human to its essential elements by incineration.

(b) The repositioning or moving of the body or remains during incineration to facilitate the process.

(c) The processing of the remains after removal from the cremation chamber pursuant to Section 7010.3.

(Amended by Stats. 2001, Ch. 436, Sec. 7. Effective January 1, 2002.)

7010.1.

(a) "Hydrolysis" means the process by which the following two steps are taken:

(1) The reduction of the body of a deceased person to its essential organic components and bone fragments by alkaline hydrolysis. "Alkaline hydrolysis" is a process using heat or heat and applied pressure, water, and potassium hydroxide or sodium hydroxide in a hydrolysis chamber.

(2) The processing of the remains after removal from the hydrolysis chamber pursuant to Section 7010.3.

(b) This section shall become operative on July 1, 2020.

(Added by Stats. 2017, Ch. 846, Sec. 34. (AB 967) Effective January 1, 2018. Section operative July 1, 2020, by its own provisions.)

7010.3.

(a) "Processing" means the removal of foreign objects, pursuant to Section 7051, and the reduction of the particle size of cremated remains by mechanical means including, but not limited to, grinding, crushing, and pulverizing to a consistency appropriate for disposition.

(b) This section shall remain in effect only until July 1, 2020, and as of that date is repealed.

(Amended by Stats. 2017, Ch. 846, Sec. 35. (AB 967) Effective January 1, 2018. Repealed as of July 1, 2020, by its own provisions. See later operative version added by Stats. 2017, Ch. 846.)

7010.3.

(a) "Processing" means the removal of foreign objects, pursuant to Section 7051, and the reduction of the particle size of cremated remains or hydrolyzed human remains by mechanical means including, but not limited to, grinding, crushing, and pulverizing to a consistency appropriate for disposition.

(b) This section shall become operative on July 1, 2020.

(Repealed (in Sec. 35) and added by Stats. 2017, Ch. 846, Sec. 36. (AB 967) Effective January 1, 2018. Section operative July 1, 2020, by its own provisions.)

7010.5.

"Residue" means human ashes, bone fragments, prostheses, and disintegrated material from the chamber itself, imbedded in cracks and uneven spaces of a cremation chamber, that cannot be removed through reasonable manual contact with sweeping or scraping equipment. Material left in the cremation chamber, after the completion of a cremation, that can be reasonably removed shall not be considered "residue."

(Amended by Stats. 2001, Ch. 436, Sec. 8. Effective January 1, 2002.)

7010.7.

(a) "Scattering" means the authorized dispersal of cremated remains at sea, in other areas of the state, or commingling in a defined area within a dedicated cemetery, in accordance with this part.

(b) This section shall remain in effect only until July 1, 2020, and as of that date is repealed.

(Amended by Stats. 2017, Ch. 846, Sec. 37. (AB 967) Effective January 1, 2018. Repealed as of July 1, 2020, by its own provisions. See later operative version added by Stats. 2017, Ch. 846.)

7010.7.

(a) "Scattering" means the authorized dispersal of cremated remains or hydrolyzed human remains at sea, in other areas of the state, or commingling in a defined area within a dedicated cemetery, in accordance with this part.

(b) This section shall become operative on July 1, 2020.

(Repealed (in Sec. 37) and added by Stats. 2017, Ch. 846, Sec. 38. (AB 967) Effective January 1, 2018. Section operative July 1, 2020, by its own provisions.)

7011.

(a) "Inurnment" means placing cremated remains in a cremated remains container suitable for placement, burial, or shipment.

(b) This section shall remain in effect only until July 1, 2020, and as of that date is repealed.

(Amended by Stats. 2017, Ch. 846, Sec. 39. (AB 967) Effective January 1, 2018. Repealed as of July 1, 2020, by its own provisions. See later operative version added by Stats. 2017, Ch. 846.)

7011.

(a) "Inurnment" means placing cremated remains or hydrolyzed human remains in a cremated remains container or hydrolyzed human remains container suitable for placement, burial, or shipment.

(b) This section shall become operative on July 1, 2020.

(Repealed (in Sec. 39) and added by Stats. 2017, Ch. 846, Sec. 40. (AB 967) Effective January 1, 2018. Section operative July 1, 2020, by its own provisions.)

7011.2.

(a) "Placement" means the placing of a container holding cremated remains in a crypt, vault, or niche.

(b) This section shall remain in effect only until July 1, 2020, and as of that date is repealed.

(Amended by Stats. 2017, Ch. 846, Sec. 41. (AB 967) Effective January 1, 2018. Repealed as of July 1, 2020, by its own provisions. See later operative version added by Stats. 2017, Ch. 846.)

7011.2.

(a) "Placement" means the placing of a container holding cremated remains or hydrolyzed human remains in a crypt, vault, or niche.

(b) This section shall become operative on July 1, 2020.

(Repealed (in Sec. 41) and added by Stats. 2017, Ch. 846, Sec. 42. (AB 967) Effective January 1, 2018. Section operative July 1, 2020, by its own provisions.)

7012.

"Entombment" means the process of placing human remains in a crypt or vault.

(Amended by Stats. 2001, Ch. 436, Sec. 10. Effective January 1, 2002.)

7013.

"Burial" means the process of placing human remains in a grave.

(Amended by Stats. 2001, Ch. 436, Sec. 11. Effective January 1, 2002.)

7014.

"Grave" means a space of earth in a burial park, used, or intended to be used, for the disposition of human remains.

(Amended by Stats. 2001, Ch. 436, Sec. 12. Effective January 1, 2002.)

7015.

(a) "Crypt" or "vault" means a space in a mausoleum of sufficient size, used or intended to be used, to entomb uncremated human remains.

(b) This section shall remain in effect only until July 1, 2020, and as of that date is repealed.

(Amended by Stats. 2017, Ch. 846, Sec. 43. (AB 967) Effective January 1, 2018. Repealed as of July 1, 2020, by its own provisions. See later operative version added by Stats. 2017, Ch. 846.)

7015.

(a) "Crypt" or "vault" means a space in a mausoleum of sufficient size, used or intended to be used, to entomb human remains that have been neither cremated nor hydrolyzed.

(b) This section shall become operative on July 1, 2020.

(Repealed (in Sec. 43) and added by Stats. 2017, Ch. 846, Sec. 44. (AB 967) Effective January 1, 2018. Section operative July 1, 2020, by its own provisions.)

7016.

(a) "Niche" means a space in a columbarium used, or intended to be used, for the placement of cremated human remains.

(b) This section shall remain in effect only until July 1, 2020, and as of that date is repealed.

(Amended by Stats. 2017, Ch. 846, Sec. 45. (AB 967) Effective January 1, 2018. Repealed as of July 1, 2020, by its own provisions. See later operative version added by Stats. 2017, Ch. 846.)

7016.

(a) "Niche" means a space in a columbarium used, or intended to be used, for the placement of cremated human remains or hydrolyzed human remains.

(b) This section shall become operative on July 1, 2020.

(Repealed (in Sec. 45) and added by Stats. 2017, Ch. 846, Sec. 46. (AB 967) Effective January 1, 2018. Section operative July 1, 2020, by its own provisions.)

7017.

(a) "Hydrolysate" means the resultant liquid from the hydrolysis of human remains, which liquid is a sterile, benign, micronutrient-rich solution consisting of sugars, salts, peptides, and amino acids. Hydrolysate and calcium phosphate "ashes" are the two end results from the alkaline hydrolysis process.

(b) This section shall become operative on July 1, 2020.

(Added by Stats. 2017, Ch. 846, Sec. 47. (AB 967) Effective January 1, 2018. Section operative July 1, 2020, by its own provisions.)

7018.

"Cemetery authority" includes cemetery association, corporation sole, limited liability company, or other person owning or controlling cemetery lands or property.

(Amended by Stats. 2008, Ch. 114, Sec. 3. Effective January 1, 2009.)

7019.

"Cemetery corporation," "cemetery association," or "cemetery corporation or association," means any corporation now or hereafter organized which is or may be authorized by its articles to conduct any one or more or all of the businesses of a cemetery, but do not mean or include a corporation sole.

(Enacted by Stats. 1939, Ch. 60.)

7020.

"Cemetery business," "cemetery businesses," and "cemetery purposes" are used interchangeably and mean any and all business and purposes requisite to, necessary for, or incident to, establishing, maintaining, operating, improving, or conducting a cemetery, interring human remains, and the care, preservation, and embellishment of cemetery property, including, but not limited to, any activity or business designed for the benefit, service, convenience, education, or spiritual uplift of property owners or persons visiting the cemetery.

(Amended by Stats. 1955, Ch. 595.)

7021.

"Directors" or "governing body" means the board of directors, board of trustees, or other policymaking body of a cemetery association.

(Amended by Stats. 2001, Ch. 436, Sec. 15. Effective January 1, 2002.)

7022.

"Lot," "plot," or "interment plot" means space in a cemetery, used or intended to be used for the interment of human remains. Such terms include and apply to one or more than one adjoining graves, one or more than one adjoining crypts or vaults, or one or more than one adjoining niches.

(Enacted by Stats. 1939, Ch. 60.)

7023.

"Plot owner," "owner," or "lot proprietor," means any person in whose name an interment plot stands of record as owner, in the office of a cemetery authority.

(Amended by Stats. 1939, Ch. 339.)

7024.

"Permit for Disposition of Human Remains" includes "burial permit" and is a permit, issued pursuant to law, for the interment, disinterment, removal, reinterment or transportation of human remains.

(Amended by Stats. 1957, Ch. 363.)

7025.

"Disposition" means the interment of human remains within California, or the shipment outside of California, for lawful interment or scattering elsewhere, including release of remains pursuant to Section 103060.

(Amended by Stats. 1996, Ch. 1023, Sec. 190. Effective September 29, 1996.)

CHAPTER 2. General Provisions [7050.5 - 7055]

(Chapter 2 enacted by Stats. 1939, Ch. 60.)

7050.5.

(a) Every person who knowingly mutilates or disinters, wantonly disturbs, or willfully removes any human remains in or from any location other than a dedicated cemetery without authority of law is guilty of a misdemeanor, except as provided in Section 5097.99 of the Public Resources Code. The provisions of this subdivision shall not apply to any person carrying out an agreement developed pursuant to subdivision (l) of Section 5097.94 of the Public Resources Code or to any person authorized to implement Section 5097.98 of the Public Resources Code.

(b) In the event of discovery or recognition of any human remains in any location other than a dedicated cemetery, there shall be no further excavation or disturbance of the site or any nearby area reasonably suspected to overlie adjacent remains until the coroner of the county in which the human remains are discovered has determined, in accordance with Chapter 10 (commencing with Section 27460) of Part 3 of Division 2 of Title 3 of the Government Code, that the remains are not subject to the provisions of Section 27491 of the Government Code or any other related provisions of law concerning investigation of the circumstances, manner and cause of any death, and the recommendations concerning the treatment and disposition of the human remains have been made to the person responsible for the excavation, or to his or her authorized representative, in the manner provided in Section 5097.98 of the Public Resources Code. The coroner shall make his or her determination within two working days from the time the person responsible for the excavation, or his or her authorized representative, notifies the coroner of the discovery or recognition of the human remains.

(c) If the coroner determines that the remains are not subject to his or her authority and if the coroner recognizes the human remains to be those of a Native American, or has reason to believe that they are those of a Native American, he or she shall contact, by telephone within 24 hours, the Native American Heritage Commission.

(Amended by Stats. 1987, Ch. 404, Sec. 1.)

7051.

(a) Every person who removes any part of any human remains from any place where it has been interred, or from any place where it is deposited while awaiting interment or cremation, with intent to sell it or to dissect it, without authority of law, or written permission of the person or persons having the right to control the remains under Section 7100, or with malice or wantonness, has committed a public offense that is punishable by imprisonment pursuant to subdivision (h) of Section 1170 of the Penal Code.

(b) This section shall not prohibit the removal of foreign materials, pacemakers, or prostheses from cremated remains by an employee of a licensed crematory prior to final processing of ashes. Dental gold or silver, jewelry, or mementos, to the extent that they can be identified, may be removed by the employee prior to final processing if the equipment is such that it will not process these materials. However, any dental gold and silver, jewelry, or mementos that are removed shall be returned to the urn or cremated remains container, unless otherwise directed by the person or persons having the right to control the disposition.

(c) This section shall remain in effect only until July 1, 2020, and as of that date is repealed.

(Amended by Stats. 2017, Ch. 846, Sec. 48. (AB 967) Effective January 1, 2018. Repealed as of July 1, 2020, by its own provisions. See later operative version added by Stats. 2017, Ch. 846.)

7051.

(a) Every person who removes any part of any human remains from any place where it has been interred, or from any place where it is deposited while awaiting interment, cremation, or hydrolysis, with intent to sell it or to dissect it, without authority of law, or written permission of the person or persons having the right to control the remains under Section 7100, or with malice or wantonness, has committed a public offense that is punishable by imprisonment pursuant to subdivision (h) of Section 1170 of the Penal Code.

(b) This section shall not prohibit the removal of foreign materials, pacemakers, or prostheses from cremated remains or hydrolyzed human remains by an employee of a licensed crematory or licensed hydrolysis facility prior to final processing of remains. Dental gold or silver, jewelry, or mementos, to the extent that they can be identified, may be removed by the employee prior to final processing if the equipment is such that it will not process these materials. However, any dental gold and silver, jewelry, or mementos that are removed shall be returned to the urn, cremated remains container, or hydrolyzed human remains container, unless otherwise directed by the person or persons having the right to control the disposition.

(c) This section shall become operative on July 1, 2020.

(Repealed (in Sec. 48) and added by Stats. 2017, Ch. 846, Sec. 49. (AB 967) Effective January 1, 2018. Section operative July 1, 2020, by its own provisions.)

7051.5.

(a) Every person who removes or possesses dental gold or silver, jewelry, or mementos from any human remains without specific written permission of the person or persons having the right to control those remains under Section 7100 is punishable by imprisonment pursuant to subdivision (h) of Section 1170 of the Penal Code. The fact that residue and any unavoidable dental gold or dental silver, or other precious metals remain in the cremation chamber or other equipment or any container used in a prior cremation is not a violation of this section.

(b) This section shall remain in effect only until July 1, 2020, and as of that date is repealed.

(Amended by Stats. 2017, Ch. 846, Sec. 50. (AB 967) Effective January 1, 2018. Repealed as of July 1, 2020, by its own provisions. See later operative version added by Stats. 2017, Ch. 846.)

7051.5.

(a) Every person who removes or possesses dental gold or silver, jewelry, or mementos from any human remains without specific written permission of the person or persons having the right to control those remains under Section 7100 is punishable by imprisonment pursuant to subdivision (h) of Section 1170 of the Penal Code. The fact that residue and any unavoidable dental gold or dental silver, or other precious metals remain in the cremation chamber, hydrolysis chamber, or other equipment or any container used in a prior cremation or hydrolysis is not a violation of this section.

(b) This section shall become operative on July 1, 2020.

(Repealed (in Sec. 50) and added by Stats. 2017, Ch. 846, Sec. 51. (AB 967) Effective January 1, 2018. Section operative July 1, 2020, by its own provisions.)

7052.

(a) Every person who willfully mutilates, disinters, removes from the place of interment, or commits an act of sexual penetration on, or has sexual contact with, any remains known to be human, without authority of law, is guilty of a felony. This section does not apply to any person who, under authority of law, removes the remains for reinterment, or performs a cremation.

(b) For purposes of this section, the following definitions apply:

(1) "Sexual penetration" means the unlawful penetration of the vagina or anus, however slight, by any part of a person's body or other object, or any act of sexual contact between the sex organs of a person and the mouth or anus of a dead body, or any oral copulation of a dead human body for the purpose of sexual arousal, gratification, or abuse.

(2) "Sexual contact" means any willful touching by a person of an intimate part of a dead human body for the purpose of sexual arousal, gratification, or abuse.

(c) This section shall remain in effect only until July 1, 2020, and as of that date is repealed.

(Amended by Stats. 2017, Ch. 846, Sec. 52. (AB 967) Effective January 1, 2018. Repealed as of July 1, 2020, by its own provisions. See later operative version added by Stats. 2017, Ch. 846.)

7052.

(a) Every person who willfully mutilates, disinters, removes from the place of interment, or commits an act of sexual penetration on, or has sexual contact with, any remains known to be human, without authority of law, is guilty of a felony. This section does not apply to any person who, under authority of law, removes the remains for reinterment, or performs a cremation or hydrolysis.

(b) For purposes of this section, the following definitions apply:

(1) "Sexual penetration" means the unlawful penetration of the vagina or anus, however slight, by any part of a person's body or other object, or any act of sexual contact between the sex organs of a person and the mouth or anus of a dead body, or any oral copulation of a dead human body for the purpose of sexual arousal, gratification, or abuse.

(2) "Sexual contact" means any willful touching by a person of an intimate part of a dead human body for the purpose of sexual arousal, gratification, or abuse.

(c) This section shall become operative on July 1, 2020.

(Repealed (in Sec. 52) and added by Stats. 2017, Ch. 846, Sec. 53. (AB 967) Effective January 1, 2018. Section operative July 1, 2020, by its own provisions.)

7052.5.

(a) Notwithstanding the provisions of Section 7052, cremated remains may be removed from the place of interment for disposition as provided in Section 7054.6 or for burial at sea as provided in Section 7117.

(b) This section shall remain in effect only until July 1, 2020, and as of that date is repealed.

(Amended by Stats. 2017, Ch. 846, Sec. 54. (AB 967) Effective January 1, 2018. Repealed as of July 1, 2020, by its own provisions. See later operative version added by Stats. 2017, Ch. 846.)

7052.5.

(a) Notwithstanding the provisions of Section 7052, cremated remains or hydrolyzed human remains may be removed from the place of interment for disposition as provided in Section 7054.6 or for burial at sea as provided in Section 7117.

(b) This section shall become operative on July 1, 2020.

(Repealed (in Sec. 54) and added by Stats. 2017, Ch. 846, Sec. 55. (AB 967) Effective January 1, 2018. Section operative July 1, 2020, by its own provisions.)

7053.

Every person who arrests, attaches, detains, or claims to detain any human remains for any debt or demand, or upon any pretended lien or charge, or fails to release any human remains, the personal effects, or any certificate or permit required under Division 102 (commencing with Section 102100) that is in his or her possession or control forthwith upon the delivery of authorization for the release signed by the next of kin or by any person entitled to the custody of the remains, is guilty of a misdemeanor.

(Amended by Stats. 2003, Ch. 874, Sec. 34. Effective January 1, 2004.)

7054.

(a) (1) Except as authorized pursuant to the sections referred to in subdivision (b), every person who deposits or disposes of any human remains in any place, except in a cemetery, is guilty of a misdemeanor.

(2) Every licensee or registrant pursuant to Chapter 12 (commencing with Section 7600) of Division 3 of the Business and Professions Code and the agents and employees of the licensee or registrant, or any unlicensed person acting in a capacity in which a license from the Cemetery and Funeral Bureau is required, who, except as authorized pursuant to the sections referred to in subdivision (b), deposits or disposes of any human remains in any place, except in a cemetery, is guilty of a misdemeanor that shall be punishable by imprisonment in a county jail not exceeding one year, by a fine not exceeding ten thousand dollars ($10,000), or both that imprisonment and fine.

(b) Cremated remains may be disposed of pursuant to Sections 7054.6, 7116, 7117, and 103060.

(c) Subdivision (a) of this section shall not apply to the reburial of Native American remains under an agreement developed pursuant to subdivision (l) of Section 5097.94 of the Public Resources Code, or implementation of a recommendation or agreement made pursuant to Section 5097.98 of the Public Resources Code.

(d) This section shall remain in effect only until July 1, 2020, and as of that date is repealed.

(Amended by Stats. 2017, Ch. 846, Sec. 56. (AB 967) Effective January 1, 2018. Repealed as of July 1, 2020, by its own provisions. See later operative version added by Stats. 2017, Ch. 846.)

7054.

(a) (1) Except as authorized pursuant to the sections referred to in subdivision (b), every person who deposits or disposes of any human remains in any place, except in a cemetery, is guilty of a misdemeanor.

(2) Every licensee or registrant pursuant to Chapter 12 (commencing with Section 7600) of Division 3 of the Business and Professions Code and the agents and employees of the licensee or registrant, or any unlicensed person acting in a capacity in which a license from the Cemetery and Funeral Bureau is required, who, except as authorized pursuant to the sections referred to in subdivision (b), deposits or disposes of any human remains in any place, except in a cemetery, is guilty of a misdemeanor that shall be punishable by imprisonment in a county jail not exceeding one year, by a fine not exceeding ten thousand dollars ($10,000), or both that imprisonment and fine.

(b) Cremated remains or hydrolyzed human remains may be disposed of pursuant to Sections 7054.6, 7116, 7117, and 103060.

(c) Subdivision (a) of this section shall not apply to the reburial of Native American remains under an agreement developed pursuant to subdivision (l) of Section 5097.94 of the Public Resources Code, or implementation of a recommendation or agreement made pursuant to Section 5097.98 of the Public Resources Code.

(d) This section shall become operative on July 1, 2020.

(Repealed (in Sec. 56) and added by Stats. 2017, Ch. 846, Sec. 57. (AB 967) Effective January 1, 2018. Section operative July 1, 2020, by its own provisions.)

7054.1.

(a) No cremated remains shall be removed from the place of cremation, nor shall there be any charge for the cremation, unless the cremated remains have been processed so that they are suitable for inurnment within a cremated remains container or an urn. Every contract for cremation services shall include specific written notification of the processing to the person having the right to control the disposition of the remains under Section 7100.

(b) This section shall remain in effect only until July 1, 2020, and as of that date is repealed.

(Amended by Stats. 2017, Ch. 846, Sec. 58. (AB 967) Effective January 1, 2018. Repealed as of July 1, 2020, by its own provisions. See later operative version added by Stats. 2017, Ch. 846.)

7054.1.

(a) No cremated remains or hydrolyzed human remains shall be removed from the place of cremation or hydrolysis, nor shall there be any charge for the cremation or hydrolysis, unless the cremated remains or hydrolyzed human remains have been processed so that they are suitable for inurnment within a cremated remains container, hydrolyzed human remains container, or an urn. Every contract for cremation or hydrolysis services shall include specific written notification of the processing to the person having the right to control the disposition of the remains under Section 7100.

(b) This section shall become operative on July 1, 2020.

(Repealed (in Sec. 58) and added by Stats. 2017, Ch. 846, Sec. 59. (AB 967) Effective January 1, 2018. Section operative July 1, 2020, by its own provisions.)

7054.3.

Notwithstanding any other provision of law, a recognizable dead human fetus of less than 20 weeks uterogestation not disposed of by interment shall be disposed of by incineration.

(Added by Stats. 1971, Ch. 377.)

7054.4.

Notwithstanding any other provision of law, recognizable anatomical parts, human tissues, anatomical human remains, or infectious waste following conclusion of scientific use shall be disposed of by interment, incineration, or any other method determined by the state department to protect the public health and safety.

As used in this section, "infectious waste" means any material or article which has been, or may have been, exposed to contagious or infectious disease.

(Amended by Stats. 1972, Ch. 883.)

7054.6.

(a) Except as provided in subdivision (b), cremated remains may be removed in a durable container from the place of cremation or interment and kept in or on the real property owned or occupied by a person described in Section 7100 or any other person, with the permission of the person with the right to disposition, or the durable container holding the cremated remains may be kept in a church or religious shrine, if written permission of the church or religious shrine is obtained and there is no conflict with local use permit requirements or zoning laws, if the removal is under the authority of a permit for disposition granted under Section 103060. The placement, in any place, of six or more cremated remains under this section does not constitute the place a cemetery, as defined in Section 7003.

(b) Notwithstanding any other provision of law, cremated remains may be placed in one or more keepsake urns. Keepsake urns shall be kept as authorized by the person or persons with the right to control disposition pursuant to Section 7100, provided that a permit for disposition of human remains pursuant to Section 103060 is issued by the local registrar for each keepsake urn designating the home address of each person receiving a keepsake urn and a permit fee pursuant to Section 103065 is paid. No keepsake urn shall be subject to Section 8345. For purposes of this section, a keepsake urn shall mean a closed durable container that will accommodate an amount of cremated remains not to exceed one cubic centimeter.

(c) Prior to disposition of cremated remains, every licensee or registrant pursuant to Chapter 12 (commencing with Section 7600) of Division 3 of the Business and Professions Code, and the agents and employees of the licensee or registrant shall do all of the following:

(1) Remove the cremated remains from the place of cremation in a durable container.

(2) Keep the cremated remains in a durable container.

(3) Store the cremated remains in a place free from exposure to the elements.

(4) Responsibly maintain the cremated remains.

(d) This section shall remain in effect only until July 1, 2020, and as of that date is repealed.

(Amended by Stats. 2017, Ch. 846, Sec. 60. (AB 967) Effective January 1, 2018. Repealed as of July 1, 2020, by its own provisions. See later operative version added by Stats. 2017, Ch. 846.)

7054.6.

(a) Except as provided in subdivision (b), cremated remains or hydrolyzed human remains may be removed in a durable container from the place of cremation, hydrolysis, or interment and kept in or on the real property owned or occupied by a person described in Section 7100 or any other person, with the permission of the person with the right to disposition, or the durable container holding the cremated remains or hydrolyzed human remains may be kept in a church or religious shrine, if written permission of the church or religious shrine is obtained and there is no conflict with local use permit requirements or zoning laws, if the removal is under the authority of a permit for disposition granted under Section 103060. The placement, in any place, of six or more cremated remains or hydrolyzed human remains under this section does not constitute the place a cemetery, as defined in Section 7003.

(b) Notwithstanding any other provision of law, cremated remains or hydrolyzed human remains may be placed in one or more keepsake urns. Keepsake urns shall be kept as authorized by the person or persons with the right to control disposition pursuant to Section 7100, provided that a permit for disposition of human remains pursuant to Section 103060 is issued by the local registrar for each keepsake urn designating the home address of each person receiving a keepsake urn and a permit fee pursuant to Section 103065 is paid. No keepsake urn shall be subject to Section 8345. For purposes of this section, a keepsake urn shall mean a closed durable container that will accommodate an amount of cremated remains or hydrolyzed human remains not to exceed one cubic centimeter.

(c) Prior to disposition of cremated remains or hydrolyzed human remains, every licensee or registrant pursuant to Chapter 12 (commencing with Section 7600) of Division 3 of the Business and Professions Code, and the agents and employees of the licensee or registrant shall do all of the following:

(1) Remove the cremated remains or hydrolyzed human remains from the place of cremation or hydrolysis in a durable container.

(2) Keep the cremated remains or hydrolyzed human remains in a durable container.

(3) Store the cremated remains or hydrolyzed human remains in a place free from exposure to the elements.

(4) Responsibly maintain the cremated remains or hydrolyzed human remains.

(d) This section shall become operative on July 1, 2020.

(Repealed (in Sec. 60) and added by Stats. 2017, Ch. 846, Sec. 61. (AB 967) Effective January 1, 2018. Section operative July 1, 2020, by its own provisions.)

7054.7.

(a) Except with the express written permission of the person entitled to control the disposition of the remains, no person shall:

(1) Cremate the remains of more than one person at the same time in the same cremation chamber, or introduce the remains of a second person into a cremation chamber until incineration of any preceding remains has been terminated and reasonable efforts have been employed to remove all fragments of the preceding remains. The fact that there is residue in the cremation chamber or other equipment or any container used in a prior cremation is not a violation of this section.

(2) Dispose of or scatter cremated remains in a manner or in a location that the remains are commingled with those of another person. This paragraph shall not apply to the scattering of cremated remains at sea from individual containers or to the disposal in a dedicated cemetery of accumulated residue removed from a cremation chamber or other cremation equipment.

(3) Place cremated or uncremated remains of more than one person in the same container or the same interment space. This paragraph shall not apply to the following:

(A) Interment of members of the same family in a common container designed for the cremated remains of more than one person.

(B) Interment in a space or container that has been previously designated at the time of sale as being intended for the interment of remains of more than one person.

(C) Disposal in a dedicated cemetery of residue removed from a cremation chamber or other cremation equipment.

(b) Written acknowledgement from the person entitled to control the disposition of the cremated remains shall be obtained by the person with whom arrangements are made for disposition of the remains on a form that includes, but is not limited to, the following information: "The human body burns with the casket, container, or other material in the cremation chamber. Some bone fragments are not combustible at the incineration temperature and, as a result, remain in the cremation chamber. During the cremation, the contents of the chamber may be moved to facilitate incineration. The chamber is composed of ceramic or other material which disintegrates slightly during each cremation and the product of that disintegration is commingled with the cremated remains. Nearly all of the contents of the cremation chamber, consisting of the cremated remains, disintegrated chamber material, and small amounts of residue from previous cremations, are removed together and crushed, pulverized, or ground to facilitate inurnment or scattering. Some residue remains in the cracks and uneven places of the chamber. Periodically, the accumulation of this residue is removed and interred in a dedicated cemetery property, or scattered at sea." The acknowledgment shall be filed and retained, for at least five years, by the person who disposes of or inters the remains.

(c) Any person, including any corporation or partnership, knowingly violating any provision of this section is guilty of a misdemeanor.

(Amended by Stats. 1994, Ch. 570, Sec. 7. Effective January 1, 1995.)

7054.8.

(a) Except with the express written permission of the person entitled to control the disposition of the remains, no person shall do any of the following:

(1) Hydrolyze the remains of more than one person at the same time in the same hydrolysis chamber, or introduce the remains of a second person into a hydrolysis chamber until dissolution of any preceding remains has been terminated and reasonable efforts have been employed to remove all fragments of the preceding remains. The fact that there is residue in the hydrolysis chamber or other equipment or any container used in a prior hydrolysis is not a violation of this section.

(2) Dispose of or scatter hydrolyzed human remains in a manner or in such a location that the remains are commingled with those of another person. This paragraph shall not apply to the scattering of hydrolyzed human remains at sea from individual containers or to the disposal in a dedicated cemetery of accumulated residue removed from processing equipment.

(3) Place hydrolyzed human remains or other remains of more than one person in the same container or the same interment space. This paragraph shall not apply to the following:

(A) Interment of members of the same family in a common container designed for the hydrolyzed human remains of more than one person.

(B) Interment in a space or container that has been previously designated at the time of sale as being intended for the interment of remains of more than one person.

(C) Disposal in a dedicated cemetery of residue removed from processing equipment.

(b) Written acknowledgment from the person entitled to control the disposition of the hydrolyzed human remains shall be obtained by the person with whom arrangements are made for disposition of the remains on a form that includes, but is not limited to, the following information: "The human body is hydrolyzed with organic protein-based material such as wool, silk, cotton, or other protein-based material in the hydrolysis chamber. Bone fragments are not hydrolyzable and, as a result, remain in the chamber. The hydrolyzed remains will be dried and crushed, pulverized, or ground to facilitate inurnment or scattering." The acknowledgment shall be filed and retained, for at least five years, by the person who disposes of or inters the remains.

(c) A person, including any corporation or partnership, that violates any provision of this section is guilty of a misdemeanor.

(d) This section shall become operative on July 1, 2020.

(Added by Stats. 2017, Ch. 846, Sec. 62. (AB 967) Effective January 1, 2018. Section operative July 1, 2020, by its own provisions.)

7055.

(a) Every person, who for himself or herself or for another person, inters or incinerates a body or permits the same to be done, or removes any remains, other than cremated remains, from the primary registration district in which the death or incineration occurred or the body was found, except a removal by a funeral director in a funeral director's conveyance or an officer of a duly accredited medical college engaged in official duties with respect to the body of a decedent who has willfully donated his or her body to the medical college from that registration district or county to another registration district or county, or within the same registration district or county, without the authority of a burial or removal permit issued by the local registrar of the district in which the death occurred or in which the body was found; or removes interred human remains from the cemetery in which the interment occurred; or removes cremated remains from the premises on which the cremation occurred without the authority of a removal permit is guilty of a misdemeanor and punishable as follows:

545

(1) For the first offense, by a fine of not less than ten dollars ($10) nor more than five hundred dollars ($500).

(2) For each subsequent offense, by a fine of not less than fifty dollars ($50) nor more than five hundred dollars ($500) or imprisonment in the county jail for not more than 60 days, or by both.

(b) Notwithstanding subdivision (a), a funeral director of a licensed out-of-state funeral establishment may transport human remains out of this state without a removal permit when he or she is acting within the requirements specified in subdivision (b) of Section 103050.

(c) This section shall remain in effect only until July 1, 2020, and as of that date is repealed.

(Amended by Stats. 2017, Ch. 846, Sec. 63. (AB 967) Effective January 1, 2018. Repealed as of July 1, 2020, by its own provisions. See later operative version added by Stats. 2017, Ch. 846.)

7055.

(a) Every person, who for himself or herself or for another person, inters, cremates, or hydrolyzes a body or permits the same to be done, or removes any remains, other than cremated remains or hydrolyzed human remains, from the primary registration district in which the death, cremation, or hydrolysis occurred or the body was found, except a removal by a funeral director in a funeral director's conveyance or an officer of a duly accredited medical college engaged in official duties with respect to the body of a decedent who has willfully donated his or her body to the medical college from that registration district or county to another registration district or county, or within the same registration district or county, without the authority of a burial or removal permit issued by the local registrar of the district in which the death occurred or in which the body was found; or removes interred human remains from the cemetery in which the interment occurred, removes cremated remains from the premises on which the cremation occurred, or removes hydrolyzed human remains from the premises on which the hydrolysis occurred without the authority of a removal permit is guilty of a misdemeanor and punishable as follows:

(1) For the first offense, by a fine of not less than ten dollars ($10) nor more than five hundred dollars ($500).

(2) For each subsequent offense, by a fine of not less than fifty dollars ($50) nor more than five hundred dollars ($500) or imprisonment in the county jail for not more than 60 days, or by both.

(b) Notwithstanding subdivision (a), a funeral director of a licensed out-of-state funeral establishment may transport human remains out of this state without a removal permit when he or she is acting within the requirements specified in subdivision (b) of Section 103050.

(c) This section shall become operative on July 1, 2020.

(Repealed (in Sec. 63) and added by Stats. 2017, Ch. 846, Sec. 64. (AB 967) Effective January 1, 2018. Section operative July 1, 2020, by its own provisions.)

CHAPTER 3. Custody, and Duty of Interment [7100 - 7117.1]

(Chapter 3 enacted by Stats. 1939, Ch. 60.)

7100.

(a) The right to control the disposition of the remains of a deceased person, the location and conditions of interment, and arrangements for funeral goods and services to be provided, unless other directions have been given by the decedent pursuant to Section 7100.1, vests in, and the duty of disposition and the liability for the reasonable cost of disposition of the remains devolves upon, the following in the order named:

(1) An agent under a power of attorney for health care who has the right and duty of disposition under Division 4.7 (commencing with Section 4600) of the Probate Code, except that the agent is liable for the costs of disposition only in either of the following cases:

(A) Where the agent makes a specific agreement to pay the costs of disposition.

(B) Where, in the absence of a specific agreement, the agent makes decisions concerning disposition that incur costs, in which case the agent is liable only for the reasonable costs incurred as a result of the agent's decisions, to the extent that the decedent's estate or other appropriate fund is insufficient.

(2) The competent surviving spouse.

(3) The sole surviving competent adult child of the decedent or, if there is more than one competent adult child of the decedent, the majority of the surviving competent adult children. However, less than the majority of the surviving competent adult children shall be vested with the rights and duties of this section if they have used reasonable efforts to notify all other surviving competent adult children of their instructions and are not aware of any opposition to those instructions by the majority of all surviving competent adult children.

(4) The surviving competent parent or parents of the decedent. If one of the surviving competent parents is absent, the remaining competent parent shall be vested with the rights and duties of this section after reasonable efforts have been unsuccessful in locating the absent surviving competent parent.

(5) The sole surviving competent adult sibling of the decedent or, if there is more than one surviving competent adult sibling of the decedent, the majority of the surviving competent adult siblings. However, less than the majority of the surviving competent adult siblings shall be vested with the rights and duties of this section if they have used reasonable efforts to notify all other surviving competent adult siblings of their

instructions and are not aware of any opposition to those instructions by the majority of all surviving competent adult siblings.

(6) The surviving competent adult person or persons respectively in the next degrees of kinship or, if there is more than one surviving competent adult person of the same degree of kinship, the majority of those persons. Less than the majority of surviving competent adult persons of the same degree of kinship shall be vested with the rights and duties of this section if those persons have used reasonable efforts to notify all other surviving competent adult persons of the same degree of kinship of their instructions and are not aware of any opposition to those instructions by the majority of all surviving competent adult persons of the same degree of kinship.

(7) A conservator of the person appointed under Part 3 (commencing with Section 1800) of Division 4 of the Probate Code when the decedent has sufficient assets.

(8) A conservator of the estate appointed under Part 3 (commencing with Section 1800) of Division 4 of the Probate Code when the decedent has sufficient assets.

(9) The public administrator when the deceased has sufficient assets.

(b) (1) If a person to whom the right of control has vested pursuant to subdivision (a) has been charged with first- or second-degree murder or voluntary manslaughter in connection with the decedent's death and those charges are known to the funeral director or cemetery authority, the right of control is relinquished and passed on to the next of kin in accordance with subdivision (a).

(2) If the charges against the person are dropped, or if the person is acquitted of the charges, the right of control is returned to the person.

(3) Notwithstanding this subdivision, no person who has been charged with first- or second-degree murder or voluntary manslaughter in connection with the decedent's death to whom the right of control has not been returned pursuant to paragraph (2) shall have any right to control disposition pursuant to subdivision (a) which shall be applied, to the extent the funeral director or cemetery authority know about the charges, as if that person did not exist.

(c) A funeral director or cemetery authority shall have complete authority to control the disposition of the remains and to proceed under this chapter to recover usual and customary charges for the disposition when both of the following apply:

(1) Either of the following applies:

(A) The funeral director or cemetery authority has knowledge that none of the persons described in paragraphs (1) to (8), inclusive, of subdivision (a) exists.

(B) None of the persons described in paragraphs (1) to (8), inclusive, of subdivision (a) can be found after reasonable inquiry, or contacted by reasonable means.

(2) The public administrator fails to assume responsibility for disposition of the remains within seven days after having been given written notice of the facts. Written notice may be delivered by hand, United States mail, facsimile transmission, or telegraph.

(d) The liability for the reasonable cost of final disposition devolves jointly and severally upon all kin of the decedent in the same degree of kinship and upon the estate of the decedent. However, if a person accepts the gift of an entire body under subdivision (a) of Section 7155.5, that person, subject to the terms of the gift, shall be liable for the reasonable cost of final disposition of the decedent.

(e) This section shall be administered and construed to the end that the expressed instructions of the decedent or the person entitled to control the disposition shall be faithfully and promptly performed.

(f) A funeral director or cemetery authority shall not be liable to any person or persons for carrying out the instructions of the decedent or the person entitled to control the disposition.

(g) For purposes of this section, "adult" means an individual who has attained 18 years of age, "child" means a natural or adopted child of the decedent, and "competent" means an individual who has not been declared incompetent by a court of law or who has been declared competent by a court of law following a declaration of incompetence.

(h) (1) For the purpose of paragraph (1) of subdivision (a), the designation of a person authorized to direct disposition (PADD) on a United States Department of Defense Record of Emergency Data, DD Form 93, as that form exists on December 31, 2011, or its successor form, shall take first priority and be used to establish an agent who has the right and duty of disposition for a decedent who died while on duty in any branch or component of the Armed Forces of the United States, as defined by Section 1481 of Title 10 of the United States Code.

(2) This subdivision shall become operative only if the United States Department of Defense Record of Emergency Data, DD Form 93, and Section 1482(c) of Title 10 of the United States Code are amended to allow a service member to designate any person, regardless of the relationship of the designee to the decedent, as the agent who has the right of disposition of a service member's remains.

(Amended by Stats. 2011, Ch. 321, Sec. 1.5. (AB 905) Effective January 1, 2012.)

7100.1.

(a) A decedent, prior to death, may direct, in writing, the disposition of his or her remains and specify funeral goods and services to be provided. Unless there is a statement to the contrary that is signed and dated by the decedent, the directions may not be altered, changed, or otherwise amended in any material way, except as may be required by law, and shall be faithfully carried out upon his or her death, provided both of the following requirements are met: (1) the directions set forth clearly and completely the final wishes of the decedent in sufficient detail so as to preclude any material ambiguity with regard to the instructions; and, (2) arrangements for payment through trusts, insurance, commitments by others, or any other effective and binding means, have been made, so as to preclude the payment of any funds by the survivor or survivors of the deceased that might otherwise retain the right to control the disposition.

(b) In the event arrangements for only one of either the cost of interment or the cost of the funeral goods and services are made pursuant to this section, the remaining wishes of the decedent shall be carried out only to the extent that the decedent has sufficient assets to do so, unless the person or persons that otherwise have the right to control the disposition and arrange for funeral goods and services agree to assume the cost. All other provisions of the directions shall be carried out.

(c) If the directions are contained in a will, they shall be immediately carried out, regardless of the validity of the will in other respects or of the fact that the will may not be offered for or admitted to probate until a later date.

(Amended by Stats. 1998, Ch. 253, Sec. 2. Effective January 1, 1999.)

7101.

When any decedent leaves an estate in this state, the reasonable cost of interment and an interment plot of sufficient size to constitute a family plot and memorial including reasonable sums for either, or both, general and special endowment care of the plot proportionate to the value of the estate and in keeping with the standard of living adopted by the decedent prior to his demise, together with interest thereon from 60 days after the date of death, shall be considered as a part of the funeral expenses of the decedent and shall be paid as a preferred charge against his estate as provided in the Probate Code.

Reasonable costs of funeral services, together with interest thereon from 60 days after the date of death, shall be considered as a part of the funeral expenses of the decedent and shall be paid as a preferred charge against his estate as provided in the Probate Code.

If a claim for mortuary and funeral services, an interment plot or memorial is rejected the burden of proving that the cost of the funeral service, interment plot or memorial is disproportionate to the value of the estate and the standard of living adopted by the decedent while living shall be upon the executor or administrator rejecting the claim. This chapter does not prohibit any relative or friend of a decedent from assuming the duty or paying the expense of interment or the funeral services.

(Amended by Stats. 1968, Ch. 267.)

7102.

When a person is charged by law with the duty of interment he is entitled to the custody of the remains for the purpose of interment or, with respect to cremated remains, for the purpose of burial at sea in accordance with the provisions of this division; except that in any case where a coroner is required by law to investigate the cause of death, the coroner is entitled to the custody of the remains of the person whose death is the subject of investigation until the conclusion of the autopsy or medical investigation by the coroner. Any person in whose possession such remains are found, shall, upon demand by the coroner, surrender such remains to him.

(Amended by Stats. 1965, Ch. 1421.)

7103.

(a) Every person, upon whom the duty of interment is imposed by law, who omits to perform that duty within a reasonable time is guilty of a misdemeanor.

(b) Every licensee or registrant pursuant to Chapter 12 (commencing with Section 7600) of Division 3 of the Business and Professions Code, and the agents and employees of the licensee or registrant, or any unlicensed person acting in a capacity in which a license from the Cemetery and Funeral Bureau is required, upon whom the duty of interment is imposed by law, who omits to perform that duty within a reasonable time is guilty of a misdemeanor that shall be punishable by imprisonment in a county jail not exceeding one year, by a fine not exceeding ten thousand dollars ($10,000), or both that imprisonment and fine.

(c) In addition, any person, registrant, or licensee described in subdivision (a) or (b) is liable to pay the person performing the duty in his or her stead treble the expenses incurred by the latter in making the interment, to be recovered in a civil action.

(Amended by Stats. 2018, Ch. 571, Sec. 32. (SB 1480) Effective January 1, 2019.)

7104.

(a) When no provision is made by the decedent, or where the estate is insufficient to provide for interment and the duty of interment does not devolve upon any other person residing in the state or if such person can not after reasonable diligence be found within the state the person who has custody of the remains may require the coroner of the county where the decedent resided at time of death to take possession of the remains and the coroner shall inter the remains in the manner provided for the interment of indigent dead.

(b) A county exercising jurisdiction over the death of an individual pursuant to Section 27491, or who assumes jurisdiction pursuant to Section 27491.55 of the Government Code, shall be responsible for the disposition of the remains of that decedent. If the decedent is an indigent, the costs associated with disposition of the remains shall be borne by the county exercising jurisdiction.

(Amended by Stats. 1988, Ch. 1139, Sec. 2.)

7104.1.

If, within 30 days after the coroner notifies or diligently attempts to notify the person responsible for the interment of a decedent's remains which are in the possession of the coroner, the person fails, refuses, or neglects to inter the remains, the coroner may inter the remains. The coroner may recover any expenses of the interment from the responsible person.

(Amended by Stats. 2001, Ch. 436, Sec. 18. Effective January 1, 2002.)

7105.

(a) If the person or persons listed in paragraphs (1), (3), (4), (5), (6), (7), and (8) of subdivision (a) of Section 7100 who would otherwise have the right to control the disposition and arrange for funeral goods and services fails to act, or fails to delegate his

or her authority to act to some other person within seven days of the date when the right and duty devolves upon the person or persons, or in the case of a person listed in paragraph (2) of subdivision (a) of Section 7100, within 10 days of the date when the right and duty devolves upon the person, the right to control the disposition and arrange for funeral goods and services shall be relinquished and passed on to the person or persons of the next degree of kinship in accordance with subdivision (a) of Section 7100.

(b) If the person or persons listed in paragraphs (1), (3), (4), (5), (6), (7), and (8) of subdivision (a) of Section 7100 who would otherwise have the right to control the disposition and arrange for funeral goods and services cannot be found within seven days of the date when the right and duty devolves upon the person or persons, or in the case of a person listed in paragraph (2) of subdivision (a) of Section 7100, within 10 days of the date when the right and duty devolves upon the person, after reasonable inquiry, the right to control the disposition and arrange for funeral goods and services shall be relinquished and passed on to the person or persons of the next degree of kinship in accordance with subdivision (a) of Section 7100.

(c) If any persons listed in paragraphs (1), (3), (4), (5), (6), (7), and (8) of subdivision (a) of Section 7100 who would otherwise have equal rights to control the disposition and arrange for funeral goods and services fail to agree on disposition and funeral goods and services to be provided within seven days of the date on which the right and duty of disposition devolved upon the persons, a funeral establishment or a cemetery authority having possession of the remains, or any person who has equal right to control the disposition of the remains may file a petition in the superior court in the county in which the decedent resided at the time of his or her death, or in which the remains are located, naming as a party to the action those persons who would otherwise have equal rights to control the disposition and seeking an order of the court determining, as appropriate, who among those parties will have the control of disposition and to direct that person to make interment of the remains. The court, at the time of determining the person to whom the right of disposition will vest, shall, from the remaining parties to the action, establish an alternate order to whom the right to control disposition will pass if the person vested with the right to control disposition fails to act within seven days.

(d) If the person vested with the duty of interment has criminal charges pending against him or her for the unlawful killing of the decedent, in violation of Section 187 of, or subdivision (a) or (b) of Section 192 of, the Penal Code, the person or persons with the next highest priority prescribed by Section 7100 may petition a court of competent jurisdiction for an order for control of the disposition of the decedent's remains. For this purpose, it shall be conclusively presumed that the petitioner is the person entitled to control the disposition of the remains if the petitioner is next in the order of priority specified in Section 7100.

(Amended by Stats. 2016, Ch. 39, Sec. 1. (SB 1284) Effective January 1, 2017.)

7106.

A cemetery authority may seek an order providing for the interment of the remains of one or more decedents. Where a proceeding is commenced involving the remains of more than one decedent the allegations of the petition shall separately state the facts as to each, and the court may make a separate order as to each.

(Enacted by Stats. 1939, Ch. 60.)

7107.

Notice of the time and place of the hearing on the petition shall be given as the court may direct. Upon the hearing the court shall make its order providing for the interment of the remains in such manner, at such time, and at such place as the court may determine to be just and proper, and for the best interests of the public health.

(Enacted by Stats. 1939, Ch. 60.)

7108.

If the coroner is directed to make such interment he shall make it in the manner provided by law for the interment of the indigent dead.

(Amended by Stats. 1939, Ch. 339.)

7109.

The court shall allow costs and reasonable attorney's fees to a prevailing plaintiff against all defendants, other than the coroner.

(Amended by Stats. 2001, Ch. 436, Sec. 19. Effective January 1, 2002.)

7110.

Any person signing any authorization for the interment or cremation of any remains warrants the truthfulness of any fact set forth in the authorization, the identity of the person whose remains are sought to be interred or cremated, and his or her authority to order interment or cremation. He or she is personally liable for all damage occasioned by or resulting from breach of such warranty.

(Amended by Stats. 1993, Ch. 1232, Sec. 23. Effective January 1, 1994.)

7111.

A cemetery authority or crematory may make an interment or cremation of any remains upon the receipt of a written authorization of a person representing himself or herself to be a person having the right to control the disposition of the remains pursuant to Section 7100.

A cemetery authority or crematory is not liable for cremating, making an interment, or for other disposition of remains permitted by law, pursuant to that authorization, unless it has actual notice that the representation is untrue.

(Amended by Stats. 2002, Ch. 819, Sec. 7. Effective January 1, 2003.)

7112.

No action shall lie against any cemetery authority relating to the cremated remains of any person which have been left in its possession for a period of one year, unless a written contract has been entered into with the cemetery authority for their care or unless permanent interment has been made.

No licensed funeral director shall be liable in damages for the lawful disposition of any cremated human remains.

(Amended by Stats. 1993, Ch. 1232, Sec. 25. Effective January 1, 1994.)

7113.

A cemetery authority or licensed funeral director or a licensed hospital or its authorized personnel may permit or assist, and a physician may perform, an autopsy of any remains in its or his custody if the decedent, prior to his death, authorizes an autopsy in his will or other written instrument, or upon the receipt of a written authorization, telegram, or a verbal authorization obtained by telephone and recorded on tape or other recording device, from a person representing himself to be any of the following:

(a) The surviving spouse; (b) a surviving child or parent; (c) a surviving brother or sister; (d) any other kin or person who has acquired the right to control the disposition of the remains; (e) a public administrator; (f) a coroner or any other duly authorized public officer. A cemetery authority or a licensed funeral director or a licensed hospital or its authorized personnel is not liable for permitting or assisting, and a physician is not liable for performing, an autopsy pursuant to such authorization unless he or it has actual notice that such representation is untrue at the time the autopsy is performed. If such authorization is contained in a will, the autopsy may be performed regardless of the validity of the will in other respects or of the fact that the will may not be offered for or admitted to probate until a later date.

This section shall not authorize the obtaining of a verbal authorization by telephone and recorded on tape or other recording device for an autopsy of a deceased person if it is made known to the physician who is to perform the autopsy that the deceased was, at the time of his death, a member of a religion, church, or denomination which relies solely upon prayer for the healing of disease.

(Amended by Stats. 1971, Ch. 99.)

7114.

Any person who performs, permits or assists at, an autopsy on a dead body without having first obtained (a) the authorization of the deceased in writing, including, but not limited to, the last will of the deceased; or (b) the authorization in writing of the person designated by Section 7100 of this code as having the right to control the disposition of the remains of the deceased; or (c) in the case of a cemetery authority or a licensed funeral director or a licensed hospital or its agents or a physician, the written or verbal authorization described in Section 7113 or 7151.6 of this code, is guilty of a misdemeanor, except that this section shall not be applicable to the performance of an autopsy by the coroner or other officer authorized by law to perform autopsies.

(Amended by Stats. 1972, Ch. 1048.)

7116.

(a) Cremated remains may be scattered in areas where no local prohibition exists, provided that the cremated remains are not distinguishable to the public, are not in a container, and that the person who has control over disposition of the cremated remains has obtained written permission of the property owner or governing agency to scatter on the property. A state or local agency may adopt an ordinance, regulation, or policy, as appropriate, authorizing, consistent with this section, or specifically prohibiting, the scattering of cremated human remains on lands under the agency's jurisdiction. The scattering of the cremated remains of more than one person in one location pursuant to this section shall not create a cemetery pursuant to Section 7003 or any other provision of law.

(b) This section shall remain in effect only until July 1, 2020, and as of that date is repealed.

(Amended by Stats. 2017, Ch. 846, Sec. 65. (AB 967) Effective January 1, 2018. Repealed as of July 1, 2020, by its own provisions. See later operative version added by Stats. 2017, Ch. 846.)

7116.

(a) Cremated remains or hydrolyzed human remains may be scattered in areas where no local prohibition exists, provided that the cremated remains or hydrolyzed human remains are not distinguishable to the public, are not in a container, and that the person who has control over disposition of the cremated remains or hydrolyzed human remains has obtained written permission of the property owner or governing agency to scatter on the property. A state or local agency may adopt an ordinance, regulation, or policy, as appropriate, authorizing, consistent with this section, or specifically prohibiting, the scattering of cremated human remains or hydrolyzed human remains on lands under the agency's jurisdiction. The scattering of the cremated remains or hydrolyzed human remains of more than one person in one location pursuant to this section shall not create a cemetery pursuant to Section 7003 or any other provision of law.

(b) This section shall become operative on July 1, 2020.

(Repealed (in Sec. 65) and added by Stats. 2017, Ch. 846, Sec. 66. (AB 967) Effective January 1, 2018. Section operative July 1, 2020, by its own provisions.)

7117.

(a) Cremated remains may be taken by boat from any harbor in this state, or by air, and scattered at sea. Cremated remains shall be removed from their container before the remains are scattered at sea.

(b) Any person who scatters at sea, either from a boat or from the air, any cremated human remains shall, file with the local registrar of births and deaths in the county nearest the point where the remains were scattered, a verified statement containing the name of the deceased person, the time and place of death, the place at which the cremated remains were scattered, and any other information that the local registrar of births and deaths may require. The first copy of the endorsed permit shall be filed with the local registrar of births and deaths within 10 days of disposition. The third copy shall be returned to the office of issuance.

(c) For purposes of this section, the phrase "at sea" includes the inland navigable waters of this state, exclusive of lakes and streams, provided that no such scattering may take place within 500 yards of the shoreline. This section does not allow the scattering of cremated human remains from a bridge or pier.

(d) Notwithstanding any other provision of this code, the cremated remains of a deceased person may be scattered at sea as provided in this section and Section 103060.

(e) This section shall remain in effect only until July 1, 2020, and as of that date is repealed.

(Amended (as amended by Stats. 2017, Ch. 846, Sec. 67) by Stats. 2018, Ch. 92, Sec. 138. (SB 1289) Effective January 1, 2019. Repealed as of July 1, 2020, by its own provisions. See later operative version added by Stats. 2017, Ch. 846.)

7117.

(a) Cremated remains or hydrolyzed human remains may be taken by boat from any harbor in this state, or by air, and scattered at sea. Cremated remains or hydrolyzed human remains shall be removed from their container before the remains are scattered at sea.

(b) Any person who scatters at sea, either from a boat or from the air, any cremated human remains or hydrolyzed human remains shall file with the local registrar of births and deaths in the county nearest the point where the remains were scattered, a verified statement containing the name of the deceased person, the time and place of death, the place at which the cremated remains or hydrolyzed human remains were scattered, and any other information that the local registrar of births and deaths may require. The first copy of the endorsed permit shall be filed with the local registrar of births and deaths within 10 days of disposition. The third copy shall be returned to the office of issuance.

(c) For purposes of this section, the phrase "at sea" includes the inland navigable waters of this state, exclusive of lakes and streams, provided that no such scattering may take place within 500 yards of the shoreline. This section does not allow the scattering of cremated human remains or hydrolyzed human remains from a bridge or pier.

(d) Notwithstanding any other provision of this code, the cremated remains or hydrolyzed human remains of a deceased person may be scattered at sea as provided in this section and Section 103060.

(e) This section shall become operative on July 1, 2020.

(Amended (as added by Stats. 2017, Ch. 846, Sec. 68) by Stats. 2018, Ch. 92, Sec. 139. (SB 1289) Effective January 1, 2019.)

7117.1.

(a) Notwithstanding subdivision (a) of Section 7117, cremated remains may be transferred from a durable container into a scattering urn no more than seven days before scattering the cremated remains at sea from a boat. For purposes of this section, "scattering urn" means a closed container containing cremated remains that will dissolve and release its contents within four hours of being placed at sea.

(b) This section shall not be construed to allow the use of a scattering urn when the cremated remains are to be scattered by a plane over land or at sea.

(Added by Stats. 2012, Ch. 79, Sec. 1. (AB 1777) Effective January 1, 2013.)

CHAPTER 3.5. Uniform Anatomical Gift Act [7150 - 7151.40]

(Chapter 3.5 repealed and added by Stats. 2007, Ch. 629, Sec. 2.)

7150.

This chapter shall be known, and may be cited, as the Uniform Anatomical Gift Act.

(Repealed and added by Stats. 2007, Ch. 629, Sec. 2. Effective January 1, 2008.)

7150.10.

(a) As used in this chapter, the following terms have the following meanings:

(1) "Adult" means an individual who is at least 18 years of age.

(2) "Agent" means an individual who meets either of the following criteria:

(A) He or she is authorized to make health care decisions on the principal's behalf by a power of attorney for health care.

(B) He or she is expressly authorized to make an anatomical gift on the principal's behalf by any other record signed by the principal.

(3) "Anatomical gift" means a donation of all or part of a human body to take effect after the donor's death for the purpose of transplantation, therapy, research, or education.

(4) "Decedent" means a deceased individual whose body or part is or may be the source of an anatomical gift. The term includes a stillborn infant and, subject to restrictions imposed by law other than this chapter, a fetus.

(5) "Disinterested witness" means a witness other than the spouse, child, parent, sibling, grandchild, grandparent, or guardian of the individual who makes, amends, revokes, or refuses to make an anatomical gift, or another adult who exhibited special care and concern for the individual. The term does not include a person to which an anatomical gift could pass under Section 7150.50.

(6) "Document of gift" means a donor card or other record used to make an anatomical gift. The term includes a statement recorded on the Donate Life California Organ and Tissue Donor Registry or other donor registry.

(6.5) "Domestic partner" means a person who is registered under Section 297 of the Family Code, or otherwise recognized under the law of any state as a domestic partner.

(7) "Donor" means an individual whose body or part is the subject of an anatomical gift.

(8) "Donor registry" means a database that contains records of anatomical gifts and amendments to or revocations of anatomical gifts, including, but not limited to, the Donate Life California Organ and Tissue Donor Registry.

(9) "Driver's license" means a license or permit issued by the Department of Motor Vehicles to operate a vehicle, whether or not conditions are attached to the license or permit.

(10) "Eye bank" means a person that is licensed, accredited, or regulated under federal or state law to engage in the recovery, screening, testing, processing, storage, or distribution of human eyes or portions of human eyes.

(11) "Guardian" means a person appointed by a court to make decisions regarding the support, care, education, health, or welfare of an individual. The term does not include a guardian ad litem.

(12) "Hospital" means a facility licensed as a hospital under the law of any state or a facility operated as a hospital by the United States, a state, or a subdivision of a state.

(13) "Identification card" means an identification card issued by the Department of Motor Vehicles.

(14) "Know" means to have actual knowledge.

(15) "Minor" means an individual who is under 18 years of age.

(16) "Organ procurement organization" means a person designated by the Secretary of the United States Department of Health and Human Services as an organ procurement organization.

(17) "Parent" means a parent whose parental rights have not been terminated.

(18) "Part" means an organ, an eye, or tissue of a human being. The term does not include the whole body.

(19) "Person" means an individual, corporation, business trust, estate, trust, partnership, limited liability company, association, joint venture, public corporation, government or governmental subdivision, agency, or instrumentality, or any other legal or commercial entity.

(20) "Physician" means an individual authorized to practice medicine or osteopathy under the law of any state.

(21) "Procurement organization" means an eye bank, organ procurement organization, or tissue bank.

(22) "Prospective donor" means an individual who is dead or near death and has been determined by a procurement organization to have a part that could be medically suitable for transplantation, therapy, research, or education. The term does not include an individual who has made a refusal.

(23) "Reasonably available" means able to be contacted by a procurement organization, without undue effort, and willing and able to act in a timely manner consistent with existing medical criteria necessary for the making of an anatomical gift.

(24) "Recipient" means an individual into whose body a decedent's part has been, or is intended to be, transplanted.

(25) "Record" means information that is inscribed on a tangible medium or that is stored in an electronic or other medium and is retrievable in perceivable form.

(26) "Refusal" means a record created under Section 7150.30 that expressly states an intent to bar other persons from making an anatomical gift of an individual's body or part.

(27) "Sign" means, to do either of the following with the present intent to authenticate or adopt a record:

(A) Execute or adopt a tangible symbol.

(B) Attach to or logically associate with the record an electronic symbol, sound, or process.

(28) "State" means a state of the United States, the District of Columbia, Puerto Rico, the United States Virgin Islands, or any territory or insular possession subject to the jurisdiction of the United States.

(29) "Technician" means an individual determined to be qualified to remove or process parts by an appropriate organization that is licensed, accredited, or regulated under federal or state law. The term includes an enucleator.

(30) "Tissue" means a portion of the human body other than an organ or an eye. The term does not include blood, unless a blood sample is needed for the purpose of research or education.

(31) "Tissue bank" means a person that is licensed, accredited, or regulated under federal or state law to engage in the recovery, screening, testing, processing, storage, or distribution of tissue.

(32) "Transplant hospital" means a hospital that furnishes organ transplants and other medical and surgical specialty services required for the care of transplant patients.

(b) This chapter applies to an anatomical gift or amendment to, revocation of, or refusal to make an anatomical gift, whenever made.

(Added by Stats. 2007, Ch. 629, Sec. 2. Effective January 1, 2008.)

7150.15.

Subject to Section 7150.35, an anatomical gift of a donor's body or part may be made during the life of the donor for the purpose of transplantation, therapy, research, or education in the manner provided in Section 7150.20 by any of the following individuals:

(a) The donor, if the donor is an adult or if the donor is a minor and is either of the following:

(1) An emancipated minor.

(2) Between 15 and 18 years of age, only upon the written consent of a parent or guardian.

(b) An agent of the donor, provided that the power of attorney for health care or other record expressly permits the agent to make an anatomical gift.

(Added by Stats. 2007, Ch. 629, Sec. 2. Effective January 1, 2008.)

7150.20.

(a) A donor may make an anatomical gift through any of the following:

(1) By authorizing a statement or symbol indicating that the donor has made an anatomical gift to be imprinted on the donor's driver's license or identification card and included on a donor database registry.

(2) Directly through the Donate Life California Organ and Tissue Donor Registry Internet Web site.

(3) In a will.

(4) During a terminal illness or injury of the donor, by any form of communication that clearly expresses the donor's wish, addressed to at least two adults, at least one of whom is a disinterested witness. The witnesses shall memorialize this communication in a writing and sign and date the writing.

(5) As provided in subdivision (b).

(b) A donor or other person authorized to make an anatomical gift under Section 7150.15 may make a gift by a donor card or other record signed by the donor or other person making the gift or by authorizing that a statement or symbol, indicating that the donor has made an anatomical gift, be included on a donor registry. If the donor or other person is physically unable to sign a record, the record may be signed by another individual at the direction of the donor or other person and shall comply with all of the following:

(1) Be witnessed by at least two adults, at least one of whom is a disinterested witness, who have signed at the request of the donor or the other person.

(2) State that it has been signed and witnessed as provided in paragraph (1).

(c) Revocation, suspension, expiration, or cancellation of a driver's license or identification card upon which an anatomical gift is indicated does not invalidate the gift.

(d) An anatomical gift made by will takes effect upon the donor's death whether or not the will is probated. Invalidation of the will after the donor's death does not invalidate the gift.

(e) Notwithstanding subdivision (i) of Section 7150.65, a document of gift may designate a particular physician to carry out the recovery procedures. In the absence of this designation, or if the designee is not reasonably available or is deemed by the organ procurement organization not to be qualified to perform the required procedure, the organ procurement organization may authorize another physician or technician to carry out the recovery.

(Added by Stats. 2007, Ch. 629, Sec. 2. Effective January 1, 2008.)

7150.25.

(a) Subject to Section 7150.35, a donor or other person authorized to make an anatomical gift under Section 7150.15 may amend or revoke an anatomical gift by either of the following:

(1) A record signed by any of the following and recorded in a donor registry database:

(A) The donor.

(B) The other person.

(C) Subject to subdivision (b), another individual acting at the direction of the donor or of the other person, if the donor or other person is physically unable to sign.

(2) A later-executed document of gift that amends or revokes a previous anatomical gift or portion of an anatomical gift, either expressly or by inconsistency.

(b) A record signed pursuant to subparagraph (C) of paragraph (1) of subdivision (a) shall comply with all of the following:

(1) It shall be witnessed by at least two adults, at least one of whom is a disinterested witness, who have signed at the request of the donor or the other person.

(2) It shall state that it has been signed and witnessed as provided in paragraph (1).

(c) Subject to Section 7150.35, a donor or other person authorized to make an anatomical gift under Section 7150.15 may revoke an anatomical gift by the destruction of the document of gift or cancellation of the document of gift on a donor database registry, or the portion of the document of gift used to make the gift, with the intent to revoke the gift.

(d) A donor may amend or revoke an anatomical gift that was not made in a will by any form of communication during a terminal illness or injury addressed to at least two adults, at least one of whom is a disinterested witness. The witnesses shall memorialize this communication in a writing and sign and date the writing.

(e) A donor who makes an anatomical gift in a will may amend or revoke the gift in the manner provided for amendment or revocation of wills or as provided in subdivision (a).

(Added by Stats. 2007, Ch. 629, Sec. 2. Effective January 1, 2008.)

7150.30.

(a) An individual may refuse to make an anatomical gift of the individual's body or part by any of the following:

(1) A record signed by either of the following:

(A) The individual.

(B) Subject to subdivision (b), another individual acting at the direction of the individual if the individual is physically unable to sign.

(2) The individual's will, whether or not the will is admitted to probate or invalidated after the individual's death.

(3) Any form of communication made by the individual during the individual's terminal illness or injury addressed to at least two adults, at least one of whom is a disinterested witness. The witnesses shall memorialize this communication in a writing and sign and date the writing.

(b) A record signed pursuant to subparagraph (B) of paragraph (1) of subdivision (a) shall comply with both of the following:

(1) It shall be witnessed by at least two adults, at least one of whom is a disinterested witness, who have signed at the request of the individual.

(2) It shall state that it has been signed and witnessed as provided in paragraph (1).

(c) An individual who has made a refusal may amend or revoke the refusal by any of the following:

(1) In the manner provided in subdivision (a) for making a refusal.

(2) By subsequently making an anatomical gift pursuant to Section 7150.20 that is inconsistent with the refusal.

(3) By destroying or canceling the record evidencing the refusal, or the portion of the record used to make the refusal, with the intent to revoke the refusal.

(d) Except as otherwise provided in subdivision (h) of Section 7150.35, in the absence of an express, contrary indication by the individual set forth in the refusal, an individual's unrevoked refusal to make an anatomical gift of the individual's body or part bars all other persons from making an anatomical gift of the individual's body or part.

(e) Notwithstanding any provision to the contrary, including, but not limited to, Section 7150.40, only an individual shall make an anatomical gift of all or part of that individual's body or pacemaker, if it is made known that the individual, at the time of death, was a member of a religion, church, sect, or denomination that relies solely upon prayer for healing of disease or that has religious tenets that would be violated by the disposition of the human body or parts or pacemakers for the purposes of transplantation, therapy, research, or education.

(Added by Stats. 2007, Ch. 629, Sec. 2. Effective January 1, 2008.)

7150.35.

(a) Except as otherwise provided in subdivision (g) and subject to subdivision (f), in the absence of an express, contrary indication by the donor, a person other than the donor is barred from making, amending, or revoking an anatomical gift of a donor's body or part if the donor made an anatomical gift of the donor's body or part under Section 7150.20 or an amendment to an anatomical gift of the donor's body or part under Section 7150.25.

(b) A donor's revocation of an anatomical gift of the donor's body or part under Section 7150.25 is not a refusal and does not bar another person specified in Section 7150.15 or 7150.40 from making an anatomical gift of the donor's body or part under Section 7150.20 or 7150.45.

(c) If a person other than the donor makes an unrevoked anatomical gift of the donor's body or part under Section 7150.20 or an amendment to an anatomical gift of the donor's body or part under Section 7150.25, another person may not make, amend, or revoke the gift of the donor's body or part under Section 7150.45.

(d) A revocation of an anatomical gift of a donor's body or part under Section 7150.25 by a person other than the donor does not bar another person from making an anatomical gift of the body or part under Section 7150.20 or 7150.45.

(e) In the absence of an express, contrary indication by the donor or other person authorized to make an anatomical gift under Section 7150.15, an anatomical gift of a part is neither a refusal to give another part nor a limitation on the making of an anatomical gift of another part at a later time by the donor or another person.

(f) In the absence of an express, contrary indication by the donor or other person authorized to make an anatomical gift under Section 7150.15, an anatomical gift of a part for one or more of the purposes set forth in Section 7150.15 is not a limitation on the making of an anatomical gift of the part for any of the other purposes by the donor or any other person under Section 7150.20 or 7150.45.

(g) Notwithstanding subdivision (a), an individual who is between 15 and 18 years of age may make an anatomical gift for any purpose authorized in this chapter, may limit an anatomical gift to one or more of those purposes, may refuse to make an anatomical gift, or may amend or revoke an anatomical gift, only upon the written consent of the parent or guardian. If a donor who is an unemancipated minor dies, a parent of the donor who is reasonably available may revoke or amend an anatomical gift of the donor's body or part.

(Added by Stats. 2007, Ch. 629, Sec. 2. Effective January 1, 2008.)

7150.40.

(a) Subject to subdivisions (b) and (c), and unless barred by Section 7150.30 or 7150.35, an anatomical gift of a decedent's body or part for the purpose of transplantation, therapy, research, or education may be made by any member of the following classes of persons who is reasonably available, in the following order of priority:

(1) An agent of the decedent at the time of death who could have made an anatomical gift under subdivision (b) of Section 7150.15 immediately before the decedent's death.

(2) The spouse or domestic partner of the decedent.

(3) Adult children of the decedent.

(4) Parents of the decedent.

(5) Adult siblings of the decedent.

(6) Adult grandchildren of the decedent.

(7) Grandparents of the decedent.

(8) An adult who exhibited special care and concern for the decedent during the decedent's lifetime.

(9) The persons who were acting as the guardians or conservators of the person of the decedent at the time of death.

(10) (A) Any other person having the authority to dispose of the decedent's body, including, but not limited to, a coroner, medical examiner, or hospital administrator, provided that reasonable effort has been made to locate and inform persons listed in paragraphs (1) to (9), inclusive, of their option to make, or object to making, an anatomical gift.

(B) Except in the case where the useful life of the part does not permit, a reasonable effort shall be deemed to have been made when a search for the persons has been underway for at least 12 hours. The search shall include a check of local police missing persons records, examination of personal effects, and the questioning of any persons visiting the decedent before his or her death or in the hospital, accompanying the decedent's body, or reporting the death, in order to obtain information that might lead to the location of any persons listed.

(b) If there is more than one member of a class listed in paragraph (1), (3), (4), (5), (6), (7), or (9) of subdivision (a) entitled to make an anatomical gift, an anatomical gift may be made by a member of the class unless that member or a person to which the gift may pass under Section 7150.50 knows of an objection by another member of the class. If an objection is known, the gift may be made only by a majority of the members of the class who are reasonably available.

(c) A person shall not make an anatomical gift if, at the time of the decedent's death, a person in a prior class under subdivision (a) is reasonably available to make, or to object to the making of, an anatomical gift.

(Added by Stats. 2007, Ch. 629, Sec. 2. Effective January 1, 2008.)

7150.45.

(a) A person authorized to make an anatomical gift under Section 7150.40 may make an anatomical gift by a document of gift signed by the person making the gift or by that person's oral communication that is electronically recorded or is contemporaneously reduced to a record and signed by the individual receiving the oral communication.

(b) Subject to subdivision (c), an anatomical gift by a person authorized under Section 7150.40 may be amended or revoked orally or in a record by any member of a prior class who is reasonably available. If more than one member of the prior class is reasonably available, the gift made by a person authorized under Section 7150.40 may be amended or revoked as follows:

(1) Amended only if a majority of the reasonably available members agree to the amending of the gift.

(2) Revoked only if a majority of the reasonably available members agree to the revoking of the gift or if they are equally divided as to whether to revoke the gift.

(c) A revocation under subdivision (b) is effective only if, before an incision has been made to remove a part from the donor's body or before invasive procedures have begun to prepare the recipient, the procurement organization, transplant hospital, or physician or technician knows of the revocation.

(Added by Stats. 2007, Ch. 629, Sec. 2. Effective January 1, 2008.)

7150.50.

(a) An anatomical gift may be made to any of the following persons named in the document of gift:

(1) A hospital, accredited medical school, dental school, college, university, or organ procurement organization, for research or education.

(2) Subject to subdivision (b), an individual designated by the person making the anatomical gift if the individual is the recipient of the part.

(3) An eye bank, or tissue bank.

(b) If an anatomical gift to an individual under paragraph (2) of subdivision (a) cannot be transplanted into the individual, the part passes in accordance with subdivision (g) in the absence of an express, contrary indication by the person making the anatomical gift.

(c) If an anatomical gift of one or more specific parts, or of all parts, is made in a document of gift that does not name a person described in subdivision (a) but identifies the purpose for which an anatomical gift may be used, all of the following rules shall apply:

(1) If the part is an eye and the gift is for the purpose of transplantation or therapy, the gift passes to the appropriate eye bank.

(2) If the part is tissue and the gift is for the purpose of transplantation or therapy, the gift passes to the appropriate tissue bank.

(3) If the part is an organ and the gift is for the purpose of transplantation or therapy, the gift passes to the appropriate organ procurement organization as custodian of the organ.

(4) If the part is an organ, an eye, or tissue and the gift is for the purpose of research or education, the gift passes to the appropriate procurement organization.

(d) For the purpose of subdivision (c), if there is more than one purpose of an anatomical gift set forth in the document of gift but the purposes are not set forth in any priority, the gift shall be used for transplantation or therapy, if suitable. If the gift cannot be used for transplantation or therapy, the gift may be used for research or education.

(e) If an anatomical gift of one or more specific parts is made in a document of gift that does not name a person described in subdivision (a) and does not identify the purpose of the gift, the gift shall be used only for transplantation or therapy, and the gift passes in accordance with subdivision (g).

(f) If a document of gift specifies only a general intent to make an anatomical gift by words such as "donor," "organ donor," or "body donor," or by a symbol or statement of similar import, the gift may be used for transplantation, therapy, research, or education, and the gift passes in accordance with subdivision (g).

(g) For purposes of subdivisions (b), (e), and (f) all of the following rules shall apply:

(1) If the part is an eye, the gift passes to the appropriate eye bank.

(2) If the part is tissue, the gift passes to the appropriate tissue bank.

(3) If the part is an organ, the gift passes to the appropriate organ procurement organization as custodian of the organ.

(h) An anatomical gift of an organ for transplantation or therapy, other than an anatomical gift under paragraph (2) of subdivision (a), passes to the organ procurement organization as custodian of the organ.

(i) If an anatomical gift does not pass pursuant to subdivisions (a) to (h), inclusive, or the decedent's body or part is not used for transplantation, therapy, research, or education, custody of the body or part passes to the person under obligation to dispose of the body or part.

(j) A person shall not accept an anatomical gift if the person knows that the gift was not effectively made under Section 7150.20 or 7150.45 or if the person knows that the decedent made a refusal under Section 7150.30 that was not revoked. For purposes of this subdivision, if a person knows that an anatomical gift was made on a document of gift, the person is deemed to know of any amendment or revocation of the gift or any refusal to make an anatomical gift on the same document of gift.

(k) Except as otherwise provided in paragraph (2) of subdivision (a), nothing in this chapter affects the allocation of organs for transplantation or therapy.

(Added by Stats. 2007, Ch. 629, Sec. 2. Effective January 1, 2008.)

7150.55.

(a) All of the following persons shall make a reasonable search of an individual who the person reasonably believes is dead or near death for a document of gift or other information identifying the individual as a donor or as an individual who made a refusal:

(1) A law enforcement officer, firefighter, paramedic, or other emergency rescuer finding the individual.

(2) If no other source of the information is immediately available, a hospital, as soon as practical after the individual's arrival at the hospital.

(b) If a document of gift or a refusal to make an anatomical gift is located by the search required by paragraph (1) of subdivision (a) and the individual or deceased individual to whom it relates is taken to a hospital, the person responsible for conducting the search shall send the document of gift or refusal to the hospital.

(c) A person is not subject to criminal or civil liability for failing to discharge the duties imposed by this section, but may be subject to administrative sanctions.

(Added by Stats. 2007, Ch. 629, Sec. 2. Effective January 1, 2008.)

7150.60.

(a) A document of gift need not be delivered during the donor's lifetime to be effective.

(b) Upon or after an individual's death, a person in possession of a document of gift or a refusal to make an anatomical gift with respect to the individual shall allow examination and copying of the document of gift or refusal by a person authorized to make or object to the making of an anatomical gift with respect to the individual or by a person to which the gift could pass under Section 7150.50.

(Added by Stats. 2007, Ch. 629, Sec. 2. Effective January 1, 2008.)

7150.65.

(a) When a hospital refers an individual at or near death to a procurement organization, the organization shall make a reasonable search of the records of the Donate Life California Organ and Tissue Donor Registry and any donor registry that it knows exists for the geographical area in which the individual resides to ascertain whether the individual has made an anatomical gift.

(b) A procurement organization shall be allowed reasonable access to information in the records of the Donate Life California Organ and Tissue Donor Registry to ascertain whether an individual who is at or near death is a donor. Personally identifiable information on a donor registry about a donor shall not be used or disclosed without the express consent of the donor or the person that made the anatomical gift for any purpose other than to determine, at or near death of the donor or a prospective donor, whether the donor or prospective donor has made, amended, or revoked an anatomical gift. A procurement organization shall not sell the information obtained from the donor registry. A procurement organization shall also comply with all state and federal laws with respect to the protection of a donor's or prospective donor's personally identifiable information.

(c) When a hospital refers an individual at or near death to a procurement organization, the organization may conduct any reasonable examination necessary to ensure the medical suitability of a part that is or could be the subject of an anatomical gift for transplantation, therapy, research, or education from a donor or a prospective donor. During the examination period, measures necessary to ensure the medical suitability of the part may not be withdrawn unless the hospital or procurement organization knows that the individual expressed a contrary intent.

(d) Unless prohibited by law other than this chapter, at any time after a donor's death, the person to which a part passes under Section 7150.50 may conduct any reasonable examination necessary to ensure the medical suitability of the body or part for its intended purpose.

(e) Unless prohibited by law other than this chapter, an examination under subdivision (c) or (d) may include an examination of all medical and dental records of the donor or prospective donor.

(f) Upon the death of a minor who was a donor or had signed a refusal, unless a procurement organization knows the minor is emancipated, the procurement organization shall conduct a reasonable search for the parents of the minor and provide the parents with an opportunity to revoke or amend the anatomical gift or revoke the refusal.

(g) Upon referral by a hospital under subdivision (a), a procurement organization shall make a reasonable search for any person listed in Section 7150.40 having priority to make an anatomical gift on behalf of a prospective donor. If a procurement organization receives information that an anatomical gift to any other person was made, amended, or revoked, it shall promptly advise the other person of all relevant information.

(h) Subject to subdivision (i) of Section 7150.50, and Section 7151.20, the rights of the person to which a part passes under Section 7150.50 are superior to the rights of all others with respect to the part. The person may accept or reject an anatomical gift in whole or in part. Subject to the terms of the document of gift and this chapter, a person that accepts an anatomical gift of an entire body may allow embalming, burial, or cremation, and use of remains in a funeral service. If the gift is of a part, the person to which the part passes under Section 7150.50, upon the death of the donor and before

embalming, burial, or cremation, shall cause the part to be removed without unnecessary mutilation.

(i) Except as provided in subdivision (e) of Section 7150.20, neither the physician who attends the decedent at death nor the physician who determines the time of the decedent's death may participate in the procedures for removing or transplanting a part from the decedent.

(j) A physician or technician may remove a donated part from the body of a donor that the physician or technician is qualified to remove.

(Added by Stats. 2007, Ch. 629, Sec. 2. Effective January 1, 2008.)

7150.70.

Each hospital in this state shall enter into agreements or affiliations with procurement organizations for coordination of procurement and use of anatomical gifts.

(Added by Stats. 2007, Ch. 629, Sec. 2. Effective January 1, 2008.)

7150.75.

(a) Except as otherwise provided in subdivision (b), a person that, for valuable consideration, knowingly purchases or sells a part for transplantation or therapy, if removal of a part from an individual is intended to occur after the individual's death, is guilty of a felony and is subject to a fine not exceeding fifty thousand dollars ($50,000), or imprisonment not exceeding five years, or both the fine and imprisonment.

(b) A person may charge a reasonable amount for the removal, processing, preservation, quality control, storage, transportation, implantation, or disposal of a part.

(Added by Stats. 2007, Ch. 629, Sec. 2. Effective January 1, 2008.)

7150.80.

(a) A person that acts in accordance with this chapter or with the applicable anatomical gift law of another state, or attempts in good faith to do so, is not liable for the act in a civil action or criminal prosecution.

(b) Neither the person making an anatomical gift nor the donor's estate is liable for any injury or damage that results from the making or use of the gift.

(c) In determining whether an anatomical gift has been made, amended, or revoked under this chapter, a person may rely upon representations of an individual listed in paragraphs (2) to (8), inclusive, of subdivision (a) of Section 7150.40 relating to the individual's relationship to the donor or prospective donor, unless the person knows that the representation is untrue.

(Added by Stats. 2007, Ch. 629, Sec. 2. Effective January 1, 2008.)

7150.85.

(a) A document of gift is valid if executed in accordance with any of the following:

(1) This chapter.

(2) The laws of the state or country where it was executed.

(3) The laws of the state or country where the person making the anatomical gift was domiciled, has a place of residence, or was a national at the time the document of gift was executed.

(b) If a document of gift is valid under this section, the law of this state governs the interpretation of the document of gift.

(c) A person may presume that a document of gift or amendment of an anatomical gift is valid unless that person knows that it was not validly executed, or that it was revoked.

(Added by Stats. 2007, Ch. 629, Sec. 2. Effective January 1, 2008.)

7150.90.

(a) The California organ procurement organizations designated pursuant to Section 273 and following of Title 42 of the United States Code, are hereby authorized to establish a not-for-profit entity that shall be designated the California Organ and Tissue Donor Registrar, which shall establish and maintain the California Organ and Tissue Donor Registry, to be known as the Donate Life California Organ and Tissue Donor Registry. The registry shall contain information regarding persons who have identified themselves as organ and tissue donors upon their death. The registrar shall be responsible for developing methods to increase the number of donors who enroll in the registry.

(b) The registrar shall make available to the federally designated organ procurement organizations (OPOs) in California and the state licensed tissue and eye banks information contained in the registry regarding potential donors on a 24-hour-a-day, seven-day-a-week basis. This information shall be used to expedite a match between identified organ and tissue donors and potential recipients.

(c) The registrar may receive voluntary contributions to support the registry and its activities.

(d) The registrar shall submit an annual written report to the State Public Health Officer and the Legislature that includes all of the following:

(1) The number of donors on the registry.

(2) The changes in the number of donors on the registry.

(3) The nonidentifiable information, as specified in subparagraph (C) of paragraph (9) of subdivision (b) of Section 12811 of the Vehicle Code, of donors as may be determined by information provided on the donor registry forms pursuant to Sections 12811 and 13005 of the Vehicle Code.

(4) The nonidentifiable information, as specified in subparagraph (C) of paragraph (9) of subdivision (b) of Section 12811 of the Vehicle Code, of donors as may be determined by information transmitted to the registry pursuant to Section 1798.90.1 of the Civil Code to identify an individual as a registered organ donor.

(Amended by Stats. 2014, Ch. 569, Sec. 2. (AB 2399) Effective January 1, 2015.)

7151.10.

(a) As used in this section the following terms have the following meanings:

(1) "Advance health care directive" means a power of attorney for health care or a record signed by a prospective donor containing the prospective donor's direction concerning a health care decision for the prospective donor.

(2) "Declaration" means a record signed by a prospective donor specifying the circumstances under which a life-support system may be withheld or withdrawn from the prospective donor.

(3) "Health care decision" means any decision made regarding the health care of the prospective donor.

(b) If a prospective donor has a declaration or advance health care directive and the terms of the declaration or directive and the express or implied terms of a potential anatomical gift are in conflict with regard to the administration of measures necessary to ensure the medical suitability of a part for transplantation or therapy, the prospective donor's attending physician and prospective donor shall confer to resolve the conflict. If the prospective donor is incapable of resolving the conflict, an agent acting under the prospective donor's declaration or directive, or, if none, or the agent is not reasonably available, another person authorized by law other than this chapter to make health care decisions on behalf of the prospective donor, shall act for the donor to resolve the conflict. The conflict shall be resolved as expeditiously as possible. Information relevant to the resolution of the conflict may be obtained from the appropriate procurement organization and any other person authorized to make an anatomical gift for the prospective donor under Section 7150.40. Before resolution of the conflict, measures necessary to ensure the medical suitability of the part shall not be withheld or withdrawn from the prospective donor if withholding or withdrawing the measures is not contraindicated by appropriate end-of-life care.

(Added by Stats. 2007, Ch. 629, Sec. 2. Effective January 1, 2008.)

7151.15.

(a) A county coroner shall cooperate with procurement organizations to maximize the opportunity to recover anatomical gifts for the purpose of transplantation, therapy, research, or education.

(b) If a county coroner receives notice from a procurement organization that an anatomical gift might be available or was made with respect to a decedent whose body is under the jurisdiction of the coroner and a post mortem examination or investigation is going to be performed, unless the coroner denies recovery in accordance with Section 7151.20, the coroner or designee shall conduct a post mortem examination or investigation of the body or the part in a manner and within a period compatible with its preservation for the purposes of the gift.

(c) A part shall not be removed from the body of a decedent under the jurisdiction of a coroner for transplantation, therapy, research, or education unless the part is the subject of an anatomical gift. The body of a decedent under the jurisdiction of the coroner shall not be delivered to a person for research or education unless the body is the subject of an anatomical gift. This subdivision does not preclude a coroner from performing the medicolegal investigation upon the body or parts of a decedent under the jurisdiction of the coroner.

(d) Notwithstanding any other law, when an anatomical gift might be available or has been made by a person whose death is imminent due to the lawful withdrawal of medical treatment and if that person's body, post mortem, will be subject to the coroner's jurisdiction pursuant to Section 27491 of the Government Code, a procurement organization may notify a coroner of the anatomical gift, and a coroner shall accept the notification, whenever that notification will facilitate the coroner's ability to conduct a postmortem examination or investigation of the body or the part in a manner and within a period compatible with its preservation for the purposes of the gift.

(Amended by Stats. 2013, Ch. 341, Sec. 2. (AB 1297) Effective January 1, 2014.)

7151.20.

(a) On request from a qualified procurement organization, the county coroner may permit the removal of organs that constitute an anatomical gift from a decedent who died under circumstances requiring an inquest by the coroner.

(b) If no autopsy is required, the organs to be removed may be released to the qualified procurement organization.

(c) If an autopsy is required and the county coroner determines that the removal of the organs will not interfere with the subsequent course of an investigation or autopsy, the organs may be released for removal. The autopsy shall be performed following the removal of the organs.

(d) If a county coroner is considering withholding one or more organs of a potential donor for any reason, the county coroner, or his or her designee, upon request from a qualified organ procurement organization, shall be present during the procedure to remove the organs. The county coroner, or his or her designee, may request a biopsy of those organs or deny removal of the organs if necessary. If the county coroner, or his or her designee, denies removal of the organs, the county coroner may do any of the following:

(1) In the investigative report, explain in writing the reasons for the denial.

(2) Provide the explanation to the qualified organ procurement organization.

(e) If the county coroner, or his or her designee, is present during the removal of the organs, the qualified procurement organization requesting the removal of the organ shall reimburse the county of the coroner, or his or her designee, for the actual costs incurred in performing the duty specified in subdivision (d), if reimbursement is requested by the county coroner. The payment shall be applied to the additional costs incurred by the county coroner's office in performing the duty specified in subdivision (d).

(f) The health care professional removing organs from a decedent who died under circumstances requiring an inquest shall file with the county coroner a report detailing the condition of the organs removed and their relationship, if any, to the cause of death.

(Added by Stats. 2007, Ch. 629, Sec. 2. Effective January 1, 2008.)

7151.25.

In applying and construing this uniform act, consideration shall be given to the need to promote uniformity of the law with respect to its subject matter among states that enact it.

(Added by Stats. 2007, Ch. 629, Sec. 2. Effective January 1, 2008.)

7151.30.

This act modifies, limits, and supersedes the Electronic Signatures in Global and National Commerce Act (15 U.S.C. Sec. 7001 et seq.), but does not modify, limit or supersede Section 101(a) of that act (15 U.S.C. Sec. 7001), or authorize electronic delivery of any of the notices described in Section 103(b) of that act (15 U.S.C. Sec. 7003(b)).

(Added by Stats. 2007, Ch. 629, Sec. 2. Effective January 1, 2008.)

7151.35.

(a) No hospital, physician and surgeon, procurement organization, or other person shall determine the ultimate recipient of an anatomical gift based upon a potential recipient's physical or mental disability, except to the extent that the physical or mental disability has been found by a physician and surgeon, following a case-by-case evaluation of the potential recipient, to be medically significant to the provision of the anatomical gift.

(b) Subdivision (a) shall apply to each part of the organ transplant process. The organ transplant process includes, but is not limited to, all of the following:

(1) The referral from a primary care provider to a specialist.

(2) The referral from a specialist to a transplant center.

(3) The evaluation of the patient for the transplant by the transplant center.

(4) The consideration of the patient for placement on the official waiting list.

(c) A person with a physical or mental disability shall not be required to demonstrate postoperative independent living abilities in order to have access to a transplant if there is evidence that the person will have sufficient, compensatory support and assistance.

(d) The court shall accord priority on its calendar and handle expeditiously any action brought to seek any remedy authorized by law for purposes of enforcing compliance with this section.

(e) This section shall not be deemed to require referrals or recommendations for, or the performance of, medically inappropriate organ transplants.

(f) As used in this section "disabilities" has the same meaning as used in the federal Americans with Disabilities Act of 1990 (42 U.S.C. Sec. 12101 et seq., P.L. 101-336).

(Added by Stats. 2007, Ch. 629, Sec. 2. Effective January 1, 2008.)

7151.36.

(a) A hospital, physician and surgeon, procurement organization, or other person shall not determine the ultimate recipient of an anatomical gift based solely upon a potential recipient's status as a qualified patient, as defined in Section 11362.7, or based solely upon a positive test for the use of medical marijuana by a potential recipient who is a qualified patient, as defined in Section 11362.7, except to the extent that the qualified patient's use of medical marijuana has been found by a physician and surgeon, following a case-by-case evaluation of the potential recipient, to be medically significant to the provision of the anatomical gift.

(b) Subdivision (a) shall apply to each part of the organ transplant process. The organ transplant process includes, but is not limited to, all of the following:

(1) The referral from a primary care provider to a specialist.

(2) The referral from a specialist to a transplant center.

(3) The evaluation of the patient for the transplant by the transplant center.

(4) The consideration of the patient for placement on the official waiting list.

(c) The court shall accord priority on its calendar and handle expeditiously any action brought to seek any remedy authorized by law for purposes of enforcing compliance with this section.

(d) This section shall not be deemed to require referrals or recommendations for, or the performance of, medically inappropriate organ transplants.

(Added by Stats. 2015, Ch. 51, Sec. 1. (AB 258) Effective January 1, 2016.)

7151.40.

(a) If there has been an anatomical gift, a technician may remove any donated parts and an enucleator may remove any donated eyes or parts of eyes, after determination of death by a physician and surgeon.

(b) Following the final disposition of the remains of the donor, upon request of a person specified in Section 7100, the donee shall return the cremated remains of the donor at no cost to the person specified in Section 7100, unless the donor has previously designated otherwise in the document of gift. A person who knowingly returns the cremated remains of a person other than the donor to a person specified in Section 7100 shall be punished by imprisonment in the county jail for not more than one year.

(c) Residual anatomical materials and human remains donated to hospitals, organ procurement organizations, accredited medical schools, dental schools, colleges, or universities for educational, research, transplantation, or therapeutic use that are no longer useful or needed for those purposes, may be disposed of by those entities through cremation, in the same manner as medical waste, and without additional burial permit requirements if the donor has specifically waived subdivision (b) of Section 7151.40.

(Added by Stats. 2007, Ch. 629, Sec. 2. Effective January 1, 2008.)

CHAPTER 3.55. Organ and Tissue Donation Information and Procedures [7158 - 7158.3]

(Chapter 3.55 added by Stats. 1998, Ch. 457, Sec. 5.)

7158.

(a) The Controller shall prepare, or cause to be prepared, an organ donor information brochure for insertion in all payroll warrants issued by the Controller for the March 1999 pay period, and for every March pay period thereafter, in recognition of National Organ and Tissue Awareness Week, which occurs in April of each year.

(b) In lieu of developing an organ donor brochure pursuant to subdivision (a), the Controller may use a brochure developed by a regional organ donor organization. The Controller shall screen for appropriateness for wide distribution.

(Added by Stats. 1998, Ch. 457, Sec. 5. Effective January 1, 1999.)

7158.1.

(a) As a part of its ongoing audit and review process, the Licensing and Certification Division of the State Department of Health Services shall audit for the existence of organ and tissue procurement procedures for all inpatient hospital facilities. The audit shall include a determination of whether these procedures are in place in the facility, whether the procedures are operational and functioning, and whether the procedures are being used. The department shall not be required to audit for the effectiveness of the procedures. No additional audits shall be required for purposes of this section. Instead, the department shall add an organ and tissue audit element to its regular ongoing audits of inpatient facilities.

(b) For purposes of this chapter, "organ and tissue procurement procedures" shall include protocols required to be developed pursuant to Section 7184. The audit criteria shall, at a minimum, include all of the following:

(1) That the protocols have been developed.

(2) That the protocols are operational.

(3) That notification requirements to next of kin or other individuals as set forth in Section 7151 and to organ procurement organizations are within a timeframe that is consistent with the maintenance of the organs for the purpose of transplantation.

(c) The absence of any of the required organ and tissue procurement procedures at any facility shall be noted by the division, and included in a written audit report or site review summary. In the event that an audit or facility review is conducted in conjunction with review by a national accreditation agency, and that agency prepares a report, the department shall request that the information required by this section with respect to organ and tissue procurement procedures be included in the report prepared by the national accreditation agency. In this event, the department shall not be required to prepare a separate report.

(Added by Stats. 1998, Ch. 457, Sec. 5. Effective January 1, 1999.)

7158.2.

Every health care service plan contract that is issued, amended, delivered, or renewed on or after July 1, 1999, shall provide, upon enrollment and annually thereafter, a notice to subscribers in the evidence of coverage, health plan newsletter, or any direct plan communication to subscribers, information regarding organ donation options. This notice shall inform subscribers of the societal benefits of organ donations and the method whereby they may elect to be an organ or tissue donor.

(Added by Stats. 1998, Ch. 457, Sec. 5. Effective January 1, 1999.)

7158.3.

(a) The following definitions shall apply for purposes of this section:

(1) "Cosmetic surgery" means surgery that is performed to alter or reshape normal structures of the body in order to improve appearance.

(2) "Donee" means a hospital, as defined in paragraph (12) of subdivision (a) of Section 7150.10, or an organ procurement organization, as defined in paragraph (16) of subdivision (a) of Section 7150.10, or a tissue bank licensed pursuant to Chapter 4.1 (commencing with Section 1635) of Division 2.

(3) "Reconstructive surgery" means surgery performed to correct or repair abnormal structures of the body caused by congenital defects, developmental abnormalities, trauma, infection, tumors, or disease to do either of the following:

(A) To improve function.

(B) To create a normal appearance, to the extent possible.

(b) For purposes of accepting anatomical gifts, as defined in paragraph (3) of subdivision (a) of Section 7150.10, a donee shall do all of the following:

(1) Revise existing informed consent forms and procedures to advise a donor or, if the donor is deceased, the donor's representative, that tissue banks work with both nonprofit and for-profit tissue processors and distributors, that it is possible that donated skin may be used for cosmetic or reconstructive surgery purposes, and that donated tissue may be used for transplants outside of the United States.

(2) The revised consent form or procedure shall separately allow the donor or donor's representative to withhold consent for any of the following:

(A) Donated skin to be used for cosmetic surgery purposes.

(B) Donated tissue to be used for applications outside of the United States.

(C) Donated tissue to be used by for-profit tissue processors and distributors.

(3) A donee shall be deemed to have complied with paragraph (2) by designating tissue that has been donated with specific restrictions on its use. Once the donee transfers the tissue to a separate entity, the donee's responsibility for compliance with any restrictions on the tissue ceases.

(4) The donor may recover, in a civil action against any individual or entity that fails to comply with this subdivision, civil penalties to be assessed in an amount not less than one thousand dollars ($1,000) and not more than five thousand dollars ($5,000), plus court costs, as determined by the court. A separate penalty shall be assessed for each individual or entity that fails to comply with this subdivision. Any civil penalty provided under this paragraph shall be in addition to any license revocation or suspension, if appropriate, authorized under subdivision (c).

(5) If the consent of the donor or donor's representative is obtained in writing, the donee shall offer to provide the donor or donor's representative with a copy of the completed consent form. If consent is obtained by telephone, the donee shall advise the donor or donor's representative that the conversation will be audio recorded for verification and enforcement purposes, and shall offer to provide the donor or donor's representative with a written copy of the recorded telephonic consent form.

(c) Violation of this section by a licensed health care provider constitutes unprofessional conduct.

(d) This section shall not apply to the removal of sperm or ova pursuant to Section 2260 of the Business and Professions Code.

(Amended by Stats. 2015, Ch. 303, Sec. 300. (AB 731) Effective January 1, 2016.)

CHAPTER 3.56. Altruistic Living Donor Registry Act [7152 - 7152.2]

(Chapter 3.56 added by Stats. 2010, Ch. 217, Sec. 1.)

7152.

This chapter shall be known, and may be cited, as the Altruistic Living Donor Registry Act of 2010.

(Added by Stats. 2010, Ch. 217, Sec. 1. (SB 1395) Effective January 1, 2011.)

7152.1.

(a) The Legislature finds and declares all of the following:

(1) More than 20,000 Californians are currently waiting for a lifesaving organ transplant, and over 17,000 of those individuals are waiting for a kidney transplant. Based on the current trend in organ donations, one in three of those waiting for a transplant will die. In 2009, 5,874 Americans died while waiting for a transplant.

(2) On a national level, the number of organ donors increased by 3 percent from the years 2008 to 2009, while the number of organ donors in California decreased by 2 percent during this same time period. In 2009, there were only 798 cadaveric donors and 734 living donors in California.

(3) A decrease in organ donors results in longer stays on the national organ transplant waiting list and, consequently, more deaths among those patients who are waiting.

(4) The national organ transplant waiting list, which is maintained by the United Network for Organ Sharing, is growing at the rate of approximately 40,000 persons per year. A name is added to this national database every 13 minutes.

(5) Since 2005, more than six million Californians have registered to donate their organs and tissue upon death.

(6) However, no registry exists in California for those individuals who wish to be an altruistic living organ donor.

(b) The use of anatomical gifts, and the donation of organs for the purpose of transplantation, are of great value to the citizens of California and may save or prolong the life, or improve the health of, extremely ill and dying individuals.

(c) It is the intent of the Legislature to increase the number of individuals who identify themselves as potential organ donors. It is further the intent of the Legislature to establish a statewide Altruistic Living Donor Registry to expedite the match between organ donors and recipients and to encourage charitable contributions to support the registry.

(Added by Stats. 2010, Ch. 217, Sec. 1. (SB 1395) Effective January 1, 2011.)

7152.2.

(a) The California organ procurement organizations designated pursuant to Section 273 and following of Title 42 of the United States Code, are hereby authorized to establish a not-for-profit entity that shall be designated the Altruistic Living Donor Registrar, which shall establish and maintain the Altruistic Living Donor Registry. The registry shall contain information regarding persons who have identified themselves as altruistic living kidney donors. The donor registry shall be designed to promote and assist live kidney donations, including donor chains, paired exchanges, and nondirected donations. The registrar shall be responsible for developing methods to increase the number of donors who enroll in the registry.

(b) The registrar shall make available to the federally designated organ procurement organizations (OPOs) and transplant centers in California information contained in the registry regarding potential altruistic living donors. This information shall be used to expedite a match between identified organ donors and potential recipients.

(c) The registrar may receive voluntary contributions to support the registry and its activities.

(d) The registrar shall collect and make all of the following information relating to altruistic kidney donations available to the public:

(1) The number of donors on the registry.

(2) The changes in the number of donors on the registry.

(3) The general characteristics of donors.

(e) The registrar may also authorize the registry to include persons who identify themselves as altruistic living donors of organs and tissue other than kidneys to be added to the registry, upon a finding by the Federal Centers for Medicare and Medicaid Services and the United Network for Organ Sharing that the donation is generally regarded as safe and without a significant risk of complications, and would not adversely affect the health of the donor. Upon a finding pursuant to this subdivision, the registrar shall notify the appropriate policy committees of the Legislature.

(Added by Stats. 2010, Ch. 217, Sec. 1. (SB 1395) Effective January 1, 2011.)

CHAPTER 3.6. Organ Transplants [7160-7160.]

(Chapter 3.6 added by Stats. 1990, Ch. 1507, Sec. 2.)

7160.

(a) The State Department of Health Services shall consult with the Legislature on or before December 31, 1991, to evaluate and make recommendations to improve the effectiveness of organ transplantation for the general public and in minority communities and low-income communities in California.

Data to be considered may include, but not be limited to:

(1) The number of persons waiting for organ transplants.

(2) The number of available organ donors.

(3) The number of hospitals performing transplants and type of transplants.

(4) The percentage of medically insured transplant recipients.

(5) The percentage of Medi-Cal funded transplant recipients.

(6) The waiting time for transplantation.

(7) Factors used to determine eligibility for organ transplantation.

(8) Referral rates of patients to transplant centers.

(9) The number of persons accepted by transplant centers.

(10) The cost of recovery, processing, and distribution of the donated organs.

(11) The cost of transplantation operations.

(12) The financial impact of an organ donation upon the donor and the donor's family.

(13) Survival rates of patients receiving organ transplants.

(14) Hospital compliance with Section 7184.

(b) In compiling data, the department may utilize various sources, including, but not limited to, the local organ procurement organizations, the United Network for Organ Sharing, and the Association of Organ Procurement Organizations.

(Added by Stats. 1990, Ch. 1507, Sec. 2.)

CHAPTER 3.7. Death [7180 - 7184.5]

(Chapter 3.7 added by Stats. 1982, Ch. 810, Sec. 2.)

ARTICLE 1. Uniform Determination of Death Act [7180- 7180.]

(Article 1 added by Stats. 1982, Ch. 810, Sec. 2.)

7180.

(a) An individual who has sustained either (1) irreversible cessation of circulatory and respiratory functions, or (2) irreversible cessation of all functions of the entire brain, including the brain stem, is dead. A determination of death must be made in accordance with accepted medical standards.

(b) This article shall be applied and construed to effectuate its general purpose to make uniform the law with respect to the subject of this article among states enacting it.

(c) This article may be cited as the Uniform Determination of Death Act.

(Repealed and added by Stats. 1982, Ch. 2.)

ARTICLE 2. Confirmation of Death [7181 - 7184.5]

(Article 2 added by Stats. 1982, Ch. 810, Sec. 2.)

7181.

When an individual is pronounced dead by determining that the individual has sustained an irreversible cessation of all functions of the entire brain, including the brain stem, there shall be independent confirmation by another physician.

(Repealed and added by Stats. 1982, Ch. 810, Sec. 2.)

7182.

When a part of the donor is used for direct transplantation pursuant to the Uniform Anatomical Gift Act (Chapter 3.5 (commencing with Section 7150)) and the death of the donor is determined by determining that the individual has suffered an irreversible cessation of all functions of the entire brain, including the brain stem, there shall be an independent confirmation of the death by another physician. Neither the physician making the determination of death under Section 7155.5 nor the physician making the independent confirmation shall participate in the procedures for removing or transplanting a part.

(Repealed and added by Stats. 1982, Ch. 810, Sec. 2.)

7183.

Complete patient medical records required of a health facility pursuant to regulations adopted by the department in accordance with Section 1275 shall be kept, maintained, and preserved with respect to the requirements of this chapter when an individual is pronounced dead by determining that the individual has sustained an irreversible cessation of all functions of the entire brain, including the brain stem.

(Added by Stats. 1982, Ch. 810, Sec. 2.)

7184.

(a) Each general acute care hospital shall develop a protocol for identifying potential organ and tissue donors. The protocol shall require that any deceased individual's next of kin or other individual, as set forth in Section 7151, at or near the time of notification of death be asked whether the deceased was an organ donor or if the family is a donor family. If not, the family shall be informed of the option to donate organs and tissues pursuant to Chapter 3.5 (commencing with Section 7150) of Part 1 of Division 7. With the approval of the designated next of kin or other individual, as set forth in Section 7151, the hospital shall then notify an organ and tissue procurement organization and cooperate in the procurement of the anatomical gift or gifts. The protocol shall encourage reasonable discretion and sensitivity to the family circumstances in all discussions regarding donations of tissue or organs. The protocol may take into account the deceased individual's religious beliefs or obvious nonsuitability for organ and tissue

donation. In the event an organ and tissue procurement organization does not exist in a region, the hospital shall contact an organ or a tissue procurement organization, as appropriate. Laws pertaining to notification of the coroner shall be complied with in all cases of reportable deaths.

(b) A general acute care hospital shall comply with subdivision (a) or (c) as a condition of participation in the Medi-Cal program contained in Chapter 7 (commencing with Section 14000) of Part 3 of Division 9 of the Welfare and Institutions Code.

(c) Notwithstanding subdivision (a), the protocol may alternately provide for the hospital to contact an organ and tissue procurement organization at the time a potential organ and tissue donor is identified, and for the trained personnel of the organ and tissue procurement organization to make the inquiries described in subdivision (a) of the deceased individual's next of kin or other individual as set forth in Section 7151.

(Amended by Stats. 1992, Ch. 583, Sec. 4. Effective January 1, 1993.)

7184.5.

(a) In conjunction with entering into any agreement with any coroner or medical examiner for release and removal of organs from bodies within that official's custody and to further the purposes of Section 27491.45 of the Government Code, a procurement organization shall develop a protocol for organ recovery, as appropriate, that provides sufficient information on the medical and injury status of the deceased to permit release and removal of organs without undue prejudice to that official's investigation of, or inquiry into, the cause of death.

(b) The protocol described in subdivision (a) shall be subject to approval by the coroner or medical examiner before release or removal of organs and shall provide for the following:

(1) Relevant information on the deceased to be given to the coroner or deputy coroner at the time of the initial request for permission to recover internal organs, including, but not limited to:

(A) Information identifying the deceased.

(B) Date and time of pronouncement of brain death.

(C) Name of procurement organizations and coordinator.

(D) Organs requested.

(E) Organ donor number and hospital.

(F) Apparent cause and manner of death.

(G) A brief description of alleged circumstances surrounding the death to the extent they are known at the time.

(H) The law enforcement agency and the name of the investigating officer handling the case.

(2) The following information, to be recorded by the organ procurement coordinator at the time of requesting permission for organ removal:

(A) The name of the deputy coroner contacted.

(B) The name of the pathologist contacted by the deputy coroner.

(C) Whether permission for removal was obtained at the time, including the date and time if permission was obtained.

(D) The coroner's case number assigned by the deputy coroner.

(E) If the request for organ removal is refused, the reason given for the refusal.

(3) A checklist to be completed prior to recovery of any organ by the procurement organization coordinator with the assistance, if necessary, of a physician attending the deceased, that includes, at a minimum, all of the following:

(A) medical record review to insure documentation of external injuries, fractures, and internal injuries.

(B) In cases of suspected child abuse, whether:

(i) A child abuse consult was obtained.

(ii) A computerized axial tomographic scan or magnetic resonance image of the head was obtained.

(iii) A radiological skeletal survey was done.

(iv) The presence or absence of visible injury to the back of the scalp, ears, nose, and mouth, or retinal hemorrhage has been documented.

(v) A coagulation screen report was in the deceased's records.

(C) A photographic record of visible external injuries.

(D) Admitting blood sample, if available, and the date and time the sample was drawn.

(4) A checklist of items to be provided to the coroner's office when the deceased's body is released after completion of organ recovery, including, but not limited to, all of the following:

(A) A copy of the deceased's medical records.

(B) Film documenting abnormal findings, if used.

(C) The information recorded pursuant to the requirements of this subdivision.

(D) A sample of the deceased's blood, if taken on admission.

(5) A form, completed by the physician and surgeon, technician, or team performing the organ recovery procedure and signed by the physician and surgeon, that describes in sufficient detail all of the following:

(A) Tests used to determine the suitability for transplantation of all organs recovered.

(B) Documentation of injuries and other abnormalities, if any, noted or occurring during the organ recovery procedure.

(C) The date and time organ recovery was started.

(D) Any other information on the state of the deceased's body or organs that the physician and surgeon, technician, or team believes may assist the coroner in his or her investigation or inquiry.

(c) The requirements of subdivision (a) shall not apply in any county that does not have a Level II trauma facility, as defined in Section 1798.160 and the regulations adopted pursuant thereto.

(d) Notwithstanding any other provision of law, a health care provider may release the information described in this section to the procurement organization, the coroner, or the medical examiner.

(e) For purposes of this section, "organ" or "organs" means internal whole organs, including, but not limited to, the heart, kidneys, the liver, and lungs, but does not include eyes, skin, or other similar tissue.

(Added by Stats. 1996, Ch. 827, Sec. 3. Effective January 1, 1997.)

CHAPTER 4. Disposal of Unclaimed Dead [7200 - 7208]

(Chapter 4 enacted by Stats. 1939, Ch. 60.)

7200.

Every head of a public institution, city or county undertaker, or state, county, or city officer having charge or control of remains to be interred at public expense shall use due diligence to notify the relatives of the decedent. In the absence of any known relative of the decedent desiring to direct the disposition of the remains in a manner other than provided in this chapter, and upon written request of the state department that these notices are required for a definite period specified in the request, that officer shall notify the state department immediately after the lapse of twenty-four hours after death, stating, whenever possible, the name, age, sex, and cause of death of the decedent.

(Amended by Stats. 2001, Ch. 436, Sec. 21. Effective January 1, 2002.)

7201.

The person in charge of a public institution in which the decedent was an inmate shall transmit upon request, to the state department or to any person designated by it, a brief medical history of the unclaimed dead for purpose of identification and permanent record, which records shall be open to inspection by any State or county official or prosecuting attorney.

(Enacted by Stats. 1939, Ch. 60.)

7202.

The unclaimed dead retained by the State department for scientific or educational purposes shall be embalmed and disposed of in accordance with the instructions of the State department. Such unclaimed dead shall be held for a period of thirty days by those to whom they may have been assigned for scientific or educational purposes, subject to claim and identification by any authenticated relative of the decedent for purpose of interment or other disposition in accordance with the directions of such relative.

(Enacted by Stats. 1939, Ch. 60.)

7203.

The bodies of the unclaimed dead retained by the State department shall be used solely for the purpose of instruction and study in the promotion of medical, chiropractic, and embalming education and science within the State.

(Enacted by Stats. 1939, Ch. 60.)

7204.

All persons receiving unclaimed dead for educational purposes shall bear all reasonable expense incurred in the preservation and transportation of the dead and shall keep a permanent record of bodies received, giving the identification number, the name, age, sex, nationality, and race, if possible, together with the place of last residence of the decedent and the source and disposition, with dates, of the body.

(Enacted by Stats. 1939, Ch. 60.)

7205.

It is unlawful for any person, unless specifically authorized by law, to hold a post mortem examination of any unclaimed dead without the express permission of the State department.

(Enacted by Stats. 1939, Ch. 60.)

7206.

Any person authorized by law to perform post mortem examinations shall permit, with the consent of relatives, or in the absence of such relatives, with the consent of the State department, any representative of the anatomical or pathological departments of an incorporated medical, chiropractic, or osteopathic school or college to obtain at the time of the necropsy, such material in a recent state as may be needed for scientific purposes, if the material is not required for the legal purposes of the State.

(Enacted by Stats. 1939, Ch. 60.)

7207.

Whenever, through the failure of any person to notify the State department, or promptly to deliver the body of a deceased indigent as required by the State department, such body becomes unfit for scientific or educational purposes, the State department shall so certify and the remains shall be interred at the expense of those guilty of such noncompliance.

(Enacted by Stats. 1939, Ch. 60.)

7208.

Every person who unlawfully disposes, uses, or sells the body of an unclaimed dead person, or who violates any provision of this chapter is guilty of a misdemeanor.

(Enacted by Stats. 1939, Ch. 60.)

CHAPTER 5. Embalming and Transportation [7300 - 7355]

(Chapter 5 enacted by Stats. 1939, Ch. 60.)

ARTICLE 1. Embalming [7300 - 7304]

(Article 1 enacted by Stats. 1939, Ch. 60.)

7300.

No person shall embalm the body of any person who has died from an unknown cause, except with the permission of the coroner.

(Amended by Stats. 1951, Ch. 560.)

7301.

No embalmer shall embalm a dead human body when he has information reasonably indicating crime in connection with the death until permission of the coroner has been obtained.

(Amended by Stats. 1977, Ch. 1257.)

7302.

Every funeral director and embalmer shall immediately report to the local health officer every contagious case on which the funeral director or embalmer may be called.

(Enacted by Stats. 1939, Ch. 60.)

7303.

No embalmer shall embalm a dead human body when he has information reasonably indicating the death has occurred while the deceased was driving or riding in a motor vehicle, or as a result of the deceased being struck by a motor vehicle, until permission of the coroner, his appointed deputy coroner, or a judge in the county, if there is no coroner, has been obtained.

(Added by Stats. 1970, Ch. 1355.)

7304.

No embalmer shall embalm a dead body without obtaining written or oral permission of a person who has the right to control the disposition of the remains pursuant to Section 7100, except that prior authorization is not required if embalming is necessary in order to comply with applicable laws or regulations, or is necessary to avoid irreparable deterioration of the dead body, in which case, a good faith effort shall be made to obtain permission.

(Added by Stats. 1978, Ch. 530.)

ARTICLE 2. Transportation [7355- 7355.]

(Article 2 enacted by Stats. 1939, Ch. 60.)

7355.

(a) Except as provided in subdivision (b), the bodies of persons who have died from any cause shall not be received for transportation by a common carrier unless the body has been embalmed and prepared by a licensed embalmer and placed in a sound casket and enclosed in a transportation case.

(b) A dead body, which cannot be embalmed or is in a state of decomposition, shall be received for transportation by a common carrier if the body is placed in an airtight metal casket enclosed in a strong transportation case or in a sound casket enclosed in an airtight metal or metal-lined transportation case.

(Amended by Stats. 1973, Ch. 574.)

PART 2. DISINTERMENT AND REMOVAL [7500 - 8030]

(Part 2 enacted by Stats. 1939, Ch. 60.)

CHAPTER 1. General Provisions [7500 - 7528]

(Chapter 1 enacted by Stats. 1939, Ch. 60.)

ARTICLE 1. Permits [7500 - 7502]

(Article 1 enacted by Stats. 1939, Ch. 60.)

7500.

No remains of any deceased person shall be removed from any cemetery, except upon written order of the health department having jurisdiction, or of the superior court of the county in which such cemetery is situated. A duplicate copy of the order shall be maintained as a part of the records of the cemetery. Any person who removes any remains from any cemetery shall keep and maintain a true and correct record showing:

(a) The date such remains were removed.

(b) The name and age of the person removed, when these particulars can be conveniently obtained and the place to which the remains were removed.

(c) The cemetery and the plot therein in which such remains were buried.

If the remains are disposed of other than by interment, a record shall be made and kept of such disposition. The person making the removal shall deliver to the cemetery authority operating the cemetery from which the remains were removed, a true, full and complete copy of such record.

(Enacted by Stats. 1939, Ch. 60.)

7501.

A cemetery authority shall not remove or permit the removal of any interred remains, unless a permit for the removal has been issued by the local registrar of the district in which the premises are located, and delivered to the cemetery authority. Any person entitled by law to remove any remains may apply to the local registrar for a permit to remove them. The local registrar shall issue a permit, which in all cases, shall specify the name of a cemetery where the remains shall be interred, and shall retain a copy, except that if cremated remains are to be buried at sea as provided in Section 7117 of this code, the permit shall so specify and indicate the county where the fact of burial at sea shall be reported.

(Amended by Stats. 1965, Ch. 1421.)

7502.

In the disinterment, transportation and removal of human remains under Chapter 4 of this part a cemetery authority need not obtain a separate permit for the disinterment, transportation or removal of the remains of each person, but disinterment, transportation and removal of human remains shall be made subject to reasonable rules and regulations relative to the manner of disinterring, transporting or removing such remains as may be adopted by the board of health or health officer of the city or city and county in which the cemetery lands are situated.
(Enacted by Stats. 1939, Ch. 60.)

ARTICLE 2. Consent to Removal [7525 - 7528]

(Article 2 enacted by Stats. 1939, Ch. 60.)

7525.
The remains of a deceased person may be removed from a plot in a cemetery with the consent of the cemetery authority and the written consent of one of the following in the order named:
(a) The surviving spouse.
(b) The surviving children.
(c) The surviving parents.
(d) The surviving brothers or sisters.
(Enacted by Stats. 1939, Ch. 60.)

7526.
If the required consent can not be obtained, permission by the superior court of the county where the cemetery is situated is sufficient.
(Enacted by Stats. 1939, Ch. 60.)

7527.
Notice of application to the court for such permission shall be given, at least ten days prior thereto, personally, or at least fifteen days prior thereto if by mail, to the cemetery authority and to the persons not consenting, and to every other person or association on whom service of notice may be required by the court.
(Enacted by Stats. 1939, Ch. 60.)

7528.
This article does not apply to or prohibit the removal of any remains from one plot to another in the same cemetery or the removal of remains by a cemetery authority from a plot for which the purchase price is past due and unpaid, to some other suitable place; nor does it apply to the disinterment of remains upon order of court or coroner.
(Enacted by Stats. 1939, Ch. 60.)

CHAPTER 3. Removal of All Remains: Cities of 1500–100,000 [7600- 7600.]

(Chapter 3 enacted by Stats. 1939, Ch. 60.)

7600.
The governing body of any city having a population of more than fifteen hundred and not exceeding one hundred thousand, may, by ordinance, and under such rules and regulations as it may adopt, provide for the disinterring and removal of all human remains from cemeteries in which no interments have been made for a period of two years, which are within the city, or owned and controlled by the city and located without its boundaries.
(Enacted by Stats. 1939, Ch. 60.)

CHAPTER 4. Removal of All Remains: Cities and Cities and Counties Over 100,000 [7700 - 8005]

(Chapter 4 enacted by Stats. 1939, Ch. 60.)

ARTICLE 1. Power of Municipality [7700 - 7701]

(Article 1 enacted by Stats. 1939, Ch. 60.)

7700.
The governing body of any city or city and county, having a population of more than one hundred thousand persons, may order the disinterment and removal of all human remains interred in all or any part of any cemetery of more than five acres in extent situated within its limits, where the right of interment in the cemetery has been prohibited by law for a period of fifteen years or more, whenever the governing body, by ordinance, declares that the further maintenance of all or any part of the cemetery as a burial place for the human dead threatens or endangers the health, safety, comfort or welfare of the public and demands the disinterment and removal beyond the limits of the city, or city and county, of the human remains interred therein.
(Enacted by Stats. 1939, Ch. 60.)

7701.
The governing body of such city or city and county may in any ordinance ordering or directing the disinterment and removal of such remains prescribe reasonable rules and regulations governing the manner of making disinterments and removals and providing for reinterment in cemeteries outside the city or city and county limits.
The ordinance shall prescribe a reasonable time of not less than two years in which the removal of remains may be made by the cemetery authority, or by the owners or holders of interment spaces, or by the relatives or friends of those whose remains are interred in the cemetery, and may also provide that if the remains are not removed within the period fixed, the city or city and county will itself proceed to remove the remains and reinter them in another cemetery or cemeteries outside the city or city and county limits.
(Enacted by Stats. 1939, Ch. 60.)

ARTICLE 2. Declaration of Intention by Cemetery Authority [7725 - 7726]

(Article 2 enacted by Stats. 1939, Ch. 60.)

7725.
The cemetery authority of any cemetery from which human remains are ordered removed by an ordinance adopted in accordance with this chapter, may declare its intention and purpose to disinter and remove the remains in accordance with the ordinance, and to reinter the remains in another cemetery or cemeteries outside the limits of the city or city and county, or to deposit the removed remains in a memorial mausoleum or columbarium.
In the case of a cemetery corporation or association the procedure for such declaration shall be by resolution of the governing body of the corporation or association, ratified and approved by a majority vote of the lot owners or holders at any regular meeting of the corporation or association, or at a meeting specially called for the purpose.
(Enacted by Stats. 1939, Ch. 60.)

7726.
Any resolution or declaration of intention to disinter and remove human remains pursuant to this chapter adopted or declared by any cemetery authority shall specify and declare that at any time after the expiration of ten months from and after the first publication of the notice of the resolution or declaration, the human remains then remaining in all or any part of the cemetery will be removed by the cemetery authority.
(Enacted by Stats. 1939, Ch. 60.)

ARTICLE 3. Notice of Intention [7735 - 7739]

(Article 3 enacted by Stats. 1939, Ch. 60.)

7735.
Notice of a declaration of intention to remove the human remains from all or any part of any cemetery shall be given by publication in a newspaper of general circulation published in the city, or city and county, in which the cemetery or the portion from which removals are to be made is situated. Publication shall be at least once a week for two successive months.
(Enacted by Stats. 1939, Ch. 60.)

7736.
The notice shall be entitled "Notice of Declaration of Intention to Remove Human Remains from _____ (insert name of cemetery) in accordance with the provisions of Ordinance No. _____ (insert number) of the _____ (insert name of city, or city and county) adopted _____ (insert date)" and shall specify a date not less than ten months after the first publication when the cemetery authority causing the notice to be published will proceed to remove the remains then remaining in such cemetery or the portion from which removals are to be made.
(Enacted by Stats. 1939, Ch. 60.)

7737.
Copies of the notice shall within ten days after the first publication be posted in at least three conspicuous places in the cemetery or the portion from which removals are to be made.
(Enacted by Stats. 1939, Ch. 60.)

7738.
A copy of the notice shall be mailed to every person who owns, holds, or has the right of interment in, any plot in the cemetery or part affected, whose name appears upon the records of the cemetery. The notice shall be addressed to the last known post-office address of the plot owner as it appears from the records of the cemetery, and if his address does not appear or is not known, then to him at the city, or city and county, in which the cemetery land is situated.
(Enacted by Stats. 1939, Ch. 60.)

7739.
The notice shall also be mailed to each known living heir at law of any person whose remains are interred in the cemetery, if his address is known.
(Enacted by Stats. 1939, Ch. 60.)

ARTICLE 4. Special Notice to Relative or Friend [7750 - 7754]

(Article 4 enacted by Stats. 1939, Ch. 60.)

7750.
At any time before the date fixed for the removal of remains by the cemetery authority, any relative or friend of any person whose remains are interred in the cemetery from which removals are to be made may give the cemetery authority written notice that he desires to be present when the remains are disinterred or are reinterred.
(Enacted by Stats. 1939, Ch. 60.)

7751.
The notice to the cemetery authority shall specify:
(a) The name of the person whose remains are to be disinterred.
(b) As accurately as possible, the plot where the remains are interred.
(c) The date of interment.
(d) An address at which the required notices may be given by the cemetery authority.
(Enacted by Stats. 1939, Ch. 60.)

7752.
The notice may be delivered, or forwarded by registered mail, to the office or principal place of business of the cemetery authority proposing to make removals.
(Enacted by Stats. 1939, Ch. 60.)

7753.
After receipt of such notice before the date fixed for the removal of the remains by the cemetery authority, it shall give written notice to the person requesting it of the time when the remains shall be disinterred and of the time when and the place where they will be

reinterred. This notice shall be given by delivery, or by mail, to the person requesting it at least ten days prior to the date specified for the disinterment of the remains.
(Enacted by Stats. 1939, Ch. 60.)

7754.

Whenever a request of notice is given by a relative or friend, the cemetery authority shall not disinter the remains referred to until the notice of the time of disinterment is given the relative or friend, as provided in this article.
(Enacted by Stats. 1939, Ch. 60.)

ARTICLE 5. Removals by Relatives or Friends [7800 - 7805]
(Article 5 enacted by Stats. 1939, Ch. 60.)

7800.

At any time prior to the removal by a cemetery authority of the remains of any person, any relative or friend of the decedent may voluntarily remove and dispose of the remains.
(Enacted by Stats. 1939, Ch. 60.)

7801.

The person desiring to cause the removal shall, prior to removal, deliver to the cemetery authority an affidavit stating the name of the decedent whose remains it is desired to remove and, so far as is known to affiant, the date of burial and the names and places of residence of the heirs at law of the decedent. If the person desiring to cause the removal is not an heir at law of the person whose remains he desires to remove, the removal shall not be made by him until he has delivered to the cemetery authority the written consent of a majority of the known heirs at law of the decedent who are residents of this State. The statements in the affidavit are sufficient evidence of the number, names, and residences of the heirs at law for all of the purposes of this article, and the written consent of the majority of the heirs at law named in the affidavit is sufficient authority for the cemetery authority to permit the removal of the remains.
(Enacted by Stats. 1939, Ch. 60.)

7802.

Removal of all remains in a plot without the filing of an affidavit of consent may be caused by any of the following:
(a) The purchaser or owner of the plot.
(b) The purchaser or owner of the right of interment in the plot.
(c) Any one of joint purchasers or owners of the plot or of the right of interment in the plot.
(Enacted by Stats. 1939, Ch. 60.)

7803.

If the right, title or interest of any grantee of any plot or of the right of interment therein has passed by succession to the heir or heirs at law of the grantee without distribution by order of court, the heir or heirs at law may remove the remains of persons interred in the plot. The affidavit of any heir at law setting out the facts of heirship shall be accepted by the cemetery authority as sufficient evidence of the fact of the transfer.
(Enacted by Stats. 1939, Ch. 60.)

7804.

Whenever remains are removed by a relative or friend of a decedent, under the provisions of this chapter, the person causing the removal is entitled to remove any vault, monument, headstone, coping or other improvement appurtenant to the interment space from which the remains have been removed. The affidavit or written consent given under the provisions of this chapter are sufficient authority for the cemetery authority to permit the removal of any such appurtenance.
(Enacted by Stats. 1939, Ch. 60.)

7805.

If such appurtenances remain on the plot for more than ninety days after the removal of the last human remains, they may be removed and disposed of by the cemetery authority, and thereafter no person claiming any interest in the plot, or any such appurtenance shall maintain in any court any action in relation to any such appurtenance.
(Enacted by Stats. 1939, Ch. 60.)

ARTICLE 6. Removal by Cemetery Authority [7850 - 7852]
(Article 6 enacted by Stats. 1939, Ch. 60.)

7850.

After the completion of notice, and after the expiration of the period of ten months specified in the notice, any cemetery authority may cause the removal of all human remains interred in the cemetery or portion from which the remains have been ordered removed, and may reinter such remains in other cemeteries in this State where interments are permitted, without further notice to any person claiming any interest in the cemetery, or portion affected, or in the remains interred therein.
(Enacted by Stats. 1939, Ch. 60.)

7851.

Whenever any remains are removed from any cemetery or portion of a cemetery pursuant to this chapter by a cemetery authority, they shall be transported to and reinterred in a cemetery in an adjoining county where interments by the cemetery authority are permitted.
(Enacted by Stats. 1939, Ch. 60.)

7852.

The remains of each person reinterred shall be placed in a separate and suitable receptacle and decently and respectfully interred under rules and regulations adopted by the cemetery authority making the removal.
(Enacted by Stats. 1939, Ch. 60.)

ARTICLE 7. Disposal of Lands [7900 - 7906]
(Article 7 enacted by Stats. 1939, Ch. 60.)

7900.

Whenever human remains have been ordered removed under this chapter, and the cemetery authority has made and published notice of intention to remove such remains, the portions of the cemetery in which no interments have been made, and those portions from which all human remains have been removed, may be sold, mortgaged, or otherwise encumbered as security for any loan or loans made to the cemetery authority.
(Enacted by Stats. 1939, Ch. 60.)

7901.

No order of any court shall be required prior to the making of any such sale, mortgage, or other encumbrance of such lands; but any sale of such cemetery lands made by any cemetery corporation or association controlled by a governing body shall be fairly conducted and the price paid shall be fair and reasonable and all such sales shall be confirmed, as to the fairness and reasonableness of the price paid, by the superior court of the county in which the lands are situated.
(Enacted by Stats. 1939, Ch. 60.)

7902.

Petitions for confirmation of sales shall be made to the superior court of the county or city and county in which the lands are situated, and the clerk of the court shall fix a day for and give notice of hearing in accordance with the provisions of Section 1230 of the Probate Code.
(Amended by Stats. 1988, Ch. 113, Sec. 11. Effective May 25, 1988. Section operative July 1, 1988, by its own provisions.)

7903.

If prior to the adoption of an ordinance pursuant to this chapter any cemetery authority has in good faith entered into any agreement to sell or has granted any option to buy all or any portion of its cemetery lands for a price reasonable at the time the agreement to sell was made, or the option granted, the superior court shall confirm the sale at the price stipulated in the agreement to sell or the option to buy.
(Enacted by Stats. 1939, Ch. 60.)

7904.

After the removal of all human remains interred in any part or the whole of the cemetery lands, the cemetery authority may file for record in the office of the county recorder of the county or city and county in which the lands are situated a written declaration reciting that all human remains have been removed from the lands described in the declaration. The declaration shall be acknowledged in the manner of the acknowledgment of deeds to real property by the president and secretary, or other corresponding officers of the cemetery authority, or by the person owning or controlling the cemetery lands, and thereafter any deed, mortgage, or other conveyance of any part of such lands is conclusive evidence in favor of any grantee or mortgagee named in it, and his successor or assigns, of the fact of the complete removal of all human remains therefrom.
(Enacted by Stats. 1939, Ch. 60.)

7905.

With the approval of the governing body of the city or city and county in which the cemetery lands are situated, sufficient lands may be reserved from any cemetery lands from which the human remains have been removed to erect a mausoleum or columbarium for the reinterment of disinterred remains, to provide sufficient grounds around it, and to preserve such historical vaults or monuments as the cemetery authority may determine to be proper or necessary.
(Enacted by Stats. 1939, Ch. 60.)

7906.

After all remains have been removed from a cemetery in accordance with Chapters 3 and 4, Part 2, Division VII of this code, the dedication may be removed from all or any part of such cemetery lands by an order and decree of the superior court of the county in which the property is situated, in a proceeding brought for that purpose and upon notice of hearing and proof satisfactory to the court:
(a) That all bodies have been removed, or that no interments were made; and
(b) That the property is no longer used or required for interment purposes.
(Added by Stats. 1939, Ch. 1032.)

ARTICLE 8. Use of Funds [7925 - 7933]
(Article 8 enacted by Stats. 1939, Ch. 60.)

7925.

Money payable or to become payable as the purchase price or on account of the purchase price of unused lands, or lands from which all remains have been removed is not subject to enforcement of a money judgment, but shall be used exclusively for any or all of the following purposes:
(a) Acquisition of lands and improvements for cemetery purposes.
(b) Disinterment, removal, and reinterment of bodies, pursuant to this chapter.
(c) Endowment care of graves, markers, and cemetery embellishments.
(d) The payment of expenses incidental to the disinterment, removal, and reinterment.
(e) Any other purpose consistent with the objects for which the cemetery authority owning the cemetery is created or organized.
(Amended by Stats. 1982, Ch. 497, Sec. 122. Operative July 1, 1983, by Sec. 185 of Ch. 497.)

7926.

Whenever any cemetery corporation or association has declared for removal and has published notice of its intention to make removals under this chapter, it may employ any money in its treasury to defray the expense of removal, including:
(a) The expense of purchasing or otherwise providing a suitable place for the interment of remains in any other cemetery.
(b) The expenses of disinterment, transportation and reinterment.

(c) The expenses of removal and disposal of vaults, monuments, headstones, copings, or other improvements.

(d) All necessary expenses incident to the sale or mortgaging of any land from which removals have been made.

(e) All other expenses necessarily incurred in carrying out the removal, and reinterment, or disposing of remains so removed.

(f) All expenses incident to any of the above purposes.

(Enacted by Stats. 1939, Ch. 60.)

7927.

From the money remaining in the treasury of the cemetery corporation or association after completing the removal and reinterment of the remains from its cemetery lands and the payment of all incidental expenses, the cemetery corporation or association shall set aside an adequate endowment care fund for the maintenance and care of the cemetery in which the remains have been interred.

(Amended by Stats. 1951, Ch. 176.)

7928.

After making provisions for an endowment care fund to provide for maintenance and care, the governing body of the cemetery corporation or association may use such portion of the funds then remaining as it may determine to be just and fair in reimbursing those who voluntarily and at their own cost and expense removed the remains of friends or relatives from the cemetery lands from which the remains were ordered removed. Such reimbursement shall not be greater in amount than the average cost to the cemetery corporation or association for removals directly made by it.

(Amended by Stats. 1951, Ch. 176.)

7929.

Any balance remaining in the fund may be used for such other purposes as the cemetery corporation or association may lawfully declare.

(Enacted by Stats. 1939, Ch. 60.)

7930.

Whenever any cemetery corporation or association having a governing body has caused the removal of remains from all or any portion of its cemetery and has funds in its treasury which are not required for other purposes, it may set aside, invest, use, and apply from such unexpended funds such sum as, in the judgment of the governing body, it is necessary or expedient to provide for the perpetual or other care or improvement of any cemetery in which the disinterred remains may be reinterred.

(Enacted by Stats. 1939, Ch. 60.)

7931.

In lieu of itself investing, using or applying the funds for care or improvement, the cemetery corporation or association may transfer the funds to any other corporation under such conditions and regulations as in the judgment of the governing body will insure their application to the purposes of care or improvement.

(Enacted by Stats. 1939, Ch. 60.)

7932.

Before any such transfer of funds is made, the cemetery corporation or association shall obtain an order authorizing the transfer from the superior court of the county where the cemetery or portion from which the remains were removed is situated.

(Enacted by Stats. 1939, Ch. 60.)

7933.

The order shall be obtained upon petition of the cemetery corporation or association, after such notice by publication as the court may direct, and any member or former plot owner may support or oppose the granting of the order by affidavit or otherwise. Before making the order, proof shall be made to the satisfaction of the court that notice has been given and that it is for the best interests of the cemetery corporation or association that the transfer be made.

(Enacted by Stats. 1939, Ch. 60.)

ARTICLE 9. New Land, Mausoleum or Columbarium [7950 - 7955]

(Article 9 enacted by Stats. 1939, Ch. 60.)

7950.

Whenever any cemetery authority owning or controlling cemetery lands from which remains are to be removed has acquired the possession or use of any cemetery for the purpose of providing a place for the reinterment of human remains removed under this chapter, new lands may be surveyed and subdivided into plots, avenues, and walks for cemetery purposes; and any mausoleum and columbarium may be divided into crypts or niches.

(Enacted by Stats. 1939, Ch. 60.)

7951.

Plots, crypts, or niches may be sold to persons desiring to make reinterments.

(Enacted by Stats. 1939, Ch. 60.)

7952.

The governing body of any cemetery corporation or association may receive and accept as part or full consideration for the purchase price of new plots full or partial releases of rights in or to the whole or any part of the assets of the corporation or association other than the plot conveyed to the purchaser. Any retransfer to the cemetery corporation or association of any plot in the cemetery from which the removal of the human remains is to be made operates as such release.

(Enacted by Stats. 1939, Ch. 60.)

7953.

After the removal and reinterment of remains disinterred from any cemetery the cemetery authority shall cause to be erected upon or imbedded in any plot in which any remains are reinterred a suitable permanent marker identifying the remains.

(Enacted by Stats. 1939, Ch. 60.)

7954.

The cemetery authority shall prepare a complete map or plat describing and showing the location and subdivision into plots of the cemetery lands where remains are reinterred, or a plan of any mausoleum or columbarium in which such remains are interred; and there shall be attached to each plan a description of the name, where known, of each person whose remains are reinterred, and the plot in the cemetery, or the niche or compartment in the mausoleum or columbarium where such remains are reinterred.

(Enacted by Stats. 1939, Ch. 60.)

7955.

The map or plan shall be kept on file in the office of the cemetery authority and shall at all times be open to inspection by the relatives or friends of deceased persons whose remains are reinterred therein.

(Enacted by Stats. 1939, Ch. 60.)

ARTICLE 10. Taxation [7975- 7975.]

(Article 10 enacted by Stats. 1939, Ch. 60.)

7975.

When any law or ordinance requires that the remains interred in any cemetery be removed and reinterred elsewhere, no county, town or political subdivision in which the reinterment of disinterred remains takes place, shall charge for any permit or levy a tax of any nature for the reinterment.

(Enacted by Stats. 1939, Ch. 60.)

ARTICLE 11. Religious Observances [7980- 7980.]

(Article 11 enacted by Stats. 1939, Ch. 60.)

7980.

The heirs, relatives or friends of any decedent whose remains have been interred in any cemetery owned, governed or controlled by any religious corporation or by any church or religious society of any denomination or by any corporation sole administering temporalities of any religious denomination, society or church, or owned, governed or controlled by any person or persons as trustee or trustees for any religious denomination, society or church shall not disinter, remove, reinter or dispose of any such remains except in accordance with the rules, regulations and discipline of such religious denomination, society or church.

The officers, representatives or agents of the church or religious society shall be the sole judge of the requirements of the rules, regulations and discipline of such religious denomination, society or church.

(Enacted by Stats. 1939, Ch. 60.)

ARTICLE 12. Removal by Counties [8000 - 8005]

(Article 12 added by Stats. 1947, Ch. 586.)

8000.

If it appears to the board of supervisors of any county owning a county cemetery that:

(a) It is necessary that the property be used for other purposes, and

(b) The cemetery is located on a portion of the site of an existing county institution maintained for the relief of the indigent, sick and afflicted, and

(c) Adequate facilities are otherwise provided for by the county for the burial of the indigent dead;

the board may, by following the procedure contained in this article, order the disinterment and removal of all humam remains interred in such cemetery.

(Amended by Stats. 1961, Ch. 303.)

8001.

Any resolution or declaration for abandonment adopted and made under the provisions of this article shall specify and declare that at any time after the expiration of 60 days after the first publication of the notice of declaration of intended abandonment and removal, the human remains then remaining in the cemetery will be removed by the county owning the cemetery. Notice of the declaration of intended abandonment of the cemetery and proposed removal of the human remains interred therein shall be given to all persons interested therein by publication in the newspaper of general circulation published in the county determined by the board of supervisors most likely to give notice to the parties concerned. Publication shall be made once a week for four consecutive times. The notice shall be entitled "Notice of Declaration of Abandonment of Lands for Cemetery Purposes and of Intention to Remove Human Bodies Interred Therein," and shall specify a date not less than 60 days after the first publication of the notice when the county controlling the cemetery lands and causing the notice to be published will proceed to remove the human remains then remaining in such cemetery. Notice shall also be mailed to any known living heir-at-law of any person whose remains are interred in the cemetery when the address of the heir is known.

(Added by Stats. 1947, Ch. 586.)

8002.

At any time before the date fixed for the removal of the remains by the county owning or controlling such cemetery land, any relative or friend of any person whose remains are interred in the cemetery may voluntarily remove the remains and reinter the same as he may desire.

(Added by Stats. 1947, Ch. 586.)

8003.

After the publication and mailing of the notice mentioned in Section 8001 of this code and after the expiration of the 60 days specified in the notice, the county shall have the power to cause the removal of all human remains interred in the cemetery about to be abandoned and to cause the reinterment in other cemeteries of the county in which burials are permitted, without further notice to any persons claiming an interest in the remains therein interred.

(Added by Stats. 1947, Ch. 586.)

8004.

Whenever the remains of any person shall be removed from any abandoned cemetery by the county owning such abandoned cemetery, such remains shall be transported and reinterred in a separate and suitable receptacle. After the removal and reinterment of human bodies disinterred from an abandoned cemetery, the county owning or controlling the abandoned cemetery lands shall cause to be erected upon or imbedded in any lot or plot wherein such body is reinterred a suitable permanent marker identifying the remains with as much particularity as is available to such county and shall prepare a complete record of the name of each person, where known, and the lot or plot where the body is reinterred and such record shall be kept in the office of the board of supervisors of the county making such removals and reinterments and shall at all times be open to the relatives and friends of those so reinterred.

(Added by Stats. 1947, Ch. 586.)

8005.

After the removal of all human remains the property may be used, managed and controlled by the board of supervisors as other county property.

(Added by Stats. 1947, Ch. 586.)

CHAPTER 5. California Native American Graves Protection and Repatriation [8010 - 8030]

(Chapter 5 added by Stats. 2001, Ch. 818, Sec. 1.)

ARTICLE 1. General Provisions [8010 - 8011]

(Article 1 added by Stats. 2001, Ch. 818, Sec. 1.)

8010.

This chapter shall be known, and may be cited as the California Native American Graves Protection and Repatriation Act of 2001.

(Added by Stats. 2001, Ch. 818, Sec. 1. Effective January 1, 2002.)

8011.

It is the intent of the Legislature to do all of the following:

(a) Provide a seamless and consistent state policy to ensure that all California Indian human remains and cultural items be treated with dignity and respect.

(b) Apply the state's repatriation policy consistently with the provisions of the Native American Graves Protection and Repatriation Act (25 U.S.C. Sec. 3001 et seq.), which was enacted in 1990.

(c) Facilitate the implementation of the provisions of the federal Native American Graves Protection and Repatriation Act with respect to publicly funded agencies and museums in California.

(d) Encourage voluntary disclosure and return of remains and cultural items by an agency or museum.

(e) Provide a mechanism whereby lineal descendants and culturally affiliated California Indian tribes that file repatriation claims for human remains and cultural items under the Native American Graves Protection and Repatriation Act (25 U.S.C. Sec. 3001 et seq.) or under this chapter with California state agencies and museums may request assistance from the commission in ensuring that state agencies and museums are responding to those claims in a timely manner and in facilitating the resolution of disputes regarding those claims.

(f) Provide a mechanism whereby California tribes that are not federally recognized may file claims with agencies and museums for repatriation of human remains and cultural items.

(Added by Stats. 2001, Ch. 818, Sec. 1. Effective January 1, 2002.)

ARTICLE 2. State Cultural Affiliation and Repatriation [8012 - 8021]

(Article 2 added by Stats. 2001, Ch. 818, Sec. 1.)

8012.

As used in this chapter, terms shall have the same meaning as in the federal Native American Graves Protection and Repatriation Act (25 U.S.C. Sec. 3001 et seq.), as interpreted by federal regulations, except that the following terms shall have the following meaning:

(a) "Agency" means a division, department, bureau, commission, board, council, city, county, city and county, district, or other political subdivision of the state, but does not include a school district.

(b) "Burial site" means, except for cemeteries and graveyards protected under existing state law, a natural or prepared physical location, whether originally below, on, or above the surface of the earth, into which human remains were intentionally deposited as a part of the death rites or ceremonies of a culture.

(c) "Commission" means the Native American Heritage Commission, established pursuant to Section 5097.91 of the Public Resources Code.

(d) "Cultural items" shall have the same meaning as defined by Section 3001 of Title 25 of the United States Code, except that it shall mean only those items that originated in California.

(e) "Control" means having ownership of human remains and cultural items sufficient to lawfully permit a museum or agency to treat the object as part of its collection for purposes of this chapter, whether or not the human remains and cultural items are in the physical custody of the museum or agency. Items on loan to a museum or agency from

another person, museum, or agency shall be deemed to be in the control of the lender, and not the borrowing museum or agency.

(f) "State cultural affiliation" means that there is a relationship of shared group identity that can reasonably be traced historically or prehistorically between members of a present-day California Indian Tribe, as defined in subdivision (j), and an identifiable earlier tribe or group. Cultural affiliation is established when the preponderance of the evidence, based on geography, kinship, biology, archaeology, linguistics, folklore, oral tradition, historical evidence, or other information or expert opinion, reasonably leads to such a conclusion.

(g) "Inventory" means an itemized list that summarizes the collection of human remains and associated funerary objects in the possession or control of an agency or museum. This itemized list may be the inventory list required under the federal Native American Graves Protection and Repatriation Act (25 U.S.C. Sec. 3001 et seq.).

(h) "Summary" means a document that summarizes the collection of unassociated funerary objects, sacred objects, or objects of cultural patrimony in the possession or control of an agency or museum. This document may be the summary prepared under the federal Native American Graves Protection and Repatriation Act (25 U.S.C. Sec. 3001 et seq.).

(i) "Museum" means an entity, including a higher educational institution, excluding school districts, that receives state funds.

(j) "California Indian tribe" means any tribe located in California to which any of the following applies:

(1) It meets the definition of Indian tribe under the federal Native American Graves Protection and Repatriation Act (25 U.S.C. Sec. 3001 et seq.).

(2) It is not recognized by the federal government, but is indigenous to the territory that is now known as the State of California, and both of the following apply:

(A) It is listed in the Bureau of Indian Affairs Branch of Acknowledgement and Research petitioner list pursuant to Section 82.1 of Title 25 of the Federal Code of Regulations.

(B) It is determined by the commission to be a tribe that is eligible to participate in the repatriation process set forth in this chapter. The commission shall publish a document that lists the California tribes meeting these criteria, as well as authorized representatives to act on behalf of the tribe in the consultations required under paragraph (3) of subdivision (a) of Section 8013 and in matters pertaining to repatriation under this chapter. Criteria that shall guide the commission in making the determination of eligibility shall include, but not be limited to, the following:

(i) A continuous identity as an autonomous and separate tribal government.

(ii) Holding itself out as a tribe.

(iii) The tribe as a whole has demonstrated aboriginal ties to the territory now known as the State of California and its members can demonstrate lineal descent from the identifiable earlier groups that inhabited a particular tribal territory.

(iv) Recognition by the Indian community and non-Indian entities as a tribe.

(v) Demonstrated membership criteria.

(k) "Possession" means having physical custody of human remains and cultural items with a sufficient legal interest to lawfully treat the human remains and cultural items as part of a collection. The term does not include human remains and cultural items on loan to an agency or museum.

(l) "Preponderance of the evidence" means that the party's evidence on a fact indicates that it is more likely than not that the fact is true.

(Amended by Stats. 2015, Ch. 24, Sec. 6. (SB 83) Effective June 24, 2015.)

8013.

(a) Any agency or museum that has possession or control over collections of California Native American human remains and associated funerary objects shall complete an inventory of all these remains and associated funerary objects and, to the extent possible based on all information possessed by the agency or museum, do all of the following:

(1) Identify the geographical location, state cultural affiliation, and the circumstances surrounding their acquisition.

(2) List in the inventory the human remains and associated funerary objects that are clearly identifiable as to state cultural affiliation with California Indian tribes. These items shall be listed first in order to expedite the repatriation of these items.

(3) List the human remains and associated funerary objects that are not clearly identifiable as to cultural affiliation but that, given the totality of circumstances surrounding their acquisition and characteristics are determined by a reasonable belief to be human remains and associated funerary objects with a state cultural affiliation with one or more California Indian tribes. Consult with California Indian tribes believed by the agency or museum to be affiliated with the items, during the compilation of the inventory as part of the determination of affiliation. If the agency or museum cannot determine which California Indian tribes are believed to be affiliated with the items, then tribes that may be affiliated with the items shall be consulted during the compilation of the inventory.

(b) Any agency or museum that has possession or control over collections of California Indian unassociated funerary objects, sacred objects, or objects of cultural patrimony shall provide a written summary of the objects based upon available information held by the agency or museum. The summary shall describe the scope of the collection, kinds of objects included, reference to geographical location, means and period of acquisition, and state cultural affiliation, where readily ascertainable. The summary shall be in lieu of an object-by-object inventory. Each agency or museum, following preparation of a summary pursuant to this subdivision, shall consult with California Indian tribes and tribally authorized government officials and traditional religious leaders.

(c) Each agency or museum shall complete the inventories and summaries required by subdivisions (a) and (b) by January 1, 2003, or within one year of the date on which the commission issues the list of California Indian tribes provided for under paragraph (2) of subdivision (i) of Section 8012, whichever is later. To the extent that this section requires the inventory and summary to include items not required to be included in the inventory and summary under the federal Native American Graves Protection and Repatriation Act (25 U.S.C. Sec. 3001 et seq.), the agency or museum shall supplement its inventory and summary under this section to include those additional items.

(d) Upon request of a California Indian tribe, a museum or agency shall supply additional available documentation to supplement the information required by subdivisions (a) and (b). For purposes of this paragraph, "documentation" means a summary of existing museum or agency records, including inventories or catalogs, relevant studies, or other pertinent data for the limited purpose of determining the geographical origin, cultural affiliation, and basic facts surrounding the acquisition and accession of California Native American human remains and cultural items subject to this section. This section shall not be construed to authorize the completion or initiation of any scientific study of human remains or cultural items.

(e) Within 90 days of completing the inventory and summary specified in subdivisions (a) and (b), the agency or museum shall provide a copy of the inventory and summary to the commission. The commission shall, in turn, publish notices of completion of summaries and inventories on its Web site for 30 days, and make the inventory and summary available to any requesting tribe or state affiliated tribe.

(f) The inventory and summary specified in subdivisions (a) and (b) shall be completed by all agencies and museums that have possession or control of Native American human remains or cultural items, regardless of whether the agency or museum is also subject to the requirements of the federal Native American Graves Protection and Repatriation Act (25 U.S.C. Sec. 3001 et seq.). Any inventory or summary, or any portion of an inventory or summary, that has been created to meet the requirements of the Native American Graves Protection and Repatriation Act (25 U.S.C. Sec. 3001 et seq.) may be used to meet the requirements of this chapter, if appropriate.

(g) Any agency or museum that has completed inventories and summaries on or before January 1, 2002, as required by the federal Native American Graves Protection and Repatriation Act (25 U.S.C. Sec. 3001 et seq.) shall be deemed to be in compliance with this section provided that the agency or museum does both of the following:

(1) Provide a copy of the inventories and summaries to the commission by July 1, 2002, or within 30 days of the date on which the commission is formed, whichever is later.

(2) Prepare supplementary inventories and summaries as necessary to comply with subdivisions (a) and (b) for those portions of their collections that originate from California and that have not been determined to be culturally affiliated with federally recognized tribes which, in the case of inventories, are those portions of the collections of an agency or museum that have been identified on their inventories under the federal Native American Graves Protection and Repatriation Act (25 U.S.C. Sec. 3001 et seq.) as "culturally unidentifiable," by January 1, 2003, or within one year of the date on which the commission issues the list of California Indian tribes provided for under paragraph (2) of subdivision (j) of Section 8012, whichever is later.

(h) If the agency or museum determines that it does not have in its possession or control any human remains or cultural items, the agency or museum shall, in lieu of an inventory or summary, state that finding in a letter to the commission at the commission's request.

(i) Following completion of the initial inventories and summaries specified in subdivisions (a) and (b), each agency or museum shall update its inventories and summaries whenever the agency or museum receives possession or control of human remains or cultural items that were not included in the initial inventories and summaries. Upon completion, the agency or museum shall provide a copy of its updated inventories and summaries to the commission. Nothing in this section shall be construed to mean that a museum or agency may delay repatriation of items in the initial inventory until the updating of all inventories and summaries is completed.

(Added by Stats. 2001, Ch. 818, Sec. 1. Effective January 1, 2002.)

8014.

A tribe claiming state cultural affiliation and requesting the return of human remains and cultural items listed in the inventory or summary of an agency or museum or that requests the return of human remains and cultural items that are not listed in the inventory but are believed to be in the possession or control of the agency or museum in the state shall do both of the following:

(a) File a written request for the human remains and cultural items with the commission and the agency or museum believed to have possession or control.

(b) Provide evidence that would establish that items claimed are cultural items and are culturally affiliated with the California Indian tribe making the claim. Evidence of cultural affiliation need not be provided in cases where cultural affiliation is reasonably established by the inventory or summary or a finding by a federal or state agency, published in the Federal Register, in compliance with the federal Native American Graves Protection and Repatriation Act (25 U.S.C. Sec. 3001 et seq.).

(Amended by Stats. 2018, Ch. 823, Sec. 2. (AB 2836) Effective January 1, 2019.)

8015.

(a) Upon receiving a written request for repatriation of an item on the inventory, the commission shall forward a copy of the request to the agency or museum in possession of the item, if the criteria specified in subdivision (b) of Section 8016 have been met. At this time, the commission shall also publish the request for repatriation on its Web site for 30 days. If there are no other requests for a particular item and there is not unresolved objection pursuant to subdivision (c) of Section 8016 within 90 days of the date of distribution and publication of the inventory or summary and completion of any federal Native American Graves Protection and Repatriation Act (25 U.S.C. Sec. 3001 et seq.) repatriation process related to the item, the agency or museum in possession of the item

shall repatriate the requested item to the requesting party. This repatriation shall occur within 30 days after the last day of the 90-day period, or on a date agreed upon by all parties.

(b) Nothing in this section shall be construed to prohibit any requesting party, a tribe, an agency, or a museum from coordinating directly with each other on repatriation, or to prohibit the repatriation at any time of any undisputed items to the requesting party prior to completion of any requirements set forth in this chapter. The commission shall receive, for their records, copies of all repatriation agreements and shall have the power to enforce these agreements.

(Added by Stats. 2001, Ch. 818, Sec. 1. Effective January 1, 2002.)

8016.

(a) If there is more than one request for repatriation for the same item, or there is a dispute between the requesting party and the agency or museum, or if a dispute arises in relation to the repatriation process, the commission shall notify the affected parties of this fact and the cultural affiliation of the item in question shall be determined in accordance with this section.

(b) An agency or museum receiving a repatriation request pursuant to subdivision (a) shall repatriate human remains and cultural items if all of the following criteria have been met:

(1) The requested human remains or cultural items meet the definitions of human remains or cultural items that are subject to inventory requirements under subdivision (a) of Section 8013.

(2) The state cultural affiliation of the human remains or cultural items is established as required under subdivision (f) of Section 8012.

(3) The agency or museum is unable to present evidence that, if standing alone before the introduction of evidence to the contrary, would support a finding that the agency or museum has a right of possession to the requested cultural items.

(4) None of the exemptions listed in Section 10.10(c) of Title 43 of the Federal Code of Regulations apply.

(5) All other applicable requirements of regulations adopted under the federal Native American Graves Protection and Repatriation Act (25 U.S.C. Sec. 3001 et seq.), contained in Part 10 of Title 43 of the Code of Federal Regulations, have been met.

(c) Within 30 days after notice has been provided by the commission, the museum or agency shall have the right to file with the commission any objection to the requested repatriation, based on its good faith belief that the requested human remains or cultural items are not culturally affiliated with the requesting California tribe or are not subject to repatriation under this chapter.

(d) The disputing parties shall submit documentation describing the nature of the dispute, in accordance with standard mediation practices and the commission's procedures, to the commission, which shall, in turn, forward the documentation to the opposing party or parties. The disputing parties shall meet within 30 days of the date of the mailing of the documentation with the goal of settling the dispute.

(e) If, after meeting pursuant to subdivision (d), the parties are unable to settle the dispute, the commission, or a certified mediator designated by the commission in accordance with paragraph (2) of subdivision (n) of Section 5097.94 of the Public Resources Code, shall mediate the dispute.

(f) Each disputing party shall submit complaints and supporting evidence to the commission or designated mediator and the other opposing parties detailing their positions on the disputed issues in accordance with standard mediation practices and the commission's mediation procedures. Each party shall have 20 days from the date the complaint and supporting evidence were mailed to respond to the complaints. All responses shall be submitted to the opposing party or parties and the commission or designated mediator.

(g) The commission or designated mediator shall review all complaints, responses, and supporting evidence submitted. Within 20 days after the date of submission of responses, the commission or designated mediator shall hold a mediation session and render a decision within seven days of the date of the mediation session.

(h) When the disposition of any items are disputed, the party in possession of the items shall retain possession until the mediation process is completed. No transfer of items shall occur until the dispute is resolved.

(i) Tribal oral histories, documentation, and testimonies shall not be afforded less evidentiary weight than other relevant categories of evidence on account of being in those categories.

(j) If the parties are unable to resolve a dispute through mediation, the dispute shall be resolved by the commission. The determination of the commission shall be deemed to constitute a final administrative remedy. Any party to the dispute seeking a review of the determination of the commission is entitled to file an action in the superior court seeking an independent judgment on the record as to whether the commission's decision is supported by a preponderance of the evidence. The independent review shall not constitute a de novo review of a decision by the commission, but shall be limited to a review of the evidence on the record. Petitions for review shall be filed with the court not later than 30 days after the final decision of the commission.

(Amended by Stats. 2015, Ch. 24, Sec. 7. (SB 83) Effective June 24, 2015.)

8017.

If there is a committee or group of tribes authorized by their respective tribal governments to accept repatriation of items originating from their region and culturally affiliated with those tribal governments, then the items may be repatriated to those groups.

(Added by Stats. 2001, Ch. 818, Sec. 1. Effective January 1, 2002.)

8018.

An agency or museum that repatriates human remains and cultural items in good faith pursuant to this chapter is not liable for claims by an aggrieved party or for claims of breach of a fiduciary duty or the public trust or of violation of state law that are inconsistent with this chapter. No action shall be brought on behalf of the state or any other entity or person for damages or for injunctive relief for a claim of improper disposition of human remains or cultural items if the agency or museum has complied with the provisions of this chapter.
(Added by Stats. 2001, Ch. 818, Sec. 1. Effective January 1, 2002.)

8019.

Nothing in this section shall be construed to prohibit the governing body of a California Indian tribe or group authorized by Section 8017 from expressly relinquishing control over any human remains or control or title to any cultural item.
(Added by Stats. 2001, Ch. 818, Sec. 1. Effective January 1, 2002.)

8020.

Notwithstanding any other provision of law, and upon the request of any party or an intervenor, the commission or designated mediator may close part of a mediation session to the public if the commission or designated mediator finds that information required at the mediation session may include identification of the specific location of a burial site, human remains and cultural items or that information necessary for a determination regarding repatriation may compromise or interfere with any religious practice or custom.
(Added by Stats. 2001, Ch. 818, Sec. 1. Effective January 1, 2002.)

8021.

The filing of an appeal by either party automatically stays an order of the commission or a designated mediator on repatriation of human remains and cultural items.
(Added by Stats. 2001, Ch. 818, Sec. 1. Effective January 1, 2002.)

ARTICLE 3. University of California Implementation [8025 - 8028.5]
(Article 3 added by Stats. 2018, Ch. 823, Sec. 3.)

8025.

(a) In order to better implement the federal Native American Graves Protection and Repatriation Act (25 U.S.C. Sec. 3001 et seq.), the Regents of the University of California shall not use state funds for the handling or maintenance of Native American human remains and cultural items unless the regents do all the following:
(1) Facilitate the establishment, composition, and function of systemwide and campus-level committees, established pursuant to Section 8026, with respect to reviewing and advising the university on matters related to the university's implementation of legal requirements to make repatriations or dispositions of Native American human remains and cultural items.
(2) (A) Adopt and implement systemwide policies regarding the culturally appropriate treatment of Native American human remains and cultural items while in the possession of a University of California campus or museum, including policies regarding research requests and testing following the submission of a request for repatriation.
(B) Adopt and implement clear and transparent policies and procedures on the systemwide requirements for submitting claims for the repatriation of human remains and cultural items, demonstrating cultural affiliation, notification to tribes of human remains and cultural items deemed culturally affiliated but that are not subject to a current repatriation claim, dispute resolution regarding repatriation claims, and any other relevant subject governed by the federal Native American Graves Protection and Repatriation Act (25 U.S.C. Sec. 3001 et seq.) and this chapter.
(C) Adopt or amend systemwide University of California museum deaccessioning policies to explicitly provide for the deaccession of collections containing Native American human remains and cultural items to effect the timely and respectful repatriation of those items pursuant to valid claims submitted by a California Indian tribe.
(D) Adopt systemwide University of California policies and procedures for the identification and disposition of culturally unidentifiable human remains and cultural items as required by the federal Native American Graves Protection and Repatriation Regulations (43 C.F.R. Part 10). Those policies shall include updates to existing inventories in order to determine whether cultural affiliation can be determined, or to confirm that the human remains are "culturally unidentifiable" as defined in paragraph (2) of subsection (e) of Section 10.2 of Part 10 of Title 43 of the Code of Federal Regulations.
(3) Develop all policies and procedures pursuant to paragraph (2) in consultation with California Native American tribes on the contact list maintained by the Native American Heritage Commission. Each California Indian tribe that is on the contact list shall be invited to consult on the proposed policies and procedures. For purposes of this section, "consultation" has the same meaning as defined in Section 65352.4 of the Government Code.
(4) Timely submit the policies and procedures adopted pursuant to paragraph (2) to the commission, so they may review and comment upon them pursuant to subdivision (q) of Section 5097.94 of the Public Resources Code by July 1, 2019.
(5) Implement the systemwide policies adopted pursuant to paragraph (2) by January 1, 2020, and implement any campus policies within one year after the adoption of the systemwide policies.
(6) Ensure that each campus Native American Graves Protection and Repatriation Act Implementation Committee implements the policies and procedures adopted pursuant to paragraph (2).
(7) Adopt procedures to support appeals and dispute resolution in cases where a tribe disagrees with a campus determination regarding repatriation or disposition of human remains or cultural items directly to the systemwide Native American Graves Protection and Repatriation Act Implementation and Oversight Committee.
(b) A campus of the University of California may adopt policies to supplement the systemwide policies adopted pursuant to paragraph (2), if the campus determines that

individual circumstances involving that campus are not adequately addressed in the adopted and approved systemwide policies, in consultation with California Native American tribes. A policy or procedure adopted by a campus pursuant to this subdivision shall not conflict with the approved systemwide policies.
(Added by Stats. 2018, Ch. 823, Sec. 3. (AB 2836) Effective January 1, 2019.)

8026.

(a) (1) As a condition for using state funds to handle and maintain Native American human remains and cultural items, the Regents of the University of California shall establish a systemwide Native American Graves Protection and Repatriation Act Implementation and Oversight Committee, which shall also be known as the U.C. NAGPRA Committee.
(2) The membership of the committee shall be as follows:
(A) Two voting members of an Indian tribe as described in paragraph (1) of subdivision (j) of Section 8012, meeting the requirements of subdivision (c).
(B) One voting member of an Indian tribe as described in paragraph (2) of subdivision (j) of Section 8012, meeting the requirements of subdivision (c), or if none is available, a member of an Indian tribe as described in paragraph (1) of subdivision (j) of Section 8012, meeting the requirements of subdivision (c).
(C) Four voting members from the University of California. Not fewer than two of these members shall be affiliated with an American Indian or Native American Studies program and each of these members shall meet the requirements of subdivision (d).
(D) One nonvoting member from each campus of the University of California that is subject to the federal Native American Graves Protection and Repatriation Act (25 U.S.C. Sec. 3001 et seq.). Each of these nonvoting members shall meet the requirements of subdivision (d).
(3) The regents or the regents' designee shall appoint members to the committee upon nomination by the commission.
(b) (1) The Regents of the University of California shall not use state funds for the handling or maintenance of Native American human remains and cultural items unless each campus of the University of California that is subject to the federal Native American Graves Protection and Repatriation Act (25 U.S.C. Sec. 3001 et seq.) establishes a campus Native American Graves Protection and Repatriation Act Implementation Committee, which shall also be known as the NAGPRA Committee for that campus.
(2) The membership of the campus committee shall be as follows:
(A) Two voting members of an Indian tribe as described in paragraph (1) of subdivision (j) of Section 8012, meeting the requirements of subdivision (c).
(B) One voting member of an Indian tribe as described in paragraph (2) of subdivision (j) of Section 8012, meeting the requirements of subdivision (c), or if none is available, a member of an Indian tribe as described in paragraph (1) of subdivision (j) of Section 8012, meeting the requirements of subdivision (c).
(C) Three voting members from the University of California. At least one of these members shall be affiliated with an American Indian or Native American Studies program and each of these members shall meet the requirements of subdivision (d).
(3) The regents or the regents' designee shall appoint members to the committees upon nomination by the commission.
(4) All claims for repatriation or claims of any violation of the policies and procedures adopted pursuant to Section 8025 shall be submitted to the campus Native American Graves Protection and Repatriation Act Implementation Committee for determination.
(c) (1) A voting member of a California Indian tribe shall be an elder, spiritual leader, tribal leader, or tribal member, as designated by the governing body of the individual's tribe, with a minimum of five years' prior experience in any of the following:
(A) Repatriation of human remains and cultural items pursuant to the federal Native American Graves Protection and Repatriation Act (25 U.S.C. Sec. 3001 et seq.).
(B) Cultural resources protection under tribal, state, and federal law.
(C) Consultation with state and federal entities and agencies.
(2) Preference shall be given to members of a California Indian tribe. If no members of a California Indian tribe meeting the qualifications of paragraph (1) are available, members of other tribes may serve.
(d) (1) A representative of the University of California shall meet the following criteria:
(A) Have a graduate degree in either Archaeology, Anthropology, Native American Studies, Ethnic Studies, Law, Sociology, Environmental Studies, or History, with a focus in California.
(B) Have a minimum of five years' experience working in his or her field of study.
(2) Preference shall be given to members who have demonstrated, through their professional experience, the ability to work in collaboration with Native American tribes successfully on issues related to repatriation or museum collection management.
(3) In the event that candidates from the University of California are not available or do not meet the criteria of paragraph (1), the University of California representative positions may be filled by retired emeriti of the University of California who meet the criteria of paragraph (1).
(Added by Stats. 2018, Ch. 823, Sec. 3. (AB 2836) Effective January 1, 2019.)

8027.

The Regents of the University of California may delegate responsibilities pursuant to this article to the President of the University of California or another person determined to be appropriate.
(Added by Stats. 2018, Ch. 823, Sec. 3. (AB 2836) Effective January 1, 2019.)

8028.

The California State Auditor, in accordance with Chapter 6.5 (commencing with Section 8543) of Division 1 of Title 2 of the Government Code, shall conduct an audit commencing in the year 2019 and again in 2021 regarding the University of California's

compliance with the federal Native American Graves Protection Repatriation Act (25 U.S.C. Sec. 3001 et seq.) and this chapter. The State Auditor shall report its findings to the Legislature and to all other appropriate entities.
(Added by Stats. 2018, Ch. 823, Sec. 3. (AB 2836) Effective January 1, 2019.)
8028.5.
The provisions of this article are severable. If any provision of this article or its application is held invalid, that invalidity shall not affect other provisions or applications that can be given effect without the invalid provision or application.
(Added by Stats. 2018, Ch. 823, Sec. 3. (AB 2836) Effective January 1, 2019.)

ARTICLE 4. Penalties and Enforcement Procedures [8029 - 8030]
(Article 4 added by Stats. 2001, Ch. 818, Sec. 1.)
8029.
(a) Any agency or museum that fails to comply with the requirements of this chapter may be assessed a civil penalty by the commission, not to exceed twenty thousand dollars ($20,000) for each violation, pursuant to regulations adopted by the commission. A penalty assessed under this section shall be determined on the record after the opportunity for a hearing.
(b) In assessing a penalty under this section, the commission shall consider the following factors, in addition to any other relevant factors, in determining the amount of the penalty:
(1) The archaeological, historical, or commercial value of the item involved.
(2) The cultural and spiritual significance of the item involved.
(3) The damages suffered, both economic and noneconomic, by the aggrieved party.
(4) The number of violations that have occurred.
(c) If any agency or museum fails to pay a civil penalty pursuant to a final order issued by the commission and the time for judicial review has passed or the party subject to the civil penalty has appealed the penalty or after a final judgment has been rendered on appeal of the order, the Attorney General shall act on behalf of the commission to institute a civil action in an appropriate court to collect the penalty.
(d) An agency or museum shall not be subject to civil penalties for actions taken in good faith to comply with the federal Native American Graves Protection and Repatriation Act (25 U.S.C. Sec. 3001 et seq.).
(Added by Stats. 2001, Ch. 818, Sec. 1. Effective January 1, 2002.)
8030.
The provisions of this chapter are severable. If any provision of this chapter or its application is held invalid, that invalidity shall not affect other provisions or applications that can be given effect without the invalid provision or application.
(Added by Stats. 2001, Ch. 818, Sec. 1. Effective January 1, 2002.)

DIVISION 8. CEMETERIES [8100 - 9703]

(Division 8 enacted by Stats. 1939, Ch. 60.)

PART 1. GENERAL PROVISIONS [8100 - 8124]

(Part 1 enacted by Stats. 1939, Ch. 60.)

CHAPTER 1. Definitions [8100- 8100.]

(Heading of Chapter 1 amended by Stats. 2001, Ch. 436, Sec. 22.)
8100.
The definitions set forth in Chapter 1 (commencing with Section 7000) of Part 1 of Division 7 shall be applicable to this division.
(Amended by Stats. 2001, Ch. 436, Sec. 23. Effective January 1, 2002.)

CHAPTER 2. Vandalism [8102 - 8103]

(Chapter 2 enacted by Stats. 1939, Ch. 60.)
8102.
Any person violating any provision of this chapter is liable, in a civil action by and in the name of the cemetery authority, to pay all damages occasioned by his unlawful acts. The sum recovered shall be applied in payment for the repair and restoration of the property injured or destroyed.
(Enacted by Stats. 1939, Ch. 60.)
8103.
The provisions of this chapter do not apply to the removal or unavoidable breakage or injury, by a cemetery authority, of any thing placed in or upon any portion of its cemetery in violation of any of the rules or regulations of the cemetery authority, nor to the removal of anything placed in the cemetery by or with the consent of the cemetery authority which has become in a wrecked, unsightly, or dilapidated condition.
(Enacted by Stats. 1939, Ch. 60.)

CHAPTER 3. Records [8110 - 8112]

(Chapter 3 enacted by Stats. 1939, Ch. 60.)
8110.
The person in charge of any premises on which interments or cremations are made shall keep a record of all remains interred or cremated and of the interment of remains on the premises under his charge, in each case stating the name of each deceased person, place of death, date of interment, and name and address of the funeral director.
(Enacted by Stats. 1939, Ch. 60.)
8111.
The records shall at all times be open to official inspection.
(Enacted by Stats. 1939, Ch. 60.)
8112.
Records required to be kept under Division 7 (commencing with Section 7000) or this division may be kept in original form or by photocopy, microfilm, microfiche, laser disc, or any other method that can produce an accurate reproduction of the original record.
(Added by Stats. 1993, Ch. 1232, Sec. 26. Effective January 1, 1994.)

CHAPTER 3.5. Requirements for Burials [8113 - 8113.7]

(Chapter 3.5 added by Stats. 1992, Ch. 828, Sec. 1.)
8113.
(a) This chapter shall apply to all cemeteries, including, but not limited to, public cemeteries, private cemeteries, and cemeteries operated by religious organizations, or fraternal or beneficial associations or societies.
(b) This chapter shall supersede any conflicting rules or regulations established by any entity that manages or operates a cemetery in this state, including, but not limited to, a city, a county, a city and county, a public cemetery district, a cemetery authority, a private corporation, or any organization, association, or society managing or operating a cemetery.
(Added by Stats. 1992, Ch. 828, Sec. 1. Effective January 1, 1993.)
8113.1.
(a) Except as provided in subdivisions (b) and (c), there shall be no less than 18 inches of dirt or turf on top of all vaults or caskets as measured at the time of burial.
(b) Cremated remains placed in an urn or urn vault and covered with at least three-quarters of an inch of concrete, brass, granite, marble, or metal plate, affixed to the urn or urn vault shall be exempt from the requirement of subdivision (a).
(c) In the case of consensual double burials, the casket or vault that is on top shall be covered with at least 12 inches of dirt or turf as measured at the time of burial.
(d) In a case of extreme hardship, upon request of the next of kin or other person responsible for making the burial arrangements for the deceased, a burial of less than 18, but not less than 12 inches may be provided.
(Added by Stats. 1992, Ch. 828, Sec. 1. Effective January 1, 1993.)
8113.3.
(a) This chapter shall not apply to mausoleums, crypts, vaults, or other burial structures designed and constructed to be installed without an earthen cover.
(b) Preexisting and presold vaults and lawn crypts that were in place on January 1, 1993, or for which sales agreements have been executed prior to that date, shall not be subject to this chapter.
(Added by Stats. 1992, Ch. 828, Sec. 1. Effective January 1, 1993.)
8113.4.
Cemeteries shall be liable for the costs of reburial of any remains improperly interred in already occupied graves or interred with less than the amount of turf, dirt, or other covering, as required by this chapter, for burials occurring after January 1, 1993.
(Added by Stats. 1992, Ch. 828, Sec. 1. Effective January 1, 1993.)
8113.5.
(a) Except with the express written permission of the person entitled to control the disposition of the remains, or in the case of a double burial consented to by both parties, no person shall knowingly or willfully inter the remains of more than one body in a single plot, or place a casket or other human remains in an already occupied grave.
(b) Violation of subdivision (a) is a crime punishable as follows:
(1) A first offense, or a second offense not committed within a year of the first, is punishable as a misdemeanor by imprisonment in a county jail not exceeding one year.
(2) A second offense committed within a year of the first offense is punishable as a misdemeanor or a felony by imprisonment in a county jail not exceeding one year, or pursuant to subdivision (h) of Section 1170 of the Penal Code.
(3) A third or subsequent offense shall be punishable as a felony by imprisonment pursuant to subdivision (h) of Section 1170 of the Penal Code.
(Amended by Stats. 2011, Ch. 15, Sec. 143. (AB 109) Effective April 4, 2011. Operative October 1, 2011, by Sec. 636 of Ch. 15, as amended by Stats. 2011, Ch. 39, Sec. 68.)
8113.6.
Notwithstanding any other provision of law, any cemetery that violates any of the requirements of this chapter shall be subject to disciplinary action by the Cemetery and Funeral Bureau.
(Amended by Stats. 2000, Ch. 568, Sec. 244. Effective January 1, 2001.)
8113.7.
Notwithstanding any other provision of law, the statute of limitations for any individual's criminal violation of Section 8113.5 shall begin to run at the time the violation is discovered.
(Added by Stats. 1996, Ch. 371, Sec. 1. Effective January 1, 1997.)

CHAPTER 4. Local Regulation of Cemeteries [8115- 8115.]

(Chapter 4 added by Stats. 1976, Ch. 525.)

8115.

The governing body of any city or county, in the exercise of its police power, may by ordinance prescribe such standards governing burial, inurnment, and entombment and such standards of maintenance for cemeteries, including mausoleums and columbariums, as it shall determine to be reasonably necessary to protect the public health or safety, assure decent and respectful treatment of human remains, or prevent offensive deterioration of cemetery grounds, structures, and places of interment. Such standards may be made applicable to every public and private cemetery within the city or county. Nothing in this section supersedes any provision of this division or Division 7 (commencing with Section 7000) or authorizes the adoption of local standards in conflict with such provisions, except that city or county ordinances adopted pursuant to this section shall prevail over the rules and regulations of any private or public cemetery to the extent of any conflict.

(Added by Stats. 1976, Ch. 525.)

CHAPTER 4.5. Maintenance of Cemetery Grounds [8117 - 8118]

(Chapter 4.5 added by Stats. 2013, Ch. 635, Sec. 3.)

8117.

Hose bibs are approved for use at cemeteries supplied with disinfected tertiary treated recycled water.

(Added by Stats. 2013, Ch. 635, Sec. 3. (AB 803) Effective January 1, 2014.)

8118.

A cemetery supplied with disinfected tertiary treated recycled water that installs a hose bib in an area subject to access by the general public shall post signage and labeling visible to the general public that the water is nonpotable. The signage and labeling shall be regularly inspected by the water purveyor, as defined in Section 512 of the Water Code, to ensure that the general public has proper notice of this fact.

(Added by Stats. 2013, Ch. 635, Sec. 3. (AB 803) Effective January 1, 2014.)

CHAPTER 5. Change In Use [8120- 8120.]

(Chapter 5 added by Stats. 1988, Ch. 1440, Sec. 2.)

8120.

(a) On or after January 1, 1990, the cemetery authority shall provide written notice to each person who purchases or agrees to purchase interment rights in the cemetery of that person's ability to receive notice, pursuant to Section 65096 of the Government Code, of a proposed change in the use of the cemetery for other than cemetery purposes. Irrespective of any other provisions of the law, this section refers to all cemeteries in the State of California.

(b) The written notice shall be substantially as follows:

"State law gives you the right to know about future plans to use this cemetery for any other purpose. If you want to receive information about a future change, you must contact the local planning office and pay a small fee."

(Added by Stats. 1988, Ch. 1440, Sec. 2.)

CHAPTER 6. Veteran's Commemorative Property [8122 - 8124]

(Chapter 6 added by Stats. 2012, Ch. 774, Sec. 1.)

8122.

For purposes of this chapter, the following definitions shall apply:

(a) "Veteran" means a living or deceased person who meets all of the following conditions:

(1) Either served in the active military or naval service of the United States during a war in which the United States was engaged, or served in active duty in a force of any organized state militia, not including the inactive National Guard and not including the California National Guard when in an inactive, full-time status.

(2) Was released from the service otherwise than by dishonorable discharge or was furloughed to the reserve.

(b) "Veteran's commemorative property" means any monument, headstone, marker, memorial, plaque, statue, vase, urn, flagholder, badge, or shield that meets all of the following conditions:

(1) Identifies or commemorates any veteran or group of veterans, including, but not limited to, any veterans' organization or any military unit, company, battalion, or division.

(2) Is located in any cemetery.

(Added by Stats. 2012, Ch. 774, Sec. 1. (AB 1225) Effective January 1, 2013.)

8123.

(a) Except as provided in subdivision (b) and Section 8124, no person or entity shall sell, trade, or transfer veteran's commemorative property.

(b) Any person, unincorporated association, cemetery corporation, or religious corporation, except a municipal corporation described in Section 8137, that owns or controls a cemetery where any veteran's commemorative property has been placed that wishes to sell, trade, or transfer veteran's commemorative property shall petition the superior court in the county in which the veteran's commemorative property is located for permission to sell, trade, or transfer all or any part of the veteran's commemorative property. The court may approve the sale, trade, or transfer of the veteran's commemorative property under any of the following conditions:

(1) The veteran's commemorative property is at reasonable risk of physically deteriorating so that it will become unrecognizable as identifying or commemorating the

veteran or group of veterans originally identified or commemorated thereby and the veteran's commemorative property that is to be sold, traded, or transferred is replaced at its original site by a fitting replacement commemorative property, monument, or marker that appropriately identifies and commemorates the veteran or group of veterans.

(2) The veteran's commemorative property is proposed to be sold, traded, or transferred to a suitable person that will preserve the current condition of the veteran's commemorative property and place the veteran's commemorative property in a suitable place that will commemorate the veteran or group of veterans.

(3) The petitioner needs to sell, trade, or transfer the veteran's commemorative property to ensure that sufficient funds are available to suitably maintain the cemetery where the veteran's commemorative property was placed, and the specific lot, plot, grave, burial place, niche, crypt, or other place of interment of a veteran or group of veterans, so that the place will retain the respect that these hallowed places deserve.

(4) If the veteran's commemorative property to be sold, traded, or transferred is reasonably known to the petitioner to have been donated to the petitioner by any veterans' organization, historical organization, civic organization, or an individual, the sale, trade, or transfer shall have been consented to by that veterans' organization, historical organization, civic organization, or individual.

(5) If the petitioner is not the owner of the veteran's commemorative property that is to be sold, traded, or transferred, the petitioner is authorized by the owner of the veteran's commemorative property to engage in the sale, trade, or transfer.

(6) By operation of any other law authorizing the sale, trade, or transfer of the veteran's commemorative property.

(c) A petition under subdivision (b) shall be filed with the clerk of the superior court. Upon receipt of the petition, the clerk shall fix the time and date for the hearing. The date fixed for the hearing shall be within a reasonable time after the petition is filed.

(d) The petitioner shall serve notice of the hearing and a copy of the petition upon the persons and entities mentioned in paragraphs (1) to (6), inclusive, of subdivision (e) who could reasonably be ascertained and contacted by the petitioner and upon any other person as may be directed by the court. Service of the notice of hearing and petition shall be made in a manner and by a date as shall be specified by the court.

(e) At the hearing held pursuant to subdivision (c), the following persons and entities, or their representatives, may be heard:

(1) The petitioner.

(2) Any person, other than the petitioner, who is the owner of the veteran's commemorative property in question.

(3) Any veterans' organization, historical organization, civic organization, or individual that donated the veteran's commemorative property in question to the petitioner.

(4) The family of each veteran at whose lot, plot, grave, burial place, niche, crypt, or other place of interment the veteran's commemorative property in question is or was placed.

(5) The Division of Veterans Services within the Department of Veterans Affairs.

(6) The Department of Parks and Recreation.

(7) Any other member of the public who would like to offer written or oral testimony.

(f) Testimony may be heard in person or by counsel or submitted in writing.

(g) An order of the court granting the petition, in whole or in part, or modifying the petition, may, at the discretion of the court, specify the manner in which the petitioner is to use or apply the proceeds of the sale, trade, or transfer. In particular, but not by way of limitation, if the petitioner is an unincorporated association or corporation that is subject to the Nonprofit Corporation Law (Division 2 (commencing with Section 5000) of Title 1 of the Corporations Code), any order of the court granting the petition, in whole or in part, or modifying the petition, may, at the discretion of the court, specify that the petitioner deposit the proceeds of the sale, trade, or transfer in the permanent maintenance fund maintained by the petitioner pursuant to the Nonprofit Corporation Law.

(h) A person who violates any provision of this section is guilty of a misdemeanor punishable by a fine of not less than one hundred dollars ($100) or more than one thousand dollars ($1,000) or by imprisonment in a county jail for not less than 10 days or more than six months, or by both that fine and imprisonment; and in addition is liable for all costs, expenses, and disbursements paid or incurred by the person prosecuting the case.

(Added by Stats. 2012, Ch. 774, Sec. 1. (AB 1225) Effective January 1, 2013.)

8124.

Nothing in this chapter shall be interpreted to prohibit a cemetery corporation or funeral establishment from selling new veteran's commemorative property on either an at-need or pre-need basis.

(Added by Stats. 2012, Ch. 774, Sec. 1. (AB 1225) Effective January 1, 2013.)

PART 2. PUBLIC CEMETERIES [8125 - 8137]

(Part 2 enacted by Stats. 1939, Ch. 60.)

CHAPTER 1. General Provisions [8125 - 8137]

(Chapter 1 enacted by Stats. 1939, Ch. 60.)

8125.

Incorporated cities, and for unincorporated towns the supervisors of the county, may survey, lay out, and dedicate for burial purposes not exceeding five acres of public lands situated in or near the city or town. The survey, description, and a certified copy of the order made constituting the land a cemetery shall be recorded in the recorder's office of the county in which it is located.

(Amended by Stats. 1939, Ch. 339.)

8125.5.

The City of Simi Valley may survey, lay out, dedicate, own, and operate for burial purposes, or may purchase, or receive by gift or donation, five acres or more of public lands to be used as a public cemetery.

(Added by Stats. 2008, Ch. 126, Sec. 1. Effective January 1, 2009.)

8126.

The title to lands situated in or near any city and used by the inhabitants without interruption as a cemetery for five years is vested in the inhabitants of the city and the lands shall not be used except as a public cemetery.

(Amended by Stats. 1939, Ch. 339.)

8127.

The inhabitants of any city may by subscription or otherwise purchase or receive by gift or donation, lands not exceeding five acres to be used as a cemetery, the title to be vested in the inhabitants, which lands when once dedicated to use for burial purposes, shall not thereafter be used for any other purpose.

(Amended by Stats. 1939, Ch. 339.)

8128.

The governing body having control of a public cemetery shall require a register of name, age, birthplace, date of death, and burial of every body interred therein, to be kept by the sexton or other officer. The register shall be open to public inspection.

(Enacted by Stats. 1939, Ch. 60.)

8129.

The public cemeteries of cities, towns, or neighborhoods or of fraternal or beneficial associations or societies shall be inclosed and laid off into plots.

(Enacted by Stats. 1939, Ch. 60.)

8130.

The general management, conduct, and regulation of burials, the disposition of plots, and keeping the plots in order, are under the jurisdiction and control of the city owning the cemetery.

(Amended by Stats. 1939, Ch. 339.)

8131.

If not owned by a city or by a fraternal or beneficial association or society, public cemeteries are under the jurisdiction and control of the board of supervisors of the county in which they are situated.

(Enacted by Stats. 1939, Ch. 60.)

8132.

Public cemeteries of fraternal or beneficial associations or societies are under the jurisdiction of and controlled and managed by the associations or societies or by trustees appointed by them.

(Enacted by Stats. 1939, Ch. 60.)

8133.

The authorities having jurisdiction and control of cemeteries may make and enforce general rules and regulations, and appoint sextons or other officers to enforce obedience to the rules and regulations, with such powers and duties regarding the cemetery as may be necessary.

(Enacted by Stats. 1939, Ch. 60.)

8134.

No streets, alleys, or roads shall be opened or laid out within the boundary lines of any cemetery located in whole or in part within the lines of any city or city and county where burials in the cemetery have been had within five years prior thereto, without the consent of the person owning and controlling the cemetery.

(Added by Stats. 1953, Ch. 83.)

8135.

Notwithstanding any other provision of law, the Department of Water Resources may sell plots in any cemetery which is owned by the department on a nonendowment care basis to a relative of the third degree or less of any person buried in such cemetery.

(Added by Stats. 1968, Ch. 816.)

8136.

Any city, including a chartered city, that owns and operates a cemetery may maintain a proceeding in the superior court of the county in which the cemetery is located to have any plot in the cemetery declared abandoned if the present owner of the plot is unknown to the city and a period of at least 50 years has passed since any portion of the plot has been used for interment purposes. The proceeding shall be initiated and conducted in the same manner as prescribed by Section 9069, except that any reference in that section to a public cemetery district shall be deemed to be a reference to the city for purposes of this section.

(Amended by Stats. 2003, Ch. 57, Sec. 3.5. Effective January 1, 2004.)

8137.

A cemetery owned and operated by a city, county, or city and county shall not engage in the business of selling monuments or markers, and its officers and employees who manage, operate, or otherwise maintain such cemetery on a day-to-day basis shall not engage in the private business of selling monuments or markers.

(Added by Stats. 1980, Ch. 161.)

PART 3. PRIVATE CEMETERIES [8250 - 8829]

(Part 3 enacted by Stats. 1939, Ch. 60.)

CHAPTER 1. General Provisions [8250 - 8253]

(Chapter 1 enacted by Stats. 1939, Ch. 60.)

8250.

Except as provided in subdivision (c) of this section, the provisions of this part do not apply to any of the following:

(a) Any religious corporation, church, religious society or denomination, a corporation sole administering temporalities of any church or religious society or denomination, or any cemetery organized, controlled, and operated by any of them.

(b) Any public cemetery.

(c) Any private or fraternal burial park not exceeding 10 acres in area, heretofore established; provided, however, (1) that the provisions of Chapter 6 (commencing at Section 8800) and Chapter 7 (commencing at Section 8825) of this part are applicable thereto, and (2) all of the provisions of this part shall apply to any such cemetery that collects a care, maintenance or embellishment deposit or funds for commodities or services.

(Amended by Stats. 1972, Ch. 1269.)

8250.5.

As used in Section 8250 of this code, a public cemetery is a cemetery owned and operated by a city, county, city and county, or public cemetery district.

(Added by Stats. 1953, Ch. 386.)

8251.

The provisions of this part do not affect the corporate existence of any cemetery organized under any law then existing prior to August 14, 1931, and as to such cemeteries, and their rights, the laws under which the corporation was organized and existed and under which such rights became vested are applicable.

(Enacted by Stats. 1939, Ch. 60.)

8252.

It is unlawful for any corporation, copartnership, firm, trust, association, or individual to engage in or transact any of the businesses of a cemetery within this state except by means of a corporation or limited liability company duly organized for these purposes.

(Amended by Stats. 2008, Ch. 114, Sec. 4. Effective January 1, 2009.)

8253.

The powers, privileges, duties and restrictions conferred and imposed upon any corporation, firm, copartnership, association, trust or individual, existing and doing business under the laws of this State, are hereby enlarged or modified as each particular case may require to conform to the provisions of this part notwithstanding anything to the contrary in their respective articles of incorporation, charter or other evidence of organization.

(Enacted by Stats. 1939, Ch. 60.)

CHAPTER 2. Operation and Management [8275 - 8382]

(Chapter 2 enacted by Stats. 1939, Ch. 60.)

ARTICLE 1. General Provisions [8275 - 8279]

(Article 1 enacted by Stats. 1939, Ch. 60.)

8275.

Any private corporation authorized by its articles so to do, may establish, maintain, manage, improve, or operate a cemetery, and conduct any or all of the businesses of a cemetery, either for or without profit to its members or stockholders.

(Enacted by Stats. 1939, Ch. 60.)

8276.

Charges made by a cemetery authority for foundations, for setting of or permitting the setting of, or for endowment care of, grave markers or monuments, shall be uniform whether the marker or monument sale was made by the cemetery authority or by another person, firm, or corporation. The amount charged for the marker or monument, the foundation, the setting, permitting the setting and the deposit for endowment care, shall be separately stated, in the contract of sale, when applicable.

(Added by Stats. 1961, Ch. 711.)

8277.

Every contract of a cemetery authority, including contracts executed in behalf thereof by a cemetery broker or salesperson, which provides for the sale by the cemetery authority of an interment plot or any service or merchandise, shall be in writing and shall contain all of the agreements of the parties. The contract shall include and disclose the following:

(a) The total contract price.

(b) Terms of payment, including any promissory notes or other evidences of indebtedness.

(c) An itemized statement of charges including, as applicable, the following:

(1) Charges for an interment plot.

(2) Charges for performing burial, entombment, or inurnment.

(3) Charges for a monument or marker.

(4) Charges for any services to be rendered in connection with any religious or other observance at the site of interment or in any facility maintained by the cemetery.

(5) Amounts to be deposited in any endowment care or special care fund.

(6) Charges for any insurance to be provided in connection with the contract.

(7) Any other charges, which shall be particularized.

(8) Space and location sold.

(Amended by Stats. 2003, Ch. 874, Sec. 35. Effective January 1, 2004.)

8278.

In addition to any right of rescission which the purchaser may have under law, a purchaser entering into a contract with a cemetery broker, salesman, or authority for the provision of an interment plot or any service or merchandise, may cancel such contract without payment of a revocation fee or other penalty, within five calendar days after the purchaser signs it, by giving written notice of cancellation to the seller at the address specified in the contract. The notice need not be in any particular form, but shall indicate the purchaser's intent not to be bound by the contract. Notice of cancellation, if given by mail, is effective when deposited in the mail properly addressed with postage prepaid. Every such contract shall contain in immediate proximity to the space reserved for the purchaser's signature, in a size equal to at least 10-point bold type, the following statement: "You, the purchaser, may cancel this transaction at any time prior to midnight of the fifth calendar day after the date of this transaction, provided no interment or substantial service or merchandise has been provided hereunder. To cancel, deliver or mail written notice of your intent to (name and address of cemetery authority or cemetery broker)."

Upon receipt of a valid notice of cancellation pursuant to this section, the cemetery authority or broker having custody of any money or property paid or transmitted by the purchaser on account of the preneed interment contract shall return such money or property to the purchaser. The cemetery authority or broker shall promptly notify the trustee if any such money or property has been transmitted thereto prior to receipt of the notice of cancellation. It shall be unlawful for any person to retain money or property received from a purchaser under such contract more than five business days after receiving or being apprised of a valid notice of cancellation.

Notwithstanding other provisions of this section, the right of cancellation granted hereby shall not be applicable if an interment has been made, or substantial services or merchandise provided, under the terms of the contract. This section shall supersede existing provisions of Sections 1689.6 to 1689.11, inclusive, of the Civil Code.

(Added by Stats. 1976, Ch. 729.)

8279.

A cemetery authority shall comply with the Mausoleum and Columbarium Law (Part 5 (commencing with Section 9501)).

(Added by Stats. 1999, Ch. 207, Sec. 1. Effective January 1, 2000.)

ARTICLE 2. Rules and Regulations [8300 - 8309]

(Article 2 enacted by Stats. 1939, Ch. 60.)

8300.

(a) A cemetery authority may make, adopt, amend, add to, revise, or modify, and enforce rules and regulations for the use, care, control, management, restriction and protection of all or any part of its cemetery and for the other purposes specified in this article.

(b) The cemetery authority's power includes, but is not limited to, the following:

(1) Restricting and limiting the use of all property within its cemetery.

(2) Regulating the uniformity, class, and kind of all markers, monuments, and other structures within the cemetery and its subdivisions, but shall not require, as a condition to the erection of a marker, monument, or other structure within the cemetery, that the marker, monument, or other structure be purchased from or through the cemetery authority.

(3) Prohibiting the erection of monuments, markers, or other structures in or upon any portion of the cemetery.

(4) Regulating or prohibiting monuments, effigies, and structures within any portion of the cemetery and provide for their removal.

(5) Regulating or preventing the introduction or care of plants or shrubs within the cemetery.

(6) Preventing interment in any part of the cemetery of human remains not entitled to interment and preventing the use of interment plots for purposes violative of its restrictions or rules and regulations.

(7) Regulating the conduct of persons and preventing improper assemblages in the cemetery.

(8) Making and enforcing rules and regulations for all other purposes deemed necessary by the cemetery authority for the proper conduct of the business of the cemetery, for the transfer of any plot or the right of interment, and the protection and safeguarding of the premises, and the principles, plans, and ideals on which the cemetery is conducted.

(Amended by Stats. 2001, Ch. 436, Sec. 25. Effective January 1, 2002.)

8301.5.

(a) Nothing in Section 8301 shall be construed to permit a cemetery authority to discriminate against any person based upon race or gender regarding the use of any property within the cemetery.

(b) The Legislature recognizes, however, that although discrimination against persons based upon race or gender is prohibited, there are strong cultural, social, and other proper reasons for people to seek to continue association with certain groups even in death.

(c) In the same way that a family may purchase contiguous plots to ensure that family members will be buried in close proximity to one another, and in the same way that a religious group may, similarly, establish and operate a cemetery for its members, or that

veterans groups may establish and operate cemeteries for veterans, the law recognizes that members of cultural, social, or other groups with strong ties are not precluded from establishing and operating cemeteries for the purpose of furthering their desire to continue to associate after interment.

(d) The urge to associate even after death also stems from an intense social and cultural need to ensure that people are connected with their past, and also to ensure that the graves and surrounding grounds are kept, tended, adorned, and embellished according to the desires and beliefs of the decedent, family, or group.

(e) The Legislature also recognizes, that the creation or operation of a cemetery for a particular group by necessity entails some exclusionary aspects. However, the exclusionary aspects are permitted only to the extent that the purpose and effect is to include persons, as set forth in this section, rather than to exclude persons based upon race or gender.

(f) Although it is, indeed, a difficult task to permit creation and operation of cemeteries that may exclude persons that are not within the social, cultural, or other group while also assuring that the cemetery is not discriminating based upon race or gender, strong public policy compels that we perform the task. To prohibit all association limitations in the creation and operation of cemeteries would certainly ensure that no discrimination based upon race or gender occurred; however, it would be overbroad in that it would preclude activity that is not so motivated and that does not have that effect.

(g) Therefore, subdivision (a) does not preclude the establishment or operation of cemeteries for the purposes set forth in this section to the extent that, and so long as the purpose and effect is to further a sincere and bona fide association interest, rather than to discriminate against persons on the basis of race or gender.

(h) Nothing in this section applies to Native American tribal burial grounds or cemeteries that, pursuant to federal law, are not subject to state jurisdiction.

(Added by Stats. 1996, Ch. 769, Sec. 1. Effective January 1, 1997.)

8309.

The rules and regulations shall be plainly printed or typewritten and maintained subject to inspection in the office of the cemetery authority or in such place or places within the cemetery as the cemetery authority may prescribe.

(Enacted by Stats. 1939, Ch. 60.)

ARTICLE 3. Police Power [8325- 8325.]

(Article 3 enacted by Stats. 1939, Ch. 60.)

8325.

Persons designated by a cemetery authority have the powers of arrest as provided in Section 830.7 of the Penal Code for the purpose of maintaining order, enforcing the rules and regulations of the cemetery association, the laws of the state, and the ordinances of the city or county, within the cemetery over which he has charge, and within such radius as may be necessary to protect the cemetery property.

(Amended by Stats. 1980, Ch. 1340.)

ARTICLE 4. Records [8330 - 8331]

(Article 4 enacted by Stats. 1939, Ch. 60.)

8330.

A record shall be kept of every interment showing the date the human remains were received, the date of interment, the name and age of the person interred, when these particulars can be conveniently obtained, and the plot in which interment was made.

(Enacted by Stats. 1939, Ch. 60.)

8331.

A record shall be kept of the ownership of all plots in the cemetery which have been conveyed by the cemetery authority and of all transfers of plots in the cemetery. Transfer of any plot, heretofore or hereafter made, or any right of interment, shall be complete and effective when recorded on the books of the cemetery authority.

(Amended by Stats. 1982, Ch. 176, Sec. 1.)

ARTICLE 5. Operation of Crematories [8341 - 8347]

(Article 5 enacted by Stats. 1939, Ch. 60.)

8341.

All cremated remains not disposed of in accordance with this chapter, within one year, shall be interred.

(Amended by Stats. 1993, Ch. 1232, Sec. 27. Effective January 1, 1994.)

8342.

No crematory shall make or enforce any rules requiring that human remains be placed in a casket before cremation or that human remains be cremated in a casket, nor shall a crematory refuse to accept human remains for cremation for the reason that they are not in a casket. Every director, officer, agent or representative of a crematory who violates this section is guilty of a misdemeanor. Nothing in this section shall be construed to prohibit the requiring of some type of container or disposal unit.

(Added by Stats. 1971, Ch. 1027.)

8343.

A crematory shall maintain on its premises, or other business location within the State of California, an accurate record of all cremations performed, including all of the following information:

(a) Name of referring funeral director, if any.

(b) Name of deceased.

(c) Date of cremation.

(d) Name of cremation chamber operator.

(e) Time and date that body was inserted in cremation chamber.

(f) Time and date that body was removed from cremation chamber.

(g) Time and date that final processing of cremated remains was completed.

(h) Disposition of cremated remains.

(i) Name and address of authorizing agent.

(j) The identification number assigned to the deceased pursuant to Section 8344.

(k) A photocopy of the disposition permit filed in connection with the disposition.

This information shall be maintained for at least 10 years after the cremation is performed and shall be subject to inspection by the Cemetery and Funeral Bureau.

(Amended by Stats. 2000, Ch. 568, Sec. 245. Effective January 1, 2001.)

8344.

A crematory shall maintain an identification system allowing identification of each decedent beginning from the time the crematory accepts delivery of human remains until the point at which it releases the cremated remains to a third party. After cremation, an identifying disk, tab, or other permanent label shall be placed within the urn or cremated remains container before the cremated remains are released from the crematory. Each identification disk, tab, or label shall contain the license number of the crematory and shall have a unique number that shall be recorded on all paperwork regarding the decedent's case and in the crematory log. Each crematory shall maintain a written procedure for identification of remains. The identification requirements pertaining to an identifying disk, tab, or other label to be placed within the urn or cremated remains container shall not apply to cremated remains placed in a keepsake urn pursuant to subdivision (b) of Section 7054.6 if space does not permit.

On or after March 1, 1994, any crematory that fails, when requested by an official of the bureau to produce a written procedure for identification of remains, shall have 15 working days from the time of the request to produce an identification procedure for review by the chief of the Cemetery and Funeral Bureau. The license of the crematory shall be suspended pursuant to Chapter 5 (commencing with Section 11500) of Part 1 of Division 3 of Title 2 of the Government Code, if no identification procedure is produced for review after 15 working days have elapsed.

(Amended by Stats. 2010, Ch. 415, Sec. 35. (SB 1491) Effective January 1, 2011.)

8344.5.

(a) Except as provided in subdivision (b), a crematory regulated by the Cemetery and Funeral Bureau shall knowingly cremate only human remains in cremation chambers, along with the cremation container, personal effects of the deceased, and no more than a negligible amount of chlorinated plastic pouches utilized for disease control when necessary.

(b) (1) Notwithstanding any other law, a crematory regulated by the Cemetery and Funeral Bureau also may incinerate one or more American flags, under the following conditions:

(A) Incineration of the flag or flags is performed separately from the cremation of human remains, as provided in subdivision (a).

(B) Incineration of the flag or flags is in accordance with Section 8(k) of Title 4 of the United States Code.

(C) Incineration of the flag or flags occurs within one week before or after any of the following:

(i) Memorial Day.

(ii) Flag Day.

(iii) Independence Day.

(2) Nothing in this subdivision shall be construed to attempt to restrict or otherwise infringe upon any person's right to free expression under the First Amendment to the United States Constitution.

(Amended by Stats. 2013, Ch. 205, Sec. 1. (SB 119) Effective January 1, 2014.)

8344.6.

(a) A crematory that incinerates an American flag or flags pursuant to Section 8344.5 shall maintain on its premises an accurate record of all American flags incinerated as specified in Section 8344.5, including all of the following information:

(1) Name of the organization or person requesting incineration of the flag or flags.

(2) Date of incineration of the flag or flags.

(3) Name of the cremation chamber operator.

(4) Time and date that the flag or flags were inserted in the cremation chamber.

(5) Time and date that the flag or flags were removed from the cremation chamber.

(6) Weight of the ashes of the flag or flags after being removed from the cremation chamber.

(7) Disposition of the ashes of the incinerated flag or flags.

(b) This information shall be maintained in the crematory log for at least 10 years after the incineration of an American flag or flags and shall be subject to inspection by the Cemetery and Funeral Bureau.

(Added by Stats. 2013, Ch. 205, Sec. 2. (SB 119) Effective January 1, 2014.)

8345.

If a cremated remains container is of insufficient capacity to accommodate all cremated remains of a given deceased, the crematory shall provide a larger cremated remains container at no additional cost, or place the excess remains in a secondary cremated remains container and attach the second container, in a manner so as not to be easily detached through incidental contact, to the primary cremated remains container for interment, scattering, or other disposition by the person entitled to control the disposition.

(Added by Stats. 1993, Ch. 1232, Sec. 31. Effective January 1, 1994.)

8345.5.

A crematory shall not accept human remains for cremation unless the remains meet all of the following requirements:

(a) The remains shall be in a cremation container, as defined.

(b) The cremation container shall be labeled with the identity of the decedent.

(Added by Stats. 1993, Ch. 1232, Sec. 32. Effective January 1, 1994.)

8346.

Within two hours after a crematory licensed by the State of California takes custody of a body that has not been embalmed, it shall refrigerate the body at a temperature not greater than 50 degrees Fahrenheit unless the cremation process will begin within 24 hours of the time that crematory took custody.

(Amended by Stats. 1994, Ch. 570, Sec. 10. Effective January 1, 1995.)

8346.5.

Every crematory operator, or duly authorized representative shall provide to any person who inquires in person, a written, or printed list of prices for cremation and storage, cremation containers, cremated remains containers and urns, and requirements for cremation containers. This information shall be provided over the telephone when requested. Commencing July 1, 1994, any written or printed list shall identify the crematorium and shall contain, at a minimum, the current address and phone number of the Cemetery and Funeral Bureau in 8-point boldface type, or larger.

(Amended by Stats. 2000, Ch. 568, Sec. 248. Effective January 1, 2001.)

8347.

(a) The crematory licensee, or his or her authorized representative shall provide instruction to all crematory personnel involved in the cremation process. This instruction shall lead to a demonstrated knowledge on the part of an employee regarding identification procedures used during cremation, operation of the cremation chamber and processing equipment and all laws relevant to the handling of a body and cremated remains. This instruction shall be outlined in a written plan maintained by the crematory licensee for inspection and comment by an inspector of the Cemetery and Funeral Bureau.

(b) No employee shall be allowed to operate any cremation equipment until he or she has demonstrated to the licensee or authorized representative that he or she understands procedures required to ensure that health and safety conditions are maintained at the crematory and that cremated remains are not commingled other than for acceptable residue, as defined. The crematory licensee shall maintain a record to document that an employee has received the training specified in this section.

(c) On or after March 1, 1994, any crematory that fails, when requested by an official of the bureau, to produce a written employee instruction plan, or record of employee training for inspection, shall have 15 working days from the time of the request to produce a plan or training record for review by the chief of the Cemetery and Funeral Bureau. The license of the crematory shall be suspended, pursuant to Chapter 5 (commencing with Section 11500) of Part 1 of Division 3 of Title 2 of the Government Code, if no plan or training record is produced for review after 15 working days have elapsed.

(Amended by Stats. 2000, Ch. 568, Sec. 249. Effective January 1, 2001.)

ARTICLE 6. Contract Limitations [8350 - 8351]

(Article 6 enacted by Stats. 1939, Ch. 60.)

8350.

Unless otherwise limited by the law under which created, cemetery authorities shall in the conduct of their business have the same powers granted by law to corporations in general, including the right to contract such pecuniary obligations within the limitation of general law as may be required, and may secure them by mortgage, deed of trust, or otherwise upon their property.

(Enacted by Stats. 1939, Ch. 60.)

8351.

All mortgages, deeds of trust, and other liens of any nature, hereafter contracted, placed or incurred upon property which has been and was at the time of the creation or placing of the lien, dedicated as a cemetery pursuant to this part, or upon property which is afterwards, with the consent of the owner of any mortgage, trust deed, or lien, dedicated to cemetery purposes pursuant to this part, shall not affect or defeat the dedication, but the mortgage, deed of trust or other lien is subject and subordinate to such dedication and any and all sales made upon foreclosure are subject and subordinate to the dedication for cemetery purposes.

(Enacted by Stats. 1939, Ch. 60.)

ARTICLE 7. Restrictions on Officers [8360 - 8362]

(Article 7 enacted by Stats. 1939, Ch. 60.)

8360.

No director or officer of any cemetery authority shall directly or indirectly, for himself or as the partner or agent of others, borrow any funds of the corporation or association, nor may he become an indorser or surety for loans to others, nor in any manner be an obligor for money borrowed of or loaned by the corporation or association, nor shall a corporation of which a director or an officer is a stockholder, or in which either of them is in any manner interested, borrow any of the funds of the corporation or association.

(Enacted by Stats. 1939, Ch. 60.)

8361.

The office of any director or officer who acts or permits action contrary to this article immediately thereupon becomes vacant.

(Enacted by Stats. 1939, Ch. 60.)

8362.

Every director or officer authorizing or consenting to a loan, and the person who receives a loan, in violation of this article are severally guilty of a misdemeanor.

(Enacted by Stats. 1939, Ch. 60.)

ARTICLE 8. Hydrolysis Facilities [8370 - 8382]

(Article 8 added by Stats. 2017, Ch. 846, Sec. 69.)

8370.

All hydrolyzed human remains not disposed of in accordance with this chapter, within one year, shall be interred.

(Added by Stats. 2017, Ch. 846, Sec. 69. (AB 967) Effective January 1, 2018. Section operative July 1, 2020, pursuant to Sec. 8382.)

8372.

A hydrolysis facility shall not make or enforce any rules requiring that human remains be placed in a casket before hydrolysis or that human remains be hydrolyzed in a casket, nor shall a hydrolysis facility refuse to accept human remains for hydrolysis for the reason that they are not in a casket. Every director, officer, agent, or representative of a hydrolysis facility who violates this section is guilty of a misdemeanor. Nothing in this section shall be construed to prohibit the requiring of some type of container or disposal unit, as specified in Section 7006.6.

(Added by Stats. 2017, Ch. 846, Sec. 69. (AB 967) Effective January 1, 2018. Section operative July 1, 2020, pursuant to Sec. 8382.)

8374.

(a) A hydrolysis facility shall maintain on its premises, or other business location within the state, an accurate record of all hydrolyses performed, including all of the following information:

(1) Name of the referring funeral director, if any.

(2) Name of the deceased.

(3) Date of the hydrolysis.

(4) Name of the hydrolysis chamber operator.

(5) Disposition of the hydrolyzed human remains.

(6) Time and date that the body was inserted into the hydrolysis chamber.

(7) Time and date that the body was removed from the hydrolysis chamber.

(8) Time and date that final processing of the hydrolyzed human remains was complete.

(9) Name and address of the authorizing agent.

(10) Identification number assigned to the deceased, pursuant to Section 8376.

(11) A photocopy of the disposition permit filed in connection with the disposition.

(12) Any documentation of compliance with appropriate environmental and safety laws.

(13) Body mass of the deceased, along with temperature, time duration, and pressure at which the hydrolysis was performed.

(b) A hydrolysis facility shall maintain on its premises, or other business location within the state, records of the maintenance performed on the hydrolysis chamber.

(c) Information described in this section shall be maintained for at least 10 years after the hydrolysis is performed and shall be subject to inspection by the Cemetery and Funeral Bureau.

(Added by Stats. 2017, Ch. 846, Sec. 69. (AB 967) Effective January 1, 2018. Section operative July 1, 2020, pursuant to Sec. 8382.)

8376.

(a) A hydrolysis facility shall maintain an identification system allowing identification of each decedent beginning from the time the hydrolysis facility accepts delivery of human remains until the point at which it releases the hydrolyzed human remains to a third party. After hydrolysis, an identifying disk, tab, or other permanent label shall be placed with the urn or hydrolyzed human remains container before the hydrolyzed human remains are released from the hydrolysis facility. Each identification disk, tab, or label shall contain the license number of the hydrolysis facility and shall have a unique number that shall be recorded on all documents regarding the decedent and in the hydrolysis log. Each hydrolysis facility shall maintain a written procedure for identification of remains. The identification requirements pertaining to an identifying disk, tab, or other label to be placed within the urn or hydrolyzed human remains container shall not apply to hydrolyzed human remains placed in a keepsake urn pursuant to subdivision (b) of Section 7054.6 if space does not permit.

(b) A hydrolysis facility that fails, when requested by an official of the Cemetery and Funeral Bureau, to produce a written procedure for identification of remains shall have 15 working days from the time of the request to produce an identification procedure for review by the chief of the Cemetery and Funeral Bureau. The license of the hydrolysis facility shall be suspended pursuant to Chapter 5 (commencing with Section 11500) of Part 1 of Division 3 of Title 2 of the Government Code, if no identification procedure is produced for review after 15 working days have elapsed.

(Added by Stats. 2017, Ch. 846, Sec. 69. (AB 967) Effective January 1, 2018. Section operative July 1, 2020, pursuant to Sec. 8382.)

8378.

Within two hours after a licensed hydrolysis facility takes custody of a body that has not been embalmed, it shall refrigerate the body at a temperature not greater than 50 degrees Fahrenheit, unless the hydrolysis process will begin within 24 hours of the time that the hydrolysis facility took custody.

(Added by Stats. 2017, Ch. 846, Sec. 69. (AB 967) Effective January 1, 2018. Section operative July 1, 2020, pursuant to Sec. 8382.)

8380.

(a) The hydrolysis facility licensee, or its authorized representatives, shall provide instruction to all hydrolysis facility personnel involved in the hydrolysis process. This instruction shall lead to a demonstrated knowledge on the part of an employee regarding identification procedures used during hydrolysis, operation of the hydrolysis chamber and processing equipment, safe work practices and procedures for the handling of corrosive materials, and all laws relevant to the handling of a body and hydrolyzed human remains. This instruction shall be outlined in a written plan maintained by the hydrolysis facility licensee for inspection and comment by an inspector of the Cemetery and Funeral Bureau.

(b) No employee shall be allowed to operate any hydrolysis equipment until the employee has demonstrated to the certified manager of a licensed hydrolysis facility or authorized representative of the licensee that the employee understands the procedures required to ensure that health and safety conditions are maintained at the hydrolysis facility and that hydrolyzed human remains are not commingled other than for acceptable residue, as defined. The hydrolysis facility licensee shall maintain a record to document that an employee has received the training specified in this section.

(c) A hydrolysis facility that fails, when requested by an official of the bureau, to produce a written employee instruction plan or record of employee training for inspection shall have 15 working days from the time of the request to produce a plan or training record for review by the chief of the Cemetery and Funeral Bureau. The license of a hydrolysis facility shall be suspended, pursuant to Chapter 5 (commencing with Section 11500) of Part 1 of Division 3 of Title 2 of the Government Code, if no plan or training record is produced for review after 15 working days have elapsed.

(Added by Stats. 2017, Ch. 846, Sec. 69. (AB 967) Effective January 1, 2018. Section operative July 1, 2020, pursuant to Sec. 8382.)

8382.

This article shall become operative on July 1, 2020.

(Added by Stats. 2017, Ch. 846, Sec. 69. (AB 967) Effective January 1, 2018. Section operative July 1, 2020, pursuant to Sec. 8382. Note: Operative date affects Article 8, commencing with Section 8370.)

CHAPTER 3. Acquisition, Dedication and Sale [8500 - 8585]

(Chapter 3 enacted by Stats. 1939, Ch. 60.)

ARTICLE 1. Acquisition of Property [8500 - 8501]

(Article 1 enacted by Stats. 1939, Ch. 60.)

8500.

Cemetery authorities may take by purchase, donation or devise, property consisting of lands, mausoleums, crematories, and columbariums, or other property within which the interment of the dead may be authorized by law.

(Enacted by Stats. 1939, Ch. 60.)

8501.

Any cemetery authority which is described in Section 23701c of the Revenue and Taxation Code or is a corporation sole may acquire by eminent domain any property necessary to enlarge and add to an existing cemetery for the burial of the dead and the grounds thereof.

(Added by Stats. 1975, Ch. 1240.)

ARTICLE 2. Declaration of Intention [8525 - 8526]

(Article 2 enacted by Stats. 1939, Ch. 60.)

8525.

A cemetery authority may execute a declaration acknowledged so as to entitle it to be recorded, describing the property and declaring its intention to use all or part of the property for cemetery purposes.

(Enacted by Stats. 1939, Ch. 60.)

8526.

The declaration may be filed for record in the office of the recorder of the county in which the property is situated, and from the date of filing the declaration is constructive notice of the use for which the property is intended.

(Enacted by Stats. 1939, Ch. 60.)

ARTICLE 3. Dedication [8550 - 8561]

(Article 3 enacted by Stats. 1939, Ch. 60.)

8550.

Every cemetery authority, from time to time as its property may be required for interment purposes, shall:

(a) In case of land, survey and subdivide it into sections, blocks, plots, avenues, walks or other subdivisions; make a good and substantial map or plat showing the sections, plots, avenues, walks or other subdivisions, with descriptive names or numbers.

(b) In case of a mausoleum, or crematory and columbarium it shall make a good and substantial map or plat on which shall be delineated the sections, halls, rooms, corridors, elevations, and other divisions, with descriptive names or numbers.

(c) The maps or plats shall be clearly and legibly drawn, printed, or reproduced by a process guaranteeing a permanent record in black on tracing cloth or polyester base film. If ink is used on a polyester base film, the ink surface shall be coated with a suitable substance to insure permanent legibility. The size of each sheet shall be 18 by 26 inches or as otherwise prescribed by the county recorder or local agency. A marginal line shall be drawn completely around each sheet, leaving an entire blank margin of one inch. The scale of the map shall be large enough to show all details clearly and enough sheets shall be used to accomplish this end. The particular number of the sheets and the total number of sheets comprising the map shall be stated on each of the sheets and its relationship to each adjoining sheet shall be clearly shown.

(d) Upon modification of an existing section after January 1, 1990, or development of a new section after January 1, 1990, the cemetery authority shall amend and file with the county recorder or local agency the maps or plats as described in subdivisions (a), (b), and (c). Within 12 months of the initial sale, the cemetery authority shall file with the county recorder or local agency the map or plat. For purposes of this subdivision, "section" means a burial space, mausoleum, or columbarium.

(Amended by Stats. 1997, Ch. 142, Sec. 7. Effective January 1, 1998.)

8551.

The cemetery authority shall file the map or plat in the office of the recorder of the county in which all or a portion of the property is situated. The cemetery authority shall also file for record in the county recorder's office a written declaration of dedication of the property delineated on the plat or map, dedicating the property exclusively to cemetery purposes.

(Enacted by Stats. 1939, Ch. 60.)

8552.

The declaration shall be in such form as the cemetery authority may prescribe, and shall be subscribed by the president or vice president, and the secretary, or other persons whom the cemetery authority may authorize, and shall be acknowledged so as to entitle it to be recorded.

(Enacted by Stats. 1939, Ch. 60.)

8553.

Upon the filing of the map or plat and the filing of the declaration for record, the dedication is complete for all purposes and thereafter the property shall be held, occupied, and used exclusively for a cemetery and for cemetery purposes.

(Enacted by Stats. 1939, Ch. 60.)

8554.

When reservation is made in the declaration of dedication, any part or subdivision of the property so mapped and platted may, by order of the directors, be resurveyed and altered in shape and size and an amended map or plat filed, so long as such change does not disturb the interred remains of any deceased person.

(Enacted by Stats. 1939, Ch. 60.)

8555.

The filed map or plat and the recorded declaration are constructive notice to all persons of the dedication of the property to cemetery purposes.

(Enacted by Stats. 1939, Ch. 60.)

8556.

The county recorder of the county in which a map or plat is filed shall index the map or plat in the general index giving reference to date of filing and number or to book and page so that it may easily be found. The recorder may bind the maps or plats in special books or in his books of maps of subdivisions. The fee for filing and indexing said map or plat shall be the same as provided for subdivided land under Section 27372 of the Government Code.

(Amended by Stats. 1957, Ch. 1865.)

8557.

The county recorder of the county in which a declaration of dedication is filed shall record it in the official records of his office and index it in the general index.

(Amended by Stats. 1957, Ch. 954.)

8558.

After property is dedicated to cemetery purposes pursuant to this chapter, neither the dedication, nor the title of a plot owner, shall be affected by the dissolution of the cemetery authority, by nonuser on its part, by alienation of the property, by any incumbrances, by sale under execution, or otherwise except as provided in this chapter.

(Enacted by Stats. 1939, Ch. 60.)

8559.

Dedication to cemetery purposes pursuant to this chapter is not invalid as violating any laws against perpetuities or the suspension of the power of alienation of title to or use of property, but is expressly permitted and shall be deemed to be in respect for the dead, a provision for the interment of human remains, and a duty to, and for the benefit of, the general public.

(Enacted by Stats. 1939, Ch. 60.)

8560.

After dedication pursuant to this chapter, and as long as the property remains dedicated to cemetery purposes, no railroad, street, road, alley, pipe line, pole line, or other public thoroughfare or utility shall be laid out, through, over, or across any part of it without the consent of the cemetery authority owning and operating it, or of not less than two-thirds of the owners of interment plots.

(Enacted by Stats. 1939, Ch. 60.)

8560.5.

No streets, alleys, or roads shall be opened or laid out within the boundary lines of any cemetery located in whole or in part within the lines of any city or city and county, where burials in the cemetery have been had within five years prior thereto, without the consent of the person owning and controlling the cemetery.

(Added by Stats. 1953, Ch. 83.)

8561.

All property dedicated pursuant to this chapter, including roads, alleys, and walks, is exempt from public improvement assessments and is exempt from enforcement of a money judgment against an individual owner of an interment plot to the extent provided in Section 704.200 of the Code of Civil Procedure.

(Amended by Stats. 1982, Ch. 497, Sec. 123. Operative July 1, 1983, by Sec. 185 of Ch. 497.)

ARTICLE 4. Sale of Plots [8570 - 8574]

(Article 4 enacted by Stats. 1939, Ch. 60.)

8570.

After filing the map or plat and recording the declaration of dedication, a cemetery authority may sell and convey plots subject to such rules and regulations as may be then in effect or thereafter adopted by the cemetery authority, and subject to such other and further limitations, conditions and restrictions as may be inserted in or made a part of the declaration of dedication by reference, or included in the instrument of conveyance of such plot.

(Amended by Stats. 1939, Ch. 339.)

8571.

(a) All plots, the use of which has been conveyed by deed or certificate of ownership as a separate plot, are indivisible except with the consent of the cemetery authority, or as provided by law.

(b) A plot, the use of which has been conveyed by deed or certificate of ownership as a family plot, thereby becomes inalienable and shall be held as a family plot of the owner.

(Amended by Stats. 2001, Ch. 436, Sec. 34. Effective January 1, 2002.)

8572.

All conveyances made by a cemetery authority shall be signed by the president or the vice president, and the secretary, or by other officers authorized by the cemetery authority.

(Enacted by Stats. 1939, Ch. 60.)

8573.

Any cemetery authority or its agents who sell, offer for sale, contract to sell, or negotiate the sale of mausoleum crypts before the receipt of a certificate of occupancy as provided for in Sections 9591 and 9592 shall:

(a) Set forth in each contract a specific period of time within which the building or structure shall be completed.

(b) Set forth in each contract that the purchaser has the right of exchange for similar interment property and, in the event completion is not accomplished as set forth in (a) above, except upon the proclamation of a national emergency, guarantee the refund of the purchase price.

(c) Provide adequate financial provision for the construction cost of the mausoleum or the refund of the sales price to the purchaser until such time as a certificate of occupancy has been received.

(Added by Stats. 1957, Ch. 1635.)

8574.

For a violation of any provision of Section 8573, the bureau may temporarily suspend or permanently revoke the license of any cemetery licensee and may order the reservation or escrowing of assets of the cemetery authority to the extent deemed necessary to satisfy the cost of construction of the structure or building.

(Amended by Stats. 2000, Ch. 568, Sec. 250. Effective January 1, 2001.)

ARTICLE 5. Removal of Dedication [8580 - 8581]

(Article 5 enacted by Stats. 1939, Ch. 60.)

8580.

Property dedicated to cemetery purposes shall be held and used exclusively for cemetery purposes, unless and until the dedication is removed from all or any part of it by an order and decree of the superior court of the county in which the property is situated, in a proceeding brought by the cemetery authority for that purpose and upon notice of hearing and proof satisfactory to the court:

(a) That no interments were made in or that all interments have been removed from that portion of the property from which dedication is sought to be removed.

(b) That the portion of the property from which dedication is sought to be removed is not being used for interment of human remains.

(Amended by Stats. 1939, Ch. 1032.)

8581.

The notice of hearing provided in section 8580 shall be given by publication once a week for at least three consecutive weeks in a daily newspaper of general circulation in the county where said cemetery is located, and the posting of copies of the notice in three conspicuous places on that portion of the property from which the dedication is to be removed. Said notice shall:

(a) Describe the portion of the cemetery property sought to be removed from dedication.

(b) State that all remains have been removed or that no interments have been made in the portion of the cemetery property sought to be removed from dedication.

(c) Specify the time and place of the hearing.

(Added by Stats. 1939, Ch. 1032.)

ARTICLE 6. Transfer of Cemetery Ownership [8585- 8585.]

(Article 6 added by Stats. 1976, Ch. 728.)

8585.

(a) Whenever ownership of any cemetery authority is proposed to be transferred, the cemetery authority shall notify the Cemetery and Funeral Bureau in the Department of Consumer Affairs. A change in ownership, for purposes of this section, shall be deemed to occur whenever more than 50 percent of the equitable ownership of a cemetery authority is transferred in a single transaction or in a related series of transactions to one or more persons, associations, or corporations. The notice shall specify the address of the principal offices of the cemetery authority, and whether it will be changed or unchanged, and shall specify the name and address of each new owner and the stockholders. A person or entity that knowingly provides false information shall be subject to a civil penalty for each violation in the minimum amount of two thousand five hundred dollars ($2,500) and the maximum amount of twenty-five thousand dollars ($25,000). An action for a civil penalty under this provision may be brought by any public prosecutor in the name of the people of the State of California and the penalty imposed shall be enforceable as a civil judgment.

(b) Notice of the change of ownership shall be published in a newspaper of general circulation in the county in which the cemetery is located. The notice shall specify the address of the principal offices of the cemetery authority, whether changed or unchanged, and shall specify the name and address of each new owner and each stockholder owning more than 5 percent of the stock of each new owner.

(c) If there is a change of ownership pursuant to this section, the existing certificate of authority shall lapse and a new certificate of authority shall be obtained from the Cemetery and Funeral Bureau. No person shall purchase a cemetery, including purchase at a sale for delinquent taxes, or purchase more than 50 percent of the equitable ownership of a cemetery authority without having obtained a certificate of authority from the Cemetery and Funeral Bureau prior to the purchase of the cemetery or the ownership interest in the cemetery authority.

(d) Every cemetery authority shall post and continuously maintain at each public entrance to the cemetery a sign specifying the current name and address of the cemetery authority, a statement that the name and address of each director and officer of the cemetery authority may be obtained by contacting the Cemetery and Funeral Bureau, and shall have either of the following:

(1) The address of the Cemetery and Funeral Bureau.

(2) A statement that the address of the Cemetery and Funeral Bureau is available at the office of the cemetery authority.

(e) The signs shall be at least 16 inches high and 24 inches wide and shall be prominently mounted upright and vertical.

(f) The Cemetery and Funeral Bureau shall suspend the certificate of authority of any cemetery authority that is in violation of this section. No person shall obtain a certificate of authority under intentionally false or misleading statements and no person shall delegate authority of ownership under this section, except to another person licensed by the bureau. The certificate may be reinstated only upon compliance with these requirements.

(Amended by Stats. 2008, Ch. 490, Sec. 3. Effective January 1, 2009.)

CHAPTER 4. Property Rights [8600 - 8680]

(Chapter 4 enacted by Stats. 1939, Ch. 60.)

ARTICLE 1. General Provisions [8600 - 8605]

(Article 1 enacted by Stats. 1939, Ch. 60.)

8600.

All plots conveyed to individuals are presumed to be the sole and separate property of the owner named in the instrument of conveyance.

(Amended by Stats. 1939, Ch. 339.)

8601.

The spouse of an owner of any plot containing more than one interment space has a vested right of interment of his remains in the plot and any person thereafter becoming the spouse of the owner has a vested right of interment of his remains in the plot if more than one interment space is unoccupied at the time the person becomes the spouse of the owner.

(Amended by Stats. 1939, Ch. 339.)

8602.

No conveyance or other action of the owner without the written consent or joinder of the spouse of the owner divests the spouse of a vested right of interment, except that a final decree of divorce between them terminates the vested right of interment unless otherwise provided in the decree.

(Amended by Stats. 1939, Ch. 339.)

8603.

If no interment is made in an interment plot which has been transferred by deed or certificate of ownership to an individual owner, or if all remains previously interred are lawfully removed, upon the death of the owner, unless he has disposed of the plot either in his will by a specific devise or by a written declaration filed and recorded in the office of the cemetery authority, the plot descends to the heirs at law of the owner subject to the rights of interment of the decedent and his surviving spouse.

(Enacted by Stats. 1939, Ch. 60.)

8604.

Cemetery property passing to an individual by reason of the death of the owner is exempt from all inheritance taxes.

(Enacted by Stats. 1939, Ch. 60.)

8605.

An affidavit by a person having knowledge of the facts setting forth the fact of the death of the owner and the name of the person or persons entitled to the use of the plot pursuant to this chapter, is complete authorization to the cemetery authority to permit the use of the unoccupied portions of the plot by the person entitled to the use of it.

(Enacted by Stats. 1939, Ch. 60.)

ARTICLE 2. Joint Tenants [8625 - 8629]

(Article 2 enacted by Stats. 1939, Ch. 60.)

8625.

In a conveyance to two or more persons as joint tenants each joint tenant has a vested right of interment in the plot conveyed.

(Enacted by Stats. 1939, Ch. 60.)

8626.

Upon the death of a joint tenant, the title to the plot held in joint tenancy immediately vests in the survivors, subject to the vested right of interment of the remains of the deceased joint tenant.

(Enacted by Stats. 1939, Ch. 60.)

8627.

Cemetery property held in joint tenancy is exempt from the provisions of the Probate Code relating to proceedings for establishing the fact of death of a person whose death affects title to real property.

(Amended by Stats. 1983, Ch. 201, Sec. 2.)

8628.

An affidavit by any person having knowledge of the facts setting forth the fact of the death of one joint tenant and establishing the identity of the surviving joint tenants named in the deed to any plot, when filed with the cemetery authority operating the cemetery in which the plot is located, is complete authorization to the cemetery authority to permit the use of the unoccupied portion of the plot in accordance with the directions of the surviving joint tenants or their successors in interest.

(Enacted by Stats. 1939, Ch. 60.)

8629.

When there are several owners of a plot, or of rights of interment in it, they may designate one or more persons to represent the plot and file written notice of designation with the cemetery authority. In the absence of such notice or of written objection to its so doing, the cemetery authority is not liable to any owner for interring or permitting an interment in the plot upon the request or direction of any coowner of the plot.

(Enacted by Stats. 1939, Ch. 60.)

ARTICLE 3. Family Interment Plots [8650 - 8653]

(Article 3 enacted by Stats. 1939, Ch. 60.)

8650.

(a) Whenever an interment of the remains of a member or of a relative of a member of the family of the record owner or of the remains of the record owner is made in a plot transferred by deed or certificate of ownership to an individual owner, the plot shall become the family plot of the owner.

(b) If the owner dies without making disposition of the plot either in his or her will by a specific devise, or by a written declaration filed and recorded in the office of the cemetery authority, any unoccupied portions of the plot shall pass according to the laws of intestate succession as set forth in Sections 6400 to 6413, inclusive, of the Probate Code.

(c) As of January 1, 2002, any unoccupied portions of a family plot that became inalienable pursuant to this section as it read on December 31, 2001, shall no longer be inalienable and shall pass according to the laws of intestate succession as set forth in Sections 6400 to 6413, inclusive, of the Probate Code. No sale, transfer, or donation of any unused portion of a family plot made alienable under this subdivision shall be made unless all persons entitled to interment in the family plot under Sections 8651 and 8652 are deceased or have expressly waived in writing the right to be interred in the family plot.

(d) The seller of a cemetery plot shall notify the buyer that unused portions of a family plot may pass through intestate succession unless written disposition is made by the buyer and may be sold, transferred, or donated by the buyer's heirs. The seller shall notify the buyer of the effect of a future transfer, sale, or donation of the unused portion of a family plot on any endowment for care or maintenance of the plot that the buyer may purchase in conjunction with the purchase of the cemetery plot.

(Amended by Stats. 2001, Ch. 516, Sec. 1. Effective January 1, 2002.)

8650.5.

An affidavit executed by a person who is the owner of the plot by virtue of the laws of intestate succession or by his or her attorney-in-fact, setting forth the fact of the death of the owner, the absence of a disposition of the plot by the owner in his or her will by a specific devise, the name of the person or persons who have rights to the plot under the intestate succession laws of the state, and the consent of that person or those persons to the sale of the plot by the cemetery authority, shall constitute complete authorization to the cemetery authority to permit any sale of the unoccupied portions of the plot.

(Added by Stats. 2001, Ch. 516, Sec. 2. Effective January 1, 2002.)

8651.

In a family plot one grave, niche or crypt may be used for the owner's interment; one for the owner's surviving spouse, if any, who by law has a vested right of interment in it; and in those remaining, if any, the parents and children of the deceased owner in order of death may be interred without the consent of any person claiming any interest in the plot.

(Enacted by Stats. 1939, Ch. 60.)

8652.

If no parent or child survives, the right of interment goes in the order of death first, to the spouse of any child of the record owner and second, in the order of death to the next heirs at law of the owner or the spouse of any heir at law.

(Enacted by Stats. 1939, Ch. 60.)

8653.

Any surviving spouse, parent, child or heir who has a right of interment in a family plot may waive such right in favor of any other relative, or spouse of a relative of either the deceased owner or of his spouse, and upon such waiver the remains of the person in whose favor the waiver is made may be interred in the plot.

(Amended by Stats. 1945, Ch. 848.)

ARTICLE 4. Vested Right of Interment [8675 - 8676]

(Article 4 enacted by Stats. 1939, Ch. 60.)

8675.

A vested right of interment may be waived and is terminated upon the interment elsewhere of the remains of the person in whom vested.

(Enacted by Stats. 1939, Ch. 60.)

8676.

No vested right of interment gives to any person the right to have his remains interred in any interment space in which the remains of any deceased person having a prior vested right of interment have been interred, nor does it give any person the right to have the remains of more than one deceased person interred in a single interment space in violation of the rules and regulations of the cemetery in which the interment space is located.
(Enacted by Stats. 1939, Ch. 60.)

ARTICLE 5. Voluntary Establishment of Inalienability [8680- 8680.]
(Article 5 enacted by Stats. 1939, Ch. 60.)
8680.
A cemetery authority may take and hold any plot conveyed or devised to it by the plot owner so that it will be inalienable, and interments shall be restricted to the persons designated in the conveyance or devise.
(Enacted by Stats. 1939, Ch. 60.)

CHAPTER 5. Endowment and Special Care [8700 - 8785]
(Heading of Chapter 5 amended by Stats. 1951, Ch. 176.)

ARTICLE 1. Care of Old Cemeteries [8700 - 8715]
(Article 1 enacted by Stats. 1939, Ch. 60.)
8700.
In addition to those cemeteries to which this part does not apply, this article does not apply to abandoned cemeteries nor to cemeteries in which interments are prohibited.
(Enacted by Stats. 1939, Ch. 60.)
8701.
Whenever a majority of the plots in all or any part of a cemetery established prior to August 14, 1931, has been sold without the owner having made provision for the establishment of an adequate endowment care fund for its care, maintenance, and embellishment, the avenues, roadways, walks, driveways, alleys, streets and parks in it may be vacated or altered and replatted into plots which may be sold for interment purposes pursuant to this article.
(Amended by Stats. 1951, Ch. 176.)
8702.
Application for the alteration or vacation or replatting of all or any portion of an alley, street, avenue, walk, driveway, or park, for plots in the cemetery shall be made to the superior court in the county in which all or any portion of the property is situated.
(Enacted by Stats. 1939, Ch. 60.)
8703.
The application may be by the cemetery authority owning or operating the cemetery or if there is no cemetery authority operating the cemetery, by twenty or more plot owners.
(Enacted by Stats. 1939, Ch. 60.)
8704.
The petition shall be verified and shall specify the facts of such ownership and shall state the reasons for the proposed change and what provisions have theretofore been made for the endowment care of the cemetery.
(Amended by Stats. 1951, Ch. 176.)
8705.
There shall be presented with the petition a plat of the cemetery and the proposed replat which shall clearly indicate the proposed changes.
(Enacted by Stats. 1939, Ch. 60.)
8706.
The petition shall be filed with the clerk of the superior court, and the clerk shall fix the time for hearing not less then thirty nor more than sixty days from the date of filing.
(Enacted by Stats. 1939, Ch. 60.)
8707.
Notice of the hearing shall be given by publishing a copy of the notice in a newspaper of general circulation near the cemetery in the county in which the property is situated, once a week for three consecutive weeks prior to the date of hearing.
(Enacted by Stats. 1939, Ch. 60.)
8708.
Copies of the notice shall be posted in three conspicuous places within the cemetery.
(Enacted by Stats. 1939, Ch. 60.)
8709.
The notice shall:
(a) Be addressed to all persons owning or interested in plots in the cemetery but need not name them.
(b) Set forth in a general way the proposed changes.
(c) Set forth the reasons stated in the petition for making the changes.
(d) State the time when the hearing of the petition will be had.
(e) State that a plat showing the proposed changes is on file with the clerk of the court.
(Enacted by Stats. 1939, Ch. 60.)
8710.
At the time fixed for the hearing, the court shall hear and consider any evidence introduced in favor of and all objections to the changes and may allow the proposed changes and replat in whole or in part, or may order and allow modifications of the proposed changes. The hearing may be continued from time to time by order of court.
(Amended by Stats. 1939, Ch. 339.)
8711.

The cemetery authority or other person directed by the court shall accept the newly created plots and shall sell and convey them only for interment purposes.
(Amended by Stats. 1957, Ch. 79.)
8713.
The vacation of an alley, avenue, roadway, walk, driveway, street, or park adjacent to a privately owned plot does not vest any interest in the owner of the plot to the vacated portion; but the adjacent owner shall, for 10 days after the date of the order of vacation, have the right to purchase the new plots.
(Amended by Stats. 1957, Ch. 79.)
8714.
In allowing any damages to any plot owner for such vacation, the court shall take into consideration the benefit to be received from endowment care.
(Amended by Stats. 1951, Ch. 176.)
8715.
The provisions of this article are hereby declared to be a necessary exercise of the police power of the State in order to preserve and keep existing cemeteries as resting places for the dead and to preserve cemeteries from becoming unkept and places of reproach and desolation in the communities in which they are located. The taking of roadways, alleys, walks, avenues, driveways, streets and parks for the purposes and by the method in this section specified, regardless of the private character of the association or person applying therefor, is hereby declared an exercise of the right of eminent domain in behalf of the public health, safety, comfort, pleasure, protection, and historic instruction to present and future generations.
(Enacted by Stats. 1939, Ch. 60.)

ARTICLE 2. Care of Active Cemeteries [8725 - 8748]
(Article 2 enacted by Stats. 1939, Ch. 60.)
8725.
A cemetery authority that maintains a cemetery may place its cemetery under endowment care and establish, maintain, and operate an endowment care fund. Endowment care and special care funds consisting of trust funds created by irrevocable trust agreements may be commingled for investment and the net income therefrom shall be divided between the endowment care and special care funds in the proportion that each fund contributed to the principal sum invested. Special care funds derived from trusts created by a revocable agreement shall not be commingled for investment and shall be accounted for separately from all other funds. The funds may be held in the name of the cemetery authority, its directors, or in the name of the trustees appointed by the cemetery authority.
(Amended by Stats. 2017, Ch. 750, Sec. 2. (AB 926) Effective January 1, 2018.)
8726.
(a) The principal of all funds for endowment care shall be invested and the income only may be used for the care, maintenance, and embellishment of the cemetery in accordance with the provisions of law and the resolutions, bylaws, rules, and regulations or other actions or instruments of the cemetery authority and for no other purpose. Endowment and special care funds shall be maintained separate and distinct from all other funds and the trustees shall keep separate records thereof.
(b) For purposes of this article, the following definitions shall apply:
(1) "Income" means distribution under either the net income distribution method or the unitrust distribution method.
(2) "Unitrust distribution method" means an income distribution method where the net income amount, known as the unitrust amount, is no more than 5 percent of the fair market value of the trust assets.
(Amended by Stats. 2017, Ch. 750, Sec. 3. (AB 926) Effective January 1, 2018.)
8726.1.
(a) If a cemetery authority establishes an endowment care fund, the fund shall be subject to a net income distribution method that requires all of the following:
(1) The trustee of the endowment care fund shall create a reserve from which principal losses may be replaced by setting aside a reasonable percentage of the income from the fund.
(2) The trustee may also set aside, out of income or net capital gains from investments, reserves for future maintenance, repair, replacement, or restoration of property or embellishments in the cemetery that may be necessary or desirable as a result of wear, deterioration, accident, damage, or destruction.
(3) The total amount of these reserves for maintenance, repair, and restoration shall not at any time exceed 10 percent of the endowment care fund.
(4) As used in this section, "net capital gains" means the amount by which cumulative realized capital gains since the establishment of the endowment care fund exceed the sum of cumulative realized capital losses since the establishment of the endowment care fund and capital gains previously set aside in reserve.
(5) Additions to the reserve in any year from net capital gains shall not exceed one-half the difference between the capital gains and the capital losses during the year.
(6) Net capital gains not set aside in reserve in any given year shall become a part of the principal of the endowment care fund.
(b) Notwithstanding subdivision (a), a cemetery authority may convert its endowment care fund from a net income distribution method to a unitrust distribution method if it obtains prior approval from the Cemetery and Funeral Bureau pursuant to Section 8726.2.
(Amended by Stats. 2017, Ch. 750, Sec. 4. (AB 926) Effective January 1, 2018.)
8726.2.
(a) On or after January 1, 2020, a cemetery authority, its board of trustees, or its corporate trustee may apply to the Cemetery and Funeral Bureau to convert its

endowment care fund from a net income distribution method to a unitrust distribution method.

(b) The bureau shall approve the application described in subdivision (a) only if all of the following conditions are met:

(1) The cemetery authority, its board of trustees, or its corporate trustee provides the investment objectives of the trust and those objectives promote the mutual goals of (A) growing the principal assets to sufficiently cover the cost of future and ongoing care and maintenance of the cemetery and (B) generating income to support the cemetery, as described in Section 8726.

(2) Evidence is provided that the cemetery authority, its board of trustees, or its corporate trustee will invest and manage the trust under the prudent investor rule, as described in Article 2.5 (commencing with Section 16045) of Chapter 1 of Part 4 of Division 9 of the Probate Code.

(3) The cemetery authority, its board of trustees, or its corporate trustee demonstrates sufficient knowledge and expertise in investing and managing the endowment care fund under the unitrust distribution method.

(4) The unitrust amount is no more than 5 percent of the fair market value of the endowment care fund, determined by averaging the net fair market value of the assets as of the last trading day for each of the three preceding fiscal years.

(5) A reserve is created for future maintenance, repair, restoration of property, or embellishments in the cemetery for use when the endowment fund has inadequate funds for full distribution, as described in subparagraph (C) of paragraph (6). The cemetery authority, its board of trustees, or its corporate trustee may set aside a portion of the unitrust amount for the reserve.

(6) (A) The distribution of the unitrust amount may be made to the cemetery authority on a monthly, quarterly, semiannual, or annual basis, unless the endowment care fund has inadequate funds for full distribution.

(B) An endowment care fund has inadequate funds for full distribution if either of the following events occur:

(i) The fair market value of the endowment care fund, after the distribution, is less than 80 percent of the aggregate fair market value of the endowment care fund as of the end of the immediate preceding fiscal year.

(ii) The endowment care fund is less than the cumulative total of all principal contributions to the fund since inception.

(C) (i) If the endowment care fund has inadequate funds for full distribution, the distribution shall be limited to the lesser of net income distribution or an amount no more than a unitrust distribution of 1.5 percent of the fair market value of the assets as of the last trading day for each of the three preceding fiscal years.

(ii) The cemetery authority, its board of trustees, or its corporate trustee may draw from the reserve described in paragraph (5) only during a fiscal year where there are inadequate funds for full distribution. An amount drawn from the reserve during that fiscal year shall be the lesser of the difference between the unitrust amount described in paragraph (4) and the limited distribution amount described in clause (i), or one-third of the total amount of the reserve.

(7) Notwithstanding Section 8733 or 8733.5, the compensation of the trustee shall be reasonable and shall not exceed 0.1 percent of the net fair market value of the assets as of the last trading day for each of the three preceding fiscal years.

(8) The cemetery authority has submitted all annual reports, pursuant to Section 7612.6 of the Business and Professions Code, for the previous five consecutive years.

(c) The bureau shall deny a cemetery authority's application if the bureau has found any of the conditions described in subdivisions (a) to (f), inclusive, of Section 7613.9 of the Business and Professions Code.

(d) To assist the bureau in making its determination, the cemetery authority, its board of trustees, or its corporate trustee shall provide all relevant trust documents, including a proposed trust instrument, if available. If relevant trust documents become available after the bureau makes a determination, the cemetery authority, its board of trustees, or its corporate trustee shall provide it to the bureau.

(e) (1) The bureau shall review on an annual basis whether a cemetery authority continues to meet the conditions of approval, described in subdivision (b), for the use of the unitrust distribution method.

(2) If a cemetery authority is determined not to meet the original conditions of approval described in subdivision (b), or has failed to file an annual report pursuant to Section 7612.6 of the Business and Professions Code, the cemetery authority may be required to revert to the use of the net income distribution method.

(f) The bureau may adopt rules to administer this section and ensure compliance, including, but not limited to, reporting requirements.

(g) The bureau shall evaluate the effectiveness of this section and report at its next two hearings before the Joint Sunset Review Oversight Hearings of the Assembly Committee on Business and Professions and Senate Committee on Business, Professions and Economic Development that occurs after January 1, 2018.

(Added by Stats. 2017, Ch. 750, Sec. 5. (AB 926) Effective January 1, 2018.)

8728.

The cemetery authority may from time to time adopt plans for the general care, maintenance, and embellishment of its cemetery, and charge and collect from all subsequent purchasers of plots such reasonable sum as, in the judgment of the cemetery authority, will aggregate a fund, the reasonable income from which will provide care, maintenance and embellishment.

(Amended by Stats. 1951, Ch. 176.)

8729.

Upon payment of the purchase price and the amount fixed as a proportionate contribution for endowment care, there may be included in the deed of conveyance or by separate instrument an agreement to use the income from such endowment care fund for the care, maintenance, and embellishment in accordance with the plan adopted, for the cemetery and its appurtenances to the proportionate extent the income received by the cemetery authority from the contribution will permit.

(Amended by Stats. 1951, Ch. 176.)

8730.

Upon the application of an owner of any plot, and upon the payment by him of the amount fixed as a reasonable and proportionate contribution for endowment care a cemetery authority may enter into an agreement with him to use the income from such fund for the care of his plot and its appurtenances.

(Amended by Stats. 1951, Ch. 176.)

8731.

(a) The cemetery authority may appoint a board of trustees of not less than three in number as trustees of its endowment care fund. The members of the board of trustees shall hold office subject to the direction of the cemetery authority.

(b) If within 30 days after notice of nonreceipt by the Cemetery and Funeral Bureau or other agency with regulatory authority over cemetery authorities, the cemetery authority fails to file the report required by Section 7612.6 of the Business and Professions Code, or if the report is materially not in compliance with law or the endowment care fund is materially not in compliance with law, the cemetery authority may be required to appoint as sole trustee of its endowment care fund under Section 8733.5, any bank or trust company qualified under the provisions of the Banking Law (Division 1 (commencing with Section 99) of the Financial Code) to engage in the trust business. That requirement may be imposed by the Cemetery and Funeral Bureau or other agency with regulatory authority over cemetery authorities, provided that the cemetery authority has received written notice of the alleged violation and has been given the opportunity to correct the alleged violation, and there has been a finding of a material violation in an administrative hearing.

(c) (1) Each member of the board of trustees shall provide signatory acknowledgment of understanding of the role of a trustee in managing trust funds in the following areas:

(A) Trustee duties, powers, and liabilities as contained in Part 4 (commencing with Section 16000) of Division 9 of the Probate Code.

(B) Reporting and regulatory requirements contained in Article 1.5 (commencing with Section 7611) of Chapter 12 of Division 3 of the Business and Professions Code.

(C) Provisions related to the care of active cemeteries contained in Chapter 5 (commencing with Section 8700) of Part 3 of Division 8.

(2) The signatory acknowledgment shall be retained by the cemetery authority during the duration of the trustee's term of office.

(Amended by Stats. 2018, Ch. 571, Sec. 33. (SB 1480) Effective January 1, 2019.)

8732.

Not more than one member of the board of trustees of an endowment care fund may have a proprietary interest in the cemetery authority.

(Repealed and added by Stats. 1976, Ch. 729.)

8732.1.

Each individual trustee of an endowment care fund shall be a resident of this State, and a corporate trustee shall be qualified to do business in this State.

(Added by Stats. 1955, Ch. 595.)

8733.

No sum in excess of 5 percent of the net income derived from an endowment care fund, or special care fund, or both, in any year shall be paid as compensation to the board of trustees for its services as trustee. This amount shall be the total compensation from the fund to be paid to a trustee for services. For purposes of this section, "net income" means the amount of income remaining after reasonable administrative expenses, including bookkeeping, postage, taxes, and other costs directly related to generating income to the trust fund, have been deducted from the gross income derived from the fund.

(Amended by Stats. 1997, Ch. 142, Sec. 10. Effective January 1, 1998.)

8733.5.

In lieu of the appointment of a board of trustees of its endowment care fund, any cemetery authority may appoint as sole trustee of its endowment care fund any bank or trust company qualified under the provisions of the Banking Law (Division 1 (commencing with Section 99) of the Financial Code) to engage in the trust business. If a cemetery authority appoints a bank or trust company, the sum paid to the bank or trust company may exceed 5 percent of the net income derived from the endowment care fund, or special care fund, or both, notwithstanding Section 8733.

(Amended by Stats. 1997, Ch. 142, Sec. 11. Effective January 1, 1998.)

8734.

(a) Except as provided in subdivisions (b), (c), and (d), the board of trustees or corporate trustee of an endowment care fund or one or more special care funds shall file a fidelity bond executed by an admitted surety insurer with the Cemetery and Funeral Bureau in the amount of fifty thousand dollars ($50,000), guaranteeing payment to each such fund of any monetary loss incurred by the fund occasioned by acts of fraud or dishonesty by the trustees or trustee. The board of trustees or corporate trustee of both an endowment care fund and one or more special care funds need file only one such bond.

(b) Any cemetery authority which has a fidelity bond on all officers and employees issued by an admitted surety insurer and which by its terms would cover any acts of fraud or dishonesty by the trustees or corporate trustee of its endowment and special care funds need not file a separate bond with the Cemetery and Funeral Bureau as provided in subdivision (a), but shall submit to the Cemetery and Funeral Bureau satisfactory evidence of such a fidelity bond. Such fidelity bond, except as provided in subdivision (c), shall provide at least fifty thousand dollars ($50,000) specifically designated to guarantee payment of any monetary loss incurred by the endowment care or special care funds of the cemetery authority occasioned by any acts of fraud or dishonesty by the board of trustees or corporate trustee thereof.

(c) Upon application, the Cemetery and Funeral Bureau may reduce the amount of the bond required pursuant to this section if moneys in the endowment care fund and special care funds administered by the applicant board of trustees or corporate trustee are substantially less than fifty thousand dollars ($50,000). In such cases, the Cemetery and Funeral Bureau may permit filing of a bond pursuant to subdivision (a) or (b) which, while the bond is on file, is not less than the aggregate amount of all moneys in the endowment care fund and special care funds administered by the applicant. If the Cemetery and Funeral Bureau permits exceptions pursuant to this subdivision, it shall adopt procedures to assure that affected bonds do not fall below such amount.

(d) The trustees or corporate trustee of an endowment care fund or special care fund shall take no action respecting trust funds unless there is on file with the bureau a bond as required by this section. The Cemetery and Funeral Bureau may suspend the certificate of authority of any cemetery authority having endowment or special care funds with respect to which there is no bond on file with the bureau as required by this section, or whenever such a bond falls below the amount required by this section.

(e) Any state or national bank authorized to engage in the trust business pursuant to Division 1 (commencing with Section 99) of the Financial Code shall be exempt from the requirements of this section.
(Amended by Stats. 2000, Ch. 568, Sec. 253. Effective January 1, 2001.)
8735.
A cemetery authority which has established an endowment care fund may take, receive, and hold as a part of or incident to the fund any property, real, personal or mixed, bequeathed, devised, granted, given or otherwise contributed to it for its endowment care fund.
(Amended by Stats. 1951, Ch. 176.)
8736.
The endowment care fund and all payments or contributions to it are hereby expressly permitted as and for charitable and eleemosynary purposes. Endowment care is a provision for the discharge of a duty due from the persons contributing to the persons interred and to be interred in the cemetery and a provision for the benefit and protection of the public by preserving and keeping cemeteries from becoming unkept and places of reproach and desolation in the communities in which they are situated.
(Amended by Stats. 1951, Ch. 176.)
8737.
No payment, gift, grant, bequest, or other contribution for general endowment care is invalid by reason of any indefiniteness or uncertainty of the persons designated as beneficiaries, nor is the fund or any contribution to it invalid as violating any law against perpetuities or the suspension of the power of alienation of title to property.
(Amended by Stats. 1951, Ch. 176.)
8738.
An endowment care cemetery is one which has deposited in its endowment care fund the minimum amounts heretofore required by law and shall hereafter have deposited in its endowment care fund at the time of or not later than completion of the initial sale not less than the following amounts for plots sold or disposed of:
(a) Four dollars and fifty cents ($4.50) a square foot for each grave.
(b) Seventy dollars ($70) for each niche.
(c) Two hundred twenty dollars ($220) for each crypt; provided, however, that for companion crypts, there shall be deposited two hundred twenty dollars ($220) for the first crypt and one hundred ten dollars ($110) for each additional crypt.
(d) Seventy dollars ($70) for the cremated remains of each deceased person scattered in the cemetery at a garden or designated open area that is not an interment site subject to subdivision (a).
(Amended by Stats. 2008, Ch. 545, Sec. 1. Effective January 1, 2009.)
8738.1.
In addition to the requirements of Section 8738 any endowment care cemetery hereafter established shall also have deposited in its endowment care fund the additional sum of twenty-five thousand dollars ($25,000), or thirty-five thousand dollars ($35,000) if established on or after January 1, 1977, before disposing of any plot or making any sale thereof.
(Amended by Stats. 1976, Ch. 525.)
8738.2.
The endowment care fund under the provisions of this code shall be kept separate and apart from all other cemetery funds. Separate records and books shall be kept of the endowment care fund. The amount to be deposited in the endowment care fund shall be separately shown on the original purchase agreement and a copy delivered to the purchaser. In the sale of cemetery property, no commission shall be paid a broker or salesman on the amount deposited by the purchaser in the fund.
(Added by Stats. 1955, Ch. 595.)
8739.
A nonendowment care cemetery is one that does not have deposited in an endowment care fund the minimum amounts required by law.
(Amended by Stats. 1951, Ch. 176.)
8739.1.

Any cemetery established, on or after September 7, 1955, or excluded from the exemption provided in subdivision (c) of Section 8250 by virtue of paragraph (2) of such subdivision, shall be an endowment care cemetery.
(Amended by Stats. 1972, Ch. 1269.)
8740.
A cemetery which otherwise complies with Section 8738 may be designated an endowment care cemetery even though it contains a small section which may be sold without endowment care, if the section is separately set off from the remainder of the cemetery and if signs are kept prominently placed around the section designating the same as a "nonendowment care section" in legible black lettering at least four inches high. There shall be printed at the head of all contracts, agreements, statements, receipts and certificates of ownership or deeds referring to plots in the section the phrase "nonendowment care" in lettering of a size and style to be approved by the Cemetery and Funeral Bureau.
No new "nonendowment care" sections shall be established, nor an existing one enlarged in an endowment care cemetery.
(Amended by Stats. 2000, Ch. 568, Sec. 254. Effective January 1, 2001.)
8741.
Each endowment care cemetery shall post in a conspicuous place at or near the entrance of the cemetery and at its administration building and readily accessible to the public, a legible sign that shall contain the following information in the order and manner set forth below:
(a) A heading containing the words "endowment care"—which shall appear in a minimum of one-inch letters.
(b) The statement, "This is an endowment care interment property."
(Amended by Stats. 2006, Ch. 124, Sec. 2. Effective January 1, 2007.)
8743.
Each nonendowment care cemetery or the Cemetery and Funeral Bureau shall post in a conspicuous place in the office or offices where sales are conducted and in a conspicuous place at or near the entrance of the cemetery or its administration building and readily accessible to the public, a legible sign with lettering of a size and style to be approved by the Cemetery and Funeral Bureau that shall contain the following information in the order and manner set forth below:
(a) A heading containing the words "nonendowment care."
(b) This is a nonendowment care interment property.
(Amended by Stats. 2000, Ch. 568, Sec. 255. Effective January 1, 2001.)
8744.
There shall be printed at the head of all contracts, agreements, statements, receipts, literature and other publications of nonendowment care cemeteries the following form:
"This institution is operated as a 'nonendowment care' interment property."
The phrase "nonendowment care" shall be of a size and style to be approved by the Cemetery and Funeral Bureau.
(Amended by Stats. 2000, Ch. 568, Sec. 256. Effective January 1, 2001.)
8745.
All the information appearing on the signs and report filed in the cemetery office shall be revised annually and verified by the president and secretary, or two officers authorized by the cemetery authority.
(Added by Stats. 1939, Ch. 339.)
8746.
Any person, partnership, corporation, association, or his, her, or its agents or representatives, who shall violate any of the provisions of this article, except as provided in Section 8785, or make any willful or false statement appearing on a sign, contract, agreement, receipt, statement, literature or other publication shall be guilty of a misdemeanor.
(Amended by Stats. 1982, Ch. 897, Sec. 1.)
8747.5.
Each cemetery shall at all times maintain and keep within the State of California all books, accounts, records, cash and evidences of investments of its general and special care funds. They shall be readily available for inspection and examination by the Cemetery and Funeral Bureau in accordance with the provisions of the Business and Professions Code.
(Amended by Stats. 2000, Ch. 568, Sec. 257. Effective January 1, 2001.)
8748.
Where an endowment care mausoleum or mausoleum-columbarium is operated within an endowment care cemetery and the cemetery corporations or cemetery authorities owning or operating each merge and consolidate into one cemetery authority or corporation, the endowment care funds established by each may be consolidated and merged into one endowment care fund. Such merger shall be accomplished by the execution of a declaration of trust by the successor cemetery authority or corporation, which declaration shall provide:
(a) That the assets of each endowment care fund shall be merged and consolidated into one endowment care fund which shall be held and administered by the directors of the successor cemetery authority or the trustees appointed by them for the care, maintenance, and embellishment of both cemeteries in accordance with the provisions of this code.
(b) That the income from such endowment care funds shall be used for the general care, maintenance, and embellishment for the cemetery as a whole, or, if the income from such consolidated fund is to be divided between such mausoleum or mausoleum-columbarium and cemetery, the proportion or manner in which it is to be divided.
(c) That it accepts and will administer all special care funds for the purpose for which they were established and in accordance with the provisions of this code.

The declaration of trust shall be approved by all of the trustees of each endowment care fund and by the directors of the cemetery authority or corporation appointing such trustees, which approval shall be endorsed upon such declaration of trust. The declaration of trust shall not be effective unless and until approved by the Cemetery and Funeral Bureau.

An executed copy of such declaration of trust so approved shall be filed with the Cemetery and Funeral Bureau and in the office of the cemetery authority or corporation owning or operating such cemetery, where it shall be available for inspection by any owner of property therein.

Upon approval of the declaration of trust by the Cemetery and Funeral Bureau, the assets and liabilities of such endowment care funds shall be deemed merged and consolidated into one endowment care fund, and the trustees of, or appointed by, the cemetery authority or corporation handling such funds shall be immediately vested with the title to all of the assets and subject to all of the liabilities thereof. The trustees of the endowment care funds which have been thus merged or consolidated shall be relieved of any obligations or duties arising subsequent to such merger or consolidation.
(Amended by Stats. 2000, Ch. 568, Sec. 258. Effective January 1, 2001.)

ARTICLE 3. Investment of Endowment Funds [8750 - 8751.1]
(Heading of Article 3 amended by Stats. 1951, Ch. 176.)

8750.
Endowment care funds shall not be used for any purpose other than to provide through income only for the reserves authorized by law and for the endowment care of the cemetery in accordance with the resolutions, by-laws, rules and regulations or other actions or instruments of the cemetery authority.
(Amended by Stats. 1951, Ch. 176.)

8751.
The funds shall be invested and reinvested, and kept invested in:
(a) Bonds of the United States or this state, or of any county, city and county, or city in this state.
(b) Bonds legal for investment for savings banks in this state.
(c) First mortgages or first trust deeds on improved real estate.
(d) Income producing improved real estate in any city or city and county in this state.
(e) Investment certificates in any savings and loan association organized, existing and doing business under the laws of this state.
(f) Investments of the type enumerated for domestic incorporated insurers in Article 3, Chapter 2, Part 2, of Division 1 of the Insurance Code of this state.
(g) By deposit in a bank which is insured by the Federal Deposit Insurance Corporation.
(h) Shares of a duly chartered and insured federal savings and loan association.
(Amended by Stats. 1977, Ch. 496.)

8751.1.
In addition to the requirements of Section 8751, the funds may be invested and reinvested and kept invested in investments of the type and in the manner as provided in Part 4 (commencing with Section 16000) of Division 9 of the Probate Code.
(Amended by Stats. 1990, Ch. 79, Sec. 12.)

ARTICLE 4. Special Care [8775 - 8779.5]
(Article 4 enacted by Stats. 1939, Ch. 60.)

8775.
A cemetery authority which has established an endowment care fund may also take and hold any property bequeathed, granted, or given to it in trust to apply the principal, or proceeds, or income to either or all of the following purposes:
(a) Improvement or embellishment of all or any part of the cemetery or any lot in it.
(b) Erection, renewal, repair, or preservation of any monument, fence, building, or other structure in the cemetery.
(c) Planting or cultivation of trees, shrubs, or plants in or around any part of the cemetery.
(d) Special care or ornamenting of any part of any plot, section, or building in the cemetery.
(e) Any purpose or use not inconsistent with the purpose for which the cemetery was established or is maintained.
(Amended by Stats. 1951, Ch. 176.)

8776.
The sums paid in or contributed to the fund authorized by this article are hereby expressly permitted as and for a charitable and eleemosynary purpose. Such contributions are a provision for the discharge of a duty due from the persons contributing to the person or persons interred or to be interred in the cemetery and likewise a provision for the benefit and protection of the public by preserving, beautifying, and keeping cemeteries from becoming unkept and places of reproach and desolation in the communities in which they are situated. No payment, gift, grant, bequest, or other contribution for such purpose is invalid by reason of any indefiniteness or uncertainty of the persons designated as beneficiaries in the instruments creating the fund, nor is the fund or any contribution to it invalid as violating any law against perpetuities or the suspension of the power of alienation of title to property.
(Enacted by Stats. 1939, Ch. 60.)

8777.
All money or property received by a cemetery authority for deposit in a special care fund shall be placed in the custody of the trustee or trustees thereof within 30 days after receipt by the cemetery authority. The corpus of special care trusts shall be invested and reinvested and kept invested as authorized by Section 8778.
(Added by Stats. 1976, Ch. 729.)

8778.
The following shall be eligible investments for all special care trusts:
(a) Bonds of the United States or this state, or of any county, city, or city and county in this state.
(b) Bonds that are legal investments for commercial banks in this state.
(c) Certificates of deposit or other interest-bearing accounts in any bank in this state insured by the Federal Deposit Insurance Corporation.
(d) Investment certificates or shares in any state or federally chartered savings and loan association insured by the Federal Savings and Loan Insurance Corporation.
(e) Investments in first trust deeds on improved real estate, provided that the loans require monthly amortization of principal and interest and are fully amortized within 30 years or the term of the loan, whichever comes first. No loan shall be made to the cemetery authority, to the director, officer, or stockholder of a cemetery authority, or trustees of the special care funds, or to partners, relatives, agents, or employees thereof.
(f) Any investment that is lawful for endowment care funds under Sections 8751 and 8751.1.
(Amended by Stats. 2007, Ch. 307, Sec. 1. Effective January 1, 2008.)

8778.5.
Each special care trust fund established pursuant to this article shall be administered in compliance with the following requirements:
(a) (1) The board of trustees shall honor a written request of revocation by the trustor within 30 days upon receipt of the written request.
(2) Except as provided in paragraph (3), the board of trustees upon revocation of a special care trust may assess a revocation fee on the earned income of the trust only, the amount of which shall not exceed 10 percent of the trust corpus, as set forth in subdivision (c) of Section 2370 of Title 16 of the California Code of Regulations.
(3) If, prior to or upon the death of the beneficiary of a revocable special care trust, the cemetery authority is unable to perform the services of the special care trust fund agreement, the board of trustees shall pay the entire trust corpus and all earned income to the beneficiary or trustor, or the legal representative of either the beneficiary or trustor, without the imposition of a revocation fee.
(b) Notwithstanding subdivision (d) of Section 2370 of Title 16 of the California Code of Regulations, the board of trustees may charge an annual fee for administering a revocable special care trust fund, which may be recovered by administrative withdrawals from current trust income, but the total administrative withdrawals in any year shall not exceed 4 percent of the trust balance.
(c) Notwithstanding Section 8785, any person, partnership, or corporation who violates this section shall be subject to disciplinary action as provided in Article 6 (commencing with Section 7686) of Chapter 12 of Division 3 of the Business and Professions Code, or by a civil fine not exceeding five hundred dollars ($500), or by both, as determined by the Cemetery and Funeral Bureau and shall not be guilty of a crime.
(Amended by Stats. 2018, Ch. 571, Sec. 34. (SB 1480) Effective January 1, 2019.)

8779.
Nothing in this article shall require liquidation or transmutation of any lawful investment existing on December 31, 1976, but any reinvestment shall be governed by Section 8778, and any interest or other increment actually received on account of such an investment shall be reinvested only as provided in Section 8778.
(Added by Stats. 1976, Ch. 729.)

8779.5.
Each special care fund established pursuant to this article shall be held in trust and managed by either the board of trustees of the cemetery authority's endowment care fund or by a board of trustees meeting the qualifications prescribed by this chapter for such a board of trustees. However, nothing in this section shall be construed to modify the terms of any special care trust established prior to January 1, 1977.
(Added by Stats. 1976, Ch. 729.)

ARTICLE 5. Misrepresentation as to Endowment [8780 - 8781]
(Heading of Article 5 amended by Stats. 1951, Ch. 176.)

8780.
No person, partnership, corporation, association, or his, her, or its agents or representatives, shall sell, offer for sale, or advertise any plot under representation that the plot is under endowment care, before an endowment care fund has been established for the cemetery in which the plot is situated.
(Amended by Stats. 1982, Ch. 897, Sec. 3.)

8781.
It shall be unlawful for a cemetery authority, its officers, employees or agents, or a cemetery broker or salesman to represent that an endowment care fund or any other fund set up for maintaining care is perpetual or permanent.
(Added by renumbering Section 8747 by Stats. 1982, Ch. 897, Sec. 2.)

ARTICLE 6. Penalties [8785 - 8785.]
(Article 6 added by Stats. 1982, Ch. 897, Sec. 4.)

8785.
Any person, partnership, or corporation administering, managing, or having responsibility for endowment care or special care funds who violates the provisions of this chapter relating to the collection, investment, or use of those funds shall be punished either by imprisonment in a county jail for a period not exceeding six months or by fine not exceeding five hundred dollars ($500), or by both such imprisonment and fine, or by imprisonment pursuant to subdivision (h) of Section 1170 of the Penal Code for 16 months, or two or three years. If the violator is a cemetery licensee or the holder of a certificate of authority, he, she, or it shall be subject to disciplinary action as provided in

Article 6 (commencing with Section 7686) of Chapter 12 of Division 3 of the Business and Professions Code.
(Amended by Stats. 2018, Ch. 571, Sec. 35. (SB 1480) Effective January 1, 2019.)

CHAPTER 7. Abandonment [8825 - 8829]

(Chapter 7 added by Stats. 1957, Ch. 862.)

8825.

A city or county having a nonendowment care cemetery within its boundaries which threatens or endangers the health, safety, comfort or welfare of the public may, by resolution of its governing board, if not more than 10 human dead bodies have been interred therein for a period of five years immediately preceding the date of the resolution, declare the abandonment of the cemetery as a place of future interment, but shall permit interment therein of any person who is an owner of a plot in the cemetery on the date of adoption of the resolution or who otherwise has a right of interment in the cemetery which is vested on such date. The resolution may provide for the removal of such copings, improvements, and embellishments which the governing board finds to be a threat or danger to the health, safety, comfort, or welfare of the public.
(Amended by Stats. 1977, Ch. 288.)

8826.

The resolution for abandonment adopted under the provisions of this chapter shall specify and declare that at any time after the expiration of 60 days after the first publication of notice of declaration of intended abandonment, the city or county in which the cemetery is located will remove such copings, improvements, and embellishments which are found to be a threat or danger to the health, safety, comfort, or welfare of the public. Notice shall be given to all persons interested therein by publication in a newspaper of general circulation published in the county or city. Publication shall be pursuant to Section 6064 of the Government Code.
(Amended by Stats. 1959, Ch. 1241.)

8827.

After the publication mentioned in Section 8826 of this code and after the expiration of the 60 days specified in the notice, the city or county shall remove such copings, improvements, and embellishments which have been found to be a threat or danger to the health, safety, comfort, or welfare of the public.
(Amended by Stats. 1959, Ch. 1241.)

8828.

After the work which the governing body, in its discretion, finds necessary and practicable has been completed, the governing body shall immediately thereafter, by resolution, which shall contain a legal description of the cemetery, dedicate such abandoned cemetery as a pioneer memorial park and may cause to be erected a suitable central memorial honoring those who have been interred in the cemetery.
Upon recordation of the resolution with the county recorder of the county in which the cemetery is located, fee title to the cemetery shall vest in the city or county as the case may be. The governing body may bring an action to quiet title to the cemetery, and in the absence of fraud the resolution and the fact of recordation shall be conclusive evidence of fee title to the cemetery.
Any county or city acquiring fee title to a cemetery under this section shall only use the property for the purpose of establishing and maintaining a pioneer memorial park.
(Amended by Stats. 1970, Ch. 543.)

8829.

Thereafter the city or county shall maintain said pioneer memorial park so that it will not endanger the health, safety, comfort, or welfare of the public.
(Added by Stats. 1957, Ch. 862.)

PART 4. PUBLIC CEMETERY DISTRICTS [9000 - 9093]

(Part 4 repealed and added by Stats. 2003, Ch. 57, Sec. 5.)

CHAPTER 1. General Provisions [9000 - 9007]

(Chapter 1 added by Stats. 2003, Ch. 57, Sec. 5.)

9000.

This part shall be known and may be cited as the Public Cemetery District Law.
(Repealed and added by Stats. 2003, Ch. 57, Sec. 5. Effective January 1, 2004.)

9001.

(a) The Legislature finds and declares all of the following:
(1) There is a continuing need to provide for the respectful and cost-effective interment of human remains to meet the cultural, economic, religious, and social needs of California's diverse communities.
(2) The Legislature authorized the creation of public cemetery districts in 1909 to assume responsibility for the ownership, improvement, expansion, and operation of cemeteries and the provision of interment services from fraternal, pioneer, religious, social, and other organizations that were unable to provide for those cemeteries.
(3) For nearly a century, public cemetery districts have provided communities with the means to publicly finance the ownership, improvement, expansion, and operation of public cemeteries and the provision of interment services, particularly in rural and formerly rural communities.

(4) Interment customs and practices have changed since the creation of the public cemetery districts but communities continue to need the means to own, improve, expand, and operate public cemeteries that provide respectful and cost-effective interments.
(b) In enacting this part, it is the intent of the Legislature to create and continue a broad statutory authority for a class of special districts that can own, improve, expand, and operate public cemeteries that provide respectful and cost-effective interments.
(c) It is also the intent of the Legislature that local officials adapt the powers and procedures provided by this part to meet the diversity of local conditions and circumstances.
(Repealed and added by Stats. 2003, Ch. 57, Sec. 5. Effective January 1, 2004.)

9002.

The definitions in Chapter 1 (commencing with Section 7000) of Part 1 of Division 7 apply to this part. Further, as used in this part, the following terms have the following meanings:
(a) "Active militia" means the active militia as defined by Section 120 of the Military and Veterans Code.
(b) "Armed services" means the armed services as defined by Section 18540 of the Government Code.
(c) "Board of trustees" means the legislative body of a district.
(d) "District" means a public cemetery district created pursuant to this part or any of its statutory predecessors.
(e) "Domestic partner" means two adults who have chosen to share one another's lives in an intimate and committed relationship of mutual caring, and are qualified and registered with the Secretary of State as domestic partners in accordance with Division 2.5 (commencing with Section 297) of the Family Code.
(f) "Family member" means any spouse, by marriage or otherwise, domestic partner, child or stepchild, by natural birth or adoption, parent, brother, sister, half-brother, half-sister, parent-in-law, brother-in-law, sister-in-law, nephew, niece, aunt, uncle, first cousin, or any person denoted by the prefix "grand" or "great", or the spouse of any of these persons.
(g) "Firefighter" means a firefighter as defined by Section 1797.182.
(h) (1) "Interment right" means the rights held by the owner to use or control the use of a plot authorized by this part, for the interment of human remains, including both of the following rights:
(A) To determine the number and identity of any person or persons to be interred in the plot within a cemetery in conformance with all applicable regulations adopted by the cemetery district.
(B) To control the placement, design, wording, and removal of memorial markers in compliance with all applicable regulations adopted by the cemetery district.
(2) An interment right is a transferable property interest, and is governed by Chapter 5.5 (commencing with Section 9069.10).
(i) "Nonresident" means a person who does not reside within a district or does not pay property taxes on property located in a district.
(j) "Peace officer" means a peace officer as defined by Section 830 of the Penal Code.
(k) "Principal county" means the county having all or the greater portion of the entire assessed value, as shown on the last equalized assessment roll of the county or counties, of all taxable property within a district.
(l) "Voter" means a voter as defined by Section 359 of the Elections Code.
(Amended by Stats. 2017, Ch. 561, Sec. 110. (AB 1516) Effective January 1, 2018.)

9003.

(a) This part provides the authority for the organization and powers of public cemetery districts. This part succeeds the former Part 4 (commencing with Section 8890), as added by Chapter 60 of the Statutes of 1939, as subsequently amended, and any of its statutory predecessors.
(b) Any public cemetery district formed pursuant to the former Part 4 or any of its statutory predecessors that was in existence on January 1, 2004, shall remain in existence as if it has been organized pursuant to this part.
(c) Any indebtedness, special tax, benefit assessment, fee, election, ordinance, resolution, regulation, rule, or any other action of a district taken pursuant to the former Part 4 or of any of its statutory predecessors which was taken before January 1, 2004, shall not be voided solely because of any error, omission, informality, misnomer, or failure to comply strictly with this part.
(Repealed and added by Stats. 2003, Ch. 57, Sec. 5. Effective January 1, 2004.)

9004.

This part is necessary to protect the public health, safety, and welfare, and shall be liberally construed to effectuate its purposes.
(Repealed and added by Stats. 2003, Ch. 57, Sec. 5. Effective January 1, 2004.)

9005.

If any provision of this part or the application of any provision of this part in any circumstance or to any person, city, county, special district, school district, the state, or any agency or subdivision of the state is held invalid, that invalidity shall not affect other provisions or applications of this part that can be given effect without the invalid provision or application of the invalid provision, and to this end the provisions of this part are severable.
(Repealed and added by Stats. 2003, Ch. 57, Sec. 5. Effective January 1, 2004.)

9006.

(a) Any action brought to determine the validity of the organization or of any action of a district shall be brought pursuant to Chapter 9 (commencing with Section 860) of Title 10 of Part 2 of the Code of Civil Procedure.

(b) Any judicial review of an action taken pursuant to this part shall be conducted pursuant to Chapter 2 (commencing with Section 1084) of Title 1 of Part 3 of the Code of Civil Procedure.

(Added by Stats. 2003, Ch. 57, Sec. 5. Effective January 1, 2004.)

9007.

(a) Except as provided in this section, territory, whether incorporated or unincorporated, whether contiguous or noncontiguous, may be included in a district. Territory that is already within a public cemetery district or another type of special district that provides cemetery facilities and services shall not be included within a public cemetery district.

(b) Except as provided in this part, the Cortese-Knox-Hertzberg Local Government Reorganization Act of 2000, Division 3 (commencing with Section 56000) of Title 5 of the Government Code, shall govern any change of organization or reorganization of a district. In the case of any conflict between that division and this part, the provisions of this part shall prevail.

(c) A district shall be deemed an "independent special district," as defined by Section 56044 of the Government Code, except when a county board of supervisors has appointed itself as the board of trustees.

(Added by Stats. 2003, Ch. 57, Sec. 5. Effective January 1, 2004.)

CHAPTER 2. Formation [9010 - 9014]

(Chapter 2 added by Stats. 2003, Ch. 57, Sec. 5.)

9010.

A new district may be formed pursuant to this chapter.

(Repealed and added by Stats. 2003, Ch. 57, Sec. 5. Effective January 1, 2004.)

9011.

(a) A proposal to form a new district may be made by petition. The petition shall do all of the things required by Section 56700 of the Government Code. In addition, the petition shall:

(1) Set forth the methods by which the district will be financed, including but not limited to special taxes, special benefit assessments, and fees.

(2) Propose a name for the district.

(3) Specify the size of the initial board of trustees and the method of their appointment.

(b) The petitions, the proponents, and the procedures for certifying the sufficiency of the petitions shall comply with Chapter 2 (commencing with Section 56700) of Part 3 of Division 3 of Title 5 of the Government Code. In the case of any conflict between that chapter and this chapter, the provisions of this chapter shall prevail.

(c) The petition shall be signed by not less than 25 percent of the registered voters residing in the area to be included in the district, as determined by the local agency formation commission.

(Added by Stats. 2003, Ch. 57, Sec. 5. Effective January 1, 2004.)

9012.

(a) Before circulating any petition, the proponents shall publish a notice of intention which shall include a written statement not to exceed 500 words in length, setting forth the reasons for forming the district and the methods by which the district will be financed. The notice shall be published pursuant to Section 6061 of the Government Code in one or more newspapers of general circulation within the territory proposed to be included in the district. If the territory proposed to be included in the district is located in more than one county, publication of the notice shall be made in at least one newspaper of general circulation in each of the counties.

(b) The following shall be signed by a representative of the proponent, and shall be in substantially the following form:

"Notice of Intent to Circulate Petition

"Notice is hereby given of the intention to circulate a petition proposing to form the _____ [name of the district]. The reasons for forming the proposed district are: _____. The method(s) by which the proposed district will be financed are: _____."

(c) Within five days after the date of publication, the proponents shall file with the executive officer of the local agency formation commission of the principal county a copy of the notice together with an affidavit made by a representative of the newspaper in which the notice was published certifying to the fact of the publication.

(d) After the filing required pursuant to subdivision (c), the petition may be circulated for signatures.

(Added by Stats. 2003, Ch. 57, Sec. 5. Effective January 1, 2004.)

9013.

(a) A proposal to form a new district may also be made by the adoption of a resolution of application by the legislative body of any county or city that contains the territory proposed to be included in the district. Except for the provisions regarding the signers, signatures, and the proponents, a resolution of application shall contain all of the matters specified for a petition in Section 9011.

(b) Before adopting a resolution of application, the legislative body shall hold a public hearing on the resolution. Notice of the hearing shall be published pursuant to Section 6061 of the Government Code in one or more newspapers of general circulation within the county or city. At least 20 days before the hearing, the legislative body shall give mailed notice of its hearing to the executive officer of the local agency formation commission of the principal county. The notice shall generally describe the proposed formation of the district and the territory proposed to be included in the district.

(c) At the hearing, the legislative body shall give any person an opportunity to present his or her views on the resolution.

(d) The clerk of the legislative body shall file a certified copy of the resolution of application with the executive officer of the local agency formation commission of the principal county.

(Added by Stats. 2003, Ch. 57, Sec. 5. Effective January 1, 2004.)

9014.

(a) Once the proponents have filed a sufficient petition or a legislative body has filed a resolution of application, the local agency formation commission shall proceed pursuant to Part 3 (commencing with Section 56650) of Division 3 of Title 5 of the Government Code.

(b) Notwithstanding any other provision of law, a local agency formation commission shall not approve a proposal that includes the formation of a district unless the commission determines both of the following:

(1) That the public interest requires the formation of the proposed district.

(2) That the proposed district will have sufficient revenues to carry out its purposes.

(c) Notwithstanding paragraph (2) of subdivision (b), a local agency formation commission may approve a proposal that includes the formation of a district where the commission has determined that the proposed district will not have sufficient revenue, provided that the commission conditions the approval on the approval by the voters of special taxes or approval by the property owners of special benefit assessments that will generate those sufficient revenues. The commission shall provide that if the voters do not approve the special taxes or if the property owners do not approve the special benefit assessments, the proposed district shall not be formed.

(d) If the local agency formation commission approves the proposal for the formation of a district, then, notwithstanding Section 57007 of the Government Code, the commission shall proceed pursuant to Part 4 (commencing with Section 57000) of Division 3 of Title 5 of the Government Code.

(e) Notwithstanding Section 57075 of the Government Code, the local agency formation commission shall take one of the following actions:

(1) If a majority protest exists in accordance with Section 57078 of the Government Code, the commission shall terminate proceedings.

(2) If no majority protest exists, the commission shall either:

(A) Order the formation subject to the approval by the voters.

(B) Order the formation subject to the approval by the voters of a special tax or the approval by the property owners of a special benefit assessment, pursuant to subdivision (c).

(f) If the local agency formation commission orders the formation of a district pursuant to paragraph (2) of subdivision (e), the commission shall direct the board of supervisors to direct county officials to conduct the necessary elections on behalf of the proposed district.

(Added by Stats. 2003, Ch. 57, Sec. 5. Effective January 1, 2004.)

CHAPTER 3. Board of Trustees [9020 - 9031]

(Chapter 3 added by Stats. 2003, Ch. 57, Sec. 5.)

9020.

A legislative body of at least three members known as the board of trustees shall govern every district. The board of trustees shall establish policies for the operation of the district. The board of trustees shall provide for the faithful implementation of those policies which is the responsibility of the employees of the district.

(Added by Stats. 2003, Ch. 57, Sec. 5. Effective January 1, 2004.)

9021.

Within 30 days after the effective date of the formation of a district, a board of trustees shall be appointed as follows:

(a) In the case of a district that contains territory in a single county, the board of supervisors shall appoint three or five persons to the board of trustees.

(b) In the case of a district that contains territory in more than one county, the board of supervisors of the principal county shall appoint three or five persons from any county in which the district is located to the board of trustees.

(Added by Stats. 2003, Ch. 57, Sec. 5. Effective January 1, 2004.)

9022.

(a) Each person appointed by a board of supervisors to be a member of a board of trustees shall be a voter in the district.

(b) All trustees shall exercise their independent judgment on behalf of the interests of the residents, property owners, and the public as a whole in furthering the purposes and intent of this part. The trustees shall represent the interests of the public as a whole and not solely the interests of the board of supervisors that appointed them.

(Added by Stats. 2003, Ch. 57, Sec. 5. Effective January 1, 2004.)

9023.

(a) The initial board of trustees of a district formed on or after January 1, 2004, shall be determined pursuant to this section.

(b) The persons appointed to the initial board of trustees shall meet on the first Monday after 45 days after the effective date of the formation of the district.

(c) At the first meeting of the initial board of trustees, the trustees shall classify themselves by lot into two classes, as nearly equal as possible. The term of office of the class having the greater number shall expire at noon on the first Monday in January that is closest to the fourth year from the appointments made pursuant to Section 9021. The term of office of the class having the lesser number shall expire at noon on the first Monday in January that is closest to the second year from the appointments made pursuant to Section 9021.

(Added by Stats. 2003, Ch. 57, Sec. 5. Effective January 1, 2004.)

9024.

(a) Except as provided in subdivision (b) of this section, subdivision (c) of Section 9023, and subdivision (d) of Section 9026, the term of office for a member of the board of trustees shall be for a term of four years and until the appointment and qualification of the successor. Terms of office commence at noon on the first Monday in January.

(b) For districts formed before January 1, 2004, where the members of the board of trustees are not serving staggered terms, the board of supervisors shall stagger the terms of the trustees and to accomplish this purpose shall appoint trustees, on or after January 1, 2004, for terms of less than four years. However, a board of supervisors shall not reduce the term of office of a trustee once the trustee has been appointed to that term, whether the appointment was made before, on, or after January 1, 2004.

(c) Any vacancy in the office of a member appointed to a board of trustees shall be filled promptly pursuant to Section 1779 of the Government Code. Any person appointed to fill a vacant office shall fill the balance of the unexpired term.

(Added by Stats. 2003, Ch. 57, Sec. 5. Effective January 1, 2004.)

9025.

(a) A board of trustees may adopt a resolution requesting the board of supervisors of the principal county to increase or decrease the number of members of the board of trustees. The resolution shall specify the number of members for which the board of trustees requests the increase or decrease.

(b) Within 60 days of receiving a resolution adopted pursuant to subdivision (a), the board of supervisors shall consider the resolution at a public hearing. The board of supervisors shall give notice of its hearing by publishing a notice pursuant to Section 6061 of the Government Code in at least one newspaper of general circulation within the jurisdiction of the district at least 10 days before the hearing. In addition, the board of supervisors shall mail the notice at least 10 days before the hearing to the district and any other person who has filed written request for notice with the clerk of the board of supervisors.

(c) At its hearing, the board of supervisors shall receive and consider any written or oral comments regarding the resolution. After receiving and considering those comments, the board of supervisors may adopt a resolution that orders the increase or decrease in the number of members of the board of trustees.

(d) If the board of supervisors adopts a resolution that orders an increase in the number of members of the board of trustees, the board of supervisors shall promptly appoint a person or persons to the board of trustees and specify their term of office, consistent with the requirements of this part. If the board of supervisors adopts a resolution that orders a decrease in the number of members of the board of trustees, the board of supervisors shall designate the trustee or trustees whose office shall be eliminated at the termination of the trustee's current term of office. Any trustee whose office is designated to be eliminated shall continue to serve until his or her term expires.

(Repealed and added by Stats. 2003, Ch. 57, Sec. 5. Effective January 1, 2004.)

9026.

(a) The board of supervisors of the principal county may appoint itself to be the board of trustees of a district and the board of supervisors may divest itself of that authority, pursuant to this section.

(b) In the case of a district that has a board of trustees appointed by the board of supervisors, the board of supervisors may adopt a resolution declaring its intention to appoint itself to be the board of trustees of the district. In the case of a district where the board of supervisors has appointed itself to be the board of trustees, the board of supervisors may adopt a resolution declaring its intention to divest itself of that authority.

(c) Within 60 days of adopting a resolution adopted pursuant to subdivision (b), the board of supervisors shall hold a public hearing on the question whether the board of supervisors should govern the district. The board of supervisors shall give notice of its hearing by publishing a notice pursuant to Section 6061 of the Government Code in at least one newspaper of general circulation within the jurisdiction of the district at least 10 days before the hearing. In addition, the board of supervisors shall mail the notice at least 10 days before the hearing to the district and any other person who has filed written request for notice with the clerk of the board of supervisors.

(d) At its hearing, the board of supervisors shall receive and consider any written or oral comments regarding a resolution adopted pursuant to subdivision (b). At the conclusion of the hearing, the board of supervisors shall make a finding regarding the value of written protests filed and not withdrawn and take one of the following actions:

(1) In the case of a district that has a board of trustees appointed by the board of supervisors:

(A) If the written protests filed and not withdrawn are less than 10 percent of the registered voters of the district, the board of supervisors may by a majority vote adopt a resolution terminating the appointed board of trustees and appointing itself as the board of trustees of the district. In that case, the terms of any trustees appointed by the board of supervisors shall terminate immediately.

(B) If the written protests filed and not withdrawn are 10 percent or more of the registered voters of the district, the board of supervisors may determine that the proposed change in governance is necessary to protect the public health, safety, and welfare. If the board of supervisors makes that determination, the board of supervisors may override those protests and by a four-fifths vote adopt a resolution terminating the appointed board of trustees and appointing itself as the board of trustees of the district. In that case, the terms of any trustees appointed by the board of supervisors shall terminate immediately.

(C) If the written protests filed and not withdrawn are 10 percent or more of the registered voters of the district and if the board of supervisors does not adopt a

resolution pursuant to paragraph (B), the board of supervisors shall adopt a resolution that terminates the proceedings to change the governance of the district.

(2) In the case of a district where the board of supervisors has appointed itself to be the board of trustees:

(A) If the written protests filed and not withdrawn are less than 10 percent of the registered voters of the district, the board of supervisors may by a majority vote adopt a resolution divesting itself of that authority. In that case, the board of supervisors shall promptly appoint persons as members of the board of trustees pursuant to this part.

(B) If the written protests filed and not withdrawn are 10 percent or more of the registered voters of the district, the board of supervisors may determine that the proposed change in governance is necessary to protect the public health, safety, and welfare. If the board of supervisors makes that determination, the board of supervisors may override those protests and by a four-fifths vote adopt a resolution divesting itself of that authority. In that case, the board of supervisors shall promptly appoint persons as members of the board of trustees pursuant to this part.

(C) If the written protests filed and not withdrawn are 10 percent or more of the registered voters of the district and if the board of supervisors does not adopt a resolution pursuant to paragraph (B), the board of supervisors shall adopt a resolution that terminates the proceedings to change the governance of the district.

(Added by Stats. 2003, Ch. 57, Sec. 5. Effective January 1, 2004.)

9027.

(a) A local agency formation commission, in approving either a consolidation of districts or the reorganization of two or more districts into a single district, may, pursuant to subdivisions (k) and (n) of Section 56886 of the Government Code, change the number of members on the board of trustees of the consolidated or reorganized district, provided that the resulting number of trustees shall be an odd number but not less than five.

(b) Upon the expiration of the terms of the members of the board of trustees of the consolidated or reorganized district whose terms first expire following the effective date of the consolidation or reorganization, the total number of members on the board of trustees shall be reduced until the number equals the number of members determined by the local agency formation commission.

(c) Notwithstanding subdivision (c) of Section 9024, in the event of a vacancy on the board of trustees of the consolidated or reorganized district at a time when the number of members of the board of trustees is greater than the number determined by the local agency formation commission, the vacancy shall not be filled and the membership of the board of trustees shall be reduced by one member.

(Added by Stats. 2003, Ch. 57, Sec. 5. Effective January 1, 2004.)

9028.

(a) At the first meeting of the initial board of trustees of a newly formed district, and in the case of an existing district not later than the first meeting of every calendar year, the board of trustees shall elect its officers.

(b) The officers of a board of trustees are a chairperson, vice chairperson, and a secretary. The chairperson and vice chairperson shall be trustees. The secretary may be either a trustee or a district employee. A board of trustees may create additional officers and elect members to those positions. No trustee shall hold more than one office.

(c) Except as provided in Section 9077, the county treasurer of the principal county shall act as the district treasurer. The county treasurer shall receive no compensation for the receipt and disbursement of money of the district.

(Added by Stats. 2003, Ch. 57, Sec. 5. Effective January 1, 2004.)

9029.

A board of trustees shall meet at least once every three months. Meetings of the board of trustees are subject to the provisions of the Ralph M. Brown Act, Chapter 9 (commencing with Section 54950) of Part 1 of Division 2 of Title 5 of the Government Code.

(Added by Stats. 2003, Ch. 57, Sec. 5. Effective January 1, 2004.)

9030.

(a) A majority of the board of trustees shall constitute a quorum for the transaction of business.

(b) Except as otherwise specifically provided to the contrary in this part, a recorded vote of a majority of the total membership of the board of trustees is required on each action.

(c) The board of trustees shall act only by ordinance, resolution, or motion.

(d) The board of trustees shall keep a record of all of its acts, including financial transactions.

(e) The board of trustees shall adopt rules for its proceedings.

(Added by Stats. 2003, Ch. 57, Sec. 5. Effective January 1, 2004.)

9031.

(a) The board of trustees may provide, by ordinance or resolution, that each of its members may receive compensation in an amount not to exceed one hundred dollars ($100) for attending each meeting of the board. A member of the board of trustees shall not receive compensation for more than six meetings of the board in a calendar month. Commencing January 1, 2019, if the district compensates its members for more than four meetings in a calendar month, the board of trustees shall annually adopt a written policy describing, based on a finding supported by substantial evidence, why more than four meetings per calendar month are necessary for the effective operation of the district.

(b) The board of trustees, by ordinance adopted pursuant to Chapter 2 (commencing with Section 20200) of Division 10 of the Water Code, may increase the amount of compensation received for attending meetings of the board.

(c) In addition, members of the board of trustees may receive their actual and necessary traveling and incidental expenses incurred while on official business other than a meeting of the board.

(d) A member of the board of trustees may waive any or all of the payments permitted by this section.

(e) For the purposes of this section, a meeting of the board of trustees includes, but is not limited to, regular meetings, special meetings, closed sessions, emergency meetings, board field trips, district public hearings, or meetings of a committee of the board.

(f) For purposes of this section, the determination of whether a trustee's activities on any specific day are compensable shall be made pursuant to Article 2.3 (commencing with Section 53232) of Chapter 2 of Part 1 of Division 2 of Title 5 of the Government Code.

(g) Reimbursement for these expenses is subject to Sections 53232.2 and 53232.3 of the Government Code.

(Amended by Stats. 2018, Ch. 170, Sec. 1. (AB 2329) Effective January 1, 2019.)

CHAPTER 4. Powers [9040 - 9056]

(Chapter 4 added by Stats. 2003, Ch. 57, Sec. 5.)

9040.

(a) A district may own, operate, improve, and maintain cemeteries and provide interment services within its boundaries.

(b) A district shall maintain the cemeteries owned by the district.

(c) The district that owns a cemetery shall have exclusive jurisdiction and control over its maintenance and management.

(Added by Stats. 2003, Ch. 57, Sec. 5. Effective January 1, 2004.)

9041.

A district shall have and may exercise all rights and powers, expressed or implied, necessary to carry out the purposes and intent of this part, including, but not limited to, all of the following powers:

(a) To sue and be sued.

(b) To acquire by purchase, eminent domain, grant, gift, lease, or other lawful means, any real property within the district or any personal property that may be necessary or proper to carry out the purposes and intent of this part.

(c) To sell, lease, or otherwise dispose of any real or personal property. A board of trustees may exchange equivalent properties if the board determines that the exchange is in the best interests of the district.

(d) To donate any surplus real or personal property to any public agency or nonprofit organizations.

(e) To engage necessary employees, to define their qualifications and duties, and to provide a schedule of compensation for performance of their duties.

(f) To engage counsel and other professional services.

(g) To enter into and perform all necessary contracts.

(h) To borrow money, give security therefore, and purchase on contract, as provided in this part.

(i) To adopt a seal and alter it at pleasure.

(j) To adopt ordinances following the procedures of Article 7 (commencing with Section 25120) of Chapter 1 of Part 2 of Division 2 of Title 3 of the Government Code.

(k) To adopt and enforce rules and regulations for the administration, maintenance, operation, and use of cemeteries.

(l) To enter joint powers agreements pursuant to the Joint Exercise of Powers Act, Chapter 5 (commencing with Section 6500) of Division 7 of Title 1 of the Government Code.

(m) To provide insurance pursuant to Part 6 (commencing with Section 989) of Division 3.6 of Title 1 of the Government Code.

(n) To provide training to trustees that will assist in the governance of the district.

(o) To appoint one or more advisory committees to make recommendations for the ownership, improvement, expansion, and the operation of cemeteries owned by the district and the provision of interment services.

(p) To take any and all actions necessary for, or incidental to, the powers expressed or implied by this part.

(Added by Stats. 2003, Ch. 57, Sec. 5. Effective January 1, 2004.)

9042.

(a) When acquiring, improving, or using any real property, a district shall comply with Article 5 (commencing with Section 53090) of Chapter 1 of Part 1 of Division 2 of Title 5 and Article 7 (commencing with Section 65400) of Chapter 1 of Division 1 of Title 7 of the Government Code.

(b) When disposing of surplus land, a district shall comply with Article 8 (commencing with Section 54220) of Chapter 5 of Part 1 of Division 2 of Title 5 of the Government Code.

(Added by Stats. 2003, Ch. 57, Sec. 5. Effective January 1, 2004.)

9043.

(a) A district shall have perpetual succession.

(b) A board of trustees may, by a two-thirds vote of its total membership, adopt a resolution to change the name of the district. The name shall contain the words "public cemetery district" or "cemetery district." The resolution shall comply with the requirements of Chapter 23 (commencing with Section 7530) of Division 7 of Title 2 of the Government Code. Within 10 days of its adoption, the board of trustees shall file a copy of its resolution with the Secretary of State, the county clerk, the board of supervisors, and the local agency formation commission of each county in which the district is located.

(c) A district may destroy a record, paper, or document pursuant to Chapter 7 (commencing with Section 60200) of Division 1 of Title 6 of the Government Code, unless the board of trustees determines that there is a need for its retention. In determining whether there is a need for retaining a document, the board of trustees shall consider future public need, the effect on statutes of limitation, and historical significance. This subdivision does not apply to records of interments that are governed by Section 9064.

(Added by Stats. 2003, Ch. 57, Sec. 5. Effective January 1, 2004.)

9044.

(a) Each district shall adopt policies and procedures, including bidding regulations, governing the purchase of supplies and equipment. Each district shall adopt these policies and procedures by rule or regulation pursuant to Article 7 (commencing with Section 54201) of Chapter 5 of Division 2 of Title 5 of the Government Code.

(b) A district may request the Department of General Services to make purchases of materials, equipment, or supplies on its behalf pursuant to Section 10298 of the Public Contract Code.

(c) A district may request the purchasing agent of the principal county to make purchases of materials, equipment, or supplies on its behalf pursuant to Article 7 (commencing with Section 25500) of Chapter 5 of Division 2 of Title 3 of the Government Code.

(d) A district may request the purchasing agent of the principal county to contract with persons to provide projects, services, and programs authorized by this part pursuant to Article 7 (commencing with Section 25500) of Chapter 5 of Division 2 of Title 3 of the Government Code.

(Added by Stats. 2003, Ch. 57, Sec. 5. Effective January 1, 2004.)

9045.

(a) The Myers-Milias-Brown Act, Chapter 10 (commencing with Section 3500) of Division 4 of Title 1 of the Government Code applies to all districts.

(b) A board of trustees may adopt an ordinance establishing an employee relations system that may include, but is not limited to, a civil service system or a merit system.

(Added by Stats. 2003, Ch. 57, Sec. 5. Effective January 1, 2004.)

9046.

A board of trustees may require any employee or officer to be bonded. The district shall pay the cost of the bonds.

(Added by Stats. 2003, Ch. 57, Sec. 5. Effective January 1, 2004.)

9047.

A board of trustees may provide for any programs for the benefit of its employees and members of the board of trustees pursuant to Chapter 2 (commencing with Section 53200) of Part 1 of Division 2 of Title 5 of the Government Code.

(Added by Stats. 2003, Ch. 57, Sec. 5. Effective January 1, 2004.)

9048.

A district may authorize the members of its board of trustees and its employees to attend professional, educational, or vocational meetings, and pay their actual and necessary traveling and incidental expenses while on official business. The payment of expenses pursuant to this section may be in addition to the payments made pursuant to Section 9031.

(Added by Stats. 2003, Ch. 57, Sec. 5. Effective January 1, 2004.)

9049.

A district may sell interment rights in its cemeteries, columbariums, and mausoleums, subject to the limitations of this part.

(Added by Stats. 2003, Ch. 57, Sec. 5. Effective January 1, 2004.)

9050.

(a) A district may acquire, construct, improve, maintain, or repair a columbarium for the placement of cremated remains.

(b) A district shall comply with the Mausoleum and Columbarium Law, Part 5 (commencing with Section 9501).

(c) A district that sells interment rights in a columbarium shall require a deposit to be made in the endowment care fund pursuant to Section 9065.

(Added by Stats. 2003, Ch. 57, Sec. 5. Effective January 1, 2004.)

9051.

(a) A district may acquire, maintain, or repair a mausoleum for crypt entombment that was completed on or before May 1, 1937. A district may construct additions to the mausoleum.

(b) Notwithstanding subdivision (a), the Visalia Public Cemetery District may acquire and manage the mausoleum originally constructed by the City of Visalia in 1965.

(c) Notwithstanding subdivision (a), the Arroyo Grande Cemetery District may allow a private mausoleum, as defined by Section 9504.5. The cost of construction and maintenance shall be completely borne by the person or persons for whom the private mausoleum is constructed. That person or persons shall contribute to a special care trust fund an amount of money that, when invested, will provide a return sufficient to assure adequate maintenance of the private mausoleum. The district shall not use public funds to construct, maintain, or repair a private mausoleum.

(d) Notwithstanding subdivision (a), a district may allow a private mausoleum, as defined by Section 9504.5, if the mausoleum was completed on or before January 1, 2003.

(e) A district shall comply with the Mausoleum and Columbarium Law, Part 5 (commencing with Section 9501).

(Added by Stats. 2003, Ch. 57, Sec. 5. Effective January 1, 2004.)

9052.

(a) A district may require that monuments or markers shall be placed at interment plots.

(b) A district may adopt minimum requirements for the permanency of monuments or markers.

(c) A district may cause to be purchased and placed suitable permanent monuments or markers at the interment plots of indigents, persons whose estates are insufficient to pay for the monuments or markers, or persons who have no responsible survivors to pay for the monuments or markers. A district may accept gifts or donations for the exclusive purpose of purchasing and placing these monuments or markers.

(d) A district, a member of the board of trustees, a district officer, or a district employee shall not engage in the business of selling monuments or markers.

(Added by Stats. 2003, Ch. 57, Sec. 5. Effective January 1, 2004.)

9053.

A district may sell accessory and replacement objects that are necessary or convenient to interments, including but not limited to burial vaults, liners, and flower vases, but excluding monuments or markers.

(Added by Stats. 2003, Ch. 57, Sec. 5. Effective January 1, 2004.)

9054.

(a) A district may use or lease land acquired for a future cemetery for an enterprise if all of the following conditions apply:

(1) The district has filed with the county recorder a declaration of intention to use the land for a cemetery.

(2) The amount of land is reasonably necessary for the district's future requirements.

(3) The enterprise is consistent with the applicable regulations of the city or county in which the land is located.

(4) The enterprise does not permit the conduct of funeral or cemetery functions not authorized by this part.

(5) The enterprise does not prevent the future use of the land as a cemetery.

(b) A district may lease land acquired for future cemetery use to a public agency for recreational use, provided that the district has filed with the county recorder a declaration of intention to use the land for a cemetery.

(c) Nothing in this part authorizes a district to acquire or retain real property that is not reasonably necessary for the district's future requirements.

(Added by Stats. 2003, Ch. 57, Sec. 5. Effective January 1, 2004.)

9055.

(a) A district may convey a cemetery owned by the district to any cemetery authority, pursuant to this section.

(b) The board of trustees of a district that proposes to convey a cemetery owned by the district to a cemetery authority shall adopt a resolution of intention that contains:

(1) A description of the cemetery that the district proposes to convey.

(2) The name of the cemetery authority to which the district proposes to convey the cemetery.

(3) An appendix that reports the cemetery's current assets and current liabilities and contains a reasonable projection of the district's ability to finance the ownership, improvement, expansion, and operation of the cemetery in the future.

(4) The terms and conditions of the proposed conveyance. The terms and conditions shall require all of the following:

(A) The cemetery authority maintain the cemetery as a endowment care cemetery pursuant to Sections 8738 and 8738.1.

(B) Appropriate consideration, as determined by the board of trustees.

(C) A restriction in the deed that conveys the cemetery to the cemetery authority that will permit the district or another public agency as the district's successor in interest to enter the cemetery and perform any repairs, restoration, or maintenance that the district or its successor deems necessary to protect the public interest, and will require the cemetery authority to reimburse the district or its successor for those costs.

(D) Any other terms and conditions that the board of trustees determines to be necessary to protect the public interest in the cemetery.

(5) A declaration that the proposed conveyance is in the public interest and in the best interests of the district.

(c) The board of trustees shall send its resolution of intention to the board of supervisors of the principal county.

(d) Within 60 days of receiving a resolution of intention adopted pursuant to subdivision (b), the board of supervisors shall hold a public hearing on the proposed conveyance. The board of supervisors shall give notice of its hearing by publishing a notice pursuant to Section 6064 of the Government Code in at least one newspaper of general circulation within the jurisdiction of the district with the first day of publication at least 30 days before the hearing. The board of supervisors shall post the public notice in at least three public places within the jurisdiction of the district, at least 30 days before the hearing. One of the public places shall be at the cemetery that the district proposes to convey, and one of the public places shall be at the offices of the district. In addition, the board of supervisors shall mail the notice at least 30 days before the hearing to the district, the cemetery authority, and any other person who has filed written request for notice with the clerk of the board of supervisors.

(e) At its hearing, the board of supervisors shall receive and consider any written or oral comments regarding the proposed conveyance of the cemetery. At the conclusion of the hearing, the board of supervisors shall make a finding regarding the value of written protests filed and not withdrawn and take one of the following actions:

(1) If the written protests filed and not withdrawn are at least 50 percent of the registered voters of the district or property owners owning at least 50 percent of the assessed value of the land within the district, the board of supervisors shall adopt a resolution that terminates the proceedings to convey the cemetery.

(2) If the written protests filed and not withdrawn are less than 50 percent of the registered voters of the district or property owners owning less than 50 percent of the assessed value of the land within the district, the board of supervisors may by a four-fifths vote adopt a resolution that concurs in the conveyance of the cemetery to the cemetery authority.

(f) The board of supervisors shall send copies of its resolution adopted pursuant to subdivision (e) to the district and the cemetery authority.

(g) If the board of supervisors adopts a resolution that concurs in the proposed conveyance of the cemetery, the board of trustees may order the conveyance of the cemetery to the cemetery authority, subject to the terms and conditions set by the board of trustees and concurred in by the board of supervisors.

(Added by Stats. 2003, Ch. 57, Sec. 5. Effective January 1, 2004.)

9056.

(a) A district may dedicate real property or an interest in real property owned by the district to another public agency for use as roads or utility rights-of-way, including but not limited to water, sewer, drainage, gas or electricity transmission, or communications purposes, pursuant to this section.

(b) The board of trustees of a district that proposes to dedicate real property or an interest in real property owned by the district to another public agency shall adopt a resolution of intention that contains:

(1) A description of the real property or interest in real property.

(2) The name of the public agency to which the district proposes to dedicate the property.

(3) The terms and conditions, including any consideration, of the proposed dedication.

(4) Findings, based on substantial evidence in the record:

(A) That the real property has never been used for interments.

(B) That no interment rights have been sold or leased for the real property.

(C) That the district does not need the property for cemetery purposes.

(5) A statement of the reason or reasons for the proposed dedication.

(6) A declaration that the proposed dedication is in the public interest and in the best interests of the district.

(c) Within 60 days of adopting a resolution of intention pursuant to subdivision (b), the board of trustees shall hold a public hearing on the proposed dedication. The board of trustees shall give notice of its hearing by publishing a notice pursuant to Section 6061 of the Government Code in at least one newspaper of general circulation within the jurisdiction of the district at least 10 days before the hearing. The board of trustees shall post the public notice in at least three public places within the jurisdiction of the district, at least 10 days before the hearing. One of the public places shall be at the real property that the district proposes to dedicate, and one of the public places shall be at the offices of the district. In addition, the board of trustees shall mail the notice at least 10 days before the hearing to the other public agency and any other person who has filed written request for notice with the board of trustees.

(d) If the board of trustees adopts a resolution that dedicates the real property to another public agency, the board of trustees shall promptly execute a deed of dedication and send the deed to the other public agency. The dedication is effective when the other public agency records the deed of dedication with the county recorder of the county in which the real property is located.

(Added by Stats. 2003, Ch. 57, Sec. 5. Effective January 1, 2004.)

CHAPTER 5. Interments [9060 - 9069]

(Chapter 5 added by Stats. 2003, Ch. 57, Sec. 5.)

9060.

(a) A district shall limit interment in a cemetery owned by the district to interment in the ground, in columbariums, and in mausoleums, as provided in this part.

(b) A district shall limit interments to:

(1) Persons who are residents of the district.

(2) Persons who are former residents of the district and who acquired interment rights while they were residents of the district.

(3) Persons who pay property taxes on property located in the district.

(4) Persons who formerly paid property taxes on property located in the district and who acquired interment rights while they paid those property taxes.

(5) Eligible nonresidents of the district, as provided in this chapter.

(6) Persons who are family members of any person described in this subdivision.

(Added by Stats. 2003, Ch. 57, Sec. 5. Effective January 1, 2004.)

9061.

(a) A district may inter a person who is not a resident of the district or a person who does not pay property taxes on property located in the district in a cemetery owned by the district if all of the following apply:

(1) The district has an endowment care fund that requires at least the minimum payment set pursuant to Section 9065.

(2) The district requires the payment of a nonresident fee set pursuant to Section 9068. A board of trustees may adopt a written policy that permits waiving the payment of the nonresident fee for a nonresident who had purchased an interment right while a resident or a taxpayer.

(3) The person meets the conditions listed in one or more of subdivisions (b) through (e).

(b) A person is an eligible nonresident pursuant to paragraph (5) of subdivision (b) of Section 9060 if the person is a family member of a person who is already interred in a cemetery owned by the district or is a family member of a person who has acquired interment rights in a cemetery owned by a district.

(c) A person is an eligible nonresident pursuant to paragraph (5) of subdivision (b) of Section 9060 if all of the following apply:

(1) The person was a resident of the district or paid property taxes on property located in the district for continuous period of at least five years, a portion of which time period shall have occurred within the 10 years immediately before the person's death.

(2) The district receives a written request for the interment of the person from a person who is a resident of the district or who pays property taxes on property located within the district, and the person submitting the written request is not a trustee, officer, or employee of the district and is not a funeral director or an employee of a funeral director.

(3) The board of trustees determines that the cemetery has adequate space for the foreseeable future.

(d) A person is an eligible nonresident pursuant to paragraph (5) of subdivision (b) of Section 9060 if all of the following apply:

(1) The person was a resident of this state at the time of death.

(2) There is no private cemetery within a straight-line radius of 15 miles of the person's residence.

(3) There is no private cemetery nearer to the person's residence than the nearest cemetery owned by the district.

(4) The distances shall be measured in a straight line from the person's residence to the nearest private cemetery and the nearest cemetery owned by the district.

(e) A person is an eligible nonresident pursuant to paragraph (5) of subdivision (b) of Section 9060 if all of the following apply:

(1) The person died while either:

(A) Serving in the Armed Forces or the active militia, or

(B) In the line of duty as a peace officer or firefighter.

(2) The board of trustees determines that the cemetery has adequate space for the foreseeable future.

(Added by Stats. 2003, Ch. 57, Sec. 5. Effective January 1, 2004.)

9062.

Notwithstanding Section 9060, the board of trustees may contract with any county in which the district is located to inter persons for whose interment the county is responsible pursuant to Chapter 10 (commencing with Section 27460) of Division 2 of Title 3 of the Government Code or Chapter 3 (commencing with Section 7100) of Part 1 of Division 7 of this code, if all of the following apply:

(a) The board of trustees determines that the cemetery has adequate space for the foreseeable future.

(b) The district has an endowment care fund that requires at least the minimum payment set pursuant to Section 9065.

(c) The contract requires the county to pay the costs of the interment, including a payment to the district's endowment care fund.

(Added by Stats. 2003, Ch. 57, Sec. 5. Effective January 1, 2004.)

9063.

Notwithstanding Section 9060, the Oroville Cemetery District may use its cemetery on Feather River Boulevard, north of Oro Dam Boulevard for up to a total of 100 interments, for interment in the ground of any person who is not a resident of the district if all of the following apply:

(a) The board of trustees determines that the cemetery has adequate space for the foreseeable future.

(b) The district has an endowment care fund that requires at least the minimum payment set pursuant to Section 9065.

(c) The district requires the payment of a nonresident fee set pursuant to Section 9068.

(Added by Stats. 2003, Ch. 57, Sec. 5. Effective January 1, 2004.)

9063.3.

Notwithstanding Sections 9060 and 9061, the Happy Homestead Cemetery District located in the City of South Lake Tahoe in the County of El Dorado may inter residents of the Nevada communities of Glenbrook, Cave Rock, Skyland, Zephyr Cove, Round Hill, Elk Point, Kingsbury, and Stateline in the cemeteries in the district if all of the following apply:

(a) The Happy Homestead Cemetery District Board of Trustees determines that the district's cemeteries have adequate space for the foreseeable future.

(b) The district has an endowment care fund that requires a contribution for every interment of at least the minimum amount set pursuant to Sections 8738, 9065, and 9068.

(c) The district requires the payment of a nonresident fee set pursuant to Section 9068.

(Added by Stats. 2016, Ch. 242, Sec. 1. (AB 1658) Effective January 1, 2017.)

9063.5.

Notwithstanding Section 9060, the Elsinore Valley Cemetery District may use the portion of its cemetery formerly known as Home of Peace for up to a total of 536 interments, for interment in the ground of any person who meets the criteria for burial in that area but is not a resident of the district if all of the following apply:

(a) The board of trustees determines that the cemetery has adequate space for the foreseeable future.

(b) The district has an endowment care fund that requires at least the minimum payment set pursuant to Section 9065.

(c) The district requires the payment of a nonresident fee set pursuant to Section 9068.

(Added by Stats. 2010, Ch. 40, Sec. 1. (AB 1969) Effective January 1, 2011.)

9063.7.

Notwithstanding Section 9060, the Davis Cemetery District may use its cemetery at 820 Pole Line Road, Davis, for up to a total of 500 interments, for interment in the ground of any person who is not a resident or a property taxpayer of the district if all of the following apply:

(a) The board of trustees determines that the cemetery has adequate space for the foreseeable future.

(b) The district has an endowment care fund that requires at least the minimum payment set pursuant to Section 9065.

(c) The district requires the payment of a nonresident fee set pursuant to Section 9068.

(Added by Stats. 2011, Ch. 111, Sec. 1. (AB 966) Effective January 1, 2012.)

9063.9.

Notwithstanding Sections 9060 and 9061, the Cottonwood Cemetery District in Shasta County, the Anderson Cemetery District in Shasta County, the Halcumb Cemetery District in Shasta County, the Kern River Valley Cemetery District in Kern County, and the Silveyville Cemetery District in Solano County may use their cemeteries for up to a total of 400 interments each, not to exceed 40 interments each per calendar year, for interment in the ground or a columbarium of any person who is not a resident or a property taxpayer of any cemetery district, and who does not qualify for that interment pursuant to Section 9061, if all of the following apply:

(a) The board of trustees determines that the district's cemetery has adequate space for the foreseeable future.

(b) The district has an endowment care fund that requires a contribution for every interment of at least the minimum amount set pursuant to Sections 8738 and 9065.

(c) The district requires the payment of a nonresident fee set pursuant to Section 9068.

(Amended by Stats. 2014, Ch. 276, Sec. 1. (SB 1291) Effective January 1, 2015.)

9064.

(a) The board of trustees shall cause to be prepared and maintained accurate and current records of:

(1) The cemeteries owned by the district, showing the location of the sites where persons have acquired interment rights, including the names and addresses of the persons who have acquired these interment rights, and the location of plots where interment rights are available for acquisition.

(2) All remains interred in cemeteries owned by the district, including the name of each person, his or her age at the time of death, place of death, date of interment, the interment plot, and the name and address of the funeral director.

(b) A district may keep the records required by this section in their original form or by any other method that can produce an accurate reproduction of the original record.

(Added by Stats. 2003, Ch. 57, Sec. 5. Effective January 1, 2004.)

9065.

(a) The board of trustees shall create an endowment care fund.

(b) The board of trustees shall require a payment into the endowment care fund for each interment right sold. The amount of the payment shall be not less than the minimum amounts set by Section 8738.

(c) The board of trustees may require a payment into the endowment care fund for each interment where no payment has previously been made. The amount of the payment shall be not less than the minimum amounts set by Section 8738.

(d) The board of trustees may pay into the endowment care fund any money from the district's general fund and from any other sources which is necessary or expedient to provide for the endowment care of the cemeteries owned by the district.

(e) The board of trustees shall not spend the principal of the endowment care fund.

(f) The board of trustees shall cause the income from the endowment care fund to be deposited in an endowment income fund and spent solely for the care of the cemeteries owned by the district.

(Added by Stats. 2003, Ch. 57, Sec. 5. Effective January 1, 2004.)

9066.

The board of trustees shall cause the principal of the endowment care fund to be invested and reinvested in any of the following:

(a) Securities and obligations designated by Section 53601 of the Government Code.

(b) Obligations of the United States or obligations for which the faith and credit of the United States are pledged for the payment of principal and interest. These shall not be limited to maturity dates of one year or less.

(c) Obligations issued under authority of law by any county, municipality, or school district in this state for which are pledged the faith and credit of that county, municipality, or school district for the payment of principal and interest, if within 10 years immediately preceding the investment that county, municipality, or school district was not in default for more than 90 days in the payment of principal or interest upon any legally authorized obligations issued by it.

(d) Obligations of the State of California or those for which the faith and credit of the State of California are pledged for the payment of principal and interest.

(e) Interest-bearing obligations issued by a corporation organized under the laws of any state, or of the United States, provided that they bear a Standard and Poor's financial rating of AAA at the time of the investment.

(f) Certificates of deposit or other interest-bearing accounts in any state or federally chartered bank or savings association, the deposits of which are insured by the Federal Deposit Insurance Corporation.

(Amended by Stats. 2009, Ch. 332, Sec. 75.4. (SB 113) Effective January 1, 2010.)

9067.

The board of trustees may cause the funds deposited in the endowment income fund pursuant to subdivision (f) of Section 9065 that are not required for the immediate care of the cemeteries owned by the district to be invested in the securities and obligations designated by Section 53601 of the Government Code.

(Added by Stats. 2003, Ch. 57, Sec. 5. Effective January 1, 2004.)

9068.

(a) The board of trustees shall adopt a schedule of fees for interments in cemeteries owned by the district and for other necessary and convenient services.

(b) The board of trustees shall also adopt a schedule of fees for nonresidents. The board of trustees shall set these fees at an amount that at least equals the amount of fees charged to residents or taxpayers and shall include a nonresident fee of at least 15 percent of that amount.

(Added by Stats. 2003, Ch. 57, Sec. 5. Effective January 1, 2004.)

9069.

(a) A district may seek the abandonment of an interment plot in a cemetery owned by the district pursuant to this section.

(b) The board of trustees shall file a petition with the superior court of the principal county which contains all of the following:

(1) An identification of the interment plot that the district desires to be declared abandoned.

(2) A statement that the district has made a diligent search to locate the present owner of the interment plot.

(3) A statement that the present owner of the interment plot is unknown to the district.

(4) A statement that, to the best knowledge of the district, at least 50 years have passed since any portion of the interment plot has been used for interment purposes.

(5) A statement that, after a reasonable physical investigation of the interment plot, the interment plot has not been used for the interment of human remains.

(6) A request that the court declare the interment plot abandoned.

(c) Upon the filing of a petition pursuant to subdivision (b), the clerk of the superior court shall set a time for a hearing on the petition.

(d) After the clerk of the superior court has set the hearing, the district shall give notice of the court's hearing. The notice shall identify the interment plot that the district desires to be declared abandoned, state the name and address of the last known owner of the interment plot, state that the court will hold a hearing to determine whether to declare the interment plot abandoned, and state the time and place of the court's hearing. The district shall give notice of the court's hearing by publishing a notice pursuant to Section 6061 of the Government Code in at least one newspaper of general circulation within the jurisdiction of the district at least 10 days before the hearing. The district shall post the public notice in at least three public places within the jurisdiction of the district, at least 10 days before the hearing. One of the public places shall be at the interment plot that the district desires to be declared abandoned, and one of the public places shall be at the offices of the district. In addition, the district shall mail the notice by certified mail, return receipt requested, at least 10 days before the hearing to the last known owner of the interment plot.

(e) At the time set for the hearing, the superior court shall hear and consider any evidence that is introduced in favor or, and any objections to, the abandonment of the interment plot. The court may continue its hearing from time to time. The court shall determine from the evidence presented whether the facts stated in the district's petition are true. The court shall dismiss any portion of the district's petition if the court determines that any of the facts stated in that portion of the petition are not true, or if the court determines the identity of the present owner of the interment plot. If the court determines that the facts stated in the district's petition are true, the court may order that the interment plot shall be deemed abandoned and full title shall revert to the district. The superior court's order shall not become final until one year after the date on which the court made its order.

(f) Within 30 days after the date on which the superior court made its order, the district shall give notice of the court's order. The notice shall identify the interment plot that the district desires to be declared abandoned, state the name and address of the last known owner of the interment plot, and state the date on which the court's order will be final. The district shall give notice of the court's order by publishing a notice pursuant to Section 6061 of the Government Code in at least one newspaper of general circulation within the jurisdiction of the district. The district shall post the public notice in at least three public places within the jurisdiction of the district. One of the public places shall be at the interment plot that the district desires to be declared abandoned, and one of the public places shall be at the offices of the district. In addition, the district shall mail the notice by certified mail, return receipt requested, to the last known owner of the interment site.

(g) At any time before the superior court's order becomes final, any person may petition the court to reopen the proceeding. Upon receiving a petition and after giving notice to the district, the court may reopen the proceeding. The court may hear and consider any additional evidence regarding the facts in the district's petition. The court may amend its previous order. If the court determines that any of the facts stated in any portion of the district's petition are not true, or if the court determines the identify of the present owner of the interment plot, the court shall dismiss that portion of the district's petition.

(h) The interment plot shall be deemed abandoned on the date on which the superior court's order becomes final. The district shall record the court's order in the office of the county recorder of the county in which the interment plot is located. Upon recordation of the court's order, the district is the owner of the interment plot and the district may resell the interment rights.

(i) If, after the proceedings taken pursuant to this section, the district discovers the presence of human remains in the interment plot, the district shall make reasonable efforts to identify the remains. The district shall close and appropriately mark the interment plot. The district shall offer the new owner of the interment rights in that interment plot comparable interment rights in another interment plot. The district shall not be liable for any claims for damages if the district has proceeded pursuant to this section.

(Added by Stats. 2003, Ch. 57, Sec. 5. Effective January 1, 2004.)

CHAPTER 5.5. Interment Rights [9069.10 - 9069.40]

(Chapter 5.5 added by Stats. 2016, Ch. 592, Sec. 2.)

9069.10.

An interment right does not include the right for disinterment of human remains except on consent of the cemetery district and the written consent of the surviving spouse, child, parent, or sibling, in that order of priority.

(Added by Stats. 2016, Ch. 592, Sec. 2. (SB 1179) Effective January 1, 2017.)

9069.15.

(a) This chapter does not apply to, or prohibit, the removal of remains from one plot to another in the same cemetery or the removal of remains by a cemetery district upon the written order of any of the following:

(1) The superior court of the county in which the cemetery is located.

(2) The coroner having jurisdiction of the location of the cemetery.

(3) The health department having jurisdiction of the cemetery.

(b) The cemetery district shall maintain a duplicate copy of an order pursuant to subdivision (a).

(c) The cemetery district shall retain a true and correct record of a removal of remains pursuant to subdivision (a) that includes all of the following:

(1) The date the remains were removed.

(2) The name and the age at death of the person whose remains were removed if available.

(3) The cemetery and plot from which the remains were removed.

(4) (A) If the removed remains are reinterred, the plot number, cemetery name, and location to which the remains were reinterred.

(B) If the removed remains are disposed of other than by being reinterred, a record of the alternate disposition.

(5) If the removed remains are reinterred at the cemetery, the date of reinterment.

(d) The person making the removal shall deliver to the cemetery district operating the cemetery from which the remains were removed a true, full, and complete copy of the record containing all of the information specified in subdivision (c).

(Added by Stats. 2016, Ch. 592, Sec. 2. (SB 1179) Effective January 1, 2017.)

9069.20.

(a) An interment right provides a transferable property interest to the person listed as the owner in the records of the cemetery district, subject to any written designation to the contrary signed by the owner and deposited with the cemetery district, or to the owner's successor pursuant to either this section or subdivision (a) of Section 9069.25. An interment right shall not be construed as conferring title to the property burdened by the transferable property interest.

(b) The owner of record of an interment right may designate in writing the person or persons, other than the owner of record, who may be interred in the plot to which the owner holds the interment right.

(c) The owner of an interment right shall, at the time of purchase, designate a successor owner or owners of the interment right in a signed written designation deposited with the district.

(d) Use of an interment right transferred from the owner to a successor pursuant to subdivision (c) shall be made in compliance with applicable provisions of state and local law, and of applicable requirements or policies established by the district board of trustees.

(Added by Stats. 2016, Ch. 592, Sec. 2. (SB 1179) Effective January 1, 2017.)

9069.25.

(a) If the owner of an interment right dies without making a valid and enforceable disposition of the interment right by a specific devise in a testamentary device, or by a written designation pursuant to subdivision (c) of Section 9069.20, the interment right shall pass according to the laws of intestate succession as set forth in Sections 6400 to 6413, inclusive, of the Probate Code. In the event that the owner has no heirs at law, the district shall follow the abandonment procedures established under Section 9069.

(b) A surviving spouse, registered domestic partner, child, parent, or heir who has an interment right pursuant to this section may waive that interment right in favor of any other relative of the deceased owner or spouse of a relative of the deceased owner.

(Added by Stats. 2016, Ch. 592, Sec. 2. (SB 1179) Effective January 1, 2017.)

9069.30.

When a public cemetery district acts to transfer ownership rights or make an interment on the basis of the affidavit, given under penalty of perjury pursuant to Section 9069.35, the district, and any employee or trustee of the district, shall not be liable for any claims, losses, or damages asserted in any action unless the district had actual knowledge that the facts stated in writing are false.

(Added by Stats. 2016, Ch. 592, Sec. 2. (SB 1179) Effective January 1, 2017.)

9069.35.

A person who purports to be the successor owner of an interment right shall execute a written affidavit declaring, under penalty of perjury, all of the following:

(a) He or she is the person entitled to succeed to the interment right pursuant to Section 9069.20.

(b) He or she has exerted all reasonable efforts to find other persons who may have an equal or higher claim to succeed to the interment right.

(c) He or she is unaware, to the best of his or her knowledge, of any opposition challenging his or her right to succeed to the interment right.

(Added by Stats. 2016, Ch. 592, Sec. 2. (SB 1179) Effective January 1, 2017.)

9069.40.

Upon the sale to a person of a plot in a cemetery within a district, the district shall notify the purchaser, in writing, of any interment rights, that this chapter governs the succession of ownership of the interment rights, and the district's duly adopted policies, rules, and regulations governing the use, sale, or other transfer of interment rights.

(Added by Stats. 2016, Ch. 592, Sec. 2. (SB 1179) Effective January 1, 2017.)

CHAPTER 6. Finances [9070 - 9079]

(Chapter 6 added by Stats. 2003, Ch. 57, Sec. 5.)

9070.

(a) On or before August 30 of each year, the board of trustees shall adopt a final budget, which shall conform to the accounting and budgeting procedures for special districts contained in Subchapter 3 (commencing with Section 1031.1) of, and Article 1 (commencing with Section 1121) of Subchapter 4 of Division 2 of Title 2 of the California Code of Regulations.

(b) The board of trustees may divide the annual budget into categories, including, but not limited to:

(1) Maintenance and operation.

(2) Employee compensation.

(3) Interest and redemption for indebtedness.

(4) Restricted reserves for the following categories:

(A) Endowment income fund.

(B) Capital outlay.

(C) Pre-need.

(D) Contingencies.

(5) Unallocated general reserve.

(c) The board of trustees shall forward a copy of the final budget to the auditor of each county in which the district is located.

(Added by Stats. 2003, Ch. 57, Sec. 5. Effective January 1, 2004.)

9071.

(a) In its annual budget, the board of trustees may establish one or more restricted reserves. When the board of trustees establishes a restricted reserve, it shall declare the exclusive purposes for which the funds in the reserve may be spent. The funds in the restricted reserve shall be spent only for the exclusive purposes for which the board of trustees established the restricted reserve. The reserves shall be maintained according to generally accepted principles.

(b) Any time after the establishment of a restricted reserve, the board of trustees may transfer any funds to that restricted reserve.

(c) If the board of trustees finds that the funds in a restricted reserve are no longer required for the purpose for which the restricted reserve was established, the board of trustees may, by a four-fifths vote of the total membership of the board of trustees, discontinue the restricted reserve or transfer the funds that are no longer required from the restricted reserve to the district's general fund.

(Added by Stats. 2003, Ch. 57, Sec. 5. Effective January 1, 2004.)

9072.

(a) On or before July 1 of each year, the board of trustees shall adopt a resolution establishing its appropriations limit and make other necessary determinations for the following fiscal year pursuant to Article XIII B of California Constitution and Division 9 (commencing with Section 7900) of the Government Code.

(b) Pursuant to subdivision (c) of Section 9 of Article XIII B of the California Constitution, this section shall not apply to a district that existed on January 1, 1978, and that did not, as of the 1977-78 fiscal year, levy an ad valorem tax on property in excess of twelve and one-half cents ($0.125) per one hundred dollars ($100) of assessed value.

(Added by Stats. 2003, Ch. 57, Sec. 5. Effective January 1, 2004.)

9073.

The auditor of each county in which a district is located shall allocate to the district its share of property tax revenue pursuant to Chapter 6 (commencing with Section 95) of Part 0.5 of Division 1 of the Revenue and Taxation Code.

(Added by Stats. 2003, Ch. 57, Sec. 5. Effective January 1, 2004.)

9074.

(a) A district may accept any grants, goods, money, property, revenue, or services from any federal, state, regional, or local agency or from any person for any lawful purpose of the district.

(b) Except as provided by Section 9077, all moneys received or collected by a district shall be paid into a separate fund in the county treasury on or before the 10th day of the month following the month in which the district received or collected the money.

(c) In addition to any other existing authority, a district may borrow money and incur indebtedness pursuant to Article 7 (commencing with Section 53820), Article 7.4 (commencing with Section 53835), Article 7.5 (commencing with Section 53840), Article 7.6 (commencing with Section 53850), and Article 7.7 (commencing with Section 53859) of Chapter 4 of Part 1 of Division 2 of Title 5 of the Government Code.

(Amended by Stats. 2010, Ch. 699, Sec. 25.2. (SB 894) Effective January 1, 2011.)

9075.

All claims for money or damages against a district are governed by Part 3 (commencing with Section 900) and Part 4 (commencing with Section 940) of Division 3.6 of Title 1 of the Government Code.

(Added by Stats. 2003, Ch. 57, Sec. 5. Effective January 1, 2004.)

9076.

(a) All claims against a district shall be audited, allowed, and paid by the board of trustees by warrants drawn on the county treasurer.

(b) As an alternative to subdivision (a), the board of trustees may instruct the county treasurer to audit, allow, and draw his or her warrant on the county treasury for all legal claims presented to him or her and authorized by the board of trustees.

(c) The county treasurer shall pay the warrants in the order in which they are presented.

(d) If a warrant is presented for payment and the county treasurer cannot pay it for want of funds in the account on which it is drawn, the treasurer shall endorse the warrant,

"NOT PAID BECAUSE OF INSUFFICIENT FUNDS" and sign his or her name and the date and time the warrant was presented. From that time until it is paid, the warrant bears interest at the maximum rate permitted pursuant to Article 7 (commencing with Section 53530) of Chapter 3 of Part 1 of Division 2 of Title 5 of the Government Code.

(Added by Stats. 2003, Ch. 57, Sec. 5. Effective January 1, 2004.)

9077.

(a) Notwithstanding Section 9076, a district that has total annual revenues greater than five hundred thousand dollars ($500,000) may withdraw its funds from the control of the county treasurer pursuant to this section.

(b) The board of trustees shall adopt a resolution that does each of the following:

(1) States its intent to withdraw its funds from the county treasury.

(2) Adopts a procedure for the appointment of a district treasurer. The board of trustees may appoint the district treasurer. The board of trustees may appoint the district treasurer, or the board of trustees may delegate the appointment of the district to the district's general manager. The district treasurer may be a member of the board of trustees, the secretary of the board of trustees, the general manager, or a district employee.

(3) Fixes the amount of the bond for the district treasurer and other district employees who will be responsible for handling the district's finances.

(4) Adopts a system of accounting and auditing that shall completely and at all times show the district's financial condition. The system of accounting and auditing shall adhere to generally accepted accounting principles.

(5) Adopts a procedure for drawing and signing warrants, provided that the procedure adheres to generally accepted accounting principles. The procedures shall provide that bond principal and salaries shall be paid when due. The procedure may provide that warrants to pay claims and demands need not be approved by the board of trustees before payment if the district treasurer determines that the claims and demands conform to the district's approved budget.

(6) Designates a bank or a savings and loan association as the depositary of the district's funds. A bank or savings and loan association may act as a depositary, paying agent, or fiscal agency for the holding or handling of the district's funds, notwithstanding the fact that a member of the board of trustees whose funds are on deposit in that bank or savings and loan association is an officer, employee, or stockholder of that bank or saving and loan association, or of a holding company that owns any of the stock of that bank or savings and loan association.

(c) The board of trustees and the board of supervisors of the principal county shall determine a mutually acceptable date for the withdrawal of the district's funds from the county treasury, not to exceed 15 months from the date on which the board of trustees adopts its resolution.

(d) In implementing this section, the district shall comply with Article 1 (commencing with Section 53600) and Article 2 (commencing with Section 5360) of Chapter 4 of Part 1 of Division 2 of Title 5 of the Government Code. Nothing in this section shall include the district treasurer from depositing the district's funds in the county treasury of the principal county or the State Treasury pursuant to Article 11 (commencing with Section 16429.1) of Chapter 2 of Part 2 of Division 4 of Title 2 of the Government Code.

(e) The district treasurer shall make annual or more frequent written reports to the board of trustees, as the board of trustees shall determine, regarding the receipts and disbursements and balances in the accounts controlled by the district treasurer. The district treasurer shall sign the reports and file them with the secretary.

(Added by Stats. 2003, Ch. 57, Sec. 5. Effective January 1, 2004.)

9078.

A district may, by resolution, establish a revolving fund pursuant to Article 15 (commencing with Section 53950) of Chapter 4 of Part 1 of Division 2 of Title 5 of the Government Code. The maximum amount of the revolving fund shall not exceed either of the following:

(a) One thousand dollars ($1,000) if the purpose of the revolving fund is to make change and pay small bills directly.

(b) One hundred ten percent of one-twelfth of the district's adopted budget for the current fiscal year if the purpose of the revolving fund is to pay any authorized expenditures of the district.

(Amended by Stats. 2009, Ch. 332, Sec. 75.7. (SB 113) Effective January 1, 2010.)

9079.

(a) The board of trustees shall provide for regular audits of the district's accounts and records and the district's endowment care fund pursuant to Section 26909 of the Government Code.

(b) The board of trustees shall provide for the annual financial reports to the Controller pursuant to Article 9 (commencing with Section 53890) of Chapter 4 of Part 1 of Division 2 of Title 5 of the Government Code.

(Added by Stats. 2003, Ch. 57, Sec. 5. Effective January 1, 2004.)

CHAPTER 7. Alternative Revenues [9080 - 9083]

(Chapter 7 added by Stats. 2003, Ch. 57, Sec. 5.)

9080.

Whenever a board of trustees determines that the amount of revenues available to the district or any of its zones is inadequate to meet the costs of providing facilities, programs, projects, and services, the board of trustees may raise revenues pursuant to this chapter or any other provision of law.

(Added by Stats. 2003, Ch. 57, Sec. 5. Effective January 1, 2004.)

9081.

A district may levy special taxes pursuant to either of the following:

(a) Article 3.5 (commencing with Section 50075) of Chapter 1 of Part 1 of Division 1 of Title 5 of the Government Code. The special taxes shall be applied uniformly to all taxpayers or all real property within the district, except that unimproved property may be taxed at a lower rate than improved property.

(b) The Mello-Roos Community Facilities Act of 1982, Chapter 2.5 (commencing with Section 53311) of Part 1 of Division 2 of Title 5 of the Government Code.

(Added by Stats. 2003, Ch. 57, Sec. 5. Effective January 1, 2004.)

9082.

(a) Whenever a board of trustees determines that it is necessary to incur a general obligation bond indebtedness for the acquisition or improvement of real property, the board of trustees may proceed pursuant to Article 11 (commencing with Section 5790) of Chapter 4 of Division 5 of the Public Resources Code. For the purposes of that article, the board of trustees shall be considered the board of directors of the district.

(b) Notwithstanding subdivision (a), a district shall not incur indebtedness that exceeds 2 percent of the assessed value of all taxable property in the district at the time the bonds are issued.

(Added by Stats. 2003, Ch. 57, Sec. 5. Effective January 1, 2004.)

9083.

(a) In addition to the other fees authorized by this part, a board of trustees may charge a fee to cover the cost of any other service that a district provides or the cost of enforcing any regulation for which the fee is charged. No fee charged pursuant to this section shall exceed the costs reasonably borne by the district in providing the service or enforcing the regulation for which the fee is charged.

(b) Notwithstanding Section 6103 of the Government Code, a board of trustees may charge a fee authorized by this section to other public agencies.

(c) A board of trustees may charge residents or persons who pay property taxes on property located in the district a fee authorized by this section that is less than the fee that it charges to nonresidents or nontaxpayers.

(d) A board of trustees may authorize district employees to waive the payment, in whole or part, of a fee authorized by this section when the board of trustees determines that payment would not be in the public interest. Before authorizing any waiver, the board of trustees shall adopt a resolution that specifies the policies and procedures governing waivers.

(Added by Stats. 2003, Ch. 57, Sec. 5. Effective January 1, 2004.)

CHAPTER 8. Zones [9090 - 9093]

(Chapter 8 added by Stats. 2003, Ch. 57, Sec. 5.)

9090.

(a) Whenever a board of trustees determines that it is in the public interest to provide different services, to provide different levels of services, or to raise additional revenues within specific areas of the district, it may form one or more zones pursuant to this chapter.

(b) The board of trustees shall initiate proceedings for the formation of a new zone by adopting a resolution that does all of the following:

(1) States that the proposal is made pursuant to this chapter.

(2) Sets forth a description of the boundaries of the territory to be included in the zone.

(3) States the different services, the different levels of services, or the additional revenues that the district will provide.

(4) Sets forth the methods by which those services or level of service will be financed.

(5) States the reasons for forming the zone.

(6) Proposes a name or number for the zone.

(c) A proposal to form a new zone may also be initiated by a petition signed by not less than 10 percent of the registered voters residing within the proposed zone. The petition shall contain all of the matters required by subdivision (b).

(d) Upon the adoption of a resolution or the receipt of a valid petition, the board of trustees shall fix the date, time, and place for the public hearing on the formation of the zone. The district shall publish notice of the hearing, including the information required by subdivision (b), pursuant to Section 6061 of the Government Code in one or more newspapers of general circulation in the district. The district shall mail the notice at least 45 days before the date of the hearing to all owners of property within the proposed zone. The district shall post the notice in at least three public places within the territory of the proposed zone.

(Added by Stats. 2003, Ch. 57, Sec. 5. Effective January 1, 2004.)

9091.

(a) At the hearing, the board of trustees shall hear and consider any protests to the formation of a zone pursuant to this chapter. The board of trustees shall terminate the proceedings, if at the conclusion of the hearing, it determines either of the following:

(1) More than 50 percent of the total number of voters residing within the proposed zone have filed and not withdrawn written objections to the formation.

(2) Property owners who own more than 50 percent of the assessed value of all taxable property within the proposed zone have filed written and not withdrawn objections to the formation.

(b) If the board of trustees determines that the written objections have been filed and not withdrawn by 50 percent or less of those voters or property owners, then the board of trustees may proceed to form the zone.

(c) If the resolution or petition for formation of a zone proposes that the zone use special taxes, special benefit assessments, fees for property-related services, or general obligation bonds to finance its purposes, the board of trustees shall proceed according to

law. If the voters or property owners do not approve those funding methods, the zone shall not be formed.

(Added by Stats. 2003, Ch. 57, Sec. 5. Effective January 1, 2004.)

9092.

(a) A board of trustees may change the boundaries of a zone or dissolve a zone by following the procedures in Sections 9090 and 9091.

(b) Except as provided in Section 56886 of the Government Code, a local agency formation commission shall have no power or duty to review and approve or disapprove a proposal to form a zone, a proposal to change the boundaries of a zone, or a proposal to dissolve a zone.

(Added by Stats. 2003, Ch. 57, Sec. 5. Effective January 1, 2004.)

9093.

(a) As determined by the board of trustees and pursuant to the requirements of this part, a zone may provide any service at any level or levels within its boundaries that the district may provide.

(b) As determined by the board of trustees and pursuant to the requirements of this part, a zone may exercise any fiscal powers within its boundaries that the district may exercise.

(c) Any special taxes, special benefit assessments, fees, or general obligation bonds which are intended solely for the support of projects, services, or programs within a zone shall be levied, assessed, and charged within the boundaries of that zone.

(Added by Stats. 2003, Ch. 57, Sec. 5. Effective January 1, 2004.)

PART 5. MAUSOLEUMS AND COLUMBARIUMS [9501 - 9677]

(Part 5 repealed and added by Stats. 1955, Ch. 1349.)

CHAPTER 1. General Provisions [9501 - 9513]

(Chapter 1 added by Stats. 1955, Ch. 1349.)

9501.

This part shall be known and may be cited as the Mausoleum and Columbarium Law.

(Amended by Stats. 1993, Ch. 350, Sec. 1. Effective January 1, 1994.)

9502.

The purpose of this part is to insure the durability and permanence of mausoleums and columbariums by requiring that they be constructed of such material and workmanship as determined by modern mausoleum-columbarium engineering science, the minimum requirements for which are set forth in this part.

(Repealed and added by Stats. 1955, Ch. 1349.)

9503.

Unless the provision or the context otherwise requires, the definitions and general provisions set forth in this chapter govern the construction of this part.

(Repealed and added by Stats. 1955, Ch. 1349.)

9504.

"Mausoleum" includes any building or structure, used or intended to be used, for the interment of human remains. A columbarium may be built within a mausoleum.

(Amended by Stats. 1993, Ch. 350, Sec. 2. Effective January 1, 1994.)

9504.5.

"Private mausoleum or columbarium" shall be a freestanding structure which:

(a) Is constructed for use by the members of any one group, and not for the sale of space therein to any other person.

(b) Does not contain crypts for the interment of more than 12 uncremated human remains, and a columbarium, niches for the interment of not more than 20 cremated human remains.

(c) Is not constructed for occupancy by any person except in the course of making an interment.

(Added by Stats. 1994, Ch. 1152, Sec. 6. Effective January 1, 1995.)

9505.

"Companion crypts" or "nest of crypts" means two or more crypts entered through a single crypt opening.

(Added by Stats. 1955, Ch. 1349.)

9506.

"Columbarium" includes any building or structure, used or intended to be used, for the interment of cremated human remains.

(Added by Stats. 1955, Ch. 1349.)

9507.

"Uniform Building Code" means the 1991 Edition of the Uniform Building Code, with 1992 amendments, adopted and published by the International Conference of Building Officials.

(Amended by Stats. 1993, Ch. 350, Sec. 3. Effective January 1, 1994.)

9508.

"The Uniform Plumbing Code" means the 1991 Edition of the Plumbing Code, with 1992 amendments, adopted and published by the International Association of Plumbing and Mechanical Officials.

(Amended by Stats. 1993, Ch. 350, Sec. 4. Effective January 1, 1994.)

9509.

"National Electrical Code" means the 1990 Edition of the National Electrical Code, with 1992 amendments, adopted and published by the National Fire Protection Association.

(Amended by Stats. 1993, Ch. 350, Sec. 5. Effective January 1, 1994.)

9510.
"Incombustible Material" means and includes any material having an ignition temperature higher than 1,000 degrees Fahrenheit.
(Added by Stats. 1955, Ch. 1349.)

9511.
"Type I Construction" includes the type of construction designated and specified as Type I Building Construction in the Uniform Building Code.
(Added by Stats. 1955, Ch. 1349.)

9512.
The provisions of this part shall not apply to any structure or building used or intended to be used for the interment of human remains all portions of which are below the ground.
(Added by Stats. 1955, Ch. 1349.)

9513.
(a) The provisions of this part shall apply to any cemetery that acquires, constructs, improves, maintains, or repairs a mausoleum or columbarium.
(b) The provisions of this part shall apply to any public cemetery district that acquires, constructs, improves, maintains, or repairs a columbarium.
(Added by Stats. 1999, Ch. 207, Sec. 3. Effective January 1, 2000.)

CHAPTER 2. Enforcement [9525 - 9528]
(Chapter 2 added by Stats. 1955, Ch. 1349.)

9525.
The building department of every city or city and county shall enforce the provisions of this part within such city or city and county. "Building department" or "department" means the department, bureau, or officer charged with the enforcement of laws or ordinances regulating the erection, construction or alteration of buildings.
(Repealed and added by Stats. 1955, Ch. 1349.)

9526.
The department, officer or officers of a county who are charged with the enforcement of laws or ordinances regulating the erection, construction or alteration of buildings, shall enforce the provisions of this part within such county but outside the territorial limits of any city.
(Repealed and added by Stats. 1955, Ch. 1349.)

9527.
Any city or county may, by ordinance, designate any department or officer to enforce any portion of this part.
(Repealed and added by Stats. 1955, Ch. 1349.)

9528.
In any city where there is no department or officer charged with or designated for the enforcement of this part, the appropriate department, officer or officers of the county in which such city is located shall enforce this part.
In any county where there is no department or officer charged with or designated for the enforcement of this part, this part shall be enforced by the county engineer, if there is a county engineer, and if not, then by the county surveyor.
(Repealed and added by Stats. 1955, Ch. 1349.)

CHAPTER 3. Permits and Plans [9550 - 9580]
(Chapter 3 added by Stats. 1955, Ch. 1349.)

ARTICLE 1. General Provisions [9550- 9550.]
(Article 1 added by Stats. 1955, Ch. 1349.)

9550.
It is unlawful for any person to construct, or cause or permit to be constructed upon any property belonging to or controlled by him, any mausoleum or columbarium, or to make any alterations or changes or do any reconstruction work upon, in or to any building or structure for use as a mausoleum or columbarium without first having applied for and procured a separate building permit for each such mausoleum, columbarium, building or structure, or alteration, from the department or official charged with the enforcement of this part.
(Repealed and added by Stats. 1955, Ch. 1349.)

ARTICLE 2. Application, Permit and Certificate of Occupancy [9560 - 9565]
(Article 2 added by Stats. 1955, Ch. 1349.)

9560.
A person desiring a permit shall file a written application with the department or official charged with the enforcement of this part on forms furnished by it. The application shall:
(a) Show in detail the proposed erection, construction, reconstruction, or alteration.
(b) State the name and address of the owner.
(c) State the name and address of the architect, structural engineer, or contractor, if any.
(d) State that the plans and specifications are true and contain a correct description of the proposed work.
(e) Give any other data or information required by the department.
(Repealed and added by Stats. 1955, Ch. 1349.)

9561.
The application shall be accompanied by:
(a) Two full, true and complete sets of plans showing in detail the work proposed and whether it is for new work, reconstruction, or alteration.
(b) Two sets of specifications describing the proposed work.

(c) The plans of the lot or land on which the building is proposed to be erected, reconstructed, or altered.
(d) The written approval of the plans and specifications and consent to the proposed erection, construction, reconstruction, or alteration, executed by the cemetery authority owning or operating the cemetery in which the work is to be performed.
(Amended by Stats. 1957, Ch. 796.)

9562.
The department shall cause all plans, specifications, and statements to be examined, and, if they conform to the provisions of this part, shall issue a permit.
(Repealed and added by Stats. 1955, Ch. 1349.)

9563.
The department may, from time to time, approve changes in any plans, specifications, or statements, previously approved if the changes are in conformity with the provisions of this part.
(Repealed and added by Stats. 1955, Ch. 1349.)

9564.
The issuance or granting of a permit or approval is not a permit or approval of a violation of any provision of this part.
(Repealed and added by Stats. 1955, Ch. 1349.)

9565.
A true copy of the plans, specifications, and other information submitted or filed upon which a permit is issued, with the approval of the department with which they are filed, stamped or written on the copy, and signed by the officer or officers authorizing the permit, shall be kept upon the premises of the building for which the permit is issued from the commencement of the work until final completion and acceptance, and shall be subject to inspection at all times by proper authorities.
(Added by Stats. 1955, Ch. 1349.)

ARTICLE 3. Cancellation of Permit [9575- 9575.]
(Article 3 added by Stats. 1955, Ch. 1349.)

9575.
In the case of any refusal, or neglect of the person to whom a permit or approval has been issued to comply with all of the provisions of this part, or in case any false statement or misrepresentation is made in any of the plans, specifications or statements submitted or filed for the permit or approval, the department shall revoke or cancel any permit or approval it has previously issued.
(Repealed and added by Stats. 1955, Ch. 1349.)

ARTICLE 4. Expiration of Permit [9580- 9580.]
(Article 4 added by Stats. 1955, Ch. 1349.)

9580.
Every permit or approval under which no work is done within one year from the date of issuance expires by limitation and a new permit shall be obtained before the work may proceed.
(Amended by Stats. 1993, Ch. 350, Sec. 7. Effective January 1, 1994.)

CHAPTER 4. Inspection and Approval [9590 - 9592]
(Chapter 4 added by Stats. 1955, Ch. 1349.)

9590.
When the work is completed in accordance with plans, specifications, and statements previously made and upon which the permit or approval was issued, the owner or contractor shall notify the department.
(Repealed and added by Stats. 1955, Ch. 1349.)

9591.
The department shall inspect or cause the work to be inspected, and shall issue a certificate of occupancy if the work has been performed in accordance with the approved plans, specifications, and statements, and in conformity with the provisions of this part; and if not, it shall refuse to issue the certificate.
(Repealed and added by Stats. 1955, Ch. 1349.)

9592.
When it is found that the building or structure is structurally complete, upon request, a temporary certificate of occupancy shall be issued by the department for the use of a portion or portions of a mausoleum or columbarium for interment of human remains prior to the completion of the entire building or structure.
(Added by Stats. 1955, Ch. 1349.)

CHAPTER 5. Construction [9600 - 9647]
(Chapter 5 added by Stats. 1955, Ch. 1349.)

ARTICLE 1. General Provisions [9600 - 9603]
(Article 1 added by Stats. 1955, Ch. 1349.)

9600.
No mausoleum or columbarium shall be constructed and no existing building or structure shall be altered for use as a mausoleum or columbarium unless the entire building or structure, including any portion to be used for any other purpose, is in conformity with the minimum requirements set forth in this chapter. Any addition to or alteration of any existing mausoleum or columbarium shall conform to the minimum requirements set forth in this chapter.
(Repealed and added by Stats. 1955, Ch. 1349.)

9600.5.

The Cemetery and Funeral Bureau may, in addition to the construction methods and standards allowed in this chapter, adopt regulations for the construction of private mausoleums or private columbariums, which at a minimum, include the following:

(a) Standards for design and construction for seismic load protection.

(b) Methods of construction, including solid granite construction.

(c) Methods of sealing to prevent leakage from crypts.

(d) Ventilation of crypts.

(e) Types of incombustible materials which may be used in construction.

(Amended by Stats. 2000, Ch. 568, Sec. 259. Effective January 1, 2001.)

9600.6.

Private mausoleums or columbariums may be constructed in conformance with the methods and standards set forth in this chapter or in conformance with the construction methods and standards as adopted by the Cemetery and Funeral Bureau.

(Amended by Stats. 2000, Ch. 568, Sec. 260. Effective January 1, 2001.)

9601.

All mausoleums or columbariums shall be of Type I Construction as specified in the Uniform Building Code, except as otherwise provided in this chapter.

(Repealed and added by Stats. 1955, Ch. 1349.)

9602.

Plumbing in all mausoleums or columbariums shall conform to the provisions of the Uniform Plumbing Code.

(Repealed and added by Stats. 1955, Ch. 1349.)

9603.

Electrical work in all mausoleums or columbariums shall conform to the provisions of the National Electrical Code.

(Repealed and added by Stats. 1955, Ch. 1349.)

ARTICLE 2. Structural and Material Requirements of Community Mausoleums and Columbariums [9625 - 9647]

(Heading of Article 2 amended by Stats. 1957, Ch. 796.)

9625.

Every mausoleum or columbarium shall be designed and constructed to conform to the earthquake provisions of the Uniform Building Code.

(Amended by Stats. 1993, Ch. 350, Sec. 8. Effective January 1, 1994.)

9626.

Except as otherwise provided in this chapter, all materials used in the construction, ornamentation, or embellishment of mausoleums or columbariums shall be incombustible. This section shall not apply to crypt vents, temporary openings or partitions, interior doors, fixtures, furniture, or furnishings.

(Amended by Stats. 1993, Ch. 350, Sec. 9. Effective January 1, 1994.)

9627.

All structural framework shall be of cast-in-place reinforced concrete, or of structural steel sections, or of concrete over metal decking; provided, however, all footings, bearing walls, floor slabs and roofs shall be of cast-in-place reinforced concrete or of concrete over metal decking only. All structural framework shall be designed and constructed in accordance with the Uniform Building Code.

(Amended by Stats. 1993, Ch. 350, Sec. 10. Effective January 1, 1994.)

9628.

All floors shall be designed and constructed for a live load of not less than 100 pounds per square foot.

(Repealed and added by Stats. 1955, Ch. 1349.)

9629.

Footings shall be designed and constructed to conform to the requirements of the Uniform Building Code or specifications of a licensed geotechnical engineer.

(Amended by Stats. 1993, Ch. 350, Sec. 11. Effective January 1, 1994.)

9630.

Floor slabs placed on earth shall be constructed of reinforced concrete designed by a licensed structural or civil engineer to include control joints at appropriate intervals to minimize cracks as well as appropriate vapor and moisture barriers as specified by a licensed geotechnical engineer.

(Amended by Stats. 1993, Ch. 350, Sec. 12. Effective January 1, 1994.)

9631.

Where any wall is constructed against a bank of earth, rock, or other porous material, or where crypts are adjacent to an outside building wall below grade, the wall shall be adequately waterproofed. Before backfilling, a waterproofed wall shall have a protection board placed against it to prevent damage to the waterproofing during backfilling.

(Amended by Stats. 1993, Ch. 350, Sec. 13. Effective January 1, 1994.)

9632.

Except as provided in Section 9633, all crypt walls and crypt floor slabs shall be constructed of cast-in-place, reinforced concrete; crypt walls shall conform to structural design but shall be not less than three and one-half inches in thickness, and crypt floor slabs shall be not less than three inches in thickness.

(Amended by Stats. 1993, Ch. 350, Sec. 14. Effective January 1, 1994.)

9633.

Horizontal and vertical partitions separating crypts comprising companion crypts or a nest of crypts entered through a single crypt opening may be constructed of precast reinforced concrete; provided, the horizontal partitions are not less than one and one-half inches in thickness and the vertical nonbearing partitions are not less than one inch in thickness, and vertical partitions bearing any load are not less than three inches in thickness, and provided the crypt walls enclosing the nest of crypts are constructed as required in Section 9632. Crypts shall be vented at roof level of the structure, and vents

shall continue to a gravel filled trench below the floor of the bottom crypt to provide adequate circulation of air. Nonstructural horizontal and vertical partitions separating columbarium niches may be constructed of precast reinforced concrete or other incombustible material.

(Amended by Stats. 1993, Ch. 350, Sec. 15. Effective January 1, 1994.)

9634.

Each crypt, including each crypt in a companion crypt or in a nest of crypts referred to in Section 9633, shall be designed for a total live load of 600 pounds.

(Repealed and added by Stats. 1955, Ch. 1349.)

9635.

(a) All individual crypt openings shall be sealed with a solid panel of precast concrete, not less than 1 1/2 inches thick, fiber reinforced cement board not less than 7/16 inch thick, or other incombustible material that meets all of the following requirements:

(1) A minimum density of 80 pounds per cubic foot.

(2) A minimum modulus of rupture of 270 pounds per square inch.

(3) A minimum compressive strength of 2500 pounds per square inch.

(4) A rating that conforms to Underwriters Laboratories fire hazard class 1.

(b) All panels shall be securely set in with a high quality, nonflammable, resilient, and nonhardening urethane, silicone base, or other appropriate sealant for permanent sealing after interment is made in the crypt. Seal panels shall be set independent of crypt fronts.

(Amended by Stats. 1993, Ch. 350, Sec. 16. Effective January 1, 1994.)

9636.

All marble floors shall be constructed on a bed of mortar or mastic placed on the floor subslab, with an approved additive to retard efflorescence.

(Amended by Stats. 1993, Ch. 350, Sec. 17. Effective January 1, 1994.)

9637.

All interior or exterior veneers shall be of stone, cast stone, granite, travertine, or marble, or other material allowed in the Uniform Building Code for type I construction. Cast stone shall meet all requirements for cast stone set forth in the Uniform Building Code.

(Amended by Stats. 1993, Ch. 350, Sec. 18. Effective January 1, 1994.)

9638.

Material for exterior trim, including exterior crypt and niche fronts, shall be travertine, serpentine marble, or grade A exterior type marble or granite, only.

(Amended by Stats. 1993, Ch. 350, Sec. 19. Effective January 1, 1994.)

9639.

Joints shall be of uniform thickness and when mortar is used it shall be raked out as work progresses and on completion of installation joints shall be brushed, thoroughly cleaned, wet and carefully filled and pointed.

(Repealed and added by Stats. 1955, Ch. 1349.)

9640.

Grout used for joints and pointing shall conform with the requirements of the Uniform Building Code.

(Repealed and added by Stats. 1955, Ch. 1349.)

9641.

Masonry veneer shall be attached to the supporting wall in accordance with the requirements of the Uniform Building Code.

(Repealed and added by Stats. 1955, Ch. 1349.)

9642.

All base, architraves, wainscoting and all other vertical work other than crypt fronts shall be securely anchored in place with rods, clips, or other suitable anchoring devices of materials as specified in Section 9643. All clips shall be countersunk into the joint surface and set in nonstaining cement or epoxy.

(Amended by Stats. 1993, Ch. 350, Sec. 20. Effective January 1, 1994.)

9643.

All interior and exterior fastenings for hangers, clips, doors, and other objects shall be of copper base alloy, aluminum, copper or stainless steel of adequate gauges and shall be installed to meet or exceed the seismic requirements of the Uniform Building Code.

(Amended by Stats. 1993, Ch. 350, Sec. 21. Effective January 1, 1994.)

9644.

All exterior materials used for doors, window frames, skylights, gutters, downspouts, flashings or embellishment shall be of copper, copper base alloy, aluminum, stainless steel, or other corrosion resistant material of gauges structurally determined.

(Amended by Stats. 1993, Ch. 350, Sec. 22. Effective January 1, 1994.)

9645.

In the event that during a national emergency, as proclaimed by the Governor for purposes of this section, none of the materials listed in Sections 9643 and 9644 are obtainable, the department may permit the use of galvanized iron or other durable materials.

(Amended by Stats. 1993, Ch. 350, Sec. 23. Effective January 1, 1994.)

9646.

Roofs shall be constructed of cast-in-place reinforced concrete, and any roof covering shall be "Fire Retardant" in conformity with the requirements of type I construction.

(Amended by Stats. 1993, Ch. 350, Sec. 24. Effective January 1, 1994.)

9647.

All skylight frames shall be fabricated in conformance with structural requirements, and shall contain wire glass, tempered glass, or plastic of comparable strength and durability.

(Amended by Stats. 1993, Ch. 350, Sec. 25. Effective January 1, 1994.)

CHAPTER 6. Penalties [9675 - 9677]

(Chapter 6 added by Stats. 1955, Ch. 1349.)

9675.

Every person who violates any provision of this part is guilty of a misdemeanor, punishable by fine of not less than one hundred dollars ($100) nor more than one thousand dollars ($1,000) or by imprisonment in a county jail not less than 10 days nor more than six months, or by both; and in addition is liable for all costs, expenses, and disbursements paid or incurred by the department or person prosecuting the case. (Amended by Stats. 1983, Ch. 1092, Sec. 156. Effective September 27, 1983. Operative January 1, 1984, by Sec. 427 of Ch. 1092.)

9676.

Every owner or operator of a mausoleum or columbarium erected in violation of this part is guilty of maintaining a public nuisance and upon conviction is punishable by a fine of not less than five hundred dollars ($500) nor more than five thousand dollars ($5,000) or by imprisonment in a county jail for not less than one month nor more than six months, or by both; and in addition is liable for all costs, expenses and disbursements paid or incurred by the department or person prosecuting the case. Each calendar month during which such public nuisance exists constitutes a separate offense.

The costs, expenses, and disbursements shall be fixed by the court having jurisdiction of the case.

(Repealed and added by Stats. 1955, Ch. 1349.)

9677.

The penalties of this chapter shall not apply as to any building which, at the time of issuance of a permit for the construction thereof was in compliance with the laws then existing, if its use is not in violation of the laws for the protection of public health. (Repealed and added by Stats. 1955, Ch. 1349.)

PART 6. PET CEMETERIES [9700 - 9703]

(Part 6 added by Stats. 1984, Ch. 1093, Sec. 1.)

9700.

The owner of property may dedicate the property to pet cemetery purposes by a notarized dedication recorded with the county recorder of the county in which the property is situated on or after January 1, 1985. The dedication document shall specify the length of time for which the dedication is made. Dedicated property shall be held and used exclusively for pet cemetery purposes, unless and until the dedication is removed from all or any part of the property by an order and decree of the superior court of the county in which the property is situated, in a proceeding brought by the pet cemetery owners for the purpose of removing the pet cemetery dedication and upon notice of hearing and proof satisfactory to the court of both of the following:

(a) That no interments were made in, or that all interments have been removed from, that portion of the property from which the dedication is sought to be removed.

(b) That the pet cemetery owners have received written authorization from those persons whose pets have been buried in the cemetery, or their heirs or assignees, to remove the dedication from their respective plots or to disinter the pet for removal to another plot location. The written authorization may or may not be given for legal consideration.

(Amended by Stats. 1986, Ch. 263, Sec. 1.)

9701.

All mortgages, deeds of trust, and other liens of any nature, hereafter contracted, placed, or incurred upon property which has been, and was at the time of the creation or placing of the lien, dedicated as a pet cemetery, or upon property which is afterwards, with the consent of the owner of any mortgage, trust deed, or lien, dedicated to pet cemetery purposes, shall not affect or defeat the dedication to pet cemetery purposes, but the mortgage, trust deed, or other lien is subject and subordinate to that dedication and any and all sales made upon foreclosure are subject and subordinate to the dedication for pet cemetery purposes.

(Added by Stats. 1984, Ch. 1093, Sec. 1.)

9702.

If a dedication is made pursuant to Section 9700, the pet cemetery owners shall charge an endowment maintenance fee to persons whose pets will be buried in the cemetery on and after the date of this act, in addition to any burial fee. This maintenance fee shall be charged only at the time of the burial and shall be not less than twenty-five dollars ($25). Proceeds from these maintenance fees shall be placed by the pet cemetery owners into an endowment care or similar trust fund, the entirety of which shall be used for the perpetual maintenance of the pet cemetery.

(Added by Stats. 1984, Ch. 1093, Sec. 1.)

9703.

(a) A pet cemetery owner may dispose of the remains of any pet which has been left for more than seven days at the pet cemetery if arrangements have not been made with the pet cemetery owner for the disposition of the pet.

(b) A pet cemetery owner shall post a notice conspicuous to the public on the cemetery site stating that the remains of any pet which has been left for more than seven days at the pet cemetery may be disposed of if arrangements have not been made with the cemetery owner for the disposition of the pet.

(Added by Stats. 1991, Ch. 490, Sec. 1.)

DIVISION 10. UNIFORM CONTROLLED SUBSTANCES ACT [11000 - 11651]

(Division 10 repealed and added by Stats. 1972, Ch. 1407.)

CHAPTER 1. General Provisions and Definitions [11000 - 11033]

(Chapter 1 added by Stats. 1972, Ch. 1407.)

11000.

This division shall be known as the "California Uniform Controlled Substances Act." (Repealed and added by Stats. 1972, Ch. 1407.)

11001.

Unless the context otherwise requires, the definitions in this chapter govern the construction of this division.

(Repealed and added by Stats. 1972, Ch. 1407.)

11002.

"Administer" means the direct application of a controlled substance, whether by injection, inhalation, ingestion, or any other means, to the body of a patient for his immediate needs or to the body of a research subject by any of the following:

(a) A practitioner or, in his presence, by his authorized agent.

(b) The patient or research subject at the direction and in the presence of the practitioner.

(Repealed and added by Stats. 1972, Ch. 1407.)

11003.

"Agent" means an authorized person who acts on behalf of or at the direction of a manufacturer, distributor, or dispenser. It does not include a common or contract carrier, public warehouseman, or employee of the carrier or warehouseman.

(Repealed and added by Stats. 1972, Ch. 1407.)

11004.

"Attorney General" means the Attorney General of the State of California.

(Repealed and added by Stats. 1972, Ch. 1407.)

11005.

"Board of Pharmacy" means the California State Board of Pharmacy.

(Repealed and added by Stats. 1972, Ch. 1407.)

11006.5.

"Concentrated cannabis" means the separated resin, whether crude or purified, obtained from cannabis.

(Amended by Stats. 2017, Ch. 27, Sec. 113. (SB 94) Effective June 27, 2017.)

11007.

"Controlled substance," unless otherwise specified, means a drug, substance, or immediate precursor which is listed in any schedule in Section 11054, 11055, 11056, 11057, or 11058.

(Added by Stats. 1987, Ch. 1174, Sec. 1. Effective September 26, 1987.)

11008.

"Customs broker" means a person in this state who is authorized to act as a broker for any of the following:

(a) A person in this state who is licensed to sell, distribute, or otherwise possess any controlled substance.

(b) A person in any other state who ships any controlled substance into this state.

(c) A person in this state or any other state who ships or transfers any controlled substance through this state.

(Repealed and added by Stats. 1972, Ch. 1407.)

11009.

"Deliver" or "delivery" means the actual, constructive, or attempted transfer from one person to another of a controlled substance, whether or not there is an agency relationship.

(Added by Stats. 1972, Ch. 1407.)

11010.

"Dispense" means to deliver a controlled substance to an ultimate user or research subject by or pursuant to the lawful order of a practitioner, including the prescribing, furnishing, packaging, labeling, or compounding necessary to prepare the substance for that delivery.

(Repealed and added by Stats. 1972, Ch. 1407.)

11011.

"Dispenser" means a practitioner who dispenses.

(Repealed and added by Stats. 1972, Ch. 1407.)

11012.

"Distribute" means to deliver other than by administering or dispensing a controlled substance.

(Repealed and added by Stats. 1972, Ch. 1407.)

11013.

"Distributor" means a person who distributes. The term distributor also includes warehousemen handling or storing controlled substances and customs brokers.

(Repealed and added by Stats. 1972, Ch. 1407.)

11014.

"Drug" means (a) substances recognized as drugs in the official United States Pharmacopoeia, official Homeopathic Pharmacopoeia of the United States, or official National Formulary, or any supplement to any of them; (b) substances intended for use in the diagnosis, cure, mitigation, treatment, or prevention of disease in man or animals; (c) substances (other than food) intended to affect the structure or any function of the body of man or animals; and (d) substances intended for use as a component of any article specified in subdivision (a), (b), or (c) of this section. It does not include devices or their components, parts, or accessories.

(Repealed and added by Stats. 1972, Ch. 1407.)

11014.5.

(a) "Drug paraphernalia" means all equipment, products and materials of any kind which are designed for use or marketed for use, in planting, propagating, cultivating, growing, harvesting, manufacturing, compounding, converting, producing, processing, preparing, testing, analyzing, packaging, repackaging, storing, containing, concealing, injecting, ingesting, inhaling, or otherwise introducing into the human body a controlled substance in violation of this division. It includes, but is not limited to:

(1) Kits designed for use or marketed for use in planting, propagating, cultivating, growing, or harvesting of any species of plant which is a controlled substance or from which a controlled substance can be derived.

(2) Kits designed for use or marketed for use in manufacturing, compounding, converting, producing, processing, or preparing controlled substances.

(3) Isomerization devices designed for use or marketed for use in increasing the potency of any species of plant which is a controlled substance.

(4) Testing equipment designed for use or marketed for use in identifying, or in analyzing the strength, effectiveness, or purity of controlled substances.

(5) Scales and balances designed for use or marketed for use in weighing or measuring controlled substances.

(6) Containers and other objects designed for use or marketed for use in storing or concealing controlled substances.

(7) Hypodermic syringes, needles, and other objects designed for use or marketed for use in parenterally injecting controlled substances into the human body.

(8) Objects designed for use or marketed for use in ingesting, inhaling, or otherwise introducing cannabis, cocaine, hashish, or hashish oil into the human body, such as:

(A) Carburetion tubes and devices.

(B) Smoking and carburetion masks.

(C) Roach clips, meaning objects used to hold burning material, such as a cannabis cigarette, that has become too small or too short to be held in the hand.

(D) Miniature cocaine spoons, and cocaine vials.

(E) Chamber pipes.

(F) Carburetor pipes.

(G) Electric pipes.

(H) Air-driven pipes.

(I) Chillums.

(J) Bongs.

(K) Ice pipes or chillers.

(b) For the purposes of this section, the phrase "marketed for use" means advertising, distributing, offering for sale, displaying for sale, or selling in a manner which promotes the use of equipment, products, or materials with controlled substances.

(c) In determining whether an object is drug paraphernalia, a court or other authority may consider, in addition to all other logically relevant factors, the following:

(1) Statements by an owner or by anyone in control of the object concerning its use.

(2) Instructions, oral or written, provided with the object concerning its use for ingesting, inhaling, or otherwise introducing a controlled substance into the human body.

(3) Descriptive materials accompanying the object which explain or depict its use.

(4) National and local advertising concerning its use.

(5) The manner in which the object is displayed for sale.

(6) Whether the owner, or anyone in control of the object, is a legitimate supplier of like or related items to the community, such as a licensed distributor or dealer of tobacco products.

(7) Expert testimony concerning its use.

(d) If any provision of this section or the application thereof to any person or circumstance is held invalid, it is the intent of the Legislature that the invalidity shall not affect other provisions or applications of the section which can be given effect without the invalid provision or application and to this end the provisions of this section are severable.

(Amended by Stats. 2017, Ch. 27, Sec. 114. (SB 94) Effective June 27, 2017.)

11015.

"Federal bureau" means the Drug Enforcement Administration of the United States Department of Justice, or its successor agency.

(Amended by Stats. 1992, Ch. 978, Sec. 2. Effective January 1, 1993.)

11016.

"Furnish" has the same meaning as provided in Section 4048.5 of the Business and Professions Code.

(Repealed and added by Stats. 1972, Ch. 1407.)

11017.

"Manufacturer" has the same meaning as provided in Section 4034 of the Business and Professions Code.

(Added by Stats. 1972, Ch. 1407.)

11018.

"Cannabis" means all parts of the plant Cannabis sativa L., whether growing or not; the seeds thereof; the resin extracted from any part of the plant; and every compound, manufacture, salt, derivative, mixture, or preparation of the plant, its seeds or resin. It does not include either of the following:

(a) Industrial hemp, as defined in Section 11018.5.

(b) The weight of any other ingredient combined with cannabis to prepare topical or oral administrations, food, drink, or other product.

(Amended by Stats. 2017, Ch. 27, Sec. 115. (SB 94) Effective June 27, 2017. Note: This section was amended on Nov. 8, 2016, by initiative Prop. 64.)

11018.1.

"Cannabis products" means cannabis that has undergone a process whereby the plant material has been transformed into a concentrate, including, but not limited to, concentrated cannabis, or an edible or topical product containing cannabis or concentrated cannabis and other ingredients.

(Amended by Stats. 2017, Ch. 27, Sec. 116. (SB 94) Effective June 27, 2017. Note: This section was added on Nov. 8, 2016, by initiative Prop. 64.)

11018.2.

"Cannabis accessories" means any equipment, products or materials of any kind which are used, intended for use, or designed for use in planting, propagating, cultivating, growing, harvesting, manufacturing, compounding, converting, producing, processing, preparing, testing, analyzing, packaging, repackaging, storing, smoking, vaporizing, or containing cannabis, or for ingesting, inhaling, or otherwise introducing cannabis or cannabis products into the human body.

(Amended by Stats. 2017, Ch. 27, Sec. 117. (SB 94) Effective June 27, 2017. Note: This section was added on Nov. 8, 2016, by initiative Prop. 64.)

11018.5.

(a) "Industrial hemp" means a crop that is limited to types of the plant Cannabis sativa L. having no more than three-tenths of 1 percent tetrahydrocannabinol (THC) contained in the dried flowering tops, whether growing or not; the seeds of the plant; the resin extracted from any part of the plant; and every compound, manufacture, salt, derivative, mixture, or preparation of the plant, its seeds or resin produced therefrom.

(b) Industrial hemp shall not be subject to the provisions of this division or of Division 10 (commencing with Section 26000) of the Business and Professions Code, but instead shall be regulated by the Department of Food and Agriculture in accordance with the provisions of Division 24 (commencing with Section 81000) of the Food and Agricultural Code, inclusive.

(Amended by Stats. 2018, Ch. 986, Sec. 8. (SB 1409) Effective January 1, 2019. Note: This section was amended on Nov. 8, 2016, by initiative Prop. 64.)

11019.

"Narcotic drug" means any of the following, whether produced directly or indirectly by extraction from substances of vegetable origin, or independently by means of chemical synthesis, or by a combination of extraction and chemical synthesis:

(a) Opium and opiate, and any salt, compound, derivative, or preparation of opium or opiate.

(b) Any salt, compound, isomer, or derivative, whether natural or synthetic, of the substances referred to in subdivision (a), but not including the isoquinoline alkaloids of opium.

(c) Opium poppy and poppy straw.

(d) Coca leaves and any salt, compound, derivative, or preparation of coca leaves, but not including decocainized coca leaves or extractions of coca leaves which do not contain cocaine or ecgonine.

(e) Cocaine, whether natural or synthetic, or any salt, isomer, derivative, or preparation thereof.

(f) Ecgonine, whether natural or synthetic, or any salt, isomer, derivative, or preparation thereof.

(g) Acetylfentanyl, the thiophene analog thereof, derivatives of either, and any salt, compound, isomer, or preparation of acetylfentanyl or the thiophene analog thereof.

(Amended by Stats. 1985, Ch. 1098, Sec. 1. Effective September 27, 1985.)

11020.

"Opiate" means any substance having an addiction-forming or addiction-sustaining liability similar to morphine or being capable of conversion into a drug having addiction-forming or addiction-sustaining liability. It does not include, unless specifically designated as controlled under Chapter 2 (commencing with Section 11053) of this division, the dextrorotatory isomer of 3-methoxy-n-methylmorphinan and its salts (dextromethorphan). It does include its racemic and levorotatory forms.

(Added by Stats. 1972, Ch. 1407.)

11021.

"Opium poppy" means the plant of the species Papaver somniferum L., except its seeds.

(Added by Stats. 1972, Ch. 1407.)

11022.

"Person" means individual, corporation, government or governmental subdivision or agency, business trust, estate, trust, partnership, limited liability company, or association, or any other legal entity.

(Amended by Stats. 1994, Ch. 1010, Sec. 159. Effective January 1, 1995.)

11023.

"Pharmacy" has the same meaning as provided in Section 4035 of the Business and Professions Code.

(Added by Stats. 1972, Ch. 1407.)

11024.

"Physician," "dentist," "podiatrist," "pharmacist," "veterinarian," and "optometrist" means persons who are licensed to practice their respective professions in this state. (Amended by Stats. 2000, Ch. 676, Sec. 6. Effective January 1, 2001.)

11025.

"Poppy straw" means all parts, except the seeds, of the opium poppy, after mowing. (Added by Stats. 1972, Ch. 1407.)

11026.

"Practitioner" means any of the following:

(a) A physician, dentist, veterinarian, podiatrist, or pharmacist acting within the scope of a project authorized under Article 1 (commencing with Section 128125) of Chapter 3 of Part 3 of Division 107, a registered nurse acting within the scope of a project authorized under Article 1 (commencing with Section 128125) of Chapter 3 of Part 3 of Division 107, a certified nurse-midwife acting within the scope of Section 2746.51 of the Business and Professions Code, a nurse practitioner acting within the scope of Section 2836.1 of the Business and Professions Code, or a physician assistant acting within the scope of a project authorized under Article 1 (commencing with Section 128125) of Chapter 3 of Part 3 of Division 107 or Section 3502.1 of the Business and Professions Code, or an optometrist acting within the scope of Section 3041 of the Business and Professions Code.

(b) A pharmacy, hospital, or other institution licensed, registered, or otherwise permitted to distribute, dispense, conduct research with respect to, or to administer, a controlled substance in the course of professional practice or research in this state.

(c) A scientific investigator, or other person licensed, registered, or otherwise permitted, to distribute, dispense, conduct research with respect to, or administer, a controlled substance in the course of professional practice or research in this state. (Amended by Stats. 2001, Ch. 289, Sec. 10. Effective January 1, 2002.)

11027.

(a) "Prescription" means an oral order or electronic transmission prescription for a controlled substance given individually for the person(s) for whom prescribed, directly from the prescriber to the furnisher or indirectly by means of a written order of the prescriber.

(b) "Electronic transmission prescription" includes both image and data prescriptions. "Electronic image transmission prescription" is any prescription order for which a facsimile of the order is received by a pharmacy from a licensed prescriber. "Electronic data transmission prescription" is any prescription order, other than an electronic image transmission prescription, which is electronically transmitted from a licensed prescriber to a pharmacy. (Amended by Stats. 1994, Ch. 26, Sec. 241. Effective March 30, 1994.)

11029.

"Production" includes the manufacture, planting, cultivation, growing, or harvesting of a controlled substance. (Added by Stats. 1972, Ch. 1407.)

11029.5.

"Security printer" means a person approved to produce controlled substance prescription forms pursuant to Section 11161.5. (Added by Stats. 2003, Ch. 406, Sec. 2. Effective January 1, 2004.)

11030.

"Ultimate user" means a person who lawfully possesses a controlled substance for his own use or for the use of a member of his household or for administering to an animal owned by him or by a member of his household. (Added by Stats. 1972, Ch. 1407.)

11031.

"Wholesaler" has the same meaning as provided in Section 4038 of the Business and Professions Code. (Added by Stats. 1972, Ch. 1407.)

11032.

If reference is made to the term "narcotics" in any law not in this division, unless otherwise expressly provided, it means those controlled substances classified in Schedules I and II, as defined in this division. If reference is made to "restricted dangerous drugs" not in this division, unless otherwise expressly provided, it means those controlled substances classified in Schedules III and IV. If reference is made to the term "marijuana" in any law not in this division, unless otherwise expressly provided, it means cannabis as defined in this division. (Amended by Stats. 2017, Ch. 27, Sec. 119. (SB 94) Effective June 27, 2017.)

11033.

As used in this division, except as otherwise defined, the term "isomer" includes optical and geometrical (diastereomeric) isomers. (Added by Stats. 1985, Ch. 21, Sec. 2. Effective April 2, 1985.)

CHAPTER 2. Standards and Schedules [11053 - 11058]

(Chapter 2 added by Stats. 1972, Ch. 1407.)

11053.

The controlled substances listed or to be listed in the schedules in this chapter are included by whatever official, common, usual, chemical, or trade name designated. (Added by Stats. 1972, Ch. 1407.)

11054.

(a) The controlled substances listed in this section are included in Schedule I.

(b) Opiates. Unless specifically excepted or unless listed in another schedule, any of the following opiates, including their isomers, esters, ethers, salts, and salts of isomers, esters, and ethers whenever the existence of those isomers, esters, ethers, and salts is possible within the specific chemical designation:

(1) Acetylmethadol.
(2) Allylprodine.
(3) Alphacetylmethadol (except levoalphacetylmethadol, also known as levo-alpha-acetylmethadol, levomethadyl acetate, or LAAM).
(4) Alphameprodine.
(5) Alphamethadol.
(6) Benzethidine.
(7) Betacetylmethadol.
(8) Betameprodine.
(9) Betamethadol.
(10) Betaprodine.
(11) Clonitazene.
(12) Dextromoramide.
(13) Diampromide.
(14) Diethylthiambutene.
(15) Difenoxin.
(16) Dimenoxadol.
(17) Dimepheptanol.
(18) Dimethylthiambutene.
(19) Dioxaphetyl butyrate.
(20) Dipipanone.
(21) Ethylmethylthiambutene.
(22) Etonitazene.
(23) Etoxeridine.
(24) Furethidine.
(25) Hydroxypethidine.
(26) Ketobemidone.
(27) Levomoramide.
(28) Levophenacylmorphan.
(29) Morpheridine.
(30) Noracymethadol.
(31) Norlevorphanol.
(32) Normethadone.
(33) Norpipanone.
(34) Phenadoxone.
(35) Phenampromide.
(36) Phenomorphan.
(37) Phenoperidine.
(38) Piritramide.
(39) Proheptazine.
(40) Properidine.
(41) Propiram.
(42) Racemoramide.
(43) Tilidine.
(44) Trimeperidine.
(45) Any substance which contains any quantity of acetylfentanyl (N-[1-phenethyl-4-piperidinyl] acetanilide) or a derivative thereof.
(46) Any substance which contains any quantity of the thiophene analog of acetylfentanyl (N-[1-[2-(2-thienyl)ethyl]-4-piperidinyl] acetanilide) or a derivative thereof.
(47) 1-Methyl-4-Phenyl-4-Propionoxypiperidine (MPPP).
(48) 1-(2-Phenethyl)-4-Phenyl-4-Acetyloxypiperidine (PEPAP).

(c) Opium derivatives. Unless specifically excepted or unless listed in another schedule, any of the following opium derivatives, its salts, isomers, and salts of isomers whenever the existence of those salts, isomers, and salts of isomers is possible within the specific chemical designation:

(1) Acetorphine.
(2) Acetyldihydrocodeine.
(3) Benzylmorphine.
(4) Codeine methylbromide.
(5) Codeine-N-Oxide.
(6) Cyprenorphine.
(7) Desomorphine.
(8) Dihydromorphine.
(9) Drotebanol.
(10) Etorphine (except hydrochloride salt).
(11) Heroin.
(12) Hydromorphinol.
(13) Methyldesorphine.
(14) Methyldihydromorphine.
(15) Morphine methylbromide.
(16) Morphine methylsulfonate.
(17) Morphine-N-Oxide.
(18) Myrophine.
(19) Nicocodeine.
(20) Nicomorphine.
(21) Normorphine.

(22) Pholcodine.

(23) Thebacon.

(d) Hallucinogenic substances. Unless specifically excepted or unless listed in another schedule, any material, compound, mixture, or preparation, which contains any quantity of the following hallucinogenic substances, or which contains any of its salts, isomers, and salts of isomers whenever the existence of those salts, isomers, and salts of isomers is possible within the specific chemical designation (for purposes of this subdivision only, the term "isomer" includes the optical, position, and geometric isomers):

(1) 4-bromo-2,5-dimethoxy-amphetamine—Some trade or other names: 4-bromo-2,5-dimethoxy-alpha-methylphenethylamine; 4-bromo-2,5-DMA.

(2) 2,5-dimethoxyamphetamine—Some trade or other names: 2,5-dimethoxy-alpha-methylphenethylamine; 2,5-DMA.

(3) 4-methoxyamphetamine—Some trade or other names: 4-methoxy-alpha-methylphenethylamine, paramethoxyamphetamine, PMA.

(4) 5-methoxy-3,4-methylenedioxy-amphetamine.

(5) 4-methyl-2,5-dimethoxy-amphetamine—Some trade or other names: 4-methyl-2,5-dimethoxy-alpha-methylphenethylamine; "DOM"; and "STP."

(6) 3,4-methylenedioxy amphetamine.

(7) 3,4,5-trimethoxy amphetamine.

(8) Bufotenine—Some trade or other names: 3-(beta-dimethylaminoethyl)-5-hydroxyindole; 3-(2-dimethylaminoethyl)-5 indolol; N,N-dimethylserolonin, 5-hydroxy-N,N-dimethyltryptamine; mappine.

(9) Diethyltryptamine—Some trade or other names: N,N-Diethyltryptamine; DET.

(10) Dimethyltryptamine—Some trade or other names: DMT.

(11) Ibogaine—Some trade or other names: 7-Ethyl-6,6beta, 7,8,9,10,12,13-octahydro-2-methoxy-6,9-methano-5H-pyrido [1',2':1,2] azepino [5,4-b] indole; Tabernantheiboga.

(12) Lysergic acid diethylamide.

(13) Cannabis.

(14) Mescaline.

(15) Peyote—Meaning all parts of the plant presently classified botanically as Lophophora williamsii Lemaire, whether growing or not, the seeds thereof, any extract from any part of the plant, and every compound, manufacture, salts, derivative, mixture, or preparation of the plant, its seeds or extracts (interprets 21 U.S.C. Sec. 812(c), Schedule 1(c)(12)).

(16) N-ethyl-3-piperidyl benzilate.

(17) N-methyl-3-piperidyl benzilate.

(18) Psilocybin.

(19) Psilocyn.

(20) Tetrahydrocannabinols. Synthetic equivalents of the substances contained in the plant, or in the resinous extractives of Cannabis, sp. and/or synthetic substances, derivatives, and their isomers with similar chemical structure and pharmacological activity such as the following: delta 1 cis or trans tetrahydrocannabinol, and their optical isomers; delta 6 cis or trans tetrahydrocannabinol, and their optical isomers; delta 3,4 cis or trans tetrahydrocannabinol, and its optical isomers.

Because nomenclature of these substances is not internationally standardized, compounds of these structures, regardless of numerical designation of atomic positions covered.

(21) Ethylamine analog of phencyclidine—Some trade or other names: N-ethyl-1-phenylcyclohexylamine, (1-phenylcyclohexyl) ethylamine, N-(1-phenylcyclohexyl) ethylamine, cyclohexamine, PCE.

(22) Pyrrolidine analog of phencyclidine—Some trade or other names: 1-(1-phenylcyclohexyl)-pyrrolidine, PCP, PHP.

(23) Thiophene analog of phencyclidine—Some trade or other names: 1-[1-(2 thienyl)-cyclohexyl]-piperidine, 2-thienyl analog of phencyclidine, TPCP, TCP.

(e) Depressants. Unless specifically excepted or unless listed in another schedule, any material, compound, mixture, or preparation which contains any quantity of the following substances having a depressant effect on the central nervous system, including its salts, isomers, and salts of isomers whenever the existence of those salts, isomers, and salts of isomers is possible within the specific chemical designation:

(1) Mecloqualone.

(2) Methaqualone.

(3) Gamma hydroxybutyric acid (also known by other names such as GHB; gamma hydroxy butyrate; 4-hydroxybutyrate; 4-hydroxybutanoic acid; sodium oxybate; sodium oxybutyrate), including its immediate precursors, isomers, esters, ethers, salts, and salts of isomers, esters, and ethers, including, but not limited to, gammabutyrolactone, for which an application has not been approved under Section 505 of the Federal Food, Drug, and Cosmetic Act (21 U.S.C. Sec. 355).

(f) Unless specifically excepted or unless listed in another schedule, any material, compound, mixture, or preparation which contains any quantity of the following substances having a stimulant effect on the central nervous system, including its isomers:

(1) Cocaine base.

(2) Fenethylline, including its salts.

(3) N-Ethylamphetamine, including its salts.

(Amended by Stats. 2017, Ch. 27, Sec. 120. (SB 94) Effective June 27, 2017.)

11055.

(a) The controlled substances listed in this section are included in Schedule II.

(b) Any of the following substances, except those narcotic drugs listed in other schedules, whether produced directly or indirectly by extraction from substances of vegetable origin, or independently by means of chemical synthesis, or by combination of extraction and chemical synthesis:

(1) Opium, opiate, and any salt, compound, derivative, or preparation of opium or opiate, with the exception of naloxone hydrochloride (N-allyl-14-hydroxy-nordihydromorphinone hydrochloride), but including the following:

(A) Raw opium.

(B) Opium extracts.

(C) Opium fluid extracts.

(D) Powdered opium.

(E) Granulated opium.

(F) Tincture of opium.

(G) Codeine.

(H) Ethylmorphine.

(I) (i) Hydrocodone.

(ii) Hydrocodone combination products with not more than 300 milligrams of dihydrocodeinone per 100 milliliters or not more than 15 milligrams per dosage unit, with one or more active nonnarcotic ingredients in recognized therapeutic amounts.

(iii) Oral liquid preparations of dihydrocodeinone containing the above specified amounts that contain, as its nonnarcotic ingredients, two or more antihistamines in combination with each other.

(iv) Hydrocodone combination products with not more than 300 milligrams of dihydrocodeinone per 100 milliliters or not more than 15 milligrams per dosage unit, with a fourfold or greater quantity of an isoquinoline alkaloid of opium.

(J) Hydromorphone.

(K) Metopon.

(L) Morphine.

(M) Oxycodone.

(N) Oxymorphone.

(O) Thebaine.

(2) Any salt, compound, isomer, or derivative, whether natural or synthetic, of the substances referred to in paragraph (1), but not including the isoquinoline alkaloids of opium.

(3) Opium poppy and poppy straw.

(4) Coca leaves and any salt, compound, derivative, or preparation of coca leaves, but not including decocainized coca leaves or extractions which do not contain cocaine or ecgonine.

(5) Concentrate of poppy straw (the crude extract of poppy straw in either liquid, solid, or powder form which contains the phenanthrene alkaloids of the opium poppy).

(6) Cocaine, except as specified in Section 11054.

(7) Ecgonine, whether natural or synthetic, or any salt, isomer, derivative, or preparation thereof.

(c) Opiates. Unless specifically excepted or unless in another schedule, any of the following opiates, including its isomers, esters, ethers, salts, and salts of isomers, esters, and ethers whenever the existence of those isomers, esters, ethers, and salts is possible within the specific chemical designation, dextrorphan and levopropoxyphene excepted:

(1) Alfentanyl.

(2) Alphaprodine.

(3) Anileridine.

(4) Bezitramide.

(5) Bulk dextropropoxyphene (nondosage forms).

(6) Dihydrocodeine.

(7) Diphenoxylate.

(8) Fentanyl.

(9) Isomethadone.

(10) Levoalphacetylmethadol, also known as levo-alpha-acetylmethadol, levomethadyl acetate, or LAAM. This substance is authorized for the treatment of narcotic addicts under federal law (see Part 291 (commencing with Section 291.501) and Part 1308 (commencing with Section 1308.01) of Title 21 of the Code of Federal Regulations).

(11) Levomethorphan.

(12) Levorphanol.

(13) Metazocine.

(14) Methadone.

(15) Methadone-Intermediate, 4-cyano-2-dimethylamino-4, 4-diphenyl butane.

(16) Moramide-Intermediate, 2-methyl-3-morpholino-1, 1-diphenylpropane-carboxylic acid.

(17) Pethidine (meperidine).

(18) Pethidine-Intermediate-A, 4-cyano-1-methyl-4-phenylpiperidine.

(19) Pethidine-Intermediate-B, ethyl-4-phenylpiperidine-4-carboxylate.

(20) Pethidine-Intermediate-C, 1-methyl-4-phenylpiperidine-4-carboxylic acid.

(21) Phenazocine.

(22) Piminodine.

(23) Racemethorphan.

(24) Racemorphan.

(25) Sufentanyl.

(d) Stimulants. Unless specifically excepted or unless listed in another schedule, any material, compound, mixture, or preparation which contains any quantity of the following substances having a stimulant effect on the central nervous system:

(1) Amphetamine, its salts, optical isomers, and salts of its optical isomers.

(2) Methamphetamine, its salts, isomers, and salts of its isomers.

(3) Dimethylamphetamine (N,N-dimethylamphetamine), its salts, isomers, and salts of its isomers.

(4) N-Ethylmethamphetamine (N-ethyl, N-methylamphetamine), its salts, isomers, and salts of its isomers.

(5) Phenmetrazine and its salts.

(6) Methylphenidate.

(7) Khat, which includes all parts of the plant classified botanically as Catha Edulis, whether growing or not, the seeds thereof, any extract from any part of the plant, and every compound, manufacture, salt, derivative, mixture, or preparation of the plant, its seeds, or extracts.

(8) Cathinone (also known as alpha-aminopropiophenone, 2-aminopropiophenone, and norephedrone).

(e) Depressants. Unless specifically excepted or unless listed in another schedule, any material, compound, mixture, or preparation which contains any quantity of the following substances having a depressant effect on the central nervous system, including its salts, isomers, and salts of isomers whenever the existence of those salts, isomers, and salts of isomers is possible within the specific chemical designation:

(1) Amobarbital.

(2) Pentobarbital.

(3) Phencyclidines, including the following:

(A) 1-(1-phenylcyclohexyl) piperidine (PCP).

(B) 1-(1-phenylcyclohexyl) morpholine (PCM).

(C) Any analog of phencyclidine which is added by the Attorney General by regulation pursuant to this paragraph.

The Attorney General, or his or her designee, may, by rule or regulation, add additional analogs of phencyclidine to those enumerated in this paragraph after notice, posting, and hearing pursuant to Chapter 3.5 (commencing with Section 11340) of Part 1 of Division 3 of Title 2 of the Government Code. The Attorney General shall, in the calendar year of the regular session of the Legislature in which the rule or regulation is adopted, submit a draft of a proposed bill to each house of the Legislature which would incorporate the analogs into this code. No rule or regulation shall remain in effect beyond January 1 after the calendar year of the regular session in which the draft of the proposed bill is submitted to each house. However, if the draft of the proposed bill is submitted during a recess of the Legislature exceeding 45 calendar days, the rule or regulation shall be effective until January 1 after the next calendar year.

(4) Secobarbital.

(5) Glutethimide.

(f) Immediate precursors. Unless specifically excepted or unless listed in another schedule, any material, compound, mixture, or preparation which contains any quantity of the following substances:

(1) Immediate precursor to amphetamine and methamphetamine:

(A) Phenylacetone. Some trade or other names: phenyl-2 propanone; P2P; benzyl methyl ketone; methyl benzyl ketone.

(2) Immediate precursors to phencyclidine (PCP):

(A) 1-phenylcyclohexylamine.

(B) 1-piperidinocyclohexane carbonitrile (PCC).

(Amended by Stats. 2018, Ch. 589, Sec. 1. (AB 2783) Effective January 1, 2019.)

11056.

(a) The controlled substances listed in this section are included in Schedule III.

(b) Stimulants. Unless specifically excepted or unless listed in another schedule, any material, compound, mixture, or preparation that contains any quantity of the following substances having a stimulant effect on the central nervous system, including its salts, isomers (whether optical, position, or geometric), and salts of those isomers whenever the existence of those salts, isomers, and salts of isomers is possible within the specific chemical designation:

(1) Those compounds, mixtures, or preparations in dosage unit form containing any stimulant substances listed in Schedule II which compounds, mixtures, or preparations were listed on August 25, 1971, as excepted compounds under Section 1308.32 of Title 21 of the Code of Federal Regulations, and any other drug of the quantitative composition shown in that list for those drugs or that is the same except that it contains a lesser quantity of controlled substances.

(2) Benzphetamine.

(3) Chlorphentermine.

(4) Clortermine.

(5) Mazindol.

(6) Phendimetrazine.

(c) Depressants. Unless specifically excepted or unless listed in another schedule, any material, compound, mixture, or preparation that contains any quantity of the following substances having a depressant effect on the central nervous system:

(1) Any compound, mixture, or preparation containing any of the following:

(A) Amobarbital

(B) Secobarbital

(C) Pentobarbital

or any salt thereof and one or more other active medicinal ingredients that are not listed in any schedule.

(2) Any suppository dosage form containing any of the following:

(A) Amobarbital

(B) Secobarbital

(C) Pentobarbital

or any salt of any of these drugs and approved by the federal Food and Drug Administration for marketing only as a suppository.

(3) Any substance that contains any quantity of a derivative of barbituric acid or any salt thereof.

(4) Chlorhexadol.

(5) Lysergic acid.

(6) Lysergic acid amide.

(7) Methyprylon.

(8) Sulfondiethylmethane.

(9) Sulfonethylmethane.

(10) Sulfonmethane.

(11) Gamma hydroxybutyric acid, and its salts, isomers and salts of isomers, contained in a drug product for which an application has been approved under Section 505 of the Federal Food, Drug, and Cosmetic Act (21 U.S.C. Sec. 355).

(d) Nalorphine.

(e) Narcotic drugs. Unless specifically excepted or unless listed in another schedule, any material, compound, mixture, or preparation containing any of the following narcotic drugs, or their salts calculated as the free anhydrous base or alkaloid, in limited quantities as set forth below:

(1) Not more than 1.8 grams of codeine per 100 milliliters or not more than 90 milligrams per dosage unit, with an equal or greater quantity of an isoquinoline alkaloid of opium.

(2) Not more than 1.8 grams of codeine per 100 milliliters or not more than 90 milligrams per dosage unit, with one or more active, nonnarcotic ingredients in recognized therapeutic amounts.

(3) Not more than 1.8 grams of dihydrocodeine per 100 milliliters or not more than 90 milligrams per dosage unit, with one or more active nonnarcotic ingredients in recognized therapeutic amounts.

(4) Not more than 300 milligrams of ethylmorphine per 100 milliliters or not more than 15 milligrams per dosage unit, with one or more active, nonnarcotic ingredients in recognized therapeutic amounts.

(5) Not more than 500 milligrams of opium per 100 milliliters or per 100 grams or not more than 25 milligrams per dosage unit, with one or more active, nonnarcotic ingredients in recognized therapeutic amounts.

(6) Not more than 50 milligrams of morphine per 100 milliliters or per 100 grams, with one or more active, nonnarcotic ingredients in recognized therapeutic amounts.

(f) Anabolic steroids and chorionic gonadotropin. Any material, compound, mixture, or preparation containing chorionic gonadotropin or an anabolic steroid (excluding anabolic steroid products listed in the "Table of Exempt Anabolic Steroid Products" (Section 1308.34 of Title 21 of the Code of Federal Regulations), as exempt from the federal Controlled Substances Act (Section 801 and following of Title 21 of the United States Code)), including, but not limited to, the following:

(1) Androisoxazole.

(2) Androstenediol.

(3) Bolandiol.

(4) Bolasterone.

(5) Boldenone.

(6) Chlormethandienone.

(7) Clostebol.

(8) Dihydromesterone.

(9) Ethylestrenol.

(10) Fluoxymesterone.

(11) Formyldienolone.

(12) 4-Hydroxy-19-nortestosterone.

(13) Mesterolone.

(14) Methandriol.

(15) Methandrostenolone.

(16) Methenolone.

(17) 17-Methyltestosterone.

(18) Methyltrienolone.

(19) Nandrolone.

(20) Norbolethone.

(21) Norethandrolone.

(22) Normethandrolone.

(23) Oxandrolone.

(24) Oxymestrone.

(25) Oxymetholone.

(26) Quinbolone.

(27) Stanolone.

(28) Stanozolol.

(29) Stenbolone.

(30) Testosterone.

(31) Trenbolone.

(32) Human clorionic gonadotropin (hCG), except when possessed by, sold to, purchased by, transferred to, or administered by a licensed veterinarian, or a licensed veterinarian's designated agent, exclusively for veterinary use.

(g) Ketamine. Any material, compound, mixture, or preparation containing ketamine.

(h) Hallucinogenic substances. Any of the following hallucinogenic substances: dronabinol (synthetic) in sesame oil and encapsulated in a soft gelatin capsule in a drug product approved by the federal Food and Drug Administration.

(Amended by Stats. 2018, Ch. 589, Sec. 2.5. (AB 2783) Effective January 1, 2019.)

11057.

(a) The controlled substances listed in this section are included in Schedule IV.

(b) Schedule IV shall consist of the drugs and other substances, by whatever official name, common or usual name, chemical name, or brand name designated, listed in this section.

(c) Narcotic drugs. Unless specifically excepted or unless listed in another schedule, any material, compound, mixture, or preparation containing any of the following narcotic drugs, or their salts calculated as the free anhydrous base or alkaloid, in limited quantities as set forth below:

(1) Not more than 1 milligram of difenoxin and not less than 25 micrograms of atropine sulfate per dosage unit.

(2) Dextropropoxyphene (alpha-(+)-4-dimethylamino-1, 2-diphenyl-3-methyl-2-propionoxybutane).

(3) Butorphanol.

(d) Depressants. Unless specifically excepted or unless listed in another schedule, any material, compound, mixture, or preparation which contains any quantity of the following substances, including its salts, isomers, and salts of isomers whenever the existence of those salts, isomers, and salts of isomers is possible within the specific chemical designation:

(1) Alprazolam.

(2) Barbital.

(3) Chloral betaine.

(4) Chloral hydrate.

(5) Chlordiazepoxide.

(6) Clobazam.

(7) Clonazepam.

(8) Clorazepate.

(9) Diazepam.

(10) Estazolam.

(11) Ethchlorvynol.

(12) Ethinamate.

(13) Flunitrazepam.

(14) Flurazepam.

(15) Halazepam.

(16) Lorazepam.

(17) Mebutamate.

(18) Meprobamate.

(19) Methohexital.

(20) Methylphenobarbital (Mephobarbital).

(21) Midazolam.

(22) Nitrazepam.

(23) Oxazepam.

(24) Paraldehyde.

(25) Petrichoral.

(26) Phenobarbital.

(27) Prazepam.

(28) Quazepam.

(29) Temazepam.

(30) Triazolam.

(31) Zaleplon.

(32) Zolpidem.

(e) Fenfluramine. Any material, compound, mixture, or preparation which contains any quantity of the following substances, including its salts, isomers (whether optical, position, or geometric), and salts of those isomers, whenever the existence of those salts, isomers, and salts of isomers is possible:

(1) Fenfluramine.

(f) Stimulants. Unless specifically excepted or unless listed in another schedule, any material, compound, mixture, or preparation which contains any quantity of the following substances having a stimulant effect on the central nervous system, including its salts, isomers (whether optical, position, or geometric), and salts of those isomers is possible within the specific chemical designation:

(1) Diethylpropion.

(2) Mazindol.

(3) Modafinil.

(4) Phentermine.

(5) Pemoline (including organometallic complexes and chelates thereof).

(6) Pipradrol.

(7) SPA ((-)-1-dimethylamino-1,2-diphenylethane).

(8) Cathine ((+)-norpseudoephedrine).

(g) Other substances. Unless specifically excepted or unless listed in another schedule, any material, compound, mixture or preparation which contains any quantity of pentazocine, including its salts.

(Amended by Stats. 2008, Ch. 292, Sec. 2. Effective January 1, 2009.)

11058.

(a) The controlled substances listed in this section are included in Schedule V.

(b) Schedule V shall consist of the drugs and other substances, by whatever official name, common or usual name, chemical name, or brand name designated, listed in this section.

(c) Narcotic drugs containing nonnarcotic active medicinal ingredients. Any compound, mixture, or preparation containing any of the following narcotic drugs, or their salts calculated as the free anhydrous base or alkaloid, in limited quantities as set forth below, which shall include one or more nonnarcotic active medicinal ingredients in sufficient proportion to confer upon the compound, mixture, or preparation valuable medicinal qualities other than those possessed by narcotic drugs alone:

(1) Not more than 200 milligrams of codeine per 100 milliliters or per 100 grams.

(2) Not more than 100 milligrams of dihydrocodeine per 100 milliliters or per 100 grams.

(3) Not more than 100 milligrams of ethylmorphine per 100 milliliters or per 100 grams.

(4) Not more than 2.5 milligrams of diphenoxylate and not less than 25 micrograms of atropine sulfate per dosage unit.

(5) Not more than 100 milligrams of opium per 100 milliliters or per 100 grams.

(6) Not more than 0.5 milligram of difenoxin and not less than 25 micrograms of atropine sulfate per dosage unit.

(d) Buprenorphine.

(Amended by Stats. 1986, Ch. 63, Sec. 1. Effective April 23, 1986.)

CHAPTER 3. Regulation and Control [11100 - 11111]

(Chapter 3 added by Stats. 1972, Ch. 1407.)

ARTICLE 1. Reporting [11100 - 11111]

(Article 1 added by Stats. 1972, Ch. 1407.)

11100.

(a) Any manufacturer, wholesaler, retailer, or other person or entity in this state that sells, transfers, or otherwise furnishes any of the following substances to any person or entity in this state or any other state shall submit a report to the Department of Justice of all of those transactions:

(1) Phenyl-2-propanone.

(2) Methylamine.

(3) Ethylamine.

(4) D-lysergic acid.

(5) Ergotamine tartrate.

(6) Diethyl malonate.

(7) Malonic acid.

(8) Ethyl malonate.

(9) Barbituric acid.

(10) Piperidine.

(11) N-acetylanthranilic acid.

(12) Pyrrolidine.

(13) Phenylacetic acid.

(14) Anthranilic acid.

(15) Morpholine.

(16) Ephedrine.

(17) Pseudoephedrine.

(18) Norpseudoephedrine.

(19) Phenylpropanolamine.

(20) Propionic anhydride.

(21) Isosafrole.

(22) Safrole.

(23) Piperonal.

(24) Thionyl chloride.

(25) Benzyl cyanide.

(26) Ergonovine maleate.

(27) N-methylephedrine.

(28) N-ethylephedrine.

(29) N-methylpseudoephedrine.

(30) N-ethylpseudoephedrine.

(31) Chloroephedrine.

(32) Chloropseudoephedrine.

(33) Hydriodic acid.

(34) Gamma-butyrolactone, including butyrolactone; butyrolactone gamma; 4-butyrolactone; 2(3H)-furanone dihydro; dihydro-2(3H)-furanone; tetrahydro-2-furanone; 1,2-butanolide; 1,4-butanolide; 4-butanolide; gamma-hydroxybutyric acid lactone; 3-hydroxybutyric acid lactone and 4-hydroxybutanoic acid lactone with Chemical Abstract Service number (96-48-0).

(35) 1,4-butanediol, including butanediol; butane-1,4-diol; 1,4-butylene glycol; butylene glycol; 1,4-dihydroxybutane; 1,4-tetramethylene glycol; tetramethylene glycol; tetramethylene 1,4-diol with Chemical Abstract Service number (110-63-4).

(36) Red phosphorus, including white phosphorus, hypophosphorous acid and its salts, ammonium hypophosphite, calcium hypophosphite, iron hypophosphite, potassium hypophosphite, manganese hypophosphite, magnesium hypophosphite, sodium hypophosphite, and phosphorous acid and its salts.

(37) Iodine or tincture of iodine.

(38) Any of the substances listed by the Department of Justice in regulations promulgated pursuant to subdivision (b).

(b) The Department of Justice may adopt rules and regulations in accordance with Chapter 3.5 (commencing with Section 11340) of Part 1 of Division 3 of Title 2 of the Government Code that add substances to subdivision (a) if the substance is a precursor to a controlled substance and delete substances from subdivision (a). However, no regulation adding or deleting a substance shall have any effect beyond March 1 of the year following the calendar year during which the regulation was adopted.

(c) (1) (A) Any manufacturer, wholesaler, retailer, or other person or entity in this state, prior to selling, transferring, or otherwise furnishing any substance specified in subdivision (a) to any person or business entity in this state or any other state, shall require (i) a letter of authorization from that person or business entity that includes the currently valid business license number or federal Drug Enforcement Administration (DEA) registration number, the address of the business, and a full description of how the substance is to be used, and (ii) proper identification from the purchaser. The manufacturer, wholesaler, retailer, or other person or entity in this state shall retain this information in a readily available manner for three years. The requirement for a full description of how the substance is to be used does not require the person or business entity to reveal their chemical processes that are typically considered trade secrets and proprietary information.

(B) For the purposes of this paragraph, "proper identification" for in-state or out-of-state purchasers includes two or more of the following: federal tax identification number; seller's permit identification number; city or county business license number; license issued by the State Department of Public Health; registration number issued by the federal Drug Enforcement Administration; precursor business permit number issued by the Department of Justice; driver's license; or other identification issued by a state.

(2) (A) Any manufacturer, wholesaler, retailer, or other person or entity in this state that exports a substance specified in subdivision (a) to any person or business entity located in a foreign country shall, on or before the date of exportation, submit to the Department of Justice a notification of that transaction, which notification shall include the name and quantity of the substance to be exported and the name, address, and, if assigned by the foreign country or subdivision thereof, business identification number of the person or business entity located in a foreign country importing the substance.

(B) The department may authorize the submission of the notification on a monthly basis with respect to repeated, regular transactions between an exporter and an importer involving a substance specified in subdivision (a), if the department determines that a pattern of regular supply of the substance exists between the exporter and importer and that the importer has established a record of utilization of the substance for lawful purposes.

(d) (1) Any manufacturer, wholesaler, retailer, or other person or entity in this state that sells, transfers, or otherwise furnishes a substance specified in subdivision (a) to a person or business entity in this state or any other state shall, not less than 21 days prior to delivery of the substance, submit a report of the transaction, which includes the identification information specified in subdivision (c), to the Department of Justice. The Department of Justice may authorize the submission of the reports on a monthly basis with respect to repeated, regular transactions between the furnisher and the recipient involving the substance or substances if the Department of Justice determines that a pattern of regular supply of the substance or substances exists between the manufacturer, wholesaler, retailer, or other person or entity that sells, transfers, or otherwise furnishes the substance or substances and the recipient of the substance or substances, and the recipient has established a record of utilization of the substance or substances for lawful purposes.

(2) The person selling, transferring, or otherwise furnishing any substance specified in subdivision (a) shall affix his or her signature or otherwise identify himself or herself as a witness to the identification of the purchaser or purchasing individual, and shall, if a common carrier is used, maintain a manifest of the delivery to the purchaser for three years.

(e) This section shall not apply to any of the following:

(1) Any pharmacist or other authorized person who sells or furnishes a substance upon the prescription of a physician, dentist, podiatrist, or veterinarian.

(2) Any physician, dentist, podiatrist, or veterinarian who administers or furnishes a substance to his or her patients.

(3) Any manufacturer or wholesaler licensed by the California State Board of Pharmacy that sells, transfers, or otherwise furnishes a substance to a licensed pharmacy, physician, dentist, podiatrist, or veterinarian, or a retail distributor as defined in subdivision (h), provided that the manufacturer or wholesaler submits records of any suspicious sales or transfers as determined by the Department of Justice.

(4) Any analytical research facility that is registered with the federal Drug Enforcement Administration of the United States Department of Justice.

(5) A state-licensed health care facility that administers or furnishes a substance to its patients.

(6) (A) Any sale, transfer, furnishing, or receipt of any product that contains ephedrine, pseudoephedrine, norpseudoephedrine, or phenylpropanolamine and which is lawfully sold, transferred, or furnished over the counter without a prescription pursuant to the federal Food, Drug, and Cosmetic Act (21 U.S.C. Sec. 301 et seq.) or regulations adopted thereunder. However, this section shall apply to preparations in solid or liquid dosage form, except pediatric liquid forms, as defined, containing ephedrine, pseudoephedrine, norpseudoephedrine, or phenylpropanolamine where the individual transaction involves more than three packages or nine grams of ephedrine, pseudoephedrine, norpseudoephedrine, or phenylpropanolamine.

(B) Any ephedrine, pseudoephedrine, norpseudoephedrine, or phenylpropanolamine product subsequently removed from exemption pursuant to Section 814 of Title 21 of the United States Code shall similarly no longer be exempt from any state reporting or permitting requirement, unless otherwise reinstated pursuant to subdivision (d) or (e) of Section 814 of Title 21 of the United States Code as an exempt product.

(7) The sale, transfer, furnishing, or receipt of any betadine or povidone solution with an iodine content not exceeding 1 percent in containers of eight ounces or less, or any tincture of iodine not exceeding 2 percent in containers of one ounce or less, that is sold over the counter.

(8) Any transfer of a substance specified in subdivision (a) for purposes of lawful disposal as waste.

(f) (1) Any person specified in subdivision (a) or (d) who does not submit a report as required by that subdivision or who knowingly submits a report with false or fictitious information shall be punished by imprisonment in a county jail not exceeding six months, by a fine not exceeding five thousand dollars ($5,000), or by both the fine and imprisonment.

(2) Any person specified in subdivision (a) or (d) who has previously been convicted of a violation of paragraph (1) shall, upon a subsequent conviction thereof, be punished by imprisonment pursuant to subdivision (h) of Section 1170 of the Penal Code, or by imprisonment in a county jail not exceeding one year, by a fine not exceeding one hundred thousand dollars ($100,000), or by both the fine and imprisonment.

(g) (1) Except as otherwise provided in subparagraph (A) of paragraph (6) of subdivision (e), it is unlawful for any manufacturer, wholesaler, retailer, or other person to sell, transfer, or otherwise furnish a substance specified in subdivision (a) to a person under 18 years of age.

(2) Except as otherwise provided in subparagraph (A) of paragraph (6) of subdivision (e), it is unlawful for any person under 18 years of age to possess a substance specified in subdivision (a).

(3) Notwithstanding any other law, it is unlawful for any retail distributor to (i) sell in a single transaction more than three packages of a product that he or she knows to contain ephedrine, pseudoephedrine, norpseudoephedrine, or phenylpropanolamine, or (ii) knowingly sell more than nine grams of ephedrine, pseudoephedrine, norpseudoephedrine, or phenylpropanolamine, other than pediatric liquids as defined. Except as otherwise provided in this section, the three package per transaction limitation or nine gram per transaction limitation imposed by this paragraph shall apply to any product that is lawfully sold, transferred, or furnished over the counter without a prescription pursuant to the federal Food, Drug, and Cosmetic Act (21 U.S.C. Sec. 301 et seq.), or regulations adopted thereunder, unless exempted from the requirements of the federal Controlled Substances Act by the federal Drug Enforcement Administration pursuant to Section 814 of Title 21 of the United States Code.

(4) (A) A first violation of this subdivision is a misdemeanor.

(B) Any person who has previously been convicted of a violation of this subdivision shall, upon a subsequent conviction thereof, be punished by imprisonment in a county jail not exceeding one year, by a fine not exceeding ten thousand dollars ($10,000), or by both the fine and imprisonment.

(h) For the purposes of this article, the following terms have the following meanings:

(1) "Drug store" is any entity described in Code 5912 of the Standard Industrial Classification (SIC) Manual published by the United States Office of Management and Budget, 1987 edition.

(2) "General merchandise store" is any entity described in Codes 5311 to 5399, inclusive, and Code 5499 of the Standard Industrial Classification (SIC) Manual published by the United States Office of Management and Budget, 1987 edition.

(3) "Grocery store" is any entity described in Code 5411 of the Standard Industrial Classification (SIC) Manual published by the United States Office of Management and Budget, 1987 edition.

(4) "Pediatric liquid" means a nonencapsulated liquid whose unit measure according to product labeling is stated in milligrams, ounces, or other similar measure. In no instance shall the dosage units exceed 15 milligrams of phenylpropanolamine or pseudoephedrine per five milliliters of liquid product, except for liquid products primarily intended for administration to children under two years of age for which the recommended dosage unit does not exceed two milliliters and the total package content does not exceed one fluid ounce.

(5) "Retail distributor" means a grocery store, general merchandise store, drugstore, or other related entity, the activities of which, as a distributor of ephedrine, pseudoephedrine, norpseudoephedrine, or phenylpropanolamine products, are limited exclusively to the sale of ephedrine, pseudoephedrine, norpseudoephedrine, or phenylpropanolamine products for personal use both in number of sales and volume of sales, either directly to walk-in customers or in face-to-face transactions by direct sales. "Retail distributor" includes an entity that makes a direct sale, but does not include the parent company of that entity if the company is not involved in direct sales regulated by this article.

(6) "Sale for personal use" means the sale in a single transaction to an individual customer for a legitimate medical use of a product containing ephedrine, pseudoephedrine, norpseudoephedrine, or phenylpropanolamine in dosages at or below that specified in paragraph (3) of subdivision (g). "Sale for personal use" also includes the sale of those products to employers to be dispensed to employees from first-aid kits or medicine chests.

(i) It is the intent of the Legislature that this section shall preempt all local ordinances or regulations governing the sale by a retail distributor of over-the-counter products containing ephedrine, pseudoephedrine, norpseudoephedrine, or phenylpropanolamine. (Amended by Stats. 2012, Ch. 867, Sec. 3. (SB 1144) Effective January 1, 2013.)

11100.05.

(a) In addition to any fine or imprisonment imposed under subdivision (f) of Section 11100 or subdivision (j) of Section 11106 of the Health and Safety Code, the following drug cleanup fine shall be imposed:

(1) Ten thousand dollars ($10,000) for violations described in paragraph (1) of subdivision (f) of Section 11100.

(2) One hundred thousand dollars ($100,000) for violations described in paragraph (2) of subdivision (f) of Section 11100.

(3) Ten thousand dollars ($10,000) for violations described in subdivision (j) of Section 11106.

(b) At least once a month, all fines collected under this section shall be transferred to the State Treasury for deposit in the Clandestine Drug Lab Clean-up Account. The transmission to the State Treasury shall be carried out in the same manner as fines collected for the state by a county.

(Amended by Stats. 2005, Ch. 468, Sec. 2. Effective January 1, 2006.)

11100.1.

(a) Any manufacturer, wholesaler, retailer, or other person or entity in this state that obtains from a source outside of this state any substance specified in subdivision (a) of Section 11100 shall submit a report of that transaction to the Department of Justice 21 days in advance of obtaining the substance. However, the Department of Justice may authorize the submission of reports within 72 hours, or within a timeframe and in a manner acceptable to the Department of Justice, after the actual physical obtaining of a specified substance with respect to repeated transactions between a furnisher and an obtainer involving the substances, if the Department of Justice determines that the obtainer has established a record of utilization of the substances for lawful purposes. This section does not apply to any person whose prescribing or dispensing activities are subject to the reporting requirements set forth in Section 11164; any manufacturer or wholesaler who is licensed by the California State Board of Pharmacy and also registered with the federal Drug Enforcement Administration of the United States Department of Justice; any analytical research facility that is registered with the federal Drug Enforcement Administration of the United States Department of Justice; or any state-licensed health care facility.

(b) (1) Any person specified in subdivision (a) who does not submit a report as required by that subdivision shall be punished by imprisonment in a county jail not exceeding six months, by a fine not exceeding five thousand dollars ($5,000), or by both that fine and imprisonment.

(2) Any person specified in subdivision (a) who has been previously convicted of a violation of subdivision (a) who subsequently does not submit a report as required by subdivision (a) shall be punished by imprisonment pursuant to subdivision (h) of Section 1170 of the Penal Code, or by imprisonment in a county jail not exceeding one year, by a fine not exceeding one hundred thousand dollars ($100,000), or by both that fine and imprisonment.

(Amended by Stats. 2011, Ch. 15, Sec. 146. (AB 109) Effective April 4, 2011. Operative October 1, 2011, by Sec. 636 of Ch. 15, as amended by Stats. 2011, Ch. 39, Sec. 68.)

11101.

The State Department of Justice shall provide a common reporting form for the substances in Section 11100 which contains at least the following information:

(a) Name of the substance.

(b) Quantity of the substance sold, transferred, or furnished.

(c) The date the substance was sold, transferred, or furnished.

(d) The name and address of the person buying or receiving such substance.

(e) The name and address of the manufacturer, wholesaler, retailer, or other person selling, transferring, or furnishing such substance.

(Amended by Stats. 1974, Ch. 1072.)

11102.

The Department of Justice may adopt all regulations necessary to carry out the provisions of this part.

(Added by Stats. 1974, Ch. 1072.)

11103.

The theft or loss of any substance regulated pursuant to Section 11100 discovered by any permittee or any person regulated by the provisions of this chapter shall be reported in writing to the Department of Justice within three days after the discovery.

Any difference between the quantity of any substance regulated pursuant to Section 11100 received and the quantity shipped shall be reported in writing to the Department of Justice within three days of the receipt of actual knowledge of the discrepancy.

Any report made pursuant to this section shall also include the name of the common carrier or person who transports the substance and date of shipment of the substance.

(Amended by Stats. 1997, Ch. 397, Sec. 3. Effective January 1, 1998.)

11104.

(a) Any manufacturer, wholesaler, retailer, or other person or entity that sells, transfers, or otherwise furnishes any of the substances listed in subdivision (a) of Section 11100 with knowledge or the intent that the recipient will use the substance to unlawfully manufacture a controlled substance is guilty of a felony.

(b) Any manufacturer, wholesaler, retailer, or other person or entity that sells, transfers, or otherwise furnishes any laboratory glassware or apparatus, any chemical reagent or solvent, or any combination thereof, or any chemical substance specified in Section 11107.1, with knowledge that the recipient will use the goods or chemical substance to unlawfully manufacture a controlled substance, is guilty of a misdemeanor.

(c) Any person who receives or distributes any substance listed in subdivision (a) of Section 11100, or any laboratory glassware or apparatus, any chemical reagent or solvent, or any combination thereof, or any chemical substance specified in Section

11107.1, with the intent of causing the evasion of the recordkeeping or reporting requirements of this article, is guilty of a misdemeanor.

(Amended by Stats. 2005, Ch. 468, Sec. 4. Effective January 1, 2006.)

11104.5.

Any person who knowingly or intentionally possesses any laboratory glassware or apparatus, any chemical reagent or solvent, or any combination thereof, or any chemical substance specified in paragraph (36) or (37) of subdivision (a) of Section 11100, Section 11107, or Section 11107.1, with the intent to manufacture a controlled substance, is guilty of a misdemeanor.

(Amended by Stats. 2005, Ch. 468, Sec. 5. Effective January 1, 2006.)

11105.

(a) It is unlawful for any person to knowingly make a false statement in connection with any report or record required under this article.

(b) (1) Any person who violates this section shall be punished by imprisonment pursuant to subdivision (h) of Section 1170 of the Penal Code, or by imprisonment in a county jail not exceeding one year, or by a fine not exceeding five thousand dollars ($5,000), or by both that fine and imprisonment.

(2) Any person who has been previously convicted of violating this section and who subsequently violates this section shall be punished by imprisonment pursuant to subdivision (h) of Section 1170 of the Penal Code for two, three, or four years, or by a fine not exceeding one hundred thousand dollars ($100,000), or by both that fine and imprisonment.

(Amended by Stats. 2011, Ch. 15, Sec. 147. (AB 109) Effective April 4, 2011. Operative October 1, 2011, by Sec. 636 of Ch. 15, as amended by Stats. 2011, Ch. 39, Sec. 68.)

11106.

(a) (1) (A) Any manufacturer, wholesaler, retailer, or any other person or entity in this state that sells, transfers, or otherwise furnishes any substance specified in subdivision (a) of Section 11100 to a person or business entity in this state or any other state or who obtains from a source outside of the state any substance specified in subdivision (a) of Section 11100 shall submit an application to, and obtain a permit for the conduct of that business from, the Department of Justice. For any substance added to the list set forth in subdivision (a) of Section 11100 on or after January 1, 2002, the Department of Justice may postpone the effective date of the requirement for a permit for a period not to exceed six months from the listing date of the substance.

(B) An intracompany transfer does not require a permit if the transferor is a permittee. Transfers between company partners or between a company and an analytical laboratory do not require a permit if the transferor is a permittee and a report as to the nature and extent of the transfer is made to the Department of Justice pursuant to Section 11100 or 11100.1.

(C) This paragraph shall not apply to any manufacturer, wholesaler, or wholesale distributor who is licensed by the California State Board of Pharmacy and also registered with the federal Drug Enforcement Administration of the United States Department of Justice; any pharmacist or other authorized person who sells or furnishes a substance upon the prescription of a physician, dentist, podiatrist, or veterinarian; any state-licensed health care facility, physician, dentist, podiatrist, veterinarian, or veterinary food-animal drug retailer licensed by the California State Board of Pharmacy that administers or furnishes a substance to a patient; or any analytical research facility that is registered with the federal Drug Enforcement Administration of the United States Department of Justice.

(D) This paragraph shall not apply to the sale, transfer, furnishing, or receipt of any betadine or povidone solution with an iodine content not exceeding 1 percent in containers of eight ounces or less, or any tincture of iodine not exceeding 2 percent in containers of one ounce or less, that is sold over the counter.

(2) Except as provided in paragraph (3), no permit shall be required of any manufacturer, wholesaler, retailer, or other person or entity for the sale, transfer, furnishing, or obtaining of any product which contains ephedrine, pseudoephedrine, norpseudoephedrine, or phenylpropanolamine and which is lawfully sold, transferred, or furnished over the counter without a prescription or by a prescription pursuant to the federal Food, Drug, and Cosmetic Act (21 U.S.C. Sec. 301 et seq.) or regulations adopted thereunder.

(3) A permit shall be required for the sale, transfer, furnishing, or obtaining of preparations in solid or liquid dosage form containing ephedrine, pseudoephedrine, norpseudoephedrine, or phenylpropanolamine, unless (A) the transaction involves the sale of ephedrine, pseudoephedrine, norpseudoephedrine, or phenylpropanolamine products by retail distributors as defined by this article over the counter and without a prescription, or (B) the transaction is made by a person or business entity exempted from the permitting requirements of this subdivision under paragraph (1).

(b) (1) The department shall provide application forms, which are to be completed under penalty of perjury, in order to obtain information relating to the identity of any applicant applying for a permit, including, but not limited to, the business name of the applicant or the individual name, and if a corporate entity, the names of its board of directors, the business in which the applicant is engaged, the business address of the applicant, a full description of any substance to be sold, transferred, or otherwise furnished or to be obtained, the specific purpose for the use, sale, or transfer of those substances specified in subdivision (a) of Section 11100, the training, experience, or education relating to this use, and any additional information requested by the department relating to possible grounds for denial as set forth in this section, or by applicable regulations adopted by the department.

(2) The requirement for the specific purpose for the use, sale, or transfer of those substances specified in subdivision (a) of Section 11100 does not require applicants or

permittees to reveal their chemical processes that are typically considered trade secrets and proprietary business information.

(c) Applicants and permittees shall authorize the department, or any of its duly authorized representatives, as a condition of being permitted, to make any examination of the books and records of any applicant, permittee, or other person, or visit and inspect the business premises of any applicant or permittee during normal business hours, as deemed necessary to enforce this chapter.

(d) An application may be denied, or a permit may be revoked or suspended, for reasons which include, but are not limited to, the following:

(1) Materially falsifying an application for a permit or an application for the renewal of a permit.

(2) If any individual owner, manager, agent, representative, or employee for the applicant who has direct access, management, or control for any substance listed under subdivision (a) of Section 11100, is or has been convicted of a misdemeanor or felony relating to any of the substances listed under subdivision (a) of Section 11100, any misdemeanor drug-related offense, or any felony under the laws of this state or the United States.

(3) Failure to maintain effective controls against the diversion of precursors to unauthorized persons or entities.

(4) Failure to comply with this article or any regulations of the department adopted thereunder.

(5) Failure to provide the department, or any duly authorized federal or state official, with access to any place for which a permit has been issued, or for which an application for a permit has been submitted, in the course of conducting a site investigation, inspection, or audit; or failure to promptly produce for the official conducting the site investigation, inspection, or audit any book, record, or document requested by the official.

(6) Failure to provide adequate documentation of a legitimate business purpose involving the applicant's or permittee's use of any substance listed in subdivision (a) of Section 11100.

(7) Commission of any act which would demonstrate actual or potential unfitness to hold a permit in light of the public safety and welfare, which act is substantially related to the qualifications, functions, or duties of a permitholder.

(8) If any individual owner, manager, agent, representative, or employee for the applicant who has direct access, management, or control for any substance listed under subdivision (a) of Section 11100, willfully violates or has been convicted of violating, any federal, state, or local criminal statute, rule, or ordinance regulating the manufacture, maintenance, disposal, sale, transfer, or furnishing of any of those substances.

(e) Notwithstanding any other provision of law, an investigation of an individual applicant's qualifications, or the qualifications of an applicant's owner, manager, agent, representative, or employee who has direct access, management, or control of any substance listed under subdivision (a) of Section 11100, for a permit may include review of his or her summary criminal history information pursuant to Sections 11105 and 13300 of the Penal Code, including, but not limited to, records of convictions, regardless of whether those convictions have been expunged pursuant to Section 1203.4 of the Penal Code, and any arrests pending adjudication.

(f) The department may retain jurisdiction of a canceled or expired permit in order to proceed with any investigation or disciplinary action relating to a permittee.

(g) The department may grant permits on forms prescribed by it, which shall be effective for not more than one year from the date of issuance and which shall not be transferable. Applications and permits shall be uniform throughout the state, on forms prescribed by the department.

(h) Each applicant shall pay at the time of filing an application for a permit a fee determined by the department which shall not exceed the application processing costs of the department.

(i) A permit granted pursuant to this article may be renewed one year from the date of issuance and, annually thereafter, following the timely filing of a complete renewal application with all supporting documents, the payment of a permit renewal fee not to exceed the application processing costs of the department, and a review of the application by the department.

(j) Selling, transferring, or otherwise furnishing or obtaining any substance specified in subdivision (a) of Section 11100 without a permit is a misdemeanor or a felony.

(k) (1) No person under 18 years of age shall be eligible for a permit under this section.

(2) No business for which a permit has been issued shall employ a person under 18 years of age in the capacity of a manager, agent, or representative.

(l) (1) An applicant, or an applicant's employees who have direct access, management, or control of any substance listed under subdivision (a) of Section 11100, for an initial permit shall submit with the application one set of 10-print fingerprints for each individual acting in the capacity of an owner, manager, agent, or representative for the applicant, unless the applicant's employees are exempted from this requirement by the Department of Justice. These exemptions may only be obtained upon the written request of the applicant.

(2) In the event of subsequent changes in ownership, management, or employment, the permittee shall notify the department in writing within 15 calendar days of the changes, and shall submit one set of 10-print fingerprints for each individual not previously fingerprinted under this section.

(Amended by Stats. 2005, Ch. 468, Sec. 6. Effective January 1, 2006.)

11106.5.

(a) The Department of Justice, or an administrative law judge sitting alone as provided in subdivision (h), may upon petition issue an interim order suspending any permittee or imposing permit restrictions. The petition shall include affidavits that demonstrate, to the satisfaction of the department, both of the following:

(1) The permittee has engaged in acts or omissions constituting a violation of this code or has been convicted of a crime substantially related to the permitted activity.

(2) Permitting the permittee to operate, or to continue to operate without restrictions, would endanger the public health, safety, or welfare.

(b) No interim order provided for in this section shall be issued without notice to the permittee, unless it appears from the petition and supporting documents that serious injury would result to the public before the matter could be heard on notice.

(c) Except as provided in subdivision (b), the permittee shall be given at least 15 days' notice of the hearing on the petition for an interim order. The notice shall include documents submitted to the department in support of the petition. If the order was initially issued without notice as provided in subdivision (b), the permittee shall be entitled to a hearing on the petition within 20 days of the issuance of the interim order without notice. The permittee shall be given notice of the hearing within two days after issuance of the initial interim order, and shall receive all documents in support of the petition. The failure of the department to provide a hearing within 20 days following issuance of the interim order without notice, unless the permittee waives his or her right to the hearing, shall result in the dissolution of the interim order by operation of law.

(d) At the hearing on the petition for an interim order, the permittee may do the following:

(1) Be represented by counsel.

(2) Have a record made of the proceedings, copies of which shall be available to the permittee upon payment of costs computed in accordance with the provisions for transcript costs for judicial review contained in Section 11523 of the Government Code.

(3) Present affidavits and other documentary evidence.

(4) Present oral argument.

(e) The department, or an administrative law judge sitting alone as provided in subdivision (h), shall issue a decision on the petition for interim order within five business days following submission of the matter. The standard of proof required to obtain an interim order pursuant to this section shall be a preponderance of the evidence standard. If the interim order was previously issued without notice, the department shall determine whether the order shall remain in effect, be dissolved, or be modified.

(f) The department shall file an accusation within 15 days of the issuance of an interim order. In the case of an interim order issued without notice, the time shall run from the date of the order issued after the noticed hearing. If the permittee files a notice of defense, the hearing shall be held within 30 days of the agency's receipt of the notice of defense. A decision shall be rendered on the accusation no later than 30 days after submission of the matter. Failure to comply with any of the requirements in this subdivision shall dissolve the interim order by operation of law.

(g) Interim orders shall be subject to judicial review pursuant to Section 1094.5 of the Code of Civil Procedure and shall be heard only in the superior court in and for the County of Sacramento, San Francisco, Los Angeles, or San Diego. The review of an interim order shall be limited to a determination of whether the department abused its discretion in the issuance of the interim order. Abuse of discretion is established if the respondent department has not proceeded in the manner required by law, or if the court determines that the interim order is not supported by substantial evidence in light of the whole record.

(h) The department may, in its sole discretion, delegate the hearing on any petition for an interim order to an administrative law judge in the Office of Administrative Hearings. If the department hears the noticed petition itself, an administrative law judge shall preside at the hearing, rule on the admission and exclusion of evidence, and advise the department on matters of law. The department shall exercise all other powers relating to the conduct of the hearing, but may delegate any or all of them to the administrative law judge. When the petition has been delegated to an administrative law judge, he or she shall sit alone and exercise all of the powers of the department relating to the conduct of the hearing. A decision issued by an administrative law judge sitting alone shall be final when it is filed with the department. If the administrative law judge issues an interim order without notice, he or she shall preside at the noticed hearing, unless unavailable, in which case another administrative law judge may hear the matter. The decision of the administrative law judge sitting alone on the petition for an interim order is final, subject only to judicial review in accordance with subdivision (g).

(i) (1) Failure to comply with an interim order issued pursuant to subdivision (a) or (b) shall constitute a separate cause for disciplinary action against any permittee, and may be heard at, and as a part of, the noticed hearing provided for in subdivision (f). Allegations of noncompliance with the interim order may be filed at any time prior to the rendering of a decision on the accusation. Violation of the interim order is established upon proof that the permittee was on notice of the interim order and its terms, and that the order was in effect at the time of the violation. The finding of a violation of an interim order made at the hearing on the accusation shall be reviewed as a part of any review of a final decision of the department.

(2) If the interim order issued by the department provides for anything less than a complete suspension of the permittee and the permittee violates the interim order prior to the hearing on the accusation provided for in subdivision (f), the department may, upon notice to the permittee and proof of violation, modify or expand the interim order.

(j) A plea or verdict of guilty or a conviction after a plea of nolo contendere is deemed to be a conviction within the meaning of this section. A certified record of the conviction shall be conclusive evidence of the fact that the conviction occurred. The department may take action under this section notwithstanding the fact that an appeal of the conviction may be taken.

(k) The interim orders provided for by this section shall be in addition to, and not a limitation on, the authority to seek injunctive relief provided in any other provision of law.

(Amended by Stats. 2012, Ch. 867, Sec. 4. (SB 1144) Effective January 1, 2013.)

11106.7.

(a) The Department of Justice may establish, by regulation, a system for the issuance to a permittee of a citation which may contain an order of abatement or an order to pay an administrative fine assessed by the Department of Justice, if the permittee is in violation of any provision of this chapter or any regulation adopted by the Department of Justice pursuant to this chapter.

(b) The system shall contain the following provisions:

(1) Citations shall be in writing and shall describe with particularity the nature of the violation, including specific reference to the provision of law or regulation of the department determined to have been violated.

(2) Whenever appropriate, the citation shall contain an order of abatement fixing a reasonable time for abatement of the violation.

(3) In no event shall the administrative fine assessed by the department exceed two thousand five hundred dollars ($2,500) for each violation. In assessing a fine, due consideration shall be given to the appropriateness of the amount of the fine with respect to such factors as the gravity of the violation, the good faith of the permittee, and the history of previous violations.

(4) An order of abatement or a fine assessment issued pursuant to a citation shall inform the permittee that if the permittee desires a hearing to contest the finding of a violation, that hearing shall be requested by written notice to the department within 30 days of the date of issuance of the citation or assessment. Hearings shall be held pursuant to Chapter 5 (commencing with Section 11500) of Part 1 of Division 3 of Title 2 of the Government Code.

(5) In addition to requesting a hearing, the permittee may, within 10 days after service of the citation, request in writing an opportunity for an informal conference with the department regarding the citation. At the conclusion of the informal conference, the department may affirm, modify, or dismiss the citation, including any fine levied or order of abatement issued. The decision shall be deemed to be a final order with regard to the citation issued, including the fine levied and the order of abatement. However, the permittee does not waive its right to request a hearing to contest a citation by requesting an informal conference. If the citation is dismissed after the informal conference, the request for a hearing on the matter of the citation shall be deemed to be withdrawn. If the citation, including any fine levied or order of abatement, is modified, the citation originally issued shall be considered withdrawn and a new citation issued. If a hearing is requested for a subsequent citation, it shall be requested within 30 days of service of that subsequent citation.

(6) Failure of a permittee to pay a fine within 30 days of the date of assessment or comply with an order of abatement within the fixed time, unless the citation is being appealed, may result in disciplinary action being taken by the department. If a citation is not contested and a fine is not paid, the full amount of the assessed fine shall be added to the renewal of the permit. A permit shall not be renewed without payment of the renewal fee and fine.

(c) The system may contain the following provisions:

(1) A citation may be issued without the assessment of an administrative fine.

(2) Assessment of administrative fines may be limited to only particular violations of the law or department regulations.

(d) Notwithstanding any other provision of law, if a fine is paid to satisfy an assessment based on the finding of a violation, payment of the fine shall be represented as satisfactory resolution of the matter for purposes of public disclosure.

(e) Administrative fines collected pursuant to this section shall be deposited in the General Fund.

(f) The sanctions authorized under this section shall be separate from, and in addition to, any other administrative, civil, or criminal remedies; however, a criminal action may not be initiated for a specific offense if a citation has been issued pursuant to this section for that offense, and a citation may not be issued pursuant to this section for a specific offense if a criminal action for that offense has been filed.

(g) Nothing in this section shall be deemed to prevent the department from serving and prosecuting an accusation to suspend or revoke a permit if grounds for that suspension or revocation exist.

(Added by Stats. 2003, Ch. 142, Sec. 1. Effective January 1, 2004.)

11107.

(a) Any manufacturer, wholesaler, retailer, or other person or entity in this state that sells to any person or entity in this state or any other state, any laboratory glassware or apparatus, any chemical reagent or solvent, or any combination thereof, where the value of the goods sold in the transaction exceeds one hundred dollars ($100) shall do the following:

(1) Notwithstanding any other law, in any face-to-face or will-call sale, the seller shall prepare a bill of sale which identifies the date of sale, cost of product, method of payment, specific items and quantities purchased, and the proper purchaser identification information, all of which shall be entered onto the bill of sale or a legible copy of the bill of sale, and shall also affix on the bill of sale his or her signature as witness to the purchase and identification of the purchaser.

(A) For the purposes of this section, "proper purchaser identification" includes a valid motor vehicle operator's license or other official and valid state-issued identification of the purchaser that contains a photograph of the purchaser, and includes the residential or mailing address of the purchaser, other than a post office box number, the motor vehicle license number of the motor vehicle used by the purchaser at the time of purchase, a description of how the substance is to be used, and the signature of the purchaser.

(B) The seller shall retain the original bill of sale containing the purchaser identification information for five years in a readily presentable manner, and present the bill of sale containing the purchaser identification information upon demand by any law enforcement officer or authorized representative of the Attorney General. Copies of these bills of sale obtained by representatives of the Attorney General shall be maintained by the Department of Justice for a period of not less than five years.

(2) (A) Notwithstanding any other law, in all sales other than face-to-face or will-call sales the seller shall maintain for a period of five years the following sales information: the name and address of the purchaser, date of sale, product description, cost of product, method of payment, method of delivery, delivery address, and valid identifying information.

(B) For the purposes of this paragraph, "valid identifying information" includes two or more of the following: federal tax identification number; resale tax identification number; city or county business license number; license issued by the State Department of Public Health; registration number issued by the federal Drug Enforcement Administration; precursor business permit number issued by the Department of Justice; motor vehicle operator's license; or other identification issued by a state.

(C) The seller shall, upon the request of any law enforcement officer or any authorized representative of the Attorney General, produce a report or record of sale containing the information in a readily presentable manner.

(D) If a common carrier is used, the seller shall maintain a manifest regarding the delivery in a readily presentable manner and for a period of five years.

(b) This section shall not apply to any wholesaler who is licensed by the California State Board of Pharmacy and registered with the federal Drug Enforcement Administration of the United States Department of Justice and who sells laboratory glassware or apparatus, any chemical reagent or solvent, or any combination thereof, to a licensed pharmacy, physician, dentist, podiatrist, or veterinarian.

(c) A violation of this section is a misdemeanor.

(d) For the purposes of this section, the following terms have the following meanings:

(1) "Laboratory glassware" includes, but is not limited to, condensers, flasks, separatory funnels, and beakers.

(2) "Apparatus" includes, but is not limited to, heating mantles, ring stands, and rheostats.

(3) "Chemical reagent" means a chemical that reacts chemically with one or more precursors, but does not become part of the finished product.

(4) "Chemical solvent" means a chemical that does not react chemically with a precursor or reagent and does not become part of the finished product. A "chemical solvent" helps other chemicals mix, cools chemical reactions, and cleans the finished product.

(Amended by Stats. 2012, Ch. 867, Sec. 5. (SB 1144) Effective January 1, 2013.)

11107.1.

(a) Any manufacturer, wholesaler, retailer, or other person or entity in this state that sells to any person or entity in this state or any other state any quantity of sodium cyanide, potassium cyanide, cyclohexanone, bromobenzene, magnesium turnings, mercuric chloride, sodium metal, lead acetate, palladium black, hydrogen chloride gas, trichlorofluoromethane (fluorotrichloromethane), dichlorodifluoromethane, 1,1,2-trichloro-1,2,2-trifluoroethane (trichlorotrifluoroethane), sodium acetate, or acetic anhydride shall do the following:

(1) (A) Notwithstanding any other provision of law, in any face-to-face or will-call sale, the seller shall prepare a bill of sale which identifies the date of sale, cost of sale, method of payment, the specific items and quantities purchased and the proper purchaser identification information, all of which shall be entered onto the bill of sale or a legible copy of the bill of sale, and shall also affix on the bill of sale his or her signature as witness to the purchase and identification of the purchaser.

(B) For the purposes of this paragraph, "proper purchaser identification" includes a valid driver's license or other official and valid state-issued identification of the purchaser that contains a photograph of the purchaser, and includes the residential or mailing address of the purchaser, other than a post office box number, the motor vehicle license number of the motor vehicle used by the purchaser at the time of purchase, a description of how the substance is to be used, the Environmental Protection Agency certification number or resale tax identification number assigned to the individual or business entity for which the individual is purchasing any chlorofluorocarbon product, and the signature of the purchaser.

(C) The seller shall retain the original bill of sale containing the purchaser identification information for five years in a readily presentable manner, and present the bill of sale containing the purchaser identification information upon demand by any law enforcement officer or authorized representative of the Attorney General. Copies of these bills of sale obtained by representatives of the Attorney General shall be maintained by the Department of Justice for a period of not less than five years.

(2) (A) Notwithstanding any other law, in all sales other than face-to-face or will-call sales the seller shall maintain for a period of five years the following sales information: the name and address of the purchaser, date of sale, product description, cost of product, method of payment, method of delivery, delivery address, and valid identifying information.

(B) For the purposes of this paragraph, "valid identifying information" includes two or more of the following: federal tax identification number; resale tax identification number; city or county business license number; license issued by the State Department of Public Health; registration number issued by the federal Drug Enforcement Administration; precursor business permit number issued by the Department of Justice; driver's license; or other identification issued by a state.

(C) The seller shall, upon the request of any law enforcement officer or any authorized representative of the Attorney General, produce a report or record of sale containing the information in a readily presentable manner.

(D) If a common carrier is used, the seller shall maintain a manifest regarding the delivery in a readily presentable manner for a period of five years.

(b) Any manufacturer, wholesaler, retailer, or other person or entity in this state that purchases any item listed in subdivision (a) of Section 11107.1 shall do the following:

(1) Provide on the record of purchase information on the source of the items purchased, the date of purchase, a description of the specific items, the quantities of each item purchased, and the cost of the items purchased.

(2) Retain the record of purchase for three years in a readily presentable manner and present the record of purchase upon demand to any law enforcement officer or authorized representative of the Attorney General.

(c) (1) A first violation of this section is a misdemeanor.

(2) Any person who has previously been convicted of a violation of this section shall, upon a subsequent conviction thereof, be punished by imprisonment in a county jail not exceeding one year, by a fine not exceeding one hundred thousand dollars ($100,000), or both the fine and imprisonment.

(Amended by Stats. 2012, Ch. 867, Sec. 6. (SB 1144) Effective January 1, 2013.)

11107.2.

(a) Except as otherwise provided in subdivision (b), it is unlawful for a manufacturer, wholesaler, reseller, retailer, or other person or entity to sell to any customer any quantity of nonodorized butane.

(b) The limitations in subdivisions (a) shall not apply to any of the following transactions:

(1) Butane sold to manufacturers, wholesalers, resellers, or retailers solely for the purpose of resale.

(2) Butane sold to a person for use in a lawful commercial enterprise, including, but not limited to, a volatile solvent extraction activity licensed under Division 10 (commencing with Section 26000) of the Business and Professions Code or a medical cannabis collective or cooperative described in subdivision (b) of Section 11362.775 of this code, operating in compliance with all applicable state licensing requirements and local regulations governing that type of business.

(3) The sale of pocket lighters, utility lighters, grill lighters, torch lighters, butane gas appliances, refill canisters, gas cartridges, or other products that contain or use nonodorized butane and contain less than 150 milliliters of butane.

(4) The sale of any product in which butane is used as an aerosol propellant.

(c) (1) Any person or business that violates subdivision (a) is subject to a civil penalty of two thousand five hundred dollars ($2,500).

(2) The Attorney General, a city attorney, a county counsel, or a district attorney may bring a civil action to enforce this section.

(3) The civil penalty shall be deposited into the General Fund if the action is brought by the Attorney General. If the action is brought by a city attorney, the civil penalty shall be paid to the treasurer of the city in which the judgment is entered. If the action is brought by a county counsel or district attorney, the civil penalty shall be paid to the treasurer of the county in which the judgment is entered.

(d) As used in this section, the following definitions shall apply:

(1) "Customer" means any person or entity other than those described in paragraphs (1) and (2) of subdivision (b) that purchases or acquires nonodorized butane from a seller during a transaction.

(2) "Nonodorized butane" means iso-butane, n-butane, butane, or a mixture of butane and propane of any power that may also use the words "refined," "pure," "purified," "premium," or "filtered," to describe the butane or butane mixture, which does not contain ethyl mercaptan or a similar odorant.

(3) "Sell" or "sale" means to furnish, give away, exchange, transfer, deliver, surrender, distribute, or supply, in exchange for money or any other consideration.

(4) "Seller" means any person, business entity, or employee thereof that sells nonodorized butane to any customer within this state.

(e) This section shall become operative on July 1, 2019.

(Added by Stats. 2018, Ch. 595, Sec. 1. (AB 3112) Effective January 1, 2019. Section operative July 1, 2019, by its own provisions.)

11110.

(a) It shall be an infraction, punishable by a fine not exceeding two hundred fifty dollars ($250), for any person, corporation, or retail distributor to willfully and knowingly supply, deliver, or give possession of a drug, material, compound, mixture, preparation, or substance containing any quantity of dextromethorphan (the dextrorotatory isomer of 3-methoxy-N-methylmorphinan, including its salts, but not including its racemic or levorotatory forms) to a person under 18 years of age in an over-the-counter sale without a prescription.

(b) It shall be prima facie evidence of a violation of this section if the person, corporation, or retail distributor making the sale does not require and obtain bona fide evidence of majority and identity from the purchaser, unless from the purchaser's outward appearance the person making the sale would reasonably presume the purchaser to be 25 years of age or older.

(c) Proof that a person, corporation, or retail distributor, or his or her agent or employee, demanded, was shown, and acted in reasonable reliance upon, bona fide evidence of majority and identity shall be a defense to any criminal prosecution under this section. As used in this section, "bona fide evidence of majority and identity" means a document issued by a federal, state, county, or municipal government, or subdivision or agency thereof, including, but not limited to, a motor vehicle operator's license, California state identification card, identification card issued to a member of the Armed Forces, or other form of identification that bears the name, date of birth, description, and picture of the person.

(d) (1) Notwithstanding any other provision of this section, a retail clerk who fails to require and obtain proof of age from the purchaser shall not be guilty of an infraction pursuant to subdivision (a) or subject to any civil penalties.

(2) This subdivision shall not apply to a retail clerk who is a willful participant in an ongoing criminal conspiracy to violate this section.

(Added by Stats. 2011, Ch. 199, Sec. 1. (SB 514) Effective January 1, 2012.)

11111.

A person, corporation, or retail distributor that sells or makes available products containing dextromethorphan, as defined in subdivision (a) of Section 11110, in an over-the-counter sale without a prescription shall, if feasible, use a cash register that is equipped with an age-verification feature to monitor age-restricted items. The cash register shall be programmed to direct the retail clerk making the sale to request bona fide evidence of majority and identity, as described in subdivision (c) of Section 11110, before a product containing dextromethorphan may be purchased.

(Added by Stats. 2011, Ch. 199, Sec. 2. (SB 514) Effective January 1, 2012.)

CHAPTER 4. Prescriptions [11150 - 11209]

(Chapter 4 added by Stats. 1972, Ch. 1407.)

ARTICLE 1. Requirements of Prescriptions [11150 - 11180]

(Article 1 added by Stats. 1972, Ch. 1407.)

11150.

No person other than a physician, dentist, podiatrist, or veterinarian, or naturopathic doctor acting pursuant to Section 3640.7 of the Business and Professions Code, or pharmacist acting within the scope of a project authorized under Article 1 (commencing with Section 128125) of Chapter 3 of Part 3 of Division 107 or within the scope of Section 4052.1, 4052.2, or 4052.6 of the Business and Professions Code, a registered nurse acting within the scope of a project authorized under Article 1 (commencing with Section 128125) of Chapter 3 of Part 3 of Division 107, a certified nurse-midwife acting within the scope of Section 2746.51 of the Business and Professions Code, a nurse practitioner acting within the scope of Section 2836.1 of the Business and Professions Code, a physician assistant acting within the scope of a project authorized under Article 1 (commencing with Section 128125) of Chapter 3 of Part 3 of Division 107 or Section 3502.1 of the Business and Professions Code, a naturopathic doctor acting within the scope of Section 3640.5 of the Business and Professions Code, or an optometrist acting within the scope of Section 3041 of the Business and Professions Code, or an out-of-state prescriber acting pursuant to Section 4005 of the Business and Professions Code shall write or issue a prescription.

(Amended by Stats. 2014, Ch. 319, Sec. 5. (SB 1039) Effective January 1, 2015.)

11150.2.

(a) Notwithstanding any other law, if cannabidiol is excluded from Schedule I of the federal Controlled Substances Act and placed on a schedule of the act other than Schedule I, or if a product composed of cannabidiol is approved by the federal Food and Drug Administration and either placed on a schedule of the act other than Schedule I, or exempted from one or more provisions of the act, so as to permit a physician, pharmacist, or other authorized healing arts licensee acting within his or her scope of practice, to prescribe, furnish, or dispense that product, the physician, pharmacist, or other authorized healing arts licensee who prescribes, furnishes, or dispenses that product in accordance with federal law shall be deemed to be in compliance with state law governing those acts.

(b) For purposes of this chapter, upon the effective date of one of the changes in federal law described in subdivision (a), notwithstanding any other state law, a product composed of cannabidiol may be prescribed, furnished, dispensed, transferred, transported, possessed, or used in accordance with federal law and is authorized pursuant to state law.

(c) This section does not apply to any product containing cannabidiol that is made or derived from industrial hemp, as defined in Section 11018.5 and regulated pursuant to that section.

(Added by Stats. 2018, Ch. 62, Sec. 3. (AB 710) Effective July 9, 2018.)

11150.6.

Notwithstanding Section 11150.5 or subdivision (a) of Section 11054, methaqualone, its salts, isomers, and salts of its isomers shall be deemed to be classified in Schedule I for the purposes of this chapter.

(Added by Stats. 1984, Ch. 22, Sec. 1. Effective March 1, 1984.)

11151.

A prescription written by an unlicensed person lawfully practicing medicine pursuant to Section 2065 of the Business and Professions Code, shall be filled only at a pharmacy maintained in the hospital which employs such unlicensed person.

(Amended by Stats. 1986, Ch. 248, Sec. 144.)

11152.

No person shall write, issue, fill, compound, or dispense a prescription that does not conform to this division.

(Added by Stats. 1972, Ch. 1407.)

11153.

(a) A prescription for a controlled substance shall only be issued for a legitimate medical purpose by an individual practitioner acting in the usual course of his or her professional practice. The responsibility for the proper prescribing and dispensing of controlled substances is upon the prescribing practitioner, but a corresponding responsibility rests with the pharmacist who fills the prescription. Except as authorized by this division, the following are not legal prescriptions: (1) an order purporting to be a prescription which is issued not in the usual course of professional treatment or in legitimate and authorized research; or (2) an order for an addict or habitual user of controlled substances, which is issued not in the course of professional treatment or as part of an authorized narcotic treatment program, for the purpose of providing the user with controlled substances, sufficient to keep him or her comfortable by maintaining customary use.

(b) Any person who knowingly violates this section shall be punished by imprisonment pursuant to subdivision (h) of Section 1170 of the Penal Code, or in a county jail not exceeding one year, or by a fine not exceeding twenty thousand dollars ($20,000), or by both that fine and imprisonment.

(c) No provision of the amendments to this section enacted during the second year of the 1981–82 Regular Session shall be construed as expanding the scope of practice of a pharmacist.

(Amended by Stats. 2011, Ch. 15, Sec. 148. (AB 109) Effective April 4, 2011. Operative October 1, 2011, by Sec. 636 of Ch. 15, as amended by Stats. 2011, Ch. 39, Sec. 68.)

11153.5.

(a) No wholesaler or manufacturer, or agent or employee of a wholesaler or manufacturer, shall furnish controlled substances for other than legitimate medical purposes.

(b) Anyone who violates this section knowing, or having a conscious disregard for the fact, that the controlled substances are for other than a legitimate medical purpose shall be punishable by imprisonment pursuant to subdivision (h) of Section 1170 of the Penal Code, or in a county jail not exceeding one year, or by a fine not exceeding twenty thousand dollars ($20,000), or by both that fine and imprisonment.

(c) Factors to be considered in determining whether a wholesaler or manufacturer, or agent or employee of a wholesaler or manufacturer, furnished controlled substances knowing or having a conscious disregard for the fact that the controlled substances are for other than legitimate medical purposes shall include, but not be limited to, whether the use of controlled substances was for purposes of increasing athletic ability or performance, the amount of controlled substances furnished, the previous ordering pattern of the customer (including size and frequency of orders), the type and size of the customer, and where and to whom the customer distributes the product.

(Amended by Stats. 2011, Ch. 15, Sec. 149. (AB 109) Effective April 4, 2011. Operative October 1, 2011, by Sec. 636 of Ch. 15, as amended by Stats. 2011, Ch. 39, Sec. 68.)

11154.

(a) Except in the regular practice of his or her profession, no person shall knowingly prescribe, administer, dispense, or furnish a controlled substance to or for any person or animal which is not under his or her treatment for a pathology or condition other than addiction to a controlled substance, except as provided in this division.

(b) No person shall knowingly solicit, direct, induce, aid, or encourage a practitioner authorized to write a prescription to unlawfully prescribe, administer, dispense, or furnish a controlled substance.

(Amended by Stats. 1982, Ch. 1403, Sec. 1.)

11155.

Any physician, who by court order or order of any state or governmental agency, or who voluntarily surrenders his controlled substance privileges, shall not possess, administer, dispense, or prescribe a controlled substance unless and until such privileges have been restored, and he has obtained current registration from the appropriate federal agency as provided by law.

(Added by Stats. 1972, Ch. 1407.)

11156.

(a) Except as provided in Section 2241 of the Business and Professions Code, no person shall prescribe for, or administer, or dispense a controlled substance to, an addict, or to any person representing himself or herself as such, except as permitted by this division.

(b) (1) For purposes of this section, "addict" means a person whose actions are characterized by craving in combination with one or more of the following:

(A) Impaired control over drug use.

(B) Compulsive use.

(C) Continued use despite harm.

(2) Notwithstanding paragraph (1), a person whose drug-seeking behavior is primarily due to the inadequate control of pain is not an addict within the meaning of this section.

(Amended by Stats. 2006, Ch. 350, Sec. 8. Effective January 1, 2007.)

11157.

No person shall issue a prescription that is false or fictitious in any respect.

(Added by Stats. 1972, Ch. 1407.)

11158.

(a) Except as provided in Section 11159 or in subdivision (b) of this section, no controlled substance classified in Schedule II shall be dispensed without a prescription meeting the requirements of this chapter. Except as provided in Section 11159 or when dispensed directly to an ultimate user by a practitioner, other than a pharmacist or pharmacy, no controlled substance classified in Schedule III, IV, or V may be dispensed without a prescription meeting the requirements of this chapter.

(b) A practitioner specified in Section 11150 may dispense directly to an ultimate user a controlled substance classified in Schedule II in an amount not to exceed a 72-hour supply for the patient in accordance with directions for use given by the dispensing practitioner only where the patient is not expected to require any additional amount of the controlled substance beyond the 72 hours. Practitioners dispensing drugs pursuant to this subdivision shall meet the requirements of subdivision (f) of Section 11164.

(c) Except as otherwise prohibited or limited by law, a practitioner specified in Section 11150, may administer controlled substances in the regular practice of his or her profession.

(Amended by Stats. 1980, Ch. 1223.)

11158.1.

(a) Except when a patient is being treated as set forth in Sections 11159, 11159.2, and 11167.5, and Article 2 (commencing with Section 11215) of Chapter 5, pertaining to the treatment of addicts, or for a diagnosis of chronic intractable pain as used in Section 124960 of this code and Section 2241.5 of the Business and Professions Code, a prescriber shall discuss all of the following with the minor, the minor's parent or guardian, or another adult authorized to consent to the minor's medical treatment before directly dispensing or issuing for a minor the first prescription in a single course of treatment for a controlled substance containing an opioid:

(1) The risks of addiction and overdose associated with the use of opioids.

(2) The increased risk of addiction to an opioid to an individual who is suffering from both mental and substance abuse disorders.

(3) The danger of taking an opioid with a benzodiazepine, alcohol, or another central nervous system depressant.

(4) Any other information required by law.

(b) This section does not apply in any of the following circumstances:

(1) If the minor's treatment includes emergency services and care as defined in Section 1317.1.

(2) If the minor's treatment is associated with or incident to an emergency surgery, regardless of whether the surgery is performed on an inpatient or outpatient basis.

(3) If, in the prescriber's professional judgment, fulfilling the requirements of subdivision (a) would be detrimental to the minor's health or safety, or in violation of the minor's legal rights regarding confidentiality.

(c) Notwithstanding any other law, including Section 11374, failure to comply with this section shall not constitute a criminal offense.

(Added by Stats. 2018, Ch. 693, Sec. 13. (SB 1109) Effective January 1, 2019.)

11159.

An order for controlled substances for use by a patient in a county or licensed hospital shall be exempt from all requirements of this article, but shall be in writing on the patient's record, signed by the prescriber, dated, and shall state the name and quantity of the controlled substance ordered and the quantity actually administered. The record of such orders shall be maintained as a hospital record for a minimum of seven years.

(Added by Stats. 1972, Ch. 1407.)

11159.1.

An order for controlled substances furnished to a patient in a clinic which has a permit issued pursuant to Article 13 (commencing with Section 4180) of Chapter 9 of Division 2 of the Business and Professions Code, except an order for a Schedule II controlled substance, shall be exempt from the prescription requirements of this article and shall be in writing on the patient's record, signed by the prescriber, dated, and shall state the name and quantity of the controlled substance ordered and the quantity actually furnished. The record of the order shall be maintained as a clinic record for a minimum of seven years. This section shall apply only to a clinic that has obtained a permit under the provisions of Article 13 (commencing with Section 4180) of Chapter 9 of Division 2 of the Business and Professions Code.

Clinics that furnish controlled substances shall be required to keep a separate record of the furnishing of those drugs which shall be available for review and inspection by all properly authorized personnel.

(Amended by Stats. 2004, Ch. 695, Sec. 52. Effective January 1, 2005.)

11159.2.

(a) Notwithstanding any other provision of law, a prescription for a controlled substance for use by a patient who has a terminal illness may be written on a prescription form that does not meet the requirements of Section 11162.1 if the prescription meets the following requirements:

(1) Contain the information specified in subdivision (a) of Section 11164.

(2) Indicate that the prescriber has certified that the patient is terminally ill by the words "11159.2 exemption."

(b) A pharmacist may fill a prescription pursuant to this section when there is a technical error in the certification required by paragraph (2) of subdivision (a), provided that he or she has personal knowledge of the patient's terminal illness, and subsequently returns the prescription to the prescriber for correction within 72 hours.

(c) For purposes of this section, "terminally ill" means a patient who meets all of the following conditions:

(1) In the reasonable medical judgment of the prescribing physician, the patient has been determined to be suffering from an illness that is incurable and irreversible.

(2) In the reasonable medical judgment of the prescribing physician, the patient's illness will, if the illness takes its normal course, bring about the death of the patient within a period of one year.

(3) The patient's treatment by the physician prescribing a controlled substance pursuant to this section primarily is for the control of pain, symptom management, or both, rather than for cure of the illness.

(d) This section shall become operative on July 1, 2004.

(Amended by Stats. 2005, Ch. 487, Sec. 1. Effective January 1, 2006.)

11161.

(a) When a practitioner is named in a warrant of arrest or is charged in an accusatory pleading with a felony violation of Section 11153, 11154, 11156, 11157, 11170, 11173, 11350, 11351, 11352, 11353, 11353.5, 11377, 11378, 11378.5, 11379,

11379.5, or 11379.6, the court in which the accusatory pleading is filed or the magistrate who issued the warrant of arrest shall, upon the motion of a law enforcement agency which is supported by reasonable cause, issue an order which requires the practitioner to surrender to the clerk of the court all controlled substance prescription forms in the practitioner's possession at a time set in the order and which prohibits the practitioner from obtaining, ordering, or using any additional prescription forms. The law enforcement agency obtaining the order shall notify the Department of Justice of this order. Except as provided in subdivisions (b) and (e) of this section, the order shall remain in effect until further order of the court. Any practitioner possessing prescription forms in violation of the order is guilty of a misdemeanor.
(b) The order provided by subdivision (a) shall be vacated if the court or magistrate finds that the underlying violation or violations are not supported by reasonable cause at a hearing held within two court days after the practitioner files and personally serves upon the prosecuting attorney and the law enforcement agency that obtained the order, a notice of motion to vacate the order with any affidavits on which the practitioner relies. At the hearing, the burden of proof, by a preponderance of the evidence, is on the prosecution. Evidence presented at the hearing shall be limited to the warrant of arrest with supporting affidavits, the motion to require the defendant to surrender controlled substance prescription forms and to prohibit the defendant from obtaining, ordering, or using controlled substance prescription forms, with supporting affidavits, the sworn complaint together with any documents or reports incorporated by reference thereto which, if based on information and belief, state the basis for the information, or any other documents of similar reliability as well as affidavits and counter affidavits submitted by the prosecution and defense. Granting of the motion to vacate the order is no bar to prosecution of the alleged violation or violations.
(c) The defendant may elect to challenge the order issued under subdivision (a) at the preliminary examination. At that hearing, the evidence shall be limited to that set forth in subdivision (b) and any other evidence otherwise admissible at the preliminary examination.
(d) If the practitioner has not moved to vacate the order issued under subdivision (a) by the time of the preliminary examination and he or she is held to answer on the underlying violation or violations, the practitioner shall be precluded from afterwards moving to vacate the order. If the defendant is not held to answer on the underlying charge or charges at the conclusion of the preliminary examination, the order issued under subdivision (a) shall be vacated.
(e) Notwithstanding subdivision (d), any practitioner who is diverted pursuant to Chapter 2.5 (commencing with Section 1000) of Title 7 of Part 2 of the Penal Code may file a motion to vacate the order issued under subdivision (a).
(f) This section shall become operative on November 1, 2004.
(Amended by Stats. 2005, Ch. 487, Sec. 2. Effective January 1, 2006.)

11161.5.

(a) Prescription forms for controlled substance prescriptions shall be obtained from security printers approved by the Department of Justice.
(b) The department may approve security printer applications after the applicant has provided the following information:
(1) Name, address, and telephone number of the applicant.
(2) Policies and procedures of the applicant for verifying the identity of the prescriber ordering controlled substance prescription forms.
(3) Policies and procedures of the applicant for verifying delivery of controlled substance prescription forms to prescribers.
(4) (A) The location, names, and titles of the applicant's agent for service of process in this state; all principal corporate officers, if any; all managing general partners, if any; and any individual owner, partner, corporate officer, manager, agent, representative, employee, or subcontractor of the applicant who has direct access to, or management or control of, controlled substance prescription forms.
(B) A report containing this information shall be made on an annual basis and within 30 days after any change of office, principal corporate officers, managing general partner, or of any person described in subparagraph (A).
(5) (A) A signed statement indicating whether the applicant, any principal corporate officer, any managing general partner, or any individual owner, partner, corporate officer, manager, agent, representative, employee, or subcontractor of the applicant who has direct access to, or management or control of, controlled substance prescription forms, has ever been convicted of, or pled no contest to, a violation of any law of a foreign country, the United States, or any state, or of any local ordinance.
(B) The department shall provide the applicant and any individual owner, partner, corporate officer, manager, agent, representative, employee, or subcontractor of the applicant who has direct access to, or management or control of, controlled substance prescription forms, with the means and direction to provide fingerprints and related information, in a manner specified by the department, for the purpose of completing state, federal, or foreign criminal background checks.
(C) Any applicant described in subdivision (b) shall submit his or her fingerprint images and related information to the department, for the purpose of the department obtaining information as to the existence and nature of a record of state, federal, or foreign level convictions and state, federal, or foreign level arrests for which the department establishes that the applicant was released on bail or on his or her own recognizance pending trial, as described in subdivision (l) of Section 11105 of the Penal Code. Requests for federal level criminal offender record information received by the department pursuant to this section shall be forwarded to the Federal Bureau of Investigation by the department.
(D) The department shall assess against each security printer applicant a fee determined by the department to be sufficient to cover all processing, maintenance, and investigative costs generated from or associated with completing state, federal, or foreign background checks and inspections of security printers pursuant to this section with respect to that applicant; the fee shall be paid by the applicant at the time he or she submits the security printer application, fingerprints, and related information to the department.
(E) The department shall retain fingerprint impressions and related information for subsequent arrest notification pursuant to Section 11105.2 of the Penal Code for all applicants.
(c) The department may, within 60 calendar days of receipt of the application from the applicant, deny the security printer application.
(d) The department may deny a security printer application on any of the following grounds:
(1) The applicant, any individual owner, partner, corporate officer, manager, agent, representative, employee, or subcontractor for the applicant, who has direct access, management, or control of controlled substance prescription forms, has been convicted of a crime. A conviction within the meaning of this paragraph means a plea or verdict of guilty or a conviction following a plea of nolo contendere. Any action which a board is permitted to take following the establishment of a conviction may be taken when the time for appeal has elapsed, the judgment of conviction has been affirmed on appeal, or when an order granting probation is made suspending the imposition of sentence, irrespective of a subsequent order under the provisions of Section 1203.4 of the Penal Code.
(2) The applicant committed any act involving dishonesty, fraud, or deceit with the intent to substantially benefit himself, herself, or another, or substantially injure another.
(3) The applicant committed any act that would constitute a violation of this division.
(4) The applicant knowingly made a false statement of fact required to be revealed in the application to produce controlled substance prescription forms.
(5) The department determines that the applicant failed to demonstrate adequate security procedures relating to the production and distribution of controlled substance prescription forms.
(6) The department determines that the applicant has submitted an incomplete application.
(7) As a condition for its approval as a security printer, an applicant shall authorize the Department of Justice to make any examination of the books and records of the applicant, or to visit and inspect the applicant during business hours, to the extent deemed necessary by the board or department to properly enforce this section.
(e) An approved applicant shall submit an exemplar of a controlled substance prescription form, with all security features, to the Department of Justice within 30 days of initial production.
(f) The department shall maintain a list of approved security printers and the department shall make this information available to prescribers and other appropriate government agencies, including the Board of Pharmacy.
(g) Before printing any controlled substance prescription forms, a security printer shall verify with the appropriate licensing board that the prescriber possesses a license and current prescribing privileges which permits the prescribing of controlled substances with the federal Drug Enforcement Administration (DEA).
(h) Controlled substance prescription forms shall be provided directly to the prescriber either in person, by certified mail, or by a means that requires a signature signifying receipt of the package and provision of that signature to the security printer. Controlled substance prescription forms provided in person shall be restricted to established customers. Security printers shall obtain a photo identification from the customer and maintain a log of this information. Controlled substance prescription forms shall be shipped only to the prescriber's address on file and verified with the federal Drug Enforcement Administration or the Medical Board of California.
(i) Security printers shall retain ordering and delivery records in a readily retrievable manner for individual prescribers for three years.
(j) Security printers shall produce ordering and delivery records upon request by an authorized officer of the law as defined in Section 4017 of the Business and Professions Code.
(k) Security printers shall report any theft or loss of controlled substance prescription forms to the Department of Justice via fax or email within 24 hours of the theft or loss.
(l) (1) The department shall impose restrictions, sanctions, or penalties, subject to subdivisions (m) and (n), against security printers who are not in compliance with this division pursuant to regulations implemented pursuant to this division and shall revoke its approval of a security printer for a violation of this division or action that would permit a denial pursuant to subdivision (d) of this section.
(2) When the department revokes its approval, it shall notify the appropriate licensing boards and remove the security printer from the list of approved security printers.
(m) The following violations by security printers shall be punishable pursuant to subdivision (n):
(1) Failure to comply with the Security Printer Guidelines established by the Security Printer Program as a condition of approval.
(2) Failure to take reasonable precautions to prevent any dishonest act or illegal activity related to the access and control of security prescription forms.
(3) Theft or fraudulent use of a prescriber's identity in order to obtain security prescription forms.
(n) A security printer approved pursuant to subdivision (b) shall be subject to the following penalties for actions leading to the denial of a security printer application specified in subdivision (d) or for a violation specified in subdivision (m):
(1) For a first violation, a fine not to exceed one thousand dollars ($1,000).

(2) For a second or subsequent violation, a fine not to exceed two thousand five hundred dollars ($2,500) for each violation.

(3) For a third or subsequent violation, a filing of an administrative disciplinary action seeking to suspend or revoke security printer approval.

(o) In order to facilitate the standardization of all prescription forms and the serialization of prescription forms with unique identifiers, the Department of Justice may cease issuing new approvals of security printers to the extent necessary to achieve these purposes. The department may, pursuant to regulation, reduce the number of currently approved security printers to no fewer than three vendors. The department shall ensure that any reduction or limitation of approved security printers does not impact the ability of vendors to meet demand for prescription forms.

(Amended by Stats. 2018, Ch. 479, Sec. 2. (AB 1753) Effective January 1, 2019.)

11161.7.

(a) When a prescriber's authority to prescribe controlled substances is restricted by civil, criminal, or administrative action, or by an order of the court issued pursuant to Section 11161, the law enforcement agency or licensing board that sought the restrictions shall provide the name, category of licensure, license number, and the nature of the restrictions imposed on the prescriber to security printers, the Department of Justice, and the Board of Pharmacy.

(b) The Board of Pharmacy shall make available the information required by subdivision (a) to pharmacies and security printers to prevent the dispensing of controlled substance prescriptions issued by the prescriber and the ordering of additional controlled substance prescription forms by the restricted prescriber.

(Added by Stats. 2003, Ch. 406, Sec. 7. Effective January 1, 2004.)

11162.1.

(a) The prescription forms for controlled substances shall be printed with the following features:

(1) A latent, repetitive "void" pattern shall be printed across the entire front of the prescription blank; if a prescription is scanned or photocopied, the word "void" shall appear in a pattern across the entire front of the prescription.

(2) A watermark shall be printed on the backside of the prescription blank; the watermark shall consist of the words "California Security Prescription."

(3) A chemical void protection that prevents alteration by chemical washing.

(4) A feature printed in thermochromic ink.

(5) An area of opaque writing so that the writing disappears if the prescription is lightened.

(6) A description of the security features included on each prescription form.

(7) (A) Six quantity check off boxes shall be printed on the form so that the prescriber may indicate the quantity by checking the applicable box where the following quantities shall appear:

1–24

25–49

50–74

75–100

101–150

151 and over.

(B) In conjunction with the quantity boxes, a space shall be provided to designate the units referenced in the quantity boxes when the drug is not in tablet or capsule form.

(8) Prescription blanks shall contain a statement printed on the bottom of the prescription blank that the "Prescription is void if the number of drugs prescribed is not noted."

(9) The preprinted name, category of licensure, license number, federal controlled substance registration number, and address of the prescribing practitioner.

(10) Check boxes shall be printed on the form so that the prescriber may indicate the number of refills ordered.

(11) The date of origin of the prescription.

(12) A check box indicating the prescriber's order not to substitute.

(13) An identifying number assigned to the approved security printer by the Department of Justice.

(14) (A) A check box by the name of each prescriber when a prescription form lists multiple prescribers.

(B) Each prescriber who signs the prescription form shall identify themselves as the prescriber by checking the box by the prescriber's name.

(15) A uniquely serialized number, in a manner prescribed by the Department of Justice in accordance with Section 11162.2.

(b) Each batch of controlled substance prescription forms shall have the lot number printed on the form and each form within that batch shall be numbered sequentially beginning with the numeral one.

(c) (1) A prescriber designated by a licensed health care facility, a clinic specified in Section 1200, or a clinic specified in subdivision (a) of Section 1206 that has 25 or more physicians or surgeons may order controlled substance prescription forms for use by prescribers when treating patients in that facility without the information required in paragraph (9) of subdivision (a) or paragraph (3).

(2) Forms ordered pursuant to this subdivision shall have the name, category of licensure, license number, and federal controlled substance registration number of the designated prescriber and the name, address, category of licensure, and license number of the licensed health care facility the clinic specified in Section 1200, or the clinic specified in Section 1206 that has 25 or more physicians or surgeons preprinted on the form. Licensed health care facilities or clinics exempt under Section 1206 are not required to preprint the category of licensure and license number of their facility or clinic.

(3) Forms ordered pursuant to this section shall not be valid prescriptions without the name, category of licensure, license number, and federal controlled substance registration number of the prescriber on the form.

(4) (A) Except as provided in subparagraph (B), the designated prescriber shall maintain a record of the prescribers to whom the controlled substance prescription forms are issued, that shall include the name, category of licensure, license number, federal controlled substance registration number, and quantity of controlled substance prescription forms issued to each prescriber. The record shall be maintained in the health facility for three years.

(B) Forms ordered pursuant to this subdivision that are printed by a computerized prescription generation system shall not be subject to subparagraph (A) or paragraph (7) of subdivision (a). Forms printed pursuant to this subdivision that are printed by a computerized prescription generation system may contain the prescriber's name, category of professional licensure, license number, federal controlled substance registration number, and the date of the prescription.

(d) Within the next working day following delivery, a security printer shall submit via web-based application, as specified by the Department of Justice, all of the following information for all prescription forms delivered:

(1) Serial numbers of all prescription forms delivered.

(2) All prescriber names and Drug Enforcement Administration Controlled Substance Registration Certificate numbers displayed on the prescription forms.

(3) The delivery shipment recipient names.

(4) The date of delivery.

(Amended by Stats. 2019, Ch. 4, Sec. 1. (AB 149) Effective March 11, 2019.)

11162.2.

(a) Notwithstanding any other law, the uniquely serialized number described in paragraph (15) of subdivision (a) of Section 11162.1 shall not be a required feature in the printing of new prescription forms produced by approved security printers until a date determined by the Department of Justice, which shall be no later than January 1, 2020.

(b) Specifications for the serialized number shall be prescribed by the Department of Justice and shall meet the following minimum requirements:

(1) The serialized number shall be compliant with all state and federal requirements.

(2) The serialized number shall be utilizable as a barcode that may be scanned by dispensers.

(3) The serialized number shall be compliant with current National Council for Prescription Drug Program Standards.

(Added by Stats. 2019, Ch. 4, Sec. 2. (AB 149) Effective March 11, 2019.)

11162.5.

(a) Every person who counterfeits a prescription blank purporting to be an official prescription blank prepared and issued pursuant to Section 11161.5, or knowingly possesses more than three counterfeited prescription blanks, shall be punished by imprisonment pursuant to subdivision (h) of Section 1170 of the Penal Code or by imprisonment in a county jail for not more than one year.

(b) Every person who knowingly possesses three or fewer counterfeited prescription blanks purporting to be official prescription blanks prepared and issued pursuant to Section 11161.5, shall be guilty of a misdemeanor punishable by imprisonment in a county jail not exceeding six months, or by a fine not exceeding one thousand dollars ($1,000), or by both that fine and imprisonment.

(Amended by Stats. 2011, Ch. 15, Sec. 150. (AB 109) Effective April 4, 2011. Operative October 1, 2011, by Sec. 636 of Ch. 15, as amended by Stats. 2011, Ch. 39, Sec. 68.)

11162.6.

(a) Every person who counterfeits a controlled substance prescription form shall be guilty of a misdemeanor punishable by imprisonment in a county jail for not more than one year, by a fine not exceeding one thousand dollars ($1,000), or by both that imprisonment and fine.

(b) Every person who knowingly possesses a counterfeited controlled substance prescription form shall be guilty of a misdemeanor punishable by imprisonment in a county jail not exceeding six months, by a fine not exceeding one thousand dollars ($1,000), or by both that imprisonment and fine.

(c) Every person who attempts to obtain or obtains a controlled substance prescription form under false pretenses shall be guilty of a misdemeanor punishable by imprisonment in a county jail not exceeding six months, by a fine not exceeding one thousand dollars ($1,000), or by both that imprisonment and fine.

(d) Every person who fraudulently produces controlled substance prescription forms shall be guilty of a misdemeanor punishable by imprisonment in a county jail not exceeding six months, by a fine not exceeding one thousand dollars ($1,000), or by both that imprisonment and fine.

(e) This section shall become operative on July 1, 2004.

(Added by Stats. 2003, Ch. 406, Sec. 10. Effective January 1, 2004. Section operative July 1, 2004, by its own provisions.)

11164.

Except as provided in Section 11167, no person shall prescribe a controlled substance, nor shall any person fill, compound, or dispense a prescription for a controlled substance, unless it complies with the requirements of this section.

(a) Each prescription for a controlled substance classified in Schedule II, III, IV, or V, except as authorized by subdivision (b), shall be made on a controlled substance prescription form as specified in Section 11162.1 and shall meet the following requirements:

(1) The prescription shall be signed and dated by the prescriber in ink and shall contain the prescriber's address and telephone number; the name of the ultimate user or

research subject, or contact information as determined by the Secretary of the United States Department of Health and Human Services; refill information, such as the number of refills ordered and whether the prescription is a first-time request or a refill; and the name, quantity, strength, and directions for use of the controlled substance prescribed.

(2) The prescription shall also contain the address of the person for whom the controlled substance is prescribed. If the prescriber does not specify this address on the prescription, the pharmacist filling the prescription or an employee acting under the direction of the pharmacist shall write or type the address on the prescription or maintain this information in a readily retrievable form in the pharmacy.

(b) (1) Notwithstanding paragraph (1) of subdivision (a) of Section 11162.1, any controlled substance classified in Schedule III, IV, or V may be dispensed upon an oral or electronically transmitted prescription, which shall be produced in hard copy form and signed and dated by the pharmacist filling the prescription or by any other person expressly authorized by provisions of the Business and Professions Code. Any person who transmits, maintains, or receives any electronically transmitted prescription shall ensure the security, integrity, authority, and confidentiality of the prescription.

(2) The date of issue of the prescription and all the information required for a written prescription by subdivision (a) shall be included in the written record of the prescription; the pharmacist need not include the address, telephone number, license classification, or federal registry number of the prescriber or the address of the patient on the hard copy, if that information is readily retrievable in the pharmacy.

(3) Pursuant to an authorization of the prescriber, any agent of the prescriber on behalf of the prescriber may orally or electronically transmit a prescription for a controlled substance classified in Schedule III, IV, or V, if in these cases the written record of the prescription required by this subdivision specifies the name of the agent of the prescriber transmitting the prescription.

(c) The use of commonly used abbreviations shall not invalidate an otherwise valid prescription.

(d) Notwithstanding subdivisions (a) and (b), prescriptions for a controlled substance classified in Schedule V may be for more than one person in the same family with the same medical need.

(e) (1) Notwithstanding any other law, a prescription written on a prescription form that was otherwise valid prior to January 1, 2019, but that does not comply with paragraph (15) of subdivision (a) of Section 11162.1, or a valid controlled substance prescription form approved by the Department of Justice as of January 1, 2019, is a valid prescription that may be filled, compounded, or dispensed until January 1, 2021.

(2) If the Department of Justice determines that there is an inadequate availability of compliant prescription forms to meet demand on or before the date described in paragraph (1), the department may extend the period during which prescriptions written on noncompliant prescription forms remain valid for a period no longer than an additional six months.

(Amended by Stats. 2019, Ch. 4, Sec. 3. (AB 149) Effective March 11, 2019.)

11164.1.

(a) (1) Notwithstanding any other provision of law, a prescription for a controlled substance issued by a prescriber in another state for delivery to a patient in another state may be dispensed by a California pharmacy, if the prescription conforms with the requirements for controlled substance prescriptions in the state in which the controlled substance was prescribed.

(2) All prescriptions for Schedule II, Schedule III, and Schedule IV controlled substances dispensed pursuant to this subdivision shall be reported by the dispensing pharmacy to the Department of Justice in the manner prescribed by subdivision (d) of Section 11165.

(b) Pharmacies may dispense prescriptions for Schedule III, Schedule IV, and Schedule V controlled substances from out-of-state prescribers pursuant to Section 4005 of the Business and Professions Code and Section 1717 of Title 16 of the California Code of Regulations.

(Amended by Stats. 2013, Ch. 400, Sec. 5. (SB 809) Effective January 1, 2014.)

11164.5.

(a) Notwithstanding Section 11164, if only recorded and stored electronically, on magnetic media, or in any other computerized form, the pharmacy's or hospital's computer system shall not permit the received information or the controlled substance dispensing information required by this section to be changed, obliterated, destroyed, or disposed of, for the record maintenance period required by law, once the information has been received by the pharmacy or the hospital and once the controlled substance has been dispensed, respectively. Once the controlled substance has been dispensed, if the previously created record is determined to be incorrect, a correcting addition may be made only by or with the approval of a pharmacist. After a pharmacist enters the change or enters his or her approval of the change into the computer, the resulting record shall include the correcting addition and the date it was made to the record, the identity of the person or pharmacist making the correction, and the identity of the pharmacist approving the correction.

(b) Nothing in this section shall be construed to exempt any pharmacy or hospital dispensing Schedule II controlled substances pursuant to electronic transmission prescriptions from existing reporting requirements.

(Amended by Stats. 2016, Ch. 484, Sec. 55. (SB 1193) Effective January 1, 2017.)

11165.

(a) To assist health care practitioners in their efforts to ensure appropriate prescribing, ordering, administering, furnishing, and dispensing of controlled substances, law enforcement and regulatory agencies in their efforts to control the diversion and resultant abuse of Schedule II, Schedule III, and Schedule IV controlled substances, and for statistical analysis, education, and research, the Department of Justice shall, contingent upon the availability of adequate funds in the CURES Fund, maintain the Controlled Substance Utilization Review and Evaluation System (CURES) for the electronic monitoring of, and Internet access to information regarding, the prescribing and dispensing of Schedule II, Schedule III, and Schedule IV controlled substances by all practitioners authorized to prescribe, order, administer, furnish, or dispense these controlled substances.

(b) The Department of Justice may seek and use grant funds to pay the costs incurred by the operation and maintenance of CURES. The department shall annually report to the Legislature and make available to the public the amount and source of funds it receives for support of CURES.

(c) (1) The operation of CURES shall comply with all applicable federal and state privacy and security laws and regulations.

(2) (A) CURES shall operate under existing provisions of law to safeguard the privacy and confidentiality of patients. Data obtained from CURES shall only be provided to appropriate state, local, and federal public agencies for disciplinary, civil, or criminal purposes and to other agencies or entities, as determined by the Department of Justice, for the purpose of educating practitioners and others in lieu of disciplinary, civil, or criminal actions. Data may be provided to public or private entities, as approved by the Department of Justice, for educational, peer review, statistical, or research purposes, if patient information, including any information that may identify the patient, is not compromised. Further, data disclosed to any individual or agency as described in this subdivision shall not be disclosed, sold, or transferred to any third party, unless authorized by, or pursuant to, state and federal privacy and security laws and regulations. The Department of Justice shall establish policies, procedures, and regulations regarding the use, access, evaluation, management, implementation, operation, storage, disclosure, and security of the information within CURES, consistent with this subdivision.

(B) Notwithstanding subparagraph (A), a regulatory board whose licensees do not prescribe, order, administer, furnish, or dispense controlled substances shall not be provided data obtained from CURES.

(3) The Department of Justice shall, no later than July 1, 2020, adopt regulations regarding the access and use of the information within CURES. The Department of Justice shall consult with all stakeholders identified by the department during the rulemaking process. The regulations shall, at a minimum, address all of the following in a manner consistent with this chapter:

(A) The process for approving, denying, and disapproving individuals or entities seeking access to information in CURES.

(B) The purposes for which a health care practitioner may access information in CURES.

(C) The conditions under which a warrant, subpoena, or court order is required for a law enforcement agency to obtain information from CURES as part of a criminal investigation.

(D) The process by which information in CURES may be provided for educational, peer review, statistical, or research purposes.

(4) In accordance with federal and state privacy laws and regulations, a health care practitioner may provide a patient with a copy of the patient's CURES patient activity report as long as no additional CURES data are provided and keep a copy of the report in the patient's medical record in compliance with subdivision (d) of Section 11165.1.

(d) For each prescription for a Schedule II, Schedule III, or Schedule IV controlled substance, as defined in the controlled substances schedules in federal law and regulations, specifically Sections 1308.12, 1308.13, and 1308.14, respectively, of Title 21 of the Code of Federal Regulations, the dispensing pharmacy, clinic, or other dispenser shall report the following information to the Department of Justice as soon as reasonably possible, but not more than seven days after the date a controlled substance is dispensed, in a format specified by the Department of Justice:

(1) Full name, address, and, if available, telephone number of the ultimate user or research subject, or contact information as determined by the Secretary of the United States Department of Health and Human Services, and the gender, and date of birth of the ultimate user.

(2) The prescriber's category of licensure, license number, national provider identifier (NPI) number, the federal controlled substance registration number, and the state medical license number of any prescriber using the federal controlled substance registration number of a government-exempt facility, if provided.

(3) Pharmacy prescription number, license number, NPI number, and federal controlled substance registration number.

(4) National Drug Code (NDC) number of the controlled substance dispensed.

(5) Quantity of the controlled substance dispensed.

(6) International Statistical Classification of Diseases, 9th revision (ICD-9) or 10th revision (ICD-10) Code, if available.

(7) Number of refills ordered.

(8) Whether the drug was dispensed as a refill of a prescription or as a first-time request.

(9) Date of origin of the prescription.

(10) Date of dispensing of the prescription.

(11) The serial number for the corresponding prescription form, if applicable.

(e) The Department of Justice may invite stakeholders to assist, advise, and make recommendations on the establishment of rules and regulations necessary to ensure the proper administration and enforcement of the CURES database. All prescriber and dispenser invitees shall be licensed by one of the boards or committees identified in subdivision (d) of Section 208 of the Business and Professions Code, in active practice in California, and a regular user of CURES.

(f) The Department of Justice shall, prior to upgrading CURES, consult with prescribers licensed by one of the boards or committees identified in subdivision (d) of Section 208 of the Business and Professions Code, one or more of the boards or committees identified in subdivision (d) of Section 208 of the Business and Professions Code, and any other stakeholder identified by the department, for the purpose of identifying desirable capabilities and upgrades to the CURES Prescription Drug Monitoring Program (PDMP).

(g) The Department of Justice may establish a process to educate authorized subscribers of the CURES PDMP on how to access and use the CURES PDMP.

(h) (1) The Department of Justice may enter into an agreement with any entity operating an interstate data sharing hub, or any agency operating a prescription drug monitoring program in another state, for purposes of interstate data sharing of prescription drug monitoring program information.

(2) Data obtained from CURES may be provided to authorized users of another state's prescription drug monitoring program, as determined by the Department of Justice pursuant to subdivision (c), if the entity operating the interstate data sharing hub, and the prescription drug monitoring program of that state, as applicable, have entered into an agreement with the Department of Justice for interstate data sharing of prescription drug monitoring program information.

(3) Any agreement entered into by the Department of Justice for purposes of interstate data sharing of prescription drug monitoring program information shall ensure that all access to data obtained from CURES and the handling of data contained within CURES comply with California law, including regulations, and meet the same patient privacy, audit, and data security standards employed and required for direct access to CURES.

(4) For purposes of interstate data sharing of CURES information pursuant to this subdivision, an authorized user of another state's prescription drug monitoring program shall not be required to register with CURES, if he or she is registered and in good standing with that state's prescription drug monitoring program.

(5) The Department of Justice shall not enter into an agreement pursuant to this subdivision until the department has issued final regulations regarding the access and use of the information within CURES as required by paragraph (3) of subdivision (c).
(Amended by Stats. 2018, Ch. 479, Sec. 4.5. (AB 1753) Effective January 1, 2019.)
11165.1.

(a) (1) (A) (i) A health care practitioner authorized to prescribe, order, administer, furnish, or dispense Schedule II, Schedule III, or Schedule IV controlled substances pursuant to Section 11150 shall, before July 1, 2016, or upon receipt of a federal Drug Enforcement Administration (DEA) registration, whichever occurs later, submit an application developed by the department to obtain approval to electronically access information regarding the controlled substance history of a patient that is maintained by the department. Upon approval, the department shall release to that practitioner the electronic history of controlled substances dispensed to an individual under his or her care based on data contained in the CURES Prescription Drug Monitoring Program (PDMP).

(ii) A pharmacist shall, before July 1, 2016, or upon licensure, whichever occurs later, submit an application developed by the department to obtain approval to electronically access information regarding the controlled substance history of a patient that is maintained by the department. Upon approval, the department shall release to that pharmacist the electronic history of controlled substances dispensed to an individual under his or her care based on data contained in the CURES PDMP.

(B) An application may be denied, or a subscriber may be suspended, for reasons which include, but are not limited to, the following:

(i) Materially falsifying an application to access information contained in the CURES database.

(ii) Failing to maintain effective controls for access to the patient activity report.

(iii) Having his or her federal DEA registration suspended or revoked.

(iv) Violating a law governing controlled substances or any other law for which the possession or use of a controlled substance is an element of the crime.

(v) Accessing information for a reason other than to diagnose or treat his or her patients, or to document compliance with the law.

(C) An authorized subscriber shall notify the department within 30 days of any changes to the subscriber account.

(D) Commencing no later than October 1, 2018, an approved health care practitioner, pharmacist, and any person acting on behalf of a health care practitioner or pharmacist pursuant to subdivision (b) of Section 209 of the Business and Professions Code may use the department's online portal or a health information technology system that meets the criteria required in subparagraph (E) to access information in the CURES database pursuant to this section. A subscriber who uses a health information technology system that meets the criteria required in subparagraph (E) to access the CURES database may submit automated queries to the CURES database that are triggered by predetermined criteria.

(E) Commencing no later than October 1, 2018, an approved health care practitioner or pharmacist may submit queries to the CURES database through a health information technology system if the entity that operates the health information technology system can certify all of the following:

(i) The entity will not use or disclose data received from the CURES database for any purpose other than delivering the data to an approved health care practitioner or pharmacist or performing data processing activities that may be necessary to enable the delivery unless authorized by, and pursuant to, state and federal privacy and security laws and regulations.

(ii) The health information technology system will authenticate the identity of an authorized health care practitioner or pharmacist initiating queries to the CURES database and, at the time of the query to the CURES database, the health information technology system submits the following data regarding the query to CURES:

(I) The date of the query.

(II) The time of the query.

(III) The first and last name of the patient queried.

(IV) The date of birth of the patient queried.

(V) The identification of the CURES user for whom the system is making the query.

(iii) The health information technology system meets applicable patient privacy and information security requirements of state and federal law.

(iv) The entity has entered into a memorandum of understanding with the department that solely addresses the technical specifications of the health information technology system to ensure the security of the data in the CURES database and the secure transfer of data from the CURES database. The technical specifications shall be universal for all health information technology systems that establish a method of system integration to retrieve information from the CURES database. The memorandum of understanding shall not govern, or in any way impact or restrict, the use of data received from the CURES database or impose any additional burdens on covered entities in compliance with the regulations promulgated pursuant to the federal Health Insurance Portability and Accountability Act of 1996 found in Parts 160 and 164 of Title 45 of the Code of Federal Regulations.

(F) No later than October 1, 2018, the department shall develop a programming interface or other method of system integration to allow health information technology systems that meet the requirements in subparagraph (E) to retrieve information in the CURES database on behalf of an authorized health care practitioner or pharmacist.

(G) The department shall not access patient-identifiable information in an entity's health information technology system.

(H) An entity that operates a health information technology system that is requesting to establish an integration with the CURES database shall pay a reasonable fee to cover the cost of establishing and maintaining integration with the CURES database.

(I) The department may prohibit integration or terminate a health information technology system's ability to retrieve information in the CURES database if the health information technology system fails to meet the requirements of subparagraph (E), or the entity operating the health information technology system does not fulfill its obligation under subparagraph (H).

(2) A health care practitioner authorized to prescribe, order, administer, furnish, or dispense Schedule II, Schedule III, or Schedule IV controlled substances pursuant to Section 11150 or a pharmacist shall be deemed to have complied with paragraph (1) if the licensed health care practitioner or pharmacist has been approved to access the CURES database through the process developed pursuant to subdivision (a) of Section 209 of the Business and Professions Code.

(b) A request for, or release of, a controlled substance history pursuant to this section shall be made in accordance with guidelines developed by the department.

(c) In order to prevent the inappropriate, improper, or illegal use of Schedule II, Schedule III, or Schedule IV controlled substances, the department may initiate the referral of the history of controlled substances dispensed to an individual based on data contained in CURES to licensed health care practitioners, pharmacists, or both, providing care or services to the individual.

(d) The history of controlled substances dispensed to an individual based on data contained in CURES that is received by a practitioner or pharmacist from the department pursuant to this section is medical information subject to the provisions of the Confidentiality of Medical Information Act contained in Part 2.6 (commencing with Section 56) of Division 1 of the Civil Code.

(e) Information concerning a patient's controlled substance history provided to a practitioner or pharmacist pursuant to this section shall include prescriptions for controlled substances listed in Sections 1308.12, 1308.13, and 1308.14 of Title 21 of the Code of Federal Regulations.

(f) A health care practitioner, pharmacist, and any person acting on behalf of a health care practitioner or pharmacist, when acting with reasonable care and in good faith, is not subject to civil or administrative liability arising from any false, incomplete, inaccurate, or misattributed information submitted to, reported by, or relied upon in the CURES database or for any resulting failure of the CURES database to accurately or timely report that information.

(g) For purposes of this section, the following terms have the following meanings:

(1) "Automated basis" means using predefined criteria to trigger an automated query to the CURES database, which can be attributed to a specific health care practitioner or pharmacist.

(2) "Department" means the Department of Justice.

(3) "Entity" means an organization that operates, or provides or makes available, a health information technology system to a health care practitioner or pharmacist.

(4) "Health information technology system" means an information processing application using hardware and software for the storage, retrieval, sharing of or use of patient data for communication, decisionmaking, coordination of care, or the quality, safety, or efficiency of the practice of medicine or delivery of health care services, including, but not limited to, electronic medical record applications, health information exchange systems, or other interoperable clinical or health care information system.

(5) "User-initiated basis" means an authorized health care practitioner or pharmacist has taken an action to initiate the query to the CURES database, such as clicking a button, issuing a voice command, or taking some other action that can be attributed to a specific health care practitioner or pharmacist.
(Amended by Stats. 2017, Ch. 607, Sec. 1. (AB 40) Effective October 9, 2017.)
11165.2.

(a) The Department of Justice may conduct audits of the CURES Prescription Drug Monitoring Program system and its users.

(b) The Department of Justice may establish, by regulation, a system for the issuance to a CURES Prescription Drug Monitoring Program subscriber of a citation which may contain an order of abatement, or an order to pay an administrative fine assessed by the Department of Justice if the subscriber is in violation of any provision of this chapter or any regulation adopted by the Department of Justice pursuant to this chapter.

(c) The system shall contain the following provisions:

(1) Citations shall be in writing and shall describe with particularity the nature of the violation, including specific reference to the provision of law or regulation of the department determined to have been violated.

(2) Whenever appropriate, the citation shall contain an order of abatement establishing a reasonable time for abatement of the violation.

(3) In no event shall the administrative fine assessed by the department exceed two thousand five hundred dollars ($2,500) for each violation. In assessing a fine, due consideration shall be given to the appropriateness of the amount of the fine with respect to such factors as the gravity of the violation, the good faith of the subscribers, and the history of previous violations.

(4) An order of abatement or a fine assessment issued pursuant to a citation shall inform the subscriber that if the subscriber desires a hearing to contest the finding of a violation, a hearing shall be requested by written notice to the CURES Prescription Drug Monitoring Program within 30 days of the date of issuance of the citation or assessment. Hearings shall be held pursuant to Chapter 5 (commencing with Section 11500) of Part 1 of Division 3 of Title 2 of the Government Code.

(5) In addition to requesting a hearing, the subscriber may, within 10 days after service of the citation, request in writing an opportunity for an informal conference with the department regarding the citation. At the conclusion of the informal conference, the department may affirm, modify, or dismiss the citation, including any fine levied or order of abatement issued. The decision shall be deemed to be a final order with regard to the citation issued, including the fine levied or the order of abatement which could include permanent suspension to the system, a monetary fine, or both, depending on the gravity of the violation. However, the subscriber does not waive its right to request a hearing to contest a citation by requesting an informal conference. If the citation is affirmed, a formal hearing may be requested within 30 days of the date the citation was affirmed. If the citation is dismissed after the informal conference, the request for a hearing on the matter of the citation shall be deemed to be withdrawn. If the citation, including any fine levied or order of abatement, is modified, the citation originally issued shall be considered withdrawn and a new citation issued. If a hearing is requested for a subsequent citation, it shall be requested within 30 days of service of that subsequent citation.

(6) Failure of a subscriber to pay a fine within 30 days of the date of assessment or comply with an order of abatement within the fixed time, unless the citation is being appealed, may result in disciplinary action taken by the department. If a citation is not contested and a fine is not paid, the subscriber account will be terminated.

(A) A citation may be issued without the assessment of an administrative fine.

(B) Assessment of administrative fines may be limited to only particular violations of law or department regulations.

(d) Notwithstanding any other provision of law, if a fine is paid to satisfy an assessment based on the finding of a violation, payment of the fine shall be represented as a satisfactory resolution of the matter for purposes of public disclosure.

(e) Administrative fines collected pursuant to this section shall be deposited in the CURES Program Special Fund, available upon appropriation by the Legislature. These special funds shall provide support for costs associated with informal and formal hearings, maintenance, and updates to the CURES Prescription Drug Monitoring Program.

(f) The sanctions authorized under this section shall be separate from, and in addition to, any other administrative, civil, or criminal remedies; however, a criminal action may not be initiated for a specific offense if a citation has been issued pursuant to this section for that offense, and a citation may not be issued pursuant to this section for a specific offense if a criminal action for that offense has been filed.

(g) Nothing in this section shall be deemed to prevent the department from serving and prosecuting an accusation to suspend or revoke a subscriber if grounds for that suspension or revocation exist.

(Added by Stats. 2011, Ch. 418, Sec. 5. (SB 360) Effective January 1, 2012.)

11165.3.
The theft or loss of prescription forms shall be reported immediately by the security printer or affected prescriber to the CURES Prescription Drug Monitoring Program, but no later than three days after the discovery of the theft or loss. This notification may be done in writing utilizing the approved Department of Justice form or may be reported by the authorized subscriber through the CURES Prescription Drug Monitoring Program. (Amended by Stats. 2012, Ch. 867, Sec. 7. (SB 1144) Effective January 1, 2013.)

11165.4.
(a) (1) (A) (i) A health care practitioner authorized to prescribe, order, administer, or furnish a controlled substance shall consult the CURES database to review a patient's controlled substance history before prescribing a Schedule II, Schedule III, or Schedule IV controlled substance to the patient for the first time and at least once every four months thereafter if the substance remains part of the treatment of the patient.

(ii) If a health care practitioner authorized to prescribe, order, administer, or furnish a controlled substance is not required, pursuant to an exemption described in subdivision (c), to consult the CURES database the first time he or she prescribes, orders, administers, or furnishes a controlled substance to a patient, he or she shall consult the CURES database to review the patient's controlled substance history before subsequently prescribing a Schedule II, Schedule III, or Schedule IV controlled substance to the patient and at least once every four months thereafter if the substance remains part of the treatment of the patient.

(B) For purposes of this paragraph, "first time" means the initial occurrence in which a health care practitioner, in his or her role as a health care practitioner, intends to prescribe, order, administer, or furnish a Schedule II, Schedule III, or Schedule IV controlled substance to a patient and has not previously prescribed a controlled substance to the patient.

(2) A health care practitioner shall obtain a patient's controlled substance history from the CURES database no earlier than 24 hours, or the previous business day, before he or she prescribes, orders, administers, or furnishes a Schedule II, Schedule III, or Schedule IV controlled substance to the patient.

(b) The duty to consult the CURES database, as described in subdivision (a), does not apply to veterinarians or pharmacists.

(c) The duty to consult the CURES database, as described in subdivision (a), does not apply to a health care practitioner in any of the following circumstances:

(1) If a health care practitioner prescribes, orders, or furnishes a controlled substance to be administered to a patient while the patient is admitted to any of the following facilities or during an emergency transfer between any of the following facilities for use while on facility premises:

(A) A licensed clinic, as described in Chapter 1 (commencing with Section 1200) of Division 2.

(B) An outpatient setting, as described in Chapter 1.3 (commencing with Section 1248) of Division 2.

(C) A health facility, as described in Chapter 2 (commencing with Section 1250) of Division 2.

(D) A county medical facility, as described in Chapter 2.5 (commencing with Section 1440) of Division 2.

(2) If a health care practitioner prescribes, orders, administers, or furnishes a controlled substance in the emergency department of a general acute care hospital and the quantity of the controlled substance does not exceed a nonrefillable seven-day supply of the controlled substance to be used in accordance with the directions for use.

(3) If a health care practitioner prescribes, orders, administers, or furnishes a controlled substance to a patient as part of the patient's treatment for a surgical procedure and the quantity of the controlled substance does not exceed a nonrefillable five-day supply of the controlled substance to be used in accordance with the directions for use, in any of the following facilities:

(A) A licensed clinic, as described in Chapter 1 (commencing with Section 1200) of Division 2.

(B) An outpatient setting, as described in Chapter 1.3 (commencing with Section 1248) of Division 2.

(C) A health facility, as described in Chapter 2 (commencing with Section 1250) of Division 2.

(D) A county medical facility, as described in Chapter 2.5 (commencing with Section 1440) of Division 2.

(E) A place of practice, as defined in Section 1658 of the Business and Professions Code.

(4) If a health care practitioner prescribes, orders, administers, or furnishes a controlled substance to a patient currently receiving hospice care, as defined in Section 1339.40.

(5) (A) If all of the following circumstances are satisfied:

(i) It is not reasonably possible for a health care practitioner to access the information in the CURES database in a timely manner.

(ii) Another health care practitioner or designee authorized to access the CURES database is not reasonably available.

(iii) The quantity of controlled substance prescribed, ordered, administered, or furnished does not exceed a nonrefillable five-day supply of the controlled substance to be used in accordance with the directions for use and no refill of the controlled substance is allowed.

(B) A health care practitioner who does not consult the CURES database under subparagraph (A) shall document the reason he or she did not consult the database in the patient's medical record.

(6) If the CURES database is not operational, as determined by the department, or when it cannot be accessed by a health care practitioner because of a temporary technological or electrical failure. A health care practitioner shall, without undue delay, seek to correct any cause of the temporary technological or electrical failure that is reasonably within his or her control.

(7) If the CURES database cannot be accessed because of technological limitations that are not reasonably within the control of a health care practitioner.

(8) If consultation of the CURES database would, as determined by the health care practitioner, result in a patient's inability to obtain a prescription in a timely manner and thereby adversely impact the patient's medical condition, provided that the quantity of the controlled substance does not exceed a nonrefillable five-day supply if the controlled substance were used in accordance with the directions for use.

(d) (1) A health care practitioner who fails to consult the CURES database, as described in subdivision (a), shall be referred to the appropriate state professional licensing board solely for administrative sanctions, as deemed appropriate by that board.

(2) This section does not create a private cause of action against a health care practitioner. This section does not limit a health care practitioner's liability for the negligent failure to diagnose or treat a patient.

(e) This section is not operative until six months after the Department of Justice certifies that the CURES database is ready for statewide use and that the department has adequate staff, which, at a minimum, shall be consistent with the appropriation authorized in Schedule (6) of Item 0820-001-0001 of the Budget Act of 2016 (Chapter 23 of the Statutes of 2016), user support, and education. The department shall notify the Secretary of State and the office of the Legislative Counsel of the date of that certification.

(f) All applicable state and federal privacy laws govern the duties required by this section.

(g) The provisions of this section are severable. If any provision of this section or its application is held invalid, that invalidity shall not affect other provisions or applications that can be given effect without the invalid provision or application.

(Added by Stats. 2016, Ch. 708, Sec. 3. (SB 482) Effective January 1, 2017. Section operative on October 2, 2018, pursuant to subdivision (e).)

11165.5.

(a) The Department of Justice may seek voluntarily contributed private funds from insurers, health care service plans, qualified manufacturers, and other donors for the purpose of supporting CURES. Insurers, health care service plans, qualified manufacturers, and other donors may contribute by submitting their payment to the Controller for deposit into the CURES Fund established pursuant to subdivision (c) of Section 208 of the Business and Professions Code. The department shall make information about the amount and the source of all private funds it receives for support of CURES available to the public. Contributions to the CURES Fund pursuant to this subdivision shall be nondeductible for state tax purposes.

(b) For purposes of this section, the following definitions apply:

(1) "Controlled substance" means a drug, substance, or immediate precursor listed in any schedule in Section 11055, 11056, or 11057 of the Health and Safety Code.

(2) "Health care service plan" means an entity licensed pursuant to the Knox-Keene Health Care Service Plan Act of 1975 (Chapter 2.2 (commencing with Section 1340) of Division 2 of the Health and Safety Code).

(3) "Insurer" means an admitted insurer writing health insurance, as defined in Section 106 of the Insurance Code, and an admitted insurer writing workers' compensation insurance, as defined in Section 109 of the Insurance Code.

(4) "Qualified manufacturer" means a manufacturer of a controlled substance, but does not mean a wholesaler or nonresident wholesaler of dangerous drugs, regulated pursuant to Article 11 (commencing with Section 4160) of Chapter 9 of Division 2 of the Business and Professions Code, a veterinary food-animal drug retailer, regulated pursuant to Article 15 (commencing with Section 4196) of Chapter 9 of Division 2 of the Business and Professions Code, or an individual regulated by the Medical Board of California, the Dental Board of California, the California State Board of Pharmacy, the Veterinary Medical Board, the Board of Registered Nursing, the Physician Assistant Committee of the Medical Board of California, the Osteopathic Medical Board of California, the State Board of Optometry, or the California Board of Podiatric Medicine.

(Added by Stats. 2013, Ch. 400, Sec. 8. (SB 809) Effective January 1, 2014.)

11165.6.

A prescriber shall be allowed to access the CURES database for a list of patients for whom that prescriber is listed as a prescriber in the CURES database.

(Added by Stats. 2018, Ch. 274, Sec. 1. (AB 2086) Effective January 1, 2019.)

11166.

No person shall fill a prescription for a controlled substance after six months has elapsed from the date written on the prescription by the prescriber. No person shall knowingly fill a mutilated or forged or altered prescription for a controlled substance except for the addition of the address of the person for whom the controlled substance is prescribed as provided by paragraph (3) of subdivision (b) of Section 11164.

(Amended by Stats. 2003, Ch. 406, Sec. 19. Effective January 1, 2004.)

11167.

Notwithstanding subdivision (a) of Section 11164, in an emergency where failure to issue a prescription may result in loss of life or intense suffering, an order for a controlled substance may be dispensed on an oral order, an electronic data transmission order, or a written order not made on a controlled substance form as specified in Section 11162.1, subject to all of the following requirements:

(a) The order contains all information required by subdivision (a) of Section 11164.

(b) Any written order is signed and dated by the prescriber in ink, and the pharmacy reduces any oral or electronic data transmission order to hard copy form prior to dispensing the controlled substance.

(c) The prescriber provides a written prescription on a controlled substance prescription form that meets the requirements of Section 11162.1, by the seventh day following the transmission of the initial order; a postmark by the seventh day following transmission of the initial order shall constitute compliance.

(d) If the prescriber fails to comply with subdivision (c), the pharmacy shall so notify the Department of Justice in writing within 144 hours of the prescriber's failure to do so and shall make and retain a hard copy, readily retrievable record of the prescription, including the date and method of notification of the Department of Justice.

(e) This section shall become operative on January 1, 2005.

(Amended by Stats. 2012, Ch. 867, Sec. 8. (SB 1144) Effective January 1, 2013.)

11167.5.

(a) An order for a controlled substance classified in Schedule II for a patient of a licensed skilled nursing facility, a licensed intermediate care facility, a licensed home health agency, or a licensed hospice may be dispensed upon an oral or electronically transmitted prescription. If the prescription is transmitted orally, the pharmacist shall, prior to filling the prescription, reduce the prescription to writing in ink in the handwriting of the pharmacist on a form developed by the pharmacy for this purpose. If the prescription is transmitted electronically, the pharmacist shall, prior to filling the prescription, produce, sign, and date a hard copy prescription. The prescriptions shall contain the date the prescription was orally or electronically transmitted by the prescriber,

the name of the person for whom the prescription was authorized, the name and address of the licensed skilled nursing facility, licensed intermediate care facility, licensed home health agency, or licensed hospice in which that person is a patient, the name and quantity of the controlled substance prescribed, the directions for use, and the name, address, category of professional licensure, license number, and federal controlled substance registration number of the prescriber. The original shall be properly endorsed by the pharmacist with the pharmacy's state license number, the name and address of the pharmacy, and the signature of the person who received the controlled substances for the licensed skilled nursing facility, licensed intermediate care facility, licensed home health agency, or licensed hospice. A licensed skilled nursing facility, a licensed intermediate care facility, a licensed home health agency, or a licensed hospice shall forward to the dispensing pharmacist a copy of any signed telephone orders, chart orders, or related documentation substantiating each oral or electronically transmitted prescription transaction under this section.

(b) This section shall become operative on July 1, 2004.

(Repealed (in Sec. 23) and added by Stats. 2003, Ch. 406, Sec. 24. Effective January 1, 2004. Section operative July 1, 2004, by its own provisions.)

11170.

No person shall prescribe, administer, or furnish a controlled substance for himself.

(Repealed and added by Stats. 1972, Ch. 1407.)

11171.

No person shall prescribe, administer, or furnish a controlled substance except under the conditions and in the manner provided by this division.

(Repealed and added by Stats. 1972, Ch. 1407.)

11172.

No person shall antedate or postdate a prescription.

(Repealed and added by Stats. 1972, Ch. 1407.)

11173.

(a) No person shall obtain or attempt to obtain controlled substances, or procure or attempt to procure the administration of or prescription for controlled substances, (1) by fraud, deceit, misrepresentation , or subterfuge; or (2) by the concealment of a material fact.

(b) No person shall make a false statement in any prescription, order, report, or record, required by this division.

(c) No person shall, for the purpose of obtaining controlled substances, falsely assume the title of, or represent himself to be, a manufacturer, wholesaler, pharmacist, physician, dentist, veterinarian, registered nurse, physician's assistant, or other authorized person.

(d) No person shall affix any false or forged label to a package or receptacle containing controlled substances.

(Amended by Stats. 1977, Ch. 843.)

11174.

No person shall, in connection with the prescribing, furnishing, administering, or dispensing of a controlled substance, give a false name or false address.

(Repealed and added by Stats. 1972, Ch. 1407.)

11175.

No person shall obtain or possess a prescription that does not comply with this division, nor shall any person obtain a controlled substance by means of a prescription which does not comply with this division or possess a controlled substance obtained by such a prescription.

(Amended by Stats. 1976, Ch. 896.)

11179.

A person who fills a prescription shall keep it on file for at least three years from the date of filling it.

(Amended by Stats. 1976, Ch. 896.)

11180.

No person shall obtain or possess a controlled substance obtained by a prescription that does not comply with this division.

(Added by Stats. 1972, Ch. 1407.)

ARTICLE 2. Prescriber's Record [11190 - 11192]

(Article 2 added by Stats. 1972, Ch. 1407.)

11190.

(a) Every practitioner, other than a pharmacist, who prescribes or administers a controlled substance classified in Schedule II shall make a record that, as to the transaction, shows all of the following:

(1) The name and address of the patient.

(2) The date.

(3) The character, including the name and strength, and quantity of controlled substances involved.

(b) The prescriber's record shall show the pathology and purpose for which the controlled substance was administered or prescribed.

(c) (1) For each prescription for a Schedule II, Schedule III, or Schedule IV controlled substance that is dispensed by a prescriber pursuant to Section 4170 of the Business and Professions Code, the prescriber shall record and maintain the following information:

(A) Full name, address, and the telephone number of the ultimate user or research subject, or contact information as determined by the Secretary of the United States Department of Health and Human Services, and the gender, and date of birth of the patient.

(B) The prescriber's category of licensure and license number; federal controlled substance registration number; and the state medical license number of any prescriber using the federal controlled substance registration number of a government-exempt facility.

(C) NDC (National Drug Code) number of the controlled substance dispensed.

(D) Quantity of the controlled substance dispensed.

(E) ICD-9 (diagnosis code), if available.

(F) Number of refills ordered.

(G) Whether the drug was dispensed as a refill of a prescription or as a first-time request.

(H) Date of origin of the prescription.

(2) (A) Each prescriber that dispenses controlled substances shall provide the Department of Justice the information required by this subdivision on a weekly basis in a format set by the Department of Justice pursuant to regulation.

(B) The reporting requirement in this section shall not apply to the direct administration of a controlled substance to the body of an ultimate user.

(d) This section shall become operative on January 1, 2005.

(e) The reporting requirement in this section for Schedule IV controlled substances shall not apply to any of the following:

(1) The dispensing of a controlled substance in a quantity limited to an amount adequate to treat the ultimate user involved for 48 hours or less.

(2) The administration or dispensing of a controlled substance in accordance with any other exclusion identified by the United States Health and Human Service Secretary for the National All Schedules Prescription Electronic Reporting Act of 2005.

(f) Notwithstanding paragraph (2) of subdivision (c), the reporting requirement of the information required by this section for a Schedule II or Schedule III controlled substance, in a format set by the Department of Justice pursuant to regulation, shall be on a monthly basis for all of the following:

(1) The dispensing of a controlled substance in a quantity limited to an amount adequate to treat the ultimate user involved for 48 hours or less.

(2) The administration or dispensing of a controlled substance in accordance with any other exclusion identified by the United States Health and Human Service Secretary for the National All Schedules Prescription Electronic Reporting Act of 2005.

(Amended by Stats. 2006, Ch. 286, Sec. 5. Effective January 1, 2007.)

11191.

The record shall be preserved for three years.

Every person who violates any provision of this section is guilty of a misdemeanor.

(Amended by Stats. 1976, Ch. 896.)

11192.

In a prosecution for a violation of Section 11190, proof that a defendant received or has had in his possession at any time a greater amount of controlled substances than is accounted for by any record required by law or that the amount of controlled substances possessed by a defendant is a lesser amount than is accounted for by any record required by law is prima facie evidence of a violation of the section.

(Amended by Stats. 1976, Ch. 637.)

ARTICLE 3. Copies of Prescriptions [11195- 11195.]

(Article 3 added by Stats. 1972, Ch. 1407.)

11195.

Whenever the pharmacist's copy of a controlled substance prescription is removed by a peace officer, agent of the Attorney General, or inspector of the Board of Pharmacy, or investigator of the Division of Investigation of the Department of Consumer Affairs for the purpose of investigation or as evidence, the officer or inspector or investigator shall give to the pharmacist a receipt in lieu thereof.

(Added by Stats. 1972, Ch. 1407.)

ARTICLE 4. Refilling Prescriptions [11200 - 11201]

(Article 4 added by Stats. 1972, Ch. 1407.)

11200.

(a) No person shall dispense or refill a controlled substance prescription more than six months after the date thereof.

(b) No prescription for a Schedule III or IV substance may be refilled more than five times and in an amount, for all refills of that prescription taken together, exceeding a 120-day supply.

(c) No prescription for a Schedule II substance may be refilled.

(Amended by Stats. 1992, Ch. 616, Sec. 2. Effective January 1, 1993.)

11201.

A prescription for a controlled substance, except those appearing in schedule II, may be refilled without the prescriber's authorization if the prescriber is unavailable to authorize the refill and if, in the pharmacist's professional judgment, failure to refill the prescription might present an immediate hazard to the patient's health and welfare or might result in intense suffering. The pharmacist shall refill only a reasonable amount sufficient to maintain the patient until the prescriber can be contacted. The pharmacist shall note on the reverse side of the prescription the date and quantity of the refill and that the prescriber was not available and the basis for his judgment to refill the prescription without the prescriber's authorization. The pharmacist shall inform the patient that the prescription was refilled without the prescriber's authorization, indicating that the prescriber was not available and that, in the pharmacist's professional judgment, failure to provide the drug might result in an immediate hazard to the patient's health and welfare or might result in intense suffering. The pharmacist shall inform the prescriber within a reasonable period of time. Prior to refilling a prescription pursuant to this section, the pharmacist shall make every reasonable effort to contact the prescriber.

The prescriber shall not incur any liability as the result of a refilling of a prescription pursuant to this section.

(Added by Stats. 1977, Ch. 1211.)

ARTICLE 5. Pharmacists' Records [11205 - 11209]

(Article 5 added by Stats. 1972, Ch. 1407.)

11205.

The owner of a pharmacy or any person who purchases a controlled substance upon federal order forms as required pursuant to the provisions of the Federal "Comprehensive Drug Abuse Prevention and Control Act of 1970," (P.L. 91-513, 84 Stat. 1236), relating to the importation, exportation, manufacture, production, compounding, distribution, dispensing, and control of controlled substances, and who sells controlled substances obtained upon such federal order forms in response to prescriptions shall maintain and file such prescriptions in a separate file apart from noncontrolled substances prescriptions. Such files shall be preserved for a period of three years.

(Amended by Stats. 1976, Ch. 896, Sec. 24.)

11206.

Filed prescriptions shall constitute a transaction record that, together with information that is readily retrievable in the pharmacy pursuant to Section 11164 shall show or include the following:

(a) The name(s) and address of the patient(s).

(b) The date.

(c) The character, including the name and strength, quantity, and directions for use of the controlled substance involved.

(d) The name, address, telephone number, category of professional licensure, and the federal controlled substance registration number of the prescriber.

(Amended by Stats. 1988, Ch. 398, Sec. 5.)

11207.

(a) No person other than a pharmacist as defined in Section 4036 of the Business and Professions Code or an intern pharmacist, as defined in Section 4030 of the Business and Professions Code, who is under the personal supervision of a pharmacist, shall compound, prepare, fill or dispense a prescription for a controlled substance.

(b) Notwithstanding subdivision (a), a pharmacy technician may perform those tasks permitted by Section 4115 of the Business and Professions Code when assisting a pharmacist dispensing a prescription for a controlled substance.

(Amended by Stats. 2004, Ch. 695, Sec. 53. Effective January 1, 2005.)

11208.

In a prosecution under this division, proof that a defendant received or has had in his possession at any time a greater amount of controlled substances than is accounted for by any record required by law or that the amount of controlled substances possessed by the defendant is a lesser amount than is accounted for by any record required by law is prima facie evidence of guilt.

(Added by Stats. 1972, Ch. 1407.)

11209.

(a) No person shall deliver Schedule II, III, or IV controlled substances to a pharmacy or pharmacy receiving area, nor shall any person receive controlled substances on behalf of a pharmacy unless, at the time of delivery, a pharmacist or authorized receiving personnel signs a receipt showing the type and quantity of the controlled substances received. Any discrepancy between the receipt and the type or quantity of controlled substances actually received shall be reported to the delivering wholesaler or manufacturer by the next business day after delivery to the pharmacy.

(b) The delivery receipt and any record of discrepancy shall be maintained by the wholesaler or manufacturer for a period of three years.

(c) A violation of this section is a misdemeanor.

(d) Nothing in this section shall require a common carrier to label a package containing controlled substances in a manner contrary to federal law or regulation.

(Amended by Stats. 1988, Ch. 918, Sec. 6.)

CHAPTER 5. Use of Controlled Substances [11210 - 11256]

(Chapter 5 added by Stats. 1972, Ch. 1407.)

ARTICLE 1. Lawful Medical Use Other Than Treatment of Addicts [11210 - 11213]

(Article 1 added by Stats. 1972, Ch. 1407.)

11210.

A physician, surgeon, dentist, veterinarian, naturopathic doctor acting pursuant to Section 3640.7 of the Business and Professions Code, or podiatrist, or pharmacist acting within the scope of a project authorized under Article 1 (commencing with Section 128125) of Chapter 3 of Part 3 of Division 107 or within the scope of Section 4052.1, 4052.2, or 4052.6 of the Business and Professions Code, or registered nurse acting within the scope of a project authorized under Article 1 (commencing with Section 128125) of Chapter 3 of Part 3 of Division 107, or physician assistant acting within the scope of a project authorized under Article 1 (commencing with Section 128125) of Chapter 3 of Part 3 of Division 107, or naturopathic doctor acting within the scope of Section 3640.5 of the Business and Professions Code, or an optometrist acting within the scope of Section 3041 of the Business and Professions Code may prescribe for, furnish to, or administer controlled substances to his or her patient when the patient is suffering from a disease, ailment, injury, or infirmities attendant upon old age, other than addiction to a controlled substance.

The physician, surgeon, dentist, veterinarian, naturopathic doctor acting pursuant to Section 3640.7 of the Business and Professions Code, or podiatrist, or pharmacist acting within the scope of a project authorized under Article 1 (commencing with Section 128125) of Chapter 3 of Part 3 of Division 107 or within the scope of Section 4052.1, 4052.2, or 4052.6 of the Business and Professions Code, or registered nurse acting within the scope of a project authorized under Article 1 (commencing with Section 128125) of Chapter 3 of Part 3 of Division 107, or physician assistant acting within the scope of a project authorized under Article 1 (commencing with Section 128125) of Chapter 3 of Part 3 of Division 107, or naturopathic doctor acting within the scope of Section 3640.5 of the Business and Professions Code, or an optometrist acting within the scope of Section 3041 of the Business and Professions Code shall prescribe, furnish, or administer controlled substances only when in good faith he or she believes the disease, ailment, injury, or infirmity requires the treatment.

The physician, surgeon, dentist, veterinarian, or naturopathic doctor acting pursuant to Section 3640.7 of the Business and Professions Code, or podiatrist, or pharmacist acting within the scope of a project authorized under Article 1 (commencing with Section 128125) of Chapter 3 of Part 3 of Division 107 or within the scope of Section 4052.1, 4052.2, or 4052.6 of the Business and Professions Code, or registered nurse acting within the scope of a project authorized under Article 1 (commencing with Section 128125) of Chapter 3 of Part 3 of Division 107, or physician assistant acting within the scope of a project authorized under Article 1 (commencing with Section 128125) of Chapter 3 of Part 3 of Division 107, or a naturopathic doctor acting within the scope of Section 3640.5 of the Business and Professions Code, or an optometrist acting within the scope of Section 3041 of the Business and Professions Code shall prescribe, furnish, or administer controlled substances only in the quantity and for the length of time as are reasonably necessary.

(Amended by Stats. 2014, Ch. 319, Sec. 6. (SB 1039) Effective January 1, 2015.)

11211.

In order to provide a supply of controlled substances as may be necessary to handle emergency cases, any hospital which does not employ a resident pharmacist and which is under the supervision of a licensed physician, may purchase controlled substances on federal order forms for such institution, under the name of such hospital, such supply to be made available to a registered nurse for administration to patients in emergency cases, upon direction of a licensed physician.

(Added by Stats. 1972, Ch. 1407.)

11212.

Persons who, under applicable federal laws or regulations, are lawfully entitled to use controlled substances for the purpose of research, instruction, or analysis, may lawfully obtain and use for such purposes those substances classified in paragraphs (45) and (46) of subdivision (b) of Section 11054 of the Health and Safety Code, upon registration with and approval by the California Department of Justice for use of those substances in bona fide research, instruction, or analysis.

That research, instruction, or analysis shall be carried on only under the auspices of the individual identified by the registrant as responsible for the research. Complete records of receipts, stocks at hand, and use of these controlled substances shall be kept.

The Department of Justice may withdraw approval of the use of such substances at any time. The department may obtain and inspect at any time the records required to be maintained by this section.

(Added by Stats. 1985, Ch. 1098, Sec. 1.5. Effective September 27, 1985.)

11213.

Persons who, under applicable federal laws or regulations, are lawfully entitled to use controlled substances for the purpose of research, instruction, or analysis, may lawfully obtain and use for such purposes such substances as are defined as controlled substances in this division, upon approval for use of such controlled substances in bona fide research, instruction, or analysis by the Research Advisory Panel established pursuant to Section 11480 and 11481.

Such research, instruction, or analysis shall be carried on only under the auspices of the head of a research project which has been approved by the Research Advisory Panel pursuant to Section 11480 or Section 11481. Complete records of receipts, stocks at hand, and use of these controlled substances shall be kept.

(Added by Stats. 1972, Ch. 1407.)

ARTICLE 2. Treatment of Addicts for Addiction [11215 - 11223]
(Article 2 added by Stats. 1972, Ch. 1407.)

11215.

(a) Except as provided in subdivision (b), any narcotic controlled substance employed in treating an addict for addiction shall be administered by:

(1) A physician and surgeon.

(2) A registered nurse acting under the instruction of a physician and surgeon.

(3) A physician assistant licensed pursuant to Chapter 7.7 (commencing with Section 3500) of Division 2 of the Business and Professions Code acting under the patient-specific authority of his or her physician and surgeon supervisor approved pursuant to Section 3515 of the Business and Professions Code.

(b) When acting under the direction of a physician and surgeon, the following persons may administer a narcotic controlled substance orally in the treatment of an addict for addiction to a controlled substance:

(1) A psychiatric technician licensed pursuant to Chapter 10 (commencing with Section 4500) of Division 2 of the Business and Professions Code.

(2) A vocational nurse licensed pursuant to Chapter 6.5 (commencing with Section 2840) of Division 2 of the Business and Professions Code.

(3) A pharmacist licensed pursuant to Chapter 9 (commencing with Section 4000) of Division 2 of the Business and Professions Code.

(c) Except as permitted in this section, no person shall order, permit, or direct any other person to administer a narcotic controlled substance to a person being treated for addiction to a controlled substance.

(Amended by Stats. 1995, Ch. 455, Sec. 6. Effective September 5, 1995.)

11217.

Except as provided in Section 11223, no person shall treat an addict for addiction to a narcotic drug except in one of the following:

(a) An institution approved by the State Department of Health Care Services, and where the patient is at all times kept under restraint and control.

(b) A city or county jail.

(c) A state prison.

(d) A facility designated by a county and approved by the State Department of Health Care Services pursuant to Division 5 (commencing with Section 5000) of the Welfare and Institutions Code.

(e) A state hospital.

(f) A county hospital.

(g) A facility licensed by the State Department of Health Care Services pursuant to Division 10.5 (commencing with Section 11750).

(h) A facility as defined in subdivision (a) or (b) of Section 1250 and Section 1250.3.

A narcotic controlled substance in the continuing treatment of addiction to a controlled substance shall be used only in those programs licensed by the State Department of Health Care Services pursuant to Article 1 (commencing with Section 11839) of Chapter 10 of Part 2 of Division 10.5 on either an inpatient or outpatient basis, or both.

This section does not apply during emergency treatment, or where the patient's addiction is complicated by the presence of incurable disease, serious accident, or injury, or the infirmities of old age.

Neither this section nor any other provision of this division shall be construed to prohibit the maintenance of a place in which persons seeking to recover from addiction to a controlled substance reside and endeavor to aid one another and receive aid from others in recovering from that addiction, nor does this section or this division prohibit that aid, provided that no person is treated for addiction in a place by means of administering, furnishing, or prescribing of controlled substances. The preceding sentence is declaratory of preexisting law.

Neither this section or any other provision of this division shall be construed to prohibit short-term narcotic detoxification treatment in a controlled setting approved by the director and pursuant to rules and regulations of the director. Facilities and treatment approved by the director under this paragraph shall not be subject to approval or inspection by the Medical Board of California, nor shall persons in those facilities be required to register with, or report the termination of residence with, the police department or sheriff's office.

(Amended by Stats. 2013, Ch. 22, Sec. 17. (AB 75) Effective June 27, 2013. Operative July 1, 2013, by Sec. 110 of Ch. 22.)

11217.5.

Notwithstanding the provisions of Section 11217, a licensed physician and surgeon may treat an addict for addiction in any office or medical facility which, in the professional judgment of such physician and surgeon, is medically proper for the rehabilitation and treatment of such addict. Such licensed physician and surgeon may administer to an addict, under his direct care, those medications and therapeutic agents which, in the judgment of such physician and surgeon, are medically necessary, provided that nothing in this section shall authorize the administration of any narcotic drug.

(Added by Stats. 1972, Ch. 1407.)

11218.

A physician treating an addict for addiction may not prescribe for or furnish to the addict more than any one of the following amounts of controlled substances during each of the first 15 days of that treatment:

(a) Eight grains of opium.

(b) Four grains of morphine.

(c) Six grains of Pantopon.

(d) One grain of Dilaudid.

(e) Four hundred milligrams of isonipecaine (Demerol).

(Amended by Stats. 2002, Ch. 543, Sec. 1. Effective January 1, 2003.)

11219.

After 15 days of treatment, the physician may not prescribe for or furnish to the addict more than any one of the following amounts of controlled substances during each day of the treatment:

(a) Four grains of opium.

(b) Two grains of morphine.

(c) Three grains of Pantopon.

(d) One-half grain of Dilaudid.

(e) Two hundred milligrams of isonipecaine (Demerol).

(Amended by Stats. 2002, Ch. 543, Sec. 2. Effective January 1, 2003.)

11220.

At the end of 30 days from the first treatment, the prescribing or furnishing of controlled substances, except medications approved by the federal Food and Drug Administration for the purpose of narcotic replacement treatment or medication-assisted treatment of substance use disorders, shall be discontinued.

(Amended by Stats. 2017, Ch. 223, Sec. 1. (AB 395) Effective January 1, 2018.)

11222.

In any case in which a person is taken into custody by arrest or other process of law and is lodged in a jail or other place of confinement, and there is reasonable cause to believe

that the person is addicted to a controlled substance, it is the duty of the person in charge of the place of confinement to provide the person so confined with medical aid as necessary to ease any symptoms of withdrawal from the use of controlled substances. In any case in which a person, who is participating in a narcotic treatment program, is incarcerated in a jail or other place of confinement, he or she shall, in the discretion of the director of the program, be entitled to continue in the program until conviction.
(Amended by Stats. 1995, Ch. 455, Sec. 11. Effective September 5, 1995.)

11223.
Notwithstanding any other provision of law, a physician and surgeon who is registered with the federal Attorney General pursuant to Section 823(g) of Title 21 of the United States Code may provide treatment for addiction pursuant to this federal law.
(Added by Stats. 2010, Ch. 93, Sec. 1. (AB 2268) Effective January 1, 2011.)

ARTICLE 3. Veterinarians [11240 - 11241]
(Heading of Article 3 renumbered from Article 4 by Stats. 1985, Ch. 1098, Sec. 2.)

11240.
No veterinarian shall prescribe, administer, or furnish a controlled substance for himself or any other human being.
(Added by Stats. 1972, Ch. 1407.)

11241.
A prescription written by a veterinarian shall state the kind of animal for which ordered and the name and address of the owner or person having custody of the animal.
(Added by Stats. 1972, Ch. 1407.)

ARTICLE 4. Sale Without Prescription [11250 - 11256]
(Heading of Article 4 renumbered from Article 5 by Stats. 1985, Ch. 1098, Sec. 3.)

11250.
(a) No prescription is required in case of the sale of controlled substances at retail in pharmacies by pharmacists to any of the following:
(1) Physicians.
(2) Dentists.
(3) Podiatrists.
(4) Veterinarians.
(5) Pharmacists acting within the scope of a project authorized under Article 1 (commencing with Section 128125) of Chapter 3 of Part 3 of Division 107, or registered nurses acting within the scope of a project authorized under Article 1 (commencing with Section 128125) of Chapter 3 of Part 3 of Division 107, or physician assistants acting within the scope of a project authorized under Article 1 (commencing with Section 128125) of Chapter 3 of Part 3 of Division 107.
(6) Optometrist.
(b) In any sale mentioned in this article, there shall be executed any written order that may otherwise be required by federal law relating to the production, importation, exportation, manufacture, compounding, distributing, dispensing, or control of controlled substances.
(Amended by Stats. 2003, Ch. 426, Sec. 4. Effective January 1, 2004.)

11251.
No prescription is required in case of sales at wholesale by pharmacies, jobbers, wholesalers, and manufacturers to any of the following:
(a) Pharmacies as defined in the Business and Professions Code.
(b) Physicians.
(c) Dentists.
(d) Podiatrists.
(e) Veterinarians.
(f) Other jobbers, wholesalers or manufacturers.
(g) Pharmacists acting within the scope of a project authorized under Article 1 (commencing with Section 128125) of Chapter 3 of Part 3 of Division 107, or registered nurses acting within the scope of a project authorized under Article 1 (commencing with Section 128125) of Chapter 3 of Part 3 of Division 107, or physician assistants acting within the scope of a project authorized under Article 1 (commencing with Section 128125) of Chapter 3 of Part 3 of Division 107.
(h) Optometrists.
(Amended by Stats. 2003, Ch. 426, Sec. 5. Effective January 1, 2004.)

11252.
All wholesale jobbers, wholesalers, and manufacturers, mentioned in this division shall keep, in a manner readily accessible, the written orders or blank forms required to be preserved pursuant to federal law relating to the production, importation, exportation, manufacture, compounding, distributing, dispensing, or control of controlled substances.
(Added by Stats. 1972, Ch. 1407.)

11253.
The written orders or blank forms shall be preserved for at least three years after the date of the last entry made.
(Amended by Stats. 1976, Ch. 896.)

11255.
The taking of any order, or making of any contract or agreement, by any traveling representative or employee of any person for future delivery in this state, of any controlled substance constitutes a sale within the meaning of this division.
(Added by Stats. 1972, Ch. 1407.)

11256.
Within 24 hours after any purchaser in this state gives any order for a controlled substance classified in Schedule II to, or makes any contract or agreement for purchases from or sales by, an out-of-state wholesaler or manufacturer of any controlled substances

for delivery in this state, the purchaser shall forward to the Attorney General by registered mail a true and correct copy of the order, contract, or agreement.
(Added by Stats. 1972, Ch. 1407.)

CHAPTER 6. Offenses and Penalties [11350 - 11392]

(Chapter 6 added by Stats. 1972, Ch. 1407.)

ARTICLE 1. Offenses Involving Controlled Substances Formerly Classified as Narcotics [11350 - 11356.5]
(Heading of Article 1 amended by Stats. 1973, Ch. 1078.)

11350.
(a) Except as otherwise provided in this division, every person who possesses (1) any controlled substance specified in subdivision (b), (c), (e), or paragraph (1) of subdivision (f) of Section 11054, specified in paragraph (14), (15), or (20) of subdivision (d) of Section 11054, or specified in subdivision (b) or (c) of Section 11055, or specified in subdivision (h) of Section 11056, or (2) any controlled substance classified in Schedule III, IV, or V which is a narcotic drug, unless upon the written prescription of a physician, dentist, podiatrist, or veterinarian licensed to practice in this state, shall be punished by imprisonment in a county jail for not more than one year, except that such person shall instead be punished pursuant to subdivision (h) of Section 1170 of the Penal Code if that person has one or more prior convictions for an offense specified in clause (iv) of subparagraph (C) of paragraph (2) of subdivision (e) of Section 667 of the Penal Code or for an offense requiring registration pursuant to subdivision (c) of Section 290 of the Penal Code.
(b) Except as otherwise provided in this division, whenever a person who possesses any of the controlled substances specified in subdivision (a), the judge may, in addition to any punishment provided for pursuant to subdivision (a), assess against that person a fine not to exceed seventy dollars ($70) with proceeds of this fine to be used in accordance with Section 1463.23 of the Penal Code. The court shall, however, take into consideration the defendant's ability to pay, and no defendant shall be denied probation because of his or her inability to pay the fine permitted under this subdivision.
(c) Except in unusual cases in which it would not serve the interest of justice to do so, whenever a court grants probation pursuant to a felony conviction under this section, in addition to any other conditions of probation which may be imposed, the following conditions of probation shall be ordered:
(1) For a first offense under this section, a fine of at least one thousand dollars ($1,000) or community service.
(2) For a second or subsequent offense under this section, a fine of at least two thousand dollars ($2,000) or community service.
(3) If a defendant does not have the ability to pay the minimum fines specified in paragraphs (1) and (2), community service shall be ordered in lieu of the fine.
(d) It is not unlawful for a person other than the prescription holder to possess a controlled substance described in subdivision (a) if both of the following apply:
(1) The possession of the controlled substance is at the direction or with the express authorization of the prescription holder.
(2) The sole intent of the possessor is to deliver the prescription to the prescription holder for its prescribed use or to discard the substance in a lawful manner.
(e) This section does not permit the use of a controlled substance by a person other than the prescription holder or permit the distribution or sale of a controlled substance that is otherwise inconsistent with the prescription.
(Amended (as amended by Proposition 47) by Stats. 2017, Ch. 269, Sec. 4. (SB 811) Effective January 1, 2018. Note: This section was amended on Nov. 4, 2014, by initiative Prop.47.)

11350.5.
(a) Except as otherwise provided in this division, every person who possesses a controlled substance specified in paragraph (3) of subdivision (e) of Section 11054 of this code with the intent to commit sexual assault shall be punished by imprisonment pursuant to subdivision (h) of Section 1170 of the Penal Code.
(b) For purposes of this section, "sexual assault" means conduct in violation of Section 243.4, 261, 262, 286, 287, or 289 of, or former Section 288a of, the Penal Code.
(Added by Stats. 2018, Ch. 423, Sec. 35. (SB 1494) Effective January 1, 2019.)

11351.
Except as otherwise provided in this division, every person who possesses for sale or purchases for purposes of sale (1) any controlled substance specified in subdivision (b), (c), or (e) of Section 11054, specified in paragraph (14), (15), or (20) of subdivision (d) of Section 11054, or specified in subdivision (b) or (c) of Section 11055, or specified in subdivision (h) of Section 11056, or (2) any controlled substance classified in Schedule III, IV, or V which is a narcotic drug, shall be punished by imprisonment pursuant to subdivision (h) of Section 1170 of the Penal Code for two, three, or four years.
(Amended by Stats. 2011, Ch. 15, Sec. 152. (AB 109) Effective April 4, 2011. Operative October 1, 2011, by Sec. 636 of Ch. 15, as amended by Stats. 2011, Ch. 39, Sec. 68.)

11351.5.
Except as otherwise provided in this division, every person who possesses for sale or purchases for purposes of sale cocaine base, which is specified in paragraph (1) of subdivision (f) of Section 11054, shall be punished by imprisonment pursuant to subdivision (h) of Section 1170 of the Penal Code for a period of two, three, or four years.
(Amended by Stats. 2014, Ch. 749, Sec. 3. (SB 1010) Effective January 1, 2015.)

11352.

(a) Except as otherwise provided in this division, every person who transports, imports into this state, sells, furnishes, administers, or gives away, or offers to transport, import into this state, sell, furnish, administer, or give away, or attempts to import into this state or transport (1) any controlled substance specified in subdivision (b), (c), or (e), or paragraph (1) of subdivision (f) of Section 11054, specified in paragraph (14), (15), or (20) of subdivision (d) of Section 11054, or specified in subdivision (b) or (c) of Section 11055, or specified in subdivision (h) of Section 11056, or (2) any controlled substance classified in Schedule III, IV, or V which is a narcotic drug, unless upon the written prescription of a physician, dentist, podiatrist, or veterinarian licensed to practice in this state, shall be punished by imprisonment pursuant to subdivision (h) of Section 1170 of the Penal Code for three, four, or five years.

(b) Notwithstanding the penalty provisions of subdivision (a), any person who transports any controlled substances specified in subdivision (a) within this state from one county to another noncontiguous county shall be punished by imprisonment pursuant to subdivision (h) of Section 1170 of the Penal Code for three, six, or nine years.

(c) For purposes of this section, "transports" means to transport for sale.

(d) This section does not preclude or limit the prosecution of an individual for aiding and abetting the commission of, or conspiring to commit, or acting as an accessory to, any act prohibited by this section.

(Amended by Stats. 2014, Ch. 54, Sec. 7. (SB 1461) Effective January 1, 2015.)

11352.1.

(a) The Legislature hereby declares that the dispensing and furnishing of prescription drugs, controlled substances, and dangerous drugs or dangerous devices without a license poses a significant threat to the health, safety, and welfare of all persons residing in the state. It is the intent of the Legislature in enacting this provision to enhance the penalties attached to this illicit and dangerous conduct.

(b) Notwithstanding Section 4321 of the Business and Professions Code, and in addition to any other penalties provided by law, any person who knowingly and unlawfully dispenses or furnishes a dangerous drug or dangerous device, or any material represented as, or presented in lieu of, any dangerous drug or dangerous device, as defined in Section 4022 of the Business and Professions Code, or who knowingly owns, manages, or operates a business that dispenses or furnishes a dangerous drug or dangerous device or any material represented as, or presented in lieu of, any dangerous drug or dangerous device, as defined in Section 4022 of the Business and Professions Code without a license to dispense or furnish these products, shall be guilty of a misdemeanor. Upon the first conviction, each violation shall be punishable by imprisonment in a county jail not to exceed one year, or by a fine not to exceed five thousand dollars ($5,000), or by both that fine and imprisonment. Upon a second or subsequent conviction, each violation shall be punishable by imprisonment in a county jail not to exceed one year, or by a fine not to exceed ten thousand dollars ($10,000), or by both that fine and imprisonment.

(Amended by Stats. 2000, Ch. 350, Sec. 1. Effective September 8, 2000.)

11352.5.

The court shall impose a fine not exceeding fifty thousand dollars ($50,000), in the absence of a finding that the defendant would be incapable of paying such a fine, in addition to any term of imprisonment provided by law for any of the following persons:

(1) Any person who is convicted of violating Section 11351 of the Health and Safety Code by possessing for sale 14.25 grams or more of a substance containing heroin.

(2) Any person who is convicted of violating Section 11352 of the Health and Safety Code by selling or offering to sell 14.25 grams or more of a substance containing heroin.

(3) Any person convicted of violating Section 11351 of the Health and Safety Code by possessing heroin for sale or convicted of violating Section 11352 of the Health and Safety Code by selling or offering to sell heroin, and who has one or more prior convictions for violating Section 11351 or Section 11352 of the Health and Safety Code.

(Amended by Stats. 1983, Ch. 223, Sec. 1.)

11353.

Every person 18 years of age or over, (a) who in any voluntary manner solicits, induces, encourages, or intimidates any minor with the intent that the minor shall violate any provision of this chapter or Section 11550 with respect to either (1) a controlled substance which is specified in subdivision (b), (c), or (e), or paragraph (1) of subdivision (f) of Section 11054, specified in paragraph (14), (15), or (20) of subdivision (d) of Section 11054, or specified in subdivision (b) or (c) of Section 11055, or specified in subdivision (h) of Section 11056, or (2) any controlled substance classified in Schedule III, IV, or V which is a narcotic drug, (b) who hires, employs, or uses a minor to unlawfully transport, carry, sell, give away, prepare for sale, or peddle any such controlled substance, or (c) who unlawfully sells, furnishes, administers, gives, or offers to sell, furnish, administer, or give, any such controlled substance to a minor, shall be punished by imprisonment in the state prison for a period of three, six, or nine years.

(Amended by Stats. 2000, Ch. 8, Sec. 6. Effective March 29, 2000.)

11353.1.

(a) Notwithstanding any other provision of law, any person 18 years of age or over who is convicted of a violation of Section 11353, in addition to the punishment imposed for that conviction, shall receive an additional punishment as follows:

(1) If the offense involved heroin, cocaine, cocaine base, or any analog of these substances and occurred upon the grounds of, or within, a church or synagogue, a playground, a public or private youth center, a child day care facility, or a public swimming pool, during hours in which the facility is open for business, classes, or school-related programs, or at any time when minors are using the facility, the defendant shall, as a full and separately served enhancement to any other enhancement provided in paragraph (3), be punished by imprisonment in the state prison for one year.

(2) If the offense involved heroin, cocaine, cocaine base, or any analog of these substances and occurred upon, or within 1,000 feet of, the grounds of any public or private elementary, vocational, junior high, or high school, during hours that the school is open for classes or school-related programs, or at any time when minors are using the facility where the offense occurs, the defendant shall, as a full and separately served enhancement to any other enhancement provided in paragraph (3), be punished by imprisonment in the state prison for two years.

(3) If the offense involved a minor who is at least four years younger than the defendant, the defendant shall, as a full and separately served enhancement to any other enhancement provided in this subdivision, be punished by imprisonment in the state prison for one, two, or three years, at the discretion of the court.

(b) The additional punishment provided in this section shall not be imposed unless the allegation is charged in the accusatory pleading and admitted by the defendant or found to be true by the trier of fact.

(c) The additional punishment provided in this section shall be in addition to any other punishment provided by law and shall not be limited by any other provision of law.

(d) Notwithstanding any other provision of law, the court may strike the additional punishment provided for in this section if it determines that there are circumstances in mitigation of the additional punishment and states on the record its reasons for striking the additional punishment.

(e) As used in this section the following definitions shall apply:

(1) "Playground" means any park or recreational area specifically designed to be used by children which has play equipment installed, including public grounds designed for athletic activities such as baseball, football, soccer, or basketball, or any similar facility located on public or private school grounds, or on city, county, or state parks.

(2) "Youth center" means any public or private facility that is primarily used to host recreational or social activities for minors, including, but not limited to, private youth membership organizations or clubs, social service teenage club facilities, video arcades, or similar amusement park facilities.

(3) "Video arcade" means any premises where 10 or more video game machines or devices are operated, and where minors are legally permitted to conduct business.

(4) "Video game machine" means any mechanical amusement device, which is characterized by the use of a cathode ray tube display and which, upon the insertion of a coin, slug, or token in any slot or receptacle attached to, or connected to, the machine, may be operated for use as a game, contest, or amusement.

(5) "Within 1,000 feet of the grounds of any public or private elementary, vocational, junior high, or high school" means any public area or business establishment where minors are legally permitted to conduct business which is located within 1,000 feet of any public or private elementary, vocational, junior high, or high school.

(6) "Child day care facility" has the meaning specified in Section 1596.750.

(f) This section does not require either that notice be posted regarding the proscribed conduct or that the applicable 1,000-foot boundary limit be marked.

(Amended by Stats. 1993, Ch. 556, Sec. 1. Effective January 1, 1994.)

11353.4.

(a) Any person 18 years of age or older who is convicted for a second or subsequent time of violating Section 11353, as that section applies to paragraph (1) of subdivision (f) of Section 11054, where the previous conviction resulted in a prison sentence, shall, as a full and separately served enhancement to the punishment imposed for that second or subsequent conviction of Section 11353, be punished by imprisonment in the state prison for one, two, or three years.

(b) If the second or subsequent violation of Section 11353, as described in subdivision (a), involved a minor who is 14 years of age or younger, the defendant shall, as a full and separately served enhancement to any other enhancement provided in this section, be punished by imprisonment in the state prison for one, two, or three years, at the discretion of the court.

(c) The additional punishment provided in this section shall not be imposed unless the allegation is charged in the accusatory pleading and admitted by the defendant or found to be true by the trier of fact.

(d) The additional punishment provided in this section shall be in addition to any other punishment provided by law and shall not be limited by any other provision of law.

(e) Notwithstanding any other provision of law, the court may strike the additional punishment provided for in this section if it determines that there are circumstances in mitigation of the additional punishment and states on the record its reasons for striking the additional punishment.

(Added by Stats. 1993, Ch. 586, Sec. 1. Effective January 1, 1994.)

11353.5.

Except as authorized by law, any person 18 years of age or older who unlawfully prepares for sale upon school grounds or a public playground, a child day care facility, a church, or a synagogue, or sells or gives away a controlled substance, other than a controlled substance described in Section 11353 or 11380, to a minor upon the grounds of, or within, any school, child day care facility, public playground, church, or synagogue providing instruction in preschool, kindergarten, or any of grades 1 to 12, inclusive, or providing child care services, during hours in which those facilities are open for classes, school-related programs, or child care, or at any time when minors are using the facility where the offense occurs, or upon the grounds of a public playground during the hours in which school-related programs for minors are being conducted, or at any time when minors are using the facility where the offense occurs, shall be punished by imprisonment pursuant to subdivision (h) of Section 1170 of the Penal Code for five, seven, or nine years. Application of this section shall be limited to persons at least five years older than the minor to whom he or she prepares for sale, sells, or gives away a controlled substance.

(Amended by Stats. 2011, Ch. 15, Sec. 155. (AB 109) Effective April 4, 2011. Operative October 1, 2011, by Sec. 636 of Ch. 15, as amended by Stats. 2011, Ch. 39, Sec. 68.)

11353.6.

(a) This section shall be known, and may be cited, as the Juvenile Drug Trafficking and Schoolyard Act of 1988.

(b) Any person 18 years of age or over who is convicted of a violation of Section 11351.5, 11352, or 11379.6, as those sections apply to paragraph (1) of subdivision (f) of Section 11054, or of Section 11351, 11352, or 11379.6, as those sections apply to paragraph (11) of subdivision (c) of Section 11054, or of Section 11378, 11379, or 11379.6, as those sections apply to paragraph (2) of subdivision (d) of Section 11055, or of a conspiracy to commit one of those offenses, where the violation takes place upon the grounds of, or within 1,000 feet of, a public or private elementary, vocational, junior high, or high school during hours that the school is open for classes or school-related programs, or at any time when minors are using the facility where the offense occurs, shall receive an additional punishment of three, four, or five years at the court's discretion.

(c) Any person 18 years of age or older who is convicted of a violation pursuant to subdivision (b) which involves a minor who is at least four years younger than that person, as a full and separately served enhancement to that provided in subdivision (b), shall be punished by imprisonment pursuant to subdivision (h) of Section 1170 of the Penal Code for three, four, or five years at the court's discretion.

(d) The additional terms provided in this section shall not be imposed unless the allegation is charged in the accusatory pleading and admitted or found to be true by the trier of fact.

(e) The additional terms provided in this section shall be in addition to any other punishment provided by law and shall not be limited by any other provision of law.

(f) Notwithstanding any other provision of law, the court may strike the additional punishment for the enhancements provided in this section if it determines that there are circumstances in mitigation of the additional punishment and states on the record its reasons for striking the additional punishment.

(g) "Within 1,000 feet of a public or private elementary, vocational, junior high, or high school" means any public area or business establishment where minors are legally permitted to conduct business which is located within 1,000 feet of any public or private elementary, vocational, junior high, or high school.

(Amended by Stats. 2011, Ch. 15, Sec. 156. (AB 109) Effective April 4, 2011. Operative October 1, 2011, by Sec. 636 of Ch. 15, as amended by Stats. 2011, Ch. 39, Sec. 68.)

11353.7.

Except as authorized by law, and except as provided otherwise in Sections 11353.1, 11353.6, and 11380.1 with respect to playgrounds situated in a public park, any person 18 years of age or older who unlawfully prepares for sale in a public park, including units of the state park system and state vehicular recreation areas, or sells or gives away a controlled substance to a minor under the age of 14 years in a public park, including units of the state park system and state vehicular recreation areas, during hours in which the public park, including units of the state park system and state vehicular recreation areas, is open for use, with knowledge that the person is a minor under the age of 14 years, shall be punished by imprisonment in state prison for three, six, or nine years.

(Amended by Stats. 2012, Ch. 43, Sec. 13. (SB 1023) Effective June 27, 2012.)

11354.

(a) Every person under the age of 18 years who in any voluntary manner solicits, induces, encourages, or intimidates any minor with the intent that the minor shall violate any provision of this chapter or Section 11550, who hires, employs, or uses a minor to unlawfully transport, carry, sell, give away, prepare for sale, or peddle (1) any controlled substance specified in subdivision (b), (c), or (e), or paragraph (1) of subdivision (f) of Section 11054, specified in paragraph (14), (15), or (20) of subdivision (d) of Section 11054, or specified in subdivision (b) or (c) of Section 11055, or specified in subdivision (h) of Section 11056, or (2) any controlled substance classified in Schedule III, IV, or V which is a narcotic drug, or who unlawfully sells, furnishes, administers, gives, or offers to sell, furnish, administer, or give, any such controlled substance to a minor shall be punished by imprisonment in the state prison.

(b) This section is not intended to affect the jurisdiction of the juvenile court.

(Amended by Stats. 2000, Ch. 8, Sec. 7. Effective March 29, 2000.)

11355.

Every person who agrees, consents, or in any manner offers to unlawfully sell, furnish, transport, administer, or give (1) any controlled substance specified in subdivision (b), (c), or (e), or paragraph (1) of subdivision (f) of Section 11054, specified in paragraph (13), (14), (15), or (20) of subdivision (d) of Section 11054, or specified in subdivision (b) or (c) of Section 11055, or specified in subdivision (h) of Section 11056, or (2) any controlled substance classified in Schedule III, IV, or V which is a narcotic drug to any person, or who offers, arranges, or negotiates to have any such controlled substance unlawfully sold, delivered, transported, furnished, administered, or given to any person and who then sells, delivers, furnishes, transports, administers, or gives, or offers, arranges, or negotiates to have sold, delivered, transported, furnished, administered, or given to any person any other liquid, substance, or material in lieu of any such controlled substance shall be punished by imprisonment in the county jail for not more than one year, or pursuant to subdivision (h) of Section 1170 of the Penal Code.

(Amended by Stats. 2011, 1st Ex. Sess., Ch. 12, Sec. 4. (AB 17 1x) Effective September 21, 2011. Operative October 1, 2011, by Sec. 46 of Ch. 12.)

11356.

As used in this article "felony offense," and "offense punishable as a felony" refer to an offense prior to October 1, 2011, for which the law prescribes imprisonment in the state prison, or for an offense on or after October 1, 2011, imprisonment in either the state prison or pursuant to subdivision (h) of Section 1170 of the Penal Code, as either an alternative or the sole penalty, regardless of the sentence the particular defendant received.

(Amended (as amended by Stats. 2011, Ch. 15) by Stats. 2011, Ch. 39, Sec. 2. (AB 117) Effective June 30, 2011. Operative October 1, 2011, pursuant to Secs. 68 and 69 of Ch. 39.)

11356.5.

(a) Any person convicted of a violation of Section 11351, 11352, 11379.5, or 11379.6 insofar as the latter section relates to phencyclidine or any of its analogs which is specified in paragraph (21), (22), or (23) of subdivision (d) of Section 11054 or in paragraph (3) of subdivision (e) of Section 11055, who, as part of the transaction for which he or she was convicted, has induced another to violate Section 11351, 11352, 11379.5, or 11379.6 insofar as the latter section relates to phencyclidine or its analogs, shall be punished as follows:

(1) By an additional one year in prison if the value of the controlled substance involved in the transaction for which the person was convicted exceeds five hundred thousand dollars ($500,000).

(2) By an additional two years in prison if the value of the controlled substance involved in the transaction for which the person was convicted exceeds two million dollars ($2,000,000).

(3) By an additional three years in prison if the value of the controlled substance involved in the transaction for which the person was convicted exceeds five million dollars ($5,000,000).

(b) For purposes of this section, "value of the controlled substance" means the retail price to the user.

(Amended by Stats. 1995, Ch. 377, Sec. 1. Effective January 1, 1996.)

ARTICLE 2. Cannabis [11357 - 11362.9]

(Heading of Article 2 amended by Stats. 2017, Ch. 27, Sec. 121.)

11357.

(a) Except as authorized by law, possession of not more than 28.5 grams of cannabis, or not more than eight grams of concentrated cannabis, or both, shall be punished or adjudicated as follows:

(1) Persons under 18 years of age are guilty of an infraction and shall be required to:

(A) Upon a finding that a first offense has been committed, complete four hours of drug education or counseling and up to 10 hours of community service over a period not to exceed 60 days.

(B) Upon a finding that a second offense or subsequent offense has been committed, complete six hours of drug education or counseling and up to 20 hours of community service over a period not to exceed 90 days.

(2) Persons at least 18 years of age but less than 21 years of age are guilty of an infraction and punishable by a fine of not more than one hundred dollars ($100).

(b) Except as authorized by law, possession of more than 28.5 grams of cannabis, or more than eight grams of concentrated cannabis, shall be punished as follows:

(1) Persons under 18 years of age who possess more than 28.5 grams of cannabis or more than eight grams of concentrated cannabis, or both, are guilty of an infraction and shall be required to:

(A) Upon a finding that a first offense has been committed, complete eight hours of drug education or counseling and up to 40 hours of community service over a period not to exceed 90 days.

(B) Upon a finding that a second or subsequent offense has been committed, complete 10 hours of drug education or counseling and up to 60 hours of community service over a period not to exceed 120 days.

(2) Persons 18 years of age or older who possess more than 28.5 grams of cannabis, or more than eight grams of concentrated cannabis, or both, shall be punished by imprisonment in a county jail for a period of not more than six months or by a fine of not more than five hundred dollars ($500), or by both that fine and imprisonment.

(c) Except as authorized by law, a person 18 years of age or older who possesses not more than 28.5 grams of cannabis, or not more than eight grams of concentrated cannabis, upon the grounds of, or within, any school providing instruction in kindergarten or any of grades 1 to 12, inclusive, during hours the school is open for classes or school-related programs is guilty of a misdemeanor and shall be punished as follows:

(1) A fine of not more than two hundred fifty dollars ($250), upon a finding that a first offense has been committed.

(2) A fine of not more than five hundred dollars ($500), or by imprisonment in a county jail for a period of not more than 10 days, or both, upon a finding that a second or subsequent offense has been committed.

(d) Except as authorized by law, a person under 18 years of age who possesses not more than 28.5 grams of cannabis, or not more than eight grams of concentrated cannabis, upon the grounds of, or within, any school providing instruction in kindergarten or any of grades 1 to 12, inclusive, during hours the school is open for classes or school-related programs is guilty of an infraction and shall be punished in the same manner provided in paragraph (1) of subdivision (b).

(Amended by Stats. 2017, Ch. 253, Sec. 15. (AB 133) Effective September 16, 2017. Note: This section was amended on Nov. 4, 2014, by initiative Prop. 47, and on Nov. 8, 2016, by initiative Prop. 64.)

11357.5.

(a) Every person who sells, dispenses, distributes, furnishes, administers, or gives, or offers to sell, dispense, distribute, furnish, administer, or give, or possesses for sale any synthetic cannabinoid compound, or any synthetic cannabinoid derivative, to any person, is guilty of a misdemeanor, punishable by imprisonment in a county jail not to exceed six months, or by a fine not to exceed one thousand dollars ($1,000), or by both that fine and imprisonment.
(b) Every person who uses or possesses any synthetic cannabinoid compound, or any synthetic cannabinoid derivative, is guilty of a public offense, punishable as follows:
(1) A first offense is an infraction punishable by a fine not exceeding two hundred fifty dollars ($250).
(2) A second offense is an infraction punishable by a fine not exceeding two hundred fifty dollars ($250) or a misdemeanor punishable by imprisonment in a county jail not exceeding six months, a fine not exceeding five hundred dollars ($500), or by both that fine and imprisonment.
(3) A third or subsequent offense is a misdemeanor punishable by imprisonment in a county jail not exceeding six months, or by a fine not exceeding one thousand dollars ($1,000), or by both that fine and imprisonment.
(c) As used in this section, the term "synthetic cannabinoid compound" refers to any of the following substances or an analog of any of the following substances:
(1) Adamantoylindoles or adamantoylindazoles, which includes adamantyl carboxamide indoles and adamantyl carboxamide indazoles, or any compound structurally derived from 3-(1-adamantoyl)indole, 3-(1-adamantoyl)indazole, 3-(2-adamantoyl)indole, N-(1-adamantyl)-1H-indole-3-carboxamide, or N-(1-adamantyl)-1H-indazole-3-carboxamide by substitution at the nitrogen atom of the indole or indazole ring with alkyl, haloalkyl, alkenyl, cyanoalkyl, hydroxyalkyl, cycloalkylmethyl, cycloalkylethyl, 1-(N-methyl-2-piperidinyl)methyl, 2-(4-morpholinyl)ethyl, or 1-(N-methyl-2-pyrrolidinyl)methyl, 1-(N-methyl-3-morpholinyl)methyl, or (tetrahydropyran-4-yl)methyl group, whether or not further substituted in the indole or indazole ring to any extent and whether or not substituted in the adamantyl ring to any extent, including, but not limited to, 2NE1, 5F-AKB-48, AB-001, AKB-48, AM-1248, JWH-018 adamantyl carboxamide, STS-135.
(2) Benzoylindoles, which includes any compound structurally derived from a 3-(benzoyl)indole structure with substitution at the nitrogen atom of the indole ring with alkyl, haloalkyl, cyanoalkyl, hydroxyalkyl, alkenyl, cycloalkylmethyl, cycloalkylethyl, 1-(N-methyl-2-piperidinyl)methyl, 2-(4-morpholinyl)ethyl, or 1-(N-methyl-2-pyrrolidinyl)methyl, 1-(N-methyl-3-morpholinyl)methyl, or (tetrahydropyran-4-yl)methyl group, whether or not further substituted in the indole ring to any extent and whether or not substituted in the phenyl ring to any extent, including, but not limited to, AM-630, AM-661, AM-679, AM-694, AM-1241, AM-2233, RCS-4, WIN 48,098 (Pravadoline).
(3) Cyclohexylphenols, which includes any compound structurally derived from 2-(3-hydroxycyclohexyl)phenol by substitution at the 5-position of the phenolic ring by alkyl, haloalkyl, cyanoalkyl, hydroxyalkyl, alkenyl, cycloalkylmethyl, cycloalkylethyl, 1-(N-methyl-2-piperidinyl)methyl, 2-(4-morpholinyl)ethyl, or 1-(N-methyl-2-pyrrolidinyl)methyl, 1-(N-methyl-3-morpholinyl)methyl, or (tetrahydropyran-4-yl)methyl group, whether or not further substituted in the cyclohexyl ring to any extent, including, but not limited to, CP 47,497, CP 55,490, CP 55,940, CP 56,667, cannabicyclohexanol.
(4) Cyclopropanoylindoles, which includes any compound structurally derived from 3-(cyclopropylmethanoyl)indole, 3-(cyclopropylmethanone)indole, 3-(cyclobutylmethanone)indole or 3-(cyclopentylmethanone)indole by substitution at the nitrogen atom of the indole ring, whether or not further substituted in the indole ring to any extent, whether or not substituted on the cyclopropyl, cyclobutyl, or cyclopentyl rings to any extent.
(5) Naphthoylindoles, which includes any compound structurally derived from 3-(1-naphthoyl)indole or 1H-indol-3-yl-(1-naphthyl)methane by substitution at the nitrogen atom of the indole ring by alkyl, haloalkyl, cyanoalkyl, hydroxyalkyl, alkenyl, cycloalkylmethyl, cycloalkylethyl, 1-(N-methyl-2-piperidinyl)methyl, 2-(4-morpholinyl)ethyl group, 1-(N-methyl-2-pyrrolidinyl)methyl, 1-(N-methyl-3-morpholinyl)methyl, or (tetrahydropyran-4-yl)methyl group, whether or not further substituted in the naphthyl ring to any extent, including, but not limited to, AM-678, AM-1220, AM-1221, AM-1235, AM-2201, AM-2232, EAM-2201, JWH-004, JWH-007, JWH-009, JWH-011, JWH-015, JWH-016, JWH-018, JWH-019, JWH-020, JWH-022, JWH-046, JWH-047, JWH-048, JWH-049, JWH-050, JWH-070, JWH-071, JWH-072, JWH-073, JWH-076, JWH-079, JWH-080, JWH-081, JWH-082, JWH-094, JWH-096, JWH-098, JWH-116, JWH-120, JWH-122, JWH-148, JWH-149, JWH-164, JWH-166, JWH-180, JWH-181, JWH-182, JWH-189, JWH-193, JWH-198, JWH-200, JWH-210, JWH-211, JWH-212, JWH-213, JWH-234, JWH-235, JWH-236, JWH-239, JWH-240, JWH-241, JWH-242, JWH-258, JWH-262, JWH-386, JWH-387, JWH-394, JWH-395, JWH-397, JWH-398, JWH-399, JWH-400, JWH-412, JWH-413, JWH-414, JWH-415, JWH-424, MAM-2201, WIN 55,212.
(6) Naphthoylnaphthalenes, which includes any compound structurally derived from naphthalene-1-yl-(naphthalene-1-yl) methanone with substitutions on either of the naphthalene rings to any extent, including, but not limited to, CB-13.
(7) Naphthoylpyrroles, which includes any compound structurally derived from 3-(1-naphthoyl)pyrrole by substitution at the nitrogen atom of the pyrrole ring by alkyl, haloalkyl, cyanoalkyl, hydroxyalkyl, alkenyl, cycloalkylmethyl, cycloalkylethyl, 1-(N-methyl-2-piperidinyl)methyl, 2-(4-morpholinyl)ethyl, or 1-(N-methyl-2-pyrrolidinyl)methyl, 1-(N-methyl-3-morpholinyl)methyl, or (tetrahydropyran-4-yl)methyl group, whether or not further substituted in the pyrrole ring to any extent and whether or not substituted in the naphthyl ring to any extent, including, but not limited to, JWH-030, JWH-031, JWH-145, JWH-146, JWH-147, JWH-150, JWH-156, JWH-243, JWH-244, JWH-245, JWH-246, JWH-292, JWH-293, JWH-307, JWH-308, JWH-309, JWH-346, JWH-348, JWH-363, JWH-364, JWH-365, JWH-367, JWH-368, JWH-369, JWH-370, JWH-371, JWH-373, JWH-392.
(8) Naphthylmethylindenes, which includes any compound containing a naphthylideneindene structure or which is structurally derived from 1-(1-naphthylmethyl)indene with substitution at the 3-position of the indene ring by alkyl, haloalkyl, cyanoalkyl, hydroxyalkyl, alkenyl, cycloalkylmethyl, cycloalkylethyl, 1-(N-methyl-2-piperidinyl)methyl, 2-(4-morpholinyl)ethyl, or 1-(N-methyl-2-pyrrolidinyl)methyl, 1-(N-methyl-3-morpholinyl)methyl, or (tetrahydropyran-4-yl)methyl group, whether or not further substituted in the indene ring to any extent and whether or not substituted in the naphthyl ring to any extent, including, but not limited to, JWH-171, JWH-176, JWH-220.
(9) Naphthylmethylindoles, which includes any compound structurally derived from an H-indol-3-yl-(1-naphthyl) methane by substitution at the nitrogen atom of the indole ring by alkyl, haloalkyl, cyanoalkyl, hydroxyalkyl, alkenyl, cycloalkylmethyl, cycloalkylethyl, 1-(N-methyl-2-piperidinyl)methyl, 2-(4-morpholinyl)ethyl, or 1-(N-methyl-2-pyrrolidinyl)methyl, 1-(N-methyl-3-morpholinyl)methyl, or (tetrahydropyran-4-yl)methyl group, whether or not further substituted in the indole ring to any extent and whether or not substituted in the naphthyl ring to any extent, including, but not limited to, JWH-175, JWH-184, JWH-185, JWH-192, JWH-194, JWH-195, JWH-196, JWH-197, JWH-199.
(10) Phenylacetylindoles, which includes any compound structurally derived from 3-phenylacetylindole by substitution at the nitrogen atom of the indole ring with alkyl, haloalkyl, cyanoalkyl, hydroxyalkyl, alkenyl, cycloalkylmethyl, cycloalkylethyl, 1-(N-methyl-2-piperidinyl)methyl, 2-(4-morpholinyl)ethyl, or 1-(N-methyl-2-pyrrolidinyl)methyl, 1-(N-methyl-3-morpholinyl)methyl, or (tetrahydropyran-4-yl)methyl group, whether or not further substituted in the indole ring to any extent and whether or not substituted in the phenyl ring to any extent, including, but not limited to, cannabipiperidiethanone, JWH-167, JWH-201, JWH-202, JWH-203, JWH-204, JWH-205, JWH-206, JWH-207, JWH-208, JWH-209, JWH-237, JWH-248, JWH-249, JWH-250, JWH-251, JWH-253, JWH-302, JWH-303, JWH-304, JWH-305, JWH-306, JWH-311, JWH-312, JWH-313, JWH-314, JWH-315, JWH-316, RCS-8.
(11) Quinolinylindolecarboxylates, which includes any compound structurally derived from quinolin-8-yl-1H-indole-3-carboxylate by substitution at the nitrogen atom of the indole ring with alkyl, haloalkyl, benzyl, halobenzyl, alkenyl, haloalkenyl, alkoxy, cyanoalkyl, hydroxyalkyl, cycloalkylmethyl, cycloalkylethyl, (N-methylpiperidin-2-yl)alkyl, (4-tetrahydropyran)alkyl, or 2-(4-morpholinyl)alkyl, whether or not further substituted in the indole ring to any extent, whether or not substituted in the quinoline ring to any extent, including, but not limited to, BB-22, 5-Fluoro-PB-22, PB-22.
(12) Tetramethylcyclopropanoylindoles, which includes any compound structurally derived from 3-tetramethylcyclopropanoylindole, 3-(1-tetramethylcyclopropyl)indole, 3-(2,2,3,3-tetramethylcyclopropyl)indole or 3-(2,2,3,3-tetramethylcyclopropylcarbonyl)indole with substitution at the nitrogen atom of the indole ring by an alkyl, haloalkyl, cyanoalkyl, hydroxyalkyl, alkenyl, cycloalkylmethyl, cycloalkylethyl, 1-(N-methyl-2-piperidinyl)methyl, 2-(4-morpholinyl)ethyl, 1-(N-methyl-2-pyrrolidinyl)methyl, 1-(N-methyl-3-morpholinyl)methyl, or (tetrahydropyran-4-yl)methyl group whether or not further substituted in the indole ring to any extent and whether or not substituted in the tetramethylcyclopropanoyl ring to any extent, including, but not limited to, 5-bromo-UR-144, 5-chloro-UR-144, 5-fluoro-UR-144, A-796,260, A-834,735, AB-034, UR-144, XLR11.
(13) Tetramethylcyclopropane-thiazole carboxamides, which includes any compound structurally derived from 2,2,3,3-tetramethyl-N-(thiazol-2-ylidene)cyclopropanecarboxamide by substitution at the nitrogen atom of the thiazole ring by alkyl, haloalkyl, benzyl, halobenzyl, alkenyl, haloalkenyl, alkoxy, cyanoalkyl, hydroxyalkyl, cycloalkylmethyl, cycloalkylethyl, (N-methylpiperidin-2-yl)alkyl, (4-tetrahydropyran)alkyl, or 2-(4-morpholinyl)alkyl, whether or not further substituted in the thiazole ring to any extent, whether or not substituted in the tetramethylcyclopropyl ring to any extent, including, but not limited to, A-836,339.
(14) Unclassified synthetic cannabinoids, which includes all of the following:
(A) AM-087, (6aR,10aR)-3-(2-methyl-6-bromohex-2-yl)-6,6,9-t rimethyl-6a,7,10,10a-tetrahydrobenzo[c]chromen-1-ol.
(B) AM-356, methanandamide, including (5Z,8Z,11Z,14Z)—[(1R)-2-hydroxy-1-methylethyl]icosa-5,8,11,14-tetraenamide and arachidonyl-1'-hydroxy-2'-propylamide.
(C) AM-411, (6aR,10aR)-3-(1-adamantyl)-6,6,9-trimethyl-6 a,7,10,10a-tetrahydrobenzo[c]chromen-1-ol.
(D) AM-855, (4aR,12bR)-8-hexyl-2,5,5-trimethyl-1 ,4,4a,8,9,10,11,12b-octahydronaphtho[3,2-c]isochromen-12-ol.
(E) AM-905, (6aR,9R,10aR)-3-[(E)-hept-1-enyl]-9-(hydroxymethyl)-6,6-dimethyl-6a,7,8,9,10,10a-hexahydrobenzo[c]chromen-1-ol.
(F) AM-906, (6aR,9R,10aR)-3-[(Z)-hept-1-enyl]-9-(hydroxymethyl)-6,6-dimethyl-6a,7,8,9,10,10a-hexahydrobenzo[c]chromen-1-ol.
(G) AM-2389, (6aR,9R,10aR)-3-(1-hexyl-cyclobut-1-yl)-6 a,7,8,9,10,10a-hexahydro-6,6-dimethyl-6H-dibenzo[b,d]pyran-1 ,9 diol.
(H) BAY 38-7271, (-)-(R)-3-(2-Hydroxymethylindanyl-4-o xy)phenyl-4,4,4-trifluorobutyl-1-sulfonate.
(I) CP 50,556-1, Levonantradol, including 9-hydroxy-6-methyl-3 -[5-phenylpentan-2-yl]oxy-5,6,6a,7,8,9,10,10a-octahydrophenant hridin-1-yl]acetate; [(6S,6aR,9R, 10aR)-9-hydroxy-6-methyl-3-[(2R)-5-phenylpentan-2-yl]oxy-5,6,6a,7,8,9,10,10a-octahydrophenanthridin-1-yl]acetate; and [9-hydroxy-6-methyl-3-[5-phenylpentan-2-yl]oxy-5,6,6a,7,8,9,10,10a-octahydrophenanthridin-1-yl]acetate.
(J) HU-210, including (6aR,10aR)-9-(hydroxymethyl)-6,6-d imethyl-3-(2-methyloctan-2-yl)-6a,7,10,10a-tetrahydrobenzo[c] chromen-1-ol; [(6aR,10aR)-9-(hydroxymethyl)-6,6-dimethyl-3-(2-methyl octan-2-yl)-6a,7,10,10a-tetrahydrobenzo[c]chromen-1-o l and 1,1-Dimethylheptyl-11-hydroxytetrahydrocannabinol.

(K) HU-211, Dexanabinol, including (6aS, 10aS)-9-(hydroxy methyl)-6,6-dimethyl-3-(2-methyloctan-2-yl)-6a,7,10,10a-t etrahydrobenzo[c]chromen-1-ol and (6aS, 10aS)-9-(hydroxy methyl)-6,6-dimethyl- 3-(2-methyloctan-2-yl)-6a,7,10,10a-t etrahydrobenzo[c]chromen-1-ol.

(L) HU-243, 3-dimethylheptyl-11-hydroxyhexahydrocannabinol.

(M) HU-308, [(91R,2R,5R)-2-[2,6-dimethoxy-4-(2-methyloctan-2 -yl)phenyl]-7,7-dimethyl-4-bicyclo[3.1.1]hept-3-enyl]methanol.

(N) HU-331, 3-hydroxy-2-[(1R,6R)-3-methyl-6-(1-m ethylethenyl)-2-cyclohexen-1-yl]-5-pentyl-2,5-cyclohexadiene-1 ,4-dione.

(O) HU-336, (6aR,10aR)-6,6,9-trimethyl-3-pentyl-6a,7,10,10a-t etrahydro-1H-benzo[c]chromene-1,4(6H)-dione.

(P) JTE-907, N-(benzol[1,3]dioxol-5-ylmethyl)-7-methoxy-2-o xo-8-pentyloxy-1,2-dihydroquinoline-3-carboxamide.

(Q) JWH-051, ((6aR,10aR)-6,6-dimethyl-3-(2-methyloctan-2-y l)-6a,7,10,10a-tetrahydrobenzo[c]chromen-9-yl)methanol.

(R) JWH-057 (6aR,10aR)-3-(1,1-dimethylheptyl)-6a,7,10,10a-t etrahydro-6,6,9-trimethyl-6H-Dibenzo[b,d]pyran.

(S) JWH-133 (6aR,10aR)-3-(1,1-Dimethylbutyl)-6a,7,10,10a-t etrahydro -6,6,9-trimethyl-6H-dibenzo[b,d]pyran.

(T) JWH-359, (6aR,10aR)- 1-methoxy- 6,6,9-trimethyl- 3-[(2R)-1 ,1,2-trimethylbutyl]-6a,7,10,10a-tetrahydrobenzo[c]chromene.

(U) URB-597 [3-(3-carbamoylphenyl)phenyl]-N-cyclohexylcarb amate.

(V) URB-602 [1,1'-Biphenyl]-3-yl-carbamic acid, cyclohexyl ester; OR cyclohexyl [1,1'-biphenyl]-3-ylcarbamate.

(W) URB-754 6-methyl-2-[(4-methylphenyl)amino]-4H-3,1-b enzoxazin-4-one.

(X) URB-937 3'-carbamoyl-6-hydroxy-[1,1'-biphenyl]-3-yl cyc lohexylcarbamate.

(Y) WIN 55,212-2, including (R)-(+)-[2,3-dihydro-5-methyl-3 -(4-morpholinylmethyl)pyrrolo[1,2,3-de]-1,4-benzoxazin-6-yl]-1 -napthalenylmethanone and [2,3-Dihydro-5-methyl-3-(4-morp holinylmethyl)pyrrolo[(1,2,3-de)-1,4-benzoxazin-6-yl]-1-n apthalenylmethanone.

(d) The substances or analogs of substances identified in subdivision (c) may be lawfully obtained and used for bona fide research, instruction, or analysis if that possession and use does not violate federal law.

(e) As used in this section, "synthetic cannabinoid compound" does not include either of the following:

(1) Any substance for which there is an approved new drug application, as defined in Section 505 of the federal Food, Drug, and Cosmetic Act (21 U.S.C. Sec. 355) or which is generally recognized as safe and effective for use pursuant to Section 501, 502, and 503 of the federal Food, Drug, and Cosmetic Act and Title 21 of the Code of Federal Regulations.

(2) With respect to a particular person, any substance for which an exemption is in effect for investigational use for that person pursuant to Section 505 of the federal Food, Drug, and Cosmetic Act (21 U.S.C. Sec. 355), to the extent that the conduct with respect to that substance is pursuant to the exemption.

(Amended by Stats. 2016, Ch. 624, Sec. 2. (SB 139) Effective September 25, 2016.)

11358.

Each person who plants, cultivates, harvests, dries, or processes cannabis plants, or any part thereof, except as otherwise provided by law, shall be punished as follows:

(a) Each person under the age of 18 who plants, cultivates, harvests, dries, or processes any cannabis plants shall be punished in the same manner provided in paragraph (1) of subdivision (b) of Section 11357.

(b) Each person at least 18 years of age but less than 21 years of age who plants, cultivates, harvests, dries, or processes not more than six living cannabis plants shall be guilty of an infraction and a fine of not more than one hundred dollars ($100).

(c) Each person 18 years of age or over who plants, cultivates, harvests, dries, or processes more than six living cannabis plants shall be punished by imprisonment in a county jail for a period of not more than six months or by a fine of not more than five hundred dollars ($500), or by both that fine and imprisonment.

(d) Notwithstanding subdivision (c), a person 18 years of age or over who plants, cultivates, harvests, dries, or processes more than six living cannabis plants, or any part thereof, except as otherwise provided by law, may be punished by imprisonment pursuant to subdivision (h) of Section 1170 of the Penal Code if any of the following conditions exist:

(1) The person has one or more prior convictions for an offense specified in clause (iv) of subparagraph (C) of paragraph (2) of subdivision (e) of Section 667 of the Penal Code or for an offense requiring registration pursuant to subdivision (c) of Section 290 of the Penal Code.

(2) The person has two or more prior convictions under subdivision (c).

(3) The offense resulted in any of the following:

(A) Violation of Section 1052 of the Water Code relating to illegal diversion of water.

(B) Violation of Section 13260, 13264, 13272, or 13387 of the Water Code relating to discharge of water.

(C) Violation of Section 5650 or 5652 of the Fish and Game Code relating to waters of the state.

(D) Violation of Section 1602 of the Fish and Game Code relating to rivers, streams, and lakes.

(E) Violation of Section 374.8 of the Penal Code relating to hazardous substances or Section 25189.5, 25189.6, or 25189.7 of the Health and Safety Code relating to hazardous waste.

(F) Violation of Section 2080 of the Fish and Game Code relating to endangered and threatened species or Section 3513 of the Fish and Game Code relating to the Migratory Bird Treaty Act, or Section 2000 of the Fish and Game Code relating to the unlawful taking of fish and wildlife.

(G) Intentionally or with gross negligence causing substantial environmental harm to public lands or other public resources.

(Amended by Stats. 2017, Ch. 27, Sec. 123. (SB 94) Effective June 27, 2017. Note: This section was amended on Nov. 8, 2016, by initiative Prop. 64.)

11359.

Every person who possesses for sale any cannabis, except as otherwise provided by law, shall be punished as follows:

(a) Every person under the age of 18 who possesses cannabis for sale shall be punished in the same manner provided in paragraph (1) of subdivision (b) of Section 11357.

(b) Every person 18 years of age or over who possesses cannabis for sale shall be punished by imprisonment in a county jail for a period of not more than six months or by a fine of not more than five hundred dollars ($500), or by both such fine and imprisonment.

(c) Notwithstanding subdivision (b), a person 18 years of age or over who possesses cannabis for sale may be punished by imprisonment pursuant to subdivision (h) of Section 1170 of the Penal Code if:

(1) The person has one or more prior convictions for an offense specified in clause (iv) of subparagraph (C) of paragraph (2) of subdivision (e) of Section 667 of the Penal Code or for an offense requiring registration pursuant to subdivision (c) of Section 290 of the Penal Code;

(2) The person has two or more prior convictions under subdivision (b); or

(3) The offense occurred in connection with the knowing sale or attempted sale of cannabis to a person under the age of 18 years.

(d) Notwithstanding subdivision (b), a person 21 years of age or over who possesses cannabis for sale may be punished by imprisonment pursuant to subdivision (h) of Section 1170 of the Penal Code if the offense involves knowingly hiring, employing, or using a person 20 years of age or younger in unlawfully cultivating, transporting, carrying, selling, offering to sell, giving away, preparing for sale, or peddling any cannabis.

(Amended by Stats. 2017, Ch. 27, Sec. 124. (SB 94) Effective June 27, 2017. Note: This section was amended on Nov. 8, 2016, by initiative Prop. 64.)

11360.

(a) Except as otherwise provided by this section or as authorized by law, every person who transports, imports into this state, sells, furnishes, administers, or gives away, or offers to transport, import into this state, sell, furnish, administer, or give away, or attempts to import into this state or transport any cannabis shall be punished as follows:

(1) Persons under the age of 18 years shall be punished in the same manner as provided in paragraph (1) of subdivision (b) of Section 11357.

(2) Persons 18 years of age or over shall be punished by imprisonment in a county jail for a period of not more than six months or by a fine of not more than five hundred dollars ($500), or by both such fine and imprisonment.

(3) Notwithstanding paragraph (2), a person 18 years of age or over may be punished by imprisonment pursuant to subdivision (h) of Section 1170 of the Penal Code for a period of two, three, or four years if:

(A) The person has one or more prior convictions for an offense specified in clause (iv) of subparagraph (C) of paragraph (2) of subdivision (e) of Section 667 of the Penal Code or for an offense requiring registration pursuant to subdivision (c) of Section 290 of the Penal Code;

(B) The person has two or more prior convictions under paragraph (2);

(C) The offense involved the knowing sale, attempted sale, or the knowing offer to sell, furnish, administer, or give away cannabis to a person under the age of 18 years; or

(D) The offense involved the import, offer to import, or attempted import into this state, or the transport for sale, offer to transport for sale, or attempted transport for sale out of this state, of more than 28.5 grams of cannabis or more than four grams of concentrated cannabis.

(b) Except as authorized by law, every person who gives away, offers to give away, transports, offers to transport, or attempts to transport not more than 28.5 grams of cannabis, other than concentrated cannabis, is guilty of an infraction and shall be punished by a fine of not more than one hundred dollars ($100). In any case in which a person is arrested for a violation of this subdivision and does not demand to be taken before a magistrate, that person shall be released by the arresting officer upon presentation of satisfactory evidence of identity and giving his or her written promise to appear in court, as provided in Section 853.6 of the Penal Code, and shall not be subjected to booking.

(c) For purposes of this section, "transport" means to transport for sale.

(d) This section does not preclude or limit prosecution for any aiding and abetting or conspiracy offenses.

(Amended by Stats. 2017, Ch. 27, Sec. 125. (SB 94) Effective June 27, 2017. Note: This section was amended on Nov. 8, 2016, by initiative Prop. 64.)

11361.

(a) A person 18 years of age or over who hires, employs, or uses a minor in unlawfully transporting, carrying, selling, giving away, preparing for sale, or peddling any cannabis, who unlawfully sells, or offers to sell, any cannabis to a minor, or who furnishes, administers, or gives, or offers to furnish, administer, or give any cannabis to a minor under 14 years of age, or who induces a minor to use cannabis in violation of law shall be punished by imprisonment in the state prison for a period of three, five, or seven years.

(b) A person 18 years of age or over who furnishes, administers, or gives, or offers to furnish, administer, or give, any cannabis to a minor 14 years of age or older in violation of law shall be punished by imprisonment in the state prison for a period of three, four, or five years.

(Amended by Stats. 2017, Ch. 27, Sec. 126. (SB 94) Effective June 27, 2017.)

11361.1.

(a) The drug education and counseling requirements under Sections 11357, 11358, 11359, and 11360 shall be:

(1) Mandatory, unless the court finds that such drug education or counseling is unnecessary for the person, or that a drug education or counseling program is unavailable;

(2) Free to participants, and shall consist of at least four hours of group discussion or instruction based on science and evidence-based principles and practices specific to the use and abuse of cannabis and other controlled substances.

(b) For good cause, the court may grant an extension of time not to exceed 30 days for a person to complete the drug education and counseling required under Sections 11357, 11358, 11359, and 11360.

(Amended by Stats. 2017, Ch. 27, Sec. 127. (SB 94) Effective June 27, 2017. Note: This section was added on Nov. 8, 2016, by initiative Prop. 64.)

11361.5.

(a) Records of any court of this state, any public or private agency that provides services upon referral under Section 1000.2 of the Penal Code, or of any state agency pertaining to the arrest or conviction of any person for a violation of Section 11357 or subdivision (b) of Section 11360, or pertaining to the arrest or conviction of any person under the age of 18 for a violation of any provision of this article except Section 11357.5, shall not be kept beyond two years from the date of the conviction, or from the date of the arrest if there was no conviction, except with respect to a violation of subdivision (d) of Section 11357, or any other violation by a person under the age of 18 occurring upon the grounds of, or within, any school providing instruction in kindergarten or any of grades 1 to 12, inclusive, during hours the school is open for classes or school-related programs, the records shall be retained until the offender attains the age of 18 years at which time the records shall be destroyed as provided in this section. A court or agency having custody of the records, including the statewide criminal databases, shall provide for the timely destruction of the records in accordance with subdivision (c), and those records shall also be purged from the statewide criminal databases. As used in this subdivision, "records pertaining to the arrest or conviction" shall include records of arrests resulting in the criminal proceeding and records relating to other offenses charged in the accusatory pleading, whether the defendant was acquitted or charges were dismissed. The two-year period beyond which records shall not be kept pursuant to this subdivision does not apply to any person who is, at the time at which this subdivision would otherwise require record destruction, incarcerated for an offense subject to this subdivision. For such persons, the two-year period shall commence from the date the person is released from custody. The requirements of this subdivision do not apply to records of any conviction occurring before January 1, 1976, or records of any arrest not followed by a conviction occurring before that date, or records of any arrest for an offense specified in subdivision (c) of Section 1192.7, or subdivision (c) of Section 667.5, of the Penal Code.

(b) This subdivision applies only to records of convictions and arrests not followed by conviction occurring before January 1, 1976, for any of the following offenses:

(1) A violation of Section 11357 or a statutory predecessor thereof.

(2) Unlawful possession of a device, contrivance, instrument, or paraphernalia used for unlawfully smoking cannabis, in violation of Section 11364, as it existed before January 1, 1976, or a statutory predecessor thereof.

(3) Unlawful visitation or presence in a room or place in which cannabis is being unlawfully smoked or used, in violation of Section 11365, as it existed before January 1, 1976, or a statutory predecessor thereof.

(4) Unlawfully using or being under the influence of cannabis, in violation of Section 11550, as it existed before January 1, 1976, or a statutory predecessor thereof.

(A) A person subject to an arrest or conviction for those offenses may apply to the Department of Justice for destruction of records pertaining to the arrest or conviction if two or more years have elapsed since the date of the conviction, or since the date of the arrest if not followed by a conviction. The application shall be submitted upon a form supplied by the Department of Justice and shall be accompanied by a fee, which shall be established by the department in an amount which will defray the cost of administering this subdivision and costs incurred by the state under subdivision (c), but which shall not exceed thirty-seven dollars and fifty cents ($37.50). The application form may be made available at every local police or sheriff's department and from the Department of Justice and may require that information which the department determines is necessary for purposes of identification.

(B) The department may request, but not require, the applicant to include a self-administered fingerprint upon the application. If the department is unable to sufficiently identify the applicant for purposes of this subdivision without the fingerprint or without additional fingerprints, it shall so notify the applicant and shall request the applicant to submit any fingerprints which may be required to effect identification, including a complete set if necessary, or, alternatively, to abandon the application and request a refund of all or a portion of the fee submitted with the application, as provided in this section. If the applicant fails or refuses to submit fingerprints in accordance with the department's request within a reasonable time which shall be established by the department, or if the applicant requests a refund of the fee, the department shall promptly mail a refund to the applicant at the address specified in the application or at any other address which may be specified by the applicant. However, if the department

has notified the applicant that election to abandon the application will result in forfeiture of a specified amount which is a portion of the fee, the department may retain a portion of the fee which the department determines will defray the actual costs of processing the application, provided the amount of the portion retained shall not exceed ten dollars ($10).

(C) Upon receipt of a sufficient application, the Department of Justice shall destroy records of the department, if any, pertaining to the arrest or conviction in the manner prescribed by subdivision (c) and shall notify the Federal Bureau of Investigation, the law enforcement agency which arrested the applicant, and, if the applicant was convicted, the probation department which investigated the applicant and the Department of Motor Vehicles, of the application.

(c) Destruction of records of arrest or conviction pursuant to subdivision (a) or (b) shall be accomplished by permanent obliteration of all entries or notations upon the records pertaining to the arrest or conviction, and the record shall be prepared again so that it appears that the arrest or conviction never occurred. However, where (1) the only entries upon the record pertain to the arrest or conviction and (2) the record can be destroyed without necessarily effecting the destruction of other records, then the document constituting the record shall be physically destroyed.

(d) Notwithstanding subdivision (a) or (b), written transcriptions of oral testimony in court proceedings and published judicial appellate reports are not subject to this section. Additionally, no records shall be destroyed pursuant to subdivision (a) if the defendant or a codefendant has filed a civil action against the peace officers or law enforcement jurisdiction which made the arrest or instituted the prosecution and if the agency which is the custodian of those records has received a certified copy of the complaint in the civil action, until the civil action has finally been resolved. Immediately following the final resolution of the civil action, records subject to subdivision (a) shall be destroyed pursuant to subdivision (c) if more than two years have elapsed from the date of the conviction or arrest without conviction.

(Amended by Stats. 2018, Ch. 92, Sec. 140. (SB 1289) Effective January 1, 2019. Note: This section was amended on Nov. 8, 2016, by initiative Prop. 64.)

11361.7.

(a) Any record subject to destruction or permanent obliteration pursuant to Section 11361.5, or more than two years of age, or a record of a conviction for an offense specified in subdivision (a) or (b) of Section 11361.5 which became final more than two years previously, shall not be considered to be accurate, relevant, timely, or complete for any purposes by any agency or person. The provisions of this subdivision shall be applicable for purposes of the Privacy Act of 1974 (5 U.S.C. Section 552a) to the fullest extent permissible by law, whenever any information or record subject to destruction or permanent obliteration under Section 11361.5 was obtained by any state agency, local public agency, or any public or private agency that provides services upon referral under Section 1000.2 of the Penal Code, and is thereafter shared with or disseminated to any agency of the federal government.

(b) No public agency shall alter, amend, assess, condition, deny, limit, postpone, qualify, revoke, surcharge, or suspend any certificate, franchise, incident, interest, license, opportunity, permit, privilege, right, or title of any person because of an arrest or conviction for an offense specified in subdivision (a) or (b) of Section 11361.5, or because of the facts or events leading to such an arrest or conviction, on or after the date the records of such arrest or conviction are required to be destroyed by subdivision (a) of Section 11361.5, or two years from the date of such conviction or arrest without conviction with respect to arrests and convictions occurring prior to January 1, 1976. As used in this subdivision, "public agency" includes, but is not limited to, any state, county, city and county, city, public or constitutional corporation or entity, district, local or regional political subdivision, or any department, division, bureau, office, board, commission or other agency thereof.

(c) Any person arrested or convicted for an offense specified in subdivision (a) or (b) of Section 11361.5 may, two years from the date of such a conviction, or from the date of the arrest if there was no conviction, indicate in response to any question concerning his prior criminal record that he was not arrested or convicted for such offense.

(d) The provisions of this section shall be applicable without regard to whether destruction or obliteration of records has actually been implemented pursuant to Section 11361.5.

(Added by Stats. 1976, Ch. 952.)

11361.8.

(a) A person currently serving a sentence for a conviction, whether by trial or by open or negotiated plea, who would not have been guilty of an offense, or who would have been guilty of a lesser offense under the Control, Regulate and Tax Adult Use of Marijuana Act had that act been in effect at the time of the offense may petition for a recall or dismissal of sentence before the trial court that entered the judgment of conviction in his or her case to request resentencing or dismissal in accordance with Sections 11357, 11358, 11359, 11360, 11362.1, 11362.2, 11362.3, and 11362.4 as those sections have been amended or added by that act.

(b) Upon receiving a petition under subdivision (a), the court shall presume the petitioner satisfies the criteria in subdivision (a) unless the party opposing the petition proves by clear and convincing evidence that the petitioner does not satisfy the criteria. If the petitioner satisfies the criteria in subdivision (a), the court shall grant the petition to recall the sentence or dismiss the sentence because it is legally invalid unless the court determines that granting the petition would pose an unreasonable risk of danger to public safety.

(1) In exercising its discretion, the court may consider, but shall not be limited to evidence provided for in subdivision (b) of Section 1170.18 of the Penal Code.

(2) As used in this section, "unreasonable risk of danger to public safety" has the same meaning as provided in subdivision (c) of Section 1170.18 of the Penal Code.

(c) A person who is serving a sentence and is resentenced pursuant to subdivision (b) shall be given credit for any time already served and shall be subject to supervision for one year following completion of his or her time in custody or shall be subject to whatever supervision time he or she would have otherwise been subject to after release, whichever is shorter, unless the court, in its discretion, as part of its resentencing order, releases the person from supervision. Such person is subject to parole supervision under Section 3000.08 of the Penal Code or post-release community supervision under subdivision (a) of Section 3451 of the Penal Code by the designated agency and the jurisdiction of the court in the county in which the offender is released or resides, or in which an alleged violation of supervision has occurred, for the purpose of hearing petitions to revoke supervision and impose a term of custody.

(d) Under no circumstances may resentencing under this section result in the imposition of a term longer than the original sentence, or the reinstatement of charges dismissed pursuant to a negotiated plea agreement.

(e) A person who has completed his or her sentence for a conviction under Sections 11357, 11358, 11359, and 11360, whether by trial or open or negotiated plea, who would not have been guilty of an offense or who would have been guilty of a lesser offense under the Control, Regulate and Tax Adult Use of Marijuana Act had that act been in effect at the time of the offense, may file an application before the trial court that entered the judgment of conviction in his or her case to have the conviction dismissed and sealed because the prior conviction is now legally invalid or redesignated as a misdemeanor or infraction in accordance with Sections 11357, 11358, 11359, 11360, 11362.1, 11362.2, 11362.3, and 11362.4 as those sections have been amended or added by that act.

(f) The court shall presume the petitioner satisfies the criteria in subdivision (e) unless the party opposing the application proves by clear and convincing evidence that the petitioner does not satisfy the criteria in subdivision (e). Once the applicant satisfies the criteria in subdivision (e), the court shall redesignate the conviction as a misdemeanor or infraction or dismiss and seal the conviction as legally invalid as now established under the Control, Regulate and Tax Adult Use of Marijuana Act.

(g) Unless requested by the applicant, no hearing is necessary to grant or deny an application filed under subdivision (e).

(h) Any felony conviction that is recalled and resentenced under subdivision (b) or designated as a misdemeanor or infraction under subdivision (f) shall be considered a misdemeanor or infraction for all purposes. Any misdemeanor conviction that is recalled and resentenced under subdivision (b) or designated as an infraction under subdivision (f) shall be considered an infraction for all purposes.

(i) If the court that originally sentenced the petitioner is not available, the presiding judge shall designate another judge to rule on the petition or application.

(j) Nothing in this section is intended to diminish or abrogate any rights or remedies otherwise available to the petitioner or applicant.

(k) Nothing in this and related sections is intended to diminish or abrogate the finality of judgments in any case not falling within the purview of the Control, Regulate and Tax Adult Use of Marijuana Act.

(l) A resentencing hearing ordered under the Control, Regulate and Tax Adult Use of Marijuana Act shall constitute a "post-conviction release proceeding" under paragraph (7) of subdivision (b) of Section 28 of Article I of the California Constitution (Marsy's Law).

(m) The provisions of this section shall apply equally to juvenile delinquency adjudications and dispositions under Section 602 of the Welfare and Institutions Code if the juvenile would not have been guilty of an offense or would have been guilty of a lesser offense under the Control, Regulate and Tax Adult Use of Marijuana Act.

(n) The Judicial Council shall promulgate and make available all necessary forms to enable the filing of the petitions and applications provided in this section.
(Added November 8, 2016, by initiative Proposition 64, Sec. 8.7.)

11361.9.

(a) On or before July 1, 2019, the Department of Justice shall review the records in the state summary criminal history information database and shall identify past convictions that are potentially eligible for recall or dismissal of sentence, dismissal and sealing, or redesignation pursuant to Section 11361.8. The department shall notify the prosecution of all cases in their jurisdiction that are eligible for recall or dismissal of sentence, dismissal and sealing, or redesignation.

(b) The prosecution shall have until July 1, 2020, to review all cases and determine whether to challenge the recall or dismissal of sentence, dismissal and sealing, or redesignation.

(c) (1) The prosecution may challenge the resentencing of a person pursuant to this section when the person does not meet the criteria established in Section 11361.8 or presents an unreasonable risk to public safety.

(2) The prosecution may challenge the dismissal and sealing or redesignation of a person pursuant to this section who has completed his or her sentence for a conviction when the person does not meet the criteria established in Section 11361.8.

(3) On or before July 1, 2020, the prosecution shall inform the court and the public defender's office in their county when they are challenging a particular recall or dismissal of sentence, dismissal and sealing, or redesignation. The prosecution shall inform the court when they are not challenging a particular recall or dismissal of sentence, dismissal and sealing, or redesignation.

(4) The public defender's office, upon receiving notice from the prosecution pursuant to paragraph (3), shall make a reasonable effort to notify the person whose resentencing or dismissal is being challenged.

(d) If the prosecution does not challenge the recall or dismissal of sentence, dismissal and sealing, or redesignation by July 1, 2020, the court shall reduce or dismiss the conviction pursuant to Section 11361.8.

(e) The court shall notify the department of the recall or dismissal of sentence, dismissal and sealing, or redesignation and the department shall modify the state summary criminal history information database accordingly.

(f) The department shall post general information on its Internet Web site about the recall or dismissal of sentences, dismissal and sealing, or redesignation authorized in this section.

(g) It is the intent of the Legislature that persons who are currently serving a sentence or who proactively petition for a recall or dismissal of sentence, dismissal and sealing, or redesignation pursuant to Section 11361.8 be prioritized for review.
(Added by Stats. 2018, Ch. 993, Sec. 1. (AB 1793) Effective January 1, 2019.)

11362.

As used in this article "felony offense," and offense "punishable as a felony" refer to an offense prior to July 1, 2011, for which the law prescribes imprisonment in the state prison, or for an offense on or after July 1, 2011, imprisonment in either the state prison or pursuant to subdivision (h) of Section 1170 of the Penal Code, as either an alternative or the sole penalty, regardless of the sentence the particular defendant received.
(Amended by Stats. 2011, Ch. 15, Sec. 163. (AB 109) Effective April 4, 2011. Operative October 1, 2011, by Sec. 636 of Ch. 15, as amended by Stats. 2011, Ch. 39, Sec. 68.)

11362.1.

(a) Subject to Sections 11362.2, 11362.3, 11362.4, and 11362.45, but notwithstanding any other provision of law, it shall be lawful under state and local law, and shall not be a violation of state or local law, for persons 21 years of age or older to:

(1) Possess, process, transport, purchase, obtain, or give away to persons 21 years of age or older without any compensation whatsoever, not more than 28.5 grams of cannabis not in the form of concentrated cannabis;

(2) Possess, process, transport, purchase, obtain, or give away to persons 21 years of age or older without any compensation whatsoever, not more than eight grams of cannabis in the form of concentrated cannabis, including as contained in cannabis products;

(3) Possess, plant, cultivate, harvest, dry, or process not more than six living cannabis plants and possess the cannabis produced by the plants;

(4) Smoke or ingest cannabis or cannabis products; and

(5) Possess, transport, purchase, obtain, use, manufacture, or give away cannabis accessories to persons 21 years of age or older without any compensation whatsoever.

(b) Paragraph (5) of subdivision (a) is intended to meet the requirements of subsection (f) of Section 863 of Title 21 of the United States Code (21 U.S.C. Sec. 863(f)) by authorizing, under state law, any person in compliance with this section to manufacture, possess, or distribute cannabis accessories.

(c) Cannabis and cannabis products involved in any way with conduct deemed lawful by this section are not contraband nor subject to seizure, and no conduct deemed lawful by this section shall constitute the basis for detention, search, or arrest.
(Amended by Stats. 2017, Ch. 27, Sec. 129. (SB 94) Effective June 27, 2017. Note: This section was added on Nov. 8, 2016, by initiative Prop. 64.)

11362.2.

(a) Personal cultivation of cannabis under paragraph (3) of subdivision (a) of Section 11362.1 is subject to the following restrictions:

(1) A person shall plant, cultivate, harvest, dry, or process plants in accordance with local ordinances, if any, adopted in accordance with subdivision (b).

(2) The living plants and any cannabis produced by the plants in excess of 28.5 grams are kept within the person's private residence, or upon the grounds of that private residence (e.g., in an outdoor garden area), are in a locked space, and are not visible by normal unaided vision from a public place.

(3) Not more than six living plants may be planted, cultivated, harvested, dried, or processed within a single private residence, or upon the grounds of that private residence, at one time.

(b) (1) A city, county, or city and county may enact and enforce reasonable regulations to regulate the actions and conduct in paragraph (3) of subdivision (a) of Section 11362.1.

(2) Notwithstanding paragraph (1), a city, county, or city and county shall not completely prohibit persons engaging in the actions and conduct under paragraph (3) of subdivision (a) of Section 11362.1 inside a private residence, or inside an accessory structure to a private residence located upon the grounds of a private residence that is fully enclosed and secure.

(3) Notwithstanding paragraph (3) of subdivision (a) of Section 11362.1, a city, county, or city and county may completely prohibit persons from engaging in actions and conduct under paragraph (3) of subdivision (a) of Section 11362.1 outdoors upon the grounds of a private residence.

(4) Paragraph (3) shall become inoperative upon a determination by the California Attorney General that adult use of cannabis is lawful in the State of California under federal law, and an act taken by a city, county, or city and county under paragraph (3) is unenforceable upon the date of that determination by the Attorney General.

(5) For purposes of this section, "private residence" means a house, an apartment unit, a mobile home, or other similar dwelling.
(Amended by Stats. 2017, Ch. 27, Sec. 130. (SB 94) Effective June 27, 2017. Note: This section was added on Nov. 8, 2016, by initiative Prop. 64.)

11362.3.

(a) Section 11362.1 does not permit any person to:

(1) Smoke or ingest cannabis or cannabis products in a public place, except in accordance with Section 26200 of the Business and Professions Code.

(2) Smoke cannabis or cannabis products in a location where smoking tobacco is prohibited.

(3) Smoke cannabis or cannabis products within 1,000 feet of a school, day care center, or youth center while children are present at the school, day care center, or youth center, except in or upon the grounds of a private residence or in accordance with Section 26200 of the Business and Professions Code and only if such smoking is not detectable by others on the grounds of the school, day care center, or youth center while children are present.

(4) Possess an open container or open package of cannabis or cannabis products while driving, operating, or riding in the passenger seat or compartment of a motor vehicle, boat, vessel, aircraft, or other vehicle used for transportation.

(5) Possess, smoke, or ingest cannabis or cannabis products in or upon the grounds of a school, day care center, or youth center while children are present.

(6) Manufacture concentrated cannabis using a volatile solvent, unless done in accordance with a license under Division 10 (commencing with Section 26000) of the Business and Professions Code.

(7) Smoke or ingest cannabis or cannabis products while driving, operating a motor vehicle, boat, vessel, aircraft, or other vehicle used for transportation.

(8) Smoke or ingest cannabis or cannabis products while riding in the passenger seat or compartment of a motor vehicle, boat, vessel, aircraft, or other vehicle used for transportation except as permitted on a motor vehicle, boat, vessel, aircraft, or other vehicle used for transportation that is operated in accordance with Section 26200 of the Business and Professions Code and while no persons under 21 years of age are present.

(b) For purposes of this section, the following definitions apply:

(1) "Day care center" has the same meaning as in Section 1596.76.

(2) "Smoke" means to inhale, exhale, burn, or carry any lighted or heated device or pipe, or any other lighted or heated cannabis or cannabis product intended for inhalation, whether natural or synthetic, in any manner or in any form. "Smoke" includes the use of an electronic smoking device that creates an aerosol or vapor, in any manner or in any form, or the use of any oral smoking device for the purpose of circumventing the prohibition of smoking in a place.

(3) "Volatile solvent" means a solvent that is or produces a flammable gas or vapor that, when present in the air in sufficient quantities, will create explosive or ignitable mixtures.

(4) "Youth center" has the same meaning as in Section 11353.1.

(c) Nothing in this section shall be construed or interpreted to amend, repeal, affect, restrict, or preempt laws pertaining to the Compassionate Use Act of 1996.

(Amended by Stats. 2017, Ch. 27, Sec. 131. (SB 94) Effective June 27, 2017. Note: This section was added on November 8, 2016, by initiative Proposition 64.)

11362.4.

(a) A person who engages in the conduct described in paragraph (1) of subdivision (a) of Section 11362.3 is guilty of an infraction punishable by no more than a one-hundred-dollar ($100) fine; provided, however, that persons under 18 years of age shall instead be required to complete four hours of a drug education program or counseling, and up to 10 hours of community service, over a period not to exceed 60 days once the drug education program or counseling and community service opportunity are made available to the person.

(b) A person who engages in the conduct described in paragraph (2), (3), or (4) of subdivision (a) of Section 11362.3 is guilty of an infraction punishable by no more than a two-hundred-fifty-dollar ($250) fine, unless that activity is otherwise permitted by state and local law; provided, however, that a person under 18 years of age shall instead be required to complete four hours of drug education or counseling, and up to 20 hours of community service, over a period not to exceed 90 days once the drug education program or counseling and community service opportunity are made available to the person.

(c) A person who engages in the conduct described in paragraph (5) of subdivision (a) of Section 11362.3 is subject to the same punishment as provided under subdivision (c) or (d) of Section 11357.

(d) A person who engages in the conduct described in paragraph (6) of subdivision (a) of Section 11362.3 is subject to punishment under Section 11379.6.

(e) A person who violates the restrictions in subdivision (a) of Section 11362.2 is guilty of an infraction punishable by no more than a two-hundred-fifty-dollar ($250) fine.

(f) Notwithstanding subdivision (e), a person under 18 years of age who violates the restrictions in subdivision (a) of Section 11362.2 shall be punished under paragraph (1) of subdivision (b) of Section 11357.

(g) (1) The drug education program or counseling hours required by this section shall be mandatory unless the court makes a finding that the program or counseling is unnecessary for the person or that a drug education program or counseling is unavailable.

(2) The drug education program required by this section for persons under 18 years of age shall be free to participants and provide at least four hours of group discussion or instruction based on science and evidence-based principles and practices specific to the use and abuse of cannabis and other controlled substances.

(h) Upon a finding of good cause, the court may extend the time for a person to complete the drug education or counseling, and community service required under this section.

(Amended by Stats. 2018, Ch. 92, Sec. 141. (SB 1289) Effective January 1, 2019. Note: This section was added on Nov. 8, 2016, by initiative Prop. 64.)

11362.45.

Section 11362.1 does not amend, repeal, affect, restrict, or preempt:

(a) Laws making it unlawful to drive or operate a vehicle, boat, vessel, or aircraft, while smoking, ingesting, or impaired by, cannabis or cannabis products, including, but not limited to, subdivision (e) of Section 23152 of the Vehicle Code, or the penalties prescribed for violating those laws.

(b) Laws prohibiting the sale, administering, furnishing, or giving away of cannabis, cannabis products, or cannabis accessories, or the offering to sell, administer, furnish, or give away cannabis, cannabis products, or cannabis accessories to a person younger than 21 years of age.

(c) Laws prohibiting a person younger than 21 years of age from engaging in any of the actions or conduct otherwise permitted under Section 11362.1.

(d) Laws pertaining to smoking or ingesting cannabis or cannabis products on the grounds of, or within, any facility or institution under the jurisdiction of the Department of Corrections and Rehabilitation or the Division of Juvenile Justice, or on the grounds of, or within, any other facility or institution referenced in Section 4573 of the Penal Code.

(e) Laws providing that it would constitute negligence or professional malpractice to undertake any task while impaired from smoking or ingesting cannabis or cannabis products.

(f) The rights and obligations of public and private employers to maintain a drug and alcohol free workplace or require an employer to permit or accommodate the use, consumption, possession, transfer, display, transportation, sale, or growth of cannabis in the workplace, or affect the ability of employers to have policies prohibiting the use of cannabis by employees and prospective employees, or prevent employers from complying with state or federal law.

(g) The ability of a state or local government agency to prohibit or restrict any of the actions or conduct otherwise permitted under Section 11362.1 within a building owned, leased, or occupied by the state or local government agency.

(h) The ability of an individual or private entity to prohibit or restrict any of the actions or conduct otherwise permitted under Section 11362.1 on the individual's or entity's privately owned property.

(i) Laws pertaining to the Compassionate Use Act of 1996.

(Amended by Stats. 2017, Ch. 27, Sec. 133. (SB 94) Effective June 27, 2017. Note: This section was added on Nov. 8, 2016, by initiative Prop. 64.)

11362.5.

(a) This section shall be known and may be cited as the Compassionate Use Act of 1996.

(b) (1) The people of the State of California hereby find and declare that the purposes of the Compassionate Use Act of 1996 are as follows:

(A) To ensure that seriously ill Californians have the right to obtain and use marijuana for medical purposes where that medical use is deemed appropriate and has been recommended by a physician who has determined that the person's health would benefit from the use of marijuana in the treatment of cancer, anorexia, AIDS, chronic pain, spasticity, glaucoma, arthritis, migraine, or any other illness for which marijuana provides relief.

(B) To ensure that patients and their primary caregivers who obtain and use marijuana for medical purposes upon the recommendation of a physician are not subject to criminal prosecution or sanction.

(C) To encourage the federal and state governments to implement a plan to provide for the safe and affordable distribution of marijuana to all patients in medical need of marijuana.

(2) Nothing in this section shall be construed to supersede legislation prohibiting persons from engaging in conduct that endangers others, nor to condone the diversion of marijuana for nonmedical purposes.

(c) Notwithstanding any other provision of law, no physician in this state shall be punished, or denied any right or privilege, for having recommended marijuana to a patient for medical purposes.

(d) Section 11357, relating to the possession of marijuana, and Section 11358, relating to the cultivation of marijuana, shall not apply to a patient, or to a patient's primary caregiver, who possesses or cultivates marijuana for the personal medical purposes of the patient upon the written or oral recommendation or approval of a physician.

(e) For the purposes of this section, "primary caregiver" means the individual designated by the person exempted under this section who has consistently assumed responsibility for the housing, health, or safety of that person.

(Added November 5, 1996, by initiative Proposition 215, Sec. 1.)

11362.9.

(a) (1) It is the intent of the Legislature that the state commission objective scientific research by the premier research institute of the world, the University of California, regarding the efficacy and safety of administering cannabis, its naturally occurring constituents, and synthetic compounds, as part of medical treatment. If the Regents of the University of California, by appropriate resolution, accept this responsibility, the University of California shall create a program, to be known as the California Cannabis Research Program, hosted by the Center for Medicinal Cannabis Research. Whenever "California Marijuana Research Program" appears in any statute, regulation, or contract, or in any other code, it shall be construed to refer to the California Cannabis Research Program.

(2) The program shall develop and conduct studies intended to ascertain the general medical safety and efficacy of cannabis and, if found valuable, shall develop medical guidelines for the appropriate administration and use of cannabis. The studies may examine the effect of cannabis on motor skills, the health and safety effects of cannabis, cannabinoids, and other related constituents, and other behavioral and health outcomes.

(b) The program may immediately solicit proposals for research projects to be included in the cannabis studies. Program requirements to be used when evaluating responses to its solicitation for proposals shall include, but not be limited to, all of the following:

(1) Proposals shall demonstrate the use of key personnel, including clinicians or scientists and support personnel, who are prepared to develop a program of research regarding the general medical efficacy and safety of cannabis.

(2) Proposals shall contain procedures for outreach to patients with various medical conditions who may be suitable participants in research on cannabis.

(3) Proposals shall contain provisions for a patient registry.

(4) Proposals shall contain provisions for an information system that is designed to record information about possible study participants, investigators, and clinicians, and deposit and analyze data that accrues as part of clinical trials.

(5) Proposals shall contain protocols suitable for research on cannabis, addressing patients diagnosed with acquired immunodeficiency syndrome (AIDS) or human immunodeficiency virus (HIV), cancer, glaucoma, or seizures or muscle spasms associated with a chronic, debilitating condition. The proposal may also include research on other serious illnesses, provided that resources are available and medical information justifies the research.

(6) Proposals shall demonstrate the use of a specimen laboratory capable of housing plasma, urine, and other specimens necessary to study the concentration of cannabinoids in various tissues, as well as housing specimens for studies of toxic effects of cannabis.

(7) Proposals shall demonstrate the use of a laboratory capable of analyzing cannabis, provided to the program under this section, for purity and cannabinoid content and the capacity to detect contaminants.

(c) In order to ensure objectivity in evaluating proposals, the program shall use a peer review process that is modeled on the process used by the National Institutes of Health, and that guards against funding research that is biased in favor of or against particular outcomes. Peer reviewers shall be selected for their expertise in the scientific substance and methods of the proposed research, and their lack of bias or conflict of interest regarding the applicants or the topic of an approach taken in the proposed research. Peer reviewers shall judge research proposals on several criteria, foremost among which shall be both of the following:

(1) The scientific merit of the research plan, including whether the research design and experimental procedures are potentially biased for or against a particular outcome.

(2) Researchers' expertise in the scientific substance and methods of the proposed research, and their lack of bias or conflict of interest regarding the topic of, and the approach taken in, the proposed research.

(d) If the program is administered by the Regents of the University of California, any grant research proposals approved by the program shall also require review and approval by the research advisory panel.

(e) It is the intent of the Legislature that the program be established as follows:

(1) The program shall be located at one or more University of California campuses that have a core of faculty experienced in organizing multidisciplinary scientific endeavors and, in particular, strong experience in clinical trials involving psychopharmacologic agents. The campuses at which research under the auspices of the program is to take place shall accommodate the administrative offices, including the director of the program, as well as a data management unit, and facilities for detection and analysis of various naturally occurring and synthetic cannabinoids, as well as storage of specimens.

(2) When awarding grants under this section, the program shall utilize principles and parameters of the other well-tested statewide research programs administered by the University of California, modeled after programs administered by the National Institutes of Health, including peer review evaluation of the scientific merit of applications.

(3) The scientific and clinical operations of the program shall occur partly at University of California campuses and partly at other postsecondary institutions that have clinicians or scientists with expertise to conduct the required studies. Criteria for selection of research locations shall include the elements listed in subdivision (b) and, additionally, shall give particular weight to the organizational plan, leadership qualities of the program director, and plans to involve investigators and patient populations from multiple sites.

(4) The funds received by the program shall be allocated to various research studies in accordance with a scientific plan developed by the Scientific Advisory Council. As the first wave of studies is completed, it is anticipated that the program will receive requests for funding of additional studies. These requests shall be reviewed by the Scientific Advisory Council.

(5) The size, scope, and number of studies funded shall be commensurate with the amount of appropriated and available program funding.

(f) All personnel involved in implementing approved proposals shall be authorized as required by Section 11604.

(g) Studies conducted pursuant to this section shall include the greatest amount of new scientific research possible on the medical uses of, and medical hazards associated with, cannabis. The program shall consult with the Research Advisory Panel analogous agencies in other states, and appropriate federal agencies in an attempt to avoid duplicative research and the wasting of research dollars.

(h) The program shall make every effort to recruit qualified patients and qualified physicians from throughout the state.

(i) The cannabis studies shall employ state-of-the-art research methodologies.

(j) The program shall ensure that all cannabis used in the studies is of the appropriate medicinal quality. Cannabis used by the program may be obtained from the National Institute on Drug Abuse or any other entity authorized by the appropriate federal agencies, the Attorney General pursuant to Section 11478, or may be cultivated by the program pursuant to applicable federal and state laws and regulations.

(k) The program may review, approve, or incorporate studies and research by independent groups presenting scientifically valid protocols for medical research, regardless of whether the areas of study are being researched by the committee.

(l) (1) To enhance understanding of the efficacy and adverse effects of cannabis as a pharmacological agent, the program shall conduct focused controlled clinical trials on the usefulness of cannabis in patients diagnosed with AIDS or HIV, cancer, glaucoma, or seizures or muscle spasms associated with a chronic, debilitating condition. The program may add research on other serious illnesses, provided that resources are available and medical information justifies the research. The studies shall focus on comparisons of both the efficacy and safety of methods of administering the drug to patients, including inhalational, tinctural, and oral, evaluate possible uses of cannabis as a primary or adjunctive treatment, and develop further information on optimal dosage, timing, mode of administration, and variations in the effects of different cannabinoids and varieties of cannabis or synthetic compounds that simulate the effects of naturally occurring cannabinoids. The studies may also focus on examining testing methods for detecting harmful contaminants in cannabis, including, but not limited to, mold, bacteria, and mycotoxins that could cause harm to patients.

(2) The program shall examine the safety of cannabis in patients with various medical disorders, including the interaction of cannabis with other drugs, relative safety of inhalation versus oral forms, and the effects on mental function in medically ill persons.

(3) The program shall be limited to providing for objective scientific research to ascertain the efficacy and safety of cannabis as part of medical treatment, and should not be construed as encouraging or sanctioning the social or recreational use of cannabis.

(m) (1) Subject to paragraph (2), the program shall, prior to approving proposals, seek to obtain research protocol guidelines from the National Institutes of Health and shall, if the National Institutes of Health issues research protocol guidelines, comply with those guidelines.

(2) If, after a reasonable period of time of not less than six months and not more than a year has elapsed from the date the program seeks to obtain guidelines pursuant to paragraph (1), no guidelines have been approved, the program may proceed using the research protocol guidelines it develops.

(n) In order to maximize the scope and size of the cannabis studies, the program may do any of the following:

(1) Solicit, apply for, and accept funds from foundations, private individuals, and all other funding sources that can be used to expand the scope or timeframe of the cannabis studies that are authorized under this section. The program shall not expend more than 5 percent of its General Fund allocation in efforts to obtain money from outside sources.

(2) Include within the scope of the cannabis studies other cannabis research projects that are independently funded and that meet the requirements set forth in subdivisions (a) to (c), inclusive. In no case shall the program accept funds that are offered with any conditions other than that the funds be used to study the efficacy and safety of cannabis as part of medical treatment.

(o) (1) Within six months of the effective date of this section, the program shall report to the Legislature, the Governor, and the Attorney General on the progress of the cannabis studies.

(2) Thereafter, the program shall issue a report to the Legislature every 24 months detailing the progress of the studies. The interim reports required under this paragraph shall include, but not be limited to, data on all of the following:

(A) The names and number of diseases or conditions under study.

(B) The number of patients enrolled in each study, by disease.

(C) Any scientifically valid preliminary findings.

(p) If the Regents of the University of California implement this section, the President of the University of California, or the president's designee, shall appoint a multidisciplinary Scientific Advisory Council, not to exceed 15 members, to provide policy guidance in the creation and implementation of the program. Members shall be chosen on the basis of scientific expertise. Members of the council shall serve on a voluntary basis, with reimbursement for expenses incurred in the course of their participation. The members shall be reimbursed for travel and other necessary expenses incurred in their performance of the duties of the council.

(q) No more than 10 percent of the total funds appropriated may be used for all aspects of the administration of this section.

(r) This section shall be implemented only to the extent that funding for its purposes is appropriated by the Legislature.

(s) Money appropriated to the program pursuant to subdivision (e) of Section 34019 of the Revenue and Taxation Code shall only be used as authorized by the Control, Regulate and Tax Adult Use of Marijuana Act (AUMA).

(t) This section does not limit or preclude cannabis-related research activities at any campus of the University of California.

(Amended by Stats. 2019, Ch. 802, Sec. 1. (AB 420) Effective October 12, 2019. Note: Sections 11362.7 to 11362.85 are in Article 2.5, which follows this section.)

ARTICLE 2.5. Medical Marijuana Program [11362.7 - 11362.85]
 (Article 2.5 added by Stats. 2003, Ch. 875, Sec. 2.)

11362.7.
For purposes of this article, the following definitions shall apply:

(a) "Attending physician" means an individual who possesses a license in good standing to practice medicine, podiatry, or osteopathy issued by the Medical Board of California, the California Board of Podiatric Medicine, or the Osteopathic Medical Board of California and who has taken responsibility for an aspect of the medical care, treatment, diagnosis, counseling, or referral of a patient and who has conducted a medical examination of that patient before recording in the patient's medical record the physician's assessment of whether the patient has a serious medical condition and whether the medical use of cannabis is appropriate.

(b) "Department" means the State Department of Public Health.

(c) "Person with an identification card" means an individual who is a qualified patient who has applied for and received a valid identification card pursuant to this article.

(d) "Primary caregiver" means the individual, designated by a qualified patient, who has consistently assumed responsibility for the housing, health, or safety of that patient, and may include any of the following:

(1) In a case in which a qualified patient or person with an identification card receives medical care or supportive services, or both, from a clinic licensed pursuant to Chapter 1 (commencing with Section 1200) of Division 2, a health care facility licensed pursuant to Chapter 2 (commencing with Section 1250) of Division 2, a residential care facility for persons with chronic life-threatening illness licensed pursuant to Chapter 3.01 (commencing with Section 1568.01) of Division 2, a residential care facility for the elderly licensed pursuant to Chapter 3.2 (commencing with Section 1569) of Division 2, a hospice, or a home health agency licensed pursuant to Chapter 8 (commencing with Section 1725) of Division 2, the owner or operator, or no more than three employees who are designated by the owner or operator, of the clinic, facility, hospice, or home health agency, if designated as a primary caregiver by that qualified patient or person with an identification card.

(2) An individual who has been designated as a primary caregiver by more than one qualified patient or person with an identification card, if every qualified patient or person with an identification card who has designated that individual as a primary caregiver resides in the same city or county as the primary caregiver.

(3) An individual who has been designated as a primary caregiver by a qualified patient or person with an identification card who resides in a city or county other than that of the primary caregiver, if the individual has not been designated as a primary caregiver by any other qualified patient or person with an identification card.

(e) A primary caregiver shall be at least 18 years of age, unless the primary caregiver is the parent of a minor child who is a qualified patient or a person with an identification card or the primary caregiver is a person otherwise entitled to make medical decisions under state law pursuant to Section 6922, 7002, 7050, or 7120 of the Family Code.

(f) "Qualified patient" means a person who is entitled to the protections of Section 11362.5, but who does not have an identification card issued pursuant to this article.

(g) "Identification card" means a document issued by the department that identifies a person authorized to engage in the medical use of cannabis and the person's designated primary caregiver, if any.

(h) "Serious medical condition" means all of the following medical conditions:

(1) Acquired immune deficiency syndrome (AIDS).

(2) Anorexia.

(3) Arthritis.

(4) Cachexia.

(5) Cancer.

(6) Chronic pain.

(7) Glaucoma.

(8) Migraine.

(9) Persistent muscle spasms, including, but not limited to, spasms associated with multiple sclerosis.

(10) Seizures, including, but not limited to, seizures associated with epilepsy.

(11) Severe nausea.

(12) Any other chronic or persistent medical symptom that either:

(A) Substantially limits the ability of the person to conduct one or more major life activities as defined in the federal Americans with Disabilities Act of 1990 (Public Law 101-336).

(B) If not alleviated, may cause serious harm to the patient's safety or physical or mental health.

(i) "Written documentation" means accurate reproductions of those portions of a patient's medical records that have been created by the attending physician, that contain the information required by paragraph (2) of subdivision (a) of Section 11362.715, and that the patient may submit as part of an application for an identification card.

(Amended by Stats. 2017, Ch. 775, Sec. 112. (SB 798) Effective January 1, 2018.)

11362.71.

(a) (1) The department shall establish and maintain a voluntary program for the issuance of identification cards to qualified patients who satisfy the requirements of this article and voluntarily apply to the identification card program.

(2) The department shall establish and maintain a 24-hour, toll-free telephone number that will enable state and local law enforcement officers to have immediate access to information necessary to verify the validity of an identification card issued by the department, until a cost-effective Internet Web-based system can be developed for this purpose.

(b) Every county health department, or the county's designee, shall do all of the following:

(1) Provide applications upon request to individuals seeking to join the identification card program.

(2) Receive and process completed applications in accordance with Section 11362.72.

(3) Maintain records of identification card programs.

(4) Utilize protocols developed by the department pursuant to paragraph (1) of subdivision (d).

(5) Issue identification cards developed by the department to approved applicants and designated primary caregivers.

(c) The county board of supervisors may designate another health-related governmental or nongovernmental entity or organization to perform the functions described in subdivision (b), except for an entity or organization that cultivates or distributes cannabis.

(d) The department shall develop all of the following:

(1) Protocols that shall be used by a county health department or the county's designee to implement the responsibilities described in subdivision (b), including, but not limited to, protocols to confirm the accuracy of information contained in an application and to protect the confidentiality of program records.

(2) Application forms that shall be issued to requesting applicants.

(3) An identification card that identifies a person authorized to engage in the medical use of cannabis and an identification card that identifies the person's designated primary caregiver, if any. The two identification cards developed pursuant to this paragraph shall be easily distinguishable from each other.

(e) No person or designated primary caregiver in possession of a valid identification card shall be subject to arrest for possession, transportation, delivery, or cultivation of medicinal cannabis in an amount established pursuant to this article, unless there is probable cause to believe that the information contained in the card is false or falsified, the card has been obtained by means of fraud, or the person is otherwise in violation of the provisions of this article.

(f) It shall not be necessary for a person to obtain an identification card in order to claim the protections of Section 11362.5.

(Amended by Stats. 2017, Ch. 27, Sec. 135. (SB 94) Effective June 27, 2017.)

11362.712.

(a) Commencing on January 1, 2018, a qualified patient must possess a physician's recommendation that complies with Article 25 (commencing with Section 2525) of Chapter 5 of Division 2 of the Business and Professions Code. Failure to comply with this requirement shall not, however, affect any of the protections provided to patients or their primary caregivers by Section 11362.5.

(b) A county health department or the county's designee shall develop protocols to ensure that, commencing upon January 1, 2018, all identification cards issued pursuant to Section 11362.71 are supported by a physician's recommendation that complies with Article 25 (commencing with Section 2525) of Chapter 5 of Division 2 of the Business and Professions Code.

(Added November 8, 2016, by initiative Proposition 64, Sec. 5.1.)

11362.713.

(a) Information identifying the names, addresses, or social security numbers of patients, their medical conditions, or the names of their primary caregivers, received and contained in the records of the State Department of Public Health and by any county public health department are hereby deemed "medical information" within the meaning of the Confidentiality of Medical Information Act (Part 2.6 (commencing with Section 56) of Division 1 of the Civil Code) and shall not be disclosed by the department or by any county public health department except in accordance with the restrictions on disclosure of individually identifiable information under the Confidentiality of Medical Information Act.

(b) Within 24 hours of receiving any request to disclose the name, address, or social security number of a patient, their medical condition, or the name of their primary caregiver, the State Department of Public Health or any county public health agency shall contact the patient and inform the patient of the request and if the request was made in writing, a copy of the request.

(c) Notwithstanding Section 56.10 of the Civil Code, neither the State Department of Public Health, nor any county public health agency, shall disclose, nor shall they be ordered by agency or court to disclose, the names, addresses, or social security numbers of patients, their medical conditions, or the names of their primary caregivers, sooner than the 10th day after which the patient whose records are sought to be disclosed has been contacted.

(d) No identification card application system or database used or maintained by the State Department of Public Health or by any county department of public health or the county's designee as provided in Section 11362.71 shall contain any personal information of any qualified patient, including, but not limited to, the patient's name, address, social security number, medical conditions, or the names of their primary caregivers. Such an application system or database may only contain a unique user identification number, and when that number is entered, the only information that may be provided is whether the card is valid or invalid.

(Added November 8, 2016, by initiative Proposition 64, Sec. 5.2.)

11362.715.

(a) A person who seeks an identification card shall pay the fee, as provided in Section 11362.755, and provide all of the following to the county health department or the county's designee on a form developed and provided by the department:

(1) The name of the person and proof of his or her residency within the county.

(2) Written documentation by the attending physician in the person's medical records stating that the person has been diagnosed with a serious medical condition and that the medicinal use of cannabis is appropriate.

(3) The name, office address, office telephone number, and California medical license number of the person's attending physician.

(4) The name and the duties of the primary caregiver.

(5) A government-issued photo identification card of the person and of the designated primary caregiver, if any. If the applicant is a person under 18 years of age, a certified copy of a birth certificate shall be deemed sufficient proof of identity.

(b) If the person applying for an identification card lacks the capacity to make medical decisions, the application may be made by the person's legal representative, including, but not limited to, any of the following:

(1) A conservator with authority to make medical decisions.

(2) An attorney-in-fact under a durable power of attorney for health care or surrogate decisionmaker authorized under another advanced health care directive.

(3) Any other individual authorized by statutory or decisional law to make medical decisions for the person.

(c) The legal representative described in subdivision (b) may also designate in the application an individual, including himself or herself, to serve as a primary caregiver for the person, provided that the individual meets the definition of a primary caregiver.

(d) The person or legal representative submitting the written information and documentation described in subdivision (a) shall retain a copy thereof.

(Amended by Stats. 2017, Ch. 27, Sec. 136. (SB 94) Effective June 27, 2017.)

11362.72.

(a) Within 30 days of receipt of an application for an identification card, a county health department or the county's designee shall do all of the following:

(1) For purposes of processing the application, verify that the information contained in the application is accurate. If the person is less than 18 years of age, the county health department or its designee shall also contact the parent with legal authority to make medical decisions, legal guardian, or other person or entity with legal authority to make medical decisions, to verify the information.

(2) Verify with the Medical Board of California or the Osteopathic Medical Board of California that the attending physician has a license in good standing to practice medicine or osteopathy in the state.

(3) Contact the attending physician by facsimile, telephone, or mail to confirm that the medical records submitted by the patient are a true and correct copy of those contained in the physician's office records. When contacted by a county health department or the county's designee, the attending physician shall confirm or deny that the contents of the medical records are accurate.

(4) Take a photograph or otherwise obtain an electronically transmissible image of the applicant and of the designated primary caregiver, if any.

(5) Approve or deny the application. If an applicant who meets the requirements of Section 11362.715 can establish that an identification card is needed on an emergency basis, the county or its designee shall issue a temporary identification card that shall be valid for 30 days from the date of issuance. The county, or its designee, may extend the temporary identification card for no more than 30 days at a time, so long as the applicant continues to meet the requirements of this paragraph.

(b) If the county health department or the county's designee approves the application, it shall, within 24 hours, or by the end of the next working day of approving the application, electronically transmit the following information to the department:

(1) A unique user identification number of the applicant.

(2) The date of expiration of the identification card.

(3) The name and telephone number of the county health department or the county's designee that has approved the application.

(c) The county health department or the county's designee shall issue an identification card to the applicant and to his or her designated primary caregiver, if any, within five working days of approving the application.

(d) In any case involving an incomplete application, the applicant shall assume responsibility for rectifying the deficiency. The county shall have 14 days from the receipt of information from the applicant pursuant to this subdivision to approve or deny the application.

(Added by Stats. 2003, Ch. 875, Sec. 2. Effective January 1, 2004.)

11362.735.

(a) An identification card issued by the county health department shall be serially numbered and shall contain all of the following:

(1) A unique user identification number of the cardholder.

(2) The date of expiration of the identification card.

(3) The name and telephone number of the county health department or the county's designee that has approved the application.

(4) A 24-hour, toll-free telephone number, to be maintained by the department, that will enable state and local law enforcement officers to have immediate access to information necessary to verify the validity of the card.

(5) Photo identification of the cardholder.

(b) A separate identification card shall be issued to the person's designated primary caregiver, if any, and shall include a photo identification of the caregiver.

(Added by Stats. 2003, Ch. 875, Sec. 2. Effective January 1, 2004.)

11362.74.

(a) The county health department or the county's designee may deny an application only for any of the following reasons:

(1) The applicant did not provide the information required by Section 11362.715, and upon notice of the deficiency pursuant to subdivision (d) of Section 11362.72, did not provide the information within 30 days.

(2) The county health department or the county's designee determines that the information provided was false.

(3) The applicant does not meet the criteria set forth in this article.

(b) Any person whose application has been denied pursuant to subdivision (a) may not reapply for six months from the date of denial unless otherwise authorized by the county health department or the county's designee or by a court of competent jurisdiction.

(c) Any person whose application has been denied pursuant to subdivision (a) may appeal that decision to the department. The county health department or the county's designee shall make available a telephone number or address to which the denied applicant can direct an appeal.

(Added by Stats. 2003, Ch. 875, Sec. 2. Effective January 1, 2004.)

11362.745.

(a) An identification card shall be valid for a period of one year.

(b) Upon annual renewal of an identification card, the county health department or its designee shall verify all new information and may verify any other information that has not changed.

(c) The county health department or the county's designee shall transmit its determination of approval or denial of a renewal to the department.

(Added by Stats. 2003, Ch. 875, Sec. 2. Effective January 1, 2004.)

11362.755.

(a) Each county health department or the county's designee may charge a fee for all costs incurred by the county or the county's designee for administering the program pursuant to this article.

(b) In no event shall the amount of the fee charged by a county health department exceed one hundred dollars ($100) per application or renewal.

(c) Upon satisfactory proof of participation and eligibility in the Medi-Cal program, a Medi-Cal beneficiary shall receive a 50 percent reduction in the fees established pursuant to this section.

(d) Upon satisfactory proof that a qualified patient, or the legal guardian of a qualified patient under the age of 18, is a medically indigent adult who is eligible for and participates in the County Medical Services Program, the fee established pursuant to this section shall be waived.

(e) In the event the fees charged and collected by a county health department are not sufficient to pay for the administrative costs incurred in discharging the county health department's duties with respect to the mandatory identification card system, the Legislature, upon request by the county health department, shall reimburse the county health department for those reasonable administrative costs in excess of the fees charged and collected by the county health department.

(Amended November 8, 2016, by initiative Proposition 64, Sec. 5.3.)

11362.76.

(a) A person who possesses an identification card shall:

(1) Within seven days, notify the county health department or the county's designee of any change in the person's attending physician or designated primary caregiver, if any.

(2) Annually submit to the county health department or the county's designee the following:

(A) Updated written documentation of the person's serious medical condition.

(B) The name and duties of the person's designated primary caregiver, if any, for the forthcoming year.

(b) If a person who possesses an identification card fails to comply with this section, the card shall be deemed expired. If an identification card expires, the identification card of any designated primary caregiver of the person shall also expire.

(c) If the designated primary caregiver has been changed, the previous primary caregiver shall return his or her identification card to the department or to the county health department or the county's designee.

(d) If the owner or operator or an employee of the owner or operator of a provider has been designated as a primary caregiver pursuant to paragraph (1) of subdivision (d) of Section 11362.7, of the qualified patient or person with an identification card, the owner or operator shall notify the county health department or the county's designee, pursuant to Section 11362.715, if a change in the designated primary caregiver has occurred.

(Added by Stats. 2003, Ch. 875, Sec. 2. Effective January 1, 2004.)

11362.765.

(a) Subject to the requirements of this article, the individuals specified in subdivision (b) shall not be subject, on that sole basis, to criminal liability under Section 11357, 11358, 11359, 11360, 11366, 11366.5, or 11570. This section does not authorize the individual to smoke or otherwise consume cannabis unless otherwise authorized by this article, nor shall anything in this section authorize any individual or group to cultivate or distribute cannabis for profit.

(b) Subdivision (a) shall apply to all of the following:

(1) A qualified patient or a person with an identification card who transports or processes cannabis for his or her own personal medical use.

(2) A designated primary caregiver who transports, processes, administers, delivers, or gives away cannabis for medical purposes, in amounts not exceeding those established in subdivision (a) of Section 11362.77, only to the qualified patient of the primary caregiver, or to the person with an identification card who has designated the individual as a primary caregiver.

(3) An individual who provides assistance to a qualified patient or a person with an identification card, or his or her designated primary caregiver, in administering medicinal cannabis to the qualified patient or person or acquiring the skills necessary to cultivate or administer cannabis for medical purposes to the qualified patient or person.

(c) A primary caregiver who receives compensation for actual expenses, including reasonable compensation incurred for services provided to an eligible qualified patient or person with an identification card to enable that person to use cannabis under this article, or for payment for out-of-pocket expenses incurred in providing those services, or both, shall not, on the sole basis of that fact, be subject to prosecution or punishment under Section 11359 or 11360.

(Amended by Stats. 2017, Ch. 27, Sec. 137. (SB 94) Effective June 27, 2017.)

11362.768.

(a) This section shall apply to individuals specified in subdivision (b) of Section 11362.765.

(b) No medicinal cannabis cooperative, collective, dispensary, operator, establishment, or provider who possesses, cultivates, or distributes medicinal cannabis pursuant to this article shall be located within a 600-foot radius of a school.

(c) The distance specified in this section shall be the horizontal distance measured in a straight line from the property line of the school to the closest property line of the lot on which the medicinal cannabis cooperative, collective, dispensary, operator, establishment, or provider is to be located without regard to intervening structures.

(d) This section shall not apply to a medicinal cannabis cooperative, collective, dispensary, operator, establishment, or provider that is also a licensed residential medical or elder care facility.

(e) This section shall apply only to a medicinal cannabis cooperative, collective, dispensary, operator, establishment, or provider that is authorized by law to possess, cultivate, or distribute medicinal cannabis and that has a storefront or mobile retail outlet which ordinarily requires a local business license.

(f) Nothing in this section shall prohibit a city, county, or city and county from adopting ordinances or policies that further restrict the location or establishment of a medicinal cannabis cooperative, collective, dispensary, operator, establishment, or provider.

(g) This section does not preempt local ordinances, adopted prior to January 1, 2011, that regulate the location or establishment of a medicinal cannabis cooperative, collective, dispensary, operator, establishment, or provider.

(h) For the purposes of this section, "school" means any public or private school providing instruction in kindergarten or any of grades 1 to 12, inclusive, but does not include any private school in which education is primarily conducted in private homes.
(Amended by Stats. 2017, Ch. 27, Sec. 138. (SB 94) Effective June 27, 2017.)

11362.769.

Indoor and outdoor medical cannabis cultivation shall be conducted in accordance with state and local laws. State agencies, including, but not limited to, the Department of Food and Agriculture, the State Board of Forestry and Fire Protection, the Department of Fish and Wildlife, the State Water Resources Control Board, the California regional water quality control boards, and traditional state law enforcement agencies shall address environmental impacts of medical cannabis cultivation and shall coordinate, when appropriate, with cities and counties and their law enforcement agencies in enforcement efforts.
(Amended by Stats. 2016, Ch. 32, Sec. 66. (SB 837) Effective June 27, 2016.)

11362.77.

(a) A qualified patient or primary caregiver may possess no more than eight ounces of dried cannabis per qualified patient. In addition, a qualified patient or primary caregiver may also maintain no more than six mature or 12 immature cannabis plants per qualified patient.

(b) If a qualified patient or primary caregiver has a physician's recommendation that this quantity does not meet the qualified patient's medical needs, the qualified patient or primary caregiver may possess an amount of cannabis consistent with the patient's needs.

(c) Counties and cities may retain or enact medicinal cannabis guidelines allowing qualified patients or primary caregivers to exceed the state limits set forth in subdivision (a).

(d) Only the dried mature processed flowers of female cannabis plant or the plant conversion shall be considered when determining allowable quantities of cannabis under this section.

(e) A qualified patient or a person holding a valid identification card, or the designated primary caregiver of that qualified patient or person, may possess amounts of cannabis consistent with this article.
(Amended by Stats. 2017, Ch. 27, Sec. 139. (SB 94) Effective June 27, 2017.)

11362.78.

A state or local law enforcement agency or officer shall not refuse to accept an identification card issued pursuant to this article unless the state or local law enforcement agency or officer has probable cause to believe that the information contained in the card is false or fraudulent, or the card is being used fraudulently.
(Amended by Stats. 2017, Ch. 27, Sec. 142. (SB 94) Effective June 27, 2017.)

11362.785.

(a) Nothing in this article shall require any accommodation of medicinal use of cannabis on the property or premises of a place of employment or during the hours of employment or on the property or premises of a jail, correctional facility, or other type of penal institution in which prisoners reside or persons under arrest are detained.

(b) Notwithstanding subdivision (a), a person shall not be prohibited or prevented from obtaining and submitting the written information and documentation necessary to apply for an identification card on the basis that the person is incarcerated in a jail, correctional facility, or other penal institution in which prisoners reside or persons under arrest are detained.

(c) This article does not prohibit a jail, correctional facility, or other penal institution in which prisoners reside or persons under arrest are detained, from permitting a prisoner or a person under arrest who has an identification card, to use cannabis for medicinal purposes under circumstances that will not endanger the health or safety of other prisoners or the security of the facility.

(d) This article does not require a governmental, private, or any other health insurance provider or health care service plan to be liable for a claim for reimbursement for the medicinal use of cannabis.

(Amended by Stats. 2017, Ch. 27, Sec. 143. (SB 94) Effective June 27, 2017.)

11362.79.

This article does not authorize a qualified patient or person with an identification card to engage in the smoking of medicinal cannabis under any of the following circumstances:
(a) In a place where smoking is prohibited by law.
(b) In or within 1,000 feet of the grounds of a school, recreation center, or youth center, unless the medicinal use occurs within a residence.
(c) On a schoolbus.
(d) While in a motor vehicle that is being operated.
(e) While operating a boat.
(Amended by Stats. 2017, Ch. 27, Sec. 144. (SB 94) Effective June 27, 2017.)

11362.795.

(a) (1) Any criminal defendant who is eligible to use cannabis pursuant to Section 11362.5 may request that the court confirm that he or she is allowed to use medicinal cannabis while he or she is on probation or released on bail.

(2) The court's decision and the reasons for the decision shall be stated on the record and an entry stating those reasons shall be made in the minutes of the court.

(3) During the period of probation or release on bail, if a physician recommends that the probationer or defendant use medicinal cannabis, the probationer or defendant may request a modification of the conditions of probation or bail to authorize the use of medicinal cannabis.

(4) The court's consideration of the modification request authorized by this subdivision shall comply with the requirements of this section.

(b) (1) Any person who is to be released on parole from a jail, state prison, school, road camp, or other state or local institution of confinement and who is eligible to use medicinal cannabis pursuant to Section 11362.5 may request that he or she be allowed to use medicinal cannabis during the period he or she is released on parole. A parolee's written conditions of parole shall reflect whether or not a request for a modification of the conditions of his or her parole to use medicinal cannabis was made, and whether the request was granted or denied.

(2) During the period of the parole, where a physician recommends that the parolee use medicinal cannabis, the parolee may request a modification of the conditions of the parole to authorize the use of medicinal cannabis.

(3) Any parolee whose request to use medicinal cannabis while on parole was denied may pursue an administrative appeal of the decision. Any decision on the appeal shall be in writing and shall reflect the reasons for the decision.

(4) The administrative consideration of the modification request authorized by this subdivision shall comply with the requirements of this section.
(Amended by Stats. 2017, Ch. 27, Sec. 145. (SB 94) Effective June 27, 2017.)

11362.8.

A professional licensing board shall not impose a civil penalty or take other disciplinary action against a licensee based solely on the fact that the licensee has performed acts that are necessary or appropriate to carry out the licensee's role as a designated primary caregiver to a person who is a qualified patient or who possesses a lawful identification card issued pursuant to Section 11362.72. However, this section shall not apply to acts performed by a physician relating to the discussion or recommendation of the medical use of cannabis to a patient. These discussions or recommendations, or both, shall be governed by Section 11362.5.
(Amended by Stats. 2017, Ch. 27, Sec. 146. (SB 94) Effective June 27, 2017.)

11362.81.

(a) A person specified in subdivision (b) shall be subject to the following penalties:
(1) For the first offense, imprisonment in the county jail for no more than six months or a fine not to exceed one thousand dollars ($1,000), or both.
(2) For a second or subsequent offense, imprisonment in the county jail for no more than one year, or a fine not to exceed one thousand dollars ($1,000), or both.

(b) Subdivision (a) applies to any of the following:
(1) A person who fraudulently represents a medical condition or fraudulently provides any material misinformation to a physician, county health department or the county's designee, or state or local law enforcement agency or officer, for the purpose of falsely obtaining an identification card.
(2) A person who steals or fraudulently uses any person's identification card in order to acquire, possess, cultivate, transport, use, produce, or distribute cannabis.
(3) A person who counterfeits, tampers with, or fraudulently produces an identification card.
(4) A person who breaches the confidentiality requirements of this article to information provided to, or contained in the records of, the department or of a county health department or the county's designee pertaining to an identification card program.

(c) In addition to the penalties prescribed in subdivision (a), a person described in subdivision (b) may be precluded from attempting to obtain, or obtaining or using, an identification card for a period of up to six months at the discretion of the court.

(d) In addition to the requirements of this article, the Attorney General shall develop and adopt appropriate guidelines to ensure the security and nondiversion of cannabis grown for medicinal use by patients qualified under the Compassionate Use Act of 1996.
(Amended by Stats. 2017, Ch. 27, Sec. 147. (SB 94) Effective June 27, 2017.)

11362.82.

If any section, subdivision, sentence, clause, phrase, or portion of this article is for any reason held invalid or unconstitutional by any court of competent jurisdiction, that portion shall be deemed a separate, distinct, and independent provision, and that holding shall not affect the validity of the remaining portion thereof.
(Added by Stats. 2003, Ch. 875, Sec. 2. Effective January 1, 2004.)

11362.83.

Nothing in this article shall prevent a city or other local governing body from adopting and enforcing any of the following:

(a) Adopting local ordinances that regulate the location, operation, or establishment of a medicinal cannabis cooperative or collective.

(b) The civil and criminal enforcement of local ordinances described in subdivision (a).

(c) Enacting other laws consistent with this article.

(Amended by Stats. 2017, Ch. 27, Sec. 148. (SB 94) Effective June 27, 2017.)

11362.84.

The status and conduct of a qualified patient who acts in accordance with the Compassionate Use Act shall not, by itself, be used to restrict or abridge custodial or parental rights to minor children in any action or proceeding under the jurisdiction of family or juvenile court.

(Added November 8, 2016, by initiative Proposition 64, Sec. 5.4.)

11362.85.

Upon a determination by the California Attorney General that the federal schedule of controlled substances has been amended to reclassify or declassify cannabis, the Legislature may amend or repeal the provisions of this code, as necessary, to conform state law to such changes in federal law.

(Amended by Stats. 2017, Ch. 27, Sec. 149. (SB 94) Effective June 27, 2017. Note: Section 11362.9 is in Article 2, following Section 11362.5. Note: This section was added on Nov. 8, 2016, by initiative Prop. 64.)

ARTICLE 3. Peyote [11363- 11363.]

(Article 3 added by Stats. 1972, Ch. 1407.)

11363.

Every person who plants, cultivates, harvests, dries, or processes any plant of the genus Lophophora, also known as peyote, or any part thereof shall be punished by imprisonment in the county jail for a period of not more than one year or the state prison. (Amended by Stats. 1976, Ch. 1139.)

ARTICLE 4. Miscellaneous Offenses and Provisions [11364 - 11376.5]

(Article 4 added by Stats. 1972, Ch. 1407.)

11364.

(a) It is unlawful to possess an opium pipe or any device, contrivance, instrument, or paraphernalia used for unlawfully injecting or smoking (1) a controlled substance specified in subdivision (b), (c), or (e) or paragraph (1) of subdivision (f) of Section 11054, specified in paragraph (14), (15), or (20) of subdivision (d) of Section 11054, specified in subdivision (b) or (c) of Section 11055, or specified in paragraph (2) of subdivision (d) of Section 11055, or (2) a controlled substance that is a narcotic drug classified in Schedule III, IV, or V.

(b) This section shall not apply to hypodermic needles or syringes that have been containerized for safe disposal in a container that meets state and federal standards for disposal of sharps waste.

(c) Until January 1, 2021, as a public health measure intended to prevent the transmission of HIV, viral hepatitis, and other bloodborne diseases among persons who use syringes and hypodermic needles, and to prevent subsequent infection of sexual partners, newborn children, or other persons, this section shall not apply to the possession solely for personal use of hypodermic needles or syringes if acquired from a physician, pharmacist, hypodermic needle and syringe exchange program, or any other source that is authorized by law to provide sterile syringes or hypodermic needles without a prescription.

(Amended by Stats. 2014, Ch. 331, Sec. 8. (AB 1743) Effective January 1, 2015.)

11364.5.

(a) Except as authorized by law, no person shall maintain or operate any place of business in which drug paraphernalia is kept, displayed or offered in any manner, sold, furnished, transferred or given away unless such drug paraphernalia is completely and wholly kept, displayed or offered within a separate room or enclosure to which persons under the age of 18 years not accompanied by a parent or legal guardian are excluded. Each entrance to such a room or enclosure shall be signposted in reasonably visible and legible words to the effect that drug paraphernalia is kept, displayed or offered in such room or enclosure and that minors, unless accompanied by a parent or legal guardian, are excluded.

(b) Except as authorized by law, no owner, manager, proprietor or other person in charge of any room or enclosure, within any place of business, in which drug paraphernalia is kept, displayed or offered in any manner, sold, furnished, transferred or given away shall permit or allow any person under the age of 18 years to enter, be in, remain in or visit such room or enclosure unless that minor person is accompanied by one of his or her parents or by his or her legal guardian.

(c) Unless authorized by law, no person under the age of 18 years shall enter, be in, remain in, or visit any room or enclosure in any place of business in which drug paraphernalia is kept, displayed or offered in any manner, sold, furnished, transferred, or given away unless accompanied by one of his or her parents or by his or her legal guardian.

(d) As used in this section, "drug paraphernalia" means all equipment, products, and materials of any kind which are intended for use or designed for use, in planting, propagating, cultivating, growing, harvesting, manufacturing, compounding, converting, producing, processing, preparing, testing, analyzing, packaging, repackaging, storing, containing, concealing, injecting, ingesting, inhaling, or otherwise introducing into the human body a controlled substance. "Drug paraphernalia" includes, but is not limited to, all of the following:

(1) Kits intended for use or designed for use in planting, propagating, cultivating, growing, or harvesting of any species of plant which is a controlled substance or from which a controlled substance can be derived.

(2) Kits intended for use or designed for use in manufacturing, compounding, converting, producing, processing, or preparing controlled substances.

(3) Isomerization devices intended for use or designed for use in increasing the potency of any species of plant which is a controlled substance.

(4) Testing equipment intended for use or designed for use in identifying, or in analyzing the strength, effectiveness, or purity of controlled substances.

(5) Scales and balances intended for use or designed for use in weighing or measuring controlled substances.

(6) Diluents and adulterants, such as quinine hydrochloride, mannitol, mannite, dextrose, and lactose, intended for use or designed for use in cutting controlled substances.

(7) Separation gins and sifters intended for use or designed for use in removing twigs and seeds from, or in otherwise cleaning or refining, cannabis.

(8) Blenders, bowls, containers, spoons, and mixing devices intended for use or designed for use in compounding controlled substances.

(9) Capsules, balloons, envelopes, and other containers intended for use or designed for use in packaging small quantities of controlled substances.

(10) Containers and other objects intended for use or designed for use in storing or concealing controlled substances.

(11) Hypodermic syringes, needles, and other objects intended for use or designed for use in parenterally injecting controlled substances into the human body.

(12) Objects intended for use or designed for use in ingesting, inhaling, or otherwise introducing cannabis, cocaine, hashish, or hashish oil into the human body, such as the following:

(A) Metal, wooden, acrylic, glass, stone, plastic, or ceramic pipes with or without screens, permanent screens, hashish heads, or punctured metal bowls.

(B) Water pipes.

(C) Carburetion tubes and devices.

(D) Smoking and carburetion masks.

(E) Roach clips, meaning objects used to hold burning material, such as a cannabis cigarette that has become too small or too short to be held in the hand.

(F) Miniature cocaine spoons, and cocaine vials.

(G) Chamber pipes.

(H) Carburetor pipes.

(I) Electric pipes.

(J) Air-driven pipes.

(K) Chillums.

(L) Bongs.

(M) Ice pipes or chillers.

(e) In determining whether an object is drug paraphernalia, a court or other authority may consider, in addition to all other logically relevant factors, the following:

(1) Statements by an owner or by anyone in control of the object concerning its use.

(2) Prior convictions, if any, of an owner, or of anyone in control of the object, under any state or federal law relating to any controlled substance.

(3) Direct or circumstantial evidence of the intent of an owner, or of anyone in control of the object, to deliver it to persons whom he or she knows, or should reasonably know, intend to use the object to facilitate a violation of this section. The innocence of an owner, or of anyone in control of the object, as to a direct violation of this section shall not prevent a finding that the object is intended for use, or designed for use, as drug paraphernalia.

(4) Instructions, oral or written, provided with the object concerning its use.

(5) Descriptive materials, accompanying the object which explain or depict its use.

(6) National and local advertising concerning its use.

(7) The manner in which the object is displayed for sale.

(8) Whether the owner, or anyone in control of the object, is a legitimate supplier of like or related items to the community, such as a licensed distributor or dealer of tobacco products.

(9) The existence and scope of legitimate uses for the object in the community.

(10) Expert testimony concerning its use.

(f) This section shall not apply to any of the following:

(1) Any pharmacist or other authorized person who sells or furnishes drug paraphernalia described in paragraph (11) of subdivision (d) upon the prescription of a physician, dentist, podiatrist, or veterinarian.

(2) Any physician, dentist, podiatrist, or veterinarian who furnishes or prescribes drug paraphernalia described in paragraph (11) of subdivision (d) to his or her patients.

(3) Any manufacturer, wholesaler, or retailer licensed by the California State Board of Pharmacy to sell or transfer drug paraphernalia described in paragraph (11) of subdivision (d).

(g) Notwithstanding any other provision of law, including Section 11374, violation of this section shall not constitute a criminal offense, but operation of a business in violation of the provisions of this section shall be grounds for revocation or nonrenewal of any license, permit, or other entitlement previously issued by a city, county, or city and county for the privilege of engaging in such business and shall be grounds for denial of any future license, permit, or other entitlement authorizing the conduct of such business or any other business, if the business includes the sale of drug paraphernalia.

(Amended by Stats. 2017, Ch. 27, Sec. 151. (SB 94) Effective June 27, 2017.)

11364.7.

(a) (1) Except as authorized by law, any person who delivers, furnishes, or transfers, possesses with intent to deliver, furnish, or transfer, or manufactures with the intent to deliver, furnish, or transfer, drug paraphernalia, knowing, or under circumstances where one reasonably should know, that it will be used to plant, propagate, cultivate, grow, harvest, compound, convert, produce, process, prepare, test, analyze, pack, repack, store, contain, conceal, inject, ingest, inhale, or otherwise introduce into the human body a controlled substance, except as provided in subdivision (b), in violation of this division, is guilty of a misdemeanor.

(2) A public entity, its agents, or employees shall not be subject to criminal prosecution for distribution of hypodermic needles or syringes or any materials deemed by a local or state health department to be necessary to prevent the spread of communicable diseases, or to prevent drug overdose, injury, or disability to participants in clean needle and syringe exchange projects authorized by the public entity pursuant to Chapter 18 (commencing with Section 121349) of Part 4 of Division 105.

(b) Except as authorized by law, any person who manufactures with intent to deliver, furnish, or transfer drug paraphernalia knowing, or under circumstances where one reasonably should know, that it will be used to plant, propagate, cultivate, grow, harvest, manufacture, compound, convert, produce, process, prepare, test, analyze, pack, repack, store, contain, conceal, inject, ingest, inhale, or otherwise introduce into the human body cocaine, cocaine base, heroin, phencyclidine, or methamphetamine in violation of this division shall be punished by imprisonment in a county jail for not more than one year, or in the state prison.

(c) Except as authorized by law, any person, 18 years of age or over, who violates subdivision (a) by delivering, furnishing, or transferring drug paraphernalia to a person under 18 years of age who is at least three years his or her junior, or who, upon the grounds of a public or private elementary, vocational, junior high, or high school, possesses a hypodermic needle, as defined in paragraph (7) of subdivision (a) of Section 11014.5, with the intent to deliver, furnish, or transfer the hypodermic needle, knowing, or under circumstances where one reasonably should know, that it will be used by a person under 18 years of age to inject into the human body a controlled substance, is guilty of a misdemeanor and shall be punished by imprisonment in a county jail for not more than one year, by a fine of not more than one thousand dollars ($1,000), or by both that imprisonment and fine.

(d) The violation, or the causing or the permitting of a violation, of subdivision (a), (b), or (c) by a holder of a business or liquor license issued by a city, county, or city and county, or by the State of California, and in the course of the licensee's business shall be grounds for the revocation of that license.

(e) All drug paraphernalia defined in Section 11014.5 is subject to forfeiture and may be seized by any peace officer pursuant to Section 11471 unless its distribution has been authorized pursuant to subdivision (a).

(f) If any provision of this section or the application thereof to any person or circumstance is held invalid, it is the intent of the Legislature that the invalidity shall not affect other provisions or applications of this section which can be given effect without the invalid provision or application and to this end the provisions of this section are severable. (Amended by Stats. 2018, Ch. 34, Sec. 7. (AB 1810) Effective June 27, 2018.)

11365.

(a) It is unlawful to visit or to be in any room or place where any controlled substances which are specified in subdivision (b), (c), or (e), or paragraph (1) of subdivision (f) of Section 11054, specified in paragraph (14), (15), or (20) of subdivision (d) of Section 11054, or specified in subdivision (b) or (c) or paragraph (2) of subdivision (d) of Section 11055, or which are narcotic drugs classified in Schedule III, IV, or V, are being unlawfully smoked or used with knowledge that such activity is occurring.

(b) This section shall apply only where the defendant aids, assists, or abets the perpetration of the unlawful smoking or use of a controlled substance specified in subdivision (a). This subdivision is declaratory of existing law as expressed in People v. Cressey (1970) 2 Cal. 3d 836. (Amended by Stats. 1991, Ch. 551, Sec. 1.)

11366.

Every person who opens or maintains any place for the purpose of unlawfully selling, giving away, or using any controlled substance which is (1) specified in subdivision (b), (c), or (e), or paragraph (1) of subdivision (f) of Section 11054, specified in paragraph (13), (14), (15), or (20) of subdivision (d) of Section 11054, or specified in subdivision (b), (c), paragraph (1) or (2) of subdivision (d), or paragraph (3) of subdivision (e) of Section 11055, or (2) which is a narcotic drug classified in Schedule III, IV, or V, shall be punished by imprisonment in the county jail for a period of not more than one year or the state prison. (Amended by Stats. 1991, Ch. 492, Sec. 1.)

11366.5.

(a) Any person who has under his or her management or control any building, room, space, or enclosure, either as an owner, lessee, agent, employee, or mortgagee, who knowingly rents, leases, or makes available for use, with or without compensation, the building, room, space, or enclosure for the purpose of unlawfully manufacturing, storing, or distributing any controlled substance for sale or distribution shall be punished by imprisonment in the county jail for not more than one year, or pursuant to subdivision (h) of Section 1170 of the Penal Code.

(b) Any person who has under his or her management or control any building, room, space, or enclosure, either as an owner, lessee, agent, employee, or mortgagee, who knowingly allows the building, room, space, or enclosure to be fortified to suppress law enforcement entry in order to further the sale of any amount of cocaine base as specified in paragraph (1) of subdivision (f) of Section 11054, cocaine as specified in paragraph

(6) of subdivision (b) of Section 11055, heroin, phencyclidine, amphetamine, methamphetamine, or lysergic acid diethylamide and who obtains excessive profits from the use of the building, room, space, or enclosure shall be punished by imprisonment pursuant to subdivision (h) of Section 1170 of the Penal Code for two, three, or four years.

(c) Any person who violates subdivision (a) after previously being convicted of a violation of subdivision (a) shall be punished by imprisonment pursuant to subdivision (h) of Section 1170 of the Penal Code for two, three, or four years.

(d) For the purposes of this section, "excessive profits" means the receipt of consideration of a value substantially higher than fair market value. (Amended by Stats. 2011, Ch. 15, Sec. 164. (AB 109) Effective April 4, 2011. Operative October 1, 2011, by Sec. 636 of Ch. 15, as amended by Stats. 2011, Ch. 39, Sec. 68.)

11366.6.

Any person who utilizes a building, room, space, or enclosure specifically designed to suppress law enforcement entry in order to sell, manufacture, or possess for sale any amount of cocaine base as specified in paragraph (1) of subdivision (f) of Section 11054, cocaine as specified in paragraph (6) of subdivision (b) of Section 11055, heroin, phencyclidine, amphetamine, methamphetamine, or lysergic acid diethylamide shall be punished by imprisonment pursuant to subdivision (h) of Section 1170 of the Penal Code for three, four, or five years. (Amended by Stats. 2011, Ch. 15, Sec. 165. (AB 109) Effective April 4, 2011. Operative October 1, 2011, by Sec. 636 of Ch. 15, as amended by Stats. 2011, Ch. 39, Sec. 68.)

11366.7.

(a) This section shall apply to the following:

(1) Any chemical or drug.

(2) Any laboratory apparatus or device.

(b) Any retailer or wholesaler who sells any item in paragraph (1) or (2) of subdivision (a) with knowledge or the intent that it will be used to unlawfully manufacture, compound, convert, process, or prepare a controlled substance for unlawful sale or distribution, shall be punished by imprisonment in a county jail for not more than one year, or in the state prison, or by a fine not exceeding twenty-five thousand dollars ($25,000), or by both that imprisonment and fine. Any fine collected pursuant to this section shall be distributed as specified in Section 1463.10 of the Penal Code. (Amended by Stats. 1994, Ch. 979, Sec. 1. Effective January 1, 1995.)

11366.8.

(a) Every person who possesses, uses, or controls a false compartment with the intent to store, conceal, smuggle, or transport a controlled substance within the false compartment shall be punished by imprisonment in a county jail for a term of imprisonment not to exceed one year or pursuant to subdivision (h) of Section 1170 of the Penal Code.

(b) Every person who designs, constructs, builds, alters, or fabricates a false compartment for, or installs or attaches a false compartment to, a vehicle with the intent to store, conceal, smuggle, or transport a controlled substance shall be punished by imprisonment pursuant to subdivision (h) of Section 1170 of the Penal Code for 16 months or two or three years.

(c) The term "vehicle" means any of the following vehicles without regard to whether the vehicles are private or commercial, including, but not limited to, cars, trucks, buses, aircraft, boats, ships, yachts, and vessels.

(d) The term "false compartment" means any box, container, space, or enclosure that is intended for use or designed for use to conceal, hide, or otherwise prevent discovery of any controlled substance within or attached to a vehicle, including, but not limited to, any of the following:

(1) False, altered, or modified fuel tanks.

(2) Original factory equipment of a vehicle that is modified, altered, or changed.

(3) Compartment, space, or box that is added to, or fabricated, made, or created from, existing compartments, spaces, or boxes within a vehicle. (Amended by Stats. 2011, Ch. 15, Sec. 166. (AB 109) Effective April 4, 2011. Operative October 1, 2011, by Sec. 636 of Ch. 15, as amended by Stats. 2011, Ch. 39, Sec. 68.)

11367.

All duly authorized peace officers, while investigating violations of this division in performance of their official duties, and any person working under their immediate direction, supervision or instruction, are immune from prosecution under this division. (Added by Stats. 1972, Ch. 1407.)

11367.5.

(a) Any sheriff, chief of police, the Chief of the Division of Law Enforcement, or the Commissioner of the California Highway Patrol, or a designee thereof, may, in his or her discretion, provide controlled substances in his or her possession and control to any duly authorized peace officer or civilian drug detection canine trainer working under the direction of a law enforcement agency, provided the controlled substances are no longer needed as criminal evidence and provided the person receiving the controlled substances, if required by the federal Drug Enforcement Administration, possesses a current and valid federal Drug Enforcement Administration registration which specifically authorizes the recipient to possess controlled substances while providing substance abuse training to law enforcement or the community or while providing canine drug detection training.

(b) All duly authorized peace officers, while providing substance abuse training to law enforcement or the community or while providing canine drug detection training, in performance of their official duties, and any person working under their immediate direction, supervision, or instruction, are immune from prosecution under this division.

(c) (1) Any person receiving controlled substances pursuant to subdivision (a) shall maintain custody and control of the controlled substances and shall keep records regarding any loss of, or damage to, those controlled substances.

(2) All controlled substances shall be maintained in a secure location approved by the dispensing agency.

(3) Any loss shall be reported immediately to the dispensing agency.

(4) All controlled substances shall be returned to the dispensing agency upon the conclusion of the training or upon demand by the dispensing agency.

(Amended by Stats. 2012, Ch. 867, Sec. 9. (SB 1144) Effective January 1, 2013.)

11368.

Every person who forges or alters a prescription or who issues or utters an altered prescription, or who issues or utters a prescription bearing a forged or fictitious signature for any narcotic drug, or who obtains any narcotic drug by any forged, fictitious, or altered prescription, or who has in possession any narcotic drug secured by a forged, fictitious, or altered prescription, shall be punished by imprisonment in the county jail for not less than six months nor more than one year, or in the state prison.

(Amended by Stats. 1990, Ch. 43, Sec. 1.)

11370.

(a) Any person convicted of violating Section 11350, 11351, 11351.5, 11352, 11353, 11355, 11357, 11359, 11360, 11361, 11363, 11366, or 11368, or of committing any offense referred to in those sections, shall not, in any case, be granted probation by the trial court or have the execution of the sentence imposed upon him or her suspended by the court, if he or she has been previously convicted of any offense described in subdivision (c).

(b) Any person who was 18 years of age or over at the time of the commission of the offense and is convicted for the first time of selling, furnishing, administering, or giving a controlled substance which is (1) specified in subdivision (b), (c), (e), or paragraph (1) of subdivision (f) of Section 11054, specified in paragraph (14), (15), or (20) of subdivision (d) of Section 11054, or specified in subdivision (b) or (c) of Section 11055, or (2) which is a narcotic drug classified in Schedule III, IV, or V, to a minor or inducing a minor to use such a controlled substance in violation of law shall not, in any case, be granted probation by the trial court or have the execution of the sentence imposed upon him or her suspended by the court.

(c) Any previous conviction of any of the following offenses, or of an offense under the laws of another state or of the United States which, if committed in this state, would have been punishable as such an offense, shall render a person ineligible for probation or suspension of sentence pursuant to subdivision (a) of this section:

(1) Any felony offense described in this division involving a controlled substance specified in subdivision (b), (c), (e), or paragraph (1) of subdivision (f) of Section 11054, specified in paragraph (13), (14), (15), or (20) of subdivision (d) of Section 11054, or specified in subdivision (b) or (c) of Section 11055.

(2) Any felony offense described in this division involving a narcotic drug classified in Schedule III, IV, or V.

(d) The existence of any previous conviction or fact which would make a person ineligible for suspension of sentence or probation under this section shall be alleged in the information or indictment, and either admitted by the defendant in open court, or found to be true by the jury trying the issue of guilt or by the court where guilt is established by a plea of guilty or nolo contendere or by trial by the court sitting without a jury.

(Amended by Stats. 1986, Ch. 1044, Sec. 13.5.)

11370.1.

(a) Notwithstanding Section 11350 or 11377 or any other provision of law, every person who unlawfully possesses any amount of a substance containing cocaine base, a substance containing cocaine, a substance containing heroin, a substance containing methamphetamine, a crystalline substance containing phencyclidine, a liquid substance containing phencyclidine, plant material containing phencyclidine, or a hand-rolled cigarette treated with phencyclidine while armed with a loaded, operable firearm is guilty of a felony punishable by imprisonment in the state prison for two, three, or four years. As used in this subdivision, "armed with" means having available for immediate offensive or defensive use.

(b) Any person who is convicted under this section shall be ineligible for diversion or deferred entry of judgment under Chapter 2.5 (commencing with Section 1000) of Title 6 of Part 2 of the Penal Code.

(Amended by Stats. 1996, Ch. 1132, Sec. 1. Effective January 1, 1997.)

11370.2.

(a) Any person convicted of a violation of, or of a conspiracy to violate, Section 11351, 11351.5, or 11352 shall receive, in addition to any other punishment authorized by law, including Section 667.5 of the Penal Code, a full, separate, and consecutive three-year term for each prior felony conviction of, or for each prior felony conviction of conspiracy to violate, Section 11380, whether or not the prior conviction resulted in a term of imprisonment.

(b) Any person convicted of a violation of, or of a conspiracy to violate, Section 11378.5, 11379.5, 11379.6, or 11383 shall receive, in addition to any other punishment authorized by law, including Section 667.5 of the Penal Code, a full, separate, and consecutive three-year term for each prior felony conviction of, or for each prior felony conviction of conspiracy to violate, Section 11380, whether or not the prior conviction resulted in a term of imprisonment.

(c) Any person convicted of a violation of, or of a conspiracy to violate, Section 11378 or 11379 with respect to any substance containing a controlled substance specified in paragraph (1) or (2) of subdivision (d) of Section 11055 shall receive, in addition to any other punishment authorized by law, including Section 667.5 of the Penal Code, a full,

separate, and consecutive three-year term for each prior felony conviction of, or for each prior felony conviction of conspiracy to violate, Section 11380, whether or not the prior conviction resulted in a term of imprisonment.

(d) The enhancements provided for in this section shall be pleaded and proven as provided by law.

(e) The conspiracy enhancements provided for in this section shall not be imposed unless the trier of fact finds that the defendant conspirator was substantially involved in the planning, direction, execution, or financing of the underlying offense.

(f) Prior convictions from another jurisdiction qualify for use under this section pursuant to Section 668.

(Amended by Stats. 2017, Ch. 677, Sec. 1. (SB 180) Effective January 1, 2018.)

11370.4.

(a) Any person convicted of a violation of, or of a conspiracy to violate, Section 11351, 11351.5, or 11352 with respect to a substance containing heroin, cocaine base as specified in paragraph (1) of subdivision (f) of Section 11054, or cocaine as specified in paragraph (6) of subdivision (b) of Section 11055 shall receive an additional term as follows:

(1) Where the substance exceeds one kilogram by weight, the person shall receive an additional term of three years.

(2) Where the substance exceeds four kilograms by weight, the person shall receive an additional term of five years.

(3) Where the substance exceeds 10 kilograms by weight, the person shall receive an additional term of 10 years.

(4) Where the substance exceeds 20 kilograms by weight, the person shall receive an additional term of 15 years.

(5) Where the substance exceeds 40 kilograms by weight, the person shall receive an additional term of 20 years.

(6) Where the substance exceeds 80 kilograms by weight, the person shall receive an additional term of 25 years.

The conspiracy enhancements provided for in this subdivision shall not be imposed unless the trier of fact finds that the defendant conspirator was substantially involved in the planning, direction, execution, or financing of the underlying offense.

(b) Any person convicted of a violation of, or of conspiracy to violate, Section 11378, 11378.5, 11379, or 11379.5 with respect to a substance containing methamphetamine, amphetamine, phencyclidine (PCP) and its analogs shall receive an additional term as follows:

(1) Where the substance exceeds one kilogram by weight, or 30 liters by liquid volume, the person shall receive an additional term of three years.

(2) Where the substance exceeds four kilograms by weight, or 100 liters by liquid volume, the person shall receive an additional term of five years.

(3) Where the substance exceeds 10 kilograms by weight, or 200 liters by liquid volume, the person shall receive an additional term of 10 years.

(4) Where the substance exceeds 20 kilograms by weight, or 400 liters by liquid volume, the person shall receive an additional term of 15 years.

In computing the quantities involved in this subdivision, plant or vegetable material seized shall not be included.

The conspiracy enhancements provided for in this subdivision shall not be imposed unless the trier of fact finds that the defendant conspirator was substantially involved in the planning, direction, execution, or financing of the underlying offense.

(c) The additional terms provided in this section shall not be imposed unless the allegation that the weight of the substance containing heroin, cocaine base as specified in paragraph (1) of subdivision (f) of Section 11054, cocaine as specified in paragraph (6) of subdivision (b) of Section 11055, methamphetamine, amphetamine, or phencyclidine (PCP) and its analogs exceeds the amounts provided in this section is charged in the accusatory pleading and admitted or found to be true by the trier of fact.

(d) The additional terms provided in this section shall be in addition to any other punishment provided by law.

(e) Notwithstanding any other provision of law, the court may strike the additional punishment for the enhancements provided in this section if it determines that there are circumstances in mitigation of the additional punishment and states on the record its reasons for striking the additional punishment.

(Amended by Stats. 1998, Ch. 425, Sec. 1. Effective January 1, 1999.)

11370.6.

(a) Every person who possesses any moneys or negotiable instruments in excess of one hundred thousand dollars ($100,000) which have been obtained as the result of the unlawful sale, possession for sale, transportation, manufacture, offer for sale, or offer to manufacture any controlled substance listed in Section 11054, 11055, 11056, 11057, or 11058, with knowledge that the moneys or negotiable instruments have been so obtained, and any person who possesses any moneys or negotiable instruments in excess of one hundred thousand dollars ($100,000) which are intended by that person for the unlawful purchase of any controlled substance listed in Section 11054, 11055, 11056, 11057, or 11058 and who commits an act in substantial furtherance of the unlawful purchase, shall be punished by imprisonment in a county jail for a term not to exceed one year, or by imprisonment pursuant to subdivision (h) of Section 1170 of the Penal Code for two, three, or four years.

(b) In consideration of the constitutional right to counsel afforded by the Sixth Amendment to the United States Constitution and Section 15 of Article 1 of the California Constitution, when a case charged under subdivision (a) involves an attorney who accepts a fee for representing a client in a criminal investigation or proceeding, the prosecution shall additionally be required to prove that the moneys or negotiable instruments were accepted by the attorney with the intent to participate in the unlawful conduct described in subdivision (a) or to disguise or aid in disguising the source of the funds or the nature of the criminal activity.

(c) In determining the guilt or innocence of a person charged under subdivision (a), the trier of fact may consider the following in addition to any other relevant evidence:

(1) The lack of gainful employment by the person charged.

(2) The expert opinion of a qualified controlled substances expert as to the source of the assets.

(3) The existence of documents or ledgers that indicate sales of controlled substances.

(Amended by Stats. 2011, Ch. 15, Sec. 167. (AB 109) Effective April 4, 2011. Operative October 1, 2011, by Sec. 636 of Ch. 15, as amended by Stats. 2011, Ch. 39, Sec. 68.)

11370.9.

(a) It is unlawful for any person knowingly to receive or acquire proceeds, or engage in a transaction involving proceeds, known to be derived from any violation of this division or Division 10.1 with the intent to conceal or disguise or aid in concealing or disguising the nature, location, ownership, control, or source of the proceeds or to avoid a transaction reporting requirement under state or federal law.

(b) It is unlawful for any person knowingly to give, sell, transfer, trade, invest, conceal, transport, or maintain an interest in, or otherwise make available, anything of value which that person knows is intended to be used for the purpose of committing, or furthering the commission of, any violation of this division or Division 10.1 with the intent to conceal or disguise or aid in concealing or disguising the nature, location, ownership, control, or source of the proceeds or to avoid a transaction reporting requirement under state or federal law.

(c) It is unlawful for any person knowingly to direct, plan, organize, initiate, finance, manage, supervise, or facilitate the transportation or transfer of proceeds known to be derived from any violation of this division or Division 10.1 with the intent to conceal or disguise or aid in concealing or disguising the nature, location, ownership, control, or source of the proceeds or to avoid a transaction reporting requirement under state or federal law.

(d) It is unlawful for any person knowingly to conduct a transaction involving proceeds derived from a violation of this division or Division 10.1 when the transaction is designed in whole or in part to conceal or disguise the nature, location, source, ownership, or control of the proceeds known to be derived from a violation of this division or Division 10.1 with the intent to conceal or disguise or aid in concealing or disguising the nature, location, ownership, control, or source of the proceeds or to avoid a transaction reporting requirement under state or federal law.

(e) A violation of this section shall be punished by imprisonment in a county jail for not more than one year or in the state prison for a period of two, three, or four years, by a fine of not more than two hundred fifty thousand dollars ($250,000) or twice the value of the proceeds or property involved in the violation, whichever is greater, or by both that imprisonment and fine. Notwithstanding any other provision of law, each violation of this section shall constitute a separate, punishable offense without limitation.

(f) This section shall apply only to a transaction, or series of related transactions within a 30-day period, involving over twenty-five thousand dollars ($25,000) or to proceeds of a value exceeding twenty-five thousand dollars ($25,000).

(g) In consideration of the constitutional right to counsel afforded by the Sixth Amendment to the United States Constitution and Section 15 of Article 1 of the California Constitution, this section is not intended to apply to the receipt of, or a related transaction involving, a fee by an attorney for the purpose of providing advice or representing a person in a criminal investigation or prosecution.

(h) For the purposes of this section, the following terms have the following meanings:

(1) "Proceeds" means property acquired or derived directly or indirectly from, produced through, or realized through any violation of this division or Division 10.1.

(2) "Transaction" includes a purchase, sale, trade, loan, pledge, investment, gift, transfer, transmission, delivery, deposit, withdrawal, payment, electronic, magnetic, or manual transfer between accounts, exchange of currency, extension of credit, purchase or sale of any monetary instrument, or any other acquisition or disposition of property by whatever means effected.

(3) "Represented by a law enforcement officer" means any representation of fact made by a peace officer as defined in Section 7 of the Penal Code, or a federal officer described in subsection (e) of Sections 1956 and 1957 of Title 18 of the United States Code, or by another person at the direction of, or with the approval of, that peace officer or federal officer.

(Amended by Stats. 1993, Ch. 589, Sec. 89. Effective January 1, 1994.)

11371.

Any person who shall knowingly violate any of the provisions of Section 11153, 11154, 11155, or 11156 with respect to (1) a controlled substance specified in subdivision (b), (c), or (d) of Section 11055, or (2) a controlled substance specified in paragraph (1) of subdivision (b) of Section 11056, or (3) a controlled substance which is a narcotic drug classified in Schedule III, IV, or V, or who in any voluntary manner solicits, induces, encourages or intimidates any minor with the intent that such minor shall commit any such offense, shall be punished by imprisonment pursuant to subdivision (h) of Section 1170 of the Penal Code, or in a county jail not exceeding one year, or by a fine not exceeding twenty thousand dollars ($20,000), or by both such fine and imprisonment.

(Amended by Stats. 2011, Ch. 15, Sec. 168. (AB 109) Effective April 4, 2011. Operative October 1, 2011, by Sec. 636 of Ch. 15, as amended by Stats. 2011, Ch. 39, Sec. 68.)

11371.1.

Any person who shall knowingly violate any of the provisions of Section 11173 or 11174 with respect to (1) a controlled substance specified in subdivision (b), (c), or (d) of Section 11055, or (2) a controlled substance specified in paragraph (1) of subdivision (b) of Section 11056, or (3) a controlled substance which is a narcotic drug classified in Schedule III, IV, or V, or who in any voluntary manner solicits, induces, encourages or intimidates any minor with the intent that such minor shall commit any such offense, shall be punished by imprisonment pursuant to subdivision (h) of Section 1170 of the Penal Code, or in a county jail not exceeding one year.

(Amended by Stats. 2011, Ch. 15, Sec. 169. (AB 109) Effective April 4, 2011. Operative October 1, 2011, by Sec. 636 of Ch. 15, as amended by Stats. 2011, Ch. 39, Sec. 68.)

11372.

(a) In addition to the term of imprisonment provided by law for persons convicted of violating Section 11350, 11351, 11351.5, 11352, 11353, 11355, 11359, 11360, or 11361, the trial court may impose a fine not exceeding twenty thousand dollars ($20,000) for each offense. In no event shall a fine be levied in lieu of or in substitution for the term of imprisonment provided by law for any of these offenses.

(b) Any person receiving an additional term pursuant to paragraph (1) of subdivision (a) of Section 11370.4, may, in addition, be fined by an amount not exceeding one million dollars ($1,000,000) for each offense.

(c) Any person receiving an additional term pursuant to paragraph (2) of subdivision (a) of Section 11370.4, may, in addition, be fined by an amount not to exceed four million dollars ($4,000,000) for each offense.

(d) Any person receiving an additional term pursuant to paragraph (3) of subdivision (a) of Section 11370.4, may, in addition, be fined by an amount not to exceed eight million dollars ($8,000,000) for each offense.

(e) The court shall make a finding, prior to the imposition of the fines authorized by subdivisions (b) to (e), inclusive, that there is a reasonable expectation that the fine, or a substantial portion thereof, could be collected within a reasonable period of time, taking into consideration the defendant's income, earning capacity, and financial resources.

(Amended by Stats. 2002, Ch. 787, Sec. 2. Effective January 1, 2003.)

11372.5.

(a) Every person who is convicted of a violation of Section 11350, 11351, 11351.5, 11352, 11355, 11358, 11359, 11361, 11363, 11364, 11368, 11375, 11377, 11378, 11378.5, 11379, 11379.5, 11379.6, 11380, 11380.5, 11382, 11383, 11390, 11391, or 11550 or subdivision (a) or (c) of Section 11357, or subdivision (a) of Section 11360 of this code, or Section 4230 of the Business and Professions Code shall pay a criminal laboratory analysis fee in the amount of fifty dollars ($50) for each separate offense. The court shall increase the total fine necessary to include this increment.

With respect to those offenses specified in this subdivision for which a fine is not authorized by other provisions of law, the court shall, upon conviction, impose a fine in an amount not to exceed fifty dollars ($50), which shall constitute the increment prescribed by this section and which shall be in addition to any other penalty prescribed by law.

(b) The county treasurer shall maintain a criminalistics laboratories fund. The sum of fifty dollars ($50) shall be deposited into the fund for every conviction under Section 11350, 11351, 11351.5, 11352, 11355, 11358, 11359, 11361, 11363, 11364, 11368, 11375, 11377, 11378, 11378.5, 11379, 11379.5, 11379.6, 11380, 11380.5, 11382, 11383, 11390, 11391, or 11550, subdivision (a) or (c) of Section 11357, or subdivision (a) of Section 11360 of this code, or Section 4230 of the Business and Professions Code, in addition to fines, forfeitures, and other moneys which are transmitted by the courts to the county treasurer pursuant to Section 11502. The deposits shall be made prior to any transfer pursuant to Section 11502. The county may retain an amount of this money equal to its administrative cost incurred pursuant to this section. Moneys in the criminalistics laboratories fund shall, except as otherwise provided in this section, be used exclusively to fund (1) costs incurred by criminalistics laboratories providing microscopic and chemical analyses for controlled substances, in connection with criminal investigations conducted within both the incorporated or unincorporated portions of the county, (2) the purchase and maintenance of equipment for use by these laboratories in performing the analyses, and (3) for continuing education, training, and scientific development of forensic scientists regularly employed by these laboratories. Moneys in the criminalistics laboratory fund shall be in addition to any allocations pursuant to existing law. As used in this section, "criminalistics laboratory" means a laboratory operated by, or under contract with, a city, county, or other public agency, including a criminalistics laboratory of the Department of Justice, (1) which has not less than one regularly employed forensic scientist engaged in the analysis of solid-dose controlled substances, and (2) which is registered as an analytical laboratory with the Drug Enforcement Administration of the United States Department of Justice for the possession of all scheduled controlled substances. In counties served by criminalistics laboratories of the Department of Justice, amounts deposited in the criminalistics laboratories fund, after deduction of appropriate and reasonable county overhead charges not to exceed 5 percent attributable to the collection thereof, shall be paid by the county treasurer once a month to the Controller for deposit into the state General Fund, and shall be excepted from the expenditure requirements otherwise prescribed by this subdivision.

(c) The county treasurer shall, at the conclusion of each fiscal year, determine the amount of any funds remaining in the special fund established pursuant to this section after expenditures for that fiscal year have been made for the purposes herein specified. The board of supervisors may, by resolution, assign the treasurer's duty to determine the amount of remaining funds to the auditor or another county officer. The county treasurer shall annually distribute those surplus funds in accordance with the allocation scheme for distribution of fines and forfeitures set forth in Section 11502.

(Amended by Stats. 2005, Ch. 158, Sec. 23. Effective January 1, 2006.)

11372.7.

(a) Except as otherwise provided in subdivision (b) or (e), each person who is convicted of a violation of this chapter shall pay a drug program fee in an amount not to exceed one hundred fifty dollars ($150) for each separate offense. The court shall increase the total fine, if necessary, to include this increment, which shall be in addition to any other penalty prescribed by law.

(b) The court shall determine whether or not the person who is convicted of a violation of this chapter has the ability to pay a drug program fee. If the court determines that the person has the ability to pay, the court may set the amount to be paid and order the person to pay that sum to the county in a manner that the court believes is reasonable and compatible with the person's financial ability. In its determination of whether a person has the ability to pay, the court shall take into account the amount of any fine imposed upon that person and any amount that person has been ordered to pay in restitution. If the court determines that the person does not have the ability to pay a drug program fee, the person shall not be required to pay a drug program fee.

(c) The county treasurer shall maintain a drug program fund. For every drug program fee assessed and collected pursuant to subdivisions (a) and (b), an amount equal to this assessment shall be deposited into the fund for every conviction pursuant to this chapter, in addition to fines, forfeitures, and other moneys which are transmitted by the courts to the county treasurer pursuant to Sections 11372.5 and 11502. These deposits shall be made prior to any transfer pursuant to Section 11502. Amounts deposited in the drug program fund shall be allocated by the administrator of the county's drug program to drug abuse programs in the schools and the community, subject to the approval of the board of supervisors, as follows:

(1) The moneys in the fund shall be allocated through the planning process established pursuant to Sections 11983, 11983.1, 11983.2, and 11983.3.

(2) A minimum of 33 percent of the fund shall be allocated to primary prevention programs in the schools and the community. Primary prevention programs developed and implemented under this article shall emphasize cooperation in planning and program implementation among schools and community drug abuse agencies, and shall demonstrate coordination through an interagency agreement among county offices of education, school districts, and the county drug program administrator. These primary prevention programs may include:

(A) School- and classroom-oriented programs, including, but not limited to, programs designed to encourage sound decisionmaking, an awareness of values, an awareness of drugs and their effects, enhanced self-esteem, social and practical skills that will assist students toward maturity, enhanced or improved school climate and relationships among all school personnel and students, and furtherance of cooperative efforts of school- and community-based personnel.

(B) School- or community-based nonclassroom alternative programs, or both, including, but not limited to, positive peer group programs, programs involving youth and adults in constructive activities designed as alternatives to drug use, and programs for special target groups, such as women, ethnic minorities, and other high-risk, high-need populations.

(C) Family-oriented programs, including, but not limited to, programs aimed at improving family relationships and involving parents constructively in the education and nurturing of their children, as well as in specific activities aimed at preventing drug abuse.

(d) Moneys deposited into a drug program fund pursuant to this section shall supplement, and shall not supplant, any local funds made available to support the county's drug abuse prevention and treatment efforts.

(e) This section shall not apply to any person convicted of a violation of subdivision (b) of Section 11357 of the Health and Safety Code.

(Amended by Stats. 2002, Ch. 545, Sec. 1.5. Effective January 1, 2003.)

11373.

(a) Whenever any person who is otherwise eligible for probation is granted probation by the trial court after conviction for a violation of any controlled substance offense under this division, the trial court shall, as a condition of probation, order that person to secure education or treatment from a local community agency designated by the court, if the service is available and the person is likely to benefit from the service.

If the defendant is a minor, the trial court shall also order his or her parents or guardian to participate in the education or treatment to the extent the court determines that participation will aid the education or treatment of the minor.

If a minor is found by a juvenile court to have been in possession of any controlled substance, in addition to any other order it may make, the juvenile court shall order the minor to receive education or treatment from a local community agency designated by the court, if the service is available and the person is likely to benefit from the service, and it shall also order his or her parents or guardian to participate in the education or treatment to the extent the court determines that participation will aid the education or treatment of the minor.

(b) The willful failure to complete a court ordered education or treatment program shall be a circumstance in aggravation for purposes of sentencing for any subsequent prosecution for a violation of Section 11353, 11354, or 11380. The failure to complete an education or treatment program because of the person's inability to pay the costs of the program or because of the unavailability to the defendant of appropriate programs is not a willful failure to complete the program.

(Amended by Stats. 1992, Ch. 185, Sec. 1. Effective January 1, 1993.)

11374.

Every person who violates or fails to comply with any provision of this division, except one for which a penalty is otherwise in this division specifically provided, is guilty of a misdemeanor punishable by a fine in a sum not less than thirty dollars ($30) nor more than five hundred dollars ($500), or by imprisonment for not less than 15 nor more than 180 days, or by both.

(Added by Stats. 1972, Ch. 1407.)

11374.5.

(a) Any manufacturer of a controlled substance who disposes of any hazardous substance that is a controlled substance or a chemical used in, or is a byproduct of, the manufacture of a controlled substance in violation of any law regulating the disposal of hazardous substances or hazardous waste is guilty of a public offense punishable by imprisonment pursuant to subdivision (h) of Section 1170 of the Penal Code for two, three, or four years or in the county jail not exceeding one year.

(b) (1) In addition to any other penalty or liability imposed by law, a person who is convicted of violating subdivision (a), or any person who is convicted of the manufacture, sale, possession for sale, possession, transportation, or disposal of any hazardous substance that is a controlled substance or a chemical used in, or is a byproduct of, the manufacture of a controlled substance in violation of any law, shall pay a penalty equal to the amount of the actual cost incurred by the state or local agency to remove and dispose of the hazardous substance that is a controlled substance or a chemical used in, or is a byproduct of, the manufacture of a controlled substance and to take removal action with respect to any release of the hazardous substance or any items or materials contaminated by that release, if the state or local agency requests the prosecuting authority to seek recovery of that cost. The court shall transmit all penalties collected pursuant to this subdivision to the county treasurer of the county in which the court is located for deposit in a special account in the county treasury. The county treasurer shall pay that money at least once a month to the agency that requested recovery of the cost for the removal action. The county may retain up to 5 percent of any assessed penalty for appropriate and reasonable administrative costs attributable to the collection and disbursement of the penalty.

(2) If the Department of Toxic Substances Control has requested recovery of the cost of removing the hazardous substance that is a controlled substance or a chemical used in, or is a byproduct of, the manufacture of a controlled substance or taking removal action with respect to any release of the hazardous substance, the county treasurer shall transfer funds in the amount of the penalty collected to the Treasurer, who shall deposit the money in the Illegal Drug Lab Cleanup Account, which is hereby created in the General Fund in the State Treasury. The Department of Toxic Substances Control may expend money in the Illegal Drug Lab Cleanup Account, upon appropriation by the Legislature, to cover the cost of taking removal actions pursuant to Section 25354.5.

(3) If a local agency and the Department of Toxic Substances Control have both requested recovery of removal costs with respect to a hazardous substance that is a controlled substance or a chemical used in, or is a byproduct of, the manufacture of a controlled substance, the county treasurer shall apportion any penalty collected among the agencies involved in proportion to the costs incurred.

(c) As used in this section the following terms have the following meaning:

(1) "Dispose" means to abandon, deposit, intern, or otherwise discard as a final action after use has been achieved or a use is no longer intended.

(2) "Hazardous substance" has the same meaning as defined in Section 25316.

(3) "Hazardous waste" has the same meaning as defined in Section 25117.

(4) For purposes of this section, "remove" or "removal" has the same meaning as set forth in Section 25323.

(Amended by Stats. 2011, Ch. 15, Sec. 170. (AB 109) Effective April 4, 2011. Operative October 1, 2011, by Sec. 636 of Ch. 15, as amended by Stats. 2011, Ch. 39, Sec. 68.)

11375.

(a) As to the substances specified in subdivision (c), this section, and not Sections 11377, 11378, 11379, and 11380, shall apply.

(b) (1) Every person who possesses for sale, or who sells, any substance specified in subdivision (c) shall be punished by imprisonment in the county jail for a period of not more than one year or state prison.

(2) Every person who possesses any controlled substance specified in subdivision (c), unless upon the prescription of a physician, dentist, podiatrist, or veterinarian, licensed to practice in this state, shall be guilty of an infraction or a misdemeanor.

(c) This section shall apply to any material, compound, mixture, or preparation containing any of the following substances:

(1) Chlordiazepoxide.
(2) Clonazepam.
(3) Clorazepate.
(4) Diazepam.
(5) Flurazepam.
(6) Lorazepam.
(7) Mebutamate.
(8) Oxazepam.
(9) Prazepam.
(10) Temazepam.
(11) Halazepam.
(12) Alprazolam.
(13) Propoxyphene.
(14) Diethylpropion.
(15) Phentermine.
(16) Pemoline.
(17) Fenfluramine.
(18) Triazolam.

(Amended (as amended by Stats. 1992, Ch. 616) by Stats. 2001, Ch. 838, Sec. 2. Effective January 1, 2002. Superseded on operative date of amendment by Stats. 1996, Ch. 109, as further amended by Sec. 1 of Stats. 2001, Ch. 838.)

11375.

(a) As to the substances specified in subdivision (c), this section, and not Sections 11377, 11378, 11379, and 11380, shall apply.

(b) (1) Every person who possesses for sale, or who sells, any substance specified in subdivision (c) shall be punished by imprisonment in the county jail for a period of not more than one year or state prison.

(2) Every person who possesses any controlled substance specified in subdivision (c), unless upon the prescription of a physician, dentist, podiatrist, or veterinarian, licensed to practice in this state, shall be guilty of an infraction or a misdemeanor.

(c) This section shall apply to any material, compound, mixture, or preparation containing any of the following substances:

(1) Chlordiazepoxide.

(2) Clonazepam.

(3) Clorazepate.

(4) Diazepam.

(5) Flurazepam.

(6) Lorazepam.

(7) Mebutamate.

(8) Oxazepam.

(9) Prazepam.

(10) Temazepam.

(11) Halazepam.

(12) Alprazolam.

(13) Propoxyphene.

(14) Diethylpropion.

(15) Phentermine.

(16) Pemoline.

(17) Triazolam.

(Amended (as amended by Stats. 1996, Ch. 109) by Stats. 2001, Ch. 838, Sec. 1. Effective January 1, 2002. Amendments conditionally operative as provided in Stats. 1996, Ch. 109, Sec. 3.)

11375.5.

(a) Every person who sells, dispenses, distributes, furnishes, administers, or gives, or offers to sell, dispense, distribute, furnish, administer, or give, any synthetic stimulant compound specified in subdivision (c), or any synthetic stimulant derivative, to any person, or who possesses that compound or derivative for sale, is guilty of a misdemeanor, punishable by imprisonment in a county jail not to exceed six months, or by a fine not to exceed one thousand dollars ($1,000), or by both that fine and imprisonment.

(b) Every person who uses or possesses any synthetic stimulant compound specified in subdivision (c), or any synthetic stimulant derivative, is guilty of a public offense, punishable as follows:

(1) A first offense is an infraction punishable by a fine not exceeding two hundred fifty dollars ($250).

(2) A second offense is an infraction punishable by a fine not exceeding two hundred fifty dollars ($250) or a misdemeanor punishable by imprisonment in a county jail not exceeding six months, a fine not exceeding five hundred dollars ($500), or by both that fine and imprisonment.

(3) A third or subsequent offense is a misdemeanor punishable by imprisonment in a county jail not exceeding six months, or by a fine not exceeding one thousand dollars ($1,000), or by both that fine and imprisonment.

(c) Unless specifically excepted, or contained within a pharmaceutical product approved by the United States Food and Drug Administration, or unless listed in another schedule, subdivisions (a) and (b) apply to any material, compound, mixture, or preparation which contains any quantity of a substance or analog of a substance, including its salts, isomers, esters, or ethers, and salts of isomers, esters, or ethers whenever the existence of such salts, isomers, esters, or ethers, and salts of isomers, esters, or ethers is possible, that is structurally derived from 2-amino-1-phenyl-1-propanone by modification in one of the following ways:

(1) By substitution in the phenyl ring to any extent with alkyl, alkoxy, alkylenedioxy, haloalkyl, or halide substituents, whether or not further substituted in the phenyl ring by one or more other univalent substituents.

(2) By substitution at the 3-position with an alkyl substituent.

(3) By substitution at the nitrogen atom with alkyl or dialkyl groups, or by inclusion of the nitrogen atom in a cyclic structure.

(d) This section shall not prohibit prosecution under any other provision of law.

(Amended by Stats. 2016, Ch. 624, Sec. 3. (SB 139) Effective September 25, 2016.)

11375.7.

(a) Unless otherwise excluded pursuant to this section, a person charged with a misdemeanor pursuant to paragraph (3) of subdivision (b) of Section 11357.5 or paragraph (3) of subdivision (b) of Section 11375.5 shall be eligible to participate in a preguilty plea drug court program, as described in Section 1000.5 of the Penal Code.

(b) Notwithstanding any other law, a positive test for use of a controlled substance, any other drug that may not be possessed without a prescription, or alcohol shall not be grounds for dismissal from the program, unless the person is not making progress in the program. The court shall consider a report or recommendation of the treatment provider in making this determination. It shall be presumed that a person engaged in a program is

making progress, unless that presumption is defeated by clear and convincing evidence. The person may offer evidence or an argument that he or she would benefit from and make progress in a different program or mode. If the court so finds, it may place the person in a different treatment program.

(c) Notwithstanding any other law, the following persons are excluded from participation in the program under this section:

(1) A person with a history of violence that indicates that he or she presents a current risk of violent behavior currently or during the treatment program. This ground for exclusion shall be established by clear and convincing evidence.

(2) A person required to register as a sex offender pursuant to Section 290, unless the court finds by clear and convincing evidence that the person does not present a substantial risk of committing sexual offenses currently or through the course of the program and the person would benefit from the program, including that treatment would reduce the risk that the person would sexually reoffend.

(3) A person who the treatment provider concludes is unamenable to any and all forms of drug treatment. The defendant may present evidence that he or she is amenable to treatment and the court may retain the person in the program if the court finds that the person is amenable to treatment through a different provider or a different mode of treatment.

(d) Notwithstanding any other law, a prior conviction for an offense involving a controlled substance or drug that may not be possessed without a prescription, including a substance listed in Section 11357.5 or 11375.5, is not grounds for exclusion from the program, unless the court finds by clear and convincing evidence that the person is likely to engage in drug commerce for financial gain, rather than for purposes of obtaining a drug or drugs for personal use.

(Amended by Stats. 2017, Ch. 561, Sec. 112. (AB 1516) Effective January 1, 2018.)

11376.

Upon the diversion or conviction of a person for any offense involving substance abuse, the court may require, in addition to any or all other terms of diversion or imprisonment, fine, or other reasonable conditions of sentencing or probation imposed by the court, that the defendant participate in and complete counseling or education programs, or both, including, but not limited to, parent education or parenting programs operated by community colleges, school districts, other public agencies, or private agencies.

(Added by Stats. 1996, Ch. 210, Sec. 1. Effective January 1, 1997.)

11376.5.

(a) Notwithstanding any other law, it shall not be a crime for a person to be under the influence of, or to possess for personal use, a controlled substance, controlled substance analog, or drug paraphernalia, if that person, in good faith, seeks medical assistance for another person experiencing a drug-related overdose that is related to the possession of a controlled substance, controlled substance analog, or drug paraphernalia of the person seeking medical assistance, and that person does not obstruct medical or law enforcement personnel. No other immunities or protections from arrest or prosecution for violations of the law are intended or may be inferred.

(b) Notwithstanding any other law, it shall not be a crime for a person who experiences a drug-related overdose and who is in need of medical assistance to be under the influence of, or to possess for personal use, a controlled substance, controlled substance analog, or drug paraphernalia, if the person or one or more other persons at the scene of the overdose, in good faith, seek medical assistance for the person experiencing the overdose. No other immunities or protections from arrest or prosecution for violations of the law are intended or may be inferred.

(c) This section shall not affect laws prohibiting the selling, providing, giving, or exchanging of drugs, or laws prohibiting the forcible administration of drugs against a person's will.

(d) Nothing in this section shall affect liability for any offense that involves activities made dangerous by the consumption of a controlled substance or controlled substance analog, including, but not limited to, violations of Section 23103 of the Vehicle Code as specified in Section 23103.5 of the Vehicle Code, or violations of Section 23152 or 23153 of the Vehicle Code.

(e) For the purposes of this section, "drug-related overdose" means an acute medical condition that is the result of the ingestion or use by an individual of one or more controlled substances or one or more controlled substances in combination with alcohol, in quantities that are excessive for that individual that may result in death, disability, or serious injury. An individual's condition shall be deemed to be a "drug-related overdose" if a reasonable person of ordinary knowledge would believe the condition to be a drug-related overdose that may result in death, disability, or serious injury.

(Added by Stats. 2012, Ch. 338, Sec. 2. (AB 472) Effective January 1, 2013.)

ARTICLE 5. Offenses Involving Controlled Substances Formerly Classified as Restricted Dangerous Drugs [11377 - 11382.5]

(Heading of Article 5 amended by Stats. 1973, Ch. 1078.)

11377.

(a) Except as authorized by law and as otherwise provided in subdivision (b) or Section 11375, or in Article 7 (commencing with Section 4211) of Chapter 9 of Division 2 of the Business and Professions Code, every person who possesses any controlled substance which is (1) classified in Schedule III, IV, or V, and which is not a narcotic drug, (2) specified in subdivision (d) of Section 11054, except paragraphs (13), (14), (15), and (20) of subdivision (d), (3) specified in paragraph (11) of subdivision (c) of Section 11056, (4) specified in paragraph (2) or (3) of subdivision (f) of Section 11054, or (5) specified in subdivision (d), (e), or (f) of Section 11055, unless upon the prescription of a physician, dentist, podiatrist, or veterinarian, licensed to practice in this state, shall be punished by imprisonment in a county jail for a period of not more than one year, except that such person may instead be punished pursuant to subdivision (h) of Section 1170 of the Penal Code if that person has one or more prior convictions for an offense specified in clause (iv) of subparagraph (C) of paragraph (2) of subdivision (e) of Section 667 of the Penal Code or for an offense requiring registration pursuant to subdivision (c) of Section 290 of the Penal Code.

(b) The judge may assess a fine not to exceed seventy dollars ($70) against any person who violates subdivision (a), with the proceeds of this fine to be used in accordance with Section 1463.23 of the Penal Code. The court shall, however, take into consideration the defendant's ability to pay, and no defendant shall be denied probation because of his or her inability to pay the fine permitted under this subdivision.

(c) It is not unlawful for a person other than the prescription holder to possess a controlled substance described in subdivision (a) if both of the following apply:

(1) The possession of the controlled substance is at the direction or with the express authorization of the prescription holder.

(2) The sole intent of the possessor is to deliver the prescription to the prescription holder for its prescribed use or to discard the substance in a lawful manner.

(d) This section does not permit the use of a controlled substance by a person other than the prescription holder or permit the distribution or sale of a controlled substance that is otherwise inconsistent with the prescription.

(Amended (as amended by Proposition 47) by Stats. 2017, Ch. 269, Sec. 6. (SB 811) Effective January 1, 2018. Note: This section was amended on Nov. 4, 2014, by initiative Prop. 47.)

11377.5.

(a) Except as otherwise provided in this division, every person who possesses any controlled substance specified in paragraph (11) of subdivision (c) of, or subdivision (g) of, Section 11056 of this code, or paragraph (13) of subdivision (d) of Section 11057 of this code, with the intent to commit sexual assault, shall be punished by imprisonment pursuant to subdivision (h) of Section 1170 of the Penal Code.

(b) For purposes of this section, "sexual assault" means conduct in violation of Section 243.4, 261, 262, 286, 287, or 289 of, or former Section 288a of, the Penal Code.

(Amended by Stats. 2018, Ch. 423, Sec. 36. (SB 1494) Effective January 1, 2019.)

11378.

Except as otherwise provided in Article 7 (commencing with Section 4110) of Chapter 9 of Division 2 of the Business and Professions Code, a person who possesses for sale a controlled substance that meets any of the following criteria shall be punished by imprisonment pursuant to subdivision (h) of Section 1170 of the Penal Code:

(1) The substance is classified in Schedule III, IV, or V and is not a narcotic drug, except the substance specified in subdivision (g) of Section 11056.

(2) The substance is specified in subdivision (d) of Section 11054, except paragraphs (13), (14), (15), (20), (21), (22), and (23) of subdivision (d).

(3) The substance is specified in paragraph (11) of subdivision (c) of Section 11056.

(4) The substance is specified in paragraph (2) or (3) of subdivision (f) of Section 11054.

(5) The substance is specified in subdivision (d), (e), or (f), except paragraph (3) of subdivision (e) and subparagraphs (A) and (B) of paragraph (2) of subdivision (f), of Section 11055.

(Amended by Stats. 2013, Ch. 76, Sec. 110. (AB 383) Effective January 1, 2014.)

11378.5.

Except as otherwise provided in Article 7 (commencing with Section 4211) of Chapter 9 of Division 2 of the Business and Professions Code, every person who possesses for sale phencyclidine or any analog or any precursor of phencyclidine which is specified in paragraph (21), (22), or (23) of subdivision of Section 11054 or in paragraph (3) of subdivision (e) or in subdivision (f), except subparagraph (A) of paragraph (1) of subdivision (f), of Section 11055, shall be punished by imprisonment pursuant to subdivision (h) of Section 1170 of the Penal Code for a period of three, four, or five years.

(Amended by Stats. 2011, Ch. 15, Sec. 173. (AB 109) Effective April 4, 2011. Operative October 1, 2011, by Sec. 636 of Ch. 15, as amended by Stats. 2011, Ch. 39, Sec. 68.)

11379.

(a) Except as otherwise provided in subdivision (b) and in Article 7 (commencing with Section 4211) of Chapter 9 of Division 2 of the Business and Professions Code, every person who transports, imports into this state, sells, furnishes, administers, or gives away, or offers to transport, import into this state, sell, furnish, administer, or give away, or attempts to import into this state or transport any controlled substance which is (1) classified in Schedule III, IV, or V and which is not a narcotic drug, except subdivision (g) of Section 11056, (2) specified in subdivision (d) of Section 11054, except paragraphs (13), (14), (15), (20), (21), (22), and (23) of subdivision (d), (3) specified in paragraph (11) of subdivision (c) of Section 11056, (4) specified in paragraph (2) or (3) of subdivision (f) of Section 11054, or (5) specified in subdivision (d) or (e), except paragraph (3) of subdivision (e), or specified in subparagraph (A) of paragraph (1) of subdivision (f), of Section 11055, unless upon the prescription of a physician, dentist, podiatrist, or veterinarian, licensed to practice in this state, shall be punished by imprisonment pursuant to subdivision (h) of Section 1170 of the Penal Code for a period of two, three, or four years.

(b) Notwithstanding the penalty provisions of subdivision (a), any person who transports any controlled substances specified in subdivision (a) within this state from one county to another noncontiguous county shall be punished by imprisonment pursuant to subdivision (h) of Section 1170 of the Penal Code for three, six, or nine years.

(c) For purposes of this section, "transports" means to transport for sale.

(d) Nothing in this section is intended to preclude or limit prosecution under an aiding and abetting theory, accessory theory, or a conspiracy theory.

(Amended by Stats. 2014, Ch. 54, Sec. 8. (SB 1461) Effective January 1, 2015.)

11379.2.

Except as otherwise provided in Article 7 (commencing with Section 4211) of Chapter 9 of Division 2 of the Business and Professions Code, every person who possesses for sale or sells any controlled substance specified in subdivision (g) of Section 11056 shall be punished by imprisonment in the county jail for a period of not more than one year or in the state prison.

(Added by Stats. 1991, Ch. 294, Sec. 5.)

11379.5.

(a) Except as otherwise provided in subdivision (b) and in Article 7 (commencing with Section 4211) of Chapter 9 of Division 2 of the Business and Professions Code, every person who transports, imports into this state, sells, furnishes, administers, or gives away, or offers to transport, import into this state, sell, furnish, administer, or give away, or attempts to import into this state or transport phencyclidine or any of its analogs which is specified in paragraph (21), (22), or (23) of subdivision (d) of Section 11054 or in paragraph (3) of subdivision (e) of Section 11055, or its precursors as specified in subparagraph (A) or (B) of paragraph (2) of subdivision (f) of Section 11055, unless upon the prescription of a physician, dentist, podiatrist, or veterinarian licensed to practice in this state, shall be punished by imprisonment pursuant to subdivision (h) of Section 1170 of the Penal Code for a period of three, four, or five years.

(b) Notwithstanding the penalty provisions of subdivision (a), any person who transports for sale any controlled substances specified in subdivision (a) within this state from one county to another noncontiguous county shall be punished by imprisonment pursuant to subdivision (h) of Section 1170 of the Penal Code for three, six, or nine years.

(c) For purposes of this section, "transport" means to transport for sale.

(d) This section does not preclude or limit prosecution for any aiding and abetting or conspiracy offenses.

(Amended by Stats. 2015, Ch. 77, Sec. 2. (AB 730) Effective January 1, 2016.)

11379.6.

(a) Except as otherwise provided by law, every person who manufactures, compounds, converts, produces, derives, processes, or prepares, either directly or indirectly by chemical extraction or independently by means of chemical synthesis, any controlled substance specified in Section 11054, 11055, 11056, 11057, or 11058 shall be punished by imprisonment pursuant to subdivision (h) of Section 1170 of the Penal Code for three, five, or seven years and by a fine not exceeding fifty thousand dollars ($50,000).

(b) Except when an enhancement pursuant to Section 11379.7 is pled and proved, the fact that a person under 16 years of age resided in a structure in which a violation of this section involving methamphetamine occurred shall be considered a factor in aggravation by the sentencing court.

(c) Except when an enhancement pursuant to Section 11379.7 is pled and proved, the fact that a violation of this section involving methamphetamine occurred within 200 feet of an occupied residence or any structure where another person was present at the time the offense was committed may be considered a factor in aggravation by the sentencing court.

(d) The fact that a violation of this section involving the use of a volatile solvent to chemically extract concentrated cannabis occurred within 300 feet of an occupied residence or any structure where another person was present at the time the offense was committed may be considered a factor in aggravation by the sentencing court.

(e) Except as otherwise provided by law, every person who offers to perform an act which is punishable under subdivision (a) shall be punished by imprisonment pursuant to subdivision (h) of Section 1170 of the Penal Code for three, four, or five years.

(f) All fines collected pursuant to subdivision (a) shall be transferred to the State Treasury for deposit in the Clandestine Drug Lab Clean-up Account, as established by Section 5 of Chapter 1295 of the Statutes of 1987. The transmission to the State Treasury shall be carried out in the same manner as fines collected for the state by the county.

(Amended by Stats. 2015, Ch. 141, Sec. 1. (SB 212) Effective January 1, 2016.)

11379.7.

(a) Except as provided in subdivision (b), any person convicted of a violation of subdivision (a) of Section 11379.6 or Section 11383, or of an attempt to violate subdivision (a) of Section 11379.6 or Section 11383, as those sections relate to methamphetamine or phencyclidine, when the commission or attempted commission of the crime occurs in a structure where any child under 16 years of age is present, shall, in addition and consecutive to the punishment prescribed for the felony of which he or she has been convicted, be punished by an additional term of two years in the state prison.

(b) Any person convicted of a violation of subdivision (a) of Section 11379.6 or Section 11383, or of an attempt to violate subdivision (a) of Section 11379.6 or Section 11383, as those sections relate to methamphetamine or phencyclidine, where the commission of the crime causes any child under 16 years of age to suffer great bodily injury, shall, in addition and consecutive to the punishment prescribed for the felony of which he or she has been convicted, be punished by an additional term of five years in the state prison.

(c) As used in this section, "structure" means any house, apartment building, shop, warehouse, barn, building, vessel, railroad car, cargo container, motor vehicle, housecar, trailer, trailer coach, camper, mine, floating home, or other enclosed structure capable of holding a child and manufacturing equipment.

(d) As used in this section, "great bodily injury" has the same meaning as defined in Section 12022.7 of the Penal Code.

(Added by Stats. 1996, Ch. 871, Sec. 1. Effective January 1, 1997.)

11379.8.

(a) Any person convicted of a violation of subdivision (a) of Section 11379.6, or of a conspiracy to violate subdivision (a) of Section 11379.6, with respect to any substance containing a controlled substance which is specified in paragraph (21), (22), or (23) of subdivision (d) of Section 11054, or in paragraph (1) or (2) of subdivision (d) or in paragraph (3) of subdivision (e) or in paragraph (2) of subdivision (f) of Section 11055 shall receive an additional term as follows:

(1) Where the substance exceeds three gallons of liquid by volume or one pound of solid substances by weight, the person shall receive an additional term of three years.

(2) Where the substance exceeds 10 gallons of liquid by volume or three pounds of solid substance by weight, the person shall receive an additional term of five years.

(3) Where the substance exceeds 25 gallons of liquid by volume or 10 pounds of solid substance by weight, the person shall receive an additional term of 10 years.

(4) Where the substance exceeds 105 gallons of liquid by volume or 44 pounds of solid substance by weight, the person shall receive an additional term of 15 years.

In computing the quantities involved in this subdivision, plant or vegetable material seized shall not be included.

(b) The additional terms provided in this section shall not be imposed unless the allegation that the controlled substance exceeds the amounts provided in this section is charged in the accusatory pleading and admitted or found to be true by the trier of fact.

(c) The additional terms provided in this section shall be in addition to any other punishment provided by law.

(d) Notwithstanding any other provision of law, the court may strike the additional punishment for the enhancements provided in this section if it determines that there are circumstances in mitigation of the additional punishment and states on the record its reasons for striking the additional punishment.

(e) The conspiracy enhancements provided for in this section shall not be imposed unless the trier of fact finds that the defendant conspirator was substantially involved in the direction or supervision of, or in a significant portion of the financing of, the underlying offense.

(Amended by Stats. 1998, Ch. 425, Sec. 3. Effective January 1, 1999.)

11379.9.

(a) Except as provided by Section 11379.7, any person convicted of a violation of, or of an attempt to violate, subdivision (a) of Section 11379.6 or Section 11383, as those sections relate to methamphetamine or phencyclidine, when the commission or attempted commission of the offense causes the death or great bodily injury of another person other than an accomplice, shall, in addition and consecutive to any other punishment authorized by law, be punished by an additional term of one year in the state prison for each death or injury.

(b) Nothing in this section shall preclude prosecution under both this section and Section 187, 192, or 12022.7, or any other provision of law. However, a person who is punished under another provision of law for causing death or great bodily injury as described in subdivision (a) shall not receive an additional term of imprisonment under this section.

(Amended by Stats. 1998, Ch. 936, Sec. 2. Effective September 28, 1998.)

11380.

(a) Every person 18 years of age or over who violates any provision of this chapter involving controlled substances which are (1) classified in Schedule III, IV, or V and which are not narcotic drugs or (2) specified in subdivision (d) of Section 11054, except paragraphs (13), (14), (15), and (20) of subdivision (d), specified in paragraph (11) of subdivision (c) of Section 11056, specified in paragraph (2) or (3) or subdivision (f) of Section 11054, or specified in subdivision (d), (e), or (f) of Section 11055, by the use of a minor as agent, who solicits, induces, encourages, or intimidates any minor with the intent that the minor shall violate any provision of this article involving those controlled substances or who unlawfully furnishes, offers to furnish, or attempts to furnish those controlled substances to a minor shall be punished by imprisonment in the state prison for a period of three, six, or nine years.

(b) Nothing in this section applies to a registered pharmacist furnishing controlled substances pursuant to a prescription.

(Amended by Stats. 2001, Ch. 841, Sec. 8. Effective January 1, 2002.)

11380.1.

(a) Notwithstanding any other provision of law, any person 18 years of age or over who is convicted of a violation of Section 11380, in addition to the punishment imposed for that conviction, shall receive an additional punishment as follows:

(1) If the offense involved phencyclidine (PCP), methamphetamine, lysergic acid diethylamide (LSD), or any analog of these substances and occurred upon the grounds of, or within, a church or synagogue, a playground, a public or private youth center, a child day care facility, or a public swimming pool, during hours in which the facility is open for business, classes, or school-related programs, or at any time when minors are using the facility, the defendant shall, as a full and separately served enhancement to any other enhancement provided in paragraph (3), be punished by imprisonment in the state prison for one year.

(2) If the offense involved phencyclidine (PCP), methamphetamine, lysergic acid diethylamide (LSD), or any analog of these substances and occurred upon, or within 1,000 feet of, the grounds of any public or private elementary, vocational, junior high school, or high school, during hours that the school is open for classes or school-related programs, or at any time when minors are using the facility where the offense occurs, the defendant shall, as a full and separately served enhancement to any other enhancement provided in paragraph (3), be punished by imprisonment in the state prison for two years.

(3) If the offense involved a minor who is at least four years younger than the defendant, the defendant shall, as a full and separately served enhancement to any other enhancement provided in this subdivision, be punished by imprisonment in the state prison for one, two, or three years, at the discretion of the court.

(b) The additional punishment provided in this section shall not be imposed unless the allegation is charged in the accusatory pleading and admitted by the defendant or found to be true by the trier of fact.

(c) The additional punishment provided in this section shall be in addition to any other punishment provided by law and shall not be limited by any other provision of law.

(d) Notwithstanding any other provision of law, the court may strike the additional punishment provided for in this section if it determines that there are circumstances in mitigation of the additional punishment and states on the record its reasons for striking the additional punishment.

(e) The definitions contained in subdivision (e) of Section 11353.1 shall apply to this section.

(f) This section does not require either that notice be posted regarding the proscribed conduct or that the applicable 1,000-foot boundary limit be marked.

(Amended by Stats. 1993, Ch. 556, Sec. 3.5. Effective January 1, 1994.)

11380.7.

(a) Notwithstanding any other provision of law, any person who is convicted of trafficking in heroin, cocaine, cocaine base, methamphetamine, or phencyclidine (PCP), or of a conspiracy to commit trafficking in heroin, cocaine, cocaine base, methamphetamine, or phencyclidine (PCP), in addition to the punishment imposed for the conviction, shall be imprisoned pursuant to subdivision (h) of Section 1170 of the Penal Code for an additional one year if the violation occurred upon the grounds of, or within 1,000 feet of, a drug treatment center, detoxification facility, or homeless shelter.

(b) (1) The additional punishment provided in this section shall not be imposed unless the allegation is charged in the accusatory pleading and admitted by the defendant or found to be true by the trier of fact.

(2) The additional punishment provided in this section shall not be imposed if any other additional punishment is imposed pursuant to Section 11353.1, 11353.5, 11353.6, 11353.7, or 11380.1.

(c) Notwithstanding any other provision of law, the court may strike the additional punishment provided for in this section if it determines that there are circumstances in mitigation of the additional punishment and states on the record its reasons for striking the additional punishment. In determining whether or not to strike the additional punishment, the court shall consider the following factors and any relevant factors in aggravation or mitigation in Rules 4.421 and 4.423 of the California Rules of Court.

(1) The following factors indicate that the court should exercise its discretion to strike the additional punishment unless these factors are outweighed by factors in aggravation:

(A) The defendant is homeless, or is in a homeless shelter or transitional housing.

(B) The defendant lacks resources for the necessities of life.

(C) The defendant is addicted to or dependent on controlled substances.

(D) The defendant's motive was merely to maintain a steady supply of drugs for personal use.

(E) The defendant was recruited or exploited by a more culpable person to commit the crime.

(2) The following factors indicate that the court should not exercise discretion to strike the additional punishment unless these factors are outweighed by factors in mitigation:

(A) The defendant, in committing the crime, preyed on homeless persons, drug addicts or substance abusers who were seeking treatment, shelter or transitional services.

(B) The defendant's primary motive was monetary compensation.

(C) The defendant induced others, particularly homeless persons, drug addicts and substance abusers, to become involved in trafficking.

(d) For the purposes of this section, the following terms have the following meanings:

(1) "Detoxification facility" means any premises, place, or building in which 24-hour residential nonmedical services are provided to adults who are recovering from problems related to alcohol, drug, or alcohol and drug misuse or abuse, and who need alcohol, drug, or alcohol and drug recovery treatment or detoxification services.

(2) "Drug treatment program" or "drug treatment" has the same meaning set forth in subdivision (b) of Section 1210 of the Penal Code.

(3) "Homeless shelter" includes, but is not limited to, emergency shelter housing, as well as transitional housing, but does not include domestic violence shelters. "Emergency shelter housing" is housing with minimal support services for homeless persons in which residency is limited to six months or less and is not related to the person's ability to pay. "Transitional housing" means housing with supportive services, including self-sufficiency development services, which is exclusively designed and targeted to help recently homeless persons find permanent housing as soon as reasonably possible, limits residency to 24 months, and in which rent and service fees are based on ability to pay.

(4) "Trafficking" means any of the unlawful activities specified in Sections 11351, 11351.5, 11352, 11353, 11354, 11378, 11379, 11379.6, and 11380. It does not include simple possession or drug use.

(Amended by Stats. 2011, Ch. 15, Sec. 177. (AB 109) Effective April 4, 2011. Operative October 1, 2011, by Sec. 636 of Ch. 15, as amended by Stats. 2011, Ch. 39, Sec. 68.)

11381.

As used in this article "felony offense" and offense "punishable as a felony" refer to an offense prior to October 1, 2011, for which the law prescribes imprisonment in the state prison, or for an offense on or after October 1, 2011, imprisonment in either the state prison or pursuant to subdivision (h) of Section 1170 of the Penal Code, as either an alternative or the sole penalty, regardless of the sentence the particular defendant received.

(Amended (as amended by Stats. 2011, Ch. 15) by Stats. 2011, Ch. 39, Sec. 3. (AB 117) Effective June 30, 2011. Operative October 1, 2011, pursuant to Secs. 68 and 69 of Ch. 39.)

11382.

Every person who agrees, consents, or in any manner offers to unlawfully sell, furnish, transport, administer, or give any controlled substance which is (a) classified in Schedule III, IV, or V and which is not a narcotic drug, or (b) specified in subdivision (d) of Section 11054, except paragraphs (13), (14), (15), and (20) of subdivision (d), specified in paragraph (11) of subdivision (c) of Section 11056, or specified in subdivision (d), (e), or (f) of Section 11055, to any person, or offers, arranges, or negotiates to have that controlled substance unlawfully sold, delivered, transported, furnished, administered, or given to any person and then sells, delivers, furnishes, transports, administers, or gives, or offers, or arranges, or negotiates to have sold, delivered, transported, furnished, administered, or given to any person any other liquid, substance, or material in lieu of that controlled substance shall be punished by imprisonment in the county jail for not more than one year, or pursuant to subdivision (h) of Section 1170 of the Penal Code.

(Amended by Stats. 2011, 1st Ex. Sess., Ch. 12, Sec. 5. (AB 17 1x) Effective September 21, 2011. Operative October 1, 2011, by Sec. 46 of Ch. 12.)

11382.5.

All controlled substances in Schedules I, II, III, IV, and V, in solid or capsule form, except for such controlled substances in the possession or inventory of a wholesaler, retailer, or pharmacist on January 1, 1975, shall not be sold, furnished, or distributed in this state unless they have on the controlled substance if in solid form, or on the capsule if in capsule form, an identifying device, insignia, or mark of the manufacturer of such controlled substance. However, the exception for such controlled substances in the possession or inventory of a wholesaler, retailer, or pharmacist shall not be available to any wholesaler, retailer, or pharmacist under the control or jurisdiction of a manufacturer of controlled substances.

This section shall not apply to a pharmacist who, in accordance with applicable state law, compounds such controlled substance in the course of his practice as a pharmacist for direct dispensing by him upon a prescription of any person licensed to prescribe such controlled substances.

(Added by Stats. 1974, Ch. 926.)

ARTICLE 6. Precursors of Phencyclidine (PCP) and Methamphetamine [11383 - 11384]

(Heading of Article 6 amended by Stats. 2006, Ch. 646, Sec. 1.)

11383.

(a) Any person who possesses at the same time any of the following combinations, a combination product thereof, or possesses any compound or mixture containing the chemicals listed in the following combinations, with the intent to manufacture phencyclidine (PCP) or any of its analogs specified in subdivision (d) of Section 11054 or subdivision (e) of Section 11055, is guilty of a felony and shall be punished by imprisonment pursuant to subdivision (h) of Section 1170 of the Penal Code for two, four, or six years:

(1) Piperidine and cyclohexanone.
(2) Pyrrolidine and cyclohexanone.
(3) Morpholine and cyclohexanone.

(b) Any person who possesses the optical, positional, or geometric isomer of any of the compounds listed in this section, with the intent to manufacture these controlled substances is guilty of a felony and shall be punished by imprisonment pursuant to subdivision (h) of Section 1170 of the Penal Code for two, four, or six years:

(1) Phencyclidine (PCP).
(2) Any analog of PCP specified in subdivision (d) of Section 11054, or in subdivision (e) of Section 11055.

(c) Any person who possesses any compound or mixture containing piperidine, cyclohexanone, pyrrolidine, morpholine, 1-phenylcyclohexylamine (PCA), 1-piperidinocyclohexanecarbonitrile (PCC), or phenylmagnesium bromide (PMB) with the intent to manufacture phencyclidine, is guilty of a felony and shall be punished by imprisonment pursuant to subdivision (h) of Section 1170 of the Penal Code for two, four, or six years.

(d) Any person who possesses immediate precursors sufficient for the manufacture of piperidine, cyclohexanone, pyrrolidine, morpholine, or phenylmagnesium bromide (PMB) with the intent to manufacture phencyclidine, is guilty of a felony and shall be punished by imprisonment pursuant to subdivision (h) of Section 1170 of the Penal Code for two, four, or six years.

(e) This section does not apply to drug manufacturers licensed by this state or persons authorized by regulation of the Board of Pharmacy to possess those substances or combinations of substances.

(Amended by Stats. 2011, Ch. 15, Sec. 179. (AB 109) Effective April 4, 2011. Operative October 1, 2011, by Sec. 636 of Ch. 15, as amended by Stats. 2011, Ch. 39, Sec. 68.)

11383.5.

(a) Any person who possesses both methylamine and phenyl-2-propanone (phenylacetone) at the same time with the intent to manufacture methamphetamine, or who possesses both ethylamine and phenyl-2-propanone (phenylacetone) at the same time with the intent to manufacture N-ethylamphetamine, is guilty of a felony and shall be punished by imprisonment pursuant to subdivision (h) of Section 1170 of the Penal Code for two, four, or six years.

(b) (1) Any person who, with the intent to manufacture methamphetamine or any of its analogs specified in subdivision (d) of Section 11055, possesses ephedrine or pseudoephedrine, or any salts, isomers, or salts of isomers of ephedrine or pseudoephedrine, or who possesses a substance containing ephedrine or pseudoephedrine, or any salts, isomers, or salts of isomers of ephedrine or pseudoephedrine, or who possesses at the same time any of the following, or a combination product thereof, is guilty of a felony and shall be punished by imprisonment pursuant to subdivision (h) of Section 1170 of the Penal Code for two, four, or six years:

(A) Ephedrine, pseudoephedrine, norpseudoephedrine, N-methylephedrine, N-ethylephedrine, N-methylpseudoephedrine, N-ethylpseudoephedrine, or phenylpropanolamine, plus hydriodic acid.

(B) Ephedrine, pseudoephedrine, norpseudoephedrine, N-methylephedrine, N-ethylephedrine, N-methylpseudoephedrine, N-ethylpseudoephedrine, or phenylpropanolamine, thionyl chloride and hydrogen gas.

(C) Ephedrine, pseudoephedrine, norpseudoephedrine, N-methylephedrine, N-ethylephedrine, N-methylpseudoephedrine, N-ethylpseudoephedrine, or phenylpropanolamine, plus phosphorus pentachloride and hydrogen gas.

(D) Ephedrine, pseudoephedrine, norpseudoephedrine, N-methylephedrine, N-ethylephedrine, N-methylpseudoephedrine, N-ethylpseudoephedrine, chloroephedrine and chloropseudoephedrine, or phenylpropanolamine, plus any reducing agent.

(2) Any person who, with the intent to manufacture methamphetamine or any of its analogs specified in subdivision (d) of Section 11055, possesses hydriodic acid or a reducing agent or any product containing hydriodic acid or a reducing agent is guilty of a felony and shall be punished by imprisonment pursuant to subdivision (h) of Section 1170 of the Penal Code for two, four, or six years.

(c) Any person who possesses the optical, positional, or geometric isomer of any of the compounds listed in this section, with the intent to manufacture any of the following controlled substances, is guilty of a felony and shall be punished by imprisonment pursuant to subdivision (h) of Section 1170 of the Penal Code for two, four, or six years:

(1) Methamphetamine.
(2) Any analog of methamphetamine specified in subdivision (d) of Section 11055.
(3) N-ethylamphetamine.

(d) Any person who possesses immediate precursors sufficient for the manufacture of methylamine, ethylamine, phenyl-2-propanone, ephedrine, pseudoephedrine, norpseudoephedrine, N-methylephedrine, N-ethylephedrine, phenylpropanolamine, hydriodic acid or a reducing agent, thionyl chloride, or phosphorus pentachloride, with the intent to manufacture methamphetamine, is guilty of a felony and shall be punished by imprisonment pursuant to subdivision (h) of Section 1170 of the Penal Code for two, four, or six years.

(e) Any person who possesses essential chemicals sufficient to manufacture hydriodic acid or a reducing agent, with the intent to manufacture methamphetamine, is guilty of a felony and shall be punished by imprisonment pursuant to subdivision (h) of Section 1170 of the Penal Code for two, four, or six years.

(f) Any person who possesses any compound or mixture containing ephedrine, pseudoephedrine, norpseudoephedrine, N-methylephedrine, N-ethylephedrine, phenylpropanolamine, hydriodic acid or a reducing agent, thionyl chloride, or phosphorus pentachloride, with the intent to manufacture methamphetamine, is guilty of a felony and shall be punished by imprisonment pursuant to subdivision (h) of Section 1170 of the Penal Code for two, four, or six years.

(g) For purposes of this section, a "reducing agent" for the purposes of manufacturing methamphetamine means an agent that causes reduction to occur by either donating a hydrogen atom to an organic compound or by removing an oxygen atom from an organic compound.

(h) This section does not apply to drug manufacturers licensed by this state or persons authorized by regulation of the Board of Pharmacy to possess those substances or combinations of substances.

(Amended by Stats. 2011, Ch. 15, Sec. 180. (AB 109) Effective April 4, 2011. Operative October 1, 2011, by Sec. 636 of Ch. 15, as amended by Stats. 2011, Ch. 39, Sec. 68.)

11383.6.

(a) Any person who possesses at the same time any of the following combinations, a combination product thereof, or possesses any compound or mixture containing the chemicals listed in the following combinations, with the intent to sell, transfer, or otherwise furnish those chemicals, combinations, or mixtures to another person with the knowledge that they will be used to manufacture phencyclidine (PCP) or any of its analogs specified in subdivision (d) of Section 11054 or subdivision (e) of Section 11055 is guilty of a felony and shall be punished by imprisonment pursuant to subdivision (h) of Section 1170 of the Penal Code for 16 months, two, or three years:

(1) Piperidine and cyclohexanone.
(2) Pyrrolidine and cyclohexanone.
(3) Morpholine and cyclohexanone.

(b) Any person who possesses the optical, positional, or geometric isomer of any of the compounds listed in this section with the intent to sell, transfer, or otherwise furnish the isomer to another person with the knowledge that they will be used to manufacture these controlled substances is guilty of a felony and shall be punished by imprisonment pursuant to subdivision (h) of Section 1170 of the Penal Code for 16 months, two, or three years:

(1) Phencyclidine (PCP).
(2) Any analog of PCP specified in subdivision (d) of Section 11054, or in subdivision (e) of Section 11055.

(c) Any person who possesses any compound or mixture containing piperidine, cyclohexanone, pyrrolidine, morpholine, 1-phenylcyclohexylamine (PCA), 1-piperidinocyclohexanecarbonitrile (PCC), or phenylmagnesium bromide (PMB) with the intent to sell, transfer, or otherwise furnish the compound or mixture to another person with the knowledge that it will be used to manufacture phencyclidine is guilty of a felony and shall be punished by imprisonment pursuant to subdivision (h) of Section 1170 of the Penal Code for 16 months, two, or three years.

(d) Any person who possesses immediate precursors sufficient for the manufacture of piperidine, cyclohexanone, pyrrolidine, morpholine, or phenylmagnesium bromide (PMB) with the intent to sell, transfer or otherwise furnish the immediate precursors to another person with the knowledge that they will be used to manufacture phencyclidine is guilty of a felony and shall be punished by imprisonment pursuant to subdivision (h) of Section 1170 of the Penal Code for 16 months, two, or three years.

(e) This section does not apply to drug manufacturers licensed by this state or persons authorized by regulation of the Board of Pharmacy to possess those substances or combinations of substances.

(Amended by Stats. 2011, Ch. 15, Sec. 181. (AB 109) Effective April 4, 2011. Operative October 1, 2011, by Sec. 636 of Ch. 15, as amended by Stats. 2011, Ch. 39, Sec. 68.)

11383.7.

(a) Any person who possesses both methylamine and phenyl-2-propanone (phenylacetone) at the same time with the intent to sell, transfer, or otherwise furnish those chemicals to another person with the knowledge that they will be used to manufacture methamphetamine, or who possesses both ethylamine and phenyl-2-propanone (phenylacetone) at the same time with the intent to sell, transfer, or otherwise furnish those chemicals to another person with the knowledge that they will be used to manufacture methamphetamine is guilty of a felony and shall be punished by imprisonment pursuant to subdivision (h) of Section 1170 of the Penal Code for 16 months, two, or three years.

(b) (1) Any person who possesses ephedrine or pseudoephedrine, or any salts, isomers, or salts of isomers of ephedrine or pseudoephedrine, or who possesses a substance containing ephedrine or pseudoephedrine, or any salts, isomers, or salts of isomers of ephedrine or pseudoephedrine, or who possesses at the same time any of the following, or a combination product thereof, with the intent to sell, transfer, or otherwise furnish those chemicals, substances, or products to another person with the knowledge that they will be used to manufacture methamphetamine or any of its analogs specified in subdivision (d) of Section 11055 is guilty of a felony and shall be punished by imprisonment pursuant to subdivision (h) of Section 1170 of the Penal Code for 16 months, two, or three years:

(A) Ephedrine, pseudoephedrine, norpseudoephedrine, N-methylephedrine, N-ethylephedrine, N-methylpseudoephedrine, N-ethylpseudoephedrine, or phenylpropanolamine, plus hydriodic acid.

(B) Ephedrine, pseudoephedrine, norpseudoephedrine, N-methylephedrine, N-ethylephedrine, N-methylpseudoephedrine, N-ethylpseudoephedrine, or phenylpropanolamine, thionyl chloride and hydrogen gas.

(C) Ephedrine, pseudoephedrine, norpseudoephedrine, N-methylephedrine, N-ethylephedrine, N-methylpseudoephedrine, N-ethylpseudoephedrine, or phenylpropanolamine, plus phosphorus pentachloride and hydrogen gas.

(D) Ephedrine, pseudoephedrine, norpseudoephedrine, N-methylephedrine, N-ethylephedrine, N-methylpseudoephedrine, N-ethylpseudoephedrine, chloroephedrine and chloropseudoephedrine, or phenylpropanolamine, plus any reducing agent.

(2) Any person who possesses hydriodic acid or a reducing agent or any product containing hydriodic acid or a reducing agent with the intent to sell, transfer, or otherwise furnish that chemical, product, or substance to another person with the knowledge that they will be used to manufacture methamphetamine or any of its analogs specified in subdivision (d) of Section 11055 is guilty of a felony and shall be punished by imprisonment pursuant to subdivision (h) of Section 1170 of the Penal Code for 16 months, two, or three years.

(c) Any person who possesses the optical, positional, or geometric isomer of any of the compounds listed in this section with the intent to sell, transfer, or otherwise furnish any of the compounds to another person with the knowledge that they will be used to manufacture these controlled substances is guilty of a felony and shall be punished by imprisonment pursuant to subdivision (h) of Section 1170 of the Penal Code for 16 months, two, or three years:

(1) Methamphetamine.

(2) Any analog of methamphetamine specified in subdivision (d) of Section 11055.

(3) N-ethylamphetamine.

(d) Any person who possesses immediate precursors sufficient for the manufacture of methylamine, ethylamine, phenyl-2-propanone, ephedrine, pseudoephedrine, norpseudoephedrine, N-methylephedrine, N-ethylephedrine, phenylpropanolamine, hydriodic acid or a reducing agent, thionyl chloride, or phosphorus pentachloride, with the intent to sell, transfer, or otherwise furnish these substances to another person with the knowledge that they will be used to manufacture methamphetamine is guilty of a felony and shall be punished by imprisonment pursuant to subdivision (h) of Section 1170 of the Penal Code for 16 months, two, or three years.

(e) Any person who possesses essential chemicals sufficient to manufacture hydriodic acid or a reducing agent with the intent to sell, transfer, or otherwise furnish those chemicals to another person with the knowledge that they will be used to manufacture methamphetamine is guilty of a felony and shall be punished by imprisonment pursuant to subdivision (h) of Section 1170 of the Penal Code for 16 months, two, or three years.

(f) Any person who possesses any compound or mixture containing ephedrine, pseudoephedrine, norpseudoephedrine, N-methylephedrine, N-ethylephedrine, phenylpropanolamine, hydriodic acid or a reducing agent, thionyl chloride, or phosphorus pentachloride, with the intent to sell, transfer, or otherwise furnish that compound or mixture to another person with the knowledge that they will be used to manufacture methamphetamine is guilty of a felony and shall be punished by imprisonment pursuant to subdivision (h) of Section 1170 of the Penal Code for 16 months, two, or three years.

(g) For purposes of this section, a "reducing agent" for the purposes of manufacturing methamphetamine means an agent that causes reduction to occur by either donating a hydrogen atom to an organic compound or by removing an oxygen atom from an organic compound.

(h) This section does not apply to drug manufacturers licensed by this state or persons authorized by regulation of the Board of Pharmacy to possess those substances or combinations of substances.

(Amended by Stats. 2011, Ch. 15, Sec. 182. (AB 109) Effective April 4, 2011. Operative October 1, 2011, by Sec. 636 of Ch. 15, as amended by Stats. 2011, Ch. 39, Sec. 68.)

11384.

The Board of Pharmacy shall, by regulation, authorize such persons to possess any combinations of substance specified in subdivision (a) or (b) of Section 11383 as it determines need and will use such substance for a lawful purpose.

(Amended by Stats. 1976, Ch. 1116.)

ARTICLE 7. Mushrooms [11390 - 11392]

(Article 7 added by Stats. 1985, Ch. 1264, Sec. 2.)

11390.

Except as otherwise authorized by law, every person who, with intent to produce a controlled substance specified in paragraph (18) or (19) of subdivision (d) of Section 11054, cultivates any spores or mycelium capable of producing mushrooms or other material which contains such a controlled substance shall be punished by imprisonment in the county jail for a period of not more than one year or in the state prison.

(Added by Stats. 1985, Ch. 1264, Sec. 2.)

11391.

(a) Except as otherwise authorized by law, every person who transports, imports into this state, sells, furnishes, gives away, or offers to transport, import into this state, sell, furnish, or give away any spores or mycelium capable of producing mushrooms or other material which contain a controlled substance specified in paragraph (18) or (19) of subdivision (d) of Section 11054 for the purpose of facilitating a violation of Section 11390 shall be punished by imprisonment in the county jail for a period of not more than one year or in the state prison.

(b) For purposes of this section, "transport" means to transport for sale.

(c) This section does not preclude or limit prosecution for any aiding and abetting or conspiracy offenses.

(Amended by Stats. 2015, Ch. 77, Sec. 3. (AB 730) Effective January 1, 2016.)

11392.

Spores or mycelium capable of producing mushrooms or other material which contains psilocyn or psyocylin may be lawfully obtained and used for bona fide research, instruction, or analysis, if not in violation of federal law, and if the research, instruction, or analysis is approved by the Research Advisory Panel established pursuant to Sections 11480 and 11481.

(Added by Stats. 1985, Ch. 1264, Sec. 2.)

CHAPTER 6.5. Analogs [11400 - 11401]

(Chapter 6.5 added by Stats. 1988, Ch. 712, Sec. 4.)

11400.

The Legislature finds and declares that the laws of this state which prohibit the possession, possession for sale, offer for sale, sale, manufacturing, and transportation of controlled substances are being circumvented by the commission of those acts with respect to analogs of specified controlled substances which have, are represented to have, or are intended to have effects on the central nervous system which are substantially similar to, or greater than, the controlled substances classified in Sections 11054 and 11055 and the synthetic cannabinoid compounds defined in Section 11357.5, of which they are analogs. These analogs have been synthesized by so-called "street chemists" and imported into this state from other jurisdictions as precursors to, or substitutes for, controlled substances and synthetic cannabinoid compounds, due to the nonexistence of applicable criminal penalties. These analogs present grave dangers to the health and safety of the people of this state. Therefore, it is the intent of the Legislature that a controlled substance or controlled substance analog, as defined in Section 11401, be considered identical, for purposes of the penalties and punishment specified in Chapter 6 (commencing with Section 11350), to the controlled substance in Section 11054 or 11055 or the synthetic cannabinoid compound defined in Section 11357.5 of which it is an analog.

(Amended by Stats. 2017, Ch. 561, Sec. 113. (AB 1516) Effective January 1, 2018.)

11401.

(a) A controlled substance analog shall, for the purposes of Chapter 6 (commencing with Section 11350), be treated the same as the controlled substance classified in Section 11054 or 11055 or the synthetic cannabinoid compound defined in Section 11357.5 of which it is an analog.

(b) Except as provided in subdivision (c), the term "controlled substance analog" means either of the following:

(1) A substance the chemical structure of which is substantially similar to the chemical structure of a controlled substance classified in Section 11054 or 11055 or a synthetic cannabinoid compound defined in Section 11357.5.

(2) A substance that has, is represented as having, or is intended to have a stimulant, depressant, or hallucinogenic effect on the central nervous system that is substantially similar to, or greater than, the stimulant, depressant, or hallucinogenic effect on the central nervous system of a controlled substance classified in Section 11054 or 11055 or a synthetic cannabinoid compound defined in Section 11357.5.

(c) The term "controlled substance analog" does not mean any of the following:

(1) A substance for which there is an approved new drug application as defined under Section 505 of the federal Food, Drug, and Cosmetic Act (21 U.S.C. Sec. 355) or that is generally recognized as safe and effective for use pursuant to Sections 501, 502, and 503 of the federal Food, Drug, and Cosmetic Act (21 U.S.C. Secs. 351, 352, and 353) and Section 330 and following of Title 21 of the Code of Federal Regulations.

(2) With respect to a particular person, a substance for which an exemption is in effect for investigational use for that person under Section 505 of the federal Food, Drug, and Cosmetic Act (21 U.S.C. Sec. 355), to the extent that the conduct with respect to that substance is pursuant to the exemption.

(3) A substance, before an exemption as specified in paragraph (2) takes effect with respect to the substance, to the extent the substance is not intended for human consumption.

(Amended by Stats. 2017, Ch. 561, Sec. 114. (AB 1516) Effective January 1, 2018.)

CHAPTER 7. Department of Justice [11450 - 11454]

(Heading of Chapter 7 amended by Stats. 2012, Ch. 867, Sec. 10.)

11450.

The Attorney General may, in conformity with the State Civil Service Act, Part 2 (commencing with Section 18500), Division 5, Title 2 of the Government Code, employ such agents, chemists, clerical, and other employees as are necessary for the conduct of the affairs of the Department of Justice in carrying out its responsibilities specified in this division.

(Added by renumbering Section 11452 by Stats. 1974, Ch. 1403.)

11454.

The Attorney General and the agents appointed by him, when authorized so to do by the Attorney General, may expend such sums as the Attorney General deems necessary in the purchase of controlled substances for evidence and in the employment of operators to obtain evidence.

The sums so expended shall be repaid to the officer making the expenditures upon claims approved by the Attorney General and subject to postaudit by the Department of Finance. The claims when approved shall be paid out of the funds appropriated or made available by law for the support or use of the Department of Justice.

(Amended by Stats. 1974, Ch. 1403.)

CHAPTER 8. Seizure and Disposition [11469 - 11495]

(Chapter 8 added by Stats. 1972, Ch. 1407.)

11469.

In order to ensure the proper utilization of the laws permitting the seizure and forfeiture of property under this chapter, the Legislature hereby establishes the following guidelines:

(a) Law enforcement is the principal objective of forfeiture. Potential revenue must not be allowed to jeopardize the effective investigation and prosecution of criminal offenses, officer safety, the integrity of ongoing investigations, or the due process rights of citizens.

(b) No prosecutor's or sworn law enforcement officer's employment or salary shall be made to depend upon the level of seizures or forfeitures he or she achieves.

(c) Whenever appropriate, prosecutors should seek criminal sanctions as to the underlying criminal acts which give rise to the forfeiture action.

(d) Seizing agencies shall have a manual detailing the statutory grounds for forfeiture and all applicable policies and procedures. The manual shall include procedures for prompt notice to interestholders, the expeditious release of seized property, where appropriate, and the prompt resolution of claims of innocent ownership.

(e) Seizing agencies shall implement training for officers assigned to forfeiture programs, which training should be ongoing.

(f) Seizing agencies shall avoid any appearance of impropriety in the sale or acquisition of forfeited property.

(g) Seizing agencies shall not put any seized or forfeited property into service.

(h) Unless otherwise provided by law, forfeiture proceeds shall be maintained in a separate fund or account subject to appropriate accounting controls and annual financial audits of all deposits and expenditures.

(i) Seizing agencies shall ensure that seized property is protected and its value preserved.

(j) Although civil forfeiture is intended to be remedial by removing the tools and profits from those engaged in the illicit drug trade, it can have harsh effects on property owners in some circumstances. Therefore, law enforcement shall seek to protect the interests of innocent property owners, guarantee adequate notice and due process to property owners, and ensure that forfeiture serves the remedial purpose of the law.

(Added by Stats. 1994, Ch. 314, Sec. 1. Effective August 19, 1994.)

11470.

The following are subject to forfeiture:

(a) All controlled substances which have been manufactured, distributed, dispensed, or acquired in violation of this division.

(b) All raw materials, products, and equipment of any kind which are used, or intended for use, in manufacturing, compounding, processing, delivering, importing, or exporting any controlled substance in violation of this division.

(c) All property except real property or a boat, airplane, or any vehicle which is used, or intended for use, as a container for property described in subdivision (a) or (b).

(d) All books, records, and research products and materials, including formulas, microfilm, tapes, and data which are used, or intended for use, in violation of this division.

(e) The interest of any registered owner of a boat, airplane, or any vehicle other than an implement of husbandry, as defined in Section 36000 of the Vehicle Code, which has been used as an instrument to facilitate the manufacture of, or possession for sale or sale of 14.25 grams or more of heroin, or a substance containing 14.25 grams or more of heroin, or 14.25 grams or more of a substance containing heroin, or 28.5 grams or more of Schedule I controlled substances except cannabis, peyote, or psilocybin; 10 pounds dry weight or more of cannabis, peyote, or psilocybin; or 28.5 grams or more of cocaine, as specified in paragraph (6) of subdivision (b) of Section 11055, cocaine base as specified in paragraph (1) of subdivision (f) of Section 11054, or methamphetamine; or a substance containing 28.5 grams or more of cocaine, as specified in paragraph (6) of subdivision (b) of Section 11055, cocaine base as specified in paragraph (1) of subdivision (f) of Section 11054, or methamphetamine; or 57 grams or more of a substance containing cocaine, as specified in paragraph (6) of subdivision (b) of Section 11055, cocaine base as specified in paragraph (1) of subdivision (f) of Section 11054, or methamphetamine; or 28.5 grams or more of Schedule II controlled substances. An interest in a vehicle which may be lawfully driven on the highway with a class C, class M1, or class M2 license, as prescribed in Section 12804.9 of the Vehicle Code, shall not be forfeited under this subdivision if there is a community property interest in the vehicle by a person other than the defendant and the vehicle is the sole class C, class M1, or class M2 vehicle available to the defendant's immediate family.

(f) All moneys, negotiable instruments, securities, or other things of value furnished or intended to be furnished by any person in exchange for a controlled substance, all proceeds traceable to such an exchange, and all moneys, negotiable instruments, or securities used or intended to be used to facilitate any violation of Section 11351, 11351.5, 11352, 11355, 11359, 11360, 11378, 11378.5, 11379, 11379.5, 11379.6, 11380, 11382, or 11383 of this code, or Section 182 of the Penal Code, or a felony violation of Section 11366.8 of this code, insofar as the offense involves manufacture, sale, possession for sale, offer for sale, or offer to manufacture, or conspiracy to commit at least one of those offenses, if the exchange, violation, or other conduct which is the basis for the forfeiture occurred within five years of the seizure of the property, or the filing of a petition under this chapter, or the issuance of an order of forfeiture of the property, whichever comes first.

(g) The real property of any property owner who is convicted of violating Section 11366, 11366.5, or 11366.6 with respect to that property. However, property which is used as a family residence or for other lawful purposes, or which is owned by two or more persons, one of whom had no knowledge of its unlawful use, shall not be subject to forfeiture.

(h) (1) Subject to the requirements of Section 11488.5 and except as further limited by this subdivision to protect innocent parties who claim a property interest acquired from a defendant, all right, title, and interest in any personal property described in this section shall vest in the state upon commission of the act giving rise to forfeiture under this chapter, if the state or local governmental entity proves a violation of Section 11351, 11351.5, 11352, 11355, 11359, 11360, 11378, 11378.5, 11379, 11379.5, 11379.6, 11380, 11382, or 11383 of this code, or Section 182 of the Penal Code, or a felony violation of Section 11366.8 of this code, insofar as the offense involves the manufacture, sale, possession for sale, offer for sale, offer to manufacture, or conspiracy to commit at least one of those offenses, in accordance with the burden of proof set forth in paragraph (1) of subdivision (i) of Section 11488.4 or, in the case of cash or negotiable instruments in excess of twenty-five thousand dollars ($25,000), paragraph (4) of subdivision (i) of Section 11488.4.

(2) The operation of the special vesting rule established by this subdivision shall be limited to circumstances where its application will not defeat the claim of any person, including a bona fide purchaser or encumbrancer who, pursuant to Section 11488.5, 11488.6, or 11489, claims an interest in the property seized, notwithstanding that the interest in the property being claimed was acquired from a defendant whose property interest would otherwise have been subject to divestment pursuant to this subdivision.

(Amended by Stats. 2017, Ch. 27, Sec. 152. (SB 94) Effective June 27, 2017.)

11470.1.

(a) The expenses of seizing, eradicating, destroying, or taking remedial action with respect to, any controlled substance or its precursors shall be recoverable from:

(1) Any person who manufactures or cultivates a controlled substance or its precursors in violation of this division.

(2) Any person who aids and abets or who knowingly profits in any manner from the manufacture or cultivation of a controlled substance or its precursors on property owned, leased, or possessed by the defendant, in violation of this division.

(b) The expenses of taking remedial action with respect to any controlled substance or its precursors shall also be recoverable from any person liable for the costs of that remedial action under Chapter 6.8 (commencing with Section 25300) of Division 20 of the Health and Safety Code.

(c) It shall be necessary to seek or obtain a criminal conviction for the unlawful manufacture or cultivation of any controlled substance or its precursors prior to the entry of judgment for the recovery of expenses. If criminal charges are pending against the defendant for the unlawful manufacture or cultivation of any controlled substance or its precursors, an action brought pursuant to this section shall, upon a defendant's request, be continued while the criminal charges are pending.

(d) The action may be brought by the district attorney, county counsel, city attorney, the State Department of Health Care Services, or Attorney General. All expenses recovered pursuant to this section shall be remitted to the law enforcement agency which incurred them.

(e) (1) The burden of proof as to liability shall be on the plaintiff and shall be by a preponderance of the evidence in an action alleging that the defendant is liable for expenses pursuant to paragraph (1) of subdivision (a). The burden of proof as to liability shall be on the plaintiff and shall be by clear and convincing evidence in an action alleging that the defendant is liable for expenses pursuant to paragraph (2) of subdivision (a). The burden of proof as to the amount of expenses recoverable shall be on the plaintiff and shall be by a preponderance of the evidence in any action brought pursuant to subdivision (a).

(2) Notwithstanding paragraph (1), for any person convicted of a criminal charge of the manufacture or cultivation of a controlled substance or its precursors there shall be a presumption affecting the burden of proof that the person is liable.

(f) Only expenses which meet the following requirements shall be recoverable under this section:

(1) The expenses were incurred in seizing, eradicating, or destroying the controlled substance or its precursors or in taking remedial action with respect to a hazardous substance. These expenses may not include any costs incurred in use of the herbicide paraquat.

(2) The expenses were incurred as a proximate result of the defendant's manufacture or cultivation of a controlled substance in violation of this division.

(3) The expenses were reasonably incurred.

(g) For purposes of this section, "remedial action" shall have the meaning set forth in Section 25322.

(h) For the purpose of discharge in bankruptcy, a judgment for recovery of expenses under this section shall be deemed to be a debt for willful and malicious injury by the defendant to another entity or to the property of another entity.

(i) Notwithstanding Section 526 of the Code of Civil Procedure, the plaintiff may be granted a temporary restraining order or a preliminary injunction, pending or during trial, to restrain the defendant from transferring, encumbering, hypothecating, or otherwise disposing of any assets specified by the court, if it appears by the complaint that the plaintiff is entitled to the relief demanded and it appears that the defendant may dispose of those assets to thwart enforcement of the judgment.

(j) The Legislature finds and declares that civil penalties for the recovery of expenses incurred in enforcing the provisions of this division shall not supplant criminal prosecution for violation of those provisions, but shall be a supplemental remedy to criminal enforcement.

(k) Any testimony, admission, or any other statement made by the defendant in any proceeding brought pursuant to this section, or any evidence derived from the testimony, admission, or other statement, shall not be admitted or otherwise used in any criminal proceeding arising out of the same conduct.

(l) No action shall be brought or maintained pursuant to this section against a person who has been acquitted of criminal charges for conduct that is the basis for an action under this section.

(Amended by Stats. 2016, Ch. 831, Sec. 1. (SB 443) Effective January 1, 2017.)

11470.2.

(a) In lieu of a civil action for the recovery of expenses as provided in Section 11470.1, the prosecuting attorney in a criminal proceeding may, upon conviction of the underlying offense, seek the recovery of all expenses recoverable under Section 11470.1 from:

(1) Any person who manufacturers or cultivates a controlled substance or its precursors in violation of this division.

(2) Any person who aids and abets or who knowingly profits in any manner from the manufacture or cultivation of a controlled substance or its precursors on property owned, leased, or possessed by the defendant, in violation of this division. The trier of fact shall make an award of expenses, if proven, which shall be enforceable as any civil judgment. If probation is granted, the court may order payment of the expenses as a condition of probation. All expenses recovered pursuant to this section shall be remitted to the law enforcement agency which incurred them.

(b) The prosecuting attorney may, in conjunction with the criminal proceeding, file a petition for recovery of expenses with the superior court of the county in which the defendant has been charged with the underlying offense. The petition shall allege that the defendant had manufactured or cultivated a controlled substance in violation of Division 10 (commencing with Section 11000) of the Health and Safety Code and that expenses were incurred in seizing, eradicating, or destroying the controlled substance or its precursors. The petition shall also state the amount to be assessed. The prosecuting attorney shall make service of process of a notice of that petition to the defendant.

(c) The defendant may admit to or deny the petition for recovery of expenses. If the defendant admits the allegations of the petition, the court shall rule for the prosecuting attorney and enter a judgment for recovery of the expenses incurred.

(d) If the defendant denies the petition or declines to admit to it, the petition shall be heard in the superior court in which the underlying criminal offense will be tried and shall be promptly heard following the defendant's conviction on the underlying offense. The

hearing shall be held either before the same jury or before a new jury in the discretion of the court, unless waived by the consent of all parties.

(e) At the hearing, the burden of proof as to the amount of expenses recoverable shall be on the prosecuting attorney and shall be by a preponderance of the evidence.

(f) For the purpose of discharge in bankruptcy, a judgment for recovery of expenses under this section shall be deemed to be a debt for willful and malicious injury by the defendant to another entity or to the property of another entity.

(Added by Stats. 1983, Ch. 931, Sec. 2.)

11470.3.

(a) Section 11470 shall be applicable to property owned by, or in the possession of, minors.

(b) The procedures for the forfeiture of property that comes within Section 11470 shall be applicable to minors.

(c) Notwithstanding the provisions of this chapter, if a petition has been filed alleging that the minor is a person described in Section 602 of the Welfare and Institutions Code because of a violation which is the basis for the seizure and forfeiture of property under this chapter, any related forfeiture hearing shall be continued until the adjudication of the petition. The forfeiture hearing shall not be conducted in juvenile court.

(Added by Stats. 1988, Ch. 1358, Sec. 2.)

11470.4.

The provisions of this chapter apply to any minor who has been found to be a person described in Section 602 of the Welfare and Institutions Code because of a violation of Section 11351, 11351.5, 11352, 11355, 11366, 11366.5, 11366.6, 11378.5, 11379, 11379.5, 11379.6, or 11382.

(Added by Stats. 1988, Ch. 1249, Sec. 1.)

11471.

Property subject to forfeiture under this division may be seized by any peace officer upon process issued by any court having jurisdiction over the property. Seizure without process may be made if any of the following situations exist:

(a) The seizure is incident to an arrest or a search under a search warrant.

(b) The property subject to seizure has been the subject of a prior judgment in favor of the state in a criminal injunction or forfeiture proceeding based upon this division.

(c) There is probable cause to believe that the property is directly or indirectly dangerous to health or safety.

(d) There is probable cause to believe that the property was used or is intended to be used in violation of this division.

(e) Real property subject to forfeiture may not be seized, absent exigent circumstances, without notice to the interested parties and a hearing to determine that seizure is necessary to preserve the property pending the outcome of the proceedings. At the hearing, the prosecution shall bear the burden of establishing that probable cause exists for the forfeiture of the property and that seizure is necessary to preserve the property pending the outcome of the forfeiture proceedings. The court may issue seizure orders pursuant to this section if it finds that seizure is warranted or pendente lite orders pursuant to Section 11492 if it finds that the status quo or value of the property can be preserved without seizure.

(f) Where business records are seized in conjunction with the seizure of property subject to forfeiture, the seizing agency shall, upon request, provide copies of the records to the person, persons, or business entity from whom such records were seized.

(Amended by Stats. 1994, Ch. 314, Sec. 4. Effective August 19, 1994.)

11471.2.

(a) State or local law enforcement authorities shall not refer or otherwise transfer property seized under state law authorizing the seizure of property to a federal agency seeking the adoption of the seized property by the federal agency for proceeding with federal forfeiture under the federal Controlled Substances Act. Nothing in this section shall be construed to prohibit the federal government, or any of its agencies, from seizing property, seeking forfeiture under federal law, or sharing federally forfeited property with state or local law enforcement agencies when those state or local agencies work with federal agencies in joint investigations arising out of federal law or federal joint task forces comprised of federal and state or local agencies. Nothing in this section shall be construed to prohibit state or local law enforcement agencies from participating in a joint law enforcement operation with federal agencies.

(b) Except as provided in this subdivision and in subdivision (c), a state or local law enforcement agency participating in a joint investigation with a federal agency shall not receive an equitable share from the federal agency of all or a portion of the forfeited property or proceeds from the sale of property forfeited pursuant to the federal Controlled Substances Act unless a defendant is convicted in an underlying or related criminal action of an offense for which property is subject to forfeiture as specified in Section 11470 or Section 11488, or an offense under the federal Controlled Substances Act that includes all of the elements of an offense for which property is subject to forfeiture as specified in Sections 11470 and 11488. In any case in which the forfeited property is cash or negotiable instruments of a value of not less than forty thousand dollars ($40,000) there shall be no requirement of a criminal conviction as a prerequisite to receipt by state or local law enforcement agencies of an equitable share from federal authorities.

(c) If the defendant has been arrested and charged in an underlying or related criminal action or proceeding for an offense described in subdivision (b) and willfully fails to appear as required, intentionally flees to evade prosecution, or is deceased, there shall be no requirement of a criminal conviction as a prerequisite to receipt by state or local law enforcement agencies of an equitable share from federal authorities.

(Added by Stats. 2016, Ch. 831, Sec. 2. (SB 443) Effective January 1, 2017.)

11471.5.

A peace officer making a seizure pursuant to Section 11471 shall notify the Franchise Tax Board where there is reasonable cause to believe that the value of the seized property exceeds five thousand dollars ($5,000).

(Added by Stats. 1987, Ch. 924, Sec. 1.5. Effective September 22, 1987.)

11472.

Controlled substances and any device, contrivance, instrument, or paraphernalia used for unlawfully using or administering a controlled substance, which are possessed in violation of this division, may be seized by any peace officer and in the aid of such seizure a search warrant may be issued as prescribed by law.

(Added by renumbering Section 11473 by Stats. 1980, Ch. 1019.)

11473.

(a) All seizures under provisions of this chapter, except seizures of vehicles, boats, or airplanes, as specified in subdivision (e) of Section 11470, or seizures of moneys, negotiable instruments, securities, or other things of value as specified in subdivision (f) of Section 11470, shall, upon conviction of the owner or defendant, be ordered destroyed by the court in which conviction was had.

(b) Law enforcement may request of the court that certain uncontaminated science equipment be relinquished to a school or school district for science classroom education in lieu of destruction.

(Amended by Stats. 1994, Ch. 979, Sec. 2. Effective January 1, 1995.)

11473.5.

(a) All seizures of controlled substances, instruments, or paraphernalia used for unlawfully using or administering a controlled substance which are in possession of any city, county, or state official as found property, or as the result of a case in which no trial was had or which has been disposed of by way of dismissal or otherwise than by way of conviction, shall be destroyed by order of the court, unless the court finds that the controlled substances, instruments, or paraphernalia were lawfully possessed by the defendant.

(b) If the court finds that the property was not lawfully possessed by the defendant, law enforcement may request of the court that certain uncontaminated instruments or paraphernalia be relinquished to a school or school district for science classroom education in lieu of destruction.

(Amended by Stats. 1994, Ch. 979, Sec. 3. Effective January 1, 1995.)

11474.

A court order for the destruction of controlled substances, instruments, or paraphernalia pursuant to the provisions of Section 11473 or 11473.5 may be carried out by a police or sheriff's department, the Department of Justice, the Department of the California Highway Patrol, or the Department of Alcoholic Beverage Control. The court order shall specify the agency responsible for the destruction. Controlled substances, instruments, or paraphernalia not in the possession of the designated agency at the time the order of the court is issued shall be delivered to the designated agency for destruction in compliance with the order.

(Amended by Stats. 1999, Ch. 787, Sec. 7. Effective January 1, 2000.)

11475.

Controlled substances listed in Schedule I that are possessed, transferred, sold, or offered for sale in violation of this division are contraband and shall be seized and summarily forfeited to the state. Controlled substances listed in Schedule I, which are seized or come into the possession of the state, the owners of which are unknown, are contraband and shall be summarily forfeited to the state.

(Added by Stats. 1972, Ch. 1407.)

11476.

Species of plants from which controlled substances in Schedules I and II may be derived which have been planted or cultivated in violation of this division, or of which the owners or cultivators are unknown, or which are wild growths, may be seized and summarily forfeited to the state.

(Added by Stats. 1972, Ch. 1407.)

11477.

The failure, upon demand by a peace officer of the person in occupancy or in control of land or premises upon which the species of plants are growing or being stored, to produce an appropriate registration, or proof that he is the holder thereof, constitutes authority for the seizure and forfeiture of the plants.

(Amended by Stats. 1980, Ch. 1019.)

11478.

Cannabis may be provided by the Attorney General to the heads of research projects which have been registered by the Attorney General, and which have been approved by the research advisory panel pursuant to Section 11480.

The head of the approved research project shall personally receipt for such quantities of cannabis and shall make a record of their disposition. The receipt and record shall be retained by the Attorney General. The head of the approved research project shall also, at intervals and in the manner required by the research advisory panel, report the progress or conclusions of the research project.

(Amended by Stats. 2017, Ch. 27, Sec. 153. (SB 94) Effective June 27, 2017.)

11479.

Notwithstanding Sections 11473 and 11473.5, at any time after seizure by a law enforcement agency of a suspected controlled substance, except in the case of growing or harvested cannabis, that amount in excess of 10 pounds in gross weight may be destroyed without a court order by the chief of the law enforcement agency or a designated subordinate. In the case of growing or harvested cannabis, that amount in excess of two pounds, or the amount of cannabis a medicinal cannabis patient or

designated caregiver is authorized to possess by ordinance in the city or county where the cannabis was seized, whichever is greater, may be destroyed without a court order by the chief of the law enforcement agency or a designated subordinate. Destruction shall not take place pursuant to this section until all of the following requirements are satisfied:

(a) At least five random and representative samples have been taken, for evidentiary purposes, from the total amount of suspected controlled substances to be destroyed. These samples shall be in addition to the 10 pounds required above. When the suspected controlled substance consists of growing or harvested cannabis plants, at least one 2-pound sample or a sample in the amount of medicinal cannabis a medicinal cannabis patient or designated caregiver is authorized to possess by ordinance in the city or county where the cannabis was seized, whichever is greater, shall be retained. This sample may include stalks, branches, or leaves. In addition, five representative samples of leaves or buds shall be retained for evidentiary purposes from the total amount of suspected controlled substances to be destroyed.

(b) Photographs and videos have been taken that reasonably and accurately demonstrate the total amount of the suspected controlled substance to be destroyed.

(c) The gross weight of the suspected controlled substance has been determined, either by actually weighing the suspected controlled substance or by estimating that weight after dimensional measurement of the total suspected controlled substance.

(d) The chief of the law enforcement agency has determined that it is not reasonably possible to preserve the suspected controlled substance in place, or to remove the suspected controlled substance to another location. In making this determination, the difficulty of transporting and storing the suspected controlled substance to another site and the storage facilities may be taken into consideration.

Subsequent to any destruction of a suspected controlled substance pursuant to this section, an affidavit shall be filed within 30 days in the court that has jurisdiction over any pending criminal proceedings pertaining to that suspected controlled substance, reciting the applicable information required by subdivisions (a), (b), (c), and (d) together with information establishing the location of the suspected controlled substance, and specifying the date and time of the destruction. In the event that there are no criminal proceedings pending that pertain to that suspected controlled substance, the affidavit may be filed in any court within the county that would have jurisdiction over a person against whom those criminal charges might be filed.

(Amended by Stats. 2017, Ch. 27, Sec. 154. (SB 94) Effective June 27, 2017.)

11479.1.

(a) Notwithstanding the provisions of Sections 11473, 11473.5, and 11479, at any time after seizure by a law enforcement agency and identification by a forensic chemist or criminalist of phencyclidine, or an analog thereof, that amount in excess of one gram of a crystalline substance containing phencyclidine or its analog, 10 milliliters of a liquid substance containing phencyclidine or its analog, two grams of plant material containing phencyclidine or its analog, or five hand-rolled cigarettes treated with phencyclidine or its analog, may be destroyed without a court order by the chief of the law enforcement agency or a designated subordinate. Destruction shall not take place pursuant to this section until all of the following requirements are satisfied:

(1) At least one gram of a crystalline substance containing phencyclidine or its analog, 10 milliliters of a liquid substance containing phencyclidine or its analog, two grams of plant material containing phencyclidine or its analog, or five hand-rolled cigarettes treated with phencyclidine or its analog have been taken as samples from the phencyclidine or analog to be destroyed.

(2) Photographs have been taken which reasonably demonstrate the total amount of phencyclidine or its analog to be destroyed.

(3) The gross weight of the phencyclidine or its analog has been determined by actually weighing the phencyclidine or analog.

(b) Subsequent to any destruction of phencyclidine or its analog, an affidavit shall be filed within 30 days in the court which has jurisdiction over any pending criminal proceedings pertaining to that phencyclidine or its analog, reciting the applicable information required by paragraphs (1), (2), and (3) of subdivision (a), together with information establishing the location of the phencyclidine or analog and specifying the date and time of the destruction. In the event that there are no criminal proceedings pending which pertain to that phencyclidine or analog, the affidavit may be filed in any court within the county which would have jurisdiction over a person against whom these criminal charges might be filed.

(Amended by Stats. 2002, Ch. 787, Sec. 4. Effective January 1, 2003.)

11479.2.

Notwithstanding the provisions of Sections 11473, 11473.5, 11474, 11479, and 11479.1, at any time after seizure by a law enforcement agency of a suspected controlled substance, except cannabis, any amount, as determined by the court, in excess of 57 grams may, by court order, be destroyed by the chief of a law enforcement agency or a designated subordinate. Destruction shall not take place pursuant to this section until all of the following requirements are satisfied:

(a) At least five random and representative samples have been taken, for evidentiary purposes, from the total amount of suspected controlled substances to be destroyed. Those samples shall be in addition to the 57 grams required above and each sample shall weigh not less than one gram at the time the sample is collected.

(b) Photographs have been taken which reasonably demonstrate the total amount of the suspected controlled substance to be destroyed.

(c) The gross weight of the suspected controlled substance has been determined, either by actually weighing the suspected controlled substance or by estimating such weight after dimensional measurement of the total suspected controlled substance.

(d) In cases involving controlled substances suspected of containing cocaine or methamphetamine, an analysis has determined the qualitative and quantitative nature of the suspected controlled substance.

(e) The law enforcement agency with custody of the controlled substance sought to be destroyed has filed a written motion for the order of destruction in the court which has jurisdiction over any pending criminal proceeding in which a defendant is charged by accusatory pleading with a crime specifically involving the suspected controlled substance sought to be destroyed. The motion shall, by affidavit of the chief of the law enforcement agency or designated subordinate, recite the applicable information required by subdivisions (a), (b), (c), and (d), together with information establishing the location of the suspected controlled substance and the title of any pending criminal proceeding as defined in this subdivision. The motion shall bear proof of service upon all parties to any pending criminal proceeding. No motion shall be made when a defendant is without counsel until the defendant has entered his or her plea to the charges.

(f) The order for destruction shall issue pursuant to this section upon the motion and affidavit in support of the order, unless within 20 days after application for the order, a defendant has requested, in writing, a hearing on the motion. Within 10 days after the filing of that request, or a longer period of time upon good cause shown by either party, the court shall conduct a hearing on the motion in which each party to the motion for destruction shall be permitted to call and examine witnesses. The hearing shall be recorded. Upon conclusion of the hearing, if the court finds that the defendant would not be prejudiced by the destruction, it shall grant the motion and make an order for destruction. In making the order, the court shall ensure that the representative samples to be retained are of sufficient quantities to allow for qualitative analyses by both the prosecution and the defense. Any order for destruction pursuant to this section shall include the applicable information required by subdivisions (a), (b), (c), (d), and (e) and the name of the agency responsible for the destruction. Unless waived, the order shall provide for a 10-day delay prior to destruction in order to allow expert analysis of the controlled substance by the defense.

Subsequent to any destruction of a suspected controlled substance pursuant to this section, an affidavit shall be filed within 30 days in the court which ordered destruction stating the location of the retained, suspected controlled substance and specifying the date and time of destruction.

This section does not apply to seizures involving hazardous chemicals or controlled substances in mixture or combination with hazardous chemicals.

(Amended by Stats. 2017, Ch. 27, Sec. 155. (SB 94) Effective June 27, 2017.)

11479.5.

(a) Notwithstanding Sections 11473 and 11473.5, at any time after seizure by a law enforcement agency of a suspected hazardous chemical, the chemical's container, or any item contaminated with a hazardous substance believed to have been used or intended to have been used in the unlawful manufacture of controlled substances, that amount in excess of one fluid ounce if liquid, or one avoirdupois ounce if solid, of each different type of suspected hazardous chemical, its container, and any item contaminated with a hazardous substance may be disposed of without a court order by the seizing agency. For the purposes of this section, "hazardous chemical" means any material that is believed by the chief of the law enforcement agency, or his or her designee, to be toxic, carcinogenic, explosive, corrosive, or flammable, and that is believed by the chief of the law enforcement agency, or his or her designee, to have been used or intended to have been used in the unlawful manufacture of controlled substances.

(b) Destruction pursuant to this section of suspected hazardous chemicals or suspected hazardous chemicals and controlled substances in combination, or the chemical containers and items contaminated with a hazardous substance, shall not take place until all of the following requirements are met:

(1) At least a one ounce sample is taken from each different type of suspected hazardous chemical to be destroyed.

(2) At least a one ounce sample has been taken from each container of a mixture of a suspected hazardous chemical with a suspected controlled substance.

(3) Photographs have been taken which reasonably demonstrate the total amount of suspected controlled substances and suspected hazardous chemicals to be destroyed.

(4) The gross weight or volume of the suspected hazardous chemical seized has been determined.

(5) Photographs have been taken of the chemical containers and items contaminated with a hazardous substance that reasonably demonstrate their size.

(c) Subsequent to any disposal of a suspected hazardous chemical, its container, or any item contaminated with a hazardous substance pursuant to this section, the law enforcement agency involved shall maintain records concerning the details of its compliance with, and reciting the applicable information required by paragraphs (1), (2), (3), (4), and (5) of subdivision (b), together with the information establishing the location of the suspected hazardous chemical, its container, and any item contaminated with a hazardous substance, and specifying the date and time of the disposal.

(d) (1) Subsequent to any destruction of a suspected controlled substance in combination with a hazardous chemical or any item contaminated with a hazardous substance pursuant to this section, an affidavit containing applicable information required by paragraphs (1), (2), (3), (4), and (5) of subdivision (b) shall be filed within 30 days in the court that issued the search warrant.

(2) If the disposed materials were seized without a warrant, an affidavit containing applicable information required by paragraphs (1), (2), (3), (4), and (5) of subdivision (b) shall be filed in the court that has jurisdiction over any criminal proceedings pertaining to the suspected controlled substance after the criminal proceedings are initiated.

(e) A law enforcement agency responsible for the disposal of any hazardous chemical shall comply with the provisions of Chapter 6.5 (commencing with Section 25100) of Division 20 of the Health and Safety Code, as well as all applicable state and federal statutes and regulations.

(Amended by Stats. 2002, Ch. 443, Sec. 1. Effective January 1, 2003.)

11480.

(a) The Legislature finds that there is a need to encourage further research into the nature and effects of cannabis and hallucinogenic drugs and to coordinate research efforts on such subjects.

(b) There is a Research Advisory Panel that consists of a representative of the State Department of Health Services, a representative of the California State Board of Pharmacy, the State Public Health Officer, a representative of the Attorney General, a representative of the University of California who shall be a pharmacologist, a physician, or a person holding a doctorate degree in the health sciences, a representative of a private university in this state who shall be a pharmacologist, a physician, or a person holding a doctorate degree in the health sciences, a representative of a statewide professional medical society in this state who shall be engaged in the private practice of medicine and shall be experienced in treating controlled substance dependency, a representative appointed by and serving at the pleasure of the Governor who shall have experience in drug abuse, cancer, or controlled substance research and who is either a registered nurse, licensed pursuant to Chapter 6 (commencing with Section 2700) of Division 2 of the Business and Professions Code, or other health professional. The Governor shall annually designate the private university and the professional medical society represented on the panel. Members of the panel shall be appointed by the heads of the entities to be represented, and they shall serve at the pleasure of the appointing power.

(c) The Research Advisory Panel shall appoint two special members to the Research Advisory Panel, who shall serve at the pleasure of the Research Advisory Panel only during the period Article 6 (commencing with Section 11260) of Chapter 5 remains effective. The additional members shall be physicians and surgeons, and who are board certified in oncology, ophthalmology, or psychiatry.

(d) The panel shall annually select a chairperson from among its members.

(e) The panel may hold hearings on, and in other ways study, research projects concerning cannabis or hallucinogenic drugs in this state. Members of the panel shall serve without compensation, but shall be reimbursed for any actual and necessary expenses incurred in connection with the performance of their duties.

(f) The panel may approve research projects, which have been registered by the Attorney General, into the nature and effects of cannabis or hallucinogenic drugs, and shall inform the Attorney General of the head of the approved research projects that are entitled to receive quantities of cannabis pursuant to Section 11478.

(g) The panel may withdraw approval of a research project at any time, and when approval is withdrawn shall notify the head of the research project to return any quantities of cannabis to the Attorney General.

(h) The panel shall report annually to the Legislature and the Governor those research projects approved by the panel, the nature of each research project, and, where available, the conclusions of the research project.

(Amended by Stats. 2017, Ch. 27, Sec. 156. (SB 94) Effective June 27, 2017.)

11481.

The Research Advisory Panel may hold hearings on, and in other ways study, research projects concerning the treatment of abuse of controlled substances.

The panel may approve research projects, which have been registered by the Attorney General, concerning the treatment of abuse of controlled substances and shall inform the chief of such approval. The panel may withdraw approval of a research project at any time and when approval is withdrawn shall so notify the chief.

The panel shall, annually and in the manner determined by the panel, report to the Legislature and the Governor those research projects approved by the panel, the nature of each research project, and where available, the conclusions of the research project.

(Added by Stats. 1972, Ch. 1407.)

11483.

No provision of this division shall be construed to prohibit the establishment and effective operation of a narcotic treatment program licensed pursuant to Article 4 (commencing with Section 11885) of Chapter 1 of Part 3 of Division 10.5.

(Amended by Stats. 1995, Ch. 455, Sec. 12. Effective September 5, 1995.)

11485.

Any peace officer of this state who, incident to a search under a search warrant issued for a violation of Section 11358 with respect to which no prosecution of a defendant results, seizes personal property suspected of being used in the planting, cultivation, harvesting, drying, processing, or transporting of cannabis, shall, if the seized personal property is not being held for evidence or destroyed as contraband, and if the owner of the property is unknown or has not claimed the property, provide notice regarding the seizure and manner of reclamation of the property to any owner or tenant of real property on which the property was seized. In addition, this notice shall be posted at the location of seizure and shall be published at least once in a newspaper of general circulation in the county in which the property was seized. If, after 90 days following the first publication of the notice, no owner appears and proves his or her ownership, the seized personal property shall be deemed to be abandoned and may be disposed of by sale to the public at public auction as set forth in Article 1 (commencing with Section 2080) of Chapter 4 of Title 6 of Part 4 of Division 3 of the Civil Code, or may be disposed of by transfer to a government agency or community service organization. Any profit from the sale or transfer of the property shall be expended for investigative services with respect to crimes involving cannabis.

(Amended by Stats. 2017, Ch. 27, Sec. 157. (SB 94) Effective June 27, 2017.)

11488.

(a) Any peace officer of this state, subsequent to making or attempting to make an arrest for a violation of Section 11351, 11351.5, 11352, 11355, 11359, 11360, 11378, 11378.5, 11379, 11379.5, 11379.6, or 11382 of this code, or Section 182 of the Penal Code insofar as the offense involves manufacture, sale, purchase for the purpose of sale, possession for sale or offer to manufacture or sell, or conspiracy to commit one of those offenses, may seize any item subject to forfeiture under subdivisions (a) to (f), inclusive, of Section 11470. The peace officer shall also notify the Franchise Tax Board of a seizure where there is reasonable cause to believe that the value of the seized property exceeds five thousand dollars ($5,000).

(b) Receipts for property seized pursuant to this section shall be delivered to any person out of whose possession such property was seized, in accordance with Section 1412 of the Penal Code. In the event property seized was not seized out of anyone's possession, receipt for the property shall be delivered to the individual in possession of the premises at which the property was seized.

(c) There shall be a presumption affecting the burden of proof that the person to whom a receipt for property was issued is the owner thereof. This presumption may, however, be rebutted at the forfeiture hearing specified in Section 11488.5.

(Repealed and added by Stats. 1994, Ch. 314, Sec. 9. Effective August 19, 1994.)

11488.1.

Property seized pursuant to Section 11488 may, where appropriate, be held for evidence. The Attorney General or the district attorney for the jurisdiction involved shall institute and maintain the proceedings.

(Amended by Stats. 1994, Ch. 314, Sec. 10. Effective August 19, 1994.)

11488.2.

Within 15 days after the seizure, if the peace officer does not hold the property seized pursuant to Section 11488 for evidence or if the law enforcement agency for which the peace officer is employed does not refer the matter in writing for the institution of forfeiture proceedings by the Attorney General or the district attorney pursuant to Section 11488.1, the officer shall comply with any notice to withhold issued with respect to the property by the Franchise Tax Board. If no notice to withhold has been issued with respect to the property by the Franchise Tax Board, the officer shall return the property to the individual designated in the receipt therefor or if the property is a vehicle, boat, or airplane, it shall be returned to the registered owner.

(Amended by Stats. 1990, Ch. 1200, Sec. 3.)

11488.4.

(a) (1) Except as provided in subdivision (j), if the Department of Justice or the local governmental entity determines that the factual circumstances do warrant that the moneys, negotiable instruments, securities, or other things of value seized or subject to forfeiture come within the provisions of subdivisions (a) to (g), inclusive, of Section 11470, and are not automatically made forfeitable or subject to court order of forfeiture or destruction by another provision of this chapter, the Attorney General or district attorney shall file a petition of forfeiture with the superior court of the county in which the defendant has been charged with the underlying criminal offense or in which the property subject to forfeiture has been seized or, if no seizure has occurred, in the county in which the property subject to forfeiture is located. If the petition alleges that real property is forfeitable, the prosecuting attorney shall cause a lis pendens to be recorded in the office of the county recorder of each county in which the real property is located.

(2) A petition of forfeiture under this subdivision shall be filed as soon as practicable, but in any case within one year of the seizure of the property which is subject to forfeiture, or as soon as practicable, but in any case within one year of the filing by the Attorney General or district attorney of a lis pendens or other process against the property, whichever is earlier.

(b) Physical seizure of assets shall not be necessary in order to have that particular asset alleged to be forfeitable in a petition under this section. The prosecuting attorney may seek protective orders for any asset pursuant to Section 11492.

(c) The Attorney General or district attorney shall make service of process regarding this petition upon every individual designated in a receipt issued for the property seized. In addition, the Attorney General or district attorney shall cause a notice of the seizure, if any, and of the intended forfeiture proceeding, as well as a notice stating that any interested party may file a verified claim with the superior court of the county in which the property was seized or if the property was not seized, a notice of the initiation of forfeiture proceedings with respect to any interest in the property seized or subject to forfeiture, to be served by personal delivery or by registered mail upon any person who has an interest in the seized property or property subject to forfeiture other than persons designated in a receipt issued for the property seized. Whenever a notice is delivered pursuant to this section, it shall be accompanied by a claim form as described in Section 11488.5 and directions for the filing and service of a claim.

(d) An investigation shall be made by the law enforcement agency as to any claimant to a vehicle, boat, or airplane whose right, title, interest, or lien is of record in the Department of Motor Vehicles or appropriate federal agency. If the law enforcement agency finds that any person, other than the registered owner, is the legal owner thereof, and that ownership did not arise subsequent to the date and time of arrest or notification of the forfeiture proceedings or seizure of the vehicle, boat, or airplane, it shall forthwith send a notice to the legal owner at his or her address appearing on the records of the Department of Motor Vehicles or appropriate federal agency.

(e) When a forfeiture action is filed, the notices shall be published once a week for three successive weeks in a newspaper of general circulation in the county where the seizure was made or where the property subject to forfeiture is located.

(f) All notices shall set forth the time within which a claim of interest in the property seized or subject to forfeiture is required to be filed pursuant to Section 11488.5. The notices shall explain, in plain language, what an interested party must do and the time in which the person must act to contest the forfeiture in a hearing. The notices shall state what rights the interested party has at a hearing. The notices shall also state the legal consequences for failing to respond to the forfeiture notice.

(g) Nothing contained in this chapter shall preclude a person, other than a defendant, claiming an interest in property actually seized from moving for a return of property if that person can show standing by proving an interest in the property not assigned subsequent to the seizure or filing of the forfeiture petition.

(h) (1) If there is an underlying or related criminal action, a defendant may move for the return of the property on the grounds that there is not probable cause to believe that the property is forfeitable pursuant to subdivisions (a) to (g), inclusive, of Section 11470 and is not automatically made forfeitable or subject to court order of forfeiture or destruction by another provision of this chapter. The motion may be made prior to, during, or subsequent to the preliminary examination. If made subsequent to the preliminary examination, the Attorney General or district attorney may submit the record of the preliminary hearing as evidence that probable cause exists to believe that the underlying or related criminal violations have occurred.

(2) Within 15 days after a defendant's motion is granted, the people may file a petition for a writ of mandate or prohibition seeking appellate review of the ruling.

(i) (1) With respect to property described in subdivisions (e) and (g) of Section 11470 for which forfeiture is sought and as to which forfeiture is contested, the state or local governmental entity shall have the burden of proving beyond a reasonable doubt that the property for which forfeiture is sought was used, or intended to be used, to facilitate a violation of one of the offenses enumerated in subdivision (f) or (g) of Section 11470.

(2) In the case of property described in subdivision (f) of Section 11470, except cash, negotiable instruments, or other cash equivalents of a value of not less than forty thousand dollars ($40,000), for which forfeiture is sought and as to which forfeiture is contested, the state or local governmental entity shall have the burden of proving beyond a reasonable doubt that the property for which forfeiture is sought meets the criteria for forfeiture described in subdivision (f) of Section 11470.

(3) In the case of property described in paragraphs (1) and (2), where forfeiture is contested, a judgment of forfeiture requires as a condition precedent thereto, that a defendant be convicted in an underlying or related criminal action of an offense specified in subdivision (f) or (g) of Section 11470 which offense occurred within five years of the seizure of the property subject to forfeiture or within five years of the notification of intention to seek forfeiture. If the defendant is found guilty of the underlying or related criminal offense, the issue of forfeiture shall be tried before the same jury, if the trial was by jury, or tried before the same court, if trial was by court, unless waived by all parties. The issue of forfeiture shall be bifurcated from the criminal trial and tried after conviction unless waived by all the parties.

(4) In the case of property described in subdivision (f) of Section 11470 that is cash or negotiable instruments of a value of not less than forty thousand dollars ($40,000), the state or local governmental entity shall have the burden of proving by clear and convincing evidence that the property for which forfeiture is sought is such as is described in subdivision (f) of Section 11470. There is no requirement for forfeiture thereof that a criminal conviction be obtained in an underlying or related criminal offense.

(5) If there is an underlying or related criminal action, and a criminal conviction is required before a judgment of forfeiture may be entered, the issue of forfeiture shall be tried in conjunction therewith. In such a case, the issue of forfeiture shall be bifurcated from the criminal trial and tried after conviction unless waived by the parties. Trial shall be by jury unless waived by all parties. If there is no underlying or related criminal action, the presiding judge of the superior court shall assign the action brought pursuant to this chapter for trial.

(j) The Attorney General or the district attorney of the county in which property is subject to forfeiture under Section 11470 may, pursuant to this subdivision, order forfeiture of personal property not exceeding twenty-five thousand dollars ($25,000) in value. The Attorney General or district attorney shall provide notice of proceedings under this subdivision pursuant to subdivisions (c), (d), (e), and (f), including:

(1) A description of the property.

(2) The appraised value of the property.

(3) The date and place of seizure or location of any property not seized but subject to forfeiture.

(4) The violation of law alleged with respect to forfeiture of the property.

(5) (A) The instructions for filing and serving a claim with the Attorney General or the district attorney pursuant to Section 11488.5 and time limits for filing a claim and claim form.

(B) If no claims are timely filed, the Attorney General or the district attorney shall prepare a written declaration of forfeiture of the subject property to the state and dispose of the property in accordance with Section 11489. A written declaration of forfeiture signed by the Attorney General or district attorney under this subdivision shall be deemed to provide good and sufficient title to the forfeited property. The prosecuting agency ordering forfeiture pursuant to this subdivision shall provide a copy of the declaration of forfeiture to any person listed in the receipt given at the time of seizure and to any person personally served notice of the forfeiture proceedings.

(C) If a claim is timely filed, then the Attorney General or district attorney shall file a petition of forfeiture pursuant to this section within 30 days of the receipt of the claim. The petition of forfeiture shall then proceed pursuant to other provisions of this chapter, except that no additional notice need be given and no additional claim need be filed.
(k) If in any underlying or related criminal action or proceeding, in which a petition for forfeiture has been filed pursuant to this section, and a criminal conviction is required before a judgment of forfeiture may be entered, the defendant willfully fails to appear as required, there shall be no requirement of a criminal conviction as a prerequisite to the forfeiture. In these cases, forfeiture shall be ordered as against the defendant and judgment entered upon default, upon application of the state or local governmental entity. In its application for default, the state or local governmental entity shall be required to give notice to the defendant's attorney of record, if any, in the underlying or related criminal action, and to make a showing of due diligence to locate the defendant. In moving for a default judgment pursuant to this subdivision, the state or local governmental entity shall be required to establish a prima facie case in support of its petition for forfeiture.
(Amended by Stats. 2016, Ch. 831, Sec. 3. (SB 443) Effective January 1, 2017.)
11488.5.
(a) (1) Any person claiming an interest in the property seized pursuant to Section 11488 may, unless for good cause shown the court extends the time for filing, at any time within 30 days from the date of the last publication of the notice of seizure, if that person was not personally served or served by mail, or within 30 days after receipt of actual notice, file with the superior court of the county in which the defendant has been charged with the underlying or related criminal offense or in which the property was seized or, if there was no seizure, in which the property is located, a claim, verified in accordance with Section 446 of the Code of Civil Procedure, stating his or her interest in the property. An endorsed copy of the claim shall be served by the claimant on the Attorney General or district attorney, as appropriate, within 30 days of the filing of the claim. The Judicial Council shall develop and approve official forms for the verified claim that is to be filed pursuant to this section. The official forms shall be drafted in nontechnical language, in English and in Spanish, and shall be made available through the office of the clerk of the appropriate court.
(2) Any person who claims that the property was assigned to him or to her prior to the seizure or notification of pending forfeiture of the property under this chapter, whichever occurs last, shall file a claim with the court and prosecuting agency pursuant to Section 11488.5 declaring an interest in that property and that interest shall be adjudicated at the forfeiture hearing. The property shall remain under control of the law enforcement or prosecutorial agency until the adjudication of the forfeiture hearing. Seized property shall be protected and its value shall be preserved pending the outcome of the forfeiture proceedings.
(3) The clerk of the court shall not charge or collect a fee for the filing of a claim in any case in which the value of the respondent property as specified in the notice is five thousand dollars ($5,000) or less. If the value of the property, as specified in the notice, is more than five thousand dollars ($5,000), the clerk of the court shall charge the filing fee specified in Section 70611 of the Government Code.
(4) The claim of a law enforcement agency to property seized pursuant to Section 11488 or subject to forfeiture shall have priority over a claim to the seized or forfeitable property made by the Franchise Tax Board in a notice to withhold issued pursuant to Section 18817 or 26132 of the Revenue and Taxation Code.
(b) (1) If at the end of the time set forth in subdivision (a) there is no claim on file, the court, upon motion, shall declare the property seized or subject to forfeiture pursuant to subdivisions (a) to (g), inclusive, of Section 11470 forfeited to the state. In moving for a default judgment pursuant to this subdivision, the state or local governmental entity shall be required to establish a prima facie case in support of its petition for forfeiture. There is no requirement for forfeiture thereof that a criminal conviction be obtained in an underlying or related criminal offense.
(2) The court shall order the money forfeited or the proceeds of the sale of property to be distributed as set forth in Section 11489.
(c) (1) If a verified claim is filed, the forfeiture proceeding shall be set for hearing on a day not less than 30 days therefrom, and the proceeding shall have priority over other civil cases. Notice of the hearing shall be given in the same manner as provided in Section 11488.4. Such a verified claim or a claim filed pursuant to subdivision (j) of Section 11488.4 shall not be admissible in the proceedings regarding the underlying or related criminal offense set forth in subdivision (a) of Section 11488.
(2) The hearing shall be by jury, unless waived by consent of all parties.
(3) The provisions of the Code of Civil Procedure shall apply to proceedings under this chapter unless otherwise inconsistent with the provisions or procedures set forth in this chapter. However, in proceedings under this chapter, there shall be no joinder of actions, coordination of actions, except for forfeiture proceedings, or cross-complaints, and the issues shall be limited strictly to the questions related to this chapter.
(d) (1) At the hearing, the state or local governmental entity shall have the burden of establishing, pursuant to subdivision (i) of Section 11488.4, that the owner of any interest in the seized property consented to the use of the property with knowledge that it would be or was used for a purpose for which forfeiture is permitted, in accordance with the burden of proof set forth in subdivision (i) of Section 11488.4.
(2) No interest in the seized property shall be affected by a forfeiture decree under this section unless the state or local governmental entity has proven that the owner of that interest consented to the use of the property with knowledge that it would be or was used for the purpose charged. Forfeiture shall be ordered when, at the hearing, the state or local governmental entity has shown that the assets in question are subject to forfeiture pursuant to Section 11470, in accordance with the burden of proof set forth in subdivision (i) of Section 11488.4.
(e) The forfeiture hearing shall be continued upon motion of the prosecution or the defendant until after a verdict of guilty on any criminal charges specified in this chapter and pending against the defendant have been decided. The forfeiture hearing shall be conducted in accordance with Sections 190 to 222.5, inclusive, Sections 224 to 234, inclusive, Section 237, and Sections 607 to 630, inclusive, of the Code of Civil Procedure if a trial by jury, and by Sections 631 to 636, inclusive, of the Code of Civil Procedure if by the court. Unless the court or jury finds that the seized property was used for a purpose for which forfeiture is permitted, the court shall order the seized property released to the person it determines is entitled thereto.
If the court or jury finds that the seized property was used for a purpose for which forfeiture is permitted, but does not find that a person claiming an interest therein, to which the court has determined he or she is entitled, had actual knowledge that the seized property would be or was used for a purpose for which forfeiture is permitted and consented to that use, the court shall order the seized property released to the claimant.
(f) All seized property which was the subject of a contested forfeiture hearing and which was not released by the court to a claimant shall be declared by the court to be forfeited to the state, provided the burden of proof required pursuant to subdivision (i) of Section 11488.4 has been met. The court shall order the forfeited property to be distributed as set forth in Section 11489.
(g) All seized property which was the subject of the forfeiture hearing and which was not forfeited shall remain subject to any order to withhold issued with respect to the property by the Franchise Tax Board.
(Amended by Stats. 2016, Ch. 831, Sec. 4. (SB 443) Effective January 1, 2017.)
11488.6.
(a) If the court or jury at the forfeiture hearing finds that the property is forfeitable pursuant to Section 11470, but does not find that a person having a valid ownership interest, which includes, but is not limited to, a valid lien, mortgage, security interest, or interest under a conditional sales contract acquired such interest with actual knowledge that the property was to be used for a purpose for which forfeiture is permitted, and the amount due such person is less than the appraised value of the property, such person may pay to the state or the local governmental entity which initiated the forfeiture proceeding the amount of the equity, which shall be deemed to be the difference between the appraised value and the amount of the lien, mortgage, security interest, or interest under a conditional sales contract. Upon such payment, the state or local governmental entity shall relinquish all claims to the property. If the holder of the interest elects not to make such payment to the state or local governmental entity, the property shall be deemed forfeited to the state or local governmental entity and the ownership certificate shall be forwarded. The appraised value shall be determined as of the date judgment is entered on a wholesale basis either by agreement between the legal owner and the governmental entity involved, or if they cannot agree, then by the inheritance tax appraiser for the county in which the action is brought. A person having a valid ownership interest, which includes, but is not limited to, a valid lien, mortgage, security interest, or interest under a conditional sales contract shall be paid the appraised value of his or her interest in accordance with the provisions of Section 11489.
(b) If the amount due to a person having a valid ownership interest, which includes, but is not limited to, a valid lien, mortgage, security interest, or interest under a conditional sales contract is less than the value of the property and the person elects not to make payment to the governmental entity, the property shall be sold at public auction by the Department of General Services or by the local governmental entity which shall provide notice of such sale by one publication in a newspaper published and circulated in the city, community, or locality where the sale is to take place.
(c) The proceeds of sale pursuant to subdivision (b) shall be first distributed in accordance with the provisions of Section 11489.
(Amended by Stats. 1994, Ch. 314, Sec. 16. Effective August 19, 1994.)
11489.
Notwithstanding Section 11502 and except as otherwise provided in Section 11473, in all cases where the property is seized pursuant to this chapter and forfeited to the state or local governmental entity and, where necessary, sold by the Department of General Services or local governmental entity, the money forfeited or the proceeds of sale shall be distributed by the state or local governmental entity as follows:
(a) To the bona fide or innocent purchaser, conditional sales vendor, or mortgagee of the property, if any, up to the amount of his or her interest in the property, when the court declaring the forfeiture orders a distribution to that person.
(b) The balance, if any, to accumulate, and to be distributed and transferred quarterly in the following manner:
(1) To the state agency or local governmental entity for all expenditures made or incurred by it in connection with the sale of the property, including expenditures for any necessary costs of notice required by Section 11488.4, and for any necessary repairs, storage, or transportation of any property seized under this chapter.
(2) The remaining funds shall be distributed as follows:
(A) Sixty-five percent to the state, local, or state and local law enforcement entities that participated in the seizure distributed so as to reflect the proportionate contribution of each agency.
(i) Fifteen percent of the funds distributed pursuant to this subparagraph shall be deposited in a special fund maintained by the county, city, or city and county of any agency making the seizure or seeking an order for forfeiture. This fund shall be used for the sole purpose of funding programs designed to combat drug abuse and divert gang activity, and shall wherever possible involve educators, parents, community-based

organizations and local businesses, and uniformed law enforcement officers. Those programs that have been evaluated as successful shall be given priority. These funds shall not be used to supplant any state or local funds that would, in the absence of this clause, otherwise be made available to the programs.

It is the intent of the Legislature to cause the development and continuation of positive intervention programs for high-risk elementary and secondary schoolage students. Local law enforcement should work in partnership with state and local agencies and the private sector in administering these programs.

(ii) The actual distribution of funds set aside pursuant to clause (i) is to be determined by a panel consisting of the sheriff of the county, a police chief selected by the other chiefs in the county, and the district attorney and the chief probation officer of the county.

(B) Ten percent to the prosecutorial agency which processes the forfeiture action.

(C) Twenty-four percent to the General Fund. Notwithstanding Section 13340 of the Government Code, the moneys are hereby continuously appropriated to the General Fund. Commencing January 1, 1995, all moneys deposited in the General Fund pursuant to this subparagraph, in an amount not to exceed ten million dollars ($10,000,000), shall be made available for school safety and security, upon appropriation by the Legislature, and shall be disbursed pursuant to Senate Bill 1255 of the 1993–94 Regular Session, as enacted.

(D) One percent to a private nonprofit organization composed of local prosecutors which shall use these funds for the exclusive purpose of providing a statewide program of education and training for prosecutors and law enforcement officers in ethics and the proper use of laws permitting the seizure and forfeiture of assets under this chapter.

(c) Notwithstanding Item 0820-101-469 of the Budget Act of 1985 (Chapter 111 of the Statutes of 1985), all funds allocated to the Department of Justice pursuant to subparagraph (A) of paragraph (2) of subdivision (b) shall be deposited into the Department of Justice Special Deposit Fund–State Asset Forfeiture Account and used for the law enforcement efforts of the state or for state or local law enforcement efforts pursuant to Section 11493.

All funds allocated to the Department of Justice by the federal government under its Federal Asset Forfeiture program authorized by the Comprehensive Crime Control Act of 1984 may be deposited directly into the Narcotics Assistance and Relinquishment by Criminal Offender Fund and used for state and local law enforcement efforts pursuant to Section 11493.

Funds which are not deposited pursuant to the above paragraph shall be deposited into the Department of Justice Special Deposit Fund–Federal Asset Forfeiture Account.

(d) All the funds distributed to the state or local governmental entity pursuant to subparagraphs (A) and (B) of paragraph (2) of subdivision (b) shall not supplant any state or local funds that would, in the absence of this subdivision, be made available to support the law enforcement and prosecutorial efforts of these agencies.

The court shall order the forfeiture proceeds distributed to the state, local, or state and local governmental entities as provided in this section.

For the purposes of this section, "local governmental entity" means any city, county, or city and county in this state.

(e) This section shall become operative on January 1, 1994.

(Amended by Stats. 1997, Ch. 241, Sec. 3. Effective January 1, 1998.)

11490.

The provisions of this division relative to forfeiture of vehicles, boats, or airplanes shall not apply to a common carrier, or to an employee acting within the scope of his employment in the enforcement of this division.

(Added by renumbering Section 11498 by Stats. 1983, Ch. 948, Sec. 29.)

11491.

Nothing in this chapter shall be construed to extend or change decisional law as it relates to the topic of search and seizure.

(Added by renumbering Section 11499 by Stats. 1983, Ch. 948, Sec. 30.)

11492.

(a) Concurrent with, or subsequent to, the filing of the petition, the prosecuting agency may move the superior court for the following pendente lite orders to preserve the status quo or value of the property alleged in the petition for forfeiture:

(1) An injunction to restrain all interested parties and enjoin them from transferring, encumbering, hypothecating, or otherwise disposing of that property.

(2) Appointment of a receiver to take possession of, care for, manage, and operate the assets and properties so that the property may be maintained and preserved.

(3) Order an interlocutory sale of the property named in the petition when the property is liable to perish, to waste, or to be significantly reduced in value, or when the expenses of maintaining the property are disproportionate to the value thereof, and the proceeds thereof shall be deposited with the court or as directed by the court pending determination of the forfeiture proceeding.

(b) No preliminary injunction may be granted, receiver appointed, or interlocutory sale ordered without notice to the interested parties and a hearing to determine that the order is necessary to preserve the property named in the petition, pending the outcome of the proceedings, and that there is probable cause to believe that the property is subject to forfeiture under Section 11470. However, a temporary restraining order may issue pending that hearing pursuant to the provisions of Section 527 of the Code of Civil Procedure.

(c) Notwithstanding any other provision of law, the court in granting these motions may order a surety bond or undertaking to preserve the property interests of the interested parties.

(Amended by Stats. 1997, Ch. 241, Sec. 4. Effective January 1, 1998.)

11493.

There is hereby created in the General Fund the Narcotics Assistance and Relinquishment by Criminal Offender Fund. The fund shall be administered by an advisory committee which shall be appointed by the Attorney General and which shall be comprised of three police chiefs, three sheriffs, two district attorneys, one private citizen, and an official of the Department of Justice who shall serve as the executive officer.

The money in the fund shall be available, upon appropriation by the Legislature, for distribution by the advisory committee to local and state law enforcement agencies in support of general narcotic law enforcement efforts.

(Amended by Stats. 2007, Ch. 176, Sec. 61. Effective August 24, 2007.)

11494.

In the case of any property seized or forfeiture proceeding initiated before January 1, 1994, the proceeding to forfeit the property and the distribution of any forfeited property shall be subject to the provisions of this chapter in effect on December 31, 1993, as if those sections had not been repealed, replaced, or amended.

(Repealed and added by Stats. 1994, Ch. 314, Sec. 22. Effective August 19, 1994.)

11495.

(a) The funds received by the law enforcement agencies under Section 11489 shall be deposited into an account maintained by the Controller, county auditor, or city treasurer. These funds shall be distributed to the law enforcement agencies at their request. The Controller, auditor, or treasurer shall maintain a record of these disbursements which records shall be open to public inspection, subject to the privileges contained in Sections 1040, 1041, and 1042 of the Evidence Code.

(b) Upon request of the governing body of the jurisdiction in which the distributions are made, the Controller, auditor, or treasurer shall conduct an audit of these funds and their use. In the case of the state, the governing body shall be the Legislature.

(c) Each year, the Attorney General shall publish a report that sets forth the following information for the state, each county, each city, and each city and county:

(1) The number of forfeiture actions initiated and administered by state or local agencies under California law, the number of cases adopted by the federal government, and the number of cases initiated by a joint federal-state action that were prosecuted under federal law.

(2) The number of cases and the administrative number or court docket number of each case for which forfeiture was ordered or declared.

(3) The number of suspects charged with a controlled substance violation.

(4) The number of alleged criminal offenses that were under federal or state law.

(5) The disposition of cases, including no charge, dropped charges, acquittal, plea agreement, jury conviction, or other.

(6) The value of the assets forfeited.

(7) The recipients of the forfeited assets, the amounts received, and the date of the disbursement.

(d) The Attorney General shall develop administrative guidelines for the collection and publication of the information required in subdivision (c).

(e) The Attorney General's report shall cover the calendar year and shall be made no later than July 1 of each year.

(Amended by Stats. 2019, Ch. 364, Sec. 9. (SB 112) Effective September 27, 2019.)

CHAPTER 9. Collection and Disposition of Fines [11500 - 11508]

(Chapter 9 added by Stats. 1972, Ch. 1407.)

11500.

The district attorney, or any person designated by him, of the county in which any violation of this division is committed shall conduct all actions and prosecutions for the violation.

However, the Attorney General, or special counsel employed by the Attorney General for that purpose, may take complete charge of the conduct of such actions or prosecutions. The Attorney General may fix the compensation to be paid for the service and may incur such other expense in connection with the conduct of the actions or prosecutions as he may deem necessary. No attorney employed as special counsel shall receive as compensation more than three thousand five hundred dollars ($3,500) in any one year.

(Repealed and added by Stats. 1972, Ch. 1407.)

11501.

The State of California, or any political subdivision thereof, may maintain an action against any person or persons engaged in the unlawful sale of controlled substances for the recovery of any public funds paid over to such person or persons in the course of any investigation of violations of this division. All proceedings under this section shall be instituted in the superior court of the county where the funds were paid over, where the sale was made, or where the defendant resides. Notwithstanding Section 483.010 of the Code of Civil Procedure, in any action under this section, a writ of attachment may be issued, without the showing required by Section 485.010 of the Code of Civil Procedure, in the manner provided by Chapter 5 (commencing with Section 485.010) of Title 6.5 of Part 2 of the Code of Civil Procedure to attach any funds paid over or any other funds on the defendant's person at the time of his arrest.

(Amended by Stats. 1974, Ch. 1516.)

11502.

(a) All moneys, forfeited bail, or fines received by any court under this division shall as soon as practicable after the receipt thereof be deposited with the county treasurer of the county in which the court is situated. Amounts so deposited shall be paid at least once a month as follows: 75 percent to the State Treasurer by warrant of the county auditor drawn upon the requisition of the clerk or judge of the court to be deposited in the State

Treasury on order of the Controller; and 25 percent to the city treasurer of the city, if the offense occurred in a city, otherwise to the treasurer of the county in which the prosecution is conducted.

(b) Any money deposited in the State Treasury under this section that is determined by the Controller to have been erroneously deposited therein shall be refunded by him or her out of any moneys in the State Treasury that are available by law for that purpose.

(Amended by Stats. 2016, Ch. 31, Sec. 161. (SB 836) Effective June 27, 2016.)

11503.

Judges and magistrates who collect fines or forfeitures under this division shall keep a record thereof, and, upon the imposition of any such fine or forfeiture, shall at least monthly transmit a record of it to the county auditor. The county auditor shall transmit a record of the imposition, collection and payment of such fines or forfeitures to the State Controller at the time of transmittal of each warrant to the State Treasurer pursuant to this article.

(Repealed and added by Stats. 1972, Ch. 1407.)

11504.

When an imprisonment has been imposed for a violation of this division, and before the termination of the sentence, the defendant is released by the vacation of the sentence of imprisonment and the imposition of a fine or forfeiture instead, the fine or forfeiture shall be recorded and accounted for in the same manner as though it had been imposed in the first instance.

(Repealed and added by Stats. 1972, Ch. 1407.)

11505.

Whenever a fine has been imposed for violation of this division, and before the full payment of the fine a sentence of imprisonment is imposed instead, the imprisonment shall be recorded and accounted for to the county auditor.

(Added by Stats. 1972, Ch. 1407.)

11506.

The State Controller shall check the reports and records received by him with the transmittals of fines and forfeitures and whenever it appears that fines or forfeitures have not been transmitted the county auditor shall and the State Controller may bring suit to enforce their collection or transmittal, or both.

(Added by Stats. 1972, Ch. 1407.)

11507.

The official bond of any judge or magistrate is liable for his failure to transmit the fines or forfeitures imposed by him under this division.

(Added by Stats. 1972, Ch. 1407.)

11508.

The records kept by a judge or magistrate under this division are open to public inspection, and may be checked by the State Controller, the Attorney General, the district attorney of the particular county, or the state bureau.

(Added by Stats. 1972, Ch. 1407.)

CHAPTER 9.5. Loitering for Drug Activities [11530 - 11538]

(Chapter 9.5 added by Stats. 1995, Ch. 981, Sec. 2.)

11530.

As used in this subdivision, the following terms have the following meanings:

(a) "Loiter" means to delay or linger without a lawful purpose for being on the property and for the purpose of committing a crime as opportunity may be discovered.

(b) "Public place" means an area open to the public or exposed to public view and includes streets, sidewalks, bridges, alleys, plazas, parks, driveways, parking lots, automobiles, whether moving or not, and buildings open to the general public, including those which serve food or drink, or provide entertainment, and the doorways and entrances to buildings or dwellings and the grounds enclosing them.

(Added by Stats. 1995, Ch. 981, Sec. 2. Effective January 1, 1996.)

11532.

(a) It is unlawful for any person to loiter in any public place in a manner and under circumstances manifesting the purpose and with the intent to commit an offense specified in Chapter 6 (commencing with Section 11350) and Chapter 6.5 (commencing with Section 11400).

(b) Among circumstances that may be considered in determining whether a person has the requisite intent to engage in drug-related activity are that the person:

(1) Acts as a "look-out."

(2) Transfers small objects or packages for currency in a furtive fashion.

(3) Tries to conceal himself or herself or any object that reasonably could be involved in an unlawful drug-related activity.

(4) Uses signals or language indicative of summoning purchasers of illegal drugs.

(5) Repeatedly beckons to, stops, attempts to stop, or engages in conversations with passersby, whether on foot or in a motor vehicle, indicative of summoning purchasers of illegal drugs.

(6) Repeatedly passes to or receives from passersby, whether on foot or in a motor vehicle, money or small objects.

(7) Is under the influence of a controlled substance or possesses narcotic or drug paraphernalia. For the purposes of this paragraph, "narcotic or drug paraphernalia" means any device, contrivance, instrument, or apparatus designed or marketed for the use of smoking, injecting, ingesting, or consuming cannabis, hashish, PCP, or any controlled substance, including, but not limited to, roach clips, cigarette papers, and rollers designed or marketed for use in smoking a controlled substance.

(8) Has been convicted in any court within this state, within five years prior to the arrest under this chapter, of any violation involving the use, possession, or sale of any of the substances referred to in Chapter 6 (commencing with Section 11350) or Chapter 6.5 (commencing with Section 11400), or has been convicted of any violation of those provisions or substantially similar laws of any political subdivision of this state or of any other state.

(9) Is currently subject to any order prohibiting his or her presence in any high drug activity geographic area.

(10) Has engaged, within six months prior to the date of arrest under this section, in any behavior described in this subdivision, with the exception of paragraph (8), or in any other behavior indicative of illegal drug-related activity.

(c) The list of circumstances set forth in subdivision (b) is not exclusive. The circumstances set forth in subdivision (b) should be considered particularly salient if they occur in an area that is known for unlawful drug use and trafficking, or if they occur on or in premises that have been reported to law enforcement as a place suspected of unlawful drug activity. Any other relevant circumstances may be considered in determining whether a person has the requisite intent. Moreover, no one circumstance or combination of circumstances is in itself determinative of intent. Intent must be determined based on an evaluation of the particular circumstances of each case.

(Amended by Stats. 2017, Ch. 27, Sec. 158. (SB 94) Effective June 27, 2017.)

11534.

If any section, subdivision, sentence, clause, phrase, or portion of this chapter is for any reason held invalid or unconstitutional by any court of competent jurisdiction, that portion shall be deemed a separate, distinct, and independent provision, and that holding shall not affect the validity of the remaining portion thereof.

(Added by Stats. 1995, Ch. 981, Sec. 2. Effective January 1, 1996.)

11536.

A violation of any provision of this chapter is a misdemeanor.

(Added by Stats. 1995, Ch. 981, Sec. 2. Effective January 1, 1996.)

11538.

Nothing in this chapter shall prevent a local governing body from adopting and enforcing laws consistent with this chapter. Where local laws duplicate or supplement this chapter, this chapter shall be construed as providing alternative remedies and not to preempt the field.

(Added by Stats. 1995, Ch. 981, Sec. 2. Effective January 1, 1996.)

CHAPTER 9.8. Treatment [11545- 11545.]

(Chapter 9.8 added by Stats. 2000, Ch. 815, Sec. 1.)

11545.

The Legislature hereby finds and declares that licensed physicians, experienced in the treatment of addiction, should be allowed and encouraged to treat addiction by all appropriate means.

(Added by Stats. 2000, Ch. 815, Sec. 1. Effective January 1, 2001.)

CHAPTER 10. Control of Users of Controlled Substances [11550 - 11595]

(Chapter 10 added by Stats. 1972, Ch. 1407.)

ARTICLE 1. Addicts [11550 - 11555]

(Article 1 added by Stats. 1972, Ch. 1407.)

11550.

(a) A person shall not use, or be under the influence of any controlled substance that is (1) specified in subdivision (b), (c), or (e), or paragraph (1) of subdivision (f) of Section 11054, specified in paragraph (14), (15), (21), (22), or (23) of subdivision (d) of Section 11054, specified in subdivision (b) or (c) of Section 11055, or specified in paragraph (1) or (2) of subdivision (d) or in paragraph (3) of subdivision (e) of Section 11055, or (2) a narcotic drug classified in Schedule III, IV, or V, except when administered by or under the direction of a person licensed by the state to dispense, prescribe, or administer controlled substances. It shall be the burden of the defense to show that it comes within the exception. A person convicted of violating this subdivision is guilty of a misdemeanor and shall be sentenced to serve a term of not more than one year in a county jail. The court may also place a person convicted under this subdivision on probation for a period not to exceed five years.

(b) (1) A person who is convicted of violating subdivision (a) when the offense occurred within seven years of that person being convicted of two or more separate violations of that subdivision, and refuses to complete a licensed drug rehabilitation program offered by the court pursuant to subdivision (c), shall be punished by imprisonment in a county jail for not less than 180 days nor more than one year. In no event does the court have the power to absolve a person convicted of a violation of subdivision (a) who is punishable under this subdivision from the obligation of spending at least 180 days in confinement in a county jail unless there are no licensed drug rehabilitation programs reasonably available.

(2) For the purpose of this section, a drug rehabilitation program is not reasonably available unless the person is not required to pay more than the court determines that he or she is reasonably able to pay in order to participate in the program.

(c) (1) The court may, when it would be in the interest of justice, permit a person convicted of a violation of subdivision (a) punishable under subdivision (a) or (b) to complete a licensed drug rehabilitation program in lieu of part or all of the imprisonment in a county jail. As a condition of sentencing, the court may require the offender to pay all or a portion of the drug rehabilitation program.

(2) In order to alleviate jail overcrowding and to provide recidivist offenders with a reasonable opportunity to seek rehabilitation pursuant to this subdivision, counties are encouraged to include provisions to augment licensed drug rehabilitation programs in their substance abuse proposals and applications submitted to the state for federal and state drug abuse funds.

(d) In addition to any fine assessed under this section, the judge may assess a fine not to exceed seventy dollars ($70) against a person who violates this section, with the proceeds of this fine to be used in accordance with Section 1463.23 of the Penal Code. The court shall, however, take into consideration the defendant's ability to pay, and a defendant shall not be denied probation because of his or her inability to pay the fine permitted under this subdivision.

(e) (1) Notwithstanding subdivisions (a) and (b) or any other law, a person who is unlawfully under the influence of cocaine, cocaine base, heroin, methamphetamine, or phencyclidine while in the immediate personal possession of a loaded, operable firearm is guilty of a public offense punishable by imprisonment in a county jail for not exceeding one year or in state prison.

(2) As used in this subdivision "immediate personal possession" includes, but is not limited to, the interior passenger compartment of a motor vehicle.

(f) Every person who violates subdivision (e) is punishable upon the second and each subsequent conviction by imprisonment in the state prison for two, three, or four years.

(g) This section does not prevent deferred entry of judgment or a defendant's participation in a preguilty plea drug court program under Chapter 2.5 (commencing with Section 1000) of Title 6 of Part 2 of the Penal Code unless the person is charged with violating subdivision (b) or (c) of Section 243 of the Penal Code. A person charged with violating this section by being under the influence of any controlled substance which is specified in paragraph (21), (22), or (23) of subdivision (d) of Section 11054 or in paragraph (3) of subdivision (e) of Section 11055 and with violating either subdivision (b) or (c) of Section 243 of the Penal Code or with a violation of subdivision (e) shall be ineligible for deferred entry of judgment or a preguilty plea drug court program.
(Amended by Stats. 2014, Ch. 819, Sec. 1. (AB 2492) Effective January 1, 2015.)

11551.
(a) Whenever any court in this state grants probation to a person who the court has reason to believe is or has been a user of controlled substances, the court may require as a condition to probation that the probationer submit to periodic tests by a city or county health officer, or by a physician and surgeon appointed by the city or county health officer with the approval of the Attorney General, to determine, by whatever means is available, whether the probationer is addicted to a controlled substance.

In any case provided for in this subdivision, the city or county health officer, or the physician and surgeon appointed by the city or county health officer with the approval of the Attorney General shall report the results of the tests to the probation officer.

(b) In any case in which a person is granted parole by a county parole board and the person is or has been a user of controlled substances, a condition of the parole may be that the parolee undergo periodic tests as provided in subdivision (a) and that the county or city health officer, or the physician and surgeon appointed by the city or county health officer with the approval of the Attorney General, shall report the results to the board.

(c) In any case in which any state agency grants a parole to a person who is or has been a user of controlled substances, it may be a condition of the parole that the parolee undergo periodic tests as provided in subdivision (a) and that the county or city health officer, or the physician and surgeon appointed by the city or county health officer with the approval of the Attorney General, shall report the results of the tests to such state agency.

(d) The cost of administering tests pursuant to subdivisions (a) and (b) shall be a charge against the county. The cost of administering tests pursuant to subdivision (c) shall be paid by the state.

(e) The state department, in conjunction with the Attorney General, shall issue regulations governing the administering of the tests provided for in this section and providing the form of the report required by this section.
(Added by Stats. 1972, Ch. 1407.)

11552.
In any case in which a person has been arrested for a criminal offense and is suspected of being addicted to a controlled substance, a law enforcement officer having custody of such person may, with the written consent of such person, request the city or county health officer, or physician appointed by such health officer pursuant to Section 11551, to administer to the arrested person a test to determine, by whatever means is available whether the arrested person is addicted to a controlled substance, and such health officer or physician may administer such test to such arrested person.
(Added by Stats. 1972, Ch. 1407.)

11553.
The fact that a person is or has been, or is suspected of being, a user of cannabis is not alone sufficient grounds upon which to invoke Section 11551 or 11552.

This section shall not be construed to limit the discretion of a judge to invoke Section 11551 or 11552 if the court has reason to believe a person is or has been a user of narcotics or drugs other than cannabis.
(Amended by Stats. 2017, Ch. 27, Sec. 159. (SB 94) Effective June 27, 2017.)

11554.
The rehabilitation of persons addicted to controlled substances and the prevention of continued addiction to controlled substances is a matter of statewide concern. It is the policy of the state to encourage each county and city and county to make use, whenever applicable, of testing procedures to determine addiction to controlled substances or the absence thereof, and to foster research in means of detecting the existence of addiction to controlled substances and in medical methods and procedures for that purpose.
(Added by Stats. 1972, Ch. 1407.)

11555.
The Attorney General is directed to promote and sponsor the use by agencies of local government of the provisions of this article. The Attorney General may assist such agencies to establish facilities for, and to train personnel to conduct testing procedures pursuant to Section 11551, and may conduct demonstrations thereof for limited periods. For these purposes the Attorney General may procure such medical supplies, equipment, and temporary services of physicians and qualified consultants as may reasonably be necessary. Subject to the availability of funds appropriated for the purpose, the Attorney General may contract with any county or city and county which undertakes to establish facilities and a testing program pursuant to Section 11551, and such contract may provide for payment by the state of such costs of initially establishing and demonstrating such program as the Attorney General may approve.
(Repealed and added by Stats. 1972, Ch. 1407.)

ARTICLE 2. Substance Abuse Treatment Control Units [11560 - 11565]
(Heading of Article 2 amended by Stats. 1992, Ch. 465, Sec. 1.)

11560.
The Department of Corrections and the Department of the Youth Authority are authorized to establish substance abuse treatment control units in state correctional facilities or training schools or as separate establishments for any study, research, and treatment that may be necessary for the control of the addiction or habituation, or imminent addiction or habituation, to controlled substances or alcohol of persons committed to the custody of the Director of Corrections or the Director of the Youth Authority.
(Amended by Stats. 1992, Ch. 465, Sec. 2. Effective January 1, 1993.)

11561.
When the parole authority concludes that there are reasonable grounds for believing that a person on parole is addicted or habituated to, or is in imminent danger of addiction or habituation to, controlled substances or alcohol, it may, in accordance with procedures used to revoke parole, issue an order to detain or place the person in a substance abuse treatment control unit for a period not to exceed 90 days. The order shall be a sufficient warrant for any peace officer or employee of the Department of Corrections to return the person to physical custody. Detention pursuant to the order shall not be deemed a suspension, cancellation, or revocation of parole until the parole authority so orders pursuant to Section 3060 of the Penal Code. A parolee taken into physical custody pursuant to Section 3060 of the Penal Code may be detained in a substance abuse treatment control unit established pursuant to this article.

No person on parole shall be placed in a substance abuse treatment control unit against his or her will.
(Amended by Stats. 2003, Ch. 468, Sec. 5. Effective January 1, 2004.)

11562.
When the Youth Authority concludes that there are reasonable grounds for believing that a person committed to its custody, and on parole, is addicted or habituated to, or is in imminent danger of addiction or habituation to, controlled substances or alcohol, it may, in accordance with procedures used to revoke parole, issue an order to detain or place that person in a substance abuse treatment control unit for not to exceed 90 days. The order shall be a sufficient warrant for any peace officer or employee of the Department of the Youth Authority to return to physical custody that person. Detention pursuant to the order shall not be deemed a suspension, cancellation, or revocation of parole unless the Youth Authority so orders pursuant to Section 1767.3 of the Welfare and Institutions Code.

With the consent of the Director of Corrections, the Director of the Youth Authority may, pursuant to this section, confine the addicted or habituated or potentially addicted or habituated person, over 18 years of age, in a substance abuse treatment control unit established by the Department of Corrections.

No person committed to the custody of the Youth Authority and on parole shall be placed in a substance abuse treatment control unit against his or her will.
(Amended by Stats. 1992, Ch. 465, Sec. 4. Effective January 1, 1993.)

11563.
When the parole authority concludes that there are reasonable grounds for believing that a woman on parole is addicted or habituated to, or is in imminent danger of addiction or habituation to, controlled substances or alcohol, it may, in accordance with procedures used to revoke parole, issue an order to detain or place the person in a substance abuse treatment control unit for a period not to exceed 90 days. The order shall be a sufficient warrant for any peace officer or employee of the Department of Corrections to return the person to physical custody . Detention pursuant to the order shall not be deemed a suspension, cancellation, or revocation of parole until such time as the parole authority so orders pursuant to Section 3060 of the Penal Code. A parolee taken into physical custody pursuant to Section 3060, 6043, or 6044 of the Penal Code may be detained in a substance abuse treatment control unit established pursuant to this article.

No woman on parole shall be placed in a substance abuse treatment control unit against her will.
(Amended by Stats. 1992, Ch. 695, Sec. 6. Effective September 15, 1992.)

11564.
The authority granted to the parole authority and to the Department of the Youth Authority in no way limits Sections 3060 and 3325 of the Penal Code.
(Amended by Stats. 1992, Ch. 695, Sec. 7. Effective September 15, 1992.)

11565.

For purposes of this article, "parole authority" has the same meaning as described in Section 3000 of the Penal Code.
(Added by Stats. 1992, Ch. 695, Sec. 8. Effective September 15, 1992.)

ARTICLE 3. Abatement [11570 - 11587]
(Article 3 added by Stats. 1972, Ch. 1407.)

11570.
Every building or place used for the purpose of unlawfully selling, serving, storing, keeping, manufacturing, or giving away any controlled substance, precursor, or analog specified in this division, and every building or place wherein or upon which those acts take place, is a nuisance which shall be enjoined, abated, and prevented, and for which damages may be recovered, whether it is a public or private nuisance.
(Amended by Stats. 1986, Ch. 1043, Sec. 1.5.)

11571.
If there is reason to believe that a nuisance, as described in Section 11570, is kept, maintained, or exists in any county, the district attorney or county counsel of the county, or the city attorney of any incorporated city or of any city and county, in the name of the people, may, or any citizen of the state resident in the county, in his or her own name, may, maintain an action to abate the nuisance and to perpetually enjoin the person conducting or maintaining it, and the owner, lessee, or agent of the building or place in or upon which the nuisance exists from directly or indirectly maintaining or permitting the nuisance.
(Amended by Stats. 2010, Ch. 570, Sec. 3. (AB 1502) Effective January 1, 2011.)

11571.1.
(a) Nothing in this article shall prevent a local governing body from adopting and enforcing laws, consistent with this article, relating to drug abatement. Where local laws duplicate or supplement this article, this article shall be construed as providing alternative remedies and not preempting the field.
(b) Nothing in this article shall prevent a tenant from receiving relief against a forfeiture of a lease pursuant to Section 1179 of the Code of Civil Procedure.
(Repealed and added by Stats. 2009, Ch. 244, Sec. 7. (AB 530) Effective January 1, 2010.)

11571.5.
For purposes of this article, an action to abate a nuisance may be taken by the city attorney or city prosecutor of the city within which the nuisance exists, is kept, or is maintained. An action by a city attorney or city prosecutor shall be accorded the same precedence as an action maintained by the district attorney of the county.
(Added by Stats. 1986, Ch. 182, Sec. 1.)

11572.
Unless filed by the district attorney, or the city attorney of an incorporated city, the complaint in the action shall be verified.
(Amended by Stats. 1987, Ch. 1076, Sec. 3.)

11573.
(a) If the existence of the nuisance is shown in the action to the satisfaction of the court or judge, either by verified complaint or affidavit, the court or judge shall allow a temporary restraining order or injunction to abate and prevent the continuance or recurrence of the nuisance.
(b) A temporary restraining order or injunction may enjoin subsequent owners, commercial lessees, or agents who acquire the building or place where the nuisance exists with notice of the temporary restraining order or injunction, specifying that the owner of the property subject to the temporary restraining order or injunction shall notify any prospective purchaser, commercial lessee, or other successor in interest of the existence of the order or injunction, and of its application to successors in interest, prior to entering into any agreement to sell or lease the property. The temporary restraining order or injunction shall not constitute a title defect, lien, or encumbrance on the real property.
(Amended by Stats. 2002, Ch. 1057, Sec. 2. Effective January 1, 2003.)

11573.5.
(a) At the time of application for issuance of a temporary restraining order or injunction pursuant to Section 11573, if proof of the existence of the nuisance depends, in whole or part, upon the affidavits of witnesses who are not peace officers, upon a showing of prior threats of violence or acts of violence by any defendant or other person, the court may issue orders to protect those witnesses, including, but not limited to, nondisclosure of the name, address, or any other information which may identify those witnesses.
(b) A temporary restraining order or injunction issued pursuant to Section 11573 may include closure of the premises pending trial when a prior order or injunction does not result in the abatement of the nuisance. The duration of the order or injunction shall be within the court's discretion. In no event shall the total period of closure pending trial exceed one year. Prior to ruling on a request for closure the court may order that some or all of the rent payments owing to the defendant be placed in an escrow account for a period of up to 90 days or until the nuisance is abated. If the court subsequently orders a closure of the premises, the money in the escrow account shall be used to pay for relocation assistance pursuant to subdivision (d). In ruling upon a request for closure, whether for a defined or undefined duration, the court shall consider all of the following factors:
(1) The extent and duration of the nuisance at the time of the request.
(2) Prior efforts by the defendant to comply with previous court orders to abate the nuisance.
(3) The nature and extent of any effect which the nuisance has upon other persons, such as residents or businesses.

(4) Any effect of prior orders placing displaced residents' or occupants' rent payments into an escrow account upon the defendant's efforts to abate the nuisance.
(5) The effect of granting the request upon any resident or occupant of the premises who is not named in the action, including the availability of alternative housing or relocation assistance, the pendency of any action to evict a resident or occupant, and any evidence of participation by a resident or occupant in the nuisance activity.
(c) In making an order of closure pursuant to this section, the court may order the premises vacated and may issue any other orders necessary to effectuate the closure. However, all tenants who may be affected by the order shall be provided reasonable notice and an opportunity to be heard at all hearings regarding the closure request prior to the issuance of any order.
(d) In making an order of closure pursuant to this section, the court shall order the defendant to provide relocation assistance to any tenant ordered to vacate the premises, provided the court determines that the tenant was not actively involved in the nuisance activity. The relocation assistance ordered to be paid by the defendant shall be in the amount necessary to cover moving costs, security deposits for utilities and comparable housing, adjustment in any lost rent, and any other reasonable expenses the court may deem fair and reasonable as a result of the court's order.
(e) At the hearing to order closure pursuant to this section, the court may make the following orders with respect to any displaced tenant not actively involved in the nuisance:
(1) Priority for senior citizens, physically handicapped persons, or persons otherwise suffering from a permanent or temporary disability for claims against money for relocation assistance.
(2) Order the local agency seeking closure pursuant to this section to make reasonable attempts to seek additional sources of funds for relocation assistance to displaced tenants, if deemed necessary.
(3) Appoint a receiver to oversee the disbursement of relocation assistance funds, whose services shall be paid from the escrow fund.
(4) Where a defendant has paid relocation assistance pursuant to subdivision (d), the escrow account under subdivision (b) may be released to the defendant and no appointment under paragraph (3) shall be made.
(f) (1) The remedies set forth pursuant to this section shall be in addition to any other existing remedies for nuisance abatement actions, including, but not limited to, the following:
(A) Capital improvements to the property, such as security gates.
(B) Improved interior or exterior lighting.
(C) Security guards.
(D) Posting of signs.
(E) Owner membership in neighborhood or local merchants' associations.
(F) Attending property management training programs.
(G) Making cosmetic improvements to the property.
(H) Requiring the owner or person in control of the property to reside in the property until the nuisance is abated. The order shall specify the number of hours per day or per week the owner or person in control of the property must be physically present in the property. In determining this amount, the court shall consider the nature and severity of the nuisance.
(2) At all stages of an action brought pursuant to this article, the court has equitable powers to order steps necessary to remedy the problem and enhance the abatement process.
(Amended by Stats. 2002, Ch. 1057, Sec. 3. Effective January 1, 2003.)

11574.
On granting the temporary writ the court or judge shall require an undertaking on the part of the applicant to the effect that the applicant will pay to the defendant enjoined such damages, not exceeding an amount to be specified, as the defendant sustains by reason of the injunction if the court finally decides that the applicant was not entitled to the injunction.
(Amended by Stats. 1982, Ch. 517, Sec. 275.)

11575.
The action shall have precedence over all other actions, except criminal proceedings, election contests, hearings on injunctions, and actions to forfeit vehicles under this division.
(Repealed and added by Stats. 1972, Ch. 1407.)

11575.5.
In any action for abatement instituted pursuant to this article, all evidence otherwise authorized by law, including evidence of reputation in a community, as provided in the Evidence Code, shall be admissible to prove the existence of a nuisance.
(Added by Stats. 1988, Ch. 1525, Sec. 2.)

11576.
If the complaint is filed by a citizen it shall not be dismissed by him or for want of prosecution except upon a sworn statement made by him and his attorney, setting forth the reasons why the action should be dismissed, and by dismissal ordered by the court.
(Repealed and added by Stats. 1972, Ch. 1407.)

11577.
In case of failure to prosecute the action with reasonable diligence, or at the request of the plaintiff, the court, in its discretion, may substitute any other citizen consenting thereto for the plaintiff.
(Added by Stats. 1972, Ch. 1407.)

11578.
If the action is brought by a citizen and the court finds there was no reasonable ground or cause for the action, the costs shall be taxed against him.

(Added by Stats. 1972, Ch. 1407.)

11579.

If the existence of the nuisance is established in the action, an order of abatement shall be entered as part of the judgment in the case, and plaintiff's costs in the action are a lien upon the building or place. The lien is enforceable and collectible by execution issued by order of the court.

(Added by Stats. 1972, Ch. 1407.)

11580.

A violation or disobedience of the injunction or order for abatement is punishable as a contempt of court by a fine of not less than five hundred dollars ($500) nor more than ten thousand dollars ($10,000), or by imprisonment in the county jail for not less than one nor more than six months, or by both.

A contempt may be based on a violation of any court order including failure to pay relocation assistance. Notwithstanding any other provision of law, any fines assessed for contempt shall first be held by the court and applied to satisfaction of the court's order for relocation assistance pursuant to subdivision (d) of Section 11573.5.

Evidence concerning the duration and repetitive nature of the violations shall be considered by the court in determining the contempt penalties.

(Amended by Stats. 1988, Ch. 1525, Sec. 3.)

11581.

(a) If the existence of the nuisance is established in the action, an order of abatement shall be entered as a part of the judgment, which order shall direct the removal from the building or place of all fixtures, musical instruments, and other movable property used in conducting, maintaining, aiding, or abetting the nuisance and shall direct their sale in the manner provided for the sale of chattels under execution.

(b) (1) The order shall provide for the effectual closing of the building or place against its use for any purpose, and for keeping it closed for a period of one year. This subdivision is intended to give priority to closure. Any alternative to closure may be considered only as provided in this section.

(2) In addition, the court may assess a civil penalty not to exceed twenty-five thousand dollars ($25,000) against any or all of the defendants, based upon the severity of the nuisance and its duration.

(3) One-half of the civil penalties collected pursuant to this section shall be deposited in the Restitution Fund in the State Treasury, the proceeds of which shall be available only upon appropriation by the Legislature to indemnify persons filing claims pursuant to Article 1 (commencing with Section 13959) of Chapter 5 of Part 4 of Division 3 of Title 2 of the Government Code, and one-half of the civil penalties collected shall be paid to the city in which the judgment was entered, if the action was brought by the city attorney or city prosecutor. If the action was brought by a district attorney, one-half of the civil penalties collected shall be paid to the treasurer of the county in which the judgment was entered.

(c) (1) If the court finds that any vacancy resulting from closure of the building or place may create a nuisance or that closure is otherwise harmful to the community, in lieu of ordering the building or place closed, the court may order the person who is responsible for the existence of the nuisance, or the person who knowingly permits controlled substances to be unlawfully sold, served, stored, kept, or given away in or from a building or place he or she owns, to pay damages in an amount equal to the fair market rental value of the building or place for one year to the city or county in whose jurisdiction the nuisance is located for the purpose of carrying out drug abuse treatment, prevention, and education programs. If awarded to a city, eligible programs may include those developed as a result of cooperative programs among schools, community agencies, and the local law enforcement agency. These funds shall not be used to supplant existing city, county, state, or federal resources used for drug prevention and education programs.

(2) For purposes of this subdivision, the actual amount of rent being received for the rental of the building or place, or the existence of any vacancy therein, may be considered, but shall not be the sole determinant of the fair market rental value. Expert testimony may be used to determine the fair market rental value.

(d) This section shall become operative on January 1, 1996.

(Amended by Stats. 2003, Ch. 62, Sec. 183. Effective January 1, 2004.)

11582.

While the order of abatement remains in effect, the building or place is in the custody of the court.

(Added by Stats. 1972, Ch. 1407.)

11583.

For removing and selling the movable property, the officer is entitled to charge and receive the same fees as he would for levying upon and selling like property on execution; and for closing the premises and keeping them closed, a reasonable sum shall be allowed by the court.

(Added by Stats. 1972, Ch. 1407.)

11584.

The proceeds of the sale of the movable property shall be applied as follows:

First—To the fees and costs of the removal and sale.

Second—To the allowances and costs of closing and keeping closed the building or place.

Third—To the payment of the plaintiff's costs in the action.

Fourth—The balance, if any, to the owner of the property.

(Added by Stats. 1972, Ch. 1407.)

11585.

If the proceeds of the sale of the movable property do not fully discharge all of the costs, fees, and allowances, the building and place shall then also be sold under execution

issued upon the order of the court or judge and the proceeds of the sale shall be applied in like manner.

(Added by Stats. 1972, Ch. 1407.)

11586.

(a) If the owner of the building or place has not been guilty of any contempt of court in the proceedings, and appears and pays all costs, fees, and allowances that are a lien on the building or place and files a bond in the full value of the property conditioned that the owner will immediately abate any nuisance that may exist at the building or place and prevent it from being established or kept thereat within a period of one year thereafter, the court, or judge may, if satisfied of the owner's good faith, order the building or place to be delivered to the owner, and the order of abatement canceled so far as it may relate to the property.

(b) The release of property under the provisions of this division does not release it from any judgment, lien, penalty, or liability to which it may be subject.

(Amended by Stats. 1982, Ch. 517, Sec. 276.)

11587.

Whenever the owner of a building or place upon which the act or acts constituting the contempt have been committed, or the owner of any interest therein, has been guilty of a contempt of court, and fined in any proceedings under this division, the fine is a lien upon the building or place to the extent of his interest in it.

The lien is enforceable and collectible by execution issued by order of the court.

(Added by Stats. 1972, Ch. 1407.)

ARTICLE 4. Registration of Controlled Substance Offenders [11590 - 11595]
(Article 4 added by Stats. 1972, Ch. 1407.)

11590.

(a) Except as provided in subdivisions (c) and (d), any person who is convicted in the State of California of any offense defined in Section 11350, 11351, 11351.5, 11352, 11353, 11353.5, 11353.7, 11354, 11355, 11357, 11358, 11359, 11360, 11361, 11363, 11366, 11366.5, 11366.6, 11368, 11378, 11378.5, 11379, 11379.5, 11379.6, 11380, 11380.5, 11383, or 11550, or subdivision (a) of Section 11377, or any person who is discharged or paroled from a penal institution where he or she was confined because of the commission of any such offense, or any person who is convicted in any other state of any offense which, if committed or attempted in this state, would have been punishable as one or more of the above-mentioned offenses, shall within 30 days of his or her coming into any county or city, or city and county in which he or she resides or is temporarily domiciled for that length of time, register with the chief of police of the city in which he or she resides or the sheriff of the county if he or she resides in an unincorporated area.

For persons convicted of an offense defined in Section 11377, 11378, 11379, or 11380, this subdivision shall apply only to offenses involving controlled substances specified in paragraph (12) of subdivision (d) of Section 11054 and paragraph (2) of subdivision (d) of Section 11055, and to analogs of these substances, as defined in Section 11401. For persons convicted of an offense defined in Section 11379 or 11379.5, this subdivision shall not apply if the conviction was for transporting, offering to transport, or attempting to transport a controlled substance.

(b) Any person who is convicted in any federal court of any offense which, if committed or attempted in this state would have been punishable as one or more of the offenses enumerated in subdivision (a) shall within 30 days of his or her coming into any county or city, or city and county in which he or she resides or is temporarily domiciled for that length of time, register with the chief of police of the city in which he or she resides or the sheriff of the county if he or she resides in an unincorporated area.

(c) This section does not apply to a conviction of a misdemeanor under Section 11357, 11360, or 11377.

(d) The registration requirements imposed by this section for the conviction of offenses defined in Section 11353.7, 11366.5, 11366.6, 11377, 11378, 11378.5, 11379, 11379.5, 11379.6, 11380, 11380.5, or 11383, shall apply to any person who commits any of those offenses on and after January 1, 1990.

(Amended by Stats. 1990, Ch. 1417, Sec. 2. Effective September 28, 1990. Superseded on operative date of amendment by Stats. 1995, Ch. 714.)

11590.

(a) Except as provided in subdivisions (c) and (d), any person who is convicted in the State of California of any offense defined in Section 11350, 11351, 11351.5, 11352, 11353, 11353.5, 11353.7, 11354, 11355, 11357, 11358, 11359, 11360, 11361, 11363, 11366, 11366.5, 11366.6, 11368, 11370.1, 11378, 11378.5, 11379, 11379.5, 11379.6, 11380, 11380.5, 11383, or 11550, or subdivision (a) of Section 11377, or any person who is discharged or paroled from a penal institution where he or she was confined because of the commission of any such offense, or any person who is convicted in any other state of any offense which, if committed or attempted in this state, would have been punishable as one or more of the above-mentioned offenses, shall within 30 days of his or her coming into any county or city, or city and county in which he or she resides or is temporarily domiciled for that length of time, register with the chief of police of the city in which he or she resides or the sheriff of the county if he or she resides in an unincorporated area.

For persons convicted of an offense defined in Section 11377, 11378, 11379, or 11380, this subdivision shall apply only to offenses involving controlled substances specified in paragraph (12) of subdivision (d) of Section 11054 and paragraph (2) of subdivision (d) of Section 11055, and to analogs of these substances, as defined in Section 11401. For persons convicted of an offense defined in Section 11379 or 11379.5, this subdivision shall not apply if the conviction was for transporting, offering to transport, or attempting to transport a controlled substance.

(b) Any person who is convicted in any federal court of any offense which, if committed or attempted in this state would have been punishable as one or more of the offenses enumerated in subdivision (a) shall, within 30 days of his or her coming into any county or city, or city and county, in which he or she resides or is temporarily domiciled for that length of time, register with the chief of police of the city in which he or she resides or the sheriff of the county if he or she resides in an unincorporated area.

(c) This section does not apply to a conviction of a misdemeanor under Section 11357, 11360, or 11377.

(d) The registration requirements imposed by this section for the conviction of offenses defined in Section 11353.7, 11366.5, 11366.6, 11370.1, 11377, 11378, 11378.5, 11379, 11379.5, 11379.6, 11380, 11380.5, or 11383, shall apply to any person who commits any of those offenses on and after January 1, 1990.

(Amended by Stats. 1995, Ch. 714, Sec. 1. Effective January 1, 1996. Operative upon appropriation of funds as prescribed by Sec. 2 of Ch. 714.)

11591.

Every sheriff, chief of police, or the Commissioner of the California Highway Patrol, upon the arrest for any of the controlled substance offenses enumerated in Section 11590, or Section 11364, insofar as that section relates to paragraph (12) of subdivision (d) of Section 11054, of any school employee, shall, provided that he or she knows that the arrestee is a school employee, do one of the following:

(a) If the school employee is a teacher in any of the public schools of this state, the sheriff, chief of police, or Commissioner of the California Highway Patrol shall immediately notify by telephone the superintendent of schools of the school district employing the teacher and shall immediately give written notice of the arrest to the Commission on Teacher Credentialing and to the superintendent of schools in the county where the person is employed. Upon receipt of the notice, the county superintendent of schools and the Commission on Teacher Credentialing shall immediately notify the governing board of the school district employing the person.

(b) If the school employee is a nonteacher in any of the public schools of this state, the sheriff, chief of police, or Commissioner of the California Highway Patrol shall immediately notify by telephone the superintendent of schools of the school district employing the nonteacher and shall immediately give written notice of the arrest to the governing board of the school district employing the person.

(c) If the school employee is a teacher in any private school of this state, the sheriff, chief of police, or Commissioner of the California Highway Patrol shall immediately notify by telephone the private school authority employing the teacher and shall immediately give written notice of the arrest to the private school authority employing the teacher.

(Amended by Stats. 2003, Ch. 536, Sec. 1. Effective January 1, 2004.)

11591.5.

Every sheriff or chief of police, upon the arrest for any of the controlled substance offenses enumerated in Section 11590, or Section 11364, insofar as that section relates to paragraph (9) of subdivision (d) of Section 11054, of any teacher or instructor employed in any community college district shall immediately notify by telephone the superintendent of the community college district employing the teacher or instructor and shall immediately give written notice of the arrest to the Office of the Chancellor of the California Community Colleges. Upon receipt of such notice, the district superintendent shall immediately notify the governing board of the community college district employing the person.

(Added by Stats. 1983, Ch. 1032, Sec. 3.)

11592.

Any person who, on or after the effective date of this section is discharged or paroled from a jail, prison, school, road camp, or other institution where he or she was confined because of the commission or attempt to commit one of the offenses described in Section 11590 shall, prior to such discharge, parole, or release, be informed of his or her duty to register under that section by the official in charge of the place of confinement and the official shall require the person to read and sign such form as may be required by the Department of Justice, stating that the duty of the person to register under this section has been explained to him or her. The official in charge of the place of confinement shall obtain the address where the person expects to reside upon his or her discharge, parole, or release and shall report that address to the Department of Justice. The official in charge of the place of confinement shall give one copy of the form to the person, and shall send two copies to the Department of Justice, which, in turn, shall forward one copy to the appropriate law enforcement agency having local jurisdiction where the person expects to reside upon his or her discharge, parole, or release.

(Amended by Stats. 2007, Ch. 130, Sec. 162. Effective January 1, 2008.)

11593.

Any person who, on or after the effective date of this section is convicted in the State of California of the commission or attempt to commit any of the above-mentioned offenses and who is released on probation or discharged upon payment of a fine shall, prior to such release or discharge, be informed of his duty to register under Section 11590 by the court in which he has been convicted and the court shall require the person to read and sign such form as may be required by the Department of Justice, stating that the duty of the person to register under this section has been explained to him. The court shall obtain the address where the person expects to reside upon his release or discharge and shall report within three days such address to the Department of Justice. The court shall give one copy of the form to the person, and shall send two copies to the Department of Justice, which, in turn, shall forward one copy to the appropriate law enforcement agency having local jurisdiction where the person expects to reside upon his discharge, parole, or release.

(Amended by Stats. 1974, Ch. 1403.)

11594.

The registration required by Section 11590 shall consist of (a) a statement in writing signed by such person, giving such information as may be required by the Department of Justice, and (b) the fingerprints and photograph of such person. Within three days thereafter the registering law enforcement agency shall forward such statement, fingerprints and photograph to the Department of Justice.

If any person required to register hereunder changes his residence address he shall inform, in writing within 10 days, the law enforcement agency with whom he last registered of his new address. The law enforcement agency shall, within three days after receipt of such information, forward it to the Department of Justice. The Department of Justice shall forward appropriate registration data to the law enforcement agency having local jurisdiction of the new place of residence.

All registration requirements set forth in this article shall terminate five years after the discharge from prison, release from jail or termination of probation or parole of the person convicted. Nothing in this section shall be construed to conflict with the provisions of Section 1203.4 of the Penal Code concerning termination of probation and release from penalties and disabilities of probation.

Any person required to register under the provisions of this section who shall knowingly violate any of the provisions thereof is guilty of a misdemeanor.

The statements, photographs and fingerprints herein required shall not be open to inspection by the public or by any person other than a regularly employed peace or other law enforcement officer.

(Amended by Stats. 1974, Ch. 1403.)

11595.

The provisions of former Article 6 (commencing with Section 1850) of Chapter 7 of Division 10 of this code, which is repealed by the act that adds this article, including Section 11850 as amended by Chapter 796 of the Statutes of 1972, shall remain in effect as to any person who comes within such provisions.

Notwithstanding Section 9605 of the Government Code, the changes which are made in former Section 11850 by Chapter 796 of the Statutes of 1972 shall be effective and operative for the purposes of this section.

(Added by Stats. 1972, Ch. 1407.)

CHAPTER 11. Educational Programs [11600 - 11605]

(Chapter 11 added by Stats. 1972, Ch. 1407.)

11600.

The Attorney General, the Board of Pharmacy, and other agencies shall carry out educational programs designed to prevent and deter misuse and abuse of controlled substances. In connection with these programs, he may do all of the following:

(a) Promote better recognition of the problems of misuse and abuse of controlled substances within the regulated industry and among interested groups and organizations.

(b) Assist the regulated industry and interested groups and organizations in contributing to the reduction of misuse and abuse of controlled substances.

(c) Consult with interested groups and organizations to aid them in solving administrative and organizational problems.

(d) Assist in the education and training of state and local law enforcement officials in their efforts to control misuse and abuse of controlled substances.

(Added by Stats. 1972, Ch. 1407.)

11601.

The Attorney General shall encourage research on misuse and abuse of controlled substances. In connection with the research, and in furtherance of the enforcement of this division, he or she may do all of the following:

(a) Develop new or improved approaches, techniques, systems, equipment, and devices to strengthen the enforcement of this division.

(b) Enter into contracts with public agencies, institutions of higher education, and private organizations or individuals for the purpose of conducting demonstrations or special projects that bear directly on misuse and abuse of controlled substances.

(c) (1) Authorize hospitals and trauma centers to share information with local law enforcement agencies, the Emergency Medical Services Authority, and local emergency medical services agencies about controlled substance overdose trends.

(2) The information provided by hospitals and trauma centers pursuant to this subdivision shall include only the number of overdoses and the substances suspected as the primary cause of the overdoses. Any information shared pursuant to this subdivision shall be shared in a manner that ensures complete patient confidentiality.

(Amended by Stats. 2014, Ch. 491, Sec. 3. (SB 1438) Effective January 1, 2015.)

11602.

The Attorney General may enter into contracts for educational and research activities without performance bonds.

(Added by Stats. 1972, Ch. 1407.)

11603.

The Attorney General, with the approval of the Research Advisory Panel, may authorize persons engaged in research on the use and effects of controlled substances to withhold the names and other identifying characteristics of individuals who are the subjects of the research. Persons who obtain this authorization are not compelled in any civil, criminal, administrative, legislative, or other proceeding to identify the individuals who are the subjects of research for which the authorization was obtained.

(Added by Stats. 1972, Ch. 1407.)

11604.

The Attorney General, with the approval of the Research Advisory Panel, may authorize the possession and distribution of controlled substances by persons engaged in research. Persons who obtain this authorization are exempt from state prosecution for possession and distribution of controlled substances to the extent of the authorization. (Added by Stats. 1972, Ch. 1407.)

11605.

(a) Commencing with the 1991–92 fiscal year, the Attorney General, in consultation with the Governor's Policy Council on Alcohol and Drug Abuse, shall conduct a biennial survey of drug and alcohol use among pupils enrolled in grades 7, 9, and 11. The survey shall assess all of the following:

(1) The frequency and type of substance abuse.

(2) The age of first use and intoxication.

(3) Pertinent attitudes and experiences of pupils.

(4) The experience of pupils with school-based drug and alcohol prevention programs.

(5) As an optional component, the survey may examine the risk factors associated with school dropouts.

(b) The biennial survey shall be based on a statewide sample of pupils enrolled in grades 7, 9, and 11 and shall be consistent with the surveys conducted by the office of the Attorney General in the 1985–86, 1987–88, and 1989–90 fiscal years.

(c) The Attorney General shall release the findings of the survey on or before May of each even-numbered year and shall prepare and distribute a report on the survey to the Legislature, the Governor, the Superintendent of Public Instruction, law enforcement agencies, school districts, and interested members of the general public.

(d) In conducting the survey, the Attorney General shall ensure that the confidentiality of participating school districts and pupils shall be maintained. Pupil questionnaires and answer sheets shall be exempt from the public disclosure requirements prescribed by Chapter 3.5 (commencing with Section 6250) of Division 7 of Title 1 of the Government Code.

(e) Persons reporting data pursuant to the requirements of this article shall not be liable for damages in any action based upon the use or misuse of pupil surveys that are mailed or otherwise transmitted to the Attorney General, or his or her designee.

(f) The requirements prescribed by this article shall continue to be funded with the existing resources of the Attorney General.

(Added by Stats. 1990, Ch. 1332, Sec. 1.)

CHAPTER 12. Clandestine Laboratory Enforcement Program [11640 - 11647]

(Chapter 12 added by Stats. 1986, Ch. 1029, Sec. 1.)

11640.

The Legislature finds and declares that there has been a recent and rapid expansion in clandestine laboratories illegally producing a variety of controlled substances. These are increasingly sophisticated operations, frequently located in rural areas or working across jurisdictional lines, which pose substantial dangers to the general public from fire, explosion, and the toxic chemicals involved. The controlled substances these laboratories produce, such as analogs of fentanyl, phencyclidine, and methamphetamine, are extremely difficult to detect and analyze and have caused numerous deaths and serious injuries to those who use them.

The Legislature further finds and declares that, given the number and nature of clandestine laboratories, local law enforcement officials in most jurisdictions lack the training, specialized equipment, and resources to adequately enforce existing law. As a result, the public is increasingly endangered by the laboratories themselves while the controlled substances they produce pose a grave danger to those who use them.

It is the intent of the Legislature in establishing the Clandestine Laboratory Enforcement Program to provide increased funding for special training, equipment, personnel, and financial assistance to state and local law enforcement officials targeted on the investigation and prosecution of clandestine laboratories. The program shall also increase public awareness of the problems posed by clandestine laboratories and the products they produce.

(Added by Stats. 1986, Ch. 1029, Sec. 1.)

11641.

The Department of Justice shall establish a Clandestine Laboratory Enforcement Program to assist state and local law enforcement and prosecutorial agencies in apprehending and prosecuting persons involved in the unlawful manufacture of controlled substances. (Added by Stats. 1986, Ch. 1029, Sec. 1.)

11642.

(a) To the extent moneys are available therefor, the Controller, in accordance with criteria and procedures which shall be adopted by the Department of Justice, may reimburse counties with a population under 1,750,000 for costs of prosecuting violations, attempts to violate, or conspiracies to violate Section 11100, 11100.1, 11104, 11105, 11379.6, or 11383 initiated after January 1, 1987. Funding under this subdivision shall not exceed twenty-five thousand dollars ($25,000) for each prosecution or joint prosecution assisted. All funds allocated to a county under this subdivision shall be distributed by it only to its prosecutorial agency, to be used solely for investigation and prosecution of these offenses. Funds distributed under this subdivision shall not be used to supplant any local funds that would, in the absence of this subdivision, be made available to support the prosecutorial efforts of counties.

Cases wholly financed or reimbursed under any other state or federal program including, but not limited to, the Asset Forfeiture Program (Section 11489), the Major Narcotic Vendors Prosecution Law (Section 13881 of the Penal Code), or the California Career

Criminal Apprehension Program (Section 13851 of the Penal Code), shall not be entitled to reimbursement under this subdivision.

(b) To the extent moneys are available therefor, the Controller, in accordance with criteria and procedures which shall be adopted by the Department of Justice, may reimburse counties with a population under 1,750,000 for law enforcement personnel expenses, not exceeding ten thousand dollars ($10,000) per case, incurred in the investigation of violations, attempts to violate, or conspiracies to violate Section 11100, 11100.1, 11104, 11105, 11379.6, or 11383 initiated after January 1, 1987. All funds allocated to a county under this subdivision shall be distributed by it only to its law enforcement agency to be used solely for investigation and detection of these offenses. Funds distributed under this subdivision shall not be used to supplant any local funds that would, in the absence of this subdivision, be made available to support the law enforcement efforts of counties. Cases financed or reimbursed under any other state or federal program, including, but not limited to, the Asset Forfeiture Program, (Section 11489), the California Career Criminal Apprehension Program (Section 13851 of the Penal Code), or the federal Asset Forfeiture Program (21 U.S.C. Sec. 881), shall not be entitled to reimbursement under this subdivision.

(c) (1) To the extent moneys are available therefor, the Controller, in accordance with criteria and procedures which shall be adopted by the Department of Justice, may reimburse counties with a population under 1,750,000 for costs incurred by, or at the direction of, state or local law enforcement agencies to remove and dispose of or store toxic waste from the sites of laboratories used for the unlawful manufacture of a controlled substance.

(2) The local law enforcement agency or Department of Justice shall notify the local health officer within 24 hours of the seizure of a laboratory used for the unlawful manufacture of a controlled substance. The local health officer shall either:

(A) Make a determination as to whether the site poses an immediate threat to public health and safety, and if so, shall undertake immediate corrective action.

(B) Notify the State Department of Health Services.

As used in this section, "counties" includes any city within a county with a population of less than 1,750,000.

The Department of Justice may adopt emergency regulations consistent with this section and the Administrative Procedure Act.

(Amended by Stats. 1991, Ch. 929, Sec. 1.)

11643.

To the extent moneys are available therefor, the Department of Justice shall do the following:

(a) In cooperation with the Commission on Peace Officer Standards and Training provide advanced training to state and local law enforcement personnel on the unique skills, such as detection and identification of chemical substances, and safety precautions, such as safe handling, storage, and disposal of toxic substances, necessary to investigate clandestine laboratories illegally manufacturing controlled substances.

(b) Make safety equipment, such as protective clothing and breathing apparatus, available to local law enforcement officials, as needed, on a case-by-case basis in connection with investigation and abatement of laboratories illegally manufacturing controlled substances.

(c) Establish enhanced enforcement teams assigned to the investigation of clandestine laboratories illegally manufacturing controlled substances, particularly targeting cabals operating in multiple local jurisdictions. These teams shall include special agents trained in investigating clandestine laboratories, criminalists to analyze the chemicals involved, auditors to conduct financial investigations and initiate forfeiture proceedings pursuant to Chapter 8 (commencing with Section 11470) where warranted, and analysts to monitor the overall pattern and network of these clandestine laboratories across the state, to develop further cases, and to target law enforcement efforts where needed.

(Amended by Stats. 2012, Ch. 867, Sec. 11. (SB 1144) Effective January 1, 2013.)

11644.

To the extent moneys are available therefor, the Crime Prevention Center of the Department of Justice shall prepare and disseminate informational materials on the unique dangers posed by clandestine laboratories and the controlled substances they produce. The Crime Prevention Center shall increase public awareness in areas such as the health dangers created by the laboratories themselves, including how to identify and report them, and the unusual effects and dangers of synthetic substances such as analogs of fentanyl, MPPP, phencyclidine, and methamphetamines.

(Added by Stats. 1986, Ch. 1029, Sec. 1.)

11646.

The Attorney General shall adopt rules and regulations for the administration and enforcement of this chapter.

(Added by Stats. 1986, Ch. 1029, Sec. 1.)

11647.

(a) The Crank-Up Task Force Program is hereby created within the Department of Justice as part of the Clandestine Laboratory Enforcement Program with responsibility for establishing, conducting, supporting, and coordinating crank-up task forces composed of state and local law enforcement agencies targeting the investigation, seizure, and cleanup of clandestine laboratories used to manufacture methamphetamine.

(b) The department shall coordinate all investigations undertaken by task forces operating under the Crank-Up Task Force Program with all local agencies having law enforcement responsibilities within the jurisdictions involved. The department also shall solicit participation by appropriate federal agencies with task force investigations whenever possible.

The department shall provide staffing and logistical support for the crank-up task forces, supplying special agents, criminal intelligence analysts, forensic experts, financial auditors, equipment, and funding to the task forces as needed.

(c) Local law enforcement agencies participating in the Crank-Up Task Force Program shall be reimbursed by the department for personnel overtime costs and equipment or supplies required for task force activities.

(Amended by Stats. 2012, Ch. 867, Sec. 12. (SB 1144) Effective January 1, 2013.)

CHAPTER 13. Miscellaneous [11650 - 11651]

(Chapter 13 added by Stats. 1972, Ch. 1407.)

11650.

(a) Prosecution for any violation of law occurring prior to the effective date of this division is not affected or abated by this division. If the offense being prosecuted is similar to one set out in Chapter 6 (commencing with Section 11350) of this division, then the penalties under Chapter 6 (commencing with Section 11350) apply if they are less than those under prior law.

(b) Civil seizures or forfeitures and injunctive proceedings commenced prior to effective date of this division are not affected by this division.

(c) All administrative proceedings pending under prior laws which are superseded by this division shall be continued and brought to a final determination in accord with the laws and rules in effect prior to the effective date of this division. Any substance controlled under prior law which is not listed within Schedules I through V, is automatically controlled without further proceedings and shall be listed in the appropriate schedule.

(d) This division applies to violations of law, seizures and forfeiture, injunctive proceedings, administrative proceedings and investigations which occur on or after the effective date of this division.

(Amended by Stats. 1993, Ch. 589, Sec. 90. Effective January 1, 1994.)

11651.

Any orders and regulations promulgated pursuant to any law affected by this division and in effect on the effective date of this division, not in conflict with it continue in effect until modified, superseded, or repealed.

(Repealed and added by Stats. 1972, Ch. 1407.)

DIVISION 10.2. DRUG DEALER LIABILITY ACT [11700 - 11717]

(Division 10.2 added by Stats. 1996, Ch. 867, Sec. 1.)

11700.

This division shall be known and may be cited as the Drug Dealer Liability Act.

(Added by Stats. 1996, Ch. 867, Sec. 1. Effective January 1, 1997.)

11701.

The purpose of this division is to provide a civil remedy for damages to persons in a community injured as a result of the use of an illegal controlled substance. These persons include parents, employers, insurers, governmental entities, and others who pay for drug treatment or employee assistance programs, as well as infants injured as a result of exposure to controlled substances in utero ("drug babies"). This division will enable them to recover damages from those persons in the community who have joined the marketing of illegal controlled substances. A further purpose of this division is to shift, to the extent possible, the cost of the damage caused by the existence of the market for illegal controlled substances in a community to those who illegally profit from that market. The further purpose of this division is to establish the prospect of substantial monetary loss as a deterrent to those who have not yet entered into the distribution market for illegal controlled substances. The further purpose is to establish an incentive for users of illegal controlled substances to identify and seek payment for their own treatment from those dealers who have sold illegal controlled substances to the user in the past.

(Added by Stats. 1996, Ch. 867, Sec. 1. Effective January 1, 1997.)

11702.

The Legislature finds and declares all of the following:

(a) Although the criminal justice system is an important weapon against the marketing of illegal controlled substances, the civil justice system can and must also be used. The civil justice system can provide an avenue of compensation for those who have suffered harm as a result of the marketing and distribution of illegal controlled substances. The persons who have joined the marketing of illegal controlled substances should bear the cost of the harm caused by that market in the community.

(b) The threat of liability under this division serves as an additional deterrent to a recognizable segment of the network for illegal controlled substances. A person who has assets unrelated to the sale of illegal controlled substances, who markets illegal controlled substances at the workplace, who encourages friends to become users, among others, is likely to decide that the added cost of entering the market is not worth the benefit. This is particularly true for a first-time, casual dealer who has not yet made substantial profits. This division provides a mechanism for the cost of the injury caused by illegal drug use to be borne by those who benefit from illegal drug dealing.

(c) This division imposes liability against all participants in the marketing of illegal controlled substances, including small dealers, particularly those in the workplace, who are not usually the focus of criminal investigations. The small dealers increase the number

of users and are the people who become large dealers. These small dealers are most likely to be deterred by the threat of liability.

(Added by Stats. 1996, Ch. 867, Sec. 1. Effective January 1, 1997.)

11703.

As used in this division:

(a) "Marketing of illegal controlled substances" means the possession for sale, sale, or distribution of a specified illegal controlled substance, and shall include all aspects of making such a controlled substance available, including, but not limited to, its manufacture.

(b) "Individual user of an illegal controlled substance" means the individual whose use of a specified illegal controlled substance is the basis of an action brought under this division.

(c) "Level 1 offense" means the possession for sale of less than four ounces or the sale or furnishing of less than one ounce of a specified illegal controlled substance, or the cultivation of at least 25 plants but less than 50 plants, the furnishing of more than 28.5 grams, or the possession for sale or sale of up to four pounds, of marijuana.

(d) "Level 2 offense" means the possession for sale of four ounces or more but less than eight ounces of, or the sale or furnishing of one ounce or more but less than two ounces of, a specified illegal controlled substance, or the cultivation of at least 50 but less than 75 plants, the possession for sale of four pounds or more but less than eight pounds, or the sale or furnishing of more than one pound but less than five pounds, of marijuana.

(e) "Level 3 offense" means the possession for sale of eight ounces or more but less than 16 ounces of, or the sale or furnishing of two ounces or more but less than four ounces of, a specified illegal controlled substance, or the cultivation of at least 75 but less than 100 plants, the possession for sale of eight pounds or more but less than 16 pounds, or the sale or furnishing of more than five pounds but less than 10 pounds, of marijuana.

(f) "Level 4 offense" means the possession for sale of 16 ounces or more of, or the sale or furnishing of four ounces or more of, a specified illegal controlled substance, or the cultivation of 100 plants or more of, the possession for sale of 16 pounds of, or the sale or furnishing of more than 10 pounds of, marijuana.

(g) "Participate in the marketing of illegal controlled substances" means to transport, import into this state, sell, possess with intent to sell, furnish, administer, or give away, or offer to transport, import into this state, sell, furnish, administer, or give away a specified illegal controlled substance. "Participate in the marketing of illegal controlled substances" shall include the manufacturing of an illegal controlled substance, but shall not include the purchase or receipt of an illegal controlled substance for personal use only.

(h) "Person" means an individual, governmental entity, corporation, firm, trust, partnership, or incorporated or unincorporated association, existing under or authorized by the laws of this state, another state, or a foreign country.

(i) "Period of illegal use" means, in relation to the individual user of an illegal controlled substance, the time of the individual's first illegal use of an illegal controlled substance to the accrual of the cause of action.

(j) "Place of illegal activity" means, in relation to the individual user of an illegal controlled substance, each county in which the individual illegally possesses or uses an illegal controlled substance during the period of the individual's use of an illegal controlled substance.

(k) "Place of participation" means, in relation to a defendant in an action brought under this division, each county in which the person participates in the marketing of illegal controlled substances during the period of the person's participation in the marketing of illegal controlled substances.

(l) "Specified illegal controlled substance" means cocaine, phencyclidine, heroin, or methamphetamine and any other illegal controlled substance the manufacture, cultivation, importation into this state, transportation, possession for sale, sale, furnishing, administering, or giving away of which is a violation of Section 11351, 11351.5, 11352, 11358, 11359, 11360, 11378.5, 11379.5, or 11383.

(Amended by Stats. 2005, Ch. 88, Sec. 1. Effective January 1, 2006.)

11704.

(a) A person who knowingly participates in the marketing of illegal controlled substances within this state is liable for civil damages as provided in this division. A person may recover damages under this division for injury resulting from an individual's use of an illegal controlled substance.

(b) A law enforcement officer or agency, the state, or a person acting at the direction of a law enforcement officer or agency or the state is not liable for participating in the marketing of illegal controlled substances, if the participation is in furtherance of an official investigation.

(Added by Stats. 1996, Ch. 867, Sec. 1. Effective January 1, 1997.)

11705.

(a) Any one or more of the following persons may bring an action for damages caused by an individual's use of an illegal controlled substance:

(1) A parent, legal guardian, child, spouse, or sibling of the individual controlled substance user.

(2) An individual who was exposed to an illegal controlled substance in utero.

(3) An employer of the individual user of an illegal controlled substance.

(4) A medical facility, insurer, employer, or other nongovernmental entity that funds a drug treatment program or employee assistance program for the individual user of an illegal controlled substance or that otherwise expended money on behalf of the individual user of an illegal controlled substance. No public agency other than a public agency medical facility shall have a cause of action under this division.

(5) A person injured as a result of the willful, reckless, or negligent actions of an individual user of an illegal controlled substance.

(b) A person entitled to bring an action under this section may seek damages from one or more of the following:

(1) A person who sold, administered, or furnished an illegal controlled substance to the individual user of the illegal controlled substance.

(2) A person who knowingly participated in the marketing of illegal controlled substances, if all of the following apply:

(A) The place of illegal activity by the individual user of an illegal controlled substance is within the city, city and county, or unincorporated area of the county in which the defendant's place of participation is situated.

(B) The defendant's participation in the marketing of illegal controlled substances was connected with the same type of specified illegal controlled substance used by the individual user of an illegal controlled substance, and the defendant has been convicted of an offense for that type of specified illegal controlled substance.

(C) The defendant participated in the marketing of illegal controlled substances at any time during the period the individual user of an illegal controlled substance illegally used the controlled substance.

(D) The underlying offense for the conviction of the specified illegal controlled substance occurred in the same county as the individual user's place of use.

(c) As used in subdivision (b), knowingly participated in the marketing of illegal controlled substances" means a conviction for transporting, importing into this state, selling, possessing with intent to sell, furnishing, administering, or giving away, or offering to transport, import into this state, sell, furnish, administer, or give away a specified illegal controlled substance or a quantity of marijuana specified in subdivision (e), (f), (g), or (h) of Section 11703, which are separate in time.

(d) A person entitled to bring an action under this section may recover all of the following damages:

(1) Economic damages, including, but not limited to, the cost of treatment and rehabilitation, medical expenses, loss of economic or educational potential, loss of productivity, absenteeism, support expenses, accidents or injury, and any other pecuniary loss proximately caused by the use of an illegal controlled substance.

(2) Noneconomic damages, including, but not limited to, physical and emotional pain, suffering, physical impairment, emotional distress, medical anguish, disfigurement, loss of enjoyment, loss of companionship, services and consortium, and other nonpecuniary losses proximately caused by an individual's use of an illegal controlled substance.

(3) Exemplary damages.

(4) Reasonable attorney fees.

(5) Costs of suit, including, but not limited to, reasonable expenses for expert testimony.
(Added by Stats. 1996, Ch. 867, Sec. 1. Effective January 1, 1997.)

11706.

(a) An individual user of an illegal controlled substance may not bring an action for damages caused by the use of an illegal controlled substance, except as otherwise provided in this section. An individual user of an illegal controlled substance may bring an action for damages caused by the use of an illegal controlled substance only if all of the following conditions are met:

(1) The individual personally discloses to narcotics enforcement authorities all of the information known to the individual regarding all that individual's sources of illegal controlled substances.

(2) The individual has not used an illegal controlled substance within the 30 days before filing the action.

(3) The individual continues to remain free of the use of an illegal controlled substance throughout the pendency of the action.

(b) A person entitled to bring an action under this section may seek damages only from a person who manufactured, transported, imported into this state, sold, possessed with intent to sell, furnished, administered, or gave away the specified illegal controlled substance actually used by the individual user of an illegal controlled substance.

(c) A person entitled to bring an action under this section may recover only the following damages:

(1) Economic damages, including, but not limited to, the cost of treatment, rehabilitation and medical expenses, loss of economic or educational potential, loss of productivity, absenteeism, accidents or injury, and any other pecuniary loss proximately caused by the person's use of an illegal controlled substance.

(2) Reasonable attorney fees.

(3) Costs of suit, including, but not limited to, reasonable expenses for expert testimony.
(Amended by Stats. 2005, Ch. 88, Sec. 2. Effective January 1, 2006.)

11707.

(a) A third party shall not pay damages awarded under this division, or provide a defense or money for a defense, on behalf of an insured under a contract of insurance or indemnification.

(b) A cause of action authorized pursuant to this division may not be assigned, either expressly, by subrogation, or by any other means, directly or indirectly, to any public or publicly funded agency or institution.
(Added by Stats. 1996, Ch. 867, Sec. 1. Effective January 1, 1997.)

11708.

A person, whose participation in the marketing of illegal controlled substances constitutes the following level offense, shall be rebuttably presumed to be responsible in the following amounts:

(a) For a level 1 offense, 25 percent of the damages.

(b) For a level 2 offense, 50 percent of the damages.

(c) For a level 3 offense, 75 percent of the damages.

(d) For a level 4 offense, 100 percent of the damages.
(Added by Stats. 1996, Ch. 867, Sec. 1. Effective January 1, 1997.)

11709.

(a) Two or more persons may join in one action under this division as plaintiffs if their respective actions have at least one market for illegal controlled substances in common and if any portion of the period of use of an illegal controlled substance overlaps with the period of use of an illegal controlled substance for every other plaintiff.

(b) Two or more persons may be joined in one action under this division as defendants if those persons are liable to at least one plaintiff.

(c) A plaintiff need not participate in obtaining and a defendant need not participate in defending against all the relief demanded. Judgment may be given for one or more plaintiffs according to their respective rights to relief and against one or more defendants according to their respective liabilities.
(Added by Stats. 1996, Ch. 867, Sec. 1. Effective January 1, 1997.)

11710.

(a) An action by an individual user of an illegal controlled substance is governed by the principles of comparative responsibility. Comparative responsibility attributed to the plaintiff does not bar recovery but diminishes the award of compensatory damages proportionally, according to the measure of responsibility attributed to the plaintiff.

(b) The burden of proving the comparative responsibility of the plaintiff is on the defendant, which shall be shown by clear and convincing evidence.

(c) Comparative responsibility shall not be attributed to a plaintiff who is not an individual user of a controlled substance, unless that plaintiff willfully and knowingly gave the individual user money for the purchase of the illegal controlled substance.
(Added by Stats. 1996, Ch. 867, Sec. 1. Effective January 1, 1997.)

11711.

A person subject to liability under this division has a right of action for contribution against another person subject to liability under this division. Contribution may be enforced either in the original action or by a separate action brought for that purpose. A plaintiff may seek recovery in accordance with this division and other laws against a person whom a defendant has asserted a right of contribution.
(Added by Stats. 1996, Ch. 867, Sec. 1. Effective January 1, 1997.)

11712.

(a) Proof of liability in an action brought under this division shall be shown by clear and convincing evidence. Except as otherwise provided in this division, other elements of the cause of action shall be shown by a preponderance of the evidence.

(b) (1) A person against whom recovery is sought who has a criminal conviction pursuant to state laws prohibiting the illegal sale of controlled substances or the Comprehensive Drug Abuse Prevention and Control Act of 1970 (Public Law 91-513, 84 Stats. 1236, codified at 21 U.S.C. Sec. 801 et seq.), is estopped from denying participation in the illegal market for controlled substances. Except as provided in paragraph (2), this subdivision does not affect the plaintiff's burden of proving subparagraphs (A), (B), and (C) of paragraph (2) of subdivision (b) of Section 11705.

(2) Such a conviction is also prima facie evidence of the person's participation in the marketing of a specified illegal controlled substance used by the individual user where that conviction was based upon the person's marketing of that same type of illegal controlled substance.

(c) The absence of a criminal conviction of a person pursuant to subdivision (b) against whom recovery is sought does not bar an action against that person in an action pursuant to paragraph (1) of subdivision (b) of Section 11705, or Section 11706..
(Added by Stats. 1996, Ch. 867, Sec. 1. Effective January 1, 1997.)

11713.

(a) A plaintiff under this division, subject to subdivision (c), may request an ex parte prejudgment attachment order from the court against all assets of a defendant sufficient to satisfy a potential award.

(b) Chapter 5 (commencing with Section 485.010) of Title 6.5 of Part 2 of the Code of Civil Procedure shall apply to any request under this subdivision.
(Added by Stats. 1996, Ch. 867, Sec. 1. Effective January 1, 1997.)

11714.

(a) Except as otherwise provided in this section, a claim under this division shall not be brought more than one year after the defendant furnishes the specified illegal controlled substance. A cause of action accrues under this division when a person who may recover has reason to know of the harm from use of an illegal controlled substance that is the basis for the cause of action and has reason to know that the use of an illegal controlled substance is the cause of the harm.

(b) For a defendant, the statute of limitations under this section does not expire until one year after the individual potential defendant is convicted of a criminal offense involving an illegal controlled substance or as otherwise provided by law.
(Added by Stats. 1996, Ch. 867, Sec. 1. Effective January 1, 1997.)

11715.

On motion by a governmental agency involved in an investigation or prosecution involving an illegal controlled substance, an action brought under this division shall be stayed until the completion of the criminal investigation or prosecution that gave rise to the motion for a stay of the action.
(Added by Stats. 1996, Ch. 867, Sec. 1. Effective January 1, 1997.)

11716.

No cause of action shall arise based on any act by a defendant which occurred prior to the effective date of this division.
(Added by Stats. 1996, Ch. 867, Sec. 1. Effective January 1, 1997.)

11717.

If any provision of this division or the application of any provision to any person or circumstance is held invalid, the remainder of this division and the application of such provision to any other person or circumstance shall not be affected by that invalidation. (Added by Stats. 1996, Ch. 867, Sec. 1. Effective January 1, 1997.)

DIVISION 10.5. ALCOHOL AND DRUG PROGRAMS [11750 - 11975]

(Heading of Division 10.5 amended by Stats. 2013, Ch. 22, Sec. 18.)

PART 1. CREATION OF DUTIES [11750 - 11759.5]

(Heading of Part 1 amended by Stats. 1984, Ch. 1328, Sec. 1.)

CHAPTER 1. General Provisions [11750 - 11756.8]

(Heading of Chapter 1 added by Stats. 1987, Ch. 1488, Sec. 1.)

11750.

(a) It is the intent of the Legislature that the administrative and programmatic functions of the State Department of Alcohol and Drug Programs be transferred to the State Department of Health Care Services and the State Department of Public Health effective July 1, 2013. It is further the intent of the Legislature that this transfer happen efficiently and effectively, with no interruptions in service delivery. This transfer is designed to:

(1) Consolidate within a single state department, the State Department of Health Care Services, all substance use disorder functions and programs from the State Department of Alcohol and Drug Programs.

(2) Align with federal and county partners by consolidating substance use disorder and community mental health functions and programs within one department.

(3) Promote opportunities for the improvement of health care delivery by integrating the state-level administration of substance use disorders, community mental health, and physical health to the benefit of communities and consumers with substance use disorders and cooccurring disorders.

(4) Ensure appropriate state oversight by consolidating the two key public funding sources, the Substance Abuse Prevention and Treatment Block Grant and the Drug Medi-Cal Treatment Program, for the substance use disorder system in one state department.

(5) Provide effective state leadership on substance use disorder issues by positioning the State Department of Health Care Services to serve as a unified, strong voice to advocate, at both the state and federal levels, on behalf of the needs of communities, county partners, and consumers with substance use disorders.

(b) Effective July 1, 2013, the administrative and programmatic functions that were previously performed by the State Department of Alcohol and Drug Programs are transferred to the State Department of Health Care Services and the State Department of Public Health in accordance with the act that added this section. Further, except as provided in Section 131055.2, any reference in state statute or regulation to the State Department of Alcohol and Drug Programs or the State Department of Alcohol and Drug Abuse shall refer to the State Department of Health Care Services. (Repealed and added by Stats. 2013, Ch. 22, Sec. 20. (AB 75) Effective June 27, 2013. Operative July 1, 2013, by Sec. 110 of Ch. 22.)

11751.

(a) Except as provided in Section 131055.2, the State Department of Health Care Services shall succeed to and be vested with all the duties, powers, purposes, functions, responsibilities, and jurisdiction of the former State Department of Alcohol and Drug Programs.

(b) Any reference in statute, regulation, or contract to the State Department of Alcohol and Drug Programs or the State Department of Alcohol and Drug Abuse shall refer to the State Department of Health Care Services to the extent that they relate to the transfer of duties, powers, purposes, functions, responsibilities, and jurisdiction made pursuant to this section.

(c) A contract, lease, license, or any other agreement to which the State Department of Alcohol and Drug Programs is a party shall not be made void or voidable by reason of the act that enacted this section, but shall continue in full force and effect with the State Department of Health Care Services assuming all of the rights, obligations, and duties of the State Department of Alcohol and Drug Programs with respect to the transfer of duties, powers, purposes, functions, responsibilities, and jurisdiction made pursuant to this section.

(d) (1) All unexpended balances of appropriations and other funds available for use by the State Department of Alcohol and Drug Programs in connection with any function or the administration of any law transferred to the State Department of Health Care Services pursuant to the act that enacted this section shall be available for use by the State Department of Health Care Services for the purpose for which the appropriation was originally made or the funds were originally available.

(2) The State Department of Health Care Services may, until July 1, 2017, liquidate the prior years' encumbrances previously obligated by the former State Department of Alcohol and Drug Programs. The Controller shall transfer the following Budget Act appropriations from the former State Department of Alcohol and Drug Programs to the State Department of Health Care Services for use by the State Department of Health Care Services to liquidate the prior years' encumbrances previously obligated by the former State Department of Alcohol and Drug Programs:

(A) Items 4200-001-0001, 4200-001-0139, 4200-001-0243, 4200-001-0816, 4200-001-0890, 4200-001-3113, 4200-101-0001, 4200-101-0890, 4200-102-0001, 4200-103-0001, 4200-104-0001, and 4200-104-0890 of Section 2.00 of the Budget Act of 2011 (Chapter 33 of the Statutes of 2011).

(B) Items 4200-001-0001, 4200-001-0139, 4200-001-0243, 4200-001-0816, 4200-001-0890, 4200-001-3113, 4200-101-0001, 4200-101-0890, 4200-104-0001, and 4200-104-0890 of Section 2.00 of the Budget Act of 2012 (Chapter 21 of the Statutes of 2012).

(e) All books, documents, forms, records, data systems, and property of the State Department of Alcohol and Drug Programs with respect to the transfer of duties, powers, purposes, functions, responsibilities, and jurisdiction made pursuant to this section shall be transferred to the State Department of Health Care Services.

(f) Positions filled by appointment by the Governor in the State Department of Alcohol and Drug Programs whose principal assignment was to perform functions transferred pursuant to this section shall be transferred to the State Department of Health Care Services.

(g) All employees serving in state civil service, other than temporary employees, who are engaged in the performance of functions transferred pursuant to this section, are transferred to the State Department of Health Care Services pursuant to the provisions of Section 19050.9 of the Government Code. The status, position, and rights of those persons shall not be affected by their transfer and shall continue to be retained by them pursuant to the State Civil Service Act (Part 2 (commencing with Section 18500) of Division 5 of Title 2 of the Government Code), except as to positions the duties of which are vested in a position exempt from civil service. The personnel records of all employees transferred pursuant to this section shall be transferred to the State Department of Health Care Services.

(h) Any regulation or other action adopted, prescribed, taken, or performed by an agency or officer in the administration of a program or the performance of a duty, power, purpose, function, or responsibility pursuant to this division or Division 10.6 (commencing with Section 11998) in effect prior to July 1, 2013, shall remain in effect unless or until amended, and shall be deemed to be a regulation or action of the agency to which or officer to whom the program, duty, power, purpose, function, responsibility, or jurisdiction is assigned pursuant to this section.

(i) A suit, action, or other proceeding lawfully commenced by or against any agency or other officer of the state, in relation to the administration of any program or the discharge of any duty, power, purpose, function, or responsibility transferred pursuant to this section, shall not abate by reason of the transfer of the program, duty, power, purpose, function, or responsibility under that section. (Amended by Stats. 2014, Ch. 71, Sec. 89. (SB 1304) Effective January 1, 2015.)

11751.4.

It is the intent of the Legislature to ensure the integrity of state alcohol and drug programs. (Amended by Stats. 2004, Ch. 862, Sec. 2. Effective January 1, 2005.)

11752.

As used in this division, "department" means the State Department of Health Care Services and "director" means the Director of Health Care Services. (Amended by Stats. 2013, Ch. 22, Sec. 27. (AB 75) Effective June 27, 2013. Operative July 1, 2013, by Sec. 110 of Ch. 22.)

11752.1.

(a) "County board of supervisors" includes county boards of supervisors in the case of counties acting jointly.

(b) "Agency" means the California Health and Human Services Agency.

(c) "Secretary" means the Secretary of California Health and Human Services.

(d) "Advisory board" means the county advisory board on alcohol and other drug problems established at the sole discretion of the county board of supervisors pursuant to Section 11805. If a county does not establish an advisory board, any provision of this chapter relative to the activities, duties, and functions of the advisory board shall be inapplicable to that county.

(e) "Alcohol and drug program administrator" means the county program administrator designated pursuant to Section 11800.

(f) "State alcohol and other drug program" includes all state alcohol and other drug projects administered by the department and all county alcohol and other drug programs funded under this division.

(g) "Health systems agency" means the health planning agency established pursuant to Public Law 93-641.

(h) "Alcohol and other drug problems" means problems of individuals, families, and the community that are related to the abuse of alcohol and other drugs.

(i) "Alcohol abuser" means anyone who has a problem related to the consumption of alcoholic beverages whether or not it is of a periodic or continuing nature. This definition includes, but is not limited to, persons referred to as "alcoholics" and "drinking drivers." These problems may be evidenced by substantial impairment to the person's physical, mental, or social well-being, which impairment adversely affects his or her abilities to function in the community.

(j) "Drug abuser" means anyone who has a problem related to the consumption of illicit, illegal, legal, or prescription drugs or over-the-counter medications in a manner other than prescribed, whether or not it is of a periodic or continuing nature. This definition includes, but is not limited to, persons referred to as "drug addicts." The drug-consumption-related problems of these persons may be evidenced by substantial impairment to the person's physical, mental, or social well-being, which impairment adversely affects his or her abilities to function in the community.

(k) "Alcohol and other drug service" means a service that is designed to encourage recovery from the abuse of alcohol and other drugs and to alleviate or preclude problems in the individual, his or her family, and the community.

(l) "Alcohol and other drug abuse program" means a collection of alcohol and other drug services that are coordinated to achieve the specified objectives of this part.

(m) "Driving-under-the-influence program," "DUI program," or "licensed program" means an alcohol and other drug service that has been issued a valid license by the department to provide services pursuant to Chapter 9 (commencing with Section 11836) of Part 2.

(n) "Clients-participants" means recipients of alcohol and other drug prevention, treatment, and recovery program services.

(o) "Substance Abuse and Mental Health Services Administration" means that agency of the United States Department of Health and Human Services.

(Amended by Stats. 2013, Ch. 22, Sec. 28. (AB 75) Effective June 27, 2013. Operative July 1, 2013, by Sec. 110 of Ch. 22.)

11754.

(a) The department shall be the single state agency authorized to receive any federal funds payable directly to the state by the Substance Abuse and Mental Health Services Administration to implement programs that provide services to alleviate the problems related to alcohol and other drug use.

(b) The department may receive other federal funds and expend them pursuant to this division, the Budget Act, or other statutes.

(Amended by Stats. 2004, Ch. 862, Sec. 4. Effective January 1, 2005.)

11755.

The department shall do all of the following:

(a) Adopt regulations pursuant to Section 11152 of the Government Code.

(b) Employ administrative, technical, and other personnel as may be necessary for the performance of its powers and duties.

(c) Do or perform any of the acts that may be necessary, desirable, or proper to carry out the purpose of this division.

(d) Provide funds to counties for the planning and implementation of local programs to alleviate problems related to alcohol and other drug use.

(e) Review and execute contracts for drug and alcohol services submitted for funds allocated or administered by the department.

(f) Provide for technical assistance and training to local alcohol and other drug programs to assist in the planning and implementation of quality services.

(g) Review research in, and serve as a resource to provide information relating to, alcohol and other drug programs.

(h) In cooperation with the Department of Human Resources, encourage training in other state agencies to assist the agencies to recognize employee problems relating to alcohol and other drug use that affects job performance and encourage the employees to seek appropriate services.

(i) Assist and cooperate with the Office of Statewide Health Planning and Development in the drafting and adoption of the state health plan to ensure inclusion of appropriate provisions relating to alcohol and other drug problems.

(j) In the same manner and subject to the same conditions as other state agencies, develop and submit annually to the Department of Finance a program budget for the alcohol and other drug programs, which budget shall include expenditures proposed to be made under this division, and may include expenditures proposed to be made by any other state agency relating to alcohol and other drug problems, pursuant to an interagency agreement with the department.

(k) Review and certify alcohol and other drug programs meeting state standards pursuant to Chapter 7 (commencing with Section 11830) and Chapter 13 (commencing with Section 11847) of Part 2.

(l) Develop standards for ensuring minimal statewide levels of service quality provided by alcohol and other drug programs.

(m) Review and license narcotic treatment programs.

(n) Develop and implement, in partnership with the counties, alcohol and other drug prevention strategies especially designed for youth.

(o) Develop and maintain a centralized alcohol and drug abuse indicator data collection system that shall gather and obtain information on the status of the alcohol and other drug abuse problems in the state. This information shall include, but not be limited to, all of the following:

(1) The number and characteristics of persons receiving recovery or treatment services from alcohol and other drug programs providing publicly funded services or services licensed by the state.

(2) The location and types of services offered by these programs.

(3) The number of admissions to hospitals on both an emergency room and inpatient basis for treatment related to alcohol and other drugs.

(4) The number of arrests for alcohol and other drug violations.

(5) The number of Department of Corrections and Rehabilitation, Division of Juvenile Facilities, commitments for drug violations.

(6) The number of Department of Corrections and Rehabilitation commitments for drug violations.

(7) The number or percentage of persons having alcohol or other drug problems as determined by survey information.

(8) The amounts of illicit drugs confiscated by law enforcement in the state.

(9) The statewide alcohol and other drug program distribution and the fiscal impact of alcohol and other drug problems upon the state.

Providers of publicly funded services or services licensed by the department to clients-participants shall report data in a manner, in a format, and under a schedule prescribed by the department.

(p) Issue an annual report that portrays the drugs abused, populations affected, user characteristics, crime-related costs, socioeconomic costs, and other related information deemed necessary in providing a problem profile of alcohol and other drug abuse in the state.

(q) (1) Require any individual, public or private organization, or government agency, receiving federal grant funds, to comply with all federal statutes, regulations, guidelines, and terms and conditions of the grants. The failure of the individual, public or private organization, or government agency, to comply with the statutes, regulations, guidelines, and terms and conditions of grants received may result in the department's disallowing noncompliant costs, or the suspension or termination of the contract or grant award allocating the grant funds.

(2) Adopt regulations implementing this subdivision in accordance with Chapter 3.5 (commencing with Section 11340) of Part 1 of Division 3 of Title 2 of the Government Code. For the purposes of the Administrative Procedure Act, the adoption of the regulations shall be deemed necessary for the preservation of the public peace, health and safety, or general welfare. Subsequent amendments to the adoption of emergency regulations shall be deemed an emergency only if those amendments are adopted in direct response to a change in federal statutes, regulations, guidelines, or the terms and conditions of federal grants. Nothing in this paragraph shall be interpreted as prohibiting the department from adopting subsequent amendments on a nonemergency basis or as emergency regulations in accordance with the standards set forth in Section 11346.1 of the Government Code.

(Amended by Stats. 2013, Ch. 76, Sec. 111. (AB 383) Effective January 1, 2014.)

11755.2.

(a) The department may implement a program for the establishment of group homes for alcohol and other drug abusers as provided for in Section 300x-4a of Title 42 of the United States Code.

(b) The department may establish the Resident-Run Housing Revolving Fund for the purpose of making loans to group resident-run homes in conformance with federal statutes and regulations. Any program for the purpose of making loans to group resident-run homes shall be a part of the Resident-Run Housing Revolving Fund. Any unexpended balances in a current program shall be transferred to the Resident-Run Housing Revolving Fund and be available for expenditure during the following fiscal year. Appropriations for subsequent fiscal years shall be provided in the annual Budget Act. All loan payments received from previous loans shall be deposited in the Resident-Run Housing Revolving Fund, as well as all future collections. The Resident-Run Housing Revolving Fund shall be invested in the Pooled Money Investment Fund. Interest earned shall accrue to the Resident-Run Housing Revolving Fund and may be made available for future group resident-run home loans.

(c) The department may adopt regulations as are necessary to implement this section.

(d) This section shall become inoperative on July 1, 2013.

(Amended by Stats. 2013, Ch. 22, Sec. 29. (AB 75) Effective June 27, 2013. Amending action operative July 1, 2013, by Stats. 2013, Ch. 22, Sec. 110. Section inoperative July 1, 2013, by its own provisions from this amendment.)

11756.

The department relative to the statewide alcohol and other drug program, in addition to the duties provided for in Section 11755, shall do all of the following:

(a) Cooperate with other governmental agencies and the private sector in establishing, conducting, and coordinating alcohol and other drug programs and projects pursuant to Chapter 2 (commencing with Section 11775) of Part 2.

(b) Cooperate with other state agencies to encourage appropriate health facilities to recognize, without discrimination, persons with alcohol and other drug problems who also require medical care and to provide them with adequate and appropriate services.

(c) Encourage counties to coordinate alcohol and other drug services, where appropriate, with county health and social service programs, or with regional health programs pursuant to Article 1 (commencing with Section 11820) of Chapter 5 of Part 2.

(d) Encourage the utilization, support, assistance, and dedication of interested persons in the community in order to increase the number of persons with alcohol and other drug problems who voluntarily seek appropriate services to alleviate those problems.

(e) Evaluate or require the evaluation, including the collection of appropriate and necessary information, of alcohol and other drug programs pursuant to Chapter 6 (commencing with Section 11825) of Part 2.

(f) Review and license driving-under-the-influence programs.

(g) Perform all other duties specifically required pursuant to this part.

(Amended by Stats. 2004, Ch. 862, Sec. 9. Effective January 1, 2005.)

11756.8.

(a) It is the intent of the Legislature to ensure that the impacts of the 2011 realignment of alcohol and drug program services are identified and evaluated initially and over time. It is further the intent of the Legislature to ensure that information regarding these impacts is publicly available and accessible and can be utilized to support the state's and counties' effectiveness in delivering these critical services and supports.

(b) (1) The State Department of Health Care Services shall annually report to the appropriate fiscal and policy committees of the Legislature, and publicly post, a summary of outcome and expenditure data that allows for monitoring of changes over time and indicates the degree to which programs are meeting state- and county-defined outcome measures.

(2) This report shall be submitted and posted each year by April 15 and shall contain expenditures for each county for the programs described in clauses (i) to (iv), inclusive, of subparagraph (B) of paragraph (16) of subdivision (f) of Section 30025 of the Government Code.

(3) The department shall consult with legislative staff and with stakeholders to develop a reporting format consistent with the Legislature's desired level of outcome and expenditure reporting detail.

(Amended by Stats. 2013, Ch. 22, Sec. 30. (AB 75) Effective June 27, 2013. Operative July 1, 2013, by Sec. 110 of Ch. 22.)

CHAPTER 2. Alcohol and Drug Affected Mothers and Infants [11757.50 - 11757.61]

(Chapter 2 added by Stats. 1990, Ch. 1688, Sec. 1.)

11757.50.

This chapter shall be known and may be cited as the Alcohol and Drug Affected Mothers and Infants Act of 1990.

(Added by Stats. 1990, Ch. 1688, Sec. 1. Effective September 30, 1990.)

11757.51.

The Legislature finds and declares the following:

(a) Many infants affected by alcohol or other drugs require neonatal intensive care because of low birth weight, prematurity, withdrawal symptoms, serious birth defects, and other medical problems. Alcohol or other drug affected infants are increasingly being placed in neonatal intensive care units and this care is very expensive.

(b) Alcohol and other drug affected infants place an expensive burden on the foster care system, regional centers, the public and private health care systems, and the public school system.

(c) The appropriate response to this crisis is prevention, through expanded resources for recovery from alcohol and other drug dependency. The only sure effective means of protecting the health of these infants is to provide the services needed by mothers to address a problem that is addictive, not chosen.

(d) California has women of childbearing age who abuse alcohol or other drugs. Current resources are not adequate to meet the treatment needs of these women. California cannot delay addressing the serious need in this area. California taxpayers and health care consumers currently bear the enormous financial burden of alcohol and other drug affected infants and those costs can only be contained through expansion of treatment services for women who have an alcohol or other drug dependency and prevention services for women at risk of developing an alcohol or other drug dependency.

(e) Comprehensive prevention and treatment services for both mothers and infants need to be provided in a multidisciplinary, multispecialist, and multiagency fashion, necessitating coordination by both state and local governments.

(f) Intervention strategies for women at risk of developing an alcohol or other drug dependency have proven effective and there are currently in operation programs that can be expanded and modified to meet the critical need in this area.

(Amended by Stats. 2004, Ch. 862, Sec. 12. Effective January 1, 2005.)

11757.53.

(a) The Office of Perinatal Substance Abuse is hereby established within the State Department of Health Care Services. For purposes of this chapter, "office" means the Office of Perinatal Substance Abuse.

(b) The office may do any of the following:

(1) Coordinate pilot projects and planning projects funded by the state which are related to perinatal substance abuse.

(2) Provide technical assistance to counties, public entities, and private entities that are attempting to address the problem of perinatal substance abuse.

(3) Serve as a clearinghouse of information regarding strategies and programs which address perinatal substance abuse.

(4) Encourage innovative responses by public and private entities that are attempting to address the problem of perinatal substance abuse.

(5) Review proposals of, and develop proposals for, state agencies regarding the funding of programs relating to perinatal substance abuse.

(c) The office shall adopt, amend, or repeal any reasonable rules, regulations, or standards as may be necessary or proper to carry out the purposes and intent of this chapter and to enable the office and the department to exercise the powers and perform the duties conferred upon it by this chapter.

(Amended by Stats. 2013, Ch. 22, Sec. 31. (AB 75) Effective June 27, 2013. Operative July 1, 2013, by Sec. 110 of Ch. 22.)

11757.57.

(a) The office may provide or contract for training regarding alcohol and other drug dependency to providers of health, social, educational, and support services to women of childbearing age and their children.

(b) The purpose of any training provided pursuant to subdivision (a) may be to facilitate the taking of appropriate and thorough medical and social histories of women of childbearing age in order to identify those in special need of alcohol or other drug

treatment services and to identify skills for providing case management services to alcohol and other drug using women and their infants. Additional training topics may be covered, including, but not limited to, how to develop procedures for referring those in need of alcohol and other drug treatment services and how to provide appropriate social and emotional support to, as well as developmental monitoring of, drug affected infants and children and their families.

(Amended by Stats. 2004, Ch. 862, Sec. 14. Effective January 1, 2005.)

11757.59.

(a) Funds distributed under this chapter shall be used by counties to fund residential and nonresidential alcohol and other drug treatment programs for pregnant women, postpartum women, and their children and to fund other support services directed at bringing pregnant and postpartum women into treatment and caring for alcohol and other drug exposed infants. Funds may also be used to provide case management services to alcohol and other drug abusing women and their children and special recruitment, training, and support services for foster care parents of substance exposed infants.

(b) In carrying out its responsibilities under this chapter, the office may include in its guidelines the special needs of pregnant women and postpartum women who are chemically dependent and who are in need of treatment services. These special needs include, but are not limited to, the following:

(1) Provision for medical services, which may include, but not be limited to, the following:

(A) Low-risk and high-risk prenatal care.

(B) Pediatric followup care, including preventive infant health care.

(C) Developmental followup care.

(D) Nutrition counseling.

(E) Methadone.

(F) Testing and counseling relating to AIDS.

(G) Monthly visits with a physician and surgeon who specializes in treating persons with chemical dependencies.

(2) Provision for nonmedical services, which may include, but not be limited to, the following:

(A) Case management.

(B) Individual or group counseling sessions, which occur at least once a week.

(C) Family counseling, including, but not limited to, counseling services for partners and children of the women.

(D) Health education services, including perinatal chemical dependency classes, addressing topics that include, but are not limited to, the effects of drugs on infants, AIDS, addiction in the family, child development, nutrition, self-esteem, and responsible decisionmaking.

(E) Parenting classes.

(F) Adequate child care for participating women.

(G) Encouragement of active participation and support by spouses, domestic partners, family members, and friends.

(H) Opportunities for a women-only treatment environment.

(I) Transportation to outpatient treatment programs.

(J) Followup services, which may include, but not be limited to, assistance with transition into housing in a drug-free environment.

(K) Child development services.

(L) Educational and vocational services for women.

(M) Weekly urine testing.

(N) Special recruitment, training, and support services for foster care parents of substance exposed infants.

(O) Outreach which reflects the cultural and ethnic diversity of the population served.

(Amended by Stats. 2012, Ch. 36, Sec. 5. (SB 1014) Effective June 27, 2012. Operative July 1, 2012, by Sec. 83 of Ch. 36.)

11757.61.

(a) Any county that receives funds distributed under this chapter may establish a perinatal coordinating council that consists of persons who are experts in the areas of alcohol and other drug treatment, client outreach and intervention with alcohol and other drug abusing women, child welfare services, maternal and child health services, and developmental services, and representatives from other community-based organizations.

(b) The coordination efforts provided through the council may include the following:

(1) The identification of the extent of the perinatal alcohol and other drug abuse problem in the county based on existing data.

(2) The development of coordinated responses by county health and social service agencies and departments, which responses shall address the problem of perinatal alcohol and other drug abuse in the county.

(3) The definition of the elements of an integrated alcohol and other drug abuse recovery system for pregnant women, postpartum women, and their children.

(4) The identification of essential support services to be included into the integrated recovery system defined pursuant to paragraph (3).

(5) The promotion of communitywide understanding of the perinatal alcohol and other drug abuse problem in the county and appropriate responses to the problem.

(6) The communication with policymakers at both the state and federal level about prevention and treatment needs for pregnant women, postpartum women, and their children for alcohol and other drug abuse that need to be addressed.

(7) The utilization of services that emphasize coordination of treatment services with other health, child welfare, child development, and education services.

(Amended by Stats. 2012, Ch. 36, Sec. 6. (SB 1014) Effective June 27, 2012. Operative July 1, 2012, by Sec. 83 of Ch. 36.)

CHAPTER 2.1. Women and Children's Residential Treatment Services [11757.65-11757.65.]

(Chapter 2.1 added by Stats. 2012, Ch. 36, Sec. 7.)

11757.65.

(a) The Legislature hereby finds and declares both of the following:

(1) The state has an interest in the women and children's residential treatment services (WCRTS) program.

(2) In 2012, there are eight local WCRTS programs established through grants from the federal Center for Substance Abuse Treatment, Residential Women and Children, and Pregnant and Postpartum Women Demonstration Program. WCRTS programs pursue the following four primary goals:

(A) Demonstrate that alcohol and other drug abuse treatment services delivered in a residential setting and coupled with primary health, mental health, and social services for women and children, can improve overall treatment outcomes for women, children, and the family unit as a whole.

(B) Demonstrate the effectiveness of six-month or 12-month stays in a comprehensive residential treatment program.

(C) Develop models of effective comprehensive service delivery for women and their children that can be replicated in similar communities.

(D) Provide services to promote safe and healthy pregnancies and perinatal outcomes.

(b) It is the intent of the Legislature for the following outcomes to be achieved through the WCRTS program:

(1) Preserving family unity.

(2) Promoting healthy pregnancies.

(3) Enabling children to thrive.

(4) Freeing women and their families from substance abuse.

(c) It is also the intent of the Legislature for the State Department of Health Care Services to work collaboratively with counties and the eight WCRTS programs receiving funds from the Women's and Children's Residential Treatment Services Special Account under the 2011 realignment to develop reporting requirements. It is the intent of the Legislature that, to the extent that WCRTS programs report to the counties, the counties annually report data on the outcomes achieved by the WCRTS program to the department and for the department to annually report to the appropriate budget committees of the Legislature on the fiscal and programmatic status of the WCRTS program.

(d) Any county may establish a WCRTS program designed to meet the goals and produce the same outcomes as described in this section.

(Amended by Stats. 2013, Ch. 22, Sec. 32. (AB 75) Effective June 27, 2013. Operative July 1, 2013, by Sec. 110 of Ch. 22.)

CHAPTER 2.5. Fatal Drug Overdose Information [11758 - 11758.06]

(Chapter 2.5 added by Stats. 2002, Ch. 678, Sec. 3.)

11758.

The definitions contained in this chapter shall govern the construction of this chapter, unless the context requires otherwise.

(Amended by Stats. 2004, Ch. 183, Sec. 194. Effective January 1, 2005.)

11758.03.

"Department" means the State Department of Health Care Services.

(Amended by Stats. 2013, Ch. 22, Sec. 33. (AB 75) Effective June 27, 2013. Operative July 1, 2013, by Sec. 110 of Ch. 22.)

11758.06.

(a) On or before July 1, 2004, and on or before January 1, 2009, as specified in subdivision (c), the department shall place on its Internet Web site information on drug overdose trends in California, including county and state death rates, from existing data, in order to ascertain changes in the causes or rates of fatal and nonfatal drug overdoses for the preceding five years.

(b) The information required by subdivision (a) shall include, to the extent available, data on all of the following:

(1) Trends in drug overdose death rates by county or city, or both.

(2) Suggested improvements in data collection.

(3) A description of interventions that may be effective in reducing the rate of fatal or nonfatal drug overdoses.

(c) The information required by subdivision (a) to be placed on the department's Internet Web site shall remain on the Internet Web site for a period of not less than six months. The department shall update the information required pursuant to subdivision (a) and shall place the updated information on the Internet Web site on or before January 1, 2009, for a period of not less than six months.

(d) This section shall become inoperative on July 1, 2013.

(Amended by Stats. 2013, Ch. 22, Sec. 34. (AB 75) Effective June 27, 2013. Amending action operative July 1, 2013, by Sec. 110 of Ch. 22. Section inoperative July 1, 2013, by its own provisions from this amendment.)

CHAPTER 3. County Plans and Negotiated Net Amount Contracts [11758.10 - 11758.20]

(Heading of Chapter 3 amended by Stats. 2004, Ch. 862, Sec. 21.)

11758.10.

(a) Within 60 days after notification of the final allocation of each fiscal year pursuant to Section 11814, the board of supervisors of each county requesting to contract for federal funding from the state to provide alcohol and other drug prevention, treatment, and recovery services shall submit to the department, in accordance with Section 11798, a contract for these services.

(b) The executed contract shall remain in effect to provide the basis for advance payment until the next year's contract is executed. The purpose of these county contracts shall be to provide the basis for reimbursements pursuant to this division and to coordinate services pursuant to Part 2 (commencing with Section 11760) in a manner that avoids fragmentation of services and unnecessary expenditures.

(c) A contract for alcohol and other drug abuse services shall not become final until executed by both the contracting county and the department. The contract shall be executed by September 30 of the fiscal year in which the contract will be effective, and shall cover the fiscal year period from July 1 to June 30, inclusive.

(d) The payments shall be based on appropriations made by the Legislature, and monthly payments shall be adjusted to reflect reductions and deletions made by the Legislature. The department shall have the option to either terminate or amend the contract to reflect the reduced funding. The payments shall continue at the adjusted level until the contract is amended to reflect the final Budget Act enacted for the fiscal year and the final allocation to the counties.

(Amended by Stats. 2012, Ch. 36, Sec. 8. (SB 1014) Effective June 27, 2012. Operative July 1, 2012, by Sec. 83 of Ch. 36.)

11758.20.

(a) The department shall negotiate contracts with each county that requests to enter into a contract to provide alcohol and other drug abuse services.

(b) The department shall allocate funds for the purpose of establishing a contract with each contracting county in accordance with Sections 11814 and 11817.3.

(Amended by Stats. 2012, Ch. 36, Sec. 11. (SB 1014) Effective June 27, 2012. Operative July 1, 2012, by Sec. 83 of Ch. 36.)

CHAPTER 4. Alcohol and Drug Treatment for Adolescents [11759 - 11759.5]

(Chapter 4 added by Stats. 1998, Ch. 866, Sec. 2.)

11759.

This act shall be known, and may be cited, as the Adolescent Alcohol and Drug Treatment and Recovery Program Act of 1998.

(Added by Stats. 1998, Ch. 866, Sec. 2. Effective January 1, 1999. Inoperative July 1, 2013, pursuant to Section 11759.5.)

11759.1.

The department, in collaboration with counties and providers of alcohol and other drug services, shall establish community-based nonresidential and residential recovery programs to intervene and treat the problems of alcohol and other drug use among youth.

(Amended by Stats. 2004, Ch. 862, Sec. 38. Effective January 1, 2005. Inoperative July 1, 2013, pursuant to Section 11759.5.)

11759.2.

The department, in collaboration with counties and providers of alcohol and other drug services, shall establish criteria for participation, programmatic requirements, and terms and conditions for funding. These criteria shall include, but not be limited to, local match requirements of 10 percent, either in-kind or in cash. The criteria shall also include consideration of indicators of alcohol and other drug use among youth so that funds are targeted to localities with the highest need.

(Amended by Stats. 2004, Ch. 862, Sec. 39. Effective January 1, 2005. Inoperative July 1, 2013, pursuant to Section 11759.5.)

11759.3.

Nothing in this chapter shall preclude regional approaches to service delivery by counties, including the utilization of community-based nonresidential and residential programs.

(Added by Stats. 1998, Ch. 866, Sec. 2. Effective January 1, 1999. Inoperative July 1, 2013, pursuant to Section 11759.5.)

11759.4.

Not later than January 1 of each year, the department, in collaboration with the counties and providers of alcohol and other drug services, shall report to the Legislature during budget hearings regarding the status of the implementation of this chapter.

(Amended by Stats. 2004, Ch. 862, Sec. 40. Effective January 1, 2005. Inoperative July 1, 2013, pursuant to Section 11759.5.)

11759.5.

This chapter shall become inoperative on July 1, 2013.

(Added by Stats. 2013, Ch. 22, Sec. 35. (AB 75) Effective June 27, 2013. Operative July 1, 2013, by Sec. 110 of Ch. 22. Note: Termination clause affects Chapter 4, commencing with Section 11759.)

PART 2. STATE GOVERNMENT'S ROLE TO ALLEVIATE PROBLEMS RELATED TO THE INAPPROPRIATE USE OF ALCOHOLIC BEVERAGES AND OTHER DRUG USE [11760 - 11856.5]

(Heading of Part 2 amended by Stats. 2004, Ch. 862, Sec. 43.)

CHAPTER 1. General Provisions [11760 - 11773.3]

(Chapter 1 added by Stats. 1979, Ch. 679.)

ARTICLE 1. Statement of Problems Related to the Inappropriate Use of Alcoholic Beverages and Other Drug Use and the Reasons for and Limitations on State Government's Role [11760 - 11760.2]

(Heading of Article 1 amended by Stats. 2004, Ch. 862, Sec. 44.)

11760.

The Legislature finds and declares that problems related to the inappropriate use of alcoholic beverages and other drug use adversely affect the general welfare of the people of California. These problems include, but are not limited to, the following:

(a) Substantial fatalities, permanent disability, and property damage resulting from driving under the influence. Crimes involving alcohol and other drug use are a drain on law enforcement, the courts, and the penal system.

(b) Alcoholism in the individual, which is an addiction to the drug alcohol, with its attendant deterioration of physical and emotional health and social well-being.

(c) Alcoholism and other drug use in the family with its attendant deterioration of all relationships and the well-being of family members.

(d) A risk of increased susceptibility to serious illnesses and other major health problems that ultimately create a burden on both public and private health facilities and resources.

(e) A risk of fetal alcohol syndrome.

(f) Losses in production and tax revenues due to absenteeism, unemployment, and industrial accidents.

(Amended by Stats. 2004, Ch. 862, Sec. 45. Effective January 1, 2005.)

11760.1.

The Legislature recognizes that any efforts to address the problems related to inappropriate alcohol use and other drug use are greatly hindered by:

(a) The stigmatization of persons who have alcohol and other drug problems.

(b) Denial by the individual and the community, especially among members of the professional community, sometimes referred to as gatekeepers, regarding the nature and scope of alcohol and other drug problems.

(c) Services that, if uncoordinated, often are conflicting, inappropriate, ineffective, duplicative, and wasteful of limited public and private resources.

(d) Actions and attitudes that encourage consumption of alcoholic beverages in California, which consumption leads to alcohol problems.

(e) Actions and attitudes that encourage illicit drug use.

(Amended by Stats. 2004, Ch. 862, Sec. 46. Effective January 1, 2005.)

11760.2.

The Legislature finds that state government has an affirmative role in alleviating problems related to the inappropriate use of alcoholic beverages and other drug use and that its major objective is protection of the public health and safety, particularly where problems related to inappropriate alcohol use and other drug use are likely to cause harm to individuals, families, and the community.

(Amended by Stats. 2004, Ch. 862, Sec. 47. Effective January 1, 2005.)

ARTICLE 2. Coordination of Services [11760.5 - 11760.6]

(Article 2 added by Stats. 2004, Ch. 862, Sec. 50.)

11760.5.

(a) The Legislature recognizes that alcohol and other drug abuse should be viewed and treated as a health problem, as well as a public safety problem. The alcohol and other drug abuse problem has significant public impact and must, in addition to public safety, be given community, education, social, and health attention if prevention and amelioration are to be achieved. These approaches should be coordinated into a multiagency and multifaceted program for alcohol and other drug abuse control in the counties of the state.

(b) It is the intent of the Legislature that community alcohol and other drug abuse services shall be organized through locally administered and locally controlled community alcohol and other drug abuse programs. The community alcohol and other drug abuse programs shall operate under the principle that services are designed to be equally accessible to all persons, including persons who because of differences in language, cultural differences in language, cultural traditions, or physical disabilities, confront barriers to knowing about or to using the alcohol and other drug abuse services that are offered.

(Amended by Stats. 2012, Ch. 36, Sec. 18. (SB 1014) Effective June 27, 2012. Operative July 1, 2012, by Sec. 83 of Ch. 36.)

11760.6.

It is the intent of the Legislature that the department encourage the development of high quality, cost-effective services. It is further the intent of the Legislature that poor quality, underutilized, duplicative, or marginal services be disapproved by the county.

(Added by Stats. 2004, Ch. 862, Sec. 50. Effective January 1, 2005.)

ARTICLE 3. Departmental Powers and Duties and Limitations Thereof [11772- 11772.]

(Article 3 added by Stats. 1979, Ch. 679.)

11772.

(a) (1) The department may enter into agreements and contracts with any person or public or private agency, corporation, or other legal entity, including contracts to pay these entities in advance or reimburse them for alcohol and other drug services provided to alcohol and other drug abusers and their families and communities.

(2) The department may make grants to public and private entities that are necessary or incidental to the performance of its duties and the execution of its powers. The department may pay these entities in advance or reimburse them for services provided.

(3) The Legislature directs the department to contract with any person or public or private agency, corporation, or other legal entity to perform its duties whenever that expertise is available and appropriate to utilize.

(b) Notwithstanding any other provision of this part, the department may not contract directly for the provision of alcohol and other drug services except as follows:

(1) For demonstration programs of limited duration and scope, which programs, wherever possible, shall be administered through the counties, and which shall be specifically authorized and funded by the Budget Act or other statutes.

(2) To provide supportive services, such as technical assistance, on a statewide basis, or management and evaluation studies to help assure more effective implementation of this part.

(3) When a county decides not to enter into a contract to provide alcohol and drug abuse services or programs, or both, the department shall determine the need for the services or programs, or both, and provide the services or programs, or both, directly or through contract.

(c) (1) Notwithstanding the rulemaking provisions of Chapter 3.5 (commencing with Section 11340) of Part 1 of Division 3 of Title 2 of the Government Code, the department may implement, interpret, or make specific the amendments to this section made by the act that added this subdivision by means of all-county letters, plan letters, plan or provider bulletins, or similar instructions from the department until regulations are adopted pursuant to that chapter of the Government Code.

(2) The department shall adopt emergency regulations no later than July 1, 2014. The department may subsequently readopt any emergency regulation authorized by this subdivision that is the same as or is substantially equivalent to an emergency regulation previously adopted pursuant to this section.

(3) The initial adoption of emergency regulations and the one readoption of emergency regulations authorized by this subdivision shall be deemed an emergency and necessary for the immediate preservation of the public peace, health, safety, or general welfare. Initial emergency regulations and the one readoption of emergency regulations authorized by this subdivision shall be exempt from review by the Office of Administrative Law. The initial emergency regulations and the one readoption of emergency regulations authorized by this subdivision shall be submitted to the Office of Administrative Law for filing with the Secretary of State and each shall remain in effect for no more than 180 days, by which time final regulations may be adopted.

(Amended by Stats. 2012, Ch. 36, Sec. 19. (SB 1014) Effective June 27, 2012. Operative July 1, 2012, by Sec. 83 of Ch. 36.)

ARTICLE 4. Methamphetamine Deterrence Program [11773 - 11773.3]

(Article 4 added by Stats. 2006, Ch. 662, Sec. 2.)

11773.

(a) Subject to Section 11773.1, the department shall develop and implement a statewide prevention campaign designed to deter the abuse of methamphetamine in California.

(b) (1) The department may design the campaign to deter initial and continued use of methamphetamine.

(2) The department may also design the campaign to target communities or populations that use methamphetamine at a greater rate than the general population, communities or populations in which the transmission and contraction of HIV and AIDS, hepatitis C, and other diseases is significantly related to methamphetamine use, communities or populations in which the use of methamphetamine is likely to have a negative effect on children, communities or populations at risk due to the environmental damage caused by the methamphetamine production, and any other community or population that is at a high risk of methamphetamine use or addiction.

(3) In determining the intended audience of the campaign, the department shall give priority to communities or populations in which the use of methamphetamine is most likely to be deterred by the campaign. In determining which communities or populations to include in the audience of the campaign, the department shall rely on evidence from published reports, the experience of other drug abuse prevention programs, and other relevant sources.

(c) (1) The department shall, in the implementation of the program, use a variety of media to convey its messages to its intended audiences. This media may include, but need not be limited to, television, radio, billboards, print media, and the Internet.

(2) The department may use a variety of marketing and community outreach programs to convey its message, including, but not limited to, programs at schools, fairs, conventions, and other venues.

(3) The department shall conduct and base the development of its messages on market research, including, but not limited to, opinion polling and focus groups, to determine which messages would be most effective in deterring methamphetamine use within particular communities or populations.

(d) The department may incorporate information regarding drug addiction treatment programs into messages meant for individuals who are addicted to methamphetamine.

(e) In implementing the campaign, the department shall work with public and private organizations to extend its message to a wide range of venues and media outlets.

(f) The department may contract with private or public organizations for the development and implementation of the campaign.

(g) The department shall conduct research to measure the effect of the prevention campaign and shall annually report its findings to the chairpersons of the appropriate Senate and Assembly Health committees.

(h) This section shall become inoperative on July 1, 2013.

(Amended by Stats. 2013, Ch. 22, Sec. 36. (AB 75) Effective June 27, 2013. Amending action operative July 1, 2013, by Sec. 110 of Ch. 22. Section inoperative July 1, 2013, by its own provisions from this amendment.)

11773.1.

(a) The department may accept voluntary contributions, in cash or in-kind, to pay for the costs of implementing the program under this article. Voluntary contributions shall be deposited into the California Methamphetamine Abuse Prevention Account, which is hereby created in the State Treasury. Only private moneys, donated for the purposes of this article, may be deposited into the account. Moneys in the account are hereby appropriated to the department for the purposes of this article for the 2006–07 fiscal year. The Legislature may appropriate moneys in the account for subsequent fiscal years in the annual Budget Act or any other act.

(b) Notwithstanding subdivision (a), during the 2006–07 fiscal year, the department shall develop and implement the campaign established under this article only upon a determination by the Director of Finance that sufficient private donations have been collected and deposited into the California Methamphetamine Abuse Prevention Account. If sufficient funds are collected and deposited, the Director of Finance shall file a written notice thereof with the Secretary of State.

(c) Except as provided in subdivision (b) of Section 11773.2, for purposes of this article, "sufficient private donations" means funds in the amount of at least twelve million dollars ($12,000,000).

(d) This section shall become inoperative on July 1, 2013.

(Amended by Stats. 2013, Ch. 22, Sec. 37. (AB 75) Effective June 27, 2013. Amending action operative July 1, 2013, by Sec. 110 of Ch. 22. Section inoperative July 1, 2013, by its own provisions from this amendment.)

11773.2.

(a) Notwithstanding Section 11773.1, during the 2006–07 fiscal year, the department may develop and implement a limited campaign to deter the abuse of methamphetamine by limiting the intended audience of the campaign in accordance with paragraphs (2) and (3) of subdivision (b) of Section 11773, only upon a determination by the Director of Finance that sufficient private donations have been collected and deposited into the California Methamphetamine Abuse Prevention Account. If sufficient funds are collected and deposited in the account, the Director of Finance shall file a written notice thereof with the Secretary of State.

(b) For purposes of this section, "sufficient private donations" means funds in the amount of at least five hundred thousand dollars ($500,000). Nothing in this section shall be construed to require the department to implement a campaign where the cost of the campaign would exceed the private donations available for the campaign in the California Methamphetamine Abuse Prevention Account.

(c) This section shall become inoperative on July 1, 2013.

(Amended by Stats. 2013, Ch. 22, Sec. 38. (AB 75) Effective June 27, 2013. Amending action operative July 1, 2013, by Sec. 110 of Ch. 22. Section inoperative July 1, 2013, by its own provisions from this amendment.)

11773.3.

(a) Any funds that are not expended or encumbered for purposes of this article 730 days after being deposited into the California Methamphetamine Abuse Prevention Account shall be returned to the private donor.

(b) This section shall become inoperative on July 1, 2013.

(Amended by Stats. 2013, Ch. 22, Sec. 39. (AB 75) Effective June 27, 2013. Amending action operative July 1, 2013, by Sec. 110 of Ch. 22. Section inoperative July 1, 2013, by its own provisions from this amendment.)

CHAPTER 2. Relationship of the Department to Other Governmental Agencies and the Private Sector [11775 - 11781.5]

(Chapter 2 added by Stats. 1979, Ch. 679.)

ARTICLE 1. Federal Government [11775- 11775.]

(Article 1 added by Stats. 1979, Ch. 679.)

11775.

(a) Each year the department shall apply for federal block grant funds from the federal Substance Abuse and Mental Health Services Administration and may expend those funds only upon appropriation of, and approval by, the Legislature pursuant to the Budget Act.

(b) Whenever the federal Substance Abuse and Mental Health Services Administration conditions its allocation of funds to the department in a manner which would conflict with any provision of this part, the department shall specifically describe the conflict in its application for federal funds.

(c) The department may receive other federal funds and expend them, upon appropriation by the Legislature, pursuant to this division.

(Amended by Stats. 2012, Ch. 36, Sec. 20. (SB 1014) Effective June 27, 2012. Operative July 1, 2012, by Sec. 83 of Ch. 36.)

ARTICLE 2. Other State Agencies [11776- 11776.]

(Article 2 added by Stats. 1979, Ch. 679.)

11776.

The department shall confer and cooperate with other state agencies whose responsibilities include alleviating the problems related to inappropriate alcohol use and other drug use in order to maximize the state's effectiveness and limited resources in these efforts. These agencies shall include, but are not limited to, the Departments of Alcoholic Beverage Control, Corrections and Rehabilitation, Industrial Relations, Motor Vehicles, and Rehabilitation, the State Departments of Developmental Services, Education, Public Health, and Social Services, the Employment Development Department, and the Office of Traffic Safety.

(Amended by Stats. 2013, Ch. 22, Sec. 40. (AB 75) Effective June 27, 2013. Operative July 1, 2013, by Sec. 110 of Ch. 22.)

ARTICLE 3. The Legislature [11777- 11777.]

(Article 3 added by Stats. 1979, Ch. 679.)

11777.

The Legislature, subject to the Governor's approval, has the sole authority under Section 12 of Article IV of the California Constitution to appropriate any funds, including federal funds, to the department pursuant to the Budget Act. Each year the Legislature shall review the Governor's proposed budget for the department and conduct public hearings on the proposed use and distribution of federal block grant funds as required by Section 1915(b) of the Omnibus Budget Reconciliation Act of 1981 (Public Law 97-35).

(Amended by Stats. 1984, Ch. 1328, Sec. 17.)

ARTICLE 4. Counties [11778- 11778.]

(Article 4 added by Stats. 1979, Ch. 679.)

11778.

It is the intent of the Legislature that the department and the counties maintain a cooperative partnership to assure effective implementation of the provisions of this division as described in Chapter 4 (commencing with Section 11795) of this part.

(Repealed and added by Stats. 1979, Ch. 679.)

ARTICLE 5. Private Sector [11778.9- 11778.9.]

(Article 5 added by Stats. 1979, Ch. 679.)

11778.9.

It is the intent of the Legislature that the department cooperate closely with individuals and organizations concerned with alleviating problems related to inappropriate alcohol use and other drug use. The Legislature recognizes the wealth of experience and commitment that many individuals and organizations in the community have to offer and that can enhance the effectiveness of the programs funded by the department through counties.

(Amended by Stats. 2004, Ch. 862, Sec. 55. Effective January 1, 2005.)

ARTICLE 7. Accessing Alcohol and Drug Recovery Programs for the Disenfranchised [11781 - 11781.5]

(Article 7 added by Stats. 1990, Ch. 1693, Sec. 1.)

11781.

The Legislature finds and declares all of the following:

(a) Federal, state, and local governments have the responsibility and the expressed intent to provide and ensure the accessibility of alcohol and other drug treatment, recovery, intervention, and prevention services to all individuals, with specific emphasis on women, ethnic minorities, and other disenfranchised segments of the population.

(b) The effects of inappropriate alcohol use by ethnic populations in California are increasing. Concurrently, the use of available recovery services by these populations is not in keeping with the increase of problems experienced by these populations.

(c) There is a great shortage of treatment programs available to pregnant women and their offspring. Blacks have an infant mortality rate twice that of the general population, and substance abuse only exacerbates the problem.

(d) Barriers to accessing the services available specifically include, but are not limited to, the following:

(1) Lack of educational materials appropriate to the community.

(2) Geographic isolation or remoteness.

(3) Institutional and cultural barriers.

(4) Language differences.

(5) Lack of representation by affected groups employed by public and private service providers and policymakers.

(6) Insufficient research information regarding problems and appropriate strategies to resolve the problems of access to services.

(e) While current law requires the department to develop and implement a statewide plan to alleviate problems related to inappropriate alcohol use and other drug use and to overcome the barriers to their solution, these attempts have been ineffective due to the magnitude of the task.

(Amended by Stats. 2004, Ch. 862, Sec. 56. Effective January 1, 2005.)

11781.5.

The department shall provide direction to counties and to public and private organizations serving the target populations to increase access to alcohol and other drug abuse prevention and recovery programs in all of the following ways:

(a) Assume responsibility to increase the knowledge within state agencies and the Legislature of problems affecting the target populations.

(b) Determine, compile, and disseminate information and resource needs of the counties and constituent service providers to better serve the target populations.

(c) Ensure that established state and county standards, policies, and procedures are not discriminatory and do not contribute to service accessibility barriers.

(d) Promote an understanding of ethnic and gender differences, approaches to problems, and strategies for increasing voluntary access to services by the target populations.

(e) Affirmatively coordinate with the counties for the provision of services to the target populations and to assure accountability that necessary services are actually provided.
(Amended by Stats. 2004, Ch. 862, Sec. 57. Effective January 1, 2005.)

CHAPTER 3. Research [11785 - 11787]

(Chapter 3 added by Stats. 1979, Ch. 679.)

11785.

The Legislature recognizes the importance of encouraging research to study the biological aspects of, and the social factors contributing to, problems related to the inappropriate use of alcoholic beverages and other drug use.

The Legislature further recognizes the value of interpreting and applying research results through changes in public policy.
(Amended by Stats. 2004, Ch. 862, Sec. 59. Effective January 1, 2005.)

11786.

The department may enter into contracts for special studies and research to develop the information needed for formulating policies that will reduce the incidence of alcohol and other drug use problems through promising and innovative approaches in prevention, intervention, and treatment.
(Amended by Stats. 2004, Ch. 862, Sec. 60. Effective January 1, 2005.)

11787.

The department may coordinate task forces and committees of subject-matter experts to assess and document successful practical applications suggested by research.
(Repealed and added by Stats. 1984, Ch. 1328, Sec. 21.)

CHAPTER 3.5. Resources and Information [11788 - 11794.1]

(Chapter 3.5 added by Stats. 2004, Ch. 862, Sec. 61.)

11788.

The department, with the approval of the Secretary of the Health and Human Services Agency, may contract with any public or private agency for the performance of any of the functions vested in the department by this chapter. Any department of the state is authorized to enter into such a contract.
(Added by Stats. 2004, Ch. 862, Sec. 61. Effective January 1, 2005.)

11789.

(a) The department shall be a central information resource on alcohol and other drug abuse prevention and treatment programs and on research projects with respect to alcohol and other drug abuse.

(b) The department shall collect, and act as an information exchange for, information on research and service projects completed or in progress relating to alcohol and other drug abuse, provide, to any person, institution, or public agency proposing any research or service project on that subject, information with respect to the areas in which research is needed, and evaluate programs of research, treatment, and education with respect to alcohol and other drug abuse.

(c) No state agency shall conduct any research or service project on alcohol and other drug abuse until it has provided the department with a description of its proposed project and until the department has responded with a written description of how the research or service project relates with other completed, concurrently operating, or pending research or service projects. If the department fails to provide the agency with the written description within 60 days from the date of receipt of the proposed project, the state agency may proceed to conduct the research or service project as described in the agency's proposal.
(Added by Stats. 2004, Ch. 862, Sec. 61. Effective January 1, 2005.)

11790.

The department, at the request of the county alcohol and drug program administrator, may assist local community organizations in initiating effective programs to prevent and treat alcohol and other drug abuse. The department may charge a fee for this assistance.
(Added by Stats. 2004, Ch. 862, Sec. 61. Effective January 1, 2005.)

11791.

The department may develop and implement a mass media alcohol and other drug education program involving newspapers, radio, and television in order to provide community education, develop public awareness, and motivate community action in alcohol and other drug abuse prevention, treatment, and rehabilitation.
(Added by Stats. 2004, Ch. 862, Sec. 61. Effective January 1, 2005.)

11792.

(a) The department, in consultation with the State Department of Public Health, shall distribute informational materials on the care and treatment of infants under the age of

six months who have been exposed to alcohol and other drugs. The informational materials shall include, but not be limited to, the following:

(1) The signs and symptoms of an infant who has been exposed to alcohol and other drugs.

(2) The health problems of infants who have been exposed to alcohol and other drugs.

(3) The special feeding needs of infants who have been exposed to alcohol and other drugs.

(4) The special care needs of infants who have been exposed to alcohol and other drugs, such as not overstimulating those infants who have been exposed to cocaine.

(b) The informational materials developed pursuant to subdivision (a) may be distributed through hospitals, public health nurses, child protective services, alcohol and other drug facilities, educational networks, foster parent groups, medical professional offices, Medi-Cal programs, and county interagency task force groups, as well as any other agency that the department selects.
(Amended by Stats. 2012, Ch. 36, Sec. 22. (SB 1014) Effective June 27, 2012. Operative July 1, 2012, by Sec. 83 of Ch. 36.)

11793.

The department may develop an objective program evaluation device or methodology and evaluate state-supported alcohol and other drug abuse prevention and treatment programs.
(Added by Stats. 2004, Ch. 862, Sec. 61. Effective January 1, 2005.)

11794.

The department shall, in consultation with the State Department of Education, screen and evaluate alcohol and other drug abuse books, pamphlets, literature, movies, and other audiovisual aids and may prepare and disseminate lists of recommended materials to schools, public libraries, alcohol and other drug information centers, and other public and private agencies. The department may charge a fee, not exceeding actual costs, for providing the materials.
(Added by Stats. 2004, Ch. 862, Sec. 61. Effective January 1, 2005.)

11794.1.

It is the intent of the Legislature that the department, in collaboration with the State Department of Public Health and stakeholders in the medical and treatment provider communities, work to identify methods for better informing medical doctors and other health professionals of the benefits of diagnosing and treating alcohol misuse and substance use among their patient population, including, but not limited to, improved outreach efforts at the state and local levels and the use of information dissemination strategies, where appropriate.
(Amended by Stats. 2012, Ch. 36, Sec. 23. (SB 1014) Effective June 27, 2012. Operative July 1, 2012, by Sec. 83 of Ch. 36.)

CHAPTER 4. State-County Partnership [11795 - 11819.1]

(Chapter 4 added by Stats. 1979, Ch. 679.)

ARTICLE 1. General Provisions [11795 - 11798.3]

(Article 1 added by Stats. 1979, Ch. 679.)

11795.

(a) The board of supervisors of each county may apply to the department for funds for the purpose of alleviating problems in its county related to alcohol abuse and other drug use. This part applies only to counties receiving state or federal funds allocated by the department under this part.

(b) The department shall coordinate state and local alcohol and other drug abuse prevention, care, treatment, and rehabilitation programs. It is the intent of the Legislature that the department and the counties maintain a cooperative partnership to assure effective implementation of this chapter.

(c) The Legislature grants responsibility to the county to administer and coordinate all county alcohol and other drug programs funded under this part. County alcohol and other drug programs shall account to the board of supervisors and to the state for their effective implementation. The county shall establish its own priorities for alcohol and other drug programs funded under this part, except with respect to funds that are allocated to the county for federally required programs and services.
(Amended by Stats. 2004, Ch. 862, Sec. 62. Effective January 1, 2005.)

11796.

(a) (1) Two or more counties may jointly establish county alcohol and other drug programs pursuant to Article 1 (commencing with Section 6500) of Chapter 5 of Division 7 of Title 1 of the Government Code.

(2) Any county may, by contract, furnish alcohol and other drug services to another county.

(b) Unless otherwise expressly provided for or required by the context, this part relating to county alcohol and other drug programs shall apply to alcohol and other drug programs operated jointly by two or more counties.
(Amended by Stats. 2012, Ch. 36, Sec. 24. (SB 1014) Effective June 27, 2012. Operative July 1, 2012, by Sec. 83 of Ch. 36.)

11796.1.

Except as provided in subdivision (b) of Section 11812, nothing in this part shall prevent any city or combination of cities from financing and administering directly an alcohol or other drug program or providing service by contracting with the county to provide and be reimbursed for services provided pursuant to the county alcohol and other drug program under Article 4 (commencing with Section 11810). In addition, where appropriate, any county may contract with a city, or combination of cities, to administer contracts with privately operated agencies to alleviate problems related to inappropriate alcohol use and other drug use.

(Amended by Stats. 2004, Ch. 862, Sec. 64. Effective January 1, 2005.)

11797.

(a) Funds allocated to the county pursuant to this part shall be used exclusively for county alcohol and other drug services as identified in the contract for alcohol and other drug services and shall be separately identified and accounted for.

(b) The funds contained in each county's Behavioral Health Subaccount of the Support Services Account of the Local Revenue Fund 2011 established pursuant to Section 30025 of the Government Code shall be considered state funds distributed by the principle state agency for the purposes of receipt of the federal block grant funds for prevention and treatment of substance abuse described in Subchapter XVII of Chapter 6A of Title 42 of the United States Code to the extent that these funds are used for authorized alcohol and drug prevention and treatment activities.

(Amended by Stats. 2012, Ch. 36, Sec. 25. (SB 1014) Effective June 27, 2012. Operative July 1, 2012, by Sec. 83 of Ch. 36.)

11798.

(a) Counties that apply for funds to provide alcohol and other drug abuse services shall prepare and submit a contract for alcohol and other drug abuse services to the department. The contract shall include a budget for all funds sources to be used to provide alcohol and other drug abuse services. The funds identified in the contract shall be used exclusively for county alcohol and other drug services to the extent that the activities meet the requirements for receipt of the federal block grant funds for prevention and treatment of substance abuse described in Subchapter XVII of Chapter 6A of Title 42 of the United States Code and shall be separately identified and accounted for. The county shall report utilization of those funds in an annual cost report pursuant to subdivision (b) of Section 11798.1.

(b) The contract shall include provisions to ensure both of the following:

(1) The appropriate expenditures of funds necessary to meet the requirements for receipt of federal block grant funds for prevention and treatment of substance abuse described in Subchapter XVII of Chapter 6A of Title 42 of the United States Code and other applicable federal provisions for funds.

(2) The provision of information necessary for the department to meet its oversight function, including, but not limited to, any required auditing, reporting, and data collection.

(c) The contract shall specify the type, scope, and cost of the services to be provided.

(d) The department, after consultation with county alcohol and drug program administrators, shall develop standardized forms to be used by the counties in the development and submission of the contracts. The forms shall include terms and conditions relative to county compliance with applicable laws.

(e) Performance requirements shall be included within the terms of the contract and shall include, at a minimum, all of the following:

(1) A provision for an adequate quality and quantity of service.

(2) A provision for access to services for at-risk populations.

(3) A provision requiring that all funds allocated by the state for alcohol and other drug programs shall be used exclusively for the purpose for which those funds are distributed.

(4) A provision requiring that performance be in compliance with applicable state and federal laws, regulations, and standards.

(5) Estimated numbers and characteristics of clients-participants by type of service.

(f) The contract shall include a provision that allows the department access to financial and service records of the county and contractors of the county for the purpose of auditing the requirements in the contract and establishing the data necessary to meet federal auditing and reporting requirements.

(g) The contract shall include a provision for resolution of disputed audit findings.

(h) Where two or more counties jointly establish substance use programs or where a county contracts to provide services in another county pursuant to Section 11796, information regarding the arrangement shall be included in the contract for alcohol and other drug abuse services.

(i) The contract shall include a provision requiring the county to ensure the security of client records as required by state and federal law.

(j) The contract shall be presented for public input, review, and comment, and the final contract shall be posted on the county's Internet Web site.

(k) (1) Notwithstanding the rulemaking provisions of Chapter 3.5 (commencing with Section 11340) of Part 1 of Division 3 of Title 2 of the Government Code, the department may implement, interpret, or make specific this section by means of all-county letters, plan letters, plan or provider bulletins, or similar instructions from the department until regulations are adopted pursuant to that chapter of the Government Code.

(2) The department shall adopt emergency regulations no later than July 1, 2014. The department may subsequently readopt any emergency regulation authorized by this section that is the same as or is substantially equivalent to an emergency regulation previously adopted pursuant to this section.

(3) The initial adoption of emergency regulations implementing this section and the one readoption of emergency regulations authorized by this subdivision shall be deemed an emergency and necessary for the immediate preservation of the public peace, health, safety, or general welfare. Initial emergency regulations and the one readoption of emergency regulations authorized by this section shall be exempt from review by the Office of Administrative Law. The initial emergency regulations and the one readoption of emergency regulations authorized by this section shall be submitted to the Office of Administrative Law for filing with the Secretary of State and each shall remain in effect for no more than 180 days, by which time final regulations may be adopted.

(Amended by Stats. 2013, Ch. 22, Sec. 41. (AB 75) Effective June 27, 2013. Operative July 1, 2013, by Sec. 110 of Ch. 22.)

11798.2.

(a) A county with an approved contract for alcohol and other drug abuse services shall bear the financial risk in providing any alcohol or other drug services to the population described and enumerated in the approved contract.

(b) The county shall not be precluded from contracting to purchase all or part of the delivery of alcohol and other drug services from noncounty providers.

(c) Counties receiving funds shall submit to the department statistical data, as required in the contract, and end-of-year cost data no later than November 1 following the close of the fiscal year.

(d) Whenever a county receives funds under a grant program for alcohol and other drug abuse services, as well as under the county contract from either the federal or state government, or from any other grantor, public or private, and fails to include that grant program in the county budget for its alcohol and other drug program, the director shall not thereafter approve any, or provide, advance payment claims submitted by the county for state reimbursement under this part until the contract and county budget for its alcohol and other drug program has been reviewed to include that grant program, and the revised contract and budget are approved by the director.

(e) (1) Except as provided in paragraphs (2) and (3), regulations adopted by the State Department of Alcohol and Drug Programs pursuant to former Section 11758.29 shall remain in effect unless amended or repealed by regulation adopted pursuant to this section.

(2) Notwithstanding the rulemaking provisions of Chapter 3.5 (commencing with Section 11340) of Part 1 of Division 3 of Title 2 of the Government Code, the department may implement, interpret, or make specific this section to the extent that this section differs from former Section 11758.29 by means of all-county letters, plan letters, plan or provider bulletins, or similar instructions from the department until regulations are adopted pursuant to that chapter of the Government Code.

(3) (A) The department shall adopt emergency regulations no later than July 1, 2014. The department may subsequently readopt any emergency regulation authorized by this section that is the same as or is substantially equivalent to an emergency regulation previously adopted pursuant to this section.

(B) The initial adoption of emergency regulations implementing the article and the one readoption of emergency regulations authorized by this subdivision shall be deemed an emergency and necessary for the immediate preservation of the public peace, health, safety, or general welfare. Initial emergency regulations and the one readoption of emergency regulations authorized by this section shall be exempt from review by the Office of Administrative Law. The initial emergency regulations and the one readoption of emergency regulations authorized by this section shall be submitted to the Office of Administrative Law for filing with the Secretary of State and each shall remain in effect for no more than 180 days, by which time final regulations may be adopted.

(Added by Stats. 2012, Ch. 36, Sec. 29. (SB 1014) Effective June 27, 2012. Operative July 1, 2012, by Sec. 83 of Ch. 36.)

11798.3.

The department shall review each county's contract for alcohol and other drug abuse services to determine that the contract complies with this division and with the standards adopted under this division. The department shall approve a contract that is in compliance.

(Added by Stats. 2012, Ch. 36, Sec. 30. (SB 1014) Effective June 27, 2012. Operative July 1, 2012, by Sec. 83 of Ch. 36.)

ARTICLE 2. County Administration [11800 - 11803]

(Article 2 added by Stats. 1979, Ch. 679.)

11800.

(a) The board of supervisors shall designate a health-related county agency or department that shall administer the county alcohol and other drug program. The board of supervisors or the head of the designated health-related agency or department shall appoint an alcohol and drug program administrator, who shall report to the head of the agency or department through administrative channels designated by the board of supervisors. The county alcohol and other drug program shall be placed at the same administrative level and have responsibility and authority similar to other major health programs in the county.

(b) In accordance with regulations adopted by the department, the alcohol and drug program administrator shall be qualified by his or her ability, training, and experience to administer or coordinate and monitor the county alcohol and other drug program.

(Amended by Stats. 2004, Ch. 862, Sec. 68. Effective January 1, 2005.)

11801.

The alcohol and drug program administrator, acting through administrative channels designated pursuant to Section 11795, shall do all of the following:

(a) Coordinate and be responsible for the preparation of the county contract.

(b) Ensure compliance with applicable laws relating to discrimination against any person because of any characteristic listed or defined in Section 11135 of the Government Code.

(c) Submit an annual report to the board of supervisors reporting all activities of the alcohol and other drug program, including a financial accounting of expenditures, number of persons served, and a forecast of anticipated needs for the upcoming year.

(d) Be directly responsible for the administration of all alcohol or other drug program funds allocated to the county under this part, administration of county operated programs, and coordination and monitoring of programs that have contracts with the county to provide alcohol and other drug services.

(e) Ensure the evaluation of alcohol and other drug programs, including the collection of appropriate and necessary client data and program information, pursuant to Chapter 6 (commencing with Section 11825).

(f) Ensure program quality in compliance with appropriate standards pursuant to Chapter 7 (commencing with Section 11830).

(g) Participate and represent the county in meetings of the County Behavioral Health Directors Association of California pursuant to Section 11811.5 for the purposes of representing the counties in their relationship with the state with respect to policies, standards, and administration for alcohol and other drug abuse services.

(h) Perform any other acts that may be necessary, desirable, or proper to carry out the purposes of this part.

(Amended by Stats. 2015, Ch. 455, Sec. 1. (SB 804) Effective January 1, 2016.)

11802.

(a) Money deposited in the county alcohol abuse education and prevention fund pursuant to Section 1463.25 of the Penal Code shall be jointly administered by the administrator of the county's alcohol and other drug program and the county office of education subject to the approval of the board of supervisors and the county office of education. A minimum of 33 percent of the fund shall be allocated to primary prevention programs in the schools and community. Primary prevention programs developed and implemented under this section shall emphasize cooperation in planning and program implementation of alcohol abuse education and prevention among schools and community alcohol and other drug abuse agencies. Coordination shall be demonstrated through an interagency agreement among county offices of education, school districts, and the county alcohol and drug program administrator.

(b) Programs funded, planned, and implemented under this section shall emphasize a joint school-community primary education and prevention program that may include:

(1) School and classroom-oriented programs, including, but not limited to, programs designed to encourage sound decisionmaking, an awareness of values, an awareness of alcohol and its effects, enhanced self-esteem, social and practical skills that will assist students toward maturity, enhanced or improved school climate and relationships among all school personnel and students, and furtherance of cooperative efforts of school- and community-based personnel.

(2) School- or community-based nonclassroom alternative programs, or both, including, but not limited to, positive peer group programs, programs involving youth and adults in constructive activities designed as alternatives to alcohol use, and programs for special target groups, such as women, ethnic minorities, and other high-risk, high-need populations.

(3) Family-oriented programs, including, but not limited to, programs aimed at improving family relationships and involving parents constructively in the education and nurturing of their children, as well as in specific activities aimed at preventing alcohol abuse.

(c) The money deposited under subdivision (a) shall supplement and not supplant any local funds made available to support the county's alcohol abuse education and prevention efforts.

(d) If the county has a drug abuse primary prevention program, it may choose to combine or coordinate its drug and alcohol abuse education and prevention programs.

(Amended by Stats. 2004, Ch. 862, Sec. 70. Effective January 1, 2005.)

11803.

If the county has an alcohol and other drug advisory board, the alcohol and drug program administrator, acting through administrative channels designated pursuant to Section 11795, may do either or both of the following:

(a) Provide reports and information periodically to the advisory board regarding the status of alcohol and other drug programs in the county and keep the advisory board informed regarding changes in relevant state, federal, and local laws or regulations or improvements in program design and services that may affect the county alcohol and other drug program.

(b) Provide for the orientation of the members of the advisory board, including, but not limited to, the provision of information and materials on alcohol and other drug problems and programs, planning, procedures, and site visits to local programs.

(Added by Stats. 2012, Ch. 36, Sec. 32. (SB 1014) Effective June 27, 2012. Operative July 1, 2012, by Sec. 83 of Ch. 36.)

ARTICLE 3. County Advisory Board [11805- 11805.]

(Article 3 added by Stats. 1979, Ch. 679.)

11805.

Each county may have an advisory board on alcohol and other drug problems appointed by the board of supervisors. The advisory board may be independent, be under the jurisdiction of another health-related or human services advisory board established pursuant to any provision of state law, or have the same membership as that other advisory board.

(Amended by Stats. 2004, Ch. 862, Sec. 71. Effective January 1, 2005.)

ARTICLE 4. County Alcohol and Other Drug Program [11810 - 11819.1]

(Heading of Article 4 amended by Stats. 2004, Ch. 862, Sec. 72.)

11810.

It is the intent of the Legislature to provide maximum flexibility in the use of federal and state alcohol and other drug program funds. County government is therefore given broad authority in determining the methods for encouragement of citizen participation, the scope of problem analysis, and the methods of planning for alcohol and other drug program services.

(Amended by Stats. 2004, Ch. 862, Sec. 73. Effective January 1, 2005.)

11811.

Counties shall have broad discretion in the choice of services they utilize to alleviate the alcohol and other drug problems of specific population groups and the community. Those services shall include services for alcohol and other drug abuse prevention and treatment.

(Amended by Stats. 2004, Ch. 862, Sec. 74. Effective January 1, 2005.)

11811.1.

(a) The major purpose of prevention and early intervention activities includes, but is not limited to, all of the following:

(1) To facilitate positive change in community and individual understanding, values, attitudes, environmental factors, and behavior concerning alcohol and its inappropriate use and other drug use.

(2) To reduce the likelihood of the inappropriate use of alcohol and other drugs by developing and implementing public policies designed to reduce or limit alcohol and other drug consumption.

(3) To lessen the stigmatization of persons who seek help for problems related to inappropriate alcohol use and other drug use.

(4) To provide information so that the public may make informed personal and public policy decisions regarding the inappropriate use and nonuse of alcoholic beverages and other drugs.

(5) To enlighten the "helping professions" to recognize persons with alcohol and other drug problems and to offer them appropriate services.

(6) To encourage persons to seek early help for their alcohol or other drug problems.

(b) The Legislature recognizes that the effective provision of the activities specified in subdivision (a) will result in an increased demand upon, and utilization of, existing services to alcohol and other drug abusers and their families. However, the Legislature believes that provision of effective prevention and early intervention activities over the next decade will result in saving taxpayers funds that might otherwise have to be expended for higher health and safety costs.

(Amended by Stats. 2004, Ch. 862, Sec. 75. Effective January 1, 2005.)

11811.3.

In addition to the services described in Section 11811, a county may provide other services or programs pursuant to this section, including, but not limited to, the following:

(a) (1) Occupational programs for county employees designed to help recognize employees with alcohol and other drug problems that affect their job performance and to encourage these employees to seek services to alleviate those problems.

(2) It is the intent of the Legislature to encourage every county to institute a program described in paragraph (1) for its own employees in order to set an example for the community regarding local government's attitude toward alcohol and other drug problems.

(b) (1) Counties may use funds allocated to them by the department for any other services authorized in Section 11811 or this section.

(2) It is the intent of the Legislature that counties make maximum utilization of vocational rehabilitation services, where reasonable and appropriate to do so. A county, pursuant to a resolution by the board of supervisors, may utilize funds for other authorized services pursuant to Section 11811.

(Amended by Stats. 2004, Ch. 862, Sec. 76. Effective January 1, 2005.)

11811.5.

To the extent the activities meet the provisions for receipt of the federal block grant funds for prevention and treatment of substance abuse described in Subchapter XVII of Chapter 6A of Title 42 of the United States Code and other applicable federal provisions for funds, a county may also utilize funds for the following:

(a) Planning, program development, and administration by the county. The department shall establish uniform definitions of the elements of county alcohol and other drug program administration and shall set the minimum and maximum levels of administrative services, taking into account the total funds expended pursuant to the contract.

(b) In conducting planning, evaluation, and research activities to develop and implement the county alcohol and other drug program, counties may contract with appropriate public or private agencies.

(c) Actual and necessary expenses incurred by the alcohol and drug program administrator relating to attendance at not more than four meetings each year of the administrators, any other meetings called by the director, and reasonable dues for any related activities and meetings. Each administrator of a county who receives funds under this part shall attend each quarterly meeting, unless a waiver is provided for by the department.

(Amended by Stats. 2012, Ch. 36, Sec. 33. (SB 1014) Effective June 27, 2012. Operative July 1, 2012, by Sec. 83 of Ch. 36.)

11811.6.

The department shall consult with county behavioral health directors, alcohol and drug program administrators, or both, in establishing standards pursuant to Chapter 7 (commencing with Section 11830) and regulations pursuant to Chapter 8 (commencing with Section 11835), shall consult with alcohol and drug program administrators on matters of major policy and administration, and may consult with alcohol and drug program administrators on other matters affecting persons with alcohol and other drug problems. The administrators shall consist of all legally appointed alcohol and drug administrators in the state as designated pursuant to subdivision (a) of Section 11800.

(Amended by Stats. 2015, Ch. 455, Sec. 2. (SB 804) Effective January 1, 2016.)

11811.7.

Services financed under this part shall:

(a) Be provided on a voluntary basis only, except as provided in Article 1.5 (commencing with Section 5170) of Chapter 2 of Part 1 of Division 5 of the Welfare and Institutions Code.

(b) Encourage persons utilizing services, and members of their family, to participate in community self-help groups providing ongoing support to alcohol and other drug abusers and their family members.

(c) Encourage persons suffering from alcoholism and other drug problems to abstain from the use of alcohol and illicit drugs.

(Amended by Stats. 2004, Ch. 862, Sec. 79. Effective January 1, 2005.)

11811.8.

The following costs shall not be eligible for state funding pursuant to this part:

(a) The costs involved in a peace officer bringing a person in for 72-hour treatment and evaluation.

(b) The costs of court proceedings or court-ordered evaluation pursuant to Article 3 (commencing with Section 5225) of Chapter 2 of Part 1 of Division 5 of the Welfare and Institutions Code, and the apprehension of the person ordered to evaluation when necessary.

(c) The costs of court proceedings in cases of appeal on 14-day intensive treatment.

(d) The costs of legal proceedings in conservatorship.

(e) The court costs in postcertification proceedings.

(f) The cost of providing a public defender or other court-appointed attorneys in proceedings for those unable to afford this assistance.

(Amended by Stats. 1984, Ch. 1328, Sec. 38.)

11812.

The following conditions apply to county expenditures of funds pursuant to this part:

(a) Where the services specified in the contract for alcohol and other drug abuse services are provided pursuant to other general health or social programs, only that portion of the services dealing with alcohol and other drug problems may be financed under this part.

(b) (1) Each county shall utilize available privately operated alcohol and other drug programs and services in the county prior to utilizing new county-operated programs and services, or city-operated programs and services pursuant to Section 11796.1, when the available privately operated programs and services are as favorable in quality and cost as are those operated by the county or city. When these privately operated programs and services are not available, the county shall make a reasonable effort to encourage the development of privately operated programs and services prior to developing county-operated or city-operated programs and services.

(2) The county alcohol and drug program administrator shall demonstrate to the board of supervisors, and to the department, prior to development of any new program or service, that reasonable efforts have been made to comply with paragraph (1). All available local public or private programs and services, as described in paragraph (1), that are appropriate shall be utilized prior to using services provided by hospitals.

(c) All personal information and records obtained by the county, any program that has a contract with the county, or the department pursuant to this section are confidential and may be disclosed only in those instances designated in Section 5328 of the Welfare and Institutions Code.

(1) Any person may bring an action against an individual who has willingly and knowingly released confidential information or records concerning that person in violation of this section, for the greater of the following amounts:

(A) Five hundred dollars ($500).

(B) Three times the amount of actual damages, if any, sustained by the plaintiff.

(2) (A) Any person may, in accordance with Chapter 3 (commencing with Section 525) of Title 7 of Part 2 of the Code of Civil Procedure, bring an action to enjoin the release of confidential information or records in violation of this chapter, and may in the same action seek damages as provided in this section.

(B) It is not a prerequisite to an action under this section that the plaintiff suffer or be threatened with actual damages.

(d) The department may require that each county and any public or private provider of alcohol and other drug services that receives any funds under this part provide any information requested by the department relating to any application for or receipt of federal or other nonstate funds, including fees, donations, grants, and other revenues, for alcohol and other drug abuse services provided by these agencies.

(Amended by Stats. 2012, Ch. 36, Sec. 35. (SB 1014) Effective June 27, 2012. Operative July 1, 2012, by Sec. 83 of Ch. 36.)

11812.6.

In addition to any other services authorized under this chapter, the department shall urge the county to develop within existing resources specific policies and procedures to address the unique treatment problems presented by persons who are chemically dependent and also have a mental health disorder. Priority may be given to developing policies and procedures that relate to the diagnosis and treatment of homeless persons who have mental health disorders and are chemically dependent.

(Amended by Stats. 2014, Ch. 144, Sec. 36. (AB 1847) Effective January 1, 2015.)

11813.

Nothing in this part shall prohibit a county from appropriating funds for alcohol and other drug programs and services in addition to the funds allocated by the department.

(Amended by Stats. 2004, Ch. 862, Sec. 82. Effective January 1, 2005.)

11814.

(a) The department shall issue allocations to contracting counties for alcohol and other drug programs.

(b) In issuing allocations to contracting counties, it is the intent of the Legislature that counties shall allocate all funds received pursuant to state and federal laws and regulations.

(c) The department shall estimate an allocation of federal funds available for each county to use as the basis for submission of the contract. In making allocations, the department shall base its allocations on the population of each county. However, the department shall ensure that each small population county receives a minimum amount of funds to provide adequate alcohol and other drug services. The department may take into account other factors in making the allocations, including, but not limited to, factors that relate to the level of alcohol and other drug problems in the county. No later than 45 days after introduction of the Budget Bill, the department shall notify each county regarding its preliminary allocation under this division and estimated amount of the federally required maintenance of effort statewide expenditure levels on authorized activities, as defined in the federal Substance Abuse Prevention and Treatment Block Grant funds (42 U.S.C. Sec. 300x-30), pending enactment of the Budget Bill. The 1984–85 fiscal year shall establish the base funding for the county alcohol and drug allocation for local programs. Beginning with the 1985–86 fiscal year, cost-of-living adjustments, if granted, shall be considered as tied to the base allocation established in the 1984–85 fiscal year, plus any subsequent cost-of-living adjustments. The department shall notify each county regarding its final allocation after enactment of the Budget Bill.

(d) (1) Notwithstanding any other provision in this section, the director may reduce federal funding allocations, on a dollar-for-dollar basis, to a county that has reduced or anticipates reducing expenditures in a way that would result in a decrease in the federal Substance Abuse Prevention and Treatment Block Grant funds (42 U.S.C. Sec. 300x-30).

(2) Prior to making any reductions pursuant to this subdivision, the director shall notify all counties that county underspending will reduce the federal Substance Abuse Prevention and Treatment Block Grant maintenance of effort (MOE). Upon receipt of notification, a county may submit a revision to the county budget initially submitted pursuant to subdivision (a) of Section 11798 in an effort to maintain the statewide Substance Abuse Prevention and Treatment Block Grant MOE.

(3) Pursuant to subdivision (b) of Section 11798.1, a county shall notify the department in writing of proposed local changes to the county's expenditure of funds. The department shall review and may approve the proposed local changes depending on the level of expenditures needed to maintain the statewide Substance Abuse Prevention and Treatment Block Grant MOE.

(e) (1) Notwithstanding the rulemaking provisions of Chapter 3.5 (commencing with Section 11340) of Part 1 of Division 3 of Title 2 of the Government Code, the department may implement, interpret, or make specific the amendments to this section made by the act that added this subdivision by means of all-county letters, plan letters, plan or provider bulletins, or similar instructions from the department until regulations are adopted pursuant to that chapter of the Government Code.

(2) The department shall adopt emergency regulations no later than July 1, 2014. The department may subsequently readopt any emergency regulation authorized by this section that is the same as or is substantially equivalent to an emergency regulation previously adopted pursuant to this section.

(3) The initial adoption of emergency regulations implementing the amendments to this section and the one readoption of emergency regulations authorized by this subdivision shall be deemed an emergency and necessary for the immediate preservation of the public peace, health, safety, or general welfare. Initial emergency regulations and the one readoption of emergency regulations authorized by this section shall be exempt from review by the Office of Administrative Law. The initial emergency regulations and the one readoption of emergency regulations authorized by this section shall be submitted to the Office of Administrative Law for filing with the Secretary of State and each shall remain in effect for no more than 180 days, by which time final regulations may be adopted.

(Amended by Stats. 2012, Ch. 36, Sec. 37. (SB 1014) Effective June 27, 2012. Operative July 1, 2012, by Sec. 83 of Ch. 36.)

11817.1.

The department may reallocate among counties any unexpended federal funds that occur during the fiscal year in programs or services or any allocations either not applied for by a county or not in compliance with this part. Reallocations may be made to counties by amendment to their county contracts.

(Amended by Stats. 2012, Ch. 36, Sec. 38. (SB 1014) Effective June 27, 2012. Operative July 1, 2012, by Sec. 83 of Ch. 36.)

11817.3.

(a) There shall be an appropriation from the Budget Act to the department to fund programs and services to alleviate problems related to inappropriate alcohol use or other drug use as provided for in this part. However, if the state receives additional funds from the federal government after the enactment of the Budget Act, which funds may be augmented by the Director of Finance to the appropriation described in this section in accordance with the Budget Act, then the department shall determine the amount of those funds to be used for allocation to counties, and shall allocate that amount to counties through amendments to executed contracts, within 90 days of receipt of the additional funds to support programs and services to alleviate alcohol-related and other drug-related problems as described in this subdivision. The allocation of all funds pursuant to this subdivision shall comply with federal requirements and with any requirements pursuant to Section 28.00 of the Budget Act.

(b) The requirement set forth in subdivision (a) that the department determine the amount of additional funds to be used for allocation to counties and allocate that amount to counties within 90 days, shall be waived when the 90-day period does not allow sufficient time for completion of the notification period pursuant to Section 28.00 of the Budget Act.

(Amended by Stats. 2012, Ch. 36, Sec. 39. (SB 1014) Effective June 27, 2012. Operative July 1, 2012, by Sec. 83 of Ch. 36.)

11817.6.

Payments or advances of funds to counties or other state agencies, which are properly chargeable to appropriations to the department may be made by a Controller's warrant drawn against funds appropriated to the department or funds administered by the department.

(Amended by Stats. 2012, Ch. 36, Sec. 41. (SB 1014) Effective June 27, 2012. Operative July 1, 2012, by Sec. 83 of Ch. 36.)

11817.8.

(a) It is the intent of the Legislature that the state and the counties work together to minimize audit exceptions. Audit findings as contained in the department audit reports may be appealed by counties directly to the department. Counties may retain disputed audit amounts while an audit appeal is pending and then only to the extent that the audit appeal is resolved in favor of the county and the amount is in the county's favor.

(b) The department shall audit the expenditures of counties, direct contractors, and county subcontractors. The department shall develop an annual audit plan that will identify the counties, direct contractors, and county subcontractors funded in whole or in part with the funds administered by the department. The annual audit plan shall consist of a sufficient number of audits and financial reviews to provide reasonable assurance that federal and state funds have been used for their intended purpose in accordance with applicable funding requirements and restrictions contained in statutes, regulations, and contracts.

(c) The department may conduct investigations, audits, and financial related reviews on other than a routine basis of any county, direct contractor, or county subcontractor funded in whole or in part with funds administered by the department, as the department deems necessary and appropriate.

(d) Counties may audit the expenditures of organizations funded in whole or in part with funds administered by the department.

(e) A county shall repay to the department amounts of state and federal funds found, as a result of an audit, not to have been expended in accordance with the requirements set forth in this part, federal block grant law, federal or state regulations pertaining to alcohol or other drug abuse services, and the conditions set forth in any contract for alcohol and other drug abuse services or an interagency agreement. For organizations or services and the conditions set forth in any combination of state, federal, or other public funds, where a clear audit trail shows that the source and application of these funds is not maintained, repayment shall be determined by prorating audit findings between each funding source.

(f) For those audits conducted by the department, the director shall administratively establish policies and procedures for the resolution of disputed audit findings. The department shall consult with county administrators when proposing changes in the procedures for the resolution of disputed audit findings.

(g) There is established in the State Treasury an Audit Repayment Trust Fund. The money in the fund shall be available upon appropriation by the Legislature.

(h) The department may deny or withhold payments or advances of funds to a county if the department finds, by audit or otherwise, that a program is not in compliance with this part or the contract.

(i) Notwithstanding subdivision (a) of Section 53134 of the Government Code, audits performed pursuant to this section shall be conducted by qualified state or local government auditors or independent public accountants in accordance with generally accepted governing auditing standards, as prescribed by Government Auditing Standards, issued by the Comptroller General of the United States. These audits shall be completed no later than six months after the completion of the audit fieldwork.

(j) (1) Notwithstanding the rulemaking provisions of Chapter 3.5 (commencing with Section 11340) of Part 1 of Division 3 of Title 2 of the Government Code, the department may implement, interpret, or make specific the amendments to this section made by the act that added this subdivision by means of all-county letters, plan letters, plan or provider bulletins, or similar instructions from the department until regulations are adopted pursuant to that chapter of the Government Code.

(2) The department shall adopt emergency regulations no later than July 1, 2014. The department may subsequently readopt any emergency regulation authorized by this section that is the same as or is substantially equivalent to an emergency regulation previously adopted pursuant to this section.

(3) The initial adoption of emergency regulations implementing the amendments to this section and the one readoption of emergency regulations authorized by this subdivision shall be deemed an emergency and necessary for the immediate preservation of the public peace, health, safety, or general welfare. Initial emergency regulations and the one readoption of emergency regulations authorized by this section shall be exempt from review by the Office of Administrative Law. The initial emergency regulations and the one readoption of emergency regulations authorized by this section shall be submitted to the Office of Administrative Law for filing with the Secretary of State and each shall remain in effect for no more than 180 days, by which time final regulations may be adopted.

(Amended by Stats. 2012, Ch. 36, Sec. 42. (SB 1014) Effective June 27, 2012. Operative July 1, 2012, by Sec. 83 of Ch. 36.)

11818.

(a) (1) Expenditures made by a county and a county's provider that may be reimbursed using appropriated funds include salaries of personnel, approved facilities and services provided through contract, operation, maintenance, and service costs, depreciation of county facilities as established in the State of California's Auditing Standards and Procedures for Counties, lease of facilities where there is no intention to, nor option to, purchase, and other expenditures that may be approved by the director.

(2) Expenditures made by a county and a county's provider that may not be paid using appropriated funds include expenditures for initial capital improvement, the purchase or construction of buildings, except for equipment items and remodeling expenses as may be provided in regulations of the department, compensation to members of a local advisory board on drug programs, except actual and necessary expenses incurred in the performance of official duties, and expenditures for a purpose for which state reimbursement is claimed under any other law.

(b) (1) Except as provided in Chapter 3 (commencing with Section 11758.10), the cost of services specified in the county contract shall be based upon reimbursement of actual costs as determined with standard accounting practices. The county may enter into contracts with providers at actual cost or a negotiated rate. The provider shall make available to the county information on prior years' actual cost of providing the services and actual revenues.

(2) (A) Providers that receive a combination of Medi-Cal funding and other federal or state funding for the same service element and location shall be reimbursed for actual costs as limited by Medi-Cal reimbursement requirements, as specified in Title XIX of the federal Social Security Act (42 U.S.C. Sec. 1396 et seq.), the Medicaid state plan, subdivisions (c) and (d) of Section 51516 of Title 22 of the California Code of Regulations, except that reimbursement for non-Medi-Cal reimbursable services shall not be limited by Medi-Cal rate requirements or customary charges to privately paying clients.

(B) For those providers who operate under a negotiated rate for non-Medi-Cal reimbursable services, the rates shall be treated as provisional rates, subject to yearend settlement of actual costs.

(Amended by Stats. 2012, Ch. 36, Sec. 43. (SB 1014) Effective June 27, 2012. Operative July 1, 2012, by Sec. 83 of Ch. 36.)

11818.5.

(a) Counties shall submit a cost report reflecting the expenditure of funds expended pursuant to the county contract. An annual cost report for the fiscal year ending June 30 shall be submitted to the department by November 1.

(b) Each county shall be responsible for reviewing its contracts with providers of services and the department may audit these contracts. The cost reports shall be reviewed by the department and interim settlements of claims shall be made expeditiously with each county. Final settlement shall be made at the time of audit, which shall be completed within three years of the date the cost report was accepted for interim settlement by the department. If the audit is not completed within three years, the interim settlement shall be considered as the final settlement.

(c) Counties shall report estimated numbers and characteristics of clients-participants by type of service and shall report actual numbers and characteristics of clients-participants served by type of service with the annual cost report. The department shall specify forms and procedures to be followed in reporting this information. The fiscal reporting system established pursuant to this section shall supersede the requirements of paragraph (2) of subdivision (b) of Section 16366.7 of the Government Code for a quarterly fiscal reporting system.

(Amended by Stats. 2012, Ch. 36, Sec. 44. (SB 1014) Effective June 27, 2012. Operative July 1, 2012, by Sec. 83 of Ch. 36.)

11819.1.

The Legislature recognizes the need for increased potential for coordination between county alcohol programs and local health system agencies established pursuant to Public Law 93-641. Therefore, the Legislature encourages a harmonious working relationship between local health system agencies and county alcohol programs.

(Repealed and added by Stats. 1984, Ch. 1328, Sec. 55.5.)

CHAPTER 5. State and County Relationships to Health Planning Agencies [11820-11820.]

(Chapter 5 added by Stats. 1979, Ch. 679.)

ARTICLE 1. State Agencies [11820- 11820.]

(Article 1 added by Stats. 1979, Ch. 679.)

11820.

The Legislature recognizes the potential positive impact that federal, state, and local agencies can have on the alleviation of alcohol and other drug problems through better coordinated planning and utilization of limited health resources. The Legislature encourages persons concerned with alcohol and other drug problems to become involved as much as possible in providing advice and comments on health plans of those agencies.

(Amended by Stats. 2012, Ch. 36, Sec. 45. (SB 1014) Effective June 27, 2012. Operative July 1, 2012, by Sec. 83 of Ch. 36.)

CHAPTER 6. Evaluation [11825 - 11829]

(Chapter 6 added by Stats. 1979, Ch. 679.)

ARTICLE 1. Statewide Evaluation [11825 - 11826]

(Article 1 repealed and added by Stats. 1984, Ch. 1328, Sec. 58.)

11825.

The department may establish reasonable criteria to evaluate the performance of programs and services that are described in the county contract for alcohol and other drug abuse services.

(Amended by Stats. 2012, Ch. 36, Sec. 46. (SB 1014) Effective June 27, 2012. Operative July 1, 2012, by Sec. 83 of Ch. 36.)

11826.

The department may do all of the following:

(a) Review and conduct evaluation studies of service delivery to clients in programs receiving state allocated funds.

(b) Conduct investigative reporting.

(c) Disseminate evaluation studies, reports, articles, and other reference documents.

(d) Evaluate the administration of county alcohol and other drug programs to determine whether the county provides for adequate administration of the county alcohol and other drug program.

(Amended by Stats. 2004, Ch. 862, Sec. 95. Effective January 1, 2005.)

ARTICLE 2. County Program Evaluation [11827 - 11829]

(Article 2 added by Stats. 1979, Ch. 679.)

11827.

The Legislature recognizes that local program effectiveness may be evaluated in a variety of ways, but should reflect the needs and priorities of the local community and attempt to measure the achievement of objectives determined through the planning process described in this part. The Legislature further recognizes that the conducting of these evaluations is essential to holding county alcohol and other drug programs accountable for their use of funds and increasing program effectiveness. The Legislature recognizes the beneficial results of the local evaluation process to those participating in this process. The Legislature desires to encourage experimentation and diversity in the methods utilized by counties to evaluate the county alcohol and other drug programs' achievement of their objectives, including, but not limited to, evaluations of individuals' progress, changes in utilization rates, changes in community attitudes, and measurement of specific programmatic goals in order to advance our knowledge about the effectiveness of programs in alleviating alcohol and other drug problems.

(Amended by Stats. 2012, Ch. 36, Sec. 47. (SB 1014) Effective June 27, 2012. Operative July 1, 2012, by Sec. 83 of Ch. 36.)

11828.

Each county shall ensure the evaluation of all funded programs to determine whether they have achieved their objectives as determined in the planning process. In addition, recognizing the difficulty and expense of conducting effective county alcohol and other drug program evaluation, the department may assist counties in developing evaluation designs for implementation by counties to measure progress of alcohol or other drug users, changes in community attitudes toward inappropriate alcohol use and other drug problems, changes in the incidence and prevalence of alcohol and other drug problems within the county, or other objectives identified in the planning process. The department, in cooperation with counties that choose to participate, may assist and fund counties to implement the evaluation designs developed. Counties may contract with public or private agencies and utilize funds allocated under this part for purposes of conducting the evaluations.

(Amended by Stats. 2012, Ch. 36, Sec. 48. (SB 1014) Effective June 27, 2012. Operative July 1, 2012, by Sec. 83 of Ch. 36.)

11829.

The department may disseminate information about the evaluation projects to all counties and interested persons throughout the state in order to advance the knowledge of the field about these evaluation methodologies.

(Amended by Stats. 1984, Ch. 1328, Sec. 61.)

CHAPTER 7. Quality Assurance [11830 - 11833]

(Chapter 7 repealed and added by Stats. 1984, Ch. 1328, Sec. 64.)

11830.

The department shall take the following goals and objectives into consideration in the implementation of this chapter:

(a) The significance of community-based programs to alcohol and other drug abuse recovery shall not be diminished.

(b) Opportunities for low-income and special needs populations to receive alcohol and other drug abuse recovery or treatment services shall be encouraged.

(Amended (as added by Stats. 1989, Ch. 919) by Stats. 2004, Ch. 862, Sec. 98. Effective January 1, 2005.)

11830.01.

(a) The department's death investigation policy shall be designed to ensure that a resident's death is addressed and investigated by the department in a timely manner.

(b) The telephonic and written reports of resident deaths occurring in a licensed facility that are required to be reported to the department shall include, but not be limited to, a description of the event or incident, including the time, location, and nature of the event or incident, a list of immediate actions that were taken, including persons contacted, and a description of the followup action that is planned, including, but not limited to, steps taken to prevent a future death.

(c) A telephonic report required under subdivision (b), which includes the event or incident and all information required under subdivision (b) that is known at the time of the report, shall be submitted to the department within one working day of the event or incident.

(d) A written report required under subdivision (b), which includes all information required under subdivision (b), shall be submitted to the department within seven calendar days of the event or incident.

(Added by Stats. 2014, Ch. 815, Sec. 1. (AB 2374) Effective January 1, 2015.)

11830.1.

In order to ensure quality assurance of alcohol and other drug programs and expand the availability of funding resources, the department shall implement a program certification procedure for alcohol and other drug treatment recovery services. The department, after consultation with the County Behavioral Health Directors Association of California, and other interested organizations and individuals, shall develop standards and regulations for the alcohol and other drug treatment recovery services describing the minimal level of service quality required of the service providers to qualify for and obtain state certification. The standards shall be excluded from the rulemaking requirements of the Administrative Procedure Act (Chapter 3.5 (commencing with Section 11340) of Part 1 of Division 3 of Title 2 of the Government Code). Compliance with these standards shall be voluntary on the part of programs. For the purposes of Section 2626.2 of the Unemployment Insurance Code, certification shall be equivalent to program review.

(Amended by Stats. 2015, Ch. 455, Sec. 3. (SB 804) Effective January 1, 2016.)

11830.5.

(a) The department, in consultation with the county alcohol and drug program administrators and other interested organizations and individuals, shall develop program standards specific to each type of residential and nonresidential program, to be used during its certification process. These standards shall be advisory only and are excluded from the provisions of Section 11340.5 of the Government Code and other rulemaking requirements of the Administrative Procedure Act (Chapter 3.5 (commencing with Section 11340) of Part 1 of Division 3 of Title 2 of the Government Code), and Chapter 8 (commencing with Section 11835).

(b) The program standards shall include, but not be limited to, both of the following:

(1) Recognition and characterization of different approaches and solutions to the alcohol and drug problems that the department determines have sufficient merit for a separate standard.

(2) Reference to the needs of youth, the elderly, women, pregnant women, mothers and their children, gays, lesbians, the disabled, and special populations, with recognition of innovative solutions to the problems of those special populations.

(c) The program standards shall serve as educational documents to inform the public of the current state-of-the-art in effective and cost-efficient alcohol and drug problem programming.

(Amended by Stats. 2004, Ch. 862, Sec. 100. Effective January 1, 2005.)

11831.

To the maximum extent possible, a reasonable effort to refer a client to other programs, facilities, or services is encouraged for any program or facility which is unable to accept a client after initial assessment.

(Added by Stats. 1989, Ch. 919, Sec. 4.)

11831.2.

The department shall charge a fee for the certification of programs, in accordance with Chapter 7.3 (commencing with Section 11833.01).

(Amended by Stats. 2007, Ch. 177, Sec. 7. Effective August 24, 2007.)

11831.5.

(a) Certification shall be granted by the department pursuant to this section to any qualified alcoholism or drug abuse recovery or treatment program, regardless of the source of the program's funding, upon approval of a completed application and payment of the required fee. The certification shall be valid for a period of not more than two years. The department may extend the certification period upon receipt of an application for renewal and payment of the required certification fee prior to the expiration date of the certification.

(b) The purposes of certification under this section shall be all of the following:

(1) To identify programs that exceed minimal levels of service quality, are in substantial compliance with the department's standards, and merit the confidence of the public, third-party payers, and county alcohol and drug programs.

(2) To encourage programs to meet their stated goals and objectives.

(3) To encourage programs to strive for increased quality of service through recognition by the state and by peer programs in the alcoholism and drug field.

(4) To assist programs to identify their needs for technical assistance, training, and program improvements.

(c) Certification may be granted under this section on the basis of evidence satisfactory to the department that the requesting alcoholism or drug abuse recovery or treatment program has an accreditation by a statewide or national alcohol or drug program accrediting body. The accrediting body shall provide accreditation that meets or exceeds the department's standards and is recognized by the department.

(d) Certification, or the lack thereof, shall not convey any approval or disapproval by the department, but shall be for information purposes only.

(e) The standards developed pursuant to Section 11830 and the certification under this section shall satisfy the requirements of Section 1463.16 of the Penal Code.

(f) The department and the State Department of Social Services shall enter into a memorandum of understanding to establish a process by which the Department of Alcohol and Drug Programs can certify residential facilities or programs serving primarily adolescents, as defined in paragraph (1) of subdivision (a) of Section 1502, that have programs that primarily serve adolescents and provide alcohol and other drug recovery or treatment services.

(g) Regulations adopted by the department pursuant to this section shall be adopted as emergency regulations in accordance with Chapter 3.5 (commencing with Section 11340) of Part 1 of Division 3 of Title 2 of the Government Code, and for the purposes of that chapter, including Section 11349.6 of the Government Code, the adoption of these regulations is an emergency and shall be considered by the Office of Administrative Law as necessary for the immediate preservation of the public peace, health and safety, and general welfare. Notwithstanding Chapter 3.5 (commencing with Section 11340) of Part 1 of Division 3 of Title 2 of the Government Code, including subdivision (e) of Section 11346.1 of the Government Code, any emergency regulations adopted pursuant to this section shall be filed with, but not be repealed by, the Office of Administrative Law and shall remain in effect until revised by the department. Nothing in this subdivision shall be interpreted to prohibit the department from adopting subsequent amendments on a nonemergency basis or as emergency regulations in accordance with the standards set forth in Section 11346.1 of the Government Code.

(Amended by Stats. 2007, Ch. 177, Sec. 8. Effective August 24, 2007.)

11831.6.

(a) The following persons, programs, or entities shall not give or receive remuneration or anything of value for the referral of a person who is seeking alcoholism or drug abuse recovery and treatment services:

(1) An alcoholism or drug abuse recovery and treatment facility licensed under this part.

(2) An owner, partner, officer, or director, or shareholder who holds an interest of at least 10 percent in an alcoholism or drug abuse recovery and treatment facility licensed under this part.

(3) A person employed by, or working for, an alcoholism or drug abuse recovery and treatment facility licensed under this part, including, but not limited to, registered and certified counselors and licensed professionals providing counseling services.

(4) An alcohol or other drug program certified by the department in accordance with the alcohol or other drug certification standards established pursuant to Section 11830.1.

(5) An owner, partner, officer, or director, or shareholder who holds an interest of at least 10 percent in an alcohol or other drug program certified by the department in accordance with the alcohol or other drug certification standards established pursuant to Section 11830.1.

(6) A person employed by, or working for, an alcohol or other drug program certified by the department in accordance with the alcohol or other drug certification standards established pursuant to Section 11830.1, including, but not limited to, registered and certified counselors and licensed professionals providing counseling services.

(b) Notwithstanding the rulemaking provisions of the Administrative Procedure Act (Chapter 3.5 (commencing with Section 11340) of Part 1 of Division 3 of Title 2 of the Government Code), the department may, if it deems appropriate, implement, interpret, or make specific this section by means of provider bulletins, written guidelines, or similar instructions from the department, until regulations are adopted.

(Added by Stats. 2018, Ch. 792, Sec. 2. (SB 1228) Effective January 1, 2019.)

11831.7.

(a) The department may investigate allegations of violations of Section 11831.6. The department may, upon finding a violation of Section 11831.6 or any regulation adopted pursuant to that section, do any of the following:

(1) Assess a penalty upon an alcoholism or drug abuse recovery and treatment facility licensed under this part.

(2) Suspend or revoke the license of an alcoholism or drug abuse recovery and treatment facility licensed under Chapter 7.5 (commencing with Section 11834.01), or deny an application for licensure, extension of the licensing period, or modification to a license. Article 4 (commencing with Section 11834.35) of Chapter 7.5 shall apply to any action taken pursuant to this paragraph.

(3) Assess a penalty upon an alcohol or other drug program certified by the department in accordance with the alcohol or other drug certification standards established pursuant to Section 11830.1.

(4) Suspend or revoke the certification of an alcohol or other drug program certified by the department in accordance with the alcohol or other drug certification standards established pursuant to Section 11830.1.

(5) Suspend or revoke the registration or certification of a counselor for a violation of Section 11831.6.

(b) The department may investigate allegations against a licensed professional providing counseling services at an alcoholism or drug abuse recovery and treatment program licensed, certified, or funded under this part, and recommend disciplinary actions, including, but not limited to, termination of employment at a program and suspension and revocation of licensure by the respective licensing board.

(c) Notwithstanding the rulemaking provisions of the Administrative Procedure Act (Chapter 3.5 (commencing with Section 11340) of Part 1 of Division 3 of Title 2 of the Government Code), the department may, if it deems appropriate, implement, interpret, or make specific this section by means of provider bulletins, written guidelines, or similar instructions from the department, until regulations are adopted.

(Added by Stats. 2018, Ch. 792, Sec. 3. (SB 1228) Effective January 1, 2019.)

11832.

The department may contract with private individuals or agencies to provide technical assistance and training to qualify programs for state certification.

(Repealed and added by Stats. 1984, Ch. 1328, Sec. 64.)

11832.1.

The department shall encourage the development of educational courses that provide core knowledge concerning alcohol and drug abuse problems and programs to personnel working within alcohol and drug abuse programs.

(Added by renumbering Section 11834 by Stats. 2007, Ch. 577, Sec. 14. Effective October 13, 2007. Note: This action repeats the same renumbering already applied by Stats. 2007, Ch. 177, on Aug. 24, 2007.)

11833.

(a) The department shall have the sole authority in state government to determine the qualifications, including the appropriate skills, education, training, and experience of personnel working within alcoholism or drug abuse recovery and treatment programs licensed, certified, or funded under this part.

(b) (1) Except for licensed professionals, as defined by the department, the department shall require that an individual providing counseling services working within a program described in subdivision (a) be registered with or certified by a certifying organization approved by the department to register and certify counselors.

(2) The department shall not approve a certifying organization that does not, prior to registering or certifying an individual, contact other department-approved certifying organizations to determine whether the individual has ever had his or her registration or certification revoked.

(c) If a counselor's registration or certification has been previously revoked, the certifying organization shall deny the request for registration and shall send the counselor a written notice of denial. The notice shall specify the counselor's right to appeal the denial in accordance with applicable statutes and regulations.

(d) The department shall have the authority to conduct periodic reviews of certifying organizations to determine compliance with all applicable laws and regulations, including subdivision (c), and to take actions for noncompliance, including revocation of the department's approval.

(e) (1) Notwithstanding Chapter 3.5 (commencing with Section 11340) of Part 1 of Division 3 of Title 2 of the Government Code, the department, without taking any further regulatory action, shall implement, interpret, or make specific this section by means of all-county letters, plan letters, plan or provider bulletins, or similar instructions until the time that regulations are adopted.

(2) The department shall adopt regulations by December 31, 2017, in accordance with the requirements of Chapter 3.5 (commencing with Section 11340) of Part 1 of Division 3 of Title 2 of the Government Code.

(Amended by Stats. 2014, Ch. 815, Sec. 2. (AB 2374) Effective January 1, 2015.)

CHAPTER 7.3. Licensing and Certification Program Funding [11833.01 - 11833.04]

(Chapter 7.3 added by Stats. 2007, Ch. 177, Sec. 9.)

11833.01.

This chapter applies to all programs, facilities, or services certified pursuant to Chapter 7 (commencing with Section 11830) or licensed pursuant to Chapter 7.5 (commencing with Section 11834.01), or both.

(Added by Stats. 2007, Ch. 177, Sec. 9. Effective August 24, 2007.)

11833.02.

(a) The department shall charge a fee to all programs for licensure or certification by the department, regardless of the form of organization or ownership of the program.

(b) The department may establish fee scales using different capacity levels, categories based on measures other than program capacity, or any other category or classification that the department deems necessary or convenient to maintain an effective and equitable fee structure.

(c) Licensing and certification fees shall be evaluated annually, taking into consideration the overall cost of the residential and outpatient licensing and certification activities of the department, including initial issuance, renewals, complaints, enforcement activity, related litigation, and any other program activity relating to licensure and certification, plus a reasonable reserve.

(d) The department shall submit any proposed new fees or fee changes to the Legislature for approval no later than April 1 of each year as part of the spring finance letter process. No new fees or fee changes shall be implemented without legislative approval.

(e) The department shall issue a provider bulletin pursuant to subdivision (a) of Section 11833.04 setting forth the approved fee structure. The department shall, on an annual basis, publish the current fee structure on the department's Internet Web site.

(f) Unless funds are specifically appropriated from the General Fund in the annual Budget Act or other legislation to support the division, the Licensing and Certification Division, no later than the beginning of the 2010–11 fiscal year, shall be supported entirely by federal funds and special funds.

(Amended by Stats. 2014, Ch. 31, Sec. 10. (SB 857) Effective June 20, 2014.)

11833.03.

The Residential and Outpatient Program Licensing Fund is hereby established in the State Treasury. All fees, fines, and penalties collected from residential and outpatient programs collected in accordance with this chapter shall be deposited in this fund. The money in the fund shall be available upon appropriation by the Legislature for the purposes of supporting the licensing and certification activities of the department.

(Added by Stats. 2007, Ch. 177, Sec. 9. Effective August 24, 2007.)

11833.04.

(a) Notwithstanding the rulemaking provisions of the Administrative Procedure Act, Chapter 3.5 (commencing with Section 11340) of Part 1 of Division 3 of Title 2 of the Government Code, the department may implement new fees or fee changes as approved by the Legislature pursuant to subdivision (d) of Section 11833.02 by means of provider bulletins or similar instructions from the director without taking regulatory action. The department shall notify and consult with interested parties and appropriate stakeholders regarding new fees or fee changes made pursuant to this chapter.

(b) (1) The department shall adopt regulations in accordance with Chapter 3.5 (commencing with Section 11340) of Part 1 of Division 3 of Title 2 of the Government

Code by January 1, 2016, to amend Section 10701 of Title 9 of Division 4 of Chapter 5.5 of the California Code of Regulations to be consistent with this chapter.

(2) The authority to implement Section 11833.02 and this section shall include the authority to supersede the licensing and certification fees in effect on the operative date of the act that adds this paragraph and shall continue until the department has amended Section 10701 of Title 9 of Division 4 of Chapter 5.5 of the California Code of Regulations pursuant to paragraph (1).

(Amended by Stats. 2014, Ch. 31, Sec. 11. (SB 857) Effective June 20, 2014.)

CHAPTER 7.4. Licensing and Certification Program Disclosures [11833.05- 11833.05.]

(Chapter 7.4 added by Stats. 2018, Ch. 784, Sec. 1.)

11833.05.

(a) All programs certified by the department pursuant to Chapter 7 (commencing with Section 11830) or licensed by the department pursuant to Chapter 7.5 (commencing with Section 11834.01) shall disclose to the department the following information:

(1) Ownership or control of, or financial interest in, a recovery residence.

(2) Any contractual relationship with an entity that regularly provides professional services or addiction treatment or recovery services to clients of programs licensed or certified by the department, if the entity is not part of the program licensed or certified by the department.

(b) All programs licensed or certified by the department shall make the disclosures pursuant to subdivision (a) upon initial licensure or certification, upon renewal of licensure or certification, and upon a licensed or certified program acquiring or starting a relationship that meets paragraph (1) or (2) of subdivision (a). The department may suspend or revoke the license or certification of a program for failing to disclose the information required in subdivision (a).

(c) For the purposes of this section, "recovery residence" means a residential dwelling that provides primary housing for individuals who seek a cooperative living arrangement that supports personal recovery from a substance use disorder and that does not require licensure by the department or does not provide licensable services, pursuant to Chapter 7.5 (commencing with Section 11834.01). A recovery residence may include, but is not limited to, residential dwellings commonly referred to as "sober living homes," "sober living environments," or "unlicensed alcohol and drug free residences."

(Added by Stats. 2018, Ch. 784, Sec. 1. (SB 992) Effective January 1, 2019.)

CHAPTER 7.5. Licensing [11834.01 - 11834.50]

(Chapter 7.5 added by Stats. 1984, Ch. 1667, Sec. 2.)

ARTICLE 1. General Provisions [11834.01 - 11834.18]

{ Article 1 added by Stats. 1984, Ch. 1667, Sec. 2. }

11834.01.

The department has the sole authority in state government to license adult alcoholism or drug abuse recovery or treatment facilities.

(a) In administering this chapter, the department shall issue new licenses for a period of two years to those programs that meet the criteria for licensure set forth in Section 11834.03.

(b) Onsite program visits for compliance shall be conducted at least once during the license period.

(c) The department may conduct announced or unannounced site visits to facilities licensed pursuant to this chapter for the purpose of reviewing for compliance with all applicable statutes and regulations.

(Added by renumbering Section 11834.10 by Stats. 1993, Ch. 741, Sec. 3. Effective January 1, 1994.)

11834.015.

(a) The department shall adopt the American Society of Addiction Medicine treatment criteria, or an equivalent evidence-based standard, as the minimum standard of care for licensed facilities and shall require a licensee to maintain those standards with respect to the level of care to be provided by the licensee.

(b) The department may implement, interpret, or make specific this section by means of plan or provider bulletins or similar instructions until regulations are adopted. The department shall adopt regulations by January 1, 2023.

(Added by Stats. 2018, Ch. 781, Sec. 1. (SB 823) Effective January 1, 2019.)

11834.02.

(a) As used in this chapter, "alcoholism or drug abuse recovery or treatment facility" or "facility" means any premises, place, or building that provides residential nonmedical services to adults who are recovering from problems related to alcohol, drug, or alcohol and drug misuse or abuse, and who need alcohol, drug, or alcohol and drug recovery treatment or detoxification services.

(b) As used in this chapter, "adults" may include, but is not limited to, all of the following:

(1) Mothers over 18 years of age and their children.

(2) Emancipated minors, which may include, but is not limited to, mothers under 18 years of age and their children.

(c) As used in this chapter, "emancipated minors" means persons under 18 years of age who have acquired emancipation status pursuant to Section 7002 of the Family Code.

(d) Notwithstanding subdivision (a), an alcoholism or drug abuse recovery or treatment facility may serve adolescents upon the issuance of a waiver granted by the department pursuant to regulations adopted under subdivision (c) of Section 11834.50.

(Amended by Stats. 2018, Ch. 784, Sec. 2. (SB 992) Effective January 1, 2019.)

11834.025.

(a) (1) As a condition of providing incidental medical services, as defined in subdivision (a) of Section 11834.026, at a facility licensed by the department, the facility, within a reasonable period of time, as defined by the department in regulations, shall obtain from each program participant, a signed certification described in subdivision (b) from a health care practitioner.

(2) For purposes of this chapter, "health care practitioner" means a person duly licensed and regulated under Division 2 (commencing with Section 500) of the Business and Professions Code, who is acting within the scope of practice of his or her license or certificate.

(b) The department shall develop a standard certification form for use by a health care practitioner. The form shall include, but not be limited to, a description of the alcoholism and drug abuse recovery or treatment services that an applicant needs.

(c) (1) The department shall adopt regulations, on or before July 1, 2018, to implement this section. The regulations shall be adopted in accordance with the Administrative Procedure Act (Chapter 3.5 (commencing with Section 11340) of Part 1 of Division 3 of Title 2 of the Government Code).

(2) Notwithstanding the rulemaking provisions of the Administrative Procedure Act, the department may, if it deems appropriate, implement, interpret, or make specific this section by means of provider bulletins, written guidelines, or similar instructions from the department only until the department adopts regulations.

(Added by Stats. 2015, Ch. 744, Sec. 2. (AB 848) Effective January 1, 2016.)

11834.026.

(a) As used in this section, "incidental medical services" means services that are in compliance with the community standard of practice and are not required to be performed in a licensed clinic or licensed health facility, as defined by Section 1200 or 1250, respectively, to address medical issues associated with either detoxification from alcohol or drugs or the provision of alcoholism or drug abuse recovery or treatment services, including all of the following categories of services that the department shall further define by regulation:

(1) Obtaining medical histories.

(2) Monitoring health status to determine whether the health status warrants transfer of the patient in order to receive urgent or emergent care.

(3) Testing associated with detoxification from alcohol or drugs.

(4) Providing alcoholism or drug abuse recovery or treatment services.

(5) Overseeing patient self-administered medications.

(6) Treating substance abuse disorders, including detoxification.

(b) Incidental medical services do not include the provision of general primary medical care.

(c) Notwithstanding any other law, a licensed alcoholism or drug abuse recovery or treatment facility may permit incidental medical services to be provided to a resident at the facility premises by, or under the supervision of, one or more physicians and surgeons licensed by the Medical Board of California or the Osteopathic Medical Board who are knowledgeable about addiction medicine, or one or more other health care practitioners acting within the scope of practice of his or her license and under the direction of a physician and surgeon, and who are also knowledgeable about addiction medicine, if all of the following conditions are met:

(1) The facility, in the judgment of the department, has the ability to comply with the requirements of this chapter and all other applicable laws and regulations to meet the needs of a resident receiving incidental medical services pursuant to this chapter. The department shall specify in regulations the minimum requirements that a facility shall meet in order to be approved to permit the provision of incidental medical services on its premises. The license of a facility approved to permit the provision of incidental medical services shall reflect that those services are permitted at the facility premises.

(2) The physician and surgeon and any other health care practitioner has signed an acknowledgment on a form provided by the department that he or she has been advised of and understands the statutory and regulatory limitations on the services that may legally be provided at a licensed alcoholism or drug abuse recovery or treatment facility and the statutory and regulatory requirements and limitations for the physician and surgeon or other health care practitioner and for the facility, related to providing incidental medical services. The licensee shall maintain a copy of the signed form at the facility for a physician and surgeon or other health care practitioner providing incidental medical services at the facility premises.

(3) A physician and surgeon or other health care practitioner shall assess a resident, prior to that resident receiving incidental medical services, to determine whether it is medically appropriate for that resident to receive these services at the premises of the licensed facility. A copy of the form provided by the department shall be signed by the physician and surgeon and maintained in the resident's file at the facility.

(4) The resident has signed an admission agreement. The admission agreement, at a minimum, shall describe the incidental medical services that the facility may permit to be provided and shall state that the permitted incidental medical services will be provided by, or under the supervision of, a physician and surgeon. The department shall specify in regulations, at a minimum, the content and manner of providing the admission agreement, and any other information that the department deems appropriate. The facility shall maintain a copy of the signed admission agreement in the resident's file.

(5) Once incidental medical services are initiated for a resident, the physician and surgeon and facility shall monitor the resident to ensure that the resident remains appropriate to receive those services. If the physician and surgeon determines that a change in the resident's medical condition requires other medical services or that a

higher level of care is required, the facility shall immediately arrange for the other medical services or higher level of care, as appropriate.

(6) The facility maintains in its files a copy of the relevant professional license or other written evidence of licensure to practice medicine or perform medical services in the state for the physician and surgeon and any other health care practitioner providing incidental medical services at the facility.

(d) The department is not required to evaluate or have any responsibility or liability with respect to evaluating the incidental medical services provided by a physician and surgeon or other health care practitioner at a licensed facility. This section does not limit the department's ability to report suspected misconduct by a physician and surgeon or other health care practitioner to the appropriate licensing entity or to law enforcement.

(e) A facility licensed and approved by the department to allow provision of incidental medical services shall not by offering approved incidental medical services be deemed a clinic or health facility within the meaning of Section 1200 or 1250, respectively.

(f) Other than incidental medical services permitted to be provided or any urgent or emergent care required in the case of a life threatening emergency, this section does not authorize the provision at the premises of the facility of any medical or health care services or any other services that require a higher level of care than the care that may be provided within a licensed alcoholism or drug abuse recovery or treatment facility.

(g) This section does not require a residential treatment facility licensed by the department to provide incidental medical services or any services not otherwise permitted by law.

(h) (1) On or before July 1, 2018, the department shall adopt regulations to implement this section in accordance with the Administrative Procedure Act (Chapter 3.5 (commencing with Section 11340) of Part 1 of Division 3 of Title 2 of the Government Code).

(2) Notwithstanding the rulemaking provisions of the Administrative Procedure Act, the department may, if it deems appropriate, implement, interpret, or make specific this section by means of provider bulletins, written guidelines, or similar instructions from the department until regulations are adopted.

(Added by Stats. 2015, Ch. 744, Sec. 3. (AB 848) Effective January 1, 2016.)

11834.03.

(a) A person or entity applying for licensure shall file with the department, on forms provided by the department, all of the following:

(1) A completed written application for licensure.

(2) A fire clearance approved by the State Fire Marshal or local fire enforcement officer.

(3) A licensure fee, established in accordance with Chapter 7.3 (commencing with Section 11833.01).

(b) (1) If an applicant intends to permit services pursuant to Section 11834.026, the applicant shall submit evidence of a valid license of the physician and surgeon who will provide or oversee those services, and any other information the department deems appropriate.

(2) The department shall establish and collect an additional licensure fee for an application that includes a request to provide services pursuant to Section 11834.026. The fee shall be set at an amount sufficient to cover the reasonable costs to the department of the additional assessment and investigation necessary to license facilities to provide these services, including, but not limited to, processing applications, issuing licenses, and investigating reports of noncompliance with licensing regulations.

(Amended by Stats. 2015, Ch. 744, Sec. 4. (AB 848) Effective January 1, 2016.)

11834.09.

(a) The department may issue a single license to operate an alcoholism or drug abuse recovery or treatment facility upon receipt of a completed written application, fire clearance, and licensing fee subject to the department's review and determination that the applicant can comply with this chapter and regulations adopted pursuant to this chapter.

(b) Failure to submit a completed written application, fire clearance, and payment of the required licensing fee in a timely manner shall result in termination of the department's licensure review and shall require submission of a new application by the applicant.

(c) Failure of the applicant to demonstrate the ability to comply with this chapter or the regulations adopted pursuant to this chapter shall result in departmental denial of the application for licensure.

(d) Initial licenses for new facilities shall be provisional for one year. During the term of the provisional license, the department may revoke the license for good cause. For the purposes of this section, "good cause" means failure to operate in compliance with this chapter or the regulations adopted pursuant to this chapter. A licensee may not reapply for an initial license for five years following a revocation of a provisional license.

(e) On or before July 1, 2022, the department shall adopt regulations to implement this section in accordance with the Administrative Procedure Act (Chapter 3.5 (commencing with Section 11340) of Part 1 of Division 3 of Title 2 of the Government Code).

(f) Notwithstanding the rulemaking provisions of the Administrative Procedure Act, the department may implement, interpret, or make specific this section by means of provider bulletins, written guidelines, or similar instructions, until regulations are adopted.

(Repealed and added by Stats. 2018, Ch. 775, Sec. 2. (AB 3162) Effective January 1, 2019.)

11834.10.

(a) A licensee shall not operate an alcoholism or drug abuse recovery or treatment facility beyond the conditions and limitations specified on the license.

(b) Licensed services offered or provided by a licensed alcoholism or drug abuse recovery or treatment facility, including, but not limited to, incidental medical services as defined in Section 11834.026, shall be specified on the license and provided exclusively:

(1) Within the licensed facility; or

(2) Within any facilities identified on a single license by street address.

(c) Only residents of the licensed alcoholism or drug abuse recovery or treatment facility shall receive licensed services.

(d) The department may adopt regulations to implement this section in accordance with the Administrative Procedure Act (Chapter 3.5 (commencing with Section 11340) of Part 1 of Division 3 of Title 2 of the Government Code).

(e) Notwithstanding the rulemaking provisions of the Administrative Procedure Act, the department may implement, interpret, or make specific this section by means of provider bulletins, written guidelines, or similar instructions.

(Repealed and added by Stats. 2018, Ch. 775, Sec. 4. (AB 3162) Effective January 1, 2019.)

11834.15.

The department may assess civil penalties in accordance with Sections 11834.31 and 11834.34.

(Amended by Stats. 2007, Ch. 177, Sec. 12. Effective August 24, 2007.)

11834.16.

A license shall be valid for a period of two years from the date of issuance. The department may extend the licensure period for subsequent two-year periods upon submission by the licensee of a completed written application for extension and payment of the required licensing fee prior to the expiration date shown on the license. Failure to submit to the department the required written application for extension of the licensing period, or failure to submit to the department the required licensing fee prior to the expiration date on the license, shall result in the automatic expiration of the license at the end of the two-year licensing period.

(Added by Stats. 1993, Ch. 741, Sec. 10. Effective January 1, 1994.)

11834.17.

No city, county, city and county, or district shall adopt or enforce any building ordinance or local rule or regulations relating to the subject of fire and life safety in alcoholism and drug abuse recovery facilities which is more restrictive than those standards adopted by the State Fire Marshal.

(Amended by Stats. 1989, Ch. 919, Sec. 12.)

11834.18.

(a) Nothing in this chapter shall authorize the imposition of rent regulations or controls for licensed alcoholism or drug abuse recovery or treatment facilities.

(b) Licensed alcoholism and drug abuse recovery or treatment facilities shall not be subject to controls on rent imposed by any state or local agency or other local government or entity.

(Amended by Stats. 1989, Ch. 919, Sec. 13.)

ARTICLE 2. Local Regulation [11834.20 - 11834.25]

(Article 2 added by Stats. 1984, Ch. 1667, Sec. 2.)

11834.20.

The Legislature hereby declares that it is the policy of this state that each county and city shall permit and encourage the development of sufficient numbers and types of alcoholism or drug abuse recovery or treatment facilities as are commensurate with local need.

The provisions of this article apply equally to any chartered city, general law city, county, city and county, district, and any other local public entity.

For the purposes of this article, "six or fewer persons" does not include the licensee or members of the licensee's family or persons employed as facility staff.

(Amended by Stats. 1989, Ch. 919, Sec. 15.)

11834.21.

Any person licensed under this chapter who operates or proposes to operate an alcoholism or drug abuse recovery or treatment facility, the department or other public agency authorized to license such a facility, or any public or private agency which uses or may use the services of the facility to place its clients, may invoke the provisions of this article.

This section shall not be construed to prohibit any interested party from bringing suit to invoke the provisions of this article.

(Amended by Stats. 1989, Ch. 919, Sec. 16.)

11834.22.

An alcoholism or drug abuse recovery or treatment facility which serves six or fewer persons shall not be subject to any business taxes, local registration fees, use permit fees, or other fees to which other single-family dwellings are not likewise subject. Nothing in this section shall be construed to forbid the imposition of local property taxes, fees for water service and garbage collection, fees for inspections not prohibited by Section 11834.23, local bond assessments, and other fees, charges, and assessments to which other single-family dwellings are likewise subject. Neither the State Fire Marshal nor any local public entity shall charge any fee for enforcing fire inspection regulations pursuant to state law or regulation or local ordinance, with respect to alcoholism or drug abuse recovery or treatment facilities which serve six or fewer persons.

(Amended by Stats. 1989, Ch. 919, Sec. 17.)

11834.23.

(a) Whether or not unrelated persons are living together, an alcoholism or drug abuse recovery or treatment facility that serves six or fewer persons shall be considered a residential use of property for the purposes of this article. In addition, the residents and operators of the facility shall be considered a family for the purposes of any law or zoning ordinance that relates to the residential use of property pursuant to this article.

(b) For the purpose of all local ordinances, an alcoholism or drug abuse recovery or treatment facility that serves six or fewer persons shall not be included within the definition of a boarding house, rooming house, institution or home for the care of minors, the aged, or persons with mental health disorders, foster care home, guest home, rest home, community residence, or other similar term that implies that the alcoholism or drug abuse recovery or treatment home is a business run for profit or differs in any other way from a single-family residence.

(c) This section shall not be construed to forbid a city, county, or other local public entity from placing restrictions on building heights, setback, lot dimensions, or placement of signs of an alcoholism or drug abuse recovery or treatment facility that serves six or fewer persons as long as the restrictions are identical to those applied to other single-family residences.

(d) This section shall not be construed to forbid the application to an alcoholism or drug abuse recovery or treatment facility of any local ordinance that deals with health and safety, building standards, environmental impact standards, or any other matter within the jurisdiction of a local public entity. However, the ordinance shall not distinguish alcoholism or drug abuse recovery or treatment facilities that serve six or fewer persons from other single-family dwellings or distinguish residents of alcoholism or drug abuse recovery or treatment facilities from persons who reside in other single-family dwellings.

(e) No conditional use permit, zoning variance, or other zoning clearance shall be required of an alcoholism or drug abuse recovery or treatment facility that serves six or fewer persons that is not required of a single-family residence in the same zone.

(f) Use of a single-family dwelling for purposes of an alcoholism or drug abuse recovery facility serving six or fewer persons shall not constitute a change of occupancy for purposes of Part 1.5 (commencing with Section 17910) of Division 13 or local building codes. However, nothing in this section is intended to supersede Section 13143 or 13143.6, to the extent those sections are applicable to alcoholism or drug abuse recovery or treatment facilities serving six or fewer residents.

(Amended by Stats. 2014, Ch. 144, Sec. 37. (AB 1847) Effective January 1, 2015.)

11834.24.

No fire inspection clearance or other permit, license, clearance, or similar authorization shall be denied to an alcoholism or drug abuse recovery or treatment facility because of a failure to comply with local ordinances from which the facility is exempt under Section 11834.23, if the applicant otherwise qualifies for a fire clearance, license, permit, or similar authorization.

(Amended by Stats. 1989, Ch. 919, Sec. 19.)

11834.25.

For the purposes of any contract, deed, or covenant for the transfer of real property executed on or after January 1, 1979, an alcoholism or drug abuse recovery or treatment facility which serves six or fewer persons shall be considered a residential use of property and a use of property by a single family, notwithstanding any disclaimers to the contrary.

(Amended by Stats. 1989, Ch. 919, Sec. 20.)

ARTICLE 2.5. Requirements for Licensees [11834.26 - 11834.29]

(Article 2.5 added by Stats. 1993, Ch. 741, Sec. 12.)

11834.26.

(a) The licensee shall provide at least one of the following nonmedical services:

(1) Recovery services.

(2) Treatment services.

(3) Detoxification services.

(b) The department shall adopt regulations requiring records and procedures that are appropriate for each of the services specified in subdivision (a). The records and procedures may include all of the following:

(1) Admission criteria.

(2) Intake process.

(3) Assessments.

(4) Recovery, treatment, or detoxification planning.

(5) Referral.

(6) Documentation of provision of recovery, treatment, or detoxification services.

(7) Discharge and continuing care planning.

(8) Indicators of recovery, treatment, or detoxification outcomes.

(c) A licensee shall not deny admission to any individual based solely on the individual having a valid prescription from a licensed health care professional for a medication approved by the federal Food and Drug Administration for the purpose of narcotic replacement treatment or medication-assisted treatment of substance use disorders.

(d) A licensee shall develop a plan to address when a resident relapses, including when a resident is on the licensed premises after consuming alcohol or using illicit drugs. The plan shall include details of how the treatment stay and treatment plan of the resident will be adjusted to address the relapse episode and how the resident will be treated and supervised while under the influence of alcohol or illicit drugs, as well as discharge and continuing care planning, including when a licensee determines that a resident requires services beyond the scope of the licensee. This subdivision does not require a licensee to discharge a resident.

(e) The department shall have the authority to implement subdivision (d) by bulletin or all-county or all-provider letter, after stakeholder input, until such time that regulations are promulgated. The department shall promulgate regulations to implement subdivision (d) no later than January 1, 2021.

(f) In the development of regulations implementing this section, the written record requirements shall be modified or adapted for social model programs.

(Amended by Stats. 2018, Ch. 784, Sec. 3. (SB 992) Effective January 1, 2019.)

11834.27.

(a) The department shall have the sole authority in state government to establish the appropriate minimum qualifications of the licensee or designated administrator, and the staff of a provider of any of the services specified in subdivision (a) of Section 11834.26. These qualifications may include, but not be limited to, education, skills, life experience, and training.

(b) Nothing in this section shall be construed to apply to credentialing or licensing of individuals or to certification qualifications established pursuant to Chapter 7 (commencing with Section 11833).

(Added by Stats. 1993, Ch. 741, Sec. 12. Effective January 1, 1994.)

11834.29.

Any licensee that provides recovery, treatment, or detoxification services, that is not in compliance with the requirements of this article, shall have one year from the effective date of the regulations adopted by the department pursuant to this article and pursuant to Article 5 (commencing with Section 11834.50) to comply. In the event that the licensee fails to comply, the department shall take action against the licensee pursuant to Article 4 (commencing with Section 11834.36).

(Added by Stats. 1993, Ch. 741, Sec. 12. Effective January 1, 1994.)

ARTICLE 3. Offenses [11834.30 - 11834.34]

(Article 3 added by Stats. 1988, Ch. 646, Sec. 4.)

11834.30.

No person, firm, partnership, association, corporation, or local governmental entity shall operate, establish, manage, conduct, or maintain an alcoholism or drug abuse recovery or treatment facility to provide recovery, treatment, or detoxification services within this state without first obtaining a current valid license issued pursuant to this chapter.

(Added by renumbering Section 11834.12 by Stats. 1993, Ch. 741, Sec. 6. Effective January 1, 1994.)

11834.31.

If a facility is alleged to be in violation of Section 11834.30, the department shall conduct a site visit to investigate the allegation. If the department's employee or agent finds evidence that the facility is providing alcoholism or drug abuse recovery, treatment, or detoxification services without a license, the employee or agent shall take the following actions:

(a) Submit the findings of the investigation to the department.

(b) Upon departmental authorization, issue a written notice to the facility stating that the facility is operating in violation of Section 11834.30. The notice shall include all of the following:

(1) The date by which the facility shall cease providing services.

(2) Notice that the department will assess against the facility a civil penalty of two thousand dollars ($2,000) per day for every day the facility continues to provide services beyond the date specified in the notice.

(3) Notice that the case will be referred for civil proceedings pursuant to Section 11834.32 in the event the facility continues to provide services beyond the date specified in the notice.

(c) Inform the facility of the licensing requirements of this chapter.

(d) A person or entity found to be in violation of Section 11834.30 shall be prohibited from applying for initial licensure for a period of five years from the date of the notice specified in subdivision (b).

(Amended by Stats. 2018, Ch. 775, Sec. 5. (AB 3162) Effective January 1, 2019.)

11834.32.

(a) The director may bring an action to enjoin the violation of Section 11834.30 in the superior court in and for the county in which the violation occurred. Any proceeding under this section shall conform to the requirements of Chapter 3 (commencing with Section 525) of Title 7 of Part 2 of the Code of Civil Procedure, except that the director shall not be required to allege facts necessary to show or tending to show lack of adequate remedy at law or irreparable damage or loss.

(b) With respect to any and all actions brought pursuant to this section alleging actual violation of Section 11834.30, the court shall, if it finds the allegations to be true, issue its order enjoining the alcoholism or drug abuse recovery or treatment facility from continuance of the violation.

(Added by renumbering Section 11834.30 by Stats. 1993, Ch. 741, Sec. 13. Effective January 1, 1994.)

11834.34.

(a) In addition to the penalties of suspension or revocation of a license issued under this chapter, the department may also levy a civil penalty for violation of this chapter or the regulations adopted pursuant to this chapter.

(1) The amount of the civil penalty, as determined by the department, shall not be less than two hundred fifty dollars ($250) or more than five hundred dollars ($500) per day for each violation, except where the nature or seriousness of the violation or the frequency of the violation warrants a higher penalty or an immediate civil penalty assessment, or both, as determined by the department. In no event shall a civil penalty assessment exceed one thousand dollars ($1,000) per day.

(2) A licensee that is cited for repeating the same violation within 24 months of the first violation is subject to an immediate civil penalty of five hundred dollars ($500) and seven hundred fifty dollars ($750) for each day the violation continues until the deficiency is corrected.

(3) A licensee that has been assessed a civil penalty pursuant to paragraph (2) that repeats the same violation within 24 months of the violation subject to paragraph (2) is subject to an immediate civil penalty of five hundred dollars ($500) and one thousand dollars ($1,000) for each day the violation continues until the deficiency is corrected.

(b) Prior to the assessment of any civil penalty, the department shall provide the licensee with notice requiring the licensee to correct the deficiency within the period of time specified in the notice.

(Amended by Stats. 2018, Ch. 775, Sec. 6. (AB 3162) Effective January 1, 2019.)

ARTICLE 4. Suspension and Revocation [11834.35 - 11834.45]
(Article 4 added by Stats. 1988, Ch. 646, Sec. 5.)
11834.35.
Any employee or agent of the department upon presentation of proper identification, may enter and inspect any building, premises, and records, at a reasonable time, with or without notice, to secure information regarding compliance with, or to prevent a violation of, this chapter or any regulation adopted pursuant to this chapter. Failure of the owner or operator of the building or premises to allow the employee or agent of the department to enter and inspect the building, premises, and records, shall result in the department taking legal action to gain entry by an inspection warrant issued pursuant to Title 13 (commencing with Section 1822.50) of Part 3 of the Code of Civil Procedure. The cost of any legal action required to gain entry to a licensed facility shall be borne by the owner or operator responsible for preventing the department from entering and inspecting the building, premises, and records.
(Added by Stats. 1993, Ch. 741, Sec. 19. Effective January 1, 1994.)
11834.36.
(a) The director may suspend or revoke any license issued under this chapter, as well as any other licenses issued under this chapter to operate an adult alcoholism or drug abuse recovery or treatment facility held by the same person or entity, or deny an application for licensure, extension of the licensing period, or modification to a license, upon any of the following grounds and in the manner provided in this chapter:
(1) Violation by the licensee of any provision of this chapter or regulations adopted pursuant to this chapter.
(2) Repeated violation by the licensee of any of the provisions of this chapter or regulations adopted pursuant to this chapter.
(3) Aiding, abetting, or permitting the violation of, or any repeated violation of, any of the provisions described in paragraph (1) or (2).
(4) Conduct in the operation of an alcoholism or drug abuse recovery or treatment facility that is inimical to the health, morals, welfare, or safety of either an individual in, or receiving services from, the facility or to the people of the State of California.
(5) Misrepresentation of any material fact in obtaining the alcoholism or drug abuse recovery or treatment facility license, including, but not limited to, providing false information or documentation to the department.
(6) The licensee's refusal to allow the department entry into the facility to determine compliance with the requirements of this chapter or regulations adopted pursuant to this chapter.
(7) Violation by the licensee of Section 11834.026 or the regulations adopted pursuant to that section.
(8) Failure to pay any civil penalties assessed by the department.
(b) The director may temporarily suspend any license, as well as any other licenses issued under this chapter to operate an adult alcoholism or drug abuse recovery or treatment facility held by the same person or entity, prior to any hearing when, in the opinion of the director, the action is necessary to protect residents of the alcoholism or drug abuse recovery or treatment facility from physical or mental abuse, abandonment, or any other substantial threat to health or safety. The director shall notify the licensee of the temporary suspension and the effective date of the temporary suspension and at the same time shall serve the provider with an accusation. Upon receipt of a notice of defense to the accusation by the licensee, the director shall, within 15 days, set the matter for hearing, and the hearing shall be held as soon as possible. The temporary suspension shall remain in effect until the time the hearing is completed and the director has made a final determination on the merits. However, the temporary suspension shall be deemed vacated if the director fails to make a final determination on the merits within 30 days after the department receives the proposed decision from the Office of Administrative Hearings.
(c) The department may terminate review of an application for licensure under this chapter from any person or entity that previously had a license issued under this chapter suspended or revoked for a period of five years from the date of the final decision and order.
(Amended by Stats. 2018, Ch. 784, Sec. 4. (SB 992) Effective January 1, 2019.)
11834.37.
(a) Proceedings for the suspension, revocation, or denial of a license under this chapter shall be conducted in accordance with the provisions of Chapter 5 (commencing with Section 11500) of Part 1 of Division 3 of Title 2 of the Government Code, and the department shall have all the powers granted by those provisions. In the event of conflict between this chapter and the Government Code, the Government Code shall prevail.
(b) In all proceedings conducted in accordance with this section, the standard of proof to be applied shall be by the preponderance of the evidence.
(c) The department shall commence and process licensure revocations under this chapter in a timely and expeditious manner. The Office of Administrative Hearings shall give priority calendar preference to licensure revocation hearings pursuant to this chapter, particularly revocations where the health and safety of the residents are in question.
(Amended by Stats. 1995, Ch. 938, Sec. 64.8. Effective January 1, 1996. Operative July 1, 1997, by Sec. 98 of Ch. 938.)
11834.38.
Any license suspended pursuant to this chapter may be reinstated pursuant to Section 11522 of the Government Code.
(Added by renumbering Section 11834.37 by Stats. 1993, Ch. 741, Sec. 21. Effective January 1, 1994.)

11834.39.
(a) The withdrawal of an application for a license after it has been filed with the department shall not, unless the department consents in writing to the withdrawal, deprive the department of its authority to institute or continue a proceeding against the applicant for the denial of the license upon any ground provided by law or to enter an order denying the license upon any of these grounds.
(b) The suspension, expiration, or forfeiture by operation of law of a license issued by the department, or its suspension, forfeiture, or cancellation by order of the department or by order of a court of law, or its surrender without the written consent of the department, shall not deprive the department of its authority to institute or continue a disciplinary proceeding against the licensee upon any ground provided by law or to enter an order suspending or revoking the license or otherwise taking disciplinary action against the licensee on any ground provided by law.
(Added by renumbering Section 11834.38 by Stats. 1993, Ch. 741, Sec. 22. Effective January 1, 1994.)
11834.40.
A license shall terminate by operation of law, prior to its expiration date, when any of the following conditions occur:
(a) The licensee sells or otherwise transfers the facility or the property of the facility as identified on the license, unless the transfer of ownership applies to the transfer of stock when the facility is owned by and licensed as a corporation, and when the transfer of stock does not constitute a majority change in ownership.
(b) The licensee surrenders the license to the department.
(c) The licensee moves the facility identified on the license from one location to another. The department shall develop regulations to provide for an expedited application and licensing process for a newly located facility.
(d) The licensee is a sole proprietor and the licensee dies.
(e) The licensee actually or constructively abandons the licensed facility. Constructive abandonment includes insolvency, eviction, or seizure of assets or equipment resulting in the failure to provide recovery, treatment, or detoxification services to residents.
(Added by Stats. 1993, Ch. 741, Sec. 23. Effective January 1, 1994.)
11834.45.
The civil and administrative remedies available to the department pursuant to this chapter are not exclusive, and may be sought and employed in any combination deemed advisable by the department to enforce this chapter.
(Added by renumbering Section 11834.33 by Stats. 1993, Ch. 741, Sec. 17. Effective January 1, 1994.)

ARTICLE 5. Regulations [11834.50- 11834.50.]
(Article 5 heading added by Stats. 1993, Ch. 741, Sec. 24.)
11834.50.
The department shall adopt regulations to implement this chapter in accordance with the purposes required by Section 11835. These regulations shall be adopted only after consultation with appropriate groups affected by the proposed regulations. The regulations shall include, but not be limited to, all of the following:
(a) Provision for a formal appeal process for the denial, suspension, or revocation of a license.
(b) Establishment of requirements for compliance, procedures for issuance of deficiency notices and civil penalties for noncompliance.
(c) Provision for the issuance of a waiver for an alcoholism or drug abuse recovery or treatment facility to serve not more than three adolescents, or 10 percent of the total licensed capacity, whichever is less, age 14 years and older, when a need exists and services specific to adolescents are otherwise unavailable. The regulations shall specify the procedures and criteria for granting the waiver. The procedures shall include, but not be limited to, criminal record reviews and fingerprinting.
(d) Establishment of the elements and minimum requirements for recovery, treatment, and detoxification services.
(e) Provision for an expedited process for reviewing an application for licensure when a license is terminated pursuant to subdivision (c) of Section 11834.40.
(Added by renumbering Section 11834.13 by Stats. 1993, Ch. 741, Sec. 7. Effective January 1, 1994.)

CHAPTER 8. Regulations [11835- 11835.]
(Chapter 8 added by Stats. 1979, Ch. 679.)
11835.
(a) The purposes of any regulations adopted by the department shall be to implement, interpret, or make specific the provisions of this part and shall not exceed the authority granted to the department pursuant to this part. To the extent possible, the regulations shall be written in clear and concise language and adopted only when necessary to further the purposes of this part.
(b) Except as provided in this section and Sections 11772, 11798, 11798.2, 11814, 11817.8, and 11852.5, the department may adopt regulations in accordance with the rulemaking provisions of the Administrative Procedure Act (Chapter 3.5 (commencing with Section 11340) of Part 1 of Division 3 of Title 2 of the Government Code) necessary for the proper execution of the powers and duties granted to and imposed upon the department by this part. However, these regulations may be adopted only upon the following conditions:
(1) Prior to adoption of regulations, the department shall consult with the County Behavioral Health Directors Association of California and may consult with any other appropriate persons relating to the proposed regulations.

(2) If an absolute majority of the designated county behavioral health directors who represent counties that have submitted county contracts, vote at a public meeting called by the department, for which 45 days' advance notice shall be given by the department, to reject the proposed regulations, the department shall refer the matter for a decision to a committee, consisting of a representative of the county behavioral health directors, the director, the secretary, and one designee of the secretary. The decision shall be made by a majority vote of this committee at a public meeting convened by the department. Upon a majority vote of the committee recommending adoption of the proposed regulations, the department may then adopt them. Upon a majority vote recommending that the department not adopt the proposed regulations, the department shall then consult again with the County Behavioral Health Directors Association of California and resubmit the proposed regulations to the county behavioral health directors for a vote pursuant to this subdivision.

(3) In the voting process described in paragraph (2), no proxies shall be allowed nor may anyone other than the designated county behavioral health director, director, secretary, and secretary's designee vote at the meetings.

(Amended by Stats. 2015, Ch. 455, Sec. 4. (SB 804) Effective January 1, 2016.)

CHAPTER 9. Services to Persons Convicted for Driving While Under the Influence of Alcohol and Other Drugs [11836 - 11838.11]

(Heading of Chapter 9 amended by Stats. 2004, Ch. 862, Sec. 104.)

11836.

(a) The department shall have the sole authority to issue, deny, suspend, or revoke the license of a driving-under-the-influence program. As used in this chapter, "program" means any firm, partnership, association, corporation, local governmental entity, agency, or place that has been initially recommended by the county board of supervisors, subject to any limitation imposed pursuant to subdivisions (c) and (d), and that is subsequently licensed by the department to provide alcohol or drug recovery services in that county to any of the following:

(1) A person whose license to drive has been administratively suspended or revoked for, or who is convicted of, a violation of Section 23152 or 23153 of the Vehicle Code, and admitted to a program pursuant to Section 13352, 13352.1, 23538, 23542, 23548, 23552, 23556, 23562, or 23568 of the Vehicle Code.

(2) A person who is convicted of a violation of subdivision (b), (c), (d), or (e) of Section 655 of the Harbors and Navigation Code, or of Section 655.4 of that code, and admitted to the program pursuant to Section 668 of that code.

(3) A person who has pled guilty or nolo contendere to a charge of a violation of Section 23103 of the Vehicle Code, under the conditions set forth in subdivision (c) of Section 23103.5 of the Vehicle Code, and who has been admitted to the program under subdivision (e) or (f) of Section 23103.5 of the Vehicle Code.

(4) A person whose license has been suspended, revoked, or delayed due to a violation of Section 23140, and who has been admitted to a program under Article 2 (commencing with Section 23502) of Chapter 1 of Division 11.5 of the Vehicle Code.

(b) If a firm, partnership, corporation, association, local government entity, agency, or place has, or is applying for, more than one license, the department shall treat each licensed program, or each program seeking licensure, as belonging to a separate firm, partnership, corporation, association, local government entity, agency, or place for the purposes of this chapter.

(c) For purposes of providing recommendations to the department pursuant to subdivision (a), a county board of supervisors may limit its recommendations to those programs that provide services for persons convicted of a first driving-under-the-influence offense, or services to those persons convicted of a second or subsequent driving-under-the-influence offense, or both services. If a county board of supervisors fails to provide recommendations, the department shall determine the program or programs to be licensed in that county.

(d) After determining a need, a county board of supervisors may also place one or more limitations on the services to be provided by a driving-under-the-influence program or the area the program may operate within the county, when it initially recommends a program to the department pursuant to subdivision (a).

(1) For purposes of this subdivision, a board of supervisors may restrict a program for those convicted of a first driving-under-the-influence offense to providing only a three-month program, or may restrict a program to those convicted of a second or subsequent driving-under-the-influence offense to providing only an 18-month program, as a condition of its recommendation.

(2) A board of supervisors may not place restrictions on a program that would violate a statute or regulation.

(3) When recommending a program, if a board of supervisors fails to place any limitation on a program pursuant to this subdivision, the department may license that program to provide any driving-under-the-influence program services that are allowed by law within that county.

(4) This subdivision is intended to apply only to the initial recommendation to the department for licensure of a program by the county. It is not intended to affect a license that has been previously issued by the department or the renewal of a license for a driving-under-the-influence program. In counties where a contract or other written agreement is currently in effect between the county and a licensed driving-under-the-

influence program operating in that county, this subdivision is not intended to alter the terms of that relationship or the renewal of that relationship.

(Amended by Stats. 2008, Ch. 103, Sec. 1. Effective January 1, 2009.)

11836.10.

No person, firm, partnership, association, corporation, or local governmental entity shall operate, establish, manage, conduct, or maintain a driving-under-the-influence program in this state without a current and valid license issued pursuant to this chapter.

(Amended by Stats. 1993, Ch. 1244, Sec. 4. Effective January 1, 1994.)

11836.11.

The department shall require license renewal on a biennial basis.

(Added by Stats. 1988, Ch. 1219, Sec. 3.)

11836.12.

Criteria for licensure of new or existing programs shall include all of the following:

(a) Completion of a written application containing necessary and pertinent information describing the applicant program.

(b) Demonstration by the applicant that it possesses adequate administrative, fiscal, and operational capability to operate a driving-under-the-influence program.

(c) Onsite review of the program by department staff determines that the program is clean, safe, free of alcohol or illicit drug use, and that the program adheres to applicable statutes and regulations.

(d) The program has paid all licensing fees.

(Amended by Stats. 1993, Ch. 1244, Sec. 5. Effective January 1, 1994.)

11836.14.

An initial license shall not be issued until all requirements identified in this chapter and in regulations adopted pursuant to this chapter have been met.

(Added by Stats. 1988, Ch. 1219, Sec. 5.)

11836.15.

The department shall adopt regulations to implement this chapter, in accordance with the purposes and process required in Section 11835, which shall include, but not be limited to, the following:

(a) Application requirements.

(b) Service requirements.

(c) Reporting requirements.

(d) Required staff qualifications.

(e) Management and documentation of participant records.

(f) Licensure fee assessment and collection procedures.

(Added by Stats. 1988, Ch. 1219, Sec. 6.)

11836.16.

The State Department of Health Care Services shall adopt regulations for satellite offices of driving-under-the-influence programs. The regulations shall include, but not be limited to, any limitations on where a satellite office may be located and the minimum and maximum number of clients to whom a satellite office may provide services. When adopting regulations pursuant to this section, the department shall also consider an appropriate licensing procedure for these offices. For purposes of this section, a "satellite office" is an offsite location of an existing licensed driving-under-the-influence program.

(Amended by Stats. 2013, Ch. 22, Sec. 45. (AB 75) Effective June 27, 2013. Operative July 1, 2013, by Sec. 110 of Ch. 22.)

11837.

(a) Pursuant to the provisions of law relating to suspension of a person's privilege to operate a motor vehicle upon conviction for driving while under the influence of any alcoholic beverage or drug, or under the combined influence of any alcoholic beverage and any drug, as set forth in paragraph (3) of subdivision (a) of Section 13352 of the Vehicle Code, the Department of Motor Vehicles shall restrict the driving privilege pursuant to Section 13352.5 of the Vehicle Code, if the person convicted of that offense participates for at least 18 months in a driving-under-the-influence program that is licensed pursuant to this chapter.

(b) In determining whether to refer a person, who is ordered to participate in a program pursuant to Section 668 of the Harbors and Navigation Code, in a licensed alcohol and other drug education and counseling services program pursuant to Section 23538 of the Vehicle Code, or, pursuant to Section 23542, 23548, 23552, 23556, 23562, or 23568 of the Vehicle Code, in a licensed 18-month or 30-month program, the court may consider any relevant information about the person made available pursuant to a presentence investigation, that is permitted but not required under Section 23655 of the Vehicle Code, or other screening procedure. That information shall not be furnished, however, by any person who also provides services in a privately operated, licensed program or who has any direct interest in a privately operated, licensed program. In addition, the court shall obtain from the Department of Motor Vehicles a copy of the person's driving record to determine whether the person is eligible to participate in a licensed 18-month or 30-month program pursuant to this chapter. When preparing a presentence report for the court, the probation department may consider the suitability of placing the defendant in a treatment program that includes the administration of nonscheduled nonaddicting medications to ameliorate an alcohol or controlled substance problem. If the probation department recommends that this type of program is a suitable option for the defendant, the defendant who would like the court to consider this option shall obtain from his or her physician a prescription for the medication, and a finding that the treatment is medically suitable for the defendant, prior to consideration of this alternative by the court.

(c) (1) The court shall, as a condition of probation pursuant to Section 23538 or 23556 of the Vehicle Code, refer a first offender whose concentration of alcohol in his or her blood was less than 0.20 percent, by weight, to participate for at least three months or longer, as ordered by the court, in a licensed program that consists of at least 30 hours of program activities, including those education, group counseling, and individual interview sessions described in this chapter.

(2) Notwithstanding any other provision of law, in granting probation to a first offender described in this subdivision whose concentration of alcohol in the person's blood was 0.20 percent or more, by weight, or the person refused to take a chemical test, the court shall order the person to participate, for at least nine months or longer, as ordered by the court, in a licensed program that consists of at least 60 hours of program activities, including those education, group counseling, and individual interview sessions described in this chapter.

(d) (1) The State Department of Health Care Services may specify in regulations the activities required to be provided in the treatment of participants receiving nine months of licensed program services under Section 23538 or 23556 of the Vehicle Code.

(2) Any program licensed pursuant to this chapter may provide treatment services to participants receiving at least six months of licensed program services under Section 23538 or 23556 of the Vehicle Code.

(e) The court may, subject to Section 11837.2, and as a condition of probation, refer a person to a licensed program, even though the person's privilege to operate a motor vehicle is restricted, suspended, or revoked. An 18-month program described in Section 23542 or 23562 of the Vehicle Code or a 30-month program described in Section 23548, 23552, or 23568 of the Vehicle Code may include treatment of family members and significant other persons related to the convicted person with the consent of those family members and others as described in this chapter, if there is no increase in the costs of the program to the convicted person.

(f) The clerk of the court shall indicate the duration of the program in which the judge has ordered the person to participate in the abstract of the record of the court that is forwarded to the department.

(Amended by Stats. 2013, Ch. 22, Sec. 46. (AB 75) Effective June 27, 2013. Operative July 1, 2013, by Sec. 110 of Ch. 22.)

11837.1.

(a) In utilizing any program described in Section 11837, the court may require periodic reports concerning the performance of each person referred to and participating in a program. The program shall provide the court, the Department of Motor Vehicles, and the person participating in a program with an immediate report of any failure of the person to comply with the program's rules and policies.

(b) If, at any time after entry into or while participating in a program, a participant who is referred to an 18-month program described in Section 23542 of the Vehicle Code or a 30-month program described in Section 23548, 23552, or 23568 of the Vehicle Code, fails to comply with the rules and policies of the program, and that fact is reported, the Department of Motor Vehicles shall suspend the privilege of that person to operate a motor vehicle for the period prescribed by law in accordance with Section 13352.5 of the Vehicle Code, except as otherwise provided in this section. The Department of Motor Vehicles shall notify the person of its action.

(c) If the department withdraws the license of a program, the department shall immediately notify the Department of Motor Vehicles of those persons who do not commence participation in a licensed program within 21 days from the date of the withdrawal of the license of the program in which the persons were previously participating. The Department of Motor Vehicles shall suspend or revoke, for the period prescribed by law, the privilege to operate a motor vehicle of each of those persons referred to an 18-month program pursuant to Section 23542 or 23562 of the Vehicle Code or to a 30-month program pursuant to Section 23548, 23552, or 23568 of the Vehicle Code.

(Amended (as amended by Stats. 1998, Ch. 756) by Stats. 1999, Ch. 22, Sec. 2. Effective May 26, 1999. Operative July 1, 1999, by Sec. 46 of Ch. 22.)

11837.2.

(a) (1) The court may refer persons only to licensed programs. Subject to these provisions, a person is eligible to participate in the program if the program is operating in any of the following:

(A) The county where the person is convicted.

(B) The county where the person resides.

(C) A county that has an agreement with the person's county of residence pursuant to Section 11838.

(D) A county to which a person may request transfer pursuant to subdivision (d).

(2) If a person granted probation under Section 23542 or 23562 of the Vehicle Code cannot be referred to a licensed 18-month program pursuant to this section, Section 13352.5 of the Vehicle Code does not apply.

(b) If a person has consented to participate in a licensed program and the county where the person is convicted is the same county in which the person resides, the court may order the person to participate in a licensed program within that county, or, if that county does not have a licensed program, the court may order that person to participate in a licensed program within another county, pursuant to Section 11838.

(c) If a person has consented to participate in a licensed program in the county in which that person resides or in a county in which the person's county of residence has an agreement pursuant to Section 11838, and the county where the person is convicted is not the county where the person resides, and if the court grants the person summary probation, the court may order the person to participate in a licensed program in that county. In lieu of summary probation, the court may utilize the probation officer to implement the orders of the court. If the county in which the person resides does not have a licensed program or an agreement with another county pursuant to Section 11838 and the person consents, the court may order the person to participate in a

licensed program within the county where that person is convicted or in a county with which the county has an agreement pursuant to Section 11838.

(d) Except as otherwise provided in subdivision (e), subsequent to a person's commencement of participation in a program, the person may request transfer to another licensed program (1) in the same county in which the person has commenced participation in the program, upon approval of that county's alcohol and drug program administrator, or (2) in a county other than the county in which the person has commenced participation in the program, upon approval of the alcohol and drug program administrator of the county in which the person is participating and the county to which the person is requesting transfer.

(e) Subdivision (d) does not apply (1) if the court has ordered the person to participate in a specific licensed program, unless the court orders the transfer or, (2) if the person is under formal probation, unless the probation officer consents to the transfer. The department shall establish reporting forms and procedures to ensure that the court receives notice of any program transfer pursuant to this subdivision or subdivision (d).

(f) Jurisdiction of all postconviction matters arising pursuant to this section may be retained by the court of conviction.

(g) The department, in cooperation with the Department of Motor Vehicles and the county alcohol and drug program administrators, shall establish procedures to ensure the effective implementation of this section.

(Amended by Stats. 2004, Ch. 862, Sec. 106. Effective January 1, 2005.)

11837.3.

(a) (1) Each county, through the county alcohol and drug program administrator, shall determine its ability to establish, through public or private resources, a program of alcohol and other drug education and counseling services for a person whose license to drive has been administratively suspended or revoked for, or who is convicted of, a first violation of Section 23152 or 23153 of the Vehicle Code, or who is convicted of a violation of subdivision (b), (c), (d), or (e) of Section 655 of, or Section 655.4 of, the Harbors and Navigation Code, pursuant to subdivisions (e) and (f) of Section 668 of the Harbors and Navigation Code. The program shall be self-supporting through fees collected from program participants. The program shall be of at least three months' duration and consist of at least 30 hours of direct education and counseling services. The program shall be authorized by each county and licensed by, and operated under general regulations established by, the department.

(2) (A) A county that shows the department that it has insufficient resources, insufficient potential program participants, or other material disadvantages is not required to establish a program.

(B) The department may license an alcohol and other drug education program that is less than 30 hours in length in any county where the board of supervisors has provided the showing pursuant to subparagraph (A), and the department has upheld that showing. The shorter program is subject to all other applicable regulations developed by the department pursuant to paragraph (3) of subdivision (b) of Section 11837.4.

(b) Each county that has approved an alcohol and other drug education program or programs and that is licensed by the department shall make provision for persons who can document current inability to pay the program fee, in order to enable those persons to participate. The county shall require that the program report the failure of a person referred to the program to enroll in the program to the referring court.

(c) In order to assure effectiveness of the alcohol and other drug education and counseling program, the county shall provide, as appropriate, services to ethnic minorities, women, youth, or any other group that has particular needs related to the program.

(d) (1) Any person required to successfully complete an alcohol and other drug education and counseling program as a condition of probation shall enroll in the program and, except when enrollment is required in a program that is required to report failures to enroll to the court, shall furnish proof of the enrollment to the court within the period of time and in the manner specified by the court. The person also shall participate in and successfully complete the program, and shall furnish proof of successful completion within the period of time and in the manner specified by the court.

(2) An alcohol and other drug education and counseling program shall report to the court, within the period of time and in the manner specified by the court, the name of any person who fails to successfully complete the program.

(Amended by Stats. 2004, Ch. 862, Sec. 107. Effective January 1, 2005.)

11837.4.

(a) No program, regardless of how it is funded, may be licensed unless all of the requirements of this chapter and of the regulations adopted pursuant to this chapter have been met.

(b) Each licensed program shall include, but not be limited to, the following:

(1) For the alcohol or drug education and counseling services programs specified in subdivision (b) of Section 11837, each program shall provide for close and regular face-to-face interviews. For the 18-month programs specified in subdivision (a) of Section 11837, each program shall provide for close and regular supervision of the person, including face-to-face interviews at least once every other calendar week, regarding the person's progress in the program for the first 12 months of the program and shall provide only community reentry supervision during the final six months of the program. In the last six months of the 18-month program, the provider shall monitor the participant's community reentry activity with self-help groups, employment, family, and other areas of self-improvement. Unless otherwise ordered by the court, the provider's monitoring services are limited to not more than six hours. For the 30-month programs specified in subdivision (b) of Section 23548, subdivision (b) of Section 23552, and subdivision (b) of Section 23568 of the Vehicle Code, each program shall provide for close and regular

supervision of the person, including regular, scheduled face-to-face interviews over the course of 30 months regarding the person's progress in the program and recovery from problem drinking, alcoholism, chemical dependency, or polydrug abuse, as prescribed by regulations of the department. The interviews in any of those programs shall be conducted individually with each person being supervised and shall occur at times other than when the person is participating in any group or other activities of the program. No program activity in which the person is participating shall be interrupted in order to conduct the individual interviews.

(2) (A) The department shall approve all fee schedules for the programs and shall require that each program be self-supporting from the participants' fees and that each program provide for the payment of the costs of the program by participants at times and in amounts commensurate with their ability to pay in order to enable these persons to participate. Each program shall make provisions for persons who can successfully document current inability to pay the fees. Only the department may establish the criteria and procedures for determining a participant's ability to pay. The department shall ensure that the fees are set at amounts that will enable programs to provide adequately for the immediate and long-term continuation of services required pursuant to this chapter. The fees shall be used only for the purposes set forth in this chapter, except that any profit or surplus that does not exceed the maximum level established by the department may be utilized for any purposes allowable under any other provisions of law. In its regulations, the department shall define, for the purposes of this paragraph, taking into account prudent accounting, management, and business practices and procedures, the terms "profits" and "surplus." The department shall fairly construe these provisions so as not to jeopardize fiscal integrity of the programs. The department may not license any program if the department finds that any element of the administration of the program does not assure the fiscal integrity of the program.

(B) Each program licensed by the department under this section may request an increase in the fees. The request for an increase shall initially be sent to the county alcohol and drug program administrator. The county alcohol and drug program administrator shall, within 30 days of receiving the request, forward it to the department with the administrator's recommendation that the fee increase be approved or disapproved.

(C) The administrator's recommendation shall, among other things, take into account the rationale that the program has provided to the administrator for the increase and whether that increase would exceed the profit or surplus limit established by the department.

(D) If the county alcohol and drug program administrator fails to forward the request to the department within the 30 days, the program may send the request directly to the department. In this instance, the department may act without the administrator's recommendation.

(E) The department shall, within 30 days of receiving the request pursuant to subparagraph (B) or (D) approve or disapprove the request. In making its decision, the department shall consider the matters described in subparagraph (C).

(3) The licensed programs described in paragraph (1) shall include a variety of treatment services for problem drinkers, alcoholics, chemical dependents, and polydrug abusers or shall have the capability of referring the persons to, and regularly and closely supervising the persons while in, any appropriate medical, hospital, or licensed residential treatment services or self-help groups for their problem drinking, alcoholism, chemical dependency, or polydrug abuse problem. In addition to the requirements of paragraph (1), the department shall prescribe in its regulations what other services the program shall provide, at a minimum, in the treatment of participants, which services may include lectures, classes, group discussions, group counseling, or individual counseling in addition to the interviews required by paragraph (1), or any combination thereof. However, any group discussion or counseling activity, other than classes or lectures, shall be regularly scheduled to consist of not more than 15 persons, except that they may, on an emergency basis, exceed 15, but not more than 17, persons, at any one meeting. At no time shall there be more than 17 persons in attendance at any one meeting. For the 30-month programs specified in subdivision (b) of Section 23548, subdivision (b) of Section 23552, and subdivision (b) of Section 23568 of the Vehicle Code, each licensed program shall include a method by which each participant shall maintain a compendium of probative evidence, as prescribed in the regulations of the department, on a trimonthly basis demonstrating a performance of voluntary community service by the participant, including, but not limited to, the prevention of drinking and driving, the promotion of safe driving, and responsible attitudes toward the use of chemicals of any kind, for not less than 120 hours and not more than 300 hours, as determined by the court, with one-half of that time to be served during the initial 18 months of program participation and one-half of that time to be served in the final 12 months. In determining whether or not the participant has met the objectives of the program, the compendium of evidence shall also include, and the court shall consider, the participant's demonstration of significant improvement in any of the following areas of personal achievement:

(A) Significant improvement in occupational performance, including efforts to obtain gainful employment.

(B) Significant improvement in physical and mental health.

(C) Significant improvement in family relations, including financial obligations.

(D) Significant improvement in financial affairs and economic stability.

The compendium of evidence shall be maintained by the participant for review by the program, court, probation officer, or other appropriate governmental agency. The program officials, unless prohibited by the referring court, shall make provisions for a participant to voluntarily enter, using the participant's own resources, a licensed chemical dependency recovery hospital or residential treatment program which has a valid license issued by the State of California to provide alcohol or drug services, and to receive three weeks of program participation credit for each week of that treatment, not to exceed 12

weeks of program participation credit, but only if the treatment is at least two weeks in duration. The program shall document probative evidence of this hospital or residential care treatment in the participant's program file.

(4) In order to assure program effectiveness, the department shall require, whenever appropriate, that the licensed program provides services to ethnic minorities, women, youth, or any other group that has particular needs relating to the program.

(5) The goal of each program shall be to assist persons participating in the program to recognize their chemical dependency and to assist them in their recovery.

(6) Each program shall establish a method by which the court, the Department of Motor Vehicles, and the person are notified in a timely manner of the person's failure to comply with the program's rules and regulations.

(c) No program may be licensed unless the county complies with the requirements of subdivision (b) of Section 11812. The provider of a program that offers an alcohol or drug education and counseling services program, an 18-month program, or a 30-month program or any or all of those programs described in this section shall be required to obtain only one license. The department's regulations shall specify the requirements for the establishment of each program. The license issued by the department shall identify the program or programs licensed to operate.

(d) (1) Departmental approval for the establishment of a 30-month program by a licensed 18-month program is contingent upon approval by the county alcohol and drug program administrator, based upon confirmation that the program applicant is capable of providing the service and that the fiscal integrity of the program applicant will not be jeopardized by the operation of the program.

(2) The court shall refer a person to a 30-month treatment program only if a 30-month program exists or is provided for in the jurisdiction of the court.

(e) A county or program shall not prescribe additional program requirements unless the requirements are specifically approved by the department.

(f) The department may license a program on a provisional basis.

(Amended by Stats. 2004, Ch. 862, Sec. 108. Effective January 1, 2005.)

11837.5.

(a) No person may participate in any program that has not been licensed by the department pursuant to this chapter.

(b) The department shall charge reasonable fees for licensing driving-under-the-influence programs. The department shall set the fees in an amount sufficient to cover all administrative costs incurred by the department and to reimburse the Department of Motor Vehicles for the costs of the evaluation and report required by Section 9 of Senate Bill 1344 of the 1989–90 Regular Session.

(c) The department may fine a provider who is delinquent in the payment of licensing fees. The department shall deposit fines collected from delinquent providers in the Driving-Under-the-Influence Program Licensing Trust Fund, and the revenues from the fines shall be used, upon appropriation, to offset costs incurred by the department in the administration of the program and to reimburse the Department of Motor Vehicles for the costs of the evaluation and report required by Section 9 of Senate Bill 1344 of the 1989–90 Regular Session.

(d) If a program fails to pay licensing fees or assessed fines, the department may deny an initial license or revoke an existing license.

(e) There is established in the State Treasury a Driving-Under-the-Influence Program Licensing Trust Fund. All fees, fines, and penalties collected from driving-under-the-influence programs shall be deposited in this fund. The money in the fund shall be available when appropriated by the Legislature.

(f) The department shall prepare a report on the assets, liabilities, and balance in the Driving-Under-the-Influence Program Licensing Trust Fund when the department increases program licensing fees. The report shall also include an itemized statement of income and expenses for the trust fund since the last report. The department shall submit the report to the Legislature and shall furnish a copy of the report, upon request, to any provider of a driving-under-the-influence program.

(g) Licensing fees shall be evaluated annually and based on the department's projected costs for the forthcoming fiscal year. Any excess fees remaining in the Driving-Under-the-Influence Program Licensing Trust Fund at the close of the fiscal year shall be carried forward and taken into consideration in establishment of fees for the subsequent fiscal year. If the department proposes to increase the licensing fees, the department shall justify the increase to the Legislature by showing that sufficient assets are not currently available in the Driving-Under-the-Influence Program Licensing Trust Fund and that current licensing fee collections are not sufficient to support current or planned expenses of the department for driving-under-the-influence program licensing activities.

(h) Licensing fee collection procedures, which include the assessment of fines for delinquent fee payments, shall be defined in regulations adopted pursuant to this chapter.

(Amended by Stats. 1993, Ch. 1244, Sec. 8. Effective January 1, 1994.)

11837.6.

(a) The major responsibility for assuring programmatic and fiscal integrity of each program rests with the county alcohol and drug program administrator of each county utilizing a program pursuant to this chapter.

(b) The county alcohol and drug program administrator shall assure, through monitoring at least once every six months, compliance with the applicable statutes and regulations by any licensed program within the county's jurisdiction. Whenever possible, the county monitoring shall coincide with the state licensing reviews. The county alcohol and drug program administrator shall prepare and submit, to the department and the program provider, an annual written report of findings regarding the program's compliance with applicable statutes and regulations.

(c) The county alcohol and drug program administrator shall submit a description of each licensed program as part of the county plan.

(d) The county alcohol and drug program administrator shall notify the department, within 30 days of the date that a program's license is denied, suspended or revoked, of the individuals who failed to commence participation in another licensed program within 21 days of the license denial, suspension or revocation.

(Amended by Stats. 2004, Ch. 862, Sec. 109. Effective January 1, 2005.)

11837.7.

(a) The county alcohol and drug program administrator, or the advisory board acting through the county alcohol and drug program administrator, shall inform the board of supervisors immediately if it is determined that any program is not meeting the regulations adopted by the department. The department shall be notified in writing by the county alcohol and drug program administrator of any program that is not in compliance with applicable statutes and regulations.

(b) The department, the county alcohol and drug program administrator, the chief probation officer, or their authorized representatives may enter, in a nondisruptive manner, any class, lecture, group discussion, or any other program element to observe these activities.

(c) Notwithstanding subdivision (a) of Section 11837.6, the department may audit, or contract for the auditing of, any licensed program.

(Amended by Stats. 2004, Ch. 862, Sec. 110. Effective January 1, 2005.)

11837.8.

(a) The department shall authorize each county alcohol and drug program administrator to retain, in an amount not in excess of that specified by the department, a portion of the fees charged for participation in the program that is sufficient to reimburse the county for the costs and expenses that the administrator reasonably incurs in discharging his or her duties pursuant to this chapter.

(b) A county may not use for any purpose set forth in this chapter any funds allocated to it by the department pursuant to Division 10.5 (commencing with Section 11750). The board of supervisors may authorize the use of any other funds for any purpose set forth in this chapter.

(c) Notwithstanding subdivision (b), a county with a population of 20,000 or less may utilize funds allocated by the department to establish and administer a program if the department finds that the county cannot establish a self-supporting program at reasonable cost or is unable to establish jointly a program with another county. If an exception is granted, reasonable effort shall be made by the county to observe the intent of subdivision (b) that programs be self-supporting.

(Amended by Stats. 2004, Ch. 862, Sec. 111. Effective January 1, 2005.)

11837.9.

The participation of the probation department in a program established pursuant to this chapter shall be described in the amendment to the county plan.

(Amended by Stats. 2004, Ch. 862, Sec. 112. Effective January 1, 2005.)

11838.

(a) The Legislature encourages all counties to utilize the procedure described in this chapter, but recognizes that it is not feasible for every county to establish its own programs. Accordingly, two or more counties may jointly establish programs pursuant to Section 11796 of this code or Article 1 (commencing with Section 6500) of Chapter 5 of Division 7 of Title 1 of the Government Code or may furnish by contract the program services to residents of another county pursuant to Section 11796 of this code. The board of supervisors of the county in which the program is located shall be responsible for assuring the integrity of the program as required pursuant to subdivision (a) of Section 11837.6.

(b) For the purpose of determining a person's eligibility to participate in an approved program where the person's county of residence establishes a program with another county or contracts for services pursuant to subdivision (a), the following eligibility requirements shall apply:

(1) Where two or more counties jointly establish a program pursuant to Section 11796 of this code or Article 1 (commencing with Section 6500) of Chapter 5 of Division 7 of Title 1 of the Government Code, subdivision (b) of Section 11838.2 shall apply.

(2) Where a county contracts for program services from another county, only those residents alleged to have committed a violation of Section 23152 or 23153 of the Vehicle Code on or after the date their county of residence executes a contract pursuant to subdivision (a) to provide program services to their residents shall be eligible to participate in such approved program pursuant to Section 11837.2.

Counties which contract for services pursuant to subdivision (a) of this section shall notify the department not later than 14 days following such action.

(Amended by Stats. 1982, Ch. 53, Sec. 5. Effective February 18, 1982.)

11838.1.

The department, in cooperation with the county and the Department of Motor Vehicles, shall establish uniform statewide reporting procedures and forms for the submission of any appropriate documents or information from boards of supervisors, administrators of programs, county alcohol and drug program administrators, and program participants to assure effective implementation of this chapter.

(Amended by Stats. 2004, Ch. 862, Sec. 113. Effective January 1, 2005.)

11838.3.

(a) The director may bring an action to enjoin any violation of Section 11836.10 in the superior court in and for the county in which the violation occurred. Any proceeding under the provisions of this section shall conform to the requirements of Chapter 3 (commencing with Section 525) of Title 7 of Part 2 of the Code of Civil Procedure, except

that the director shall not be required to allege facts necessary to show or tending to show lack of adequate remedy at law or irreparable damage or loss.

(b) With respect to any and all actions brought pursuant to this section alleging actual violation of Section 11836.10 the court shall, if it finds the allegations to be true, issue its order enjoining the program from continuance of the violation.

(Added by Stats. 1988, Ch. 1219, Sec. 16.)

11838.4.

(a) Notwithstanding any other provision of this chapter, any person who violates Section 11836.10 may be assessed by the department an immediate civil penalty in the amount of two hundred dollars ($200) per day of the violation. The civil penalty shall be imposed if an unlicensed program is operated and the operator refuses to seek licensure or the operator's licensure application is denied and the operator continues to operate the unlicensed program.

(b) In addition to suspension or revocation of a license issued under this chapter, the department may levy a civil penalty against any program provider who is not in compliance with statutes and regulations.

(1) The amount of the civil penalty shall not be less than twenty-five dollars ($25) or more than fifty dollars ($50) per day for each violation of this chapter except where the nature or seriousness of the violation or the frequency of the violation warrants a higher penalty or an immediate civil penalty assessment, or both, as determined by the department. In no event, shall the civil penalty assessment for noncompliance exceed one hundred fifty dollars ($150) per day, or a total of five thousand dollars ($5,000).

(2) Prior to the assessment of any civil penalty other than a civil penalty specified in paragraph (1) or (3), the program provider shall have a minimum of 30 days to correct the deficiency.

(3) Any program provider that is cited for repeating the same violation of this chapter within a 12-month period is subject to an immediate civil penalty of one hundred fifty dollars ($150) and fifty dollars ($50) for each day the violation continues until the deficiency is corrected. In no event shall the total fine exceed five thousand dollars ($5,000).

(4) The suspension, revocation, forfeiture, or surrender of a license issued by the department shall not deprive the department of its authority to institute or continue a disciplinary proceeding against a licensee upon any grounds provided for in law or to enter and order suspending or revoking the license or otherwise taking disciplinary action against the licensee.

(c) An operator may appeal the assessment to the director, and if the matter is unresolved at that stage, the operator may appeal the director's decision in accordance with Chapter 5 (commencing with Section 11500) of Part 1 of Division 3 of Title 2 of the Government Code.

(Amended by Stats. 1993, Ch. 589, Sec. 92. Effective January 1, 1994.)

11838.5.

The civil, criminal, and administrative remedies available to the department pursuant to this article are not exclusive, and may be sought and employed in any combination deemed advisable by the department to enforce this chapter.

(Added by Stats. 1988, Ch. 1219, Sec. 18.)

11838.10.

The director may suspend or revoke any license issued under this chapter, or deny an application to renew a license or to modify the terms and conditions of a license, upon any of the following grounds and in the manner provided in this chapter:

(a) Violation by the licensee of this chapter or regulations adopted pursuant to this chapter.

(b) Repeated violation by the licensee of this chapter or regulations adopted pursuant to this chapter.

(c) Aiding, abetting, or permitting the violation of, or any repeated violation of, subdivisions (a) and (b).

(d) Continued program operations jeopardize the health and welfare of participants or the public.

(e) Misrepresentation of any material fact in obtaining a multiple offender program license.

(Added by Stats. 1988, Ch. 1219, Sec. 19.)

11838.11.

(a) Proceedings for the suspension, revocation, or denial of a license under this chapter shall be conducted in accordance with Chapter 5 (commencing with Section 11500) of Part 1 of Division 3 of Title 2 of the Government Code, and the department shall have all the powers granted by these provisions. In the event of conflict between this chapter and the Government Code, the Government Code shall prevail.

(b) In all proceedings conducted in accordance with this section, the standard of proof to be applied shall be by the preponderance of the evidence.

(Added by Stats. 1988, Ch. 1219, Sec. 20.)

CHAPTER 10. Narcotic Treatment Programs [11839 - 11839.34]

(Chapter 10 added by Stats. 2004, Ch. 862, Sec. 114.)

ARTICLE 1. Narcotic Treatment Programs [11839 - 11839.22]

(Article 1 added by Stats. 2004, Ch. 862, Sec. 114.)

11839.

The department, with the approval of the Secretary of California Health and Human Services, may contract with any public or private agency for the performance of any of the functions vested in the department by this chapter. Any department of the state is authorized to enter into a contract described in this section.

(Amended by Stats. 2012, Ch. 36, Sec. 52. (SB 1014) Effective June 27, 2012. Operative July 1, 2012, by Sec. 83 of Ch. 36.)

11839.1.

The Legislature finds and declares that it is in the best interests of the health and welfare of the people of this state to coordinate narcotic treatment programs to use narcotic replacement therapy and medication-assisted treatments for substance use disorders in the treatment of addicted persons whose addiction was acquired or supported by the use of a narcotic drug or drugs, not in compliance with a physician and surgeon's legal prescription, and to establish and enforce minimum requirements for the operation of all these treatment programs in this state.

(Amended by Stats. 2017, Ch. 223, Sec. 2. (AB 395) Effective January 1, 2018.)

11839.2.

The following medications are authorized for use in narcotic replacement therapy and medication-assisted treatment by licensed narcotic treatment programs:

(a) Methadone.

(b) Levo-alpha-acetylmethadol (LAAM) as specified in paragraph (10) of subdivision (c) of Section 11055.

(c) Buprenorphine products or combination of products approved by the federal Food and Drug Administration for maintenance or detoxification of opioid dependence.

(d) Any other medication approved by the federal Food and Drug Administration for the purpose of narcotic replacement treatment or medication-assisted treatment of substance use disorders.

(e) Notwithstanding Chapter 3.5 (commencing with Section 11340) of Part 1 of Division 3 of Title 2 of the Government Code, the department may implement, interpret, or make specific this section by means of plan or provider bulletins, or similar instructions. The department shall adopt regulations by no later than January 1, 2021.

(Amended by Stats. 2017, Ch. 223, Sec. 3. (AB 395) Effective January 1, 2018.)

11839.3.

(a) In addition to the duties authorized by other statutes, the department shall perform all of the following:

(1) License the establishment of narcotic treatment programs in this state to use narcotic replacement therapy in the treatment of addicted persons whose addiction was acquired or supported by the use of a narcotic drug or drugs, not in compliance with a physician and surgeon's legal prescription, except that the Research Advisory Panel shall have authority to approve methadone or LAAM research programs. The department shall establish and enforce the criteria for the eligibility of patients to be included in the programs, program operation guidelines, such as dosage levels, recordkeeping and reporting, urinalysis requirements, take-home doses of controlled substances authorized for use pursuant to Section 11839.2, security against redistribution of the narcotic replacement drugs, and any other regulations that are necessary to protect the safety and well-being of the patient, the local community, and the public, and to carry out this chapter. A program may admit a patient to narcotic maintenance or narcotic detoxification treatment at the discretion of the medical director. The program shall assign a unique identifier to, and maintain an individual record for, each patient of the program. The arrest and conviction records and the records of pending charges against a person seeking admission to a narcotic treatment program shall be furnished to narcotic treatment program directors upon written request of the narcotic treatment program director provided the request is accompanied by a signed release from the person whose records are being requested.

(2) Inspect narcotic treatment programs in this state and ensure that programs are operating in accordance with the law and regulations. The department shall have sole responsibility for compliance inspections of all programs in each county. Annual compliance inspections shall consist of an evaluation by onsite review of the operations and records of licensed narcotic treatment programs' compliance with applicable state and federal laws and regulations and the evaluation of input from local law enforcement and local governments, regarding concerns about the narcotic treatment program. At the conclusion of each inspection visit, the department shall conduct an exit conference to explain the cited deficiencies to the program staff and to provide recommendations to ensure compliance with applicable laws and regulations. The department shall provide an inspection report to the licensee within 30 days of the completed onsite review describing the program deficiencies. A corrective action plan shall be required from the program within 30 days of receipt of the inspection report. All corrective actions contained in the plan shall be implemented within 30 days of receipt of approval by the department of the corrective action plan submitted by the narcotic treatment program. For programs found not to be in compliance, a subsequent inspection of the program shall be conducted within 30 days after the receipt of the corrective action plan in order to ensure that corrective action has been implemented satisfactorily. Subsequent inspections of the program shall be conducted to determine and ensure that the corrective action has been implemented satisfactorily. For purposes of this requirement, "compliance" shall mean to have not committed any of the grounds for suspension or revocation of a license provided for under subdivision (a) of Section 11839.9 or paragraph (2) of subdivision (b) of Section 11839.9. Inspection of narcotic treatment programs shall be based on objective criteria including, but not limited to, an evaluation of the programs' adherence to all applicable laws and regulations and input from local law enforcement and local governments. Nothing in this section shall preclude counties from monitoring their contract providers for compliance with contract requirements.

(3) Charge and collect licensure fees. In calculating the licensure fees, the department shall include staff salaries and benefits, related travel costs, and state operational and administrative costs. Fees shall be used to offset licensure and inspection costs, not to exceed actual costs.

(4) Study and evaluate, on an ongoing basis, narcotic treatment programs including, but not limited to, the adherence of the programs, to all applicable laws and regulations and the impact of the programs on the communities in which they are located.

(5) Provide advice, consultation, and technical assistance to narcotic treatment programs to ensure that the programs comply with all applicable laws and regulations and to minimize any negative impact that the programs may have on the communities in which they are located.

(6) In its discretion, to approve local agencies or bodies to assist it in carrying out this chapter provided that the department may not delegate responsibility for inspection or any other licensure activity without prior and specific statutory approval. However, the department shall evaluate recommendations made by county alcohol and drug program administrators regarding licensing activity in their respective counties.

(7) The director may grant exceptions to the regulations adopted under this chapter if he or she determines that this action would improve treatment services or achieve greater protection to the health and safety of patients, the local community, or the general public. An exception shall not be granted if it is contrary to, or less stringent than, the federal laws and regulations that govern narcotic treatment programs.

(b) It is the intent of the Legislature in enacting this section, in order to protect the general public and local communities, that take-home doses of narcotic replacement therapy medications authorized for use pursuant to Section 11839.2 shall only be provided when the patient is clearly adhering to the requirements of the program, and if daily attendance at a clinic would be incompatible with gainful employment, education, responsible homemaking, retirement or medical disability, or if the program is closed on Sundays or holidays and providing a take-home dose is not contrary to federal laws and regulations governing narcotic treatment programs. The department shall define "satisfactory adherence" and shall ensure that patients not satisfactorily adhering to their programs shall not be provided take-home doses. A narcotic treatment program medical director shall determine whether or not to dilute take-home doses.

(c) There is established in the State Treasury the Narcotic Treatment Program Licensing Trust Fund. All licensure fees collected from the providers of narcotic treatment services shall be deposited in this fund. Except as otherwise provided in this section, if funds remain in this fund after appropriation by the Legislature and allocation for the costs associated with narcotic treatment licensure actions and inspection of narcotic treatment programs, a percentage of the excess funds shall be annually rebated to the licensees based on the percentage their licensing fee is of the total amount of fees collected by the department. A reserve equal to 10 percent of the total licensure fees collected during the preceding fiscal year may be held in each trust account to reimburse the department if the actual cost for the licensure and inspection exceed fees collected during a fiscal year.

(d) Notwithstanding any provision of this code or regulations to the contrary, the department shall have sole responsibility and authority for determining if a state narcotic treatment program license shall be granted and for administratively establishing the maximum treatment capacity of a license. However, the department shall not increase the capacity of a program unless it determines that the licensee is operating in full compliance with applicable laws and regulations.

(Amended by Stats. 2017, Ch. 223, Sec. 4. (AB 395) Effective January 1, 2018.)

11839.4.

The department shall impose a civil penalty of one hundred dollars ($100) per day for a program that fails to timely submit a corrective action plan, or to timely implement any corrective action when it has been found to not be in compliance with applicable laws and regulations as required in Section 11839.3.

(Added by Stats. 2004, Ch. 862, Sec. 114. Effective January 1, 2005.)

11839.5.

In addition to the duties authorized by other provisions, the department shall be responsible for licensing narcotic treatment programs to use narcotic replacement therapy and medication-assisted treatment in the treatment of addicted persons whose addiction was acquired or supported by the use of alcohol or a narcotic drug or drugs, not in compliance with a physician and surgeon's legal prescription. No narcotic treatment program shall be authorized to use narcotic replacement therapy and medication-assisted treatment without first obtaining a license as a narcotic treatment program as provided in this chapter. The department may license narcotic treatment programs on an inpatient or outpatient basis, or both. The department may also grant a state narcotic treatment license.

(Amended by Stats. 2017, Ch. 223, Sec. 5. (AB 395) Effective January 1, 2018.)

11839.6.

(a) The department shall establish a program for the operation and regulation of office-based narcotic treatment programs. An office-based narcotic treatment program established pursuant to this section shall meet either of the following conditions:

(1) Hold a primary narcotic treatment program license.

(2) Be affiliated and associated with a primary licensed narcotic treatment program. An office-based narcotic treatment program meeting the requirement of this paragraph shall not be required to have a license separate from the primary licensed narcotic treatment program with which it is affiliated and associated.

(b) For purposes of this section, "office-based narcotic treatment program" means a program in which interested and knowledgeable physicians and surgeons provide addiction treatment services, and in which community pharmacies or medication units supply necessary medication both to these physicians and surgeons for distribution to patients and through direct administration and specified dispensing services.

(c) Notwithstanding any other law or regulation, including Section 10020 of Title 9 of the California Code of Regulations, an office-based narcotic treatment program in a remote site that is affiliated and associated with a licensed narcotic treatment program may be approved by the department, if all of the following conditions are met:

(1) A physician may provide office-based addiction services only if each office-based patient is registered as a patient in the licensed narcotic treatment program and both the licensed narcotic treatment program and the office-based narcotic treatment program ensure that all services required under Chapter 4 (commencing with Section 10000) of Division 4 of Title 9 of the California Code of Regulations for the management of narcotic addiction are provided to all patients treated in the remote site.

(2) A physician in an office-based narcotic treatment program may provide treatment for an appropriate number of patients under the appropriate United States Drug Enforcement Administration registration. The primary licensed narcotic treatment program shall be limited to its total licensed capacity as established by the department, including the patients of physicians in the office-based narcotic treatment program.

(3) The physicians in the office-based narcotic treatment program shall dispense or administer pharmacologic treatments for narcotic addiction or a substance use disorder that have been approved by the federal Food and Drug Administration for the purpose of narcotic replacement therapy or medication-assisted treatment of substance use disorders.

(4) Office-based narcotic treatment programs, in conjunction with primary licensed narcotic treatment programs, shall develop protocols to prevent the diversion of medication. The department may develop regulations to prevent the diversion of medication.

(d) For purposes of this section, "remote site" means a site that is geographically or physically isolated from any licensed narcotic treatment program. Therefore, the requirements in this subdivision regarding a remote site do not apply to an office-based narcotic treatment program that holds a primary narcotic treatment program license.

(e) In considering an office-based narcotic treatment program application, the department shall independently weigh the treatment needs and concerns of the county, city, or areas to be served by the program.

(f) Nothing in this section is intended to expand the scope of the practice of pharmacy.
(Amended by Stats. 2017, Ch. 223, Sec. 6. (AB 395) Effective January 1, 2018.)

11839.7.

(a) (1) Each narcotic treatment program authorized to use narcotic replacement therapy in this state, except narcotic treatment research programs approved by the Research Advisory Panel, shall be licensed by the department.

(2) Each narcotic treatment program, other than a program owned and operated by the state, county, city, or city and county, shall, upon application for licensure and for renewal of a license, pay an annual license fee to the department. July 1 shall be the annual license renewal date.

(3) The department shall set the licensing fee at a level sufficient to cover all departmental costs associated with licensing incurred by the department, but the fee shall not, except as specified in this section, increase at a rate greater than the Consumer Price Index. The fees shall include the department's share of pro rata charges for the expenses of state government. The fee may be paid quarterly in arrears as determined by the department. Fees paid quarterly in arrears shall be due and payable on the last day of each quarter except for the fourth quarter for which payment shall be due and payable no later than May 31. A failure of a program to pay renewal license fees by the due date shall give rise to a civil penalty of one hundred dollars ($100) a day for each day after the due date. Second and subsequent inspection visits to narcotic treatment programs that are operating in noncompliance with the applicable laws and regulations shall be charged a rate of one-half the program's annual license fee or one thousand dollars ($1,000), whichever is less, for each visit.

(4) Licensing shall be contingent upon determination by the department that the program is in compliance with applicable laws and regulations and upon payment of the licensing fee. A license shall not be transferable.

(5) (A) As used in this chapter, "quarter" means July, August, and September; October, November, and December; January, February, and March; and April, May, and June.
(B) As used in this chapter, "license" means a basic permit to operate a narcotic treatment program. The license shall be issued exclusively by the department and operated in accordance with a patient capacity that shall be specified, approved, and monitored solely by the department.

(b) Each narcotic treatment program, other than a program owned and operated by the state, county, city, or city and county, shall be charged an application fee that shall be at a level sufficient to cover all departmental costs incurred by the department in processing either an application for a new program license, or an application for an existing program that has moved to a new location.

(c) Any licensee that increases fees to the patient, in response to increases in licensure fees required by the department, shall first provide written disclosure to the patient of that amount of the patient fee increase that is attributable to the increase in the licensure fee. This provision shall not be construed to limit patient fee increases imposed by the licensee upon any other basis.
(Amended by Stats. 2013, Ch. 22, Sec. 51. (AB 75) Effective June 27, 2013. Operative July 1, 2013, by Sec. 110 of Ch. 22.)

11839.8.

The director may deny the application for initial issuance of a license if the applicant or any partner, officer, director, 10 percent or greater shareholder, or person proposed to be employed by the applicant under the authority of subdivision (c) of Section 2401 of the Business and Professions Code:

(a) Fails to meet the qualifications for licensure established by the department pursuant to this article. However, the director may waive any established qualification for licensure of a narcotic treatment program if he or she determines that it is reasonably necessary in the interests of the public health and welfare.

(b) Was previously the holder of a license issued under this article, and the license was revoked and never reissued or was suspended and not reinstated, or the holder failed to adhere to applicable laws and regulations regarding narcotic treatment programs while the license was in effect.

(c) Misrepresented any material fact in the application.

(d) Committed any act involving fraud, dishonesty, or deceit, with the intent to substantially benefit himself or herself or another or substantially injure another, and the act is substantially related to the qualification, functions, or duties of, or relating to, a narcotic treatment program license.

(e) Was convicted of any crime substantially related to the qualifications, functions, or duties of, or relating to, a narcotic treatment program license.

(f) The director, in considering whether to deny licensure under subdivision (d) or (e), shall determine whether the applicant is rehabilitated after considering all of the following criteria:

(1) The nature and severity of the act or crime.

(2) The time that has elapsed since the commission of the act or crime.

(3) The commission by the applicant of other acts or crimes constituting grounds for denial of the license under this section.

(4) The extent to which the applicant has complied with terms of restitution, probation, parole, or any other sanction or order lawfully imposed against the applicant.

(5) Other evidence of rehabilitation submitted by the applicant.

(g) With respect to any other license issued to an applicant to provide narcotic treatment services, violated any provision of this article or regulations adopted under this article that relate to the health and safety of patients, the local community, or the general public. Violations include, but are not limited to, violations of laws and regulations applicable to take-home doses of methadone, urinalysis requirements, and security against redistribution of replacement narcotic drugs. In these cases, the department shall deny the application for an initial license unless the department determines that all other licensed narcotic treatment programs maintained by the applicant have corrected all deficiencies and maintained compliance for a minimum of six months.
(Added by Stats. 2004, Ch. 862, Sec. 114. Effective January 1, 2005.)

11839.9.

(a) The director shall suspend or revoke any license issued under this article, or deny an application to renew a license or to modify the terms and conditions of a license, upon any violation by the licensee of this article or regulations adopted under this article that presents an imminent danger of death or severe harm to any participant of the program or a member of the general public.

(b) The director may suspend or revoke any license issued under this article, or deny an application to renew a license or to modify the terms and conditions of a license, upon any of the following grounds and in the manner provided in this article:

(1) Violation by the licensee of any laws or regulations of the Substance Abuse and Mental Health Services Administration or the United States Department of Justice, Drug Enforcement Administration, that are applicable to narcotic treatment programs.

(2) Any violation that relates to the operation or maintenance of the program that has an immediate relationship to the physical health, mental health, or safety of the program participants or general public.

(3) Aiding, abetting, or permitting the violation of, or any repeated violation of, any of the provisions set forth in subdivision (a) or in paragraph (1) or (2).

(4) Conduct in the operation of a narcotic treatment program that is inimical to the health, welfare, or safety of an individual in, or receiving services from, the program, the local community, or the people of the State of California.

(5) The conviction of the licensee or any partner, officer, director, 10 percent or greater shareholder, or person employed under the authority of subdivision (c) of Section 2401 of the Business and Professions Code at any time during licensure, of a crime substantially related to the qualifications, functions, or duties of, or relating to, a narcotic treatment program licensee.

(6) The commission by the licensee or any partner, officer, director, 10 percent or greater shareholder, or person employed under the authority of subdivision (c) of Section 2401 of the Business and Professions Code at any time during licensure, of any act involving fraud, dishonesty, or deceit, with the intent to substantially benefit himself or herself or another, or substantially to injure another, and that act is substantially related to the qualifications, functions, or duties of, or relating to, a narcotic treatment program licensee.

(7) Diversion of narcotic drugs. A program's failure to maintain a narcotic drug reconciliation system that accounts for all incoming and outgoing narcotic drugs, as required by departmental or federal regulations, shall create a rebuttable presumption that narcotic drugs are being diverted.

(8) Misrepresentation of any material fact in obtaining the narcotic treatment program license.

(9) Failure to comply with a department order to cease admitting patients or to cease providing patients with take-home dosages of narcotic replacement drugs.

(10) Failure to pay any civil penalty assessed pursuant to paragraph (3) of subdivision (a) of Section 11839.16 where the penalty has become final, unless payment arrangements acceptable to the department have been made.

(11) The suspension or exclusion of the licensee or any partner, officer, director, 10 percent or greater shareholder, or person employed under the authority of subdivision

(c) of Section 2401 of the Business and Professions Code from the Medicare, medicaid, or Medi-Cal programs.

(c) Prior to issuing an order pursuant to this section, the director shall ensure continuity of patient care by the program's guarantor or through the transfer of patients to other licensed programs. The director may issue any needed license or amend any other license in an effort to ensure that patient care is not impacted adversely by an order issued pursuant to this section.

(Amended by Stats. 2013, Ch. 22, Sec. 52. (AB 75) Effective June 27, 2013. Operative July 1, 2013, by Sec. 110 of Ch. 22.)

11839.10.

(a) The department shall cease review of an application for a license if either of the following occur:

(1) An application for a license indicates, or the department determines during the application inspection process, that the applicant was issued a license under this article and the prior license was revoked within the preceding two years. The department shall cease any further review of the application until two years have elapsed from the date of the revocation.

(2) An application for a license indicates, or the department determines during the application inspection process, that the applicant was denied a license or had a license suspended under this article within the preceding year. The department shall cease any further review of the application until one year has elapsed from the date of the denial or suspension.

(b) The department may cease review of an application for license renewal if either of the following occur:

(1) The applicant has not paid the required license fee.

(2) The county in which the licensee is located certifies to the department's satisfaction that there is no need for the narcotic treatment program because of a substantial decline in medically qualified narcotic treatment patients in the licensee's catchment area, or clearly demonstrates that other applicants for licensure can provide more efficient, cost-effective, and sufficient narcotic treatment services in the catchment area, or that the license should not be renewed due to one of the grounds that are enumerated in Section 11839.9.

(c) Upon cessation of review, the license shall be permitted to expire by its own terms. However, if the licensee subsequently submits the items, the absence of which led to the cessation of review, the department may reinstate the license.

(d) Cessation of review shall not constitute a denial of the application for purposes of Sections 11839.8 and 11839.9.

(Added by Stats. 2004, Ch. 862, Sec. 114. Effective January 1, 2005.)

11839.11.

A narcotic treatment program license shall automatically terminate if the Substance Abuse and Mental Health Services Administration withdraws or revokes its approval of the program, or if the United States Department of Justice, Drug Enforcement Administration, revokes the program's registration.

(Added by Stats. 2004, Ch. 862, Sec. 114. Effective January 1, 2005.)

11839.12.

Except as provided in Section 11839.16, proceedings for the suspension, revocation, or denial of a license or cessation of review of a renewal license under this article, except where there has been a failure to pay required fees, under this article shall be conducted in accordance with Chapter 5 (commencing with Section 11500) of Part 1 of Division 3 of Title 2 of the Government Code and the department shall have all the powers granted thereby. In the event of conflict between this article and the Administrative Procedure Act, the Administrative Procedure Act shall prevail.

(Added by Stats. 2004, Ch. 862, Sec. 114. Effective January 1, 2005.)

11839.13.

(a) The withdrawal of an application for a license after it has been filed with the department shall not, unless the department consents in writing to the withdrawal, deprive the department of its authority to institute or continue a proceeding against the applicant for the denial of the license upon any ground provided by law or to enter an order denying the license upon any ground provided by law.

(b) The suspension, expiration, or forfeiture by operation of law of a license issued by the department, or its suspension, forfeiture, or cancellation by order of the department or by order of a court of law, or its surrender without the written consent of the department, shall not deprive the department of its authority to institute or continue a disciplinary proceeding against the licensee upon any ground provided by law or to enter an order suspending or revoking the license or otherwise taking disciplinary action against the licensee upon any ground provided by law.

(Added by Stats. 2004, Ch. 862, Sec. 114. Effective January 1, 2005.)

11839.14.

For purposes of this article, a conviction means a plea or verdict of guilty or a conviction following a plea of nolo contendere. Any action that the department is permitted to take following the establishment of a conviction may be taken when the time for appeal has elapsed, or the judgment of conviction has been affirmed on appeal or when an order granting probation is made suspending the imposition of sentence, notwithstanding a subsequent order pursuant to Section 1203.4 or 1203.4a of the Penal Code permitting the person to withdraw his or her plea of guilty and to enter a plea of not guilty, or setting aside the verdict of guilty, or dismissing the accusation, information, or indictment. For purposes of this article, the record of conviction, or a certified copy thereof, shall be conclusive evidence of the conviction.

(Added by Stats. 2004, Ch. 862, Sec. 114. Effective January 1, 2005.)

11839.15.

The director may bring an action to enjoin the violation of Section 11839.7, or the violation of a departmental order issued pursuant to Section 11839.16, in the superior court in and for the county in which the violation occurred. Any proceeding under this section shall conform to the requirements of Chapter 3 (commencing with Section 525) of Title 7 of Part 2 of the Code of Civil Procedure. The rebuttable presumption set forth in paragraph (7) of subdivision (b) of Section 11839.9 shall be applicable. If the court finds the allegations to be true, it shall issue its order enjoining the narcotic treatment program from continuance of the violation.

(Added by Stats. 2004, Ch. 862, Sec. 114. Effective January 1, 2005.)

11839.16.

(a) (1) The director shall, in addition to any other remedy, issue an order that prohibits a narcotic treatment program from admitting new patients or from providing patients with take-home dosages of a narcotic drug if the director determines, pursuant to the compliance inspection procedures set out in paragraph (2) of subdivision (a) of Section 11839.3, that a program has done any of the following:

(A) Failed to provide adequate security measures over its narcotic drug supply as agreed in the program's approved protocol.

(B) Failed to maintain a narcotic drug reconciliation system that accounts for all incoming and outgoing narcotic drugs.

(C) Diverted narcotic drugs.

(D) Repeatedly violated one or more departmental or federal regulations governing narcotic treatment programs, which violations may subject, or may have subjected, a patient to a health or life-endangering situation.

(E) Repeatedly violated one or more departmental or federal regulations governing the provisions of take-home medication.

(F) Operated above combined licensed capacity for maintenance and detoxification programs at a single location.

(2) (A) The order becomes effective when the department serves the program with a copy of the order. The order shall state the deficiencies forming the basis for the order and shall state the corrective action required for the department to vacate the order. The order, as it pertains to subparagraph (F) only, shall automatically be vacated when the department receives the program's written notification that licensed capacity has been achieved. If the order is issued pursuant to subparagraph (A), (B), (C), (D), or (E), the department shall vacate the order when the program submits a corrective action plan that reasonably addresses the deficiency or substantially conforms to the required action set out in the order.

(B) The department shall notify the program that the corrective action plan is accepted or rejected within 10 working days after receipt of the plan. If the department rejects the corrective action plan, it shall detail its reason in writing. The department order is vacated when the department either accepts a corrective action plan and ensures substantial conformity with the required action set out in the order or fails to reject a plan within 10 working days after receipt of the plan.

(3) In addition to any other remedies, a failure of the program to comply with the order of the department under this subdivision shall give rise to a civil penalty of five hundred dollars ($500) a day for each day that the order is violated.

(4) All civil penalties collected by the department under paragraph (3) shall be deposited in the Narcotic Treatment Program Licensing Trust Fund, and shall be used to offset the department's costs associated with collecting the civil penalties, or associated with any civil, administrative, or criminal action against the program when appropriated for this purpose.

(b) (1) The director may, in addition to any other remedy, issue an order temporarily suspending a narcotic treatment program license prior to any administrative hearing for the reasons stated in subparagraphs (A) to (E), inclusive, of paragraph (1) of subdivision (a) when the department determines pursuant to the compliance inspection procedures set out in paragraph (2) of subdivision (a) of Section 11839.3, that the action is necessary to protect patients of the program from any substantial threat to their health or safety, or to protect the health or safety of the local community or the people of the State of California. Prior to issuing the order, the director shall ensure continuity of patient care by the program's guarantor or through the transfer of patients to other licensed programs. The director may issue any needed license or amend any other license in his or her effort to assure that patient care is not impacted adversely by the suspension order.

(2) The director shall notify the licensee of the temporary suspension and the effective date thereof and at the same time shall serve the licensee with an accusation. Upon receipt of a notice of defense to the accusation by the licensee, the director shall, within 15 days, set the matter for hearing, and the hearing shall be held as soon as possible, but not later than 20 days, exclusive of weekends, after receipt of the notice. The temporary suspension shall remain in effect until the hearing is completed and the director has made a final determination on the merits. However, the temporary suspension shall be deemed vacated if the director fails to make a final determination on the merits within 20 days after the original hearing has been completed. Failure to cease operating after the department issues an order temporarily suspending the license shall constitute an additional ground for license revocation and shall constitute a violation of Section 11839.8. The department shall suspend the program's license if the hearing outcome is adverse to the license. The department shall notify the program of the license suspension within five days of the director's final decision.

(c) A program may, at any time after it is served with an order, petition the superior court to review the department's issuance of an order or rejection of a corrective action plan.

(Added by Stats. 2004, Ch. 862, Sec. 114. Effective January 1, 2005.)

11839.17.

(a) In cases where a program is closing and the licensed entity that has agreed to assume temporary operation of the closing program is unable to do so, the department may assume temporary operation of the closing program or designate another licensed entity willing to do so. In cases where the licensed entity that has agreed to assume temporary operation is the subject of a pending licensing action or order issued pursuant to Section 11839.16, the department may issue an order prohibiting the entity from assuming temporary operation and may assume temporary operation of the closing program or designate another licensed entity willing to do so. This section shall not be construed to require the department or any other licensed entity to assume any of the closing programs' financial obligations.

(b) For purposes of this section, "temporary" means no more than 90 days.

(Added by Stats. 2004, Ch. 862, Sec. 114. Effective January 1, 2005.)

11839.18.

Any licensee may petition the director for waiver of licensure fees or late payment penalties for the current fiscal year based upon financial hardship. Prior to the granting of relief, the licensee shall demonstrate hardship by production of appropriate financial records. The director may, in his or her discretion, grant all or part of the relief sought, but shall consider the reasonableness of the relief in light of the other expenditures undertaken by the licensee, giving particular scrutiny to the licensee's own profits, earnings, or other compensation, and expenses such as interest, mortgage, or loan payments, as well as noncash expenses such as accruals and depreciation.

(Added by Stats. 2004, Ch. 862, Sec. 114. Effective January 1, 2005.)

11839.19.

(a) The department shall not license the establishment of a narcotic treatment program without a written application by the treatment facility that meets evaluative criteria required by the department.

(b) The department shall not require disclosure of the identity of patients or former patients or of any records containing identifying information except as provided in Section 11845.5.

(Added by Stats. 2004, Ch. 862, Sec. 114. Effective January 1, 2005.)

11839.20.

(a) It is the intent of the Legislature in licensing narcotic treatment programs to provide a means whereby the patient may be rehabilitated and will no longer need to support a dependency on opiates.

(b) It is the intent of the Legislature that each narcotic treatment program shall have a strong rehabilitative element, including, but not limited to, individual and group therapy, counseling, vocational guidance, and job and education counseling.

(c) The Legislature declares the ultimate goal of all narcotic treatment programs shall be to aid the patient in altering his or her lifestyle and eventually to eliminate the improper use of legal drugs and the use of illicit drugs.

(d) The department shall adopt any regulations necessary to ensure that every program is making a sustained effort to end the drug dependency of the patients.

(Amended by Stats. 2005, Ch. 616, Sec. 3. Effective October 6, 2005.)

11839.21.

The State Department of Health Services shall establish criteria for acceptable performance from those laboratories performing urinalysis or other body fluid analysis and shall not permit utilization of laboratories unable to meet an acceptable level of performance. The results of any performance evaluation of any laboratory shall immediately be made available to the local programs upon request. Nothing in this section shall prohibit body fluid analysis to be performed by a licensed narcotic treatment program upon approval of the State Department of Health Services.

(Added by Stats. 2004, Ch. 862, Sec. 114. Effective January 1, 2005.)

11839.22.

The state department shall require a system to detect multiple registrations by narcotic treatment program patients.

(Amended by Stats. 2014, Ch. 484, Sec. 2. (SB 973) Effective January 1, 2015.)

ARTICLE 2. Narcotic Treatment Program Body Fluids Testing [11839.23 - 11839.34]

(Article 2 added by Stats. 2004, Ch. 862, Sec. 114.)

11839.23.

The State Department of Health Services shall adopt and publish rules and regulations to be used in approving and governing the operation of laboratories engaging in the performance of tests referred to in Section 11839.24, including, but not limited to, the qualifications of the laboratory employees who perform the tests, which qualifications the department determines are reasonably necessary to ensure the competence of the laboratories and employees to prepare, analyze, and report the results of the tests.

(Added by Stats. 2004, Ch. 862, Sec. 114. Effective January 1, 2005.)

11839.24.

Substance abuse testing for narcotic treatment programs operating in the state shall be performed only by a laboratory approved and licensed by the State Department of Public Health for the performance of those tests.

(Amended by Stats. 2014, Ch. 484, Sec. 3. (SB 973) Effective January 1, 2015.)

11839.25.

Each laboratory in this state that performs the test referred to in Section 11839.24 shall be licensed by the State Director of Health Services. The laboratory, other than a laboratory operated by the state, county, city, city and county, or other public agency, or a clinical laboratory licensed pursuant to subdivision (f) of Section 1300 of the Business and Professions Code, shall, upon application for licensing, pay a fee to the State Department of Health Services in an amount to be determined by that department, which fee will reimburse the department for the costs incurred by the department in the

issuance and renewal of the licenses. On or before July 1 of each year thereafter, the laboratory shall pay to the State Department of Health Services a fee, determined by the department, for the renewal of its license.

(Added by Stats. 2004, Ch. 862, Sec. 114. Effective January 1, 2005.)

11839.26.

The State Department of Health Care Services shall enforce this article and the rules and regulations adopted pursuant to this article.

(Amended by Stats. 2013, Ch. 22, Sec. 53. (AB 75) Effective June 27, 2013. Operative July 1, 2013, by Sec. 110 of Ch. 22.)

11839.27.

The State Department of Health Services shall annually publish a list of approved and licensed laboratories engaging in the performance of tests referred to in Section 11839.24.

(Added by Stats. 2004, Ch. 862, Sec. 114. Effective January 1, 2005.)

11839.28.

Every laboratory that has been approved and for which a license has been issued shall be periodically inspected by a duly authorized representative of the State Department of Health Services. Reports of this inspection shall be prepared by the representative conducting it upon forms prepared and furnished by the State Department of Health Services and shall be filed with that department.

(Added by Stats. 2004, Ch. 862, Sec. 114. Effective January 1, 2005.)

11839.29.

Any license issued pursuant to Section 11839.25 may be suspended or revoked by the State Director of Health Services. The State Director of Health Services may refuse to issue a license to any applicant. Any proceedings under this article shall be conducted in accordance with Chapter 5 (commencing with Section 11500) of Part 1 of Division 3 of Title 2 of the Government Code, and the State Director of Health Services shall have the powers and duties granted therein.

(Added by Stats. 2004, Ch. 862, Sec. 114. Effective January 1, 2005.)

11839.30.

The State Director of Health Services may deny a license if any of the following apply to the applicant, or any partner, officer, or director thereof:

(a) The person fails to meet the qualifications established by the State Department of Health Services pursuant to this chapter for the issuance of the license applied for.

(b) The person was previously the holder of a license issued under this chapter, which license has been revoked and never reissued or was suspended and the terms of the suspension have not been fulfilled.

(c) The person has committed any act involving dishonesty, fraud, or deceit, whereby another was injured or whereby the applicant has benefited.

(Added by Stats. 2004, Ch. 862, Sec. 114. Effective January 1, 2005.)

11839.31.

The State Director of Health Services may suspend, revoke, or take other disciplinary action against a licensee as provided in this chapter, if the licensee or any partner, officer, or director thereof does any of the following:

(a) Violates any of the regulations promulgated by the State Department of Health Services pursuant to this article.

(b) Commits any act of dishonesty, fraud or deceit, whereby another is injured or whereby the licensee benefited.

(c) Misrepresents any material fact in obtaining a license.

(Added by Stats. 2004, Ch. 862, Sec. 114. Effective January 1, 2005.)

11839.32.

The State Director of Health Services may take disciplinary action against any licensee after a hearing as provided in this article by any of the following:

(a) Imposing probation upon terms and conditions to be set forth by the State Director of Health Services.

(b) Suspending the license.

(c) Revoking the license.

(Added by Stats. 2004, Ch. 862, Sec. 114. Effective January 1, 2005.)

11839.33.

All accusations against licensees shall be filed within three years after the act or omission alleged as the ground for disciplinary action, except that with respect to an accusation alleging a violation of subdivision (c) of Section 11839.31, the accusation shall be filed within two years after the discovery by the State Department of Health Services of the alleged facts constituting the fraud or misrepresentation prohibited by that section.

(Added by Stats. 2004, Ch. 862, Sec. 114. Effective January 1, 2005.)

11839.34.

After suspension or revocation of the license upon any of the grounds set forth in this article, the license shall not be reinstated or reissued within a period of one year after the effective date of suspension or revocation. After one year after the effective date of the suspension or revocation, the State Department of Health Services may reinstate the license upon proof of compliance by the applicant with all provisions of the decision as to reinstatement.

(Added by Stats. 2004, Ch. 862, Sec. 114. Effective January 1, 2005.)

CHAPTER 11. General Financial Provisions [11841- 11841.]

(Heading of Chapter 11 renumbered from Chapter 10 by Stats. 2004, Ch. 862, Sec. 115.)

(Heading of Article 3 renumbered from Article 2 by Stats. 1984, Ch. 1328, Sec. 80.)

11841.

(a) It is the intent of the Legislature that all programs funded under this part shall be partially self-supporting by raising revenues in addition to the funds allocated by the department. These revenues may include, but are not limited to, fees for services, private contributions, grants, or other governmental funds. These revenues shall be used in support of additional alcohol and other drug services or facilities.

(b) Each program funded under this part, which program provides alcohol and other drug services to individuals and their families, shall assess fees to participants in the programs. The fee requirement shall not apply to prevention and early intervention activities.

(c) Each county shall identify in its annual cost report the types and amounts of revenues raised by all the providers of services funded under this part.

(Amended by Stats. 2004, Ch. 862, Sec. 118. Effective January 1, 2005.)

CHAPTER 12. Registration of Narcotic, Alcohol, and Other Drug Abuse Programs [11842 - 11845.5]

(Chapter 12 added by Stats. 2004, Ch. 862, Sec. 119.)

11842.

As used in this chapter, "narcotic and drug abuse program" means any program that provides any service of care, treatment, rehabilitation, counseling, vocational training, self-improvement classes or courses, narcotic replacement therapy in maintenance or detoxification treatment, or other medication services for detoxification and treatment, and any other services that are provided either public or private, whether free of charge or for compensation, which services are intended in any way to alleviate the problems of narcotic addiction or habituation or drug abuse addiction or habituation or any problems in whole or in part related to the problem of narcotics addiction or drug abuse, or any combination of these problems.

(Amended by Stats. 2013, Ch. 22, Sec. 54. (AB 75) Effective June 27, 2013. Operative July 1, 2013, by Sec. 110 of Ch. 22.)

11842.5.

As used in this chapter, an alcohol and other drug abuse program includes, but is not limited to:

(a) Residential programs that provide a residential setting and services such as detoxification, counseling, care, treatment, and rehabilitation in a live-in facility.

(b) Drop-in centers that are established for the purpose of providing counseling, advice, or a social setting for one or more persons who are attempting to understand, alleviate, or cope with their problems of alcohol and other drug abuse.

(c) Crisis lines that provide a telephone answering service that provides, in whole or in part, crisis intervention, counseling, or referral, or that is a source of general drug abuse information.

(d) Free clinics that are established for the purpose, either in whole or in part, of providing any medical or dental care, social services, or treatment, or referral to these services for those persons recognized as having a problem of narcotics addiction or drug abuse. Free clinics include primary care clinics licensed under paragraph (2) of subdivision (a) of Section 1204.

(e) Detoxification centers that are established for the purpose of detoxification from drugs, regardless of whether or not narcotics, restricted dangerous drugs, or other medications are administered in the detoxification and whether detoxification takes place in a live-in facility or on an outpatient basis.

(f) Narcotic treatment programs, whether inpatient or outpatient, that offer narcotic replacement therapy and maintenance, detoxification, or other services, in conjunction with that replacement narcotic therapy.

(g) Chemical dependency programs, whether inpatient or outpatient and whether in a hospital or nonhospital setting, that offer a set program of treatment and rehabilitation for persons with a chemical dependency that is not primarily an alcohol dependency.

(h) Alcohol and other drug prevention programs that promote positive action that changes the conditions under which the drug-taking behaviors to be prevented are most likely to occur and a proactive and deliberate process that promotes health and well-being by empowering people and communities with resources necessary to confront complex and stressful life conditions.

(i) Nonspecific drug programs that have not been specifically mentioned in subdivisions (a) to (h), inclusive, but that provide or offer to provide, in whole or in part, for counseling, therapy, referral, advice, care, treatment, or rehabilitation as a service to those persons suffering from alcohol and other drug addiction, or alcohol and other drug abuse related problems that are either physiological or psychological in nature.

(Amended by Stats. 2013, Ch. 22, Sec. 55. (AB 75) Effective June 27, 2013. Operative July 1, 2013, by Sec. 110 of Ch. 22.)

11843.

The county shall establish and maintain a registry of all narcotic and drug abuse programs and alcohol and other drug abuse programs within the county in order to promote a coordination of effort in the county.

(Added by Stats. 2004, Ch. 862, Sec. 119. Effective January 1, 2005.)

11843.5.

Each narcotic and drug abuse program and alcohol and other drug abuse program in a county shall register annually with the county alcohol and drug program administrator by July 1 or within 30 days after being established.

(Added by Stats. 2004, Ch. 862, Sec. 119. Effective January 1, 2005.)

11845.5.

(a) The identity and records of the identity, diagnosis. prognosis, or treatment of any patient, which identity and records are maintained in connection with the performance of any alcohol and other drug abuse treatment or prevention effort or function conducted, regulated, or directly or indirectly assisted by the department shall, except as provided in subdivision (c), be confidential and be disclosed only for the purposes and under the circumstances expressly authorized under subdivision (b).

(b) The content of any records referred to in subdivision (a) may be disclosed in accordance with the prior written consent of the client with respect to whom the record is maintained, but only to the extent, under the circumstances, and for the purposes as clearly stated in the release of information signed by the client.

(c) Whether or not the client, with respect to whom any given record referred to in subdivision (a) is maintained, gives his or her written consent, the content of the record may be disclosed as follows:

(1) In communications between qualified professional persons employed by the treatment or prevention program in the provision of service.

(2) To qualified medical persons not employed by the treatment program to the extent necessary to meet a bona fide medical emergency.

(3) To qualified personnel for the purpose of conducting scientific research, management audits, financial and compliance audits, or program evaluation, but the personnel may not identify, directly or indirectly, any individual client in any report of the research, audit, or evaluation, or otherwise disclose patient identities in any manner. For purposes of this paragraph, the term "qualified personnel" means persons whose training and experience are appropriate to the nature and level of work in which they are engaged, and who, when working as part of an organization, are performing that work with adequate administrative safeguards against unauthorized disclosures.

(4) If the recipient of services is a minor, ward, or conservatee, and his or her parent, guardian, or conservator designates, in writing, persons to whom his or her identity in records or information may be disclosed, except that nothing in this section shall be construed to compel a physician and surgeon, psychologist, social worker, nurse, attorney, or other professional person to reveal information that has been given to him or her in confidence by members of the client's family.

(5) If authorized by a court of competent jurisdiction granted after application showing probable cause therefor, as provided in subdivision (c) of Section 1524 of the Penal Code.

(d) Except as authorized by a court order granted under paragraph (5) of subdivision (c), no record referred to in subdivision (a) may be used to initiate or substantiate any criminal charges against a client or to conduct any investigation of a client.

(e) The prohibitions of this section shall continue to apply to records concerning any individual who has been a client, irrespective of whether he or she ceases to be a client.

(Added by Stats. 2004, Ch. 862, Sec. 119. Effective January 1, 2005.)

CHAPTER 13. Narcotic and Alcohol and Other Drug Abuse Programs [11847 - 11856.5]

(Chapter 13 added by Stats. 2004, Ch. 862, Sec. 120.)

11847.

The Legislature hereby finds and declares that it is essential to the health and welfare of the people of this state that action be taken by state government to effectively and economically utilize federal and state funds for narcotic and alcohol and other drug abuse prevention, care, treatment, and rehabilitation services. To achieve this, it is necessary that all of the following occur:

(a) Existing fragmented, uncoordinated, and duplicative narcotic and alcohol and other drug abuse programs be molded into a comprehensive and integrated statewide program for the prevention of narcotic and alcohol and other drug abuse and for the care, treatment, and rehabilitation of narcotic addicts and alcohol and other drug users.

(b) Responsibility and authority for planning programs and activities for prevention, care, treatment, and rehabilitation of narcotic addicts be concentrated in the department. It is the intent of the Legislature to assign responsibility and grant authority for planning narcotic and alcoholic and other drug abuse prevention, care, treatment, and rehabilitation programs to the department whose functions shall be subject to periodic review by the Legislature and appropriate federal agencies.

(c) The department succeeds to, and is vested with, all the duties, powers, purposes, responsibilities, and jurisdiction with regard to substance abuse formerly vested in the State Department of Alcohol and Drug Programs.

(Amended by Stats. 2013, Ch. 22, Sec. 59. (AB 75) Effective June 27, 2013. Operative July 1, 2013, by Sec. 110 of Ch. 22.)

11847.1.

The department shall consult with state and local health planning bodies and encourage and promote effective use of facilities, resources, and funds in the development of integrated, comprehensive local programs for the prevention, care, treatment, and rehabilitation of narcotic and alcohol and other drug abuse.

(Added by Stats. 2004, Ch. 862, Sec. 120. Effective January 1, 2005.)

11847.2.

Any community alcohol and other drug abuse service may by contract furnish community alcohol and other drug abuse services to any other county.

(Added by Stats. 2004, Ch. 862, Sec. 120. Effective January 1, 2005.)

11847.3.

The department shall, within available resources, consult with federal, state and local agencies involved in the provision and delivery of services of prevention, care, treatment, and rehabilitation of alcohol and other drug abusers.

(Added by Stats. 2004, Ch. 862, Sec. 120. Effective January 1, 2005.)

11847.4.

The department shall provide technical assistance, guidance, and information to local governments and state agencies with respect to the creation and implementation of programs and procedures for dealing effectively with alcohol and other drug abuse prevention, care, treatment, and rehabilitation. The department may charge a fee for these services.

(Added by Stats. 2004, Ch. 862, Sec. 120. Effective January 1, 2005.)

11847.5.

The department shall establish goals and priorities for all state agencies providing narcotic and alcohol and other drug abuse services. All state governmental units operating alcohol and other drug programs or administering or subventing state or federal funds for alcohol and other drug programs shall annually set their program priorities and allocate funds in coordination with the department.

(Added by Stats. 2004, Ch. 862, Sec. 120. Effective January 1, 2005.)

11847.6.

The department shall, in the same manner and subject to the same conditions as other state agencies, develop and submit annually to the Department of Finance a program budget.

(Added by Stats. 2004, Ch. 862, Sec. 120. Effective January 1, 2005.)

11848.5.

(a) Once the negotiated rate with service providers has been approved by the county, all participating governmental funding sources, except the Medi-Cal program (Chapter 7 (commencing with Section 14000) of Part 3 of Division 9 of the Welfare and Institutions Code), shall be bound to that rate as the cost of providing all or part of the total county alcohol and other drug program as described in the county contract for each fiscal year to the extent that the governmental funding sources participate in funding the county alcohol and other drug program. Where the State Department of Health Services adopts regulations for determining reimbursement of alcohol and other drug program services formerly allowable under the Short-Doyle program and reimbursed under the Medi-Cal Act, those regulations shall be controlling only as to the rates for reimbursement of alcohol and other drug program services allowable under the Medi-Cal program and rendered to Medi-Cal beneficiaries. Providers under this section shall report to the department and the county any information required by the department in accordance with the procedures established by the director of the department.

(b) The Legislature recognizes that alcohol and other drug abuse services differ from mental health services provided through the State Department of Health Care Services and therefore should not necessarily be bound by rate determination methodology used for reimbursement of those services formerly provided under the Short-Doyle program and reimbursed under the Medi-Cal Act.

(Amended by Stats. 2012, Ch. 36, Sec. 57. (SB 1014) Effective June 27, 2012. Operative July 1, 2012, by Sec. 83 of Ch. 36.)

11849.

Expenditures incurred pursuant to this part shall be in accordance with the regulations of the director and shall be subject to payment whether incurred by direct or joint operation of the facilities and services, by provisions therefor through contract, or by other arrangement pursuant to the provisions of this chapter. The director may make investigations and audits of the expenditures as he or she may deem necessary.

(Added by Stats. 2004, Ch. 862, Sec. 120. Effective January 1, 2005.)

11849.5.

(a) In determining the amounts that may be paid, fees paid by persons receiving services or fees paid on behalf of those persons by the federal government, by the California Medical Assistance Program set forth in Chapter 7 (commencing with Section 14000) of Part 3 of Division 9 of the Welfare and Institutions Code, and by other public or private sources, shall be deducted from the costs of providing services. Whenever feasible, alcohol and other drug abusing persons who are eligible for alcohol and other drug abuse services under the California Medical Assistance Program shall be treated in a facility approved for reimbursement in that program.

(b) General unrestricted or undesignated private charitable donations and contributions made to charitable or nonprofit organizations shall not be considered as "fees paid by persons" or "fees paid on behalf of such persons" under this section and the contributions shall not be applied in determining the amounts to be paid. The unrestricted contributions shall not be used in part or in whole to defray the costs or the allocated costs of the California Medical Assistance Program.

(Added by Stats. 2004, Ch. 862, Sec. 120. Effective January 1, 2005.)

11850.

The department shall coordinate all narcotic and alcohol and other drug abuse services and related programs conducted by state agencies with the federal government, and shall ensure that there is no duplication of those programs among state agencies and that all agreements, contracts, plans, and programs proposed to be submitted by any state agency, other than the Regents of the University of California, to the federal government in relation to narcotic and alcohol and other drug abuse related problems shall first be submitted to the state department for review and approval.

(Added by Stats. 2004, Ch. 862, Sec. 120. Effective January 1, 2005.)

11850.5.

The department may require state agencies to contract with it for services to carry out the provisions of this division.

(Added by Stats. 2004, Ch. 862, Sec. 120. Effective January 1, 2005.)

11851.

The department may accept and expend grants, gifts, and legacies of money, and, with the consent of the Department of Finance, accept, manage, and expend grants, gifts, and legacies of other properties in furtherance of the purposes of this division.

(Added by Stats. 2004, Ch. 862, Sec. 120. Effective January 1, 2005.)

11851.5.

In addition to those expenditures authorized under Section 11851, expenditures shall include expenses incurred by members of the local advisory board on alcohol and other drug programs in providing alcohol and other drug program services through the implementation of an executed county contract. Payment shall be made of actual and necessary expenses of members incurred incident to the performance of their official duties and may include travel, lodging, and meals while on official business.

(Amended by Stats. 2012, Ch. 36, Sec. 58. (SB 1014) Effective June 27, 2012. Operative July 1, 2012, by Sec. 83 of Ch. 36.)

11852.5.

(a) Charges shall be made for services rendered to each person under a county contract in accordance with this section. Charges for the care and treatment of each client receiving service under a county contract shall not exceed the actual cost thereof as determined by the director in accordance with standard accounting practices. The fee requirement shall not apply to prevention and early intervention services. The director is not prohibited from including the amount of expenditures for capital outlay or the interest thereon, or both, in his or her determination of actual cost. The responsibility of a client, his or her estate, or his or her responsible relatives to pay the charges shall be determined in accordance with this section.

(b) Each county shall determine the liability of clients rendered services under a county contract, and of their estates or responsible relatives, to pay the charges according to ability to pay. Each county shall collect the charges. The county shall establish and maintain policies and procedures for making the determinations of liability and collections, by collecting third-party payments and from other sources to the maximum extent practicable. The written criteria shall be a public record and shall be made available to the department or any individual. Fees collected shall be retained at the local level and be applied toward the purchase of additional drug services.

(c) Services shall not be denied because of a client's ability or inability to pay. County-operated and contract providers of treatment services shall set and collect fees using methods approved by the county alcohol and drug program administrator. All approved fee systems shall conform to all of the following guidelines and criteria:

(1) The fee system used shall be equitable.

(2) The fee charged shall not exceed actual cost.

(3) Systems used shall consider the client's income and expenses.

(4) Each provider fee system shall be approved by the county alcohol and drug program administrator. A description of each approved system shall be on file in the county board office.

(d) To ensure an audit trail, the county or provider, or both, shall maintain all of the following records:

(1) Fee assessment schedules and collection records.

(2) Documents in each client's file showing client's income and expenses, and how each was considered in determining fees.

(e) Each county shall furnish the director with a cost report of information the director shall require to enable the director to maintain a cost-reporting system of the costs of alcohol and other drug program services in the county funded in whole or in part by funds identified in the county contract with the department. The cost-reporting system established pursuant to this section shall supersede the requirements of paragraph (2) of subdivision (b) of Section 16366.7 of the Government Code for a quarterly fiscal reporting system. An annual cost report, for the fiscal year ending June 30, shall be submitted to the department by November 1.

(f) The Legislature recognizes that alcohol and other drug programs may provide a variety of services described in this part, which services will vary depending on the needs of the communities that the programs serve. In devising a system to ensure that a county has expended its funds pursuant to an approved county contract, including the budget portions of the contract, the department shall take into account the flexibility that a county has in the provision of services and the changing nature of alcohol and other drug programs in responding to the community's needs.

(g) The department shall maintain a reporting system to ensure that counties have budgeted and expended their funds pursuant to their approved contracts.

(h) (1) Notwithstanding the rulemaking provisions of Chapter 3.5 (commencing with Section 11340) of Part 1 of Division 3 of Title 2 of the Government Code, the department may implement, interpret, or make specific the amendments to this section made by the act that added this subdivision by means of all-county letters, plan letters, plan or provider bulletins, or similar instructions from the department until regulations are adopted pursuant to that chapter of the Government Code.

(2) The department shall adopt emergency regulations no later than July 1, 2014. The department may subsequently readopt any emergency regulation authorized by this section that is the same as or is substantially equivalent to an emergency regulation previously adopted pursuant to this section.

(3) The initial adoption of emergency regulations implementing the amendments to this section and the one readoption of emergency regulations authorized by this subdivision shall be deemed an emergency and necessary for the immediate preservation of the public peace, health, safety, or general welfare. Initial emergency regulations and the one readoption of emergency regulations authorized by this section shall be exempt from review by the Office of Administrative Law. The initial emergency regulations and the one readoption of emergency regulations authorized by this section shall be submitted to the Office of Administrative Law for filing with the Secretary of State and each shall remain in effect for no more than 180 days, by which time final regulations may be adopted.
(Amended by Stats. 2012, Ch. 36, Sec. 60. (SB 1014) Effective June 27, 2012. Operative July 1, 2012, by Sec. 83 of Ch. 36.)

11853.
Counties are encouraged to contract with providers for the provision of alcohol and drug abuse services. Counties shall comply with the regulations of the department for the management of contracts with community organizations.
(Amended by Stats. 2012, Ch. 36, Sec. 61. (SB 1014) Effective June 27, 2012. Operative July 1, 2012, by Sec. 83 of Ch. 36.)

11854.
The department shall devise and implement, in consultation with the counties, a program reporting method to evidence county compliance with this part. Until that date, the department shall ensure the payment and cost-reporting system does not impair the implementation of this part.
(Added by Stats. 2004, Ch. 862, Sec. 120. Effective January 1, 2005.)

11854.5.
Each county may establish standards that meet or exceed state standards for the treatment and operation of all county-operated and county-contracted alcohol and other drug treatment facilities and services, hereafter referred to as a "quality assurance system." A "quality assurance system" is a systematic approach for the evaluation of the quality of care, which approach is designed to promote and maintain efficient, effective, and appropriate alcohol and other drug treatment services.
(Added by Stats. 2004, Ch. 862, Sec. 120. Effective January 1, 2005.)

11855.
Payments or advances of funds to cities, counties, cities and counties, or other state agencies, which funds are properly chargeable to appropriations to the department, may be made by a Controller's warrant drawn against state funds appropriated to the department or federal funds administered by the department. No more than one-twelfth of the amount to be allocated to a given entity for the fiscal year may be advanced each month.
(Added by Stats. 2004, Ch. 862, Sec. 120. Effective January 1, 2005.)

11855.5.
(a) The department may charge a reasonable fee for the certification or renewal certification of a program that voluntarily requests the certification. The fee shall be set at a level sufficient to cover administrative costs of the program certification process incurred by the department. In calculating the administrative costs the department shall include staff salaries and benefits, related travel costs, and state operational and administrative costs.
(b) The department may contract with private individuals or agencies to provide technical assistance and training to qualify programs for state certification. The department may charge a fee for these services.
(Added by Stats. 2004, Ch. 862, Sec. 120. Effective January 1, 2005.)

11856.
The department shall encourage the development of educational courses that provide core knowledge concerning alcohol and other drug problems and programs to personnel working within alcohol and other drug programs.
(Added by Stats. 2004, Ch. 862, Sec. 120. Effective January 1, 2005.)

11856.5.
The department shall conduct onsite monitoring and reviews of individual county-operated alcohol and other drug programs and alcohol and other drug program administration with emphasis on the review of county administration. The administrative reviews shall include sampling of all services, including those provided by county contract providers.
(Added by Stats. 2004, Ch. 862, Sec. 120. Effective January 1, 2005.)

PART 3. STATE GOVERNMENT'S ROLE TO ALLEVIATE PROBLEMS RELATED TO THE USE AND ABUSE OF ALCOHOL AND OTHER DRUGS [11876 - 11975]
(Heading of Part 3 amended by Stats. 2004, Ch. 862, Sec. 121.)

CHAPTER 1. General [11876- 11876.]
(Chapter 1 added by Stats. 1977, Ch. 1252.)

ARTICLE 3. Narcotic Treatment Programs [11876- 11876.]
(Article 3 repealed and added by Stats. 2004, Ch. 862, Sec. 125.5.)

11876.
The department shall inspect programs dispensing controlled substances described in subdivision (c) of Section 11839.2 to ensure that the programs are operating in compliance with applicable federal statutes and regulations, including the provisions of Part 8 of Title 42 of the Code of Federal Regulations.
(Amended by Stats. 2012, Ch. 36, Sec. 65. (SB 1014) Effective June 27, 2012. Operative July 1, 2012, by Sec. 83 of Ch. 36.)

CHAPTER 2. Community Alcohol and Other Drug Abuse Control [11970 - 11975]
(Heading of Chapter 2 amended by Stats. 2004, Ch. 862, Sec. 127.)

ARTICLE 1. Comprehensive Drug Court Implementation Act of 1999 [11970 - 11974]
(Article 1 added by Stats. 2012, Ch. 36, Sec. 67.)

11970.
(a) This article shall be known and may be cited as the Comprehensive Drug Court Implementation Act of 1999.
(b) The State Department of Alcohol and Drug Programs shall provide oversight of this article.
(c) The department and the Judicial Council shall design and implement this article through the Drug Court Partnership Executive Steering Committee established under the former Drug Court Partnership Act of 1998 pursuant to former Section 11970, for the purpose of funding cost-effective local drug court systems for adults, juveniles, and parents of children who are detained by, or are dependents of, the juvenile court.
(d) This section shall become inoperative on July 1, 2013.
(Amended by Stats. 2013, Ch. 22, Sec. 60. (AB 75) Effective June 27, 2013. Amending action operative July 1, 2013, by Sec. 110 of Ch. 22. Section inoperative July 1, 2013, by its own provisions from this amendment.)

11970.5.
(a) This article shall be known and may be cited as the Drug Court Programs Act.
(b) This section shall become operative on July 1, 2013.
(Added by Stats. 2013, Ch. 22, Sec. 61. (AB 75) Effective June 27, 2013. Adding action operative July 1, 2013, by Sec. 110 of Ch. 22. Section operative July 1, 2013, by its own provisions.)

11971.
(a) (1) At its option, a county may provide a program authorized by this article. A county that chooses to provide a program shall ensure that any funds used for the program are used in compliance with the requirements for receipt of federal block grant funds for prevention and treatment of substance abuse described in Subchapter XVII of Chapter 6A of Title 42 of the United States Code and other federal provisions governing the receipt of federal funds.
(2) The funds contained in each county's Behavioral Health Subaccount of the Support Services Account of the Local Revenue Fund 2011 may be used to fund the cost of drug court treatment programs for the purpose of applying for federal grant funds from the federal Substance Abuse and Mental Health Services Administration as described in Section 11775.
(b) If a county chooses to provide a drug court program, a county alcohol and drug program administrator and the presiding judge in the county shall develop, as part of the contract for alcohol and other drug abuse services, a plan for the operation of drug court program that shall include the information necessary for the state to ensure a county's compliance with the provisions for receipt of the federal block grant funds for prevention and treatment of substance abuse found at Subchapter XVII of Chapter 6A of Title 42 of the United States Code and other applicable federal provisions for funds.
(c) The plan shall do all of the following:
(1) Describe existing programs that serve substance abusing adults, juveniles, and parents of children who are detained by, or are dependents of, the juvenile court.
(2) Provide a local action plan for implementing cost-effective drug court systems, including any or all of the following drug court systems:
(A) Drug courts operating pursuant to Sections 1000 to 1000.5, inclusive, of the Penal Code.
(B) Drug courts for juvenile offenders.
(C) Drug courts for parents of children who are detained by, or are dependents of, the juvenile court.
(D) Drug courts for parents of children in family law cases involving custody and visitation issues.
(E) Other drug court systems that are approved by the Drug Court Partnership Executive Steering Committee.
(3) Develop information-sharing systems to ensure that county actions are fully coordinated, and to provide data for measuring the success of the local action plan in achieving its goals.
(4) Identify outcome measures that will determine the cost effectiveness of the local action plan.
(Added by Stats. 2012, Ch. 36, Sec. 67. (SB 1014) Effective June 27, 2012. Operative July 1, 2012, by Sec. 83 of Ch. 36.)

11972.
It is the intent of the Legislature that drug court programs be designed and operated in accordance with the document entitled "Defining Drug Courts: The Key Components," developed by the National Association of Drug Court Professionals and Drug Court Standards Committee (reprinted 2004). It is the intent of the Legislature that the key components of the programs include:
(a) Integration by drug courts of alcohol and other drug treatment services with justice system case processing.

(b) Promotion of public safety, while protecting participants' due process rights, by prosecution and defense counsel using a nonadversarial approach.

(c) Early identification of eligible participants and prompt placement in the drug court program.

(d) Access provided by drug courts to a continuum of alcohol, drug, and other related treatment and rehabilitation services.

(e) Frequent alcohol and other drug testing to monitor abstinence.

(f) A coordinated strategy to govern drug court responses to participants' compliance.

(g) Ongoing judicial interaction with each drug court participant is essential.

(h) Monitoring and evaluation to measure the achievement of program goals and gauge effectiveness.

(i) Continuing interdisciplinary education to promote effective drug court planning, implementation, and operations.

(j) Forging partnerships among drug courts, public agencies, and community-based organizations to generate local support and enhance drug court program effectiveness.
(Added by Stats. 2012, Ch. 36, Sec. 67. (SB 1014) Effective June 27, 2012. Operative July 1, 2012, by Sec. 83 of Ch. 36.)

11973.

(a) It is the intent of the Legislature that dependency drug courts be funded unless an evaluation of cost avoidance as provided in this section with respect to child welfare services and foster care demonstrates that the program is not cost effective.

(b) The State Department of Social Services, in collaboration with the State Department of Alcohol and Drug Programs and the Judicial Council, shall conduct an evaluation of cost avoidance with respect to child welfare services and foster care pursuant to this section. These parties shall do all of the following:

(1) Consult with legislative staff and at least one representative of an existing dependency drug court program who has experience conducting an evaluation of cost avoidance, to clarify the elements to be reviewed.

(2) Identify requirements, such as specific measures of cost savings and data to be evaluated, and methodology for use of control cases for comparison data.

(3) Whenever possible, use existing evaluation case samples to gather the necessary additional data.

(c) This section shall become inoperative on July 1, 2013.
(Amended by Stats. 2013, Ch. 22, Sec. 62. (AB 75) Effective June 27, 2013. Amending action operative July 1, 2013, by Sec. 110 of Ch. 22. Section inoperative July 1, 2013, by its own provisions from this amendment.)

11974.

(a) Notwithstanding the rulemaking provisions of Chapter 3.5 (commencing with Section 11340) of Part 1 of Division 3 of Title 2 of the Government Code, the department may implement, interpret, or make specific the amendments to this article made by the act that added this section by means of all-county letters, plan letters, plan or provider bulletins, or similar instructions from the department until regulations are adopted pursuant to that chapter of the Government Code.

(b) The department shall adopt emergency regulations no later than July 1, 2014. The department may subsequently readopt any emergency regulation authorized by this section that is the same as or is substantially equivalent to an emergency regulation previously adopted pursuant to this section.

(c) The initial adoption of emergency regulations implementing this article and the one readoption of emergency regulations authorized by this section shall be deemed an emergency and necessary for the immediate preservation of the public peace, health, safety, or general welfare. Initial emergency regulations and the one readoption of emergency regulations authorized by this section shall be exempt from review by the Office of Administrative Law. The initial emergency regulations and the one readoption of emergency regulations authorized by this section shall be submitted to the Office of Administrative Law for filing with the Secretary of State and each shall remain in effect for no more than 180 days, by which time final regulations may be adopted.
(Added by Stats. 2012, Ch. 36, Sec. 67. (SB 1014) Effective June 27, 2012. Operative July 1, 2012, by Sec. 83 of Ch. 36.)

ARTICLE 2. Drug Court Partnership Act of 2002 [11975- 11975.]
(Article 2 repealed and added by Stats. 2012, Ch. 36, Sec. 69.)

11975.

(a) This article shall be known and may be cited as the Drug Court Partnership Act of 2002.

(b) The Drug Court Partnership Program, as provided for in this article, shall be administered by the State Department of Alcohol and Drug Programs for the purpose of providing assistance to drug courts that accept only defendants who have been convicted of felonies. The department and the Judicial Council shall design and implement this program through the Drug Court Systems Steering Committee as originally established by the department and the Judicial Council to implement the former Drug Court Partnership Act of 1998 (Article 3 (commencing with Section 11970)).

(c) (1) The department shall require counties that participate in the Drug Court Partnership Program to submit a revised multiagency plan that is in conformance with the Drug Court Systems Steering Committee's recommended guidelines. Revised multiagency plans that are reviewed and approved by the department and recommended by the Drug Court Systems Steering Committee shall be funded for the 2002–03 fiscal year under this article. The department, without a renewal of the Drug Court Systems Steering Committee's original recommendation, may disburse future year appropriations to the grantees.

(2) The multiagency plan shall identify the resources and strategies for providing an effective drug court program exclusively for convicted felons who meet the requirements of this article and the guidelines adopted thereunder, and shall set forth the basis for determining eligibility for participation that will maximize savings to the state in avoided prison costs.

(3) The multiagency plan shall include, but not be limited to, all of the following components:

(A) The method by which the drug court will ensure that the target population of felons will be identified and referred to the drug court.

(B) The elements of the treatment and supervision programs.

(C) The method by which the grantee will provide the specific outcomes and data required by the department to determine state prison savings or cost avoidance.

(D) Assurance that funding received pursuant to this article will be used to supplement, rather than supplant, existing programs.

(d) Funds shall be used only for programs that are identified in the approved multiagency plan. Acceptable uses may include, but shall not be limited to, any of the following:

(1) Drug court coordinators.

(2) Training.

(3) Drug testing.

(4) Treatment.

(5) Transportation.

(6) Other costs related to substance abuse treatment.

(e) The department shall identify and design a data collection instrument to determine state prison cost savings and avoidance from this program.

(f) This section shall become inoperative on July 1, 2013.
(Amended by Stats. 2013, Ch. 22, Sec. 63. (AB 75) Effective June 27, 2013. Amending action operative July 1, 2013, by Sec. 110 of Ch. 22. Section inoperative July 1, 2013, by its own provisions from this amendment.)

DIVISION 10.6. DRUG AND ALCOHOL ABUSE MASTER PLANS [11998 - 11998.4]

(Division 10.6 added by Stats. 1988, Ch. 983, Sec. 4.)

CHAPTER 1. Long-Range Goals [11998 - 11998.4]

(Chapter 1 added by Stats. 1988, Ch. 983, Sec. 4.)

11998.

This chapter sets forth the long-range goals of a five-year master plan to eliminate drug and alcohol abuse in California. The goals of this chapter are advisory, but it is the intent of the Legislature that the goals will be addressed to the extent possible by each county and by state government. These advisory goals do not amend existing law.

Implementation of the goals of the master plan, after the state plan has been developed and issued, shall be subject to the budget review process.
(Amended by Stats. 1989, Ch. 1370, Sec. 2. Effective October 2, 1989. Inoperative July 1, 2013, pursuant to Section 11998.4.)

11998.1.

It is the intent of the Legislature that the following long-term five-year goals be achieved:

(a) With regard to education and prevention of drug and alcohol abuse programs, the following goals:

(1) Drug and alcohol abuse education has been included within the mandatory curriculum in kindergarten and grades 1 to 12, inclusive, in every public school in California.

(2) Basic training on how to recognize, and understand what to do about, drug and alcohol abuse has been provided to administrators and all teachers of kindergarten and grades 1 to 12, inclusive.

(3) All school counselors and school nurses have received comprehensive drug and alcohol abuse training.

(4) Each school district with kindergarten and grades 1 to 12, inclusive, has appointed a drug and alcohol abuse advisory team of school administrators, teachers, counselors, students, parents, community representatives, and health care professionals, all of whom have expertise in drug and alcohol abuse prevention. The team coordinates with and receives consultation from the county alcohol and drug program administrators.

(5) Every school board member has received basic drug and alcohol abuse information.

(6) Each school district has a drug and alcohol abuse specialist to assist the individual schools.

(7) Each school in grades 7 to 12, inclusive, has student peer group drug and alcohol abuse programs.

(8) Every school district with kindergarten and grades 1 to 12, inclusive, has updated written drug and alcohol abuse policies and procedures including disciplinary procedures which will be given to every school employee, every student, and every parent.

(9) The California State University and the University of California have evaluated and, if feasible, established educational programs and degrees in the area of drug and alcohol abuse.

(10) Every school district with kindergarten and grades 1 to 12, inclusive, has an established parent teachers group with drug and alcohol abuse prevention goals.

(11) Every school district has instituted a drug and alcohol abuse education program for parents.

(12) Drug and alcohol abuse training has been imposed as a condition for teacher credentialing and license renewal, and knowledge on the issue is measured on the California Basic Education Skills Test.

(13) Drug and alcohol abuse knowledge has been established as a component on standardized competency tests as a requirement for graduation.

(14) Every school district has established a parent support group.

(15) Every school district has instituted policies that address the special needs of children who have been rehabilitated for drug or alcohol abuse problems and who are reentering school. These policies shall consider the loss of schooltime, the loss of academic credits, and the sociological problems associated with drug and alcohol abuse, its rehabilitation, and the educational delay it causes.

(16) The number of drug and alcohol abuse related incidents on school grounds has decreased by 20 percent.

(b) With regard to community programs, the following goals:

(1) Every community-based social service organization that receives state and local financial assistance has drug and alcohol abuse information available for clients.

(2) All neighborhood watch, business watch, and community conflict resolution programs have included drug and alcohol abuse prevention efforts.

(3) All community-based programs that serve schoolaged children have staff trained in drug and alcohol abuse and give a clear, drug- and alcohol-free message.

(c) With regard to drug and alcohol abuse programs of the media, the following goals:

(1) The state has established a comprehensive media campaign that involves all facets of the drug and alcohol abuse problem, including treatment, education, prevention, and intervention that will result in increasing the public's knowledge and awareness of the detrimental effects of alcohol and drug use, reducing the use of alcohol and drugs, and increasing healthy lifestyle choices.

(2) The department on a statewide basis, and the county board of supervisors or its designees at the local level, have:

(A) Assisted the entertainment industry in identifying ways to use the entertainment industry effectively to encourage lifestyles free of substance abuse.

(B) Assisted the manufacturers of drug and alcohol products in identifying ways to use product advertising effectively to discourage substance abuse.

(C) Assisted television stations in identifying ways to use television programming effectively to encourage lifestyles free of substance abuse.

(3) A statewide cooperative fundraising program with recording artists and the entertainment industry has been encouraged to fund drug and alcohol abuse prevention efforts in the state.

(d) With regard to drug and alcohol abuse health care programs, the following goals:

(1) The number of drug and alcohol abuse-related medical emergencies has decreased by 4 percent per year.

(2) All general acute care hospitals and AIDS medical service providers have provided information to their patients on drug and alcohol abuse.

(3) The Medical Board of California, the Psychology Examining Committee, the Board of Registered Nursing, and the Board of Behavioral Science Examiners have developed and implemented the guidelines or regulations requiring drug and alcohol abuse training for their licensees, and have developed methods of providing training for those professionals.

(e) With regard to private sector drug and alcohol abuse programs, the following goals:

(1) A significant percentage of businesses in the private sector have developed personnel policies that discourage drug and alcohol abuse and encourage supervision, training, and employee education.

(2) Noteworthy and publicly recognized figures and private industry have been encouraged to sponsor fundraising events for drug and alcohol abuse prevention.

(3) Every public or private athletic team has been encouraged to establish policies forbidding drug and alcohol abuse.

(4) The private sector has established personnel policies that discourage drug and alcohol abuse but encourage treatment for those employees who require this assistance.

(f) With regard to local government drug and alcohol abuse programs, the following goals:

(1) Every county has a five-year master plan to eliminate drug and alcohol abuse developed jointly by the county-designated alcohol and drug program administrators, reviewed jointly by the advisory boards set forth in paragraph (2), and approved by the board of supervisors. For those counties in which the alcohol and drug programs are jointly administered, the administrator shall develop the five-year master plan. To the degree possible, all existing local plans relating to drug or alcohol abuse shall be incorporated into the master plan.

(2) Every county has an advisory board on alcohol problems and an advisory board on drug programs. The membership of these advisory boards is representative of the county's population and is geographically balanced. To the maximum extent possible, the county advisory board on alcohol problems and the county advisory board on drug programs will have representatives of the following:

(A) Law enforcement.

(B) Education.

(C) The treatment and recovery community, including a representative with expertise in AIDS treatment services.

(D) Judiciary.

(E) Students.

(F) Parents.

(G) Private industry.

(H) Other community organizations involved in drug and alcohol services.

(I) A representative of organized labor responsible for the provision of Employee Assistance Program services.

If any of these areas is not represented on the advisory bodies, the administrator designated in paragraph (1) shall solicit input from a representative of the nonrepresented area prior to the development of a master plan pursuant to paragraph (1).

(3) Every county public social service agency has established policies that discourage drug and alcohol abuse and encourage treatment and recovery services when necessary.

(4) Every local unit of government has an employee assistance program that addresses drug and alcohol abuse problems.

(5) Every local unit of government has considered the potential for drug and alcohol abuse problems when developing zoning ordinances and issuing conditional use permits.

(6) Every county master plan includes treatment and recovery services.

(6.5) Every county master plan includes specialized provisions to ensure optimum alcohol and drug abuse service delivery for handicapped and disabled persons.

(7) Every local unit of government has been encouraged to establish an employee assistance program that includes the treatment of drug and alcohol abuse-related programs.

(8) Every local governmental social service provider has established a referral system under which clients with drug and alcohol abuse problems can be referred for treatment.

(9) Every county drug and alcohol abuse treatment or recovery program that serves women gives priority for services to pregnant women.

(10) Every alcohol and drug abuse program provides AIDS information to all program participants.

(g) With regard to state and federal government drug and alcohol abuse programs, the following goals:

(1) The Department of Alcoholic Beverage Control has informed all alcohol retailers of the laws governing liquor sales and has provided training available to all personnel selling alcoholic beverages, on identifying and handling minors attempting to purchase alcohol.

(2) The Office of Emergency Services has required all applicants for crime prevention and juvenile justice and delinquency prevention funds to include drug and alcohol abuse prevention efforts in their programs.

(3) All county applications for direct or indirect drug and alcohol services funding from the department include a prevention component.

(4) The Superintendent of Public Instruction has employed drug and alcohol abuse school prevention specialists and assisted school districts with the implementation of prevention programs.

(5) The State Department of Health Care Services has staff trained in drug and alcohol abuse prevention who can assist local mental health programs with prevention efforts.

(6) The Department of the California Highway Patrol, as permitted by the United States Constitution, has established routine statewide sobriety checkpoints for driving while under the influence.

(7) The Department of Corrections and the Department of the Youth Authority have provided drug and alcohol abuse education and prevention services for all inmates, wards, and parolees. Both departments have provided drug and alcohol abuse treatment services for any inmate, ward, or parolee determined to be in need of these services, or who personally requests these services.

(8) The Department of Motor Vehicles has distributed prevention materials with each driver's license or certificate of renewal and each vehicle registration renewal mailed by the Department of Motor Vehicles.

(9) Federal prevention programs have been encouraged to follow the master plan.

(10) State licensing and program regulations for drug and alcohol abuse treatment programs have been consolidated and administered by one state agency.

(11) State treatment funding priorities have been included to specially recognize the multiple diagnosed client who would be eligible for services from more than one state agency.

(12) Every state agency has formalized employee assistance programs that include the treatment of drug and alcohol abuse-related problems.

(13) The state master plan includes specialized provisions to ensure optimum drug and alcohol abuse service delivery for handicapped and disabled persons.

(h) With regard to private sector direct service providers, the following goals:

(1) Drinking drivers programs have provided clear measurements of successful completion of the program to the courts for each court-ordered client.

(2) Sufficient drug and alcohol treatment and recovery services exist throughout the state to meet all clients' immediate and long-range needs.

(3) Each county to the extent possible provides localized alcohol and drug treatment and recovery services designed for individuals seeking assistance for polydrug abuse.

(4) Adequate nonresidential and residential services are available statewide for juveniles in need of alcohol or drug abuse services.

(5) Each provider of alcohol or drug services has been certified by the state.

(6) Drug and alcohol abuse treatment providers provide general AIDS information during treatment.

(i) With regard to supply regulation and reduction in conjunction with drug and alcohol abuse, the following goals:

(1) The California National Guard supports federal, state, and local drug enforcement agencies in counternarcotic operations as permitted by applicable laws and regulations.

(2) Each county has a drug and alcohol abuse enforcement team, designated by the board of supervisors. This team includes all components of the criminal justice system.

This team shall be responsible to the board of supervisors, shall coordinate with the drug and alcohol abuse advisory board and the county on all criminal justice matters relating to drug and alcohol abuse, and shall coordinate, and actively participate, with the county alcohol and drug program administrators throughout the development and implementation of the five-year master plan.

(3) The Office of Emergency Services, the Youth and Adult Correctional Agency, the Department of the California Highway Patrol, the Office of Traffic Safety, and the Department of Justice have established a state level drug and alcohol abuse enforcement team that includes representatives from all facets of criminal justice. The lead agency for the enforcement team has been designated by the Governor. This team advises the state and assists the local teams.

(4) The Office of Emergency Services, the Youth and Adult Correctional Agency, and the Department of Justice have, as a priority when determining training subjects, prevention seminars on drug and alcohol abuse. The Commission on Peace Officer Standards and Training has, as a priority, when determining training subjects, drug and alcohol enforcement.

(5) The Department of the California Highway Patrol, as permitted by the United States Constitution, will, in conjunction with establishing sobriety checkpoints statewide, assist local law enforcement agencies with the establishment of local programs.

(6) Counties with more than 10 superior court judgeships have established programs under which drug cases receive swift prosecution by well-trained prosecutors before judges who are experienced in the handling of drug cases.

(7) The courts, when determining bail eligibility and the amount of bail for persons suspected of a crime involving a controlled substance, shall consider the quantity of the substance involved when measuring the danger to society if the suspect is released.

(8) Drunk driving jails have been established that provide offender education and treatment during incarceration.

(9) All probation and parole officers have received drug and alcohol abuse training, including particular training on drug recognition.

(10) All parolees and persons on probation with a criminal history that involves drug or alcohol abuse have conditions of parole or probation that prohibit drug and alcohol abuse.

(11) The Judicial Council has provided training on drug and alcohol abuse for the judges.

(12) The courts, when sentencing offenders convicted of selling drugs, consider "street value" of the drugs involved in the underlying crime.

(13) Judges have been encouraged to include drug and alcohol abuse treatment and prevention services in sentences for all offenders. Judges are requiring, as a condition of sentencing, drug and alcohol abuse education and treatment services for all persons convicted of driving under the influence of alcohol or drugs.

(14) Juvenile halls and jails provide clients with information on drug and alcohol abuse.

(15) The estimated number of clandestine labs operating in California has decreased by 10 percent per year.

(16) Each local law enforcement agency has developed, with the schools, protocol on responding to school drug and alcohol abuse problems.

(17) Every county has instituted a mandatory driving-under-the-influence presentence offender evaluation program.

(Amended by Stats. 2013, Ch. 352, Sec. 337. (AB 1317) Effective September 26, 2013. Operative July 1, 2013, by Sec. 543 of Ch. 352. Inoperative July 1, 2013, pursuant to Section 11998.4.)

11998.2.

(a) "Department," as used in this division, means the State Department of Alcohol and Drug Programs.

(b) The board of supervisors of each county is encouraged to prepare and adopt a county drug and alcohol abuse master plan, pursuant to paragraph (1) of subdivision (f) of Section 11998.1, that addresses as many of the long-range goals set forth in Section 11998.1 as possible. It is the intent of the Legislature that every county master plan include quantitative outcome objectives that, at a minimum, measure progress in the areas of prevention, education, enforcement, and treatment. It is the intent of the Legislature that these objectives include measurements of:

(1) The reduction of arrests for driving under the influence of drugs or alcohol, or both.

(2) The reduction of alcohol and drug-related arrests.

(3) Increased public education on the dangers of substance abuse and the available prevention techniques including specific measurements of children, parents, and teachers who have received this education.

(4) The reduction of alcohol- and drug-related deaths and injuries.

(5) The increased number of persons successfully completing drug and alcohol abuse services.

If a county master plan is adopted, the board of supervisors or its designee shall, in conjunction with the county advisory boards as established pursuant to paragraph (2) of subdivision (f) of Section 11998.1, annually assess the progress of the county in reaching its long-range goals.

(c) Every county or public or private agency within a county that applies for state or local assistance funds for drug and alcohol abuse efforts in their program, may address, to the extent possible, any long-range goals set forth in a county drug and alcohol abuse master plan established pursuant to subdivision (b), and funding priority may be given to those entities which address these goals within their respective programs.

(d) The Governor shall designate one state agency to act as the lead agency on all drug and alcohol abuse matters.

(e) Every state agency that contracts or grants money to local jurisdictions or programs for drug and alcohol abuse services shall require the submission and shall review the contents of an approved county drug and alcohol abuse master plan, to the extent a plan has been adopted pursuant to subdivision (b).

(f) Every state agency that offers drug and alcohol abuse services or financial assistance shall report annually to the Legislature on its efforts to achieve the master plan goals provided in Section 11998.1. Individual agencies may report separately or in combination with other state agencies.

(g) The department shall send copies of this division to all state-funded social service programs that provide drug and alcohol abuse services.

(h) The department shall maintain copies of every county drug and alcohol abuse master plan for review by other state agencies and the Legislature.

(i) The Governor shall designate one statewide resource center to coordinate efforts of other resource centers statewide and to coordinate with local government and assist in their preparation of drug and alcohol abuse master plans.

(j) The department shall maintain an annually updated listing of all drug and alcohol abuse programs provided or funded by the state. Every other state agency shall regularly provide the department with current information on programs they fund or provide.

(k) The Governor's Policy Council on Drug and Alcohol Abuse shall review and consider all of the goals contained in Section 11998.1.

(Amended by Stats. 2004, Ch. 193, Sec. 91. Effective January 1, 2005. Inoperative July 1, 2013, pursuant to Section 11998.4.)

11998.3.

(a) Priority in allocating state funds for substance abuse to law enforcement agencies shall be given to those counties whose law enforcement agencies are participating in both of the following:

(1) A drug and alcohol abuse enforcement team established in accordance with paragraph (2) of subdivision (i) of Section 11998.1.

(2) Development and implementation of a county master plan pursuant to this chapter.

(b) The drug and alcohol abuse enforcement team shall adopt measures to coordinate the efforts of drug and alcohol abuse law enforcement agencies within the county.

(Repealed and added by Stats. 1990, Ch. 1610, Sec. 3. Inoperative July 1, 2013, pursuant to Section 11998.4.)

11998.4.

This division shall become inoperative on July 1, 2013.

(Added by Stats. 2013, Ch. 22, Sec. 64. (AB 75) Effective June 27, 2013. Operative July 1, 2013, by Sec. 110 of Ch. 22. Note: Termination clause affects Division 10.6, commencing with Section 11998.)

DIVISION 10.7. ILLEGAL USE OF DRUGS AND ALCOHOL [11999 - 11999.3]

(Division 10.7 added by Stats. 1989, Ch. 1429, Sec. 1.)

11999.

The Legislature finds and declares all of the following:

(a) The Legislature has established various drug- and alcohol-related programs which provide for education, prevention, intervention, treatment, or enforcement.

(b) The Legislature has classified certain substances as controlled substances and has defined the lawful and unlawful use of controlled substances which are commonly referred to as, but not limited to, anabolic steroids, marijuana, and cocaine.

(c) The Legislature has classified certain substances as imitation controlled substances which are commonly referred to as, but not limited to, designer drugs.

(d) The Legislature has determined that the possession with the intent to be under the influence, or being under the influence of toluene, or any substance or material containing toluene, or any substance with similar toxic qualities, is unlawful. Some substances or materials containing toluene, or substances with similar toxic qualities are commonly referred to, but not limited to, inhalants such as cement, glue, and paint thinner.

(e) The Legislature has determined that the purchase, possession, or use of alcohol by persons under 21 years of age is unlawful.

(f) Public and private agencies that provide information pertaining to the drug- and alcohol-related programs provide mixed messages and misinformation relating to the unlawful use of drugs and alcohol. It is the intent of the Legislature that the messages and information provided by the drug and alcohol programs promote no unlawful use of any drugs or alcohol. Mixed messages mean communications discussing how to use or when to use unlawful drugs or alcohol.

(g) Any material, curricula, teachings, or promotion of responsible use, if the use is unlawful, of drugs or alcohol is inconsistent with the law.

(h) The "no unlawful use" message applies to all drug and alcohol programs for the people of the State of California. These materials are to teach and promote that any unlawful use of drugs and alcohol is illegal and dangerous.

(Added by Stats. 1989, Ch. 1429, Sec. 1. Operative July 1, 1990, by Sec. 3 of Ch. 1429.)

11999.1.

For the purpose of this division, the following definitions apply:

(a) "Drug" means all of the following:

(1) Any controlled substance as defined in Division 10 (commencing with Section 11000).

(2) Any imitation controlled substance as defined in Chapter 1 (commencing with Section 11670) of Division 10.1.

(3) Toluene or any substance or material containing toluene or any substance with similar toxic qualities as set forth in Sections 380 and 381 of the Penal Code.

(b) "Drug- or alcohol-related program" means any program designed to reduce the unlawful use of, or assist those who engage in the unlawful use of, drugs or alcohol, whether through education, prevention, intervention, treatment, enforcement, or other means.

(c) "Local agency" shall include, but is not limited to, a county, a city, a city and county, and school district.

(d) "State agency" shall include the State Department of Health Care Services, the State Department of Education, the Department of Justice, the Office of Criminal Justice Planning, and the Office of Traffic Safety. Any other state agency or department may comply with this division.

(Amended by Stats. 2013, Ch. 22, Sec. 65. (AB 75) Effective June 27, 2013. Operative July 1, 2013, by Sec. 110 of Ch. 22.)

11999.2.

(a) Notwithstanding any other provision of law, commencing July 1, 1990, no state funds shall be encumbered by a state agency for allocation to any entity, whether public or private, for a drug- or alcohol-related program, unless the drug- or alcohol-related program contains a component that clearly explains in written materials that there shall be no unlawful use of drugs or alcohol. No aspect of a drug- or alcohol-related program shall include any message on the responsible use, if the use is unlawful, of drugs or alcohol.

(b) All aspects of a drug- or alcohol-related program shall be consistent with the "no unlawful use" message, including, but not limited to, program standards, curricula, materials, and teachings.

These materials and programs may include information regarding the health hazards of use of illegal drugs and alcohol, concepts promoting the well-being of the whole person, risk reduction, the addictive personality, development of positive self-esteem, productive decisionmaking skills, and other preventive concepts consistent with the "no unlawful use" of drugs and alcohol message.

(c) The "no unlawful use" of drugs and alcohol message contained in drug- or alcohol-related programs shall apply to the use of drugs and alcohol prohibited by law.

(d) This section does not apply to any program funded by the state that provides education and prevention outreach to intravenous drug users with AIDS or AIDS-related conditions, or persons at risk of HIV-infection through intravenous drug use.

(Added by Stats. 1989, Ch. 1429, Sec. 1. Operative July 1, 1990, by Sec. 3 of Ch. 1429.)

11999.3.

(a) A state agency that distributes state funds to an entity, whether public or private, for a drug- or alcohol-related program shall establish and provide guidelines and procedures for the entity to use to ensure compliance with this division. If the drug or alcohol program fails to satisfy the guidelines adopted by the state agency, the drug or alcohol program shall not receive state funds from the state agency. A state agency that provides or develops drug- or alcohol-related programs shall also comply with this division.

(b) Each state and local agency which distributes funds shall establish a reasonable time frame for each program to comply with the requirements of this division.

(c) A drug- or alcohol-related program that receives state funds from a local agency shall file with the local agency which distributes the state funds a written assurance signed by the person responsible for operating the drug- or alcohol-related program stating all of the following:

(1) The person understands the requirements of Section 11999.2.

(2) The person has reviewed those aspects of the program to which Section 11999.2 applies.

(3) Those aspects of the program to which Section 11999.2 applies meet the requirements of Section 11999.2.

(d) Every state or local agency distributing funds to which this division applies shall provide a process for appealing a determination to deny or terminate funding to a drug- or alcohol-related program based upon noncompliance with the requirements of this division. When funding is allocated to counties for distribution to local agencies, the director of the state agency distributing the funds shall develop and distribute to counties guidelines for the development of a local appeals process.

(e) A local agency which receives state funds from a state agency for establishing a drug- or alcohol-related program and which has discretionary authority for how the local agency spends the state funds, shall consider the requirements of Section 11999.2 in establishing the drug- or alcohol-related program.

(f) School district personnel who have authority to select and purchase instructional materials, curricula, or both, for the purpose of teaching drug or alcohol use prevention, or both, shall follow the requirements specified in Section 11999.2.

(Added by Stats. 1989, Ch. 1429, Sec. 1. Operative July 1, 1990, by Sec. 3 of Ch. 1429.)

DIVISION 10.8. SUBSTANCE ABUSE TREATMENT FUNDING [11999.4 - 11999.13]

(Division 10.8 added November 7, 2000, by initiative Proposition 36, Sec. 7.)

11999.4.

Establishment of the Substance Abuse Treatment Trust Fund

A special fund to be known as the "Substance Abuse Treatment Trust Fund" is created within the State Treasury and is continuously appropriated for carrying out the purposes of this division.

(Added November 7, 2000, by initiative Proposition 36, Sec. 7. Operative July 1, 2001, pursuant to Sec. 8 of Prop. 36.)

11999.5.

Funding Appropriation

Upon passage of this act, $60,000,000 shall be continuously appropriated from the General Fund to the Substance Abuse Treatment Trust Fund for the 2000–01 fiscal year. There is hereby continuously appropriated from the General Fund to the Substance Abuse Treatment Trust Fund an additional $120,000,000 for the 2001–02 fiscal year, and an additional sum of $120,000,000 for each such subsequent fiscal year concluding with the 2005–06 fiscal year. These funds shall be transferred to the Substance Abuse Treatment Trust Fund on July 1 of each of these specified fiscal years. Funds transferred to the Substance Abuse Treatment Trust Fund are not subject to annual appropriation by the Legislature and may be used without a time limit. Nothing in this section precludes additional appropriations by the Legislature to the Substance Abuse Treatment Trust Fund.

(Added November 7, 2000, by initiative Proposition 36, Sec. 7. Operative July 1, 2001, pursuant to Sec. 8 of Prop. 36.)

11999.6.

Moneys deposited in the Substance Abuse Treatment Trust Fund shall be distributed annually by the Secretary of California Health and Human Services through the State Department of Health Care Services to counties to cover the costs of placing persons in and providing drug treatment programs under this act, and vocational training, family counseling, and literacy training under this act. Additional costs that may be reimbursed from the Substance Abuse Treatment Trust Fund include probation department costs, court monitoring costs, and any miscellaneous costs made necessary by the provisions of this act other than drug testing services of any kind. Incarceration costs cannot be reimbursed from the fund. Those moneys shall be allocated to counties through a fair and equitable distribution formula that includes, but is not limited to, per capita arrests for controlled substance possession violations and substance abuse treatment caseload, as determined by the department as necessary to carry out the purposes of this act. The department may reserve a portion of the fund to pay for direct contracts with drug treatment service providers in counties or areas in which the director of the department has determined that demand for drug treatment services is not adequately met by existing programs. However, nothing in this section shall be interpreted or construed to allow any entity to use funds from the Substance Abuse Treatment Trust Fund to supplant funds from any existing fund source or mechanism currently used to provide substance abuse treatment. In addition, funds from the Substance Abuse Treatment Trust Fund shall not be used to fund in any way the drug treatment courts established pursuant to Article 1 (commencing with Section 11970) or Article 2 (commencing with Section 11975) of Chapter 2 of Part 3 of Division 10.5, including drug treatment or probation supervision associated with those drug treatment courts.

(Amended by Stats. 2013, Ch. 22, Sec. 66. (AB 75) Effective June 27, 2013. Operative July 1, 2013, by Sec. 110 of Ch. 22. Note: This section was added on Nov. 7, 2000, by initiative Prop. 36.)

11999.6.1.

(a) Notwithstanding any other provision of law, when the department allocates funds appropriated to the Substance Abuse Treatment Trust Fund, it shall withhold from any allocation to a county the amount of funds previously allocated to that county from the fund that are projected to remain unencumbered, up to the amount that would otherwise be allocated to that county. The department shall allow a county with unencumbered funds to retain a reserve of 5 percent of the amount allocated to that county for the most recent fiscal year in which the county received an allocation from the fund without a reduction pursuant to this subdivision.

(b) The department shall allocate 75 percent of the amount withheld pursuant to subdivision (a) in accordance with Section 11999.6 and any regulations adopted pursuant to that section, but taking into account any amount withheld pursuant to subdivision (a).

(c) The department shall reserve 25 percent of the amount withheld pursuant to subdivision (a) until all counties have submitted final actual expenditures for the most recent fiscal year. The department shall then allocate the funds reserved to adjust for actual rather than projected unencumbered funds, to the extent that the amount reserved is adequate to do so. Any balance of funds not reallocated pursuant to this subdivision shall be allocated in accordance with subdivision (e).

(d) If the department determines from actual expenditures that more funds should have been withheld from any county than were withheld pursuant to subdivision (a), it shall adjust any allocations pursuant to subdivision (e) accordingly, to the extent possible. If one or more counties fails to report actual expenditures in a timely manner, the department may, in its discretion, proceed with the available information, and may exclude any nonreporting county from any allocations pursuant to this section.

(e) If revenues, funds, or other receipts to the Substance Abuse Treatment Trust Fund are sufficient to create additional allocations to counties, through reconsideration of unencumbered funds, audit recoveries, or otherwise, the Director of Finance may authorize expenditures for the department in excess of the amount appropriated no earlier than 30 days after notification in writing of the necessity therefor is provided to the chairpersons of the fiscal committees in each house and the Chairperson of the Joint

Legislative Budget Committee, or at an earlier time that the Chairperson of the Joint Legislative Budget Committee, or his or her designee, may in each instance determine.

(f) The department may implement this section by All-County Lead Agency letters or other similar instructions, and need not comply with the rulemaking requirements of Chapter 3.5 (commencing with Section 11340) of Division 3 of Title 2 of the Government Code.
(Added by Stats. 2006, Ch. 75, Sec. 23.1. Effective July 12, 2006.)

11999.7.
Local Government Authority to Control Location of Drug Treatment Programs
Notwithstanding any other provision of law, no community drug treatment program may receive any funds from the Substance Abuse Treatment Trust Fund unless the program agrees to make its facilities subject to valid local government zoning ordinances and development agreements.
(Added November 7, 2000, by initiative Proposition 36, Sec. 7. Operative July 1, 2001, pursuant to Sec. 8 of Prop. 36.)

11999.8.
Surplus Funds
Any funds remaining in the Substance Abuse Treatment Trust Fund at the end of a fiscal year may be utilized to pay for drug treatment programs to be carried out in the subsequent fiscal year.
(Added November 7, 2000, by initiative Proposition 36, Sec. 7. Operative July 1, 2001, pursuant to Sec. 8 of Prop. 36.)

11999.9.
(a) The department shall conduct three two-year followup studies to evaluate the effectiveness and financial impact of the programs that are funded pursuant to the requirements of this act, and submit those studies to the Legislature no later than January 1, 2009, January 1, 2011, and January 1, 2013, respectively. The evaluation studies shall include, but not be limited to, a study of the implementation process, a review of lower incarcerations costs, reductions in crime, reduced prison and jail construction, reduced welfare costs, the adequacy of funds appropriated, and other impacts or issues the department can identify, in addition to all of the following:
(1) Criminal justice measures on rearrests, jail and prison days averted, and crime trends.
(2) A classification, in summary form, of rearrests as having occurred as a result of:
(A) A parole violation.
(B) A parole revocation.
(C) A probation violation.
(D) A probation revocation.
(3) A classification, in summary form, of the disposition of crimes committed in terms of whether the person was:
(A) Retained on probation.
(B) Sentenced to jail.
(C) Sentenced to prison.
(4) Treatment measures on completion rates and quality of life indicators, such as alcohol and drug used, employment, health, mental health, and family and social supports.
(5) A separate discussion of the information described in paragraphs (1) to (3), inclusive, for offenders whose primary drug of abuse was methamphetamine or who were arrested for possession or use of methamphetamine and, commencing with the report due on or before January 1, 2009, the report shall include a separate analysis of the costs and benefits of treatment specific to these methamphetamine offenders.
(b) In addition to studies to evaluate the effectiveness and financial impact of the programs that are funded pursuant to the requirements of this act, the department shall produce an annual report detailing the number and characteristics of participants served as a result of this act, and the related costs.
(Amended by Stats. 2006, Ch. 63, Sec. 3. Effective July 12, 2006. Note: This section was added on Nov. 7, 2000, by initiative Prop. 36.)

11999.10.
The department shall allocate up to 0.5 percent of the fund's total moneys each year to fund the costs of the studies required in Section 11999.9 by a public or private university.
(Amended by Stats. 2006, Ch. 63, Sec. 4. Effective July 12, 2006. Note: This section was added on Nov. 7, 2000, by initiative Prop. 36.)

11999.11.
County Reports
Counties shall submit a report annually to the department detailing the numbers and characteristics of clients-participants served as a result of funding provided by this act. The department shall promulgate a form which shall be used by the counties for the reporting of this information, as well as any other information that may be required by the department. The department shall establish a deadline by which the counties shall submit their reports.
(Added November 7, 2000, by initiative Proposition 36, Sec. 7. Operative July 1, 2001, pursuant to Sec. 8 of Prop. 36.)

11999.12.
The department shall conduct periodic audits of the expenditures made by any county that is funded, in whole or in part, with funds provided by this act. Counties shall repay to the department any funds that are not spent in accordance with the requirements of this act. The department may require a corrective action by the county in the place of repayment, as determined by the department.
(Amended by Stats. 2006, Ch. 63, Sec. 5. Effective July 12, 2006. Note: This section was added on Nov. 7, 2000, by initiative Prop. 36.)

11999.13.
Excess Funds

At the end of each fiscal year, a county may retain unspent funds received from the Substance Abuse Treatment Trust Fund and may spend those funds, if approved by the department, on drug programs that further the purposes of this act.
(Added November 7, 2000, by initiative Proposition 36, Sec. 7. Operative July 1, 2001, pursuant to Sec. 8 of Prop. 36.)

DIVISION 10.9. SUBSTANCE ABUSE TESTING AND TREATMENT ACCOUNTABILITY PROGRAM [11999.20 - 11999.25]

(Division 10.9 added by Stats. 2001, Ch. 721, Sec. 1.)

11999.20.
(a) The State Department of Alcohol and Drug Programs shall administer and award grants to counties to supplement funding provided under the Substance Abuse and Crime Prevention Act of 2000 for the purpose of funding substance abuse testing for eligible offenders. Funding shall be used to supplement, rather than supplant, funding for existing substance abuse testing programs.
(b) This section shall become inoperative on July 1, 2013.
(Amended by Stats. 2013, Ch. 22, Sec. 67. (AB 75) Effective June 27, 2013. Amending action operative July 1, 2013, by Sec. 110 of Ch. 22. Section inoperative July 1, 2013, by its own provisions from this amendment.)

11999.25.
(a) To be eligible for a grant pursuant to this division, a county shall have on file with the State Department of Alcohol and Drug Programs an approved plan for implementing the Substance Abuse and Crime Prevention Act of 2000.
(b) The county plan shall include a description of the process to be used for substance abuse treatment and substance abuse testing of probationers consistent with Sections 1210.1 and 1210.5, and substance abuse treatment and substance abuse testing of parolees consistent with Sections 3063.1 and 3063.2.
(c) The State Department of Alcohol and Drug Programs shall establish a fair and equitable distribution formula for allocating money to eligible counties.
(d) This section shall become inoperative on July 1, 2013.
(Amended by Stats. 2013, Ch. 22, Sec. 68. (AB 75) Effective June 27, 2013. Amending action operative July 1, 2013, by Sec. 110 of Ch. 22. Section inoperative July 1, 2013, by its own provisions from this amendment.)

DIVISION 11. EXPLOSIVES [12000 - 12761]

(Division 11 enacted by Stats. 1939, Ch. 60.)

PART 1. HIGH EXPLOSIVES [12000 - 12401]

(Part 1 repealed and added by Stats. 1967, Ch. 1497.)

CHAPTER 1. Definitions and Scope [12000 - 12007]

(Chapter 1 added by Stats. 1967, Ch. 1497.)

12000.
For the purposes of this part, "explosives" means any substance, or combination of substances, the primary or common purpose of which is detonation or rapid combustion, and which is capable of a relatively instantaneous or rapid release of gas and heat, or any substance, the primary purpose of which, when combined with others, is to form a substance capable of a relatively instantaneous or rapid release of gas and heat.
"Explosives" includes, but is not limited to, any explosives as defined in Section 841 of Title 18 of the United States Code and published pursuant to Section 555.23 of Title 27 of the Code of Federal Regulations, and any of the following:
(a) Dynamite, nitroglycerine, picric acid, lead azide, fulminate of mercury, black powder, smokeless powder, propellant explosives, detonating primers, blasting caps, or commercial boosters.
(b) Substances determined to be division 1.1, 1.2, 1.3, or 1.6 explosives as classified by the United States Department of Transportation.
(c) Nitro carbo nitrate substances (blasting agent) classified as division 1.5 explosives by the United States Department of Transportation.
(d) Any material designated as an explosive by the State Fire Marshal. The designation shall be made pursuant to the classification standards established by the United States Department of Transportation. The State Fire Marshal shall adopt regulations in

accordance with the Government Code to establish procedures for the classification and designation of explosive materials or explosive devices that are not under the jurisdiction of the United States Department of Transportation pursuant to provisions of Section 841 of Title 18 of the United States Code and published pursuant to Section 555.23 of Title 27 of the Code of Federal Regulations that define explosives.

(e) Certain division 1.4 explosives as designated by the United States Department of Transportation when listed in regulations adopted by the State Fire Marshal.

(f) For the purposes of this part, "explosives" does not include any destructive device, as defined in Section 16460 of the Penal Code, nor does it include ammunition or small arms primers manufactured for use in shotguns, rifles, and pistols.

(Amended by Stats. 2010, Ch. 178, Sec. 37. (SB 1115) Effective January 1, 2011. Operative January 1, 2012, by Sec. 107 of Ch. 178.)

12001.

This part does not apply to any of the following:

(a) Any person engaged in the transportation of explosives regulated by, and when subject to, the provisions of Division 14 (commencing with Section 31600) of the Vehicle Code.

(b) Small arms ammunition of .75 caliber or less when designated as a division 1.4 explosive by the United States Department of Transportation.

(c) Fireworks regulated under Part 2 (commencing with Section 12500) of this division, including, but not limited to, special effects pyrotechnics regulated by the State Fire Marshal pursuant to Section 12555.

(d) Any explosives while in the course of transportation via railroad, aircraft, water, or highway when the explosives are in actual movement and under the jurisdiction of and in conformity with regulations adopted by the United States Department of Transportation, United States Coast Guard, or the Federal Aviation Agency. However, no explosives shall be sold, given away, or delivered except as provided in Section 12120.

(e) Special fireworks classified by the United States Department of Transportation as division 1.3 explosives when those special fireworks are regulated under Part 2 (commencing with Section 12500) of this division, when a permit has been issued pursuant to regulations of the State Fire Marshal.

(f) (1) Black powder in quantities of 25 pounds or less in the hands of a retailer having a permit issued under Article 2 (commencing with Section 6066) of Chapter 2 of Part 1 of Division 2 of the Revenue and Taxation Code and in quantities of five pounds or less in the hands of all others and smokeless powder in quantities of 20 pounds or less used, possessed, stored, sold, or transported that is exempted under, or authorized by, the Federal Organized Crime Control Act of 1970 (Public Law 91-452) and applicable federal regulations thereunder.

(2) All cities, counties, and special districts and county service areas providing fire protection shall require retailers in possession of black powder to notify fire authorities.

(Amended by Stats. 1998, Ch. 478, Sec. 2. Effective January 1, 1999.)

12002.

Except when transporting explosives on highways and at safe stopping places established under the provisions of Division 14 (commencing with Section 31600) of the Vehicle Code, this part does not affect the operation of provisions of any city, county, or city and county ordinance respecting the delivery, storage, and handling of explosives which are at least as restrictive as the provisions of this part.

(Repealed and added by Stats. 1967, Ch. 1497.)

12003.

"Chief" means the Director of Forestry and Fire Protection and his or her authorized representatives, the chief of a fire department or fire protection agency maintained by a city, county, or city and county, or fire protection district and his or her authorized representatives, or the authorized representative of the United States Forest Service. In any area of the state in which there exists no organized fire protection agency responsible for the protection of the area, "chief," for the purpose of this part only, means the county sheriff and his or her authorized representatives.

On any property that is owned by the state, the "chief," for the purpose of this part, shall be the official of the fire protection agency responsible for the suppression of fires in the area. On any state property where there is no fire protection agency responsible for the suppression of fires, the "chief," for the purpose of this part, shall be the State Fire Marshal.

Upon request of the Director of Forestry and Fire Protection, the chief of a fire department or fire protection agency, or upon request of the county sheriff, the governing body of the area under the jurisdiction of the requesting chief or sheriff may designate any person as "chief" for the purposes of this part.

(Amended by Stats. 1992, Ch. 427, Sec. 90. Effective January 1, 1993.)

12004.

For the purposes of this part, the term "person" shall mean any person, organization, firm, corporation, association, city, county, city and county, and state, and shall include any of their employees and authorized representatives.

(Repealed and added by Stats. 1967, Ch. 1497.)

12005.

This part does not apply to the transportation and use of explosives by representatives of the California Highway Patrol, the State Bureau of Criminal Identification and Investigation, local police departments, sheriff's departments, and fire departments acting in their official capacity, nor shall this part apply to the transportation and use of explosives by any peace officer authorized to enforce the provisions of this part by Section 12020 when he is acting pursuant to such authority.

(Amended by Stats. 1970, Ch. 1425.)

12005.5.

(a) This part shall not apply to the possession, handling, storage, transportation, or use of not more than 10 pounds of blasting agents (division 1.5 explosives), two pounds of division 1.1, 1.2, or 1.3 explosives, or 1,000 feet of detonating cord, or any combination thereof, by authorized employees of the Department of Transportation, acting within the scope of their employment, in the pursuit of seismic explorations.

(b) The Department of Transportation may not undertake that seismic exploration, unless the fire authority having jurisdiction in the area of the proposed seismic exploration has received a written notice from the department at least 48 hours prior to the commencement of the seismic exploration. The notice shall include the time and location of the proposed seismic exploration. In addition, the employee supervising the proposed seismic exploration, or his or her designated representative, shall consult with the fire authority to determine if the proposed handling, storage, transportation, or use of explosives would constitute an unreasonable hazard to life or property. If the fire authority determines that such a hazard would arise, the department shall not engage in that handling, storage, transportation, or use of explosives.

(c) The state shall be strictly liable for any injury to any person or property proximately caused by the handling, storage, transportation, or use of explosives by the Department of Transportation for the purpose of conducting seismic exploration. All claims for damages against the state arising under this section are governed by the procedures set forth in Part 3 (commencing with Section 900) and Part 4 (commencing with Section 940) of Division 3.6 of Title 1 of the Government Code.

(Amended by Stats. 1998, Ch. 478, Sec. 3. Effective January 1, 1999.)

12006.

The provisions of this part and the regulations adopted by the State Fire Marshal pursuant to this part do not apply when the use, handling, possession, storage and transportation is subject to the requirements of the Division of Occupational Safety and Health, Department of Industrial Relations, except as the provisions of this part and the regulations adopted by the State Fire Marshal may extend beyond the scope or authority of the Division of Occupational Safety and Health, Department of Industrial Relations.

(Amended by Stats. 1981, Ch. 714.)

12007.

(a) For the purposes of this part, the term "issuing authority" shall mean either the sheriff of a county, or the chief or other head of a municipal police department of any city or city and county, or the chief of a fire department or fire protection agency, and their authorized representatives, provided that, in the event the designated issuing authority is the chief of a fire department or fire protection agency, such fire department or fire protection agency is organized with regularly paid full-time personnel. The governing body of any county, city, or city and county shall designate one of the above as the issuing authority within its jurisdiction and shall notify the State Fire Marshal of the person so designated.

(b) If the governing body of any county, city, or city and county does not designate an issuing authority pursuant to subdivision (a), the State Fire Marshal shall designate the sheriff of the county as the issuing authority.

(Amended by Stats. 1976, Ch. 1094.)

CHAPTER 2. Enforcement [12020- 12020.]

(Chapter 2 added by Stats. 1967, Ch. 1497.)

12020.

The chief and the issuing authority, as defined in Sections 12003 and 12007, respectively, shall in their areas of jurisdiction enforce the provisions of this part and the regulations adopted by the State Fire Marshal pursuant to this part.

Any peace officer, as defined in Sections 830.1, 830.2, and subdivisions (a), (e), (k), and (l) of Section 830.3 of the Penal Code, and those officers listed in Section 830.6 of the Penal Code while acting in the course and scope of their employment as peace officers may enforce the provisions of this part.

(Amended by Stats. 1990, Ch. 1695, Sec. 3.)

CHAPTER 3. General [12080 - 12092]

(Chapter 3 added by Stats. 1967, Ch. 1497.)

12080.

(a) No person shall sell, give away, or transport any explosive which has not been classified as provided in Section 12000.

(b) The State Fire Marshal, upon receiving an application from any interested party, with the concurrence of the chief in the area affected, and if he determines that such action may be taken without jeopardizing the public welfare and safety, may authorize the transportation of unclassified explosives provided all other provisions of this part are met.

(Added by Stats. 1967, Ch. 1497.)

12081.

Except as limited by Chapter 6 (commencing with Section 140) of Division 1 of the Labor Code and Section 18930 the State Fire Marshal shall prepare and adopt, in accordance with Chapter 3.5 (commencing at Section 11340) of Part 1 of Division 3 of Title 2 of the Government Code, reasonable regulations that are not in conflict with this part, relating to the sale, use, handling, possession, and storage of explosives.

The building standards adopted and submitted for approval pursuant to Chapter 4 (commencing with Section 18935) of Part 2.5 of Division 13 and the other regulations adopted by the State Fire Marshal shall do all of the following:

(a) Make reasonable allowances for storage facilities in existence when the regulations become effective. No allowance, however, shall be made for storage facilities which constitute a distinct hazard to life and property, nor shall any allowance be made for storage facilities wherein proper safeguards for the control and security of explosives cannot be maintained.

(b) Be based on performance standards wherever possible.

(c) Make reasonable allowances for the storage of gunpowder for commercial and private use. No allowance, however, shall be made for storage facilities which constitute a distinct hazard to life and property, nor shall any allowance be made for storage facilities wherein proper safeguards for the control and security of explosives cannot be maintained.

(d) Set uniform requirements for the use and handling of explosives that would apply statewide.

(e) The building standards published in the California Building Standards Code relating to storage of explosives and the other regulations adopted by the State Fire Marshal pursuant to this section shall apply uniformly throughout the state, and no city, county, city and county, or other political subdivision of this state, including, but not limited to, a chartered city, county, or city and county, shall adopt or enforce any ordinance or regulation that is inconsistent with this section.

(f) In making the regulations, the State Fire Marshal shall consider as evidence of generally accepted safety standards the publications of the National Fire Protection Association, the United States Bureau of Mines, the United States Department of Defense, and the Institute of Makers of Explosives.

(g) The regulations shall establish standards relating to the size, form, contents, and location of caution placards to be placed on or near storage facilities for division 1.1, 1.2, and 1.3 explosives as set forth in Article 77 of the Uniform Fire Code of the International Conference of Building Officials and the Western Fire Chiefs Association, Inc. or similar standards that are consistent with the United States Department of Transportation classifications, or for any explosives as defined in Section 841 of Title 18 of the United States Code and published pursuant to Section 555.23 of Title 27 of the Code of Federal Regulations.

(Amended by Stats. 2004, Ch. 247, Sec. 6. Effective August 23, 2004.)

12082.

No explosives shall be sold, furnished, or given away to any person under 21 years of age, whether such person is acting for himself or for another person, nor shall any such person be eligible to obtain any permit to receive explosives governed by the provisions of this part.

The reference to "under 21 years of age" in this section is unaffected by Section 1 of Chapter 1748 of the Statutes of 1971 or any other provision of that chapter.

(Amended by Stats. 1972, Ch. 1011.)

12083.

With the exception of the chief, the owner, a person authorized to enter by the owner, or the owner's agent, no person shall enter any explosive manufacturing plant, magazine, or vehicle containing explosives.

(Added by Stats. 1967, Ch. 1497.)

12084.

No person shall willfully discharge any firearm within 500 feet of any magazine or any explosive manufacturing plant.

(Added by Stats. 1967, Ch. 1497.)

12085.

No person shall make, possess, or transport any explosive in a manner prohibited by this part or prohibited by any ordinance of a city, county, or city and county, or prohibited by the laws or regulations governing a harbor in those areas where such ordinance, laws, or regulations apply.

(Added by Stats. 1967, Ch. 1497.)

12086.

Any theft or loss of explosives, whether from a storage magazine, a vehicle in which they are being transported, or from a site on which they are being used, or from any other location, shall immediately be reported by the person having control of such explosives to the local police or county sheriff. The local police or county sheriff shall immediately transmit a report of such theft or loss of explosives to the State Bureau of Criminal Identification and Investigation at Sacramento.

(Amended by Stats. 1970, Ch. 1425.)

12087.

No person shall abandon or otherwise dispose of any explosives in any manner which might, as the result of such abandonment or disposal, create any danger or threat of danger to life or property. Any person in possession or control of explosives required in the performance of his duties shall, when the need for such explosives no longer exists, either return the explosives to the source from which the explosives were obtained, or to an appropriate issuing authority for disposal or shall destroy the explosives in a safe manner so as not to make them available to persons who might obtain them and use them in a manner prejudicial to the safety of life and property. Magazines or temporary magazines used for storage purposes in any area where blasting is required shall, when the need for such storage no longer exists and the explosives have been removed or disposed of as above required, be removed or demolished, or signs, indicating the presence of explosives in such magazines or on the premises on which such magazines are located, shall be removed or effectively obliterated, and the issuing authority who issued the storage permit shall be immediately notified of the action taken.

(Amended by Stats. 1970, Ch. 1425.)

12088.

The contents of a package containing explosives shall be plainly marked on the outside of the package at the time the package is delivered for transportation.

It is unlawful for any person to deliver, or cause to be delivered, to any carrier for transportation any explosive under any false or deceptive marking, description, invoice, shipping order, or other declaration.

(Added by Stats. 1967, Ch. 1497.)

12089.

Except when transporting explosives received under Section 12102 of this code, every motor vehicle used in the transportation of explosives and which is subject to this part, shall have displayed thereon, signs conforming to the regulations of the United States Department of Transportation.

(Amended by Stats. 1968, Ch. 662.)

12090.

There shall not be included in any cargo of explosives any flammable or combustible liquids, acids, or corrosive liquids, oxidizers, or combustible materials, other than the explosives themselves, which may have such characteristics. Blasting caps or detonators shall not be transported upon the same vehicle with other explosives. The foregoing provisions of this section shall be subject to such exceptions as are permitted by the regulations of the United States Department of Transportation.

(Amended by Stats. 1978, Ch. 868.)

12091.

Blasting caps or similar primary explosive initiation devices shall not be transported upon any vehicle equipped with a radio transmitter or other device which may cause detonation of such primary initiators unless such blasting caps or similar primary explosive initiation devices have been tested and proved safe for transportation by laboratory approved by the State Fire Marshal and there is affixed to the shipping container of such devices a label which states all of the following:

(a) The type of primary explosive initiation devices in the container.

(b) That such devices have been tested and proved safe for transportation upon any vehicle equipped with a radio transmitter or other device which may cause detonation of such primary initiators by a laboratory approved by the State Fire Marshal.

(Amended by Stats. 1969, Ch. 568.)

12092.

Any person who violates any of the requirements prescribed by regulation adopted pursuant to Section 12081 or 12151 shall be assessed a civil penalty of up to one thousand dollars ($1,000) for each violation.

(Added by Stats. 1990, Ch. 734, Sec. 2.)

CHAPTER 4. Permits [12101 - 12112]

(Chapter 4 added by Stats. 1967, Ch. 1497.)

12101.

(a) No person shall do any one of the following without first having made application for and received a permit in accordance with this section:

(1) Manufacture explosives.

(2) Sell, furnish, or give away explosives.

(3) Receive, store, or possess explosives.

(4) Transport explosives.

(5) Use explosives.

(6) Operate a terminal for handling explosives.

(7) Park or leave standing any vehicle carrying explosives, except when parked or left standing in or at a safe stopping place designated as such by the Department of the California Highway Patrol under Division 14 (commencing with Section 31600) of the Vehicle Code.

(b) Application for a permit shall be made to the appropriate issuing authority.

(c) (1) A permit shall be obtained from the issuing authority having the responsibility in the area where the activity, as specified in subdivision (a), is to be conducted.

(2) If the person holding a valid permit for the use or storage of explosives desires to purchase or receive explosives in a jurisdiction other than that of intended use or storage, the person shall first present the permit to the issuing authority in the jurisdiction of purchase or receipt for endorsement. The issuing authority may include any reasonable restrictions or conditions which the authority finds necessary for the prevention of fire and explosion, the preservation of life, safety, or the control and security of explosives within the authority's jurisdiction. If, for any reason, the issuing authority refuses to endorse the permit previously issued in the area of intended use or storage, the authority shall immediately notify both the issuing authority who issued the permit and the Department of Justice of the fact of the refusal and the reasons for the refusal.

(3) Every person who sells, gives away, delivers, or otherwise disposes of explosives to another person shall first be satisfied that the person receiving the explosives has a permit valid for that purpose. When the permit to receive explosives indicates that the intended storage or use of the explosives is other than in that area in which the permittee receives the explosives, the person who sells, gives away, delivers, or otherwise disposes of the explosives shall ensure that the permit has been properly endorsed by a local issuing authority and, further, shall immediately send a copy of the record of sale to the issuing authority who originally issued the permit in the area of intended storage or use. The issuing authority in the area in which the explosives are received or sold shall not issue a permit for the possession, use, or storage of explosives in an area not within the authority's jurisdiction.

(d) In the event any person desires to receive explosives for use in an area outside of this state, a permit to receive the explosives shall be obtained from the State Fire Marshal.

(e) A permit may include any restrictions or conditions which the issuing authority finds necessary for the prevention of fire and explosion, the preservation of life, safety, or the control and security of explosives.

(f) A permit shall remain valid only until the time when the act or acts authorized by the permit are performed, but in no event shall the permit remain valid for a period longer than one year from the date of issuance of the permit.

(g) Any valid permit which authorizes the performance of any act shall not constitute authorization for the performance of any act not stipulated in the permit.

(h) An issuing authority shall not issue a permit authorizing the transportation of explosives pursuant to this section if the display of placards for that transportation is required by Section 27903 of the Vehicle Code, unless the driver possesses a license for the transportation of hazardous materials issued pursuant to Division 14.1 (commencing with Section 32000) of the Vehicle Code, or the explosives are a hazardous waste or extremely hazardous waste, as defined in Sections 25117 and 25115 of the Health and Safety Code, and the transporter is currently registered as a hazardous waste hauler pursuant to Section 25163 of the Health and Safety Code.

(i) An issuing authority shall not issue a permit pursuant to this section authorizing the handling or storage of division 1.1, 1.2, or 1.3 explosives in a building, unless the building has caution placards which meet the standards established pursuant to subdivision (g) of Section 12081.

(j) (1) A permit shall not be issued to a person who meets any of the following criteria:

(A) He or she has been convicted of a felony.

(B) He or she is addicted to a narcotic drug.

(C) He or she is in a class prohibited by state or federal law from possessing, receiving, owning, or purchasing a firearm.

(2) For purposes of determining whether a person meets any of the criteria set forth in this subdivision, the issuing authority shall obtain two sets of fingerprints on prescribed cards from all persons applying for a permit under this section and shall submit these cards to the Department of Justice. The Department of Justice shall utilize the fingerprint cards to make inquiries both within this state and to the Federal Bureau of Investigation regarding the criminal history of the applicant identified on the fingerprint card.

This paragraph does not apply to any person possessing a current certificate of eligibility issued pursuant to subdivisions (a) to (c), inclusive, of Section 26710 of the Penal Code or to any holder of a dangerous weapons permit or license issued pursuant to Section 31000, 32650, or 33300 of the Penal Code, or pursuant to Sections 18900 to 18910, inclusive, or Sections 32700 to 32720, inclusive, of the Penal Code.

(k) An issuing authority shall inquire with the Department of Justice for the purposes of determining whether a person who is applying for a permit meets any of the criteria specified in subdivision (j). The Department of Justice shall determine whether a person who is applying for a permit meets any of the criteria specified in subdivision (j) and shall either grant or deny clearance for a permit to be issued pursuant to the determination. The Department of Justice shall not disclose the contents of a person's records to any person who is not authorized to receive the information in order to ensure confidentiality. If an applicant becomes ineligible to hold a permit, the Department of Justice shall provide to the issuing authority any subsequent arrest and conviction information supporting that ineligibility.

(Amended by Stats. 2010, Ch. 178, Sec. 38. (SB 1115) Effective January 1, 2011. Operative January 1, 2012, by Sec. 107 of Ch. 178.)

12101.5.

This chapter does not apply to any possession or use by a person licensed as a pyrotechnic operator—special effects first class of 20 pounds or less of smokeless powder, or five pounds or less of black sporting powder, if all of the following requirements are satisfied:

(a) All such powder is for use in the pursuit of the lawful business of such licensee and not for resale, and, in the case of black sporting powder, there shall be no gift, delivery or other disposition to another person who is not licensed as a pyrotechnic operator—special effects first class. Any such licensee may sell, give, deliver, or otherwise dispose of any smokeless or black sporting powder to another such licensee.

(b) The storage, use and handling of such smokeless and black powder conforms to rules, regulations, or ordinances of authorities having jurisdiction for fire prevention and suppression in the area of such storage, use, and handling of such explosives.

(Amended by Stats. 1975, Ch. 355.)

12102.

This chapter does not apply to any possession or use of 20 pounds or less of smokeless powder, or one pound or less of black sporting powder, provided that:

(a) Smokeless powder is intended only for hand loading of small arms ammunition of .75 caliber or less.

(b) Black sporting powder is intended for loading of small arms or small arms ammunition of .75 caliber or less.

(c) All such powder is for private use and not for resale, and, in the case of black sporting powder, there shall be no gift, delivery, or other disposition to another person.

(d) The storage, use and handling of such smokeless and black powder conforms to rules, regulations, or ordinances of authorities having jurisdiction for fire prevention and suppression in the area of such storage, use, and handling of such explosives.

(Amended by Stats. 1970, Ch. 1425.)

12102.1.

Any person who sells, gives, delivers or otherwise disposes of 20 pounds or less of smokeless powder, or one pound or less of black sporting powder, shall first obtain a statement from the person who purchases or otherwise receives such powder, which statement shall include:

(a) The name, address and birth date of the person purchasing or receiving the powder.

(b) The purpose for which the powder is intended to be used, handled, stored, or possessed.

(c) The type and amount of the powder.

(d) The signature of the person purchasing or receiving the powder.

(e) The driver's license number, selective service card number, or other identifying information concerning the person purchasing or receiving the powder.

Any person furnishing a fictitious name or address or knowingly furnishing an incorrect birth date and any person violating any of the provisions of this section is guilty of a misdemeanor.

(Added by Stats. 1970, Ch. 1425.)

12103.

Application for a permit, as required under Section 12101, shall be made by filing a statement on forms prescribed by the State Fire Marshal. Such statement shall contain, but shall not necessarily be limited to, the following:

(a) The name and address of the applicant.

(b) The name and address of the employee or authorized representatives designated by the applicant as being responsible for the use, handling, storage, possession, or transportation of explosives for the applicant and whether the employee or authorized representative has been issued a blaster's license by the Division of Industrial Safety to use or handle explosives.

(c) The place where, and the purpose for which, the explosives are intended to be used, handled, stored, or possessed.

(d) The type and amount of explosives for which application is made.

(e) The signature of the applicant.

(f) The number of times purchases may be made and the frequency of such purchases.

(g) The routes, highways, and stopping places intended to be utilized in transporting the explosives.

(Amended by Stats. 1976, Ch. 1094.)

12105.

If the issuing authority finds, after reviewing the application for a permit, that the applicant possesses sufficient and adequate facilities to conduct the acts specified in the application, and that the issuance of such permit would not appear to be contrary to the public welfare and safety, he shall issue a permit authorizing the applicant to engage in such specific acts. Before issuing a permit for the storage of explosives, the issuing authority shall first inspect and approve the storage facility. No application for such a permit shall be approved by the issuing authority unless the storage facility is in strict compliance with the regulations adopted by the State Fire Marshal pursuant to Section 12081. In addition, the issuing authority may, at his discretion, require the submission of any personal information relevant to the acts for which application is made.

A permit shall not be issued until after the payment of a fee of ten dollars ($10), unless the quantity of explosives is 100 pounds or less, in which case the fee shall be two dollars ($2). The permit fee shall be equally divided and deposited into the treasury of the city, county, or city and county having jurisdiction over the issuing authority and into the State Treasury.

(Amended by Stats. 1970, Ch. 1425.)

12105.1.

Except in a case in which the issuing authority determines that the explosives are necessary because of an emergency involving a danger to persons or property, no permit shall normally be issued until one week has elapsed after application is made. If the applicant gives evidence that he has previously been issued an explosives permit pursuant to this part and if the legitimacy of the purpose for which the current application is made is clearly apparent to the issuing authority, the issuing authority may in his discretion issue a permit before one week has elapsed. If no affirmative action is taken on the application within 14 days after the application is made, the issuing authority shall explain the cause for such delay to the applicant.

(Amended by Stats. 1972, Ch. 1011.)

12105.2.

A copy of each permit issued shall be forwarded to the State Bureau of Criminal Identification and Investigation in Sacramento.

(Added by Stats. 1970, Ch. 1425.)

12106.

When required by and in amounts set forth in local ordinance, the applicant for a permit for explosives shall submit evidence that the applicant has a minimum and specified amount of funds available for the purpose of the payment of all damages to persons or property which arise from, or are caused by, the conduct of any act authorized by the permit and from which any legal judgment results.

Such evidence, when required, shall be a bond issued by an authorized surety company or a public liability insurance policy or cash or other evidence of financial security acceptable to the State Fire Marshal. The minimum amount of any such bond or insurance policy shall be determined by the appropriate issuing authority.

The provisions of this section do not apply to any public entity, as defined in Section 811.2 of the Government Code.

(Amended by Stats. 1970, Ch. 1425.)

12107.

The issuing authority shall, in the exercise of reasonable discretion, deny a permit to any person if it is his opinion that the handling or use of explosives by such person would be hazardous to property or dangerous to any person.

(Amended by Stats. 1970, Ch. 1425.)

12108.

The form of the permits shall be prescribed by the State Fire Marshal. Permits shall be numbered by the local agency issuing the permit. The permit shall include on its face the date of expiration of the permit. It shall also include a statement to the effect that any unused portion of explosives authorized by the permit shall either be returned to the source from which the explosives were obtained, destroyed, or returned to an appropriate issuing authority in accordance with Section 12087 or, in lieu thereof, application for a new permit shall be made.
(Amended by Stats. 1970, Ch. 1425.)

12109.

Except as provided in Section 12111, permits shall be valid for the period of time specified thereon.
(Repealed and added by Stats. 1967, Ch. 1497.)

12110.

No permit issued under the provisions of this chapter shall be transferable.
(Repealed and added by Stats. 1967, Ch. 1497.)

12111.

A permit may be suspended or revoked, after reasonable notice and hearing, by any chief or issuing authority in the area in which explosives are sold, used, stored, handled, or possessed, if the person to whom the permit was issued sells, uses, stores, or handles the explosives in a manner which is unlawful or which creates an unreasonable hazard to life and property.

The chief or issuing authority taking action to suspend or revoke a permit shall immediately notify the agency who issued the permit of the action taken and shall also immediately notify the State Bureau of Criminal Identification and Investigation in Sacramento.
(Amended by Stats. 1970, Ch. 1425.)

12112.

Any decision or action by any chief or issuing authority made pursuant to this part may be appealed to the governing body of the area in which such decision or action is made.
(Amended by Stats. 1970, Ch. 1425.)

CHAPTER 5. Sale or Other Disposition [12120 - 12124]

(Chapter 5 added by Stats. 1967, Ch. 1497.)

12120.

No person shall knowingly sell, give away, deliver, or otherwise dispose of any explosive to any person who does not possess a valid permit as required pursuant to Section 12101.

The provisions of this section and subdivisions (e) and (f) of Section 12122 do not apply to transactions by the Department of Defense or to the transactions of an agency or organization acting pursuant to contract with the Department of Defense.
(Amended by Stats. 1968, Ch. 662.)

12121.

Every person who possesses, stores, uses, sells, gives away, delivers, or otherwise disposes of explosives shall keep an accurate journal, record book, or a record of sale in which he shall note each possession, storage, use, sale, delivery, gift, or other disposition of an explosive and the time when such disposition is made whether in the course of business or otherwise. Such journal, record book, or the record of sale shall be kept on file for a period of not less than three years. Field records required to be kept pursuant to Section 12123 need be kept in the appropriate county only for the period of the possession, storage, use, sale, gift, delivery, or other disposition of explosives within that county, after which time the field records may be destroyed.
(Amended by Stats. 1970, Ch. 1425.)

12122.

Each notation in the journal, record book, or each record of sale, as required by Section 12121, shall legibly show:
(a) The date of each purchase or receipt, storage, use, sale, delivery, gift, or other disposition of explosives.
(b) The name and quantity of the explosives possessed, stored, used, sold, delivered, given away, or otherwise disposed of.
(c) The name, address, and business of the purchaser or transferee, where applicable.
(d) When the explosives are to be transported under Division 14 (commencing with Section 31600) of the Vehicle Code, the permit number issued by the California Highway Patrol; or when transported other than under Division 14 (commencing with Section 31600) of the Vehicle Code, the vehicle operator's license number or other comparable identification, the motor vehicle license number of the vehicle used, and the name and address of the individual to whom the explosives are to be delivered.
(e) The number of the permit to receive explosives.
(f) The name of the public agency which issued the permit and the name of the officer issuing such permit.
(Amended by Stats. 1970, Ch. 1425.)

12123.

The journal, record book or record of sale shall be kept by the person required to keep it in his principal office or place of business. It shall be at all times, on proper demand, subject to the inspection and examination of any chief or other duly authorized law enforcement official. In addition, if the principal office or place of business is located in a place other than the county within which the explosives are possessed, stored, used, sold, given away, delivered, or otherwise disposed of, field records shall be kept in that

county during the period of such possession, storage, use, sale, gift, delivery or other disposition.
(Amended by Stats. 1970, Ch. 1425.)

12124.

The keeping of a journal, record book, or record of sale required by Sections 12121, 12122, and 12123 does not apply to those persons who are rendering a delivery service under a permit issued by the California Highway Patrol pursuant to Division 14 (commencing with Section 31600) of the Vehicle Code, nor does it apply to any possessor or user of explosives not required to have a permit under Section 12102. A journal, record book, or record of sale need not be kept by anyone who is in lawful possession of an explosive and who receives and detonates all such explosives within a 24-hour period.
(Amended by Stats. 1970, Ch. 1425.)

CHAPTER 6. Storage [12150 - 12151]

(Chapter 6 added by Stats. 1967, Ch. 1497.)

12150.

Except for explosives kept only at an explosive manufacturing plant, no person shall possess, keep, or store any explosive which is not completely encased in a tight metal, wooden, or fiber container, or a container approved by the Interstate Commerce Commission.

No person having any explosives in his possession or control shall under any circumstances permit or allow any grains or particles of such explosives to be or remain on the outside of, or about, the containers in which such explosives are kept.
(Repealed and added by Stats. 1967, Ch. 1497.)

12150.5.

Every person having any blasting caps (electric or nonelectric) in his possession or control shall keep the same securely deposited in a locked approved magazine, except when taken therefrom for actual use, transportation, or sale.
(Amended by Stats. 1969, Ch. 568.)

12151.

Except while in the custody of a common carrier or in course of transportation pending delivery to a consignee, all explosives shall be kept or stored as specified in the rules or regulations adopted by the State Fire Marshal pursuant to this part.
(Repealed and added by Stats. 1967, Ch. 1497.)

CHAPTER 7. Illegal Use or Possession [12303 - 12305]

(Chapter 7 added by Stats. 1967, Ch. 1497.)

12303.

"Lawful possession of an explosive," as used in this chapter, means possessing explosives in accordance with the stated purpose and conditions of a valid permit obtained pursuant to the provisions of this part, unless such person is specifically excepted from the permit requirements by the provisions of this part.
(Amended by Stats. 1970, Ch. 1425.)

12305.

Every person not in the lawful possession of an explosive who knowingly has any explosive in his possession is guilty of a felony.
(Repealed and added by Stats. 1967, Ch. 1497.)

CHAPTER 8. Confiscation [12350 - 12355]

(Chapter 8 added by Stats. 1967, Ch. 1497.)

12350.

Except as provided in subdivision (b) of Section 12080, any unclassified explosives which are sold, given away, or transported shall be subject to immediate seizure by any chief or police official.
(Repealed and added by Stats. 1967, Ch. 1497.)

12351.

Any explosives which are illegally manufactured, sold, given away, delivered, stored, used, possessed, or transported shall be subject to immediate seizure by any chief, issuing authority, or peace officer authorized to act under Section 12020. When a permit issued pursuant to this part has expired and is not immediately renewed, any explosives in the possession of the permittee shall be subject to immediate seizure by any chief, issuing authority, or peace officer authorized to act under Section 12020, unless first destroyed by the permittee in accordance with Section 12087.
(Amended by Stats. 1970, Ch. 1425.)

12352.

When a permit issued pursuant to this part has been suspended or revoked any explosives in the possession of such permittee shall be subject to immediate seizure by the chief causing such suspension or revocation.
(Repealed and added by Stats. 1967, Ch. 1497.)

12353.

Any explosive seized under this chapter shall be stored in an approved manner and in accordance with regulations adopted by the State Fire Marshal. The person from whom such explosives have been seized may within 10 days after such seizure petition the governing body of the area in which such seizure was made to return the explosives upon the ground that such explosives were illegally or erroneously seized. Any such petition so filed shall be considered by the governing body within 15 days after filing and an oral

hearing shall be granted the petitioner if requested. Notice of the decision of the governing body shall be served upon the petitioner.
(Repealed and added by Stats. 1967, Ch. 1497.)

12354.
If the governing body finds that the explosives were illegally or erroneously seized, the explosives shall be returned to the petitioner. The determination of the governing body is final unless within 60 days of the notice served pursuant to this chapter, an action is commenced in a court of competent jurisdiction in the State of California for the recovery of the explosives seized by the chief.
(Repealed and added by Stats. 1967, Ch. 1497.)

12355.
If no petition is received by the governing body within 10 days of seizure of any explosive, or if no action is commenced in a court of competent jurisdiction in the State of California within 60 days of the notice served pursuant to this chapter, the chief may dispose of the seized explosives in any manner which will not jeopardize public welfare and safety. When any explosive is disposed of pursuant to this section, the person from whom such disposed of explosives were seized shall not have any legal redress against the chief who caused the disposal of the explosives.
(Added by Stats. 1967, Ch. 1497.)

CHAPTER 9. Penalties [12400 - 12401]
(Chapter 9 added by Stats. 1967, Ch. 1497.)

12400.
Except as provided in Chapter 7 (commencing with Section 12302), Part 1, Division 11 of the Health and Safety Code, every person who violates any provision of this part, or violates any regulation adopted by the State Fire Marshal pursuant to this part, is guilty of a misdemeanor, punishable by a fine of not more than one thousand dollars ($1,000), or by imprisonment for not more than six months, or by both such fine and imprisonment.
(Repealed and added by Stats. 1967, Ch. 1497.)

12401.
Every person who is found guilty of a felony as specified in this part is punishable by imprisonment pursuant to subdivision (h) of Section 1170 of the Penal Code, or in a county jail not exceeding one year, or by fine not exceeding ten thousand dollars ($10,000), or by both such fine and imprisonment.
(Amended by Stats. 2011, Ch. 15, Sec. 183. (AB 109) Effective April 4, 2011. Operative October 1, 2011, by Sec. 636 of Ch. 15, as amended by Stats. 2011, Ch. 39, Sec. 68.)

PART 2. FIREWORKS AND PYROTECHNIC DEVICES [12500 - 12728]
(Part 2 repealed and added by Stats. 1973, Ch. 1109.)

CHAPTER 1. General Provisions and Definitions [12500 - 12534]
(Chapter 1 added by Stats. 1973, Ch. 1109.)

12500.
This part shall be known and may be cited as the State Fireworks Law.
(Repealed and added by Stats. 1973, Ch. 1109.)

12501.
Unless the context otherwise requires, the definitions in this chapter govern the construction of this part.
(Repealed and added by Stats. 1973, Ch. 1109.)

12502.
"Advertise" means an announcement publicly with any sign, card, or notice, or by any other means, on which appears a person's name or business name style offering to sell or transfer fireworks or pyrotechnic devices, or to cause a person's name or business name style to be included in any classified advertisement or directory for the purpose of the sale or transfer of fireworks or pyrotechnic devices.
(Repealed and added by Stats. 1973, Ch. 1109.)

12503.
"Agricultural and wildlife fireworks" means fireworks designed and intended by the manufacturer to be used to prevent damage to crops or unwanted occupancy of areas by animals or birds through the employment of sound or light, or both.
(Repealed and added by Stats. 1973, Ch. 1109.)

12504.
"Flammable liquid" means any liquid whose flashpoint is 100 degrees Fahrenheit, or less, when tested pursuant to Standard D56-70 of the American Society for Testing and Materials.
(Amended by Stats. 1978, Ch. 868.)

12505.
"Dangerous fireworks" includes all of the following:
(a) Any fireworks which contain any of the following:
(1) Arsenic sulfide, arsenates, or arsenites.
(2) Boron.
(3) Chlorates, except:
(A) In colored smoke mixture in which an equal or greater amount of sodium bicarbonate is included.
(B) In caps and party poppers.

(C) In those small items (such as ground spinners) wherein the total powder content does not exceed 4 grams of which not greater than 15 percent (or 600 milligrams) is potassium, sodium, or barium chlorate.
(4) Gallates or Gallic acid.
(5) Magnesium (magnesium-aluminum alloys, called magnalium, are permitted).
(6) Mercury salts.
(7) Phosphorous (red or white except that red phosphorus is permissible in caps and party poppers).
(8) Picrates or picric acid.
(9) Thiocyanates.
(10) Titanium, except in particle size greater than 100-mesh.
(11) Zirconium.
(b) Firecrackers.
(c) Skyrockets and rockets, including all devices which employ any combustible or explosive material and which rise in the air during discharge.
(d) Roman candles, including all devices which discharge balls of fire into the air.
(e) Chasers, including all devices which dart or travel about the surface of the ground during discharge.
(f) Sparklers more than 10 inches in length or one-fourth of one inch in diameter.
(g) All fireworks designed and intended by the manufacturer to create the element of surprise upon the user. These items include, but are not limited to, auto-foolers, cigarette loads, exploding golf balls, and trick matches.
(h) Fireworks known as devil-on-the-walk, or any other firework which explodes through means of friction, unless otherwise classified by the State Fire Marshal pursuant to this part.
(i) Torpedoes of all kinds which explode on impact.
(j) Fireworks kits.
(k) Such other fireworks examined and tested by the State Fire Marshal and determined by him, with the advice of the State Board of Fire Services, to possess characteristics of design or construction which make such fireworks unsafe for use by any person not specially qualified or trained in the use of fireworks.
(Amended by Stats. 1977, Ch. 513.)

12506.
"Emergency signaling device" means a pyrotechnic device designed and intended by the manufacturer to be used as such and which provides a reasonable degree of safety to the user and does not create a fire hazard when used according to the label of instructions.
(Repealed and added by Stats. 1973, Ch. 1109.)

12507.
"End fuse" means a fuse inserted into any fireworks or pyrotechnic device at the end as distinguished from the side of such item.
(Repealed and added by Stats. 1973, Ch. 1109.)

12508.
"Exempt fireworks" means any special item containing pyrotechnic compositions which the State Fire Marshal, with the advice of the State Fire Advisory Board, has investigated and determined to be limited to industrial, commercial, agricultural use, or religious ceremonies when authorized by a permit granted by the authority having jurisdiction.
(Repealed and added by Stats. 1973, Ch. 1109.)

12509.
"Exporter" means any person who sells, consigns, or delivers fireworks located within this state for delivery, use, or sale out of this state.
(Repealed and added by Stats. 1973, Ch. 1109.)

12510.
"Fire nuisance" means anything or any act which increases, or may cause an increase of, the hazard or menace of fire, or which may obstruct, delay, or hinder, or may become the cause of any obstruction, delay, or hindrance, to the prevention or extinguishment of fire.
(Repealed and added by Stats. 1973, Ch. 1109.)

12511.
"Fireworks" means any device containing chemical elements and chemical compounds capable of burning independently of the oxygen of the atmosphere and producing audible, visual, mechanical, or thermal effects which are useful as pyrotechnic devices or for entertainment.
The term "fireworks" includes, but is not limited to, devices designated by the manufacturer as fireworks, torpedoes, skyrockets, roman candles, rockets, Daygo bombs, sparklers, party poppers, paper caps, chasers, fountains, smoke sparks, aerial bombs, and fireworks kits.
(Repealed and added by Stats. 1973, Ch. 1109.)

12512.
"Fireworks kit" means any assembly of materials or explosive substances, which is designed and intended by the seller to be assembled by the person receiving such material or explosive substance and when so assembled would come within the definition of fireworks in Section 12511.
(Repealed and added by Stats. 1973, Ch. 1109.)

12513.
"Importer" means any person who for any purpose does any of the following:
(a) Brings fireworks into this state or causes fireworks to be brought into this state.
(b) Procures the delivery or receives shipments of any fireworks into this state.
(c) Buys or contracts to buy fireworks for shipment into this state.
(Repealed and added by Stats. 1973, Ch. 1109.)

12514.

"Issuing authority" means any person who has the responsibility of evaluating the application for, and issuing, the permits required by Section 12640.
(Repealed and added by Stats. 1973, Ch. 1109.)
12515.
"Label of registration" means the label of registration of the State Fire Marshal.
(Repealed and added by Stats. 1973, Ch. 1109.)
12516.
"License" means any nontransferable authorization granted by the State Fire Marshal to engage in any activity regulated by this part.
(Repealed and added by Stats. 1973, Ch. 1109.)
12517.
"Licensee" means any person 21 years of age or older holding a fireworks license issued pursuant to Chapter 5 (commencing with Section 12570).
(Repealed and added by Stats. 1973, Ch. 1109.)
12518.
"Manufacturer" means any person who manufactures, makes, constructs, fabricates, or produces any fireworks or pyrotechnic devices, but does not include any person who assembles or fabricates any sets or mechanical pieces for public displays of fireworks, or persons operating within the scope of public display or pyrotechnic operator licenses.
(Repealed and added by Stats. 1973, Ch. 1109.)
12519.
"Model rocket" means a toy or educational device that weighs not more than 1500 grams, including the engine and any payload, that is propelled by a model rocket motor, and that conforms to the definition of "model rocket" in the 2013 edition of the "NFPA 1122: Code for Model Rocketry," or a more recent edition as adopted by the State Fire Marshal.
(Amended by Stats. 2015, Ch. 106, Sec. 1. (AB 467) Effective January 1, 2016.)
12520.
"Model rocket motor" means a rocket propulsion device using commercially manufactured solid propellant, that does not require mixing by the user, and that conforms to the definition of "model rocket motor" in the 2012 edition of the "NFPA 1125: Code for the Manufacture of Model Rocket and High Power Rocket Motors," or a more recent edition as adopted by the State Fire Marshal.
(Amended by Stats. 2015, Ch. 106, Sec. 2. (AB 467) Effective January 1, 2016.)
12521.
"Package" includes any case, container, or receptacle, used for holding fireworks, which is closed or sealed by tape, cordage, or by any other means.
(Repealed and added by Stats. 1973, Ch. 1109.)
12522.
"Permit" means the nontransferable permission granted by the public agency having local jurisdiction to a licensee for the purposes of establishing and maintaining a place where fireworks are manufactured, constructed, produced, packaged, stored, sold, exchanged, discharged, or used, or the nontransferable permission granted by the public agency having local jurisdiction or by the State Fire Marshal to a licensee for the purpose of transporting fireworks.
(Repealed and added by Stats. 1973, Ch. 1109.)
12523.
"Person" means any person, copartnership, organization, firm, corporation, association, or any combination thereof, or any city, county, city and county, and state, and shall include any of their employees and authorized representatives.
(Repealed and added by Stats. 1973, Ch. 1109.)
12524.
"Public display of fireworks" means an entertainment feature where the public or a private group is admitted or permitted to view the display or discharge of dangerous fireworks.
(Repealed and added by Stats. 1973, Ch. 1109.)
12525.
"Pyrotechnic compositions" means any combination of chemical elements or chemical compounds capable of burning independently of the oxygen of the atmosphere.
(Repealed and added by Stats. 1973, Ch. 1109.)
12526.
"Pyrotechnic device" means any combination of materials, including pyrotechnic compositions, which, by the agency of fire, produce an audible, visual, mechanical or thermal effect designed and intended to be useful for industrial, agricultural, personal safety, or educational purposes.
The term "pyrotechnic device" includes, but is not limited to, agricultural and wildlife fireworks, model rockets, exempt fireworks, emergency signaling devices, and special effects.
(Repealed and added by Stats. 1973, Ch. 1109.)
12527.
"Pyrotechnic operator" means any licensed pyrotechnic operator, who by examination, experience, and training, has demonstrated the required skill and ability in the use and discharge of fireworks as authorized by the license granted.
(Added by Stats. 1973, Ch. 1109.)
12528.
"Retailer" means any person who, at a fixed place of business, sells, transfers, or gives fireworks to a consumer or user.
(Added by Stats. 1973, Ch. 1109.)
12529.

"Safe and sane fireworks" means any fireworks which do not come within the definition of "dangerous fireworks" or "exempt fireworks."
(Added by Stats. 1973, Ch. 1109.)
12530.
"Salesman" means any person who, as an employee of a manufacturer or wholesaler, solicits, accepts, or receives an order for fireworks for a licensee or permittee.
(Added by Stats. 1973, Ch. 1109.)
12531.
"Sell" means any arrangement between two or more persons as a result of which there is a transfer of property for a consideration.
(Added by Stats. 1973, Ch. 1109.)
12532.
"Special effects" means articles containing any pyrotechnic composition manufactured and assembled, designed, or discharged in connection with television, theater, or motion picture productions, which may or may not be presented before live audiences and any other articles containing any pyrotechnic composition used for commercial, industrial, education, recreation, or entertainment purposes when authorized by the authority having jurisdiction.
(Added by Stats. 1973, Ch. 1109.)
12533.
"Wholesaler" means any person, other than an importer, exporter, or manufacturer selling only to wholesalers, who sells fireworks to a retailer or any other person for resale. It also includes any person who sells dangerous fireworks to public display permittees.
(Added by Stats. 1973, Ch. 1109.)
12534.
"Within this state" means within all territory within the boundaries of this state.
(Added by Stats. 1973, Ch. 1109.)

CHAPTER 2. Exceptions [12540 - 12541.1]
(Chapter 2 added by Stats. 1973, Ch. 1109.)
12540.
The provisions of this part shall not apply to any of the following:
(a) Explosives regulated under Part 1 (commencing with Section 12000) of Division 11.
(b) Arms and handguns defined as firearms by the Federal Gun Control Act of 1968, as well as such devices and weapons classified under Section 16460 of the Penal Code or any provision listed in Section 16590 of the Penal Code, including blank cartridge pistols of the type used at sporting events or theatrical productions.
(c) Research or experiments with rockets or missiles or the production or transportation of rockets or missiles by the Department of Defense of the United States, or by any agency or organization acting pursuant to a contract with the Department of Defense for the development and production of rockets or missiles.
(d) Paper caps which contain less than 0.25 grain of pyrotechnic composition per unit load.
(Amended by Stats. 2010, Ch. 178, Sec. 39. (SB 1115) Effective January 1, 2011. Operative January 1, 2012, by Sec. 107 of Ch. 178.)
12541.
Nothing in this part authorizes the sale, use, or discharge of fireworks in any city, county, or city and county in which the sale, use, or discharge is otherwise prohibited or regulated by law or ordinance.
(Amended by Stats. 1984, Ch. 202, Sec. 1. Effective June 19, 1984. Pursuant to Sec. 2 of Ch. 202, Section 12541.1 prevails in case of conflict.)
12541.1.
(a) A special district which provides fire protection, prevention, or suppression services may adopt an ordinance or regulation to prohibit or regulate the sale, use, or discharge of fireworks within that special district.
(b) If the county or city in which any area of the special district is located has adopted an ordinance or regulation to prohibit or regulate the sale, use, or discharge of fireworks within that county or city, the ordinance or regulation adopted by the county or city shall prevail over the ordinance or regulation adopted by the special district within any area of the special district which is within that county or city, and only the ordinance or regulation adopted by the county or city shall be operative in that area of the special district.
(c) If any area of a special district encompasses lands which are a state responsibility area, as defined in Sections 4125 and 4126 of the Public Resources Code, any regulation or prohibition of the state with respect to the sale, use, or discharge of fireworks within the state responsibility area shall prevail over any ordinance or regulation of the special district within that area.
(Added by Stats. 1984, Ch. 262, Sec. 1. Effective June 29, 1984.)

CHAPTER 3. Administration [12550 - 12558]
(Chapter 3 added by Stats. 1973, Ch. 1109.)
12550.
The State Fire Marshal shall enforce and administer this part.
(Repealed and added by Stats. 1973, Ch. 1109.)
12551.
The State Fire Marshal shall appoint deputies and employees as may be required to carry out the provisions of this part, subject to approval in the annual Budget Act.
(Amended by Stats. 2007, Ch. 563, Sec. 1. Effective January 1, 2008.)
12552.

The State Fire Marshal shall adopt regulations relating to fireworks as may be necessary for the protection of life and property not inconsistent with the provisions of this part. These regulations shall include, but are not limited to, provisions for the following:

(a) Granting of licenses and permits for the manufacture, wholesale, import, export, and sale of all classes of fireworks.

(b) Classification of fireworks and pyrotechnic devices.

(c) Registration of employees of licensees.

(d) Licenses and permits required for presentation of public displays.

(e) Granting of licenses and permits for research or experimentation with experimental or model rockets and missiles.

(f) Investigation, examination, and licensing of pyrotechnic operators of all classes.

(g) Registration of emergency signaling devices and the classification and use of exempt fireworks.

(h) Transportation of all classifications of fireworks, model rockets, emergency signaling devices, and exempt fireworks.

(Amended by Stats. 2007, Ch. 563, Sec. 2. Effective January 1, 2008.)

12553.

The State Fire Marshal shall also adopt regulations for classification of any new type of fireworks or pyrotechnic devices which have not been classified prior to January 1, 1974 and for the regulation of such fireworks in accordance with the provisions of this part.
(Repealed and added by Stats. 1973, Ch. 1109.)

12554.

The regulations adopted by the State Fire Marshal relating to fireworks and in existence on January 1, 1974 shall continue thereafter to be in effect as regulations of the State Fire Marshal until amended or repealed pursuant to the provisions of this part.
(Repealed and added by Stats. 1973, Ch. 1109.)

12555.

The State Fire Marshal or his salaried deputies may make an examination of the books and records of any licensee or permittee relative to fireworks, and may visit and inspect any building or other premises subject to the control of, or used by, the licensee or permittee for any purpose related to fireworks of any licensee or permittee at any time he may deem necessary for the purpose of enforcing the provisions of this part.
(Repealed and added by Stats. 1973, Ch. 1109.)

12556.

In addition to the obligations described in Section 13110.5, on or before July 1, 2008, the State Fire Marshal shall identify and evaluate methods to capture more detailed data relating to fires, damages, and injuries caused by both dangerous fireworks and safe and sane fireworks. These evaluation methods shall include a cost analysis related to capturing and reporting the data and shall meet or exceed the specificity, detail, and reliability of the data captured under the former California Fire Incident Reporting System (CFIRS). The State Fire Marshal shall furnish a copy of these evaluation methods to any interested person upon request.
(Added by Stats. 2007, Ch. 563, Sec. 3. Effective January 1, 2008.)

12557.

(a) The Office of the State Fire Marshal shall consult with public safety agencies and other stakeholders as deemed necessary by the State Fire Marshal and develop a model ordinance that permits local jurisdictions to adopt a streamlined enforcement and administrative fine procedures related to the possession of 25 pounds or less of dangerous fireworks. These procedures shall be limited to civil fines and as authorized pursuant to Section 53069.4 of the Government Code, and provide that the fines collected pursuant to this section shall not be subject to Section 12706. The model ordinance shall include provisions for reimbursing the Office of the State Fire Marshal for the costs associated with the disposal of seized fireworks and collecting these disposal costs as part of an administrative fine as described in subdivision (c).

(b) An ordinance of a local jurisdiction in effect on or after January 1, 2008, that is related to dangerous fireworks and is not the model ordinance described in subdivision (a) shall, as soon as practicable, comply with all of the following:

(1) The ordinance shall be amended or adopted to include provisions for cost reimbursement to the Office of the State Fire Marshal and the collection of disposal costs as part of an administrative fine as described in subdivision (c).

(2) The ordinance shall be amended or adopted to provide that the ordinance shall be limited to a person who possesses or the seizure of 25 pounds or less of dangerous fireworks.

(3) The ordinance shall be amended or adopted to provide that the fines collected pursuant to the ordinance shall not be subject to Section 12706.

(c) The State Fire Marshal shall, in consultation with local jurisdictions, develop regulations to specify a procedure on how to cover the cost to the Office of the State Fire Marshal for the transportation and disposal of dangerous fireworks that are seized by local jurisdictions. The regulations shall include, but are not limited to, all of the following:

(1) A cost recovery procedure to collect, as part of an administrative fine, the actual cost for transportation and disposal of dangerous fireworks from any person who violates a local ordinance related to dangerous fireworks.

(2) The method by which the actual cost for transportation and disposal by the Office of the State Fire Marshal will be calculated.

(3) The method, manner, and procedure the local jurisdiction is required to follow to forward the amounts collected pursuant to paragraph (1) to the State Fire Marshal.
(Added by Stats. 2007, Ch. 563, Sec. 4. Effective January 1, 2008.)

12558.

The licensee or permittee shall permit the chief of the issuing authority, or his authorized representatives, as qualified in Section 12721, to enter and inspect any building or other premises subject to the control of or used by the licensee or permittee for any purpose related to fireworks at any time for the purpose of enforcing the provisions of this part.
(Added by Stats. 1973, Ch. 1109.)

CHAPTER 4. Classification of Fireworks and Pyrotechnic Devices [12560 - 12569]

(Chapter 4 added by Stats. 1973, Ch. 1109.)

12560.

The State Fire Marshal shall classify all fireworks and pyrotechnic devices in accordance with the provisions of this chapter. No fireworks or pyrotechnic devices shall be imported, sold, or offered for sale prior to the examination and classification by the State Fire Marshal.
(Added by Stats. 1973, Ch. 1109.)

12561.

All fireworks examined by the State Fire Marshal and determined by him to come within the definition of "dangerous fireworks" in Section 12505 shall be classified as dangerous fireworks.
(Added by Stats. 1973, Ch. 1109.)

12562.

All fireworks examined by the State Fire Marshal and determined by him to come within the definition of "safe and sane fireworks" in Section 12529 shall be classified as safe and sane fireworks.
(Added by Stats. 1973, Ch. 1109.)

12563.

All fireworks examined by the State Fire Marshal and determined by him to come within the definition of "agricultural and wildlife fireworks" in Section 12503 shall be classified as agricultural and wildlife fireworks.
(Added by Stats. 1973, Ch. 1109.)

12564.

All fireworks examined by the State Fire Marshal and determined by him to come within the definition of "exempt fireworks" in Section 12508 shall be classified as exempt fireworks.
(Added by Stats. 1973, Ch. 1109.)

12565.

All fireworks or toy propellent devices containing pyrotechnic compositions examined by the State Fire Marshal and found by him or her to come within the definition of "model rocket" or "model rocket motor" in Section 12519 or 12520, respectively, shall be classified as model rocket motors.
(Amended by Stats. 2015, Ch. 106, Sec. 3. (AB 467) Effective January 1, 2016.)

12566.

All pyrotechnic devices examined by the State Fire Marshal and found by him to come within the definition of "emergency signaling devices" in Section 12506 shall be classified by the State Fire Marshal as emergency signaling devices.
(Added by Stats. 1973, Ch. 1109.)

12567.

Those fireworks classified by the State Fire Marshal as safe and sane prior to January 1, 1974 may continue to bear that designation and may be sold as safe and sane fireworks until 12 noon on July 6, 1974. All fireworks previously designated as safe and sane which are offered for sale or sold during the 1974 retail license year and thereafter shall bear the State Fire Marshal label with the classification of safe and sane fireworks.
(Added by Stats. 1973, Ch. 1109.)

12568.

The manufacturer, importer, or wholesaler shall stamp or label each case or carton of dangerous fireworks offered for sale, sold, consigned, or delivered within the state for sale or use within this state as dangerous fireworks. Each package of safe and sane fireworks shall be marked as safe and sane fireworks and shall bear the State Fire Marshal's classification label and licensee's registration number.
(Added by Stats. 1973, Ch. 1109.)

12569.

Except as provided in Section 12637 and pursuant to the provisions of Sections 12560 and 12581, fireworks or pyrotechnic devices examined and classified by the State Fire Marshal shall be submitted by manufacturers, wholesalers, and importers and exporters holding a valid license only.
(Added by Stats. 1973, Ch. 1109.)

CHAPTER 5. Licenses [12570 - 12637]

(Chapter 5 added by Stats. 1973, Ch. 1109.)

ARTICLE 1. Types of Licenses [12570 - 12579]

(Article 1 added by Stats. 1973, Ch. 1109.)

12570.

The State Fire Marshal may issue any license described in this part, subject to the regulations which he may adopt not inconsistent with the provisions of this part.
(Added by Stats. 1973, Ch. 1109.)

12571.

A manufacturer's license shall allow the manufacture of fireworks and other pyrotechnic devices of all types and the sale and transport to licensed wholesalers in California only and the sale to special effects pyrotechnic operators of materials and devices for which such pyrotechnic operators hold a valid permit.
(Added by Stats. 1973, Ch. 1109.)

12572.

A wholesaler's license allows the sale and transportation of all types of fireworks to licensed retailers, or retailers operating under a permit, licensed public display operators, and other licensed wholesalers in California only and sale to special effects pyrotechnic operators holding a valid permit and sale of exempt fireworks to those industrial and commercial concerns that possess a valid permit from the local agency having jurisdiction in the area where such fireworks are to be used or stored.
(Added by Stats. 1973, Ch. 1109.)

12573.

An importer's and exporter's license shall allow fireworks to be imported into and exported from the state. Import activity shall be limited to the sale of fireworks to licensed wholesalers and licensed manufacturers only. Export activity shall be limited to the sale of fireworks to persons outside of the state. Holders of this type of license shall not be issued or possess a public display license of any type without first securing a wholesaler's license. This section shall not require a license for a motion picture production company to transport or deliver special effects from within the state to a destination outside the state.
(Added by Stats. 1973, Ch. 1109.)

12574.

A retail sales license allows the retail sale of safe and sane fireworks for private use.
(Added by Stats. 1973, Ch. 1109.)

12575.

A public display (special) license allows the holding and conducting at various times of public displays of dangerous fireworks at a single location only.
(Added by Stats. 1973, Ch. 1109.)

12576.

A public display license (general) allows the holding and conducting of public displays of dangerous fireworks at various locations and at various times.
(Added by Stats. 1973, Ch. 1109.)

12577.

A public display license (limited) allows the performance of a single public display action of a single nature with dangerous fireworks at one location to be executed at one or more performances or exhibitions.
(Added by Stats. 1973, Ch. 1109.)

12578.

The State Fire Marshal shall adopt regulations that identify and specify the scope of each class of pyrotechnic operator license. A pyrotechnic operator license shall allow the licensee to handle, supervise, or discharge dangerous fireworks at public displays of all types, and to handle, supervise, or discharge rockets and special effects pyrotechnic devices which produce an audible or visual effect in connection with group entertainment or motion picture productions which may or may not be held before live audiences.
(Amended by Stats. 1990, Ch. 233, Sec. 1.)

12579.

All licensees may transport the class of fireworks for which they hold a valid license as provided in Section 12651.
(Added by Stats. 1973, Ch. 1109.)

ARTICLE 2. Issuance, Revocation and Renewal [12580 - 12608]
(Article 2 added by Stats. 1973, Ch. 1109.)

12580.

The State Fire Marshal may issue and renew licenses for the manufacture, import, export, sale, and use of all fireworks and pyrotechnic devices in this state.
(Added by Stats. 1973, Ch. 1109.)

12581.

Any person who desires to manufacture, import, export, sell or use fireworks, shall first make written application for a license to the State Fire Marshal on forms provided by him. Such application shall be accompanied by the annual license fee as prescribed in this chapter.
(Added by Stats. 1973, Ch. 1109.)

12582.

The application for a license shall be signed by the applicant. If the application is made by a partnership, it shall be signed by each partner of the partnership. If the application is made by a corporation, it shall be signed by an officer of the corporation and bear the corporation's seal.
(Added by Stats. 1973, Ch. 1109.)

12583.

The authorization to engage in the particular act or acts conferred by a license to a person shall extend to salesmen or other employees of such person who are registered with the State Fire Marshal. The sales personnel and other employees of licensed retailers, however, need not be registered with the State Fire Marshal. No person under the age of 18 shall sell, or handle for sale, any classification of fireworks.
(Added by Stats. 1973, Ch. 1109.)

12585.

Any applicant may withdraw his application for a license or renewal of a license and the State Fire Marshal may allow the withdrawal when he has determined that it is in the best interest of public safety or the administration of this part.
(Added by Stats. 1973, Ch. 1109.)

12586.

The suspension, expiration, or forfeiture by operation of law of a license issued by the State Fire Marshal, or its suspension, forfeiture, or cancellation by order of the State Fire Marshal or by a court of law, or its surrender to the State Fire Marshal shall not, during any period in which it may be renewed, restored, reissued, or reinstated, deprive the State Fire Marshal of his authority to institute or continue disciplinary action against the licensee upon any ground provided by law, or to enter an order suspending or revoking a license or otherwise taking disciplinary action against the licensee on any such ground.
(Added by Stats. 1973, Ch. 1109.)

12587.

A written report by the State Fire Marshal, any of his deputies, or salaried assistants, or by the chief of any city or county fire department or fire protection district or their authorized representatives, disclosing that the applicant for a license or for renewal of a license does not meet, or the premises for which the license is required do not meet, the qualifications or conditions for such license as required by this part or regulations adopted pursuant to this part, may constitute grounds for denial of any application for the license or renewal of the license.
(Added by Stats. 1973, Ch. 1109.)

12588.

The State Fire Marshal may deny, without hearing, an application for a license or renewal of a license, if within one year prior to the date of application, the State Fire Marshal has denied or revoked a license after proceedings conducted in accordance with the provisions of Chapter 5 (commencing with Section 11500) of Part 1 of Division 3 of Title 2 of the Government Code for the same applicant on the ground of violation of this part.
(Added by Stats. 1973, Ch. 1109.)

12589.

The application for any license shall become void when any of the following occurs:
(a) The State Fire Marshal has notified the applicant to appear for examination and the applicant fails to appear or fails to submit a written statement of just cause for not appearing.
(b) The applicant fails to achieve a passing score on a required examination. A minimum qualifying score shall be established by regulations pursuant to this part.
(c) The applicant has not submitted documentary evidence of his qualifications as required by regulations adopted pursuant to this part.
(d) The applicant has failed to submit evidence of insurability as required by this part.
(e) The applicant withdraws his application prior to an investigation by the State Fire Marshal to determine if the license shall be issued.
(f) The license is denied after a hearing is conducted as provided by this part.
(g) The applicant has made misrepresentations or filed false statements.
(Added by Stats. 1973, Ch. 1109.)

12590.

The State Fire Marshal may deny or revoke any license issued pursuant to this part if the State Fire Marshal finds any of the following conditions has occurred:
(a) The licensee has failed to pay the annual renewal license fee provided in this chapter.
(b) The licensee or license applicant has violated any provisions of this part or any regulations adopted by the State Fire Marshal pursuant to this part.
(c) The licensee or license applicant has created or caused a fire nuisance.
(d) The licensee has failed to keep full, complete, and accurate records or failed to file any required reports.
(e) Any fact or condition exists which, if it had existed at the time of the original application for the license reasonably would have warranted the State Fire Marshal in refusing originally to issue the license.
(f) The permit issued under Section 12640 has been rescinded or revoked by the issuing authority.
(g) Any licensee or license applicant has refused to make available to the State Fire Marshal full, complete, and accurate records.
(Amended by Stats. 1985, Ch. 622, Sec. 1.)

12591.

The State Fire Marshal may, upon three days notice, suspend any license for a period not exceeding 30 days pending investigation of any violation of the provisions of this part.
(Added by Stats. 1973, Ch. 1109.)

12592.

Any applicant who has been denied a license or renewal of a license, or any licensee who has had a license suspended, shall be entitled to a hearing in accordance with the provisions of this part.
(Added by Stats. 1973, Ch. 1109.)

12593.

Except where otherwise provided in this part, all hearings under this part shall be conducted in accordance with Chapter 5 (commencing with Section 11500) of Part 1 of Division 3 of Title 2 of the Government Code.
(Added by Stats. 1973, Ch. 1109.)

12594.

Reports on fireworks transactions or the payment of license fees or penalties required by this part shall be deemed to have been made or paid at the time they are filed with, or paid to, the State Fire Marshal, or, if sent by mail, on the date shown by the United States postmark on the envelope containing the report or payment.
(Added by Stats. 1973, Ch. 1109.)

12595.

Except as otherwise provided in Section 12599, on and after July 1, 1974, the original and annual license fee shall be for the fiscal year beginning July 1 and ending June 30 of the following year, or for the remaining portion of such fiscal year if the license is issued after the beginning of that fiscal year.
(Added by Stats. 1973, Ch. 1109.)

12596.

Any person or organization may obtain any license required by this part between January 1, 1974, and June 30, 1974, to be effective for that period only.
(Added by Stats. 1973, Ch. 1109.)
12597.
Application for renewal of a license shall be made during the license renewal period in the current license year in order to renew a license for the next following license year. The license renewal period shall begin on January 1 and end May 1 preceding the license year for which renewal is requested. A penalty of 50 percent of the basic license fee shall be assessed in all cases where the renewal fees are not paid on or before May 1, preceding the license year for which renewal is requested. This section shall not apply to retail sales licenses.
(Added by Stats. 1973, Ch. 1109.)
12598.
Every licensee who fails to renew his or her license by the time the license expires shall surrender the license to the State Fire Marshal within 10 days after the license expires.
(Amended by Stats. 1985, Ch. 622, Sec. 2.)
12599.
A retail license shall authorize a retail sale of safe and sane fireworks within this state only during the period of 12 noon on the 28th of June through 12 noon on the 6th of July of the same calendar year and such license shall expire at the end of such period. No retail license shall be issued for the license period defined in this section unless the application for such license is received by the State Fire Marshal on or before June 15 preceding the license period. A new retail sales license shall be required annually for the period specified in this section.
(Added by Stats. 1973, Ch. 1109.)
12600.
Except as provided in Section 12583, the authority to perform any acts permitted by a license issued under this part shall be limited to the licensee and shall not be transferable.
(Repealed and added by Stats. 1973, Ch. 1109.)
12601.
Except as provided in Section 12599, any license not renewed in accordance with the provisions of this part shall automatically expire at 12 midnight on June 30 of each year.
(Repealed and added by Stats. 1973, Ch. 1109.)
12602.
A license shall not be required for the retail sale, use, or discharge of agricultural and wildlife fireworks, model rocket motors, or emergency signaling devices.
(Amended by Stats. 2015, Ch. 106, Sec. 4. (AB 467) Effective January 1, 2016.)
12603.
No person or employee holding a pyrotechnic license shall be required to obtain a manufacturer's license to design, assemble, compound, use, discharge, fabricate, construct, or erect any fireworks of any class or any combination thereof when such person or employee of such person is engaged in the business of producing television, motion picture, theater, or opera productions if the fireworks are for a specific use in a particular production or are used to maintain a reasonable inventory of special effects by a special effects independent contractor.
(Repealed and added by Stats. 1973, Ch. 1109.)
12604.
Following the revocation or voluntary surrender of a license, or failure to renew his license, any person in lawful possession of lawfully acquired fireworks for which a license is required may sell or otherwise dispose of such fireworks only under supervision of the State Fire Marshal and in such a manner as he shall provide by regulations and solely to persons who are authorized to buy, possess, sell, or use such fireworks. Such disposal shall be accomplished not later than 90 days from the legal revocation, voluntary surrender, or day that the license expires. Any person possessing fireworks pursuant to this section shall report the disposition of such fireworks to the local authority who issued the storage permit within the time period specified by this section.
(Repealed and added by Stats. 1973, Ch. 1109.)
12605.
Any person found guilty of violating any of the provisions of this part is not eligible to apply for a new license, apply for a renewal of a license, or take an examination for any license for a period of one year from the date of any conviction. The State Fire Marshal may waive the provisions of this section when he finds the granting of a license will not endanger public safety.
(Repealed and added by Stats. 1973, Ch. 1109.)
12606.
Any charges against applicants for a license or against licensees which would be cause for the State Fire Marshal to initiate proceedings for revocation or denial of a license shall be filed with the State Fire Marshal within three years of the alleged act or omission.
(Repealed and added by Stats. 1973, Ch. 1109.)
12606.1.
(a) If the State Fire Marshal or his or her designee determines that the public interest and public welfare will be adequately served by permitting a person licensed under this chapter to pay a monetary penalty to the State Fire Marshal in lieu of an actual license suspension, the State Fire Marshal or his or her designee may stay the execution of all or part of the suspension if all of the following conditions are met:
(1) The violation that is the cause for the suspension did not pose, or have the potential to pose, a significant threat or risk of harm to the public.
(2) The licensee pays a monetary penalty.

(3) The licensee does not incur any other cause for disciplinary action within a period of time specified by the State Fire Marshal or his or her designee.
In making the determination, the State Fire Marshal or his or her designee shall consider the seriousness of the violation, the violator's record of compliance with the law, the impact of the determination on the licensee, the licensee's employees or customers, and other relevant factors.
(b) The State Fire Marshal or his or her designee may exercise the discretion granted under this section either with respect to a suspension ordered by a decision after a contested hearing on an accusation against the licensee or by stipulation with the licensee after the filing of an accusation, but prior to the rendering of a decision based upon the accusation. In either case, the terms and conditions of the disciplinary action against the licensee shall be made part of a formal decision of the State Fire Marshal or his or her designee.
(c) If a licensee fails to pay the monetary penalty in accordance with the terms and conditions of the decision of the State Fire Marshal or his or her designee, the State Fire Marshal or his or her designee may, without a hearing, order the immediate execution of all or any part of the stayed suspension in which event the licensee shall not be entitled to any repayment nor credit, prorated or otherwise, for money paid to the State Fire Marshal under the terms of the decision.
(d) The amount of the monetary penalty payable under this section shall not exceed two hundred fifty dollars ($250) for each day of suspension stayed nor a total of ten thousand dollars ($10,000) per decision regardless of the number of days of suspension stayed under the decision.
(e) Any monetary penalty received pursuant to this section shall be deposited in the State Fire Marshal Licensing and Certification Fund.
(f) On or before March 1 of each year, the State Fire Marshal shall make available to the public data showing the percentage of enforcement actions taken that resulted in license suspension or the assessment of monetary penalties pursuant to this section.
(Added by Stats. 2010, Ch. 161, Sec. 1. (AB 1773) Effective January 1, 2011.)
12607.
The State Fire Marshal may deny the application for a license or the application for renewal of a license filed by any person who has been convicted of a felony involving explosives or dangerous fireworks or who has been convicted as a principal or accessory in a crime against property involving arson or any other fire-related offense contained in Chapter 1 (commencing with Section 447a) of Title 13 of Part 1 of the Penal Code.
(Amended by Stats. 1979, Ch. 626.)
12608.
The authority to perform those acts conferred upon the employee of a licensee as provided for in Section 12583 may be denied to any person who has been convicted of a felony.
(Amended by Stats. 1979, Ch. 626.)

ARTICLE 3. Insurance [12610 - 12611]
(Article 3 added by Stats. 1973, Ch. 1109.)
12610.
Notwithstanding any of the provisions of the law which may require a certificate of insurance as a condition for a permit to hold a general, special, or limited public display, any person, firm, or corporation applying for a public display license shall furnish to the State Fire Marshal a policy of public liability and property damage insurance, with limits, as determined by the State Fire Marshal, which are reasonably necessary to cover possible liability for damage to property and bodily injury or damage to persons which may result from, or be caused by, the public display of fireworks, or any negligence on the part of the licensee or his or her or its agents, servants, employees, or subcontractors presenting the public display.
(Amended by Stats. 1985, Ch. 622, Sec. 3. Became operative upon adoption of regulations, as prescribed by Sec. 4 of Ch. 622.)
12611.
The certificate of insurance shall provide all of the following:
(a) That the insurer will not cancel the insured's coverage without 15 days' prior written notice to the State Fire Marshal.
(b) That the duly licensed pyrotechnic operator required by law to supervise and discharge the public display, acting either as an employee of the insured or as an independent contractor and the State of California, its officers, agents, employees, and servants are included as additional insureds, but only insofar as any operations under contract are concerned.
(c) That the state shall not be responsible for any premium or assessments on the policy.
(Added by Stats. 1973, Ch. 1109.)

ARTICLE 4. Reports [12615 - 12620]
(Article 4 added by Stats. 1973, Ch. 1109.)
12615.
All licensees, except retailers, shall maintain and make available to the State Fire Marshal full and complete, true, and accurate records showing all production, imports, exports, purchases, sales, or other disposition or consumption of fireworks by kind and class whether dangerous, safe and sane, or agricultural and wildlife fireworks.
(Added by Stats. 1973, Ch. 1109.)
12616.
The licensees shall report any theft or loss of fireworks to the State Fire Marshal within 24 hours after the discovery of theft or loss. The report shall show the quantity, type and kind, classification of fireworks and the location where the loss occurred.

(Added by Stats. 1973, Ch. 1109.)

12617.

In the event of the theft or loss of any fireworks or pyrotechnic devices, the State Fire Marshal shall notify the fire authorities in the location where the theft or loss occurred and the fire authorities shall cooperate with the State Fire Marshal in conducting a joint investigation of the circumstances.

(Added by Stats. 1973, Ch. 1109.)

12618.

Each bill of lading, manifest, and invoice issued to cover the sale and shipment of fireworks shall bear the license number of both the seller or shipper and buyer or receiver.

(Added by Stats. 1973, Ch. 1109.)

12619.

All import and export licensees shall file a notice with the State Fire Marshal prior to the arrival of any class of fireworks subject to the license he holds. The notice shall state all of the following:

(a) Estimated date of arrival.

(b) Type, kind, and quantity of fireworks.

(c) Name of carrier.

(d) Point of origin and bill of lading number.

(e) Name and address of consignee.

(f) Load number or other identification carton marks.

(Added by Stats. 1973, Ch. 1109.)

12620.

In addition to the report required under this part, the State Fire Marshal may by regulation require such additional reports from licensees or permittees as are necessary to carry out the purposes of this part, and prescribe the form, including verification of the information to be given when filing such additional reports.

(Added by Stats. 1973, Ch. 1109.)

ARTICLE 5. Fees [12630 - 12637]

(Article 5 added by Stats. 1973, Ch. 1109.)

12630.

The State Fire Marshal shall establish and collect the original and annual renewal fees for fireworks licenses required by this chapter. The fees shall not exceed the amount necessary to cover the costs incurred in the administration and enforcement of this part.

(Repealed and added by Stats. 1983, Ch. 1313, Sec. 2.)

12631.

The original and annual renewal license fee to manufacture, import, export, or wholesale, or any combination thereof, agricultural and wildlife fireworks shall be established and collected by the State Fire Marshal.

(Amended by Stats. 1983, Ch. 1313, Sec. 3.)

12632.

The original and annual renewal license fee to manufacture, import, export, or wholesale, or any combination thereof, model rocket motors shall be established and collected by the State Fire Marshal.

(Amended by Stats. 2015, Ch. 106, Sec. 5. (AB 467) Effective January 1, 2016.)

12633.

The original and annual renewal application for registration of each model of emergency signaling devices shall be made to the State Fire Marshal. A registration fee established and collected by the State Fire Marshal for each model of signaling device shall accompany each application.

(Amended by Stats. 1990, Ch. 233, Sec. 2.)

12634.

When a license to manufacture, wholesale, or import and export fireworks has been issued pursuant to Section 12571, 12572, or 12573, respectively, a separate license for the same person to manufacture, wholesale, import, or export agricultural and wildlife fireworks or model rocket motors pursuant to Section 12631 or 12632 shall not be required where the license allows the activity with respect to other fireworks.

(Amended by Stats. 2015, Ch. 106, Sec. 6. (AB 467) Effective January 1, 2016.)

12635.

All of the moneys collected pursuant to this part shall be deposited in the State Fire Marshal Licensing and Certification Fund established pursuant to Section 13137 and shall be available, when appropriated by the Legislature, to the State Fire Marshal to carry out this part.

(Amended by Stats. 1992, Ch. 306, Sec. 1. Effective January 1, 1993. Operative July 1, 1993, by Sec. 6 of Ch. 306.)

12636.

Except as otherwise provided by law, the State Fire Marshal shall charge a fee in the amount of five dollars ($5) for each certified copy of any record, document, or paper in his custody, or for certification of any document representing the content of any such record, document, or paper.

(Added by Stats. 1973, Ch. 1109.)

12637.

All fireworks or pyrotechnic devices intended for sale in this state, which are products of nonlicensed manufacturers, shall be examined and classified by the State Fire Marshal upon written application on forms provided by him. Such application shall be accompanied by a fee as follows:

(a) Ten dollars ($10) for each label of an item of identical size and design of a given lot or batch, provided that the lot or batch is identifiable by a code, serial number, shipment lot, case cargo number, etc.

A separate application and fee shall be submitted for each lot or batch. The State Fire Marshal seal and the wholesalers or importers registration number shall not be imprinted on the label until the lot or batch has been examined and classified.

(Added by Stats. 1973, Ch. 1109.)

CHAPTER 6. Permits [12640 - 12654]

(Chapter 6 added by Stats. 1973, Ch. 1109.)

12640.

In any case in which this chapter requires that a permit be obtained from the State Fire Marshal, or in any case in which the public agency having local jurisdiction requires pursuant to this chapter that a permit be obtained, a licensee shall possess a valid permit before performing any of the following:

(a) Manufacturing, importing, exporting, storing, possessing, or selling dangerous fireworks at wholesale.

(b) Manufacturing, importing, exporting, storing, or selling at wholesale or retail safe and sane fireworks or transporting safe and sane fireworks, except that a transportation permit shall not be required for safe and sane fireworks possessed by retail licensees.

(c) Manufacturing, importing, exporting, possessing, storing, transporting, using, or selling at wholesale or retail, those fireworks classified by the State Fire Marshal as agricultural and wildlife fireworks.

(d) Manufacturing, importing, exporting, possessing, storing, or selling at wholesale or retail, model rocket motors.

(e) Discharging dangerous fireworks at any place, including a public display.

(f) Using special effects.

(Amended by Stats. 2016, Ch. 86, Sec. 182. (SB 1171) Effective January 1, 2017.)

12641.

A permit, as provided in this part, shall not be required of any person to transport, purchase at retail, or use safe and sane fireworks, or to purchase at retail, use, or transport registered emergency signaling devices.

(Added by Stats. 1973, Ch. 1109.)

12642.

The effective period of the permit shall be defined in the permit and in no case shall the period of the permit exceed the valid period of the license. This section shall not prohibit the revocation of the permit by the issuing authority for just cause where a fire nuisance exists or where personal injury may occur.

(Added by Stats. 1973, Ch. 1109.)

12643.

Any licensee desiring to do any act specified in Section 12640 shall first make written application for a permit to the chief of the fire department or the chief fire prevention officer of the city or county, or to such other issuing authority which may be designated by the governing body of the city or county. In the event there is no such officer or person appointed within the area, application shall be made to the State Fire Marshal or his deputy. Applications for permits shall be made in writing at least 10 days prior to the proposed act.

(Added by Stats. 1973, Ch. 1109.)

12644.

The issuing authority shall not accept an application for a permit from any person who does not possess, and present at the time of application, evidence of a valid license to perform those acts specified on the application for the permit. When a license is not required for specific acts, the issuing authority may prescribe such reasonable conditions to qualify the applicant to receive a permit and provide for the public safety.

(Added by Stats. 1973, Ch. 1109.)

12645.

The officer to whom the application for a permit is made shall undertake an investigation and submit a report of his findings and his recommendation concerning the issuance of the permit, together with his reasons therefor, to the governing body of the city or county. The applicant for a permit to conduct a public display shall file a certificate evidencing the possession of a valid public display license with the officer making the investigation.

(Added by Stats. 1973, Ch. 1109.)

12646.

The governing body may grant or deny the permit, subject to such reasonable conditions, if any, as it shall prescribe.

(Added by Stats. 1973, Ch. 1109.)

12647.

The governing body may delegate the power to grant or deny the permit to the issuing authority to whom the application is made. In such case, the governing body shall also provide for a hearing by the governing body by which an applicant may appeal a denial of the permit. The governing body may, after such a hearing, reverse, modify, or sustain the denial.

(Added by Stats. 1973, Ch. 1109.)

12648.

The officer to whom the application for a permit for a public display of fireworks is made shall make an investigation to determine whether such a display as proposed will be of such character or so located that it may be hazardous to property or dangerous to any person. He shall, in the exercise of reasonable discretion, recommend granting or denying the permit, subject to such conditions as he may prescribe.

(Added by Stats. 1973, Ch. 1109.)

12649.

The applicant for a permit for any public display of fireworks shall, at the time of application, submit his license for inspection and furnish proof that he carries compensation insurance for his employees as provided by the laws of this state.
(Added by Stats. 1973, Ch. 1109.)

12650.
When a permit for the public display of fireworks is granted, the sale, possession, transportation, and use of fireworks for the public display is lawful for that purpose only. The permit to hold a public display shall authorize the transportation of public display fireworks between the approved routes, as specified in Section 12651, and the public display site.
(Repealed and added by Stats. 1973, Ch. 1109.)

12651.
Any person holding a valid license for the manufacture, wholesale, or import and export of dangerous fireworks or pyrotechnic devices may transport any class of fireworks or pyrotechnic devices authorized by such license. Persons holding a special effects pyrotechnic operators license may transport special effects fireworks, but the transportation of fireworks by all other pyrotechnic operator licensees shall not be permitted. The authority granted to the licensee to transport fireworks is limited to traveling upon the approved routes for the transportation of explosives designated as provided in Section 31616 of the Vehicle Code. The licensee shall also comply with Section 27903 of the Vehicle Code and equip and maintain any vehicle used to transport fireworks as required by Section 31610 of the Vehicle Code. It is the intent of the Legislature by this section to require the maximum use of the approved routes in the delivery of fireworks to the point of destination.
(Amended by Stats. 1986, Ch. 248, Sec. 146.)

12652.
When traveling between the approved routes, as specified in Section 12651, and the point of destination the licensee shall possess a transportation permit from the local fire authority having jurisdiction over the boundaries in which the off-route travel occurs. A transportation permit is not required for public display fireworks as provided in Section 12650.
(Repealed and added by Stats. 1973, Ch. 1109.)

12653.
The application for a transportation permit shall be submitted to the State Fire Marshal for the transportation of any quantity of fireworks where such transportation is outside the boundaries of the issuing authority having jurisdiction at the point of origin or such shipment originates within this state and is transported out of this state. The application for a transportation permit as required by this section shall be approved by the issuing authority having jurisdiction at the place where the shipment originates before the State Fire Marshal shall issue such transportation permit. No further permits shall be required by issuing authorities other than the authority at the point of origin where the State Fire Marshal has issued a permit pursuant to this section.
(Repealed and added by Stats. 1973, Ch. 1109.)

12654.
A transportation permit shall not be required by this part for public carriers or private carriers who each hold a valid license or permit issued pursuant to the provisions of Division 14 (commencing with Section 31600) of the Vehicle Code or Division 11 (commencing with Section 12000) of the Health and Safety Code.
(Repealed and added by Stats. 1973, Ch. 1109.)

CHAPTER 7. Violations [12670 - 12692]

(Chapter 7 added by Stats. 1973, Ch. 1109.)

12670.
It is unlawful for any person to advertise that he is in any business or venture involving fireworks or pyrotechnic devices or shall cause his name or business name style to be included in any classified advertisement or directory under a classification which includes the word fireworks, unless he is licensed pursuant to this part.
(Added by Stats. 1973, Ch. 1109.)

12671.
It is unlawful for any person to sell, offer for sale, use, discharge, possess, store, or transport any type of fireworks within this state unless the State Fire Marshal has classified and registered such fireworks.
(Added by Stats. 1973, Ch. 1109.)

12672.
It is unlawful for any person to sell, or offer for sale, safe and sane fireworks at any time outside of the period specified in Section 12599.
(Added by Stats. 1973, Ch. 1109.)

12673.
It is unlawful for any person to store any fireworks without having in his possession a valid permit as required by this part.
(Added by Stats. 1973, Ch. 1109.)

12674.
It is unlawful for any person to store or possess any fireworks for which a license is required and which has been revoked or surrendered or any license which has not been renewed and such storage or possession is held beyond the period provided for in Section 12604.
(Added by Stats. 1973, Ch. 1109.)

12675.
It is unlawful for any person to fail to record on each bill of lading, manifest or invoice issued to cover the sale or shipment of fireworks, the license number of both the seller or

shipper and the buyer or receiver, unless the sale or shipment is made to nonlicensees in accordance with the provisions of his license.
(Added by Stats. 1973, Ch. 1109.)

12676.
It is unlawful for any person to sell, transfer, give, deliver, or otherwise convey title of any dangerous fireworks, including fireworks kits, to any person in this state who does not possess and present to the seller or donor for inspection at the time of transfer, a valid permit to receive, use, or transport dangerous fireworks as provided in this part.
(Added by Stats. 1973, Ch. 1109.)

12677.
It is unlawful for any person to possess dangerous fireworks without holding a valid permit.
(Added by Stats. 1973, Ch. 1109.)

12678.
It is unlawful for any person to use or discharge agricultural and wildlife fireworks without first securing a permit as provided in this part.
(Added by Stats. 1973, Ch. 1109.)

12679.
It is unlawful for any person to store, sell, or discharge any type of fireworks in or within 100 feet of a location where gasoline or any other flammable liquids are stored or dispensed.
(Amended by Stats. 1978, Ch. 868.)

12680.
(a) Except as provided in subdivision (b) or (c), it is unlawful for any person to place, throw, discharge or ignite, or fire dangerous fireworks at or near any person or group of persons where there is a likelihood of injury to that person or group of persons or when the person willfully places, throws, discharges, ignites, or fires the fireworks with the intent of creating chaos, fear, or panic.
(b) Subdivision (a) does not apply to a person described in Section 12517 who uses special effects. For purposes of this subdivision, "special effects" means articles containing any pyrotechnic composition manufactured and assembled, designed, or discharged in connection with television, theater, or motion picture productions, which may or may not be presented before live audiences, and any other articles containing any pyrotechnic composition used for commercial, industrial, educational, recreational, or entertainment purposes when authorized by the authority having jurisdiction.
(c) Subdivision (a) does not apply to a person holding a fireworks license issued pursuant to Chapter 5 (commencing with Section 12570).
(Amended by Stats. 2000, Ch. 274, Sec. 1. Effective January 1, 2001.)

12681.
It is unlawful for any person to sell or transfer any safe and sane fireworks to a consumer or user thereof other than at a fixed place of business of a retailer for which a license and permit has been issued.
(Added by Stats. 1973, Ch. 1109.)

12682.
It is unlawful for any person to allow or permit a fire nuisance, as defined in Section 12510, to exist on any premises where any fireworks are manufactured, sold, assembled, discharged, packaged, stored, or distributed. The authority to determine that a fire nuisance exists shall be vested in those officers identified in Section 12721.
(Added by Stats. 1973, Ch. 1109.)

12683.
It is unlawful for any person to sell, use, or discharge any emergency signaling device not registered by the State Fire Marshal.
(Added by Stats. 1973, Ch. 1109.)

12684.
It is unlawful for any person to use or discharge any registered emergency signaling device in any manner other than that permitted by the instructions for use.
(Added by Stats. 1973, Ch. 1109.)

12685.
It is unlawful for any person to conduct a public display without possessing a valid permit for this purpose.
(Added by Stats. 1973, Ch. 1109.)

12686.
It is unlawful for any person to use any special effects fireworks unless he possesses a pyrotechnic operator license.
(Added by Stats. 1973, Ch. 1109.)

12687.
It is unlawful for any person to sell, transfer, give, or deliver any special effects fireworks to any person not licensed as a pyrotechnic operator.
(Added by Stats. 1973, Ch. 1109.)

12688.
It is unlawful for a person to advertise to sell or transfer any class of fireworks, including agricultural and wildlife fireworks or model rocket motors, unless he or she possesses a valid license or permit.
(Amended by Stats. 2015, Ch. 106, Sec. 8. (AB 467) Effective January 1, 2016.)

12689.
(a) It is unlawful for any person to sell, give, or deliver any dangerous fireworks to any person under 18 years of age.
(b) It is unlawful for any person who is a retailer to sell or transfer any safe and sane fireworks to a person who is under 16 years of age.

(c) Except as otherwise provided in subdivision (d), it is unlawful for any person who is a retailer to sell or transfer to a person under the age of 18 any rocket, rocket propelled projectile launcher, or similar device containing any explosive or incendiary material whether or not the device is designed for emergency or distance signaling purposes. It is also unlawful for a minor to possess such a device unless he or she has the written permission of, or is accompanied by, his or her parent or guardian while it is in his or her possession.

(d) Model rocket products including model rockets, launch systems, and model rocket motors designed, sold, and used for the purpose of propelling recoverable model rockets may be sold or transferred pursuant to regulations, adopted by the State Fire Marshal which the Fire Marshal determines are reasonably necessary to carry out the requirements of this part.

(Amended by Stats. 1983, Ch. 56, Sec. 1. Effective May 31, 1983.)

12690.

It is unlawful for any person to perform any act, or transact or attempt to transact any business, with an expired license or an expired permit where a license or permit is required for the performance of such act or transaction.

(Added by Stats. 1973, Ch. 1109.)

12691.

It is unlawful for any person to violate any provision of any regulation adopted by the State Fire Marshal pursuant to this part.

(Added by Stats. 1973, Ch. 1109.)

12692.

This chapter shall not prohibit the operations or functions of a licensed pyrotechnic operator holding a special effects license when the operations or functions are a necessary part of the production and are performed pursuant to a valid permit issued by the authority having jurisdiction.

(Amended by Stats. 1990, Ch. 233, Sec. 3.)

CHAPTER 8. Penalties [12700 - 12706]

(Chapter 8 added by Stats. 1973, Ch. 1109.)

12700.

(a) Except as provided in Section 12702 and subdivision (b), a person who violates any provision of this part, or any regulations issued pursuant to this part, is guilty of a misdemeanor, and upon conviction shall be punished by a fine of not less than five hundred dollars ($500) or more than one thousand dollars ($1,000), or by imprisonment in the county jail for not exceeding one year, or by both that fine and imprisonment.

(b) A person who violates any provision of this part, or any regulations issued pursuant to this part, by possessing dangerous fireworks shall be subject to the following:

(1) A person who possesses a gross weight, including packaging, of less than 25 pounds of unaltered dangerous fireworks, as defined in Section 12505, is guilty of a misdemeanor, and upon conviction shall be punished by a fine of not less than five hundred dollars ($500) or more than one thousand dollars ($1,000), or by imprisonment in the county jail for not exceeding one year, or by both that fine and imprisonment. Upon a second or subsequent conviction, a person shall be punished by a fine of not less than one thousand dollars ($1,000) or by imprisonment in a county jail not exceeding one year or by both that fine and imprisonment.

(2) A person who possesses a gross weight, including packaging, of not less than 25 pounds or more than 100 pounds of unaltered dangerous fireworks, as defined in Section 12505, is guilty of a public offense, and upon conviction shall be punished by imprisonment in a county jail for not more than one year, or by a fine of not less than one thousand dollars ($1,000) or more than five thousand dollars ($5,000), or by both that fine and imprisonment.

(3) A person who possesses a gross weight, including packaging, of not less than 100 pounds or more than 5,000 pounds of unaltered dangerous fireworks, as defined in Section 12505, is guilty of a public offense, and upon conviction shall be punished by imprisonment pursuant to subdivision (h) of Section 1170 of the Penal Code or a county jail for not more than one year, or by a fine of not less than five thousand dollars ($5,000) or more than ten thousand dollars ($10,000), or by both that fine and imprisonment.

(4) A person who possesses a gross weight, including packaging, of more than 5,000 pounds of unaltered dangerous fireworks, as defined in Section 12505, is guilty of a public offense, and upon conviction shall be punished by imprisonment pursuant to subdivision (h) of Section 1170 of the Penal Code, or a county jail for not more than one year, or by a fine of not less than ten thousand dollars ($10,000) or more than fifty thousand dollars ($50,000), or by both that fine and imprisonment.

(c) Subdivision (b) shall not apply to a person who holds and is operating within the scope of a valid license as described in Section 12516 or valid permit as described in Section 12522.

(Amended by Stats. 2011, Ch. 15, Sec. 184. (AB 109) Effective April 4, 2011. Operative October 1, 2011, by Sec. 636 of Ch. 15, as amended by Stats. 2011, Ch. 39, Sec. 68.)

12701.

A person is guilty of a separate offense for each day during which he or she commits, continues, or permits a violation of this part, or any order or regulation issued pursuant to this part.

(Amended by Stats. 2006, Ch. 538, Sec. 371. Effective January 1, 2007.)

12702.

Notwithstanding the provisions of Section 12700:

(a) A person who violates this part by selling, giving, or delivering any dangerous fireworks to any person under 18 years of age is guilty of a misdemeanor and upon a first conviction shall be punished as prescribed in subdivision (b) of Section 12700.

(b) Upon a second or subsequent conviction of the offense, the person shall be punished by an additional fine of five thousand dollars ($5,000), or by imprisonment in a county jail for up to one year or by both that fine and imprisonment. The person shall not be granted probation and the execution of the sentence imposed upon the person shall not be suspended by the court.

(Amended by Stats. 2007, Ch. 563, Sec. 6. Effective January 1, 2008.)

12703.

(a) The State Fire Marshal shall, in conjunction with the Department of Motor Vehicles, develop regulations and procedures to temporarily suspend the commercial motor vehicle license of a person who is operating a commercial motor vehicle while transporting unaltered dangerous fireworks, as defined in Section 12505, having a gross weight, including packaging, of 10,000 pounds or more.

(b) A driver of a commercial motor vehicle shall not operate a commercial motor vehicle for three years if the driver is convicted of transporting unaltered dangerous fireworks, as defined in Section 12505, having a gross weight, including packaging, of 10,000 pounds or more, as described in Section 15301 of the Vehicle Code.

(c) This section shall not apply to a person who holds and is operating within the scope of a valid license as described in Section 12516 or valid permit as described in Section 12522.

(Added by Stats. 2007, Ch. 563, Sec. 7. Effective January 1, 2008.)

12704.

The State Fire Marshal, at least once a year and in consultation with the Attorney General, shall serve notice to any individual or business known to supply fireworks that any unauthorized shipments of fireworks into California will result in an immediate report to federal authorities with a request for any relevant federal prosecution.

(Added by Stats. 2007, Ch. 563, Sec. 8. Effective January 1, 2008.)

12706.

Notwithstanding Section 1463 of the Penal Code, all fines and forfeitures imposed by or collected in any court of this state, except for administrative fines described in Section 12557, as a result of citations issued by a public safety agency, for any violation of subdivision (b) of Section 12700 or of any regulation adopted pursuant to subdivision (b) of Section 12700, shall be deposited, as soon as practicable after the receipt of the fine or forfeiture, with the county treasurer of the county in which the court is situated. Amounts deposited pursuant to this section shall be paid at least once a month as follows:

(a) Sixty-five percent to the Treasurer, by warrant of the county auditor drawn upon the requisition of the clerk or judge of the court, for deposit in the State Fire Marshal Fireworks Enforcement and Disposal Fund, as described in Section 12728, on order of the Controller. At the time of the transmittal, the county auditor shall forward to the Controller, on the form or forms prescribed by the Controller, a record of the imposition, collection, and payments of the fines or forfeitures.

(b) Thirty-five percent to the local public safety agency in the county in which the offense was committed to reimburse the local public safety agency for expenses, including, but not limited to, the costs for handling, processing, photographing, and storing seized dangerous fireworks.

(Added by Stats. 2007, Ch. 563, Sec. 9. Effective January 1, 2008.)

CHAPTER 9. Remedies [12720 - 12728]

(Chapter 9 added by Stats. 1973, Ch. 1109.)

12720.

Any threatened violation of any provision of this part or of any order or regulation of the State Fire Marshal issued pursuant to this part may be enjoined in a civil action brought in the name of the people of the State of California. Such actions may be instituted by the Attorney General or the district attorney of the county in which the act, practice, or transaction is about to be committed.

(Added by Stats. 1973, Ch. 1109.)

12721.

The State Fire Marshal, his or her salaried deputies, or any chief of a fire department, or his or her authorized representatives, any fire protection agency, or any other public agency authorized by statute to enforce the State Fire Marshal's regulations, may seize any fireworks described in this part. The State Fire Marshal, any chief of a fire department, any fire protection agency, or any other public agency authorized to enforce the State Fire Marshal's regulations may charge any person, firm, or corporation, whose fireworks are seized pursuant to this section, an amount which is sufficient to cover the cost of transporting, storing, and handling the seized fireworks. When the State Fire Marshal, other enforcing officer or agency described in this section, or a court determines that a person's, firm's, or corporation's fireworks are illegally or erroneously seized, or if legal proceedings do not result in a conviction for violation of any provision of this part, any funds collected pursuant to this section shall be refunded, or if charged but unpaid, canceled.

(Amended by Stats. 1984, Ch. 681, Sec. 1.)

12722.

The following fireworks may be seized pursuant to Section 12721:

(a) Those fireworks that are sold, offered for sale, possessed, stored, used, or transported within this state prior to having been examined, classified, and registered by the State Fire Marshal, except those specific items designated as samples pending examination, classification, and registration by the State Fire Marshal where the licensee provides documentary evidence that the action by the State Fire Marshal is pending.

(b) All imported fireworks possessed without benefit of the filing of notices as required by this part.

(c) Safe and sane fireworks stored in violation of the conditions required by the permit as provided in this part.

(d) Safe and sane fireworks sold or offered for sale at retail that do not bear the State Fire Marshal label of registration and firing instructions.

(e) Safe and sane fireworks sold or offered for sale at retail that are in unsealed packages or containers that do not bear the State Fire Marshal label of registration and firing instructions.

(f) Safe and sane fireworks sold or offered for sale at retail before 12 noon on the 28th day of June or after 12 noon on the sixth day of July of each year.

(g) Each safe and sane fireworks item sold or offered for sale at retail that does not have its fuse or other igniting device protected by a cap approved by the State Fire Marshal, or groups of fireworks with exposed fuses that are not enclosed in sealed packages that bear the State Fire Marshal label of registration. The State Fire Marshal shall approve the caps as he or she determines provide reasonable protection from unintentional ignition of the fireworks.

(h) Dangerous fireworks, including fireworks kits, used, possessed, stored, manufactured, or transported by a person who does not possess a valid permit authorizing an activity listed in this part.

(i) Fireworks stored or sold in a public garage or public oil station, or on any premises where gasoline or any other class 1 flammable liquids are stored or dispensed.

(j) Fireworks still possessed by a person who has just thrown any ignited fireworks at a person or group of persons.

(k) Model rocket motors or model rockets with motors possessed by a person who does not hold a valid permit.

(l) An emergency signaling device sold, offered for sale, or used that does not bear the State Fire Marshal label of registration as required by this part.

(m) Fireworks or pyrotechnic device offered for sale by a person violating this part.
(Amended by Stats. 2015, Ch. 106, Sec. 9. (AB 467) Effective January 1, 2016.)

12723.

(a) The authority seizing fireworks under the provisions of this chapter shall notify the State Fire Marshal not more than three days following the date of seizure and shall state the reason for the seizure and the quantity, type, and location of the fireworks. Fireworks, with the exception of dangerous fireworks, seized pursuant to Section 12721 shall be disposed of by the State Fire Marshal in the manner prescribed by the State Fire Marshal at any time subsequent to 60 days from the seizure or 10 days from the final termination of proceedings under the provisions of Section 12593 or 12724, whichever is later. Dangerous fireworks shall be disposed of according to procedures in Sections 12724 and 12726. Fireworks seized by any authority as defined in this chapter, other than the State Fire Marshal or his or her salaried assistants, shall be held in trust for the State Fire Marshal by that authority.

(b) This section shall become operative on January 1, 2016.
(Repealed (in Sec. 9) and added by Stats. 2015, Ch. 24, Sec. 10. (SB 83) Effective June 24, 2015. Section operative January 1, 2016, by its own provisions.)

12724.

(a) Any person whose fireworks are seized under the provisions of this chapter may, within 10 days after seizure, petition the State Fire Marshal to return the fireworks seized upon the ground that the fireworks were illegally or erroneously seized. Any petition filed pursuant to this section shall be considered by the State Fire Marshal within 15 days after filing or after a hearing granted to the petitioner, if requested. The State Fire Marshal shall advise the petitioner of his or her decision in writing. The determination of the State Fire Marshal is final unless within 60 days after seizure an action is commenced in a court of competent jurisdiction in the State of California for the recovery of the fireworks seized pursuant to this part, except as provided in subdivision (b).

(b) The determination of the State Fire Marshal is final in the case of the seizure of dangerous fireworks, unless within 20 days after the notice of the determination is mailed to the petitioner an action is commenced in a court of competent jurisdiction in the State of California for the recovery of the fireworks seized pursuant to this part.
(Amended by Stats. 1985, Ch. 629, Sec. 2.)

12725.

The State Fire Marshal, his salaried deputies, or any chief or his authorized representatives as qualified in this chapter may prevent, stop, or cause to be stopped, any public display in progress, or any proposed public display, when the location, discharge, or firing of such public display is determined by him to be hazardous to property or dangerous to the public.
(Added by Stats. 1973, Ch. 1109.)

12726.

(a) The dangerous fireworks seized pursuant to this part shall be disposed of by the State Fire Marshal in the manner prescribed by the State Fire Marshal at any time after the final determination of proceedings under Section 12724, or upon final termination of proceedings under Section 12593, whichever is later. If no proceedings are commenced pursuant to Section 12724, the State Fire Marshal may dispose of the fireworks after all of the following requirements are satisfied:

(1) A random sampling of the dangerous fireworks has been taken, as defined by regulations adopted by the State Fire Marshal pursuant to Section 12552.

(2) The analysis of the random sampling has been completed.

(3) Photographs have been taken of the dangerous fireworks to be destroyed.

(4) The State Fire Marshal has given written approval for the destruction of the dangerous fireworks. This approval shall specify the total weight of the dangerous fireworks seized, the total weight of the dangerous fireworks to be destroyed, and the total weight of the dangerous fireworks not to be destroyed.

(b) To carry out the purposes of this section, the State Fire Marshal shall acquire and use statewide mobile dangerous fireworks destruction units to collect and destroy seized dangerous fireworks from local and state agencies.

(c) If dangerous fireworks are seized pursuant to a local ordinance that provides for administrative fines or penalties and these fines or penalties are collected, the local government entity collecting the fines or penalties shall forward 65 percent of the collected moneys to the Controller for deposit in the State Fire Marshal Fireworks Enforcement and Disposal Fund, as described in Section 12728.

(d) This section shall become operative on January 1, 2016.
(Repealed (in Sec. 11) and added by Stats. 2015, Ch. 24, Sec. 12. (SB 83) Effective June 24, 2015. Section operative January 1, 2016, by its own provisions.)

12727.

(a) The State Fire Marshal shall establish regulations pursuant to the requirements and procedures established with the Office of Administrative Law to assess fees on all import and export, wholesale, and retail fireworks licensees in California to be deposited in the State Fire Marshal Fireworks Enforcement and Disposal Fund.

(b) In determining the appropriate amount of the fees described in subdivision (a), the State Fire Marshal shall consult with the fireworks industry and import and export, wholesale, and retail fireworks licensees.

(c) The total amount of the fees collected shall not exceed the reasonable costs of the statewide programs described in subdivision (c) of Section 12728.
(Added by Stats. 2007, Ch. 563, Sec. 11. Effective January 1, 2008.)

12728.

(a) The State Fire Marshal Fireworks Enforcement and Disposal Fund is hereby established in the State Treasury.

(b) All of the moneys collected pursuant to Section 12706 shall be deposited in the fund and shall be available, upon appropriation by the Legislature, to the State Fire Marshal for the exclusive use in statewide programs for the enforcement, prosecution related to, disposal, and management of seized dangerous fireworks, and for the education of public safety agencies in the proper handling and management of dangerous fireworks.

(c) All of the moneys collected pursuant to Section 12727 shall be deposited in the fund and shall be available, upon appropriation by the Legislature, to the State Fire Marshal for the exclusive use in statewide programs for all of the following:

(1) To further assist in statewide programs for the enforcement, prosecution related to, disposal, and management of seized dangerous fireworks.

(2) The education of public safety agencies in the proper handling and management of dangerous fireworks as well as safety issues involving all fireworks and explosives.

(3) Assist the State Fire Marshal in identifying and evaluating methods to capture more detailed data relating to fires, damages, and injuries caused by both dangerous and safe and sane fireworks, and to assist with funding the eventual development and implementation of those methods.

(4) To further assist in public safety and education efforts within the general public as well as public safety agencies on the proper and responsible use of safe and sane fireworks.
(Added by Stats. 2007, Ch. 563, Sec. 12. Effective January 1, 2008.)

PART 3. FLAMETHROWING DEVICES [12750 - 12761]

(Part 3 added by Stats. 2004, Ch. 496, Sec. 1.)

CHAPTER 1. Definitions and Scope [12750 - 12751]

(Chapter 1 added by Stats. 2004, Ch. 496, Sec. 1.)

12750.

For purposes of this part, the following definitions shall apply:

(a) "Flamethrowing device" means any nonstationary and transportable device designed or intended to emit or propel a burning stream of combustible or flammable liquid a distance of at least 10 feet.

(b) "Permitholder" means a person who holds a flamethrowing device permit issued pursuant to this part.
(Added by Stats. 2004, Ch. 496, Sec. 1. Effective January 1, 2005.)

12751.

This part shall not apply to the sale, purchase, possession, transportation, storage, or use of a flamethrowing device by a person if all of the following apply:

(a) The person is regularly employed by or a paid officer, employee, or member of a fire department, fire protection district, or firefighting agency of the federal government, the state, a city, a county, a city and county, district, public or municipal corporation, or political subdivision of this state.

(b) The person is on duty and acting within the course and scope of his or her employment.

(c) The flamethrowing device is used by the fire department, fire protection district, or firefighting agency described in subdivision (a) in the course of fire suppression.
(Added by Stats. 2007, Ch. 30, Sec. 1. Effective January 1, 2008.)

CHAPTER 2. Administration [12755 - 12759]

(Chapter 2 added by Stats. 2004, Ch. 496, Sec. 1.)
12755.
No person shall use or possess a flamethrowing device without a valid flamethrowing device permit issued by the State Fire Marshal pursuant to this part.
(Added by Stats. 2004, Ch. 496, Sec. 1. Effective January 1, 2005.)
12756.
The State Fire Marshal shall adopt regulations to administer this part and establish standards for the background investigation of an applicant for, and holder of, a flamethrowing device permit, and for the use, storage, and transportation of a flamethrowing device. In adopting these regulations, the State Fire Marshal shall consult with the Department of Justice regarding regulations for the use and possession of destructive devices (Chapter 12.5 (commencing with Section 970) of Division 1 of Title 11 of the California Code of Regulations). These regulations for the use and possession of destructive devices may provide suggestions for potential methods to utilize in developing standards and shall serve as guidance only. At a minimum, the regulations adopted by the State Fire Marshal shall require an applicant to possess a current, valid certificate of eligibility issued by the Department of Justice pursuant to subdivisions (a) to (c), inclusive, of Section 26710 of the Penal Code.
(Amended by Stats. 2010, Ch. 178, Sec. 40. (SB 1115) Effective January 1, 2011. Operative January 1, 2012, by Sec. 107 of Ch. 178.)
12757.
The State Fire Marshal may issue or renew a permit to use and possess a flamethrowing device only if all of the following conditions are met:
(a) The applicant or permitholder is not addicted to any controlled substance.
(b) The applicant or permitholder possesses a current, valid certificate of eligibility issued by the Department of Justice pursuant to subdivisions (a) to (c), inclusive, of Section 26710 of the Penal Code.
(c) The applicant or permitholder meets the other standards specified in regulations adopted pursuant to Section 12756.
(Amended by Stats. 2010, Ch. 178, Sec. 41. (SB 1115) Effective January 1, 2011. Operative January 1, 2012, by Sec. 107 of Ch. 178.)
12758.
(a) If the State Fire Marshal denies an application for, or the renewal of, or revokes a flamethrowing device permit, the applicant for a flamethrowing device permit or permitholder shall be entitled to a hearing conducted in accordance with Chapter 5 (commencing with Section 11500) of Part 1 of Division 3 of Title 2 of the Government Code.
(b) The State Fire Marshal shall revoke a flamethrowing device permit if the permitholder does not comply with the requirements of this part and the regulations adopted pursuant to this part.
(Added by Stats. 2004, Ch. 496, Sec. 1. Effective January 1, 2005.)
12759.
The State Fire Marshal shall establish fees pursuant to this part that shall be deposited in the State Fire Marshal Licensing and Certification Fund.
(Added by Stats. 2004, Ch. 496, Sec. 1. Effective January 1, 2005.)

CHAPTER 3. Enforcement and Penalties [12760 - 12761]

(Chapter 3 added by Stats. 2004, Ch. 496, Sec. 1.)
12760.
The State Fire Marshal shall seize any flamethrowing device in the possession of any person who does not have a valid flamethrowing device permit issued pursuant to this part.
(Added by Stats. 2004, Ch. 496, Sec. 1. Effective January 1, 2005.)
12761.
Any person who uses or possesses any flamethrowing device without a valid flamethrowing device permit issued pursuant to this part is guilty of a public offense and, upon conviction, shall be punished by imprisonment in the county jail for a term not to exceed one year, or in the state prison, or by a fine not to exceed ten thousand dollars ($10,000), or by both imprisonment and fine.
(Added by Stats. 2004, Ch. 496, Sec. 1. Effective January 1, 2005.)

DIVISION 12. FIRES AND FIRE PROTECTION [13000 - 14960]

(Division 12 enacted by Stats. 1939, Ch. 60.)

PART 1. GENERAL PROVISIONS [13000 - 13083]

(Part 1 enacted by Stats. 1939, Ch. 60.)

CHAPTER 1. Liability in Relation to Fires [13000 - 13011]

(Chapter 1 enacted by Stats. 1939, Ch. 60.)
13000.
Every person is guilty of a misdemeanor who allows a fire kindled or attended by him to escape from his control or to spread to the lands of any person other than the builder of the fire without using every reasonable and proper precaution to prevent the fire from escaping.
(Enacted by Stats. 1939, Ch. 60.)
13001.
Every person is guilty of a misdemeanor who, through careless or negligent action, throws or places any lighted cigarette, cigar, ashes, or other flaming or glowing substance, or any substance or thing which may cause a fire, in any place where it may directly or indirectly start a fire, or who uses or operates a welding torch, tar pot or any other device which may cause a fire, who does not clear the inflammable material surrounding the operation or take such other reasonable precautions necessary to insure against the starting and spreading of fire.
(Amended by Stats. 1965, Ch. 732.)
13002.
(a) Every person is guilty of a misdemeanor who throws or discharges any lighted or nonlighted cigarette, cigar, match, or any flaming or glowing substance, or any substance or thing which may cause a fire upon any highway, including any portion of the right-of-way of any highway, upon any sidewalk, or upon any public or private property. This subdivision does not restrict a private owner in the use of his or her own private property, unless the placing, depositing, or dumping of the waste matter on the property creates a public health and safety hazard, a public nuisance, or a fire hazard, as determined by a local health department, local fire department or fire district, or the Department of Forestry and Fire Protection, in which case this section applies.
(b) Every person convicted of a violation of this section shall be punished by a mandatory fine of not less than one hundred dollars ($100) nor more than one thousand dollars ($1,000) upon a first conviction, by a mandatory fine of not less than five hundred dollars ($500) nor more than one thousand dollars ($1,000) upon a second conviction, and by a mandatory fine of not less than seven hundred fifty dollars ($750) nor more than one thousand dollars ($1,000) upon a third or subsequent conviction.
The court may, in addition to the fine imposed upon a conviction, require as a condition of probation, in addition to any other condition, that any person convicted of a violation of this section pick up litter at a time and place within the jurisdiction of the court for not less than eight hours.
(Amended by Stats. 1987, Ch. 133, Sec. 1.)
13003.
Every person is guilty of a misdemeanor who uses any steam-powered logging locomotive, donkey, or threshing engine, or any other steam engine or steam boiler, in or near any forest, brush, grass, grain, or stubble land, unless the steam engine or steam boiler is provided with adequate devices to prevent the escape of fire or sparks and unless he uses every reasonable precaution to prevent the causing of fire thereby.
(Amended by Stats. 1971, Ch. 445.)
13004.
Every person is guilty of a misdemeanor who harvests grain or causes it to be harvested by means of a combined harvester, header, or stationary threshing machine, or who bales hay by means of a hay press, or harvests by means of a mechanical harvester other agricultural crops which are flammable at the time of harvest, unless he keeps at all times in a convenient place upon each machine or press, one backpack or pump-type water extinguisher of not less than four-gallon capacity fully equipped, filled with water and ready for immediate use.
(Amended by Stats. 1968, Ch. 900.)
13005.
Every person is guilty of a misdemeanor who:
(a) Sells, offers for sale, leases, or rents to any person any tractor, engine, machine, or truck equipped with an internal combustion engine that uses hydrocarbon fuels, if either:
(1) It is specifically designed for use in harvesting or moving grain or hay or for use on land covered with any other flammable agricultural crop, unless the exhaust system of the engine is equipped with a spark arrester in effective working order or the engine is constructed, equipped, and maintained for the prevention of fire pursuant to Section 4443 of the Public Resources Code.
(2) It is not specifically designed for any of the uses described in paragraph (1) but could be used for any of those uses, unless the person provides written notice to the purchaser or bailee at the time of sale or at the time of entering into the lease or rental contract stating that the use or operation of the engine on any flammable agricultural cropland is a violation of subdivision (b), unless the exhaust system is equipped with a spark arrester in effective working order or the engine is constructed, equipped, and maintained for the prevention of fire pursuant to Section 4443 of the Public Resources Code.
(b) Operates or causes to be operated any tractor, engine, machine, or truck equipped with an internal combustion engine that uses hydrocarbon fuels in harvesting or moving grain or hay, or on land covered with any other flammable agricultural crop, unless the engine is equipped with a spark arrester maintained in effective working order or the engine is constructed, equipped, and maintained for the prevention of fire pursuant to Section 4443 of the Public Resources Code.

Spark arrester, as used in this section, is as defined in Section 4442 of the Public Resources Code.

Spark arresters attached to the exhaust system of engines on equipment or vehicles, as described in this section, shall not be placed or mounted in such a manner as to allow flames or heat from the exhaust system to ignite any flammable material.

Motortrucks, truck tractors, buses, and passenger vehicles, except motorcycles, are not subject to the provisions of paragraph (2) of subdivision (a) if the exhaust system is equipped with a muffler as defined in the Vehicle Code.

(Amended by Stats. 1982, Ch. 1333, Sec. 2.)

13006.5.

Every owner, operator, lessee, or other person in charge of any apartment house, roominghouse, motel or hotel heretofore or hereafter constructed, or any occupant thereof, who becomes aware of any fire or smoldering combustion of an unwarranted or insidious nature which is not confined within equipment designed for fire or which is a hazard to the apartment house, roominghouse, motel or hotel, shall be guilty of a misdemeanor if he shall fail to report said fire or smoldering combustion without delay to the local fire department.

(Added by Stats. 1965, Ch. 733.)

13007.

Any person who personally or through another wilfully, negligently, or in violation of law, sets fire to, allows fire to be set to, or allows a fire kindled or attended by him to escape to, the property of another, whether privately or publicly owned, is liable to the owner of such property for any damages to the property caused by the fire.

(Added by Stats. 1953, Ch. 48.)

13008.

Any person who allows any fire burning upon his property to escape to the property of another, whether privately or publicly owned, without exercising due diligence to control such fire, is liable to the owner of such property for the damages to the property caused by the fire.

(Added by Stats. 1953, Ch. 48.)

13009.

(a) Any person (1) who negligently, or in violation of the law, sets a fire, allows a fire to be set, or allows a fire kindled or attended by him or her to escape onto any public or private property, (2) other than a mortgagee, who, being in actual possession of a structure, fails or refuses to correct, within the time allotted for correction, despite having the right to do so, a fire hazard prohibited by law, for which a public agency properly has issued a notice of violation respecting the hazard, or (3) including a mortgagee, who, having an obligation under other provisions of law to correct a fire hazard prohibited by law, for which a public agency has properly issued a notice of violation respecting the hazard, fails or refuses to correct the hazard within the time allotted for correction, despite having the right to do so, is liable for the fire suppression costs incurred in fighting the fire and for the cost of providing rescue or emergency medical services, and those costs shall be a charge against that person. The charge shall constitute a debt of that person, and is collectible by the person, or by the federal, state, county, public, or private agency, incurring those costs in the same manner as in the case of an obligation under a contract, expressed or implied.

(b) Public agencies participating in fire suppression, rescue, or emergency medical services as set forth in subdivision (a), may designate one or more of the participating agencies to bring an action to recover costs incurred by all of the participating agencies. An agency designated by the other participating agencies to bring an action pursuant to this section shall declare that authorization and its basis in the complaint, and shall itemize in the complaint the total amounts claimed under this section by each represented agency.

(c) Any costs incurred by the Department of Forestry and Fire Protection in suppressing any wildland fire originating or spreading from a prescribed burning operation conducted by the department pursuant to a contract entered into pursuant to Article 2 (commencing with Section 4475) of Chapter 7 of Part 2 of Division 4 of the Public Resources Code shall not be collectible from any party to the contract, including any private consultant or contractor who entered into an agreement with that party pursuant to subdivision (d) of Section 4475.5 of the Public Resources Code, as provided in subdivision (a), to the extent that those costs were not incurred as a result of a violation of any provision of the contract.

(d) This section applies to all areas of the state, regardless of whether primarily wildlands, sparsely developed, or urban.

(Amended by Stats. 1994, Ch. 444, Sec. 1. Effective January 1, 1995.)

13009.1.

(a) Any person (1) who negligently, or in violation of the law, sets a fire, allows a fire to be set, or allows a fire kindled or attended by him or her to escape onto any public or private property, (2) other than a mortgagee, who, being in actual possession of a structure, fails or refuses to correct, within the time allotted for correction, despite having the right to do so, a fire hazard prohibited by law, for which a public agency properly has issued a notice of violation respecting the hazard, or (3) including a mortgagee, who, having an obligation under other provisions of law to correct a fire hazard prohibited by law, for which a public agency properly has issued a notice of violation respecting the hazard, fails or refuses to correct the hazard within the time allotted for correction, despite having the right to do so, is liable for both of the following:

(1) The cost of investigating and making any reports with respect to the fire.

(2) The costs relating to accounting for that fire and the collection of any funds pursuant to Section 13009, including, but not limited to, the administrative costs of operating a fire suppression cost recovery program. The liability imposed pursuant to this paragraph is limited to the actual amount expended which is attributable to the fire.

(b) In any civil action brought for the recovery of costs provided in this section, the court in its discretion may impose the amount of liability for costs described in subdivision (a).

(c) The burden of proof as to liability shall be on the plaintiff and shall be by a preponderance of the evidence in an action alleging that the defendant is liable for costs pursuant to this section. The burden of proof as to the amount of costs recoverable shall be on the plaintiff and shall be by a preponderance of the evidence in any action brought pursuant to this section.

(d) Any testimony, admission, or any other statement made by the defendant in any proceeding brought pursuant to this section, or any evidence derived from the testimony, admission or other statement, shall not be admitted or otherwise used in any criminal proceeding arising out of the same conduct.

(e) The liability constitutes a debt of that person and is collectible by the person, or by the federal, state, county, public, or private agency, incurring those costs in the same manner as in the case of an obligation under a contract, expressed or implied.

(f) This section applies in all areas of the state, regardless of whether primarily wildlands, sparsely developed, or urban.

(Amended by Stats. 1987, Ch. 1127, Sec. 2.)

13009.2.

(a) In a civil action by a public agency seeking damages caused by a fire, pecuniary damages must be quantifiable and not unreasonable in relation to the prefire fair market value of the property, taking into consideration the ecological and environmental value of the property to the public. The only recoverable pecuniary damages shall be:

(1) Either the restoration and rehabilitation costs associated with bringing the damaged property back to its preinjured state or replacement or acquisition costs of equivalent value, or diminution in value of property as a result of the fire, including lost timber value, or some combination thereof.

(2) Short-term costs related to immediate damages suffered as a result of the fire, such as burned area emergency response costs, costs associated with discrete restoration activities related to repair and replacement of real property improvements, and remediation and eradication costs relative to invasive species and any other nonnative infestation caused by or exacerbated by sudden burn area conditions.

(b) In addition to the damages authorized by subdivision (a), a public agency may also recover ecological and environmental damages caused by the fire, if those damages are quantifiable, and are not redressed by the damages set forth in subdivision (a), taking into consideration the ecological and environmental value of the property to the public. Ecological and environmental damages may include:

(1) Lost recreational value.

(2) Lost interim use.

(3) Lost historical and archeological value.

(4) Damage to wildlife, wildlife habitat, water or soil quality, or plants.

(5) Damage to any rare natural features of the property.

(6) Lost aesthetic value.

(c) In assessing the reasonableness of damages under subdivision (b), the prefire fair market value of the property is relevant and one factor to be considered, in addition to the other factors listed in subdivision (b).

(d) A public agency plaintiff who claims environmental damages of any kind under subdivision (a) or (b) shall not seek to enhance any pecuniary or environmental damages recovered under this section. This section is not intended to alter the law regarding whether Section 3346 of the Civil Code or Section 733 of the Code of Civil Procedure can be used to enhance fire damages, but this section does confirm that if a public agency claims environmental damages under subdivision (a) or (b), it shall not seek to enhance any damages recovered under this section for any reason, and shall not use Section 3346 of the Civil Code or Section 733 of the Code of Civil Procedure to do so, regardless of whether those sections might otherwise apply. This section is not intended to limit or change the ability of a public agency to recover costs arising from a fire as provided in Sections 13009 and 13009.1.

(e) For purposes of this section, the term "public agency" means the United States of America or any political subdivision thereof, the State of California, any city, county, district, public agency, or any other public subdivision of the state.

(f) This section shall apply only to a civil action filed on or after the effective date of the act adding this section.

(Added by Stats. 2012, Ch. 289, Sec. 1. (AB 1492) Effective September 11, 2012.)

13009.5.

Where the Department of Forestry and Fire Protection utilizes inmate labor for fighting fires, the charge for their use, for the purpose of Section 13009, shall be set by the Director of Forestry and Fire Protection. In determining the charges, he or she may consider, in addition to costs incurred by the department, the per capita cost to the state of maintaining the inmates.

(Amended by Stats. 1992, Ch. 427, Sec. 92. Effective January 1, 1993.)

13009.6.

(a) (1) Those expenses of an emergency response necessary to protect the public from a real and imminent threat to health and safety by a public agency to confine, prevent, or mitigate the release, escape, or burning of hazardous substances described in subdivision (c) are a charge against any person whose negligence causes the incident, if either of the following occurs:

(A) Evacuation from the building, structure, property, or public right-of-way where the incident originates is necessary to prevent loss of life or injury.

(B) The incident results in the spread of hazardous substances or fire posing a real and imminent threat to public health and safety beyond the building, structure, property, or public right-of-way where the incident originates.

(2) Expenses reimbursable to a public agency under this section are a debt of the person liable therefor, and shall be collectible in the same manner as in the case of an obligation under contract, express or implied.

(3) The charge created against the person by this subdivision is also a charge against the person's employer if the negligence causing the incident occurs in the course of the person's employment.

(4) The public agencies participating in an emergency response meeting the requirements of paragraph (1) of this subdivision may designate one or more of the participating agencies to bring an action to recover the expenses incurred by all of the designating agencies which are reimbursable under this section.

(5) An action to recover expenses under this section may be joined with any civil action for penalties, fines, injunctive, or other relief brought against the responsible person or employer, or both, arising out of the same incident.

(b) There shall be deducted from any amount otherwise recoverable under this section, the amount of any reimbursement for eligible costs received by a public agency pursuant to Chapter 6.8 (commencing with Section 25300) of Division 20. The amount so reimbursed may be recovered as provided in Section 25360.

(c) As used in this section, "hazardous substance" means any hazardous substance listed in Section 25316 or subdivision (q) of Section 25501 of this code, or in Section 6382 of the Labor Code.

(d) As used in this section, "mitigate" includes actions by a public agency to monitor or model ambient levels of airborne hazardous substances for the purpose of determining or assisting in the determination of whether or not to evacuate areas around the property where the incident originates, or to determine or assist in the determination of which areas around the property where the incident originates should be evacuated.
(Amended by Stats. 2011, Ch. 603, Sec. 1. (AB 408) Effective October 8, 2011.)
13010.
Sections 13007, 13008, and 13009 of this code do not apply to nor affect any rights, duties, or causes of action in existence and accruing prior to August 14, 1931.
(Added by Stats. 1953, Ch. 48.)
13011.
Both doors of any double doors designated as the public entrance to any place of business shall be kept unlocked during normal business hours.
(Added by Stats. 1983, Ch. 267, Sec. 1.)

CHAPTER 2. Fire Equipment [13025 - 13060]

(Chapter 2 enacted by Stats. 1939, Ch. 60.)

ARTICLE 1. Standard Equipment [13025 - 13028]
(Article 1 enacted by Stats. 1939, Ch. 60.)
13025.
(a) All equipment for fire protection purposes having couplings or fittings with an inside diameter of three inches or less, purchased by any authorities having charge of public property, shall be equipped with standard threads for fire hose couplings and hydrant fittings designated as the national standard as adopted by the National Board of Fire Underwriters, which standard is designated as the standard for such equipment in this state. The State Fire Marshal shall adopt and submit building standards for approval pursuant to Chapter 4 (commencing with Section 18935) of Part 2.5 of Division 13 of this code in order to conform such building standards to the provisions of this subdivision and subdivision (b).

(b) All equipment for fire protection purposes having couplings or fittings with an inside diameter greater than three inches, if equippped with threads, shall be equipped with the standard threads prescribed in subdivision (a).

(c) All equipment for fire protection purposes having couplings or fittings with an inside diameter greater than three inches not equipped with threaded fittings or couplings shall be approved by the State Fire Marshal, with advice from the State Board of Fire Services. The proposed system of use of such nonthreaded couplings or fittings shall be submitted in detail to the State Fire Marshal who shall, with advice from the State Board of Fire Services, approve its use if mutual aid capability is assured.

(d) The State Fire Marshal shall adopt and submit building standards for approval pursuant to the provisions of Chapter 4 (commencing with Section 18935) of Part 2.5 of Division 13 of this code for any fire hydrants, including dry standpipe connections, in or on any improvement to land, which building standards define the requirements for standard threads for fire hose couplings and hydrant fittings as provided in subdivision (a) or (b).
(Amended by Stats. 1979, Ch. 1152.)
13025.5.
Any fire department maintained by the City and County of San Francisco using fire hydrant outlets with other than two-and-one-half-inch (2 ¹/₂-inch) threaded fittings shall cause any vehicle used for firefighting purposes and designed to pump water from those hydrants, that is normally used in areas of the city and county bordering the boundaries of any other public entity, as defined in Section 13050.1, providing any fire protection and suppression service, to carry a minimum of eight adapters, consisting of four increasers and four reducers, that enable the vehicle to couple its equipment and apparatus to fire hydrant outlets having two-and-one-half-inch (2 ¹/₂-inch) threaded fittings, and that enable fire equipment vehicles from other public entities using two-and-

one-half-inch (2 ¹/₂-inch) threaded fittings to couple their firefighting equipment and apparatus to fire hydrant outlets maintained by the city and county.
(Amended by Stats. 1992, Ch. 1069, Sec. 2. Effective January 1, 1993.)
13026.
The State Fire Marshal is authorized to make such changes as may be necessary to standardize all existing fire protective equipment throughout the state.
(Amended by Stats. 1980, Ch. 118.)
13027.
The State Fire Marshal shall notify industrial establishments and property owners having equipment for fire protective purposes of the changes necessary to bring their equipment into conformity with, and shall render them such assistance as may be available in converting their equipment to, standard requirements.
(Enacted by Stats. 1939, Ch. 60.)
13028.
Any person who sells or offers for sale any fire hose, hydrant, fire engine or other equipment with threaded parts, for fire protective purposes, unless it is fitted and equipped with the standard thread for fire hose couplings and hydrant fittings is guilty of a misdemeanor, punishable by a fine of not less than one hundred dollars ($100) nor more than four hundred dollars ($400), or by imprisonment in the county jail for not less than five or more than 30 days, or by both.
(Amended by Stats. 1983, Ch. 1092, Sec. 160. Effective September 27, 1983. Operative January 1, 1984, by Sec. 427 of Ch. 1092.)

ARTICLE 2. Use of Fire Equipment [13050 - 13060]
(Article 2 enacted by Stats. 1939, Ch. 60.)
13050.
The apparatus, equipment and firefighting force of any public entity may be used for the purpose of providing fire protection or firefighting services:
(a) In any other public entity with the consent of the chief administrative officer of the office or department authorized by law to provide fire protection in such other public entity.
(b) Outside the limits of any public entity.
(Amended by Stats. 1965, Ch. 1203.)
13050.1.
"Public entity" includes the state, a county, city, district, public authority, public agency, and any other political subdivision or public corporation in the state.
(Added by Stats. 1965, Ch. 1203.)
13051.
The reasonable value of the use of, and repairs and depreciation on, apparatus and equipment, and other expenses reasonably incurred in furnishing firefighting services, may constitute a charge against the public entity in which the firefighting services are furnished.
(Amended by Stats. 1965, Ch. 1203.)
13052.
(a) The public entity rendering the service may present a claim to the public entity liable therefor. If the claim is approved by the head of the fire department, if any, in the public entity to which the claim is presented, and by its governing body, it shall be paid in the same manner as other charges and if the claim is not paid, an action may be brought for its collection.
(b) Notwithstanding any other provision of this section, any claims against the state shall be presented to the Department of General Services in accordance with Part 3 (commencing with Section 900) and Part 4 (commencing with Section 940) of Division 3.6 of Title 1 of the Government Code.
(Amended by Stats. 2016, Ch. 31, Sec. 162. (SB 836) Effective June 27, 2016.)
13052.5.
The governing board of any county fire protection district may contract with any city contiguous to the district for the furnishing of fire protection to the district by such city, and the legislative body of any city may contract for the furnishing of fire protection to the district in such manner and to such extent as the legislative body may deem advisable. All of the privileges and immunities from liability which surround the activities of any city fire fighting force or department when performing its functions within the territorial limits of the city shall apply to the activities of any city fire fighting force or department while furnishing fire protection outside the city under any contract with a county fire protection district pursuant to this section.
(Added by Stats. 1953, Ch. 48.)
13053.
Whenever a fire occurs in any county or within the boundaries of any national forest which is of such proportions that it cannot be adequately handled by the forestry department or fire warden of the county or the facilities of the Department of Forestry and Fire Protection or of the United States Forest Service, the personnel, equipment, and firefighting facilities of any county may be authorized by the state forest ranger within the county or the county forester or fire warden of the county to assist in its extinguishment and control.
(Amended by Stats. 1992, Ch. 427, Sec. 93. Effective January 1, 1993.)
13054.
Where the personnel, equipment, and facilities of any county are utilized in the extinguishment or control of any fire outside its boundaries, the county furnishing its personnel, equipment, and facilities shall be reimbursed by the county in which the fire occurs in an amount in accordance with a predetermined schedule of repayments agreed upon by the boards of supervisors of the counties, or between the board of supervisors

of the county and the Department of Forestry and Fire Protection or the United States Forest Service, as the case may be.
(Amended by Stats. 1992, Ch. 427, Sec. 94. Effective January 1, 1993.)

13055.
Any public agency authorized to engage in fire protection activities, including but not limited to a fire protection district, city, city and county, or county fire department, the Department of Forestry, and the United States Forest Service, may use fire to abate a fire hazard.
(Amended by Stats. 1981, Ch. 714.)

13060.
Any public entity may place blue reflective pavement markers in any highway, street, or road for marking fire hydrant locations and water supply locations. These blue reflective pavement markers shall not be used for any other purpose. This section shall not apply to freeways or freeway ramps.
A public entity shall not place blue reflective pavement markers on a state highway unless it first obtains an encroachment permit from the Department of Transportation.
(Added by Stats. 1983, Ch. 570, Sec. 1. Effective August 29, 1983. Operative January 1, 1984, by Sec. 4 of Ch. 570.)

CHAPTER 3. FIRESCOPE Program [13070 - 13073]

(Chapter 3 added by Stats. 1989, Ch. 1364, Sec. 1.)

13070.
This chapter shall be known and may be cited as the FIRESCOPE Act of 1989.
(Added by Stats. 1989, Ch. 1364, Sec. 1.)

13071.
The Office of Emergency Services shall establish and administer a program, which shall be denominated the FIRESCOPE Program (FIrefighting RESources of California Organized for Potential Emergencies), to maintain and enhance the efficiency and effectiveness of managing multiagency firefighting resources in responding to an incident. The program shall be based on the concepts and components developed or under development by the Firescope project chartered by the United States Congress in 1972. The program shall provide for the research, development, and implementation of technologies, facilities, and procedures to assist state and local fire agencies in the better utilization and coordination of firefighting resources in responding to incidents.
(Amended by Stats. 2013, Ch. 352, Sec. 338. (AB 1317) Effective September 26, 2013. Operative July 1, 2013, by Sec. 543 of Ch. 352.)

13072.
The goal of the FIRESCOPE Program is the improvement of fire incident management and the coordination of multiagency firefighting resources on major or multiple incidents. The program shall include, but is not limited to, the following areas as part of its research, development, and implementation objectives:
(a) Improved methods to coordinate multiagency firefighting resources during major incidents.
(b) Improved methods for forecasting fire behavior.
(c) The capability to assess fire, weather, and terrain conditions at the scene of an incident.
(d) Standard fire terminology for improving incident management.
(e) Improved multiagency fire communications.
(f) Multiagency training on FIRESCOPE components and products.
(g) A common mapping system, including orthophoto maps.
(h) Improved fire information management systems.
(i) Regional operational coordination centers for regional multiagency coordination of firefighting resources.
(Added by Stats. 1989, Ch. 1364, Sec. 1.)

13073.
The Office of Emergency Services shall carry out this chapter in cooperation with the Department of Forestry and Fire Protection, including the Office of the State Fire Marshal, and with the advice of the Fire and Rescue Service Advisory Committee/FIRESCOPE Board of Directors within the Office of Emergency Services.
(Amended by Stats. 2013, Ch. 352, Sec. 339. (AB 1317) Effective September 26, 2013. Operative July 1, 2013, by Sec. 543 of Ch. 352.)

CHAPTER 4. Firefighters' Memorial [13081 - 13083]

(Chapter 4 added by Stats. 1992, Ch. 1217, Sec. 1.)

13081.
(a) The construction of a memorial to California firefighters on the grounds of the State Capitol is hereby authorized. For purposes of this chapter, the grounds of the State Capitol is that property in the City of Sacramento bounded by Ninth, Fifteenth, "L," and "N" Streets. The actual site for the memorial shall be selected by the task force after consultation with the State Office of Historic Preservation, and after consultation with, and approval of, the Department of General Services and the Historic State Capitol Commission.
(b) No state moneys shall be expended for any of the purposes specified in this chapter. Funds for the construction of the memorial shall be provided exclusively through private contributions for this purpose.
(Added by Stats. 1992, Ch. 1217, Sec. 1. Effective January 1, 1993.)

13082.
(a) The California Fire Foundation may, in consultation with the Department of General Services, prepare a plan to construct modifications to the memorial to California firefighters on the grounds of the State Capitol, which may include the construction of a new wall within the existing footprint of the memorial that would include the names of additional fallen firefighters.
(b) If the California Fire Foundation prepares a plan to modify the memorial pursuant to this section, the Department of General Services shall do all of the following:
(1) Review preliminary design plans for the modifications and identify potential maintenance concerns.
(2) Ensure that the proposed modifications comply with the requirements of the Americans with Disabilities Act of 1990 (42 U.S.C. Sec. 12101 et seq.) and other applicable safety laws and regulations.
(3) Ensure that the proposed modifications comply with the requirements of the California Environmental Quality Act (Division 13 (commencing with Section 21000) of the Public Resources Code) and any other applicable building standards for work to be carried out at the existing memorial.
(4) Review the final construction documents to ensure that all applicable requirements are met.
(5) Prepare the right-of-entry permit outlining the final area of work, final construction documents and permits, construction plans, and the name of the contractor who will perform the work, and verify that the contractor is properly licensed and insured, including maintaining adequate personal liability insurance for damage to state property.
(6) Conduct inspections of the construction performed by the contractor selected by the foundation.
(c) If the California Fire Foundation undertakes responsibility to modify the memorial to California firefighters pursuant to this section, it shall, in consultation with the Department of General Services, establish a schedule for the design and construction, implement procedures to solicit designs, devise a selection process for the choice of the design for the modifications, and report to the Joint Committee on Rules on the proposed modifications.
(d) The California Fire Foundation shall submit a plan for proposed modifications of the memorial prepared pursuant to this section to the Department of General Services and the Joint Committee on Rules for their review and approval. The California Fire Foundation shall not commence construction of any proposed modifications until the master plan of the State Capitol Park is approved and adopted by the Joint Committee on Rules, or until January 1, 2021, whichever occurs first. Any approved modifications shall not commence unless the Joint Committee on Rules and the Department of Finance have verified that sufficient private donations have been secured to complete construction of the modifications.
(e) Any modifications to the memorial carried out pursuant to a plan prepared pursuant to this section shall be funded exclusively through private donations secured by the California Fire Foundation.
(Added by Stats. 2016, Ch. 688, Sec. 1. (AB 1980) Effective January 1, 2017.)

13083.
Firefighters' memorial ceremonies, including the dedication of the memorial and any subsequent ceremonies, shall be conducted by the California Fire Foundation, in consultation with the Assembly General Research Committee on Fire, Police, Emergency, and Disaster Services.
(Added by Stats. 1992, Ch. 1217, Sec. 1. Effective January 1, 1993.)

PART 2. FIRE PROTECTION [13100 - 13263]

(Part 2 enacted by Stats. 1939, Ch. 60.)

CHAPTER 1. State Fire Marshal [13100 - 13159.10]

(Chapter 1 enacted by Stats. 1939, Ch. 60.)

ARTICLE 1. General [13100 - 13135]
(Heading of Article 1 added by Stats. 1945, Ch. 1173.)

13100.
(a) The Office of the State Fire Marshal is hereby created in the Department of Forestry and Fire Protection. The Office of the State Fire Marshal shall be administered by the State Fire Marshal, who shall be a Chief Deputy Director of Forestry and Fire Protection in accordance with paragraph (1) of subdivision (b) of Section 702 of the Public Resources Code and appointed pursuant to Section 13101 of this code.
(b) The Office of the State Fire Marshal and the State Fire Marshal in the Department of Forestry and Fire Protection succeed to, and are vested with, all of the powers, duties, responsibilities, and jurisdiction of the former Office of the State Fire Marshal and the former State Fire Marshal, as the case may be, in the State and Consumer Services Agency.
(c) Wherever any reference is made in any law to the former Office of the State Fire Marshal or to the former State Fire Marshal in the State and Consumer Services Agency pertaining to a power, duty, responsibility, or jurisdiction transferred to, and vested in, the Office of the State Fire Marshal or the State Fire Marshal in the Department of Forestry and Fire Protection, the reference shall be deemed to be a reference to, and to mean, the Office of the State Fire Marshal or the State Fire Marshal in the Department of Forestry and Fire Protection, as the case may be.

13100.1.

The functions of the office shall be to foster, promote and develop ways and means of protecting life and property against fire and panic.

13101.

The State Fire Marshal shall be appointed by the Governor with the advice and consent of the Senate and shall hold office at the pleasure of the Governor. In order to be eligible for appointment, he or she shall have had not less than eight years experience in a regularly organized fire department in this State. He or she shall be paid the annual salary provided for by Chapter 6 of Part 1 of Division 3 of Title 2 of the Government Code.

13103.

The State Fire Marshal may appoint those assistant or deputy state fire marshals as he or she may consider necessary from among active chiefs of fire departments, fire marshals of cities, counties, and districts providing fire protection, and the salaried field assistants of the State Fire Marshal.

The State Fire Marshal and the assistant or deputy state fire marshals shall exercise the functions of peace officers.

13104.

The State Fire Marshal shall aid in the enforcement of all laws and ordinances, any rules and regulations adopted under the provisions of Division 11 (commencing with Section 12000) of, and Part 1 (commencing with Section 13000) and Part 2 (commencing with Section 13100) of Division 12 of, the Health and Safety Code, and building standards adopted by the State Fire Marshal and published in the State Building Standards Code relating to fires or to fire prevention and protection.

The State Fire Marshal shall, if possible, attend, and take charge of and protect all property which may be imperiled by any fire other than:

(a) A forest, brush, or grain fire.

(b) A fire occurring within any city or town maintaining a fire department, within a fire protection district, or within a county where there is a regularly appointed county fire warden.

13104.5.

Except on property which has been deeded to the state for taxes, the Department of Forestry and Fire Protection may abate fire hazards existing on property owned, controlled, or held in trust by the state, in areas not under the jurisdiction of the Director of Forestry and Fire Protection, upon the request of the legislative body of the city, county, or city and county within which the property is situated. The cost of the abatement shall be paid out of any money in the State Treasury appropriated for that purpose.

13104.6.

The State Fire Marshal may determine the existence of a fire hazard on any property which has been deeded to the State for taxes and may serve a written notice of condemnation of the fire hazard on the State Controller, or on any person designated by the Controller. The fire hazard is then subject to removal in accordance with the law relating to removal of public nuisances on tax deeded property.

13105.

The State Fire Marshal shall encourage the adoption of fire prevention measures by means of education, engineering, and enforcement and shall prepare or cause to be prepared for dissemination information relating to the subject of fire prevention and extinguishment.

13105.2.

(a) The State Fire Marshal shall establish and operate a statewide hazardous materials training facility to be located at the Del Valle Firefighting Facility of the County of Los Angeles.

(b) Subdivision (a) shall be operative in any fiscal year only to the extent that funds are appropriated in the annual Budget Act or donated by private donors, contributed by local agencies, or provided by other funding sources for the purpose of subdivision (a). Donations by private donors, local agencies, or other sources may be in the form of money, in-kind services, or equipment. All monetary contributions received pursuant to this subdivision shall be deposited into a special deposit fund account to carry out the requirements of subdivision (a).

13105.5.

The State Fire Marshal shall establish or cause to be established a program of fire prevention training for fire prevention inspectors employed by local fire protection agencies. The training program shall be conducted on a regional basis located near such agencies which employ or contract with such inspectors.

13105.7.

(a) The State Fire Marshal may establish a schedule of fees for the inspection, approval, and listing of testing laboratories which test consumer products for fire safety that are regulated by the State Fire Marshal.

(b) The State Fire Marshal may charge the testing laboratories fees to cover the costs of the program specified in subdivision (a), including the cost of establishing the fee schedule.

13106.

During the existence of a fire, the State Fire Marshal may protect any property which is affected thereby until the arrival of the owner or claimant. If the owner or claimant does not take charge of the property within twenty-four hours, the State Fire Marshal may store it at the owner's or claimant's expense.

13107.

(a) The State Fire Marshal shall investigate every explosion or fire occurring in any state institution, state-owned building, or any building which is determined, pursuant to regulations adopted by the State Fire Marshal, to be state occupied, and every explosion or fire occurring in those areas of the state not under the jurisdiction of a legally organized fire department or fire protection district or other public entity, including, but not limited to, the state, which provides fire protection in which there is suspicion that the crime of arson or attempted arson has been committed.

(b) Upon request of the chief fire official of a legally organized fire department or fire protection district, or the governing body thereof, or upon request of the chief of a police department or the sheriff regarding a fire which occurs in an area where there is no operating arson investigation unit, the State Fire Marshal shall, within the limitation of resources and manpower established for those purposes, investigate any explosion or fire occurring within the jurisdiction of the requesting official in which there is suspicion that the crime of arson or attempted arson has been committed.

(c) The State Fire Marshal shall cooperate in the establishment of a program for training fire department personnel in arson investigation and detection.

(d) In order to carry out his or her responsibilities and duties pursuant to this section, the State Fire Marshal shall establish an arson investigation unit within his or her office, which shall be staffed with necessary personnel to perform the function for which the unit is established.

(e) If there is reason to believe that any fire or explosion investigated by the State Fire Marshal resulted from a crime or that a crime has been committed in connection with it, the State Fire Marshal shall report that fact in writing to the district attorney of the county in which the fire or explosion occurred.

13107.5.

The State Fire Marshal may investigate every break, and shall investigate every explosion or fire, involving a pipeline reported by a local agency pursuant to Chapter 5.5 (commencing with Section 51010) of Division 1 of Title 5 of the Government Code. The State Fire Marshal may immediately order any pipeline closed when it is determined to be necessary to do so in the interests of public safety. The pipeline shall remain closed until it is determined that operations may be resumed with safety or until any discovered safety defect has been remedied or repaired.

13108.

(a) Except as limited by Chapter 6 (commencing with Section 140) of Division 1 of the Labor Code and Section 18930 of this code, the State Fire Marshal shall prepare and adopt building standards, not inconsistent with existing laws or ordinances, relating to fire protection in the design and construction of the means of egress and the adequacy of exits from, and the installation and maintenance of fire alarm and fire extinguishment equipment or systems in, any state institution or other state-owned building or in any specified state-occupied building and submit those building standards to the State Building Standards Commission for approval pursuant to Chapter 4 (commencing with Section 18935) of Part 2.5 of Division 13. The State Fire Marshal shall prepare and adopt regulations other than building standards for the installation and maintenance of equipment and furnishings that present unusual fire hazards in any state institution or other state-owned building or in any specified state-occupied building. The State Fire Marshal shall adopt those regulations as are reasonably necessary to define what buildings shall be considered as state-occupied buildings.

(b) The fire chief of any city, county, city and county, or fire protection district, or that official's authorized representative, may enter any state institution or any other state-owned or state-occupied building for the purpose of preparing a fire suppression preplanning program or for the purpose of investigating any fire in a state-occupied building.

(c) Except as otherwise provided in this section, the State Fire Marshal shall enforce the regulations adopted by the State Fire Marshal and building standards relating to fire and panic safety published in the California Building Standards Code in all state-owned buildings, specified state-occupied buildings, and state institutions throughout the state. Upon written request from the chief fire official of any city, county, city and county, or fire protection district, or a Designated Campus Fire Marshal, pursuant to Section 13146, the State Fire Marshal may authorize that person and their authorized representatives, in their geographical area of responsibility, to make fire prevention inspections of state-owned or specified state-occupied buildings, other than state institutions, for the purpose of enforcing the regulations relating to fire and panic safety adopted by the State Fire Marshal pursuant to this section and building standards relating to fire and panic safety published in the California Building Standards Code. Authorization from the State Fire Marshal shall be limited to those fire departments or fire districts that maintain a fire prevention bureau staffed by paid personnel.

(d) Any requirement or order made by a chief fire official or Designated Campus Fire Marshal pursuant to this section may be appealed to the State Fire Marshal. The State Fire Marshal shall, upon receiving an appeal and subject to Chapter 5 (commencing with Section 18945) of Part 2.5 of Division 13, determine if the requirement or order made is reasonably consistent with the fire and panic safety regulations adopted by the State Fire Marshal and building standards relating to fire and panic safety published in the California Building Standards Code.

(e) For purposes of subdivisions (a) and (c), "specified state-occupied building" shall mean a building that is leased or rented by the state, in whole or in part, and is any of the following:

(1) A building where the state has entered into a build-to-suit lease.

(2) A trial court facility with a detention area.

(3) A building used by the Department of Corrections and Rehabilitation as a reentry facility.

(4) Any other building specified by the State Fire Marshal through adopted regulations.

(f) This section does not prohibit the State Fire Marshal from entering and enforcing the regulations relating to fire and panic safety adopted by the State Fire Marshal and building standards relating to fire and panic safety published in the California Building Standards Code in any publicly or privately owned building occupied by the state, in whole or in part, whenever the State Fire Marshal determines that enforcement by the State Fire Marshal is necessary for the safety of state workers or wards.

(Amended by Stats. 2019, Ch. 31, Sec. 6. (SB 85) Effective June 27, 2019.)

13108.1.

The State Fire Marshal, in consultation with the Bureau of Household Goods and Services, shall review the flammability standards for building insulation materials, including whether the flammability standards for some insulation materials can only be met with the addition of chemical flame retardants. Based on this review, and if the State Fire Marshal deems it appropriate, he or she shall, by July 1, 2015, propose for consideration by the California Building Standards Commission, to be adopted at the sole discretion of the commission, updated insulation flammability standards that accomplish both of the following:

(a) Maintain overall building fire safety.

(b) Ensure that there is adequate protection from fires that travel between walls and into confined areas, including crawl spaces and attics, for occupants of the building and any firefighters who may be in the building during a fire.

(Amended by Stats. 2018, Ch. 578, Sec. 35. (SB 1483) Effective January 1, 2019.)

13108.5.

(a) The State Fire Marshal, in consultation with the Director of Forestry and Fire Protection and the Director of Housing and Community Development, shall, pursuant to Section 18930, propose fire protection building standards for roofs, exterior walls, structure projections, including, but not limited to, porches, decks, balconies, and eaves, and structure openings, including, but not limited to, attic and eave vents and windows of buildings in fire hazard severity zones, including very high fire hazard severity zones designated by the Director of Forestry and Fire Protection pursuant to Article 9 (commencing with Section 4201) of Chapter 1 of Part 2 of Division 4 of the Public Resources Code.

(b) Building standards adopted pursuant to this section shall also apply to buildings located in very high fire hazard severity zones designated pursuant to Chapter 6.8 (commencing with Section 51175) of Part 1 of Division 1 of Title 5 of the Government Code, and other areas designated by a local agency following a finding supported by substantial evidence in the record that the requirements of the building standards adopted pursuant to this section are necessary for effective fire protection within the area.

(c) Building standards adopted pursuant to this section shall also apply to buildings located in urban wildland interface communities. A local agency may, at its discretion, include in or exclude from the requirements of these building standards any area in its jurisdiction following a finding supported by substantial evidence in the record at a public hearing that the requirements of these building standards are necessary or not necessary, respectively, for effective fire protection within the area. Changes made by a local agency to an urban wildland interface community area following a finding supported by substantial evidence in the record shall be final and shall not be rebuttable.

(d) For purposes of subdivision (c), "urban wildland interface community" means a community listed in "Communities at Risk from Wild Fires," produced by the California Department of Forestry and Fire Protection, Fire and Resource Assessment Program, pursuant to the National Fire Plan, federal Fiscal Year 2001 Department of the Interior and Related Agencies Appropriations Act (Public Law 106-291).

(Amended by Stats. 2004, Ch. 183, Sec. 195. Effective January 1, 2005.)

13108.6.

The State Fire Marshal may adopt regulations specifying the access to roof areas of commercial establishments which firefighters shall have and may limit or restrict the use of razor wire fences, chain link fences, or any other fences which would obstruct that access.

For purposes of this section, "commercial establishment" shall not include any facility of a public utility.

(Added by Stats. 1984, Ch. 632, Sec. 1.)

13108.9.

The State Fire Marshal shall adopt regulations to require a public address system with an emergency backup power system for all buildings or structures constructed on or after July 1, 1991, which are intended for public assemblies of 10,000 or more persons. The State Fire Marshal shall adopt regulations to require any existing building or structure intended for public assemblies of 10,000 or more persons which, on or after January 1, 1991, has or subsequently installs a public address system, to have an emergency backup power system for the public address system.

(Added by Stats. 1990, Ch. 1426, Sec. 1.)

13109.

The State Fire Marshal, his or her deputies, or his or her salaried assistants, the chief of any city or county fire department or fire protection district and their authorized representatives may enter any building or premises not used for dwelling purposes at any reasonable hour for the purpose of enforcing this chapter. The owner, lessee, manager or operator of any such building or premises shall permit the State Fire Marshal, his or her deputies, his or her salaried assistants and the chief of any city or county fire department or fire protection district and their authorized representatives to enter and inspect them at the time and for the purpose stated in this section.

(Amended by Stats. 1996, Ch. 332, Sec. 11. Effective January 1, 1997.)

13110.

(a) Notwithstanding any other provision of this part, the State Fire Marshal may propose, adopt, and administer the regulations that he or she deems necessary in order to ensure fire safety in buildings and structures within this state including regulations related to construction, modification, installation, testing, inspection, labeling, listing, certification, registration, licensing, reporting, operation, and maintenance. Regulations that are building standards shall be submitted to the State Building Standards Commission for approval pursuant to Chapter 4 (commencing with Section 18935) of Part 2.5 of Division 13.

(b) The Office of the State Fire Marshal may establish and collect reasonable fees necessary to implement this section, consistent with Section 3 of Article XIII A of the California Constitution.

(Added by Stats. 2013, Ch. 377, Sec. 4. (AB 433) Effective January 1, 2014.)

13110.5.

The State Fire Marshal shall gather statistical information on all fires, medical aid incidents, and hazardous materials incidents occurring within this state. The chief fire official of each fire department operated by the state, a city, city and county, fire protection district, organized fire company, or other public or private entity which provides fire protection, shall furnish information and data to the State Fire Marshal relating to each fire which occurs within his or her area of jurisdiction. The chief fire official of each fire department operated by the state shall, and the chief fire official of fire departments operated by a city, city and county, fire protection district, organized fire company, or other public or private entity which provides fire protection may, also furnish information and data to the State Fire Marshal relating to medical aid incidents and hazardous materials incidents which occur within their area of jurisdiction. The State Fire Marshal shall adopt regulations prescribing the scope of the information to be reported, the manner of reporting the information, the forms to be used, the time the information shall be reported, and other requirements and regulations as the State Fire Marshal determines necessary.

The State Fire Marshal shall annually analyze the information and data reported, compile a report, and disseminate a copy of the report, together with his or her analysis, to each chief fire official in the state. The State Fire Marshal shall also furnish a copy of his or her report and analysis to the State Emergency Medical Services Authority and any other interested person upon request.

(Amended by Stats. 1987, Ch. 345, Sec. 1.)

13110.7.

The State Fire Marshal shall establish and maintain a registry of burn injuries and deaths, and shall annually compile a statistical report of such injuries and deaths.

The director of every burn center which examines, treats, or admits a person with a burn or smoke inhalation injury or a person who suffers a burn-related death shall file a report with the State Fire Marshal describing the injury or death at the end of the examination or treatment or at the time the patient is discharged from the burn center or at the time of the patient's death.

As used in this section, the term "burn center" means an intensive care unit in which there are specially trained physicians, nursing and supportive personnel and the necessary monitoring and therapeutic equipment needed to provide specialized medical and nursing care to burned patients.

The State Fire Marshall shall, in cooperation with the burn centers, develop the form to be used in reporting information to the State Fire Marshal under this section.

(Amended by Stats. 1980, Ch. 149.)

13111.

The State Fire Marshal may adopt a model ordinance for adoption by any local agency authorized pursuant to Article 3.6 (commencing with Section 50078) of Chapter 1 of Part 1 of Division 1 of Title 5 of the Government Code to establish uniform schedules and rates for assessments for fire suppression services as provided in Section 50078.2 of the Government Code.

(Added by Stats. 1982, Ch. 1396, Sec. 18.)

13111.1.

(a) The office of the State Fire Marshal may expend money appropriated for the administration of the laws, the enforcement of which is committed to the office. Such expenditures by the office shall be made in accordance with law in carrying on the work for which such appropriations were made.

(b) A sum, not to exceed five thousand dollars ($5,000) in each fiscal year, may be withdrawn for investigative purposes from General Fund money appropriated in support of the office of the State Fire Marshal, without at the time furnishing vouchers and itemized statements. This sum shall be used as a revolving fund where cash advances are necessary, and at the close of each fiscal year, or any other time, upon demand of the Department of Finance, shall be accounted for and substantiated by vouchers and itemized statements submitted to and audited by the State Controller.

(Amended by Stats. 1978, Ch. 562.)

13111.3.

The State Department of Health shall establish and administer a program which will make loans available to private nonprofit children's institutions and private nonprofit homes for the aging which are nonprofit community care facilities for adults under subdivision (a) of Section 1502 of the Health and Safety Code from such funds as may be appropriated by the Legislature to pay the cost of the installation of automatic sprinkler systems or detectors responding to invisible products of combustion other than heat approved by the State Fire Marshal. Any loan pursuant to this section shall bear interest at a rate of 5 percent per annum and shall not be for a term exceeding 30 years.

The State Department of Health shall adopt and enforce such regulations as may be necessary for the reasonable administration of the loan program which it is required by this section to establish and administer.

(Amended by Stats. 1975, Ch. 406.)

13112.

Every person who violates any provision of this chapter, or any order, rule, or regulation made pursuant to this chapter, is guilty of a misdemeanor punishable by a fine of not less than one hundred dollars ($100) or more than five hundred dollars ($500), or by imprisonment for not more than six months, or by both.

A person is guilty of a separate offense each day during which he or she commits, continues, or permits a violation of any provision of, or any order, rule, or regulation made pursuant to, this chapter.

(Amended by Stats. 1984, Ch. 322, Sec. 1.)

13112.1.

Notwithstanding Section 1463 of the Penal Code, all fines and forfeitures imposed by or collected in any court of this state, as a result of citations issued by the State Fire Marshal or salaried deputy state fire marshals employed by the State of California, for any violation of this part or of any regulation adopted pursuant to this part, shall be deposited, as soon as practicable after the receipt of the fine or forfeiture, with the county treasurer of the county in which the court is situated. Amounts so deposited shall be paid at least once a month as follows:

(a) One-half to the Treasurer, by warrant of the county auditor drawn upon the requisition of the clerk or judge of the court, for deposit in the California Fire and Arson Training Fund, on order of the Controller. At the time of the transmittal, the county auditor shall forward to the Controller, on the form or forms prescribed by the Controller, a record of the imposition, collection, and payments of the fines or forfeitures.

(b) One-half to the county in which the offense was committed for disposition as provided in Section 1463 of the Penal Code.

(Amended by Stats. 1985, Ch. 333, Sec. 1.)

13112.2.

All revenue collected pursuant to subdivision (a) of Section 13112.1 shall be deposited in the California Fire and Arson Training Fund and shall be available, when appropriated by the Legislature, for the office of the State Fire Marshal to support fire training.

(Amended by Stats. 1985, Ch. 333, Sec. 2.)

13113.

(a) Except as otherwise provided in this section, a person, firm, or corporation shall not establish, maintain, or operate a hospital, children's home, children's nursery, or institution, home or institution for the care of people who are elderly, persons with mental health disorders or intellectual disabilities, or nursing or convalescent home, wherein more than six guests or patients are housed or cared for on a 24-hour-per-day basis unless there is installed and maintained in an operable condition in every building, or portion thereof where patients or guests are housed, an automatic sprinkler system approved by the State Fire Marshal.

(b) This section shall not apply to homes or institutions for the 24-hour-per-day care of ambulatory children if all of the following conditions are satisfied:

(1) The buildings, or portions thereof where children are housed, are not more than two stories in height and are constructed and maintained in accordance with regulations adopted by the State Fire Marshal pursuant to Section 13143 and building standards published in the California Building Standards Code.

(2) The buildings, or portions thereof housing more than six children, shall have installed and maintained in an operable condition therein a fire alarm system of a type approved by the State Fire Marshal. The system shall be activated by detectors responding to invisible products of combustion other than heat.

(3) The buildings or portions thereof do not house children with mental health disorders or children with intellectual disabilities.

(c) This section shall not apply to any one-story building or structure of an institution or home for the care of the aged providing 24-hour-per-day care if the building or structure is used or intended to be used for the housing of no more than six ambulatory aged persons. However, the buildings or institutions shall have installed and maintained in an operable condition therein a fire alarm system of a type approved by the State Fire Marshal. The system shall be activated by detectors responding to products of combustion other than heat.

(d) This section does not apply to occupancies, or any alterations thereto, located in type I construction, as defined by the State Fire Marshal, under construction or in existence on March 4, 1972.

(e) "Under construction," as used in this section, means that actual work shall have been performed on the construction site and shall not be construed to mean that the hospital, home, nursery, institution, sanitarium, or a portion thereof, is in the planning stage.

(Amended by Stats. 2014, Ch. 144, Sec. 38. (AB 1847) Effective January 1, 2015.)

13113.5.

The State Fire Marshal shall adopt regulations requiring the installation of automatic fire devices activated by products of combustion other than heat in all facilities within the scope of Sections 13143 and 13143.6, which provide 24-hour per day care, which house six or fewer persons, and which do not have automatic sprinkler systems.

(Added by Stats. 1978, Ch. 693.)

13113.6.

(a) Any person, or public or private firm, organization, or corporation, that owns, rents, leases, or manages a facility that hosts a ticketed event for live entertainment shall make an announcement of the availability of emergency exits prior to the beginning of the live entertainment.

(b) As used in this section, "facility" means a building or portion of a building having an assembly room with an occupancy load of less than 1,000 persons and a legitimate stage for the gathering together of 50 or more persons as defined pursuant to Division 2 of Section 303.1.1 of Title 24 of the California Code of Regulations (California Building Code of 2001).

(Added by Stats. 2005, Ch. 537, Sec. 1. Effective January 1, 2006.)

13113.7.

(a) (1) Except as otherwise provided in this section, smoke alarms, approved and listed by the State Fire Marshal pursuant to Section 13114 at the time of installation, shall be installed, in accordance with the manufacturer's instructions in each dwelling intended for human occupancy.

(2) For all dwelling units intended for human occupancy for which a building permit is issued on or after January 1, 2014, for alterations, repairs, or additions exceeding one thousand dollars ($1,000), the permit issuer shall not sign off on the completion of work until the permittee demonstrates that all smoke alarms required for the dwelling unit are devices approved and listed by the State Fire Marshal pursuant to Section 13114.

(3) However, if any local rule, regulation, or ordinance, adopted prior to January 1, 1987, requires installation in a dwelling unit intended for human occupancy of smoke alarms which receive their power from the electrical system of the building and requires compliance with the local rule, regulation, or ordinance at a date subsequent to the dates specified in this section, the compliance date specified in the rule, regulation, or ordinance shall, but only with respect to the dwelling units specified in this section, take precedence over the date specified in this section.

(4) Unless prohibited by local rules, regulations, or ordinances, a battery-operated smoke alarm, which otherwise met the standards adopted pursuant to Section 13114 for smoke alarms at the time of installation, satisfies the requirements of this section.

(5) A fire alarm system with smoke detectors installed in accordance with the State Fire Marshal's regulations may be installed in lieu of smoke alarms required pursuant to paragraph (1) or (2) of this subdivision, or paragraph (3) of subdivision (d).

(b) "Dwelling units intended for human occupancy," as used in this section, includes a one- or two-unit dwelling, lodging house, apartment complex, hotel, motel, condominium, stock cooperative, time-share project, or dwelling unit of a multiple-unit dwelling complex, or factory-built housing as defined in Section 19971. For the purpose of this part, "dwelling units intended for human occupancy" does not include manufactured homes as defined in Section 18007, mobilehomes as defined in Section 18008, and commercial coaches as defined in Section 18001.8.

(c) A high-rise structure, as defined in subdivision (b) of Section 13210 and regulated by Chapter 3 (commencing with Section 13210), and which is used for purposes other than as dwelling units intended for human occupancy, is exempt from the requirements of this section.

(d) (1) The owner shall be responsible for testing and maintaining alarms in hotels, motels, lodging houses, apartment complexes, and other multiple-dwelling complexes in which units are neither rented nor leased.

(2) The owner of a hotel, motel, lodging house, apartment complex, or other multiple-dwelling complex in which units are rented or leased, and commencing January 1, 2014, the owner of a single-family dwelling that is rented or leased, shall be responsible for testing and maintaining alarms required by this section as follows:

(A) An owner or the owner's agent may enter any dwelling unit, efficiency dwelling unit, guest room, and suite owned by the owner for the purpose of installing, repairing, testing, and maintaining single station smoke alarms required by this section. Except in cases of emergency, the owner or owner's agent shall give the tenants of each such unit, room, or suite reasonable notice in writing of the intention to enter and shall enter only during normal business hours. Twenty-four hours shall be presumed to be reasonable notice in absence of evidence to the contrary.

(B) At the time that a new tenancy is created, the owner shall ensure that smoke alarms are operable. The tenant shall be responsible for notifying the manager or owner if the tenant becomes aware of an inoperable smoke alarm within his or her unit. The owner or authorized agent shall correct any reported deficiencies in the smoke alarm and shall not be in violation of this section for a deficient smoke alarm when he or she has not received notice of the deficiency.

(3) On or before January 1, 2016, the owner of a dwelling unit intended for human occupancy in which one or more units are rented or leased shall install additional smoke alarms, as needed, to ensure that smoke alarms are located in compliance with current building standards. Existing alarms need not be replaced unless the alarm is inoperable. New smoke alarms installed in compliance with current building standards may be battery operated provided the alarms have been approved and listed by the State Fire Marshal for sale in the state. This paragraph shall not apply to fire alarm systems with smoke detectors, fire alarm devices that connect to a panel, or other devices that use a low-power radio frequency wireless communication signal.

(e) A violation of this section is an infraction punishable by a maximum fine of two hundred dollars ($200) for each offense.

(f) This section shall not affect any rights which the parties may have under any other provision of law because of the presence or absence of a smoke alarm.
(Amended by Stats. 2012, Ch. 420, Sec. 1. (SB 1394) Effective January 1, 2013.)
13113.8.
(a) On and after January 1, 1986, every single-family dwelling and factory-built housing, as defined in Section 19971, which is sold shall have an operable smoke alarm. At the time of installation, the alarm shall be approved and listed by the State Fire Marshal and installed in accordance with the State Fire Marshal's regulations. Unless prohibited by local rules, regulations, or ordinances, a battery-operated smoke alarm that met the standards adopted pursuant to Section 13114 for smoke alarms at the time of installation shall be deemed to satisfy the requirements of this section.
(b) On and after January 1, 1986, the transferor of any real property containing a single-family dwelling, as described in subdivision (a), whether the transfer is made by sale, exchange, or real property sales contract, as defined in Section 2985 of the Civil Code, shall deliver to the transferee a written statement indicating that the transferor is in compliance with this section. The disclosure statement shall be either included in the receipt for deposit in a real estate transaction, an addendum attached thereto, or a separate document.
(c) The transferor shall deliver the statement referred to in subdivision (b) as soon as practicable before the transfer of title in the case of a sale or exchange, or prior to execution of the contract where the transfer is by a real property sales contract, as defined in Section 2985. For purposes of this subdivision, "delivery" means delivery in person or by mail to the transferee or transferor, or to any person authorized to act for him or her in the transaction, or to additional transferees who have requested delivery from the transferor in writing. Delivery to the spouse of a transferee or transferor shall be deemed delivery to a transferee or transferor, unless the contract states otherwise.
(d) This section does not apply to any of the following:
(1) Transfers which are required to be preceded by the furnishing to a prospective transferee of a copy of a public report pursuant to Section 11018.1 of the Business and Professions Code.
(2) Transfers pursuant to court order, including, but not limited to, transfers ordered by a probate court in the administration of an estate, transfers pursuant to a writ of execution, transfers by a trustee in bankruptcy, transfers by eminent domain, or transfers resulting from a decree for specific performance.
(3) Transfers to a mortgagee by a mortgagor in default, transfers to a beneficiary of a deed of trust by a trustor in default, transfers by any foreclosure sale after default, transfers by any foreclosure sale after default in an obligation secured by a mortgage, or transfers by a sale under a power of sale after a default in an obligation secured by a deed of trust or secured by any other instrument containing a power of sale.
(4) Transfers by a fiduciary in the course of the administration of a decedent's estate, guardianship, conservatorship, or trust.
(5) Transfers from one coowner to one or more coowners.
(6) Transfers made to a spouse, or to a person or persons in the lineal line of consanguinity of one or more of the transferors.
(7) Transfers between spouses resulting from a decree of dissolution of a marriage, from a decree of legal separation, or from a property settlement agreement incidental to either of those decrees.
(8) Transfers by the Controller in the course of administering the Unclaimed Property Law provided for in Chapter 7 (commencing with Section 1500) of Title 10 of Part 3 of the Code of Civil Procedure.
(9) Transfers under the provisions of Chapter 7 (commencing with Section 3691) or Chapter 8 (commencing with Section 3771) of Part 6 of Division 1 of the Revenue and Taxation Code.
(e) No liability shall arise, nor any action be brought or maintained against, any agent of any party to a transfer of title, including any person or entity acting in the capacity of an escrow, for any error, inaccuracy, or omission relating to the disclosure required to be made by a transferor pursuant to this section. However, this subdivision does not apply to a licensee, as defined in Section 10011 of the Business and Professions Code, where the licensee participates in the making of the disclosure required to be made pursuant to this section with actual knowledge of the falsity of the disclosure.
(f) Except as otherwise provided in this section, this section shall not be deemed to create or imply a duty upon a licensee, as defined in Section 10011 of the Business and Professions Code, or upon any agent of any party to a transfer of title, including any person or entity acting in the capacity of an escrow, to monitor or ensure compliance with this section.
(g) No transfer of title shall be invalidated on the basis of a failure to comply with this section, and the exclusive remedy for the failure to comply with this section is an award of actual damages not to exceed one hundred dollars ($100), exclusive of any court costs and attorney's fees.
(h) Local ordinances requiring smoke alarms in single-family dwellings may be enacted or amended. However, the ordinances shall satisfy the minimum requirements of this section.
(i) For the purposes of this section, "single-family dwelling" includes a one- or two-unit dwelling, but does not include a manufactured home as defined in Section 18007, a mobilehome as defined in Section 18008, or a commercial coach as defined in Section 18001.8.
(Amended by Stats. 2012, Ch. 420, Sec. 2. (SB 1394) Effective January 1, 2013.)
13113.9.
(a) For the purposes of this section:

(1) "Burglar bars" are security bars located on the inside or outside of a door or window of a residential dwelling.
(2) "Residential dwelling" means a house, apartment, motel, hotel, or other type of residential dwelling subject to the State Housing Law (Part 1.5 (commencing with Section 17910) of Division 13) and a manufactured home, mobilehome, and multiunit manufactured housing as defined in the Mobilehome-Manufactured Housing Act of 1980 (Part 2 (commencing with Section 18000) of Division 13).
(b) On or before July 1, 1998, the State Fire Marshal shall develop and adopt regulations for the labeling and packaging of burglar bars addressing the requirements in the California Building Standards Code intended to promote safety in the event of a fire. For this purpose, the regulations shall include specification of the language to be printed on the packaging, the location of the language on the packaging, and the height and stroke of the print type to be utilized. The regulations shall direct the consumer or installer to contact the local fire department or local building official to determine whether the city or county requires that the burglar bars have a release mechanism on the outside for use by the fire department in the event of a fire emergency.
(c) Burglar bars shall not be sold in California at wholesale or retail unless the burglar bars are either labeled or their packaging contains the warning information specified in the regulations adopted pursuant to subdivision (b).
(d) Any contractor or installer of burglar bars shall provide the owner of the residential dwelling a copy of the warning information required pursuant to subdivision (b) prior to installing burglar bars.
(e) No person shall install unopenable burglar bars on a residential dwelling (1) where the California Building Standards Code requires openable burglar bars for emergency escape or rescue, or (2) on mobilehomes, manufactured homes, or multiunit manufactured housing unless at least one window or door to the exterior in each bedroom is openable for emergency escape or rescue.
(Amended by Stats. 1998, Ch. 730, Sec. 1. Effective January 1, 1999.)
13114.
(a) The State Fire Marshal, with the advice of the State Board of Fire Services, shall adopt regulations and standards as he or she may determine to be necessary to control the quality and installation of fire alarm systems and fire alarm devices marketed, distributed, offered for sale, or sold in this state.
(b) (1) No person shall market, distribute, offer for sale, or sell any fire alarm system or fire alarm device in this state unless the system or device has been approved and listed by the State Fire Marshal.
(2) (A) Except as provided in subparagraph (B), commencing July 1, 2014, in order to be approved and listed by the State Fire Marshal, a smoke alarm that is only operated by a battery shall contain a nonreplaceable, nonremovable battery that is capable of powering the smoke alarm for at least 10 years.
(B) This paragraph shall not apply to smoke alarms that have been ordered by, or are in the inventory of, an owner, managing agent, contractor, wholesaler, or retailer on or before July 1, 2014, until July 1, 2015.
(3) Commencing January 1, 2015, in order to be approved and listed by the State Fire Marshal, a smoke alarm shall display the date of manufacture on the device, provide a place on the device where the date of installation can be written, and incorporate a hush feature.
(4) The State Fire Marshal shall have the authority to create exceptions to paragraphs (2) and (3) through its regulatory process. The exceptions that may be considered as part of the regulatory process shall include, but are not limited to, fire alarm systems with smoke detectors, fire alarm devices that connect to a panel, or other devices that use a low-power radio frequency wireless communication signal.
(5) The State Fire Marshal shall approve the manufacturer's instructions for each smoke alarm and shall ensure that the instructions are consistent with current building standard requirements for the location and placement of smoke alarms.
(Amended by Stats. 2013, Ch. 183, Sec. 21. (SB 745) Effective January 1, 2014.)
13114.1.
To the extent that resources are available, the State Fire Marshal shall prepare and distribute for use by local agencies, community groups, and private firms, public education materials about the dangers of illegal burglar bars. These public education materials shall use multiple media, including Braille, 18-point type, cassette tape, and computer disk for those who are print impaired, and multiple languages, as the State Fire Marshal determines appropriate.
(Added by Stats. 1998, Ch. 730, Sec. 2. Effective January 1, 1999.)
13114.2.
(a) On or before January 1, 2000, the State Fire Marshal shall adopt regulations and standards to control the quality and installation of burglar bars and safety release mechanisms for emergency escape/rescue windows or doors installed, marketed, distributed, offered for sale, or sold in this state.
(b) On and after July 1, 2000, no person shall install, market, distribute, offer for sale, or sell burglar bars and safety release mechanisms for emergency escape/rescue windows or doors in this state unless the burglar bars and safety release mechanisms have been approved by a testing laboratory recognized by the State Fire Marshal.
(c) As used in this section:
(1) "Burglar bars" means security bars located on the inside or outside of a door or window of a residential dwelling.
(2) "Residential dwelling" means a house, apartment, motel, hotel, or other type of residential dwelling subject to the State Housing Law (Part 1.5 (commencing with Section 17910) of Division 13) and a manufactured home, mobilehome, and multiunit

manufactured housing as defined in the Mobilehomes-Manufactured Housing Act of 1980 (Part 2 (commencing with Section 18000) of Division 13).

(3) "Emergency escape/rescue windows or doors" means the exits required by Section 1-310.4 of the 1998 edition of the California Building Standards Code, or its successor.
(Amended by Stats. 1999, Ch. 550, Sec. 26.5. Effective September 28, 1999.)

13114.3.
(a) Notwithstanding any other provision of law, on and after January 1, 1999, no burglar bars shall be installed or maintained on any residential dwelling that is owned or leased by a public agency, unless the burglar bars meet current state and local requirements, as applicable, for burglar bars and safety release mechanisms.
(b) As used in this section:
(1) "Burglar bars" means security bars located on the inside or outside of a door or window of a residential dwelling.
(2) "Public agency" means any of the following:
(A) A state agency, department, board, or commission.
(B) The University of California.
(C) A local agency, including, but not limited to, a city, including a charter city, county, city and county, community redevelopment agency, housing authority, special district, or any other political subdivision of the state.
(3) "Residential dwelling" means a house, apartment, motel, hotel, or other type of residential dwelling subject to the State Housing Law (Part 1.5 (commencing with Section 17910) of Division 13) and a manufactured home, mobilehome, and multiunit manufactured housing as defined in the Mobilehomes-Manufactured Housing Act of 1980 (Part 2 (commencing with Section 18000) of Division 13).
(Added by Stats. 1998, Ch. 730, Sec. 4. Effective January 1, 1999.)

13114.5.
The governing body of any city or county may enact ordinances or laws imposing restrictions greater than those imposed by Sections 13113 and 13114.
(Added by Stats. 1955, Ch. 1480.)

13114.7.
(a) For the purposes of this section the following are definitions of class I and class II systems:
(1) American Water Works Association (A.W.W.A.) Manuel No. M-14 class 1—Automatic fire sprinkler systems with direct connection from public water mains only; no pumps, tanks, or reservoirs; no physical connection from other water supplies; no antifreeze or additives of any kind; and all sprinkler drains discharging to the atmosphere or other safe outlets.
(2) American Water Works Association (A.W.W.A.) Manual No. M-14 class 2—Automatic fire sprinkler systems which are the same as class 1, except that booster pumps may be installed in the connections from the street mains.
(b) Automatic fire sprinkler systems described in subdivision (a) shall not require any backflow protection equipment at the service connection other than required by standards for those systems contained in the publication of the National Fire Protection Association entitled "Installation of Sprinkler Systems" (N.F.P.A. Pamphlet No. 13, 1980 edition).
(Added by Stats. 1982, Ch. 425, Sec. 1.)

13115.
(a) It is unlawful for any person, firm or corporation to establish, maintain or operate any circus, side show, carnival, tent show, theater, skating rink, dance hall, or a similar exhibition, production, engagement or offering or other place of assemblage in or under which 10 or more persons may gather for any lawful purpose, in any tent, awning or other fabric enclosure unless a tent, awning or other fabric enclosure, and all auxiliary tents, curtains, drops, awnings and all decorative materials, are made from a nonflammable material or are treated and maintained in a flame-retardant condition. This subdivision shall not apply to tents used to conduct committal services on the grounds of a cemetery, nor to tents, awnings or other fabric enclosures erected and used within a sound stage, or other similar structural enclosure which is equipped with an overhead automatic sprinkler system.
(b) One year after the adoption of regulations by the State Fire Marshal, but not later than July 1, 1976, it shall be unlawful for any person to sell or offer for sale any tent designed and intended for use for occupancy by less than 10 persons unless the tent is made from flame-retardant fabrics or materials approved by the State Fire Marshal. One year after the adoption of regulations by the State Fire Marshal, but not later than July 1, 1976, all tents manufactured for sale in this state shall be flame retardant and shall be labeled in a manner specified by the State Fire Marshal. Any manufacturer of tents for sale in this state who fails to use flame-retardant fabrics or materials or who fails to label them as specified by the State Fire Marshal shall be strictly liable for any damage which occurs to any person as a result of a violation of this section.
(c) "Flame retardant," as used in this section, means a fabric or material resistant to flame or fire to the extent that it will successfully withstand standard fire-resistive tests adopted and promulgated by the State Fire Marshal.
(Amended by Stats. 1996, Ch. 332, Sec. 16. Effective January 1, 1997.)

13116.
Except as provided in Section 18930, the State Fire Marshal shall prepare and adopt rules and regulations establishing minimum requirements for the prevention of fire and panic in connection with the use of tents, awnings or other fabric enclosures. The State Fire Marshal shall adopt and submit building standards for approval pursuant to Chapter 4 (commencing with Section 18935) of Part 2.5 of Division 13 of this code for the purposes described in this section.
(Amended by Stats. 1979, Ch. 1152.)

13117.
(a) Any new detector or new automatic high pressure shutoff device sold by any person on or after January 1, 1987, in this state shall, prior to sale, be approved by the State Fire Marshal.
(b) For purposes of this section:
(1) "Liquefied petroleum gas" has the same meaning as that term is defined by Section 380 of the Vehicle Code.
(2) "Detector" means any electronic or mechanical device which monitors the unintended or accidental release of liquefied petroleum gas from any tank or other storage facility.
(3) "Automatic high pressure shutoff device" means a device which meets all of the following requirements:
(A) Senses excess pressure and automatically shuts off the liquefied petroleum gas supply system before the pressure reaches a danger level.
(B) At the same time, signals the shutoff with a red indicator.
(C) Prevents the unit to be reset until the high pressure problem has been corrected.
(Added by Stats. 1986, Ch. 21, Sec. 1.)

13118.
All solvents offered for sale at retail shall be labeled as required by the regulations adopted pursuant to the Federal Hazardous Substances Act (Public Law 86-813; 74 Stats. 372; 15 U.S.C., Sec. 1261, et seq.) which are in effect on January 1, 1979, or which are adopted on or after that date.
Any person, firm, or corporation in violation of the provisions of this section shall be guilty of a misdemeanor.
(Amended by Stats. 1978, Ch. 868.)

13119.
It is unlawful for any person, firm or corporation to establish, maintain or operate any night club, restaurant, cafe or any similar place where alcoholic liquors are sold for consumption on the premises, or any dance hall, skating rink, theater, motion picture theater, auditorium, school, or any other place of public assemblage used, or intended for use, as a place of amusement, entertainment, instruction, display, or exhibition, unless all drapes, hangings, curtains, drops and all other similar decorative materials that would tend to increase the fire or panic hazard, are made from a nonflammable material, or are treated and maintained in a flame-retardant condition as defined in Section 13115. The provisions of this section shall not apply to portions of the premises which are not a part of and are not directly connected with that portion of the premises used for any of the above purposes.
(Added by Stats. 1947, Ch. 1549.)

13120.
The State Fire Marshal shall establish minimum standard requirements, and shall adopt rules and regulations as are deemed necessary by him or her to properly regulate the manufacture, sale and application of flame-retardant chemicals and the sale of flame-retardant treated fabrics or materials used or intended for use in connection with any occupancy mentioned in Sections 13115 and 13119.
(Amended by Stats. 1996, Ch. 332, Sec. 17. Effective January 1, 1997.)

13121.
The State Fire Marshal shall, before approving any flame-retardant chemical, fabric or material, require that flame-retardant chemicals and flame-retardant fabrics or materials be submitted to a laboratory approved by him or her for testing in accordance with the standards established pursuant to Section 13120.
(Amended by Stats. 1996, Ch. 332, Sec. 18. Effective January 1, 1997.)

13122.
The State Fire Marshal shall promulgate and make available at cost of printing at least once each year a list of the flame-retardant chemicals, flame-retardant fabrics or materials, and flame-retardant application concerns approved by him or her. He or she may, without cost, furnish a single copy of each list to each flame-retardant chemical and application concern that is registered and approved by him or her and to all California fire officials.
(Amended by Stats. 1996, Ch. 332, Sec. 19. Effective January 1, 1997.)

13123.
The State Fire Marshal shall remove from his or her approved list the name of any flame-retardant chemicals, flame-retardant fabric or material or any flame-retardant application concern where he or she finds after a hearing that any of the following causes exists:
(a) Selling or offering for sale a flame-retardant chemical or a flame-retardant material that is inferior to that submitted for test and approval.
(b) Distributing or disseminating or causing to be distributed or disseminated, misleading or false information with respect to any flame-retardant chemical, fabric or material.
(c) Changing the flame-retardant chemical formula or methods of flame-retardant treatment without first notifying and obtaining approval of the change by, the State Fire Marshal.
(d) Using chemicals other than those shown on the State Fire Marshal's approved list.
(e) Using chemicals for the treatment of materials for which they have not been approved.
(f) Failure to adequately and properly treat a fabric or material to make it flame-retardant to the extent that it will successfully pass the flame-retardant tests established by the State Fire Marshal.
(g) Violating any minimum standard or any rule or regulation adopted pursuant to Section 13120.
The proceedings shall be conducted in accordance with Chapter 5 (commencing with Section 11500) of Part 1 of Division 3 of Title 2 of the Government Code, and the State

Fire Marshal shall have all the powers granted therein. Pending hearing and decision the State Fire Marshal may temporarily remove any name from the approved list for a period not to exceed 30 days, if he or she finds that the action is required in the public interest. In any such case the order of temporary removal shall be effective upon notice to the persons affected thereby, and a hearing shall be held and a decision issued within 30 days after the notice.
(Amended by Stats. 1994, Ch. 475, Sec. 1. Effective January 1, 1995.)
13124.
The name of any chemical, chemical concern or flame-retardant application concern whose name has been removed from the approved list shall not be restored to the approved list for a period of 90 days from the date of the removal.
(Amended by Stats. 1996, Ch. 332, Sec. 20. Effective January 1, 1997.)
13125.
The name of any chemical, chemical concern or flame-retardant application concern shall not be restored to the approved list until a new application, accompanied by a new registration fee, has been filed with the State Fire Marshal.
(Added by Stats. 1947, Ch. 1549.)
13126.
With the advice of the State Fire Advisory Board, the State Fire Marshal shall prepare and adopt rules and regulations establishing minimum standards and specific procedures for the approval of flame-retardant chemicals, flame-retardant materials and flame-retardant applicator concerns whose names are to appear on the approved list.
(Added by Stats. 1947, Ch. 1549.)
13127.
(a) Any chemical manufacturing concern, or any flame-retardant application concern, or any concern marketing a flame-retardant fabric or material that desires to have its name appear on the approved list shall first make application to the State Fire Marshal on forms provided by the State Fire Marshal.
(b) For purposes of this section, Sections 13128 and 13129:
(1) "General applicator" means a concern that engages in the business of or performs for a fee the application of a flame-retardant compound or chemical to any textile including decorative materials.
(2) "Limited applicator" means a concern that engages in the business of or performs for a fee the application of a flame-retardant compound or chemical to nontextile decorative items, including Christmas trees.
(c) (1) The annual registration fee renewal period for chemical manufacturing concerns, concerns marketing a flame-retardant fabric or material, and general applicators shall begin on January 1 and end on May 1 preceding the registration year for which the renewal is requested. A penalty of 50 percent of the listing fee shall be assessed in all cases where the renewal fees are not paid on or before May 1, preceding the registration year for which renewal is requested.
(2) The annual registration fee renewal period for limited applicators shall begin September 15 and end on October 31 preceding the registration year for which the renewal is requested. A penalty of 50 percent of the listing fee shall be assessed in all cases where the fees are not paid on or before October 31, preceding the registration year for which renewal is requested.
(d) All applications shall be accompanied by a registration fee established by the State Fire Marshal. The registration fee shall not exceed the amount necessary to cover the costs incurred by the State Fire Marshal in carrying out Sections 13120 to 13126, inclusive.
(Amended by Stats. 1996, Ch. 332, Sec. 21. Effective January 1, 1997.)
13128.
(a) The annual and renewal registration fee period for chemical manufacturing concerns, concerns marketing a flame-retardant fabric or material, and general applicators shall be for the fiscal year period from July 1 to June 30 or for the remaining portion thereof.
(b) The annual and renewal registration fee period for limited applicators shall be for the fiscal year period from November 1 to October 31 or for the remaining portion thereof.
(Amended by Stats. 1996, Ch. 332, Sec. 22. Effective January 1, 1997.)
13129.
(a) The State Fire Marshal shall remove from the approved list the names of all chemicals, chemically treated fabrics or materials and the names of all flame-retardant general applicator concerns for which renewal fees have not been paid prior to May 1 of each year.
(b) The State Fire Marshal shall remove from the approved list the names of all flame-retardant limited applicator concerns that have not paid their renewal registration fee prior to October 31 of each year.
(Amended by Stats. 1996, Ch. 332, Sec. 23. Effective January 1, 1997.)
13130.
All money collected pursuant to this chapter shall be deposited in the State Fire Marshal Licensing and Certification Fund established pursuant to Section 13137, and shall be available to the State Fire Marshal upon appropriation by the Legislature to carry out the purposes of this chapter.
(Amended by Stats. 1992, Ch. 306, Sec. 2. Effective January 1, 1993. Operative July 1, 1993, by Sec. 6 of Ch. 306.)
13131.
"Nonambulatory persons" means persons unable to leave a building unassisted under emergency conditions. It includes any person who is unable, or likely to be unable, to physically and mentally respond to a sensory signal approved by the State Fire Marshal, or an oral instruction relating to fire danger, and persons who depend upon mechanical aids such as crutches, walkers, and wheelchairs. The determination of ambulatory or nonambulatory status of persons with developmental disabilities shall be made by the Director of Social Services or his or her designated representative, in consultation with the Director of Developmental Services or his or her designated representative. The determination of ambulatory or nonambulatory status of all other disabled persons placed after January 1, 1984, who are not developmentally disabled shall be made by the Director of Social Services, or his or her designated representative.
(Amended by Stats. 1983, Ch. 1132, Sec. 1.)
13131.5.
(a) All of the following building standards shall apply to any single-story building housing nonambulatory persons which is operated as a residential care facility for the elderly and licensed to care for more than six persons:
(1) The entire building shall have installed a State Fire Marshal approved fully automatic fire extinguishing system, designed and installed in accordance with Section 2-3801(d) of Chapter 2-38 of Part 2 of Title 24 of the California Code of Regulations.
(2) The entire building shall have installed a State Fire Marshal approved and listed manual fire alarm system.
(3) The entire building shall be of at least Type V one-hour fire resistive construction, as described in Chapter 2-22 of Part 2 of Title 24 of the California Code of Regulations.
(4) A building with individual floor areas over 6,000 square feet per floor shall have an approved smoke barrier dividing the floor approximately in half, unless there is direct exiting available from each dwelling unit.
(b) All of the following building standards shall apply to any two-story building housing nonambulatory persons on a second floor, which is operated as a residential care facility for the elderly and licensed to care for more than six persons:
(1) The entire building shall have installed a State Fire Marshal approved fully automatic fire extinguishing system, designed and installed in accordance with Section 2-3801(d) of Chapter 2-38 of Part 2 of Title 24 of the California Code of Regulations.
(2) The entire building shall have installed a State Fire Marshal approved and listed automatic fire alarm system.
(3) The entire building shall be of at least Type V one-hour fire resistive construction, as described in Chapter 2-22 of Part 2 of Title 24 of the California Code of Regulations.
(4) A building with individual floor areas over 6,000 square feet per floor shall have an approved smoke barrier dividing the floor approximately in half, without regard to whether direct exiting is available from each dwelling unit.
(5) The entire building shall have at least two sets of enclosed stairways.
(c) All of the following building standards shall apply to any multistory building housing nonambulatory persons on the third, fourth, or fifth floor, which is operated as a residential care facility for the elderly and licensed to care for more than six persons:
(1) The entire building, unless otherwise exempt pursuant to subdivision (d) of Section 13113, shall have installed a State Fire Marshal approved fully automatic fire extinguishing system, designed and installed in accordance with Section 2-3801(d) of Chapter 2-38 of Part 2 of Title 24 of the California Code of Regulations.
(2) The entire building shall have installed a State Fire Marshal approved and listed automatic fire alarm system.
(3) The entire building shall be of Type II fire resistive construction, as described in Chapter 2-19 of Part 2 of Title 24 of the California Code of Regulations.
(4) A building with individual floor areas over 6,000 square feet per floor shall have an approved smoke barrier dividing the floor approximately in half, without regard to whether direct exiting is available from each dwelling unit.
(5) The entire building shall have at least two sets of enclosed stairways.
(d) All of the following building standards shall apply to any multistory building housing nonambulatory persons on floors above the fifth floor, which is operated as a residential care facility for the elderly and licensed to care for more than six persons:
(1) The entire building, unless otherwise exempt pursuant to subdivision (d) of Section 13113, shall have installed a State Fire Marshal approved fully automatic fire extinguishing system, designed and installed in accordance with Section 2-3801(d) of Chapter 2-38 of Part 2 of Title 24 of the California Code of Regulations.
(2) The entire building shall have installed a State Fire Marshal approved and listed automatic fire alarm system.
(3) The entire building shall be Type I fire resistive construction, as described in Chapter 2-18 of Part 2 of Title 24 of the California Code of Regulations.
(4) A building with individual floor areas over 6,000 square feet per floor shall have an approved smoke barrier dividing the floor approximately in half, without regard to whether direct exiting is available from each dwelling unit.
(5) The entire building shall have at least two sets of enclosed stairways.
(e) This section and the regulations adopted by the State Fire Marshal pursuant to subdivision (f) shall apply uniformly throughout the state and no city, county, city and county, or district shall adopt any ordinance, rule, or regulation which is inconsistent with this section or with the regulations adopted by the State Fire Marshal pursuant to subdivision (f).
(f) The State Fire Marshal shall adopt regulations establishing a reasonable fee, not to exceed the actual costs of inspection to the agency conducting the inspection, for the final inspection of any facility which is subject to the standards established pursuant to this section.
(g) This section shall be enforced in accordance with the division of authority prescribed in Section 13146.
(Added by Stats. 1990, Ch. 436, Sec. 1.)
13132.
Every person, firm, or corporation maintaining or operating any facility for the care of the mentally handicapped shall file a statement with the fire authority having jurisdiction within

five days of the admission or readmission of a patient stating that such patient is an ambulatory or a nonambulatory person and enumerating the reasons for such classification. Such a statement shall also be filed for each existing patient within 30 days of the effective date of this section.

Any statement required to be filed pursuant to this section shall be certified as to its correctness by the person attending such patient.

It shall be unlawful for any person, firm, or corporation required to file a statement pursuant to this section to include false statements therein. Any such act shall be in violation of this section and subject to the provisions of Section 13112.
(Added by Stats. 1971, Ch. 1407.)

13132.7.

(a) Within a very high fire hazard severity zone designated by the Director of Forestry and Fire Protection pursuant to Article 9 (commencing with Section 4201) of Chapter 1 of Part 2 of Division 4 of the Public Resources Code and within a very high hazard severity zone designated by a local agency pursuant to Chapter 6.8 (commencing with Section 51175) of Part 1 of Division 1 of Title 5 of the Government Code, the entire roof covering of every existing structure where more than 50 percent of the total roof area is replaced within any one-year period, every new structure, and any roof covering applied in the alteration, repair, or replacement of the roof of every existing structure, shall be a fire retardant roof covering that is at least class B as defined in the Uniform Building Code, as adopted and amended by the State Building Standards Commission.

(b) In all other areas, the entire roof covering of every existing structure where more than 50 percent of the total roof area is replaced within any one-year period, every new structure, and any roof covering applied in the alteration, repair, or replacement of the roof of every existing structure, shall be a fire retardant roof covering that is at least class C as defined in the Uniform Building Code, as adopted and amended by the State Building Standards Commission.

(c) Notwithstanding subdivision (b), within state responsibility areas classified by the State Board of Forestry and Fire Protection pursuant to Article 3 (commencing with Section 4125) of Chapter 1 of Part 2 of Division 4 of the Public Resources Code, except for those state responsibility areas designated as moderate fire hazard responsibility zones, the entire roof covering of every existing structure where more than 50 percent of the total roof area is replaced within any one-year period, every new structure, and any roof covering applied in the alteration, repair, or replacement of the roof of every existing structure, shall be a fire retardant roof covering that is at least class B as defined in the Uniform Building Code, as adopted and amended by the State Building Standards Commission.

(d) (1) Notwithstanding subdivision (a), (b), or (c), within very high fire hazard severity zones designated by the Director of Forestry and Fire Protection pursuant to Article 9 (commencing with Section 4201) of Chapter 1 of Part 2 of Division 4 of the Public Resources Code or by a local agency pursuant to Chapter 6.8 (commencing with Section 51175) of Part 1 of Division 1 of Title 5 of the Government Code, the entire roof covering of every existing structure where more than 50 percent of the total roof area is replaced within any one-year period, every new structure, and any roof covering applied in the alteration, repair, or replacement of the roof of every existing structure, shall be a fire retardant roof covering that is at least class A as defined in the Uniform Building Code, as adopted and amended by the State Building Standards Commission.

(2) Paragraph (1) does not apply to any jurisdiction containing a very high fire hazard severity zone if the jurisdiction fulfills both of the following requirements:

(A) Adopts the model ordinance approved by the State Fire Marshal pursuant to Section 51189 of the Government Code or an ordinance that substantially conforms to the model ordinance of the State Fire Marshal.

(B) Transmits, upon adoption, a copy of the ordinance to the State Fire Marshal.

(e) The State Building Standards Commission shall incorporate the requirements set forth in subdivisions (a), (b), and (c) by publishing them as an amendment to the California Building Standards Code in accordance with Chapter 4 (commencing with Section 18935) of Part 2.5 of Division 13.

(f) Nothing in this section shall limit the authority of a city, county, city and county, or fire protection district in establishing more restrictive requirements, in accordance with current law, than those specified in this section.

(g) This section shall not affect the validity of an ordinance, adopted prior to the effective date for the relevant roofing standard specified in subdivisions (a) and (b), by a city, county, city and county, or fire protection district, unless the ordinance mandates a standard that is less stringent than the standards set forth in subdivision (a), in which case the ordinance shall not be valid on or after the effective date for the relevant roofing standard specified in subdivisions (a) and (b).

(h) Any qualified historical building or structure as defined in Section 18955 may, on a case-by-case basis, utilize alternative roof constructions as provided by the State Historical Building Code.

(i) The installer of the roof covering shall provide certification of the roof covering classification, as provided by the manufacturer or supplier, to the building owner and, when requested, to the agency responsible for enforcement of this part. The installer shall also install the roof covering in accordance with the manufacturer's listing.

(j) No wood roof covering materials shall be sold or applied in this state unless both of the following conditions are met:

(1) The materials have been approved and listed by the State Fire Marshal as complying with the requirements of this section.

(2) The materials have passed at least 5 years of the 10-year natural weathering test. The 10-year natural weathering test required by this subdivision shall be conducted in accordance with standard 15-2 of the 1994 edition of the Uniform Building Code at a testing facility recognized by the State Fire Marshal.

(k) The Insurance Commissioner shall accept the use of fire retardant wood roof covering material that complies with the requirements of this section, used in the partial repair or replacement of nonfire retardant wood roof covering material, as complying with the requirement in Section 2695.9 of Title 10 of the California Code of Regulations relative to matching replacement items in quality, color, and size.

(l) No common interest development, as defined in Section 4100 or 6534 of the Civil Code, may require an owner to install or repair a roof in a manner that is in violation of this section. The governing documents, as defined in Section 4150 or 6552 of the Civil Code, of a common interest development within a very high fire severity zone shall allow for at least one type of fire retardant roof covering material that meets the requirements of this section.
(Amended (as amended by Stats. 2012, Ch. 181, Sec. 63) by Stats. 2013, Ch. 605, Sec. 35. (SB 752) Effective January 1, 2014.)

13133.

(a) The State Fire Marshal shall develop and adopt regulations establishing new occupancy classifications and specific fire safety standards appropriate for residential facilities, as defined in Section 1502, and residential care facilities for the elderly, as defined in Section 1569.2. Notwithstanding Sections 13143.2, 13143.5, and 13869.7, building standards adopted by the State Fire Marshal pursuant to this section and published in the State Building Standards Code relating to fire and panic safety, and other regulations adopted by the State Fire Marshal pursuant to this section, shall apply uniformly throughout the state, and no city, county, city and county, including a charter city or charter county, or fire protection district shall adopt or enforce any ordinance or local rule or regulation relating to fire and panic safety in buildings or structures subject to this section that is inconsistent with building standards adopted by the State Fire Marshal pursuant to this section and published in the State Building Standards Code relating to fire and panic safety, or other regulations adopted by the State Fire Marshal pursuant to this section.

(b) Notwithstanding subdivision (a), a city, county, city and county, including a charter city or charter county may pursuant to Section 13143.5, or a fire protection district may pursuant to Section 13869.7, adopt standards more stringent than those contained in subdivision (a) that are reasonably necessary to accommodate local climate, geological, or topographical conditions relating to roof coverings for residential care facilities for the elderly.
(Amended by Stats. 1992, Ch. 420, Sec. 1. Effective January 1, 1993.)

13135.

The State Fire Marshal shall adopt regulations for alcoholism or drug abuse recovery or treatment facilities, as defined in Section 11834.11, based on whether the residents or patients of the facilities are nonambulatory, as defined in Section 13131, and not based on the age of residents or patients of the facilities.
(Added by Stats. 1991, Ch. 415, Sec. 1.)

ARTICLE 1.5. Financial Provisions [13137 - 13139]
   (Article 1.5 added by Stats. 1992, Ch. 306, Sec. 3.)

13137.

(a) The State Fire Marshal Licensing and Certification Fund is hereby created in the State Treasury. All money in the fund is available for the support of the State Fire Marshal upon appropriation by the Legislature. All moneys collected by the State Fire Marshal pursuant to this part, pursuant to Part 2 (commencing with Section 12500) or Part 3 (commencing with Section 12750) of Division 11, and pursuant to Section 41961, shall be deposited in the fund and shall be available to the State Fire Marshal for expenditure upon appropriation by the Legislature for the purposes of this part, Part 2 (commencing with Section 12500) or Part 3 (commencing with Section 12750) of Division 11, or Section 41961, respectively.

(b) Neither this article nor any provision of this part or Part 2 (commencing with Section 12500) or Part 3 (commencing with Section 12750) of Division 11 or Section 41961 authorize fees to exceed the actual cost of administration of the programs administered by the State Fire Marshal, nor authorize the charging of fees to a particular group being regulated under a program, for the costs of regulation under another program or for the costs of a different group under the same program.
(Amended by Stats. 2004, Ch. 496, Sec. 2. Effective January 1, 2005.)

13138.

(a) For state agencies, local agencies, or private entities that are charged for the costs of fire and life safety building code inspections and related fire and life safety activities rendered by the State Fire Marshal, such as plan review, construction consulting, fire watch, and investigation, the State Fire Marshal shall charge an amount sufficient to recover the costs incurred for the fire and life safety building code inspections and those related fire and life safety activities.

(b) Upon the request of the State Fire Marshal, in the form prescribed by the Controller, the Controller shall transfer the amount of the charges for services rendered from the agency's appropriation to the appropriation for the support of the State Fire Marshal's office. The State Fire Marshal shall charge local agencies and private entities for the amount sufficient to recover the costs of the services provided.

(c) A state agency that has a dispute regarding charges for fire and life safety building code inspections provided by the State Fire Marshal shall notify the State Fire Marshal, in writing, of the dispute and the basis therefor. The State Fire Marshal shall immediately provide a credit to the state agency in the subsequent billing or billings for the amount of the charges in dispute. No further transfer of funds shall occur with respect to the

services for which charges are disputed until the dispute is resolved by the State Fire Marshal, subject to the approval of the Department of Finance.
(Amended by Stats. 2008, Ch. 760, Sec. 4. Effective September 30, 2008.)

13139.

(a) On or before January 1, 2008, the State Fire Marshal shall approve and list portable gasoline containers that are designed and constructed according to one of the following child-resistant standards:

(1) Construction and design standards that are substantially the same as the American Society for Testing and Materials (ASTM) F2517-05 standard, issued by ASTM International, or any successor standard issued by ASTM International.

(2) Construction and design standards approved by a national testing laboratory recognized by the State Fire Marshal.

(b) No person shall sell, offer for sale, or possess for sale, on or after April 1, 2008, a portable gasoline container that has not been listed and approved by the State Fire Marshal.

(c) For purposes of this section, "portable gasoline container" means any container or vessel with a nominal capacity of 10 gallons or less that is intended for reuse and is designed, used, sold, advertised, or offered for sale primarily for receiving, transporting, storing, or dispensing gasoline. "Portable gasoline container" does not include either of the following:

(1) A container or vessel permanently embossed or permanently labeled as described in Section 172.407(a) of Title 49 of the Code of Federal Regulations, as it existed on September 15, 2005, indicating containers or vessels that are solely intended for use with nonfuel or nonkerosene products.

(2) A safety can meeting the requirements of Subpart F (commencing with Section 1926.150) of Part 1926 of Title 29 of the Code of Federal Regulations, as it existed on January 1, 2008. This exception shall not apply to any safety can manufactured after October 31, 2008, unless the can contains a label or silkscreen of the words "NOT CHILDPROOF" in a conspicuous and prominent place against a contrasting background, and the type shall be clear and legible. On safety cans larger than one quart, the font size of the label wording shall be printed in at least 12-point type. On safety cans one-quart and smaller, the font size of the label wording shall be printed in at least 8-point type. All labels shall be printed in both English and Spanish.

(d) Retailers are permitted to sell through existing supplies of portable gasoline containers that have not been listed and approved for sale by the State Fire Marshal.

(e) This section shall cease to be applicable if federal fire safety standards for portable gasoline containers that preempt this section are enacted and take effect subsequent to the effective date of this statute and the State Fire Marshal so notifies the Secretary of State.
(Amended by Stats. 2008, Ch. 5, Sec. 1. Effective April 15, 2008. Section conditionally inapplicable as provided in subd. (e).)

ARTICLE 2. The State Board of Fire Services [13140 - 13147]
(Heading of Article 2 amended by Stats. 1973, Ch. 1197.)

13140.

There is hereby created in the Office of the State Fire Marshal a State Board of Fire Services which shall consist of 18 members. The State Board of Fire Services succeeds to all of the powers, duties, and responsibilities of the State Fire Advisory Board, which is hereby abolished. Whenever the term "State Fire Advisory Board" appears in any other law, it means the State Board of Fire Services.
(Amended by Stats. 1996, Ch. 332, Sec. 24. Effective January 1, 1997.)

13140.5.

The board shall be composed of the following voting members: the State Fire Marshal, the Chief Deputy Director of the Department of Forestry and Fire Protection who is not the State Fire Marshal, the Director of Emergency Services, the Chairperson of the California Fire Fighter Joint Apprenticeship Program, one representative of the insurance industry, one volunteer firefighter, three fire chiefs, five fire service labor representatives, one representative from city government, one representative from a fire district, and one representative from county government.

The following members shall be appointed by the Governor: one representative of the insurance industry, one volunteer firefighter, three fire chiefs, five fire service labor representatives, one representative from city government, one representative from a fire district, and one representative from county government. Each member appointed shall be a resident of this state. The volunteer firefighter shall be selected from a list of names submitted by the California State Firefighters Association. One fire chief shall be selected from a list of names submitted by the California Fire Chiefs' Association; one fire chief shall be selected from a list of names submitted by the Fire Districts Association of California; and one fire chief shall be selected from a list of names submitted by the California Metropolitan Fire Chiefs. One fire service labor representative shall be selected from a list of names submitted by the California Labor Federation; one fire service labor representative shall be selected from a list of names submitted by the California Professional Firefighters; one fire service labor representative shall be selected from a list of names submitted by the International Association of Fire Fighters; one fire service labor representative shall be selected from a list of names submitted by the California Department of Forestry Firefighters; and one fire service labor representative shall be selected from a list of names submitted by the California State Firefighters Association. The city government representative shall be selected from elected or appointed city chief administrative officers or elected city mayors or council members. The fire district representative shall be selected from elected or appointed directors of fire districts. The county government representative shall be selected from elected or appointed county chief administrative officers or elected county supervisors. The appointed members shall

be appointed for a term of four years. Any member chosen by the Governor to fill a vacancy created other than by expiration of a term shall be appointed for the unexpired term of the member he or she is to succeed.
(Amended by Stats. 2013, Ch. 352, Sec. 340. (AB 1317) Effective September 26, 2013. Operative July 1, 2013, by Sec. 543 of Ch. 352.)

13140.6.

A quorum of the board shall consist of not less than nine members of the board. Proxy representation shall not be permitted.
(Amended by Stats. 2001, Ch. 779, Sec. 2. Effective January 1, 2002.)

13140.7.

The State Fire Marshal shall act as chairman of the board and provide necessary staff services. A vice chairman shall be selected by majority vote of the members.
(Amended by Stats. 1973, Ch. 1197.)

13141.

The board shall meet at the call of the State Fire Marshal, or at the request of any two members, but not less than annually, and shall receive no salary. Board members shall be paid actual and necessary expenses related to activities of the board. Meetings of the board shall be announced in writing to all members at least 15 days in advance of the meeting date.
(Amended by Stats. 1983, Ch. 1313, Sec. 11.)

13142.

The board, shall from time to time make full and complete studies, recommendations, and reports to the Governor and the Legislature for the purpose of recommending establishment of minimum standards with respect to all of the following:

(a) Physical requirements, education and training of fire protection personnel appointed to positions in regularly organized fire service agencies in this state, who are to be engaged in fire protection, including, but not limited to, fire suppression, fire prevention, arson investigation, and other allied fields.

(b) Fire apparatus, equipment, hose, tools, and related items.

(c) Basic minimum courses of training and education for fire protection personnel.
(Repealed and added by Stats. 1973, Ch. 1197.)

13142.6.

(a) The board, under the direction of the vice chairperson, shall sit as a board of appeals on the application of the State Fire Marshal's regulations excepting application of building standards published in the California Building Standards Code, by the State Fire Marshal or his or her salaried assistants. When any affected person believes that the State Fire Marshal's regulations, excepting building standards, are being applied incorrectly, the person may appeal the decision of the State Fire Marshal to the board. The board shall not consider the appeal unless the matter has come to the attention of the State Fire Marshal and he or she has rendered a decision in writing. Any appeal to the board shall be made by the affected person or his or her agent in writing in the form and manner prescribed by the board. The decision of the board shall be binding upon the State Fire Marshal. Any decision made by the board shall be for the instant case only and shall not be construed as setting precedent for general application.

(b) When an affected person believes that building standards are being applied incorrectly by the State Fire Marshal or his or her salaried assistants, that person may appeal to the California Building Standards Commission pursuant to Chapter 5 (commencing with Section 18945) of Part 2.5 of Division 13 of this code.
(Amended by Stats. 1996, Ch. 332, Sec. 25. Effective January 1, 1997.)

13142.8.

When the board sits as a board of appeals:

(a) The State Fire Marshal shall not sit as a member of the board.

(b) A member of the board shall not sit as a member or participant in the decision of any particular appeal if that member has a financial or other interest which would influence his or her decision on the particular appeal.
(Amended by Stats. 1996, Ch. 332, Sec. 26. Effective January 1, 1997.)

13143.

(a) Except as provided in Section 18930, the State Fire Marshal, with the advice of the State Board of Fire Services, shall prepare, adopt, and submit building standards for approval pursuant to Chapter 4 (commencing with Section 18935) of Part 2.5 of Division 13 and shall prepare and adopt other regulations establishing minimum requirements for the prevention of fire, and for the protection of life and property against fire and panic, in any building or structure used or intended for use as an asylum, jail, mental hospital, hospital, home for the elderly, children's nursery, children's home or institution not otherwise excluded from the coverage of this subdivision, school, or any similar occupancy of any capacity, and in any assembly occupancy where 50 or more persons may gather together in a building, room, or structure for the purpose of amusement, entertainment, instruction, deliberation, worship, drinking or dining, awaiting transportation, or education, and for any laboratory or research and development facility that stores, handles, or uses regulated hazardous materials. The State Fire Marshal shall adopt and submit building standards for approval pursuant to Chapter 4 (commencing with Section 18935) of Part 2.5 of Division 13 for the purposes described in this section. Regulations adopted pursuant to this subdivision and building standards relating to fire and panic safety published in the California Building Standards Code shall establish minimum requirements relating to the means of egress and the adequacy of exits from, the installation and maintenance of fire extinguishing and fire alarm systems in, the storage and handling of combustible or explosive materials or substances, and the installation and maintenance of appliances, equipment, decorations, security bars, grills, grates, and furnishings that present a fire, explosion, or panic hazard, and the minimum requirements shall be predicated on the height and fire-resistive qualities of the building or structure and the type of occupancy for which it is to be used. The building standards and other regulations shall apply to auxiliary or accessory buildings used or intended for use with any of the occupancies mentioned in this subdivision. Violation of any building standard or other regulation shall be a violation of this chapter.

In preparing and adopting building standards for approval pursuant to Chapter 4 (commencing with Section 18935) of Part 2.5 of Division 13, and in preparing and adopting other regulations affecting public schools, the State Fire Marshal shall also secure the advice of the State Department of Education. No regulation adopted by the State Fire Marshal shall conflict with any rule, regulation, or building standard lawfully adopted or enforced by the Department of General Services pursuant to Article 3 (commencing with Section 39140) of Chapter 2 of Part 23 or Article 7 (commencing with Section 81130) of Chapter 1 of Part 49 of the Education Code.

In addition to any other requirements for location of exit signs or devices in any building or structure used or intended for use as an asylum, jail, mental hospital, hospital, home for the elderly, children's nursery, children's home or institution not otherwise excluded from the coverage of this subdivision, school, or any similar occupancy of any capacity, and in any assembly occupancy where 50 or more persons may gather together in a building, room, or structure for the purpose of amusement, entertainment, instruction, deliberation, worship, drinking or dining, awaiting transportation, or education, the State Fire Marshal shall adopt building standards pursuant to this section establishing minimum requirements for the placement of distinctive devices, signs, or other means that identify exits and can be felt or seen near the floor. Exit sign technologies permitted by the model building code upon which the California Building Standards Code is based, shall be permitted. These building standards shall be adopted before July 1, 1998, and shall apply to all newly constructed buildings or structures subject to this subdivision for which a building permit is issued, or construction commenced, if no building permit is issued, on or after January 1, 1989.

(b) Notwithstanding subdivision (a) and Section 13143.6, facilities licensed pursuant to Chapter 3 (commencing with Section 1500) of Division 2 which provide nonmedical board, room, and care for six or fewer ambulatory children placed with the licensee for care or foster family homes and family day care homes for children, licensed pursuant to Chapter 3.6 (commencing with Section 1597.50) of Division 2, with a capacity of six or fewer and providing care and supervision for ambulatory children or children two years of age or younger, or both, shall not be subject to Article 1 (commencing with Section 13100) or Article 2 (commencing with Section 13140) of this chapter or regulations adopted pursuant thereto. No city, county, or public district shall adopt or enforce any requirement for the prevention of fire, or for the protection of life and property against fire and panic, with respect to structures used as facilities specified in this subdivision, unless the requirement would be applicable to a structure regardless of the special occupancy. Nothing in this subdivision shall restrict the application of state or local housing standards to those facilities, if the standards are applicable to residential occupancies and are not based upon the use of the structure as a facility specified in this subdivision.

"Ambulatory children," as used in this subdivision, does not include nonambulatory persons, as defined in Section 13131, and relatives of the licensee or the licensee's spouse.

(c) The State Fire Marshal shall adopt building standards establishing regulations providing that all school classrooms constructed after January 1, 1990, not equipped with automatic sprinkler systems, which have metal grills or bars on all their windows and do not have at least two exit doors within three feet of each end of the classroom opening to the exterior of the building or to a common hallway used for evacuation purposes, shall have an inside release for the grills or bars on at least one window farthest from the exit doors. The window or windows with the inside release shall be clearly marked as an emergency exit, in accordance with regulations adopted by the State Fire Marshal.
(Amended by Stats. 2008, Ch. 367, Sec. 1. Effective January 1, 2009.)

13143.1.

(a) Except as provided in Section 18930, the State Fire Marshal, with the advice of the State Board of Fire Services, shall prepare, adopt, and submit building standards for approval pursuant to Chapter 4 (commencing with Section 18935) of Part 2.5 of Division 13 establishing minimum requirements for the prevention of fire and for the protection of life and property against fire and panic in any motion picture or television production facility.

(b) In accordance with Section 13143.5, this subdivision shall not limit the authority of a city, county, city and county, or special district to set, pursuant to this division, stricter standards than those adopted pursuant to this section.
(Added by Stats. 1994, Ch. 498, Sec. 1. Effective January 1, 1995.)

13143.2.

(a) Except as provided in Section 18930, the State Fire Marshal shall adopt, amend, and repeal fire safety rules and regulations, and, except as otherwise provided in this part and Part 1.5 (commencing with Section 17910) of Division 13, the State Fire Marshal shall enforce building standards published in the California Building Standards Code and those other rules and regulations adopted by the State Fire Marshal for the provision of structural fire safety and fire-resistant exits in multiple-story structures existing on January 1, 1975, let for human habitation, including, and limited to, apartment houses, hotels, and motels wherein rooms used for sleeping are let above the ground floor. The State Fire Marshal shall adopt, amend, or repeal, and shall submit building standards for approval pursuant to Chapter 4 (commencing with Section 18935) of Part 2.5 of Division 13. The rules and regulations and building standards shall provide adequate safety to the occupants and the general public, and shall be consistent with the requirements contained in subdivisions (d), (e), (f), (g), (h), (i), (k), and (l) of Section 1215 of Part 2

of the California Building Standards Code, 1990 edition, or similar successor standards of the California Building Standards Code.

Except as provided in Section 18930, the department, with the written approval of the State Fire Marshal, may allow reasonable exceptions to subdivisions (e) and (g) of Section 1215 of Part 2 of the California Building Standards Code, 1990 edition, or similar successor standards of the California Building Standards Code, to permit the continued use of existing stairs and to subdivision (l) of Section 1215 to permit equivalent protection in lieu of occupancy separations. However, the exceptions shall not impair occupant safety and shall be consistent with the legislative intent of this section.

The building standards adopted by the State Fire Marshal and submitted for approval pursuant to Chapter 4 (commencing with Section 18935) of Part 2.5 of Division 13 shall not require that interior stairs and vertical openings be enclosed in two-story buildings.

(b) Notwithstanding subdivision (a), any city, county, or city and county may adopt building standards for structural fire safety and fire-resistant exits in structures subject to this section. However, those building standards shall be substantially equivalent in fire safety to, or more stringent in fire safety than, the building standards published in the California Building Standards Code. Each city, county, or city and county adopting alternative standards shall submit a detailed statement, with supporting data, to the State Fire Marshal of the alternate standards to the state building standards and other regulations adopted by the State Fire Marshal. The State Fire Marshal shall make a finding as to whether the alternative local standards are equivalent to the requirements of the California Building Standards Code. It is the intention of the Legislature that the building standards adopted and published in the California Building Standards Code shall be consistent with the requirements for new construction contained in the Uniform Building Code, 1988 edition, as adopted by the International Conference of Building Officials or similar successor standards adopted in accordance with Section 18928, except as otherwise required by state or federal law.

(c) This section shall not apply to any apartment house, hotel, or motel existing on May 14, 1979, having floors, as measured from the top of the floor surface, used for human occupancy located more than 75 feet above the lowest floor level having building access which is subject to Chapter 3 (commencing with Section 13210) of Part 2 of Division 12 relating to high rise buildings existing on May 14, 1979.

(d) The enforcement agency shall make inspections to the extent necessary to identify the structures within its jurisdiction in violation of the rules and regulations adopted pursuant to this section, and all structures subject to this section shall be conformed to the requirements contained in those regulations.

(e) All structures governed by Part 2.7 (commencing with Section 18950) of Division 13 are exempt from the permissive authority granted by subdivision (b).
(Added by Stats. 1990, Ch. 1111, Sec. 2.)

13143.3.

The State Fire Marshal or any local public entity shall not charge any fee for enforcing the provisions of Section 13143 or regulations adopted pursuant thereto with respect to facilities providing nonmedical board, room, and care for six or less children which are required to be licensed under the provisions of Chapter 2 (commencing with Section 1250) of Division 2.
(Added by renumbering Section 13143.5 (as added by Stats. 1973, Ch. 1204) by Stats. 2015, Ch. 303, Sec. 306. (AB 731) Effective January 1, 2016.)

13143.4.

The State Fire Marshal shall adopt regulations to authorize National Fire Protection Association 704 Standard System Diamonds, as provided in the 1985 Edition of the National Fire Protection Association 704, Standard System for Identification of Fire Hazards of Materials, be displayed at entrances to buildings and other locations where hazardous materials are stored.
(Added by Stats. 1988, Ch. 1189, Sec. 1.)

13143.5.

(a) Notwithstanding Part 2 (commencing with Section 13100) of Division 12, Part 1.5 (commencing with Section 17910) of Division 13, and Part 2.5 (commencing with Section 18901) of Division 13, any city, county, or city and county may, by ordinance, make changes or modifications that are more stringent than the requirements published in the California Building Standards Code relating to fire and panic safety and the other regulations adopted pursuant to this part. Any changes or modifications that are more stringent than the requirements published in the California Building Standards Code relating to fire and panic safety shall be subject to subdivision (b) of Section 18941.5.

(b) Nothing in this section shall authorize a local jurisdiction to mandate, nor prohibit a local jurisdiction from mandating, the installation of residential fire sprinkler systems within newly constructed dwelling units or in new additions to existing dwelling units, including, but not limited to, manufactured homes as defined in Section 18007.

(c) Nothing in this section shall authorize a local jurisdiction to mandate, nor prohibit a local jurisdiction from mandating, the retrofitting of existing dwelling units for the installation of residential fire sprinkler systems, including, but not limited to, manufactured homes as defined in Section 18007.

(d) Nothing in this section shall apply in any manner to litigation filed prior to January 1, 1991, regarding an ordinance or regulation which mandates the installation of residential fire sprinkler systems within newly constructed dwelling units or new additions to existing dwelling units.

(e) This section shall not apply to fire and panic safety requirements for the public schools adopted by the State Fire Marshal pursuant to Section 13143.

(f) (1) A city, county, or city and county that adopts an ordinance relating to fire and panic safety pursuant to this section shall delegate the enforcement of the ordinance to either of the following:

(A) The chief of the fire authority of the city, county, or city and county, or his or her authorized representative.

(B) The chief building official of the city, county, or city and county, or his or her authorized representative.

(2) Any fee charged pursuant to the enforcement authority of this subdivision shall not exceed the estimated reasonable cost of providing the service for which the fee is charged, pursuant to Section 66014 of the Government Code.

(g) On or before October 1, 1991, and each October 1 thereafter, the Department of Housing and Community Development, in conjunction with the office of the State Fire Marshal, shall transmit a report to the State Building Standards Commission on the more stringent requirements, adopted by a city, county, or city and county, pursuant to this section or adopted by a fire protection district and ratified pursuant to Section 13869.7, to the building standards relating to fire and panic safety adopted by the State Fire Marshal and contained in the California Building Standards Code. The report shall be for informational purposes only and shall include a summary by the department and the office of the reasons cited as the necessity for the more stringent requirements. The report required pursuant to this subdivision shall apply to any more stringent requirements adopted or ratified on or after January 1, 1991.

(h) All structures governed by Part 2.7 (commencing with Section 18950) of Division 13 are exempt from the permissive authority granted by subdivision (a).

(Amended (as amended by Stats. 1992, Ch. 661) by Stats. 1993, Ch. 906, Sec. 12. Effective October 8, 1993. Operative January 1, 1994, by Sec. 24 of Ch. 906.)

13143.6.

(a) Except as provided in Section 18930, the State Fire Marshal, with the advice of the State Board of Fire Services, shall prepare and adopt regulations establishing minimum standards for the prevention of fire and for the protection of life and property against fire in any building or structure used or intended for use as a home or institution for the housing of any person of any age when such person is referred to or placed within such home or institution for protective social care and supervision services by any governmental agency. The State Fire Marshal shall adopt and submit building standards for approval pursuant to the provisions of Chapter 4 (commencing with Section 18935) of Part 2.5 of Division 13 for the purposes described in this section. Occupancies within the meaning of this subdivision shall be those not otherwise specified in Sections 13113 and 13143 and shall include, but are not limited to, those commonly referred to as "certified family care homes," "out-of-home placement facilities," and "halfway houses." Building standards relating to fire and panic safety published in the State Building Standards Code and other regulations adopted pursuant to this subdivision shall establish minimum requirements relating to the means of egress and the adequacy of exits, the installation and maintenance of fire extinguishing and fire alarm systems, the storage, handling, or use of combustible or flammable materials or substances, and the installation and maintenance of appliances, equipment, decorations, and furnishings that may present a fire, explosion, or panic hazard. Such minimum requirements shall be predicated on the height, area, and fire-resistive qualities of the building or structure used or intended to be used.

Any building or structure within the scope of this subdivision used or intended to be used for the housing of more than six nonambulatory persons shall have installed and maintained in proper operating condition an automatic sprinkler system approved by the State Fire Marshal. "Nonambulatory person," as used in this section, means nonambulatory person as defined in Section 13131.

The ambulatory or nonambulatory status of any developmentally disabled person within the scope of this subdivision shall be determined by the Director of Social Services or his or her designated representative, in consultation with the Director of Developmental Services or his or her designated representative.

Any building or structure within the scope of this subdivision used or intended to be used for the housing of more than six ambulatory persons shall have installed or maintained in proper operating condition an automatic fire alarm system approved and listed by the State Fire Marshal which will respond to products of combustion other than heat.

In preparing and adopting regulations pursuant to this subdivision, the State Fire Marshal shall give reasonable consideration to the continued use of existing buildings' housing occupancies established prior to March 4, 1972.

In preparing and adopting regulations pursuant to this subdivision, the State Fire Marshal shall also secure the advice of the appropriate governmental agencies involved in the affected protective social care programs in order to provide compatibility and maintenance of operating programs in this state.

Any governmental agency that refers any person to, or causes his or her placement in, any home or institution subject to this section shall, within seven days after the referral or placement, request verification of conformance to the fire safety standards adopted by the State Fire Marshal pursuant to this section from the fire authority having jurisdiction pursuant to Sections 13145 and 13146. Any referral or placement in homes or institutions subject to this section shall be subject to rescission if the fire authority having jurisdiction subsequently informs the governmental agency that it is unable to give the requested verification.

When a building or structure within the scope of this subdivision is used to house either ambulatory or nonambulatory persons, or both, and an automatic sprinkler system, approved by the State Fire Marshal, is installed, this subdivision shall not be construed to also require the installation of an automatic fire alarm system.

(b) Notwithstanding any other provision of law, facilities which are subject to the provisions of subdivision (a) and which are used for the housing of persons, none of whom are physically or mentally handicapped or nonambulatory persons within the meaning of Section 13131, shall not be required to have installed an automatic sprinkler

system or an automatic fire alarm system. In adopting regulations, or when adopting building standards for approval pursuant to Chapter 4 (commencing with Section 18935) of Part 2.5 of Division 13, affecting facilities specified in this subdivision, the State Fire Marshal shall take into consideration the ambulatory and nonhandicapped status of persons housed in such facilities.

(c) It is the intent of the Legislature that any building or structure within the scope of subdivision (a) in which there is housed any totally deaf person, shall be required by the State Fire Marshal to be equipped with fire warning devices to which such person is able to respond.

(d) The provisions of this section, building standards adopted by the State Fire Marshal pursuant to this section and published in the State Building Standards Code relating to fire and panic safety, and the other regulations adopted by the State Fire Marshal pursuant to this section shall apply uniformly throughout the State of California, and no county, city, city and county, or district shall adopt or enforce any ordinance or local rule or regulation relating to fire and panic safety in buildings or structures subject to the provisions of this section which is inconsistent with the provisions of this section, building standards published in the State Building Standards Code relating to fire and panic safety, or the other regulations adopted by the State Fire Marshal pursuant to this section.

(Amended by Stats. 1980, Ch. 118.)

13143.7.

(a) Except as provided in Section 18930, the State Fire Marshal, in consultation with the Department of Corrections and Rehabilitation, shall prepare and adopt regulations establishing minimum standards for the prevention of fire and for the protection of life and property against fire in any building or structure used or intended for use as a community correctional reentry facility, as defined in Section 6258 of the Penal Code. The State Fire Marshal shall adopt and submit building standards for approval pursuant to the provisions of Chapter 4 (commencing with Section 18935) of Part 2.5 of Division 13 for the purposes described in this section.

(b) The regulations and building standards developed pursuant to subdivision (a) shall also address buildings and structures that provide residential housing for parolees under contract with the Department of Corrections and Rehabilitation.

(Added by Stats. 2017, Ch. 363, Sec. 7. (SB 112) Effective September 28, 2017.)

13143.8.

In case of conflict between the State Fire Marshal and the local enforcement agency in the interpretation or application of the provisions, regulations, or building standards of the State Fire Marshal by local enforcement agencies as they pertain to community care facilities, upon request of the permittee or licensee of the community care facility, the State Fire Marshal shall notify the local enforcement agency in writing of the State Fire Marshal's interpretation, and if the local enforcement agency fails to apply the State Fire Marshal's interpretation, the State Fire Marshal shall conduct an adjudication hearing pursuant to Chapter 5 (commencing with Section 11500) of Part 1 of Division 3 of Title 2 of the Government Code before a hearing officer of the Office of Administrative Hearings, with the local enforcement agency as respondent, to resolve the conflict. The interpretation or application made by the hearing officer is binding on that local enforcement agency and the State Fire Marshal. The adjudication hearing shall be held within 30 days after the State Fire Marshal notifies the local enforcement agency of the interpretation, and a decision shall be rendered within 15 days of the hearing.

(Amended by Stats. 1996, Ch. 332, Sec. 28. Effective January 1, 1997.)

13143.9.

(a) The State Fire Marshal shall, in carrying out Section 13143, prepare, adopt, and submit building standards and other fire and life safety regulations for approval pursuant to Chapter 4 (commencing with Section 18935) of Part 2.5 of Division 13 establishing minimum requirements for the storage, handling, and use of hazardous materials, as defined, in the California Fire Code. The State Fire Marshal shall seek the advice of the Office of Emergency Services in establishing these requirements. This section does not prohibit a city, county, or district from adopting an ordinance, resolution, or regulation imposing stricter or more stringent requirements than a standard adopted pursuant to this section.

(b) A business that files the annual inventory form in compliance with Chapter 6.95 (commencing with Section 25500) of Division 20, including the addendum adopted pursuant to paragraph (4) of subdivision (e) of Section 25504, shall be deemed to have met the requirements of the California Fire Code regarding hazardous materials inventory statements, as adopted by the State Fire Marshal pursuant to this section.

(c) A business that is not required to file a hazardous materials inventory form pursuant to Section 25506 but that is required by the local fire chief to comply with the California Fire Code regarding hazardous materials inventory statements, as adopted by the State Fire Marshal pursuant to this section, shall, notwithstanding Chapter 6.95 (commencing with Section 25500) of Division 20, file the inventory form adopted pursuant to Section 25506 and the addendum adopted pursuant to paragraph (4) of subdivision (e) of Section 25504 with the local fire chief for purposes of complying with this requirement, if determined to be necessary by the fire chief.

(Amended by Stats. 2013, Ch. 419, Sec. 1.5. (SB 483) Effective January 1, 2014.)

13144.

The State Fire Marshal shall prepare in book or bulletin form excerpts of the laws, rules, and regulations dealing with fire and panic safety and may make single copies of such laws, rules, and regulations available, without cost, to California fire officials and to owners and managers of establishments governed by such laws, rules, and regulations.

(Amended by Stats. 1951, Ch. 1290.)

13144.1.

(a) Except as provided in Sections 18930 and 18933, the State Fire Marshal shall biennially prepare and publish listings of construction materials and equipment and methods of construction and of installation of equipment, together with the name of any person, firm, corporation, association, or similar organization designated as the manufacturer, representative, or supplier, which are in conformity with building standards relating to fire and panic safety adopted and published in the State Building Standards Code and other fire and panic safety requirements adopted by the State Fire Marshal and published in Title 19 of the California Administrative Code. The State Fire Marshal shall in alternate years prepare and publish revisions to the listings.

Copies of the listings or revisions shall be distributed by the State Fire Marshal at the costs incurred by him or her for the printing and distribution of the listings or revisions to persons who have submitted written requests for the approved listings or revisions.

The purpose of this section is to provide enforcement authorities, architects, engineers, contractors, local building officials, and any other interested persons, with a reliable and readily available source of information of construction materials, equipment, methods of construction, and installation of equipment which meet the minimum requirements established or enforced by the State Fire Marshal, pursuant to Sections 13108 and 13143. No person, firm, corporation, association, or similar organization shall be denied listing if the material to be listed is approved by a testing organization using testing procedures approved by the State Fire Marshal.

It shall not be construed that because a material, assemblies of materials, method of construction and installation of equipment have not been listed, as provided by this section, the material, assemblies of materials, method of construction and installation of equipment does not conform to the fire and panic safety requirements as published in the State Building Standards Code or in Title 19 of the California Administrative Code.

(b) The State Fire Marshal may evaluate, test, approve, disapprove, and list any other fire safety product not covered in subdivision (a).

(Amended by Stats. 1996, Ch. 332, Sec. 29. Effective January 1, 1997.)

13144.2.

Any person, firm, corporation, association, or similar organization desiring listing pursuant to Section 13144.1 shall, prior to placement on any list or revision thereto, make an original or annual renewal application to the State Fire Marshal on forms provided by the State Fire Marshal. Original applications shall be accompanied by both an application fee and a listing fee. Renewal applications shall be accompanied by a listing fee. An application for revision shall be accompanied by a revision fee.

Failure to submit an annual renewal application and listing fee shall automatically cause removal of the material, equipment, method of construction, or installation of equipment from the listings or revision thereto.

The original application fee, the listing fee, and the revision fee shall be established and collected by the State Fire Marshal. Those fees shall not exceed the costs incurred by the State Fire Marshal in conducting evaluations and tests of construction materials and equipment and methods of construction and of installation of equipment.

The annual application and listing fee renewal period shall begin on January 1 and end on May 1 preceding the listing year for which the renewal is requested. A penalty of 50 percent of the listing fee shall be assessed in all cases where the renewal fees are not paid on or before May 1, preceding the listing year for which renewal is requested.

The State Fire Marshal may designate in generic terms, without application or fee, materials or assemblies of materials classed by the State Fire Marshal as industrywide, by regulations adopted pursuant to Sections 13108 and 13143.

(Amended by Stats. 1989, Ch. 529, Sec. 3.)

13144.3.

The annual and renewal listing established by Section 13144.2 shall be for the fiscal year period from July 1 to June 30 or for the remaining portion thereof. All moneys collected from original and annual renewal fees pursuant to Section 13144.2 shall be deposited in the State Fire Marshal Licensing and Certification Fund established pursuant to Section 13137, and shall be available to the State Fire Marshal upon appropriation by the Legislature for the purposes specified in Section 13144.2.

(Amended by Stats. 1992, Ch. 306, Sec. 4. Effective January 1, 1993. Operative July 1, 1993, by Sec. 6 of Ch. 306.)

13144.4.

The State Fire Marshal may adopt regulations to implement, interpret, make specific or otherwise carry out the provisions of Sections 13144.1, 13144. 2, and 13144.3.

(Added by Stats. 1963, Ch. 1955.)

13144.5.

The State Fire Marshal shall prepare and conduct voluntary regular training sessions devoted to the interpretation and application of the laws and rules and regulations in Title 19 and Title 24 of the California Code of Regulations relating to fire and panic safety. The training sessions shall include, but need not be limited to, interpretation of the regulations pertaining to community care facilities licensed pursuant to Section 1508, to residential care facilities for the elderly licensed pursuant to Section 1569.10, and to child day care facilities licensed pursuant to Section 1596.80, in order to coordinate a consistent interpretation and application of the regulations among local fire enforcement agencies.

(Amended by Stats. 1989, Ch. 993, Sec. 5.)

13145.

The State Fire Marshal, the chief of any city, county, or city and county fire department or district providing fire protection services, or a Designated Campus Fire Marshal, and their authorized representatives, shall enforce in their respective areas building standards relating to fire and panic safety adopted by the State Fire Marshal and published in the California Building Standards Code and other regulations that have been formally adopted by the State Fire Marshal for the prevention of fire or for the protection of life and property against fire or panic.

(Amended by Stats. 2010, Ch. 370, Sec. 2. (AB 2021) Effective January 1, 2011.)

13146.

(a) The responsibility for enforcement of building standards adopted by the State Fire Marshal and published in the California Building Standards Code relating to fire and panic safety and other regulations of the State Fire Marshal shall be as follows:

(1) The city, county, or city and county with jurisdiction in the area affected by the standard or regulation shall delegate the enforcement of the building standards relating to fire and panic safety and other regulations of the State Fire Marshal as they relate to R-3 dwellings, as described in Section 310.5 of Part 2 of the California Building Standards Code, to either of the following:

(A) The chief of the fire authority of the city, county, or city and county, or the chief's authorized representative.

(B) The chief building official of the city, county, or city and county, or the official's authorized representative.

(2) The chief of any city, county, or city and county fire department or of any fire protection district, and their authorized representatives, shall enforce within its jurisdiction the building standards and other regulations of the State Fire Marshal, except those described in paragraph (1) or (4).

(3) The State Fire Marshal shall have authority to enforce the building standards and other regulations of the State Fire Marshal in areas outside of corporate cities and districts providing fire protection services.

(4) The State Fire Marshal shall have authority to enforce the building standards and other regulations of the State Fire Marshal in corporate cities and districts providing fire protection services upon request of the chief fire official or the governing body.

(5) The State Fire Marshal shall enforce the building standards and other regulations of the State Fire Marshal on all University of California campuses and properties administered or occupied by the University of California and on all California State University campuses and properties administered or occupied by the California State University. For each university campus or property the State Fire Marshal may delegate that responsibility to the person of the State Fire Marshal's choice who shall be known as the Designated Campus Fire Marshal.

(b) A fee may be charged pursuant to the enforcement authority of this section but shall not exceed the estimated reasonable cost of providing the service for which the fee is charged, pursuant to Section 66014 of the Government Code.

(Amended by Stats. 2019, Ch. 31, Sec. 7. (SB 85) Effective June 27, 2019.)

13146.1.

(a) Notwithstanding Section 13146, the State Fire Marshal, or the State Fire Marshal's authorized representative, shall inspect every jail or place of detention for persons charged with or convicted of a crime, unless the chief of any city, county, or city and county fire department or fire protection district, or that chief's authorized representative, indicates in writing to the State Fire Marshal, by June 30 of each applicable year pursuant to subdivision (b), that inspections of jails or places of detention, therein, shall be conducted by the chief, or the chief's authorized representative, and submits the reports as required in subdivision (c).

(b) The inspections shall be made at least once every two years for the purpose of enforcing the regulations adopted by the State Fire Marshal, pursuant to Section 13143, and the minimum standards pertaining to fire and life safety adopted by the Board of State and Community Corrections, pursuant to Section 6030 of the Penal Code.

(c) Reports of the inspections shall be submitted to the official in charge of the facility, the local governing body, the State Fire Marshal, and the Board of Corrections within 30 days of the inspections.

(d) The State Fire Marshal, or the State Fire Marshal's authorized representative, who performs an inspection pursuant to subdivision (a) may charge and collect a fee for the inspection from the local government. Any fee collected pursuant to this subdivision shall be in an amount, as determined by the State Fire Marshal, sufficient to pay the costs of that inspection or those related fire and life safety activities.

(Amended by Stats. 2019, Ch. 31, Sec. 8. (SB 85) Effective June 27, 2019.)

13146.2.

(a) Every city, county, or city and county fire department or district providing fire protection services required by Sections 13145 and 13146 to enforce building standards adopted by the State Fire Marshal and other regulations of the State Fire Marshal shall, annually, inspect all structures subject to subdivision (b) of Section 17921, except dwellings, for compliance with building standards and other regulations of the State Fire Marshal.

(b) A city, county, or city and county fire department or district providing fire protection services that inspects a structure pursuant to subdivision (a) may charge and collect a fee for the inspection from the owner of the structure in an amount, as determined by the city, county, or city and county fire department or district providing fire protection services, sufficient to pay the costs of that inspection.

(c) A city, county, or city and county fire department or district providing fire protection services that provides related fire and life safety activities for structures subject to subdivision (b) of Section 17921, such as plan review, construction consulting, fire watch, and investigation, may charge and collect a fee from the owner of the structure in an amount, as determined by the city, county, city and county, or district, sufficient to pay the costs of those related fire and life safety activities.

(d) The State Fire Marshal, or the State Fire Marshal's authorized representative, who inspects a structure subject to subdivision (b) of Section 17921, except dwellings, for compliance with building standards and other regulations of the State Fire Marshal, may charge and collect a fee for the inspection from the owner of the structure. The State Fire Marshal may also charge and collect a fee from the owner of the structure for related fire and life safety activities, such as plan review, construction consulting, fire watch, and investigation. Any fee collected pursuant to this subdivision shall be in an amount, as determined by the State Fire Marshal, sufficient to pay the costs of that inspection or those related fire and life safety activities.

(Amended by Stats. 2019, Ch. 31, Sec. 9. (SB 85) Effective June 27, 2019.)

13146.3.

(a) A city, county, or city and county fire department or district providing fire protection services shall inspect every building used as a public or private school within its jurisdiction, for the purpose of enforcing regulations promulgated pursuant to Section 13143, not less than once each year. The State Fire Marshal and the State Fire Marshal's authorized representatives shall make these inspections not less than once each year in areas outside of corporate cities and districts providing fire protection services.

(b) A city, county, or city and county fire department or district that, or the State Fire Marshal or the State Fire Marshal's authorized representative who, inspects a structure pursuant to subdivision (a) may charge and collect a fee for the inspection in an amount sufficient to pay the costs of that inspection.

(Amended by Stats. 2019, Ch. 31, Sec. 10. (SB 85) Effective June 27, 2019.)

13146.4.

(a) Every city or county fire department, city and county fire department, or district required to perform an annual inspection pursuant to Sections 13146.2 and 13146.3 shall report annually to its administering authority on its compliance with Sections 13146.2 and 13146.3.

(b) The report made pursuant to subdivision (a) shall occur when the administering authority discusses its annual budget, or at another time determined by the administering authority.

(c) The administering authority shall acknowledge receipt of the report made pursuant to subdivision (a) in a resolution or a similar formal document.

(d) For purposes of this section, "administering authority" means a city council, county board of supervisors, or district board, as the case may be.

(Added by Stats. 2018, Ch. 854, Sec. 1. (SB 1205) Effective January 1, 2019.)

13146.5.

The provisions of Sections 13145, 13146 and 13146.3 shall, so far as practicable, be carried out at the local level by persons who are regular full-time members of a regularly organized fire department of a city, county, or district providing fire protection services, and shall not be carried out by other persons pursuant to Section 34004 of the Government Code.

(Amended by Stats. 1980, Ch. 118.)

13146.6.

If the governing body of a city, county, or city and county fire department or district providing fire protection services relies on an all-volunteer fire department for the provision of fire protection services pursuant to Sections 13145, 13146, 13146.2, and 13146.3, they may do so through one of the following methods:

(a) They may request the State Fire Marshal to enforce the building standards and other regulations of the State Fire Marshal, in accordance with paragraph (4) of subdivision (a) of Section 13146.

(b) They may request another city, county, or city and county fire department or district providing fire protection services that has regular full-time members of a regularly organized fire department to enforce the building standards and other regulations of the State Fire Marshal.

(Added by Stats. 2019, Ch. 31, Sec. 11. (SB 85) Effective June 27, 2019.)

13147.

The regulations adopted pursuant to subdivision (a) of Section 13143 shall require that the new construction of any school building for which review and approval is required under subdivision (a) of Section 39140 of the Education Code include the placement of fire hydrants and water piping as necessary to supply the water capacity required for the fire protection of the building.

(Added by Stats. 1990, Ch. 52, Sec. 1.)

ARTICLE 3. Administration [13150 - 13153]

(Heading of Article 3 renumbered from Article 4 by Stats. 1969, Ch. 39.)

13150.

For purposes of this article, "flammable liquids" shall mean any liquid having a flashpoint below 100°F (37.8°C) and a vapor pressure not exceeding 40 pounds per square inch (absolute) at a temperature of 100°F (37.8°C). Flammable liquids may include crude oils and cutback asphalts. "Combustible liquid" shall mean a liquid having a flashpoint at or above 100°F (37.8°C), and below 200°F (93.3°C).

This does not include wine, or any other aqueous solution, having an alcoholic content less than, or equal to, 24 percent by volume. This exemption applies only if the nonalcohol portion of the aqueous solution does not fall within the definition of flammable or combustible liquid.

The provisions of this article also apply to liquids having a flashpoint of 200°F (93.3°C) or higher when such liquids, upon being heated, assume the characteristics of a flammable or combustible liquid.

(Amended by Stats. 1978, Ch. 868.)

13151.

The State Fire Marshal shall prepare and adopt regulations in accordance with the provisions of the Administrative Procedure Act (commencing with Section 11340 of the Government Code), which in his or her judgment are designed to promote the safe use of portable internal combustion engine-driven pumps used for the transfer of flammable and combustible liquids.

(Amended by Stats. 1983, Ch. 101, Sec. 113.)

13152.

The authority for the enforcement of the provisions of this article shall be in accordance with Sections 13145 and 13146, Health and Safety Code.

(Added by renumbering Section 13182 by Stats. 1969, Ch. 39.)

13153.

No person, firm, or corporation shall use, permit, or instruct any other person to use or permit, any portable internal combustion engine-driven pump used for the transfer of any flammable or combustible liquids unless such pump conforms to the regulations adopted by the State Fire Marshal.

(Amended by Stats. 1978, Ch. 868.)

ARTICLE 4. California Fire Service Training and Education Program [13155 - 13159.4]

(Article 4 added by Stats. 1977, Ch. 1248.)

13155.

This article shall be known and may be cited as the California Fire Service Training and Education Program Act.

(Added by Stats. 1977, Ch. 1248.)

13156.

The Legislature finds and declares that the purposes of this article are as follows:

(a) To reduce the costs in suffering and property loss resulting from fire through standardized fire training and education programs.

(b) To provide professional fire service training and education programs to personnel in fire departments that rely extensively on volunteers.

(c) To develop new methods and practices in the area of fire protection.

(d) To disseminate information relative to fires, techniques of firefighters, and other related subjects to all interested agencies and individuals throughout the state.

(e) To enhance the coordination of fire service training and education.

(f) To develop a coordinated and standardized plan for the control of fires and the safety of firefighters where hazardous materials are involved.

(Amended by Stats. 1983, Ch. 1313, Sec. 13.)

13157.

The California Fire Service Training and Education Program is hereby established in the office of the State Fire Marshal.

The State Fire Marshal, with policy guidance and advice from the State Board of Fire Services, shall carry out the management of the California Fire Service Training and Education Program and shall have the authority to:

(a) Promulgate and adopt rules and regulations necessary for implementation of the program.

(b) Establish the courses of study and curriculum to be used in the program.

(c) Establish prerequisites for the admission of personnel who attend courses offered in the program.

(d) Establish and collect admission fees and other fees that may be necessary to be charged for seminars, conferences, and specialized training given, which shall not be deducted from state appropriations for the purposes of this program.

(e) Collect such fees as may be established pursuant to subdivision (d) of Section 13142.4.

(Added by Stats. 1977, Ch. 1248.)

13158.

The State Fire Marshal shall employ under civil service a program manager and staff as necessary to perform the functions for which the program has been established.

All personnel of the State Fire Training Program with the Department of Education shall be eligible to transfer to appropriate positions in the California Fire Service Training and Education Program provided they meet the qualifications for those positions.

(Amended by Stats. 1996, Ch. 332, Sec. 31. Effective January 1, 1997.)

13159.

The State Fire Marshal, with policy guidance and advice from the State Board of Fire Services, shall have the following responsibilities:

(a) To make fire service training and education programs, including training and education in the use of heavy rescue equipment, available on a voluntary basis to fire departments that rely extensively on volunteers.

(b) Cooperate with the State Board of Fire Services in the development of a minimum standards program for fire service personnel and fire service instructors.

(c) Assist and cooperate with State Board of Fire Services pursuant to Section 13142.4.

(d) Verify that minimum curriculum requirements, facilities, and faculty standards for schools, seminars, or workshops operated by or for the state for the specific purpose of training fire service personnel are being met.

(e) Make or encourage studies of any aspect of fire service training and education.

(f) Determine the need for and recommend locations of regional training sites.

(g) Develop a model plan or system for use by fire departments for the control of fires and the safety of firefighters where hazardous materials are involved.

(h) Study the feasibility of establishing within the office of the State Fire Marshal, a depository of information on hazardous material characteristics for use by local fire departments and other entities that respond to emergencies.

(Amended by Stats. 1984, Ch. 1574, Sec. 3.)

13159.1.

(a) The State Fire Marshal shall establish additional training standards that include the criteria for curriculum content recommended by the Emergency Response Training

Advisory Committee established pursuant to Section 8588.10 of the Government Code, involving the responsibilities of first responders to terrorism incidents and to address the training needs of those identified as first responders.

(b) The State Fire Marshal shall contract with the California Firefighter Joint Apprenticeship Program for the development of curriculum content criteria specified in subdivision (a).

(c) Every paid and volunteer firefighter assigned to field duties in a state or local fire department or fire protection or firefighting agency may receive the appropriate training described in this section. Pertinent training previously completed by any jurisdiction's firefighters and meeting the training standards of this section may be submitted to the State Fire Marshal to assess its content and determine whether it meets the training requirements prescribed by the State Fire Marshal.

(Amended by Stats. 2006, Ch. 803, Sec. 1. Effective January 1, 2007.)

13159.15.

(a) The Division of Apprenticeship Standards, in collaboration with the California Firefighter Joint Apprenticeship Committee (CAL-JAC), shall develop a statewide firefighter preapprenticeship program designed to recruit candidates from underrepresented groups.

(b) The firefighter preapprenticeship program funded by the division shall meet both of the following objectives:

(1) Create training and curriculum based on California firefighter standards designed to prepare candidates from underrepresented groups with the skills, competencies, and mentorship needed to pass the Candidate Physical Ability Test (CPAT), and the written tests and oral components common to the California hiring process that are necessary for a candidate to be eligible for consideration and hire with fire protection agencies.

(2) Provide Emergency Medical Technician (EMT) Training to candidates from underrepresented groups, preparing them to meet the necessary minimum qualification required by the majority of fire protection agencies.

(c) CAL-JAC shall deliver the pilot classes established through the preapprenticeship program using existing facilities and training models in order to minimize the costs of the program. CAL-JAC shall provide the preapprenticeship program model to fire protection agencies. That program may include curriculum, course set up and outlines staffing and equipment requirements, and recruitment strategies developed pursuant to this section. A protection fire agency may then use those resources to establish a local preapprenticeship program for recruiting candidates from underrepresented groups.

(d) The Division of Apprenticeship Standards shall provide the oversight and technical assistance in the development of this preapprenticeship program.

(e) For purposes of this section, "underrepresented groups" means groups that CAL-JAC determines are currently underrepresented in the firefighter profession.

(Added by Stats. 2017, Ch. 344, Sec. 1. (AB 579) Effective September 28, 2017.)

13159.2.

(a) For purposes of this section, the State Fire Marshal shall be referred to as the SFM.

(b) The SFM may accept certification by the United States Department of Defense as a firefighter as an alternative for the basic SFM training and certification standards for the position of Firefighter I of the California Fire Service Training and Education Program, if the United States Department of Defense certification is accompanied by a national certification or accreditation that has been approved by the SFM and that is based on the International Fire Service Accreditation Congress, Pro Board, or other accepted third-party certification standard.

(c) If the United States Department of Defense certification is not accompanied by a national certification approved by the SFM, as described in subdivision (b), the SFM shall follow the verification process adopted pursuant to the authority provided in Sections 13157 and 13159.

(Added by Stats. 2011, Ch. 215, Sec. 1. (AB 398) Effective January 1, 2012.)

13159.4.

The State Fire Marshal shall annually review, revise as necessary, and administer the California Fire Service Training program, shall establish priorities for the use of state and federal fire service training and education funds applicable to statewide programs, other than those funds administered by the Department of Forestry and Fire Protection, and shall approve the expenditure of these funds in accordance with the established priorities. This section shall not restrict local entities from independently seeking and utilizing state and federal funds for local fire training and education needs.

(Amended by Stats. 1992, Ch. 427, Sec. 98. Effective January 1, 1993.)

ARTICLE 5. California Fire and Arson Training Act [13159.7 - 13159.10]
(Article 5 added by Stats. 1988, Ch. 653, Sec. 1.)

13159.7.

This article shall be known and may be cited as the California Fire and Arson Training Act.
(Added by Stats. 1988, Ch. 653, Sec. 1.)

13159.8.

The State Fire Marshal, with policy guidance and advice from the State Board of Fire Services, shall:

(a) Establish and validate recommended minimum standards for fire protection personnel and fire protection instructors at all career levels.

(b) Develop course curricula for arson, fire technology, and apprenticeship training for use in academies, colleges, and other educational institutions.

(c) Develop, validate, update, copyright, and maintain security over a complete series of promotional examinations based on the minimum standards established pursuant to subdivision (a).

(d) Have the authority to make the examinations developed pursuant to subdivision (c) available to any agency of the state, to any political subdivision within the state, or to any other testing organization, as he or she deems appropriate.

(e) Establish any fees which are necessary to implement this section. However, the State Fire Marshal shall not establish or collect any fees for training classes provided by the State Fire Marshal to fire protection personnel relating to state laws and regulation which local fire services are authorized or required to enforce.

(f) Promote, sponsor, and administer the California Fire Academy System.

(g) Establish procedures for seeking, accepting, and administering gifts and grants for use in implementing the intents and purposes of the California Fire and Arson Training Act.

(h) The recommended minimum standards established pursuant to subdivision (a) shall not apply to any agency of the state or any agency of any political subdivision within the state unless that agency elects to be subject to these standards.

(Added by renumbering Section 13142.4 by Stats. 1988, Ch. 653, Sec. 2.)

13159.9.

The State Fire Marshal shall:

(a) Jointly, with the California Professional Firefighters, promote participation in, sponsor, and administer the California Firefighter Joint Apprenticeship Program as the preemployment recruitment, selection, and training system to be utilized for entry level firefighters.

(b) Establish advisory committees or panels, as necessary, to assist the State Fire Marshal in carrying out his or her function under this article.

(Added by Stats. 1988, Ch. 653, Sec. 1.)

13159.10.

There is established in the State Treasury the California Fire and Arson Training Fund. All revenue collected pursuant to Section 13159.8 shall be paid into this fund and these moneys shall be available when appropriated by the Legislature for the office of the State Fire Marshal to carry out the provisions of this article.

(Added by renumbering Section 13142.5 by Stats. 1988, Ch. 653, Sec. 3.)

CHAPTER 1.5. Portable Fire Extinguishers [13160 - 13190.4]

(Chapter 1.5 added by Stats. 1968, Ch. 802.)

ARTICLE 1. General Provisions [13160 - 13162]
(Article 1 added by Stats. 1968, Ch. 802.)

13160.

With the advice of the State Fire Advisory Board, the State Fire Marshal shall adopt, in accordance with the provisions of Chapter 3.5 (commencing with Section 11340) of Part 1 of Division 3 of Title 2 of the Government Code, and administer regulations and standards as he or she may deem necessary for the protection and preservation of life and property to control the servicing, including charging, and testing, of all portable fire extinguishers for controlling and extinguishing fires, and for controlling the sale and marketing of all such devices with respect to conformance with standards of their use, capacity, and effectiveness. In adopting the regulations, the State Fire Marshal shall consider the standards of the National Fire Protection Association.

(Amended by Stats. 1983, Ch. 101, Sec. 114.)

13161.

It is the legislative intention in enacting this chapter that the provisions of this chapter and the regulations and standards adopted by the State Fire Marshal pursuant to this chapter shall apply uniformly throughout the State of California and no county, city, city or county or district shall adopt or enforce any ordinance or rule or regulation regarding portable fire extinguishers which is inconsistent with the provisions of this chapter or the regulations and standards adopted by the State Fire Marshal pursuant to this chapter.

(Repealed and added by Stats. 1968, Ch. 802.)

13162.

No person shall market, distribute, or sell any portable fire extinguisher in this state unless it meets the following requirements:

(a) It complies with regulations and standards adopted by the State Fire Marshal pursuant to Section 13160.

(b) It has been examined by and bears the label of Underwriters' Laboratories Inc. or another testing laboratory which is approved by the State Fire Marshal as qualified to test portable fire extinguishers. Any testing laboratory approved by the State Fire Marshal shall have facilities, personnel, and operating procedures equivalent to those of the Underwriters' Laboratories Inc.

(c) It does not use as an extinguishing agent any carbon tetrachloride, chlorbromomethane, or methyl bromide.

The State Fire Marshal may grant reasonable exceptions to this subdivision when the extinguisher is intended for industrial use in places to which the public is not invited or admitted. The provisions of this section apply to the state and any political subdivision thereof.

(Amended by Stats. 1979, Ch. 267.)

ARTICLE 2. Licensing [13163 - 13174]
(Article 2 added by Stats. 1968, Ch. 802.)

13163.

No person shall engage in the business of, nor perform for a fee, the servicing, charging, or testing of portable fire extinguishers without a license issued by the State Fire Marshal pursuant to this chapter expressly authorizing such person to perform such acts.

(Repealed and added by Stats. 1968, Ch. 802.)

13164.

Application for a license to engage in the business of, or perform for a fee, the servicing, charging, or testing of portable fire extinguishers shall be made in writing to the State Fire Marshal on forms provided by him and shall be accompanied by the fees prescribed in this chapter. A separate application for license shall be made for each separate place of business location of the applicant for license.

The application shall be signed by the applicant. If the application is made by a partnership, it shall be signed by each partner. If the application is made by a corporation or association other than a partnership, it shall be signed by the principal officer thereof and, in the case of applications by corporations, bear the seal of the corporation. The application shall also include written authorization by the applicant permitting the State Fire Marshal and any of his properly authorized employees to enter, examine and inspect any premises, building, room, or establishment used by the applicant in servicing, charging, or testing portable fire extinguishers to determine compliance with the provisions of this chapter and the regulations and standards adopted by the State Fire Marshal pursuant to Section 13160.

(Repealed and added by Stats. 1968, Ch. 802.)

13165.

Following receipt of the properly completed application and prescribed fees, and compliance with the provisions of this part and the regulations adopted pursuant to Section 13160, the State Fire Marshal shall issue a license.

(Repealed and added by Stats. 1968, Ch. 802.)

13166.

Original licenses shall be valid from the date of issuance through December 31st of the year in which issued. Thereafter, each license shall be renewed annually and renewals thereof shall be valid from January 1st through December 31st.

(Repealed and added by Stats. 1968, Ch. 802.)

13167.

Application for renewal shall be made on or before November 1st of the year in which the current license expires. Application for renewal shall be made in writing on forms provided by the State Fire Marshal and shall be accompanied by the prescribed fees.

(Repealed and added by Stats. 1968, Ch. 802.)

13168.

The State Fire Marshal may refuse to renew any license in the same manner and for any reason that he is authorized pursuant to Article 4 (commencing with Section 13185) of this chapter to deny an original license. The applicant shall, upon such refusal, have the same rights as are granted by Article 4 of the chapter to an applicant for an original license which has been denied by the State Fire Marshal.

(Repealed and added by Stats. 1968, Ch. 802.)

13169.

Every licensee shall notify the State Fire Marshal at his Sacramento office in writing within 15 days of any change of his address.

(Repealed and added by Stats. 1968, Ch. 802.)

13170.

Any advertisement of the servicing, charging, or testing of portable fire extinguishers constitutes prima facie evidence that the premises, business, building, room, shop, store or establishment in or upon which it appears, or to which it refers, is a separate place of business location.

(Added by Stats. 1968, Ch. 802.)

13171.

No licensee shall conduct his licensed business or solicit business under a name other than a name or names which appears on his license.

(Added by Stats. 1968, Ch. 802.)

13172.

The State Fire Marshal shall without cost, annually notify the chief fire official of each local fire authority of the name, address and license number of each firm that is licensed pursuant to this chapter. Upon request, single copies of such list shall be furnished, without cost, to a licensed person.

(Added by Stats. 1968, Ch. 802.)

13173.

The holder of any license shall submit such license for inspection upon request of the State Fire Marshal, any of his properly authorized employees, or any local fire official.

(Added by Stats. 1968, Ch. 802.)

13174.

Every licensed person shall annually, within seven days of employment and within seven days of termination of employment, report to the State Fire Marshal at his Sacramento office, the name, address, and certificate of registration number, if any, of every natural person performing any act of servicing, charging, or testing portable fire extinguishers for such licensed person.

(Added by Stats. 1968, Ch. 802.)

ARTICLE 3. Certificates of Registration [13175 - 13184]
(Article 3 added by Stats. 1968, Ch. 802.)

13175.

No natural person shall service, charge, or test any portable fire extinguisher without a certificate of registration issued by the State Fire Marshal pursuant to this chapter expressly authorizing such person to perform such acts.

The provisions of this article apply to the state, the Regents of University of California, a county, city, district, public authority, and any other political subdivision or public corporation in this state.

(Added by Stats. 1968, Ch. 802.)

13175.1.

The provisions of this article shall not apply to any person servicing, charging, or testing any portable fire extinguisher owned by such person when the portable fire extinguisher is not required by any statute, regulation, or ordinance, to be provided or installed. The provisions of this section shall not prohibit the servicing, charging, or testing of portable fire extinguishers by new employees of a licensed person for a period not to exceed 90 days provided such servicing, charging or testing is conducted in the presence of and under the direct supervision of a natural person holding a valid certificate of registration.

(Added by Stats. 1968, Ch. 802.)

13176.

Application for a certificate of registration to service, charge, or test portable fire extinguishers shall be made in writing to the State Fire Marshal on forms provided by him and shall be accompanied by the fee prescribed in this chapter. The application shall be signed by the applicant.

(Added by Stats. 1968, Ch. 802.)

13177.

The State Fire Marshal shall require all applicants for a certificate of registration to take and pass a written examination which may be supplemented by practical tests when deemed necessary, to determine the applicants knowledge of servicing, charging and testing of portable fire extinguishers.

(Added by Stats. 1968, Ch. 802.)

13178.

Following receipt of the properly completed application and prescribed fee, and the completion of the required examination, the State Fire Marshal shall issue a certificate of registration.

(Added by Stats. 1968, Ch. 802.)

13179.

Original certificates of registration shall be valid from the date of issuance through December 31st of the year in which issued. Thereafter, each certificate of registration shall be renewed annually and renewals thereof shall be valid from January 1st through December 31st.

(Added by Stats. 1968, Ch. 802.)

13180.

Application for renewal shall be made on or before November 1st of the year in which the current certificate of registration expires. Application for renewal shall be made in writing on forms provided by the State Fire Marshal and shall be accompanied by the prescribed fee.

(Added by Stats. 1968, Ch. 802.)

13181.

The State Fire Marshal may refuse to renew any certificate of registration in the same manner and for any reason that he is authorized pursuant to Article 4 (commencing with Section 13185) of this chapter to deny an original certificate of registration. The applicant shall, upon such refusal, have the same rights as are granted by Article 4 of this chapter to an applicant for an original certificate of registration which has been denied by the State Fire Marshal.

(Added by Stats. 1968, Ch. 802.)

13182.

Every certificate of registration holder shall notify the State Fire Marshal at his Sacramento office in writing within 15 days of any change of his address.

(Added by Stats. 1968, Ch. 802.)

13183.

Every natural person who services, charges, or tests any portable fire extinguisher shall affix a tag to the serviced unit. Such tag shall indicate the date upon which the service work was performed and it shall bear the signature of such natural person, and other information specified by the State Fire Marshal.

(Added by Stats. 1968, Ch. 802.)

13184.

The holder of a certificate of registration shall submit such certificate for inspection upon request of the State Fire Marshal, any of his properly authorized employees, or any local fire official.

(Added by Stats. 1968, Ch. 802.)

ARTICLE 4. Denial, Revocation, and Suspension [13185 - 13188.4]
(Article 4 added by Stats. 1968, Ch. 802.)

13185.

The issuance of a license or certificate of registration may be denied by the State Fire Marshal for any of the following reasons:

(a) The applicant is not the real person in interest.

(b) Material misrepresentation or false statement in the application.

(c) Refusal to allow inspection by the State Fire Marshal or his duly authorized employees.

(d) The applicant for a license does not have the proper or necessary facilities, including qualified personnel, to conduct the operations for which application is made.

(e) The applicant for a certificate of registration does not possess the qualifications of skill or competence to conduct the operations for which application is made as evidenced by failure to pass the examination pursuant to Article 3 (commencing with Section 13175) of this chapter.

(f) Refusal to take the examination required by Section 13177 of this chapter.

(g) The applicant has been convicted of a violation of the provisions of this chapter or the regulations adopted by the State Fire Marshal pursuant to this chapter.
(Added by Stats. 1968, Ch. 802.)

13186.

Within 30 days after receipt of notice of denial sent by the State Fire Marshal by registered or certified mail to the applicant's last address of record, the applicant may file with the State Fire Marshal a request for statement of issues. Such request shall not be deemed an answer to the statement of issues, a request for a hearing, or a notice of defense. Unless the State Fire Marshal files a statement of issues regarding the denial of the appliction within 30 days after the timely filing of such request, the license or certificate of registration shall be issued.
(Added by Stats. 1968, Ch. 802.)

13187.

When a statement of issues has been so filed, the State Fire Marshal may order denial pursuant to Chapter 5 (commencing with Section 11500), Part 1, Division 3, Title 2 of the Government Code.
(Added by Stats. 1968, Ch. 802.)

13188.

A license or certificate of registration may be suspended or revoked by the State Fire Marshal pursuant to Chapter 5 (commencing with Section 11500), Part 1, Division 3, Title 2, of the Government Code, for any of the following reasons:
(a) The applicant is not the real person in interest.
(b) Material misrepresentation or false statement in the application.
(c) Violation of any provision of this chapter or any regulation adopted by the State Fire Marshal pursuant to this chapter.
(Added by Stats. 1968, Ch. 802.)

13188.1.

The State Fire Marshal may, upon a preliminary finding of a violation of the provisions of this part, suspend any license or certificate of registration for a period not exceeding 30 days pending investigation of any violation of the provisions of this part.
(Added by Stats. 1989, Ch. 909, Sec. 2.)

13188.2.

Any applicant who has been denied a license or certificate of registration or who has had a license or certificate of registration suspended, shall be entitled to a hearing in accordance with the provisions of this part.
(Added by Stats. 1989, Ch. 909, Sec. 3.)

13188.3.

Except where otherwise provided in this part, all hearings under this part shall be conducted in accordance with Chapter 5 (commencing with Section 11500) of Part 1 of Division 3 of Title 2 of the Government Code.
(Added by Stats. 1989, Ch. 909, Sec. 4.)

13188.4.

(a) If the State Fire Marshal or his or her designee determines that the public interest and public welfare will be adequately served by permitting a person who has a license issued pursuant to Section 13165 or a certificate of registration issued pursuant to Section 13178 to pay a monetary penalty to the State Fire Marshal in lieu of a license or certificate of registration suspension, the State Fire Marshal or his or her designee may stay the execution of all or part of the suspension if all of the following conditions are met:
(1) The violation that is the cause for the suspension did not pose, or have the potential to pose, a significant threat or risk of harm to the public.
(2) The holder of the license or certificate of registration pay a monetary penalty.
(3) The holder of the license or certificate of registration does not incur any other cause for disciplinary action within a period of time specified by the State Fire Marshal or his or her designee.
In making the determination, the State Fire Marshal or his or her designee shall consider the seriousness of the violation, the violator's record of compliance with the law, the impact of the determination on the violator, the violator's employees or customers, and other relevant factors.
(b) The State Fire Marshal or his or her designee may exercise the discretion granted under this section either with respect to a suspension ordered by a decision after a contested hearing on an accusation against the holder of the license or certificate of registration or by stipulation with the holder of the license or certificate of registration after the filing of an accusation, but prior to the rendering of a decision based upon the accusation. In either case, the terms and conditions of the disciplinary action against the holder of the license or certificate of registration shall be made part of a formal decision of the State Fire Marshal or his or her designee.
(c) If a holder of the license or certificate of registration fails to pay the monetary penalty in accordance with the terms and conditions of the decision of the State Fire Marshal or his or her designee, the State Fire Marshal or his or her designee may, without a hearing, order the immediate execution of all or any part of the stayed suspension in which event the holder of the license or certificate of registration shall not be entitled to any repayment nor credit, prorated or otherwise, for money paid to the State Fire Marshal under the terms of the decision.
(d) The amount of the monetary penalty payable under this section shall not exceed two hundred fifty dollars ($250) for each day of suspension stayed nor a total of ten thousand dollars ($10,000) per decision regardless of the number of days of suspension stayed under the decision.
(e) Any monetary penalty received pursuant to this section shall be deposited in the State Fire Marshal Licensing and Certification Fund.

(f) On or before March 1 of each year, the State Fire Marshal shall make available to the public data showing the percentage of enforcement actions taken that resulted in license suspension or the assessment of monetary penalties pursuant to this section.
(Added by Stats. 2010, Ch. 161, Sec. 2. (AB 1773) Effective January 1, 2011.)

ARTICLE 5. Fees [13189 - 13190]

(Article 5 added by Stats. 1968, Ch. 802.)

13189.

(a) The original and annual renewal fee for any license or a certificate of registration issued pursuant to this chapter shall be established by the State Fire Marshal. That fee shall not exceed the amount necessary to cover the costs incurred in the administration and enforcement of this chapter.
(b) A penalty fee equal to 50 percent of the required annual license fee or certificate of registration fee shall be added to the fee in all cases where the fee for a renewal is not paid on or before November 1.
(Repealed and added by Stats. 1983, Ch. 1313, Sec. 16.)

13190.

No special fee other than that charged for an ordinary business license shall be charged for any natural person, corporation, firm, or association, by any city, county, city and county or fire protection district, for the privilege of performing acts involving servicing, charging or testing of portable fire extinguishers.
(Added by Stats. 1968, Ch. 802.)

ARTICLE 6. Enforcement [13190.1 - 13190.4]

(Article 6 added by Stats. 1968, Ch. 802.)

13190.1.

Except as provided in this article, the State Fire Marshal shall enforce in all areas of the state, the provisions of this chapter and the regulations and standards adopted by him pursuant to Section 13160.
The provisions of this chapter and the regulations and standards adopted by the State Fire Marshal pursuant to Section 13160 shall not apply to any firm or corporation not engaged in the business of servicing, charging or testing portable fire extinguishers and that maintains its own fully equipped and specially staffed fire prevention and protection department, or to any employee of any such firm or corporation while acting in the scope of his employment.
(Added by Stats. 1968, Ch. 802.)

13190.2.

Any governmental agency, including the state, and any city, county, district, or any other political subdivision or public corporation of the state, may, in their respective areas of jurisdiction, enforce ordinances, regulations, and orders adopted by such agency relating to the number, size, and type of portable fire extinguishers required to be installed or provided. Such agencies may, in their respective areas of jurisdiction, also enforce the regulations adopted by the State Fire Marshal relating to care, maintenance, and frequency of servicing, charging, and testing of portable fire extinguishers.
Nothing in this article shall diminish the enforcement responsibility and authority conferred upon any governmental agency pursuant to any other state statute.
(Added by Stats. 1968, Ch. 802.)

13190.3.

Any portable fire extinguisher that is required to be installed by any statute or ordinance shall be maintained in accordance with the regulations adopted pursuant to Section 13160.
(a) The owner or occupant of a property in which fire extinguishers are located shall be responsible for the inspection, maintenance, and recharging of the fire extinguishers.
(b) Maintenance, servicing, and recharging shall be performed by concerns licensed by the State Fire Marshal having available the appropriate servicing manual, the proper types of tools, recharge materials, lubricants, and manufacturer's recommended replacement parts or parts of equal quality.
(Amended by Stats. 1988, Ch. 615, Sec. 2.)

13190.4.

Every person who violates any provision of this chapter or any regulation adopted by the State Fire Marshal pursuant to Section 13160 is guilty of a misdemeanor punishable by a fine of not more than one thousand dollars ($1,000), or by imprisonment for not more than six months, or by both such fine and imprisonment.
A person is guilty of a separate offense each day during which he commits, continues, or permits a violation of this chapter or of any regulation adopted pursuant to this chapter.
(Added by Stats. 1968, Ch. 802.)

CHAPTER 1.8. Automatic Fire Extinguisher Systems [13195 - 13199]

(Chapter 1.8 added by Stats. 1982, Ch. 699, Sec. 1.)

13195.

The State Fire Marshal shall adopt and administer the regulations and building standards he or she deems necessary in order to (1) establish and control a program for servicing, testing, and maintaining all automatic fire extinguishing systems, including but not limited to, fire sprinkler systems, engineered and preengineered fixed extinguishing systems, standpipe systems, and water flow alarm devices and (2) establish minimum frequencies of service, inspection, and testing for the various types of automatic fire extinguishing systems. All tests of automatic sprinkler systems shall include a test of all supervisory signaling equipment that is provided to determine whether a condition exists that will impair the satisfactory operation of the system.

The regulations and building standards established by the State Fire Marshal for servicing, testing, and maintaining automatic fire extinguishing systems shall consider the requirements of the applicable standards of the National Fire Protection Association and the voluntary standards published by the State Fire Marshal entitled the "California Voluntary Standards for Residential Sprinkler Systems," dated January 1982.
(Added by Stats. 1982, Ch. 699, Sec. 1.)

13195.5.
Every automatic fire extinguishing system, including, but not limited to, fire sprinkler systems, engineered and preengineered fixed extinguishing systems, standpipe systems, and alarm and supervisory equipment attached to those systems shall be serviced, tested, and maintained in accordance with the regulations and building standards adopted by the State Fire Marshal pursuant to Section 13195.
(Added by Stats. 1982, Ch. 699, Sec. 1.)

13196.
The regulations and building standards adopted pursuant to Section 13195 shall be enforced pursuant to Sections 13145 and 13146.
(Added by Stats. 1982, Ch. 699, Sec. 1.)

13196.5.
(a) Except as provided in subdivisions (b), (c), and (d), no person shall engage in the business of servicing or testing automatic fire extinguishing systems without a license issued by the State Fire Marshal pursuant to this chapter.
(b) Persons who engage in the business of servicing or testing fire alarm devices, water flow alarm devices, or the supervisory signaling components of automatic fire extinguishing systems shall not be subject to the licensing requirements contained in this chapter.
(c) Industrial systems may be serviced or tested by, or under the supervision of, an engineer employed by a private entity who shall not be subject to the licensing requirements contained in this chapter unless he or she performs the service or testing for a fee outside of the employment relationship.
(d) Any specialty contractor, as defined in subdivision (b) of Section 7058 of the Business and Professions Code, shall not be subject to the licensing requirements contained in this chapter.
(Amended by Stats. 1985, Ch. 253, Sec. 2.)

13197.
The State Fire Marshal shall adopt regulations to establish and maintain the licensing program required by this chapter. To the extent the State Fire Marshal determines is necessary to carry out the provisions of this chapter, the regulations may provide for, but need not be limited to, requirements that the applicant for a license pass an examination or possess the qualifications necessary to perform the prescribed service, maintenance, and testing, or both.
(Added by Stats. 1982, Ch. 699, Sec. 1.)

13197.5.
A license may be denied or revoked by the State Fire Marshal for either of the following reasons:
(a) The applicant made a material misrepresentation or false statement in the application.
(b) Violation of any provision of this chapter or any regulation adopted by the State Fire Marshal pursuant to this chapter.
(Added by Stats. 1982, Ch. 699, Sec. 1.)

13197.6.
(a) If the State Fire Marshal or his or her designee determines that the public interest and public welfare will be adequately served by permitting a person licensed under this chapter to pay a monetary penalty to the State Fire Marshal in lieu of an actual license suspension, the State Fire Marshal or his or her designee may stay the execution of all or part of the suspension if all of the following conditions are met:
(1) The violation that is the cause for the suspension did not pose, or have the potential to pose, a significant threat or risk of harm to the public.
(2) The licensee pays a monetary penalty.
(3) The licensee does not incur any other cause for disciplinary action within a period of time specified by the State Fire Marshal or his or her designee.
In making the determination, the State Fire Marshal or his or her designee shall consider the seriousness of the violation, the violator's record of compliance with the law, the impact of the determination on the licensee, the licensee's employees or customers, and other relevant factors.
(b) The State Fire Marshal or his or her designee may exercise the discretion granted under this section either with respect to a suspension ordered by a decision after a contested hearing on an accusation against the licensee or by stipulation with the licensee after the filing of an accusation, but prior to the rendering of a decision based upon the accusation. In either case, the terms and conditions of the disciplinary action against the licensee shall be made part of a formal decision of the State Fire Marshal or his or her designee.
(c) If a licensee fails to pay the monetary penalty in accordance with the terms and conditions of the decision of the State Fire Marshal or his or her designee, the State Fire Marshal or his or her designee may, without a hearing, order the immediate execution of all or any part of the stayed suspension in which event the licensee shall not be entitled to any repayment nor credit, prorated or otherwise, for money paid to the State Fire Marshal under the terms of the decision.
(d) The amount of the monetary penalty payable under this section shall not exceed two hundred fifty dollars ($250) for each day of suspension stayed nor a total of ten

thousand dollars ($10,000) per decision regardless of the number of days of suspension stayed under the decision.
(e) Any monetary penalty received pursuant to this section shall be deposited in the State Fire Marshal Licensing and Certification Fund.
(f) On or before March 1 of each year, the State Fire Marshal shall make available to the public data showing the percentage of enforcement actions taken that resulted in license suspension or the assessment of monetary penalties pursuant to this section.
(Added by Stats. 2010, Ch. 161, Sec. 3. (AB 1773) Effective January 1, 2011.)

13198.
The State Fire Marshal shall adopt a schedule of fees to be paid by licensees in an amount which is necessary to cover the cost of administering and enforcing the provisions of this chapter by the State Fire Marshal. Any city or county fire department, or any district providing fire protection services may adopt a schedule of fees as required to cover the cost of enforcing the provisions of this chapter.
The annual and renewal license shall be valid for the period from January 1, to December 31.
The annual license fee renewal period shall begin on September 1 and end on November 1 preceding the license year for which the renewal is requested. A penalty of 50 percent of the license fee shall be assessed in all cases where the renewal fees are not paid on or before November 1, preceding the license year for which renewal is requested.
(Amended by Stats. 1989, Ch. 529, Sec. 4.)

13198.5.
It is the legislative intention in enacting this chapter that the provisions of this chapter and the regulations and building standards adopted by the State Fire Marshal pursuant to Section 13195 shall apply uniformly throughout the State of California, and no state agency, county, city and county, or district shall adopt or enforce any ordinance or rule or regulation regarding automatic fire extinguishing systems which is inconsistent with the provisions of this chapter or the regulations and standards adopted by the State Fire Marshal.
(Added by Stats. 1982, Ch. 699, Sec. 1.)

13199.
Any person who violates any provisions of this chapter or any regulation or building standard adopted by the State Fire Marshal pursuant to Section 13195 is guilty of a misdemeanor punishable by a fine of not more than ten thousand dollars ($10,000), or by imprisonment for not more than six months, or by both such fine and imprisonment. A person is guilty of a separate offense each day during which he or she commits, continues, or permits a violation of this chapter or any regulation or building standards adopted pursuant to this chapter.
(Added by Stats. 1982, Ch. 699, Sec. 1.)

CHAPTER 2. Clothes Cleaning Establishments [13201 - 13203]

(Chapter 2 repealed and added by Stats. 1972, Ch. 991.)
13201.
The minimum building standards for all drycleaning plants and processes in this state shall be the provisions published in the State Building Standards Code. The State Fire Marshal shall adopt regulations for protection against fire and panic safety in drycleaning plants and processes, other than building standards, reasonably consistent with the Uniform Fire Code, 1979 edition, and its referenced document, as published by the International Conference of Building Officials and the Western Fire Chiefs Association, Inc. The State Fire Marshal shall adopt building standards for such purposes, reasonably consistent with such model code, and submit such building standards for approval pursuant to Chapter 4 (commencing with Section 18935) of Part 2.5 of Division 13 of this code. Any local agency may adopt more restrictive building standards and regulations relating to fire and panic safety in drycleaning plants.
(Amended by Stats. 1979, Ch. 1152.)

13202.
Facilities which are in existence on the effective date of this section need not mandatorily conform or be made to conform with the requirements of Section 13201 for new construction if in the opinion of the enforcing authority there is a reasonable degree of fire and life safety in such facilities.
(Repealed and added by Stats. 1972, Ch. 991.)

13203.
The division of authority for the enforcement of this chapter shall be as follows:
(a) The chief of any city or county fire department or fire protection district and their authorized representatives in their respective areas on matters relating to fires and fire protection, and the State Fire Marshal outside of such areas.
(b) The local building official on matters relating to building construction.
(Repealed and added by Stats. 1972, Ch. 991.)

CHAPTER 3. High Rise Structures [13210 - 13217]

(Chapter 3 added by Stats. 1973, Ch. 946.)
13210.
As used in this chapter:
(a) "Existing high-rise structure" means a high-rise structure, the construction of which is commenced or completed prior to July 1, 1974.

(b) "High-rise structure" means every building of any type of construction or occupancy having floors used for human occupancy located more than 75 feet above the lowest floor level having building access, except buildings used as hospitals, as defined in Section 1250.

(c) "New high-rise structure" means a high-rise structure, the construction of which is commenced on or after July 1, 1974.

(Amended by Stats. 1974, Ch. 1246.)

13211.

The State Fire Marshal, with the advice of the State Board of Fire Services, shall prepare and adopt building standards relating to fire and panic safety in high-rise structures and submit such building standards for approval and publication in the State Building Standards Code pursuant to Chapter 4 (commencing with Section 18935) of Part 2.5 of Division 13 of this code. The State Fire Marshal shall prepare and adopt other regulations establishing minimum standards for the prevention of fire and for the protection of life and property against fire and panic in high-rise structures. Such regulations shall differentiate between existing high-rise structures and new high-rise structures.

(Amended by Stats. 1979, Ch. 1152.)

13212.

Subject to the provisions of Sections 25 and 18943 of this code, regulations adopted by the State Fire Marshal pursuant to Section 13211 applicable to new high-rise structures shall be adopted on or before July 1, 1974, and shall become effective July 1, 1974. Such regulations may include, but not be limited to, requirements with respect to the following elements:

(a) Automatic smoke and fire detection systems.

(b) Automatic fire extinguishing systems.

(c) An infrastructure communication system for those engaged in fire suppression activities.

(Amended by Stats. 1979, Ch. 1152.)

13213.

(a) Building standards and other regulations of the State Fire Marshal applicable to existing high-rise structures shall provide to the greatest feasible extent for the safety of occupants of the high-rise structure and persons involved in fire suppression activities. All existing high-rise structures shall be conformed to the requirements contained in such building standards and such other regulations on or before April 26, 1979.

(b) The period for compliance with such requirements may be extended upon showing of good cause for such extension if a systematic and progressive plan of correction is submitted to, and approved by, the enforcing agency. Such extension shall not exceed two years from the date of approval of such plan. Any plan of correction submitted pursuant to this subdivision shall be submitted and approved on or before April 26, 1979.

(c) This section shall not apply to structures located in a city and county if all of the following conditions exist:

(1) The structure is used solely for residential purposes.

(2) The structure contains 12 or fewer dwelling units.

(3) Each dwelling unit in the structure is owner-occupied.

(4) The structure is made of reinforced concrete.

(5) Each dwelling unit in the structure has at least two exits, one of which may be an existing exterior fire escape.

(Amended by Stats. 1980, Ch. 1378.)

13214.

The provisions of this chapter, building standards applicable to high-rise structures published in the State Building Standards Code relating to fire and panic safety, and the other regulations of the State Fire Marshal adopted pursuant to this chapter shall be enforced in the same manner as provided in Sections 13145 and 13146. The State Fire Marshal, his deputies, or his salaried assistants, the chief of any city or county fire department or district providing fire protection services, and their authorized representatives, may enter any building, premises, or portion thereof not used for dwelling purposes at any reasonable hour for the purpose of enforcing this chapter. The owner, lessee, manager, or operator of any such building or premises shall permit the State Fire Marshal, his deputies, his salaried assistants, or the chief of any city or county fire department or district providing fire protection services, or their authorized representatives, to enter and inspect the building or premises at the time and for the purpose stated in this chapter.

(Amended by Stats. 1980, Ch. 118.)

13215.

It is unlawful for any person to construct or maintain any highrise structure in violation of the provisions of this chapter, building standards published in the State Building Standards Code relating to fire or panic safety, or other regulations adopted pursuant to the provisions of this chapter. Any person who violates these provisions, standards, or regulations is guilty of a misdemeanor and, upon conviction, shall be punished by imprisonment for not to exceed six months in the county jail or by a fine not to exceed ten thousand dollars ($10,000), or both.

A person shall be guilty of a separate offense for each and every day during any portion of which any violation of any provision, standard, or regulation within this section is continued or permitted to continue by that person after the person has been notified of the violation by the appropriate enforcing agency. In addition, any condition existing in violation of any provision, standard, or regulation within this section is a public nuisance and may be summarily abated.

(Amended by Stats. 1981, Ch. 443.)

13216.

The governing body of any city or county may impose greater restrictions with respect to high-rise structures than are imposed by the building standards published in the State Building Standards Code relating to fire or panic safety or the other regulations of the State Fire Marshal adopted pursuant to this chapter.

(Amended by Stats. 1979, Ch. 1152.)

13217.

(a) A city, county, or city and county fire department or district providing fire protection services may annually inspect all highrise structures for compliance with building standards and other regulations of the State Fire Marshal. If a local agency elects to perform the inspection, the results of the inspection shall be submitted to the State Fire Marshal's office in a form and manner approved by the State Fire Marshal no later than 30 days after the date of the inspection. If the local fire department or district providing fire protection services elects not to conduct an inspection, the local fire department or district shall notify, by June 30 of each year, the State Fire Marshal of this election. If the State Fire Marshal receives this notification, the State Fire Marshal shall conduct the inspection.

(b) A local agency that, or the State Fire Marshal who, inspects a highrise structure pursuant to subdivision (a) may charge and collect a fee for the inspection from the owner of the highrise structure in an amount, as determined by the inspecting entity, sufficient to pay its costs of that inspection.

(Amended by Stats. 2019, Ch. 31, Sec. 12. (SB 85) Effective June 27, 2019.)

CHAPTER 4. Emergency Procedure Information [13220 - 13223]

(Heading of Chapter 4 amended by Stats. 1994, Ch. 1292, Sec. 1.)

13220.

The owner or operator of any of the following buildings shall provide to persons entering those buildings specific emergency procedures to be followed in the event of fire, including procedures for handicapped and nonambulatory persons:

(a) In the case of privately owned highrise structures, as defined in Section 13210, and office buildings two stories or more in height, the emergency procedure information shall be made available in a conspicuous area of the structure that is easily accessible to all persons entering the structure, designated pursuant to regulations of the State Fire Marshal.

(b) In the case of hotels and motels, as defined in subdivision (b) of Section 25503.16 of the Business and Professions Code, the emergency procedure information shall be posted in a conspicuous place in every room available for rental in the hotel or motel, or, at the option of the hotel or motel operator, it shall be provided through the use of brochures, pamphlets, video recordings, or other means, pursuant to regulations adopted by the State Fire Marshal.

(c) In the case of apartment houses two stories or more in height that contain three or more dwelling units, and where the front door opens into an interior hallway or an interior lobby area, the emergency information shall be provided as follows:

(1) Information for exiting the structure shall be posted on signs using international symbols at every stairway landing, at every elevator landing, at an intermediate point of any hallway exceeding 100 feet in length, at all hallway intersections, and immediately inside all public entrances to the building.

(2) Information shall be provided to all tenants of record, through the use of brochures, pamphlets, or video recordings, if any of these items is available, or this requirement may be satisfied pursuant to regulations adopted by the State Fire Marshal.

(3) If the owner or operator, or any individual acting on behalf of the owner or operator, of an apartment house, as described in this subdivision, negotiates a lease, sublease, rental contract, or other term of tenancy contract or agreement in any language other than English, the information required to be provided pursuant to paragraph (2) shall be provided in English, in international symbols, and in the four most common non-English languages spoken in California, as determined by the State Fire Marshal.

(d) On or before July 1, 1996, the State Fire Marshal shall adopt, for use in apartment houses described in subdivision (c), a consumer-oriented model brochure or pamphlet that includes general emergency procedure information in English, in international symbols, and in the four most common non-English languages spoken in California, as determined by the State Fire Marshal.

(e) An owner, agent, operator, translator, or transcriber who provides emergency procedure information pursuant to this section in good faith and without gross negligence shall be held harmless for any errors in the translation or transcription of that emergency information. This limited immunity shall apply only to errors in the translation or transcription and not to the providing of the information required to be provided pursuant to this section.

(f) Unless expressly stated, nothing in this section shall be deemed to require an owner or operator of any of the buildings listed in this section to provide emergency procedure information in any language other than English, or through the use of international symbols.

(Amended by Stats. 2009, Ch. 88, Sec. 63. (AB 176) Effective January 1, 2010.)

13221.

The State Fire Marshal shall adopt regulations for the furnishing of emergency procedure information according to this chapter. Those regulations may include the general contents of brochures, pamphlets, signs, or video recordings used in furnishing emergency procedure information, but shall provide for at least the following:

(a) A reference to the posting of exit plans for the structure.

(b) A general explanation of the operation of the fire alarm system of the structure.

(c) Other fire emergency procedures.
(Amended by Stats. 2010, Ch. 328, Sec. 128. (SB 1330) Effective January 1, 2011.)
13223.
Any person who violates the provisions of this chapter is guilty of a misdemeanor and upon conviction, shall be punished by a fine of not to exceed ten thousand dollars ($10,000) or imprisonment in the county jail not to exceed six months, or both.
(Added by Stats. 1981, Ch. 557.)

CHAPTER 5. Building Certification [13230 - 13234]

(Chapter 5 added by Stats. 1981, Ch. 442.)
13230.
As used in this chapter, "high rise structure" has the same meaning as defined in Section 13210.
(Added by Stats. 1981, Ch. 442.)
13233.
The owner or operator of any privately owned high rise structure shall annually certify that he or she has requested the appropriate local fire enforcing agency to conduct an inspection of the building to determine its conformance with all applicable high rise structure fire safety standards. The certification shall be submitted by letter to the State Fire Marshal.
(Added by Stats. 1981, Ch. 442.)
13234.
The State Fire Marshal may establish regulations for certification according to Section 13233, including the general form and contents of letters certifying conformance with high rise fire codes.
(Amended by Stats. 1993, Ch. 178, Sec. 3. Effective January 1, 1994.)

CHAPTER 5.5. Fire Safety Inspections of Care Facilities [13235- 13235.]

(Chapter 5.5 added by Stats. 1989, Ch. 993, Sec. 4.)
13235.
(a) Upon receipt of a request from a prospective licensee of a community care facility, as defined in Section 1502, of a residential care facility for the elderly, as defined in Section 1569.2, or of a child day care facility, as defined in Section 1596.750, the local fire enforcing agency, as defined in Section 13244, or State Fire Marshal, whichever has primary jurisdiction, shall conduct a preinspection of the facility prior to the final fire clearance approval. At the time of the preinspection, the primary fire enforcing agency shall provide consultation and interpretation of fire safety regulations, and shall notify the prospective licensee of the facility in writing of the specific fire safety regulations which shall be enforced in order to obtain fire clearance approval. A fee equal to, but not exceeding, the actual cost of the preinspection services may be charged for the preinspection of a facility with a capacity to serve 25 or fewer persons. A fee equal to, but not exceeding, the actual cost of the preinspection services may be charged for a preinspection of a facility with a capacity to serve 26 or more persons.
(b) The primary fire enforcing agency shall complete the final fire clearance inspection for a community care facility, residential care facility for the elderly, or child day care facility within 30 days of receipt of the request for the final inspection, or as of the date the prospective facility requests the final prelicensure inspection by the State Department of Social Services, whichever is later.
(Amended by Stats. 2009, 4th Ex. Sess., Ch. 12, Sec. 14. Effective July 28, 2009.)

CHAPTER 6. Propane Storage and Handling [13240 - 13244.5]

(Chapter 6 added by Stats. 1994, Ch. 1293, Sec. 1.)
ARTICLE 1. General and Definitions [13240 - 13243.6]
(Article 1 added by Stats. 1994, Ch. 1293, Sec. 1.)
13240.
This chapter shall be known, and may be cited, as the Propane Storage and Handling Safety Act.
(Added by Stats. 1994, Ch. 1293, Sec. 1. Effective January 1, 1995.)
13240.1.
For the purposes of this chapter, the following terms have the following meanings:
(a) "Propane storage system" or "system" means any tank or collection of tanks or other vessels that are intended or used for the commercial purpose of storing more than 18,000 gallons of propane.
(b) "Odorized propane" means propane to which ethyl mercaptan or any other odorizing substance is added.
(Added by Stats. 1994, Ch. 1293, Sec. 1. Effective January 1, 1995.)
13241.
Prior to January 1, 1996, the State Fire Marshal in conjunction with the Occupational Safety and Health Standards Board shall, after public hearings, adopt by reference the 1992 edition of the NFPA 58 Standard for the Storage and Handling of Liquified Petroleum Gasses, or as this 1992 edition may be subsequently amended or supplemented. It is the intent of the Legislature that the NFPA 58 Standard supersede any inconsistent state standards, including, but not limited to, Sections 470 to 494, inclusive, of Chapter 4 of Title 8 of the California Code of Regulations, except where

Sections 470 to 494, inclusive, of Chapter 4 of Title 8 of the California Code of Regulations contain a more stringent safety standard than that contained in the NFPA 58 Standard. Nothing in this section prohibits the board from adopting more stringent standards than those contained in the NFPA 58 Standard.
(Added by Stats. 1994, Ch. 1293, Sec. 1. Effective January 1, 1995.)
13242.
The State Fire Marshal, in cooperation with the Department of Industrial Relations as appropriate, shall do all of the following:
(a) Prior to January 1, 1997, inspect and certify the safety of all propane storage systems existing on January 1, 1995.
(b) Adopt regulations setting forth safety standards for the siting and construction of fixed propane storage systems. These standards shall be prepared, adopted, and submitted for approval as building standards pursuant to Chapter 4 (commencing with Section 18935) of Part 2.5 of Division 13.
(c) Adopt propane storage system fire safety compliance requirements setting forth propane fire safety handling standards relating to propane storage systems.
(d) Adopt regulations setting forth minimum training and other qualifications for personnel handling propane storage systems, including, but not limited to, continuing education requirements.
(e) Issue operator certificates to persons that comply with minimum training and other qualifications for personnel handling propane storage systems.
(f) Adopt standards setting forth minimum training and other qualifications for firefighting personnel responding to a fire involving a propane storage system.
(g) Upon completion of inspection of propane storage systems as required by subdivision (b), the Division of Occupational Safety and Health and the State Fire Marshal shall report to the Legislature on the condition of propane storage systems statewide. The report shall include identification and location of the propane storage systems inspected; identification of fire safety violations, if any, at each system inspected, and a determination of whether the fire safety violation was significant or minor. The report shall also include what remedial actions were taken, or were proposed to be taken, to correct the violations, and whether the propane storage system is in compliance with current fire safety requirements.
The Division of Occupational Safety and Health and the State Fire Marshal shall also recommend in the report, after consulting with representatives of the propane industry, any corrective or remedial legislation necessary to ensure future compliance with fire safety requirements, including, but not limited to, future fire safety inspection requirements, including the recommended frequency of these inspections.
(Added by Stats. 1994, Ch. 1293, Sec. 1. Effective January 1, 1995.)
13243.
The Department of Industrial Relations shall on or before January 1, 1996, develop a propane storage system inspection training curriculum and certification program for inspectors who are authorized to inspect propane storage system pressure vessels. The training curriculum shall include, but is not limited to, training and enforcement procedures for the NFPA 58 Standard, Article 82 of the Uniform Fire Code Standards, and the propane storage system fire safety compliance requirements adopted pursuant to subdivision (d) of Section 13242.
(Added by Stats. 1994, Ch. 1293, Sec. 1. Effective January 1, 1995.)
13243.3.
Any requirements adopted as provisions of the federal Clean Air Act (42 U.S.C. Sec. 7401 et seq.) shall supersede this measure.
(Added by Stats. 1994, Ch. 1293, Sec. 1. Effective January 1, 1995.)
13243.6.
Any costs incurred by state agencies or departments pursuant to this article, that are not funded through fees pursuant to Section 13244.5, shall be funded from existing resources.
(Added by Stats. 1994, Ch. 1293, Sec. 1. Effective January 1, 1995.)
ARTICLE 2. Liability Insurance Coverage [13244 - 13244.2]
(Article 2 added by Stats. 1994, Ch. 1293, Sec. 1.)
13244.
(a) All of the following persons or entities shall carry liability insurance set forth in subdivision (b):
(1) Any person or entity that owns or operates a business engaged in whole or in part, in the wholesale or retail sale of any energy product, liquid or vapor, which is transported or dispensed.
(2) Any person or entity engaged in the wholesale or retail sale of propane, if the activities are subject to Part 387 of Title 49 of the Code of Federal Regulations and if the activities are within the scope of the National Fire Protection Association (NFPA) Standard 58, "Standard for the Storage and Handling of Liquefied Petroleum Gases."
(3) Any person or entity engaged in the wholesale or retail sale of any energy product, liquid or vapor, which is transported or dispensed, if required by law to obtain any California hazardous materials permit based upon that activity.
(b) Persons or entities set forth in subdivision (a) shall carry liability insurance for any liability arising from that activity in an amount of no less than five hundred thousand dollars ($500,000).
(c) The liability insurance requirement of this section is a minimum and does not control over other provisions of law, if any, that may require a greater insurance coverage.
(d) The liability insurance requirement of this section does not apply to any of the following:
(1) An operation for the exchange of propane cylinders.
(2) The retail sale of propane in small propane canisters of 20 pounds or less.

(Added by Stats. 1994, Ch. 1293, Sec. 1. Effective January 1, 1995.)

13244.1.

Notwithstanding any provision of law, any person or entity that owns or operates a business engaged, in whole or in part, in the wholesale or retail sale of any energy product, liquid or vapor, which is transported or dispensed, may combine to form an insurance risk pool, or pools, for the purpose of purchasing insurance in compliance with this article.

(Added by Stats. 1994, Ch. 1293, Sec. 1. Effective January 1, 1995.)

13244.2.

If any provision of this article or the application thereof to any person or circumstances is held invalid, that invalidity shall not affect other provisions or applications of this article which can be given effect without the invalid provision or application, and to this end the provisions of this article are severable.

(Added by Stats. 1994, Ch. 1293, Sec. 1. Effective January 1, 1995.)

ARTICLE 3. Fees [13244.5- 13244.5.]

(Article 3 added by Stats. 1994, Ch. 1293, Sec. 1.)

13244.5.

The State Fire Marshal, in conjunction with local fire departments, shall determine a fee, not to exceed two hundred fifty dollars ($250) per propane storage system, to pay for the cost of the inspection and regulation of propane storage systems required by this chapter. The fees shall not exceed the cost of this inspection and regulation.

(Added by Stats. 1994, Ch. 1293, Sec. 1. Effective January 1, 1995.)

CHAPTER 7. Civil Actions to Abate Fire Hazards [13250 - 13253]

(Heading of Chapter 7 renumbered from Chapter 4 (as added by Stats. 1981, Ch. 345) by Stats. 1983, Ch. 101, Sec. 116.)

13250.

Whenever, in the judgment of the State Fire Marshal, any person has engaged in or is about to engage in any acts or practices which constitute or will constitute a violation of any provision of this part, or any rule, regulation, or order issued thereunder, at the request of the State Fire Marshal, the district attorney of the county in which such acts or practices occur or will occur or the Attorney General may make application to the superior court for an order enjoining such acts or practices, or for an order directing compliance, and upon a showing by the State Fire Marshal that such person has engaged in or is about to engage in any such acts or practices, a permanent or temporary injunction, restraining order, or other order may be granted.

(Added by Stats. 1981, Ch. 345.)

13251.

Every civil action brought under the provisions of this chapter at the request of the State Fire Marshal shall be brought by the district attorney or Attorney General in the name of the people of the State of California and any such actions relating to fire protection may be joined or consolidated.

(Added by Stats. 1981, Ch. 345.)

13252.

Any civil action brought pursuant to this chapter shall be brought in the county in which the action occurs.

(Added by Stats. 1981, Ch. 345.)

13253.

In any civil action brought pursuant to this chapter in which a temporary restraining order, preliminary injunction, or permanent injunction is sought, it shall not be necessary to allege or prove at any stage of the proceeding that irreparable damage will occur should the temporary restraining order, preliminary injunction, or permanent injunction not be issued; or that the remedy at law is inadequate, and the temporary restraining order, preliminary injunction, or permanent injunction shall issue without such allegations and without such proof.

(Added by Stats. 1981, Ch. 345.)

CHAPTER 8. Carbon Monoxide Poisoning Prevention Act of 2010 [13260 - 13263]

(Chapter 8 added by Stats. 2010, Ch. 19, Sec. 3.)

13260.

This chapter shall be known and may be cited as the Carbon Monoxide Poisoning Prevention Act of 2010.

(Added by Stats. 2010, Ch. 19, Sec. 3. (SB 183) Effective January 1, 2011.)

13261.

The Legislature finds and declares all of the following:

(a) According to the American Medical Association, carbon monoxide is the leading cause of accidental poisoning deaths in the United States. The federal Centers for Disease Control and Prevention estimate that carbon monoxide kills approximately 500 people each year and injures another 20,000 people nationwide.

(b) According to the United States Environmental Protection Agency, a person cannot see or smell carbon monoxide. At high levels carbon monoxide can kill a person in minutes. Carbon monoxide is produced whenever any fuel, such as gas, oil, kerosene, wood, or charcoal, is burned.

(c) The State Air Resources Board estimates that every year carbon monoxide accounts for between 30 and 40 avoidable deaths, possibly thousands of avoidable illnesses, and between 175 and 700 avoidable emergency room and hospital visits.

(d) There are well-documented chronic health effects of acute carbon monoxide poisoning or prolonged exposure to carbon monoxide, including, but not limited to, lethargy, headaches, concentration problems, amnesia, psychosis, Parkinson's disease, memory impairment, and personality alterations.

(e) Experts estimate that equipping every home with a carbon monoxide device would cut accident-related costs by 93 percent. Eighteen states and a number of large cities have laws mandating the use of carbon monoxide devices.

(f) Carbon monoxide devices provide a vital, highly effective, and low-cost protection against carbon monoxide poisoning and these devices should be made available to every home in California.

(g) The Homeowners' Guide to Environmental Hazards prepared pursuant to Section 10084 of the Business and Professions Code is an important educational tool and should include information regarding carbon monoxide. It is the intent of the Legislature that when the booklet is next updated as existing resources permit, or as private resources are made available, it be updated to include a section on carbon monoxide.

(Added by Stats. 2010, Ch. 19, Sec. 3. (SB 183) Effective January 1, 2011.)

13262.

For purposes of this chapter, the following definitions shall apply:

(a) "Carbon monoxide device" means a device that meets all of the following requirements:

(1) A device designed to detect carbon monoxide and produce a distinct, audible alarm.

(2) A device that is battery powered, a plug-in device with battery backup, or a device installed as recommended by Standard 720 of the National Fire Protection Association that is either wired into the alternating current power line of the dwelling unit with a secondary battery backup or connected to a system via a panel.

(3) If the device is combined with a smoke detector, the combined device shall comply with all of the following:

(A) The standards that apply to carbon monoxide alarms as described in this chapter.

(B) The standards that apply to smoke detectors, as described in Section 13113.7.

(C) The combined device emits an alarm or voice warning in a manner that clearly differentiates between a carbon monoxide alarm warning and a smoke detector warning.

(4) The device has been tested and certified, pursuant to the requirements of the American National Standards Institute (ANSI) and Underwriters Laboratories Inc. (UL) as set forth in either ANSI/UL 2034 or ANSI/UL 2075, or successor standards, by a nationally recognized testing laboratory listed in the directory of approved testing laboratories established by the Building Materials Listing Program of the Fire Engineering Division of the Office of the State Fire Marshal of the Department of Forestry and Fire Protection.

(b) "Dwelling unit intended for human occupancy" means a single-family dwelling, factory-built home as defined in Section 19971, duplex, lodging house, dormitory, hotel, motel, condominium, stock cooperative, time-share project, or dwelling unit in a multiple-unit dwelling unit building or buildings. "Dwelling unit intended for human occupancy" does not mean a property owned or leased by the state, the Regents of the University of California, or a local governmental agency.

(c) "Fossil fuel" means coal, kerosene, oil, wood, fuel gases, and other petroleum or hydrocarbon products, which emit carbon monoxide as a byproduct of combustion.

(Added by Stats. 2010, Ch. 19, Sec. 3. (SB 183) Effective January 1, 2011.)

13263.

(a) (1) The State Fire Marshal shall develop a certification and decertification process to approve and list carbon monoxide devices and to disapprove and delist previously approved devices, if necessary. The certification and decertification process shall include consideration of effectiveness and reliability of the devices, including, but not limited to, their propensity to record false alarms. The certification and decertification process shall include a review of the manufacturer's instructions and shall ensure their consistency with building standards applicable to new construction for the relevant type of occupancy with respect to number and placement.

(2) The State Fire Marshal shall charge an appropriate fee to the manufacturer of a carbon monoxide device to cover his or her costs associated with the approval and listing of carbon monoxide devices.

(b) A person shall not market, distribute, offer for sale, or sell any carbon monoxide device in this state unless the device and the instructions have been approved and listed by the State Fire Marshal.

(Added by Stats. 2010, Ch. 19, Sec. 3. (SB 183) Effective January 1, 2011.)

PART 2.7. FIRE PROTECTION DISTRICT LAW OF 1987 [13800 - 13970]

(Heading of Part 2.7 renumbered from Part 3 (as added by Stats. 1987, Ch. 1013) by Stats. 1989, Ch. 1360, Sec. 91.)

CHAPTER 1. General Provisions [13800 - 13806]

(Chapter 1 added by Stats. 1987, Ch. 1013, Sec. 11.)

13800.

This part shall be known and may be cited as the Fire Protection District Law of 1987 or as the Bergeson Fire District Law.

(Amended by Stats. 1993, Ch. 1195, Sec. 20.5. Effective January 1, 1994.)

13801.

The Legislature finds and declares that the local provision of fire protection services, rescue services, emergency medical services, hazardous material emergency response services, ambulance services, and other services relating to the protection of lives and property is critical to the public peace, health, and safety of the state. Among the ways that local communities have provided for those services has been the creation of fire protection districts. Local control over the types, levels, and availability of these services is a long-standing tradition in California which the Legislature intends to retain. Recognizing that the state's communities have diverse needs and resources, it is the intent of the Legislature in enacting this part to provide a broad statutory authority for local officials. The Legislature encourages local communities and their officials to adapt the powers and procedures in this part to meet their own circumstances and responsibilities.
(Repealed and added by Stats. 1987, Ch. 1013, Sec. 11.)
13802.
As used in this part:
(a) "City" means any city whether general law or charter, including a city and county, and including any city the name of which includes the word "town."
(b) "Day" means a calendar day.
(c) "District" means a fire protection district created pursuant to this part or created pursuant to any law which this part supersedes.
(d) "District board," means the board of directors of a district.
(e) "Employee" means any personnel of a district, including any regular or call firefighter hired and paid on a full-time or part-time basis, or any volunteer firefighter. "Employee" also includes any person who assists in the provision of any authorized emergency duty or service at the request of a person who has been authorized by the district board to request this assistance from other persons.
(f) "Principal county" means the county having all or the greater portion of the entire assessed value, as shown on the last equalized assessment roll of the county or counties, of all taxable property within a district.
(g) "Zone" means a service zone formed pursuant to Chapter 10 (commencing with Section 13950).
(Repealed and added by Stats. 1987, Ch. 1013, Sec. 11.)
13803.
(a) This part provides the authority for the organization and powers of fire protection districts. This part succeeds the Fire Protection District Law of 1961 and all of its statutory predecessors. Any fire protection district organized or reorganized pursuant to the Fire Protection District Law of 1961 or any of its statutory predecessors which was in existence on January 1, 1988, shall remain in existence as if it had been organized pursuant to this part, except that when the district board is a county board of supervisors the number and method of selection of its board of directors shall continue to be governed by the provisions of Chapter 4 (commencing with Section 13831) of the Fire Protection District Law of 1961 in effect on December 31, 1987, as if that chapter had not been repealed. Any special fire protection zone formed pursuant to Chapter 12 (commencing with Section 13991) of the Fire Protection District Law of 1961 or any of its statutory predecessors which was in existence on January 1, 1988, shall remain in existence as a service zone as if it has been formed pursuant to Chapter 10 (commencing with Section 13950).
(b) This part does not apply to any reorganization which was filed pursuant to the Fire Protection District Law of 1961 and which is pending on January 1, 1988. Those pending reorganizations may be continued and completed under, and in accordance with, the Fire Protection District Law of 1961. The repeals, amendments, and additions made by the act enacting this part shall not apply to any of those pending reorganizations, and the laws existing prior to January 1, 1988, shall continue in full force and effect as applied to those pending reorganizations.
(Repealed and added by Stats. 1987, Ch. 1013, Sec. 11.)
13804.
This part is necessary for the public health, safety, and welfare, and shall be liberally construed to effectuate its purposes.
(Repealed and added by Stats. 1987, Ch. 1013, Sec. 11.)
13805.
If any provision of this part or the application of any provision of this part in any circumstance or to any person, city, county, district, the state, or any agency or subdivision of the state is held invalid, that invalidity shall not affect other provisions or applications of this part which can be given effect without the invalid provision or application of the invalid provision, and to this end the provisions of this part are severable.
(Repealed and added by Stats. 1987, Ch. 1013, Sec. 11.)
13806.
Any action to determine the validity of the organization or of any action of a district shall be brought pursuant to Chapter 9 (commencing with Section 860) of Title 10 of Part 2 of the Code of Civil Procedure.
(Repealed and added by Stats. 1987, Ch. 1013, Sec. 11.)

CHAPTER 2. Area [13810 - 13812]

(Chapter 2 added by Stats. 1987, Ch. 1013, Sec. 11.)
13810.
Any territory, whether incorporated or unincorporated, whether contiguous or noncontiguous, may be included in a district.
(Repealed and added by Stats. 1987, Ch. 1013, Sec. 11.)
13811.

Territory which has been classified as a state responsibility area may be included in a district, except for commercial forest lands which are timbered lands declared to be in a state responsibility area. The executive officer of the local agency formation commission shall give mailed notice of the commission's hearing on any proposal to include a state responsibility area in a district, whether by annexation or formation, to the Director of Forestry and Fire Protection. The commission may approve the proposal. Upon inclusion of a state responsibility area in a district, whether by formation or annexation, the state shall retain its responsibility for fire suppression and prevention on timbered, brush, and grass-covered lands. The district shall be responsible for fire suppression and prevention for structures in the area and may provide the same services in the state responsibility area as it provides in other areas of the district.
(Amended by Stats. 1988, Ch. 465, Sec. 5. Effective August 22, 1988.)
13812.
The Cortese-Knox-Hertzberg Local Government Reorganization Act of 2000 (Division 3 (commencing with Section 56000) of Title 5 of the Government Code) shall govern any change of organization or reorganization of a district.
(Amended by Stats. 2003, Ch. 296, Sec. 23. Effective January 1, 2004.)

CHAPTER 3. Formation [13815 - 13839]

(Chapter 3 added by Stats. 1987, Ch. 1013, Sec. 11.)

ARTICLE 1. Initiation [13815 - 13822]
(Article 1 added by Stats. 1987, Ch. 1013, Sec. 11.)
13815.
A new district may be formed pursuant to this chapter.
(Amended by Stats. 2001, Ch. 176, Sec. 38. Effective January 1, 2002.)
13816.
A proposal to form a new district may be made by petition which shall do all of the following:
(a) State that the proposal is made pursuant to this article.
(b) Set forth a description of the boundaries of the territory to be included in the district.
(c) Set forth the methods by which the district will be financed.
(d) State the reasons for forming the district.
(e) Propose a name for the district.
(f) Designate no more than three persons as chief petitioners, setting forth their names and mailing addresses.
(g) State whether the formation is consistent with the sphere of influence of any affected city or affected district.
(h) Specify the number of members of the initial board of directors and the method of their selection, as provided by Article 3 (commencing with Section 13834).
(i) Request that proceedings be taken for the formation pursuant to this chapter.
(Added by Stats. 1987, Ch. 1013, Sec. 11.)
13817.
(a) Before circulating any petition, the chief petitioners shall publish a notice of intention which shall include a written statement not to exceed 500 words in length, setting forth the reasons for forming the district. The notice shall be published pursuant to Section 6061 of the Government Code in one or more newspapers of general circulation within the territory proposed to be included in the district. If the territory proposed to be included in the district is located in more than one county, publication of the notice shall be made in at least one newspaper of general circulation in each of the counties.
(b) The notice shall be signed by at least one, but not more than three, chief petitioners and shall be in substantially the following form:
"Notice of Intent to Circulate Petition
Notice is hereby given of the intention to circulate a petition proposing to form the _____ (name of the district). The reasons for the proposal are: _____."
(c) Within five days after the date of publication, the chief petitioners shall file with the executive officer of the local agency formation commission of the principal county a copy of the notice together with an affidavit made by a representative of the newspaper in which the notice was published certifying to the fact of publication.
(d) After the filing required pursuant to subdivision (c), the petition may be circulated for signatures.
(Added by Stats. 1987, Ch. 1013, Sec. 11.)
13818.
The petition shall be signed by not less than 25 percent of the registered voters residing in the area to be included in the district, as determined by the local agency formation commission pursuant to subdivision (f) of Section 56375 of the Government Code. Sections 100 and 104 of the Elections Code shall govern the signing of the petition and the format of the petition.
(Amended by Stats. 2001, Ch. 176, Sec. 39. Effective January 1, 2002.)
13819.
A petition may consist of a single instrument or separate counterparts. The chief petitioner or petitioners shall file the petition, including all counterparts, with the executive officer of the local agency formation commission of the principal county. The executive officer shall not accept a petition for filing unless the signatures have been secured within six months of the date on which the first signature was obtained and the chief petitioner or petitioners submitted the petition to the executive officer for filing within 60 days after the last signature was obtained.
(Added by Stats. 1987, Ch. 1013, Sec. 11.)
13820.
(a) Within 30 days after the date of filing a petition, the executive officer of the local agency formation commission shall cause the petition to be examined and shall prepare a

certificate of sufficiency indicating whether the petition is signed by the requisite number of signers.

(b) The executive officer shall cause the names of the signers on the petition to be compared with the voters' register in the office of the county clerk or registrar of voters and ascertain (i) the number of registered voters in the territory to be included in the district, and (ii) the number of qualified signers appearing upon the petition.

(c) If the certificate of the executive officer shows the petition to be insufficient, the executive officer shall immediately give notice by certified mail of the insufficiency to the chief petitioners. That mailed notice shall state in what amount the petition is insufficient. Within 15 days after the date of the notice of insufficiency, the chief petitioners may file with the executive officer a supplemental petition bearing additional signatures.

(d) Within 10 days after the date of filing a supplemental petition, the executive officer shall examine the supplemental petition and certify in writing the results of his or her examination.

(e) The executive officer shall sign and date a certificate of sufficiency. That certificate shall also state the minimum signature requirements for a sufficient petition and show the results of the executive officer's examination. The executive officer shall mail a copy of the certificate of sufficiency to the chief petitioners.

(Added by Stats. 1987, Ch. 1013, Sec. 11.)

13821.

(a) A proposal to form a new district may also be made by the adoption of a resolution of application by the legislative body of any county or city which contains territory proposed to be included in the district. Except for the provisions regarding the signers and signatures, and the chief petitioners, a resolution of application shall contain all of the matters specified for a petition in Section 13816. Before submitting a resolution of application, the legislative body shall conduct a public hearing on the resolution.

(b) Notice of the hearing shall be published pursuant to Section 6061 of the Government Code in one or more newspapers of general circulation within the county or city.

(c) At the hearing, the legislative body shall give any person an opportunity to present his or her views on the resolution.

(d) The clerk of the legislative body shall file a certified copy of the resolution of application with the executive officer of the local agency formation commission of the principal county.

(Amended by Stats. 1995, Ch. 529, Sec. 16. Effective October 4, 1995.)

13822.

Once the chief petitioners have filed a sufficient petition or a legislative body has filed a resolution of application, the local agency formation commission shall proceed pursuant to Chapter 5 (commencing with Section 56825) of Part 3 of Division 3 of Title 5 of the Government Code.

(Amended by Stats. 2016, Ch. 366, Sec. 20. (SB 974) Effective January 1, 2017.)

ARTICLE 2. Election [13823 - 13831]

(Article 2 added by Stats. 1987, Ch. 1013, Sec. 11.)

13823.

(a) If the local agency formation commission approves the formation of a district, with or without amendment, wholly, partially, or conditionally, the board of supervisors shall call and give notice of the election to be held in the proposed district. If the proposed district lies in more than one county, the board of supervisors shall call and give notice of the election to be held in the territory of the proposed district which lies in that county.

(b) The election shall be held on the next regular election date not less than 113 nor more than 150 days after the date the board of supervisors calls and gives notice of the election.

(c) Notice of the election shall be published pursuant to Section 6061 of the Government Code in a newspaper of general circulation circulated within the territory of the proposed district which lies in the county.

(Added by Stats. 1987, Ch. 1013, Sec. 11.)

13823.5.

After the local agency formation commission approves the formation of the district, notwithstanding Section 13823, if the board of supervisors finds that the petition filed with the executive officer of the local agency formation commission pursuant to Section 13819 has been signed by not less than 51 percent of the registered voters residing within the territory to be included within the proposed district, the board of supervisors may dispense with an election and adopt the resolution required pursuant to Section 13829. The initial members of the board of directors of the district shall be determined pursuant to Article 3 (commencing with Section 13834) of Chapter 3 of Part 3 of Division 12.

(Added by Stats. 1990, Ch. 1558, Sec. 5.)

13824.

Within five days after the district formation election has been called, the board of supervisors which has called the election shall transmit by registered mail a written notification of the election call to the executive officer of the local agency formation commission of the principal county. The written notice shall include the name and a description of the proposed district and may be in the form of a certified copy of the resolution adopted by the board of supervisors calling the district formation election. The executive officer of the local agency formation commission shall submit an impartial analysis of the proposed district formation to the officials in charge of conducting the district formation election, pursuant to Section 56859 of the Government Code.

(Added by Stats. 1987, Ch. 1013, Sec. 11.)

13825.

(a) The chief petitioners or the agency filing the resolution or any member or members of the board of supervisors authorized by the board, or any individual voter or bona fide

association of citizens entitled to vote on the district formation proposition, or any combination of these voters and associations of citizens, may file a written argument for or a written argument against the proposed district formation.

Arguments shall not exceed 300 words. Based on the time reasonably necessary to prepare and print the text of the proposition, analysis, arguments, and sample ballots and to permit the 10-day public examination period as provided in Section 9190 of the Elections Code for the particular election, the elections officials shall fix and determine a reasonable date prior to the election after which no arguments for or against the measure may be submitted for printing and distribution to the voters pursuant to Section 13826. Notice of the date fixed shall be published by the elections officials pursuant to Section 6061 of the Government Code. Arguments may be changed until and including the date fixed by the elections officials.

(b) If more than one argument for or more than one argument against the proposed district formation is filed with the elections officials within the time prescribed, the elections officials shall select one of the arguments for printing and distribution to the voters.

In selecting the arguments, the elections officials shall give preference and priority in the order named to the arguments of the following:

(1) Chief petitioners, or the agency filing the resolution.

(2) The board of supervisors, or any member or members of the board authorized by the board.

(3) Individual voters, or bona fide associations of citizens or a combination of voters and associations.

(Amended by Stats. 1994, Ch. 923, Sec. 129. Effective January 1, 1995.)

13826.

The elections officials in charge of conducting the election shall cause a ballot pamphlet concerning the district formation proposition to be voted on to be printed and mailed to each voter entitled to vote on the district formation question. Section 9190 of the Elections Code shall apply to the materials required to be contained in the ballot pamphlet.

The ballot pamphlet shall contain the following, in the order prescribed:

(a) The complete text of the proposition.

(b) The impartial analysis of the proposition, submitted by the executive officer of the local agency formation commission.

(c) The argument for the proposed district formation.

(d) The argument against the proposed district formation.

The elections officials shall mail a ballot pamphlet to each voter entitled to vote in the district formation election at least 10 days prior to the date of the election. The ballot pamphlet is "official matter" within the meaning of Section 13303 of the Elections Code.

(Amended by Stats. 1994, Ch. 923, Sec. 130. Effective January 1, 1995.)

13827.

The notice of election shall contain all of the following:

(a) The date of the election.

(b) The name of the proposed district.

(c) The purposes for which the district is to be formed.

(d) A statement that the first directors will be elected at that election who will take office or will be appointed as the case may be, if the district is formed.

(e) A description of the boundaries of the proposed district.

(Repealed and added by Stats. 1987, Ch. 1013, Sec. 11.)

13828.

(a) The formation election and the election of members of the district board, if any, shall be held and conducted in accordance with the Uniform District Election Law, Part 4 (commencing with Section 10500) of Division 10 of the Elections Code.

(b) If less than a majority of the votes cast at the election is in favor of forming the district, the board of supervisors shall declare the proceedings terminated.

(Amended by Stats. 1994, Ch. 923, Sec. 131. Effective January 1, 1995.)

13829.

If the majority of the votes cast at the election is in favor of forming the district the board or boards of supervisors shall by resolution entered on its minutes declare the district duly organized under the Fire Protection District Law, giving the name of the district, and the purposes for which it is formed, and describing its boundaries. If the district lies in more than one county, the county clerk of the principal county shall transmit a certified copy of the resolution to the county clerk of each of the other counties in which the district lies.

(Repealed and added by Stats. 1987, Ch. 1013, Sec. 11.)

13830.

If the district lies in one county, immediately after entering the resolution in the board minutes pursuant to Section 13829, the county clerk shall cause to be recorded in the office of the county recorder of the county for which he or she is county clerk a certified copy of the resolution forming the district. Thereupon, the organization of the district shall be complete.

(Amended by Stats. 1998, Ch. 829, Sec. 39. Effective January 1, 1999.)

13831.

(a) No informality in any proceeding, including informality in the conduct of any election not substantially affecting adversely the legal rights of any person, shall invalidate the formation of any district.

(b) The validity of the formation and organization of a district shall not be contested in any proceeding commenced more than 60 days after the date that the formation of the district is complete.

(Repealed and added by Stats. 1987, Ch. 1013, Sec. 11.)

(Article 3 added by Stats. 1987, Ch. 1013, Sec. 11.)

13834.
The initial board of directors of a district formed on or after January 1, 1988, shall be determined pursuant to this article.
(Repealed and added by Stats. 1987, Ch. 1013, Sec. 11.)

13835.
In the case of a district which contains only unincorporated territory in a single county, the district board may be elected or may be appointed by the county board of supervisors which may appoint itself as the district board.
(Repealed and added by Stats. 1987, Ch. 1013, Sec. 11.)

13836.
In the case of a district which contains only unincorporated territory in more than one county, the district board may be elected or may be appointed by the boards of supervisors of the counties in which the district is located. If the district board is appointed by the boards of supervisors, they shall appoint directors according to the proportionate share of population of that portion of each county within the district, provided that each board of supervisors shall appoint at least one director.
(Added by Stats. 1987, Ch. 1013, Sec. 11.)

13837.
In the case of a district which contains unincorporated territory and the territory of one or more cities:
(a) The district board may be elected or appointed by the county board of supervisors and the city councils in which the district is located. If the district board is to be appointed, the board of supervisors and the city council or councils shall appoint directors according to the proportionate share of population that portion of the county and each city within the district, provided that the board of supervisors and each city council shall appoint at least one director. The board of supervisors or city council may appoint one or more of its own members to the district board. In no case shall the number of directors exceed 11 members.
(b) Notwithstanding subdivision (a), the county board of supervisors may appoint itself as the district board, if the city council of each of the cities consents by resolution.
(Added by Stats. 1987, Ch. 1013, Sec. 11.)

13838.
In the case of a district which includes only incorporated territory within a single city, the district board may be elected or appointed by the city council which may appoint itself as the district board.
(Added by Stats. 1987, Ch. 1013, Sec. 11.)

13839.
In the case of a district which includes only incorporated territory in more than one city, the district board may be elected or appointed by the city councils in which the district is located. If the district board is appointed, the city councils shall appoint directors according to the proportionate share of population of that portion of each city within the district, provided that each city council shall appoint at least one director. The city council may appoint one or more of its own members to the district board. In no case shall the directors exceed the number permitted pursuant to Section 13842.
(Added by Stats. 1987, Ch. 1013, Sec. 11.)

CHAPTER 4. Existing Board of Directors and Officers [13840 - 13857]

(Chapter 4 added by Stats. 1987, Ch. 1013, Sec. 11.)

13840.
Every district shall be governed by a legislative body known as a board of directors.
(Repealed and added by Stats. 1987, Ch. 1013, Sec. 11.)

13841.
Except in the case where a county board of supervisors has appointed itself as the district board, each member of a district board and each member of a fire commission appointed pursuant to Section 13844 shall be a resident of the district. In addition, if the district board is elected, each member of the district board shall be a registered voter of the district. In the case of a district board which is elected by divisions, each director shall be a registered voter of the division from which he or she is elected.
(Amended by Stats. 1990, Ch. 1558, Sec. 6.)

13842.
Except in the case where a county board of supervisors or a city council has appointed itself as the district board, a district board may have three, five, seven, nine, or eleven members.
(Repealed and added by Stats. 1987, Ch. 1013, Sec. 11.)

13843.
(a) The term of office of each member of a district board is four years or until his or her successor qualifies and takes office, except as provided in subdivision (b).
(b) In the case of a district formed on or after January 1, 1988, the directors shall serve terms as provided in the Uniform District Election Law, Part 4 (commencing with Section 10500) of Division 10 of the Elections Code.
(Amended by Stats. 1994, Ch. 923, Sec. 132. Effective January 1, 1995.)

13844.
If a county board of supervisors or a city council has appointed itself as the district board, the board of supervisors or city council may delegate any or all of its powers to a fire commission composed of five or seven commissioners. In the case of a district governed by a board of supervisors, the commissioners may be councilmembers of cities which are

located in the district. The board of supervisors or city council shall determine whether the commissioners shall serve at its pleasure or for staggered terms of four years subject to removal for cause.
(Amended by Stats. 1989, Ch. 45, Sec. 1. Effective June 15, 1989.)

13845.
(a) Except in the case where a county board of supervisors or a city council has appointed itself as the district board, the number of members of a district board may be increased or decreased if a majority of the voters voting on the question are in favor of the question at a general district or special election. The question shall specify the resulting number of members of the district board.
(b) The district board may adopt a resolution placing the question on the ballot. Alternatively, upon receipt of a petition signed by at least 25 percent of the registered voters of the district, the district board shall adopt a resolution placing the question on the ballot.
(c) If the question is submitted to the voters at a general district election, the notice required by Section 12112 of the Elections Code shall contain a statement of the question to appear on the ballot. If the question is submitted to the voters at a special election, the notice of election and the ballot shall contain a statement of the question.
(d) If the voters approve of increasing the number of directors, the new members shall be elected or appointed pursuant to this chapter. If the district board is elected, the additional members may be elected at the same election.
(e) If the voters approve of decreasing the number of directors, the members of the district board continue to serve until the end of their current terms.
(f) The number of members of a district board may be changed by the local agency formation commission as a term and condition of approval by the commission of any change of organization or reorganization. Unless the Cortese-Knox-Hertzberg Local Government Reorganization Act of 2000, Division 3 (commencing with Section 56000) of Title 5 of the Government Code, otherwise requires voter approval, the change ordered by the commission does not require approval by the voters of the district.
(Amended by Stats. 2006, Ch. 588, Sec. 12. Effective January 1, 2007.)

13846.
(a) In the case of an elected district board, the directors may be elected by divisions if a majority of the voters voting upon the question are in favor of the question at a general district or special election. Conversely, in the case of a district that has an elected district board which is elected by election division, the directors may be elected at large if a majority of the voters voting upon the question are in favor of the question at a general district or special election.
(b) As used in this section, "election by division" means the election of each member of the district board by voters of only the respective election division.
(c) The district board may adopt a resolution placing the question on the ballot. Alternatively, upon receipt of a petition signed by at least 25 percent of the registered voters of the district, the district board shall adopt a resolution placing the question on the ballot.
(d) If the question is submitted to the voters at a general district election, the notice required by Section 12112 of the Elections Code shall contain a statement of the question to appear on the ballot. If the question is submitted to the voters at a special election, the notice of election and ballot shall contain a statement of the question.
(e) If the majority of voters voting upon the question approves the election of directors by divisions, the district board shall promptly adopt a resolution dividing the district into as many divisions as there are directors. The resolution shall assign a number to each division. Using the last decennial census as a basis, the divisions shall be as nearly equal in population as possible. In establishing the boundaries of the divisions the district board may give consideration to the following factors: (1) topography, (2) geography, (3) cohesiveness, contiguity, integrity, and compactness of territory, and (4) community of interests of the divisions.
(f) If the majority of voters voting upon the question approves the election of directors by division, the board members shall be elected by election divisions and each member elected shall be a resident of the election division from which he or she is elected. At the district general election following the approval by the voters of the election of directors by divisions, the district board shall assign vacancies on the board created by the expiration of terms to the respective election divisions and the vacancies shall be filled from those election divisions.
(g) If the majority of voters voting upon the question approves the election of directors at large, the district board shall promptly adopt a resolution dissolving the election divisions which had existed.
(Amended by Stats. 2006, Ch. 588, Sec. 13. Effective January 1, 2007.)

13847.
In the case of a district board elected by election divisions, the district board shall adjust the boundaries of the election divisions before November 1 of the year following the year in which each decennial federal census is taken. If at any time between each decennial federal census a change of organization alters the population of the district or the district increases or decreases the number of members of the district board, the district board shall reexamine the boundaries of its election divisions. If the district board finds that the population of any election division has varied so that the divisions no longer meet the criteria specified in subdivision (d) of Section 13846, the district board shall adjust the boundaries of the election divisions so that the divisions shall be as nearly equal in population as possible. The district board shall make this change within 60 days of the effective date of the change of organization or an increase or decrease in the number of members of the district board.
(Added by Stats. 1987, Ch. 1013, Sec. 11.)

13848.

(a) If a majority of the voters voting upon the question at a general district or special election are in favor, a district that has an appointed district board shall have an elected district board or a district that has an elected district board shall have an appointed district board.

(b) The district board may adopt a resolution placing the question on the ballot. Alternatively, upon receipt of a petition signed by at least 25 percent of the registered voters of the district, the district board shall adopt a resolution placing the question on the ballot.

(c) If the question is submitted to the voters at a general district election, the notice required by Section 12112 of the Elections Code shall contain a statement of the question to appear on the ballot. If the question is submitted to the voters at a special election, the notice of election and ballot shall contain a statement of the question.

(d) If a majority of voters voting upon the question approves of changing from an appointed district board to an elected district board, the members of the district board shall be elected at the next general district election. If a majority of voters voting upon the question approves of changing from an elected district board to an appointed district board, members shall be appointed to the district board as vacancies occur.
(Amended by Stats. 2006, Ch. 588, Sec. 14. Effective January 1, 2007.)

13849.

(a) Before circulating any petition pursuant to Section 13845, 13846, or 13848 the chief petitioners shall publish a notice of intention which shall include a written statement not to exceed 500 words in length, setting forth the reasons for the proposal. The notice shall be published pursuant to Section 6061 of the Government Code in one or more newspapers of general circulation within the district. If the district is located in more than one county, publication of the notice shall be made in at least one newspaper of general circulation in each of the counties.

(b) The notice shall be signed by at least one, but not more than three, chief petitioners and shall be in substantially the following form:

"Notice of Intent to Circulate Petition

Notice is hereby given of the intention to circulate a petition affecting the Board of Directors of the _____ (name of the district). The petition proposes that _____ (description of the proposal)."

(c) Within five days after the date of publication, the chief petitioners shall file with the secretary of the district board a copy of the notice together with an affidavit made by a representative of the newspaper in which the notice was published certifying to the fact of publication.

(d) After the filing required pursuant to subdivision (c), the petition may be circulated for signatures.
(Added by Stats. 1987, Ch. 1013, Sec. 11.)

13850.

(a) Sections 100 and 104 of the Elections Code shall govern the signing of the petition and the format of the petition.

(b) A petition may consist of a single instrument or separate counterparts. The chief petitioner or petitioners shall file the petition, together with all counterparts, with the secretary of the district board. The secretary shall not accept a petition for filing unless the signatures have been secured within six months of the date on which the first signature was obtained and the chief petitioner or petitioners submitted the petition to the secretary for filing within 60 days after the last signature was obtained.
(Amended by Stats. 1994, Ch. 923, Sec. 136. Effective January 1, 1995.)

13851.

(a) Within 30 days after the date of filing a petition, the secretary of the district board shall cause the petition to be examined and shall prepare a certificate of sufficiency indicating whether the petition is signed by the requisite number of signers.

(b) The secretary shall cause the names of the signers on the petition to be compared with the voters' register in the office of the county clerk or registrar of voters and ascertain (i) the number of registered voters in the district, and (ii) the number of qualified signers appearing upon the petition.

(c) If the certificate of the secretary shows the petition to be insufficient, the secretary shall immediately give notice by certified mail of the insufficiency to the chief petitioners. That mailed notice shall state in what amount the petition is insufficient. Within 15 days after the date of the notice of insufficiency, the chief petitioners may file with the secretary a supplemental petition bearing additional signatures.

(d) Within 10 days after the date of filing a supplemental petition, the secretary shall examine the supplemental petition and certify in writing the results of his or her examination.

(e) The secretary shall sign and date a certificate of sufficiency. That certificate shall also state the minimum signature requirements for a sufficient petition and show the results of the secretary's examination. The secretary shall mail a copy of the certificate of sufficiency to the chief petitioners.

(f) Once the chief petitioners have filed a sufficient petition, the district board shall take the actions required pursuant to Section 13845, 13846, or 13848.
(Repealed and added by Stats. 1987, Ch. 1013, Sec. 11.)

13852.

(a) Any vacancy in the office of a member appointed to the district board shall be filled pursuant to Section 1779 of the Government Code.

(b) Any vacancy in the office of a member elected to the district board shall be filled pursuant to Section 1780 of the Government Code.
(Repealed and added by Stats. 1987, Ch. 1013, Sec. 11.)

13853.

(a) Within 60 days after their initial election or appointment and after each general district election or unopposed election, the district board shall meet and elect its officers. The officers of a district board are a president, a vice president, and a secretary or clerk.

(b) The secretary or clerk may be a member of the district board. He or she may receive compensation set by the district board which shall be in lieu of any other compensation to which he or she may be entitled as a member of the district board. The district board may employ a clerk to perform the duties of the secretary.

(c) A district board may create additional officers and elect members to those positions, provided that no member of a district board shall hold more than one office.
(Repealed and added by Stats. 1987, Ch. 1013, Sec. 11.)

13854.

(a) Except as provided in subdivision (b), the county treasurer of the principal county shall act as the district treasurer and shall receive no compensation for the receipt and disbursement of money of the district.

(b) The district board may adopt a resolution appointing a district treasurer other than the county treasurer and defining the duties and compensation of the office. The district treasurer, or any other person authorized by the district board, shall draw checks or warrants to pay any demands which have been audited and approved in the manner prescribed by the district board.

(c) If the district board adopts the resolution provided by subdivision (b), the district treasurer and any other person designated by the district board shall give bonds to the district conditioned for the faithful performance of their duties. The amount of each bond shall be at least one hundred thousand dollars ($100,000) or 10 percent of the total amount of the district's final budget for the preceding fiscal year, whichever is greater. The district board shall pay the premiums on the bonds.
(Repealed and added by Stats. 1987, Ch. 1013, Sec. 11.)

13855.

A district board shall meet at least once every three months. Meetings of the board are subject to the provisions of the Ralph M. Brown Act, (Chapter 9 (commencing with Section 54950) of Part 1 of Division 2 of Title 5 of the Government Code).
(Repealed and added by Stats. 1987, Ch. 1013, Sec. 11.)

13856.

(a) A majority of the district board shall constitute a quorum for the transaction of business.

(b) The district board shall act only by ordinance, resolution, or motion. Except as specifically provided to the contrary in this part, a recorded vote by a majority of the total membership of the district board is required on each action.
(Added by Stats. 1987, Ch. 1013, Sec. 11.)

13857.

(a) Subject to subdivision (b), each member of the district board may receive compensation in an amount set by the district board not to exceed one hundred dollars ($100) for attending each meeting of the district board. The number of meetings for which a member of the board of directors may receive compensation shall not exceed six meetings in any calendar month. Commencing January 1, 2019, if the district compensates its members for more than four meetings in a calendar month, the district board shall annually adopt a written policy describing, based on a finding supported by substantial evidence, why more than four meetings per month are necessary for the effective operation of the district.

(b) The district board, by ordinance adopted pursuant to Chapter 2 (commencing with Section 20200) of Division 10 of the Water Code, may increase the compensation received by the district board members above the amount prescribed by subdivision (a).

(c) For purposes of this section, the determination of whether a director's activities on any specific day are compensable shall be made pursuant to Article 2.3 (commencing with Section 53232) of Chapter 2 of Part 1 of Division 2 of Title 5 of the Government Code.
(Amended by Stats. 2018, Ch. 170, Sec. 2. (AB 2329) Effective January 1, 2019.)

CHAPTER 5. General Powers and Duties [13860 - 13879]

(Chapter 5 added by Stats. 1987, Ch. 1013, Sec. 11.)

13860.

A district has perpetual succession.
(Repealed and added by Stats. 1987, Ch. 1013, Sec. 11.)

13861.

A district shall have and may exercise all rights and powers, expressed or implied, necessary to carry out the purposes and intent of this part, including, but not limited to, the following powers:

(a) To sue and be sued.

(b) To acquire any property, including water facilities for providing fire protection, within the district by any means, to hold, manage, occupy, dispose of, convey and encumber the property, and to create a leasehold interest in the property for the benefit of the district.

(c) To acquire by eminent domain any property necessary to carry out any of its powers or functions.

(d) To appoint necessary employees, to define their qualifications and duties, and to provide a pay schedule for performance of their duties.

(e) To employ counsel.

(f) To enter into and perform all necessary contracts pursuant to Article 53 (commencing with Section 20810) of Part 3 of Division 2 of the Public Contract Code.

(g) To adopt a seal and alter it at pleasure.

(h) To adopt ordinances following the procedures of Article 7 (commencing with Section 25120) of Chapter 1 of Part 2 of Division 2 of Title 3 of the Government Code.

(i) To establish and enforce rules and regulations for the administration, operation, and maintenance of the services listed in Section 13862.

(j) To enter joint powers agreements pursuant to Chapter 5 (commencing with Section 6500) of Division 7 of Title 1 of the Government Code.

(k) To provide insurance pursuant to Part 6 (commencing with Section 989) of Division 3.6 of Title 1 of the Government Code.

(Amended by Stats. 1988, Ch. 465, Sec. 7. Effective August 22, 1988.)

13862.

A district shall have the power to provide the following services:

(a) Fire protection services.

(b) Rescue services.

(c) Emergency medical services.

(d) Hazardous material emergency response services.

(e) Ambulance services, pursuant to Division 2.5 (commencing with Section 1797).

(f) Any other services relating to the protection of lives and property.

(Repealed and added by Stats. 1987, Ch. 1013, Sec. 11.)

13863.

(a) A district may enter into mutual aid agreements with any federal or state agency, any city, county, city and county, special district, or federally recognized Indian tribe.

(b) A district may also enter into mutual aid agreements with any private firm, corporation, or federally recognized Indian tribe that maintains a full-time fire department. The firm, corporation, or federally recognized Indian tribe, or any of its employees, shall have the same immunity from liability for civil damages on account of personal injury to or death of any person or damage to property resulting from acts or omissions of its fire department personnel in the performance of the provisions of the mutual aid agreement as is provided by law for the district and its employees, except when the act or omission occurs on property under the control of the firm, corporation, or federally recognized Indian tribe.

(Amended by Stats. 1998, Ch. 17, Sec. 1. Effective April 14, 1998.)

13864.

A district may lease or rent any property from an employee, including but not limited to, vehicles or equipment.

(Repealed and added by Stats. 1987, Ch. 1013, Sec. 11.)

13865.

A district may join any local, state, or national group or association which promotes the preservation of life and property from the hazards of fire and other disasters.

(Repealed and added by Stats. 1987, Ch. 1013, Sec. 11.)

13866.

A district may authorize its directors and employees to attend professional or vocational meetings and pay their actual and necessary traveling and incidental expenses while on official business. Reimbursement for these expenses is subject to Sections 53232.2 and 53232.3 of the Government Code.

(Amended by Stats. 2005, Ch. 700, Sec. 15. Effective January 1, 2006.)

13867.

The acquisition of any equipment for fire protection purposes shall conform to the standardization provisions of Article 1 (commencing with Section 13025) of Chapter 2 of Part 1.

(Repealed and added by Stats. 1987, Ch. 1013, Sec. 11.)

13868.

(a) A district board shall keep a record of all its acts, including its financial transactions.

(b) A district may destroy a record pursuant to Chapter 7 (commencing with Section 60200) of Division 1 of Title 6 of the Government Code.

(Amended by Stats. 2005, Ch. 158, Sec. 24. Effective January 1, 2006.)

13869.

A district may adopt a fire prevention code by reference pursuant to Article 2 (commencing with Section 50022) of Chapter 1 of Part 1 of Division 1 of Title 5 of the Government Code. For that purpose, the district board shall be deemed a legislative body and the district shall be deemed a local agency.

(Repealed and added by Stats. 1987, Ch. 1013, Sec. 11.)

13869.7.

(a) Any fire protection district organized pursuant to Part 2.7 (commencing with Section 13800) of Division 12 may adopt building standards relating to fire and panic safety that are more stringent than those building standards adopted by the State Fire Marshal and contained in the California Building Standards Code. For these purposes, the district board shall be deemed a legislative body and the district shall be deemed a local agency. Any changes or modifications that are more stringent than the requirements published in the California Building Standards Code relating to fire and panic safety shall be subject to subdivision (b) of Section 18941.5.

(b) Any fire protection district that proposes to adopt an ordinance pursuant to this section shall, not less than 30 days prior to noticing a proposed ordinance for public hearing, provide a copy of that ordinance, together with the adopted findings made pursuant to subdivision (a), to the city, county, or city and county where the ordinance will apply. The city, county, or city and county, may provide the district with written comments, which shall become part of the fire protection district's public hearing record.

(c) The fire protection district shall transmit the adopted ordinance to the city, county, or city and county where the ordinance will apply. The legislative body of the city, county, or city and county, may ratify, modify, or deny an adopted ordinance and transmit its determination to the district within 15 days of the determination. Any modification or denial of an adopted ordinance shall include a written statement describing the reasons for any modifications or denial. No ordinance adopted by the district shall be effective until ratification by the city, county, or city and county where the ordinance will apply. Upon ratification of an adopted ordinance, the city, county, or city and county, shall file a copy of the findings of the district, and any findings of the city, county, or city and county, together with the adopted ordinance expressly marked and identified to which each finding refers, with the Department of Housing and Community Development.

(d) Nothing in this section shall authorize a district to mandate, nor prohibit a district from mandating, the installation of residential fire sprinkler systems within newly constructed dwelling units or in new additions to existing dwelling units, including, but not limited to, manufactured homes as defined in Section 18007.

(e) Nothing in this section shall authorize a district to mandate, nor prohibit a district from mandating, the retrofitting of existing dwelling units for the installation of residential fire sprinkler systems, including, but not limited to, manufactured homes as defined in Section 18007.

(f) Nothing in this section shall apply in any manner to litigation filed prior to January 1, 1991, regarding an ordinance or regulation which mandates the installation of residential fire sprinkler systems within newly constructed dwelling units or in new additions to existing dwelling units.

(g) This section shall not apply to fire and panic safety requirements for the public schools adopted by the State Fire Marshal pursuant to Section 13143.

(h) (1) A city, county, or city and county that ratifies an ordinance relating to fire and panic safety pursuant to this section shall delegate the enforcement of the ordinance to either of the following:

(A) The chief of the fire protection district that adopted the ordinance, or his or her authorized representative.

(B) The chief building official of the city, county, or city and county, or his or her authorized representative.

(2) Any fee charged pursuant to the enforcement authority of this subdivision shall not exceed the estimated reasonable cost of providing the service for which the fee is charged, pursuant to Section 66014 of the Government Code.

(Amended by Stats. 1993, Ch. 906, Sec. 13. Effective October 8, 1993. Operative January 1, 1994, by Sec. 24 of Ch. 906.)

13870.

(a) Notwithstanding any other provision of law, a district board or its authorized representative may issue a written order to correct or eliminate a fire hazard or life hazard.

(b) Any person who has been ordered to immediately correct or eliminate a fire hazard or life hazard pursuant to subdivision (a) and who believes that strict compliance with the order would cause undue hardship may, within 10 days, present a written request to the district board requesting a hearing on and a review of the order. The request shall state the reasons for making the request.

(c) Within 30 days of the receipt of a written request pursuant to subdivision (b), the district board or its authorized representative shall hold a hearing. The board may modify, vacate, or affirm the order.

(Repealed and added by Stats. 1987, Ch. 1013, Sec. 11.)

13871.

(a) Any citation issued by a district for violation of a fire prevention code or a district ordinance may be processed pursuant to subdivision (d) of Section 17 of the Penal Code.

(b) Every person who fails or refuses to correct or eliminate a fire or life hazard after written order of a district board or its authorized representative is guilty of a misdemeanor.

(c) Every person who falsely personates a member of a district board or an officer or employee of a district is guilty of a misdemeanor.

(d) Every misdemeanor is punishable pursuant to Section 19 of the Penal Code.

(Repealed and added by Stats. 1987, Ch. 1013, Sec. 11.)

13872.

A district may, by ordinance, authorize its fire chief, or his or her duly authorized representative, to issue citations for the misdemeanors specified in Section 13871. The provisions of Chapter 5C (commencing with Section 853.5) of Title 4 of Part 2 of the Penal Code shall apply.

(Amended by Stats. 2001, Ch. 176, Sec. 40. Effective January 1, 2002.)

13872.5.

The fire chief of a city, city and county, or county fire department, or his or her authorized representative, has the same authority as specified in Sections 13870 to 13872, inclusive, to issue a written order to correct or eliminate a fire hazard or life hazard, hold hearings and modify, vacate, or affirm those orders, and issue citations if so authorized by ordinance of the city, city and county, or county. This section does not limit or affect any authority of a fire chief or authorized representative of a fire chief under any local ordinance.

(Added by Stats. 1988, Ch. 1589, Sec. 3.)

13873.

Employees of a district shall have the powers of peace officers while engaged in the prevention and suppression of fires and the protection and preservation of life and property, including, but not limited to, actions associated with rescue services, emergency medical services, hazardous material emergency response services, and ambulance services.

(Repealed and added by Stats. 1987, Ch. 1013, Sec. 11.)

13874.

If a district board has adopted regulations for the control of open fires, no person shall burn any material without a permit. A district shall not issue a permit to burn any material which would not be permitted by an air pollution control district or an air quality management district, or any other state or federal agency.
(Repealed and added by Stats. 1987, Ch. 1013, Sec. 11.)
13875.
A district may prepare and disseminate information and operate educational programs, including, but not limited to, those which help to prevent fire, eliminate life hazards, and prepare for medical emergencies.
(Repealed and added by Stats. 1987, Ch. 1013, Sec. 11.)
13876.
A district board may adopt a resolution to change the name of the district. The resolution shall comply with the requirements of Chapter 23 (commencing with Section 7530) of Division 7 of Title 1 of the Government Code. Within 10 days of its adoption, the district board shall file a copy of the resolution with the county clerk, and the board of supervisors and the local agency formation commission of each county in which the district is located.
(Amended by Stats. 1998, Ch. 829, Sec. 40. Effective January 1, 1999.)
13877.
A district board may authorize the use of any vehicle, apparatus, or equipment outside the district, subject to any terms and conditions it prescribes.
(Repealed and added by Stats. 1987, Ch. 1013, Sec. 11.)
13878.
A district may contract with any person or public agency to provide district services to territory which is outside the district. A contract shall provide for payment in advance.
(Repealed and added by Stats. 1987, Ch. 1013, Sec. 11.)
13879.
A district board may abate hazardous weeds and rubbish pursuant to Part 5 (commencing with Section 14875). For that purpose, the district board shall be deemed to be a "board of supervisors" and district employees shall be deemed to be the "persons" designated by Section 14890.
(Repealed and added by Stats. 1987, Ch. 1013, Sec. 11.)

CHAPTER 6. Elections [13885 - 13887]

(Chapter 6 added by Stats. 1987, Ch. 1013, Sec. 11.)
13885.
Except as otherwise provided in this part, districts are subject to the Uniform District Election Law, Part 4 (commencing with Section 10500) of Division 10 of the Elections Code.
(Amended by Stats. 1994, Ch. 923, Sec. 137. Effective January 1, 1995.)
13886.
A district board may require that its election of district board members be held on the same day as the statewide general election pursuant to Section 10404 of the Elections Code.
(Amended by Stats. 1994, Ch. 923, Sec. 138. Effective January 1, 1995.)
13887.
The expense of an election on the question of the formation of a district shall be paid by the county if the proposition fails. If the formation is approved, the expense shall be a charge against the district and repaid to the county from the first moneys collected by the district. The expense of all other elections shall be a charge against the district.
(Added by Stats. 1987, Ch. 1013, Sec. 11.)

CHAPTER 7. Finance [13890 - 13906]

(Chapter 7 added by Stats. 1987, Ch. 1013, Sec. 11.)
13890.
On or before June 30 of each year, a district board shall adopt a preliminary budget which shall conform to the accounting and budgeting procedures for special districts contained in Subchapter 3 (commencing with Section 1031.1) of, and Article 1 (commencing with Section 1121) of Subchapter 4 of, Chapter 2 of Division 2 of Title 2 of the California Code of Regulations.
(Amended by Stats. 1999, Ch. 550, Sec. 27. Effective September 28, 1999. Operative January 1, 2000, by Sec. 33 of Ch. 550.)
13891.
On or after July 1 of each year, the amounts set forth in the preliminary budget, except obligations for fixed assets and new permanent employee positions, are deemed appropriated until the district board adopts the final budget. If the district board has not adopted a preliminary budget, the amounts deemed appropriated shall be based on the budget of the preceding year, excluding fixed assets and new permanent employee positions.
(Added by Stats. 1987, Ch. 1013, Sec. 11.)
13892.
If the district board determines that the amount of revenue for the coming fiscal year will be inadequate to meet the amount of expenditures needed to protect life and property, the preliminary budget shall propose methods of raising adequate revenues or reducing services.
(Repealed and added by Stats. 1987, Ch. 1013, Sec. 11.)
13893.
(a) On or before June 30 of each year, a district board shall publish a notice stating all of the following:

(1) That it has adopted a preliminary budget which is available for inspection at a time and place within the district specified in the notice.
(2) The date, time, and place when the board will meet to adopt the final budget and that any person may appear and be heard regarding any item in the budget or regarding the addition of other items.
(b) The notice shall be published pursuant to Section 6061 of the Government Code in at least one newspaper of general circulation in the district. The first publication shall be at least two weeks before the date of the meeting. If there is no newspaper published in the district, the notice shall be posted in three public places in the district at least two weeks before the date of the meeting.
(Amended by Stats. 1993, Ch. 1195, Sec. 21. Effective January 1, 1994.)
13894.
At the time and place specified for the meeting, any person may appear and be heard regarding any item in the budget or regarding the addition of other items. The hearing on the preliminary budget may be continued from time to time.
(Repealed and added by Stats. 1987, Ch. 1013, Sec. 11.)
13895.
On or before October 1 of each year, after making any changes in the preliminary budget, the board shall adopt a final budget. The final budget shall establish its appropriation limit pursuant to Division 9 (commencing with Section 7900) of Title 1 of the Government Code. A copy of the final budget shall be forwarded to the auditor of each county in which the district is located.
(Repealed and added by Stats. 1987, Ch. 1013, Sec. 11.)
13896.
The auditor of each county in which a district is located shall allocate to the district its share of property tax revenue pursuant to Chapter 6 (commencing with Section 95) of Part 0.5 of Division 1 of the Revenue and Taxation Code.
(Repealed and added by Stats. 1987, Ch. 1013, Sec. 11.)
13897.
A district may borrow money and incur indebtedness pursuant to the authority contained in Article 7 (commencing with Section 53820), Article 7.4 (commencing with Section 53835), Article 7.5 (commencing with Section 53840), Article 7.6 (commencing with Section 53850), and Article 7.7 (commencing with Section 53859), of Chapter 4 of Part 1 of Division 2 of Title 5 of the Government Code.
(Amended by Stats. 2010, Ch. 699, Sec. 25.3. (SB 894) Effective January 1, 2011.)
13898.
A district may accept any revenue, money, grants, goods, or services from any federal, state, regional, or local agency or from any person for any lawful purpose of the district.
(Added by Stats. 1987, Ch. 1013, Sec. 11.)
13899.
All taxes and assessments levied under this chapter shall be computed and entered on the county assessment roll and collected at the same time and in the same manner as other county taxes. When collected, the taxes and assessments shall be paid into the county treasury for the use of the district. Except as provided in Section 13854, the county may deduct its costs for this service pursuant to Section 29142 of the Government Code.
(Added by Stats. 1987, Ch. 1013, Sec. 11.)
13900.
At any regular meeting or properly noticed special meeting, a district board by two-thirds majority vote of the total membership of the district board may make available for appropriation any of the following:
(a) Balances in appropriations for contingencies, including accretions from cancellations of appropriations.
(b) Designations and reserves no longer required for the purpose for which intended, excluding the general reserve, balance sheet reserves, and reserve for encumbrances.
(c) Amounts which are either in excess of anticipated amounts or not specifically set forth in the budget derived from any or anticipated increases in available financing.
(Added by Stats. 1987, Ch. 1013, Sec. 11.)
13901.
If it finds that an emergency affects the ability of a district to furnish adequate fire protection services, rescue services, emergency medical services, hazardous material emergency response services, ambulance services, or other services relating to the protection of lives and property, a district board, by resolution adopted by a two-thirds vote of the total membership of the district board, may provide the moneys which have been received but not specifically set forth as revenue in the adopted final budget be made available for appropriation and expenditure during the current fiscal year.
(Repealed and added by Stats. 1987, Ch. 1013, Sec. 11.)
13902.
(a) A district board may establish a reserve for capital outlays and shall declare the purposes for which the reserve is to be used.
(b) At any time, the district board may transfer to its reserve for capital outlays any unencumbered surplus reserve remaining at the end of a fiscal year.
(c) A capital outlay reserve shall be used only for the purposes specified by the district board. However, if a district board finds at the time it adopts its final budget that the reserve is no longer required, it may, by unanimous vote, discontinue the reserve or transfer any balance to the district's general fund.
(Repealed and added by Stats. 1987, Ch. 1013, Sec. 11.)
13903.

(a) All claims for money or damages against a district are governed by Part 3 (commencing with Section 900) and Part 4 (commencing with Section 940) of Division 3.6 of Title 1 of the Government Code.

(b) Claims against a district shall be audited, allowed, and paid by order of the district board.

(c) As an alternative to subdivision (b), a district board may instruct the county auditor to audit, allow, and draw his or her warrant on the county treasurer for all legal claims presented to him or her and authorized by the district board.

(d) The warrants shall be paid in the order in which they are presented.

(Repealed and added by Stats. 1987, Ch. 1013, Sec. 11.)

13904.

If a warrant is presented to the district treasurer for payment and the treasurer cannot pay it for want of funds in the account on which it is drawn, the treasurer shall endorse the warrant "NOT PAID BECAUSE OF INSUFFICIENT FUNDS" and sign his or her name and indicate the date and time the warrant was presented. From that time until it is paid, the warrant bears interest at the maximum rate permitted pursuant to Article 7 (commencing with Section 53530) of Chapter 3 of Part 1 of Division 2 of Title 5 of the Government Code.

(Repealed and added by Stats. 1987, Ch. 1013, Sec. 11.)

13905.

Notwithstanding Section 13903, a district board may adopt a resolution ordering the establishment of a petty cash fund to pay small bills directly. The resolution shall designate all of the following:

(a) The maximum amount of the fund, not to exceed five hundred dollars ($500).

(b) The purposes for which the fund may be spent.

(c) The officer or employee who is authorized to spend the fund and who will account for it.

(d) The officer or employee who is authorized to draw a warrant on the district treasury to establish the fund and who is authorized to draw additional warrants to reimburse the fund. Each warrant drawn to reimburse the fund shall contain an itemized account of expenditures.

(Repealed and added by Stats. 1987, Ch. 1013, Sec. 11.)

13906.

(a) A district may acquire any necessary property by purchase or purchase on contract with money borrowed pursuant to this section.

(b) The amount of indebtedness to be incurred shall not exceed an amount equal to three times the actual income from property taxes received pursuant to Section 13896 for the fiscal year preceding the year in which the indebtedness is incurred. Any indebtedness shall be repaid within 10 years from the date on which it is incurred. An indebtedness shall bear interest at a rate which shall not exceed the rate permitted under Article 7 (commencing with Section 53530) of Chapter 3 of Part 1 of Division 2 of Title 5 of the Government Code.

(c) An indebtedness shall be authorized by resolution adopted by a two-thirds majority vote of the total membership of the district board.

(Repealed and added by Stats. 1987, Ch. 1013, Sec. 11.)

CHAPTER 8. Alternative Revenues [13910 - 13919]

(Chapter 8 added by Stats. 1987, Ch. 1013, Sec. 11.)

13910.

Whenever the district board determines that the amount of revenue available to the district or any of its zones is inadequate to meet the costs of providing services pursuant to Section 13862, the board may raise revenues pursuant to this chapter or any other provision of law.

(Repealed and added by Stats. 1987, Ch. 1013, Sec. 11.)

13911.

A district may levy a special tax pursuant to Article 3.5 (commencing with Section 50075) of Chapter 1 of Part 1 of Division 1 of Title 5 of the Government Code.

(Repealed and added by Stats. 1987, Ch. 1013, Sec. 11.)

13912.

A district may levy a special tax pursuant to the Mello-Roos Community Facilities Act of 1982, Chapter 2.5 (commencing with Section 53311) of Part 1 of Division 2 of Title 5 of the Government Code.

(Repealed and added by Stats. 1987, Ch. 1013, Sec. 11.)

13913.

A district may levy a special tax pursuant to Article 16 (commencing with Section 53970) of Chapter 4 of Part 1 of Division 2 of Title 5 of the Government Code. However, the tax shall not require a higher rate of payment or other measure of tax on the part of new construction than on the part of other real property.

(Repealed and added by Stats. 1987, Ch. 1013, Sec. 11.)

13914.

A district may levy an assessment for fire suppression services pursuant to Article 3.6 (commencing with Section 50078) of Chapter 1 of Part 1 of Division 1 of Title 5 of the Government Code.

(Repealed and added by Stats. 1987, Ch. 1013, Sec. 11.)

13915.

A district may levy assessments to finance capital improvements pursuant to the Improvement Act of 1911, Division 7 (commencing with Section 5000), the Improvement Bond Act of 1915, Division 10 (commencing with Section 8500), and the Municipal Improvement Act of 1913, Division 12 (commencing with Section 10000) of the Streets and Highways Code.

(Repealed and added by Stats. 1987, Ch. 1013, Sec. 11.)

13916.

(a) A district board may charge a fee to cover the cost of any service which the district provides or the cost of enforcing any regulation for which the fee is charged. No fee shall exceed the costs reasonably borne by the district in providing the service or enforcing the regulation for which the fee is charged. A district board shall not charge a fee on new construction or development for the construction of public improvements or facilities or the acquisition of equipment.

(b) The district board shall adopt an ordinance establishing a schedule of fees. Before either approving an increase in an existing fee or initially imposing a new fee, the district board shall publish notice of its intention to establish a schedule of fees pursuant to Section 6066 of the Government Code. The notice shall state the time and place of the meeting, including a general explanation of the matter to be considered, and a statement that the data required by subdivision (d) is available.

(c) The district board shall mail the notice of the meeting at least 14 days before the meeting to any interested party who has filed a written request with the district board for mailed notice of the meeting on new or increased fees. Any written request for mailed notice is valid for one year from the date on which it is filed unless a renewal request is filed. Renewal requests for mailed notice shall be filed on or before April 1 of each year. The district board may establish a reasonable annual charge for sending these notices based on the estimated cost of providing that service.

(d) At least 10 days before the meeting, the district board shall make available to the public, data indicating the amount of cost, or estimated cost, required to provide the service or the cost of enforcing any regulation for which the fee is charged and the revenue sources anticipated to provide the service or the cost of enforcing any regulation, including general fund revenues.

(e) Any costs incurred by a district in conducting the meeting required by this section may be recovered from fees charged for the service or the cost of enforcing any regulation which were the subject of the meeting.

(f) At the meeting, the district board shall hear and consider any objections or protests to the proposed schedule of fees.

(Repealed and added by Stats. 1987, Ch. 1013, Sec. 11.)

13917.

A district board may charge residents or taxpayers of the district a fee authorized pursuant to Section 13916 which is less than the fee which it charges to nonresidents or nontaxpayers of the district.

(Amended by Stats. 1988, Ch. 465, Sec. 9. Effective August 22, 1988.)

13918.

Notwithstanding Section 6103 of the Government Code, a district board may charge a fee authorized pursuant to Section 13916 to other public agencies.

(Repealed and added by Stats. 1987, Ch. 1013, Sec. 11.)

13919.

A district board may waive payment of a fee authorized pursuant to Section 13916 when it determines that payment would not be in the public interest. Before waiving payment of any fee, a district board shall adopt a resolution which specifies the policies and procedures governing waivers.

(Repealed and added by Stats. 1987, Ch. 1013, Sec. 11.)

CHAPTER 9. General Obligation Bonds [13925 - 13938]

(Chapter 9 added by Stats. 1987, Ch. 1013, Sec. 11.)

13925.

Whenever a district board determines that it is necessary to incur a general obligation bonded indebtedness for the acquisition or construction of any real property or other capital expense or for funding or refunding of any outstanding indebtedness, the district board shall adopt a resolution making determinations and calling an election on a proposition to incur indebtedness and to issue general obligation bonds.

(Repealed and added by Stats. 1987, Ch. 1013, Sec. 11.)

13926.

The resolution shall state:

(a) The purpose for which the proposed debt is to be incurred, which may include expenses for the authorization, issuance, and sale of bonds.

(b) The amount of debt to be incurred.

(c) The maximum term of the bonds, not to exceed 30 years.

(d) The maximum rate of interest to be paid, not to exceed the maximum rate permitted pursuant to Article 7 (commencing with Section 53530) of Chapter 3 of Part 1 of Division 2 of Title 5 of the Government Code.

(e) The measure to be submitted to the voters.

(f) The date the election will be held.

(g) Any other matters that are required pursuant to the Uniform District Election Law, Part 4 (commencing with Section 10500) of Division 10 of the Elections Code.

(Amended by Stats. 1994, Ch. 923, Sec. 139. Effective January 1, 1995.)

13927.

The election shall be conducted pursuant to the Uniform District Election Law, Part 4 (commencing with Section 10500) of Division 10 of the Elections Code.

(Amended by Stats. 1994, Ch. 923, Sec. 140. Effective January 1, 1995.)

13928.

If two-thirds of voters voting upon the proposition favor incurring the indebtedness and issuing the bonds, the district board may adopt resolutions to issue bonds for all or any part of the amount of the indebtedness.
(Repealed and added by Stats. 1987, Ch. 1013, Sec. 11.)
13929.
The district board may provide for the issuance of bonds in any amounts, in any series, and on any terms, provided that they do not exceed the limits approved by the voters.
(Repealed and added by Stats. 1987, Ch. 1013, Sec. 11.)
13930.
The district board shall adopt a resolution prescribing the form and denomination of the bonds and any coupons. The resolution shall specify the dates on which all or any part of the principal shall become due and payable. The payment of the first installment or principal may be deferred for a maximum period not to exceed five years from the date on which the district board issues the first bonds or first bonds in each series.
(Repealed and added by Stats. 1987, Ch. 1013, Sec. 11.)
13931.
The district board may provide for the call and redemption of bonds before their maturity at times and prices and upon any other terms as it specifies. A bond shall not be subject to call or redemption before maturity unless it contains a recital to that effect or unless a statement to that effect is printed on it.
(Repealed and added by Stats. 1987, Ch. 1013, Sec. 11.)
13932.
The principal and interest of the bonds shall be payable in lawful money of the United States at the office of the district treasurer or any other place, at the option of the bondholder.
(Repealed and added by Stats. 1987, Ch. 1013, Sec. 11.)
13933.
(a) The bonds shall be dated, numbered consecutively, and be signed by the president of the district board and the district treasurer. The district treasurer shall sign any coupons. Any signatures or countersignatures may be mechanically reproduced by any means, except that one of the signatures shall be signed by hand.
(b) If the president of the district board or the district treasurer whose signature appears on a bond or coupon ceases to hold that office before the delivery of the bonds or the coupons to the purchaser, the signature is nevertheless valid and sufficient for any purpose as if the president or treasurer had remained in office until the delivery of the bonds or coupons.
(Repealed and added by Stats. 1987, Ch. 1013, Sec. 11.)
13934.
(a) Before selling the bonds or coupons, the district board shall give notice inviting sealed bids. At a minimum, the district board shall publish notice at least once in a newspaper of general circulation in the district at least 10 days before the deadline for receiving the bids.
(b) The district board shall award the sale of the bonds to the highest responsible bidder.
(c) If the district board does not receive any bids or if it determines that the bids received are not satisfactory as to price or responsibility of the bidders, it may reject all bids, if any, and either readvertise or sell the bonds at private sale.
(Repealed and added by Stats. 1987, Ch. 1013, Sec. 11.)
13935.
(a) All premiums and accrued interest received from the sale of the bonds shall be deposited with the district treasurer in a special bond service fund to be used for the payment of the principal of and interest on the bonds, and the remainder of the proceeds of the bonds shall be placed to the credit of the proper improvement fund and applied exclusively to the purpose and object recited in the proposition approved by the voters.
(b) When the purpose and object have been accomplished, any moneys remaining in the improvement fund shall be transferred to the special bond service fund. When the purpose and object have been accomplished and all principal and interest on the bonds have been paid, any balance of money then remaining shall be transferred to the general fund of the district.
(Repealed and added by Stats. 1987, Ch. 1013, Sec. 11.)
13936.
Any general obligation bonds issued by a district have the same force, value, and use as bonds issued by a city and the bonds and the interest on the bonds are exempt from all taxation within the State of California.
(Repealed and added by Stats. 1987, Ch. 1013, Sec. 11.)
13937.
A district shall not incur a bonded indebtedness in excess of 10 percent of the assessed value of all taxable property within the district.
(Repealed and added by Stats. 1987, Ch. 1013, Sec. 11.)
13938.
(a) After incurring a general obligation indebtedness, and annually thereafter until the indebtedness is paid or until there is a sum in the district treasury in a special bond service fund set apart for that purpose sufficient to meet all payments of principal and interest on that indebtedness as it becomes due, the district board shall adopt a resolution directing the county tax collector to levy a tax on behalf of the district.
(b) The tax shall be in addition to all other taxes levied by and for the district and shall be collected in the same manner and at the same time as county taxes. A county may recover its costs as provided by Section 29142 of the Government Code.

(c) The rate of the tax shall be fixed to result in proceeds which are sufficient to pay any principal and interest which will become due before the next proceeds of a tax to be levied will be available.
(Amended by Stats. 2001, Ch. 176, Sec. 41. Effective January 1, 2002.)

CHAPTER 10. Service Zones [13950 - 13956]

(Chapter 10 added by Stats. 1987, Ch. 1013, Sec. 11.)
13950.
(a) Whenever a district board determines that it is in the public interest to provide different services, to provide different levels of service, or to raise additional revenues within specific areas of the district, it may form one or more service zones pursuant to this chapter.
(b) The district board shall initiate proceedings for the formation of a new zone by adopting a resolution which shall do all of the following:
(1) State that the proposal is made pursuant to this chapter.
(2) Set forth a description of the boundaries of the territory to be included in the zone.
(3) State the different services, different levels of service, or additional revenues which the zone will provide.
(4) Set forth the methods by which those services or levels of service will be financed.
(5) State the reasons for forming the zone.
(6) Propose a name or number for the zone.
(7) Fix the date, time, and place for the public hearing on the formation of the zone.
(c) The district board shall publish notice of the hearing, including the information required by subdivision (b), pursuant to Section 6061 of the Government Code in one or more newspapers of general circulation in the district. The district board shall mail the notice to all owners of property within the proposed zone. The district board shall post the notice in at least three public places within the territory of the proposed zone.
(d) At the hearing, the district board shall hear and consider any protests to the formation of the zone. At the conclusion of the hearing, the district board may adopt a resolution ordering the formation of the zone.
(Repealed and added by Stats. 1987, Ch. 1013, Sec. 11.)
13951.
A district board may change the boundaries of a service zone or dissolve a zone by following the procedures in Section 13950.
(Repealed and added by Stats. 1987, Ch. 1013, Sec. 11.)
13952.
A local agency formation commission shall have no power or duty to review and approve or disapprove a proposal to create a service zone, a proposal to change the boundaries of a zone, or a proposal to dissolve a zone.
(Repealed and added by Stats. 1987, Ch. 1013, Sec. 11.)
13953.
As determined by the district board, a service zone may provide any service at any level within its boundaries which the district may provide.
(Repealed and added by Stats. 1987, Ch. 1013, Sec. 11.)
13954.
As determined by the district board and pursuant to the requirements of this part, a service zone may exercise any fiscal powers within its boundaries that the district may exercise.
(Repealed and added by Stats. 1987, Ch. 1013, Sec. 11.)
13955.
Any taxes, special taxes, assessments, or fees which are intended solely for the support of services within a zone shall be levied, assessed, and collected only within the boundaries of the zone.
(Added by Stats. 1987, Ch. 1013, Sec. 11.)
13956.
To assist it in the operation of a service zone, the district board may appoint one or more advisory groups composed of persons who reside in or own property in the zone.
(Added by Stats. 1987, Ch. 1013, Sec. 11.)

CHAPTER 11. Employee Relations [13960 - 13970]

(Chapter 11 added by Stats. 1987, Ch. 1013, Sec. 11.)
13960.
(a) The Meyers-Milias-Brown Act, Chapter 10 (commencing with Section 3500) of Division 4 of Title 1 of the Government Code applies to all fire protection districts.
(b) Chapter 4 (commencing with Section 1960) of Part 7 of Division 2 of the Labor Code applies to all fire protection districts.
(Added by Stats. 1987, Ch. 1013, Sec. 11.)
13961.
(a) A district board may adopt an ordinance establishing an employee relations system.
(b) "Employee relations system" as used in this chapter means a civil service system or a merit system.
(Added by Stats. 1987, Ch. 1013, Sec. 11.)
13962.
(a) Upon receipt of a petition proposing an employee relations system for employees of the district, signed by at least 10 percent of the registered voters of the district, the

district board shall either adopt an ordinance providing for the employee relations system, or adopt an ordinance subject to the approval of the voters of the district.

(b) District employees may circulate the petitions described in subdivision (a) at any time when they are not on duty.

(c) If the question is submitted to the voters at a general district election, the notice required by Section 12112 of the Elections Code shall contain a statement of the question to appear on the ballot. If the question is submitted to the voters at a special election, the notice of election and ballot shall contain a statement of the question.

(d) The question placed before the voters shall call for a "Yes" or "No" vote and shall be in substantially the following form:

"Shall the ordinance of the Board of Directors of the _____ (name of the district), adopting an employee relations system for the employees of the district, be approved?"

(e) If a majority of the voters voting on the question approve of the question, the ordinance shall go into effect.

(Amended by Stats. 2006, Ch. 588, Sec. 15. Effective January 1, 2007.)

13963.

When more than one district is governed by the same board of directors, the district board may do all of the following:

(a) Adopt the same set of employee relations rules, regulations, and procedures for any or all districts.

(b) Authorize one examination for any or all districts for each classification of employment, establish one eligibility list, permit qualified candidates to transfer from one district to another, and allow requested changes in assignment.

(c) Adopt one seniority list to be used in the layoff of all employees of any or all districts. Persons laid off due to lack of work shall be eligible for reemployment and shall be reemployed in preference to the employment of new applicants. The district board may set a time limit on the use of this seniority list.

(Added by Stats. 1987, Ch. 1013, Sec. 11.)

13964.

If a county board of supervisors has appointed itself as the district board, it may change to district status any employee of a county fire warden department and the status of any district employee may be changed to that of a county employee, subject to charter provisions relating to employee relations, and the rules, regulations, and procedures of the employee relations system of the employer county.

(Added by Stats. 1987, Ch. 1013, Sec. 11.)

13965.

If the civil service commission or body performing employee relations functions for a district finds that a person has been employed by a city or another district which has, or any portion of which has, been annexed to, included within, or contracts with, the district for all fire protection, rescue, or emergency medical services, in a position classification the duties of which and qualifications for which are substantially the same as those of any position classification in the district, at the request of the district board, the civil service commission or other body may certify, without examination, that person as eligible to hold that district position classification or any lower position classification for which the person is qualified and which would not result in a lower level of salary than was received by the person immediately before the annexation, inclusion, or contract. If a person is employed by the district after certification without examination by the civil service commission or other body because of his or her employment in a position classification of similar duties by a city or district, all time employed in that city or district shall be considered as time employed by the district, to determine seniority rights and salary rates.

(Added by Stats. 1987, Ch. 1013, Sec. 11.)

13966.

(a) In the case of a district where the Board of Supervisors of the County of Santa Clara has appointed itself as the district board of a district, the district board may call an election to be held in the district for the purpose of submitting to the voters of the district the question of whether the district board may provide for a system of binding arbitration for the resolution of impasses in employer-employee relations.

(b) Where the district has created service zones, the election specified in subdivision (a) shall be held only in those zones in which the district provides direct fire protection and not in those zones in which fire protection is provided by contract with other agencies.

(Added by Stats. 1987, Ch. 1013, Sec. 11.)

13967.

A district board may require any employee of the district to be bonded. The district shall pay the cost of the bonds.

(Added by Stats. 1987, Ch. 1013, Sec. 11.)

13968.

A district board may provide for any programs for the benefits of its employees or members of the district board, pursuant to Chapter 2 (commencing with Section 53200) of Part 1 of Division 2 of Title 5 of the Government Code.

(Added by Stats. 1987, Ch. 1013, Sec. 11.)

13969.

A district board shall train all employees of the district who are expected to provide services pursuant to Section 13862, except those whose duties are primarily clerical or administrative, to administer first aid and cardiopulmonary resuscitation, as required pursuant to Section 1797.182. A district board may provide any other training programs for its employees.

(Added by Stats. 1987, Ch. 1013, Sec. 11.)

13970.

A fire protection district shall be considered a "fire district" to grant leaves of absence in lieu of temporary disability payments pursuant to Article 7 (commencing with Section 4850) of Chapter 2 of Part 2 of Division 4 of the Labor Code.

(Added by Stats. 1987, Ch. 1013, Sec. 11.)

PART 4. FIRE COMPANIES IN UNINCORPORATED TOWNS [14825 - 14860]

(Part 4 enacted by Stats. 1939, Ch. 60.)

CHAPTER 1. Organization [14825 - 14833]

(Chapter 1 enacted by Stats. 1939, Ch. 60.)

14825.

(a) Fire companies in unincorporated towns may be organized by filing a certificate signed by the foreman or presiding officer and by the secretary, with the Fire and Rescue Operational Area Coordinator in the same county, or other county agency as designated by ordinance of the county board of supervisors.

(b) Fire companies in incorporated cities may be organized, subject to any local ordinance established pursuant to Section 14832, by filing a certificate signed by the foreman or presiding officer and by the secretary, with the city council or other agency as designated by ordinance of the city council and with the Fire and Rescue Operational Area Coordinator in the same county as the city.

(Amended by Stats. 2008, Ch. 65, Sec. 1. Effective January 1, 2009.)

14826.

The certificate shall set forth the following matters:

(a) The date of organization.

(b) The name of the company.

(c) The names of the officers.

(d) The roll of active volunteer firefighters and those volunteer firefighters on leave.

(e) Where an ordinance has been adopted pursuant to Section 14831, a copy of the determination of the board of supervisors pursuant to Section 14831.

(Amended by Stats. 2008, Ch. 65, Sec. 2. Effective January 1, 2009.)

14827.

The certificate shall be filed by February 1 of each year. The board of supervisors may, by ordinance, require an updated or second filing each year.

(Amended by Stats. 2008, Ch. 65, Sec. 3. Effective January 1, 2009.)

14828.

There shall not be in any one unincorporated town more than one company for each one thousand inhabitants, but one company may be allowed in any town where the population is less than one thousand.

(Enacted by Stats. 1939, Ch. 60.)

14829.

An engine company may consist of not more than 65 certificate members; a hook-and-ladder company of not more than 65 certificate members; a hose company of not more than 25 certificate members; and a rescue squad company of not more than 25 certificate members.

(Amended by Stats. 1979, Ch. 517.)

14830.

Every fire company shall choose or elect a foreman, or president, who is the presiding officer, and a secretary and treasurer.

(Amended by Stats. 2008, Ch. 65, Sec. 4. Effective January 1, 2009.)

14831.

The board of supervisors of a county that has a population of 400,000 or more on or after January 1, 1985, may, by ordinance, regulate the formation and continued existence of fire companies. The board of supervisors may authorize the formation of any new fire company within the county where it determines that a reasonable level of fire services does not already exist and where the provision of supplemental or competing fire services by any other entity would not result in the mismanagement of emergencies or in confusion to those seeking aid.

The board of supervisors may order that any fire companies formed pursuant to this part may continue to exist upon making the determination that the circumstances stated above exist. The board of supervisors may, by ordinance, establish additional regulations and criteria for the establishment and ongoing operation of fire companies organized pursuant to this part.

(Amended by Stats. 2010, Ch. 67, Sec. 1. (SB 902) Effective January 1, 2011.)

14832.

The city council of an incorporated city may, by ordinance, regulate the formation and continued existence of fire companies providing services within its city.

(Added by Stats. 2008, Ch. 65, Sec. 5. Effective January 1, 2009.)

14833.

Fire company vehicles granted exempt California vehicle registration or displaying exempt California license plates shall be properly insured, marked, and identified as a fire company vehicle. The fire company shall not allow those vehicles to be loaned, rented, or used for personal pleasure or by for-profit businesses for private economic gain of a business or contractor. This limitation is not intended to prohibit or hinder the fire company's legitimate use of fire company vehicles for emergency services, including contract arrangements or agreements to provide temporary emergency services or standby services to organizations or governmental agencies requesting those services.

(Added by Stats. 2008, Ch. 65, Sec. 6. Effective January 1, 2009.)

CHAPTER 2. Powers and Duties [14835 - 14845]

(Chapter 2 enacted by Stats. 1939, Ch. 60.)

14835.

Every fire company may establish and adopt bylaws and regulations, and impose penalties, not exceeding five dollars or expulsion for each offense.

(Enacted by Stats. 1939, Ch. 60.)

14836.

Every fire company regularly organized may adopt a seal, having upon it the arms of the State, and the name of the company to which it belongs.

(Enacted by Stats. 1939, Ch. 60.)

14837.

The seal shall be under the control of and for the use of the secretary, and be by him affixed to exempt certificates, certificates of active membership, and such other documents as the by-laws provide.

(Enacted by Stats. 1939, Ch. 60.)

14838.

The secretary of every company having a seal shall take the constitutional oath of office and give a bond as the bylaws provide for the faithful performance of his or her duties.

(Amended by Stats. 2008, Ch. 65, Sec. 7. Effective January 1, 2009.)

14839.

The secretary shall keep a record of all certificates of exemption or active membership, their date, and to whom issued; and when the company has no seal, the clerk shall keep similar entries of certificates issued to obtain county clerk's certificates.

(Enacted by Stats. 1939, Ch. 60.)

14840.

Every certificate is prima facie evidence of the facts stated in it.

(Enacted by Stats. 1939, Ch. 60.)

14841.

The chief or ranking officer of every fire company shall inquire into the cause of, and keep a record of, every fire occurring in the town.

(Amended by Stats. 2008, Ch. 65, Sec. 8. Effective January 1, 2009.)

14842.

The chief or ranking officer shall aid in the enforcement of all fire ordinances, examine buildings in process of erection, report violations of ordinances relating to prevention or extinguishment of fires, and when directed by the proper authorities institute prosecutions therefor.

(Amended by Stats. 2008, Ch. 65, Sec. 9. Effective January 1, 2009.)

14843.

The chief or ranking officer shall perform other duties as may be by proper authority imposed upon him or her.

(Amended by Stats. 2008, Ch. 65, Sec. 10. Effective January 1, 2009.)

14844.

Every chief, if any, shall attend all fires with his or her badge of office conspicuously displayed.

(Amended by Stats. 2008, Ch. 65, Sec. 11. Effective January 1, 2009.)

14845.

The chief or ranking officer shall prevent injury to, take charge of, and preserve all property rescued from fires, and return the property to its owner on the payment of the expenses incurred in saving and keeping it.

(Amended by Stats. 2008, Ch. 65, Sec. 12. Effective January 1, 2009.)

CHAPTER 3. Exemptions [14855 - 14860]

(Chapter 3 enacted by Stats. 1939, Ch. 60.)

14855.

The active volunteer firefighters of volunteer fire companies or departments regularly organized and recognized by the Fire and Rescue Operational Area Coordinator or the county board of supervisors are exempt from military duty, except in case of war, invasion, or insurrection.

(Amended by Stats. 2008, Ch. 65, Sec. 13. Effective January 1, 2009.)

14856.

The burden of providing proof of eligibility for the privileges and exemptions of Section 14855 shall be the responsibility of the volunteer firefighter with the reasonable cooperation of his or her department.

(Repealed and added by Stats. 2008, Ch. 65, Sec. 15. Effective January 1, 2009.)

14860.

Every officer of a fire company or department who willfully issues or causes to be issued any certificate of exemption to a person not entitled to it, is guilty of a misdemeanor.

(Amended by Stats. 2008, Ch. 65, Sec. 19. Effective January 1, 2009.)

PART 4.5. Use of Privately Contracted Private Fire Prevention Resources [14865 - 14868]

(Part 4.5 added by Stats. 2018, Ch. 636, Sec. 1.)

14865.

It is the intent of the Legislature to provide for the highest level of safety for firefighters and the communities they protect by regulating the use of privately contracted private fire prevention resources. Nothing in this part shall be construed or otherwise interpreted to authorize public agencies to contract for firefighting services or other first response services. The Legislature finds and declares that firefighting and fire protection services are a municipal function and a public good to be provided by public agencies and their employees.

(Added by Stats. 2018, Ch. 636, Sec. 1. (AB 2380) Effective January 1, 2019.)

14866.

For purposes of this part, the following terms have the following meanings:

(a) "Department" means the Department of Forestry and Fire Protection.

(b) "Office" means the Governor's Office of Emergency Services.

(Added by Stats. 2018, Ch. 636, Sec. 1. (AB 2380) Effective January 1, 2019.)

14867.

(a) The office, in collaboration with the department and the board of directors of the FIRESCOPE Program, established pursuant to Chapter 3 (commencing with Section 13070) of Part 1, shall develop standards and regulations for any privately contracted private fire prevention resources operating during an active fire incident in California.

(b) (1) In developing standards and regulations, the office shall consider private resource utilization guidelines developed by the FIRESCOPE Program, pursuant to Chapter 3 (commencing with Section 13070) of Part 1.

(2) Regulations developed pursuant to subdivision (a) shall include, but not be limited to, the following requirements:

(A) A privately contracted private fire prevention resource shall heed all evacuation warnings and leave the evacuation area when prompted, until the area is reopened or until they have received incident command authorization to reenter or stay in the area.

(B) A privately contracted private fire prevention resource shall check in with incident command before entering an area.

(C) A privately contracted private fire prevention resource shall be equipped with a Global Positioning System (GPS) tracking device so its liaison at incident command, as described in subparagraph (D), and incident command, can locate the privately contracted private fire prevention resource in the event of an evacuation. The Global Positioning System used by the privately contracted private fire prevention resource shall be compatible with the state's incident management and situational awareness tracking system.

(D) A privately contracted private fire prevention resource shall have a liaison at incident command that is available to incident command at all times and can contact the privately contracted private fire prevention resource at any time.

(E) (i) A privately contracted private fire prevention resource shall monitor incident command radio frequencies assigned to a particular incident, as permitted under Part 90 of Title 47 of the Code of Federal Regulations.

(ii) The regulations shall include a prohibition on a privately contracted private fire prevention resource from communicating on incident command radio frequencies, without prior approval from incident command.

(F) A privately contracted private fire prevention resource shall, whenever possible, focus on prefire treatment activities and pretreatment of values-at-risk and other nonemergency activities outside of a restricted area to ensure safety, clear command and control, and minimize potential liability issues.

(Added by Stats. 2018, Ch. 636, Sec. 1. (AB 2380) Effective January 1, 2019.)

14868.

(a) The office, in collaboration with the department and the board of directors of the FIRESCOPE Program, shall develop regulations to govern the use of equipment used by privately contracted private fire prevention resources during an active fire incident. The regulations shall include, but not be limited to, the following:

(1) All equipment shall be clearly labeled nonemergency.

(2) Privately contracted private fire prevention resource vehicles shall not use emergency lights or sirens.

(3) Privately contracted private fire prevention resource vehicles shall not have any labeling that indicates emergency personnel or fire department.

(b) The office may consult with both private sector entities that provide privately contracted private fire prevention resources and public sector fire agencies before developing the regulations as required by this section.

(Added by Stats. 2018, Ch. 636, Sec. 1. (AB 2380) Effective January 1, 2019.)

PART 5. ABATEMENT OF HAZARDOUS WEEDS AND RUBBISH [14875 - 14922]

(Heading of Part 5 amended by Stats. 1970, Ch. 154.)

CHAPTER 1. General Provisions [14875 - 14876]

(Chapter 1 enacted by Stats. 1939, Ch. 60.)

14875.

"Weeds," as used in this part, means vegetation growing upon streets, sidewalks, or private property in any county, including any fire protection district and may include any of the following:

(a) Vegetation that bears seeds of a downy or wingy nature.

(b) Vegetation that is not pruned or is otherwise neglected so as to attain such large growth as to become, when dry, a fire menace to adjacent improved property.

(c) Vegetation that is otherwise noxious or dangerous.

(d) Poison oak and poison ivy when the conditions of growth are such as to constitute a menace to the public health.

(e) Dry grass, stubble, brush, litter, or other flammable material which endangers the public safety by creating a fire hazard in an urbanized portion of an unincorporated area which has been zoned for single and multiple residence purposes.
(Amended by Stats. 2005, Ch. 260, Sec. 2. Effective January 1, 2006.)

14876.
Weeds may be declared a public nuisance and may be abated as provided in this part.
(Enacted by Stats. 1939, Ch. 60.)

CHAPTER 2. Resolution [14880 - 14884]

(Chapter 2 enacted by Stats. 1939, Ch. 60.)

14880.
Whenever weeds are growing upon any street, sidewalk, or on private property in any county, the board of supervisors, by resolution, may declare the weeds a public nuisance.
(Enacted by Stats. 1939, Ch. 60.)

14881.
The resolution shall refer, by the name under which it is commonly known, to the street, highway, or road upon which the nuisance exists, upon which the sidewalks are located, or upon which the private property affected fronts or abuts or nearest to which the private property is located.
(Enacted by Stats. 1939, Ch. 60.)

14882.
If the private property fronts or abuts upon more than one street, highway, or road, it is necessary to refer to only one of the streets, highways, or roads.
(Enacted by Stats. 1939, Ch. 60.)

14883.
The resolution shall describe the property upon which, or in front of which the nuisance exists by describing the property by reference to the tract, block, lot, code area and parcel number as used in the records of the county assessor or in accordance with the map used in describing property for taxation purposes. No other description is necessary.
(Amended by Stats. 1959, Ch. 1534.)

14884.
Any number of streets, highways, roads, or parcels of private property may be included in one resolution.
(Enacted by Stats. 1939, Ch. 60.)

CHAPTER 3. Notice to Destroy Weeds [14890 - 14902]

(Chapter 2 enacted by Stats. 1939, Ch. 60.)

ARTICLE 1. Persons Authorized to Give Notice [14890- 14890.]
(Article 1 enacted by Stats. 1939, Ch. 60:)

14890.
The board of supervisors shall designate the person to give notice to destroy weeds. This may be any one of the following:
(a) The county agricultural commissioner.
(b) The county forester.
(c) The county board of forestry.
(d) Any other officer, board, or commission.
(Enacted by Stats. 1939, Ch. 60.)

ARTICLE 2. Contents of Notice [14891 - 14892]
(Article 2 enacted by Stats. 1939, Ch. 60.)

14891.
The notices shall be headed "Notice to destroy weeds," in words not less than one inch in height.
(Enacted by Stats. 1939, Ch. 60.)

14892.
The notice shall be substantially in the following form:

NOTICE TO DESTROY WEEDS.

Notice is hereby given that on the _____ day of _____, 19__, the board of supervisors of _____ county passed a resolution declaring that noxious or dangerous weeds were growing upon or in front of the property on, or nearest to _____ street (or road), in said county, and more particularly described in said resolution and that the same constitute a public nuisance which must be abated by the removal of said noxious or dangerous weeds, otherwise they will be removed and the nuisance will be abated by the county authorities, in which case the cost of such removal shall be assessed upon the lots and lands from which or in front of which such weeds are removed, and such cost will constitute a lien upon such lots or lands until paid. Reference is hereby made to said resolution for further particulars.

All property owners having any objections to the proposed removal of such weeds are hereby notified to attend a meeting of the board of supervisors of said county, to be held (give date), when their objections will be heard and given due consideration.
Dated this _____ day of _____, 19__.

(*Title of officer, board or commission causing notices to be posted.*)

(Enacted by Stats. 1939, Ch. 60.)

ARTICLE 3. Posting and Publishing Notice [14893 - 14896]
(Heading of Article 3 amended by Stats. 1959, Ch. 60.)

14893.
The notices shall be conspicuously posted in front of the property on which or in front of which the nuisance exists, or if the property has no frontage upon any street, highway or road then upon the portion of the property nearest to a street, highway or road, or most likely to give actual notice to the owner.
(Enacted by Stats. 1939, Ch. 60.)

14894.
The notices shall be posted not more than one hundred feet in distance apart, but at least one notice shall be posted on each lot or parcel.
(Enacted by Stats. 1939, Ch. 60.)

14895.
Notice of the hearing prescribed in Section 14892 shall be published once in a newspaper of general circulation printed and published in the county, not less than 10 days prior to the date of the hearing.
(Added by Stats. 1959, Ch. 60.)

14896.
As an alternative to posting and publication, notice in the form required in Section 14892 may be mailed to the property owners as their names and addresses appear from the last equalized assessment role, or as they are known to the clerk.
(Added by Stats. 1977, Ch. 579.)

ARTICLE 4. Hearing on Notice [14898 - 14899]
(Article 4 enacted by Stats. 1939, Ch. 60.)

14898.
At the time stated in the notices, the board of supervisors shall hear and consider all objections or protests, if any, to the proposed removal of weeds, and may continue the hearing from time to time.
(Enacted by Stats. 1939, Ch. 60.)

14899.
Upon the conclusion of the hearing the board shall allow or overrule any or all objections, whereupon the board shall acquire jurisdiction to proceed and perform the work of removal, and the decision of the board on the matter is final, except as provided in Sections 14920 and 14921 of this code.
(Amended by Stats. 1941, Ch. 69.)

ARTICLE 5. Proceedings After Hearing on Notice [14900 - 14902]
(Article 5 enacted by Stats. 1939, Ch. 60.)

14900.
After final action is taken by the board on the disposition of any protests or objections or in case no protests or objections are received, the board shall order the officer, board or commission causing the notices to be posted to abate the nuisance, or to cause it to be abated by having the weeds removed.
(Enacted by Stats. 1939, Ch. 60.)

14900.5.
If the nuisance is seasonal and recurrent, the board of supervisors shall so declare. Thereafter, such seasonal and recurring weeds shall be abated every year without the necessity of any further hearing.
(Added by Stats. 1939, Ch. 1018.)

14900.6.
In the case of weeds which have previously been declared to constitute a seasonal and recurring nuisance, it is sufficient to mail a post card notice to the owners of the property as they and their addresses appear upon the current assessment roll.

The notice shall refer to and describe the property and shall state that noxious or dangerous weeds of a seasonal and recurrent nature are growing on or in front of the property, and that the same constitute a public nuisance which must be abated by the removal of said noxious or dangerous weeds, and that otherwise they will be removed and the nuisance will be abated by the county authorities, in which case the cost of such removal shall be assessed upon the lot and lands from which or in front of which such weeds are removed and that such cost will constitute a lien upon such lots or lands until paid.
(Added by Stats. 1939, Ch. 1018.)

14901.
The officer, board or commission, and his or its assistants, deputies, employees, or contracting agents, or other representatives may enter upon private property for the purpose of removing the weeds.
(Enacted by Stats. 1939, Ch. 60.)

14902.
Before the arrival of the officer, board, or commission, or their representatives, any property owner may remove weeds at his or her own expense. Nevertheless, in any case in which an order to abate is issued, the board by resolution or motion may further order that a special assessment and lien be imposed pursuant to Section 14912. In that case the assessment and lien shall be limited to the costs incurred by the responsible agency in enforcing abatement upon the parcels, including investigation, boundary determination, measurement, clerical, and other related costs.
(Amended by Stats. 1982, Ch. 352, Sec. 3.)

CHAPTER 4. Expense of Abatement [14905 - 14922]

(Chapter 4 enacted by Stats. 1939, Ch. 60.)

ARTICLE 1. Determination and Notice [14905 - 14906]

(Article 1 enacted by Stats. 1939, Ch. 60.)

14905.

The officer, board or commission abating the nuisance shall keep an account of the cost of abatement in front of or on each separate parcel of land and shall render an itemized report in writing to the board of supervisors showing the cost of removing the weeds on or in front of each separate lot or parcel of land, or both.

(Enacted by Stats. 1939, Ch. 60.)

14906.

Before the report is submitted to the board of supervisors, a copy of it shall be posted for at least three days on or near the chamber door of the board with a notice of the time when the report will be submitted to the board for confirmation.

(Amended by Stats. 1959, Ch. 60.)

ARTICLE 2. Hearing on Report [14910 - 14912]

(Article 2 enacted by Stats. 1939, Ch. 60.)

14910.

At the time fixed for receiving and considering the report, the board shall hear it and any objections of any of the property owners liable to be assessed for the work of abatement.

(Enacted by Stats. 1939, Ch. 60.)

14911.

Thereupon the board may make such modifications in the report as it deems necessary, after which, by order or resolution, the report shall be confirmed.

(Enacted by Stats. 1939, Ch. 60.)

14912.

The amount of the costs for abating the nuisance in front of or upon the various parcels of the land mentioned in the report as confirmed and the amount of the costs incurred by the responsible agency in enforcing abatement upon the parcels, including investigation, boundary determination, measurement, clerical and other related costs, shall constitute special assessments against the respective parcels of land, and are a lien on the property for the amount of the respective assessments. Such lien attaches upon recordation in the office of the county recorder of the county in which the property is situated of a certified copy of the resolution of confirmation. The assessment may be collected at the same time and in the same manner as ordinary municipal ad valorem taxes are collected, and shall be subject to the same penalties and the same procedure and sale in case of delinquency as provided for such taxes. All laws applicable to the levy, collection and enforcement of municipal ad valorem taxes shall be applicable to such assessment, except that if any real property to which such lien would attach has been transferred or conveyed to a bona fide purchaser for value, or if a lien of a bona fide encumbrancer for value has been created and attaches thereon, prior to the date on which the first installment of such taxes would become delinquent, then the lien which would otherwise be imposed by this section shall not attach to such real property and the costs of abatement and the costs of enforcing abatement, as confirmed, relating to such property shall be transferred to the unsecured roll for collection.

(Amended by Stats. 1982, Ch. 352, Sec. 4.)

ARTICLE 3. Collection of Expenses [14915 - 14922]

(Article 3 enacted by Stats. 1939, Ch. 60.)

14915.

A copy of the report, as confirmed, shall be turned over to the auditor of the county, on or before the tenth day of August following such confirmation, and the auditor shall enter the amounts of the respective assessments against the respective parcels of land as they appear on the current assessment roll.

(Amended by Stats. 1939, Ch. 354.)

14916.

The tax collector shall include the amount of the assessment on bills for taxes levied against the respective lots and parcels of land.

(Enacted by Stats. 1939, Ch. 60.)

14917.

Thereafter the amounts of the assessments shall be collected at the same time and in the same manner as county taxes are collected, and are subject to the same penalties and the same procedure and sale in case of delinquency as provided for ordinary county taxes.

(Enacted by Stats. 1939, Ch. 60.)

14918.

All laws applicable to the levy, collection and enforcement of county taxes are applicable to such special assessment taxes.

(Enacted by Stats. 1939, Ch. 60.)

14919.

The county tax collector may, in his discretion, issue separate bills for such special assessment taxes and separate receipts for collection on account of such assessments.

(Enacted by Stats. 1939, Ch. 60.)

14920.

All or any portion of any such special assessment, penalty or costs heretofore or hereafter entered, shall on order of the board of supervisors be canceled by the auditor if uncollected, or, except in the case provided for in subdivision (e) hereof, refunded by the county treasurer if collected, if it or they were entered, charged or paid:

(a) More than once;

(b) Through clerical error;

(c) Through the error or mistake of the board of supervisors or of the officer, board or commission designated by them to give notice or to destroy the weeds, in respect to any material fact, including the case where the cost report rendered and confirmed as hereinbefore provided shows the county abated the weeds but such is not the actual fact;

(d) Illegally;

(e) On property acquired after the lien date by the State or by any county, city, school district or other political subdivision and because of this public ownership not subject to sale for delinquent taxes.

(Added by Stats. 1941, Ch. 69.)

14921.

No order for a refund under the foregoing section shall be made except on a claim:

(a) Verified by the person who paid the special assessment, his guardian, executor, or administrator;

(b) Filed within three years after making of the payment sought to be refunded.

The provisions of this section do not apply to cancellations.

(Added by Stats. 1941, Ch. 69.)

14922.

The lien, whether bonds issued to represent the assessment or otherwise, shall be subordinate to all fixed special assessment liens previously imposed upon the same property, but it shall have priority over all fixed special assessment liens which may thereafter be created against the property. The lien of a reassessment and of a refunding assessment shall be the same as the original assessment to which it relates. A supplemental assessment is a new assessment.

(Added by Stats. 1963, Ch. 1465.)

PART 6. ABATEMENT OF HAZARDOUS WEEDS AND RUBBISH: ALTERNATIVE PROCEDURE [14930 - 14931]

(Part 6 added by Stats. 1970, Ch. 154.)

14930.

The board of supervisors may, by ordinance, compel the owner, lessee, or occupant of buildings, grounds, or lots in the county, to remove dirt, rubbish, weeds, or other rank growths from such property and adjacent sidewalks. If the owner, lessee, or occupant defaults, after notice prescribed by such ordinance, the board may authorize the removal or destruction of the dirt, rubbish, weeds, or rank growths at his expense by a county officer. The board may, by ordinance, prescribe a procedure for such removal or destruction and make the expense a lien upon the real property in accordance with Section 25845 of the Government Code.

(Added by Stats. 1970, Ch. 154.)

14931.

The ordinance may require or provide any of the following:

(a) Require and provide for the removal of grass, weeds, or other obstructions from the sidewalks, parkings, or streets and make the cost of removal a lien upon the abutting property.

(b) Require or provide for the removal from property, lands, or lots of all weeds, rubbish, or other material dangerous or injurious to neighboring property or the health or welfare of residents of the vicinity and make the cost of removal a lien upon the property.

(c) Provide for the enforcement of the lien by the sale of the property or otherwise.

(Added by Stats. 1970, Ch. 154.)

PART 7. CIGARETTE LIGHTERS [14940 - 14943]

(Part 7 added by Stats. 1991, Ch. 904, Sec. 1.)

14940.

The Legislature finds and declares that unreasonable risks of death and serious bodily injury are caused by fires started by the operation of cigarette lighters by children. The Legislature further finds and declares that these risks are sufficiently severe to require the enactment of standards to reduce the risks.

(Added by Stats. 1991, Ch. 904, Sec. 1.)

14941.

As used in this part, the following terms shall have the following meanings:

(a) "Cigarette lighter" means a device used to light cigarettes, cigars, and pipes, but does not mean a match. "Cigarette lighter" includes a device, such as a watch, that may be used to light cigarettes, cigars, and pipes even though it is primarily used for other purposes. "Cigarette lighter" does not include lighters that are refillable and have a gross fueled weight of at least 35 grams.

(b) "Operate" means the ability to cause a cigarette lighter to ignite.

(c) "Special design" means a design of a cigarette lighter that results in the cigarette lighter being significantly difficult for children under five years of age to operate.

(Added by Stats. 1991, Ch. 904, Sec. 1.)

14942.

(a) The State Fire Marshal shall adopt regulations by January 1, 1994, that specify standards for the special design of cigarette lighters, using an 80 percent acceptance criterion with respect to safety features that prevent operation of the lighters by children five years of age or younger. The State Fire Marshal shall select a test protocol from those which have been submitted, on or before the effective date of this act, to the Consumer Products Safety Commission of the United States. If federal standards for the special design of cigarette lighters are adopted, the federal standard shall take precedence over a regulation adopted pursuant to this section, and the regulation shall have no force or effect.

(b) Each manufacturer shall provide for the testing of its products that are subject to this section, through laboratories approved by the State Fire Marshal, and shall bear the cost of product testing according to the approved plan and test protocol. The State Fire Marshal may collect fees from manufacturers to pay for the application and approval process in conjunction with administering this section. Fees collected pursuant to this section shall be deposited into the Cigarette Lighter Safety Account in the General Fund, which is hereby created. Moneys in that account shall be available, upon appropriation by the Legislature, for reimbursement of the State Fire Marshal's costs in processing applications and approvals under this section. This section shall remain operative only if and when federal standards for the special design of cigarette lighters for the purpose stated in this section are not in effect.

(Added by Stats. 1991, Ch. 904, Sec. 1. Inoperative, by its own provisions, when federal standards are in effect.)

14943.

(a) No person shall sell, offer for sale, or distribute a cigarette lighter that does not comply with the standards adopted by the State Fire Marshal pursuant to Section 14942.

(b) Any person who violates subdivision (a) is guilty of an infraction and shall be punished by a fine of up to one hundred dollars ($100) for each cigarette lighter that is sold in violation of subdivision (a).

(c) This section shall not become operative until the State Fire Marshal adopts standards pursuant to Section 14942 and shall be operative only when those regulations are in effect as provided in subdivision (a) of Section 14942.

(Added by Stats. 1991, Ch. 904, Sec. 1. Section operative, by its own provisions, only when state regulations specified in Section 14942 are in effect.)

PART 8. CIGARETTES [14950 - 14959]

(Part 8 added by Stats. 2005, Ch. 633, Sec. 2.)

14950.

(a) This part shall be known, and may be cited, as the California Cigarette Fire Safety and Firefighter Protection Act.

(b) As used in this part, the following terms have the following meanings:

(1) "Cigarette" means a cigarette as defined in Section 30003 of the Revenue and Taxation Code, but does not include a little cigar. "Little cigar" means any roll of tobacco wrapped in a leaf of tobacco or any substance containing tobacco and weighing not more than three pounds per thousand.

(2) "Department" means the California Department of Tax and Fee Administration.

(3) "Distributor" means a distributor as defined in Section 30011 of the Revenue and Taxation Code.

(4) "Manufacturer" means any of the following:

(A) An entity that manufactures or otherwise produces cigarettes or causes cigarettes to be manufactured or produced anywhere that the manufacturer intends to be sold in the state, including cigarettes intended to be sold in the United States through an importer.

(B) The first purchaser anywhere that intends to resell in the United States cigarettes manufactured anywhere that the original manufacturer or maker does not intend to be sold in the United States.

(C) An entity that becomes a successor of an entity described in subparagraph (A) or (B).

(5) "Offer to sell" means to offer or agree to sell.

(6) "Package" means package as defined in Section 30015 of the Revenue and Taxation Code.

(7) "Quality control and quality assurance program" means the laboratory procedures implemented to ensure that operator bias, systematic and nonsystematic methodological errors, and equipment-related problems do not affect the results of the testing. This program ensures that the testing repeatability remains within the required repeatability values stated in paragraph (5) of subdivision (a) of Section 14952 for all test trials used to certify cigarettes in accordance with this part.

(8) "Repeatability" means the range of values within which the repeat results of cigarette test trials from a single laboratory will fall 95 percent of the time.

(9) "Retailer" means a person who engages in the sale of cigarettes, but not for the purpose of resale.

(10) "Sale" or "sell" means any transfer, exchange, or barter, in any manner or by any means whatever, or any agreement for these purposes. The giving of cigarettes as samples, prizes, or gifts, and the exchanging of cigarettes for any consideration other than money are considered sales.

(11) "Stamp and meter impression" means stamp and meter impression as defined in Section 30018 of the Revenue and Taxation Code.

(12) "Wholesaler" means a wholesaler as defined in Section 30016 of the Revenue and Taxation Code.

(Amended by Stats. 2018, Ch. 613, Sec. 1. (SB 1408) Effective January 1, 2019.)

14951.

(a) A person shall not sell, offer, or possess for sale in this state cigarettes not in compliance with the following requirements:

(1) The cigarettes are tested by the manufacturer in accordance with the test method prescribed in subdivision (a) of Section 14952.

(2) The cigarettes meet the performance standard specified in subdivision (b) of Section 14952.

(3) The cigarettes meet the marking requirement of Section 14954.

(4) A written certification is filed by the manufacturer with the State Fire Marshal in accordance with Section 14953.

(b) This section does not prohibit distributors, wholesalers, or retailers from selling their inventory of cigarettes existing on January 1, 2007, if both of the following conditions are met:

(1) The distributors, wholesalers, or retailers can establish that California tax stamps or meter impressions were affixed to the cigarettes pursuant to Section 30163 of the Revenue and Taxation Code before January 31, 2007.

(2) The distributors, wholesalers, or retailers can establish that the inventory was purchased before January 1, 2007, in comparable quantity to the inventory purchased during the same period of 2005.

(Amended by Stats. 2018, Ch. 613, Sec. 2. (SB 1408) Effective January 1, 2019.)

14952.

(a) (1) Testing of cigarettes shall be conducted in accordance with the American Society of Testing and Materials (ASTM) Standard E2187-04, "Standard Test Method for Measuring the Ignition Strength of Cigarettes." However, a subsequent ASTM Standard Test Method may be adopted upon finding that the subsequent method does not result in a change in the percentage of full-length burns exhibited by any tested cigarette when compared to the percentage of full-length burns that the same cigarette would exhibit when tested in accordance with ASTM Standard E2187-04 and the testing requirements in paragraphs (2) to (5), inclusive, and the performance standard specified in subdivision (b).

(2) Testing shall be conducted on 10 layers of filter paper.

(3) Forty replicate tests shall comprise a complete test trial for each cigarette tested.

(4) The performance standard required by subdivision (b) shall only be applied to a complete test trial.

(5) Laboratories conducting testing in accordance with this subdivision shall implement a quality control and quality assurance program that includes a procedure that will determine the repeatability of the testing results. The repeatability value shall be no greater than 0.19 pursuant to subdivision (b).

(b) When tested in accordance with subdivision (a), no more than 25 percent of the cigarettes tested in a test trial shall exhibit full-length burns.

(c) Each cigarette listed in a certification submitted pursuant to Section 14953 that uses lowered permeability bands in the cigarette paper to achieve compliance with the performance standard set forth in subdivision (b) shall have at least two nominally identical bands on the paper surrounding the tobacco column. At least one complete band shall be located at least 15 millimeters from the lighting end of the cigarette. For cigarettes on which the bands are positioned by design, there shall be at least two bands fully located at least 15 millimeters from the lighting end and 10 millimeters from the filter end of the tobacco column or 10 millimeters from the labeled end of the tobacco column for a nonfiltered cigarette.

(d) The manufacturer or manufacturers of a cigarette that cannot be tested in accordance with the test method prescribed in subdivision (a) may employ a test method and performance standard for that cigarette that is equivalent to the performance standard prescribed in subdivision (b). The manufacturer or manufacturers may employ that test method and performance standard to certify that cigarette pursuant to Section 14953. All other applicable requirements of this part shall apply to the manufacturer or manufacturers of that cigarette.

(e) This section does not require additional testing if cigarettes are tested consistent with this section for any other purpose.

(f) In order to ensure compliance with the performance standard specified in subdivision (b), data from testing conducted by manufacturers to comply with this performance standard shall be kept on file by these manufacturers for a period of three years after the initial date of certification and for a period of three years after each recertification required by subdivision (c) of Section 14953 and shall be sent to the State Fire Marshal and the Attorney General upon his or her request.

(g) This section shall be implemented in accordance with the implementation and substance of the New York Fire Safety Standards for Cigarettes that are effective on June 28, 2004.

(Added by Stats. 2005, Ch. 633, Sec. 2. Effective January 1, 2006. Operative January 1, 2007, by Section 14960.)

14953.

(a) Each manufacturer shall submit a written certification to the State Fire Marshal attesting that each cigarette listed in the certification has been tested in accordance with subdivision (a) of Section 14952 and meets the performance standard set forth in subdivision (b) of that section.

(b) Each cigarette listed in the certification shall be described with the following information:

(1) Brand.

(2) Style (for example, light, ultra light).

(3) Length in millimeters.

(4) Circumference in millimeters.

(5) Flavor (for example, menthol, chocolate) if applicable.

(6) Filter or nonfilter.

(7) Package description (for example, soft pack, box).

(8) Marking approved in accordance with Section 14954.

(c) Each cigarette certified under this section shall be recertified every three years.

(d) Manufacturers certifying cigarettes in accordance with this section shall provide a copy of the certifications to all distributors and wholesalers to which they sell cigarettes and shall also provide sufficient copies of an illustration of the cigarette packaging marking utilized by the manufacturer pursuant to Section 14954 for each retailer to which the distributors and wholesalers sell cigarettes. Distributors and wholesalers shall provide a copy of these cigarette packaging markings received from manufacturers to all retailers to which they sell cigarettes.
(Added by Stats. 2005, Ch. 633, Sec. 2. Effective January 1, 2006. Operative January 1, 2007, by Section 14960.)

14954.
(a) Cigarettes that are certified by a manufacturer in accordance with Section 14953 shall be marked on the packaging and case to indicate compliance with the requirements of this part. Marking shall be in 8-point type or larger and consist of one of the following:
(1) Modification of the universal product code to include a visible mark printed at or around the area of that code. The mark may consist of alphanumeric or symbolic characters permanently stamped, engraved, embossed or printed in conjunction with the universal product code.
(2) Any visible combination of alphanumeric or symbolic characters permanently stamped, engraved, or embossed upon the cigarette packaging or cellophane wrap.
(3) Printed, stamped, engraved, or embossed text on the cigarette packaging that indicates that the cigarettes meet California standards.
(b) Before a certified cigarette can be sold in the state, a manufacturer shall submit its proposed marking to the State Fire Marshal. The State Fire Marshal shall approve the marking upon a finding that it is compliant with the criteria outlined in subdivision (a). Proposed markings shall be deemed approved if the State Fire Marshal fails to act within 10 business days of receiving a proposed marking. A marking in use and approved for the sale of cigarettes in the State of New York shall be deemed approved.
(c) A manufacturer must use only one marking and must apply this marking uniformly for all packagings, including, but not limited to, packages, cartons, and cases, and brands marketed by that manufacturer.
(d) A manufacturer who modifies its marking shall notify the State Fire Marshal of this change and submit to the State Fire Marshal a copy of the new marking which shall comply with subdivisions (a) and (b).
(Added by Stats. 2005, Ch. 633, Sec. 2. Effective January 1, 2006. Operative January 1, 2007, by Section 14960.)

14955.
(a) A manufacturer or any other person or entity that knowingly sells or offers to sell cigarettes other than through retail sale in violation of this part is subject to a civil penalty not to exceed ten thousand dollars ($10,000) for each sale.
(b) A retailer, distributor, or wholesaler that knowingly sells or offers to sell cigarettes in violation of this part shall be subject to the following:
(1) A civil penalty not to exceed five hundred dollars ($500) for each sale or offer for sale in which the total number of cigarettes sold or offered for sale does not exceed 50 packages of cigarettes.
(2) A civil penalty not to exceed one thousand dollars ($1,000) for each sale or offer for sale in which the total number of cigarettes sold or offered for sale exceeds 50 packages of cigarettes.
(c) The civil penalties imposed pursuant to subdivisions (a) and (b) shall be deposited in the Cigarette Fire Safety and Firefighter Protection Fund.
(d) In addition to any other penalty prescribed by law, any corporation, partnership, sole proprietor, limited partnership, or association engaged in the manufacture of cigarettes that knowingly makes a false certification pursuant to Section 14953 shall be subject to a civil penalty not to exceed ten thousand dollars ($10,000) for each false certification.
(e) A person who violates any other provision in this part shall be subject to a civil penalty not to exceed one thousand dollars ($1,000) for each violation. Any cigarettes that have been sold or offered for sale that do not comply with the performance standard required by Section 14952 shall be deemed contraband per se and subject to seizure and disposal by the department or a law enforcement agency.
(f) The Attorney General may bring an action on behalf of the people of the state to restrain further violations of this part and for any other relief that may be appropriate. In any action by the Attorney General to enforce this act, the Attorney General shall be entitled to recover costs of investigation, expert witness fees, costs of the action, and reasonable attorney's fees.
(g) It shall be a defense in any action for civil penalties, that a distributor, wholesaler, retailer, or a person in the stream of commerce relied in good faith on the manufacturer's certificate or marking that the cigarettes comply with this part.
(Amended by Stats. 2018, Ch. 613, Sec. 3. (SB 1408) Effective January 1, 2019.)

14956.
(a) Inspections may be made at any place where cigarettes are sold, offered for sale, or stored or at any site where there is evidence of a violation of subdivision (a) of Section 14951.
(b) Manufacturers, distributors, wholesalers, and retailers shall permit an employee of the department, upon presentation of the appropriate identification and credentials, to enter into, and to conduct an inspection of, any building, facility, site, or place described in subdivision (a).
(c) Any person that refuses to allow an inspection authorized under this section is subject to the penalty imposed by Section 14958.
(Amended by Stats. 2018, Ch. 613, Sec. 4. (SB 1408) Effective January 1, 2019.)

14957.

Upon discovery by the department or a law enforcement agency that a person offers or possesses for sale, or has made a sale of, cigarettes in violation of subdivision (a) of Section 14951, the department or that law enforcement agency may seize and dispose of those cigarettes possessed in violation of this part as contraband per se.
(Amended by Stats. 2018, Ch. 613, Sec. 5. (SB 1408) Effective January 1, 2019.)

14958.
Any person who knowingly fails or refuses to allow an inspection by the department, pursuant to Section 14956, is subject to a civil penalty not to exceed one thousand dollars ($1,000) for each failure or refusal.
(Amended by Stats. 2018, Ch. 613, Sec. 6. (SB 1408) Effective January 1, 2019.)

14959.
This part shall cease to be applicable if federal fire safety standards for cigarettes that preempt this act are enacted and take effect subsequent to the effective date of this act and the State Fire Marshal so notifies the Secretary of State.
(Added by Stats. 2005, Ch. 633, Sec. 2. Effective January 1, 2006. Operative January 1, 2007, by Section 14960.)

DIVISION 12.5. BUILDINGS USED BY THE PUBLIC [16000 - 16604]

(Division 12.5 added by Stats. 1972, Ch. 1130.)

CHAPTER 2. Essential Services Buildings [16000 - 16023]

(Chapter 2 added by Stats. 1985, Ch. 1521, Sec. 1.)

ARTICLE 1. General Provisions [16000 - 16001]
(Article 1 added by Stats. 1985, Ch. 1521, Sec. 1.)
16000.
This chapter shall be known and may be cited as the Essential Services Buildings Seismic Safety Act of 1986.
(Added by Stats. 1985, Ch. 1521, Sec. 1.)

16001.
It is the intent of the Legislature that essential services buildings, which shall be capable of providing essential services to the public after a disaster, shall be designed and constructed to minimize fire hazards and to resist, insofar as practical, the forces generated by earthquakes, gravity, and winds. It is also the intent of the Legislature that the structural systems and details set forth in working drawings and specifications be carefully reviewed by the responsible enforcement agencies using qualified personnel, and that the construction process be carefully and completely inspected. In order to accomplish these purposes, the Legislature intends to provide for the establishment of building standards for earthquake, gravity, fire, and wind resistance based upon current knowledge, and intends that procedures for the design and construction of essential services buildings be subjected to qualified design review and construction inspection. It is further the intent of the Legislature that the nonstructural components vital to the operation of essential services buildings shall also be able to resist, insofar as practical, the forces generated by earthquakes, gravity, fire, and winds. The Legislature recognizes that certain nonstructural components housed in essential services buildings, including, but not limited to, communications systems, main transformers and switching equipment, and emergency backup systems, are essential to facility operations and that these nonstructural components should be given adequate consideration during the design and construction process to assure, insofar as practical, continued operation of the building after a disaster.
(Added by Stats. 1985, Ch. 1521, Sec. 1.)

ARTICLE 2. Definitions [16002 - 16008]
(Article 2 added by Stats. 1985, Ch. 1521, Sec. 1.)
16002.
Unless the context otherwise requires, the definitions in this article govern the construction of this chapter.
(Added by Stats. 1985, Ch. 1521, Sec. 1.)

16003.
"Architect" means a person who is certified under Chapter 3 (commencing with Section 5500) of Division 3 of the Business and Professions Code.
(Added by Stats. 1985, Ch. 1521, Sec. 1.)

16004.
"Civil engineer" means a person who is registered as a civil engineer under Chapter 7 (commencing with Section 6700) of Division 3 of the Business and Professions Code.
(Added by Stats. 1985, Ch. 1521, Sec. 1.)

16005.
"Construction or alteration" includes any construction of, addition to, reconstruction of, or alteration to any essential services building.
(Added by Stats. 1985, Ch. 1521, Sec. 1.)

16006.
"Enforcement agency" means the agency of a city, city and county, or county responsible for building safety within its jurisdiction. The office of the State Architect is the enforcement agency for state-owned facilities or facilities leased by the state.
(Added by Stats. 1985, Ch. 1521, Sec. 1.)

16007.

"Essential services building" means any building, including buildings designed and constructed, for public agencies used, or designed to be used, or any building a portion of which is used or designed to be used, as a fire station, police station, emergency operations center, California Highway Patrol office, sheriff's office, or emergency communication dispatch center.

(Added by Stats. 1985, Ch. 1521, Sec. 1.)

16008.

"Structural engineer" means a person who is authorized to use the title structural engineer under Chapter 7 (commencing with Section 6700) of Division 3 of the Business and Professions Code.

(Added by Stats. 1985, Ch. 1521, Sec. 1.)

ARTICLE 3. General Requirements and Administration [16009 - 16016]
(Article 3 added by Stats. 1985, Ch. 1521, Sec. 1.)

16009.

The appropriate enforcement agency which meets the requirements of Sections 16017 and 16018 shall review the design and inspect the construction of essential services buildings or the reconstruction, alteration, or addition to any essential services building to the extent it deems necessary to ensure that:

(1) When the enforcement agency is a local agency, drawings and specifications comply with the locally adopted editions of the model codes, as defined in Section 18916, the administrative regulations contained in Part 1 (commencing with Section 1-101) of Title 24 of the California Code of Regulations, and the regulations contained in Part 2 (commencing with Section 101), except for Chapters 23 to 30, inclusive, and Chapter 47 of Title 24 of the California Code of Regulations.

(2) When the enforcement agency is the Office of the State Architect, that drawings and specifications comply with all parts of the State Building Standards Code, as contained in Title 24 of the California Code of Regulations, as adopted by that agency.

(3) For the protection of life and property that the work of construction has been performed in accordance with the approved drawings and specifications and this chapter.

(Amended by Stats. 1990, Ch. 72, Sec. 1.)

16010.

Essential services buildings of one-story Type V and Type II N construction that are 2,000 square feet or less in floor area are exempt from the provisions of this chapter.

(Added by Stats. 1985, Ch. 1521, Sec. 1.)

16010.5.

Notwithstanding any other law, the inclusion of office space for or an emergency dispatch center of the Department of the California Highway Patrol in any building constructed, restored, rehabilitated, renovated, or reconstructed pursuant to Article 5.2 (commencing with Section 9112) or Article 5.6 (commencing with Section 9125) of Chapter 1.5 of Part 1 of Division 2 of Title 2 of the Government Code shall not subject any part of those projects to this chapter or any rule, regulation, standard, or requirement promulgated or enforced by the Division of the State Architect pursuant to this chapter.

(Added by Stats. 2019, Ch. 29, Sec. 118. (SB 82) Effective June 27, 2019.)

16011.

Unless a contract for the construction or alteration of an essential services building is entered into prior to July 1, 1986, before adopting any drawings or specifications for the essential services building, the governing board, authority, owner, corporation, or other agency proposing to construct any essential services building shall submit the design calculations, drawings, and specifications of the essential services buildings to the appropriate enforcement agency. The enforcement agency shall stamp the drawings and specifications if the construction or alteration is approved by the enforcement agency. Included with the stamp shall be the signature of the qualified person referred to in Section 16018 or Section 16019.

(Added by Stats. 1985, Ch. 1521, Sec. 1.)

16012.

In each case, the application for approval of the drawings and specifications for essential services buildings shall be accompanied by comprehensive and complete drawings, design calculations, and specifications, and required fees, all of which shall comply with the requirements prescribed by the enforcement agency. This review shall not preclude incremental submission and approval of drawings and specifications.

(Added by Stats. 1985, Ch. 1521, Sec. 1.)

16013.

The enforcement agency shall approve or reject all drawings and specifications for the construction or the alteration of all essential services buildings, and in doing so, shall review the design calculations, drawings, and specifications to ensure compliance with the requirements of this chapter. A record shall be kept by the enforcement agency indicating that design calculations, drawings, and specifications have been reviewed and conform with:

(1) When the enforcement agency is a local agency, the locally adopted editions of the model codes, as defined in Section 18916, the administrative regulations contained in Part 1 (commencing with Section 1-101) of Title 24 of the California Code of Regulations, and the regulations contained in Part 2 (commencing with Section 101), except for Chapters 23 to 30, inclusive, and Chapter 47 of Title 24 of the California Code of Regulations.

(2) When the enforcement agency is the Office of the State Architect, all parts of the State Building Standards Code, as contained in Title 24 of the California Code of Regulations and adopted by that agency.

(Amended by Stats. 1990, Ch. 72, Sec. 2.)

16014.

(a) Except as otherwise provided in subdivision (b), drawings and specifications submitted pursuant to this chapter for construction, reconstruction, remodeling, additions, or alterations which affect structural elements of structures in existence on January 1, 1986, shall be based upon an assessment of the geological conditions of the site and the potential for earthquake damage, relying upon geologic and engineering investigations and studies by personnel who are competent to report on geologic conditions and their potential for causing earthquake damage. One-story Type V and Type II N construction of 4,000 square feet or less shall be exempt from this section, unless the project is within a special studies zone established pursuant to Section 2622 of the Public Resources Code.

(b) The requirements of subdivision (a) may be waived by the enforcement agency if it determines that these requirements for the proposed essential services building project are unnecessary and would not be beneficial to the safety of the public.

(Added by Stats. 1985, Ch. 1521, Sec. 1.)

16015.

All drawings and specifications shall be prepared under the responsible charge of an architect, civil engineer, or structural engineer, who shall sign all drawings and specifications for approval of the enforcement agency. Observation of the work of construction shall be under the general responsible charge of the same architect, civil engineer, or structural engineer when feasible, as determined by the enforcement agency, except that if drawings and specifications do not involve architectural or structural conditions, the drawings and specifications may be prepared and the work of construction may be administered by a registered professional engineer qualified in the branch of engineering that is appropriate to the drawings, specifications, estimates, and work of construction.

(Added by Stats. 1985, Ch. 1521, Sec. 1.)

16016.

Except as provided in Section 16011, on and after July 1, 1986, construction of an essential services building shall not begin unless the drawings and specifications comply with this chapter and the requirements prescribed by the enforcement agency and approval of those drawings and specifications has been obtained from the enforcement agency.

(Added by Stats. 1985, Ch. 1521, Sec. 1.)

ARTICLE 4. Qualifications and Reporting [16017 - 16022.5]
(Article 4 added by Stats. 1985, Ch. 1521, Sec. 1.)

16017.

During construction or alteration of an essential services building, the building owner shall provide for, and the local enforcement agency shall require, competent, adequate, and detailed inspection by a qualified inspector. To be qualified, inspectors shall have an adequate level of expertise and experience in the subject matter for which they have responsibilities for inspection as prescribed by this section. Qualification shall include current certification by the International Conference of Building Officials; or qualifications as an inspector meeting the requirements of subdivision (a) of Section 305 and subdivision (b) of Section 306 of, the 1982 Edition of the Uniform Building Code. Additionally, the architect, civil engineer, or structural engineer responsible for designing the essential services facility is qualified to inspect construction of the facility.

(Added by Stats. 1985, Ch. 1521, Sec. 1.)

16017.5.

(a) Notwithstanding any provision of law to the contrary, including, but not limited to, Part 6 (commencing with Section 8000) of Division 4 of the Civil Code, the Department of General Services may issue a stop work order when construction work on an essential services facility is not being performed in accordance with existing law and would compromise the structural integrity of the building, thereby endangering the public safety. The Department of General Services shall allow construction of incidental and minor nonstructural additions or nonstructural alterations without invoking its stop work authority.

(b) A public board, body, or officer whose construction work on an essential services facility is subject to a stop work order issued pursuant to subdivision (a) shall not be held liable in any action filed against the public board, body, or officer for stopping work as required by the stop work order, or for any delays caused by compliance with the stop work order, except to the extent that an error or omission by the public board, body, or officer is the basis for the issuance of the stop work order.

(Amended by Stats. 2010, Ch. 697, Sec. 38. (SB 189) Effective January 1, 2011. Operative July 1, 2012, by Sec. 105 of Ch. 697.)

16018.

An enforcement agency is qualified to undertake the review of plans, drawings, and specifications for essential services buildings if the enforcement agency has an architect, civil engineer, or structural engineer on its staff or under contract who is responsible for all design review conducted by the enforcement agency and the record prepared under Section 16013.

(Added by Stats. 1985, Ch. 1521, Sec. 1.)

16019.

A jurisdiction whose enforcement agency does not meet the qualifications specified in Sections 16017 and 16018 shall obtain necessary qualified personnel to meet the requirements of this chapter by contracting with other public agencies, private sector firms, or individuals qualified to perform the necessary services.

(Added by Stats. 1985, Ch. 1521, Sec. 1.)

16020.

Periodically, as the work of construction or alteration progresses and whenever the enforcement agency requires, except as exempt under Section 16010, the architect, civil engineer, or structural engineer in general responsible charge of the work of construction, and the registered engineer shall make a report, duly verified by him or her through periodic review of construction, showing that the work during the period covered by the report has been performed and that the materials used and installed are in accordance with the approved drawings and specifications, setting forth any detailed statements of fact required by the enforcement agency.

"Periodic review of construction," as used in this section and as applied to the architect, civil engineer, or structural engineer and the registered engineer, means the knowledge which is obtained from periodic visits to the project site of reasonable frequency for the purpose of general observation of the work, and also which is obtained from the reporting of others as to the progress of the work, testing of materials, inspection and superintendence of the work that is performed between those periodic visits of the architect, civil engineer, or structural engineer, or the registered engineer. The exercise of reasonable diligence to obtain the facts is required. The term "periodic review of construction" does not include responsibility for superintendence of construction processes, site conditions, operations, equipment, personnel, or the maintenance of a safe place to work or any safety in, on, or about the site of work.
(Added by Stats. 1985, Ch. 1521, Sec. 1.)

16021.

Periodically, as the work of construction or alteration progresses and whenever the enforcement agency requires, except as exempt under Section 16010, the inspector on the work and the contractor shall each make a report, duly verified by him or her, showing in his or her own personal knowledge, that the work during the period covered by the report has been performed and that the materials used and installed are in accordance with the approved drawings and specifications, setting forth any detailed statements of fact required by the enforcement agency.

"Personal knowledge" as applied to the inspector, means the actual personal knowledge which is obtained from his or her personal continuous inspection of the work of construction in all stages of its progress at the site where he or she is responsible for inspection and when work is carried out away from the site, that personal knowledge which is obtained from the reporting of others of the testing or inspection of materials and workmanship for compliance with plans, specifications, or applicable standards. The exercise of reasonable diligence to obtain the facts is required.

"Personal knowledge," as applied to the contractor, means the personal knowledge which is obtained from the construction of the building. The exercise of reasonable diligence to obtain the facts is required.
(Added by Stats. 1985, Ch. 1521, Sec. 1.)

16022.

The State Architect shall do all of the following:
(a) Observe the implementation and administration of this chapter.
(b) Establish and adopt, in consultation with the League of Cities, County Supervisors Association, and California Building Officials, those regulations deemed necessary for carrying out this chapter.
(c) Provide advice and assistance to local jurisdictions regarding essential services buildings.
(d) Hear appeals relative to the administration of this chapter.
The State Architect may establish an advisory committee to assist the State Architect with his or her responsibilities under this chapter. The State Architect shall periodically inform the Seismic Safety Commission and the State Fire Marshal with respect to the implementation and the administration of this chapter.
(Added by Stats. 1985, Ch. 1521, Sec. 1.)

16022.5.

Following completion of construction of a state-owned or state-occupied essential services building, the State Fire Marshal may conduct regular inspections of those buildings for compliance with building standards relating to fire and panic safety.
(Added by Stats. 2019, Ch. 31, Sec. 13. (SB 85) Effective June 27, 2019.)

ARTICLE 5. Offenses [16023- 16023.]
(Article 5 added by Stats. 1985, Ch. 1521, Sec. 1.)

16023.

Any person who willfully violates this chapter is guilty of a misdemeanor.
(Added by Stats. 1985, Ch. 1521, Sec. 1.)

CHAPTER 3. Earthquake Hazard Mitigation Technologies [16100 - 16110]

(Chapter 3 added by Stats. 1989, Ch. 988, Sec. 1.)

16100.

As used in this chapter:
(a) "Earthquake hazard mitigation technologies" includes, but is not limited to, seismic isolation, energy dissipation, ductility, damping systems, and other technologies which endeavor to reasonably protect buildings and nonstructural components, building contents, and functional capability from earthquake damage. Earthquake hazard mitigation technologies do not include those technologies with detailed code provisions in the 1988 edition of the model codes as defined in Section 18916.
(b) "Life cycle cost" includes, but is not limited to, the present value of the cost of initial construction, earthquake insurance premiums, operating and maintenance costs, physical earthquake damage cost to the facility, and related earthquake disruption costs including, but not limited to, loss of production or loss of business anticipated over the projected useful life of the building.

(c) "Peer review" is a review conducted by a multidisciplinary group of experienced technical professionals, including, but not limited to, architects and structural and geotechnical engineers who have recognized expertise in the design and performance of earthquake hazard mitigation technologies, who are independent of the subject of the review, and who are peers with the same professional registration as that of the design professionals responsible for the subject of the review.
(d) "Public agency" means any state agency, any county, city and county, city, regional agency, public district, redevelopment agency, or any other political subdivision.
(Added by Stats. 1989, Ch. 988, Sec. 1.)

16101.

(a) The Seismic Safety Commission, in cooperation with the State Architect, shall develop a state policy on acceptable levels of earthquake risk for new and existing state-owned buildings and submit their policy to the Legislature for consideration by January 1, 1991.
(b) The State Architect, in conjunction with state agency owners and operators of buildings, shall identify activities carried out within state-owned buildings which are necessary for postearthquake operation.
(Added by Stats. 1989, Ch. 988, Sec. 1.)

16102.

(a) The State Architect shall develop and adopt by January 1, 1992, regulations for the application of earthquake hazard mitigation technologies to buildings which do all of the following:
(1) Prescribe design criteria and performance standards with the objective of reasonably ensuring the limitation of earthquake damage or the continuous operational capability of buildings with earthquake hazard mitigation technologies, or both.
(2) Determine the procedure for estimating the life cycle costs of a building designed and constructed according to the provisions of this chapter.
(3) Establish the criteria for determining the suitability of earthquake hazard mitigation technology as compared to conventional construction considering project-specific design requirements and life cycle costs.
(b) The advisory board established pursuant to Section 16022 shall advise the State Architect in the development of regulations for this chapter.
(Added by Stats. 1989, Ch. 988, Sec. 1.)

16103.

(a) The State Architect shall seek the advice and cooperation of appropriate state agencies, structural and earthquake engineering professional organizations, the California Building Officials, the International Conference of Building Officials, and other professional organizations or associations to carry out the provisions of this section.
(b) The State Architect shall encourage technical and professional societies to conduct forums and seminars to increase the understanding of design professionals and building officials about new earthquake hazard mitigation technologies.
(c) The State Architect shall encourage state and federal governments, the University of California, other state agencies, the private educational institutions and the private sector to increase the availability of earthquake research funds and equipment, including, but not limited to, shake tables. The State Architect shall encourage the development of educational materials for earthquake hazard mitigation technologies.
(d) The State Architect, in cooperation with structural engineering professional organizations, shall submit the regulations developed according to this chapter to the International Conference of Building Officials for consideration of adoption in future model codes, as defined in Section 18916, by August 1, 1993.
(Added by Stats. 1989, Ch. 988, Sec. 1.)

16104.

(a) The State Architect shall select suitable buildings and provide direction and supervision for the use of earthquake hazard mitigation technologies on three buildings owned by the Department of General Services, or other state-owned buildings proposed by another state agency, as demonstration projects. Buildings owned by the University of California, the California State University, the Department of Corrections, or other state agencies may be proposed as demonstration projects by the respective state agency but are subject to the approval of the State Architect for selection as a demonstration project and review by the State Architect according to provisions of this chapter.
(b) One demonstration project shall be a new building and two projects shall be existing buildings.
(c) It is in the best interest of the state that these demonstration projects should be fully instrumented and monitored by the Strong Motion Instrumentation Program (Chapter 8 (commencing with Section 2700) of Division 2 of the Public Resources Code) of the Division of Mines and Geology. The Strong Motion Instrumentation Program is encouraged to instrument these demonstration projects. The State Architect shall consult with the Strong Motion Instrumentation Program prior to the selection of demonstration projects.
It is the intent of the Legislature that the cost of instrumentation be funded by the appropriation that funds the construction of the building.
(Added by Stats. 1989, Ch. 988, Sec. 1.)

16106.

(a) The State Architect shall develop and publish informational material describing the anticipated earthquake performance of new and existing buildings afforded by current and earlier building codes, the threat of earthquakes, and earthquake hazard mitigation technologies. This information shall be made available to the federal government, public agencies, and the public to assist building owners, occupants, and managers to better understand the anticipated earthquake performance of buildings.
(b) The State Architect shall provide information by various methods, including publications and seminars, to insurance companies, building owners, and the general

public explaining the significant reductions in damage to buildings and contents which may be effected through the use of earthquake hazard mitigation technologies with the objective of encouraging the use of these technologies, reducing earthquake damage and disruption, and reducing insurance premiums for earthquake peril coverage.
(Added by Stats. 1989, Ch. 988, Sec. 1.)

16107.

(a) The University of California, the California State University, the Department of Corrections, and public agencies are encouraged to develop and implement policies and performance standards according to lowest reasonable life cycle costs in a similar manner to Section 16101.

(b) No provision of this chapter shall apply to the Regents of the University of California unless the regents, by resolution, make the provision applicable.
(Added by Stats. 1989, Ch. 988, Sec. 1.)

16107.5.

No provision of this chapter or the regulations adopted pursuant thereto, shall reduce, alter, or diminish the authority of the design professional who signs the plans and specifications for a project subject to this chapter.
(Added by Stats. 1989, Ch. 988, Sec. 1.)

16108.

(a) Private and public agency building owners and developers may, and are encouraged to, use the provisions of this chapter for new and existing buildings. Private and public agency building owners and developers are encouraged to consider the building standards enacted by local governments for building reconstruction pursuant to Article 4 (commencing with Section 19160) of Chapter 2 of Part 3 of Division 13.

(b) The State Architect, using the advisory committee defined in Section 16022 shall review the suitability of the candidate buildings for earthquake hazard mitigation technologies upon request from building owners or developers, public agencies, or design professionals and shall review the adequacy of the project-specific design and earthquake performance criteria and report its findings to the appropriate public agency prior to the approval of design concepts, preliminary design criteria, geotechnical reports, and ground response reports by the appropriate public agency.

(c) The advisory committee established pursuant to Section 16022 shall be used by the State Architect to perform a peer review of the earthquake hazard mitigation technologies for a project at the State Architect's discretion or at the request of a building owner, design professional, or responsible public agency. The State Architect may add to the advisory committee additional peers for a particular project from a list of recognized experts in the field of earthquake hazard mitigation technologies.

(d) An appropriate fee for all reviews by the State Architect and advisory committee shall be established by the State Architect and paid for by building owners prior to reviews. The fees established pursuant to this subdivision shall not exceed the actual costs of performing the individual peer review.

(e) No local agency may require any private or public agency, building owner or developer, or their design professionals, to comply with the provisions of this chapter as a condition of local agency review, permitting, or approval.
(Added by Stats. 1989, Ch. 988, Sec. 1.)

16109.

In the event that a project involving buildings utilizing earthquake mitigation technologies and other new seismic resistant design technologies requires design review and plan approval by more than one public agency, the Coordinating Council of the Building Standards Commission shall, to the maximum extent feasible, consolidate the various hearings which may be required in order to minimize the time required for the hearings. This consolidation shall be for procedural purposes only and shall not be construed as consolidating the statutory responsibilities of the public agencies conducting the consolidated hearings.
(Amended by Stats. 2004, Ch. 193, Sec. 93. Effective January 1, 2005.)

16110.

The State Architect shall periodically inform the Seismic Safety Commission with respect to the implementation and administration of this chapter.
(Added by Stats. 1989, Ch. 988, Sec. 1.)

CHAPTER 3.5. School Buildings [16500-16500.]

(Heading of Chapter 3.5 renumbered from Chapter 3 (as added by Stats. 1989, Ch. 953, Sec. 2) by Stats. 2015, Ch. 303, Sec. 307.)

16500.

The State Architect shall adopt guidelines applicable to substandard conditions of school buildings, as defined in Section 17283 of the Education Code, which guidelines shall take into consideration the unique design, use, safety needs, and construction of the school buildings.
(Amended by Stats. 2015, Ch. 303, Sec. 308. (AB 731) Effective January 1, 2016.)

CHAPTER 4. Public Postsecondary Buildings [16600 - 16604]

(Chapter 4 added by Stats. 1990, Ch. 1511, Sec. 1.)

16600.

(a) The State Architect and the State Building Standards Commission, in consultation with, and with the concurrence of, the University of California, the California State University, the Structural Engineers Association of California, and the Seismic Safety Commission, shall develop and adopt building seismic retrofit guidelines for state buildings, including those owned by the University of California and by the California State University, by January 1, 1993.

(b) Building seismic retrofit guidelines shall include provisions for the abatement of falling hazards that are structural or nonstructural components of buildings and that pose serious threats to life, including, but not limited to, parapets, appendages, cornices, hanging objects, and building cladding.

(c) Building seismic retrofit guidelines shall include provisions for the strengthening of structures of buildings, or the means necessary to reduce the response of a building to ground shaking during an earthquake, so as to significantly reduce the hazards to life, while concomitantly providing for safe egress of occupants during and immediately after an earthquake.

(d) Building seismic retrofit guidelines shall be consistent with the state Historical Building Code (Part 2.7 (commencing with Section 18950), Division 13) and shall include provisions for the preservation of historical buildings.

(e) Building seismic retrofit guidelines shall incorporate building seismic retrofit standards developed pursuant to Sections 8875.5 and 8879.5 of the Government Code.

(f) The State Architect and the State Building Standards Commission, in cooperation with the University of California, the California State University, the Structural Engineers Association of California, and the Seismic Safety Commission, shall develop and adopt seismic retrofit building standards for state buildings, including those owned by the University of California and by the California State University by July 1, 1996. The standards for state buildings owned by the University of California and the California State University shall not be more stringent than the standards for other state buildings.

(g) The State Architect and the State Building Standards Commission, in cooperation with the Structural Engineers Association of California, shall submit the regulations, findings, and data developed according to this chapter to model code writing agencies and organizations for review and development into code format for consideration and adoption into future model codes, as defined in Section 18916, by August 1, 1997.
(Added by Stats. 1990, Ch. 1511, Sec. 1.)

16601.

(a) The State Building Standards Commission shall review and approve the guidelines adopted by the State Architect and the State Building Standards Commission pursuant to Section 16600 by January 1, 1994, and take administrative actions to make the guidelines applicable to all state buildings, including those owned by the University of California or the California State University.

(b) The State Building Standards Commission shall review and approve the seismic retrofit building standards as developed by the State Architect and the State Building Standards Commission pursuant to Section 16600 by July 1, 1997, and take administrative actions to make the standards applicable to all state buildings, including those owned by the University of California or the California State University.
(Added by Stats. 1990, Ch. 1511, Sec. 1.)

16603.

No provision of this chapter shall apply to the University of California except to the extent that the Regents of the University of California, by resolution, make that provision applicable.
(Added by Stats. 1990, Ch. 1511, Sec. 1.)

16604.

It is the intent of the Legislature that funds to carry out the provisions of this chapter in the amount of thirty thousand dollars ($30,000) be provided as follows:

(a) The sum of fifteen thousand dollars ($15,000) from the June 1990 Higher Education Capital Outlay Bond Fund pursuant to Chapter 14.4 (commencing with Section 67345) of Part 40 of the Education Code, known as the Higher Education Bond Act of June 1990.

(b) The sum of fifteen thousand dollars ($15,000) from the Earthquake Safety and Public Buildings Rehabilitation Fund of 1990 pursuant to Chapter 12.47 (commencing with Section 8878.50) of Division 1 of Title 2 of the Government Code, known as the Earthquake Safety and Public Buildings Rehabilitation Bond Act of 1990.
(Added by Stats. 1990, Ch. 1511, Sec. 1.)